WESTERN CIVILIZATION

THIRD EDITION

WESTERN CIVILIZATION

A Social and Cultural History

THIRD EDITION

Combined Edition

MARGARET L. KING

Brooklyn College and the Graduate Center
City University of New York

Prentice Hall Inc., Upper Saddle River, NJ. 07458

Published 2006 by Prentice Hall Inc.
A Division of Pearson Education
Upper Saddle River, New Jersey 07458

A CIP catalog record for this book is available from the
Library of Congress.
ISBN 0-13-192956-9

10 9 8 7 6 5 4 3 2 1

This book was designed and produced by
LAURENCE KING PUBLISHING LTD.,
London, www.laurenceking.co.uk

Every effort has been made to contact the copyright
holders, but should there be any errors or omissions,
Laurence King Publishing Ltd. would be pleased to insert
the appropriate acknowledgment in any subsequent
printing of this publication.

Design: Ian Hunt Design
Cover Design: Ian Hunt Design
Picture Research: Peter Kent
Maps: Andrea Fairbrass and Ailsa Heritage
Printed in Hong Kong

Cover: Chardin, *The Young Schoolmistress,* 1740
(oil on canvas).

CONTENTS

PART ONE

BEFORE THE WEST
The Inhabited World from the
First Civilizations to Alexander the Great

(PREHISTORY–300 B.C.E.)

CHAPTER 1

STONE, BRONZE, AND WORD
Prehistory and Early Civilizations

(2 MILLION–500 B.C.E.)

CHAPTER 2

ARMIES AND EMPIRES
Politics and Power in the Bronze and Iron Ages

(3500–300 B.C.E.)

PART TWO
THE ORIGINS OF THE WEST
From Roman Dominion to the New
Peoples of Europe

(300 B.C.E–1300 C.E.)

CHAPTER 5
OUR SEA
The Mediterranean World in the
Hellenistic and Early Roman Eras

(300–27 B.C.E.)

CHAPTER 6
PAX ROMANA
Society, State, and Culture in
Imperial Rome

(27 B.C.E.–500 C.E.)

CHAPTER 10
THE SPIRITUAL SWORD
Religion and Culture in the Middle Ages

(500–1500)

CHAPTER 11
IN THE NAME OF PROFIT
Cities, Merchants, and Trade in
the Middle Ages

(1000–1500)

PART FOUR

THE WEST EXPANDS
The Self, the State, the World

(1200–1750)

CHAPTER 12

CITY LIFE
Public and Private Life in the
Late Medieval Cities

(1200–1500)

CHAPTER 13

REBIRTH IN ITALY
The Civilization of the Italian Renaissance

(1300–1550)

CHAPTER 14

OF ONE CHURCH, MANY
Protestant Reformation and
Catholic Reform

(1500–1650)

CHAPTER 15
ABSOLUTE POWER
War and Politics in Early Modern Europe

1500–1750)

CHAPTER 16
EUROPE REACHES OUT
Global Voyages and Cultural Encounters

(1500–1750)

PART SIX
THE WEST BECOMES MODERN
Industrialization, Imperialism, Ideologies
(1750–1914)

CHAPTER 20
REVOLT AND REORGANIZATION IN EUROPE
From Absolute Monarchy to
the Paris Commune
(1750–1871)

CHAPTER 21
MACHINES IN THE GARDEN
The Industrialization of the West
(1750–1914)

CHAPTER 22
LIVES OF THE OTHER HALF
Western Society in an Industrial Age
(1750–1914)

CHAPTER 23
THE CONCERT OF EUROPE
Mass Politics and the Triumph of the State
(1815–1914)

CHAPTER 24
THE WESTERN IMPERIUM
European Migration, Settlement, and
Domination around the Globe
(1750–1914)

PART SEVEN

TOWARD A NEW WEST
Post-War, Post-Modern, Post-Industrial

(1914–2000)

CHAPTER 25

STORM, STRESS, AND DOUBT
European Culture from Classicism to Modernism

(1780–1914)

CHAPTER 26

THE MIGHTY ARE FALLEN
The Trauma of World War I

(1914–1920)

CHAPTER 27
THE TRIUMPH OF UNCERTAINTY
Cultural Innovation, Social Disruption, and
Economic Collapse
(1915–1945)

CHAPTER 28
STATES IN CONFLICT
Communism, Fascism, Democracy,
and the Crisis of World War II
(1917–1945)

CHAPTER 29
THE END OF IMPERIALISM
Decolonization and Statebuilding
around the Globe
(1914–1990s)

CHAPTER 30

BACK FROM ARMAGEDDON
From the Bomb to the Internet

(1945–1990)

EPILOGUE:
THE FUTURE OF THE WEST
(SINCE 1990)

WITNESSES

TIMELINES

Society, Politics, and Economy	Religion and Ideas	Europe and the Americas
Rulers, Nations, Warfare, and Revolution	Civilization, Art, and Science	Africa, the Middle East, Asia, and Oceania

Beyond the West

MAPS

WINDOWS ON

'Windows on the Web' activities extend the scope of the Windows On feature by combining documents, images, and Web-based material to explore concepts and problems in more depth. Each Windows on the Web activity can be found at **www.prenhall.com/king**

PREFACE

On September 11, 2001, four squads of suicidal terrorists hijacked four planes, and piloted them towards four monuments that symbolized the achievements and strivings of American society. Three hit their targets; one crashed before it could do so, brought down by the prompt and courageous intervention of some of the doomed passengers. Nearly 4,000 people died in the four incidents, including hundreds of citizens of foreign nations resident in this country.

Within weeks, the United States was at war in Afghanistan, and within eighteen months in Iraq, in a "War on Terror" claiming to target not nations or peoples, but terrorists and their protectors. The President of the United States and his principal allies, including most notably British Prime Minister Tony Blair, in defiance of the United Nations, have defined these preemptive campaigns as a battle for freedom against radical Islam. In their view, not two civilizations, but two sets of principles, are bitterly engaged.

As these terrifying events have unfolded, the concept of "Western civilization" has been mentioned rather more than it usually is in our bold and boisterous national discourse. Somehow, many felt these 9/11 attacks on the US were strikes at the fundamental structures of Western society: not just objections to American foreign policy, or resentment of American success, but a more basic blow to the values that sustain the democratic societies of the Western world. The issue continues to be mentioned, by voices on the Left and on the Right, who debate whether "freedom," that quintessential Western value, can be exported or imposed on another culture and civilization.

It is possible that many goods will proceed from the horror of September 11, and that one of them may be a renewed interest in the development of the West. The third edition of this book therefore begins with some very basic questions: where, and what, is the West?

WHERE IS THE WEST?

When I teach the introductory history course at Brooklyn College of the City University of New York, I start each semester by asking my students "Where is the West?" I send an unfortunate victim to the map of the world mounted on the back wall of the room. A finger roams around the continents of the globe. The class suggests many possibilities: western Europe? The western hemisphere? The wild west? The search goes on all semester—a search of special complexity for the many students who, speaking tens of languages, professing all the world's major religions, and hailing from all its inhabited continents, have no association by birth with Western civilization. To

begin, I tell my students about Greenwich, England, where the Prime Meridian begins.

Visitors gathered outside the gates of the old Royal Observatory in Greenwich, England, may read a sign announcing that they now stand "at the center of time and space." From that spot an imaginary line circles the earth from pole to pole, slicing the globe in half. The two halves are the Eastern and the Western hemispheres. The line is the Prime Meridian, the first and last of the infinite series of lines of longitude by which any location on the globe, East or West, can be accurately denoted by its precise variation in hours, minutes, and seconds from Greenwich time.

The packs of schoolchildren who come to Greenwich are often photographed grinning as they stand astride the Prime Meridian—each with one foot in the East and one in the West. Yet both feet are in England, in Europe, and in the zone of Western Civilization. Part of England and most of Europe (and all of Australia and New Zealand) lie in the Eastern hemisphere. Yet they belong to the West. A good fraction of Africa lies in the Western hemisphere. Yet it does not belong to the West. The people of the nations of Latin America lie in the western hemisphere, accept an official language which is European, and adhere for the most part to the Roman Catholic Church—is their civilization "Western?" Or does a struggling economy, or a large population of peoples of mixed indigenous and African heritage, mark them as non-Western?

What is the West? It isn't the "west" of the old movies, where for a brief moment cowboys prowled the frontier, and the native peoples of North America resisted the incursions of Europeans arriving from the East. It isn't the "west" of the Cold War era (1945–1991; see Chapter 30) when eastern and western zones of Europe adhered to different ideologies, and the boundary between their mental and political battles was designated by an Iron Curtain in part mythical, in part real. It is not only the zone of western, Catholic Christianity (which includes Poland, a nation solidly in "eastern" Europe), but embraces also the nations whose majorities embrace eastern, Orthodox Christianity: Greece, Serbia, perhaps even Russia. The West is not defined by any number of terms which contain, in their designations, the word "west": the Western hemisphere, the North American West, or Western Europe. What is the West? It is not, in fact, a place.

Neither is the West a specific people, or race, or set of nations. Although all of the nations of Europe are Western, so too are other nations far away—the nations of the Americas, Australasia, and the Asian zones of Russia—that were settled by Europeans

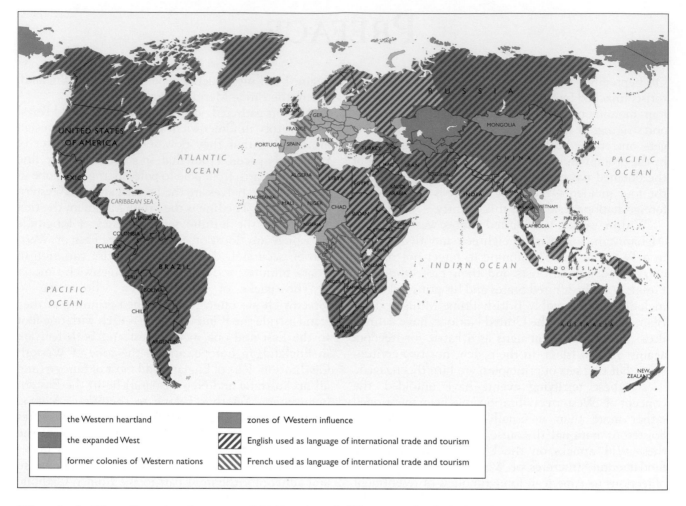

Where is the West: *Shown here is one way of thinking about the West geographically. Its heartland is Europe, where the cultural, social, and political traditions of the West developed their modern form after about 1000 C.E. "The expanded West" includes regions of European settlement, where Western civilization was transplanted from Europe after 1500 but where it has since developed in modified form because of contacts with other peoples. "Former colonies of Western nations" include those regions where Western civilization was imposed upon other nations, nations now largely liberated from colonial rule but still retaining some features of that civilization. Finally, areas designated as "zones of Western influence" have been largely free of any period of direct domination by Western nations, but have to a greater or lesser extent adopted selected Western political and economic institutions.*

who bore with them, along with their tools and skills, the elements of their civilization. In these scattered zones of Western civilization, and in the European homeland now as well, as migrations of peoples have altered its original population, people of greatly different origins—Asian, African—have adopted aspects of Western civilization. Just as anybody may learn French, or become a Methodist, anyone who so chooses may adopt and transmit the civilization of the West. Although at times in the Western past, theorists argued that civilization was linked to what was then, erroneously, called "race," the events of the last century have at long last obliterated those notions. Among the millions destroyed in the maelstrom of genocidal war were those considered to be by race outside the bounds of Western civilization; but their language and values were solidly Western, and their appeals for justice recapitulate the patterns of Western thought.

WHAT, THEN, IS THE WEST?

The West is a body of ideas, values, customs, and beliefs. These were forged over a period of centuries on the continent of Europe, which lay to the west of the then more advanced civilizations of the East. They triumphed during the centuries of European expansion: from approximately 1000 to 1900 of the Common Era, when Western values followed Western merchants, travelers, armies, and governors into every other corner of the inhabited globe. They are what the West means, and they are truly the meaning of the West.

Here are a few of the many concepts that have made the West and that constitute its core meaning:
• The principle of human dignity: that all human beings are equal in worth (if not in talents, beauty, or size), that they possess rights which cannot be taken away, and that to the greatest possible degree they are free.

• The ideal of justice: that no person should be unfairly privileged above another.
• The value of democracy: that the power to shape the future of a community belongs to its people as a whole and not to arbitrarily selected leaders.
• The method of rationalism, which assumes that all phenomena (even those pertaining to God, essence, or spirit) may be subject to the critical scrutiny of the human mind.
• The inclination to progress, to work toward goals to be achieved in the future.
• The habit of self-examination, which encourages human beings to examine themselves seriously and often to test whether they have fulfilled their promise and their responsibilities.

These, among others, are the habits and values that together characterize Western civilization, and which have caused it to develop in the directions it has—the very habits and values that have provoked the enemies to strike cruelly and violently against the innocent citizens of New York City and Washington DC on September 11, 2001.

THE WEST AND THE REST OF THE WORLD

We learn more about the Western world when we also examine the rest of the world. Some features of Western civilization are not unique to the West. They appear also in the cultural systems of other people around the globe, although not all of them appear in the same way in any other civilization. In many cases, particularly in the era of its origins, the West borrowed customs and ideas from the civilizations of Asia and Africa. More recently, a fully developed Western culture has lent, shared, or imposed its values on those civilizations and the newer ones of the Western hemisphere (see map, facing page).

This book will frequently pause in its narration of Western development to consider key aspects of non-Western civilizations, in the past and now. The ancient civilizations of the Mediterranean region, which confer upon the later West its first patterns of urbanization and political rule, its religious traditions and its alphabet, are, of course, considered. But so, too, are the ancient and medieval civilizations of China, India, Africa, and the Americas (Chapters 1, 2, 8, and 16). In the modern era, this book considers at length not only the process by which Western nations came to control much of the globe in the nineteenth century (Chapter 24), but also how colonized regions freed themselves from that domination in the twentieth (Chapter 29). To isolate the West from other regions which have helped shape it, and upon which it has impacted, makes no sense—especially in an age which is now no longer dominated by the West but is truly **global**.

A global perspective transcends any claims for the superiority of one civilization to another. The civilization of the West is the focus of this book not because it is better (arguable) or because it is ours (it is not "ours" to many Americans by virtue of birth), but because it embodies principles of permanent value that will survive as long as there are those who learn them, reflect on them, and teach them to future generations, in the West and elsewhere in the world.

CHANGES TO THE THIRD EDITION

Drawing on the comments of the many reviewers of the earlier editions of *Western Civilization: A Social and Cultural History*, a number of changes and enhancements appear in this new edition.
• Volume 2 now starts with a Prologue that reviews the history of Western civilization from its origins through the Reformation. It introduces in condensed form the people, places, and concepts students will need to know (if they have not studied the material of Volume 1) to understand the history of the West in modern times.
• The epilogue for Volume 2 has been thoroughly revised and expanded. It now includes new material on globalization and anti-globalization, free trade, genocide and the prosecution of war crimes, and the "War on Terror."
• The chapter openers now invite students to read with questions about key issues, rather than announce topics and themes.
• The *Timelines* have been thoroughly reworked for greater clarity.
• Accompanying the maps in this edition are thought-provoking questions designed to encourage students to make connections between the maps and the text.
• Each chapter ends with *Questions to Consider* which in asking students "why" things happened as they did, guide them in reviewing the contents of the chapter.
• The bibliographies have been extensively revised, streamlined, and brought up-to-date.

ACKNOWLEDGMENTS

The single name of the author appearing on the title page disguises the reality that I have had many guides and helpers in the creation of this book. I am grateful to the staff at Laurence King Publishing (Rada Radojicic, Ian Hunt, Lesley Henderson, Lee Greenfield, Judy Rasmussen, and especially Laurence King) who have had confidence in the project, assisted it in every way, and alternately soothed and bullied its restive author.

At Prentice Hall I would also like to thank Yolanda deRooy, President of the Humanities and Social Sciences Division, Charlyce Jones-Owen,

Editorial Director for the Humanities and Social Sciences, and especially Charles Cavaliere, Executive Editor, who has been a fund of good ideas.

My colleagues in the History Department at Brooklyn College, especially Leonard Gordon, have contributed ideas and criticisms for which I am immensely grateful; as has former colleague Michael Mendle, now in the History Department at the University of Alabama (Tuscaloosa), former student and associate Michael Sappol, now at the National Library of Medicine (Bethesda, Maryland); and Brooklyn staffer Brian Bonhomme, now at the University of Arkansas, a young scholar whose insight

and imagination contributed greatly to all the chapters of the second volume.

My severest critics and most valiant sustainers have been my sons and my husband—David, Jeremy, and Robert Kessler. They have waited patiently for the day when the stacks of books on the floor of my study return to their home on library shelves, and normalcy to our household.

Margaret L. King
Brooklyn College and the Graduate Center
City University of New York

The author and publisher would like to thank the many scholars and teachers whose thoughtful and often detailed comments helped to shape this book.

John F. Battick, University of Maine
Wood Bouldin, Villanova University
Linda Bregstein, Mercer Community College
Blaine T. Browne, Broward Community College
Amy Burnett, University of Nebraska-Lincoln
Jack Cargill, Rutgers University
Anna Clark, University of North Carolina at Charlotte
Cyndia Susan Clegg, Pepperdine University
Jessica A. Coope, University of Nebraska Lincoln
Tim Crain, University of Wisconsin-Milwaukee
Gerald Danzer, University of Illinois at Chicago
Meaghan N. Duff, Western Kentucky University
Steven Fanning, University of Illinois at Chicago
Allan Fletcher, Boise State University
Neal Galpern, University of Pittsburgh
Richard Gerberding, University of Alabama
Gay Gullickson, University of Maryland
Charles W. Hope, Tarrant County Junior College
Jeff Horn, Stetson University
David Hudson, California State University, Fresno
Patrick Kelly, Adelphi University
Herbert Luft, Pepperdine University
Eleanor McCluskey, Broward Community College
Andrew McMichael, Western Kentucky University
Mavis Mate, University of Oregon

John Mauer, Tri-County Technical College
Marion S. Miller, University of Illinois at Chicago
Joseph R. Mitchell, Howard Community College
Jim Murray, University of Cincinnati
Jasonne Grabher O'Brien, University of Kansas
Michael G. Paul, Boston College
William Percy, University of Massachusetts, Boston
Mary Pickering, San Jose State University
John Powell, Penn State University at Erie
Thomas Preisser, Sinclair Community College
Carole A. Putko, San Diego State University
Timothy A. Ross, Arkansas State University
Brian Rutishauser, Fresno City College
Linda Bregstein Scherr, Mercer County Community College
Roger Schlesinger, Washington State University
Hugo B. Schwyzer, Pasadena City College
James Smither, Grand Valley State University
Francis Stackenwalt, East Central University
Emily Sohmer Tai, Queensborough Community College
Robert W. Thurston, Miami University
Michael Weiss, Linn-Benton Community College
William Benton Whisenhunt, College of DuPage
Steven Jay White, University of Kentucky Lexington Community College
Norman J. Wilson, Methodist College
Jennifer Wynot, Metropolitan State College of Denver
Michael Zirinsky, Boise State University.

PICTURE CREDITS

All numbers refer to page numbers (t=top; b=bottom; l=left; r=right; c=center)

CHAPTER 1

3 Venus of Willendorf, c.25,000-21,000 B.C.E. Naturhistorisches Museum Vienna; 6 AKG London; 7l, 15, 22tr Hirmer Fotoarchiv, Munich; 7r Craig & Marie Mauzy, Athens; 12b Werner Forman Archive, London; 14 Spectrum Colour Library, London; 22tl India Office, London; 22b American School of Classical Studies

CHAPTER 2

31 detail of 45t; 37 Hirmer Fotoarchiv, Munich; 40, 45br Craig & Marie Mauzy, Athens; 41 Spectrum Colour Library, London

CHAPTER 3

57 detail of 79b; 61tl Louisa Eldridge McBurney Gift Fund, 1953, (53.11.6); 61br, 63t RMN-Hervè Lewandowski, Paris; 63b Bildarchiv Preussicher Kulturbesitz, Berlin; 75t Fletcher Fund, 1931, (31.11.10); 76 Hirmer Fotoarchiv, Munich

CHAPTER 4

83 detail of 99; 88l Fletcher Fund, 1932; 89 Fotografica Foglia, Naples; 92l Hirmer Fotoarchiv, Munich; 92c Alison Frantz; 97t Hulton Getty, London; 97c TAP © Archaeological Receipts Fund; 99 Bildarchiv Preussicher Kulturbesitz, Berlin

CHAPTER 5

111 The Battle of Issos (detail), Pompei, 2nd century B.C.E. Museo Archeologico Nazionale, Naples/Fotografica Foglia Naples; 115 Robert Harding, London; 116t Vincenzo Pirozzi, Rome; 116b Araldo Da Luca, Rome; 121, 127 Araldo De Luca, Rome; 123 AKG London

CHAPTER 6

139 detail of 161; 142, 143, 148tr, 148br Alinari; 152 Scala; 153, 161 Vincenzo Pirozzi, Rome; 154 Paul M.R. Maeyaert, Mont de l'Enclus (Orroir), Belgium; 155cl Fotografica Foglia, Naples

CHAPTER 7

167 Christ Pantocrator (detail) 6th century C.E./AKG London; 170 Vincenzo Pirozzi, Rome; 171 Christies Images; 172 RMN, Paris; 174 Werner Forman Archive, London; 175 Sonia Halliday, Weston Turville, UK; 179c Alinari; 184l Scala; 184r Araldo De Luca, Rome; 186 A.F. Kersting, London

CHAPTER 8

195 Ludovisi Sarcophagus (detail) c.250 C.E. Museo Nazionale Rome; 197t Alinari; 197b Hirmer Fotoarchiv, Munich; 198, 207b Spectrum Colour Library, London; 202 Bridgeman Art Library; 206 Sonia Halliday, Weston Turville, UK; 207t Cameraphoto Arte, Venice; 223t Aerofilms, Hertfordshire; 223bl Justin Kerr, New York; 223br Werner Forman Archive, London

CHAPTER 9

229 Les Très Riches Heures du Duc de Berry (detail), 1413-16, ms. 65, fol.6v, Museè Condè/Giraudon, Paris; 234 Alinari; 239t Frank Blackwell, Oxfordshire; 241 Spectrum Colour Library, London; 244r Giraudon, Paris

CHAPTER 10

257 detail of 262l; 259t Studio Fotografico Quattrone, Florence; 261 Wim Cox, Cologne; 264 Hirmer Fotoarchiv, Munich; 265, 286 Paul M.R. Maeyaert, Mont de l'Enclus (Orroir), Belgium; 272l

Art Resource, New York; 272r Scala; 274 AKG London; 277r photo: C. Vignaud

CHAPTER 11

289 detail of 291; 291 RMN-Daniel Arnaudet, Paris; 292 Scala; 303t Alain Lonchampt/CNMHS, Paris; 305 Bridgeman Art Library

CHAPTER 12

323 Gentile Bellini, Procession of the Cross in Piazza San Marco (detail), 1496, Galleria dellíAccademia/Cameraphoto Arte Venice; 325 Higginson/Private Collection, London; 326-7 Studio Fotografico Quattrone, Florence; 328 CNMHS, Paris; 329t A.F. Kersting, London; 329b Bildarchiv Foto Marburg; 334, 336 AKG London; 344, 346 Scala

CHAPTER 13

353 Michelangelo, David, 1501-4 Galleria dellíAccademia, Florence/ Studio Fotografico Quattrone, Florence; 355, 359r, 367t, 371, 376, 377 Scala; 359bl RMN, Paris; 363, 397, 373 Studio Fotografico Quattrone, Florence; 367b Cameraphoto Arte, Venice; 370 Raffaello Bencini, Florence

CHAPTER 14

383 Hans Holbein the Younger, Erasmus of Rotterdam, c.1520, Louvre, Paris/RMN-Hervè Lewandowski; 386 Mary Evans Picture Library, London; 388 Bridgeman Art Library; 391tl, 403l, 410b, 413tr Higginson/Private Collection; 402 Scala; 405 Spectrum Colour Library, London; 410t RMN-Michäfe Bellot, Paris; 411 photo: J.-C. Ducret; 413bl Araldo Da Luca, Rome; 413br Images/Charles Walker Collection, London

CHAPTER 15

417 The Battle of Pavia (detail), 1525, Museo di Capodimonte/Scala; 419t AKG London; 419b Mary Evans Picture Library, London; 420 English Heritage Photo Library; 432b Cameraphoto Arte, Venice; 436 RMN-Jean/Lewandowski, Paris; 443t RMN-Gèrard Blot, Paris; 443b Institut Amatller DíArt Hispànic, Barcelona

CHAPTER 16

447 detail of 450; 450 Artothek, Peissenberg; 451 © Patrimonio Nacional, Madrid; 453tr, 468, 475 Mary Evans Picture Library, London; 453b, 469b Hulton Getty, London; 460t AKG London; 469t Bridgeman Art Library

CHAPTER 17

483 Rembrandt, sketch of a woman reading (detail), 1634, Library of Congress; 484t, 498 AKG London; 486 Science Museum/Science and Society Picture Library, London; 487 Scala, Florence; 491l from Charles Singer, *The Discovery of the Circulation of the Blood*, London, 1956, courtesy Mr. A.W. Singer; 491r, 507tl Wellcome Institute Library, London; 499 photo: © Metropolitan Museum of Art, New York. Harris Brisbane Dick Fund, 1930 (30.67.2); 504 RMN-Hervé Lewandowski; 507bl Mary Evans Picture Library, London; 507r from Hevelius, *Machinae Coelestis*; 508t RMN-Arnaudet; 508b RMN-Gérard Blot

CHAPTER 18

513 detail of 532; 516 © Paul M. R. Maeyaert, Mont de l'Encus (Orroir), Belgium; 517 RMN-Gérard Blot; 522 RMN-R.G. Ojeda; 523 AKG London; 525 Giraudon, Paris; 531tl © Studio Fotografico Quattrone, Florence; 531tr Bibliothèque Nationale, France; 531b The State Hermitage Museum, St. Petersburg, Russia/with the assistance of Petrushka Ltd, Moscow; 534 photo:Ursula Seitz-Gray; 538t The Art Archive, London; 538b Bulloz, Paris

LITERARY CREDITS

Augsburg Fortress: from *Luther's Works*, Volume 31, edited by Harold J. Grimm (Muhlenberg Press, 1957), © 1957 Fortress Press; **Beacon Press**: from *The Broken Spears* by Miguel Leon-Portilla (Beacon Press, 1992), © 1962, 1990 by Miguel Leon-Portilla; Expanded and Updated Edition © 1992 by Miguel Leon-Portilla; **Nancy Birdsall**: from "Life is Unfair: Inequality in the World", in *Foreign Policy*, Number 111 (Summer, 1998); **Blackwell Publishers**: "Decree of the Provveditori alla Sanità, February 22, 1522" from *Venice: A Documentary History, 1450-1630*, edited by David Chambers and Brian Pullan (Blackwell, 1992); **Georges Borchardt Inc**: from *The Kingdom of Memory* by Elie Wiesel (Elirion, 1990); **Burns & Oates Ltd**: from "Edict of Milan" by Constantine, with Licinius, in *Church and State Through the Centuries*, edited by S. Ehler and J. Morrall (Burns & Oates/Newman Press, 1954); **Center for Reformation & Renaissance Studies, University of Toronto**: from "On the Removal of Images" by Andreas Karlstadt in *A Reformation Debate: Three Treatises in Translation* by Bryan Mangrum and Giuseppe Scavizzi (CRRS, 1991); **Michel Chossudovsky**: from "Global Poverty in the Late 20th Century", in *Journal of International Affairs*, Volume 52, No. 1 (Fall, 1998); **Columbia University Press**: from "New Chronicle" by Giovanni Villani in *Medieval Trade in the Mediterranean World: Illustrative Documents*, edited by Robert S. Lopez and Irving W. Raymond (Columbia University Press, 1955), © 1955 Columbia University Press; from "Res gestae divi Augusti" by Augustus, "Letters" by Pliny the Younger, "History of Rome" by Livy, "The Elements of Oratory" by Quintilian, "Histories, 4" by Sallust, "Dialogue on Oratory" by Tacitus, and "Theodosian Code" by Emperor Theodosius, in *Roman Civilization: Selected Readings*, edited by Naphtali Lewis and Meyer Reinhold (Columbia University Press, 1990), © 1990 Columbia University Press; **Continuum Publishing Company**: from *The Devastation of the Indies: A Brief Account* by Bartolemé de las Casas, edited by Herma Briffault (The Seabury Press/Continuum, 1974), © 1974 by The Seabury Press; **DharmaNet International**: from *The Edicts of King Asoka*, translated by Ven. S. Dhammika (Dharma Net edition, 1993); **Dover Publications Inc**: from *Malleus maleficarum* by Heinrich Krämer and James Sprenger, translated by Montague Summers (1928; Dover Publications, 1971); **The Gioi Publishers**: from "Declaration of Independence of the Democratic Republic of Vietnam" by Ho Chi Minh from *Selected Writings* by Ho Chi Minh (Hanoi: Foreign Languages Publishing House, 1977); **Elizabeth Hadas**: from "Edict on Prices" by Diocletian, preface to the "Institutes" by Justinian, "Moral Epistles" by Seneca, and "Histories" by Tacitus in *A History of Rome*, edited by Moses Hadas (Doubleday, 1956), © Estate of Moses Hadas; **HarperCollins Publishers Inc**: from *A History of Their Own: Women in Europe from Prehistory to the Present, Volume 2* by Bonnie S. Anderson and Judith P. Zinsser (Harper & Row, 1988); **HMSO**: from *Documents on British Foreign Policy, 1919-1939*, edited by E. L. Woodward and Rohan Butler. 3rd Series (HMSO, 1954); **Johns Hopkins University Press**: from Livy in *Women's Life in Greece and Rome: A Source Book in Translation*, edited by Mary R. Lefkowitz and Maureen B. Fant (Johns Hopkins University Press, 1982); **Houghton Mifflin Company**: from *Mein Kampf* by Adolf Hitler, translated by Ralph Manheim (Houghton Mifflin, 1943), © 1943, renewed 1971 by Houghton Mifflin Company; **Nikki Keddie**: "On the Importance of Science" by Al-Afghani from *Islamic Response to Imperialism: Political and Religious Writings of Sayyid Jam I al-Din n al-Afghani*, edited/translated by Nikki Keddie (University of California Press, 1983); **Kendall/Hunt Publishing Company**: from "Nemean VI" by Pindar in *Ancient Greece: Documentary Perspectives*, edited by Stylianos Spyridakis and Bradley Nystrom (Kendall/Hunt Publishing, 1985), © 1985 by Kendall/Hunt Publishing Company; **Manchester University Press**: from "Cronica de Don Manuel" by Damiao de Gois in *The Jews in Western Europe, 1440-1600*, translated by John Edwards (Manchester University Press, 1994); **The New York Review of Books**: from Vaclav Havel's Address to the Canadian Senate and House of Commons (April 29, 1999), translated by Paul Wilson, from *The New York Review of Books* (June 10, 1999), © NYREV Inc; **The Orion Publishing Group**: from *The Condition of the Working Class in England, 1844* by Friedrich Engels, in *Engels, Manchester and the Working Class* by S. Marcus (Weidenfeld & Nicolson, 1974); **Oxford University Press**: from "The Institutes of the Christian Church" by John Calvin in *Documents of the Christian Church*, edited by Henry Bettenson (Oxford University Press, 1952); from "The Goodman of Paris" in *Le Menagier de Paris*, edited by Georgine E. Brereton and Janet M. Ferrier (Clarendon Press, 1981); **Oxford University Press Inc**: from "Eurocentrism Revisited, 1994" in *Cultures in Conflict: Christians, Muslims, and Jews in the Age of Discovery* by Bernard Lewis (Oxford University Press, 1995), © 1995 by Oxford University Press Inc; **Pegasus Press**: from "On the Equal or Unequal Sin of Adam and Eve" by Isotta Nogarola in *Her Immaculate Hand*, edited by Margaret King and Albert Rabil (SUNY, 1992); **Penguin Putnam Inc**: from *Notes from Underground and the Grand Inquisitor* by Fyodor Dostoevsky, translated by Ralph E. Matlaw, translation © 1960, 1988 by E. P. Dutton; **Penguin UK**: from *The Book of the Courtier* by Baldassare Castiglione, translated by George Bull (Penguin Classics, 1967), © George Bull, 1967; from *The Prince* by Niccolo Machiavelli, translated by George Bull (Penguin Classics, 1961; third revised edition, 1981), © George Bull, 1961, 1975, 1981; from "Agricola" from *The Agricola and the Germania* by Tacitus, translated by H. Mattingly, revised by S.A. Handford (Penguin Classics, 1948; revised edition, 1971), © The Estate of H. Mattingly, 1948, 1970; S. A. Handford, 1970; from *The Life of Saint Teresa of Avilla by Herself*, translated by J. M. Cohen (Penguin Classics, 1957), © J. M. Cohen, 1957; from *The Peloponnesian War* by Thucydides, translated by Rex Warner (Penguin Classics, 1954), © Rex Warner, 1954; **Prentice-Hall Inc**: from *A Documentary Survey of the French Revolution*, translated by J. H. Stewart (Macmillan, 1951), © 1951; "The Attack of King Industry" by Dalpatram Kavi, translated by Howard Spodek and Chimanbhai Privedi, in *The World's History* by Howard Spodek (Prentice-Hall, 1998), © 1998 by Prentice Hall; **Princeton University Press**: from *Ancient Near Eastern Texts Relating to the Old Testament*, edited by James B. Pritchard, 2nd edition, revised, © 1950, 1955, 1964, renewed 1978 by Princeton University Press; **Random House Archive & Library**: from "Epic of Gilgamesh", translated by R. Temple, in *He Who Saw Everything: A Verse Translation of Gilgamesh* (Rider Books, 1991); from "The Medea" by Euripedes in *The Great Plays of Euripedes*, translated by Rex Warner (The Bodley Head/Signet), © 1958 and renewed © 1986 by Rex Warner; **Random House Inc**: from *Restless Days* by Lilo Linke, © 1935 by Alfred A. Knopf Inc and renewed 1963 by Lilo Linke; from *Preparing for the Twenty-First Century* by Paul Kennedy (Random House, 1993), © 1993 by Paul Kennedy; **Salman Rushdie**: from article on Islam in *The New York Times* (November 2, 2001); **Amartya Sen**: from "A World Not Neatly Divided" in *The New York Times* (November 23, 2001); **Simon & Schuster Inc**: from *Hope Against Hope: A Memoir* by Nadezhda Mandelstam, translated by Max Hayward (Macmillan, 1970), © 1970 Atheneum Publishers, English translation © 1970 Atheneum Publishers; from *The Clash of Civilizations and the Remaking of World Order* by Samuel P. Huntington (Simon & Schuster, 1996), © 1996 by Samuel P. Huntington; **Teachers College Press**: from "De ingenius moribus" by Pier Paolo Vergerio in *Vittorino da Feltre and Other Humanist Educators* by W. H. Woodward (Teachers College Press, 1964), © 1964 Teachers College, Columbia University; **Thames & Hudson Ltd**: from *The Origins of War: From the Stone Age to Alexander the Great* by Arthur Ferrill (Thames & Hudson, 1985); **University of California Press**: from *History of a Voyage to the Land of Brazil, Otherwise Called America* by Jean de Léry, edited/translated by Janet Whatley (University of California Press 1990),

THE MEANING OF THE WEST,
EXAMINED IN A LIVELY NEW EDITION OF

WESTERN CIVILIZATION

A Social and Cultural History

AVAILABLE IN THE FOLLOWING FORMATS:

Combined Edition
Chapters 1–30

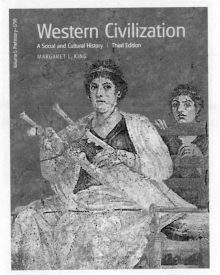

Volume I
Prehistory to 1750
Chapters 1–16

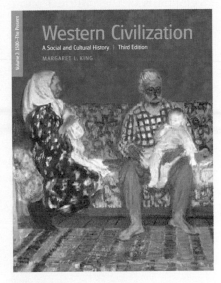

Volume 2
1500 to the Present,
Chapters 15–30

ORGANIZATION

Because this book gives special attention to the history of culture and society, its organization is topical. Some chapters focus on politics, others on society, others on religion or ideas. Often two or three chapters in succession will deal with the same historical period, but from different topical vantage points. The chapters on the Middle Ages, for instance, examine the whole of that thousand-year period, stressing first politics and society (Chapter 9), then religion and ideas (Chapter 10), then commerce and urbanization (Chapter 11). A topical division has the virtue that students are introduced systematically to the variety of ways that historians study the past.

The consequence of a focus on social and cultural themes is a deemphasis of the political narrative. That shift of priorities parallels the tendency of historical scholarship since 1960, which has elevated the richness of multiple themes, and highlighted the many voices of past reality. Accordingly, attention is paid to the experience of workers, the poor, and marginalized groups (modifying the traditional emphasis on rulers and elites), to the changing roles of women and children, to the structure and growth of cities, to war as

***Exekias,* Achilles and Penthesilea on amphora, c. 540 B.C.E.**

***Quinten Massys,* A Moneylender and his Wife, 1514**

an expression of social values, to religious experience and behavior (as well as doctrine and organization), to popular and high culture, to the settings of intellectual discourse and the role of the powerful in shaping culture.

Although the development of states, the sequence of rulers, and the chain of wars and peace treaties are included, they are in briefer format than in most texts. No more than one of five chapters is devoted primarily to political discussion (Chapters 2, 15, 20, 23, 26, 29); only six others contain large sections dedicated to political narrative (Chapters 3, 5, 6, 9, 19, 28). Nearly two-thirds of the whole centers on social and cultural themes. Some chapters are particularly dedicated to language, religion, and ideas (Chapters 1, 4, 6, 7, 10, 13, 14, 17, 25, 27); others to social or economic problems, including world trade, migrations, urbanization, social structures, technology, development, and the environment (Chapters 3, 9, 11, 12, 16, 18, 21, 22, 30).

A topical organization means that students must read, and teachers must teach, different chapters in different ways. But in all cases, that reading and teaching is supported by maps, graphical, visual, and documentary materials that bring the material to life, and aid the student in gaining a rich and up-to-date vision of the past, and in developing an appreciation of Western civilization that is based not only on the recitation of its triumphs of war and state, but also on the impressive foundations of its social and cultural heritage.

Gustave Caillebotte, Rainy Day, 1876–1877

FEATURES OF THE THIRD EDITION

PART THREE

THE WEST TAKES FORM

Medieval Society, Politics, Economy, and Culture (500–1500)

Peasants and nobles created the society of the European Middle Ages. As Roman institutions crumbled and waves of invaders destroyed communities, medieval peasants devised new patterns of agricultural work and life, generally on the manors, or large estates, of noble landholders. The nobles, as an elite group of military men, warded off invaders and struggled among themselves for power.

Amid the bounds of mainly local authority, the first European kingdoms emerged, and kings employed violence and persuasion to assert their authority over nobles. The Crusades sent knightly armies east to the Levant (Palestine and Syria, on the eastern Mediterranean shores), while knights who stayed home at court developed the rituals of chivalry. In the late medieval centuries, which were gripped by famine and plague, peasant rebellions against landholders were frequent.

Providing cohesion to the disparate communities of Europe was the Catholic Church, centered in Rome under the pope, whose authority was at its height around 1300 after a process of reform, centralization, and resistance to the encroachments of secular rulers. A powerful Church summoned Christians to respect celibacy, the priestly administration of the sacraments, and the examples of saints and martyrs; and it disciplined those who strayed from orthodoxy. Providing access to libraries and schools, the Church trained most of Europe's intellectuals, who elaborated a rational system of theology and laid the foundations for modern philosophical, political, legal, and scientific thought.

As monarchical and ecclesiastical institutions crystallized, a new social group and setting emerged: merchants and towns. By 1300, towns stretching from the Mediterranean to the North Sea coasts housed artisans, merchants, bankers, and entrepreneurs. By 1500, their commercial ventures, extending to Africa, the Middle East, and Asia, made Europe rich and ready to expand.

9 Workers, Warriors, and Kings
Politics and Society in the Middle Ages, 800–1500

10 The Spiritual Sword
Religion and Culture in the Middle Ages, 500–1500

11 In the Name of Profit
Cities, Merchants, and Trade in the Middle Ages, 1000–1500

227

110

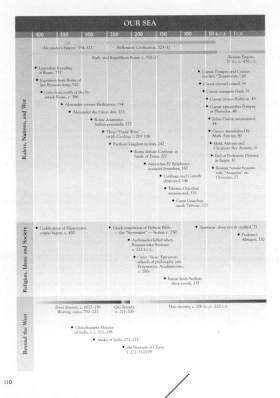

Part Opener

Western Civilization is divided into seven parts that group the chapters into a cohesive, thematic framework. Part-opening essays set the stage for discussions that follow.

Chapter Opener Timeline

Organized thematically, and arranged into color-coded sections, chapter-opening timelines show the chronology of major events and developments.

US debtor nations, 1914-25

industrial unemployment, 1931-36:

countries reaching a maximum of 15-25%

countries reaching a maximum of 26-50%

Map Opener

Map openers add a geographical and spatial dimension to each chapter's narrative. Inset maps put the the West in global perspective.

Contrasting colors, and a simple key, give clear information to ensure that the map is readily understood by students.

Map 8.1 Migrants, Raiders, and Conquerors, 100–800 C.E.: *Beginning in the first century C.E., nomadic peoples of the central Asian steppes began to expand both west and east, disrupting civilization in both the Mediterranean region and in China. China resisted determinedly, and had attained some stability by around 600. In the west, the movement of Asian peoples triggered the dispersion first of Germanic, and then of Slavic peoples, which was to cut western Europe off from the Mediterranean and the Eastern Roman Empire centered at Constantinople, and to result in the failure of Roman rule in the west. (Compare Map 6.3, p. 160, showing the region when Rome, governed from its single capital, held unquestioned dominion over the region; and Map 8.2, p. 205, showing the position of successor kingdoms to western Rome.) What attracted these invaders into the Roman Empire?*

KEY QUESTIONS

◆ **Power and Civilization:** Why did the rulers of ancient civilization wage war? What kinds of weapons and armies did they have to do so?

◆ **Bronze Age Kingdoms in Egypt and Mesopotamia:** Which of the rival states emerged victorious in Mesopotamia? How successful were Egypt's pharaohs in maintaining power?

◆ **Bronze Age Kingdoms in the Aegean and the Levant:** What were the characteristics of the Hittite and Mycenaean civilizations? What calamities beset the Levant and the Aegean around 1200 B.C.E.?

◆ **Iron Age Empires of the Middle East:** What made Assyria a particularly dangerous neighbor?

◆ **Bronze and Iron Age Kingdoms in East and South Asia:** What characteristics of later Chinese civilization emerged under the Shang, Zhou, and Qin emperors? What role did the Aryan invasion play in the development of civilization in India?

◆ **The Birth of the West:** How and why did Mycenaean rule in the Aegean region end? What kind of civilization emerged in its stead?

Key Questions

Key questions open each chapter and ask students to consider important problems before engaging with the narrative.

Maps

In each chapter, a range of colorful maps (many featuring topography) help students to place events in their geographical context. Throughout the book, they chart the political, social, and economic changes that have taken place globally during the course of Western civilization. Accompanying each map, a question asks students to interpret information and relate it to the text.

The Genealogy of Writing

Development of early writing
— pictographic
— hieroglyphic
— cuneiform
— alphabetic
— probable relationship between scripts

A system of writing was a feature of every ancient civilization. Although some still remain undeciphered, many writing systems have been decoded, enabling us to get a close-up view of life in the distant past. Writing began as pictures, or pictographs, which symbolized ideas increasingly unrelated to the object depicted. The alphabet developed from the simplified pictograph to represent not a thing but a single sound, which could be assembled with other sounds to form words. Source: R. Whitehouse and J. Wilkins, The Making of Civilization: History Discovered through Archaeology (New York: Alfred A. Knopf, 1986).

Illustrated Information

Numerous tables, charts, and graphs display information visually. Complex processes and data are presented in an easy-to-read format that facilitates student learning.

Patterns of European Economic Development: 1850–1873

	1850	1869	1873
Britain			
Railroad	6,621	15,145	16,082
Coal	37,500	97,066	112,604
Steam power	1,290		4,040
Pig iron	2,249	5,446	6,566
Raw cotton	266.8	425.8	565.1
Germany			
Railroad	3,639	10,834	14,842
Coal	5,100	26,774	36,392
Steam power	260	2,480	
Pig iron	212	1,413	2,241
Raw cotton	17.1	64.1	117.8
France			
Railroad	1,869	10,518	11,500
Coal	7,225	21,432	24,702
Steam power	370	1,850	
Pig iron	406	1,381	1,382
Raw cotton	59.3	93.7	55.4
Belgium			
Railroad	531	1,800	2,335
Coal	3,481	7,822	10,219
Steam power	70	350	
Pig iron	145	535	607
Raw cotton	10.0	16.3	18.0

By five measures of economic development—total railroad mileage (statute miles), coal production (1000 metric tons), steam power capacity (1000 horsepower), pig iron output (1000 metric tons), and raw cotton consumption (1000 metric tons)—Britain outpaced her three leading European rivals from 1850 to 1873. The gap narrowed, however, especially between Germany and Britain. Note Germany's sevenfold increase in coal production, compared to Britain's threefold increase, and Germany's sevenfold increase in cotton consumption, compared to Britain's, which slightly more than doubled. Source: Based on D. Landes, The Unbound Prometheus (Cambridge: Cambridge University Press, 1969), p. 194.

Captions give a concise overview of visually presented information.

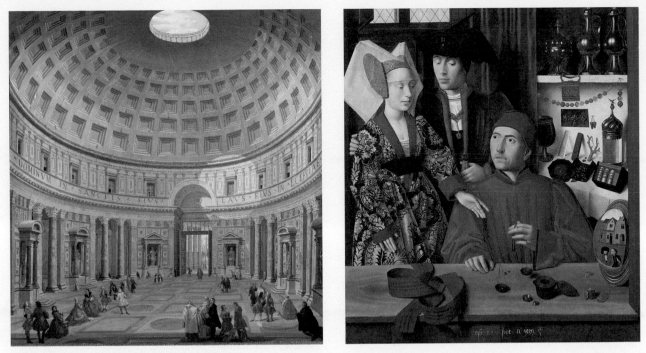

High Quality Art Reproductions

A stunning gallery of art focuses on the diverse experiences of people throughout Western history.

WINDOWS ON
Revolution in Fashion

Pre-Revolution fashion worn by the upper-middle class, 1780

Pre-Revolution dress of the working class, c.1780

The momentous changes wrought by the French Revolution are written, among other ways, in how men and women dressed before and after the event. Shown here at top left are a representative couple of the upper-middle class just prior to the Revolution. She wears an elaborate flounced and frilled dress; he a vest, jacket, and culottes, or knee-length pants, which come to an end below the knee, atop silk stockings and elegant, heeled shoes. Modest though their dress is—aristocratic and courtly fashion was much more elaborate—it would become less showy after the Revolution ran its course. To their right is a working-class couple of the same era, dressed far more simply. Note especially the man's characteristic trousers, or sans-culottes, which extend, never gathered, below the knee to the ankles. The image upper right depicts soldiers and other participants in the Revolution in 1793–1794, the year of the Reign of Terror. Only the military drummer retains the culottes of the pre-Revolutionary era. At lower left, a wealthy couple strut the latest fashion at the climactic moment of the Revolution, 1794, just

Fashion worn by the Incroyables, or Unbelievables, 1794

Revolutionaries, 1793–94

before the fall of Robespierre and the institution of the Directory. These represent the Incroyables, or Unbelievables, the fast set of Revolutionary Paris at a tricky, transitional moment. At lower right, in a parlor scene from 1839, the effects of

Revolution on fashion are displayed. The men, whether in military or sober civilian dress, now wear trousers like the proletarian sans-culottes that their ancestors would have disdained, while the woman, still beautifully attired, has moderated her frills and flounces. (top left: Private Collection; right: Costumes Historiques de la France; below left: Private Collection; Facing page, top: Private Collection; Facing page, below: Private Collection)

Did men's or women's fashions change more over these two generations? Why?

Post-Revolutionary fashion, 1839

600

601

 To continue your investigation of this topic, please go to www.prenhall.com/king for the related **WINDOWS** on the **WEB** activity

'Windows On' boxes

Windows On boxes illuminate subjects of high interest by gathering together a range of provocative visual sources.

'Windows on the Web' activities extend the scope of the Windows On feature by combining documents, images, and Web-based material to explore concepts and problems in more depth. Each Windows on the Web activity can be found at **www.prenhall.com/king**

Phalanx and Legion

The Greek Phalanx
= heavily armed infantry formed in close, deep ranks, with spears overlapping and shields touching.

The Roman Legion
= the largest unit of the Roman army, comprising 10 cohorts (400–600 men each)

1 maniple of *hastati* (approx. 100 young, heavily armed hoplites)

1 maniple of *principes* (approx. 100 hoplites of prime age)

1 maniple of *triarii* (approx. 100 veteran hoplites)

120 velites (lightly armed infantry)

30 cavalry

The Roman legion = 4000–6000 men, organized in 10 cohorts; led by 1 commander, 6 tribunes, 1 prefect, 1 legate, and 60 centurions

'How Many' *boxes*

Unique to Western Civilization, How Many? boxes present useful data clearly and visually.

Women Protest against Husbands and Predators

In the sixteenth century, women's voices were finally heard—after centuries of near silence. Their works were composed mostly in the vernacular, which unlike Latin did not require an advanced education. The printing press made possible the publication of many copies, circulated widely, as in the case of Moderata Fonte's The Worth of Women represented in the first excerpt here. Women artists, too, became more conspicuous, as in the case of Artemisia Gentileschi, represented in the second excerpt. Both women protest against the actions of men: the first, broadly and theoretically, condemning them for "usurping" women's rights; the second, concretely and particularly, testifying in a trial against a man who raped her.

A Venetian woman lambasts the tyranny of men (1592): If men usurp our rights, should we not complain and declare that they have wronged us? Or if we are their inferiors in status, but not in worth, this is an abuse that has been introduced into the world and that men have then, over time, gradually translated into law and custom; and it has become so entrenched that they claim ... that the status they have gained through their bullying is theirs by right. ... And we would suffer it. ... if they did not insist on exerting such absolute control over us and in such an arrogant manner, treating us like slaves who cannot take a step without asking their permission or say a word without their jumping down our throats. ... As fathers, as brothers, as sons or husbands or lovers or whatever other relationship they have to us, they all abuse us, humiliate us, and do all they can to harm and annihilate us.
(Moderata Fonte (Modesta da Pozzo), *The Worth of Women, Wherein is Clearly Revealed their Nobility and their Superiority to Men*, 1592; ed. and trs. V. Cox, 1997)

Artemisia Gentileschi, painter, testifies at the trial of her rapist (1612): Agostino put his head on my breast ... and said: "Let's walk together a while, because I hate sitting down." ... After we had walked around two or three times, each time going by the bedroom door, when we were in front of the bedroom door, he pushed me in and locked the door. He then threw me onto the edge of the bed, pushing me with a hand on my breast. ... Lifting my clothes, which he had a great deal of trouble doing, he placed a hand with a handkerchief at my throat and on my mouth to keep me from screaming. ... I felt a strong burning and it hurt very much, but because he held my mouth I couldn't cry out. However, I tried to scream as best I could.
I scratched his face and pulled his hair and ... I even removed a piece of flesh. ... And after he had done his business he got off me. When I saw myself free, I went to the table drawer and took a knife and moved toward Agostino saying: "I'd like to kill you with this knife because you have dishonored me."
(From M. D. Garrard, *Artemisia Gentileschi*, 1989)

'Witnesses' *boxes*

Bringing to life the events narrated in the text, authentic voices from the past provide personal accounts of social and political change. Brief headnotes introduce the documents and place them in comparative perspective.

Books and Pamphlets from the French Revolution

Emmanuel Sieyès	*What Is the Third Estate?* (1789)
Edmund Burke	*Reflections on the Revolution in France* (1790)
Olympe de Gouges	*Declaration of the Rights of Woman and the Citizen* (1791)
Tom Paine	*Rights of Man* (1791)
Mary Wollstonecraft	*A Vindication of the Rights of Woman* (1792)

Key Books by Key Leaders

Vladimir Ilyich Lenin	*What Is To Be Done?* (1902)
Adolf Hitler	*Mein Kampf (My Struggle)* (1925)
Winston Churchill	*The Speeches of Winston Churchill* (1941–1945)

'Must Reads' *boxes*

Must Reads boxes list books of exceptional importance to the meaning of the West—books students may wish to read.

Fading Empires in Africa

Patrice Lumumba (1925–1961), first premier of the state of Zaire (formerly the Congo) upon Belgian withdrawal in 1960, but assassinated by rivals in 1961.

Joseph (Sese Seko) Mobutu (1930–1997), seized power in Zaire after Lumumba's death, and held it for 32 years, with US support.

Kwame Nkrumah (1909–1972), pan-Africanist prime minister of Ghana upon its independence in 1957, and president in 1960; ousted by a military coup in 1967.

Robert Mugabe (1924–), Marxist leader of Rhodesian revolutionary party which ousted prime minister Ian Smith; became head of nation re-named Zimbabwe.

Desmond Tutu (1931–), South African Anglican archbishop who aroused world outrage against the segregationist apartheid policy of the white Afrikaner government of South Africa; winner of the 1984 Nobel Prize.

Nelson Mandela (1918–), leader of African National Congress imprisoned in 1964 and released in 1960; in 1994, won election to the presidency of South Africa.

Muammar el-Qaddafi (1942–), seized power in Libya in 1969 after toppling the pro-Western monarchy, nationalizing foreign petroleum assets, and, during the Cold War, accepting Soviet aid and arms.

'Who's Who' *boxes*

Important figures are identified and listed in Who's Who boxes, and their principal contributions noted.

Conclusion

THE EARLIEST CIVILIZATIONS AND THE MEANING OF THE WEST

Much of what distinguishes human life today was first attained by the ancient people of the first civilizations. The ability to control nature, to manage food production, to build cities, to conduct trade, to develop technology, to understand science and mathematics, to create works of literature, to establish systems of law, and to ask thoughtful questions about the cosmos and our place in it—all of these were bequeathed to later generations by the first civilizations, and to the "West" specifically by the ancient civilizations of the Middle East. These civilizations offer lessons as well about the organization of the state and the fragility of power. The next chapter will consider this other dimension of life in antiquity.

'Conclusion' *boxes*

Conclusion boxes look at how the events discussed in each chapter influenced the course of Western civilization, and provide insights into their consequences.

Stone, Bronze, and Word, 2 million–500 B.C.E. **29**

QUESTIONS TO CONSIDER

1. What would you consider to be the most important biological or behavioral change in the evolution of the human species from hominid to *homo sapiens*?

2. How would you explain the very rapid development in human skills and social organization since the last Ice Age?

3. The earliest civilizations in human history all grew up in river valleys. What opportunities or challenges did that location present to those societies?

4. Why is the possession of the skill of writing seen as an essential benchmark of civilization?

5. What are the questions that ancient peoples asked to which myth and religion gave answers?

SUGGESTED RESOURCES

Bergmann, Martin S., *In the Shadow of Moloch: The Sacrifice of Children and its Impact on Western Religions* (New York: Columbia University Press, 1991). An eye-opening account of the ritual convention of child sacrifice and its shaping of ancient cultures.

Burkert, Walter, *Creation of the Sacred: Tracks of Biology in Early Religions* (Cambridge MA: Harvard University Press, 1996). Proposes that ancient religious practices are a natural and perhaps necessary development from human biology, thus explaining the universality of many features of religion, such as the practice of sacrifice and a sense of guilt.

Cavalli-Sforza, Luigi Luca, *Genes, Peoples, and Languages*, trans. Mark Seielstad (New York: Farrar, Straus & Giroux; North Point Press, 2000). Linking complex genetic and linguistic evidence, Cavalli-Sforza proposes to map the history of the migrations of all the world's peoples.

Cross, Frank Moore, *Canaanite Myth and Hebrew Epic: Essays in the History of the Religion of Israel* (Cambridge, MA.: Harvard University Press, 1973; reprint 1997). Traces continuities between early Israelite religion and its underlying Canaanite culture. Explores re-emergence of Canaanite mythic material in the apocalypticism of early Christianity and the Dead Sea Scrolls.

Diamond, Jared, *Guns, Germs and Steel: The Fates of Human Societies* (New York: W.W. Norton, 1997). A brilliant exploration of the geographical and material conditions that permitted Eurasian civilizations to advance and gain dominance.

Fagan, Brian M., *The Journey from Eden: The Peopling of Our World* (London: Thames & Hudson, 1990). A critical overview of theories of human origin, arguing on the basis of recent historical, paleoanthropological, and genetic research that fully modern humans evolved in Africa and from there colonized the rest of the world.

Hodder, Ian, *The Domestication of Europe: Structure and Contingency in Neolithic Societies* (Cambridge, MA: Basil Blackwell, 1990). A bold if controversial attempt to reconstruct human societies in the Near East and Europe at the end of the Ice Age.

Leakey, Richard and Roger Lewin, *Origins Reconsidered: In Search of What Makes Us Human* (New York: Doubleday, 1992). Reflections of a renowned paleoanthropologist on his own discoveries of early hominid life in East Africa. Leakey incorporates ideas from philosophy, anthropology, molecular biology, and linguistics to investigate not only how we evolved anatomically but how we acquired the qualities that make us human: consciousness, creativity, and culture.

Leeming, David A., & Jake Page, *Goddess: The Myths of the Female Divine* (Oxford: Oxford University Press, 1994). A biography of the "goddess," the compelling, commanding, threatening female divinity revered by human populations from the Ice Age to modern times, showing how ancient themes endure in modern religion and psychology.

Leick, Gwendolyn, *Mesopotamia: the Invention of the City* (London: Allen Lane, 2001; rpt. Penguin, 2003). Elicits from the evidence of textiles, jeweled artifacts, and literary texts the structure and interactions of the world's first cities.

Martin, Henri Jean (trans. Lydia G. Cochrane), *The History and Power of Writing* (Chicago: University of Chicago Press, 1995). A comprehensive study by a preeminent scholar of the book. Examines the technologies, forms, and structures of writing throughout history.

McElvaine, Robert S., *Eve's Seed: Biology, the Sexes, and the Course of History* (New York: McGraw Hill, 2000). Fills in the history between the culmination of human evolution and the establishment of civilization, a period when women's role was dominant before envious men overturned power relations.

Nissen, Hans J., *The Early History of the Ancient Near East, 9000–2000 B.C.* (Chicago: University of Chicago Press, 1988). A balanced political and cultural history of Mesopotamia, based on archaeological sources and analysis of material culture.

The Indus Valley civilization:
http://www.historyofindia.com/indus.html
http://www.harappa.com/har/har0.html

The Analects of Confucius:
http://classics.mit.edu/Confucius/analects.html

Bible tools—text and history:
http://bible.crosswalk.com

💿 **Western Civilization Documents CD-ROM**

1.1 New Theories about Human Development
1.2 An Egyptian Hymn to the Nile
1.3 The Epic of Gilgamesh
1.4 Hammurabi's Law Code
1.7 The Instruction of the Ptah-hotep

End of chapter matter

Review Questions stimulate critical thought and understanding. A list of documents on the Documents CD-ROM, correlated by chapter, provides students with opportunities for further inquiry. Suggested Resources direct students to further study by recommending books and websites.

SUPPLEMENTS FOR

WESTERN CIVILIZATION

Third Edition

PRINT SUPPLEMENTS

The Instructor's Manual with Test Item File combines teaching resources with testing material. The Instructor's manual includes chapter outlines, overviews, key concepts, discussion questions, and audiovisual resources. The Test Item File offers a menu of multiple choice, true-false, essay, and map questions for each chapter. A collection of blank maps can be photocopied and used for map testing or other class exercises.

History Notes (Volumes I and II) provides, for each chapter, a list of chapter objectives, study exercises, and multiple-choice, short-answer, and essay questions. In addition, each chapter includes a number of specific map questions and exercises.

 Produced in collaboration within Dorling Kindersley, **The Prentice Atlas of Western Civilization** includes approximately 100 maps fundamental to the study of world history—from early hominids to the twenty-first century.

Documents in Western Civilization (Volumes I and II) is a collection of additional primary source documents that underscore the themes outlined in the text. Each document is accompanied by a headnote and study questions.

Prentice Hall is pleased to provide adopters of *Western Civilization* with an opportunity to recreate significant discounts when copies of the text are bundled with titles from the prestigious Penguin Classics Series.

Transparencies provide instructors with full-color transparency actetates of all maps, charts, and graphs in the text for use in the classroom.

Understanding and Answering Essay Questions suggests helpful analytical tools for understanding different types of essay questions, and provides precise guidelines for preparing well-crafted essay answers.

Reading Critically About History This brief guide prepares students with helpful strategies for reading a history textbook.

MEDIA RESOURCES

The Companion Website™
www.prenhall.com/king
The Companion Website™ works in tandem with the text to help students use the Internet to enrich their understanding of Western civilization. Built around the primary subtopics of each chapter, it includes study questions, map exercises, and "Windows on the Web" activities.

Western Civilization Documents CD-ROM Bound in every new copy of *Western Civilization*, and organized by the main periods in history, the Western Civilization Documents CD-ROM contains over 200 primary sources in an easily-navigable PDF file. Each document is accompanied by essay questions that allow students to read the sources via the CD-ROM and respond online via a dedicated website.

Prentice Hall OneSearch with Research Navigator: History 2005 This brief guide focuses on developing critical-thinking skills necessary for evaluating and using online sources. It provides a brief introduction to navigating the Internet with specific references to History web sites. It also provides an access code and instruction on using Research Navigator, a powerful research tool that provides access to three exclusive databases of reliable source material: ContentSelect Academic Journal Database, the New York Times Search by Subject Archive, and Link Library.

 Prentice Hall Western Civilization Image Library Bringing together over 1000 images—many never before digitized—this innovative new CD-ROM organizes images of fine art, culture, photographs, posters, and cartoons, allowing instructors to efficiently export the material into customized PowerPoint lectures or other presentation platforms.

Test Manager a commerical-quality computerized, test management program is available for Windows and Macintosh environments. This allows instructors to select items from the Test Item File in the Instructor's Manual and design their own exams.

PART ONE
BEFORE THE WEST

The Inhabited World from the First Civilizations to Alexander the Great (d. 323 B.C.E.)

The Western world has not always existed; in fact, it is rather new. Many things needed to happen before there was a "West." It was necessary for the human species to evolve from earlier primates; to learn to grow food and live in villages; and to develop the first civilizations. Those civilizations formed about five to six thousand years ago far away from Europe (the heartland of the "West") in Asia and Africa. They are recognized by certain features: a high level of organization; a political system, or state, ruled by kings or priests; technical achievements such as the crafting of bronze metal implements or the use of the wheel; the ability to write, and so to record knowledge and remember the past. Even when living in simpler communities, people had demonstrated advanced skills and a creative imagination; but the capacity of peoples in the earliest civilizations to invent tools, organize systems, store information, and express feeling, beliefs, and ideas immeasurably expanded the possibilities of life for human beings everywhere in the world.

Several other civilizations emerged through contact with these earliest civilizations (while at least two, in China and the Americas, developed independently). One was that of the Israelites, whose worship of a single just God distinguished them from many of their neighbors. Another was that of the Greeks, although its characteristic forms developed some centuries later. From their mythological traditions, the Greeks developed philosophy, science, and drama, while modern concepts of the state and people's rights derive from the unique model of the Greek city. The beliefs of the Israelites and ideas of the Greeks would count among the cultural foundations of the West.

In the fourth century B.C.E., Alexander the Great of Macedonia conquered the cities of Greece, and the empires of Persia and Egypt. Under his successors Greek civilization became established throughout the ancient Mediterranean world.

1 Stone, Bronze, and Word
Prehistory and Early Civilizations, 2m–500 B.C.E.

2 Armies and Empires
Politics and Power in the Bronze and Iron Ages, 3500–300 B.C.E.

3 The Greek *Polis*
The New Politics of Ancient Greece, 1000–300 B.C.E.

4 The School of Hellas
Poetry, Ideas, and the Arts in Ancient Greece, 800–300 B.C.E.

STONE, BRONZE, AND WORD

	2.5m	100,000	10,000	5000	3500	3000	2500	2000	1500	1000	500 B.C.E.*

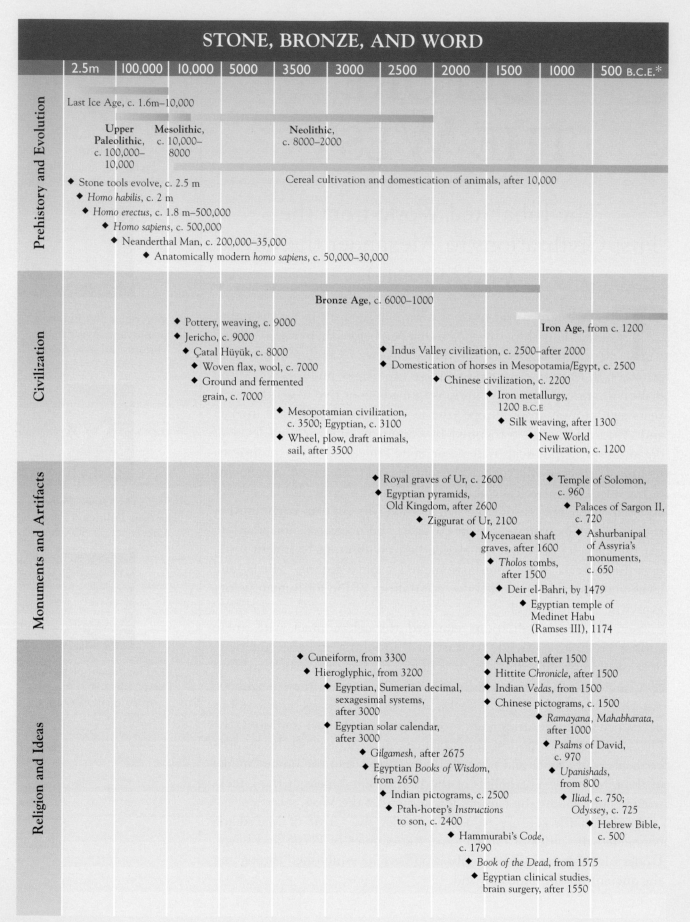

Prehistory and Evolution

Last Ice Age, c. 1.6m–10,000

Upper Paleolithic, c. 100,000–10,000 **Mesolithic,** c. 10,000–8000 **Neolithic,** c. 8000–2000

◆ Stone tools evolve, c. 2.5 m

Cereal cultivation and domestication of animals, after 10,000

◆ *Homo habilis*, c. 2 m

◆ *Homo erectus*, c. 1.8 m–500,000

◆ *Homo sapiens*, c. 500,000

◆ Neanderthal Man, c. 200,000–35,000

◆ Anatomically modern *homo sapiens*, c. 50,000–30,000

Civilization

Bronze Age, c. 6000–1000

Iron Age, from c. 1200

◆ Pottery, weaving, c. 9000

◆ Jericho, c. 9000

◆ Çatal Hüyük, c. 8000

◆ Indus Valley civilization, c. 2500–after 2000

◆ Woven flax, wool, c. 7000

◆ Domestication of horses in Mesopotamia/Egypt, c. 2500

◆ Ground and fermented grain, c. 7000

◆ Chinese civilization, c. 2200

◆ Iron metallurgy, 1200 B.C.E

◆ Mesopotamian civilization, c. 3500; Egyptian, c. 3100

◆ Silk weaving, after 1300

◆ Wheel, plow, draft animals, sail, after 3500

◆ New World civilization, c. 1200

Monuments and Artifacts

◆ Royal graves of Ur, c. 2600

◆ Temple of Solomon, c. 960

◆ Egyptian pyramids, Old Kingdom, after 2600

◆ Palaces of Sargon II, c. 720

◆ Ziggurat of Ur, 2100

◆ Mycenaean shaft graves, after 1600

◆ Ashurbanipal of Assyria's monuments, c. 650

◆ *Tholos* tombs, after 1500

◆ Deir el-Bahri, by 1479

◆ Egyptian temple of Medinet Habu (Ramses III), 1174

Religion and Ideas

◆ Cuneiform, from 3300

◆ Alphabet, after 1500

◆ Hieroglyphic, from 3200

◆ Hittite *Chronicle*, after 1500

◆ Egyptian, Sumerian decimal, sexagesimal systems, after 3000

◆ Indian *Vedas*, from 1500

◆ Chinese pictograms, c. 1500

◆ Egyptian solar calendar, after 3000

◆ *Ramayana, Mahabharata,* after 1000

◆ *Gilgamesh*, after 2675

◆ *Psalms* of David, c. 970

◆ Egyptian *Books of Wisdom*, from 2650

◆ *Upanishads*, from 800

◆ Indian pictograms, c. 2500

◆ *Iliad*, c. 750; *Odyssey*, c. 725

◆ Ptah-hotep's *Instructions* to son, c. 2400

◆ Hebrew Bible, c. 500

◆ Hammurabi's *Code*, c. 1790

◆ *Book of the Dead*, from 1575

◆ Egyptian clinical studies, brain surgery, after 1550

*Before Common Era
Note: timelines illustrate only major periods, movements, and events covered in the chapter or part.

1

STONE, BRONZE, AND WORD

Prehistory and Early Civilizations

2 MILLION–500 B.C.E.

core areas of earliest civilizations

KEY QUESTIONS

◆ **Before History:** Where and when did the human species come into existence? How did humans live, and what tools, crafts, and technologies did they invent?

◆ **Civilization and the City:** Where did civilizations begin, and why? What are the necessary ingredients of a civilization?

◆ **Writing, Language, and Consciousness:** Why did people invent writing, and how did they use it?

◆ **From Sacrifice to Conscience:** What did ancient peoples believe about the cosmos? What gods, spirits, or forces controlled it, and how could humans approach them?

The Unbinding of Isaac An old man, Abraham, led his cherished son Isaac to a hilltop, obedient to the God who had ordered him long ago to leave the land of his birth. He drew a knife and laid wood for the fire, in preparation for the unimaginable deed he had been commanded to do. The deity demanded a sacrifice, Abraham's son must die. Satisfied by Abraham's steadfastness, and before the slaughter could take place, God sent a messenger to tell Abraham that he should set the child free. Abraham seized a ram caught in a nearby thicket, sacrificed the animal, and released his child.

Written down nearly 3000 years ago, this story originated even earlier, not long after the appearance of the first human **civilization**. It is recorded in the Bible (Genesis 22:1–13), known also as the Hebrew Bible, the Old Testament, Scripture ("what is written"), or the Word, the fundamental book of the Western world. The story of Abraham and Isaac marks a key moment in the civilizing process. The value of human life, the strength of human love, the power of the will are all recognized in that moment when Isaac was rescued from the sacrificial knife. The unbinding of Isaac is preconditioned by the spiritual, or psychological, unbinding of Abraham. Freed from the fear of the unknown that drove his contemporaries to placate the gods, Abraham may trust, love, reflect, and choose between good and evil.

By the time the story of Abraham and Isaac was recorded, at least some members of the human **species** had completed one phase of a long journey, and entered the era of civilization: they had settled in villages and cities, used metal tools and weapons, learned to write and, equipped with words, to reason about the human condition. That journey extended over the vast expanse of time that had passed since the first appearance on earth of the human species about 500,000 years before. It is the subject of this chapter.

BEFORE HISTORY

The universe began some 15 billion years ago. The planet Earth took form as long as 4.5 billion years ago. The first living cells developed nearly 4 billion years ago. About halfway into the last billion years the first animals walked on land—dinosaurs and early mammals. About 65 million years ago, the mammals flourished, evolving in many ways. Some 55 million years ago, the first primates appeared, the group of mammals to which humans belong. Between 5 and 6 million years ago evolved the first human-like primate (or **hominid**). This critical development occurred in Africa in the Old World, the land mass made up of the three continents of Africa, Asia, and Europe.

The Arrival of the Human Being

The increased size of fossil skulls tells us that between 1 and 2 million years ago, these African hominids developed significantly larger brains. This distinction identified a new being, recognizably human and thus called by the genus name *Homo*—Latin for "man" or "human." The first species of human was called **Homo habilis** or "skilled man," which referred to the ability to make tools from stone. The second, **Homo erectus**, was so called because scientists at first believed that this was the first primate to walk on two legs, with a fully upright posture. It is now known that earlier hominids had also walked in this way.

Homo sapiens, or "wise man," probably evolved from *Homo erectus*. Until recently it was believed that *Homo sapiens* developed independently in several parts of the world, from populations of *Homo erectus* that had migrated from Africa. Today it is generally believed that *Homo sapiens* originated only in Africa, as many as 2 million years ago, or as few as 200,000 years ago. Many authorities put the date at about 500,000 years ago (see *How Many?*).

Homo sapiens had a body and brain like ours. His hands were equipped with a prehensile thumb more dexterous than that of his primate ancestors, which could grasp and manipulate tools to do work. His brain could link words with ideas to create language. He could chip rock into a hatchet to kill his prey, or wield two sticks to start a fire in which to roast his victim. She could gather fruits and grains found growing wild to share with her mate and her children, whom she kept close by her longer than mothers in the animal kingdom.

The evolution of early forms of *Homo* and their migration to the Middle East, Asia, and Europe

HOW MANY?

From Then to Now

Approximate years B.C.E. (Before Common Era)

15,000,000,000	birth of the universe
4–5,000,000,000	formation of the earth
500,000,000	first land animals
55,000,000	first primates
6–5,000,000	first hominids
2,000,000	*Homo habilis*
1,800,000	*Homo erectus*
last 500,000	*Homo sapiens*
last 50,000–30,000	anatomically modern *Homo sapiens*

occurred during the Stone Age, so named after the material—pebbles and stones—from which humans made the tools used to hunt and dig and defend themselves. The Stone Age, which extends from about 2.5 million to 5000 years ago, is further divided into "old," "middle," and "new" periods. Using Greek terms, scientists refer to these respectively as Paleolithic, Mesolithic, and Neolithic. The **Paleolithic** was by far the longest, reaching to within 10,000 years of our own time.

Toward the end of the Paleolithic period, "Neanderthal man" appeared, probably a distinct species of *Homo* rather than a sub species of *Homo sapiens*. They were named after the Neander Valley in western Germany where their skeletal remains were first found. Neanderthalers lived scattered throughout Europe and southwest Asia, from perhaps 200,000 to 35,000 years ago. They made their homes in caves, hunted in packs, and appeased the spirits of nature— so the evidence suggests—with ceremonies that have left traces in the heaps of skulls and bones of the bears they revered. They gathered around fires, wore clothing, and buried their dead with tools and ornaments to accompany them to the afterworld. Their behavior implies a belief in a form of afterlife. Beginning with the Neanderthals, human beings have known that they are born to die, and that awareness shaped their culture. The rite of burial marks the appearance of religion within the human population.

Undisputably a form of *Homo sapiens* were the Cro-Magnon humans, so called after the site in southern France where their remains were first discovered. When they evolved at least 30,000 years ago, similar anatomically modern humans had already emerged in Africa and Asia. But European Cro-Magnons were extraordinarily creative. They used tools more refined than those of the Neanderthalers. They sewed clothes from animal skins, using needles of bone. They crafted statuettes of plump women with exaggerated breasts and bellies, who may have represented the source of life and new birth. Cro-Magnon artists adorned their cave walls with paintings of beasts whom the hunters had vanquished, or wished to vanquish. Some of the finest of these cave paintings can be seen at Lascaux, in France, illustrated on p. 6 and Altamira, in Spain. They bear witness to the emerging creative power of the human mind.

With Cro-Magnon humans, and their counterparts around the world, the evolution of humankind, as it exists today, was nearly complete. The human species that dominates the earth today is technically called *Homo sapiens sapiens*, indicating a supreme level of intelligence; some scientists prefer the term "anatomically modern *Homo sapiens*." Nevertheless, modern humans have learned to apply that brainpower in ever more sophisticated ways. Intelligence is essential to human nature, creating the capacity for **culture** or learned behavior, including social customs, religion, language, and the arts. Their capacity for culture distinguishes human beings from their close relatives, the apes—even more so than a dexterous thumb or an erect posture.

As humans evolved, so did the conditions in which they lived. Between about 1.6 million and 10,000 years ago, the Arctic ice cap repeatedly expanded over the land masses of the northern hemisphere. During this period, called the Pleistocene era, glaciers flowed into the valleys of the temperate zones of Asia, Europe, and North America. These ice ages made life hard for humans and animals alike, and they often migrated in search of warmer climes. The spread of glaciers also resulted in low sea levels, as ice deposits on the land surface stole water from the rivers and oceans. Coastal areas extended farther into the sea than they do today, and land outcroppings or bridges that have since disappeared under the sea made possible the human colonization of Australia and the Western Hemisphere—every continent except Antarctica.

Settling Down

The final recession of the ice cap, around 10,000 years ago, was a turning point in the evolution of human culture. As the climate warmed, human beings entered a new phase of their development—the **Neolithic**, or New Stone Age. During this era, they made important discoveries which radically changed their way of living and laid the foundations for the development of civilization. These achievements of the Neolithic age, made gradually over millennia, cumulatively amount to the most dramatic change in the way human beings lived until the modern era.

Foremost among the discoveries of the Neolithic period are farming and animal husbandry. In early human communities men hunted for food and the women gathered it: picking fruits from trees and bushes, gleaning grain from fields sown with seeds borne by animals or wind, digging edible roots from the earth. For almost all of human history, food was found in grassland or forest, growing wild or running free. Only recently have foodstuffs been deliberately cultivated. In the 5000 years after the end of the last Ice Age (about 10,000 years ago), human beings learned to control the plant and animal resources upon which their survival depended. That process is called "domestication."

It was probably a woman who first observed that a kernel she had neglected to pick and that happened to fall on soft, damp soil, soon germinated and formed a new plant. Countless people may have observed that process before one of them thought to break up the earth with a tool—probably only a stick—and sow it with grain. When she did so, agriculture began. It was a discovery of monumental importance for the human species. Now human beings—driven, perhaps,

Bull Worship: *The religious rituals of early peoples are not completely understood. We do know that tens of thousands of years ago and all over the globe, they revered figures representing fertility—male and female, human and animal, such as these powerful bulls painted on a cave wall in southern France by a Neolithic hunter about 100 centuries before civilization began. (Lascaux, France, 16,000–10,000 B.C.E.)*

by the overpopulation of their homeland into areas less productive—could cultivate the land, produce their own food, settle in one place, form stable communities, and increase in population. These were the preconditions of further achievements.

Agriculture was first enduringly established in the highlands of the Middle East after 8000 B.C.E. Fields of wheat, millet, oats, and, especially, barley fed the growing population of that region. The cultivation of these and a variety of other crops extended gradually into Asia Minor, southeast Europe, northern Africa, and Asia.

Three to four thousand years later, inhabitants of northern China and the Indus Valley and of The Americas, independently discovered how to sow and harvest. They grew wheat, millet, and rice in Asia, maize (corn) and potatoes in the Americas. From these centers, agricultural technology spread around the globe and eventually to nearly all its inhabitants—all but the fraction of about 1 percent who still live in hunting-and-gathering communities.

Neolithic farmers prepared their grains—ancestors of the kinds consumed today—to make a palatable food by boiling, soaking, pounding, and grinding them, as is known from the grinding stones discovered in several sites. They stewed the grains in water to form a porridge, molded them into a loaf or a cake for baking, and brewed them to make a fermented sludge, the precursor of modern beer. For thousands of years in all the civilizations of the globe, such foodstuffs were the basis, or staple, of the human diet.

Perhaps even before the first grain crops were cultivated, some animals had been trained and bred to suit the needs of human masters. Donkeys and horses learned to accept a bit, and dogs to follow the hunt. Early attempts to domesticate other animals, such as stags, antelopes, and lions, failed; and many centuries passed before the camel was tamed. But other animals—cows, goats, sheep, pigs, and fowl— soon proved their usefulness. Herding animals for later slaughter was an alternative to hunting. Beasts intended for future consumption grazed in open pastures or ate plant foods grown for their fodder. Sheep and cows, goats and pigs provided early livestock farmers, or pastoralists, with clothing and milk as well as meat. Eventually, humans learned to use strong animals, such as oxen, water buffalo, and horses, to haul loads and help them with their work.

Caring for crops and animals entailed a new way of life for the first farmers. They settled down in one place. They built shelters close to the fields, using the reeds and clay or timber and stones of the land about them. They clustered into communities larger than the groups of thirty or so persons whose tasks had been simply to hunt and gather. The new villagers numbered in the hundreds, even the thousands.

Traces of Neolithic villages exist in the Middle East at Jericho (9000 B.C.E., Jordan River valley), Jarmo (7000 B.C.E., modern Iraq), and Çatal Hüyük in Asia Minor (8000 B.C.E, modern Turkey). These may have been the first villages. By 8000 B.C.E. in Jericho, closely packed, round, mud-brick houses covered 4 acres (1.6 ha.) and housed a population of around 2000. For defense against invasion by wild beasts or other humans, the residents erected walls; these measured nearly 10 feet (3 m.) thick and 12 feet (3.6 m.)

Mother Goddesses

Hittite and Minoan art:
The numerous prehistoric figurines of female figures promising fertility (see also p. 3) reappeared in more sophisticated form thousands of years later. Shown here are two figures from the Bronze Age: a Hittite bronze statuette of a mother with child (left) and a decorated earthenware (faience) figure depicting a Minoan snake goddess, or attendant, from Knossos, c. 1600 B.C.E. (below). (below: Archaeological Museum, Herakleion, Crete)

Mother and child *(left),*
Horoztepe, c. 2100–2000
B.C.E.

The Diet of Early Civilizations

Middle East	barley, wheat, rye, lentils
China	rice, millet, soy beans
Africa	yam, millet, rice, sorghum
Americas	cocoa, maize (corn), tomatoes

accessed via a ladder through a window or roof opening. Within, religious worship seems to have been organized around a building (forty shrines on nine building levels) apparently designed for that purpose. The inhabitants adorned their temple with the heads of bulls and triple images of a fertility goddess in her youth, prime, and old age.

Artisans and Specialists

Of the human inhabitants of the globe, a small fraction were now farmers, herders, and villagers, better fed, housed, and protected than their hunting and gathering forebears. Soon these communities began to develop technical skills which enabled them to make their lives more comfortable and secure. The most competent or powerful assumed positions of leadership and undertook the task of placating the gods.

To store the products of their harvests, early farmers devised baskets and pots made of the same materials, reeds and clay, that they used to build their huts. The development of pottery skills—a major advance, as pots could be used to store grain and liquids—took place some 8000 years ago in the Old World zones of advanced human culture, from North Africa to Japan. In the Americas this innovation came independently and later—at around 2000 B.C.E.

Potters then learned to shape their products on a turning wheel—an object used for this purpose even before it was used as a means of transport. They learned to select the best clay and to make the clay vessels harder and more durable by heating them at a certain temperature for the right length of time. They took the time to decorate the clay before firing, producing useful vessels that were also works of art. When villages disappeared,

high, and were guarded from a watchtower. In the seventh millennium—that is, in the thousand-year period from 7000 to 6000 B.C.E.—the smaller village of Jarmo, perched on a hillside in the Zagros Mountains, boasted a watchtower rising to a height of 40 feet (12 m.), built of stone and set in stone walls.

Çatal Hüyük sprawled over 32 acres (13 ha.) and had a population of between 5000 and 7000 by the sixth millennium B.C.E. Here archaeologists have unearthed evidence of woven cloth, intricate stone weaponry, and technically advanced pottery. The crafters of these goods lived in a complex of connected homes, each

Minoan snake goddess, Knossos,
c. 1600 B.C.E.

Map 1.1 Agriculture and Urbanization: From the Neolithic Era to the Era of the First Civilizations: *After the icecap began to recede about 10,000 years ago, farming spread to every part of the globe. Where the crops were most abundant, some people were freed from farm labor for other tasks. Here advanced civilizations began at four different points and times: Mesopotamia, Egypt, India, and China. Why did these civilizations all take form along river valleys?*

fragments of the pots were buried in the soil underneath ash and dust and stone. Archaeologists today read in these deposits a record of the inhabitants' ways of life.

Other workers learned to process plant or animal fibers to form linen, cotton, wool, and (in China) silk, spinning the fibers into thread, then weaving them into cloth. Both of these textile-manufacturing tasks were nearly always performed by women. Spinning was accomplished by first wrapping a raw fiber around a simple stick, the distaff, then drawing a strand from the distaff and winding it onto a turning, weighted stick, the spindle. The thread could then be woven into cloth. A simple loom allowed the first weavers to craft both plain fabrics and more intricately patterned textiles. Villagers could put aside the animal skins that had warmed their ancestors and clothe themselves in light and flexible fabric.

Spinning, weaving, and sewing were women's work. In those early pre-agricultural communities where distinctions of sex roles were already established, women contributed as gatherers to feeding the family. As in traditional societies today, they may have provided 60 to 80 percent of the food supply. Women's role changed upon crossing the threshold to an agricultural society. Now men took on the jobs of farming—the hard work of herding and plowing (for the ox-drawn plow soon replaced the woman's hoe). Women took responsibility for the household and its numerous tasks: textile production, food preparation, water carrying, and the bearing and rearing of children.

This simple division of labor into farming and domestic work was gradually replaced by a more complex one, as some people became specialists in particular tasks. Among them were potters and tool-makers. While other villagers farmed and herded, the labor of these experts was freed for the highly skilled work that they alone could perform. Other specialists also emerged: managers who coordinated village labor; warriors, expert in fighting; priests who proclaimed the will of the gods.

Neolithic peoples feared and revered forces of nature with an attitude we call "worship." Those terrifying forces included the shifting winds and recurrent sun, flood and fire, lightning and thunder, the sheer heights of trees and mountains, the mysterious depths of caves, the new life of the springtime, and the inexplicable phenomenon of human birth from the body of a woman—all these were recognized as the work of a god. Gods had their own concerns. But human beings could summon their attention with gifts, with **icons**, with charms, with chants.

In this regard Neolithic people differed little from their Paleolithic ancestors, whose caves and graves yield evidence of artifacts used to claim the attention of the gods. Some ancient peoples revered the bull as an emblem of potency and painted or sculpted images of the beast. Others worshiped a goddess whose good will furthered both human and plant fertility. Archaeological sites worldwide have yielded a harvest of little statues of goddesses or magical figures, endowed with ample breasts, hips, and abdomens and sometimes shown in the act of suckling or giving birth (two examples are shown on p. 7). The bodies of these "Venuses" (so called later after the Roman goddess of love) symbolize the power of women to bring forth life and, by extension, the power of nature to provide all things bountifully.

To possess such images and to please the spirits they represented was the core of early religion. Some men and women took on the role of communicating the will of the gods and arranging for its fulfillment. These were the priests and priestesses, shamans or medicine men, prophets and prophetesses who mediated between the divine and the human. Since their services were thought to be necessary if the fields were to bear fruit and if new generations of human beings were to be born, priests and priestesses held special status in Neolithic societies. They remained important in the civilizations that soon emerged.

CIVILIZATION AND THE CITY

About 6000 years ago, some complex Neolithic societies crossed the threshold between pre-history and history and formed the first civilizations. These societies consisted of concentrated populations, a complex social organization, and advanced technical skills. Their peoples joined together to drain or irrigate the soil, to sow and harvest and serve the gods, as directed by their priests. They lived in walled cities, ruled by kings and defended by armies. They built temples, tombs, and palaces for gods and rulers, and lived in families that resembled ours. Their more efficient farming yielded a surplus of food, so that some workers were freed to pursue other tasks. They began to forge metals—first bronze, then iron—into weapons and tools, and they learned to write. Now they could use language to keep records of their possessions and lists of their kings; and soon, to convey their visions, fears, and longings, to speculate about the cosmos, and to develop moral thought.

The First Civilizations

As the chart on p. 10 shows, civilizations developed at different times at five points on the globe: in four river valleys of the Old World and on the coasts of the New World. The earliest of these arose in the river valleys of the Middle East—an area reaching from the Nile to the Tigris and Euphrates rivers and called the Fertile Crescent: the first in Mesopotamia (modern Iraq), around 3500 B.C.E.; the second in Egypt, around 3000 B.C.E. Another civilization arose around 2500 B.C.E. in the valley of the Indus River, in south Asia (in modern Pakistan), and around 2200 B.C.E. a further Asian civilization developed in the valley of the Yellow River (Huang He) (in modern China). In c. 1200 B.C.E. the first **Amerindian** civilizations developed along the Pacific coast of South America and in Mexico (see Chapter 8).

From the nuclei of the first four Old World civilizations developed all the subsequent civilizations of Afro-Eurasia and their offspring in the New World, Australia, and Oceania. The first New World civilizations were succeeded by later and more splendid Amerindian empires.

But what about the West? Paradoxically, the civilization we call "Western" did not begin in the West: not in Europe, where its culture was refined, nor in the Western Hemisphere whose Amerindian civilizations Westerners would later destroy (see Chapter 16). "Western" civilization, rather, derives from the civilizations of ancient Asia (Mesopotamia) and Africa (Egypt). During the first three millennia of the history of civilization, Europe lagged far behind these areas in development.

In the valleys formed by the Tigris and Euphrates (the region called Mesopotamia) and Nile rivers, the soil was potentially very fertile. Crops would grow abundantly in the hot climate, but only if they had the right amount of water. In both regions, the crucial task of water management required coordinated labor.

In Egypt, where rainfall was practically unknown, the Nile River made a fertile valley of what would otherwise be a parched and sterile desert. The Nile flooded its banks every summer and receded every fall. This inundation created a green strip on both banks about 15 miles (24 km.) wide. Here plant and animal life flourished, ripe for human exploitation. The deposit of alluvial soil formed an ideal bed for the cultivation of grains, which Egypt produced in quantities so great that its surplus regularly fed other peoples of the ancient world.

To take full advantage of the Nile waters, the Egyptians developed a system of storage pools. When the land was flooded, peasants rowed around to these pools, shutting the vents to trap some of the water. After the river had receded, the plowing and sowing took place, as shown on p. 12, under the direction of supervisors; keeping the growing crops watered entailed carrying water from the pools to the fields. Although much hard labor was involved, the reliability of the annual flood enabled the Egyptians to farm efficiently and productively. Writing in the fifth century B.C.E. the Greek historian Herodotus described the good fortune of the Egyptians (somewhat oversimplifying the case): "They obtain the fruits of the field with less trouble than any other people in the world … the husbandman waits till the river has of its own accord spread itself over the fields and withdrawn again to its bed, and he sows his plot of ground … after which he has only to await the harvest." Benefitting from this bountiful harvest, the Egyptian population tripled between 3000 and 1250 B.C.E.

Mesopotamian peasants faced a tougher task. Unlike the Nile, the Tigris and Euphrates rivers flooded unpredictably, furiously, and dangerously. When they were calm, it was necessary to carry water

The First Civilizations

Civilization	Time	Continent/Region	Waterway	Features
Mesopotamia	after 3500 B.C.E.	Asia	Tigris and Euphrates Rivers	ziggurat, Hammurabi's *Code*
Egypt	after 3100 B.C.E.	Africa	Nile River	pyramid, *Book of the Dead*
Indus	after 2500 B.C.E.	Asia	Indus River	citadels and bathhouses, mother goddess
China	after 2200 B.C.E.	Asia	Yellow River	bronze ritual vessels, Confucius
Olmec	after 1200 B.C.E.	Mesoamerica		temples, giant head monuments

or channel it from the river to the fields. Laborers constructed dams to hold back the flood-waters and canals to channel them. Managers and foremen organized the workforce for the diverse jobs of sowing and harvesting, building, and irrigation.

The Earliest Cities

True cities developed in all the early civilizations. They housed large populations, with distinct groups of rulers and workers. They were surrounded by walls which encompassed palace or temple complexes as well as the homes of ordinary families. In these cities artisans pursued their crafts. They learned to forge bronze and, later, to cast iron to make tools and weapons. This was the first major technological innovation since a human being first used a stone to kill a beast or ward off an enemy.

By the early third millennium B.C.E., the Sumerians, the founders of the first civilization in southern Mesopotamia, dominated the southern zone of the Tigris-Euphrates Valley from a dozen walled city-states. The walls of the city of Uruk, which by 2700 B.C.E. had a population of about 50,000 people, had a circumference of over 5 miles (8 km.), and its inner ramparts were more than 12 feet (3.6 m.) thick. The city of Ur was enclosed by thick walls, with a circumference of more than a mile (1.6 km.). Ur had some 25,000 residents, and the population of its surrounding area may have been 200,000. Among smaller cities, Lagash may have numbered 19,000, and Umma 16,000 residents. Although small by modern standards, these cities are comparable in size to many medieval European towns.

Within the walls of a Mesopotamian city were jumbled tenements amid unpaved pathways, a few avenues, and public squares. The ordinary artisan lived in a one-story building of mud-brick consisting of a few rooms opening onto a communal courtyard. The rich man's house, whose blank brick walls (built thick to ward off heat) were both plastered and whitewashed, had two stories and a dozen rooms

opening onto an interior courtyard. It had a kitchen, shrines, and reception areas, with walls and floors covered by rugs or mats. The family's dead were often buried below the house, though sometimes in cemeteries outside the city walls.

When civilization first emerged in Egypt, it did so in a form quite different from that in Mesopotamia. As elsewhere in the Fertile Crescent, walled cities were established as centers of trade. By 3100 B.C.E., Egypt's kings, or pharaohs, had destroyed these cities and created a centralized state. After that time, Egyptians lived in villages governed directly by the pharaoh. The pharaohs' administrative centers at Thebes and Memphis were a form of capital city, and they were inhabited by a huge staff of bureaucrats and temple priests.

Sometime after 2500 B.C.E., a third Old World civilization began to arise along the Indus River valley in the Indian subcontinent. Although its origins were independent, it was in contact with Middle Eastern civilizations by both land and sea routes. As in Mesopotamia, cities were centrally important features of the Indus civilization. Its two principal cities were Mohenjo-daro, in the lower Indus Valley, and Harappa, almost 400 miles (644 km.) to the northeast. Their populations extended to 30–40,000, and included merchants, artisans, and farmers. Dominated by a citadel complex enclosing temples and other public buildings, these unwalled cities were peaceful centers of agriculture. Below the high citadels, the lower cities were built neatly on a grid pattern formed by streets as much as 30 feet (9 m.) wide. The streets had gutters; cleanliness and an efficient water supply were clearly important to these people. Their houses contained plumbing systems to carry water and waste from or to external cisterns, drains, and sewers. Mohenjo-daro also had a public bathhouse. Despite a glorious start, the Indus civilization vanished completely after 2000 B.C.E.. This civilization that so respected water may have been weakened by flood and drought before falling prey to the armies of invading **Aryans** (see Chapter 2).

Populations

Global populations	about **4,000,000** 10,000 B.C.E.
	about **6,000,000,000** in 2000 C.E.
City populations	about **2000** in Jericho, 8000 B.C.E.
	about **50,000** in Uruk, after 3000 B.C.E.
	about **1,000,000** in Rome, first century C.E.

By the time the civilization of the Indus Valley disappeared, a fourth Old World civilization had emerged along the Yellow River (Huang He) in eastern China. The region soon came under the domination of city-states headed by well-armed warlords. Together these Yellow River cities constituted an urban zone which nurtured industries and entrepreneurs.

By about 1550 B.C.E., the city of Anyang was established as the capital of the first known **dynasty** of Chinese rulers, the Shang (see Chapter 2). An earlier Shang capital, dating from about 1700 B.C.E., lies buried underneath modern Zhengzhou. Unlike Anyang, which had no wall, this was a walled rectangle with a perimeter of about 4 miles (7 km.). In size it compares with the larger cities of Mesopotamia, but like the Egyptian capitals, it was a center of administration not commerce. Merchants and food-producers lived outside the walls, with the houses, workshops, and tombs of the workers. Within the walls dwelt the privileged **elite** of kings, officials, and priests who directed the business of civilization.

Tools and Trade

Urban life was one of the hallmarks of civilization. So also was the manufacture of metals. The technological breakthrough was achieved with bronze, the first alloy that could be used to make effective tools and weapons. Neolithic workers had extracted copper from its ore from at least the eighth millennium B.C.E., but this soft metal had limited uses. About the time the first cities were forming in the Middle East, metal-workers discovered the secret of casting bronze, an alloy of copper and other elements, usually tin. Now miners in remote regions unearthed ores which merchants shipped to the cities. There artisans extracted copper from its ore and fused it with tin to produce bronze. From bronze could be crafted the sharp-edged implements that have lent their name to the whole era: the **Bronze Age.**

Bronze was too expensive to replace stone for agricultural use. It was a luxury metal, used to create the implements of war and ritual required by the two dominant social groups, nobles and priests. Nevertheless, its manufacture and distribution fueled the commerce of the ancient world, and in its working—riveting, soldering, hammering, and decoration—people's artistic vision was expressed.

Between the societies of the Middle East and the Indus River valley there was frequent contact, allowing the spread of bronze manufacture from one civilization to another. But the Chinese, remote from this contact, probably discovered the technique on their own. Cast bronze vessels were a central feature of Shang civilization—striking for their intricate design (unmatched elsewhere in antiquity), and great beauty. Far away in the New World Amerindian civilizations bronze metallurgy also developed independently, but much later (around 1100 C.E.)

Iron, a stronger metal than bronze, came into use only after 1200 B.C.E., long after the beginning of the Bronze Age. To forge useful iron implements, it was necessary not merely to extract the metal from the ore, but also to develop techniques to harden it. Artisans working in the Hittite Empire (see Chapter 2) in Asia Minor learned to combine the raw metal with a small percentage of carbon, a process called carburizing. This process, together with high and sustained heat, yielded tough iron implements, both cheaper and more durable than those of bronze.

Once the forging of iron was perfected, iron tools spread throughout the Middle East (although not to the exclusion of bronze weapons), used not only by elite warriors but also by common laborers. The iron plowshare opened a new era in agriculture, while iron spears made warfare more lethal. Iron manufacture was developed much later in China and Africa. It was never developed by Amerindians, who used stone.

As they developed advanced metallurgical techniques, Bronze and Iron Age peoples also extended the trade networks begun by their Neolithic ancestors, who had traded natural and manufactured goods sometimes over very great distances. Merchants now procured the raw materials needed by artisans and distributed their manufactured goods. The invention of the sail, soon after 3500 B.C.E., aided the expansion of trade. Using as roadways the same rivers that watered the fields, merchants organized the transport of stone and metal, of pots and tools, of grain and weapons between cities.

To transport merchandise to markets isolated from waterways, Bronze Age merchants utilized the wheel (see p. 12), which was invented around the same time as the sail. Wheeled carts replaced heavy sledges, whose load had overtaxed draft animals. After 2000 B.C.E., when camels were at last domesticated in the Middle East, merchants led caravans across the deserts and plateaus to distribute goods from the

Arabian Peninsula and the Indian subcontinent. Pack animals carried goods overland between China and India and across the belly of Eurasia.

By river, ocean, road, and desert, Old World merchants transported grain and wine and oil, the produce of the farms, decorative pottery, ores and finished implements, and ornaments made of metal and gems. They traded silk from China, cotton cloth from India, and linen and **papyrus** (see above) from Egypt—the latter produced from the reeds that grew wild in the Nile. The system of trade routes established in antiquity endured until the opening of the Atlantic and Pacific trade routes in the sixteenth century by Europeans (see Chapter 16).

The Social Hierarchy

Even Neolithic villages had chiefs and priests, artisans and workers, warriors and weavers. In the cities of the first civilizations, the differentiation of the population according to skill and rank became more pronounced. A **hierarchy** developed, a vertically arranged sequence of social groups. The process by which social groups became defined and arranged in hierarchical patterns is called **stratification**.

At the top of the social hierarchy were those who ruled: priests and priestesses, nobles and kings. The members of this privileged elite lived in palaces, or administered temple buildings and land. On their death, some were buried in spectacular tombs built by great armies of ordinary men to perpetuate their status in the next world. At the bottom of the social hierarchy were slaves, who owned nothing. In between these two levels were merchants and artisans, laborers and scribes, wives, widows, and children.

The imprint of social division is seen in the collections of laws that survive from various Mesopotamian cities. The most famous of these is the code of the Babylonian king Hammurabi (c. 1792–1750 B.C.E.), based on Sumerian legal traditions (see *Witnesses*, p. 13, and *Windows On*, p. 22). These codes define crime and punishment according to the social position of the perpetrator and the victim. A poor man assaulting a rich man might pay with his life, whereas a rich man could assault a poor man and be subject only to a fine. A rich man who stole another man's animals would be fined three times more heavily than a poor thief—and both would be put to death if unable to pay their fines.

Lower than the poor man in the social hierarchy was the slave. The first slaves were the products of war, survivors made captive after one city or kingdom defeated another. Initially, women and children predominated among slave captives; men usually were slaughtered. Other slaves were taken from among the poor of the native population. For example, debtors might sell themselves, or, more often, their wives, or their children, who were sold into slavery to pay their debts. That practice further blurred the line dividing the condition of women or children from that of slaves or prostitutes, for which conditions women and children were likely recruits.

Two types of slaves could be found in ancient societies—those who served private families, and those used by temples and palaces as agricultural workers, stewards, or prostitutes. Most household slaves performed domestic tasks, but some acquired training in marketable skills and worked at a profit, which filled the pockets of their owners. Domestic slaves often bought their own freedom. The slavery practiced in these first civilizations—although intrinsically cruel, as all slavery is—was arguably much milder than that later found in Rome or in the Americas.

Nobles and kings derived their authority from their status as warriors. Priests and priestesses derived theirs from their power (as they claimed) to communicate with the gods. Performing sacred tasks, some of which predated the advent of civilization, they informed mortals of the immortals' demands, and appeased those deities with rites and human or animal sacrifices. A goddess might be represented by a priestess. Just as priests were often of the same rank or blood as kings and nobles, so priestesses were often women drawn from the highest class and in some cases from royalty.

Breaking the Law

The creation of law is one of the great achievements of civilized societies. Below are extracts from two famous ancient law codes. The first comes from the laws codified under Hammurabi, the Babylonian king, based on even older Sumerian legal traditions. These laws are characterized (as were many ancient law codes) by attention to the status of the victim or perpetrator as well as to the nature of the crime: if the victim is of low, or the perpetrator of high rank, the penalty is generally less. The laws of the Hebrews, which deal with the plain matters of everyday life—including food conventions and relations with servants—are framed by higher moral and religious laws, still considered sacred by millions of Jews and Christians today. The faithful believe that they were conveyed directly by God to Moses, who led them from slavery to freedom.

Hammurabi's laws vary with the social condition of the criminal and his victim (c. 1790 B.C.E.):

Personal injuries, class by class:

196 If a nobleman has destroyed the eye of a member of the aristocracy, they shall destroy his eye.

198 If he has destroyed the eye of a commoner ..., he shall pay one mina of silver.

199 If he has destroyed the eye of a nobleman's slave ..., he shall pay one-half [the slave's] value.

229 If a builder constructed a house for a nobleman but did not make his work strong, with the result that the house which he built collapsed and so has caused the death of the owner of the house, that builder shall be put to death.

230 If it has caused the death of a son of the owner of the house, they shall put the son of that builder to death.

231 If it has caused the death of a slave of the owner of the house, he shall give slave for slave to the owner of the house.

Fathers and sons:

188 If a member of the artisan class took a son as a foster child and has taught him his handicraft he may never be reclaimed.

189 If he has not taught him his handicraft, that foster child may return to his father's house.

195 If a son has struck his father, they shall cut off his hand.

On noble marriages:

128 If a nobleman acquired a wife, but did not draw up the contracts for her, that woman is no wife.

129 If the wife of a nobleman has been caught while lying with another man, they shall bind them and throw them into the water ...

142 If a woman so hated her husband that she has declared, "You may not have me," ... that woman, without incurring any blame at all, may take her dowry and go off to her father's house.

(From "Code of Hammurabi," *Ancient Near Eastern Texts relating to the Old Testament*, 2e, ed. J. B. Pritchard, 1955)

Yahweh's commandments are for all:

You shall have no other gods before me.
You shall not make for yourself a graven image, or
   any likeness of anything that is in
   heaven above, or that is in the earth beneath, or
   that is in the water under the
   earth; you shall not bow down to them or serve
   them ...
You shall not kill.
You shall not commit adultery.
      You shall not steal.
      (Exodus 20: 3–4, 13–15)

As they presided over the temples that housed their gods, priests and priestesses oversaw the warehousing of their society's wealth. Ancient peoples struggled hard to satisfy their gods. However hard the peasant labored, however well the artisan wrought, however fearlessly the merchant ventured forth to trade in distant lands, they were mere servants of the will of the gods. These workers bore to the temples a fat share of the produce of the earth, or the bounty of trade and manufacture, all commandeered by the priests for use of the deity—or by the priests themselves, who lived on this largesse. Their offerings were received in the temple precinct, a self-sufficient inner city. The god owned slaves and received taxes; leased such equipment as plows, wagons, and boats to the workers; stored wealth in the temple warehouse; and managed flocks of cattle or sheep. In Sumer especially, all of society was organized around the management of the gods' property.

The great religious importance of temples to ancient society was matched by the originality of their architectural design and the heroic feat of their construction. Beginning about 2900 B.C.E. and continuing until the sixth century B.C.E., the civilizations of Mesopotamia built distinctive structures called ziggurats for their gods. Artificial hills made of mud-brick, with sides ascending stepwise from foot to summit, these structures were elaborate bases for the temple at the peak. The temple was the "house of the god," lifted so high it seemed to sit in heaven, while the stepped hill suggested a staircase leading to the upper world of the gods. The ziggurat at Ur constructed by the king Ur-Nammu around 2100 B.C.E.,

shown on p. 15, rose to a height of about 80 feet (24 m.). Built in Babylon around 600 B.C.E., the ziggurat of Etemenanki rose 300 feet (92 m.), its commanding presence visible above the surrounding plain. This structure may have been the model for the biblical "Tower of Babel" (Genesis 11:1–9).

In their different way, the pyramids of Egypt expressed that society's concept of the divine. The pyramid was not a temple, but the tomb of the pharaoh, the god-king himself, who would return after his death to the heavens from which he had come. His resurrection ensured the continued processes of life and creation: the river's flood, the sun's warmth, the crops' growth, the social order. Unlike the ziggurat, the pyramid had smooth sides and was built of stone. Broad at the surface of the earth, it soared confidently toward the sphere of heaven, from which royal power derived. The precise geometry of its form succinctly expressed the Egyptian idea of the relations of earth and sky, of right and justice.

Most of the great pyramids were built for Egypt's earliest pharaohs, those who reigned between about 2700 and 2200 B.C.E. Later pharaohs were buried in less spectacular tombs, choosing instead to have themselves immortalized by vast temple complexes. Erected in the name of the sun-god Amon-Ra (or Re), the temple of Karnak (c. 1320–1237 B.C.E.) was designed so that on two mornings a year the sun's rays penetrated deep inside the temple to illuminate the statues that at all other times stood unseen in interior darkness. The royal temple at Medinet Habu (built to honor the conquering pharaoh Ramses III, c. 1198–1155 B.C.E.) required a staff of governors and

Tombs and Temples

Pyramids of Menkure, Khafre, and Khufu: *Ancient civilizations recruited immense labor forces to build monuments suitable for the worship of their gods or the welfare of their rulers. On this page and the following are two examples from the third millennium* B.C.E. *Below is a photograph of the Giza group of pyramids for Menkure, Khafre, and Khufu (or Cheops), with the latter, dating from c.2570–2530* B.C.E. *in the foreground.*

Ziggurat of Ur-Nammu:
To the left is the Sumerian ziggurat built by Ur-Nammu, king of Ur around 2112 B.C.E., *in a photograph taken during the monument's excavation. Although contemporary, Khufu's pyramid and Ur-Nammu's ziggurat were built for different purposes: the first to house the body of a divine ruler intended for immortality, the second to support a temple for the worship of a god.*

officials, housed with scribes within the temple precincts. Temple bureaucrats managed acres of land and herds of cattle, fleets, and workshops, fifty-six Egyptian towns and nine foreign cities.

The temple built in Jerusalem by King Solomon of the Israelites was small, compared to the gigantic temples of Egypt, for example. According to the biblical account (in 1 Kings chapter 6; see *Witnesses*, p. 16), it was 60 cubits long, 20 broad, and 30 high (or 88 by 29 by 44 feet [27 × 8.8 × 13 m.], using 17½ inches [44 cm.] as the approximate length of that ancient unit). However, it was made of the richest materials. Built of stone, it was paneled inside with precious cedar, overlaid with gold, and embellished with sculpture. King Solomon's building fulfilled the pledge of his father David to build a house for the Ark of the Covenant, the wooden chest that housed the Law, which forms the basis of Judaism.

Besides building temples, pyramids, and ziggurats to honor the gods and provide for their own afterlife, ancient rulers built splendid residences for themselves. The palace of King Sargon II of Assyria (in northern Mesopotamia) contained 209 rooms. The 71-room palace at the late Assyrian capital of Nineveh housed the superb library of King Ashurbanipal (r. c. 688–627 B.C.E.). Adorned with relief sculptures of lion hunts and other fierce subjects, it proclaimed the king's prowess in war, as well as his role as a patron of arts and literature.

Fathers, Women, and Children

Just as ancient society was arranged in hierarchical patterns, so also was the family, the basic unit of society. Prehistoric peoples had grouped themselves in **clans**, which worshiped a common ancestor. Clan organization persisted into the era of civilization. But increasingly, as agricultural communities found that the control of property was the key to survival, nuclear family units became more important and the wider network of kin less so. In the early cities, people lived in a family: a small group of closely related

persons dominated by one man, father and husband. His subjects were his wife and children.

Among the ancient civilizations, Egypt offered women and children the fairest treatment. Egyptian relief sculptures, wall paintings, and papyrus illustrations often depict families—mother, father, child—united in perfect harmony and even equality. Women had the same legal rights as men and the same claim on the afterlife. They could enjoy high social status, although they could hold no public position. The high valuation of women in Egypt was matched by the high valuation of children, implied by the amulets children were given to wear to protect them from danger. Children of both sexes were nurtured, and almost all children were raised.

Outside Egypt, women's condition was less satisfactory. Women were excluded from public life—a pattern that endured, with few exceptions, in east and west, Old World and New, until recent times. Marriage and motherhood constituted a woman's life, yet she (and her husband) had little say in selecting a mate. Fathers, or parents acting together, arranged the marriages of their daughters and sons. Contracts, often required for a valid marriage, specified exchanges of property: given by the bride's family to a desirable groom, by the groom's to a valuable bride. Marriage was an economic arrangement that answered the aspirations of families—for status, for offspring, for allies. It was not designed to suit the inclinations of the individuals whose lives it affected.

Once married, a woman was subject to her husband's authority, as she had previously been to her father's. She could not act independently in society, although in some communities she could hold property. In some societies husbands could flog or mutilate even high-status wives they believed to be disobedient. In exchange for obedience, a woman received protection, a critical factor in determining her status. In Assyrian society, a married woman was always veiled: only those without male protection went unveiled. The veil declared women's relationships to men—their husbands, their fathers, and their brothers—and

WITNESSES

Skyscrapers of the Past

Among the earliest monuments created by human beings are the temples of the gods and the tombs or palaces of kings. In these three passages are described the building of three famous structures: an Egyptian pyramid, a royal tomb for a divine monarch; the first temple of the Israelites in Jerusalem, by King Solomon; the splendid renovation of the palace in Ninevah of the Assyrian King Ashurbanipal.

The Greek historian Herodotus describes an Egyptian pyramid (c. 450 B.C.E.): [Cheops] closed the temples, and forbade the Egyptians to offer sacrifice, compelling them instead to labour, one and all, in his service. Some were required to drag blocks of stone down to the Nile from the quarries ...; others received the blocks after they had been conveyed in boats across the river ... One hundred thousand men laboured constantly, and were relieved every three months by a fresh lot. It took ten years' oppression of the people to make the causeway for the conveyance of the stones ... The pyramid itself was twenty years in building. It is a square, 800 feet each way, and the height the same, built entirely of polished stone, fitted together with the utmost care.
(Herodotus, *Persian Wars*; ed. G. Rawlinson, 1924)

Solomon's temple (Jerusalem) according to the Hebrew Bible: So Solomon built the house [of the Lord], and finished it. He lined the walls of the house on the inside with boards of cedar; from the floor of the house to the rafters of the ceiling, he covered them on the inside with wood; and he covered the floor of the

house with boards of cypress. He built twenty cubits of the rear of the house with boards of cedar from the floor to the rafters, and he built this within as an inner sanctuary, as the most holy place ... The inner sanctuary he prepared in the innermost part of the house to set there the ark of the Lord ... and he overlaid it with pure gold.
(1 Kings 6:14–16, 19–20)

Ashurbanipal rebuilds his Assyrian private apartments at Nineveh (c. 650 B.C.E.): At that time, ... the private apartment of the palace in Nineveh, the noble city, beloved of Ninlil, which Sennacherib, king of Assyria, the father of the father, my begetter, had built for his royal abode, ... its walls had given way. I, Ashurbanipal ... tore down its ruined portions ... In a favorable month, on an auspicious day, I laid its foundations upon that terrace and built its brickwork ..., I put down its floor, I laid its mud walls ... The kings of Arabia, who had violated the oaths sworn to me, whom I had taken alive in the midst of battle with my own hands, I made to carry the basket and headpad, and to do taskwork, for the building of those apartments. Molding its bricks, performing labor upon it, they passed their days to the accompaniment of music. Amidst gladness and rejoicing I completed it from its foundation to its top ... [and] filled it with splendid furnishings.
(From D. D. Luckenbill, *Ancient Records of Assyria and Babylon*, 1968)

---

thereby their social value. Unveiled women were considered outcast and available for exploitation.

Just as they had little choice in entering a marriage, women had little choice in its dissolution. In Mesopotamia and the Near East, a man could divorce his wife summarily and return her in disgrace to her father's house. The ancient Israelites considered such a woman irreparably defiled. In Babylon, a high-status woman could divorce her husband for sufficient cause, but she too returned with her bridal property to her father's house. In China, a wife who was not obedient to her husband's family was sent home, disgraced.

Once admitted to her husband's family, a woman was considered to belong to that family. If her husband died she was expected, in many societies, neither to leave nor to remarry. If she were allowed to remarry it was to a near male relative of her deceased husband. By that strategy, the family alliance originally secured by the marriage would be continued. These restrictions were all the more pressing if the woman, while married, had borne a child. Rarely did a woman take away with her the child of her dead husband. In India and China, sanctions against

remarriage were especially severe. In some cases (a custom practiced especially among the elites), an Indian widow surrendered herself to be burned on her husband's funeral pyre in the infamous (to Westerners) custom of *sati* (or *suttee*), an expression of woman's absolute loyalty to man.

Harsh as were the restrictions that encircled wife or widow, her status was higher than that of an unmarried woman not under male protection: a prostitute, a slave, or simply a woman without property. The rape or assault of a married woman was judged a more serious offense than the same crime directed against a slave woman or prostitute. If an assault caused a woman to miscarry, the punishment was heavier if the victim was of high status. In Babylon, the fine for such an assault on the daughter of a noble was double that for an assault on the daughter of a merchant. Physical crimes against women were understood to be actually crimes against men, whose female property was thus damaged.

According to Babylonian law, if a man and a woman were caught in adultery, both could be killed. A woman who was accused of adultery could prove her innocence by jumping into the river and managing not to drown. A man's situation was different. Adultery was construed as a man having sex with another man's *wife*, not simply with another woman. The penalty for this was death. If, however, a man's lover was neither another man's legitimate wife nor his virgin daughter—in other words, his property—he could freely have sex with her.

Marriage customs in ancient societies often allowed polygamy and concubinage. In the Middle East, men could have more than one legal wife—the custom of polygamy. Or they could have one wife and one or more concubines. The latter were usually slaves but lived as though married to a householder. Examples of these arrangements abound in the Hebrew Bible. Abraham's wife Sarah urged upon him the concubine Hagar, a slave woman, to be the mother of Abraham's son Ishmael before she gave birth to Isaac. Jacob, Abraham's grandson, had two wives, the sisters Leah and Rachel, and also fathered children by the female slaves given to each by their father.

In Babylonian law, the status of concubines relative to the first, free-born wife varied with their fertility. Once a concubine had borne a child to the husband, she could not be sold by the first wife. The children of such concubines were raised as free-born members of the family, whereas a child born to a slave but fathered by a man outside the family unit was marked as a slave. Concubinage thus offered slave women a chance for higher status.

The ability of women to bear children gave them what status they possessed in ancient societies. But not all children were welcomed. Fathers might sell their children into slavery, or "expose" (that is, abandon) unwanted infants. By contrast, if a woman aborted her own child, she might be executed. Abandoned infants often died. Those who survived might be claimed from the crossroads or dumps where they had been left. The lucky ones would be raised by other families as servants or dependents, the less fortunate (male and female) by managers of brothels as prostitutes.

Infanticide, although rare in Egypt, was especially common in eastern Asia and India. In these areas, evidence of disproportionately high numbers of men attests to the widespread infanticide of females. Girls caused great expense because of the dowries they were expected to provide. (The dowry was a sum of money by which the bride's natal family discharged its obligations to support a daughter.) Also, they could not carry on the family line. To preserve the honor and property of their families, they were often abandoned.

By contrast, property-owning families greatly valued their healthy male children. In the cities of the Middle East, upper-class fathers educated their sons for high-level occupations, while merchants and artisans placed theirs out as apprentices. Family farms and family businesses were jointly operated by men and their sons, who expected to inherit family wealth. But

All in the Family

Were human relations the same or different 3,000 years ago? These brief statements—an Egyptian woman's love for her husband, a Jewish man's expectations of a wife, and an Egyptian father's advice to his son—sound familiar to us, despite the great dissimilarities between the societies in which these speakers lived and our own.

An Egyptian in love:
> My god, my husband, I come to you.
> It is pleasant to go into the pool and
> I rejoice that you wish me
> To plunge in and bathe before you.
> I let you see my beauty
> In a tunic of fine royal linen
> When it is wet
> I go into the water with you
> And emerge with a red fish for you
> Pulsating in my hands.
> I lay it on my breast.
> O my man, my brother,
> Come and see me!

(From B. Watterson, *Women in Ancient Egypt*, 1991)

A good Hebrew wife:
> A good wife who can find?
>   She is far more precious than jewels.
> The heart of her husband trusts in her,
>   and he will have no lack of gain ...
> She seeks wool and flax,
>   and works with willing hands ...
> Strength and dignity are her clothing,
>   and she laughs at the time to come.
> She opens her mouth with wisdom,
>   and the teaching of kindness is on her tongue.

(Proverbs 31:10–11, 13, 25–26)

An Egyptian father advises his son to become a scribe: I have considered violent manual labor—give your heart to letters ... I have seen the blacksmith, directing his foundrymen, but I have seen the metal-worker at his toil before a blazing furnace ... And every carpenter who works or chisels, has he any more rest than the plowman? ... The weaver sitting in a closed-up hut has a lot that is worse than that of a woman. His thighs are drawn up close to his breast, and he cannot breathe fully ... Verily there is no occupation than which better cannot be found except the calling of the scribe which is the best of all ... One day spent in the chamber of instruction is better for you than eternity outside it; the works thereof endure like the mountains ...

(From J. B. Bernal, *Science in History*, 1969; modernized)

boys also faced some of the same restrictions faced by women. They were completely under their father's control. The penalty was severe for a son's crime against his father.

WRITING, LANGUAGE, AND CONSCIOUSNESS

Slaves, children, women, and the poor participated scarcely at all in the greatest cultural achievement of antiquity: the invention of writing. Its development is shown on p. 19. Art in verbal form could and did exist without writing, in poetry and song and story repeated orally and transmitted over many generations. But writing allows words to be preserved, reviewed, and analyzed. Writing furthered the development of critical thought, the "storage" of thought in texts inscribed on durable surfaces, and the communication of those thoughts to later generations. From this point onward, people speak to us directly, in words, rather than their tangible remains—however eloquent these may be. Hence the period before the invention of writing, in a given society, is called "prehistoric." With the written word, history became possible.

Words and Pictures

Human beings learned to write so as to keep lists: lists of the measures of grain stored in the gods' treasury, records of fees owed to the god by the citizens, inventories of tools and ornaments, records of planetary motion or the rise and fall of river waters threatening flood or drought. The first surviving written documents (from Sumer, around 3300 B.C.E.) record the sale of cattle and sheep, milk and grain. Of the tens of thousands of inscribed tablets found in that region, more than 90 percent deal with commercial transactions.

To make lists, it was necessary to learn to write. Priests, the guardians of temple wealth, were the first list makers and the first scribes. To transmit the complex art of writing to others, the priests formed schools for scribes. Bureaucrats and entrepreneurs sent their sons to these schools, the first in human history, so that they might master the new and crucial skill. Sumerian schools enrolled children of the city elites (governors, temple administrators, tax officials, scribes, and accountants) for instruction in writing. Their textbooks, mathematical tables, and dictionaries, some of which have survived, provide evidence of the process of teaching and learning 4000 years ago. In Egypt, the pharaoh's huge bureaucracy offered an appealing career to ambitious young people and learning to write was the prerequisite.

The first writing was based on **pictographs**. A pictograph is a simplified picture of an object: an ox, a house, a serpent. By 3000 B.C.E., thousands of such pictographs were in use in Mesopotamia and in Egypt.

Mesopotamian scribes recorded pictographs by pressing the point of a wedge-shaped (**cuneiform**) stylus in a wet clay tablet, which was then left to harden and form a durable document. Thousands of these tablets have been unearthed.

Egyptian scribes painted pictograms called **hieroglyphs** (Greek: "sacred carving") on walls, carved them in stone, or wrote them on papyrus. Papyrus, a valued commodity of ancient trade, was manufactured from woven strips of fibers found in the pithy stem of the papyrus plant which grew along the Nile. Papyrus panels laid end to end and pasted together produced a roll, the standard book of antiquity. From Mesopotamian cuneiform and Egyptian hieroglyph derive all the writing systems of the ancient Mediterranean world and their modern descendants.

Other systems of writing developed independently outside the Middle East, in Asia and the Americas. By about 2500 B.C.E., the Indus Valley civilization had created a pictographic language, which died with the civilization that produced it. By 1500 B.C.E., the Chinese had developed a pictographic system with about 2000 characters. Later rulers standardized and preserved the precious legacy. Though modified, this Chinese system of writing has never since gone out of use. Amerindian civilizations also independently developed writing (see Chapters 8, 16).

Once invented, writing spread from people to people as neighboring communities on the fringes of the first civilizations eagerly borrowed this practical art. Mesopotamian kingdoms all adapted cuneiform to communicate the words of their own languages. It was used for Sumerian as well as for the **Semitic** languages Akkadian, Ugaritic, and Aramaic. (Semitic was a family of languages from Africa and Southwest Asia, which also featured Amharic, Arabic, and Hebrew). Egyptian scribes learned Akkadian, and Ugaritic texts were known to scribes of the Aegean region. Words, techniques, and symbols passed easily from group to group across the sites of Old World civilizations.

Mastery of ancient pictographs required powerful memory and great patience. Scribes were tempted to simplify the original elaborate pictures by reducing their detail and altering their forms in the direction of a flowing script. Egyptian scribes developed two levels of simplified hieroglyphic writing: the **hieratic** (or "priestly") and **demotic** (or "popular"). Meanwhile, Mesopotamian scribes developed new scripts in which the graphic image represented the initial sound associated with an object: a **phonogram**. At first, these figures represented syllables; later, the sounds of individual consonants.

As the pictograph yielded to the phonogram, so the phonogram ultimately led to the alphabet. Soon after 1500 B.C.E., the priestly scribes of the city of Ugarit (in present-day Ras Shamra) in northern Syria (whose population spoke a mixture of Semitic as well as Indo-European languages) assigned single

The Genealogy of Writing

Development of early writing

- ▬ pictographic
- ▬ hieroglyphic
- ▬ cuneiform
- ▬ alphabetic
- ▬ probable relationship between scripts

MESOPOTAMIA

EGYPT

3000 B.C.E.

Pictographs

Hieroglyphs

Cuneiform

INDIA

2500 B.C.E.

Indus script

Pictographs

AEGEAN

2000 B.C.E.

Hieroglyphic script

SYRIA/ PALESTINE

ANATOLIA

1500 B.C.E.

Linear A script

Hurrian cuneiform

Hittite cuneiform

Linear B script

first alphabets

CHINA

Hittite Hieroglyphic

Phoenician

1000 B.C.E.

EUROPE

Latin script

earliest Greek alphabetic inscription

500 B.C.E.

MESOAMERICA

Zapotec

Etruscan script

Greek alphabetic script

Brahmin script (India)

1 C.E.

Mayan script

A system of writing was a feature of every ancient civilization. Although some still remain undeciphered, many writing systems have been decoded, enabling us to get a close-up view of life in the distant past. Writing began as pictures, or pictographs, which symbolized ideas increasingly unrelated to the object depicted. The alphabet developed from the simplified pictograph to represent not a thing but a single sound, which could be assembled with other sounds to form words.
Source: R. Whitehouse and J. Wilkins, *The Making of Civilization: History Discovered through Archaeology* (New York: Alfred A. Knopf, 1986).

consonantal sounds to thirty cuneiform signs. This set of figures and sounds was the first true alphabet. In an alphabet, each figure denotes not an object, nor an idea, nor a syllable, but an individual sound. A few figures can be combined flexibly in any number of patterns to represent the sounds of any words in the language—and in other languages, too. Easy to learn, an alphabet facilitated commerce with other peoples. It threatened the status of the scribes, however, whose rare and specialized skills were no longer needed.

At about the same time, the scribes of neighboring Phoenicia created a modified set of twenty-two signs based on Egyptian hieroglyphs. Abandoning the wedge-shaped stylus, they could write the figures of their alphabet with pen and ink on papyrus. This material had first been introduced to the Phoenician harbor city of Byblos and from there exported to Greece. The Greeks called papyrus *byblos*, after this port, and the word yielded in their language the word for "book" (*biblion*) and in ours the word for "the book," the Bible. The Phoenician alphabetic script, modified, also passed to the Greeks (who added symbols for vowel sounds), to the Romans and Etruscans, to the Persians and speakers of Aramaic and Hebrew, and to modern Hindi, Arabic, and European languages.

Languages and Peoples

Writing is a tool. It can be used, and was used in antiquity, to record a variety of languages. Languages are much more. They are an expression of the life, beliefs, and history of a community. People who share the same language are united in a way that is different from kinship by blood or common loyalty to a ruler or constitution but, in its own way, just as strong.

The skill of writing, once attained, has never been lost to the human species. But individual human communities that once were literate have subsequently lost the ability to write. Similarly, a language may "die," in the sense that no one speaks it anymore, although scholars may study it. Sumerian, Egyptian, Hittite, Phoenician, and ancient Greek are all "dead" languages; Latin has all but died, apart from some use in medicine, law, and Christian music. But many modern languages are derived from ancient ones.

The different languages spoken by the people of ancient civilizations fall into several distinct groups, or families. The oldest languages spoken by civilized persons were Sumerian and Egyptian. The former, unrelated to any modern language, disappeared completely when its speakers were absorbed by other groups. Ancient Egyptian stemmed from the "Hamitic" family of north African languages (so called after Ham, one of the three sons of Noah in the Hebrew Bible).

Closely related to the Hamitic are the "Semitic" languages (so called after Shem, Ham's older brother). These prevailed in the Fertile Crescent after the Sumerian period. The ancient peoples of the Middle East known as Akkadians and Amorites, Canaanites and Assyrians, Israelites and Aramaeans all spoke Semitic languages. The common language of Mesopotamia in the second millennium B.C.E. was Akkadian. In the first millennium, it was Aramaic. These languages were used for communication between different groups, even by peoples who retained their own language among themselves.

Most languages spoken in the West today (in Europe and the lands of European settlement) are distinct in origin from the Hamitic and Semitic languages of ancient Egypt and Mesopotamia. They mostly descend from those spoken by nomadic tribes who originated in the steppes of Eurasia between the Black and Caspian seas. These are called **Indo-European** languages, grouped as a family because they share many elements of basic vocabulary. Derived from them are classical Greek and Latin and their descendants, and the Celtic, Germanic, and Slavic languages of the European peoples who settled from the Alps to the Arctic. Other members of the Indo-European family are Persian, spoken by settlers on the Iranian plateau, and many Indian languages (classical Sanskrit, modern Hindi, and Urdu).

The grouping of peoples by language traditions is distinct from racial or ethnic classification. The human species has traditionally been divided into **races**—although many geneticists now question the validity of that classification, finding that the genes shared by visibly different peoples are vastly more numerous than the genes that cause them to have a distinctive appearance. The Caucasoid, Mongoloid, and Negroid races (which some specialists would divide into many sub groups) are no longer understood as biologically distinct species, but as groups of people who share certain physical traits that are transmitted genetically. They include features such as skin color, shape of head, and blood type.

Races (in this sense) emerged late in the process of human evolution but well before the first civilizations. Racial divisions do not coincide with language or culture or degree of technical achievement. Caucasoid peoples may speak Indo-European or Semitic (or other) languages, for example; and not all speakers of Semitic tongues are Caucasoid. And although some speakers of ancient Indo-European tongues called themselves Aryans, there is no Aryan race—a notion created by nineteenth-century race theorists and adopted with catastrophic consequences by the dictator Adolf Hitler (see Chapter 28).

How linguists learned to read the languages of antiquity is an intriguing detective story. In 1821, Jean-François Champollion (1790–1832), completing work begun by Thomas Young (1773–1829), deciphered the hieroglyphs carved on the Rosetta Stone, the prize brought back from Egypt by a French army under Napoleon. The partly eroded stone displayed a document dated to 196 B.C.E. written in three scripts: hieroglyphs, Egyptian demotic, and Greek. Because the Greek was familiar to European scholars, it was the key to interpreting the Egyptian, and so reading other Egyptian texts. In a similar way, the British soldier Henry Rawlinson (1810–1895) deciphered carvings on a rock face in Behistun in present-day Iran. Comparing the texts inscribed in three languages (Old Perisian, Elamite, and Babylonian), he succeeded, by 1850, in making the Persian and Babylonian texts legible to modern scholars. (The

Elamite text was finally deciphered by scholars early in the twentieth century.) Another ancient script, the Linear B of the ancient Mycenaeans—who lived in Greece and its neighboring islands in the second millennium B.C.E.—was decoded only recently. In the 1950s, the British linguist Michael Ventris (1922–1956) studied the clay tablets accidentally burned in the devastation of Mycenaean cities around 1200 B.C.E. After lengthy analysis of the script, Ventris discovered that the language recorded was an early form of Greek. His work finally unlocked the history of the warrior civilization whose exploits and values are recorded in the *Iliad* by Homer (see Chapter 4). Another ancient script from this region, Linear A, is still undeciphered.

Words and Ideas

Written language was first used to make lists; soon, ancient scribes employed their skills to publish royal decrees and codes of law which, like the kings themselves, were considered divine. They inscribed these laws on tablets and stone.

The first law codes from ancient Sumer are lost, or survive only in fragments. But extant still is the Babylonian law code, assembled by Hammurabi around 1790 B.C.E., inscribed on tablets called **stelae**, and displayed in several cities for all to consult. The code of Hammurabi is the most extensive surviving set of laws created until the compilation of Roman law ordered by the emperor Justinian at the end of the ancient era (see Chapter 8).

Hammurabi's pronouncements aimed to replace tribal systems of blood vengeance with a system of compensations. For each offense a punishment, corporal or monetary, is specified. As was often the case in ancient societies, these punishments were proportional to social status and gender. The code does not deal only with crime. Of its 282 regulations, about one-third deal with land tenure and commercial transactions, and one-quarter with the family.

Hammurabi claimed that he received these laws from the god Shamash, who is depicted with the king on the stone slab, or **stele**, on which the laws were inscribed (see *Windows On*, p. 22). Later, other Middle Eastern civilizations produced laws. These included the Assyrians, whose law codes also survive, and the Israelites, whose laws, recorded in the Hebrew Bible, are fundamental to modern Judaism.

There is no comparable document of legal thought from the civilization of Egypt. There the pharaoh himself was the law. He embodied the principal of *Ma'at*, or cosmic justice. No legal system was required where the pharaoh's living word took its place.

Ancient civilizations also laid the foundations of science. Priests and scribes observed planetary motions, measured the passage of time and the surface of the earth, and studied and healed disease.

Babylonian mathematicians devised the multiplication table and certain theorems of geometry. They could calculate squares of numbers and square roots, exponents and percentages, and, in their **sexagesimal** system (based on the sacred number 60) of reckoning quantities, they divided the year into twelve months, the circle into 360 degrees, and the hour into 60 minutes, all divisions that are still in use. From observations of the moon, Babylonian scientists developed a calendar based on the lunar cycle of 28 days.

In Egypt, the annual flooding of the Nile encouraged observers to devise a solar calendar of 365 days, the basis of our own. The faceless plain created each year by the receding river encouraged the development of another skill, that of surveying. Medicine and surgery developed from Egyptian religion as tools in the struggle against ever-present demons. Descriptions of surgical operations (of which forty-eight survive) reveal that Egyptian practitioners performed abortions and explored the cavity of the skull.

The human venture of writing could have stopped with lists, laws, and numbers; indeed for nearly 1000 years it did. But in the first millennium B.C.E. some scribes discovered in writing the tool for a deeper exploration of the meaning of their lives. They began to write down the **myths** and legends of their people, producing the first documents of literature and, in due course, of history. Epics and chronicles of the experience of the Aryans (India) and Akkadians, the Israelites and the Hittites were inscribed on clay tablets and papyrus rolls. The first libraries numbered among their treasures works from earlier civilizations.

In the ruined library of the Assyrian king Ashurbanipal at Nineveh was found one of the key surviving texts of the Babylonian epic *Gilgamesh*, the first major surviving work of world literature, recorded on 12 tablets in 3000 lines of cuneiform (see *Witnesses*, p. 23). Son of the goddess Ninsun and himself called "two-thirds god, one-third man," the legendary hero Gilgamesh was probably based on an actual King Gilgamesh of Uruk, in Sumer, who reigned around 2675 B.C.E. and is credited with establishing its powerful walls. According to the story, Gilgamesh journeys abroad in search of adventure, accompanied by his friend Enkidu. When Enkidu dies, Gilgamesh struggles with his great sorrow and greater fear of death. Setting out again, this time on a quest for immortality, he returns home, sobered by his new-found understanding of the grim limits of the human condition, to perform his duty as sovereign.

Much of ancient literature was religious. Hymns and prayers, incantations and charms meant to sway the will of a thousand deities fill many clay tablets and sheets of papyrus. The Egyptian *Book of the Dead* is only one collection of a genre known as "wisdom literature," of which there are also samples in the Hebrew Bible. This literature consists of meditations on the conditions of human life and its destiny. The

Laws as Hard as Stone

Pillar of Asoka, third century B.C.E.

***Stele of Hammurabi, c. 1790–1750** B.C.E.*

In the Hebrew Bible Moses is recorded as receiving the Law, or Ten Commandments, inscribed by God himself on stone tablets. Similarly, ancient legislators, sometimes portrayed as recipients of divine favor, had their laws inscribed on the most durable materials available: stone and bronze. Shown here (left) are the basalt stele containing Hammurabi's Code, representing the king receiving the laws from the god Shamash; a limestone pillar inscribed with the Laws of Asoka (far left); and a stone with a law code inscription from Crete (below). (left: Louvre, Paris)

Given that most people were illiterate, why do you think that rulers went to such ends to publish display inscriptions?

***Law code inscription** (below), **Dreros, Crete, c. 600** B.C.E.*

Bible contains many other genres of literature: poetry and history, law and prophecy.

The **brahman** priests who were the guardians of the sacred texts of Indian civilization transmitted orally (they were committed to writing only in the first millennium C.E.) the four sacred *Vedas* and the commentaries upon these known as the *Upanishads*. Two epics of that era—the *Ramayana* and the *Mahabharata*—retell the experience of legendary princes and warriors and are laced with mystical theology and stories of the gods. The *Mahabharata*, a vast anthology, incorporates the *Bhagavad-Gita* ("Song of God"), in itself a classic of Indian religious thought.

Thus the invention of writing enabled ancient civilizations to record the achievements of heroes and observations of scholars, to announce ethical and legal standards for successful community life, and to express their highest aspirations.

SACRIFICE, MYTH, AND CONSCIENCE

Ancient peoples inherited the custom of sacrifice from prehistoric times. The gods required sustenance, and were fed on the altars with the scarce foodstuffs offered up by worshipers hoping to avert their fury. In time, worshipers created myths, stories about the gods that helped explain the workings of the cosmos. By the last millennium before the Common Era, some communities of the Middle East and Asia developed new understandings of the divine. They believed that what was required of them was not only the sacrifice of beast or wealth, but obedience or faith, and good behavior. That understanding is expressed in the biblical account of Abraham, who was permitted to sacrifice a ram and spare his son Isaac. Abraham's faith alone satisfied his God.

He Who Saw Everything

King Gilgamesh of Uruk, in Sumer, who reigned more than 3,000 years ago, is also the subject of the first major epic in world literature. Its themes, first expressed in the language and rhythms of a culture now lost, are the themes endlessly explored by the human imagination: the quest for glory, the poignancy of friendship and love, the purpose of life, and the meaning of death.

Gilgamesh will strive for glory (after 2675 B.C.E.):
"If I fall, I shall have made my name;
'Gilgamesh,' they will say, 'against fierce Huwawa
Has fallen!' And long after,
My descendants born in my house
Shall honour my name …
I will ready my hand,
I will fell the cedar trees.
I will make my name a name that endures!"
(*Epic of Gilgamesh*, 28, Tablet III; trs. R. Temple, 1991)

Gilgamesh grieves for his friend Enkidu and commissions a statue (after 2675 B.C.E.):
"O Enkidu, my younger friend,
How you hunted the wild ass in the hills,
Chased the panther on the steppe!
We,
We two,
Have conquered all, climbed all …
What is this sleep that has now come over you?
You have gone dark and cannot hear me!"
But Enkidu does not raise his head.
Gilgamesh felt for his heartbeat
But there was none.
Then he drew a veil across Enkidu's face
As if he were a bride.
He roared like a lioness

Who has had her cubs taken from her.
Backwards and forwards he went before his friend,
And tore his hair, …
He tore off his beautiful clothes,
Flung them down
As though they were filth …
Then Gilgamesh proclaimed unto the land:
"Come smith, come workman,
Come fashioner of copper,
Come worker in gold,
Come inscriber in metal!
Shape you the image of my friend!
My friend whose stature is beyond compare;
May his breast be lapis lazuli,
May his body be of gold …"
(*Epic of Gilgamesh*, 80–81, Tablet VIII)

Gilgamesh contemplates the end for which he, too, is born (after 2675 B.C.E.):
"Fearing death, I roam over the steppe.
The fate of my friend
Lies heavy upon me,
On distant ways I roam the steppe.
The fate of Enkidu, my friend,
Lies heavy upon me.
How can I be silent?
How be still?
My friend whom I loved has turned to clay!
And I,
Shall I too, like him,
Lie down,
Never to rise—
Never again—
For ever and ever?"
(*Epic of Gilgamesh*, 108, Tablet X)

MUST READS

Books of the Ancient World

Gilgamesh	(after 2675 B.C.E.)
Ptah-hotep	*Instructions to his Son* (c. 2400 B.C.E.)
Hammurabi	*Code of Law* (c. 1790 B.C.E.)
Upanishads	(from 800 B.C.E.)
Hebrew Bible	(first codified from older materials, c. 500 B.C.E.)

Gods of Earth and Sky

The same storm gods and flood gods, round and full-breasted earth mothers, fierce and fertile bulls worshiped by Neolithic peoples were worshiped still by the peoples of the first civilizations. These gods looked like human beings or animals or both; many of the Egyptian gods had human bodies and animal heads. The gods resided in splendid and costly temples, on mountain tops, or in trees, streams, or oceans. They were immortal and numberless.

Ancient peoples shared and exchanged their gods and goddesses, just as they did their writing and metallurgical techniques. The whole ancient world teemed with a multiplicity of deities. The gods of a friendly neighbor or conquered foe were adopted or fused with native gods in a process called **syncretism**.

In Mesopotamia, the Sumerians revered Enlil and Anu, gods of storms and the atmosphere, and Enki, the god of wisdom and water. They worshiped fertility goddesses such as the earth mother Ninhursag, and the goddess of love and war, Ishtar, and the ubiquitous bull, whom the heroes Gilgamesh and Enkidu fought and vanquished. The Babylonians and Assyrians worshiped the sun gods Shamash and Assur (or Ashur). Assur was also associated with storms and with war.

Some of the most important Egyptian gods and goddesses personified the sun and moon and the river Nile. The gods Ra and Aten represented the sun in different aspects, rising or setting. Amon was the chief god of Thebes. Through his association with Ra, as Amon-Ra he became a sun god and the official king of the gods. At one moment, in the reign of Akhenaten, he had to fight for supremacy with Aten, god of the solar disk. Hathor was the Egyptian goddess of love, joy, and music, and was represented variously as a lovely woman and as a great golden cow, crowned with a solar disk. Osiris, god of justice, and his consort Isis, goddess of the moon and of fertility, were related to the worship of the pharaoh.

The Semitic Canaanites, who dwelt on the eastern Mediterranean shore (see Chapter 2) worshiped fertility gods with orgiastic rites, which attracted many of their Israelite neighbors but outraged the prophets. Like the Sumerians, they worshiped Ishtar, whom they called Astarte. Their chief deity, El, one of many gods bearing this name, was represented as a bull. Late into antiquity, the fifth century C.E., adherents still worshiped these deities by washing their bodies in the blood of slaughtered bulls, or having sexual union with temple prostitutes. From Palestine, these rites spread to the Hittites and the Assyrians, to the Phoenicians and their far-flung colonies, and finally to Greece and Rome.

The Indo-European Hittites, rulers of Asia Minor during the second millennium B.C.E. (see Chapter 3), proclaimed themselves the "people of a thousand gods." Among these were deities of the sky and the earth: a weather god (the "king of heaven"), a sun goddess, her son, god of the harvest, and the Canaanite Baal. The people of Crete, the Minoans, appear to have had no temples, although shrines have been found in some of their palaces. They also worshiped divine spirits on mountain tops, in caves, and in sacred groves. They celebrated a mother goddess and fertile bull with dancing and games in which young men and bare-breasted women participated, some of whom may have been sacrificial victims. The Mycenaean Greeks also worshiped fertility goddesses, and a sky god known later as Zeus, chief of all the Greek gods.

To the east, on the Indian subcontinent, during the formative years of Hinduism, people worshiped gods of thunder and lightning, fire and dawn, as well as the fertility goddesses inherited from the lost Indus civilization and from the indigenous peoples of the Ganges region. In China, ancestor worship was the most important form of religious observance. Nature gods and demons abounded, but they were later disdained by the philosophies that edged out traditional religion in that vast empire. In addition to worship of their ancestors, many Chinese revered semi-historical figures: the Three Sovereigns, the Five Emperors, founders of their well-managed kingdom.

Appeasing the Gods

Ancient peoples attempted to appease the gods and goddesses, and thereby bring order to their world, by offering sacrifices. The spirits of forest and desert, the gods of sun and moon, required grain, wine, or meat. If neglected, they would strike out furiously at their human subjects, whose very reason for existence was to satisfy the needs of divine beings. To the altars of their temples people brought their offerings. Here priests scattered grain and spilled wine, slew rams and goats to feed the greedy powers of the other world with the smell of roasted meat. The Persians sacrificed the horses central to the culture of their nomadic ancestors, and the Chinese developed complicated rituals of sacrifice in which a bronze-cast vessel of distinctive shape was used for each ritual substance. In some cultures, elaborate rules of cleanliness and order evolved, a kind of sacrificial behavior undertaken in honor of the deity. Among the Israelites and Hindus, for example, only certain foods might be eaten, in certain vessels and with certain companions.

Some gods demanded more than a sheep or a pigeon or spilled wine. They required a human sacrifice: a young man or woman, or a child. Both the Hebrew Bible and Greek mythology record traces of these sacrifices: Abraham was prepared to offer up his son Isaac at God's command, and King Agamemnon permitted his daughter Iphigenia to be slaughtered on the altar of an angry Greek god. In Shang China and in Canaan during the formative years of Israel and Judah, human beings were sacrificed to the gods. In the royal tombs of Sumerian Ur and the Shang city of Anyang were found, scattered around the body of the king, the remains of courtiers, slaves, and animals sacrificed in tribute to the dead monarch. In the Phoenician city of Carthage, crowds of children were surrendered by their parents for sacrifice into the hands of the officiating priests.

Explaining the Cosmos

Besides making sacrifices to the gods, ancient peoples created myths about them, in an attempt to make sense of the universe, to find order in the cosmos. In their sacred books (notably the *Enuma Elish*, c. 2000 B.C.E.), the Sumerians depicted the process of creation. According to this myth, the gods emerged from chaos and proceeded to create order, fighting battles over mysterious forces of darkness, monsters of chaos and death. Victorious, they arranged the universe neatly, with a heaven and an earth, in a form their worshipers understood as a box. The god's task was to keep the universe in order, in a perpetual repetition of the the creation of the cosmos.

The Sumerians' creation myth was transmitted to later peoples of the Middle East. These included the Israelites, who wove parts of the Sumerian creation legend into their own Bible. Another Sumerian tale, that of a universal flood that extinguished all human life except for a few individuals, also reappears in the biblical story of Noah and the Ark. That legend is first encountered in the epic *Gilgamesh* described above. In *Gilgamesh*, too, the hero's friend Enkidu is fashioned by the gods from clay, as the biblical Yahweh creates Adam.

The Sumerians also developed, from their ancient fertility beliefs, rituals celebrating resurrection and rebirth. In April, the month of resurgent growth, they celebrated their main festival: a ritual marriage of king and priestess, followed by the king's apparent death, representing the marriage and death of the god Dumuzi. His consort Inanna searches the bleak underworld for him, and he achieves a glorious resurrection. The goal of this festival was to ensure the fecundity of the earth. Elsewhere the same ritual was performed with a different cast of characters such as the Babylonian Shamash and the Canaanite Tammuz. Later echoes of this myth would be found in the Greek story of Persephone (see Chapter 4), and in the Christian narrative of the death and resurrection of Jesus of Nazareth (see Chapter 7).

Egyptian religion centered on the belief in immortality, related to notions of rebirth and resurrection. The soil's abundance encouraged that belief, and the dry desert conditions permitted the preservation of bodies. It was thought that the pharaoh, associated with the god Horus (son of Osiris, god of death, rebirth, and justice), was resurrected after death and rose as Horus to be united with Osiris. At first, immortality was seen as being the special destiny of the pharaoh. Eventually it was understood to be available to all faithful and just servants of the divine will.

In the second millennium B.C.E. the pharaoh Amenhotep IV (c. 1379–c. 1362 B.C.E.) abandoned the **polytheism** of his people and took a step toward **monotheism**. He changed his name to Akhenaten (meaning "he who serves Aten" or "the glory" or "the delight of Aten") to signal his intent to worship one God above all: the god of the setting sun, represented by a winged solar disk. His hymn of praise is quoted in *Witnesses*, p. 26.

Akhenaten practiced the reformed rites of his deity at a new capital he built called Akhetaten (meaning "horizon of Aten"), today's Tell el-Amarna. There he was joined in a life of worship by his children and his queen Nefertiti, who was renowned for her beauty. He or his priests composed moving hymns to their deity, including a hymn of praise to Aten as creator of the world. As a work of ancient religious literature, it deserves to be placed alongside the creation accounts of the Sumerians and the Hebrews.

Good and Evil

In a few ancient religious communities, the force of the divine was fundamentally reconceived. Not merely a master (or mistress) who demanded sacrifice, or a participant in cosmic dramas of creation and resurrection, the deity was identified with a single force for goodness, truth, and justice.

To arrive at that notion, it was necessary to conceive of one, not many deities—the conception of monotheism. Akhenaten was not really a monotheist. For him, Aten was not the only god, but *his* God, who showed special favor to him and his family. The more conservative priests continued to worship Amon-Ra, and Akhenaten's successors quickly reinstated conventional forms of Egyptian religion. It would take another thousand years for true monotheism to develop. It arose among the Israelites, who struggled for centuries to define themselves as worshipers of

Forms of Worship

The gods ruled the first human civilizations, and they were fearsome beings. As these civilizations matured, however, so did people's understandings of the cosmos, and the relationship between divine power, the true, and the good. The four passages here give voice to four different understandings of divinity. In the first, an Egyptian pharaoh speaks of his relationship with the sun god Aten, identified as the one or principal all-powerful deity. In the second, a Mesopotamian goddess is portrayed as the powerful and universal force of nature. In the third, the Hebrew god is revealed as not merely powerful, but intimately in contact with the worshiping psalmist. In the fourth, the Four Noble Truths of Buddhism are explained, which define a way of life that touches the infinite.

Pharaoh Akhenaten adores his Creator, the Sun (c. 1362 B.C.E.):

> Thou appearest beautifully on the horizon of
> heaven,
> Thou living Aten, the beginning of life!
> When thou art risen on the eastern horizon,
> Thou has filled every land with thy beauty …
> When thou settest in the western horizon,
> The land is in darkness, in the manner of death …
> Darkness is a shroud, and the earth is in stillness,
> For he who made them rests in his horizon …
> The world came into being by thy hand,
> According as thou hast made them.
> When thou hast risen they live,
> When thou settest they die.
> Thou art lifetime thy own self,
> For one lives only through thee.

(From J. B. Pritchard ed., *Ancient Near Eastern Texts relating to the Old Testament*, 2e, 1955)

The Mesopotamian goddess Inanna sings her own praises: I am Nature, the universal Mother, mistress of all the elements, primordial child of time, sovereign of all things spiritual, queen of the dead, queen also of the immortals, the single manifestation of all gods and goddesses that are … Though I am worshiped in many aspects, known by countless names, and propitiated with all manner of different rites, yet the whole round earth venerates me … and the Egyptians who excel in ancient learning and worship me with ceremonies proper to my godhead, call me by my true name, namely, Queen Isis.

(*ibid.*, 3e, 1969, supplement)

Psalm 63: 1–8:

[1]O God, you are my God, I seek you, my soul thirsts for you; my flesh faints for you, as in a dry and weary land where there is no water. [2]So I have looked upon you in the sanctuary, beholding your power and glory. [3]Because your steadfast love is better than life, my lips will praise you. [4]So I will bless you as long as I live; I will lift up my hands and call on your name. [5]My soul is satisfied as with a rich feast, and my mouth praises you with joyful lips [6]when I think of you on my bed, and meditate on you in the watches of the night; [7]for you have been my help, and in the shadow of your wings I sing for joy. [8]My soul clings to you; your right hand upholds me.

Buddhism's Four Noble Truths (c. 500 B.C.E.): This is the Noble Truth of Sorrow. Birth is sorrow, age is sorrow, disease is sorrow, death is sorrow, contact with the unpleasant is sorrow, separation from the pleasant is sorrow, every wish unfulfilled is sorrow—in short all the five components of individuality are sorrow.

And this is the Noble Truth of the Arising of Sorrow. [It arises from] thirst, which leads to rebirth, which brings delight and passion, and seeks pleasure now here, now there—the thirst for sensual pleasure, the thirst for continued life, the thirst for power.

And this is the Noble Truth of the Stopping of Sorrow. It is the complete stopping of that thirst, so that no passion remains, leaving it, being emancipated from it, being released from it, giving no place to it.

And this is the Noble Truth of the Way which Leads to the Stopping of Sorrow. It is the Noble Eightfold Path—Right Views, Right Resolve, Right Speech, Right Conduct, Right Livelihood, Right Effort, Right Recollection, and Right Meditation.

(From A. L. Basham, *The Wonder that Was India*, 1954)

Yahweh distinct from the cultists who surrounded them in Canaan (see Chapter 2).

According to the Bible, the Israelites' journey to monotheism did not follow a straight line. In imitation of the neighboring Canaanites, some of Abraham's descendants worshiped images of their deity Baal, and they may have celebrated the feasts of indigenous fertility goddesses with ritual prostitution and even human sacrifice. Some, as was charged, may have brutalized the poor and homeless and wallowed in luxury. They were accused of all these crimes by the prophets, the Israelites' spiritual leaders, who may have demanded meticulous obedience to religious law. Micah and Hosea and Amos, Isaiah and Jeremiah and others warned their people, in a stream of eloquence, that Israel's neglect of God's will would lead to its destruction.

In the end, the Israelites suffered the fate of which the prophets had warned—devastation and exile (see Chapter 2). Those deported to Babylon in 586 B.C.E. continued to live in exile for nearly fifty years, clinging to their memories of nationhood. With no temple

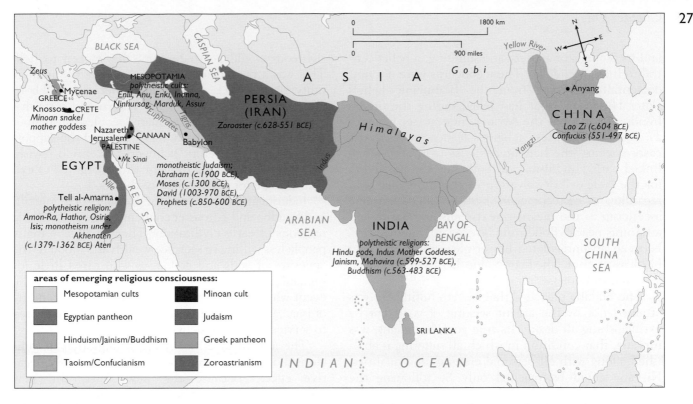

Map 1.2 Old and New Religions: *Ancient peoples were animists or polytheists, revering the spirits of nature or deities understood to control natural forces. From late in the second millennium* B.C.E., *critics and innovators began to forge new religious outlooks that were spiritually more inward and psychologically more demanding.* Why did major shifts in religious consciousness follow upon the foundation of civilizations?

or homeland, their leaders came to believe that an omnipotent God had no need of temples or kingdoms but demanded only righteous obedience. At some point thereafter, the mature Jewish faith emerged. It was a true ethical monotheism, the first such religion in the history of humankind.

The bedraggled remnant of the Israelites who returned from Babylonian exile to the Persian province of Judah in 538 B.C.E. had forged a new relationship with their Lord. Jews, as they were now called (after Judah), continued to make sacrifices of beasts and birds. But now it was, rather, strict observance of the Law that defined a Jew. According to Jewish tradition, the Law referred to a body of laws, which Yahweh himself had conveyed to Moses, leader of the Hebrew-speaking tribes who fled Egypt for the land of Canaan. Yahweh inscribed the commandments on stone tablets on the summit of Mount Sinai in the Arabian desert. The Law consisted of a body of dietary and domestic regulations. It also included principles of the highest ethical nature, intoned with the sonorous "thou shalt" or "thou shalt not" of the commandments. A righteous God was worshiped by righteous action. The nation that first proclaimed this notion had a revolutionary impact on future generations. It had defined ethical behavior as the central purpose of human life.

Independently, in China, in India, and in Iran, other sages sought in the divine realm a revelation of truth or justice or enlightenment. For the Chinese, the universe was simply the expression of the forces of nature (heaven, sun, earth, grain). No mystery, no sin, no apocalypse, could even be imagined in

a system where the central challenge was to conform to the harmony already prevailing in the world. To achieve that harmony, one followed "the Way" or *Tao*. Taoism is the religion, or philosophy, that underlies most other patterns of Chinese thought.

The sage Lao Zi (born c. 604 B.C.E.) taught his followers how to reach the enlightenment of the Tao through a moral regimen promoting quiet and unassertive behavior. Two generations later, the master-teacher Kong Fuzi (551–479 B.C.E.; anglicized as "Confucius") would offer another path to enlightened, ethical behavior, specifically in the context of government. Confucius formed his views in an age of political stress, when there was great longing for the imagined good government of past regimes. His principles, which avoided the worship of gods or the pursuit of metaphysics, constituted a system of ethics for the ruling class. Public officials, he taught, must demonstrate high skill, loyalty, honesty, and selflessness. Since virtue existed independent of status, such rulers could come from any rank of society. This notion, common in modern democratic societies, was original with Confucius.

In India, two noblemen, both contemporaries of Confucius, taught followers the means of reaching higher knowledge and tranquillity. These are the two sages Nataputta Vardhamana (traditionally 599–527 B.C.E.), known as the "hero" or Mahavira, founder of Jainism, and Siddhartha Gautama (c. 563–c. 483 B.C.E.), known as the Buddha, originator of Buddhism.

Both Mahavira and the Buddha were concerned with freeing the soul from the endless cycle of rebirth and its burdens of anxiety and suffering, a belief central to Indian religions. These concerns were not fundamentally different from the Brahmanic beliefs (later Hinduism) that had jelled during the fifteen hundred years since the Aryan conquest (see Chapter 2). But both of these religious leaders opposed the **caste** system—the hereditary division into classes—linked with Hinduism, and both saw the possibility for the "release" or salvation of the individual soul regardless of caste or class. Jainism valued extreme asceticism as the means of extinguishing desire and attaining peace. Buddhism favored a "middle way" between an unregulated life of pleasure-seeking and bleak asceticism. The Four Noble Truths of Buddhism are cited in *Witnesses* on p. 26.

The Buddha preached that human fulfillment was attained not by the ardent seeking of goals but by extinguishing all desire. Its true goal, he taught, was **nirvana**, that condition in which all suffering is abolished, along with all personal cravings and qualities. Nirvana could be reached only by following the Eightfold Path of right behavior: in understanding, aspiration, speech, livelihood, ethics, action, thought, and contemplation. Buddha's message succeeded abroad, in east and southeast Asia, spread by missionaries over many centuries. In India, it lost its appeal and became reabsorbed into Hinduism.

The Persian religious reformer Zoroaster (or Zarathustra; c. 628–c. 551 B.C.E.), who was active a century before either Buddha or Confucius, also preached a religion based on righteous conduct. Crusading at first against the corrupt priests known as Magi, who performed the rites of Persian polytheism, he acknowledged only one God, Ahura Mazda ("Wise Lord"), proclaiming him the supreme deity of truth and light. This deity, resembling in some ways both the Egyptian Aten and the Jewish Yahweh, is opposed by a counter-force of evil and darkness, called Angra Mainyu. Throughout past, present, and future, for nine millennia in all, the two struggle. In the end, that struggle will result in victory for the good.

In the universe as conceived by Zoroaster, each individual would face a judgment after death; the righteous would go to heaven, the wicked to hell. This was a new idea in antiquity, where the immortality of the gods was assumed but the stubborn mortality of human beings was known as a certainty. Zoroastrianism appealed to many peoples throughout the Middle East, and at home it enjoyed the support of the Persian emperors. It lingered to enrich Jewish, Christian, and Islamic thought with its hatred of evil and its hope for the triumph of the good.

Judaism and Taoism and the messages of Confucius and Buddha and Zoroaster challenged the polytheistic religions of early civilization. They also made many people less willing to sacrifice wealth and blood to the appetites of gods and goddesses who cared little for humankind. This was the change represented by the event with which this chapter opened: the unbinding of Isaac, freed from the fate of sacrifice but committed to service of the divine will.

The advent of ethically-based monotheistic religions did, however, have at least one seriously negative effect. Because the new deity, the new righteousness, the new heaven were thoroughly masculine, women had even less status than under polytheism. Goddesses—and the priestesses ministering to them—disappeared.

Polytheism continued to flourish in many later civilizations, notably those of Greece and Rome—and in our own time in India, in the Hindu religion. And the Mother Goddess has survived in many guises, all over the world. The Egyptian goddess Isis (see Chapter 7), whose cult flourished in late Roman times, inspired many of the images associated with the Virgin Mary, mother of Jesus. The reverence accorded her by Christians (especially in the Roman Catholic and Orthodox churches) testifies to the enduring strength of the maternal principle in religion.

At the beginning of human civilization, the gods of prehistoric times were securely established as guardians of the known. By the end of the first millennium before the Common Era, among some peoples, these manifold gods had become one God, or one Principle or Source, identified with all the good toward which the human spirit would strive.

Conclusion
THE EARLIEST CIVILIZATIONS AND THE MEANING OF THE WEST

Much of what distinguishes human life today was first attained by the ancient people of the first civilizations. The ability to control nature, to manage food production, to build cities, to conduct trade, to develop technology, to understand science and mathematics, to create works of literature, to establish systems of law, and to ask thoughtful questions about the cosmos and our place in it—all of these were bequeathed to later generations by the first civilizations, and to the "West" specifically by the ancient civilizations of the Middle East. These civilizations offer lessons as well about the organization of the state and the fragility of power. The next chapter will consider this other dimension of life in antiquity.

QUESTIONS TO CONSIDER

1. What would you consider to be the most important biological or behavioral change in the evolution of the human species from hominid to *homo sapiens?*

2. How would you explain the very rapid development in human skills and social organization since the last Ice Age?

3. The earliest civilizations in human history all grew up in river valleys. What opportunities or challenges did that location present to those societies?

4. Why is the possession of the skill of writing seen as an essential benchmark of civilization?

5. What are the questions that ancient peoples asked to which myth and religion gave answers?

SUGGESTED RESOURCES

Bergmann, Martin S., *In the Shadow of Moloch: The Sacrifice of Children and its Impact on Western Religions* (New York: Columbia University Press, 1993). An eye-opening account of the ritual convention of child sacrifice and its shaping of ancient cultures.

Burkert, Walter, *Creation of the Sacred: Tracks of Biology in Early Religions* (Cambridge MA: Harvard University Press, 1996). Proposes that ancient religious practices are a natural and perhaps necessary development from human biology, thus explaining the universality of many features of religion, such as the practice of sacrifice and a sense of guilt.

Cavalli-Sforza, Luigi Luca, *Genes, Peoples, and Languages*, trans. Mark Seielstad (New York: Farrar, Straus & Giroux; North Point Press, 2000). Linking complex genetic and linguistic evidence, Cavalli-Sforza proposes to map the history of the migrations of all the world's peoples.

Cross, Frank Moore, *Canaanite Myth and Hebrew Epic: Essays in the History of the Religion of Israel* (Cambridge, MA.: Harvard University Press, 1973; reprint 1997). Traces continuities between early Israelite religion and its underlying Canaanite culture. Explores re-emergence of Canaanite mythic material in the apocalypticism of early Christianity and the Dead Sea Scrolls.

Diamond, Jared, *Guns, Germs and Steel: The Fates of Human Societies* (New York: W.W. Norton, 1997). A brilliant exploration of the geographical and material conditions that permitted Eurasian civilizations to advance and gain dominance.

Fagan, Brian M., *The Journey from Eden: The Peopling of Our World* (London: Thames & Hudson, 1990). A critical overview of theories of human origin, arguing on the basis of recent historical, paleoanthropological, and genetic research that fully modern humans evolved in Africa and from there colonized the rest of the world.

Hodder, Ian, *The Domestication of Europe: Structure and Contingency in Neolithic Societies* (Cambridge, MA: Basil Blackwell, 1990). A bold if controversial attempt to reconstruct human societies in the Near East and Europe at the end of the Ice Age.

Leakey, Richard and Roger Lewin, *Origins Reconsidered: In Search of What Makes Us Human* (New York: Doubleday, 1992). Reflections by a renowned paleoanthropologist on his own discoveries of early hominid life in East Africa. Leakey incorporates ideas from philosophy, anthropology, molecular biology, and linguistics to investigate not only how we evolved anatomically but how we acquired the qualities that make us human: consciousness, creativity, and culture.

Leeming, David A. & Jake Page, *Goddess: The Myths of the Female Divine* (Oxford: Oxford University Press, 1994). A biography of the "goddess," the compelling, commanding, threatening female divinity revered by human populations from the Ice Age to modern times, showing how ancient themes endure in modern religion and psychology.

Leick, Gwendolyn, *Mesopotamia: the Invention of the City* (London: Allen Lane, 2001; rpt. Penguin, 2003). Elicits from the evidence of textiles, jeweled artifacts, and literary texts the structures and interactions of the world's first cities.

Martin, Henri Jean (trans. Lydia G. Cochrane), *The History and Power of Writing* (Chicago: University of Chicago Press, 1995). A comprehensive study by a preeminent scholar of the book. Examines the technologies, forms, and structures of writing throughout history.

McElvaine, Robert S., *Eve's Seed: Biology, the Sexes, and the Course of History* (New York: McGraw Hill, 2000). Fills in the history between the culmination of human evolution and the establishment of civilization, a period when women's role was dominant before envious men overturned power relations.

Nissen, Hans J., *The Early History of the Ancient Near East, 9000–2000 B.C.* (Chicago: University of Chicago Press, 1988). A balanced political and cultural history of Mesopotamia, based on archaeological sources and analysis of material culture.

The Indus Valley civilization:
http://www.historyofindia.com/indus.html
http://www.harappa.com/har/har0.html

The *Analects* of Confucius:
http://classics.mit.edu/Confucius/analects.html

Bible tools—text and history:
http://bible.crosswalk.com

◉ Western Civilization Documents CD-ROM

1.1 New Theories about Human Development
1.2 An Egyptian Hymn to the Nile
1.3 The Epic of Gilgamesh
1.5 Hammurabi's Law Code
1.7 The Instruction of the Ptah-hotep

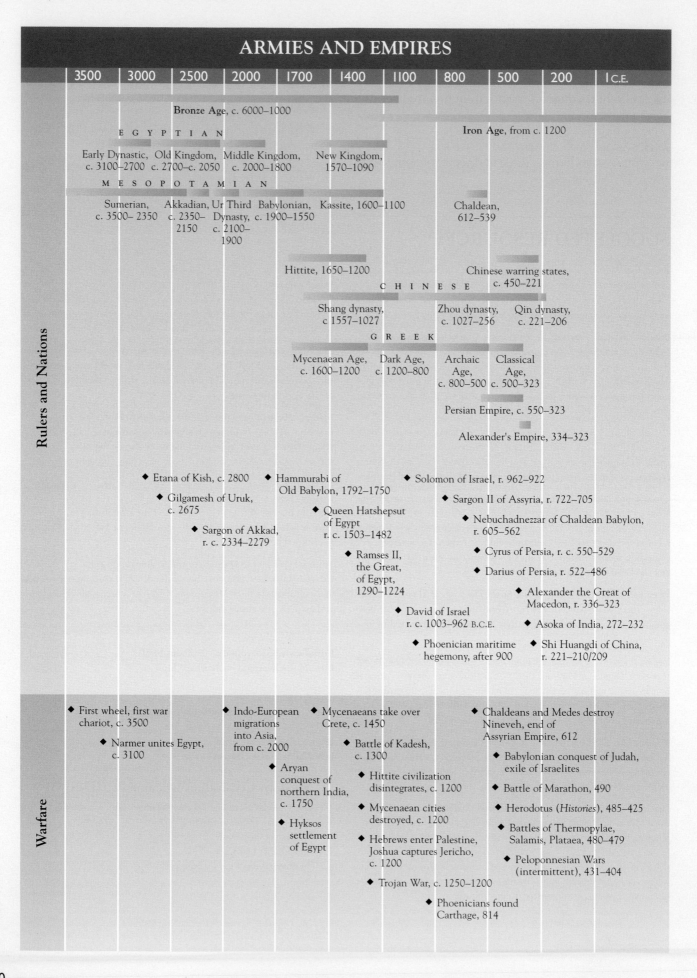

ARMIES AND EMPIRES

| 3500 | 3000 | 2500 | 2000 | 1700 | 1400 | 1100 | 800 | 500 | 200 | 1 C.E. |

Bronze Age, c. 6000–1000

Iron Age, from c. 1200

E G Y P T I A N

Early Dynastic, Old Kingdom, Middle Kingdom, New Kingdom,
c. 3100–2700 c. 2700–c. 2050 c. 2000–1800 1570–1090

M E S O P O T A M I A N

Sumerian, Akkadian, Ur Third Babylonian, Kassite, 1600–1100
c. 3500– 2350 c. 2350– Dynasty, c. 1900–1550
2150 c. 2100–
1900

Chaldean,
612–539

Hittite, 1650–1200

Chinese warring states,
c. 450–221

C H I N E S E

Shang dynasty, Zhou dynasty, Qin dynasty,
c 1557–1027 c. 1027–256 c. 221–206

G R E E K

Mycenaean Age, Dark Age, Archaic Classical
c. 1600–1200 c. 1200–800 Age, Age,
c. 800–500 c. 500–323

Persian Empire, c. 550–323

Alexander's Empire, 334–323

Rulers and Nations

◆ Etana of Kish, c. 2800   ◆ Hammurabi of   ◆ Solomon of Israel, r. 962–922
Old Babylon, 1792–1750
◆ Gilgamesh of Uruk,   ◆ Sargon II of Assyria, r. 722–705
c. 2675
◆ Queen Hatshepsut   ◆ Nebuchadnezzar of Chaldean Babylon,
◆ Sargon of Akkad,   of Egypt   r. 605–562
r. c. 2334–2279   r. c. 1503–1482
◆ Cyrus of Persia, r. c. 550–529
◆ Ramses II,
the Great,   ◆ Darius of Persia, r. 522–486
of Egypt,
1290–1224   ◆ Alexander the Great of
Macedon, r. 336–323
◆ David of Israel
r. c. 1003–962 B.C.E.   ◆ Asoka of India, 272–232

◆ Phoenician maritime   ◆ Shi Huangdi of China,
hegemony, after 900   r. 221–210/209

Warfare

◆ First wheel, first war   ◆ Indo-European   ◆ Mycenaeans take over   ◆ Chaldeans and Medes destroy
chariot, c. 3500   migrations   Crete, c. 1450   Nineveh, end of
into Asia,   Assyrian Empire, 612
◆ Narmer unites Egypt,   from c. 2000   ◆ Battle of Kadesh,
c. 3100   c. 1300   ◆ Babylonian conquest of Judah,
◆ Aryan   exile of Israelites
conquest of   ◆ Hittite civilization
northern India,   disintegrates, c. 1200   ◆ Battle of Marathon, 490
c. 1750
◆ Mycenaean cities   ◆ Herodotus (Histories), 485–425
◆ Hyksos   destroyed, c. 1200
settlement   ◆ Battles of Thermopylae,
of Egypt   ◆ Hebrews enter Palestine,   Salamis, Plataea, 480–479
Joshua captures Jericho,
c. 1200   ◆ Peloponnesian Wars
(intermittent), 431–404
◆ Trojan War, c. 1250–1200

◆ Phoenicians found
Carthage, 814

2

ARMIES AND EMPIRES

Politics and Power in the
Bronze and Iron Ages

3500–300 B.C.E.

core areas of Old World civilizations,
c.3500-1000 BCE

secondary civilized areas, c.1000-500 BCE

KEY QUESTIONS

◆ **Power and Civilization:** Why did the rulers of
ancient civilization wage war? What kinds of
weapons and armies did they have to do so?

◆ **Bronze Age Kingdoms in Egypt and
Mesopotamia:** Which of the rival states emerged
victorious in Mesopotamia? How successful were
Egypt's pharaohs in maintaining power?

◆ **Bronze Age Kingdoms in the Aegean and the
Levant:** What were the characteristics of the
Hittite and Mycenaean civilizations? What
calamities beset the Levant and the Aegean
around 1200 B.C.E.?

◆ **Iron Age Empires of the Middle East:** What
made Assyria a particularly dangerous neighbor?

◆ **Bronze and Iron Age Kingdoms in East and
South Asia:** What characteristics of later
Chinese civilization emerged under the Shang,
Zhou, and Qin emperors? What role did the
Aryan invasion play in the development of
civilization in India?

◆ **The Birth of the West:** How and why did
Mycenaean rule in the Aegean region end? What
kind of civilization emerged in its stead?

During the reign of King Xerxes of Persia (r. 486–465 B.C.E.), two citizens of the ancient Greek city of Sparta journeyed to the Persian court on an official mission. It was the custom for visitors to prostrate themselves before the King of Kings, as Xerxes called himself. Ordered to do so, the Spartans refused "and said they would never do any such thing, even were their heads thrust down to the ground; for it was not their custom to worship men ..." The Spartans' refusal to abase themselves before a king announces a theme that would recur often in the history of the Western world.

Long before these Spartans faced the Persian monarch, who could have ordered their execution with a nod of his head, the power of kings, who reigned in nearly all the civilized regions of the globe, had grown vigorous and irresistible. Their taste for war wrought devastation and enslaved multitudes. Their need for weapons to fight these wars spurred innovation and trade. Their zeal for glory inspired great tombs and monuments, which also testify to the genius of the artists who made them. Their quest for domination led to the creation of larger and larger empires. The struggles that resulted from this accumulation of power in the hands of kings forcefully shaped the course of civilization.

POWER AND CIVILIZATION

Kings appeared almost as soon as civilization began. They reigned in most nations of the world for some 5000 years, until, early in the twentieth century, world war started to close the chapter on most kings. Until then, the history of world politics is largely the history of **monarchy**, or "the rule of one." Ancient monarchs were mostly male, and nearly divine. They were gods, they claimed, or became gods, or took the place of gods (see *Witnesses*, p. 33). Although religion buttressed monarchy, kings still imposed their will by force. They forged empires and held power by accumulating weapons and waging war. Some of these important rulers are listed in *Who's Who* on pp. 34, 37, 48, 49, and 50.

Kings, Queens, and Priests

Monarchy developed partly from the religious beliefs of early civilizations. People believed that they were governed by the gods, represented by their priests. Such societies are called **theocracies**. Gradually the rule of priests gave way to that of a single person, although the priests remained a privileged group. This individual cast himself as a representative of the gods, or the son of a god, or even a god himself.

The Egyptian pharaoh was believed to rise from death in the form of the god Horus, son of the divine judge Osiris, and to reign with him eternally. This divine afterlife is expressed in the pyramid, a monument whose clear, converging lines bridge earth and heaven. The superhuman status of King Sargon of Akkad (r. c. 2334–2279 B.C.E.) is indicated by his having been miraculously rescued in infancy from a basket set adrift on the Euphrates River (like the biblical story of Moses). Hammurabi (c. 1792–1750) was depicted receiving directly from the Supreme God, Shamash, the code of laws he published (see *Windows On*, p. 22). Assyrian kings were priests of the warrior god Assur, and Hittite kings, called "Sun" while alive, were hailed as gods upon their death. Chinese monarchs claimed to rule by the mandate of heaven.

Rarely did a woman rule in her own right from the outset. The biblical judge and perhaps mythical prophetess Deborah (Judges: 4–5), and the legendary Amazon queens (see Chapter 3) were thought to have done so. Most monarchs were male. Where the legitimate male ruler had died or was still a child, his widow or mother might rule in his stead. Hatshepsut of Egypt (r. c. 1503–1482 B.C.E.), Summuramat of Assyria (ninth century B.C.E.) (the legendary Semiramis), and Artemisia (fifth century B.C.E.) of Halicarnassus (a city in Asia Minor) were **surrogate**, or substitute, rulers of this kind.

Apart from their claims to divinity, kings acquired power through their military skills. Violence threatened early societies. Even before human communities grew from village to city, people preyed upon each other. Paleolithic remains show that the stone weapons used to bring down bear and bull were also used to smash human skulls and limbs: evidence of homicide, at least, if not of battle. Skeletons from Neolithic times, in mass graves and marked by multiple injuries, testify to the invention of organized war.

Even the oldest towns archaeologists have explored had thick walls and tall watchtowers (see Chapter 1). These structures guarded town dwellers from attack not only from wild beasts roaming outside the walls, but other humans like themselves. Especially fit and skilled men were chosen to hold the battlements and direct the defense, or to lead and pursue an assault. Some of these war chiefs became kings. Their fellow warriors became the nobility, professionals equipped with the finest weapons.

Weapons and Warriors

The earliest weapons were only the sticks and stones that early humans found readily at hand, but during the Neolithic age and the first civilizations weapons became increasingly sophisticated and effective. With the mace (stone head, wooden handle) Neolithic warriors could smash their enemies, and with a carved stone dagger stab them. With a sling

The Idea of the King

The kings who ruled ancient civilizations claimed extraordinary powers; the whole later history of politics can be seen, in part, as the story of the moderation of, or restraint on, the kingly power possessed by ancient monarchs. The first passage is from an edict of the reforming Buddhist king of India, Asoka, who sets forth a different ideal: that of the monarch's responsibility for the welfare of his people. The second and third passages testify to the high claims of the monarchs of Egypt and Persia. The fourth contains a warning against the power of kings by the Hebrew judge Samuel, who would anoint David and Saul as kings of Israel.

King Asoka issues an edict about the duty of the ruler for the welfare of his people (c. 250 B.C.E.): In the past, state business was not transacted nor were reports delivered to the king at all hours. But now I have given this order, that at any time, whether I am eating, in the women's quarters, the bed chamber, the chariot, ... the park or wherever, reporters are to be posted with instructions to report to me the affairs of the people so that I might attend to these affairs wherever I am. And ... when urgent business presses itself ..., if disagreement or debate arises in the Council, then it must be reported to me immediately. ... Truly, I consider the welfare of all to be my duty, and the root of this is exertion and the prompt despatch of business. There is no better work than promoting the welfare of all the people and whatever efforts I am making is to repay the debt I owe to all beings to assure their happiness in this life, and attain heaven in the next. Therefore this ... edict has been written to last long and that my sons, grandsons and great-grandsons might act in conformity with it for the welfare of the world.
(From The Edicts of King Asoka, trans. Ven. S. Dhammika, 1993)

Obey the divine pharaoh:
He is Re [the sun], by whose beams one sees,
   He is the one who illumines the Two Lands
[of Egypt] more than the sun disc.

He is one who makes the land greener than [does] a high Nile,
   For he has filled the Two Lands with strength and life ...
He whom the king has loved will be a revered one,
   But there is no tomb for a rebel against his majesty,
   And his corpse is cast into the water.
(From J. B. Pritchard ed., Ancient Near Eastern Texts relating to the Old Testament, 2e, 1955)

Darius, king of Persia, says who he is (c. 500 B.C.E.): A great god is Ahuramazda, who created this earth, who created yonder sky, who created man, who created happiness for man, who made Darius king, one king of many, one lord of many. I am Darius the Great King, King of Kings, King of countries containing all kinds of men, King in this great earth far and wide, son of Hystaspes, an Achaemenian, a Persian, son of a Persian, an Aryan, having Aryan lineage ... Ahuramazda, when he saw this earth in commotion, thereafter bestowed it upon me, made me king; I am king ... This which has been done, all that by the will of Ahuramazda I did.
(From R. G. Kent, Old Persian: Grammar, Texts, Lexicon, 2e, 1953)

Advised by Yahweh, Samuel warns the Israelites about kings: So Samuel reported all the words of the Lord to the people who were asking him for a king. He said, "These will be the ways of the king who will reign over you: he will take your sons and appoint them to his chariots and to be his horsemen, and to run before his chariots; and he will appoint for himself commanders of thousands and commanders of fifties, and some to plow his ground and to reap his harvest, and to make his implements of war and the equipment of his chariots. He will take your daughters to be perfumers and cooks and bakers ... He will take one-tenth of your flocks, and you shall be his slaves. And in that day you will cry out because of your king, whom you have chosen for yourselves; but the Lord will not answer you in that day."
(1 Samuel 8:10–18)

of wood and leather they could hurl a small stone, or with a wooden bow they could launch a wooden arrow tipped in stone.

These primitive weapons remained effective even into later ages when metal began to be used. According to the Bible, the Israelite youth David opposed the Philistine hero Goliath with sling and stone. "Am I a dog," Goliath sneered, "that you come to me with sticks?" But David's simple weapon prevailed over the Philistine's bronze sword (I Samuel 17:41–50). Centuries later, the Roman army, the most formidable military force of the ancient world, still massed slingers, whose missiles were of stone, and bowmen in its rear lines.

But metal was better. The sharp edge of a bronze weapon allowed a warrior to penetrate (rather than smash) the body of his enemy. The stone dagger would break if it met resistance, but the long bronze sword ripped through flesh. The bronze-bladed axe could do much more damage than the mace. Wheeled chariots staffed with spearmen were deadlier than a line of bowmen, even those equipped with bronze arrowheads. Iron weapons mimicked those of bronze, but were cheaper and stronger. Hence iron made possible the multiplication of weapons and of wars.

Weapons were not only useful, they were also a form of wealth, whose possession conferred status. Military equipment was elaborate and expensive.

Besides weapons, it included pieces of armor: shin-plates (greaves) and chestplate, shield and helmet, each piece invested with the glamour of rarity and power. These objects were buried with monarchs as tokens of their rank. The artisan or peasant possessed little bronze, as it was rarely used to make the implements of their daily life. Although it gave its name to the whole age, it was in fact the attribute only of the rich who ruled.

Like their kings, the upper-class warriors of the first civilizations came to the field armed in bronze—one form of wealth. For their prowess, they were rewarded with land or treasure. For millennia, the social order of noble warriors would rank higher than that of any laborer—merchant, farmer, or artisan.

Waging War

Then, as now, these warriors dealt in mass destruction. They devastated cities, the centers of civilization, and ravaged whole populations, who faced the alternatives of death or **slavery**. The colossal walls around a city could not offer total protection. The population could be surrounded and starved and those sturdy walls breached—by surrender, by storming, or by treachery. Then the unleashed invading army would run through the streets to loot and burn. Many accounts of ancient battles depict the storm and sack of cities (see *Witnesses*, p. 36). According to the Bible, Jericho was seized (its walls felled by the sound of trumpets) by the Israelites under Joshua, who "put everyone to the sword, men and women, young and old, and also cattle, sheep, and asses" (Joshua 6:21). Ur, in Sumer, was devastated by Sargon of Akkad in c. 2000 B.C.E., and Troy, according to legend, was sacked and ravaged by the Greeks, its men killed and its women enslaved (see Chapter 4).

The captors of a city might kill or deport the vanquished king, along with his brothers and sons, advisors and noble retinue, and other prominent persons, such as the temple priests and the skilled artisans. Sometimes the entire population was killed, or exiled to another city, to vanish as a people. Some of the lost kingdoms and lost peoples of the ancient world, such as the Indus Valley civilization, may have disappeared in this way. Alternatively, the male inhabitants of the conquered city might be slain, but the captive women and children would have been brought home to labor as servants, concubines, and prostitutes (see Chapter 1)—history's first slaves.

From the outset of civilization, war and peace were seen as the poles of human experience. An oblong box from ancient Sumer, known as the "Royal Standard of Ur," is decorated in mosaic with scenes of war on one side, those of peace on the other. In the same way, war and peace are the alternate modes of life depicted on the shield made by the god Hephaistos for the warrior Achilles, as recounted in the *Iliad* (18:478–613), the eighth-century epic poem attributed to Homer (see Chapter 4).

Kings and nobles, armies bristling with bronze weapons, the consolidation of states, the destruction of cities and even whole populations—all these were well-established in early antiquity. Over three millennia, a ceaseless cycle of warfare caused the appearance and disappearance of human communities as monarchs built or acquired their kingdoms, their dynasties, and empires.

BRONZE AGE KINGDOMS IN EGYPT AND MESOPOTAMIA

From the birth of the Bronze Age until about 1200 B.C.E., rulers of single cities expanded their authority over surrounding lands, creating kingdoms for themselves (see Map 2.1). The first to do so were the pharaohs of Egypt, who created a unified kingdom that would endure for nearly 3000 years. Meanwhile the war chiefs of the Sumerian cities extended their rule over neighboring communities, to be engulfed in turn by kings based in Akkad and Babylon. These Bronze Age kingdoms were the earliest to form in the history of humankind. They were pioneers in the concentration of power, the extension of rule, and the control of subject populations. Directly or indirectly, their model has influenced most of the world's subsequent political systems.

Egypt and its Pharaohs

The pharaohs came to power by absorbing the small communities of the region. Before civilization began, people of the Nile River valley clustered in towns headed by local chiefs. These clusters were scattered throughout the region, extending deep into the upper Nile zone of present-day Sudan, known in antiquity as Nubia. Some chiefs were sovereign over a single town, some over several. In time, these separate communities were absorbed into two kingdoms: those of Upper Egypt to the south, and Lower Egypt to the

WHO'S WHO

In Egypt

Narmer (r. c. 3100 B.C.E.) (traditionally called Menes) King who unites Egypt.

Hatshepsut (r. c. 1503–1482 B.C.E.) Pharaoh of Egypt, one of the few ancient queens to hold sovereign power.

Ramses II the Great (1290–1224 B.C.E.) Pharaoh of Egypt, who extends Egyptian power into Palestine and contends with the Hittites at Kadesh.

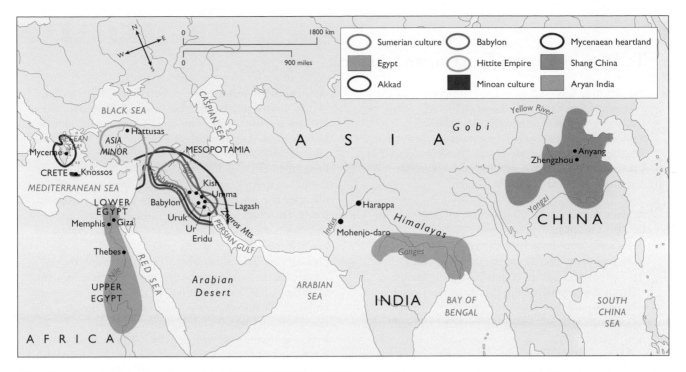

Map 2.1 Bronze Age Empires of the Old World, 3500–1200 B.C.E.: *Rulers and dynasties contended with each other, and the form, core, and extent of their domains shifted constantly.* Why do states rise and fall often, but civilizations endure?

north. The identity of the rulers of these two adjoining kingdoms remains unknown.

By 3100 B.C.E., these kingdoms were united under a single ruler, King Narmer (traditionally called Menes). Where there had been many kings, then two, there was now one. Narmer's achievement was announced and celebrated with complex imagery as shown on the Palette of Narmer on p. 37. He was depicted as wearing two crowns: the peaked White Crown and flatter Red Crown, of Upper and Lower Egypt respectively. The symbol of Narmer's clan, the falcon, was associated with the god Horus, a divine association strengthening his claim to sovereignty.

Narmer established the capital of his kingdom at Memphis in Lower Egypt, not far from the site, at Giza, where later pharaohs would raise the greatest of the pyramids. Under his successors, of the First and Second dynasties, Egypt grew in size, prosperity, and technical expertise, including the arts of building and writing. By about 2700 B.C.E. the main features of Egyptian civilization were established.

The pharaohs of the following five centuries—a period known as the Old Kingdom—enjoyed absolute power (see *Witnesses*, p. 33). Even during the political changes of later periods, Egyptian life and culture remained remarkably stable. The annual flooding of the Nile was a constant factor that regulated economic life, and the pharaoh in every dynasty personified the principle of cosmic constancy and justice expressed by the word *Ma'at*.

The pharaohs of the Middle Kingdom (who ruled from about 2050 to nearly 1800 B.C.E.) pursued a mainly defensive military strategy. Already protected by the desert to the west and the Red Sea to the east, they needed a minimal force to guard the frontier.

When Egypt was settled around 1700 B.C.E. by a nomadic people called the Hyksos, the newcomers met little resistance. Taking possession of Egypt, these "Kings of foreign lands" ruled from Avaris, in the eastern delta, for about 150 years. Then, beginning in about 1570 B.C.E., a new line of pharaohs gained power, launching the New Kingdom (1570–1090 B.C.E.). They expelled the Hyksos and pursued a strategy of expansion which continued to the brink of the **Iron Age**. After a confrontation with the Hittites in the 1200s, Egypt ceased to expand. Later, successive conquests by the Persians, Macedonians, Romans, Arabs, and Turks would put Egypt under foreign domination for the better part of 2000 years.

Mesopotamian Kingdoms

The first pharaohs of Egypt created a large, centralized state. The earliest kings of lower Mesopotamia, in contrast, ruled cities: one, two, or perhaps as many as ten. But although they had relatively modest powers over a small area, these kings were revered for their achievements and allegedly divine attributes.

Among the earliest written documents we possess are "king lists" from Sumer, the first political power of ancient Mesopotamia. The first ruler noted in these chronicles was Etana (c. 2800 B.C.E.) of the city of Kish, described as "he who stabilized all the lands" and as having later "ascended to heaven."

Sumer did not have dynasties, in the modern sense of the word (unless a family could establish a

To War in Sumer, Canaan, and Assyria

Ancient war was total war. The conquering army razed the walls of the enemy city, looted and raped, slaughtered combatants and innocents, and enslaved whole populations. Some scenes of these conflicts are given here: the destruction of Sumerian Ur, the Israelite conquest of Jericho, and, in three separate boastful reports, the devastation wrought by Assyrian kings.

A poet laments the destruction of the city of Ur (c. 2000 B.C.E.):

> Its walls were breached; the people groan.
> In its lofty gates, where they were wont to
>   promenade, dead bodies were lying about;
> In its boulevards, where the feasts were celebrated,
>   scattered they lay ...
> Ur—its weak and its strong perished through
>   hunger;
> Mothers and fathers who did not leave their houses,
>   were overcome by fire;
> The young lying on their mothers' laps, like fish
>   were carried off by the waters. ...

(From J. B. Pritchard ed., *Ancient Near Eastern Texts relating to the Old Testament*, 2e, 1955)

Joshua and the Israelites take the city of Jericho with a shout: On the seventh day they rose early, at dawn, and marched around the city in the same manner seven times. ... And at the seventh time, when the priests had blown the trumpets, Joshua said to the people, "Shout! For the Lord has given you the city. The city and all that is in it shall be devoted to the Lord for destruction. ... " So the people shouted, and the trumpets were blown. As soon as the people heard the sound of the trumpets, they raised a great shout, and the wall fell down flat; so the people charged straight ahead into the city and captured it. Then they devoted to destruction by the edge of the sword all in the city, both men and women, young and old, oxen, sheep and donkeys.
(Joshua 6:15–17, 20–21)

Tiglathpileser I reports his conquests (c. 1100 B.C.E.): Assur and the great gods, who have made my kingdom great, and who have bestowed might and power as a ... gift, commanded that I should extend the boundary of their land, and they intrusted to my hand their mighty weapons, the storm of battle. Lands, mountains, cities, and princes, the enemies of Arrus, I have brought under my sway, and have subdued their territories. With sixty kings ... I fought, and established (my) victorious might over them. I was without an equal in battle, or a rival in the fight. I enlarged the frontier of my land, and all of their lands I brought under my sway.
(From D. D. Luckenbill ed., *Ancient Records of Assyria and Babylonia I*, 1968)

Assurnasirpal puts down a revolt (c. 870 B.C.E.): While I was staying in the land of Kutmuki, they brought me the word: "The city of Suru of Bit-Halupe has revolted, they have slain Hamatai, their governor, and Ahiababa, the son of nobody, whom they have brought from Bit-Adini, they have set up as king over them." ... to the city of Bit-Halupe I drew near, and the terror of the splendor of Assur, my lord, overwhelmed them. The chief men and the elders of the city, to save their lives, came forth into my presence and embraced my feet, saying: 'If it is thy pleasure, slay! If it is thy pleasure, let live! That which thy heart desireth, do!' Ahiababa, the son of a nobody, whom they had brought from Bit-Adini, I took captive. In the valor of my heart and with the fury of my weapons I stormed the city. All the rebels they seized and delivered them up ... Azi-ilu I set over them as my own governor. I built a pillar over against his city gate, and I flayed all the chief men who had revolted, and I covered the pillar with their skins; some I walled up within the pillar, some I impaled upon the pillar on stakes, and others I bound to stakes round about the pillar; many within the border of my own land I flayed, and I spread their skins upon the walls; and I cut off the limbs of the officers, of the royal officers who had rebelled. Ahiababa I took to Nineveh, I flayed him, I spread his skin upon the wall of Nineveh.
(From A. Ferrill, *Origins of War: From the Stone Age to Alexander the Great*, 1985)

Sennacherib triumphs over Hezekiah (c. 688 B.C.E.): As to Hezekiah, the Jew, who did not submit to my yoke, I laid siege to 46 of his strong cities, walled forts; and to the countless small villages in their vicinity, and conquered them by means of well-stamped ramps and battering-rams brought near to the walls combined with the attack by foot soldiers, using mines, breeches as well as sapper work. I drove out 200,150 people, young and old, male and female, horses, mules, donkeys, camels, big and small cattle beyond counting ... Himself I made a prisoner in Jerusalem, his royal residence, like a bird in a cage. ... Hezekiah himself, whom the terror-inspiring splendour of my lordship had overwhelmed ... did send me, later, to Nineveh, my lordly city, together with 30 talents of gold, 800 talents of silver, precious stones, antimony, large cuts of red stone, couches, inlaid with ivory ... daughters, concubines, male and female musicians.
(From H. V. F. Winstone, *Uncovering the Ancient World*, 1986)

WHO'S WHO

In Mesopotamia

Etana of Kish (r. c 2800 B.C.E.) first Sumerian ruler to form a kingdom beyond his own city.

Gilgamesh of Uruk (c. 2675 B.C.E.) Sumerian king whose deeds are recorded in history's oldest epic, *Gilgamesh*.

Sargon of Akkad (r. c. 2334–2279 B.C.E.) conquers Sumerian cities and builds the first empire.

Hammurabi of Babylon (r. 1792–1750 B.C.E.) Amorite king, famed for his *Code of Laws* (c. 1790 B.C.E.).

dynasty), but a "kingship," which passed from one city to another. After Kish's heyday, the kingship passed to the city of Uruk, which nurtured some renowned kings. Among them was Dumuzi, identified with a god who dies and is resurrected. Better known, however, was Dumuzi's successor, Gilgamesh. As immortalized in legend, the hero Gilgamesh symbolized the tragedy of human existence. The historical Gilgamesh ruled Uruk at about the time the kings of Ur also gained prominence, in about 2675 B.C.E. There would follow the kings of Lagash and Umma

and Eridu, each of whom was a divinely appointed ruler of a different Sumerian city.

Another king of Uruk, Lugalzaggesi ("lugal" meant "king"), was captured after twenty years of military triumph and brought in chains to the city of Nippur as the booty of King Sargon the Great. By 2331 B.C.E., Sargon had conquered and unified many of the cities of the Tigris-Euphrates Valley and beyond, from the Syrian tip of the Fertile Crescent down to the Persian Gulf. He thereby achieved for the region a consolidation comparable to Narmer's earlier unification of Egypt.

An imaginative administrator and clever fashioner of his own image, Sargon built a new capital c. 2300 B.C.E., called Akkad, which had a population of about 5400. Here, he presided over a huge court of nobles and officials. Akkad gave its name to Akkadian, the civilization founded by Sargon, and also to the Semitic language spoken by its people. For 1000 years Akkadian was the universal tongue of the Middle East.

The Akkadian conquerors imposed their language on the vanquished Sumerians. Yet, in a pattern that would often be repeated, the Akkadians were themselves "conquered." They adopted many of the innovations of Sumerian life, and so perpetuated the civilization of their victims. The wheel and the sailing boat, myth and poetry, ceramic and metallurgical techniques, agricultural methods and reckoning of

Victory in Egypt *(Palette of Narmer, front and back): Narmer, king of Upper Egypt, became the first pharaoh and began the political history of Egyptian civilization by conquering the lands of his rival, the king of Lower Egypt (c. 3100 B.C.E.). On the front of the slate palette commemorating the victory from Hierakonpolis (left), Narmer seizes his enemy by the hair and raises his mace to strike. Below his feet are represented two of his defeated foes. (Egyptian Museum, Cairo)*

weights and measures developed by the civilization of Sumer, and above all its system of writing were used by the Akkadians as well. Cuneiform writing, which had recorded the Sumerian language (now dead), passed into the service of a Semitic language which even today has many relatives.

Like all other kingdoms, Sargon's eventually fell—in the reign of his descendant Naramsin, around 2250 B.C.E. Now, wrote a contemporary, Akkad's "canalboat towpaths grew nothing but weeds," the chariot roads were overgrown, and "no human being walks because of the wild goats, vermin, snakes, and mountain scorpions." The Sumerian cities briefly revived around 2100 B.C.E. under the leadership of the Third Dynasty of Ur. Then, early in the second millennium B.C.E., control of the region was seized by Babylon, capital of a Semitic people called the Amorites. The Amorites migrated from Syria to the Mesopotamian valley around 1900 B.C.E. and established themselves not far from Akkad. Among their kings was the renowned Hammurabi, codifier of the laws (see Chapter 1).

After 1600 B.C.E., other rulers displaced the descendants of Hammurabi in the Mesopotamian heartland. Dynasty yielded to dynasty over 1500 years, leaving behind destroyed cities, lost peoples, and memories of great deeds. Meanwhile, new and energetic kingdoms were forming farther west, in Asia Minor and around the Mediterranean.

BRONZE AGE KINGDOMS IN THE AEGEAN AND THE NEAR EAST

While the power of Mesopotamian and Egyptian monarchs was at its zenith, peoples speaking Indo-European languages spread into many parts of Europe and Asia. Their strong kingdoms would challenge those of the senior civilizations, while they easily overcame their lesser rivals. Of these new kingdoms, the Mycenaean and Hittite were the first to flourish.

The Arrival of the Indo-Europeans

By 2000 B.C.E., the long migrations of Indo-European speakers from their barren homelands north of the Black and Caspian seas ended, and they settled in new and more hospitable regions closer to the centers of civilization (see Chapter 1 and Map 2.2). They had pushed west and northwest into Europe as far as Iceland; south and east into India; south into Iran; and south and west into the Balkans, Greece, and Asia Minor. They brought with them new gods and goddesses, swift horses, and a militarist tradition.

Indo-European peoples brought to their new homes a religion centered on the worship of a preeminent sky god, the wielder of lightning and thunder. This deity appears among the Aryan settlers of India with the name Dyaus Pitar, among the Greeks as Zeus, among the Romans as Jupiter (note the similarity in the sounds of the names).

Indo-European tribesmen were master horsemen. Hitching a light cart to their racing mounts, they created the chariot of ancient warfare. Unlike the noble warriors of Mesopotamia or Egypt, they followed chiefs into battle who owed no allegiance to an all-powerful king. When the united tribes needed a leader, the chiefs together chose one of their number, who ruled with only a limited mandate and no expectation of hereditary succession.

The culture of the newcomers—their language, use of horses, and patterns of authority—impressed itself on the peoples among whom they settled. At the same time, the natives' culture supplied elements

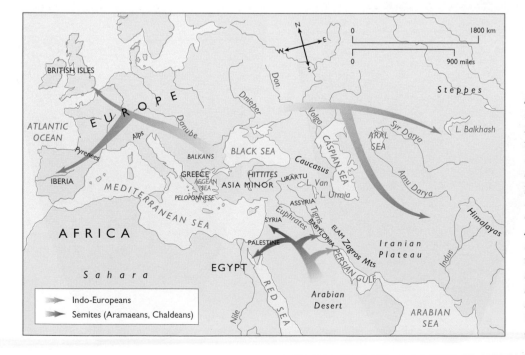

Map 2.2 Semitic and Indo-European Speakers, 3000–2000 B.C.E.: *Although the pioneers of civilization, the Sumerians, spoke a language now extinct, most of the founders of the Middle-Eastern kingdoms spoke either a Semitic (or related Afro-Asiatic) or an Indo-European language. During the third and second millennia B.C.E., speakers of both language groups were on the move.* Why do some languages become dominant over others?

that the invaders' lacked. The word "ocean," absent from the vocabulary of a people whose entire past was on the land-locked **steppes**, was borrowed from the Mediterranean people they conquered. The word *thalassa*, meaning "sea," was absorbed into early Greek from the non-Indo-European language of the indigenous Aegean people.

Civilizations of the Aegean and Asia Minor

Two Indo-European kingdoms grew to dominate the region around the Aegean Sea. One, the Mycenaean, occupied part of the Greek mainland and its islands; the other, the Hittite, controlled the area of Asia Minor. Both were characterized by strong monarchies and an aggressive program of expansion.

The Indo-Europeans who migrated south through the Balkans and settled in mainland Greece were the ancestors of the Greeks. Intermingling with native populations, whom they easily subdued, they created a new civilization, discovered only in the last hundred years or so. It is called Mycenaean, after **Mycenae**, the name given by archaeologists to one of the chief cities excavated and one which may possibly be the kingdom of Mycenae in Homer's *Iliad*. Other Mycenaean sites have been located at Thebes (not to be confused with the Egyptian city of that name) and at Tiryns, Pylos, Corinth, and Athens.

Mycenaean civilization revered horses and cherished weapons. The treasuries of kings were packed with the implements of war, crafted in bronze—helmets, shields, swords, knives, the parts of chariots. The same objects were found in the tombs of Mycenaean kings, as was the mask depicted on p. 40. These took two forms: shaft graves under the earth (c. 1600 B.C.E.) and after about 1500 B.C.E. "beehive" or **tholos** tombs, huge earthwork mounds constructed on the surface. More than eighty of these monuments have been uncovered, the largest reaching to a height of over 43 feet (13 m.).

The military focus of Mycenaean civilization is visible in the fortified palaces of its kings. Mycenaean monarchs ruled self-sufficient but loosely allied city-states. The king's residence was a complex arranged around the central hall where the business of state was managed. Here the king and his consort sat enthroned before a sacred hearth, symbolic of the hearth of the whole city. Other rooms and storehouses radiating around the central hall housed an army of bureaucrats, who administered the king's land, treasure, and trading ventures.

Beyond the royal precinct was the city itself, populated mainly by artisans, and enclosed by massive stone walls pierced by an imposing gate, as shown in *Windows On* on pp. 44–5. Outside the walls were the lands worked by peasants but owned by the priests and the kings' warrior companions.

The primary source of wealth for the kings and their companions was the booty taken by raiding other communities in the Aegean region. Profits came also from trade. Mycenaeans participated in the commercial networks of the eastern Mediterranean in the second millennium B.C.E. Their sailing ships reached Crete and Asia Minor, Egypt, and the eastern shore of the Mediterranean. Their excellent pottery, decorated with their favorite themes of men in battle, circulated all over the region. An example is shown in *Windows On* on p. 61.

The roaming Mycenaeans absorbed many important lessons from neighboring peoples. Above all, they were influenced by the Minoan civilization, the first to develop in Europe, which was established around 2200 B.C.E. on the island of Crete, south of the Greek mainland. Cretan kings lived in expansive palace complexes that extended up to three acres (1.2 ha.) and had two or three stories. Palace walls were painted with **frescoes** and these rooms were supplied with bathrooms, running water, and sewage systems. Within the royal precincts were organized the region's food supply and manufactures, the inventories carefully documented on clay tablets. Or so it is presumed: the tablets cannot be read, as the language spoken on Crete has not been deciphered.

Crete had no true cities, no walls, and no fortifications—unique in these respects among the civilizations of the ancient Middle East. Its commercial relations with the Syrian cities and the ports of Egypt suggest strong cultural links with those regions. Around 1450 B.C.E., Mycenaean Greeks conquered Crete and inherited its cultural traditions. For the next two centuries, the lands west of the Aegean were under the power of the Mycenaean kings, until these also perished.

Across the Aegean Sea, the Indo-European people called the Hittites established their own kingdom in the mountainous interior of Asia Minor (modern Turkey). This was the first civilization not located on a river or the ocean coast. By 1500 B.C.E., the Hittites had established their capital at Hattusas (modern Bogazköy). In that inhospitable setting, possessing only thin soil, the Hittites nevertheless organized themselves as a rich and powerful nation. They seem to have been the first people to smelt iron successfully (although their warriors continued to use armor and weapons made of bronze).

Innovators in iron technology, the Hittites showed themselves willing to learn skills from their neighbors. They were the first major Indo-European people to absorb, to a substantial degree, Mesopotamian culture: writing, religion, political organization, and more. The Hittites were earnest recorders of commercial and administrative data, as the 10,000 or so of their surviving cuneiform tablets attest. In the political arena, their conception that a "covenant," like a contract, defined the relations between ruler and was to charge through enemy lines). He was protected by a bodyguard of seasoned troops.

Under later rulers, Hittite forces reached far enough south and east to harry the rulers of Babylon. To the south and west, the Hittites struggled with Egypt for dominance in the Near Eastern region known as Canaan.

Near Eastern Rivalries and the End of the Bronze Age

Sandwiched between the Hittites, the Mesopotamian kingdoms, and Egypt, small communities of Semitic peoples flourished in Canaan. In the second millennium Canaan was culturally rich and commercially vigorous, but militarily weak. Into this power vacuum the Hittites pushed from the north, the Egyptians from the south.

In the southern part of Canaan, an area later known as Palestine, the Canaanites farmed and herded sheep and clustered in walled cities such as Jericho and Jerusalem. Their religion and culture, including cuneiform writing, were similar to those of neighboring Mesopotamia.

Farther north lay the cities of Syria and Phoenicia (akin to modern Lebanon), which were the commercial crossroads of the ancient Middle East. Through Damascus and Ugarit, Sidon, Byblos, and Tyre streamed the wealth of Egypt and Mesopotamia. Because of the crucial location and cosmopolitan culture of these cities, innovations made here in spoken and written language had an impact on the whole region of the Middle East. In Syria, scribes developed the alphabetic script now used in modified form by many modern languages. The same scribes recorded oral myths and legends of the Canaanite peoples which were circulating through the region.

Following their expulsion of the Hyksos, in about 1570 B.C.E., the Egyptians had pursued an aggressive policy of foreign conquest. In warfare they adopted the horse-drawn chariot introduced by the Hyksos (who had themselves perhaps copied it from the Hittites). Formidably armed, they pushed northeast into Canaan and beyond.

ruled may underlie the conception found in the Hebrew Bible of a "covenant" between God and his "chosen people."

Like other Indo-European peoples, the warlike Hittites were, by tradition, expert horsemen and chariot drivers. From their ancestors they had also inherited the tribal custom of electing their kings. These rulers were selected by a council of nobles and, unlike other Middle Eastern monarchs, could not claim divinity or divine favor. No ruler could hold secure power, nor establish a dynasty and an enduring regime. Around 1520 B.C.E., this practice was modified. King Telipinus seized the throne, then compelled the Hittite chiefs to recognize a unified and hereditary dynasty. Under a king who could command their allegiance, the Hittites posed the first challenge to the dominance of Mesopotamia and Egypt.

Within two centuries of Telipinus's coup, Hittite power had grown to rival that of Egypt. King Suppiluliumas (r. c. 1380–1346) was even invited by the young widow of the pharaoh Tutankhamen to send one of his sons to be her husband. Although the marriage never materialized, and the Hittites thus failed to secure a profitable alliance, they pursued power more forcefully, expanding into the neighboring regions of northern Mesopotamia and Syria. Suppiluliumas himself went into battle with an army of about 30,000, which included infantry and chariots (equipped with heavy three-man crews whose task

Chinese warriors: *In northern China the emperor Shi Huangdi was buried with 7000 lifesize terracotta statues of the soldiers, servants, horses, and chariots he wished to protect him in the afterlife, 210* B.C.E..

not so much peace as limits to the exploitation of the powerless by competing powers. It is important as a model of the kind of agreement that can be made between different sovereign states. Also, its expressions of peace and material commitment evoke other covenants that were found in ancient civilization, such as that in the Hebrew Bible between Yahweh and the children of Israel.

As the rivalry of the Egyptians and the Hittites drew to a close, the civilizations of the Aegean were on the brink of disaster. Under Mycenaean domination after 1450 B.C.E., Minoan civilization dwindled and disappeared. Not long thereafter, during the years 1250 to 1100 B.C.E., the Mycenaean cities of the mainland, already weakened by social and political stresses, succumbed to invasions, or revolutions, or both. The result was devastation; the Mycenaean centers were literally incinerated. It was the heat of the fire at Pylos around 1200 B.C.E. that accomplished the baking—and thus the preservation—of clay tablets inscribed with royal accounts. After this disaster, the population of Mycenaean cities and even the number of inhabited sites dropped sharply—the population of Pylos fell to 10 percent of what it had been, while the number of Mycenaean sites in the area of Laconia dropped from thirty to seven, in Boeotia from twenty-seven to three. Of 320 sites inhabited in the 1300s, only 40 were known two centuries later. Of the major cities, Athens alone survived, weak and depopulated. The Mycenaean civilization to which it had once belonged vanished utterly.

Shortly before the Mycenaean cities crumbled, they may have joined forces around 1250 B.C.E. to raid Troy. Troy was a city on the Aegean cost of Asia Minor, not far from the Hellespont (the strait separating Greece from Asia Minor and the gateway to Black Sea ports). Six cities stood successively on the same point of land, each abandoned or destroyed in turn before there developed the rather poor one that was the target of the Mycenaean raid. The siege and capture of Troy by the Mycenaeans lingered in folk memory during the period of the "Dark Ages" which followed the collapse of the civilization of the Mycenaean kings. The story reappeared in the epic

One of these New Kingdom pharaohs, Hatshepsut, is the first known of the queens who ruled effectively as surrogates for male relatives. Daughter and wife of deceased pharaohs, Hatshepsut began her reign (c. 1503) by acting as regent for her minor stepson and nephew Thutmose III. When he reached adulthood, she usurped his rule. Her claim to full power is expressed by the honorary beard with which she is depicted in painting and sculpture. She arranged for the celebration of her achievement with a mortuary temple at Deir el-Bahri, one of the great architectural sites on the Nile in Upper Egypt. The reliefs carved on the walls, including those celebrating her divine birth (she considered herself the daughter, through her human mother, of the god Amen) were defaced by order of her successor, Thutmose III.

Hatshepsut herself launched no wars of conquest, but Thutmose III (r. 1479–1447 B.C.E.) engaged in many. With these conquests he created a new imperial role for Egypt. He penetrated western Asia seventeen times, reaching the Euphrates River. Once content to use military force only to police their frontier, Egypt was now, like other kingdoms of the ancient world, organized as a military state.

For the next century and a half after Thutmose's death in 1447 B.C.E., the Egyptians and the Hittites struggled for supremacy in Palestine. The pharaoh Ramses II (r. 1290–1224) finally faced the Hittites at Kadesh in about 1300 B.C.E., a battle that left neither party a victor. The lines of battle are shown on the chart on p. 52. He settled with his Hittite opponents in 1269 B.C.E. in a written treaty of peace—the first known to historians—which survives today in both Hittite and Egyptian versions (see *Witnesses*, p. 42).

This agreement, which established separate spheres of influence in Syria and Palestine, achieved

The Quiet Voice of Peace

*A*mid the warfare endemic in the ancient world, some indications of a desire for peace
do appear. In the first of the passages here, a historic treaty is arranged between the
Egyptians and the Hittites, the 3000-year-old archetype of subsequent peace treaties in
human history. In the second, the Greek poet Homer, who lived some 500 years later,
sketches an ideal picture of a world at peace, which is engraved, ironically, on the shield
of the hero Achilles, fighter par excellence.

The Egyptians and the Hittites make peace (c. 1269 B.C.E.): Behold, Hattusils,
the Great Prince of Hatti, has set himself in a regulation with User-maat-Re
Setep-en-Re, the great ruler of Egypt, beginning from this day, to cause that good
peace and brotherhood occur between us forever, while he is in brotherhood with me
and he is at peace with me, and I am in brotherhood with him and I am at peace with
him forever. ... The land of Egypt, with the land of Hatti, shall be at peace and in
brotherhood like unto us forever. Hostilities shall not occur between them forever.
(J. B. Pritchard ed., *Ancient Near Eastern Texts relating to the Old Testament*, 2e, 1955)

A vision of peace on the shield of Achilles (c. 750 B.C.E.):
>   On it [Hephaistos] wrought in all their beauty two cities of mortal
>   men. And there were marriages in one, and festivals.
>   They were leading the brides along the city from their maiden chambers
>   under the flaring of torches, and the loud bride song was arising.
>   The young men followed the circles of the dance, and among them
>   the flutes and lyres kept up their clamour as in the meantime
>   the women standing each at the door of her court admired them. ...
>   But around the other city were lying two forces of armed men
>   shining in their war gear.
>   (Homer, *Iliad*, 18:490–496, 508–509; ed. R. Lattimore, 1951)

poem believed to have been composed by a blind man
named Homer around 750 B.C.E. (see Chapter 4).
This is the *Iliad*, a sacred book to the ancient Greeks
and a classic of Western civilization.

The years around 1200 B.C.E. brought upheaval
to other kingdoms of the late Bronze Age. Piratic
"Sea Peoples" raided Egypt and threatened the eastern Mediterranean coast. Among these were the
Philistines, speakers of an Indo-European language,
who had migrated from their Aegean homes to settle
on the coast of Canaan. Other invaders, the Indo-
European Phrygians, attacked the Hittites, whose civilization, like that of the Mycenaeans, vanished. Both
civilizations were forgotten until rediscovered by
twentieth-century archaeologists.

The great Bronze Age empires were now dead or in
eclipse. In the Iron Age that followed, new nations
would contend for power in the Middle East. Iron Age
empires are shown on Map 2.3.

IRON AGE EMPIRES OF THE MIDDLE EAST

In the centuries of turmoil following 1200 B.C.E.,
the small nations along the eastern Mediterranean
held the stage in the Middle East. Pioneers of culture
and commerce, they seized a brief moment of glory
before the iron-wielding giants of late antiquity—
Assyria, Babylonia, and Persia—overpowered them.
By the middle of the sixth century B.C.E., the Indo-
European Persians had created an empire that united
and dominated most of the region, including the
whole of Egypt and Mesopotamia, where the first
civilizations began.

Philistines, Israelites, and Phoenicians

Sometime after 1200 B.C.E., two different peoples, the
Philistines and Israelites, arrived in Canaan. The
Philistines were expert fighters, well equipped with
iron tools and weapons. The Israelites were endowed
with a religious and ethical tradition that constituted
the world's first major monotheism. Farther north a
diverse people joined together as the Phoenicians to
develop a different kind of empire—an empire of
commerce—facilitated by their navigational, industrial, and communications skills.

Philistines and Israelites   The Philistines arrived
by sea and established a dominion along the coastal
plain, an area that, from the eleventh century B.C.E.
onward, was called Palestine. The Hebrew-speaking

peoples who would be known first as Israelites and later as Jews arrived from the Sinai Desert. According to the Book of Exodus (chapters 1–15), these were led by Joshua, lieutenant of Moses (who had died during the forty-year migration from his native Egypt). Moses not only had led his people out of Egypt, but also had bestowed upon them, carved in stone, the law code decreed by their one God.

The Israelites, who believed that they were descended from Abraham (whom their tradition depicted as an immigrant to Canaan around 1900 B.C.E.), thought of Canaan as their homeland despite generations of slavery in Egypt. In around 1200 B.C.E. they finally returned to Canaan.

Convinced that they were obeying God's will, the Hebrew-speaking migrants founded the nation of Israel. Joshua's dramatic capture of Jericho (see Chapter 1 and *Witnesses*, p. 36) was allegedly accomplished by faith and the sound of trumpets. In reality, detachments of armed men were required to carve out a domain in a land already thickly settled with inhabitants. Organized after the death of Joshua as a

loose confederation of twelve tribes under military leaders called "judges," the Israelites labored persistently to erode the significant power of the Canaanites who dwelled between the Jordan River and the Mediterranean shore.

At the same time, Israelite armies contended with the Philistines who also aimed to relieve the Canaanites of their villages and cities. Disciplined and aggressive, heavily armed with weapons of iron and bronze, the Philistines were extremely formidable opponents of the nomadic Israelites. Despite the Philistines' superior strength, they were subdued in the tenth century by King David of the Israelites. The Philistines' power waned from then on. In the end they retained sovereignty over only five city-states: Gaza, Ashkelon, Ashdod, Gath, and Ekron.

King David was the successor to the first king, Saul. Saul himself had been anointed by the priest Samuel around 1020 B.C.E. although Samuel had warned the Israelites against kings (see *Witnesses*, p. 33) when the inadequacy of the rule of the "judges" became apparent. King David (r. c. 1003–962 B.C.E.)

Map 2.3 Iron Age Empires of the Old World, after 1200 B.C.E.: *Peoples and states of the Iron Age displaced each other as they gained and lost territory and supremacy. If Assyrians were the ancient masters of military technology, why were the Persians able to defeat them?*

Soldiers besieging a city (probably in Babylon), from Nimrud, 728 B.C.E.

Hand axe, Gray's Inn, London, c. 250,000 B.C.E.

Archers and hoplites hunting lions, bronze dagger, Mycenae c. 1550–1450 B.C.E.

Our human ancestors engaged in violence even before they learned to form or sew clothing, as we see from the stone hand-held axe (top left), a weapon which is a quarter of a million years old. More sophisticated is the ornate carving on the bronze dagger blade, from a shaft grave at Mycenae. As soldiers besiege a city (above) one soldier holds a body shield in front of himself and two others in an early example of teamwork. The relief (below) shows horses and chariot being used in warfare. (Top left: British Museum, London: top right: British Museum, London; center: National Archaeological Museum, Athens; below: British Museum, London)

What are the modern equivalents of the stone axe, the shield, the chariot, the bow-and-arrow, and the siege ladder?

King Ashurnasirpal in chariot, from Nimrud, c. 865 B.C.E.

44

Assyrian army attacking the city Upa, believed to be the city of Medes 728 B.C.E.

By the first millennium B.C.E., the notoriously aggressive Assyrians had developed powerful engines of war. The relief (top left) features a line of archers on the right, soldiers scaling the enemy's fortifications with siege ladders, and a wheeled assault chariot assigned with the task of breaching the city's gate. Not long afterwards, the Greeks developed the phalanx, a line of citizen soldiers who charged into battle as though they were a single machine of war, held together by discipline and high morale.

In the relief (center left) a schematic view of a circular fortified camp shows food being prepared and a priest in a flat hat examining entrails of sacrifice. To the right horses are being groomed while, to the far right, a guard stands watch. Depicted on a vase (below left) is a rank of Mycenaean foot-soldiers, with helmets, shields, and spears. Defense was as important as offense. The massive stone Lion Gate to the citadel of Mycenae (below right) assertively expressed the military determination of its masters.

(top: British Museum, London; center: British Museum, London; below left: National Archaeoligical Museum, Athens)

Lion Gate, Mycenae, 1500–1300 B.C.E.

Fortified camp, Nimrud, 870–860 B.C.E.

Greek vase, from Mycenae, c. 1300 B.C.E.

 To continue your investigation of this topic, please go to www.prenhall.com/king for the related **WINDOWS** on the **WEB** activity

unified the Israelites into a nation. He captured the city of Jerusalem from its Canaanite inhabitants and established it as his capital. Here he hoped to build a temple to Yahweh that would house the Ark of the Covenant, the shrine containing the two stone tablets inscribed with the Ten Commandments.

David's objectives were realized by his son and successor, Solomon (r. 962–922 B.C.E.). Surrounded by soldiers and advisers, a bureaucracy and a harem, Solomon reigned in splendor. He built the temple and fortified and adorned the capital, including some magnificent royal palaces. This extravagance (at odds with his legendary wisdom) was resented by his heavily-taxed subjects, and on his death the kingdom split into two parts. The northern state comprised ten of the twelve original tribes and was known as the kingdom of Israel. The southern state, centered on the temple at Jerusalem and comprising the other two tribes, was known as the kingdom of Judah.

The people of Judah would later become known as Jews, and their religion as Judaism. By the time of Solomon, many of the formative experiences of the Jewish people had already occurred (see Chapter 1). But their ethical, monotheistic faith had yet to reach maturity. It would do so during the period of exile that followed the defeat of both Israel and Judah by, respectively, Assyria and Babylon.

While the kingdoms of Israel and Judah were still taking shape in Palestine, the communities to the north crystallized. These were peopled by Semitic natives, Philistine and Canaanite refugees from the south, and Aramaean immigrants from desert regions to the east. The latter established strongholds throughout the region (in modern-day Syria), including the important commercial center of Damascus. Their language, Aramaic, replaced Akkadian as the common language of the Middle East, and would become the official language of the Persian empire. This language maintained its primacy into the period of Greek domination.

The Phoenicians The Phoenicians, another Canaanite people, were established in the narrow zone west of Syria between the Lebanon mountains and the Mediterranean coast (modern Lebanon). Along that coast stood their principal cities: Tyre, Byblos, and Sidon. The Phoenicians continued to practice the religious rites of Canaan, which included child and animal sacrifice and temple prostitution. At the same time, they possessed the most advanced culture of the whole region. The best-skilled sailors of antiquity (their navigation guided by sightings of the North Star), the Phoenicians not only traded with the coastal cities of the eastern Mediterranean but also colonized its western shores. They founded Carthage on the north coast of Africa (modern Tunis) in 814 B.C.E., and reached as far west as Spain and the mouth of the Atlantic.

Wherever they traveled, the Phoenicians purveyed a reddish-purple dye extracted from a marine snail of the genuses *Murex* or *Purpura* (from which the name "purple" is derived). So costly was Tyrian purple that the color became associated with power. Cherished by royalty and nobility, who alone could afford it, the dye colored the robes of kings and, later—in the form of a modest stripe—the white togas of Roman senators. The Phoenicians also exported cedar from the forests of Lebanon and transported luxury goods from remoter parts of Asia. They spread abroad the alphabetic script their ancestors had devised, and supplied ancient empires with mercenary warriors. Yet these enterprising, literate, and wealthy Phoenicians were no match for the later empires that successively dominated the Mediterranean and the Middle East from the seventh century B.C.E.

Assyria, Babylon, and Persia

The Iron Age dawned in about 1200 B.C.E. when the iron-smelting technology developed by the Hittites began to spread rapidly through the Middle East. Iron was now available to make swords and spears and knives for a whole army. So equipped, an opportunistic king could rule not only a kingdom but an empire.

The Assyrians The kings of Assyria were the first to exploit iron for this purpose. Located at the northern bend of the Fertile Crescent, the cities of Assur and Nineveh successively served as capitals for Assyrian kings. The Semitic people they ruled had been established there since the third millennium B.C.E. and had absorbed the main features of Mesopotamian culture. From the thirteenth to the tenth centuries, they had been harassed by the Hurrians of Mittani (a people probably originating in Armenia before their expansion into Anatolia and Mesopotamia), and challenged by the Aramaean tribes of the northern Euphrates and Syria. Now, beginning in about 900 B.C.E., they began to expand into neighboring kingdoms. The Hittites were gone. There was room for a new, aggressive contender in this maelstrom of nations.

The Assyrians were equipped with an experienced army, unprecedented weapon strength, and relentless ferocity. For the Assyrians, war was a profession and a commitment, as the name of their first capital indicated: for Assur was the Assyrian god of war and chief god in their pantheon. Their art, too, glorified war. Their cult of strength is expressed by the bulls and lions, crouching, leaping, and dying, some bearded and half-human, carved in relief or monumentalized in statues in their palace complexes. These savage creatures and their human companions told the stories of Assyrian conquest.

The ferocity expressed in those images was not lost on the peoples unlucky enough to fall to the Assyrian advance. Assyrian kings went to war each year, and viciously subdued the conquered. King Assurnasirpal II (r. c. 884–859 B.C.E.) excelled in the ruthless tactics that won Assyria infamy (see *Witnesses*, p. 36). In the wake of victory, he ordered the mass deportation of whole populations. These captives were brought back to Assyria as slave laborers and set to work building the walls, towers, and palaces on which was brazenly proclaimed in sculpted relief the relentless power of their masters.

Each monarch surrounded himself with a personal bodyguard or security force—the troops, as these kings often described them, "who in a place hostile or friendly never leave my feet." In addition to these, the monarch commanded a standing army of faithful Assyrians, and a "grand army," numbering some 100,000 to 200,000—certainly the largest assembled to that date—which included auxiliaries drawn from conquered provinces.

At the head of this force marched standard-bearers and priests. At the rear followed engineers, specialists in Assyrian technology, with equipment for bridge- and road-building, portable ramps, and battering rams. In between were ranks of heavy and light infantry, spearmen, archers, and slingers. Here, too, were chariot and cavalry units, for the Assyrians brought the management of horses in warfare to a new level of efficiency. The later armies of the Persians, of the Macedonians, and of the Romans profited from Assyrian innovations in tactical military organization.

To this vast human and material force, the Assyrians added psychological weapons: they deliberately broadcast far and wide warnings of their brutal tactics. Such warnings of rape and mayhem and massacre often sufficed to deter a defeated enemy from harassing the conqueror with guerrilla counterattacks. Better still was to release a few wounded prisoners of high rank to describe to their compatriots the might of the conqueror: "Their leaders, men who understood battle and who had fled before my weapons," crowed Sargon II (r. 722–705 B.C.E.), "drew near to them covered with the venom of death, and recounted to them the glory of Assur, … so that they became like dead men."

In the eighth century B.C.E., the Assyrian king Tiglathpileser III (r. 745–727 B.C.E.) seized the Aramaean kingdom centered at Damascus, in north Syria, and pushed into Arabia. A successful conqueror, he was also an efficient manager. He built roads, started a postal service, and trimmed provincial government. His successors Shalmaneser V (r. 727–722 B.C.E.) and Sargon II destroyed the northern kingdom of Israel and deported its people. The tens of thousands of captives said to have been marched back to Assyria to slave on construction projects subsequently lost their national identity. These were the "Ten Lost Tribes" of the ancient Israelites. The Assyrians recolonized Israel's former territory (now known as Samaria) with foreigners, and these intermingled with the resident population to form the "Samaritan" culture (despised in the time of Jesus for its lukewarm or lapsed Judaism).

Sargon's son Sennacherib (r. 705–681 B.C.E.), having relocated the Assyrian capital to Nineveh, crushed the Phoenicians, north of Samaria, and captured forty of the fortified cities of the kingdom of Judah, whose king, Hezekiah (r. 787–699 B.C.E.), was stranded in Jerusalem. By the end of the seventh century B.C.E., the Assyrians controlled all the lands arching upward from Egypt, through Palestine and Asia Minor, and down to the Persian Gulf.

Although known for power and cruelty, Assyria made some important cultural contributions to the ancient world. Its huge cities were filled with vital, awe-inspiring sculpture commissioned by Assyrian kings. From Nineveh, their later capital, Assyria's conquest-hungry rulers managed state affairs with competence and even benevolence. Their skills built the first true empire, encompassing not only related peoples and kingdoms but a **polyglot** assortment of unrelated states. The Assyrians encouraged the general use of the Aramaic language throughout their domain (in preference to their native Akkadian), and through this medium, the accumulated culture of the whole of Mesopotamia was disseminated.

Among the cultural achievements of the Assyrians, none exceeds those of King Ashurbanipal (r. 668–631 B.C.E.), who died only nineteen years before the extinction of the Assyrian Empire. This grandson of the conqueror Sennacherib created at Nineveh a major research library. It contained about 22,000 clay tablets, consisting mainly of literature useful for magicians and priests. But it also included, on twelve tablets, the Akkadian version of the epic of *Gilgamesh* which is our main source of this work. Editions of other works of literature were standardized by the critical skills of Assyrian scribes, who also recorded the deeds of their kings. Ashurbanipal ordered his agents to gather works of which there were not yet any copies known in their homeland: "If you hear of any tablet or ritualistic text that is suitable for the palace," he instructed them, "seek it out, secure it, and send it here." His empire fell, but many of the works from his library survive.

The Babylonians Assyria aroused the envy of its neighbors. In 612 B.C.E., the two independent nations of the Chaldeans, centered at Babylon, and the Medes, centered at Ecbatana, united to defeat the oppressor. The allied forces captured and obliterated Nineveh, visiting upon it the same savage destruction that the Assyrians had so often inflicted on the cities of their foes.

As fruits of victory, the Chaldeans assumed the domination of the Fertile Crescent, while the Medes consolidated their power on the Iranian plateau, to

WHO'S WHO

Hittites, Israelites, and Assyrians

Suppululiumas (c.1380–1346 B.C.E) the Hittites' greatest king expands their boundaries.

David (1003–962 B.C.E) unites the Hebrew-speaking kingdoms of Israel and Judah, and founds city of Jerusalem.

Solomon (962–922 B.C.E.) David's son; erects the first temple at Jerusalem.

King Assurnasirpal (r. 884–859 B.C.E.) launches military terror tactics; begins process of Assyrian expansion.

King Ashurbanipal (r. 668–631 B.C.E) last Assyrian king; palace-builder and creator of one of the first great libraries.

the north. Among the other main contenders for power in the Middle East were a fading Egypt and the new state of the Lydians, in Asia Minor. Babylonian armies wrested Syria and Palestine from the pharaoh, whom they defeated at Carchemish (in modern Turkey) in 605 B.C.E., and asserted their authority in that corridor.

In 597 B.C.E., the Babylonians suppressed a revolt in Judah, deporting the king, his family, and 8000 leaders. When the remnant of the nation rebelled a second time, the Babylonians spared no one. In 586 B.C.E., they seized Jerusalem and blinded King Zedekiah and his sons so that they could cause no more trouble. The nation of the Jews (excepting the poorest, who were left behind) was marched to captivity in Babylon, where for forty-seven years two generations of priests and scholars would reflect on the meaning of their history and their exile.

Babylon at this brief moment of its supremacy—between the fall of Nineveh in 612 B.C.E. and its conquest by the Persians in 539 B.C.E.—was a cosmopolitan city, filled with boulevards and lovely parks. Bold public buildings formed a palace complex and temple precinct, on whose glazed brick walls strode fantastic beasts. According to legend, King Nebuchadnezzar II (or Nebuchadrezzar; r. 605–562 B.C.E.) built in his palace for his consort Amytis, a Median princess, the Hanging Gardens, constructed on stone arches above ground and watered by the Euphrates through a sophisticated engineering system. Babylon was both a center of luxury and the cultural capital of the Middle East. Here philosophers observed the heavens and created astronomy, which later they would teach to the Greeks.

The study of astronomy caught the imagination of King Nabonidus (r. 556–539 B.C.E.), who was one of Nebuchadnezzar's successors. Nabonidus was an ardent adherent of a moon cult. As a scholar, like Ashurbanipal of Assyria, and as a mystic, like Akhenaten of Egypt, he promoted his heretical cult over the objections of the priests of the traditional and heretofore unchallenged god Marduk. These priests took advantage of the King's unpopularity—in a time when Babylon was afflicted by famine and illness—to lead an uprising against him. He was forced into exile, leaving his son Belshazzar as regent.

The Persians   In 539 B.C.E., the priests conspired to open the gates of Babylon to the Persian army waiting outside the walls. The Persians seized Babylon and its empire and established their sway over the whole Middle East. These events are the subject of the Book of Daniel, in which the Jewish scholar Daniel decodes for Belshazzar the fatal "writing on the wall" which tells of the impending fall of his kingdom.

The craft of empire building that the Hittites had learned from Mesopotamia, that Egypt learned from the Hyksos and the Hittites, that Assyria learned from its warrior neighbors, the Medes learned from Assyria, and the Persians borrowed from the Medes. During the last generations of Assyrian kings, the Medes, with their subjects and dependents, including, ironically, the Persians, had been building a desert state to the east of Assyria. By 625 B.C.E., they had become an independent kingdom under their king Cyaxerxes (r. 625–585 B.C.E.). In 612 B.C.E., they joined the Chaldeans in the sack of Nineveh. Before their forces were able to venture farther westward, the Persian subject king Cyrus II, called the Great (r. c. 550–529 B.C.E.), ousted the Median king in a swift *coup d'état*. He then set about expanding his domain. Within the next twenty years the Persians created an empire reaching from the Mediterranean to the Indus River.

As the Assyrians excelled at war, the Persians excelled at domination, thanks largely to their policy of toleration. The kings who ruled from 550 to 486 B.C.E.—Cyrus, Cambyses, Darius—all permitted their subjects to practice their native customs and religions. This policy won the support of the conquered, or at least made the condition of servitude more endurable. Tolerance of the ethnic and cultural distinctiveness of each people was a new value in the political world of antiquity—a principle that would endure, if often violated, into our own time.

Cyrus conquered Lydia in about 546 B.C.E., and Babylonia, Palestine, and Syria in 539–538 B.C.E. He liberated the Jews from their "Babylonian Captivity," as this exile became known, and allowed them to return to their homeland (now re-organized as the Persian province of Judaea) to reestablish their temple and their reinvigorated faith. Cambyses (r. 529–522 B.C.E.) conquered Egypt in 525 B.C.E., terminating the independence of that most enduring of kingdoms. Darius (r. 522–486 B.C.E.) pushed into Europe north of the Black Sea and across the Aegean, into the Balkans.

Persians and Chaldeans (Babylon)

Nebuchadnezzer (r. 605–562 B.C.E.) conqueror of Judah; deports the Jewish people wholesale to his splendid city of Babylon, capital of the short-lived Chaldean Empire.

Cyrus (r. 550–529 B.C.E.) seizes leadership from the Medes for the Persian people and conquers much of the Middle East, including Babylon.

Darius (r. 522–486 B.C.E.) launches Persian attempt to conquer Greece.

King Darius set a new standard in the efficient governing of an empire. He directly controlled only his ceremonial capital, Persepolis (in modern Iran). From his administrative capital at Susa, Darius governed his vast empire through officials called **satraps**, each of whom had charge of a province. The satraps collected the tribute due the King of Kings (as the Persian rulers styled themselves) and kept the peace, closely watched by the military commanders of local garrisons and financial officers that Darius also appointed in each province.

The tireless Darius read the reports submitted in writing by all three sets of officials and cross-checked to make sure that they were all in agreement. In addition, he appointed traveling inspectors to supervise all of the provincial officials. To enable this network of officials and bureaucrats to function, he had an immense highway system constructed. The Royal Road (which the Romans would later imitate; see Chapter 6) stretched across the empire from Susa to Sardis (in modern Turkey), spanning a vast 1000 miles (1600 km.).

The Persian conquest of the ancient Middle East was decisive. The Persians had forged into a political and cultural unity the proliferating kingdoms of an earlier era, the culmination of a struggle for empire that had engaged the Middle East from the creation of the first civilizations. That political and cultural unity persisted even as—in the centuries that followed—Persian rule succumbed to Greek and Parthian, Sassanid and Roman, Arab and Turkish leadership.

BRONZE AND IRON AGE KINGDOMS IN EAST AND SOUTH ASIA

While Egyptians, Hittites, Assyrians, Persians, and others were competing for power in the Middle East, advanced civilizations coalesced in east and south Asia (see Map 2.1). Around 1557 B.C.E., the Shang rulers of China established a kingdom on the Yellow River (Huang He). Later dynasties refined the principles and mechanisms of Chinese rule, which were, by the end of the Han dynasty (220 C.E.) the most advanced in the world. In India, Aryan conquerors invading around 1750 B.C.E. created a civilization that briefly achieved political unification.

Heaven's Mandate in China

Over nearly 2000 years, Chinese monarchs labored to create a strong, centralized kingdom. It was the divine will, they believed, that such political unity be achieved, and they ruled by the command or "mandate" of heaven.

Around 1557 B.C.E. in east Asia, the Shang kings conquered and unified the cities of the Yellow River (Huang He) valley, establishing themselves as rulers of this region. Central to their government was a dynastic cult, managed by priests, which involved the worship of the royal ancestors upon whose favor the welfare of the state depended. As in the Middle East and the Aegean, royal tombs were loaded with the various trappings of power: treasures of jewels and bronze and even, in one case, a whole chariot with its horse and driver.

Shang rulers were supported by a nobility as well as a priesthood. As in the Middle East, the nobility consisted of trusted warriors, who followed the king into battle, riding in chariots and wielding spear and bow. In return for their loyal service, they expected, and received, gifts of land and valuables.

During the eleventh century B.C.E., a tribe from the northwest, specialists in breeding and deploying horses, overwhelmed the Shang and established the Zhou dynasty (to 221 B.C.E.). Coming to power as conquerors, they asserted their legitimacy by claiming to rule by the special will, or "mandate," of Heaven—a claim that would be repeated by Chinese rulers over the next 3000 years. The Zhou monarchy was precarious, however, unable to control a powerful nobility obsessed with war. The conflicts between these warlords culminated in the period of the Warring States (c. 450–221 B.C.E.), which overshadowed the last years of the weakened Zhou dynasty.

Despite weak kings and restive nobles, China flourished under the Zhou dynasty. Over the 800-plus years of its tenure, the population grew and commerce flourished, as did the many schools of philosophy that sprang to life. Several philosophical schools prescribed political goals strikingly absent from the Zhou regime: a strong central government, the rule of law, and a well-trained, selfless, and peaceable class of government officials. This last recommendation was particularly dear to Confucius.

Those noisy schools of thought would be silenced by the short-lived Qin dynasty (221–206 B.C.E.). The Qin came to power amid the chaos of late Zhou rule, about the time that iron replaced bronze in the

In China and India

Chandragupta Maurya (r. 321–298 B.C.E.) carves out an empire in northern India.

Asoka (r. 272–232 B.C.E.) grandson of Chandragupta; renounces war to take up good works and promote Buddhism.

Shi Huangdi (r. 221–210/209 B.C.E.) foremost emperor of brief Qin dynasty which gives China its name; launches the building of the Great Wall and has philosophical books burned.

region. The Qin crushed local warlords and restored order, establishing thirty-six territories, each commanded by trained officials loyal only to the emperor, chosen for their talent and their freedom from ties of clan and friendship. Throughout the country, standard systems were established for weights and measures, for writing, for the value of coins, and even for the width of the axle of each cart that traveled on the country's well-planned roads.

Also standardized was the life of the mind. A halt was called to the splendid profusion of philosophical thought of the late Zhou era—for that had been the classical age when Chinese thinkers produced a "Hundred Schools of Flowers" and Confucius and Lao Zi flourished. Only technical books and manuals were now permitted, friendly to imperial rule and housed in the imperial library. In 213 B.C.E. the first Qin emperor, Shi Huangdi (r. 221–210/209 B.C.E.), ordered burned the books he didn't like—any that did not concern such practical matters as agriculture, medicine, or magic. When scholars protested against this destruction, 460 of them were executed and thrown into a common grave.

Such tyrannical behavior must be weighed against Shi Huangdi's most famous achievement: the Great Wall which joined together a series of walls previously built by local magnates to ward off external enemies. Standing 25 feet (7.6 m.) high, 20 feet (6.1 m.) wide, and equipped with 25,000 towers, the Great Wall extends 1400 miles (2253 km.). Equally astonishing, in a different way, is Shi Huangdi's mausoleum. Within this vast tomb is buried, along with the Emperor's own body, an army of more than 7000 life-size statues of warriors made of terracotta and bronze (see p. 41). Soon after Shi Huangdi's death, Qin rule was replaced by the Han dynasty, who carried forward the achievements of their predecessors.

Aryans and Emperors in India

Spreading southeast into India from around 1750 B.C.E., Indo-European peoples established a new civilization in the Ganges River valley. These newcomers conquered the survivors of the Indus civilization, which had probably begun to fail even before the newcomers arrived, as well as the indigenous peoples of northern India. These Indo-Europeans called themselves "Aryans." The ancient connotations of the word were "honor" and "liberty," but in modern history its association with Nazi racial theory has lent it an unfortunate meaning. The same word is echoed in "Iran," the region settled by the Indo-European peoples who eventually came to be known as the Medes and Persians.

The Aryans were relentless warrior-charioteers who worshiped war gods such as the storm god Indra, who also conquered with horse and chariot. Memories of the age of Aryan conquest are stored in the later epic poems *Mahabharata* and *Ramayana*, classics of world literature. The civilization that emerged, a blend of the customs of Aryans and natives, is notable not only for its epic literature but also for its religious creativity. This creativity is displayed in the literature of the Vedic age, which followed the conquest. That age is named for the *Vedas*, or hymns, which were its first cultural product, and which culminate in the *Upanishads* with their yearning for other-worldly enlightenment. The Vedas were transmitted orally for more than a thousand years until writing was reinvented on the subcontinent.

The guardians of this tradition at once religious, literary, and ethnic were the brahmans, or priests, who formed an elite social class. In the pattern of social hierarchy that the brahmans prescribed, they themselves occupied the first rank. Below them in descending order were the classes of warriors, merchants, farmers, and laborers, and, in last place, the servile "untouchables," those with no social identity whatsoever. Within each category, females were ranked as inferior to males.

This brahmanic system did not exist in reality. But a hierarchical social structure far more complex did develop in which every individual belonged by birth to a particular social unit, or *jati*, loosely grouped within the brahmanic categories. That identification strictly limited his or her opportunities for social mobility or advancement—more so than the barriers that separated the classes of most other societies. People lived, intermarried, and even ate with members of their caste and no other. Originating in the Vedic age, these boundaries solidified into the **caste** system that in modern times so troubled observers from the more democratic nations of the West.

The sub-continent of India resisted unification; its civilization developed in the Vedic period without a centralized state structure. But by around 300 B.C.E. Chandragupta Maurya (r. 321–298 B.C.E.) had founded the Mauryan Empire in northern India; a true Golden Age emerged. Chandragupta was a near-contemporary of Alexander the Great (see below), whose followers had occupied and then left the Indus region. Chandragupta conquered the lands vacated by the Greeks, and established an empire extending from the Himalayan passes to the Bay of Bengal.

Chandragupta's achievement was overshadowed by that of his grandson Asoka (r. 272–232 B.C.E.), one of the most renowned of India's rulers (see *Witnesses*, p. 33). After some initial military ventures which he later regretted, Asoka, a convert to Buddhism, instituted the "Law of Piety." Renouncing war and promoting peace, he followed its enlightened precepts over his reign's last three decades. Out of respect for animal life, he ate only vegetables. He built inns, parks, hospitals, and veterinary clinics. His agents traveled extensively, supervising local administrations and guaranteeing the equitable treatment of his subjects. He himself traveled frequently and widely to ensure the observance of his laws. These he had inscribed in stone on tall limestone pillars erected throughout his dominions for all to view. Asoka's empire endured only fifty years after his death.

THE BIRTH OF THE WEST

A century before the ascendancy of Shi Huangdi in China or Asoka in India, a European empire had displaced the Persian Empire, marking the first entry of a Western power into the contest of nations. This empire was the creation of an obscure Balkan prince known to history as Alexander the Great (356–323 B.C.E.). By the time of his death, a little more than two centuries after Cyrus the Great swept to power, Alexander had established his supremacy in his native Macedonia, in mainland Greece, and over the ancient nations of the Middle East. But Alexander's Empire was grounded in more than his matchless talent and the might of his army. It had as its foundation the whole civilization of classical Greece. That civilization had evolved quietly over the previous four centuries.

Greece, Europe, and the West

In the age of the Sumerians and Egyptians, or that of the Hittites and Assyrians, there was no "Greece." The Mycenaeans who dominated the Aegean region during the second millennium B.C.E. spoke a language now known to be an early form of Greek. After the close of Mycenaean civilization and the interval of the Dark Ages, there emerged a new and distinctive Greek-speaking civilization. That civilization was called "**Hellenic**" by its contemporaries and, later, "Greek," by the Romans and their successors. Influenced by the traditions of neighboring Africa and Asia, which in turn it would dramatically and radically transform, Hellenic civilization would even more profoundly influence the later civilizations of Europe and of the Islamic world.

What we call "Western Civilization" today has its roots in ancient Greece, although the Greeks, at first, did not see themselves as "Western"—and indeed made no distinction between "West" and "East." Southeastern Europe belonged to the same cultural world as western Asia and northeastern Africa. Indeed, although the nation we call Greece belongs (apart from its islands) to the European mainland, ancient Greece included settlements on the coast of Asia Minor, as well as colonies throughout the Mediterranean and Black Sea regions. The poet Homer was born on the Asian, not the European, shore of the Aegean. The *Iliad*, Homer's epic tale of the siege and destruction of Troy, shows no conception of the Asian enemy as alien. The Trojans (as the poet imagined them) lived in a Greek city, worshiped Greek gods, and shared Greek funeral customs and concepts of personal honor.

About 300 years after Homer composed his epic *Iliad*, the Greeks' first historian, Herodotus (485–425 B.C.E.), wrote the Western world's first history. Like Homer, Herodotus viewed the Greek realm as part of the Near East. His inquiry into the origins of his people opens with a leisurely tour of the civilizations of the eastern Mediterranean. But it is with Herodotus that the "West" first distinguishes itself from the "East." He identifies as the critical event of his age the Persian Wars fought in the first decades of the fifth century B.C.E., in which a few Greek cities opposed that great empire. Persian armies twice crossed over the barrier of the Aegean between Asia and Europe, and were twice repulsed by the Greeks. When the tiny armies of the defiant Greek cities vanquished the hordes of the Persian imperial army, the ways of the "West" (as Herodotus and his contemporaries saw these events) triumphed over those of the "East." This bloody war fought with iron weapons was not only a political struggle, but a war between competing visions of human society and aspiration.

The civilization that Herodotus knew was a relatively young one, by the standards of the ancient world, although it had its roots in the much older one of Mycenaea. With the destruction or decline of Mycenaean centers after 1200 B.C.E., the elaborate palace communities, the advanced skills of a multiplicity of artisans, the ability to write were all lost. In the villages of mainland Greece, only a few potters and smiths continued to ply their trade. Their manufactures were used only by the local population of farmers and fishermen, for trade had ceased. And those farmers and fishermen faced starvation.

This period of poverty and chaos, known as the "Dark Ages," lasted four centuries. Then, in about 800 B.C.E., the dawn lifted on a scattering of small cities both on the mainland and, across the Aegean, on the western shore of Asia Minor. In most of these cities, the traditional form of government, monarchy, had been abandoned. Instead, networks of wealthy landowners ruled the city, their comfortable farms occupying the best valley land outside the city walls. These aristocrats made laws and debated them, decided for war or peace, and settled disputes among the citizens. In due course they created formal councils and assemblies and sometimes even juries, with rules for their selection: in effect, a constitution.

These cities were not democracies in the modern sense of the term. Many people (women, children, and slaves) were excluded from political life. Freedom belonged not to the individual but to the community. Yet even with these limitations, the political life of these Greek cities was remarkably free—with citizens and their leaders devoted to the Greek way of life and hostile to kings, and wary of tyrants. The chasm between civic life in Greece and in any Mediterranean or Middle Eastern land was enormous. It was dramatized by the response made by the Spartans when ordered to prostrate themselves before the Persian king Xerxes. To do so was to submit, and this they would not do.

To protect their way of life, many Greek cities were willing to go to war against any power that threatened. The threat eventually came from the Persians—ironically, of all the great imperial powers the most tolerant, the most adaptive, the most favorable to the development of human potential. Yet there remained a crucial difference between the two counterposed civilizations. The vast empire of Persia sought to grow, whereas the small cities of Greece sought to remain free.

The Persian Wars, the struggle between Greeks and Persians (which took place mainly from 499 to 479 B.C.E., then dragged on for another thirty years) began when some of the Greek cities on the shore of Asia Minor rose in rebellion against Persian overlordship, which had been imposed by Cyrus the Great in his great sweep through the region. The mainland Greek city of Athens, aided by Eretria, sent an armed fleet to assist the rebels—an act that would rankle with the Persians even after they had subdued the uprising and wooed back the allegiance of the rebel cities.

Determined to punish Athens for aiding the rebels, King Darius decided to establish, at least theoretically, his sovereignty on the Greek mainland. He sent agents to the Greek cities demanding earth and water, the material symbols of submission to his rule. Many Greek cities capitulated. They saw no danger of effective intervention by the distant monarch and wished to avoid a potentially disastrous conflict. From Athens and Sparta, Darius received a quite different response: they murdered his emissaries and set about preparing for war.

The spectacle of these two small cities, with their correspondingly small armies, preparing to fight the massed armies of the world's greatest empire seems amazing even now, 2500 years later. The shrewd Athenians and Spartans could have had no illusions

Battles of Kadesh and Marathon

KADESH, c. 1300 B.C.E.

Ramses' troops
Hittite infantry
Ramses' household troops
Kadesh
Hittite chariot reserve
Hittite infantry
Division of Ptah
Orontes River
Wood of Robaui

A typical war chariot at Kadesh

MARATHON, 490 B.C.E.

Decelea
Persian troops
Swamp
Plain of Marathon
Greek troops
Persian fleet
Mt. Pentelicon

A typical hoplite at Marathon

about their own strength relative to the Persians. The audacity of their stance compels admiration. Even more astonishing is what happened in 490 B.C.E. at Marathon, a village on the Attic peninsula of mainland Greece, where the Athenians, with an army of only 10,000 citizens, plus 1000 allies, turned back some 25,000 Persian soldiers. The defenders had better weapons and armor; moreover, they were fighting to defend their homeland—always an advantage. Finally, they had Miltiades, a steel-nerved adventurer whose strategy was to invite a Persian assault at the center of the Greek line in order to smash the enemy between its heavy and dangerous wings (see battle plan).

Ten years later, at the instigation of Darius' successor, Xerxes, the Persians returned, more determined than before to conquer Greece and punish Athens. This time they crossed the Hellespont by a bridge of linked, contiguous ships (engineered by their cooperative Phoenician subjects, trade rivals of the Greeks) and marched south through Macedon and Thessaly toward the lands dominated by Athens and Sparta. A small Spartan force of 300 crack citizen troops plus 700 of their allies resisted the advancing Persians at the pass of Thermopylae, fighting until they were all slain. The poet Simonides (c. 506–467 B.C.E.) composed their epitaph:

> *Tell them in Lacedaemon [Sparta], passer-by:*
> *Carrying out their orders, here we lie.*

Still the Persians continued their march on Athens, where the cagey statesman Themistocles (c. 528–462 B.C.E.), recognizing impending and irresistible disaster, had persuaded the citizens to flee to the offshore island of Salamis. The Athenians abandoned their city and temples to sack and to the torch. The Greek fleet bottled up their Persian opponents in the narrow channel between island and mainland and destroyed more than half of the Persian ships by ramming them with the iron-tipped prows of their warships (triremes) as described in *Witnesses* opposite. Xerxes watched, despaired, and turned home. The army he left behind was defeated at Plataea the following year. Although sporadic fighting would continue until 449 B.C.E., with Athens leading the resistance against Persian domination, the Persians no longer posed any serious threat to the Greeks.

From City-State to Empire

Over the next generation, Athens did not merely lead the anti-Persian alliance but effectively dominated it. The coastal city and island states that had formerly been co-equals were absorbed, briefly, into an Athenian Empire. Based on naval power first amassed by Themistocles and later extended by Cimon, the son of Miltiades, this alliance was meant to be a permanent bulwark against the menacing despotism to

Greeks at War

Although the Greek poet Homer could imagine a peaceful world (see the Witness box, p. 42), the Greeks were not peaceful; nor did they become less violent as they became more civilized as the creators of magnificent works of science, philosophy, and literature. In these two passages, the tragic playwright Aeschylus and the historian Thucydides describe two incidents from the wartorn fifth-century B.C.E., one of the most glorious periods—in terms of cultural achievement—in human history.

The Persian defeat at Salamis (480 B.C.E.), according to the playwright Aeschylus (c. 480 B.C.E.):
First the floods of Persians held the line,
But when the narrows choked them, and rescue hopeless,
Smitten by prows, their bronze jaws gaping,
Shattered entire was our fleet of oars.
The Grecian warships, calculating, dashed
Round, and encircled us; ships showed their belly:
No longer could we see the water, charged
With ships' wrecks and men's blood.
Corpses glutted beaches and the rocks. ...
... never in a single day
So great a number died.
(Aeschylus, *Persians*, 411–421, 431–432; eds. D. Grene, R. Lattimore, trs. S. G. Benardete, 1992)

Describing revolution at Corcyra in northwestern Greece, Thucydides diagnoses human nature as prone to violence and treachery (c. 420 B.C.E.): During seven days ..., the Corcyraeans were engaged in butchering those of their fellow-citizens whom they regarded as their enemies: and although the crime imputed was that of attempting to put down the democracy, some were slain also for private hatred, others by their debtors because of the monies owed to them. Death thus raged in every shape; and, as usually happens at such times, there was no length to which violence did not go; sons were killed by their fathers, and suppliants dragged from the altar or slain upon it; while some were even walled up in the temple of Dionysus and died there.

So bloody was the march of the revolution, and the impression which it made was the greater as it was one of the first to occur. Later on, one may say, the whole Hellenic world was convulsed. ... The sufferings which revolution entailed upon the cities were many and terrible, such as have occurred and always will occur, as long as the nature of mankind remains the same. ... In peace and prosperity states and individuals have better sentiments, because they do not find themselves suddenly confronted with imperious necessities; but war takes away the easy supply of daily wants, and so proves a rough master, that brings most men's characters to a level with their fortunes.
(Thucydides, *Peloponnesian War*, 3:81–82; ed. J. Crawley, 1951)

the east. Called the Delian League (478–404 B.C.E.), because its combined treasure was originally stored on the island of Delos, it became increasingly dominated by the Athenians, who found it a valuable source of revenue. Athens, which at Marathon had heroically defended its own freedom, became (it seemed to onlookers) the exploiter and oppressor of other once-free cities.

With the diminished Persian threat, Athens' allies became restive, and Sparta, in particular, cast a worried eye on the magnificence of its former friend. With its wealth and maritime allies, Athens had the advantage at sea and (it seemed) could be defeated only by an opponent with a comparably strong navy. Sparta, with its dominion over much of the Peloponnesus (the southern Greek peninsula) and alliance with other major cities, possessed a reputably unbeatable army and an impregnable position. Over nearly thirty years these two antagonists hammered each other in a war that was punctuated by internal disasters on both sides (such as an outbreak of plague in Athens described in *Witnesses*, p. 53), periods of truce, and outbursts of atrocities. This was the Peloponnesian War (fought intermittently 431–404 B.C.E.). It closed the century in which Greece achieved the highest cultural attainments of its history.

The two major cities of Greece had exhausted themselves in the Peloponnesian War and were now vulnerable to foreign aggression. As normality seemed to return, a power emerged to the north that would challenge the cities that once had faced the might of Persia. The new player in the game of Greek—and eventually world—politics was Macedonia.

Cities that had refused to sacrifice their autonomy even to other Greeks (let alone Persians) soon bent to the superior power of Philip II (r. 359–336 B.C.E.) of Macedon. To the Greeks, Macedonia was a crude and backward land, and Philip hateful simply by virtue of being a king. But that despised monarch ruled a unified nation and marched at the head of the most up-to-date army of the day. He was unstoppable. From the outset of his reign until his assassination twenty-three years later, he conquered all the cities of Greece: oligarchies and democracies alike.

Philip's ambition had been to conquer Greece. That of his son and successor, Alexander, was to conquer the world. He began with the Persians. Once, the Persians had amassed a huge army in a vain attempt to breach the Aegean and conquer Greece. Now, with his army of Macedonians and Greeks, Alexander would pay the Persians a return visit.

Astoundingly, Alexander won. His forces overran Asia Minor and the Middle East, pushing beyond the Himalayan passes to the shore of the Indus; they reached deep down the Nile River into southern Egypt. They combined the strength of the Greek phalanx where soldiers were organized in row upon tight row, as shown in *How Many?* on p. 128 with the machinery that the Persians had borrowed from the Assyrians and a tactical genius that exploited each geographical advantage, adapted to each variation in terrain, and boldly attacked fortifications that were believed impregnable.

Just as Persia had absorbed all that the Assyrians and the Hittites before them had once ruled, and more, Alexander absorbed all the realms of the Persians, as well as the whole of Greece. By Alexander's death in 323 B.C.E., the empire he had created was the largest ever known. It contained a greater diversity of communities and languages than had any previous state. It would exert an enduring cultural influence upon successor states—Rome, Byzantium, Islam (see Chapters 5 and 8)—and their modern descendants.

Conclusion
THE CONTEST FOR EMPIRE AND THE MEANING OF THE WEST

During the first 3000 years of civilization, armies and empires reigned. One armed state after another would emerge to dominate, and sometimes destroy, its neighbors. From Africa to Asia, from the Bronze Age to the Iron Age, kings led their armies in an endless struggle for power, sometimes winning a brief ascendancy for a century or more. With Alexander the Great, Europe for the first time entered the contest for ascendancy.

Alexander's conquests mark a new ascendancy for Europe—one that had been foreshadowed by Greek victories in the Persian Wars. Ironically, those earlier victories represented not a claim for empire but a claim for freedom—a refusal to bow to power expressed also in the proud words of the Spartan emissaries to King Xerxes, with which this chapter opened.

New political and cultural principles were introduced into the heritage of the West by the Greeks who had withstood the advancing might of the Persian Empire. These principles were in tension with the lust for empire. In the political sphere, they asserted the right of human communities to independence and self-determination. In the cultural sphere, they included high ethical and intellectual standards which more than once in the later history of the West would present a challenge to those who sought world domination at all costs.

QUESTIONS TO CONSIDER

1. In an age before luxury cars and condominiums, what were the symbols of status and prestige that distinguished kings and nobles from ordinary people?

2. Why did kingdoms rise and fall in Mesopotamia, but endure securely, even when dynasties occasionally changed, in Egypt?

3. The Mycenaeans and the Phoenicians were both societies based on commerce—one Aegean, one Levantine. In what ways were they different?

4. Why were the Persians able to defeat the Assyrians, a society structured around military needs and ambitions?

5. How did ancient Chinese philosophy and the nature of Chinese politics interrelate? Were rulers more attuned to philosophical issues in China than in other ancient states?

SUGGESTED RESOURCES

Aubet, Maria Eugenia (trans. Mary Turton), *The Phoenicians and the West: Politics, Colonies, and Trade* (Cambridge: Cambridge University Press, 1993). Shows how recent archaeological research has changed our understanding of the relationship of Phoenicia and its colonies to local Iron Age communities.

Basham, A. L., *The Wonder that was India: A Study of the History and Culture of the Indian Subcontinent before the Coming of the Muslims*, 3rd ed. (London: Sidgwick & Jackson, 1985). A survey of the civilization of classical India, prehistory to end of first millennium C.E., covering state, society, everyday life, religion, arts, language, and literature.

Crawford, Harriet, *Sumer and the Sumerians* (Cambridge: Cambridge University Press, 1991). A review of social and technological developments from 3800 through 2000 B.C.E..

Drews, Robert, *The End of the Bronze Age: Changes in Warfare and the Catastrophe ca. 1200 BC* (Princeton: Princeton University Press, 1993). Offers a largely military explanation for the collapse of the great Bronze Age states, whose chariot warfare was vulnerable to infantry assaults.

Hanson, Victor Davis, *History of Warfare: the Wars of the Ancient Greeks* (London: Cassell, 2002). A complete history of Greek warfare from the Dark Ages through Alexander the Great, profiling the military technology, strategy, and culture in which Greek civilization excelled.

Johnson, Paul, *The Civilization of Ancient Egypt* (London: Weidenfeld and Nicolson, 2000). The whole 3,000-year course of Egyptian history, highlighting the simplicity and effectiveness of its theocratic government, the role played by an esoteric system of hieroglyphic writing in maintaining the privileged order of priests and scribes, and the cultural effects of the high status of women.

Mallory, J. P., *In Search of the Indo-Europeans: Language, Archaeology, and Myth* (New York: Thames & Hudson, 1989). An introduction to the history of the Indo-Europeans and the problematic history of Indo-European studies.

O'Connell, Robert L., *Ride of the Second Horseman: The Birth and Death of War* (Oxford: Oxford University Press, 1995). A survey of human experience of war, from the Ice Age to the present.

Postgate, J. N., and Nicholas Postgate, *Early Mesopotamia: Society and Economy at the Dawn of History* (London/New York: Routledge, 1994). Integrates historical and archaeological data drawn from specialist literature; scholarly yet readable.

Raaflaub, Kurt & Nathan Rosenstein, *War and Society in the Ancient and Medieval Worlds: Asia, the Mediterranean, Europe, and MesoAmerica* (Cambridge, MA: Harvard University Press, 2000). A multi-authored work that studies the interface of war and society from the third millennium B.C.E. through about 1000 C.E. in the Asian, European, and American regions of early civilization.

Robins, Gay, *Women in Ancient Egypt* (Cambridge: Harvard University Press, 1993). An introduction to the history of women of all classes in ancient Egyptian society and culture.

Sandars, N. K., *The Sea Peoples: Warriors of the Ancient Mediterranean, 1250–1150 B.C.* (London: Thames & Hudson, 1985). An account of migrating peoples known as Land and Sea Peoples, arguing that disparate groups combined to cause the collapse of Bronze Age civilizations in the eastern Mediterranean.

Wood, Michael, *In Search of the Trojan War* (rev. ed.; Berkeley: University of California Press, 1998). Fascinating account of the city of Troy and the struggle with Greece as revealed in recent archeological exploration.

Xueqin, Li (trans. K. C. Chang), *Eastern Zhou and Qin Civilizations* (New Haven: Yale University Press, 1985). Covers 1500 years of Chinese history from 1700 through 200 B.C.E., discussing the shift from stone to bronze to iron, the development of a complex strictly ranked society, and the unification of the Chinese state.

Timeline of Egyptian military technology:
www.anthro.mankato.msus.edu/prehistory/egypt/military/tech.html

Sun Tzu, *The Art of War* (earliest known guide to warfare, from ancient China): **http://eawc.evansville.edu/anthology/artwar.htm**

⊙ Western Civilization Documents CD-ROM

1.4 Hittite Laws
1.6 Laws of the Hebrews
2.1 Laws Relating to Women
2.2 Homer from the Iliad

THE GREEK POLIS

800	700	600	500	400	300	200 B.C.E.

Archaic Age, c. 800–500   Classical Age, c. 500–323   Hellenistic Civilization, c. 323–31

Greek colonization, c. 750–600   Persian Empire, 550–323

Alexander's Empire, 334–323

Early and Republican Rome, c. 550–27

Rulers, Nations, and War

◆ Peisistratus, tyrant of Athens, comes to power, 546

◆ Peloponnesian War ends, 404

◆ Thebes defeats Sparta at Leuctra, 371

◆ Persian invasion repelled at Marathon, 490

◆ Thebes defeats Sparta at Mantinea, 362

◆ Philip II defeats Athens, allies, at battle of Chaeronea, 338

◆ Pericles presides in Athens, 454–429

◆ Alexander the Great, r. 336–323

◆ Deaths of Aristotle, Demosthenes, 322

Society, Politics, and Ideas

◆ Homer's *Iliad*, c. 750, *Odyssey*, c. 725

◆ Hesiod's *Works and Days*, c. 700

◆ Alphabet used to write Greek, c. 700

◆ Spartan constitution established, c. 700

◆ Solon is archon in Athens, 594/3

◆ Aegina issues first Greek coin, the drachma, 575

◆ Cleisthenes reforms Athenian constitution, 508

◆ Common treasury of Delian League removed to Athens, 454

◆ Pericles' "funeral oration," 431

◆ Socrates arrested, tried, executed, 399

Beyond the West

Zhou dynasty, c. 1027–256

Chinese warring states, 450–221

Qin dynasty, c. 221–206

◆ Chandragupta Maurya of India, r. c. 321–298

◆ Asoka of India, 272–232

◆ Shi Huangdi of China, r. 221–210/209

56

3

THE GREEK POLIS

The New Politics of Ancient Greece

1000–300 B.C.E.

Mycenaean cultural area, c.1250 BCE

area of Greek colonization, c.700 BCE

KEY QUESTIONS

◆ **The Formation of the *Polis*:** Why did the Greeks form *poleis*, or city-states, rather than monarchies?

◆ **Justice and the *Polis*:** What did justice mean in the Greek *poleis*? Who were considered citizens, and to what extent were they able to participate in ruling the state?

◆ **Private Life:** What place did women and children inhabit in the Greek household? What activities were limited to men? What was the importance of the gymnasium and the symposium?

The Obedience of Socrates One short, ugly, and unassuming man commanded the intellectual life of Athens when it was still the leading city of ancient Greece: the philosopher Socrates. In 399 B.C.E., Socrates was arrested, charged with "impiety," convicted, and sentenced to death. He had lured the young, it was said, from their reverence for the old gods and values.

Socrates' friends begged him to escape, but he refused. He had been judged by the laws of the city. These laws were sacred: they enshrined the principle that the task of the human community is to establish justice. Socrates took from the prison guard the offered cup of poison, drank it, and died. That final act of obedience to the rule of law was the last lesson he had to teach. Socrates' reverence for the laws of his city is a key to understanding the achievement of Greek civilization. Greek civilization centered around the *polis* (plural *poleis*) or city-state. The Greek *poleis* were the cradles of the Western world.

THE FORMATION OF THE *POLIS*

Despite relentless poverty, the consequence of unyielding soil, the Greeks showed evidence early on of energy, inventiveness, and genius. By the end of the period called the Greek "Dark Ages" (c. 1200–800 B.C.E.), they had thrown off the yoke of kings and priests, created rich new literary and visual forms, wandered abroad to live and trade, and developed at home new ways to govern and defend themselves. During what is called the "Archaic" age of Greek civilization (about 800 to about 500 B.C.E.), they gave birth to the *polis*, and became the first **citizens** of the Western world.

Rich and Poor in a Poor Land

The *poleis* emerged toward the end of the Greek "Dark Ages," which followed the collapse of Mycenaean centers in c. 1200 B.C.E. Dark Age villagers lived in isolation, producing clothing and pottery only for their own use, using the crude implements forged by the smith to cook, to fight, to hunt, and to plow. Clustered in small communities bounded by craggy hill and rocky coast, they turned inward upon themselves. In the disparate intonations of the local dialects they told stories about their gods and what they remembered about their past. At once barred and yet sheltered from the world beyond the hill, they were loyal to their village, its people, its speech, and its way of life. Although they spoke different dialects—Dorian, Ionian, Aeolian—they thought of themselves as Hellenes (our word "Greek" is a legacy of the Romans' *Graecus*), and the Greek-speaking world as **Hellas**.

Even as Greek civilization developed in distinct poleis, it was unified by its common language.

The Greek villagers labored hard and ate little. The land they worked was stingy—thin, rocky, depleted by overuse. While every Greek farmer wished for a son who would take over the right to toil on his land, he did not want many sons. There was not enough land and not enough food. The only remedy for poverty was work, advised the poet Hesiod (c. 700 B.C.E.) in his account of village life entitled *Works and Days*:

> Work! Work, and then Hunger will not be your
> companion ...
> Let there be order and measure in your own work
> until your barns are filled with the season's harvest.
> Riches and flocks of sheep go to those who work.

Some villagers owned more and better land than others—not much more, nor much better. These privileged proprietors may have been the descendants of Mycenaean kings or tribal chiefs. They were the ancestors of the aristocrats who would lead the transformation of Greece from a backwater of Mediterranean civilization into a paragon of political and cultural innovation. Wealth gave the greater landowners prestige and power. They settled disputes among the villagers, there being no law beyond their judgments. These decisions concerned what a modern lawyer would call civil cases such as disputes about land or livestock. Criminal matters were handled without benefit of court, by sword and dagger. The victim or the victim's family demanded compensation for the crime, in the form of treasure or the life of the perpetrator. Crime and criminal were apparent to all, and vengeance was swift and exact.

Village society of the Greek Dark Ages had no great kings ruling from vast palaces. Some landowners bore the title of "king"; but these "kings" were tillers of the soil and masters of herds, more like the war chiefs of Neolithic towns than the monarchs of Babylon or Persia to the east. Landowners also served as priests, performing the sacrifices of chosen beasts to satisfy ever-hungry deities. But unlike the priests of their forbears, they did not live in temple complexes managing the wealth of the gods or demanding tribute from fearful worshipers. The poverty of the Greeks could not support priests and kings. Poverty was a tyrant to the Greeks. It was also their liberator.

The Homeric epics, the *Iliad* and the *Odyssey*, depict the meager authority of the Greek "kings" in the years between the Mycenaean collapse and the appearance of the *polis*. In the *Iliad* (composed about 750 B.C.E.), the Greek war effort against the rival kingdom of Troy is headed by a squad of loosely leagued petty kings without clear channels of command. Agamemnon, the acknowledged chief, must bully his colleagues into action, or gather them for long debates in order to arrive at consensus.

The *Odyssey* (composed about 725 B.C.E.) describes the experiences of Odysseus, one of the heroes of the *Iliad*, on his journey home from the Trojan War. Both Homer and Odysseus fear the world lying beyond the boundaries of Greek culture: it is ruled by dagger-toothed monsters and one-eyed giants, vengeful deities and seductive cannibals, witches who cast spells and an angry cosmos armed with destructive storm and hungry whirlpool. When the hero, naked and scarred, finally reaches his home (more a large farmhouse than a palace) together with his son Telemachus and aided by his great bow he must massacre the uncouth princes who have occupied the premises. This king has no greater authority over his nobles than that exercised by his bow.

The Coming of the Archaic Age

It was the ordinary potter who created the first harbinger of the flowering of Greek culture—a simple vase. This was a pot of graceful contour, bare of decoration except for a few plain lines. Its style is known as "Proto-Geometric," as it anticipated the more richly decorated Geometric style that would follow (see *Windows On*, p. 61). The understatement of this object is profound yet wholly original and breathtakingly lovely. These qualities would characterize the artistic and intellectual products of the civilization that crystallized in the Archaic age that now opened.

Two centuries earlier, around 1000 B.C.E., Greeks pressed by hunger had ventured out in tiny fishing vessels in search of more fertile land to the east, across the Aegean Sea. They established Greek-speaking communities on the Aegean islands and along the western shore of Asia Minor. There, they continued to worship the same gods, remember the same heroes, follow the same customs, and speak the same language as their fellow Greeks on the mainland. Language, in particular, was the line of demarcation between these transplanted Greeks and the **barbarians** in whose midst they lived. To the Greeks, a "barbarian" was simply a person who could not speak Greek but

Map 3.1 Cities of the Greek Homeland: *Centuries after the destruction of most of the Mycenaean cities on the Greek mainland in c. 1200 B.C.E., new centers, or* poleis, *arose amid the villages and farms of the Greek-speaking* ethnoi *("peoples"). Why do you think autonomous* poleis *developed in Greece, rather than a unified kingdom?*

barked meaningless (to them) syllables or chirped "bar-bar" like mindless birds. Whereas, for them, a civilized person was distinguished by the ability to speak the language in which a great literature had been created.

Although the Greeks of Asia Minor shared a language distinct from that of their "barbarian" neighbors, they spoke different dialects of Greek. Reflecting the pattern of settlement that prevailed in the homeland, these dialects were distributed with Dorian in the south, Aeolian in the far north, and Ionian in between (see Map 2.3). The Ionian dialect came to dominate in Asia Minor and set the standard for Greek-speaking settlers there. The Ionian culture that subsequently developed in that region over the next few centuries was not only thoroughly Greek but more advanced than that of the mainland. Here the *polis* was born and developed.

A *polis* generally developed when one or several villages coalesced around a common religious center. The cult celebrated a local deity (usually a goddess) as patron, and built for this deity a wooden temple on a high hill, called the *acropolis*. At the foot of that hill was a flat, clear area: the **agora**. Here people brought goods to market for exchange, wealthy landowners listened to civil disputes, and citizens gathered together for debate.

The Greek *polis* was an association of people united by place, by custom, by principle. It was not primarily an administrative or commercial center like the cities of Egypt or the Middle East, centered on palace or temple. The Greeks of the *polis* were rooted in the land they owned, on which they labored. They united to carry on a distinct way of life: to celebrate their principal gods, to decide between war and peace, to organize for mutual defense. The Greek *polis* was a gathering of those who defined and pursued shared goals—a group of people rather than an institution. The language used by contemporaries in referring to the *poleis* is significant: not Athens, but "the Athenians" opposed the Persians at Marathon; not Sparta but "the Spartans" supported **oligarchy** throughout Hellas. The Greek city was not a place, but a people.

The emergence of hundreds of *poleis* during the Archaic age enriched the Aegean world (see Map 3.1). The number of inhabited sites on the mainland, which had been reduced to a fraction of their level during the Mycenaean civilization, now began to rise rapidly, and their populations increased. By 700 B.C.E., the population of Attica (the region surrounding and including the city of Athens), had increased more than sevenfold from its low during the Dark Ages. On the peripheries of the zone of *polis* formation, social organization was by tribe and clan grouped into *ethnoi*. These communities considered themselves Greek and interacted with the *poleis* throughout the period. But social and cultural leadership belonged to the *poleis*.

Council, Assembly, and Phalanx

The people ruled the *polis*. Not all of them, sometimes only a very few; yet some consortium or committee drawn from the people organized city life. The primacy of the people resulted from the demotion of kings, which had occurred before the opening of the Archaic age (see Chapter 2). Ghosts of the earlier institution of kingship persisted in the organization of some *poleis*. Sparta retained the office of "king" and had in fact two kings simultaneously (probably reflecting an earlier alliance between two villages). They were generals who did not rule.

In Athens, one of the nine "leaders" (or archons) of the community was called the "king archon." He performed religious functions only—the vestige of a king who was the vestige of a priest. The priesthood itself, as a separate and privileged social class, had disappeared. Although the Greek world knew both priests and priestesses, these were either ordinary citizens performing special rites on ceremonial occasions, or inspired oracles attached to particular deities, public places, and temples. They did not constitute a priesthood such as that which had dominated Sumer or managed the Egyptian temple complex at Medinet Habu.

In the absence of monarchs, the Greek people devised for themselves a primitive machinery of government, or constitution. Their assembly, the first political institution of the early *polis*, had origins in earlier times. Even among Neolithic peoples, some sort of assembly probably met to approve actions proposed by a warlord. In early Hittite society, the assembly elected the king, although later the monarchy was hereditary, as in neighboring states (see Chapter 2). Homer describes in the *Iliad* assemblies held by the Achaean leaders (as he named the war chiefs now understood to be the kings of Mycenaean cities) in the struggle against Troy. In the Archaic age Corinthians, Thebans, Athenians, and citizens of other *poleis* practiced in their assemblies, in the *agora*, the skills of argument and debate, which would henceforth indelibly mark Greek culture.

The assembly was too large a body to examine a serious problem in depth. In Athens, the place set aside for the assembly could hold up to 6000. For this reason, some kind of guiding committee or council was formed to discuss issues in more detail. Nearly everywhere this more select body was made up of major landowners—men (never women) of the traditional nobility who firmly established themselves as a ruling elite. In some *poleis*, another criterion for admission to the council was advanced age. By the mechanisms of assembly and council, the *poleis* made decisions without the authority of monarch or priesthood.

The citizens also needed to develop a system of defense. In other societies, war was the responsibility

**Octopus vase,
from Mycenae,
1200–1125** B.C.E.

**Proto-
Geometric
amphora,
c. 950** B.C.E.

Hellenic civilization can be traced by observing the evolution of vases which served as useful utensils, ritual objects, prized works of art, and objects of trade. A Mycenaean vase (above) from the pre-Hellenic period features strong organic forms in its depiction of octopi and fish.

After the disappearance of Mycenaean centers in the twelfth century B.C.E., Athenian potters slowly began to create Proto-Geometric vases, typically stern and bare (above right).

Two centuries later, crowded linear patterns spread over the surface of this Athenian Geometric krater from the early Archaic age (below right).

From flourishing Corinth in the later Archaic period comes this krater (below left), depicting in black-figure terms part of a marriage procession. Black figure describes pottery in which the decoration is black on a red background. In contrast, the later red-figure pottery from the sixth and fifth century B.C.E. was decorated with red on a black background (see p. 63). (above: Metropolitan Museum of Art; upper right: Kerameikos Museum, Athens; below right: Louvre, Paris; below left: Vatican Museum, Rome)

Why do you think vase design in ancient Greece became more simple and austere, lacking human or animal forms, before it became freely descriptive and realistic?

**Geometric
krater, from
Athens,
c. 800** B.C.E.

**Black-figure
krater, Corinth,
c. 560** B.C.E.

To continue your investigation of this topic, please go to www.prenhall.com/king for the related **WINDOWS** on the **WEB** activity

of kings. In the Dark Ages wars were fought by heavily armed aristocrats, often in single combat. The Greeks of the Archaic age, however, made war the responsibility of the people. In doing so, they transformed the methods of warfare. Whereas other armies of the time depended on cavalry and lightly-armed infantry, the Greeks developed the **phalanx**: a block of men, standing shoulder to shoulder, packed solidly for rows, defended by a wall of shields held by each soldier over his own left side and his comrade's right. These soldiers of the phalanx were genuine "citizen soldiers," called **hoplites**, after the newly devised double-gripped shield (*hoplon*) that each held. The success of the formation (which spelled life or death for the community) depended on the willingness of each man to fight and thereby sustain the courage of his neighbor. The *polis* was the assembly of its people. The phalanx was the *polis* at war.

Only fairly prosperous male citizens could be hoplites; for the soldier had to pay for the expensive bronze armor that gave the phalanx its muscle. Despite this restriction, the phalanx was much less exclusive than the old **aristocracy** which was made up of wealthy landowners. Men of middling prosperity served as hoplites, assuming new risks which brought new privileges—full citizenship and full participation in the state. Poorer men, too, might fight for the *polis*. They served as light infantry and archers, and, in those *poleis* that developed navies, as sailors and oarsmen. They were counted as citizens, like the hoplites, but were generally not admitted to the highest offices.

Battles between hoplite armies, scheduled between sowing time and harvest, were quick and decisive. The forces faced each other on the level, fertile ground in dispute, which then became the prize of the victor. The loser fled. Such wars occurred regularly in Greece, from the first imperial conquests of the Spartans, in the eighth century B.C.E., to the constant battering of city against city in the fifth and

fourth centuries B.C.E. which ended in the Macedonian conquest. The phalanx maintained its dominance throughout this period, the tactics of war changing only in the fourth century B.C.E. under the generalship of Epaminondas from Thebes, Philip II of Macedonia, and Philip's son Alexander the Great.

The hoplite soldier was one of the first exports of Archaic Greece. Because too many men competed to feed their wives, children, and extended families from the thin soil of Greece, younger or disinherited sons and orphaned boys often sold their services abroad, to the kings of the Middle East. Some of those in the employ of the Egyptian pharaoh Psammetichos II (r. 595–589 B.C.E.) carved their names (like modern graffitists) on the legs of a colossal statue of Ramses II at Abu Simbel on the Nile River in southern (Upper) Egypt (591 B.C.E.). Greek mercenaries serving in armies throughout the Mediterranean region learned and profited much from wealthier and more advanced civilizations.

Colonization, Commerce, and Manufacturing

Overpopulation—or hunger—also impelled some Greeks to emigrate from the mainland and found colonies overseas. This period of colonization (extending from about 750 to 600 B.C.E.) resulted in the Greek domination of the northern rim of the Mediterranean as far west as Spain, as well as the coasts of the northern Aegean and Black seas as shown on Map 3.2. These regions became part of Hellas—as the Greeks referred to their own civilization—as had the earlier settlements on the west coast of Asia Minor.

Like its "mother city" or **metropolis** (the "mother" *polis* that established a colony), the Greek colony was from inception a *polis*—a self-contained political unit, a community of new citizens acting autonomously and aiming at economic self-sufficiency. The parent city recruited the colonists, funded the expedition, provided the necessary ships, and secured the good will of the patron god or goddess. Once the migrants were replanted on new soil, the parent city's function disappeared. The homeland was remembered fondly, and maintained its cultural influence, but the new *polis* claimed full autonomy.

Most of the colonies were coastal, just as most of the *poleis* of the Greek mainland were close to the sea. A lively exchange of goods developed among these settlements, a commercial advance to match the urban one. Olive oil and wine, staples of the Mediterranean diet, flowed out from areas of abundant production. Potters shipped their vases to the ports of the Middle East, Egypt, Italy, and the western Mediterranean. There, merchants bought and sold slaves and purchased the mineral resources Greece craved: amber and tin from the west and north, copper from Cyprus, and iron from Asia Minor. To feed their growing cities the Greeks imported wheat from the regions of the Black Sea, Sicily, and Egypt. From the more advanced civilizations to the east and south came luxury goods: fine ivories and elaborate metalwork, rugs and cushions, spices and perfume. Knowledge and skills, other gods and customs, the secrets of astronomy and mathematics, the techniques of coinage and the alphabet, all found their way back to Greece with the trading ships and returning mercenaries.

Ingots of precious metals were already used as a medium of exchange in the seventh century B.C.E. Around 650 B.C.E. stamped coins were first introduced, probably in Lydia (Asia Minor). These "croesids" (so named after King Croesus, r. 560–546) were circulated by the Persians, who after overrunning Lydia and capturing Croesus, imitated them with their own gold "darics" (after the monarch Darius). Around 575 B.C.E., Aegina became the first Greek *polis* to issue a stamped silver drachma (called a "turtle," after the city mascot on its face). Soon other Greek *poleis* minted their own coins stamped with figures relating to their city's myths and traditions: Corinth its "colts," for example, and Athens its "owls." These coins eased the exchange of goods in both local and international markets. Daily purchases were made in obols, a bronze currency; in the fifth century, a worker's wage reached a drachma per day (literally a "handful" of obols). The value of a ship's cargo or a nobleman's fortune was measured in minas and talents (respectively 100 and 6000 drachmas).

Like coinage, writing was an important commercial tool, as the merchants who brought the Phoenician alphabet to Greece clearly recognized. Now Greek producers could track inventories, as had the Mycenaean scribes. The new alphabet, extended to include vowel signs, was much simpler to learn than the old Mycenaean system of writing based on the graphic representation of syllables (see Chapter 1). The ordinary merchant, or even his intelligent slave assistant, could record transactions, send business letters, and report the various sights seen on a commercial venture.

Merchants occupied an uncomfortable place in Greek society. They were the agents of the commerce that brought wealth to Greece and fueled its achievements. Yet they were perceived as outsiders in the *polis*, which was understood as a community of farmers. Few farmers turned from the land in order to engage in the world of commerce. The great landowners almost never did so. Those who engaged in manufacture and commerce—working "seated and in the shade," as the historian Xenophon (c. 430–c. 354 B.C.E.) sneered—were looked down upon by the landowners. The ideal state, chided the philosopher Aristotle (384–322 B.C.E.), cannot allow its citizens to "live a mechanic or a mercantile life (for such a life is ignoble and inimical to virtue)."

Most merchants were foreigners, immigrants to the *polis* who formed a separate class of resident non-citizens, the "**metics**." Metics supported the *polis*, in Athens paying an annual head tax (twelve drachmas for men, six for women) and serving in the army. They could own personal property, but not land or houses. They could appear in law courts, but could not represent their own interests. Nor could they become citizens—the most serious liability of all—or hold office or join in the deliberations of the assembly. Barred from public life (for Greeks, the life that mattered the most), many Athenian metics settled in the commercial neighborhood of the port of Piraeus not far from the city. There they established workshops employing artisans, most of whom were slaves.

Slavery burgeoned in Greece as the *poleis* grew larger and required non-farm labor. At first, slaves

Working in Classical Greece

Clay statuette: *Fundamental to Greek life was agricultural work. In this figure from Boeotia, sixth century B.C.E., a man is plowing with the aid of two oxen. (Louvre, Paris)*

Red-figure cup: *The laborers shown in this red-figure Athenian cup, c. 480 B.C.E., are heating and hammering bronze in order to produce a statue of a man, who is also shown, on the far left, headless, but otherwise just like his fabricators. (Staatliche Museen, Berlin)*

were recruited from the ranks of abandoned children and captive peoples. These first slaves were mostly women, who spun and wove cloth, carted water, and doubled as concubines. Later, as the slave trade developed, slaves were bought and sold in auctions, held in the *agora* as they were for other commodities. Here a strong adult worker from Syria or Thrace might cost 200 or 300 drachmas, a child less than 100. Those who wished a slave's services on a limited basis might rent one from a slaveowner. Slavedealing was an acceptable occupation for an Athenian citizen, even though other commerce was despised. Many reputable gentlemen grew wealthy on income from the rented labor of their slaves.

Slaves were the engine of the Greek economy. Unskilled slaves loaded and unloaded ships; skilled ones produced the commodities of trade. Intelligent slaves were employed as record keepers, scribes, accountants, managers, bankers, and entrepreneurs. Slaves worked alongside metic and citizen workers in building the Parthenon and Erechtheum in Athens, and 300 Scythian slaves armed with bows and arrows constituted the Athenian police force. (The Scythians were a largely nomadic people who settled successively but temporarily in Asia Minor, southern Russia, and north of the Black Sea.) The Greeks did not subscribe to the notion that the slave was incompetent or untrustworthy. Yet the slave was considered the property of an owner, not because of his or her race (slaves in Greece were generally "barbarian" but resembled their masters in many racial characteristics), but because of his or her "nature." To Aristotle, a slave was an "instrument," ranking in the family hierarchy between children and inanimate objects. Slaves were naturally inferior, for "some people are marked out from the moment of birth to rule or to be ruled."

Most slaves worked in commerce, industry, and construction, supervised by metics. Others were servants; a rich man might require a staff of fifty, and even a poor citizen wanted one or two. More rarely, slaves were farmhands. Greece never employed the large contingents of agricultural slaves employed in the Roman Empire or in the United States before the Civil War. The worst fate for a slave was to be sent to work in the mines, where they worked prostrate for hours on end to extract ore, endured the terrible heat of smelting, which was done on the spot, and suffered appalling living conditions. The silver which enriched the *poleis* relied on the work of the slaves.

By contrast, some of the slaves who rose in commerce and industry to manage banks or businesses became wealthy enough to buy their own freedom. Yet in Greece, freed slaves (like metics) hardly ever acquired the political rights of native-born citizens. Membership in the *polis* was too precious a privilege, its citizens felt, to share with non-Greeks and other supposed inferiors.

The Cityscape

The spirit of the *polis* pervaded its physical structure. At its center stood *acropolis* and *agora*, the city's heart, combining the religious, political, and commercial strivings of the citizenry. Those at Athens are shown on p. 65. Scattered about the *agora* were a variety of public buildings: shrines, temples, fountains, storehouses, meeting houses, and **stoa**, or free-standing colonnades, sometimes called "porticos." On market days this commercial center would also contain temporary structures, such as the tables on which bankers counted out their coins. Such variety was typical of the Greek city. Regularity in the pattern of streets or the shape of houses was not esteemed by city builders until a much later date (see Chapter 5).

Shrines were everywhere, within the city and out in the country, in public spaces and interspersed among urban dwellings, wherever custom and tradition demanded recognition for some encounter of the human with the divine. A shrine consisted of an altar and a bit of sacred land marked by boundaries—a gate or wall or simple stone markers. Often the shrine became a temple, the most important architectural innovation of the Greeks (see Chapter 4). Temple building accompanied the establishment of the *polis*. Nearly forty temples had been constructed by 600 B.C.E., nearly ninety more in the next century.

Other prominent features of the Greek city were **gymnasiums** and stadiums. These were open spaces, placed as nature dictated at the center, in the suburb, in residential zones, or wherever a flat, clear space could be found to allow physical training and exercise, unadorned except by groves of trees and a sprinkling of shrines. The theater, a Greek invention, was initially another open space where singers and dancers performed in celebration of some god. This unpaved, flat, and roughly circular surface was often located at the foot of a hill on which spectators sat to view the proceedings. In time, stone seats for the audience were constructed or carved out of the native rock.

Acropolis and *agora*, shrine and temple, gymnasium and stadium and theater—these were the main structures of the *polis*. Private houses were nondescript, a jumble of rooms, bundled together along a disorderly network of streets. The great palace architecture of the Minoans and Mycenaeans, long forgotten, could offer no pattern for rich man's house or council building. Also forgotten were the great walls and gates of Mycenae. Almost as an afterthought, the Greek citizens threw a circuit of walls around the mass of their buildings, but these were only lightly fortified, if at all, and played little part in defining the *polis*.

In the featureless houses of the *polis* lived people of all classes, intermixed: rich and poor, citizen and

The Agora and Acropolis

Plan of the Athenian agora:
The citizens of Athens shopped, did their banking, talked about the news or the latest ideas, and sacrificed to the gods in the market zone or agora—the physical center of civic life. They also attended religious rituals on the Acropolis (below).

Plan of the Acropolis, Athens
(below): **The Parthenon (1), Erechtheum (2), Propylaia (3), and Temple of Athena Nike (4), whose reconstruction, 447–420** B.C.E., *marked a high point in Athens' development as a major city.*

N

Dipylon Gate
Altar
Poikile Stoa
Eridanos River
Royal Stoa
St Philip
Hadrian St
shops
12 Gods
Courtroom
Eschara
Dikasts' Ballots
Stoa of Zeus
seats
Hedhaisteion
Great Drain
Orchestra
Private houses & shops
Kolonos Agoraios
Old Bouleuterion
Street of the Panathenaia
Tholos
Race Track
Boundary Stones of Agora
The Eponymous Heroes?
Evrysakeion St
small buildings
Piraeus Gate
Strategion?
Law Courts
South Stoa I
Acropolis
House
Mint
Shrine
S.E. Fountain House
Prison

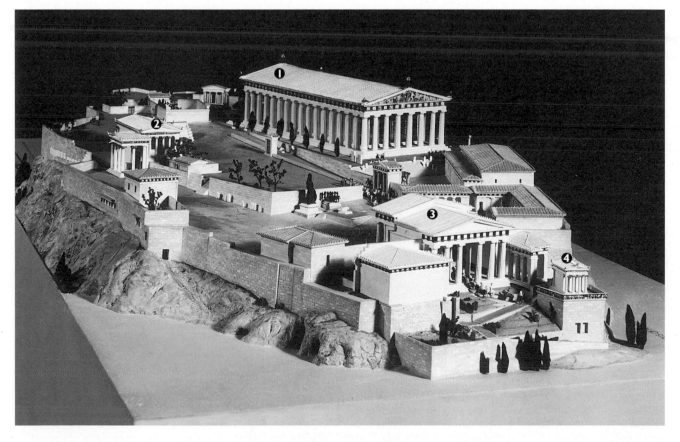

foreigner, free and slave. The total population was small. A population of 4000 or 5000 free men and women was common, and few cities exceeded 40,000. To these figures should be added at least an equal number of foreigners and slaves. Athens at its peak in 431 B.C.E. was the largest city by far, having a combined urban and rural population of 310,000. This number comprised 172,000 free men and women (of whom less than half lived in Athens and its harbor town of Piraeus), 28,000 metics (concentrated in Piraeus), and 110,000 slaves. Of this total, approximately 15 percent—between 40,000 and 50,000 adult males—were citizens who directed the course of both city and empire. The remaining 85 percent—slaves, foreigners, children, and women—had no voice in Athenian public life.

The free male citizens of the Greek *polis* were those whom the philosopher Aristotle had in mind when he asserted that "man is a political animal," or an animal capable of living in a city. Communities of no more than 100,000 citizens—not too small and not too large—should join, Aristotle advised, for "the purpose of living the good life after the manner of a political community." Nothing was more crucial to that ideal of the good life than justice. In pursuit of that preeminent value, the *polis* took form.

JUSTICE AND THE *POLIS*

Like modern cities, the Greek *polis* included rich people and poor ones. In the ancient world no fabric of laws or values had limited the right of the wealthy and powerful to exploit subordinates. The *polis*-dwelling Greeks were the first people in the Western world to formulate such a notion—that of **isonomia**, or "equality before the law." That guarantee in no way implied the leveling of social classes, and it never extended to non-citizens. Yet it was a lofty principle which, from the Archaic through the next age, the Classical (about 500 to 323 B.C.E.), prevailed in many of the *poleis*, notably in Sparta and Athens. Extracts from Greek writings on law and justice are given in *Witnesses* on pp. 67 and 70.

Law and Tyranny

On a sparse diet of barley and lentils varied with figs, grapes, and garlic, the Greek peasant struggled to survive. The poorest men owned the least land (about one-third of the arable land around Athens in the Archaic period). They were often the victims of those who owned the most (those of the hoplite class or better, who together possessed two-thirds of the land).

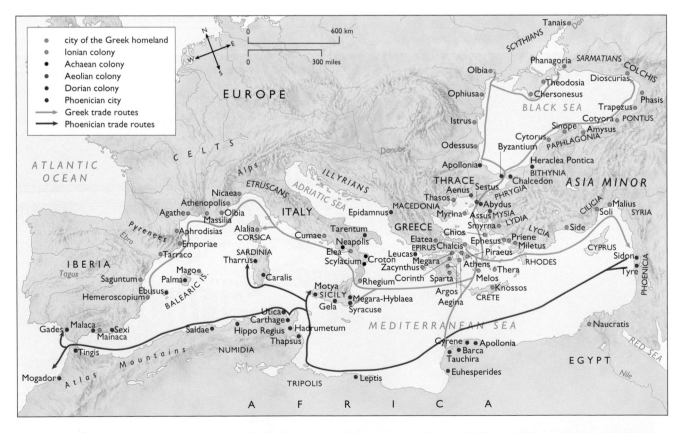

Map 3.2 Greek Colonization and Trade: *"Hellas" consisted of the Greek-speaking world. At first, Hellenes lived on the mainland of modern Greece, clustering in and near their distinctive poleis. Later, those poleis sent out colonists, who created new cities loosely related to their "mother cities" or metropoleis in the homeland. "Hellas" embraced all its cities, colonies, and ventures—all sites of Greek culture, even when not located in Greece.* **Why was Greek civilization so unified, even though its states were scattered around the Aegean and Mediterranean region?**

Resources were slight, population pressure was great, and the wealthy would not yield to the demands of the poor: to release them from their debts, to give more seed or lend more tools, or to give up their own land. The magistrates to whom the poor man turned for justice were landowners, too, and more inclined to protect the interests of the rich than to defend the poor from exploitation.

In earlier societies, poor peasants locked in conflict with rich landowners often sank into serfdom—dependents often immobilized by debt who owed the landowners produce and service. In Greece at least a few of the peasants were able to climb into the political class, the circle of those who debated the issues of state and made decisions. These few achieved this status because rich and poor alike came to agree that the *polis* should guarantee its citizens "equality before the law."

The principle of equality before the law was established only after long social conflict. Especially in the early days of the *poleis*, there was strife between the various classes or factions within Greek society: the nobly born (the *aristoi*, "the best," from which term derives our word "aristocracy"), the wealthy few (the *oligoi*, from which comes the English "oligarchy"), and the people (the *demos*, from which the English "**democracy**"). In any *polis*, one of these groups asserted itself as dominant. At the peak of its development, Corinth was an oligarchy, Athens a democracy. In the late Archaic age, social conflict often led to **tyranny**.

Tyranny was a distinctively Greek phenomenon. It meant the rule of an illegitimate ruler, the tyrant, who seized power and held it by violence. Thus it was quite different from monarchy: the rule of a legitimate king (however ruthless), descended from a royal lineage. Both forms of rule were autocratic (with power concentrated in a single figure), but whereas monarchy can be seen as legitimate because right to rule inheres in the figure holding power, tyranny is not.

Tyranny was a new force in Greek politics. In early Greece the term implied innovation and energy in state-formation, and even had a "democratic" tinge—the tyrant, though himself an aristocrat, often came to power with the support of the *demos*, the ordinary people. In some cases tyrants were prudent and competent rulers whose policies benefited the people.

During the sixth century B.C.E., tyrants ruled Corinth and Athens. In Corinth, the tyrant Cypselus expelled the arrogant noble clan of the Bacchiadae, redistributing their wealth to satisfy the urgent land hunger of the *demos*, who propelled him to power.

On Law and Justice, I

The publication of law codes was important for the citizens of the Greek poleis, as it was for other ancient communities. The poet Homer describes a scene in which justice is being exercised by acknowledged public authorities. The poet Hesiod paints a stark contrast between the unjust—those whose "verdicts are crooked"—and the just, who "know neither hunger nor ruin." The historian Herodotus reports the conversation of a Greek exile to the Persian king, in which the former explains the mystery of the Spartans' courage: it is because the law is their master.

Elders adjudicate in a scene on the shield of Achilles (c. 750 B.C.E.):
The people were assembled in the market place, where a quarrel
had arisen, and two men were disputing over the blood price
for a man who had been killed. One man promised full restitution
in a public statement, but the other refused, and would accept nothing.
Both then made for an arbitrator, to have a decision;
and people were speaking up on either side, to help both men.
But the heralds kept the people in hand, as meanwhile the elders
were in session on benches of polished stone in the sacred circle …
The two men rushed before these, and took turns speaking their cases,
and between them lay on the ground two talents of gold, to be given
to that judge who in this case spoke the straightest opinion.
(Homer, *Iliad*, 18:497–504, 506–508; ed. R. Lattimore, 1951)

Hesiod on prosperity for those who do justice (c. 700 B.C.E.):
Justice howls when she is dragged by bribe-devouring men
whose verdicts are crooked when they sit in judgment.
Weeping and clothed in mist, she follows through the cities
and dwellings of men, and visits ruin on those
who twist her straight ways and drive her out.
But those who give straight verdicts and follow justice …,
live in a city that blossoms, a city that prospers.
Then youth-nurturing peace comes over the land, and Zeus
who sees afar does not decree for them the pains of war.
Men whose justice is straight know neither hunger nor ruin,
but amid feasts enjoy the yield of their labors.
(Hesiod, *Works and Days*; ed. R. Lattimore, 1960)

Damaratus explains to Xerxes how Spartans obey the law (c. 450 B.C.E.):
So … the Spartans, when they fight singly, are as good men as any in the world, and when they fight in a body, are the bravest of all. For though they be free men, they are not in all respects free; Law is the master whom they own, and this master they fear more than your subjects fear you. Whatever it commands they do; and its commandment is always the same; it forbids them to flee in battle, whatever the number of their foes, and requires them to stand firm, and either to conquer or die.
(Herodotus, *Histories*, 7:104; ed. G. Rawlinson, 1924)

Cypselus then spurred an economic renewal which established Corinth as the foremost commercial center in Greece, destroying Athenian preeminence, if only temporarily. Under Cypselus and his successors, Corinth also minted its own coins, supported poetry and the arts, began a major project of temple construction, and launched a famous festival celebrated with athletic games. The commercial class that benefited from these projects became the sturdy core of a new ruling class. This ruling class, or oligarchy, survived the tyrant, his son Periander (c. 628–588 B.C.E.), and his grandnephew Psammetichus, whose assassination in about 586 B.C.E. closed the chapter on tyranny in Corinth.

After having failed twice to make himself tyrant, Peisistratus of Athens (c. 605–527 B.C.E.) succeeded on his third attempt, around 546 B.C.E. Like Cypselus, he enjoyed the support of the *demos*, whom he favored with many benefits. Without changing existing political structures, this tyrant exiled all his aristocratic rivals and critics, confiscated their lands, and distributed plots of land from this store of confiscations to poorer citizens. He improved the city's water supply and developed new sources of revenue from customs duties and the city-owned silver mines at Laurium. Moreover, he was an active promoter of cultural life, in ways that benefited not only Athens but the whole of Greece.

Poetry was the main form of cultural expression in sixth-century Greece. The epic of wandering minstrels and the lyric of the leisured nobility were chanted or sung to private audiences in rich men's homes. Peisistratus democratized poetry by providing public settings for its recitation. He elevated two festivals, in particular, to state holidays: the Great Panathenaea for Athena, the city's patroness, and the City Dionysia for Dionysus, the god of wine and unrestrained revelry. The Panathenaea featured the public recitation of Homer's verse. Under Peisistratus, not only did Homer become the poet of Athens and all of Greece, but the words of his epics were transcribed, possibly for the first time, using the alphabet recently arrived from Phoenicia. Originally, the Dionysiac festival had been celebrated in the country with lively and ribald song and dance. Now relocated to the center of Athens, it was transformed into a public performance, from which developed the drama, both tragic and comic (see Chapter 4).

After Peisistratus' death in 527 B.C.E., his sons Hipparchus (assassinated in 514 B.C.E.) and Hippias continued his policies. Deposed in 510 B.C.E., Hippias took refuge in Persia, which welcomed disgruntled Greek leaders. In 490 B.C.E. he returned with the Persian invading force, hoping a Persian victory would lead to his reinstatement. The battle, at Marathon, turned against him and his Persian armies, and the founders of the new government established after his deposition were victorious.

The Greek tyrants made some positive contributions to the *poleis* in the Archaic age; they mustered public support, fostered public institutions, and nurtured public values. The irony is that, in so doing, they created the state, a political organism distinct from the personal rule and will of a monarch or any other single individual. Though popular at first, the tyrant was ultimately hated. Nowhere did a tyrant succeed in establishing a dynasty lasting more than three generations. In these formative years of the political life of the West, the Greeks collectively made a momentous decision: they chose to be governed not by rulers but by laws. The future of the *polis* would lie in the hands of the legislator.

Lawmakers of Sparta and Athens

During the Archaic age, legislators shared the stage with tyrants. Sometimes competently, always autocratically, tyrants ruled the people of the Greek *poleis*, elevating their own agendas above any existing political customs or values. Legislators, by contrast, forged the laws by which the citizens, or one group of citizens, ruled a *polis*. Those laws pertained both to criminal and to civil matters—to murder, assault, and feud, but also to transactions in the marketplace and the relations of masters and servants. Of the political structures, or constitutions, created by such legislators, the most famous are those of Sparta and Athens.

Sparta   The earliest lawmaker was said to be Lycurgus of Sparta, a figure wrapped in legend. Whether or not he actually existed (possibly during the seventh century B.C.E.), he is credited with the creation of institutions that existed for many centuries. According to tradition, succeeding lawmakers bestowed upon Spartans the "Great Rhetra," or "enactment." This brief and cryptic document underlay the principles of the Spartan constitution. In the seventh century B.C.E., Sparta had achieved victory in a series of wars (begun the previous century) waged for the domination of the adjacent and fertile region of Messenia.

Victory brought its burdens. Having conquered hundreds of thousands of free Messenian peasants, the Spartan citizens found it necessary to keep them captive. Over nearly 350 years they pursued a policy of suppression and terror, reducing the conquered Messenians to **helots**, near-slaves, of the state. The helots were forced to labor on plots of land assigned in equal proportion to the handful of Spartan citizens called the "peers" or "equals." The poet Tyrtaeus (fl. c. 685–668 B.C.E.) described the helots' labors: "Like donkeys worn out with huge burdens, compelled by a terrible necessity, they bring to their masters a half of all the fruits of the earth."

The "Great Rhetra" defined the institutions Sparta needed in order to survive as a permanently armed garrison state. Like other Greek *poleis*, it was ruled by a council of thirty men, five annually elected executives, and an assembly of all the citizens. The novelty of the Spartan constitution lay in its mirroring of Spartan society. Elsewhere in Greece the citizenry included landowners and peasants and artisans. In Sparta, all citizens were equal by law, and all were soldiers. Distinctions between rich and poor were erased among the citizen "peers" or "equals," who jointly ruled the oppressed helots and the loosely allied citizens of neighboring *poleis*. These neighbors (to whom were left the functions of manufacture and trade, as those of agriculture were left to the helots) possessed a limited form of citizenship: they were expected to fight in the Spartan army, but had no political rights.

From around 550 B.C.E., the Spartan "equals" subjected themselves to a harsh regime, organized according to ancient structures of tribe and brotherhood. From age seven to age fifty, Spartan males lived with their comrades in military camps—not in private households with their wives and children. At age thirty, they were admitted to the assembly and allowed greater freedom to visit their marital homes. Meanwhile, they ate in common eating clubs, slept in barracks, and passed their days (when they were not at war) in drill, singing, and dancing—the sum total of their cultural activity. Engaging neither in agriculture nor commerce, their business was warfare. Intellectual, domestic, and economic life were subordinated to the needs of a male society perpetually ready for battle. This manner of life was expected to instill the virtues necessary so that Spartans might behave as the poet Tyrtaeus, spokesman for the city's militarist values, advised:

> *For no man ever proves himself a good man in war*
> *Unless he can endure to face the blood and the*
> *slaughter,*
> *go close against the enemy and fight with his hands.*

Sparta's constitution made it, by the mid-sixth century, the most powerful *polis* in Greece. What kind of system was it? The Greeks considered Sparta an oligarchy, and indeed the city supported oligarchies among its allies and occasionally intervened to impose them elsewhere. But it also fitted other descriptions. It was democratic, in that the Spartan citizens accepted a leveling of condition, and became true "equals" in duty to the state and in submission to its laws. It was communistic in that property ownership was a right subordinated to the needs of the community: all shared in the produce of the land (worked by others), owned by no individual (at least not before the fourth century B.C.E.). It was aristocratic, in that the Spartans ruled as a nobility over the intimidated helots and neighboring cities. It was imperialistic, in that it depended on the subjugation of another people. It was totalitarian, in that all rights were

---

> ### MUST READS
>
> ## The World of the Greek poleis
>
> **Herodotus** *History*
>
> **Thucydides** *History of the Peloponnesian War*
>
> **Aristotle** *The Constitution of Athens*
>
> **Xenophon** *Oeconomicus (The Housholder)*
>
> **Plutarch** *Lives,* especially of *Lycurgus, Themistocles, Pericles*
>
> **Arrian** *Life of Alexander the Great*

subordinated to nationalist and militaristic goals. This curious society has been much admired by the philosopher Plato (c. 427–347 B.C.E.), among other fantasizers of ideal commonwealths. But was it just? It was—but only for the "equals," a restricted and ever-shrinking class. In contrast, the Athenian lawmakers—Draco, Solon, Cleisthenes—came closer to organizing a truly just society.

Athens During the seventh century B.C.E. nine magistrates called archons ruled Athens, all of them members of the landowning class. These men (who comprised the council called the Areopagus) laid down the laws—and they were the laws, for outside of their personal judgment and memory there was no repository of the principles of justice. In about 621 B.C.E. the lawmaker Draco first organized this body of legal custom and had the laws inscribed on stone for the benefit of a *demos* who wanted to know them and, apparently, knew how to read. The publication of laws, wherever it occurs, is a landmark. It records the moment when people are given the means of knowing the otherwise mysterious rules by which they are governed. As the later playwright Euripides wrote, "When the laws are written down, weak and rich men get equal justice; the weaker, when abused, can respond to the prosperous in kind, and the small man with justice on his side defeats the strong." Draco's legacy to the small man of Athens was knowledge of the laws, and thus the possibility of justice.

Those of Draco's laws that survive concern criminal acts—principally homicide, the pressing legal issue of early societies. They define transgressions and assign punishments—of such severity that later political writers gave the name "draconian" to a very harsh punishment. Draco's achievement, however, pales next to that of Solon (c. 640–559 B.C.E.), an aristocrat and archon who, responding to the pleas of the *demos*, managed to rebuild Athenian society on new principles (see *Witnesses*, p. 70). If he had not done so, Athens might have become another Sparta, dedicated to the repression of a subject serf population.

On Law and Justice, II

These passages on law and justice give evidence again of the immense importance for the Greeks of the ideal of justice. The archon Solon explains how he managed to balance the demands of competing factions in Athens, protecting both. The philosopher Socrates, in prison, refuses to allow his friends to secure his freedom, lest he violate the laws of the city that had reared him. The philosopher Aristotle argues that the human being is perfected by law and justice—without which he is "the most unscrupulous and savage of animals."

Solon explains his just settlement of factional struggles between rich and poor in Athens (c. 594/3 B.C.E.):

> I gave the people as much privilege as they have a right to:
>> I neither degraded them from rank nor gave them free hand;
> and for those who already held the power and were envied for money,
>> I worked it out that they also should have no cause for complaint.
> I stood there holding my sturdy shield over both the parties;
>> I would not let either side win a victory that was wrong.

(Solon, *Greek Lyrics*, 2e, 20; ed. R. Lattimore, 1960)

In prison, Socrates imagines that the personified Laws of Athens call upon him to obey them, and not, by escaping, to evade a sentence of death (360 B.C.E.): You, Socrates, are breaking the covenants and agreements which you made with us at your leisure, not in any haste or under any compulsion or deception, but having had seventy years to think of them, during which time you were at liberty to leave the city, if we were not to your mind, or if our covenants appeared to you to be unfair. You had your choice, and might have gone either to Lacedaemon or Crete, which you often praise for their good government, or to some other Hellenic or foreign State. Whereas you, above all other Athenians, seemed to be so fond of the State, or, in other words, of us her laws (for who would like a State that has no laws?), that you never stirred out of her: the halt, the blind, the maimed, were not more stationary in her than you were. And now you run away and forsake your agreements. Not so, Socrates, if you will take our advice; do not make yourself ridiculous by escaping out of the city.

(Plato, *Crito*, trans. Benjamin Jowett)

Aristotle argues that humans are excellent creatures when embracing justice, but evil when lacking it; and for this reason they should belong to a state (c. 330 B.C.E.): Therefore the impulse to form a partnership of this kind [that is, a state] is present in all men by nature; but the man who first united people in such a partnership was the greatest of benefactors. For as man is the best of the animals when perfected, so he is the worst of all when sundered from law and justice. For unrighteousness is most pernicious when possessed of weapons, and man is born possessing weapons for the use of wisdom and virtue, which it is possible to employ entirely for the opposite ends. Hence when devoid of virtue man is the most unscrupulous and savage of animals ... Justice on the other hand is an element of the state; for judicial procedure, which means the decision of what is just, is the regulation of the political partnership.

(Aristotle, *Politics*, 1.1.12, 1253, 32–38; ed. H. Rackham, 1932)

When Solon was elected chief archon in 594 B.C.E., the poorest peasants of Attica were in danger of slipping into serfdom. Each year they borrowed seed and tools. If they could not repay the value of that debt, they lost possession of their land, mortgaged to wealthy landowners. Driven deeper into debt, the least fortunate of these mortgaged life itself to satisfy their creditors: they sold their children, their wives, and themselves into slavery. Many were resold abroad. These lost Athenians were recovered by Solon. He issued a call for their return, sent agents abroad to identify and reclaim them, and provided funds for the purchase of their freedom.

As a further step in his policy, called the "lifting off of burdens," Solon cancelled existing debts—thereby abolishing the quasi-serfdom of the poor peasant.

Witness to his success (as he announced in the verses he later composed) was the "Black Earth" herself, freed of the stones inscribed with notices of debt which had pierced her surface:

I took away the mortgage stones stuck in her breast,
and she, who went a slave before, is now set free.

Next on Solon's agenda was a program to rebuild the economy. He promoted the export of oil and wine, which could be produced in surplus and sold abroad for cash; but he discouraged the export of wheat, for shortages of this grain meant famine. He invited artisans to relocate to Athens. The excellent work of Athenian potters soon invigorated the ceramic industry, in particular, and the influx of these and other skilled artisans allowed Athens to reestablish the commercial primacy it had yielded to Corinth. To encourage the use of all native talent, Solon directed that each man must teach a trade to his son. If he did not, his son would have no moral or legal responsibility to sustain his parent in old age.

To prevent a recurrence of the pernicious war between rich and poor, Solon revised the Athenian constitution to give the less privileged a voice in the political process. "I stood there holding my sturdy shield over both the parties," reflected Solon, referring to the rich and poor; "I would not let either side win a victory that was wrong." He classified the citizenry into four grades from the richest to poorest. At the top were the "men of five hundred bushels" (in annual yield of wheat); next,

the "three hundred-bushel men," or horsemen; third, the "two hundred-bushel men" or "men of the line," wealthy enough to arm themselves as hoplites; fourth, the simple, even landless, "workers." Previously, the top rank of these social groups had held exclusive power.

With wealth, not birth, as the determinant of social status, the old aristocratic system gave way. Solon opened the archonship to men of the second rank, and apparently created a council of 400 persons to be drawn from all ranks except the lowest. By this constitution, Solon did not institute full democracy, in the modern sense, but he came close to doing so.

Solon enacted his revolutionary program swiftly. His work completed, he performed a last notable deed: he resigned, before he himself might be tempted to become a tyrant, or before the *demos* might desire to make him one. The Roman dictator Julius Caesar also declined the crowns offered him. But he did not renounce power so decisively as did his Athenian predecessor.

Two generations later (the interlude marked by Peisistratus' tyranny), the aristocrat Cleisthenes (fl. c. 508 B.C.E.) carried Solon's work of social reconstruction forward in the direction of democracy. Whereas for Solon the great threat to the Athenian *polis* was greed, for Cleisthenes it was the ancient authority of clans, brotherhoods, and tribes. These groups promoted the rule of the great aristocratic families. To counter the power of clan and tribe, Cleisthenes devised a wholly new system of social organization. Its basic unit was the *deme* (from the

Map 3.3 Athens, its Allies and Enemies, c. 430 B.C.E.: *Athens was the only major city of Attica, a triangular region projecting to the southeast from central Greece. By 500 B.C.E., the city dominated the region. Fifty years later, as center of the Athenian Empire, it dominated constellations of mainland, overseas, and island cities as well. The capital city was itself a democracy that had been reorganized by Cleisthenes (c. 508 B.C.E.) so that representatives to its council were chosen from a social cross-section without regard to earlier tribal solidarities.* **What common interests drew the members of the Athenian empire together?**

Greek *demos*), or village. Before Cleisthenes, a young Athenian was registered in a *phratry*, or brotherhood, to which he belonged by virtue of birth. Now he would be registered in a deme by virtue of residence. Cleisthenes thus removed from the realm of politics the dimensions of kinship and hereditary rights, and approached closer to his ideal of *isonomia*—equality before the law.

The next step was to reconstitute the traditional tribe (of which there were four) according to new principles. The *polis* was divided into thirty regions or "thirtieths," each formed from several contiguous demes. These thirtieths were then grouped into three zones of ten thirtieths each: those of the plain, those of the city, and those of the coast. From the thirty divisions, ten new "tribes" were assembled to replace the four traditional ones, each consisting of three thirtieths in all and one from each of the three geographical zones—thus attaining a balance of rich plain dwellers, poor hill dwellers, and the middling sort of the coasts in each tribe. Each of the 10 tribes chose by lot 50 representatives to a council of 500 citizens (an expansion of the one Solon presumably created of 400), and served as a governing committee of that council for one-tenth of each year.

Cleisthenes' redefinition of the tribe was, in fact, a masterly act of social restructuring. In the world's first democracy, men could no longer claim the right to rule others by reason of blood and association. Tribes were composed of citizens from demes that varied in wealth, background, and interest, and politics was open to a process of decision-making based on argument and debate rather than origin and custom.

A final ingredient to the democratized constitution was **ostracism**, possibly another invention of Cleisthenes. This device, which was first used in 487 B.C.E., answered the need of citizens who recognized that a *polis* in which the *demos* ruled was vulnerable to seduction by tyrants. To forestall the rise of any tyrant, each year the citizens would assemble to vote whether there was a man in Athens dangerous to the state. They did so by inscribing a name on a shard of pottery, or *ostrakon*, the most available form of stationery—hence the term "ostracism." Whoever won this prize of unpopularity (some years, there was no candidate) would be exiled for ten years, whether or not he had committed any crime.

Justice in the Classical Age

During the Classical age—from about 500 to 323 B.C.E.—the Greek *poleis* flourished, at first, under the constitutions forged by legislators of the Archaic age; then they declined from the impact of war and misrule. The experience of Athens, in particular, traced a spectacular trajectory to glorious fruition and then to inglorious old age.

Athens was fortunate in its leaders. Solon originated the concept of the responsibility of the *polis* to its citizens. Cleisthenes created the structure by which citizens could rule the *polis*. Over the following (fifth) century, a series of leaders guided Athens. Aristides, Xanthippus, and Themistocles were leaders of the Athenian state in the critical years following the Battle of Marathon in 490 B.C.E. After 480 B.C.E., the general Cimon policed the seas and secured the primacy of Athens in the Aegean. Toward mid-century, the democrats Ephialtes and Pericles held sway. Ephialtes was assassinated, and in 443 B.C.E. Pericles (c. 495–429 B.C.E.) assumed the leadership of Athens, now the foremost state of the Greek world.

Under Pericles the Athenian democracy and the Athenian Empire reached their maximum development, as shown on Map 3.3. The democracy matured to such an extent that any Athenian citizen might aspire to a one-year term on the Council of Five Hundred. Annual selections by lot filled 700 government positions (not counting places on the 600-man juries)—enough jobs to give every citizen a chance to hold public office at least once in his lifetime. Public officials and jurors received salaries, which ensured that the poor as well as the rich could participate in government. The archonship was still restricted to men of the three highest classes by wealth, but archons were now selected by lot, in order to ensure the most open selection and widest distribution of the honor. Moreover, the archonship was now only an honor, its authority having been transferred to the more broadly based council. Real leadership was exercised by a board of ten generals, elected by popular vote each year. It was to this office that Pericles was reelected by the will of the *demos* every year from 443 to 429 B.C.E.

The citizens of Athens reaped other material benefits during Pericles' administration. In 454 B.C.E., the Athenians had removed the treasure of the Delian league to the capital at Athens, ostensibly to protect it. There Pericles tapped it at will, not only for the costs of defense but also for the private use of Athens. The Persians had destroyed the Athenian temples in 480 B.C.E.; shouldn't the monies gathered to rebuff the Persians be used to rebuild them, and more splendidly? The temples were magnificently rebuilt: the Parthenon and Erechtheum, both dedicated to the patron goddess Athena and each adorned with a statue of this deity; the temple to Nike, goddess of Victory; the Propylaea, or entrance gate to the Acropolis on the west. The ruins that stand on the Acropolis today still impress the viewer with the genius of their makers and the noble spirit of the civilization that produced them. A reconstruction of the Acropolis is shown on p. 65.

The leader of this democratic yet imperialistic *polis* was an idealistic aristocrat. Pericles was the friend of artists and thinkers: Sophocles the dramatist and Phidias the sculptor, Herodotus the historian, Protagoras the sophist (a teacher of philosophy or rhetoric noted for clever argumentation), Anaxagoras the philosopher, and Aspasia, Pericles' learned mistress. An imperious strategist at times, yet a democrat at heart, Pericles never boasted in public but led from the background. No document records his own words, but the contemporary historian Thucydides (c. 471–400 B.C.E.) may have been present at the speech Pericles gave in 431 B.C.E., and he reported its unforgettable message (see *Witnesses*, right).

In this speech, known to later generations as his "Funeral Oration," Pericles commemorated the dead of the first year of the Peloponnesian War by celebrating the city for which they had died—its independence, its democratic system, its encouragement of individual expression, its love of beauty and wisdom. Athens was, he maintained, the center of Greek culture, home to poets and philosophers, historians and sculptors, the focus of all discussion. It was by its example, he proclaimed, the "school," or "educator" of Hellas, the universe of Greek *poleis*.

Of Pericles' Athens, however, we may ask the question: Was it just? For the citizens, yes: this group, which included rich and poor, city and country-dweller, idler and artisan, attained an unprecedented level of political privilege. But excluded from the citizenry was more than half the population of Attica: foreigners, slaves, women, and children. Also excluded were the residents of the subject cities of the Athenian Empire. Any assessment of Athenian democracy must recognize the injustice suffered by the great number of the excluded. Nevertheless, the achievement of true political equality for much of the Athenian citizenry was unprecedented.

When Pericles delivered the "Funeral Oration," the Peloponnesian War had already begun. The Athens that surrendered to Sparta a generation later, in 404 B.C.E., was a ghost of the city that Pericles celebrated. Sparta stripped Athens of parts of her walls and her ships. It tried to smother her political institutions, imposing, briefly, an oligarchical government; called by the unhappy Athenians the rule of the "Thirty Tyrants," soon rejected in favor of a revived democracy. In the post-war period, Athenian democracy reached its zenith while Athenian power diminished. The citizens voted themselves ever-expanding government services, collected regular pay for government jobs, and sued each other in the law courts. They ignored the impending threat to the city's autonomy—the growing power of Macedonia, which loomed larger after the mid-fourth century.

Sparta, meanwhile, in the very flush of victory lost its heart as a military power. In 371 B.C.E., it was beaten decisively (at Leuctra, in Boeotia), in the aimless struggle among the *poleis* that filled these years after the Peloponnesian conflict. The victorious city was Thebes, a newcomer to the first rank of the *poleis*. Theban success was owed to the innovations of her military commander Epaminondas (c. 418–362 B.C.E.), the first Greek captain to do something new with the phalanx since its creation some four centuries earlier. Massing his hoplites at fifty deep on one wing, he crushed the Spartan troops, heretofore thought invincible. Over four hundred out of seven

WITNESSES

Pericles

In his "Funeral Oration" for the dead fallen in war, Pericles clarifies the reasons for the greatness of Athens— for which her citizens are proud to die (431 B.C.E.).

[O]ur system of government does not copy the institutions of our neighbours. ... Our constitution is called a democracy because power is in the hands not of a minority but of the whole people. When it is a question of settling private disputes, everyone is equal before the law; when it is a question of putting one person before another in positions of public responsibility, what counts is not membership of a particular class, but the actual ability which the man possesses. No one, so long as he has it in him to be of service to the state, is kept in political obscurity because of poverty. ...

Then there is a great difference between us and our opponents, in our attitude towards military security. ... Our city is open to the world, and we have no periodical deportations in order to prevent people observing or finding out secrets which might be of military advantage to the enemy. This is because we rely, not on secret weapons, but on our own real courage and loyalty. There is a difference, too, in our educational systems. The Spartans, from their earliest boyhood, are submitted to the most laborious training in courage; we pass our lives without all these restrictions, and yet are just as ready to face the same dangers as they are. ... Our love of what is beautiful does not lead to extravagance; our love of the things of the mind does not make us soft. We regard wealth as something to be properly used, rather than as something to boast about. As for poverty, no one need to be ashamed to admit it: the real shame is in not taking practical measure to escape from it. ... Taking everything together then, I declare that our city is an education to Greece. ... This, then, is the kind of city for which these men, who could not bear the thought of losing her, nobly fought and nobly died. Its greatness derives from the freedom of its citizens, which permits them to excel in many enterprises, and suits them to respond flexibly to any crisis that might arise. Pericles contrasts that freedom and flexibility with the rigor and regulation of Spartan society.

(From Thucydides, *Peloponnesian War*, 2:36, 39–42; ed. R. Warner, 1954)

WHO'S WHO

Lawmakers of Athens

Solon (639–c. 550 B.C.E.) lawgiver who "lifted burdens" from the Athenian poor and established a representative council that limited the arbitrariness of the archons.

Cleisthenes (c. 570–c. 507 B.C.E.) developed a new system of social organization for Athens based on place of residence, not clan allegiance, and thus promoted the development of democracy.

Pericles (c. 498–429 B.C.E.) presided for a generation over the Athenian city and Empire, under whose patronage and leadership it reached a cultural pinnacle.

hundred Spartan soldiers was killed at Leuctra (not to mention the devastation of allies and auxiliaries), including hundreds of Spartan officers. The humiliation was repeated in 362 B.C.E. at Mantinea. The "equals"—that privileged group of Spartan citizens—had, during the three centuries of their ascendancy, admitted no new families to their ranks. In the preceding century, their number had plummeted from about 5000 to 1000. The losses at Leuctra and Mantinea delivered a blow that crippled Sparta.

Thebes held the stage only briefly. For three years it had held, as hostage, a young prince who learned military arts there. In 359 B.C.E., this young man, Philip, became the second Macedonian king of that name. He promptly undertook a program of conquest, seizing cities around the northern Aegean and in Euboea, east of Athens. At Chaeronea, in 338 B.C.E., he smashed Athens and her allies, who had rallied too late to stop his advance. Athens had apparently forgotten what it had understood clearly in the years before Marathon—that life under a foreign master would crush her own identity. She rushed to support Philip, and in an act of great irony, made this foreign monarch a citizen.

City by city, region by region, Philip absorbed the once proud and autonomous *poleis*. Henceforth, although the Greek cities continued to exist, they never regained the quality of public life that they had known when free. Under Philip's son Alexander the Great Greece would be swept back into the world of monarchs and empires.

PRIVATE LIFE OF THE POLIS

In their public life, the ancient Greeks sought *isonomia* (equality before the law) and access to justice for rich and poor (though they did not generally, as in Sparta, eliminate social distinctions among citizens). The private life of the Greek *polis*, in contrast, was characterized by a great inequality between male and female. Women were subordinated to men to an extraordinary degree. Even the domestic space that they occupied was clearly separated from the open and public space occupied by men.

The Household: Woman's Place

The public life of the *polis* was based on distinctive patterns of private life, whose fundamental unit was the *oikos*, or household. The need to preserve the *oikos* in an environment of continuing scarcity was the overwhelming concern of its head, always a male. This need triggered the anxiety that underlay the social organization of the *polis*.

The *oikos* consisted of a man, his wife and children, and related and unrelated dependents including slaves. The philosopher Aristotle defines these household members in his *Politics*, in a descending hierarchy from free adults to children and slaves to animals and even tools: a continuous system of superior and inferior being headed by a dominant male, since "the male is by nature superior and the female inferior, the male ruler and the female subject."

The *oikos* was **patrilineal** in origin and purpose, and **patriarchal** in character. A patrilineal family traces its foundation to a male forebear on the father's side. It considers as descendants only males. Female offspring are valued insofar as they marry men whose families, also patrilineal, are useful friends or allies to her family of birth (her natal family). In patrilineal families, all individuals (including children of both sexes) are asked to conform to the need for survival in the male line. Patrilineal families may also be patriarchal. In a patriarchy, not only is the bloodline traced through the father's ancestors, but power within the family and over all its members is exercised by a senior male.

The elevation of the male head-of-household in Greek society was matched by a derogation of the woman. The attitude is apparent in the works of Greek philosophers and poets. Aristotle may have spoken for common opinion when he stated that "we should look upon the female state as being as it were a deformity, though one which occurs in the ordinary course of nature." The tragedian Aeschylus, in his *Eumenides*, denied women's role even in reproduction. The god Apollo explains to the goddess Athena:

> *The mother is no parent of that which is called her child, but only nurse of the new-planted seed that grows. The parent is he who mounts.*

For Homer, women were valuable as sexual objects and as artisans: like the seven women the king Agamemnon offered the warrior Achilles, "the work of whose hands is blameless, ... who in their beauty surpassed the races of women." The poet Hesiod

Working Women

Greek pottery: *Shown here are characteristic forms of women's work. This detail from a lekythos or flask by the Amasis painter, c. 540* B.C.E. *(above), shows women spinning and weaving at home. On this three-handled black-figure water jar (hydria) by the Priam painter, c. 520* B.C.E.*, women are shown carrying water from the fountain in jugs (below). (top: Metropolitan Museum of Art; below: Museum of Fine Arts, Boston, William/Francis Warden Fund)*

Priam painter, Black-figure hydria, c. 520 B.C.E.

Nevertheless, women did have their champions. For Plato, capable women were suitable candidates for political rule. The ruling class of "Guardians," in the ideal state he outlines in his *Republic*, includes women who are expected to procreate more exceptional leaders. Here his views reflected to some extent the social reality of Sparta, which he admired, where women had somewhat greater freedom than in other cities and participated fully in athletic training. The tragedians portrayed female characters of extraordinary depth and power. Aeschylus created the magnificent but wily and dangerous Clytemnestra, and Sophocles the courageous Antigone. Euripides depicted giants of womankind: the implacable Medea, driven by insane jealousy to kill her children; the love-wracked Phaedra rejected by her stepson Hippolytus; the eloquent Hecuba, weeping for Troy and for her slaughtered grandson Astyanax.

Such commanding women may have reigned in tragic theater, but they were nowhere to be found in Classical Greek society. The sharp divergence between the dramatic portrayal of women and their actual social role defies explanation. Perhaps some women, though confined to a domestic role, impressed at least some men with their high capacity, and the tragic playwrights and poets report this rare and exceptional woman. Or perhaps the tragedians echo a tradition of female leadership (dating back to Mycenaean times) wholly lost by the Classical age in which they wrote. Whatever the explanation of the discrepancy between literature and life, the status of women in Classical Greece was low.

Generally, girls were married young (at about age fifteen, soon after attaining puberty) to considerably older men (about age thirty) chosen by their families. This age difference, which strengthens the imbalance of power within the family, is characteristic of patriarchal families. The wife's duties included obedience to her husband, who made most decisions of family life. They also included childbearing. Over her twenty to thirty years of fertility (if she did not die young in childbirth), a woman was expected to give birth to several children, including a male heir.

Although subordinate to her husband, a woman held some authority as a result of the useful labor she performed. Examples of tasks are shown here on the flask and water jar. In peasant families, she sowed and harvested, ground grain, carried water, milked and herded, gathered and stored surpluses. In wealthy families, she was a manager of household supplies, of tools and wardrobe, of slaves. In all households, she was the producer of textiles, performing the tasks of spinning, weaving, and embroidering, which from earliest times had been a female province.

Engaged in such labor, a woman spent her life first in her father's household and then in her husband's: each in turn was her "lord." She could not choose to

described Pandora, the first woman, according to Greek mythology, as "an evil for mortal men," the "tempting snare" from whom descends the race of "wicked womenfolk." The great misogynist Simonides of Amorgos compared women to pigs, dogs, asses, horses, and monkeys, finding worthwhile only the woman who was like a bee, thrifty and productive: "To her alone no blame is attached, … She grows old cherishing a husband who cherishes her, … She does not take pleasure in sitting among the women / when they are discussing sex."

remain single and live in her own house, or even at home. She could be divorced by her husband (though she could not, under any circumstances, choose to divorce him). In that case, she would be returned, with her dowry, to her father's house.

Just as the wife in a Greek household was subordinate to her husband, children were the subjects of their parents, and especially of their fathers, from the very moment of birth. The father had exclusive power to decide whether or not a child was to be accepted into the household. A child might be unwanted because resources were scarce, or because the family already numbered sufficient children or children of that sex. The unwanted child would then be "exposed"—left unprotected in a public place.

Often, the exposed child died. Sometimes he or she was claimed by other adults. Childless couples might take abandoned children into their households. Families who needed hands to assist with domestic tasks, or managers of workshops or brothels equally in search of inexpensive labor might also take them in. In none of these cases was a child "adopted,"in the modern sense. As the child was transferred from his or her original family to another one, his or her status sank from family member to subordinate. It is likely that most of the abandoned children who survived were enslaved.

The father who decided to expose his child thus condemned his own offspring to death, servitude, or slavery. These destinies more often greeted girls than boys. Female infanticide may account for the unnaturally high ratio of males to females in the population, while the practice of feeding girls less than boys may have resulted in girls' greater rate of natural death in childhood. Girls were also exposed more often than boys, though abandoned boys, as well as girls, were pressed into sex slavery—sometimes undergoing first the further humiliation of castration (a procedure which, in the absence of antibiotics, was also extremely dangerous). The plentiful supply of abandoned children meant that fewer foreign slaves were required. Slavedealers kept watch over the usual places of abandonment.

Along with evidence of infanticide and abandonment, there is evidence that many children were treasured by their parents. That sentiment is known from literary sources in which parents' love for children is described. Parental love is also documented by the gravestones whose inscriptions express the grief of fathers and mothers at the loss of their young children. Children were carefully reared. Mothers generally nursed their own babies. As was the near-universal custom in the ancient Mediterranean region,

Women's Lives

Life and death: *Confined to their houses, the wives and daughters of Greek citizens led quiet lives. Here we glimpse some moments, as on this grave stele (above) depicting a lady and her maid studying her jewels, Athens, late fourth century* B.C.E.; *and on this stone relief from the "Ludovisi throne" (below) where a woman emerging from the bath is robed by her servants, Rome, fifth century* B.C.E. *(above: National Archaeological Museum, Athens; below: Museo Nazionale delle Terme, Rome)*

Girl playing the lyre: *In leisure hours, a woman might sing to the lyre, a stringed instrument which accompanied the recitation of "lyric" poetry, another Greek innovation. Such musical activity was considered respectable for women in ancient Greece; not so the flute. Women flute-players were often slaves or prostitutes who entertained men at banquets and drinking parties.* (Antiken Sammlungen, Munich)

children were swaddled (wrapped tightly in cloth) at birth, parents probably believing they were protecting their infants. Nurseries were equipped with a variety of toys, feeding bowls, potties, and all the other cheerful paraphernalia found wherever children are cherished and protected.

Loving parents often had to face the sorrow of natural infant death. The mortality rate in ancient Greece ranged around 30 to 40 percent for the first year of life. Children were helpless before infection, to which inadequate nutrition left them even more vulnerable. Epidemic disease (or "plague") ravaged the very young. On average, each female would give birth to five or six children, of whom only two or three might reach adulthood. Life expectancy (about forty-five for men, thirty-six for women) was low largely because of the toll of death on the very young. A male who reached thirty years of age might hope to live to fifty or sixty. But most men had already died by age thirty, and even more women, due to frequent childbirth.

Since adults often died young, families were frequently disrupted by the death of a mother or father. A complete nuclear family, often posed today as the ideal basis of human society, was rare in ancient Greece. A mother's death most often meant the father's remarriage and the children's adjustment to a stepmother. A father's death meant the dissolution of the family, the removal of the children to another household of their father's ancestral line, and the loss of the mother, who returned to her natal family. These were normal, not exceptional, dislocations.

One particular form of family disruption was unique to Greece. It was triggered by the phenomenon of the *epikleros*: the surviving member and sole daughter of a household whose patriarch had died. All household wealth devolved to her. Being a woman, however, she could not inherit. According to Greek law and custom, she must be married to another male of the same line: her father's brother, cousin, nephew. The choice was not hers, nor even his. She was to marry the male closest to her in biological relationship, immediately and without exception. This practice was observed even when it required the new husband first to divorce his own wife.

The obligatory marriage of an *epikleroi* was only one Greek institution in which the economic concerns of the household impinged upon the lives of women. Another was the custom of the dowry. In Greece, as in most ancient civilizations, a woman was married to a man only upon payment of a dowry. In accepting it, the groom's parents assumed the burden of protecting a new family member. The ability to provide a dowry established capacity for marriage. The dowry institution assumes that the woman will not inherit, in her own right, household property, which is reserved for her brothers.

In the urban household of citizen families (specifically in Athens, the city for which evidence is available), women were strictly segregated from men. All women—the wife and mother, her husband's female relations, the female slaves, together with children of both sexes—lived in the *gynaeceum*, or "women's quarters." This set of rooms, sealed with a locked door, was physically remote from those in which adult men slept, ate, and met with their fellows. It was remote, too, from the *agora*, where men met to discuss the news or do the shopping—for men shopped, while women stayed at home.

The *gynaeceum* enfolded the lives of women. It was here that the endless spinning, weaving, sewing, washing, and mending were accomplished. Here women prepared food and planned meals, although they did not usually join the male household members at mealtimes. Children were raised in the *gynaeceum*, surrounded by the conversation and the concerns of women. That setting was limiting but appropriate for girls, whose destiny it was to reenact the lives their mothers lived. What were the effects on the men who shaped the public life of Greece of an early childhood spent exclusively in the company of their mothers and their maids?

Women were, however, permitted to leave their homes to participate in the religious festivals that dotted the calendar. They danced and sang and carried ritual objects in processions. Often their activities were gender related: girls might carry baskets of wool or dolls representing babies as symbols

WITNESSES

Women's Lives

Like the ideal woman envisioned in the Hebrew Bible (see Witnesses, chapter 1, p. 17), Greek women were expected to please their husbands by tending the household. This ideal is expressed in the third passage by the philosopher and historian Xenophon. As in all ancient societies, women also fulfilled expectations in their roles as mothers. That role occasions the more complex images of women as mothers offered in the first two passages by the poet Homer and the playwright Euripides. Homer's Andromache is poignantly aware of her own and her child's vulnerability if her warrior husband can no longer protect her. Euripides' Medea has been abandoned by her husband, and imagines she will be forced to leave her children—whom she will in fact, in the end, destroy.

Andromache, wife of the Trojan hero Hector, begs him to remain home and not lead the fighting, for her sake and her son's (c. 750 B.C.E.):

[She] stood close beside him, letting her tears fall,
and clung to his hand and called him by name and spoke to him: "Dearest,
your own great strength will be your death, and you have no pity
on your little son, nor on me, ill-starred, who soon must be your widow;
for presently the Achaians, gathering together,
will set upon and kill you; and for me it would be far better
to sink into the earth when I have lost you ...
... you are father to me, and my honoured mother,
you are my brother, and you it is who are my young husband.
Please take pity upon me then, stay here on the rampart,
that you may not leave your child an orphan, your wife a widow. ...
(Homer, *Iliad*, 6:405–411, 429–432; ed. R. Lattimore, 1951)

Thinking she must leave her children, Medea laments (c. 431 B.C.E.):

... I am going in exile to another land
Before I have seen you happy and taken pleasure in you,
Before I have dressed your brides and made your marriage beds
And held up the torch at the ceremony of wedding. ...
What was the purpose, children, for which I reared you?
For all my travail and wearing myself away?
They were sterile, those pains I had in the bearing of you.
Oh surely once the hopes in you I had, poor me,
were high ones: you would look after me in old age,
and when I died would deck me well with your own hands;
A thing which all would have done. Oh but now it is gone,
That lovely thought. For, once I am left without you,
Sad will be the life I'll lead and sorrowful for me.
And you will never see your mother again with
your dear eyes, gone to another mode of living.
(Euripedes, *Medea*, 1024–1027, 1029–1039; eds. D. Grene, R. Lattimore, 1951)

Xenophon's householder explains to his wife how she is to keep order in the household (c. 390 B.C.E.): How good it is to keep one's stock of utensils in order, and how easy to find a suitable place in a house to put each set in. ... And what a beautiful sight is afforded by boots of all sorts and conditions ranged in rows! How beautiful it is to see cloaks of all sorts and conditions kept separate, or blankets, or brazen vessels, or table furniture! Yes, no serious man will smile when I claim that there is beauty in the order even of pots and pans set out in neat array. ... There is nothing, in short, that does not gain in beauty when set out in order. ...
(Xenophon, *Oeconomicus*, 8:18–19; ed. E. C. Marchant, 1923)

of their roles, whereas boys engaged in athletic contests. Some festivals were especially linked to women. The "maenads" were women ("mad-women") whose wild and uncontrolled dancing celebrated the god Dionysus. For the Great Panathenaea, selected girls wove a new robe to be worn by the image of the patron goddess Athena. At the Thesmophoria, celebrating the fertility goddesses Demeter and Persephone, women set up their own city, for three brief days near the *agora*, from which men were excluded. There they performed magic rituals to ensure fertility. But these festal occasions were brief interruptions in a life spent almost entirely within the home.

Beyond the Household: Male Space

If the household environment of the *gynaeceum* seems limiting, so, too, do other elements of the private lives of the Greeks: their food, their clothing, their schooling. Of the latter, girls received none beyond the knowledge of the language and customs of their people, transmitted by the women of the household. Older boys went to school, accompanied by a slave called a **pedagogue**, to a master who taught music, gymnastics, and the essential tools of reading and writing (see Chapter 4).

Both men and women wore simple clothing: a tunic or a robe, longer or shorter, variously gathered and fastened. Only the wealthy dyed their clothes (their choice restricted to only a few colors, including the costly Phoenician purple), and few people even washed them more than occasionally. An adult might own only one or two such costumes. A set of clothes might cost as much (in current values) as a personal computer or a used car. The Greeks ate as simply as they dressed, consuming a sparse diet of porridge, porridge, and porridge, enriched with goat cheese, a few olives or figs, as well as an occasional piece of meat.

While women were isolated in the private household, men moved in the public realm, where they might

Gender Wars

Amazons and Greeks: *The struggle between Greek heroes and the female Amazon warriors was a central theme of Greek art, adorning no less a monument than the Parthenon in Athens. Here is a battle scene from the monument of Mausolus of Caria. This relief was possibly by Scopas, a great Greek sculptor of the fourth century B.C.E.* (British Museum, London)

participate in a variety of wholly male organizations. The oldest of these were the ancestral tribes and phratries, networks of men related by blood or by hereditary ties originating in military comradeship. Each newborn son was registered in a phratry, already admitted by virtue of blood and gender to a social network long before he was able to recognize its import.

The other male networks that pervaded Greek society were based on friendship. The action of Homer's *Iliad* revolves around one such friendship: that between Achilles and Patroclus. Slain by the Trojan hero Hector, Patroclus is honored by Achilles. Such male friendships flourished in a military setting, where young men trained together and fought together, united in danger and victory.

In Crete and Sparta, where Archaic military customs survived into the Classical age, young men in arms lived together and were encouraged to form deep ties, possibly homosexual ones. These were also the ties that inspired the fighters in the Sacred Band of Thebes (fourth century B.C.E.). "A band that is held together by the friendship between lovers is indissoluble and not to be broken," wrote the moralist Plutarch (c. 46–120 C.E.), "since the lovers are ashamed to play the coward before their beloved, and the beloved before their lovers, and both stand firm in danger to protect each other." Elsewhere, too, military training and exploits were the setting for important male associations.

The gymnasium was another setting for such relationships—similar in kind because athletics were viewed in part as a preparation for war. From adolescence through old age, Greek men exercised at the gymnasium. Here they also conversed and debated

Achilles and Penthesilia: *In another struggle between a hero and an Amazon, the sculptor Exekias shows the Greek Achilles and the Amazon queen Penthesilea on a black-figure amphora, c. 540 B.C.E.* (British Museum, London)

matters of public or intellectual interest—as Socrates instructed young boys in the interlude between games in Plato's dialogue *Lysis*. In the same way, schools were a setting for close relationships among groups of boys and men—both the grammar schools of Athens and the philosophical schools launched by that city's great philosophers Plato and Aristotle.

Preeminent among the all-male gatherings of Greek society was the drinking party, or **symposium**. Some of the earliest and finest Greek poetry to survive consists of drinking songs, composed by men engaged in that pastime during leisurely evenings. In private homes, the business of conversation, eating, and drinking (and sexual play with prostitutes or boys) took place in a special "men's room," which respectable women did not enter. Spartan citizens ate together, apart from wives and children, in eating clubs, which continued in another milieu the camaraderie of military exercise. An Athenian drinking party is depicted in Plato's brilliant dialogue entitled the *Symposium*. Here unfolds a rich complex of ideas that might be heard where men, by themselves, sat together in fellowship and freely conversed.

The Greek city can in some ways be seen as a club to which only men belonged. From Homer to Plato, a portrait emerges of an essentially masculine culture. Anthropologists also point to elements of civic ritual that denote a high valuation of the masculine, almost amounting to an obsession with male potency. Before every Athenian house, for example, there stood a "herm," a monument to the god Hermes consisting of the head of the god mounted on a square stone pillar from which projected at the mid-point a swollen, erect phallus. Participants in the festal processions that celebrated the god Dionysus carried huge and prominent terracotta penises. Actors in the comedies of Aristophanes probably also sported over-sized leather phalluses, which they tapped or swung or raised as suggested by the script. Perhaps this phallic display is not surprising in a culture whose deities—notably the supreme Zeus—regularly engaged in seduction, adultery, incest, and heterosexual, homosexual, and pederastic rape. This behavior was unashamedly depicted with precision and grace on the exquisite painted vases sold in local and international markets.

Alongside the glorification of unrestrained male sexuality, Greek art celebrated men's power over women. The band of sculpted reliefs on the west side of the Parthenon in Athens, now nearly destroyed, depicts the legendary victory, at the time of the city's foundation, of the Athenian hoplites over the mythical female warriors known as Amazons. Amazons shunned the company of men and constructed their own nation, which they defended by their own prowess. In the Parthenon scenes, as in numerous other portrayals of battles against Amazons—on the frieze of the Temple of Apollo at Bassae, on the throne of Zeus at Olympia, on the Athenian treasury

at Delphi, and elsewhere—these fierce women are not merely defeated: they are mangled, humiliated, and annihilated. Two examples are shown on p. 79.

The hostility to women expressed in Greek art and literature, and the importance given to the relationships between men, point to the widespread practice of homosexuality in Greece. The patterns of homosexual relationships differ, however, from those familiar in Western society today. In Greece, older men formed relationships with adolescents over twelve and not yet twenty. These relationships, although deplored by some, were generally seen as beneficial for both parties. It was believed that the young, having been deprived of close relationships with their own fathers, were guided by their older lovers toward understanding and high achievement. When the young man himself entered full adulthood, he in turn would seek an adolescent male companion. These homosexual liaisons in no way were seen to interfere with the heterosexual pursuits of marriage, fatherhood, and household management.

Neither homosexual relationships nor marriage, moreover, ruled out heterosexual relationships with prostitutes and *hetaerae*, or "courtesans." Prostitutes were generally slaves who also performed the roles of servant and entertainer. The *hetaerae*, often foreigners, were elegant and brilliant women who could offer to men companionship of the sort not provided by wives, who were confined by the social limits of the *gynaeceum*. Pericles and Alexander the Great had relationships with *hetaerae*. Pericles' mistress Aspasia was a constant companion, an intellectual who composed speeches and debated issues of philosophy. When she was tried for the grave crime of "impiety," he defended her tearfully before the jury, and in defiance of his own laws, he had his son by her legitimated.

The private life of the Greeks was ordered in a way that best supported their public life. The isolation and subordination of women was complemented by the intricately layered networks linking together the men who created the world's first democracies and laid the bases for later Western political theory. The "people" who were served by those political institutions and theories, however, were defined in markedly narrow and exclusionary terms—a definition restricted by class, by ethnic origin, and by gender. Such deep contradictions must be confronted in any consideration of the achievement of the ancient *polis*.

Conclusion
THE GREEK *POLIS* AND THE MEANING OF THE WEST

Planted on sparse soil and cultivated by hungry men, the Greek *polis*—though it granted justice to some and not to all—was a remarkable achievement. For the Greek experiment has nourished later attempts of Western civilization to create a just society. In modern times, it continues to underlie that quest wherever it occurs, in the West and in the wider world.

QUESTIONS TO CONSIDER

1. The Greek *poleis* generally formed around an acropolis, a hilltop religious site. Was this pattern characteristic of ancient cities? What other kinds of city were there?

2. The Archaic Age revered men who were lawgivers, like Solon or the legendary Lyrurus, not powerful kings. What does this preference say about the nature of Greek society?

3. Why did Cleisthenes seek to destroy tribalism, the set of relationships formed by real or imaginary kinship relations, in his reforms of the Athenian state?

4. In ancient Greece, intellectual discussion often occurred in two settings: the male-only drinking party (symposium), and the male-only gymnasium. Are these today generally the settings of philosophical discourse? Were the women's quarters of the private household equally the setting of intellectual discussion?

SUGGESTED RESOURCES

Blundell, Sue, *Women in Ancient Greece* (Cambridge: Harvard University Press, 1995). A recent overview of a topic largely ignored until 1975, but now addressed in an abundance of studies.

Cartledge, Paul, *The Spartans: the World of the Warrior-Heroes of Ancient Greece, from Utopia to Crisis and Collapse* (Woodstock, NY : Overlook Press, 2003). Thorough history of Spartan politics and society, from Lycurgus to Roman times.

Davidson, James N., *Courtesans and Fishcakes: the Consuming Passions of Classical Athens* (New York: St. Martin's, 1998). Shows how fun-loving Athenians enjoyed food, drink, and sex, and especially fish.

Davies, J.K., *Democracy and Classical Greece*, 2nd ed. (Cambridge, MA: Harvard University Press, 1993). Recent and authoritative study of how—and to what extent—democracy emerged in fifth-century Greece.

Garland, Robert, *The Greek Way of Life: From Conception to Old Age* (New York: Cornell University Press, 1990). An imaginative account of the life-cycle of Classical and Hellenistic men and women, which discusses changing attitudes toward various phases of life.

Golden, Mark, *Children and Childhood in Classical Athens* (Baltimore: Johns Hopkins University Press, 1990). A persuasive reconstruction using archeological and documentary evidence of the lives of one of the most overlooked groups in Greek society—young children.

Halperin, David M., John J. Winkler, and Froma I. Zeitlin, eds., *Before Sexuality: The Construction of Erotic Experience in the Ancient Greek World* (Princeton: Princeton University Press, 1990). Fifteen authors examine Greek sexuality in relation to myth, law, medicine, and language, in order to comprehend how it functioned in a cultural context fundamentally different from our own.

Hanson, Victor David, *The Other Greeks: The Family Farm and the Agrarian Roots of Western Civilization* (Berkeley: University of California Press, 1994). Argues that the real Greek innovation—which explains much about the Greek state and civilization—was the family farm, the nursery of concepts of individual rights.

Hunter, Virginia J., *Policing Athens: Social Control in the Attic Lawsuits, 420–320* B.C.E. (Princeton: Princeton University Press, 1994). Fascinating exploration of how Athenian society regulated itself by community moral "policing" through the gossip of women and slaves, and the infliction of private as well as public punishments.

Kagan, Donald, *Pericles of Athens and the Birth of Democracy* (New York: Free Press, 1990). One of many studies of the fifth-century Greek world by a leading U.S. expert, focused on the critical Athenian leader Pericles as the creator of the democratic ethos.

Kurke, Leslie, *Coins, Bodies, Games and Gold: The Politics of Meaning in Archaic Greece* (Princeton: Princeton University Press, 1999). Traces the cultural symbols linked to the emergence of coinage in the Greek Archaic Age, building an ideological basis for the egalitarian *polis* system.

Murray, Oswyn, *Early Greece*, 2nd ed. (Cambridge, MA: Harvard University Press, 1993). Masterful account of the emergence of the *polis* system, and the patterns of cultural and social life that it supported.

Pomeroy, Sarah B., *Families in Classical and Hellenistic Greece: Representations and Realities* (Oxford: Clarendon Press, 1997). With a superb command of sources, Pomeroy studies the Greek family across centuries and regions, including patterns of inheritance and the meaning of death and work.

Sealey, Raphael, *Demosthenes and his Time: A Study in Defeat* (Oxford: Oxford University Press, 1993). Studies the unraveling of the Athenian democratic paradigm and the world of the *polis* as Macedonia reached for and seized power in the fourth century.

Guide to classical Athens: society, economy, culture, politics:
http://www.fhw.gr/chromos/05/en

Everyday life in ancient Greece:
http://www.ibiscom.com/ancientgreece.htm

◯ Western Civilization Documents CD-ROM

2.4 Tyrtaues, The Spartan Creed
2.5 Education and the Family in Sparta

THE SCHOOL OF HELLAS

800	700	600	500	400	300	200 B.C.E.

Civilization and War

Greek Dark Age, c. 1200–800   Archaic Age, c. 800–500   Classical Age, c. 500–323   Hellenistic Civilization, c. 323–31

Persian Empire, 550–323

Greek colonization,
c. 750–600

Alexander's Empire, 334–323

Early and Republican Rome, c. 550–27

Art, Religion, and Ideas

◆ Geometric pottery, c. 1000–700

◆ First Olympic Games

◆ Homer composes epics
Iliad, c. 750, *Odyssey*, c. 725

◆ Hesiod, poet (*Works and
Days, Theogony*), c. 700

◆ Alphabet used to write Greek,
c. 700

◆ Tyrtaeus of Sparta, poet, general,
fl. c. 650

◆ Sappho of Mitylene, poet,
c. 612–580

◆ Archaic *kouros, kore*,
c. 600–500

◆ Pythagoras, philosopher,
fl. c. 530

◆ Aeschylus, playwright (*Oresteia* trilogy),
c. 525–456

◆ Attic black-figure pottery peaks,
succeeded by red-figure, c. 500–400

◆ Sophocles, playwright (*Antigone,
Oedipus Rex, Oedipus at Colonus*),
496–406

◆ Phidias, sculptor, fl. c. 490–430

◆ Euripides, playwright
(*Trojan Women, Electra, Medea*),
c. 485–407

◆ Herodotus, historian (*Histories*),
c. 484–425

◆ Sophists Protagoras (c. 484–415)
and Gorgias (c. 483–376)

◆ Socrates, philosopher, 470–399

◆ Thucydides, historian, c. 460–400

◆ Democritus, philosopher, c. 460–370

◆ Aristophanes, playwright (*The Clouds,
The Frogs, Lysistrata*), c. 450–385

◆ Isocrates, orator, 436–338

◆ Leucippus, philosopher, fl. c. 435

◆ Pericles' funeral oration, 431

◆ Plato, philosopher (*Symposium, Republic*),
428–347; founds Athenian Academy

◆ Aristotle, philosopher (*Politics*), 384–322;
founds Athenian Lyceum, 335

◆ Demosthenes, orator, 384–322

◆ Praxiteles, sculptor, fl. c. 340

◆ Aristotle dies, 322

Beyond the West

Chinese warring states, 450–221

Zhou dynasty, c. 1027–256

Qin dynasty, c. 221–206

◆ Phoenician maritime
hegemony, after 900

◆ Chandragupta Maurya of India,
r. c. 321–298

◆ Asoka of India, 272–232

◆ Shi Huangdi
of China,
r. 221–210/209

CHAPTER

4

THE SCHOOL OF HELLAS

Poetry, Ideas, and the Arts in
Ancient Greece

800–300 B.C.E.

Greek homeland and colonies,
c.800-300 BCE

KEY QUESTIONS

◆ **The Birth of the Greek Gods:** How did the
Greeks imagine their gods? In what ways did they
differ from mortals?

◆ **Discovering Humanity:** What are the
understandings of the human condition that the
Greeks presented in their epic, lyric, and
dramatic poetry? In what way were these original?

◆ **To Know and to Love to Know:** What are the
Greek contributions to Western philosophy,
science, history, social science, pedagogy, and
rhetoric? What is unique about the intellectual
traditions they developed?

The Life of Reason "Intelligence, above all else, **is** man," wrote the philosopher Aristotle. Reason makes human beings human. The life of the mind is the true source of happiness. Aristotle died in 322 B.C.E., the year after Alexander the Great succumbed to disease and drink in the heart of his Asian empire. The philosopher's claim that the mind's activity is life, that reason is the distinctively human quality, is the product of several centuries of Greek thought whose originality was nurtured by the world of the polis.

Centuries before Aristotle wrote down these words, unnamed storytellers of the Dark Ages had transformed the religious fears and otherworldly visions of preliterate Greeks into myths that even today form part of the imaginative legacy of Western civilization. Later, poets and artists of the Archaic and Classical ages turned to considering the place of the human being on earth and the nature of earth itself. Their deep and imaginative seeking stimulated the development of philosophy, which was distinguished by the **rationalism**—acceptance of reason as supreme authority in the determination of truth—that has come to mark Western thought, but a few steps removed from the choral dances of heroes and the birth of the gods.

THE BIRTH OF THE GREEK GODS

The life of reason envisioned by Aristotle originated in the world of myth created by the Greek imagination before the onset of the Greek tradition of poetry or philosophy. The omnipresence of the gods, their immunity to death, the supremacy of the sky god all preconditioned later Greek thought, while the worship of the gods established the framework, as well, of Greek art and customs.

Myths and Mythmakers

Myths are stories that humans invent to explain their experiences. Over the centuries, the Greek myths were told by the old to the young and by mothers to children, and sung by wandering bards to avid listeners. In the seventh and sixth centuries B.C.E., when singing and storytelling gave way to books and alphabets, poets wrote the myths down. Some of those works still survive. Mythology reveals what the Greeks thought of their gods and the universe.

For the Greeks, the essence of the gods was that they were **immortal**, "deathless," free from the ordinary law of nature that applied to all other creatures, and in particular to humans. Gods could also traverse great distances instantaneously, hear human appeals over such distances, and disguise themselves magically.

Aside from these distinctions, the Greek gods and goddesses resembled mortals. They were **anthropomorphic**, meaning they looked and behaved like humans, but to an extreme degree, possessing exceptional beauty and great sensitivity. Greek deities set a standard that human worshipers longed to achieve.

In the myths humans often encountered gods. The gods appeared to mortals in person, disguised as other men and women or wrapped in supernatural mists or clouds. Thus disguised, they aided mortals or punished them. They seduced, raped, and kidnapped mortal men, women, and children, and fathered or mothered half-divine offspring who were nearly as remarkable as their supernatural parents.

Greek deities thus differed markedly from those of neighboring civilizations in Asia and Africa. The gods of the East tended to be remote, invisible, often monstrous: multi-limbed or multi-breasted, animal-headed. Such awesome beings were approached only by professional priests, who alone knew how to communicate with them, and how, by elaborate ritual, to appease these unfathomable divinities. By contrast, Greek priests did not form a separate professional class. They performed a minimal role, and their rites required only an open-air altar, a special rock or tree, or a space set aside as sacred. Their gods demanded simple sacrifices: the offering of a cup of wine or a sacrificial beast, whose flesh was then given to the hungry worshipers to eat.

The presence of immortal gods did not stimulate in the Greeks, as it did in the Egyptians, an obsession with death and with the afterlife. The dead were dead. Their souls (for they did have souls, the Greeks believed) sometimes lingered in the vicinity of the grave, and demanded offerings of food and drink. That duty accomplished, the living preferred to celebrate life. With song, games, and dance they celebrated their deities in themselves.

The Greek gods were a motley group, an assortment of deities recruited from the numerous different peoples of the region. Some had been worshiped by the indigenous peoples who dwelled on the Greek mainland before the Indo-European speakers arrived from the north early in the second millennium B.C.E. Some were the gods of those newcomers. Some were the gods of neighbors on the eastern rim of the Mediterranean, of the Hittites and their successors in Asia Minor, of the Phoenicians and Babylonians in the Near East, and of the Egyptians. The names of these gods were changed as they entered the Greek pantheon.

These multitudinous deities promoted the fertility of the earth or represented the forces of nature: thunder, sky, and water. Zeus hurled his thunderbolts and lived on mountaintops, lofty and powerful. Poseidon roared and roiled the fearful waters of the oceans and rivers. Goddesses, too, had their distinct functions and attributes. Athena was, paradoxically, the goddess

WITNESSES

Who the Gods Are

The profound understanding that the Greeks developed of human nature was complemented by their view of the gods. The gods were deathless; human beings would die. That stark opposition encouraged the Greeks to conceive both of the mightiness of the powers beyond human control, and the nobility of human efforts to achieve greatness in the face of death. Here Pindar summons his listeners to "rival the Immortals," while Homer attributes to the supreme god, Zeus, an extraordinary conception of his own power.

The poet Pindar explains the difference between the immortal gods and humans destined to "run"—that is, to die (c. 460 B.C.E.):

There is a race of men
and a race of gods,
but both received the breath of life
from the same mother.
It is only power in all things
that separates us;
for men are as nothing,
while the brazen heavens remain forever
the secure abode of the gods.
Still, through the power of mind
or the strength of our bodies
we can rival the Immortals,
though we know not
what destiny awaits us in day or night,
what race fate has decreed
we shall run.
(Pindar, *Nemean VI*, 1–16; eds. S. Spyridakis, B. Nystrom, 1985)

Zeus declares that he is the greatest of the gods:

"Hear me, all you gods and all you goddesses: hear me
while I speak forth what the heart within my breast urges. ...
Come, you gods, make this endeavor, that you all may learn this.
Let down out of the sky a cord of gold; lay hold of it
all you who are gods and all who are goddesses, yet not
even so can you drag down Zeus from the sky to the ground, not
Zeus the high lord of counsel, though you try until you grow
    weary.
Yet whenever I might strongly be minded to pull you,
I could drag you up, earth and all and sea and all with you,
then fetch the golden rope about the horn of Olympos
and make it fast, so that all once more should dangle in mid air.
So much stronger am I than the gods, and stronger than
    mortals."
(Homer, *Iliad*, 8:5–6, 18–27; ed. R. Lattimore, 1951)

Artemis, were versions of the fertility goddesses long revered by humankind—as were the numerous nymphs, dryads (minor deities), "seasons," "fates," and "Muses," who breathed life into the human imagination. These deities of the earth, of its unknown depths and of its surface fruitfulness, appealed to worshipers with their promise of abundance.

From their various origins, the gods and goddesses of sky and storm and earth came to live together in the Greek imagination and to reign supreme over mortals, but not in equality. The gods of the conquerors edged out the gods of the conquered. The male sky god Zeus claimed precedence over the many female deities who had reappeared in the Archaic age as the patron goddesses of the new *poleis*. These changes resulted in a reorganization of the society of the gods into a hierarchy of male over female, sky over earth. That reorganization was accomplished before the Dark Ages and is codified in the words of Homer and Hesiod, the first Greek poets known to us.

In the *Iliad* and the *Odyssey*, the two epic poems ascribed to him, Homer gave the Greek deities their lasting definition. He named them, sketched their personalities, and plotted their relationships to each other and to the supreme and exalted Zeus. They were one "family" and lived together on Mount Olympus (in northern Greece), where "in the tall sky" the mother of the earthly hero Achilles, seeking help for her son, found Zeus "sitting upon the highest peak of rugged Olympus." The gods spent their endless days feasting and playing, quarreling and making love, and observing the life of mortals.

Of this pack of spoiled, child-like deities, Zeus was supreme. In Homer's narrative of the Trojan War (see Chapter 2 and *Witnesses*, left) it is Zeus who holds a golden balance beam to decide whether the Greeks or their opponents will win. Achilles, steeling himself to reenter the battle he had spurned in anger, draws from his chest of precious possessions the splendid cup he used to pour libations to Zeus alone. When Zeus is challenged by his brother god Poseidon, he sends Poseidon a stern message of his superiority:

*I am far greater than he is
in strength, and elder born.*

of war and of wisdom, also of handicrafts. Because she was a virgin goddess, her temple in Athens was called the Parthenon, after the Greek for "virgin," *parthenos*. Aphrodite was the goddess of love and beauty; Artemis, of the moon and hunting. Demeter and her daughter, Persephone, were associated with grain and fruitfulness. However, all these female deities, including the supposedly virginal Athena and

The Deathless Gods

The Greeks thought of their gods descending in generations (like their human families), beginning with Uranus.
M. = married

Uranus (M.* Gaia), Father of the Gods and son of Gaea (Earth)

Mnemosyne · Phoebe · Thia · Hyperion · Themis · Rhea · Crios · Japet · Tethys · Oceanus · Coeus

9 Muses · Selene · Helios · Eos · Cronus (M. Rhea) · Epimetheus · Atlas · Prometheus · Metis · Leto

Hestia · Demeter · Hera (M. Zeus) · Zeus · Poseidon · Hades

Aphrodite · Persephone · Hermes · Hephaestus · Ares · Athena · Apollo · Artemis · Dionysus

And when the Olympians display too great partisanship for the mortals on the Trojan plain, Zeus calls an assembly and announces that he alone is in charge.

> *Now let no female divinity, nor male god either,*
> *presume to cut across the way of my word, but*
> * consent to it*
> *all of you…*

he thunders, and threatens grave reprisals if they disobey: "So much stronger am I than the gods, and stronger than mortals."

Homer's younger contemporary Hesiod (fl. c. 705 B.C.E.), a very different poet, enlarged the Greeks' conception of the gods by describing their origins and history. For this purpose, he borrowed from the literature of a non-Greek and pre-Homeric people—the Hittites—two epic myths of creation. These described the struggles of the gods for supremacy and the eventual triumph of a chief deity. Hesiod adapted this Hittite legend to Greek concepts and characters in his *Theogony,* or "Birth of the Gods."

Here Hesiod tells the story of "how the gods and the earth came into being, the rivers, the boundless sea with its raging swell, and the glittering stars, and the wide sky above," and "of the gods born of them to whom death never comes." Earth, or "Gaia," and Sky, "Uranus," were formed from the void of the beginning of things—Chaos itself. From the marriage of Earth and Sky there descended over generations all the races of gods and humans as shown in *Who's Who* on p. 86. Aided by his mother, Rhea, Zeus overturned his father, Cronus, and defeated his rivals to achieve supreme universal power. From the material of Greek myth and Hittite cosmology—study of the universe—Hesiod supplied the missing foundations of Greek theology.

Worshiping the Gods

In Greek religion, as in all ancient religions, the gods were fearsome beings whose good will was sought through the offering of gifts, especially that of a creature sacrificed on an altar (see Chapter 1). The temple was the house of the god, awesome and sacrosanct. Designed more as a residence than as a place of worship, the temple contained a statue of the resident god or goddess in an inner room, or *cella*. In temples of the eighth century B.C.E., the *cella* was approached through a porch supported by two columns—an arrangement that suggests the megaron of the Mycenaean kings and may have been modeled on it.

Over the next few centuries the Greek temple would develop into what may be the most influential building type in the history of Western architecture. Just as the institutions of the Greek *polis* have shaped the modern West, so the forms and decorative elements of the Greek temple have shaped its visual, constructed world.

The most distinctive feature of the temple is the column, which soon began to be used in rows to form a colonnade, often running around the entire building. The first columns were made of wood—the walls being of mud-brick. Later, the Greeks began to construct temples of stone, including the white marble with which parts of Greece are richly endowed. Several different styles of column evolved: the simple Doric; the taller Ionic, with its scrolled capital; the elegant Corinthian, with its intricately carved capital of acanthus leaves. Each type of column supported its own style of entablature, including a projecting cornice and a frieze, which might be decorated with relief carvings of gods, goddesses, and mortals illustrating the central myths of the community. Some of the finest examples of Greek sculpture to survive are remnants of temples.

The artistry of the decoration was matched by the mathematical precision that informed every part of the building. Proportions were carefully calculated to achieve the greatest sense of harmony and serenity. This included the use of optical tricks, or refinements, such as the slight swelling in an apparently straight column which prevents it from looking concave.

The Parthenon in Athens is the most famous of all Greek temples. An earlier temple to Athena, begun under the tyrant Peisistratus, was partially completed when the Persians destroyed all the buildings on the Acropolis in 480 B.C.E. From 443 to 429 B.C.E., Pericles drained vast sums from the Athenian treasury to build the new one. The sculptor Phidias (fl. c. 490–430 B.C.E.), one of the first artists known by name, erected in its interior a huge gold and ivory statue of the goddess. Carved in **relief** on the temple surfaces were scenes of Athena's birth; her foundation of the city of Athens; mythical battles between Greeks and barbarians, Athenians and Persians; and the solemn processional of the Great Panathenaea, the festival in honor of the goddess. Although the Parthenon was badly damaged in 1687 C.E. by a

---

Achilles

Achilles, the hero of Homer's epic Iliad, *has a choice of a long and prosperous life in obscurity, or a brief life of heroic achievement. Here he ponders those possibilities, recognizing the advantages of the former choice. In the end, however, he will choose glory and death—and thus set a standard of heroism for all subsequent Western culture (750 B.C.E.).*

The hero Achilles wonders whether to go home (c. 750 B.C.E.):
"Fate is the same for the man who holds back, the same if he fights hard.
We are all held in a single honor, the brave with the weaklings.
A man dies still if he has done nothing, as one who has done much.
Nothing is won for me, now that my heart has gone through its afflictions
in forever setting my life on the hazard of battle. ...
.... For not
worth the value of my life are all the possessions they fable
were won for Ilion, that strong-founded citadel, in the old days
when there was peace, before the coming of the sons of the Achaians; ...
.... Of possessions
cattle and fat sheep are things to be had for the lifting,
and tripods can be won, and the tawny high heads of horses,
but a man's life cannot come back again, it cannot be lifted
nor captured again by force, once it has crossed the teeth's barrier.
For my mother Thetis the goddess of the silver feet tells me
I carry two sorts of destiny toward the day of my death. Either,
if I stay here and fight beside the city of the Trojans,
my return home is gone, but my glory shall be everlasting;
but if I return home to the beloved land of my fathers,
the excellence of my glory is gone, but there will be a long life
left for me, and my end in death will not come to me quickly.
And this would be my counsel to others also, to sail back
home again. ..."
(Homer, *Iliad*, 9: 318–322, 400–403, 405–418; ed. R. Lattimore, 1951)

The Beauty of Man

Greek sculpture: *Lamenting the carnage underway in distant Troy, the old men of Argos who form the chorus of Aeschylus' tragedy Agamemnon weep for the "young men in their beauty," dead on the field of battle. Greek sculptors, most of them anonymous, labored to depict the beauty of the nude body and profound spirit of the knowing, heroic male. Here (left) is an example from Attica c. 600 B.C.E. of the kouros genre developed during the Archaic age. The term kouros, which is from the Greek word for "boy," denotes a type of standing male figure, typically carved in marble and usually commemorative in nature. (Metropolitan Museum of Art)*

Egyptian sculpture: *The Greek kouros was inspired by the Egyptian relief, c. 2500 B.C.E. (above) and free-standing sculpture. The kouros differs from the Egyptian relief in its solid and more lifelike qualities. (Egyptian Museum, Cairo)*

Venetian bomb, which exploded the gunpowder stored there by Turkish occupiers, it still stands after more than 2400 years, an elegant composition of horizontal and vertical lines (not one of which is absolutely straight), simple and perfect in its beauty.

The rationality of the Greek temple forms mirrored the rationality of the society of the gods as Homer and Hesiod depicted it, imposing poetic discipline upon the riotous throng of deities inherited from Greek prehistory. Yet in the minds of the Greek people the unknown still held its terrors. A manic irrationality counterbalanced the rational spirit of Greek religion. Dreams and omens, visions and possessions reminded people of the awful power of the divine. Many sought to defeat their enemies or woo their lovers with charms, amulets, and wax figures pierced with pins. In 413 B.C.E. the Athenian general Nicias lost a whole fleet, his men, and his own life

Doryphorus: *This Roman marble copy of Doryphorus (Spearbearer) shows a later Classical rendition of the nude male figure by Polyclitus, c. 440 B.C.E., derived from Greek models. This figure stands with the weight of the body now carried on one leg. The attached "tree trunk" was added by the copyist because bronze (the original medium of the statue) can stand on its own more easily than marble. (National Archaeological Museum, Naples)*

during the Peloponnesian War because the dreadful omen of an eclipse of the moon delayed his retreat from the harbor of Syracuse in Sicily.

Communities feared the "pollution" (called *miasma*) caused by the spilling of blood or other impious acts, which placed them at risk of divine vengeance. A case of pollution required that acts of purification be performed by the responsible individual or even by the whole city. Trials for "impiety," as in fifth-century Athens, protected the city from the wrath of the gods against a community harboring skeptics, atheists, and religious nonconformists.

In the rural villages, especially, but also among urban sophisticates, the gods of the underworld had many worshipers, who sought in a variety of **mystery cults** to gain contact with the fundamental forces of creation, of spirit, of life itself. The adherents of Demeter, foremost of the earth mothers, reenacted in their ritual observances her grief for her child, Kore or Persephone, who had been snatched into the underworld by Hades and whose release in springtime signified both an abundant harvest and a resurrection of the dead. Pilgrims streamed to Eleusis outside Athens, the center for this cult which promised its initiates secret knowledge (hence "mystery").

Other mystery cults introduced from Asia also appealed to the spiritually hungry and socially dispossessed—especially to women, whose opportunity for religious experience in conventional Olympian religion was limited. Fertility was largely a female principle, because of the primal association of women, generation, and birth. Mystery religions often centered on such themes, and highlighted goddesses linked to sexual and agricultural reproduction. Many seekers were attracted to the Orphic movement, named after the legendary musician Orpheus, who had sought to recover his wife, Eurydice, from the underworld. Orphism consisted of a cluster of ideas about the immortality of the soul and promised enhanced, renewed, or eternal life.

Two gods who came late to the Greeks, Apollo and Dionysus (imported respectively from Asia and Thrace, northeast of the zone of mainland Greek *poleis*) won considerable attention. Although known to Homer, these new gods became fully established in the Greek pantheon shortly after his time. The temples of Apollo, a god associated with prophecy, with intellect, with law, with profound beauty of spirit and body, became pan-Hellenic cult centers: the nearest thing in the history of Greece to an established church. Apollo's priestess at Delphi (known as the "Pythia," or "pythoness" because Apollo killed a giant female snake there) uttered, from a deep trance, prophecies in scrambled verse which were regularly sought and pondered in the various *poleis*. Inscribed on the shrine, according to contemporary witnesses, were two statements summing up official Greek wisdom: "Know yourself," and "Nothing in excess."

In contrast, excess was actively encouraged in the worship of Dionysus (also known as Bacchus), a fertility god associated with wine. Having partaken liberally of this liquid, his adherents (generally women) danced and ran in the open air, on hilltops, possessed, they believed, by the spirit of the god.

The disturbingly frenzied character and the great popularity of the Dionysian cult induced statesmen to civilize it—to mitigate its excess and to incorporate it into the normal cycle of urban religion. In Athens, Peisistratus organized the worship of Dionysus in the regular festivals known as the City Dionysia. At these festivals were performed songs and dances imported from village celebrations—notably the "goat dance," from which derives the Greek *tragoedia* and our word "**tragedy**." Soon the singing and dancing evolved into the chorus of tragic theater. And so, ironically, from the primitive rites of the god Dionysus evolved that form of poetry and thought that has, in the history of the West, most poignantly explored the universal predicament of all humans: to be alive but destined ultimately to die.

DISCOVERING HUMANITY

The poets who explored the grip exerted by the gods on human consciousness also examined, in the epic, lyric, and dramatic forms that they created, the depths of human nature. The cultivation and visual representation of the body also furthered that examination. The Greek inquiry into human nature began at the same point as the Greek study of the divine. It began with Homer and Hesiod.

Homer and Hesiod

Why did the Greeks treasure Homer? In delightful Olympian scenes, he portrayed their beautiful and immortal gods. He reminded them of their glorious, long-gone, and nearly forgotten Mycenaean past, naming the heroes they saw as ancestors. He took them to the battlefield where Achaean (or Greek) and Trojan heroes pierced, pounded, impaled, and slaughtered each other, models of skill and valor. Homer made war the business of life and the matter of history: henceforth, war was the theater in which human excellence would be tested and would triumph. Amid the clangor and tumult, he depicted for the first time in literature, in the figure of the Achaean hero Achilles, the struggles and contradictions of human existence.

The *Iliad*, as its author states in his opening line, is about the anger of Achilles, who has been dishonored by the supreme commander of the Achaean army, Agamemnon. The latter has taken away Achilles' concubine Briseis—perhaps for good reason—but Achilles' skill had won her fair and square. Achilles withdraws from the battle to sulk, and consequently the Achaean forces are desperately weakened and forced to retreat. Agamemnon and his commanders beg Achilles to return to the battle, but he will not. He plays the lyre and sings, considering whether a quiet life at home contemplating his fields would not be preferable to the life of battle (see *Witnesses*, p. 87).

Achilles stands aloof from the conflict until his companion, Patroclus, is slain by the Trojan leader Hector. Now he will act, but he is a different man from the one who spurned Agamemnon. He acts knowing that he has chosen death over life. His sole purpose is to exact his revenge and meet his destiny with dignity. He avenges Patroclus' death by slaying Hector. He then drags the body in the dust, seven times around the walls of Troy, buries Patroclus magnificently, then tempers his anger and returns the body of his slaughtered foe to King Priam, Hector's father. In the span of the *Iliad*'s more than 16,000 lines, the war has neither started nor closed, Achilles' life has neither begun nor ended, but a human personality has grown to understand the meaning of life and the purpose of death.

Until they were written down in the sixth century B.C.E., the verses of Homer were kept alive by the *rhapsodes*, traveling bards or minstrels whose special craft was the recitation of these myth-laden stories from prehistory. The poet Hesiod, who is believed to have been active a generation after Homer, may have been, briefly, one of these wandering *rhapsodes*. Steeped in that poetry, Hesiod stood one day on the summit of Mount Helicon, not far from his farm, and experienced a vision of the Muses. They inspired him, as he tells us, to become a poet.

Like Homer, Hesiod grappled in his verse with the meaning of human existence. But he did so in terms of his own daily life and that of other struggling farmers, crafting a quite different heroic ideal—the heroism of the ordinary. Unlike the *Theogony*, which addressed cosmic issues, his *Works and Days* addressed social ones. It describes the burdens borne by human beings who labor in the face of certain death and the cruel injustice of the powerful. The ordinary farmer, not the valiant warrior, is Hesiod's hero. The limits of human experience are touched by those who spend their days plowing and harvesting and who crave, as the fruit of their labor, justice:

> *This is the law Zeus laid down for men,*
> *but fish and wild beasts and winged birds*
> *know not of justice and so eat one another.*
> *Justice, the best thing there is, he gave to men. ...*

Lyric Poets: Personal and Civic Lives

A century after Hesiod, in the seventh century B.C.E., a new group of poets emerged as the leaders of Greek thought. These were poets of the emerging *poleis*. While not ignoring war or labor, their verse focused more often on their personal concerns as men—and one woman—forging an existence in a complex society. Their experiences were as varied as the cities where they lived and the circles of their friends. To express their new outlook, these authors created a new form of poetry, called "lyric." Brief and expressive, it was composed to be sung to the lyre, a small stringed instrument, in small gatherings, instead of chanted, like Homer and Hesiod's verse, to the public. Those earlier bards were addressing the nation of the Hellenes, all those who spoke Greek. The newer poets wrote for each other and for people like them: the leisured, cultivated aristocrats of the cities.

Archilochus (714–676 B.C.E.), from the Aegean island of Paros, is one of the earliest of the lyric poets whose work is extant. Illegitimate son of an aristocratic father and a slave mother, Archilochus lived on the fringes of fine society—an adventurer and mercenary, given to outrageous behavior. His poetry displays his aversion to traditional codes and values. One verse sounds an unheroic note, which must have seemed discordant in a world imbued with the warrior ethos of the *Iliad*. Part of an expedition that joined battle with some fearsome Thracians, Archilochus turned and ran:

> *Some Thracian has the shield I left behind,*
> *My trusty shield—I had to—in a wood.*
> *Well, I have saved my life; so never mind*
> *That shield; I'll get another just as good.*

Archilochus' intensely personal tone is soon heard again in two other poets, one male and one female, who were both well-born citizens of Mitylene, on the Aegean island of Lesbos: Alcaeus (fl. 620 B.C.E.) and Sappho (c. 612–c. 580 B.C.E.). A prominent citizen, Alcaeus portrays in his verse the concerns of the male aristocrat: his hatred for his political rivals, his

MUST READS

A Sampling of the Greek Classics

Homer	*Iliad, Odyssey*
Hesiod	*Theogony, Works and Days*
Pindar	*Odes*
Aeschylus	*Prometheus Bound, Agamemnon*
Sophocles	*Antigone, Oedipus Rex*
Euripides	*Trojan Women, Hippolytus*
Aristophanes	*Clouds, Lysistrata*
Plato	*Apology, Symposium*
Aristotle	*Nicomachean Ethics, Poetics*
Demosthenes	*Orations*

fascination with the paraphernalia of war, and his delight in the comradeship of the *symposium*, or drinking party, where words and ideas flow freely.

Sappho may epitomize the circle of aristocratic women in Mitylene—but we have no way of knowing whether that is so. Her voice is unique, and her figure solitary, the only female poet of antiquity from whom more than a few scraps of verse survive ... and only a few more, at that. Sappho wrote of love and beauty with a passion unsurpassed for 2000 years. Perhaps her isolation from the concerns of war and politics left her free to explore these themes. She makes clear her distaste for the usual business of men: "Some say the fairest thing on earth is a troop of horsemen, others a band of foot-soldiers, others a squadron of ships. But I say the fairest thing is the beloved."

No man in Greek antiquity described the experience of love like Sappho: "When I even see you, my voice stops, my tongue is broken, a thin flame runs beneath all my skin, my eyes are blinded, there is thunder in my ears, the sweat pours from me, I tremble through and through, I am paler than grass, and I seem like one dead." To some, the emotional impact of these lines is greater because the words are probably addressed to another woman, one of Sappho's pupils.

The poet headed an informal school for upper-class girls, sent to learn the refinements of song and dance and manners (for these were the substance of Greek education at that time). They came to Sappho, who admired their beauty, nourished all, and loved some, then lost them to new, young husbands. So Sappho, poet of Lesbos, is the world's most famous Lesbian, and the reason why that term is used to describe women whose sexual desires are for other women. The idea has seemed variously repulsive, unimportant, or titillating to later readers, who agree, nevertheless, on the poet's brilliance.

The outlook of Tyrtaeus (fl. c. 650 B.C.E.) of mainland Sparta, in contrast, is resolutely male. Active as a general and a poet during the Messenian wars (c. 640–630 B.C.E.), Tyrtaeus was the architect of a warrior code for that city's aristocrats. Sparta could survive only if the "equals," the elite citizen class, maintained her military readiness at a constant pitch of ferocity. Tyrtaeus' words spurred them on to this state, as in this celebration of heroic death:

> *The youth's fair form is fairest when he dies.*
> *Even in his death the boy is beautiful,*
> *The hero boy who dies in his life's bloom....*
> *More sacred than in life, more beautiful by far,*
> *Because he perished on the battlefield.*

In Tyrtaeus' verse, Homeric values are refashioned for the life of the *polis*. In the sixth century B.C.E., Athens' first known poet (and great statesman), Solon, follows Hesiod in exploring the theme of justice. Solon held that the moral force of justice would

Worthy Maidens

Kore, c. 510 B.C.E.

Caryatid, Erectheum, Acropolis, Athens, c. 420–410 B.C.E.

Contrast the female figures depicted here with those on page 7; what changes in civilizational values may have occurred that explain the differences in these representations?

Cnidos Aphrodite (Imperial Roman copy of Greek original)

In contrast to the heroic male youths depicted by Greek artists, female figures sculpted in the Archaic period—the genre of the kore (Greek word for "maiden")—bespoke dignity, restraint, and silence. The progress from earlier to later concepts of the female form are illustrated in these three figures: a kore from the Athenian Acropolis (left); a female figure, or Caryatid (center), merged with a column and bearing the weight of the roof of the Erectheum, Athens; and a late-Classical statue of Aphrodite (right), the goddess of beauty, now a realistic nude who covers her revealed body. (left: Acropolis Museum, Athens; right: Capitoline Museum, Rome)

 To continue your investigation of this topic, please go to www.prenhall.com/king for the related WINDOWS on the WEB activity

not permit the powerful to crush the powerless. Evil men "go on stealing, by force or deception each from the other, nor do the solemn commitments of Justice keep them in check …," but Justice keeps track, "and in her time she returns to exact a full revenge."

Tragedy and Comedy: The Myth Transformed

With Solon, the inward gaze of the lyric poets turned outward again. Employing lyric verse to probe the soul of the city, he anticipated the Athenian poets who would, soon after his death, create dramatic tragedy and further the Greek exploration of the human spirit. These writers studied anew the body of myth preserved by the epic poets Homer and Hesiod. They not only retold the tales; they asked bold and horrifying questions about the human and divine players.

It was from the ritual dance and song of the Dionysiac festival that drama evolved, during the sixth century B.C.E. The dancers (ordinary citizens who diligently rehearsed for weeks) constituted the chorus, and the open space on which they danced, at first only a section of the *agora*, was called the *orchestra*. Poets composed the music as well as the words, and taught and directed the performers (always men, even for female characters). The chorus master managed and funded the project. Funding a dramatic production was one of the two principal ways (the other was the outfitting of a ship) in which the rich were expected to support the state.

On the slopes around the orchestra sat the spectators—a large audience including most of the citizen population. This audience listened carefully enough to be able to vote for the best performance of the several offered over three days. Ordinary citizens thus acted as literary critics and judges as well as observers. Later centuries saw the construction of spectator seating, and a stone building that served as set and backdrop. From the beginning, the performers wore costumes, including special shoes which elevated them above their ordinary stature and brightly colored masks with exaggerated features.

Tragedy According to Aristotle, the first tragedies were entirely choral—the events described or related by groups of singers. Who wrote these dramas is uncertain; however, the first recorded winner of a form of tragedy (in c. 534 B.C.E.) was a playwright named Thespis (in whose memory actors are sometimes called "thespians"). Thespis was the first to introduce an actor—the author himself—who broke away from the chorus of singers and dancers to deliver spoken individual lines. Once a separate actor appeared, so did the possibility of dialogue. Two generations later, the poet Aeschylus (c. 525–456 B.C.E.) introduced a second actor: now two characters could interact with each other, as well as an individual character with the chorus. That innovation allowed the dramatic confrontations of tragedy as we know it. At Greek tragedy's fullest development, no more than three speaking actors shared the stage.

With this skeletal cast of characters but with extraordinary power of language, the tragic poets reopened ancient myths. Aeschylus explored the story of Agamemnon, the leader of the Greek forces at Troy, who had returned triumphant to his homeland only to be murdered by his faithless wife, Clytemnestra. She held against him the grievance that he had sacrificed their young daughter, Iphigenia, like a beast on the altar in order to win the favor of the goddess Artemis for his military venture. The story and its consequences over two generations are told in a series of three plays—a "trilogy"—which would have been performed in a continuous sequence at the Dionysia. The trilogy is called the *Oresteia* (so named after Orestes, Agamemnon's son, who will avenge his father), and consists of the *Agamemnon*, the *Choëphoroe* ("Libation Bearers), and the *Eumenides* ("Furies").

These brief plays probe such problems as the justice of war; competing public and private claims on the individual's conscience; the nature of monarchy, tyranny, and democracy; the duties of children to father and mother, of parents to children; the rival loves of mother and nurse; and the forgiveness of sin. One unforgettable scene from the *Agamemnon* gives a taste of the whole. Clytemnestra, having lured Agamemnon into his bath, trapped him in his luxurious robe, and slaughtered him, appears proudly to proclaim the deed with terrible "I" sentences announcing both strength and guilt: "I stand now where I struck him down. … Thus have I wrought, and I will not deny it now. … I struck him twice."

The strength of Antigone, heroine of Sophocles' play of that name, is of a different sort. Following Aeschylus in the sequence of tragic authors, Sophocles (496–406 B.C.E.) was the popular victor of as many as twenty-four dramatic contests. Where Aeschylus interested himself in broad and multiple themes, Sophocles focused intensely on individual human characters. In *Antigone*, he draws on a Theban cycle of legend alluded to, but not recounted, by Homer. Polyneices of Thebes, the exiled son of King Oedipus, has been killed, a traitor to his own city. The new King of Thebes, Creon, has ordered that he be left unburied. But Polyneices' sister Antigone insists on burying him so that his spirit may find rest.

Creon had ordained that death would be the punishment for burying a traitor. Didn't she know the law? asked Creon. Not the gods but a man had made that law, Antigone responded:

> *Nor did I think your orders were so strong*
> *that you, a mortal man, could over-run*
> *the gods' unwritten and unfailing laws. …*

So not through fear of any man's proud spirit
would I be likely to neglect these laws. ...
I knew that I must die. ...

Creon has Antigone sealed up alive. She hangs her-self. In this tragedy, tremendous and irreconcilable forces clash, shown as male and female polarities: the claims of the state on its citizens as against those of the gods, the claims of human and divine law, the claims of love.

Euripides (c. 485–407 B.C.E.), in his lifetime the least popular of these three tragedians, had a darker vision. His genius was recognized after his death when, in a bleaker age, spectators and readers more readily confronted the harsh truths he projects. Euripides was skeptical about the gods, pessimistic about the future, outraged by war, tormented by the pain inflicted by some humans upon others, especially upon the weakest, and obsessed with untangling the inner workings and secrets of the human mind. With such heavy thoughts he retired young to the island of Salamis, not far from Athens, to live as a recluse, with only the company of his library. Later he moved even farther away, to Macedonia, in the north, where he composed the last of his ninety-two plays, named a prizewinner after its author's death.

Euripides ransacked the material of myth for themes to develop in his original way. He developed, for instance, the legend of the hero Jason, who sailed with his loyal band of companions, the Argonauts, to retrieve the magical Golden Fleece from a distant city bordering the Black Sea. From this material Euripides fashioned the portrait of the ferocious Medea, Jason's spurned wife, who took her revenge on her disloyal husband by murdering their children. From the stories of Theseus, legendary king of Athens, he crafted the tortured triangle of that hero, of his wife, Phaedra, her desperate and unrequited love of her stepson Hippolytus, and Hippolytus' punishment of death as ordered by his vengeful father.

Moved by the massacre (in 415 B.C.E.) of the residents of the island of Melos by leaders of his own city, Euripides elaborated from the Trojan legend the drama of the *Trojan Women*. Slavery was the fate awaiting the women and children of a captured city; death, that of its men. Euripides requires his audience to listen to the pain of the captured. The prophetess Cassandra and Hector's wife, Andromache, are both carried away to degradation. Hector's son Astyanax is hurled from the city walls, his cries echoing offstage. The boy's grandmother, Hecuba, is left on stage to stroke his dead body—and to make the audience realize the dimensions of tragedy beyond even death.

Comedy While Euripides composed his painful dis-sections of human feelings, the comic playwright Aristophanes (c. 450–c. 385 B.C.E.) turned a cynical eye on Athenian society. Although **comedy** devel-oped later than tragedy, it also derived from the worship of Dionysus. It evolved from the Dionysiac processions characterized by sexual play and costumes equipped with oversized phalluses, lest the god's association with fertility and the absurd be missed. By 486 B.C.E., comic drama had emerged from this carnival. By mid-century, it had its own festive season, the Lenaea, to match tragedy's Dionysia.

It was the purpose of Greek comedy to point out the defects of public life. This mission Aristophanes pursued with relish. His works are the only complete comedies to survive from Ancient Greece. They are hilariously funny—full of slapstick, puns, lewd asides, and sheer craziness. They are also biting critiques of the Athenian world during the years when it slid into brutality and thoughtlessness.

Aristophanes blamed the decay of Athens on a failure of culture. The elevated values of the old aris-tocracy were being undermined by the war frenzy of the masses, the vulgarity of thick-witted politicians, and above all, in his view, the dangerous novelties of a new generation of unprincipled teachers. In *The Clouds*, Aristophanes mocked the Sophists (among whom he wrongly numbered Socrates) for seducing the Athenian young away from the traditional values of piety, reverence, and fitness. These teachers taught the young to worship not the gods, but the Clouds—evanescent things, having no permanent form and tempting the mind to wild fantasies.

Athenian theater flourished for a century, during which many hundreds of plays were performed. The

---

HOW MANY?

The First Athletic Competitions

4	The period of years between each set of games (an Olympiad)
1	The number of events (the stade) in the earliest known athletic competition at Olympia (776 B.C.E.)
210	The length of the track in yards (192m) for the earliest track event (the stade)
500	The number of gallons of olive oil in the amphora awarded to the winner of the stade
600	The value in drachmas of 500 gallons of olive oil, equivalent to about two years' wages for a mason or carpenter
393	The date (C.E.) of the abolition of the games
1	The number of female spectators (the Priestess of Demeter)
0	The number of female competitors

plays of only four authors survive—those of Aeschylus, Sophocles, Euripides, and Aristophanes. Of the approximately 300 plays they wrote, there survive today 7 by the first, 7 by the second, 19 by the third, and 11 by the fourth. The whole body of Greek drama still extant fits on a very small bookshelf. Yet is is the matrix of all subsequent theater in the West, and it has influenced all of Western literature.

The Perfect Body

While Greek playwrights explored the human condition, their compatriots aimed to perfect the human body through an activity they found equally important: gymnastics. Gymnastic exercise helped build bodies that were healthy, powerful, and beautiful. These goals were achieved principally by men. (In Sparta, an exception, women also engaged in physical training.) The cultivation of perfect male bodies, delectable to the gods, was a central to Greek culture.

Gymnastics were a part of the daily routine of all those who had the leisure to engage in them. After a morning of work, the citizen would put in several hours of physical training: running, jumping, wrestling, and the throwing of spear or discus, all of which disciplines were performed in the nude. Some activities are shown in *Windows On* on pp. 96–7. Such athletic activity was considered desirable for all, and essential for the leader of the state.

Gymnastic training formed a major part of education, constituting half of the elementary curriculum. (The other half was "music," or poetry, an academic subject which included what would today be called grammar and literature as well as metrics and music. In the fourth century, the two most famous schools of philosophy, the Academy and the **Lyceum**, were founded adjacent to two of Athens' suburban gymnasia.

In their striving for physical perfection, Greek athletes competed vigorously, engaging in a struggle—a struggle to win, psychologically akin to the struggle of the tragic hero who combats an overwhelming destiny. The athlete's striving also related to the Greek pursuit of war. War and games were both athletic encounters. To lose the first was to suffer death. To lose the second was to suffer shame. To win, in either case, was glorious. Winning or losing spelled the meaning of the individual's existence.

Gymnastics and war were related in another way. The former prepared a man for the latter. Citizens who kept fit through gymnastics constituted a citizen army ready to defend the *polis*. Pericles pointed out in his "Funeral Oration" that Athenian males kept themselves in a state of readiness for war through their pleasant sports activities—in contrast to the dour Spartans who insisted on a conventional military drill. Gymnastics were a civic version of war.

The central role gymnastics would play in Greek civilization at its zenith was prefigured in Homer's *Iliad*. When Achilles has vanquished Hector and returned to the Achaean camp, he organizes a festival of funeral games for his martyred beloved, Patroclus. Chariot races, boxing, wrestling, running, dueling, archery: these sports absorbed the Achaean contestants as much as battle, which they closely resembled. To the reader unfamiliar with the role played by gymnastics in Greek culture, the devotion of more than 600 lines of verse to these activities is unfathomable.

Games in honor of Patroclus were not only mock battles but also sacred rites. Like song and dance, athletic performance was a mode of worshiping the gods. About the time that Homer described the funeral of Patroclus (the traditional date is 776 B.C.E.), athletic contestants from different cities met at Zeus' sacred city Olympia. These games were the first to be called "Olympic" and were the ancestors of today's Olympic Games. Other athletic festivals were launched by rival cities; for example, the Isthmian games were sponsored by Corinth in honor of its patron god, Poseidon. The games were ceremonies of worship, in honor of which the Greeks agreed to a holy truce for the protection of participants and spectators.

The winner (often a Spartan, whose whole life was dedicated to the culture of the body) became a hero whose achievement honored his family and, even more than that, his *polis*. He won valuable trophies in recognition of his victory, and when he went home he was guaranteed a lifetime of free meals at public expense. A sixth-century winner from Sybaris, in Italy, was able to construct a shrine to Athena with a fraction of his prize money.

Wealthy winners, or their families, might also hire a poet to commemorate a victory. Pindar (c. 522–c. 440 B.C.E.) specialized in writing odes for athletic heroes. These odes say little about the race. Instead, they celebrate as divine gifts the spiritual and physical prowess of the hero—and heap disgrace on the unfortunate losers, who receive "no glad home-coming":

> They, when they meet their mothers,
> Have no sweet laughter around them, moving delight.
> In back streets, out of their enemies' way.
> They cower; for disaster has bitten them.

The idealization of the male body that underlies the Greek sports culture is also fundamental to the evolution of its art. When the crude products of Dark Age artisans gave way to a new generation of pottery, its decoration consisted of the simplest and most austere lines (see Chapter 3). This Proto-Geometric style was followed by increasingly complex but still mainly linear decoration, which often included angular, highly stylized representations of human beings. This is known as the Geometric style.

Many of the pots in Geometric style were unearthed near Athens' Dipylon Gate. Crafted in the eighth century B.C.E., these colossal vases (nearly as

Wrestling, boxing, and athletics: *The importance in Greek culture of athletic competition cannot be overstated. Those who had leisure to do so exercised daily in the gymnasium. Athletic competitions were held at religious festivals, an indication of their universal meaning. The relief above shows wrestlers in competition c. 500 B.C.E. (above), while a black-figure amphora of 530 B.C.E. (below) shows boxers competing as its main image, with a smaller image of wrestling above. (above: National Archaeological Museum, Athens; below: British Museum)*

Black-figure amphora, 530 *B.C.E.*

Here are scenes of men racing (above), and of a Spartan girl engaging in races--called the Heraia—specifically designated for women. The central image, from the later Hellenistic era, is of a young rider on a racing steed. (above: Metropolitan Museum of Art; center: National Archaelogical Museum, Athens; below: British Museum, London)

The Greek propensity for exercise in the nude surprised other peoples (who lived in climates just as warm). Why do you think they adopted this custom?

Bronze jockey of Artemision, Hellenistic, 2nd-century B.C.E.

Bronze figurine, late-6th century B.C.E.

 To continue your investigation of this topic, please go to www.prenhall.com/king for the related **WINDOWS** on the **WEB** activity

tall as an adult human) were funeral objects, ordered by wealthy patrons who wished to make drink offerings to the spirits of their dead. Accordingly, they often depicted funerals. These pots represent an early step toward establishing the human form as the proper subject of the visual arts.

That development presaged a dramatic change in the style of pottery decoration. During the seventh century, when the potters of Corinth temporarily took the lead away from Athens in ceramic art, the vase surface erupted in a riot of plant and animal forms: pouncing lions, bellowing cattle, devilish monsters. The motifs were Eastern, copied from the ivories and metalwork of Egyptian, Assyrian, and Phoenician luxuries that passed through the port of Corinth. In the sixth century, the Athenians responded with ballets of black figures painted on a reddish background.

These Athenian figures were different. They were fully formed human beings, engaged in the full range of human acts from farming to weaving to dancing to love. The painted dramas continued to be produced in the Classical age, yet were more refined and detailed in the red-figure pottery (developed about 530–480 B.C.E.). On these pots, the artist inscribed the outlines of the figures in the red clay and painted the background black—thus reversing the black-figure procedure. The surfaces of these pots became the screen for varied images of contemporary life: scenes from the gymnasium and the *symposium*, war and athletics, domestic and farm work, sexual activity of all varieties, amusements innocent and lurid. Some are shown on the cups illustrated on p. 63 and p. 99.

Meanwhile other artisans began to carve from stone, or cast in bronze, freestanding statues of the human figure. The first such statue-type to emerge in Greece—of the young male nude, the **kouros**, or boy—belongs to the Archaic age. It is the commonest form of sculpture, and sets the pattern for all successive forms. Once introduced, the pattern sparked imitation: *kouroi* (plural of *kouros*) date from the seventh century B.C.E., when the genre was new, but five times as many—157—are known from the sixth century B.C.E. The *kouros* was based on Egyptian models, transformed with an unmistakably Greek face as shown on p. 88. Bones and muscles appear to move beneath the surface, the legs seem to bear weight and walk, the torso to fill with breath and the statue with life.

The female counterpart of the *kouros* was the statue of the **kore**, or young woman as seen in *Windows On*, p.92. This, too, derived from Eastern models and was given new life by Greek artists. The *kore* statue, like the *kouros*, enjoyed growing popularity in ancient Greece: 35 are known from the seventh century B.C.E., and 144 from the sixth century B.C.E. Both were remarkable innovations in the history of sculpture. But the *kouros* exceeded the *kore* as an artistic creation. His nude figure was individualized, whereas her clothed figure tended toward the anonymity of the sculpted women, called caryatids, that served as columns to hold up the roof of a temple porch. He, not she, was seen as the prototype of human beauty: for the Greeks, the beauty of men was tantamount to beauty itself.

From the *kouros* and *kore* figures of the sixth century B.C.E. developed the realistic yet refined sculpture of the fifth and later centuries. Anonymous artisans and even some masters whose names are known—Phidias, Praxiteles, Scopas—created both freestanding and relief sculpture in stone and bronze, some life-size and some larger than life-size. In their surviving works, and in copies made by the Romans, we find eloquent testimony to the Greeks' reverence for the dignity and grace of the human being.

TO KNOW AND TO LOVE TO KNOW

By the sixth century B.C.E., to the Greek cultural world of myth and art, poetry and games, entered a series of thinkers who yearned to understand the universe. They came from all over the Greek world, as shown on Map 4.1. The first philosophers began to seek the foundations of reality in matter or spirit, while the first historians sought to explain human events, looking at cultures and individuals (rather than the gods) as motive forces. Professional speakers and teachers redefined the scope of useful knowledge and perfected the skills by which to learn how to succeed in human affairs. Orators helped communities decide matters of law and custom, and war and peace, while the philosophers of the Classical age, building on the achievement of their predecessors, probed the nature of the cosmos and the state, the natural world and the soul, the realms of ethics, language, and art.

Presocratic Knowers and Seekers

One group of Greek thinkers thrust the gods aside and rejected myth as the explanation of things. These are called the **Presocratics**, for they predate the figure of Socrates, the teacher of Plato, the teacher of Aristotle, who was to inaugurate a new phase in the history of thought. From the work of the Presocratics derives—to give only the short list—science and philosophy, theories of law and government, history, ethics, and psychology. There being no professions yet of science and philosophy, these thinkers were called "knowers," "knowers of many things," and "the wise."

The Presocratics began to make their mark in the sixth century B.C.E., one century after Archilochus, two after Homer, and in the same part of the Greek world: the Ionian coast of Asia Minor and its islands, whose cities had extensive contacts with Middle Eastern cultures. Their investigations were continued first by the Greeks of Italy, and only in the late fifth century B.C.E. by mainland Greeks.

Paideia: Transmitting Greek Culture

Red-figure cup: *In early Greece, "education" consisted of learning to farm, or hunt, or to craft tools, weapons, or pots. With the use of the alphabet in a more sophisticated society, it became necessary to transmit Greek language and values to new generations—a mission summed up in* paideia, *meaning not merely education in the modern sense but also acculturation. Among the propertied, it became common to send boys to study with a grammar-master. Scenes from Greek education are depicted on this fifth-century* B.C.E. *cup by the sculptor Douris where, from right to left in the first half (above), a boy learns to play the lyre, then reads from a manuscript page held by the master while his pedagogue waits. In the second half (below), the boy learns to play the flute and to write, watched, again, by the pedagogue.* (Staatliche Museen, Berlin)

Xenophanes of Colophon (in Asia Minor; fl. c. 540 B.C.E.) waged a relentless attack on the mythic conception of reality as he journeyed for sixty-seven years around the Greek world to recite his poems and share his wisdom. His poetry was different from the lyric, the epic, the tragic, or the comic: it was about the nature of reality, of human life, and of the gods. Xenophanes dismissed as absurd the multifarious gods and goddesses of myth. Foolish mortals believe "that the gods are born, and that they have clothes and speech and bodies like their own"; "But if cattle and horses or lions had hands, or were able to draw with their hands and do the works that men can do, horses would draw the forms of the gods like horses, and cattle like cattle. …"

Although Xenophanes rejected the deities of Olympus, he detected a spiritual substratum to all of reality: deity itself. "One" existed who was omniscient and omnipotent, commander of the universe which was regulated for the good: "one god, greatest among gods and men, in no way similar to mortals either in body or in thought" (see *Witnesses*, p. 100). The monotheism of Xenophanes is an exception to the polytheism of the Greeks.

While Xenophanes challenged the assumptions of polytheism, the three thinkers of the **Milesian school** (so called because they were all citizens of Miletus, in Asia Minor) invented what we call science. These were Thales (fl. c. 585 B.C.E.), Anaximander (c. 610–546 B.C.E.), and Anaximenes (fl. c. 550 B.C.E.). Their school was not an institution with a building, deans, and janitors, but simply a gathering of those who conversed about the same kinds of things.

The Milesian sages all rejected mythic explanations of the origins and causes of things, and sought better ones. Thales proposed that water was the universal medium: from it, he thought, all matter had been formed, and it continued to sustain the life of all earthly creatures. He was thus what we call a **materialist,** one who believes that reality itself is formed of an original material substance.

Anaximander and Anaximenes also named fundamental substances, but different ones, as the fabric of creation. For Anaximander, that substance was the *apeiron,* or "the Boundless": an infinite and nonperceptible primal mass in never-ending motion within which the universal opposites of heat and cold and wet and dry worked to generate the first creatures. For Anaximenes, the first substance was air, alternately thinning and thickening as pulled by opposing universal forces; from this derived both matter and spirit. Working without laboratories or textbooks and not thinking to conduct experiments, these theorists nevertheless approached the conclusions of modern scientists—that certain universal substances underlie all matter, whose interactions cause change and form.

According to Pythagoras (fl. c. 530 B.C.E.), the nature of things was determined not by a material substratum but by fundamental spiritual and logical relationships. Pythagoras was born on the Aegean island of Samos but worked in Croton (Italy) in the late sixth century B.C.E. As a religious leader, Pythagoras instructed his followers to observe strictly a number of rituals and taboos, and taught the transmigration of human souls after death. He was also an inspired mathematician, profiting from the work of Babylonian and Egyptian predecessors. Pythagoras is most famous for generalizing an ancient theorem for calculating the hypotenuse of a right angle—a theorem still named after him "Pythagorean."

Investigating the relations between numbers and musical harmonies, Pythagoras found that the fourth, fifth, and octave of a musical note were produced by plucking a lyre string respectively three-quarters, two-thirds and one-half the length of the string producing the initial sound. The relations between the lengths of the lyre string can thus be expressed in ratios that add up to ten—a number that Pythagoras represented as a figure controlling both number and shape, the spatial expression of a perfect number reflecting the underlying structure of the universe.

Heraclitus of Ephesus (in Asia Minor; fl. c. 500 B.C.E.) believed the key to the structure of the universe is change itself. Life is a constant struggle between opposite forces that are always shifting, yet always the same in the constancy of their oppositions, and therefore a check on what would otherwise be chaos. The universe is a never-ending fire, in which is found the unity of the opposites, the oneness behind antagonistic substances.

Responding to Heraclitus' theory of change, Parmenides of Elea (in Italy; c. 510–c. 450 B.C.E.) posited a single spiritual reality at the heart of the universe. What Parmenides calls "IT," or being, is an unmoving, perfect, eternal spiritual center completely removed from nonbeing, which cannot exist: for if **IT IS**, then that which is not, is not. Parmenides' intense consciousness of Reality itself would have a long future in Western thought. Presented in a long poem, much of which survives, his ideas are remarkable as an early exercise in purely abstract thought—pure reason. An extract is given in *Witnesses* above.

The Milesians had been materialists, for whom reality had a substantial, material basis. Pythagoras and Parmenides were idealists, for whom reality

WITNESSES

Presocratic Thinkers on Reality

What is real? The Greeks were the first thinkers to pursue an answer to that question through rigorous reasoning that has survived in written form. Here two of those early philosophers posit their visions of the real, and they are similar. For Parmenides, the real is Being itself, "entire, immovable and without end"; for Xenophanes, it is God, all of whom at once "sees," "thinks," and "hears."

Parmenides—Being is that which is immovable and without end (c. 470 B.C.E.): One way only is left to be spoken of, that it *is*; and on this way are full many signs that what *is* is uncreated and imperishable, for it is entire, immovable and without end. It *was* not in the past, nor *shall* it be, since it *is* now, all at once, one, continuous … Nor shall I allow you to say or to think, "from that which is not"; for it is not to be said or thought that it is not . … for if it came into being, it is not, nor if it is going to be in the future. So coming into being is extinguished and perishing unimaginable.
(Parmenides, no. 347; from G. S. Kirk, J. E. Raven, *Presocratic Philosophers*)

Xenophanes—The one, supreme god (c. 530 B.C.E.): One god, greatest among gods and men, in no way similar to mortals either in body or in thought.

Always he remains in the same place, moving not at all; nor is it fitting for him to go to different places at different times, but without toil he shakes all things by the thought of his mind.

All of him sees, all thinks, and all hears.
(Xenophanes, nos. 173, 174, 175; eds. G. S. Kirk, J. E. Raven)

existed in an abstract realm, apart from matter. In the following generation materialism returned in the persons of Empedocles (fl. c. 445 B.C.E.; from Acragas in Sicily), Anaxagoras (c. 500–c. 428 B.C.E.; from Clazomenae in Asia Minor), Leucippus (fl. c. 435 B.C.E.; from Miletus in Asia Minor), and Democritus (c. 460–370 B.C.E.; from Abdera in northern Greece). Empedocles posited four basic elements (earth, air, fire, and water) from which all natural things were composed. These were subject to change and mixture through the powerful force of two principles of unification and disintegration: Love and Strife.

For Anaxagoras, the universe was made up of small and countless "seeds" governed by the rule of "mind." Those "seeds" are a foreshadowing of atomic theory, while that "mind" is reminiscent of Parmenides: "All other things have a portion of everything, but Mind is infinite and self-ruled, and is mixed with nothing but is all alone by itself." Anaxagoras' claim (inspired by the sight of a falling meteor) that the sun was a huge burning rock as big as the Peloponnese got him into trouble with the authorities, who charged him

Map 4.1 The Geography of Thought, c. 750–320 B.C.E.: *The poets and orators, scientists and philosophers, historians and dramatists who created the monuments of thought that make ancient Greece memorable came from all over the Greek world—from Asia Minor in the east to Sicily in the west. An extraordinary number, however, came from Athens. What features of life in Athens encouraged intellectual innovation?*

with impiety. He was living in Athens at the time, a friend of Pericles, whose political enemies aimed to strike at their adversary by discrediting the philosopher. Anaxagoras was forced to flee.

What Anaxagoras called "seeds," Leucippus and his follower Democritus called "atoms." These were infinite in number and form, unchanging in substance, hurtling and crashing through a void—not exactly what modern science has to say about the atom, but in its time a revolutionary concept. In this view of the universe Anaxagoras' controlling "Mind" had no place. The Democritean cosmos is irrational, and the tiny volatile atoms govern themselves and it.

History, Sophistry, and Oratory

While the inquiries of the Presocratics gave birth to philosophy and science, their rational method spurred the development of new groups of thinkers. Historians, Sophists, and orators turned the skeptical methods of the Presocratics to the problem of the past and present conduct of human society.

History Herodotus (c. 484–425 B.C.E.), whose distinction between "West" and "East" has already been noted, was the first major Greek historian. He traveled throughout the Mediterranean to gain insight into the peoples who affected the dramatic confrontation between Persia and Greece. Scythian burial customs, the astronomical lore of the Babylonians, courtly practices of the Persians—all were important to him.

In these researches, Herodotus invented a new discipline, the one that is practiced in the volume now before you: history. History, however, did not mean to him what it means now. In Greek, the word *historia* meant simply "inquiry": history originally was not the answer to a question but the process of seeking the answer. Why bother to seek? Herodotus announced his purpose in the opening words of his *History*: it is to preserve "from decay the remembrance of what men have done" and to prevent "the great and wonderful actions of the Greeks and the Barbarians from losing their due [measure] of glory."

Herodotus displays a skepticism reminiscent of Xenophanes. But whereas the latter simply scoffed at the absurd figures of the gods, Herodotus dutifully reported, but went on record as doubting, supernatural explanations. In response to the story that in the topmost chamber of the highest tower in Babylon a god slept with a woman provided for his comfort, the historian remarked: "but I do not believe it." When Xerxes' ships were wracked by storms, Herodotus wrote, "At length the [priests], by offering victims to the winds, and charming them with the help of conjurers, while at the same time they sacrificed to Thetis and the Nereids, succeeded in laying the storm four days after it first began." Then he added: "or perhaps it ceased of itself."

The goal of Thucydides (c. 460–c. 400 B.C.E.), the other renowned Greek historian, was similar to that of Herodotus: to understand the beginning and consequences of a war. But the men, and the wars, were

Thucydides

The historian Thucydides, most famous for his reporting of political struggle and violence (see Chapter 2, p. 53), is also an accurate observer of events caused by no human agency. Here is an excerpt of his famous description of the plague (its nature is controversial) that descended on Athens in 430 B.C.E, the year after Pericles delivered his funeral oration for the first year's dead (see p. 73).

Not many days after [the Lacedaemonian invasion of] … Attica the plague first began to show itself among the Athenians. It was said that it had broken out in many places previously …; but a pestilence of such extent and mortality was nowhere remembered. … It first began, it is said, in the parts of Ethiopia above Egypt, and thence descended into Egypt and Libya. … Suddenly falling upon Athens, it first attacked the population in Piraeus … and afterwards appeared in the upper city, when the deaths became much more frequent. All speculation as to its origin and its causes, if causes can be found adequate to produce so great a disturbance, I leave to other writers, whether lay or professional; for myself, I shall simply set down its nature, and explain the symptoms by which perhaps it may be recognized by the student, if it should ever break out again. This I can the better do, as I had the disease myself, and watched its operation in the case of others. As a rule, … there was no ostensible cause; but people in good health were all of a sudden attacked by violent heats in the head, and redness and inflammation in the eyes, the inward parts, such as the throat or tongue, becoming bloody and emitting an unnatural and fetid breath. These symptoms were followed by sneezing and hoarseness, after which the pain soon reached the chest, and produced a hard cough. When it fixed in the stomach, it upset it; and discharges of bile of every kind named by physicians ensued, accompanied by very great distress. In most cases also an ineffectual retching followed, producing violent spasms, which in some cases ceased soon after, in others much later. Externally the body was not very hot to the touch, nor pale in its appearance, but reddish, livid, and breaking out into small pustules and ulcers. But internally it burned so that the patient could not bear to have on him clothing or linen even of the very lightest description; or indeed to be otherwise than stark naked. … The body meanwhile did not waste away so long as the distemper was at its height, but held out to a marvel against its ravages; so that when they succumbed, as in most cases, on the seventh or eighth day to the internal inflammation, they had still some strength in them. But if they passed this stage, and the disease descended further into the bowels, inducing a violent ulceration there accompanied by severe diarrhoea, this brought on a weakness which was generally fatal. … By far the most terrible feature in the malady was the dejection which ensued when any one felt himself sickening, for the despair into which they instantly fell took away their power of resistance, and left them a much easier prey to the disorder; besides which, there was the awful spectacle of men dying like sheep, through having caught the infection in nursing each other. This caused the greatest mortality. On the one hand, if they were afraid to visit each other, they perished from neglect; indeed many houses were emptied of their inmates for want of a nurse: on the other, if they ventured to do so, death was the consequence …

(Thucydides, *Peloponnesian War*, 2:47.3–51.5; trans. R. Crawley)

different to the extent that, for a second time, history was invented anew. The Persian war was for Herodotus an epic confrontation between freedom and slavery. For Thucydides, the struggle between Athens and Sparta called the Peloponnesian War was a doomed and meaningless battle (though perhaps inevitable) between peoples already corrupted in spirit whose only outcome could be catastrophe. "Love of power," he grimly pronounced, "operating through greed and through personal ambition, was the cause of all these evils." Human psychology, he believed, was the motor that drove history forward.

The disaster unfolds, in Thucydides' presentation, in a series of intensely dramatic scenes. A social revolution in Corcyra, a Corinthian colony, is described in all its murderous and soul-destroying horror (see *Witnesses*, p. 53). The debate between the islanders of Melos and the Athenians who wished to dominate them displays the cold logic of power and ends in the enslavement of men, women, and children.

The departure of the Athenian fleet for adventures in Sicily is depicted as the tragic escapade of men who should have anticipated, but did not, the devastation that lay ahead. Every one of the survivors of the battles that followed faced incarceration and death by exposure, starvation, and disease. All these horrors are foreshadowed by paired events which occurred soon after the outset of the war. The first was Pericles' uplifting funeral speech for the first dead. The second was the plague that struck Athens shortly afterward and which, over three years, ravaged its population, killing one-third of its troops and Pericles himself, and leaving survivors demoralized. Thucydides' description is given in *Witnesses*, above.

The historian who wrote of these tragedies was scrupulous in his testing of sources and relentless in his pursuit of evidence. More than Herodotus, Thucydides rejects supernatural or even implausible explanations for events, seeking the springs of action in the decisions of the human minds that controlled the course of history. These he framed in speeches which he claimed were based on words that he heard or which had been reliably reported to him, but which he may have crafted to sound as though they had been uttered. In composing these speeches, he added the skills of the artist to those of the historian.

Thucydides was an Athenian of prominent family, distantly related to Miltiades, the hero of Marathon. He fought as a soldier in the war until 426 B.C.E. when he was exiled from his own city. From that distant vantage point, Thucydides was able both to describe war realistically and to understand its power to determine the future of human beings. His commitment to analyze the course and meaning of war has this defect: that he recognizes no history except the history of antagonistic states. For centuries to come, in the tradition of Herodotus and Thucydides, history was understood to be the history of empires and kingdoms and cities and the men who ruled them.

The Sophists Thucydides probably learned to write his chilling speeches from a new breed of specialist, the "Sophists." The original meaning of the Greek word *sophistes* was "expert" or "wise man," but it soon came to mean one who knew about, or talked about, or peddled wisdom. The Sophists were makers of speeches, and speech-making played a central role in Greek life. Like the bards of the Archaic age who traveled from city to city to recite the epics of Homer, the Sophists journeyed about the Greek world to display their talents, even addressing crowds of spectators at athletic festivals. They announced their arrival in each new locale with an elaborate speech, which was an exemplar of their eloquence and a form of job résumé: an invitation to the listener to employ the speaker. For the Sophists not only made speeches but taught others to make them—for a stiff fee.

The students who flocked to the Sophists did not aspire to knowledge, as did those who gathered around Thales or Pythagoras. They were often the sons of ambitious Greek citizens who aimed to participate in political life. Without training, they could not debate in the assembly, or defend friends or accuse opponents. The ability to make persuasive, dynamic speeches was a prerequisite of power. To gain that skill, many turned to the Sophists.

The Sophists taught another useful skill: that of devising deceitful or manipulative arguments. In addition to teaching the technique of building an argument, they also taught the technique of subverting their opponent's—to the dismay of cultural conservatives like Aristophanes and sticklers for the truth like Socrates. The willingness of the Sophists to adjust facts for practical ends was based on a profound transformation of values—just as their critics had feared. Many of them were atheists. Neither the Olympian gods and their myths nor the gods of the earth and their grip on natural forces impressed the Sophists. Their standards of behavior were eerily modern. "Is this action useful?" they might ask, not "Is it right?"; "Will this idea produce the desired response?" not "Is this the truth?"

The Sophist Protagoras of Abdera, in northern Greece (c. 484–c. 415 B.C.E.), came to Athens in the mid-fifth century B.C.E. and joined the brilliant circle around Pericles, which also included Aspasia, Anaxagoras, and Socrates. The philosopher Plato provides a full portrait of him in the dialogue entitled *Protagoras*. In addition, two of Protagoras' telling statements survive. The first expresses not merely skepticism about the existence of the gods, but sheer indifference to the possibility that they might exist: "Concerning the gods I cannot know either that they exist or that they do not exist, or what form they might have, for there is much to prevent one's knowing: the obscurity of the subject and the shortness of man's life." The second statement announces that truth and falsehood are not absolutes fixed by nature or the gods but relatives determined by the human mind: "Of all things the measure is man, of things that are that they are, and of things that are not that they are not." If man is the measure of all things, Protagoras' opponents feared, then standards of truth and falsehood, right and wrong, fall away.

It was said that to teach a young man such wisdom, Protagoras might charge 1000 drachmas: a worker's wages for three years. On such fees the Sophist Gorgias of Leontini, in Sicily (c. 483–376 B.C.E.), became rich. Gorgias claimed to be able to argue any case either way and to vindicate the unjust as well as the just cause. He demonstrated this in a piece of rhetoric entitled the *Encomium of Helen*. Here he argued the innocence of the woman blamed for embroiling the Greeks in the Trojan War: she was the victim of persuasion—in the same way that the Sophists' audience was a victim of their eloquence. No one can resist the power of speech, "which by means of the finest and most invisible body effects the divinest works," and must be acknowledged "a powerful lord" by the Greeks, who otherwise acknowledged none.

In his book *On Non-Being*, or *On What is Not*, Gorgias parodied the Presocratic thinkers whose ideas were often reported in books entitled *On Being, On Nature*, or *On What Is*. Here he announces the unknowability of anything for certain—a stance that leaves a Sophist with a clear field: "Nothing exists... even if it exists it is inapprehensible to man... even if it is apprehensible, still it is without a doubt incapable of being expressed or explained to the next man." With the possibility of rational knowledge of nature thus discarded, nothing is left but tissues of words. Of these, the Sophists were masters.

The Sophists' desertion of fixed standards of moral goodness or rational truth has been much lamented. Yet their achievement was considerable. By broadening the definition of what there was to know and what was worth knowing, they paved the way for many learned disciplines: the humanities and social sciences; the studies of language and meaning, of society and politics and of human behavior. The Sophists, finally, were the first professional educators, and very popular ones. Young men left the gymnasium and the stadium to attend to the sparkling words of the Sophists. These schools resemble ours far more closely than did the "school" of Thales or even the "school" of Plato. Under such instruction, young men were trained to assume leadership in their cities.

Oratory The elaboration by the Sophists of the discipline of prose composition paved the way for the professional orators who flourished in Athens in the last century of her independence. The long-lived Isocrates (436–338 B.C.E.), a speechwriter and (in the Sophist tradition) a teacher of oratory, was an elegant stylist, whose prose set a standard of Greek rhetoric. His speeches circulated in writing as models for composition. Demosthenes (384–322 B.C.E.) was a fierce and effective orator who spoke often in the law courts and councils of Athens during the years when her democracy reached its peak.

During the three generations between the end of the Peloponnesian War (404 B.C.E.) and the Greeks' defeat at Chaeronea by Philip of Macedon (338 B.C.E.), which brought an end to their independence, even the poorest Athenian citizens could participate in government. Only a few of them had received the education that was the privilege of the old aristocrats, or the expressive training offered by the Sophists. To present a defense or bring a suit, they required the services of an orator. Most of the surviving speeches of the fourth-century B.C.E. orators are private commissions of this sort. Others, however, deal with the tremendous issues of foreign policy the Athenians faced as the power of Macedon loomed ever larger.

To that threat Isocrates and Demosthenes had two different reactions. Isocrates' views are outlined in a famous speech entitled *Panegyricus*, in which he urges the Greek states to unite under Macedonian overlordship and turn to fight the still-mighty Persian Empire: "It is much more glorious to fight against the King for his empire," he chided, "than to contend against each other for the hegemony [of Greece]."

Demosthenes urged resistance to the Macedonian advance in a series of speeches delivered between 351 and 338 B.C.E.: three called the *Olynthiacs*, occasioned by the capture of the city of Olynthus, and four called *Philippics*, directed against the Macedonian king. While Philip advanced in summer and winter alike, intent on the domination of Greece, Demosthenes argued, Athenians thought only of their bribes and perquisites. There might still be a chance, he thundered in 351 B.C.E.: "If you will adopt this principle now, though you did not do so before, and if each citizen who can and ought to give his service to the state is ready to give it . . . , if, put bluntly, you will become your own masters and each cease expecting to do nothing himself while his neighbor does everything for him, then, God willing, you will recover

your own, get back what has been frittered away, and turn the tables on Philip." The plea didn't work, and Philip advanced exactly as Demosthenes had forecast.

Philosophers—Lovers of Wisdom

By the time of Isocrates and Demosthenes in the fourth century B.C.E., the world of myth had diminished. Both of these men were heirs to the pragmatism of the Sophists, the realism of the historians, the skepticism of the Presocratics, as both men were shaped by the events that led to the collapse of the free *polis* in Greece. Also shaped by these cultural and political circumstances were the three men—Socrates, Plato, Aristotle—whose achievement it is to have invented philosophy: the "love of wisdom" or "love of truth," a ceaseless striving to know.

The new "**philosophers**" (*philosophoi*) asked the same questions as had their predecessors, especially the Presocratics, called "the wise" (*sophoi*): What is the universe made of? Is it substance or spirit, being or nonbeing? Is it one or many? Does it change? Is it in motion? What causes it to change or move? What causes it to stop? Is there any order in the cosmos? How do we know what it is—or anything that we know? Are there gods? What do they do? What meaning does human existence have in the cosmic system? What is the purpose of human life? What is the best form of state?

Socrates Socrates (470–399 B.C.E.) asked questions and wouldn't give answers. Claiming to know nothing, he challenged those who claimed to know everything or even something, and thus to be wise. Socrates did not give speeches or take fees for lessons (as his opponents falsely charged) and he attacked the Sophists for doing so. He sauntered to the *agora* and the gymnasium, as though he had nothing of importance to do, and engaged in conversation with the young men of Athens. He wrote nothing himself.

Socrates' method can be observed in the dialogues written by his pupil Plato. In his dialogue with Meno, Socrates asks that gentleman what virtue is. Meno responds that there are many kinds of virtue: the virtue of a man, of a woman, and many others. Gracefully, Socrates recoils from the spate of words: "I seem to be in luck. I wanted one virtue and I find that you have a whole swarm of virtues to offer." The implication is clear: Meno hasn't the slightest idea, in spite of his costly sophistic education, what virtue is.

A second Platonic dialogue, the *Symposium*, describes a drinking party at which the guests each give extemporaneous speeches in honor of love. The poet Agathon, the host, gives the most exquisite, his language sporting the excesses of contemporary drama and sophistic oratory. Then Socrates is asked to speak. He begins by praising Agathon's presentation, which he could never, he demurs, hope to equal. But, he

Plato's "Allegory of the Cave"

THE CAVE

The fire

The roadway

Diffused daylight

The rough ascent to sunlight

Source: From *The Great Dialogues of Plato*, trs. W. H. D. Rouse. Courtesy Dutton Signet/Penguin Books.

wonders, was it his job to speak beautifully about love (as Agathon had done), or to speak the truth? None of those, he implies, who had spoken had approached the real issue, which was the nature of love. Again, Socrates exposes the ignorance of others as a necessary step to finding what is actually the case.

Searching after truth is often dangerous, and for Socrates it was fatal. In 399 B.C.E. he was accused of "impiety": of having neglected religious duties and corrupted the young of Athens. The accusers demanded the death penalty. Socrates defended himself with the same kind of reasoning that had so charmed the gentlemen of the gymnasia and street corners. He was found guilty by a vote of 281 to 220. By a second and more emphatic vote of 300–201, the jury condemned him to death by poisoning. His friends proposed to bribe the jailors. Socrates refused. He died a martyr, at the hands of a democracy and by majority vote, to the principle of truth.

Plato Socrates' death shocked his younger friend Plato (428–347 B.C.E.). Plato's earliest works describe the trial and death of his mentor, and nearly all the later ones memorialize him. They are composed as dialogues between Socrates and his friends or acquaintances, dramatic reenactments of the open-air conversations in which the older man dazzled his hearers for nearly fifty years. Plato was both philosopher and dramatist, perpetual student of the questing Socrates, and pioneer of new regions of thought.

Plato believed that ultimate truths really existed and could be known. These were the Ideas of things: supernatural like the gods, unchanging like the "It" posited by Parmenides, invulnerable to the destructive

criticism of the Sophists, apprehensible by the mind like the truths that Socrates sought behind meaningless chatter. To know these Ideas was the supreme purpose of life. The philosopher would be led by love of the beautiful: beyond beautiful things to the idea of the Beautiful and the Ideas themselves, formers and sustainers of the universe. Only philosophers were capable of the pure apprehension of Ideas. Ordinary people (as Plato explained in his "allegory of the cave" in the seventh book of his *Republic*), quoted in *Witnesses* on p. 106 saw only the shadows of images of things, like the fleeting and distorted images cast by a campfire on the wall of a cave.

Such lofty thinking did not blind Plato to the realities of life in the world. Believing that the philosopher should act and not just observe, he journeyed to Syracuse on the island of Sicily in 387 B.C.E., to guide the political education of the heir to the tyrant of that city. He opposed the Sophists' notion that, all things being relative, the ideal of justice was, too. In the *Republic*, he outlined an ideal state where justice was administered by carefully chosen philosopher-kings, male and female—for women, Plato held, were capable of excellence. Later in life, sobered by his experience of the decline of the *polis*, he wrote in his *Laws* a more sour sketch of how political life should be ordered. Never did he despair of justice, but he did despair of human benevolence.

On his return from a last, disheartening expedition to Sicily, Plato purchased a small park just outside Athens, where he founded a school: the "Academy." Not only a group of thinkers but also the institution in which they worked, Plato's Academy is the ancestor of academies, research institutes, and universities,

Plato and Aristotle on the Nature of Knowing

Ancient Greek philosophy culminates in the work of Plato and Aristotle, teacher and student, whose works in their sum outline the branches of philosophical thought to be pursued by Western thinkers for the next 2,400 years. In these passages, Plato presents his "allegory of the cave" to show that human beings think they know the truth when they in fact see only shadows of truth; and Aristotle speaks of the importance of knowledge: "the activity of our intelligence constitutes . . .complete happiness."

Plato—Humans, like prisoners in a cave who see only shadows, know nothing of reality (c. 380 B.C.E.): Picture men dwelling in a sort of subterranean cavern with a long entrance open to the light on its entire width. Conceive them as having their legs and necks fettered from childhood, so that they remain in the same spot, able to look forward only, and prevented by the fetters from turning their heads. Picture further the light from a fire burning higher up and at a distance behind them, and between the fire and the prisoners and above them a road along which a low wall has been built, as the exhibitors of puppet shows have partitions before the men themselves, above which they show the puppets. ... See also, then, men carrying past the wall implements of all kinds that rise above the wall, and human images and shapes of animals as well, wrought in stone and wood, and every material, some of these bearers presumably speaking and others silent. ... Then in every way such prisoners would deem reality to be nothing else than the shadows of the artificial objects. ...
(Plato, *Republic*, 7:514–515; ed. P. Shorey, 1982)

Aristotle—The greatest happiness lies in pursuing the life of the mind, since "intelligence *is* man" (c. 335 B.C.E.): [The activity of the mind] is not only the highest—for intelligence is the highest possession we have in us, and the objects which are the concern of intelligence are the highest objects of knowledge—but also the most continuous: we are able to study continuously more easily than to perform any kind of action. ... Again, study seems to be the only activity which is loved for its own sake. For while we derive a greater or a smaller advantage from practical pursuits beyond the action itself, from study we derive nothing beyond the activity of studying. ... [I]t follows that the activity of our intelligence constitutes the complete happiness of man. ... In other words, a life guided by intelligence is the best and most pleasant for man, inasmuch as intelligence, above all else, is man. Consequently, this kind of life is the happiest.
(Aristotle, *Nicomachean Ethics*, 1177–1178; ed. M. Ostwald, 1985)

and of the people who teach there, perform experiments, and pursue research. There Plato taught for nearly forty years, surrounded by friends and students (women as well as men, so long as they met the high prerequisites). Disciples carried on his work for nine centuries thereafter, until the Academy was suppressed by the Emperor Justinian (in 529 C.E.).

Aristotle A dozen years after Plato's death another school, the Lyceum, was founded by his restive student Aristotle (384–322 B.C.E.). Born at Stagira, in northern Greece, Aristotle grew up in the swelling shadow of Macedonia. There his father, Nicomachus, became physician to King Philip II. The young Aristotle moved to Athens in 367 B.C.E. to study at Plato's Academy. On the founder's death in 347 B.C.E. (and at a time when persons tinged with Macedonian relations were unwelcome in Athens), he moved to the court of the tyrant Hermeias of Atarneus (in Asia Minor), another of Plato's students. Three years later, Aristotle journeyed to Mitylene, on the island of Lesbos, off the coast of Asia Minor, where he befriended Theophrastus, who was to be his eventual successor. It was another short stay. From 342 B.C.E., Aristotle was in Pella, the capital of Macedonia, serving as tutor to the future world conqueror Alexander the Great. In 335 B.C.E., with Athens now under Macedonian control, he established there his new philosophical school, rival to the nearby Academy.

The Lyceum resembled a modern research institute. It received a subsidy, in the form of a huge gift (800 talents) from Alexander. It provided office, library, and laboratory space, and areas for teaching, spirited lunches, and private contemplation. Aristotle often taught as he walked the paths and arcades that crossed the property; hence he and his followers were called "Peripatetics," meaning "walking about." At the Lyceum Aristotle systematized the branches of Western philosophy.

Aristotle's approach to knowledge was different from that of Socrates and Plato, in that it was based on observable phenomena. To this end, he collected and classified data: thousands of species of marine life; 158 constitutions of Greek cities. From such a wealth of material, Aristotle established the study of biology and politics. On the basis of his data, he proceeded to theoretical statements. Like the modern manipulator of a database, Aristotle understood that classifying information made certain kinds of knowledge possible.

Upon the basis of classified data about the political structures of the Greek states, Aristotle established in his *Politics* forms of government that are still in use: monarchy, aristocracy, and democracy. Reared when the Greek *polis* was a vital reality, he argued that the city was a community of households, and superior to both family and individual: "For the whole must necessarily be prior to the parts." Individuals are

The Anatomy of Virtue and Vice

Extreme/Excess = Vice	Mean/Moderation = Virtue	Extreme/Deficiency = Vice
Confidence	Courage	Fear
Self-indulgence	Self-control	Insensitivity
Extravagance	Generosity	Stinginess
Vanity	Honor	Small-mindedness
Anger	Gentleness	Apathy
Boastfulness	Truthfulness	Self-deprecation

Source: Aristotle, *Nicomachean Ethics*, 2: 6–7

not unimportant: but what is good "for a nation and for states is nobler and more divine."

On the issues of change, motion, and the universe, Aristotle synthesized in his works on physics and metaphysics the insights of his Presocratic predecessors into a model of his own. Distinguishing matter from form, motion from rest, what was "lower" from what was "higher," being from becoming, cause from effect, he hypothesized a universal system, which was directed by its own laws to rational and worthy ends. It had a creator, too: the one God, life and thought itself, "a living being, eternally most good; and therefore life and a continuous eternal existence belong to God; for that is what God is." (See *Witnesses*, p. 106).

The human mind, according to Aristotelian psychology, shared in the eternity and rationality of the divine. This was not to say that the human being was all mind. Aristotle saw that human life consisted in a balance of good things: citizenship in a just city, the enjoyment in moderation of wealth and leisure and food and sex and friendship and other pleasures. In his *Ethics* he outlined his ideal: that virtue lies in moderation, in the choice of the mean between extremes of behavior. Nevertheless, the final happiness of the human being lies in the contemplation of truth, the absorption of his or her mind into the one eternal and incorporeal mind. Life is the activity of the mind: "Intelligence, above all else, is man."

Here in the fourth century B.C.E. Greek thought reaches its culmination. The *polis* had nurtured an explosion of intellectual life. The result was the elevation of reason as the one distinctively human quality. Over four centuries, Greek minds had explored the meaning of human existence, wandering far from inherited myths and memories to create vast systems of thought which have since then been modified and criticized but never cast aside.

These systems of thought endured, but the world of the *polis* was dying. In 323 B.C.E., Alexander died and Athens reverberated with anti-Macedonian feeling—boding ill for Aristotle, with his Macedonian connections. On the verge of being charged with the same crime of "impiety" that had threatened Anaxagoras and killed Socrates, he fled to the Macedonian stronghold of Chalkis—saving the Athenians from the charge, he commented wryly, of sinning a second time against philosophy. The next year he died. In this same year Demosthenes, encouraging a Greek revolt, was condemned to death by Alexander's successors, fled Athens, and committed suicide. Hereafter in the Greek-speaking world, the theater would flourish, gymnasia would stand in every city, the verses of Homer and Hesiod would be pounded into the heads of schoolchildren, and philosophers would philosophize. But the greatest era of creation was over.

Conclusion
THE LIFE OF REASON AND THE MEANING OF THE WEST

Pericles called Athens the "school of Hellas." By that statement he meant that his city's advanced and refined culture set a standard for the whole Greek-speaking region. Although Athens dominated Classical culture, other cities also contributed to the astonishing flowering of science and philosophy, poetry and rhetoric, pedagogy and scholarship achieved by Greek civilization. Over the course of four centuries, Greek poets and thinkers had expanded their intellectual world through the elaboration of myth, the exploration of the human condition, and the analysis of the natural and supernatural world about them—the latter analysis resulting in the rejection of the same mythic vision with which the cultural journey began. As a result of this inquiry, by the end of the Classical era the foundations of all subsequent Western thought had been laid.

QUESTIONS TO CONSIDER

1. The Greeks conceived of their gods both as very like humans, and yet as fundamentally unlike humans. How could they hold these seemingly contradictory views?

2. What are the questions that Greek mythology left unanswered and that early Greek science and philosophy tried to resolve?

3. What did ordinary Greek spectators learn from watching tragedies performed? What education or experiences did they share that made it possible for them to understand these complex dramas?

4. How did the comedy of Aristophanes differ from our own conception of comedy? Do you think people you know today would be amused by one of Aristophanes' plays?

5. To what extent is Socrates, who challenged the Sophists, himself a Sophist?

SUGGESTED RESOURCES

Barnes, Jonathan, *The Presocratic Philosophers* (London: Routledge & Kegan Paul, 1982). A survey of Presocratic writings, going from Hesiod to the Atomists, with essays on each major author or school. Contains useful summaries and analyses of Presocratic arguments.

Burkert, Walter, *Greek Religion: Archaic and Classical* (Cambridge, MA: Harvard University Press, 1985). A thorough account of rituals, religious organization, deities, beliefs of Greek religion from the Neolithic to the Classical period. Discusses mystery cults, mythological narratives, philosophical religion, and death ritual.

Easterling, P. E., and J. V. Muir, eds. *Greek Religion and Society* (Cambridge, MA: Harvard University Press, 1985). A thoughtful, wide-ranging collection of essays on the cultural meaning of Greek religion. Discusses poetry, death beliefs, temples and other sites of worship, religious festivals, divination, art, and the challenge to Greek religion posed by the Sophists.

Garland, Robert, *Introducing New Gods: The Politics of Athenian Religion* (Ithaca: Cornell University Press, 1992). Not all gods, or myths, were ancient; here the process is explored by which new gods and their cults were introduced to the surprisingly modern world of fifth-century Athens.

Golden, Mark, *Sport and Society in Ancient Greece* (Cambridge: Cambridge University Press, 1998). A comprehensive study of the purpose of Greek athletics—religious, political, and personal.

Hunt, Peter, *Slaves, Warfare, and Ideology in the Greek Historians* (Cambridge: Cambridge University Press, 1998). Although the Greeks mobilized slave contingents for war, as did many ancient societies, Herodotus and Thucydides tended to overlook their role, which is here rescued from the silence created by anti-slave ideology.

Lateiner, Donald, *The Historical Method of Herodotus* (Toronto: University of Toronto Press, 1992). A sophisticated but accessible study of Herodotus as a creative historian. Discusses his selection and organization of material and structure and patterns of interpretation.

Lefkowitz, Mary R., *Women in Greek Myth* (Baltimore: Johns Hopkins University Press, 1986). Countering recent feminist interpretations of Greek mythology as fiercely misogynist, this amply documented study contends that Greek myths present, in their context, a balanced view of women's personalities and capacities.

Morgan, Catherine, *Athletes and Oracles: The Transformation of Olympia and Delphi in the Eighth Century* B.C. (Cambridge: Cambridge University Press, 1990). A fascinating study of the connection between athletics and religion forged in the early years of the development of Greek culture, which continued to nurture Greek ways of understanding the world into the Hellenistic era.

Pickard-Cambridge, A. W., John Gould, and David M. Lewis, eds. *The Dramatic Festivals of Athens* (Oxford: Clarendon Press of Oxford University Press, 1988). Detailed descriptions of actors, choruses, audiences, and settings of Athenian tragedy, comedy, mime, and song.

Poliakoff, Michael D., *Combat Sports in the Ancient World: Combat, Violence and Culture* (New Haven: Yale University Press, 1987). The Greek gymnasium was a training ground equally for the disparate activities of philosophy and war. Here Poliakoff examines the ways in which Greek athleticism was centrally related to the defensive strategy of the *polis*.

Robb, Kevin, *Literacy and Paideia in Ancient Greece* (Oxford: Oxford University Press, 1994). Fascinating study of how Greek civilization evolved, first before all others in the world, but only slowly over four centuries, from an oral to an alphabetic mode of communication and thought.

Stewart, Andrew, *Art, Desire, and the Body in Ancient Greece* (Cambridge: Cambridge University Press, 1997). Considers the Greek fascination with the naked body as an expression of Greek society and mentality.

Vlastos, Gregory, *Socrates: Ironist and Moral Philosopher* (Ithaca: Cornell University Press, 1991). A riveting, erudite study of Socrates' style and moral philosophy.

Ancient Olympic sports:
http://www.perseus.tufts.edu/Olympics/sports.html

About Sappho and her poetry:
http://www.sappho.com/poetry/historical/sappho.html

Plato's *Dialogues*: discussion, biography, bibliography, links:
http://www.plato.evansville.edu

Aristotle: discussion, biography, bibliography, links:
http://www.knuten.liu.se/~bjoch501/philosophers/ari.html

⦿ Western Civilization Documents CD-ROM

2.3 Historical Methods: Thucydides
2.6 Poetry: Sappho
2.7 Alcaeus
3.1 The Apology from Plato
3.2 Aristotle, Nichomachean Ethics
3.3 Aristotle's Will
3.4 Drama: Antigone
3.5 Pericles' Funeral Oration

PART TWO

THE ORIGINS OF THE WEST

From Roman Dominion to the New Peoples of Europe (300 B.C.E.–1300 C.E.)

Greek dominion over the Mediterranean world, the achievement of Alexander the Great, yielded within two centuries to the sterner domination of Rome. As a republic (c. 500-27 B.C.E.), Rome extended its control over the Mediterranean region, while developing social and political institutions that would endure in the Western world. As an empire, it brought peace and prosperity, at first, to its subjects; later, it increasingly brought exploitation and war.

Before the western zone of the Roman Empire succumbed to invasions by nomadic tribes in 476 C.E., its civilization had matured to embody in art and literature the accumulated vision of the ancient Mediterranean world. And although Roman might had dispersed the Jews of Palestine, Christianity, an offshoot of Judaism, became the official religion of the Empire. As it did so, however, the frontiers, defended by an enormous and non-Roman army, began to fail.

As Germanic tribes settled in the western parts of Europe that were once Roman, a Christianized Rome lived on in the Greek-speaking, eastern zone of the Empire, centered at Constantinople (formerly Byzantium). This eastern Roman or Byzantine Empire endured until 1453. It was then overcome by a Turkish people, the Ottomans, who had adopted the religion and civilization of Islam.

Islam arose in the seventh century C.E., the creation of the Arab prophet Muhammad. Expanding across North Africa and the Middle East, and into Asia and Africa, Islam developed an advanced civilization that built upon the achievements of Greece, India, and China.

As the three successors of Rome (European kingdoms, Byzantium, and Islam) established themselves, other civilizations prospered in Asia, Africa, and the Americas. By the end of the first millennium C.E., the human species had expanded to inhabit the whole of the globe except Antarctica, and advanced civilizations flourished on five out of the seven continents.

5 Our Sea
The Mediterranean World in the Hellenistic and Early Roman Eras, 300–27 B.C.E.

6 Pax Romana
Society, State, and Culture in Imperial Rome, 27 B.C.E.–500 C.E.

7 Pagans, Jews, and Christians
Religions of the Mediterranean World, 500 B.C.E.–500 C.E.

8 After Antiquity
New Peoples of Europe and Other Peoples of the World, 300–1300 C.E.

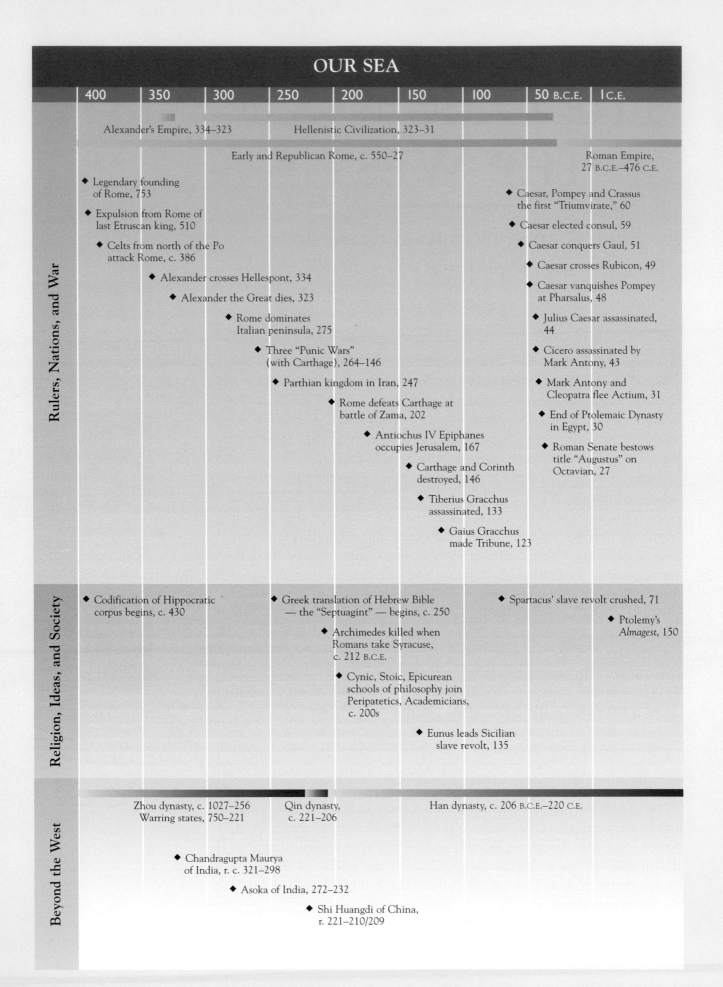

OUR SEA

	400	350	300	250	200	150	100	50 B.C.E.	1 C.E.

Alexander's Empire, 334–323   Hellenistic Civilization, 323–31

Early and Republican Rome, c. 550–27

Roman Empire,
27 B.C.E.–476 C.E.

Rulers, Nations, and War

◆ Legendary founding
of Rome, 753

◆ Expulsion from Rome of
last Etruscan king, 510

◆ Celts from north of the Po
attack Rome, c. 386

◆ Alexander crosses Hellespont, 334

◆ Alexander the Great dies, 323

◆ Rome dominates
Italian peninsula, 275

◆ Three "Punic Wars"
(with Carthage), 264–146

◆ Parthian kingdom in Iran, 247

◆ Rome defeats Carthage at
battle of Zama, 202

◆ Antiochus IV Epiphanes
occupies Jerusalem, 167

◆ Carthage and Corinth
destroyed, 146

◆ Tiberius Gracchus
assassinated, 133

◆ Gaius Gracchus
made Tribune, 123

◆ Caesar, Pompey and Crassus
the first "Triumvirate," 60

◆ Caesar elected consul, 59

◆ Caesar conquers Gaul, 51

◆ Caesar crosses Rubicon, 49

◆ Caesar vanquishes Pompey
at Pharsalus, 48

◆ Julius Caesar assassinated,
44

◆ Cicero assassinated by
Mark Antony, 43

◆ Mark Antony and
Cleopatra flee Actium, 31

◆ End of Ptolemaic Dynasty
in Egypt, 30

◆ Roman Senate bestows
title "Augustus" on
Octavian, 27

Religion, Ideas, and Society

◆ Codification of Hippocratic
corpus begins, c. 430

◆ Greek translation of Hebrew Bible
— the "Septuagint" — begins, c. 250

◆ Archimedes killed when
Romans take Syracuse,
c. 212 B.C.E.

◆ Cynic, Stoic, Epicurean
schools of philosophy join
Peripatetics, Academicians,
c. 200s

◆ Eunus leads Sicilian
slave revolt, 135

◆ Spartacus' slave revolt crushed, 71

◆ Ptolemy's
Almagest, 150

Beyond the West

Zhou dynasty, c. 1027–256
Warring states, 750–221

Qin dynasty,
c. 221–206

Han dynasty, c. 206 B.C.E.–220 C.E.

◆ Chandragupta Maurya
of India, r. c. 321–298

◆ Asoka of India, 272–232

◆ Shi Huangdi of China,
r. 221–210/209

CHAPTER 5

OUR SEA

The Mediterranean World in the Hellenistic and Early Roman Eras

300–27 B.C.E.

the Hellenistic world after the death of Alexander, 323 BCE

Roman Empire, c.100 BCE

KEY QUESTIONS

◆ **Around the Mediterranean:** What happened to the empire of Alexander the Great on his death? What societies could be found on the fringes of the Hellenistic world?

◆ **Becoming Greek:** What impact did Greek civilization have on the native cultures of the Mediterranean region? What effect did these changes have on scholars, scientists, and philosophers?

◆ **Rome: From Village to Nation:** How was Rome able to establish its autonomy? What kind of institutions did it establish once it became free?

◆ **Rome: from West to East:** What advantages did Rome have, and what strategies did it pursue that enabled it to establish dominance on the Italian peninsula, in North Africa, and in Greece?

◆ **Rome: from Republic to Empire:** Why did the Roman Republic fall, and give way to an imperial monarchy?

Caesar's Words and the Roman Sea
Following his successful campaign in Asia Minor in 47 B.C.E., the Roman general Julius Caesar (100–44 B.C.E.) described his achievement in a single sentence: Veni, vidi, vici ("I came, I saw, I conquered"). These three short Latin words convey the unrelenting efficiency of the Roman advance. Over the past three centuries, Rome had grown from village to **cosmopolis**, the chief city of the Mediterranean world. The Roman Empire encircled the Mediterranean sea, once dominated by older Middle Eastern and Greek civilizations. By the opening of the Common Era, that sea was Roman, and the Romans called it mare nostrum, "our sea."

AROUND THE MEDITERRANEAN

Before Caesar, there was Alexander the Great (356–323 B.C.E.); the Roman conquest of the Mediterranean lands rested on the Macedonian Greek conquest. Alexander's swift advance through the eastern Mediterranean conveyed much of the surrounding territory into the hands of Greek-speaking Macedonian rulers, whose struggles and policies dominated the remaining autonomous cities and nations of the region. The leading powers of the western Mediterranean, though independent in their development, were also linked to eastern centers. The whole of the Mediterranean grew together to form a unified civilization, its unity the unexpected and remarkable fruit of a remarkable military conquest.

Hellenistic Civilization and the Eastern Mediterranean

Alexander and his successors reshaped the eastern Mediterranean politically, reorganizing boundaries, displacing rulers, and establishing cities (see Map 5.1). And they did so culturally, planting Greek customs and language. This civilization, beginning with Alexander and extending up to 30 B.C.E. and the onset of Roman domination, is called "**Hellenistic**"—unlike the pre-Alexandrian age known as "Hellenic."

Alexander came to the throne in 336 B.C.E., over the body of his murdered father, Philip II. He commanded a superb army based on the fast and flexible Macedonian phalanx, whose soldiers were equipped with spears longer and deadlier than those of the traditional Greek hoplite. This army consisted of 15,000 disciplined infantrymen, 25,000 light-armed auxiliaries and mercenaries, and 5000 cavalry, Alexander's "Companions." With the army marched a staff of secretaries, sages, and philosophers, servants of a prince who slept each night with the text of the *Iliad* (annotated by his tutor, Aristotle) under his pillow.

In 334 B.C.E., Alexander crossed the Hellespont, the narrow straits between Europe and Asia, through which the Persian King Xerxes had passed, seeking dominion over the Greeks, nearly 150 years before. Now Alexander intended to subdue Persia. In a series of battles from Asia Minor to Mesopotamia—at the Granicus River, at Issus, at Tyre, and at Gaugamela—Greek tactics outweighed greater Persian numbers. When Alexander's troops were checked at the Phoenician city of Tyre, which resisted their siege for seven months, the Persian king Darius III eventually sought an honorable peace. Alexander's highest-ranking general, Parmenion, sent a message that if he were Alexander, he would accept. "And I, too," answered Alexander scornfully, "if I were Parmenion." Alexander went on to take Tyre. By 331 B.C.E., he had conquered all that Darius possessed—including the mother, wife, children, and treasure of that monarch, who was butchered by his own guard.

From 330 to 324 B.C.E., Alexander marched across the Iranian plateau, east to the Himalayas and over the Khyber Pass to the Indus River. He had traversed 22,000 miles (35,420 km.) and won every battle along the route when on June 10, 323 B.C.E., at the age of thirty-two, he died of fever and drink in the heart of his empire. He had made no arrangements for the transfer of power. "Let the job go," he reportedly gasped on his deathbed, "to the strongest."

After Alexander's death, his generals struggled mightily for this prize. They eventually split it into three portions, over which they and their descendants reigned. To the south, a dynasty of kings named Ptolemy ruled Egypt, as the pharaohs had done before. To the east the Seleucid dynasty ruled an empire comprising Syria, Babylon, and Persia. The Antigonids ruled Macedonia to the north, dominating the Greek mainland.

The Ptolemies pressed the 7 million peasants who farmed the Nile valley to the limit of their capacity. Their overseers managed systems of irrigation and drainage, and experimented with new crops, crop rotation, and fertilizers, in order to maximize their master's profits and their own chances for promotion. Some of the profits were creamed off by **tax farmers**, private agents who paid themselves what they could from the sums demanded of the peasants. Sporadic rebellions by the exploited peasants were suppressed by the Ptolemies' Greek mercenaries.

The Ptolemies held monopolies on essential commodities (salt, oil, cloth, papyrus), which they protected with tariff barriers (tax duties on imports and exports). Trade flourished, nevertheless. Ships throughout the Mediterranean docked at the new capital, Alexandria, which was dominated by a 328-foot (100 m) high lighthouse, the Pharos.

Founded by Alexander himself (whose tomb there was a tourist attraction), Alexandria was the world's largest commercial center, teeming with merchants, bureaucrats, and artisans. By the first century B.C.E. it counted one million inhabitants from diverse national, cultural, and racial origins. Here were Syrians and Egyptians, Jews and Greeks, living in elegant town houses and crowded tenements. These surrounded public buildings approached by paved avenues and illuminated at night. The Ptolemies established botanical gardens and a zoo, the world's largest library and first **museum**, or "temple of the Muses," an institute of scientific research.

Hellenistic Egypt thrived longer than its sister kingdoms. At its peak in the third century B.C.E., it declined in the second, dwindled to the status of a Roman dependency, and ceased to be in 30 B.C.E. with the suicide of Cleopatra VII, the last of the Ptolemies.

Embracing more nations and peoples than Egypt, the lands of the Middle East proved a greater challenge to the Seleucids. Still, these Macedonian rulers did manage to impose order on a tumultuous empire and protected the trade caravans that wound their way toward Asia across desert and plateau. Pressed from the east by the Parthians (an Asian people from the Caspian region), and from the west by the Ptolemies, their empire had shrunk by 100 B.C.E. to a slim corridor on the Mediterranean's eastern coast (Syria–Lebanon). A Roman army under the general

Pompey devoured that remnant in 63 B.C.E. Macedonians of the Antigonid dynasty dominated mainland Greeks. Other Greek *poleis* pursued their own civic lives under Antigonid domination until, after 167 B.C.E., Rome seized Macedonian Greece.

Adjacent to the Seleucid and Antigonid realms, several independent kingdoms and city-states emerged. On the coast of Asia Minor, King Attalus I (241–197 B.C.E.) created his city-kingdom at Pergamum, which rivaled Alexandria as a center of culture. Rising from the huddle of commoners' houses, the hallmark buildings of a Greek *polis*, including a theater, a temple, a library, and not one but three gymnasia, climbed the hill to the royal palace complex on the ridge. The plan is shown on p. 114, the ruins on p. 115. There stood the altar of Zeus "the Savior," its 400-foot (122 m.) frieze celebrating the victory of Olympian gods over primal "Giants," and of the Greeks over the barbarians. When the last Attalid king died childless in 133 B.C.E., he willed his prosperous kingdom to Rome, which still had to fight until 129 B.C.E. for it.

The island state of Rhodes flourished nearby, a center for banking and for the study of rhetoric. It acted as the policeman of the eastern Mediterranean, purging the seas of pirates. Over its busy harbor

Map 5.1 *Persia, Greece, and Alexandrian Successors, 334–240* B.C.E.: *The multinational empire of Persia had twice invaded Greece when, in 334 B.C.E., Alexander of Macedon crossed the Hellespont, vanquished Darius III, and dismembered the Persian state in just three years. Upon Alexander's death in 323 B.C.E., his generals and their descendants competed for his empire. By 276 B.C.E., the Antigonid, Seleucid, and Ptolemaic dynasties ruled Macedon and Greece, the Near and Middle East, and Egypt until Roman expansion absorbed them all during the last two centuries B.C.E. By that time, Greek values had already penetrated the whole Mediterranean region. Why was Rome attracted to the eastern Mediterranean lands?*

The City-Kingdom

Plan of Pergamum: Near the coast of Asia Minor, King Attalus I created his city-kingdom at Pergamum (third-second century B.C.E.)—one distinguished enough to challenge Athens and Alexandria for preeminence in architecture, sculpture, and learning. The city contained the buildings of a Greek polis with three gymnasia and domestic buildings lower down the hill and a royal palace complex on the ridge. This plan of the upper city shows the palace, theater, and Altar of Zeus.

towered the Colossus, a statue 120 feet (33 m.) high of the sun god Helios. The earthquake that destroyed the Colossus in 226 B.C.E. also weakened the city. A much later earthquake, in about 155 C.E., ruined it. No longer a commercial center, it became a provincial Roman capital.

In the eastern reaches of Iran (Persia), the Parthians established an independent kingdom in the third century B.C.E.. Grown prosperous from the caravan traffic across the region, the Parthians pushed westward to the Euphrates River in 129 B.C.E., leaving only Syria and Palestine under Seleucid rule.

The interior of Asia Minor, including its Black Sea rim, was never completely tamed: not by Alexander, not by the Seleucids, and not by Rome. Here reigned the semi-Hellenized kings of Bithynia, Pontus, and Cappadocia, and the more isolated Galatians, descendants of Celtic invaders who had crossed from Europe in 278 B.C.E.

The Western Mediterranean and Beyond

While eastern Mediterranean lands had produced one great civilization after another, the inhabitants of the western Mediterranean gathered in tribes and lived in villages, dwarfed by their eastern neighbors.

By the time of the Alexandrian conquest, however, this area had begun to develop. The flourishing centers at Carthage (North Africa) and Etruria (central Italy) were engaged actively in trade, both with the more sophisticated East and with the promising hinterlands of Europe and North Africa. Through these connections, the western Mediterranean, too, was brought into the circle of advancing civilization.

Founded by Phoenicians from Tyre around 800 B.C.E., Carthage soon surpassed its mother city as a commercial center and controlled the north African shore of the Mediterranean. Spanish minerals and other European exports passed through Carthage, which guarded the Mediterranean at its narrow

mid-point, across from Sicily. The light-skinned Berbers of North Africa, the native peasantry exploited by the Carthaginians, were little affected before the latter's arrival by the encroachment of civilization. To the east lay Ptolemaic Egypt, and the burgeoning Kushite kingdom up the Nile valley.

In southern Italy and Sicily, the Greek colonies (called Magna Graecia, or "Greater Greece," by the Romans) struggled for autonomy against Carthage across the sea and Etruria to the north. There, in the region between the Tiber and Arno rivers, the Etruscans by 800 B.C.E. had created a vigorous city-state civilization based on their iron resources, manufacturing skills, and fertile soil. While metalworkers produced tools and ornaments, engineers developed techniques of drainage and construction, anticipating Roman expertise in these areas.

Etruria's cities were federated in a league ruled by a monarch who was also a priest, general, and judge. A committee of magistrates advised him, while prosperous aristocrats dominated a population of **serfs**. The pleasurable lives of those aristocrats are depicted in painting and sculpture. Women participated fully in the revelry and are often shown alongside their husbands, proud and self-sufficient—a posture that scandalized the Greeks. Descent in Etruscan society may even have been traced through the female line.

The life-loving Etruscans were also obsessed with death. They arranged their elaborately sculpted sarcophagi in huge cities of the dead, whence their spirits descended to a grim afterworld inhabited by demons. To ward off the malice of these demons, Etruscan priests called "augurs" were engaged to determine whether conditions were favorable for any venture. They did so by inspecting the livers of sacrificial beasts or by tracking the phenomena of thunder and lightning. They encircled cities and sacred places with ritual boundaries, and occasionally sought to appease angry deities with human sacrifices—the victims obtained through duels of mortal combat.

The origins of Etruscan civilization are uncertain. Had the Etruscans come from Asia Minor, as Herodotus maintained? They were more advanced than their Italian neighbors, and they spoke a different, non-Indo-European language, which has never been fully deciphered. It was written in the Greek alphabet, which the Etruscans borrowed, with other customs, from their Greek trading partners. Among these, the Etruscans adopted many of the Greek anthropomorphic gods—including Zeus, Hera, and Athena. They constructed temples (mostly of wood), adorned on one face, in the Greek style, with columns, pediments, and frieze, but otherwise enclosed, in accord with their own ideal of sacred spaces. Just as the Etruscans learned much from the Greeks, they transmitted many of their traditions to Rome: their gods, the forms of their temples, the elaborate rules of augury, their engineering techniques and architectural innovations (notably the arch), their sacred boundaries and bloody sacrifices, the possibility of female autonomy.

Much of Europe was inhabited by less-advanced farming peoples or nomads: on the Italian peninsula, by the Oscans, Umbrians, Venetians, and Latins; north of the Alps and on the Iberian peninsula, by the Celts; to the east of the Celtic homelands, by the Germans of northern Europe. Still farther east lived the Scythians of the Crimean region, who traded with the Greek settlements on the Black Sea, exchanging their fine metal ornaments and their slaves for manufactured goods.

The Greeks, Persians, Phoenicians, and Etruscans who ringed the Mediterranean all participated in commerce, as did the neighboring peoples on the margins of civilization. Trade boomed in the century following Alexander's death, encouraged by the outpouring of Persian treasure. Greek coins circulated throughout the region, while bankers at Rhodes converted currency and bullion and issued letters of credit. The commodities of ancient commerce—slaves and pots, incense and perfume, spices, ivories, gems, wine and olive oil, copper and tin, papyrus and glass, silver and gold, and above all, wheat—flowed across the Mediterranean. They were carried by ever-larger ships which docked in well-designed harbors funded by adroit entrepreneurs. Caravan routes connected the Nile and the Red Sea, traversed mainly by camel trains. Routes to India, both across Afghanistan and up the Persian Gulf, were heavy with traffic. From at least the second century B.C.E., caravans traveled east and west on the Silk Road.

Not only goods but also people circulated through these prosperous regions. Travel was a popular activity for an adventurous elite, who were equipped with well-written guidebooks. Explorers probed the Caspian Sea and the Indian subcontinent, the shores of the Indian Ocean and Persian Gulf, the islands of the Atlantic, the upper Nile and Sudan regions, and the west coast of Africa. In the fourth century B.C.E., Pytheas of Massalia, a Greek colony (Marseille), circumnavigated distant Britain, encountering icy fog so dense that the elements of nature fused in a nameless mass: "The earth, the sea, and all the elements are held in suspension; and this is a sort of bond to hold all together, which you can neither walk nor sail upon." He had reached, he thought, the end of the inhabited world.

The whole Mediterranean world—European, African, and Asian—was now very nearly one: an **oecumene**. The region tended naturally to unity by its

Pergamum: *This photograph shows a southwesterly view of Pergamum from the top of the theater to the lower town and surrounding terrain. The theater was a prominent building in the upper city and emphasized the theatricality of the whole setting.*

geography, its climate, and its access to the sea. Its political unity was the culmination of the spread of civilization from the nuclei of Mesopotamia and Egypt in the third millennium B.C.E. Between Alexander's death in 323 B.C.E. and Cleopatra's in 30 B.C.E., it became culturally unified as well.

BECOMING GREEK

The Hellenistic civilisation that flourished in the Mediterranean *oecumene* was characterized by the vigorous growth of city life and an enormous outpouring of literary, philosophical, and scientific work. Eventually, when the Hellenistic states succumbed to

Rome over the last two centuries B.C.E., the culture of that new participant in the world of nations was indelibly stamped by the ideas and forms of Hellenistic civilization.

Hellenistic Cities

During this period the Greek city entered a new phase of development. Political life proceeded on a local level as it had before—though the loss of autonomy and the constant surveillance by Macedonian overlords left the citizens to debate only such peripheral issues as the funding of theater construction or the hiring of schoolteachers.

Beyond the boundaries of the Greek homeland, new Greek cities sprang up. Alexander founded as many as seventy cities, while the Seleucids founded nearly eighty colonies, settled by Greek subjects. These new communities were named for towns in faraway Macedonia (Pella, Edessa, Amphipolis) or for the conquerors (Alexandria, Seleucia, and Antioch—of which there were several, named for Seleucid kings called Antiochus). Storehouses of Greek culture suspended in alien territory, these cities possessed many familiar institutions: councils and assemblies and magistrates, the trappings of democracy. A royal governor represented the monarchy and limited political activity to the purely local level.

Professional architects planned the new cities, following the principles introduced by the fifth-century Greek town planner Hippodamus. The new planned cities, in

Etruscans at War and at Leisure

Men at war (above): Fed by contacts with Greek cities and the eastern Mediterranean region, Etruscan art conveyed deep emotion. This handle of an Etruscan bronze chest from Praeneste, fourth century B.C.E., is composed of two soldiers carrying their dead comrade between them—the functional verticals and horizontals serving to emphasize both the contrast and the links between the survivors and the fallen. (National Museum, Villa Giulia, Rome)

Man and wife: In this Etruscan sarcophagus (coffin) from Veii, c. 520 B.C.E., a man and his wife recline together on their marriage bed, the woman wrapped in her husband's protective presence. The sculpted bed forms the lid of their sarcophagus, so that their love and their death are combined in one monument. (National Museum, Villa Giulia, Rome)

HOW MANY?

City Sizes

Sumerian	10–40,000
Indus	c. 40,000
Athens	100–200,000
Carthage	100–200,000
Rome	c. 1 million
Alexandria	c. 1 million
Provincial cities	10–20,000

contrast to the older, haphazardly constructed *poleis*, were organized in a rectangular grid of streets encompassing all the key components of city life: *agora* and temple, gymnasia and theaters, residences, harbors, and docks. These impressive monuments, set in their checkerboard frame, proclaimed throughout the region the dominance of Greek culture.

The major Hellenistic cities were multiethnic, multiracial, and multicultural. Amid such diversity, participation in the *oecumene* displaced identification based on city or nation. Place of origin and native customs mattered less than wealth, which mattered a great deal. An elite of leisured town dwellers, their wealth derived from land or investments, funded the buildings and temples, games and theatrical performances that graced urban life. Beneath them in the social hierarchy thrived merchants and bankers, physicians and intellectuals, and skilled artisans. Members of these trades and professions, as well as groups of foreign nationals or coreligionists (i.e. worshipers of the same gods) formed associations providing companionship and social benefits from pooled funds.

Alongside the rich and well-heeled lived masses of the poor and unfree, whose conditions worsened in the centuries after Alexander. Daily wages declined for the ordinary laborer, and slaves and serfs were subjected to new burdens. Peasant and slave revolts disturbed city and countryside and the sleep of monarchs. While Hellenistic society softened national and racial distinctions to an unprecedented degree, the gap between rich and poor became all the more pronounced.

Women in the Hellenistic World

Upper-class women enjoyed unusual freedom in the Hellenistic city—especially in Egypt, where, although they were not considered equal to men, women enjoyed greater respect than in other parts of the ancient Middle East. Cosmopolitan influences eroded the traditional Greek attitude toward women. Greek society was previously based on the *oikos* (household) and the *polis*, in both of which women played a subordinate role. In the Hellenistic world of autonomous individuals, those constraints no longer operated.

In particular, the consorts of rulers now acquired a high status. Among the Macedonian queens whose personalities influenced events was Olympias, the mother of Alexander, executed for political maneuverings. Other Macedonian queens supported religious innovations, founding cults and building temples. Most of these queens owed their station to marriage. However, the most famous of them, Cleopatra VII (69–30 B.C.E.), became queen of Egypt in her own right, first sharing the throne, successively, with two of her brothers (whom she married in turn, as was the custom). Seductive and clever, she secured her own sovereignty through alliances with Julius Caesar and Mark Antony, Roman general and statesman who fought under Caesar in Gaul (54–50 B.C.E.).

Several women won fame as poets, artists, and philosophers during the Hellenistic age. Late in the fourth century B.C.E., Erinna of Telos composed an exquisite 300-line poem, later entitled *The Distaff*, in memory of a friend who had recently married and died. The first well-authenticated female poet since Sappho, she managed to achieve a rudimentary education. Eurydice of Hierapolis (western Anatolia) somehow gained her education: already a mother "of young and lusty sons," she "by her diligence attained to learn letters, wherein lies buried all our lore," as we read in her epitaph.

Elite women were avid readers of love poetry and romances, and attended theatrical performances of the genre called "New Comedy" (to distinguish it from the "Old Comedy" of Aristophanes), in which the dilemmas of ordinary private life took center stage. The playwright Menander (c. 343–c. 292 B.C.E.) wove play after play around such matters as dowry and inheritance, marital and extramarital sex.

Yet patriarchal families still limited women's options, and those limits began in infancy. Hellenistic families were small, often numbering only one or two sons, and rarely including more than one daughter. That pattern suggests that infanticide, especially of females, was widely practiced. As one contemporary observed, "Everyone, even a poor man, raises a son; everyone, even a rich man, exposes a daughter." Another instructed his wife by letter: "If you chance to bear a child and it is a boy, let it be; if it is a girl, expose it." Of the families who migrated to Miletus in Asia Minor from Athens around 228–200 B.C.E., statistics survive for 79; among them were 118 sons and 28 daughters. Delphic inscriptions referring to some 600 families and dating from the next century reveal that only six reared more than one daughter. The absent women form a bleak, silent chorus on the Hellenistic stage.

118

WITNESSES

Roman Women

One of the first expressions that history offers of the organized protest of women against government is reported here by Livy, who describes the demonstration of wealthy Roman women against the restrictions upon them under the Oppian Law, and the speech made by the revered statesman, Cato the Elder, urging against any accommodation to women's taste for luxury, and presumptions against the state (195 B.C.E.).

During the Second Punic War, men and women were barred from the ostentatious display of wealth. When the war ended in 201 B.C.E., rich men resumed their habits of luxury, but women continued to be barred by the Oppian Law from that behavior. Six years later, they protested:

The matrons, whom neither counsel nor shame nor their husbands' orders could keep at home, blockaded every street in the city and every entrance to the Forum. As the men came down to the Forum, the matrons besought them to let them, too, have the luxuries they had enjoyed before. ...

The consul Marcus Porcius Cato (the Elder) spoke against their plea for the repeal of the Oppian law, and warned against female claims for sovereignty:

If each man of us, fellow citizens, had established that the right and authority of the husband should be held over the mother of his own family, we should have less difficulty with women in general; now, at home our freedom is conquered by female fury, here in the Forum it is bruised and trampled upon, and because we have not contained the individuals, we fear the lot. ... Our ancestors did not permit women to conduct any—not even private—business without a guardian; they wanted them to be under the authority of parents, brothers, or husbands. Even now let them snatch at the government and meddle in the Forum and our assemblies. ... If they are victorious now, what will they not attempt? As soon as they begin to be your equals, they will have become your superiors.

Other speakers took the other position, and the women persisted in their protest. The Oppian Law was repealed.
(Livy, 34:1–8; eds., trs. M. R. Lefkowitz, M. B. Fant, 1982)

The Mixing of Cultures

Greek colonists and expatriates transplanted their own way of life into foreign lands. In particular, the world of the eastern Mediterranean was transformed by the Greek rituals of athletic exercise and the simplified but still powerful Greek language. At the same time, voyaging Greeks grafted some of the political and religious institutions of the East onto their own cultural traditions.

In gymnasia constructed in the cities of the eastern Mediterranean, men exercised in the nude, as they had in Athens or Corinth, and barbarian newcomers who wished to attach themselves to the Greek elite were pressed to adopt that custom—a sign of Hellenistic culture. The gymnasium developed into a new form: originally merely an open field, it was now a complex of exercise rooms, baths, and stadium.

The native inhabitants also needed to learn Greek—the common tongue, or **koine**, of the Mediterranean world, which had largely displaced the earlier Aramaic language. Its distribution is shown on Map 5.2 below. In Egypt, peasants continued to speak their ancestral language, but Greek was used among

Map 5.2 Transnational Languages of the Mediterranean World, 1000 B.C.E.–300 C.E.: The hybrid cultures of the ancient Mediterranean world adopted three successive languages as a means of communicating across political boundaries: Aramaic until the Alexandrian conquest; Greek until the Roman; and Latin until the third century C.E., when it would yield again to Greek in the eastern Mediterranean while flourishing in western Europe until c. 1800 C.E. Why was Greek language dominance able to outlast the Roman conquest?

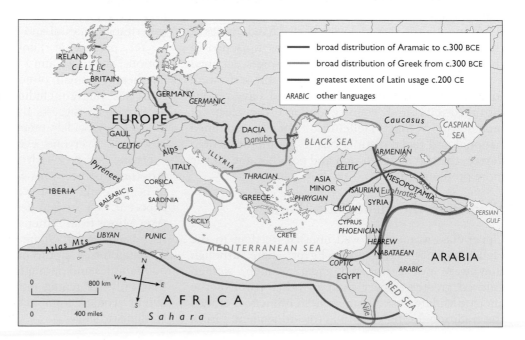

the elites. In the first century B.C.E., the Roman author Cicero remarked that Greek was known everywhere: it was read "in nearly all nations."

Hellenization also entailed the translation into Greek of works of literature of the subject cultures and the writing of their history in that language. The priest Manetho of Egypt (fl. 280 B.C.E.) wrote a Greek history of his nation that remains an authoritative record of its dynasties and rulers. The Babylonian priest Berossus did the same for his nation. Around 250 B.C.E., the ruler of Egypt is said to have commissioned in Alexandria a board of Jewish scholars (seventy, as legend has it) to translate scriptures into Greek. The text is the *Septuagint*, or "the book of seventy." While such writers remained Egyptian or Babylonian or Jewish, they were now also Greeks.

The elite members of conquered peoples gave their children Greek names, wore Greek clothing, and adopted Greek models for ritual and worship. At the same time, Greek leaders borrowed customs from the people they ruled. The result was a hybrid civilization defined by Greek language and culture, but open to the diversity resident in native populations.

Among the customs adopted by the conquerors was the characteristic eastern form of government: absolute monarchy. Although the Macedonians had always lived under a monarchy, they found alien the veneration of kings practiced in the lands they occupied. Nevertheless, Alexander quickly adopted this custom, assuming the Persian title "king of kings" and the Egyptian "pharaoh." From 327 B.C.E. onward, he ordered his visitors to prostrate themselves before him, in the Persian custom; and in 324 B.C.E. he announced to the Greeks of the mainland the news of his deification—where it was received with consternation. "If Alexander wishes to be a god, we grant that he is a god," read a Spartan decree. "Let him be the son of Zeus and of Poseidon too, if he wishes it," snapped Demosthenes. After his death, Alexander was worshiped as a god by Greeks and Asians alike.

Greek expatriates readily acquired the religious beliefs of their hosts—the Olympians having failed as deities because they were too much like mortals, because they offered no chance of salvation, because their authority had been challenged by the speculations of the philosophers and the criticism of the Sophists, because they found no worshipers when uprooted from the *polis*. In contrast, the deities of the Middle East promised life and renewal. The dead and reborn gods of the ancient Caananites still lived in the cults of the Phoenicians, Syrians, and Egyptians.

The process of syncretism, or blending of diverse religious traditions, intensified in the Hellenistic period (see Chapter 7). The Greek Zeus became identified with the Egyptian Amon-Re and the Babylonian Baal, while the Egyptian mother-goddess Isis stood for several female deities of the Middle East and for the Olympians Hera and Demeter. The Macedonian pharaoh Ptolemy I (d. 282 B.C.E.) concocted a new god, "Sarapis," a version of the Egyptian Osiris. The temple of Sarapis in Alexandria, which housed a mechanical model of the god, was in its time a huge attraction.

Neither the old gods of the East nor the Olympians of the Greeks could win the allegiance of the Jews. Released from their Babylonian exile in 538 B.C.E., they had returned to their homeland, their religious faith matured by the experience of exile. There they rebuilt the temple in Jerusalem and forged the textual and ritual foundations of the Jewish religion. Rigorous followers of scriptural law, they shunned alien customs. Above all, they feared losing their young to the seductive customs of the Greeks, epitomized by the gymnasium and its idealization of the nude male human form.

The Seleucid King Antiochus IV Epiphanes ("the god made manifest") (d. 164 B.C.E.) was determined to bring Judaea (as the Greeks called the Jewish homeland) to heel and compel the Jews to accept Greek cultural supremacy. Supported by Jewish Hellenists, he occupied Jerusalem in 167 B.C.E. Antiochus intended to establish a gymnasium and school in Jerusalem and to rename the city after himself, Antioch. He ordered the Jews to eat pork (prohibited by their law) and forbade them to possess the Torah, their sacred scriptures, or circumcise their sons (a time-honored custom signifying their membership in the Jewish community). He set up a statue of Zeus in the temple, and burned there in sacrifice an offering (to the Jews detestable) of pigs: the "abomination of desolation."

In response, Mattathias and his sons, of the priestly family of the Hasmoneans, took to the mountains with a handful of supporters to oppose the Seleucid regime with "guerrilla" tactics. In December 164 B.C.E., Mattathias' eldest son Judah, called Maccabee ("the Hammer"), celebrated the first Hanukkah: a Jewish festival created (without scriptural authority, some later complained) to mark the recovery and purification of the temple. Judah was slain, and his brothers felled in turn until the survivor, Simon, reached an agreement in 142 B.C.E. with Antiochus' successor, Demetrius II, after Simon became High Priest. Judaea was granted a fragile autonomy in the Seleucid empire.

Books, Science, and Philosophy

While some Jews struggled against Hellenization and others made their peace with it, educated Greek elites strove to extend and preserve their cultural heritage. The Hellenistic era saw an explosion of creative work in literary and technical fields and the creation of institutions in which the products of the human imagination could be studied, reflected upon, and transmitted to later generations.

Such an institution was the library at Alexandria, which held a matchless collection, properly catalogued, of more than 500,000 papyrus rolls (the bound book wasn't yet invented), and housed a community of scholars who studied the literary works of Greece. The poet Timon of Phlius (c. 320–c. 230 B.C.E.), mockingly described their enterprise: while consuming the wealth of Egypt, he wrote, they "scribbled" on papyrus "in the bird-coop of the Muses."

Pergamum's library (about 200,000 rolls) ranked second to Alexandria's. Egyptian rulers were so envious of its collection that they banned the export of papyrus to Pergamum. That city's scribes learned to prepare sheepskin to make writing material. Known as "Pergamene paper," or parchment, this would remain in use in Europe throughout the Middle Ages.

Hellenistic artists created huge monuments in honor of their monarchs. They also provided the aristocrats and middle classes with more modest sculptures and paintings to adorn their gardens and houses. Whereas Classical artists had aimed to depict ideal beauty, their Hellenistic successors depicted exactly what they saw: the ordinary and the weird, the beautiful and the deformed; human bodies asleep, at play, drunk, or dying. An example is shown below. Even wealthy patrons learned to accept realistic portraits which revealed defects.

The scholars of the Hellenistic world preserved the intellectual heritage of antiquity for later generations. They studied, commented upon, and edited the Classical Greek texts and created supplementary texts such as chronologies, dictionaries, bibliographies, and textbooks. They divided each of Homer's epics into the twenty-four books that still constitute modern editions. They compiled the works of poets and playwrights and drew up lists of the "best" works. Their copying and recopying of these chosen texts ensured their later survival. With few exceptions, those that did not win the attention of Hellenistic scholars are lost to readers today.

The heart of a Hellenistic education lay in the reading of the corpus of literary works prepared by these scholars—a different enterprise from Greek education in the Classical era. It was more strictly literary, though it took place in the traditional setting (the gymnasium), which now functioned more like a modern school. In alien lands, the institution of the school preserved Greek culture and transmitted it to subsequent

Lysippos, Apoxyomenos,
c. 320 B.C.E.

generations of children, who were enduringly stamped with the Greek world-view.

In these schools, children (including some girls) aged seven to fourteen learned letters, syllables, and words, by repetition. Older boys aged fourteen to eighteen mastered the core curriculum of Classical works. Graduates who wished for a higher education (there being as yet no university) traveled to Athens, Rhodes, or Cnidus (in Asia Minor) or Cos (in the Aegean Sea) to study philosophy, rhetoric, or medicine with the scholars and physicians in those centers.

While Hellenistic teachers perpetuated knowledge, Hellenistic scientists, mathematicians, and physicians were engaged in expanding it (see *Who's Who*, p. 122). Aristotle had established the method of systematic observation that first made science possible. Now increased contacts with the "barbarian" sciences of Babylon and Egypt stimulated Greek thinkers, many of whom enjoyed the patronage of monarchs. In this environment, science prospered in the two centuries after Alexander.

Hellenistic Science The greatest scientific achievement was in astronomy. Eudoxus of Cnidus (c. 390–c. 340 B.C.E.) showed that the planets moved in circular patterns on distinctive paths. Heraclides of Pontus (c. 390–310 B.C.E.) learned that the earth rotated on its own axis, and that Mercury and Venus both revolved around the sun. Aristarchus of Samos (c. 310–230 B.C.E.) proposed that the planets revolved around a fixed sun,

The Hellenistic Vision

A range of feeling: Like Etruscan art, Hellenistic art expressed strong emotions—but the former represented the daily range of sentiments in a restrained key, while the latter tended to the loud representation of extreme feeling, often of unusual persons or dramatic moments. The Roman copy of a bronze Greek original of an athlete scraping his arm (left), the Apoxyomenos by Lysippos, c. 320 B.C.E., can be contrasted with earlier representations in Greek art (see pp. 88, 92). The later artists highlighted individual personalities in a manner the earlier ones avoided and indeed would not have understood. (left: Vatican Museums, Rome) beyond which stood fixed stars. His views lost out to the more geocentric, or earth-centered, hypothesis. Centuries later, Nicholas Copernicus (1473–1543) would revive Aristarchus' theory and open the doors of modern science (see Chapter 17).

The distant fixed stars posited by Aristarchus interested Hipparchus of Nicaea in Anatolia (fl. 161–126 B.C.E.), who produced a catalogue of 850 of them and "left the heavens as a legacy to all mankind." Hipparchus calculated within a second of the modern figure the length of the lunar month and contributed to the bizarre readings of planetary motion by which Hellenistic scientists tried to "save the phenomena"—that is, to explain erratic planetary motion so as to preserve the principle of the earth's centrality. Hipparchus' work would be continued by Ptolemy (c. 90–168 C.E.), whose codification of that geocentric system (in the *Almagest*, around 150 C.E.) was orthodox astronomy until Copernicus.

The mathematician Euclid (c. 325–250 B.C.E.) outlined the fundamentals of plane geometry in his *Elements*, which would remain the standard text for the next 2000 years. Eratosthenes of Cyrene in modern Libya (c. 285–194 B.C.E.) applied mathematics to the study of geography. He calculated the circumference of the earth (which he knew to be round) at a nearly accurate 25,000 miles (40,250 km.). His plan of the world is illustrated in *Windows On*, p. 123.

The mathematician and engineer Archimedes of Syracuse (c. 287–211 B.C.E.) calculated the value of *pi* (the ratio of the circumference of a circle to its diameter) and invented integral calculus. In a more practical vein, he invented the water screw—a device consisting of a screw inside a cylinder—which made possible the irrigation of dry land and the pumping of ship holds or mines, and also the compound pulley, which powered various other devices. Archimedes was famous for his role in the defense of Syracuse against the Romans in 213–211 B.C.E. It was his gamut of machines that kept the Romans at bay, including a system of mirrors that intensified the sun's rays and caused them to set the invaders' ships afire. When the city was taken, the command was given to take Archimedes alive. But he had already

been murdered by a common soldier, annoyed by the scientist's imperturbability in the presence of Roman power. In accordance with his own wishes, Archimedes' grave was marked by a cylinder enclosing a sphere, accompanied by an inscription defining the ratio between their two surfaces and volumes—a discovery he considered his greatest achievement.

Other Hellenistic scientists studied the ills of the human body. In the second half of the fifth century B.C.E., Hippocrates of Cos (c. 460–c. 358 B.C.E.) had pioneered the science of medicine based on meticulous observation and careful record-keeping. From about 430 to 330 B.C.E., his followers produced what moderns call the Hippocratic Corpus: a collection of about sixty treatises on surgery and gynecology, dietetics and epilepsy, diagnostics, and more.

Hellenistic physicians extended the work of the Hippocratic school. Herophilus of Chalcedon in northwestern Anatolia (c. 330–260 B.C.E.) dissected corpses to explore the sensory nervous system, understood the function of the brain, learned that the arteries carried blood, and identified the ovaries of females. Erasistratus (c. 315–240 B.C.E.) from Ceos in the Aegean described the function of the heart, distinguished between sensory and motor nerves, and challenged the Hippocratic theory that health was governed by the interaction of four qualities, or "humors"—a theory that still prevailed for many centuries. Despite the empirical work of physicians, ordinary people placed their trust in magic, not science, and illness was treated with potions, charms, and prayers to the healing god Asclepius.

Hellenistic Philosophy Philosophy was still centered in Athens: the birthplace of democracy, now in its twilight years the home of philosophers. The followers of Aristotle (called "Peripatetics," meaning "walking about," based on Aristotle's habit of teaching while strolling around the Lyceum school) and Plato (called "Academics," after Plato's founding of the Academy), continued their studies until Emperor Justinian closed both schools in the sixth century C.E. Aristotle's student Theophrastus of Eresus in Anatolia (371–288 B.C.E.)

A Gaul slays himself over his dying wife: *Desperate action and emotion reach a climax in this marble copy of a Hellenistic group, late third century B.C.E., portraying a Gaul committing suicide rather than surrender. The Gaul has already killed his wife to prevent her becoming a slave.* (Museo delle Terme, Rome)

Hellenistic and Roman Authors, Scientists, Philosophers

ASTRONOMERS

Eudoxus (c. 390–c. 340 B.C.E.) claimed planets move in circular patterns on distinctive paths.

Heraclides (c. 390–310 B.C.E.) showed that earth rotates on own axis.

Aristarchus (c. 310–230 B.C.E.) proposed that planets revolve around fixed sun.

Hipparchus (fl. 161–126 B.C.E.) compiled catalog of stars.

MATHEMATICIANS

Euclid (c. 325–250 B.C.E.) outlined fundamentals of plane geometry.

Eratosthenes of Cyrene (285–194 B.C.E.) applied mathematics to study of geography.

Archimedes of Syracuse (287–211 B.C.E.) calculated value of *pi* and invented calculus.

SCIENTISTS

Hippocrates of Cos (c. 460–c. 358 B.C.E.) pioneered science of medicine based on observation.

Herophilus (c. 330–260 B.C.E.) studied nervous system.

Erasistratus (c. 315–240 B.C.E.) described function of heart.

PHILOSOPHERS

Diogenes (412–323 B.C.E.) founded Cynic school.

Epicurus (341–270 B.C.E.) founded Epicurean school.

Zeno (335–263 B.C.E.) founded Stoic school.

WRITERS

Plautus (254–184 B.C.E.) comedy playwright.

Terence (c. 195–159 B.C.E.) comedy playwright.

Cicero (106–43 B.C.E.) orator and author.

---

pioneered the scientific approach that characterized the later Peripatetics. The thinking of the Academy evolved from Plato's idealism, to a skepticism that refused to accept virtually any statement as unarguably true, to a mysticism ("Neoplatonism") based on the primacy of the Light, the Good, the One—easily identified with the Christian God or with the principal deity of some pagan religions. Skepticism also developed independently, its views summed up in the writings of Sextus Empiricus in the second century C.E.

The philosophers Diogenes, Epicurus, and Zeno founded respectively the new Cynic, Epicurean, and Stoic schools. Diogenes of Sinope in northern Anatolia (c. 412–323 B.C.E.) proposed to live without possessions or responsibilities, in order to avoid the hypocrisy of the merchant or politician; in short, he lived "like a dog" (for that is what "cynic" means), and advised others to do so too.

Epicurus (341–270 B.C.E.) proposed that people should pursue what they were inclined to pursue anyway—pleasure. But that true pleasure consisted in tranquility, intellectual pursuits, the company of friends. All these were to be found in withdrawing from the maelstrom of society. Safe from the torments of competition and desire, the Epicurean sage was also safe from the more distant sources of unease: the fear of the gods, the fear of death. "Death, the most terrifying of evils," he wrote, "is nothing to us; for as long as we exist death is not present with us, and when death comes then we no longer exist."

Just as death lost its fearsomeness for the Epicurean, the cosmos itself threatened no ills. It was nothing but a flash of hurtling atoms let loose in a void (here Epicurus was influenced by Democritus), without malice because without meaning. The gods, if they existed at all, did nothing. Realizing these truths, the individual could achieve a tranquil state marked by the absence of distress and desire. Epicurus defined this ideal in 300 volumes of tortured prose, lost except for fragments, and preached it to his disciples in his pleasant Athenian garden.

The most successful of the schools of Hellenistic philosophy, Stoicism, presented a moral ideal, offered a cosmic theory, and championed the dignity of the human spirit and unity of the human race. Its founder, Zeno (335–263 B.C.E.), and his followers urged the individual to seek his own destiny and happiness, as Epicurus did—but to do so by pursuing "virtue," the habitual practice of acts worthy of a true gentleman, or statesman. The steady cultivation of virtue would allow the good man to rise above all emotions through the greater development of the inner self.

According to Zeno, that inner self contained a divine spark, a fragment of the fire that governed the cosmos, a force identified with reason. The wise man who lived according to virtue also lived in harmony with the cosmos, ordered and purposeful in its design. Since each individual possessed that spark initially to the same extent, no person was by nature greater than any other; conversely, no person could be considered, by nature, a slave. All human beings were equal, and

The Worlds of Eratosthenes and Archimedes

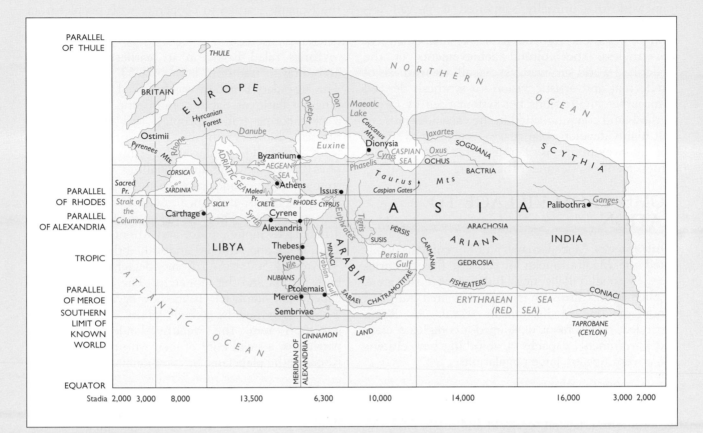

PARALLEL OF THULE

THULE

BRITAIN

EUROPE

Hyrcanian Forest

Ostimii

Pyrenees Mts.

Rhone

Danube

Dnieper

Don

Maeotic Lake

Caucasus Mts

NORTHERN OCEAN

SCYTHIA

Jaxartes

SOGDIANA

Euxine

Dionysia

CASPIAN SEA

Oxus

OCHUS

BACTRIA

Byzantium

AEGEAN SEA

Phaselis

Cyrus

CORSICA

Sacred Pr.

SARDINIA

ADRIATIC SEA

Malea

Athens

Pr. CRETE

Issus

Taurus

Mts

Caspian Gates

PARALLEL OF RHODES

Strait of the Columns

SICILY

RHODES

CYPRUS

ASIA

Palibothra

Ganges

PARALLEL OF ALEXANDRIA

Carthage

Cyrene

Syrtis

Euphrates

Tigris

PERSIS

ARACHOSIA

ARIANA

INDIA

Alexandria

LIBYA

Thebes

Syene

Nile

MINACI

Arabian Gulf

ARABIA

Persian Gulf

SUSIS

CARMANIA

GEDROSIA

TROPIC

NUBIANS

PARALLEL OF MEROE

Ptolemais

Meroe

ATLANTIC OCEAN

SABAEI

CHATRAMOTITAE

FISHEATERS

ERYTHRAEAN SEA (RED SEA)

CONIACI

SOUTHERN LIMIT OF KNOWN WORLD

Sembrivae

CINNAMON

LAND

TAPROBANE (CEYLON)

MERIDIAN OF ALEXANDRIA

EQUATOR

Stadia 2,000 3,000 8,000 13,500 6,300 10,000 14,000 16,000 3,000 2,000

Eratosthenes, plan of the world, c. 215 B.C.E.

At the height of Hellenistic civilization in the third century B.C.E., when infant Rome was embarking on its first foreign ventures, scientists made remarkable progress toward understanding their world in mathematical and mechanical terms—progress that would soon slow down and not resume again in the Western world for eighteen centuries. Among those scientists were Eratosthenes of Alexandria, whose plan of the world (above) testifies to his capacity to extend his thoughts beyond the obvious and tangible, and Archimedes, bold mathematician and inventor of many machines, whose discovery of the principle of specific gravity is alluded to here in this later German woodcut. Legendarily, it was when Archimedes was in his bathtub, and noted how his body displaced the water, that the solution for the problem came to him.

What practical use could be made of Archimedes' discovery?

Archimedes in his bath, sixteenth-century German woodcut

To continue your investigation of this topic, please go to www.prenhall.com/king for the related **WINDOWS** on the **WEB** activity

society should recognize their universal partnership, or "brotherhood." Zeno delivered these admonitions from the *stoa*, or arcaded, free-standing porch in the *agora* at Athens—whence the term "Stoic."

While Hellenistic culture flourished, the political framework that initially supported it proved less durable. Alexander's empire began to dissolve as soon as he died. By 100 B.C.E., it had collapsed. Nevertheless, the cultural achievements of the Hellenized world survived. Above all, its synthesis of intellectual and artistic vision—a synthesis derived from earlier civilizations but systematized by Greek methods and communicated in the capacious prose of that highly developed language—remained to stimulate later civilizations. Perhaps this was the true achievement of Alexander the Great.

ROME: FROM VILLAGE TO NATION

While Greeks, Macedonians, and Phoenicians dominated the Mediterranean in the last five centuries B.C.E., a small village near Italy's west coast grew, rebelled against Etruscan masters, devoured Italy, and conquered the Mediterranean world. As Rome expanded, the Romans developed a complex society and government, capable of absorbing new citizens and governing very large populations.

Early Days

According to a legend, very old and surely false, the city of Rome was originally founded by the Trojan refugee Aeneas, son of the goddess Venus by the noble Anchises. Two of his descendants, twin baby boys named Romulus and Remus, were abandoned in the wilderness by a jealous uncle who usurped their inheritance. There, they were nurtured by a she-wolf and survived to establish the city on one of the seven hills clustered near the easiest ford of the river Tiber. Romulus killed his brother Remus, gave his name to the settlement, and became its first king.

So much for legend. At about the time Romulus is supposed to have killed Remus, in 753 B.C.E., a village community formed around the Palatine Hill, one of seven on which the city would be built. Near the base of this hill was an open space called the Forum, where cattle grazed and men assembled to decide the relative merits of war or peace. Other communities developed on the remaining hills (see Map 5.3). By about 600 B.C.E., the seven hills had coalesced into a single town. Its inhabitants now thought of themselves as Romans, distinct from neighboring Latin tribes from whom they originated and whose language they spoke. Their small city was situated in Italy's central triangular plain, called Latium, which is formed by the Apennine Mountains as they wander from the Tyrrhenian Sea on the

west coast to the Adriatic on the east, south to the toe of the Italian boot and across the straits to Sicily. Unlike the Greek *poleis*, which developed in isolation created by the physical barriers of mountains and sea, Rome lay exposed to its neighbors. Consequently, the Romans learned to cooperate with peoples from other nearby cities—while learning also how to defend themselves.

Kings ruled Rome in its earliest days: seven, according to tradition, between 753 and 509 B.C.E. The legendary Romulus was followed by three other kings of Latin or Sabine origin (the Sabines being a neighboring Italian people), and then by three Etruscan kings. From the Etruscans, the Romans learned to build temples and worship anthropomorphic gods (gods with human qualities and form); how to map the skies and inspect the prophetic livers of sacrificed beasts; and how to drain swamps and organize magistracies. They erected on the Capitoline Hill a temple to Jupiter, Juno, and Minerva (the Greek Zeus, Hera, and Athena) and walled their city.

Around 500 B.C.E., Rome detached itself from both Etruria and the monarchy. The Etruscans were expelled, or simply left. Rome now became a republic: a state governed by a body of its citizens. Those governors were the wealthy landowners, called **patricians**, a small elite of men who ruled the other Romans, the **plebeians**, or commoners.

Family and Society in Early Rome

Roman society was rooted in the ancient social organizations of tribe, clan, and family, which subordinated women, children, and slaves to one dominant male householder.

A Roman was a member of a tribe and a clan as well as of a family. Clan identification remained strong in Rome into the late Republic, at least among the landowning classes. The name of a Roman male citizen had three components: the name of the individual (Gaius, Quintus, Publius, etc.); the name of the clan (Julius, Cornelius, Fabius); and the name of the family within the clan. Gaius Julius Caesar, the general and dictator, had the personal name Gaius, the clan name Julius, and family name Caesar.

Identification with the clan was fostered by the worship of ancestors, the basis of Roman religion (see Chapter 7). The father of each family was the priest of the family cult, which venerated the ancestral spirits (a patrician holding the heads of his ancestors is shown on p. 127). Wax masks or (later) sculpted busts of these forebears were displayed in the household, adjacent to the central hall or *atrium*. These were silent participants in household rites and were carried in religious processions to honor the dead and cement their bonds with the living. When a Roman noble died, male family members went in a procession to the funeral wearing these ancestral masks, and in

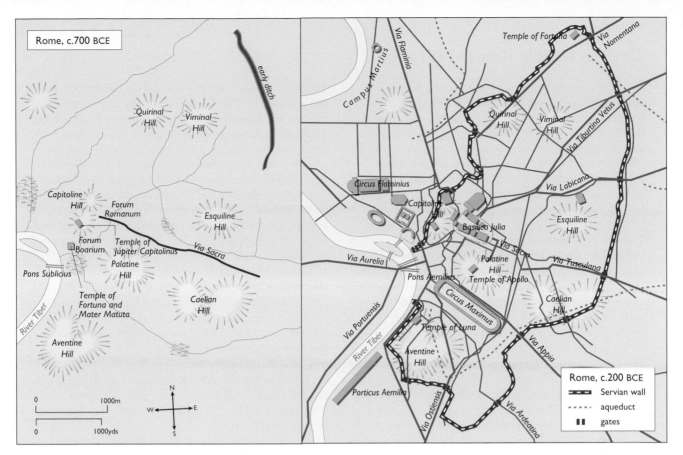

Map 5.3 Rome before the Empire (c. 700–200 B.C.E.): *Rome enjoyed a favorable location: a cluster of seven hills, excellent for defense, on the banks of the Tiber River, a conduit of trade and information. Originally a village centered on the Forum Boarium (a field for the grazing of cattle), by the third century B.C.E. it had grown into a considerable town, equipped with walls, gates, streets, and public buildings. Rome was not a seaport: how might that be an advantage, or a disadvantage?*

ghostly array listened to a kinsman or friend deliver an oration commemorating the achievements of the deceased and his forebears.

The father of each family, the *paterfamilias*, held absolute power over other family members who lived under his protection, literally under his *manus* or hand. He determined whether an infant was to live or not, ceremonially raising an accepted child from the ground where it was placed for his judgment. He governed his wife and children, relatives and slaves, with absolute authority, holding over each household member the power of life and death. A wife caught in adultery, a disobedient child, he could sell into slavery, or even kill.

Fathers fostered close ties with their children, who imitated and obeyed these fearsome elders. Education, conducted primarily by fathers and mothers, consisted in the inculcation of one virtue, that of **pietas**. Quite different from our "piety," this was a selfless regard for the father and ancestors and a determination to protect and continue the lineage. "I ... sought to equal the deeds of my father," reads an epitaph expressing the values of *pietas*; "I maintained the glory of my ancestors, my honors have ennobled my stock."

A Roman girl bore only one name: the feminine form of her father's clan name. Thus Julia was the daughter of Julius, Pompeia of Pompeius. All daughters bore the same name, but might be distinguished

with the addition of "second" (*secunda*) or "third" (*tertia*). Sons received individual names, but bore the same clan and family names as their fathers: thus Lucius, son of the general Publius Cornelius Scipio (236–183 B.C.E.), was called Lucius Cornelius Scipio. Names reflected the close ties the Romans made between fathers and daughters, and fathers and sons.

The mission of the family was to preserve itself in the male line and to transmit property down through the generations. Originally, property descended to sons only, and only to those born of legitimate marriages. Aside from gifts, daughters received only a dowry, which was always managed by a male: husband, father, brother, or guardian. Childless men might adopt sons of their peers so as to have a legitimate male heir, or bequeath the inheritance to **agnates** (male relatives in the paternal line). Sons or agnates inherited not only property, but also the responsibility to perpetuate the "sacred things" of each family—a religious obligation. If there were no surviving sons or agnates, the responsibility fell to the freed slaves of the family, who adopted the family name and identity.

The mothers of early Rome transmitted community values to their children. Unlike Greek women, Roman women were never sequestered in separate rooms from male family members. Yet, though respected for their maternal role, they received little

The Irresistible Roman Advance

During the last two centuries B.C.E., Rome became a power recognized not only in Italy but throughout the Mediterranean world. The first of these passages (from the Biblical book of Maccabees) indicates how the Jews at this time perceived the Romans, remarkable both for their many conquests and for their republican form of government. The second, by the Roman historian Sallust, imagines how the increasingly arrogant behavior of the Romans must have appeared to a ruler of an eastern kingdom.

The fame of Roman power and governance reaches Judas Maccabeus, leader of Jewish resistance to Greek overlords, in Judaea (c. 160 B.C.E.): Now Judas heard of the fame of the Romans, that they were very strong and were well-disposed toward all who made an alliance with them. ... He had been told of their wars and of the brave deeds that they were doing among the Gauls. ... what they had done in the land of Spain. ... They also had defeated Antiochus the Great, king of Asia, who went to fight against them with one hundred twenty elephants and with cavalry and chariots and a very large army. He was crushed by them. ... Yet for all this not one of them has put on a crown or worn purple as a mark of pride, but they have built for themselves a senate chamber, and every day three hundred and twenty senators constantly deliberate concerning the people, to govern them well.
(1 Maccabees, 8:1–13)

In the words of the historian Sallust, King Mithridates of Pontus describes the corruption and cruelty of Roman rulers to a potential ally, King Tigranes of Armenia (c. 30 B.C.E.): The Romans have one inveterate motive for making war upon all nations, peoples, and kings, namely, a deep-seated desire for domination and riches. Therefore they first began a war with Philip, king of Macedon, after pretending to be his friends. ... When Antiochus came to his aid, they craftily diverted him by conceding Asia to him, and then, after Philip's power had been broken, Antiochus was stripped of all the territory this side of Taurus and of 10,000 talents. Next Perseus, Philip's son, ... they took under their protection ..., and then those masters of craft and artists in treachery caused his death from want of sleep, since they had compacted not to kill him. Eumenes ... they ... [transformed] from a king into the most wretched of slaves [and] led his son Aristonicus in triumph like an enemy because he had sought to occupy his father's throne and took possession of Asia. Finally, on the death of Nicomedes, they snatched away Bithynia, although [his widow Queen] Nysa ... unquestionably had a son. ...
(Sallust, *Histories*, 4, fragment 69; trs. M. Reinhold, N. Lewis)

---

public recognition and only limited freedom. Given by their fathers to their husbands at an early age (as young as twelve), women of the early Republic lived under the rule—the *manus*—of their new masters. Their property passed entirely into his ownership.

Eventually the Romans evolved alternative forms of marriage, which allowed the wife greater freedom to move in society and to own property. Free marriage became more common among the upper classes in the later Republic. In this arrangement a woman still received a dowry, which was administered by a male; but the male was her father or his agent, rather than her husband. In effect, the woman often gained control of the administration of that dowry as though it were her own property. Ownership of property gave elite women greater status within their families.

Affluent households also included slaves. These victims of war, abandonment, and sale worked largely as farmhands and household servants. Their numbers swelled enormously during the period of Rome's military expansion. Many were high-status slaves from Greece or farther east, equipped with desirable artisan or intellectual skills. Their wares and services could be sold at a profit. Their masters might even establish them in shops and allow them considerable independence. Less gifted slaves worked as agricultural laborers on the expanding farms (the **latifundia**, or "broad fields") of wealthy Roman and other Italian landowners. Domestic and skilled slaves were often granted their freedom in recognition of their services, or were allowed to purchase it. The freeing of a slave, or **manumission**, was practiced throughout antiquity but especially in Rome, where freedmen enjoyed unique privileges. Adopting the clan name of their masters, they practised the ancestor cult of their former proprietors. They acquired limited political rights, and their descendants inherited full citizen status. A freedman's son could vote even when a non-Roman Italian landholder could not.

A wealthy Roman householder also exercised authority over his "clients"—people farther down the social scale who depended on him in various ways. The reciprocal ties between patron and client were hereditary and enduring. The patron defended his clients in legal matters, interceded for them with the public authorities, and advised them in private and public affairs. The client visited his patron regularly and contributed toward the cost of a wedding, or an election bid, or a ransom. Poor clients climbed to the mansions planted on the hills of Rome to greet their patrons, collect a cash handout, and accompany them to meetings in the Forum. A patron's importance was indicated by the magnitude of this client escort.

The Organization of Power

Early Romans devised a system of councils and assemblies able to provide effective government and to adapt to changing circumstances. As in Britain today, their constitution was unwritten: a body of accumulated laws and customs. The organization of the army, mirroring that of government and society, involved the participation of all adult male citizens.

Under the Republic, Rome came to be ruled by elite landowners. Its Senate (literally "a gathering of old men"), which had advised the ancient kings, was made up at first exclusively of patricians. When the last kings left, the Senate remained to formulate policy for the young state. It continued to meet for more than one thousand years until its obliteration in the sixth century C.E.

Executive power resided in the magistracy of the consulate. Two **consuls** were elected each year to preside over the Senate and to head the army. For that purpose they were granted **imperium**: the right to rule absolutely outside Rome itself, over Roman soldiers and subject peoples.

In the early Republic, the *censor* (one of two elected every four, later five, years, each serving only eighteen months) administered the *census*—a regular count of the population, providing data necessary in constituting the army, the assemblies, and the Senate. In addition, the censor established eligibility for the Senate, and could

The living dead—patrician with heads of ancestors: *The Roman virtue of* pietas, *connoting not "piety" but rather reverence for ancestors, and the practice of honoring them through the* mos maiorum, *the "customs of our ancestors," attest to the deep bond held by Roman citizens with those from whom they were descended. Wealthier Romans kept wax masks of these forebears in their homes, and paraded with them through the streets on the occasion of a funeral. Later, they commissioned artists to sculpt lifelike busts of their ancestors, greatly increasing the production of realistic portraiture that was a characteristic genre of Roman art. Here a prominent Roman holds the busts of two of his forefathers, c. 15* C.E.—*the living and the dead all equally captured in stone. (Palazzo dei Conservatori, Rome)*

eject any person from that body for improper behavior. The one-year office of *praetor*—of which there were eight by the end of the Republic—consisted of administering justice, and serving as a general and/or provincial governor. Like the consulate, this office conferred *imperium*.

In time, two other offices were added: those of *quaestor* and *aedile*. The quaestor was a financial officer, while the aedile administered temple properties and managed the provision of public entertainments and entitlements. In an emergency, the consuls, advised by the Senate, could choose a *dictator*, who possessed extraordinary powers for a period limited to just six months.

Priests, also considered part of the government, held their title for life; they were charged to ensure scrupulous adherence to Roman traditions. The *pontifex maximus* (the chief priest, literally the "greatest bridge-maker" between human beings and the gods) had to be of patrician descent and to observe certain ritual laws. Such requirements of class and ritual purity were also applied to other priestly ranks, such as the augurs, and the vestal virgins.

All these officials were elected by the "Centuriate Assembly." That body included all the citizens of Rome down to the very poorest. But it was dominated absolutely by the wealthiest because of its voting procedure. The citizen population gathered and each man took his place in one of 193 "centuries" (from *centum*, a hundred—because each originally included 100 men), which were grouped in turn into six classes. The first century of the first class contained the wealthiest men in Rome; the last century, comprising the sixth and lowest class, contained the poorest. Voting proceeded century by century, from the top down. If the first ninety-eight centuries voted unanimously in the affirmative or negative, a majority was reached and the voting stopped—even though the poorer citizens had not yet voiced their will.

The centuriate organization of the assembly derived from the centuriate organization of the army. When the army

Phalanx and Legion

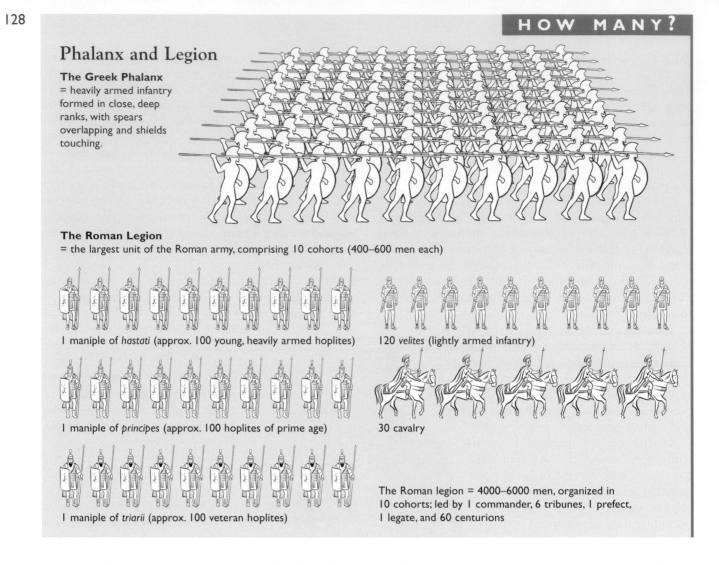

The Greek Phalanx
= heavily armed infantry formed in close, deep ranks, with spears overlapping and shields touching.

The Roman Legion
= the largest unit of the Roman army, comprising 10 cohorts (400–600 men each)

1 maniple of *hastati* (approx. 100 young, heavily armed hoplites)

1 maniple of *principes* (approx. 100 hoplites of prime age)

1 maniple of *triarii* (approx. 100 veteran hoplites)

120 *velites* (lightly armed infantry)

30 cavalry

The Roman legion = 4000–6000 men, organized in 10 cohorts; led by 1 commander, 6 tribunes, 1 prefect, 1 legate, and 60 centurions

---

assembled for battle or review on the Field of Mars (the war god), immediately outside the city, it was ordered into centuries. As in the hoplite armies of Greece and Etruria, each warrior's wealth determined his place in the military system. Those who could afford to equip themselves with helmet, breastplate, spear, and shield held the highest rank, and were deployed in the first centuries. The remaining citizens eligible for war, outfitted to the extent of their fortunes as light infantrymen armed with javelins or daggers or as skirmishers, filled the remaining centuries. The very poorest citizens were not enlisted in the army. They were called the **proletarians** ("bearers of children"), because their only service to the state was to reproduce and thereby provide new generations of citizens.

Thus the Roman citizenry arrayed in the Centuriate Assembly resembled the Roman army arrayed for battle (with the exception that the proletarians were recognized as citizens, but not as soldiers). The military organization was adapted to a political one. And the military origin of the assembly explains why wealth played a decisive role in the political system. The wealthy who formed the first lines of battle—and took the greatest risks—were those who voted first, and held the greatest power, in the assembly.

The Roman army took the field organized into legions. The legion was subdivided into smaller units: "maniples" or "cohorts." Its organization is shown in *How Many?*, above. Participants were recruited from those aged between seventeen and forty-six, and served for sixteen (later twenty) years. By the time of Hannibal's invasion of Italy in 218 B.C.E., the Romans could mobilize more than 100,000 men, including legionaries and lighter-armed auxiliaries recruited from the non-citizen population.

Plebeian Gains

From the first days of the Republic, plebeian Romans pressed for increased representation in government and enhanced social freedoms. Even wealthy plebeians were barred from the Senate, from public office, and from marriage with patricians.

Wealthy patricians belonged to the higher ranks of the Centuriate Assembly, and so did some wealthy plebeians. Beginning in the fifth and fourth centuries, plebeian leaders launched what later historians have dramatically named the Struggle of the Orders. It was not until the end of the third century B.C.E., however, that the barriers to a dramatic plebeian advance dissolved and plebeians gained their true objectives. The wealthiest plebeians would now merge with the patrician order to form a powerful new ruling class: that of the office-holding "nobility."

The plebeian advance began with the clever tactic of secession, which they employed several times over two centuries. Plebeians withdrew from the city, refusing to bear arms (the most powerful card they held), swore mutual loyalty, and established their own temple, temple administrators (the *aediles*), and priesthood. They created two new powerful magistrates (later ten) called *tribunes*. The tribunes were granted the status of sacrosanctity: dedicated to the gods, they were considered holy, and anyone who laid a hand on them could be summarily killed without fear of divine or human justice. Thus protected from patrician vengeance, the tribunes could veto actions of the patrician magistrates deemed injurious to their emerging social order.

Plebeian leaders also demanded the publication of the laws. In about 450 B.C.E., patrician magistrates acceded to this demand and codified the laws. They may also, as later authors assert, have inscribed them on twelve tables, which were placed in the Forum for all to consult. The originals of these Twelve Tables do not survive, but they were in the minds of generations of Romans who, as schoolchildren, were required to memorize them. Excerpts contained in later historical works depict early republican Roman society and its already sophisticated concepts of law.

Plebeian leaders created a new assembly paralleling the Centuriate Assembly, in which their votes had greater weight: the "Tribal Assembly." This was based on an ancient tribal assembly, and it featured a majority of plebeians. The new assembly contained the same Roman population that constituted the Centuriate Assembly but was divided into "tribes"— at first twenty, later thirty-five. Crucially, the system of voting was different. One tribe voted at a time (the order of voting being decided by lot). A majority of eleven (later eighteen) voting yes or no controlled the decision. Patricians were excluded from the assembly (only because tribunes could only convene plebeians), leaving a body called the Plebeian Council, presided over by a tribune. The Plebeian Council was a very powerful body that could exercise a nearly democratic force in the republican machinery. In 287 B.C.E. this council obtained the right to pass laws binding on all Romans.

In the meantime, plebeian leaders also gained access to the high magistracies leading to the consulate. Eventually, plebeians served alongside patricians as consuls, praetors, and quaestors. As the first two titles conferred *imperium*, plebeians as well as patricians could lead the Roman army in battle and, eventually, rule provinces and the empire itself. Plebeians who won election to the city's chief offices became members of the "senatorial order," and becoming a Consul conferred nobility on their family.

By the time the plebeian order had achieved these goals, Rome itself had grown from a village to a nation. It would soon be an empire.

ROME: FROM WEST TO EAST

Without having any preexisting plan to do so, in the fourth century B.C.E. Rome began a career of military conquest that would result in its domination of all of the Mediterranean region. Its conquests began in Italy, extended south and west, especially to Carthage and Spain, then east to the kingdoms of the successors of Alexander as shown in Maps 5.4 and 5.5. As it progressed, the Roman advance became unstoppable, driven not so much by a need for self-defense as by the zeal to conquer. The engine of conquest transformed not only the conquered territories, but also the values of the conqueror (see *Witnesses*, p. 126).

Italy, Carthage, and the West

At first, Rome looked only to secure its position in Italy and to defend itself against possible aggressors.

Once they had expelled the Etruscans, the Romans subdued the neighboring Aequi and Volsci tribes then struck back at their old Etruscan neighbors by seizing one of their foe's principal towns, Veii. Thereafter, Etruscan power diminished as Roman power expanded. The next challenge came from a new quarter. In 386 B.C.E., the Celts (called Gauls by the Romans) who dwelled north of the river Po (in northern Italy) invaded Rome, sacked the city, and terrorized its people. Rallied by the patrician consul Marcus Furius Camillus (the conqueror of Veii, d. 365 B.C.E.), the Romans counterattacked. They drove off the Celts and laid the foundation of their empire.

The victorious Camillus, acting as dictator, constructed a ring of protective walls around Rome and reorganized the army. He discarded the phalanx formation (see p. 128) for the more flexible maniple, whose soldiers held javelins—lighter than hoplite spears. Rome was now ready for war.

Assisted by a league of Latin tribes, Rome subdued central Italy. By 300 B.C.E., Rome had disbanded the league and asserted dominion. According to the geographer Strabo (c. 64 B.C.E.—after 21 C.E.), the Latins were "struck with amazement" at Roman military strength, by which "all became subjects."

At this stage Rome was a gentle conqueror. She extended to her Latin allies some of the privileges of citizenship. In addition, Latins were invited to form colonies in lands newly conquered by Rome. In these they were autonomous and gained full citizenship rights. Rather than crush a vanquished people, the Romans welcomed them into their fellowship.

In three terrible wars from 343 to 290 B.C.E., the Romans defeated the Samnites, a hill-people of southeastern Italy. These, too, were incorporated into the

Map 5.4 Roman Expansion in Italy, 500–80 B.C.E.: In 500 B.C.E., Rome was a small town subject to Etruscan kings which was situated on a peninsula shared with native tribes and Carthaginian and Greek strangers. By 275 B.C.E., Rome had gained its independence and established direct territorial control in the center of the peninsula and on the western coast. Over the next two centuries, Rome had engulfed Italy, its dominion made visible by the network of roads that radiated from Rome across the entire region. By 90 B.C.E., free Italians were made Roman citizens. How was Rome able to unify the many different peoples who lived on the Italian peninsula?

growing Roman Empire by the strategies of alliance, colonization, and grants of partial citizenship. The Greek cities of southern Italy, not waiting for a Roman attack, preemptively declared war. They had hired the forces of King Pyrrhus of Epirus, on the Greek mainland, who arrived with a well-trained army of 25,000 men and 20 war elephants. He overpowered the Romans in 280 and 279 B.C.E., but only after suffering severe losses himself and by unleashing the fury of his awesome beasts. This was a "Pyrrhic" victory—one achieved with such damage that it is tantamount to defeat. Pyrrhus went home, having accomplished little. The Greek cities soon accepted Roman hegemony.

By 264 B.C.E., Roman power extended from the Po River to the toe of Italy, jutting deep into the central Mediterranean. The only other major power in the region, the Carthaginians, took notice. After a clash between the two forces in Sicily, Carthage declared war on Rome. Three wars were required to decide who would hold sovereignty in the western Mediterranean, and to achieve the destruction of the

city of Carthage. In these Punic Wars, as they were called (after the Latin name for the Carthaginians, *Punici*–or "Phoenicians"), Rome waged an epochal struggle. At the outset, Rome was an Italian power and could have remained only that. With the end of the Wars, Rome controlled the western Mediterranean. In the course of these wars, the Romans more than once launched and lost their navies, sacrificed the lives of thousands of citizens and allies, and saw generals thought invincible lured into ambush, blinded by mist, or tricked by decoy armies.

Four brilliant Carthaginian generals of the same clan, the Barcids, led the assault on Rome in the first two Punic wars: Hamilcar, his son-in-law Hasdrubal, and his sons Hannibal and (again) Hasdrubal. The most famous was Hannibal (247–183/182 B.C.E.), who launched the second Punic War when he invaded the Italian heartland after crossing the seemingly impregnable Alps. With thirty-seven elephants and a massive infantry force, he won victory upon victory as he descended from the Po to the south. Arrayed against him were Rome's finest leaders, who found that the African could not be defeated in a head-on battle. Only Quintus Fabius Maximus succeeded, by harrying the enemy, in stemming Hannibal's advance.

The consul Publius Cornelius Scipio (236–183 B.C.E.), who had been stationed in Spain, slipped across the straits between Sicily and Africa, and marched on Carthage. The desperate citizens recalled Hannibal. His Carthaginian forces met the Romans at Zama, not far from the capital, in 202 B.C.E. Undefeated in Italy, Hannibal lost the war at home. The victorious Romans stripped Carthage of its territories, its wealth, and its international prestige. Rome had triumphed in the west, and Scipio acquired another surname: Africanus, the conqueror of Africa.

There was no need for a third Punic War (149–146 B.C.E.), except in the minds of Rome's elder statesmen, who feared a resurgence of Carthaginian power. Marcus Porcius Cato, called "the Elder" (234–149 B.C.E.), former consul, as well as censor, author, and moralist, harangued the Senate regularly with the pronouncement "Carthage must be destroyed." It was an already weakened Carthage that faced the Roman army sent to execute that mission in 149 B.C.E. The besieged citizens resisted, starving and unarmed, for three years. In 146 B.C.E., the remaining Carthaginians were captured or killed, the city burned to the ground, the ground itself spread with salt to prevent its renewal. The triumphant Roman general was another Scipio, called Aemilianus, and surnamed (like his adoptive grandfather) Africanus.

The first Punic War (264–241 B.C.E.) gave the Romans Sicily, the fertile island off Italy's toe. The second (218–201 B.C.E.) gave them Spain and a foothold in Africa. The third (149–146 B.C.E.) opened all of North Africa to Roman domination. From these new lands, Rome was immeasurably enriched. Both Sicily and Africa were breadbaskets, producers of wheat, which the Romans needed in quantity. Spain's lodes of ore and, above all, its silver mines were an unimaginable treasure which, once discovered,

---

Defenders of the Roman Ideal

The roster of Roman heroes includes those notable for their self-control or self-sacrifice, as well as those known for their record of military successes. Among them are Cato the Elder, whose self-restraint is commended by the later Greek biographer Plutarch; Tiberius Gracchus, whose efforts to improve the conditions of the Roman poor are described also by Plutarch; and the orator Cicero, who at great personal risk publicly denounced the dictatorship of Mark Antony.

Plutarch describes the virtues of the statesman Cato the Elder (c. 80 C.E.): He gained, in early life, a good habit of body by working with his own hands, and living temperately, and serving in war … For his general temperance … and self-control, he really deserves the highest admiration. For when he commanded the army, he never took for himself, and those who belonged to him, above three bushels of wheat for a month, and somewhat less than a bushel and a half a day of barley for his baggage-cattle. … Yet, though he seemed thus easy and sparing to all who were under his power, he on the other hand showed most inflexible severity and strictness in what related to public justice, so that the Roman government never seemed more terrible, nor yet more mild, than under his administration.
(Plutarch, *Lives*; trs. Dryden, rev. A. H. Clough 1875)

When Tiberius Gracchus advocated a program for land reform to requisition lands from the rich and redistribute them to the poor, the rich launched a campaign against him (c. 80 C.E.): But they had no success. For Tiberius … was quite invincible. Whenever the people crowded around the rostra, he would take his place there and speak on behalf of the poor. "The wild beasts of Italy," he would say, "have their own dens as places of repose and refuge, but the men who fight and die for their country enjoy nothing more in it than the air and light, having no houses or settlements of their own, they must wander from place to place with the wives and children. The army commanders are guilty of a ridiculous error when they exhort the common soldiers to defend their sepulchers and altars, for not one among so many Romans has an ancestral altar or tomb. They fight and die to maintain the luxury and wealth of other men. They are called the masters of the world, but they have not one foot of ground to call their own."
(Plutarch, *Lives*; trs. Dryden, rev. A. H. Clough 1875)

Cicero denounces Mark Antony's dictatorship (43 B.C.E.): But today, this very day that now is, this very moment when I am speaking, defend your conduct during this very moment, if you can. Why is the Senate surrounded by a belt of armed men? Why are your henchmen listening to me sword in hand? … Why do you bring Ityreans, the most barbarous of all tribes, into the forum armed with arrows? He says he does so as a guard. Is it not better to perish a thousand times than to be unable to live in one's own city without an armed guard? But believe me, there is no protection in that— a man must be defended by the affection and good will of his fellow-citizens, not by arms. The Roman people will take them from you, will wrest them from your hands—may it be while we are still safe! … The name of peace is sweet, the thing itself is a blessing. But between peace and slavery there is a wide difference. Peace is liberty in tranquility; slavery is the worst of all evils—to be repelled, if need be, not only by war but even by death.
(Cicero, *Second Philippic*, 112–119; ed. N. M. Bailkey, 1996)

were brutally seized from the region's barbarian inhabitants for the benefit of Rome.

Rome also looked north. Roman armies seized Cisalpine Gaul (the region between the Po and the Alps), completing the conquest of the Italian mainland. Then they reached over the Alps, where they met new nations of barbarians: Germans and Britons. The general Gaius Julius Caesar mastered Gaul (modern France, Belgium, and the Rhineland) by 51 B.C.E. after eight years of battle and maneuver. He encountered the Germans but did not pursue them, and crossed to Britain but did not stay. Rome had tasted the possibilities of the north, and would return under the emperors to export its version of peace.

Greece and the East

Meanwhile, richer prizes awaited Rome in the eastern Mediterranean: first in Greece, and then beyond, in the Middle East and Egypt.

Even before the victory at Zama, the Romans had peered across the Adriatic toward Greece, where two city leagues (the Aetolian and the Achaean) struggled with the Macedonian kingdom to the north. The leagues now invited the Seleucid king in Syria to assist them against Macedonia. Persuaded by her allies (the island state of Rhodes and the little Pergamene monarchy), who were fearful of Seleucid aggression (and annoyed with Macedonia for its support of Carthage during the second Punic War), Rome then intervened.

Over seventy years, the Romans fought four Macedonian wars. At first they did not seek domination over Greece. Instead, they proclaimed the liberation of the Greek cities, intending that a system of competing powers would check the Macedonian kings. But the Greek states were unruly, and Rome had begun to develop a taste for conquest. At Pydna, on the frontiers of Macedonia, in 168 B.C.E., the Roman legions under Lucius Aemilius Paullus (henceforth "Macedonicus"; d. 160 B.C.E.) defeated the Macedonian king, Perseus. All of Greece was subsequently swept into Roman hands, the conquerors announcing their power unambiguously by the wholesale enslavement in a single day of 150,000 inhabitants of Epirus. The point was underscored in 146 B.C.E. by the obliteration of the city of Corinth.

The Romans had crossed several barriers in absorbing Greece, mental as well as real. Hitherto, Rome had waged wars to defend its interests. Henceforth, it would fight to extend its empire. When the Romans faced the Greeks, moreover, they faced a people of superior culture. The civilization of the vanquished would profoundly change the thought and values of the victors.

Beyond Greece, the Near East beckoned. The king of Pergamum sought protection from the king of Pontus on his eastern flank, and from his Seleucid neighbor to the south—the latter squeezed by Parthian newcomers pressing from Iran. Rome imposed order, making clients of the Egyptian Ptolemies and fencing in the Seleucid monarchs. When in 168 B.C.E. Antiochus IV (the opponent of the Maccabees) approached Alexandria with hostile intent, the Roman legate drew his sword and marked a circle around the king in the sand, commanding him to disavow his ambitions before stepping beyond it. Thus the new masters of Egypt publicly humiliated one of the great kings of the East.

Gnaeus Pompeius Magnus (106–48 B.C.E.; anglicized as Pompey) completed the job of subduing this region. By 63 B.C.E., he had crushed Pontus, abolished the Seleucid Empire, and reorganized Judaea as a Roman province. In 30 B.C.E., Egypt fell to Octavian, Caesar's heir and Rome's future emperor (Augustus). Rome had come full circle: clockwise, from Carthage, through northwest Africa and Spain, Gaul and Greece, Asia Minor and the Middle East, and, returning to Africa, to Egypt. The Mediterranean was now a Roman sea.

The Roman sweep of the Mediterranean was startling. Who was this new Western power? How could it unseat the established masters of that world? A Greek taken hostage after Pydna undertook to explain the Roman phenomenon to his countrymen. This was Polybius of Megalopolis (c. 200–c. 118 B.C.E.) in the Peloponnesus, subsequently tutor and companion of Scipio Aemilianus, the son of Polybius' captor. His history of Rome from 220 to 146 B.C.E. (of which only parts survive) is a portrait of irresistible state power. Her leaders' virtue, her military genius, her balanced constitution, he proposed, allowed Rome to outstrip all competitors and resist normal patterns of growth and decay, which otherwise prevailed in the world of nations.

When Polybius arrived in Rome to become the pet of high-society intellectuals, Greek influence could be felt everywhere. Greek New Comedy played in the theater, rewritten for a Roman audience by the playwrights Plautus (254–184 B.C.E.) and Terence (195–159 B.C.E.). Greek philosophy grabbed the attention of bright adolescents, who journeyed to Athens to study at the source. Stoic philosophers brought to Rome the tenets of the school that most meshed with that city's spirit. Teachers of rhetoric, fixtures of every major Hellenistic city, founded schools in Rome where future senators mastered new skills. In noblemen's homes Greek schoolmasters, captive slaves, taught Romans the international language of culture. At aristocratic houses the witty and elegant gathered to discuss new books and to consult the rolls from captured libraries. Greek statues graced the halls and gardens of the wealthy.

Many Roman leaders deplored the conquest of the Roman aristocracy by the Greek imagination. None did so more angrily than Cato the Elder (234–149

B.C.E.), who as censor attempted to stem the tide of what he considered immoral Greek values. Greek philosophy must go, he argued: "Theirs is a vile race, and an unruly one," whose literature may be worth looking at, but not closely. When the lectures of the Greek philosophers Carneades and Diogenes took Rome by storm, Cato expelled them from the city—this though he sent his son to study philosophy in Athens.

ROME: FROM REPUBLIC TO EMPIRE

Cato was probably right. Rome could not expand and conquer (whatever Polybius thought) without becoming transformed itself. By the end of the Republic, the experience of empire-building had transformed Roman institutions, Roman values, and the Roman people. The city that had begun its career by renouncing monarchy became the capital of a world empire, and subject to an emperor.

Changing Social Patterns

The provinces the Romans conquered they governed badly. Whether the lure was bushels of wheat or bars of silver, or statuary and libraries, greedy and corrupt governors milked the wealth of subject territories.

So blatant was this theft that Rome established a court system—the Extortion Court—specifically to try officials charged by provincials with such crimes. However, the jury designated to hear those charges was generally made up of senators, with the same interests as the accused governors. In such an environment, corruption was the norm and honesty the exception. Writing in the fifth century C.E., when Roman depredations had long gone unchecked, Saint Augustine of Hippo (354–430 C.E.) concluded that empires were only "robbery on a grand scale."

Even had the provincial governors been honest, their subjects would have suffered from Roman rule. Rome lacked the machinery to administer an empire. A mere twenty or thirty magistrates, together with the Senate and the assemblies, ruled the city, Italy, and the Empire. The jobs of provincial administration (tax-collecting, road-building, importing, exporting) were auctioned to Roman entrepreneurs rich enough to undertake large projects. These men were *publicans*, who performed public services on commission. Some took only modest profits, but others equaled the worst of their senatorial counterparts and mercilessly bled the provinces.

Publicans belonged to the class of *equestrians*, which gained prominence in the late Republic. In earlier years, equestrians were men wealthy enough to

Map 5.5 Roman Imperialism in the Republican Era, 264–31 B.C.E.: *Having absorbed much of Italy by 264 B.C.E., Rome proceeded to confront other Mediterranean powers over the next two centuries. Its victories were hard-won but astonishing. By 100 B.C.E., Rome held most of the western Mediterranean region as well as the Balkans, Greece, and parts of Asia Minor. By 31 B.C.E., it had acquired the ancient centers of civilization in the Near East, Egypt, and parts of North Africa. It was a republic, but at the same time it was an empire.* **How were the Romans able to communicate with all the parts of their vast empire?**

be rated with the cavalry in the Centuriate Assembly. Later, a minimum requirement of 400,000 *sesterces* (a *sestertius* coin equalled a quarter of a *denarius*) established eligibility for equestrian status. Equestrians were often as wealthy as the aristocracy whose sons formed the senatorial elite. Unlike the aristocracy, equestrians did not seek political office or a place in the Senate. The aristocracy who did so were barred from engaging in commerce, and it was commerce that interested the equestrians. They were a nonpolitical class of moneymakers, who profited from moneylending, trade, and public contracting.

During the late Republic, independent subsistence farmers, who had fought in the legions that won Rome her empire, were declining in number and prosperity. In some areas they were swallowed up by the large landowners: Roman senators and equestrians, and the Latin and other Italian aristocracy. Big men advanced at the expense of the small because they were able to take advantage of the burgeoning numbers of slaves: a consequence of empire.

The slave population swelled with imports of human cargo from conquered territories: 20,000 at one blow from Africa in 256 B.C.E.; 25,000 from Agrigentum, Sicily, in 262 B.C.E.; 150,000 from Epirus in 167 B.C.E.; 1,000,000 allegedly seized in Gaul by Julius Caesar. Laboring on Sicilian and Italian *latifundia*, this slave force was an unwilling army, rarely freed (unlike domestic and artisan slaves), impelled by force.

The slave hordes of the *latifundia* often rebelled—twice in such numbers that seasoned troops were deployed to suppress them. In 135 B.C.E., Sicilian slaves rebelled under the Syrian-born Eunus, amassing an army of 70,000 men before they were crushed in 131 B.C.E.. In 73–71 B.C.E., the Thracian gladiator Spartacus led a polyglot army of 90,000 desperate slaves on raids up and down the Italian peninsula. The general Marcus Licinius Crassus (d. 53 B.C.E.) destroyed the rebels, underscoring the message with a mass crucifixion of 6000 survivors along the Appian Way, the highway to Rome.

Small farmers who could not compete with the large plantations mortgaged their land, gave up in despair and, landless, migrated to Rome. Here perhaps they might become part of the floating mass of unemployed slum-dwellers, the **plebs**. This urban proletariat lived to eat and be entertained. In order to achieve this goal, they sold the one commodity they possessed: their vote. The capital belonged to the idle poor, the very rich, and the slaves.

A man of the plebs was not welcome in the army. He could not be disciplined, commanders feared. But with fewer small farmers, it was necessary to find a new social group from which to recruit soldiers. A solution was discovered by the general and consul Gaius Marius (c. 157–86 B.C.E.), an equestrian from a family that had never before held high office (thus that rarity, a "new man"). Marius brought into his

The Career of the Roman Republic

Polybius   *The Histories*

Livy   *The History of Rome*

Plutarch   *Lives*, especially of *Tiberius and Gaius Gracchus, Julius Caesar*

Sallust   *The Conspiracy of Catiline*

Cicero   *Orations, On the Republic*

army a new breed of men: the old proletarians. Men of this class had once made up one-half the population of old Rome: poor men without property or patrons, lumped as a mass into the last of the 193 centuries of the Centuriate Assembly. The proletarians whom Marius admitted to his army had one overriding loyalty: to the general who gave them a job, a mission, and the promise of a fat bonus upon retirement.

Returning soldiers expected that bonus: a piece of land to compensate for years of military service abroad. Marius' promises unleashed from his veterans a pressing demand for land, when most available land had been gobbled up by the large landowners to be cultivated by slaves or entrepreneurial tenant farmers.

To some extent, a serious program of colonization could meet this demand. Retired soldiers settled in the Po Valley, on the island of Sicily, or in North Africa. Far from Rome, they retained their citizenship, and served as a permanent reserve garrison in subject territory. Colonization was a useful but insufficient tool. To provide the veterans with land, it became necessary to take it from somebody else.

The Last Century of the Republic

During Rome's early expansion within Italy, new lands acquired from conquered neighbors were designated as "public land." Over the years, public land had been absorbed by large landowners or tenants who had made it their own. Those holdings could be reclaimed by the state and distributed in small allotments to retired soldiers—or they might be given to the landless poor of the city of Rome, who might repeople the class of smallholders. The latter proposal, called the "Agrarian Law," was the idea of Tiberius Sempronius Gracchus (d. 133 B.C.E.). It sparked the revolution that ended with the dismantling of the Republic.

The extraordinary lives of Tiberius and his brother Gaius Sempronius Gracchus did much to shape the history of the last phase of the Roman Republic. According to legend, their mother, Cornelia (the daughter of the elder Scipio Africanus and sister of Aemilius Paullus, victor at Pydna in 168 B.C.E.), when asked to display her jewels, pointed to her two sons and replied, "These are my jewels." A cultivated matron and known author, Cornelia raised and educated her sons herself. The monument eventually erected for her in Rome noted not only her parentage (as was usual) but her maternity (which was unprecedented): "Cornelia, daughter of Africanus, [mother] of the Gracchi." That monument rightly awards their mother some of the credit for the achievements of the Gracchi brothers.

It was while serving as a tribune in 133 B.C.E., that Tiberius Gracchus proposed the "Agrarian Law." An aristocrat himself, his aim was conservative: to bolster the peasant population, which had borne the burdens of Rome's expansion by being unable to compete with large slave-owners. His proposal angered his peers in the Senate, for whom land redistribution was anathema—even if it involved only public land and the appropriations were modest. Their refusal to sacrifice their property or their privilege would ultimately spell their demise as a political class.

Another tribune, a puppet of the senatorial elite, vetoed Tiberius' proposed law. Tiberius then unprecedentedly called for a special election to unseat the dissenting tribune, which secured passage of the law. He further appropriated for the use of the land commission set up by his law (whose members were people he could trust—himself, his brother, and his father-in-law) the treasury of the kingdom of Pergamum, recently willed to Rome. Finally, Tiberius outraged his opponents by (against all precedent) running for reelection. Incited by the Senate, a mob stabbed him to death. It was the first of the political assassinations of this troubled era.

Ten years later (123 B.C.E.), Tiberius' brother Gaius (d. 121 B.C.E.) became tribune and undertook a still more radical program. Continuing Tiberius' land distributions, he also ordered the distribution of cheap grain to the plebs, planned colonization programs for veterans, and proposed the extension of Roman citizenship to Latins, and of Latin rights to Italians. He introduced a reformed system for tax collection in Asia and for the prosecution in Rome of corrupt provincial governors. Opposition to some of these measures gathered force, and in 121 B.C.E. the Senate enacted a *senatus consultum ultimum*, or "Final Decree," which authorized the consul to impose martial law and destroy anyone perceived as an enemy of the state. In the fighting that followed, Gaius committed suicide to escape the shame of execution.

With their broad vision, bold programs, and tragic deaths, the Gracchi brothers opened a new era of republican politics. Henceforth, those who refused to surrender privilege in order to heal the pain of Roman society called themselves the **Optimates**, the "best." Those who courted the masses were known as the **Populares**, the "popular" or "people's" party. The rigidity of the Optimate position and the ruthlessness of the Popular leaders hastened the downfall of the Republic.

The laws of the Gracchi and the governance, while consul, of Marius cost senators some of their privileges (and, in some cases, their lives). They regained their privileges when Lucius Cornelius Sulla (c. 138–79 B.C.E.), once Marius' lieutenant, established himself as Dictator for the Reconstitution of the Republic, a post he held from 82 to 80 B.C.E. Posting the names of his opponents in the Forum, Sulla invited their murder and saw to the confiscation of their wealth. These **proscriptions**, as they were called, resulted in the butchery of some 10,000 men and the redefinition of the ruling class.

Julius Caesar

A general with an army behind him had great power—more so if it were an army of landless men whose futures depended on the skill and success of their leader. In the last half-century of the Republic (up to 31 B.C.E.), generals held sway. Crassus and Pompey—two of Sulla's lieutenants who between them had vanquished the slave Spartacus, cleared the Mediterranean of pirates, suppressed rebellion in Spain, and acquired a large chunk of the Middle East, dominated Rome for the next generation. They were soon joined by Julius Caesar (100–44 B.C.E.), the greatest general of all.

From 65 to 59 B.C.E., Caesar served as aedile, chief priest, praetor, governor of Spain, and consul. In 60 B.C.E. he joined forces with Crassus and Pompey to form the First **Triumvirate**, an unofficial alliance dedicated essentially to their mutual advantage. On stepping down from the consulship in 59 B.C.E., he assumed command of the armies in Cisalpine and Transalpine Gaul. By 50 B.C.E. he had subdued these regions. Meanwhile, the "First Triumvirate" had crumbled: Crassus died fighting the Parthians in 53 B.C.E., and Pompey betrayed Caesar's policies to become the darling of the Senate. Fearful that Caesar would return to Rome as a conqueror, the Senate, early in 49 B.C.E., appointed another general to succeed him in Gaul and ordered him to lay down his arms. Defying that command, Caesar led one of his legions across the Rubicon River at the southern boundary of his province, in an act tantamount to a declaration of war. Pompey and the senators fled, abandoning the state treasury, which Caesar found useful when he occupied the capital.

Caesar pursued Pompey and vanquished his superior force at Pharsalus, in Macedonia, in 48 B.C.E. Pompey then fled to Egypt, where he was murdered by order of the Ptolemaic king, and Caesar proceeded to rule the empire as Perpetual Dictator. This title he preferred to that of king, which he refused, placing the proffered crown instead on a statue of the god

Jupiter. Caesar reformed provincial administration, extended citizenship to deserving provincial elites, provided free grain and entertainment to the urban plebs, opened the Senate to eager equestrians, settled his veterans on colonial and public land, and in these and other ways seriously addressed the social problems that had first prompted the Gracchi brothers in their heroic attempts at reform. Caesar was a brilliant administrator as well as a brilliant general. But the Republic was dead.

Among the senators who had opposed Caesar and championed Pompey were the younger Marcus Porcius Cato (95–46 B.C.E.), great-grandson of Cato the Elder, and Marcus Tullius Cicero (106–43 B.C.E.), orator, author, and (though a timid man) dedicated republican. Cato possessed high principles, honed by a superior education in the Greek classics and Stoic philosophy. The best advocate the Optimates could put forward, he was self-righteous, nostalgic for the old Republic, and committed to protecting the authority of the senatorial order. After Pompey's defeat, Cato commanded an army that faced Caesar and lost at Thapsus (North Africa) in 46 B.C.E. Rather than submit to the enemy, he killed himself at Utica—considered the most eloquent suicide of the age.

Cicero, a moderate, had feared Caesar's return in 49 B.C.E., but was reconciled with the general, who bore no grudge against his former opponent. Cicero spent the next five years far from the Forum, writing his celebrated works: *On Duties, Tusculan Disputations, On the Orator, The Republic, On the Nature of the Gods.* In these treatises and dialogues, he distilled the Roman outlook on society and politics in prose that would become a standard of composition for two millennia. In these works, too, he translated into Latin the key concepts of Greek philosophy. It was in Ciceronian Latin that Greek thought first won the attention of Europe's philosophers in the age of the Renaissance. His numerous orations and more than 900 letters taught later generations to think and feel like Romans. This dedicated intellectual was an unlikely martyr. A martyr he became.

Caesar died on March 15, 44 B.C.E., stabbed twenty-three times by conspirators led by Marcus Junius Brutus (c. 85–42 B.C.E.). Caesar's lieutenants Marcus Antonius (83–30 B.C.E; anglicized as Mark Antony) and Marcus Aemilius Lepidus (d. 13/12 B.C.E.), intent on vengeance, seized command of Rome. The murderers dispersed. Antony and Lepidus were joined by the adolescent Gaius Octavius (63 B.C.E.–14 C.E.), renamed, according to Caesar's will (adopting him as son and heir), Gaius Julius Caesar Octavianus (anglicized as Octavian). The three formed the Second Triumvirate, dedicated like the first to the promotion of its members and the mastery of Rome.

At the top of the Second Triumvirate's agenda (though Octavian regretted it) was the assassination of Cicero. For that scholar had stood in the Forum on fourteen occasions after Caesar's murder and with piercing eloquence denounced Mark Antony as a traitor to Rome, as quoted in *Witnesses* on p. 131. Those speeches he called Philippics: an allusion to Demosthenes' orations against Philip of Macedon. Cicero was slain by Antony's soldiers while attempting, reluctantly and too late, to flee. Antony ordered his head and hands (with which he had spoken and written the *Philippics*) to be nailed to the rostrum in the same Forum where he had delivered his orations.

The Second Triumvirate defeated Caesar's assassins in Spain and Greece, then turned on each other. Lepidus was pushed aside. Octavian and Mark Antony fought a duel to the death, the latter aided by the last Ptolemaic monarch, Caesar's one-time lover Cleopatra. Losing their nerve during the naval battle of Actium (off the Greek coast) in 31 B.C.E., Mark Antony and Cleopatra fled to Egypt, and Octavian won the field. The next year, the two fugitives were both suicides. After 27 B.C.E., Octavian ruled Rome: not as consul or dictator, but as Caesar Augustus. He had made the Roman sea his own.

Conclusion
THE ROMAN SEA AND THE MEANING OF THE WEST

With the conquests of Alexander the Great, the Greek world engrossed the whole of the eastern Mediterranean world. The Hellenic culture of the Greek Classical age blended with local cultures to produce Hellenistic civilization. To the west, Carthage and Etruria emerged as new centers of civilization related to the ancient Middle East and open to the Hellenistic synthesis. In Etruria's shadow, Latins centered at Rome won independence from Etruscan domination and began to forge the institutions that constituted the Roman Republic. From the fourth to the first century B.C.E., Rome extended its sovereignty throughout Italy, North Africa, and the regions of the Alexandrian conquest, and claimed the Mediterranean Sea as *mare nostrum,* "our sea."

The whole product of civilization that had accumulated on the shores of that sea became part of the Roman heritage, which passed in time to other Europeans who carried forward the cultural tradition of the West. A fusion of the successive strata of the Asian, African, Greek, and Latin imaginations, that heritage was to outlive both the Roman Republic and the Empire.

QUESTIONS TO CONSIDER

1. Why did Alexander cross the Hellespont to attempt the conquest of the Persian empire?

2. How were Hellenistic cities different from the *poleis* of ancient Greece?

3. How could Hellenistic civilization—thought, literature, art—be so inventive and imaginative, when the Hellenistic states were largely repressive monarchies?

4. What was unique about the small city of Rome that enabled it to become master of Italy and the whole Mediterranean region?

5. What was the legacy of the Gracchi brothers, both for Rome and later times?

SUGGESTED RESOURCES

Bradley, Keith R., *Slavery and Society at Rome* (Cambridge: Cambridge University Press, 1994). Examines Roman slavery as a social institution from the last two centuries of the Republic through the first two of the Empire, noting comparisons with later slave systems.

Canfora, Luciano, *The Vanished Library: A Wonder of the Ancient World* trans. Martin Ryle; Berkeley–Los Angeles (University of California Press, 1990). Imaginative and elegant reconstruction of the Hellenistic intellectual world, and particularly of the legendary library at Alexandria created by the Ptolemies to hold all the world's books.

Casson, Lionel, *Libraries in the Ancient World* (New Haven: Yale University Press, 2002). The history of the book, of reading, and of book collections from Mesopotamia to the end of Roman times, with a close look necessarily at the great libraries of the Hellenistic era.

Cribiore, Raffaella, *Gymnastics of the Mind: Greek Education in Hellenistic and Roman Egypt* (Princeton: Princeton University Press, 2001). How people learned to read and what they read in Hellenistic and Roman Egypt and throughout the Mediterranean region.

Dixon, Suzanne, *The Roman Family* (Baltimore: John Hopkins University Press, 1992). Scholarly synthesis of the latest views on law and marriage, household and servitude, women and children, and life-cycle stages in Roman society.

Green, Peter, *Alexander of Macedon 356–323 B.C.: A Historical Biography* (Berkeley: University of California Press, 1992). Portrays Alexander as a brilliant but brutally single-minded general, a man capable of patricide or the massacre of civilians.

Holt, Frank L., *Alexander the Great and the Mystery of the Elephant Medallions* (Berkeley: University of California Press, 2003). How Alexander promoted his own self-image in the design of silver medallions recovered from Iraq and Afghanistan, depicting him in mythic and heroic poses.

Horden, Peregrine & Nicholas Purcell, *The Corrupting Sea: A Study of Mediterranean History* (Oxford: Blackwell, 2000). Studies the interaction between people and the environment in the Mediterranean region during prehistory, antiquity, and the Middle Ages.

Kyle, Donald G., *Spectacles of Death in Ancient Rome* (London: Routledge, 1998). Studies the slaughter of humans and beasts in the Roman arena, as spectacle, as institution, and as religious rite.

Lintott, Andrew, *The Constitution of the Roman Republic* (Oxford: Clarendon Press, 1999). A comprehensive study of the political system that allowed a village to become an empire.

Millar, Fergus, *The Crowd in Rome in the Late Republic* (Ann Arbor: University of Michigan Press, 1998). How the crowd made law in the last century of the Republic, drawn into the vortex of the Forum to be wooed by competing politicians who needed the populace to legislate.

Mitchell, Richard E., *Patricians and Plebeians: The Origin of the Roman State* (Ithaca: Cornell University Press, 1990). A controversial account of the patricians as a hereditary religious elite, de-emphasizing the patrician/plebeian struggle.

Parenti, Michael, *The Assassination of Julius Caesar: A People's History of Ancient Rome* (New York: the Free Press, 2003). Explores the street politics of the late republic, and the involvement of those below the nobility in Caesar's assassination.

Wallace-Hadrill, Andrew, *Houses and Society in Pompeii and Herculaneum* (Princeton: Princeton University Press, 1994). A revisionist history of Pompeii and Herculaneum, based on archaeological evidence.

Watson, Alan, *The Spirit of Roman Law* (Athens GA: University of Georgia Press, 1995). An intellectual framework of lawmakers in Rome, from around 451 B.C.E. to around 235 C.E.

Alexander the Great on the web:
http:/ancienthistory.about.com/msubalexander.htm?once=true8
http://www.pbs.org/mpt/alexander/index.html

Archimedes: inventions, problems, and solutions:
http://www.mcs.drexel.edu/~crorres/Archimedes/contents.html

Julius Caesar, resources:
http://www.virgil.org/caesar

⊙ Western Civilization Documents CD-ROM

3.6 On the Murder of Eratosthenes
4.1 The Speech of Camillus
4.2 Women in Roman Politics
4.3 Slaves in the Roman Countryside
4.4 Appian of Alexandria
4.5 Polybius; "Why Romans and Not Greeks Govern the World"
4.6 Cicero: The Laws
4.7 A Marriage Contract

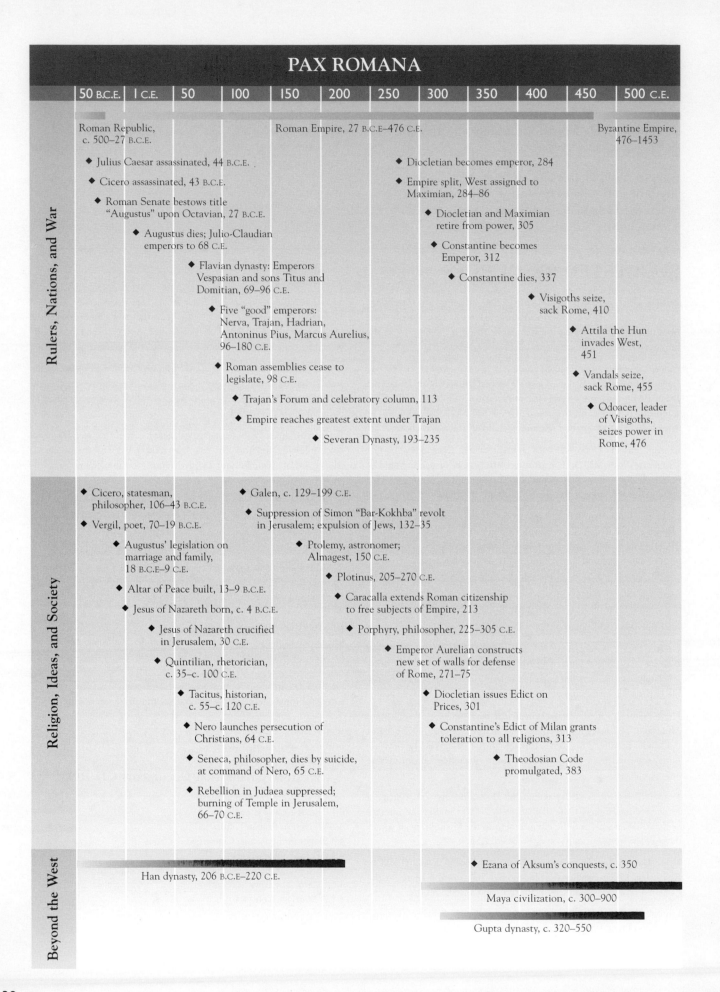

PAX ROMANA

| | 50 B.C.E. | I C.E. | 50 | 100 | 150 | 200 | 250 | 300 | 350 | 400 | 450 | 500 C.E. |

Rulers, Nations, and War

Roman Republic, c. 500–27 B.C.E.

Roman Empire, 27 B.C.E.–476 C.E.

Byzantine Empire, 476–1453

- ◆ Julius Caesar assassinated, 44 B.C.E.
- ◆ Cicero assassinated, 43 B.C.E.
- ◆ Roman Senate bestows title "Augustus" upon Octavian, 27 B.C.E.
- ◆ Augustus dies; Julio-Claudian emperors to 68 C.E.
- ◆ Flavian dynasty: Emperors Vespasian and sons Titus and Domitian, 69–96 C.E.
- ◆ Five "good" emperors: Nerva, Trajan, Hadrian, Antoninus Pius, Marcus Aurelius, 96–180 C.E.
- ◆ Roman assemblies cease to legislate, 98 C.E.
- ◆ Trajan's Forum and celebratory column, 113
- ◆ Empire reaches greatest extent under Trajan
- ◆ Severan Dynasty, 193–235

- ◆ Diocletian becomes emperor, 284
- ◆ Empire split, West assigned to Maximian, 284–86
- ◆ Diocletian and Maximian retire from power, 305
- ◆ Constantine becomes Emperor, 312
- ◆ Constantine dies, 337
- ◆ Visigoths seize, sack Rome, 410
- ◆ Attila the Hun invades West, 451
- ◆ Vandals seize, sack Rome, 455
- ◆ Odoacer, leader of Visigoths, seizes power in Rome, 476

Religion, Ideas, and Society

- ◆ Cicero, statesman, philosopher, 106–43 B.C.E.
- ◆ Vergil, poet, 70–19 B.C.E.
- ◆ Augustus' legislation on marriage and family, 18 B.C.E.–9 C.E.
- ◆ Altar of Peace built, 13–9 B.C.E.
- ◆ Jesus of Nazareth born, c. 4 B.C.E.
- ◆ Jesus of Nazareth crucified in Jerusalem, 30 C.E.
- ◆ Quintilian, rhetorician, c. 35–c. 100 C.E.
- ◆ Tacitus, historian, c. 55–c. 120 C.E.
- ◆ Nero launches persecution of Christians, 64 C.E.
- ◆ Seneca, philosopher, dies by suicide, at command of Nero, 65 C.E.
- ◆ Rebellion in Judaea suppressed; burning of Temple in Jerusalem, 66–70 C.E.

- ◆ Galen, c. 129–199 C.E.
- ◆ Suppression of Simon "Bar-Kokhba" revolt in Jerusalem; expulsion of Jews, 132–35
- ◆ Ptolemy, astronomer; Almagest, 150 C.E.
- ◆ Plotinus, 205–270 C.E.
- ◆ Caracalla extends Roman citizenship to free subjects of Empire, 213
- ◆ Porphyry, philosopher, 225–305 C.E.
- ◆ Emperor Aurelian constructs new set of walls for defense of Rome, 271–75
- ◆ Diocletian issues Edict on Prices, 301
- ◆ Constantine's Edict of Milan grants toleration to all religions, 313
- ◆ Theodosian Code promulgated, 383

Beyond the West

- ◆ Ezana of Aksum's conquests, c. 350

Han dynasty, 206 B.C.E.–220 C.E.

Maya civilization, c. 300–900

Gupta dynasty, c. 320–550

CHAPTER 6

PAX ROMANA

Society, State, and Culture in Imperial Rome

27 B.C.E.–500 C.E.

NORTH SEA

Elbe *Vistula* *Dnieper*

SLAVS

SCYTHIANS

BRITAIN

Rhine

GERMANIA

EUROPE

DACIA

BLACK SEA

GAUL

Loire

NORICUM

Danube

BITHYNIA AND PONTUS

ATLANTIC OCEAN

RHAETIA

PANNONIA

MOESIA

CAPPADOCIA

Rhône

Alps

ILLYRICUM

THRACIA

GALATIA

Po

ITALY

MACEDONIA

ASIA

CILICIA

SYRIA

CORSICA

• Rome

CYPRUS

Pyrenees

Ebro

SPAIN

Tagus

SARDINIA

ACHAIA

CRETE

JUDAEA

MEDITERRANEAN SEA

ARABIA

SICILY

MAURETANIA

Atlas Mts

NUMIDIA

AFRICA

CYRENAICA

EGYPT

Nile

Roman Empire, 2nd century CE

SLAVS people

KEY QUESTIONS

◆ **The New Imperium:** How was Rome able to establish peace generally within the empire, when in the capital the emperors were often disliked and distrusted?

◆ **Upper Classes and Other Classes:** Why did Roman society become more heterogeneous in the first two centuries of the empire? How were masses and elites able to coexist?

◆ **The Culture of Imperial Rome:** Why did Roman thought and literature enter a decline when the standard of living was high and social mobility possible?

◆ **Holding the Frontier:** How did Rome attempt to manage the growing problem of the imperial frontier? How successful was the strategy?

Peace, Roman Style At the limit of the inhabited world, reports the historian Tacitus (c. 56–118 C.E.), a rebel chieftain rallied his followers to defy Rome in the name of freedom. The Romans had pacified Britain, he charged, by devastating it. "To robbery, butchery, and rapine, they give the lying name of 'government'; they create a desolation, and call it peace."

Tacitus' narrative, composed in about 105–110 C.E., dramatizes the nature of Roman power, both creative and destructive (it is further quoted in *Witnesses* on p. 141). During the 500 years of the Republic, Rome acquired an empire. In the 250 years following Augustus' ascension to power in 27 B.C.E., that empire reached its zenith. It conferred upon its subjects the *pax romana* ("Roman peace"), purchased by conquest and secured with bloodshed. Over the next 250 years the peace failed. Rome's power was insufficient to stave off devastation in the land of its origin, or transformation in the eastern lands it had conquered.

THE NEW IMPERIUM

Octavian, later called Augustus (r. 27 B.C.E.–14 C.E.), conferred peace, order, and beauty upon the city and empire of Rome. His testimony is quoted in *Witnesses* on p. 141. His leadership also inaugurated an unprecedented concentration of authority in one person. He became "prince," the first among formerly equal citizens, and "emperor," the latter word itself (the Latin ***imperator***) taking on enlarged and ominous meaning from the nature of his rule. The Roman *imperator*, henceforth, was no mere general, wielding *imperium* in conquered lands, but the ruler of the Mediterranean world.

Augustus was succeeded first by members of his own family, then later by outsiders who acceded to imperial power by the will of the army or the Senate, by violence, or simply by luck. From Augustus' death in 14 C.E. until the middle of the third century, these rulers shaped the administration of an imperial monarchy. The principal emperors are listed in *Who's Who* on p. 144.

Augustus, the First Citizen

After Caesar's assassination in 44 B.C.E., Octavian waged war: first against Caesar's murderers, then against fellow triumvirs Mark Antony and Lepidus, now his rivals. After the battle of Actium in 31 B.C.E. and the deaths of Antony and Cleopatra, Octavian consolidated his control of Egypt, Greece, Syria, and Asia Minor. In 29 B.C.E., he returned to Rome, having established his leadership out of the ruins of the Republic. The Senators celebrated, but with some anxiety. Would he become dictator, like Caesar? Or

king, like the other rulers in the Mediterranean region? Or would he, like his predecessor Sulla, having reorganized matters in Rome, retire in order to concentrate on writing his memoirs? Octavian chose another course altogether.

Octavian took his time and established his authority gradually. The army was behind him, and during the civil wars he had obtained an oath of allegiance from all Italians. Employing the extraordinary powers granted him as military commander, he reduced the number of senators from 900 to 600 (during most of the Republic the number had stood at 300)—thus eliminating many of those appointed by his great-uncle Julius Caesar. And he reduced the legions from 60 to 28. Then in 27 B.C.E., he went before the Senate and announced that he had restored the Republic.

Octavian allowed the Senate (unconvinced that his intentions were so benign) to name him "Augustus" ("revered") and, later, **princeps** ("first citizen"). These were titles of respect, not offices of the Republic; and they were more valuable than mere offices. By the time of his death the "Principate" was established; an empire directed by a "first citizen" who still acknowledged the validity of republican forms, but with increasingly less conviction. In effect, Octavian—now Augustus—had not restored the Republic but created a monarchy.

Octavian assumed other titles which permitted him covertly to direct the organs of government. In 23 B.C.E., he surrendered the consulate (which gave him military authority, the *imperium*) bestowed on him in 27 B.C.E. by a grateful Senate. He accepted instead the *maius imperium* ("greater authority"), which meant that as proconsul, or provincial governor, he held authority over other proconsuls and could intervene in those provinces governed by the Senate. He now controlled both military and political institutions throughout the Empire.

The Senate's further grant of tribunician powers—as a patrician, he could not hold the office of tribune—reaped other benefits. He could initiate or veto legislation in the Senate and popular assemblies; he was immune from arrest or punishment; and he enjoyed the popular support generally accorded tribunes, traditionally the advocates of the people. As chief priest, he associated himself with the sacred rituals of republican Rome. He appointed priests conscientiously and saw to the construction of temples. Among them was one dedicated to his preferred deity, Apollo, whose temple and enormous statue he erected beside his modest palace on the Palatine Hill. Another he constructed for his adoptive father Caesar, who had recently been declared a god.

As Augustus laid the foundations of the imperial monarchy, an inattentive observer might have accepted the fiction that the Republic had indeed been temporarily restored. After a generation of civil war, the Senate and assemblies again met, issued

Imperial Power in the Words of Emperor Augustus and Tacitus

These passages provide two different views of Roman rule in the first century of the Empire. In the first, Augustus, the first of the emperors, describes his own significant achievements as a liberator, conqueror, and benefactor of the Roman people. In the second, in words imagined by the historian Tacitus, the leader of a British rebellion describes the Romans' insatiable greed and lust for conquest.

The emperor Augustus describes his achievements (c. 14 C.E.): 1. At the age of nineteen, on my own initiative and at my own expense, I raised an army by means of which I liberated the Republic, which was oppressed by the tyranny of a faction. ... 3. I waged many wars throughout the whole world by land and by sea, both civil and foreign, and when victorious I spared all citizens who sought pardon. ... About 500,000 Roman citizens were under military oath to me. ... 15. To the Roman plebs I paid 300 sesterces apiece in accordance with the will of my father; and in my fifth consulship, I gave each 400 sesterces in my own name out of the spoils of war; ... in my eleventh consulship I made twelve distributions of food out of grain purchased at my own expense. ... These largesses of mine reached never less than 250,000 persons. ... 17. Four times I came to the assistance of the treasury with my own money, transferring to those in charge of the treasury 150,000,000 sesterces. ... 20. I repaired the Capitol and the theater of Pompey with enormous expenditures on both works, without having my name inscribed on them. I repaired the conduits of the aqueducts which were falling into ruin in many places because of age. ... 34. In my sixth and seventh consulships, after I had put an end to the civil wars, having attained supreme power by universal consent, I transferred the state from my own power to the control of the Roman senate and people. For this service of mine I received the title of Augustus by decree of the senate. ...
(Augustus, *Res gestae divi Augusti*, nos. 1, 3, 15, 17, 20, 34; ed. N. Lewis, M. Reinhold 1966)

In words supplied by the historian Tacitus, Calgacus, leader of rebellious Britons, calls for resistance to Roman imperialism (c. 105–110 C.E.): When I consider the motives we have for fighting and the critical position we are in, I have a strong feeling that the united front you are showing today will mean the dawn of liberty for the whole of Britain. You have mustered to a man, and all of you are free. ... Out of sight of subject shores, we kept even our eyes free from the defilement of tyranny. We, the most distant dwellers upon earth, the last of the free, have been shielded till today by our very remoteness and by the obscurity in which it has shrouded our name. Now, the farthest bounds of Britain lie open to our enemies; and what men know nothing about they always assume to be a valuable prize. But there are no more nations beyond us; nothing is there but waves and rocks, and the Romans, more deadly still than these—for in them is an arrogance which no submission or good behaviour can escape. Pillagers of the world, they have exhausted the land by their indiscriminate plunder, and now they ransack the sea. A rich enemy excites their cupidity; a poor one, their lust for power. East and West alike have failed to satisfy them. They are the only people on earth to whose covetousness both riches and poverty are equally tempting. To robbery, butchery, and rapine, they give the lying name of "government"; they create a desolation and call it peace.
(Tacitus, *Agricola*, no. 30; ed. H. Mattingly, rev. S. A. Handford 1970)

---

decrees, and held elections. Over the next five centuries, however, these republican gestures were to fade to mere vestiges. They were already failing by the end of Augustus' reign. The Senate had usurped many functions of the unruly plebeian assemblies which had supported the Gracchi and later revolutionaries. Under Augustus, senatorial decrees acquired the force of law. The assemblies, ceding that function to the Senate, ceased to legislate after 98 C.E. Elections for the higher magistrates were also shifted from the assemblies to the less democratic Senate.

As republican institutions withered, Augustus created imperial ones. Secretaries, drawn from his own vast ranks of slaves and freedmen, kept accounts of his personal fortune—much greater than the ancient "Treasure of Saturn," the store of public wealth administered by the Senate (Saturn was father of the Roman gods). He placed the army under his control. Each of its 250,000 to 300,000 soldiers swore a personal oath to him. A separate Praetorian Guard of nine citizen **cohorts** kept close watch over Italy and Rome and in the immediate vicinity of the ruler.

In the provinces, imperial interests were managed by officials called procurators who were drawn from the secondary elite of the equestrian order (see Chapter 5). Newly created officials called prefects took responsibility for five key tasks: to head the ruler's personal military guard (the Praetorian Prefect); to manage the city of Rome (the Urban Prefect); to head the city's seven semi-military cohorts of police and fire forces; to monitor the city's grain supply; and to rule Egypt, Rome's breadbasket. Although the Urban Prefect was of senatorial status, all the other officials were equestrians.

His claim to have restored the Republic was a fiction, yet Augustus could legitimately claim many impressive achievements. Shortly before he died he described these in his *Res gestae* ("My Deeds"). "At the age of nineteen, ... I raised an army by means of which I liberated the Republic," claimed the aged emperor. He distributed largesse to the Roman plebs, funded the public treasury, built temples, and repaired aqueducts. He provided for shows in which gladiators fought (in the public arena for the entertainment of spectators) or wild beasts were butchered by the thousands. He drove out pirates and expanded the frontiers, established colonies of army veterans, and appropriated for Rome the wealth of the Nile.

His contemporaries loved Augustus for having restored peace. "The civil wars were ended after twenty years," wrote the historian Velleius Paterculus; "foreign wars suppressed, peace restored, the frenzy of arms everywhere lulled to rest. ..." Cultivating that association, Augustus constructed the "Altar of Peace" in the Roman Forum. In this monument imperial imagery commingles with the sacred, expressing in stone the lofty message of an old man who, in his youth, had ravaged the people of Rome and murdered the leaders of the expiring Republic. One of the reliefs is shown below.

Emperors Good and Bad: Augustus to the Severi

Augustus saw his children and grandchildren die, and outlived two of his appointed heirs: his trusted comrade and son-in-law Marcus Vipsanius Agrippa (c. 63 B.C.E.–12 C.E.), and his beloved nephew, Marcus Claudius Marcellus (c. 42–23 B.C.E.). As he approached his own impending demise, the matter of succession loomed. By now there was no thought of relinquishing power; the Republic would never be truly restored. Augustus must be followed by another Augustus, of his extended family, if not of his own blood. The mantle fell on Tiberius (r. 14–37 C.E.): the son of Augustus' consort, Livia, by her first husband, a member of the Claudian clan.

To cement the relationship, Augustus grudgingly adopted Tiberius as son and heir, merging the ancient Julian and Claudian clans, his own and his wife's. In 14 C.E., upon Augustus' death at age seventy-six, Tiberius became emperor. Efficient, surly, and autocratic, Tiberius scaled down the citizen assemblies, bullied the Senate, and hoarded gold and silver for the imperial treasury. He also held the frontiers Augustus had attained and supervised his provincial administrators. If his personality had not been so frosty, and if his sexual eccentricities had not been so offensive, he might have been better liked. He was not, upon his death, made a god. Instead, the populace rejoiced, shouting "Into the Tiber with Tiberius."

The new emperor was Gaius (r. 37–41 C.E.), called "Caligula," or "little boot," a nickname from the days when he was an endearing child. As an adult, he was dangerous and probably insane. The soldiers of the Praetorian Guard murdered him, designating as successor the one surviving adult male of the Julio-Claudian line: the scholar Claudius (r. 41–54 C.E.). This elderly man, seemingly inept and chronically ill, nevertheless saw to the conquest of Britain, the construction of the lighthouse at the port of Ostia, and the creation of an imperial bureaucracy. He, too, was murdered: by his fourth wife, Agrippina (15–59 C.E.), a great-granddaughter of Augustus.

Agrippina promoted her own son Nero for the imperial title, even murdering Britannicus (Claudius' son by a previous marriage) to assure Nero's future. Her maneuvers met with due reward: Nero had her murdered, his soldiers ripping open the womb from which Nero had sprung. As mad as Caligula, Nero (r. 54–68 C.E.), let the now well-oiled machinery of empire churn on while he declaimed, strummed his lyre, and even leaped into the arena to contend, like the gladiators, with savage beasts. When a great fire destroyed much of Rome in 64 C.E., he blamed it on the Christians, thus launching the first major persecution of what was then a despised sect. Four years later, having aroused the opposition of the Praetorian Guard, he fled Rome, accompanied by his concubine and his nurse. These loyal servants assisted him to commit suicide and avoid assassination.

Imperial Power

Altar of Peace: *The emperors employed cultural as well as political strategies to announce and bolster their power, as seen here in objects associated with the successful emperors Augustus, Vespasian, and Trajan. In the marble-relief on the Ara Pacis ("Altar of Peace"), Rome, 13–9 B.C.E., a mother goddess is surrounded by images of abundant fertility—the fruits of the peace won by Augustus.*

Imperial Philanthropy: This detail from a relief on the triumphal arch erected in honor of Trajan in Benevento, 114–117 C.E., shows the emperor distributing gifts of food to the children of the poor.

Senate moved quickly to appoint the next emperor in 96: a senator like themselves, an old man with no sons, the gentle and capable Nerva (r. 96–98 C.E.).

Five emperors had now reigned as descendants, if only indirectly, of Julius Caesar. Now the last of the Julio-Claudian dynasty was dead. In the absence of a legitimate heir to power, the legions were all too ready to provide for the succession. The four armies dispersed through the provinces selected four generals in turn as emperor in the single year 68–69 C.E.. As each emperor claimed the throne, only to be replaced by the next strong man, senators and ordinary citizens trembled in Rome.

The end of the "Year of the Four Emperors" found the last of them, the experienced and sensible Titus Flavius Vespasianus (r. 69–79 C.E.; anglicized as Vespasian) alive, secure, and in charge.

In the remaining ten years of his life, Vespasian enlarged the Senate with recruits from the provinces, favored skilled equestrians over freedmen in the bureaucracy, enriched the treasury, and tamed the dangerous security force Augustus had created, the Praetorian Guard. A relief after Caligula and Nero, this prudent penny-pincher shunned the glossy attributes of power. As he died, his whispered last words mocked the pretensions of his deified predecessors: "My, I think I am becoming a god." Vespasian had already arranged for the succession of his sons: his family or anarchy, he had warned the Senate. Vespasian's sons reigned in turn: Titus briefly (r. 79–81 C.E.), quickly followed by Domitian (r. 81–96 C.E.). Fascinated by his own power, Domitian was obsessed with possible conspiracies directed against him by the senators, whom he bullied and persecuted. Spies and informers, paid from the imperial purse, identified potential conspirators. Domitian compelled the Senate to participate in the prosecution of these alleged enemies of the state—and even to condemn the books they wrote. Jointly emperor and senators purged the ranks of the Senate, sending many to their deaths for "treason." Ironically, the autocrat who called for this bloodletting did not escape the fate he most feared. He, too, was murdered, by conspirators who had escaped the notice of imperial spies. The

With Nerva began a series of five emperors who succeeded each other by a nondynastic principle over nearly a century (from 96 to 180 C.E.). Each appointed his successor during his lifetime. Nerva named the general Trajan (r. 98–117 C.E.). Trajan appointed his own cousin Hadrian (r. 117–138 C.E.). Hadrian reluctantly named the dutiful Antoninus (r. 138–161 C.E.), commanding Antoninus to adopt as his sons and joint successors the latter's nephew Marcus (later called Marcus Aurelius; r. 161–180 C.E.) and also Lucius Verus, the son of the candidate Hadrian would have preferred. Under these rulers, the Empire reached its maximum extent, its frontiers were fortified, trade flourished, the treasury swelled, the fusion of Greek and Roman culture was accomplished, and the city of Rome became more beautiful than ever. The Senate relaxed, unaware that its power had evaporated. The *pax romana* reached its zenith.

Marcus Aurelius was a philosopher as well as an emperor, and he ruled capably and diligently. Yet all his mental prowess could not avert the problems that befell Rome in the late second century. Barbarian tribes gnawed at Italy's northern frontier, while armies returning from the East brought a deadly plague to the capital—which could not be halted. Lucius Verus died in 169 C.E., and Marcus Aurelius proposed his own son Commodus to replace him.

It was a terrible mistake. An unstable megalomaniac who wished to be a gladiator, Commodus (r. 180–192 C.E.) became emperor on Marcus Aurelius' death in 180 C.E. and retained power for twelve years before he was strangled by an assassin. Two emperors reigned briefly, then the army intervened with its own candidate: the Punic general Septimius Severus (r. 193–211 C.E.). Severus was able, in a reign of nearly twenty years, to reassert Roman military strength at vulnerable border points and to rebuild the treasury, depleted by Commodus' excesses.

Severus was succeeded by three members of his Afro-Syrian family. The Severan dynasty ended in 235 C.E. with the murder of Alexander Severus and

Principal Players in the Imperial Roman Succession

	Emperor	Dates	Reign
1	Augustus	63 B.C.E.–14 C.E.	27 B.C.E.–14 C.E.
2	Tiberius	42 B.C.E.–37 C.E.	14–37 C.E.
3	Vespasian	9–79 C.E.	69–79 C.E.
4	Antoninus Pius	86–161	138–161
5	Marcus Aurelius	121–180	161–180
6	Commodus	161–192	180–192
7	Septimius Severus	c. 145–211	193–211
8	Diocletian	245–313	284–305
9	Constantine	c. 285–337	312–337

his mother—the partner, if not the mastermind, of his reign and mother (so she claimed) of the "Armies, Senate, Fatherland, and whole Human Race."

Inside the Imperial Monarchy

By this time the Roman Republic was forgotten, its revival out of the question. For the second time in the history of the West, monarchy had replaced a government where the citizens—at least some of them—had ruled. Before his death in 323 B.C.E., Alexander had reintroduced monarchy to the world of the Greek *polis*. Augustus reintroduced it to Rome. For now, the experience of self-government was lost except in the books that recorded its history. Until the end of antiquity in the West, emperors ruled.

The emperor went through the formality of presenting his decrees to the Senate, which promptly approved them. Still sporting togas trimmed in purple, like their predecessors of republican days, the new class of senators was a shadow of the old. The old nobility had been ravaged by revolution and purges. Equestrians or provincials, the new senators were loyal to the monarch who promoted them. The emperor now ruled with the advice of a council of bureaucrats, mostly equestrian. From that class also came the officers of the army—from which, beginning in the mid-third century C.E., senators were barred.

Imperial administration lay in the hands of secretaries, accountants, and other bureaucrats who handled finances, letter-writing, minutes-taking, and record-keeping. Augustus' office staff was composed of his own slaves and freedmen. Claudius created a more elaborate bureaucracy, also staffed with freedmen of his household. Later emperors replaced Claudius' freedmen with equestrians. This bureaucracy was subdivided into departments like those of a modern state: finance, foreign affairs, domestic administration. As republican institutions deteriorated, this civil service managed the business of empire.

Law was a central concern of the Roman people. In the Republic, schoolboys had memorized the laws, legendarily inscribed on the Twelve Tables. Prospective senators were amateur lawyers who began their careers by testifying as character witnesses, defending family members, clients, or friends, or prosecuting a defendant charged with a private or public crime. Summaries of the legal issues involved in these cases and records of the precedents they established became the basis of later Roman law. To these were added senatorial edicts and laws voted in the assemblies. Private citizens called **jurisprudents** (men learned in the law but holding no official magistracy) advised private persons.

Under the emperors, law and lawmaking changed. New laws originated with the emperor and his council, not the Assembly or the Senate (who still ratified them). The jurisprudents were now professionals in the imperial bureaucracy, whose documentation and analysis of past decisions constituted a system of law. Imperial jurisprudents began the process of codification under Hadrian. Under Marcus Aurelius this resulted in a textbook of Roman law: the *Institutes*. Later experts under the Severan rulers created original new theories about the relation of civil law (*jus civile*) to the "law of nations" (*jus gentium*) and the "law of nature" (*jus naturale*) (see Chapters 17, 19). Modern thinkers would draw on these concepts to argue that some rights are universal and inalienable—the concept underlying all democratic constitutions.

The final codification of Roman law was achieved in the sixth century under the emperor Justinian in the *Corpus juris civilis* (*The Collected Civil Law*) which became a source of much of the law of the modern West (see Chapter 8). In this body of law as developed over the next 1000 years is distilled Rome's contribution to the world in the area of government.

The growing sophistication of the legal system coexisted with ancient patterns of monarchy. The emperors were worshiped as gods—in Rome only after their death (at first) but in the eastern provinces while living. The custom of king worship was a continuation of Hellenistic custom, in which kings were worshiped as benefactors: providers of protection, food, relief from taxes, or a new set of walls. They acquired surnames such as "savior" or "doer of good deeds" or "the god made manifest."

In Rome, the worship of the ruler was introduced tentatively. After his death, Julius Caesar was declared a god, a designation plausible to his subjects because his family was thought to be descended from the deities Mars and Venus. Still, some Romans resisted—as did Cicero, who scoffed at the **deification** of a man who had been buried by his family in the ordinary way. Such scruples soon disappeared. Augustus was worshiped in the East during his lifetime, and deified by the Senate at his death—one senator solemnly attesting that he had seen the deceased ascend to heaven. Domitian was addressed in his lifetime as "lord and god." The divinity of later emperors was celebrated in temples and sanctuaries throughout the realm. In the ceremony of **apotheosis**, the deification of a deceased emperor was announced by the release to the heavens of an eagle caged above the funeral pyre. Astonishingly, this rite continued to be practiced even for Christian emperors.

Under Augustus, all subjects and citizens swore loyalty to the emperor, pledging their own persons and calling down upon their children and their descendants "utter ruin and utter destruction" if they violated that pledge. The monarchization of Rome implicit was accomplished by the time of the Severan emperors. Individuals might act freely in their personal or economic lives. Only the emperor was free to participate in the political realm. The Empire—Augustus' new *imperium*—bestowed a hollow peace on Rome: one disguising the loss of civic freedom. It was a sad benefit to confer upon a people whose history had begun with the expulsion of a tyrant.

UPPER CLASSES AND OTHER CLASSES

In the social realm, as well as the political, the imperial regime brought both advantages and drawbacks. On the one hand, the old senatorial elite suffered terribly under the emperors, both from direct and concerted repression and from a long-term waning of influence. On the other, a new elite of equestrian entrepreneurs found a role in the imperial bureaucracy alongside its already established position in commerce and public contracting.

Social opportunities also improved for other, less privileged Romans. The status of elite women, of children, and of slaves improved slightly. The ranks of "freed" persons, male and female, increased, and also fed the rolls of new citizens, once their own children, one generation removed from slavery, claimed their right of full citizenship. Now extended to larger and larger groups outside Rome and even outside Italy, citizenship meant little politically—the right to vote being meaningless under an increasingly authoritarian monarchy. But it did enhance status and bestow commercial privileges. And for those citizens who lived in the capital, it also conferred the right to free grain and free and lurid entertainments.

Senators and Equestrians

The emergence of the imperial monarchy most severely affected the members of the old senatorial order. While members of this elite faced declining opportunities, other Romans of the equestrian order actually experienced a rise in status.

The Senate's deliberations, debates, and divisions still filled the long hours, but the conclusions were predetermined: they would be those that the master wished. The memory of their decimation during the years of civil war discouraged any senatorial initiative. To defy the emperor was to be vulnerable to a charge of *laesa maiestas*, "injured majesty": it was considered a capital crime even to criticize the ruler.

The demoralized nobility embarked on its own extinction: unable to resist the advance of imperial power, the senators were not even able to reproduce themselves. Their population dwindled. Few married, or they divorced; or if they married, they remained childless. The practice of celibacy may have caused this sterility, or more probably the widespread practice of birth control, or the equally widespread exposure of unwanted infants.

To staunch the hemorraging of the senatorial ranks, Augustus proposed over the period from 18 B.C.E. to 9 C.E. a package of laws extending special privileges to upper-class fathers of children. Acknowledging that children were a financial burden—boys requiring an expensive education and allowances commensurate with their rank, girls needing dowries—Augustus offered cash bonuses, tax exemptions, and opportunities for political advancement to aristocratic fathers. Conversely, childless men were penalized, and unmarried heirs heavily taxed. Elite women with three or more children were fully emancipated—free, that is, to handle all property transactions without a male guardian as intermediary. Augustus' legislation extended to the private sexual behavior of the upper classes as he attempted to promote traditional models of family life as shown in *Witnesses* on p. 146. Heretofore adultery (defined exclusively as the wife's violation of marriage vows) had been punished within the family, at the discretion of the *paterfamilias*. Now it became a crime: one that implicated many upper-class matrons and their partners. Married men who engaged in sex outside marriage were free of the charge of adultery, so long as their lovers were of a lower social class. Any male, married or unmarried, who engaged in sex with an unmarried woman of the elite was guilty of *stuprum*, or "fornication": a new criminal offense. Augustus' moral zeal was unrelenting. He exiled his daughter and his granddaughter, both bearing the distinguished clan name of Julia, for adultery.

Augustus' pro-family legislation failed. Augustus himself died with no direct heir of his own blood, as did many of his successors. Domitian and Septimius Severus attempted to revive Augustus' legislation, with equally poor results. Their attempts could not promote the biological survival of the nobility or check its flight from politics. Its place would be filled by new men filtering up from lower social ranks.

Family Values in Imperial Rome

How people in the past felt about their families and loved ones is difficult to assess —even in the case of the Romans, for whom we have rich literary, historical, and legal sources. The four excerpts here give a glimpse of the private world in a society that sometimes seems very like, sometimes very remote, from our own. In the first, the historian Suetonius describes the laws made by Augustus to promote and preserve families. The second reveals the sentiments of an upper-class author, Pliny the Younger, towards his wife. The third, by the poet Juvenal, reflecting the sophisticated lives of elite Romans, mocks women and marriage both. The fourth is from the law codes issued by the much later emperor Theodosius, whose Christian outlook is displayed in legislation against the sale of children.

The emperor Augustus tries to strengthen families with new legislation (c. 9 C.E.): He revised existing laws and enacted some new ones, for example, on extravagance, on adultery and chastity, on bribery, and on the encouragement of marriage among the various classes of citizens. Having made somewhat more stringent changes in the last of these than in the others, he was unable to carry it out because of an open revolt against its provisions, until he had abolished or mitigated a part of the penalties. ... When the knights even then persistently called for its repeal at a public show, he sent for the children of [the popular hero] Germanicus and exhibited them, some in his own lap and some in their father's, intimating by his gestures and expression that they should not refuse to follow that young man's example. And on finding that the spirit of the law was being evaded by betrothal with immature girls and by frequent changes of wives, he shortened the duration of betrothals and set a limit on divorce.
(Suetonius, *De Vita Caesarum*, 34; trans. J. C. Rolfe, 1920)

Pliny the Younger writes lovingly to his wife (c. 100 C.E.): Never have I chafed more impatiently under my engagements which have prevented me from accompanying you on your journey to Campania to convalesce and from following immediately after you. For at this moment I particularly want to be with you; I want to believe the evidence of my eyes and see what you are doing to look after your strength and your little self, whether in fact you are enjoying to the full the peace and the pleasures and the richness of the place. ... I beg you therefore all the more earnestly to be kind to my fears and to send me a letter, or even two letters, every day. While I am reading it, I shall worry less: when I have finished it, my fears will at once return.
(Pliny the Younger, *Letters*; ed. R. H. Barrow, 1949)

Satirist Juvenal urges a friend not to marry (c. 120 C.E.):
... Postumus, are you *really*
Taking a wife? You used to be sane enough ...
Why endure such bitch-tyranny when rope's available
By the fathom, when all those dizzying top-floor windows
Are open for you, when there are bridges handy
To jump from? Supposing none of these exits catches
Your fancy, isn't it better to sleep with a pretty boy?
Boys don't quarrel all night, or nag you for little presents
While they're on the job. ...
(Juvenal, *Satire 6*)

The law code under Emperor Theodosius bans the sale of children (383 C.E.): XI.xvii.1: A law shall be written on bronze or waxed tablets or on linen cloth, and posted throughout all the municipalities of Italy, to restrain the hands of parents from infanticide. ... [I]f any parent should report that he has offspring which on account of poverty he is unable to rear, there shall be no delay in issuing food and clothing, since the rearing of a new-born infant can not tolerate a delay. ... XI.xvii.2: We have learned that provincials suffering from scarcity of food and lack of sustenance are selling or pledging their children. Therefore, if any such person is found who is sustained by no substance of family possessions and is supporting his children with hardship and difficulty, he shall be assisted through our fisc before he becomes a prey to calamity. ... For it is repugnant to our customs to allow any person to be destroyed by hunger or rush forth to the commission of a shameful deed.
(Theodosian Code, 11:27:1–2; ed. N. Lewis, M. Reinhold, 1966)

Equestrians, meanwhile, who under the Republic had performed valuable services as publicans and entrepreneurs, now participated in the imperial bureaucracy and council, and in intelligence and diplomatic and fiscal services. They might be employed as accountants in the provinces, or hold one of the prefectures created by the emperor, or serve as officers in the army. From Italians and provincials of equestrian rank the emperors also replenished the ranks of the Senate.

Wives, Mothers, and Children

The senatorial and equestrian orders made up the class designated *honestior* ("more honorable") by Roman law (see Chapter 5). Women of this social class were granted extraordinary freedom in the early Empire—resembling in their status, but exceeding in privilege, even the upper-class women of the Hellenistic East. The form of marriage by which a woman passed from her father's to her husband's authority—marriage with *manus*—had been replaced by a form of free marriage. Women who married remained theoretically under the authority of their father or guardian, who retained supervision of the dowry wealth that wives brought their husbands. Thus women possessed (if only through male relatives) an independence conferred by wealth that they had not known in earlier eras. Augustus' "law concerning children," moreover, liberated elite women who had borne at least three legitimate children from all restrictions of guardianship.

Romans developed a concept of companionate marriage similar to the modern one, in which spouses are seen as loving partners. The biographer Plutarch (c. 50–120 C.E.) considered married love the highest form of friendship. The author Pliny the Younger (c. 61–112 C.E.) vividly expressed in his letters to his wife his great affection for her (see *Witnesses*, p. 146)—an affection implicit in his sharing with her the drafts of his works, for her comment. A greater respect for wives may explain the extension of the concept of the family to include relatives on the wife's side (cognates) as well as those in the male or agnate line.

Old restraints and new freedoms characterized the lives of upper-class wives. On the one hand, they were largely confined to their homes, where they were still expected to spend much of their time spinning—and in epitaphs and letters, many women were congratulated for their excellent work with wool! On the other hand, some matrons were active in public life, attending banquets and literary readings, where they might even discourse on philosophy or recite their own poems. Less gifted women might accompany their husbands to the games and races and mock battles in the Colosseum, proclaiming their status in society with the brilliance of their jewels.

A widow was expected to wait ten months after a spouse's death before remarriage (widowers didn't have to wait at all). The widow who renounced remarriage was more greatly honored. Such women were rare. More is heard of the lively widows preferred as lovers by young aristocrats.

During the Empire, divorce was easy and common. Either partner could divorce the other by repudiation: one merely informed the other of the step. Upon divorce, women (or their families) reclaimed their dowries. Among the ranks of the divorced were Julius Caesar, Pompey, Cicero, Augustus, Tiberius, and Nero; and divorce reached epidemic proportions in the generations thereafter. Some women, remarked the philosopher Seneca (c. 3 B.C.E.–65 C.E.), reckoned the year not by the names of the consuls (as was traditional) but by those of their husbands.

The wives and mothers of emperors, often echoing the pattern of Hellenistic queens, enjoyed fame and power. Livia, Augustus' wife for fifty-two years, received the title "Augusta" and was deified by her grandson Claudius. She helped groom her son Tiberius for power. Agrippina, wife and murderer of Claudius, promoted her own son Nero. Trajan's wife, Plotina, may have engineered the succession of his cousin Hadrian, a great favorite of hers whom she continued to advise. Her influence was acknowledged in Hadrian's funeral oration for the dynamic empress: "She often made requests of me," declared the emperor, "and I never once refused her anything."

The four Julias of the Severan dynasty—the wife of Septimius Severus, her sister, and her two daughters—were stalwart women. The first survived her husband to wield the power behind the throne of their son Caracalla—after the latter had murdered her other son as she held him in her arms. This capable woman managed the treasury, attempted government reform, encouraged religious tolerance, and patronized both philosophy and law. After her son Caracalla's assassination in 217 C.E., she starved herself to death. She was soon avenged by her sister, who engineered the succession in turn of her two grandsons: the bizarre Elagabalus (who took the name of the Asian solar deity he favored) and the docile Alexander Severus, both closely monitored by their mothers.

The efforts of highly placed mothers for the advancement of their sons is one small part of the story of family life in imperial Rome. Similar behavior is found in nonimperial families. The mother of Saint Augustine (354–430 C.E.), Monica (a devout Christian, who also achieved sainthood), groomed him for a career in the civil service, praying both for his soul and for his professional success. The author Seneca discoursed on philosophy with his mother, Helvetia, who had been forbidden by her husband to study that lofty subject. Such glimpses of maternal initiative suggest, at least among the elite, close ties between mothers and sons.

Among the elites, nurses, too, may have played a significant role in the lives of young Romans. The nurse began as a wet nurse: a woman who, having recently borne a child herself, was lactating and available to provide nourishment to other women's infants. She did so, if she were free, for a price. More often, she was a slave. Frequently, she was Greek-speaking, which was desirable, as the child would thereby easily learn the language considered, for its cultural value, superior to Latin.

Wet nurses often stayed with the household for years, continuing to nurture and support the young children whom they had once nourished. With what feelings the nurse contemplated the child who was her social superior, who had replaced her own offspring (by compulsion of poverty or slavery) in her life, can only be guessed. In a few cases, adult Romans expressed their profound affection for the nurses who had raised them.

Upper-class Roman men treasured their daughters. They became close to their daughters' husbands, and often preferred the children of their daughters to

Not only the deeds of emperors, but also the personal relations of ordinary people are recorded in Roman monuments. This tomb sculpture (left) shows a freedman (center) with his wife and child (left). The child is called her father's "delight" in the inscription below the figures. This relief (right) of a well-known merchant depicts the merchant's shop, with five standing clerks (including one woman, a slave, shown in profile) and two seated customers. The funerary relief (below right) shows a man holding a portrait bust. (left: Deutsches Archaeologisches Institut; right: Uffizi, Florence; below, Villa Albani, Rome)

What typically Roman cultural value is expressed in this last representation?

Funerary relief of Sextitius Selprimus, Rome, first century C.E.

Funerary relief, Rome, first century C.E.

Funerary relief, Rome, mid–1st century C.E.

To continue your investigation of this topic, please go to www.prenhall.com/king for the related WINDOWS on the WEB activity

On Education and Oratory

Whereas Cicero, Livy, and Virgil were deeply immersed in politics during the last years of the Republic, cultural life in the first century of the Empire became more detached from the political realm, and at the same time both more varied and more legislated. The orator Quintilian became a schoolmaster, who taught young Romans the fundamentals of rhetoric and wrote a book on the topic, the source of the first of the first passage here. His contemporary, the historian Tacitus, laments the loss of political freedom that had permitted the originality and spontaneity of an older generation of orators.

Quintilian on children's potential to learn (c. 90 C.E.): I would, therefore, have a father conceive the highest hopes of his son from the moment of his birth. If he does so, he will be the more careful about the groundwork of his education. For there is absolutely no foundation for the complaint that but few men have the power to take in the knowledge that is imparted to them, and that the majority are so slow of understanding that education is a waste of time and labor. On the contrary, you will find that most are quick to reason and ready to learn. ... Those who are dull and unteachable are as abnormal as prodigious births and monstrosities and are but few in number. ... But, it will be urged, there are differing degrees of intellectual ability. Undoubtedly, I reply, and there will be a corresponding variation in actual accomplishment; but that there are any who gain nothing from education, I absolutely deny.
(Quintilian, *The Elements of Oratory*, 1:1–3; eds. N. Lewis, M. Reinhold 1966)

Tacitus explains why oratory flags when dictators rule (c. 90 C.E.): Great oratory is like a flame: it needs fuel to feed it, movement to fan it, and it brightens as it burns. At Rome too the eloquence of our forefathers owed its development to the same conditions. For although the orators of today have also succeeded in obtaining all the influence that it would be proper to allow them under settled, peaceable, and prosperous political conditions, yet their predecessors in those days of unrest and unrestraint seemed to accomplish more when, in the general ferment and without the strong hand of a single ruler, a speaker's political wisdom was measured by his power of carrying conviction to the unstable populace. ... [A]s long as the constitution was unsettled, so long as the country kept wearing itself out with factions and dissensions and disagreements, so long as there was no peace in the Forum, no harmony in the senate, no restraint in the courts, no respect for authority ... the growth of eloquence was doubtless sturdier just as untilled soil produces certain vegetation in greater luxuriance. But the benefit derived from the eloquence of the Gracchi did not make up for what the country suffered from their laws, and too dearly did Cicero pay by the death he died for his renown in oratory.
(Tacitus, *Dialogue on Oratory*, 36–40; eds. N. Lewis, M. Reinhold 1966)

---

those of their sons. The harsh paternal authority of the early Republic had faded. Boys, too, were freer of the paternal yoke in the imperial centuries. A father could not sell into slavery a son he had acknowledged as his own, and the killing of a son was seen as murder, the equivalent of killing a parent. Still, the boy remained economically subject to his father for many years, not acceding to full adulthood until his father's death—an event sometimes anxiously awaited as the springboard to financial and personal autonomy.

As in Greece, there were more boys than girls, more men than women—that different sex ratio indicating the widespread elimination of females in all classes, by exposure, by the preferential feeding of males, and as a result of young women's death in childbirth or as a result of abortion. Throughout the Empire, it was rare for a family to have more daughters than sons. Children of both sexes born out of wedlock, ill, or deformed, were regularly exposed. Indeed, children must have been exposed in quantity to explain the widespread childlessness of adults, to which both histories and epitaphs of the rich and poor attest. The high incidence of child mortality is not sufficient to do so.

"Exposure" consisted of abandoning children in public places: typically, on heaps of garbage or dung. Here they might die of hunger and cold. Alternatively, they might be picked up by ordinary folk or professional slavedealers. In the former case, the "adopted" child became an **alumnus** of the family—not a true child but a valued servant trained in the skills necessary to assist the household economy. Epitaphs testify to the great number of these *alumni* (more often male than female), many cherished by their surrogate parents. The child's status was theoretically determined by that of his biological mother—free or slave—but was often unknown because of the silence of the dungheap. If a slave, or presumed a slave, the child could be freed (manumitted), but never, having begun life in the womb of a slave, legally adopted. If picked up by the slavedealer, a foundling of either sex would be sold as a servant or laborer or to the brothel manager as a prostitute.

The lot of children improved in the later Empire. Domitian prohibited the castration and prostitution of children. From the reign of his successor, Nerva, until that of Septimius Severus, a system of relief for poor children, funded by the profits on low-interest loans, maintained at least 5000 children at a time in some 40 Italian cities. By the late third century, the abandonment of a child was considered an act of murder. In the late Empire, under Christian influence, infanticide and abortion were harshly condemned.

The condition of children, especially their vulnerability to abandonment, touches on two other aspects of private life in Rome: misogyny and homosexuality. The lesser value of women is witnessed by the presumed rate of female infanticide. The hatred of women (expressed in the literature of the aristocracy) reached a peak in the imperial centuries at the same time, ironically, as they achieved their greatest freedom. Meanwhile, the practice of male homosexuality (so central to Greek culture) became more prevalent—reflecting, among other factors, the easy availability of young male slaves and *alumni*.

Freedmen, Slaves, and the Poor

The circumstances of birth determined to which half of Roman society a child would belong. The few children of the legitimate marriages of members of the elites belonged to the class of *honestiores* (the "more honorable"). The many children of the legitimate marriages of the poor, the children of concubinage relationships, and the children of slaves all indiscriminately belonged to the class of the *humiliores* ("more humble"). From the second century, these two social groups acquired legal definition, adding to the preexisting social distinctions between free and slave, citizen and noncitizen. *Honestiores* and *humiliores* were treated differently in civil and criminal cases. Penalties such as torture, condemnation to the mines, crucifixion, or consignment to the wild beasts of the arena were reserved for humbler folk.

The *humiliores* included three groups: freedmen (and freedwomen), slaves, and the plebs (poor but free citizens). Of these, freedmen held the highest position in Roman society. It was a class made up of freed slaves who, uniquely in the ancient world, became citizens without taint in the second generation. Freedman status lasted only a generation; even then the freedman had only partial citizen rights. A freedman's children and grandchildren were free to enter into Roman society at any level to which their skills could bring them. They could intermarry with other Roman citizens. By the second century, many senators and equestrians numbered among their family, a mere one or two generations back, a freedman ancestor—and in the previous generation a slave.

Freedmen were numerous and powerful. Although they constituted only about 5 percent of Rome's total population, they were especially visible because their industry and zeal rewarded them with wealth and status. Their numbers swelled from the rapid rate of manumission—explainable perhaps by the fact that highly motivated freedman artisans were more valuable to upper-class families than slaves. So common became the practice of manumission that the slave population in the city of Rome declined rapidly. Augustus attempted to stem the tide of manumissions (although he also opposed the abuse of slaves). Yet the freedman population continued to grow, filling the ranks of the shopkeepers and artisans and their collegial organizations.

Since few women practiced as artisans or had any trade beyond spinning and weaving, they were less likely to be manumitted. However, a freedwoman who subsequently bore at least four children gained the legal status of a freeborn woman and economic independence. For women of both classes, high fertility opened up an avenue to higher economic status.

Freedmen continued after manumission to have special ties to former owners, resembling the traditional Roman tie between client and patron. They took on the clan name of those owners, and visited them on a daily basis to offer their homage. Should the noble family die without heirs, it was the family's freedmen who were pledged to carry on the worship of its ancestors. If a noble family faced extinction because of a lack of children, a possible remedy was to adopt the child of a family freedman—but not the freedman himself, or the freedwoman, for he or she had been born a slave. The freedman, indeed, might have to free his own child, if that child were born to a slave concubine, and await grandchildren if he wished for progeny with full citizen status. A freedman lived more often with women in concubinage than in legitimate marriage, whether the woman was slave, freed, or freeborn.

The possibility of manumission offered hope to skilled slaves. Most urban slaves were artisans, producers of goods for local consumption and export. They received an allowance from their masters (rather than a wage) in compensation for their labor. While city slaves looked to manumission, the slaves who had worked on the land were replaced by poor tenant farmers called **coloni**. Rome still housed many slaves—some working as domestic servants in the houses of the rich or imperial families, others pressed into prostitution or trained as gladiators. But increasingly their offspring joined the society of freedmen.

Legislation introduced by Augustus, Claudius, Domitian, Hadrian, Antoninus Pius, and others attended to the protection of slaves. If sick and neglected by their masters, they were to be manumitted; if they were mistreated, their masters would be charged before the urban prefect of Rome. They were not to be castrated for use in brothels, sold into prostitution or into the gladiatorial schools, nor executed by the sole judgment of their masters without a confirming investigation by the proper authorities.

Still the condition of a slave was low. Slaves called as witnesses were examined under torture: how else could one guarantee the truth of their testimony?

Lives of Slaves and Masters

Underlying the patterns of social life was the institution of slavery. Here the philosopher Seneca, with a very modern outlook, notes that "slavery" can be seen as an existential, as well as a social condition (no great consolation to the slave). Pliny the Younger tells the story of a wealthy man's murder by his slaves, which, without comment, raises questions about the justice, or at least the viability, of the institution of slavery.

Philosopher Seneca discourses on slavery, and finds character to be the real determinant of the human condition (c. 60 C.E.): Remember, if you please, that the man you call slave sprang from the same seed, enjoys the same daylight, breathes like you, lives like you, dies like you. You can as easily conceive him a free man as he can conceive you a slave. ... Treat your slave with compassion, even with courtesy; admit him to your conversation, your planning, your society. Here the genteel will protest loudly and unanimously, "Nothing could be more degrading or disgusting!" ... "What is the upshot? Am I to bring all slaves to my table?" No more than all free men. But if you imagine I would exclude some because their work is dirty, that muleteer for example, or that cowhand, you are mistaken. I value them not by their jobs but by their character; a man gives himself his own character, accident allots his job. ... "He is a slave!" But perhaps a free man in spirit. "He is a slave!" Shall that count against him? Show me a man who is not; one is a slave to lust, another to greed, another to ambition, all to fear. ... Voluntary slavery is the meanest of all.

(Seneca, *Moral Epistles*, no. 47; ed. M. Hadas 1956)

Pliny the Younger narrates the incident of slaves who killed their master (c. 90 C.E.): Here is the terrible story ... of how Larcius Macedo, a man of praetorian rank, was treated by his slaves. To be sure, he was a haughty and cruel master, who remembered too little— or rather, only too well—that his own father was once a slave. He was bathing at his villa near Formiae. Suddenly slaves surrounded him, one seized him by the throat, another struck him in the face, another pommeled him on the chest, the stomach, and even, shocking to relate, on the private parts; and when they thought he was lifeless, they threw him onto the hot floor, to see if he was alive. He, either unconscious or pretending to be, lay stretched out and motionless, giving the impression that death was complete. Then, finally, they carried him out as if he had fainted with the heat. Faithful slaves received him, and his concubines rushed up, wailing and shrieking. ... [H]e opened his eyes and moved his body to show, since it was now safe, that he was alive. ... He himself was with difficulty kept alive a few days, and did not die without the consolation of revenge.

(Pliny the Younger, *Letters*, 3:14; eds. N. Lewis, M. Reinhold 1966)

Stewards of households or villas were almost always slaves: unlike free citizens, they could, under torture, be made to confess to embezzlement. Slaves, unable to contract legitimate marriages, could have neither wives nor children. Female slaves more often escaped the horrendous conditions of the fields and the mines, but in other ways they suffered as much as males. Their skills were largely limited to domestic tasks and textile production. Consequently, their labor was less valued. Market values reflect that fact. Female slaves cost less: in the time of Emperor Diocletian (243–313 C.E.) about two-thirds to three-fourths the price of a man.

Roman households had fewer female than male slaves. Those few were considered sexually available to their masters (as were, indeed, young males). They were frequently (perhaps because of their many pregnancies) sold away from the master's family. If so, they were forced to leave their own children—who were considered slaves, whatever the status of their fathers, having been carried in the womb of a slave. Many were sold into prostitution, or to the inns and cookshops whose unskilled female servants were amateur prostitutes. Taverns and brothels were the bleak reservoir of unfree Roman women.

One class of Roman citizens enjoyed untrammeled freedom, if little wealth. These were the Roman citizens who made up the city's underclass: the plebs, meaning "people," or even "mob." As in the Republic, citizenship gave the plebs the right to vote, however meaningless that might now be. The plebs had done little but grow since the time of the Gracchi, when cheap, subsidized grain was first made available. Now the grain was free, and the citizens were no longer motivated to work—an activity considered better left to lower status people: slaves and freedmen. Some 200,000 to 250,000 male citizens received the daily gift of grain, which supported (when one adds women and children) more than half the urban population of about one million.

Not only did the plebs count on the distribution of grain, but they insisted as well (if the rulers wished no riots) on increasingly gaudy and frequent entertainments. Their idleness left them available for the many entertainments offered throughout the year. Performances of mime and the chariot races in the Circus Maximus were especially popular. So were the blood sports: gladiatorial combats often pursued to the death and "hunts" in which wild beasts, kept hungry for the occasion, tore at each other or at the bodies of condemned men and women sent into the arena. Did a people who had gained world leadership because of an exceptional capacity for violence require staged displays of contrived violence to retain their sense of control?

Such events were the prime attraction of the Colosseum, shown below, which was erected in 80 C.E. on the site of the hated Nero's palace. They continued to fascinate the Romans into the Christian era. "He saw the blood and he gulped down savagery," wrote Saint Augustine of one of his contemporaries who became a leader of the new church. For the urban poor, such pleasures were counted among the chief benefits of living in Rome. "The people which once bestowed imperium, fasces [symbols of authority], legions, everything, now forgoes such activities and has but two passionate desires: bread and circus games," observed the satirist Juvenal (c. 60–130 C.E.).

The dispossession of the plebs, stripped of an active political role, like the humiliation of the senators, served the interests of the imperial monarchy. At the same time, the regime's patronage of equestrians, the promotion of freedmen, and the easing of the reins on some of the most disadvantaged—women, children, and slaves—made the epoch of the *pax romana* one of social opportunity as well as of decline.

THE CULTURE OF IMPERIAL ROME

Roman culture reached its apex in the era of the *pax romana*. The city of Rome acquired new spaciousness and splendor, befitting its status as the foremost city of the civilized world. The system of roads, sewers, and aqueducts begun in the Republic now served ample domestic residences, both utilitarian and palatial, and numerous public buildings: baths, colonnades, and amphitheaters, all embellished with statues, arches, and columns. Digesting the inheritance of Greek literature, Roman literature flourished. Trained in Greek and Latin letters, in rhetoric and philosophy, educated Romans enjoyed Latin epics and plays, treatises and speeches, in which Greek forms were adapted to Roman cultural requirements. Yet this florescence was increasingly tinged by a tone of despair, reflecting political demoralization and the threat of invasion by hostile tribes.

Buildings and Waterways

During its first four centuries, Rome was a modest city. Its circuit of walls, embracing the seven hills, was intersected by the Sacred Way, which led from the Forum to the temple of Jupiter on the Capitoline Hill. In the last decades of the Republic, the city's spaces expanded, boasted more buildings and sprouted adornments. Scattered throughout the open spaces were Greek statues, both originals brought from Greece and Sicily and copies made by Roman artisans. The great fire of 64 C.E. destroyed much of the city's center and created space for more building ventures, among them the Colosseum.

Intensive building began with Pompey and Caesar. The former added a theater seating 40,000 people, and the latter began improvements to the Forum. Augustus completed Caesar's projects and added a panoply of temples to the city's fabric. He boasted that he had found Rome a city of brick and left it a city of marble. Already the largest city in the Mediterranean world, Rome became the most splendid.

The emperor Trajan added his own forum, adjacent to those areas already constructed, which overpowered them in grandeur. Completed between 109 and 113 C.E., it consisted of a covered area bounded by a **basilica**, or public assembly hall, and two libraries—one dedicated to Latin and the other to Greek texts. The semicircular plans of the latter echoed the form

Roman Monuments

The Colosseum:
Under the emperors, Rome sprouted arches and columns, temples and theaters, palaces and bathhouses. The Colosseum, built 72–80 C.E. on the site of the hated Nero's palace, housed many of the gladiatorial contests and races so popular with members of all classes. The interior of the surviving structure shows the basement pens and passageways.

Temple of Mars Ultor:
From the Roman Forum, a complex built up from republican through imperial times, are shown (left) the ruins of the Temple of Mars Ultor, late first century B.C.E., and a drawing (below) depicting how the Temple would have appeared.

of the scrolls within. They were adorned with busts of great authors of the past. The central space of Trajan's Forum was punctuated by a marble column almost 90 feet (27 m.) high, commemorating the emperor's campaigns in Dacia (modern Romania), the culmination of Rome's military expansion.

While temples and palaces beautified the city (see above and pp. 170 and 171), the Romans' genius for practical building works and their synthesis of form and function were best displayed by their system of aqueducts and sewers shown on Map 6.1. This system was almost as old as Rome itself. Some of the sewers, including the famous Cloaca Maxima, began as Etruscan drainage tunnels. The first aqueducts, which piped fresh water from the countryside to the city, dated from the fourth century B.C.E. By the reign of Augustus, eleven had been constructed. His lieutenant Agrippa added three more, along with 700 basins and 500 fountains. Agrippa also upgraded the sewers, which he explored, it is said, by boat.

Hundreds of miles of aqueducts brought water into the city, supplying public drinking fountains and baths; the overflow was diverted into the sewers. The baths, which contained a series of pools at different temperatures, were more than an aid to cleanliness. They were social and recreational centers.

Baths, aqueducts, and sewers, the Forum, and the Colosseum served all groups in the population. In contrast, domestic building reflected the gulf between *honestiores* and *humiliores*. The urban poor lived in tenements several stories high, shoddily built, inadequately supplied with light, air, heat, or water (only the ground floor benefited from the public water supply), vulnerable to fire. Each tenement building generally featured, on the ground floor, shops open to the street. Above were warrens of apartments consisting of featureless rooms without baths or kitchens. In the fourth century, Rome is said to have contained more than 46,000 of these tenements, in contrast to fewer than 2000 homes of the rich.

The wealthy lived in private town houses similar to the ones shown in *Windows On* on p. 155. These were one story high and built around a central courtyard, called an **atrium**, lit by a roof opening. Stables and storage rooms, servants' rooms and baths, dining rooms and bedrooms served the functions of the household. One house was not enough; a rich man might own several. "Say where I may call upon you, say in what quarter I may look for you," the poet Martial implored one of his wealthy patrons, as the latter circulated among his establishments.

A City, an Empire, a World

Other nations had boundaries, wrote the poet Ovid, but Rome was "*urbs et orbis idem*"—at the same time one city and the whole world. During the early Empire, Rome had a population of about one million—superseding Alexandria as the largest city in the Mediterranean world. Of its residents, many were non-Roman and even non-Italian foreigners. About 400,000 were slaves.

In the time of Augustus, Italy had a population of four or five million Roman citizens, plus two to three million slaves. At Rome's zenith (around 200 C.E.), the population of the whole Empire—slave, citizen, and free—was about 50 million. Although most lived on the land, we know more about those who dwelled in cities. The Roman Empire was a network of cities, at whose center stood the capital city itself.

The Hellenistic cities of the East—such as Alexandria, Antioch, Carthage, Ephesus, Smyrna, and Pergamum—were nodes of Roman power. To these established centers were added new cities in Italy and in the western provinces of Europe and Africa. In these latter regions, veteran colonies or army camps might form the nuclei of cities where none had existed before. New or old, the cities of the Empire modeled themselves on Rome. The Greek cities added Roman basilicas and baths to their centers, already packed with gymnasia, theaters, and marketplaces. The new cities of the Empire were equipped with amphitheaters, forums, and temples, basilicas, baths, and aqueducts funded by the local aristocracy or by imperial largesse. Each city (a large one counted between 100,000 and 200,000 citizens) had its own magistrates and justice system, its own assembly, elections, and charter.

The Empire adopted the Hellenistic commercial system, itself derived from ancient patterns of trade. Pots from Greece, Italy, and now Gaul traveled throughout the Mediterranean. So did olive oil from Spain, Italy, and Greece; wheat from Sicily, Egypt, and the Black Sea; wine from Gaul, Italy, and Greece; minerals from Spain and Britain; spices and perfumes, ivory and silk from the Middle East, India, and China.

Neither the commodities nor the techniques of production changed under the Empire. Yet the volume of trade increased. A web of paths and roads and sea routes, shown on Map 6.2, linked large and small localities into one Eurasian world—prefiguring the global village we inhabit today. On land and by sea, camels and sailboats directed by Roman, Greek, Arab, Persian, Indian, and Chinese entrepreneurs carried goods east and west across the great expanse from Spain to the Far East. Roman merchandise and coins reached the interior of Arabia, India, the Malay peninsula, Vietnam, China. A representative of emperor Marcus Aurelius reached the Chinese court in the second century.

Most commerce was seaborne. Indian and even Chinese ships traveled the Red Sea; from Red Sea and Persian Gulf ports, more than 100 ships per year loaded with goods from the Mediterranean and the African and European hinterlands took sail for India. Within two or three months, a ship could travel from Rome to Carthage, Alexandria, Antioch, or Ephesus. More ships carried more goods around the Mediterranean and nearby waterways in the late Republic and early Empire than at any time for the next 1000 years. (From the third century Italy's exports decreased as its colonies became more self-sufficient.) The commercial system of the late Roman world endured into the modern era, when it was outpaced by new systems centered on the Atlantic and Pacific oceans.

Land travel was slow (20 to 40 miles [32–64 km.] per day was an achievement) and not always safe. The roads themselves, however, were excellent. Roman roads linked the capital to the farthest outposts of the Empire, facilitating rapid communications and the transport of armies and military supplies.

Roman infrastructure: *In addition to freestanding monuments, Roman engineers designed aqueducts, roads, and bridges that extended throughout the empire, structures unsurpassed until recent times, as beautiful as they were functional. Seen here is the splendid aqueduct bridging the River Gardon, known as the Pont du Gard, near Nîmes, France.*

Pont du Gard, Nîmes, late first century B.C.E.

Patrician townhouse plan

peristyle · courtyard · atrium · impluvium · vestibule · entryway

Lifestyles of the Wealthy: Villa and Townhouse

Wealthy Romans developed luxurious styles of townhouses and country villas that were closer to the lifestyles of rulers than to the dismal dwellings of the poor. Shown here are a plan of a patrician townhouse (above) and the atrium of one of the fine houses of Pompeii (left).

What message might be communicated to a visitor standing in the atrium, or entrance hallway, of a Roman townhouse?

House of the Silver Wedding atrium, Pompeii, early first century C.E.

Bedroom, Boscoreale villa, near Pompeii, first century B.C.E.

This reconstruction drawing (right) of a villa complex shows the magnificent main residence and the simpler farm buildings beyond its garden walls. The owner may also have had a house in a neighboring town. This bedroom (above right) at Boscoreale shows the fine furniture and rich wall paintings that decorated such buildings. (Metropolitan Museum of Art)

Reconstruction of a villa complex

To continue your investigation of this topic, please go to www.prenhall.com/king for the related **WINDOWS** on the **WEB** activity

Road-building, too, was a legacy from the Etruscans. By 312 B.C.E. a road had been constructed leading south from Rome to Capua (later to Brindisi); it was named the Via Appia, or Appian Way, after the censor Appius Claudius, who supervised the project. More than 800 years later, the historian Procopius of Caesarea in Anatolia described how the stones were smoothed, made flat and shaped, and joined together without mortar: "And they were fastened together so securely and the joints were so firmly closed," he marveled, "that they give the appearance … not of being fitted together, but of having grown together."

The Via Appia was joined by the Via Flaminia, begun around 220 B.C.E., which crossed the Apennines to the Adriatic, and by the Via Aemilia, from Rimini to Piacenza along the western edge of the Po plain. In 20 B.C.E. Augustus set up at one end of the Forum a stone column called the Golden Milestone. The bronze plaques attached to it announced the distances from Rome to all the main cities of the Empire.

The network of roads carried information and armies, travelers and merchants. It bound together capital and satellite cities, Greek east and Latin west, center and periphery. Building on earlier unities of the Hellenistic kingdoms, Rome had achieved a greater unity, due to its unusual aptitude for absorbing the people it conquered. That pattern began with the absorption of Latin and Sabine tribes in the early Republic. In the late Republic, all Italians gained full citizenship, and in the early Empire, citizenship was extended to the elites of many provincial towns. Rome's outreach culminated in 212 C.E., when the

Emperor Caracalla (the better to collect his taxes) bestowed citizenship on every free male within the Empire's boundaries. Now one could be just as Roman in Syria or Spain as in the Po Valley or Rome itself.

The leaders of Rome came from all over the Roman Empire. The historian Livy was from the northern Po Valley. The writers Seneca, Martial, and Quintilian all came from Spain, as did the emperors Trajan and Hadrian. The Emperor Septimius Severus was African; so were the writers Fronto and Apuleius, and the Christians Tertullian and Saint Augustine. Country of origin was forgotten in the *orbis* of Rome. A Latin, or political, dimension had been added to the Hellenistic notion of *oecumene* (see Chapter 5), the community of the inhabited world.

Map 6.1 Imperial Rome, 27 B.C.E.–300 C.E.: Under the emperor Augustus Rome was at the same time a great metropolis and the capital of the Empire: "urbs et orbis," a city and the whole world. Already a populous center of government and trade, the city under the emperors became star-studded with theaters and baths, temples and arches, markets and libraries, palaces and racecourses. It was served by an intricate network of roads and aqueducts and protected, when dangers mounted in the third century C.E., by a huge circuit of walls (see also Map 5.3). Why did Rome acquire a new wall in the third century?

Map 6.2 The Roman Trade System (c. 200 C.E.): *From Britain in the northwest, to the fringes of the African Sahara in the south, to India in the east, Roman ships and Roman merchants journeyed on their mission to supply necessities (wheat, olive oil) and luxuries (perfumes, spices, gems, and textiles) to the center of the Empire—and news of other cultures, and deadly epidemic diseases. Encompassing the earlier trade empires of western Asia and the western Mediterranean, the Roman trading system foreshadows the one that developed during the European Middle Ages, to be dominated successively by Arabs and Italians. Why were most goods transported by water, when the Romans had a superior road system?*

Roman Literature in Florescence and Decay

A universal culture based on a common literature was the earlier achievement of Hellenistic civilization, which now became the Roman as well, and was exported to all the new provinces of the West. Children of the elites were taught by nurses and pedagogues, and sent to school to learn to read and write from the grammar teacher, who was generally Greek and often a slave. Learning (first in Greek, then in Latin, even for Romans) was by memorization and repetition, enforced by frequent beatings.

Classic works of literature were used as spellers and as textbooks of geography, history, religion, music, and science. Students bound for high positions went on to study rhetoric and even philosophy. This training marked the student as an educated and cultured person who, from whatever region he came, could converse freely anywhere in the Empire with anyone of his class. Such an education conferred status.

While only the wealthy achieved the fine veneer imparted by the schools of rhetoric and philosophy,

even ordinary people learned the rudiments of reading and writing. In sculpture, the educational level of the elite man would often be represented by a scroll. The literate commoner would be represented holding tablets on which were recorded prices and inventories. Literacy among artisans and shopkeepers is witnessed by graffiti found in ancient ruins. It is also indicated by the epitaphs that these commoners left behind—more than 100,000 of them, mostly from the first two centuries C.E. Planted along the roads outside the city walls, these inscriptions begged the reader to attend to the story of the person who spoke from the grave.

Greek literature flagged in the late Hellenistic period, but revived in the early Empire as shown in *How Many?* on p. 158. Strabo the geographer (64 B.C.E.–21 C.E.), Plutarch the biographer and moralist (c. 46–c. 120 C.E.), Ptolemy the astronomer (d. 180 C.E.), Galen the physician (129–199 C.E.), the Neoplatonic philosophers Porphyry (225–c. 305 C.E.) and Plotinus (205–270 C.E.); all these created works which would be studied for centuries. Strabo distinguished for later ages the regions of Europe, Asia, and Africa, while Ptolemy's *Almagest* codified ancient astronomical knowledge. Galen's medical works (twenty-one volumes survive) in their Latin and Arabic versions dominated the Middle Ages and Renaissance, the same eras that responded to the Neoplatonist identification of God with the One, the Good, the Beautiful, the Light. Plutarch narrated in his forty-eight extant *Lives* the accomplishments of the great leaders of Greece and Rome. Pairing forty-four of these biographies in twenty-two pairs, in which a Greek hero was matched with a Roman one, he claimed the parallelism of Greco-Roman culture.

The early Republic had produced little in the way of literature. Most authors were Greeks of Italian or Sicilian background, or Romans who dutifully followed Greek models. Much of this early literature is lost. Roman literature began a steady development in the second century B.C.E., when Cato the Elder wrote about agriculture and composed a book of maxims for his son. In the following century, the poet Lucretius (c. 94–c. 55/51 B.C.E.) expressed the principles of Epicurean thought in six books of luminous Latin verse entitled *De rerum natura* ("On the Nature of Things"). The same century was graced above all by Cicero (see Chapter 5), both a transmitter of Greek learning and an original Roman thinker. Cicero's enormous production of treatises, dialogues, letters, and orations opens up the richest period of Latin literature: the Golden Age.

Golden Age and Decline   The great confidence in the future stimulated by Augustus' achievements set the stage for the supreme literary work of the Golden, or Augustan, Age. Three of the finest writers of this era were all identified with Augustus: the poets Horace (65–8 B.C.E.) and Vergil (70–19 B.C.E.) and the historian Livy (59 B.C.E.–17 C.E.). The low-born Horace was bankrolled by Augustus through his agent Maecenas (c. 70–8 B.C.E.), an equestrian aesthete and full-time literary patron. At a secluded villa purchased with Maecenas' money, Horace composed his famous *Odes* celebrating Roman life and character. Vergil celebrated the Roman state with religious fervor in his epic *Aeneid*, retelling the story of the city's supposed founding by a son of Troy. In his fourth *Eclogue*, Vergil proclaimed Augustus as savior in messianic language which Christian scholars later took as evidence that Vergil was "a soul Christian by nature." Livy celebrated the deeds of the ancients, whose virtues set the ideal still admired by Romans, though no longer practiced. The achievement of these authors was to forge a tradition distinctively Roman, even though built on forms established by Greek predecessors.

After the death of Augustus, the refined Latin prose of the early Empire continued to sparkle in literary works for two more centuries, but the spirit of literature changed greatly. As the future clouded over, authors concentrated on practical matters and on digesting the lessons of the past. That practical orientation is illustrated in such works as Columella's *On Country Life*, a twelve-volume guide to farm management; or Pliny the Elder's *Natural History*, an encyclopedia of more or less true information; or even Quintilian's *The Elements of Oratory*, on proper rhetorical training. Reflection on past history is evidenced in the brilliant but painful *Histories* and *Annals* of Tacitus, grieving the loss of the Republic; or his exquisite *Germania* and *Agricola*, covert exercises, disguised as anthropology and biography, on the meaning of liberty.

Curiously it was the historian Tacitus, rather than the professional rhetorician and educator Quintilian (an imperial employee), who diagnosed the cultural disease from which the Empire suffered: it was the decline of oratory, directly related to the loss of political freedom (see *Witnesses*, p. 149). Taught in the schools by the tedious recitation of mock orations on absurd set topics, rhetoric had become a stale relic of the age when Cicero, at imminent risk of his life, delivered his *Philippics* in the Forum. Because there was no opportunity to speak the truth, Tacitus argued, the one literary genre in which Rome had especially excelled died with the coming of the Caesars.

The other literary genres met their own deaths following the demise of oratory. After the second century, few new Latin works were considered fit to be numbered among the "classics." Great works in Latin were yet to be created: but they were Christian, and the import of their message was to despair of Rome and to trust in God. The flow of Roman eloquence, which had coursed freely under Augustus, had slowed to nothing and left barrenness behind.

HOW MANY?

Absolute Decline in Greek and Roman Literary Production

Authors in Loeb, Oxford, and Teubner Libraries (assigned to period by date of death minus ten years).
Source: R. MacMullen, *Corruption and the Decline of Rome* (New Haven–London: Yale University Press, 1988).

According to Tacitus, the present sterility was a direct outcome of the loss of freedom instituted by Augustus himself. While acknowledging that Augustus brought an end to the lawlessness that followed Julius Caesar's power grab, Tacitus maintained that the price for the restoration of order, monarchy, was too high. "Thenceforth," concluded the embittered writer, "our bonds were tighter."

A spiritual aridity characterized Roman culture even as the Empire basked in peace, grew in wealth, and reached its peak years of growth. People sought out new and more satisfying forms of religious experience (see Chapter 7), and new philosophical consolations. Such a collapse in the realm of spirit may explain the grim words of the Stoic philosopher Seneca (tutor and adviser to Nero who eventually, on that despot's order, took his own life) on the ready availability of freedom: "Look at that precipice—a descent to freedom; that sea, that river, that well—at the bottom of each there is freedom. That stunted, parched, unfruitful tree; freedom hangs from its branches. Your neck, your throat, your heart—escape-routes from slavery, all of them. ... If you are looking for a way to freedom, any vein in your body will do."

The spiritual impoverishment of late Roman culture is expressed in this dismal equation of death with liberty and slavery with life. Meanwhile, Rome came to face a problem more severe than the loss of freedom: that of survival.

HOLDING THE FRONTIER

During the *pax romana* of the first two centuries C.E., the Roman Empire reached its maximum extent. Its borders were secure, trade flourished; the lives of city dwellers, even including plebs, were enhanced by comforts and refinements, while those of the peasants, never easy, were not evidently harsher. Then, in the third century, the tide turned. A deep and persistent crisis took hold. Prosperity faded; poetry and philosophy languished. The borders could be held only by enormous efforts involving a desperate reorganization of the army, the economy, and the machinery of the state. Thenceforth, until the final collapse of authority in the Western Empire in the late 400s, although Rome survived, it bled. A new city took form in the Greek-speaking eastern zone of the Empire, which was to transmit some remnants of Roman culture into the next age. In the western, Latin zone, the old city of Rome fell to invaders, who plundered and consumed it. The survival of Roman civilization rested insecurely in the hands of the expanding Christian Church.

Defending the Boundaries

In the second century C.E., Rome's dominion included all the lands of the Mediterranean as well as much of western Europe beyond the Alps. By the third century, its extensive borders were at risk.

The first major setback to Roman expansion came under Augustus. Roman armies plunged northeast into Europe, where in 9 C.E., the troops of the general Publius Quinctilius Varus were slaughtered by the horsemen of the German leader Arminius (Hermann), a former Roman "auxiliary" commander (a foreign commander in the service of Rome), who ambushed them in the Teutoburg Forest (near Osnabrück). Varus committed suicide. Legions XVII, XVIII, and XIX of Augustus' twenty-eight legions were lost, an enduring reproach to Roman ambition.

Augustus' successor, Tiberius, assumed the inglorious task of holding a frontier with less ambitious dimensions. He labored to secure the line formed by the Rhine and Danube rivers, slicing across Europe from the North to the Black Sea. Claudius acquired Britain in 43 B.C.E., a task previously attempted by Caesar in 55–54 B.C.E.

The need to secure the lower Danube brought Trajan to Dacia, in the Balkans, to discipline that people's rebellious king. The vicious wars of 101–102 C.E. and subsequent treaties of 105–106 C.E. reduced the Dacian king to client status. Roman settlers arrived to colonize the area, achieving the domestication of that region (where today the Romanian language, descended from Latin, is still spoken). A further benefit was the profit from the Dacian gold mines, which poured into Rome and into Trajan's pockets. Trajan's Column in the Roman Forum shown on p. 161 commemorates his Dacian victory, depicted with splendid narrative detail in carved reliefs winding upward along the length of the monument.

Trajan also confronted the Parthians, who had overrun Iran and now pushed against the Empire's eastern border. Roman armies seized Arab caravan routes, quarreled over Armenia, and invaded Mesopotamia, where they seized (for a while) the town of Ctesiphon, capital of Parthia, and set up a puppet prince. The Empire reached its greatest extent in 117 C.E., as shown on Map 6.3. But what Trajan had acquired in remote eastern lands, some of his successors abandoned.

Not so Trajan's cousin and chosen successor, Hadrian, who adopted a different strategy. His aim was to hold the forty-three provinces that his predecessors had won—as much as could be prudently conserved. Parthia was forgotten for the moment. In the rest of the East and on the African coast, it was necessary only to maintain a stable position.

To the north, Hadrian adopted a militantly defensive position. Where his predecessors had warred with the fierce Celts in the remotest north of Britain, Hadrian retreated southward and built a mammoth wall across the island, through what are now the northernmost counties of England. The ruins of Hadrian's Wall still stand. Along the Rhine and

Map 6.3 The Roman Empire at its Apex, 117 C.E.: *By the time of Emperor Trajan's death in 117 C.E., the Roman Empire had reached its greatest limit. Later emperors chose to defend, garrison, or even contract the frontiers, rather than continue to press against irresistible forces—the German tribes in northern Europe, and the Parthians and Sassanids in Iran—or unbridgeable obstacles—the Atlantic ocean and the African Sahara. Why were some peoples able to resist the Roman advance?*

Danube line, he ordered permanent fortifications built and garrisoned. To all the frontiers he sent troops, which he inspected regularly, keeping them out of war but war-ready. One war Hadrian could not avoid was in the troublesome province of Judaea. There, a rebellion under the Jewish leader Bar-Kokhba in 132–135 C.E. was suppressed with horrific slaughter.

Hadrian's strategy of holding the frontier became permanent. It was pursued by prudent sacrifices of land, generous alliances with alien peoples, and the outpouring of military personnel from the center to the periphery of the Empire. Whereas the task of the Empire during its first two centuries was to acquire more provinces, its task over the next three centuries was to defend them. The task proved impossible.

Redefining the Army

To hold the frontiers required the reorganization of the army, the institution on which the Roman system was based and in which the state of Rome itself was most clearly reflected. Its increasing size is outlined in *How Many?* on p. 162.

From the time of the early Republic, Rome's army was composed of legions of four to six thousand citizens of the appropriate census classes, commanded by officers from the nobility. Backing up the legions were auxiliary forces (foreign troops in the service of Rome). In the late Republic, after the innovations of

Marius and the extension of citizenship to all Italians, the legionaries were drawn from poorer census classes, and the auxiliaries from more distant and alien regions. Meanwhile, the army gained political importance. It helped boost such figures as Marius and Sulla, Pompey and Caesar, who acquired political power because of their military strength (see Chapter 5).

During the civil wars, the legionary forces of Octavian and Mark Antony swelled from about 80,000 to more than 400,000. After the defeat of Antony and Cleopatra at Actium in 30 B.C.E., Octavian (now Augustus) demobilized, retiring almost half the legionaries with cash bonuses or grants of land. The remaining soldiers were organized in 28 legions (5500 to 6000 men each), reduced to 25 legions after the disaster at Teutoburg. An equally large force—150,000 men—was provided by auxiliaries organized in cohorts of about 1000 men each. In addition, each army marched with a supply train and machines for sieges and defense. The legionaries served twenty years, after which they retired with the usual bonuses. Auxiliaries served twenty-five years, receiving at discharge a grant of citizenship which allowed foreign-born sons to enter the legions.

The army of the early Republic cost nothing: each citizen supplied his own food, weapons, and armor. Not so under the Empire. Feeding, transporting, and paying its legions and auxiliaries was the biggest charge on the Roman treasury. The imperial systems

Narrative in stone: *Completed in Rome in 113 C.E., the column built to celebrate the conquests of the emperor Trajan soared nearly 100 feet high, circled by 23 spirals that extended more than 200 meters and displayed 2500 figures—a panorama that documents the scale and complex organization of Rome's imperial expansion. The lower bands of spiral relief depict the imperial troops advancing along the Danube river, with a Roman camp shown in the top band of the column.*

of coinage and taxation were structured to manage the giant military machine. The biggest drain was in coin. Caesar doubled the pay of common soldiers, and Augustus raised pay for centurions (non-noble officers) and provided legionaries with bonuses on discharge of 3000 *denarii* (75,000 *sestercii*): more than ten times the annual pay of 225 *denarii* (5625 *sestercii*). Domitian raised the annual figure to 300 *denarii*, and Septimus Severus to almost 500 *denarii*. Praetorian guards were paid more than twice that. These figures reflect a high rate of inflation and an increased dependence on the military.

By Hadrian's reign (117–138 C.E.), the army was no longer seen as a mobile striking force but was largely stationed in semi-permanent positions on the frontier. Roman soldiers became builders of camps and designers of fortifications, engineers and farmers, who sometimes neglected the business of war in the quest for maximum security. Augustus' twenty-five legions were distributed in this way: three in Spain, eight on the Rhine, seven on the Danube, four in Syria, two in Egypt, and one in Africa (the III Augusta legion, stationed there for more than 300 years). The greater stability of Africa and Egypt is indicated by the smaller number of legions needed to hold it. The volatility of the Rhine–Danube line to the north and northeast, on the other hand, and the weakness of the Syrian border are reflected in the heavy arming of those regions.

Towns sprang up around the semi-permanent army camps planted on the frontiers. The towns supported magistracies and law courts, commerce and theaters, baths and games. The language spoken in these communities was the rough Latin of the average soldier. That uncouth figure was a principal agent of Romanization in the European part of the Empire. Veterans were also effective agents of Romanization

in the colonies they peopled upon retirement. At the same time that the legions were a Romanizing force, the army itself became less Roman and increasingly "barbarized," as its soldiers acquired the language and customs of the people among whom they settled and with whom they intermarried. By the late Empire, legionaries were no longer recruited primarily from Rome or even from Italy: after 300 C.E., fewer than 20 percent came from Italy. Auxiliaries were recruited not merely from non-Italian but even from alien communities: from the warlike peoples on the fringes of the Empire, kin to the tribal peoples who threatened the frontier. By the last years of the Empire, whole groups of foreign peoples were allowed to penetrate that boundary and settle within it. At that point, invasion was scarcely necessary. Rome itself had become the home of European peoples who roamed the forests and grasslands beyond the zone of civilization.

Managing the Crisis

In the last two centuries of the Empire, the emperors scrambled to manage the economic and military crisis as indicated in *Witnesses* on p. 163. Some of them responded brilliantly, flexibly reinventing the administrative machinery to deal with new realities, just as their predecessor Augustus had done. Even these heroic efforts at adaptation, however, were unsuccessful.

In the fifty years between the death of Alexander Severus and the reign of Diocletian (284–305 C.E.), at least eighteen men held the title of emperor. One of these, Aurelian, constructed, in 274 C.E., a new set of walls around Rome to secure it—an act that demonstrated at the same time his prudence and the grave collapse of order. By such desperate measures, these near-forgotten emperors attempted to stem the tide of barbarian invasion, the decay of civic institutions, and the decline of the rural economy. The plain-speaking but brilliant Diocletian managed—but just barely—to keep in check the inner strains and external stress that beset the Empire.

Never had the army been more important. It did not merely protect the state. Rather, the state existed to support the army, as all other objectives rolled into the single imperative of defense. The auxiliary forces,

Army Organization

The Roman army that had conquered Carthage, Greece, and the eastern Mediterranean lands numbered only a few tens of thousands of soldiers recruited from among Roman or Italian citizens. That army quintupled in size during the Civil Wars. Once normalcy had been restored, Augustus demobilized many of the legionaries—reducing the force, after the Teutoburg disaster, to 25 legions—while recruiting many "auxiliary" soldiers from non-citizen provincials and tribal peoples of the frontier. Under his successors, who established fixed maximum borders for the Empire and planted soldier garrisons to defend them, the overall force rose to a maximum of about 500,000—a vast army not to be seen again in Europe until the eighteenth century. The maintenance of that force (whose annual pay had doubled since the days of Augustus) drained the wealth of the Empire.

ARMY SIZE AT VARIOUS POINTS:

Before Julius Caesar's death (44 B.C.E.) about 80,000 Roman legionaries

Under Octavian and Mark Antony (during Civil Wars 43–31 B.C.E.) about 40,000 Roman legionaries

Under Augustus (after Teutoburg 9 C.E.) about 150,000 Roman legionaries, plus about 150,000 auxiliaries

Around 400 C.E. about 500,000 total forces

adept in the skills required to deal with the barbarians, now mattered more than the legions. Heavy cavalry edged out infantry in importance, foreshadowing medieval styles of warfare. German recruits prevailed in both the mobile cavalry forces that accompanied each emperor and the troops stationed on the frontier. By 400 C.E., 500,000 men were serving in arms—a force nearly double that of Augustus' army, exceeding even the peak numbers of the civil war years.

To fund the army, the state became a machine for the generation of tax revenues, waging a relentless raid on the meager resources of the poor. "No man shall possess any property that is tax-exempt," read the Theodosian Code of 383 C.E.. New methods of land assessment increased the flow of revenues from the countryside. The sums due the government, based on an annual budget, were announced on a regular schedule. Ceilings were established for prices and wages in order to control inflation, which was driven by the debasement of the currency. A negative side effect of price fixing was to dim initiative, thus contributing to the already plummeting volume and value of trade.

Roman coins, prized throughout the ancient world, were used to carry on trade and to pay taxes. Under Augustus, the metal content (gold, silver, bronze, copper) was fixed for the various coins: the *aureus*, the *denarius*, the *sestertius*, the *as*, and the *dupondius*. Upon these standardized coins were stamped the emperor's profile and a variety of symbols of his achievements. The value of these splendid coins began to deteriorate in the third century, as the emperors allowed the currency to be debased and as inflation ate at its value. Quality coins fell out of circulation, to be melted down or simply hoarded, while the corrupt currency continued to circulate. This tendency, together with the Western Empire's negative trade balance with the East led, especially in the West, to the near-disappearance of coins and a slide into a barter economy.

The cities suffered economic decline. That decline put pressure on the **decurions**—the elite class in the outlying cities who were responsible for municipal functions. Once the decurions had been the proud patrons of civic life. By ancient custom, they funded public monuments and services: theatrical performances, council halls, shipbuilding, roads and bridges, athletic games, and even the statues by which their own accomplishments were publicly commemorated. The decurions were also responsible for collecting taxes and feeding the Roman treasury. Whole families were assigned municipal responsibilities on a hereditary basis. The decurions could not escape these obligations, nor could their sons—except by fleeing altogether, a remedy they chose as Rome continued to decline. From fourth-century Antioch a mournful voice complained, speaking of the citizen elite, that "we used to be six hundred … but now we are sixty."

Seeking relief, decurions fled the cities; some of the cities, fearful of depredations, relocated to more secure hilltop sites, well fortified with walls and towers. In the countryside, great tracts of land lay waste, abandoned, the result of rapid depopulation, the erosion of the soil, and the devastations of the army. Overburdened peasants were required to guard—and pay taxes on—the land abandoned by their neighbors. The great landowners alone remained prosperous, living on the accumulated produce of their tenants, who were by now for the most part hopelessly in debt. In exchange for the right to farm the land and to claim the master's protection, these tenants, the *coloni*, willingly surrendered much of their freedom. They were the immediate ancestors of the serfs of medieval Europe.

The emperors, too, withdrew from urban society to their court, where they spoke mainly with their officials and advisers and slaves. These made up a small council, the chief members of which were called *comites*, or "companions" (in medieval times, "counts"). From this court emanated all public decrees. An elaborate ritual developed to enhance the

Crisis and Response in Late Imperial Rome

By the fourth and fifth centuries C.E., Roman institutions were crumbling. Emperors Diocletian and Theodosius attempted to stave off crises by issuing regulatory edicts, such as those excerpted here: Diocletian's capping prices, and Theodosius's restricting the mobility of rural workers and municipal officeholders. Yet Roman institutions weakened nevertheless, inviting the invasion of tribal peoples, whose devastation of the city of Rome is lamented in the third passage by the Christian author Jerome.

In his "Edict on Prices," the emperor Diocletian explains why the state must intervene to protect citizens from the avarice of profiteers (301 C.E.): Avarice boundless and frenzied, with no consideration for humankind, multiplies its spreading grasp like wildfire, not by years or months or days but every hour and minute. Since the unrestrained madness of lust will take no thought for the common welfare, since only necessity ... can check the seething and torrential avarice of unscrupulous exploiters ... in view of this situation we who are protectors of humankind have resolved that justice should intervene as arbiter ...
(Diocletian, "Edict on Prices"; ed. M. Hadas 1956)

The law code promulgated under the emperor Theodosius issues certain restrictions on the semi-dependent peasants (called *coloni*) and on the class of municipal officeholders (called *decurions*) (383 C.E.): 5.17.1.1: Coloni ... who meditate flight must be bound with chains and reduced to a servile condition. ... 5.19.1: There is no doubt that coloni do not have the right to alienate the fields that they cultivate [or] ... transfer them to others without the advice and knowledge of their patrons. 12.1.13: Since ... the municipal councils are being left desolate by those persons who are obligated to them through birth status... we order all municipal councils to be admonished that if they should apprehend any persons with less than twenty terms of service in governmental offices ... they shall drag such persons back to the municipal councils.
(Theodosian Code, 5.17.11, 5.19.1, 12.1.13; ed. B. Tierney 1973)

Saint and scholar Jerome, quoting Vergil, describes Rome plundered by the tribe of Visigoths (410 C.E.): A terrible rumor has arrived from the West. Rome is besieged. ... The City is taken which took the whole world. It had perished of famine before it died by the sword, and only a few captives were found. The fury of the hungry sought out horrible food; men tore each other to pieces; a mother did not spare her infant at the breast and ate what she had brought forth a little before. ...

What tongue can tell the slaughter of that night?
What eyes can weep the sorrows and affright?
An ancient and imperial city falls. ...
(Jerome, Letter 127,12; trs. J. Hillgarth, 1986; Vergil, *Aeneid*, 2.361–365, 369; trs. Dryden)

---

figure of the emperor, who was displayed, bejeweled, like a deity on earth. Diocletian was no longer *princeps*, "first citizen;" he was, and was addressed as, *dominus*, or "lord." He was an absolute monarch who ruled not by persuading but by dominating—hence the naming of this phase of the Empire as the "Dominate," as opposed to the earlier "Principate." He and his successors resorted to terror to enforce their domination; like Valens (376–378 C.E.), who, it was said, held "death at the tip of his tongue."

More and more, the emperor resembled an eastern monarch of the age before the Greeks. Indeed, he established himself in the East, more secure than the unstable West, which was vulnerable to tribal pressures. Diocletian appointed Maximian to police that region as a partner equal to himself and with the same title: "Augustus." Each Augustus had a lieutenant designated his heir, each one entitled "Caesar." By this organization of four rulers, two senior and two junior (called the tetrarchy, or "rule of four"), Diocletian aimed both to secure all zones of the Empire and to ensure an orderly succession. He stepped down, as he had said he would, in 305 C.E., and waited for the planned succession to take place. The plan failed. The two caesars and several others vied to be sole monarch. Chaos once again ruled, east and west.

Constantine's City and *The City of God*

The Emperor Constantine, called "the Great" (r. 312–337 C.E.), once again united and pacified the Empire—if briefly. He governed it now from a new city in the Eastern Empire, "Constantinople." The Empire survived by changing its character: it was now led from a Greek-speaking Rome ensconced in the eastern Mediterranean.

As the legitimate successor of Maximian, Diocletian's partner in the West, Constantine had battled his way to power by 312 C.E.. By 324, he had succeeded in ousting his co-ruler, abandoned the tetrarchy, and claimed sole authority. Nevertheless, Constantine preserved much of Diocletian's imperial reorganization. He followed Diocletian toward the east, establishing his new capital in the old Greek city of Byzantium on the Bosporus. Grandly renamed Constantinople, after himself, it reflected the changing image of the Empire, now a repressive state under an absolutist king.

Constantine was the first Roman emperor to become a Christian. His formal conversion took place only on his deathbed, but in spirit he had already embraced Christianity much earlier than this. In 313, his Edict of Milan extended toleration to all religions, including Christianity and Judaism, thus ending the terrible persecutions that Diocletian had instituted toward the end of his reign for the security of the realm. Constantine followed the endless discussions of theologians over various fine points of doctrine: the humanity of Christ, the motherhood of Mary, the possibility of free will (see Chapter 7). When he died in 337, the Empire had already become more Christian than pagan.

Under Constantine's successors—with one exception, Julian (r. 361–363)—Christianity continued to flourish. With the accession to the throne of Theodosius (r. 380–395), Christians rejoiced; for Theodosius (whom they called "the Great") did what two centuries earlier would have been inconceivable: he made Christianity the official religion. The very religion that had been seen as a threat to the Empire was now its refuge. So severe and pathless was the crisis that confronted Rome that the army was not sufficient to rescue it. The peace imposed by Roman power from the time of Augustus and maintained by its legions had disintegrated. It could not be reestablished by military means.

The "New Rome" planted at Constantinople would endure on the foundations laid by Diocletian and Constantine for one thousand years more (see Chapters 10, 11). But the old Rome, and the whole western sector of the Empire, decayed and fell prey to hungry newcomers—Visigoths, Ostrogoths, Vandals, Huns, and Franks. In 410, the Visigoth king Alaric I invaded Italy and sacked Rome. A contemporary description is given in *Witnesses* on p. 163. In 451, the Huns rammed through northern Italy, spreading desolation. One by one, the garrisons that had held the frontier gave way—as they did on the Danube border, when the soldiers ceased to be paid and "the military units were abolished together with the frontier." In 455, Rome was sacked again, by the Vandals. In 476, the Germanic warrior Odoacer deposed the reigning western emperor and declared himself king of Italy. "Rome fell to the Goths in the 1164th year after its foundation," was the terse comment of the English scholar the Venerable Bede (c. 673–735), writing when Rome was only a memory.

Long before Odoacer captured Rome, the western Empire was dead. Saint Augustine (who died during the Vandal invasion of North Africa in 430) had pronounced it doomed in 410, when the capital was sacked by the Visigoths under Alaric. It was this catastrophe that impelled Augustine to write his monumental work *The City of God*. In that work, he dissected the inadequacies of Roman paganism and the Roman state: the "city of man," which compared unfavorably to the community of believers gathered in the "city of God." His analysis would lead the way to later understandings of human society and the state by such diverse thinkers as Hobbes (English political philosopher, 1588–1679), Hegel (German philosopher, 1770–1831), and Darwin (British naturalist, 1809–1882).

Like Tacitus, Augustine exposed what he saw as the fraudulence of the great Empire: it was a blood-stained arena where the strong destroyed the weak, "a sea wherein men devour one another in turn like fish." Far from benefiting its citizens, the megalithic state torments them with crime, sedition, and war, "from the occurrence of which states are rarely free, from the apprehension of them never." An organization designed for the hoarding and spending of wealth, the business of the state is robbery, and that of large states (in Augustine's unforgettable judgment), "robbery on a grand scale." In Rome, "the lust for possession . . . triumphed in the persons of a few men of exceptional power, only to reduce and exhaust the remainder and, ultimately, to impose upon them the yoke of servitude." While the state may confer certain cultural benefits, it does so at an enormous cost in the spilling of human blood: "its victories are deadly or at any rate deathly."

Conclusion
THE ROMAN PEACE AND THE MEANING OF THE WEST

Observing the ruins of the crumbling Empire, Augustine argued that true peace (peace of the spirit, peace for eternity) was to be found only in communion with a transcendent God. Many, over the next two thousand years, would agree with him. But the Roman Peace—Augustus' *pax romana*—was not, though it failed, a meaningless episode in the building of the West.

The Roman Peace was actually a permanent condition of war, waged hot and cold on the borders of Empire far from the center. There, over five centuries, Roman emperors struggled to save Roman institutions by transmuting and subverting them. As they struggled, and though they lost, Roman generals and soldiers, landowners and poets and, eventually, bishops (see Chapter 7), brought the products of ancient culture to the peoples of Europe and planted the Latin language in fields far from Rome before French, German, or English were born. By their agency, and protected by the formidable power of the imperial state, a bridge was built between the ancient Mediterranean and unformed, unsettled Europe. Across that bridge, the cultural heritage of the ancient world traveled north to nurture that civilization that we call the West.

QUESTIONS TO CONSIDER

1. How well did Augustus evaluate his own reign as *princeps* in his memoirs (the *Res gestae*)?

2. How could the Empire function so successfully during its first two centuries when so many of its rulers were personally corrupt or tyrannical?

3. What was the nature of the order of "freedmen" in imperial Rome? What functions did they perform, and why did they become so influential?

4. What were the effects of having different approaches to justice for "honorable" and "less honorable" citizens?

5. Why did the emperors limit the extent of the frontier, rather than expand the military, to deal with the threats from tribal peoples on the periphery?

SUGGESTED RESOURCES

Ariès, Philippe and Georges Duby, eds., *A History of Private Life*, vol 1: *From Pagan Rome to Byzantium*, trans. Arthur Goldhammer (Cambridge, MA: Belknap Press of Harvard University Press, 1987). These essays discuss family structures and private life, domestic architecture, and the presuppositions underlying private life.

Boatwright, Mary Taliaferro, *Hadrian and the City of Rome* (Princeton: Princeton University Press, 1987). A solid and readable study of city planning and construction in imperial Rome, emphasizing the emperor Hadrian's building program and administrative reforms.

Burns, Thomas S., *Barbarians within the Gates of Rome: A Study of Roman Military Policy and the Barbarians, ca. 375–425 A.D.* (Bloomington: Indiana University Press, 1995). Studies a critical half-century where Roman policy changed step by fatal step—fatal for the survival of the Empire—from allowing Germans to fight in Roman armies to allowing them to fight under their own kings, upon whom Roman leaders, in turn, became dependent.

Cameron, Averil, *The Mediterranean World in Late Antiquity, A.D. 395–600* (London: Routledge, 1993). Excellent up-to-date overview of the two centuries of Roman disintegration, including ample consideration of both the eastern and western zones of empire.

Evans, John K., *War, Women, and Children in Ancient Rome* (London: Routledge, 1991). Surveys the effects of imperialism on the status of propertied women, working women in towns and the countryside, and ties between parents and children.

MacMullen, Ramsay, *Romanization in the Time of Augustus* (New Haven: Yale University Press, 2000). Attributes the rapid Romanization of the provinces to the imitation of Roman ways by local populations amid whom Roman military units were stationed.

Mellor, Ronald, *Tacitus* (London: Routledge, 1991). Thorough presentation of the thought and craft of the great first-century historian which makes a persuasive case for Tacitus as moralist, psychologist, and political analyst, as well as literary artist.

Southern, Pat & Karen Ramsey Dixon, *The Late Roman Army* (New Haven: Yale University Press, 1996). How the Roman army and its managers from Septimius Severus to the last throes of the Empire addressed multiple crises by adjusting systems of funding, recruitment, fortification, and tactics until it could fend off disaster no longer.

Sullivan, J. P., *Literature and Politics in the Age of Nero* (Ithaca: Cornell University Press, 1985). An insightful study of the profound influence of patronage and politics on literature during Nero's reign.

Treggiari, Susan, *Roman Marriage: Iusti coniuges from the Time of Cicero to the Time of Ulpian* (Oxford: Clarendon Press of Oxford University Press, 1991). Exhaustive study of legal and other sources yields a comprehensive understanding of the functioning of marriage in the various social classes of the Empire.

Wells, Peter S., *The Battle That Stopped Rome: Emperor Augustus, Arminius, and the Slaughter of the Legions in the Teutoburg Forest* (New York: Norton, 2003). Dissection of the events and characters involved in the terrible battle of 9 C.E. (resulting in a loss of 20,000 men) that kept the Romans from expanding beyond the Rhine for the rest of the ancient period.

Williams, Aeryk. *The Reach of Rome: A History of the Roman Imperial Frontier, First to Fifth Centuries A.D.* (New York: St. Martin's Press, 1997). Examines the 4,000 miles of the Roman frontier, how it was established and how defended by walls, garrisons, and natural objects.

Yavetz, Zvi, *Plebs and Princeps* (Oxford: Oxford University Press, 1988). An account of how Julio-Claudian emperors gained the support of the plebs through grain supply, entertainments, and clemency.

Zanker, Paul, *The Power of Images in the Age of Augustus* (Ann Arbor: University of Michigan Press, 1988). Studies the visual imagery of the Roman state and identity under Augustus.

Chronology of Roman History, Trojan War to Byzantine Empire (Forum Romanum):
http://www.geocities.com/Athens/Forum/6946/history.html

Diotima: materials for the study of women in antiquity:
http://www.stoa.org/diotima

The destruction of Pompeii, 79 C.E.:
http://www.ibiscom/pompeii.html

⦿ **Western Civilization Documents CD-ROM**

5.1 Augustus' Moral Legislation
5.2 A Satirical View of Women

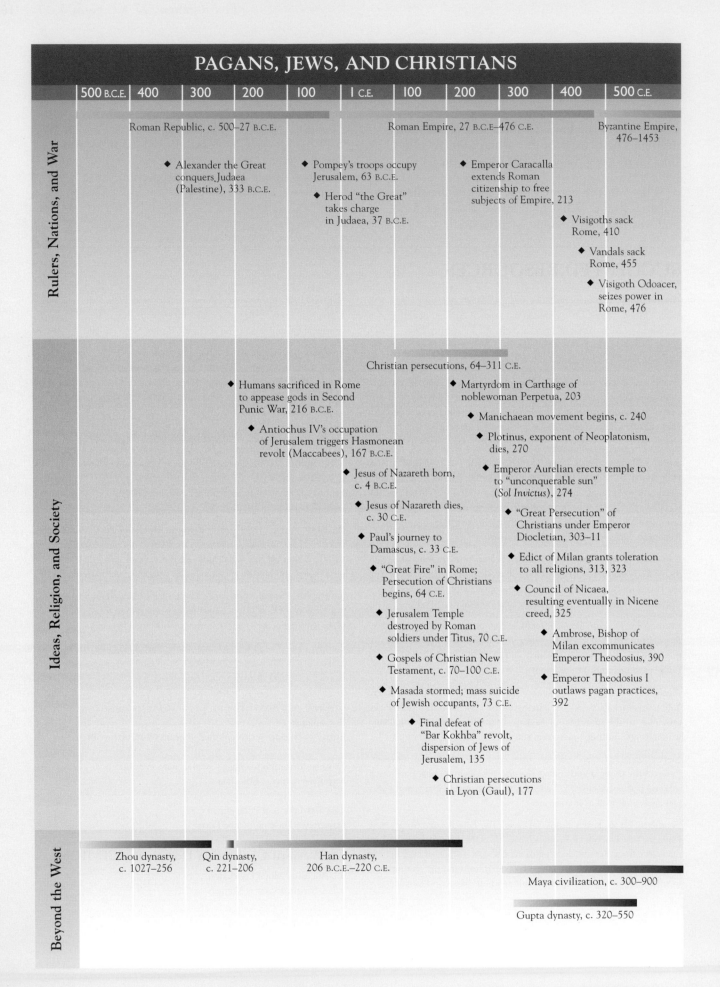

PAGANS, JEWS, AND CHRISTIANS

| 500 B.C.E. | 400 | 300 | 200 | 100 | I C.E. | 100 | 200 | 300 | 400 | 500 C.E. |

Rulers, Nations, and War

Roman Republic, c. 500–27 B.C.E.

Roman Empire, 27 B.C.E–476 C.E.

Byzantine Empire, 476–1453

◆ Alexander the Great conquers Judaea (Palestine), 333 B.C.E.

◆ Pompey's troops occupy Jerusalem, 63 B.C.E.

◆ Herod "the Great" takes charge in Judaea, 37 B.C.E.

◆ Emperor Caracalla extends Roman citizenship to free subjects of Empire, 213

◆ Visigoths sack Rome, 410

◆ Vandals sack Rome, 455

◆ Visigoth Odoacer, seizes power in Rome, 476

Ideas, Religion, and Society

Christian persecutions, 64–311 C.E.

◆ Humans sacrificed in Rome to appease gods in Second Punic War, 216 B.C.E.

◆ Antiochus IV's occupation of Jerusalem triggers Hasmonean revolt (Maccabees), 167 B.C.E.

◆ Jesus of Nazareth born, c. 4 B.C.E.

◆ Jesus of Nazareth dies, c. 30 C.E.

◆ Paul's journey to Damascus, c. 33 C.E.

◆ "Great Fire" in Rome; Persecution of Christians begins, 64 C.E.

◆ Jerusalem Temple destroyed by Roman soldiers under Titus, 70 C.E.

◆ Gospels of Christian New Testament, c. 70–100 C.E.

◆ Masada stormed; mass suicide of Jewish occupants, 73 C.E.

◆ Final defeat of "Bar Kokhba" revolt, dispersion of Jews of Jerusalem, 135

◆ Christian persecutions in Lyon (Gaul), 177

◆ Martyrdom in Carthage of noblewoman Perpetua, 203

◆ Manichaean movement begins, c. 240

◆ Plotinus, exponent of Neoplatonism, dies, 270

◆ Emperor Aurelian erects temple to to "unconquerable sun" (*Sol Invictus*), 274

◆ "Great Persecution" of Christians under Emperor Diocletian, 303–11

◆ Edict of Milan grants toleration to all religions, 313, 323

◆ Council of Nicaea, resulting eventually in Nicene creed, 325

◆ Ambrose, Bishop of Milan excommunicates Emperor Theodosius, 390

◆ Emperor Theodosius I outlaws pagan practices, 392

Beyond the West

Zhou dynasty, c. 1027–256

Qin dynasty, c. 221–206

Han dynasty, 206 B.C.E.–220 C.E.

Maya civilization, c. 300–900

Gupta dynasty, c. 320–550

7

PAGANS, JEWS, AND CHRISTIANS

Religions around the Mediterranean

500 B.C.E.–500 C.E.

Roman Empire, 2nd century CE

SLAVS people

KEY QUESTIONS

◆ **Roman Gods:** How did Roman religion change under the influence of imperial expansion and immigration from the provinces?

◆ **Judaism in Transition:** How did the dispersed Jews of Palestine adapt following the destruction of the Second Temple and the suppression of the Bar-Kochba revolt?

◆ **Origins of Christianity:** What currents of contemporary religious thought were incorporated into the new Christian religion?

◆ **Progress of Christianity:** How did a persecuted religion succeed in becoming the dominant religion of the Roman Empire?

The Unknown God In Athens, where the latest intellectual fad caused tongues to wag and where every new god found a worshiper, there stood one altar—in case any deity had been slighted—to the "unknown god." Here Paul of Tarsus, a follower of the crucified teacher Jesus of Nazareth, preached a sermon around the midpoint of the first century C.E. "What therefore you worship as unknown, this I proclaim to you. The God who made the world and everything in it ... does not live in shrines made by human hands, nor is he served by human hands, as though he needed anything, since he himself gives to all mortals life and breath and all things." The god who was unknown to the Athenians, Paul told his audience, was the Jewish God, revealed in Jesus.

The doctrine Paul preached gave birth to Christianity: the religion that today has more followers than any other on the globe and that has fundamentally shaped the experience of the Western world. Unknown to the Athenians of the first century, it would go on to triumph throughout the Roman Empire before that power fell in the West. It triumphed for several reasons: because it responded to human needs not addressed by ancient polytheistic religions; because it reached populations broader than those responding to its parent religion, Judaism; and because, as it developed within Rome's harsh bosom, it adopted the principles of organization established by that once-successful state.

The polytheistic religions of the ancient world—many of which found their way to Rome itself—will be the first concern of this chapter. Within that polytheistic universe, Judaism developed, insisting on the awesome presence in the cosmos of only one God, whose action in the world was revealed in sacred Hebrew scripture, and who made moral demands on his worshipers. From Judaism, finally, emerged Christianity, which added to the monotheism, the scriptural tradition, and the ethical principles of its parent religion the figure of Jesus the Christ, or Savior, or Messiah. With its promise of **salvation** and eternal life, and with the support of some of the greatest minds and most effective leaders of the era, Christianity flourished in the fading Roman world.

ROMAN GODS

Like most other ancient peoples, the Romans were polytheists who revered gods of earth and sky and the spirits animating their natural world. The evolution of Roman polytheism is as outlined in *Who's Who* on p. 172. At first, Roman villagers worshiped the deities of their households and fields. As Rome developed, its citizens embraced the gods of the peoples they conquered and imitated. Later, Romans experimented with exotic cults that promised salvation to troubled souls, or looked to elevated philosophies that offered a different path toward the same spiritual peace. By the fourth century, with Christianity ascendant, the Romans who still worshiped many gods were called pagans: "country-dwellers." These simple villagers clung to ancestral ways when most urbanites had abjured polytheism and embraced the one God of ancient Israel and the new church.

Ancestral Ways

The religion of the early Romans was simpler than that of the Christians or Jews, simpler even than that of other Indo-European peoples. Common to most Indo-European groups was a powerful sky god: the Greek Zeus, the Hindu Indra, the Persian Ahura Mazda, the Viking Odin (see Chapter 1). An anthropomorphic deity, with human forms and human attributes, he caused storms, thunder and lightning, and ruled the other deities, approximating, in some cases, the one God of the monotheistic faiths. In the Greek and Viking traditions especially, a rich body of myth grew up around thundering sky gods.

In the earliest days, before Rome's exposure to Etruscan customs, the Romans did not worship a supreme sky god. Nor did they conceive of their gods in human form, or develop a mythology. Instead, they worshiped a multitude of spirits: mystic forces embedded in nature. There were gods, or spirits, of plowing, of harvest, of the boundaries between farms, of the hearth, the doorway, and the granary. Most important were the beings who safeguarded the household and were worshiped daily in the domestic cult: the *lares* (deified spirits of dead ancestors) and *penates* (gods of the household stores). Each day the family honored these deities with ritual acts and sacrificial offerings.

The important role of the household in Roman religion mirrors the role of the *paterfamilias*, its head, in Roman society. The religion of the Roman state was the religion of the household writ large. Certain rites had to be performed, certain duties fulfilled, if the community was to thrive. The Latin word for religion—*religio*, meaning a bond between humans and gods—connotes the scrupulous fulfilment of obligation, the union of human beings in their duty to the divine. If all due rites were paid to the deities, there would be peace with the gods, among the gods, and among human beings: "the peace of the gods." If not, all was at risk. No public business was to be undertaken, no war prosecuted unless proper deities had been consulted and rituals conducted.

Among the Etruscan religious practices the Romans inherited was that of divination. Some Etruscan priests predicted future events by examining the livers of sacrificed beasts. Others examined the movements of birds or other natural phenomena.

Another Etruscan religious concept was that of sacred space. The boundaries of Etruscan cities were marked with special rituals, and their temples, although modeled on those of the Greeks, were erected in a reserved spatial realm defined by ancillary buildings.

The Romans borrowed and blended these features of Etruscan ritual with their worship of the spirits of the granary and the hearth. Accordingly, the early Romans marked the boundary of their city with a sacred ritual to ensure its protection by spirits. Until the practice was abolished by Christian emperors, the

young men of the city, stripped naked, ran the circuit of Rome in a ritual that promised security and abundance. On festal days (of which there were about 100 each year), public business was not to be conducted. State priests published a calendar of these days to prevent infractions, which would anger the gods.

Roman religion was greatly concerned with the preeminent business of war. One god's function was to announce whether the city was at war or at peace. This was Janus, the god of the city's doorways. The door of his temple was open in peacetime and closed

Faith and Skepticism in Roman Religion

The Romans regarded religion very seriously, taking care to show due reverence to the gods by observing all obligations and following rituals meticulously; in return, they expected that the gods would protect their households and city. Those attitudes find expression in the passages by Livy and Plutarch, later historians describing behavior dictated by traditional religion: the self-devotion to the gods (exemplified by the sacrifice of P. Decius Mus), and the guardianship of the purity of the Vestal Virgins. In contrast, the third passage by the poet and Epicurean convert Lucretius is wholly skeptical. For Lucretius, the atomic "science" of Epicurean philosophy was a consolation to human beings who need no longer fear the afterworld or the vengeance of the gods.

To save Rome, P. Decius Mus devotes himself to the gods of the underworld (340 B.C.E.): In the confusion of this movement Decius the consul called out to Marcus Valerius in a loud voice: "We have need of the gods' help, Marcus Valerius. Come therefore, state pontiff of the Roman people, dictate the words, that I may devote myself to save the legions." The pontiff bade him don the purple-bordered toga and, with veiled head and one hand thrust out from under the toga and touching his chin, stand upon a spear that was laid under his feet and say as follows: "Janus, Jupiter, Father Mars. …, ye gods in whose power are both we and our enemies, … I invoke and worship you, … that you may prosper the might and the victory of the Roman people, … and visit the foes of the Roman people … with fear, shuddering and death. As I have pronounced the words, even so … do I devote the legions and auxiliaries of the enemy, together with myself to the divine Manes and to the Earth." … He then girded himself …, and vaulting, armed, upon his horse, plunged into the thick of the enemy. …
(Livy, *History of Rome*, 8.9.4–10; eds. N. Lewis, M. Reinhold, 1966)

Plutarch describes the punishment assigned to a Vestal Virgin (one of the priestesses assigned to guard the perpetual flame of Rome), who has broken her vow of chastity (c. 110 C.E.): [A Vestal who] has broken her vow of chastity is buried alive … [under] a little mound of earth … [where] a narrow room is con-structed, to which a descent is made by stairs; here they prepare a bed, and light a lamp, and leave a small quantity of victuals, such as bread, water, a pail of milk, and some oil. … The culprit herself is put in a litter, which they cover over, and tie her down with cords on it, so that nothing she utters may be heard. They then take her to the Forum; all people silently go out of the way as she passes, and such as follow accompany the bier with solemn and speechless sorrow; and, indeed, there is not any spectacle more appalling, nor any day observed by the city with greater appearance of gloom and sadness. When they come to the place of execution, the officers loose the cords, and then the Pontifex Maximus [the chief priest] … brings out the prisoner, … and placing her upon the steps that lead down to the cell, turns away his face with the rest of the priests; the stairs are drawn up after she has gone down, and a quantity of earth is heaped up over the entrance to the cell. … This is the punishment of those who break their vow of virginity.
(Plutarch, "Life of Numa" in William Stearns Davis, ed., *Readings in Ancient History*, 1912–13)

The poet Lucretius explains why mortal humans need have no fears; the world is ruled by the forces of nature alone, and there are no gods who have power over us (c. 55 B.C.E.):
This fright, this night of the mind, must be dispelled
not by the rays of the sun, nor day's bright spears,
but by the face of nature and her laws.
And this is her first, from which we take our start:
nothing was ever by miracle made from nothing.
You see, all mortal men are gripped by fear
because they see so many things on earth
and in the sky, yet can't discern their causes
and hence believe that they are acts of god.
But in all this, when we have learned that nothing
can come from nothing, then we shall see straight through
to what we seek: whence each thing is created
and in what manner made, without god's help.
(Lucretius, *De rerum natura*; trs. F. O. Copley 1977)

in wartime. War was undertaken only after consulting with religious experts such as diviners—called augurs or *haruspices* (singular *haruspex*)—who studied the movements of birds, clouds, and wind, and the organs of sacrificed beasts to judge whether the time was auspicious for battle, as shown on p. 172. *Fetial* priests were responsible for the ethics of war. Because Romans were not to fight except in self-defense, it was the fetials' duty to determine whether a proposed war was legitimate or not (they generally thought it was). When the time came for battle, Roman priests accompanied the army and exhorted the deities of the enemy city to flee before the attack. With terrifying gravity, the priests proclaimed those alien gods doomed if they did not defect to the victor.

The priests who performed such rituals were elected from among the "fathers," those heads of families who belonged to the order of patricians. Organized in groups, each responsible for a different element of the Roman cult, the priests established the calendar, supervised worship, and authorized the building of temples or the admission of new deities. Chief of all the priests was the *pontifex maximus*, a title that has lived on as the Latin name for the head of the Roman Catholic Church.

In addition to the male priests drawn from the patrician crust of Roman society, a group of six patrician women was charged with the performance of one important duty. That duty was to tend the flame (rekindled every March) that burned on the communal hearth in honor of Vesta, the patron goddess of the city. The women designated for this task (mostly young girls from leading families) were required to be virgins at the time of their selection and, by law, to remain so until they resigned their office (permissible after age forty), or died. These were the vestal virgins: the pure "daughters" of the city of Rome. The punishment was severe for those vestals discovered to have broken their vows: they were buried alive. It happened only rarely—for the last time during the reign of the emperor Domitian. "There is no spectacle in the world more terrifying," wrote the moralist Plutarch (46–120 C.E.), "and in Rome no day of comparable horror (see *Witnesses*, p. 169)."

Besides the six vestals, other women also participated in the Roman cult. As in Greece, religious celebration was one of the avenues for female participation in public life. Women danced, prayed, adorned their houses, and joined in processions. The annual worship of Ceres, the goddess of grain, for example, could be celebrated only by women. During the Second Punic War, these rites were canceled; so many women were in mourning for lost husbands and sons that there were not enough available to serve the goddess.

The Greeks of the southern Italian peninsula worshiped the Olympian gods of their homeland: Zeus, Apollo, Athena, Ares, Hermes. These cults became

A Temple for all the gods

The Pantheon *(left, right): By the second century C.E., Roman building techniques had matured considerably, as seen in the Pantheon, Rome, the temple to all the gods erected under the emperor Hadrian, c. 118 C.E. Built of marble, brick, and concrete, the most prominent feature of this temple was the enormous dome, its expanse pierced in the center by a round window (oculus) that admitted light to the spacious interior. This interior was captured in 1740 (facing page) by the Italian painter Giovanni Paolo Pannini. (facing page: National Gallery of Art, Washington D.C. Samuel H. Kress Collection)* known to the Romans both directly from the Greeks resident in Italy and indirectly from the Etruscans, who had absorbed Greek customs in earlier centuries. The Romans soon adopted these deities, who looked and behaved like human beings. They built a temple on the Capitoline Hill to Jupiter, Juno, and Minerva (the Roman designations for the Greek gods Zeus, Hera, and Athena), which became the center of Roman religious life. In the temple consecrated to these three gods were deposited the books of prophecies announced by the Cumaean sibyl (from Italian Cumae), one of Rome's revered female prophets.

The anthropomorphic gods of hearth and household now encountered the anthropomorphic gods of a kindred yet very different people. The temples of the indigenous and the imported deities shared the same sacred zone: those dedicated to Janus and Vesta stood adjacent to those dedicated to Jupiter or Apollo. Native Roman traditions merged with adopted Greek ones, and Greek myth was Romanized.

New Religious Impulses

This early Roman religion—a mixture of Greek imagination, Etruscan practice, and ancestral Roman cult—faced a severe challenge during the last years of the third century B.C.E., in the Second Punic War, when the Carthaginian general Hannibal ravaged

Sacrifice and prophecy: In Roman as in many ancient polytheistic cultures the sacrifice of an animal on the altar was a central religious ritual. Also important for the Romans was the practice derived from the Etruscans: the expert examination of the sacrificed beast's entrails for signs that predicted favorable or unfavorable outcomes for intended actions. These ritual events are depicted in this first century bowl, showing a bull being sacrificed. (Louvre)

The sacrifice of a bull, first century B.C.E.

Italy (see Chapter 5). While wives, widows, and orphans were left at home alone to till the land, virtually all adult males were enrolled in the army. Routs, massacres, and retreats followed from encounters with the African general, along with a mounting death toll among the Romans and their Latin allies. In 216 B.C.E., the Carthaginians trapped and butchered a Roman force of 60,000; only 10,000 men

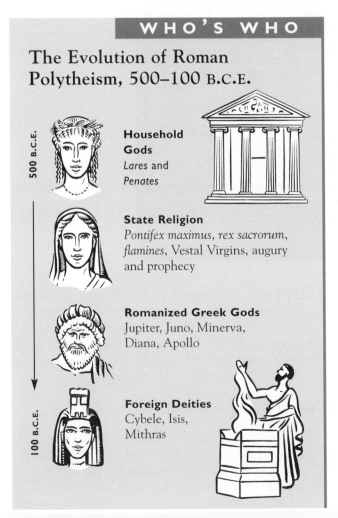

WHO'S WHO

The Evolution of Roman Polytheism, 500–100 B.C.E.

500 B.C.E.

Household Gods
Lares and *Penates*

State Religion
Pontifex maximus, *rex sacrorum*, *flamines*, Vestal Virgins, augury and prophecy

Romanized Greek Gods
Jupiter, Juno, Minerva, Diana, Apollo

100 B.C.E.

Foreign Deities
Cybele, Isis, Mithras

escaped. Reaching deep into their past for a suitable response to this seemingly inexplicable disaster, the Romans sacrificed human victims to appease the gods for the last time in their history—two men and two women (according to the historian Livy), Greeks and Celts, buried alive in the cattle market.

When Hannibal's forces paraded outside the gates of Rome, some Romans, gripped by fear, sought strength in new forms of religious experience. Foremost among these was the cult of Cybele: the *Magna Mater* (Great Mother). In 204 B.C.E., a Roman delegation brought back from Pessinus (in Asia Minor) a black stone sacred to Cybele. Her cult and that of her dead and reborn consort Attis were celebrated each spring with orgiastic rites, performed by castrated male priests, the Galli (a profession barred to Roman citizens until the reign of the emperor Claudius, r. 41–54 C.E.).

Around the same time, the Greek god Dionysus (or Bacchus) began to be celebrated in Rome. As the god of wine, this deity was worshiped with noisy and orgiastic festivals (known as Bacchanals) that grieved the senatorial fathers who had already bent their principles to the arrival of the Great Mother.

Rome's further conquests in the East meant that more and more foreign religious cults found their way back to Rome. Traditionalists distrusted their exotic message and sometimes bizarre practices—especially since they often appealed to slaves, who could participate as equals in cultic rites and even become priests. The historian Sallust (86–34 B.C.E.) lamented that greed had driven morality from Rome and replaced it with "pride, cruelty, neglect of the gods, and total materialism." It was the neglect of religion, Cicero maintained, that had brought the civil wars upon the Romans. But these voices could not prevail against the appeal of exotic cultural forms that appeared to offer certainties about this world and the other. Compared to these, the Roman cults of hearth and house seemed irrelevant.

The man who once had consented to Cicero's murder came later to defend, like him, the worship of the ancient gods. Augustus believed that traditional worship would help preserve the "customs of our ancestors," the virtues that had made Rome great. As *pontifex maximus*, he revived the Roman cults and oversaw a program of temple construction. Yet even as he defended traditional religion, Augustus, too, was a religious innovator. He chose as his personal deity Apollo—among the Greeks, the god of the intellect, and patron of the rational approach to human existence, but also (as a result of Hellenistic syncretism) assimilated to the sun gods of eastern cults.

Augustus' patronage of Apollo encouraged later emperors to choose a personal god, and served to break down the solidity of the ancient Roman tradition. So did the creation of a priesthood dedicated to Augustus' imperial cult, which was practiced after Augustus' death in the Hellenistic lands where king-worship was an established practice (see Chapter 6). Just as Augustus, as restorer of the Republic, sealed its death sentence, so Augustus, champion of ancestral virtues, helped open the path to the unrestrained syncretism of the imperial centuries.

Later Roman Religion

In the early Empire, the religious traditions of the Mediterranean world continued to fuse. To be sure, the official cults of the Greek *poleis* and the Roman state remained distinctive, as did Judaism. Otherwise, the deities of West and East were interchanged to such an extent that their ethnic origins were forgotten. This process of syncretism (the blending of diverse religious traditions) resulted in the elevation of some deities to near universal status. One example of this is the amalgamation of Sarapis from the Egyptian Osiris with various other deities of the ancient East. The syncretic process flourished under Roman rule, which tolerated all forms of religious expression that were not perceived as threatening to the power of the state.

Not only did ancient cults blend by the process of syncretism, but ancient "mystery religions" found new popularity in Rome during the early Empire. These promised a secret knowledge or special experience of the divine realm which could lead to individual illumination. The mystery religions appealed especially to the swollen populations of the cities of the Hellenistic and Roman eras.

In earlier antiquity, religion tended to be communal: the household, the village, the city gained by the worship of specific gods. In later antiquity, religion tended to become personal: the individual hoped to experience the benefits of worship and was more willing to risk his or her personal security to gain that benefit. The former kind of religious system was ideally suited to peasant communities, with their strong ties to the land. The latter suited the cities, where diverse populations were offered many religious options, where individuals often felt isolated amid the crowd and were vulnerable to promises of salvation, and where the boredom of the rich and the desperation of the poor both sought remedies in devotion.

The goddess Isis attracted many worshipers over the centuries, especially women. She was understood as the universal and compassionate mother, often depicted with her consort Osiris (sometimes Sarapis) or holding her infant son Horus, as shown on p. 174. Her priests were a regular clergy, robed in white, who daily administered rituals of purification. They baptized new initiates, who were thereby cleansed from sin and expected to pass through a final judgment by Sarapis and enter into eternal life. There are elements here of belief and ritual that anticipate mature Christianity.

People also worshiped the Sun, which had been personified as a deity by the Egyptians and the Hittites, among others. In late antiquity, the worship of the Sun gained such popularity that it almost became a universal religion—in the place not long after to be filled by Christianity. Augustus' worship of Apollo, in this era a Sun deity, has been noted. Hadrian's Pantheon (built c. 118 C.E. to celebrate all the gods) especially exalted the Sun, the light of which shone through the special opening in the building's huge domed roof.

In the third century C.E. the Severan emperors and their wives also worshiped the Sun. The emperor Aurelian (r. 270–275 C.E.) made sun worship the central feature of the state religion, erecting a temple to Sol Invictus, the Invincible Sun (in 274 C.E.). The emperor Constantine (r. 312–337 C.E.) worshiped the Sun until his victory over a rival claimant to the Empire at the Battle of the Milvian Bridge (312 C.E.), which he believed was due to Christ's favor. The birthday of Sol Invictus was celebrated annually on December 25 (approximately at the winter solstice). The same date served as the birthday of the god Mithras, and would be adopted by Christians for the celebration of the birth of their Savior.

The Persian deity Mithras was one of the many solar gods of the imperial era. Brought home to Rome by Pompey's troops, Mithras became a favorite among the Roman soldiers, who worshiped him in barracks, garrisons, and frontier camps. A heroic champion against evil (a reflection of his Zoroastrian origins), Mithras appealed to those who often faced danger and death. The faithful (exclusively male) gathered to worship their deity in his temple, in the center of which was a sculpted image of the god slaying a bull, from whose body all living things were thought to be created. Initiation involved progress through seven stages, including a ritual washing in the spilled blood of a sacrificial beast. Full members participated in communal meals at which consecrated bread and wine were consumed. Through these they gained unity with the god, and hoped for an eternity in Heaven. In these practices, there were prefigurations of Christianity.

While many Romans sought to enrich their lives through religion, others looked to magic. Religion involved reverence for the gods and the performance of required duties or rituals. Magic offered control over divine spirits and natural forces with the aim of increasing personal power. Magic manipulated the supernatural realm and could (it was believed) arrange love affairs, cure diseases, tell the future, and even murder an enemy.

Magic was the science of the unlearned. For the learned, astrology offered an opportunity to penetrate (so they thought) otherwise unknowable secrets of the universe. Astrology used the knowledge of the motion of the stars and planets to predict the future and understand the present. As the planets circled the earth, they also (apparently) influenced earthly events. They did so according to their position in the sky relative to the earth, to the other planets, and to the signs of the zodiac (a set of twelve constellations each at the zenith during a different period of the year). Astrologers could use their knowledge to forecast the future, as magicians could use their charms and incantations to shape it.

Other religious beliefs derived from the learned traditions. The ancient Zoroastrians had seen the universe as a stage for a struggle between gods of Good and Evil (see Chapter 1). That **dualism**, which supported such religious beliefs as immortality and the Devil, survived into later antiquity and beyond. It influenced some Jewish authors of the last centuries B.C.E. and reemerged in the theology of the Persian prophet Mani (216–276 C.E.). Mani preached that the struggle between the forces of Light and Darkness would be decided by a Savior (whom he identified with Jesus). Mani's teachings survived in the Manichean religion, which had many adherents—including the young Saint Augustine before his conversion to Christianity—during the first few centuries C.E. Mani was crucified as a heretic by the Zoroastrians.

The Neoplatonists were the late successors to Plato, the great Athenian philosopher (see Chapter 4). They developed a secular theology that appealed to the skeptical intellectuals of the late Empire. The Egyptian-born Plotinus (205–270 C.E.) envisioned a transcendent force of the One, or First Principle: being that exists beyond number, thought, motion, or time. From the One there radiates all of existence, in ever-widening circles, to its farthest limit: the Many, creatures locked in time and space. Nearest to the One is the Universal Mind; and immediately below it, Universal Soul. The individual human being can hope, through the cultivation of his own soul or mind, to reach the One in an experience of intimate union. Plotinus' philosophy, developed for oral instruction, is recorded in the six books of *Enneads*, by his pupil Porphyry of Tyre (234–305 C.E.).

In the last Roman centuries, philosophy became an alternative to religion, more a guide for existence than a method for the rational investigation of the cosmos. That tendency could already be seen in the work of Lucretius, Cicero, and Seneca. These were popularizers, whose aim was to make available to literate but practical Romans the visions of the ancient philosophers—all of them Greek. Lucretius' enormous verse exposition of Epicurean philosophy, *On the Nature of Things*, assured his compatriots in moving and insistent tones that they need not fear death. On the one hand, the universe itself would never die, as all substance was eternal. On the other, humans would die without consequence, with no prospect of afterlife or punishment or pain, since all souls were mortal.

The eclectic Cicero drew on all the philosophical schools. In *De natura deorum* he encapsulated the Academic, the Peripatetic, the Epicurean, and the Stoic views of the nature of the universe, the role of the gods, and the role of the human being. In his *Tusculan Disputations* and *On Duties* and other works, he explored Greek insights into the interactions of human society and the predicaments of the soul.

Divine Mothers

Isis and Horus *(left): Just as Roman religion was syncretistic, readily absorbing the deities and beliefs of other religious traditions practiced in the Mediterranean world, so also was Christianity, which grafted Greek, Roman, and other ancient ideas and practices onto the original stem of Judaism. The worship of the Egyptian goddess Isis (left), the loving mother of Horus, was widely practiced in Rome, as shown in this sculpture c. 1400 B.C.E. (Schimmel Collection, New York)*

Virgin and Child *(right): When Jesus, the central figure of emerging Christianity, became paired in artistic representations with his mother Mary—as shown in this apse mosaic from Hosias Loukas, Greece, c. 1020 C.E.—the resulting image could resemble those of the Greeks, Romans, or Egyptians.*

Seneca's moral essays and letters popularized Stoicism (see Chapter 5)—of all the ancient philosophies the one most congenial to the Romans. He chided his readers about the emptiness of their lives, and nudged them to a deeper understanding of humanity. Each person had within him or her a spark of the divine fire, Seneca wrote reassuringly: "God is near you, he is with you, he is within you. ... A holy spirit indwells within us, one who marks our good and bad deeds, and is our guardian. ..."

The second-century emperor Marcus Aurelius retold in his diary all that ancient philosophy could offer as a guide to daily life, to the encounter with evil and with chance, and to the imminence of death. That the emperor's work *To Himself* (later referred to as his *Meditations*) seems weak testifies to the exhaustion of the intellectual tradition begun with Thales, Anaximander, and Anaximenes (see Chapter 4). For spirits in search of nurture, the two monotheistic faiths—Judaism and Christianity—offered more.

JUDAISM IN TRANSITION

On returning to Judah after 538 B.C.E. from their exile in Babylon, the Jews reorganized the life of their community under new leaders in accord with their ancient traditions. Over the next several centuries, they lived under the Persians, the Greeks, and the Romans in turn, struggling to maintain their unique religious and cultural identity. At some points, that struggle became violent. And the era ended in violence, in 135 C.E., two generations after the Temple at Jerusalem was destroyed for the last time. Thenceforth, Jewish faith and culture would survive only in exile, in scattered communities around the ancient Mediterranean and beyond, under the guidance of learned teachers, **rabbis**, whose knowledge of scripture constituted a standard for daily life (see Map 7.1).

The Jewish State Under Foreign Overlords

When Cyrus the Great of Persia destroyed the Babylonian Empire in 539 B.C.E., he allowed the thousands of Jews exiled there to return to their land of Judah. Governors and priests led the restored community in the crystallization of a Jewish way of life based on the sacred writings of the **Torah**. Among these towered Nehemiah (d. 415 B.C.E.) and Ezra "the Scribe" (fl. c. 458 B.C.E.). Nehemiah, an effective administrator, oversaw the building of the walls of the city that Nebuchadnezzar had demolished. Ezra organized the compilation of Hebrew writings (probably some part of the Pentateuch, the first five biblical books—perhaps only Deuteronomy). From a wooden pulpit, he read the law aloud and stirred the Jewish people to commit to the covenant with an almighty God that it defined. With that determination (as distinct from the already long history of the Jewish people) the history of Judaism begins.

Alexander's conquest of 333 B.C.E. shook the newly formed Jewish community. The Ptolemies of Egypt invited Jews to settle in Alexandria, and ruled Judaea (as it was known to the Greeks) benevolently. Later, the Seleucid rulers of Syria challenged the Ptolemaic presence in Judaea, and Antiochus III (r. 223–187 B.C.E.) finally unseated the Egyptians and took command of the region. The Jewish hero Mattathias, of the Hasmonean clan, along with his sons, successfully resisted the Hellenizing crusade of Antiochus IV Epiphanes. By 142 B.C.E., his last surviving son, Simon, held the title of high priest over an autonomous Jewish state within the fading Seleucid Empire.

After 63 B.C.E., authority seeped from the high priest Hyrcanus to his adviser, Antipater (an Idumaean or Edomite, whose people—related to the Jews but traditionally hostile to them—had been recently converted to Judaism). Herod, one of Antipater's sons, gained supremacy in 37 B.C.E. and ruled an expanded Judaea until his death in 4 B.C.E. A generous patron of building and the arts, Herod (called "the Great") was known for both his exceptional brutality and his great competence. He was the last person to command an autonomous Jewish state until the twentieth-century leaders of Israel. Herod's successors were titular rulers until 70 C.E., when the Second Temple, which Herod had rebuilt and adorned, fell to Roman conquerors, who destroyed it. A description is given in *Witnesses* on p. 177.

Herod's successors were rulers in name only, for Rome now controlled Judaea. Just as external politics had introduced the Jews to the Greeks, so they introduced the Jews to the Romans. During the years of Hasmonean rule in Judaea, the Roman presence loomed in nearby Asia Minor, Syria, and Egypt. In 63 B.C.E., Pompey reached Jerusalem and entered its temple, penetrating to the inner sanctum known as the Holy of Holies, heretofore the unique prerogative of the high priest on the holiest day of Yom Kippur.

Roman procurators and tax-collectors ruled Judaea. Herod's successors followed Roman directives as they clung to remnants of their autonomy: Herod even built a temple in Samaria for the celebration of the imperial cult, as well as an athletic complex (hateful to some Jews) in Jerusalem. Nevertheless, the Jewish community flourished. As of the census of 48 C.E., there may have been as many as 2 million Jews within Palestine and 7 million within the Empire; a large proportion, perhaps as much as 15 percent of the population of that cosmopolitan state was Jewish.

Under Roman rule, the high priest in Jerusalem and the members of the Sanhedrin, or council, avoided politics and concerned themselves with strictly religious matters. Of these there were many.

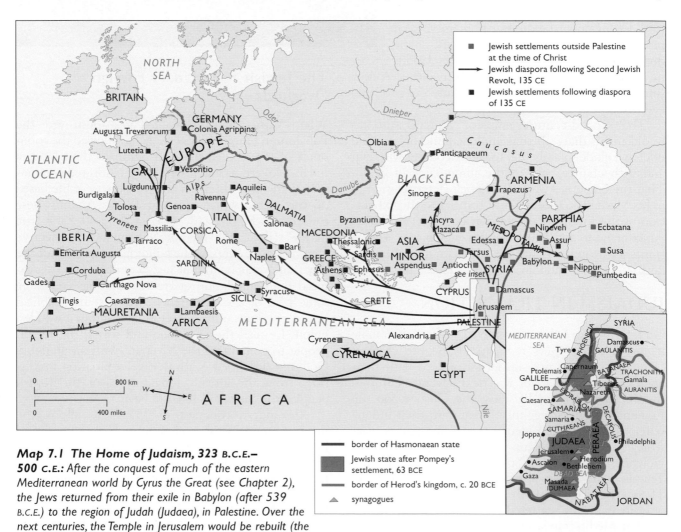

Map 7.1 The Home of Judaism, 323 B.C.E.–500 C.E.: *After the conquest of much of the eastern Mediterranean world by Cyrus the Great (see Chapter 2), the Jews returned from their exile in Babylon (after 539 B.C.E.) to the region of Judah (Judaea), in Palestine. Over the next centuries, the Temple in Jerusalem would be rebuilt (the Second Temple). Meanwhile, Jewish communities also flourished throughout the Fertile Crescent, Alexandria, and Cyrene; and after 135 C.E., also in Europe—the communities of the Diaspora, or "dispersion." How were the Jews able to maintain their traditions in the Diaspora?*

Jerusalem Destroyed, and Lamented

The Temple in Jerusalem, built by Solomon around 960 B.C.E. (see Chapter 1), had represented the center of the world for the Jews, and also the site for ritual and sacrifice. It was destroyed by the Babylonian king Nebuchadnezzar in 587 B.C.E., and a second temple was built to replace it when the large community of Jews who had been exiled to Babylonia were liberated by the Persian King Cyrus and returned to Jerusalem. It was destroyed again by a Roman army in 70 C.E., a loss that would transform Jewish life forever. In the first passage, the historian Tacitus describes the Roman destruction of the Second Temple. The second is a prophet's lamentation for the destruction of the First Temple by Nebuchadnezzar.

When Vespasian, who had been conducting the war against the Jews, returned to Rome in 70 C.E. to become emperor, he left his son Titus to pursue the siege of Jerusalem—which ended in the storming and burning of the temple: Titus pitched his camp before the walls of Jerusalem, and displayed his legions in battle order. The Jews formed their line close under the walls. … The temple had its own walls, like a citadel. … The founders had foreseen frequent wars because of differences from other peoples, and had prepared for protracted siege. … It is recorded that the besieged, of every age and both sexes, amounted to 600,000. All who could bore arms. … Men and women showed equal perseverance: they feared life more than death if they should be forced to leave their country. …

About the fifth hour of the following day the Jews were overpowered and shut up in the inner court of the temple, whereupon Titus withdrew, resolved to attack the following dawn with his whole force and gain the temple. … [At this point] one of the soldiers, awaiting no order and feeling no dread at such a deed but yielding to some demonic impulse, snatched a brand from the burning timbers and … hurled the fire through a little golden door which gave access to the rooms around the sanctuary on the north. As the flames shot up the Jews raised a cry worthy of the disaster and scurried to the rescue. …

[Titus] Caesar was unable to restrain the frenzy of his soldiers, and the fire got the upper hand. With his officers, he stepped in and saw the holy of holies and its contents. … One of the men who had made his way in … thrust a brand into the hinges of the gate. At once, a flame shot up from the interior and Caesar and his officers withdrew; now there was no one to prevent those outside from spreading the fire. And so, against Caesar's wishes, the temple was burned down.
(Tacitus, *Histories*, 5.11; ed. M. Hadas 1956)

Once before the destruction of the temple in 70 C.E., Jerusalem had been devastated—when it fell to the Babylonian king Nebuchadnezzar in 587 B.C.E. On that occasion, a prophet lamented its downfall:

How lonely sits the city
    that once was full of people!
How like a widow she has become,
    she that was great among the nations!
She that was a princess among the provinces
    has become a vassal.

Her foes have become the masters,
    her enemies prosper,
because the Lord has made her suffer
    for the multitude of her transgressions;
her children have gone away,
    captives before the foe.

Jerusalem remembers,
    in the days of her affliction and wandering,
all the precious things
    that were hers in days of old.
When her people fell into the hand of the foe,
    and there was no one to help her,
the foe looked on mocking
    over her downfall.
(Lamentations, 1:1,5,7)

During the Hasmonean and Herodian eras, two parties of Jewish thought emerged with different views of the relative value of written and oral tradition and with different outlooks upon the law and worship: the **Sadducees** and **Pharisees**.

Sadducees, Pharisees, and Essenes The wealthy Sadducees (the term derives from Zadok, high priest under David) were prominent in the Sanhedrin and dedicated themselves to the performance of the Temple cult. They recognized the written Torah as final and authoritative, resisting new ideas which, as they saw it, threatened the timelessness of the ritual performance. Because many of them came from the elite of Jewish society, they were inclined to support the balance of power established between foreign overlords and the native rulers.

The Pharisees (the term means "separated" or "distinct"), their natural opponents, differed from the Sadducees above all in their recognition of an oral tradition of law, handed down from Moses, that had validity alongside scripture. Holding that the observance of the law, more than the practice of the Temple cult, was central to Judaism, they developed a liturgy for worship in the synagogue based on scriptural readings and prayer. They closely examined points of law, often by disputations, foreshadowing some aspects of post-Temple Judaism. Some Pharisees

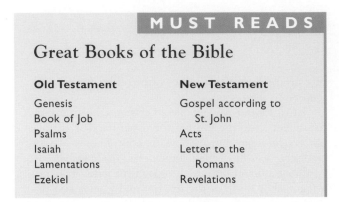

MUST READS

Great Books of the Bible

Old Testament	New Testament
Genesis	Gospel according to
Book of Job	St. John
Psalms	Acts
Isaiah	Letter to the
Lamentations	Romans
Ezekiel	Revelations

accepted the idea of an afterlife for the pious and of the **resurrection** of the body, perhaps influenced by Greek and Zoroastrian thought. In addition, the Pharisees elaborated the concept of the **Messiah** as an ideal future leader who would bring the reign of divine justice to the earth. That concept was an extension of what can be read in the Hebrew Bible about the Messiah (meaning "one who is anointed"); references are striking but few.

Associated with the Pharisees were the scribes and rabbis, or teachers. The scribes were laymen learned in scripture, who could define the conduct required by a strict reading of biblical law. The rabbis, the heirs of the Pharisees, were learned men who read and commented upon the Torah in the synagogues of the Jewish world, in Judaea and beyond. Their activity marked the emerging importance to the Jewish community of the **synagogue**—a place of study, assembly, and prayer, as contrasted with the Temple in Jerusalem, which was a holy place for ritual acts and sacrifice. Two great rabbis taught in Herod's reign: Hillel (c. 30 B.C.E.–10 C.E.) and his contemporary Shammai (c. 50 B.C.E.–30 C.E.), forerunners of a great tradition. The rabbis preserved the tradition of Pharisaic observance of the law when the high priests and Sadducees were no more, and Judaism was guided by its teachers.

Contemporaries of the Sadducees and the Pharisees were the Essenes (the term means "holy" or "pious"), members of one of the Jewish **sects** that flourished in the Herodian age. Highly disciplined, ascetic observers of the law, they withdrew into wilderness communities to pursue a religious life and, expecting the imminent arrival of the Messiah, to prepare for a cosmic war to ensue—similar to the Zoroastrian prediction of a conflict between the Children of Light and the Children of Darkness.

The most famous Essene community was at Qumran, near the northern tip of the Dead Sea. In 1947, scrolls from Qumran that recorded the community's sacred work and apocalyptic vision were found buried in caves. Among these Dead Sea Scrolls, a fragment of which is illustrated on p. 179 were copies, mostly fragments, of nearly all the canonical books of Hebrew scripture, the oldest still extant.

Resentment of Roman power simmered in the Jewish community of the Herodian age. In the countryside, especially, some rebels plotted the random assassination of Roman officials and collaborators. Such groups gathered force and men, setting the stage for the great rebellions of the first two centuries C.E.— the most serious ones the Romans would experience—and their terrible consequences.

The Revolts and Rabbinical Judaism

The first of these rebellions resulted in the destruction of the temple refounded by Nehemiah. The second resulted in the devastation of Judaea.

Rebellion first broke out in 66 C.E., triggered by the Roman desecration of the Temple. To suppress the revolt, the emperor Nero sent his experienced general Vespasian. Jewish leaders seized the Temple, and Vespasian prepared to besiege the city. In 68 C.E., Nero killed himself, and the Empire was claimed by four successors in turn. Returning to Rome to claim the imperial title for himself, Vespasian left his son Titus to complete the siege of Jerusalem.

Titus stormed the Temple heights, and, failing to weaken the walls with his formidable war machines, burned the gates. The fire spread. The complex was obliterated, and Roman soldiers sacked Jerusalem. The destruction of the Second Temple was the second great national tragedy of the Jewish people, comparable to their long-ago captivity in Babylon (see *Witnesses*, p. 177). Refugees from Jerusalem streamed into the countryside, north to Galilee, east to Mesopotamia, and south to Egypt, where they did not forget their suffering or the principles for which they stood.

The Roman army had seized all Jewish fortifications they encountered en route to Jerusalem. When they came to Galilee, in the north of the Jewish state, the defending Jewish general Joseph, or Josephus (37–c. 100 C.E.), quickly sized up the strength of the Roman force sent against him and surrendered. Soon he was to be found amid the councils of the Roman leadership. Detested by many of his coreligionists for his apostasy, Josephus nevertheless performed a valuable service for them, recording the narrative (flawed by some self-protective inaccuracies) of Jewish life in this age and of the inexorable Roman advance.

One flawed story he tells is the tragic one of Masada. A group of Zealots (a faction that fervently resisted the Roman presence) and their families had taken refuge there, in Herod's fortified mountaintop palace, south of Jerusalem near the Dead Sea. Well-supplied, this rump of the Jewish resistance was able to hold out for three years. In 73 C.E., the Romans stormed the citadel and found almost all the belligerents dead. The men had killed their wives and children and then themselves. They had chosen suicide before submission to Rome. Only a handful of women and children survived, hidden in a cistern.

Dead Sea Scrolls

Ancient Jewish Life

Practices and beliefs very different from those of the Romans and other ancient polytheists characterized the ancient and still-living religion of Judaism. From its earliest formation, Judaism was a religion of the "book," the "Bible," the name taken from the Greek word for book. The Dead Sea Scrolls (top) are the earliest extant portions of the Bible read by first-century Jews (in this case, those belonging to the ascetic community of Essenes at Qumran).

The stone relief from the Arch of Titus in Rome (center) depicts a procession of Roman soldiers carrying the Menorah, the seven-branched candelabrum borne in the Hanukkah celebration to commemorate the Maccabean revolt against Greek overlords.

The fresco (below) is from one of the synagogues around which Jewish worship centered, especially after the fall of the Second Temple in 70 C.E.. It depicts the wheeled Ark of the Covenant (carrying the sacred books) shattering and scattering pagan idols.
(top: Israel Museum, Jerusalem; below: National Archaeological Museum, Damascus)

What relation might there be between the Jewish faith in the power of the written word—subsequently inherited by Christianity—and the development of Western thought?

Arch of Titus, Rome, c. 81 C.E.

Wheeled Ark of the Covenant, Dura-Europos, Syria, c. 245 C.E.

 To continue your investigation of this topic, please go to www.prenhall.com/king for the related **WINDOWS** on the **WEB** activity

179

The Roman repression of the revolt of 66–70 C.E. was severe, but its severity did not prevent recurrences. In 117 C.E., during Trajan's reign, Roman troops brutally suppressed a concerted rebellion of the Egyptian Jews, with huge losses on both sides. Trajan's successor, Hadrian, who was determined to discipline the Jews, introduced unprecedented forms of discrimination against them—including a ban on circumcision, central to the Jewish way of life. Like Antiochus IV Epiphanes, whose attempts to Hellenize Jewish culture had been thwarted by Maccabean resistance, Hadrian attempted to Romanize the Jews. Above all, he insisted on their participation in the imperial cult, from which they had been previously excused.

Hadrian's behavior provoked a last rebellion in Palestine (as Judaea was called after 70 C.E.): that of Simon, dubbed Bar Kokhba, or "Son of the Star," by the rabbi Akiba ben Joseph. When the revolt was suppressed in 135 C.E., Bar Kokhba was executed, Akiba (according to legend) horribly tortured to death, and many other of the rabbinical leaders martyred. On the site of ruined Jerusalem stood Hadrian's new capital of Aelia Capitolina. This was a Roman city to which, except for one day a year, Jews were not even admitted. Judaea was ravaged, and more than half a million people were killed. Jews were now a minority in their homeland. The history of Judaism would develop henceforth primarily outside the Jewish homeland.

The **Diaspora**, or "scattering," of the Jewish people had begun long before Bar Kokhba's rebellion. The Assyrians deported the Ten Lost Tribes from Israel. The Babylonian king Nebuchadnezzar deported a large number of Jewish people to Mesopotamia. When they were permitted to return to Judaea (Judah) by Cyrus the Great, some stayed. These formed the nucleus of the Babylonian community of Jews which grew eventually to equal and exceed the Palestinian remnant.

After the death of Alexander and before the arrival of the Romans, many Jews had migrated to Egypt, North Africa and the Arabian peninsula, to Asia Minor, and even to Europe. In Roman times there were sizable Jewish communities in Athens and Corinth, in Greece; in Rome and Milan, in Italy; in Córdoba and Gades, in Spain; in Marseille and Lyon, in Gaul; in Cologne and Ratisbon, on the fringes of the German wilderness. In these remote places, Jews were united by their allegiance to the Torah and, once it was formulated, to the **Talmud**.

The Torah had been completed before the Herodian era. But the literary product of Jewish experience continued to grow. The Talmud was the creation of the rabbis, who took command of the destiny of Judaism after the destruction of the Second Temple and the devastation of the Bar Kokhba rebellion. The **Mishnah** was a legal casebook that commented upon orally transmitted law, put together by the patriarchs of the Sanhedrin (in Jabneh and Usha, in Galilee) during the second century C.E. **Midrash** consisted of stories and sermons elaborating biblical material. The Talmud consisted of these and of further *Halachah* (laws) and *Agada* (narratives), as well as more informal discussions about proper Jewish life, and a miscellany of folklore, science, literature, and history, recording the experience of a people frequently challenged desperately by events but never left spiritless.

The Talmud was compiled in the third and fourth centuries C.E., first by the rabbis of Palestine (the *Palestinian Talmud*) and more than a century later, independently, by those of Mesopotamia (the *Babylonian Talmud*). These works were the basis for the forged unity of the Jewish people, homeless and stateless, dispersed over three continents. The Talmud was the creation not of priests, but of scholars equipped with knowledge and intelligence. As a result, the Jewish hero henceforth was neither king nor conqueror, but student. The people he led were not a nation but—more resourceful, more lasting—a spiritual community.

After the catastrophes of 117 and 135 C.E., the Jewish population of the Empire, though diminished, remained a vigorous presence and—after Hadrian's decrees lapsed—were allowed to practice their religion undisturbed. When Caracalla extended Roman citizenship to all free subjects of the Empire in 212 C.E., the Jews enjoyed, alongside polytheists, all the privileges of that status. With the exception of Hadrian, moreover, the emperors did not insist on Jewish participation in the imperial cult. Constantine's Edict of Milan of 313 C.E. extended toleration to all religions, specifically naming Judaism among those encompassed by the new decree.

Yet the attitude of many Romans toward Jews was highly critical. Roman authors often made negative allusions to the Jews, as when Tacitus (c. 55–120 C.E.) complained: "Most Jews were convinced that … those who came forth from Judaea should possess the world." Nonetheless, many Romans—including some of the elite and many women—were attracted to Judaism. These converts supported the local synagogues, studied the Torah, observed the Sabbath, and accepted the dietary restrictions. For such adherents, the learned Philo of Alexandria (c. 20 B.C.E.–45 C.E.), or "Philo Judaeus" (Philo the Jew) harmonized Plato and the *Septuagint* (the Greek version of the Bible read outside Palestine). Philo argued that Greek philosophy and Judaism could be reconciled, that philosophy preceded and supported theology.

The uneasy coexistence of Romans and Jews was threatened by the emergence of a new religious community, Christianity. Persecuted at first, then favored, it insisted upon and won preeminence within the Roman world. Christian preeminence was to spell new disadvantages for Judaism.

ORIGINS OF CHRISTIANITY

The Christian religion originated when Rome was at its zenith. Roman emperors, generals, and nobles knew nothing of the lives of the people of Judaea, a province of the Empire. Those people suffered under Roman domination while believing that, one day, a servant of their one God would redeem them. In the reign of Augustus, a man was born among them whom a few followers at first, but ultimately most of the Roman world, acknowledged as that redeemer. The religion that came to be known as Christianity formed around the singular figure of Jesus of Nazareth. Propelled by the Greek-speaking Jew Paul of Tarsus, Christianity spread beyond Judaea and the eastern shores of the Mediterranean, reaching all the way to imperial Rome itself.

Jesus of Nazareth

Christianity developed from the message preached and enacted by Jesus (4 B.C.E.–c. 30 C.E.), a Jew from Nazareth in Galilee. His parents observed Jewish law and ritual and he himself was learned in scripture. These facts are known from the accounts of Jesus' life in the **Gospels** of the Christian **New Testament**.

The Gospels were compiled in the latter part of the first century C.E., more than a generation after Jesus' death. They are not scientific biographies but interpretative narratives, based on oral reports and lost earlier sources. They were written in the Greek of the *oecumene*, rather than the Hebrew or vernacular Aramaic of the Palestinian region. On the whole, they are acknowledged as giving fairly sound evidence about many of events. The authors identified as Mark, Luke, Matthew, and John (in the order of the composition of their works) transmitted a living faith based upon a real historical figure: the Jew Jesus.

When Jesus was about thirty years old, the Gospel authors report, he met one of the self-appointed holy men who were a feature of late Hellenistic Judaism. The visionary was his cousin John, called "the Baptist" because he ritually blessed his followers as they washed in the river Jordan, symbolizing their renunciation of sin. In the tradition of the prophets of Israel, John denounced the ways of the world and called his listeners to repent or turn away from guilty lives.

Jesus was one of those baptized by John. God himself acknowledged the event, according to the Gospels: "And just as he was coming up out of the water, he saw the heavens torn apart and the Spirit descending like a dove on him. And a voice came from heaven, 'You are my Son, the Beloved; with you I am well pleased.'" From this moment, Jesus' mission begins. For the next three years (probably 27–30 C.E.), he traveled through Judaea, Samaria, and Galilee, gathering disciples, performing miracles of healing, and preaching to crowds of followers.

Jesus' central message was similar to John's: the Kingdom of Heaven was coming, in which God would reign on earth as in heaven, punish those who had strayed from his way, and gather up the true believers in his love. His worshipers should pray for the coming of that kingdom, which Jesus made it his mission to announce: "Then Jesus went about all the cities and villages, teaching in their synagogues, and proclaiming the good news of the kingdom. ..." In his **parables**, or instructive stories, Jesus likened the kingdom of God to a variety of familiar and organic things that were joyously capable of growth: a mustard seed, sprouting grain, little children.

Jesus' announcement to the faithful of the coming of the Kingdom of God was a message well within the framework of Hellenistic Judaism. His idea of who the faithful were, however, was new and surprising. They were not the powerful, but the weak; not the rich, but the poor; not the wise, but the ignorant; not only those who were strong or healthy, but those who were sick and disabled; not only men, but women; not only adults, but children; not the established, but the homeless and the lost. According to the Gospel writers, Jesus proposed a revolution in the valuation of the human being: one implicit in Judaism, but unknown in all the polytheisms of the ancient world.

According to Jesus, the meek would inherit the Kingdom of God, and he called the meek to be his disciples. The disciple Peter was a fisherman, and Matthew a despised tax-collector. Jesus conversed with prostitutes and women considered unclean, with children (generally ignored in antiquity), with **Gentiles** (non-Jews avoided by faithful Jews), and with Samaritans (who had lapsed from **orthodoxy**). Those whom others condemned Jesus recommended as models of behavior: the prostitute who loved more than the Pharisee, the Samaritan who tended with compassion an injured and abandoned man ignored by two members of the Judaean elite.

Jesus also healed the sick: a stream of the blind and paralyzed, limping and bleeding, dying and dead. The figure of the healer endowed with special spiritual powers was often lionized in the Hellenistic era. Yet Jesus was different: he healed by forgiving sins and admonishing demons of madness and despair. It was not magic but faith, the Gospel authors claimed, that healed the sick who knew Jesus.

Just as he elevated faith over magic, Jesus placed love over law, subtly shifting emphasis in the values established by scriptural tradition. That tradition centered on law: God's gift of the commandments and the community's obedience to them. The tradition also distinguished itself among ancient religions by an emphasis on acts of love and mercy. Jesus does not depart from his tradition when he speaks of the great power of love. Yet he takes a small but significant step in placing love before and above the law, which was the cornerstone of Jewish life.

Map 7.2 The Growing Christian Realm, 30–c. 500 C.E.: *When Jesus was crucified, the "church," or assembly of followers, was resident in Jerusalem. Among their enemies was the rabbinical student Saul or (to use his Greek name) Paul. Following his experience of conversion on the road to Damascus, Paul became a promoter of the new beliefs. In Antioch, his converts first came to be known as "Christians." Over the approximately thirty years of his missionary career, Paul added many Christians to the church, which subsequently made significant progress. By 313 C.E., Christianity was a tolerated religion, and by 600, when the Roman state in the west had been disrupted, it was the official religion of the majority of those living within the former boundaries of the Empire. What appeal did Christianity have for the citizens of the Roman Empire?*

Jesus' ministry extended from his baptism until his last entry to Jerusalem, where he had gone to celebrate the holiday of Passover, five days before his death. The events of that last week are laden with meaning for Christians—and also for Jews, on whom these same events inflicted a legacy of pain.

On the day he entered Jerusalem (according to the Gospel accounts), Jesus was greeted by crowds of ordinary people who hailed him—an ordinary man—as the Messiah. For four days he preached in Jerusalem, visited the Temple, and talked with his disciples and friends. The evening of the fifth day, Thursday, was the start of the Passover feast. Jesus celebrated it with his twelve closest disciples in the room of a house lent by a friend. In the course of the ritual meal, Jesus warned his followers of his impending death. He then blessed the bread and wine, which were the staples of the Passover feast, and distributed them to his disciples with the message to take and eat and drink: "This is my Body, which is given for you. Do this in

remembrance of me. …" (Luke 22: 19), "Drink from [this cup], all of you; for this is my Blood of the new covenant, which is poured out for many for the forgiveness of sins" (Matthew 26: 27–28).

These words predicted Jesus' imminent death and influenced the ritual by which later Christians would remember him. This meal—Jesus' last, called by Christians the Last Supper—was later seen as the institution of the Eucharist, the central act of Christian worship. It is re-created regularly in churches of all sorts: Roman Catholic; Eastern, Russian, and Armenian Orthodox; and many Protestant churches.

The Gospels report that Judas Iscariot, one of the disciples present at the Last Supper, had already agreed to point Jesus out to his enemies. Later that evening, after Jesus had gone into the Garden of Gethsemane to pray about the grim destiny that he foresaw, Judas pointed him out to the guards—with a kiss—according to Matthew and Luke. Jesus was brought before the Sanhedrin. Seen as a danger to the Jewish community, he was sent before the Roman procurator, the governor of Judaea, who alone could condemn a man to death. The procurator, Pontius Pilatus, or Pilate (known as a harsh judge of upstart leaders and fomenters of riot), condemned Jesus to be tortured and crucified. The execution occurred at midday, on Friday.

That Jesus of Nazareth was crucified during Pontius Pilate's procuratorship in Judaea (26–36 C.E.) is a secure historical fact. It is also exceedingly probable that some Jews, including some Jewish leaders, urged his death—although most others played no part at all in these events, and some were his enthusiastic followers to the last. For centuries, the crucifixion story was a source of anti-Semitic prejudice among some groups of Christians, who blamed all Jews for the death of one man whom they recognized as both innocent and divine. Matthew notoriously invites that conclusion when he portrays the cruel Pilate saying self-righteously, "I am innocent of this man's blood," and the crowd responding, "His blood be on us and on our children!"

Because they shaped the narrative of Jesus' mission during a time of hostile relations between Jews and Christians, the Gospel writers encouraged their gentile converts to blame the Jews as a whole. That interpretation of the events of the last days of Jesus' life is now rejected by most Christians and churches, including the largest, the Roman Catholic church.

Jesus was crucified on Friday, and buried in a tomb a follower had prepared for himself. Christians believe that on the following Sunday morning (celebrated as Easter) he was resurrected: that he rose bodily from the dead, walked the earth again, and thereafter returned to God. The Gospel accounts testify to the resurrection: an angel announces that Jesus has risen; the resurrected Jesus invites his skeptical follower Thomas to touch the wound in his side, as proof that it is really he, restored to life.

It was reported that fifty days after the Passover at which he had eaten his Last Supper (on the day of the Jewish feast of Shavuot, or Pentecost), a startling experience shook Jesus' followers. They were gathered in Jerusalem, reflecting on the meaning of their departed master's life, when "suddenly from heaven there came a sound like the rush of a violent wind, and it filled the entire house where they were sitting. Divided tongues, as of fire, appeared among them, and a tongue rested on each of them. All of them were filled with the Holy Spirit and began to speak in other languages..." (Acts 2: 2–4).

The disciples believed that they had been sent the divine force of the Holy Spirit as consolation for the loss of Jesus. This event is recorded in a fifth book of the Christian New Testament, the Acts of the Apostles. The Acts also records other occasions on which early Christians (as the followers of Jesus were soon called) were visited by the Holy Spirit. Most dramatic among those occasions was the experience of the tentmaker Paul of Tarsus (d. c. 67 C.E.), the one most responsible, after Jesus himself, for the creation of the Christian religion.

Paul's Mission

Paul's achievement was to spread the news of Jesus' ministry and to elucidate its meaning to the Jews of the Diaspora as well as, even more significantly, to non-Jews. By expanding the Christian mission beyond the small Jewish communities of the Mediterranean world to gentile populations, Paul added enormously to the new religion's potential for success.

Paul was a Jew (born Saul) from one of the Diaspora communities of Asia Minor. A faithful observer of the law, he studied in Jerusalem with the eminent rabbi and Pharisee Gamaliel. Initially, Paul was an enemy of the early followers of Jesus, "breathing threats and murder against the disciples of the Lord," according to Luke (Acts 9: 1). As an enemy of the infant Christian sect, he had watched the stoning of Stephen, the first **martyr** (one who willingly suffers for a belief) of the church. Rioters had laid their robes at Paul's feet, while he stood by and "approved [of Stephen's death]" (Acts 8: 1).

Committed to eradicating the **heresy** (religious doctrine at variance with accepted doctrine), as he saw it, spread by Jesus' followers, Paul visited the various communities of Jews. It was on such a mission (around 33 C.E.) to the Jews of Damascus, in Syria, that Paul experienced (as recorded in Acts 9: 3–8) the profound vision that changed his life. He fell prostrate on the road, struck blind, and heard a voice say: "Saul, Saul, why do you persecute me?" Taken into the town, he was reluctantly tended by a Christian. Soon he could see again, and he, too, became a converted Christian. No more a persecutor of the new sect, Paul now became its greatest advocate.

In the 40s C.E., Paul set out on a series of three missionary expeditions, extending over twenty years, which took him and the new faith from Jerusalem to Rome. He preached first to the Jews of Syria, Cyprus, and Asia Minor, and then increasingly to the Gentiles of the Near East and Greece. The letters he wrote to the churches he founded (the Epistles) form a substantial part of the New Testament. They helped nurture the Christian communities at Ephesus, Colossae, and Galatia, all in Asia Minor; at Corinth, Philippi, and Thessalonica, in Greece and Macedonia; and eventually in Rome.

By the time Paul undertook his journeys, the followers of Jesus were known as Christians: followers, that is, of "the anointed one," *Christos* in Greek, the equivalent of the Jewish "Messiah." But these early Christians considered themselves Jews. The disciples in Jerusalem insisted upon strict observance of Jewish

The Christian Way

Ruler and Redeemer: *By the end of the fourth century C.E., the Roman Empire was a Christian empire. The heroic ideal of classical antiquity, exemplified in the early first-century statue of the emperor Augustus of Prima Porta (right) had yielded to a new ideal of the silent and mysterious redeemer, Jesus Christ— as shown in this sixth-century C.E. mosaic from Ravenna (left). Even the medium makes a difference—the three-dimensional stone sculpture describing the worldly ruler, but the flat, glistening mosaic surface more suitably portraying the incarnate God.*
(right: Vatican Museums, Rome)

Augustus of Prima Porta, early first century C.E.

law as part of the obedience to the new creed. That requirement was a barrier to the recruitment of Gentiles to the new religion—which, by the authority of Jesus himself, claimed a mission to the non-Jew. "Go therefore and make disciples of all nations," Jesus had commanded in the account of the Gospel author Matthew (28: 19). His disciple Peter, instructed in a vision that what was unclean by Jewish law could be sanctified by God, opened the infant church to gentile converts. Paul advanced that venture when he found the Jews of the Diaspora hostile to his message but the Gentile adherents of the synagogues accessible. These he converted in great numbers. By Paul's death, around 67 C.E., the church was becoming more Gentile than Jewish.

The mission to the Gentiles was the key to Christianity's ultimate success. It was facilitated by the compromise Paul made with the Jerusalem Christians on the matter of Jewish law. The requirements of the law included dietary rules, ritual procedures, and the all-important bodily sign of circumcision. Gentile adherents were reluctant to assume the full burden of the law that devolved by birth onto the Jew. Paul persuaded the Jerusalem church to agree to this formulation: that new converts should be required only to abstain "from things polluted by idols and from fornication and from whatever has been strangled and from blood" (Acts 15: 20). In other words, they did not need to follow all the requirements of Jewish law in order to become Christians. Paul was required to give proof of his own orthodoxy by undergoing a rite of purification.

While Paul acted as a negotiator between the different worlds of Gentile and Jewish Christians, he was also elaborating a theology—still fundamental to Christian belief—centered on the issue of law, its relation to sin, and the abrogation of both by Jesus the Christ. All the requirements of the law, according to Paul, were satisfied by the death of the man who was also the Son of God: he had expiated the sins of humanity. Moreover, his resurrection carried the promise of eternal life to all those who accepted the expiation of sin effected by his supreme sacrifice. That acceptance was an act of faith, the expiation or righting of all wrongs. The followers of Jesus the Christ (although by no means free to act immorally or licentiously) were freed from the law because they were "justified," or made righteous, by faith—a concept that would later become central for the sixteenth-century German Protestant reformer Martin Luther. "Therefore, since we are justified by faith," wrote Paul, "we have peace with God through our Lord Jesus Christ" (Romans 5: 1). In the love of Jesus Christ is the Christian's assurance of eternal salvation: "Who will separate us from the love of Christ? Will hardship, or distress, or persecution, or famine, or nakedness, or peril, or sword? … For I am convinced that neither death, nor life, nor angels, nor rulers, nor things present, nor things to come, nor powers, nor height, nor depth, nor anything else in all creation, will be able to separate us from the love of God in Christ Jesus our Lord" (Romans 8: 35, 38–39).

Paul's supreme confidence in the love of God withstood the trials of danger and persecution. In 58 C.E., he returned to Jerusalem. There he preached in Hebrew (instead of the Greek of his missionary journeys) to an angry crowd. Accused of blasphemy in bringing a Gentile into the forbidden part of the Temple, he was remanded to Roman authorities and detained at Caesarea, the Roman administrative capital on the Mediterranean coast. Two successive Roman governors avoided making any decision about him. Paul insisted on bringing his case to Rome—an appeal which, as a Roman citizen, he was entitled to make. Transferred to the capital, he spent at least two years in prison. According to Christian tradition, he was condemned following a trial probably instigated by rivals in the Jewish Christian community in Rome, and executed around 67 C.E. He left behind him the germ cells of the world's most influential religion.

PROGRESS OF CHRISTIANITY

When Paul was a student in Jerusalem, and watched Stephen become the first martyr of a new faith, a few followers of Jesus, who still thought of themselves as Jews, formed the small matrix of the Christian Church. When Paul died, small communities of Christians, many of gentile origin, practiced their new faith amid the Greek and Jewish communities of the Mediterranean east. Over the next few centuries, the Christian churches grew in members, in moral force, in intellectual power, and in political status. By the time the western Roman Empire was weakening, Christianity was rooted, east and west, as the dominant religion of the Roman people and the official faith of an empire. Its expansion is shown on Map 7.2 and in *How Many?* on p. 192.

The Early Church

The early Christians were mostly Greek-speaking city-dwellers of the eastern Mediterranean world: artisans and laborers and household slaves. Paul took note of the humble status of his flock when he wrote to the Christians of Corinth: "Not many of you were wise by human standards, not many were powerful, not many were of noble birth. But … God chose what is weak in the world to shame the strong; God chose what is low and despised in the world … so that no one might boast in the presence of God" (I Corinthians 1: 26–29). The second-century polytheist Celsus (fl. c. 175–181 C.E.) mocked the low estate of the new Christians: "Let no one educated, no one wise, no one sensible draw near. … But as for anyone ignorant, anyone stupid, anyone uneducated, anyone who is a child, let him come boldly."

The humbler members of society may have been attracted to Christianity because of its universalism: all who accepted baptism in Christ were considered equal. "For in Christ Jesus you are all children of God through faith. … There is no longer Jew or Greek," wrote Paul, "there is no longer slave or free, there is no longer male and female; for all of you are one in Christ Jesus" (Galatians 3: 28).

The promise that there was "neither male nor female" in the new religion must have attracted women, who were among the most loyal early Christians. Already in the first generation (as narrated in Acts), the churches thrived under the protection of female patrons. In Philippi, Paul and Luke stayed in the house of Lydia (apparently a widow), "a worshiper of God" and a "dealer in purple cloth" (Acts 16: 14). Having heard Paul's message, this evidently wealthy woman was baptized with her whole household. Aquila and Priscilla, a Jewish couple expelled by the emperor Claudius from Rome, became Paul's converts. He stayed with them in Corinth, where they helped establish the church there. The wife is noted as much as the husband by Paul, who, in his letter to that community, sends greetings from them in Asia: "Aquila and Prisc[illa], together with the church in their house, greet you warmly in the Lord" (I Corinthians 16: 19).

Elsewhere Paul recommends to the Roman church the deaconess Phoebe: "I commend to you our sister Phoebe, a deacon of the church at Cenchreae, so that you may welcome her in the Lord ..., for she has been a benefactor of many and of myself as well" (Romans 16: 1–2). The tradition of female participation continued into the fourth century, when Christianity had won wide support among upper-class women—not least among them Helen (d. c. 328), the mother of the emperor Constantine.

Charity did not begin with Christianity. In the Greek *poleis* and in the Roman Republic, wealthy patrons had supported poor suppliants or clients. Such patrons also funded public benefits in their cities: they paid for theatrical and athletic spectacles, religious festivals, ships, and palaces, statues to adorn public spaces and grain to feed the hungry in times of scarcity. Professionals, artisans, and laborers gathered in guilds, and other groups organized by their ethnic or religious allegiances pooled their resources to provide mutual support and alms to the desperate.

These Greco-Roman benevolent institutions were exceeded by those of the Jews, who sustained the needy in their communities. The systematic and generous philanthropy of the early Christians continued

The Christian basilica: *Christians required a new space in which to worship God, and the Christian basilica was developed that combined the architecture of the Roman law courts with the traditions of the Jewish synagogue. The great basilica of Santa Maria Maggiore, Rome, c. 440 C.E., is flanked by two aisles, the majestically proportioned nave clearly suggesting the grandeur of the basilican style of architecture.*

these earlier traditions. The churches aided the poor and sick, widows, orphans, and children (working to make abandonment, abortion, and infanticide illegal) and slaves (who were urged, nonetheless, to accept their status as legitimate).

The main goal of worship in ancient religious practices was to make a human or animal sacrifice to a deity on an altar. The altar could stand independently, or within a temple, which was understood as the house of a god. Among early Christians, who worshiped in private houses or even, when endangered, in underground catacombs, altar and sacrifice gave way to common prayer and celebration. Once Christianity became a legal religion, it required a new physical space: not one to house its deity (whose house was "not made with hands") but one that could accommodate a community joined to give thanks for Jesus' life, death, and resurrection. Christians adapted a kind of building already in existence: the Roman basilica. Originally designed as a place of assembly for judicial or commercial purposes, the basilica became the fundamental unit of Christian architecture.

The basilica provided a large central space lit by high windows—an example is shown on p. 186. The rectangular, vaulted building developed side aisles and focused attention on the eastern end of the longitudinal axis, where stood an altar backed by a sunlit apse. The spaciousness, the height, the clear orientation, and the light operated to provide an ideal place for worship, subordinating the individual to the group and to an ideal beyond them all. By the fourth century, Christian churches in basilican form had been erected all over the Empire. In some areas, almost the only buildings constructed were ecclesiastical.

The fourth-century basilicas of Saint Peter and Saint John Lateran in Rome and the Church of the Holy Wisdom (Santa Sophia) in Constantinople were built under Constantine's direction. His mother, Helen, built a church on the alleged site of Jesus' ascension (the Mount of Olives) in Jerusalem and another on the presumed site of Jesus' birth in Bethlehem—discovering in the excavations (according to legend) the cross on which he died. Soon every major city had a church. Within them developed the **liturgy** of Christian worship (much of it borrowed from Judaism), the performance of sacraments, the vocabulary of ceremony, vestments, and accessories that would characterize mature Christianity.

The first churches were informal gatherings of the faithful. They were led by elders or "presbyters" and deacons: the former charged with the spiritual guidance of the community, the latter with the administration of charity. As larger Christian communities formed, leaders called bishops presided over all the churches in a city and surrounding area. Possessing greater authority because of their social status or learning, they took precedence over local leaders in the institution of the church. The bishops imitated the secular government in administrative style and court ritual. As bishops (always men) asserted control over local communities, women were relegated to supportive roles in the institution of the church.

Persecutions and Controversies

While Christian communities grew, distaste for the new sect remained strong among the Roman elites. They found the Jews more like themselves in that they worshiped the god of their ancestors. Christians, by contrast, all converts at the outset, and without ancestral authority, were seen as peculiar and secretive. And worse: Christians engaged (so Roman critics believed or found it convenient to believe) in magic, incest, drunkenness, and cannibalism. As one Christian writer put it: "They gather together ignorant persons from the lowest dregs, and credulous women, easily deceived as their sex is, and organize a rabble of unholy conspirators, leagued together in nocturnal associations and by ritual fasts and barbarous foods, not for the purpose of some sacred rite but for the sake of sacrilege—a secret tribe that shuns the light, silent in public but talkative in secret places."

They seemed, according to Tacitus, to be possessed by a "baneful superstition" and to have a "hatred of the human race"—in fact, because they avoided the company of their pagan neighbors, for fear of being infected by their beliefs. In the second century, the aesthete Celsus (in his *On True Doctrine*) expounded the Greco-Roman case against Christianity, and in the fifth century, the philosopher Porphyry (in his vitriolic *Against the Christians*, 448 C.E.), both vaunting the humane values of late pagan thought against what they saw as Christian incivility.

Persecution Avid dislike of Christians periodically erupted in persecution. Judaism had bequeathed to the world as models of martyrdom the Maccabees, the zealots of Masada, and the faithful rabbis of the days of Bar Kokhba. Beginning in the first century C.E., Christian martyrdom had increased spectacularly by the third century, when thousands of Christians went to their death rather than participate in the imperial cult. Two accounts are given in *Witnesses* on p. 188. The sacrifice of these convinced Christians helped to energize the survivors. "Nothing whatever is accomplished by your cruelties," the theologian Tertullian (c. 160–c. 240 C.E.) boasted to Roman oppressors. "We multiply whenever we are mown down by you; the blood of Christians is [like] seed."

Tertullian was right: martyrdom was indeed stupendously successful. The spectacle of Christians so committed to their faith that they chose to die rather than make the slightest compromise with the demands of the secular world impressed even highborn Romans. The martyrs' courage affirmed these Romans' own stoic values—as when the theologian

Christians to the Lions

The Roman persecution of Christians began in the first century C.E., *continued intermittently for more than 200 years, and peaked under the emperor Diocletian— yet Christianity still grew. As the African theologian Tertullian commented, the blood of martyrs, whose self-sacrifice inspired confidence and recruited new followers, was the "seed" of the Church. These passages describe two impressive incidents where Christian witnesses willing to die for their faith defied persecution: the martyrdoms of the bishop Polycarp and the noblewoman Perpetua.*

Polycarp, Bishop of Smyrna, declining to compromise with power or to flee it, is burned alive, a martyr to the Christian faith (c. 155 C.E.): And when finally he was brought up, there was a great tumult on hearing that Polycarp had been arrested. ... The proconsul ... tried to persuade him to deny [the faith], saying, "Have respect to your age"—and other things that customarily follow this, such as, "Swear by the fortune of Caesar; change your mind; say, 'Away with the atheists!' " [by which he meant the Christians].

But Polycarp looked with earnest face at the whole crowd of lawless heathen in the arena, and motioned to them with his hand. Then, groaning and looking up to heaven, he said, "Away with the atheists!" [by which he meant his persecutors].

But the proconsul was insistent and said: "Take the oath, and I shall release you. Curse Christ."

Polycarp said: "Eighty-six years I have served him, and he never did me any wrong. How can I blaspheme my King who saved me?" ...

But the proconsul said: "I have wild beasts. I shall throw you to them, if you do not change your mind."

But [Polycarp] said: "Call them. For repentance from the better to the worse is not permitted us; but it is noble to change from what is evil to what is righteous. ..."

And when he had said these things and many more besides he was inspired with courage and joy, and his face was full of grace. ... The proconsul was astonished, and sent his own herald into the midst of the arena to proclaim three times: "Polycarp has confessed himself to be a Christian." When this was said ... the entire crowd ... shouted with uncontrollable anger. ... Straightway then, they set about him the material prepared for the fire. ... And with his hands put behind him and tied, like a noble ram out of a great flock ready for sacrifice, a burnt offering ready and acceptable to God, he looked up to heaven and said: "Lord God almighty, ... I praise thee, I bless thee, I glorify thee, through the eternal and heavenly High Priest, Jesus Christ, thy beloved Servant, through whom be glory to thee with him and Holy Spirit both now and unto the ages to come. Amen." And when he had concluded the Amen and finished his prayer, the men attending to the fire lighted it. ...

(The Martyrdom of St. Polycarp, Bishop of Smyrna, c. 155 C.E., as told in the letter of the Church of Smyrna to the Church of Philomelium, 9:2–15:1; ed. J. Richardson 1970)

The noblewoman and martyr Perpetua, slaughtered by beasts in the arena at Carthage on 7 March 203, chronicled her imprisonment (during which she gave birth to a child) in her own words. Here, in the last passage of her memoir, she describes the vision she experienced (in which she becomes a man and vanquishes her enemy) the day before her execution: ...

I saw in a vision that Pomponius the deacon had come hither to the door of the prison, and knocked hard upon it. And I went out to him and opened to him. ... And he said to me: Perpetua, we await thee; come. And he took my hand. ... At last with much breathing hard we came to the amphitheatre, and he led me into the midst of the arena. And he said to me: Be not afraid; I am here with thee and labour together with thee. And he went away. And I saw much people watching closely. And because I knew that I was condemned to the beasts I marvelled that beasts were not sent out against me. And there came out against me a certain ill-favored Egyptian with his helpers, to fight with me. ... And I was stripped, and I became a man. ... And there came forth a man of very great stature, so that he overpassed the very top of the amphitheatre, ... bearing a rod like a master of gladiators, and a green branch whereon were golden apples. And he besought silence and said: The Egyptian, if he shall conquer this woman, shall slay her with the sword; and if she shall conquer him, she shall receive this branch. And he went away. And we came nigh to each other, and began to buffet one another. ... And I rose up into the air and began so to smite him as though I trod not the earth. But when I saw that there was yet delay, I ... caught his head, and he fell upon his face; and I trod upon his head. And the people began to shout, and my helpers began to sing. And I went up to the master of gladiators and received the branch. And he kissed me and said to me: Daughter, peace be with thee. And I began to go with glory to the gate called the Gate of Life.

And I awoke; and I understood that I should fight, not with beasts but against the devil; but I knew that mine was the victory.

Thus far I have written this, till the day before the games; but the deed of the games themselves let him write who will.

(Perpetua, from J. Geary ed., *Passion of Perpetua*, 1989, 83–89; ed. W. H. Shewring, 1931)

Justin confronted his persecutors at his own martyrdom (c. 165 C.E.): "You indeed may be able to kill us, but you cannot harm us."

Nero blamed the Christians for the Great Fire of 64 C.E., which marked the beginning of his downfall. To appease the Roman populace, he sent hundreds of Christians into the arena to be slain by gladiators or hungry beasts. During a later persecution, Tertullian angrily remarked, "If the Tiber reaches the walls, if the Nile does not rise to the fields, if the sky doesn't move or the earth does, if there is famine, if there is plague, the cry is at once: 'The Christians to the lions!' "

Around 110 C.E., the emperor Trajan cautioned the author Pliny the Younger, governor of Bithynia, in Asia Minor, not to act too zealously to pursue Christians: if they superficially conformed to the Roman state cult, they were to be left alone. Yet later in the same century, the high-minded Marcus Aurelius permitted the slaughter of Christians in the arena of Lyon in Gaul (in 177 C.E.). Men should be willing to face death, reflected the philosophical emperor, but not "out of crude obstinacy, like the Christians." In the arena at Lyon women, too, faced death willingly—going to their crucifixion, wrote an observer, in an ecstasy of union with Christ.

Around 249–50 C.E., the emperor Decius (r. 249–251 C.E.) commanded every suspected Christian to perform at least once the sacrificial rites of the imperial cult. In 303 C.E., Diocletian and his caesar, or deputy, Galerius launched the Great Persecution, in an attempt to stamp out the new faith, which had by now been adopted by a tenth of the Empire's population and was seen as an enemy of old Roman values. The persecution lasted eight years, raging most fiercely in the east, where it consumed some 3000 believers. Its aim was to root out the new faith: to suppress its churches, its clergy, its followers.

Controversy and Heresy The persecutions extended over nearly 250 years and consumed perhaps 100,000 victims. Nevertheless, martyrdom did not weaken the Church. Neither did the controversies it carried on through its spokesmen—theologians and scholars later collectively given the name "Fathers of the Church". The Church faced three opponents: the Roman world (which stood for polytheism and for the learned tradition); the Jews (from whom the Christians had sprung); and heretics (dissenters from the emerging orthodoxy of the Church). Out of these controversies the Fathers evolved the doctrines that still underlie Christian theology.

The Fathers attempted to build a bridge between Christianity (perceived as a sect followed by illiterates) and the high Classical tradition. One of them was Justin of Neapolis, in Samaria (c. 100–c. 165 C.E.), martyred around 165 C.E. and thus known to history as Justin Martyr. Justin wrote two *Apologies* for Christianity against the intellectuals who assailed it.

Portraying the new faith as reasonable, he invited his enemies to join the community of those who sought peace. As for the Classical tradition that Christians were accused of undervaluing, he revered it and proposed to enlist the learning of the past in the service of the future: "Whatever things were rightly said among all men are the property of us Christians."

Clement of Alexandria (c. 150–c. 215 C.E.) headed a Christian school in which Classical learning was studied as a tool for the advancement of the new faith. His pupil Origen of Alexandria (c. 185–c. 254 C.E.), a philosopher in the Platonic tradition, defended the Christian church against the Roman advocate Celsus. Origen's defense provided at last a rational foundation for the tenets of the new religion, sophisticated enough to interest its detractors. Justin, Clement, and Origen (all writing in Greek) established the Christian approach to Classical culture and to the intellectual life generally. Although the anti-intellectual alternative was voiced—most succinctly by Tertullian, who thundered, "What has Athens to do with Jerusalem?", that is, philosophy with faith—it was these scholars' formulation that endured. While Christians rejected the paganism of the Roman world, they embraced, enlarged, and transmitted its culture. Their decision to do so would help to shape the development of civilization in the West.

By the end of the first century C.E., most Christians were Gentiles. The Jews themselves, led by the rabbis who now guided their community, had expelled Jewish Christians from their fellowship. Before the two religions parted course, Christians had taken much from the Jews: the idea of the Sabbath, the priests' vestments, and the chants and hymns of the choir. Most important, they adopted the whole of the Hebrew Bible, which formed the **Old Testament**

WHO'S WHO

Fathers of the Church

Clement of Rome, late 1st century C.E.; bishop of Rome c. 88–101

Justin Martyr (Justin of Neapolis), c. 100–c. 165 C.E., Rome

Tertullian, c. 155/160–after 220 C.E., Carthage (modern Tunis)

Origen, c. 185–c. 254 C.E., Caesarea (coast of modern Israel)

John Chrysostom, c. 347–407 C.E., Antioch

Jerome, c. 347–419/420 C.E., Palestine (Bethlehem)

Augustine, 354–430 C.E., Hippo (modern Annaba, Algeria)

companion to their own scriptures, the New Testament. The Jewish foundation of Christianity was an incontrovertible fact recognized thereafter, if reluctantly, by the official church. That debt did not preclude opposition to Judaism and even active anti-Semitism in the Christian community.

Justin established the case for Christianity against Judaism in his *Dialogue with Trypho*. He was not alone: several early Christian writers wrote similar books. The tone became angrier around 400 C.E., when the eloquent Saint John Chrysostom (c. 354–407 C.E.) delivered in Antioch eight *Sermons against the Jews and Gentiles*. Accusing the Jews of the murder of Jesus, Chrysostom's fierce diatribes provide many of the arguments that supported anti-Semitism in later centuries (see Chapters 24, 25, 28).

As they defined their position vis-à-vis pagan and Jewish communities, Christian intellectuals faced new opponents on another flank: heretics within their own ranks. In its early years, Christianity could have followed a different course from the one firmly established by the end of the fifth century. Each of these other possible directions came to be labeled a "heresy" by the thinkers who battled to establish Christian principles about the nature of God, of Jesus, and of the human being.

Gnostics believed that they had received a special *gnosis*, or "knowledge," which set them apart from other worshipers. Montanists (followers of the second-century C.E. prophet Montanus) revered inspired prophets within the church, whose utterances they saw as authoritative. In both cases, an inequality of status was admitted to the Christian community. Christian leaders rejected this notion: all were equally sinners, they argued, all equally saved by the crucifixion and resurrection of Christ. Knowledge of God came from his revelation of himself in scripture and in the person of Jesus, God's Son.

In the fourth century, a new crop of heresies arose. These revolved around the nature of Jesus and his mother, Mary. If Jesus was the son of God, how could he also be human? If he was human, how could he also be God? The Arians (followers of the priest Arius [c. 260–336 C.E.]) believed Jesus was a human being, godlike, but separate in nature from the divine. The opposition to the Arians was led by another bishop, Saint Athanasius (c. 295–373 C.E.), who endured persecution and exile before his formulation of the nature of Jesus—that he was both fully human and fully divine—triumphed as the central tenet of Christian orthodoxy. The Athanasian position was hammered out at a council of the leaders of the church, held in Nicaea, in Asia Minor, which was called by the emperor Constantine in 325 C.E. Its resolution was eventually enunciated in the Nicene Creed, still recited by most Catholic Christians today. These two positions were differentiated linguistically by a single letter: the "i" in the Greek word defining the nature of Christ. For the Arians, Christ's nature was similar to that of God: *homoiousios*. For the Athanasians, it was identical: *homoousios*. Subsequent councils ratified the Athanasian principle.

Although the Arian doctrine had been defeated, Arian worshipers persisted in what was seen as their error. It never completely disappeared. In the meantime, yet another movement emerged—that of the Monophysites, who believed that Christ had only one nature (*monophysite* means "one nature"), which was divine. The Nestorians (followers of the bishop Nestorius [d. c. 451 C.E.]) upheld a more complex view: that Mary, a mere human being, could have given birth only to Jesus' human nature, which was a kind of shell enclosing his divine nature. These positions were duly debated and rejected.

Two more bishops lent their names to heresies defeated in the fourth century: Donatus (d. c. 355 C.E.) and Pelagius (fl. 380–410 C.E.). The former refused to acknowledge as effective certain sacred rites (called **sacraments**) when performed by members of the clergy who had, during the persecutions, momentarily repudiated their faith rather than face martyrdom. The orthodox response was that the sacraments were effective whatever the moral condition of the officiating clergyman.

Pelagius argued that human beings exercising their free will (although aided by divine **grace**) could work their own salvation. The orthodox retorted that all human beings were sinful and could be saved only by the gift of grace bestowed upon those who accepted Jesus' sacrifice. In both of these heresies, the issue was not so much the nature of God, or Jesus, but the nature of the human being.

The Triumph of Christianity

The councils, the debates, the books, and the sermons together constructed the edifice of Christian theology. It was based on the Bible, both Old and New Testaments. It honored and acknowledged the preceding Jewish tradition. It saw human nature as basically good but utterly debased by sin and in need of divine rescue. It saw God as omnipotent, and Jesus as fully God yet fully human.

The difficult relationship between an omnipotent God and God incarnate in Jesus was articulated in the central and difficult doctrine of the **Trinity**: the notion that God was threefold (or triune, "three in one"). In God were included the persons of the Father, the Son, and the Holy Spirit. All were in God, all were eternal, and each, when acting separately, was wholly God. The trinitarian concept is complex and rests on intricate philosophical reasoning. But it remains fundamental to Christianity.

The culminating statement of the doctrine of the Trinity was the work of Saint Augustine (354–430), arguably the most important and most brilliant of

Christianity Victorious

Christianity did not become the religion of the Roman Empire overnight, but by a series of steps, each involving a conscious decision. Three of those decisions are highlighted in these passages. In the first, Emperor Constantine makes Christian worship legal. In the second, Emperor Theodosius establishes Christianity as the official religion of the Empire. In the third, the scholar Augustine makes a personal decision—in contrast to the preceding official ones—in favor of Christianity.

The emperor Constantine and his associate Licinius issue the Edict of Milan (313 C.E.), permitting free Christian worship: We, Constantinus and Licinius the Emperors ... give both to Christians and to all others free facility to follow the religion which each may desire. ... [and decree that] no one who has given his mental assent to the Christian persuasion or to any other which he feels to be suitable to him should be compelled to deny his conviction, so that the Supreme Godhead ..., whose worship we freely observe, can assist us in all things with his wonted favour and benevolence. Wherefore ... it is our pleasure that all restrictions which were previously put forward in official pronouncements concerning the sect of the Christians should be removed, and that each one of them who freely and sincerely carries out the purpose of observing the Christian religion may endeavour to practice its precepts without any fear or danger. ...
(From S. Ehler, J. Morrall eds., *Church and State through the Centuries*, 1954)

The Code of the emperor Theodosius I establishes Christianity as the sole official religion in the imperial capital of Constantinople, and assigns penalties for pagan practices (392 C.E.): *Theodosian Code, 16.1.2 (380):* It is Our will that all the peoples who are ruled by the administration of Our Clemency shall practice that religion which the divine Peter the Apostle transmitted to the Romans. ...

Theodosian Code, 16.10.25 (435): We interdict all persons of criminal pagan mind from the accursed immolation of victims, from damnable sacrifices, and from all other such practices that are prohibited by the authority of the more ancient sanctions. We command that all their fanes, temples and shrines, if even now any remain entire, shall be destroyed by the command of the magistrates, and shall be purified by the erection of the sign of the venerable Christian religion. ...
(*Theodosian Code*, 440, 476; ed. C. Pharr)

Torn between dissatisfaction with his past life and doubts about Christianity, Augustine hears the message that will resolve his uncertainties and lead to his conversion (c. 400 C.E.): I was saying these things and weeping in the most bitter contrition of my heart, when, lo, I heard the voice as of a boy or girl, I know not which, coming from a neighboring house, chanting, and oft repeating, "Take up and read; take up and read." Immediately my countenance was changed, and I began most earnestly to consider whether it was usual for children in any kind of game to sing such words; nor could I remember ever to have heard the like. So, restraining the torrent of my tears, I rose up, interpreting it no other way than as a command to me from Heaven to open the book, and to read the first chapter I should light upon. ... So quickly I returned to the place where Alypius was sitting; for there I had put down the volume of the apostles, when I rose thence. I grasped, opened, and in silence read that paragraph on which my eyes first fell—"Not in rioting and drunkenness, not in chambering and wantonness, not in strife and envying; but put ye on the Lord Jesus Christ, and make not provision for the flesh, to fulfil the lusts thereof." Nor further would I read, nor did I need; for instantly, as the sentence ended—by a light, as it were, of security infused into my heart—all the gloom of doubt vanished away.
(Augustine, *Confessions*, 1: 19–20; ed. J. G. Pilkington 1896)

the Christian Fathers. He has already been encountered as the author of the massive *City of God*. His *Confessions*, an autobiography (the first) constructed as a lengthy prayer, reveals an understanding of the human psyche that has left its mark on later generations. An extract is given in *Witnesses* above. His *On the Trinity*, his commentaries on Scripture, and his many other works form a monument of Christian doctrine fed by the preceding centuries of debate and illumined by Augustine's peerless originality, literary style, and power of expression. Moreover, he was a master of Latin—which by the fifth century had become the international language of the West, as Greek was of the East.

In the early years of the Empire, learned Romans used Greek as well as Latin. Greek reigned supreme in the eastern Mediterranean, where the various elites nevertheless mastered Latin as the language of politics and administration. By the fourth century, the Empire had split into Latin and Greek zones, centered respectively at Rome (and later Milan or Ravenna) and Constantinople. This process of separation was under way precisely during the years of the formation of Christian theology. Its creators, the Church Fathers, became distinguished as Greek- or Latin-speaking, Eastern or Western. The early Fathers were Greek-speaking. The cantankerous Tertullian (who died a Montanist heretic), a Latin author, was the first of a series of Latin-speaking Fathers who created the Latin tradition that would over the next centuries serve as the crucible of Western thought.

Constantine's Edict of Milan (313) declared Christianity a legal religion in the western Roman Empire. A decree of 323 extended that order to the

HOW MANY?

Converts to Christianity

Year	Number of Christians	Percent of population
40	1,000	0.0017
50	1,400	0.0023
100	7,530	0.0126
150	40,490	0.07
200	217,795	0.36
250	1,171,356	1.9
300	6,299,832	10.5
350	33,882,008	56.6

This projection of the extraordinary growth of Christianity is based on figures relating to the urban populations within the Roman Empire in the period 40–350 C.E., assuming a total population of 60 million people.
Source: Philip F. Esler, *The Early Christian World* (Routledge, 2000).

East. Within a century, Christianity was elevated to the status of an official religion. It had pursued an extraordinary path from target of persecution to object of tolerance to identification with the state.

In the middle of the fourth century, the emperor Julian (r. 361–363), known as "the Apostate," attempted to stem the tide of Christian expansion and to restore the glory of pagan philosophy. Although he was raised as a Christian, his youthful training was overwhelmed by his later Classical education and his resentment of the Christianizing members of Constantine's family, who had slaughtered all those of his own family except himself. He outlawed Christian teaching of the Classics and restored to the Senate house in Rome the statue of the pagan god of Victory.

Julian was the last non-Christian emperor of the ancient world. In 382, the emperor Gratian (the first emperor not to bear the ancient title of *pontifex maximus*) removed the restored statue of Victory from the Senate. In 391, Theodosius ordered the destruction of the pagan temples of Alexandria, the center of the late imperial culture; in 392, he banned all pagan sacrifices throughout the Empire. In 391, (possibly Christian) mobs in Alexandria burned the city's great library and in 415 a Christian mob murdered Hypatia (370–415), female philosopher and mathematician.

Justinian (r. 527–565) closed the schools of pagan philosophy and decreed that only baptized Christians could be citizens.

As the Empire became more Christian, the Church grew more like an empire. The power of church leaders increased. Because they were all male, their advancement entailed the exclusion of women from public roles in the churches. In the East, the Christian hierarchy was subordinated to the emperor. In the West, where public governance was fading, the bishops were in command. In 390, the bishop of Milan, Saint Ambrose (c. 340–397), had banned the emperor Theodosius from the sacraments of the Church (an order of excommunication), and forced him to do penance to lift the ban. By the fifth century, the bishop of Rome (now called "**pope**," from *papa*, or "father," and *pontifex maximus*) played the role of the emperor. Pope Innocent I (r. 401–417) negotiated with the Goth Alaric; later, Pope Leo I (r. 440–461) persuaded the Hun Attila in 451 to halt his Italian campaign and spare the city of Rome.

When the Empire faded, the Church was there in its place; as one scholar has written, the Church "outthought it, outwrote it, and outlived it." The Unknown God, born in Galilee and preached by Paul to Athenian bystanders, had won.

Conclusion

Roman Gods, the One God, and the Meaning of the West

It was Paul's genius that plucked the Unknown God, one of many, from the pantheon of the Greco-Roman world, and persuaded his audience that he was the one God of the universe. Belief in the one God, inherited from his worshipers in ancient Judaea and adopted by the followers of Jesus of Nazareth, separates the later fully developed Western civilization from the ancient world that gave it birth. As much as the culture of Greece and Rome, itself the bearer of the culture of still earlier civilizations, the beliefs and traditions of the first monotheistic religions, Judaism and Christianity, helped form the West.

QUESTIONS TO CONSIDER

1. How significant were the Etruscan influences on early Roman religion?

2. Why would Romans be attracted to the foreign cults of Cybele (the Great Mother, from Asia Minor) or Isis (from Egypt)?

3. Why did exile play an important role in the development of Jewish thought and tradition? What changes followed the dispersion of the Jews from Palestine as a result of their resistance to Rome?

4. Why was Paul a particularly effective communicator of the beliefs of the new Christian religion?

5. Between 50 C.E. and 350 C.E., the number of Christians in the Roman empire rose from 1,400 to nearly 34 million. What do you think was the most important factor in that growth?

SUGGESTED RESOURCES

Athanassiadi, Polymnia & Michael Frede, eds., *Pagan Monotheism in Late Antiquity* (Oxford: Clarendon Press, 2000). Studies of late ancient pagan monotheism, a literary tradition that was the context for the development of Jewish, Christian, and Islamic monotheism.

Brown, Peter, *Authority and the Sacred: Aspects of the Christianisation of the Roman World* (Cambridge: Cambridge University Press, 1996). This examines the work of Christian leaders as negotiators between the new faith and traditional ways of dealing with the supernatural.

Chilton, Bruce, *Rabbi Jesus: The Jewish Origin of Christianity* (New York: Doubleday, 2000). Based on recent archeological research, recreates world of first-century Palestine and situates Jesus within the social customs, political world, and religious controversies of the Jewish community—and especially that of Galilee, with its own tradition of personal communication with God.

Curran, John R., *Pagan City and Christian Capital: Rome in the Fourth Century* (Oxford: Oxford University Press, 2000). Traces how the city itself became christianized by new building and a new morale.

Dzielska, Maria, *Hypatia of Alexandria*, trans. F. Lyra (Harvard: Harvard University Press, 1995). Reconstruction of the life of the fabled mathematician, philosopher, and teacher, a pagan scholar caught in the conflicts among Alexandrian Christians, tragically murdered in 415.

Feldman, Louis H., *Jew and Gentile in the Ancient World: Attitudes and Interactions from Alexander to Justinian* (Princeton: Princeton University Press, 1993). Interactions of Jews and gentiles especially in the diaspora, exploring the Jewish community's ability to attract converts through the fifth century of the new era.

Gruen, Erich S., *Heritage and Hellenism: The Reinvention of Jewish Tradition* (Berkeley-Los Angeles: University of California Press, 1998). Traces how the Jews of the Hellenistic world learned and transformed the genres and ideas of the dominant Greek culture, at the same time enriching and extending the Jewish tradition.

Hopkins, Keith, *A World Full of Gods: Pagans, Jews, and Christians in the Roman Empire* (London: Weidenfeld & Nicolson, 1999; New York: Free Press, 2000). A bold historiographical experiment mixing fictional characters, speculation, and scholarship, the author asks but does not quite answer why Christianity prevailed over pagan rites, mystery cults, Gnostic rivals, Greek philosophy, and Hellenized Judaism.

MacMullen, Ramsay, *Christianity and Paganism in the Fourth to Eighth Centuries* (New Haven: Yale University Press, 1997). Shows that Christianity did not triumph suddenly and nearly over paganism, but prevailed only after a long period of interaction, in which paganism resisted the Christian advance and Christianity became to some extent assimilated to pagan practices and outlooks.

Salisbury, Joyce E., *Perpetua's Passion: The Death and Memory of a Young Roman Woman* (New York–London: Routledge, 1997). Raised in a wealthy, still-pagan household, the young mother of an infant son, Perpetua enthusiastically welcomed martyrdom in a famous moment that is here placed solidly in the context of the magical and mystical passions of the third century.

Segal, Alan F., *Paul the Convert: The Apostolate and Apostasy of Saul the Pharisee* (New Haven/London: Yale University Press, 1990). Argues that Jewish history can be illuminated by examining Paul's writings.

Tripolitis, Antonia, *Religions of the Hellenistic-Roman Age* (Grand Rapids: W.B. Eerdmans, 2002). Current synthesis of the late-ancient religious traditions, including Hellenistic Judaism, Gnosticism, and Mithraism to the establishment of Christianity.

Watson, Alan, *Jesus: A Profile* (Atlanta: University of Georgia Press, 1998). A controversial examination of the Gospels, depicting Jesus as a charismatic individual who demanded personal faith from his followers.

Dictionaries of Greek and Latin mythological characters (Forum Romanum and Oracle):
http://www.geocities.com/Athens/Forum/6946/mythology
http://www.geocities.com/Athens/Oracle/5545/index.html

Timeline of Jewish history (University of California Davis):
http://www.philo.ucdavis.edu/zope/home/bruce//RST23/chart.html

Chronology of the early church:
http://www.gospelcoom.net/chi/EARLYF/earlychs.shtml

🔘 Western Civilization Documents CD-ROM

5.3 Traditional Roman Religious Practice
5.4 The Gospel According to Luke
5.5 The Letter of Paul to the Romans
5.6 Defining the Christian Woman
5.7 "What Has Jerusalem to do with Athens?"

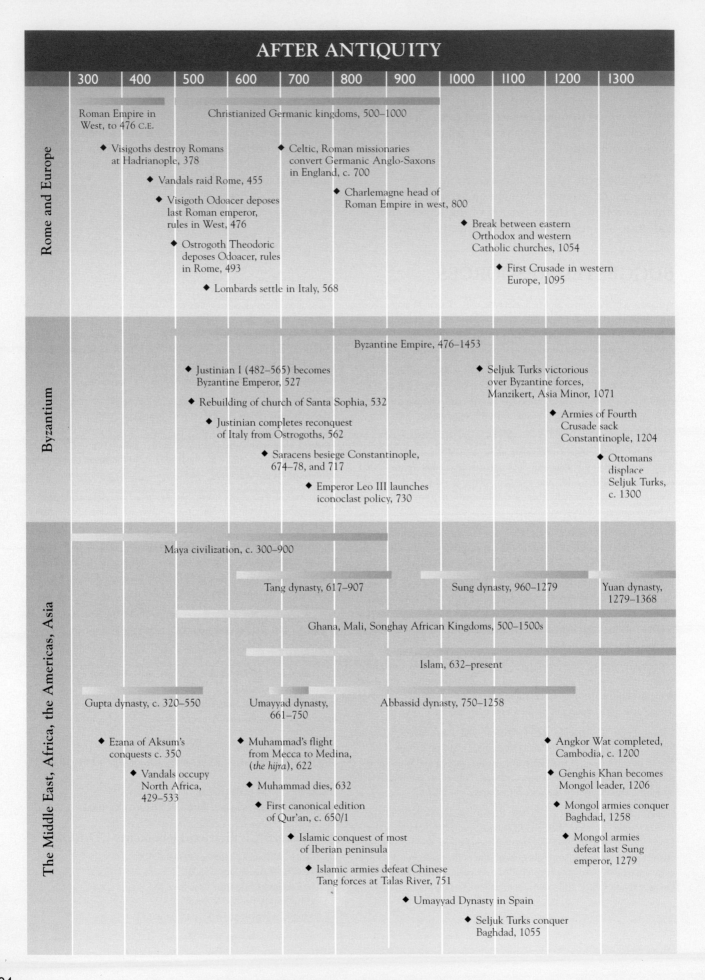

AFTER ANTIQUITY

| 300 | 400 | 500 | 600 | 700 | 800 | 900 | 1000 | 1100 | 1200 | 1300 |

Rome and Europe

Roman Empire in West, to 476 C.E.

Christianized Germanic kingdoms, 500–1000

◆ Visigoths destroy Romans at Hadrianople, 378

◆ Vandals raid Rome, 455

◆ Visigoth Odoacer deposes last Roman emperor, rules in West, 476

◆ Ostrogoth Theodoric deposes Odoacer, rules in Rome, 493

◆ Lombards settle in Italy, 568

◆ Celtic, Roman missionaries convert Germanic Anglo-Saxons in England, c. 700

◆ Charlemagne head of Roman Empire in west, 800

◆ Break between eastern Orthodox and western Catholic churches, 1054

◆ First Crusade in western Europe, 1095

Byzantium

Byzantine Empire, 476–1453

◆ Justinian I (482–565) becomes Byzantine Emperor, 527

◆ Rebuilding of church of Santa Sophia, 532

◆ Justinian completes reconquest of Italy from Ostrogoths, 562

◆ Saracens besiege Constantinople, 674–78, and 717

◆ Emperor Leo III launches iconoclast policy, 730

◆ Seljuk Turks victorious over Byzantine forces, Manzikert, Asia Minor, 1071

◆ Armies of Fourth Crusade sack Constantinople, 1204

◆ Ottomans displace Seljuk Turks, c. 1300

The Middle East, Africa, the Americas, Asia

Maya civilization, c. 300–900

Tang dynasty, 617–907

Sung dynasty, 960–1279

Yuan dynasty, 1279–1368

Ghana, Mali, Songhay African Kingdoms, 500–1500s

Islam, 632–present

Gupta dynasty, c. 320–550

Umayyad dynasty, 661–750

Abbassid dynasty, 750–1258

◆ Ezana of Aksum's conquests c. 350

◆ Vandals occupy North Africa, 429–533

◆ Muhammad's flight from Mecca to Medina, (the hijra), 622

◆ Muhammad dies, 632

◆ First canonical edition of Qur'an, c. 650/1

◆ Islamic conquest of most of Iberian peninsula

◆ Islamic armies defeat Chinese Tang forces at Talas River, 751

◆ Umayyad Dynasty in Spain

◆ Seljuk Turks conquer Baghdad, 1055

◆ Angkor Wat completed, Cambodia, c. 1200

◆ Genghis Khan becomes Mongol leader, 1206

◆ Mongol armies conquer Baghdad, 1258

◆ Mongol armies defeat last Sung emperor, 1279

CHAPTER 8

AFTER ANTIQUITY

New Peoples of Europe and Other Peoples of the World

300–1300 C.E.

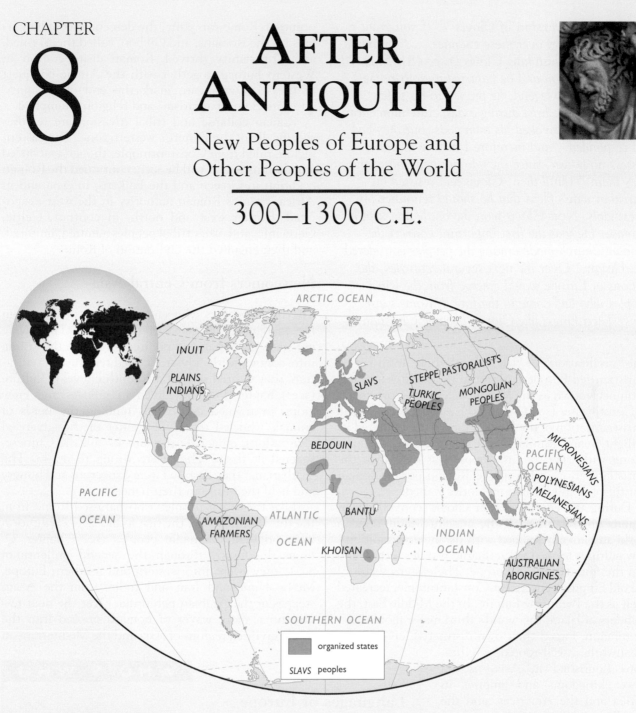

KEY QUESTIONS

◆ **The "Triumph of Barbarism and Religion":** What were the weaknesses of the late Roman Empire that allowed less-advanced peoples to enter and assume command?

◆ **Byzantium:** The Enduring Empire: Why was the eastern Empire, centered at Byzantium—now Constantinople—able to endure while the western Empire crumbled?

◆ **Islam: From Arabian Desert to World Stage:** What explains the momentous force of Islam as it expanded rapidly across North Africa and eastward into Asia?

◆ **Beyond the West:** Why did peoples from the Old World fan out to all continents except Antarctica? To what extent did they create civilizations like those of Afro-Eurasia?

The Conversion of Clovis *"If you grant me victory over these enemies ...,"* promised the Frankish king Clovis (r. c. 481–511), *"I will believe in you and be baptized in your name."* So, according to legend, he prayed to his wife's protector Jesus Christ during a desperate moment in battle. He had invoked his own gods, but they had not responded: *"and therefore I believe that they possess no power, since they do not help those who obey them."* Until then, Clovis had resisted his Christian wife's pleas that he should renounce his forest idols. Now Clovis won the battle and kept his promise. He was the first important convert the Roman Church made among the peoples considered *"barbarian."* Over the next several centuries, the nations of Europe would emerge from the tribal peoples who had come to the fore in Rome's last days. Their kings, like Clovis, became Christian.

The civilization of the West took form in a Christianized Europe during the thousand years after antiquity known as the Middle Ages. The conversion of Constantine (see Chapter 7) was decisive for the Christianization of the Roman Empire as it entered its twilight years. Similarly, the conversion of Clovis (along with 3000 of his troops) was crucial to the Christianization of Europe, as Roman power, Roman institutions, and Roman memories waned.

During the centuries after Clovis' conversion, in regions on the fringe of the ancient Mediterranean world and already imbued with its ancient traditions, new cultures formed as Germanic peoples settled and laid the foundations of Europe. The eastern sector of the old Empire, centered at Constantinople, recreated itself as the Byzantine Empire. In the Middle East, the founders of Islam, the world's third major monotheistic religion, forged their own distinctive civilization. Meanwhile, well-rooted civilizations flourished in Asia, as did newer kingdoms and empires in Africa and the Americas, and the world's peoples explored every habitable region of the globe.

THE "TRIUMPH OF BARBARISM AND RELIGION"

The eighteenth-century historian Edward Gibbon (1737–1794) held that Rome's decline was accomplished by "the triumph of barbarism and religion." What Gibbon saw as an explanation for Rome's collapse (which it was not) may be seen as simply a description of what occurred: Rome was gone, the descendants of barbarians (as the Romans, and Gibbon, called them) ruled, and Christianity thrived. Roman disintegration in Western Europe, together with the Arabic conquest of the Mediterranean, mark the end of antiquity. After its close, "barbarism" and religion triumphed.

Roman collapse and tribal invasion are features specifically of the Empire's western zone. The eastern region, ruled from Constantinople, though embattled and diminished, as will be seen, continued the Roman tradition in Greece and the Balkans, in Asia and in Africa, even as Roman authority in the west evaporated. Farther west and north, in contrast, Celtic, Germanic, and other tribal peoples admired, imitated, and then engulfed the civilization of Rome.

Newcomers from Central Asia

The tribal peoples who engulfed Europe came from the margins of Eurasia's civilized core. They were pre-state, pre-urban and preliterate. Before they came into contact with advanced Mediterranean civilization, they existed only at a Neolithic level of culture (see Chapter 1). They lived in villages and grew crops, or roamed as nomads tending the herds of animals who fed them. The elites of the advanced civilizations, especially the Greeks and the Chinese, sneered at them. They were wrong to do so. The "barbarians" they despised were dangerous and hungry and held the future in their hands.

Like the tribal peoples who harassed Rome from the third century C.E., the first founders of civilization were originally nomadic peoples (see Chapter 1). From the fourth through the second millennium B.C.E. they swept into western and southern Europe, Mesopotamia and Iran and India, from the Asian steppes or the Arabian peninsula. Over the next few millennia, more waves of nomads pressed into the newly civilized regions of Asia and the Mediterranean

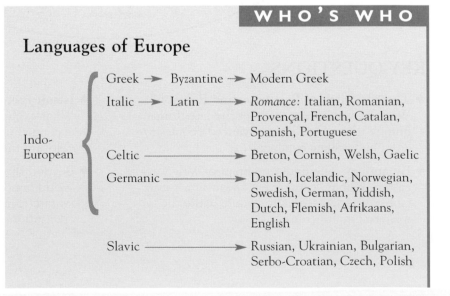

WHO'S WHO

Languages of Europe

Indo-European:
- Greek → Byzantine → Modern Greek
- Italic → Latin → *Romance*: Italian, Romanian, Provençal, French, Catalan, Spanish, Portuguese
- Celtic → Breton, Cornish, Welsh, Gaelic
- Germanic → Danish, Icelandic, Norwegian, Swedish, German, Yiddish, Dutch, Flemish, Afrikaans, English
- Slavic → Russian, Ukrainian, Bulgarian, Serbo-Croatian, Czech, Polish

Roman and German Leaders

The column of Marcus Aurelius: *The spectrum of relations between the Romans and the Germanic peoples who invaded the Western Empire is hinted at in this relief from the column of Emperor Marcus Aurelius, 121–180 C.E., depicting Roman soldiers beheading German prisoners.*

world. Searching for a better place to live, they followed the gradient of the great steppes downward toward land that was warmer and wetter, or where rich, walled cities lay ready for sacking.

Among them were the Celts. By 500 B.C.E., the Celts had settled down in central and western Europe: in Switzerland, Germany, and Austria, in modern France and Belgium. As time went on, they moved north into Ireland and Britain and south into Spain and Portugal. Their languages (of the Indo-European family) have left traces in Breton, Gaelic, and Welsh still heard in parts of France and Britain. The Celts built villages and grew crops, practicing an ancient religion under the guidance of their priests, or *druids*. The druids (some of whom may have been women) practiced magic, wrote a language as yet undeciphered, presided over ritual sacrifices of human beings and beasts, and preached the resurrection of the body. They advised the chieftains and educated their sons.

In 390 B.C.E., the Celts of Gaul (modern France) attacked northern Italy, burned the infant city of Rome, and fell before the counterassault of the patrician general Camillus. A century later, they were rebuffed in Asia Minor by the kings of Pergamum, who celebrated in sculpture their victory over the Celtic invaders. A contingent of the same Gauls founded the nation called "Galatia" in the interior of Asia Minor, where, three centuries later, the apostle Paul founded a church.

The Romans pacified many of the Celtic territories. Resistant at first, the Celts of Spain and Gaul eventually yielded to Roman rule, adopting the customs and language of their overlords. The Celts of Britain, conquered last, were less completely Romanized. They often rebelled against the foreign presence—as they

did in 60 C.E. under the fierce Queen Boudicca of the Iceni tribe. The Roman emperor Hadrian constructed his famous wall (c. 120 C.E.), shown on p. 198, to define the frontier between the zones of Roman domination and of unconquered natives. In 407 C.E., no longer able to hold that frontier, Roman armies abandoned Britain. Soon the British were overrun by new Germanic peoples, while Roman customs and language were forgotten. But Roman walls, roads, and camps—even baths and foundations of villas—still remain, witnesses to the Roman conquest.

Meanwhile, tribes speaking Germanic languages (another Indo-European branch) and living on the shores of the Baltic Sea moved into central Europe. In their migrations, their tribal divisions multiplied. Those in the north would develop the Nordic dialects, ancestral to the modern Scandinavian tongues. They, too, would migrate, but later, as the feared Vikings:

Flavius Stilicho: *The Germanic Vandal general employed by the Romans, Flavius Stilicho is represented in Roman dress on this ivory panel from Monza, Italy.*

Frontier Defenses

The Great Wall of China: *The crisis caused by the movements of nomadic steppes peoples, which triggered equally vast movements by other peoples, developed from the first century C.E. and affected both China in the east and Rome in the west. The Great Wall of China was the famous achievement of Shi Huangdi (r. c. 221–210 B.C.E.), who ordered the joining together of previously built walls to defend China against foreign incursions. The Great Wall extends 1400 miles (2253 km.) and is studded with many towers which served as signaling stations, warning of the approach of enemies.*

Hadrian's Wall: *Three centuries after the building of the Great Wall of China, the Roman emperor Hadrian (76–138 C.E.) sponsored the building of a wall from west to east across the narrow neck of the northern part of England. Hadrian's wall both consolidated Roman possessions and provided a strategic defense line, with a small fort every mile, and 12 substantial garrison posts across the 73-mile (118 km.) span of the frontier.*

east to Russia, and west to France, England, Ireland, and Iceland. The German peoples who settled in southern Russia spoke Gothic. Those who moved into western Europe gave birth to modern German.

By 300 C.E., German tribes were arrayed along the Roman frontier marked by the Rhine and Danube rivers: Franks and Alamanni, Vandals and Goths (split into western Visigoths and eastern Ostrogoths), Burgundians, Saxons, Lombards, and others. The historian Tacitus, who admired the freedom of the Germans while he scorned their simplicity, named tens of these tribes, describing their outlandish costume, surly drinking bouts, and untarnished strength.

Tacitus also described German society, in meticulous detail (see *Witnesses*, p. 204). The knotted coiffure he described as characteristic of the tribe called the Suebi, for instance, adorns a skull archaeologists unearthed in the German state of Schleswig. Modern archaeologists and anthropologists have explored buried villages and bogs (which have yielded human remains, perhaps of sacrificial victims) that provide tangible evidence of German tribal customs.

Germans were grouped by tribe (the "**folk**"), clan, and family. Ten or twenty families formed a clan, and groups of clans lived together in villages. A number of these were grouped for military or judicial purposes as the "hundred." German men were warriors and herders, counting their wealth in booty and in cattle. They left agriculture to women and to prisoners of war, who used a simple wooden plow to score the heavy northern soil. Women were responsible (as elsewhere) for spinning and weaving, but they also accompanied their menfolk into battle, goading them on to feats of valor. A German husband could have several wives and some concubines. German laws witness that the chastity of German women (much admired by Tacitus) was honored, and its violation harshly punished.

Laws were customary and unwritten. Fixed remedies of vengeance or compensation were set for different categories of crime. Each individual had a price: the **wergeld**. Women, children, old men, and warriors in their prime were assigned wergelds according to their perceived usefulness to society. Rather than taking vengeance on a murderer, the victim's family might instead accept the wergeld in compensation. These payments reduced the overall level of violence in the community.

Chiefs or kings, who were elected by an assembly of the folk for their perceived strength and courage, administered this legal system. Often the king came from a distinguished or "royal" family. Around him clustered a band of elite warriors united to him by oaths of loyalty. The Romans called this band the *comitatus*, or group of companions. These companions foreshadow the vassals of later European kings, who swore oaths of loyalty to their rulers. In addition to his personal band, the king could call on all his tribesmen to fight. All were joined to him, as to the tribe, by pledges of loyalty.

Across the Asian steppes dwelled other peoples, who threatened China, India, and Rome. These included Scythians and Sarmatians near the Black Sea, and Parthians near the Caspian—from where they descended to take over Persia from the Seleucid kings. In central Asia roamed the Altaic- or Turkic-speaking tribes of future conquerors: Huns, Mongols, Turks. From these descended the Kushans, who briefly established rule in the Indian Punjab in the early centuries C.E. Of the same origin were the Hsiung-Nu (the Huns), who prompted Shi Huangdi, in the third century B.C.E., to build the Great Wall as a defence against intruders. Later the Huns turned west to dislodge the Goths from the Dnieper-Danube region and to push into the rich lands of Italy. The Mongols would eventually erupt west, east, and south, to dominate the Eurasian core and shape the future of Russia, China, and western Asia.

Romanization, Invasion, and Rule

Tribal peoples positioned close to the Roman frontier learned to be just like Romans. For centuries, they lived as admiring neighbors, trading their coarse wares for Roman handicrafts and learning to use iron tools and weapons and to haul their belongings in wheeled carts. Often German warriors were recruited as auxiliary soldiers. Some of these Roman-trained warriors returned to their people to lead rebellions against their old commanders. One such was Arminius ("Hermann"), who defeated Varus in the Teutoburg forest in 9 C.E.. Other Germans spent time within Roman boundaries as captives, slaves, or visitors.

Admiration turned to desire. The wealth of Rome was a magnet, especially to people who were starving. The Germans asked the emperors for permission to cross the frontier. Often they were permitted to do so, settling on wasteland or collecting cash subsidies from a state in need of capable mercenaries. If the Romans told the newcomers to stay out, they came anyway: groups of 20,000 to 100,000, who would then form part of the populations they conquered.

After 300 C.E., the accumulated energy of these roaming and expanding populations spilled over the barriers of the Roman frontier, as indicated on Map 8.1. The Huns were the catalyst. Expelled from China, these expert horsemen and bowmen pushed westward across the steppe. After arriving in south Russia in 355, they went on to ravage the Ostrogothic kingdom, between the Don and Dnieper rivers, around 376. The neighboring Visigoths asked the Roman emperor Valens at Constantinople for permission, which he granted, to cross the Danube and take refuge within imperial borders. An extraordinary step had been taken in admitting a whole people across the frontier. Imperial agents abused and cheated the migrants, offering to supply the starving refugees with dog meat at the price of one woman or child per dog. The Visigoths rose up in protest, destroying the imperial forces at Hadrianople (modern Edirne, in Turkey) in 378. The battle marked the first serious encounter between Romans and newcomers in which the newcomers won. Other such encounters would follow.

Over the century, waves of expanding peoples—migrants, raiders, and conquerors—pounded the western Empire. The Visigoths left the Balkans and pushed on into Italy itself, where the emperor now huddled behind the walls of Ravenna in northern Italy on the Adriatic, protected by swamps and fortifications. The emperor Honorius employed his Vandal commander-in-chief, Stilicho (r. 359–408), portrayed on p. 197 as a bulwark against the Visigoths. When Stilicho was murdered, on his master's instructions, in 408, Honorius (r. 384–423) was left on his own to address the threat of invasion.

In this he failed utterly. The Visigoth king Alaric (r. c. 395–410), having been refused permission to occupy Austria, proceeded, in 410, to attack Rome. "Rome, the mistress of the world," wrote the contemporary Christian heretic Pelagius, "shivered, crushed with fear, at the sound of the blaring trumpets and the howling of the Goths." The invaders left the city with booty of gold and silver, bolts of silk, jewelry, and portable household furnishings. Resettled in southern Gaul in 418, these restless people soon crossed the Pyrenees and occupied northern Spain.

The Huns, who had driven the Ostrogoths and Visigoths from the Danube Valley, now stormed westward to forage for food and treasure within the boundaries of the Roman Empire. Stopped near Troyes, in Gaul, in 451, their young chief Attila (r. 435–453) turned back to raid northern Italy the following year. There he was met by Leo I, the Roman pope, and a delegation, whose offers of tribute (added to the Huns' own difficulties with famine and disease) caused the invaders to withdraw to the north in 452.

The Vandals invaded next, also driven by hunger. Under their king, Gaiseric (r. 428–477), they swept into Spain, arriving ahead of the Visigoths. Their ultimate goal was prosperous Africa, Rome's breadbasket. Despite attempts to keep from the invaders either boats or knowledge of shipbuilding, the Vandals commandeered the craft they needed, and in 429 all of them, numbering more than 80,000, sailed across the Straits of Gibraltar to North Africa. Over the next ten years they struck across the Mediterranean coast of Africa to Carthage, which they captured in 439, establishing a kingdom that lasted almost a century thereafter. From their North African base, they attacked Rome by sea in 455. It was the second time in fifty years that the capital was looted.

In 476, the German Odoacer (r. 476–493), head of a tribal auxiliary force in the Roman army, rebelled with his troops against his commander. Made "king" by his followers, Odoacer proceeded to Rome and deposed the child emperor Romulus Augustulus. The Roman state in the west had been a ghost for nearly a century. Odoacer's coup merely made absolutely plain the deterioration that was already accomplished. The eastern emperor, Zeno, commissioned Theodoric (r. 493–526), the king of the Ostrogoths (who had by now migrated to the west) to unseat Odoacer. Theodoric accomplished this feat in 493, sealing the usurpation with the murder of Odoacer and his son. Romans no longer ruled the Empire in the west.

Europe Transformed

The Romans still didn't know they had lost. Nor did the conquerors realize they had won. Rome itself still

Map 8.1 Migrants, Raiders, and Conquerors, 100–800 C.E.: *Beginning in the first century C.E., nomadic peoples of the central Asian steppes began to expand both west and east, disrupting civilization in both the Mediterranean region and in China. China resisted determinedly, and had attained some stability by around 600. In the west, the movement of Asian peoples triggered the dispersion first of Germanic, and then of Slavic peoples, which was to cut western Europe off from the Mediterranean and the Eastern Roman Empire centered at Constantinople, and to result in the failure of Roman rule in the west. (Compare Map 6.3, p. 160, showing the region when Rome, governed from its single capital, held unquestioned dominion over the region; and Map 8.2, p. 205, showing the position of successor kingdoms to western Rome.)* What attracted these invaders into the Roman Empire?

stood amid the splendid, crumbling monuments of its youth. Italy lived as before. Although bishops and popes now guided a thoroughly Christianized world, the great landowners still called their leaders "senator" and studied Greek and Roman classics in the libraries of their villas. Theodoric prudently enlisted the senators in his service. Among them were the cultivated Romans Cassiodorus and Boethius.

Cassiodorus (c. 490–585) recorded Theodoric's correspondence, and wrote in elegant Latin a *History of the Goths* (now lost, except for a later abridgment). Having served the Ostrogoths for more than thirty years, he retired in 538 to found a monastery in southern Italy, and to copy the manuscript books that were the legacy of the Roman way of life.

His colleague in Theodoric's service, Boethius (c. 480–524), was accused of treason, imprisoned, and eventually executed. The author of a treatise on music and translator of important works of Aristotle and Plato, Boethius composed in prison his *Consolation of Philosophy*. In this last product of Roman thought, the ghostly figure of "Philosophy" visits the tormented Boethius in his cell. Boethius recounts his miseries, and she diagnoses the disease: he had sought the Highest Good in pleasures, advancements, and wealth, where it could not be found. That supreme reward, which alone could satisfy the longing of the human soul, was to be found only in the mind. Boethius' work announces a turn toward the inner life, which would be a hallmark of the thought of the medieval age to come.

Germanic Kingdoms The Ostrogothic kingdom in Italy lasted from Theodoric's accession in 493 until the emperor Justinian's reconquest of Italy, completed finally in 562—to be followed only a few years later by the new invaders, the Lombards. The Vandal kingdom in North Africa was also relatively short-lived: from the 429 invasion until Justinian's reconquest of that region in 533. By the end of the sixth century, these kingdoms had all vanished, while the Visigoths held Toulouse, in southern Gaul, and then Spain from 418 until the Arab conquest in 711.

In the meantime, other peoples to the north had penetrated Roman frontiers to establish a second generation of kingdoms. The Lombards, arriving in 568, founded a kingdom in northern Italy that lasted for two centuries. As Roman authority waned in Britain, German-speaking Saxons, Angles, and Jutes from across the Channel invaded, destroying churches and monasteries as they progressed, zealous champions of their ancient polytheistic culture. By 700, Christian missionaries from Ireland and Rome had converted the descendants of these invaders—who were a church before they were a nation. Their story was told by the contemporary scholar and saint Bede (c. 673–735), called "Venerable," in his *Ecclesiastical History of the English People*. Meanwhile,

Conquerors of Rome

Arminius (Hermann; d. 19 C.E.) German chief; defeats Roman general Varus in the Teutoburg forest in 9 C.E., destroying three legions and halting the conquest of Germany.

Alaric (r. 395–410) leader of the Visigoths; attacks and sacks Rome in 410, provoking in response Saint Augustine's explanatory *City of God*.

Attila (r. 435–453) leader of the Huns; ravages Germany, Gaul, and northern Italy in 451–452, before being persuaded to turn back.

Gaiseric (r. 428–477) leader of the Vandals: leads the force that sweeps through Spain to North Africa in 429, takes Carthage in 439, and attacks Rome in 455.

Odoacer (r. 476–493) Visigothic king; deposes Western emperor Romulus Augustulus and rules as king at Rome.

Theodoric (r. 493–526) "the Great," king of the Ostrogoths; with blessing of Eastern Emperor Zeno crosses the Alps and retakes Italy from Odoacer (r. 488–493), whom he assassinated, and reigns as king at Rome.

Germanic Burgundians infiltrated southeastern Gaul, and Franks moved into the north.

In 481 or 482, the vigorous leader Clovis took charge of the Frankish kingdom. Its turbulent career would be described by Bishop Gregory of Tours (538–594) in his *History of the Franks*. Clovis and his descendants, called "Merovingians" (after their patriarch Merovech), ruled until 751, when Pepin, the king's minister, deposed the last of them and assumed the royal title. Pepin's line was "Carolingian," after his father Charles (Carolus in Latin) Martel (i.e. "the Hammer"; 688?–741). In 732 Charles Martel had driven Arab Muslim invaders back at Poitiers—the high-water mark of their penetration of western Europe. Pepin's son was also called Charles: Charles "the Great," or Charlemagne (r. 768–814).

Germanic newcomers settled among Roman citizens gingerly, displacing but not crushing the natives. They occupied one-third to two-thirds of the land, and governed their own people by Germanic law—which was often codified and committed to writing in the Latin of the vanquished Romans. The Romans, meanwhile, maintained their own laws and customs. The two societies dwelt side by side, at first neither intermingling nor intermarrying. Eventually, they blended. They used as a common language the simple Latin of late Roman times, which absorbed some Germanic words and concepts—except in distant

Britain, more resolutely Germanic in speech. In Spain, Portugal, France, and Italy (as well as Romania and parts of Switzerland) the rough provincial Latin of the Roman inhabitants developed into the **Romance** languages spoken in these countries today.

Arians and Catholics Some of the tribal peoples who descended on the western Empire were already Christians: Arian Christians (see Chapter 7). The Goth Ulfilas (c. 311–382) had learned this heresy in Constantinople, where he was consecrated bishop in 341. When he returned to his people, he brought the new religion and a new alphabet. He translated parts of the Bible into Gothic and adapted the Greek alphabet to write it down. Gothic Arianism spread to neighboring peoples. The kingdoms of the Vandals, the Ostrogoths, and the Visigoths were all Arian.

The Romans, in contrast, were staunch catholics. They adhered, to the key Christian doctrines, notably those proclaimed in the Nicene Creed (see Chapter 7); and they were obedient to the bishop of Rome, the pope. The Anglo-Saxons of Britain and the Franks of northern Gaul were both converted from polytheism to Latin catholicism. These tribes, especially the Franks, became the allies of the Church in the Christianization of Europe. When the Roman popes despaired of Byzantine aid against the Lombards in

Protecting ancestral graves: *This tomb guardian figure, c. 386–534 C.E., was crafted by the nomadic Asian Mongols, later raiders of Europe. (Inner Mongolia Museum, Hahehaote)*

the eighth century, they called on the kings of the Franks to defend the faith. Thus, a long tradition of Church–state interdependence was born in the West.

The Task of Preservation As newcomers settled in the world that had been Roman, Roman intellectuals tried to keep Roman literature alive. As Christian converts, they had at first shied away from the body of Classical works forming the foundation of the Greco-Roman curriculum. It was laden with allusions to a pagan world now repudiated, whose religious and sexual customs were equally repugnant. But by now these converts had made their peace with the Classics, which they read, copied, abridged, and raided. The great task of preservation began.

Although the literature of the past was prized, it was no longer understood. As the task of preservation progressed, complexity of thought declined. A curtain had dropped between the new world of Germanic kingdoms and Christian orthodoxy and the old world of elevated language, erudition, and empire. The *Etymologies* of the Spanish scholar-bishop Saint Isidore of Seville (c. 560–636), an encyclopedia of the "origins" of things, contained shreds and fragments of the whole ancient literary tradition. It had lost the coherent vision of antiquity and exemplifies the

The Fringes of Civilization

The Wild and the Tame: *Not only the great civilizations, but also peoples on the fringes of civilization produced artifacts of great beauty. This pectoral, or necklace, by a Scythian craftsman, fourth century B.C.E., depicts in the first band foals and calves feeding and a man milking sheep. In contrast, the lower band shows wild animals—boars, lions, and winged beasts—attacking each other. (Historical Museum, Kiev)*

A King's helmet: *Excavated from a trove of grave-goods at Sutton Hoo on England's east coast, c. 660* C.E., *was this Saxon helmet. With other objects like hinged clasps and brooches, it was buried in a ship under a mound which served as a memorial to an East Anglian king.* (British Museum)

process of intellectual decay. The conquest had done its work. "Barbarism" won, and a chasm yawned between past and present.

The debasement of literary culture paralleled a loss of population, a decline of urban life, the collapse of commerce, the disappearance of currency, an increase in lawlessness, and a deep isolation: these features characterized a period once called the "Dark Ages." It is called so no longer. Historians now recognize that the deep changes of the sixth through ninth centuries laid the foundations of modern European culture. The period was more one of transition than of decline, as the focus of European life shifted from the Mediterranean to the forested interior of western Europe. The shift from oil (the fruit of the olive consumed throughout the Mediterranean) to butter (processed from the milk of Europe's cows) marked a new departure in Western civilization.

BYZANTIUM: THE ENDURING EMPIRE

As Rome languished in the west, Rome in the east, centered at Constantinople, flourished and would endure for a millennium to come. Thoroughly Roman before it became detached from the Latin West, the eastern Empire sought for two centuries to reestablish the western domain. Then it turned inward and eastward, and spoke only Greek. Now known as the

Byzantine Empire, it was to survive confrontation with the forces of Islam, as well as its own internal religious conflicts, until 1453. During that time, it was the center of a commercial network linking interior regions of Russia and western Asia with Mediterranean ports, and the principal home of the preservation of ancient Greek culture.

The Eastern Empire to the Autocracy of Justinian

The split between West and East began early. The Latinization of the eastern Mediterranean had never been so thorough as the Latinization of North Africa or Western Europe. The emperor Hadrian had encouraged Greek culture to reassert itself. After Commodus, many Roman emperors were of eastern origin. These and other factors encouraged the break between the two halves of the Empire.

The two men who rescued Rome from its third-century depression were also those who precipitated the divorce between West and East. Both were Latin-speaking Westerners. Diocletian divided the administration of the Empire between the two regions. Constantine established an eastern capital at Constantinople (formerly Byzantium). With the death of Theodosius the Great in 395, imperial unity broke down irrevocably. His sons ascended to separate western and eastern thrones. The division between East and West had been a cultural reality since the second century and an administrative one since the third. Now it was absolute. A century and a half later, while the Ostrogoths ruled Italy, in the east Justinian (r. 527–565) was to establish the full autocracy of the Byzantine emperor. He is shown with his retinue on p. 207.

Justinian the Autocrat   The pharaohs of ancient Egypt and the Persian "king of kings" had pointed the way to autocracy. Earlier Roman emperors revived such claims, and Diocletian especially, seeking to impose order, exalted himself as "lord." But with Justinian the evolution of the emperor's role from "first citizen" to absolute monarch reached its culmination. In establishing this autocracy, Justinian was motivated at least partly by an incident early in his reign that challenged his authority.

Justinian often attended the horse races at the Hippodrome in Constantinople. In 532, the audience began a riot against his repressive regime. These were the Nika riots, so named after the shout "*nika!*" (meaning "win!") so often heard at the races. After the trauma of this rebellion (suppressed by his versatile agent Belisarius, c. 505–565, who trapped and massacred the insurgents), Justinian was now even more committed to autocracy.

His partner in this venture was his wife, the intelligent Theodora (c. 497–548). Unusually for a queen,

The Coming of the Germans

The culture and society of the Germans differed markedly from those of the Romans, as the Roman historian Tacitus expertly notes in his ethnography—the first of its kind—of those tribal nations, of which some extracts are given in the first passage. The different values of the Germans, captured in Tacitus's narrative, is also recognized in their laws and customs, as in the excerpts from the laws of the Salian Franks.

The Roman historian Tacitus describes, with some amusement and with some admiration, the customs of the Germans (c. 105–110 C.E.):

7. They choose their kings by birth, their generals for merit. These kings have not unlimited or arbitrary power, and the generals do more by example than by authority. If they are energetic, if they are conspicuous, if they fight in the front, they lead because they are admired. But to reprimand, to imprison, even to flog, is permitted to the priests alone. ... They also carry with them into battle certain figures and images taken from their sacred groves. And what most stimulates their courage is, that their squadrons or battalions, instead of being formed by chance or by a fortuitous gathering, are composed of families and clans. Close by them, too, are those dearest to them, so that they hear the shrieks of women, the cries of infants. ...

11. About minor matters the chiefs deliberate, about the more important the whole tribe. Yet even when the final decision rests with the people, the affair is always thoroughly discussed by the chiefs. They assemble, except in the case of a sudden emergency, on certain fixed days, either at new or at full moon; for this they consider the most auspicious season for the transaction of business. ... When the multitude think proper, they sit down armed. Silence is proclaimed by the priests, who have on these occasions the right of keeping order. Then the king or the chief, according to age, birth, distinction in war, or eloquence, is heard. ... If his sentiments displease them, they reject them with murmurs; if they are satisfied, they brandish their spears. The most complimentary form of assent is to express approbation with their spears.

14. When they go into battle, it is a disgrace for the chief to be surpassed in valour, a disgrace for his followers not to equal the valour of the chief. And it is an infamy and a reproach for life to have survived the chief, and returned from the field. To defend, to protect him, to ascribe one's own brave deeds to his renown, is the height of loyalty. The chief fights for victory; his vassals fight for their chief ...

(Tacitus, *The Agricola and Germania*; trans. A. J. Church and W. J. Brodribb, 1877)

The laws of the Salian Franks, written down beginning in the seventh century from oral traditions, assign monetary penalties, graded according to the social status of victim and perpetrator, for assault and murder; note especially the heavy punishment assigned to the murderer of a male child, or a woman capable of bearing children:

Title XIV. Concerning Assault and Robbery: 1. If any one have assaulted and plundered a freeman, and it be proved on him, he shall be sentenced to 2500 denars, which make 63 shillings. 2. If a Roman have plundered a Salian Frank, the above law shall be ordered. 3. But if a Frank have plundered a Roman, he shall be sentenced to 35 shillings ...

Title XVII. Concerning Wounds: 1. If any one have wished to kill another person, and the blow have missed, he on whom it was proved shall be sentenced to 2500 denars, which make 63 shillings. 2. If any person have wished to strike another with a poisoned arrow, and the arrow have glanced aside, and it shall be proved on him: he shall be sentenced to 2500 denars, which make 63 shillings. 3. If any person strike another on the head so that the brain appears, and the three bones which lie above the brain shall project, he shall be sentenced to 1200 denars, which make 30 shillings. 4. But if it shall have been between the ribs or in the stomach, so that the wound appears and reaches to the entrails, he shall be sentenced to 1200 denars-which make 30 shillings... 6. But if a freeman strike a freeman with his fist so that blood does not flow, he shall be sentenced for each blow—up to 3 blows to 120 denars, which make 3 shillings.

Title XXIV. Concerning the Killing of Little Children and Women: 1. If any one have slain a boy under 10 years ... he shall be sentenced to 24000 denars, which make 600 shillings ... 3. If any one have hit a free woman who is pregnant, and she dies, he shall be sentenced to 28000 denars, which makes 700 shillings. 6. If any one have killed a free woman after she has begun bearing children, he shall be sentenced to 24000 denars, which make 600 shillings. 7. After she can have no more children, he who kills her shall be sentenced to 8000 denars, which make 200 shillings.

("The Salic Law," in Ernest F. Henderson, *Select Historical Documents of the Middle Ages*, 1910) especially in ancient times, she began life near the bottom of the social ladder (her father was reported variously to be a circus bear-trainer or a horse-stable owner) and descended further. If not actually a prostitute when Justinian met her, she was engaged in no respectable trade. In later life, perhaps recalling her origins, she founded a hostel for reformed prostitutes. Theodora was an active empress, whom Justinian consulted frequently. She is famous for her advice to him during the Nika riots. If he wished to flee, she said, "yonder is the sea, and there are the ships." She herself would stay, regardless of risk; "purple [the color of royalty] makes an excellent shroud."

Freed from the poverty of her youth, Theodora enjoyed the opulence of the imperial court, where she was served, witnesses report, by as many as 4000 attendants. The luxury, the rituals, the obeisance of courtiers matched the claims of imperial status. Access to the emperor was controlled by slaves and eunuchs (thought to be asexual and therefore trustworthy). Intrigues abounded. These, and observations about the private lives of the principals, are recorded in the scandalous and elegant *Secret History* of the court historian Procopius (c. 500–565).

Justinian's civil servants were highly educated men from middling or immigrant backgrounds. They formed a bureaucracy which collected taxes, governed the provinces, and watched the treasury, enriched by the profits from state monopolies such as that of the luxury fabric silk. Justinian's bureaucrats were expected to labor ceaselessly in the interests of the emperor, emulating Marinus of Syria, adviser to Justinian's predecessor Anastasius (r. 491–518), who even at night kept "a pen-and-ink stand hanging beside his bedside, and a lamp burning by his pillow, so that he could write down his thoughts on a roll."

Church and State   Justinian was head of the church as well as of the government. In these roles, he followed the examples of his predecessors Constantine and Theodosius the Great, who had called councils, debated with bishops, and refereed dogmatic squabbles. Now that pattern of ecclesiastical leadership became fixed. In a law of 535 Justinian announced that the state possessed two powers, both granted by God: those pertaining to the priesthood and those pertaining to politics—meaning that the emperor was empowered to lead the church as much as the state.

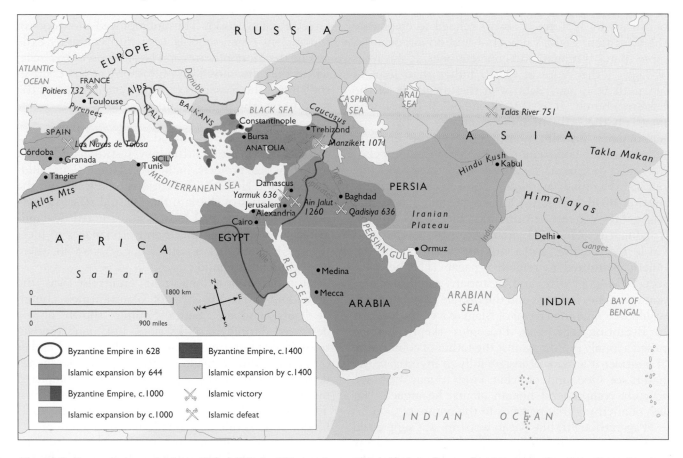

Map 8.2 Byzantium and Islam, 500–1400: *By 500 C.E., the eastern half of the Roman Empire was on its way to becoming the Byzantine Empire: Greek-speaking and eastward-facing. After 632, the new Islamic civilization challenged Byzantium militarily and economically. The period from 800 to 1453 saw the still greater expansion of Islamic civilization, which reached into regions beyond its Mediterranean origin. At the same time, after some recovery in the ninth century, Byzantium gradually deteriorated to the position of a weak state on the fringe of Islam, and it fell to the assault of Islamic Ottoman Turks. What accounts for the rapid and wide expansion of Islam on three continents?*

Byzantium and Islam

Basilica of Santa Sophia: *Christian Byzantium and Islamic caliphates nurtured grand architectural projects and exquisitely decorated interior surfaces, the latter affected by cultural norms—for Islam forbade the representation of human or animal figures in religious contexts, whereas these were essential to the didactic purposes of Christian art. The most impressive building of Justinian's reign was Santa Sophia in Constantinople (Istanbul), built 532–537. The four minarets were added when the basilica was converted into a mosque with the Turkish capture of the city in 1453 C.E.*

Byzantine Christianity was different from that evolving in the West. The East had concurred in the orthodox definition about the human and divine natures of Jesus the Christ crystallized by the Council of Nicaea in 325. Yet it always tended to emphasize the Christian Savior's universal and divine qualities more than his human and concrete ones. It was Jesus as *Logos* ("the Word of God") rather than Jesus of Nazareth (the man) who won the allegiance of the Eastern church. It is this disembodied Christ who floats on the brilliant mosaic surfaces of Byzantine monuments: an all-powerful ruler of the universe more than the compassionate healer of the Gospels.

Under Justinian, Byzantine Christianity became not just the only legal religion but a colossal force permitting no opposition. Officials pressured Jews and pagans to convert. Justinian's chief legal adviser, Tribonian (c. 470–544), architect of the *Corpus Iuris Civilis* (see below), was a striking exception: he was quietly permitted to remain a pagan. The heretical sects of Monophysites and Nestorians established separate churches in Egypt and the Middle East; later they would welcome the arrival of Islam as a counterweight to Byzantine repression. Procopius' skeptical voice raised a lonely protest against the tether of conformity: "I consider it a mark of insane folly to investigate the nature of God and of what kind it may be." We scarcely comprehend human affairs, he argued; "far less of anything that pertains to the nature of God."

Pagan thought, like pagan worship, was suppressed under Justinian. In 529, he closed down the Academy and the Lyceum in Athens, the schools that had been opened 900 years before by Plato and Aristotle. Meanwhile, in Constantinople there flourished the Christian school founded by the emperor Theodosius II (r. 408–50) in 425, with a staff of eight professors of Greek and Latin rhetoric, ten of Greek and Latin

grammar, one of philosophy, and two of jurisprudence. Here and at Alexandria and Gaza (in Palestine), orthodox Christian doctrine was taught by Christian teachers, along with the standard curriculum of the Greco-Roman world. The unemployed professors of the ancient pagan schools went into voluntary exile among the Monophysites and Nestorians, or to Persia, where they discoursed on philosophy at the court of the king of the Sassanids (ethnic Persian rulers of the region since the third century C.E.).

Buildings and Laws   In addition to his work of establishing Christian orthodoxy, Justinian undertook more practical projects, including his ambitious building program. He had fortifications rebuilt around the shrunken cities of the late Empire and near the perilous frontiers. He had hostels constructed near **pilgrimage** sites, and hospitals and orphanages to meet the needs of Christian conscience. Above all, there were churches to build.

Justinian's most important enterprise was the rebuilding, from 532 C.E., of Constantine's church of "holy wisdom," Santa Sophia, shown above, destroyed during the Nika riots. Justinian's renovations (funded by treasure snatched from the Vandals of North Africa) made Santa Sophia the largest domed church of the age. Viewing the completed monument, Justinian exclaimed (referring to the First Temple of the Jews): "Solomon, I have outdone you!" Under Turkish rule, it was redesigned as a mosque.

Larger than its nearest rivals, Alexandria and Antioch (Rome had shrunk to about 30,000 by the late sixth century), Constantinople under Justinian was at its peak, the foremost city of the eastern Empire. A center of international trade as well as church and government, it was home to a population of between 300,000 and 400,000 Asians and Slavs,

Jews and Romans, both Latin- and Greek-speaking. A fifth-century document catalogues its major features: among them 14 palaces, 4388 residential houses, 8 public and 153 private baths, 2 theaters, not counting the Hippodrome; 20 public and 120 private bakeries, and 14 churches, all guarded by 65 night-watchmen and 560 firemen.

More lasting than any building was the great law code compiled at Justinian's direction: the whole legacy of Roman experience of the administration of justice. The collection and analysis of the law had been the ongoing concern of the great jurists of the second and third centuries. Two earlier codes had been gathered under Diocletian, and Theodosius II had seen to the publication of the Theodosian Code of 438. Yet the job needed to be done again: new legislation needed to be ordered, contradictory or out-of-date laws eliminated, and the relevant commentaries of legal experts organized in a useful way.

The *Corpus Iuris Civilis* ("The Collected Civil Law") consisted of four parts: the *Code*, a revised compilation of laws, the preface to which is quoted in *Witnesses* on p. 208; the *Digest*, containing summaries of the opinions of the classical jurists; the *Institutes*, a legal textbook; and the *Novels*, a compilation of the new laws issued after 533, when the *Code* was completed. Justinian left no monument to his achievement more important for the history of the West than the *Corpus Iuris Civilis*, in which he proclaimed the primacy of law above even emperors: "the subordination of sovereignty under the law is a greater thing than the imperial power itself." This acknowledgment of the superior authority of law is a rare statement of monarchical principle.

Roman law was written in Latin. Justinian was by birth a Latin speaker, and Latin remained during his reign the official language of the Byzantine court. But in the *Corpus Iuris Civilis*, Latin had its last day in the East. Soon the language of imperial administration, of the church, and of scholarship would be Greek.

Justinian's jurists achieved more than his generals. A year after suppressing the Nika riots, Belisarius set

Justinian and his retinue:
The splendid mosaics in San Vitale, Ravenna, crafted c. 547 show the Byzantine emperor Justinian with his retinue. Justinian in fact never went to Ravenna, but the mosaic was intended to serve as his substitute and as an important visual reminder of his power.

Dome of the Rock: *The first major enterprise of Islamic architecture was the Dome of the Rock in Jerusalem, built 688–691. With its gold dome and elaborate tilework, it departed significantly from plainer earlier mosques.*

out to reconquer the western half of the Empire, accompanied by his staff historian, Procopius, who would report the entire operation in his *History of the Wars of Justinian*. At first, all went well. Belisarius reconquered North Africa from the Vandals in 533, and he and another general, Narses (c. 480–574), reconquered much of Italy between 535 and 561. The African mission achieved its goals. The wealth seized from Carthage and Rome by the Vandals was recovered, and the native, Romanized elites welcomed Byzantine overlordship. This arrangement would endure about a century, after which Africa was absorbed into the new power of Islam. The Italian reconquest, in contrast, was bloody and troubled. In the end, only Ravenna, Rome, and Sicily were securely held for Byzantium. The rest of Italy succumbed in 568 to the invading Lombards.

Byzantium after Justinian

These losses in the west were followed by devastating losses in the north and east. The Byzantine Empire would never again be so large as it was under Justinian. Slavic peoples seized the Balkans in the sixth and seventh centuries, while nomadic Bulgars and Avars ravaged the northern frontier. Persians, under Sassanid leadership, threatened Byzantium's eastern flank from 609 to 622. Then the still more powerful force of Islam challenged the bastions of the Empire. Armies of **Saracens** (as Muslim Arabs were called by the Greek-speaking Byzantine chroniclers) swept away Byzantine defenses in Egypt, Palestine, and Syria, and besieged Constantinople regularly from 674 to 678 and again in 717. The defenders sprayed or pumped "Greek fire" (a flammable brew of petroleum, sulfur, and pitch) on enemy ships, saving the capital from capture. But the borders of the Empire were shrinking.

Three hundred and fifty years later, Islamic armies would return—not the Saracens as before, but the Seljuk Turks, who had seized power from the caliphs of Baghdad. Turkish armies defeated Byzantine forces decisively at Manzikert, Asia Minor, in 1071, removing much of that region from Byzantine domination. Emperor Alexius I Comnenus (r. 1081–1118) asked the pope for help, and brought on his head the avalanche of the Crusades. Soldiers poured out from western Europe ready to fight the "infidel" who had captured the holy sites in Jerusalem. A century later, in 1204, the Crusaders turned on their Christian brethren in Constantinople. When a Byzantine regime was restored later in the same century, it had fewer than two centuries more to endure. Ottoman Turks, manning the first warships ever to be mounted with guns, seized the last remnant of the Roman Empire in 1453. Today Istanbul—as Constantinople was renamed in 1930—is the major city of the modern nation of Turkey.

WITNESSES

The Byzantines in Charge

These two passages give brief glimpses into the exercise of imperial power in Byzantium. In the first, the sixth-century Emperor Justinian explains the importance of the monumental compilation of law called the Corpus Iuris Civilis, *completed under his direction. In the second, the daughter of a later emperor, the twelfth-century conqueror Alexius, explains how he delegated the tasks of ordinary government to his mother.*

In the preface to the *Institutes,* a part of the *Corpus Iuris Civilis* containing the codification of Roman law, the emperor Justinian explains the nature of the whole work (c. 540): In the name of Our Lord Jesus Christ ... to the youth desirous of studying the law. ... Having removed every inconsistency from the sacred constitutions hitherto inharmonious and confused, we extended our care to the immense volumes of the older jurisprudence, and have now completed a work of which we once despaired. When this had been done, we [ordered the completion of] ... a book of Institutes. ... Receive then these laws... and show yourselves so learned ... that ... you may have ability to govern such portions of the state as may be entrusted to you.
(Justinian, preface to the *Institutes*; ed. M. Hadas 1956)

Anna Comnena, chronicler of the reign of her father, the emperor Alexius, describes his entrusting civil power to his mother, her grandmother Anna Dalassena (c. 1120): My father reserved for himself the waging of wars against the barbarians, while he entrusted to his mother the administration of state affairs, the choosing of civil servants, and the fiscal management of the empire's revenues and expenses. ... For my grandmother really had the gift of conducting the affairs of state. She knew so well how to organize and administer that she was capable of governing not only the Roman Empire but also every other kingdom under the sun. ...
(Anna Comnena, *Alexiad*; ed. P. Thiébaux 1987)

During the centuries from Justinian's reign in the sixth century until the collapse of the Byzantine Empire in the fifteenth, the cities of the Empire weakened and failed. The profits of trade drained eastward, and coins fell out of circulation. The concern with security was obsessive, as "fortifications replaced men." Alexandria and Antioch withered, and lesser cities disappeared altogether. Constantinople itself declined: hit by plague in 542 and by other disasters thereafter, its population decreased in the eighth century to fewer than 50,000 residents. Two centuries later it had regained some prosperity and had a

Comparative City Sizes and Plans, c. 800–1000

Baghdad, Iraq *300–500,000*

Córdoba, Spain *500,000*

Aachen, Germany *2000–3000*

Chang'an, China *1,000,000*

Constantinople (modern Istanbul), Turkey *300–400,000*

Teotihuacán, Mexico *100,000*

population of several hundred thousand; but the city that fell to the Turks in 1453 was a small mercantile center whose population had again shrunk to 50,000.

The Iconoclastic Controversy and the Emperor Irene   An early religious crisis greatly influenced the culture of Byzantium. In 730—precisely when Islam threatened Byzantium with annihilation—the puritanical Emperor Leo III (r. 717–741) launched a war on the holy images, or icons, treasured by the pious as aids to devotion. Leo and other like-minded people in the Eastern church condemned the use of icons as a violation of the Second Commandment, against idolatry. Their opponents considered icons valuable means of apprehending the divine. The policy of **iconoclasm** (meaning "the smashing of images") was ultimately reversed. Yet it created irreparable tensions with the West and encouraged the eventual and enduring rift between the Roman Catholic and Eastern Orthodox churches (see Chapter 10).

The decision, in 787, by the Council of Nicaea to restore icons to homes and churches was prompted by Irene (r. 780–802), mother of the future emperor Constantine VI and regent during his minority (780–91). This determined woman wanted to rule herself, rather than yield to her son. On being proclaimed emperor in 790, Constantine confined his mother to house arrest. When she seized power in 797, Irene ordered her son captured, blinded, and killed; she then ruled in her own right for five years. The Frankish king Charlemagne is reported to have proposed marriage to her in 802, intending perhaps to reunite the eastern and western remnants of ancient Rome. That possibility alarmed high officials in Constantinople, who deposed Irene in 802. She died in exile a year later.

Court scribes, not having dealt before with a female ruler, referred to Irene as "emperor," a ruler in her own right; the term verbally differentiates her from "empresses," who were merely consorts. Despite the exalted status achieved by Irene and by Theodora and other empress-consorts, for most women conditions under Byzantine domination resembled those of Hellenistic or Roman society. Women could still be executed for adultery, be summarily divorced, testify in court only about matters concerning children and family, and lose guardianship of their children upon remarriage. These were the measures of women's legal and sexual status. The boundary of a woman's life remained the walls of her home.

Scholarship, Male and Female   Amid conflicts and crises both internal and external, Byzantine scholars kept ancient knowledge alive. Many of the best manuscripts of Greek philosophy and literature—nearly the whole of what is now known, barring the papyrus fragments recovered in modern times from Egypt— were produced in Constantinople. That achievement was the work of earnest bishops, committed teachers, and leisured aristocrats, whose Greek was native and natural. For these scholars, there was no need for the kind of "Renaissance" (or "rebirth") that occurred later in the West. However, some authors or books became more fashionable than others, and occasionally fits of editorial enthusiasm saw to the purging of "errors" that had crept into the text.

Although the goal of Byzantine scholarship was more to preserve the wisdom of the ancients than to develop new learning, one or two exceptional individuals did flourish in this age. Michael Psellus (1018–1096), author of treatises on science and mathematics, rhetoric, law, and history, wrote compellingly of his discovery of the works of the ancient philosophers: "Having found philosophy extinct in its practitioners, I revived it by my own efforts. …Since, however, I heard it said that Greece had achieved great things in philosophy, … [a]fter reading some commentators on this science, I learned from them the road to knowledge: one referred me to another, the inferior to the superior … and so, finally, to Aristotle and Plato."

At least two women joined in the intellectual life of Byzantium. The poet Icasia (b. c. 810) sparkled briefly in court circles before she retired to spend the rest of her life in a convent. Of even higher social position was Anna Comnena (1083–1153), the eldest daughter of the emperor Alexis I Comnenus.

Comnena wrote a biography of her father in fifteen books (an extract is given in *Witnesses* on p. 208): a significant historical work, based on Classical models and contemporary sources. Strikingly, Comnena says nothing about women's inner experience in the Byzantine milieu. Her record would surely have been interesting. This Byzantine princess mastered Classical literature clandestinely, while confined within her house. As a child she cherished hopes of deposing her brother and succeeding her father on the imperial throne. She was forced instead to spend her mature years, like Icasia, in a convent. Comnena wrote not a word of those constraints as she penned the record of her father's achievements.

Byzantine scholarship discouraged innovation. Learned men copied, memorized, edited, commented upon, and stored classic texts. Within two centuries after the death of Justinian, leadership in science and philosophy had passed to the Islamic world. After the twelfth century, philosophy found a home in Europe, built by those the ancients had called "barbarians."

ISLAM: FROM ARABIAN DESERT TO WORLD STAGE

As Rome faded in the west and revived in new guise in the eastern Mediterranean, in that region where the world's first civilizations took root there emerged a new faith and a new culture: that of Islam, the third to develop of the world's monotheistic religions. Shaped at first by the Arab prophet Muhammad and his followers, it spread by force and by persuasion throughout the main centers of ancient Eurasian civilization and to farther regions beyond. Many non-Arabs were converted to Islam, which offered its followers the spiritual experience of a transcendent God while providing moral principles.

The Formation of Islam

When the western Empire yielded to the Ostrogoths, what had been one world became two. Soon it would become three. Less than a century after Odoacer seized Rome, in the city of Mecca, on the Arabian Peninsula not far from the Red Sea, was born the creator of a new religion and a new world civilization: Muhammad ibn Abdullah (c. 570–632). His followers were called Muslims ("those who submit"), and the faith they followed Islam ("submission" to God's will). Islam was the third child—after Byzantium and western Europe—of the Roman world. The three were united by their common past, rooted in the history of the ancient Mediterranean; and by their common monotheism, rooted in scripture.

By trade, Muhammad was a merchant who journeyed with the caravans of the Arabian desert north of Syria. By birth, he was a worshiper of the many gods of his homeland, although he learned much from Judaism and Christianity. When Muhammad was about forty, he had a vision in which the angel Gabriel (the same who appeared to the Virgin Mary in Luke's Gospel account) appeared to him and made known to him the will of the one God, called (in Arabic) Allah. By this experience Muhammad was transformed into the prophet of Allah—called simply the Prophet by Muslims. The record of his communion with Allah is the substance of the **Qur'an** (the word means "reading" or "reciting"), the holy book of Islam.

After some initial setbacks, the new monotheism Muhammad espoused made rapid progress. Muhammad's first converts were members of his immediate circle: his wife, Khadijah; his friend, Abu Bakr; and a Meccan merchant, Umar. These were his supporters in the city of Mecca, where, at first, the Prophet had mostly enemies. So hostile was the reception to his new gospel that in 622 Muhammad fled from Mecca to Medina, 240 miles (386 km.) distant. The flight, which marks the first year of the Islamic calendar, is called the *hijra*.

In Medina, the new religion planted its roots. Muhammad enrolled enough enthusiastic believers in the one God to take control in Medina and to enable a return in 630 to what would become the Muslim holy city of Mecca. The Ka'ba, the city's central temple, was cleansed of its idols. The ancient black stone it housed, revered in local polytheism, became the holy object that every Muslim hoped someday to

WITNESSES

The Civilization of Islam

Among the controversial principles of Islam is that of jihad, or holy war. The obligation of jihad is described here from the Islamic scripture, the Qur'an, which also contains many other ethical and spiritual principles that are the foundations of Islamic civilization. That civilization was richly productive during the period that European historians call the "Middle Ages" of scholars, scientists, and philosophers. Among the greatest of these is Avicenna, an excerpt of whose Autobiography is given here.

The Qur'an prescribes *Jihad*, the Holy War for Islam, an obligation of the whole community (c. 640): When you meet those who are infidels, strike their necks until you have overwhelmed them, tighten their bonds, and then release them, either freely or for ransom, when war lays down its burdens. Those who are killed in the path of God, he does not let their good deeds go for nothing. (Qur'an, XLVII, 4/4–5; ed. N. Lewis, 1983)

More than for conquest, Islamic civilization is known for its great achievements in the sphere of the philosophy of science. Here Avicenna (980–1037) describes the early training that helped make him one of the foremost Islamic thinkers: By the time I was ten I had mastered the Koran [Qur'an] and a great deal of literature, ... [There followed training in philosophy] ... [then] ... I took to reading texts by myself ... [mastering logic, geometry and astronomy] ... I now occupied myself with mastering the various texts and commentaries on natural science and metaphysics, until all the gates of knowledge were open to me. Next I desired to study medicine, and proceeded to read all the books that have been written on this subject. ... At the same time I continued ... to study and dispute on law, being now sixteen years of age. (Avicenna, *Autobiography*, ed. C. Brand, 1969; trs. A. J. Arberry, *Avicenna on Theology*, 1951)

touch; according to legend it had been given to Adam on his leaving paradise. Modern Muslims still strive to make, someday, a pilgrimage to Mecca. During the prayers that are said five times every day, they turn their faces to the city of Muhammad's birth.

When Muhammad died in 632, Islam spread among the Arabic nomads of the Sinai peninsula, the Bedouins. Bedouin society was based on the groupings of family, clan, and tribe similar to those encountered among the early Greeks and Romans, the nomads of the steppes, and the villagers of the north. These small groups gathered under the authority of leaders called sheiks. They created vibrant poetry in the language that became the classic language of Islam, and worshiped many gods and imagined the interventions of genies, or *jinns*. To the Bedouins, Islam offered a novel political, social, and ethical ideal.

Arab herdsmen were important agents in the commercial system of the ancient world, conveying by camel caravans the goods of Asia from Indian Ocean ports to depots on the Mediterranean coast. In their journeys, they encountered Jewish and Christian, Monophysite, Nestorian, and Zoroastrian believers in a transcendent God. All had an impact on the concepts of Islam, a religion of high ethical content and great depth, numbering today more than 900 million adherents.

The faith of Islam centers on the Qur'an. About the length of the New Testament, it was committed to writing around 650 or 651, within a generation of the Prophet's death. In 114 *suras* ("chapters"), it enjoins absolute obedience upon its followers to the will of one single God, called Allah, as revealed through his prophet Muhammad: "God, there is no God but he, the living, the self-subsistent." Islam accepts the messages of the Hebrew Bible and the Christian New Testament, and reveres the earlier prophets Isaiah and Jeremiah, the patriarchs Abraham and Moses, and, as witnesses, Jesus and Mary of Nazareth.

Islam requires its followers to adhere to the Five Pillars of Islam. These are (1) to accept with conviction the core principle of the faith, that there is no God but Allah and that his prophet is Muhammad; (2) to pray five times each day; (3) to fast during daylight hours in the holy month of Ramadan; (4) to give alms to the poor; and (5) to go at least once in a lifetime as a pilgrim to Mecca and visit the Ka'ba.

Islam provided rules governing virtually every aspect of life: commerce, family life, personal behavior. These rules banned usury and set high standards of fairness in economic life. They forbade gambling and the consumption of all pork and alcohol. They granted women and children protections unknown in earlier pagan society.

Still, women enjoyed fewer opportunities than men. Although they could own property, they could not divorce their husbands (who could obtain divorce at will) and were severely punished for violating premarital virginity or marital chastity. Men were limited to four wives (plus as many concubines as they chose). Respectable women were to be veiled in public, a practice in Middle Eastern society going back to the Assyrians (see Chapter 1). Although most women were powerless to change their condition, the wives, daughters, and sisters of Islamic rulers were often able to wield considerable influence.

The **mosque** is the Islamic place of worship and the central building of an Islamic city. It generally consists of a court with fountain for ritual purification, a hall of prayer, and one or more towers, called minarets, from which the call to prayer is issued. Decorated with intricate metalwork, mosaic floors and walls, and sinuous columns, some mosques rivaled the great cathedrals of medieval Europe (see Chapter 10) in architectural splendor. Nowhere in a mosque is the human form represented. According to Islam (as in Judaism), the work of God as creator of humanity must not be imitated by human hands.

Unlike most religions of the late ancient world, Islam had no priests. Instead, religious experts called *'ulamâ* emerged. These were not priests, but preachers, judges, teachers, and other experts in the Muslim tradition, who extracted from the implications of the words of the Prophet a theological system. In every locality, a *qâdî* served as a judge in civil and criminal cases and as arbiter of all disputes. He represented at once Islamic orthodoxy, political authority, and social and economic custom. Law, as announced by the *'ulamâ* and the *qâdî*, reflected the principles of Islam in every action of the lives of the faithful.

Some Muslims did not accept the interpretation of tradition provided by the *'ulamâ*. Among these were the **Shiites** (who would be counterposed to the **Sunni** respecters of the mainstream tradition). The Shiites were followers of Muhammad's son-in-law Ali, the fourth **caliph** (a ruler understood to be a successor of Muhammad) of the Arab Muslims. Groups of Shiites survived in independent communities, where they resisted the secularizing tendencies of governments. They were concentrated for the most part in Persia, as they are in modern Iran. Another group of Muslims were the Sufi: ascetics and mystics, whose inner conviction and charismatic healing inspired many converts and assisted in the worldwide diffusion of Islam.

The first Muslims spread the faith by "holy war," or **jihad** (see *Witnesses*, p. 211). Within a few generations, however, Islamic policy shifted from coercion to toleration. Practitioners of other faiths in conquered territory were not forcibly converted, although these **infidels** had to pay a burdensome tax. Freedom from that tax, along with the possibility of full participation in Islamic society, encouraged many to acquiesce willingly to conversion and to adopt the Arabic language and culture of their conquerors. Christians and Jews in Islamic lands were generally not harassed. As "people of the book" (the Bible), they even enjoyed the respect of Muslim leaders as children of Abraham and co-worshipers of the one God.

Arabic Expansion under the Caliphs

The beliefs and customs of Islam gained a large following in part because of its political structure and military prowess. Immediately after Muhammad's death began the first dynasties of caliphs who flourished for three centuries before stumbling on to extinction another three centuries later. The caliphs provided direction and pursued the conquests that made Islam a religion not of Arabs alone, but of many other peoples of Africa and Asia.

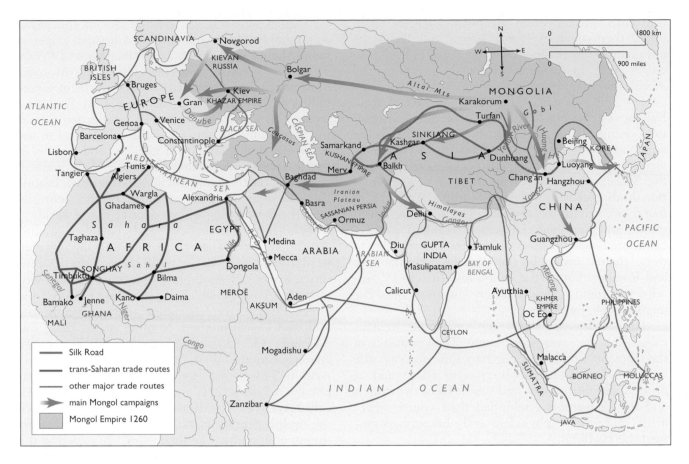

Map 8.3 Africa and Asia: Pathways of Trade, to 1300 C.E.: *As Byzantium and Islam faced each other in the Mediterranean region, African states and cities crystallized, stimulated by trade opportunities overland across the Sahara, and by sea across the Indian and Persian oceans. Why was the Silk Road an overland route, enormously important for the Eurasian trading system?*

Muhammad's friend Abu Bakr was the first leader of Islam (from 632 to 634) after the Prophet himself. He rallied the leaders of the Arabian cities, and compelled the compliance of desert sheiks. By the time of his death, just two years after Muhammad's, the Arabian Peninsula was united. Earnest Muslims were ready to spread the new faith.

Under the second caliph, Umar (r. 634–644), Bedouin Muslims seized much of the territory once dominated by the Persian emperor: Mesopotamia, Iran, Syria, Palestine, and Egypt. Some of this territory was grabbed from the weakened Byzantine Empire (including the holy site of Jerusalem in 638); the rest from the Sassanid dynasty (the ethnic Persian rulers of the region since the third century C.E.). The conquerors learned from the conquered. Byzantine and Sassanid administrative systems became the model for caliphal government. The still vital Zoroastrianism of the Persian regime seeped into Islam, as it had into Judaism and Christianity.

Umar and his two successors, Uthman and Ali, were all assassinated: in 644, 656, and 661, respectively. A struggle then ensued between Sunni traditionalists and Shiite followers of Ali, with the victory going to the former. The Umayyad dynasty quickly established its authority from its capital, Damascus, and ruled throughout the lands of Islam from 661 until 750. Under their leadership, Islam became a far-flung civilization, centered on flourishing cities and bountiful courts.

The conquests resumed. Umayyad armies swept victoriously through North Africa, the Iberian peninsula, and, in Asia, the Caucasus region and Indus Valley. They met resistance at two points of entry to the European continent. Byzantium saved itself, rebuffing naval expeditions sent against Constantinople in 674–678 and 717. In 732, Charles Martel turned back the attempt to penetrate the Frankish kingdom. Islam had extended into Europe for the moment as far is it might. In Asia, it held the frontier against Chinese expansion. In 751, at the Talas River, near Samarkand, Islamic forces fought and won a decisive victory against the expansive force of Tang China.

By that year, the Umayyad dynasty had fallen to Abu al-Abbas (r. 750–754), who claimed to be the successor of Muhammad. To prove it, he marched out of Persia to Damascus and murdered all but one of the surviving males of the Ummayad clan. The Abbasid caliphate would now govern the lands of Islam until the tenth century, when separatist dynasties established themselves in North Africa and Iberia. Its power sapped by the increasing authority of local governors and the generals of its slave armies, the Abbasid remnant ruled in the east until 1258.

The Abbasids removed the capital eastward, from Damascus to Baghdad. This relocation mirrored a cultural change within Islam. No more did an Arab elite dominate foreigners. The Arab leaders of Islam now merged with the surviving aristocracies of Persia and the Mediterranean shore to create a new international ruling class in which all Muslims, Arab or not, found opportunity to advance. The resulting multiethnic and multinational society required a giant, centralized administrative system—comparable to those created earlier by the Persians, Macedonians, and Romans. Under the caliph and his chief counselor, the grand vizier, hereditary governors ruled the many Islamic provinces.

The Mediterranean, which once the Romans called "our sea," was now Islamic. The commerce of the ancient world continued to flow through the cities of the eastern Mediterranean coasts and at other nodes farther east and south. Here the caliphs and their governors established their courts, where artists and writers, physicians and philosophers pursued their callings.

Foremost among these cities was Baghdad, a center of international trade founded in 762 and called the "city of peace." A plan is shown in *How Many?* on p. 209. The city was polyglot, multireligious, multiethnic: Arabic, Persian, and Aramaic were spoken; Jews, Christians, and Zoroastrians coexisted with Muslims; Syrians and Turks, Greeks and Arabs competed for advancement. Reaching, in the ninth century, a population of between 300,000 and 500,000, Baghdad was the largest city in the Fertile Crescent; the largest in the Mediterranean since Rome and Alexandria, now in their fading glory; the largest in the world outside China.

Islamic Civilization

As they tended to their empire-building, the Umayyad and Abbasid caliphs also nurtured Islamic civilization. As early as the eighth century there rose in Jerusalem the mosque called the Dome of the Rock, shown on p. 207 and in Damascus the Great Mosque, blending the borrowed forms of Byzantium and Persia in a new Islamic architectural language. The Arabic poetic tradition flourished in new urban and court settings. The collection of classic stories entitled in English *The Arabian Nights* had been written by the time of the Abbasid Harun al-Rashid (r. 786–809). In 802 Harun al-Rashid sent his royal contemporary Charlemagne an elephant named Abul Abaz as a pet: a creature as strange to that Frankish king as the refined culture of the caliphate.

The ancient schools and libraries of the pagan world that had been shut down by Christian emperors found shelter in Antioch and Damascus and Persia. There they revived again under Umayyad patronage. Muslim scholars translated the key works of Greek philosophy, science, and medicine into Arabic, a medium in which they fueled an intellectual flowering. Resident at the courts of the caliphs and in the academies that sprang up at Córdoba and Seville, in Spain; Cairo and Damascus, on the Mediterranean coast; and Baghdad and Bukhara, farther east, Islamic thinkers from the ninth through twelfth centuries were the most daring and productive in the world.

Scholars in Damascus and Baghdad studied Aristotle's works when these were still unknown in western Europe. From the tenth through twelfth centuries, a series of Arab philosophers wrote commentaries on Aristotle which digested and explored the Greek thinker's understanding of the cosmos, the soul, and logical method. Notable among these was Al-Farabi (d. 950); Ibn Sina (980–1037), called Avicenna in the West (who claimed to have read Aristotle's *Metaphysics* forty times) whose autobiography quoted on p. 211; and Ibn Rushd (1126–1198), called Averroës. The death of Averroës at the close of the twelfth century marks the end of Islamic leadership in philosophy. The torch would be passed to the university professors of once-laggard western Europe.

During the same period, Arab thinkers also developed the ancient Greek legacy in science and medicine. Al-Kindi (c. 800–c. 870) performed experiments with light and heat, color and optics, perfumes and drugs. Al-Razi (c. 865–932), called Rhazes in the Latin-speaking West, wrote a classic treatise distinguishing smallpox and measles. Avicenna established the medical curriculum which endured until displaced by Western medical science in the nineteenth century.

Other Islamic thinkers explored the astrological and agricultural treatises of Indian scholars. It was from India that Islamic mathematicians imported the system of numerals we use today: one through nine plus zero—a system based on powers of ten (today's decimal system) which permitted complex calculations. These "Arabic" numerals, formed in their distinctive hand, were borrowed by the West after 1300 and replaced (generally) the more cumbersome Roman numerals. Arab mathematicians also invented the advanced mathematics that is known by its Arabic name as algebra.

From China came an invention as important for the history of thought as the philosophy of Greece or the mathematics of India: paper. Among the captives taken by the Muslims after the Battle of Talas, in central Asia in 751, were Chinese artisans skilled in paper-making. Their instruction made possible the wide availability of paper, and of knowledge, throughout Islam and the West.

Islam Becomes Global

After the tenth century, when its culture achieved its zenith, the political unity of Islam was shattered. Independent caliphates ruled in Spain, North Africa, and Persia. Meanwhile, new peoples arrived from the Asian steppes: successively Seljuk Turks, Ottoman Turks, and Mongols. They fought for the caliphs as foreign mercenaries. Then they took charge.

The Seljuk Turks, a pastoral people originally from northern Persia led by a dynasty of that name, conquered Baghdad in 1055. Imposing their dominion over the eastern wing of Islam, they pushed west to the Mediterranean and into Asia Minor, where, at Manzikert in 1071, they inflicted defeat on the Byzantine army. Two centuries later, Seljuk authority weakened, enabling a renegade Turkish band called "Ottoman" after their leader, Uthman, to claim leadership in 1300, and to pursue further conquests in Asia Minor and Europe. In the meantime, the Mongols, another group of Asian tribespeople, had penetrated the Middle East from the 1220s. In 1258 they captured Baghdad, ravaging the city (and killing its last caliph). Mongol rule put an end to Islamic theocracy. The caliphs still presided as religious leaders and judges under non-Arabic Seljuk and Ottoman overlords, who became Muslims themselves.

While eastern Islamic lands once ruled by Arab caliphs fell to the Turks and the Mongols, Islam itself spread peaceably to other regions of the world. Muslim traders touring the commercial centers of the Mediterranean Sea, the Indian Ocean, and the African Sahara brought with them their law, their faith, and their way of life. Through their activity, and that of Sufi mystics who acted as missionaries, Islam spread from the Mediterranean shore across the Iranian plateau into India and the East Indies; across North Africa to western Sudan and south along the east African coast; across the Mediterranean to European Spain and the Balkans. Its expansion is shown on Map 8.2.

Thus, long before Christianity, Islam became a global religion. Most Muslims live in south and southeast Asia, far from the Saudi desert. Indonesia has the world's largest Muslim population: about 150 million. Another 300 million live in Pakistan, Bangladesh, and India. More than two-thirds of the world's Muslims live outside the Middle East where Islam began. More than four-fifths are non-Arabs. Yet five times a day, they pray in that Semitic tongue to the God of the Arab prophet Muhammad.

BEYOND THE WEST

While the civilizations of Islam, Byzantium, and Europe were forming, different cultures and civilizations developed in Africa, in Asia, and in the Americas as indicated in *Witnesses*, p. 216. These emerged independently of the traditions in the Fertile Crescent and around the Mediterranean. Neither "ancient" nor "medieval", they exist in a timeframe apart from the Western one. Yet it is important to understand their career in the first millennium C.E., for the West—which increasingly meant Europe—would soon confront these distant and alien worlds.

African Tribes, Cities, and Kingdoms

As civilizations formed in Egypt and Mesopotamia, most native Africans developed the skills of farming and herding animals typical of the Neolithic era (see Chapter 1). During an unusual period of very high moisture in the Sahara and to the south, bringing greater fertility to the land, these peoples increased in population and prosperity. One African community, bordering southern Egypt, achieved an advanced level of civilization.

The black African civilizations of Kush, Meroë, and Aksum developed immediately to the south of Egypt as ruled by native pharaohs, Greek Ptolemies, and Roman emperors. The kingdom of Kush, which had emerged by 1000 B.C.E. along the upper Nile, sent rhinoceros horns and leopard skins, ebony and ivory, and mercenaries and slaves north to Egypt in exchange for Egyptian linen and payprus. From the pharaohs, Kushite monarchs learned the skills of statecraft, pyramid construction, and hieroglyphic writing. Kushite society was hardy enough, when Egyptian society deteriorated, to take over the senior civilization. Its king Piankhi and his successors ruled Egypt for a little over a century as the Twenty-Fifth Dynasty (c. 719–663 B.C.E.), until overrun and defeated by the Assyrian Empire.

Defeated in Egypt in 663 B.C.E., the former pharaoh Tanutamon reestablished Kushite civilization at the new capital of Meroë, where it flourished into the fourth century C.E. This region enjoyed fertile, well-watered soil and a position on the trade routes that led to the Red Sea and the commercial network beyond. Most important, it possessed rich deposits of iron ore which the Kushites learned to exploit—leaving a litter of furnaces and slag heaps for archaeologists to discover and admire. From Meroë's iron factories, knowledge of iron-working spread to other regions of Africa. Africa proceeded to the Iron Age without pausing for the Bronze.

Around 350 C.E., Emperor Ezana (r. 320–350) of neighboring Aksum (modern Ethiopia) destroyed the city and temples and storehouses of Meroë. His people (mostly Christian) were a mixture of African Kushitic-speakers and Semitic-speaking Arab migrants from across the Red Sea. The merchants of Aksum were intermediaries in trade between western and eastern Asia. Indian ships sailed to African Red Sea ports, where Aksumite merchants exchanged for their goods the products of Syria, Palestine, Egypt,

Africa and Asia: Glimpses of the World beyond the West

These three passages give brief glimpses of other non-Western civilizations that flourished from late antiquity into the period of the European Middle Ages: those of East Africa, Buddhist India, and Japan. In the first passage, a traveler describes how an African king is revered by his subjects. In the second, a Chinese pilgrim searches for Buddhist sacred writings in India. In the third, a famous woman author describes in her fictional Tales of Genji *the competition among the ladies of the court for the favor of the emperor.*

The learned Ibn Battuta (1304–1368), an Arab Muslim who chronicled his travels, describes his encounter with an East African chief: The ceremonial at the [public] session of this king is as follows. He takes his seat on a platform carpeted and decorated with silken fabrics; to right and left of him are the men-at-arms, those nearest him holding swords and shields, and next to them the bowmen; in front of them to the right and left are the chamberlain and the officers of government and the private secretary. ... When the sultan takes his seat they cry with one voice *Bismillah*, and when he rises they do the same, so that all those in the audience-hall know the moment of his rising and the moment of his sitting.
(Ibn Battuta, *Travels 1325–1354*; ed. H. A. R. Gibb, 1986)

The Chinese monk Fa-Hsien (fl. 399–414) searches for traces of the Buddha and the Buddhist sacred writings during his journey to India (402 onwards): [In Patna.] Here, in the mahayana monastery, [Fa-Hsien] found a copy of the Vinaya ... rules—those which were observed in the first Great Council, while Buddha was still in the world. ... He further got the transcript of the ... sarvastivadah rules,—those which are observed by the communities of monks in the land of Ts'in; which also have all been handed down orally from master to master without being committed to writing. ... In consequence (of this success in his quest) [Fa-Hsien] stayed here for three years, learning Sanskrit books and the Sanskrit speech and writing out the Vinaya rules.
(Fa-Hsien, *A Record of Buddhistic Kingdoms, an Account of his Travels in India and Ceylon (399–414) in search of the Buddhist Books of Discipline*; trs., ed. J. Legge, 1965)

Lady Murasaki's (978–1014) *Tale of Genji* **describes the intrigues of the Japanese court and the deadly business, managed by women behind the scenes, of inheriting the throne:** In a certain reign there was a lady not of the first rank whom the emperor loved more than any of the others. The grand ladies with high ambitions thought her a presumptuous upstart, and lesser ladies were still more resentful. She survived despite her troubles ... [and] bore the emperor a beautiful son, a jewel beyond compare.

With the birth of the son, it became yet clearer that [the mother] was the emperor's favorite. The mother of the eldest son began to feel uneasy. If she did not manage carefully, she might see the new son designated crown prince. ...
(Murasaki Shikubu, *The Tale of Genji*, 11th century; trs. E. G. Seidensticker, 1985)

and Mesopotamia. Ethiopians traded overland as well, west across the Sahara to the gold- and salt-producing regions of the western Sudan. When the Aksumite kingdom declined around 800, its people left behind *stelae*: tall needle-shaped monuments crafted in stone using skills the original Arab settlers had brought from their homeland, as shown on p. 223.

Once a hospitable pasture, the Sahara had become, by the third millennium B.C.E., dry and waste. Its inhabitants dispersed southward, to the grasslands that stretched west to east across the continent, and farther south, to the rain forests of the center. Carrying with them their farming skills and iron tools, these Negroid migrants drove before them weaker tribes, hunters and gatherers still, who took refuge in remote pockets of the interior. Many of these migrants were ancestors of modern speakers of the Bantu languages that predominate today in sub-Saharan Africa. They lived in small communities dominated by "big men," leaders of extraordinary wealth in wives, children, and cattle, who could therefore command local obedience.

Caucasoid Arabs and Berbers (now Muslim) dwelling far to the north on the Mediterranean shore took control of the Sahara. Though a desert, the Sahara served as a highway (its main vehicle the camel caravan) from the African interior to Mediterranean and Indian Ocean ports. The caravans journeyed to the Sudanese kingdoms in western Africa, in the grasslands south of the Sahara called the Sahel, where resources of gold, other minerals, and agricultural products encouraged the successive growth, after 900, of three native African civilizations.

These were the three kingdoms of Ghana, Mali, and Songhay, which from about 500 through the 1500s dominated in turn the region between the Niger and Senegal river valleys of the western Sudan. Ruled by revered and powerful kings, who claimed to be in touch with a multitude of deities, these autonomous African states developed advanced administrative machinery and military strength. Exchanging Saharan salt for gold and other goods, Arab traders brought these commodities to Mediterranean ports to exchange them in turn for Asian and European products. A by-product of trade was religious conversion; Islam became securely planted as the religion of the western Sudan.

On the east African coast of the Indian Ocean (from modern Somalia to Mozambique), cities established by native Bantu migrants during the first millennium C.E. participated in the brisk trade that developed after 1100 between the Mediterranean zone, India, and east Asia (see Map 8.3). Islamic Arab merchants acted as intermediaries, whose architecture and language left their stamp on African civilization—especially on the Swahili language, which predominated in the region. Arab trading ships sailed the Indian Ocean, following the prevailing winds, in a pattern that intensified as India also became drawn into the sphere of Islamic civilization. The commercial sector of the east African coast stimulated the growth of interior kingdoms, like that of Zimbabwe, which supplied ivory and other tropical products to merchants for re-export to distant ports.

Unity and Disunity in India

Soon after 200 B.C.E., the northern Indian Empire established by Chandragupta Maurya fragmented (see Chapter 2). For 500 years thereafter, the Indian subcontinent possessed no single unified state. Instead, many regional kingdoms and principalities developed, whose elites practiced diverse forms of a religion now called Hinduism and shared a sacred literature recited orally on ritual occasions and recorded in classic Sanskrit (accessible only to a literate and exclusive few). Amid this diversity of political and cultural forms, commerce flourished. The merchants of India exported fine cotton cloth, pearls and exotic woods (teak and sandalwood), iron and copper, gold and silver. They transshipped spices and silks from eastern Asia to ports on the Red Sea and the Persian Gulf, and overland to Mediterranean depots. The prosperous coastal cities of India, in turn, were a lure to the fleets that set out from Arabia and Africa across the Indian Ocean.

Around 320 C.E., the Gupta dynasty established a unified Indian state in the same part of India—the Ganges River valley—that had given birth to the earlier Mauryan Empire. Gupta kings ruled a belt of territory extending from the Indus in the west to the Bay of Bengal in the east. Their empire lasted about two centuries, falling prey in the fifth century C.E. to nomadic invaders, the Huns. By the mid-sixth century the Guptas had retreated to their homeland on the Ganges and abandoned the west to the invaders. Thenceforth, until the establishment of the Muslim Mughal Empire after 1526, India was once again the home of multiple states and kingdoms, no one of which dominated the whole of the subcontinent. Despite political disunity, cultural life (which had reached a new height under Gupta patronage) continued to flourish all the same in a true golden age.

In the first millennium C.E., Indian culture achieved its classic stage. Brahman scholars preserved and studied ancient Sanskrit literature (see Chapter 1). Respected teachers of that Vedic tradition, called *gurus*, taught the male children of the three upper castes of Indian society. Girls of the elites often learned to read and write, and some composed literary works (see p. 218). Indian sages wrote on law and political theory, in which they distinguished between just and unjust conquest and exhorted kings to rule justly. Astronomers determined that the earth rotated on its axis and calculated the length of the solar year, while mathematicians calculated the value of *pi* and laid the basis for the decimal system of numbers.

Hinduism also flourished in the post-Mauryan period. The caste system became increasingly complex as new peoples and occupations were assigned their niche in the hierarchy and as the Brahmans exercised their dominance. The gods of the northern region, now a vast pantheon composed of Aryan and non-Aryan deities, spread to the south as well. Among the populace below the elite, religious devotions increased in form and earnestness, as temple-building proceeded vigorously and worshipers undertook frequent pilgrimages to offer homage to their gods. Of the many deities revered in ceremony and incarnated in sculpture, two stood out: Shiva, the storm god, creator and destroyer of the universe; and Vishnu, whose incarnations as Rama and Krishna were the subject of epics. The fertile goddesses of earlier antiquity returned, usually represented as consorts of male deities. Hinduism dominated Indian culture from the Mauryans in the fourth century B.C.E. until the arrival of the Muslim Moghuls in the sixteenth century. It overshadowed the Buddhist and Jain traditions, while at the same time absorbing the ideas of these faiths.

Meanwhile, Buddhism, which had prospered under the patronage of the Mauryan king Asoka, splintered thereafter into many sects, among which two main branches emerged: the "Greater" and "Lesser Vehicle," Mahayana and Hinayana. The Hinayana, closer to the original form of Buddhism, traveled on Indian trade routes to Ceylon (modern Sri Lanka), the East Indies (the Malaysian archipelago and Indonesia), and Indochina. The Mahayana tradition, a more popular form of Buddhism, would have been in some ways unrecognizable to the founder. It admitted numerous deities (including the Buddha himself), centered around temple worship and rituals, and featured leaders called *boddhisattvas*: holy men committed to the service of humanity. Missionaries carried Mahayana Buddhism to China, Korea, and Japan, where it flourished after India itself had settled back into its native Hinduism.

Asian Arts

An Indian woman writing: *As Islam and Christianity, eastern or Roman, determined the course of the development of the arts in the Mediterranean region and in Europe, in Asia secular as well as religious matter informed architecture, sculpture, painting, and the decorative arts. This sculpture, tenth-eleventh century, is from Khajurāho, the capital of a small central Indian kingdom, and shows a woman engaged in writing. (Indian Museum, Calcutta)*

A Chinese view of Spring: *This Chinese landscape executed in ink and light color on silk was painted by Guo Xi in 1072 during the Sung dynasty. (National Palace Museum, Taipei)*

China and its Neighbors

China, once it was unified by the Qin dynasty, remained a centralized state for nearly 2000 years. Its political history is the history of a sequence of dynasties interspersed with briefer periods of fragmentation and discord. After the death of the last Qin emperor, Shi Huangdi, the Han dynasty ruled (with a brief interruption) for more than 400 years (206 B.C.E.–220 C.E.)—contemporary with Rome at its height. Han emperors (ruling, as they believed, by the mandate of heaven) reinforced the northern frontier, pressured by nomadic peoples whom they called "barbarians." At the same time, they extended China's boundaries west into Mongolia and Tibet, south into Vietnam, and northeast to Korea.

Han, Tang, Sung, and Yuan Dynasties Han rule was marked by economic well-being and cultural resurgence. Under the Qin, China had become the most populous nation in the world. Under the Han, population continued to increase to about 60 million—comparable to that of the Roman Empire. Foreign trade flourished, not only east (to Korea and Japan) and south (to north Vietnam), but west across Eurasia, traveling on the Silk Road through central Asia to the Mediterranean shore. Imperial agents supervised the silk industry, and the cloth served—as did coins or measures of grain—as a unit of value.

The great profits of foreign trade reflected domestic commercial and technological success. Canals joining the two river systems of the Yellow (Huang He) and the Yangzi reached the capital at Chang'an and made commerce safe and easy through the country's central corridor. Public granaries collected surpluses to cushion the impact of famines. Under the Han, the tax burden was less onerous and the justice system less harsh than under the Qin. Inventions included the wheelbarrow, the water lift (for irrigation), the stirrup, and paper. Made from rags, bark, and other cheap materials, paper soon spread throughout Asia, the Islamic world, and Europe.

Whereas the Qin had promoted the "legalist" school of philosophers as the most supportive of the imperial mission, Han emperors embraced Confucianism. The old books—those that had escaped burning by Shi Huangdi in 213 B.C.E.—were taken out of hiding, copied, and studied. Thereafter the precepts of Confucius became the official doctrine of the Chinese state.

Confucian works formed the body of knowledge that state officials were expected to master. Bureaucrats were required first of all to be scholars, trained in the Confucian body of ideas. "Exceptional work demands exceptional men," declared the emperor Wu Ti (r. 141–86 B.C.E.). "We therefore command the various district officials to search for men of brilliant and exceptional talents, to be our generals, our ministers, and our envoys to distant states." These scholarly paragons, trained in special schools, took rigorous examinations to qualify for government service: "Parents, however much they love a child," wrote a later poet, cannot ensure his future; "only the examiner can bring the youth to notice. ..." As a consequence of this strict training, Han officials and the Han state were the most efficient anywhere.

Confucianism was primarily an educational program which embodied high ethical ideals. It was not a religion, although in popular practice some sacrifices were offered to the ancient sage, and his memory was venerated. This popularized form of Confucianism coexisted with the religions of Han China, primarily Taoism and Buddhism. Taoism continued to attract adherents, with its nature mysticism and magical adjuncts and vague promises of immortality. Buddhism, a newcomer, also won many adherents, converted by Indian missionaries.

Japanese Buddhist temple complex: *This photograph shows the Buddhist temple complex at Horyuji, Nara, Japan, 670 C.E., one of the earliest Japanese Buddhist temple complexes. Surrounded by a wall, it included a lecture hall (Kodo) and a pagoda.*

Interest in Buddhism resulted in a classic work of contemporary description. Around 400 C.E., the Chinese scholar Fa-hsien journeyed to India. There he remained for ten years, in the company of Buddhist monks and scholars, copying their sacred texts, which he translated from Sanskrit into Chinese. Other scholars wrote history. The courtier Sima Qian (c. 145–85 B.C.E.) chronicled 3000 years of Chinese history in his *Records of the Grand Historian.* Ban Zhao (c. 32–102 C.E.) (a woman, the daughter and sister of historians) helped write a history of the reigning Han dynasty. She also wrote a treatise on female decorum, *Lessons for Women,* amid whose bleak prescripts she included a plea for the education of girls.

Nearly four centuries of political disorder followed the fall of the Han in 221 C.E., as a series of short-lived regimes (the "Six Dynasties") ruled different parts of China and nomadic peoples invaded through the northern frontier to settle in old Han centers. Confucian culture, in temporary eclipse, along with the centralized empire it supported, was overshadowed by Buddhism, which traveled along the trade routes from India. Taoism also resurged during this period of disunion.

By the late sixth century C.E., China was reunited under the brief Sui dynasty (581–618). For three centuries thereafter, the Tang dynasty (618–907) ruled a reconstituted China. Emperor T'ai-tsung (626–49) reformed the imperial administration and pushed the boundaries of China westward. His successor, the Empress Wu (r. 649–705), continued his work for more than fifty years, holding not only the title of ruler but (at least during the last fifteen years of her reign) real power in her own hands. China's westward movement finally halted in 751, when, at the Talas River, Arab Muslims defeated the armies of Empress Wu's grandson.

The Tang capital at Chang'an was a planned city, holding a million people, with another million in the immediate suburbs—by the eighth century C.E., the world's largest city. The imperial complex of office and palace occupied a precinct of several square miles in the north of the city, reached by a ceremonial road. From here, Confucian scholars governed the great expanse of China, while the emperor and his court enjoyed a luxurious way of life in the palace. "Behind those vermilion gates meat and wine go to waste / While out on the road lie the bones of men frozen to death," wrote the poet Li Po (701–762), who had lived at court before his own impoverishment and disgrace. The rest of the city housed residences, temples, gardens, and marketplaces where merchants from many nations exchanged their goods. Yet Chang'an was vulnerable. It was sacked, pillaged, and burned during the invasions that accompanied the destruction of the Tang regime in 907.

Anarchy reigned again until the establishment in 960 of a new imperial dynasty: the Sung (960–1279).

MUST READS

Travellers, Founders, and Commentators

Sima Qian (c. 145–c. 85 B.C.E.)	*Records of the Grand Historian*
Ban Zhao (c. 32–102 C.E.)	*Lessons for Women*
St. Augustine (354–430)	*City of God*
Boethius (c. 480–524)	*Consolation of Philosophy*
Procopius (c. 500–565)	*Secret History*
Gregory of Tours (538–594)	*History of the Franks*
Isidore of Seville (c. 560–636)	*Etymologies*
The Venerable Bede (c. 673–735)	*Ecclesiastical History of the English People*
	The Qur'an *The Arabian Nights*
Anna Comnena (1083–c. 1153)	*Alexiad*

The Sung set a new standard of government efficiency. Managed from the capital at Kaifeng, its bureaucracy was fed by about 200 graduates each year from Confucian schools. They represented the top 20 percent who succeeded in the elaborate examination system, now the only method by which a young man, even a prosperous one, could secure a government position.

Commerce thrived under the Sung. The growing fashion for tea drinking, begun in the eighth century C.E., necessitated the circulation of that product, as well as the development of fine porcelain (to which Westerners would give the name "china"), which joined silk as a major export commodity. The abacus, a Chinese invention, facilitated commercial transactions, and a water-powered bellows improved iron production. Continuing a pattern that had begun under the Tang, the center of Chinese prosperity and culture shifted southward. The cultivation of rice (a southern crop) edged out millet (the northern staple).

Other Chinese innovations included the compass, facilitating navigation on the high seas; the block printing press, permitting the publication of both books and money; and gunpowder, used for firework displays and not (until the fourteenth century) for military use. Cartography, medical research, and literature flourished. Some 5000 poets composed during the Sung centuries, while painters depicted the region's striking landscapes. A revived Confucianism dealt with metaphysical issues as well as politics and morals. Some women received an education from

their fathers and brothers—an asset valued for its future usefulness in raising their sons. Many Chinese women found that their position declined as marriage options narrowed. Among the elite, girls were made to bind their feet from an early age so that they would remain small and render the mature woman more sexually desirable—and less mobile.

The last Sung emperor died in 1279 in the final standoff between Chinese troops and Mongol armies. The Mongols were fierce steppe nomads who had, for 3000 years, menaced the Eurasian civilizations. In the thirteenth century, these herders of sheep and goats, survivors of the stark cold of their high plateau, mounted their shaggy horses to ride off in three directions: to China, where they successfully established the brief Yuan dynasty (1271–1368); to Islamic western Asia, where they settled in modern Afghanistan, Iraq, and Iran; and to Russia, where (called the "Golden Horde") they ousted the princes of Kiev and ruled for more than two centuries. By 1259 their vast empire reached from Asia Minor to the Pacific Ocean.

The Mongol armies were the best on earth at that time. Exceptionally mobile, organized in disciplined units by decimal principles, skilled in reconnaissance, spying, and communications over long distances, they could sustain themselves in the field on long campaigns, their reserves of horses providing milk, blood, and meat. From the Chinese, they learned to make catapults and incendiary missiles. From the Turkic-speaking, Muslim Uighur, their neighbors on the central Asian plain, they learned to write. From their native customs they developed one of the great premodern law codes, the Yasa, which dealt sensibly with criminal, commercial, and civil matters. It ensured that the Mongols' ferocious conquest led to effective political settlement.

Gifted leaders were the key factor in the initial success of the Mongol advance. Raised in conditions severe even for a Mongol, the warrior Temuchin was appointed chief by his fellows in 1206 with the title of "universal leader," or Genghis (or Jenghiz) Khan (1167–1227). Genghis was the first leader of the Mongol invaders who seized much of Asia in the thirteenth century. His grandson Kublai (r. 1260–1294), the fifth Great Khan, completed the conquest of China. In 1267 Kublai Khan removed the Mongolian capital from the western outpost of Karakorum (its ruins situated in the modern Mongolian People's Republic) to the vicinity of modern Beijing. There, in 1275, he welcomed the Venetian merchant Marco Polo and his companions. Polo's account of his Chinese journey is the first landmark of the western European encounter with Asia. Meanwhile, although China succumbed to the Mongols, the Mongols did not disturb the refined patterns of Chinese customs and governance. Chinese influence continued even under these alien rulers to spread powerfully to the neighboring peoples of east and southeast Asia.

Map 8.4 The Chinese world, seventh to eighth centuries: *While in western Europe, after 500* C.E., *Roman civilization was in retreat, the Chinese empire proceeded, to expand its influence in east Asia. This map of China under the T'ang dynasty shows the area directly dominated by China, and the areas under its military, cultural, and economic influence. The inset map shows T'ang expansion into the rich trading zone of the south China sea and, some centuries later, the path that would be taken by Mongols originating in central Asia when they swept into and came to dominate the empire.* How was China able to dominate, and accultrate, its neighbors to the east, west, and south?

China's Neighbors in Asia and the Pacific   From the first centuries C.E., Chinese influence transformed the lives of the simple hunting, fishing, and farming peoples of Korea, Japan, and north Vietnam. Both Korea and Japan formed independent states on the Chinese model. Korean institutions adhered strictly to Chinese patterns. Confucianism was deeply entrenched, and the Chinese system of writing, and for centuries even its language, was employed for official documents and laws. By contrast, Japanese civilization, although permeated by Chinese influence (transmitted by Korean intermediaries), was not wholly determined by it. Here warrior nobles from great court families dominated, their lives of leisure inspiring an abundance of literary and artistic works. These aristocrats circulated around an emperor alternately revered and resisted, whose claim to legitimate rule was buttressed by his supposed descent from an ancient sun goddess. In Japan, Buddhism was more successful than Confucianism. Originally the home of **Shintoism**, a traditional polytheism of nature spirits and ancestor worship, Japan developed a rich Buddhist culture which accommodated native religious customs. A Japanese Buddhist temple complex is shown on p. 219.

In north Vietnam, Chinese overlordship shaped a culture based on Chinese patterns, which informed its government, arts, religion, and language. In other parts of Indochina, Indian culture—brought by merchants and missionaries, not conquerors—had a great impact. The greatest religious center of the region was Hindu, not Confucian or Buddhist; this was the huge temple complex at Angkor Wat, built in the twelfth century C.E. by Cambodian kings. Even when freed from foreign domination, the kingdoms of Indochina remained within either the Chinese or the Indian cultural zone.

Off the Asian coasts on Pacific islands and archipelagoes lived peoples isolated from the advanced civilizations of the mainland. Beginning as long as 35,000 years ago, but according to other models perhaps only 5 to 6,000 years ago, migrants from southeast Asia ventured into the Pacific Ocean to settle in island homelands: the East Indies (including the Malaysian and Indonesian archipelagoes) and the Philippines, Australasia and Melanesia, Micronesia, and Polynesia (collectively Oceania). Meanwhile, other Asian peoples crossed the Siberian land-bridge to the Western Hemisphere, where they continued migrating throughout its two vast continents (see below, and Chapter 16). As a result, by about 1000 C.E. the habitation of the globe had reached its zenith. People were planted in all parts of the globe where the human race still makes a home.

Inhabitants of Indonesia, poised between the Indian and Pacific oceans, supplied Indian and Arab traders with spices and other exotic products from at least the first millennium C.E. Inhabitants of the Philippines began to come into contact with advanced civilizations from the fourteenth century, and those of Australia did so from the seventeenth (see Chapter 16). But those on the remote islands of the Pacific, wholly isolated, remained until modern times at a Stone Age level of culture.

American Migrations and Civilizations

Asian hunters migrated across the land-bridge between Siberia and Canada as long as 36,000 years ago, although many experts argue only in the last 20,000 years. They were in pursuit of the big game herds that wandered the tundra of North America. As the glaciers of the last Ice Age receded, they continued to move southward and eastward. In Mesoamerica (modern Mexico and Central America) and in northwest South America around 7000 years ago, some of the natives learned to cultivate maize (corn) and potatoes, the staples of the Amerindian diet. Population increased, languages multiplied, and organized societies developed around religious cult centers, headed by priests.

Map 8.5 shows the early development of Amerindian civilizations. The oldest, that of the Olmecs, began to take shape around 1200 B.C.E. and reached its height by 400 B.C.E. These people inhabited the fertile southeastern tail of Mexico. Although the Olmecs did not develop cities, they did have lively commercial networks and a system of writing. Olmec society had priests, who supervised the building of large pyramidal earth mounds as worship centers, and aristocrats, whose rich possessions were buried in their tombs. Its farmers lived in huts, grew maize and beans, and made clay pots and tiny statues. We do not know who created the most stunning monuments of the Olmec world: giant human heads, with lifelike features carved of stone and looming up to 9 feet (2.7 m.) tall on the flat lowlands.

After Olmec civilization faded, soon after reaching its zenith, other cultures flourished in Mesoamerica and elsewhere in the Americas. Temple complexes high in the Andes (modern Peru) and the artifacts found in the villages of the Adena-Hopewell culture (in the midwestern United States), the multistory residences (or pueblos) of the southwest, and the ceremonial mounds of native Mississippian farmers all testify to the presence of advanced societies in the Western Hemisphere long before the arrival of European conquerors after 1492. The more advanced peoples of Meso- and South America used metal and developed writing, formed stratified societies and practiced elaborate religious rites. These were the precursors of the most brilliant of the early Amerindian civilizations: the Mayan, which began to form in the Yucatán peninsula (modern Mexico and Guatemala) in the last three centuries B.C.E. It flourished later during a "classic" phase, from about 300 to 900 C.E., which paralleled the formative years of western

A Roundup of World Monuments

Stonehenge, England, c. 2100–2000 B.C.E.

Remote from the Eurasian centers of civilization, other peoples engaged in monumental architecture. Great structures, wonderfully expressive by their massive size and simple forms, were created by the inhabitants of ancient Britain, the Mayans of the Americas, and the Ethiopians of Aksum. Here are shown Stonehenge (right) on Salisbury Plain in England; the stepped pyramid at Tikal (below) in present Guatemala; and an Aksumite pillar in East Africa (below right).

What do these ancient monuments have in common with each other, and with the ziggurats (see p. 15) and pyramids (see p. 14) of the Mediterranean region?

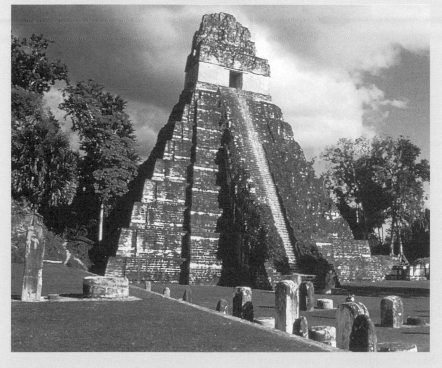

Tikal, Guatemala, before 800 C.E.

Aksumite pillar, East Africa, fourth–fifth century

 To continue your investigation of this topic, please go to www.prenhall.com/king for the related **WINDOWS** on the **WEB** activity

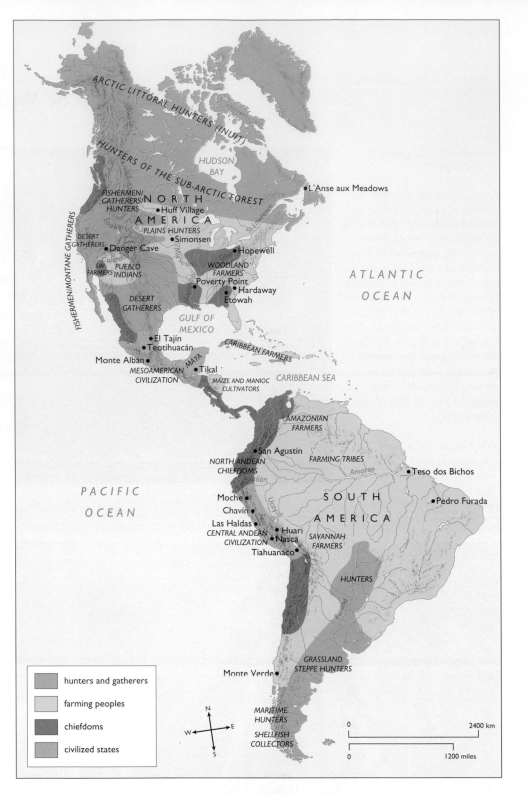

Map 8.5 A World Apart: Amerindian Cultures and Civilizations, to 1000: *By the year 1000, the Western Hemisphere was home to hundreds of Amerindian societies ranging in development from Stone-Age cultures to civilizations possessing writing and advanced metallurgical skills, and speaking vernaculars belonging to more than twenty unrelated language families. Though the classical Mayan civilization had passed its zenith by 1000, the Mayan and Andean cultural zones continued to be centers from which high skills were diffused to surrounding areas. In those two zones, the Aztec and Inca civilizations would emerge in the fifteenth and sixteenth centuries, on the brink of the era of European (particularly Spanish) conquest (see Chapter 16). Why did advanced civilization develop only in Mesoamerica and the Andaean regions?*

European civilization, and endured through a decline that extended into the seventeenth century. Its descendants survive to this day in Yucatán.

Heirs to Olmec civilization, the Maya developed an efficient agricultural system involving extensive irrigation projects to produce the maize that was central to their diet and way of life. Maize surpluses permitted the development of elites: nobles, priests, warriors, merchants, and artisans, whose responsibilities were not directly related to agricultural production. This complex society supported a rich intellectual and artistic life.

The Maya invented an ideographic system of writing which has recently been deciphered—the only natives of the Western Hemisphere to do so. The Spanish invaders found many Mayan writings—and destroyed many. Bishop Diego de Landa (c. 1524–1579), whose eyewitness account of the Spanish conquest of Yucatán in the 1500s survives, reported seeing many books written in their strange (to him) characters: "And, as they contained nothing in which there was not to be seen superstition and lies of the devil, we burned them all … which [the natives] regretted to an amazing degree, and which caused them affliction."

Despite the efforts of the conquerors to destroy them, quantities of Mayan writing exist.

The Maya developed a calendar based on the 365-day solar year that was more accurate than the one then used in Europe. They possessed advanced mathematics which included the concepts of place value and the all-important zero. They built bustling cities and huge stepped pyramids on the high inland plateau of Yucatán as shown on p. 223. They left traces of their artistry in stone and plaster sculpture and vivid murals featuring, alongside scenes of gaiety and celebration, other scenes of violence and victory and human sacrifice. Organized in a grid pattern encompassing homes for rich and poor as well as temples, courts, and markets, their central city of Teotihuacán housed a population, around 600, of some 125,000. Its largest structure was the mammoth Temple of the Sun, larger than the pyramids of Egypt. Smaller step-pyramids abounded, in the capital itself and at scattered sites obtruding from the cover of jungle foliage. The Maya's cities mysteriously disappeared, along with most other vital features of their civilization, after around 900. But their heritage lived on in later Amerindian cultures, such as the Aztecs defeated in every way by Cortés (see Chapter 16), and among their distant posterity, who survived the later Spanish conquest despite its cruelties, and even today preserve their identity.

Conclusion

THE ANCIENT WORLD, ITS LEGACY, AND THE MEANING OF THE WEST

By the end of the first millennium C.E., the human species had made an appearance in every part of the globe hospitable to human life. Advanced civilizations were established on five of the seven continents— all but solitary Australia and frigid Antarctica. From their centers travelers, peddlers, refugees, conquerors, and slaves carried the arts of civilization to human communities around the planet. Of these communities, those of Europe were among the poorest—lacking the sophistication and wealth of the Byzantine, Islamic, and Chinese empires, the formidable strength of the Mongols. But they stood poised for an explosion of cultural energy that would soon boost them to the front rank of nations.

Today Europe encompasses, among others, the nations of Great Britain and France, Belgium and the Netherlands, Spain and Sweden, Hungary and Poland, Russia and Italy. In the years following the disintegration of Rome, Europe was a backwater, and these nations did not exist. They would emerge over the centuries that extend between antiquity and the era of European mastery: the period Europeans call the Middle Ages.

Those years after antiquity—the Middle Ages—begin with the "triumph of barbarism and religion" and end with the transformation of Europe in the era of the Renaissance and the Reformation. They span almost one thousand years. During those years Europe would create the civilization called "Western": grounded in the experience of antiquity yet profoundly original. The elements of which it was formed were preeminently two, both ancient in origin: a religious tradition rooted in Judaism and developed as Christianity; and a cultural tradition deriving from Greece and elaborated by Rome. Those two distinct traditions blended throughout the early history of the West, whenever Christian intellectuals embraced with renewed vision the Greco-Roman heritage. They did so at peak moments, the first of which occurred as early as the eighth century C.E.

A Frankish king presided over that cultural renewal, the leader of one of the warrior tribes who had penetrated Roman defenses, and a successor to Clovis with whose momentous conversion this story began. The king was Charles the Great (in French, Charlemagne; in Latin, Carolus Magnus). And the renewal is named, after him, the Carolingian Renaissance. Its makers reached back into the past whose experience was concretized in church liturgy and in libraries. These scholars gathered at the king's court in Aachen (in modern Germany; Aix-la-Chapelle in French) with their leader Alcuin of York (c. 732–804), director of the palace school. They organized the copying and distribution of books, so that new generations could learn to preach the word of God and manage the business of the king.

In the libraries of the Frankish kingdom trained monks copied the works of Cicero and Seneca and others. They did so in a clear and lucid script (the Carolingian minuscule) which is the ancestor of the type used in the printed books of the Western world. More, they punctuated the text (as the Romans never had) for sense, and adorned the margins with splendid and ebullient paintings called "**illuminations**." Their manuscripts (the word means "written by hand") were bound between hard covers and were the first true books. Scattered over Europe, these books were the principal source of subsequent Western thought. Barbarism and religion may have triumphed, but the legacy of Greece and Rome, poured by the careful and loving hands of Christian monks into the vessels of their books, was never lost.

QUESTIONS TO CONSIDER

1. Why did the Germans settled within and on the borders of the Roman Empire not share the Roman understandings of law, justice, and the state?

2. Why was the compilation of Justinian's *Corpus Iuris Civilis* around the turn of the sixth century C.E. so important a moment of political and intellectual history? To what extent are the norms of a society preserved in its laws?

3. Why did Islamic scholars incorporate Greek philosophy in their own theoretical works of philosophy, science and medicine, and what was the effect of the incorporation of Greek thought?

4. Why did India remain, despite the rather brief periods of Mauryan and Guptan unity, largely disunited into the modern era, while China maintained a highly centralized state?

SUGGESTED RESOURCES

Armstrong, Karen, *Islam: A Short History* (New York: Modern Library, 2000). Synopsis of the whole history of Islam, from the flight of the prophet Muhammad to encounters with the West in the modern era.

Bulliet, Richard W., *Islam: The View from the Edge* (Cambridge: Cambridge University Press, 1993). An interesting synthesis of Islamic social history, arguing that local developments are, in the final analysis, more important than central political history.

Chaudhuri, K.N., *Trade and Civilization in the Indian Ocean: An Economic History from the Rise of Islam to 1750* (Cambridge: Cambridge University Press, 1997). Compact history of the trade networks across the Indian Ocean, demonstrating the lively mercantile interactions of Asians, Arabs, and others.

Evans, J. A. S., *The Age of Justinian: The Circumstances of Imperial Power* (London: Routledge & Kegan Paul, 1996). A history of the reign of Justinian, with attention to the theological issues that split the empire and left deep divisions after Justinian's death.

Fairbank, John King, *China: A New History* (Harvard: Belknap Press, 1992). Comprehensive, up-to-the-minute history of China from antiquity to the present.

Herrin, Judith, *Women in Purple: Rulers of Medieval Byzantium* (Princeton: Princeton University Press, 2001). Studies three fascinating empresses of the eighth and ninth centuries who ruled like men and shaped imperial policy.

Keay, John, *India: A History* (New York: HarperCollins, 2000). A comprehensive historical portrait of the many peoples and civilization of India from the ancient Harappan culture to modern times.

Liebeschuetz, J. H. W. G., *Decline and Fall of the Roman City* (Oxford: Oxford University Press, 2001). Looks at building, bureaucracies, finances, and culture, to trace the decline of the Roman cities after 400 C.E.

Munro-Hay, S. C., *An African Civilization: The Axumite Kingdom of Northern Ethiopia* (Stanford, CA: Stanford University Press, 1989). A solid introduction to the ancient Aksumite Kingdom, based on recent archaeological discoveries, literary evidence, and inscriptions.

Sharer, Robert J., *The Ancient Maya*, 5th ed. (Stanford, CA: Stanford University Press, 1994). The standard account of the first mature American civilization.

Treadgold, Warren, *A History of the Byzantine State and Society* (Stanford: Stanford University Press, 1997). Overview, especially good on the processes of Christianization and related cultural change.

Wallace-Hadrill, J.M., *The Barbarian West: 400–1000* (New York: Barnes & Noble, 1998). Useful overview of the different groups of tribal peoples settled in Europe and their interactions during the whole of the late ancient and early medieval periods.

Wells, Peter S., *The Barbarians Speak: How the Conquered Peoples Shaped Roman Europe* (Princeton: Princeton University Press, 1999). Uses a range of archeological evidence to reconstruct the culture of the Celtic and German peoples as they observed and responded to the Roman advance.

History of Islam, with timeline, and discussion of current events in Islamic world:
http://members.nbci.com/romaioi/women.htm

A brief chronology of Islam (Northpark University):
http:/campus.northpark.edu/history/WebChron/Islam/Islam.html

Byzantine civilization, sources, and links:
http://members.nbci.com/romaioi

Byzantine women:
http://members.nbci.com/romaioi/women.htm

Introduction to the civilization of India:
http://www.interknowledge.com/india/index.html

A brief history of China, with timelines (University of Maryland):
http:/www-chaos.umd.edu/history/toc.html

A guide to major Mesoamerican civilizations (University of Minnesota):
http://www.harappa.com/har/har0.html
http:www.angelfire.com/ca/humanorigins/index.html

◉ Western Civilization Documents CD-ROM

6.1 Portrait of a Visigothic King
6.2 Corpus Juris Civilis
6.3 The Koran
6.4 Baghdad: City of Wonders
6.5 A Christian's Description of the Mongols

PART THREE

THE WEST TAKES FORM

Medieval Society, Politics, Economy, and Culture (500–1500)

9 Workers, Warriors, and Kings
Politics and Society in the Middle Ages, 800–1500

10 The Spiritual Sword
Religion and Culture in the Middle Ages, 500–1500

11 In the Name of Profit
Cities, Merchants, and Trade in the Middle Ages, 1000–1500

Peasants and nobles created the society of the European Middle Ages. As Roman institutions crumbled and waves of invaders destroyed communities, medieval peasants devised new patterns of agricultural work and life, generally on the manors, or large estates, of noble landholders. The nobles, as an elite group of military men, warded off invaders and struggled among themselves for power.

Amid the bounds of mainly local authority, the first European kingdoms emerged, and kings employed violence and persuasion to assert their authority over nobles. The Crusades sent knightly armies east to the Levant (Palestine and Syria, on the eastern Mediterranean shores), while knights who stayed home at court developed the rituals of chivalry. In the late medieval centuries, which were gripped by famine and plague, peasant rebellions against landholders were frequent.

Providing cohesion to the disparate communities of Europe was the Catholic Church, centered in Rome under the pope, whose authority was at its height around 1300 after a process of reform, centralization, and resistance to the encroachments of secular rulers. A powerful Church summoned Christians to respect celibacy, the priestly administration of the sacraments, and the examples of saints and martyrs; and it disciplined those who strayed from orthodoxy. Providing access to libraries and schools, the Church trained most of Europe's intellectuals, who elaborated a rational system of theology and laid the foundations for modern philosophical, political, legal, and scientific thought.

As monarchical and ecclesiastical institutions crystallized, a new social group and setting emerged: merchants and towns. By 1300, towns stretching from the Mediterranean to the North Sea coasts housed artisans, merchants, bankers, and entrepreneurs. By 1500, their commercial ventures, extending to Africa, the Middle East, and Asia, made Europe rich and ready to expand.

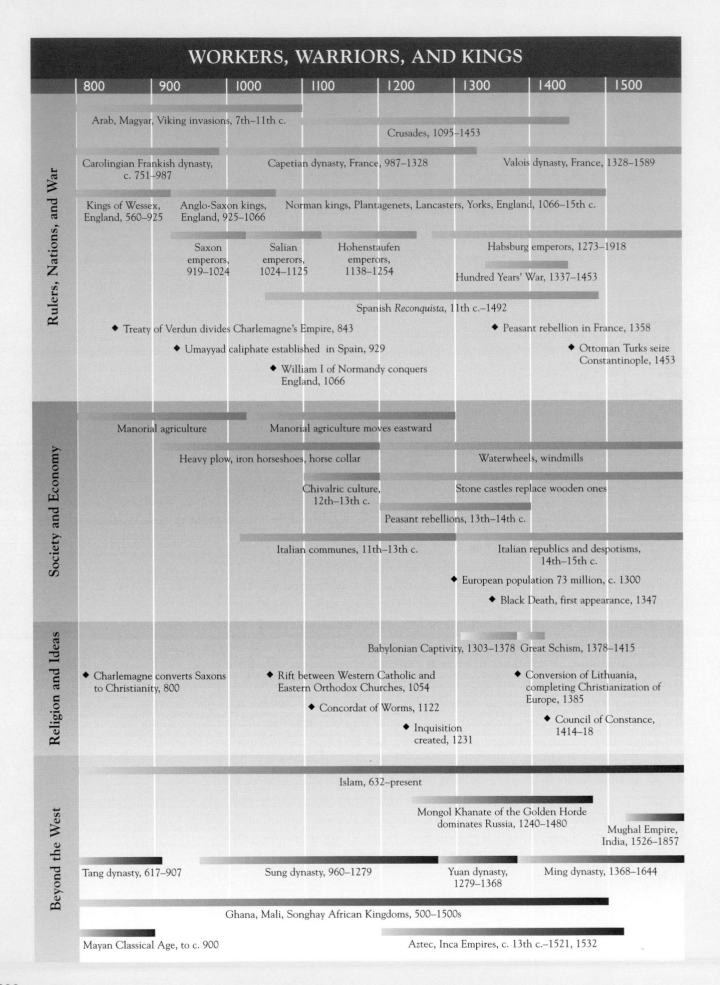

WORKERS, WARRIORS, AND KINGS

	800	900	1000	1100	1200	1300	1400	1500

Rulers, Nations, and War

Arab, Magyar, Viking invasions, 7th–11th c.

Crusades, 1095–1453

Carolingian Frankish dynasty, c. 751–987

Capetian dynasty, France, 987–1328

Valois dynasty, France, 1328–1589

Kings of Wessex, England, 560–925

Anglo-Saxon kings, England, 925–1066

Norman kings, Plantagenets, Lancasters, Yorks, England, 1066–15th c.

Saxon emperors, 919–1024

Salian emperors, 1024–1125

Hohenstaufen emperors, 1138–1254

Habsburg emperors, 1273–1918

Hundred Years' War, 1337–1453

Spanish *Reconquista*, 11th c.–1492

◆ Treaty of Verdun divides Charlemagne's Empire, 843

◆ Peasant rebellion in France, 1358

◆ Umayyad caliphate established in Spain, 929

◆ Ottoman Turks seize Constantinople, 1453

◆ William I of Normandy conquers England, 1066

Society and Economy

Manorial agriculture

Manorial agriculture moves eastward

Heavy plow, iron horseshoes, horse collar

Waterwheels, windmills

Chivalric culture, 12th–13th c.

Stone castles replace wooden ones

Peasant rebellions, 13th–14th c.

Italian communes, 11th–13th c.

Italian republics and despotisms, 14th–15th c.

◆ European population 73 million, c. 1300

◆ Black Death, first appearance, 1347

Religion and Ideas

Babylonian Captivity, 1303–1378 Great Schism, 1378–1415

◆ Charlemagne converts Saxons to Christianity, 800

◆ Rift between Western Catholic and Eastern Orthodox Churches, 1054

◆ Conversion of Lithuania, completing Christianization of Europe, 1385

◆ Concordat of Worms, 1122

◆ Inquisition created, 1231

◆ Council of Constance, 1414–18

Beyond the West

Islam, 632–present

Mongol Khanate of the Golden Horde dominates Russia, 1240–1480

Mughal Empire, India, 1526–1857

Tang dynasty, 617–907

Sung dynasty, 960–1279

Yuan dynasty, 1279–1368

Ming dynasty, 1368–1644

Ghana, Mali, Songhay African Kingdoms, 500–1500s

Mayan Classical Age, to c. 900

Aztec, Inca Empires, c. 13th c.–1521, 1532

CHAPTER
9
WORKERS, WARRIORS, AND KINGS

Politics and Society in the Middle Ages

800–1500

KEY QUESTIONS

◆ **Workers:** What kind of work did medieval workers do? What obstacles did they face?

◆ **Warriors:** Why was a warrior class needed in the Middle Ages? How did they prepare for their role, and how did they occupy their leisure?

◆ **Kings:** How did medieval kings manage to enhance their authority? Why were some more successful than others?

Piers, the Plowman *The peasant hero of* The Vision of Piers Plowman *(probably by the fourteenth-century English poet William Langland, c. 1330–c. 1400) bewailed in eloquent verse the world's injustice and his own poverty: "I have no penny," he cried, when Hunger asked for an offering, "to buy pullets, nor geese nor pigs," but only the food of the poor—cheese, beans, grain. The poor, Piers lamented, are like "prisoners in cells ... charged with children and overcharged by landlords."*

> *What they may spare in spinning they spend on rental,*
> *On milk, or on meal to make porridge,*
> *To still the sobbing of the children at mealtime.*

The fictional Piers represents many millions of workers who could not always feed themselves or their children; for hunger haunted Europe during much of the Middle Ages (as it did most people in all regions of the world before modern times). Yet, over the seven centuries from the age of Charlemagne to that of the Renaissance, a new and vigorous civilization emerged. It devised systems of agriculture appropriate to the damp, heavy soil north of the Alps. It molded the social groups needed to perform its work, to defend its boundaries, to create laws and administer justice. As its social and political organizations crystallized, Europe reconstructed its networks of commerce and generated ideas and cultural institutions. Thanks to these achievements, by the beginning of the sixteenth century, Europeans were in a position to dominate the world stage.

The foundations of this greatness were laid, to a great extent, by members of three social groups: the agricultural workers known as serfs and peasants; the warriors, who constituted the class of nobles; and the kings, who consolidated their authority and forged the framework of the modern nations of Europe. (The contributions of other—**clergy**, scholars, and merchants—will be examined in later chapters.)

WORKERS

Of the achievements of the Middle Ages, those in farming were the earliest and most fundamental. They were accomplished by peasants, who made up 90 percent or more of all Europeans. These workers invented the techniques of medieval agriculture, felled forests for settlement, and built stable village communities. They also launched rebellions, increasingly frequent, of those who worked against those who commanded.

Serfs, Peasants, and Poverty

In the early Middle Ages, until about 1200, most peasants became serfs, dependent laborers on their masters' lands. After that time, many serfs in western Europe were able to win their freedom. In the east, the process worked in reverse; there, by the late Middle Ages, after about 1300, many previously free peasants were enserfed.

As in antiquity, peasants had to struggle to produce the minimum necessary for survival. The soil was stubborn and unpredictable. To yield crops, it had to be loosened with a stick or a plow—a wooden or iron blade that scratched or sliced or turned the earth and was drawn by human or animal power. Even when soil was manipulated in this way, it still needed enrichment—from decayed plant matter or manure dropped by animals or spread by workers. It needed watering, by nature or by human artifice, by rain or flood. At times the earth was stingy. The rains did not come, or they washed away the topsoil, or the sun did not warm the growing crops. At such times during the Middle Ages there was **famine**, and the peasant and his family might starve to death. If they survived, they might fall victim, in their weakened state, to an **epidemic**.

Nature imposed these hardships of stubborn soil, bad weather, and disease. Human beings imposed others. Landholders, whose extensive properties protected them from the starvation and, to some extent, the disease that threatened the ordinary laborer, added to the peasants' suffering. The landholder might lend seed or lease tools to the peasant in exchange for a share of the crop. The price for that assistance was high: one-third or one-half of the yield. In good years, the peasant paid his due. In bad years, he fell into debt. Then he was likely to become a serf.

The agricultural economy of medieval Europe was characterized largely by the phenomenon of serfdom. A serf was neither free nor slave. Many were the descendants of late Roman peasants and slaves. By the last centuries of the Roman era, many peasants had already fallen into a desperate condition, forced into dependency by the relentless demands of landholders and tax collectors. These oppressed smallholders of late antiquity were called *coloni*, in Latin, or "settlers"; they were peasants who had surrendered their freedom in order to gain the right to stay on the land and farm it. Unlike slaves, they could not be sold, or even removed from the land they had bargained sacrificially to win. But neither could they leave and seek a different occupation, or richer soil, elsewhere. Meanwhile, slaves escaped their servitude. Amid chaos and disintegration, they ascended, ironically, to the condition of serfdom.

As invasions hammered Europe and public institutions disintegrated, thousands of former slaves and formerly free peasants turned to landholders, with whom they made contracts of serfdom. They and their descendants, they promised, would labor on the great man's land and contribute to his stores specified "dues," defined as quantities of crops and animals or labor service. In exchange, they and their

January page of a calendar showing plowing, eleventh century

The heavy plow, which could dig deep and turn over dense northern soils, was the key to medieval agriculture. This illustration (above) from a manuscript calendar shows a plow drawn by four oxen.

Compare this with a modern sketch of the medieval mechanism (below).

The ridges and furrows arrayed in strips characteristic of medieval agriculture are revealed in this aerial photograph of an English field at Padbury (right).
(top: British Library, London; right: Cambridge University Collection, England)

What effects might the invention and use of the heavy plow have had on medieval economy and society?

Padbury, England

To continue your investigation of this topic, please go to www.prenhall.com/king for the related **WINDOWS** on the **WEB** activity

231

descendants, they were assured, could count on certain services performed by the lord. He would protect their right to the land, provide justice, and defend them from invaders. The promise of protection lured peasants to surrender their freedom and assume the dues and burdens of serfdom.

Although most medieval peasants became serfs, some remained free, and some who had been serfs won their freedom. Free status persisted where the lords were not so powerful. In parts of what is today Germany, or in the sparse, hilly land on Europe's northern fringe, there were few great landowners, and free ownership of land by peasants remained common. In modern France and England, in contrast, where powerful lords dominated nearly all available land, serfdom advanced swiftly. But in these lands the early establishment of governmental authority and an official administration of justice made possible its equally quick decline. After about 1200, French and English serfs were able to sell a surplus or market a skill. They purchased their freedom and were serfs no longer. Farther east, even in those areas where the free ownership of land had previously been common, peasants subsequently were pressed into serfdom.

Working the Land

During the early Middle Ages, the serfs of northern Europe worked soil that was more difficult to till, but also more fertile, than the land around the Mediterranean. A series of innovations in plowing and managing the soil made European agriculture productive.

North of the Alps, the soil demanded a different pattern of land cultivation from that common in the ancient civilizations ringing the Mediterranean Sea. The Mediterranean climate was warm, the soil thin, but easily cultivated with a lightweight plow, the terrain hilly. Here the olive tree and vine were the major crops, while grain was imported from fertile Egypt and Sicily. To the north, the climate was cool and wet, the soil heavy, damp, and deep, the land a forested plain from the Atlantic shore eastward into modern Russia. Once the forests were cleared, that rich and well-watered plain was suitable for growing grain. The peasants of this region developed new techniques to meet the demands of climate and topography.

By about 1000, they had developed a heavy plow, called the moldboard plow, the key to Europe's future prosperity. Drawn by a pair of yoked oxen or a team of horses, this powerful implement pierced the tough skin of the northern soil, sheared the grass at the roots, turned the sliced soil, and mounded it alongside the deep furrow (see *Windows On*, p. 231). The deep cultivation of the soil accomplished by the heavy plow permitted the intensive cultivation of grains. By the beginning of the fourteenth century, thanks to this invention, grain yields had climbed to a peak that would not be surpassed until the eighteenth.

To mill the grain, serfs used human or animal power, but also that of waterwheels (and later, windmills), described in *Witnesses* on p. 235. Although known to antiquity and in the east, waterwheels were first fully exploited by medieval peasants. On the land of the monks of Saint Germain-des-Prés (in modern Paris) as early as the ninth century, 59 water-driven mills were operating. In 1086, the agents of King William the Conqueror of England counted 5624 mills in 34 English counties. Later in the Middle Ages the wheel's power was used for brewing, fulling of cloth, and papermaking. The last of these processes, though invented by the Chinese and spread by Muslims, was mechanized only by Europeans.

Oxen are strong but slow workers; horses are brisk and dependable. But the ancients, who harnessed their horses the way they yoked their broad-shouldered oxen, never were able to utilize horsepower effectively. The horse hauling a full load was strangled by his harness. By the ninth century medieval peasants had learned to employ a device imported from the Asian steppes—a rigid, padded collar. Equipped with such a collar, the horse could pull heavy loads without choking. At about the same time, peasants began to equip their beasts with another device, also Asian in origin—iron shoes nailed to the hoof. Now teams of horses with armored hoofs and hitched in teams could work faster than the cheaper, clumsier ox. Energetic horses freed human labor, which could now be applied to tasks requiring skill and intelligence. And peasants who lived scattered about within an ox's stroll of their fields began to cluster in villages, where they developed a rich rural culture that persisted well into modern times.

Another useful innovation was neither a machine nor a device but a method—that of **fallowing**. Peasants learned that planting the same crops on the same fields year after year inevitably resulted in the impoverishment of the soil. Leaving one-half of the soil idle, or fallow, for a season enriched it. This practice allowed nutrients to be reintroduced through the normal processes (which people then lacked the scientific knowledge to understand) of the decay of vegetable matter and the interaction of elements in the soil with those in the air.

In some regions, peasants developed a more refined fallowing process, the three-field system, as shown on p. 233. They left only one-third of the land fallow. They planted a second third in winter with a staple but soil-depleting grain, and the final third in the spring in an alternate crop (often one of the legumes, whose roots release soil-enriching nitrogen, such as peas, beans, alfalfa, acacia, and peanuts). The peasants' collective decision to leave one-third of their land fallow won them better yields and more robust health. These fallowing techniques were possible only for those peasants of northern Europe who dwelled on the region's great plain. In the Mediterranean climate,

The Three-Field Cycle

	1st Year				2nd Year				3rd Year			
	W	S	S	F	W	S	S	F	W	S	S	F
Field 1	🌱🌱🌱	🌱🌱🌱	🌱🌱🌱	⌐		🌱🌱🌱	🌱🌱🌱	⌐				🌱🌱🌱
Field 2		🌱🌱🌱	🌱🌱🌱	⌐				🌱🌱🌱	🌱🌱🌱	🌱🌱🌱	🌱🌱🌱	⌐
Field 3			🌱🌱🌱	🌱🌱🌱	🌱🌱🌱	🌱🌱🌱	⌐			🌱🌱🌱	🌱🌱🌱	⌐

Winter Planting 🌱🌱🌱   Spring Planting 🌱🌱🌱   Harvesting ⌐

Medieval peasants developed the three-field cycle of plowing, sowing, and harvesting that maximized the yield from northern Europe's heavy soil and cold, damp climate. Here are depicted an "ideal" or "typical" manor, with three fields divided into strips capable of being plowed in a single pass, and a calendar showing the staggered tasks required in the three fields.

there was insufficient rainfall for a spring crop of legumes to supplement the winter yield of wheat.

This rich soil and these technical innovations made Europe a producer of grain sufficient not only to sustain population levels but even to support population growth. By 1300, Europe had achieved a prosperity that would not be surpassed for centuries.

Manor, Village, and Household

The rotation of fallow and cultivated land, and of grain and legume crops, characterized a medieval plantation, often called a **manor**. Although there was no "typical" manor, most in the prosperous regions of western Europe possessed—in addition to open

Peasant labor: *The biblical Adam and Eve are depicted in this stone relief from the façade of the cathedral in Modena, Italy, early twelfth century. They have just been expelled from the Garden of Eden and are now at work, hoeing.*

fields—forest, common grazing lands, a manor house with the lord's demesne, or private land, and one or more parish churches and peasant villages.

The lord's house was normally the largest structure on the manor. Often it was fortified and called a **castle**. In the early years, the castle was a plain wooden tower. By the thirteenth century, it was an imposing stone pile (if the proprietor was wealthy) containing a spacious hall and kitchen, for feeding large numbers of people, a private chapel, and various bedchambers. In some cases the manor "house" was actually a monastery, inhabited by a community of monks (see Chapter 10). The Church controlled a significant portion of the land of Europe. Its monasteries governed that land much as did the medieval lord. Monks, pledged to poverty under the rule of their abbot, warehoused crops and directed the labor of serfs. The great monastery of Bobbio, in northern Italy, for instance, had 650 serfs in its employ.

The other structures on the manor formed the village: the one-roomed houses of the serfs, the church, and a mill to grind essential grain. Around these stretched blocks of land divided according to purpose: first, common land for the grazing of the animals of all members of the community; second, forest reserved for the lord and his peers and for the peasants' pigs, who rooted for nourishment on its floor; and third, open fields, the pattern for medieval cultivation.

The requirements of the plow encouraged the patterning of the land into great open fields, divided into long, narrow strips. These strips, visible in the photograph in *Windows On* on p. 231, were as long as possible, so that a plow could move in one direction without turning, and as narrow as the swath the plow cut through the soil. An individual serf might have the right to the produce of various strips of land scattered over the fields—some in fallow, some in grain, some in low, wet land, some in high, light soil.

While certain strips were assigned to each peasant for the sustenance of his household, others were reserved to the lord of the manor for the stocking of his storehouses. But all were worked by teams of peasants who cooperated in providing the tremendous labor demanded by the heavy plow. This organization of agricultural production was adapted to the needs of the laborers and the nature of their tools.

The manorial organization of agriculture prevailed in the level and well-ordered lands of northwestern Europe—France, England, and western Germany. On the northern, eastern, and southern fringes of Europe's central plain—among the Celtic peoples of Iceland, Ireland, Scotland, and in northern Scandinavia, in Spain, the Balkans, Russia, and eastern Europe—this system failed to gain a foothold. These areas continued to suffer invasions, or remained outside the zone of Latin Christianity longer, or were too hilly for the use of the plow. Here free peasants on lone farms or in scattered hamlets scraped what they could from the soil or tended sheep and goats.

A manor was a community of laborers subject to the rule of the lord or the abbot, and his agent, the steward. These masters demanded contributions in kind of plant or animal produce, as well as labor dues, which consisted of farming the lord's demesne, building and mending the manor's roads and walls, clearing forest, hauling goods, or personal service. The goods and services required of the laborers varied from master to master and from manor to manor. So did the style of the landholder's exactions—fair and equitable in some cases, abusive in others.

Some of the laborers on the manor were engaged in work other than farming. A prosperous manor had its own blacksmith, who made the few necessary iron implements: plowshares (the part of the plow that cuts the furrow) and hoes, hammerheads and chisels, knives and pots. The miller was another key figure, one whose honesty was critical: Did he return in flour all the grain that was brought to the mill, less the small share that was his pay? The steward might be a member of the lesser nobility, but occasionally he was drawn from the peasant population. He might exercise his considerable power for his own advancement as much as for the benefit of the landholder.

The manor had to clothe itself as well as feed itself. In medieval Europe, as nearly everywhere else, women performed the work of producing textiles—generally wool or linen—for clothing. Peasant wives, grandmothers, and daughters carried on the perennial tasks of spinning and weaving and sewing. On small manors they worked in their huts. On larger manors, they produced textiles for the use of the whole population in a central workshop called the *gynaeceum*, or "women's quarters"—a term derived from the Greek word for the women's quarters of a citizen's house (see Chapter 3). That earlier gynaeceum, too, had among its other functions the responsibility for textile production.

Serf women also assisted with farmwork—even with the heavy plowing, although they more often

Country Life

The moments of medieval rural life sketched here give some idea of its variety and dynamism. The first passage shows Frankish King Charlemagne ordering an inventory of his manors. The second depicts a waterwheel in operation. The third describes an uprising of discontented peasants.

Charlemagne orders his stewards to make an inventory of his manors (c. 800): We desire that each steward shall make an annual statement of all our income, ...; of the pigs, of the rents, of the obligations and fines; ... of the mills, of the forest, of the fields ...; of the hay, firewood, torches, planks and other kinds of lumber; of the waste lands; ... of the wool, flax and hemp; ... of the hens and eggs; of the geese; ... of the colt and fillies. They shall make all these known to us, set forth separately and in order, at Christmas, so that we may know what and how much of each thing we have.
(Charlemagne, *De Villis*; trs., ed. J. H. Robinson, 1904)

A monk describes the working of a waterwheel which provides power to mill grain and full cloth: The stream first hurls itself impetuously at the mill where ... it strains ... to crush the wheat beneath the weight of the millstones, then to shake the fine sieve which separates flour from bran ... One by one it lifts and drops the heavy pestles, the fullers' great wooden hammers. ... How many horses would be worn out, how many men would have weary arms if this graceful river, to whom we owe our clothes and food, did not labour for us. ...
(From J. Gimpel, *The Medieval Machine: The Industrial Revolution of the Middle Ages* 1976)

The peasants of northern France rise up in revolt (1358): They banded together and went off, ... unarmed except for pikes and knives, to the house of a knight who lived near by. They broke in and killed the knight, with his lady and his children, big and small, and set fire to the house. Next they went to another castle and did much worse; for, having seized the knight and bound him securely to a post, several of them violated his wife and daughter before his eyes. Then they killed the wife, who was pregnant, and the daughter and all the other children, and finally put the knight to death with great cruelty and burned and razed the castle. They did similar things in a number of castles and big houses, and their ranks swelled until there were a good six thousand of them.
(Froissart, *Chronicles*; ed., trs. G. Brereton 1968)

Back in the village, they brewed ale from barley, milled grain, baked bread, cooked and preserved foods by salting or drying, and tended small garden patches of vegetables and herbs. Their housekeeping tasks were minimal because their huts had dirt floors, no windows, few implements other than the cooking pot, and scarcely any furniture beyond a table and some stools.

In these rude huts the peasant family gathered after work for the brief leisure before sunset and sleep. They ate a supper of bread—of wheat, if they were fortunate—which was the largest part of their diet, perhaps accompanied by a soup or stew of vegetables flavored with garden herbs; only the rich had spices. Peasants in the north drank beer; in the south, wine. Occasionally they ate cheese from sheep, goats, or cows. They ate meat rarely, and then most often pork or mutton from the superfluous or elderly beasts slaughtered before the onset of winter, when no fodder could be spared to feed them. In those unlit evenings they may have told stories to entertain each other, creating and transmitting the folk traditions of Europe. They slept together, parents and children—generally not on a bed, an expensive item of property. Children alert enough to do so witnessed the sexual relations between their parents or others in pairings of which no record remains.

In this casual manner, children learned all the things they needed to know for the course of their short lives. The death toll was especially high in the first year or two of life. Those who survived infancy were quickly integrated into peasant existence. They followed their mother in her work until they were old enough to perform small tasks, such as feeding the chickens, rounding up the sheep, carrying messages. By eight or nine, boys and girls learned the ways of adult work from, respectively, their fathers and mothers. Adolescence as we know it today—a time of turmoil when the young person constructs his or her future social identity—did not exist. Childhood flowed into adulthood as skills matured and strength grew. Adult lives were scarcely longer than the course of childhood, as life expectancies hovered around 30 or 40 years, much like in Ancient Greece—barely half that of the modern North American or European (although those who survived infancy and epidemic might live into old age).

The flowing continuity of peasant life unfolded in a regular sequence from generation to generation. The rhythm of the seasons determined the framework of plowing, sowing, maintaining, harvesting, and storing from spring to autumn, and, in the harsh winter, of making and repairing tools to prepare for the spring. The celebrations of the church punctuated the rhythms of agricultural life. Saints' days littered the calendar, numerous enough to serve the same purpose as modern weekends. On these days, work ceased, and the villagers gathered for festivals as boisterous as their stores of food and drink allowed.

gathered hay or carefully gleaned the scattered kernels of grain left behind by teams of male harvesters. They brought their babies with them into the fields, or let their toddlers run on the **common** while they and the older children watched the sheep or fed the chickens.

Map 9.1 Settlement and Invasion, 700–1300: *From 500 to 1000, Romanized and Christianized Europeans settled down to cultivate their lands. Beginning around 700, they were beset by waves of invasion from the north, east, and south: by Vikings originating in Scandinavia; by Magyars and Mongols originating in central Asia; and by Arabs originating in North Africa. By 1000, many of the invaders were absorbed into the European culture, and Europeans themselves began a steady advance outward from their center: south into the Iberian peninsula in the first phase of the "Reconquest"; eastward through Germany, then east and north into the Slavic regions on the Baltic sea. What might explain the European urge for expansion after the year 1000?*

In a world where even the landholder was generally illiterate, the medieval serf received no schooling. The manor priest, often as ignorant as the peasants, offered little instruction but performed the rituals that led the way from birth to death. Knowledge and poetry, customs and beliefs, and the fruits of experience lived in songs and stories told by mothers to children, who matured rapidly and might die swiftly, but not before they had repeated the stories and sung the songs to the next cohort of the young. From generation to generation, that wisdom and that ignorance survived, distilled in adages and tales and in the melodic fragments that have inspired much of the Western musical tradition. These folk traditions would yield to the printed book and, in the nineteenth century, to mass education, and many, apart from those recorded by scholars, would disappear.

Expansion, Crisis, and Protest

Parallel with the seemingly changeless pattern of village life, many changes were, in fact, taking place. After around 1200, western Europe experienced dynamic growth, underwent economic crisis, suffered the devastations of the plague, and saw frequent outbreaks of peasant rebellion.

The biggest change was the increase in population, as indicated in *How Many* on p. 237. The productivity of the land, tended by the plow and nursed by fallowing, and greater prosperity, meant that people live a longer; that healthier mothers, fertility enhanced by ample diets, gave birth to more children; and that children more often survived. From around the year 700, when Rome had withered but Charlemagne had not yet begun his work of cultural renewal, to around

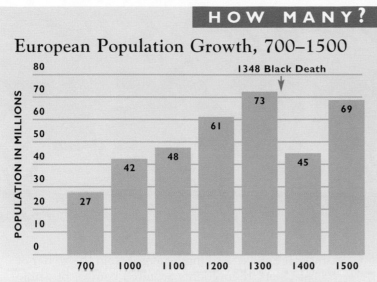

European Population Growth, 700–1500

1348 Black Death

The European population sagged from a high during the Roman Empire around 200 C.E. to a low during the seventh to ninth centuries. It then surged forward around 1000 to a new peak just before the onslaught of the Black Death. Having then lost a third to a half of its population, and still vulnerable to new outbreaks of plague, the European population recovered slowly and had not yet reached its pre-plague high before the end of the Middle Ages.
Source: B. H. Slicher van Bath, *The Agrarian History of Western Europe*, A.D. 500–1850 (New York: St. Martin's Press, 1963).

in eastern Germany. Claiming the wilderness for the plow was the epic tale of medieval agriculture, and the peasant was its hero.

The explosive growth of western Europe halted around 1300. The years that followed brought cycles of famine and disease. The most serious famine was the prolonged one of 1315–1317, in part the result of an epochal cooling of the climate. In these years, cold, wet winters were followed by cool, sterile summers. Famine paved the way for disease, culminating in the terrible onslaught of the Black Death, which ravaged Europe from south to north in 1347–1351 and would recur in every generation until the eighteenth century.

The Black Death took so many lives that a labor shortage developed in some regions, benefiting, ironically, the peasants who survived. They could now negotiate a good price for their labor. Many bargained for freedom, and won. Others began to dream of bettered conditions, and some began to risk their lives to fight for them. While hopes of change swept through their communities, peasants armed with their simple tools revolted against their lords—most dramatically in France and England.

In 1358, peasants in parts of France rebelled against the imposition of ever-higher taxes and other burdens. Tales of rape and torture, murder and cannibalism reached the royal court in Paris, which was itself threatened by an urban revolt (see *Witnesses*, p. 235). In 1381, English peasants, aroused by the peasant priest John Ball (d. 1381), joined in an uprising that flourished in the southeast region of that kingdom. Most peasant rebellions had as their objective the amelioration of farmers' contracts with their lords, rather than the dismantling of the apparatus of lordship. Ball reached further, preaching the equality of all people, in an age unready for such claims. He urged the confiscation of church lands and their redistribution to peasants, and the abolition of serfdom. For his revolutionary activity, Ball was imprisoned several times; but his message found an audience.

In June 1381, an angry mob under the peasant leader Wat Tyler (d. 1381) marched on London, where the king resided, plundering the mansions of the privileged that lay in their way. They released Ball from prison. The king and his retinue met Tyler and his men for negotiations, in the course of which Tyler was slain. By mid-July, Ball was hanged, his corpse mutilated in judicial revenge, and his protest silenced.

Clasped in the rhythms of nature, slaves of the soil and servants of the landholders, the peasants produced the first wealth that fueled Europe's expansion. By the end of the medieval era, a few began to ask a fundamental question—silenced at the time, but not forever: By what right do some rule, compelling others to obey?

the year 1300, when medieval Europe reached the height of its prosperity, its population grew from approximately 27 million to 73 million. The growth of the advanced European centers is impressive. Between the arrival of William the Conqueror (1066) and the plague called the Black Death (1347–1351), the combined population of England, Scotland, and Wales tripled, reaching a peak of between 5 and 6 million. During that time, France grew to 20 million persons, not far short of its population at the outbreak of the French Revolution in 1789 and one-half its population in 1940 at the beginning of World War II. Even the poorer eastern regions experienced population growth. Poland, for instance, grew dramatically from 1.25 million to 3.1 million between 1340 and 1580. This increase in population was largely due to the labor and initiative of the peasant.

Territorial expansion followed upon population growth. Prodded by their lords, the peasants of western Europe undertook the enormous task of clearing for cultivation the forests and swamps of the eastern region. At the beginning of the Middle Ages, most of Europe was wilderness. Only the fields within the boundaries of the old Roman Empire were regularly cultivated. Many of these reverted to waste during the years of invasion. Around 800, the emperor Charlemagne launched an eastward migration with the conquest of German Saxony and its forced conversion to Christianity. Around 1000, Europeans completed the conquest of the soil within the western region and began pushing the boundary of the zone of settlement to the Elbe River and beyond to the Oder

Nobles Armed for War

Fighting with the lance: *War was a nobleman's job. Until the nineteenth century, the possession of a sword announced elite status—an attitude inherited from the Middle Ages when only noblemen could afford armor, weapons, and horses. On these pages are images of armed nobles. The eleventh-century Bayeux Tapestry colorfully depicts the Norman conquest of England (1066). The section shown reveals the defining characteristics of medieval knights: they are armored, they ride horses, and they wield long spears called* **lances.** (Bayeux Tapestry Museum, by special permission of the City of Bayeux)

WARRIORS

The masters of the land (apart from clergy) constituted, according to region, between 1 percent and 10 percent of the population. These were the nobles of Europe, those men who possessed the tools of war and the skill to use them. Their military skills enabled them to snatch the greater part of the power, status, and wealth that could be accrued in a world bereft of cities and schools and dominated by chaos. They seized command of great chunks of Europe's land, claiming them by birthright, by the commission of a higher lord, or by simple force. These lands they defended from invaders as warlike as themselves. Once possessed of Europe's land, they guarded their wealth and strove to pass it undiminished to their heirs. Like other elite groups, they developed their own code of values and sponsored a cultural program suited to their position. These were the values of chivalry and a culture of the court.

Nobles, Knights, and Lords

Over some five centuries, as the Roman state died and no new one could take form, Europe suffered recurrent invasions of warriors from the east, south, and north, as Map 9.1 shows. In this vacuum of authority, the first European nobles performed the single most essential governmental function: that of defense. Granted the right to do so by kings, or claiming that right by virtue of their strength, they assumed judicial and other administrative functions as well. The lands they possessed they also governed, claiming the obedience and dues of their serfs. Nobles without land did not govern, but they did fight, offering their skills and their counsel to lords greater than they and forming part of these great lords' households and retinue. In time, nobles took steps to secure heritable title to their lands within their branch of their family.

The medieval nobles were the counts or "companions" of the chiefs of the Germanic tribes that spread through Europe. As kings emerged from the welter of tribal chiefs, their counts acquired control of whole regions ("counties") on their behalf, where they administered justice and executed royal decrees. As a reward for such services, they were granted land; for money—if there was any available—was of no use where there was little commerce. Other nobles were assigned to hold border areas, or marches, and were entitled "marquess" or "marquis." Others, called "dukes," were usually rulers of small regions, not quite kingdoms. Beneath the duke, marquess, and count (in England, an earl) were their loyal supporters, who followed them in battle and formed the lesser ranks of the nobility: viscounts, barons, and **knights**.

From duke to knight, all of these nobles were essentially warriors, and all fought on horseback. Beginning in the eighth century, they adopted a distinctive mode of warfare. It depended on the development of the stirrup, an invention of the nomads of the great Asian plains, which reached western Europe around 730. With his feet in stirrups, the horseman more easily held his seat. He could withstand a thrust from a mounted opponent attacking even at full force. Instead of throwing his spear at his enemy, he could hold it firmly under his armpit, knowing that the powerful momentum of horse and rider would give his spear's (or lance's) piercing tip a more deadly power. From the eighth through the fourteenth centuries, cavalry outstripped infantry, and the mounted warrior, or knight, ruled the land.

The knight rode to war on his horse and wielded, as his chief weapon, not the sword of the Romans but a lance, a long sharpened wooden spear held extended as he charged into battle. The power of a charging horseman armed with a lance was formidable—the medieval equivalent of a modern tank with blasting guns. Squadrons of knights encountering each other in this way fought until they were unhorsed, or their lances splintered or were wrested from their hands. A vest of interlinked chains—"chain mail"—might protect them from the assault of the lance (later in the Middle Ages, plate armor offered more protection). If captured alive they were generally ransomed. Payment was made to the victor by the vanquished knight's family, lord, or friends.

Knights fought in wars, and even when there was no war. They honed their skills in the uncleared forests, the nobleman's preserve. Their dogs and hawks helped these idle soldiers track deer and wild boar in a perpetual war against nature (one effect of which being that nobles dined excessively on meat). Alternatively, knights without real wars to fight might engage in mock ones. Tournaments, staged in times of peace by noblemen or kings, were more than sporting events; they were a form of controlled warfare. Groups of knights attacked each other in a melee that resembled the chaos of battle. In the joust, the predecessor of the duel, one knight faced another in personal combat, the outcome of which might decide an important issue. Only toward the end of the Middle Ages did the lance and sword of the knight begin to yield—though it survived in the ritualized tournament—to the longer range and fearful power of the projectile crossbow, longbow, and gun.

Nobles in general were fighters. Many, in addition, held land. A few held high judicial and administrative authority, granted by a ruler. These three sources of noble privilege—military service, land tenure, and administrative authority—were distinct but intersecting. Only a few nobles possessed all three assets, while many boasted only their military standing.

Men considered noble because of their military role actively sought to acquire land, the major source of wealth in the Middle Ages. They might possess it absolutely, in freehold, or might have the right to use and dispose of the products of the land granted to them by another noble, a king, or an agent of the Church. Although that right was not equal to possession, noble tenants often achieved the same end by making the right itself permanent and heritable by their descendants. Thus nobility, originally the professional order of military experts, came to be, in effect, a class of hereditary landholders.

From the twelfth century, as professional jurists in Italy began the task of recovering and reinterpreting Roman law for medieval social conditions, a technical language was fitted to the arrangements of noble land tenure. Land held by a noble in **usufruct** and

granted by another noble, or a king or an agent of the Church, was often called a **fief**. The nobleman receiving the fief was then called the **vassal** of the person or institution granting it. In exchange for the fief, he owed military and administrative services. Sometimes the fiefholder was wealthy and powerful; granted a large and lucrative fief, he was obliged in return to administer this large territory, and his military obligation consisted of supplying a company of men. But sometimes he was only a knight or baron, whose small fief required him to provide his lord merely with "aid and counsel": personal military service and free advice.

The understanding between lord and vassal was between two persons of similar status who each expected to gain an important benefit. The lord acquired a soldier, adviser, loyal supporter. The vassal acquired land, the right to rule that land, and to take the yield from the labor of its serfs. The relation between lord and vassal was wholly distinct from that between lords and serfs, where the two parties were of widely different social status. The interlocking arrangements between lords and serfs and lords and vassals, demonstrated in the passages in *Witnesses*, below, are sometimes called (but with too great an implication of formal organization) the "**feudal system**" or "**feudalism**."

These terms are now best avoided because they give an impression of symmetry and order to social relationships that were quite unsystematic and forged,

WITNESSES

Vassals and Serfs

In the turbulent Middle Ages, individuals of all social levels might seek security and protection from powerful men. Rural laborers entering into such a contract might become serfs; modest landowners seeking out a patron became the "vassal" (the "boy") of that "lord" (the master of land and people). These two excerpts show a landowner assuming vassal status in the ninth century; and another winning freedom from servitude in the more prosperous thirteenth century.

A charter of Louis the Pious grants privileges to a faithful vassal (815): A certain faithful man of ours, named John has come before us and commended himself to us; and he has asked our permission to occupy and take possession of whatever our father and we ourselves have granted to him, together with possession of whatever he or his sons have occupied and possessed in the past. … And all these things he and his sons shall hold as a gift from us; they and their posterity shall hold them from us free from rent and free from all molestation.
(From R. C. Cave, H. C. Coulson, *A Source Book for Medieval Economic History*, 1936)

Richard, Abbot of Peterborough, frees a serf (1278): Let all know that we have manumitted and liberated from all yoke of servitude William, the son of Richard of Wythington whom previously we have held as our born bondman, with his whole progeny and all his chattels, so that neither we nor our successors shall be able to require or exact any right or claim in the said William, his progeny, or his chattels. But the same William with his whole progeny and all his chattels will remain free and quit and without disturbance, exaction, or any claim on the part of us or our successors by reason of any servitude, forever.
(From J. H. Robinson, *Translations and Reprints from the Original Sources of European History*, 1897)

in fact, in an environment of radical disorder. Medieval society was not so much a hierarchy as a web of interlocking rights and obligations; or, as one scholar has colorfully expressed it, not so much a layer cake, in which each social stratum retained a separate identity, as the English dessert called a trifle—"its layers … blurred, and the sherry of accepted values soaked through."

The desire to make land tenures heritable encouraged the reorganization of noble families. After about 1000, noblemen increasingly defined their kin on the male side alone. By emphasizing that agnatic lineage, they limited the numbers of claimants to property, and assisted them in preserving it intact for male heirs. Often only one son—generally the eldest, in the system known as **primogeniture**—was designated to inherit the bulk of landed property, while the others were assisted in gaining positions in the Church or as landless retainers of other nobles. Daughters were excluded from inheritance in those noble families adopting an agnatic definition of lineage. They were assigned a **dowry** in lieu of an equal share of the inheritance, sufficient to make them eligible to marry a man of acceptable rank, or to enter the religious life, for which a fee was required.

Noblewomen served the interests of their families by marrying or not marrying, as instructed. Unmarried, they could assist their families with prayers from behind convent walls, or even gain prominence as abbesses. Married, they served as links to other noble families whose political and military support could be vital. If the alliance formed by the marriage was no longer useful, the marriage could be dissolved (assuming cooperative clerics could be found to arrange this) and the young woman remarried to a more promising husband. Although women appear to have been much disadvantaged by these arrangements, in fact some noblewomen gained considerable authority under certain circumstances: as proprietors of noble courts; as **regents** (or political guardians of their minor sons); and as surrogate rulers in the absence of their husbands. Blanche of Castile was one such regent: from 1226 until 1236, she competently ruled France until her son Louis IX (destined to be one of the most effective of the French kings) ascended the throne. Women could not rule in their own right; but as surrogates for their husbands, they often demonstrated a complete capacity for leadership.

The administrative authority conferred with land tenure varied considerably. Noble landholders collected dues in goods and labor from their serfs. In addition, sometimes for fees stipulated in ancient contracts, they approved marriages, served as guardians for orphans and widows, and supervised the inheritance of land tenures upon death. The extent of a lord's right to rule varied. The knight who administered a manor could certainly punish a serf for theft, and could issue orders about the use of the mill or the

Dover Castle: *Castles began as defensive positions erected in the tumultuous ninth and tenth centuries when invasions were a constant threat. They began as mere mounds of earth; then they were constructed as mounds of earth topped with wooden towers. By the twelfth century, castles were built of stone, and those of the wealthier nobles were sometimes luxurious complexes which housed the lord, his family, and his many retainers. This photograph (left) shows Dover Castle in England, which was begun in the Norman period.*

maintenance of the road. A high-ranking nobleman with extensive lands might possess the right of "high justice," the right to punish wrongdoing with death. This right was symbolized by the presence on the manor of a gallows.

A great nobleman on his lands resembled a king in his kingdom—particularly at a time when kingdoms were tiny and kings frail. Such nobles housed their own retainers, who followed them in battle, and might ignore kings altogether when it suited them to do so. These great lords expressed their power in their castles. Originally built of wood, by the eleventh century of stone, these fortified structures featured a central tower, or keep, and outbuildings, the complex protected by ditches, moats, and gates. As indicated in the photograph of Dover Castle shown above. A garrison of their knights guarded the tower. When invasion threatened, nobles and peasants and animals sheltered within the strong walls and there survived the passing of the storm—or suffered sack and massacre if the castle were taken by force. By 1300 or 1400, castles sometimes resembled great stone cities, centers of administration as well as bulwarks against invasion. As kings became more powerful in the late Middle Ages, the noblemen's proud towers were sometimes razed by royal overlords who sought to draw all authority into their own hands.

Courts and Courtly Culture

Although they did not yet value reading and writing, the European nobility nevertheless developed a refined cultural code. As invasions ceased and prosperity increased, the courts of the higher nobles were sites for the nurturance of chivalric values, the sentiments of loyalty and love, and high standards of decorum. Elevation of thought and sentiment characterized the courts of the later Middle Ages, even

while these most privileged people lacked all the basic comforts that are now taken for granted.

Beginning in the 1100s, with the encouragement of the Church, of leisured noblewomen, and of the poets and storytellers who loitered about the great courts, the young noblemen who wandered from court to court in search of employment and adventure were challenged to learn something new. They were asked to become gentlemen, observers of the code of **chivalry**. "Chivalry" was a set of values proposed to soften aristocratic culture, otherwise centered on war and acquisition. It held rough warriors to standards of behavior enforced by sentiments of loyalty and honor. It designated certain groups worthy of protection—widows, orphans, noblewomen, clerics, noncombatants—and decreed that certain places and times—churches and holy days—were not to be violated by bloodshed. It insisted that noblemen loyally serve their lords and, equally, their ladies. For the first time in European history, women were raised to high status, in theory at least, and deemed worthy to receive special attention from men.

Noblemen who subscribed to the code of chivalry were considered to be "gentle" (hence our word "gentleman") and to exhibit "gentility." In time, gentility required medieval noblemen and noblewomen to adopt the forms of modern behavior embraced by the name of "civility." Customs now generally accepted as signs of proper behaviour in the Western world, such as using a handkerchief, deferring to another person at table or in a doorway, bowing, or shaking hands, derive from the patterns of behavior invented at the medieval court.

Chivalric values and the postures of civility coexisted with a still unrefined style of life. Life in a castle was more comfortable than life in a serf's hut; yet (by our standards) it was rude. Most of the activities of daily life took place within the great hall: a vast room, poorly lit, barely heated, and sparsely furnished. When times were good and the hunt was productive, food was ample—and so was drink. But amenities were few and privacy nonexistent. Until late in the Middle Ages, food was consumed without forks, only with knives and fingers; napkins evolved even later. The lord's family had separate sleeping quarters, but other courtiers found a bench or stretch of floor in the hall on which to spend the night.

In this austere setting, entertainers amused the company and celebrated the manners and exploits of their patrons. By the twelfth century, wandering poets called minstrels or troubadours sang epics of the exploits of heroic nobles in war or in love. This oral culture is reminiscent of early Greece when Homer composed his epics from the fragments of earlier poetic traditions. But the medieval epics were quickly written down, and their composers were master craftsmen (and occasionally craftswomen), concerned with the accurate transmission of their work.

Courtly Love The romantic love celebrated by the poets of the Middle Ages was a new phenomenon, called courtly love because it was cultivated in the grander courts of western Europe. Its nature is explained in *Witnesses* on p. 243. Courtly love was limited to members of the aristocracy and limited, in its life span, to the eleventh to thirteenth centuries (though its legacy endures today). It was characterized by the longing of a young man for an unattainable woman. The man was typically a younger son without property of his own, who sought advancement at court. The woman might be unattainable because she was socially superior to the longing knight, because her virginity could not be violated, or because she was already married. Most of the love relationships encompassed by the phenomenon of courtly love were adulterous, many were unconsummated, and many were fictitious. Far more real were the forgotten sexual encounters between noblemen and lower-class women, victims of rape rather than objects of adoration, and rarely the subjects of poems.

Why and how did the phenomenon of courtly love become established? And why is it important? Among several possible answers, historians often mention these. In an era of frequent warfare, the husbands of high-ranking noblewomen were absent for long periods, and vassals resident at their courts may have been tempted to think about obtaining their master's wife as a precious prize. Or perhaps the values of courtly love controlled and civilized the lustful impulses of vassals at court, bringing them to heel in obedience.

Courtly love is important because of its influence on all subsequent literature in the European languages. And this literature has shaped the Western tradition of romantic love. The yearning and the courting which were celebrated by a small social elite of the high Middle Ages, have for several centuries

been accepted by ordinary people as the normal course of events leading to a sexual relationship—with the significant difference that the relationship now often includes marriage. Thus, the experience of love as it is understood in the Western world was first explored by the medieval nobility.

Women enthusiastically promoted courtly love. The wives, mothers, and daughters of great noblemen encouraged the knights of their courts to listen to the troubadours, staged the contests of love that the cult encouraged, and were often the objects of the romantic obsessions of their vassals. Queen Eleanor of Aquitaine (c. 1122–1204), who was married in turn to the king of France and the king of England, was the granddaughter of a man who was not only a patron but a poet himself. She grew up amid the courtly games of love and knew them intimately.

Women and Power Courtly love intrigues might amuse a medieval noblewoman whose experience was much harsher. For most of their lives noblewomen were pawns in the political strategies of fathers and husbands. They were married, sometimes at young ages, to the nobleman or king with whom their father considered an association most advantageous. With puberty, they were expected to give birth, for all the years of their fertility—perhaps twenty-five, if not cut short by death in childbirth, the commonest cause of death for women of childbearing age.

Noblewomen did not breastfeed their own infants but employed wet nurses. As a result, they did not experience the contraceptive effects of lactation and could expect to face a rapid cycle of pregnancy, birth, and new pregnancy. The burden of reproduction was inevitable because of the social assumptions of European noblemen. Although a nobleman's wife brought him fine properties or valuable alliances, her most important function was to produce a male heir—one who survived the perils of childhood. If a wife failed to do so, her husband might renounce her, with or without the approval of the Church.

Although noblewomen were powerless to choose husbands, homes, and way of life, the circumstances of medieval life often gave them power. When their husbands were away, women acted as their surrogates and were accorded due respect. If the family castle were attacked while her husband was away at war, the noblewoman defended it, directing the troops and standing in the zone of the battle, as depicted in the manuscript illumination on p. 239. If her husband were held for ransom in another lord's prison, she could call his retainers to meet to give counsel, to reaffirm their loyalty, and to raise funds. Most notably, noblewomen could rule lands for years after the death of their lords, while a young heir grew to adulthood. Young kings, too, often learned their leadership skills from a mother who, as regent, governed the kingdom after the death of the monarch.

Noblewomen as Mothers and Lovers

Most medieval women—like most women throughout history—were mothers. Did they feel towards their children as mothers do today? The first two passages here suggest that they did. The first is by a ninth-century noblewoman who wrote a book to advise her exiled son, because she could not herself be with him. The second is by a prominent twelfth-century cleric, who fondly remembers his mother's affection for him. In contrast, the third passage concerns the passionate love between adult men and women, which medieval elites considered as existing only outside the institution of marriage.

The ninth-century noblewoman Dhuoda opens the book of advice written for her exiled son William: Having noticed that most women in this world are able to live with and enjoy their children, but seeing myself, Dhuoda, living far away from you, my dear son William, filled with anxiety because of this, and with the desire to be of aid to you, I am sending you this little manual, written by me, for your scrutiny and education, rejoicing in the fact that, though I am absent in body, this little book will recall to your mind, as you read it, the things you are required to do for my sake.
(From K. M. Wilson, *Medieval Women Writers*, 1984; trs. J. Marchand)

Abbot Guibert of Nogent (12th century) praises his mother: Yet you know, Almighty One, with what purity and holiness in obedience to you she raised me, how greatly she provided me with the care of nurses in infancy and of masters and teachers in boyhood, with no lack even of fine clothes for my little body, so that I seemed to equal the sons of kings and counts in indulgence. ...
(From J. F. Benton, *Self and Society in Medieval France: The Memoirs of Abbot Guibert of Nogent, 1064–c. 1125*)

In the words of Andrew the Chaplain (12th century), a nobleman explains to a noblewoman the nature of courtly love: But I am greatly surprised that you wish to misapply the term "love" to that marital affection which husband and wife are expected to feel for each other after marriage, since everybody knows that love can have no place between husband and wife. ... For what is love but an inordinate desire to receive passionately a furtive and hidden embrace? But what embrace between husband and wife can be furtive, I ask you, since they may be said to belong to each other. ...
(Andreas Capellanus, *Art of Courtly Love*; ed. J. J. Parry, 1941)

It was a fortunate mother who was able to nurture her young son at home. Many noblewomen saw their sons leave home at an early age to live in other households, as the passage reproduced in *Witnesses* above reveals. The child might be sent there to learn courtly graces and skills away from parental interference. In the early Middle Ages, especially, he often served as a hostage—his father having guaranteed a certain course of behavior by sending his child to live with a skeptical and possibly hostile lord. If the father failed to keep his promise, the child might be put to death, paying the price of his parent's duplicity. In such ways mothers often lost the company of their young sons. Their daughters more often stayed home, to learn from their mothers the skills of managing the intricacies of an aristocratic household until their own marriages.

In addition to the skills of conversation, household management, and defense, noblewomen acquired the traditional skills of textile production. Like peasant women on the manor, noblewomen spun thread and wove cloth. Whereas peasants wove the crude fabrics worn by ordinary folk, however, the lady created the fine tissues worn at court—embroidered and embellished or interwoven with silver or gold—and the bright banners held by knights in battle or a joust. One product of medieval women's needlework is the Bayeux Tapestry. When Duke William of Normandy ventured across the English Channel in 1066 to win the throne of England, the events of the conquest were recorded (tradition holds) by his wife and her companions on an embroidered strip of cloth (not, in fact, a tapestry) 230 feet (76 meters) long.

Defending the Kingdoms and the Faith

It was the nobleman's job to fight. It was a job he performed regularly, as medieval Europe was wracked by virtually constant warfare interrupted by respites of peace. Much of the fighting was internal, disruptive, and unnecessary, as nobles or kings competed with each other for land or advantage. Other warfare was necessary to defend the newly emerging communities of Europe against outsiders. Still other campaigns were fought to defend the interests, as it was thought, of Christians by rescuing the Holy Land from newly arrived Turkish overlords, or wresting the Iberian peninsula from Muslim rule, or completing the conversion of the peoples of Europe to Christianity.

Invaders The first struggles pitted young European communities against invaders from east, south, and north. From 500 to 700, while the memory of Roman rule was still vivid, Celts, Romans, and Greeks tried in vain to fend off Gothic and Vandal, Lombard and Frankish, Angle and Saxon invaders. Once settled, these erstwhile invaders in turn wheeled around to face new intruders: Avars (eventually destroyed), Slavs, and Bulgars, who settled down on Europe's eastern periphery. From 700 to 1000, new generations of combatants arrived to continue the onslaught.

The first of these were the "Moors," North African Muslims of mixed Arab and Berber descent (see Chapter 8). In 711 they moved northward into the

Count Dirk II of Holland and his wife, Hildegard, 940–970

European noblemen were deeply concerned with the continuation of their lineage. Their wives, noblewomen of equivalent birth and fortune, were partners in a conjugal unit upon which the future of the lineage depended. These images give a hint of the solidarity that could be achieved by the noble couple. This manuscript (above) shows Count Dirk II of Holland and his wife Hildegard jointly donating a book to the Egmont monastery.

This sculpture (right) shows the crusader knight Hugo I of Vaudémont locked in a single stone block with his wife.
(top: Koninklijke Bibliothek, The Hague; right: Musée des Monuments Français, Paris)

Why might women born into the noble households of their fathers have identified willingly with the lineage interests of their husbands?

Hugo I of Vaudémont and his wife, after 1163, Church of the Cordeliers, Nancy, France

To continue your investigation of this topic, please go to www.prenhall.com/king for the related **WINDOWS** on the **WEB** activity

244

Iberian peninsula (modern Spain and Portugal), which they quickly conquered. A century later, Arab invaders called, Saracens by contemporaries, struck at the southern coastline of Europe. They seized the island of Crete in 824 and thus confronted the Byzantine lords of the Aegean Sea. Three years later, Arabs conquered Byzantine outposts on the island of Sicily, effectively curtailing Greek influence in the western Mediterranean. Arab raiders had already helped themselves to numerous Mediterranean islands lying between Italy and Spain. From these posts they could contemplate further movements toward the mainland. The possession of these Mediterranean bases stimulated trade, which at first profited the conquerors but eventually benefited even the Europeans, whose ships traveled the ancient sea.

After 899, eastern Europe was attacked by the Magyars, ancestors of modern Hungarians who spoke a rare (non-Indo-European) Finno-Ugric language. These nomads raced across the Eurasian steppe as had the Germanic tribes and Huns before them. The Magyars' advance was stopped only by the combined forces of the Frankish king Otto I (r. 936–973) at the Battle of Lechfeld (in southeastern Germany) in 955. Like the Bulgars and the Slavs, the Magyars retreated a little eastward, settled and stayed.

In the 800s and 900s, the Vikings, or "Northmen," descended from the Scandinavian lands (modern Norway, Denmark, and Sweden). The Vikings were traders who roamed the Baltic and North seas and founded commercial depots on their coasts. When circumstances changed, they adapted easily to piracy. Spurred by poverty and overpopulation, they sailed swiftly along the shores of Europe in their elegantly designed long, shallow boats. Darting up rivers, deep into the centers of developing civilization, they raided, burned, and pillaged monasteries and villages, raping, kidnaping, and sometimes killing the inhabitants.

In time, the Viking incursions changed in nature. Instead of small groups of raiders, large armies arrived, headed by rulers seeking permanent settlement. In 911, one of these won from the cowering king of France a duchy of his own at the mouth of the river Seine— later known as Normandy. Another settled with his followers in a large section of eastern England (later designated as the Danelaw), and collected tribute from Anglo-Saxon peoples who had settled there not so long before. Others, mostly from Sweden and known as Varangians, journeyed down the Dvina and Dnieper river systems to settle in the western part of European Russia, where they established a capital at Kiev.

When the pressure of Viking incursions waned, European nobles proceeded to wage war against each other. These were profitable battles for clever landholders. They could build up their territorial holdings, their retinues, and their status. Over the generations, men of little property became great lords, and great lords fell to insignificance.

Crusaders Other noble warriors took part in a series of wars that would span three centuries and more, far from the European homeland. These were the Crusades (see Map 9.2), fought in the name of the cross on which Jesus had died in Jerusalem (and which pilgrims to that city used as an emblem on their clothing). Several circumstances combined to launch these wars of conquest. The embattled emperors of Byzantium, their own territories falling like dominoes to Turkish invaders, had requested assistance from the West. A newly vigorous, reformed papacy sought to extend the realm of **Christendom** and to arouse the faith of its followers. Italian traders, sparsely outfitted and meagerly supplied, sought to gain a presence in a Mediterranean dominated by Arab competitors. Landless knights, the younger sons of Europe's now-established nobility, sought land, adventure, and opportunities for advancement.

The event that triggered the first Crusade was the fall, in 1071, of the city of Jerusalem—holy to Christians, Muslims, and Jews—to the Seljuk Turks. An Asian people who had usurped the sovereignty of the Arab caliphs of Baghdad in 1055, the Seljuks had then advanced westward and northward. After their victory over the Byzantine army at Manzikert in 1071, they went on to conquer much of Asia Minor, the buffer between the Byzantine capital at Constantinople and the centers of Islamic civilization.

With Constantinople now endangered, the pope saw an opportunity to play a larger role in the eastern Mediterranean. In 1095 Pope Urban II issued a call to the nobility of Europe—not to defend the Byzantine remnant of the Roman Empire, but to recapture Jerusalem itself, as a Christian act meriting the remission of all sins. "God wills it!" shouted his followers. Large crusader armies set out under nobles ready to profit from any opportunities that battle afforded. In 1099 they captured Jerusalem, where they massacred both Muslim and Jewish inhabitants. Seizing the coastal strip that forms part of the modern nations of Syria, Lebanon, and Israel, the crusaders established states on a European model which would endure into the thirteenth century in the midst of a Greek, Turkish, Arab, and Islamic world.

When the crusader state of Edessa fell to the Turks in 1144, Church leaders launched the Second Crusade (1147–1148). It failed to achieve any useful end. The recapture of Jerusalem in 1187, by Saladin, the king of Egypt and Syria (r. 1186–1193), precipitated the Third Crusade (1189–1192), which was headed by three of Europe's monarchs: Frederick Barbarossa of the Holy Roman Empire, Philip Augustus of France, and Richard I, "the Lion-Hearted," of England. Little was accomplished. Jerusalem remained lost (although the theoretical right of pilgrims to visit that capital was assured), along with most other crusader possessions.

The major beneficiaries of the first three Crusades were the Italian trading cities who ferried supplies to

Map 9.2 Seljuk Advance and the Crusades, 1071–1204: *The Seljuk Turks, having defeated the Byzantines in 1071 at Manzikert, threatened Constantinople. European armies traveled east in successive ventures—the Crusades—beginning in 1096. The first arrivals established a short-lived Latin Kingdom in the Near East which had tremendous impact on European culture and commerce. In 1204, crusaders traveling eastward to recapture Jerusalem were diverted by Venetian paymasters to the conquest of Constantinople. What were the motivations of the Christians who took the long journey to the Levant in the First through Fourth Crusades?*

the troops. One of these, Venice, was the principal actor in the Fourth Crusade (1202–1204), which the Venetians diverted in 1204 to serve their own interests. With a ruthlessness at odds with every Christian precept, Venice employed the crusader army to capture, sack, and control Constantinople, the home of Eastern Orthodox Christianity and purported ally of the western European force. The result was—as Venice intended—to enhance its own commercial foothold in the eastern Mediterranean.

A bizarre variation on the crusading idea was the so-called Children's Crusade (1212), in which thousands of children, aged between ten and fourteen,

set off to retake Jerusalem themselves. Virtually all its little soldiers died or were taken into slavery long before reaching the east. Later Crusades gave opportunity for glory to eager noblemen, kings, and popes, but failed to reassert the dominance of Latin leaders. The whole crusade movement closed painfully and finally in 1453, when the Ottoman Turks (successors to the Seljuks) overran the region and seized Constantinople. Its magnificent church of Santa Sophia was converted into a mosque. The crusading spirit was not dead; it would reemerge in various guises in later European ventures against non-Christians all over the globe (see Chapter 16).

Although the Crusades did not succeed in their original objective—the permanent conquest of the Holy Land for Christendom—they had enormous consequences for the development of Europe. Knights and kings had contact with a world outside Europe, and learned much from an alien and in many ways superior culture. Italian ship captains and sailors took command of the Mediterranean Sea, and brought the luxury goods of Asia back to European ports while they mastered the techniques of international commerce. With the Crusades begins the opening up of Europe to the outer world which has continued steadily since that time.

By 1300, crusading zeal had slackened, while the nobility of western Europe had reached the zenith of its military prowess. Another great conflict—the Hundred Years' War (1337–1453)—absorbed the attention of the knights of France and England intermittently over the last years of the Middle Ages. It caused great devastation in France, while leaving the political situation little changed. England, the aggressor, possessed considerable French territory at the beginning of the struggle, only a foothold at its close. In 1453, devastated France set about to repair its wounds and reform its monarchy. The English then entered upon the debilitating Wars of the Roses (1455–1485), which saw rival claimants to the throne and their noble supporters savage each other over two generations, until in that country, too, rebuilding began.

One outcome of the Hundred Years' War was to retire the weapons and tactics of medieval warfare, and with them the assumption of knightly invincibility. They were surpassed on the battlefield in three signal contests all won by massed English infantrymen equipped with their native longbow. At Crécy in 1346, at Poitiers in 1356, and at Agincourt in 1415, the English defeated superior numbers of French. That third victory conveyed a lesson that the new French king, Charles VII (r. 1422–1461), at last absorbed. Before the curtain was drawn on the war in 1453, he had constructed a national army on the basis of infantry and artillery units. Between the English tactical innovations and the French model of military organization, modern warfare took root from the last stale conflict of the Middle Ages (see Chapter 15).

KINGS

In the early Middle Ages, warrior nobles had seized leadership at a time when chaos and invasion prevailed, often overshadowing the petty kings of Europe. Over the next five centuries kings emerged as sovereigns of the new nations of Europe. Seeking to maximize their own authority, these powerful leaders also sought to bring order to the fragmentary and quarreling communities of their region. They cobbled together orderly states by enlisting the cooperation of

nobles and commoners. In doing so, they borrowed the administrative methods of the Roman Church, which shared the goal of bringing order to Europe, or availed themselves of the skills of its prelates. Most of the modern nations of Europe originated from the ordered domains of medieval lords who compelled others to regard them as kings. What follows is a survey of the progress of monarchy in the core regions of Europe—France, England, and the German lands—and on its periphery.

Charlemagne's Empire

Charlemagne (r. 768–814) was the greatest figure of the Carolingian dynasty which had seized power over the Frankish kingdom from the Merovingian dynasty installed by Clovis. He has already been introduced as the architect of the ninth-century cultural renewal called the "Carolingian Renaissance," a key moment in the formation of Western civilization (see Chapter 8). Had he accomplished nothing more, this Charles would have deserved his title Charlemagne, or "Charles the Great." Other accomplishments as significant in the realm of politics, however, secure him that honor. Charlemagne harnessed the might of his nobles, choosing able men—as many as 250 counts—and supervising them systematically. He sent out to the far reaches of his domain special agents who scrutinized the performance of the nobles and listened to appeals from the aggrieved. His treasurers and secretaries kept careful records of the people and products in his own domains. Decrees specified just how the harvest should be counted, and under what circumstances serf women should work.

Like others whom history has deemed "Great," Charlemagne was also a conqueror. He extended the limits of the Frankish kingdom deep into Italy, down to the Pyrenees, and east beyond the Rhine into the land the Romans had called "Germany," the home of still-pagan Saxon tribes whom he forcibly converted to Christianity. Charlemagne's empire at its height comprised much of modern Italy and Germany, and all of modern Belgium, the Netherlands, Austria, and Switzerland, in addition to buffer zones, or marches, in northern Spain and eastern Europe.

Charlemagne's interventions in Italy won him the support of the Church, which could no longer rely on the protection of the emperor in the east. In 774 Charlemagne assisted the pope, Adrian I, by conquering the kingdom of the Lombards and so releasing the papacy from their domination. In 799, he came to the assistance of Pope Leo III, the near-victim of a Roman conspiracy, and had him reinstated. On Christmas Day, 800, in Rome, Leo crowned Charlemagne "emperor of the Romans"—a title better than that of king, for as emperor he became the successor to the successors of the great Augustus. This revival of the Western Empire would be the basis of the concept, still to mature, of a Holy Roman Empire, a Christianized European simulacrum of ancient Rome.

At the time of his death, Charlemagne ruled vast territories from which many of the future states of western Europe would be carved. On his death in 814, his empire descended to his one son, Louis the Pious (r. 814–840), and then to his three grandsons. Their squabbles over the division of that inheritance, begun even before the death of their father, fractured the unified state Charlemagne had erected. These disputes were resolved in the Treaty of Verdun, one of Europe's earliest, in 843. By its terms, Charles the Bald (r. 843–877) received the western zone, consisting largely of parts of modern France; Louis the German (r. 817–875) received the eastern zone, consisting largely of parts of modern Germany; and Lothair (r. 843–855) received the narrow ribbon of territories running between the two. Those territories included parts of modern Belgium, the oft-disputed provinces of Alsace, Lorraine, and Burgundy, and patches of northern and central Italy. Each heir received a slice of the empire Charlemagne had built, and now was no more.

France: The Patient Capetians

In the western zone of Charlemagne's empire, the developing kingdom of France, his descendants struggled for 150 years to hold power. When the last Carolingian king died in 987, the nobles bypassed his available Carolingian descendants and elected one of their own company to succeed to the throne. Their choice was deliberate: a weak king posed no threat to lords intent on expanding their own power.

The man they chose was Hugh Capet (r. 987–996), whose realm consisted initially of the minuscule territory called the Ile de France ("island of France") in which sat the then obscure town of Paris. Hugh soon died, but he had a son, and so on for fourteen successions—an unequaled example of dynastic success. The sheer biological tenacity of these Capetian kings was perhaps the most important ingredient of their achievement. Confounding the expectations of the great lords, Hugh Capet's descendants held the monarchy for more than 300 years.

With the conquest, in 1202–1204, of the duchy of Normandy and other territories, the reigning Capetian, Philip II (called "Philip Augustus"; r. 1179–1223), was now master of a state that was beginning to look like France and was the leading nation of Europe. Paris was a populous city, with paved streets and new wall, a royal fortress (the Louvre), a partially completed cathedral (Notre Dame); and it was home of one of Europe's first and most influential universities. These achievements must be credited to Philip Augustus, who also centralized royal administration and finances.

The successors of Philip Augustus continued to expand the territory, efficiency, and prestige of France. In 1302–1303, his great great-grandson Philip IV (called "the Fair"; r. 1285–1314) presided over the first Estates-General, one of the representative assemblies that are the ancestors of modern Western congresses and parliaments. Philip's ruthless acquisition of some of the wealth of the Church for the royal coffers (his nickname refers to his good looks, not to any sense of fairness) enhanced both his financial and his political position. His three sons succeeded him in turn, the last of the Capetian line. Their cousin, the first of the Valois dynasty, ascended the throne as Philip VI (r. 1328–1350) in 1328.

The first century or so of Valois rule was dominated by the Hundred Years' War with England, which brought foreign occupation and the devastation of the countryside. Yet postwar recovery came swiftly under Charles VII. That vacillating young man had received his crown through the efforts of Joan of Arc (see Chapter 10), but lived to reorganize France's army, its finances, and its relationship with

WHO'S WHO

Kings, Queens, and Peasants

Alfred the Great, King of Wessex (849–899) scholar and patron who held off the Danes during the Viking invasions and laid the foundations for the English monarchy.

Otto I the Great, Emperor (912–973) established the Holy Roman Empire in Germany and met the Magyar onslaught at Lechfeld (955).

William I (the Conqueror) of England (1027–1087) led a successful invasion of England in 1066 and established the Norman monarchy, the foundation of modern English governance.

Eleanor of Aquitaine (1122?–1204) divorced and remarried; a political pawn who grew powerful enough to gain both respect and hatred; mother of two kings of England, Richard I and John.

Philip IV the Fair, King of France (1268–1314) asserted royal power against the papacy.

John Ball and Wat Tyler (died 1381) peasant rebels in England.

Ivan III the Great, Grand Duke of Moscow (1440–1505) threw off Mongol domination; reined in the nobles and pronounced Moscow to be the "Third Rome."

Ferdinand II, King of Aragon (r. 1479–1516) and Isabella, Queen of Castile (r. 1474–1504) as joint rulers, they completed the Reconquest, expelled the Jews, and sent Columbus westward across the Atlantic.

Crowning the king: *Medieval kings gradually elevated themselves above their noblemen by military power, financial maneuvering, and deft use of symbols and rituals. Yet by the end of the Middle Ages nobles and even commoners began to resist by asserting rights and creating new constitutional principles. This fourteenth-century manuscript shows the coronation of a king, with ecclesiastical and secular lords. The vessels near his shoulder held the oil with which he was anointed.* (Master and Fellows of Corpus Christi College, Cambridge, England)

and undoing the process of Christianization. Saxon kings proceeded to form their own miniature kingdoms (Wessex, Essex, Sussex, and Mercia); they accepted Christianity in the sixth and seventh centuries as a result of two waves of missionary effort, from, respectively, Ireland and Rome.

In the late ninth century, the king of Wessex ("West Saxony") remained as the one strong Anglo-Saxon leader in a land largely occupied by Danes. King Alfred (r. 871–899), called the Great, not only ruled the nation that was the germ of modern England and began the process of reconquest from the Danes but also, like Charlemagne, instituted a cultural revival, patronizing scholars and furthering education. A Latin scholar himself, he translated into English such fundamental works as Boethius' *Consolation of Philosophy* and the *Pastoral Care* of Pope Gregory the Great (c. 540–604), a manual outlining the duties of priests. In doing so, he helped to create what would become the language of Chaucer (c. 1345–1400) and Shakespeare (1564–1616).

Under Alfred's leadership, a unified English kingdom took form (neatly organized into administrative units called "shires"), with one established religion and one accepted code of law. The Danes were confined to a region in northern and eastern England called the Danelaw. Alfred's England was the first nation of Europe since Rome to achieve such integration. Although the unity would be disturbed after Alfred's death (899), it would soon be regained under a new line of kings.

Alfred's successors continued the struggle against invaders. For a brief period in the eleventh century, the Danish monarch Cnut (or Canute; r. 1016–1035) dominated the English kingdom. After several years of instability, the Anglo-Saxon king Edward (r. 1042–1066), called "the Confessor" in recognition of his exceptional piety, regained the kingdom.

On Edward's death in 1066, two claimants for his throne presented themselves simultaneously: his brother-in-law Harold (who immediately resumed the endless job of repelling invaders from the north) and his kinsman William, Duke of Normandy. According to William, Harold himself had sworn to uphold his claim. When Harold showed no sign of stepping aside, William promptly launched an invasion of England. Harold had no sooner defeated a combined force of English rebels and Norwegians at Stamford Bridge in the north when he was summoned to Hastings on the Channel coast in the south to meet the Norman army. He was crushed. The Normans and their descendants have held the throne of England (apart from 1649–1660; see Chapter 15) ever since.

William was not only a successful soldier but an efficient ruler. He seized the lands of virtually all the English lords and parceled them out to his own followers. As he did so, he reorganized the conditions of land tenure on the Norman model, so that most of the

Rome. His son Louis XI (r. 1461–1483) continued in the tradition of his most effective predecessors: he expanded the territory of France, fending off neighbors and enemies alike, centralized the bureaucracy, increased the flow of revenue, and encouraged industrial and commercial growth.

England: The Heritage of Conquest

The building of the English nation was a task already begun by the descendants of Angle, Saxon, and Danish invaders over the five centuries before 1066. In that year, Duke William of Normandy (in modern France; r. 1066–1087), himself a descendant of Viking raiders, invaded the island; within about five years he had made the kingdom his own. William and his successors asserted royal authority, establishing systems for the collection of taxes, the summoning of armies, and the administration of justice. By 1500, despite the long disruption of the Wars of the Roses, tiny England was one of the best-managed nations in Europe.

During the chaotic 400s, the Saxons, Angles, and Jutes, all northern Germanic peoples, had overrun Britain, destroying the remains of Roman settlement major lords owed obedience directly to the king. His officials compiled a systematic inventory of English land, down to the number of cattle on each manor (called the Domesday Book, presumably because there was no appeal against it, just as there would be none on Doomsday). The Norman knights who acquired land tenures by William's actions owed allegiance directly to him. Boldly, William had managed to establish structures of authority linked to land-holding, ensuring that in England power remained centered in the king.

William's successors continued to centralize systems of law. Royal officials travelling to local courts established the supremacy of royal justice and created the **common law**. Compounded of both customary and Roman elements, common law was the law that would be enforced by the king's courts. It came to override local custom and became common to all inhabitants. It has had a continuous history from the twelfth century to the present.

Equally fundamental was the Norman monarchy's reordering of finances. From every corner of England, officials brought taxes due the king to the Exchequer, the office of the treasurer at Winchester (later relocated to Westminster, in London). There, a method of accounting was employed that was meaningful even to the illiterate stewards of the day. Wooden sticks notched to indicate the amount tendered were split in two, one half remaining with the royal treasurer, the other returning with the local representative. These sticks, called "tallies," performed essentially the same function as multi-paged carbon forms do today. An unbroken record of these transactions extends from the twelfth century onward.

William's conquest of England gave the king ascendancy over the nobility, making England the first European state to balance the principles of centralization of power and local governance. Some 150 years later, in 1215, the barons of England who were restive under the autocratic King John (r. 1199–1216), compelled that monarch to sign an agreement known as *Magna Carta* ("Great Charter"). It too aimed at a balance between the power of the king and the prerogatives of his nobility.

Although the *Magna Carta* was concerned only with regulating the relations between kings and lords, this medieval document stated principles that would later be brilliantly developed for wider purposes. It stated for the first time the guarantee that lies at the heart of the Anglo-American concept of freedom: that "no free man shall be arrested, or imprisoned, or deprived of his property, or outlawed, or exiled, ... unless by legal judgment of his peers or by the law of the land." Two other principles developed from clauses of the *Magna Carta* gained prominence in the seventeenth century, when the revolutionary movements began that yielded the English constitution and its offspring in the United

WITNESSES

Kings at Work

In contrast to later periods, in the turbulent Middle Ages many people looked to kings to administer order and justice. The first two passages praise the English King Henry II and French King Louis IX for doing just that. The third argues that a harmonious world can only be achieved by obedience to a powerful monarch.

The chronicler William of Newburgh describes the ascension of Henry II of England (1154): In the year 1154, Henry ... came into England ... [and] received there his hereditary kingdom, ... was consecrated king with the holy oil, while all the people throughout the kingdom exclaimed, "Long live the king!" Having experienced the unhappiness of the former reign in which so many evils had arisen, all hoped for better things from the new king, especially since ... a great zeal for justice seemed to possess him, and since he already gave the appearance of a great leader in his very first acts. ... Especially did he take care of the public order, and that the strength of the law might be felt again in England. ...
(From E. P. Cheyney, *Readings in English History drawn from the Original Sources*, 1935)

The thirteenth-century French King Louis IX administers justice (c. 1280): In summer, after hearing mass, the king often went to the wood of Vincennes, where he would sit down with his back against an oak, and make us sit all around him. Those who had any suit to present could come to speak to him without hindrance from an usher or any other person. The king would address them directly, and ask: "Is there any one here who has a case to be settled?" Those who had one would stand up. Then he would say: "Keep silent all of you, and you shall be heard in turn, one after the other."
(Jean de Joinville: "The Life of St. Louis," *Chronicles of the Crusades*; ed. M. R. B. Shaw 1963)

The Florentine poet Dante argues that a powerful monarch is necessary for the good of the world (1310/1316): A single kingdom. ... should have one king who rules and governs it. If not, not only do those living in the kingdom not achieve their goals, but the kingdom itself also falls into ruin. ... The whole human race is ordered to one end, ... [and] should have one ruler or sovereign who can be called the "Monarch" or "Emperor." And so it is evident that for the world's well-being there is necessary a Monarchy or Empire.
(Dante, *Monarchia*; ed. P. G. Ricci, 1965, trs. M. L. King 1997)

States. These are the principles that the king was not to pass laws without consulting those who would be compelled to obey them; and that the king was subject to the law of the whole land. The *Magna Carta* did not create a modern democracy. But it enunciated assumptions that would become essential to modern democratic constitutions.

John's grandson Edward I (r. 1272–1307) extended the principle of consultation. It had been commonplace for the king to consult with the lords of his realm (who constituted a *curia*, or court) in a session called a *parliamentum* (literally, a session for "talking together"). John had run into trouble when he failed to do this. Three times in the reign of John's son Henry III (r. 1216–1272), the parliament met with enhanced membership, including elected representatives of the knights of each shire and, twice, with representatives of the town (called burgesses). Henry's grandson Edward remembered this practice and turned it from a device for managing a crisis to a feature of government for preventing one. Edward's Model Parliament of 1295 is an important landmark in the development of that assembly. Not long after his death, the knights and burgesses assembled in London in what became the House of Commons, while the great lords continued to meet together in what came to be called the House of Lords. Both chambers of Parliament continue to sit to this day.

From Henry II (who ascended in 1154) through Richard III (who was killed in 1485), members of the Plantagenet, Lancaster, and York branches of William the Conqueror's family ruled England in turn. The 1300s and 1400s were occupied by their struggles for supremacy, accompanied by conspiracy, murder, and warfare. During the same period, the English kings fought in France in the Hundred Years' War. Despite the turbulence of this era, English institutions—the monarchy and system of shires, the common law, the courts of justice, and Parliament—all survived. By the end of the Middle Ages, England was a small kingdom compared to populous France. But it was well organized and prepared to assume an important role in the world of nations that would follow.

The Empire: Two Romes in Conflict

Although Charlemagne's empire was split up after his death, the idea of a Western European Empire—a successor to Rome—lived on. Charlemagne's grandson Lothair, ruler of the central kingdom, retained the title of emperor. But the further partitioning of this middle kingdom under his successors left a power vacuum in this region, and during the tenth century, the eastern Frankish kingdom (modern Germany) asserted its own right to be considered the heir to Rome. In this it received, at first, the support of the papacy; but conflict soon emerged between these two powers. The Rome of the popes had political and territorial ambitions over and above its spiritual role as the seat of Latin Christendom, while the new secular, or temporal, "Rome" of the German emperors not only competed with the Church in the political realm but also assumed some ecclesiastical powers. Its claims to supremacy are expressed in the titles that came in the thirteenth century to preface that of "Empire": "Holy" and "Roman."

During the one hundred years or so following Charlemagne's death in 814, the eastern Frankish kingdom had suffered both from repeated invasions from the east and from political fragmentation within its boundaries. In the absence of a strong central monarchy, the German dukes managed the defense of their own lands and ultimately took it on themselves to elect their kings. When Louis (called "the Child"), the last of Charlemagne's descendants to rule this kingdom, died in 911, the dukes elected as king one of the weakest of their number, Conrad of Franconia (r. 911–918). On his death, seeing the losses incurred by Conrad's ineffectiveness, they elected the strongest: Henry the Fowler, Duke of Saxony (r. 919–936). Henry's successors included the most brilliant ruler of the century, Otto I, victor over the Magyars at Lechfeld, who was crowned emperor by the pope in 962. In 1024, the imperial election went to a different Conrad, founder of the Salian line, which reigned until 1125, through the whole period of papal reform (see Chapter 10), which was to present a challenge to imperial ambitions.

In the absence of a dynastic monarchy, in which power descended on hereditary lines, no unified government or generalized system of law took hold in the imperial lands. The ruler was never able to subordinate the dukes and other great nobles whose interests tended to undermine the structure of government power. Instead, the German emperors looked to the Church as a source of loyal and skilled administrators. These could serve the emperor as the territorial lords could not. The choice was logical, but it had a flaw. Beginning in the eleventh century, the popes opposed the control of clerical offices to further the interests of a secular state. The tension between empire and papacy mounted. It climaxed in 1076, during the reign of Henry IV (r. 1056–1106) when the pope forced the Emperor to yield on the issue of the appointment of clergy by secular rulers.

No longer permitted to exploit the expertise of the clergy for political purposes, Henry's successors sought other ways to consolidate their power. In the German lands, they won the cooperation of territorial lords and free cities. They aimed at center the empire, however, in Italy, where imperial sovereignty might be established, rather than in Germany, where all such attempts seemed to fail. These were the ambitions of Frederick I and II, two rulers of the Hohenstaufen dynasty which held the imperial title from 1138 to 1254. The former tried but failed to establish his sovereignty in northern Italy. The latter did establish a power base in southern Italy, where he had been born and where, as the son of a German father and a Sicilian mother (of Sicily's Norman royal house), he had a cosmopolitan background suitable for this polyglot, ethnically mixed region. But after his death the papacy and its allies among the northern Italian city-states threw off the German imperial yoke.

By the mid-fifteenth century, the Habsburg family had gained preeminence as the imperial rulers of the German lands. In 1477, the future emperor Maximilian (r. 1493–1519) married Mary, the heiress to the rich duchy of Burgundy and attached county of Flanders. Their son Philip married Joanna, the heiress to the Spanish kingdoms of Aragon and Castile and became Philip I of Spain. Their eldest son, Charles, not only inherited Spain, which he ruled as Charles I from 1516, but also became emperor, as Charles V, from 1519 until his death in 1556. With title to Spain, the Netherlands, Burgundy, and the German realm, he was the greatest monarch on the continent.

The moment of imperial supremacy in Europe soon passed. The Habsburg realms were divided in two, with Spain going its own way and the German Habsburgs continuing the tradition of the empire. The failure of the empire to assume a strong role in the post-medieval world began with its foundation. Although it was medieval Europe's dominant political structure, the empire never achieved the organizational sophistication of little England or the wealth and muscle of France. Despite the luster of the "Roman" name, these monarchs were unable to concentrate power in their hands or to establish a single dynasty that ruled by hereditary right, or to disenfranchise the other territorial lords of the huge Germanic domain. By the eighteenth century the empire was something of a joke—in the scornful but apt judgment of the French writer Voltaire (1694–1778), it was "neither holy, nor Roman, nor an Empire." In 1806, it ceased to be.

The European Core and Periphery

As Map 9.3 indicates, the German lands and the kingdoms of England and France constituted the core regions of western, Christian Europe in the Middle Ages. Here lordship was most developed, the manorial system was most deeply entrenched, and the foundations of modern monarchical states were laid. Around the periphery of this European core, other political units were forming. But they followed courses tied to their differing origins and circumstances.

Stretching northeastward from France along the English Channel and North Sea were the Low Countries of Flanders and Holland (in modern Belgium and the Netherlands). Already in late antiquity, cloth made by the people of Flanders was a valuable commodity of international trade when Europe had scarcely any other. Later, the towns of the Low Countries were pioneers in international commerce in the northern European waterways. Alternately subject to the kings of France and to the emperors of the German lands, these areas did not develop their own monarchies during the Middle Ages. Instead, their flourishing towns were subject to the local governance of secular or ecclesiastical lords.

Along the northwestern rim of Europe, Ireland and Scotland (inhabited by peoples of Celtic origin) and Iceland (settled by the Vikings during the ninth and tenth centuries) retained their ancient organization by clan and tribe—and would do so into recent times. The Scandinavian homelands, as has been seen, gave birth to the Viking raids and migrations, while developing their distinctive culture. In this era the Viking sagas were compiled—the last European folk epics—and the Norwegian, Danish, and Swedish people established monarchies of their own.

The Swedish Varangians, who had expanded into Russia from the early 800s and vanquished the resident Slavs, established their capital at Kiev. Christianized by Byzantine missionaries, Kievan Russia grew wealthy from trade with Constantinople. The Kievan state fell to the Mongol invasion that hammered Asia and Europe in the thirteenth century. Organized as the Khanate of the Golden Horde, the Mongols dominated Russia from 1240 to 1480.

In the fourteenth century, Ivan I (r. 1328–1341), the native prince of Moscow, gained the confidence of Mongol overlords and succeeded in undermining their governance. Under his rule, the Grand Duchy of Moscow emerged as the center of Russian civilization and the germ of the modern state of Russia. A century later, Ivan III (r. 1462–1505), called "the Great," won independence from Mongol domination and gained sovereignty over the other Russian princes. Married to the niece of the last Byzantine emperor (whose realm had fallen to the Turks in 1453), he pronounced Moscow the successor to Constantinople as the central Christian see—the "Third Rome." His grandson Ivan IV (1533–1584) pursued the imagery further, naming himself head of the Eastern Orthodox Church and taking the title of *Tsar* ("Caesar").

Among some of Russia's neighbors, too, Christianization led to the development of young monarchies. Soon after the year 1000, in Poland, Hungary, and Bulgaria, kingdoms were established. The Baltic lands, extending from Denmark to Russia along the Baltic Sea, were a special case. Still pagan in 1000, this last European frontier became the special mission of the order of Teutonic Knights, who slowly established Christian worship and Western governance in the region. The most concerted resistance to conversion came from Lithuania, which expanded after 1300 to include parts of Russia, Belarus (Byelorussia), and Ukraine. Once joined to Poland by dynastic ties in 1383, Lithuania at last accepted Roman Catholic Christianity and joined its neighbors in becoming part of European Christendom. Deep in eastern Europe, the culture of Prussia, Lithuania, Latvia, and Estonia was Western.

Although it had been Christian before the Middle Ages began, Mediterranean Europe did not form independent monarchies as early as other parts of western Europe. The unification of Italy achieved by the Romans in the first century B.C.E., then shattered in the fifth century C.E., would not be restored for fourteen hundred years. During the Middle Ages, Italy was an ever-shifting patchwork of jurisdictions. The kingdom established by the Lombards and taken over by Charlemagne gradually withered after the ninth century. The Byzantine outposts at Ravenna and in southern Italy and Sicily were lost to that Empire in the Middle Ages. In this vacuum of authority, territorial lords and local towns took charge.

In the eleventh century, the new island city of Venice in the northeast retained a titular loyalty to Byzantium. To the interior, the areas of Lombardy and Tuscany were the home of flourishing towns. These were ruled by a consortium of local lords and urban merchant elites, who were amassing the capital that would launch the European commercial revolution. Some were also creating political institutions that would help shape the modern state system. Across the center of the peninsula stretched the belt of the Papal States. Patched together from donations fictitious and real and ruled, sometimes directly, sometimes only nominally, by the pope, the Papal States lasted until 1870. The last vestige of these holdings, today's Vatican City, is an independent state within the boundaries of Italy's capital at Rome. Southern Italy and Sicily formed yet another region, heavily influenced by its Greek and Arab populations, ruled successively by Norman, German, French, and Spanish monarchs. Its cultural variety made it a fertile source

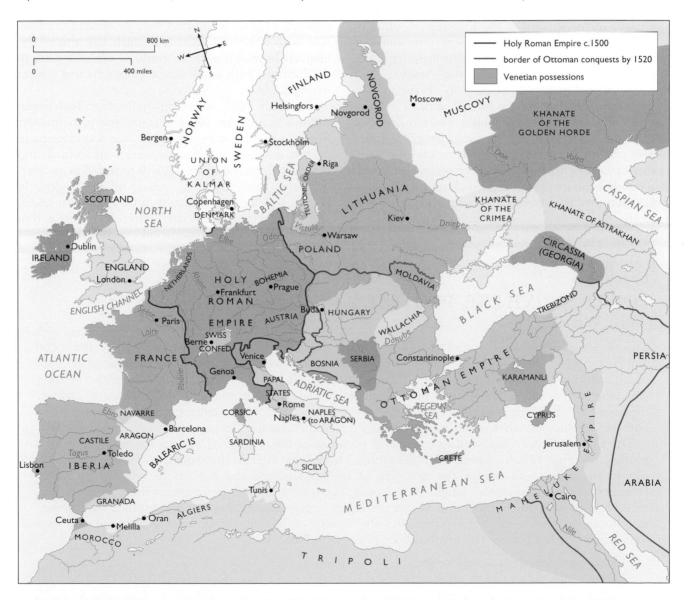

Map 9.3 European States in 1453: *The process of state-building that had occupied European rulers during the Middle Ages produced a constellation of kingdoms, principalities, and city-states very different in 1453 than it had been in 500 or during the later phase (beginning in the eighth century) of invasion (see Map 9.1, p. 236). In 1453, which European state might an observer think would be most likely to gain dominance over the others? Why?*

of innovations in thought and literature that helped shape the civilization of late-medieval Europe.

To Italy's east, the small states of the Balkan region broke free of Byzantium during the era of the Crusades, then became subject to the Ottoman Turks from the late fourteenth century. To the west, the Iberian peninsula was the setting for a dramatic confrontation of Arabic and European cultures. There, from the fifth century, Visigothic invaders had established a unified kingdom under their Arian Christian monarchs (converted to Catholic Christianity by 600). The Visigoth kingdom was home to an early medieval civilization that flourished when the rest of Europe had reached a cultural nadir. The promising career of the Visigothic realm was cut short in 711 C.E., when Islamic invaders from North Africa conquered nearly the whole of the peninsula. The only Christian settlements that survived were Léon and Asturias, far to the north in the shadow of the Pyrenees Mountains. Charlemagne established the region just south of the Pyrenees as a Spanish "march," or frontier buffer state, the germ of the later kingdom of Aragon.

The Islamic state established in Iberia in 711 became a separate caliphate in 929 under Umayyad rule. Islamic Spain was the major western depot of Mediterranean trade and an unsurpassed cultural center. At a time when the crude noble and royal courts of Europe to the north kept records, if at all, through the labors of one or two clerics, the Islamic cities promoted the creation of poetry and music, philosophy and law and medicine with the participation of Muslim, Jewish, and Christian scholars.

By 1100, the Christian states in the north of Spain had begun the enormous task of "*Reconquista*," the reconquest of the whole peninsula from Islamic rule. Led by the kingdom of Castile (founded in 1035), this project succeeded, by 1252, in bringing most of the Iberian lands under a variety of Christian dominions. The final Islamic stronghold of Granada fell to Christian forces in 1492. It did so after a concerted offensive mounted by the two monarchs of Aragon and Castile, respectively Ferdinand (r. 1479–1516) and Isabella (r. 1474–1504), whose marriage permitted their joint rule from 1479 and the concentration of military strength needed for that purpose. The royal pair clinched their military victory with a cultural show of force: a purge of all non-Christian elements. They expelled from the kingdom all unconverted Muslims and Jews (whose leaders were closely identified with the Muslim regime). This accomplished, they proceeded to persecute with notorious cruelty, through the arm of the Spanish **Inquisition**, those converts whose loyalty to the Catholic faith and the new monarchy was subject to any doubt.

In about 1000, medieval civilization had begun to form in a cluster of small states and principalities in the west of Europe. By 1300, the foundations of modern England and France were well formed, and the Holy Roman Empire was still regarded as an overmastering state. By 1500, nearly all the regions of Europe had formed the bases of their modern states, and were participants in the Western civilization that was the product of the medieval experience.

Conclusion

POWER, PRIVILEGE, PROTEST, AND THE MEANING OF THE WEST

The privileges of the nobility and the power of kings forged in the Middle Ages would shape the social and political life of the West into the modern era. They emerged in response to the conditions of chaos and destitution left after the collapse of Roman authority. Together, nobles and kings provided security and developed Europe's fundamental judicial and governmental institutions. By 1500, the states and territories of Europe were prepared to foster the development of European culture, technology, and economy—a development that would enable the tiny continent to extend influence throughout the globe.

The whole edifice of medieval society rested, however, on the labor of its workers—mostly serfs bound to the land. They benefited from the order Europe's leaders created. At the same time they suffered, subject to the vagaries of nature, the exactions of landholders, and the restrictions imposed by rulers. Peasants rebelled against the weight of authority, but their rebellions were everywhere, in time, suppressed. In fourteenth-century England, one of the last of these medieval uprisings culminated in the confrontation between established power and the masses of human beings who questioned the very foundations of that power. The revolutionary priest John Ball asked:

> When Adam delved [dug] and Eve span,
> Who was then the gentleman?

This verse must have sparked the imagination of peasants who, like Piers the Plowman, struggled to feed their children as the lords of the earth accumulated wealth and power. The extinction of aristocratic privilege and royal power was already anticipated in these words.

QUESTIONS TO CONSIDER

1. Why was the heavy plow so important a tool in the conquest of European soil?

2. How do you think peasant communities made decisions about patterns of planting (two-field, three-field) and land rights?

3. Why were horses and the hunt centrally important for noble identity?

4. In what way does the art of courtly love help civilize the medieval European nobility?

5. In what way did medieval kingdoms resemble a modern state? In what ways did they not?

SUGGESTED RESOURCES

Abulafia, David, *Frederick II: A Medieval Emperor* (London: Pimlico, 1992). A landmark biography, balancing the weaknesses and strengths of this remarkable medieval monarch.

Bartlett, Robert, *The Making of Europe: Conquest, Colonization, and Cultural Change, 950–1350* (London: Penguin, 1994). Shows how backward Europe expanded from center to periphery and created a common culture by the fourteenth century, poised for expansion.

Cheyette, Frederic L., *Ermengard of Narbonne and the World of the Troubadours* (Ithaca: Cornell University Press, 2001). Portrait of a woman warrior and practitioner of the arts of courtly love illuminating the feudal society of twelfth-century Languedoc (southern France).

France, John, *Western Warfare in the Age of the Crusades, 1000-1300* (Ithaca: Cornell University Press, 1999). Studies the technology of war and actual battles within the framework of medieval economic and political structures.

Freedman, Paul H., *Image of the Medieval Peasant as Alien and Exemplary* (Stanford: Stanford University Press, 1998). Examines the range of the representations of the peasant from the Carolingian period through the sixteenth century, embodying the attitudes both of the peasants themselves and of those who enserfed them.

Harding, Alan, *Medieval Law and the Foundations of the State* (Oxford: Oxford University Press, 2002). Argues that the concept of the state evolved from medieval systems of law and measures taken for the protection of property.

Howell, Margaret, *Eleanor of Provence: Queenship in Thirteenth-Century England* (Malden, MA: Blackwell, 1998). Portrays the life of a medieval queen, consort of Henry III, who was enmeshed in politics, war, and diplomacy, and who powerfully influenced, even as she struggled with, her even more important son, Edward I.

Madden, Thomas F., *A Concise History of the Crusades* (Totowa, NJ: Rowman & Littlefield, 1999). Clear and up-to-date overview, examining why the crusaders left Europe to fight in the Middle East, and how the conflict affected the Byzantine and Islamic East.

Magnusson, Roberta J., *Water Technology in the Middle Ages: Cities, Monasteries, and Waterworks after the Roman Empire* (Baltimore: Johns Hopkins University Press, 2001). Shows how gravity-driven water-flow systems, generally spurred by private initiatives, continued to provide water and remove waste from Roman times, long before the modern world dawned.

Moore, R.I., *The First European Revolution* (Basil Blackwell, 2000). Argues that Europe underwent its first and most important transformation 1000–1300, when masses of people were recruited by competing elites into the political process.

Pennington, Kenneth, *The Prince and the Law 1200–1600: Sovereignty and Rights in the Western Legal Tradition* (Berkeley and Los Angeles: University of California Press, 1993). Traces how European jurists developed concepts of common law roughly universal in Western Europe, which understood that the powers of sovereigns were limited both by the rights of subjects and the demands of natural (and divine) law.

Reynolds, Susan, *Fiefs and Vassals: The Medieval Evidence Reinterpreted* (Oxford: Oxford University Press, 1994). Bold and controversial reconceptualization of property rights and law in medieval Europe, arguing that the formal rules of "feudalism" derived from academic and legal texts, and never existed until monarchical centralization encouraged them, in real life.

Rösener, Werner, *Peasants in the Middle Ages* (New York: Polity Press, 1996). A study of Central European peasants, including house and farmyard, clothing, labor, sociability, kinship, relationships with lords, legal status, rebellions, and the late medieval crisis.

Rosenthal, Joel T., *Patriarchy and Families of Privilege in Fifteenth-Century England* (Philadelphia: University of Pennsylvania Press, 1991). Examination of kinship patterns among noble, gentry, and mercantile families in England, highlighting wider kin networks, the importance of patriarchy, and the condition of widows.

Vale, Malcolm, *The Princely Court: Medieval Courts and Culture in North-West Europe 1270–1380* (Oxford: Oxford University Press, 2001). Explores the social relations and culture of the princely courts of France, Flanders, and England in the thirteenth and fourteenth centuries.

ORB: the OnLine Reference Book for Medieval Studies (Medieval Academy, Kalamazoo):
http:orb.rhodes.edu/default.html

King René d'Anjou's tournament book, in English—how to conduct a medieval tournament (Princeton):
http://www.princeton.edu/~ezb/rene/renehome.html

Eleanor of Aquitaine, extraordinary medieval queen, brief biography:
http://www.womeninworldhistory.com/heroine2.html

◉ Western Civilization Documents CD-ROM

6.6 Contracts Between Lords and Vassals
6.7 The Book of Emperors and Kings, Charlemagne and Pope Leo III
8.1 Manorial Court Records

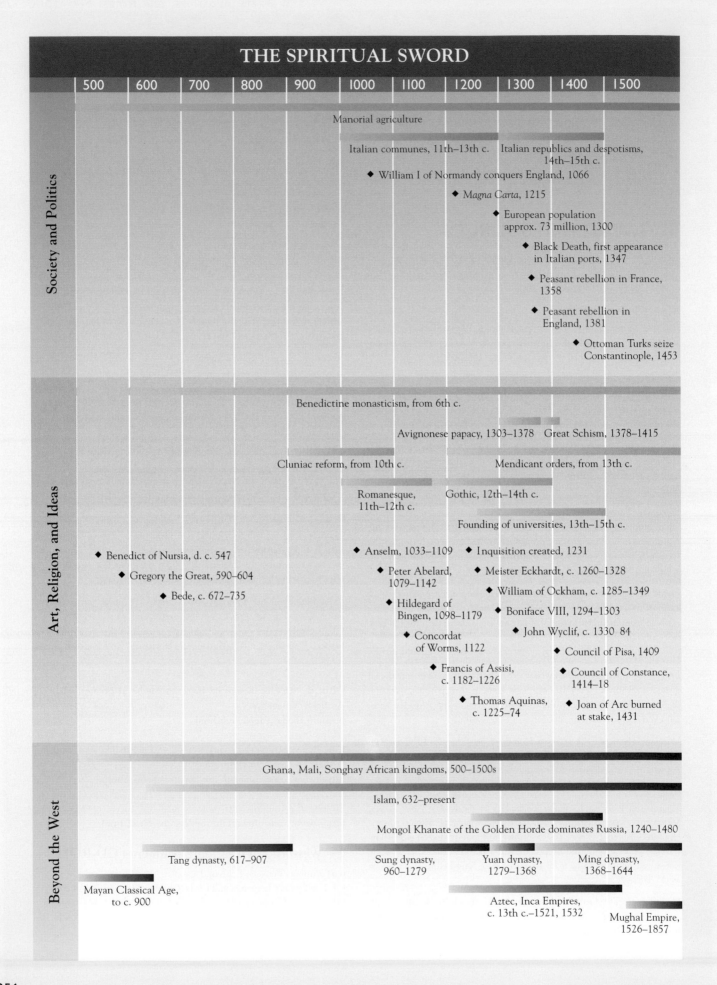

THE SPIRITUAL SWORD

| | 500 | 600 | 700 | 800 | 900 | 1000 | 1100 | 1200 | 1300 | 1400 | 1500 |

Society and Politics

Manorial agriculture

Italian communes, 11th–13th c.   Italian republics and despotisms, 14th–15th c.

◆ William I of Normandy conquers England, 1066

◆ *Magna Carta*, 1215

◆ European population approx. 73 million, 1300

◆ Black Death, first appearance in Italian ports, 1347

◆ Peasant rebellion in France, 1358

◆ Peasant rebellion in England, 1381

◆ Ottoman Turks seize Constantinople, 1453

Art, Religion, and Ideas

Benedictine monasticism, from 6th c.

Avignonese papacy, 1303–1378   Great Schism, 1378–1415

Cluniac reform, from 10th c.   Mendicant orders, from 13th c.

Romanesque, 11th–12th c.   Gothic, 12th–14th c.

Founding of universities, 13th–15th c.

◆ Benedict of Nursia, d. c. 547

◆ Gregory the Great, 590–604

◆ Bede, c. 672–735

◆ Anselm, 1033–1109   ◆ Inquisition created, 1231

◆ Peter Abelard, 1079–1142   ◆ Meister Eckhardt, c. 1260–1328

◆ William of Ockham, c. 1285–1349

◆ Hildegard of Bingen, 1098–1179   ◆ Boniface VIII, 1294–1303

◆ Concordat of Worms, 1122   ◆ John Wyclif, c. 1330–84

◆ Council of Pisa, 1409

◆ Francis of Assisi, c. 1182–1226   ◆ Council of Constance, 1414–18

◆ Thomas Aquinas, c. 1225–74   ◆ Joan of Arc burned at stake, 1431

Beyond the West

Ghana, Mali, Songhay African kingdoms, 500–1500s

Islam, 632–present

Mongol Khanate of the Golden Horde dominates Russia, 1240–1480

Tang dynasty, 617–907   Sung dynasty, 960–1279   Yuan dynasty, 1279–1368   Ming dynasty, 1368–1644

Mayan Classical Age, to c. 900

Aztec, Inca Empires, c. 13th c.–1521, 1532   Mughal Empire, 1526–1857

CHAPTER

10

THE SPIRITUAL SWORD

Religion and Culture in the Middle Ages

500–1500

KEY QUESTIONS

◆ **Renunciation of the Body:** Why were many men willing to give up their wealth, family, and mobility, and subject themselves to the strict regime of monasticism? Did women who became nuns make the same kinds of decisions, and lead the same kinds of lives?

◆ **Church and State:** How was the church able to maintain its independence from nobles and kings?

◆ **The Church and the People:** How was the experience of ordinary Christians different from that of the clergy? In what way did they participate in Christian worship and observance?

◆ **The Mind's Road to God:** How did Christianity affect the development of medieval thought? What kinds of institutions developed to train medieval thinkers, both secular and religious?

Power and spirit "Pardon me," Saint Catherine of Siena wrote to the lethargic Pope Gregory XI in 1376, for "what I have said to you and am saying; I am constrained by the Sweet Primal Truth to say it. His [God's] will ... demands that you execute justice. ... Since He has given you authority and you have assumed it, you should use your virtue and power; and if you are not willing to use it, it would be better for you to resign what you have assumed. ..."

With these words, a holy woman rebuked the Pope, the head of the Roman Catholic Church and spiritual leader of the majority of European Christians of her time. She was summoning him to return with the papal court to Rome, understood to be the proper home of the Church, from Avignon, where a flourishing papacy enjoyed special favors from the French king. Both Saint Catherine and Pope Gregory, who is portrayed on the ivory book cover on p. 259 were figures of vast authority—possessors of different but equally mysterious and formidable powers. They represent two extremes of the meaning of medieval Christianity—she represented the inward spirit of the believer, while he represented the institutional structures of the Catholic Church.

Medieval Europe was overwhelmingly Christian: it was, indeed, Christendom, a civilization defined by the creed liturgy, and institutions of the Latin church. The Church constrained individuals, it battled with kings and waged war with enemies, it corrected social ills, it influenced the patterns of Western thought. The charisma and the decisions of some popes swayed millions of people. The values and ideas of Christianity shaped the inner lives of Europeans of all social groups. At the same time, the doctrines and decrees of the clergy, a hierarchy of Christian professionals, shaped political, educational, and charitable institutions.

Christianity's impact on inner lives and their social behavior is the first theme of this chapter. The Church taught the renunciation of the body and the disciplining of the will. As its institutions developed through a process of internal self-examination and reform, the Latin church confronted the kings and princes of Europe and demanding that they, too, the lords of the earth, acknowledge ecclesiastical supremacy. Meanwhile, church intellectuals developed an all-encompassing theology which absorbed and Christianized the philosophical traditions they had inherited from antiquity as well as those of neighboring Islamic and Jewish cultures. In so doing, they elaborated methods of argument and proof that would outlast even the propositions they articulated. The great edifice of theological thought created and developed by medieval clerics, ironically, prepared the West for its breakthroughs in rational, **secular**, and scientific thought. Some of the important figures of the period are listed in *Who's Who* on p. 280.

RENUNCIATION OF THE BODY

Medieval Christianity's great success may be due in part to its radical departure from Classical values in insisting upon the separation of spirit from flesh and the renunciation of the body. As early as the first century C.E., Christian theologians embraced the principle that the body must be renounced for the sake of the spirit's salvation. In forging this ascetic ideal over the next few centuries, Christianity diverged from both Judaism and Islam, the two other world monotheisms. The institution of **monasticism**, which matured in western Europe from the fifth century C.E. (somewhat earlier in the Greek-speaking East), both limited and institutionalized the practice of asceticism. Monasticism in turn shaped the social and intellectual lives of medieval Europeans.

Origins of Christian Asceticism

Early Christian thinkers developed a radically ascetic program. It prized virginity over marriage (and certainly over any sexual relations outside marriage). It exalted martyrdom, the willingness to die rather than renounce the faith. It canonized saints, or holy persons, revered after their deaths in recognition of the heroic sacrifices they had made or the miracles they had apparently worked while alive. Virginity, martyrdom, sanctity all involved the denial of the needs of the body.

Jesus himself was no enemy of the body. He acknowledged the urgent human need for food, as he demonstrated in the miracle of the loaves and fishes, when he fed thousands of his listeners from one meager meal. He commanded his disciples in the wheatfields to pick and eat, even though it was the sabbath (when Jews were forbidden to work). He welcomed women followers, a violation of ancient norms that construed women as irremediably sensual creatures, and expressed willingness to forgive the violation of sexual limits.

In these respects, Jesus did not, as his later followers did, advocate a renunciation of the body. Yet Jesus did demand sacrifice, a renunciation of the worldly delights bought with wealth and power. To the rich man who had fulfilled all the commandments, he assigned one further task—to surrender all his wealth. To the powerful Sadducees and Pharisees he proclaimed that the meek, not the powerful, would inherit the earth. Moreover, he submitted to the ultimate renunciation of the body when he offered up his body unprotestingly to torture and crucifixion.

The importance of bodily renunciation became more prominent with the Christian missionary Paul of Tarsus. Paul distinguished sharply between body and spirit, insisting that the latter was superior to the former. The spirit turned to God, he said, but the flesh rebelled. "For I know that nothing good dwells … in my flesh," lamented Paul; "I see in my members another law at war with the law of my mind. … Wretched man that I am! Who will rescue me from this body of death?" Paul inherited from Greek thought the split between body and spirit, and introduced to Christianity a new hierarchy—the overwhelming superiority of spirit to body.

Paul's understanding of pure spirit and deceitful flesh profoundly influenced early Christian thought and practice. In quest of the higher good of the spirit, Christians renounced their homes, families, and ordinary comforts. A few deeply committed disciples fled to the deserts of Egypt and the Middle East to live in isolation. Here these hermits made amends for past sins by abusing their bodies and practicing an asceticism which they believed would prepare them for perfect communion with God.

Christian hermits were generally male, but Christian women also sought to approach God through the renunciation of the body. In antiquity women were understood as sexual beings—those who through sexual union gave birth to new generations. Women who rejected that sexual role implicitly declared themselves to be wholly transformed and ready for perfection. The spirituality and holiness of these virgins brought glory to the whole Christian community. Saint Ambrose, an early Church Father, described them as "gardens heavy with the scent of flowers, like shrines filled with solemn worship, like

The Bishop of Assisi and Francis of Assisi: *In this fourteenth-century fresco from the Basilica of Saint Francis of Assisi, the Bishop of Assisi covers the nakedness of Francis (later Saint Francis of Assisi) after he stripped off his clothes and hurled them at his father whose values he rejected.*

altars that touch their priests with holy awe." Many widows, too, embraced the celibate life. Often groups of these women established female religious communities, including one at Bethlehem, Jesus' birthplace. Their way of life was considered "above nature, and beyond common human living," a realm beyond marriage and childbirth, wealth and property.

The assumption that virginity brought one closer to holiness applied to men as well as women. The same men who encouraged women to deny their bodies also struggled themselves with the demand of celibacy. Saints Ambrose and Jerome urged virginity upon all male aspirants to the holy life. Saint Augustine detailed in his *Confessions* the difficulties he had faced in submitting to its demands: "Make me chaste," he cried to God in one anguished moment, "but not yet."

Martyrdom The willingness to suffer for one's religious beliefs defined martyrdom—the surrender to death in witness of faith. Like hermits and virgins, Christian martyrs—created by persecutions under Roman emperors—elevated spirit over body. In imitation of Jesus, they sacrificed their flesh for the sake of their own souls and the spiritual welfare of the church. In appreciation of their sacrifice, Christian communities revered the martyrs, who, they believed, were made holy, or "sanctified," by their ultimate sacrifice. Many of these martyrs were among the first Christians to be proclaimed saints, or canonized.

Forms of Sainthood

Gregory the Great: *Medieval sainthood took many forms. This image from an ivory book cover, tenth century, shows Gregory the Great (Pope Gregory I) seated at his writing-desk and receiving the word of God from the dove on his shoulder. (Kunsthistorisches Museum, Vienna)*

After death, the bodies of the saints became holy objects. Believers began to worship at their graves, or to treasure their material remains—pieces of clothing or even bodily **relics**, such as bones or portions of their persecuted flesh. Special tombs were built for their remains, which were believed to have special properties, including that of immunity to decay. The reverence for the lost personality easily slipped toward the worship of his or her bodily remains. Sometimes that worship seemed to work miracles, which were interpreted as the signs of sanctity. Even in the absence of a miracle, Christians believed that the deceased saint now lived close to God, and that, having once had bodily form, he or she could serve as an intermediary between the human world of the flesh and the eternal realm of spirit. If approached rightly, it was believed that saints would intercede with God for aid or forgiveness. Thus, paradoxically, a part of the body—despised in life—became, in death, an object of veneration.

These attitudes toward the bodies of particular individuals were new. The ancients generally viewed corpses as unclean and capable of polluting the precincts in which they were laid. For that reason, Greeks and Romans preferred to bury their dead outside the city walls. Christian reverence for the bodies of the holy reversed popular attitudes toward death. For the ancients, the body was beautiful in life but terrifying in death. For Christians, the body was detestable in life, but in death (the pure death of the believer) it was glorious. By about 500 C.E., European Christians, who now buried their dead close about their places of worship at the center of their communities, revered the saints and treasured their bodily relics.

Monasticism and the Christian Mission

By the fourth century C.E., the impulse for holiness had found a new means of expression. The persecutions had ended, and with them the opportunity for martyrdom. The ascetic life still beckoned, but the response to that call shifted. Men began to explore the spiritual life not as isolated individuals, but in groups, as monks. During the early medieval centuries, monks living in communities founded throughout Europe enriched the Church's liturgy, read, copied, and stored books, taught children, treated the sick, and housed the superfluous members of noble families. Monasticism attracted many thousands of people during the Middle Ages, becoming one of that era's foremost institutions.

While the ascetic ideal remained central to monastic life, it was not the only purpose served by communities of holy men (and women). In his two *Rules* for monks, Saint Basil of Caesarea (c. 330–379) stressed the humanity of the communal life and the centrality of study to the monastic mission.

Cassiodorus (already encountered as the secretary of the Ostrogoth king Theodoric), in his monastic retirement at Vivarium, on Italy's "heel," devoted himself to transcribing numerous religious manuscripts. He gathered there one of the world's foremost libraries, which would one day help to reinvigorate intellectual life.

Most important for the development of monasticism in western Europe was the work of the Roman nobleman Benedict of Nursia (c. 480–c. 550). As his native Italy was being devastated by Justinian's reconquest, Benedict defined monastic life as a rational alternative to the turmoil of the secular world. Basil, Cassiodorus, and Benedict, established the main features of life in a monastery: study and contemplation, prayer and chant, and, in some cases, productive work in service to the poor and ill of the community.

Saint Benedict's compact *Rule for Monks* outlined in seventy-three chapters the organization of the Christian community. He called it a beginners' guide, and it served more to restrain excess than to demand any sacrifice. An extract is given in *Witnesses* on p. 266. He reduced the demands of early monastic life to three, which each and every monk must vow to assume—poverty, chastity, and obedience. Thenceforth, those who took monastic vows were considered "regular"—meaning they followed a rule, or *regula*. They were distinct from the priests and bishops, who were called the secular clergy because they lived in the *seculum*, the world.

Monastic communities formed under the *Rule* of Saint Benedict sprang up throughout Europe. They formed in the old Roman lands, as many Christians left the decaying cities to join communities of their fellow believers in searching for an indestructible truth. In the new lands wrested from the wilderness or from invasion, the monasteries served as fortresses of established culture.

Monasticism took root with special success on the remote island of Ireland, recently and profoundly converted to Christianity through the efforts in part of Saint Patrick (c. 390–c. 461). Here a particularly strict form of monasticism arose under the *Rule* of Saint Columban (543–615). This Irish saint demanded absolute obedience and ceaseless austerities: "Let [the monk] come weary and as if sleep-walking to his bed, and let him be forced to rise while his sleep is not yet finished." In the seventh century, Irish missionaries helped convert the Anglo-Saxon peoples and exported to the Continent their high standards of dedication and intellectual life.

As *Windows On* on p. 261 shows, the main task of the monks was the glorification of God in communal worship. Seven times a day (including twice in the night), Benedictine monks assembled in their chapel to chant liturgical prayers and Old Testament psalms. They chanted in simple but expressive melodies, derived from Jewish practice and Greek theory, which

The Monastery and the Monastic Day

1 Church	9 Workshops	17 *Scriptorium* and
2 Cloister	10 Brewery and	library
3 Infirmary	bakery	18 Dormitory
4 Chapel	11 Stables	19 Refectory
5 Novitiate	12 Animal pens	20 Kitchens
6 Orchard/	13 Hostel	21 Cellars
Cemetery	14 Guesthouse	22 Hospice for the
7 Garden	15 School	poor
8 Barn	16 Abbot's house	23 Baths and latrines

Plan of the Monastery of Saint Gall

The medieval monastery was a complete world, whose facilities provided for the monk's needs and whose rituals structured his mental universe. The plan of the monastery of Saint Gall in Switzerland is shown (above), together with a reconstruction (below). The monks' day was divided between periods for divine service (song and prayer in the chapel), for work (manual, administrative or intellectual), and for meals and sleep, as shown in the daily plan (right).

What attraction might the monastic life have had for young men who would otherwise have become warriors and knights?

A Summer's Day for a Medieval Monk	
MIDNIGHT	Sing *Matins* in church
	Sleep
6 A.M.	Sing *Prime* in church
	Eat breakfast
	Study or manual labor
9 A.M.	Mass in church
10 A.M.	Meeting of the Chapter (council of monks)
11 A.M.	High Mass in church
12 NOON	Dinner
	Rest
2 P.M.	Sing *Nones* in church
	Work
4 P.M.	Sing *Vespers* in church
	Work
6 P.M.	Supper
7 P.M.	Sing *Compline* in church
	Sleep
The winter schedule was adjusted to the hours of daylight	

Reconstruction of the Monastery of Saint Gall

To continue your investigation of this topic, please go to www.prenhall.com/king for the related **WINDOWS** on the **WEB** activity

later evolved into increasingly complex patterns. Called plainsong or Gregorian chant, because it was linked to the work of Pope Gregory I, "the Great" (r. 590–604), the monastic chant of the Latin church is the origin of the formal tradition of Western music.

When not performing the central duty of worship, Benedictine monks were expected to work—their duties including housekeeping, study, teaching, medical service, and hard physical labor in the fields. Amid the poverty and disruption of medieval Europe there was no way for a community of Christians to sustain life except by farming. As conditions improved, the monks employed others to grow their food—serfs attached to the monastic lands or ordinary men pledged to the monastery but not full members of the community. One effect of the Benedictine labor requirement, even when it was no longer strictly observed, was to establish the principle of the dignity of work. If the Christian served God even as he labored, then labor itself was sanctified.

There was also mental work to be done. The European monasteries were the chief repositories of books that had survived the collapse of Roman authority in the west—and such repositories were the only link between the European wilderness and ancient culture. The more learned monks studied and, more importantly, copied these works. Their reverence for these Latin texts, which they did not always understand, is visible in the brilliant illustrations with which they decorated the margins, the chapter-opening capital letters, and the title pages of their books. Those illustrations, called miniatures or illuminations, were the major form of artistic expression in early medieval Europe. The copyists and illuminators were trained in the monastery schools—which for centuries, with few exceptions, were the only ones in Europe.

Convents Monasticism was not exclusively male. Female monasteries, or convents, were also established throughout Europe. Their residents, called nuns, were often unmarried or widowed noblewomen. Although some women entered the conventual life unwillingly, many others found in convents the opportunity for education and spiritual enrichment. Both types appear in *Witnesses* on p. 278.

Like monks, nuns also took vows of poverty, chastity, and obedience and passed their days in prayer and work (see the illustrations on this page and p. 263). An abbess governed their convent, usually a woman of great authority: "noble in wisdom and holiness, as well as noble by birth," wrote one advisor.

Cloistered Nuns

Nuns singing: *The convent was a complete world for medieval nuns. They are shown singing in this fifteenth-century psaltery of Henry VI. (British Library, London)*

Claricia, by herself: *Like monks, nuns copied and illustrated manuscript books. The initial letter Q can be seen in this manuscript, c. 1200, by the nun Claricia. On the tail of this letter Claricia has represented herself as a female scribe. (Walters Art Gallery)*

In the early Middle Ages, monasteries often consisted of a male and a female house adjacent to each other, administered by an abbess. In these "dual monasteries," the prominent role of the abbess, truly parallel to the abbot of all-male institutions, underscored the equality (later lost) of the male and female monastic mission. Yet there were fundamental differences. Because only men could be priests, and only priests could administer the sacraments, female convents required the services of these professionals from a neighboring monastery or church.

Abbesses might be women of great skill and even great learning. An outstanding example was Hildegard of Bingen (1098–1179), renowned as a scholar, a visionary, a composer, and a leader. Founder of her own convent (in 1150), she wrote a play, a treatise on natural science and medicine (as understood in that day), and her important *Scivias*, describing the visions that presented themselves to her inner senses. "I do not hear these things … with my external ears," she wrote, "nor do I perceive them by the thoughts of my heart, nor by any combination of my five senses—but rather in my soul, with my external eyes open, so that I … alertly see them by day and by night." The spirit itself commanded her to record them: "For the benefit of mankind, do not relinquish your pen! Write down what your inner eye has seen and your inner ear has heard. …"

Places of Refuge Increasingly, monasteries served as a refuge for upper-class noblemen. Repentant or elderly nobles often retired to monasteries, believing that the cloistered life was the only alternative to certain damnation. Thus one nobleman stated in the charter by which he donated his property to the monastery he entered: "Acknowledging the enormity of my sins and … fearing the dread condemnation of the reprobate, … I fly to the harbor of safety."

Monasteries also provided a refuge for children. The monastic life was an alternative career for those not destined to share in the inheritance of property. In the early Middle Ages, it was common for families to commit to monasteries very young children, along with a monetary donation. This system of "offering up" or oblation of children to a religious house benefited both parties. It gave the monasteries a steady stream of novice monks or nuns, who could easily be trained to monastic service. It gave noble families a means of reducing family size and future claims on inheritance. At the same time, it conferred upon these families the spiritual benefits accrued from the prayers of their children, who now worked for their parents' salvation.

There is no way of knowing how many children disliked the monastic life, from which they would never escape, or how many were cruelly denied all possibility of choosing their own destiny. But many such children later thrived, among them the Anglo-Saxon scholar Bede (c. 672–735), called "the Venerable." A skilled historian, prolific writer, and fertile thinker, he produced a study of chronology that promoted the now nearly universal method of dividing the calendar from the presumed date of the birth of Jesus. Bede had no regrets about his childhood: "I have spent all my life in this monastery," he wrote, "applying myself with all my might to the study of the Scriptures; and … it has always been my delight to learn or to teach or to write."

Monastic Reform and Transformation

Along with a steady supply of high-ranking novices, monastic institutions received a steady influx of wealth—partly from benefactions, or charitable donations, and partly from the products of their lands. That wealth posed a problem for an institution based on the principle of renunciation. Monks were pledged to poverty, yet the monasteries in which they lived became wealthy. By the late Middle Ages, the Church controlled a considerable portion of all the land of Europe.

This wealth nourished corruption. Monks accustomed to fine food and drink, luxurious surroundings, the company of the powerful, and dazzling ritual displays abandoned the regimen of simple duties and plain food. During the troubled ninth and tenth centuries, when they were isolated in remote houses within a world beset by invasion and disorder, the monks became lax in performing even basic duties. Critics recalled the essential mission of monasticism,

Guda, by herself: *This self-portrait of the nun Guda appears in an illuminated manuscript,* Homilia super Evangilia, *late twelfth century. Here Guda describes herself as a scribe, artist, and sinner. (Stadt-und-Universitätsbibliothek, Frankfurt)*

its renunciation of the body and the world. Pressure for reform swelled, spearheaded by determined abbots. Map 10.2 shows the centers of monastic reform.

An early program of reform took place in the Abbey of Cluny, in eastern France, which was founded in 910. In 927, its abbot, Odo (879–942) launched a reform movement that would have repercussions beyond his own monastery, or order, or age. First, he reestablished strict standards within his own community, insisting on the performance of constant communal prayer (exceeding the Benedictine guideline, which called only for intermittent prayer service). Then he agreed to supervise other houses that petitioned him for help in achieving the same goals. Soon, reformed monasteries, all linked by a common submission to the authority of the abbot at Cluny, who in turn was directly responsible to the pope, spread throughout the region. These in turn attracted new patrons and their benefactions. Cluny became the center of medieval monasticism, and from there flowed an energy for reform that reached Rome.

Patrons rushed to associate themselves with the greater purity of the reformed Cluniac order. Their donations enriched its monasteries, whose residents readily prayed for the souls of the great men and women whose endowments they enjoyed. With that newly acquired wealth, several Cluniac monasteries rebuilt their churches in the first major architectural style of the Middle Ages: the **Romanesque**.

A Romanesque church resembled the basilican style of church begun in early Christianity. These included a long hall, or nave, often flanked by side aisles, surmounted by a flat or tunnel-vaulted roof, and climaxed (usually in the east) by a semicircular or polygonal **apse** or an **ambulatory**, a curved aisle behind the altar, used originally for processions. To this plain and stately format, the Cluniac builders added elaborate sculptural embellishment. The columns and capitals supporting the upper interior walls of the nave and the moldings surrounding the round-arched windows and doors on the exterior were decorated with intertwined plant, animal, and human

Romanesque Style

Poitiers Cathedral:
Romanesque architecture was dominant in Europe from the ninth to the twelfth century and derived from ancient Roman precedents. The style was characterized by massive architectural forms, as shown here in this view of the west front of Poitiers Cathedral, c. 1130–1145.

Autun Cathedral: *Romanesque style is also characterized by its energetic, expressive sculptural decoration, as in this scene of the torment of souls in hell from the* **tympanum** *(drum), part of the facade decoration of Autun Cathedral. Saint Bernard criticized the ebullience of Romanesque style, which he feared would distract monks from their studies:*
". . . what is that ridiculous monstrosity doing? what is that deformed beauty and that beautiful deformity? those unclean monkeys? those ferocious lions? . . . on all sides one sees such a rich and amazing variety of forms that it is more pleasing to read the marbles than the manuscripts."

forms. These decorative forms were united by complex themes reflecting the main preoccupations of the era—salvation and damnation and the Last Judgment, the majesty of Jesus Christ as judge, the giant confrontation of the human and divine. Such carvings also decorated cathedrals, as shown in the figure above and on p. 264.

The impassioned saints, the grinning demons, the florid patterns of Romanesque sculpture were symptomatic of the problem with the Church, charged a new generation of critics. They argued that the elaborate sculptural decoration of Cluniac churches distracted people from true religion. New twelfth-century reform efforts included those of the Carthusians and the Cistercians, both in France. The Carthusian reform laid new austerities on the monks, who were to maintain strict silence and live and sleep in a solitary cell (in which they were to keep, ready at hand, parchment, pen and ink, and ruler; for every Carthusian was required to be a scholar). The Cistercian order aimed to return to the original simplicity of the Benedictine ideal. Its churches were denuded of adornment, and the requirement to do manual work

was strictly enforced. The special mission of the Cistercians was to clear and reclaim the wastelands that still littered the surface of Europe.

The Mendicant Orders Reform efforts culminated in the thirteenth-century innovation of the **mendicant** orders, which transformed monasticism by creating an alternative to it. Mendicant friars—called "brothers," rather than monks—pledged themselves to service in a world that was no longer poor, no longer exclusively rural, and no longer simple. The growth of cities of a vigor unimaginable in the days of Benedict called for radically new forms of Christian mission. It was a young Italian, the son of a wealthy cloth merchant, but later known to the world as Saint Francis of Assisi (c. 1182–1226) who first defined that new venture. Francis began by giving away his possessions to the poor, whereupon his father disowned him. According to legend, Francis then stripped himself of all his finery in the market square of his native town of Assisi and, wearing a cloak donated by the bishop of Assisi, journeyed forth in poverty to seek God, as illustrated on p. 259. Francis urged that poverty was central to true reform. For twenty years, he and his loyal followers devoted themselves to "spiritual poverty." They wandered from village to village and town to town, begging for food, offering service, and preaching in their "lofty poverty" a gospel focused on the humility of Jesus. With neither monastic house nor endowment, the Franciscans were the pioneers of a form of Christian devotion adapted to thirteenth-century life—mobile and urban—just as Benedictinism had suited those of the sixth.

Among the followers of Francis of Assisi was a young noblewoman, Clare, who was converted by him and founded a female order, the "Poor Clares," the counterpart of Francis' own order of Franciscans. (The "Clares," however, remained cloistered and could not follow the mendicant life of their Franciscan brothers.)

Not long after Francis' death, the Franciscan movement began to encounter a familiar obstacle: wealth. The stupendously rich merchant leaders of the Italian cities respected the deep spirituality of the Franciscans. Their generous gifts flowed into an order that had, at the outset, neither treasury nor administrative center. These soon appeared, causing a rift among the Franciscans.

The "Conventual" Franciscans became managers of wealth, and adjusted Francis' rule—the pope concurring—to suit its new condition. The friars who refused to compromise and maintained strictly their founder's injunction to poverty were called "Observant" or "Spiritual" Franciscans. The absolute standard of poverty, though it accorded perfectly with scripture, implicitly challenged the practices of property management essential to the institutional Church, which made it a dangerous idea in the eyes of that organization. The pope declared the Observants heretical. Many were burned at the stake.

Before these internal tensions weakened the Franciscan mission, a contemporary of Francis of Assisi, the Spanish nobleman Dominic Guzmán of Castile (c. 1170–1221) inaugurated another movement of itinerant friars. Like Francis, Dominic saw that a new form of Christian service was required to meet the needs of the society of his day. He, too, pledged his followers to poverty. But Dominic had a further mission: to teach orthodox Christian doctrine and to prevent the spread of false or heretical views. Dominicans became not only teachers but also inquisitors—agents of the church in the identification and prosecution of heresy.

The launching of the Inquisition in the thirteenth century marks the culmination of a period of change in the medieval church. The Catholic Church, rooted in Rome, where once Senate and emperor had held sway, and led by an effective hierarchy of clerical administrators, had become an institution of unprecedented power. Establishing policy and issuing decrees, church leaders now often found themselves in conflict with kings and princes whose claims for authority they sought to control.

CHURCH AND STATE

While monasticism evolved with changes in medieval society, the relations of the Church with the political powers of Europe also shifted. In the early Middle Ages, the institutions of the Church performed the functions abandoned by the Roman state. Lords and princes availed themselves of churchmen's skills of management and literacy, with the effect that many of the higher clergy became attached to the interests of secular rulers. Under church leadership, Europeans battled with Muslim Turks in the Crusades for access to the Holy Land (see Chapter 9), and defined their differences with the Eastern church and with their own Jewish populations. The Catholic Church acted like a state, or provided aid to the rulers of states, while those rulers employed churchmen as their secretaries and advisers. Thus, by the twelfth century, political and ecclesiastical functions were thoroughly intertwined.

Beginning around 1000, the papacy had led an extensive reform movement which established the independence of the clergy from secular government and society. Now, as the Middle Ages reached maturity, the powerful papacy forgot its original mission and warded off efforts to restrict its power by subordinating the pope to the authority of representative councils. As the institutional Church grew in wealth and power, the needs of the ordinary Christian were often forgotten.

Popes and Kings: The Era of Cooperation

By the fourth century C.E., when the Roman world was turning Christian, the bishops of the great ancient cities of Rome, Constantinople, Alexandria, and Antioch had gained preeminence over all others. Of these, only Rome lay in the Latin-speaking west. The bishop of Rome represented special authority

---

WITNESSES

Monastic Life and Mendicant Spirituality

Monasticism was a primary institution of the medieval world, offering stability to its members, and solace and services to those beyond its doors. Benedict, the author of the first passage, lays down guidelines for a meaningful life in religious community. Seven centuries later, some observant Christians sought a different kind of spiritual experience—not of stability and labor, but of service in the world, and a more passionate connection to God and his creation. Francis of Assisi, the pioneer of this later "mendicant" movement, is the author of this prayer of praise to God, closely identified with nature.

Benedict sets limits on work and wealth for monks (c. 536): Idleness is the great enemy of the soul, therefore the monks should always be occupied, either in manual labor or in holy reading. The hours for these occupations should be arranged according to the seasons . ... But if the conditions of the locality or the needs of the monastery, such as may occur at harvest time, should make it necessary to labor longer hours, they shall not feel themselves ill-used, for true monks should live by the labor of their own hands, as did the apostles and the holy fathers. ...

The sin of owning private property should be entirely eradicated from the monastery. No one shall presume to give or receive anything except by the order of the abbot; no one shall possess anything of his own, books, papers, pens, or anything else; for monks are not to own even their own bodies and wills to be used at their own desire, but are to look to the father [abbot] of the monastery for everything.
(St. Benedict, *Rule*, c. 536; eds. O. J. Thatcher, E. H. McNeal, 1905)

Francis of Assisi exalts God in nature (13th century):
Praise be to Thee, my Lord, with all Thy creatures,
Especially to my worshipful brother sun,
The which lights up the day, and through him dost Thou brightness give;
And beautiful is he and radiant with splendour great;
Of Thee, most High, signification gives.

. . .

Praised be my Lord for our sister, mother earth,
The which sustains and keeps us
And brings forth diverse fruits with grass and flowers bright.
(St. Francis, "The Canticle of the Sun"; ed. P. Robinson, 1906)

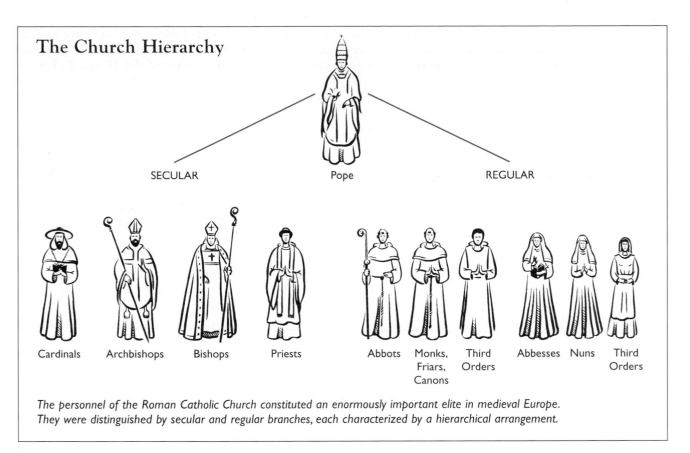

The Church Hierarchy

Pope

SECULAR   Pope   REGULAR

Cardinals   Archbishops   Bishops   Priests   Abbots   Monks, Friars, Canons   Third Orders   Abbesses   Nuns   Third Orders

The personnel of the Roman Catholic Church constituted an enormously important elite in medieval Europe. They were distinguished by secular and regular branches, each characterized by a hierarchical arrangement.

because of the association with Saint Peter, one of Jesus' twelve disciples, who was believed to have been executed in that capital during Nero's persecution. Jesus had granted Peter authority over the church, it was thought, when he pronounced these words: "You are Peter [in the original Aramaic phrase, *Caipha*, meaning "rock" and in Latin translation *Petrus*, or rock] and on this rock I will build my church." Peter transferred that authority (it was believed) to all subsequent bishops of Rome. In time, these prelates assumed the title of "pope," meaning "father." They also assumed the functions of rulers, as Roman authority crumbled and no one was left in charge.

The emergence of the papacy as a major institution began with the Roman bishop Leo I (r. 440–461), called "the Great," later canonized. Amid the many crises of the fifth century, the figure of Pope Leo towers. He was a serious theologian, a prolific author, and a dauntless leader. When Attila the Hun swept into northern Italy in 452 intent on conquest (though weakened by sickness), Leo and a small delegation of churchmen conferred with him. According to legend, it was the pope's pleas that deflected the bellicose chieftain from his path.

At the end of the next century, another pope later called "Great" led the Church. Gregory (r. 590–604), the son of a Roman senator, grew up in an Italy devastated by the Gothic wars and beset by Lombard invasions. As a scholar, Gregory encapsulated Christian teachings in works that were easily

mastered by a barely literate clergy. More, he established the role and duties of priests and bishops in an environment where secular authority had practically vanished. These two achievements helped prepare the West for the great isolation that prevailed in the early Middle Ages, and helped extend Christian institutions to the farthest reaches of Europe (it was Gregory's mission that finally achieved the conversion of Anglo-Saxon England). By the time of his death, the principle that the pope was head of the Church not only in Rome or in Italy but in the whole of Latin-speaking Europe had been clearly asserted.

Yet the popes had to concern themselves especially with Italy, lest the Church be swallowed up by the conflicts that boiled there after the Lombard takeover. They sought the protection of the Eastern emperor, who still controlled footholds in Sicily, the south, and Venice. When that aid became undependable, the popes sought military aid from another secular ruler, Pepin, the king of the Franks, who was both strong and a Catholic. In 754 and again in 756, Pepin was invited into Italy to dispel the Lombard threat to Rome. Pepin's son and successor, Charlemagne, twice went to Italy to secure the pope's safety.

By 800, the papacy had acquired, through Frankish intervention, control over a belt of territory (in addition to smaller, scattered possessions) running from sea to sea across central Italy. This region, called the Papal States, enabled the papacy to both feed and defend itself. Meanwhile, Italy, which had already experienced invasion by the Gauls, the Ostrogoths, the Huns, and the Lombards, had learned to expect periodic irruptions of armies led by northern kings over the Alpine frontier.

In the ninth and tenth centuries, the Church at Rome continued to work with the emerging monarchs of the European nations for their mutual benefit. The pope expected priests to be supported by the secular power. At the same time, he expected secular rulers to respect the autonomy of the Church—its property, its personnel, and its laws. Secular rulers, in turn, helped select church leaders in their own lands and employed clergy (for years the only literate persons in Europe) in their own administrations. This symbiotic relationship of Church and state endured until about 1000. Thereafter, it changed, as both Church and state sought to expand their power.

The Militant Church

After the millennium year 1000, a confident Church within a confident Christendom, no longer fearful of persecution or invasion, began to show its strength, as indicated on Map 10.1. It struck out against Islam in a series of holy wars, the Crusades, and defined its position relative to European Jews and Eastern Orthodox Christians. Christian society then turned aggressively on its fellow monotheists in confrontations supported and sometimes led by the Church. Opening the door to an era of intolerance, these events witness the readiness of the Church to assert its authority within Europe and beyond.

The Crusades were fought by European knights against Turkish dominion of lands considered holy (see Chapter 9 and Map 9.2). But it was the newly powerful papacy that instigated and orchestrated these wars. The First Crusade (1095–1099) was triggered by an appeal to the pope from the Byzantine emperor, under threat from the Seljuk Turks. The pope, Urban II (r. 1088–1099), saw several good reasons to hurl an army of European knights against the Muslim Turks, whose advance put Christian pilgrimage routes to the Holy Land at risk. A foreign war, moreover, would mobilize Christian sentiments in the west, would channel the aggression of western warriors in a useful direction, and might possibly result in the recovery of Jerusalem, the Holy City, which had been occupied by Seljuk Turks in 1071. In 1095, at Clermont (in France), Urban exhorted the people to join the Crusade. Thousands of poor pilgrims and armored knights set out from the European heartlands. Europe had begun to expand its authority, impelled in part by the leadership of the Church.

Military Orders One sign of the aggressive posture of Christianity in the crusading era was the birth of military-monastic orders. Two of these were inspired by the need to provide security and medical care for the pilgrims who flooded the Holy Land after its conquest in the First Crusade. They were the Hospitallers (the "Knights of the Order of the Hospital of Saint John") and the Templars ("Knights of the Temple"). Members of these orders took monastic vows but wore arms and led a military life.

Both orders were expelled from the Holy Land after the Turks reconquered the region in the thirteenth century. The Hospitallers relocated to the islands of Cyprus, then Rhodes, and finally Malta. The Templars returned to Europe, immensely wealthy from their activity as protectors of Crusader treasure. Their control of thousands of castles and manors in France aroused the greed of the French king, Philip IV (r. 1285–1314). He accused the Templars of abominable crimes, tortured and executed their leaders, and confiscated property. In cooperation with the French monarchy, the Church dissolved the order.

A third order, the Teutonic Knights, established themselves in the thirteenth century in the German lands of eastern Prussia. Their mission was to Christianize the last pagan territory of Europe—a form of crusade itself, though in a different geographical arena. The Teutonic Knights dominated the Baltic area from Gdansk (in modern Poland) to Estonia, and presided over the colonization of the region by German settlers. They were dissolved in the sixteenth century during the Protestant Reformation.

Intolerance The era of the Crusades occasioned a shift in the Church's relationship with Islam (see Chapter 8). Islamic society had successfully absorbed both Christians and Jews, because they considered them, like themselves, "people of the book," co-believers in one God and in his prophets, from Abraham to Moses to Jesus—albeit not Muhammad. In Islamic regions both communities were tolerated, although they were required to pay special taxes. Christians were less tolerant toward Islam, but had little opportunity to confront it in the early Middle Ages. After 1000, that confrontation began on several fronts. In Spain, Christian leaders began the long "Reconquest" of the Iberian peninsula from Moorish domination. In the Mediterranean, the navies of Pisa and Genoa, with papal aid, swept aside Saracen fleets and raided North African cities. In the south of Italy, Norman knights supported by the pope wrested Sicily from Saracen hands. Then, beginning with the First Crusade, Christian soldiers faced the Muslim Turks in a struggle over what both considered holy land.

At the same time, Christian relations with Judaism also became more hostile. Officially, the Church viewed Judaism as the matrix from which Christianity had been born. For this reason, it was stipulated that Jews were not to be harmed or forcibly converted to Christianity. Despite that official stance of grudging toleration, ordinary Christians sometimes behaved differently. The First Crusade opened

Map 10.1 Christianity and other World Religions, to 1500: *Over many centuries, Christianity spread from Constantinople and Rome; from Celtic Ireland, Anglo-Saxon England, and the eastern Frankish kingdom; from Moscow and Novgorod. As Christianity expanded from its Mediterranean homeland to the remotest boundaries of Europe, it took its place as a major world religion. In the inset map above, it appears that the boundaries of major religious traditions correspond to the boundaries of the advanced Old World civilizations: why?*

with massacres of Jews in the German Rhineland, an expression, at this exceptionally intense moment, of endemic hostility toward neighbors perceived as alien. Anti-Semitism broke out frequently thereafter,

as Jews continued to be stigmatized in popular culture and even in learned treatises as monstrous, greedy, and bloodthirsty. Throughout medieval Europe rulers expelled Jews from their lands—from England in

Papal Supremacy, Clerical Reform, and Conciliar Resistance

What kind of an institution would the Church become? Who would be in charge? These questions pressed urgently from the eleventh through the sixteenth century. These three passages contain three different claims to authority. In the first, the pope asserts his authority even over the emperor, the greatest of secular rulers. In the second, a church official reports to his superiors about the lax behavior of some cathedral canons, who will be required to reform. In the third, a council of prelates and scholars announces that it has its "power directly from Christ," and can therefore exercise it even over popes.

Pope Gregory VII insists on papal supremacy (1075), decreeing:
1. That the Roman church was founded by God alone.
2. That the Roman pontiff alone can with right be called universal.
3. That he alone can depose or reinstate bishops.

. . .

8. That he alone may use the imperial insignia.
9. That of the pope alone all princes shall kiss the feet.
10. That his name alone shall be spoken in the churches.
11. That this is the only name in the world.
12. That it may be permitted to him to depose emperors.

. . .

19. That he himself may be judged by no one.

(Gregory VII, *Dictatus papae*, 1075, 1:121–125; ed. E. F. Henderson, 1892)

Eudes de Rigaud describes the lax obedience of the clergy (1248): We visited the Chapter of Rouen [attached to the cathedral], and found that they talk in choir contrary to rule. The clergy wander about the church, and talk in the church with women, during the celebration of divine service. The statute regarding the entrance [of lay folk] into the choir is not kept. The psalms are run through too rapidly, without due pauses. ... Moreover, the clergy leave the choir without reason, before the end of the service already begun; and, to be brief, many other of the statutes written on the board in the vestry are not kept. The chapter revenues are mismanaged.

(Eudes de Rigaud, "Register of Visitations," 1248; ed., trs. G. G. Coulton, 1892)

Decree of the Council of Constance, claiming authority even over popes (1415): This holy synod of Constance, constituting a general council, does hereby ordain, ratify, enact, decree, and declare the following:

First, it declares that ... it has its power directly from Christ, and that all persons of whatever rank or dignity, even a Pope, are bound to obey it in matters relating to faith and the end of the Schism and the general reformation of the Church of God in head and members.

Further, it declares that any person of whatever position, rank or dignity, even a Pope, who contumaciously refuses to obey the mandates, statutes, ordinances, or regulations enacted or to be enacted by this holy synod, or by any other general council lawfully assembled, ... shall, unless he repents, be subject to condign penalty and duly punished. ...

("Decrees of the Council of Constance," 1415; trs. L. R. Loomis 1961)

1290 (under Edward I); from France in 1306 (under Philip IV); from Spain, horribly, in 1492 (under Ferdinand and Isabella); from Portugal, on the Spanish model, in 1497. The Jewish communities migrated: from the Iberian peninsula to the eastern Mediterranean and North Africa; and from the north, eastward to the German and Slavic lands of Europe, where great numbers lived until the Holocaust of the twentieth century (see Chapters 24, 28).

When the crusading era opened, the Roman Church had split from the Eastern Orthodox Church, whose official leader, or patriarch, reigned in Constantinople under the protection of the Byzantine Empire. As early as the fourth century, doctrinal and philosophical differences could be observed between western (Latin-speaking) and eastern (Greek-speaking) leaders of the church. Thus, their respective churches developed, quite early, separate intellectual traditions. From the fifth through the seventh centuries, the Catholic Church often appealed to the Eastern emperor for political support but in vain. In the eighth and ninth centuries, finding itself increasingly isolated, it turned instead to the Frankish king. That era coincided with the episode of iconoclasm in the Eastern Church, decried by the popes (see Chapter 8).

Relations between the two churches foundered irremediably over a single clause in the formulation of the Nicene Creed. The Western Church insisted that the Holy Spirit (one of the three members of the Trinity) proceeded from the Father *and* the Son. The Eastern theologians insisted that the Spirit proceeded from the Father only. In 1054, leaders of the two churches excommunicated each other. The rift endures. The break with the Eastern Church left the pope the unrivaled Christian leader in the west.

In the meantime, Byzantine missionaries had brought their form of Christianity to the Slavic peoples of Europe inhabiting the eastern part of the continent from the Baltic to the Balkans. Byzantine missionaries reached Bulgaria in the ninth century, and Russia in the tenth. In the 860s, the missionary Saint Cyril (c. 827–869) devised from Greek characters an alphabet (named, after him, Cyrillic) in which to write the Slavic language (which heretofore had had no written form). Thereafter the saints' lives could be read by the new converts, just as the beautiful icons representing their faces could be venerated. Among the Slavic practitioners of Eastern Christianity were the ancestors of modern Russians. After Constantinople fell to the Ottoman Turks in 1453, the independent Russian Church preserved the Eastern Orthodox tradition.

Reform and Confrontation

As it proceeded to distinguish itself from other faiths, the Catholic Church undertook a thorough self-examination, inspired by the monastic reform begun at Cluny. In the same way that the Cluniac abbots insisted on monastic discipline, the Church in Rome (beginning shortly before 1100) announced stringent standards of personal behavior for the secular clergy. They were to remain strictly celibate (abstaining completely from sexual contacts) and to fulfill their pastoral responsibilities. Church offices were not to be sold or conferred upon relatives, friends, or favorites. Above all, authority was to be centered at Rome, and church personnel and funds were to be strictly reserved for the purposes of the Church.

The papal reform effort placed the Church at loggerheads with secular rulers on matters regarding the selection, appointment, and **investiture** of bishops—investiture being the process by which an office, either secular or ecclesiastical, was conferred. A new bishop was invested by being given the ring and staff that symbolized his clerical office. Because bishops and other church officials had both spiritual and temporal authority, confusion reigned as to who was entitled to appoint them and perform the ceremony of investiture. In the ninth and tenth centuries, the appointment and investiture of church officials had been the prerogative of secular rulers, but this right was now reclaimed for the Church by the papacy, who saw lay investiture of clergy as a major impediment to the establishment of church autonomy. The shift in policy especially affected the German emperors, whose political power rested on the bishops and lesser clerics, and who wanted able, skilled men to serve the interests of their state.

Also included in the papal reform agenda was the enforcement of moral standards with regard to the sexual behavior of the clergy and to the sale of church offices. In the early Middle Ages, celibacy had been thought desirable but not essential for the secular clergy. Many priests had concubines who acted virtually as wives, or engaged in other illicit forms of heterosexual behavior; homosexuality, too, appears to have been tolerated. Not only were the heterosexual alliances of priests increasingly considered improper, but they threatened church property, which might be lost to the illegitimate sons of errant priests. With church reform, celibacy became a requirement. Almost as common as the failure of priestly chastity was the sale of church offices, called **simony**, or their bestowal upon unworthy or juvenile relatives, called **nepotism**. These corrupt practices often resulted in the conveyance of church responsibilities to unqualified candidates who endangered both the effectiveness and the wealth of the Church. They, too, were now condemned.

One eleventh-century pope—one of the greatest in the history of the papacy—is particularly associated with the reform thrust of the mature medieval Church. Born Hildebrand, he was elected to the papacy as Gregory VII in 1073, having developed his reform program under the two previous popes. His principal target was the German emperor, Henry IV. In 1075, Pope Gregory wrote about his condemnation of lay investiture and his conception of papal authority in his register known as *Dictatus papae* ("The Pope's Decree"), quoted in *Witnesses* on p. 270. It declared, among other things:

> *That all princes shall kiss the feet of the pope.*
> *That he may be permitted to depose emperors.*
> *That he himself may be judged by no one.*

In 1076, Henry assembled his bishops and got them to declare their independence of the pope. Gregory responded by excommunicating Henry. The decree of **excommunication** was a sanction of utmost gravity, cutting the Christian off from the sacraments and ordinary social relations; and, when a monarch was excommunicated, releasing his subjects from allegiance to him. Thus it humiliated and incapacitated the German emperor, whose authority was fragile and whose barons now found it convenient to rebel. In the winter of 1077, in a hauntingly memorable scene, Henry stood for three days as a barefoot penitent outside the castle at Canossa, in Tuscany, where the papal party was en route to an assembly where the emperor's status would be discussed. The pope granted Henry **absolution**. For the moment, the papacy had outpaced in authority the secular monarchy.

The moment of reconciliation quickly passed. Years of papal-imperial conflict ensued; and in 1084 Henry IV succeeded in deposing his old adversary. Gregory died the following year, affirming, in the words of the psalmist, "I have loved justice and hated iniquity, therefore I die in exile."

The emperor's son and successor, Henry V (r. 1106–1125), continued to battle with popes. In 1122, he and the reigning pope, Calixtus II (r. 1119–1124) agreed to the Concordat of Worms (a city in the southwest of modern Germany), a landmark accord that settled at last the issue of lay investiture. The emperor guaranteed the free election of clergy and renounced any role in their investiture with ring and staff. The pope granted the emperor the right to be present at elections and to invest those elected with their lay responsibilities. In effect, this document described a new and enduring balance between church and secular powers—in the metaphor of the day, two "swords." The Church held the spiritual and archbishop differed over the issue of punishing "criminous clerics"—churchmen accused of crimes, who were tried and convicted in church courts. Henry wanted them to be punished by secular authorities, to which Becket refused to assent. The king later charged Becket with financial improprieties while serving as his chancellor, and Becket went into exile rather than submit to trial in a secular court. The pope intervened, belatedly, on behalf of his archbishop. On Becket's return, he again offended the king, and Henry complained aloud of his troublesome prelate. In 1170, four of his knights—spontaneously perhaps, or too hastily responding to the king's instruction—slaughtered Becket in his own cathedral at Canterbury—murder compounded by sacrilege. England acquired in Becket a saint, and Canterbury became a pilgrimage site. Henry did **penance** and acknowledged church authority.

Church and State

Thomas à Becket: *The clashes between popes and emperors, bishops and kings, are represented vividly by the manuscript illumination (Ramsey Abbey, England, c. 1316) of the murder of Thomas à Becket, Archbishop of Canterbury and martyr of the English Church. (Pierpont Morgan Library)*

sword and authority in all matters pertaining to faith. The empire held the temporal sword and authority in all matters related to the security of the realm and the administration of justice among **laypeople**. The pope would choose his bishops, but the emperor might suggest his own candidates. The pope would invest the new cleric, then the emperor would charge him with his secular responsibilities. The principle had been announced—and would eventually prevail in the West—that Church and state were distinct.

The settlement at Worms was precarious, as soon became apparent in a different setting. King Henry II (1154–1189) of England had among his closest advisers the shrewd churchman Thomas à Becket (1118–1170). When, in 1162, Becket assumed the highest ecclesiastical office in the land, that of Archbishop of Canterbury, his behavior changed profoundly. No longer the cooperative royal servant, he was now the guardian of ecclesiastical rights. King

Pinturicchio, Pope Pius II at Ancona: *The papal role in fostering the Crusade effort is depicted by Pinturicchio in a fresco in Siena Cathedral, c. 1500, showing Pope Pius II assembling forces (in 1464) for a last vain attempt to reconquer the Holy Land from the Ottoman Turks.*

Born ten years before Becket's murder and made pope in 1198, Innocent III (r. 1198–1216) was a worthy successor to Gregory VII as an intellectual, reformer, and opponent of lay encroachment on ecclesiastical authority. Just as spirit reigned over body, he maintained, popes held rightful preeminence over secular princes—a belief he put into action on several occasions, one being when he excommunicated King John of England for interfering with the process of papal appointments. The principle of papal supremacy was acknowledged by the French, Spanish, and German monarchs, from whom Innocent demanded obedience.

At the opening of the fourteenth century, pope and monarch clashed again, this time in France. Here the issue was not investiture or judicial rights but money. King Philip IV (the Fair) planned to tap church wealth to restore the national treasury. In 1302 Pope Boniface VIII (r. 1294–1303) hurled at Philip the decree *Unam Sanctam*, which declared the supremacy of the Church over secular monarchs. Philip ordered his agents to depose the pope; they pursued him to Anagni, the town of his birth, where he had taken refuge, and proceeded to terrorize him. The townspeople rescued Boniface, but he died soon after, no doubt hurried along by his ordeal. The French king proclaimed the autonomy of the church in France from papal intervention. Philip IV's humiliation of Boniface in 1303, some two centuries after Pope Gregory's triumph over Henry IV in 1077, is a significant measure of the decline of papal authority in the later Middle Ages.

Popes and Councils

Following the death of Boniface, papal authority continued to wane. The next pope, Clement V (r. 1305–1314), was a Frenchman and Philip's puppet. He established himself and his court in the southern town of Avignon (then a papal possession, now part of France). Ordinary Christians were disheartened. For the first time, the head of the Catholic Church was no longer at Rome. Later critics of the papacy named the period of French residence (1309–1377) the "Babylonian Captivity" of the Church, recalling the image of the exile of the Israelites in Babylon in the sixth century B.C.E (see Chapter 2). It was the first phase of a period in which an increasingly corrupt and worldly papacy asserted its power in the face of mounting popular resentment.

During the Avignon years, and continuing a trend begun in the thirteenth century, the Church came to resemble a modern corporation. It employed an enormous staff of secretaries and treasurers and handled great sums of money. It reformed its administration, organized its bureaucracy, and improved its methods of accountancy. Presenting a model for growing monarchies to imitate, the papacy became the foremost monarchy in Europe. Some observers were impressed; others resented its political ambitions.

The Great Schism The pope belonged in Rome—so nearly everyone but the king of France believed. In 1377, persuaded by voices such as that of Catherine of Siena, Pope Gregory XI returned to Rome accompanied by his court and the College of Cardinals, high-ranking prelates whose unique privilege it is to elect popes. On Gregory's death in 1378, these cardinals (pressured by a Roman mob) elected his successor—an Italian—in Rome. Then, dissatisfied with their candidate, they repudiated him and elected a French pope, with whom they returned to Avignon. In Rome, however, the first candidate continued to reign, claiming supremacy and surrounded by a newly appointed College of Cardinals. The Church was now divided—in a state of **schism**.

Throughout Europe, nations, principalities, and cities now aligned themselves with one or the other pope. In 1409, at a council of clerical delegates and university theologians held at Pisa, the two then-reigning popes were deposed and a third was elected. Since neither of the deposed prelates recognized the authority of the council, they refused to step down. As a result, there were three popes. The scandalous "Great Schism," as the period of a divided church was called, lasted from 1378 to 1417. During those years, some Christians began to wonder whether they needed a pope at all.

Council of Constance The schism came to an end by actions taken at another council, held at Constance (in modern Switzerland) from 1414 to 1418 under the stern gaze of Sigismund, the Holy Roman Emperor (r. 1411–1437). The council's goals were three: to end the schism, to check the spread of heresy, to reform the Church. With nearly all the important leaders of the Church as well as university experts in theology and church law participating, it resolved the schism by deposing all three popes and electing (in 1417) the reliable Martin V (r. 1417–1431). It also, notoriously, condemned as a heretic the Czech scholar and visionary John Huss (c. 1372–1415), who was burned at the stake.

Before disbanding, those assembled at Constance decreed that the Church was to be governed not by the pope alone but by regularly held councils made up of persons like themselves (see *Witnesses* p. 270). Once the popes were solidly established at Rome, however, and getting ever richer, they resisted. A council was held beginning in 1431 (at Basel, in Switzerland), which degenerated into hostilities between pope and councilors. In 1437 another council convened—first at Ferrara, in Italy, then in Florence when Ferrara was struck by plague. It was dedicated to conversations with prelates from the Eastern Orthodox Church. Terrified at the Turkish advance, which was in its final stage, the emperor at Constantinople had sent that delegation hoping that reconciliation would yield western military assistance for his embattled capital. Despite a compromise, the rift between the two churches was not healed. Constantinople fell in 1453. In the west, the conciliar movement faded under the eagle eye of a now-potent pope.

In the century following the elevation of Martin V at the Council of Constance, the papacy became increasingly powerful, wealthy, and corrupt. The centralized bureaucracy collected taxes from every corner of Christendom. The wealth funded the rebuilding of Rome, the creation of a fine library at the Vatican, the defense of the Papal States, a network of ambassadors and agents, and even the preparations for a last futile Crusade. The popes, the cardinals, and the bishops, well compensated for duties they left others to perform, promoted their friends, nephews, and illegitimate children to lucrative offices. The Catholic Church had strayed far from the example of simplicity and sincerity presented by the biblical Jesus. To many, it seemed to have abandoned ordinary Christians, and especially those that Jesus had especially recommended: the poor and the forgotten.

THE CHURCH AND THE PEOPLE

Most people at this time were unaware of the papacy's accumulation of wealth and power, or the scandalous behavior of the various popes. Their knowledge of the Church was based only on the rhythms and rituals of the Christian year and their acquaintance with the parish priest. Even the dedicated lives of the monks and nuns in nearby monasteries and convents seemed remote to ordinary villagers and townsfolk. A few, however, lived extraordinary lives. Craving a deeper religious experience, they were drawn to **mysticism**, or to heresy, or to the movements of pious lay people that flourished in the later Middle Ages.

The Pattern of Christian Life

Most medieval Christians knew the tenets of the Church only as told them by a village priest—often a peasant like themselves, uneducated and unaware. Those who lived in the towns and cities that developed after 1000 knew the priest of their immediate neighborhood or parish, the bishop and semimonastic **canons** of the cathedral, and the friars who preached in the market squares and begged in the streets. The wealthy nobleman was tended by his own priest or chaplain, who officiated in the private chapel of his castle. In village, city, or castle, the priest celebrated the **mass** by which Christians experienced union with the Deity, and administered other sacraments by which they received the grace of God and some assurance of salvation.

Only an ordained priest could officiate at the mass, in which bread and wine—the elements—were believed to be transformed into the body and blood of Christ. Worshipers consuming those transformed elements (by 1300, only the bread called "the host" was offered to the **laity**) were believed to be in communion with Christ. This ritual event, called the Eucharist, was one of the seven sacraments of the Church.

A sacrament in the Catholic and Orthodox churches is a ritual act conveying grace to the worshiper. Four others mark stages in human life—baptism, which incorporates a child into the church; confirmation, by which a child affirms his or her faith; marriage, which joins male and female in a legitimate relationship; and anointing, or extreme unction, which prepared a dying person for eternity. The other two sacraments are ordination, by which a man is made a priest; and penance, which follows a person's confession of their sins. The priest assigns an act of penance to be performed in order to atone for a particular sin and obtain absolution, the forgiveness of that sin.

The crucified Jesus: *The central event of the Christian religion is the crucifixion of Jesus, represented frequently over the medieval centuries in every available medium. Here is shown an ornate crucifix from fourteenth-century France. (Musei Civici, Padua)*

To medieval Christians (and to some Christians today), penance and absolution were matters of supreme importance. Those whose sins had been confessed and absolved looked forward to life after death in Heaven. Those who died burdened with serious sins would be doomed to Hell, a place of eternal punishment. These were the poles that defined the universe of the medieval Christian. The faithful were instructed about these destinies in words and forms, in the preachers' sermons and in the stone and wooden sculptures and stained-glass windows of the churches. Fears of Hell were somewhat lessened, however, by the possibility of spending some term of the afterlife in Purgatory.

From late antiquity to the thirteenth century, the concept of Purgatory gradually developed as a third realm to which the soul might be temporarily consigned. Here the Christian who was not entirely sinless could expiate his or her sins and still eventually achieve admission to Heaven. He or she could be helped along by the intercession of the saints or of the Virgin Mary, or by the prayers of the faithful still on earth. Some careful planners left bequests in their wills to pay for the performance of masses for the welfare of their souls in Purgatory. These could help. But the Christian who wished to gain Heaven and avoid Hell must attend mass, receive the sacraments, confess, and receive absolution for sins. Thus priests were the gatekeepers of salvation.

Guidebooks called "penitentials" assigned punishments to those who had sinned. In the early Middle Ages, an adulterer or murderer might be assigned a long and difficult penance—years of fasting on bread and water, for instance, or confinement. In the later period, available acts of penance also included gifts to the Church for the building of a hospital or a chapel—attractive alternatives to persons of middling wealth, just as great noblemen of earlier times had found it beneficial to found a monastery.

A form of penance popular with repentant sinners throughout the period was the pilgrimage (which for knights could take the form of a Crusade). A long and hazardous journey to Jerusalem or a somewhat shorter one to the Shrine of Saint James of Compostela (in Spain) or that of Saint Thomas à Becket at Canterbury (in England) or to Rome might atone for a mountain of sins. At these sites, the penitent could revere the body or part of the body—the relic, sometimes only a knucklebone or a tooth—of a saint, who could intercede with God for forgiveness of sins.

The many sins were classified in seven categories: pride, envy, anger, greed, lust, gluttony, and a spiritual apathy dangerous to the soul called sloth. Although all were evil, the emphasis in the confessional often fell on lust—illicit sexual desire and sexual misconduct. Confessors asked adult men and women about adultery and prostitution, male adolescents about masturbation, and females about secret pregnancies.

They asked husbands and wives whether they had performed intercourse only for the purpose of procreation, and if they had done so according to acceptable guidelines established by church scholars. They queried women about obedience to parents or husbands, and men about homosexual behavior. Homosexuality was considered not only a sin but, in some regions and periods, a crime punishable by death. Yet it was common in the exclusively male community of the monastic clergy.

Baptism was expected to follow birth promptly. The death of an unbaptized infant condemned the soul of the unfortunate to a zone on the margins of Hell, called limbo—and threatened survivors with contamination. Clerical experts also condemned abortion and infanticide; abandoned infants were considered a responsibility of the Church. The dying were to confess their sins, making a "good death" so that they might enter Heaven or, at least, Purgatory. Those who died unbaptized or excommunicate or as a result of suicide were denied burial in sacred ground.

Marriage was considered not only a sacrament of the Church but also a secular institution involving the transfer of property between families. For those who bestowed or received wealth in a marriage agreement, the moment when the contract was signed or when the bride was conducted to her husband's house might be considered the moment of marriage. The Church attempted to bring marriage customs under its jurisdiction. It insisted on the equal importance of the man's and the woman's intention to marry. Each had to consent freely to the arrangement, and it was their freely exchanged words, when followed by consummation, that were regarded as establishing the marriage. Around the beginning of the thirteenth century, it became the custom for this exchange of vows to be conducted in front of or inside the church building and to receive the blessing of a priest. However, the marriage ceremony was not wholly standardized until the sixteenth century, when both Protestants and Catholics insisted on church control of the institution.

Although the Church regulated the lives of most Christians, it especially controlled those of women. Clerical authors considered women—in the pattern of Eve, who had led Adam to sin in the Garden of Eden—to be the origin of all sin (see *Windows On*, p. 277). From this assumption emerged a clerical and long-enduring misogyny. Women's bodies were condemned for luring men into vice. The monastic reformer Odo of Cluny exclaimed: "How can we desire to embrace such a sack of dung?" Women were deceitful, lustful, incapable of reason. They had to be confined to domesticity and to carefully guarded chastity. A special target of preachers and confessors, women were portrayed as an ever-present danger. Summing up the Church's view of women, a cleric warned, "Woe unto this sex, which knows nothing of awe, goodness, or friendship, and which is more to be feared when loved than when hated!" Of that sex also, ironically, was the Virgin Mary, revered by medieval Christians, and the subject of many works of prayer and art, as illustrated on p. 175.

As it battled against the dangers posed by women, as it was believed, to the health of the soul, the medieval Church also struggled with the relics of paganism—the customs and beliefs surviving among European communities from the days before Christianization. Many of the attributes of ancient gods had become attached to revered saints. The old legends and rituals were gradually assimilated into Christian practices. As late as the eighteenth century, in some quiet villages and enclaves, people who were nominally Christian displayed vestiges of pre-Christian religious behavior—evident in their faith in charms or spells or special objects—despite the rigorous intervention of priests and inquisitors.

If the Church intruded in many ways upon the lives of Christians, it also provided services that were otherwise unavailable. The Church cared for the ill, the poor, the hungry, the widowed and orphaned. In the early Middle Ages, monasteries served as hospitals and hostelries in the absence of any others. With the expansion of urban life, later in the Middle Ages, the Church expanded its mission, establishing hospitals and orphanages and homes for abandoned wives and destitute widows. Here the pious and the saintly, by their concern, their labor, and their donations, might give expression to charity.

Extraordinary Christians

Although the lives of ordinary people were saturated with Christian meanings and regulated by Christian instruction, some individuals found even this degree of religiosity inadequate to their spiritual needs. They yearned for a deeper, more complete experience of God. Some of them were later canonized as saints, whose holy works could transfer holiness to those who revered them. Some were mystics, who sought in the interior self a union with the divine. Some were heretics, who urged that God be sought outside the norms and boundaries of Catholic orthodoxy. Some lived outwardly normal lives in the world while they privately devoted themselves to a higher standard of devotion than did their neighbors. Men, women, laity, and clergy, these extraordinary Christians added to the rich texture of medieval life.

During the Middle Ages, the pattern of sainthood shifted, as *How Many?* on this page indicates. In the early Christian centuries, martyrs, theologians, and missionaries were canonized. In the high Middle Ages, many saints were healers and feeders; their care for the poor and the abandoned was understood as the sign of their sanctity. At the same time, female saints became more numerous. The percentage of women among the saints rose from just under 10 percent around 1100, to 15 percent around 1250, to 24 percent by 1300, to 29 percent for the fifteenth century.

Female sanctity differed from male sanctity. Female saints tended more than males to explore the inner life. They engaged in mystic contemplation, experienced divine visions, struggled with demons, and uttered prophecies. More than men, too, they engaged in extreme forms of asceticism. They confined themselves to cells, had themselves whipped, tormented their bodies, drank pus from the festering wounds of lepers, and starved themselves.

HOW MANY?

630 Saints

SAINTS' BIRTHPLACES

	Century of Saints' Death				
	11th	12th	13th	14th	15th
British Isles	19	20	10	2	2
Low Countries	8	11	6	1	2
France	23	37	24	11	7
Italy	26	35	79	74	53
Iberia	11	13	12	3	9
Scandinavia	1	9	1	3	0
Holy Roman Empire, Switzerland	32	27	22	7	4
Eastern Europe	7	0	4	5	4
Non-European	1	1	1	1	2
Total (630)	128	153	159	107	83

SAINTS' PROFESSIONS

	Century of Saints' Death				
	11th	12th	13th	14th	15th
Popes, cardinals	4	3	4	2	3
Bishops, archbishops	31	42	28	8	7
Abbots, abbesses, priors, prioresses	34	49	26	14	20
Lesser clerics	19	18	35	32	18
Tertiaries	5	0	8	15	5
Lay people	35	41	58	36	30
Total (630)	128	153	159	107	83

Source: D. Weinstein & R. M. Bell, *Saints and Society: The Two Worlds of Western Christendom, 1000–1700* (Chicago: University of Chicago Press, 1982)

Radegund dining, kneeling, and praying, late eleventh century

Berthold Fürtmayr, The Tree of Life and Death, Salzburger Missale, c. 1481

Eve and Mary represented for medieval people the polar possibilities for women: wicked Eve, who brought damnation upon humankind, or holy Mary, who almost redeems Eve's wickedness. Depicted in this miniature of the Garden of Eden (left) are these two figures of female possibility.

In this manuscript (right) is depicted the eleventh-century holy woman Radegund, a follower of Mary. She is seen here kneeling in her chapel, sitting at table reluctantly with her husband, and (below) abandoning her husband's bed in order to pray on the hard floor.
(left: Bayerische Staatsbibliothek, Munich; right: Médiathèque François Mitterrand, Poitiers)

What might have attracted elite women like Radegund to a life of renunciation and sacrifice?

To continue your investigation of this topic, please go to www.prenhall.com/king for the related **WINDOWS** on the **WEB** activity

Holy Women

For women as well as men, the religious life could offer a refuge, or an opportunity for study and spiritual development; and for some, whose commitment was shallow, a stress-free life with opportunities for indulgence and sociability. In the first passage, the seventh-century queen Etheldreda deliberately chooses a religious life over a secular one. In the second, the fourteenth-century mystic Beatrice of Nazareth describes in vivid and sensual language her relationship to God. In the third, the fourteenth-century English poet Geoffrey Chaucer sketches as a fictional character a shallow and self-centered nun.

Etheldreda marries King Egfrid and becomes a nun (7th century): King Egfrid married Etheldreda, a daughter of Anna, King of the East Angles. ... Although she lived with him for twelve years, she preserved the glory of perpetual virginity, which fact is absolutely vouched for by Bishop Wilfrid of blessed memory, of whom I made enquiry when some people doubted it. He said that Egfrid promised to give estates and much money to anyone who could persuade the queen to consummate the marriage. ... For a long time Etheldreda begged the king to allow her to retire from worldly affairs and serve Christ the only true King in a convent. And having at last obtained his reluctant consent, she entered the convent of the Abbess Ebba, king Egfrid's aunt. ... A year later she was herself made Abbess of Elge [Ely], where she built a convent and became the virgin mother of many virgins vowed to God, displaying the pattern of a heavenly life in word and deed.
(Bede, *History of the English Church and People*, Bk. 4, Ch. 19, 660; ed. L. Sherley-Price, 1955)

Beatrice of Nazareth describes the experience of loving God (14th century): At times love throws off all restraint, it surges forth with such power and sets the heart beating so fast and furious that it feels wounded through and through, and those wounds are constantly reopened, each day more searing and painful than the last. The veins seem to open, the blood to run out, the marrow to wither. Bones crack, the chest explodes, the throat is parched. One's face and limbs burn inwardly with the sovereign rage of love. Sometimes it is as though an arrow were passing through the heart and into the throat, causing loss of consciousness; at other times it is like a fire that consumes everything in its vicinity. Such is the violence to which the soul is subjected, such is the effect on it of unrestrained and pitiless love, which wants and devours all things.
(Beatrice of Nazareth, *The Seven Kinds of Love*, 14th c.; ed. E. Petroff, trs. E. Colledge, 1986)

The English poet Geoffrey Chaucer describes a different kind of nun—aristocratic, vain, and shallow (c. 1387–1400):
Full well she sang the services divine,
Intoning through her nose, becomingly;
And fair she spoke her French, and fluently,
After the school of Stratford-at-the-Bow,
For French of Paris was not hers to know.
At table she had been well taught withal,
And never from her lips let morsels fall,
Nor dipped her fingers deep in sauce, but ate
With so much care the food upon her plate
That never driblet fell upon her breast.
(Chaucer, *Canterbury Tales*, The Prioress, c. 1387–1400; trs. J. U. Nicholson, 1934)

Besides caring for the needy, medieval saints and other holy men and women peered deep into themselves, where they found a spiritual life and an openness to God not possible in the busy and practical world. Their mysticism belongs to a distinct kind of religious experience encountered in many religions. The Buddha and his followers in quest of Nirvana participated in mystical experiences, as did the Muslim Sufis, whose insight was so compelling a force in the spread of Islam.

In Christian mysticism, the worshiping self was understood to merge with the reality of God. As Saint Bernard of Clairvaux (1090–1153), a leading exponent of the mystical knowledge of God, described: "For in a certain way you lose yourself, as if you were not." Another mystic was the German Dominican Meister Eckhardt (c. 1260–c. 1328). Female mystics were active, too: the deep passion of Elizabeth of Schönau and Mechthild of Magdeburg probably informed the work of Eckhardt. The female

recluse Julian of Norwich (1342–d. after 1416) explored the meaning of a God who contained both female and male principles: "God almighty is our kindly Father, and God-all-wisdom is our kindly Mother, ... which is all one God, one Lord." The mystical experience of Beatrice of Nazareth is described in *Witnesses* on this page.

Prophets, unlike mystics, concerned themselves with the state of affairs on earth and within Christendom. Their inner experience and deep convictions led them to critique the present and predict the course of things to come. A burst of prophecy accompanied the crossing of the millennium in the year 1000. Later prophets were self-appointed critics of the secular world, such as Joachim of Fiore (c. 1130–c. 1201). This nobly born, former Cistercian abbot predicted the imminent end of his age and the birth of a new one which would be guided by genuinely spiritual monks (the corrupt priests of his day having been ousted) in a universal sabbath for the human race. Joachim's ideas, which were judged heretical, continued to circulate long after his death, in a popular book entitled *The Everlasting Gospel*.

Heresy and Unorthodoxy Among the prophets, mystics, and saintly people were those whom authorities labeled heretics, deviants from orthodox belief. The first heresies dated from the earliest centuries of the church—those of the Arians and Pelagians, Montanists and Nestorians, which proposed alternate formulations of the Church's creed. Medieval heresies were different. They opposed the Church itself. Their centers are shown on Map 10.2.

The heretics called Waldensians took their name from Peter Waldo (d. c. 1184), a merchant of Lyons, who gave up all his possessions (about 1176) and pledged himself to a life of poverty. His followers, too, embraced a simple life, similar to that later followed by the Franciscans. Unlike the Franciscans, who did not so plainly challenge church institutions and were able to persuade the pope to approve their order, the Waldensians challenged the doctrine of Purgatory and saw no need for priests. In 1211, eighty of the faithful were burned in Strasbourg, inaugurating a persecution that would extend for centuries.

Even more critical of the mainstream Church were the Albigensians, centered at Albi, in France. Their views can be traced to the Manicheanism of the early Christian era. Repudiating the Church and the priesthood, the Albigensians—also called Cathars—rejected the flesh, and with it marriage and procreation. They believed that the Christian's aim, attainable only by an elite few, was to achieve a perfect purity in this life as a condition of salvation. The "perfect" who succeeded in meeting these stern demands constituted a kind of alternate priesthood, who could bestow the yearned-for "consolation," a bestowal of sacred grace. Despite the extraordinary demands of this faith, it won widespread support in the south of France, especially from the nobility, a few of whom became converts. It was so successful that in 1208 the Church in Rome launched a crusade against

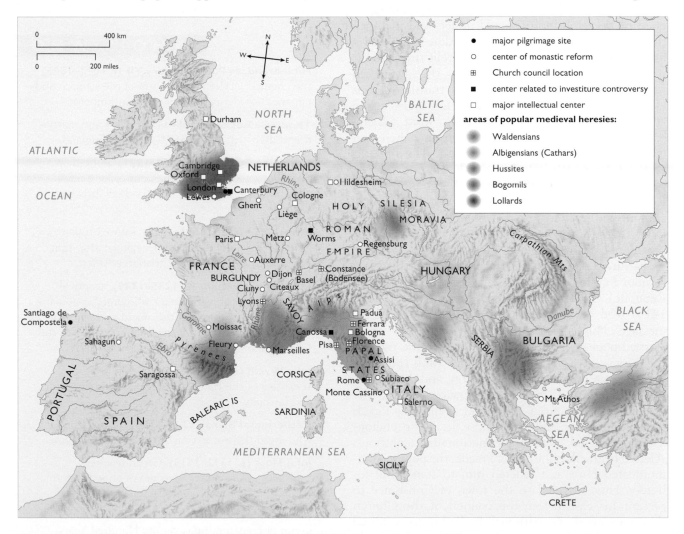

Map 10.2 Religious centers and centers of heresy, to 1500: *The great events of Christian history in western Europe were also events that influenced the political, social, and cultural lives of Europeans. The sites of reform initiative, of conflict between rulers and prelates, of pilgrimages and councils, of the centers of heresy and intellectual life, are all major landmarks in the fascinating development of Western civilization.* **The sites of greatest religious and intellectual importance seem to be concentrated along a diagonal from Italy to southeastern England; why?**

the heretics—one of several, culminating in one led by the French king, Louis VIII, in 1225–1226. That war resulted in the near-extermination of Albigensian adherents and won the region for France. But it failed to eradicate the heresy. Dominican friars set themselves to that task as agents of the Inquisition, begun by papal order in 1231 precisely for this purpose.

A century later, John Wyclif (c. 1330–1384), one of Catholic orthodoxy's most formidable opponents, was born in England. He studied and taught at Oxford University, seldom leaving its precincts before 1381 (although he acquired a number of ecclesiastical benefices), just three years before his death. This churchman and scholar denied papal claims to earthly authority and attacked the Church's priestly and sacramental structure. Worse, as the official Church viewed it, his message was heard with interest by king and Parliament. Still worse, it reached the common people, including artisans and merchants, among whom it gained a significant following.

Wyclif believed that Scripture was the source of all truth and that even ordinary human beings, if enlightened by the Holy Spirit, could understand it. Since the only Bible available in the Middle Ages was a fourth-century Latin translation, Wyclif translated it into English. As growing numbers of the laity could read the English, the effect of his translation was electrifying. Wyclif inspired many followers, called "Lollards" (from the Middle Dutch word *lollaerd*, "mutterer," applied to various pious but heretical groups who "muttered" their prayers). The Lollards endured long after Wyclif's death, despite intense persecution, up to the time of the Protestant Reformation (see Chapter 14). Wyclif himself was admonished to silence in 1378, and died a few years later. In 1428, his body was exhumed and burnt—a posthumous punishment for heresy.

Far from England, in the section of the Holy Roman Empire called Bohemia (the modern Czech Republic), the schoolmaster John Huss (c. 1372–1415) read Wyclif's books and began to spread his message. Huss preached to the people and wrote learned books against the clergy and for the right of the laity to take communion in both kinds (both the wine, normally reserved to the clergy, and the bread). His message won a large following among the Bohemians, who, from 1388, had available a Czech translation of the Bible and whose desire for religious reform mingled with their nationalist ambitions. Alerted by the Archbishop of Prague, the pope excommunicated Huss and ordered him to stand trial for heresy. Huss traveled to the town of Constance to present his case before the council of the Church then meeting there. Although he had been promised a safe-conduct by the emperor Sigismund himself, the document provided was merely a passport. When Huss arrived in Constance, he was condemned as a heretic, imprisoned, and tortured. Finally he was burned at the stake and his ashes scattered on the waters of the Rhine, lest any relic remain for followers to revere. Even so, the Hussite movement survived and even thrived, until—like Lollardy and Waldensianism—it merged with the many strands of the Protestant Reformation (see Chapter 14).

Many heretics were women. They were attracted to the Albigensian and Lollard messages, and even to other, more extreme, movements. Why the inordinate appeal of **heterodoxy** among those who, for the most part, were the patient bearers of culture and transmitters of the mainstream Catholic faith? It is possible that heterodoxy gave opportunities for personal expression that orthodoxy did not. Such was probably the explanation for the career of Marguerite Porete.

The Flemish Marguerite Porete (?–c. 1310) expressed in more than 60,000 words some deeply heretical notions. Excerpts from her book *The Mirror of Simple Souls* were examined by scholars at the University of Paris, who found much to condemn in her notions of the annihilation of the soul and its

WHO'S WHO

Hildebrand, as Pope Gregory VII (r. 1073–1085) the engineer of the papal reform of the Church and opponent of Henry IV, Holy Roman Emperor.

Thomas à Becket (1118–1170) saint and martyr, friend then critic of Henry II, King of England.

Dominic of Castile (c. 1170–1221) sainted Spanish founder of the mendicant order named after him, and champion of orthodox Christian doctrine.

Francis of Assisi (1182?–1226) sainted Italian founder of the mendicant order named after him, and advocate of absolute Christian poverty.

William of Ockham (c. 1285–1349) skeptical English philosophical thinker who urged systematic investigation of things of this world and reverence for the absolute power of the divine; wielder of the logical Razor; opponent of the papal monarchy.

John Wyclif (c. 1330–1384) English professor, translator of the Bible, advocate of church reform and lay piety.

Catherine of Siena (1347–1380) Italian saint who urged the restoration of the papacy to Rome.

John Huss (c. 1372–1415) Czech teacher, translator of the Bible, advocate of church reform and lay piety; burned at Constance as a heretic.

Joan of Arc (c. 1412–1431) peasant visionary; savior of French military during Hundred Years' War; taken captive, tried, and burned as a witch and heretic; canonized 1920.

identification with the divine: "Now this soul is a blank, because it sees its nothingness by fullness of divine knowledge, which makes it a blank, makes it a void. ..." Into this void comes God, who "sees himself in the Soul ... by means of his divine majesty." In another time and place Porete might have been thought a mystic, or even a saint; instead, she was burned at the stake.

Joan of Arc (c. 1412–1431) also defied orthodox norms and suffered condemnation for heresy. A pious and illiterate girl from the French countryside, she grew up during the Hundred Years' War between France and England. In 1429, Joan presented herself to the uncrowned king of France, Charles VII, and announced that she had been sent by God to defeat the English. Fully armed and dressed as a man, this seventeen-year-old girl fought with the French forces at Orléans, and so inspired them that within three days they had lifted the seven-month-long siege of that city. Subsequently, she stood by King Charles at his coronation in Rheims. In 1430, she was captured and remanded to the enemy—Charles making no attempt to win her release. Handed over to the Inquisition in Rouen (who, though French, supported the English), Joan was imprisoned, tortured, intimidated, and, in the course of a ten-week-trial, interrogated, chiefly over the nature of the "voices"—of saints, she maintained—that had guided her actions. In the end, the court condemned her as a heretic and a witch and had her burned in the market square of Rouen. Five hundred years later, in 1920, the Church declared her a saint.

Other women were inclined by their religious yearnings to join communities of the faithful. By the late Middle Ages, however, female monasticism was in serious decline, hemmed in by ecclesiastical regulations and avoided by women seeking greater scope for their spiritual lives. Some women were attracted to heresy or a solitary mysticism, but others wanted to devote themselves to a communal Christian life without taking vows. Many chose to live in lay communities, where they supported themselves and others, performed Christian service, and engaged in prayer and study. From the end of the twelfth century, beginning in the Low Countries, women called Beguines congregated in such communities, called *béguinages*; later, Beguine houses were established in the various towns of the prosperous German Rhineland. Between 1250 and 1350, about 100 of them were founded in Cologne, housing about 1,000 women. Those in Strasbourg housed about 600. The movement of these pious laywomen anticipates other lay movements, involving both men and women, of the late Middle Ages. Of these perhaps the most influential called themselves the "Brethren of the Common Life."

Followers of the Dutch reformer and mystic Gerhard Groote (1340–1384) joined together as the "Brethren of the Common Life" to foster a simpler, more sincere piety than was found, they felt, in the official Church. Their brotherhood was part of the larger movement of the *devotio moderna*, or "New Devotion." The Brethren supported the education of young people bound for clerical service, and influenced scholars of the next generation. Their views are most fully expressed in *The Imitation of Christ*, which may have been written by the shadowy Thomas à Kempis (1379–1431), who was associated with them. In some ways their beliefs approximate those of the followers of Wyclif and Huss, deemed heretical, and anticipate some aspects of the Protestant Reformation.

THE MIND'S ROAD TO GOD

While Christianity dominated the lives of ordinary people and, even more, those of saints and religious reformers, it also ruled the lives of intellectuals. Rather than through mystical experience or a pious, communal life, they sought a road to God built on thought and reason.

Christian rationalism was developed further in medieval Europe than in any other culture. It nurtured the tradition of high medieval philosophy. It opened the paths to modern science and political thought, in which the West would make major contributions. It was cultivated in the schools and universities of the Middle Ages, wholly new institutions which grew up in the shelter of the monastery and the cathedral.

School and University

It was thanks to the Church that the practice of reading, reflecting, and writing survived in medieval Europe. Christianity was based on a written tradition, and the Church required trained experts to guide the faithful in the worship of God. Clerics were virtually the only literate people in the early Middle Ages. (Our word "clerk" derives from "cleric," or "churchman.") They learned to read and write in schools created for the purpose of training servants of the Church.

For centuries, the principal schools in Europe were monastic schools. At first, they taught only monks, many of them child oblates. Their curriculum consisted of learning to read and write Latin, using fragments of the books drawn from monastic libraries. In time, the monastic schools also taught persons destined for the secular clergy. After 1000, new schools were formed for this purpose, attached to the cathedrals of some larger cities, especially in northern France (Laon, Rheims, Paris). Their graduates would become priests and bishops themselves, or advisers and secretaries to kings. The purpose of monastic education was thus different from that of the cathedral schools. The monks wished to preserve the Christian tradition and to reflect upon its meaning. The cathedral schools wished to develop skills of rational analysis for men who needed to accomplish things. From these schools developed the intellectual movement called **Scholasticism**.

Scholasticism can be identified by its characteristic method of reasoning, evidenced in the **disputation**, which derived from the circumstances of medieval education. Instruction in medieval schools was oral, as books were scarce. The presentation of arguments developed a form suited for oral delivery, the disputation. A kind of structured debate, the disputation required each of two participants to present arguments for or against a proposed statement, or thesis. The disputation required mastery of language and knowledge, the ability to speak and think quickly and sharply, and psychological qualities of determination and combativeness. It was a superb training ground for the mind—the intellectual counterpart of the medieval tournament.

The method of reasoning used in oral disputation or in written books was **dialectic**. In the dialectical method, a problem was proposed, arguments pro and con presented and evaluated, and a conclusion reached. At the close of the argument, medieval authors would often add the triumphant words "*quod erat demonstrandum*," abbreviated Q.E.D., meaning "which was the thing that had to be proved," and was now resolved. This dialectical method of reasoning was pursued in virtually every subject matter—philosophy, theology, law, and medicine, the premier disciplines of the age.

Peter Abelard   In Paris, a quarrelsome teacher named Peter Abelard (1079–1142) cultivated an even bolder critical style. Abelard attracted students from all over Europe, who flocked to hear penetrating critiques of other men's ideas from the man who considered himself "the only philosopher remaining in the world." Abelard's challenging notion of truth is illustrated in his *Sic et Non* ("Yes And No"). Here a series of controversial views from the Church Fathers are presented and assessed by arguments pro and con. No conclusion follows. Abelard deliberately left these matters open to trouble later thinkers and inspire further exploration. A critical thinker rather than a builder of systems, Abelard is representative of the first phase of Scholasticism.

Abelard is also known for his involvement with Héloïse (c. 1098–1164), one of the most tragic love stories of the era. The niece of Fulbert, the cleric with whom Abelard boarded, Héloïse became Abelard's student and then his lover. When she got pregnant, she refused to stay with him, which would have cut short his promising intellectual career. Learning of the clandestine marriage performed at Abelard's insistence over Héloïse's objections, Fulbert had Abelard seized, beaten, and castrated. Thus mutilated and

---

MUST READS

Books to Remember

Benedict of Nursia (c. 480–c. 550)   *Rule for Monks*

Peter Abelard (1079–1142)   *Sic et Non* (Yes and No)

Hildegard of Bingen (1098–1179)   *Scivias* (Visions)

Joachim of Fiore (c. 1130–c. 1201)   *Everlasting Gospel*

St. Thomas Aquinas (c. 1225–1274)   *Summa Theologica* (Compendium of Theology)

Marguerite Porete (?–c. 1310)   *Mirror of Simple Souls*

---

shamed, Abelard sought refuge and peace in a monastery. Letters exchanged between Abelard and Héloïse—perhaps genuine, although their authenticity cannot be proved—testify to their continuing love. But Abelard refused to have further personal relations with Héloïse, who became abbess of the convent he founded. While the story reveals much about Abelard, it is also a record of the experience of an educated woman. Her story is known not only from the letters, but from one of the most absorbing books of the era, Abelard's own autobiography, one of the earliest in the Western tradition.

Universities   Abelard helped establish Paris as a center of learning. It would soon become the site of one of Europe's foremost universities. In earlier civilizations there had been centers of learning—Plato's Academy and Aristotle's Lyceum in Athens, the Museum at Alexandria, and the schools of Byzantium. Centers of Islamic civilization, including Córdoba, Damascus, and Baghdad, housed similar places of learning. In western Europe, medieval universities established the pattern for the institutions of higher education still functioning in the modern world. Map 10.2 shows the principal intellectual centers.

The word "university" originally meant a guild, or an association of professors or students. They banded together to establish who was eligible to teach, then to set standards for instruction—the courses offered, when and how often professors would teach, what subjects needed to be mastered for a student to be certified at an elementary or advanced level. The medieval institution did not at first have its own campus or buildings. It was a group of persons in search of, or ready to provide, knowledge, and who, to that end, agreed to certain regulations.

Universities were exclusively for men. Most developed from monastic and cathedral schools, and as such were clerical institutions—and the clergy (except for cloistered nuns, who did not attend schools) were all male. (Universities did not begin to admit women until late in the nineteenth century.) The religious origins of the university are visible even today. They are seen in the "quad" or quadrangle, reminiscent of the cloister, and in the style of academic robes still worn at official events. They live on also in the titles of the degrees awarded (Bachelor and Master of Arts, Doctor of Philosophy), which marked the attainments of the clerical scholar.

The University of Paris was officially established by royal charter in 1200. The two major universities in England, Oxford and Cambridge, soon followed. In the thirteenth and fourteenth centuries, several universities were founded in the sprouting cities of north Italy, and both the medical school at Salerno and the law school at Bologna were even older than the University of Paris. In the fourteenth and fifteenth centuries, universities sprang up rapidly throughout the German lands (where fourteen were established between 1386 and 1506) and throughout central Europe. When Europeans settled in the Americas after 1500, they brought the university tradition with them.

One characteristic of the medieval university that distinguished it from the monastic and cathedral school, was the granting of degrees. Degrees were granted to those who had completed a prescribed sequence of courses and public demonstrations of mastery. They were offered in four subject areas: the elementary area of arts (including language, logic, and philosophy) and the advanced areas of law (**canon** or civil), theology, and medicine. Of these, the greatest was theology, considered to be the culmination of the other disciplines, on whose intellectual foundations it was firmly grounded. The medieval schools and universities saw no contradiction between matters of faith and the life of the mind.

The Age of Faith and Reason

The Middle Ages has often been called the "age of faith." But it was just as surely an age of reason. The example of the eleventh-century philosopher and saint Anselm illustrates very well how the profound faith of medieval people could be joined to a relentless rationalism.

Saint Anselm (c. 1033–1109) already believed that God existed when he set out to prove it. Yet belief was not enough—enough for salvation, perhaps, but not for him. He wanted to understand: "I believe," he proclaimed in his famous formulation, "so that I may understand." Anselm searched for the mind's road to God. The result of his intellectual quest is the "ontological proof" (ontology is the study of the nature of existence) of the existence of God.

It works like this: (1) I have in my understanding a concept of God—that is, of "a being than which nothing greater can be conceived." (2) But it cannot be that a being "than which nothing greater can be conceived" exists *only* in the understanding. (3) If it existed only in the understanding, I could conceive of a being that is greater: a being that exists also in reality. (4) But it is impossible that there can be a conception greater than the conception of "a being than which nothing greater can be conceived." (5) Therefore that being exists not only in the understanding but also in reality, and that being is God. (6) God, furthermore, cannot be conceived not to exist; for if I conceive of being whose nonexistence is possible, then I could also conceive of a being greater still (one which could exist), and this latter being would truly be God. For medieval thinkers, reason and faith meet perfectly in this proof; for the correspondence between their interior, mental life and what existed in fact in the external world seemed to them to be absolute.

Anselm and his many successors shaped the mental world of the Middle Ages and of the modern West. A variety of circumstances prepared Europeans to take the lead in critical, rational thought after the twelfth century. First, Europe was defined by Christianity, a religion based on a book, the Bible, inherited from Judaism and extended by its own authors, which invited constant study and reflection. Second, the Fathers of the Church in the first centuries C.E. chose to embrace the whole of the Classical tradition, Greek and Latin, and to synthesize it with Christian doctrine. Third, monasticism from the start deemed as a preeminent objective the collection, transcription, and study of books and reliably transmitted the linguistic skills necessary to pursue this objective. Fourth, in its universities Europe provided a place for the prolonged study that intellectual creation requires. Finally, in the twelfth and thirteenth centuries, contacts with Arabic, Greek, and Jewish cultures provided materials and insights that stimulated several centuries of creative thought. Of these, the most important was certainly the recovery of the works of Aristotle.

The Aristotelian Revival The works of Aristotle, studied throughout antiquity, were still available during the Middle Ages in Constantinople (in their original Greek) and at the major centers of Islamic culture (where they were read both in Greek and in Arabic translation). Aside from the simpler logical works, they were not well known in western Europe. Beginning in the twelfth century, Jewish and Christian scholars based in Spain, in southern Italy, and in Constantinople began to acquire Aristotelian texts and translate them from the Greek and the Arabic into a serviceable, technical Latin. In addition to this flood of Aristotle, translations of three of Plato's dialogues reached the Christian West.

Not only did Christian Europeans acquire Aristotelian texts, but they read some of the Islamic and Jewish works that had been based on the Greek philosophical tradition. Of these, the scientific and philosophical works of Avicenna and Averröes were central to the development of scholastic thought. They focused on problems raised by the combined Platonic, Aristotelian, and Neoplatonic tradition—within a monotheistic framework—about the meaning of "essence" and "existence," the status of the individual soul, the rule of freedom or necessity, the relation between God and nature. More strictly Aristotelian was the work of the Jewish philosopher and physician Maimonides (Moses ben Maimon) (1135–1204). Forced by persecutions to leave Córdoba, then under Moorish domination, he lived in Egypt as a physician in the royal court and leader of the Jewish community. His *Guide for the Perplexed* (written in Arabic around 1204) contained a synthesis of ancient and theistic ideas. These were important issues for Christians who wished to make sense of the universe in which they lived without denying the truths taught them by faith.

Through the filters of Islamic and Jewish philosophy, and directly from the Greek, as well, the ideas of Aristotle reshaped the mental world of Christian Europe. Previously, the text that was the mainstay of their study was the Bible—rich in literary image and meaning, but poor in the abstract ideas that appealed to masters of disputation. Aristotle provided books on logical method, which became the new basis for arguing and proving propositions. Moreover, Aristotle provided a complete system of **metaphysics** (the study of the essential nature of reality), physics, political theory, and ethics that, however alien in origin, could be attached to fundamental Christian conceptions. Aristotle's understanding of a just ruler or of sexual moderation agreed with Christian notions of goodness and virtue. Aristotle's Prime Mover (an unmoved force which moves the universe) could be identified with God, and the whole of his metaphysical and physical model could be employed to explain a God-driven universe. The university professors, now voracious consumers of Aristotle, became the ancestors of our scientists and political theorists, ethicists, and logicians, as well as of our philosophers and theologians.

Saint Thomas Aquinas Perhaps the best known of these scholastic thinkers is Saint Thomas Aquinas (c. 1225–1274). An Italian nobleman and Dominican friar, Thomas wrote (among other works) two very large books establishing Christian theology on a systematic philosophical basis which are still read today by those capable of appreciating the author's vast understanding: the *Summa theologica* ("Compendium of Theology"), and the *Summa contra gentiles* ("Compendium against the Gentiles," an argument against the pagan construction of reality, quoted in *Witnesses* on p. 285). Thomas envisions a completely rational universe run by a rational God, in which the experience of the senses provides reliable knowledge and evil is not a force in itself but the absence of the good. Like Anselm and Maimonides, he presented important proofs of God's existence, which could be known through reason. Although his ideas were once suspected of heresy, they are now considered official doctrines of the Catholic Church and one of the grandest structures of thought in world history.

The English scholar and bishop (of Lincoln) Robert Grosseteste (c. 1175–1253) took Aristotle in a different direction—toward the consideration of the phenomena of the natural world—thus opening the road to modern scientific thought, based on mathematics rather than dialectic, and informed by a direct reading of Greek texts. Grosseteste saw God as light, and understood knowledge to be a form of illumination. But his theory of light was scientific as well as mystical: Grosseteste saw light as the basis of the whole of the physical universe, and experimental optics ("optics" is the scientific investigation of light and vision) as the key to its understanding. His approach (continued by his equally renowned student Roger Bacon, c. 1214–1294) identifies him as an early practitioner of the scientific method.

Another Englishman, the Franciscan William of Ockham (c. 1285–c. 1349), opened the final phase of medieval Scholasticism. By the fourteenth century, Aristotelianism and its implications had been well digested, and reaction set in. Was the God of creation and of revelation really so rational? Were the truths of faith and reason truly harmonious? Ockham's response to such questions was skeptical, and his answers disclose a waning of faith in cosmic or ecclesiastical or political order. His thinking had tremendous impact on later philosophy, theology, and politics (see Chapters 14, 15).

In the field of philosophy, Ockham was an **empiricist**, accepting the reality of things as perceived by the senses—a position essential for the development of science. Opposing the tendency toward unnecessary elaboration in the explanation of phenomena, he insisted on a principle not original with him but called ever afterward "Ockham's Razor"—that one should not postulate the existence of a greater number of factors than will suffice to explain a phenomenon. The rule can be judiciously wielded in many areas even today.

In theology, Ockham insisted on the dignity, power, and unknowability of the divine. By what right did men dictate to God how he conducted the business of the cosmos? God's will and power were alike absolute and undisclosed to humankind except through the actions of his creatures. Ockham's insistence on the unlimited power of the divine would be echoed in late mysticism and heresy, but even more powerfully in the theology of the Protestant reformers (see Chapter 14).

Ockham's daring views were suspect to church officials, particularly because he was a professed supporter of the Spiritual Franciscans (as opposed to the Conventual Franciscans), who were deemed heretical. In 1328, he was condemned by a papal inquisition at Avignon, whereupon he fled to Munich (modern Germany) with the aid of the emperor Louis of Bavaria. He was then joined by other heterodox intellectuals united in their opposition to what they saw as papal tyranny: John of Jandun (c. 1286–1328) and Marsiglius of Padua (c. 1280–c. 1343). Ockham and his fellow exiles helped lay the intellectual groundwork for the burgeoning of state power of the coming centuries.

In Munich, under imperial protection, Ockham dedicated himself to philosophical work and to destroying the theory of papal supremacy. Undeterred by a 1328 order of excommunication, Ockham declared the interfering Pope John XXII (r. 1316–1334) a heretic. Where the pope had claimed supremacy even in temporal affairs, Ockham argued the autonomy of the secular state. At the beginning of the Middle Ages, Saint Augustine had proclaimed the failure of the state and the triumph of the kingdom of God. At its close, Ockham declared church power fraudulent and hailed the supreme authority of the secular ruler. The circle had been completed.

The Glory of Gothic

Ockham challenged the earlier medieval assumption that the mind's activity could lead the seeker to God. The same assumption had reached full and public expression in a new style of architecture which emerged late in the twelfth century, when Scholasticism was reaching its innocent heights.

WITNESSES

Schools and Scholars

By the thirteenth century in medieval Europe, Christian thought had developed in a markedly rational direction under the influence of a renewed study of Roman law and Greek (especially Aristotelian) philosophy. Students, mostly clerics, flocked to study this new synthesis of scriptural truths and logical methods at centers called "universities." These passages variously reflect the nature of the scholarly pursuit at such institutions. The first describes the not-always admirable behavior of university students in thirteenth-century Paris. The second shows a teacher announcing his plans for the semester, promising "to teach you faithfully and in a kindly manner." The third exemplifies the style and substance of the work of the philosopher, saint, and university professor Thomas Aquinas, for whom what was true and what was reasonable must necessarily coincide.

The cleric and bishop Jacques de Vitry skeptically describes student life at the new university in Paris (early 13th century): Almost all the students at Paris, foreigners and natives, did absolutely nothing except learn or hear something new. Some studied merely to acquire knowledge, which is curiosity; others to acquire fame, which is vanity; others still for the sake of gain, which is cupidity and the vice of simony. Very few studied for their own edification, or that of others. They wrangled and disputed not merely about the various sects or about some discussions; but the differences between the countries also caused dissensions, hatreds and virulent animosities among them, and they impudently uttered all kinds of affronts and insults against one another.
(Jacques de Vitry, *Letters*, 13th c.; ed. N. Downs, 1959)

Odofredus explains to his students at the university of Bologna how he intends to teach them the *Corpus Juris Civilis*, or Compendium of Civil Law (c. 1250):

If you please, I will begin the *Old Digest* on the eighth day or thereabouts after the feast of St. Michael [September 29] and I will finish it entire … in the middle of August or thereabouts. The *Code* I will always begin within about a fortnight of the feast of St. Michael and I will finish it … on the first of August or thereabouts. … And so all scholars including the unskilled and novices will be able to make good progress with me, for they will hear their text as a whole, nor will anything be left out, as was once done in this region, indeed was the usual practice. … For it is my purpose to teach you faithfully and in a kindly manner. … And if any law is deserving of a review by reason of its fame or difficulty, I shall reserve it for an afternoon review.
(Odofredus, c. 1250; ed. L. Thorndike, 1944)

The philosopher and saint Thomas Aquinas explains that the truth uncovered by reason is in harmony with the truth taught by faith (1258–1260): Now, although the truth of the Christian faith which we have discussed surpasses the capacity of the reason, nevertheless that truth that the human reason is naturally endowed to know cannot be opposed to the truth of the Christian faith. For that with which the human reason is naturally endowed is clearly most true; so much so, that it is impossible for us to think of such truths as false. Nor is it permissible to believe as false that which we hold by faith, since this is confirmed in a way that is so clearly divine. Since, therefore, only the false is opposed to the truth, as is clearly evident from an examination of their definitions, it is impossible that the truth of faith should be opposed to those principles that the human reason knows naturally.
(St. Thomas Aquinas, *Summa contra gentiles*, 1258–1260; ed. A. Thompson, 1980, trs. A. Pegis, 1955)

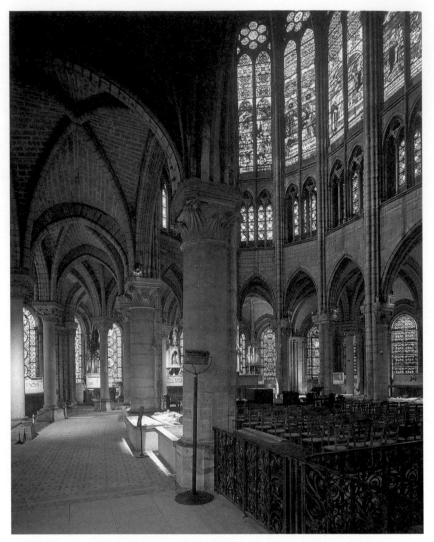

Gothic style—Abbey Church of St. Denis:
Gothic architecture is full of light and apparently weightless, in comparison to the Romanesque. Where Romanesque was characterized by intricate sculptural forms, Gothic is characterized by harmonious compositions in stained glass, their effect wrought by light and color, as revealed in the apse and ambilatory of the church at St. Denis. Begun in 1140, the church pioneers Gothic style.

Arising in the cities, adjacent to the schools and universities, marketplaces and courts it would challenge the earlier Romanesque style and stand as arguably the greatest artistic achievement of the mature Middle Ages.

The **Gothic** style (so named by some various eighteenth-century critics, who disapproved of it) replaced the round arch, inherited from antiquity, with a pointed arch. This is composed of two intersecting arcs that appear to soar upward, like the trees of northern forests, to the source of light and grace. Another characteristic of the Gothic style was the presence of light, achieved by allotting less space to wall and more to window. The windows, generally pointed like the related arches, were glazed with hundreds of tiny panes of richly colored glass conveying the narratives and messages of scripture.

A third characteristic of the Gothic was the accentuation of clear, daring structural elements. As the style developed, the wall thinned, the light intensified, and builders learned to brace this weaker structure with graceful external supports called flying buttresses, which added to the lace-like beauty of the whole. Just as the purpose and presence of these supports were acknowledged without embarrassment, the structural forms of the interior—pillars, columns, ribs—were boldly highlighted. It was as though the builder's aim was to clarify the process of building, just as the aim of the whole Church was to clarify for people's edification the nature of God's creation.

Romanesque had suited monasticism at its height: brooding and mysterious. Gothic suited an energized Europe: vibrant with change, daring in vision, refined and logical, pursuing a road to God expressed in stone and light surging powerfully and elegantly upward. "The very world," wrote a contemporary, "had shaken herself and cast off her old age and [was] clothing herself everywhere in a white garment of churches."

Conclusion
THE MEDIEVAL CHURCH AND THE MEANING OF THE WEST

In our secular modern world, it is easy to forget the Christian contribution to the formation of Western civilization. But that contribution is profound. Guided by leaders of exceptional talent, the Church shaped the values, institutions, customs, ideas, and styles of the Middle Ages over the course of one thousand years. Those values, which once fed nearly all of Europe's people, have not been obliterated, but reside still in the consciousness of those who are building the modern world—even those who reject the moral codes and doctrinal formulas of Christianity. Just as Saint Catherine of Siena summoned Gregory XI to be mindful of his duties, so the Christian past summons the heirs to Western civilization to be conscious of their standards of thought and behavior. It is, even today, a spiritual sword.

QUESTIONS TO CONSIDER

1. Why did the principle of the renunciation of the body appeal to large numbers of Christians during late antiquity and the early Middle Ages? Would it be equally appealing today?

2. How would the experience of nuns in convents differ from that of monks in monasteries?

3. In what way did the papacy benefit from the reform of the church in the eleventh and twelfth centuries?

4. Was the sacramental system an aid to or a burden on ordinary medieval people?

5. Why would Christian thinkers embrace the rationalism of the Aristotelian tradition, and see it as supportive of, not antithetical to, faith?

SUGGESTED RESOURCES

Brentano, Robert, *A New World in a Small Place: Church and Religion in the Diocese of Rieti, 1188–1378* (Berkeley–Los Angeles: University of California Press, 1994.) Meticulous, original study of how church, religion, and society are transformed by the arrival of the Franciscans in one small Italian diocese under the rule of its enterprising bishops.

Brown, Peter, *The Body and Society: Men, Women, and Sexual Renunciation in Early Christianity* (London: Faber, 1990). A study of early Christian attitudes toward sexuality and the body.

Bynum, Caroline Walker, *Holy Feast and Holy Fast: The Religious Significance of Food to Medieval Women* (Berkeley: University of California Press, 1987). An original exploration of the importance of food, food imagery, and fasting among medieval religious women.

Clanchy, M.T., *Abelard: A Medieval Life* (Malden, MA: Blackwell, 1997). Comprehensive and up-to-date biography of this key figure in the making of scholasticism, the most important intellectual expression of the Middle Ages and the medieval Church.

Clark, Anne L., *Elisabeth of Schönau: A Twelfth-Century Visionary* (Philadelphia: University of Pennsylvania Press, 1992). Explores how the literary works of a twelfth-century mystic (often ignored in favor of Hildegard of Bingen) illuminate women's relationships to the male-dominated social, religious, and intellectual worlds.

Cowdrey, H.E.J., *Pope Gregory VII, 1073–1085* (Oxford: Clarendon Press, 1998). The new standard biography of the pope who came from humble origins and who revolutionized the medieval church.

Geary, Patrick, *Living with the Dead in the Middle Ages* (Ithaca, NY: Cornell University Press, 1995). Explores the nature of popular piety by tracking the "exchange and interaction between the living and the dead" in the early to high Middle Ages, when the reverence for saints called for the possession of part or whole of the bodies of the saints.

Grant, Edward, *God and Reason in the Middle Ages* (Cambridge: Cambridge University Press, 2001). Argues that the European "age of reason" began in the universities of the Middle Ages, wrongly considered an era of credulity and superstition.

Hayes, Dawn Marie, *Body and Sacred Place in Medieval Europe, 1100–1389* (New York: Routledge, 2003). Shows how medieval church buildings and furnishings acted as metaphors of the human body.

Iogna-Prat, Dominique, *Order and Exclusion: Cluny and Christendom Face Heresy, Judaism, and Islam (1000–1150)*, trans. Graham Robert Edwards (Ithaca: Cornell University Press, 2002). How the Cluniac movement helped construct the notion of Christendom by the psychological seclusion of heretics, Jews, and Muslims.

Johnson, Penelope D., *Equal in Monastic Profession: Religious Women in Medieval France* (Chicago: University of Chicago Press, 1991). A social history of French nunneries, focusing on their organization, the social origins of the nuns, relations with bishops, and monasteries.

Lawrence, C.H., *The Friars: The Impact of the Early Mendicant Movement on Western Society* (New York: Longman, 1994). Discusses the importance of the new orders of mendicant friars in medieval religious experience and society.

Radding, Charles M. & William W. Clark, *Medieval Architecture, Medieval Learning: Builders and Masters in the Age of Romanesque and Gothic* (New Haven: Yale University Press, 1994). Argues that the two successive styles of Romanesque and Gothic were analogous to developments in medieval philosophy.

Simons, Walter, *Cities of Ladies: Beguine Communities in the Medieval Low Countries, 1200–1565* (Philadelphia: University of Pennsylvania Press, 2001). Traces the evolution of the Beguine movement of lay, pious women from its informal beginnings to formalized communities.

St. Benedict's *Rule for Monks*: Order of St. Benedict gateway page and texts:
http://www.osb.org/rb

HildegardofBingen.org, for materials on the most famous of the medieval women saints:
http://www.uni-mainz.de/~horst/hildegard

Works by/about philosopher Robert Grosseteste (funded British Academy):
http://www.grosseteste.com

Western Civilization Documents CD-ROM

6.8 St. Patrick's Confession

7.1 Gregory VII's Letter to the Bishop of Metz

7.2 Benedict of Nursia: The Rule

7.3 Duke William of Aquitaine: Foundation Charter for the Abbey of Cluny

7.4 Beha-ed-Din: Richard I Massacres Prisoners

7.5 Unam Sanctum

7.6 Penitentials

7.7 The Siege of Lisbon

8.4 St. Thomas Aquinas: Summa Contra Gentiles

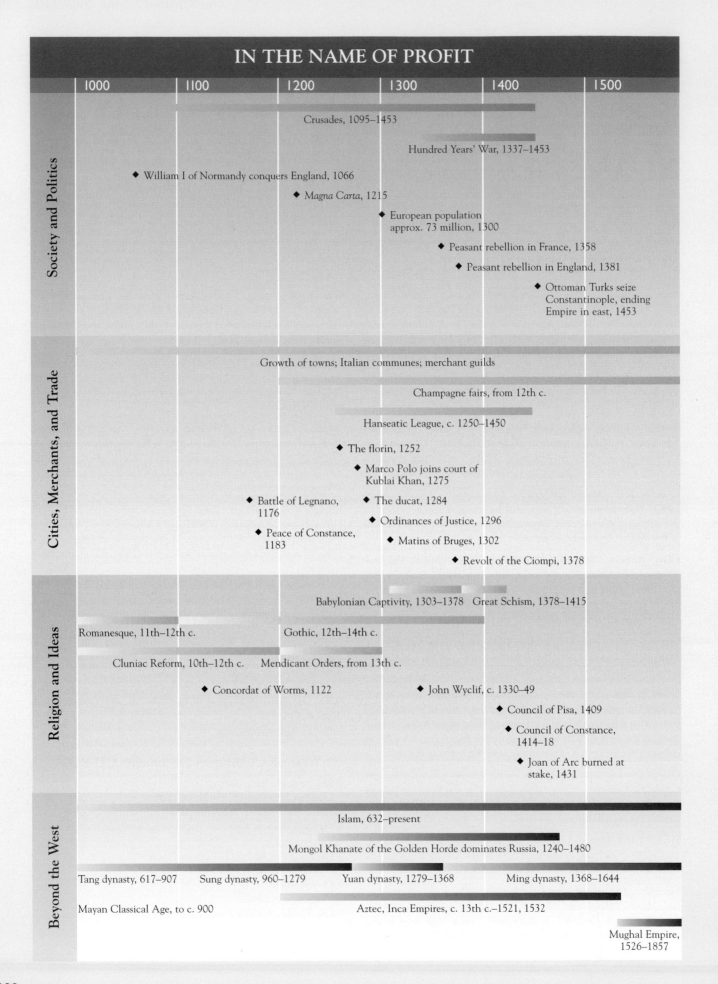

IN THE NAME OF PROFIT

1000	1100	1200	1300	1400	1500

Society and Politics

Crusades, 1095–1453

Hundred Years' War, 1337–1453

◆ William I of Normandy conquers England, 1066

◆ Magna Carta, 1215

◆ European population approx. 73 million, 1300

◆ Peasant rebellion in France, 1358

◆ Peasant rebellion in England, 1381

◆ Ottoman Turks seize Constantinople, ending Empire in east, 1453

Cities, Merchants, and Trade

Growth of towns; Italian communes; merchant guilds

Champagne fairs, from 12th c.

Hanseatic League, c. 1250–1450

◆ The florin, 1252

◆ Marco Polo joins court of Kublai Khan, 1275

◆ Battle of Legnano, 1176

◆ The ducat, 1284

◆ Ordinances of Justice, 1296

◆ Peace of Constance, 1183

◆ Matins of Bruges, 1302

◆ Revolt of the Ciompi, 1378

Religion and Ideas

Babylonian Captivity, 1303–1378   Great Schism, 1378–1415

Romanesque, 11th–12th c.   Gothic, 12th–14th c.

Cluniac Reform, 10th–12th c.   Mendicant Orders, from 13th c.

◆ Concordat of Worms, 1122

◆ John Wyclif, c. 1330–49

◆ Council of Pisa, 1409

◆ Council of Constance, 1414–18

◆ Joan of Arc burned at stake, 1431

Beyond the West

Islam, 632–present

Mongol Khanate of the Golden Horde dominates Russia, 1240–1480

Tang dynasty, 617–907   Sung dynasty, 960–1279   Yuan dynasty, 1279–1368   Ming dynasty, 1368–1644

Mayan Classical Age, to c. 900   Aztec, Inca Empires, c. 13th c.–1521, 1532

Mughal Empire, 1526–1857

CHAPTER 11

IN THE NAME OF PROFIT

Cities, Merchants, and Trade
in the Middle Ages

1000–1500

major trading centers

KEY QUESTIONS

◆ **Money and Merchants:** Why did money begin to circulate more freely? How were some individuals able to amass great wealth?

◆ **Cities and Towns:** How did new cities form in Europe? How were medieval European cities different from those of the ancient world?

◆ **Artisans and Entrepreneurs:** What were the main purposes of merchant guilds, and how did they differ from craft guilds? In what ways did the interests of artisans differ from those of merchants?

◆ **The World of Commerce:** What skills and behaviors did Italian merchants learn from the Arab merchants who dominated Mediterranean trade until about the year 1000? How were they able to gain mastery of the Mediterranean system?

The creed of Francesco Datini It was the custom of Francesco Datini (c. 1335–1410), merchant of Prato, to head the records of his transactions with the invocation "In the name of God and of profit." "Money is all the help you have," said another Tuscan merchant. "It is your defense, honor, profit, and adornment." "Florins are the best of kin," the kind who never give you any trouble, wrote the Sienese poet Cecco Angiolieri (c. 1260–1312) speaking of the newly minted gold coins that Western entrepreneurs used to buy more than their share of the world's luxuries. These statements breathe a spirit distant from church and manor. Beginning around 1000, Europeans began to sell, acquire, hoard, spend, and crave in a project of economic expansion that has lasted into this century. By 1500, their activity had propelled Europe all the way from last place to first in the race for the world's goods.

It was money that fueled the transformation of Europe, and the merchants who traded goods for money were certainly the vehicles of that transformation. As they concentrated their activities at the intersections of key trade routes, they caused towns to form and ripen into cities, the dynamic centers of commerce. Within those cities, and gathered into **guilds**, **artisans** produced the goods that were bought and sold, while the great international **entrepreneurs** of the age forged new commercial techniques and a new mental world.

MONEY AND MERCHANTS

Merchants made the profits that transformed Europe from a commercial backwater to a commercial superpower. A merchant sells a commodity for a price greater than its cost to him (rarely her). His profit is the difference between the two amounts. Early in the Middle Ages that merchant was merely a peddler who carried his goods in his saddlepack, traveling from village to village. It was a precarious living. Often he was the target of bandits and marauders.

Later, the merchant was typically a dealer traveling with a group of other dealers who shared risks and costs. Eventually, he might even be a merchant prince, directing the buying and selling operations of a host of agents located throughout Europe, Africa, the Middle East, and Asia. The career of one merchant is described in *Witnesses* on p. 293. From the peddler's slim profit margin to the international entrepreneur's fat one came wealth that circulated, slowly at first, in small streams of silver coins, and later, torrentially, in gold **florins** and **ducats**. Those currents expanded the possibilities that life could offer even the humblest peasant.

Economic Crisis and Recovery

Even before incursions of tribal raiders and settlers overwhelmed the Roman west wealth had begun to seep away to the east. The economy of the late Roman Empire slumped into a downturn which, in the western zone, proved irreversible (see Chapter 6). Gold and silver leaked to the depots of Constantinople, Antioch, and Alexandria, to be exchanged for the fine products of Asia—oils and perfumes, spices, silk, ivory, and other exotic products. In its declining years, the Roman economy sank under the weight of a serious trade imbalance. Commerce slowed dangerously in the west, to revive only after a lapse of centuries.

The early Middle Ages saw a near-eclipse of trade. Bandits and pirates roamed at will, unchecked by Roman legions or auxiliaries, endangering merchant shipments by road or water. Roads and bridges were no longer maintained and fell into disrepair. Water routes became even more dangerous after 700, when Arab ships claimed the Mediterranean, and in the ninth and tenth centuries, when Vikings prowled the northern seas and rivers (one of their ships is shown on p. 302). Merchant enterprises in the imperiled cities dwindled and merchants quickly dispersed. By the ninth century, even the names of merchants or references to trade have virtually disappeared from written records. The trade that did exist must surely have suffered from political disarray—there were no judges available to enforce contracts and no financial officials to regulate the **minting** of new coins or the conversion of currency.

Already drained of **bullion** by the reckless spending on foreign luxuries during the late Empire, Europe, under its newly formed principalities, lost its remaining currency reserves to hoarding. Gold coins were stored as treasure or melted down to make the gorgeous objects that warriors displayed on their person (belt buckles and sword hilts) and that priests displayed on their altars (crucifixes and reliquaries). The little wealth that Europe possessed was frozen and immobilized, unavailable for trade. Small silver coins of little value were sufficient until the thirteenth century, when the florins and ducats of the great Italian cities established gold and silver as different standards of value.

Barter As coins disappeared, trade was conducted by means of barter: things were exchanged for things—so many chickens for so much grain, a percentage of the crop to pay the Church's **tithe**, or tax, the use of the lord's mill for a sack of flour. Such trade was almost purely local. Neither chickens nor sacks of flour were transported over large distances. Medieval peasants saw the boundaries of their own manor or village as the limit of their economic world.

If small sums were measured in chickens and sacks of barley, large sums were measured in land. Even a king paid an administrator in this way, by giving him the use of a certain quantity of land for a period of time. In exchange for the land given him in usufruct, as this arrangement was called, the recipient often owed the lord or king who had granted it specified services—military, advisory, managerial (see Chapter 9). On the land-user's death, the gift might become hereditary, his heir continuing to owe services, in theory at least, to the lord who conferred the benefit (or to his descendants). In the same way, the serf on the manor was rewarded for his labor by the right to use land that he did not own.

In this economic setting, where most trade was by barter and most payment was in land use, a few daring men traveled about buying and selling their wares—no more than could be carried in one wagon or two saddlebags. From the Mediterranean ports of Italy, Spain, and southern France, these peddlers journeyed north to the local markets of the interior. The first traders of the medieval West were Syrians and Jews with close ties to the Levant, the chief marketplace of Mediterranean civilization. They traveled "from the East to the West and from the West to the East by land as well as by sea [from the] land of the Franks" to Egypt and Constantinople, according to an Arab geographer of the ninth century.

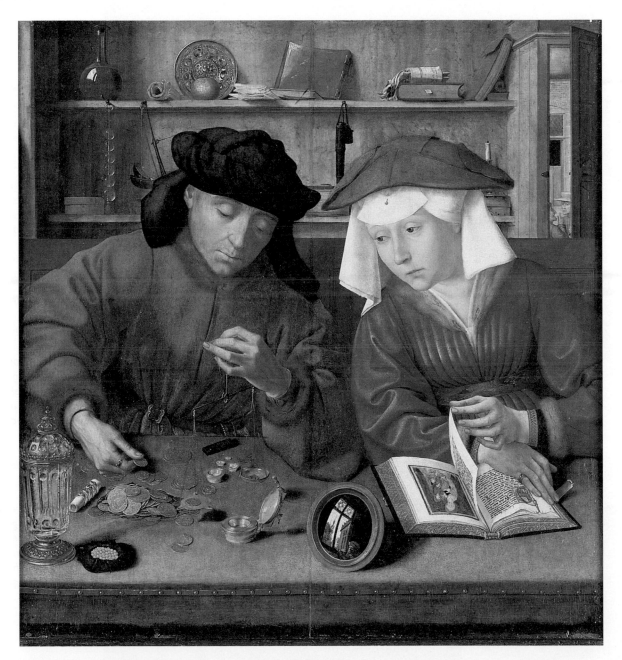

Quinten Massys, A Moneylender and his Wife: *The conflicting demands of spiritual and worldly matters is illustrated in this fifteenth-century painting of a woman distracted from perusing a religious text by her husband weighing coins in a balance.* (Louvre, Paris)

The disruption of maritime trade in the west, following the Islamic conquests and new prohibitions against the Jews caused many thousands of these merchants to vanish eastward across the Mediterranean to more welcoming lands.

By the tenth century, some Europeans, dislodged from the soil by population pressure or misfortune, had learned of the great profit to be gained from buying things cheaply and selling them dearly. Among these were Vikings, or Norsemen (kin to the raiders who beset monasteries and villages), who packed up the produce of their farms and villages, once the harvest was in, and journeyed through the various ports of the North Sea in order to sell it. From such enterprising traders came the makers of the medieval towns and, ultimately, the great merchants of the later Middle Ages.

Fairs In the absence of permanent markets, traveling merchants brought their goods to depots where, for a few days or a few weeks a year, an open-air market was held. In the twelfth century, the count of Champagne, one of the greatest landholders in the Frankish lands, realized how he could profit from inviting a great confluence of these merchants to buy and sell in his territory. The county of Champagne

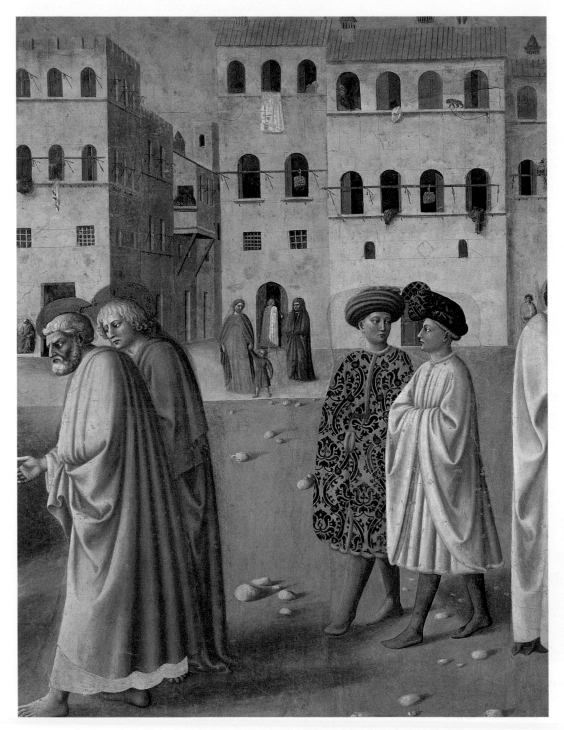

Masaccio, Resurrection of Tabitha: *The frescoes painted by Masolinoda Panicale and his more talented assistant—who was known by his sobriquet Masaccio—for the wealthy Felice Brancacci in the church of the Carmine in Florence described incidents from the life of disciple Peter as though they had occurred in a contemporary Florentine setting. Shown here is a detail of two fashionably dressed merchants engaged in conversation in a medieval street setting. Peter heals a disabled beggar to the left. (Church of Carmine, Florence)*

Wandering Merchants and Flourishing Towns

The individual initiative and willingness to assume risk displayed by the earliest medieval merchants helped build up a trade network and, in time, an urban grid which, by 1300, supported a vital, prosperous economy. These passages describe, first, the solitary ventures of an eleventh-century merchant and, second, the enormous wealth of the merchants of early fourteenth-century Florence, who had formed themselves into several specialized guilds to further their interests.

The profitable journeys of merchant Godric of Finchale (1070): At first, he lived as a chapman [peddlar] …, going on foot and carrying the smallest wares; then he travelled abroad, first to St. Andrews in Scotland and then for the first time to Rome. On his return, … he began to launch upon bolder courses, and to coast frequently by sea to the foreign lands that lay around him. Thus … he traded in many divers wares and … made great profit in all his bargains, and gathered much wealth in the sweat of his brow; for he sold dear in one place the wares which he had bought elsewhere at a small price.
(Reginald of Durham, *Life of Godric of Finchale*, 1070; ed. G. G. Coulton, 1918)

The chronicler Giovanni Villani describes the business enterprises of Florence (1335–1338): The workshops of the *Arte della Lana* [wool guild] were 200 or more, and they made from 70,000 to 80,000 pieces of cloth, which were worth more than 1,200,000 gold florins. … And more than 30,000 persons lived by it. … The *fondachi* [businesses] of the *Arte di Calamala* [finished cloth guild] … were some twenty, and they imported yearly more than 10,000 pieces of cloth, worth 300,000 gold florins. … The banks of money-changers were about eighty. The gold coins which were struck amounted to some 350,000 gold florins and at times 400,000 [yearly]. … There were then in Florence 146 bakeries.
(Giovanni Villani, *New Chronicle*, 1335–1338, Bk. XI; eds. I. Raymond, R. Lopez, 1955)

was ideal for this purpose, lying just at the point where river boats traveling up the Rhone, Saône, and Seine Rivers could go no farther. Saleable goods could be unloaded from the boats and brought directly for display at the Champagne fairs.

Six fairs were held annually at various towns of Champagne, in addition to others elsewhere in France and nearby Flanders (in modern Belgium and northeastern France). At the midpoint of the main axis of European trade from the North Sea to the Mediterranean, which led on to Russia and Constantinople respectively, they served until the fourteenth century as Europe's greatest clearinghouse. In the following century, international fairs were held in Geneva (in modern Switzerland), Frankfurt, and Nuremberg (both in Germany). By this time, new and revitalized cities had also become centers of trade.

The great fairs, such as those in Champagne, were international markets. Here the goods of the east were available as well as European goods such as salt, metals, food, and wool. They were distinct from the local markets and fairs in which villagers exchanged the products of their farms. The two economies persisted side by side—the local economy of the manor, and the long-distance economy of the merchants.

The Flow of Money

Having purchased goods at the fairs of western Europe, itinerant merchants returned to the depots where they had acquired the eastern goods offered in exchange, and sold the European products for cash.

Some of that cash they exchanged immediately for new commodities to carry back to the interior of western Europe. Some of it was not used for purchases but was taken back to Europe, and so a small trickle of coin began to circulate from center to center; in time the trickle broadened into a stream of silver. That stream, flowing like blood through the body, would revive the European economy. Nobles with ready cash spent it on new luxuries; serfs with cash—acquired by extra labor—could purchase their own liberation. While coin worked its swift magic, however, its abundance alarmed the guardians of Christian morality, who read in Scripture that the poor were destined to inherit the earth.

The silver coins that circulated among European markets were of various kinds. Each type needed to be measured for conversion into the units of currency minted by other communities. A new figure—the moneychanger—took his place at the fairs. Merchants with currency of diverse origins came to the moneychanger to have their metal tested and their coin weighed. Kings and the great lords took an interest in guaranteeing the quality of coin produced in their domains.

The moneychanger was often a moneylender as well. If so, he was often a Jew. Jewish merchant communities had formed in England and France and the German lands, from which their trading ventures extended into eastern Europe. Where their services were especially valued they were protected by local authorities, and allowed to possess property. Some converted to Christianity and merged with the local population. But many kept their ancient faith, building synagogues and continuing, under their rabbis, a long tradition of learning and remembrance. By the twelfth century, Jews in the small English city of Lincoln had a stone-built community house. In the German city of Cologne at about the same time, there were forty-eight Jewish households.

The reason why Jews were the main moneylenders in the Middle Ages (at least before 1300) was that the Christian religion prohibited **usury**. "Usury" was defined as lending money at interest, since charity required lending to any in need without charge. Since the prohibition against usury is in the Old Testament (Leviticus 25:35–37; Deuteronomy 23:19–20) it applied, theoretically, to both Jews and Christians. But Jews, although they did not take interest within their own community, were compelled to take it from others in order to earn a livelihood, being barred from most occupations in the Christian community—dealing with "others" as they were not permitted to deal with "brothers." Another group that felt free to trade usuriously were the merchants of Lombardy, in northern Italy (so named because it had earlier been occupied by the Lombards). Lombard merchants, though professed Christians, disregarded church law against lending money at interest and seemed fearless of the associated punishment. Their example may have encouraged other Christian merchants to lend money.

Church law condemned not only usury but also overcharging. Theologians posed the abstract rule of the "just price," a price for commodities that fairly rewarded the seller for his labor but did not unfairly burden the buyer in his need. Their speculations about the costs of labor and materials and the factor of risk foreshadow later economic theories of capitalism and socialism (see Chapters 21, 25).

By the thirteenth century, Italian merchants had overcome their reluctance to lend money at interest or take high percentages of profit—if not their sense of guilt. Having encountered banks in their journeys to the Middle East, where these institutions were well established, they became not merely moneychangers or moneylenders but bankers—possessors of great wealth, exchangers of vast sums, engineers of currency conversion on a large scale. While worrying at times whether they could manage to do so, these men hoped to serve both God and profit.

The Worth of Wealth

Bankers were among the vanguard of businessmen who, in an era overshadowed by the Christian preference for poverty, lived according to the principle of the peerless worth of wealth. They were at odds with the norms of medieval society in other ways as well. While most Europeans were knit together by their common village life or their dependency upon a lord, town dwellers were, at first, socially undefined. They did not belong to one of the three main groups of medieval society: they did not fight, they did not plow the fields, they did not lead the faithful to salvation. They made things, bought things, sold things—tasks little known to earlier medieval society. But in the construction of Western society these men (and a few women) who were without lords or masters, these kings of account books and warehouses, were as important as the canniest monarchs and emperors. Three examples of outstandingly successful merchants will display their outlook.

Datini and Barbarigo One of the leading merchants of fourteenth-century Italy was Francesco Datini (c. 1335–1410) of Prato, a small town near Florence. He spent his youth apprenticed to an Italian businessman in Avignon, where the papal court was located for much of the fourteenth century. In about 1385, he returned to Prato a rich man and joined its guild of silk merchants. He then set up a business in Florence, dealing not only in silk but in all sorts of other items from Europe and beyond, including leather from Córdoba, Spain, wheat from Sicily, cloves from the East Indies. Rather than travel himself, he had agents in the cities where his business was done. Datini shared profits with these agents, but always retained the senior position. With the fortune he made from his investments, he bought houses and farms in the Tuscan countryside outside Florence. His extraordinary command of detail is witnessed by the extensive records that survive—574 books of accounts and 153,000 other business records.

Two generations later, a struggling Venetian nobleman, Andrea Barbarigo (1418–1449), rescued his family fortunes from the morass into which they had fallen as the result of a single disastrous shipwreck.

Barbarigo acquired woolen cloth from England and the Netherlands, oil from Valencia, in Spain, and cotton cloth from Asia, all of which he sold in Venice at a neat profit. Like Datini, he stayed home and directed the operations of his business, engaging agents abroad with whom he shared his profits, never allowing too great a portion of his assets to be involved in any single venture.

Jacques Cœur Barbarigo's contemporary Jacques Cœur (c. 1395–1456) was born to a commercial family in the French city of Bourges. He began his career in 1427, voyaging to the eastern Mediterranean and establishing the trade connections that would make him one of the richest men of the age. Obtaining a papal dispensation that permitted him to trade with non-Christians in Egypt and Syria, Cœur transported, by his own fleet of four **galleys** and three smaller vessels, the high-profit goods that were the staple of Mediterranean commerce— silks and spices, armor and furs, feathers and ivory. One of his galleys is depicted on p. 303. A staff of 300 supervised warehouses at Marseilles, Paris, Tours, and other French centers, and arranged for the sale of his merchandise throughout northwestern Europe.

Unlike Barbarigo and Datini—both citizens of independent city-states—Jacques Cœur belonged to a nation just emerging from the Hundred Years' War under a monarch striving to forge a modern centralized state. When Cœur undertook his first ventures, the French king, Charles VII, was a desperate refugee from his own capital city. In later years, as France struggled free of foreign domination, Cœur stood by the now-confident king, a trusted servant who provided much of the money needed to pursue these aims. Grateful for Cœur's support and acumen, the king drew him into royal service, made him a member of the council, conferred upon him the insignia of nobility, promoted his children, and made him master of the royal mint—a position both sensitive and lucrative.

Meanwhile, Cœur was the universal moneylender at the French court. He lent to the king, the queen, the nobles, building up good will and dangerous resentment at the same time. When the king's mistress Agnès Sorel died in childbirth, in 1450, Jacques Cœur was accused of having poisoned her. After a cycle of torture and forced confession, the merchant paid a huge fine, suffered the confiscation of all his wealth, and was banished from France. The king used Cœur's money to recapture the stubborn English stronghold in the French city of Bordeaux. Cœur died fighting the Turks on the Aegean island of Chios, a captain in the papal navy.

Before his fall from power, Cœur had built a mansion in Bourges befitting his wealth and circumstances. From the front, it looked like a commercial house, with warehouse facilities on the ground floor. From the back, it looked like a castle. The architecture expressed the ambivalence of a merchant's place in late medieval society: imbedded in, yet aloof from, the world of knights and nobles.

The merchants and bankers of the Middle Ages were the first agents of Europe's great expansion over the coming centuries. Their activity radiated out from the towns and cities in which they gathered to live, to bargain, and to profit.

CITIES AND TOWNS

During the late Roman Empire, the once-populous cities of western Europe bled and dwindled (see Chapter 6). People left them in order to avoid taxes and responsibilities and even honors, which came at a heavy price. City walls, now mere shells, enclosed areas too large for the population that remained. Yet these shrunken cities would revive in the three centuries after 1000, and new cities would emerge alongside them. These European towns fostered the growth of institutions that were the foundations of modern civilization.

Urban Decline and Revival

The city of Rome itself typified this urban decline. From about a million at the height of the Empire, the population of Rome dropped to less than half that in the mid-fifth century, then to about 50,000 after Justinian's devastating war against the Goths a hundred years later. In the thirteenth century, its population numbered scarcely 35,000. The whole population of the city could have found seats in the Colosseum. By the fourteenth century it had fallen even further, to about 20,000.

Beyond the Alps, in Gaul, Britain, and elsewhere, Roman towns wasted to ruins. "The work of giants moldreth away," wrote one Anglo-Saxon poet of the decline of a Roman outpost in Britain: roofs collapsed, towers crumbled, gates were breached, "battered ramparts … shorn away and ruined." Opportunists salvaged the well-dressed stones from ancient crumbled buildings to build their new cathedrals and fortifications. Beyond the limits of Rome's former rule, there were not even ruined cities. Instead, there was only a virgin wilderness of dense forest and swampy wasteland.

From this depressing landscape, there began to arise, in the eleventh century, an urban civilization. Cities emerged in various places: within the shells of the old Roman centers, amid the wastelands of central and eastern Europe, around the castles of the great lords, as shown on p. 297. Wherever they emerged, they introduced new energies, opened new possibilities, and presented new challenges to a world in which warriors, workers, and kings had just managed to achieve stability.

Many cities developed around the households of bishops, who remained in the old Roman centers as imperial authority declined, representatives of the now-mighty Church. This household consisted of the bishop, his secretaries and clerks, servants and artisans, priests and canons (members of a cathederal chapter or collegiate church) who sang the daily offices, and, in time, the students and teachers of the cathedral school. The bishop's extensive church property was farmed by serfs for the benefit of the whole household. This land was a natural focus for a weekly or monthly market for the exchange of local produce, where surplus crops were traded with the community just like for any landlord.

Merchants from distant places occasionally came offering rare and expensive goods. Some of them settled together, forming a commercial community not far from the cathedral precincts, content to live under the rule of the bishop. Other merchants followed, as did landowners who wished a house in town and peasants from nearby villages who had escaped from serfdom or bought their freedom with the profits of their labor. Originally, the merchants' "town" was very much distinct from the bishop's nearby "city." In time they drew together, and the same wall expanded to enclose them both.

Burgs Other cities formed around the fortified castles of the European countryside. These offered to local villagers a reliable defense against raid and assault. They had other advantages as well. They held stores of grain in case of a protracted siege, and the local lord or prince provided justice. These advantages attracted merchants fearful of insecurity and disorder. Some merchants ceased to wander, settled down, and built their houses and shops outside the castle walls in a development called a *suburbium*—the first **suburbs**— meaning "below [that is, outside] the walls."

A fortified place that served as a mercantile center was called *bourg* in French, *burg* in German, *borgo* in Italian, and *borough* in English. In time the word came to signify the city that grew straggling outside its walls. Its residents were called **burghers** or *bourgeois*. In these fragile merchant settlements began the career of the European ***bourgeoisie***—a class of enterprising merchants, bankers, and long-distant traders. Like the residents of the cathedral city, they would in due course erect a stone wall with ramparts and gates around their new settlement, absorbing the smaller circle of fortification that was the original burg. While merchant colonies tended to cluster around the bishop's see in areas once under Roman domination, the burg-centered city was more typical in

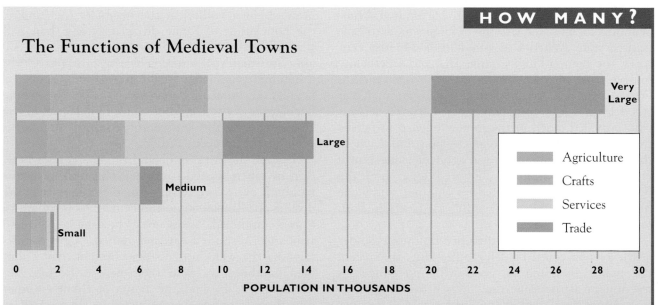

HOW MANY?

The Functions of Medieval Towns

Very Large

Large

Medium

Small

Legend:
- Agriculture
- Crafts
- Services
- Trade

POPULATION IN THOUSANDS (0 2 4 6 8 10 12 14 16 18 20 22 24 26 28 30)

This is a schematic representation of the kinds of functions performed in four sizes of medieval towns: very large (c. 28,000); large (c. 14,000); medium (c. 7000); and small (c. 2000). The small size, to modern eyes, of even "very large" towns should be noted. Europe's great vitality came from its numerous, interlinked, but modest commercial centers, most of them less than one mile in diameter. The tasks represented here are "trade" (buying and selling); "services" (inns and taverns, banking, professional services); "crafts" (artisan production such as shoes, textiles, wood and metal work); and agriculture. The agricultural function becomes increasingly less important as town size grows, and the trade function—the central activity of a commercial society—increases at the most rapid rate of all four functions as town size expands from "small" to "very large." The "trade" function of a small town is virtually invisible. For a medium town, it might absorb 1000 (15%) of 7000 residents; of a large town, 4000 (29%) of 14,000 residents; of a very large town, 8000 (again 29%) of 28,888. The "service" function also increases notably, from 29% to 36% to 40%. The "craft" function declines from 43% to 29% as town size increases from medium to very large.

Source: Norman J. G. Pounds, *An Economic History of Medieval Europe* (London: Longman, 1974), p. 255, fig. 6.7.

How Cities Grew

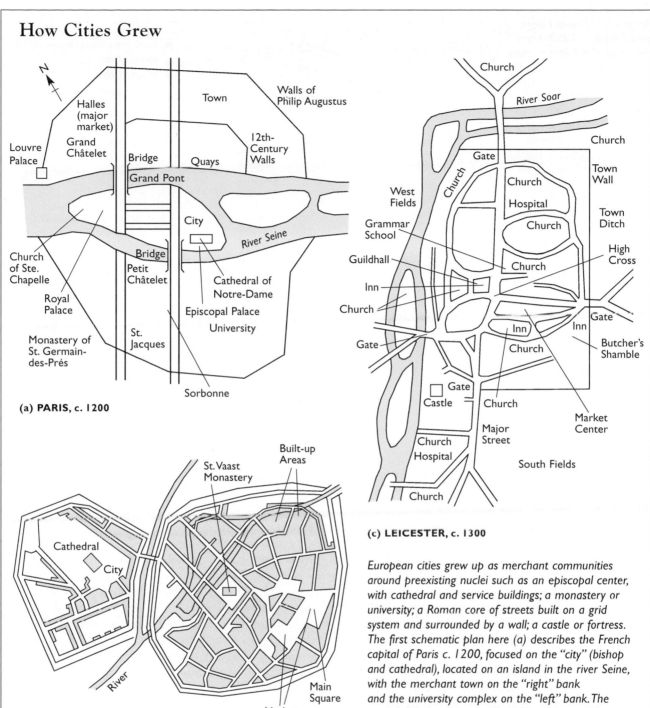

(a) PARIS, c. 1200

N

Louvre Palace
Halles (major market)
Grand Châtelet
Town
Walls of Philip Augustus
12th-Century Walls
Bridge
Quays
Grand Pont
City
River Seine
Bridge
Petit Châtelet
Church of Ste. Chapelle
Royal Palace
Cathedral of Notre-Dame
Episcopal Palace
University
Monastery of St. Germain-des-Prés
St. Jacques
Sorbonne

(b) ARRAS, c. 1435

St. Vaast Monastery
Built-up Areas
Cathedral
City
River
Main Square
Market Squares

(c) LEICESTER, c. 1300

Church
River Soar
Church
Gate
Church
Town Wall
West Fields
Church
Hospital
Town Ditch
Church
Grammar School
High Cross
Guildhall
Church
Inn
Church
Gate
Inn
Inn
Gate
Butcher's Shamble
Gate
Church
Market Center
Castle
Church
Hospital
Major Street
South Fields
Church

European cities grew up as merchant communities around preexisting nuclei such as an episcopal center, with cathedral and service buildings; a monastery or university; a Roman core of streets built on a grid system and surrounded by a wall; a castle or fortress. The first schematic plan here (a) describes the French capital of Paris c. 1200, focused on the "city" (bishop and cathedral), located on an island in the river Seine, with the merchant town on the "right" bank and the university complex on the "left" bank. The second (b) shows the northern French town of Arras c. 1435, in which the town is an addendum to the cathedral center, or "city" across the river. The third (c) shows the English town of Leicester c. 1300, a merchant center addendum to the castle complex commanding the river edge. All three are typical medieval cities enclosed by walls and built in relation to rivers that flow through them (Arras and Paris) or along one boundary (Leicester).

Map 11.1 Towns Large and Small, c. 1350: From the shells of old Roman cities, around cathedrals and castles, amid farmlands newly cleared for the plow, after 1000 European merchant communities expanded and established thriving towns. As the chart opposite shows, most towns in Europe were small. Why do we find large cities—Córdoba and Constantinople—in Islamic Spain and the Byzantine Empire? Why are the other large European cities c. 1350 all in Italy?

northern and central Europe. The great cloth towns of Flanders, for instance—Bruges, Ghent, Ypres, Lille, and others—began as burgs.

New towns Some towns were created wholly new. They might be planted in rural areas by a nobleman wishing to cultivate new soil. The peasant farmers attracted to these areas were granted personal freedom and a charter establishing civic autonomy. They formed a kind of rural bourgeoisie, to whose settlements commerce and industry eventually migrated. The proliferation of "new towns" marks the effects of the growth of commerce and urbanization on even the rural landscape. Their presence is especially conspicuous in central and eastern Europe, areas opened up by colonization efforts after about 1200.

The cities formed within Roman walls soon outgrew the original enclosure and new rings of walls of greater dimensions had to be built. In prosperous cities, this process occurred more than once. Dynamic Florence extended its walls repeatedly. The ancient Roman ring was replaced by a larger medieval one, which was also outgrown and replaced in the fourteenth century by a third set of walls. Those walls, 5 miles (8 km.) in circumference, and capable of housing its maximum population of some 100,000, stood until the 1860s. Likewise in 1240, neighboring Pistoia built its third and final circuit of walls, which mark the maximum growth of the medieval town.

Cities that formed as merchant colonies outside fortified sites were also encircled by walls—in this case brand-new. At first these were mere mounds of earth or wooden palisades, in the north at least, but

soon the art of building in stone was learned from the Mediterranean south. Whatever the type of town, eventually all of its constituent parts—merchant quarter, lord's castle, cathedral precinct—were united in a common whole and ringed by a common stone circuit of wall.

By 1200, much of western Europe (and, to a lesser extent, eastern Europe) was speckled with cities constructed within Roman walls or around castles, or sprung up at a crossroads or ford or confluence of waterways. The framework of cities by now far surpassed that during the Roman occupation. Although western Europe had as yet no huge metropolises, such as Constantinople and Baghdad, its web of small and densely-packed centers constituted an urban network of great productive capacity and flexibility. By 1300, as much as 10 percent of the population of western Europe lived in cities. After that time few new towns were founded, and existing towns rarely extended their walls farther.

Towns and their populations are indicated on Map 11.1 and *How Many?* on p. 299. Cities remained small throughout the Middle Ages. At their peak, around 1300, many numbered between 10,000 and 20,000 persons. Only the giant Italian cities of Florence, Milan, Genoa, Naples, and Venice reached 100,000, while the largest northern cities, Paris and London, housed only about 80,000 and 40,000 persons respectively (the latter expanded over the 12,000 that William the Conqueror found in 1066). Of the 50 or so major German towns around 1400, 35 had populations of 10,000 or less. Of the 15 that exceeded that figure, Cologne was the largest, with 30,000, followed by Lübeck, with 25,000, and Strasbourg, Nuremberg, and Danzig (modern Gdansk, in Poland), with about 20,000. Other major cities in this era included Prague (in today's Czech Republic), which reached 30,000 to 40,000; Ghent and Bruges (in Belgium), with 60,000 and 45,000 respectively; Toulouse, Bordeaux, Rouen, and Lyons (in France), which surpassed 25,000. Barcelona, in Christian Spain, reached about 35,000, while in Islamic Spain, Seville and Granada exceeded 50,000, and Córdoba half a million. Cities with populations over 20,000 generally engaged in long-distance commerce as well as the manufacture of goods. Smaller towns tended to produce for local markets, and agriculture played a significantly larger role than manufacture in their economy.

The Bourgeoisie The first townspeople—the burghers, or bourgeoisie—were undoubtedly the children or descendants of serfs. They could scarcely have come from any other class of medieval society. Yet by virtue of having detached themselves from the land, they had become free. Serfs who managed to escape to a city, and who remained there unreported for a term of "a year and a day," were generally protected by city law and not returned to serfdom. Moreover, they were considered not only free but

(legally at least) equal; there were no differentiations in the status of freemen. That fact lent meaning to the German proverb "*Stadtluft macht frei*," that the air of the city makes one free. The towns were havens of freedom and autonomy, to the extent that those concepts could be understood in a hierarchical society.

The societies of free men in the burgeoning cities promptly sought charters from the lords who held dominion over the land—whether noble, king, or Church—defining their special standing in medieval society (see *Witnesses*, p. 300). Kings especially found it useful to protect the cities whose merchants had access to ready cash. City charters established the privileges and exemptions of the urban community, along with its obligations. The townspeople might be granted the privilege of creating and administering their own laws, or of commuting to money payments the labor and military service owed the lord, or of being exempt from the gate and road tolls that the nobility exacted everywhere, which were grave impediments to trade. They sought the precious privileges also sought by territorial lords—to hold a market, to mint coins, to collect tolls.

Once freed from subjection to overlords and from irksome dues and services, the burghers of the medieval cities proceeded to establish their own

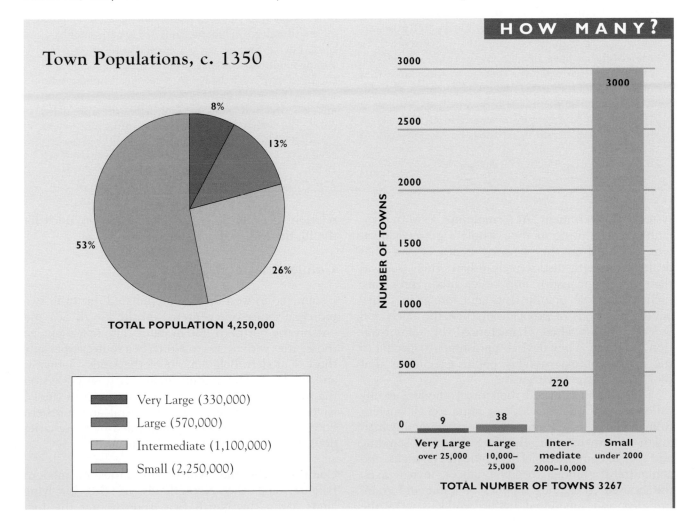

Town Populations, c. 1350

8%
13%
26%
53%

TOTAL POPULATION 4,250,000

■ Very Large (330,000)
■ Large (570,000)
■ Intermediate (1,100,000)
■ Small (2,250,000)

HOW MANY?

NUMBER OF TOWNS

3000			3000
2500			
2000			
1500			
1000			
500			
0	9	38	220

Very Large over 25,000	Large 10,000–25,000	Intermediate 2000–10,000	Small under 2000

TOTAL NUMBER OF TOWNS 3267

Town Statutes and Troubles

The nodes of medieval economic life were the towns, which were carved out of a rural landscape by the energy of the merchant citizens aided by legal charters granted by feudal overlords, who sometimes lost all authority over the townspeople. In the first passage, the Count of Flanders grants a charter to the town of St. Omer, a charter that is particularly generous in freeing the citizens of taxes and toll liabilities, a great boost to commercial development. The second describes the citizens of the self-governing commune of the Italian city of Volterra swearing mutual loyalty. The third is a report by a hostile witness of the revolt of the commune of the merchants of French Laon against their overlord, the bishop, who was supported by members of the nobility.

William Clito, Count of Flanders, grants a Charter offering valuable tax relief to the town of St. Omer, 1127: I, William, by the grace of God, Count of Flanders, not wishing to reject the petition of the citizens of St. Omer ... grant them the laws written below, and command that those laws remain inviolate. 1. First that to every man I will show peace, and I will protect and defend them with good will just as I do my other men ... 9. All who dwell within the walls of St. Omer, or who dwell there in the future, I make free from *cavagium*, i.e., from head-tax, and from suit of court ... 11. Moreover they have asked the king of France and Ralph of Peronne that wherever they go in their lands they may be free of toll, transit dues, and passage; I wish this to be granted to them ... 13. As I wish the citizens of Flanders to be free henceforward from all customs [taxes], I shall require from them no *scot*, or *taille*, or forced loan.
(From J. M. Kemble, *The Saxons in England*, 1965)

Oath of the citizens of Volterra to obey their magistrates, meet in assembly, and to rise to defend the city: I ... swear on the holy gospels of God to observe and fulfill and never violate by fraud each and every order which the consuls [chief magistrates] or podestà [judge] of Volterra should have me obey. ... Likewise, if I should hear the great bell sound once the call to assembly I shall come to the public meeting without arms, and I shall remain in good faith until the end of the meeting. ... Likewise, if I should hear the two great bells sounding the call to assembly I shall appear at the designated place armed. ...
(*Volterra Statutes*; eds. J. Mundy, P. Reisenberg, 1958)

Abbot Guibert of Nogent describes the revolt of the commune of Laon against the bishop and his noble allies (1166): The next day, ... behold there arose a disorderly noise throughout the city, men shouting "Commune!" and again through the middle of the chapel of the Blessed Mary ... citizens now entered the Bishop's court with swords, battle-axes, bows and hatchets, and carrying clubs and spears, a very great company. As soon as this sudden attack was discovered, the nobles rallied from all sides to the Bishop. ... In this rally Guiimon ... , an aged nobleman of handsome presence and guiltless character, armed only with shield and spear, ran out through the church and as he entered the Bishop's hall, was the first to fall, struck on the back of the head with a battle-axe by a certain Rainbert, who was his fellow-citizen. ... Next the outrageous mob attacking the Bishop and howling before the walls of his palace, he with some who were succoring him fought them off by hurling of stones and shooting of arrows.
(Guibert of Nogent, *Autobiography*, 1166; ed. C. C. Swinton Bland, 1925)

systems of government. As a **commune**, a sworn community constituting in their whole a power equivalent to lordship, they created codes of law that dealt amply with distinctively urban crime (such as theft and vandalism), and other urban problems, such as the role of transients and foreigners. They devised methods of proof other than the duels and ordeals that elsewhere characterized the administration of justice. They devised punishments specific to the urban context, notably public executions that took place in the town square.

Town leaders created their own officials, usually called mayors or "consuls," in imitation of ancient Rome. They elected a representative council, which might in turn have an elaborate system of standing and special committees. These officials, councils, and committees attended to city finances, levied taxes, warehoused emergency supplies of water and grain, initiated and supervised public works, saw to the relations between laity and clergy, and provided for the ill, the widowed, and the rootless young.

Commercial Zones

Commerce in western Europe radiated out from two principal zones: one centered on the North Sea and one on the northern Italian plain. The first included those cities with access to North Sea routes, especially those of modern Belgium, the Netherlands, Germany, and England. The second included those poised on the Mediterranean coast, on the tributaries of the Po River, or on Alpine passes to central and northern Europe. The commercial system ruled by these cities flourished into the seventeenth century.

Commerce in the North The cities of modern Belgium and the Netherlands in the low-lying lands along the North Sea were among the first outside Italy to spring into activity. As early as the time of Charlemagne, cloth-makers of this region produced an especially fine "Frisian" wool (of which Charlemagne was proud to send a sample to the Caliph Harun-al-Rashid, in exchange for the elephant the latter had tendered as a gift). Frisian cloth was one of the few manufactures traded at that time. The region was also enriched by the commercial activity of the Norsemen, who established merchant colonies there in the ninth and tenth centuries. As these enterprising northerners discovered that commerce yielded wealth more safely and reliably than raiding, they extended their network northwestward to Iceland, eastward to Russia, and from there southward to Constantinople. All of these contacts invigorated the economic life of the Netherlands. After 1000, the Viking depots of this northern region yielded their primacy to the flourishing centers at Bruges, Ghent, Ypres, and elsewhere.

The Hanseatic League After 1200, with the opening up of eastern Europe and the continued extension of trade avenues, commercial networks around the North and Baltic seas reorganized for long-distance ventures. A group of port cities leagued together for the more effective transport of goods and the security of their merchants. This alliance, which united northern Europe into one economic unit between about 1250 and 1450, was known as the Hanseatic League (*hansa* means guild or company). It had its own flag, was governed by its own laws, and exercised diplomacy with foreign governments.

At its peak in the fourteenth century, the League included some eighty cities and extended from Bruges in the west to Novgorod (in Russia) to the east. Between lay the German towns of Hamburg, Lübeck, Rostock, Danzig, and others. Across this system flowed the exchange of goods: English wool to Flanders, where it was woven into cloth, some of which was traded for the raw materials of Scandinavia and Russia (furs, amber, herring, hunting falcons, and timber) and the fine goods and gold coin brought from the larger market of Constantinople.

Hanseatic commerce had brought prosperity to the cities of southern Germany, most notably Nuremberg. Nuremberg exchanged its armor and swords, wrought

Medieval Town: *Many medieval European towns took form within the walls of old Roman settlements—as was clearly the case of medieval Arles, shown here in an engraving of 1686. Arles was built within the remains of the colosseum that Roman settlers had built in antiquity. The structure that had served as an arena for games and races was transformed into city walls.* (British Library, London)

Ships and Shipbuilding

The Arsenal: *Ships and shipbuilders made it possible for Italian merchants to dominate Mediterranean trade after 1100. This plan shows the Venetian "Arsenal" as it stood around 1560, Europe's largest shipbuilding operation until modern times.*

Powder, charcoal, and sulphur, storehouses

Covered basins

Eleven covered dry docks

Lumber yard

Covered dry docks, basins

Area for drawing up galleys on land

Newest Arsenal

Covered dry docks

Covered dry docks

Covered dry docks

Old Arsenal

Rio delle Seghe

a
b
c

d

e

g

f

New Arsenal

Eleven covered dry docks, two covered basins

Shops and storerooms

Arms room

Office

Rio dell' Arsenale

Tana

Rio della Tana

Mastmakers' shop

Workers on gun carriages, small parts, etc.

Ironsmiths' foundries

N

a Doge's galley
b Storeroom for oars
c Storeroom for tow
d Admiral's storeroom
e Oarmakers' shop
f Gunmakers' foundry
g Three artillery sheds

Viking ship: *As trade routes developed, so ships were built to transport money and goods back and forth across the Old World. This Viking ship from Oseberg, early ninth century, was capable of swift, accurate navigation of stormy northern waters. (University Museum, Oslo)*

from metals mined in the region, for the goods of eastern Europe and northern Italy. By 1500, Nuremberg had become the foremost trading city of the German lands. Nearby Augsburg and Frankfurt were also energized in this way.

London was one of the outlying ports of call for Hanseatic merchants. Their market in that city flourished until the end of the fifteenth century. Here English merchants mingled with foreigners and participated, from their remote corner of Europe, in the commercial web that reached from their own Thames River to the Mediterranean Sea. A twelfth-century observer was struck by the exotic wares that reached the London market: "The Arabian sends gold. … The Scythian brings arms, and from the rich fat lands of Babylon comes oil of palms. … the men of Norway and Russia [send] furs and sables; nor is China absent with purple silk."

Commerce in Italy Nowhere in Europe, however, was there a greater concentration of flourishing towns and cities than in northern Italy. Despite urban depopulation and the splintering of authority throughout the region, some city traditions lingered from the ancient Roman era. Milan, Lucca, Padua, Florence, and others descended from cities once

A ship of Jacques Coeur: *This round galley of the fifteenth-century merchant prince Jacques Cœur is depicted on stained glass.* (Bourges Museum, France)

Sailing ship: *Ships sailed from the Islamic Middle East to China and back, transporting silks and spices to ports such as Alexandria where the Europeans bought these luxury goods. Such a ship is shown in this manuscript illumination from Al-Hariri's* Tales of Fiction, *1237, showing the stitched planking of the vessel, Arabs manning the rigging, and the faces of Arab passengers at the portholes.* (Bibliothèque Nationale, Paris)

inhabited by toga-clad senators. These cities revived early—soon after 900—and steadily progressed. Venice led them all.

Never a Roman city, Venice had its origins in the chaos of the early medieval invasions. Refugees from northeast Italy, not trusting even in their walled fortifications, fled from the mainland to settle on the sandbars and marshes and shifting islets of the Adriatic lagoon. Here they fished. After 900, they began to sell their catch and supplies of salt as well, which they farmed on the shores of the abundant sea around them. They carried these cheap commodities to nearby coastal settlements and to inland villages on the tributaries of the Po River. In exchange they acquired the grain they could not grow in their watery domain.

By 1000 the Venetians had formed a government (theoretically under Byzantine rule) and a fleet. With their ships they brought to Constantinople the plain but useful products of the west—wine and wheat, timber and salt, and (though the trade was officially forbidden to Christians) slaves from the Slavic settlements on the eastern Adriatic coast. From

Constantinople they sailed home with the sumptuous fabrics produced in Byzantine workshops and spices from far Asia. Back in Europe, nobles and kings awaited hungrily these luxurious imports.

The Venetians soon outstripped their masters in Constantinople and dominated the trade routes of the Adriatic. By the fourteenth century, their administrative and market center on the island of Rialto had become the greatest emporium in the west. "Merchandise flows through this noble city even as water flows from the fountains," wrote the chronicler Martino da Canale, "and the salt water runs though it and round it and in all places save in the houses and the streets. ... You may find within this fair town many men ... who buy and sell, and money changers and citizens of all crafts, and therewith mariners of all sorts, and ships to carry them to all lands and galleys to lay low their enemies."

Late in the eleventh century, Genoa and Pisa burst into activity, equipped with their own war galleys, with which to join in the Italian infiltration of Mediterranean trade. Their fleets traveled to Arab ports from Tripoli (modern Libya) to Morocco on the North African coast, which they opened up by force even before Urban II launched the First Crusade in 1095. The military support of Genoese and Pisan warships was essential to the conquest of Jerusalem and the surrounding territory, which was the chief result of this Crusade. Afterward, the Genoese and Pisans, like the Venetians, established merchant colonies of their nationals in Constantinople and throughout the eastern Mediterranean.

After 1100, the towns of Lombardy fed by Pisa and Genoa on the west coast of Italy and by Venice on the east, began to swell with people and products. Watered by the broad Po River, the fertile Lombard plain produced amply the agricultural goods that could be exchanged for the new commodities brought by merchants from the coasts. Towns and cities sprang up densely along the river banks, along the Italian rim of the Alps, just to the north, and the slope of the Apennines to the south. From the northernmost centers, such as Milan, which edged out the other contenders for eminence, merchant caravans crossed the Alps by passes now cleared of bandits and properly maintained. Once over the mountain barriers, they sought the river valley routes to the interior. These Lombard merchants soon became a well-known presence in the commercial centers of western Europe.

Urban Revolution in Northern Italy

In Italy, particularly, the burgeoning of mercantile centers had important political consequences. The nascent Lombard towns joined together to defend themselves, when central authorities were too weak to do so, and to advance their special interests against those of their masters. Some northern Italian cities developed republican patterns of government, and a few managed to retain these for a century or more. None survived Venice, whose republic did not fall until 1797—to the French conqueror Napoleon (see Chapter 20), who boasted that he would ravage Venice as Attila the Hun had intended to ravage Rome, and did so. The precedent of self-government that the Italian republics posed to the nations of modern Europe did not go ignored.

The Lombard towns were not only numerous, but populous—numbering in the range of 10,000 to 25,000 inhabitants. There were no powerful kings in northern Italy, and the cities, welcoming within their walls the nobles of the countryside, became centers of authority. Merchant leaders (who lived rather like lords) joined forces with noble town dwellers (who dabbled in trade). These alliances—sometimes amiable and sometimes tense and perilous—served to gain control over both city and region and to construct a politics ruled by law and administered by representatives of the governing elite. From as early as the 1080s until 1138, sixteen Italian towns declared themselves independent communes, ruled not by bishops or lords but by sworn associations of merchant and noble citizens.

The Lombard League In 1167, these towns joined together to form the Lombard League. Its purpose—unlike that of the Hanseatic League—was to provide a common defense. The threat that rallied the cities was the power of the Holy Roman Emperor, who periodically asserted his claim to the overlordship of northern Italy, dating back to the times of Charlemagne. The now-sophisticated leaders of the Lombard cities believed that both their autonomy and their profit margins were threatened by the prospect of rule by a monarch insensitive to the needs and aspirations of urban populations.

The man whose ambitions so threatened the Lombard merchants was the emperor Frederick I, called "Barbarossa" ("red-beard"), of the Hohenstaufen dynasty. Determined to execute the imperial claim to rule as king in Italy, Barbarossa (r. 1152–1190) entered Italy six times. He declared his sovereignty at the **Diet** (assembly) of Roncaglia in 1158; then, backed up by a knightly army, he attempted to place imperial agents in the rebel Italian cities. In a convincing show of force in 1162, he razed Milan to the ground. Formed in response to these acts of aggression, the Lombard League was ready when Barbarossa marched south to Italy in 1174, and defeated him at Legnano in 1176. In the peace treaty of 1183, the League gained a historic victory for the Italian cities and delivered an early challenge from self-governing peoples to the principle of monarchy.

Guelfs and Ghibellines The Peace of Constance of 1183, which established peace between the Italian cities and the Holy Roman emperors, did not entirely settle the hostility between them. For centuries, emperors claimed Italy as their own, while the Italian cities—after their rare moment of cooperation in the Lombard League—struggled separately for economic and political autonomy. When imperial designs for expansion spelled danger, however, they found it useful to join forces, especially with the Empire's greatest enemy, the papacy (see Chapter 10).

Supporters of the imperial party in Italy were called "Ghibellines," and those of the papal party "Guelfs." Although alliances shifted, Italy's nobility tended to be Ghibelline, and the merchants of its major commercial cities tended to be Guelf. The pope, who now headed a great bureaucracy needed bankers and tax-collectors, and the merchants obliged.

During the thirteenth century, Florence was the preeminent Guelf republic. As a reward for their city's loyalty to the Guelf cause, Florentine bankers were commissioned as papal agents. Throughout Europe they collected the rich tax revenues destined for Rome, and skimmed their due percentage from the top. The wealth they brought to Florence stimulated the city's already-thriving industry of cloth production and refinishing, described in *Witnesses*, p. 293, and *Windows On*, p. 306.

In 1250, some of the city's foremost merchants led the citizenry in a revolt against local noble magnates, aligned with the Ghibellines. In 1250 they formed a republic, called the "Primo Popolo," or the "First People's Government." Two years later the Florentines celebrated their triumph by minting the first gold coin to rival Byzantine currency in Mediterranean commerce. Named after the city of its birth, the florin, along with its cousin the ducat, first

minted in Venice in 1284 (and named after the *dux*, or *doge*, who presided over the city's republican institutions), replaced the coins of Constantinople and Islam as the principal currency of western Europe for the purchase of costly commodities. General purchases were still made with silver coins.

After further wrangling, the Florentine republic was finally constituted in 1267 as a Guelf merchant state, run by an oligarchy of prominent citizens. Establishing laws that protected the interests of merchant rulers against noble landholders in 1296, the new government gave orders to tear down the towers of the nobles (built for defence against rival families) which dominated the city. When the jagged skyline posed by the fortified towers of a hereditary aristocracy fell to the discipline of law imposed by a merchant elite, Europe was on the threshold of a new age. Commercial growth would lead to political and social transformation.

ARTISANS AND ENTREPRENEURS

Cities and towns were the sites of commercial growth and political innovation in the Middle Ages. They were also home to the workers and businessmen whose activity made both happen.

Some of the goods sold at a profit by European merchants were grown from the soil, fished from the sea or rivers, or mined from the earth. But the most profitable goods were produced by the artful labor of human hands. Those laborers were skilled craftspeople, or artisans. Some artisans sold their own products in their own workshop, generally the front room of their homes. Others worked for merchants

Oar makers at work: *Guilds existed for the production of goods as various as cloth and oars; oars and other wooden components are shown in this fifteenth-century painting of a medieval guild sign. (Museo Correr, Venice)*

The Florentine Wool Cloth Industry, Thirteenth Century

Spinning the thread

Weaving the cloth

Florentine wool workshops were a prototype of modern industrial production. Tasks were subdivided and performed by human labor, as shown here: spinning the thread (distaff and wheel), performed mostly by women (above); weaving cloth, horizontal loom (left); combing and fulling the woven cloth (below). (For dyeing see p. 309).

What different levels of skill did these various occupations require? Which required the most expensive equipment?

Combing the cloth

Fulling the cloth

To continue your investigation of this topic, please go to www.prenhall.com/king for the related **WINDOWS** on the **WEB** activity

who organized large-scale industrial enterprises. These merchant entrepreneurs, their artisan employees, and independent **master** artisans often struggled to be heard in the medieval city; and sometimes struggled to exclude the others from power.

Medieval Industry: Textiles, Mining, and Shipbuilding

It was the productive capacity of the expanding medieval cities that made them formidable. Unlike the cities of Greek and Roman antiquity, which considered commercial and industrial functions inferior to political and military ones, medieval cities were engines of production.

The most important product of European manufacture was cloth. The textile industry produced the wealth that powered Europe's commercial achievements during the period from 1000 to 1300, and centuries later stimulated the industrialization of modern Europe (see Chapter 21). Its modest origins gave little sign of this great outcome. In the early Middle Ages, cloth was produced at home, by serf women and noblewomen. On the larger manors, women workers were gathered into a central workshop, the *gynaeceum*. Much of the cloth made in such home workshops was crude. After 1000, while households continued to produce cloth for local use, the new towns and cities became centers of textile production. As quality improved with the concentration of textile production in the towns, cloth became Europe's most important export, the basis for its emerging preeminence.

Linen was the first fabric produced in Europe of a quality fine enough to serve as a commodity of long-distance trade. It was processed from flax, which grew in marshy regions of the Low Countries, an area that won an early primacy in textile production. Burghers and nobles might wear undergarments of linen or spread their beds or tables with sheets of the fine fabric—hence even today, the shelves on which sheets and tablecloths are stored are called "linen closets" even though few people still use linen for those purposes. A tenth-century Arab geographer saw especially fine samples of this fabric in Naples and wrote that the like could not be found in any other country: "There is no craftsman in any other workshop in the world who is able to manufacture it."

Silk was even more of a luxury than linen. Originally imported from Asia via depots in Syria, Constantinople, or Egypt, this luxury textile was, by the late Middle Ages, being domestically produced—in Italy at Lucca and later in Venice, Florence, Bologna, and Milan, and in south-central France in Lyons. The nobility and high clergy were among the first attracted to silk, but soon the town dwellers of Italy and northern Europe developed an appetite for splendidly woven and decorated silks. Few consumers

---

WITNESSES

Commercial Contracts

Essential to the growth of trade was the development of tools of credit. In the first excerpt, an individual receives a loan from another and promises to return the amount with a sum of interest buried in the final payment. In the second, a sedentary partner contributes twice the amount of the active partner in a colleganza contract, while they agree to share all profits from the venture equally, "without fraud and evil device." Both contracts have the effect of rewarding the lender without utilizing the term "interest," considered to be usury, and against church law.

A contract explicitly mentioning interest equivalent to 20 per cent per year, forbidden by church law (Genoa, July 16, 1161): I, Embrone, have taken in loan from you, Salvo of Piacenza, £100 Genoese, for which I shall pay you or your messenger ... £120 within in one year; but if I wish to pay the aforesaid £100 and accrued interest before the next feast of the Purification, you must accept them and for that purpose have your messenger in Genoa. If I do not so observe [these conditions], I promise you, making the stipulation, the penalty of the double.
(From R. Lopez, I. Raymond, eds., *Medieval Trade in the Mediterranean World*, 1955)

A Venetian *Commenda* agreement between a seagoing merchant and a passive partner (Venice, August, 1073): I, Giovanni Lissado of Luprio, ... have received in *collegantia* [partnership commitment] from you, Sevasto Orefice, ... £200 [Venetian]. And I myself have invested £100 in it. And with this capital ... we have [acquired] two shares ... in the ship of which Cosmiro da Molino is captain. And I am under obligation to bring all of this with me ... to Thebes ... Indeed, by this agreement and understanding of ours I promise to put to work this entire [capital] and to strive the best way I can. Then, if the capital is saved, we are to divide whatever profit the Lord may grant us from it by exact halves, without fraud and evil device. ... And if all these goods are lost because of the sea or of [hostile] people ... neither party ought to ask any of them from the other; if, however, some of them remain, in proportion as we invested so shall we share.
(From R. Lopez, I. Raymond, eds., *Medieval Trade in the Mediterranean World*, 1955)

could afford this fine product, but those few yielded large profits for manufacturers and merchants.

Medieval industry was based not upon these luxury fabrics, however, but upon a humbler textile: wool. Sheared from the coats of English and Spanish sheep, processed and refined in Flemish, Italian, and, later, English workshops, wool furnished the peasant's tunic and the patrician's robe, and it traveled to foreign markets to fetch a tidy profit for Western merchants. Matted, filthy clumps of raw wool were transformed into gold by European workers and merchants, and by the bankers who financed the industry.

Once the raw wool reached the hands of artisans, it underwent a series of operations: cleaning, combing, spinning, weaving, fulling (shrinking and thickening for expensive cloth), dyeing, and finishing, as shown in *Windows On*, p. 306. Some of these tasks, such as weaving and dyeing, required considerable skill, while others, such as cleaning and spinning, were menial. Often these unskilled tasks were performed in nearby country villages, where women especially were available at low wages to prepare the thread for city weavers.

So many women were spinners that they became permanently identified with that labor. The word **"spinster,"** which today signifies a woman who has never married, recalls the medieval woman (especially the young unmarried girl or dependent widowed relative) who spent much of her life spinning. She twisted the fibers between her fingers, adding one fiber at a time to a thread that gradually increased in density and length. By the thirteenth century, an early form of spinning wheel (probably invented in India) was available, powered by a hand crank. But it was not always used. Armies of women workers continued to wind and twist raw fiber into thread with their tools of **distaff** and **spindle** which were everywhere the symbols of the female gender.

Weavers made up perhaps the largest group of urban craftworkers. By the high Middle Ages, most of them were men, who displaced women as the looms grew in size and capacity. From the thirteenth century, the mammoth horizontal loom replaced the simple vertical ones traditionally used in home workshops. The new loom stretched a **warp** as long as 164 feet (50 meters), across which the **woof**, or weft, progressed, thrown by a pedal-operated **shuttle**.

Spinning and weaving were the principal operations of cloth production. The cloth was also fulled and beaten to make it thick, then stretched into proper shape. The fabric's nap was raised with teasing, using a spiky plant called a teasel, then shorn smooth. Last, it was colored in any of a number of bright hues by one of the many available vegetable and animal dyes, which penetrated the fibers with the aid of the metallic compound alum (aluminum potassium sulfate), another commodity essential to the industry, also used as an astringent and in dyeing and tanning.

After textiles, the most important European industries were the mining of metals and production of metal goods. Iron was mined throughout Europe, as were tin, lead, and copper. Silver mined in remote mountains of northern Germany helped build that region's prosperity. Southern German cities specialized in metal products, as did Milan—above all in the manufacture of armor and weapons—as one recent historian has observed, an "illustration of the inferiority of the west in every craft except those of war." Outside of these metalworking centers, the craft was practiced at a more basic level in every European city or town, where blacksmiths labored to produce tools. Even remote manors boasted a blacksmith (his skill perhaps shared by several villages), who supplied the plowshares and hoes agricultural production.

Shipbuilding was an increasingly important industry. The poet Dante (1265–1321) visited Venice's famous dockyard, the Arsenal, which he described:

> *… the winter through*
> *there boils the sticky pitch to caulk the seams*
> *of the sea-battered bottoms. …*

The operation Dante described was Europe's largest industrial enterprise. Founded in 1104, the Venetian Arsenal (the word, derived from Arabic, testifies to contacts with Islamic) grew at its height in the early sixteenth century to enclose 60 acres (24 hectares) of the city's land, as shown on p. 302. Here were built and launched the Venetian merchant and war fleets which dominated the Mediterranean, outstripping Muslim, Byzantine, and other Italian competitors.

Guilds and Their Functions

The Arsenal was huge, and it was unique. Most medieval production, by contrast, took place in a small workshop, usually within the master's home, where artisans labored to produce the modest commodities needed in daily life—barrels, bread, shoes, and the like. These simpler artisans joined "craft guilds," distinct from the "merchant guilds" that developed earlier in the period of commercial revival.

The great entrepreneurs—those who got raw fiber or metallic ores into the hands of workers, who transported finished cloth or brought tools and arms to markets in Europe and abroad, who invested in workshops, equipment, and mines, or funded expensive commercial ventures, who managed the exchange of high-quality goods across the boundaries of county, country, or continent—probably belonged to the town's merchant guild, which represented the interests of merchants rather than artisans. This body was known by different names all over Europe—"guild" and "hansa" most common in the north, "brotherhood," "company," or "society" in Italy.

Management and labor—a guildmaster supervises the dyeing of cloth: *By the thirteenth century specific craftsman's guilds began to emerge. These guilds issued regulations that covered everything from protecting the welfare of deceased members' families to ensuring quality of production. This fifteenth-century Flemish manuscript illumination shows a guildmaster of the dyer's guild supervising men dyeing cloth. (British Library, London)*

At first, merchant guilds were undifferentiated by the merchandise they sold. In time, especially in larger cities, an early merchants' association did become differentiated by industry. In Florence, the more elite merchants belonged to one of seven "major" guilds. These included the bankers, cloth merchants, spice dealers, and goldsmiths. Their status was distinct from the retailers, who sold cheaper commodities in local markets, and from artisans such as bakers, brewers, and blacksmiths. They were called the *popolo grasso* (the "fat people") because of their wealth and social prominence.

The members of merchants' or upper guilds were those who negotiated city charters with the leaders of medieval society and thus became the city's governors. The urban elite became a "patriciate"—not a nobility, with its ancestral military associations, but an urban ruling class. As it assumed near-permanent control of the higher offices and responsibilities of leadership, the patriciate became hereditary and jealous of its authority, and especially in Venice rarely permitted new men to break into their circle. These men, the source of much of the city's wealth through donations or forced loans, were also the main patrons of building and the arts.

The lesser traders and artisans produced what they sold, performing both functions within the walls of their own house. They gathered in the craft guilds.

Their roster varied from city to city, but bakers, brewers, and barrelmakers generally figured among them, along with makers of purses and hats, and even physicians and **notaries** (the trained professionals who drew up deeds, contracts, wills, and other types of important documents).

These guild members worked not for a wage but for the profit on the goods they produced. They were both capitalists, who invested in workshop, tools, and materials, and laborers, equipped with special skills. Skill was critical in the medieval industrial system, the success of which rested on the performance of each individual worker. To assure the high quality of the products, the craft guilds insisted on rigorous observance of minimum standards in manufacture.

Guilds also concerned themselves with quantities—the exact weight and measure of goods sold, and the precise value of coin tendered. Together with the town governments, they helped overcome the weakening of standards that had occurred throughout Europe after the disappearance of Roman authority. Of particular concern to the towns was the minting of reliable coins, especially silver, in which virtually all wages and most local purchases were paid. Eventually towns were equally careful about gold, used in long-distance transactions and standardized, from the late thirteenth century, by the Florentine florin and Venetian ducat.

Guilds regulated the training of new workers. Training began with **apprenticeship**, in which a young boy was apprenticed to a guild master—one who had established his credentials and been admitted to the guild. The period of apprenticeship was from seven to fourteen years. At the end of that term, the apprentice would become a journeyman, so called because he worked by the day (in French, *journée*). When the journeyman could demonstrate his superior skills—in some towns by completing a "masterpiece"—he might be admitted to the guild as a master, but only if the guild approved of the person and was willing to accept new members. By the later Middle Ages, entrance to a guild was often limited to the sons of masters (and, until her remarriage or death, to his widow and her new husband). The craft guild was far from being the ancestor of the modern labor union, as it is often wrongfully described. It protected the interests of the owner-employer, not the worker.

In return for their members' compliance with tough standards, the guilds bestowed upon them the privilege of monopoly. Non-members could not engage in the trade except as apprentices or journeymen. Prices were set at a level considered "just." That regulation limited competitive practices such as price-cutting, and prevented the free floating of prices in accord with shifts in supply or demand. Workshops were small, and guild rulers kept them that way, limiting the amount of equipment, such as looms and furnaces, that any master might have. Such restrictions prevented one master from too far outstripping the others and breaking the fellowship of the guild circle.

If guild regulations assured quality of production, they also discouraged competition and may have prevented or retarded the development of new and more productive modes of manufacture. During the last two centuries of their existence—into the 1700s—the guilds' effect on the pace of commerce was chilling.

Guilds served other functions besides economic ones. They were a kind of "brotherhood" (although they did enrol some women), with a sense of solidarity, of common purpose and identity, similar to other overlapping communal and confraternal gatherings so frequent in medieval society (see Chapter 12). In the towns, in fact, guilds served many of the functions performed elsewhere by the village community or the protective church. Members gathered for banquets, assumed the responsibility to fund civic or religious festivals, staged processions and plays. They pooled funds for the funeral expenses of members and their families, and insured the protection of members' widows and orphans. Above all, the personal associations made through the guilds yielded practical benefits and were emotionally sustaining.

Diversity and Conflict

Commercial expansion resulted in the diversification of economic activity and the increased likelihood of conflict. Workers skilled and unskilled, merchants small and great, entrepreneurs local and international, patrician managers and subordinate laborers were arrayed against each other by their social and political interests even as they labored together, increasing the wealth of their cities and of Europe.

While the guilds functioned to ensure conformity and standardization within each craft, the number of enterprises in the medieval towns and cities mushroomed. Florence's 14 "minor" guilds numbered twice as many as the "major" guilds and encompassed a broad range of occupations. By the late Middle Ages, Cologne had a population of about 30,000 and as many as 45 guilds. Those enrolled in the woolen cloth industry were most numerous, but the city also supported 122 master goldsmiths. In 1292 Paris had 130 regulated professions, including 22 each in textiles and metallurgy and 18 in foodstuffs and consumable materials such as firewood, and employed more than 5000 artisans. In 1322, the French city of Toulouse counted 177 butchers, while Milan, with a population of about 75,000, counted 300 bakeries. Little Carcassonne (in France), with a population of 9500 in 1304, boasted 63 notaries.

Working Women Most women worked in medieval Europe, even in the cities, dominated though they were by the jealous guild structure and male-oriented patriciates. They worked as "butchers, chandlers, ironmongers, net-makers, shoe-makers, glovers, girdlers, haberdashers, purse-makers, cap-makers, skinners, bookbinders, gilders, painters, silk-weavers and embroiderers, spiciers [dealers in spices], smiths and goldsmiths. …" They entered these trades as laborers, after an apprenticeship with a female instructor, usually arranged by a father or his surrogate. Or they gained entry as the wife, daughter, or widow of a master. In addition, women were often vendors of goods produced in family workshops, as shown on this page. Some women labored as prostitutes, a profession considered legal and necessary throughout most of Europe; many of them were organized in guilds, with an exclusively female membership. At the lowest level of the pay scale, women worked for a small daily wage as spinners of thread.

The most privileged female worker was the wife or widow or daughter of a guild master in the northern European cities. These women engaged in skilled and high-status work. They often supervised other workers as well—daughters, apprentices, journeymen—and so gained habits of authority. Although barred by law from buying and selling goods, or handling money without the approval of husband or guardian, women often circumvented such regulations. Because they generally worked in the home,

Going to market—*a woman selling fish:* *Like the husband-and-wife bankers shown on page 291, medieval merchants and artisans often produced or sold goods from workshops or shopfronts located in homes. This manuscript illumination from 1385 shows a woman selling fish from a shopfront.* (Österreichische Nationalbibliothek, Vienna)

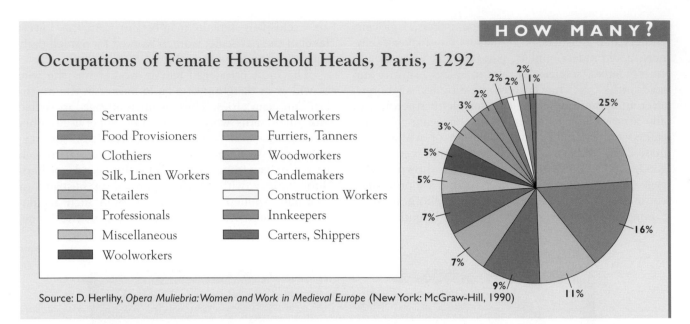

HOW MANY?

Occupations of Female Household Heads, Paris, 1292

- Servants
- Food Provisioners
- Clothiers
- Silk, Linen Workers
- Retailers
- Professionals
- Miscellaneous
- Woolworkers
- Metalworkers
- Furriers, Tanners
- Woodworkers
- Candlemakers
- Construction Workers
- Innkeepers
- Carters, Shippers

25%
16%
11%
9%
7%
7%
5%
5%
3%
3%
2%
2%
2%
2%
1%

Source: D. Herlihy, *Opera Muliebria: Women and Work in Medieval Europe* (New York: McGraw-Hill, 1990)

they could tend to a variety of other household needs as well as to the rearing of their children.

In some trades—especially in luxury garment trades such as gold-spinning and silk-weaving, the embroidery of bags and gloves and headdresses—the guild may have been dominated by women. In others, such as weaving or dyeing, women were enrolled in guilds because of their connection to male members. Most often, these women were widows, who maintained the family enterprise until the maturity of a male heir, or who married an ambitious journeyman until they took over the master's role.

Women workers generally accepted the marginal roles assigned to most of them in medieval cities. Male workers consigned to such positions, on the other hand, often seethed with resentment, and that resentment sometimes exploded into riot or rebellion. The level of conflict rose in the later Middle Ages as the wealthier merchants consolidated their positions and excluded lower-level artisans from important civic roles. In the later thirteenth century, unrest between merchants and artisans broke out in seven of the most important cities of northern Italy and in five of those in Flanders, as well as in Barcelona and smaller Spanish and French towns.

These revolts were not democratic revolutions. The rebellious laborers sought access to guild membership or privileges, not the recognition of principles of political equality or civil rights. Those who gained admittance to guilds, or who were permitted to form their own guilds, could well be ready to exclude others from the same privilege. Yet the language of rebellion was not forgotten, and the clamor of medieval workers for economic rights would echo in the revolutions of later centuries.

Workers' Revolts Toward the end of the fourteenth century, weavers in Cologne challenged patrician

dominance and won changes in the political constitution. Indeed, weavers' revolts were then commonplace in the textile-producing towns of Germany. The Parisian merchant Etienne Marcel, fired by the stress of war as well as by social and political resentments, led a revolt of fellow citizens against the government at about the same time as the peasant Jacquerie of 1358 (see Chapter 9).

Flanders and the Netherlands were densely studded with cloth-producing cities where a large labor force was harshly subordinated to a jealous patriciate. Not surprisingly, throughout the fourteenth century Flemish workers joined in major revolts. In 1302, workers turned on the French allies of their patrician masters in an event dubbed the "Matins of Bruges" (a "wake-up call," alluding to the *matins*, or early morning prayers, of medieval monks). It was followed up two months later with a stunning victory at Courtrai over an army of knights. In 1311 and 1319 in Ghent and in 1326 in Bruges, cloth weavers banded against their city governments. In 1381, workers from Ghent, Ypres, and Bruges defied the count of Flanders, only to be crushed the following year. The artisan leaders of these movements were heroes in the eyes of their contemporaries and forerunners of the champions of later revolutions.

The *Ciompi* In 1378, the wool workers of Florence rose up against guildmasters and governors in the most famous workers' revolt of the age.

The Florentine system of textile production was the most advanced in Europe. Merchants imported in quantity fine English wool and beautiful dyes, from which the highest-quality cloth could be made. They processed the raw wool in a series of steps that anticipate the mass production patterns of modern times. They controlled the whole process of production through a network of agents, owning and directing it

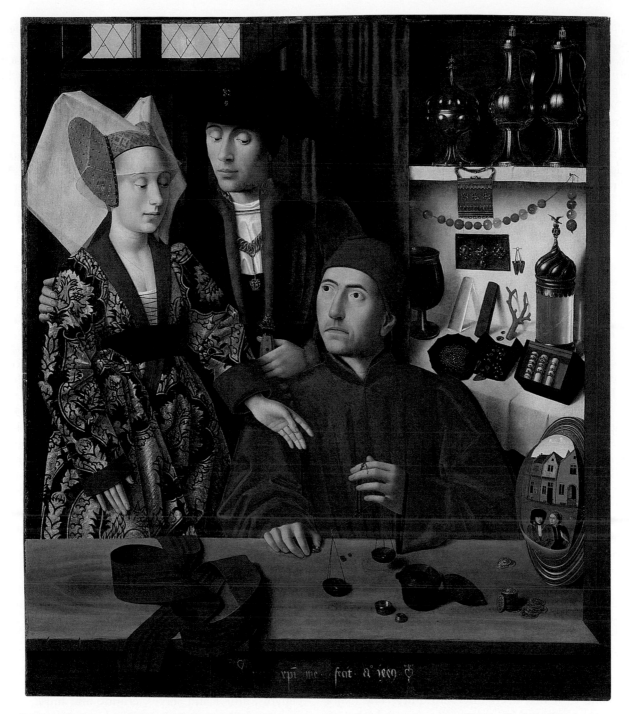

***Petrus Christus*, A Goldsmith in his Shop:** *This painting from 1449 shows a goldsmith (possibly Saint Eloi, the patron saint of goldsmiths) at work in his home workshop. Note the elegantly dressed couple come to examine the artisan's elegantly crafted and highly expensive goods—and the mirror that reflects the life of the town outside.* (The Metropolitan Museum of Art, Robert Lehman Collection, 1975, 1.110)

themselves. The wool was washed in the Arno River, transferred to the countryside for spinning, brought back to an army of urban pieceworkers for weaving, sent out to workshops for dyeing and to the fulling mills for further processing, and finally sent to the central factory for packaging prior to export. The process involved many transfers of goods and a hierarchy of personnel, from the supervisors and skilled workers down to the ordinary laborers, called the *ciompi* ("people of God").

In Florentine society, where wealth was power, the *ciompi* ranked lower even than the members of smaller guilds. In 1378, encouraged by a faction of dissident patricians, but led by one of their own, the wool-comber Michele de Lando, the *ciompi* seized the Florentine government and made Lando chief executive, or *gonfaloniere* (literally, the "standard-bearer"). The *ciompi*'s demand was reasonable—they wished to be admitted to the guild structure, which provided access to government. In response, the guild structure expanded to add three new guilds of wool workers to the twenty-one existing guilds. By this modification, the common workers of Florence became eligible for political office. Having achieved this end, Lando resigned from office.

Within a few weeks, the rebellion was suppressed. Some constitutional changes remained in place until 1382, when disgruntled conservatives from the "minor" guilds joined the elites in restoring the old guild structure, and the control of a narrow oligarchy of "major" guildsmen was asserted. The aspirations of the common workers were defeated. Of the *ciompi* leaders, 161 were executed. Lando himself died in peace and obscurity.

The social unrest of the late Middle Ages left workers where they were before—with those who produced the goods having little share of the wealth and power they had helped to create.

THE WORLD OF COMMERCE

As cities grew and production expanded, European commerce reached the ports of the eastern Mediterranean and the remote depots of Asia and Africa, as Map 11.2 shows. This expansion of trade, which some historians call a "commercial revolution," was a major step toward European economic primacy in the Old World.

By the end of the Middle Ages, Italian merchant venturers had achieved that primacy. And although the Italians would soon lose control of the Mediterranean, European supremacy in trade was maintained by their Spanish, Dutch, English, and French successors, who shifted the economic activity westward to the Atlantic Ocean. The tools and methods they would employ were those developed by Italians in the Middle Ages.

Italy and the Old World Commercial System

In 1000, the Eurasian trade network was essentially the same as it had been since antiquity. The major ports of the eastern Mediterranean were world depots, exchanging goods from Middle Eastern civilizations, Africa, Europe, and south and east Asia. This network had been dominated in turn by the Phoenicians, the Greeks, the Carthaginians, and the Romans, who established their supremacy in the Mediterranean in the first millennium B.C.E. As Rome's economic supremacy declined, Constantinople—the capital of the Eastern, or Byzantine, Empire—took charge. The Arab caliphates soon challenged Constantinople, their ships dominating the Mediterranean from about 700 to about 1000.

Thereafter European, and especially Italian, convoys swept Arab fleets aside and took command of what had once been the Roman sea (see Chapter 5).

Italian merchants established residential colonies at key points on the Mediterranean. Nor did their supremacy end at the Mediterranean shore but reached out across the belly of Eurasia, pressing forward by land as well as by sea in the tireless quest for profit.

Byzantium and the Arabs In the seventh and eighth centuries Arab conquests in the Middle East, North Africa, and Spain posed a threat to Byzantium. After that, the Mediterranean was dotted with Arab vessels warily avoiding and sometimes confronting the Byzantine fleets, which held their own in the Aegean region and the approaches to the Black Sea. In the ninth and tenth centuries, as Viking raiders terrified northern Europe, Arab forces further extended their realm. They not only seized Crete and Sicily, but grabbed footholds in southern Italy, and attacked Marseilles and the Christian Spanish city of Barcelona.

Constantinople was a major Mediterranean port as well as an imperial capital. Byzantine ships sailed regularly to the Black Sea and Asia Minor and toured the Aegean islands, southern Italy, and the Adriatic shores. The city exported wine and oil and the lustrous silk fabrics made in government-run workshops from raw silk acquired from Asia. It imported ordinary wheat to feed its population as well as spices, papyrus, and exotic luxury items. Facilitating this commerce were the splendid gold coins that marked Byzantine authority and prestige on the Mediterranean Sea— the bezants, successor to the Roman solidus.

Paradoxically, the Arab irruption into Mediterranean trade produced a net gain for Europe, because it brought Europeans into contact, gradually, with the outside world. Islamic explorers, merchants, and sailors knit the Middle East to Africa (including regions south of the Sahara, previously unexplored by advanced Mediterranean cultures), to Russia (from which Islamic silver currency and goods made their way to the North Sea), and to India and East Asia. One observer listed, among the products arriving from distant suppliers, ostriches and panthers, gems and papyrus, armor and slaves, ermine and musk, combs and pomegranates, cuirasses and jasmine ointment, pistachios and pearls—commodities for consumers who lacked nothing. The words *bazaar* and *arsenal*, *admiral* and *risk*, all Arabic in origin, suggest the significant impact of Islamic control of international commerce at this time.

In 762, Abbasid caliphs transferred their capital from Damascus to Baghdad. Located on the Tigris River the new capital thus had access to the Persian Gulf, which led to the Indian Ocean. From here Islamic traders swept across the Indian Ocean and beyond to the ports of India, Sri Lanka, Malaysia, Vietnam, and China. One of their ships is illustrated on p. 303. According to a tenth-century chronicler, the caliph announced, on the founding of Baghdad,

"Here is no distance between us and China. Everything on the sea can come to us."

Some things came from China overland by the old Silk Road, its stretch across the Middle Eastern plateau kept clear of raiders by the Abbasids as it had been earlier by the Sassanids and Parthians (see Chapter 8). The road reached west to the Mediterranean shore, where merchants transshipped the raw fiber and luxury fabrics to other ports.

Meanwhile, Islamic merchants extended their African ventures. From the Middle East, ships sailed the Persian Gulf to the eastern shore of Africa to take on cargoes of ivory, feathers, exotic woods, and slaves. From North Africa, merchants traveled overland into the sub-Saharan interior. They were lured by unimaginably rich deposits of gold mined in the western Sudan and managed by the kings of Ghana, Mali, and Songhai (see Chapter 8). The gold-starved Byzantine merchants, whose bezants flowed at a dangerous rate to eastern depots, snapped up this precious commodity, paying a heavy toll to the Arab traders who hauled it from the remote African interior.

The Varangians Both Constantinople and Islam profited from trade with the Varangians, centered at Kiev (modern Ukraine). In the ninth century, these descendants of Viking invaders had established themselves in fortified communities called *gorods* along the Dvina and Dnieper river valleys. The most famous of these—Novgorod—flourished for centuries as the easternmost port of call of Hanseatic ships. Even in the early Middle Ages, the Varangian settlements connected the bleak desert of northern Europe to the flourishing civilizations of western Asia.

From their *gorods*, Varangian overlords collected tribute from the Slavic peoples who had settled in

---

Faraway Places

In the medieval world, merchants traveled far to obtain the valuable luxury goods desired by the wealthy and powerful at home. In the first passage, King Richard of England, while on crusade in the Holy Land, captures a whole caravan of merchant goods. In the second, a Florentine merchant describes the journey to China for his fellow merchants. In the third, the Venetian merchant Marco Polo describes the prosperity of Beijing, where he spent many years serving the Chinese emperor.

Forces led by King Richard of England capture a merchant caravan in the Holy Land, 1192: By this defeat the pride of the Turks was entirely cast down, and their boldness effectually repressed; whilst the caravan, with all its riches, became the spoil of the victors. Its guards surrendered to our soldiers ... and stretching forth their hands in supplication, they implored for mercy, on condition only that their lives should be spared. They led the yoked horses and camels by the halter, and offered them to our men, and they brought mules loaded with spices of different kinds, and of great value; gold and silver; cloaks of silk; purple and scarlet robes, ... besides arms and weapons of divers forms; coats of mail, ... costly cushions, pavilions, tents, biscuit, bread, barley, grain, meal, and a large quantity of conserves and medicines; basins, bladders, chess-boards; silver dishes and candlesticks; pepper, cinnamon, sugar, and wax; ... an immense sum of money, and an incalculable quantity of goods, such as had never before ... been taken at one and the same time, in any former battle.
("Geoffrey de Vinsauf's Itinerary of Richard I and Others, to the Holy Land"; trs., ed. H. G. Bohn, *Chronicles of the Crusades*, 1848)

Francesco Pegolotti advises merchants traveling to Cathay [China] (Florence, 1310/1340): The road leading from Tana to Cathay is quite safe both by day and by night, according to what the merchants report who have used it—except that if the merchant should die along the road, ... everything would go to the lord of the country where the merchant dies. ... It is reckoned that from Tana to Sarai the road is less safe than all the rest of the journey. But should there be sixty men [in the caravan], [even] when the road is in its worst condition you would travel as safely as [if you were] in your own home.
(From R. S. Lopez, I. W. Raymond, trs., *Medieval Trade in the Mediterranean World*, 1955)

***The Book of Ser Marco Polo the Venetian* (1298) concerning the kingdoms and marvels of the east—the city of Cambaluc (Beijing):** You must know that the city of Cambaluc has such a multitude of houses, and such a vast population inside the walls and outside, that it seems quite past all possibility. There is a suburb outside each of the gates, which are twelve in number; and these suburbs are so great that they contain more people than the city itself. ... In those suburbs lodge the foreign merchants and travellers ... who have come to bring presents to the Emperor, or to sell articles at Court, or because the city affords so good mart to attract traders. ... To this city are brought articles of greater cost and rarity, and in greater abundance of all kinds, than to any other city in the world. For people of every description, and from every region, bring things (including all the costly wares of India, as well as the fine and precious goods of Cathay [China] itself with its provinces). ... As a sample, I tell you, no day in the year passes that there do not enter the city 1000 cart-loads of silk alone. ...
(Marco Polo, *The Book of Ser Marco Polo the Venetian*, 1298; trs. H. Yule, ed. G. B. Parks, 1929, modernized)

the region during the late Roman period. Having no productive agriculture of their own, the Varangians seized the produce of the Slavs, as well as furs and skins, honey and amber. They also took human beings as tribute from the Slavs. (In most European languages, the word for "slave" is derived from "Slav.") The slave trade was central to the development of Russian commerce. Loaded with such goods, Varangian river rafts floated downriver to the Black Sea and on to Constantinople, or eastward via the Volga to the Caspian Sea and the Islamic center at Baghdad. Until the mid-eleventh century, these traders were pagan, so no Christian proscriptions barred either the slave trade or commerce with Muslims. By the tenth century, the profits of this trade had enriched Kiev, the center of Russian civilization until the Mongol onslaught in the thirteenth century (see Chapter 9). Hoards of Greek and Arab coins were stored in Russia and Scandinavia.

From the seventh through the tenth centuries, western Europeans contributed little to the international commercial system that thrived on the Mediterranean and stretched to Africa and Asia. But Arab, Jewish, and Syrian merchants visited the Mediterranean ports of Spain, France, and Italy, and some penetrated to the fairs of the interior. Here they acquired the few, cheap, bulky goods the West had to offer—salt and fish, raw wool and some finished linen, timber, tin, and iron. European elites in turn bought luxuries from the east, in the small quantities that they could afford with their few silver coins and their ever-diminishing treasure of gold. These luxuries included spices, perfumes, medicinal herbs, silk, and other luxury fabrics.

The Italians By the eleventh century, Italian fleets had begun to claim their piece of Mediterranean commerce. Venetian ships hugged the Adriatic shores en route to and from Constantinople, while Pisan and Genoese raids announced the intent of their merchants to gain footholds in both North Africa and the Middle East. After the Crusades began in 1095, Italian ships carried armies and supplies to the eastern Mediterranean and planted colonies of their nationals in the region. The Italian presence became so great that a considerable fraction of the population of Constantinople consisted of resident Italian merchants.

Although the Crusaders failed to hold Jerusalem, by the thirteenth century the Mediterranean was dominated, as in Roman days, by people speaking Romance languages. Genoese merchants emerged as the major presence in the northern Aegean, carrying cargoes of alum from Asia Minor to supply the cloth workshops of Florence and other textile-producing centers. The Venetians controlled trade with Egypt and Syria, having secured bases in the Aegean, especially Crete. Spices were their chief cargo, especially pepper, prized and expensive, the importation of which remained in Venetian hands into the sixteenth century. These two Italian giants became fierce rivals in the thirteenth and fourteenth centuries, as they competed for control of markets in the Black Sea and access to Russia, and were often at war. A final war in 1379–1380 resulted in a hard-won victory for Venice.

The Italian grip on Mediterranean commerce was tight, but their merchants generally halted at the eastern Mediterranean. There, Asian products, brought by Arab or Jewish intermediaries, were purchased for shipment to the west. In 1271, Marco Polo (c. 1254–1324) accompanied his father and uncle, both Venetian merchants, on a trip to Asia, including China, which the older men had visited a few years earlier (becoming among the first Europeans to do so). There Marco lived for seventeen years (1275–1292), working for the emperor Kublai Khan, which he describes in *Witnesses* on p. 315. Those eventful years included a three-year stint as governor of Yangchow, a city with a population of more than one million. Of this city, Marco later wrote: "It surpasses in grandeur, wealth and beauty, every other city in the world." In a Genoese prison, after his return to Italy in 1295, Polo dictated his memoirs. His experience marked Europe's first reliably documented encounter with cultures beyond the Mediterranean and pointed the way to future such ventures.

But Italian hegemony in the Mediterranean was to face a new challenge in the fifteenth century, when Constantinople fell to the Ottoman Turks. By 1300 the Ottoman Turks, a new power in Asia Minor, named after their dynasty of rulers, were advancing aggressively toward Constantinople. In 1350, they seized Nicaea, the last Byzantine foothold in Asia Minor. Soon they arrived on the Balkan peninsula, overwhelming the Serbs at Kosovo in 1389. In the following century, they absorbed the whole of the Balkans and the islands of the Aegean, then reached to Syria and Egypt to the south, and toward Vienna to the north. In 1453, they captured Constantinople, the fortress city once believed to be impregnable. Rome had truly died with the seizing of its last eastern outpost. An Islamic nation had established itself in southeastern Europe. Italian supremacy in the Mediterranean was doomed.

Venice proceeded cheerfully to do business with the "heathen" Turks despite papal condemnation. Yet Ottoman fleets continued to expand in the Aegean, the Adriatic, and the Mediterranean, gobbling up Italian islands and depots. Control of the pepper trade slipped to the Portuguese, who had begun to probe the Atlantic shores of Africa and opened up an oceanic trade link to Asia. Soon those nation states of Europe with windows on the Atlantic would snatch commercial leadership from the Italians and build an even greater engine for generating profits.

The Tools of Trade

Although they would come to surpass their Italian predecessors, the merchants of northern Europe were greatly indebted to these pioneering traders who had developed both the tools and methods of commercial success.

Ships Over some three centuries, the Italians became master shipbuilders and sailors. Their ships—no bigger than the 130-foot (40-m.)-long grain transports of ancient Rome—had a rudder (a northern European invention of about 1200), which afforded precision in steering; articulated sails, which permitted the exploitation of winds from any direction; and improved charts, which guided adventurous sailors through unfamiliar territory.

Two types of vessel emerged: the swift longship, or galley and the heavier, capacious round ship. The galley was powered by oars (manned by ordinary laborers or condemned criminals) and supplementary sails and could race through seas ridden with pirates or enemy fleets. But much of its interior was occupied by the crew and the rowing decks, so little space remained for cargo. These fast, safe ships were operated only by the larger and wealthier cities, and they carried mainly luxury goods. The round ship was cheaper, slower, and spacious. It carried a smaller crew, including, for security, a few crossbowmen. Its vast hold could accommodate such bulky goods as wheat and alum, metals and wool, salt and timber. The humble round merchantman, relying entirely on sail power, was true ancestor of the ships that later carried Europeans to the Americas.

Map 11.2 Trade Networks, to 1500: *Money and goods circulated through the Old World, transported by Chinese, Arab, Byzantine, and western European ships. By the close of the Middle Ages, the latter had achieved dominance, Venetians foremost among them.* **What particular advantages did Venice have in the competition for world trade?**

Venice developed the greatest fleets of the late Middle Ages, edging out the Genoese and the late-comer Florentines (who acquired Pisa and Livorno, on the coast, in the early 1400s). Her Arsenal could complete four or five galleys every two years, supplying her merchant complements of seven to ten galleys for the routes to Syria, Egypt, and Flanders. Her "great galley," introduced in 1290, was immense: 120 to 150 feet (37–46 meters) long, it carried a crew of up to 200, its oarsmen arrayed on 25 to 30 benches each side in banks of two or three. The mightiest ships of the west, these were used in long voyages until the mid-sixteenth century, when sails displaced oars.

Law and Bookkeeping Together with merchants, goods, and ships, other important components of the economic expansion were notaries and lawyers, who created the culture that supported the mechanisms of trade. Building on the expertise of canon (that is, church) lawyers, civil lawyers explored the Roman legal tradition for precepts applicable to commerce, while notaries drew up the documents that met the standards so developed. Merchants, too, learned to read and sign contracts and to keep records of inventories and transactions. In the commercial centers of Europe, but especially in Italy, a new secular and commercial culture began to flourish.

Merchants faced a variety of problems, three of which were solved by the creation of new contractual forms. First, they needed to be able to transfer funds without actually exchanging large quantities of currency. Second, they needed to raise capital for merchant ventures. Third, they needed to charge interest—though the practice was forbidden by the church—on such capital loans.

The bill of exchange solved the first problem. This performed the function of the modern check or its equivalent. A merchant in one city instructed his agents in another to release a specified sum in the currency of that locality to another merchant. The

---

WITNESSES

How and How Not to Succeed in Business

As important for business as buying and selling itself are certain intellectual or cultural traits acquired by merchants, which allow them to make prudent judgments. The first of these passages consists of a merchant's advice to other merchants about careful record-keeping. The second sternly condemns a fellow merchant for attempting too much, and ending up in bankruptcy.

Benedetto Cotrugli's advice on business methods (Naples, 1458): The pen is an instrument so noble and excellent that it is absolutely necessary ... to merchants. ... And when you see a merchant to whom the pen is a burden ..., you may say that he is not a merchant. And [a good merchant] not only must be skilled in writing but also must keep his records ... methodically. ... Mercantile records are the means to remember all that a man does, and from whom he must have, and to whom he must give, and the costs of wares, and the profits, and the losses, and every other transaction on which the merchant is at all dependent. ...

Therefore the merchant ought to keep three books, that is, the ledger ..., the journal ..., and the memorandum. ... And the ledger ought to have its alphabetical [index] through which one may quickly find any account written in the said ledger. ...

In the journal you shall reconstruct methodically all [your] capital, item by item, and you shall carry it forward in the ledger. ... And when you have finished writing the said ledger, you shall settle all accounts opened in it, extract from them all balances ... to the debit or likewise to the credit. ...

In the memorandum you ought to note every evening or morning before you leave your home every-thing you have traded and transacted on that day because of your commerce. ... And you should further note that you ought to keep always with you a small notebook ... in which you shall note day by day and hour by hour even the minute [detail] of your transactions, so that later you may at your best convenience create accounts in the memorandum book or the journal ... then carry them forward into the ledger daily. ...

And therefore I warn and encourage any merchant to take pleasure in knowing how to keep his books well and methodically. ... Otherwise your commerce will be chaos, a confusion of Babel—of which you must beware if you cherish your honor and your substance.
(Benedetto Cotrugli, *On Commerce and the Perfect Merchant*, 1458; eds. R. Lopez, I. Raymond, 1955)

Chronicler Francesco da Molin describes the bankruptcy of a wealthy Pisan merchant (1584): He had built up much credit by his many business transactions, but in truth it was based on his reputation alone and not upon his capital, for this market and the city of Venice are naturally very much inclined to love and trust in appearances. Hence, heaping business upon business, his reach exceeding his grasp, he suffered the fate of almost all those who want to be bigger than other men. With his fall came the fall of the bank, because its creditors ... all wanted to be satisfied at the same time. The bank kept going for a few days, ... but in the end the crowd of creditors increased and the bank collapsed and failed, to the detriment of numberless people and great damage to this market.
(Francesco da Molin, *Compendio ... delle cose che reputero degni di venerne particolar memoria*, 1584; eds. D. Chambers, B. Pullan, 1992)

second merchant, rather than collecting the funds, could acquire credit with the agent for the purchase of goods which he could then exchange elsewhere. The bill of exchange also served to provide short-term credit, and permitted merchants to exploit differences in currency values between markets.

With such documents in circulation, little currency changed hands. Instead, merchants kept records of transactions in "money of account," a theoretical currency. Medieval commerce conceived of value abstractly and exchanged instruments of credit as comfortably as in the modern world.

To raise capital for commercial ventures, merchants developed a variety of partnership arrangements. In a true partnership, the parties pooled their capital, shared risks, and divided profit in proportion to their contributions. In other varieties of partnership, such as the one cited in *Witnesses* on p. 307, a passive party contributed all or part of the capital and received a stipulated share of the profit, but did not travel with the merchandise. He was in fact an investor, rather than a merchant.

To circumvent the prohibition against charging interest, merchants levied extra charges by building interest charges invisibly into the bill of exchange; payment to the distant merchant would correspond to the value of the merchandise in foreign currency plus an additional percentage. They also concealed interest in loan contracts. The investor was repaid not merely the amount advanced, but an additional amount ostensibly in compensation for risk or for services. Such mechanisms had precedents in Byzantine, Islamic, Roman, Greek, and Babylonian practices. But by 1300, Italian merchants, lawyers, and bankers had made these practices much more sophisticated.

By the early fourteenth century, the merchants who watched revenues flow in and expenditures spill out had elaborated from Arab models a new method of keeping track of them—double-entry bookkeeping. Still in use today (its principles still underlie computerized systems), this method of accounting revolutionized commercial practice. Linked credit and debit entries were posted in a journal in columns aligned

> ### MUST READS
> ## Books to Remember
>
> | | |
> |---|---|
> | **Luca Pacioli** | *Summa de arithmetica* (*Compendium of Arithmetic*) (1494) |
> | **Francesco Pegolotti** | *Pratica della mercatura* (*Practical Business Methods*) |
> | **Marco Polo** | *Milione* ("Million," memoirs of his journey to China) (c. 1298) |

side by side, with cross references to other ledgers or customers' accounts, as required, and with an alphabetical index at the end. These detailed ledgers enabled merchants to gain their virtual monopoly of western Europe's foreign trade.

Fifteenth-century handbooks taught merchants commercial practices. The *Compendium of Arithmetic* (1494) by Luca Pacioli, a friar and mathematician, contained a section on accountancy. Francesco Pegolotti's *Practical Business Methods* advised on currencies and measures and how to get by abroad. The importance of good penmanship was emphasized by Benedetto Cotrugli in *On Commerce and the Perfect Merchant* (1458). "The pen is an instrument so noble and excellent that it is absolutely necessary … to merchants … And when you see a merchant to whom the pen is a burden or who is inept with the pen, you may say that he is not a merchant (see *Witnesses*, p. 318)."

These handbooks taught merchants how to succeed in business with diligence and precision. With these attitudes, commercial instruments and fine sailing ships and skilled navigators, merchants introduced Europe to the world and its wealth, the taste of which awakened ardent appetites. Europe would now be integrated into a world economy, which it would one day dominate in the name of God, and of profit.

Conclusion
MERCHANTS, MONEY, AND THE MEANING OF THE WEST

Kings and emperors, priests and scribes, peasants, prophets, and poets made the ancient world. Those who prayed, those who fought, and those who plowed created the civilization of early medieval Europe. But among the later developers of that civilization were also European merchants, who teased a profit from the sale of goods, who opened the dikes and floodgates of an agrarian economy to the rush of cash, who built cities that were monuments to entrepreneurial ingenuity and greed. They accumulated the wealth, and—just as important—they developed the techniques and mental habits that enabled the West to breach the borders of Europe and explore the world. The quest for profit was the dynamo that powered the expansion of Western civilization after 1500.

QUESTIONS TO CONSIDER

1. Why did some moneylenders, bankers, and merchants begin to defy the church's rule against usury from about the twelfth century? Why did it take several centuries before they did so?

2. What was, from the very start, different about living in a city? What attracted people to live and work there?

3. Why were the northern Italian cities able to league together and win partial autonomy from both Pope and Emperor? What made Italy unique?

4. Why was the textile industry central to the medieval economy?

5. Who benefited and who lost with the appearance of merchant and craft guilds?

SUGGESTED RESOURCES

Abu-Lughod, Janet L., *Before European Hegemony: The World System, A.D. 1250–1350* (Oxford: Oxford University Press, 1989). A view of the medieval world as an interdependent, decentralized world system made possible by the decline of a previous world system.

Clarke, Helen & Björn Ambrosiani, *Towns in the Viking Age* (New York: St. Martin's, 1991). Uses archeological evidence to reconstruct the history of commercial towns from Ireland to Novgorod from late Roman times to the eleventh century.

Crosby, Alfred W., *The Measure of Reality: Quantification and Western Society, 1250–1600* (Cambridge: Cambridge University Press, 1997). The European habit of quantification is identified as the precondition for Europe's later expansion and world dominance.

Dyer, Christopher, *Making a Living in the Middle Ages: the People of Britain 850–1520* (New Haven: Yale University Press, 2002). Shows ordinary people making rational economic choices as they responded to natural and political pressures and changes in social life.

Epstein, Steven A., *Wage Labor and Guilds in Medieval Europe* (Chapel Hill: University of North Carolina Press, 1991). Original study of the apprenticeship system that developed within the framework of medieval guilds and prepared the way for modern wage labor.

Herlihy, David, *Opera muliebria: Women and Work in Medieval Europe* (Philadelphia: Temple University Press, 1990). A thoughtful reconstruction of the kinds of women's work in medieval society.

Hohenberg, Paul M. and Lynn Hollen Lees, *The Making of Urban Europe, 1000–1994*, 2nd ed. (Cambridge: Harvard University Press, 1995). Unique history of the whole span of European urbanization from the first significant commercial settlements to recent times.

Howell, Martha C., *Women, Production, and Patriarchy in Late Medieval Cities* (Chicago: University of Chicago Press, 1986). An examination of women workers in Leiden and Cologne.

Jones, Philip, *The Italian City-State: From Commune to Signoria* (Oxford: Clarendon Press of Oxford University Press, 1997). An authoritative and up-to-date synthesis.

Kaye, Joel, *Economy and Nature in the Fourteenth Century: Money, Market Exchange, and the Emergence of Scientific Thought* (Cambridge: Cambridge University Press, 1998). Argues that the resurgence of the monetary economy in medieval Europe encouraged the development of scientific thinking.

Larner, John, *Marco Polo and the Discovery of the World* (New Haven: Yale University Press, 2000). Discusses the pivotal role of Polo's book for later geographical thought and exploration.

Mueller, Reinhold, *The Venetian Money Market: Banks, Panics and the Public Debt, 1200–1500* (Baltimore: Johns Hopkins University Press, 1997). The second and final volume of a comprehensive study of the financial system of Venice, examining the trajectory from moneychanging to banking, bank failures, and bank underwriting of government functions through public loans.

Nicholas, David, *The Growth of the Medieval City: from Late Antiquity to the Early Fourteenth Century* (Addison Wesley Longman, 1997). A recent synthesis by an expert in the highly urbanized region of Flanders.

Swanson, Heather, *Medieval Artisans: An Urban Class in Late Medieval England* (Oxford: Basil Blackwell, 1989). Examines craft production, the place of artisans in municipal government, relations between artisans and the merchant class, and political subordination.

Medieval English towns, town histories, study of office-holding, links (ORB):
http://orb.rhodes.edu/encyclop/culture/towns/towns.html

Francesco Datini, merchant of Florence, brief biography and images (Istituto Datini):
http://www.istitutodatini.it/schede/datini/eng/fdatini.htm

⚙ Western Civilization Documents CD-ROM

8.2 "The Sports of the City"
8.3 College Life: Between Students and their Fathers
8.5 Guilds: Regulating the Craft
8.6 "For the Honor of the Guild"
8.7 The Ideal Wife of a Merchant

PART FOUR

THE WEST EXPANDS

The Self, the State, the World (1200–1750)

From 1200–1750, Europe's unique urban civilization fostered wealth and innovation. The precocious cities of northern Italy, in particular, nurtured the artists and intellectuals who created the brilliant cultural movement of the "Renaissance." Drawing on the literary and artistic legacy of the ancient world, they laid the foundations for the modern development of European thought and expression, an enterprise aided by the new technology of the printing press.

As the Renaissance reached its zenith, criticism of clerical corruption, ecclesiastical finances, and the sacramental system of the Roman Catholic Church exploded into the rival movement of the Protestant Reformation. Diversified into a spectrum of beliefs and institutions, Protestantism spread rapidly, sometimes supported, and sometimes suppressed by powerful emerging states. In response to Protestant advance, the Catholic Church reaffirmed its authority, rededicating itself to its mission at home and abroad.

As the coherence of medieval civilization yielded to these disruptive cultural currents, the European monarchies claimed a new sovereignty over that of the modern nation state. Their rulers possessed, or hoped to possess, absolute power. To assert that claim, they fielded huge armies, equipped with guns and cannon, ordered in squares, rows, or columns, and drilled to fire on command. Some theorists defended the monarch's divine right to rule, a right proclaimed in ritual and images; others proposed the countervailing notion of the rights of citizens.

European civilization was content no longer, after 1500, to remain within its borders. Venturing across the unknown Atlantic, explorers, conquerors, entrepreneurs, and Old World refugees opened two new continents to European settlement. Others traded in Asia and Africa amid civilizations that, for now, thought little of these western visitors who would soon deem themselves lords of the world.

12 City Life
Public and Private Life in the Late Medieval Cities, 1200–1500

13 Rebirth in Italy
The Civilization of the Italian Renaissance, 1300–1550

14 Of One Church, Many
Protestant Reformation and Catholic Reform, 1500–1650

15 Absolute Power
War and Politics in Early Modern Europe, 1500–1750

16 Europe Reaches Out
Global Voyages and Cultural Encounters, 1500–1750

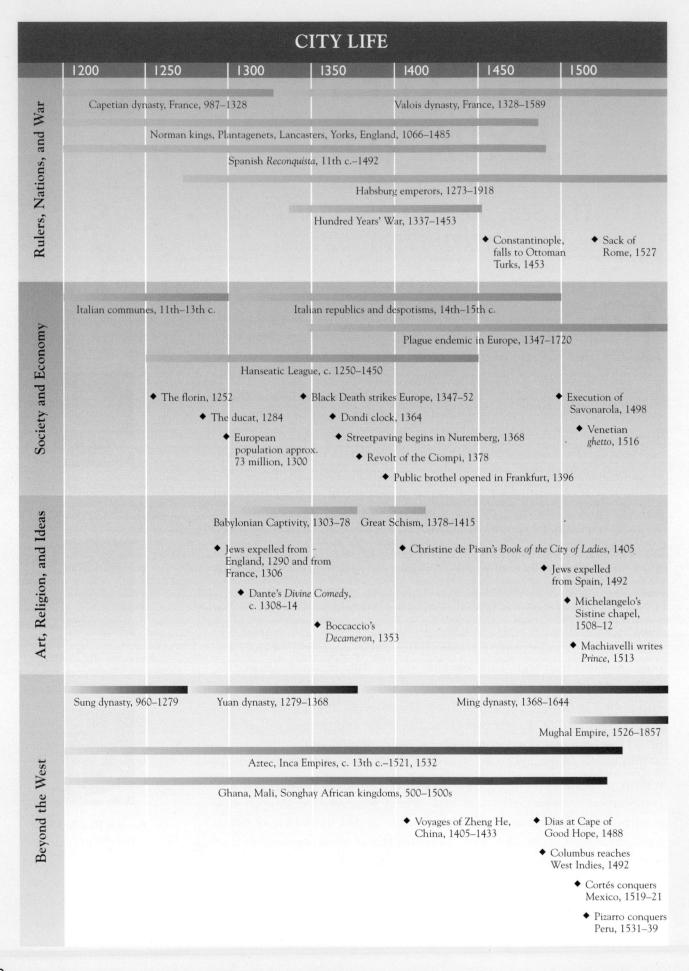

CITY LIFE

	1200	1250	1300	1350	1400	1450	1500

Rulers, Nations, and War

Capetian dynasty, France, 987–1328

Valois dynasty, France, 1328–1589

Norman kings, Plantagenets, Lancasters, Yorks, England, 1066–1485

Spanish *Reconquista*, 11th c.–1492

Habsburg emperors, 1273–1918

Hundred Years' War, 1337–1453

◆ Constantinople, falls to Ottoman Turks, 1453

◆ Sack of Rome, 1527

Society and Economy

Italian communes, 11th–13th c.

Italian republics and despotisms, 14th–15th c.

Plague endemic in Europe, 1347–1720

Hanseatic League, c. 1250–1450

◆ The florin, 1252

◆ Black Death strikes Europe, 1347–52

◆ Execution of Savonarola, 1498

◆ The ducat, 1284

◆ Dondi clock, 1364

◆ European population approx. 73 million, 1300

◆ Streetpaving begins in Nuremberg, 1368

◆ Venetian *ghetto*, 1516

◆ Revolt of the Ciompi, 1378

◆ Public brothel opened in Frankfurt, 1396

Art, Religion, and Ideas

Babylonian Captivity, 1303–78   Great Schism, 1378–1415

◆ Jews expelled from England, 1290 and from France, 1306

◆ Christine de Pisan's *Book of the City of Ladies*, 1405

◆ Jews expelled from Spain, 1492

◆ Dante's *Divine Comedy*, c. 1308–14

◆ Michelangelo's Sistine chapel, 1508–12

◆ Boccaccio's *Decameron*, 1353

◆ Machiavelli writes *Prince*, 1513

Beyond the West

Sung dynasty, 960–1279

Yuan dynasty, 1279–1368

Ming dynasty, 1368–1644

Mughal Empire, 1526–1857

Aztec, Inca Empires, c. 13th c.–1521, 1532

Ghana, Mali, Songhay African kingdoms, 500–1500s

◆ Voyages of Zheng He, China, 1405–1433

◆ Dias at Cape of Good Hope, 1488

◆ Columbus reaches West Indies, 1492

◆ Cortés conquers Mexico, 1519–21

◆ Pizarro conquers Peru, 1531–39

CHAPTER 12

CITY LIFE

Public and Private Life in the Late Medieval Cities

1200–1500

[Map of Europe showing cities: Hamburg, Antwerp, London, Bruges, Paris, Strasbourg, Nuremberg, Augsburg, Lyons, Milan, Genoa, Florence, Venice, Rome, with seas and geographic features labeled including NORTH SEA, BALTIC SEA, ATLANTIC OCEAN, ENGLISH CHANNEL, EUROPE, ASIA, BLACK SEA, CASPIAN SEA, MEDITERRANEAN SEA, AFRICA, TYRRHENIAN SEA, ADRIATIC SEA, AEGEAN SEA, Ural Mts, Carpathian Mts, Balkan Mts, Caucasus, Pyrenees, Alps, Apennines, and rivers Thames, Seine, Loire, Rhine, Elbe, Oder, Vistula, Dvina, Dniester, Dnieper, Don, Volga, Danube, Po, Rhone, Ebro, Tagus, Irmak. Islands: CORSICA, SARDINIA, SICILY, CRETE, CYPRUS, BALEARIC IS.]

KEY QUESTIONS

◆ **The Urban Landscape:** What were the key structures and spaces of the medieval urban landscape?

◆ **Public Life:** What kind of public events and rituals involved the diverse groups of urban dwellers?

◆ **Private Life:** How did medieval citizens arrange their households and raise their families? How did women's experiences differ from men's?

◆ **The City and the Book:** Outside of the universities, the cities were the main setting for the reading and writing of books; who were the medieval authors who lived in or wrote about cities? How did their works reflect the urban environment?

Urbanity As soon as towns began to spring up in medieval Europe, the "city slicker" began to mock the "country bumpkin." The poet and scholar Brunetto Latini (c. 1220–1294), an advocate of urban life, commended the town-dweller who rides "in a stately manner," and urged newer arrivals to emulate his poise:

> . . . . . . *Guard against moving*
> *Like a man from the country;*
> *Don't squirm like an eel, go self-assuredly*
> *Through the streets and people.*

Town-dwellers developed customs, speech, and perceptions, superior (as they saw it) to those of peasant villagers. To be of the city was to be "urbane"—well-mannered, polished, and sophisticated.

The citizens' prejudice had some basis in fact. Although the culture of western Europe first took form in monastery, castle, and village, its later development was conditioned by life in the city. Amid the packed **urban** landscape and busy public life, townspeople inhabited a very different world from that of the peasants, monks, and mounted warriors outside the walls.

The previous chapter traced the development of towns in their commercial aspects. But what was life like within these towns? Visually, the town presented a marked contrast to the fields and villages that surrounded it. As the illustrations opposite show, the urban landscape was marked by gates, towers, and steeples, twisting roads and welcoming open spaces, public and private buildings, and the crowded districts of the poor. Here, city people carried on their public life of celebration, service, and suffering, and their private lives of marrying and child-rearing. The mental world of the city, so different from the court or university, would also powerfully shape Western civilization.

THE URBAN LANDSCAPE

Like most medieval towns, the German city of Nuremberg in the fifteenth century was encircled by a wall, shown on p. 325. Entry to the town was through one of four huge gates—as few as two in smaller towns, or as many as eight in larger ones. Heavy chains and iron clamps secured these gates at night or in time of danger. If these could not deter an intruder, there was an extra barrier: the portcullis. "Vertical bars and drop gates fitted with needle-sharp bronze spikes can be thrust down upon invaders," reports the scholar and poet Conrad Celtis (1459–1508) "and, throwing them to the ground, pierce their bodies through." Its portcullis shut, the town was an island,

secure from the assaults, the business, and the ways of the outside. All who came to the city passed through the ferocious barrier of the city gate.

That gate and the wall it sealed marked the boundary between city and country—never absolute, for goods and people flowed regularly across that limit, yet still distinct. Outside the walls lay the country landscape, a gentle undulation of cultivated fields, striped by the plow. Within was a boisterous chorus: crowded, noisy, and in motion. Within the stone circle of walls, city people moved faster than the folk in the country. Time was short and space was tight, and both were worth money.

Time and Spaces

Church bells tolled and clocks chimed to measure the working day for medieval town dwellers. Similarly, the rich patterns of buildings, streets, and open spaces shaped their consciousness.

Work began at dawn for town dwellers, summoned by the ringing of church bells. They rang at intervals all day until the toll of curfew at nightfall. Bells called people to prayer or to face an emergency; they marked the opening and closing of markets, sent

Urban Forms

From the Tower to London Bridge: *This fifteenth-century view of London shows the city wall and royal Tower in the foreground. In the background is London Bridge with its many houses spanning the River Thames. (British Library, London)*

civic officials to their deliberations, and announced executions. The spaces of time that stretched between the tolling of the bells were a commodity to be saved, and certainly not wasted.

During the fourteenth century clocks replaced bells in the larger and wealthier cities. A town clock was installed in Florence in 1325, Milan in 1335, and Geneva in 1353. In 1370, the French king, Charles V, ordered that all the bells of Paris coordinate with the clock at the royal palace. By this ruling the musical bells were subordinated to the modern tempo of mechanical motion. The precise partitioning of time coordinated with the psychology of the merchant, for whom the new machines imposed on the flow of natural rhythms time that was measured, orderly, and precise. The clock was an instrument, commented an English monk, "by which the people rule themselves."

Regulated by the arithmetic of passing hours, the town dweller's mentality was also shaped by the visual grammar of urban forms: the city's compact mass of buildings and its streets. Again, Nuremberg is typical; by the fifteenth century the perimeter of its wall enclosed more than 500 streets and thousands of buildings. Both individuals and corporations (guilds and **confraternities**, church and government councils) organized the construction of buildings of wood, brick, or stone. Few still stand that are older than the thirteenth century, but their outlines can be deduced from documents or later structures that do survive.

The halls of the guilds declared the success of those who labored to produce and sell. That is the boastful spirit observed in the lines of the Cloth Hall of Ypres and of Orsanmichele in Florence. Not far from the guildhall was the market square, the nerve center of the medieval city. The "haymarket" or "fishmarket" or "flowermarket" provided a space to buy and sell, but also to dance or to repent, to shout down a leader or welcome a guest, hear a sermon or plot a rebellion.

Church and Town Hall Towns were also centers of the life of the spirit. Throughout a medieval city were scattered the buildings that marked the presence of the Church. At or near the center stood a cathedral or another large church. Built with the love and labor of citizens for the glory of God, cathedrals and churches were also built for the glory of the prosperous bourgeoisie, who provided the materials, appointed the masters, and paid the bills, and whose family and guild chapels intruded upon the sacred space, alongside those of nobility and important clergy, lining the nave and encircling the high altar.

The great cathedrals represented only a fraction of church construction. Churches proliferated as the population grew, each serving the surrounding neighborhood, or parish, and most dedicated to one or another of the saints. The 200,000 residents of thirteenth-century Milan were divided into 115 parishes: no inhabitant was expected to journey far to hear mass. In the parish church and adjacent churchyard citizens were baptized, married, and buried, and here they settled the contracts that made up the web of commerce, sworn to by witnesses on sacred relics.

Monasteries and convents stood at the edge of the city or just beyond its walls. Convents housed mostly wealthy women, along with their servants. Whereas traditional monasticism was rural in origin, but found a place in the city, the mendicant orders of the Franciscans and Dominicans embraced an urban mission from the start. As part of the core of city life, they staked out their claim at once to the cheap land on the city's fringe.

In Paris, the Dominicans and the Franciscans found homes in the then-suburban expanses of the Left Bank, around the nucleus of the growing university. In Nuremberg, the Franciscan complex had been built outside the circuit of the walls that stood at the time of its foundation, but hugged the inner perimeter of the expanded late-medieval walls. In the same way, in Florence, the Franciscans, Dominicans, and Augustinians established their orders beyond the city walls, to be eventually encompassed within a still-larger circuit. They occupied, as at Paris, the sparsely settled areas of the city where dwelt the poor and restive masses who particularly responded to their message.

Not far from the commercial zone of market and guildhall and the ecclesiastical centers of monastery and cathedral stood the imposing public buildings that housed the government. The councilors of Siena explained the need for such grand structures: "It is a matter of honor for each city that its rulers and officials should occupy beautiful and honorable buildings. ... This is a matter of great importance for the prestige of the city." The patricians of Bruges deliberated in

Nuremberg within its walls: *This woodcut from Hartmann Schedel's Liber Chronicarum, 1493, shows the sloped roofs of tightly packed buildings mounting the hill from city gate to castle.*

Ambrogio Lorenzetti, The Effects of Good Government in the City and the Country: *This fresco (Palazzo Pubblico, 1338–1339) by the Italian artist Ambrogio Lorenzetti encompasses a peaceful country landscape and well-regulated urban scene, clearly contrasted and separated by the city's walls and gates.*

the Old Hall; those of hilltop Volterra, Italy, in the Palazzo dei Priori (Priors' Palace); those of Florence in the Palazzo del Popolo ("palace of the people"; now called the Palazzo Vecchio, or "old palace"); those of Venice in the Doge's Palace (the Doge was the title of the city's elective presiding head), adjacent to the Piazza and the basilica of San Marco: "the most beautiful square in the world," pronounced one of the city chroniclers, "and ... the most beautiful church in the world."

Houses Not to be outdone by Church, corporation, or council, the town's leading merchants proclaimed their status by building themselves houses as splendid as their considerable fortunes would allow. The ordinary merchant lived comfortably, though he shared his premises with commercial bustle and the business of strangers. His house might have shop and warehouse on the ground floor, hall with kitchen and pantry on the second, and bedchambers on the third, furnished with multiple beds for master's family and servants alike. Beds were shared by parents and children, masters and servants, merchants and workmen,

occasioning a kind of interaction among diverse groups unacceptable—even unthinkable—today.

Fireplaces provided heat on every floor of multistory houses, served by chimneys (an improvement on the hole in the roof of peasant establishments). This heating system was so improved over those of earlier periods that it made city life comfortable, whereas hitherto winter was only "a period of stupefied hibernation." The new fireplaces not only took smoke out of a room, but could be modified to radiate heat into the room before taking it out of the building. Windows still lacked glass, but were closed against the elements by oiled cloth or parchment; at night, shutters protected the house against harsh cold and unlawful entry. Likewise, hefty doors locked or barred at night, kept out cold and strangers.

Floors were strewn with rushes—green in summer, dried into hay by winter—food for fire. Walls were finished with plaster or wood paneling and, in affluent homes, hung with tapestries. These added color and texture while protecting against drafts. The toilet? A chamber pot, emptied the next morning from the window, or a shed over a ditch in the rear garden—next to the neighbor's property line—served the purpose. Better-equipped homes had a privy near the bedrooms, from which a chute conducted waste to a pit in the cellar.

An ordinary burgher's house was usually built as part of a row of attached houses, backed by a series of gardens or a common green. The grand houses of important merchants were mostly free-standing. The thirteenth-century Florentine moralist Brunetto Latini admired the houses of the grand burghers of France, "great and spacious and painted, their fair chambers wherein they have joy and delight," and the splendid gardens adjacent to them. These homes set a new standard of luxury and, still more novel, of privacy—featuring that most precious of innovations, a private bedroom, at least for the master of the house and his wife.

The town houses of urban patricians and those of ordinary merchants differed not only in scale and elegance, but even in function. The ground floor of the average tradesman's or master craftsman's house was devoted to his trade. It included a shop or workshop, perhaps also an office for bookkeeping and a storeroom. By contrast, the residence of a rich merchant was dedicated to the display of wealth rather than its production, and kept separate from the workshop. Cosimo de' Medici (1389–1464), for example,

Florentine financier and unofficial ruler, built his splendid palace apart from his place of business, the family's famous bank, left behind in the heart of the old town. The divorce of home life and work life begins with these great merchants, the first commuters of the western world. (An exception was Venice, where the ground floors of the great merchants' palaces opened onto dank canals and were used for loading and unloading).

The Italian writer Leonardo Bruni (c. 1370–1444) had in mind the palaces of rich merchants when he described their "entrance courts, halls, pavements, banquet halls ... [and] the curtains, arches, the paneled ceilings and richly decorated hung ceilings ... beautiful chambers decorated with fine furniture, gold, silver and brocaded hangings and precious carpets." He claimed that in Florence (which included some of the richest men in Europe), such buildings were found in every street and neighborhood: "Just as blood is spread throughout the entire body, so fine architecture and decoration are diffused throughout the whole city (see *Witnesses* on p. 331)."

Nearby, in crowded houses near the center of town or in cave-like recesses under the walls, lived the small craftsman or aspiring journeyman, the poor worker and his family, the destitute widow and her children (if they had not been dispatched as servants

Walls, Halls, and Towers

Aigues Mortes, France, thirteenth century

Medieval towns were often sited for defense purposes. The thirteenth-century walled city of Aigues Mortes (right) in southern France, is symmetrically proportioned, which the flat landscape allows. By contrast, another walled French town of around the same period, Carcassone (below) is sited on a plateau and the walls are built to fit its shape.

Public buildings in the Gothic style added grandeur to medieval cities. The great vaulting structure of Westminster Hall (opposite) in London accentuates the beauty of windows intricate with tracery. In the flamboyant Gothic style, Brussels Town Hall has ornate turrets, high windows, balconies and small bell towers. The tall tower bears a shrine, upon which sits Archangel Michael, the patron saint of the city.

Why would designers of merchant halls borrow architectural elements from churches?

Carcassone, France, twelfth to thirteenth centuries

Westminster Hall, London, 1397–1399

Brussels Town Hall, Belgium, fifteenth century

 To continue your investigation of this topic, please go to www.prenhall.com/king for the related **WINDOWS** on the **WEB** activity

or laborers). The poorest of these inhabited a miserable space in tenements. Others occupied a room in a rich man's house, or a lean-to shack thrown against cathedral walls, or a small room adjoining the master's workshop. They paid rent drawn from daily wages to live in these places without the merest amenities: "For a poor man who has no money," wrote one twelfth-century author, "does not sit by a fire, nor sit at a table, rather he eats on his lap."

Houses of rich and poor alike were jumbled together, without zoning restrictions or social or stylistic barriers. Public and private, ecclesiastical and municipal buildings stood side-by-side, as did the grand and the tiny, the ornate and the plain. New buildings required little advance planning or cash investment: no installations for sewerage, electricity, or telephones were needed. Space could easily be extended upward by adding a new story, or outward by tearing down a wall. Cities could increase quickly in area and density, as space was emptied or filled. The medieval town dweller saw no impropriety in the haphazardness of such construction, the juxtaposition of

shacks and palaces, warehouses and cathedrals. In 1300 still a hodgepodge lined with the faceless tenements of the poor and punctuated by the towers of the great, Florence became in the fourteenth century one of the first cities to impose order on the medieval cluster of forms.

The vigorous interplay of buildings and towers, of private and public, of sacred and civic, of urgent chimes and bells created a world full of energy.

On the Street

The pathways of urban life were the network of streets, bridges, and rivers, snaking past the imposing buildings in the shadow of the towers. Townspeople worked, governed, prayed, and slept indoors, but city life was lived in the streets. Narrow, winding, and dirty, the city streets knit together miscellaneous structures in an integrated system.

City streets were meant for pedestrians, who could walk across even the largest cities in twenty or thirty minutes. Begun as cattle paths or the beds of ancient streams or the contours of hill and valley, they formed organic patterns—except where the tight grid of a preexistent Roman town imposed an abstract order. Often they grew in a starfish or web pattern, as arterial roads led out from the center to the city gates. Streets were wide enough to accommodate the tradesman's wagon but no wider. Sometimes they shrank to narrow tunnels almost entirely covered by the projecting upper stories of the buildings on either side.

City Time

Dondi's clock (left and right): *The mechanism of the Paduan Giovanni de' Dondi's astronomical clock (1364) is known from the author's own detailed descriptions, available in several surviving manuscripts which provide the earliest-known illustrations of mechanical clocks. A modern reconstruction is shown here (left), together with a sketch of the mechanism (right) from one of the Dondi manuscripts, fourteenth century.* (left: Smithsonian Institution, Museum of American History; right: Bodleian Library, Oxford)

The Splendors of Florence and Venice

By the fifteenth century, some leading cities had become extraordinarily wealthy, powerful, and beautiful, developing in each case a unique architecture and sense of space appropriate to its location, its governance, the taste of its elites, and its mercantile activities. Here two renowned authors describe their own cities of Florence and Venice, the first stressing the buildings and street system of the former, the second the unique situation of the latter, a series of linked islands afloat in a lagoon in the Adriatic Sea.

Leonardo Bruni praises the buildings of Florence (1404): What in the world is so splendid and magnificent as the architecture of Florence? ... In other places perhaps one or at the most two streets in the entire city are filled with important buildings, while the rest of the town is so devoid of architectural distinction. ... But in our city there is really no street, no quarter that does not possess spacious and ornate buildings. ... The sort of careful scrutiny that brings shame to other cities only serves to raise the esteem held for Florence, for behind the walls of the buildings of Florence there are no fewer ornaments and no less magnificence than there is outside; nor is any one street better decorated or more handsome than another, but every quarter shares in the beauty of the city. Hence, just as blood is spread throughout the entire body, so fine architecture and decoration are diffused throughout the whole city.
(Leonardo Bruni, "Panegyric," 1404; eds. B. Kohl, J. Witt, 1978)

Marino Sanudo describes the glories of Venice (1493): The city of Venice is a free city, a common home to all men, and it has never been subjugated by anyone, as have been all other cities. ... This city, amidst the billowing waves of the sea, stands on the crest of the main, almost like a queen restraining its force. It is situated in salt water and built there, because before there were just lagoons, and then, wanting to expand, firm ground was needed for the building of palaces and houses. These are being constructed all the time; they are built above the water by a very ingenious method of driving piles, so that the foundations are in water. Every day the tide rises and falls, but the city remains dry. At times of very low tides, it is difficult to go by boat to wherever one wants. The city is about 7 miles in circumference; it has no surrounding walls, no gates which are locked at night, no sentry keeping watch as other cities have for fear of enemies; it is so very safe at present, that no one can attack or frighten it. For it takes pride of place before all others, if I may say so, in prudence, fortitude, magnificence, benignity and clemency. ... To conclude, this city was built more by divine than human will.
(Marino Sanudo, "Laus urbis venetae," 1493; eds. D. Chambers, B. Pullan, 1992)

As the rivers along and across which cities grew became incorporated in the urban fabric, they needed to be crossed by bridges. On some of these bridges rose towers and churches, **hospitals** and shops, homes and schools. Paris's Pont au Change ("Commerce Bridge") once sheltered about 120 moneychangers and goldsmiths, while Florence's Ponte Vecchio ("Old Bridge"), built in 1345 and still preserved today, was designed from the first to house shops. Rents from bridge residents, along with donations received from passersby, paid for maintenance and new construction. Cheaper bridges made of wood were vulnerable to fire and flood and were replaced by durable stone wherever funds allowed. London Bridge was reconstructed in stone by 1209; Venice's splendid Rialto Bridge only in 1588.

Sanitation Paving the streets eased traffic and helped control the filth of the city. Road paving began in Paris as early as 1185, but only the streets that led to the city gates were so improved. Lübeck, in Germany, paved its main streets in 1310; Nuremberg hers from 1368; Florence paved them all between 1235 and 1339, which made that city "more clean, and more beautiful, and more healthy," reports her leading chronicler, Bruni. English municipalities set standards for the maintenance of roads, policing those laborers who neglected to dig down to lay a proper substructure. Unchecked, such lazy workers would lay new pavement over old layers to such a height, supervisors complained, that one had to step down in order to enter home or church.

Water for washing and bathing was hauled from nearby streams, drawn from public wells, collected from rainwater in cisterns, or, in some cases, piped in from distant sources. The water-starved hill towns of Italy built aqueducts to bring in water, which was then dispersed through wells and fountains. Not only useful amenities, these were civic focal points and often very imposing—as was Perugia's Fontana Maggiore ("Great Fountain"), completed in 1278, which was adorned with reliefs by the sculptor Nicola Pisano (c. 1220–c. 1278) and his son Giovanni. Public bathhouses abounded: there were 12 in Nuremberg, 15 in Frankfurt, 17 in Augsburg; 26 in Paris. Medieval townspeople bathed regularly—in contrast to their descendants in the sixteenth through eighteenth centuries, who feared that water might spread infection and preferred perfume and powder (if they could afford such luxuries) to soap and water.

In patrician houses, washbasins of copper and even silver held water for washing. Most people wore heavy wool garments which they rarely washed, but servants and professional laundresses washed linens for bed and table in large cisterns—or, illegally, in the wells and rivers. It was the merchant's responsibility to clothe his servants and apprentices decently (as it was a husband's to clothe his wife). One London tailor was sent to prison on a charge of ill-treatment, which included that of having forced a boy to sleep in a bed "foule shirtyd & full of vermin."

Although city leaders knew about the value of cleanliness, they did not always achieve it. Bruni praised Florence for its excellence in this regard: "Surely this city is unique and singular in all the world because you will find here nothing that is disgusting to the eye, offensive to the nose, or filthy under foot." Any other city, in contrast, "is so dirty that the filth created during the night is seen in the early morning by the population and trampled under foot in the streets. Really can one think of anything worse than this?"

The omnipresence of the privy, the coexistence of humans with animals destined for work and for slaughter, and the insufficiency of paving made sanitation an intractable problem. Through open gutters flowed dirty water from kitchen and tavern, animal dung, the refuse of dyeing vats, the entrails of butchered animals, the heads of fish and the corpses of dogs, cats, and horses: an accumulation horrible to see and worse to smell. The waste products of the butcher and—worse—the dyer flowed into rivers and canals: as at Antwerp, where citizens complained that the polluted water of the canals killed thirsty horses. Official street sweepers and overseers, hired rakers, carters, and scavengers labored to reduce the mountains of dirt. Pigs ran loose, to glean what they could from the wondrous leavings in the street. The Italian writer Petrarch (1304–1374), usually deferential, berated the ruler of Padua: "This city … so outstanding in its many glories, is being transformed—with you looking on and not stopping it, as you easily could—into a horrid and ugly pasture by rampaging herds of pigs!"

Fire and Crime Fire was a worse menace than vagrant pigs or open dungheaps. Every town knew this purgative killer and mindless agent of urban renewal. Most houses were built of wood, and filled with flammable furnishings—even including the paint on the walls. If one house burned, an entire district was at risk. Rouen burned six times within twenty-five years; and in a single year—1188—fire attacked the French cities of Rouen (again), Troyes, Beauvais, Provins, Arras, Poitiers, and Moissac. A conflagration in Florence in 1304 destroyed 1700 buildings, another in Nuremberg in 1340 more than 400. Lübeck was burned to the ground in 1157, and in

Padua, in 1174, 2614 houses—three-quarters of the residences—were destroyed. In an attempt to prevent such calamities, city governments issued regulations prescribing fireproof materials and stipulating the hours when fires could be lit. Firefighting systems were organized. But where no means existed for the conveyance of water, they could do little.

Municipalities also struggled with accident and evildoing. Watchmen toured the unlit streets at night, charged to pursue and arrest suspected felons. Bruges, with a population (before the Black Death) of some 35,000, maintained a police force of 27. In 1422, the English city of Coventry hired 24 constables for a population of some 5000, and giant London, in 1461, employed 285 watchmen. To police its population of about 100,000, Venice required several government agencies: magistrates called the "gentlemen of the night" performed this service at the local neighborhood level. In smaller towns, the duty of "watch and ward" (as it was called in England) was passed in rotation to all male burghers. The streets belonged to everyone.

PUBLIC LIFE

In this urban complex of buildings and streets, diverse groups of people lived together observing their separate customs. At the same time, the whole city engaged in public celebration and suffered together in times of calamity, as all benefited from the institutions of public charity that aimed to ameliorate the conditions of the least fortunate urban dwellers.

Foreigners, Friends, and Outcasts

Because of the diversity of the city's population, life within its walls offered ample opportunity for violence and disorder. Just as rich and poor crowded together, workers and merchants, slaves and servants, men without roots and women without families, so also—especially in the case of larger cities—did members of different national groups: the French, Flemish, and Germans in London and Novgorod; Turks, Slavs, Germans, and Greeks in Venice and Genoa. These outsiders gathered in closed communities under their own leaders and laws. Germans representing the towns of the Hanseatic League (see Chapter 11) formed a stable community at London's Steelyard, while the Greeks and Dalmatians of Venice formed autonomous societies centered on two churches called respectively "Saint George of the Greeks" and "Saint George of the Slavs."

Jews Regarded as strangers wherever they settled, Jews were the ethnic community most widely encountered in European cities. Gathering in the shadow of the town synagogue, they maintained their own social and religious customs while sharing wherever possible in the surrounding cultural world. This was not always possible. As Christian Europe developed its own merchants to carry on functions for which Jewish traders were once valued, resentment swelled against perceived "outsiders." Native Christians blamed the Jews in their midst for accidents or disasters, or held them guilty of imaginary and horrible crimes. Although sporadically, and fiercely, persecuted in the spate of massacres that accompanied the Crusades, Jewish communities fared relatively well in medieval Europe into the twelfth century. Then economic resentments and psychological fears took over. Their status in the centers of trade and industry began a downturn that would last for centuries.

Jews were subject to special restrictions. An Avignonese law of 1243 proclaimed that "Jews or whores shall not dare to touch with their hands either bread or fruit put out for sale. ..." In Lübeck, a chronicler commented, there were no Jews; "there

is no need of them either." In Florence in 1463, a limit of 70 was placed on the number of Jews that were allowed in the city—"to prevent any large concentration ... or a greater number than is necessary"—and all adult members of the community were required to wear a distinguishing sign: a yellow "O," which "shall be worn on the left breast, over the clothing in a visible place. ..." Nevertheless, all religious practices were permitted, in this decree, and religious and scholarly books might be "possessed, read, studied, and copied."

Many Jewish communities suffered doubly during the Black Death: not only from the disease itself but also from the fury of Christian neighbors, as described in *Witnesses* beneath. Having already been expelled from England and France (in 1290 and 1306, respectively), Jews were driven from many cities, victims of the notion that they had caused the disease. In 1349, they were expelled from Nuremberg, where the whole

---

WITNESSES

Jews and Medieval Cities

The communities of Jews scattered throughout Europe's towns and cities were occasionally tolerated, as official pronouncements said they must be. They were also occasionally, but horribly, persecuted, often by mobs made unsteady by crisis conditions, or sometimes instigated by those who would profit most by their rivals, or their creditors', removal. In the first passage, Pope Gregory X urges the toleration of the Jews. In the second, a chronicler reports the vicious massacre of the Jewish population of Strasbourg.

Pope Gregory X (1271–1276) clarifies the Church's official policy of toleration toward the Jews of Europe: The Jews ... ought not to suffer any disadvantage in those [privileges] which have been granted them ... we therefore admit their petition and offer them the shield of our protection through the clemency of Christian piety. ...

We decree moreover that no Christian shall compel them or any one of their group to come to baptism unwillingly. ... Moreover no Christian shall presume to seize, imprison, wound, torture, mutilate, kill, or inflict violence on them. ... In addition, no one shall disturb them in any way during the celebration of their festivals, whether by day or by night, with clubs or stones or anything else. ...

Since it happens occasionally that some Christians lose their Christian children, the Jews are accused by their enemies of secretly carrying off and killing these same Christian children and of making sacrifices of the heart and blood if these very children. ... And most falsely do these Christians claim that the Jews have secretly and furtively carried away these children and killed them, and that the Jews offer sacrifice from the

heart and the blood of these children. ... We decree, therefore, ... that Jews seized under such a silly pretext be freed from imprisonment, and that they shall not be arrested henceforth on such a miserable pretext, unless—which we do not believe—they be caught in the commission of the crime. We decree that no Christian shall stir up anything new against them, but that they should be maintained in that status and position in which they were in the time of our predecessors, from antiquity till now.
(Pope Gregory X, *Letter*; ed. B. Tierney, 2e, 1973)

Jacob von Königshofen on Strasbourg's Jewry (1349): In the matter of this plague the Jews throughout the world were reviled and accused in all lands of having caused it through the poison which they are said to have put into the water and the wells ... and for this reason the Jews were burnt ... from the Mediterranean into Germany, but not in Avignon, for the pope protected them. ...

On Saturday ... they burnt the Jews on a wooden platform in the cemetery. ... Many small children were taken out of the fire and baptized against the will of their fathers and mothers. And everything that was owed to the Jews was cancelled, and the Jews had to surrender all pledges and notes that they had taken for debts. The council, however, took the cash that the Jews possessed and divided it among the working-men proportionately. The money was indeed the thing that killed the Jews. If they had been poor and if the feudal lords had not been in debt to them, they would not have been burnt. ...
(Jacob von Königshofen, *Chronicle*, 1349; eds. J. Ross, M. McLaughlin, 1949)

City People

Massacre of the Jews of Cologne: *The persecution of the Jews of Cologne is shown in this illustration from a contemporary chronicle, the* Liber Chronicarum Mundi, *Nuremberg, 1493.*

Jewish quarter and synagogue were immediately razed. The Jews of Basel (in modern Switzerland) were herded together on an island in the Rhine and burned, while the town council, to drive the point home, prohibited their future resettlement in that city for 200 years. Some 2000 Jews of Strasbourg (now in France) were burned—purely to free the lords from debt, suggests a contemporary witness. "The money was indeed the thing that killed the Jews. If they had been poor and if the feudal lords had not been in debt to them, they would not have been burnt." Jews could save themselves by converting, but they usually resisted that act, which would result in their destruction as a people and as a faith. Parents condemned to death reportedly hurled their children into the flames to prevent their being seized and baptized into an alien religion.

The Jews of the German lands suffered many massacres during the plague years. Persecutions surged again in the fifteenth century, as illustrated above. After 1424 in Cologne, and 1435 in Rhineland Speyer, no Jews were allowed. Between the effects of plague and persecution, the Jewish population of the Iberian peninsula was reduced to one-fourth its former size; then from 1492 to 1496 all Jews were commanded to convert or to leave. The Inquisition notoriously persecuted those Jews who had converted, if they lapsed into the observance of Jewish rituals.

With the significant exception of the Spanish Inquisition, the Church urged restraint upon the Christian population with respect to the Jews in their midst (see *Witnesses* on p. 333). The Jews were to be able to practice their religion freely, and to enjoy limited rights in society. Eventually, it was believed—on the eve of the Apocalypse—their conversion would be accomplished. In the meantime, they were to be unmolested. Ordinary Christians, however, did not always accept the policy officially formulated. It was in vain that the Church pointed out that Jews, too, died of the plague; common people held them responsible. If a child died or disappeared under mysterious circumstances, people blamed the Jews. Such "ritual murder" charges became "blood libels" when Christians accused Jews of using the blood of these allegedly kidnapped and murdered children. One such fantastic charge was that they mixed the blood with the unleavened bread, or matzoh, used during the Jewish holy days of Passover.

Jews suffered wave upon wave of persecution, despite Pope Gregory X's ruling in 1272 that "no Christian shall presume to seize, imprison, wound, torture, mutilate, kill, or inflict violence on [the Jews]," or "compel them or any one of their group to come to baptism unwillingly." Later Clement VI, reigning (1343–1352) during the plague years, rebuked those who shed "the blood of Jews, whom Christian piety accepts and sustains." European **anti-Semitism** developed in the communities of medieval Europe, even as the Church forbade physical attacks against Jews and deplored the accusations of ritual murder, often with the participation of churchmen.

City governments found it useful to make Jews welcome when their services as moneylenders or pawnbrokers or physicians were needed. Yet they did not include Jews fully as members of society. In time, in addition to requirements of special dress, some cities allocated special neighborhoods for Jewish residents. The first organized precinct of this sort was the **ghetto** of Venice, founded in 1516—the one from which the word "ghetto" originated.

The Venetian dialect word "ghetto" (derived from *gettare*, "to cast") originally designated an iron foundry, the site of which became the locus of the Jewish community newly permitted to stay within city limits. Ghetto residents (there were as many as 5000 at its height) had frequent and sometimes cordial relations with Christian merchants, scholars, and patricians. Within their walls, they freely followed their own rites (requiring the importation and preparation of special foods in order to observe the dietary laws). Yet those walls were also a prison: the gates were locked at nights and during certain Christian holidays, purportedly for the security of ghetto residents. Over later centuries, ghettoes were established in other cities, eventually becoming a commonplace of Jewish social life within European Christendom.

Prostitutes Prostitutes, like Jews, had a precarious place in the medieval town. One is depicted on p. 335. In some places, prostitutes were required to wear distinctive dress—a headdress or a telltale color—to set them apart from respectable citizens. Often their brothels were cautiously located outside the walls.

A Prostitute's Trade: *In the well-furnished bedchamber depicted in this sixteenth-century engraving after Lucas van Leyden, a client fondles a prostitute as she reaches for his payment.* (Warburg Institute, London)

Elsewhere, prostitution was openly acknowledged and even fostered. In Italy, public brothels were opened in Venice in 1360, in Florence in 1403, and in Siena in 1421. In Germany, Frankfurt led the way in 1396, Nuremberg by 1400, Munich by 1433, Memmingen (in Bavaria) by 1454, and Strasbourg by 1469. In France, Dijon opened its "Great House" in 1385, and Toulouse operated a municipal brothel from 1363 or 1372.

Nobles A considerably grander city enclave, found especially in Italy, was formed by the associations of noble clans. Members of the nobility who settled within the city during the period of formation and built their own houses there led their lives, as much as possible, as though they were still in the country and masters of all about them. In the close confines of the city, they carried on the feuds and fights that occupied them elsewhere. In Italy they even endowed their houses with fortified towers, always on the ready for an attack. Their towers afforded a view of the region, warehoused weapons, and sheltered dependents. Noblemen's towers soared over the roofs of burgher dwellings, creating a skyline of verticals anticipating modern skylines such as that of Manhattan in New York City. Eventually, municipal governments tore down the anomalous towers. Some 140 were dismantled in Rome in the 1250s, while

in Florence, hundreds were sawn off to an altitude that matched the reduced status of nobles in a merchant republic. But in the little Tuscan town of San Gimignano, 13 towers survive today to bristle menacingly against the horizon.

Neighbors For most town dwellers the important associations were those of parish, neighborhood, and friendship. In Florence, the formula of "kin, neighbors, and friends" was routinely used to define the networks that mattered. The patrician Gino Capponi advised his sons to "stick together above all else with your neighbors and your kinsmen, and serve your friends within and without the city." A town's neighborhoods—Rome's thirteen *rioni*, Florence's sixteen *gonfaloni*, Venice's six *sestieri*, Nuremberg's eight *viertel*—actively fostered social life. In Genoa, clusters of people who hailed from the same country village reproduced the intimacy of their former life in a tightly packed urban colony. In Venice, wealthy people gave gifts to poor neighbors who shared the same courtyard. Especially among women, barred from the public communities of market or government, the neighborhood courtyard offered a buzz of news and advice among friends and neighbors.

The desperately poor belonged nowhere and to no group. The disabled or unemployed or those newly arrived from a famine-ridden countryside pressed into the city. Vagrants and migrants formed an underclass of shifting dimensions. In Nuremberg, out of a population of about 30,000 in 1449–1450, nearly one-third were refugees without permanent residence. In Florence, the wretchedly poor or "destitute," as distinguished from the working poor, made up nearly one-third of the population. These rootless folk worked if they found work, begged if they could not, and slept in the shadow of the houses of the wealthy.

The different kinds of people who inhabited the towns—foreigners and visitors, Jews, beggars, and prostitutes, friends, kin, and neighbors—enriched the experience of urban life, just as did the variety of its visual forms.

Special Days

The everyday activity of a medieval town often gave way to the heightened activity of special days, when work ceased and the streets filled with throngs of spectators and participants. From every parish, and courtyards, quarters, and wards, city people poured into central public spaces for the celebration of special events—religious festivals, public ceremonies, and executions.

The calendar of religious festivals supplied ample occasion for spectacle and display. Throughout Europe, religious dramas, originally produced in churches, later out of doors, were performed on various holy days. In England, the "mystery" plays celebrating

Corpus Christi (the feast of the "body of Christ") were among the most important. The feast of Saint Firmin was celebrated in Pamplona (Spain) by a parade of giant characters representing Moors and Normans and the running of bulls through the streets. A horse race marked the celebration in Florence of the festal day of Saint John the Baptist, its patron saint, and in Siena (the famous "Palio"), on the day after the Feast of the Assumption of the Virgin, in the city's huge Piazza del Campo.

The tournament, a ritual of the knightly class, was adapted for town use. In imitation of noblemen, common soldiers and rich merchants donned special tournament armor. Patricians formed special societies of urban chivalry—such as Bruges' "Order of the White Bear," whose pudgy mascot carved in stone adorns a niche of the patrician meeting house, the Poortersloge. The marriage of the son of the Doge Francesco Foscari in Venice in 1441 was celebrated by a tournament in which mercenary captains vied with each other to capture mock wooden castles.

When no celebration was in the offing, the townspeople might enjoy an execution. Venetians gathered to watch the hanging, caging, or decapitation of the condemned between the Columns of Justice in the Piazza San Marco. Here, in 1432, died the

Piero della Francesca, Pregnant Madonna: *As depicted in this fresco by Piero della Francesca in Monterchi, Italy, c. 1410, the stature accorded the pregnant woman is suggested by the serene and dignified figure of the Virgin Mary, who is about to give birth to the Savior.*

mercenary captain Francesco Carmagnola, trapped by the notorious Council of Ten (part of the Venetian government), who claimed to have found evidence of his collusion with the enemy. As momentous was the execution in Florence in 1498 of the Dominican leader and prophet Girolamo Savonarola (1452–1498), who was condemned for heresy. Criminals met their fate in Bruges before the market square's belfry, adorned with a statue of Saint Michael driving out Satan.

On one occasion, the townspeople of Mons (France), temporarily short of local criminals, bought a condemned thief "for the pleasure of seeing him quartered"—at which event, reported a contemporary, "the people rejoiced more than if a new holy body had risen from the dead." The citizens of Nuremberg accompanied the targets of their judicial vengeance to a place beyond the walls, where the machines necessary to hang, burn, draw and quarter, behead, or drown the victim were masterfully assembled by the public executioner. Justice was then served, a historian observed, "amid the noise of the crowd and the smell of frying pork sausages from the butchers' stalls put up for the occasion."

Town dwellers also assembled to witness the ceremonial entrances of rulers and dignitaries. It was the custom for the kings of France, having been crowned and anointed at Rheims, to process through the whole city of Paris en route to the royal palace. In 1440 the entrance to Bruges of its Burgundian lord, Duke Philip the Good, was followed in full splendor by 136 Hanseatic merchants, 48 Spaniards, 40 Milanese, 40 Venetians, 12 Lucchese (citizens of Lucca), 36 Genoese, 22 Florentines, and scatterings of others. Great exits, too, attracted a crowd. The whole city turned out for the funerals, in Florence, of the English-born mercenary captain John Hawkwood (1394) and the chancellor Coluccio Salutati (1406); in Venice the burials of the doges were attended by the whole population. Witnesses of the funeral of King Charles VII of France in 1461 saw the procession of luminaries attired in deepest mourning: "and because of the great sorrow and grief they exhibited for the death of their master," wrote one of them, "many tears were shed and lamentations uttered throughout the town."

Other moments, sacred and political, were celebrated with a processional of ranked groups of citizens and corporations. In Bruges, on solemn occasions, the people bore the city's collection of saints' relics through the town and around the walls, followed by civic officials, mounted knights, and resident foreign merchants. For weeks during the year 1412, the citizens of Paris processed daily, seeking victory for their king, then engaged in the grim struggle of the Hundred Years' War. Those who marched or looked on wept "piteously, with many tears, in great devotion," while the rain poured down relentlessly, in what one contemporary described as the "most touching processions in the memory of men."

At Nuremberg, crowds gathered each May to view the imperial regalia, which had been deposited in the city for safekeeping in 1424: gilded and jeweled scepters, crowns, orbs, clasps, and stirrups, and sacred relics, including the lance that had opened Jesus' side (it was thought) and one of the nails that fixed him to the cross. Venetian processions celebrated the transcendent role of their own doge and state over both emperor and pope. The doge's preeminence was symbolized in objects known as the *trionfi*, or "triumphs"—a white candle, lead seals, banners, a sword, gold ring, ceremonial umbrella, and silver trumpets—the gifts (legendarily) bestowed upon the doge in 1177 by the then pope, Alexander III. Twelve times a year, for sacred feasts and state events, these *trionfi* were paraded through the Piazza San Marco in processions of unmatched splendor and a discipline elsewhere unknown, reported one observer, "in the best order imaginable."

In such public ceremonies, the town dwellers, who were united by their residence within the walls, by their ties to the producers and sellers of goods, by their neighborhood and family and group allegiances, were further bound together by the mutual experience of celebrating—not only the glory of the saints or the triumph of justice but the excellence of their own city.

Charity

The sense of unity experienced by the citizens expressed itself also in charitable activity. To a remarkable degree, medieval town dwellers cared for their neighbors, their associates, and even the most unfortunate of their fellow citizens.

From its earliest days, the Church had taken seriously Jesus' command to "feed my sheep"—to care for the sick, the hungry, and the deserted. To do so in an urban setting required the creation of new institutions. The urban public organized itself in a variety of corporations for pious purposes. The lay confraternity, an association of men and women linked by a common mission or obligation, combined spiritual observance and charitable service. The craft guilds had social and fraternal functions as well as professional ones, providing for the burial of members and their kin and the saying of penitential prayers for the souls of the departed. They also dispensed charity, helped construct public works, planned and produced mystery plays, and supported schools. Residential communities of holy women (see Chapter 10) or networks of pious laymen also dispensed charity and organized schools.

The great numbers of the poor made such charitable service necessary. To feed the poor, tend the ill, house the deserted wife or homeless widow, nurture the abandoned infant, or provide a dowry for a fatherless girl, townspeople created hospitals and asylums. Almshouses for the destitute and **hospices** for the aged were among the biggest public buildings of the medieval city. Foundling homes received the unwanted infants left at their doorsteps. Similar institutions welcomed women seeking refuge from neglectful husbands, engaged them in productive work, and prepared them for return to society.

Hospitals were the most conspicuous of these institutions. Built by pious lay donors or monastic foundations, the hospitals provided for the great numbers of the ill, who were cared for by volunteers from the lay confraternities or semireligious orders. Most German towns had two—one for "lepers" (victims of Hansen's Disease) and one for victims of other diseases; while populous Breslau, with 15, offered one hospital for every 2000 residents. Thirty hospitals, affording more than 1000 beds (each shared by several patients), served 90,000 residents of Florence, and the French city of Toulouse boasted 7 leprosariums and 13 general-purpose hospitals. An astonishing 200 hospitals in England tended exclusively to lepers.

Most hospitals housed only a dozen or so patients, but some were, by medieval standards, enormous. The Hôtel Dieu ("God's House") in Paris, begun in the 1190s, had by 1260 extended to include 375 feet (114 m.) of patient wards. The largest was Milan's Ospedale Maggiore (the "Greater Hospital"), begun in 1456 and completed in the seventeenth century. Consisting of a rectangular block about 920 by 350 feet (280 by 107 m.), it was divided internally into two wings, one for men, one for women, and was equipped with a latrine for each bed.

The people who funded this charitable activity were the same merchants whose aggressive profit-seeking built the cities, who were as deliberate in their giving as in their taking. Patterns of charity are revealed in their wills. While most made bequests to the traditional religious institutions of parish and monastery, of 660 persons making wills in Siena between 1205 and 1500, approximately 15 percent aided hospitals and confraternities. In Pistoia (Italy), philanthropists supported hospitals and religious organizations in preference to the traditional institutions of monastery and cathedral. Gifts to hospitals are a signpost of the concern medieval townspeople felt for those disadvantaged in the present world: a spirit one scholar has called "civic Christianity."

Plague

The medieval philanthropists who did so much to relieve those in pain were helpless against the greatest emergency of the Middle Ages: the plague. The plague known as the "Black Death" struck in 1347 and did not die out until the eighteenth century. It was the single greatest natural disaster in the history of the West. It was especially severe in towns and had an enduring effect on urban life. Map 12.1 shows the extent of the plague.

Originating in Asia, the plague may have been caused by the deadly bacterium, *Yersinia pestis*, and entered western Europe through busy Italian ports. Spread by the bite of an infected flea which lived in the hair of the black rat, it caused swellings or buboes (hence "bubonic," as one variety of the plague is termed) in the armpits and the groin of its victims. The accompanying hemorrhage turned dark; thus the name "Black Death." In an even more deadly variant form, pneumonic plague, the bacterium was airborne and highly contagious. Even before the advent of the plague, European peoples had been weakened—in body, in morale—by a sequence of poor harvests and famine (see Chapter 9). The population was thus

especially vulnerable to the disease, which struck down from 25 to 45 percent of the inhabitants of Europe before 1400, wiping out whole generations, and stripping the crowded cities with special savagery.

In Italy, the disease took the lives of about two-thirds of the populations of Bologna and Venice, 30 to 40 percent of Pisa and Genoa, one-half of Orvieto and Florence. Sixteen times in the thirteenth and fourteenth centuries pestilence devastated Florence, as described in *Witnesses* on p. 340. Nearby Pistoia suffered twelve bouts of plague between 1313 and 1458. The onslaught of 1400 devoured half that city's population, and of the dead nearly three-fourths (1140 of 1625) were children. A chronicler of the first 1348 attack witnessed the massacre of the young of Siena: "And I, Agnolo di Tura, called the Fat, buried my five children with my own hands." The old were

Map 12.1 The Progress of the Plague, 1347–1353: *Originating in Asia and extending to Constantinople by 1347, the plague invaded Italy in 1347–1348 and spread north, west, and east on the European continent through 1353. It would return sporadically and irregularly for centuries to come.* What resources did medieval people have to halt the spread of contagion?

also at special risk: 70 percent of the 52,000 plague victims at Siena in 1348 were elderly.

The plague traveled over the Alps from late 1348, and struck northern Europe with equal ferocity. England may have lost up to half her population—"in every parish a great multitude (see *Witnesses* on p. 340)." In France, Avignon, then seat of the papacy, lost more than 50 percent of its people, Paris one-third. In Flanders and the Netherlands the mortality rate was typically 20 to 30 percent. Most German towns lost 25 to 50 percent, but in little Bremen, 6966 individuals, known and identified, were lost: close to two-thirds of that population. Even remote parts of Europe were hard-hit. The plague wrought such havoc in Scandinavia that the king of Sweden proclaimed, "By it, most of our countrymen are dead." An Irish Franciscan described the siege of his country, while being himself "as if among the dead, waiting till death do come"; he left blank parchment ready for a future chronicler to record the outcome, "if by chance anyone may be left in the future, and any child of Adam may escape this pestilence and continue the work thus commenced."

Doctors could neither cure nor prevent the disease. The level of medical expertise can be gauged from the fact that Gentile of Foligno, a physician at the University of Padua, ascribed the plague to planetary motions which caused "poisonous material [to be] generated about the heart and the lungs." Yet medical services were sought and paid for, and many professionals dutifully tended the sick at great personal risk to themselves. One doctor described his experience with a patient in Lucca during the outbreak of 1373: "I cared for [this woman] with the greatest devotion, constantly, both day and night, six or eight times a day. She died of the worst kind of plague, and the most contagious: that involving spitting blood. This went on for four entire days. I would never have treated her for money, but for love alone."

Not all physicians were so devoted. Many escaped to the countryside or declined to serve. In Florence, so many young men of elite families now sought other and safer careers that the profession of medicine became the business of foreign immigrants. In Brescia in 1477, according to one chronicler, the ill perished because of lack of medical care: "The physicians were few in number, and nearly all succumbed while in service." In 1479, the Italian city of Pavia hired Giovanni Ventura as a municipal plague doctor. His contract specified that he must "treat all patients and visit infected places as it shall be found to be necessary," and that he would be suitably rewarded "according to how he shall behave himself." If he died in the course of his duties—"may God forbid it"—his heirs would be relieved of the obligation of restoring the salary he collected in advance. That salary was remuneration high enough, apparently, "to attract a doctor to a job which bordered on suicide."

Like the historian Thucydides (see Chapter 4), witness to a different but similarly lethal epidemic in ancient Athens, the poet and scholar Giovanni Boccaccio (1313–1375) described how moral values and human affection crumbled in the presence of ubiquitous death. In his account (which may have embroidered upon reality to some extent) terrified fathers abandoned their own children, daughters their own parents. Physicians neglected the sick, and grave-diggers cast the carcasses of the lost into unmarked and unconsecrated graves. The devastation wrought by the Black Death is a reminder of how fragile is the shell of civilization, and how easily ruptured by crisis, tragedy, and dislocation.

From 1347 until 1720, the plague struck anew each generation of Europeans. City populations shrank markedly after the first onslaught, and each new episode eroded population gains (although slow net growth was achieved after 1500). The fear of disease darkened the urban landscape for centuries.

PRIVATE LIFE

Despite the devastating effects of the plague on family life, the family remained a vital organism for urban Europeans, a refuge against danger, the matrix of social values, the core community in a social world made up of interlocking rings of diverse communities. In western and northern Europe it was a nuclear family, centered on a married couple who together established a household independent of their elders. For women, especially, marriage was the central reality of life. Instructed by their fathers, the Church, and their husbands in turn, women carried on the business of the household and bore responsibility for the critical tasks of bearing and raising children.

Although marriage was common to all social classes, among the middle and upper classes it differed in involving the transfer of property. Thus it was a concern for merchants and tradesmen, for whom, like the nobility, the preservation of property across the generations was of the utmost importance.

Marrying for Love and Money

Today, young people generally marry because they are in love. In medieval Europe, they married to perpetuate the human species and, in some cases, to preserve family wealth. Marriage was a supremely serious matter, requiring proper behavior (as defined by the Church, by law, by families) of both spouses and obedience and diligence, particularly of wives.

The Church considered that a marriage had been constituted whenever a man and a woman expressed to each other words of consent. These words might be uttered in private, and the marriage would be valid whether or not the family approved, or whether a priest was present. Love, in its broader sense, was

The Assault of the Plague

The epidemic of bubonic plague known as the "Black Death" struck Europe for several years beginning in 1347, and then recurred periodically for another 400 years. Two of those who witnessed its onslaught are represented, although their vivid descriptions must be understood as literary constructions and cannot be considered to be wholly accurate. They convey, nevertheless, a sense of the devastation of human life caused by the epidemic.

Giovanni Boccaccio, who survived the plague in Florence (1348), describes the disease and its effect on the people: In the year of Our Lord 1348 the deadly plague broke out in the great city of Florence, most beautiful of Italian cities. ... The plague had arisen in the East some years before, causing the death of countless human beings. It spread without stop from one place to another, until, unfortunately, it spread over the West. Neither knowledge nor human foresight availed against it, though the city was cleansed of much filth by chosen officers in charge and sick persons were forbidden to enter it. ...

At the onset of the disease both men and women were afflicted by a sort of swelling in the groin or under the armpits which sometimes attained the size of a common apple or egg. ... From these two starting points the boils began in a little while to spread and appear generally all over the body.

Afterwards, the manifestation of the disease changed into black or livid spots on the arms, thighs and the whole person. ... Like the boils, which had been and continued to be a certain indication of coming death, these blotches had the same meaning for everyone on whom they appeared. ... Neither the advice of physicians nor the virtue of any medicine seemed to help or avail in the cure of these diseases. ... The fact was that not only did few recover, but on the contrary almost everyone died within three days of the appearance of the signs. ...

More wretched still were the circumstances of the common people and, for a great part, for the middle class, for, confined to their homes either by hope of safety or by poverty, and restricted to their own sections, they fell sick daily by thousands. There, devoid of help or care, they died almost without redemption. A great many breathed their last in the public streets, day and night; a large number perished in their homes, and it was only by the stench of their decaying bodies that they proclaimed their death to their neighbors. Everywhere the city was teeming with corpses.
(Giovanni Boccaccio, *Decameron*, 1348–1353; trs. F. Winwar, 1955)

Henry Knighton observes the arrival of plague in England (1348): In this year [1348] and in the following one there was a general mortality of men throughout the whole world. ... Then that most grievous pestilence penetrated the coastal regions [of England] by way of Southampton, and came to Bristol, and people died as if the whole strength of the city were seized by sudden death. For there were few who lay in their beds more than three days or two and a half days; then that savage death snatched them about the second day. In Leicester, in the little parish of St. Leonard, more than three hundred and eighty died; in the parish of the Holy Cross, more than four hundred, and in the parish of St. Margaret in Leicester, more than seven hundred. And so in each parish, they died in great numbers. ...

During this same year, there was a great mortality of sheep everywhere in the kingdom; in one place and in one pasture, more than five thousand sheep died and became so putrefied that neither beast nor bird wanted to touch them. And the price of everything was cheap, because of the fear of death; there were very few who took any care for their wealth, or for anything else. ... After the aforesaid pestilence, many buildings, both large and small, in cities, towns, and villages had collapsed, and had completely fallen to the ground in the absence of inhabitants. Likewise, many small villages and hamlets were completely deserted; there was not one house left in them, but all those who had lived in them were dead. It is likely that many such hamlets will never again be inhabited. ... Moreover, both the magnates of the kingdom and the other lesser lords who had tenants, remitted something from the rents, lest the tenants should leave, because of the lack of servants and the dearth of things. ... They either had to excuse them entirely or had to fix them in a laxer manner at a small rent, lest ... the land everywhere remain completely uncultivated. And all foodstuffs and all necessities became exceedingly dear. ...
(Henry Knighton, *Compilation of Events in England*, Book VI; eds. J. Ross, P. McLaughlin, 1949)

understood to be at the center of family life, a bond of mutual affection making wife and husband equal partners in the act of marriage (although the wife nevertheless was expected to remain subordinate to her husband in practical affairs). The Church posed one model for the medieval household: the companionate model, the joining of spiritual equals.

Owners of property posed another: the patriarchal model. The family patriarchy was a miniature society in which the male "partner" exercised authority over wife, children, servants, and others. Its purpose was to preserve and transmit property from fathers to sons. Like the families of Greece and Rome, those of the medieval nobility were patriarchies. Merchants adopted the same pattern of family structure, husbanding their resources for the benefit of male heirs and the continuity of the lineage.

Husbanding resources meant restricting inheritance. In many regions of Europe, and consistently in England, only the eldest son inherited. Younger sons were provided for, where possible, by guidance into lucrative careers at royal courts, in knightly armies, or in the Church. Or they were sent out with their parents' blessing to "seek their fortune."

Daughters faced a different prospect. They were excluded from the inheritance lest they remove wealth from the father's lineage on marrying into that of a stranger. Instead, girls received when they married a set sum, a dowry, which was their only and final claim upon paternal wealth. Invariably less than an equal share of the **patrimony** (familial wealth), the dowry could, however, be a sizable sum of money, and might include clothing, jewelry, investments, and even land. At the death of the endowed woman, the dowry passed to whomever she designated: often to her children. In this way, dowry wealth was subtracted from her father's "line" and grafted upon her husband's.

What happened if the woman's husband died? If she was young enough to remarry, she returned to her father's house. Her husband's family was responsible for returning the dowry to the wife's family of birth, where it might be used a second time to purchase a good marriage. If she did not return to her father but stayed with her husband's family, the dowry, too, would remain with her and pass to her designated heirs.

Prudent fathers were torn between responsibility to a child and duty to the patrimony. They calculated carefully before assigning a dowry to a daughter, for the drainage of wealth could be ruinous: "girls do not make families but rather 'unmake' them," warned Marguerita Datini (wife of the merchant Francesco Datini, c. 1335–1410). Often the decision was made not to arrange for a daughter to marry but to send her instead to a convent. Convents also required a dowry of new entrants. But the conventual dowry was much smaller than the marital dowry. The parsimony of many fathers populated European convents with nuns whose piety was less than ardent.

Although theoretically the wife's property, the dowry was used and administered (but not owned) by her husband, who alone was viewed as competent to do so. A married woman is "a kind of infant," wrote an English lawyer; her husband, he continued, is "her prime mover, without whom she cannot do much at home, and less abroad." In Italy, it was commonly understood that no wife could make a contract without the consent of her husband. And the code of the German **duchy** of Saxony declared that "when a man takes a wife, he also takes all her goods into his power by right of guardianship."

Among less prosperous people, too, the destinies of male and female children were radically different. At an age as young as seven, a boy might be apprenticed to a craftsman to learn a trade or sent off to a wealthier family as a domestic servant—choices narrowing the range of future opportunities. Poor girls were also dispatched from the family as workers or servants—but with lower pay and status than their brothers. Girls also faced the further dilemma of marriage. To marry, they needed a dowry. If neither their father nor their employer provided one, they labored to accumulate one themselves. Without a dowry—with rare exceptions—a girl did not marry.

Towns had virtually no place for unmarried women (unless cloistered, or under religious vows). The proportion of unmarried women was well under 10 percent in the larger towns, probably less in smaller ones. These women needed to be disposed of in some way. Some girls were dowered by the town or by a benefactor. Some found in domestic service an alternative to marriage. Others—some burdened with illegitimate children—sought refuge in one of the many asylums medieval towns provided for the deserted and the widowed, reformed prostitutes and unwed mothers. Others might live with a family: their father's or someone else's. The "families" of the affluent included—in addition to those related by blood—servants and foster children, retired widows or widowers, apprentices and journeymen.

Domestic Duties Most households were led by a husband who commanded, while his wife obeyed and labored, as described in *Witnesses* on p. 342. Delineating the duties of a housewife in the fourteenth century, the anonymous "Goodman of Paris" advised a young woman to keep the fire smokeless and the bedchamber free of fleas. She was to see to her husband's comfort, "and I pray you keep him in clean linen, for that is your business." Husbands must labor hard in the world "and journey hither and thither, in rain and wind, in snow and hail, now drenched, now dry, now sweating, now shivering, ill-fed, ill-lodged, ill-warmed and ill-bedded." In these trials he would be sustained by thoughts of the care his wife would provide: "to be unshod before a good fire, to have his feet washed and fresh shoes and hose, to be given good food and drink. ... And the next day fresh shirts and garments."

The housewife was expected to spin and weave, care for children and servants, purchase and store supplies, entertain guests, and tend the ill. "She takes care of the granary and keeps it clean, she takes care of the oil-jars ...," wrote the popular preacher Saint Bernardino (1380–1444). "She sees to the salted meat ... she sees to the spinning and the weaving [and] to the whole house." In childhood, advised an expert on household management, a girl should be taught "everything about the house, to make bread, clean capons, sift, cook, launder, make beds, weave French

Family Life

The intimate relations between people of the past can't quite be comprehended by people living today, when women and children (in modern Western nations) have been liberated from the power of fathers and husbands. Yet parallels do exist. In the first passage, a wife is advised to stifle her complaints and allow her husband to remain "lord and master" of his household. In the second, mothers are urged to nurse and rear their own children. In the third, a widow advises her absent son about his health and his conduct far away from home.

The Goodman of Paris shows how a wife must yield to her husband (c. 1393): And if you cannot move him [your husband] that he turn his wrath from you, take heed that you make not plaint thereof to your friends or to others, so that he may perceive it, for he will think the less of you and will remember it another time; but go you into your chamber and weep gently and softly in a low voice, and make your plaint to God; and thus do all wise ladies. And if perchance he be prone to wrath against another person less near unto him, do you wisely restrain him. ...

Whereof I say unto you that it behoveth good ladies, subtly, cautiously and gently, to counsel and restrain their husbands from the follies and silly dealings whereunto they see them drawn and tempted, and in no wise to think to turn them aside by lording over them, not by loud talk, by crying to their neighbours or in the street, by blaming them, by making plaint to their friends and parents, nor by other masterful means. For all this bringeth nought but irritation and the making of bad worse, for the heart of man findeth it hard to be corrected by the domination and lordship of a woman, and know that there is no man so poor nor of so small value that would not be lord and master when he is wed.

(*The Goodman of Paris*, c. 1393; ed. J. Adams, 1969)

Francesco Barbaro advises mothers to nurse their own children (1415): In pregnancy the same blood of which women are otherwise cleansed in their monthly effusions is held back. This time, following the laws of nature, the fetus is nourished by this blood until the time of birth arrives. Then, as in all animals who give birth, the nourishment of milk is supplied. For this, Nature has made breasts, which, like bountiful fountains, nourish the young child and help it to grow gradually in all its parts. Moreover, women have been given two breasts so that if they have twins they may easily suckle and nourish them together. All these things have been thus provided with great wisdom, but they still might seem to have been done in vain except that Nature has also instilled in women an incredible love and affection for their offspring. Here the special care and diligence of Nature can be observed, for while she has placed the nipples of other animals under their stomachs, in women she has affixed them on their breasts so that they may feed their children milk and fondle them with embrace at the same time, kiss them easily and comfortably, and, as they say, receive them to their bosoms.

Thus Nature has assigned to women the duty of bearing and rearing children not only by necessity but also with her singular goodwill and love. ... Therefore, women ought to consider it best, very honorable, and commendable to suckle their own children, whom they should nourish with great love, fidelity, and diligence; or they may commit this part of their duty to well-trained nurses who will esteem and care for the infants, not with a pretended enthusiasm nor out of mercenary consideration.

(Francesco Barbaro, "On Wifely Duties," 1415; eds. B. Kohl, J. Witt, 1978)

Alessandra Strozzi entreats her son to write often and to do as she says (1447): Do not wonder if I do not write to you often, as I am immersed in Caterina's affairs. I shall compensate for my silence when Matteo learns to write. You should not emulate me. Send me a letter with every courier, even if you say no more than that you and Niccolò are well. I do not know how you are conducting yourself in your affairs. God knows of my unhappiness when I learned that you could not come to see me while visiting Livorno; such displeasure can only be expressed orally and not in writing. May it please God that I see you again in good health before I die. Above all, my son, make certain to behave well so that, while last year you caused me so much grief by your poor behavior, now you may give me consolation. Consider well your position, and reflect upon all the benefits that Niccolò has rendered to you. You will then realize that you should kiss the earth on which he walks. You are more obligated to him than to your father and mother for all that he has done for you; no one else would have done the same. You should not be ungrateful to him for his past and present favours. I do not wish to say anything more, for you must be able to understand. You are not a little boy any more, as last July you were already 19. Above all, save some money. You will need it because your conditions are even worse than you think. Nor do I wish to say anything more in this letter. May God keep you from evil. ... And if you are the treasurer of your company behave honourably, keep your hands clean so that I may not suffer more pain than I already did in the past.

(Alessandra Strozzi, *Lettere di una gentildonna fiorentina del secolo XV ai figliuoli esuli*, 1447; ed. A. Molho, 1969) purses, embroider, cut wool and linen clothes, put new feet onto socks. ..." The wife who cheerfully met these expectations was genuinely appreciated. "These are so useful to us, so convenient, / That if they were lacking, the good order of life would be diminished," wrote the eleventh-century poet and bishop Marbode. "Of all the things that God has provided / For human benefit ... there is nothing lovelier, / Nothing better, than a good wife ..." More frequently encountered than such expressions of appreciation were attacks on woman's character. They were, claimed the anonymous fifteenth-century author of *Fifteen Joys of Marriage*, domineering, lascivious, flighty, demanding. Insatiable and devious, he continued, women make the putative joys of marriage the "greatest torments, pains, sorrows, and sufferings to be found on earth, than which no others are worse or more continuous, except the cutting off of one's limbs."

Women who did not meet a husband's expectations could be beaten—in moderation, moralists urged. A regional French law code stated the general principle: "Provided he neither kills nor maims her, it is legal for a man to beat his wife when she wrongs him—for instance, when she is about to surrender her body to another man, when she contradicts or abuses him, or when she refuses, like a decent woman, to obey his reasonable commands." Even if women were not physically abused, they were limited to the sphere of the household and (in artisan circles) the marketplace, and carefully supervised. In Italy, upper-class women lived virtually under house arrest, rarely leaving except, with chaperone in tow, to visit their peers or go to church. The "**honor**" or reputation of the family was at stake if a wife's chastity were suspect or a daughter lost her virginity.

Not only fathers and husbands, but magistrates and churchmen also kept a close watch on women's behavior. **Sumptuary** laws defined, among other levels of consumption, the limits of appropriate dress. Although these applied to men also, they chiefly targeted women. They admonished women to dress modestly and in accord with their social standing, lest those of lower social rank overreach themselves by sporting the furs, velvets, and jewels of the privileged. Observing that young women formerly dressed modestly, the Italian storyteller Franco Sacchetti (c. 1330–1400) complained that now they "go attired like common women, wearing caps, and collars and strings round their necks, with divers kinds of beasts hung upon their breasts." The purpose of much of this finery—especially the jewels—was to announce the status of the husband, whose property it remained. "The very goods which a man giveth to his wife, are still his own, her chair, her bracelets, her apparel, are all the goodman's goods. ..."

Those moralists who insisted on propriety in dress also defined the limits of women's sexual behavior. The fifteenth-century Sienese friar Cherubino forbade intercourse on Sunday, during Lent, on the day of taking holy communion, during menstruation (given to women by God "to humble you," Cherubino explained), pregnancy ("or else you are worse than beasts"), or lactation. Intercourse should not be too frequent (a risk to health); it should be performed face to face; without the use of hands or mouth to stimulate the genitals ("And you call this *holy matrimony?*"); without obscenity, visible nudity, violence, or insult.

Ejaculation outside the body, recognized by Cherubino as a method of birth control, was deemed a sin. As for "place," Cherubino is explicit: "You must come together in those generative parts, ordained by God for that purpose, for generation," and intercourse achieved with any other organs is considered to be a mortal sin: "You must not consent to so great a sin; rather let yourself be beaten, rather than be forced to do this. And if ... your husband batters you, submit with good will; for you would die a martyr, and you would go surely to eternal life."

Like the other sexual prohibitions imposed by church doctrine, this one was guided by the principle that sexual intercourse occurred only for the sake of procreation. "Coitus is only permitted for the sake of offspring," pronounced the fourteenth-century physician Bernard de Gordon. If its goal were not the generation of new life, it should not occur at all.

Childbirth and Childrearing

Caring for a newborn infant and rearing the young child were seen as a mother's responsibility, performed so as to meet the expectation of her husband, the Church, and society at large.

Most women faced a future of frequent conception, pregnancy, and childbirth. Elite women married in their adolescence, and poorer women in their mid-twenties. Once married, they experienced a cycle of childbirth and nursing and childbirth again. Poor women gave birth every twenty-four to thirty months on average, rich women as often as every year. Rich women were enormously fertile. The wealthier households of Italian cities, for instance, reared more than twice as many children as the poorest.

For a brief moment, the patrician woman who gave birth to a legitimate child was favored with an assortment of elaborate honors. Her bedchamber, for example, might be richly adorned with the finest textiles—linen and silks intricately embroidered with gold thread. Even to be pregnant won a woman recognition. In Piero della Francesca's (c. 1420–1492) painting of the pregnant Virgin (see p. 336), the lovely young woman proudly points to her belly in which she is carrying the infant Christ, signifying to her viewers not only the miracle of his conception but also the prestige enjoyed by the ordinary woman soon to bring forth life.

The realities of childbirth were, of course, somewhat less delightful than the attendant honors suggested. If the unborn child were illegitimate, the mother faced both shame and poverty. Even married women had much to fear in the painful and dangerous process of giving birth. Many women died in childbed, a factor that explains the relatively high mortality rates, compared to those for men, for the years from puberty to menopause.

If childbirth was full of risk, so was infant life. Infants and children died at an appalling rate, especially in the cities. In the countryside, the rate of mortality for children under five was 25 to 30 percent; in large cities, that figure climbed to 40 to 50 percent. In fifteenth-century Florence, of the children born to well-off families, 45 percent died before the age of twenty. The death of children figured sadly in the histories of many prominent families. Of the twenty-one children of the sixteenth-century Nuremberg patrician Konrad Paumgartner, only nine married and had children. From about 1400 to about 1600, sixty-five children were born into the Rorach family of Frankfurt. Of these, eighteen died before their fathers did, and only twelve married. Of the twenty children born to the first three wives of the fifteenth-century Florentine merchant Gregorio Dati, only five survived; of the six to which his fourth wife gave birth, three survived.

Did parents learn from the deaths of children not to hope and not to love too much? Perhaps; but some at least grieved each loss. The Florentine Alessandra Macinghi Strozzi wrote that the death of her son Matteo in 1459 caused her to suffer "the greatest pain in my heart that I have ever experienced." When Gregorio Dati's three-month-old son died in 1411, he wrote poignantly of the "very attractive baby boy" that "God was pleased to call the child very shortly to Himself," where he could now intercede with God for the benefit of his parents' souls.

Surplus Children Some children were unwanted. Measures were taken to control birth through contraception or abortion, measures that the Church vehemently condemned. Saint Bernardino (1380–1444) believed that these diabolic practices were so widespread as to result in the damnation of a great many souls: "I believe that very few of those in the married state will be saved. Out of 1000 marriages, 999 … are of the devil." Friar Cherubino believed that some women tried to prevent conception or achieve abortion, and that when those attempts failed, "then

***Ghirlandaio*, Birth of the Virgin, 1486–1490:** *Ghirlandaio's lavish and stately depiction of the Virgin birth—which most certainly would not have happened in a luxurious palace decorated with a row of naked boys, or putti—reveals the characteristic feature of childbirth in pre-modern Europe. It was a collective event, and one which involved only women, and many of them. Here midwives and servants prepare to bathe (or to baptize) the infant, as neighbors arrive to observe and to pay their respects to the hero of the day: the mother, elevated in her bed, who surveys with lordly interest the care taken of the baby to whom she has just given birth. (Santa Maria Novella, Florence)*

when the creature is born, they beat it, and would want to see it dead, so that they can be free to go freely about their business, here and there."

Sometimes, in desperation, women did kill the infants for whom they could not care. Infanticide was considered a grave crime meriting the death penalty. It was the only crime other than witchcraft for which women faced capital punishment. Often infanticide went undetected, disguised as a case of "overlaying"—death caused when a sleepy or drunken parent or nurse rolled over in bed and suffocated a fragile child.

Unwanted children were more often abandoned than murdered. "How many infants ...," Boccaccio wailed, "are given over to the forests, how many to the wild animals and to the birds!" Although Boccaccio bemoaned the practice, abandonment was not considered sinful. In an era when poor families with too many children to feed faced starvation, and when wealthy families with too many heirs faced the dissipation of their wealth, it was considered a plausible method of family limitation. Often the abandoned babies were "found," and put to work as a servant or a prostitute, or foster child. The generally small size of poor families and the vast numbers of servants, some of them very young, can be explained in part by the practice of abandoning children.

One solution to the problem of child abandonment was the foundling hospital. Several of these institutions dedicated to the care of unwanted children were founded as early as the seventh and eighth centuries, in France, Germany, and Italy. Noteworthy foundling hospitals were established in Venice and Florence, in the fourteenth and fifteenth centuries. The task, however, was insuperable, and their resources were insufficient. The foundlings were very young, mostly female (more often unwanted than boys), and not yet weaned. These infants needed to be sent out to **wet nurses** in the country, as there was no adequate substitute for breastfeeding. Often they did not survive the experience. Death rates were around 50 percent at Florence's "Hospital of the Innocents" in the fifteenth century. In Lyons and Paris, foundling hospitals amounted to, in one critic's words, "a veritable system of social infanticide."

Like any other infants at this time, the abandoned babies in the municipal hospital needed to be breastfed for eighteen to twenty-four months. Other food and drink were often contaminated or indigestible, even if they could be fed to a nursling; human milk alone was suitable, giving adequate immunity. Most women must have spent much of their time nursing babies—especially poor women, since wealthy ones often avoided this task. The words of the Italian fifteenth-century physician Paolo Bagellardo imply that social distinction: "If the infant is a child of the poorer class, let it be fed on its mother's milk." Despite the fact that, as one pediatric historian has written, "almost every writer on the subject points out the desirability of maternal suckling," most elite women declined to nurse their babies as shown by the passage quoted in *Witnesses* on p. 342.

The wet nurses who sustained upper-class babies and foundlings entrusted to them were, of necessity, lactating women who had recently given birth themselves, who had consigned their own offspring (if it still lived) to another's care (perhaps for even lower pay). Employers (generally fathers or their agents) took great pains to select a suitable nurse. They considered the health, age, and character of the candidate, the magnitude of her breasts, and the consistency of the product. "It should be white, sweet to taste and free from any unnatural savour," counseled one expert, "not too watery and not too thick." A drop placed on a fingernail should be dense enough to hold its form. Milk was to be examined thus diligently because it was distilled, physicians believed, from the nurse's blood, and was thus imbued with her character. As much as her speech and behavior, it would shape, for better or worse, the character of the nursling.

Thus, in the medieval city, male heads of households made the decisions that framed the lives of women, whose behavior was strictly regulated, and of children, whose very existence was precarious. Their scrutiny was searching and their right to command unquestioned. The openness and vitality otherwise characteristic of the town did not apply to the intimacy of private life.

THE CITY AND THE BOOK

From the thirteenth century, urban households began to acquire books. Merchants and artisans and their wives learned to read, and reading encouraged them to think about more than their money and their shops. In the towns and cities of medieval Europe, for the first time since antiquity, laymen and even women learned to read and sent their children to school. As those institutions matured, the intellectual world of the medieval city began to produce great books of its own.

Learning and Literacy

The child's first teacher was his mother. Once weaned from the nurse the child was left, until the age of seven, in the care of his or her mother, from whom he acquired his basic knowledge of his own society and culture. From her, the child, male or female, received religious and moral values, and even, in elite circles, some reading and writing. But maternal education was insufficient to prepare townspeople for the tasks of business and government. These necessary skills were provided by schools.

In order to manage their accounts and plan their business ventures, medieval merchants needed, first, to know how to read. In the early Middle Ages that competence had been the prerogative of the clergy, who monopolized the few schools. The townspeople of Europe were the first to break the clerical monopoly on learning, recognizing the crucial value of education in formulating business transactions and keeping records.

By the thirteenth century, most European merchants could read and write. By 1500, the wives of many London merchants were literate also. In 1262, the Lübeck city council created the Saint James School to teach Latin to sons of citizens. In Paris around 1400, the moralist Christine de Pisan urged mothers of the artisan class to have their children "taught first at school by educated people so that they may know how better to serve God," before having them apprenticed to a trade.

In Italy, many children of townspeople attended some sort of school, if only, as in the case of some girls, to learn to sew. High rates of literacy resulted; for example, in Venice in 1587, one-third of all boys and a little more than one-tenth of all girls were literate. In the case of the boys, literacy was largely the fruit of attendance at **vernacular** "abacus schools" (so named after the device that facilitated high-speed arithmetical calculation). Those schools trained young boys to read and write, to do arithmetic, and to keep the books, as a commercial career required. These schools were set up, much like shops, by independent schoolmasters, who thrived only to

the extent that their pupils learned. Such masters were numerous. In fourteenth-century Venice (with a population of about 100,000), between 130 and 165 teachers were laboring at any given time to inculcate a basic curriculum.

The masters ran their schools without the intervention of a "board of education" or any plan from above. Students went early in the morning to spend a long day, all year round. There were no readers or workbooks. The texts they used were the books that parents had at home: moral books, the Gospels, saints' lives, or tales of knights and dragons and battles. Boys also learned "abacus"—not the use of the ancient abacus itself but rather the practical mathematics imported from Arab centers in the thirteenth century. This study comprised arithmetic, algebra, and geometry, and used the numerals still known today as "arabic" rather than the clumsy Roman symbols they replaced. The student of abacus could convert currencies (which varied from city to city), calculate the inheritance due to each member of a family, or compute the annual profits and losses in his father's business.

Some cities established a "public" school, "for the common good." Quite different in purpose from the "abacus" school, these Latin "grammar" schools, staffed by one or two experts, offered an advanced

The City and the Book

Benozzo Gozzoli, Saint Augustine Given to the Grammar Master: *In this fresco by Benozzo Gozzoli (San Gimignano, Italy, 1465) Saint Augustine as a child is being taken to school by his parents, suggesting what that experience might have been like for a city boy.*

Giovanni Boccaccio, A Woman Copying a Manuscript: *A few women did master literacy, as appears in this image in a fifteenth-century French manuscript of Boccaccio's* Le Livre des clercs et nobles femmes, *in which a well-dressed woman copies a book in a well-equipped study.* (Bibliothèque Nationale, Paris)

curriculum designed to prepare a select group of future managers and the sons of patricians. ("Grammar" included the formal study of Latin and Classical literature.) "Since the knowledge of grammar is the origin and foundation of all virtue and knowledge," read the founding document of the school of Lucca in 1371, "it is not only useful but necessary to locate a qualified man who will teach the young and guide their behavior." The city fathers of Treviso, Italy, asserted in 1524 that "nothing else can dignify and exalt a city so much as higher education." In wealthier households, a private tutor offered a similar curriculum. Status and wealth determined what training a boy would receive. Whether obtained in public, at a school, or in private, from a tutor, education was bought.

Class as well as gender limited education for girls. Girls of the middle classes did learn to read, as the figure above shows, but rarely at schools. Female instructors might train them in needlework, as well as the rudiments of reading and arithmetic. Upper-class girls might acquire a Classical education from their fathers, their brothers, or their brothers' tutors.

Although Latin learning among women was rare, city women of the elite classes were avid readers of works written in the vernacular languages of the people—works of devotion (approved by educators) and of romance (disdained). The latter could corrupt a young woman with thoughts of unregulated love or distract her mind from domestic duties. "If you have a female child," warned the fourteenth-century

Florentine moralist Paolo da Certaldo, "set her to sewing and not to reading, for it is not suitable for a female to know how to read unless she is going to be a nun. ..."

In time merchants' sons even went to the university. Their attendance at these temples of abstract thought marked a breakthrough: as recently as the thirteenth century, when the first universities were in their infancy, almost all students were "clerks," members of the clergy (if only the minor clergy), destined for jobs in church or royal **chanceries**. But the knowledge offered by the universities had a far wider appeal. Training in law and medicine (also studied by clerks) would open up lucrative careers. From university lecture halls came the skilled physicians and lawyers, the administrators, managers, letter-writers, and diplomats of a vigorous urban culture. After 1400, many of the patrician leaders of the larger cities possessed university degrees. The town clerks of Germany were now more likely to be laymen than clergy, university graduates from the burgher class.

The language of the university was Latin, and those young patricians seeking an academic degree necessarily mastered it. But such mastery was rare. Most literate townspeople read vernacular books. The greatest storytellers of the fourteenth century—

Bartolomé Murillo, Saint Anne Teaching the Virgin to Read: *This seventeenth-century painting by Murillo shows the child Mary learning to read at the knee of her mother Saint Anne.* (Prado, Madrid)

the Englishman Geoffrey Chaucer and the Italian Giovanni Boccaccio—were avidly read by literate members of the merchant classes, who were their main audience. In the case of Boccaccio, whose *Decameron* was dedicated to a noblewoman, the targeted audience was not only bourgeois, but female: "Most gracious ladies," the narrator began.

Favorite Books

The favorite books of the town-dwellers were all about knights: courtly epics and romantic tales derived from the troubadour tradition. Shopkeepers and their wives delighted in tales of ancient Troy, of King Arthur and his comrades, of Charlemagne and Roland, according to legend the king's most trusted knight. The characters of chivalric romance spilled into daily life as merchants adorned the walls of their houses with tapestries and frescoes depicting scenes from the quest of the legendary Holy Grail (the lost chalice thought to have been used by Jesus), or named their daughters after literary heroines—Isolde and Guinevere. The popular French poem *The Romance of the Rose* (completed 1275–1280) provided both romantic fantasy and keen bourgeois observation— and more than a little hostility toward women.

Although they loved romances, city folk also treasured devotional books: collections of prayers and psalms, lives of the saints, works of moral admonition. In Italy, the *Flower of Virtue* (written between 1300 and 1323) served for leisure reading and instruction alike. It consisted of about forty chapters, each illustrating with a lively story a vice and its dangers or a virtue and its rewards. Sebastian Brant's monumental *Ship of Fools* of 1494 provided an encyclopedia of medieval characters and clever satire of contemporary greed and pettiness.

"How-to" books on manners and household management were also standard fare for the bourgeois reader. In Italy, and especially in Florence, patricians composed such works for their sons. These memoirs gave advice about making sound investments, weaving political alliances, and choosing a spouse, interspersed with memorable events of family history or lists of the birth and baptismal dates of offspring. The general tone is exemplified by Giovanni Morelli's admonition to his sons (in his memoirs composed between 1393 and 1421), after he had retold a cautionary tale of fiscal irresponsibility: "I decided to write this down ... as a warning that no one ... should ever divest himself of his property or rights either from fear, flattery, or any other motive."

Accumulated wisdom was also handed on to children by their mothers. Women who owned books (one historian has discovered as many as 186 laywomen who did in the fourteenth and fifteenth centuries) might bequeath them to their daughters in their wills. The Frenchwoman Christine de Pisan (1365–1430)

addressed to her fatherless son a book entitled *Moral Instructions*. Though she dedicated no such work to her daughter, she nevertheless argued staunchly for the education of women. "If it were customary to send little girls to school and teach them the same subjects as are taught to boys, they would learn just as fully and would understand the subtleties of all arts and sciences. Indeed maybe they would understand them better. ..." Her own father, a royal physician and astronomer, had approved of her studies, although her mother, "who held the usual feminine ideas on the matter," wanted Christine "to spend her time spinning." She did not. Having received a rudimentary education from her father, she pursued her studies as a girl in the library of the king of France and as a wife and widow among her own books. She became the first professional female writer of the modern age.

Christine de Pisan and the *City of Ladies*

Christine de Pisan was not only a learned city woman, but an author who wrote about women and cities. Her *Book of the City of Ladies* (completed 1405) envisions the mystical building of a "city" of the mind in which the heroes are women. The story opens in the author's study, as she recalls the many (male) authors who had written disparagingly of the female sex. She wondered "how it happened that so many different men—and learned men among them—have been and are so inclined to express ... so many wicked insults about women and their behavior." So many books, and so much agreement: "it seems they all speak from one and the same mouth."

As Christine falls into despair, three celestial ladies—Reason, Rectitude, and Justice—appear before her. It is jealousy, resentment, and error that drive male authors to demean women, they explained. Why then, the author asks, do women not defend themselves from these slanders? That task, Lady Rectitude replies, is to be assigned to Christine. She must write a book in defense of women—and build a city that will be their fortress and their monument. Her mission will be to protect the good women of past, present, and future, and to house them forever. "Thus, fair daughter," explains Lady Reason, "the prerogative among women has been bestowed on you to establish and build the City of Ladies [which] will be extremely beautiful, without equal, and of perpetual duration in the world." This city will be their indomitable castle. Wielding the "pick of her understanding," Christine will build it herself, using the tools provided by her advisers: mortar, a ruler, and a balance, the instruments, respectively, of builders, mathematicians, and judges. Men have built the cities of the past; in heaven, God has His. Now there would tower also a city for women.

Yet that city exists only in the imagination. More popular than her *Book of the City of Ladies*, Christine's

Book of Three Virtues (also called *The Treasure of the City of Ladies*) describes the real settings of women's lives—court, city, village. *Three Virtues* outlines the duties appropriate to women in different social categories: royalty, the high nobility, and all the lower social orders—including women of the bourgeoisie, artisanry, and peasantry. In each category, women are enjoined to exemplary behavior and hard work, keeping to their own particular stations in life.

Wives of merchants should wear "handsome, fine, and modest clothing," and beware of dressing beyond their station. "It is very great folly," chides the first modern feminist, "to dress up in clothes more suitable for someone else. ... It is to [women's] advantage and it is their best course of action to wear their rightful clothing, each woman according to her own position." As for the wives of artisans "who live in cities and fine towns," far from tending to luxury, they face

the omnipresent risk of descent into poverty. They must be "very painstaking and diligent if they wish to have the necessities of life," encouraging husbands and workers alike "to get to work early in the morning and work until late, for mark our words, there is no trade so good that if you neglect your work you will not have difficulty putting bread on the table."

Unlike city women of high and low estate, the hard-working peasant wife had no one to advise her. Christine de Pisan reaches out in particular to such women, deprived of the commerce and conversation of the city: "Listen, simple women who live in villages, in low country or in mountains, who cannot often hear what the Church prescribes to every person for his salvation. ... Remember our lessons addressed to you, if it happens to reach your ears, so that ignorance, which can deceive you through lack of knowing more, will not deprive you of salvation." For Christine, it is ignorance, above all other evils, that imperils women, but especially those who have not the good fortune to live in cities.

Dante the Florentine

Like de Pisan, the great Italian vernacular poet Dante Alighieri (1265–1321) was shaped by the life of the city. Dante was born into a substantial Florentine family during the time of that city's birth as a Guelf power, ruled by the party of the "people" (as opposed to the "fat ones," as ordinary citizens described the elite, or patriciate). But the Guelfs, once in power, split into the factions of "Whites" and "Blacks"—more moderate and more radical, respectively. Allied with the former, Dante was on the losing side when the Blacks seized control in 1301. Being absent from the city at the time, he prudently stayed away. His voluntary absence turned into unwilling exile, which lasted until his death.

Even before that turning point of his life, Dante had emerged as the city's foremost poet. From two sources of inspiration—the figure of Beatrice, a woman he loved who came to represent the salvation he craved, and the ideal of a Holy Roman Empire that would truly emulate the kingdom of Heaven—he derived the theoretical bases of his most important work, *The Divine Comedy*. This epic (c. 1308–1314) records Dante's spiritual loss and his self-discovery in the experience of exile and maps out his conception of the afterlife and the course of his own path to God. It is also concerned with the rise and fall of cities: his hopes for his own city of Florence, his despair over the condition of Italian cities in general, and his vision of the heavenly city, realm of perfection.

The shadow of Florence falls on this grandest of Dante's works and colors the poet's journey through the realms of the afterlife—Hell, Purgatory, and Heaven. In his voyage, he encounters many citizens of his native city. Passing through the circle of Hell

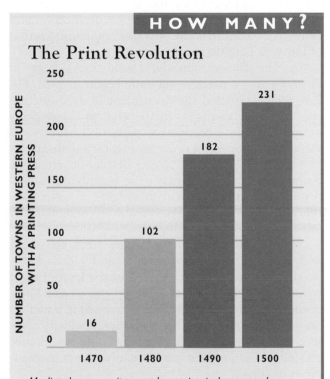

HOW MANY?

The Print Revolution

NUMBER OF TOWNS IN WESTERN EUROPE WITH A PRINTING PRESS

Year	Number
1470	16
1480	102
1490	182
1500	231

Medieval manuscripts rarely survive in large numbers. We know for instance that Wolfram von Eschenbach's Parvizal *was a popular work because over 80 copies have come down to us; about 60 copies of Chaucer's* Canterbury Tales *survive. With the advent of the printing press, however, came the bestseller. In the last three decades of the fifteenth century Thomas à Kempis's* De imitatione Christi *(The Imitation of Christ) passed through 99 editions of up to 200 copies each. At the beginning of the following century Erasmus's* Adagia *passed through 34 editions of 1,000 copies each.*

Sources: S.H. Steinberg, *Five Hundred Years of Printing* (Harmondsworth, Middlesex: Penguin Books 1955); W.T. Berry and H.E. Poole, *Annals of Printing: a chronological encyclopedia from the earliest times to 1950* (London: Blandford Publishing, 1966)

Books to Remember

Dante Alighieri	*Divine Comedy* (1314)
Giovanni Boccaccio	*Decameron* (1353)
Anonymous	*The Goodman of Paris* (around 1393)
Christine de Pisan	*Book of the City of Ladies* (1404–1405)

reserved for gluttons, Dante is hailed by Ciacco, a Florentine. Like all the dead, Ciacco is gifted with the ability to foretell the future; and at Dante's request he predicts the future course of internecine conflict in Florence and makes known to the poet the locations in the nether regions of Hell of other countrymen.

Dante goes on to encounter these Florentines: friends, enemies, and neighbors from the earthly city that had nurtured so much evil and so many evildoers. Faced with eternal torment, they think of themselves still as citizens of Florence. Among the heretics Dante encounters is the Florentine nobleman Farinata degli Uberti. Doubly imprisoned in Hell and in the tomb that will become at the end of time his eternal sarcophagus, Farinata remains proudly Florentine in his outlook despite God and fate: "Erect, / he rose above the flame, great chest, great brow; / he seemed to hold all Hell in disrespect."

Lower still in Hell and nearer its vortex, Dante is surprised to find Ser Brunetto Latini, one of his teachers, among the sodomites (as male homosexuals were termed). Dante learns from this prominent patrician and moralist of his own fate: he will be ground between the factions that struggled over the identity of the city. The conflict between factions that dominated Dante's Florence, as it later would Machiavelli's, is in the forefront of the poet's mind even as he plumbs the lowest depths of the afterworld.

In Purgatory and Paradise, there are more reminders of the urban world. The spirits Dante encounters still identify with their earthly cities and issue dire warnings about the danger of civic strife. The poet Vergil, Dante's companion and guide through Hell and Purgatory, encounters a fellow Mantuan: a near-contemporary of Dante's named Sordello. The compatriots greet each other affectionately: "O Mantuan," cries the latter, "I am Sordello / of your own country," and embraces Vergil. The encounter spurs Dante to reflect on his torn country, Italy, and his own city of Florence. Beset by factional strife, Florence had destroyed itself: "[you have] hacked your own limbs off, and sewed them on."

In Paradise, Dante meets his own ancestor, Cacciaguida, who recalls the city in a simpler age: "Florence, within her ancient walls secure … / lived in sweet peace, her sons sober and pure." Florence was then unbloodied by the factionalism that sent Dante into exile: "the red dye of division." Later Dante concludes that the only just community is that of Heaven: here there are no factions.

In *The Divine Comedy*, Dante looks back at Florence after a twenty-year exile begun in 1301. His love for his city and his resentment of its shortcomings permeate its pages. In the end, as Cacciaguida prophesies, Dante becomes a "party of [his] own"—a vigorous proponent of unity against factionalism.

Factionalism was a great defect of city life. Another was plague, which more harshly devastated populations in towns than in villages. Another was the pressing problem of poverty, more urgent in the urban than the rural setting.

Yet the life of the city, where time was short and precious, where opportunity and profits beckoned, offered intense pleasures. Not the least of these were those of the intellect. City life encouraged forms of thought different from those nourished in a monastic school or university. Town dwellers read with pleasure and studied for advancement. The world they created would produce great triumphs over the centuries to come.

Conclusion

CITY LIFE AND THE MEANING OF THE WEST

Within their walls, city people thought differently than country people, and moved faster. The rich visual forms of the city and the constant activity of its public life continually inspired them (even as their private lives were closely controlled by patriarchs and moralists). In this vital setting, there emerged a distinctively urban culture. Townspeople forged the culture of Europe as much as the monks in their abbeys, knights in their castles, and peasants in their crude huts. Moreover, it was the cities that gave birth to the ideas and the patterns of life that would rupture the fabric of medieval European culture, and set the West on the road to a new consciousness. Soon after Dante penned his *Divine Comedy*, and before Christine de Pisan created her visionary city, northern Italy, Europe's most urban region, would produce the cultural transformation that historians call the "Renaissance."

QUESTIONS TO CONSIDER

1. Why do people desire privacy? Did the desire for privacy, do you think, encourage the creation of private spaces in the urban dwellings of the wealthy, or did the creation of new spaces trigger the sense of privacy?

2. Do urban settings tend to promote tolerance of the diverse groups that settle there? If not, why not?

3. Why does city life promote different kinds of recreation, use of leisure, and charitable activity than does life in the country?

4. Why would city life promote a different kind of literature than life on a rural manor?

5. Would it be more likely that women gain an education in a city, or in the countryside? Why?

SUGGESTED RESOURCES

Atkinson, Clarissa W., *The Oldest Vocation: Christian Motherhood in the Middle Ages* (Ithaca: Cornell University Press, 1991). An interesting survey of medieval motherhood; treats motherhood both as an ideology and an institution.

Cohn, Jr., Samuel K., *The Black Death Transformed: Disease and Culture in Early Renaissance Europe* (London: Arnold. 2002). Offers a radical—and convincing—new understanding of the cause, nature, and immediate effects of the plague.

Dean, Trevor & K. J. P. Lowe, eds., *Marriage in Italy, 1300–1650* (Cambridge: Cambridge University Press, 1998). Defines the Italian case of rules and patterns of marriage at a time when the family determined the destinies of children, especially daughters.

Erler, Mary C., *Women, Reading, and Piety in Late Medieval England* (Cambridge: Cambridge University Press, 2002). Identifies women owners of books, and traces the circulation of books among them, situation female readership within family and community networks.

Farmer, Sharon, *Surviving Poverty in Medieval Paris: Gender, Ideology, and the Daily Lives of the Poor* (Ithaca: Cornell University Press, 2002). Demonstrates how care of the poor was affected by the assumed neediness and worthiness of the afflicted along lines of gender and status.

Hanawalt, Barbara A., *Growing up in Medieval London: The Experience of Childhood in History* (Oxford: Oxford University Press, 1993). This text reconstructs the condition of urban children, including apprenticeship, wardship, inheritance.

Hanawalt, Barbara & Kathryn Reyerson, eds., *City and Spectacle in Medieval Europe* (Minneapolis: University of Minnesota Press, 1994). Twelve essays offering vivid accounts and explanations of public ritual events in English, French, Flemish, Spanish, and Italian settings.

Herlihy, David, *Medieval Households* (Cambridge, MA: Harvard University Press, 1985). An introduction to the history of the domestic family, from the late Roman period to about 1500 C.E., concentrating on Tuscany.

Hollander, Robert, *Dante: A Life in Works* (New Haven: Yale University Press, 2001). An intellectual biography of the poet reconstructed from an exhaustive reading of the whole gamut of his works.

Karras, Ruth Mazo, *Common Women: Prostitution and Sexuality in Medieval England* (Oxford: Oxford University Press, 1996). A synthesis of the legal and social framework for prostitution in medieval England.

Musacchio, Jacqueline Marie, *The Art and Ritual of Childbirth in Renaissance Italy* (New Haven: Yale University Press, 1999). A woman's birthing a child was one of the peak moments of her life, assessed here through the range and meaning of the objects that surrounded the ritual of birth.

Nirenberg, David, *Communities of Violence: Persecution of Minorities in the Middle Ages* (Princeton: Princeton University Press, 1996). Finds the origin of mob violence and Jews and Muslims, prostitutes and lepers not in popular intolerance but elite attempts to define society.

Richards, Earl Jeffrey, ed., *Reinterpreting Christine De Pisan* (Athens: University of Georgia Press, 1992). Seventeen diverse essays about the work of Christine de Pisan and the origins of feminist thought.

Stow, Kenneth R., *Alienated Minority: The Jews of Medieval Latin Europe* (Cambridge, MA: Harvard University Press, 1992). An overview of medieval Jewry in France, Spain, and Italy, from antiquity through the reign of Pope Paul IV.

Christine de Pisan, brief biography:
http://www.distinguishedwomen.com/biographies/pisan.html

Bibliographies of women writers of the Middle Ages (University of Calgary):
http://www.ucalgary.ca/library/subjects/HIST/womenwriters.html

Dante Alighieri on the Web: **http://www.greatdante.net**

Western Civilization Documents CD-ROM

9.1 The Flagellants
9.5 How They Died
9.6 Workers Revolt: The Demands of the Ciompi

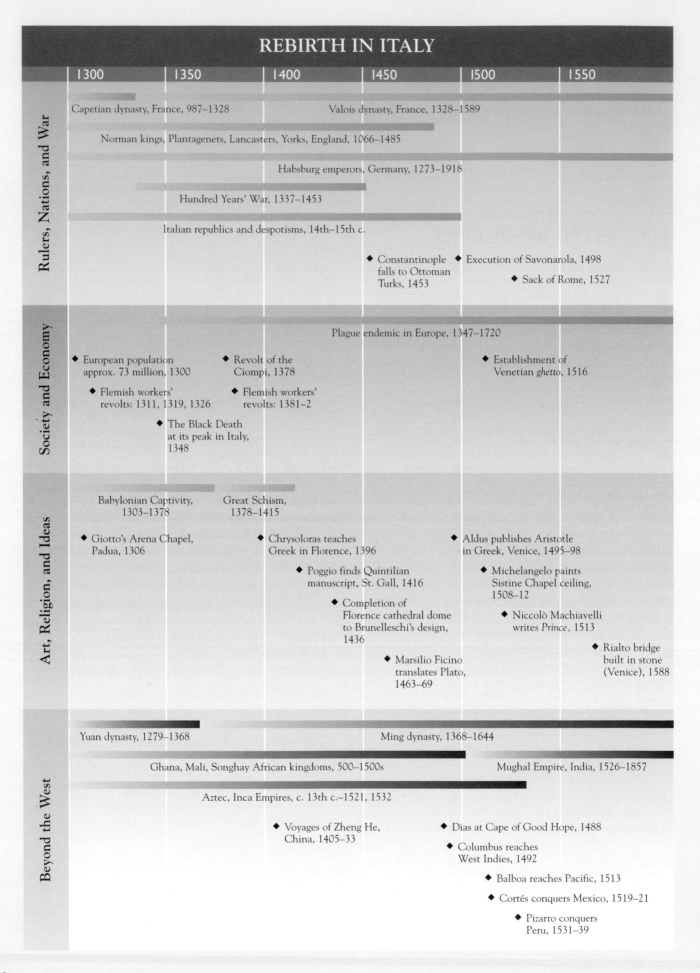

CHAPTER 13

REBIRTH IN ITALY

	1300	1350	1400	1450	1500	1550

Rulers, Nations, and War

Capetian dynasty, France, 987–1328

Valois dynasty, France, 1328–1589

Norman kings, Plantagenets, Lancasters, Yorks, England, 1066–1485

Habsburg emperors, Germany, 1273–1918

Hundred Years' War, 1337–1453

Italian republics and despotisms, 14th–15th c.

◆ Constantinople falls to Ottoman Turks, 1453

◆ Execution of Savonarola, 1498

◆ Sack of Rome, 1527

Society and Economy

Plague endemic in Europe, 1347–1720

◆ European population approx. 73 million, 1300

◆ Revolt of the Ciompi, 1378

◆ Establishment of Venetian *ghetto*, 1516

◆ Flemish workers' revolts: 1311, 1319, 1326

◆ Flemish workers' revolts: 1381–2

◆ The Black Death at its peak in Italy, 1348

Art, Religion, and Ideas

Babylonian Captivity, 1303–1378

Great Schism, 1378–1415

◆ Giotto's Arena Chapel, Padua, 1306

◆ Chrysoloras teaches Greek in Florence, 1396

◆ Aldus publishes Aristotle in Greek, Venice, 1495–98

◆ Poggio finds Quintilian manuscript, St. Gall, 1416

◆ Michelangelo paints Sistine Chapel ceiling, 1508–12

◆ Completion of Florence cathedral dome to Brunelleschi's design, 1436

◆ Niccolò Machiavelli writes *Prince*, 1513

◆ Marsilio Ficino translates Plato, 1463–69

◆ Rialto bridge built in stone (Venice), 1588

Beyond the West

Yuan dynasty, 1279–1368

Ming dynasty, 1368–1644

Ghana, Mali, Songhay African kingdoms, 500–1500s

Mughal Empire, India, 1526–1857

Aztec, Inca Empires, c. 13th c.–1521, 1532

◆ Voyages of Zheng He, China, 1405–33

◆ Dias at Cape of Good Hope, 1488

◆ Columbus reaches West Indies, 1492

◆ Balboa reaches Pacific, 1513

◆ Cortés conquers Mexico, 1519–21

◆ Pizarro conquers Peru, 1531–39

CHAPTER

13

REBIRTH IN ITALY

The Civilization of the Italian Renaissance

1300–1550

KEY QUESTIONS

◆ **The Rebirth of Classical Antiquity:** Why did the study of the classics stimulate new kinds of thinking?

◆ **Italian Renaissance Settings:** How did Renaissance civilization develop differently in the republics, such as Florence and Venice, and the courts, such as Milan, Urbino, or Rome?

◆ **Italian Renaissance Profiles:** Of the five figures profiled (Giotto, Pico, Valla, Nogarola, and Machiavelli), which relates most to the classical tradition? Which departs the most from it?

Born Again *In 1416, the noted scholar Poggio Bracciolini (1381–1459) and his friends found, in a Swiss monastery, the long-lost complete text of a book by the first-century* C.E. *Roman orator Quintilian—the* Institutio oratoria *("The Training of an Orator"). Here, in the oblivion of a monastic library, wrote Poggio, intentionally confounding the author and the book, "he was being kept prisoner." The searchers found the "prisoner ... still safe and sound" amid a heap of valuable and neglected volumes, "though filthy with mold and dust ... in a sort of foul and gloomy dungeon at the bottom of one of the towers." At the sight of "countless books ... kept like captives and the library neglected and infested with dust, worms, soot," wrote one of Poggio's companions, "we all burst into tears." The humanist Leonardo Bruni (1370–1444) sent congratulations from Florence: "For Quintilian, who used to be mangled and in pieces will recover all his parts through you. ..."*

These fifteenth-century book hunters recovered Quintilian's work, Quintilian's mind, and, in a sense, Quintilian himself, only fragments of whose work had been known during the previous centuries. In effect, Quintilian was "born again." In different ways, other books of distant antiquity were "reborn" in Italy in the first phase of the cultural movement that historians call the **Renaissance**. Not only the books, but also the art and ideas, the politics and law, the thoughts and the values of Greek and Roman antiquity were "reborn" in the period 1300–1550 as Europeans created a new synthesis of ancient and Judeo-Christian cultures. In that combined heritage the subsequent cultural achievements of the West are securely rooted.

The people who lived during the Renaissance (the French word for "rebirth") did not use that term, or its equivalent in their own language (in Italian, *Rinascimento*; in German, *Wiederbelebung*), but considered their own era as one of "renewal" (in the scholars' preferred Latin, *renovatio*). This renewal, or rebirth, followed an age that most of them considered one of absolute darkness, a "Middle Age" that lay between the glorious past and their own era.

The "Renaissance" began in Italy, home to the most urbanized and commercialized society in Europe apart from Byzantium. In the thriving Italian cities, great wealth provided great opportunities for cultural expression and for the employment of artists and scholars to accomplish it. Here the rediscovery and rebirth of Classical antiquity was achieved. This achievement inaugurated a new phase in Western civilization, and set it on the road to modernity. Renaissance scholars' explorations of the past led them to examine contemporary concerns as well, better understood with the tools of Classical literature, they believed, than with those of medieval theology or philosophy. Those concerns were different in each city (in republics such as Florence and Venice; in large principalities such as Milan and Naples; in small ones such as Mantua, Ferrara, and Urbino; and at the papal court in Rome) and shaped by the interests of both creators and patrons.

In these various settings individuals of extraordinary genius—an unusually large group over a few brief generations—emerged to create the culture of the Renaissance. Of these individuals, profiles of five, whose careers were distinguished by great originality and significance, are examined toward the end of this chapter: one painter, one philosopher, two humanists, and one historian and political thinker. These individuals, four male and one female, span the era from the fourteenth through the sixteenth centuries. They and their contemporaries among Italy's artists, scholars, and patrons created the culture of the Renaissance that diverged from the main patterns of medieval culture and defined the framework of thought and feeling that has continued into the modern age.

THE REBIRTH OF CLASSICAL ANTIQUITY

It was the humanists above all—scholars such as Poggio Bracciolini—who led the drive to restore the literary world of Classical antiquity. Important ones are listed in *Who's Who* on p. 356. The humanists (mostly men, and mostly laymen) developed the capacity to read, understand, discuss, imitate, and value the written legacy of Greece and Rome. These skills were developed through the mastery of what they called, in Latin, the *studia humanitatis*, or "studies of humanity," roughly comparable to what are now called the humanities. These included the studies of Latin (and sometimes Greek) grammar, poetry, rhetoric, history, and moral philosophy.

The humanists first emerged in Italy in the late 1300s as an elite group of intellectuals charged with the administrative, diplomatic, and **rhetorical** functions of the cities and the Church. They became teachers as well, training humanists like themselves, both Italian and foreign, for literary and practical careers; and training the children of wealthy patricians and powerful rulers who were persuaded that the skills taught by the humanists groomed intelligent and capable leaders.

While performing their various official tasks, the humanists also labored to recover Classical texts and their forgotten meanings. Those texts, in turn, took on new life as the humanists employed these Classical forms in order to inquire about the cosmos, the self, and society.

Vittore Carpaccio, Saint Augustine in his Study, 1460–c.1526: *Surrounded by his books, his pens, his votive candles, and a lap dog, in a magnificent Renaissance setting, the fourth-century saint, Augustine, attends to a voice or vision from the divine realm. The painting is intended to convey the humanist ideal of the fulfillment the scholar achieves in the pursuit of the life of the mind.* (Scuola di S. Giorgio degli Schiavoni, Venice)

Recovering the Past

The humanists gathered the books of the ancient Greco-Roman world to master its languages. The book-hunters, such as Poggio Bracciolini, exemplify those who learned to understand the ancient past. Like all humanists, they had a mastery of Latin and sense of history that gave them access to a culture distant from theirs in time and outlook. Fewer humanists acquired Greek, but their contributions, too, were essential.

Poggio found the manuscript of Quintilian's *The Training of an Orator* in the monastery of Saint Gall, in Switzerland, not far from the city of Constance, where high-ranking prelates gathered in council discussed church unity and the threat of heresy. But these were not the matters that concerned Poggio and his friends, secretaries in attendance on Pope John XXIII (an "antipope," deposed in 1415). In search of lost books, they scoured the libraries of venerable monasteries. In such expeditions not only Quintilian's work but those of other Roman authors were brought to light. Humanist book-hunters "rescued" Cicero from bondage, and "discovered" the theologian Lactantius, the philosopher Lucretius,

the architect Vitruvius, the novelist Petronius, the grammarian Priscian, and the playwright Plautus.

In fact, this process of discovery was begun much earlier, as *How Many* on p. 379 shows. Two generations before the rescue of Quintilian, the poet Petrarch (Francesco Petrarca; 1304–1374) had already launched the recovery of antiquity: its texts, its artifacts and monuments, its mental world. Petrarch was the third of three fourteenth-century Italian authors, known to their fellow Florentines as the three "crowns" of literary culture. The others were Dante and Boccaccio (see Chapter 12). All three mined antiquity for models of excellence in human behavior and for insight into the purpose of human life. Of these, Petrarch especially understood the passions that moved those ancient figures and found in them an unsurpassed greatness of spirit. In the preface to his collection of biographies entitled *On Great Men*, Petrarch explained that only the ancients, not his contemporaries, were great. The lives of the latter are material for "satire, not history," he wrote; if they won fame, it was only because they were lucky.

So deep a bond did Petrarch feel with the men of antiquity that occasionally he spoke to them directly.

He addressed letters dated from "the world above" to Cicero, Seneca, Quintilian, Vergil, and Homer, in the realm of the dead. He apologized to Homer (see Chapter 4) for intruding on his time: "I realize how very far removed you are, and I fear lest it may be annoying to you to read so lengthy a letter in the dim light of the lower world." For this Renaissance author, the Greek poet seemed still to be alive.

Petrarch knew Homer by reputation only, for he could not read Greek. He had tried to learn it, without success. Greek manuscripts—including the works of Plato—sat on his shelves, admired but unread. Petrarch's friend the scholar and storyteller Giovanni Boccaccio (1313–1375) also longed to know Greek, but failed. During the 1390s, the visit of the Byzantine scholar and diplomat Manuel Chrysoloras (1350–1415) spurred in Italy the successful study of that ancient tongue. The Greek works that are read in translation today were first made available through the efforts of Renaissance scholars to learn a forgotten language.

Knowledge of Classical Greek had largely disappeared from western Christian Europe after the collapse of Roman hegemony; the modern Greek used by some Italian merchants in commercial dealings was quite a different language. Although some Greek works were known in Latin translation, original Greek texts were not studied in medieval Europe outside of Byzantium and Islamic Spain. If parts of Quintilian, Cicero, and Tacitus were "missing" during the Middle Ages—Latin works on history, on philosophy, on rhetoric—even more deeply "lost" were the tragedies, orations, histories, and dialogues of such Greek authors as Euripides, Demosthenes, Plato, and Thucydides. Like the Latin volumes, these were missing from the shelves of monastery libraries. Had they been available, few people in Europe could have read them.

Even the Latin of the ancients was difficult for medieval scholars. Classical Latin was fluent and complex, whereas contemporary Latin employed a workaday vocabulary and simplified grammar. It was suitable for contracts and treaties, brief communications, handbooks and dictionaries, summaries and lists. But the scribes of courts and abbeys could not fully comprehend the texts of the orator Cicero, let alone the elaborate prose of the historian Tacitus. Scholars based in Italy's busy cities, immersed in the flow of ideas and languages, would in time learn to write the Latin of Cicero, and understand the dense structure of Tacitus.

The culture and traditions of antiquity also were strange to medieval readers. The names of the gods and goddesses, heroines and heroes were perplexing, the names even of the rivers and mountains a mystery. Moreover, the dominance of Christian ideals and images posed a barrier to the understanding of the pre-Christian past. The ideals and the style of Classical Greece and Rome had vanished from

memory. These ancient values were to be reborn (as forgotten books were recovered) through the efforts of the Italian humanists.

The Humanist Program

Besides reading and rereading the Classics, the humanists taught others to read them as well. For those who found the reading difficult, they wrote commentaries. For those who could not learn Latin and Greek, they translated the originals into Italian, French, English, German, and Spanish. These translations provided the vernacular languages of modern Europe with a wealth of new concepts and images, forgotten forms and genres.

By making ancient ideas accessible to contemporary readers, the humanists were the first modern scholars. Through their labors, the surviving fruit of antiquity was transmitted to the modern world. They learned to write history from Classical authors, becoming the first secular historians of Europe. Their scholarly activity is the bedrock of modern literature, modern philosophy and theology, and even modern science.

Renaissance humanists were also creators of new values, suitable for a new age. They lived in a dynamic society centered on cities built on commerce and industry, and they served its leaders. They were secretaries to the merchants of Florence and Venice and to the princes of Milan and Ferrara. Or they were high-ranking patricians, who in their leisure time read and composed works for others to read. Or they were (less frequently) the sisters or daughters of those patricians. They were the teachers of these secretaries, these noblemen, and these merchants. The humanist culture of the Renaissance inevitably reflects the values of the elite society that nurtured it.

For medieval scholars, the residents of cloisters and universities, **contemplation** had been the ideal: quiet and solitary thought. Many humanists shared that outlook—among them Petrarch, who championed the superiority of the solitary life (although decidedly not the monastic one). More often, however, Renaissance humanists focused on the ideas necessary for the active life, and on the moral concerns of city-dwellers. They sought the kind of practical knowledge useful to men of affairs—merchants, bankers, politicians. These humanists admired the active more than the contemplative life. This dimension of their work had been labeled by later scholars "**civic humanism**"—humanism adapted to life in a city. "Civic humanism" was an important dimension, but only one dimension, of Renaissance humanism, which also pursued problems defined by medieval thinkers.

Philosophical Dimensions of Humanism

The perspective of the "civic humanist" is evident in Renaissance discussions of the nature of the human being. Traditionalists viewed human beings as sinful. The humanists countered that God created human beings "in His image and likeness" and declared them "good" (Genesis 1:26–27, 31): only a little less than angels. Herein the humanists proposed the notion of the "dignity of man", as shown in *Witnesses* on p. 358 and *Windows On*, p. 359. Behind the creation of that notion lay another kind of revolution: the humanist revolt against dialectic and the supremacy of Aristotelian metaphysics in favor of rhetoric and the espousal of Plato's ideas.

"How does man resemble God?" asked Florentine humanist, scholar, and statesman Gianozzo Manetti

(1396–1459). The answer: in his activity. Human beings freely enjoy and manipulate the beauty that God has bestowed upon them and imitate the Creator in their own creations. Consider, urged Manetti, what men have produced: "all homes, all towns, all cities, finally all buildings in the world"; paintings, sculpture, arts, sciences, discoveries, "all the different kinds of languages and literatures." In such creativity lies the worth of humanity—its "dignity."

Manetti's views exemplify the strand of Renaissance thought that valued will over intellect, doing over knowing. If will precedes intellect, then the discipline of "rhetoric," which persuades people to do the good, is to be preferred to philosophy, which simply informs them of the truth. Truth acquires life only when communicated in the vivid language that can move the will. As Petrarch proclaimed, "It is better to will the good than to know the truth." Thus poetry, which teaches "other men to speak," wrote another humanist, is—rather than philosophy—the "most fertile mother of all knowledge."

The philosophy the humanists opposed was that of the medieval schoolmen: the clerics who taught theology and philosophy in the universities, and wrought the vast compendia ("summations" or *summae*) of all that was known. The intricate demonstrations of Scholasticism repelled the humanists. But they did not oppose all philosophy. Renaissance thinkers, in fact, rescued from ignorance (as they saw it) the two greatest of the ancient philosophers: Plato and Aristotle (see Chapter 4).

It was from Cicero that the humanists first learned of Plato's immense importance. Then, soon after 1400, the first generation of humanists trained in Greek (largely through the efforts of Chrysoloras) made direct contact with this most profound philosopher. A few years later, Greek scholars laden with books and skills began migrating to Italy from Constantinople, around the time of its fall to the Turks in 1453. Now the way was prepared for the heroic work of Marsilio Ficino (1433–1499): the publication of all of Plato's surviving works.

Son of the physician to Cosimo de' Medici (1389–1464), the de facto ruler of Florence, Ficino acquired the mastery of Greek (as well as the philosophical and humanistic disciplines) necessary for this massive enterprise. Between 1463 and 1469, he translated the text of Plato into Latin, adding his own valuable commentaries to some works. In 1484 the work was printed (thanks to the recent development of the printing press in Germany) for circulation throughout Europe. Ficino and friends recreated Plato's Academy in their gatherings and conversations. Its members discussed serious ideas at lively *symposia*, in imitation of Greek models, and regularly celebrated their hero's supposed birthday.

With the revival of Platonism came the rebirth also of Neoplatonism, a philosophical school of late antiquity. More mystical than Platonic philosophy, Neoplatonism speculated about the unity of the cosmos and the possibility for the human intellect of perfect identification with the divine. As they had in the early centuries C.E., such ideas both resembled and departed from orthodox Christian views of humanity, divinity, and the natural world. They would have a profound and lasting impact upon developments over the next three centuries in science and literature.

Unlike Plato, most of whose works were not read in medieval Europe, Aristotle had circulated in Europe since the twelfth century, in translations from the original Greek or from Arabic versions. These medieval translations, used by the schoolmen in constructing a Christian philosophy, the humanists scorned as incorrect and inelegant.

Now the translation of Aristotle was undertaken again—this time by humanists expert in Greek. Other scholars strove to rescue the master from Latin altogether. One Venetian humanist taught Aristotle in Greek, hoping "to converse" with Aristotle "as though he were alive and in our midst." Between 1495 and 1498, the printer Aldo Manuzio (also called, in Latin, Aldus Manutius; c. 1450–1515) published in five volumes all of Aristotle's works in the original Greek.

WITNESSES

Defining the Self

Among the many projects and themes of the humanists, one has fascinated contemporary and later audiences: that of the "dignity of man," the worthiness of the human being. The humanists Leon Battista Alberti and Giovanni Pico della Mirandola here address that issue. Alberti talks of the striving for excellence that he understands to be the main task of the human being. Pico creates a mythic creation story, based on the Biblical book of Genesis, to isolate a central characteristic of the human condition: free will, the freedom to choose how to act—and to bear the consequences of one's actions.

Leon Battista Alberti sees life as a race in which merit and effort win honor and glory—and idleness and incapacity win shame (1443): Let us suppose a great regatta were being organized in the harbor of Venice, a display of many ships with a multitude of participants. Suppose you were the captain of one of the ships. ... You would strive mightily to reach the goal, where the garlands and trophies of victory were stored and where the prizes and honors were given out to the winning contestants. You would want your ship to share with no more than two others in the first three prizes. ... The other participants in the race, however, would remain unknown. No one would speak of them. These contestants might perhaps have been better off if they had remained on land, taking no active part. They might have been judging, laughing, criticizing the slowness and tardiness of others as much as they liked instead of having, so to speak, shown only languorous enthusiasm in the race. As it is, they find themselves far from admired, indeed they are generally mocked. In the race of human life and the general contest for honor and glory, ... it is best to hope and desire and fight wholeheartedly for a place among the first, if not the first place. One must surpass entirely that obscure and forgotten crowd behind. One must struggle with all the force and cunning at his disposal for a certain fame and a measure of glory.
(Leon Battista Alberti, *On the Family*, 1443; from R. N. Watkins, 1989)

Giovanni Pico della Mirandola explains how each man determines his own nature (1486): *[After God had created all other creatures of sea and land, he turned to the creation of the human being, whose nature he left indeterminate, totally at the disposition of the individual's free will.]* At last the best of artisans ordained that the creature to whom He had been able to give nothing proper to himself should have joint possession of whatever had been peculiar to each of the different kinds of being. He therefore took man as a creature of indeterminate nature and, assigning him a place in the middle of the world, addressed him thus: "Neither a fixed abode not a form that is thine alone nor any function peculiar to thyself have we given thee, Adam, to the end that according to thy longing and according to thy judgment thou mayest have and possess what abode, what form, and what functions thou thyself shalt desire. The nature of all other beings is limited and constrained within the bounds of laws prescribed by Us. Thou, constrained by no limits, in accordance with thine own free will, in whose hand We have placed thee, shalt ordain for thyself the limits of thy nature. We have set thee at the world's center that thou mayest from thence more easily observe whatever is in the world. We have made thee neither of heaven nor of earth, neither mortal nor immortal, so that with freedom of choice and with honor, as though the making of thyself, thou mayest fashion thyself in whatever shape thou shalt prefer. Thou shalt have the power to degenerate into the lower forms of life, which are brutish. Thou shalt have the power, of thy soul's judgment, to be reborn into the higher forms, which are divine."
(Giovanni Pico della Mirandola, *Oration on the Dignity of Man*, 1486; from E. Cassirer, et al, 1989, trs. E. L. Forbes)

Leonardo da Vinci, **Man in a Circle and a Square,** *c. 1485*

Piero della Francesca, **Resurrection,** *Sansepolcro, 1450s*

Michelangelo, Rebellious Slave, *1513*

The notion of human dignity was realized in Renaissance art just as it was in Renaissance humanism, as can be seen in the few examples offered here.

Leonardo da Vinci's study of the human body (above left) shows the perfect figure defining the limits of the square and the circle, and of the perfect cosmos these inscribed figures represent.

In this late-1450s fresco of the Resurrection (above) in the Town Hall at Sansepolcro, Piero della Francesca depicts Christ as a superb human form.

The Rebellious Slave sculpted by Michelangelo (left) for the tomb of Julius II has, as a human being, the consciousness of freedom that drives him to struggle free from the imprisoning block of stone. (top left: Accademia, Venice; right: Pinacoteca Comunale, Sansepolcro; left: Louvre, Paris)

What—other than their nudity—do these three figures have in common?

To continue your investigation of this topic, please go to www.prenhall.com/king for the related **WINDOWS** on the **WEB** activity

Humanism and Society

The humanists also studied their own social world. As they did so, they adapted traditional concepts of moral virtue to the context of urban society. Moral philosophy was one of the disciplines of the "studies of humanity" promoted by the humanists. In their hands, moral philosophy turned to issues of pressing social concern: the limits of avarice; the determinants of social status; the goal of political action; the nature of the family; the role of women.

Poggio Bracciolini posed an economic ethos unthinkable in the Middle Ages in his **dialogue** *On Avarice*. Christianity, in theory, urged the value of poverty over wealth. Medieval preachers (not all of them, but those whom Poggio mocked) warned darkly about the evil of greed. But Renaissance culture was built on the Renaissance city; and the Renaissance city was built—if not on greed—certainly on credit, investment, interest, and profit.

The dialogue form, a favorite device of humanists based on the Classical genre, permitted an author to present two or more competing viewpoints and argue for each plausibly without committing himself to any explicit (or unpopular) point of view. Poggio uses the device to advantage, allowing different speakers to expound traditional and modern arguments about the acquisition of wealth. He programs one provocative speaker to counter the Christian consensus by pointing out the good side of greed. Unlike lust (always harmful, he maintains) greed is sometimes beneficial. "Avarice does not subvert the soul, upset the mind, or impede the study of literature and the acquisition of knowledge." Only the rich can benefit the communities in which they live. Without the wealth accumulated by ambitious men, willing to spend it, "No one would build churches or colonnades; all artistic activity would cease, and confusion would result ... if everyone were satisfied with only enough for himself. ... What are cities, states, provinces, and kingdoms, ... if not the workshops of avarice?"

Poggio's dialogue *On Nobility* boldly addressed a social issue of immense significance for centuries to come: by what right do some men rule over others?

On Studies

A central concern for humanists was the structure of the curriculum of studies for young people. Should they be oriented towards practical, mercantile, clerical, or bureaucratic careers? Or curricula be aimed at broadening the mind and developing the character of young people, male and even (a daring project for the age) female? The humanists opted for the latter, developing the curriculum of the "studies of humanity," which we would today call, with some approximation, the "liberal arts." Here Pier Paolo Vergerio advocates such a program of studies for his pupils, and Leonardo Bruni does so for a prominent noblewoman.

Pier Paolo Vergerio advocates a liberal education and the value of books (c. 1404): We call those studies *liberal* which are worthy of a free man; those studies by which we attain and practice virtue and wisdom; that education which calls forth, trains and develops those highest gifts of body and of mind which ennoble men, and which are rightly judged to rank next in dignity to virtue only. For to a vulgar temper gain and pleasure are the one aim of existence, to a lofty nature, moral worth and fame. It is, then, of the highest importance that even from infancy this aim, this effort, should constantly be kept alive in growing minds. For I may affirm with fullest conviction that we shall not have attained wisdom in our later years unless in our earliest we have sincerely entered upon the search. ...

In [books] are contained the records of the great achievements of men; the wonders of Nature; the works of Providence in the past, the key to her secrets of the future. And, most important of all, this Knowledge is not liable to decay. With a picture, an inscription, a coin, books share a kind of immortality. In all these memory is, as it were, made permanent. ...

How bright a household is the family of books! ... In their company is no noise, no greed, no self-will; at a word they speak to you, at a word they are still; to all our requests their response is ever ready and to the point. Books indeed are a higher—a wider, more tenacious—memory, a store-house which is the common property of us all.

(Pier Paolo Vergerio, *De ingenuis moribus*, c. 1404; from W. H. Woodward, E. F. Rice, Jr., rev. ed., 1964)

Leonardo Bruni advises Battista Malatesta to gain knowledge and verbal proficiency (1424): To sum up what I have endeavoured to set forth. ... Proficiency in literary form, not accompanied by broad acquaintance with facts and truths, is a barren attainment; whilst information however vast, which lacks all grace of expression, would seem to be put under a bushel or partly thrown away. Indeed, one may fairly ask what advantage it is to profess profound and varied learning if one cannot convey it in language worthy of the subject. Where, however, this double capacity exists—breadth of learning and grace of style—we allow the highest title to distinction and to abiding fame. If we review the great names of ancient literature, Plato, Democritus, Aristotle, Theophrastus, Varro, Cicero, Seneca, Augustine, Jerome ... we shall find it hard to say whether we admire more their attainments or their literary power.

(Leonardo Bruni, *De studiis et litteris*, 1424; ibid, 1964)

Traditionally in Europe, the nobility was defined by ability to bear arms, a capacity linked to birth in a privileged order of warriors. Poggio urged a new standard. Only those who are virtuous—wise, learned, productive, committed—are noble. His arguments would reappear many times in the social revolutions of later centuries.

So would those that Alamanno Rinuccini (1426–1504) expressed in his dialogue *On Liberty*. Where Poggio argued that only the wise man is noble, Rinuccini argued that only the free man can be wise. Exiled by the Medici family which had trapped Florence in its snares (as he saw it), Rinuccini argued that despotism spelled the diminution of the human spirit. Liberty is "potential or capacity": only in freedom can human greatness realize itself in creative action.

Humanists also reexamined that institution fundamental to all other social forms: the family. Francesco Barbaro (1390–1454) advised young men about the selection of a wife in his treatise *On Marriage*. She was to be chosen for her virtue, a quality considered more important than beauty or wealth. Only a virtuous woman could competently perform her responsibilities: from unquestioning love and support of her husband to proper decorum and the competent administration of the household staff. The dialogue *On the Family*, by the humanist and architect Leon Battista Alberti (1404–1472) emphasized the critical role of the father. It was he who guided the destinies of all family members, the monarch of his own little kingdom.

These humanist experts on the family were hardly sympathetic to women's own claims for productive roles and for due recognition of achievement. Most humanists, like most intellectuals of the Middle Ages and later eras, largely ignored women. There were exceptions. The educator Vittorino da Feltre (1378–1446) counted at least one young woman among his pupils: Cecilia Gonzaga, daughter of the Marquis of Mantua, who at age ten entertained visitors with her recitations in Greek and Latin. Leonardo Bruni (1370–1444) and Lauro Quirini (c. 1420–c. 1475), in letters advising two women in their studies, assumed that intelligent women could master the same skills as intelligent men. For the most part, however, women made their own way.

Some women, prodigies of Renaissance culture, acquired the difficult skills that Bruni and Quirini outlined, and joined the ranks of the humanists. A handful, no more than a score, these learned women came mostly from ruling or patrician families—often that specialized in learning or even in learning specifically for women. Four women stand out: the Veronese noblewoman Isotta Nogarola (1418–1466); the Brescian Laura Cereta (1469–1499), daughter of a physician (see *Witnesses*, p. 375); the Venetian Cass-andra Fedele (1465–1558), from a family of cultivated citizens; Olimpia Morata (1525–1555), daughter of a Ferrarese court humanist and émigré spouse of a young German Lutheran. Authors of letters, poems, orations, and treatises, they rank with the male humanists of the day.

Humanists skilled in Latin and sometimes Greek, knowledgeable in the literature of the past and conscious of current affairs, reshaped the culture of Italy. But they were not the only creators of the Italian Renaissance. They were joined by other thinkers, by artists and musicians, and by their patrons. Important ones appear in *Who's Who* on pp. 366 and 369.

ITALIAN RENAISSANCE SETTINGS

The Italian cities, where the city clock set a brisk pace and gold reigned instead of kings, were the first home of the Renaissance (see Chapter 11, 12, and Map 13.1). Here the humanists who launched the revival of ancient learning were employed as secretaries, administrators, and teachers. Here princes and bureaucrats hired architects to create buildings reminiscent of those of the ancients; artists to breathe new life into the statues and paintings that filled those buildings; and poets, playwrights, and composers to educate a new generation in the refined tastes of a renewed culture.

These patrons invested their wealth in the new culture not simply to create beauty but also to advance their own interests. The brilliant creations of Renaissance scholars, artists, and writers lent legitimacy to the rule of city councils and upstart princes in a Europe elsewhere ruled by pedigreed noblemen and monarchs. The cities that had begun their careers as laboratories of civic freedom became the stage on which a prince, with a cadre of artists and intellectuals in tow, enacted his ambitions and displayed his power. In due course, the forms thus created in the small Italian cities would be adopted by the nobles and monarchs of the great nations of Europe to enhance their authority.

The following pages survey the manifestations of Renaissance culture in two independent cities, in a series of the greater and the lesser princely courts, and in the papal court at Rome.

Florence: Capital of the Renaissance

"What city, not merely in Italy, but in all the world, is more securely placed within its circle of walls, more proud in its [palaces], more bedecked with churches, more beautiful in its architecture, more imposing in its gates, richer in piazzas, happier in its wide streets, greater in its people, more glorious in its citizenry, more inexhaustible in wealth, more fertile in its fields?" So wrote one humanist chancellor of Florence in praise of his city. Though it measured little more than a mile (1.6 km.) across, Florence was the capital of Renaissance civilization in Italy.

Many reasons have been offered for the preeminence of Florence during the Renaissance. It was a city of merchants—confident and wealthy. It was large: with some 100,000 residents prior to the Black Death in 1348 (though it sank thereafter to less than half that size), one of the largest cities in Europe. It was conscious, if distantly, of a Roman past. It was a republic, with a record of a successful democratic revolution. In addition—and inexplicably—Florence and its environs produced more of the creators of Renaissance culture than any other single setting.

Beginning around 1300, the merchants of Florence diverted some of the profits from foreign trade, banking, and cloth manufacture to the beautification of their city. In a spate of constructive energy, they built, replaced, and refurbished churches, guildhalls, palaces, marketplaces, and bridges. Two central

zones were carved out of the fabric of the medieval city: the area around the palace where the city magistrates met—the Palazzo della Signoria (now called the Palazzo Vecchio, "Old Palace"), and the complex surrounding the cathedral, or Duomo. These new urban centers, respectively political and ecclesiastical, lent majesty and purpose to the jumbled stone structures of Florence.

A piazza, or open square, was constructed in front of the remodeled Palazzo Vecchio—a clear statement of governmental power in a city where open space was rare. A new cathedral and freestanding *campanile*, or bell tower, were constructed on the site of the old cathedral, across from the baptistry, the older, freestanding building where all Florentine infants were baptized. The latter edifice was refurbished with three sets of sculpted bronze doors—two of which were executed in the fifteenth century by Lorenzo Ghiberti (1378–1455). The commission for the north

Map 13.1 Renaissance in Italy, 1300–1570: *From 1300–1570 in Italy, artists and intellectuals worked to fuse the Christian tradition (originating in antiquity but developed during the Middle Ages) with the Greco-Roman tradition in a movement fundamental for the later evolution of the modern civilization of the West: the Renaissance. This map shows the principal places that are associated with the named important figures. Why were so many figures associated with the single city of Florence?*

The Competition Panels

The Sacrifice of Isaac: *Shown here are the two panels, completed 1401–1403, submitted by Brunelleschi and Ghiberti in the competition for the commission to sculpt the bronze doors of the Florentine baptistry. While both represent "The Sacrifice of Isaac," Ghiberti's depiction (above right) is not only more fluent than Brunelleschi's (above left), but shows the would-be sacrificial victim Isaac as a magnificent human figure, honorable in his readiness to suffer without fear: another emblem of human dignity. (Museo Nazionale [Bargello], Florence)*

door was won by Ghiberti in a competition with Filippo Brunelleschi (1377–1446). Each contestant created a sample panel (see above) representing "The Sacrifice of Isaac," both of them powerful images in which the characters are treated naturalistically. But whereas in Brunelleschi's panel Isaac is shown crouching and twisted, with his father clutching his head, preparing to strike the blow, in Ghiberti's panel the boy is shown as a splendid nude, accepting his fate with Classical dignity; indeed, all the figures in Ghiberti's panel are depicted with the grace and restrained eloquence that would characterize Renaissance art. After completing the north door, Ghiberti went on to create the even more magnificent east door, known as the "Gates of Paradise."

Italian architecture had never quite abandoned Classical forms during the Middle Ages. Although many Gothic-style buildings were constructed, the Romanesque style persisted; and in Florence, by the late eleventh century, Classical motifs such as attached columns and pediments had begun to reappear. This process accelerated during the fifteenth century. Palaces displaying elements of Classical style—those of such leading families as the Medici, Rucellai, Strozzi, and Pitti—replaced the old houses in the city center. The Medici Palace shows the cautious approach of its architect Michelozzo (1396–1472). In its basic form—massive and somewhat forbidding, with roughly cut stone on the first

story—it recalls the traditional forms of civic architecture. Yet the building's symmetry, the graceful arches of its courtyard, and its imposing cornice announce the presence of a Classical sensibility.

Churches, too, acquired new elements of Classical style. The Gothic church of Santa Maria Novella was given a Classically inspired façade by Leon Battista Alberti. The contrasting interior and exterior of the church illustrate the process by which the revived antique style of the Renaissance grew out of and overlaid earlier styles. The churches of San Lorenzo and Santo Spirito, designed by Filippo Brunelleschi, were fully conceived as Classical buildings.

The same architect erected over the cathedral crossing (of **nave** and **transepts**) the splendid dome which dominates the city's skyline. Spanning a space of 138 feet (42 m.) in diameter, it was an achievement of great technical, as well as artistic, ingenuity. With the completion of the Duomo (as cathedrals are called in Italy) in 1436, Florence was visually, as well as intellectually, a Renaissance city.

Inside these new and remodeled structures, a new style of painting portrayed the world in the language preferred by patrons of the arts whose tastes were Classical and whose vision of humanity was confident. Artists rendered human figures in three dimensions (not the traditional two), engaged in motion, seemingly inhabiting a real space behind the flat panels and frames in which they were contained. These figures stood in backgrounds familiar from contemporary life: kitchens, gardens, bedrooms, piazzas, and battlefields, as the Uccello's painting below shows. The recently invented science of **perspective** made this realism possible. Artists now knew how to represent three-dimensional bodies on flat surfaces. In subject matter, most Renaissance art remained religious, depicting scenes from the Bible and the lives of the saints, although subjects from Classical mythology and even portraits of living people were beginning to appear.

Patrons of the arts, the rulers of Florence also supported literature and humanism. They read the works of Dante, Petrarch, and Boccaccio. They hired humanists to teach their sons and, sometimes, their daughters. They supported the humanists in their first discoveries and creations, and funded chairs of humanist learning at the local university. Some of them even became humanists themselves: patrician amateurs rank among Florence's most distinguished intellectuals.

In their role as government officials, the city's merchant princes employed humanists to record their debates, to compose letters destined to be read in foreign assemblies, and to formulate documents fixing the terms of war and peace. The chancellors, or chief secretaries, of Renaissance Florence were among Italy's foremost humanists. Well rewarded by their employers, they were also among the city's wealthiest and most important citizens.

The heads of the Medici family, who directed Florence from behind the scenes from 1433 to 1494, were the city's leading patrons of arts and learning. Surrounding themselves with books, paintings, and monuments and philosophers, they thus claimed a legitimacy that they could not claim by birth.

Cosimo de' Medici (1389–1464), the first of his family to assume leadership in Florence, displayed his commitment to Classical scholarship by supporting Ficino's translation of Plato. He also commissioned the rebuilding of the church of San Lorenzo, as well as the monastery of San Marco (where he housed his own remarkable collection of books, making them accessible to the public and thus creating Europe's first public library), and his own family palace. In addition, Cosimo and his son Piero employed several of the sculptors and painters who created some of the most glorious treasures of Western art, including Donatello (1386–1466) and Fra Angelico (Giovanni da Fiesole; c. 1395–1455).

Lucrezia Tornabuoni (1425–1482), wife of Piero de' Medici (r. 1464–1469), was herself a talented poet and enthusiastic patron. Perhaps it was she who inspired her son Lorenzo in his adventures of the spirit. Lorenzo de' Medici (1449–1492), called "the Magnificent," wrote excellent poetry. The brisk lines

Renaissance Style: Perspective

Paolo Uccello, The Battle of San Romano: *Uccello was one of the first painters to apply the theory of perspective to his works. This panel painting, c. 1445, is more a study of how forms (human and equine bodies, ornaments and weapons) inhabit space than it is a depiction of a battle. (National Gallery, London)*

Renaissance Style: Myth

Sandro Botticelli, Primavera: Botticelli borrows figures and themes from ancient mythology in this painting, c. 1482, to depict a hauntingly lovely scene. (Uffizi, Florence)

and charming rhymed pattern of one famous lyric passage by Lorenzo call up sensations of love's joy, the swift march of time, and death's advent:

Quant' è bella giovinezza,	How beautiful is youth,
Che si fugge tuttavia!	But it vanishes, utterly—
Chi vuol esser lieto, sia:	If you wish to be happy, be happy today;
Di doman non c'è certezza	Of tomorrow, there is no certainty.

Lorenzo brought a special flamboyance to the role of the Medici as directors of artistic endeavor. Like his father, Piero, and grandfather, Cosimo, Lorenzo promoted the major artists of the city (though he could not always afford to employ them)—among others, the remarkable Sandro Botticelli (1445–1510) and, in his youth, Michelangelo Buonarroti (1475–1564).

Influenced by the Platonism of Ficino's circle, Botticelli translated into form and color the pagan myths that the humanists unearthed from Classical literature. Even the esoteric messages found behind these myths by philosophers informed some of Botticelli's works. For example, in his renowned painting *Primavera* ("Springtime"), illustrated above, the lovely maiden at the center may represent a Christianized deity or a rational principle, perhaps "humanitas" itself, the human ideal. Contrasting with Botticelli's complexity is Michelangelo's statue of *David*, commissioned by the republican government that replaced the Medici after Lorenzo's death. In its simplicity, its heroic nudity, its confidence, it is a majestic statement of contemporary moral and aesthetic values, and perhaps the most remarkable monument of the age.

Reviewing the Medici family's enormous expenditures on **patronage** projects Lorenzo concluded that they amounted to an "incredible sum"—663,755 florins (at a time when a worker might earn 20 florins per year, or a university professor 100). It was well worth the expense to Lorenzo to acquire the glory reflected by the buildings and paintings and works of literature this money purchased. "Nor would I complain about this, for though many a man would like to have even part of that sum in his purse I think it gave great luster to the state and this money seems to be well spent and I am very satisfied."

Venice: "La Serenissima"

Unlike Florence, in which the rediscovery of Classical learning and art created a great cultural ferment, Venice adopted Renaissance ideals with caution.

Seeking to maintain a high standard of civic discipline, the rulers of "La Serenissima" ("the Most Serene" republic) imposed firm control on those who forged its intellectual culture. As a result, its humanists and its artists, the works they wrote, and even the subjects they painted, seem faceless compared to those of her sister republic. But even so, Venetian Renaissance art is graced with extraordinary beauty.

Venice's visual tradition was first Byzantine and then Gothic. As late as the fifteenth century, Venetian palaces along the Grand Canal boasted such features as quatrefoil (four-leaf clover-shaped) windows and balconies with lacy Gothic tracery—at a time when Classical forms had gained hold in Florentine architecture. The monuments to Venice's self-concept (the Doge's Palace, the basilica of San Marco, the showiest canal façades) posed an unashamed medley of forms—whimsical, exotic, echoes of ancient Constantinople or the French court. The element of fantasy in these forms was enhanced by Venice's physical setting, seemingly floating in mist and water, as described in *Witnesses* on p. 331. Eventually, however, Classical shapes began to rise above the Venetian Lagoon and along the canals—imposing new palaces and churches. Two of the latter, the churches of San Giorgio Maggiore and the Redentore, by Andrea Palladio (1508–1580), rank among the great masterpieces of Western architecture.

In painting, as in architecture, a Venetian Renaissance style evolved slowly. It was finally realized by Giovanni Bellini (c. 1430–1516), who achieved the transformation from Byzantine stiffness with a focus not on the manipulation of space and form, as in Florence, but rather on mood and feeling. The differences can be seen in Bellini's representation of the *Pietà*, shown on p. 367, which depicts the mourning over the crucified Christ by his faithful mother and his beloved disciple John. In Bellini's interpretation of this theme, Jesus has suffered not so much from his wounds as from the pain of knowledge. John turns away, a participant in the anguish of the Savior who now directs outward the wisdom yielded by the experience of death. Mary supports her dead son's hand and face with her own, united with him in body and in spirit. All three figures stand in an open sarcophagus in a ghostly landscape. Bellini's understanding of the central event of the Christian drama is quiet, contained, and profound.

Patronage in Venice was not confined to private or ecclesiastical commissions. The government commissioned works of art to adorn its public spaces: paintings of military victories or historical legend, or of the haughty lion with open book, a politicized symbol of Mark the Evangelist, the city's patron saint and one of its ubiquitous emblems. The walls of the city's *scuole* or "schools" (religious confraternities of non-noble citizens) provided a distinctive setting for some of the most charming paintings of the Renaissance, for example the painting by Gentile Bellini on p. 367.

While Venetian artists adapted themselves to the currents of Renaissance taste, the city's humanists were long bound to the particular ideology of its rulers. Two-thirds of the fifteenth-century Venetian humanists were themselves of noble birth and members of the inner circle of the city's ruling elite. These men promoted humanistic studies particularly of the type that bolstered the reputation of Venice. They themselves produced a respectable corpus of works defending the Venetian nobility, Venetian government, and Venetian values.

Typical of this group is Bernardo Giustiniani (1408–1489), a diplomat and humanist like his father, and the nephew of the city's first patriarch (its leading prelate), the revered ascetic Lorenzo Giustiniani (1380–1456). Giustiniani's *Origin of the City of Venice*

WHO'S WHO

Renaissance Artists

Giotto di Bondone (1267–1337) pioneer of Renaissance artistic style, famed especially for Arena Chapel frescoes.

Filippo Brunelleschi (1377–1446) pioneering architect of the dome of Florence cathedral and the Ospedale degli Innocenti.

Lorenzo Ghiberti (1378–1455) sculptor, winner of competition with Brunelleschi to design the bronze doors of Florence's baptistry.

Donatello (1386–1466) sculptor of *St. George*, *David*, and *Mary Magdalene*.

Fra Angelico (c. 1395–1455) Dominican monk, painter of several fresco cycles, including the *Annunciation*.

Giovanni Bellini (c. 1430–1516) one of the founders of a distinctive Renaissance style in Venetian painting, with a characteristic emphasis on feeling and color.

Sandro Botticelli (1445–1510) painter of lovely mythological scenes, especially *Primavera*.

Leonardo da Vinci (1452–1519) most versatile of Renaissance artists, a painter, sculptor, designer, inventor, scientific draftsman.

Michelangelo Buonarotti (1475–1564) painter, sculptor, architect, known especially for his frescoes in the Vatican's Sistine Chapel.

Raphael (Raffaello Sanzio) (1483–1520) painter known for his lush color and many lovely depictions of the Virgin Mary and Child; with Michelangelo provided the decoration of the Sistine Chapel.

Views from Venice

Giovanni Bellini, Dead Christ with Saint John and the Virgin: *The brothers Giovanni and Gentile Bellini provide different insights into the Venetian experience. This fifteenth-century painting is an intimate and expressive exploration of the emotions of those who first understood the meaning of Jesus' death.* (Pinacoteca di Brera, Milan)

Gentile Bellini, Procession in the Piazza San Marco *(above): This splendidly executed procession, 1496, is the best of official art—a precise rendering of the leaders of the Venetian state in their hierarchical order, framed by the resplendent space of the city's central square.* (Accademia, Venice)

is at once a fine specimen of humanist historiography and a hymn of praise to the city that both reared and exalted its author. Other humanists collected manuscripts—notably many from the Greek—and arranged for their transcription, circulation, and translation. Two priceless libraries were offered to Venice by foreigners: that of Petrarch (although the donation was never effected) and that of Cardinal John Bessarion (a treasure of Greek texts which form the basis of the city's National Library of Saint Mark).

The new craft of printing found a natural home in this city where learned men from the centers of Italy and Greece circulated more than anywhere else in Italy, and where a cultivated elite read, purchased, funded, lent, and borrowed books. In the 1460s and 1470s, the presses issued forth the Latin classics that had been so rare only two generations earlier. In the shop of the printer Aldo Manuzio, the Greek classics were prepared in unadorned clean type and with unprecedented accuracy.

In the sixteenth century, patrician intellectuals broadened the range of their endeavors to include official history and church reform; the theoretical discussion of mathematics, science, and metaphysics; and the collection of antiquities and rare books. In their "academies," special clubs where they gathered to discuss ideas and the arts, they cultivated the art of polite conversation. Countering this refined society of noble aesthetes was a swelling crowd of newcomers. Foreign and transient writers, editors, book-dealers, and teachers formed another stratum of intellectual life—one that spoke with a brusque voice disruptive of the smooth finish of Venetian culture. This circle included numerous "*poligrafi*," professional writers with sharp and dauntless pens ready for hire, and the female poets Veronica Franco (1546–1591) and Gaspara Stampa (c. 1523–1554). The elegant verse of these two courtesans (as high-status prostitutes were called) displayed not only the play of wit so prized in Venice, but the tension they were bold enough to express between male and female perspectives on love and meaning.

The republics of Florence and Venice were uniquely unfettered in their explorations of thought and form. The cities to be considered next were all centered around courts. Ruled by princes, these cities and city-states produced distinctive cultures, guided in each case by its rulers and their agents. Each would make a unique contribution to the civilization of the Renaissance.

Milan: Culture from Above

The Visconti family, who ruled Milan between 1287 and 1447, were among the first Renaissance despots to enlist intellectuals in their struggles for territorial aggrandizement. Giangaleazzo Visconti, despot, then Duke of Milan (r. 1385–1402) and Florence's fierce opponent, surrounded himself with poets and propagandists. The last of the Visconti died in 1447, and three years later the city surrendered to an illiterate mercenary captain of rare intelligence, Francesco Sforza (r. 1450–1466). This new Duke of Milan gathered about him a staff of well-trained secretaries who performed his intricate diplomacy and rewrote the history of his ascent to power, in prose and verse, in Latin and Greek.

Sforza's successors were less concerned with history and epic than with glamor and display, theater and the hunt. His son Ludovico "il Moro" (r. 1476–1505; called "the Moor," perhaps, because of his dark complexion) presided over a splendid court, adorned above all by the genius of Leonardo da Vinci (1452–1519), artist and scientist, in his own words, a "universal master of creating through his art all the qualities of the forms which nature produces. …" Painter, sculptor, engineer, architect, and set designer, Leonardo executed all the kinds of commissions that a whimsical patron could make: altarpieces and guns, stage sets that swiveled and spun around, works of art designed for destruction before the next performance. Ludovico was also the patron of the Dominican monastery of Santa Maria delle Grazie, for which Leonardo painted *The Last Supper*.

Naples: Legitimacy for Kings

In 1442 Alfonso V, the first of a line of Aragonese monarchs, seized the throne of Naples, which had long been occupied by German emperors or Frenchmen of royal blood. Like the usurping Sforza dukes of Milan, the kings of Naples sought to establish legitimacy through the cluster of scholars and artists they patronized. Once established in Naples (he already reigned in Sicily and Sardinia), Alfonso of Aragon (r. 1435–1458), dubbed "the Magnanimous," purchased the loyalty of several of Italy's leading humanists. Their first assignment was to describe in the most flattering light the deeds of their king. On generous stipends—salaries double or triple those available from other patrons—these writers also produced works on moral philosophy, astronomy, history, and biblical scholarship, as well as translations from Greek to Latin and Latin to Italian, which filled the shelves of the court library. Alfonso's son Ferrante (r. 1458–1494), although less generous than his father, employed some of the finest musicians and performers in Europe.

Ferrara, Mantua, and Urbino: The Condottiere Courts

It was not only the rulers of important states like Naples and Milan who surrounded themselves with leading artists and scholars. In the smaller cities of Mantua, Ferrara, and Urbino, the Gonzaga, the d'Este, and the Montefeltro families cultivated equally brilliant courts. The founders of all these dynasties were or had been ***condottieri*** by profession—**mercenary** captains. Their ducal titles and literary and artistic patronage were meant to legitimize regimes won by usurpation. These petty monarchs built splendid palaces, adorning the rooms with beautiful frescoes, plasterwork, and paneling, dined to music provided by Europe's finest performers of that art, acquired libraries, and listened to the orations of their court humanists in a Latin they had absorbed from the best teachers of the age. Even more than the rulers of republican Florence and Venice, or the upstart despots of Milan and Naples, they are the models, culturally, for the great monarchs who would command Europe in coming centuries and, in their courts, define that continent's standards of taste.

Ferrara   In 1429, the Ferrarese ruler Niccolò d'Este (r. 1393–1441) engaged the humanist educator Guarino da Verona (1374–1460) to bestow upon his adolescent son Leonello the polish of a Classical training. Guarino did so, establishing a school that also nourished many of the notable minds of the age. Guarino's circle soon expanded into the "Studio" of Ferrara, a still-flourishing university. Niccolò's successors followed his model of patronage, enhancing the d'Este library with ancient and humanist works and brilliantly illuminated manuscripts of vernacular works and translations.

Another of Niccolò's sons, Ercole (r. 1471–1505), married the daughter of the king of Naples, Eleonora of Aragon. A patron of the arts in general, she also amassed her own small collection of books, consisting largely of devotional works. An exception was the volume dedicated to her by the court humanist Bartolomeo Goggio, entitled *In Praise of Women*, a celebration of the whole female sex.

Eleonora's husband, Ercole ("Hercules"), commissioned costly dramatic and musical performances. He maintained a stable of musicians to create and perform serious sacred music: "two musical choruses of expert singers," a contemporary reports, "one of twenty-four young boys, and the other of more than that number of very expert professionals." Also on the d'Este payroll were the painters and architects who built and decorated their palaces—such as the Schifanoia palace, whose frescoes, although damaged, still convey the pleasure and elegance of life at the d'Este court. Great expanses of frescoed wall embellished the palaces of these petty Italian princes. Most are now unfortunately lost.

At the court of Ercole's son, one of Italy's most renowned poets, Ludovico Ariosto (1474–1533), enjoyed special favor. His epic *Orlando Furioso* is set against the background of a holy war between Charlemagne and the Saracens and portrays a magical world in which a knight is driven mad by thwarted

love and maidens are rescued and honor saved by indomitable heroes both masculine and feminine.

Mantua   At Mantua, the Gonzaga family rivaled the d'Este of Ferrara in their artistic patronage. The Marquis Gianfrancesco (r. 1407–1444) hired the humanist Vittorino da Feltre (1378–1446) to educate his sons and daughter. In 1425 Vittorino created a school, called the "House of Joy," which had features anticipating modern educational trends. About 70 children in all (for the Gonzaga children were joined by those of Mantua's nobility and Italy's scholars) withstood early morning recitations of Vergil in the cold (which Vittorino found bracing) and long mountain hikes intended to prime the intellect.

Here Cecilia Gonzaga (one of the few women in Renaissance Europe ever sent to school) mastered Greek and Latin and failed to still the love of learning that Vittorino had aroused. She refused the husband her father had selected for her. When his death bought her freedom to do so, she entered a convent, in which shelter, if nowhere else, she might pursue the studies of her youth.

The most notable patron at the Mantuan court was Isabella (1474–1539), wife of Francesco Gonzaga, and daughter of Ercole d'Este and Eleonora of Aragon. Taught by renowned humanist tutors, she mastered a Classical curriculum as well as the skills of dance, lute-playing, and witty conversation. Isabella nurtured scholars and writers, studied maps and astrology, and had frequent discussions with the court librarian. Her *Studiolo* and *Grotta*, specially decorated rooms of the palace—the Grotta lined with intarsia, or inlaid wood paneling—suggest her refined taste, although the collection of works of art they once contained (an inventory of which occupies fourteen pages in a modern edition) has long since been dispersed. It included statues, boxes, clocks, marbles, lutes, dishes, gowns, playing cards, jewels, and gold, as well as paintings by outstanding artists, including the Gonzaga court painter, Andrea Mantegna (1431–1506). He and other painters produced allegorical paintings based on Classical schemes devised by Isabella in consultation with her humanist advisers. To fill her library, she dealt directly with printers, whom she bullied about the quality of parchment and design.

Urbino Emulating his colleagues in Ferrara and Mantua, the soldier-prince of Urbino, Federigo da Montefeltro (r. 1444–1482), portrayed with his wife in the portraits below, made his mountaintop fortress one of the most civilized courts in Europe. The wealth Federigo earned through the exercise of arms (an annual fortune of 60,000 to 80,000 ducats) he bestowed on the arts of peace. His enormous ducal palace was filled with gilded chests and chairs, silver objects, silk and velvet furnishings, and resident astrologers and physicians, painters, humanists, and musicians. A lover of books, the aging *condottiere* developed one of the finest libraries on the peninsula. By 1482, this library included 1100 volumes in Latin, Greek, Hebrew, and even Coptic (a language derived from ancient Egyptian), specially bound in velvet and leather.

The court of Federigo's son Guidobaldo (r. 1482–1508) was graced by his duchess, Elisabetta Gonzaga, and her ladies-in-waiting, who helped to create the kind of setting described in *The Courtier*, by Baldassare Castiglione who spent several years at Guidobaldo's court. While the ladies presided over after-dinner games, the learned and important conversed wittily and discoursed gravely. The type of the European courtier, who would flourish from this time until the French Revolution, was born not in France or England or any other of the nations of modern Europe, but in the diminutive court of Urbino.

Rome: Reclaiming the Ancient City

Like secular princes, popes also sought to enhance their status with literary and artistic projects. Traumatized by more than a century of crisis, Rome had reached its nadir by 1417, when Martin V was elected Pope, ending the Great Schism. His successors established their authority in that city, employing in this endeavor an army of the learned and accomplished. The first step was to revive Rome's Classical past. Later, the monuments of that past and the new forms they inspired were pressed into the service of the papacy, which was now celebrated in works of art and architecture of stupendous power and scale.

The many humanists who gravitated to Rome in the service of the pope searched intently for the material relics of the ancient city. They described and

Reflections of Power

Piero della Francesca, Portraits of Federigo da Montefeltro and Bianca Sforza: *The rulers of the Italian court cities (including papal Rome) were also patrons seeking to aggrandize themselves. Reproduced here are Federigo da Montefeltro and his wife Bianca Sforza, c. 1465, whose stark profiles are elevated above the landscapes they dominate, in art as in life. (Uffizi, Florence)*

Michelangelo Buonarroti, Sistine Chapel ceiling: *The Sistine Chapel in the Vatican, Rome, was built in 1473 by Pope Sixtus IV, after whom it was named. The pope commissioned Michelangelo to paint the ceiling with frescoes of scenes from the Old Testament. Michelangelo, who worked on the ceiling and window lunettes between 1508 and 1512, had to lie on his back in cramped conditions on high scaffolding in order to paint the scenes.*

catalogued its ruins, while also establishing the historical context that gave these ruins meaning and significance. Meanwhile, the artists Donatello and Brunelleschi reconstructed the fabric of the city in drawings which measured, traced, and dissected what was left of Roman greatness.

With the elevation of Nicholas V to the papacy in 1447, Renaissance culture took root in the city. Nicholas ordered existing structures embellished, collapsed fortifications rebuilt, office complexes constructed for the secretaries, librarians, accountants, and clerks of the papal establishment. In many cases, enthusiasm triumphed over conservation. Cardinals built themselves palaces around the ancient city, carelessly erecting them on the layered ruins of past ages. While humanists peered into coverts for relics of the past and climbed ladders to read half-obliterated inscriptions, a frenzy of building tore at the remnants of old Rome, cannibalizing the very monuments that earlier generations had admired.

A humanist himself, Nicholas (r. 1447–1455) collected the volumes that today form the nucleus of the Vatican Library, one of the world's richest repositories of ancient, medieval, and Renaissance texts. He appointed a humanist as head of the library, and planned for its eventual housing in a new Vatican complex—a plan that would be realized by his successor Sixtus IV. Nicholas' successors, the humanists Pius II and Paul II, added to this treasury of books. The latter also collected antiquities—ancient bronzes, ivories, medals, coins, and cameos. Later popes added to that collection, while they erected odds and ends of ancient statuary on the Capitoline Hill and in the Vatican. Noblemen and bankers, cardinals and diplomats followed suit, littering their houses and gardens with statues and sarcophagi.

Amid this enthusiasm for all remnants of the Classical past, the monuments of Christian antiquity were joined to the papal cult. The figure of Saint Peter (who, according to tradition, was crucified in Rome) was enlisted in the network of ideas that propped up the Renaissance papacy. The popes derived their legitimacy from Jesus' commissioning of Peter, whom he dubbed the "rock" of his church. The Vatican complex on the west side of the Tiber, as planned by Nicholas V, was accordingly centered on the ancient basilica dedicated to Peter.

In 1475, Sixtus IV took up Nicholas' building program. His best-known achievement was the building of the chapel known, after him, as "Sistine" in the Vatican. The adornment of the chapel was eventually completed under Sixtus' successors by artists including Raphael (Raffaello Sanzio; 1483–1520) and Michelangelo Buonarroti. Raphael designed a set of tapestries depicting scenes from the lives of the apostles to cover the chapel's walls. They now hang in a gallery in the Vatican Museums. For the ceiling, Michelangelo executed the renowned cycle of paintings portraying the story of Creation, as well as various Old Testament figures; for the wall behind the altar, the overwhelming "Last Judgment," illustrated on p. 371. Michelangelo's concerns—about humankind, subject to death, about his own future—are compellingly expressed in smaller compass in his original design for the never-completed tomb of Pope Julius II (r. 1502–1513). The subject was to be the liberation of the soul: from its imprisonment in the body, in sin and death, to its redemption. Two struggling and dying figures, known as the "Slaves" or "Captives," represent the striving soul. Now dispersed in museums in Paris and Florence, these powerfully expressive sculptures are emblems of Michelangelo's spiritual yearnings and eloquent statements of the Renaissance concept of heroic humanity.

Michelangelo's vision was extraordinary, but he was only one genius among the many who peopled the age of the Renaissance. The wealthy and powerful people who wished to proclaim their status required the talents of many writers and artists of whom hundreds, gifted with exceptional boldness and originality, flourished over these two centuries.

ITALIAN RENAISSANCE PROFILES

The Florentine book-dealer Vespasiano da Bisticci (1421–1498) occupied the leisure hours of his retirement with a project that still amuses and enlightens modern readers: writing the *Lives of Illustrious Men*. His compilation profiles bankers and tyrants, architects and humanists, popes and courtiers. It portrays the abundant life of Renaissance society. Following Vespasiano's example in miniature, we will look closely at five of the exceptional creators of Renaissance culture.

The five chosen are Giotto (Florence); Lorenzo Valla (Rome); Isotta Nogarola (Verona); Giovanni Pico, Count of Mirandola; and Niccolò Machiavelli (Florence). They include one painter, one philosopher, two humanists, and one historian and political thinker; four men and one woman.

Giotto: Form in Space

Even his contemporaries recognized that the great artist Giotto di Bondone (1267–1337) surpassed his contemporaries in the depiction of real bodies in real space. Dante and Boccaccio celebrated him, and Petrarch bequeathed a painting by Giotto to the ruler of Padua, with this comment: "The beauty of this painting the ignorant cannot comprehend, but masters of the art marvel at it." The sixteenth-century biographer Giorgio Vasari explained Giotto's unique importance: "For after the many years during which the methods and outlines of good painting had been buried … it was Giotto alone who … rescued and

Form in Space

Giotto, The Meeting at the Golden Gate *(left): Giotto's ability to find expressive force by manipulating forms in space is signalled in this depiction of the intimate embrace of Anne and Joachim. This painting is one of a series of scenes from the life of the Virgin which Giotto painted in the Arena Chapel, Padua, 1305–1306.*

Giotto, Betrayal: *The same ability to manipulate forms is seen in* Betrayal, *also in the Arena Chapel, 1305–1306. Here the kiss is a hostile and world-changing one—as Judas' kiss points to Jesus' crucifixion and resurrection.*

restored the art. ..." Scholars have debated whether Giotto was, strictly speaking, a medieval or a Renaissance artist, since his career unfolded precisely on the boundary between the two ages. But it is indisputable that his transformation of the concept of human form was fundamental to all later Renaissance innovations in painting.

Giotto altered the canons of painting. He uniquely understood the density of meaning that could be concentrated in the human form when it was free to turn in palpable space. Rooted in assumptions of the solidity, plasticity, and expressiveness of the human form, his style would remain authoritative until the days of the Impressionists in the late nineteenth century.

The sheer attractiveness of Giotto's sturdy figures derives from their expressive quality. Without their ability to communicate meaning, their compact masses—however clear the space they occupy and brilliant the color—would have been lifeless and without consequence in the art of the Renaissance. Giotto made these figures speak. Two scenes from the cinematic sequence lining the chancel walls of the Arena Chapel in Padua exemplify Giotto's special achievement.

The Arena Chapel was a modest church built for the Paduan merchant Enrico Scrovegni on the site of ancient Roman ruins. Between 1303 and 1305, Giotto transformed its interior into a compact encyclopedia of Christian truth with a series of compelling and moving frescoes. The blue ceiling, representing Heaven itself, is studded with portraits of the Evangelists and a central Christ, his hand held up to bless his saints. At one end, on slim panels framing the triumphal arch that surrounds altar and apse, the angel Gabriel tells the Virgin that she is to be the mother of Jesus (Luke 1:36–38). At the other, Christ is depicted in glory at the Last Judgment. Between these two events the side walls present forty-eight narrative scenes of the life of Mary, the mother of Jesus, and of her son's birth, ministry, and death.

Especially forceful is the scene of the reunion of Mary's parents, Joachim and Anne, before the gates of Jerusalem, illustrated on p. 373. Since their last meeting, Joachim had been exiled for his failure to beget a child. Anne in the meantime had received the God-sent message that she would soon give birth. These contrasting experiences are forgotten in the joyful rush of greeting. Their compact figures are charged with emotion, their heads, eyes, hands, even backs reaching for joining and consummation. These bearers of truth, these vehicles of divine expression, are for Giotto above all two human beings in love.

The embrace of Joachim and Anne contrasts with that portrayed lower on the same wall of Jesus and his betrayer (see p. 373). This is the moment when Judas identifies the Savior to his enemies by a kiss. Judas leans forward slightly to clasp Jesus in his arms, the taut folds of his robe sweeping up to engulf his victim.

The assault of evil is counterposed to the positive stasis of good. Jesus stands firm, immobile in the tormented man's arms, supreme in dignity as his eyes lock with those of the traitor. His absolute calm is underscored by the chaos played out around him: torches and spears and the jumble of half-hidden faces of Roman soldiers charged to carry out the predestined arrest and execution.

In both these scenes, Giotto speaks with unprecedented insight. His aim is not only to display the narrative of Jesus' life and resurrection but to probe the human significance implicit in each encounter of that narrative. He portrays not just the skeleton of truth but its flesh and sinew; not so much religious truth, as the mysterious, glittering Byzantine icons, but human truth. For that weight of meaning, he devised bodies never seen before in paint and rarely even in sculpture, full of power and mass.

Valla and the Transformation of Values

Quite as original as Giotto, the humanist Lorenzo Valla (1407–1457) was considerably more shocking to contemporaries. He was born in Rome, the city whose masters, the papacy, he would challenge. The son and the nephew of lawyers, Valla developed to the maximum a lawyer's critical eye in a twenty-six-year career productive of bold and thoughtful works. These challenged squarely the conventional ethical and religious assumptions of his day.

While still a young man, teaching at the University of Pavia (near Milan), Valla published a dialogue *On Pleasure*, cited in *Witnesses* on p. 378. The very title was dangerous: for the prevailing ideal of Christian asceticism denied the value of pleasure. Valla's defense of pleasure was actually an insightful rereading of Christian doctrine. It is not the puritanical Christian who represses all desire who truly loves God and merits salvation, Valla argues, but the sinful, striving seeker of deeper meaning, fuller existence, paradisiacal joy. In a stroke, he rejects the ethics of the medieval confessional for the profound self-examination and transformation that later thinkers, both Christian and secular, would propose as the test of human authenticity and worth.

Valla's *On Pleasure* placed these bold notions in the mouths of his friends among the smart set of Pavia. Two years later, he prudently revised his work, altering the cast of characters (which now included two reputable clerics). Renamed *On the True and the False Good*, it exerted great influence—eventually upon the Protestant reformers Martin Luther and John Calvin (see Chapter 14).

Both Greek and Christian philosophers had generally agreed that virtue was intrinsically good and vice intrinsically evil. These central propositions Valla denied. Vice is to be avoided only because it makes its practitioner miserable: "Those who do not possess

Women and Humanism

A few—very few—of the humanists were women; and they wrote about the paradox of being women and thinking beings at the same time. Isotta Nogarola confronts that paradox by grappling with the biblical story of the expulsion of Adam and Eve from the Garden of Eden; it was Adam's fault, she argues, attempting to free all women from the intolerable burden of Eve's prior act of disobedience. Laura Cereta defends her own anomalous position as a woman intellectual by striking out at other women whom, she believes, waste themselves on trivialities.

Isotta Nogarola excuses Eve from responsibility for the Fall by conceding women's innate ignorance and moral incapacity (1451–1453): Eve sinned out of ignorance and inconstancy, and hence you contend that she sinned more gravely, because the ignorance of those things which we are obligated to now does not excuse us. ... I would concede your point if that ignorance were crude or affected. But Eve's ignorance was implanted by nature, of which nature God himself is the author and founder. In many people it is seen that he who knows less sins less, like a boy who sins less than an old man or a peasant less than a noble. ... The same is true of imperfection. For when gifts increase, greater responsibility is imposed. When God created man, from the beginning he created him perfect, and gave him a greater understanding and knowledge of truth as well as a greater depth of wisdom. Thus it was that the Lord led to Adam all the animals of the earth and the birds of heaven, so that Adam could call them by their names. For God said: "Let us make mankind in our image and likeness, and let them have dominion over the fishes of the sea, and the birds of the air, the cattle, over all the wild animals and every creature that walks on earth," making clear his own perfection. But of the woman he said: "It is not good that the man is alone; I will make him a helper like himself." ... Therefore, it appears that Adam's sin was greater than Eve's.
(Isotta Nogarola, *On the Equal or Unequal Sin of Adam and Eve* 1451–1453; from M. L. King, A. Rabil, 2e, 1992)

Laura Cereta lambastes women who follow outlandish fashion instead of building their character (1487): I would pardon the morally hopeless and even people destined for a life of crime, whom wagging tongues are accustomed to castigate with obvious fury. But I cannot tolerate the gabbing and babbling women who, burning with wine and drunkenness, harm with their petulant talk not only their sex but themselves. These mindless women—these female counselors who emerge victorious from the cookshop jar after a prodigious vote among their neighbors—hunt down with their bilious poison those women who rise to greater distinction than they. The bold and undisguised passion these women have for destruction and disgrace, this hunger of theirs for calamity, which strives to smear even those who are completely above reproach, deserves to bring a worse disgrace on itself. ... Besides, these women, being idle with time on their hands and no interests of their own, occupy themselves with keeping watch over other people's business. ... Human error causes us to be ashamed and disgusted that those women who are themselves caught in a tangle of doubt have given up hope of attaining knowledge of the humane arts, when they could easily acquire such knowledge with skill and virtue. For an education is neither bequeathed to us as a legacy, nor does some fate or other give it to us as a gift. Virtue is something that we ourselves acquire; nor can those women who become dull-witted through laziness and the sludge of low pleasure ascend to the understanding of difficult things. But for those women who believe that study, hard work, and vigilance will bring them sure praise, the road to attaining knowledge is broad.
(Laura Cereta, Letter to Lucilia Vernacula, 1487; ed, trs. D. Robin, 1997)

quiet minds are always wretched; such are robbers, thieves, murderers, gamblers, tyrants. ..." As to the notion that virtue is its own reward, "I personally have never heard a sillier idea than this one," Valla's spokesman remarked in disgust.

Valla questions assumptions held sacred even today. Is it really praiseworthy, he asks, to die for your country? What does it matter to you, when you are dead? "You undergo death because you want your country not to die, as though in your death, your country did not become dead to you. For the man deprived of his eyes, light itself is a darkness, and for the man who is extinguished in death, all things are extinguished." From the radical vantage point of the lone individual, Valla boldly reexamines even the secular piety of patriotism.

A nasty academic quarrel compelled Valla to leave Pavia and seek employment as a secretary to Alfonso "the Magnanimous" of Aragon, who was struggling to win dominion over Naples. In Alfonso's court, Valla published a series of provocative books: which challenged prevailing Catholic belief in salvation through works. These included a biography of his patron; a gem-like dialogue entitled *On Free Will*; challenges to the authority of Aristotle and the ascetic ideal fundamental to monasticism; a guidebook to correct Latin usage; and the celebrated *Falsely-Believed and Forged Donation of Constantine*.

The "Donation of Constantine," a document generally accepted as valid by jurists and church scholars from the ninth century until Valla's day, supposedly recorded a gift from the emperor Constantine (306–337) to Silvester I (314–335), Bishop of Rome—and hence to subsequent popes. According to the "Donation," Constantine gave the head of the Roman Church authority over all other bishops and patriarchs in the West, dominion over the lands of the Church in Italy, and implicit supremacy even over all secular rulers in western Christendom. It thus supported papal ambitions as the Church took its place among the competing states of Europe. According to Valla, that gift had never been made.

In a model exercise of destructive criticism, Valla exposed the "Donation" as a medieval forgery. His minute humanist analysis of the text uncovered anachronisms, inconsistencies, and errors of fact. This exposé laid the groundwork for more profound challenges to papal authority in the following century. Valla charged the popes with boundless greed and ambition. "Indeed, I have never heard or read that any of you has been deterred from striving to increase his dominion," he wrote acidly. "And this passion, this desire for immense rule agitates and torments most intensely those who are most powerful."

That the powerful might retaliate against critics, Valla knew well. In the service of truth, he was willing to run higher risks than most other men. "Many have run the risk of dying in order to defend their country on earth; shall I be afraid to risk death in order to reach the celestial fatherland? ... One must defend the cause of truth, the cause of justice, the cause of God, with steadfast courage, great confidence, and undying hope. For he who has the ability to speak well should not be considered a true orator unless he also has the courage to speak."

Valla ended his life in—of all places—Rome, which was now hospitable to the humanists. At his death there in 1457, his mother commissioned his tomb. The sarcophagus bears a conventional sculpted likeness of Valla lying supine, a peaceful expression on his face—an ironic image for a man of such a fearlessly combative spirit.

Nogarola and the Defense of Eve

Something of Valla's anger is found in the figure of Isotta Nogarola (1418–1466) of Verona, an outstanding figure among the few women humanists of the Italian Renaissance. Tutored by a student of Guarino da Verona's hired by her mother (this was quite unusual!), she engaged enthusiastically, while still a young woman, in the exchange of letters and books so central to the life of humanism. Soon, however, she became disillusioned with the world and retreated

Images of Women

Antonio del Pollaiuolo, Portrait of a Young Woman: *Beautiful women were often portrayed in Renaissance art as angels, goddesses, or graces, and featured in portraits, as of this nameless woman, 1460s. (Museo Poldi Pezzoli, Milan)*

to solitude and her studies. Unlike her medieval predecessors—the abbesses and mystics who flowered in the solitude of the convent—Nogarola did not embrace the religious life. Her solitude was that of the scholar, and not of the cloistered nun. She prefigures the women writers and thinkers of subsequent centuries whose careers took place in the world and not the cloister.

The incident that probably triggered Nogarola's withdrawal from the world was an act of slander. An anonymous detractor, in an obscene letter to his unnamed friend, alleged that she had committed incest, an act that would surely ravage a woman's reputation. The slanderer complained that "she, who sets herself no limit in this filthy lust, dares to engage so deeply in the finest literary studies," linking Nogarola's unnatural erudition (for so he viewed it) to the unnatural sexuality he alleged. A woman who attempted to enter the male preserve of humanist studies would be punished for her presumption!

Soon after this incident, Nogarola retired to her "book-lined cell" in her mother's house, where she continued her studies until her death. During these years, she engaged in a debate with the Venetian diplomat Ludovico Foscarini on the question often raised in these Christian centuries: Who was more responsible for Original Sin—Adam, who ate the forbidden fruit, or Eve, who persuaded him to do so? Eve, most authorities answered. In their answer is concealed the full weight of ancient and medieval misogyny.

Nogarola's discussion with Foscarini resulted in a dialogue of crucial importance in the history of feminist thought: *On the Equal or Unequal Sin of Adam and Eve* (see *Witnesses*, p. 375). Eve was a tremendous obstacle for women who wished to claim sexual equality. Theologians over the centuries had blamed her for submitting to the serpent and manipulating Adam, so bringing about humanity's fall from innocence. Nogarola confronts the issue directly, defending Eve and assigning the fault for the fall of Man to the first man, Adam. Yet even while she champions Eve, she deprecates women, basing her defense, paradoxically, on the supposed weakness of female nature. Created imperfect, Eve could not be held responsible for universal sin. God had made Eve ignorant; but Adam He had created perfect: "When God created man, from the beginning he created him perfect, and gave him a greater understanding and knowledge of truth as well as a greater depth of wisdom. ..."

The beleaguered Nogarola here conceded that woman was essentially inferior to man, and that all women were to bear the burden of the first defiance of God's law. She lived wrapped in the predicament of her sexual identity for the quarter-century of her voluntary solitude until her death. Her career illustrates some of the possible obstacles faced by a woman of the Renaissance who sought to participate in cultural life.

Pico della Mirandola's One Truth

While Nogarola explored the essential nature of "woman," the brilliant philosopher Giovanni Pico della Mirandola (1463–1494) brought to a climax Renaissance thinking about the nature of "man." Having mastered the traditional philosophical curriculum based on Aristotle, the young Pico thirsted for more than that relatively meager store of knowledge and added to it the study of the sage's Greek, Arabic, and medieval commentators; the works of Plato, Avicenna, and Averroes; and the medieval Jewish mystical books called the Kabbalah. At heart, he believed, all philosophies were one. The diverse tenets of all the philosophers were true, and could be united into one truth.

Above all a philosopher—a seeker of truth—Pico also participated in humanist discussions. With one friend (the Venetian Ermolao Barbaro, a formidable

scholar in his own right), Pico held a famous debate on the issue of whether rhetoric or philosophy was the better road to truth. Barbaro had written Pico a letter lambasting the "barbaric" Latin of the medieval philosophers. In his response, Pico defended his calling, and not without a humanist's eloquence. The task

***Masaccio*, Expulsion from Eden:** *More revealing of attitudes toward women is Masaccio's panel showing Adam and Eve, in the Brancacci Chapel, Florence, c. 1425. Adam is humbled by the consciousness of sin, his realization of its gravity signified by his holding his head. Eve, all emotion without understanding, bewails her condition.*

of a **rhetor**, he argued, is "to lie, to entrap, to circumvent, to practice sleight-of-hand." This "sheer mendacity" contrasts with the aim of the philosopher, "whose entire endeavor is concerned with knowing the truth and demonstrating it to others." At home in the highest society and a participant in convivial celebrations of the young, Pico wrote romantic sonnets and was occasionally in love: once he abducted a woman married to a lesser member of the Medici family. Pico also chose as his mentor the prophet Girolamo Savonarola (1452–1498), who was brought to Florence at Pico's urging. When Pico's body was laid to rest, it was clothed in imitation of Savonarola in the garb of a Dominican friar.

Before Pico's religious conversion and early death, he was involved in another scandal more serious than the one involving a Medici lady. He had called an international meeting of scholars to take place in Rome in 1487. Its task would be to bring into the harmony of the One Truth the disparate truths scattered over the spectrum of thought. To structure the debate, Pico proposed 900 theses—a gargantuan sum of philosophical propositions!

The audacity of Pico's project alarmed the Church. A commission examined his propositions for heresy and condemned seven of them, along with their unrepentant author. The judges decided that his 900 propositions were "in part heretical, in part they

---

WITNESSES

Rethinking Right and Wrong

The ethical questions raised by humanists occasioned a profound reevaluation by some authors of the nature of the human being. Whereas the religious and philosophical thought of the previous era assumed that human beings, rightly guided, would be motivated to pursue virtuous ends, here the humanist and philosopher Lorenzo Valla suggests that perhaps they are in fact motivated only by pleasure. The politician and theorist Niccolò Machiavelli suggests that they are moved only by power—or fear.

Lorenzo Valla presents the Epicurean argument that not virtue but pleasure motivates human activity (1431–1433): But now, having arrived at our conclusion ... we must speak in praise of pleasure. ... Not only the laws ... were framed for the sake of that expediency from which pleasure stems; cities and states were created for the same reason. In governing them, no prince, administrator, or king was ever chosen unless men expected great advantage from him. In addition to the arts that are called liberal, ... the innumerable other arts ... for instance, agriculture ..., architecture, weaving, painting, shipbuilding, sculpture, dyeing. In any one of these was there virtue? And what about the liberal arts? Do numbers or geometrical measurement or song shape the virtues belonging to rightful action? What about medicine, whose students seek nothing but the health of others and their own profit? ... And what is the aim of friendship? Has it been so sought for and so greatly praised by all ages and nations for any other reasons than the satisfactions arising from the performance of mutual services ..., and the joy arising from talking, listening, and doing other things in company? As for masters and servants, there is not doubt that their only is one of common advantage. What should I say about teachers and students? Those who teach cannot be devoted to their students without expecting from them remuneration or a portion of fame. ... Or let us advance to the most intimate relationship of all: what, finally, forms the link between parents and children if it is not advantage and pleasure? ... There is even less doubt concerning the love of man and wife and brothers and sisters. Marriage, in any case, and the union of male and female, seems to be born from the very womb of pleasure. ...

(Lorenzo Valla, *On Pleasure, De Voluptate*, 1431–1433; ed., trs. A. K. Hiett, M. Lorch, 1977)

Niccolò Machiavelli assumes that the prince will do what is necessary—not what is right—to gain and hold power (1513–1514): Many have dreamed up republics and principalities which have never in truth been known to exist; the gulf between how one should live and how one does live is so wide that a man who neglects what is actually done for what should be done learns the way to self-destruction rather than self-preservation. The fact is that a man who wants to act virtuously in every way necessarily comes to grief among so many who are not virtuous. Therefore if a prince wants to maintain his rule he must learn how not to be virtuous, and to make use of this or not according to need.

[Machiavelli lists some virtues considered desirable in princes: generosity, compassion, loyalty, courage, courtesy, piety, etc.] I know everyone will agree that it would be most laudable if a prince possessed all the qualities deemed to be good among those I have enumerated. But, human nature being what it is, princes cannot possess those qualities, or rather they cannot always exhibit them. So a prince should be so prudent that he knows how to escape the evil reputation attached to those vices which could lose him his state, and how to avoid those vices which are not so dangerous, if he possibly can. ... That is because, taking everything into account, he will find that some of the things that appear to be virtues will, if he practises them, ruin him, and some of the things that appear to be wicked will bring him security and prosperity.

(Niccolò Machiavelli, *The Prince*, 1513–1514; ed., trs. G. Bull, 1961)

savor of heresy; … many … are inimical to the Catholic faith and to the human race." Pico fled to France—but only after having penned a defiant *Apology*, dedicated to Lorenzo de' Medici, defending his original beliefs. Why were they deemed so dangerous? To a Christian tribunal (even in an age of clerical corruption), the great emphasis on the power of the human will and the corresponding denigration of faith and grace were profoundly shocking.

Captured and imprisoned, Pico was released at the intervention of Lorenzo de' Medici, and allowed to retire quietly to Florence for the remainder of the lightning burst that was his life. There he continued to write books—*On Being and the One*, *The Seven Days of Creation*—which maintained, as had his 900 impudent propositions, the oneness of all things.

In these works, Pico verged on a "new science, new logic, and new methods of research." He is best remembered today, however, not for these but for his *Oration on the Dignity of Man*. Pico had planned to recite this work as an introduction to the 900 theses whose publication so troubled the Church. Never delivered nor even published in Pico's lifetime, it won tumultuous fame in later centuries. For the work expresses a unique vision of the potential of the human being to create his own reality. That vision is among the key contributions of the Renaissance to present and future citizens of the globe.

By the sixth day of Creation, Pico wrote in his *Oration* (embroidering freely the account in Genesis of the creation of the world), God had already filled the heavens with stars and the earth with beasts. But He still longed to create a creature who could contemplate the splendor of the divine creation. For this purpose, He created Man, addressing him thus: "Neither a fixed abode nor a form that is yours alone nor any function peculiar to yourself have we given you, Adam." All other beings are assigned a precise nature. Man alone, granted perfect free will, may choose his own identity. "We have made you neither of heaven nor of earth, neither mortal nor immortal, so that with freedom of choice and with honor, as though the maker and molder of yourself, you may fashion yourself in whatever shape you shall prefer." Alone in the universe, the human being is free to create himself.

Machiavelli's Hard Facts

While Pico ranked human beings as little lower than God, the politician and historian Niccolò Machiavelli (1469–1527) placed them closer to the beasts: just as fierce and dangerous, but greedier and more cruel. These assumptions he expressed in his most famous book, *The Prince*, as well as in other works, especially the *Discourses on Livy* (advocating a republican form of government), the *Art of War*, the *History of Florence*, and three remarkably cynical comedies. Machiavelli's negative vision of human

---

HOW MANY?

Bibliophilia

Monastic institutions were the repositories for learning during the early medieval centuries, but at the Renaissance, with the renewed interest in classical texts and the invention of movable type, the initiative passed to private collectors and secular educational institutions.

Date	Location/Collector	Number of volumes
1162	Durham Abbey	352
1331	Christ Church, Canterbury	1,850
1338	Sorbonne, Paris	1,722
1362?	Petrarch, humanist poet	???
1372	Charles V of France	910
1436	Niccolò Niccoli, librarian to Cosimo de' Medici	800
1490	Matthias Corvinus, king of Hungary	50,000
1576	Biblioteca de el Escorial	4,000
1604	Trinity College, Dublin	4,000
1642	Bibliothèque du Roi, Paris (basis of the Bibliothèque Nationale)	6,000
1655	Collection of the Fugger family, Germany	15,000
1727	Die Nationalbibliothek, Vienna	90,000
1837	British Library, London	240,000

Source: John L. Thornton, *The Chronology of Librarianship* (London, 1941).

---

nature was based on hard facts as he knew them in the years before and after 1500. His writings would inspire political theorists whose ideas would frame the modern notion of the state.

Born in Florence to a minor patrician family, Machiavelli witnessed in young adulthood the invasion of Italy—and his own city—in 1494 by the French king Charles VIII. The democratic regime instituted in Florence thereafter soon succumbed to the spell of the theocratic friar Savonarola. Upon the prophet's fall, at the age of twenty-eight Machiavelli procured a bureaucratic position in the city's reorganized republican government.

For the next fourteen years, as a committed servant of the republican state, he wrote the letters (thousands of them) for the Ten, the committee overseeing Florence's foreign policy in these tense years. He wrote communications to army captains and city governors, and dispatched reports from some thirty diplomatic missions, as foreign troops devoured the disunited Italian peninsula bit by bit. This experience fueled Machiavelli's dim view of human nature and his dynamic vision for the future: Italy could be rescued still, but only by extraordinary means—only under a ruthless prince who could unify the nation and expel the "barbarians."

The Prince is a handbook for the man who would undertake this mission (a passage from it is quoted in *Witnesses* on p. 378). Machiavelli's models were ruthless men, praised not for their kindness but for their efficiency and power. In the political emergency suffered by Italy in the early 1500s, it was these skills that were needed to establish a state. By this yardstick, cruelty could be counted a plus. Cesare Borgia was considered cruel, acknowledged Machiavelli; "nevertheless, this cruelty of his reformed the Romagna [a province of central Italy], brought it unity, and restored order and obedience."

The prince might need to compel obedience through terror. Posing the famous question "whether it is better to be loved than feared, or the reverse," Machiavelli concludes that it is better to be feared, given the nature of humankind. "One can make this generalization about men," he wrote: "they are ungrateful, fickle, liars, and deceivers, they shun danger and are greedy for profit." They must be forced to obey. Still, it is wise to avoid their hatred. This the prince can easily do "if he abstains from the property of his subjects and citizens and from their women"; above all, from their property, "because men sooner forget the death of their father [*padre*] than the loss of their patrimony [*patrimonio*]." The author presents

such judgments with the ruthlessness of a surgeon, knife poised to salvage what he can of the suffering body of his nation.

The Prince expresses with matchless clarity Machiavelli's analysis of the condition of Italy and of humanity. It was written during the exile and enforced retirement in which the disgraced Machiavelli languished from 1512 until his death in 1527, and was addressed to the Medici, now hereditary dukes of Florence, by an author desperate to rejoin the world of action, in the hope of forgiveness and favor. In the isolation of his rural farm, he had turned to the studies that everywhere spurred the Renaissance imagination. At nightfall he withdrew to his study, and changed from his mud-stained country clothes to the "robes of court and palace":

And in this graver dress I enter the antique courts of the ancients where … I taste the food that alone is mine, for which I was born. And there I make bold and speak to them and ask the motives of their actions. And they, in their humanity, reply to me. And for the space of four hours I forget the world, remember no vexation, fear poverty no more, tremble no more at death: I am wholly absorbed in them.

Machiavelli's adult life was wholly enmeshed in the tragedy of Italy's decline. In poverty and isolation, accompanied only by his wits and the shades of ancient heroes with whom he conversed, properly attired, he watched Florence fall to the "barbarian" princes whom he hated more than he hated evil. The Italian Renaissance was not yet over, but it had reached old age.

Conclusion
THE ITALIAN RENAISSANCE AND THE MEANING OF THE WEST

The Renaissance was a peak moment in the history of the Italian people, equaled only by that of the Roman Empire. The patterns of high culture created in that resplendent era continued through the next three centuries—long after the Italian cities of the high Renaissance had succumbed to invasion, oppression, and lassitude.

Outside Italy, the Renaissance found a home in other nations. Exported over the course of two centuries by returning students and returning armies, by printed books and stolen paintings, the ideas and products of the Italian Renaissance continued to flourish, developing in two principal directions. First, the thinkers of the early Reformation—many of whom were humanists themselves—employed humanist methods and arguments in constructing their different vision of Christendom. Second, Renaissance thought, imagination, and manners found a richly receptive environment in the royal courts of the emerging national states, poised to extend their influence across the face of the globe.

The Renaissance, finally, has left its distinctive mark on the modern age, and up to the present day. Renaissance thinkers achieved a reintegration of ancient thought with the medieval tradition that constituted the rebirth, the reformulation, of Western culture. The two ancient traditions tributary to Western civilization—the Judeo-Christian and the Greco-Roman—were fused again, as they had been in late antiquity, and for the last time. From that melding descend the values fundamental to the West, even in an age when those values sometimes seem forgotten. They are neither Judeo-Christian nor Greco-Roman, but a combination of both.

QUESTIONS TO CONSIDER

1. How would you explain the surge of renewed interest in the Greek and Roman Classics during the period of the Renaissance? Is there likely to be such a revival today?

2. Why was Florence, rather than Venice, the first and major center of the Renaissance in Italy?

3. To what extent does the Renaissance develop differently in republican oligarchies (Florence, Venice) and princely courts (Ferrara, Mantua, Urbino, Rome)?

4. What is the significance of Isotta Nogarola's dialogue on Adam and Eve? Would it affect the way people lived their lives as well as the way they thought about the world?

5. Do Pico della Mirandola and Machiavelli have strikingly different, or rather similar views about the nature and capacity of the human being?

SUGGESTED RESOURCES

Brown, Patricia Fortini, *Venice and Antiquity: the Venetian Sense of the Past* (New Haven: Yale University Press, 1997). Founded only after the Roman Empire dissolved in Italy, Venice created a complex series of relationships with its Byzantine, Roman, and local past, drawing on medals and inscriptions, works of art, and literary texts.

Brucker, Gene, *Florence: The Golden Age, 1138–1737* (Berkeley–Los Angeles: University of California Press, 1998). By the Florentine expert (bar none) on either side of the Atlantic, this work offers a rich and diverse story of the city—not just the wars and changes of regime, but the people in the streets, the enterprise of the merchants, the brilliant new visions of artists and thinkers—over a full six centuries.

Burke, Peter, *The Italian Renaissance: Culture and Society in Italy* (Princeton: Princeton University Press, 1987). Defines an "elite" of intellectuals and artists, and examines them (and their audience and patrons) in social context in an attempt to discover the reasons for the clustering of talent that characterizes the Renaissance.

Goldthwaite, Richard, *Wealth and the Demand for Art in Italy, 1300–1600* (Baltimore: Johns Hopkins University Press, 1993). Considers art as a material good that became an important object of consumption for Renaissance moneymen in search of status and prestige.

Grafton, Anthony, *Commerce with the Classics: Ancient Books and Renaissance Readers* (Ann Arbor: University of Michigan Press, 1997). How Renaissance readers read the classics—where they read them, how they thought about them—including major thinkers such as Alberti, Pico, Bude, and Kepler.

Grendler, Paul F., *Schooling in Renaissance Italy: Literacy and Learning, 1300–1600* (Baltimore–London: Johns Hopkins University Press, 1989). A comprehensive intellectual and social history of primary and secondary education in early modern Italy.

Hollingsworth, Mary, *Patronage in Renaissance Italy: From 1400 to the Early Sixteenth Century* (Baltimore: Johns Hopkins University Press, 1994). How patronage worked in Florence, Venice, Rome, and the princely courts.

King, Catherine, *Renaissance Women Patrons* (Manchester: Manchester University Press, 1998). Introduces the women patrons, often widowed, who commissioned tombs, chapels, and altarpieces for their fathers, husbands, and sons, and sometimes even themselves.

Nauert, Charles G., *Humanism and the Culture of Renaissance Europe* (Cambridge: Cambridge University Press, 1995). Recent synthesis, that relates the dramatic achievements of Italian humanism to the humanist culture it engendered beyond the Alps.

Rosenberg, Charles M., *The Este Monuments and Urban Development in Renaissance Ferrara* (Cambridge: Cambridge University Press, 1997). Traces how the princes of Ferrara expressed on the cityscape monumental statements of their legitimacy and power.

Rowland, Ingrid D., *The Culture of the High Renaissance: Ancients and Moderns in Sixteenth-Century Rome* (Cambridge: Cambridge University Press, 1998). Imaginatively reconstructs the economic, civic, and religious life of Rome at the point when Renaissance culture burgeoned there, along with the evolving networks of patronage that made that flowering possible.

Thornton, Dora, *The Scholar in his Study: Ownership and Experience in Renaissance Italy* (New Haven: Yale University Press, 1998). Traces the invention of the private space where the scholars and amateurs of classical texts retreated for study.

Viroli, Maurizio, *Machiavelli* (Oxford: Oxford University Press, 1998). An up-to-date interpretation of Machiavelli's contribution, stressing his commitment to civic life and law.

Witt, Ronald G., *In the Footsteps of the Ancients: the Origins of Humanism from Lovato to Bruni* (Leiden-Boston: Brill, 2000). Pathbreaking study of early humanism in Italy, linking it to medieval French currents and the crucial contributions of participants in northern Italy's notarial culture.

Jacob Burkhardt's 1860 classic, The Civilization of the Renaissance in Italy, trans. S.G.C. Middlemore, 1878 (Boise State University): **http://www.idbsu.edu**

Francis Petrarch: works, bibliography, website links (Hanover College): **http://history.hanover.edu/early/pet.htm**

Leonardo da Vinci homepage (Boston Museum of Science): **http://www.mos.org/sln/Leonardo**

Select list of links to websites for Renaissance and Reformation Studies (University of Toronto): **http://www.library.utoronto.ca/crrs**

◉ Western Civilization Documents CD-ROM

10. 1 Petrarch: Rules for the Ruler
10.2 Machiavelli: from the Discourses
10.5 Cellini: The Artist
10.6 Marriage: A Serious Business
10.7 On Wifely Duties

OF ONE CHURCH, MANY

	1500	1525	1550	1575	1600	1625	1650

Politics and Society

Ottoman advance   Independence struggle, Netherlands, 1579–1609

French religious wars, 1562–94   Thirty Years' War, 1618–48

Plague endemic in Europe, 1347–1720

Atlantic slave trade, c. 1500–1888

◆ Sack of Rome, 1527

◆ Ottoman Turks besiege Vienna, 1529

◆ Approx. 10% of Europeans live in cities, 1600

◆ Peace of Westphalia, 1648

◆ Stock Exchange completed, Amsterdam, 1611

Art, Religion, and Ideas

First century of printing, c. 1460–1560

The Scientific Revolution, 1543–1687

◆ Erasmus' *Praise of Folly,* 1509

◆ Peace of Augsburg, 1555

◆ Luther's *Ninety-five Theses,* 1517

◆ Calvin's *Institutes of the Christian Religion,* 8e, 1559

◆ Peasants' Revolt suppressed, 1525

◆ Parliamentary Act of Uniformity, 1559

◆ Parliamentary Act of Supremacy, 1534

◆ *Index of Prohibited Books* first issued, 1559

◆ John Foxe's *Acts and Monuments,* 1563

◆ Anabaptists seize control in Münster, 1534

◆ Saint Bartholomew's Day Massacre, 1572

◆ Thomas More beheaded, 1535

◆ Formula of Concord, 1577

◆ Edict of Nantes, 1598

◆ Jesuit Order founded, 1540

◆ Roman Inquisition, 1542

◆ Council of Trent meets intermittently, 1545–1563

◆ *Book of Common Prayer,* 1549

◆ Servetus burned in Geneva, 1553

Beyond the West

Mughal Empire, India, 1526–1857

Ming dynasty, 1368–1644   Qing dynasty, 1644–1912

◆ Cortés conquers Mexico, 1519–21

◆ Drake circumnavigates globe, 1577–80

◆ Pizarro conquers Peru, 1531–39

◆ Jamestown founded, 1607

◆ Plymouth Bay Colony founded, 1620

CHAPTER 14

OF ONE CHURCH, MANY

Protestant Reformation and Catholic Reform

1500–1650

| largely Catholic | largely Orthodox |
| largely Protestant | largely Muslim |

KEY QUESTIONS

◆ **Before the Reformation:** What were the principal criticisms that reformers like Erasmus made against contemporary Christian practice?

◆ **Faith and Works:** How did Luther go beyond the goal of reforming the Church to transforming its fundamental propositions?

◆ **The Unfolding Reformation:** Why did the Reformation split into different movements? And did they win new converts?

◆ **Protestantism and Society:** What were the social effects of the adoption of Protestant Christianity?

◆ **Catholic Reform:** How did the Catholic reform movement differ from the Protestant? What were the social effects of Catholic reform?

◆ **The Reign of Intolerance:** With plural religious traditions in play, why did intolerance actually increase against perceived outsiders such as Jews, Muslims, and accused witches?

" ere I Stand ..." In 1521, the German monk Martin Luther (1483–1546) was summoned to appear before the Holy Roman Emperor Charles V (r. 1519–1556). On a table before him lay his books, fearsome to the religious and secular leaders of Europe. He was asked to repudiate them, and recant—the order normally given to an identified heretic, permitting the accused to disown his views and escape punishment. Luther refused. "I am bound by the Scriptures I have quoted," he responded, according to German words inserted in the Latin notes of the session, "and my conscience is captive to the Word of God. I cannot and will not retract anything, for it is neither safe nor right to go against conscience. I cannot do otherwise. Here I stand, may God help me, Amen."*

At that point, Luther stood a good chance of being condemned to death—his views spurned and his memory erased. Instead, he survived to lead a revolution. That revolution, called today the Protestant Reformation, ruptured the monopoly of the Roman Church over the Christians of western Europe and, in turn, spurred that Church to its own reformation. It transformed European culture and society, formed in the era of a unified Christendom, and left many churches where once there had been one.

The Reformation developed in the sixteenth century, when the Italian Renaissance had already outlived its heroic phase (see Chapter 13) and as European settlers established themselves in the Western Hemisphere (see Chapter 16). The preconditions for the Reformation included the neglect or abuse of church leaders; the quest of lay men and women for religious assurance; the opportunism of rulers, and the intellectual currents set in motion by Renaissance humanism, which liberated its participants from the Church-dominated thought systems of medieval Scholasticism (see Chapter 10).

The Reformation began in 1517, when Martin Luther first issued a list of ninety-five objections to Roman church laws and practices. Once launched, Protestantism spread throughout many parts of Europe. In its various forms, it impacted profoundly upon society—on the family, on women and children, and on the poor. Catholicism responded to the Protestant challenge, generating its own reform program and charismatic leaders. Catholic and Protestant movements alike, at this volatile moment of change and readjustment, experienced a surge of intolerance—intolerance and bigotry toward outsiders, heretics, and dissenters, and those labeled as witches, victims of their neighbors' very deepest anxiety and insecurity.

BEFORE THE REFORMATION

Long before Martin Luther confronted the emperor and declined to recant, the preconditions for his revolt were forming. The failures of the Roman Church, and the anxieties of the faithful, formed one set of those preconditions. By 1500, corruption had diminished the Church in the eyes especially of educated elites. Both church leaders and secular rulers had stifled earlier movements for fundamental change. Many Christians were skeptical of the Church and uncertain of their own salvation. They were open to the new solutions proposed by reformers.

A second precondition of the Reformation was the emergence of humanism, the principal intellectual movement of the Renaissance. Humanist thinkers squarely challenged the dominance of the Church in the realm of ideas. Humanist critics, meanwhile, called for moral reform, although they hesitated to take action against the structures of the Church. They were overtaken by the flood of events.

Christendom at Risk

The two centuries from 1300 to 1500 saw the collapse of the Church's prestige, caused by the proliferation of corrupt practices within that institution, and the growth, among lay people, of extreme or bizarre beliefs and customs, at odds with the austere prescriptions of orthodoxy. By 1500, the Church and Christendom itself were in crisis.

From the election of Pope Martin V in 1417, which marked the end of the Great Schism, to the death of Pope Leo X in 1521, the year of Luther's trial for heresy, the Roman Church reached new peaks of worldly grandeur. At great cost, it undertook to rebuild the city of Rome and construct new churches and palaces amid the ancient ruins. To pay for these building projects and to support the lavish establishments of the clergy, papal agents collected taxes from all over Europe. These demands drained a struggling peasantry, while a few privileged men benefited. Wealthy clerics clustered in Rome and spent lavishly to further their ambitions and their comforts. The secretary of the German city of Augsburg wrote ominously in 1491 of his visit to Rome: "I see that everything here can be bought from top to bottom. Intrigues, hypocrisy, adulation are highly honored, religion is debased; ... righteousness sleeps."

The offices of the Church could indeed be bought, and not only in Rome. Among laymen and clergy, abuses were rampant. Wealthy men bought lucrative church positions for their nephews or sons (the abuses of simony and nepotism). Clergymen acquired several titles at once (the practice of **pluralism**). Or they collected incomes from positions they held as bishops while they resided elsewhere and delegated their responsibilities to less eminent substitutes (the abuse

Map 14.1 German confessionalization, sixteenth to seventeenth centuries: *"Protestantism" was not a monolithic movement. Within 50 years after Luther's defiance of the Roman church, it flourished in several different varieties. This map shows that the religious divisions of Germany were nearly as numerous as the political divisions—and indeed they mirrored the religious preferences of the princes or city-states that dominated in each state. What benefits accrued from accepting the "established" (state-authorized) church, and what pressures might be experienced by the practitioners of minority religions?*

Legend:
- Roman Catholic
- Lutheran
- Calvinist
- Roman Catholic with Calvinist, Lutheran or Hussite minorities
- Lutheran with Calvinist or Roman Catholic minorities
- Calvinist with Roman Catholic or Lutheran minorities
- —— boundary of the Holy Roman Empire

of absenteeism). Or they arranged for offices to be conferred on them or their kin in the future (the abuse of reservation). Or they paid to be nominated to vacant offices. The treasury in Rome, meanwhile, grew fat from collecting the annate, the first year's revenue from these ecclesiastical offices. Besides profiting from their official positions, priests, bishops, cardinals, and even the pope kept concubines, or surrounded themselves with courtesans and prostituted boys.

Male and female monasticism were also in decline. Even the mendicant friars, created in the last surge of monastic reform, often lived comfortable lives. Although monasteries and convents included many pious men and women, they also housed people who had no true vocation or calling for the religious life. At the same time, the friars who preached to ordinary lay people ranted at them for their sins and painted vividly the tortures of Hell awaiting the unrepentant. Receptive to and terrified by such tirades, Christians often feared that their sins would merit eternal damnation or prolonged suffering in Purgatory. To avert these destinies, they could repent and receive absolution and perform penance.

They could also earn or purchase an **indulgence**, a papal letter to those who had performed an especially worthy act (such as going on a pilgrimage or making a large donation). It granted remission from punishment for sins that had not been absolved

at the time of death. This practice dated back to the early Middle Ages. It received new life in the mid-1400s when the Church decreed that indulgences could remit punishment for souls of the dead already in Purgatory, as well as those still alive who might someday find themselves in that state. After about 1500 the papal sale of indulgences accelerated. The proceeds were earmarked to pay for the building of the new Basilica of Saint Peter's and to fend off a feared invasion of the Turks.

The sale of indulgences was an extremely successful mode of fund raising because it tapped the fervent piety of the Christian public. Throughout the fourteenth and fifteenth centuries popular religious feeling had been increasingly intensifying. The number of shrines multiplied, especially those that promised miracles of healing, and the number of people going on pilgrimages likewise mounted. The use of the **rosary** as an aid in devotion and the recitation of prayers became popular. The collection and veneration of relics of the saints, a long-established practice, intensified around 1500, when the craze for relics also heightened. One famous and proud collector was Frederick III (r. 1486–1525), called "the Wise," the Elector of Saxony—later the protector of Martin Luther (an elector was one of the German princes entitled to participate in the election of the Holy Roman Emperor). Among his enormous collection of 19,000 relics were a straw from the manger in Bethlehem where Jesus was born, wood from the cross on which he had died, and the thumb of Saint Anne.

The faces of reform: The scholar Erasmus, a severe critic of the Catholic Church who nonetheless remained within its circle until his death, is depicted in a lithograph together with students, and prominent disciples. (Nederlands Geschiedenis)

These pious practices could not entirely allay people's anxiety about death or their fears of the afterlife. Skeletons figured often in paintings; references to the decay of the body appeared in poems; and the design and construction of tombs preoccupied many eminent patrons. Manuals of instruction in "the art of dying" sold well. Wealthy men and women made prudent bequests to religious communities to pay for special services for their own departed souls. For the first time, mourners clothed themselves in black and devised elaborate funeral rites.

While the higher clergy misbehaved and the pious sought comfort where they could, several reform movements developed to meet the spiritual needs of the faithful. The Waldensian, Wyclifite, and Hussite movements (see Chapter 10), all decreed heretical, distrusted the clergy and called for a deeper piety, more closely linked to the New Testament Jesus. In Italy, pious Christians joined in ritual processions to win the favor of the saints and met regularly in confraternities to worship, to do charitable service, and to perform works of penance. The Italian movements climaxed in an extraordinary four years in Florence, where the Dominican monk Girolamo Savonarola (1452–1498) persuaded the citizenry to make a "bonfire of the vanities"—to burn in public their mirrors, jewelry, works of art, books—as a sign of repentance.

The Low Countries (modern Belgium and the Netherlands) were the home of the "New Devotion," an anticlerical and anti-institutional movement of pious laymen and women influenced by the tradition of northern mysticism. Its practitioners believed that each individual should find his or her way to God through devotional reading and reflection. It was this mix of piety and books that characterizes the work of Desiderius Erasmus (c. 1466–1536), the leading intellectual of the day.

Christian Humanism

An education influenced by the "New Devotion" was one stimulus behind Erasmus' religious thought. Another, equally important, was humanism. Erasmus was the major communicator outside Italy of humanist scholarship (see Chapter 13). The dual commitment to Christian piety and humanist learning that he exemplified is known as "Christian humanism." Although Christian humanists laid some of the groundwork for the Protestant Reformation, they stopped short of a commitment to that movement.

Erasmus   Born in the city of Rotterdam (modern Netherlands), Erasmus considered himself, with reason, a citizen of the world. After spending six years in a Dutch monastery and taking holy orders, he went on to study and work in England, France, Italy, and Switzerland. He rejected the dogmatic, intolerant attitudes of his religious training, being drawn increasingly toward the scholarship of the humanists. In the early 1500s, he urged a return to the simple faith of the followers of Jesus, a set of beliefs that he called the "philosophy of Christ." The vast hierarchy of the Church, the panoply of rituals and sacraments, the worship (rather than merely reverence) of saints, the claim to forgiveness for sins through the performance of pilgrimages or the purchase of pardons—all these practices he considered unnecessary and a barrier to faith. His views reached a huge audience.

Erasmus wrote many works—sixty-five volumes—which underwent many editions and translations and were read widely throughout Europe. It was the invention of movable type that made this voluminous production possible. Perfected by John Gutenberg in the 1440s and 1450s in Mainz (modern Germany), the printing press revolutionized the dissemination of ideas. By 1500 printing presses could produce accurate and legible versions of religious and secular classics. In the past, all books had been copied by hand. They circulated in two or ten or thirty copies, each a little different because transcribed by a different writer. Only a classic, such as the orations of Cicero or the Bible, would be available in hundreds of copies—and their texts might differ significantly. After the invention of the printing press, identical copies of a single work could be purchased for a relatively modest price at one of the bookstalls that began to appear in towns. More than ever before, books could sway people's minds.

One of the bestsellers of the early 1500s was Erasmus' *Handbook of the Christian Soldier*. The book was written, the author explained, on the plea of a woman whose soldier husband's sins put him in danger of losing his soul. Erasmus offered as a remedy his own prescription for a Christian life. A person who imitated Jesus, he wrote, could achieve an experience of oneness with God. There was no need for saints or pilgrimages, popes or theologians, or even priests. Erasmus' recipe for piety plain and simple amounted to a frontal attack on the Roman Church—precisely what the author, who hoped to die in bed and not as a branded heretic, wished to avoid.

Erasmus' reputation as a troublemaker only increased when he wrote (in 1511) the *Praise of Folly*. "Folly" herself—an outlandish female personification of foolishness and irrationality—narrates this lively essay in self-praise, sharp satire, and Christian vision. She defends the "folly" of friendship and marriage, self-delusion, and even insanity against a spiritless and life-defeating rationalism. She pokes fun at schoolteachers and philosophers, bishops, cardinals, popes, priests, monks, and, most of all, theologians. She argues that religious experience, by which one deserts earthly concerns to dwell in the spirit of God, is a form of folly. The whole work is a witty exercise in indirection, a veiled but still devastating attack on a corrupt clergy and decadent Church.

Even more audacious than Folly's critique of the Church was Erasmus' edition of the New Testament (1516). In the fourth century, the whole Bible had been translated into Latin, in which version, later called the Vulgate, it circulated during the Middle Ages. But the Vulgate was occasionally inaccurate, argued Erasmus, who was influenced in this criticism by the Italian humanist Lorenzo Valla. It interposed meanings not justified by the literal text, and its inaccuracies, he believed, had led Christians astray. Erasmus' New Testament contained the authoritative Greek text and his own translation into Latin, together with his critical commentary. It could be seen as a scholarly exercise. Or it could be interpreted as an assault on the authority of the Church.

Erasmus wrote *The Education of the Christian Prince* for a privileged boy who would one day become a ruler—the future emperor Charles V. A young prince, rightly trained, argued the author, would mature to hate war, provide justice, and nurture the poor. As for ordinary children, Erasmus feared they might grow up ignorant and therefore vulnerable to the excessive formalism of the Church. The antidote he offered was, again, proper learning, and he wrote a treatise, *On Education*, advocating a rigorous yet humane course of study for the young.

Erasmus also produced a textbook: a collection of entertaining dialogues entitled *Colloquies*, designed to teach young people the rudiments of Latin as they discussed current issues. One of these dialogues, called "The Shipwreck," illustrates how Erasmus promoted his concept of true piety through his humanist work. On the bleak North Sea, sharp winds batter a little ship. The mast breaks. The captain tells his passengers that all is lost—it is just a matter of time. The voyagers pray to the saints, to whom they offer gifts of golden candlesticks or golden coin if they survive. A woman holding a child prays quietly to herself. A priest strips himself to his underclothes—so as best to be prepared to swim. The narrator of the story silently trusts to God. The mighty waves tear the ship to pieces, and the voyagers pile onto the lifeboat—which quickly sinks—or cling to splintered planks and fragments of mast. Only seven of the fifty-eight passengers find their way to shore. All those who tried to buy the favor of the saints perish. Among the survivors are the narrator, the mother and child, and the literally unfrocked priest.

This simple story unveils the false worship of saints, de-sanctifies the clergy, and depicts nature as an autonomous force not readily controlled by ritual. It amounts to a critique of contemporary religion, addressed to an unprecedently large public and energizing a whole generation of thinkers.

Erasmus' friends and correspondents, some of whom are depicted on p. 386, included many of Europe's leading intellectuals. Most important among these were his English colleagues John Colet (c. 1467–1519) and Thomas More (1478–1535), and the Spanish-born Juan Luis Vives (1492–1540), who worked in England and Louvain (or Leuven; in modern Belgium). Colet labored to introduce Greek as well as Latin studies to English education. He founded a school at Saint Paul's Cathedral in London, centered on the new humanist curriculum, reserving a few places for poor scholarship students. Vives, too, was a teacher, and briefly tutor to Princess Mary, King Henry VIII's elder daughter and future queen of England. He wrote groundbreaking works on liberal education, and specifically on women's education. The work of both Colet and Vives had a social dimension, in line with Erasmian principles: Colet was a pacifist, and Vives proposed for one Belgian town (Ypres) a complete program for poor relief.

Thomas More   The lawyer (later saint) Sir Thomas More did much to promote humanistic scholarship, training his own children in the Classics (including his daughter, Margaret More Roper, an author in her own right). The author of letters, history, biography, and religious treatises, More is best known for his slim book **Utopia**. In its pages he criticizes the social policies of contemporary England and proposes a wholly rational model society, which exists "nowhere" (the literal meaning of the Greek word *utopia*). Thomas More rose in the government of King Henry VIII to the lofty position of lord chancellor—then fell suddenly, later to be convicted of treason. His earnest Catholicism, which he would not relinquish to save his life, led him into fatal conflict with the king, who had broken with the Roman Church to solve some problems of his own.

In 1535, More was beheaded, a martyr and a Christian humanist. For the previous fifteen years, Erasmus had been maneuvering to avoid the same fate. Opposed in principle to all conflict, Erasmus especially feared conflicts caused by religious disagreement. These he could not avoid, although he did manage to die in his bed and not on the scaffold.

His own works excited the controversy he so much deplored. They were condemned in country after country, burned or defaced. Yet Erasmus remained a Catholic. In his last years, he settled in Basel (Switzerland), which he found very congenial until it officially adopted Protestantism, whereupon he transferred swiftly to Catholic Freiburg (modern Germany)—returning to Basel only when close to death. Though he refused to join the new Protestant movement (hatched, as one observer put it, from the egg Erasmus laid), he could not disown his criticism of the Roman Church.

Erasmus and his colleagues, caught up in the furor of the first phase of the Reformation, were men whose intellectual outlooks were formed by the Renaissance.

Hans Holbein the Younger, Erasmus of Rotterdam, *c.1523. Hans Holbein, the leading German artist of his generation, knew Erasmus from his youth. Both artist and author were actively involved in the printing houses, then in their dynamic first years. In 1523, Holbein painted Erasmus as a scholar in his prime at work in his study. In this later portrait, Erasmus is portrayed as the cosmopolitan senior intellectual of the age, as upstanding and elegant as the classically sculpted pillar next to which he stands, his hands, which had crafted so many books, lightly resting on a book on the edges of which appear words in Greek—"the Herculean labors"—and Latin— "of Erasmus of Rotterdam."* (Private Collection)

The two movements were very different in nature but were closely related and nearly contemporary—in Italy the Renaissance preceded the Reformation; in the north, the two movements coincided. The Renaissance was a cultural movement, fueled above all by the zeal to recover and relive the world of Classical antiquity. Its agents were intellectuals, mostly male, mostly lay people, and mostly from the middling and elite ranks of society. The Reformation was a religious movement which had enormous social and political effects. It was impelled by the spiritual needs of individuals and communities, as well as by the ambitions of opportunistic rulers and leaders. It had consequences for men and women, rich and poor, Protestants and Catholics, town dwellers and villagers, from every region of Europe. Erasmus was a Christian and a man of the Renaissance whose high principles opened the path to the Reformation, a revolution he had no desire to join.

The Erasmian blend of Renaissance humanism and Christian piety offered a promise of spiritual, educational, and social reform. However, its program was not sufficient for the challenges of that day, and so it ultimately failed. Religious tensions had already developed to the point that they called forth fundamental changes in the lives and beliefs of Christians. The unity of the one church and the one faith would soon be shattered.

FAITH AND WORKS

The following revolution had spiritual, social, and political dimensions of a magnitude Erasmus could not have imagined. The critical figure was the German monk and university professor Martin Luther, who struck at the heart of the Roman Church by questioning the whole apparatus of clergy, sacrament, and canon law. He insisted on a transformation of the individual personality resulting from a renewed commitment to the New Testament Jesus as the route to salvation (see *Witnesses*, p. 393). He stood by those beliefs before the Holy Roman Emperor, and survived to see his ideas transform Europe.

Luther's Message

For centuries, Christians had sought salvation, a reunion with God in Heaven after death, through a lifelong striving to do good deeds and avoid sin. They purged any sins they might commit through the sacramental process of confession, penance, and absolution, and thus achieved justification. Luther upset this understanding of the Christian's road to God. All people were immersed in sin, he believed, and no one could perform truly good works or avoid sinful acts. Every Christian seeking salvation must experience the forgiveness of God inwardly—the experience of faith, which itself conferred justification.

Like all conscientious Christians of his day, the young man Luther had sought assurance of salvation. He examined his conscience scrupulously: had he committed any deeds he had forgotten to confess? was there some secret sin, of which he was not even aware, that might spell his damnation? Luther was afraid of God and afraid for himself. The consequence was anxiety and despair.

While in his early twenties, Luther had joined the Augustinian order and had subsequently been ordained a priest. Later, he became a lecturer in philosophy at the University of Wittenberg, in Saxony (in modern Germany); and it was while teaching there that he found the solution to his predicament. He found it in the Epistles of Paul. "The just shall live by faith," wrote Paul (Romans 1:17); that is, they would receive from God the gift of righteousness. Luther argued that the Christian was reconciled with God, or justified, not by the performance of certain acts but by the reception of divine forgiveness: the grace of God.

The doctrine of "justification by faith alone" countered the Roman Church's assumption (later made official doctrine) that salvation could be attained by doing good works, aided by God's grace. According to the traditional outlook, sin was inevitable but could be erased by doing penance—more good works. In theory, sincere repentance was required before absolution would be granted. In practice, absolution was often granted in the absence of a repentant attitude upon the performance of a penance (such as the recitation of a prayer a certain number of times), or a donation to the Church, or the purchase of an indulgence.

This last practice seemed especially outrageous to Luther. How could the mere purchase of a letter release a sinner from punishment when God required true and perfect obedience? In 1517, aware of the approach of the indulgence salesman John Tetzel, a Dominican monk, Luther compiled a list of abuses in the contemporary Church as a series of theses, or propositions he would debate with any challenger. Luther's *Ninety-Five Theses* may not actually have been nailed to the door of Wittenberg's castle church, as legend has it. Nevertheless, they roused a clamor, as printed copies of the *Theses* flew to all parts of Europe. "No words of mine could describe the storm raised here by your books," wrote Erasmus, then in Louvain, a few months later.

Erasmus was horrified. Initially, he agreed with Luther's statements about indulgences, the bloated papacy, the excessive stress on rites and sacraments. But Erasmus feared the coming conflict and its consequences. He gradually distanced himself from Luther. In 1518, he expressed cautious approval of the German reformer's statements. In 1519 and 1529, he lamented their outspokenness. By 1524, he had rejected Luther's positions on faith and grace. These theological giants contended in a verbal duel, as Erasmus outlined his views in *On Free Will*, and Luther expressed his in the rebuttal entitled *On the Bondage of the Will*.

If human beings are not free to choose, Erasmus argued, then how can they be rewarded for good acts and punished for evil ones? Upon the freedom of the individual to make moral decisions hinges the individual's welfare and, ultimately, that of human society as well. In responding, Luther pointed to the omnipotence of God, who created the human actors of deeds good and bad. These human agents, if filled with the spirit of God, performed good acts; if not, they performed evil ones. With considerable psychological insight, Luther argued that those who did evil did not do so unwillingly but spontaneously. Such an impulse to do evil the individual "cannot, by his own strength, eliminate, restrain, or change." Although free will may operate in ordinary matters, in matters pertaining to God and salvation, "man has no free will, but is a captive, servant and bondslave, either to the will of God or to the will of the Devil."

By 1525, the profound implications of the concept of justification by faith emerged. It was in faith, rather than in works, that Christians found salvation and true liberty—a personal, interior liberty, and a liberation from the institutions of the old Church. For now each Christian was his own priest, equipped (increasingly) with a Bible translated into his own native language. Priests, bishops, monks, cardinals, nuns, and abbots, the whole splendid hierarchy of the Church, were useless. At the weekly Sunday celebration of Jesus' resurrection, not a priest but a **pastor** presided: a "shepherd," or minister, whose role was not to confer grace but to teach Scripture. Authority resided in Scripture alone, and the church consisted of a "priesthood of all believers."

The Confrontation

In the traditional Church, members of a professional priesthood saw to the spiritual growth of its adherents. Luther's concepts of justification by faith alone, of the bondage of the will, of the scriptural standard for truth, and of the priesthood of all believers challenged the status of those professionals. Prelates and theologians denounced Luther. Nevertheless, unlike John Huss and some others who had challenged the Church of Rome (see Chapter 10), Luther survived the attacks against him. Three circumstances explain his survival: his compelling message, his powerful personality, and the ambitions of the German princes and free cities, for whom conversion to the new faith meant liberation from Rome. As a result, Luther's revolt matured into a new religion.

The printing press which enabled the circulation of increasingly accurate texts also drove Luther's reform. New views now spread swiftly, in cheap and easily digested form. Luther's pamphlets could be understood by the sizable number of readers literate in the vernacular. Even those unable to read could understand the inflammatory cartoons mocking fat and greedy clergymen which were reproduced from woodcuts in pamphlets and single sheets. One is illustrated in *Windows On* on p. 391. The 30 tracts Luther wrote between 1517 and 1520 were distributed in 300,000 printed copies, each appearing in as many as 19 editions. By early 1519, his works had reached France, Spain, Italy, England, the Low Countries, and Switzerland. "I have never had such good luck with a book," the overjoyed Basel-based printer John Froben reported to Luther; he had only ten copies left.

In the single year 1520, Luther published three works that further eroded the universal authority of the Roman Church. In his *Address to the Christian Nobility of the German Nation*, he summoned local secular rulers to take charge of church matters (including social welfare and education) and participate in the reform movement he delineated. In his *Babylonian Captivity of the Church*, he denied the capacity of priests or popes to affect the relationship between individuals and God. In *On the Freedom of a Christian*, he argued that true human liberty was obtained through God's justification.

To these three angry and uncompromising pamphlets, the pope responded with an official letter or "**bull**": if Luther persisted, warned the pope, he would be excommunicated. Luther responded by burning the bull, along with the works of his adversaries, in full view of the faculty and students of Wittenberg University. Early in 1521, the pope excommunicated the rebellious monk. The emperor then summoned him before a Diet (a meeting of the imperial Reichstag, or parliament) at Worms. Upon examination Luther appeared to be guilty as charged. He refused to recant, in the memorable words quoted at the outset of this chapter.

In anticipation of Luther's arrest (which meant a likely heresy trial and death), his friends arranged his to escape. He took refuge for a year in a castle provided by the German prince of Saxony, Frederick the Wise. There Luther undertook a translation of the New Testament into German—in violation of church guidelines—so that it might be read by ordinary Christians. He subsequently completed a German translation of the whole Bible. His masterful translation helped mold the German language and encouraged Biblical translations into other vernaculars in the years that followed.

In only a few years, Luther had wrought a new theology and inspired a movement of peoples prepared to shed the customs of their childhood and of their ancestors for a different way of life. Luther explained how it happened: "I simply taught, preached, and wrote God's word; otherwise I did nothing. ... The Word did everything. ..."

Cranach the Younger, **The Last Supper of Lutherans, c. 1540**

Protestant Propaganda

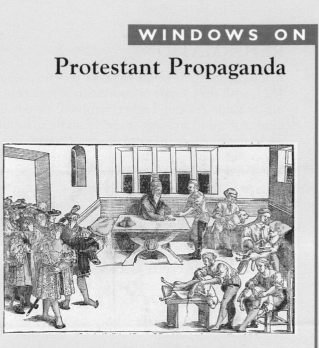

The pope and clergy fleecing sheep, c. 1530

The early reformers fought their battles in print. In inexpensive pamphlets as well as traditional, sturdy volumes, they presented their case against the old Church to ordinary people, especially of the towns, where literacy rates reached as high as 50 percent. Woodcut cartoons and narrative pictures had the desired effect on those who were not literate. In this engraving by Cranach the Younger (above left), Lutheran worshipers left and center receive the bread and wine of the Last Supper while Catholics, on the right, descend to hell; in the middle, Luther preaches the Word of God.

In the second of these scenes (above right) the pope and clergy are shown fleecing sheep, which stand for the ordinary Christian people.

On the title page of John Foxe's Acts and Monuments (left) commemorating English Protestant martyrs, Protestant worshipers are depicted in the lower left vignette listening to and revering the Word of God (in Hebrew characters at top right), while Catholic worshippers in the right vignette, hold rosary beads and march in mindless uniformity behind a clerical procession.
(top right: Graphische Sammlung Albertina, Vienna; left: Folger Shakespeare Library)

These illustrations critique both the corruption of the church (cheating the people) and what Protestants saw as false beliefs (trusting in the clergy rather than the word of God itself)—how?

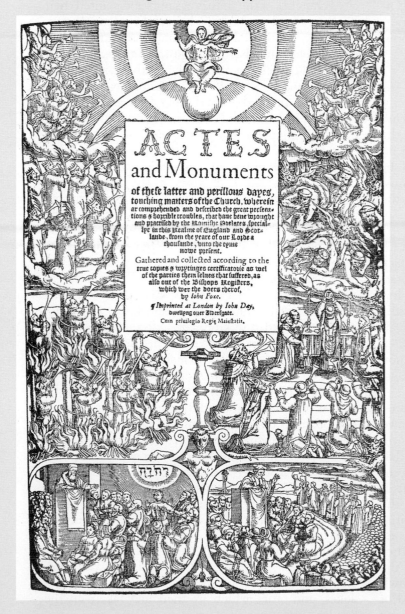

John Foxe, **Actes and Monuments, 1563**

 To continue your investigation of this topic, please go to www.prenhall.com/king for the related **WINDOWS** on the **WEB** activity

THE UNFOLDING REFORMATION

It took more than words to make this revolution. In 1522, with the climate of opinion in Wittenberg leaning towards reform, Luther returned to rebuild its form of worship and way of life. From there he and his associates oversaw the conversion of towns and their princes elsewhere in the Empire. Soon other leaders inaugurated independent reform movements in other parts of Europe—notably in the towns of Switzerland, under the leadership of Ulrich Zwingli and John Calvin. Meanwhile, rulers exploited Protestantism in order to promote their ambitions, elevating themselves as heads of the church within their own nations. Not only petty German princes, but also the kings of Denmark, Sweden, and England sought to enhance their authority by this route. Within a generation of its origin, the Reformation, now "Protestant," reinvented itself in disparate forms throughout much of Europe.

Wittenberg, Zurich, and Geneva

Luther's Wittenberg, Zwingli's Zürich, Calvin's Geneva: these were the three nurseries of the Reformation. In each, a reformer who was both an original thinker and a gifted leader, supported by committed disciples and a cooperative civic administration, led a whole community to exchange the yoke of tradition for a radically different form of religious observance.

Luther's colleagues in Wittenberg did not wait for him to return from exile before escalating their attack on Catholicism. They seized churches, smashed altars and images, and ousted uncooperative clergy. They opened the monasteries and convents, dispersing monks and urging nuns to marry. On Christmas Day, 1521, Andreas Karlstadt (c. 1480–1541) celebrated for the first time anywhere the Protestant communion instead of the Catholic mass. His call for the removal of images is quoted in *Witnesses* on p. 397.

Luther returned in 1522, reined in his associates, and led a more moderate transition to a reformed liturgy. Still, worship differed radically from the Latin mass. By 1526, it was performed in German, so that the whole congregation might understand it. It centered on the sermon, rather than on the ritual of the mass. Most crucially, the very meaning of the Eucharist was changed. In place of **transubstantiation**, the miraculous transformation of bread and wine into the body and blood of Christ, Lutherans (as they now called themselves) embraced the doctrine of the "real presence" of Christ in the elements (see below). Musically, too, the service was different. Instead of only listening to priest and choir, all joined in singing hymns, or "chorales," some of them composed, words and music, by Luther. The singers included women, whose voices had not previously been heard in the churches. Hymn singing would inspire later composers and spur new developments in Western music.

By the mid-1520s a leading clergyman of Zürich, Ulrich Zwingli (1484–1531), had started a revolution of his own. An admirer of Erasmus, Zwingli had pursued the logic of the humanist critique of medieval Christianity to the point of rebellion. Luther's ideas encouraged him further. In 1522, during the forty-day penitential fast of Lent, the Reformation in Switzerland was launched as, in Zwingli's presence, some of the city's most prominent men sat down ceremoniously to a meal of forbidden sausages.

In 1523, Zwingli composed sixty-seven articles summarizing his theological principles, based on the premise that Scripture contained the whole word of God. In 1524–1525, he and his followers purged the city's churches of the statues of saints and painted their figured walls white. In 1527, he had the splendid organ of the great cathedral removed and chopped to pieces in the belief that beautiful music promoted idolatry. Other old church practices which Luther continued—such as elaborate choral music—Zwingli banned.

Zwingli differed from Luther especially on the meaning of the Lord's Supper. For Zwingli, the event was simply a remembrance of the Last Supper, during which, stirred by symbolic representation, the believer experienced communion with God. For Luther, the bread and wine of the Supper were ("essentially and substantively") also the body and blood of Jesus. Thus he held to the doctrine of the "real presence" of Christ in the communion, while rejecting the Roman doctrine of transubstantiation. A Lutheran Last Supper is depicted in *Windows On* on p. 391. In 1527, Luther fired a bitter tract at Zwingli entitled "That These Words of Christ 'This Is My Body' Still Stand Firm Against the Fanatics." Zwingli responded in kind.

In 1529, the two combatants met in the German city of Marburg to settle the matter, which they were unable to do. By this time, other German and Swiss cities (including Basel and Strasbourg) had begun the process of reformation, and their leaders were present. Although no final agreement was reached, the stage was set for the Augsburg Confession of the following year. The terms of the Confession were composed by Luther's younger associate, Philip Melanchthon (1497–1560). The document was a moderate and minimal statement of the Lutheran position, which provided a point of focus for the diverse churches and communities that had begun to crystallize in central Europe. A later statement of Lutheran principles was reached in the 1577 Formula of Concord, endorsed by the majority of the electors, princes, dukes, and cities which by then had taken up the banner of reform.

Zwingli died in 1531, on the battlefield at Kappel (modern Germany) in one of the first wars of religion that would mark the century to come. The Zwinglian reform had made its particular contribution, but developed no further. The Calvinist movement which began soon after Zwingli's death, and borrowed much from the Swiss reformer's achievement, was quite another matter.

The French-born John Calvin (1509–1564) was on the road to reform himself when Luther's revolution broke. As a student in Paris, Calvin had been inspired by the Christian humanist Jacques Lefèvre d'Etaples, who enjoyed the patronage of the sister of the king of France, Marguerite d'Angoulême. But the royal court was less tolerant of Lutheranism, and in 1533–1534 Calvin found his life in danger for associating with reform-minded friends. It was around this time, when forced to flee Paris, that he decided Luther was right.

Once converted to the reform movement, Calvin moved swiftly. By 1536, he had written the first version of his *Institutes of the Christian Religion* outlining the basic arguments of Calvinist, or "Reformed," Protestant theology. Subsequent, larger editions were published until the final eighth one of 1559. The precepts of the *Institutes* were also contained in Calvin's

---

WITNESSES

Luther and Calvin Challenge the Church

Martin Luther and John Calvin both challenged the Roman Church fiercely and defiantly—but from different positions. Here Luther argues that faith in Jesus Christ confers a complete freedom upon the believer, who in his transformed condition acts upon his faith purely and uncompelled. Calvin argues, in contrast, that the human individual from birth has been predestined by an omnipotent God either towards salvation or damnation.

Luther defines the freedom of a Christian (1520):
Man has a twofold nature, a spiritual and a bodily one. According to the spiritual nature, which men refer to as the soul, he is called a spiritual, inner, or new man. According to the bodily nature, which men refer to as flesh, he is called a carnal, outward, or old man. ... Because of this diversity of nature the Scriptures assert contradictory things concerning the same man, since these two men in the same man contradict each other, "for the desires of the flesh are against the Spirit, and the desires of the Spirit are against the flesh," according to Gal. 5 [:17].

First, let us consider the inner man to see how a righteous, free, and pious Christian, that is, a spiritual, new, and inner man becomes what he is. It is evident that no external thing has any influence in producing Christian righteousness or freedom, or in producing unrighteousness or servitude. ... It does not help the soul if the body is adorned with the sacred robes of priests or dwells in sacred places or is occupied with sacred duties or prays, fasts, abstains from certain kinds of food, or does any work that can be done by the body and in the body. The righteousness and the freedom of the soul require something far different since the things which have been mentioned could be done by any wicked person. Such works produce nothing but hypocrites. On the other hand, it will not harm the soul if the body is clothed in secular dress, dwells in unconsecrated places, eats and drinks as others do, does not pray aloud, and neglects to do all the above-mentioned things which hypocrites can do. ...

One thing, and only one thing, is necessary for Christian life, righteousness and freedom. That one thing is the most holy Word of God, the gospel of Christ.

The Word of God cannot be received and cherished by any works whatever but only by faith. Therefore it is clear that, as the soul needs only the Word of God for its life and righteousness, so it is justified by faith alone and not any works; for if it could be justified by anything else, it would not need the Word, and consequently it would not need faith.
(Martin Luther, *On the Freedom of a Christian*, 1520; ed. J. Dillenberger, 1961)

John Calvin insists that some are predestined to eternal life, and some to damnation (1559): Book II, Chap. i. Therefore original sin is seen to be an hereditary depravity and corruption of our nature, diffused into all parts of the soul ... wherefore those who have defined original sin as the lack of the original righteousness with which we should have been endowed, no doubt include, by implication, the whole fact of the matter, but they have not fully expressed the positive energy of this sin. For our nature is not merely bereft of good, but is so productive of every kind of evil that it cannot be inactive. Those who have called it concupiscence have used a word by no means wide of the mark, if it were added (and this is what many do not concede) that whatever is in man, from intellect to will, from the soul to the flesh, is all defiled and crammed with concupiscence; or, to sum it up briefly, that the whole man is in himself nothing but concupiscence. ...

Book III, chap. xxi. No one who wishes to be thought religious dares outright to deny predestination, by which God chooses some for the hope of life, and condemns others to eternal death. ... By predestination we mean the eternal decree of God, by which He has decided in His own mind what He wishes to happen in the case of each individual. For all men are not created on a equal footing, but for some eternal life is preordained, for others eternal damnation. ...
(John Calvin, *The Institutes of the Christian Church*, 1559, Bk. II, Ch. I, Bk. III, Ch. 21; from ed. H. Bettenson, 1950)

treatises, biblical commentaries, letters, and sermons, of which more than 2000 survive.

This great body of works presents a sternly consistent theology. Like Luther, Calvin insisted on the priority of Scripture, the omnipotence of God, and the power of redemptive grace, while challenging the authority of the priesthood, sacraments, and saints. More than Luther, he stressed the power of God to govern the universe and to determine the destiny of individual human beings. Central to Calvin's theology is the doctrine of predestination: that God has determined, prior to any human action, the destiny of each human being for good or evil, salvation or damnation (see *Witnesses*, p. 393). Luther, following Saint Augustine (354–430) agreed that God had such authority. But he would not agree to Calvin's imposing statement that "eternal life is fore-ordained for some [people] and eternal damnation for others," each person "predestined either to life or to death." It was a grim message, which, ironically, strengthened the confidence of those who believed themselves among the saved, or "elect."

After leaving France, Calvin settled in Geneva (modern Switzerland) in 1536. Except for a three-year interlude, he preached weekly until his death in 1564, creating of the bourgeois citizens of Geneva a righteous Christian society as he envisioned it. An extract from the Ordinances of 1547 is given in p. 397. In Geneva, Calvinism was a complete way of life, providing a model for other new Protestant communities as to how reform doctrine could be expressed in social arrangements. Preachers guided the behavior of all citizens, and a council, or consistory, scrutinized all lapses. While directing life in Geneva, Calvin coordinated an international Reformed movement, which was unsurpassed in winning new converts and initiating social change. "The Reformation of the church is God's work," a triumphant Calvin wrote to the Emperor Charles V, "and is as independent from human hope and intention as the resurrection of the dead."

The Progress of Protestantism

In 1529, the movement acquired a name. A minority of delegates to the Diet of Speyer, which had condemned the young Lutheran movement, issued a dissenting report in its defense. This was entitled the *Protestatio*, or "protestation"; thus the term "Protestant" was born. By 1555, equipped with a name as well as an identity, Protestantism claimed most of the autonomous cities of the Holy Roman Empire and many of its principalities (small states headed by hereditary rulers). It had also reached peoples in England, France, the Netherlands, Scandinavia, and eastern Europe, as shown on Map 14.2. The map of Protestantism would not achieve clear boundaries for another hundred years and after much bloodshed.

In reaching these boundaries, Protestantism advanced in diverse ways. It expanded city by city, principality by principality, community by community. Sometimes it was instituted by the collective decision of civic leaders. Sometimes it was imposed from above, by a ruler who was himself a convert, or who saw in religious conversion an opportune tool for advancing his interests. Sometimes it came from below, from groups of peasants or artisans for whom liberation from the traditional church promised social liberation also. Sometimes a charismatic figure reminiscent of Huss or Savonarola whipped the mass of the population into a frenzied enthusiasm for reform.

The early changes in Wittenberg and Zurich provided a model for Protestant conversion which many other communities imitated. The reform program in such cases was enacted gradually as decreed by the town council. A new ritual of communion and new beliefs concerning it replaced the celebration of mass. The sacrament of confession and absolution ceased to be performed, although baptism—which, like communion, was sanctioned by Scripture—was retained. The statues of saints vanished from the churches, and Friday and Lenten fasting was forgotten. Preaching based on Scripture and in the language of the people dominated the church service. Schools taught a new set of beliefs organized in question-and-answer form as a **catechism**; the congregation, including women, sang hymns. The monasteries and convents were emptied, and the brothels were shut down.

This was the pattern of reformation in the cities of the Holy Roman Empire, where, in the absence of an overarching system of authority, Protestantism had remarkable success. A majority of the sixty-five imperial cities became Protestant either permanently or for a period (as did a majority of more than 200 smaller towns). In some cases, former clergymen of the Roman Catholic Church, now Protestant reformers, initiated the change. They were supported by the burghers. The ruling council of the town then acted officially to mandate the change. Where the Protestant cause had broad appeal, no particular party or interest group is identifiable as the initiator of city-based reform.

In the principalities of the Empire, the reformation process depended on the prince. If he became a convert to the reform movement, he mandated the reform of all the churches in his domain. If he remained loyal to the old church, so must his subjects. As a result of these princely choices, Protestantism became the established religion, and other religions were either not tolerated or subjected to disadvantages. The same model was followed by whole nations—such as England and Sweden—which became Protestant because of decisions made by their monarchs. The people at large were not consulted, although the reform may already have won many individual converts.

Thus Protestantism spread like a quilt, patch by patch: one became Protestant if one lived in a Protestant city or principality or region. The process was not entirely smooth. It was especially rocky for the principalities of the Holy Roman Empire. In 1530 the Emperor commanded the Lutherans to re-convert to Catholicism. The Lutheran cities and principalities banded together in the League of Schmalkalden (the town in which they met) and raised an army. After years of negotiation and a brief war, the Emperor acknowledged the Protestants' rights in the Peace of Augsburg of 1555. The ruler's religion was to be the religion of his people—a principle later succinctly stated in the Latin phrase "*Cuius regio, eius religio*": "Whoever rules the realm, his religion shall also prevail." Protestant states gained equal rights with Catholic states and were allowed representation in imperial councils. By 1570, well over half of the inhabitants of the Empire were Protestant.

In a region officially Roman Catholic, Protestants of any variety (Lutheran, Calvinist, or one of the smaller **sects**) formed a minority. Or a minority Protestant community might coexist with an established Protestantism of another type. Often these minority Protestant communities, being denied the use of the regular churches, met for worship and governance in "conventicles": in small groups in members' homes or in some other setting. Minority Protestantisms existed most notably in France (officially Roman Catholic) and eastern Europe (officially Catholic or Lutheran). The Puritans of England were minority Protestants within a Protestant nation whose official religion was Anglican—neither Lutheran nor Calvinist, it was similar to Roman Catholicism but owing no allegiance to Rome.

A Protestant city was often multiconfessional. Although the majority adhered to a Lutheran or Calvinist agenda, practitioners of other religions

Map 14.2 The Christian Churches in Europe in the mid-Sixteenth Century: *By the mid-sixteenth century, central and eastern Europe had dissolved into a patchwork of churches, while the northern kingdoms of England, Scotland, Denmark, and Sweden had converted solidly to Protestant denominations. Roman Catholicism held its own in the Mediterranean south and much of France. Russia remained the bulwark of the Eastern Orthodox church, while Orthodox adherents shared the Balkans with a Catholic minority and Islamic converts. Why are Protestant states predominant in the north of Europe, the Catholic regions largely in the south?*

were tolerated (although not accorded the same legal rights as conformers): other Protestants, sectarians, Roman Catholics, Jews. Typical of this pattern of reform were cities such as Nuremberg, Basel, and Strasbourg (modern France).

Protestantism and Catholicism coexisted in two regions formerly part of the Holy Roman Empire that gained their political independence in this period: in the cantons of Switzerland and the northern provinces of the Netherlands. In these regions, the divisions of the early Reformation spurred violence. In time, however, the lack of religious uniformity promoted mutual tolerance and did not prevent cooperation for national objectives. When the northern provinces of the Netherlands united to gain their independence from Spanish Habsburg rule after 1579 (see Chapter 15), both Protestant and Catholic nobles participated in the struggle.

France   France was not so fortunate. Protestant communities spread especially in its southern regions. They clustered around cities where merchant councils supported reform, as in the Empire, and around noblemen converted to the new faith for various personal and political ends. Sporadic war raged between the Protestant (called "Huguenot") and Catholic nobles until the last decades of the sixteenth century. The hostilities climaxed on the eve of Saint Bartholomew's Day (August 24) of 1572, when the principal representatives of both parties were gathered in Paris. The Catholic nobles sparked a massacre of their Protestant opponents. Smelling blood, a mob of Parisians took to the streets in pursuit of "heretics," slaying more than 3000 before the day dawned. The hysteria spread to the outer provinces, where many thousands more were slain on both sides. The Pope had a medal struck celebrating the massacre and the Catholic king of Spain rejoiced at the news.

After the Saint Bartholomew's Day Massacre, depicted on p. 411, some leading Frenchmen, deploring the effects of religious fanaticism, tried to restore political stability. Calling themselves the *"politiques"* (because their secular and purely *political* goal was to achieve order) they included both Catholics and Protestants. Among them was the Huguenot King Henry of Navarre (a region between France and Spain), who in 1589 succeeded to the throne of France as Henry IV (r. 1589–1610). After several years of Catholic resistance to his rule, he sagaciously converted to the majority faith in 1593, saying (according to some reports), "Paris is well worth a mass." Five years later, Henry issued the Edict of Nantes, which permitted his former coreligionists not merely freedom of worship but even freedom to arm themselves and to build and maintain fortifications against possible outbreaks of anti-Protestant violence. At least for a while, France peaceably contained both Protestant and Catholic communities.

England   In England, as in France, Protestantism did not advance smoothly. There, it was the king, Henry VIII (r. 1509–1547), who initiated the break with Rome. He did so in order to divorce his first wife, Catherine of Aragon (daughter of the Spanish monarchs Isabella and Ferdinand), who had failed to produce a male heir, and take a new wife—a move the pope steadfastly forbade. The king then asserted his own supremacy over the Church in England.

With the cooperation of the high clergy and with a minimum of theological debate, Parliament passed the enabling legislation whereby the king displaced the pope as head of the Church. By 1534 there was an independent Church of England, though a Protestant creed for this church had not yet been established. Indeed, by this date very few English men or women were Protestant—including Henry himself. A staunch Catholic, he had previously written a rebuttal of Lutheran beliefs, for which a grateful pope had dubbed him "Defender of the Faith." Britain's Protestant monarchs have borne this ironic accolade down to the present day.

The king's will worked through his ministers and through Parliament. In 1533, Parliament passed the Act of Restraint of Appeals, and in 1534 the Act of Supremacy, which made the king the head of the Church. The Ten Articles issued by clerical convocation in 1536 and the parliamentary Six Articles of 1539 set guidelines for correct belief. Meanwhile, the king had dissolved the monasteries and confiscated their lands and wealth thereby doubling crown revenues. Until 1553, when the Catholic Queen Mary came to the throne the plundering of the churches and monasteries—beautiful and historic stained-glass windows, statues, bells, candlesticks, and vestments, things still sacred to many—proceeded with ravenous force.

Just how Protestant the Church of England would become was an unresolved issue on Henry's death in 1547. For the next decade, England rocked between Protestantism, Catholicism, and Protestantism again. In the reign of Henry's young son Edward VI, a Protestant orthodoxy was established based on the *Book of Common Prayer* (published 1549) and the Forty-Two Articles of 1553, the year of the young king's death. Henry's daughter Mary I, succeeding Edward, reestablished the Catholic Church and persecuted non-repenting Protestants. Responsible for the death of some 300 Protestants (and the exile of many others), she won for herself the epithet "Bloody Mary."

On Mary's death in 1558, she was succeeded by her half sister Elizabeth I (1558–1603), the third surviving legitimate child of Henry VIII (although some opponents questioned her legitimacy). In 1559, Parliament passed the Act of Uniformity, once again abolishing the Catholic mass and bringing back the prayer book of 1549 as a standard for worship

The Progress of Protestantism

Protestantism progressed as diverse individuals in different settings and moved by greatly varied circumstances made a decision to substitute new beliefs and practices for old and familiar ones. These passages give a sampling of the kinds of decisions or assertions that were made. In the first, Luther's early associate Andreas Karlstadt moves to "cleanse," as he saw it, the churches of images of the saints that traditionally had been the prized objects of reverence. In the second, peasant rebels seize upon reform theology to justify their resistance to serfdom. In the third, the reformed church at Geneva—Calvin's Church—lays out regulations for daily life for members.

Andreas Karlstadt calls for the removal of images from churches (c. 1521): God's houses are buildings in which God alone should be glorified, invoked, and adored. ... Deceitful images bring death to those who worship and praise them. ... We could never deny that it is out of love that we have placed the so-called saints in churches. If we had not loved them, we would not have set them up where God alone should dwell and rule. Had we been opposed to them, we would have fled them rather than embraced them. Our deeds convict us of loving images. Have we not shown them the honour which we show exclusively to great lords? Why have we caused them to be painted and coloured, to be adorned with velvet, damask, silver, and golden robes? ... And offer them that honour and love that we do not willingly give our children, our wives, our parents, our most exalted princes and lords? Who can believe us when we say: We have not loved the idols, the carved and painted images? When our actions have betrayed us? God hates and is jealous of pictures ... and considers them an abomination, and proclaims that all men in his eyes are like the things they love. Pictures are loathsome. It follows that we also become loathsome when we love them.

Thus images bring death to those who worship or venerate them. Therefore, our temples might be rightly called murderers' caves, because in them our spirit is stricken and slain.

(Andreas Karlstadt, "On the Removal of Images," c. 1521; eds. B. D. Mangrum, G. Scavizzi, 1991)

God ordains freedom from serfdom, according to "The Twelve Articles of the Peasants" (1525): The Third Article: It has been the custom hitherto for men to hold us as their own property, which is pitiable enough, considering that Christ has delivered and redeemed us all, without exception by the shedding of his precious blood, the lowly as well as the great. Accordingly, it is consistent with Scripture, that we should be free and wish to be so. Not that we would wish to be absolutely free and under no authority. God does not teach us that we should lead a disorderly life in the lusts of the flesh, but that we should love the Lord our God and our neighbor. ... We are thus ready to yield obedience according to God's law to our elected and regular authorities in all proper things becoming to a Christian. We, therefore, take it for granted that you will release us from serfdom, as true Christians, unless it should be shown us from the Gospel that we are serfs.

("The Twelve Articles of the Peasants," 1525, no. 3; ed. J. H. Robinson, 1897)

Defining the Christian life: from Ordinances For The Regulation of the Churches Dependent Upon the Seigniory of Geneva (1547): *Blasphemy.* Whoever shall have blasphemed, swearing by the body or by the blood of our Lord, or in similar manner, he shall be made to kiss the earth for the first offence; [for the second and third offenses a monetary fine is assigned]; and for the last offence be put in the pillory for one hour. *Drunkenness* 1. That no one shall invite another to drink under penalty of [a fine]. 2. That taverns shall be closed during the sermon ... *Songs and Dances.* If anyone sings immoral, dissolute or outrageous songs, ... he shall be put in prison for three days and then sent to the consistory. ... *Games.* That no one shall play at any dissolute game or at any game whatsoever it may be, neither for gold nor silver nor for any excessive stake, upon penalty of [a fine] and forfeiture of stake played for.

(*Translations and Reprints from the Original Sources of European History*, 1898–1912; ed. George L. Burns)

and belief. Four years later, the moderate and mainstream Thirty-Nine Articles attempted to resolve religious discontents. The English state Church, which was later called Anglican, was thereby established; it posed a *via media* ("middle path"), Protestant in principle but not too distant in its ritual from Roman Catholicism.

Scotland and Ireland In neighbouring Scotland, Calvinist reformers led by John Knox (c. 1514–1572)

won converts among both the populace and the nobility, who distrusted their Catholic Stuart queen Mary (r. 1542–1568) and her Catholic French relatives and allies. By the 1560s, much of the nation, including most of its powerful nobles, was Protestant; the monarch, Catholic. After Mary's flight to England and eventual execution by Elizabeth (in 1587), Protestantism was firmly established in Scotland.

Ireland, subject to English rule, remained Catholic during the sixteenth century, but Protestantism was forcibly imposed in the next. A 1641 uprising that was partly a peasant rebellion, partly a strike for national independence, and partly a religious struggle provoked a brutal English response. Oliver Cromwell's equally brutal raid followed in 1649–1650. The 1652 Act of Settlement which concluded this cycle of rebellion and repression not only sought to establish Protestantism as the official religion but expropriated most of the land of Ireland's Catholic natives. The Irish people and their priests have felt the repercussions of these events into the twentieth century.

Scandinavia and eastern Europe With reforming preachers at their side, the Scandinavian kings of Denmark (then including Norway) and Sweden imposed Lutheranism on the German model in the 1520s and 1530s. These were the first kingdoms—as opposed to principalities—to leave the Catholic fold. Here, as in England later, religious autonomy enhanced the authority of the monarch.

By contrast, the spread of Protestantism in eastern Europe, late in the 1500s, took place because of its appeal to aristocratic opponents of centralized monarchy. For a time, Poland became largely Protestant, as its powerful nobles inclined variously to Lutheran, Calvinist, and other reformed beliefs. Protestantism had similar attractions for the nobles of Hungary, while those of Bohemia (the modern Czech Republic), some descendants of the Hussites, easily inclined to the new faith. The Protestantizing tendency of eastern Europe lasted less than two generations. By 1648, these lands had nearly all been won back for the Catholic Church.

By 1555, Protestant communities were established in Germany, Switzerland, France, Belgium, the Netherlands, Scandinavia, England, and Scotland; and, by 1600, in Poland, Bohemia, Hungary, and Austria. By the time Protestantism had achieved these gains, however, it was already being challenged by competing radical sects and countered by a reformed Catholicism.

Radical Reform

Lutherans, Calvinists, and Anglicans were able to achieve political settlements for their adherents. Other Protestant groups were unable to do so. These alternative groups, or sects, constituted the "radical reformation" and were harshly repressed even by other Protestants. Radical Protestants remained critical of both secular and ecclesiastical power. These attitudes foreshadowed some of the views that would accompany political revolution in the seventeenth and eighteenth centuries.

In 1524 to 1525, the German peasants of Thuringia rose up in a revolt that was both a rebellion against oppressive landowners and a call for religious reform (see *Witnesses*, p. 397). The peasants' leader Thomas Müntzer (c. 1489–1525) declared that lords and princes, priests and monks were all "hypocrites and worshipers of men" in whom no further faith could be placed. "I tell you the time has come for bloodshed to fall upon this impenitent and unbelieving world." Müntzer's own blood was spilled at Frankhausen in 1525, along with that of 5000 of his 9000 supporters. Armed only with farming tools, they sang hymns ("as if they were insane," commented a chronicler) as they were slaughtered by soldiers sent to put down the rebellion.

Anabaptists Müntzer is often grouped with the Anabaptists, whose umbrella sheltered a variety of Protestant movements. Beginning in the 1520s, Anabaptist communities spread from Switzerland and the southern German region to the Netherlands and England in the west, and, somewhat later, to Moravia, Bohemia, Prussia, and Poland in the east.

Anabaptists pursued a strict Biblicism, testing each element of their life and belief against the model posed in Scripture. By that biblical yardstick, Anabaptists denied the validity of infant baptism. They believed that, like Jesus himself (baptized in his thirtieth year), the baptized convert to the Christian life should be a thinking, willing adult (including adolescents as young as twelve) who genuinely confessed an experience of faith. On the basis of this belief, they underwent, and required converts to undergo, a "second baptism"—the meaning of the term "Anabaptism." By contrast, Luther, Calvin, and the other mainstream reformers accepted the traditional Church's arguments for infant baptism. Those held that a Christian identity was obtained through birth into a Christian community because of the intent of the adults present. Like their Catholic counterparts, Protestant leaders were, however, horrified by a second rite of baptism performed on adult Christians.

Anabaptists shared more than a preference for adult baptism. They opposed all authorities, secular or ecclesiastical, who sought to limit the perfect freedom of individual conscience. Champions of religious liberty, skeptical of political institutions, they anticipated the position of the United States' Bill of Rights written some 250 years later, with its clear delineation between the realms of church and state.

In sixteenth-century Europe, Anabaptist views aroused great hostility, as was evident in an episode that occurred at the German city of Münster. In 1534 Anabaptists seized the marketplace and town hall, elected their own council, and expelled Catholics and Lutherans from the city. They held all goods in common, opened all houses to all, and burned all books but the Bible. This Anabaptist flock of about 10,000 was led by the charismatic worker John of Leiden, who established a "royal" court, complete with a harem of his fifteen wives, to preside over what he proclaimed to be the New Jerusalem. His reign was brief. In 1535 an army under Münster's bishop besieged, then stormed, the city. They tortured and executed John of Leiden and his followers, tore down the city walls, and returned the residents to Catholicism.

After Münster, the Anabaptist challenge subsided. Equally detested by Protestant and Catholic establishments, Anabaptist groups endured only in a few enclaves, where they appealed to other opponents of secular regimes. Among their best-known descendants are the Moravian Brethren and Mennonites (including the Amish) of North America.

Quakers Other "radical" movements that survived the sixteenth-century persecutions, or which sprang up thereafter, also met with harsh persecution. Inward-looking reformers known as **spiritualists** included the English Society of Friends, popularly known as Quakers (because early Friends sometimes trembled with religious emotion in their meetings). Quakers refused to fight in wars, to swear oaths in court, or even to pay conventional signs of respect to highly placed members of society. They believed that each individual possessed an inner light, an extension of God Himself within the human personality. Originally excluded from public office in England and despised in colonial North America, Quakers managed to survive despite repression and still thrive on both sides of the Atlantic.

Unitarians Another group of scripturally-based religious individualists were the anti-Trinitarians or **Unitarians**, a sect founded in the early 1500s by several theologians including the Spaniard Michael Servetus (c. 1511–1553), a physician who had discovered the pulmonary circulation of the blood, who was executed at Geneva with Calvin's approval, and the Italian Faustus Socinus (1539–1604). Unitarians denied the principle, shared by Catholics and mainstream Protestants, of the threefold nature of God, expressed mystically in the persons of Father, Son, and Holy Spirit. A Unitarian hymn places these provocative words in the mouth of God: "I am one! I am not three persons, but I am one! ... I alone am!" Their author was beheaded, as other Unitarians were viciously and mercilessly hounded and persecuted. In eastern Europe, Unitarianism found a welcome, where it was protected by libertarian nobles sympathetic to its anti-establishment agenda.

Radical reform could not compete with the mainstream Protestant reform movements instituted by city governments or princes. The conservative Protestants urged obedience to political authority—or at least cooperation with rulers and magistrates. For kings, princes, and city councils, church and state must be one and must be united in the interests of the secular order.

PROTESTANTISM AND SOCIETY

The Reformation transformed the lives of ordinary men, women, and children. Under Protestantism, the household, rather than the monastery, became the ideal Christian community. Here the values of orderliness, hard work, sexual morality, economic success, and (as usual) female subordination were cultivated. More schools were created to educate the young, who required literacy if they were to read Scripture and earn salvation. The poor, the grateful recipients of the medieval Catholic charity, had little to hope for from Protestant leaders and patriarchs.

The Family, Sexuality, and Women

Protestantism reshaped the family (see *Windows On*, p. 413). No longer considered by religious leaders to be inferior to contemplative celibacy, family life became the new social ideal. In the household, the dominant male enjoyed enhanced power, even greater than before. He was the chief intermediary between his dependents and God. He led prayers, read Scripture, and enforced moral discipline upon his wife and children, other female kin, and servants. "Every man must be in his own house ... a bishop," explained one prominent Protestant preacher, "not only giving good example, but teaching according to it, rebuking and punishing vice." The household was not merely a family, but a miniature church.

While the father took on pastoral duties, Protestant pastors, who had replaced presumably celibate priests, formed families and households of their own. By 1525, all of Luther's colleagues at Wittenberg had married. Luther himself, at age forty-two, married the twenty-six-year-old Katherina von Bora, a nun who had just been released from her convent. Protestant leaders elsewhere increasingly followed suit. "It is better to make a home and teach the Word of God to one's family than to mutter frigid prayers alone in a sanctuary," thundered the radical Protestant reformer Karlstadt.

Closing the convents was high on the Protestant agenda. Luther's pamphlet entitled *Why Nuns May Leave Cloisters with God's Blessing* asserted that only "blind and mad" bishops and abbots would condemn young girls to waste away in cloisters, for "a woman is not created to be a virgin, but to conceive and bear children." Yet some women preferred to stay in convents—among them the scholar and abbess Caritas Pirckheimer, a noblewoman of Nuremberg. When, in 1525, the city council ordered her to free her nuns of their vows, she protected those who wished to stay. Only one member of the community deserted willingly to Protestantism.

Closing the brothels was often one of the first things a city council did when it embarked on becoming Protestant. In the Middle Ages, prostitution was tolerated, even encouraged and regulated. Protestant reformers, aiming to establish high moral standards, viewed the brothel as an obstruction to the new program. They determined also to control sexual behavior, targeting illegitimacy and single motherhood, premarital sex, infanticide, and sodomy.

Tied to roles as daughters and wives, Protestant women were entirely subject to men and lost the option of the convent offered by the Roman Church. As wives, their duty was to bear and raise children, as Martin Luther himself declared: "Even if they bear themselves weary, or bear themselves out … this is the purpose for which they exist." Unmarried women were at a disadvantage, where all women were understood to have as their destiny the tasks of childbearing, child-rearing, and household management. As under the old Church, daughters were to accept their parents' choice of spouse. Some Protestant reformers approved of divorce (never accepted by Catholics) for overwhelming cause—where there was adultery or impotence, abandonment or abuse.

The Protestant doctrine of the "priesthood of all believers" presumably granted women a new autonomy, in that they were free as individuals to forge their own relationship with God. In the early days of reform, some women benefited from that new principle. The wives of the early reformers participated in the Protestant **mission**, helping refugees, entertaining visiting pastors, organizing hospitals. One such was Catherine Zell (1497–1562), wife of the Strasbourg reformer Matthias Zell, who helped care for the refugees from the Peasants' War and urged toleration for Anabaptists and other sectarians.

Wealthy women might be patrons of reform. The queen of Navarre Jeanne d'Albret (r. 1555–1572), granddaughter of one king of France and mother of another (Henry IV), whom she raised as a Protestant, protected Huguenots in her realm while practicing a policy of religious liberty unique among European rulers of her day. Ordinary women often persuaded their husbands and sons to embrace Protestantism.

Women were especially active in the radical sects, many of whose leaders allowed women the role of prophet and martyr. About 300 women prophets are known to have existed in England in the 1640s and 1650s alone. Anabaptists welcomed female adherents, even to the priesthood. Spiritualists, who focused on the inner life, inspired by a spark of divine light, viewed women as the equals of men. The sixteenth-century spiritualist Ursula Jost, active in Strasbourg, had many visions of the coming end of the world, seventy-two of which were published. Margaret Fell, wife of the Quaker leader George Fox (1624–1691), announced women's right to preach in her 1666 pamphlet entitled *Women's Speaking, Justified, Proved, and Allowed of by the Scriptures*. The Quakers at first accorded women status equal to men,

although they ultimately retreated from that liberal attitude during the eighteenth century.

Even so, there was fear of women becoming involved in matters thought better left to men. The low esteem in which the sects were held by established religions was partly due to the active role taken in them by women. The only church office that women were normally permitted to hold was that of deaconess (a position charged with supplying aid to the sick and the poor). Authorities placed limits on women's discussion of religious matters and even of their thinking about them. The council of the German city of Memmingen prohibited women from discussing religion while drawing water at the well, and King Henry VIII of England officially forbade women to read the Bible.

Reaching the Young

The Protestant emphasis on Bible-reading as the means of establishing a relationship with God triggered an educational mission. Each individual must learn to read. Building on the pedagogical work of the Christian humanists, Protestant reformers opened schools. Their work would ultimately promote the ideal of universal education even after its religious purpose was no longer central.

Beginning with Luther's own town of Wittenberg, schools were established to teach all children to read and to master the rudiments of Christianity. Luther himself created a shorter and a longer catechism by which to instruct both little children and adults in the faith. The shorter catechism was used in the Lutheran schools established throughout Protestant Germany. In 1530, the reformer assessed his achievement: "Our young people, girls as well as boys, are now so well taught in catechism and Scripture that my heart grows warm as I observe children praying more devoutly and speaking more eloquently of God and Christ than, in the old days, all the learned monks and doctors."

On the secondary and university levels, Luther's younger colleague Philip Melanchthon (1497–1560) introduced rigorous academic programs which incorporated the goals of Renaissance humanism along with those of Protestant reform. Melanchthon constructed a secondary school curriculum designed to prepare the young for entry to the advanced professional programs offered in the university. New universities were founded, equipped with theological faculties for the training of future Protestant leaders.

Little was expected of girls' education, as there was no possibility whatsoever of their continuing from elementary to secondary or university education. Girls' schools taught reading, along with morality, decorum, sewing, and singing. As a direct result of Protestant educational efforts, however limited, literacy rates among women rose.

Calvinists also instituted schools to prepare young Christians for the experience of divine grace. Children went to school in remote parts of Scotland and in the English Puritan communities in Massachusetts in North America during the early 1600s. The Geneva Academy, founded in 1559, trained young men from all over Europe to lead new Calvinist communities. In Strasbourg, Johann Sturm (1507–1589), one of the leading pedagogical thinkers of Protestantism, founded a secondary school informed by both humanist and reformed agendas, which came to be influential as a model throughout western Europe. The English Society for Promoting Christian Knowledge (founded in 1698) established fifty-four charity schools to teach boys arithmetic, reading, and writing, and to teach girls "to knit their stockings and gloves," to "learn to write and to spin their clothes."

Such Protestant educational ventures spawned the systems of public education that would be firmly established in some European countries by the end of the nineteenth century, and eventually through much of the world.

The Plight of the Poor

Saint Francis of Assisi (1181–1226) had awakened the conscience of Europe when he insisted that poverty was the key to the genuine worship of God. The true Christian, he maintained, voluntarily embraced poverty, and served the poor. Here Francis renewed the commitment to the poor made by Jesus in the Gospels and acknowledged by the early founders of the Christian churches. The Roman Church acted on that understanding by creating numerous charitable organizations, especially hospitals, orphanages, and asylums for prostitutes, widowed, and abandoned or abused wives. Beggars (who were numerous in many medieval towns) were seen as an opportunity for charitable giving.

The Protestant churches took a dimmer view of the poor, especially of beggars. Jesus loved the poor, they acknowledged, and Protestantism was rooted in Scripture. But Protestants insisted that Christians exert themselves mightily to escape from poverty, just as they were to exert themselves to seek the experience of grace. (Of course, such exertions could not in themselves win salvation for the Christian, who, in Protestant theology, was justified only by faith; but they prepared the spirit for the experience of salvation.) A poor person, especially an able-bodied and youthful male, had self-evidently not exerted himself very much. Protestant towns expelled beggars. At the same time, Protestantism did create institutions to deal with poverty to replace those funded by the Roman Church. Each town or parish had to wrestle with the problem of the local poor, creating workhouses or providing for outrelief.

Precursors, Reformers, Radicals

Erasmus of Rotterdam (c. 1466–1536) Christian humanist who called for reform, but never left the Roman Church that condemned his books.

Gasparo Contarini (1483–1542) Venetian nobleman and humanist dedicated to the reform of the Roman Church; he signed with Melanchthon a moderate formulation on the issue of justification by faith repudiated by the papacy.

Martin Luther (1483–1546) defied papal excommunication and spearheaded the Protestant break from the Roman Church.

Ulrich Zwingli (1484–1531) architect of the Reform in Zürich (Switzerland), who opposed Luther's moderate stand on the sacrifice of the mass.

Thomas Müntzer (c. 1489–1525) adopting the scripturalism of radical Reform, led the Peasants' Revolt of 1524–1525.

Ignatius of Loyola (1491–1556) Spanish nobleman, he founded the Jesuit order on the principles of absolute obedience to the pope and the defense and expansion of the Roman Church.

Philip Melanchthon (1497–1560) Luther's scholarly adviser, author of the Augsburg Confession; mediated many controversies and created the pattern of Protestant higher education.

John Calvin (1509–1564) led the Reformed Church of Geneva, the capital of the European Calvinist movement.

Michael Servetus (c. 1511–1553) Spanish physician and opponent of the doctrine of the Trinity fundamental for both Protestant and Catholic believers; executed by order of the Genevan consistory.

John Foxe (1516–1587) author of *Acts and Monuments of these Latter and Perilous Days* (1563), the much-read account of English Protestant martyrs.

Charles Borromeo (1538–1584) reforming prelate of the Roman Church who attempted to form a model Christian commonwealth in the city of Milan over which he presided as Archbishop.

The peasants were one group of the poor who expected much from the Protestant reform when it first began. These tillers of the soil had been restive during the late medieval centuries, seeking relief from their ancestral dues to territorial lords and from the taxes owed the Roman Church. Expecting that liberation from priests and sacraments would lead to liberation from landlords and rulers, the German peasants, under Thomas Müntzer, mounted their rebellion. In their Twelve Articles published that year, they called for release from serfdom, access to fish, game, firewood, and common lands; modification of tenure, tax, and labor requirements; and the right of a community to choose its own pastor.

Luther at first sympathized with the peasants who had rebelled in the name of the reform, acknowledging their great hardship. The blame lay, he argued, with the lords and princes, the "blind bishops and mad priests and monks," whom he berated: "[you] flay and rob your subjects in order that you may lead a life of splendor and pride, until the poor common folk can bear it no longer." Still the proper remedy for that abuse, he argued, was not rebellion but a new spirit of kindliness on the part of the rulers, and forbearance on the part of the victims. "Suffering, suffering, cross, cross! ... For no matter how right you are," Luther counseled the peasant rebels, "it is not for a Christian to appeal to law, or to fight, but rather to suffer wrong and endure evil; there is no other way. ..."

These were Luther's calm pleas of May 1525. But his tone became harsher. In the end, the same Luther who had defied the authority of the Church could not bring himself to defy the authority of secular rulers, the guarantors of social order. In his treatise *Against the Murdering and Thieving Hordes of Peasants*, he condemned the revolt of the poor mounted in the name of Jesus. Anyone who could do so was invited to "smite, slay, and stab" the rebels. "It is just as when one must kill a mad dog; if you do not strike him, he will strike you, and a whole land with you." Protestant and Catholic princes and lords joined in crushing the revolt, with Luther's approval, in the process slaughtering thousands of rebels.

As Protestantism took form in its many settings, it supported political leaders, enforced moral guidelines, and bolstered the family, showing little indulgence for the poor and little support for women. The Roman Church, meanwhile, undertook its own reform.

CATHOLIC REFORM

Even before Luther, the clergy, intellectuals, and lay people of the Roman Church had urged reform. After the Protestant challenge, the papacy at last undertook a program of self-examination and self-discipline. Reenergized Catholic leaders now renewed their

Catholic Reform

Anonymous, The Burning of Girolamo Savonarola: *Catholic reform had many dimensions as represented in this and the next image. This anonymous painting, c. 1600, shows the execution of Savonarola, the Dominican reformer and prophet of Renaissance Florence. (Saint Mark's Museum, Florence)*

commitment to lead and serve the laity, to worship God wholeheartedly, to recover for the old faith those lost to Protestantism, and to lure to Catholic Christianity those who had never before encountered it, in Old and New Worlds alike. In all, the Catholic reformation, which is sometimes called the Counter-Reformation, amounted to a revolution as significant as the Protestant one.

The Struggle for Change

From the late 1400s, when its moral prestige was at its nadir, both laity and clergy struggled to reform the Church of Rome. Christian humanists urged a return to the simplicity of the early church; fiery preachers called for repentance and social change; and church leaders sought to restore forgotten standards of responsibility. Eventually, galvanized by the desertion of millions of its flock, the Church heard the calls for renewal. Beginning in 1545, it undertook a serious program of reform.

Christian humanism was a strong current in Spain and France even before Luther's break with Rome. Its adherents translated and commented upon biblical and early Christian texts as part of a program for the renewal of what Erasmus had called the "philosophy of Christ." The Cardinal Francisco Ximénez de Cisneros (1436–1517), confessor to Queen Isabella of Castile (r. 1474–1504) from 1492 and founder of the Spanish University of Alcalá, exemplified this approach. A diligent scholar himself, he oversaw the production of a Bible, published after his death in

1522, containing the complete text printed in parallel columns of Hebrew, Greek, Aramaic, and Latin. Such a tool for study conformed to the Erasmian program that aimed to return religion to its biblical source.

The home of the papacy as well as of the Renaissance, Italy bristled with humanists, saints, prophets, preachers, papal secretaries, and reformers of all categories. The episode of the Dominican monk Girolamo Savonarola revealed the intensity of religious feeling in Florence, the most culturally advanced city on the peninsula. Savonarola pressed Florentines of all social classes, intellectuals and artists among them, to repent of their sins, and reordered the government along republican lines consistent with his vision of a holy city. Denounced in 1498 for heresy, he was tried, condemned, and executed, as shown on p. 402. The deeper streams of spiritual yearning that he tapped would surface again in the turbulent century that followed.

More mild-tempered Christian humanists, often high-ranking clerics, were active in the early 1500s. A group of these formed the Oratories of Divine Love, voluntary associations of clerics seeking a more intense spirituality.

The Changing Church

Caspar Crayer, Saint Charles Borromeo Giving Communion to the Plague-stricken in Milan: *In this seventeenth-century Flemish painting, Bishop (later Saint) Charles Borromeo is depicted serving his flock during an epidemic of plague in Milan, while his attendant distributes coins. (Musée des Beaux-Arts, Nancy, France)*

The Complutensian Polyglot: *Shown here is a page from* The Complutensian Polyglot Bible, *product of a Catholic committee of scholars, which provides Greek, Latin, and Hebrew versions of the same scriptural passage.*

Similar ideals inspired the creation of such new orders as the highly orthodox Theatines and the Capuchins, an austere offshoot of the Franciscans.

Some theologians explored dimensions of the problem of salvation that seemed to anticipate Luther. Others attempted practical reform programs on their own; among them was the bishop Gian Matteo Giberti (1495–1543), whose diocese of Verona became a model of Christian administration. Many of these men and movements gravitated to Venice in the late 1520s and 1530s, where they were joined by refugees from Rome (sacked in 1527 by imperial troops) and a variety of visitors from abroad who shared their ideals.

After the election of the reforming Pope Paul III (r. 1534–1549), Rome became once again a magnet for prelates intent on Christian renewal. The new pope elevated many reformers to the office of cardinal. In 1537, a group of these cardinals presented to him their *Proposal for the Reformation of the Church*, blasting simony, nepotism, absenteeism, pluralism, and clerical immorality and laxity. By then, both Luther and Calvin had broken away from the Catholic Church.

Briefly in the 1520s to 1540s, Catholic reform tilted toward heresy, as intellectuals and leaders reacted to Luther's challenge. In Venice, Protestant books rolled off the presses and were snapped up by visitors, students, patricians, professionals, and artisans. In Naples, a circle of aristocratic women and adventurous clerics gathered to study scripture with the Spanish mystic and follower of Erasmus Juan de Valdés (c. 1500–1540). Valdés' views, which approached the Lutheran doctrine of justification by faith, inspired a number of erudite noblewomen and Italian clerics, some of whom fled north in 1542 to find safety in Protestant lands.

Even the loyal papal servant Gasparo Contarini (1483–1542), prime mover of the 1537 *Proposal*, found that some Lutheran views made sense. Dispatched in 1541 to the German city of Regensburg to meet with representative Protestant leaders, he and Melanchthon came to a compromise agreement on the issue of justification. It was a dangerous moment for Contarini. His *Letter on Justification*, dispatched from Regensburg to Rome, came close to the Protestant formulation. He died the next year, having narrowly escaped being charged with heresy by the newly established (in 1542) Roman Inquisition.

At first, popes and cardinals had ignored the rebellion brewing north of the Alps. By the time they set in motion the machinery to counter Protestantism and initiate a Catholic reform it was almost too late. Nevertheless, over the next twenty years, the Church would prove itself more than capable of surviving and triumphing over its many problems.

Papal Reform

The Renaissance popes remembered the Council of Constance (1414–1418) all too clearly: it had pushed aside three popes (two were deposed, one resigned) and elected its own papal candidate. After Martin V's election in 1417, reigning popes avoided councils and pursued their own business: the waging of war, the rebuilding of Rome, the accumulation of wealth. Tentative steps toward reform were few and unsuccessful. The Fifth Lateran Council, which was called by Julius II (r. 1503–1513) and which met in Rome over five years from 1512, failed to address the question of papal reform. Its main achievements were to reaffirm the bull *Unam sanctam*, asserting the authority of the pope over secular rulers and to declare officially the doctrine of the immortality

of the soul recently questioned by some university-based philosophers. The eloquent reform proposals of the Venetian reformers went unanswered. It was felt that Catholic reform would need to proceed from above, a course intimated by the Platonist scholar Egidio da Viterbo (1465–1532): "Man must be changed by religion, not religion by man." Any changes to be made would be required to respect the supremacy of the Church.

Finally in 1545, no longer able to remain deaf to the Protestant threat, the papacy summoned the council that would grapple with the serious problems facing the Church. The representatives at the Council of Trent (Trento, in northern Italy), which met intermittently in twenty-five formal sessions during the period from 1545 to 1563, undertook the complete reformulation of the Catholic position necessary if the Church were to withstand the explosive force of burgeoning Protestantism. Attendance was scant, and mostly Italian. Only thirty prelates were present at the opening session, sixty at the session where the decision was made on justification that closed the door to compromise with Protestantism, and only 255 at the closing sessions to approve and sign the various decrees. These numbers contrast sharply with the more than 1000 who had gathered at Constance in 1414.

These few delegates repudiated Protestant doctrines and reaffirmed Catholic ones. They reformed and strengthened the church hierarchy while at the same time reaffirming the primacy of the pope. They worked to establish religious uniformity and to stem the variants introduced by popular religion or overzealous mysticism or female activism. They created a new social discipline with regard to marriage, the family, and sexuality.

The matter of first importance was to counter the main Protestant tenets. Against the Lutheran doctrine of justification by faith, church leaders at Trent reaffirmed the effectiveness of good works for the soul's salvation, aided by divine grace transmitted through the sacraments. Where Protestants, following the Gospel accounts, reduced the sacraments to two (baptism and the Lord's Supper), the Catholic reformers reaffirmed the validity of all seven (penance, matrimony, confirmation, ordination, and extreme unction, in addition to those named above; see *Witnesses* on p. 407). Where Protestant reformers recognized the authority only of Scripture, Trent maintained the authority of church tradition, along with that of the Bible (in the approved Latin version), as a sound basis for doctrinal judgment.

Overriding the Protestant claims that the laity should receive the wine as well as the bread in the Eucharist, Catholic leaders reestablished the traditional boundary between laity and clergy which permitted lay people only the bread. They reaffirmed the requirement of clerical celibacy against the Protestant encouragement of clerical marriage. They restated the validity of the veneration of the saints, the efficacy of relics, the intercessory power of the Virgin Mary—all challenged by Protestant reform.

Catholic leaders listed and banned books that were thought to pose a threat to the conscience of the faithful. The list, called the *Index of Prohibited Books*, was first issued in 1559 and later regularly revised and reissued. It included prominently the name of Erasmus, who had never deserted the Roman Catholic fold. Thereafter, in Catholic Europe, all books published were required to gain the permission of church authorities. These books carried (and still do) the notation "*Imprimatur*" ("Let it be printed") as a sign of the approval. In addition to books, works of art fell under the scrutiny of ecclesiastical censors. The nudes painted on the walls and ceilings of

wealthy cardinals' palaces were decorously clothed. Simony, nepotism, pluralism, absenteeism, and other such abuses of clerical office which had angered many for centuries were all condemned by the council. It subjected sainthood to more rigorous standards and redrew the guidelines for canonization. The pious lay movements and the spontaneous expressions of spirituality that had arisen in the late Middle Ages were now to be scrutinized by well-trained and well-coordinated church officials.

Another series of reforms inaugurated at Trent pertained to the institutions of marriage and the family. Prior to Trent, the role of the Church in constituting a legal marriage was minimal. A priestly blessing might play a part in the completion of a marriage, but it was no more important than other elements, such as the betrothal contract, the exchange of gifts, or the

Saint Peter's, Rome: *The grand façade and colonnade of the basilica of Saint Peter's in the Vatican City, seat of the pope, dominates Rome. Begun by the Renaissance pope Julius II in 1506, it was completed under Paul V in 1615.*

words of consent exchanged between the new spouses. It was the marriage itself that was considered to be sacramental in character. Church leaders at Trent established a standard form of marriage, to be performed in a church and by a priest, after due notification of all members of the community who might testify to any impropriety.

The decrees of the Council of Trent affected women's lives in various ways. By reaffirming the power of the priesthood to confer grace through the sacraments the delegates effectively kept women on the margins of the religious life. Confessors strictly regulated even saintly women, and priests supervised marital conduct and familial relationships. Women's sexual lives and relationships with family members were subjects for the questions of the confessor. Even those with a religious vocation were now under stricter control. Many of the spontaneous and informal communities that had flourished in the past were eliminated. Women were limited to the formal convents of one of the established orders, which, moreover, were tightly supervised and enclosed. Although, unlike Protestant women, Catholic women still had the option of the convent, they were confined in their cloisters and barred from the opportunities that their predecessors had enjoyed in the Middle Ages.

Catholic Revival

The reorganization achieved at Trent ensured the Church's survival in the face of the Protestant challenge. At the same time, committed Catholic leaders outside the Council sought not merely for survival but for revitalization. These men and women labored as much as the reformers at Trent to create the modern Catholic Church, leading their communities, serving the poor, the sick, and the ignorant, exploring the inner recesses of the spirit, recovering Catholics lost to Protestantism, and extending the mission of the Church beyond the borders of Europe.

Reforming bishops worked to reinvent the real mission of their office. They restored churches that had fallen into disrepair, set standards for the secular clergy and members of the religious orders, and intervened with secular authorities to protect the interests of the members of their dioceses. Whereas bishops presided over a whole community, other reformers served particular groups within that community, tending the ill, the poor, the ignorant, in hospitals, orphanages, institutes, and schools. In France, saints Francis de Sales (1567–1622) and Vincent de Paul (c. 1581–1660) organized charitable missions of this sort. They also promoted the work of Saint Jane de Chantal (1572–1641), the founder, together with Francis, of the Visitation Order of nuns, and Saint Louise de Marillac (1591–1660), Vincent's disciple, founder of the Daughters of Charity (also known as the Sisters of Charity). Lay women *dévotes* ("devout

ones"), who remained unmarried but avoided the cloister, participated in these missions of teaching, nurturing, and nursing. They continued the medieval Christian mission to the poor at a time when most Protestant communities were engaged in reducing or abandoning it.

Education   Like Protestants, Catholic leaders recognized that education was vital to the success of their church. In the parishes, weekly catechism classes provided training in basic literacy for all children. Religious orders established schools for able students and offered scholarships to the poor. Convents provided schooling for the daughters of the wealthy, even those without a religious vocation, with instruction in literacy, needlework, and Catholic piety as a preparation for marriage.

In 1535, in the north Italian city of Brescia, Saint Angela Merici (c. 1474–1540) created a new order named after the legendary martyred virgin saint Ursula. The women who joined Merici's Ursulines lived, at first, not in cloistered seclusion but in their own homes, gathering together for business meetings and prayers. They devoted their days to teaching the female children of the poor. Returned to the cloister by the legislation of the Council of Trent, the Ursulines have survived as a teaching order into modern times.

Even England, now officially Protestant, produced another pioneer of female Catholic education: Mary Ward. Inspired by the example of the Jesuits (see below), Ward (1585–1645) founded, in 1609, a society later called the Institute of the Blessed Virgin Mary. By 1628, her society was running a network of eight schools for girls on the Continent (none could be founded in England), especially in central Europe, where its lay women teachers were known as the Englische Fräulein ("English young ladies"). These schools offered a rigorous secondary education grounded in the classics and the Christian tradition.

Mysticism   Other Catholics excelled in spiritual life. In Spain, saints Teresa of Avila (1515–1582; see *Witnesses*, p. 407, and *Windows On*, p. 413) and her student John of the Cross (1542–1591) were remarkable for their exploration of the inner life. Teresa's *Interior Castle* and John's *Dark Night of the Soul* describe the paths by which the soul achieves divine communion. The Spanish *Alumbrados*, or "enlightened ones," and the French Jansenists (followers of the doctrine of Cornelius Jansen, bishop of Ypres in Flanders, 1585–1638), both similar in some ways to the spiritualist vein in Protestantism (and similarly tending to heresy), assumed that each individual possessed an inner spark of divine light.

The Jesuits   The Jesuit order (the members of the Society of Jesus) combined features of these elements

Catholic Reform and Revival

The Catholic Church responded vigorously to the Protestant challenge by reaffirming its traditions and developing new forms of spiritual experience. In the first of these passages, the Council of Trent prelates reassert the validity of traditional Catholic practices. The second and third are the words of two representatives of a resurgent religious leadership: Ignatius of Loyola summons his followers to a renewed, absolute obedience to the Church; Teresa of Avila, explorer of the inner life, describes her spiritual vision.

Decrees of the Council of Trent reaffirm the validity of the sacraments in general and of the Eucharist in particular (1545–1563): *Decree on the Sacraments in General: Canon I.* If any one saith, that the sacraments of the New Law were not all instituted by Jesus Christ, our Lord; or, that they are more, or less, than seven, to wit, Baptism, Confirmation, the Eucharist, Penance, Extreme Unction, holy Orders, and Matrimony; or even that any one of these seven is not truly and properly a sacrament; let him be anathema. [note: *anathema* is a formal ecclesiastical curse of damnation.]

Canon IV. If any one saith, that the sacraments of the New Law are not necessary unto salvation, but superfluous; and that, without them, or without the desire thereof, men obtain of God, through faith alone, the grace of justification; … let him be anathema.

On the Most Holy Sacrament of the Eucharist: Canon I. If any one denieth, that, in the sacrament of the most holy Eucharist, are contained truly, really and substantially, the body and blood together with the soul and divinity of our Lord Jesus Christ, and consequently the whole Christ; but saith that He is only therein as in a sign, or in figure, or virtue; let him be anathema.

Canon II. If any one saith, that, in the sacred and holy sacrament of the Eucharist, the substance of the bread and wine remains conjointly with the body and blood of our Lord Jesus Christ, and denieth that wonderful and singular conversion of the whole substance of the wine into the Blood—the species only of the bread and wine remaining—which conversion indeed the Catholic Church most aptly calls Transubstantiation; let him be anathema.

(*The Canons and Decrees of the Sacred and Oecumenical Council of Trent*; trs. J. Waterworth, 1848, ed. E. Weber, 1990)

Ignatius of Loyola counsels his companions to obedience (1541): *Rules for Thinking with the Church.* 1. Always to be ready to obey with mind and heart, setting aside all judgment of one's own, the true spouse of Jesus Christ, our holy mother, our infallible and orthodox mistress, the Catholic Church, whose authority is exercised over us by the hierarchy. … 9. To uphold especially all the precepts of the of the Church, and not censure them in any manner; but, on the contrary, to defend them promptly, with reasons drawn from all sources, against those who criticize them.

10. To be eager to commend the decrees, mandates, traditions, rites and customs of the Fathers in the Faith or our superiors. As to their conduct; although there may not always be the uprightness of conduct that there ought to be, yet to attack or revile them in private or in public tends to scandal and disorder. Such attacks set the people against their princes and pastors; we must avoid such reproaches and never attack superiors before inferiors. The best course is to make private approach to those who have power to remedy the evil. … 13. That we may be altogether of the same mind and in conformity with the Church herself, if she shall have defined anything to be black which to our eyes appears to be white, we ought in like manner to pronounce it to be black. For we must undoubtingly believe, that the spirit of our Lord Jesus Christ, and the Spirit of the Orthodox Church His Spouse, by which Spirit we are governed and directed to Salvation, is the same; …

(Jesuits' "First Sketch," 1541; ed. J. C. Olin, 1990)

Saint Teresa of Avila describes a rapturous vision (1565): Our Lord was pleased that I should sometimes see a vision of this kind. Beside me, on the left hand, appeared an angel in bodily form, such as I am not in the habit of seeing except very rarely. Though I often have visions of angels, I do not see them. … But it was our Lord's will that I should see this angel in the following way. He was not tall but short, and very beautiful; and his face was so aflame that he appeared to be one of the highest ranks of angels, who seem to be all on fire. They must be of the kind called cherubim, but they do not tell me their names. I know very well that there is a great difference between some angels and others, and between these and others still, but I could not possibly explain it. In his hands I saw a great golden spear, and at the iron tip there appeared to be a point of fire. This he plunged into my heart several times so that it penetrated to my entrails. When he pulled it out, I felt that he took them with it, and left me utterly consumed by the great love of God. The pain was so severe that it made me utter several moans. The sweetness caused by this intense pain is so extreme that one cannot possibly wish it to cease, nor is one's soul then content with anything but God. This is not a physical, but a spiritual pain, though the body has some share in it—even a considerable share. So gentle is this wooing which takes place between God and the soul that if anyone thinks I am lying, I pray God, in His goodness, to grant him some experience of it.

Throughout the days that this lasted I went about in a kind of stupor. I had no wish to look or to speak, only to embrace my pain, which was a greater bliss than all created things could give me.

(Teresa of Avila, *The Life of Saint Teresa of Avila by Herself*, 1565; ed. J. M. Cohen, 1957)

Books that Made the Reformations

Erasmus	*Praise of Folly* (1511)
Luther	*On the Freedom of a Christian* (1520)
Calvin	*Institutes of the Christian Religion* (1536)
Loyola	*Spiritual Exercises* (1541)
Foxe	*Acts and Monuments* (1563)

of Catholic revival while dedicating itself to a particular mission: to defend papal authority and combat the enemies of the Church. That mission was defined by the Jesuits' founder, the Spanish nobleman and priest Saint Ignatius of Loyola (1491–1556).

In 1521, a cannonball wound ended Ignatius's first career as a soldier and precipitated a spiritual crisis. To prepare himself for the religious life to which he was now committed, Ignatius undertook advanced theological studies at Paris, which he completed in 1535. From Paris, he set out with six companions, who had vowed to devote themselves to a life of mission. Their object was a pilgrimage to Jerusalem, a dangerous venture at the time, which was abandoned of necessity. Instead, the travelers stopped at Venice, then moved on to Rome in 1537, on the eve of the creation of the Roman Inquisition.

In 1540, Ignatius obtained papal approval of a new order, of which he became the first head, or General—the Society of Jesus. Enlisting sixty founding members (called "Jesuits") the order was directly responsible to the pope and committed to active service of the Church. In his *Spiritual Exercises*, published in 1541, Ignatius described his inner struggle to subordinate his will to divine commands. Now he joined his deep spirituality with a commitment to practical action in the world.

The Society of Jesus was organized on a military model, with absolute obedience as its first requirement (see *Witnesses*, p. 407). How else was the authority of the Catholic Church to be reestablished where critics and dissenters had overcome it? "Your superior is to be obeyed," Ignatius enjoined his followers, "not because he is prudent, or good, or qualified by any other gift of God, but because he holds the place and the authority of God." The *Spiritual Exercises* declared, "I will believe that the white that I see is black, if the hierarchical church so defines."

By Ignatius's death in 1556, more than 1000 Jesuits were living by such principles in their work as teachers and missionaries around the world.

They set for themselves three main objectives: to develop committed Catholics in their western European homeland; to recover Protestant defectors in eastern Europe; and to win new converts in Asia, the Western Hemisphere (newly opened to Europeans), and Africa.

To achieve the first of these goals, the Jesuits created a network of prestigious schools offering a humanist education coupled with training in Catholic principles. An original, graded curriculum was designed to guide children from the earliest ages through their adolescence. By 1600 there were approximately 500 Jesuit schools. Although they admitted a few poor children on a scholarship basis, these Jesuit schools primarily enrolled the sons of the aristocracy and burgher elites, who were the future leaders of Catholic Europe.

Protestantism had won many adherents in Poland, Bohemia, Austria, and Hungary. The Jesuits won back these lands of central and eastern Europe by convincing their rulers that the Roman Catholic Church best supported their goal of national consolidation under the monarchy. In those regions, whose most revered saints included royal converts and the founders of nations, the Jesuit strategy was especially effective.

Jesuit Missions Abroad   While they sought to return Europe to the Catholic fold, the Jesuits also faced the challenge of Christian expansion. In the New World, Theatine, Franciscan, Dominican, and Augustinian missionaries were already seeking Catholic converts among the native populations when the newly formed Jesuits joined their efforts. In Asia from the 1540s, Jesuit missionaries attempted to bring Christianity to non-Christian civilizations. The Jesuits pledged "to go, without complaint, to any country …, whether to the Turk or other infidels, in India or elsewhere," and so they did, reaching India and many of the East Indian islands, Japan, and China.

Saint Francis Xavier (1506–1552), a Spanish nobleman and Ignatius's close associate, had already baptized thousands in the Portuguese colonies in India and the East Indies when, in 1549, he reached Japan, a place hardly known to Europeans. Establishing a Christian community there, he remained for two years before attempting to reach China. In this latter venture he died.

A generation later, the Jesuit Matteo Ricci (1552–1610) set off in Xavier's footsteps for the East. At the court at Beijing, he translated works of Western theology and learning, winning thousands of converts and some respect for Christianity. At the same time, impressed by the high cultural achievements of Chinese scholars, he learned their language and adopted their dress and customs. Ricci's mission, and the Jesuit endeavor in China generally, failed in the sense that it could not convert the population to Catholic Christianity. Yet the Jesuit adventure in Asia was not without effect. It formed the peaceful first chapter in the story of western Europe's interaction with the people of east Asia.

By 1600, Catholic reform had borne fruit. The institutional Church corrected the abuses that beset it, reaffirmed the authority of pope and priesthood, and commanded the obedience of Catholics. It established high standards of moral behavior for both clergy and laity, controlled the flow of books and ideas considered injurious to orthodoxy, and committed itself anew to wide-ranging programs of social service and education. Its missionaries won back to conformity whole regions of central and eastern Europe and assumed the task of extending Catholic Christianity throughout the globe.

THE REIGN OF INTOLERANCE

Both the Catholic and the Protestant movements were combative and exclusive. Both opposed groups deviating from their orthodoxies—radicals, dissenters, heretics, and presumed witches. Both demonized Turks, Jews, and Moors. And they battled each other ferociously. The abundantly creative period

---

The Persecutions

The affirmation of religious beliefs by reformers and traditionalists brought with it a surge of persecution and violence—a continuation, but also an acceleration, of the suppression of heresy and rage against "infidels" that had marked European life since the eleventh century. These passages report a massacre by a Catholic mob of presumed false converts to Christianity, and the testimony of a Protestant woman who would be executed for her beliefs, as well as the moderate voice of Erasmus revealing the absurdity, brutality, and self-deception of Christian Europe's hostility to the Muslim Turks.

The chronicle of the massacre of *conversos* in Lisbon, Portugal (1506): Some men from the lower orders who were there hauled [a worshiping New Christian, or *converso*] out of the church by his hair and killed him and immediately burned his body. ... To this disturbance many people came, to whom a friar gave a sermon, to call them together against the New Christians. After this two friars came out of the monastery with a crucifix in their hands, shouting "Heresy! Heresy!" This made such an impression on many foreigners, [who were] ordinary people, sailors from ships ... of the same [social] condition and low quality, that, more than five hundred having assembled, they began to kill all the New Christians they found in the streets. They threw the dead and dying bodies onto, and burnt them on, a bonfire which they had made. ... In this business they were helped by slaves and serving-lads, who with great diligence carted wood and other materials to light the fire. On this Easter Sunday they killed more than five hundred people.
(Damaio de Gois, *Cronica de Don Manuel*, 1506; from ed. J. Edwards, 1995)

Anne Askew describes her examination for heresy, in which her responses elevate the authority of the Bible over that of the Church (1545): I [Anne Askew] was asked how I interpreted the passage in the Book of Acts which says that God dwells not in temples made with hands. I replied that I would not cast pearls before swine. Acorns are good enough. Did I say that five lines out of the Bible are better than five masses? Yes, I get something out of the Bible, nothing out of the masses. ... At the next examination ... I was asked, If Scripture says that the bread and wine are the body of Christ will you believe it? I replied that I believe Scripture. If Scripture says they are not the body of Christ will you believe it? I replied that I believe Scripture. I believe all things as Christ and the apostles did leave them. I was asked to sign a confession that the body and blood of Christ are in substance at the mass. I said, in so far as Holy Scripture doth agree unto. At the third examination ... I wrote out for them my confession of faith: The sacramental bread was left to us to be received with thanksgiving, in remembrance of Christ's death, the only remedy of our soul's recovery; and that thereby we also receive the whole benefits and fruits of his most glorious passion. I told them that if the bread is left in a box for three months it will be mouldy, so it cannot be God. I wish neither death nor fear his might. ...
(Anne Askew; ed. R. H. Bainton, 1972)

Erasmus reproves those who want to fight the "cruel" Turks, when Christians have been cruel (1530): Whenever the ignorant mob hear the name "Turk," they immediately fly into a rage and clamour for blood, calling them dogs and enemies to the name of Christian; it does not occur to them that, in the first place, the Turks are men, and, what is more, half Christian; they never stop to consider whether the occasion of the war is just, nor whether it is practical to take up arms and thereby to provoke an enemy who will strike back with redoubled fury. ... For however cruel the deeds of the Turks, the same deeds committed against his fellow by a Christian are still more cruel. What a sight it would be if men were confronted with paintings of the atrocities which Christians have committed against Christians in the last forty years! This is all I have to say to those who do no more than scream "War on the Turks! War on the Turks!"
(Erasmus; ed. E. Rummel, 1990)

Repressing Dissent

A scene of torture: *A suspected heretic is tortured by the Venetian state's inquisitorial Holy Office in this sixteenth-century drawing by Domenico Beccafumi. The tribunal's notaries kept meticulous records of the tortures.* (Louvre, Paris)

The sacrament of penance: *Another aspect of Catholic reform (and of the Protestant Reformation) was the repression of dissent. In this illustration from Luca Bertelli's* Typus Ecclesiae Catholicae *(Venice, 1574), a priest administers the sacrament of penance (rejected by Protestantism), while defeated "heretics" including John Calvin are punished by drowning.*

of the Protestant Reformation and the Catholic Counter-Reformation was also an age of intolerance. Yet before the reform era ended, many critics were pleading vigorously for the toleration of dissent and difference.

Excluding Outsiders

For Europeans, "outsiders" were those who lived beyond the borders of Christendom, or within them as non-Christians. The Moors of Spain and Portugal; the Turks in the Balkans, western Asia, and North Africa; the Jews scattered across the Continent; all were outsiders, and all were hated.

It was especially on the Iberian peninsula and the borders of southeastern Europe that Europeans confronted many non-Christians. The Iberian kingdoms that eventually became the nations of Spain and Portugal had completed their *Reconquista* by 1492, when the last Moorish stronghold, Granada, was seized (see Chapter 9). The king and queen of Aragon and Castile, Ferdinand and Isabella, had already begun an internal *reconquista*, an ethnic cleansing of Moors and Jews. Meanwhile, the Ottoman Turks, who had captured Constantinople in 1453, surged through the Balkan peninsula and threatened Vienna, gateway to western Europe, as illustrated on p. 424. These developments fueled old fears of Jews and of Moorish and Turkish Muslims.

The Spanish Inquisition In Spain such fears spurred the creation of a new Inquisition. As early as the thirteenth century the Church had appointed special inquisitors (generally Dominicans) to investigate charges of heresy. Around 1480, Ferdinand and Isabella established the distinct organization of the Spanish Inquisition to complete the ideological task of conquest of the Iberian peninsula. From that time, and even more intensively after the 1492 conquest of Granada and the merciless expulsion of all non-converting Muslims and Jews, this task was pursued in earnest.

The Inquisition targeted for special scrutiny the Moors and Jews who converted and remained in Spain. Called respectively the *Moriscos* and *conversos*, they formed a considerable population; many of the latter, moreover, were well-educated and prosperous and held high places in the Church and the royal bureaucracy. Perpetually under suspicion of false conversion, they were virtually exterminated over the next century. Most of the Moriscos were expelled. Those of Jewish descent (there may have been close to 100,000 around 1500) were suspected of continued Jewish observance despite conversion to Christianity and were the special targets of the Spanish Inquisition. Charged with heresy, they were forced to undergo the public humiliation of an ***auto-da-fé***, or "act of faith," confronted with their alleged crime,

François Dubois, **Saint Bartholomew Day's Massacre:** *In this sixteenth-century painting, Catholic soldiers and citizens slaughter Huguenot (French Protestant) opponents, August, 1572, in Paris, perhaps encouraged by the regent queen, Catherine de' Medici.* (Musée des Beaux Arts, Lausanne, Switzerland)

and consigned to secular authorities for punishment and often execution. The Inquisition also had other targets: the *alumbrados*, Erasmian intellectuals, and actual Protestants. But the Jews were the Spanish Inquisition's main victims.

Spanish Jews, numbering in the hundreds of thousands in 1492, were all expelled or forcibly converted. Jewish communities elsewhere in Europe, where they existed, were also subjected to increasing restrictions. Venice, home of Europe's first ghetto, confined Jews to one locked section of the city and barred them from practicing certain professions. In other Italian cities, they lived in segregated communities and wore distinguishing marks on their clothing. In eastern Europe, especially Poland, Jews expelled from western regions in the Middle Ages had settled in villages and towns where they lived according to their own customs. Here they were taxed, watched, and sporadically persecuted. Throughout Europe, Jews were vulnerable to charges of the ritual murder of Christian children, products of a hysterical mythology that peaked in the age of the Reformation.

European intellectuals viewed the Jews ambivalently. A few, like the humanists Giovanni Pico della Mirandola (1463–1494) and Johannes Reuchlin (1455–1522), admired Hebrew scholarship and studied the mystical tradition called the Kabbalah. Others, however, vividly displayed their anti-Semitism. Some critics trounced Reuchlin for "Judaizing," and Luther in his old age wrote the vicious tract *On the Jews and their Lies.* Neither Erasmus nor Calvin departed cleanly from medieval anti-Judaism. Jews remained vulnerable to hostility, despite grudging acceptance by some.

The Turks European Christians were also afraid of the Ottoman Turks. During the fourteenth and fifteenth centuries, Ottoman armies pressed northward from the Middle East through Asia Minor, Greece, and the Balkans. The conquest of Constantinople in 1453 gave them a foothold in Europe of maximum strategic and commercial importance. At the battles of Kosovo (modern Serbia) in 1389, Belgrade (modern Serbia) in 1522, and Mohács (modern Hungary) in 1526, Turkish armies defeated Christian Serbs and Hungarians.

In 1529, a Turkish army stood outside Vienna. Only the hectic arrival of troops from both Catholic and Protestant German regions allowed the Austrian force of some 20,000 men to withstand the siege manned by some 200,000 Turks, whose heavy artillery repeatedly breached the fortifications. Turkish forces returned to Vienna the following year and again in 1683, to be repulsed eventually to a position only 50 miles (80 km.) short of its wall. Meanwhile Turkish and European navies clashed in a struggle for supremacy on the Mediterranean, climaxed by the victory of Spanish and Venetian galleys at Lepanto in 1571. But the victory was short-lived. Christendom was on the defensive.

The Balkan region of southeastern Europe lay under Turkish domination for some 500 years. There, most Christians (and Jews) practiced their own religion, lived under their own laws, and engaged in commerce during this period. But whereas Eastern Orthodox Christians enjoyed considerable freedom, western Catholic missionaries, usually Franciscans, suffered persecution, and many were martyred. Many natives of Bosnia and Albania found cogent reasons for conversion to Islam, and Christian boys throughout the Balkans were likely to be kidnapped, forcibly converted, and incorporated as military slaves into the elite Turkish janissary corps.

As Protestant-Catholic cooperation in the 1529 defense of Vienna demonstrated, Europeans were united in their fear and hatred of the Turks. Yet some contemporaries passed beyond this hatred sufficiently to query the behavior of Christians. Luther suggested that the repeated Turkish assaults were the just punishment of God for the sins of Christians, and should not be repulsed. Erasmus granted that the Turks committed atrocities—but so had Christian armies, and recently. "That is all I have to say to those who do no more than scream 'War on the Turks! War on the Turks!' " he wrote; let them remember that "the Turks are men" (see *Witnesses*, p. 409).

Sebastian Castellio (1515–1563), whose influential book *Concerning Heretics, Whether They Are to Be Persecuted and How They Are to be Treated* (1554) was published in 133 editions, called for toleration all around: "Let not the Jews or Turks condemn the Christians, nor let the Christians condemn the Jews or Turks, ... and let us, who are Christians, not condemn one another, but, if we are wiser than they, let us also be better and more merciful." The humanist and spiritualist Sebastian Franck (c. 1499–c. 1542) professed simply: "I have my brothers among the Turks, Papists, Jews, and all peoples," with whom "in the evening" of the Apocalypse he expected to enjoy eternity. But Europeans were not yet ready for the peaceful tolerance these pioneers recommended.

Witches and Martyrs

Intolerant of outsiders, Europeans also hated their neighbors. Within villages, towns, and nations, Catholics and Protestants, moderates and radicals persecuted each other, and waged wars along the fault lines of religious allegiance. Hostility toward those who were different, odd, or powerful resulted in fantasies of diabolic possession, and broke out in witch-hunts claiming the lives of tens of thousands of innocent victims, mostly women.

In the sixteenth and seventeenth centuries, martyrdom became as common as it had been in the early church. Missionaries in the Balkans, Asia, and the New World, Protestants in Catholic regions, Catholics in Protestant ones, and radical sectarians everywhere produced an abundant crop of new Christian martyrs—in addition to the Moors, Turks, and Jews that were killed by the Inquisition or by European armies. New rosters of martyrs fed new

---

WITNESSES

Witches

The persecution of witches, which was undoubtedly fueled by passions beyond the religious aroused by changing social patterns, is seen as part the history of religious persecution because the accused were identified as heretics who had surrendered themselves body and soul to the Devil. In the first of these passages, two Dominican clerics explain why they think that women are especially prone to witchery. In the second, an eyewitness describes the witch-hunt at Trier, in western Germany.

Heinrich Krämer and James Sprenger explain why women are especially prone to witchery (1486):
Question VI: Concerning Witches who copulate with Devils: As for the first question, why a greater number of witches is found in the fragile feminine sex than among men; it is indeed a fact that it were idle to contradict, since it is accredited by actual experience, apart from the verbal testimony of credible witnesses. ...If we inquire, we find that nearly all the kingdoms of the world have been overthrown by women. Troy, which was a prosperous kingdom, was, for the rape of one women, Helen, destroyed, and many thousands of Greeks slain. ... And so with others. Therefore it is no wonder if the world now suffers through the malice of women.

And now let us examine the carnal desires of the body itself, whence has arisen unconscionable harm to human life. ... a woman is beautiful to look upon, contaminating to the touch, and deadly to keep. ... Let us consider also her gait, posture, and habit, in which is vanity of vanities. There is no man in the world who studies so hard to please the good God as even an ordinary woman studies by her vanities to please men. ... To conclude. All witchcraft comes from carnal lust, which is in women insatiable. ...
(Heinrich Krämer, James Sprenger, *Malleus maleficarum*, 1486; ed. M. Summers, 1928)

The canon of Linden, author of a chronicle of the city of Trier, describes the witch persecutions there of the late sixteenth century: Inasmuch as it was popularly believed that the continued sterility of many years was caused by witches through the malice of the Devil, the whole country rose to exterminate the witches. This movement was promoted by many in office, who hoped wealth from the persecution. And so, from court to court throughout the towns and villages of all the diocese, scurried special accusers, inquisitors, notaries, jurors, judges, constables, dragging to trial and torture human beings of both sexes and burning them in great numbers. Scarcely any of those who were accused escaped punishment. Nor were there spared even the leading men in the city of Trier ... [who] were swept away in this ruin. ... Meanwhile notaries, copyists, and innkeepers grew rich. The executioner rode a blooded horse, like a noble of the court, and went clad in gold and silver; his wife vied with noble dames in the richness of her array. ... This persecution lasted for several years; and some of those who presided over the administration of justice gloried in the multitude of the stakes, at each of which a human being had been given to the flames. At last, though the flames were still unsated, the people grew impoverished, rules were made and enforced restricting the fees and costs of examinations and examiners, and suddenly, as when in war funds fail, the zeal of the persecutors died out.
("The Witch Persecutions", from *Translations and Reprints from the Original Sources of European History*, 1898–1912; ed. George L. Burns)

Robert Crowley, The Burning of Anne Askew, *from Confutation of Nicolas Shaxton, 1548*

*From **The Whole Book of Psalms in Four Parts,** 1563*

Different facets of women's participation in the Reformation era are illustrated here. The burning of Anne Askew, who abandoned her Catholic husband to pursue her faith, is shown in this illustration (above left). In this household scene (above right) is depicted the husband's supremacy over wife and children. Witches are shown burning at Dernburg, Germany, in a mid-sixteenth-century woodcut (below). The Catholic mystic Saint Teresa is shown in a sculpture by Bernini (left) experiencing the ecstasy of divine union. (top left: British Library, London; top right: Private Collection)

To what extent did women find new possibilities in the era of Reform?

Gianlorenzo Bernini, The Ecstasy of Saint Teresa, Cornaro Chapel, Rome, 1645–52

Witches burning, mid-sixteenth century

To continue your investigation of this topic, please go to www.prenhall.com/king for the related **WINDOWS** on the **WEB** activity

413

martyrologies, or biographical anthologies of these victims of official repression. An example is illustrated in *Windows On* on p. 391. These widely read works kept the memory of pain and persecution alive in the public mind.

The repressive capacity of early Protestantism is illustrated by the execution of Michael Servetus (c. 1511–1553), a Spanish physician. Among his other works, Servetus published anti-Trinitarian tracts, culminating in *The Restoration of Christianity*. Provocatively, he sent the unfinished manuscript to John Calvin, who refuted the arguments in the next edition of his *Institutes*. The two antagonists seemed drawn to each other: Servetus was determined to go to Geneva, and Calvin was determined to pounce on him if he did. They met at last, and Calvin prevailed. In 1553, Servetus was arrested, tried, convicted, and burned at the stake—a freethinking martyr to a revolutionary but intransigent Protestantism.

War created martyrs even more abundantly than did trials and persecutions. The Protestant Reformation ushered in an era of religious warfare that did not slow until 1648. In the lands of the Holy Roman Empire and in France, with effects extending throughout Europe, Protestants confronted Catholics on the field of battle. Religious warfare finally ended in the West only when markets and dominions replaced religion as the cause of conflict among nations.

Even amidst fighting, Protestants and Catholics agreed on one subject: witchcraft. Witches were diabolical and dangerous and should be suppressed. Today it is clear that there never was such a thing as a witch, in the medieval sense of the word: someone who has sworn a pact with the Devil, who can ride a broom, who cannibalizes children or causes plague as part of a systematic program of evil. But sixteenth- and seventeenth-century Europeans accepted the reality of witches. For about two centuries, beginning just before the Protestant revolt, the fear and distrust of witches became epidemic, as described in *Witnesses* on p. 412. This was the era of the great witch-hunt, resulting in the execution of 60,000 and the terrorization of the villages of Europe.

The story of the witch-hunt belongs here because it forms part of the history of the persecution of heresy. The witchcraft accusation touched tens of thousands of Europeans, mostly women, often the old eccentric or envied solitary or gifted but fallible healer. These unfortunates were charged with child murder, blasphemy, sexual liaisons with the Devil, and nocturnal broom-riding among other hideous and outlandish crimes. Like accused heretics, accused and unrepentant witches were tortured until they confessed—torture being a legal option in the investigation of heresy. Torture worked. Where torture was not used (or only rarely used, as in England), few confessions resulted, and few accused witches were condemned. Upon confession, victims were pressed to name their associates in diabolic activity. Like heretics, they were executed not by the Church but by the "secular arm" of the state.

The voices of learned men fanned the witch hysteria—the same humanists, lawyers, and physicians who promoted the study of the classics and the arts and sciences. German, French, and Italian writers produced comprehensive witch manuals, luridly illustrated, and two Dominican friars wrote an impressive *Hammer of Witches* (1487), a guidebook to the identification and conviction of diabolically possessed, baby-murdering, broom-flying deviants. At the same time, a few voices were raised on behalf of the accused. The physicians Johann Weyer (1515–1588) and Reginald Scot (1538–1599) argued in separate works that the witch accusation was illegitimate, and easily foisted upon depressed, aging women. The jurist Andrea Alciati (1492–1550) pointed to abuses in witch trials, and the essayist Michel de Montaigne (1533–1592) insisted that there be "sharp and luminous evidence" for witchcraft accusations: "It is putting a very high price on one's conjectures to roast a man alive for them."

Over the clamor of the witch-hunt, such voices of reason were heard at last. These enlightened critics resembled those others who cautioned against the persecution of the Jews or the Turks, or who were grieved by the slaughter and by the pointlessness of religious warfare.

Conclusion
THE PROTESTANT CHALLENGE AND THE MEANING OF THE WEST

Luther's bold stand at Worms was a revolutionary moment in the history of the West. It was the first step in a tortuous process that dismantled the cultural and religious monopoly of the Roman Church. It opened up an era of competition among churches for the consciences of Europeans, and of the redefinition of the Catholic mission. It was an era, also, of deadly intolerance, in which only a few dissonant thinkers called for mutual understanding. Amid these intersecting currents of thought and belief, the rulers of the states of Europe took advantage of religious turbulence to strengthen their positions. In the short term, the princes were the winners of the struggle for reform. Amid warfare and zealotry, which they turned to suit their purposes when they could, they began to build the nations of modern Europe.

QUESTIONS TO CONSIDER

1. Would there have been a Reformation without the Christian humanism of Erasmus?

2. Why did Luther's attack on the sale of indulgences in the Ninety-Five Theses strike at the heart of the sacramental system of the medieval church?

3. Why was the Protestant Reformation able to spread? To what extent was it attractive to masses of people, and to what extent useful to reigning monarchs?

4. Why did Protestantism diversify into so many groups, including radical groups that were persecuted both by mainstream Protestants and by Catholics?

5. Did the emergence of Protestantism lead to more opportunities for women, or to greater tolerance for unorthodox beliefs and behavior?

SUGGESTED RESOURCES

Ahlgren, Gillian, *Teresa of Avila and the Politics of Sanctity* (Ithaca: Cornell University Press, 1996). Studies Teresa's carefully constructed works which aimed to protect women's visionary experience in a restrictive and persecuting age, and shows how she thereby became the one Spanish religious woman of the era promoted to sainthood.

Benedict, Philip, *Christ's Churches Purely Reformed: A Social History of Calvinism* (New Haven: Yale University Press. 2002). An updated survey of the history of the spread of Reformed churches with special emphasis on the experience of the laity.

Briggs, Robin, *Witches and Neighbors: The Social and Cultural Context of European Witchcraft* (New York: HarperCollins, 1995; Viking; Penguin, 1996). A recent entry to the list of many excellent studies on European witchcraft, focusing on the nature of the victimized alleged witch.

Duffy, Eamon, *The Voices of Morebath: Reformation and Rebellion in an English Village* (New Haven: Yale University Press, 2001). Records the experience of villagers who resisted for decades the imposition of official Protestantism.

Gregory, Brad S., *Salvation at Stake: Christian Martyrdom in Early Modern Europe* (Cambridge MA: Harvard University Press, 1999). Probing account of the phenomenon of martyrdom suffered by the victims of both Catholic and Protestant states.

Grell, Ole Peter and Bob Scribner, eds., *Tolerance and Intolerance in the European Reformation* (Cambridge: Cambridge University Press, 1996). Essays examining the different contexts for incidents of tolerance and intolerance in all the regions of Europe, revealing no clear progression towards greater toleration on the continental level.

Kamen, Henry, *The Spanish Inquisition: A Historical Revision* (New Haven: Yale University Press, 1998). Long seen as a byword for cruel intolerance, the Spanish Inquisition, Kamen argues, does not deserve the evil reputation assigned it by nineteenth-century historians.

Levi, Anthony, *Renaissance and Reformation: the Intellectual Genesis* (New Haven: Yale University Press, 2002). Offers a revisionist view of both movements and their interrelations.

Mack, Phyllis, *Visionary Women: Ecstatic Prophecy in Seventeenth-Century England* (Berkeley–Los Angeles: University of California Press, 1992). Traces women's limited participation in the Reformation as prophets and visionaries.

Muller, Richard A., *The Unaccommodated Calvin: Studies in the Foundation of a Theological Tradition* (Oxford: Oxford University Press, 2000). Studies Calvin's thought as essential to Reformation theology, and resistant to modern analysis.

O'Malley, John W., *The First Jesuits* (Cambridge, MA: Harvard University Press, 1993). Comprehensive account of the formation of the Society of Jesuits, understood in their social context.

Scribner, Bob, Roy Porter and Mikuláš Teich, eds., *The Reformation in National Context* (Cambridge: Cambridge University Press, 1994). Thirteen essays surveying how and why Protestantism came, didn't come, or came and went, to twelve regions of Europe.

Tracy, James D., *Europe's Reformations, 1450–1650* (Totowa: Rowman & Littlefield, 1999). A careful examination of Europe's migration from a single faith to a multiplicity of confessions over two centuries, always attentive to continuities and complexities.

Zagorin, Perez, *How the Idea of Religious Toleration Came to the West* (Princeton: Princeton University Press. 2003). Zagorin argues that the idea of tolerance began with a particular strand of Protestantism, and particularly with Sebastian Castellio.(see above pp. 411–412).

Martin Luther: biography, resources, and links (Michigan State University):
http://www.educ.msu.edu

John Calvin: biography, resources, and links (Michigan State University):
http://www.educ.msu.edu

John Locke, A Letter Concerning Toleration, 1689 (University of Tenn Martin):
http://www.utm.edu/research/iep/text/locke/tolerat.htm

⊙ Western Civilization Documents CD-ROM

9.2 Propositions of Wycliffe Condemned at London
9.3 The Lollard Conclusions
9.4 Individual Heretics: Saints and Witches
11.1 Erasmus: A Diatribe Against the Pope
11.2 Luther's Ninety-Five Theses
11.3 The Act of Supremacy
11.4 A Protestant Woman Argues for Tolerance
11.5 The Edict of Nantes
11.6 The Catholic Response: The Council of Trent
11.7 The Execution of Archbishop Cranmer
11.8 A Right with Roots in the Bible
12.1 the German Peasant's Revolt
12.2 Elizabeth's Act of Uniformity
12.3 The Arrest of the Catholic Priest Edmund Campion
12.6 The Ecclesiastical Ordinances of Geneva

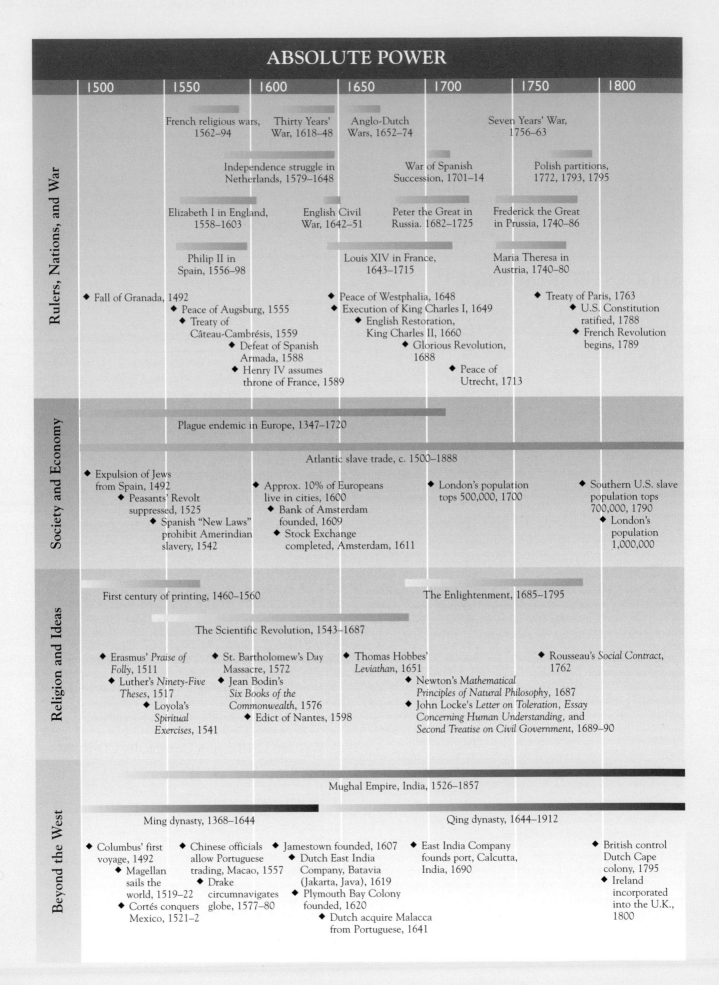

ABSOLUTE POWER

| | 1500 | 1550 | 1600 | 1650 | 1700 | 1750 | 1800 |

Rulers, Nations, and War

French religious wars, 1562–94

Thirty Years' War, 1618–48

Anglo-Dutch Wars, 1652–74

Seven Years' War, 1756–63

Independence struggle in Netherlands, 1579–1648

War of Spanish Succession, 1701–14

Polish partitions, 1772, 1793, 1795

Elizabeth I in England, 1558–1603

English Civil War, 1642–51

Peter the Great in Russia, 1682–1725

Frederick the Great in Prussia, 1740–86

Philip II in Spain, 1556–98

Louis XIV in France, 1643–1715

Maria Theresa in Austria, 1740–80

◆ Fall of Granada, 1492

◆ Peace of Augsburg, 1555

◆ Treaty of Câteau-Cambrésis, 1559

◆ Defeat of Spanish Armada, 1588

◆ Henry IV assumes throne of France, 1589

◆ Peace of Westphalia, 1648

◆ Execution of King Charles I, 1649

◆ English Restoration, King Charles II, 1660

◆ Glorious Revolution, 1688

◆ Peace of Utrecht, 1713

◆ Treaty of Paris, 1763

◆ U.S. Constitution ratified, 1788

◆ French Revolution begins, 1789

Society and Economy

Plague endemic in Europe, 1347–1720

Atlantic slave trade, c. 1500–1888

◆ Expulsion of Jews from Spain, 1492

◆ Peasants' Revolt suppressed, 1525

◆ Spanish "New Laws" prohibit Amerindian slavery, 1542

◆ Approx. 10% of Europeans live in cities, 1600

◆ Bank of Amsterdam founded, 1609

◆ Stock Exchange completed, Amsterdam, 1611

◆ London's population tops 500,000, 1700

◆ Southern U.S. slave population tops 700,000, 1790

◆ London's population 1,000,000

Religion and Ideas

First century of printing, 1460–1560

The Enlightenment, 1685–1795

The Scientific Revolution, 1543–1687

◆ Erasmus' *Praise of Folly*, 1511

◆ Luther's *Ninety-Five Theses*, 1517

◆ Loyola's *Spiritual Exercises*, 1541

◆ St. Bartholomew's Day Massacre, 1572

◆ Jean Bodin's *Six Books of the Commonwealth*, 1576

◆ Edict of Nantes, 1598

◆ Thomas Hobbes' *Leviathan*, 1651

◆ Newton's *Mathematical Principles of Natural Philosophy*, 1687

◆ John Locke's *Letter on Toleration, Essay Concerning Human Understanding,* and *Second Treatise on Civil Government*, 1689–90

◆ Rousseau's *Social Contract*, 1762

Beyond the West

Mughal Empire, India, 1526–1857

Ming dynasty, 1368–1644

Qing dynasty, 1644–1912

◆ Columbus' first voyage, 1492

◆ Magellan sails the world, 1519–22

◆ Cortés conquers Mexico, 1521–2

◆ Chinese officials allow Portuguese trading, Macao, 1557

◆ Drake circumnavigates globe, 1577–80

◆ Jamestown founded, 1607

◆ Dutch East India Company, Batavia (Jakarta, Java), 1619

◆ Plymouth Bay Colony founded, 1620

◆ Dutch acquire Malacca from Portuguese, 1641

◆ East India Company founds port, Calcutta, India, 1690

◆ British control Dutch Cape colony, 1795

◆ Ireland incorporated into the U.K., 1800

CHAPTER 15

ABSOLUTE POWER

War and Politics in Early Modern Europe

1500–1750

KEY QUESTIONS

◆ **Power and Gunpowder:** Which of the innovations in military technology and organization—the use of gunpowder, the improved design of fortifications, the deployment of infantry—was most critical?

◆ **War Games:** How important was the factor of religion in the major wars of the sixteenth through eighteenth centuries?

◆ **An Age of Kings:** How successful were European kings at getting and wielding "absolute power"?

◆ **Mirrors for Princes:** How did the growth of kingly power retard or advance the rights of citizens?

The Perfect Prince *Around the beginning of the sixteenth century, the Italian duke Cesare Borgia (1475–1507) was engaged in acquiring for himself a large chunk of central Italy. To bolster his authority in the city of Cesena, he decided to rid himself of the agent he had placed in charge of it. He waited for the right moment; "Then, one morning, Remirro's body was found cut in two pieces on the piazza …, with a block of wood and a bloody knife beside it." The brutal message had its intended effect, keeping the citizens, at least for a while, "appeased and stupefied."*

This incident was narrated by Niccolò Machiavelli (1469–1527) in his handbook for the perfect prince (see Chapter 13). For Machiavelli, the concern of a prince is to gain and hold power—by any means necessary. He should crush enemies, rather than forgive them; inflict cruelties as necessary, swiftly and all at once. His subjects need not love him; better that they fear him, since "fear is strengthened by a dread of punishment which is always effective." Such a prince might possibly, Machiavelli thought, save Italy.

Machiavelli's prince never came. Hopelessly fragmented, Italy fell to nations beyond the Alps. Those nations embodied new dimensions of power, not seen since the days of the Roman Empire—enough to consume each other and to dominate much of the rest of the world. Their ascension owed much to their ambitious kings, who exemplified the principles that Machiavelli proposed.

The period from 1500 to 1750—often called the "early modern" era—saw a great concentration of power in Europe: the power of armies, of states, and, above all, of kings. Changes in military organization and funding, as well as terrible new weapons, made their progress possible and their ambitions urgent. (*How Many* on p. 428 shows the growth in army size and casualties.) Those ambitions erupted into a series of wars, fought at first in the name of religion and later for ***raison d'état***, "reason of state." The kings and princes who profited from these wars—who taxed their subjects, reined in their fractious nobles, and compelled ordinary men to fight—not only expanded their states but maximized their power. In several states, they reached for absolute power, which would allow them to execute law without the restraint of parliament or peerage. As monarchs gathered power, abetted by prime ministers, advisers, and **courtiers**, intellectuals developed theories of monarchy justifying the power of kings to the people who had none.

POWER AND GUNPOWDER

Machiavelli's hypothetical prince was armed with acute intelligence and supreme force of will. The states of Europe armed themselves with new weapons and new military methods. By 1500, armies that depended on the force of their **infantry** had supplanted armies of mounted knights. Lance and sword gave way to **arquebus** and **pike**, then to **musket** and **bayonet** (see p. 419); the cavalry charge, to rows and columns of uniformed soldiers; the simple medieval wall, punctuated by gates and towers, to elaborate systems of fortification, designed to foil the force of cannon fire. Military leaders—now required to be management experts as much as battle chiefs—forged armies that performed on the battlefield with the precision they learned on the drill field.

Knights and Guns

On late medieval battlefields, ordinary foot soldiers had already proved themselves a match for mounted knights. In Flanders, in 1302, a mob of urban workers smashed an army of French cavalry. Afterwards, the fragments of the noble warriors' expensive arms and armor littered the "Field of Golden Spurs," as the disaster was expressively named. In 1346, at Crécy, and 1415, at Agincourt, two battlefields of the Hundred Years' War, English peasants armed with longbows, made from the flexible wood of their native yew trees, mowed down heavily armed knights.

Within a century, the advent of guns clinched the triumph of infantry over cavalry. Basically, the gun is an iron tube in which gunpowder—a mixture of potassium nitrate, sulfur, and charcoal—is exploded to fire a missile. The Chinese and the Arabs had used gunpowder since the eighth century C.E., mainly for fireworks. The Mongols who attacked Sung Chinese fortifications early in the thirteenth century exploded gunpowder-packed bamboo stalks, the ancestor of the first guns. When Mongol armies swung westward to Poland and Hungary in 1240, Europeans first experienced the deadly might of gunfire. Soon European ironworkers—who honed their skills making swords and horseshoes, metal plowshares and great church bells—learned to manufacture guns.

Around 1400, the Ottoman Turks employed German and Hungarian metalworkers to construct the cannon they fired in their advance through the Middle East and the Balkans. Cannon fire figured in the Ottoman victory at Constantinople in 1453. Europeans soon surpassed the Turks, however, developing gun technology to an extraordinary degree. Guns would be the premier tool of European explorers, conquerors, and merchants as they penetrated other continents of the globe.

In the short run, guns prompted the creation of tougher suits of armor for mounted knights. In the long run, they spelled the death of knighthood. No cavalry force could withstand the direct assault of a battery of guns, although as late as the twentieth century some were still trying to. Ordinary foot

The Tools of War

The cannon: From the mid-fifteenth century, innovations in weapons changed the nature, costs, and social implications of warfare. The most dramatic changes affected the cannon, as shown here in Four Books of Knighthood, *1528.*

soldiers armed with better and better guns formed the heart of the modern army, replacing mounted warriors as these had once replaced the ancient legion and phalanx. In the sixteenth and seventeenth centuries, ranks of arquebusiers surrounded a core of pikemen (soldiers armed with long spears). In the eighteenth, lines or columns of musketeers—their more accurate weapons fitted with bayonets which made the pike obsolete—fired in unison, in precise rhythm on command, to halt an enemy charge.

At first, guns could not fire straight or very far. The main use of the new weaponry was in big guns, used to batter down gates and walls. Huge cannon, finely adorned by the talents of engravers and sculptors, were dragged by beasts or before the besieged town or castle. Firing ball after ball, they eventually breached the defenses. The greedy horde of soldiers then swarmed in to sack, rape, and burn. Among the first to use these tactics was the French king Charles VII (r. 1422–1461), who, in 1450, drove the English from their strongholds in France at the close of the Hundred Years' War.

Siege warfare had long figured in human conflict—as testified by the protective circuit of walls that ringed some of the most ancient communities. But now the siege became newly destructive. Innocent populations, trapped within their walls, hearing the cannon fire, awaited in fear the ending that must come as walls gave way to explosive force.

Responding to the challenge of cannon fire, military engineers designed a new type of fortification. The long, exposed **curtain walls** of medieval castles and towns were vulnerable to bombardment. The squat walls of the new-style fortifications, equipped with projecting **bastions** and thickened by earthworks, as shown in the illustration on p. 420, withstood cannon fire painlessly. The triangular bastions distanced the battle from the town within, and enabled crossbowmen, **musketeers**, and riflemen to rain missiles upon attackers from two sides at once. These fortifications required fat purses and master designers—among the first of whom were Leonardo da Vinci and Michelangelo. The craft of military engineering developed sophistication as the demand for fortifications increased, and was advanced by the experience of battle.

Although the development of land warfare was crucial, much of the fighting took place at sea. Europe's expanding dominion in the world, linked together by oceans and rivers, owed much to its naval power. Here, too, firepower proved its value, giving European navies an incontestable advantage over those of other civilizations precisely when the stakes of shipborne commerce peaked. Cannon mounted on shipboard or below deck could defend merchant convoys or fight all-out naval battles.

Guns and fortifications were expensive, as were the accoutrements of the new mode of warfare. Soldiers and sailors required not only weapons, but helmets and armor, ammunition and cannonballs, powder flasks and water canteens. Armies traveled with baggage wagons and construction gear, bringing in their wake servants, wives, mistresses, children, and spare horses. In the Greek *polis* or ancient Rome or medieval Europe, the soldier came to fight bearing his own equipment. Now the principality or nation supplied that equipment. The machinery of revenue collection strained to meet the cost of outfitting forces that numbered, by 1600, tens of thousands of men.

Military Organization

The use of guns and the greater reliance on infantry constitute major changes in methods of warfare.

The gun: The gun, which later developed to become a musket with bayonet, was also an important innovation (shown here in a 1508 drawing).

The castle: *The curtain walls of medieval castles, which were incapable of withstanding cannon fire, were replaced by massive fortifications like at Deal Castle in the sixteenth century, specially designed to face artillery attack from all angles.*

But these were only part of what some scholars have called the "military revolution" of the early modern period. Military organization also developed, as gifted leaders forged the modern, professional army.

Italy   Modern warfare first unfolded in Italy, where war was a paid profession. Unlike the armies of the north, which consisted of native noblemen and their peasant auxiliaries, those of the Italian cities consisted of hired warriors, paid with cash. Managing these hired, or mercenary, armies were generals called *condottieri* ("contractors"), one of whom is depicted in *Windows On* on p. 432. The *condottieri* were strategists, economists, and engineers, as well as soldiers. They were experts at recruiting troops, keeping them paid, pitching camp, and retreating in the face of danger. They fought to fulfill their contracted terms with their paymaster state. They aimed to spill as little blood, and to face as few battles, as possible. Thus Italian warfare was an efficient tool of statecraft, but it was not especially deadly.

It was on the shrewdest of such *condottieri* that Machiavelli modeled his prince (although he deplored the use of mercenary soldiers, who he thought would always fight less well than natives). Such men as Cesare Borgia (the son and agent of Pope Alexander VI) and Francesco Sforza (1401–1466, who in 1450 became Duke of Milan) battled their way to eminence and, in the case of the latter, even to sovereign power. Their skills of military organization lifted them far above the ranks of ordinary men and close in line to the thrones of hereditary monarchs.

Switzerland   Among the mercenaries hired by the combative Italian states were soldiers from Switzerland. In that mountainous southwestern zone of the Holy Roman Empire, local regions called **cantons** had been engaged, since the late thirteenth century, in a struggle for independence. This struggle encouraged the development of native military skills. Swiss soldiers, like the hoplites of ancient Greece, fought on foot and side by side, mutually supporting each other. Armed with pikes and arrayed in tight squares from which their weapons bristled, they could withstand the cavalry charges led by the Empire's noblemen. The ordinary male citizen of a Swiss canton was nearly always of necessity a soldier. When the Swiss finally won their independence in 1499, these disciplined infantrymen sold their skills abroad.

Sweden   Far to the north, Sweden's King Gustavus II Adolphus (r. 1611–1632) led the way in creating a national standing army, rather than a knightly or mercenary one. Sweden was then a small and rather poor country whose role in European affairs before the seventeenth century was minimal. That role was changed with the outbreak of the Thirty Years' War. Gustavus Adolphus intervened in that conflict in 1630 to protect Protestant interests and to secure a footing on the south shore of the Baltic Sea. The supreme performance of his disciplined troops and mobile cannon won fame for Sweden, whose hymn-singing soldiers were forbidden by their pious king to pillage or rape—a unique prohibition in that era.

England   A generation later, the Englishman Oliver Cromwell (1599–1658), a leader of Parliamentary opposition to the king, organized the New Model Army, which defeated the Royalist forces in 1645. He personally led the military unit known as the Ironsides, men who as he said, "had the fear of God before them." Forming tight squares, their unflinching pikes projecting at set angles like a deadly, mechanical porcupine, his soldiers set a new standard for disciplined warfare.

France   Also contributing to the military revolution was France. In the mid-1400s King Charles VII reorganized the French army, building up a strong artillery and de-emphasizing the role of knights (who had once been so shamefully vanquished by England's bowmen). As knights became less important, the power of the nobility (which often challenged that of the monarch) could be curtailed. Charles ordered the castle towers of feudal strongholds cut down and extended his mandate into every pocket of regional power, seeking to create a national spirit and a national military organization.

Despite Charles's efforts, the French military remained a motley combination of individual units recruited by semi-independent generals. Then, in the later 1600s, King Louis XIV (r. 1643–1715) thoroughly reconstituted the army as an instrument of state policy. Its captains and generals became part of a hierarchy arrayed under the king's personal authority. Its soldiers wore standard uniforms, drilled and marched, and were provisioned by a central office. By

the early 1700s, intensive recruiting had resulted in an increase from 100,000 to 400,000 men, making the French army the largest in Europe.

Prussia   It was in Prussia, however, that the professionalization of the early modern army reached its zenith. Prussia was a new state, formed by the Great Elector Frederick William (1640–1688) from two non-adjacent territories—the imperial electorate of Brandenburg and the Polish duchy of Prussia. Geographically fragmented (it included several other small territories) Prussia required a powerful army for its defense. Its first ruler, the Great Elector Frederick William, made military values and needs the linchpin of his political strategy. Prudently providing for all other state expenses from the modest resources of his private purse, he dedicated all tax revenues to the maintenance of the army, while recruiting nearly the whole of the Prussian aristocracy—called the *Junkers*—to lead it. By these methods, he built the army up to 40,000 men, enormous for its time and for the size of the principality, which then numbered 1.5 million inhabitants. His successors in the next century raised that total to 200,000, one-half that of the army of France, with a population more than ten times that of Prussia.

By the eighteenth century, the miscellaneous cavalry contingents of the Middle Ages had been replaced by the modern army.

War and Diplomacy   The eighteenth-century army centered on an infantry force armed with smooth-bore muskets, descendants of the earlier arquebus, which were transformed into spears by affixing a sharp dagger or bayonet. The infantry faced an enemy who had already been ravaged by artillery teams with mobile, increasingly accurate cannon. Salaried soldiers wore centrally-issued uniforms, slept in barracks, and drilled regularly the maneuvers that they would be called upon to perform in battle. Officers of noble origin learned the art of command at military academies such as those in Paris, Saint Petersburg, or Turin (modern Italy). Conducting a siege, according to King Frederick II, the Great, of Prussia (r. 1740–1786), was a craft "like that of carpenter or clock-maker." Battle itself—unlike the whirling charges of mounted warriors or the relentless pressure of a siege—was a formal, choreographed event in which two bodies of men faced each other across an open field and fired precisely on command.

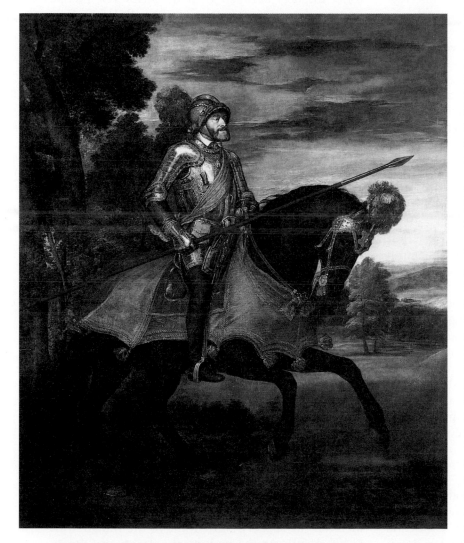

***Titian*, Charles V on Horseback, 1548:** *The Italian painter Titian (Tiziano Vecellio) painted this portrait of the Holy Roman emperor Charles V on horseback after the latter's victory in 1547 over Protestant armies at Mühlberg. The portrait evokes the energy and magnificence of the Roman emperors, to whom Charles, at this date the ruler in name of much of Europe, wished to think himself equal. (Prado, Madrid)*

Why did they fire? Because they were drilled to load, aim, and shoot in unison, and paid to do so—however meagerly and irregularly. Certainly, they did not fight for glory or territory, or for their faith; in the eighteenth century, religious differences did not spark wars. Nor did they fight from patriotism, a sentiment not yet invented. But if patriotism was not yet born, national and dynastic interests were very much alive. European wars were fought in the service of those interests, as rulers jostled for prestige, for land, and for power. To win those ends, they tolerated devastating losses of life and property, and incurred huge expenses borne by the citizenry.

Then, as now, talk was the main alternative to war. By the fourteenth century, especially in Flanders and Italy, the medieval herald, who conveyed messages between leaders, was beginning to develop into that of the modern **ambassador**. The ambassador also represented a state or ruler at the courts or assemblies of another. He brought information; conveyed messages of sympathy or congratulations; and presented terms for the settlement of disputes. Two are portrayed on *Windows On* on p. 432.

Even in the midst of hostilities, the ambassador enjoyed promises of personal security from all parties. By the sixteenth century, ambassadors were based in the main European centers and conducted negotiations between states. Those negotiations, constituting what is called **diplomacy**, prepared the peace treaties that followed upon war, or prevented war altogether. In 1619, an experienced Spanish diplomat advised that wars were no longer a test of strength, like a bullfight, to be decided by "mere battles"; "rather they depend on losing or gaining friends and allies, and it is to this end that good statesmen must turn all their attention and energy."

The citizens of *Utopia*, the ideal "nowhereland" envisioned by the sixteenth-century English writer Thomas More, did not go to war. If necessary, mercenaries were dispatched to do so. Utopian ambassadors arranged for a settlement of differences even at great financial cost. When diplomacy failed, Utopian policy called for the assassination of the enemy leader—an atrocity resorted to only to prevent the worse one of war. Europe was not yet so civilized.

WAR GAMES

Three centuries of war trace the shifts in the political configuration of Europe after 1500, as shown by Maps 15.1 and 15.2 and *How Many?* on p. 428. Cities and principalities lost to nations competing for dominance. Each sought security, territory, commercial advantages, and a share in the balance of power maintained by national leaders. Equipped with the latest military technology, rulers and statesmen employed war to reconfigure the map of Europe, playing a game that dealt its winners status, wealth, and power.

In the first phase of early modern warfare from 1500 to 1648, the enmity between two great players—France (successively under Valois and Bourbon rulers) and the House of Habsburg (Holy Roman Emperors, whose domains included Austria, Styria, Carinthia, Tyrol, the Netherlands, and Spain) stoked the fires of religious conflict. By the end of the Thirty Years' War, religious issues had waned, outpaced by political objectives. In the second phase, from 1648 to 1763, France again played a central role. Having emerged from the Thirty Years' War the most powerful nation in Europe, France ceded that title, in 1763, to the new dynamo on the world stage, Great Britain.

Wars over Faith and Turf, 1500–1648

From 1500 to 1648, religious controversies and territorial disputes between rival dynasties saw Europe in a nearly constant state of warfare. By 1500, Italy was overrun with Spanish, German, and French soldiers—"barbarians," they were called, but barbarians in such numbers as to overwhelm the once-proud Italian city-states. At the same time, the Protestant Reformation created the issues that precipitated warfare between Protestants and Catholics, especially in the Holy Roman Empire and in France. Religious differences also figured in a war for independence in the Netherlands and in a civil war in England, although these conflicts also had political dimensions. From 1618 to 1648, much of Europe became involved in the Thirty Years' War, fought largely on German soil. At its outset, religious issues were prominent. By its close, religious factors had been overshadowed by the contest between the dynasties of France and the German lands: the Bourbons and the Habsburgs.

The trends in international politics characteristic of the early modern era first emerged in Italy, where the experience of city-states prefigures that of the nations beyond the Alps. Intermittently at war, some of the principal Italian states, including Milan, Naples, Rome, Venice, and Florence, had arrived at an agreement by the Peace of Lodi in 1454. This truce aimed at maintaining a balance of power among contending nations. Within a generation, however, the five participants were at war again. Soon they looked for assistance to the nations on the far side of the Alps. Beginning in 1494, France, the Empire, and Spain sent their armies. Where the Italians had sought helpers, instead they stirred up conquerors.

The process of conquest rolled on for fifty years more on the slippery battlefronts of the Italian Wars (1494–1559). At the end, by the Treaty of Câteau-Cambrésis in 1559, the Spanish and allied imperial forces had bested the French and seized control of the peninsula. Of the major Italian states, only four remained independent: the two republics of Venice and Genoa, and the two principalities of Savoy and Tuscany (the region of which Florence was capital), now under the Grand Dukes of Tuscany, descendants of the Medici family of Renaissance days. Italy was mortally wounded, but the political system of balanced competitive states which it pioneered set the pattern for relations between European nations until World War I in the twentieth century.

As cities and nations contended on Italian soil, north of the Alps a series of conflicts arose as a consequence of the Protestant Reformation (see Chapter 14). Within the Empire, Protestant and Catholic princes and states maneuvered against and fought each other, as did Huguenot, Catholic, and *politique* nobles in France. In the German lands these wars lasted until 1555, when they ended with the Peace of Augsburg. War in France continued until the reign of Henry IV (1589–1610), drawing to a close with his conversion to Catholicism in 1593 and his issuing, in 1598, of the Edict of Nantes. These conflicts, ending in territorial settlements for Protestants and Catholics and some hope of reconciliation,

belong to the history of the Reformation. Although religion figured in other conflicts in the Netherlands, the Empire, and England, these were essentially struggles between competing nations and interests. The first was the Dutch war of independence against Spain, begun officially in 1579 (though fighting dated from 1568). The second was the Thirty Years' War (1618–1648), which began as a struggle between Protestant and Catholic rulers in the Empire, and ended as a European-wide conflict in which religious identification had lost political significance. The third was the English Civil War (1642–1651).

In the seventeen provinces of the Netherlands, in 1566, discontent with Spanish rule, especially among Protestants, gave way to full-scale protests and to riots. The Spanish responded by sending the Duke of Alba at the head of an army, to subdue these unruly subjects and administer the Inquisition. "Everyone must be made to live in constant fear of the roof breaking down over his head," ordained the Duke.

Map 15.1 The European States in 1526: *The map of Europe in the early 1500s was dominated by the House of Habsburg, while northern Italy and the German lands remained fragmented. To the east, the duchy of Muscovy was being transformed into Russia. The Ottoman Empire pressured Europe from the southeast.* Which states were best positioned for increased power and influence at this juncture in the history of Europe?

His Council of Troubles, set up to track down heretics, sentenced thousands of Protestants to death, and ordered the confiscation of many noble estates. In the face of this tyranny, Catholics and Protestants of all classes united in armed revolt.

In 1578, the more moderate Duke of Parma, sent by the Spanish to reestablish obedience, rallied the support of the largely Catholic southern provinces. These ten provinces returned to Spanish dominion calmly, and after 1713 to the Austrian Habsburgs. The seven largely Protestant northern provinces, led by Holland and Zeeland, formed the Union of Utrecht in 1579 and declared independence from Spain in 1581. Their leader was Prince William I, called "the Silent," of the House of Orange (1533–1584). Previously appointed *stadholder*, or lieutenant-governor in Holland, by the emperor Charles V, he had already begun, in the 1570s, to direct military and naval operations against Spanish rule.

The United Provinces, as they were called after 1579, were supported by England, which sent several thousand troops to assist in the struggle. It was partly to stop this support that Spain launched, in 1588, its fearsome Armada. Although the Armada boasted formidable guns, its ships were cumbersome. The sleeker, swifter English vessels, fitted with excellent guns, chased the Spanish fleet from the English Channel into the North Sea—and into oblivion. As England stood poised to enter into Continental power struggles, it perceived its success in this incident as providential.

Dutch and Spanish armies struggled until 1609, when the Twelve Years' Truce provided for a division between Catholic south and Protestant north. Dutch independence was officially recognized in 1648, and the new federal Dutch Republic took its place in the political arena. The Dutch had already greatly expanded their maritime ventures (see Chapter 16), which flourished as the English became involved in their Civil War. Emerging from that struggle, the English Parliament responded to Dutch competition by issuing the Navigation Act of 1651. This act (subsequently reissued several times) limited the shipment of goods to England to English-owned ships or the ships of the region of origin. The Navigation Acts challenged the Dutch carrying trade, the source of that Republic's wealth, and provoked war between these two Protestant powers—the First Anglo-Dutch War of 1652–54, followed by two others before 1674—who not long before had cooperated in resisting the Spanish.

The Thirty Years' War   Sparked by rebellious Protestant nobles, the Thirty Years' War developed into a general European melee involving at least seventeen sovereign powers. The war was fought largely on German soil between, on the one hand, the Habsburg dynasty (both its Austrian and Spanish branches) and, on the other, the German Protestant princes and their allies, both Protestant (Denmark, Sweden, the United Provinces) and Catholic (France). The Habsburgs stood for a strong central European empire, backed by the Roman Catholic Church. Their opponents, both Protestant and Catholic, wished for political and religious reasons to preserve the autonomy of the states composing the Holy Roman Empire—now a nearly vaporous entity.

Coursing through several phases—Bohemian, Rhineland, Dutch, Swedish, and French—as different generals and interests came to the fore, the conflict was finally settled in 1648 by the Peace of Westphalia. That treaty provided for a balance of power between the main contenders (the Habsburg and French Bourbon powers) and associates. Granting virtual sovereignty to the component German states, it dictated the effective death of the Holy Roman Empire (although the Empire lingered in name until 1806) and created a power vacuum in central Europe, threatening danger to come. Finally, the treaty

War in Action

The Turkish army at Mohacs, 1526: *This miniature painting depicts the Battle of Mohacs, in Hungary, on the campaign road to Vienna in 1526. In it, Suleiman I, "the Magnificent," is shown directing his Turkish army from behind a row of cannon.* (Topkapi Museum, Istanbul)

recognized existing religious differences, thereby signaling the end of religious warfare in Europe.

What was indisputably accomplished by thirty years of battle was the devastation of Germany: its people, of whom perhaps 20 percent died; and its towns, its commerce, its blighted economy, its ruined fields, as the woodcut below and the passage reproduced in *Witnesses* on p. 427 testify. From the German perspective alone, this may have been the most catastrophic war in modern European history.

States in Competition, 1648–1763

The Thirty Years' War brought France to the front rank of European power. As she attempted to pursue that advantage, she collided with England, which had emerged from relative insignificance in the late Middle Ages to become a major presence in Europe. As the duel between them proceeded, other rivalries were pursued by the new nations of eastern Europe (the term denoting the lands of modern Poland, the Czech Republic, Slovakia, Hungary, the eastern German region, and Austria), Prussia and Austria, the most successful remnants of the Holy Roman Empire, and a reinvigorated Russia.

By the 1660s, France possessed the largest army in Europe and nurtured vast ambitions. It sought to limit Habsburg power on its borders, and to annex nearby lands, especially Alsace-Lorraine and the southern, or Spanish, Netherlands. The French strategy was checked in 1688 by a coalition of alarmed nations. It was contained again in the War of the Spanish Succession (1701–1714), when again most of the other major European powers united to combat it.

In Bauier men not left to bury the dead, but Rattes, and mice, devoured there carcasses.

Carcasses devoured by rats and mice: *There were many tragic consequences of war. Casualties from the Thirty Years' War, 1618–48, where bodies, left unburied, were devoured by rats and mice, are shown in this woodcut from* The Lamentations of Germany, *1638. (British Library, London)*

This war was precipitated when the last Habsburg king of Spain, Charles II, died in 1700, having willed all of his possessions, to be kept intact, to the grandson of Louis XIV of France. Had the terms of the will been observed without protest, France would have dominated Europe (and much of the Western Hemisphere as well). An enormous alliance rose up against this possibility. The Peace of Utrecht of 1713 between England and France settled the conflict (although fighting continued between some parties for another year), and, together with the Peace of Rastatt (1714) drew new lines of authority in Europe. A French king of the Bourbon dynasty would rule in Spain and in Spanish America, but other Spanish dominions—principally the southern Netherlands and Spanish domains in Italy—were conveyed to Habsburg Austria. The rulers of the small states of Savoy and Prussia obtained territorial gains and the status of king, and the Dutch Republic received small concessions.

All contenders won something, but Great Britain (created by joining the crowns of England and Scotland in 1707) emerged the winner. She won the fortress of Gibraltar on the Spanish Mediterranean shore and parts of French Canada, which enabled her to pursue her maritime ambitions. Even more precious was the grant of the *asiento* ("contract") from Spain, giving Britain the right to carry African slaves to Spanish America (see Chapter 16). As a bonus, she also won a promise that France would not attempt to place a Catholic king on the British throne, which was now Protestant by law.

After some twenty-five years of relative peace, the European nations began fighting again in the 1740s, intent on gaining slips of territory and small advantages. An eight-year interlude between 1748 and 1756 was followed by the Seven Years' War (1756–1763), fought on three continents— not only in Europe but also in India and in North America, where it was known as the French and Indian War. Overarching all other issues was the continuing duel between Britain and France.

This time, the duel was fought largely overseas, as colonial possessions and foreign trade increasingly became the measure of national preeminence. By 1761, Britain had seized French possessions in India, and was poised for further ventures in the domination of that subcontinent. In 1759 a British force launched a surprise attack on the key French fortress at Quebec. After a ten-minute battle on the Plains of Abraham, outside the fortress, which the British won with disciplined musket volleys at close range, French prospects in North America were doomed. The Treaty of Paris of 1763 secured Britain's triumph over her main rival in India, in North America, and in Europe.

Eastern Europe   By 1700, three states dominated eastern Europe: Austria, Prussia, and Russia. The homeland of the Habsburg family, Austria had a strong monarchy and an expansive agenda. It absorbed Hungary, Bohemia, Transylvania, and parts of the northern Balkans, knitting its empire together through the figure of the king, who ruled as monarch in each kingdom. It held the southeast frontier of Europe against the Ottoman Turks, whose vigor had waned since the siege of Vienna in 1529, though it resurged in 1683 to threaten that outpost once again.

The kingdom of Prussia developed from the ancestral lands of the Hohenzollern family: Brandenburg, some tiny states in the Empire, and the duchy of Prussia itself. These lands were patiently acquired over generations and combined to form an independent state; it was granted the status of kingdom by the Peace of Utrecht of 1713. Farther east, Tsar Peter I (r. 1682–1725), called "the Great," who had toured the successful nations of western Europe, learned what he could, and imported trained experts to Russia, now built a new capital city on the Baltic Sea and reoriented his political goals. For the first time, Russia looked westward, ready to engage as a great power in European struggles for sovereignty.

In 1713, Prussia, along with most other European nations, had agreed to the Pragmatic Sanction. Issued by the Holy Roman Emperor Charles VI (r. 1711–1740), this provided that his daughter and heir, Maria Theresa (r. 1740–1780), would inherit all the Habsburg lands intact (although, as a woman, she was ineligible to become Holy Roman Emperor). In 1740, on the basis of no other principle than *raison d'état*, the young king of Prussia, Frederick II (r. 1740–1786) broke this agreement. Frederick needed Silesia—a prosperous province under Austrian domination. And so he took it. Other nations entered into the fray, nibbling at the Habsburg lands. By the 1748 Peace of Aix-la-Chapelle, which settled the War of the Austrian Succession, Silesia was his. A few years later, in the Seven Years' War, Austria allied itself with France and Russia, to block Prussia's further expansion. Bankrolled by Britain but left to fight on its own, Prussia stayed firm and retained its position.

In 1772, Prussia was still hungry for territory to round out the boundaries of its domain. Along with Austria and Russia, it annexed small bits of Poland, an ailing republic dominated by a fractious nobility under an elected king, fatally resistant to centralization. In 1793 and 1795, Poland's neighbors completed her dismemberment. In the final "partition," it disappeared from the map, not to be reconstituted until after World War I. Prussia, Austria, and Russia, fat with new territory, now held unrivaled domination of eastern Europe. As recently as 1500, they had been overshadowed by the Holy Roman Empire, now in tatters; by the Ottoman Empire, in retreat through the Balkans; and by Poland, devoured whole.

During the early modern era, the violence that had characterized medieval Europe in an era of invasion became the official tool of the state. As a result, the map of Europe was radically altered as winners took their prizes and losers shrank behind their borders. Soon after 1500, the Italian cities yielded their primacy, as Machiavelli had feared, to more powerful nations beyond the Alps. By 1600, the most potent states in Europe were monarchies poised on the Atlantic coast: Spain, France, and England. Emerging as major players soon thereafter were the kingdom of Sweden, the newly constituted Dutch Republic, and the German electorate of Brandenburg, subsequently the kingdom of Prussia. Meanwhile, the Holy Roman Empire withered, while the Habsburg dynasty, which had long held the imperial title, raised its hereditary domain of Austria to international importance. Portugal, the rising star of the early 1500s, languished, and Poland was obliterated. Led by a series of tsars, who considered themselves the successors of Roman Caesars, Russia moved into the European arena.

AN AGE OF KINGS

As the nations of Europe competed, they also developed forms of government that endured into the modern era. This process usually involved the refinement of monarchy, as the ability to make laws and exercise force was concentrated in the figure of the king—or, in a few cases, the queen. Such kings were "absolute" monarchs, because they tried to rule "absolutely" (believing in complete, unrestricted powers due to their divine right), unchecked by representatives of the people. By the end of the eighteenth century, that newly evolved monarchy would be challenged and, in some places, limited. In diverse ways, monarchy developed in the direction of **absolutism** in several European countries: in Spain, France, and England in the western zone; and in Prussia, Austria, and Russia in the eastern one (see *Who's Who* on pp. 437 and 439).

Spain: Religious Zeal and Royal Absolutism

The autonomous kingdoms that formed on the Iberian peninsula in the Middle Ages were united by a common dedication to the centuries-long crusade called the *Reconquista* (see Chapter 9). After the fall of the last Moorish fortress at Granada in 1492, the Inquisition fostered the crusading spirit by pursuing lapsed converts to Christianity, as well as heretics. The same crusading spirit inspired Spanish missionaries to the Americas, to convert the native population. Before it became a nation, Spain was a culture united by its dedication to Roman Catholic orthodoxy. On this basis, kings from the fifteenth and sixteenth centuries built a strong, centralized state.

Crucial developments in this unifying process were achieved in the reigns of Ferdinand II of Aragon

(r. 1479–1516) and Isabella of Castile (r. 1474–1504), whose marriage in 1479 linked their two kingdoms. (Portugal had already taken a separate path to nationhood before the events about to be described.) Although the component states of Castile and Aragon retained their separate judicial, political, and administrative laws and institutions, a strong commonality of purpose marked the reigns of their two respective sovereigns—displayed most decidedly and dramatically by their conquest of Granada.

In 1516, on Ferdinand's death, a now-united Spain passed to his grandson, Charles I. The grandson also of the Holy Roman Emperor Maximilian I and Mary of Burgundy, Charles inherited the Habsburg lands on Maximilian's death in 1519 and, as Charles V (r. 1519–1556), became Holy Roman Emperor. A portrait of him by Titian is illustrated on p. 421.

Ruler of several states, and required to manage the Italian Wars, the consequences of the Protestant Reformation, the rivalry of France, and the threat of Turkish invasion, Charles could not concentrate exclusively on Spain. When he abdicated in 1556, the Spanish inheritance (along with title to the Netherlands and parts of Italy) passed to his son Philip, and the Habsburg lands to his brother Ferdinand I.

Under Philip II (r. 1556–1598) the Spanish state rose to an apex of wealth and influence. Outside Madrid, Philip constructed the Escorial, a combined palace and monastery, vast and austere, which is depicted on p. 443. There he worshipped daily and ruled his far-flung possessions. Aided by diplomats and spies, he worked to extend Spanish rule and to reassert Catholic orthodoxy in Europe. Those goals were not implausibly grandiose, given that the great

---

WITNESSES

The Experience of War in Fiction and Fact

Early modern Europe pioneered the war against civilians that some historians see as distinctively modern. Armies besieged walled cities, battered their walls and gates, gained entry, and loosed their soldiers to loot, murder, and rape at will. That fate is depicted vividly in the words of William Shakespeare's character Henry V, ironically the late medieval English king perceived as most heroic. It is also the fate of the city of Magdeburg, as described by its mayor, an eyewitness.

King Henry V threatens the French city of Harfleur with battery, capture, rape, and sack:

How yet resolves the Governor of the town?
This is the latest parle we will admit:
Therefore to our best mercy give yourselves,
Or, like to men proud of destruction,
Defy us to our worst; for, as I am a soldier,
A name that in my thoughts becomes me best,
If I begin the batt'ry once again,
I will not leave the half-achieved Harfleur
Till in her ashes she lie buried.
The gates of mercy shall be all shut up,
And the fleshed soldier, rough and hard of heart,
In liberty of bloody hand shall range
With conscience wide as hell, mowing like grass
Your fresh fair virgins and your flow'ring infants. ...
... Therefore, you men of Harfleur,
Take pity of your town and of your people
Whiles yet my soldiers are in my command,
Whiles yet the cool and temperate wind of grace
O'erblows the filthy and contagious clouds
Of heady murder, spoil, and villainy.
If not—why, in a moment look to see
The blind and bloody soldier with foul hand
Defile the locks of your shrill-shrieking daughters;
Your fathers taken by the silver beards,

And their most reverend heads dashed to the walls;
Your naked infants spitted upon pikes,
While the mad mothers with their howls confused
Do break the clouds, as did the wives of Jewry
At Herod's bloody-hunting slaughtermen.
What say you? Will you yield, and this avoid?
Or, guilty in defense, be thus destroyed?

(Shakespeare, *Henry V*, 1600, III. iii. 1–14, 27–43; ed. J. R. Brown, 1998)

Eyewitness Otto von Guericke, mayor of Magdeburg, describes the destruction of his city by an imperial army during the Thirty Years' War (May, 1631):
[The imperial troops and allies breached a gate and flooded into the city.] Thus it came about that the city and all its inhabitants fell into the hands of the enemy, whose violence and cruelty were due in part to their common hatred of the adherents of the Augsburg Confession, and in part to their being embittered by the chain shot which had been fired at them and by the derision and insults that the Magdeburgers had heaped upon them from the ramparts. Then was there naught but beating and burning, plundering, torture, and murder. ... Then, what with blows and threats of shooting, stabbing, and hanging, the poor people were so terrified that if they had had anything left they would have brought it forth if it had been buried in the earth or hidden away in a thousand castles. In this frenzied rage, the great and splendid city that had stood like a fair princess in the land was now, in its hour of direst need and unutterable distress and woe, given over to the flames, and thousands of innocent men, women, and children, in the midst of a horrible din of heart-rending shrieks and cries, were tortured and put to death in so cruel and shameful a manner that no words would suffice to describe, nor no tears to bewail it. . .

(*Readings in European History*, vol. 2, 1906; ed. J. H. Robinson)

wealth then pouring into Spain from its American possessions (see Chapter 16) could fund a formidable military organization. Philip succeeded in acquiring Portugal in 1580. With his marriage in 1554 to the queen of England, Mary Tudor (r. 1553–1558), came the opportunity, never realized, to add that kingdom to his other possessions and to restore it to the roster of Catholic nations.

The great success of sixteenth-century Spain faded during the seventeenth, as its silver imports from the Americas failed to enrich the nation. After 1665, the deterioration was rapid. Charles II, who ascended the throne in that year as a child, was sickly, stupid, and impotent. It was his death in 1700 that precipitated the War of the Spanish Succession, resulting in the importation to Spain of a French Bourbon dynasty. Spanish fortunes revived in the 1700s as Bourbon monarchs and ministers created administrative systems on the French model, but Spain no longer played its earlier role of foremost European monarchy.

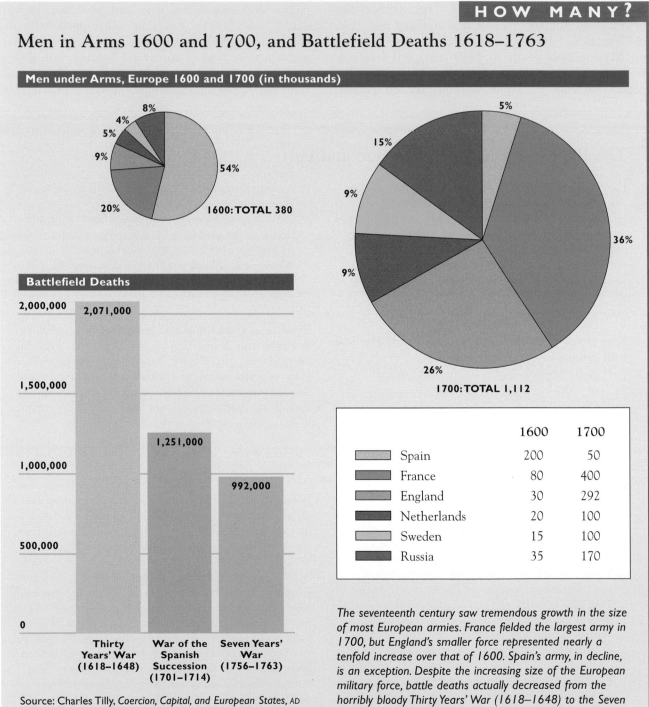

HOW MANY?

Men in Arms 1600 and 1700, and Battlefield Deaths 1618–1763

Men under Arms, Europe 1600 and 1700 (in thousands)

1600: TOTAL 380 — 54%, 20%, 9%, 5%, 4%, 8%

1700: TOTAL 1,112 — 5%, 36%, 26%, 9%, 9%, 15%

Battlefield Deaths

	Thirty Years' War (1618–1648)	War of the Spanish Succession (1701–1714)	Seven Years' War (1756–1763)
Deaths	2,071,000	1,251,000	992,000

	1600	1700
Spain	200	50
France	80	400
England	30	292
Netherlands	20	100
Sweden	15	100
Russia	35	170

The seventeenth century saw tremendous growth in the size of most European armies. France fielded the largest army in 1700, but England's smaller force represented nearly a tenfold increase over that of 1600. Spain's army, in decline, is an exception. Despite the increasing size of the European military force, battle deaths actually decreased from the horribly bloody Thirty Years' War (1618–1648) to the Seven Years' War (1756–1763), a crucial conflict that was not grossly wasteful of human life.

Source: Charles Tilly, *Coercion, Capital, and European States,* AD 990–1990 (Cambridge, MA: Basil Blackwell, 1990), pp. 79, 165–166.

Map 15.2 The European States in 1795: *France had lost to Britain in the global conflict that ended in 1763. Yet France remained a contender under its revolutionary leadership, and would soon strike out under Napoleon's leadership for hegemony in Europe. In eastern Europe, Russia, Austria, and Prussia were dominant having by 1795 partitioned and obliterated the once enormous Polish state.* What advantage does Great Britain have in 1795 relative to the other states of Europe?

France: The Apogee of Absolutism

That role fell to France, which had lain in Spain's shadow in the sixteenth century, but towered above it in the next. Thanks to a larger and more productive population, the kings of France were able to build an impressive administrative machine, field an enormous army, and claim cultural leadership in Europe.

The French kings had already traveled far along the road toward sovereignty during the medieval centuries. They had gained recognition from the feudal nobility of their preeminence in the realm, and from the pope of their rights over the French clergy—the "Gallican liberties" won by the Pragmatic Sanction of Bourges in 1438 and the Concordat of Bologna in 1516. They had defended French territorial rights against other claimants, particularly the English, against whom they ultimately prevailed in the Hundred Years' War. The ascension to the throne of Henry IV (r. 1589–1610), the first of the

Bourbon line, finally brought an end to the chaotic era of religious warfare. It also marked the opening of an especially fruitful era in the building of the French monarchy.

If Henry IV had done nothing else he would be remarkable for his promulgation in 1598 of the Edict of Nantes guaranteeing generous freedoms to his former coreligionists, the Huguenots. But Henry did much more. He saw to France's recovery from the civil wars, collected forgotten taxes and paid forgotten salaries, repaired roads and bridges and the mechanisms of government, administered justice, and promoted commerce. In the twenty-one years of his reign, he never summoned the Estates-General (an assembly of representatives of France's three **estates**, clergy, nobility, and commoners, comparable to the English Parliament). He thereby signaled the capacity of the monarch to rule without consulting a representative assembly. An unusually effective ruler, he laid the foundations for absolute monarchy in France.

After the death of Henry IV, the true ruler of France was neither his son Louis XIII (r. 1610–1643) nor his widow, Marie de' Medici (1573–1642), regent for Louis, then only nine years old. It was the nobleman and cardinal Armand Jean du Plessis, the Duke de Richelieu (1585–1642). This prudent cleric, who became secretary of state in 1616 and Louis's chief minister in 1624, devoted himself to the secular interests of the French monarchy. In the last phase of the Thirty Years' War he intervened on the Protestant side against the Catholic Habsburgs.

Cardinal Richelieu promoted commerce in France and in its overseas possessions, encouraging poor nobles to enrich themselves in business ventures and wealthy merchants to gain titles of nobility by funneling cash to the royal treasury. He reined in aristocratic pretensions, prohibited private dueling, and destroyed fortified castles not in royal service. He also stripped the Huguenot community of its right to bear arms and live in fortified towns, although he reaffirmed the freedom of worship guaranteed by Henry IV.

Cardinal Richelieu's protégé, the Italian-born Jules Mazarin (1602–1661), followed his mentor's model. Made Cardinal in 1641, Mazarin effectively ruled France from 1643 to 1661 as the chief adviser to Anne of Austria, widow of Louis XIII and regent for Louis XIV. Like Cardinal Richelieu, Mazarin managed domestic and international affairs in the interests of the French monarchy, deftly succeeding in surviving a rebellion of restive nobles and peasants called the Fronde.

The Bourbon dynasty benefited from the service of yet a third royal servant: Jean-Baptiste Colbert (1619–1683). The son of a merchant, Colbert began his career by monitoring Mazarin's investments. In 1665, recommended by his mentor, Colbert was employed by Louis XIV (r. 1643–1715) as France's chief financial minister, a position he held until his death in 1683. Colbert reduced France's debt, systematized its accounting methods, and attempted (unsuccessfully) to equalize tax burdens. Aiming at economic self-sufficiency, he encouraged commerce and discouraged misuse of natural resources, built roads and canals, set standards of quality for manufactured goods and agricultural products, increased foreign tariffs and reduced internal ones—all features of the strategy of **mercantilism**.

The French kings were brilliantly served by their ministers Richelieu, Mazarin, and Colbert. It was the genius of the third Bourbon ruler, Louis XIV, himself to raise the monarchy to a new zenith of power. Already under Henry IV, the Estates-General had ceased to function. After 1614, when a fruitless meeting of the Estates-General was dismissed, it was not summoned again until 1789. Those 175 years mark the span of royal absolutism in France—its achievement due principally to Louis XIV.

The Sun King   Louis was four years old when his father died. His mother, assisted by Mazarin, ruled in his stead. He was ten when the Peace of Westphalia was signed, preparing the ground for France's assumption of European leadership. In 1661, Mazarin died and Louis, aged twenty-two, undertook personal rule. He guided France until 1715, when he was succeeded by his great-grandson. At that point he had reigned for seventy-two years and outlived two generations, his sheer endurance unmatched by other monarchs. Heir to the achievements of Richelieu and Mazarin, Louis labored for the supremacy of France in Europe, and of the king within France.

Louis may have said, as it is reported, "I am the state." If so, it would have been an accurate statement of the role of the absolute monarch, in whom were centered all the capacities of the political realm. Louis's central role in the French state and culture was expressed visually as well as politically: in the architecture, gardens, and rituals of the royal complex he built at Versailles, twelve miles outside the ancient capital of Paris.

Beginning in the 1660s, Louis converted the small royal hunting lodge at Versailles into the most splendid palace in Europe (see p. 443). According to the statesman Montesquieu, there were "more statues in [the king's] palace gardens than there are citizens in a large town." Palace and gardens, 1400 fountains (fed by a river diverted from its natural course), a panoply of nobles, administrators, and servants (more than 10,000 in all) and nearly as many well-stabled horses—all served to furnish an image of royal grandiloquence. Ranks of courtiers and servants attended the king's daily acts, from waking up to eating dinner to strolling through the gardens or meeting with important officials. Their attendance in itself, their rank and privilege indicated by their dress and proximity to the king, was the business of the court, where all of life was a ceremony underscoring the importance of the king—*le Roi Soleil*, as he was called, "the Sun King." As the prestige of the king rose, the status of the aristocracy sank and the patterns of French culture—costume, behavior, and diet, as well as music, literature, drama, and dance—became the standard in the West.

As Louis gathered the tamed nobles of France at Versailles to dance and play, he centralized in his court the administration of justice and the determination of law, eroding the authority of regional courts and assemblies (the **parlements** and "estates"). To supervise affairs in the provinces, he dispatched bureaucrats called **intendants**, directly responsible to the crown. Royal appointees were often men from the middle classes who had purchased both their office and a title of nobility. These were members of the "nobility of the robe," to distinguish them from the ancient "nobility of the sword." In a further assertion of royal authority, Louis repealed the Edict of Nantes.

French Huguenots who wished to continue to worship as Protestants—among them many productive merchants and artisans—fled to the Dutch Republic, to England and to the Americas. An absolute monarch could not abide religious diversity.

In 1715, a child again ascended the throne of France—Louis XV (r. 1715–1774); again the country was governed by a regent. The aristocracy, which had been brought to heel by Louis XIV, now sought to recover their prestige and to curtail royal authority. The local *parlements* reasserted themselves, insisting on the right to register legislation and to assent to taxation. In this atmosphere of resurgent feudal claims, Louis XV and his grandson and successor, Louis XVI (r. 1774–1793), never enjoyed the absolute authority of their great ancestor. Louis XVI enlisted the aid of a series of capable and reform-minded finance ministers but never succeeded in winning the cooperation of the nobility. Indeed, he saw the principle of absolutism utterly defeated by the Revolution of 1789, which even cost him his life.

England: The Sharing of Power

The career of absolutism in England was different from the one it followed in Spain or France, for two principal reasons. First, England had a long tradition of the political rights of groups represented in its representative assembly, called Parliament. Second, England was, by the early 1600s, a Protestant nation; thus its kings could not bolster their authority, as did the Bourbon and Habsburg monarchs, by alignment with the Catholic Church. These realities tended against the accumulation of royal authority. Nevertheless, England achieved a strong, centralized monarchy; and, thereafter, a strong, centralized state, of which a limited monarch was titular head.

In 1485, the first king of the Tudor line, Henry VII (r. 1485–1509), acquired not only a throne, but the job of patching together a nation torn by the Wars of the Roses, fought between claimants from the York and Lancaster families. He succeeded in this task, organizing national finances, promoting trade and exploration, avoiding foreign entanglements, subduing rebellious nobles, and establishing the court of Star Chamber as a central judicial authority.

In 1509, his son Henry VIII (r. 1509–1547) succeeded him. Supported by shrewd ministers, Henry VIII pursued his father's centralizing strategies (but not his fiscal prudence). His concerns about the succession led him into a controversial series of marriages—six in all. Four of his unlucky wives were dismissed or beheaded; one died, and one survived him. The surviving progeny of these marriages were two daughters and, the youngest, a son—all of whom would accede to the throne, in 1547, 1553, and 1558 respectively: Edward (d. 1553), son of Henry's third wife, Jane Seymour; Mary (d. 1558), daughter of his first wife, Catherine of Aragon; and Elizabeth (d. 1603), daughter of his second wife, Anne Boleyn.

Great controversy surrounded the dissolution by annulment of Henry's first marriage. To effect it, Henry repudiated the pope and had himself declared the "supreme governor" of the Church in England, precipitating the Reformation in that country. His role as head of the Church enhanced Henry's authority. Later, religious controversy would flare up several times under his successors.

A child during most of his six-year reign (he died at fifteen), Edward VI was unable himself to act to shape the English monarchy. His advisers tended to the business of foreign affairs and the establishment of Protestant Christianity in England. On Edward's premature death, their labors on behalf of a Protestant Church were rendered futile. The young king's elder half sister Mary succeeded, having been passed over earlier in favor of the male heir. Granddaughter of Ferdinand and Isabella, raised by her mother an earnest Catholic, and married the year after her succession to the zealous Philip II of Spain, Mary sought to reestablish Catholicism in England. This attempt was thwarted by her death and the accession of Henry VIII's middle child, Elizabeth, whom Catholics considered illegitimate.

Elizabeth, portrayed on p. 434, overcame this liability and that of her sex in a forty-five year reign that is among the most remarkable in all of European history. A moderate Protestant, a classical scholar, and an extraordinarily intelligent leader, Elizabeth completed the task of forging an absolute monarchy begun by her Tudor forebears. Guided but not overshadowed by her very effective covey of ministers—notably Sir William Cecil (1520–1598), Sir Francis Walsingham (c. 1532–1590), and Robert Cecil (1563–1612)—she clarified the nature of English Protestantism, rallied popular support in foreign affairs, and guided financial and judicial institutions. Refusing to marry, she was able even as a woman to maintain authority in her own person and to command the respect of people and Parliament alike. Meanwhile, England's naval successes and deft diplomacy brought it recognition as a major nation.

In 1587, Elizabeth reluctantly authorized the execution—after eighteen years of imprisonment—of her cousin Mary Stuart (r. 1542–1567), the exiled queen of Scotland. (A Catholic with French ties, Mary was implicated in plots against Elizabeth just at the moment when Spain was planning to launch its Armada against England.) On her deathbed, in 1603, Elizabeth named as her successor the son of the woman she had executed, James VI, the reigning king of Scotland. As James I (r. 1603–1625), he assumed the thrones of England and Ireland as well, becoming the first of England's Stuart dynasty.

Twice a king, James was an advocate of absolutism in theory and reached for it in practice. As king in

Gentile Bellini, **Muhammad II, c. 1480**

Warriors and Peacemakers

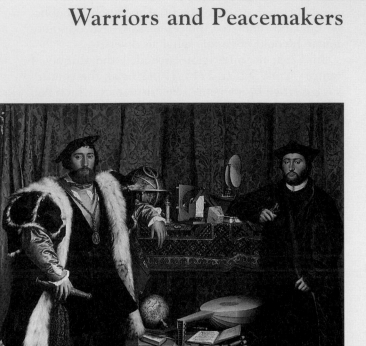

Hans Holbein, **The Ambassadors, 1533**

Gentile Bellini's portrait (above left) from the life of Muhammad II, the Ottoman Turkish ruler who conquered Constantinople and destroyed the Byzantine Empire, depicts its subject as poised and statesmanlike, in retirement from battle.

The two splendidly attired ambassadors painted by Holbein (above right), experts in the avoidance of war, are surrounded by astronomical and musical instruments, appropriately remote from the field of battle.

In contrast, the bronze statue by Verrocchio of the Italian mercenary captain Bartolommeo Colleoni (left) epitomizes the early modern warrior possessed of power and determination.
(top left: National Gallery, London; top right: National Gallery, London)

Can you identify any of the objects depicted—presumably for a reason—alongside the two ambassadors? What might they represent?

Andrea del Verrocchio, **Bartolommeo Colleoni, Venice, c. 1481–1496**

To continue your investigation of this topic, please go to www.prenhall.com/king for the related **WINDOWS** on the **WEB** activity

Scotland, he established royal authority over warring Protestant lords, his mother's Catholic friends and kin, and leaders of the Calvinist (called Presbyterian in Scotland) church. An author and scholar, he wrote in defense of royal absolutism: *The True Law of Free Monarchy*. In England, he chose to challenge or evade the authority of Parliament, acquiring the funds to manage the state and his lavish court from unpopular customs taxes or grants of monopoly.

The Parliament James antagonized included a growing number of Puritan representatives who were critical of the practices of the established Anglican Church. He also antagonized Catholics, who sought an amelioration of the civil disabilities under which they suffered. And the flagrant immorality of his court aroused general disapproval. Serious tensions persisted when James died in 1625 and his son Charles I (r. 1625–1649) succeeded.

Civil War and Commonwealth Married to a French Catholic Bourbon Charles soon revealed a tendency toward absolutism and was suspected of favoring his wife's religion. Whether or not that was so, he certainly did his best to impose the Anglican faith upon all of his subjects. His ministers took repressive measures against nonconforming Protestants, and angered the Presbyterian Scots to the point of armed rebellion. Charles followed his father's lead in relations with Parliament, ignoring it when it did not vote him funds and, not long after the French king's dissolution of the Estates-General, dismissing it altogether in 1629. Eleven years later, desperate for more funds, he recalled Parliament. In 1642, Parliament demanded to be granted greater powers, including approval of the king's ministers. Charles now raised his military standard against Parliament.

At least some of the members of the Parliament that assembled in 1640—called the Long Parliament—continued to meet until 1653 (after 1649, consisting of a remnant of some 100 members, it was called the "Rump" Parliament). They presided over a war between royalists and parliamentarians, and between Anglicans and other Protestants, which permanently changed the course of government in England. In 1649, the victorious parliamentarians created a High Court of Justice, which tried Charles for treason and condemned him to death. His execution followed. At the very moment of the triumph of royal absolutism on the Continent, the English had demonstrated the superiority of assemblies to kings. Although Charles I's sons would later reach for absolute power, the possibility of establishing such power in England had been gravely wounded.

In 1653, the leader of the parliamentary army, Oliver Cromwell (1599–1658), engineered his own elevation to "Lord Protector" of the new Commonwealth of England under a written constitution called the Instrument of Government. Cromwell enforced Puritan policies that suppressed, among other activities, theatrical performances and Sunday games on the village green. He repressed political dissent, such as that offered by the sectarian Ranters and Quakers, and harshly persecuted the Irish, whose religion and culture he attempted to crush. He did, however, favor religious tolerance within a Protestant community. Generally hated, Cromwell was a curious amalgam of religious zeal and military skill, a dictator who had destroyed a monarch. At his death in 1658, Englishmen from all sectors turned from his path and looked forward to the Restoration of the monarchy, which was accomplished in 1660.

Restoration and "Glorious Revolution" The Stuart line returned in the person of Charles II (r. 1660–1685), son of the executed Charles I. Mindful of the need to conciliate parliamentary opponents, Charles agreed to all the demands made by those groups—including a general amnesty to nearly all of those who had opposed and killed his father. He further conciliated both elites and people by setting a new cultural tone. During the Restoration, as the years of his reign are called, Puritan repression ended and the quest for pleasure was back in fashion.

Nevertheless, in the course of his reign Charles repeated the patterns that had led to friction before. He tended to Roman Catholicism, to a pro-French foreign policy, to noncooperation with Parliament, and to absolutism. Worse, as Charles had no legitimate children, his successor was his brother James, an avowed Catholic. One parliamentary faction, called "Whig," called for the exclusion of James from that inheritance, while another, called "Tory," supported the king. James in fact succeeded on Charles' death in 1685, with little opposition.

But Tories and Whigs joined in opposition to James II when, in 1688, his wife gave birth to a son, assuring the continuance of a Roman Catholic monarchy. Parliamentary leaders offered the throne jointly to Mary II (r. 1689–1694), James's elder and Protestant daughter, and her husband William III, the Prince of Orange (r. 1689–1702), zealous opponent of French expansionism in the Netherlands. William arrived with his army, the king's commanders disbanded, and James took refuge in France. These events constitute the "Glorious Revolution," a bloodless rechanneling of authority in perfect contrast to the Civil War which had resulted in the execution of a king and the elevation of a dictator.

By accepting Parliament's Declaration of Right of 1689, William and Mary accepted, as a condition of their joint rule, limits on monarchical power articulated in the Bill of Rights (also 1689). The Bill of Rights reaffirmed constitutional principles that had developed over the previous few stormy decades, providing that the king would not be able to suspend a law of Parliament nor raise taxes nor maintain an army without parliamentary consent; nor could any subject be arrested without full due legal process. Furthermore, the throne would pass to the descendants in turn of Mary and her younger sister Anne; but no Roman Catholic could ever succeed to the English monarchy. The Act of Settlement of 1701 reaffirmed these principles and extended the provisions for the succession. The Toleration Act in the same year protected the rights of non-Anglican Protestants to worship, though it continued to exclude them from political office—as Catholics had been so excluded since the Test Act of 1673. The guarantees in these key documents were added to the traditional rights of Englishmen inherited from medieval custom.

By the complicated events of the 1600s, the government of England achieved a delicate but fruitful balance between the king and Parliament, and of both with the established Anglican Church. The king could not hold absolute power, but would yield to decisions of Parliament. Kings and public officials could be neither Catholics nor non-Anglican Protestant dissenters, although private worship was tolerated (not, however, in Ireland, where Catholicism was illegal and vital). Even Jews, who had been expelled from England in 1290, had been permitted by Cromwell to return without conversion.

Over the next century, the struggle between kings and Parliament gave way to a government dominated by political parties, prominent ministers, and the policies of the Bank of England. Great Britain in the eighteenth century, under the last Stuart monarch, Anne, and the first three kings of the House of Hanover, all Georges, was a different world from that ruled by Stuart kings before 1688.

Three New Empires: The Reshaping of Eastern Europe

The Thirty Years' War left central and eastern Europe in fragments. The Holy Roman Empire was a mere shell. Its more than 300 component cities and principalities, populated largely by German speakers, proceeded to develop independently. To the east of a line formed by the Elbe River and the mountains of Bohemia, largely Slavic and Hungarian peoples lived under Polish, Russian, or Ottoman overlordship. After 1648, three strong monarchies expanded to fill the vacuum of authority in central and eastern Europe—Austria, Prussia, and Russia. The main rulers are listed in *Who's Who* on p. 439.

Austria   The Habsburgs had long ruled the principality of Austria and had held the title of Holy Roman Emperor since 1438. By 1714, these Austrian rulers had gained sovereignty over Bohemia, Hungary,

Kings and Queens

Anonymous, Elizabeth I: *The kings and queens of Europe were the subjects of celebratory art. This sixteenth-century "Rainbow Portrait" of Elizabeth I shows her possessing the authority of a ruler, youthful despite increasing age. (Hatfield House, Hertfordshire; Courtesy, Marquess of Salisbury)*

and parts of the Balkans (wrested from the Ottoman Turks by 1699), as well as, in the west, the southern Netherlands, parts of Italy, and some Mediterranean possessions (taken from Spain). They were emperors over many different peoples who spoke different languages, practiced different religions, and possessed very different historical traditions.

Although Habsburg rulers managed this disparate empire with a fair amount of skill, it continually threatened to disintegrate. Ethnic rivalries among Magyars, Germans, Czechs, Poles, Croatians, and Italians were inevitable. Religious tensions were also severe. Austria had been re-Catholicized during the Thirty Years' War, and now imposed strict Catholic uniformity in all of its possessions. Yet the Polish and Czech nobility had strong Protestant leanings, and Eastern Orthodox (and later Muslim) subjects in the Balkans resisted Catholic preeminence. Partly to win over the landowning classes, Habsburg rulers permitted the enserfment or reenserfment of the peasantry, now an oppressed group perpetually liable to restlessness and revolt.

With the Pragmatic Sanction of 1713, Charles VI attempted to guarantee the inheritance of his daughter and only heir, Maria Theresa (r. 1740–1780). Yet on her succession in 1740, she faced the aggressions of other European states which little respected a female ruler when there was so much land to be had. Nevertheless, Maria Theresa managed to hold the bulk of her lands and even acquired additional territory by the first partition of Poland in 1772.

By that date Maria Theresa was ruling jointly with her son Joseph II (r. 1765–1790). After her death in 1780, Joseph ruled alone. He continued his mother's policy of centralizing authority, attempting agrarian reforms, and making the capital, Vienna, a center for the arts and learning. But he attempted more fundamental reforms than his mother would ever have countenanced. These included, notably, the abolition of serfdom in 1781; the creation of a civil service based on the principle of merit; and the reform of the justice system, including the abolition of torture and capital punishment. These and other of Joseph's projects aroused substantial opposition and were suspended after his death in 1790.

Prussia By the time of Joseph's death, Prussia was overtaking Austria as the major power of the fading Holy Roman Empire. Piecing together the small states of Brandenburg, Prussia, and Pomerania, lands scattered across the southern coast of the Baltic Sea, the "Great Elector" Frederick William (r. 1640–1688) had assembled a small nation. He had also built up a mighty army to defend it. His successor was granted the title "King in Prussia" in 1701 and reigned as Frederick I (r. 1688–1713). Frederick's son Frederick William I (r. 1713–1740) continued in his grandfather's path, hoarding his wealth, promoting the landowning class, from which he drew his officers, and modernizing and expanding the army.

These achievements were the inheritance of his son, the capable Frederick II, the Great (r. 1740–1786). The edifice of Prussian power rested on the army. Civil servants, the middle class, the serfs, were all subordinate to its needs and to the will of the aristocracy, who led an enormous military force consisting of 200,000 soldiers out of a population of only 6 million. The prince who ruled this successful state was also a flute-player and author of note, who corresponded easily with the finest minds of the age and shared their skeptical spirit. An absolute monarch himself, Frederick thought little of the theory of the divine right of kings (see below).

Russia By the time of Frederick the Great, Russia had developed from the medieval duchy of Muscovy to become a modern state, governed by an absolute ruler. Having won independence from their Mongol overlords after 1480, the grand princes of Muscovy continued a policy of annexing adjacent territories.

Francisco de Goya, **Family of Charles IV:** *A more critical portrayal of a king and queen is seen in Goya's depiction of the Spanish royal family in 1800. The opulence of attire of Charles IV and his family does not disguise a weakness of intellect and will. (Prado, Madrid)*

Peter Paul Rubens, Marie de' Medici, Queen of France, Landing in Marseilles, 1622–25: *In 1622, Marie de' Medici, the widow of French king, Henri IV, called the Flemish artist Rubens to her court in Paris to paint a series of 21 canvases for her palace walls. Although her activities were only routine—like the one depicted in this painting—Rubens brilliantly employed mythological figures, sumptuous color and texture, and dramatic compositional strategies to elevate and glorify his patron. (Louvre)*

Under Ivan III, called "the Great" (r. 1462–1505), and Ivan IV, called "the Terrible" (r. 1533–1584), the new state of Russia became a powerful kingdom. The "Terrible" Ivan earned his designation by crushing the traditional landowner caste, the boyars, installing his own supporters as territorial lords, and supplying them with serfs. He further inspired fear when he established a corps of state spies, the *oprichniki*, the ancestor of the much-hated tsarist political police of the nineteenth century; and when, in 1581, he killed his own son in a fit of rage. Viewing himself as the heir to the Roman and Byzantine empires, Ivan had himself proclaimed "tsar" ("caesar") at his coronation in 1547. Anarchy followed his death in 1584, but in 1613, the establishment of the Romanov dynasty, destined to rule until 1917, restored stability.

Traditionally eastward-looking because of its history and because of its Orthodox Christianity, Russia turned westward under Peter I, "the Great" (r. 1682–1725). From 1689, when he ended the regency of his mother, Peter guided Russia to participation in the European cultural realm. He promoted the commercial and intellectual innovations of the West in order to develop the skills Russia needed to become a modern, sovereign state. The Church, too, was put under his control. He suppressed the old landed nobility and created a new aristocratic elite, subservient to the tsar but granted extraordinary powers over their serfs, who, since 1675, were reduced to the condition of slaves; that is, they could be bought and sold separately from the land. He required the sons of the nobles to gain a Western education, and directed the printing presses to publish newspapers and books like those read in such cities as Paris and London. He created a Baltic fleet, completely rebuilt the army, and encouraged industry (while punishing financial failure). Totally ruthless, he had his own son and heir condemned to death when that young man balked at the Tsar's cultural revolution.

By the time of Peter the Great, Russia had swollen far beyond the limits of old Muscovy. It extended eastward to the region of the Volga River, dominating the Asian descendants of the once-victorious Mongols, called Tatars. Passing the Ural Mountains, Russia reached still father across the arc of northern Asia into Siberia and to the Pacific shore. Pushing northward into the region of the Baltic Sea, it faced Sweden, which it stripped of vital territory in the Great Northern War (1700–1721). Here Peter constructed a new capital, facing west across the Gulf of Finland, named after himself: Saint Petersburg.

Pushing southward to the Black Sea, gateway to the Mediterranean, Russia faced Tatar chiefs who paid tribute to Ottoman Turkish rulers. To the west, it bordered the regions of Belarus and Ukraine, then under Polish domination. Much of this territory it acquired by the three eighteenth-century partitions of Poland accomplished under the most capable of Peter's successors, Catherine II, called "the Great" (r. 1762–1796).

A German princess by birth, Catherine came to the throne by the assassination of her husband, the grandson of Peter the Great. Although at first a committed reformer, seriously educated in political thought, she nevertheless worked to enhance the nobility's power over their serfs, at the same time insisting upon their obedience to herself. In foreign affairs she succeeded in expanding Russia's presence in the Middle East, and she acquired land from both Poland and the Ottoman Empire, including a precious outlet on the Black Sea. Considered an "enlightened" monarch, like her contemporaries in Austria and Prussia, Catherine, too, retained absolute power.

By the late eighteenth century, Europe was unique in being largely organized into nation-states (sovereign states containing a population linked by language, ethnicity, or history), and most Europeans were the subjects of monarchs who ruled, or wished to rule, absolutely. Of the continent's major political units, only Venice, the Swiss cantons, and the Dutch republic were not monarchies. Britain, though a monarchy, was a limited one, its king hedged around with constitutional restrictions. Yet although this was an age of

WHO'S WHO

Europe's Rulers in an Era of Concentrating Power, I

Charles V (r. 1519–1556, d. 1558) Habsburg emperor who briefly ruled much of Europe from the Iberian peninsula to the Ottoman border, including Italian possessions and Mediterranean islands, and much of the New World in addition.

Philip II (r. 1556–1598) Habsburg king of Spain, who from his monastic fortress (the Escorial) reigned over a Spanish Empire reaching to the New World and Italy, and defended Spanish naval supremacy and Atlantic monopoly.

Elizabeth I, "the Great" (r. 1558–1603) Queen of England who presided over the Anglican religious settlement, victory over the Spanish Armada, and the New World exploration.

Gustavus Adolphus (r. 1611–1632) King of Sweden who led reorganized Swedish army in Thirty Years' War.

Louis XIV (r. 1643–1715) King of France and patron of the court of Versailles, who best illustrates the concept of "absolute monarch," reportedly claiming: "I am the State."

Oliver Cromwell (r. 1653–1658) Parliamentary leader in English Civil War; subsequently, as Lord Protector, uncrowned ruler of England.

kings, the forces that would someday dethrone them were already gathering strength.

MIRRORS FOR PRINCES

In the thirteenth century, the saintly French King Louis IX (r. 1226–1270) had administered justice in a grove of trees, reclining against a great oak in order to hear the petitions of his subjects. In the seventeenth, his successor the "Sun King" Louis XIV was surrounded by circles of advisers and bureaucrats, laws and institutions, rituals and splendor. The four centuries that lie between saw the development of the notion of monarchy and the apparatus of the court—and, concurrently, the arguments for resistance to unjust power, and the theories of natural law and inborn rights that would in time dismantle both.

The Idea of the Prince

Almost as soon as kings appeared in Europe, writers began telling them how to rule. The same university-trained clerics who wrote on philosophy and theology wrote works on the ideal king. These "mirrors for princes," as they were called, urged moral values on the ruler: he should be kind, just, generous. The prince or king was to look into such books and see a perfected image of himself, which he was to emulate.

The idealized model of kingship projected by these works was remote from kingship in the flesh. Medieval monarchy had rested largely on force—military, judicial, personal. A theoretical understanding of the role of the sovereign, the figure in whom all authority resided, had not yet crystallized. Still less had the idea of the state as an abstract entity served by the king for the benefit of the people. From the fourteenth through seventeenth centuries, these concepts developed, culminating in the theoretical model of absolute monarchy.

The struggle between popes and emperors, originating in the eleventh century, stimulated in the fourteenth works challenging the notion of papal supremacy. Political theorists such as John of Jandun, Marsilius of Padua, and William of Ockham, as well as the poet Dante Alighieri aimed to free politics from papal ambitions and proposed the model of a universal monarchy. They observed that rulers operated in a realm of necessity separate from the realm of spirit, and made the decisions most beneficial to the state. These theories helped dismantle the secular authority of the papacy, which had peaked in the previous two centuries, and paved the way for the development of discrete secular monarchies in the two that followed.

Machiavelli's lawless prince, with whom this chapter opened, enters into consideration here. Italy, the arena where the struggle between pope and emperor took place, had no national monarchy until the nineteenth century. It was a patchwork of autonomous city republics and principalities. This region of fragmented authority and endemic violence was the context for Machiavelli's prince, a figure representing an abrupt departure from medieval tradition. He was to act unburdened by piety, compassion, or ideals of any sort. He was calculating, opportunistic, and ambitious for power. His aim was only to secure his state; the purpose of the state merely to exist, to avert conquest by another prince.

Machiavelli's contemporary Erasmus developed his own conception of the ideal monarch, in his *Education of the Christian Prince,* as well as in other treatises and letters. Like the subject of the medieval mirrors for princes, that figure was to be just, well-advised, and all-provident. But he had particularly Erasmian features, in addition: he would have a classical education, he would avoid war at all costs, and he would support with special diligence the productive middling and poorer citizens of his state. Erasmus's prince resembles not at all his Machiavellian counterpart.

Although Erasmus and Machiavelli differed in their view of the ideal monarch, they agreed that the modern world required a modern type of monarch. For Machiavelli, that new monarch, the "prince," would need to be ruthlessly focused on the problem of maintaining his power. For Erasmus, he would need to assume increased cultural, social, and economic responsibilities, and his ability to perform these primary duties would be jeopardized by the enormous costs of warfare.

Both were right. The ideal of the monarch developed by later sixteenth- and seventeenth-century theorists had both Machiavellian and Erasmian dimensions. The monarch would be truly sovereign, concentrating in himself all authority and pursuing all

---

HOW MANY?

European Wars, 1500–1763

The Italian Wars: 1494–1559 (Italian states, Papacy, Habsburg armies, France)

Dutch wars of independence: 1579–1648 (Provinces of Northern Netherlands, Spain)

Thirty Years' War: 1618–1648 (States of Holy Roman Empire [Bohemia, Palatinate], France, Austrian Habsburg Empire, Sweden)

English Civil War: 1642–1651 (England [Parliamentary and Royalist forces], Scotland)

War of the Spanish Succession: 1701–1714 (Spain, France, England, Netherlands)

Seven Years' War: 1756–1763 (Spain, France, England, Netherlands)

means necessary to further the interests of the state. At the same time, he would set standards in the cultural realm, promote the economic welfare of his subjects, secure peace and administer justice, and serve in his person as the symbol of national unity. He was an absolute monarch, who ruled by divine right.

The notion of the "divine right of kings" is implicit in the medieval worldview, with its hierarchies of perfection culminating in God. It was but a step more to declare that the king in his kingdom was comparable to God in the universe. Answering only to God, an absolute monarch might free himself of the laws passed by parliaments or urged by the Church or embodied in traditional customs. The king himself, deriving his powers from God, was the embodiment of law.

The French philosopher Jean Bodin (1530–1596) presented a classic statement of the theory of absolute monarchy in his *Six Books of the Commonwealth* of 1576 (see *Witnesses*, p. 440). Just as families fell under the authority of the father (a definition of patriarchy), so communities of families fell under the authority of the state and its prince. The sovereign power could maintain peace, make laws, ensure justice, promote well-being. He was not all-powerful, but was limited, like his subjects, by natural law. Those subjects, too, had rights, which the monarch was to respect. Bodin's theory implies an abstract state, a sovereign power embodied in the monarch but conceivable without him as an independent entity.

In his *Politics Drawn from the Very Words of Scripture* published posthumously in 1709 and quoted in *Witnesses* on p. 440, another Frenchman, Bishop Jacques-Bénigne Bossuet (1627–1704), allowed kings more authority than did Bodin. As God's representatives, kings naturally produced judgments that were reasonable and just, like the will of God. While the king conformed to the divine law that reigned over all, what he willed, in the secular state, was the law itself. Bossuet verbalized the assumptions of power made by his own prince, Louis XIV.

Across the English Channel, too, the monarch's claims for absolute power were voiced—as in the *True Law of Free Monarchy* written in 1598 by James VI of Scotland, the future James I of England. James argued for the elevation of the king's will over Parliament, law, and custom. It was precisely such a claim that caused English absolutism to fail in the next generation, when Parliament dispatched monarchy for eleven years and absolute monarchy forever.

Yet in 1651, amid the throes of that revolution, the *Leviathan* (a reference to the Biblical monster appearing in the Book of Job, chapter 41) of Thomas Hobbes (1588–1679) promoted a different kind of absolutism: that of the state itself (see *Witnesses*, p. 442). Viewing human nature in an infamously negative light, Hobbes argued that people allowed their freedom would descend to anarchy, corruption, and violence—a "state of war." They must be reined in by a "Leviathan," a stern and vigilant government (not necessarily a king), to which they voluntarily conferred their obedience in an implicit contract. Thenceforth, the state would order the lives of those made desperate because their existence was, in Hobbes' memorably succinct and sad expression, "solitary, poor, nasty, brutish, and short."

The "Monstrous Regiment of Women" As theoreticians elevated the status of the king, the question of female monarchy was reexamined. What if the heir to the throne were a woman? A woman, it was believed, was unfit to rule. She would be fickle, deceitful, incapable of leading an army, obsessed with male relationships. In France, women were legally barred from ascending the throne.

Yet the early modern era boasts many female rulers. Isabella of Castile presided jointly with her husband, Ferdinand, over the *Reconquista* and the Spanish expansion into the New World. The British Isles saw three women rulers in the sixteenth century alone: Mary I, Elizabeth I, and their cousin Mary, Queen of Scots. In seventeenth-century Sweden, Christina (r. 1632–1654; d. 1689) succeeded her father Gustavus Adolphus. In the eighteenth century, Russia had four reigning empresses: Catherine I, Anna, Elizabeth, and Catherine II. The empress Maria Theresa (r. 1740–1780) ruled the disparate German, Hungarian, and Balkan areas of the Habsburg empire. In France, where a woman could not reign, Catherine de' Medici, Marie de' Medici, and Anne of Austria all ruled France as regents for their sons, its future kings.

Facing the ascension of Elizabeth I to the throne (in the wake of Queen Mary I) and with his native Scotland under the rule of Mary Stuart, the Protestant reformer John Knox (c. 1514–1572) wrote, in 1558, his *First Blast of the Trumpet against the Monstrous Regiment of Women* (see *Witnesses*, p. 441). For Knox, women were defects in nature, and rule by women was a hideous contradiction in terms. Assembling the various misogynist views of ancient philosophers, pagan poets, the Bible, and Church Fathers, he thundered that the English and Scottish nobility were worse than "brute beasts" for tolerating female sovereignty: "for that they do to women which no male amongst the common sort of beasts can be proved to do to their female, that is, they reverence them, and quake at their presence; they obey their commandments, and that against God."

In order to withstand such criticism, women who ruled often adopted the guise of androgyny. Queen Elizabeth I of England played with such male/female images—positive ones, of course—in representing herself to her subjects. She was a prince, and manly, she asserted, even though she was female, as recorded in *Witnesses* on p. 441. She was also (she claimed) a virgin, a condition essential to avoid the attacks of her opponents, for whom female nature always inclined to lust. In her last years, she defied the limits of female sexual identification. "My sex," she said, just before her death, "cannot diminish my prestige."

Catherine de' Medici skirted the boundaries of male and female identifications in the imagery she adopted to define her position. She chose as one symbol the figure of Artemisia, an androgynous ancient warrior-heroine, who combined a female persona with masculine powers. Thus clothed in androgynous imagery, these women rulers could, like their male counterparts, claim to be princes and absolute sovereigns.

Some later female rulers readily acknowledged and even exploited their gender. Maria Theresa, devoted to her wayward husband and to her thirteen children, was the embodiment of the motherly queen, while at the same time being an outstanding monarch. Catherine the Great indulged her own sexual appetites with the same freedom shown by male monarchs, taking numerous lovers—but never allowing them to distract her from affairs of state.

Halls of Mirrors

Just as political philosophers developed the theory of absolute monarchy, architects designed spaces in which those monarchs might display their power. On grand staircases and in splendid reception rooms, such as the huge Hall of Mirrors built for Louis XIV at Versailles (and imitated in other royal courts) the king shone in glory; and those gathered around him, like glass, reflected his brilliant image. In addition to the crowds of courtiers pressing forward to catch a glimpse of majesty, the monarch was attended by poets and playwrights, composers and painters, all competing for the honor (and financial rewards) of royal patronage.

During the Middle Ages, as before, events of importance to the community had been celebrated with processions—solemn ritual marches, featuring a display of special objects. In the early modern era, kings adapted the ritual device of the procession to

---

WITNESSES

A King's Right to Rule

During the sixteenth and seventeenth centuries, kings became more powerful and theorists rushed in to justify their claims to power. Here two French theorists, writing in that nation where "absolute monarchy" reached an apogee under Louis XIV, defend the king's right to make law (Bodin) and to rule as an agent of God himself (Bossuet).

Jean Bodin argues the king's right to impose laws without consent (1576): On the other hand it is the distinguishing mark of the sovereign that he cannot in any way be subject to the commands of another, for it is he who makes law for the subject, abrogates law already made, and amends obsolete law. No one who is subject either to the law or to some other person can do this. That is why it is laid down in the civil law [Roman law] that the prince is above the law, for the word *law* in Latin implies the command of him who is invested with sovereign power. … From all of this it is clear that the principal mark of sovereign majesty and absolute power is the right to impose laws generally on all subjects regardless of their consent. …
(Jean Bodin, *Six Books of the Commonwealth*, 1576, 1:8, 10; ed. R. Brown, 1990)

Jacques-Bénigne Bossuet claims that kings are God's ministers on earth (1678): It is God who establishes kings. … Princes thus act as ministers of God and His lieutenants on earth. It is through them that he rules. … This is why we have seen that the royal throne is not the throne of a man, but the throne of God himself. … It appears from this that the person of kings is sacred, and to move against them is sacrilege. … Since their power comes from on high, kings should not believe that they are its masters and may use it as they wish; they should exercise it with fear and restraint as a thing which has come to them from God, and for which God will demand an account. …

Therefore let them respect their power, since is not theirs but the power of God, and must be used holily and religiously.
(Jacques-Bénigne Bossuet, *Politiques tirées des propres paroles de L'Ecriture sainte*, 1678; ed. W. F. Church, 1984)

A Queen's Right to Rule

Although the sovereignty of the male monarch could be vigorously defended, the sovereignty of a woman monarch remained in question. In the first passage the Scottish reformer John Knox, whose own country and neighboring England were (to his fury) ruled by queens, denies that women can exercise authority as men do. In the second, Queen Elizabeth I presents herself to the English army, and declares her readiness and capacity to rule.

John Knox blasts his trumpet against rule by women (1558): The empire of a Woman is a thing repugnant to Nature. ... For who can deny but it is repugnant to nature, that the blind shall be appointed to lead and conduct such as do see? That the weak, the sick, and impotent persons shall nourish and keep the whole and strong? And finally, that the foolish, mad, and frenetic shall govern the discrete, and give counsel to such as be sober of mind? And such be all women, compared unto man in bearing of authority. For their sight in civil regiment [government] is but blindness; their strength, weakness; their counsel, foolishness; and judgment, frenzy, if it be rightly considered.

(John Knox, *The First Blast of the Trumpet against the Monstrous Regiment of Women,* 1558; ed. D. Laing, 1864, modernized)

Queen Elizabeth addresses the troops encamped at Tilbury (9 August 1588), asserting her sovereignty even in a military situation—the naval battle against the Spanish Armada had commenced–where her enemies might hope she would weaken: I know I have the body but of a weak and feeble woman; but I have the heart and stomach of a king, and of a king of England too, and think foul scorn that Parma or Spain or any prince of Europe should dare to invade the borders of my realm; to which, rather than any dishonor should grow by me, I myself will take up arms; I myself will be your general, judge, and rewarder of every one of your virtues in the field ... not doubting but by your obedience to my general, by your concord in the camp, and your valor in the field, we shall shortly have a famous victory over those enemies of my God, of my kingdoms, and of my people.

(Elizabeth I, "To the Troops at Tilbury, 1588"; ed. G. P. Rice, Jr., 1951)

sovereign's power. The paintings on the wall, the carving of the furniture, the patterns of the glass in the window, or the carpet on the floor—all could be designed to label the space inhabited by the prince. Throughout the Middle Ages, works of art and literature had been mainly religious, whether commissioned by the Church or by a private individual. In the early modern age, in the precincts of royal power, to communicate the authority and prestige of the prince was itself the business of the arts.

To convey their grandeur, kings built palaces increasingly distinct, in size and magnificence, from the homes of the subjects they ruled. Both the Escorial, near Madrid, and Versailles, near Paris, were not mere palaces, but immense complexes engineered to express the raw fact of royal power. The Austrian princes built palaces of commensurate grandeur and Peter the Great, of Russia, built a whole city, Saint Petersburg, in his image. Even the dukes and despots of Italy and the petty German princes of the Holy Roman Empire surrounded themselves with splendor.

The arrogance of royal power is nowhere expressed so eloquently as in these palaces, whose purpose was frankly not to live or to rule but to overawe. The claim to absolute power made by the kings of Europe and portrayed in stone, glass, and gilding would be challenged by other currents of early modern culture. In time these new ideas would variously reshape monarchy or abolish it, and would make of those palaces what most of them are today: museums, displaying the customs and values of a remote past.

Roman Law and Natural Right

As European monarchs accumulated power and as writers and artists celebrated it, traditions of law evolved that variously supported or undermined royal claims to authority. Concepts of natural right, based on both legal and philosophical traditions, also emerged to pose a challenge to political absolutism.

When Roman authority evaporated in the fifth century C.E., the peoples of Europe outside the old Empire—Celtic, Germanic, and Slavic—continued to follow the customs of their ancestors: tribal law. These customs satisfactorily regulated community life and disciplined criminal behavior so long as those communities remained simple. As tribes and villages became incorporated into nations, the increased complexity of life required the development of more complex systems of law. In many parts of western Europe, the sophisticated apparatus of Roman law, which had served the needs of the largest empire of the ancient Mediterranean world, was drawn upon to alter and even replace customary law.

While medieval philosophers fitted the concepts of Christian theology into the framework of Aristotelian metaphysics, medieval jurists studied the *Code* of Justinian. Centered at Bologna from the

their purposes. When a ruler was scheduled to enter a city, a team of artists, architects, and mechanics constructed props and scenery to make the arrival more imposing. Costume, music, and the careful choreography of the prince's retinue also enhanced the effect.

In the prince's private dwelling, too, sound, imagery, and movement were designed to reflect the

The Origins of Government in the Consent of the Citizens

While some political theorists labored to bolster the theory of monarchy, others thought about why and how citizens formed themselves into a political community. Foremost among these are Thomas Hobbes and John Locke, whose very different understandings of "civil society" are still important in political thought. Here Hobbes explains why subjects should and must obey a sovereign authority (who might or might not be a monarch), while Locke explains why individuals freely sacrifice some of their rights and join forces to form a civil body.

Thomas Hobbes shows how all citizens consent to the sovereign power (1651): II.17. The only way to erect such a common power, as may be able to defend [men] from the invasion of foreigners, and the injuries of one another, and thereby to secure them in such sort, as that by their own industry, and by the fruits of the earth, they may nourish themselves and live contentedly, is, to confer all their power and strength upon one man, or upon one assembly of men, that may reduce all their wills, by plurality of voices, unto one will. ... This is more than consent, or concord; it is a real unity of them all, in one and the same person, made by covenant of every man, in such manner, as if every man should say to every man, "I authorize and give up my right of governing myself, to this man, or to this assembly of men, on this condition, that thou give up thy right to him, and authorize all his actions in like manner." This done, the multitude so united in one person is called a "commonwealth," in Latin *civitas*. This is the generation of that great LEVIATHAN, or rather, to speak more reverently, of that "mortal god," to which we owe under the "immortal God," our peace and defence. For by this authority, given him by every particular man in the commonwealth, he has the use of so much power and strength conferred on him, that by terror thereof, he is enabled to perform the wills of them all, to peace at home, and mutual aid against their enemies abroad. And in him consists the essence of the commonwealth . ...

And he that carries this person is called "sovereign," and is said to have "sovereign power"; and every one besides, his "subject."
(Thomas Hobbes, *Leviathan*, 1651, 2:17; ed. E. Weber, 1990)

John Locke explains why people will surrender their freedom to form civil government (1690): Men, being, as has been said, by nature all free, equal, and independent, no one can be put out of this estate and subjected to the political power of another without his own consent. The only way whereby anyone divests himself of his own natural liberty and puts on the bonds of civil society, is by agreeing with other men, to join and unite into a community for their comfortable, safe and peaceable living one among another, in a secure enjoyment of their properties, and a greater security against any that are not of it. ... When any number of men have so consented to make one community or government, they are thereby presently incorporated, and make one body politic, wherein the majority have a right to act and conclude the rest. ...

If man in the state of nature be so free as has been said ... why will he part with his freedom? Why will he give up this empire, and subject himself to the dominion and control of any other power? To which it is obvious to answer, that though in the state of nature he has such a right, yet the enjoyment of it is very uncertain. ... This makes him willing to quit this condition which, however free, is full of fears and continual dangers; and it is not without reason that he seeks out and is willing to join in society with others who ... unite for the mutual preservation of their lives, liberties and estates, which I call by the general name—property.

The great and chief end, therefore, of men uniting into commonwealths, and putting themselves under government, is the preservation of their property. ...
(John Locke, *The Second Treatise on Government*, 1690; ed. E. Weber, 1990)

---

twelfth century, a series of jurists wrote commentaries showing how Roman law could be applied to the patterns of Christian society and medieval communities. Soon Roman legal concepts were employed by the advisers to the kings of Europe. Roman law had been developed for a state in which power was centered in a ruler, the emperor. Its concepts were now useful to kings seeking tools by which to discipline their nobility, administer their states, and become "emperors" in their own lands. Indeed, the very concept of a "state" was made available in the language of Roman law. It was the precondition of the further development of the nations of Europe.

In England, newly revived concepts of Roman law encountered an independent tradition of common law, developed during the Middle Ages and rooted in Anglo-Saxon and Norman practice. English common law was based on the principle that previous judicial decisions, rather than codes or statutes, established right. The jury system and the system of criminal procedure based on "grand" and "petty" inquests are components of English common law. The kings of England promoted common law, which was the law administered in the kings' courts, and shaped its procedures to the benefit of royal authority. In time, they also incorporated elements of Roman law into

The Royal Palace

Pierre Patel the elder, **View of Versailles:** *In the sixteenth and seventeenth centuries, Europe's rulers built palaces to match their claims for glory. Greatest of these was Louis XIV's palace at Versailles, built between 1669 and 1686. This painting is an aerial view of the palace and its walks, fountains, and gardens.*

the tradition, especially those that tended to exalt the authority of the monarch. As elsewhere in Europe, the law of the Roman Church, or "canon law," which was modeled on Roman principles, also helped to shape common law.

If Roman law served to bolster the authority of the state and its ruler, it also conveyed another concept important in the development of modern politics: that of natural law. Roman jurists distinguished between the positive law by which Roman citizens

were bound—the "law of nations" which regulated interactions between peoples—and natural law, which mirrored eternal principles of good and evil that were intrinsic in nature. Those concepts were transmitted in Christian Europe through the work of medieval jurists, and flourished anew in the early modern era. "The law of nature is a dictate of right reason," wrote the seventeenth-century Dutch theorist Hugo Grotius (1583–1645); an act is judged morally worthy if in accord with rational nature, or

View of the Escorial: *The Spanish king Philip II's gloomier palace, the Escorial, was built outside Madrid between 1563 and 1584 more for labor and penitence than for the leisured elegance of Versailles.*

base if it is not. Human law, God's law, nature's law were all different, he maintained, but they could exist in congruence.

If medieval and Reformation thinkers wished to bring human activity into accord with divine mandates, some political thinkers of the early modern era wished to limit the state by the principles of natural law. Whereas Roman law favored state-building, the theory of natural law encouraged the building of states according to principles of right and justice which were unattached to any specific nation or people or system of belief.

Another school of political theory developed to justify resistance to states perceived as unjust. Some religious communities fostered an ethic of skepticism toward those in power, and even sanctioned disobedience to governments that violated independent standards of justice. These attitudes often prospered in radical Protestant groups, and in many cases they were extinguished as the adherents of such groups were suppressed. But similar attitudes also characterized the reformed churches radiating from Calvin's Geneva, born of a man who had himself fled a persecuting regime. "Obedience to man must not become disobedience to God," wrote that sober reformer. Next to God, Calvin acknowledged, we are subject to kings—but only so long as their command is godly. "If they command anything against Him, let it go unesteemed."

The right to resist unjust governors, cautiously but clearly stated here, is the proto-democratic germ of Calvinist political theory. The theme was not so prominent in Geneva (where Protestants were in power) as in the further reaches of the Calvinist network, where the reformers were opposed to the majority: in England, Scotland (until the late 1600s), Huguenot France, and Hungary, Poland and Bohemia before their re-conversion to Catholicism in the Thirty Years' War. Later Calvinist theorists went so far as to propose the notion that sovereignty lies in the people, who have the authority to make laws, appoint magistrates, and create kings.

It was but a step further to propose that government was based on a contract between the ruler and the ruled. Sovereignty resided in the people, who, by a kind of contract, agreed to surrender their independence in order to gain the benefits of a well-regulated state. These views form part of the famous analysis of civil government forged in the late seventeenth century by the English liberal John Locke.

A university-trained philosopher who witnessed in his youth the struggles of the English Civil War, John Locke (1632–1704) worked as secretary to a nobleman of the Whig party, which engineered the 1688 Revolution. By that time, Locke himself was living in the Dutch Republic, a center for the circulation of the latest and most daring ideas. From there in 1689–1690 he published four fundamental works: the *Letter on Toleration*, the *Essay Concerning Human Understanding*, and *Two Treatises on Civil Government*. Each was a groundbreaking work of momentous significance. The second of the two *Treatises* is specifically relevant here.

According to Locke, human beings were born absolutely free to pursue their own welfare as best they might amid the natural abundance that God provided at the Creation. All were born with fundamental rights: to life, to liberty, and to the pursuit of property. Some chose to labor diligently and acquire private property. When the others, propertyless, sought to seize what they had not labored to accumulate, the property-owners joined together to create civil government—which was, in effect, the result of a contract. That contract was reminiscent of that called for by Hobbes, but unlike his, it was reversible.

The participants chose representatives to a legislature, which reported to a king. If the government failed to perform the functions for which it was created, it could be dismantled and refounded on the original principles. If the king abused his position and interfered with the proper function of a just government, he could be removed. Locke's treatise is a roadmap at once for the creation of a society based on capitalist notions of the accumulation of property and for the founding of a government rooted in the consent and will of the people. These views passed directly to the authors of the American Declaration of Independence and inform its core principles.

Conclusion
POWER, RESISTANCE, AND THE MEANING OF THE WEST

Although Machiavelli's prince never appeared and Italy was lost, elsewhere the European monarchs of the early modern era adopted the objective that Machiavelli defined: the pursuit of power. By the mid-eighteenth century, the states of Europe were the most powerful in the world, and the rulers who governed them were, in most cases, absolute. Yet the possibility of resistance to unjust monarchy had also become apparent—in the example of the English Revolution on the one hand, and, on the other, in the philosophical vision of the proponents of natural law and social contracts. The tendencies to the concentration of power and, at the same time, to its limitation would both continue to characterize the civilization of the West, as Westerners set out to explore and to dominate the rest of the globe.

QUESTIONS TO CONSIDER

1. How did the use of gunpowder change the organization and tactics of European armies?

2. How did those changes in turn affect the developing nation states?

3. Name one major military leader of the early modern period. What innovations did he introduce, and why were they important?

4. Why did some nations lose importance, and others gain primacy during the sixteenth through eighteenth centuries?

5. Why can the Glorious Revolution be considered glorious?

SUGGESTED RESOURCES

Anderson, Fred, *Crucible of War: The Seven Years' War and the Fate of Empire in North America, 1754–1766* (New York: Knopf, 2000). Traces the events that led to the Seven Years' War and its expansion over three of the continents, which shaped the development of Britain into a world empire.

Black, Jeremy, ed., *European Warfare, 1453–1815* (New York: St. Martin's Press, 1999). Nine historians look at major conflicts in Europe—in their social, cultural, and political contexts—painting a comprehensive picture of warfare from the Ottoman conquest of Constantinople to the fall of Napoleon.

Burke, Peter, *The Fabrication of Louis XIV* (New Haven–London: Yale University Press, 1992). An imaginative analysis of the staging of the French kingship during the high point of absolutism.

DuPlessis, Robert S., *Lille and the Dutch Revolt: Urban Stability in an Era of Revolution, 1500–1582* (Cambridge–New York: Cambridge University Press, 1991). Shows that Lille remained loyal to Philip II during the Dutch revolt due to the political response of its ruling class.

Elliott, J. H. & L. W. B. Brockliss, eds., *The Age of the Favourite* (New Haven: Yale University Press, 1999). The absolute kings did not rule absolutely but shared power, tacitly, with their "favorites," men who gained importance because of their privileged access to and command over the monarch, and depicted in a variety of European settings in these essays.

Fichtner, Paula S., *Emperor Maximilian II* (New Haven: Yale University Press, 2001). Portrait of a Renaissance monarch faced by Turkish aggression, religious change, and a stubborn bureaucracy.

Frye, Susan, *Elizabeth I: The Competition for Representation* (Oxford: Oxford University Press, 1993). How Elizabeth appropriated the image-making machinery around her to advance her own construction of herself as both woman and monarch.

Knoppers, Laura L., *Constructing Cromwell: Ceremony, Portrait, and Print, 1645–1661* (Cambridge: Cambridge University Press, 2000). Describes how the revolutionary Cromwell, lacking the imprimatur of royal birth or high nobility, was represented in literary and visual texts.

Love, Ronald S., *Blood and Religion: The Conscience of Henri IV 1553–1593* (Montreal: McGill-Queen's University Press. 2001). Views the situation facing the first Bourbon king of France, raised as a Calvinist, as a choice between the obligations of lineage ("blood") and faith.

Major, J. Russell, *From Renaissance Monarchy to Absolute Monarchy: French Kings, Nobles, and Estates* (Baltimore: Johns Hopkins University Press, 1994). Considers kings, aristocrats, and assemblies in the struggle for power, with the monarchy edging ahead in the end.

Mack Holt, *The French Wars of Religion: 1562–1629* (Cambridge: Cambridge University Press, 1995). Recent synthesis that navigates and clarifies a complex episode in military and political as much as religious history.

Monod, Paul Kleber, *The Power of Kings: Monarchy and Religion in Europe, 1589–1715* (New Haven: Yale University Press, 2000). Into the age of absolutism, Monod shows, kings continued to employ religious proofs of their authority and legitimacy.

Parker, Geoffrey, *The Grand Strategy of Philip II* (New Haven: Yale University Press, 1998). Explores the vision of empire Philip II possessed, and how he made his decisions in the interest of that vision.

Parker, Geoffrey, *The Military Revolution: Military Innovation and the Rise of the West, 1500–1800*, 2nd ed. (Cambridge: Cambridge University Press, 1996). A classic description of a "military revolution" that was a major factor in Europe's achievement of global power during the early modern era.

Rowlands, Guy, *The Dynastic State and the Army under Louis XIV: Royal Service and Private Interest, 1661–1701* (Cambridge: Cambridge University Press, 2002). Studies the development of the army as an interaction between king and noble officers.

Tracy, James D., *Emperor Charles V, Impresario of War: Campaign Strategy, International Finance, and Domestic Politics* (Cambridge: Cambridge University Press, 2002). Views Charles V as caught between political and military imperatives and financial needs and limitations.

Life and Times of Queen Elizabeth I:
http://www.elizabethi.org

Louise XIV, biography (Versailles):
http://www.chateauversailles.fr/en/210.asp

Constitutional goovernment, works of all periods, including Machiavelli, Grotius, Hobbes, Locke, Bodin, and Bossuet:
http://www.constitution.org/liberlib.htm

◉ Western Civilization Documents CD-ROM

12.4 The Peace of Westphalia
13.4 Thomas Hobbes
15.1 Richelieu: Controlling the Nobility
15.2 The Sun King Shines
15.3 Louis XIV: Memoirs for the Instruction of the Dauphin
15.4 M. de la Colonie: The Battle of Schellenberg
15.5 G.M. Trevelyan: Chapter 1 from History of England
15.6 Peter the Great: Correspondence with His Son

EUROPE REACHES OUT

| 1500 | 1550 | 1600 | 1650 | 1700 | 1750 | 1800 |

Diseases ravage Amerindian populations, 1500s–1600s

Thirty Years' War, 1618–48   Anglo-Dutch Wars, 1652–74   Seven Years' War, 1756–63

English Civil War, 1642–51

Conquest and Discovery

◆ Voyages of Columbus, 1492–1504

◆ Da Gama in Calicut, Goa, 1498

  ◆ Cortés conquers Mexico, 1519–21

  ◆ Magellan sails the world, 1519–22

    ◆ Verrazano in New York harbor, 1524

    ◆ Pizarro conquers Peru, 1531–39

    ◆ Cartier explores Canada, 1534–42

      ◆ Coronado in Arizona, New Mexico, 1539–42

      ◆ Drake circumnavigates globe, 1577–80

◆ Champlain explores Canada, 1603

  ◆ Foundation of Jamestown, 1607

    ◆ Dutch East India Company, Batavia (Jakarta, Java), 1619

    ◆ Pilgrims found Plymouth Bay Colony, 1620

      ◆ Dutch acquire Malacca from Portuguese, 1641

      ◆ English Navigation Acts, 1651–96

        ◆ Marquette, Jolliet explore Mississippi valley, 1673

        ◆ De la Salle explores Mississippi region, 1682

◆ Treaty of Paris, 1763

  ◆ Stamp Act repealed, 1766

    ◆ U.S. Declaration of Independence, 1776

      ◆ U.S. Constitution, Bill of Rights ratified, 1788, 1791

Slavery and Abolition

Atlantic slave trade, 1500–1888

Plantation cultivation in Americas of sugar and tobacco, then cotton and rice

◆ Spanish "New Laws" prohibit Amerindian slavery, 1542

◆ Abolition Society founded, 1787

  ◆ Haiti independent, 1804

    ◆ Britain abolishes slave trade, 1807

    ◆ U.S. abolishes slave trade, 1808

Ideas

First century of printing, 1460–1560

The Enlightenment, 1685–1795

The Scientific Revolution, 1543–1687

◆ Martin Waldseemüller's, world map 1507

  ◆ Luther's *Ninety-five Theses*, 1517

    ◆ Copernicus's *On the Revolutions of the Heavenly Spheres*, 1543

◆ Galileo's *Dialogue Concerning the two Chief World Systems*, 1632

  ◆ Newton's *Mathematical Principles of Natural Philosophy*, 1687

  ◆ Locke's *Second Treatise on Civil Government*, 1690

◆ Rousseau's *Social Contract*, 1762

  ◆ Adam Smith's *Wealth of Nations*, 1776

Beyond the West

Ming dynasty, 1368–1644   Qing dynasty, 1644–1912

Mughal Empire, India, 1526–1857

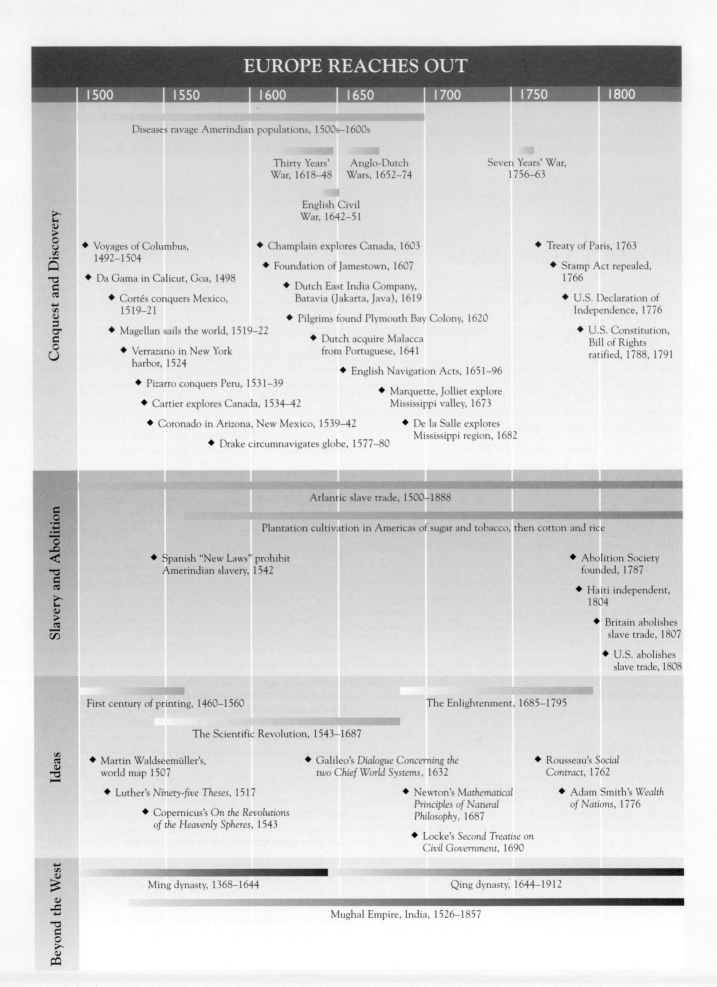

CHAPTER 16
EUROPE REACHES OUT

Global Voyages and
Cultural Encounters

1500–1750

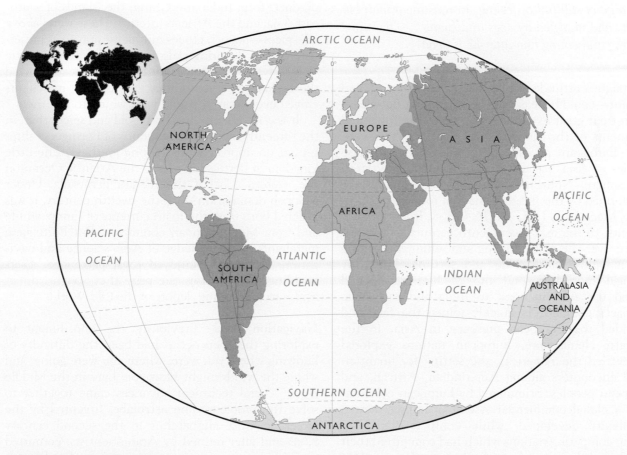

KEY QUESTIONS

◆ **The Open Seas:** Why did the exploration of the Atlantic only begin in the fifteenth century? What discovery made it possible for Europeans to reach Asian marketplaces by sea?

◆ **Brave New World:** Why were Amerindian populations unable to defend themselves against European arrivals? Why were African slaves imported to labor on newly-built plantations?

◆ **The Wealth of Nations:** What products were exchanged between the Americas and the Old World? Why did states attempt to protect or limit the exchange of some goods?

Who is the Cannibal? *The Tupinambá, wrote the sixteenth-century French essayist Michel de Montaigne (1533–1592) of the* **Amerindian** *inhabitants of Brazil, roasted and then ate their war captives. As the victims awaited their fate, they suffered without flinching the winners' abuse and mockery. A well-bred European of the ruling noble class, Montaigne did not quite admire this behavior, but neither did he condemn it. Did not Europeans perpetrate worse cruelties? "I think there is more barbarity in eating a man alive than in eating him dead," wrote Montaigne referring to then current judicial punishments, "and in tearing by torture and the rack a body still full of feeling, in roasting a man bit by bit, and mangled by dogs and swine …, than in roasting and eating him after he is dead."*

Montaigne's attitude—at once curious, skeptical, and tolerant—could have crystallized only after Europeans began their great expansion into the other inhabited continents of the globe. During that 500-year venture, European peoples encountered the diverse peoples of Asia, Africa, Australia, and the Western Hemisphere. Non-Europeans and Europeans were transformed by the interactions that followed.

As Maps 16.1, 16.3, and 16.4 show, from the mid-fifteenth to the mid-seventeenth century, Europeans ranged over the globe, buying and selling, measuring and mapping, conquering and settling. First tiny Portugal ranged beyond the Mediterranean, and around the African coast to India and east Asia. Portugal's competitors quickly joined the race and extended the European presence in Asia. In the Western Hemisphere, European nations explored and settled the Americas, the setting for unanticipated encounters among Amerindian, African, and European peoples. Stimulated by European colonization, a global commercial system of unprecedented complexity developed, while conflicts flared up among competing nations which had committed their wealth and their people, and other peoples and their wealth too, in the quest for greater profits.

THE OPEN SEAS

In the late 1400s, European ships which had rarely ventured beyond the Mediterranean Sea launched out into the open ocean: the Indian, the Pacific, and the Atlantic, called the "Ocean Sea." These waters were the key to Europe's powerful leap forward in the early modern era. They were conquered by sturdy ships, refined navigational tools, cast-iron cannon, and better maps. The tiny Iberian state of Portugal took the lead, establishing footholds in Africa, India, China, Japan, and the famed "Spice Islands" or

Moluccas (in modern Indonesia). Immense profits flowed into the port of Lisbon and the Portuguese royal treasury. Dutch, French, and English merchants followed their lure. By 1700, these nations had footholds of their own on the African coasts and in south and east Asia and the Pacific islands.

Portugal Takes the Lead

Since the earliest days of civilization, world trade had centered on the Mediterranean. In the Middle Ages, Byzantine, Arab, and Italian merchants carried across the Mediterranean goods hauled overland and over water from the three continents that surrounded it. Driving this commerce was the demand for luxury products from India and China, the islands of southeast Asia, and the African interior. These were, above all, spices—pepper, cloves, nutmeg—craved as preservatives and flavorings; also silks and cottons, exotic woods, ivory, and gems. Much as Europeans craved these luxury commodities, European merchants craved even more the gold with which to buy them.

It was in order to find both gold and spices that, in the fifteenth century, the captains of Portuguese ships set out on unprecedentedly long journeys. The little kingdom of Portugal bordered the Atlantic Ocean on the western edge of the Iberian peninsula. Under Moorish domination until the twelfth century, it was isolated both from the main currents of European life and from Mediterranean commerce. But Portuguese merchants had knowledge of Arab science and navigational tools, and enjoyed royal patronage, assets enabling them to win the prize they sought: direct access to the trading depots of the Old World.

Navigation Aids Previously, the impediment to exploring the open ocean had been the difficulty of knowing where you were, where you were going, and where the winds might blow you. Late in the Middle Ages, several technical advances came together to solve the problem. The **astrolabe**, invented by the Greek scientist Hipparchus in the second century B.C.E. and later refined by Arab scientists, permitted the navigator to measure the apparent height of a star and thus determine his latitude. Meanwhile, astronomers worked out detailed tables of the positions of the stars. These tables allowed the technician with an astrolabe to determine a ship's position.

The **quadrant** and, later, the more advanced **sextant**, also measured the altitude of heavenly bodies and thus determined position. Mechanical clocks could check the bearing of the sun—although longitude could not be measured until precision chronometers in the eighteenth century. The **compass**, used by Chinese navigators from around 1100, was adopted by Europeans, who designated as its four cardinal points the fixed directions North, South, East, and West. The device pointed to a magnetic, and therefore variable, north, rather than a true north, which limited its usefulness.

As nautical tools improved, so too did maps. **Portolan** charts gave sailing distances in clear quantities and bearings in straight lines. Lacking parallels and **meridians**, or any indication of the curvature of the earth, they could be used for enclosed seas, but not on the open oceans. Better charts became available as geographical knowledge improved.

Early in the fifteenth century, a copy of the *Geography* by the Greek scientist Ptolemy (c. 90–168 C.E.), began to circulate in western Europe, spurring the creation of a new generation of world maps. These first ventures of modern **cartography** (the science of mapmaking) sadly preserved Ptolemy's errors. He underestimated the circumference of the earth by one-sixth and imagined a huge "unknown land"

covering much of the Southern Hemisphere. Portuguese expeditions enabled cartographers to partially correct the maps and charts and called for the drawing of at least one meridian and lines of latitude. By the mid-sixteenth century, map projections regularly described the earth as a sphere, as shown in *Windows On*, p. 453. Thereafter maps were more accurate than Ptolemy's, as science and experience improved on the knowledge inherited from antiquity.

As shipbuilding also improved, so too did ships (see Chapter 11). The ships of medieval Europe were square-masted and depended on oars for maneuverability and speed. Arab ships called **dhows**, designed for the deep waters of the Indian Ocean, were rigged with triangular, or **lateen**, sails. From these two types of vessel, Spanish and Portuguese shipbuilders developed the small, fast **caravel**. The key to the caravel's

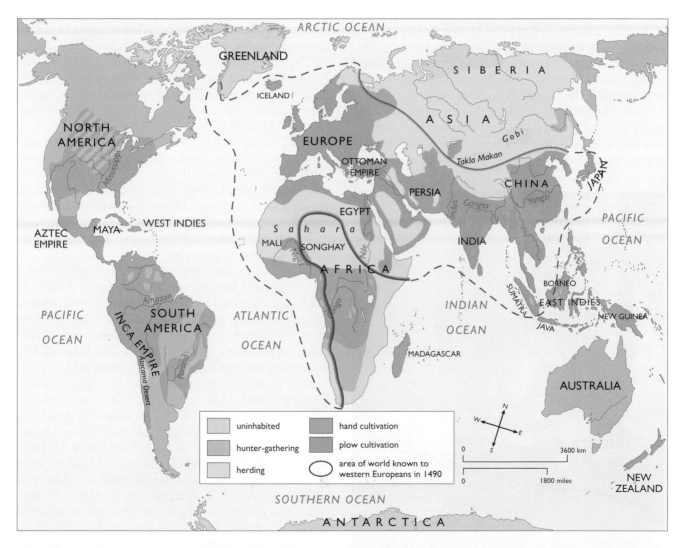

Map 16.1 World Economies and Movements of Peoples around 1500: *On the eve of European expansion, advanced economies based on cultivation with the plow were found in Europe, Asia Minor and the Near East, South and East Asia and some of the Pacific islands, and parts of Africa. Food gatherers, hand cultivators, and pastoralists occupied the rest of the inhabited globe, the major part of its surface. Beginning in the late fifteenth century, peoples from the more advanced areas began the settlement, expansion, and transformation of those unvisited areas.* Why do the regions of plow cultivation roughly correspond to the regions where the earliest civilizations developed, and where urbanization was most intense?

speed was its enlarged sail area, achieved by increasing the number of masts and rigging the middle mast with a square sail or sails, the fore and aft with lateen sails. The stern rudder, a recent innovation, allowed for quick, precise steering. Navigators learned to overcome the westerly winds of the Atlantic and to make use of wind patterns on the Indian Ocean. Because oarsmen were unnecessary, their places could be taken by sailors, cargo, or soldiers.

These superior sailing ships also developed fighting capacity. In the 1400s, they carried cannon on deck, as well as soldiers armed with crossbows and arquebuses. By the early 1500s, guns were permanently mounted between the decks so as to fire broadside through special gunports. Hulls were strengthened, and the whole structure braced by multiple decks, so that the ship could withstand enemy bombardment and cannon recoil. Wherever they went, the new men-of-war (as these warships were called) out-powered other ships and even coastal defences. "At the rumor of our coming," a Portuguese general wrote his king in 1513, "the native ships all vanished, and even the birds ceased to skim over the water." This armed, oceangoing craft made possible the European domination of the seas.

Safe, fast, and formidable, well-steered and powered entirely by sails, manned by a smaller crew but equipped to sustain long journeys, these ships constituted an improvement over the Mediterranean carriers used by the Genoese and Venetians. They brought explorers to

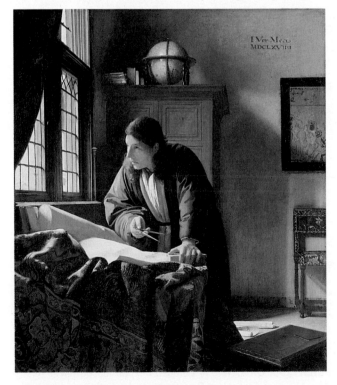

The Lure of Faraway Places

Jan Vermeer, The Geographer: *In this painting of 1669 by the Dutch artist Vermeer can be seen different articles of navigation: a compass, maps, and a globe. (Städelsches Kunstinstitut, Frankfurt)*

the New World, and escorted convoys of heavy merchant vessels across the oceans. (The "New World," designating the lands of the Western Hemisphere, was isolated from the Old World civilizations of Afro-Eurasia until Columbus' arrival in 1492.) By 1600, European ships, once inferior, were the best in the world.

The African Route The first nation to benefit from this improved technology was Portugal. Emerging from the wars of the *Reconquista*, Portugal entered upon its most glorious age around 1400, during the long reign of King John I (r. 1385–1433). John was not only a state-builder but the founder of Portugal's maritime success, even more brilliantly patronized by his brother Prince Henry the Navigator (1394–1460). In 1415, Henry participated in the Portuguese capture of Ceuta, a Moorish depot opposite Gibraltar. The next year he summoned cartographers and seamen to form an institute for navigation. Under Henry's patronage, dozens of vessels sailed straight from the shore into unknown waters, to Africa and beyond.

Plucking up the Atlantic archipelagoes of the Azores and Madeiras Islands on the way (while Spain took the Canaries), Portuguese sea captains turned south to plant garrisons along the west African shore. By the 1470s, they had founded permanent trading stations, where they loaded the gold, spices, ivory, and exotic woods of the interior on ships bound for home. Although their original objectives were gold and spices, they quickly developed an appetite for slaves. As early as 1433, Prince Henry approved the traffic in human cargoes. Soon the crown was taxing the revenues of this trade at 20 percent. The slave trade funded the Portuguese state.

Late in the fifteenth century, Portuguese exploration reached beyond the west coast of Africa. In 1488, Bartolomeu Dias (1430–1500) looped around Africa's southern tip (later named the Cape of Good Hope) and continued northeast along the further coast. Repelled by Arab merchants, and daunted by unfamiliar winds, Dias returned to Portugal.

Ten years later, and under Dias' tutelage, Vasco da Gama (c. 1460–1524) completed the mission his predecessor had launched. With four ships, he sailed past the Cape of Good Hope and into the Indian Ocean, previously the preserve of Arab merchants. In 1498, he anchored off Calicut, on the west (Malabar) coast of India, one of the main depots for the Asian spice trade, as described in *Witnesses* on p. 458. Although hostilities erupted between the Portuguese and the ruler of Calicut, Da Gama managed to return to Portugal with a quantity of pepper. That pepper signaled the accomplishment of a route to the east that started from the western coast of Europe.

Soon the Portuguese established a firm base at the city of Goa, farther north on the west coast of India. This would serve as the Asian capital of their commercial empire of "the Indies" (meaning at the time all of

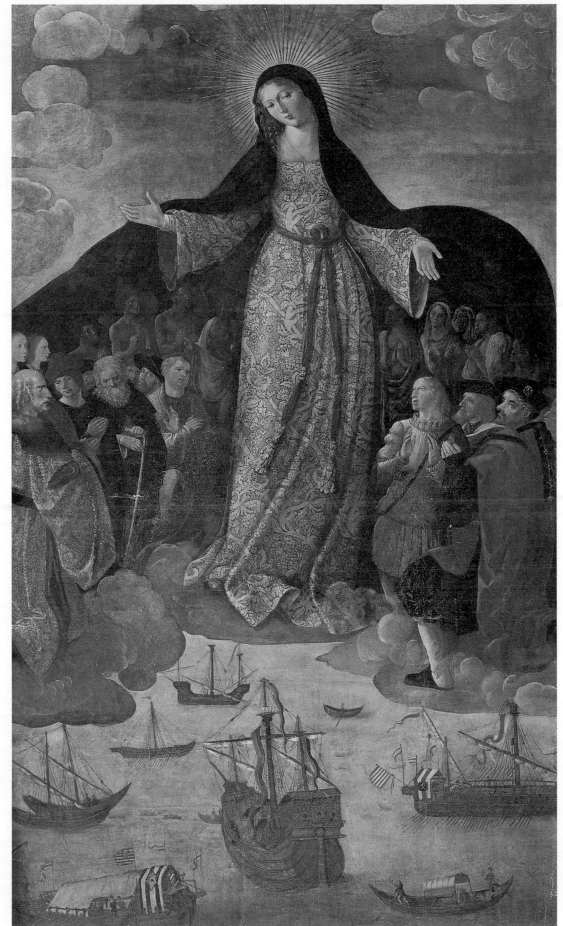

Alejo Fernandez, Our Lady of the Navigators: *This 1535 painting of the Virgin Mary as protectress of several known bold explorers (Columbus may be the figure at the left), and depicting some of the kinds of ships in which they would have sailed, was painted for the Casa de Contratación, or Trade House, in Seville, the center for New World shipping in Spain.*

Asia) which embraced merchant depots in the spice-rich Molucca islands, China, and Japan. Governor-general Afonso de Albuquerque (1453–1515) wrested the depot from Arab merchants and military forces who had long-established colonies there, committing terrible atrocities in the process. Portuguese merchants sent the precious commodities of the east directly back to Lisbon on an average of twelve ships per year. There they sold cheaply (the prices uninflated by the middle-men costs that Venice had had to pay), but at profits sufficient to make the tiny country rich. The kings of Portugal took 20 percent of the profit.

The Portuguese achievement was unprecedented. With a population of only 2 million, Portugal quickly acquired an empire vastly greater than itself. Its ships pierced the zone of Arab mercantile supremacy, crossed the Indian Ocean, and opened a European sea route to India, Indonesia, and China. The port at Lisbon now rivaled once-mighty Venice. After 1600, her mastery of the Mediterranean devalued by Portuguese competition, Venice was reduced to enjoying the small profits of Middle Eastern commerce. The future of merchant ventures lay on the open ocean.

Old World Ventures

In the early 1500s, the Dutch, English, and French followed the Portuguese into the commercial heart of the Old World, and had usurped their position by 1700. They did so by developing merchant empires, consisting of far-flung networks of garrisoned depots, often managed by **joint-stock** merchant companies which acted like nations in themselves.

Joint-stock companies were corporations more complex than the partnerships created by medieval Italian merchants. Now hundreds or thousands of individuals contributed funding for an ongoing commercial enterprise, and awaited, passively, a share of profits in return. The company itself had an identity independent of its participating partners, or share-holders. It sold its shares where merchants gathered—at the *bourse* (French for "purse"), or stock market, such as the one in Antwerp (Europe's first), founded in 1531, or the more important one in Amsterdam, completed in 1613. The company developed its own bureaucracy and hierarchy of officers and agents, and even its own security force, which looked much like a small army. A joint-stock company had the power not merely to buy and sell, but also to settle, manage, and defend a merchant **colony**.

The European agents of merchant companies pressed for trade privileges everywhere along the coasts of southern and eastern Asia. They succeeded especially well in establishing themselves in India, where most of the local rulers, possessing no naval capacity and at odds among themselves, were accustomed to commercial interaction with foreign merchants. Portuguese merchants maintained the base at

Goa until it was reclaimed by an independent India in 1961. By 1700, English and Dutch competitors had taken over Indian trade with Europe. Their various enterprises in India were organized by the English East India Company, established in 1600, and the Dutch East India Company, established in 1602 (see *How Many?*, p. 454).

India As the Portuguese, English, and Dutch planted their commercial colonies on the coasts of India, great changes occurred in the interior. Since the Gupta kings died out on the Indian subcontinent in the mid-sixth century C.E., India had split into a multitude of states and kingdoms, but it still sustained a lively commercial life. By 1192, Islamic invaders from the frontier Sind region had conquered much of northern India and established a sultanate at Delhi which gained sovereignty in the northern part of the subcontinent. Meanwhile, Arab Muslim traders established commercial depots along the coasts. The Delhi sultanate fell in 1398 to the Mongol-Turkic conqueror Tamerlane (c. 1336–1405), to be succeeded by small Muslim kingdoms. After 1526, Tamerlane's descendant Babur (1483–1530) swept in, defeated the different petty states of the north, and established the Mughal Empire. The Great Mughals, as the emperors were called, gained dominion over much of the region, creating a united empire, and presided over a blossoming of culture.

By the early 1700s, the Hindu kingdoms of the center and south reasserted themselves, however, and by mid-century, the Mughal Empire had weakened, leaving India in a disarray the British then exploited. By 1757, the English East India Company, with bases at Bombay, Madras, and Calcutta, and employing its own army and diplomats, had become the principal power in the subcontinent (see Chapter 23). Over the next century it would defeat one regional power after another until it came to rule all of India—about two-thirds directly, and one-third indirectly.

China In China, European merchants never controlled local rulers as they did in India. Prosperous China was uninterested in the goods and services proffered by Europeans. Under the Ming dynasty (which replaced the Mongol Yuan dynasty in 1368), the Chinese people were better fed, clothed, and educated, and perhaps better ruled than peoples anywhere else. Even a poor boy from one of the remote farming villages could aspire to pass the difficult examinations that permitted entrance to the ruling bureaucracy. Steeped in the ancient Confucian tradition, these mandarins advocated self-sufficiency and disdained commercial enterprises and projects of territorial expansion.

Such attitudes had not always prevailed in China. Between 1405 and 1433 (two generations before Columbus' voyages), the emperor's Muslim eunuch Zheng He had made a quite remarkable series of

Diego Homes, Portolan chart of the east coast of Africa, c. 1520

Anonymous, Amerigo Vespucci, 1673

The most important navigational device was the map. Improved world maps based on data collected by explorers provided Europeans with an entirely new concept of the globe. Shown here (above) is an example of a Portolan chart, which guided navigators before the development of modern maps. The intersecting lines connect known locations, and the coastline is drawn freehand based on the careful observation of experienced sailors.

Amerigo Vespucci, Italian navigator, is shown (above right) complete with a compass, a map, and a globe.

Hondius' sophisticated map (below) shows the route followed during Sir Francis Drake's circumnavigation of the globe in 1580.
(top left: British Library, London)

What continents shown on Hondius' map were unknown to navigators and cartographers prior to 1400? What continent is not shown at all?

Hondius, World map showing Drake's voyage (1580), seventeenth century

 To continue your investigation of this topic, please go to www.prenhall.com/king for the related **WINDOWS** on the **WEB** activity

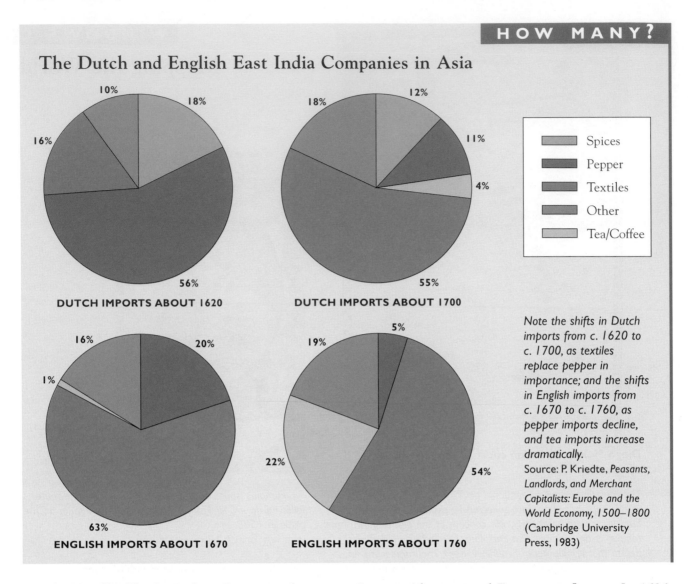

The Dutch and English East India Companies in Asia

HOW MANY?

DUTCH IMPORTS ABOUT 1620

DUTCH IMPORTS ABOUT 1700

ENGLISH IMPORTS ABOUT 1670

ENGLISH IMPORTS ABOUT 1760

Spices
Pepper
Textiles
Other
Tea/Coffee

Note the shifts in Dutch imports from c. 1620 to c. 1700, as textiles replace pepper in importance; and the shifts in English imports from c. 1670 to c. 1760, as pepper imports decline, and tea imports increase dramatically.
Source: P. Kriedte, *Peasants, Landlords, and Merchant Capitalists: Europe and the World Economy, 1500–1800* (Cambridge University Press, 1983)

expeditions through the Indian Ocean to the east African coast. On the first occasion, Zheng had sailed with a fleet of sixty-two vessels, carrying 28,000 men. Advised by mandarin officials, Chinese rulers later halted these expeditions, and even banned the building of ships. Commerce had low priority for the ruling Chinese. But Europeans yearned to sell Chinese goods to the west—especially since the decline of the ancient caravan link between the Middle East and China, through which had flowed Chinese silks and luxury products. Chinese rulers stood firm, however. They might grant Europeans a trading base, such as that gained by the Portuguese at Macao in 1557, but they continued to insulate Chinese society from Europeans.

Japan   Japanese rulers felt much the same way. From the twelfth century, Japan had been dominated by a class of warrior landowners—the **samurai**, roughly similar to the knights of medieval Europe—who owed obedience to an overlord, or shogun. Shoguns and samurai overshadowed the emperor, isolated in his court but protected from challenges by his divine descent. This

Japanese elite opposed European influence. In 1636, the Japanese abandoned all seafaring activity and sealed themselves within their borders. In the 1630s, they expelled all Europeans except the Dutch, who were allowed to dock one ship each year and remain, segregated, on an island near Nagasaki. But the Dutch were to have no contact with Japanese, nor even learn that language; and the Japanese, similarly, were prohibited from learning Dutch, with the result that the two merchant communities were forced to converse in the language of the now-absent Portuguese. The Dutch merchant colony was the main link between Japan and the West until the nineteenth century.

The Dutch Initiative   The Malay Peninsula (part of modern Malaysia), the islands of the South Pacific (including modern Indonesia and the Philippines), and other Pacific islands, including New Zealand and the continent of Australia, all became known to European merchant fleets between 1500 and 1800. The prime commercial target was the Moluccas, or Spice Islands, producers of cloves and nutmeg. In this vast Pacific region, as in India, the Portuguese were the first venturers, establishing a base at Malacca (in modern Malaysia) by 1511. But farther east the Dutch outpaced the Portuguese to win the prize. They gained title to the Moluccas by 1613, and in 1619 established an administrative center at Batavia (now Jakarta, in modern Indonesia). Dutch merchants became the main exploiters of the spice trade, and they were the first Europeans to sight New Zealand and Australia. The Dutch explorer Willem Schouten discovered the southern tip of South America in 1616 and named it Cape Hoorn (or Horn) after his birth place. In 1652 the Dutch settled the African Cape of Good Hope, indicating their leadership in world trade by their presence at these two southernmost outcroppings.

In the seventeenth century, the immense Pacific looked like a Dutch sea. How could such a tiny nation command so far-flung and efficient an empire, if only a merchant empire? The answer lay in its familiarity with the sea—a constant threat to the low-lying Dutch terrain but also a stimulus to shipbuilding. By 1600, the Dutch had 10,000 ships, which sailed the Baltic and Northern seas, as well as the Atlantic and Pacific oceans. The *fluyt* or "flyboat," a Dutch innovation, was an efficient vessel designed for inexpensive, utilitarian hauling. The Dutch became the common carriers of Europe, transporting both utilitarian and luxury goods and linking ports all over the globe. Of these entrepreneurs, the English writer Daniel Defoe (1660–1731) wrote with some awe: "They buy to sell again, take in to send out, and the greatest part of their vast commerce consists in being supplied from all parts of the world that they may supply all the world again."

From the coasts of Africa, across the Indian Ocean and on into the Pacific, merchant vessels probed the ports of the Old World. The next frontier lay on the far side of the Atlantic.

BRAVE NEW WORLD

As the human species evolved and developed communities in the Old World, the New World of the Western Hemisphere remained uninhabited. It acquired its first human immigrants around the time of the last Ice Age (which ended about 10,000 years ago). These peoples developed their own varied cultures and civilization in isolation from Old World influences. After 1492, explorers, conquerors, and settlers came in turn to the Western Hemisphere, overwhelming the New World's tens of millions of Amerindian natives, importing more than 10 million African strangers, and planting the seeds of new cultures descended from those of Europe. The New World became part of Western civilization; but its Amerindian and African inhabitants, whose labor enriched merchant and professional elites on both sides of the Atlantic, remained, to varying degrees, alienated from it.

Exploration and Conquest

The first explorers to visit the Western Hemisphere entered a world inhabited by defenseless peoples, rich in resources, and ripe for exploitation. They learned the extent and nature of the land and claimed it for the European nations that had sent them. Conquest followed exploration, resulting in the destruction of two advanced New World civilizations.

During the last Ice Age (from about 30,000 to 10,000 years before the present), Asian hunters wandered over the land bridge that stretched some 50 miles (80 km.) from Siberia (modern Russia) to Alaska—a region Europeans later called "Beringia," after the straits named for the Danish explorer Vitus Bering (1681–1741), (see Chapter 8). Others may have come from Asia by sea. These Asian migrants were the true discoverers of the lands of the Western Hemisphere. Material remains of their culture testify to their residence at various sites of North and South America from between 20,000 and 10,000 years ago.

Over thousands of years, the Amerindians migrated across the land mass to its southernmost tip, developing into numerous tribes and nations, speaking hundreds of languages. Most had not progressed beyond a Neolithic condition before the arrival of Europeans. Some remained hunters and gatherers, while others, beginning about 7000 years ago, learned to farm. More than half of them lived in Mexico and the Andes regions, where they developed, respectively, the Aztec and Inca civilizations. Perhaps 4 to 6 million lived in what is now the continental United States, and as many more in the Caribbean. In all, perhaps as many as 75 million Amerindians inhabited the Western Hemisphere before Europeans "discovered" that world and proclaimed it "new."

As early as the late tenth century, Viking sailors were exploring the waters of the north Atlantic near the coast of modern Canada. In 982 Erik the Red founded a settlement on the island of Greenland (so named by him to make it more attractive to

---

MUST READS

Tracing the Spanish Conquest of the Americas

Bernal Diaz del Castillo   *The Discovery and Conquest of Mexico (c. 1527)*

Bartolomé de las Casas   *Brief Relation of the Destruction of the Indies (1552)*

Christopher Columbus   *Diaries*

Hernán Cortés   *Letters*

colonists). A few years later some Viking sailors are believed to have accidentally discovered the Atlantic coast of North America; they reported their discovery to their compatriots in Greenland. Erik's son Leif Eriksson repeated the journey in 1003, naming the site of his landing as that of Vinland (possibly in Newfoundland). Two subsequent expeditions failed to establish a lasting settlement, and the Viking adventure was forgotten except in Greenland sagas. Nearly 500 years later, as Vasco da Gama and Dias were skirting Africa, a European expedition again arrived on the fringes of the Western Hemisphere. This time the newcomers stayed, and were followed by many others.

Columbus and the Spanish   In 1492 the Genoese sea captain Christopher Columbus (1451–1506), funded by the Spanish monarchs Ferdinand and Isabella, set out with three ships on a daring expedition on the open ocean. His goal was to sail to the rich markets of the Indies, claiming for Spain any islands or mainlands he discovered en route. Assuming that Japan and China lay only 3000 miles (4380 km.) to the west, Columbus planned to reach Asia by traversing the Atlantic. This "Admiral of the Ocean Sea" died in 1506 still thinking he had reached Asia, called the "Indies", (see Map 16.2).

In fact, Japan lay more than 13,000 miles (20,900 km.) to the west—over half the circumference of the globe. Just under 4000 miles (6440 km.) away were the continents of the Western Hemisphere. Columbus first landed on the island he named San Salvador in the Bahamas, then visited other Caribbean islands. On a second journey, he established a base on the island he named Hispaniola (now shared by Haiti and the Dominican Republic). In two subsequent voyages he reached what is now Venezuela (1498) and the shores of Central America (1502)—and realized that his expedition had encountered not just some islands, but at least one huge land mass.

Columbus wanted to find gold, as he wrote in his notebook soon after the discovery: "I do not wish to delay but to discover and go to many islands to find gold." In Hispaniola, he established a trading depot. This was the first of a circuit of fortified mercantile settlements which, within a generation, ringed the Caribbean Sea along the coasts of Mexico, Central America, northern South America, and Florida, and on various islands including Cuba.

Within weeks of his arrival in the New World, Columbus had formed an opinion of its aboriginal residents, whom he named *Indios*, or Indians, thinking he had reached the Indies, or Asia. He concluded that the native Amerindians "would make good and industrious servants" and were "fit to be ruled" (see *Witnesses*, p. 464, and illustration on p. 461). Columbus's men put the Taino natives to work hauling the goods to be sent back to Spain. Appointed viceroy of the island, Columbus sparked a native

revolt by his authoritarian rule. He was sent back to Spain in disgrace, but allowed to return again. In 1503, Queen Isabella granted his request for permission to enslave the Taino tribespeople. "Being as they are hardened in their bad habits of idolatry and cannibalism, I hereby give license and permission ... to capture them ... and to sell them and utilize their services. ..." Thus used, the Tainos were extinct within a century.

Meanwhile, Portugal laid claim to Spain's new possessions, announcing that they were an extension of the Atlantic islands of the Azores. Spain appealed to the reigning pope, Alexander VI (r. 1492–1503), who was Spanish by birth. In 1493, Alexander issued a series of papal bulls confirming Spanish possession of the new lands, and drawing an imaginary boundary between Spanish and Portuguese zones: a north-south line about 300 miles west of the Portuguese Azores. By the 1494 Treaty of Tordesillas between Spain and Portugal, the north-south line was redrawn farther west. The effect of the Treaty was that Portugal retained title to what is now Brazil, and Spain to the remaining lands of North and South America claimed by her explorers.

Papal intervention into the realm of geopolitics had a sound foundation. According to medieval theology, all property came from God. Who better to determine its allocation than the pope—according to Roman Catholic thought, God's representative on earth? Later Protestant participants in the race for New World properties were naturally unpersuaded by this line of reasoning.

Spurred by Columbus's example, a stream of explorers now journeyed across the Atlantic. Most were Italians or Portuguese in the employ of other nations. Soon after Columbus's first voyage, the Italian explorer Amerigo Vespucci (1454–1512), scion of an important commercial family of Florence and portrayed in *Windows On* on p. 453, set out in the employ of Spain and (later) Portugal. Probing the coast of South America, he found and explored some of the vast expanse of the Amazon River. He was the first to conclude that the new lands were not part of Asia but part of a previously unknown continent. He called it the "New World." The New World, ironically, was later named after him. In 1507, the German cartographer Martin Waldseemüller published an updated world map in which the New World lands were designated, in honor of the pioneering Florentine, "America."

Over the next fifty years, Spanish explorers crossed Panama to the Pacific Ocean (Vasco Nuñez de Balboa, 1475–1517), and claimed the lands of Florida (Juan Ponce de León, c. 1460–1521), Mississippi and Texas (Hernando de Soto, c. 1496–1542), Arizona and New Mexico (Francisco Vásquez de Coronado, c. 1510–1554), and California (Juan Rodríguez Cabrillo, d. 1543). Their expeditions in search of gold and of a miraculous "fountain of youth" were largely

Map 16.2 Columbus' World: *Columbus fully intended to reach Japan after a westward journey across some 3000 miles of the Atlantic—"correcting" the prevailing Ptolemaic (ancient Greek) model that placed Asia at a distance nearly three times that. What geographical entities were unknown to both Columbus and Ptolemy?*

fruitless, but they acquired for their Spanish overlords the lands of western North America stretching as far north as Utah.

The venture of the Portuguese navigator Ferdinand Magellan (c. 1480–1521) was of another sort. In Spain's employ, Magellan set out in 1519 to reach Asia. He sailed from Atlantic to Pacific through the strait near the tip of South America later named after him, the Strait of Magellan, and then across the Pacific, with a starving crew for sixty-eight days, described in *Witnesses* on p. 458, before reaching land (on the island of Guam). Touching on some islands which were later named the Philippines (after the future King Philip II of Spain), Magellan died in a battle with hostile natives. The expedition continued under the second in command. Of the five ships and 270 men who began the journey in 1519, one ship and a mere eighteen men returned in 1522. Accomplishing for the first time the feat of circumnavigating the globe, they had learned how vast was the Pacific, and how distant Asia was from Europe.

Opening up North America The other Atlantic nations now entered the race for American lands, focusing their efforts on the coast of North America. The English sent the Italian Giovanni Caboto (John Cabot, 1450–1499) with one small ship and eighteen sailors to explore in 1497. Cabot reached Newfoundland (in modern Canada), establishing a foothold on the basis of which England would later claim rights to much of North America.

Years later, the English adventurer Sir Walter Raleigh (c. 1552–1618) journeyed three times to the coast of what is now the southeastern United States—a land he named Virginia, in honor of the "Virgin Queen," Elizabeth I. On Roanoke Island (in modern North Carolina) he formed a colony, which failed. Francis Drake (c. 1540–1596), famed for his persistent raids on Spanish Atlantic commerce, repeated in 1577–1580 the feat of circumnavigation achieved first by Magellan's crew. Henry Hudson (d. 1611) explored for England Canada's immense northern bay, later named after him. For the Netherlands, Hudson explored the New York river also named after him, along which the Dutch established trading depots.

Hoping to find a "northwest passage"—an alternative northern route through the American land mass to the Pacific—the French sent the Italian navigator Giovanni da Verrazano (c. 1485–1528) in 1524 to explore the North American coast. Venturing south from Newfoundland, he entered what is now New York harbor. For over 200 years, French captains explored the Canadian coast and the Saint Lawrence, Great Lake, and Mississippi waterways as far as the Gulf of Mexico. Among the most notable were Jacques Cartier (1491–1557), Samuel de Champlain

Exploration and Conquest

The expansion of European ventures into other regions of the world was accomplished with great brutality at times, yet also, at times, with great courage. The first passage reports the Portuguese plundering of an African town. The second presents the first, disappointing attempts by Vasco da Gama to open trade at Calicut, in India. The third describes the enormous hardships suffered during a portion of the journey by a participant in Magellan's expedition to circumnavigate the globe.

João de Barros describes the sack of Mombasa, eastern Africa, by the forces of Portuguese grand-captain Dom Francisco d'Almeida (15–16 August 1505): The Portuguese attack and burn the town; the fire raged all night long, and many houses collapsed. ... [The next morning.] The Grand-Captain ordered that the town should be sacked. ... Then everyone started to plunder the town and to search the houses, forcing open the doors with axes and iron bars. ... A large quantity of rich silk and gold embroidered clothes was seized. ... [The next day] they also carried away provisions, rice, honey, butter, maize, countless camels and a large number of cattle, and even two elephants. ... There were many prisoners, and white women among them and children, and also some merchants. ...
(From G. S. P. Freeman-Grenville, *The East African Coast*, 1962)

Vasco da Gama arrives in Calicut, India (20–29 May 1498), according to an eyewitness: The king was in a small court, reclining upon a couch covered with a cloth of green velvet ... and upon this again a sheet of cotton stuff, very white and fine, more so than any linen. ... On the right side of the king stood a basin of gold, so large that a man might just encircle it with his arms. ... The canopy above the couch was all gilt. ...

On Tuesday the captain [da Gama] got ready the following things to be sent to the king, viz., twelve pieces of *lambel* [a striped cloth], four scarlet hoods, six hats, four strings of coral ... a case of sugar, two casks of oil, and two of honey. ... [The king's officials came] and when they saw the present they laughed at it, saying that it was not a thing to offer to a king, that the poorest merchant from Mecca, or any other part of India, gave more, and that if he wanted to make a present it should be in gold, as the king would not accept such things. When the captain heard this he grew sad, and said that he had brought no gold, that, moreover, he was no merchant, but an ambassador; that he gave of that which he had. ... Upon this they declared that they would not forward his presents, nor consent to his forwarding them himself.
(*A Journal of the First Voyage of Vasco da Gama, 1497–1499*; trs., ed. E. J. Ravenstein, 1848)

Eyewitness Antonio Pigafetta describes Magellan's Pacific crossing (1521): We were three months and twenty days without getting any kind of fresh food. We ate biscuit, which was no longer biscuit, but powder of biscuits swarming with worms, for they had eaten the good. It stank strongly of the urine of rats. We drank yellow water that had been putrid for many days. Rats were sold for one-half ducado apiece, and even then we could not get them. ... Had not God and His blessed mother given us so good weather we would all have died of hunger in that exceeding vast sea. ...
(From L. Wright, *Gold, Glory, and the Gospel*, 1970)

Map 16.3 European Exploration, 1450–1600: *By 1600, Spanish and Portuguese explorers and traders had established settlements and depots in South America and the Caribbean, and on the coasts of Africa, India, the Pacific islands, China, and Japan—at a time when English, Dutch, and French explorations of North America had just begun.* Why did the Portuguese take the lead in exploration?

(1567–1635), Louis Jolliet (1645–1700), along with the priest Jacques Marquette (1637–1675), and Robert de la Salle (1643–1687).

The Aztecs   Even before the English, French, and Dutch embarked on North American ventures, Spain had completed its conquest of much of the Americas. Most Amerindian communities succumbed quickly to European force. The Aztec and Inca empires, centered respectively in modern Mexico and Peru, promised serious resistance. In 1521 and 1533, two **conquistadores**, conquerors from a nation with a long history of conquest, destroyed these civilizations within a brief time and with only a handful of men.

Spain had only just completed the reconquest of the Iberian peninsula from the Moors when it set out to conquer the lands of the New World. Behind it was a

centuries-old military tradition, fueled by a religious zeal tinged deeply with intolerance. Ahead was a project that also invited the use of arms and the missionary muscle of the Roman Catholic Church. The goal of the medieval *Reconquista* was the recovery of Iberian land from foreign domination. That of the American conquest was gold. The extraction of gold from the earth—and later silver, in much greater abundance—was the major economic activity of the Spanish in the New World.

The Amerindian people who constructed the civilization that Europeans called "Aztec" (they called themselves the Mexicas) had moved into central Mexico in the middle of the thirteenth century, establishing a harsh dominion over existing tribal groups. There they claimed inheritance of the culture of the Olmecs and Maya, creators of successive Mesoamerican civilizations (see Chapter 8). On an

New World Encounters

Columbus' first voyage: *This woodcut by Giuliano Dati, 1493, depicts the imminent arrival of Columbus' ship in the Bahamas, with idealized representations of natives on the shore.*

island in the middle of Lake Texcoco, the Aztecs built their capital of Tenochtitlán (incorporated in modern Mexico City), the preeminent metropolis of pre-Conquest culture.

Tenochititlán bristled with temples, sculptures, and shrines, with palaces and schools, workshops and markets, interspersed with floating gardens and equipped with roads and movable bridges to the mainland. It had a population of about 100,000; few cities in contemporary Europe were larger or more splendid. A Spanish chronicler described the reaction of the soldiers—some of whom had seen Constantinople and the cities of Italy—who reported that "so large a market place and so full of people, and so well regulated and arranged, they had never beheld before."

The Aztecs worshiped many gods, especially a sun god having male and female attributes, the dual deity represented by an eagle on a cactus. Guided by Mayan traditions recorded in sacred picture books (for they had no written language), Aztec priests supervised religious life according to calendar cycles of worship, sacrifice, and feasting. Rite and sacrifice shaped the civilization—including human sacrifice, a celebration of the spilling of blood, in which the victim's still-beating heart was ripped from their chest and offered up to the divinity, as illustrated on this page. The need to secure sacrificial victims to appease the sun god stimulated wars of conquest. From childhood, young warriors were trained to capture rather than slay enemies, so that prisoners might be brought back for ceremonial deaths—"the flowered death by the obsidian knife"—on temple stones.

This was the civilization that fell to the conquistador Hernán Cortés (1485–1547). Arriving in 1519 with about 600 men and 11 vessels, in defiance of an order of recall from the Spanish governor of Cuba, Cortés and his troops made their way to Tenochtitlán. Having been received cordially, they proceeded to take prisoner the Aztec emperor, the oddly compliant Montezuma II (the familiar form of the name; more properly Moctezuma, r. 1502–1520). Cortés had burned his own ships, thereby closing off any escape for his men. He sallied from Tenochtitlán to meet a force of his own compatriots who had come to put an end to his mission. Defeating the leaders, he persuaded the men to return with him and pursue the conquest of Mexico.

In Cortés's absence, warfare broke out in Tenochtitlán, triggered by a Spanish massacre of a group of natives during a religious festival. Cortés returned; Montezuma died (possibly as a result of stoning by his angered people, possibly at the hands of the Spanish); and Cortés withdrew again during a "Sad Night" in which half his men were killed. Regrouping, the Spanish forces returned in 1521 to besiege the city, having constructed a fleet

Human sacrifice: *The Aztec practice of human sacrifice by excising the heart of a living victim, pictured in this sixteenth-century Florentine Codex, was condemned as barbaric by the conquerors. (Biblioteca Medicea Laurenziana, Ms. Laur. Med. Palat. 218, c. 175v, Florence)*

of twelve small oar- and sail-powered boats to do so. A few months later, after firing cannon from the decks of their ships, they seized and razed Tenochtitlán. A few Spanish soldiers armed with arquebuses and cannon achieved this military conquest (assisted by epidemic, caused by microbes for which the Aztecs had no immunity) over thousands of Mexicans armed merely with arrows and swords carved from obsidian, a volcanic glass. (An account of the Spanish forces is given in *Witnesses* on p. 464.) A cultural conquest followed. In an attempt to extinguish Aztec religion, the conquerors burned the sacred books and erected Christian churches, often on the sites of native temples.

The Incas The other great indigenous civilization was the Inca Empire at Cuzco (in modern Peru), in the Andes Mountains. The Inca domain, extending 2000 miles (3200 km.) along the Pacific coast of South America, included parts of modern Bolivia, Chile, Argentina, and Ecuador, as well as Peru. The empire had reached its greatest extent just prior to the arrival in 1531 of the Spaniard Francisco Pizarro (1475–1541), whose forces conquered and destroyed it.

The Inca emperor was an absolute monarch, whose legitimacy was marked by ceremonies of veneration for the mummies of his deceased ancestors. The emperor commanded the obedience of his subjects and was considered responsible for their welfare. The state owned virtually all property, which was sustained by the labor of the inhabitants. The agricultural wealth thus generated, and stored in an elaborate warehousing system, supported an elite of priests, government workers, and merchants, as well as the elderly, the ill, and widows. The priests managed the feasts, ceremonies, and sacrifices (including human ones) necessary to gain the favor of a roster of deities, among whom the sun god held sway.

The Incas used advanced engineering to terrace, drain, and irrigate the mountainous terrain and maximize productivity on plots as high as 9000 feet (2745 m.) above sea level. They were also expert builders, working from models rather than plans (as they had no system of writing) to create large cities. A network of roads and bridges extended more than 12,000 miles (19,000 km.), negotiating chasms, rivers, and solid rock. Metals buried in the earth, especially silver and gold, were reserved for the use of the emperor—until the arrival of Pizarro and his followers.

Pizarro arrived in Peru in 1531 with a mere 168 men, 67 horses, and 3 cannon, to assail an empire with a population of several millions and a military force of some 100,000. He captured, deceived, tortured, and executed the uncomprehending ruler Atahuallpa. Moving briskly to the capital at Cuzco, he began a conquest in which European guns and European steel swords overcame the force of wooden spears and clubs of the Incas. Pizarro's men accomplished the victory by unparalleled brutality, of which one participant has left this testimony: "I can bear witness that this is the most dreadful and cruel war in the world," in which both sides "give each other the cruelest deaths they can imagine." By 1539, the Spanish victors had quelled native resistance and established their colonial regime, subordinating almost as slaves a people who had administered one of the world's great empires. The Spanish soon opened the mines of Potosí (in modern Bolivia), an immense reservoir of silver, rich enough to supply the numerous Spanish **bullion** fleets for decades to come.

Patterns of Settlement

After the first phase of New World exploration and conquest, settlers built European communities in what seemed like an endlessly fertile expanse. The pattern of settlement varied from region to region. Two main colonial zones emerged: the southern zone, or "Latin" America (including those regions of South America, the Caribbean, and Mexico where Spanish, Portuguese, or French—all derived from Latin—are spoken); and the northern zone, including much of North America, predominantly English- and French-speaking. The southern zone was settled earlier, and its main characteristics established by 1600. The northern zone was settled in the period after 1600. The administrative blocs in both areas were called colonies, each related to its own European "mother" country, or metropolis.

Silver mines: *Once conquered, Amerindians were pressed into service as laborers. At the "Silver Mountain" mines in Potosí (modern Bolivia), as in this engraving, c. 1584, 40,000 poorly paid laborers were employed to mine the silver which was then shipped back to Spain and made into coinage. (Hispanic Society, New York)*

Latin America   By the mid-1500s, Spanish settlers had organized the main population centers of Peru and Mexico. Spanish administrators and landowners, drawn primarily from the lesser nobility of the metropolis, recreated so far as they could the culture of their homeland. Their native Spanish language soon developed into a **creole**—a colloquial language containing elements of local Amerindian and African dialects. Their cities, modeled on European cities, boasted cathedrals, palaces, theaters, printing houses, and universities (five by 1636, when the first university of Anglo-America, Harvard, was founded). The new American culture was a mixture of imported Spanish and native Amerindian customs.

The Amerindian inhabitants worked for the proprietors of the *encomiendas* (royal land grants to the conquistadors), or as domestic and agricultural laborers on *haciendas*, the large ranches or plantations owned by the Spanish-speaking elite. The natives who lived on the land granted in *encomienda* owed labor services to the proprietor—who in turn owed the laborers protection, security, religious training, and even education. Haciendas drew on the labor services both of permanent residents—often **peons**, or debt slaves—and of seasonal workers from nearby Indian villages. These arrangements seemed to promise advantage to both laborer and contractor or landowner. In practice, the laborers were abused while the proprietors got richer.

The kingdom of Castile directly ruled the Spanish colonies and closely supervised their governance. Two governors—called viceroys ("vice-kings"), respectively, of "New Spain" (modern Mexico) and Peru—administered the whole of Spanish territory (the number of viceroys increased after 1700). Each viceroy presided over a regional advisory council established in the principal cities, and sent out inspectors to report on local administrations. The position of viceroy conferred high status and attracted ambitious noblemen from Spain. There, a Council of the Indies, based in Madrid, scrutinized the records of each viceroy's service upon completion, and intervened to direct the course of colonial events.

In contrast, Portuguese settlement in the New World followed the pattern of Portuguese expansion in Africa and Asia. Garrisoned merchant colonies were planted at key locations on the coast of Brazil, as fueling stations for fleets bound for the Caribbean. Later, Portuguese governors and landowners took over the settled areas of the interior, intending to control the native population more than to establish European communities.

By the late 1500s, settlers had brought to Brazil the **plantation system** (with lands worked by slave labor under supervision) for sugar cultivation developed in the Portuguese Atlantic islands, especially the island of São Tomé, just off the African coast. English, French, and Spanish landowners later adopted this system in the Caribbean (where tobacco, generally farmed on a smaller scale and yielding lower profits, had previously been the main cash crop). The Dutch, although possessing small colonial bases in the West Indies and on the north Brazilian coast, were more interested in trade than in settlement. Their Dutch West India Company, established in 1621, organized a profitable trade in Brazil and the Caribbean. From the West Indies ports of Havana (Cuba) and San Juan (Puerto Rico), the Spanish bullion fleets took off twice each year, an irresistible lure for Dutch, English, and French raiders.

North American Colonies   After 1600, a northern zone of European settlement in the Americas established itself from Savannah (in modern Georgia) to Quebec (in modern Canada). Most of the settlers were English-speakers; some were French, German, or Dutch; there were even a few hundred Swedes. English settlement was at first organized by joint-stock companies. These obtained from the crown a charter enabling the creation of single agricultural communities, centered in Virginia and New England. Jamestown (in modern Virginia), settled by English emigrants, was founded on this pattern in 1607. The Virginia colony thrived, based as it was on the cultivation of tobacco as a cash crop.

In 1620, Plymouth (in modern Massachusetts) was the second English-speaking community to be established. The aim of the Plymouth **Separatists** (Puritans who had separated from the Church of England— later dubbed "Pilgrims") was not simply to gain farmland but also to secure the right to practice their own form of Protestant worship. Other Puritans settled the Massachusetts Bay Colony (1630), while other New England and mid-Atlantic settlements were also motivated by the quest for religious freedom.

By 1700, twelve colonies had been established (the thirteenth, Georgia, was founded in 1732), and about one-half million English-speakers dwelled in North America, equivalent to one-eighth to one-tenth of the population of England itself. Without initially planning to do so, the English had created a sizable empire abroad. Ruled theoretically by King and Parliament (although they had no representatives in Parliament), the colonies developed effective regional, representative governments.

The Dutch and French settlements more closely resembled the Portuguese pattern of coastal enclaves, and contained fewer colonists. These nationals established merchant colonies respectively in New Netherland (modern New York State) and New France (modern Canada, especially the province of Quebec). The Dutch merchants dealt in a variety of commodities, but the French (who competed with the Portuguese for fish in these northern waters) were particularly interested in the valuable furs that their hunters and traders obtained from the forested interior. French settlement was sparse. By the mid-1600s,

Committed atrocities: *The conquerors treated the native population barbarically, as in this engraving by Théodore de Bry (from Brevissima Relación, 1598, by Bartolomé de Las Casas) of Spaniards hanging and burning the inhabitants of a village.* (Bibliothèque Nationale, Paris)

The Amerindians When Columbus and his sailors first landed on San Salvador, native Amerindian Tainos greeted them with an assortment of gifts. Impressed by the Europeans' unusual appearance, the Tainos concluded that they were gods. The European newcomers were equally startled by the appearance and customs of a people they had never seen before: largely naked, with painted bodies and long hair, smoking tobacco. The Tainos lived in stable communities, in well-constructed houses equipped with hammocks—an object the Europeans had never seen. Their enemies on nearby islands, the Caribs (after whom we name the Caribbean Sea), had a reputation for ferocity—specifically for cannibalism (although this is possibly undeserved). With such terrifying and amazing stories Columbus and later visitors impressed readers back in Europe.

The millions of natives inhabiting the Western Hemisphere before the European advent consisted of hundreds of nations and tribes and peoples too diverse to be considered as a single Amerindian culture. However, they did have some things in common. Their hundreds of languages ultimately descended from a common pool of Asian languages. None of these was a written language. Only the Mayan peoples acquired the ability to record spoken language in symbols. Although this skill vanished with their decline, the Maya transmitted to successor Mesoamerican peoples—who composed sacred texts using pictographs—a memory of writing and a respect for books.

Based on collectives of family, tribe, and clan, Amerindian societies could be highly stratified, with extended lineages generally traced in the male line. Some formed federations, while others developed representative assemblies. Respected priests, or shamans, were in charge of religious rites, medicine, and magic, all of which might overlap considerably. Some groups practiced human sacrifice, often of war captives. In many, women performed agricultural work.

Amerindians wielded as weapons spears, bows, and clubs of wood, stone, and, more rarely, copper or bronze; they had no iron and no sharp-edged swords, a key factor in their military defeat. They had no horses and no pack animals for hauling heavy loads long distances (the Andean llama could bear only a light burden) or for pulling plows—and perhaps for that reason never developed the wheeled vehicles

there were only about 3000 Europeans in all of New France, many fewer than in the single English colony of Virginia. The French crown ruled its colony directly, sending military governors and financial supervisors responsible to officials in Paris.

In 1664 the Dutch lost their North American mainland possessions to their English challengers on the seas. The French would intermittently fight the British for theirs until an eventual British victory in 1763. By the time that the American War of Independence broke out in 1775 (see Chapter 19), the Atlantic region of North America was largely English both by language and tradition. Although the Spanish and the Portuguese had opened up the New World, the British eventually dominated in North America.

Religion played a major role in shaping the post-conquest civilizations of the New World. A main objective of many of the settlements, especially of the Spanish, was the conversion of Amerindian natives. In the English colonies of North America, as has been seen, a main motive for colonization was religious freedom—or freedom, in effect, from other Europeans. That impulse for liberation would express itself again, years later, when an ideology of political liberty took root in the same region. Meanwhile, the freedom sought by some colonists was steadily denied by all of them to the two "other" peoples with whom they interacted in the New World—the native Amerindians and the newcomer Africans.

Encountering Others

The "discovery" of the New World was more than the discovery by Europeans of lands previously unknown to them. It was a mutual discovery of different peoples, as European strangers, Amerindian natives, and, in time, African captives interacted. For the Amerindians, the encounter was deadly.

New World Peoples and Customs

Exploration? Expansion? Conquest? Encounter? How should the European quest for land, wealth, knowledge, and power around the globe be titled? "Encounter" is certainly a term that could be used to describe one facet of that process, as Europeans encountered peoples previously unknown to them, and as remote peoples looked at Europeans for the first time. In these passages, Christopher Columbus observes the natives of the island he called Hispaniola; the king of the Mexican Aztecs, Montezuma, hears his agents' report of the Europeans arrived in his land; and the French Huguenot explorer Jean de Léry describes the customs of the Tupinamba natives of Brazil.

From Columbus' Diary: The arrival in the New World (1492): In order that they would be friendly to us … to some of them I gave red caps, and glass beads which they put on their chests, and many other things of small value, in which they took so much pleasure and became so much our friends that it was a marvel. …

But it seemed to me that they were a people very poor in everything. All of them go around as naked as their mothers bore them. … They are very well formed, with handsome bodies and good faces. Their hair [is] coarse—almost like the tail of a horse—and short. … And some of them paint their faces, and some of them the whole body, and some of them only the eyes, and some of them only the nose. … They should be good and intelligent servants … and I believe that they would become Christians easily, for it seemed to me that they had no religion.

(Christopher Columbus, *The Diario of Christopher Columbus' First Voyage to America, 1492–1493*; ed. trs. O. Dunn, J. E. Kelley Jr., 1969)

Aztec King Motecuhzoma (Montezuma) hears his messengers' report of Cortés' men (who they think are gods), according to an Aztec account (1521): Motecuhzoma was also terrified to learn how the cannon roared, how its noise resounded, how it caused one to faint and grow deaf. The messengers told him: "A thing like a ball of stone comes out of its entrails; it comes out shooting sparks and raining fire. The smoke that comes out with it has a pestilent odor, like that of rotten mud. … If the cannon is aimed against a mountain, the mountain splits and cracks open. If it is aimed against a tree, it shatters the tree into splinters. …"

The messengers also said: "Their trappings and arms are all made of iron. They dress in iron and wear iron casques [helmets] on their heads. Their swords are iron; their bows are iron; their shields are iron; their spears are iron. Their deer [horses] carry them on their backs wherever they wish to go. These deer, our lord, are as tall as the roof of a house. … Their skin is white, as if it were made of lime. They have yellow hair, though some of them have black. … Their dogs are enormous, with flat ears and long, dangling tongues. The color of their eyes is a burning yellow; their eyes flash fire and shoot off sparks. … They bound here and there, panting, with their tongues hanging out. And they are spotted like an ocelot."

When Motecuhzoma heard this report, he was filled with terror. It was as if his heart had fainted, as if it had shriveled. It was as if he were conquered by despair.

(From M. L. Portilla, *The Broken Spears*, 1992)

Huguenot explorer Jean de Léry describes how the Tupinambá treat their war captives (1556): Now when the captive has hurled everything he could pick up near him on the ground—stones, even clods of earth—he who is to strike the blow … approaches the prisoner with, for instance, "Are you not of the nation called Margaia, which is our enemy? And have you not yourself killed and eaten of our kinsmen and our friends?" The prisoner, more fearless than before, replies in his language … "Yes, I am very strong, and have slain and eaten a great many." "… And for that reason," says he who is standing there ready to slaughter him, "since you are now in our power, you will presently be killed by men, and then roasted on the *boucan* and eaten by all the rest of us." "Very well," replies the prisoner …, "my kinsmen will avenge me in turn." … [He] who is there ready to perform this slaughter lifts his wooden club with both hands and brings down the rounded end of it with such force on the head of the poor prisoner that … I have seen some who fell stonedead on the first blow. …

(Jean de Léry, *History of a Voyage to the Land of Brazil, Otherwise called America*, 1556; trs., ed. J. Whatley, 1990)

such beasts might haul. They ate corn rather than wheat as a cereal staple. Where the climate permitted, they wore little or no clothing. They wore adornments crafted from stone and metal, shells, teeth, and feathers, and often painted their faces or bodies. Their skin was tawny.

The Amerindians worshiped many gods, among whom were gods of sun and sky like those the ancestors of the European newcomers had once worshiped. Their forests were alive with indwelling spirits—of the trees, of the eagles, of the jaguars. The land, like the air, was free for the use of all, and sacred in its generative power. To these communities, the European languages and their artifacts—treaties, contracts, documents, treatises of theology—must have seemed inexpressibly strange. The tools and weapons and clothing and armor and horses of the newcomers were awesome. Their guns were "iron which has a spirit." Their white skin seemed to be luminous. At Roanoke Island (modern North Carolina) in 1584, an eyewitness reported, the natives "wondered marvelously … at the whiteness of our skins, ever coveting to touch our breasts, and to view the same." The religious rites, institutions, and personnel—the robed priests and friars with their crucifixes and sacred vessels—must have seemed odd and overwhelming.

The customs of Amerindian communities both shocked and surprised the European newcomers. They were impressed by the nakedness of the natives, and the brilliant hues of their adornments; their unfamiliar sexual customs, their generally meager technology and (in the European sense) their illiteracy; the ferocity and (from the European viewpoint) barbarous customs of a few—the cannibalism of the Caribs and the human sacrifices of the Aztecs and Incas. These permitted the invaders to label the inhabitants of the new land "primitive"; and because primitive, inherently suited to serve the new arrivals. Even if they

Huejotzingo Codex, 1531: *Constituting part of the testimony in a lawsuit brought by the Huejotzingo people in central Mexico to the Audiencia (high court) of New Spain, this detail shows a Christian image of the Virgin and child Jesus. Surrounding it are the objects representing the items brought in tribute by Amerindian workers to their masters. (Library of Congress)*

were not to serve, they were at least expected not to impede Europeans as they settled new lands that they considered to be empty wilderness.

Nevertheless, each group learned from the other. Europeans learned to eat corn and potatoes, to smoke or sniff tobacco, to equip their ships with hammocks (an improvement over the deck in terms of comfort and hygiene), and to employ some Amerindian methods of coping with the climate and cultivating crops. Amerindians learned to use horses and guns—to such an extent that some of them fundamentally changed their way of life. They craved European goods. One native hunter who delivered cherished beaver pelts to European fur traders observed contentedly that "the beaver does everything perfectly well"; and indeed, the beaver had netted him a fortune in "kettles, hatchets, swords, knives, bread."

Some Amerindians, often those who were kidnapped by settlers, learned to speak Spanish, Portuguese, English, or French, and served as translators and interpreters. The need to teach the natives the language of the conquerors encouraged the creation of language-teaching tools. The author of the first Castilian (Spanish) grammar, published in 1492, observed correctly that "language has always been the companion of empire."

So also was religion. Dominican, Franciscan, Augustinian, and, after 1540, Jesuit missionaries accompanied the Spanish expeditions. The Jesuits were especially active in Brazil. (Suspected of pursuing an agenda hostile to the monarchy, the Jesuits were expelled from several European nations in this period, and from the Portuguese colonies in 1759, the Spanish in 1767.) Missions constituted some of the first permanent European settlements in the Spanish American periphery, beyond the main regions of settlement in Mexico and the Andes. Missions were establishments modeled on European monastery communities; they offered medical assistance and skills training to Amerindian communities while urging conversion to Christianity. On a smaller scale, Protestant missionaries also attempted the conversion of native populations. Christian beliefs, institutions, and rituals were deeply alien to Amerindian belief systems. Conversions remained largely unsuccessful in the case of the Protestants, or incomplete in the case of the Roman Catholics, where native attitudes heavily colored alien doctrines. Each Amerindian group thought of itself as "the people," or "the true people," and were not disposed to adopt the spiritual habits of alien folk they considered inferior to themselves.

Over the same centuries, as Christian clergy attempted the conversion of the Amerindians, European farmers and landowners claimed their land. The original inhabitants were sometimes, initially, tolerated. More often, they were pushed away to more remote regions of the interior, or pressed into labor service. In the latter case, they worked as virtual serfs—dependent on a European owner and paid meager wages to work the land that had once been theirs. Others were labored under hideous conditions in the gold and silver mines that fed the Spanish Empire for nearly a century, as shown on p. 461.

Amerindian workers proved an unsatisfactory labor force—resistant to regimentation, prone to disease. The debased condition of the enslaved Amerindians prompted attempts at reform. The "Laws of Burgos" of 1512–1513 limited to 150 the number of forced laborers one person could maintain in Spanish America, but tacitly sanctioned the *encomienda* system. The "New Laws" of 1542 prohibited Amerindian slavery, even of war captives, and banned the *encomiendas*. The laws were not enforced.

During these years, the problem of Amerindian servitude aroused the attention of one of the West's most original and profound moralists: the priest Bartolomé de las Casas (1474–1566). As an owner of enslaved natives, de las Casas observed the harsh treatment of the Amerindians. In 1512 or 1513, he became a priest. In 1514, he gave up his slaves and committed himself to exposing the atrocities against American natives. His opposition was based on the view that natural laws and rights were common to all peoples, Christian and non-Christian. Moreover, the Amerindians were inherently a gentle, teachable, amenable people. He felt that if priests, and not armed conquerors, were sent to the New World, the Amerindians could be guided peacefully to live as Christians in a society based on European standards. Thus de las Casas did not propose to abandon plans to settle the New World and subordinate the Amerindians—but only to accomplish those projects without brutalizing them.

De las Casas described Spanish atrocities and his proposals for ideal Amerindian communities in works written over a long lifetime: in direct appeals to the Spanish monarchs, in a history of the new territories, in memoranda to the council that administered New World affairs, in a scathing *Brief Relation of the Destruction of the Indies* (see *Witnesses*, p. 470, and the illustration on p. 463). After the composition of this work, but before its publication in 1552, he held a public debate with the theologian Juan Ginés de Sepúlveda. Sepúlveda argued that slavery was natural, that the Amerindians were inherently suited to be slaves, and that the evils that accompanied the conquest were outweighed by the greater good achieved for civilization. In response, de las Casas swayed his audience by reporting vividly the tortures of innocent natives that he had witnessed.

In the end, he convinced King Philip II of Spain. In 1573, Philip approved new regulations decreeing that the occupation of the New World was not to be considered a "conquest," and that the natives were to be treated with love. "The Indians," read the ordinance, "[are] to be pacified and indoctrinated, but in no way are they to be harmed, for all we seek is their welfare and conversion." Such decrees ruled out the actual enslavement of the Amerindian population, but could not reverse (nor was that the intention) the destruction of its pre-conquest way of life.

The brutal conquest, the hideous conditions of labor, the disruption of Amerindian communities, the dispossession of the natives from their lands were terrible events. But these are responsible for only a small fraction of the Amerindian death toll that resulted from the European arrival in the New World. The rest were victims of "microbe shock."

Before the arrival of Columbus, the approximately 75 million Amerindian inhabitants of the Western Hemisphere constituted nearly one-fifth of the world population. A little more than 50 years later, only about 10 million remained. In Mexico, a pre-conquest native population of as many as 25 million inhabitants

had, by 1600, sunk to about 1 million. The number of Caribs sank almost to zero. Most of the natives of the Western Hemisphere vanished in the first century after the arrival of the Europeans. They died from disease: smallpox, diphtheria, influenza, measles, mumps, and other illnesses. The inhabitants of the Old World had been exposed to the microbes causing these diseases, and had developed some immunity against them. New World populations, isolated from Eurasia for many millennia, had none. (Perhaps the New World retaliated; some scholars believe that syphilis, which infected Europe about the time of Columbus, originated in the Americas.) More than guns, more than abuse and dislocation, the common illnesses of Europe battered and nearly consumed the flourishing societies of the Americas. The continent became, it appeared, what the first European visitors proclaimed it to be: a wilderness.

The African Solution

Amerindians became less available as a labor force because they were deemed not subject to enslavement, because they resisted the regimentation of the mines and plantations, and because they were ravaged by disease (imported from Europe) and declining in numbers. Europeans then turned to another labor source: that of African slaves. African slavery would have enormous consequences for the later development of American culture.

Two circumstances combined to trigger the exploitation of Africans in the New World by European landowners and entrepreneurs. The first was that the Portuguese had settled the west African coast at about the same time as the opening and exploitation of the Western Hemisphere. The second was that these same Portuguese had already experimented successfully, on their recently acquired Atlantic islands, with the plantation farming of sugar using African slave labor. Once the Portuguese inaugurated sugar planting in the Western Hemisphere, the importation there of the necessary slaves was inevitable. This happened in the 1530s, in Portuguese Brazil. Soon Dutch entrepreneurs had carried the system to the West Indies, where Spanish, French, and English landowners developed into a slakeless market for slaves.

Continuing a pattern begun in the first millennium C.E., the east African coastal cities, dominated by Arab traders, looked toward the mercantile zones of the Persian Gulf and Indian Ocean. Christian Ethiopia, facing the Red Sea, was also related to those trading centers. The states of North Africa were culturally Arab; their merchants traded south across the Sahara and on the Mediterranean, where they were trade rivals of Italian, Spanish, and Portuguese merchants. Egypt, in the northeast, previously part of the Arab network, and for nearly three centuries

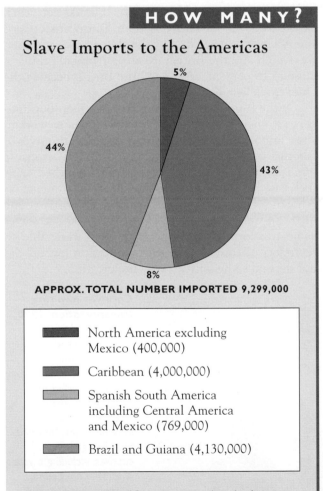

HOW MANY?

Slave Imports to the Americas

5%

43%

8%

44%

APPROX. TOTAL NUMBER IMPORTED 9,299,000

■ North America excluding Mexico (400,000)

■ Caribbean (4,000,000)

■ Spanish South America including Central America and Mexico (769,000)

■ Brazil and Guiana (4,130,000)

Of nearly ten million Africans imported to the Americas and enslaved, the greatest numbers remained in Brazil (and nearby Guiana) and the Caribbean (totalling 87% of the whole), with lesser numbers dispersed over the great areas of Spanish America and North or Anglo-America (totalling 13% of the whole).
Source: H. Spodek, *The World's History* (Upper Saddle River, NJ: Prentice Hall, 1998), p. 448

(1250–1517) governed by the Mamluk sultans, became part of the Ottoman Empire in 1517.

In contrast to northern and eastern Africa, central and south Africa was characterized by village-based societies and small states. Though geographically more remote, these communities had been involved in local and even continental trade for centuries. West Africa was the zone of the great medieval kingdoms of Ghana, Mali, and Songhay, centers for commerce in gold and salt, and was still dominated by Songhay. Other, smaller states continued to form in west Africa. From these, and from the Kongo region to the south, flowed the stream of men and (in lesser numbers) women who were involuntarily removed to labor across the Atlantic Ocean.

Slaves were the major commodity that Portuguese merchants traded from their African depots. During the Middle Ages, most of the slaves exchanged in Mediterranean markets were Asian or Slavic—whence the word "slave" and its equivalents in European languages. The supply of these victims diminished in Europe after the conquest of Constantinople by the Ottoman Turks in 1453. Black African slaves took their place, and soon were exchanged in greater numbers than Eurasian captives had been earlier. Like the ancient Romans, Arab purchasers enslaved white and black workers indiscriminately.

North African Arab dealers supplied African slaves from the continent's interior to Mediterranean markets and to the courts and cities of Islamic Africa. After the Portuguese settlement on the west coast, mainly near modern Ghana, these dealers brought slaves also to the western coastal markets, where European traders waited to purchase them. European traders also recruited slaves directly from the nations and tribes of the interior, who willingly surrendered their war captives to the care of the new entrepreneurs.

In exchange, African suppliers received textiles and hardware, especially guns. The guns permitted more war, and war produced more slaves.

From the 1440s, Portuguese ships brought African slaves to Europe. After 1503, slaves were transported across the Atlantic. Their numbers rose into the nineteenth century, to constitute the largest instance ever of the mass-transplantation of captive peoples. This trade enriched the Atlantic nations of Europe.

Different estimates are given for the numbers of slaves transported across the Atlantic, but recent research indicates the magnitude of that transshipment. Some 9 to 12 million African slaves arrived in the Western Hemisphere (in addition to one to 2 million others who died during the voyage) between the first shipment in 1503 and the last in the 1880s, as shown in *How Many?* on p. 467. The numbers were low at first (a few thousand per year in the 1500s), but mounted rapidly in the 1600s (20,000 per year) to peak in the late 1700s (nearly 100,000 per year). Before 1800, more Africans than Europeans crossed the Atlantic, carried first by the Portuguese, and then the Dutch and the British. Realizing annual profits of close to 10 percent, after 1730 the British became the chief traffickers in slaves.

Of the 9 to 12 million transported, men outnumbered women by two to one. Most were put to work in the Caribbean and South America, where the lives of laborers were short—slaves being, as one Portuguese official commented, "a commodity that died with such ease." They were swiftly replaced. The impact on African society of the steady removal of mostly young men can well be surmised. Only about 400,000 slaves came to North America, where they were able to reproduce themselves, so that plantation owners did not depend so heavily on new importation.

A SLAVE-SHED.

Captives awaiting transportation, 1890: *From around 1500, human slaves were the most important commodity that European traders exported from Africa. Often African chieftains acted as intermediaries. Depicted here is a group of captives, including a young child, who are bound, leashed, shackled, and immobilized in locked devices, awaiting whatever fate that the slavemaster may assign.* (Century Magazine, 1890)

Commerce in Human Flesh

A slave ship: In this drawing, 1789, of the slave ship **Brookes**, a slave cargo is arranged below decks for the horrific "Middle Journey" across the Atlantic. The slaves were squashed so tightly that they hardly had room to move. Contagious diseases spread quickly, leading to significant loss of life. (Wilberforce House Museum, Hull, England)

The journey was punishing. Slavers brought the bands of new slaves to the ship, stripped them, and examined them—only the strong and healthy were valuable. For eight to twelve weeks, the slaves lived below deck, chained together and lying on shelves where they could neither sit up nor move about, as shown on this page. They were exercised on the deck, in which sessions females were vulnerable to rape. The food was scarce and shared from common buckets. Disease ran rampant. Vomit, mucus, excreta, and blood pooled in the slave quarters, breeding new waves of illness, described in *Witnesses* on p. 470. Despair drove many to suicide. The dead were thrown overboard. On the other side of the Atlantic, the survivors faced the degradation of the slave markets, depicted on this page and described in *Witnesses* on p. 470. Here, many were wrenched from family members and compatriots before being dispatched to a life of forced, unremunerated labor.

The system of African slavery developed to provide labor in places where Amerindians could not or would not work, and where Europeans were unavailable. Those circumstances differed in the northern and southern zones. In the south, especially in the Caribbean, African laborers were immediately impressed into labor on the sugar plantations—indeed, the numbers of slaves shipped rose directly in proportion to the increase of sugar farming. In the north, where sugar was not a key crop, slavery was slower to develop. In Brazil in later years, coffee plantations, displacing sugar as the main form of agriculture, eventually absorbed great numbers of slaves.

In the early years of North American settlement, European immigrants farmed the lands themselves. For additional labor services, they could employ convicted felons who had been transported to the colonies in lieu of punishment at home (a phenomenon also found in the West Indies). Or they could employ **indentured servants**, who worked without wages for a contractually

defined period of years in exchange for the price of passage to the colonies and clothing, room, and board while in service. From the employment of these workers—tantamount to temporary slaves—it was not a long distance to the use of imported African slaves.

The first African laborers in the English colonies were brought to Virginia by Dutch traders in 1619, twelve years after the colony's founding. They worked as indentured servants, however. So long as tobacco—the first cash crop—was farmed on a small scale, there was little reason to resort to slaves. As late as 1660, there were only 1700 black workers in Virginia, when slaves in West Indian Barbados numbered 20,000. As tobacco plantations grew, slavery was established in Virginia. In the Carolinas, the cultivation of rice—requiring intense labor under unpleasant and dangerous conditions—also encouraged the adoption of slavery. The introduction of cotton in the warmer colonies in the early 1700s gave a further impetus to the use of slave labor. By 1700, there were 20,000 African slaves in the Chesapeake

A slave auction: A slave family is sold on the auction block in Virginia, 1861. The placard reads "Negroes for sale at Auction this day at 1 o'clock."

Voices of Protest

The slave trade, rampant within Africa for centuries before the European arrival, entered a new and horrible "Atlantic" phase for nearly four centuries thereafter, during which it supported a colonial economic system that enriched the planters and merchants who became the governors of new American states. Yet there were those who opposed it, and whose opposition, in time, led to its extinction. Here the priest Bartolomé de las Casas protests against the exploitation of the Amerindians; his intervention prefigures later protests against the evils of colonialism. More than two centuries later, the former slave Olaudah Equiano deplores the evils of slavery; and a British physician reveals the awful conditions on the ship that was to transport human cargo out of Africa and into slavery.

The Spanish Priest Bartolomé de las Casas describes the native Amerindians and condemns Spanish atrocities (1552): And of all the infinite universe of humanity, these people are the most guileless, the most devoid of wickedness and duplicity, the most obedient and faithful to their native masters and to the Spanish Christians whom they serve. ... And because they are so weak and complaisant, they are less able to endure heavy labor and soon die of no matter what malady. ... They are very clean in their persons, with alert, intelligent minds, docile and open to doctrine, very apt to receive our holy Catholic faith, to be endowed with virtuous customs, and to behave in a godly fashion. ...

[Towards these gentle people, for the last forty years, the Spaniards have been] ... acting like ravening beasts, killing, terrorizing, afflicting, torturing, and destroying the native peoples, doing all this with the strangest and most varied new methods of cruelty, never seen or heard of before, and to such a degree that this Island of Hispaniola, once so populous (having a population that I estimated to be more than three millions), has now a population of barely two hundred persons. ...

(Bartolomé de las Casas, *The Devastation of the Indies: A Brief Account*, 1552; ed. H. Briffault, 1974)

Former slave Olaudah Equiano describes the sale of his fellow slaves at auction (1789): We ... were sold after their usual manner, which is this: On a signal given ..., the buyers rush at once into the yard where the slaves are confined, and make choice of that parcel they like best. ... In this manner, without scruple, are relations and friends separated, most of them never to see each other again. ... O, ye nominal Christians! Might not an African ask you—Learned you this from your God, who says unto you, Do unto all men as you would men should do unto you? Is it not enough that we are torn from our country and friends, to toil for your luxury and lust of gain? Must every tender feeling be likewise sacrificed to your avarice? ... Why are parents to lose their children, brothers their sisters, or husbands their wives? Surely, this is a new refinement in cruelty, which ... adds fresh horrors even to the wretchedness of slavery.

("The Life of Olaudah Equiano, or Gustavus Vassa, the African," 1789; ed. A. Bontemps, 1969)

A British physician inspects slaves on a ship bound for Brazil (1843): After the first paroxysm of horror and disgust had subsided, I remarked on the poop another wretched group, composed entirely of females. Some were mothers with infants who vainly endeavoring to suck a few drops of moisture from the lank, withered, and skinny breasts of their wretched mothers ... most of them destitute even of the decency of a rag. ...

While employed in examining the negroes individually ... I obtained a closer insight into their actual condition. Many I found afflicted with a confluent smallpox, still more with purulent ophthalmia, and the majority of what remained, with dysentery, ulcers, emaciation, and exhaustion. ... Not the least distressing sight on that pest-laden deck was the negroes whom the ophthalmia had struck blind, and who cowered in seeming apathy to all that was going around. This was indeed the ultimatum of wretchedness. ... Deprived of liberty, and torn from their native country, there was nothing more of human misery but to make them the victims of a physical darkness as deep as they had already been made a moral one.

(Thomas Nelson, "Remarks on the Slavery and Slave Trade of the Brazils," 1843; from eds. P. Riley et al., 1998)

Bay region of Virginia and Maryland; by 1775, some 331,000 African slaves in the North American British colonies, outstripping the number of those on the islands of Barbados and Jamaica together. These slaves, generally better treated than in the West Indies, enjoyed a higher birth rate and lower mortality rate and were able to reproduce themselves.

New World Women   Women of all races and peoples, such as Amerindian natives and African slaves, were another kind of "other" in the New World: they did not number among the explorers, conquerors, settlers, and governors, but instead were subordinate to them. They had the main responsibility for domestic labor, and they were sexually exploited by the men of the ruling elite. Although all women shared this subordinate position, European women were by far the most privileged. The wives and daughters of upper-class men lived comfortable and protected lives. Even those who began their lives in the Americas as servants or laborers might improve their status by marrying rich planters or professional men—for women were in high demand in the largely male communities of European settlers, and found unusual opportunity for social mobility through employment or marriage.

Quite the opposite was true of Amerindian and African women. In their own cultures, they were already subordinated, and very often assigned responsibility (in addition to domestic service) for agricultural work held in low esteem. Additionally, they were vulnerable to the sexual demands of European males. Often they were coerced into such sexual relationships, ranging from rape to concubinage or marriage, from fleeting to long-term. From these sexual relationships was born a whole new population of persons of mixed ancestry. In Spanish America, where intermixture of races was common, persons with mixed Amerindian and European ancestries were called *mestizos*, meaning simply "mixed." Men and women with mixed African and European ancestries were called *mulattoes*, an insulting term derived from the Spanish word for "mule." In the West Indies, light-skinned mulattoes, often slaves, in some circumstances obtained higher status than their fully black peers and kin.

In addition to sexual services, African slave women labored hard as field hands or domestics, often, in the latter case, bearing full responsibility for the functioning of the slave-owner's household. They served as nurses for the infants and the elderly members of the slave-owner's family, and their young children were the companions of the slave-owner's heirs, until separated in adolescence.

In time, slavery received the detestation it deserved. The French theoretician Montesquieu concluded as early as 1721 that the institution of slavery was opposed to natural law (see Chapter 17). In Britain, Quakers proclaimed an ardent anti-slavery message. Later in the century, the former slave Olaudah Equiano (c. 1750–1797) raised his voice for the abolition of slavery. Using the name Gustavus Vassa given him by his English purchaser, he published his compelling autobiography in 1789. In it he described his capture in Nigeria at age eleven and the cruelties of his passage across the Atlantic, the slave market where he was sold, and the different masters for whom he labored. Eventually he bought his freedom, taught himself to read and write, settled in England, and publicized his story. In this case, one man was instrumental in changing public opinion.

The system of African slavery gradually ceased over a period of nearly a hundred years. The London-based Abolition Society, founded in 1787, and the French Declaration of the Rights of Man of 1789 spelled out the principle of the fundamental evil of slavery—which was also implicit, but without immediate fruit, in the "all men are created equal" clause of the Declaration of Independence (1776) of the new United States. In 1794, the French decreed the abolition of slavery at home and in its colonies; but the

system was later reinstated in the colonies by Napoleon and lasted until 1848. In 1804, nevertheless, the Caribbean nation of Haiti, populated almost entirely by slaves, won independence from France. In 1807 and 1808 respectively, Britain and the United States banned the slave trade. The former abolished slavery throughout the British Empire in 1838; the latter abolished it only in 1865.

In 1813, the independent government of Buenos Aires (Argentina) decreed that all children born of slaves would be deemed free, thus launching the process of emancipation in Latin America. New World slavery ended only in 1886 and 1888, when the Spanish colony of Cuba and the nation of Brazil, respectively, decreed abolition. The scar left by the institution of slavery on the societies of the new nations of the Americas was indelible. Like the metropolitan nations of Europe, the nations of the Americas are heirs of the civilization of the West—in all aspects, good and bad. We are all the descendants of societies that profited from slavery; and that fact has had persistent and inescapable consequences.

In the same way, these nations are the children of societies that dispossessed the Amerindian inhabitants of the Western Hemisphere. That heritage, too, conditions the civilization that American nations, north and south, have inherited.

THE WEALTH OF NATIONS

Just as the encounter among European, African, and Amerindian peoples shaped the cultural systems that developed in the New World, so did the economic dynamics that developed during the first hundred years of European presence in this vast region. The commercial energies of Europeans, which in previous centuries had built mercantile cities and trading empires, now produced modern capitalism. The origins of today's global economy lie in the Atlantic age that Columbus, it might be said, "discovered."

Bringing Home the Bacon

Before about 1500, Europe's foreign trade was fundamentally unbalanced. Wealthy nobles, prelates, and patricians craved the spices and gems, exquisite porcelains and finished silks found in the East. Having little of value to offer in exchange, Europe paid mostly in **specie,** with gold or silver coin. That pattern shifted after the opening of the New World. The Americas provided not only new sources of silver and gold, but also beneficial new commodities and raw materials for Europe's many manufacturing enterprises. By the 1700s the products of these enterprises had found markets in Asia. Eastern luxuries still satisfied the appetites of the rich, but other imports fed the European economy in more productive ways. By 1750, instead of draining Europe of coin, trade with other regions of the globe had, in fact, contributed to Europe's wealth.

The conquistadors, it was said, set out from Spain for "God, gold, and glory." They found gold and silver in abundance, as indicated in *How Many?* on p. 476, although not as much of the former as they would have liked. From the mid-1500s, annual shipments of bullion loaded on twenty to sixty ships escorted in convoy by two to six men-of-war left American ports for Spain (mostly) and Portugal. One-fifth of the wealth went directly to the royal treasury. From Columbus's first voyage until 1800, the New World supplied 85 percent of the world's silver and 70 percent of its gold; Spanish coins (the **reales**, each one-eighth of a **peso**, or "piece of eight") circulated worldwide.

Profitable New Crops   Meanwhile, some people saw that a potentially greater treasure was present in a plant for which Europeans developed an enormous appetite—the sugar cane. In medieval Europe, honey was the principal sweetener, and sugar was rare. It was sold only in small pellets as a pharmaceutical, the ancestor of the modern candy bar. Sugar cane grew in Arab lands, including Sicily. From there, Portuguese entrepreneurs transplanted it to their newly settled Atlantic islands in the late fifteenth century, and to Brazil early in the sixteenth. From Brazil, sugar cultivation spread to the West Indies, where it grew on plantations owned by nationals of several different countries, with the labor of African slaves.

By itself, sugar constituted a whole economy, and its cultivation was a preeminent agricultural pursuit. It became doubly profitable when merchants learned to derive molasses and rum from it. In the eighteenth century, sugar and sugar products accounted for more imports to Britain (where their consumption reached huge proportions) than all the goods of the North American mainland, or all of those from Asia.

Of greater benefit to the European diet were some native American crops that proved to be cultivable in the Old World. None was more basic than the potato. Rich in vitamins, easily grown, capable of

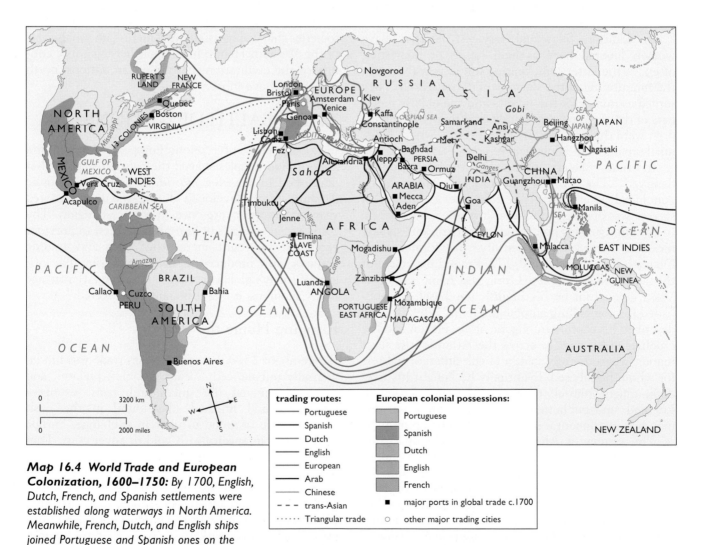

Map 16.4 World Trade and European Colonization, 1600–1750: *By 1700, English, Dutch, French, and Spanish settlements were established along waterways in North America. Meanwhile, French, Dutch, and English ships joined Portuguese and Spanish ones on the trade routes across the Indian and Pacific Oceans. Europeans had not yet fully explored the interiors of the Americas, Africa, and parts of Asia. They came to know of the existence of Australia and New Zealand only late in the eighteenth century.* **What products were exchanged as part of the Triangular trade system?**

The Profits of Trade

It was trade that enriched Europe so that Europeans might venture beyond their borders to other parts of the globe; and then trade again that enriched Europe and supported her political and cultural modernization. In these two passages, the French finance minister Jean-Baptiste Colbert and the Scottish economist Adam Smith think about the benefits of the circulation of goods in trade. For Colbert, trade will increase the nation's wealth, and thus its tax revenues, which can in turn support the nation in the event of war. For Smith, the effect of trade is the generation of wealth, and more is generated as each individual separately attempts to acquire as much of it as he can—through which selfish activity, as though by an "invisible hand," he is led to increase the wealth of the nation.

French Minister Jean-Baptiste Colbert instructs King Louis XIV about finances (1670): The palpable reward ... will be that by attracting a great quantity of wealth into the kingdom by trade, not only will you soon re-establish that due proportion between the money circulating in trade and the taxes paid by the people, but both will be increased proportionately, so that revenue will rise and the people will be in a condition to assist more effectively in the event of war or other emergency.
(Jean-Baptiste Colbert, "Mémoire au Roi sur les Finances," 1670; from ed. A. Lossky, trs. G. Symcox, 1967)

Scots economist Adam Smith criticizes mercantilist theories and argues for Free Trade and the regulation of an "Invisible Hand" (1776): The annual revenue of every society is always precisely equal to the exchangeable value of the whole annual produce of its industry. ... As every individual, therefore, endeavours as much as he can both to employ his capital in the support of domestic industry, and so to direct that industry that its produce may be of the greatest value; every individual necessarily labours to render the annual revenue of the society as great as he can. He generally, indeed, neither intends to promote the public interest, nor knows how much he is promoting it. ... [H]e intends only his own gain, and he is in this ... led by an invisible hand to promote an end which was no part of his intention. Nor is it always the worse for the society that it was not part of it. By pursuing his own interest he frequently promotes that of the society more effectually than when he really intends to promote it.
(Adam Smith, *The Wealth of Nations*, 1776; ed. E. Cannan, 1987)

---

being prepared in innumerable ways, this root vegetable which was already a prime source of nutrition (unlike sugar) for the Amerindian soon became a staple of the European (and African) diet. Its consumption in some places increasingly came to rival that of bread, which in Eurasia had held pride of place since antiquity.

Corn, tomatoes, yams, beans, squash, and cacao beans (for chocolate) and cashews also traveled to Europe, and even the ungainly turkey found some consumers on the eastern side of the Atlantic. Other North American animals were valuable not as food, but for the products they yielded. The beaver's fur (for warmth and fashion), the whale's blubber (for heat and light) were readily available in the huge forests and waters of the new continent. From a Mexican insect came the valuable dyestuff cochineal, which produced a rich red hue.

Some crops and beasts made the journey the other way. European pigs, sheep, horses, cattle, and chickens; honey bees; apple, peach, and pear trees; and, of course, wheat came with European farmers and thrived on new soil. Europeans also transplanted from Asia white rice (the Amerindian cereals were corn and wild rice), coffee and bananas, indigo (another dye), and cotton.

One other American crop added much to European culture, though nothing of benefit to its health: tobacco leaves, grown in southeastern North America. Europeans learned from Amerindian users to dry, age, and pulverize it into a powder called **snuff**, to be inhaled, or shred it into a coarse mix to be smoked in pipes, cigars, or in cigarettes, invented as early as the sixteenth century but refined in the later 1700s. This new luxury product complemented the spices, silks, porcelains, and other luxuries already imported from Asia.

European planters in warmer regions of North America experimented with crops native to tropical regions of the Old World. Rice, the staple grain of much of Asia, thrived in the marshy lands of the Carolinas, whose economy it boosted from the 1690s. Slaves first undertook its cultivation, using their experience of growing rice in Africa. The cotton plant, the source of the principal textile of the Indian subcontinent, could grow throughout the North American southeast. Cotton cultivation was already established in the 1600s, but really took off after 1800 to become the "king" of American agriculture (see Chapter 19). Both of these were plantation crops, grown by methods that were first developed for sugar cultivation in the West Indies, and absorbed the labor of African slaves. Coffee grown in Brazil also used forced labor. New World products greatly invigorated the European economy and made the Atlantic a theater of world trade as great as, and soon greater than, those of the Old World. But the old trade routes still functioned. At the height of Dutch sea trade in the 1600s, one-third of this trade was committed to the Baltic Sea, where Dutch ships had supplanted those of the medieval Hanseatic League after the late 1400s. The Baltic route, which extended from London in the west to Novgorod in the east, carried tar and timber, flax and hemp, honey, wax, and, most important, grain from the plains of eastern Europe. That ready supply of grain permitted some western European laborers to leave the soil and tend to manufacturing tasks—a precondition of subsequent industrialization.

European-made products and those transshipped from Asia—textiles above all, plus tools, furniture, nails, and tea—won ready markets on the western side of the Atlantic. The American colonists required these high-cost goods for survival and comfort and paid for them with low-cost raw materials in bulk. In the Atlantic trading system, trade was again unbalanced, but now in Europe's favor.

Trade Wars

With the creation of the Atlantic trade system, Europe's role in the global economy changed dramatically. Now she became the pivot of world trade (the nations of east Asia remaining aloof from the West for three more centuries). Her manufactures diversified, her appetite grew, her need for markets expanded, her merchant fleets swelled, and her treasuries fattened. The quest for profit, which had once driven Italian entrepreneurs to scour the Mediterranean, now drove the capitalists of Spain and Portugal, Britain and France, the Netherlands and Germany to expand their business empires to the farthest possible limits. By 1750, Europe was the wealthiest region on the globe. On the wave of this expansion, prices increased, populations soared, cities grew; and the ancient rivalries between European states increasingly gave way to a new generation of commercial competition and trade wars.

In the race for wealth, the European nation states took the lead in a departure from the medieval trade pattern, in which Italian merchants won the first fortunes of the modern West. But as navigation and commerce increasingly shifted to the Atlantic, these states developed under the aegis of newly powerful monarchies, whose rulers and chief ministers understood wealth to be the wealth of the nation.

This outlook was the outlook of mercantilism. Mercantilist strategies involved both economic and political measures, which sought to increase the nation's wealth in various ways: by encouraging domestic industries (often by grants of monopoly right), by limiting foreign imports, by assuring a favorable balance of trade, by securing ample quantities of gold and silver bullion, and by outpacing rival nations, whose increased wealth meant a relative decrease of their own. In mercantilist logic, these objectives were to be won, if necessary, by force. "Trade cannot be maintained without war, nor war without trade," pronounced an official of the Dutch East India Company, stating a commonplace of mercantilist thought.

Thus mercantilism pitted nation against nation in the race for wealth. The Portuguese were at first in the forefront, then were displaced by the Spaniards, who had meanwhile acquired the gold and silver resources of the Americas. Spanish ships laden with gold and silver attracted pirates and privateers, the semi-official raiding ships of the northern Atlantic nations which were ready to steal from Spain, but not yet to compete with her. The Spanish bullion hoards

Engines of Commerce

The great crane at Bruges: *Machines in early modern Europe speeded up enterprise but were powered by the energy of human beings or beasts, as shown in the operation by human beings of a treadmill in this sixteenth-century manuscript illumination. (Bayerisches Staatsbibliothek, Munich)*

Jhiob Berckheyde, **A general scene at the Amsterdam Stock Exchange:** *At the Amsterdam stock exchange, completed in 1613, merchants might purchase shares in the commercial and industrial enterprises that fueled the prosperity of the age.* (Private Collection)

did not enrich the nation as planned (most of the money went to foreign bankers), and by the early seventeenth century Spain had fallen behind the Dutch.

For nearly a century, the Dutch were the masters of European trade, with England and France nipping at their heels. In those years, approximately three times as many Dutch ships as English ones set off for Asia. England's several Navigation Acts, passed between 1651 and 1696, aimed at undercutting Dutch competition. In the three Anglo-Dutch wars fought between 1652 and 1674, the English navy edged ahead of the Dutch. In the next century, with France as a primary rival, the British struggled to maintain economic supremacy, which it achieved at the close of the Seven Years' War in 1763.

From 1500 to 1800, foreign trade grew steadily, as more raw materials from the New World were used for European manufacture, and as more European products found markets in the west or in Asia. By 1700, almost half of England's merchant fleet was trading with America or India—the cargoes often guaranteed by Lloyd's, a new company which set the pattern for the modern insurance industry. In the following century, British exports to other parts of the world rose from a trickle to more than a third of the whole, while imports from those lands rose to over one-half of all imports. Meanwhile, France's foreign trade trailed Britain's and the Dutch share fell behind, while Spain and Portugal were no longer serious competitors.

The profits from this commerce went to merchant capitalists, but also to small investors, who sometimes greedily participated in unwise ventures: notoriously the "Louisiana bubble" (in France) and the "South Sea bubble" (in Britain). In these early-eighteenth-century episodes, private investors, sometimes pledging family estates and life savings, purchased stock in investment ventures that promised huge profits. Speculation proceeded unchecked, the stock values collapsed, and the investors were left with nothing from the exploded "bubble."

While western Europe's large nation-states seized the leadership of European trade, other areas were

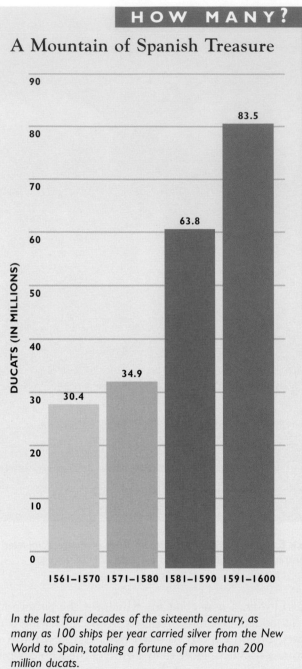

HOW MANY?

A Mountain of Spanish Treasure

DUCATS (IN MILLIONS)

- 90
- 80 — 83.5
- 70
- 60 — 63.8
- 50
- 40 — 34.9
- 30 — 30.4
- 20
- 10
- 0

1561–1570 1571–1580 1581–1590 1591–1600

In the last four decades of the sixteenth century, as many as 100 ships per year carried silver from the New World to Spain, totaling a fortune of more than 200 million ducats.
Source: De Lamar Jensen, *Reformation: Age of Reform and Revolution*, 2e (Lexington, MA–Toronto: D. C. Heath, 1992).

or the circulation of personnel. Mercantilist projects tended to enliven the manufacturing sector, stimulating certain crafts or inviting joint-stock companies to undertake new endeavors. For example, Colbert (1619–1683), finance minister to Louis XIV, encouraged a variety of manufacturing enterprises (including the famous Gobelins tapestry workshop). To promote commerce, Colbert also oversaw the construction of new roads and canals, harbors and shipyards, and built up the French navy. The failure of Spain to support its industries, especially as silver imports dwindled, helps to explain its economic decline.

The devices that promoted the wealth of nations also enriched individuals, who accumulated enough wealth to fund extensive investments. Still, the wealthy merchants of the early modern era must be distinguished from later industrial capitalists, whose great factories won them previously extraordinary profits. These earlier merchants took commodities made by others and shipped them to distant markets. Or they supervised manufacturing enterprises, especially textiles, which worked on the domestic or "putting-out" system. In this system, the merchant acquired raw materials, distributed them to country workers who labored in their own cottages, and collected the finished goods for sale. Employing men, women, and children, this system flourished into the eighteenth century. It constituted a "proto-industrial" phase of European manufacturing, featuring rural production and city-directed exchange.

Technological innovations also contributed to the growth of the European economy. By 1500, Europe already had put machines to work in productive ways. Waterwheels and windmills helped grind grain, brew ale, pump water, make paper, saw wood, and treat textiles. The circulation of goods was facilitated by the building of canal networks which in turn was made possible by the invention of locks. Changes in ship design and gun manufacture have already been noted. Over the next centuries, other new machines and industrial processes improved textile and glass manufacturing, coal mining, and iron production.

All this growth, however, had a disadvantage: rapid inflation. The injection of new quantities of bullion into the European economy, the deliberate devaluation of existing currencies, and the steady climb of the European population caused an explosion of values and prices. Prices rose for goods, while wages and rents lagged, with regional variations: in Spain, prices more than tripled in the century before 1600; in England, the prices of basic goods rose nearly sixfold during the same period. The pattern of steep price increases affected different groups differently— it allowed merchants to accumulate capital for investment in more manufacture and trade, while it mercilessly pinched peasants and urban workers.

The forward wave of commercial economy favored population increase, which in turn undergirded the

quiescent, and still mainly agrarian in character. Eastern Europe turned deliberately to more intensive agricultural production. Italy lost its commercial preeminence in trade, although some Italian cities continued to produce profitable luxury goods, such as Venetian glass and lace.

Proto-industrialization Another way to enhance the wealth of the nation was to build up its manufacturing base. The old merchant and craft guilds that had generated economic growth during the Middle Ages had become restrictive, discouraging innovation economic boom. European population generally increased until about 1600, when it surpassed for the first time the pre-Black Death level of 73 million. During the seventeenth century, population growth slowed again, owing in part to the disastrous effect of the Thirty Years' War, which reduced the population of central Europe by 30–40 percent. The marriage age increased in many regions, showing that people were adopting a familiar strategy to reduce the birth rate. Spain and Italy fell behind the north Atlantic nations, and France's rate of growth fell behind England's. In the eighteenth century, the population began again to increase as mortality rates declined. After a last outbreak of bubonic plague in Marseilles in 1720, the plague left Europe (perhaps because of unfavorable shifts in the ecology of the black rat, the critical carrier of the deadly infectious flea). The cycle of famine receded too, and the proto-industrial cottage industries, which allowed young persons to make a profit from their labor without delaying marriage, drove the numbers upward.

Despite economic growth, the steady upward pressure on prices and the increasing population brought hardship, especially to the rural poor. Grain prices rose by factors of three, four, even six, while the average price of manufactured goods merely doubled. Bread was expensive or scarce, while landowners strove to extract more labor from their workers. The real wages of agricultural workers fell catastrophically, and the force of hunger, briefly subdued in the aftermath of the Black Death, returned. The numbers of the landless increased, and beggars proliferated.

The high price of grain resulted not only from general inflationary trends but also from a shortage of good soil due to over-plowing and little fertilization. In England and the Netherlands, farmers opened up new land for cultivation of more grain. They drained low-lying lands, fenced off fields to raise stock, and systematized crop rotation to increase the yield of already-plowed soil. These practices were only slowly diffused to the rest of Europe.

Urbanization   With economic growth came urbanization, as Map 16.5 below shows. Merchants concentrated in cities, where goods changed hands, where banks held funds, where artisans labored, and where consumers purchased. In the early modern centuries, towns became cities, cities expanded. For the first

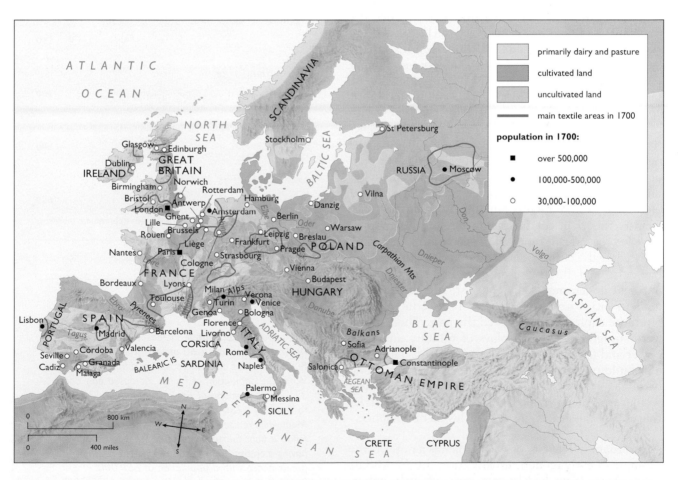

Map 16.5 European Commerce, Industry, and Urbanization, 1550–1750: *The medieval centers of commerce in Italy and Flanders expanded from the fifteenth through the eighteenth centuries, while new areas of textile production and zones of intensive mining enriched the European economic scene. Population increased overall, and especially in cities.* Which cities are approaching a population of one million in 1700, and what accounts for their enormous growth?

time, many European cities grew to exceed the largest cities previously known in the Western world (London, Paris, Naples, and Milan). Not only did large cities grow larger, but a greater proportion of Europeans lived in cities and towns; even country workers often migrated to the city for part of their lives before returning to their villages, their mental outlook forever changed. No longer islands in a world of fields, the cities were open to the countryside and linked to each other in large regional networks of economic activity.

Before 1500, few people lived in concentrations greater than 10,000. Between 1500 and 1800, the number of western European cities larger than 10,000 more than doubled (from 154 to 364). At the same time, the number of people living in those cities more than tripled (from 3,441,000 to 12,218,000). From 1500 to 1750, the percentage of Europeans living in cities of more than 10,000 inhabitants increased from 6.1 to 9.9 percent. The growth was heaviest in areas of new urbanization—western and northern Europe—rather than in Italy, whose cities had been the power centers of medieval commerce. Farther east—in Russia, for example—urbanization was minimal, and only a few towns held populations as large as 30,000.

Some individual cities mushroomed. By 1600 the populations of Seville (Spain), Lisbon (Portugal), and Antwerp (modern Belgium), all involved in transatlantic trade, had jumped to 100,000—the size previously reached only by the largest Italian cities. By the same year, the populations of London and Paris approached 200,000; by the end of the eighteenth century, they reached 800,000 and 670,000 respectively. Lyons, France's second commercial city, had nearly 100,000 inhabitants. Smaller cities, with populations hovering around 20,000, were nevertheless important centers of regional trade. The major German cities (Augsburg, Nuremberg, Cologne), subject to the political fragmentation of the Empire, never exceeded this range in the early modern period.

Medieval cities, concentrated in Italy and Flanders, had flourished in the absence of strong national governments. In contrast, the largest early modern cities were the centers of powerful nations, often the capitals. They looked the part. Their streets were straightened, for displays of military and state power and for the carriages of the wealthy. Their secular buildings—palaces, banks, **stock exchanges** and theaters—began to rival cathedrals in grandeur, both secular and sacred buildings being designed in styles that raised classical forms to new levels of opulence.

Amsterdam   The city of Amsterdam is a noteworthy example of early modern urbanization. In the Middle Ages, Amsterdam had been a town of little importance, but the political developments of the sixteenth century boosted it to eminence. Nearby Antwerp, a port city with access to the Atlantic, had preceded

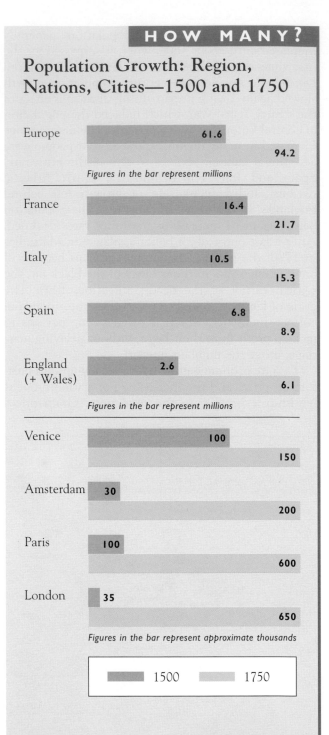

HOW MANY?

Population Growth: Region, Nations, Cities—1500 and 1750

Europe — 61.6 / 94.2
Figures in the bar represent millions

France — 16.4 / 21.7
Italy — 10.5 / 15.3
Spain — 6.8 / 8.9
England (+ Wales) — 2.6 / 6.1
Figures in the bar represent millions

Venice — 100 / 150
Amsterdam — 30 / 200
Paris — 100 / 600
London — 35 / 650
Figures in the bar represent approximate thousands

1500   1750

The population of Europe increased more than 50% (from a base of about 60 million) from 1500–1750. But nations and cities increased at different rates. While the population of France increased only about 32%, the population of England increased 135%, to reach by 1750 more than twice its 1500 figure. Meanwhile Venice, the front-ranking city of 1500, fell to a poor fourth place by 1750, when London, having increased more than twentyfold, reached preeminence with a population of 650,000.
Source: J. de Vries, *European Urbanization, 1500–1800* (Cambridge, MA: Harvard University Press, 1984)

Amsterdam as the major port (and thus the commercial and banking center) of northern Europe. It reigned supreme in the sixteenth century, when it handled much of Portuguese trade as well as the commerce of the textile manufactures of the region. But Antwerp's career suddenly declined around 1650, when the newly independent United Provinces were allowed (by the Treaty of Münster, 1648) to close the Scheldt River, the city's route to the sea. Located not far to the north of Antwerp and in closer proximity to the sea, Amsterdam took its place.

In the seventeenth and eighteenth centuries, Amsterdam was the banking center of Europe, the fulcrum of world trade. Its population grew from 30,000 in 1567 to over 200,000 by the early 1780s. Its bank, founded in 1609 on the model of the Venetian Rialto banks, issued its own gold florin. By 1700, the bank provided safety for more than 2000 depositors and the lowest interest rates in Europe (4 percent or less) on investment loans. At its stock exchange (completed 1613), illustrated on p. 475, merchants participated in ventures around the globe, trading in as many as 491 commodities by 1674 (when London, its rising competitor, dealt in 305). A weekly bulletin listed options and gave updated prices.

Even after the 1713 Peace of Utrecht, when the Netherlands fell behind the British and French as a European power, Amsterdam remained the center of European financial life. During the eighteenth century, the city lived on the capital it had accumulated over the previous 200 years, which now helped fund, at profitable rates of interest, nearly every major commercial venture in Europe.

The growing mercantilist commercial system of the sixteenth, seventeenth, and eighteenth centuries enriched European nations, swelled their towns and cities, and lavishly rewarded the merchant investors. It seemed a great success. And yet it also had many defects. The intervention of government into the business of business, while often protective, also retarded the pace of commerce. Tariffs set to shelter domestic manufactures and monopolies created by royal edict interfered with the free flow of trade and the mechanisms which, as later experts argued, allowed the market to regulate itself.

Such problems of mercantilist organization encouraged the Scottish professor Adam Smith (1723–1790) to argue for an alternative organization of manufacture and commerce. In his *Inquiry into the Nature and Causes of the Wealth of Nations* (published in 1776, the same year as the Declaration of Independence), part of which is quoted in *Witnesses* on p. 473, he argued that the absence of intervention would enhance production within the nation, as individuals pursuing their own self-interest would both yield high profits and benefit the public. Free trade policies would allow the entrepreneurs competing for foreign trade to realize the greatest possible wealth, and thus enrich the nation. Directed only by merchant interest and buyer need, "as though by an invisible hand," free trade would more greatly increase the "wealth of nations" than a trade system controlled by jealous states and governors. The nation states that had just matured in the political life of Europe were now instructed to limit themselves to defense and security. They did not easily retreat.

Conclusion
THE EXPANSION OF EUROPE AND THE MEANING OF THE WEST

From 1500 to 1750, Europe expanded beyond its earlier borders physically, economically, and psychologically. The expansion had begun even earlier, with the commercial revolution achieved by Italian merchants and the foreign adventures of the Crusades. The cultural and religious movements of the Renaissance and the Reformation, although contained within the geographical boundaries of Europe, entailed an enormous broadening of Europeans' mental horizons. Now, however, the expansion was fundamental and taking place on all fronts: it sent people of many nations around the world on new ships driven by new technology; it stimulated Europeans to reconsider their view of themselves upon contact with human communities previously unknown; it changed what ordinary people ate and wore, their work and their homes; it impacted on the lives of nearly every European, from the Dutch ship hand to the Polish peasant.

The same expansion made Europe the master of the globe. Europeans were involved in the rout of Amerindian culture, in the mass enslavement of Africans, and in the enlistment of Indian and Indonesian (if not yet east Asian) producers into the economy of the West. At the beginning of the episode of European expansion, Montaigne wrote about the Amerindian Caribs who ate their war captives. But he had already detected that, much as his fellow Europeans feared and deplored the cannibal, the cannibal had much to dread in the advent to his world of European civilization.

QUESTIONS TO CONSIDER

1. In what way were Portugal and the Dutch Republic important innovators in the age of maritime exploration?

2. To what extent was Columbus an explorer, a visionary, a governor, a merchant, a historian?

3. Why were Cortès and Pizarro able to defeat the Aztecs and Incas with so few soldiers?

4. Why and to what extent did European settlers treat imported African slaves differently from indigenous Amerindians?

5. Which nations most profited from American and Asian trade in the sixteenth through eighteenth centuries? Which lost out, and why?

6. Why did some cities grow in importance, and others retreat during the sixteenth through eighteenth centuries?

SUGGESTED RESOURCES

Axtell, James, *Beyond 1492: Encounters in Colonial North America* (Oxford: Oxford University Press, 1992). Essays on themes relating to interactions between Amerindians and Europeans.

Blackburn, Robin, *The Making of New World Slavery: From the Baroque to the Modern, 1492–1800* (New York: Verso, 1998). A discussion of New World slavery in a comparative and historical perspective.

Chaudhuri, K. N., *Asia before Europe: Economy and Civilisation of the Indian Ocean from the Rise of Islam to 1750* (New York: Cambridge University Press, 1990). A study of cultural practices and beliefs: food and drink, architecture, clothing, symbolism, land, nomadism, urbanism.

Crosby, Alfred W., *Ecological Imperialism: The Biological Expansion of Europe 900–1900* (Cambridge: Cambridge University Press, 1993). A survey of the biological impact of European contact on the Americas, Africa, Asia, Australia, and the Pacific islands.

De Vries, Jan & Ad Van der Woude, *The First Modern Economy: Success, Failure, and Perseverance of the Dutch Economy, 1500-1815* (Cambridge: Cambridge University Press, 1997). Presents the Dutch as the first to create a truly modern economy, with an integrated profitable agricultural sector, foreign trade, and capital market.

Gray, Edward G., *New World Babel: Languages and Nations in Early America* (Princeton: Princeton University Press, 1999). Studies the multiplicity of Amerindian languages at the time of the European conquest, and the impact upon them of the European tongues.

Harms, Robert, *The Diligent: A Voyage through the Worlds of the Slave Trade* (New York: Basic Books. 2002). Follows the voyages of the French slave ship *Diligent* in 1731–1732, as it pursued the triangular trade in slaves, sugar, and manufactures between the African coast, the Caribbean island of Martinique, and the French port of Vannes, based on the journal by a young officer on board.

Matar, Nabil, *Turks, Moors, and Englishmen in the Age of Discovery* (New York: Columbia University Press, 1999). Studies the consciousness of the Islamic world by the English who encountered Muslims as part of diplomatic, military, and commercial endeavors.

Pagden, Anthony, *Lords of All the World: Ideologies of Empire in Spain, Britain and France, c. 1500–c. 1800* (New Haven: Yale University Press, 1995). A brilliant and fascinating reconstruction of the different ideological traditions that authorized European conquerors to dominate other peoples.

Price, Jacob M., *Perry of London: A Family and a Firm on the Seaborne Frontier, 1615–1753* (Cambridge MA: Harvard University Press, 1992). Traces the history of one family, and firm, which imported American tobacco into Britain in the 17th and 18th centuries; reveals the connectedness of social, economic, and political power.

Rubies, Joan-Pau, *Travel and Ethnology in the Renaissance. South India through European Eyes, 1250-1625* (Cambridge: Cambridge University Press, 2001). Explores how European visitors viewed the radically different world of India, from Marco Polo to the seventeenth-century Jesuits, examining European, Muslim, and Hindu writings.

Russell, Peter, *Prince Henry "the Navigator": A Life* (New Haven: Yale University Press, 2000). The first biography in a century of the prince who fostered the mathematical and navigational research making it possible for Europe to break free of its medieval geographical boundaries.

Schmidt, Benjamin, *Innocence Abroad: the Dutch Imagination and the New World, 1570–1670* (Cambridge: Cambridge University Press, 2001). Relates the Dutch perception of the freedom and novelty of the New World with the construction at home of a new society and politics following the struggle for liberation from Spain.

Smith, Roger C., *Vanguard of Empire: Ships of Exploration in the Age of Columbus* (Oxford: Oxford University Press, 1993). Explores the advances in ship technology that allowed the Spanish and Portuguese to venture out on the deep seas for exploration and exploitation.

Thomas, Hugh, *The Slave Trade: The Story of the Atlantic Slave Trade, 1440–1870* (New York: Simon and Schuster, 1998). Splended overview written for a general audience, that evokes the whole tragedy of the Atlantic slave trade, taking into its purview the slave traders, purchasers, collaborators, and the slaves themselves.

Columbus navigation homepage:
http://www1.minn.net/~keithp
Voyages of discovery and exploration, biographies and links:
http://www.win.tue.nl/cs/fm/engels/discovery

Sir Walter Raleigh, biography, resources, and links:
http://www.britishexplorers.com

Indigenous peoples of the Americas, all regions, articles, and resources:
http://www.hartford-hwp.com

◉ Western Civilization Documents CD-ROM

10.3 Christopher Columbus
10.4 Bartholomew De Las Casas
12.7 Mercantilism: Financing Absolutism
14.1 Before Europe: The Zheng He Expeditions
14.2 From King to King: Letters from Kongo to Portugal
14.3 "The Chronicle of Peru"
14.4 The Jamestown Charter
14.5 First Contact: The English Describe Pawatah's People
14.6 The Experiences of an Indentured Servant

PART FIVE
THE WEST EXPANDS

Science, Enlightenment,
and Revolution (1500–1900)

17 The Age of Reason
Science, Schooling, and
Thought in Early Modern
Europe, 1500–1780

**18 Town, Court, and
Country**
Privilege and Poverty in Early
Modern Europe, 1500–1780

19 Inalienable Rights
Revolution and its Promises in
Anglo- and Latin America,
1500–1880

**20 Revolt and
Reorganization in Europe**
From Absolute Monarchy to
the Paris Commune,
1750–1871

The social and cultural changes of the sixteenth through eighteenth centuries formed a prelude to the great political upheavals of the eighteenth and nineteenth centuries, together bringing the West to the threshold of modernity. The first scientists constructed a new model of the cosmos, discovered by observation and described with mathematics, while philosophers refined the logical and theoretical methods needed to explore both cosmic and human realms. In the intellectual movement known as the Enlightenment, critics questioned the bases of prevailing political and social systems, while an increasingly literate public joined in the conversation.

These new ideas challenged the system of social orders inherited from the Middle Ages—the Old Regime—prompting nobles to cling to the signs of their status and bourgeois hopefuls to try to "live nobly"; the peasantry, meanwhile, suffered the effects of economic change and political ambition. Across the ocean in the Americas North and South, the civilization of the West was reinvented in a new land and among new peoples, where opportunity beckoned to those who sought refuge from the cruelties of Europe. Along the Atlantic seaboard, the first Americans to cast off the rule of kings created a new nation, while in Europe the accumulated weaknesses of the French polity led to the French Revolution, which destroyed the Old Regime without establishing a society free of its defects.

The French Revolution bred sporadic later revolutions in France and elsewhere through 1871, when the Paris Commune was violently suppressed. The other major nations of Europe mobilized to suppress such revolutionary activity, while Britain, a unique case, gradually opened its political process to widening circles of ordinary citizens. Nationalist aspirations, meanwhile, another product of the French Revolution, culminated by 1871 in the unification of Italy and Germany, which for the first time took their place among the nation states of Europe.

THE AGE OF REASON

	1450	1500	1550	1600	1650	1700	1750	1800

Scientific Developments

Scientific Revolution, 1543–1687

- Nicholas Copernicus' *On the Revolutions of the Celestial Spheres*, 1543
- Andreas Vesalius' *On the Structure of the Human Body*, 1543
- Tycho Brahe observes a comet, 1577
- Galileo makes first astronomical observations with telescope, 1609
- Johannes Kepler's *New Astronomy*, 1609
- William Harvey's *Circulation of the Blood*, 1628
- Galileo's *Dialogue Concerning the Two Chief World Systems*, 1632
- René Descartes' *Discourse on Method*, 1637
- English Royal Society founded in London, 1662
- Academy of Sciences founded in Paris, 1666
- Isaac Newton's *Mathematical Principles of Natural Philosophy (Principia)*, 1687
- Lady Mary Wortley Montagu champions smallpox innoculation in Britain, 1721

Art, Religion, and Ideas

First century of printing, c. 1460–1560

The Enlightenment, c. 1685–1789

- Peter Martyr's *Chronicles of the New World*, 1530
- Richard Hakluyt's *Principal Navigations*, 1589
- Francis Bacon's *The Advancement of Learning*, 1605
- Francis Bacon's *Novum Organum (New Method)*, 1620
- Poulain de la Barre's *On the Equality of the Two Sexes*, 1673
- Louis XIV of France revokes Edict of Nantes, 1685
- Aphra Behn's *Oroonoko*, 1688
- Locke's *Essay Concerning Human Understanding* and *Two Treatises of Government*, 1690
- Daniel Defoe's *Robinson Crusoe*, 1710
- Peter the Great of Russia creates "ciphering schools," 1714
- Montesquieu's *Spirit of Laws*, 1748
- Denis Diderot and Jean d'Alembert's *Encyclopedia*, 1751–80
- British Museum established in London, 1753
- Jean-Jacques Rousseau's *The Social Contract*, 1762
- Frederick II of Prussia decrees obligatory elementary education, 1763
- Voltaire's *Philosophical Dictionary*, 1764
- Louvre Museum opens in Paris, 1793
- Condorcet's *Sketch for a Historical Account of the Progress of the Human Mind*, 1795

Beyond the West

Mughal Empire, India, 1526–1857

Ming Dynasty, China, 1368–1644

Qing Dynasty, China, 1644–1912

- Portuguese capture Malacca (Malaysia) and the Moluccas, 1511–13
- Ferdinand Magellan claims Philippines for Spanish crown, 1521
- Japanese expel Christian missionaries, 1614
- Dutch wrest Malacca from Portuguese, 1641
- Viceroyalty of New Granada created, 1717
- Viceroyalty of Rio de la Plata created, 1776

17

THE AGE OF REASON

Science, Schooling, and Thought in Early Modern Europe

1500–1780

Legend:
- major sites of the Enlightenment
- major cities
- boundary of the Holy Roman Empire, 1648

KEY QUESTIONS

◆ **New Heavens, New Earth:** How did the notions of the cosmos and of the human body change as a result of the "Scientific Revolution"? What changes in method accompanied changes in substance?

◆ **The Lights Go On:** How did new scientific ideas affect the understanding of the state, society, and the individual's place within these?

◆ **A Little Learning:** What made possible the spread of literacy and learning even to those who did not receive advanced schooling? How did women benefit from this trend?

Descartes' Dilemma *During a pause in the Thirty Years' War (1618–1648), the French nobleman René Descartes (1596–1650) turned his mind to a basic but important question: did he in fact exist? His senses of vision and touch told him that he was alive—but could he rely upon their evidence? In an anxious mental exercise, he stripped away from his consciousness everything he knew by means of his senses. Only one clear, distinct idea remained: his doubting, thinking mind. And if he was thinking, he concluded, he must exist. He announced his conclusion: "I think, therefore I am."*

This statement in Descartes' *Discourse on Method* (1637), which is also quoted in *Witnesses* on p. 493, marks the beginning of modern **rationalism**, the principle that human reason is the source of knowledge. Where medieval rationalism had used logical arguments to prove the existence of God, Descartes would deduce God's existence from his own—the first step in a new way of thinking that would shift the attention of European thinkers from the divine to the physical world.

Descartes' thought epitomizes the intellectual culture of the early modern era. From 1500 to 1750, European thinkers remapped the universe and unveiled the workings of the human body. They created the scientific method, reformulated the rules of logic, and distinguished verifiable truth from magic and superstition. Applying the test of reason to social institutions and assumptions, they opened the door to fundamental change in the way Europeans lived. Making their ideas available to an ever-growing public, they even included in their number some women, who employed the tools of reason to advance the condition of their peers.

NEW HEAVEN, NEW EARTH: THE SCIENTIFIC REVOLUTION

During the early modern period, a series of thinkers including Descartes transformed the way Europeans viewed the universe and laid the foundations of modern scientific thought. In the Middle Ages, the universe had been seen as a closed system, controlled by God, centered on the earth and its human inhabitants. Now it became an infinite system that governed itself by immutable, natural laws.

While these scientists taught Europeans to see "a new heaven, and a new earth" (in the prophetic words of the Biblical writer of *Revelations*), others investigated the structure of the human body and the human mind—all became aspects of nature to be explored and known in their own right, not simply celebrated as evidence of God's creative powers. This expansion of the field of human inquiry, and the new

methods used to pursue it, constitute what some historians term the **Scientific Revolution**.

The Advent of Infinity

The creation of a new world system entailed a changed conceptualization of the place of the human and the divine in an immeasurable cosmos. The old model of the universe had prevailed for some 1400 years, since it was formulated by the ancient Greek mathematician, geographer, and philosopher Ptolemy (second century C.E.; see Chapter 5). It was geocentric—the earth stood at its center, circled by the planets and stars, including the sun. Complex patterns of the planetary paths were devised to make the geocentric model plausible. European philosophers of the Middle Ages added a Christian dimension to the **Ptolemaic** cosmos: they imagined the movements of

Anonymous, Portrait of Johann Kepler: *Johann Kepler (1571–1630), astronomer and imperial mathematician, lent new force to the Copernican hypothesis of a sun-centered system when he proved that the planets moved in regular and predictable ways that could be clearly explained mathematically—and thus opened a route that would lead to the work of Galileo and Newton. Also shown is a figure illustrating the first of his laws of motion in which orbits are not circles as previously believed. (Munster, Strassburg)*

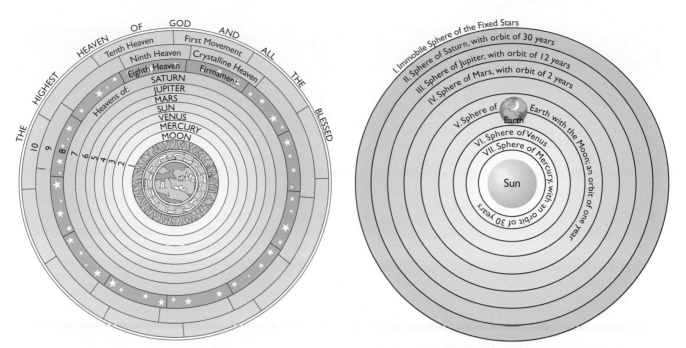

Mapping the heavens: *The Scientific Revolution saw the creation of a new cosmology (an understanding of the shape and structure of the universe). The medieval view had placed the stationary earth in the center of a finite universe composed of concentric crystalline spheres (above left). Each sphere rotated about the earth, carrying with it one or more of the heavenly bodies. God himself moved the outermost sphere, thereby causing all motion in the universe. This model was shattered by Nicholas Copernicus who in 1543 proposed that the sun was central and that the earth was the third planet from the center (above right). Copernicus retained other elements of the medieval view, however, in that his universe was still finite and composed of crystalline spheres.*

the planets and stars to describe a series of spheres within spheres, contained in a vast outer sphere on which were fixed the most remote stars. Outside the outermost sphere lay the realm of God and his angels, who guided the motion of the spheres. The diagram, top left, shows the medieval view of the universe in which the earth formed the stationary center.

Nicholas Copernicus   Nicholas Copernicus (1473–1543), a Polish cleric who had studied Greek, astronomy, and medicine in Cracow and Italian universities, was the first to challenge the Ptolemaic model. He rejected the accepted patterns of planetary motion. In his reading of Greek texts, he encountered the theory of a sun-centered system first proposed by Aristarchus of Samos in the third century B.C.E. (see Chapter 5). If the earth were understood to move around the sun, Copernicus argued, everything else fell into place: "if the motions of the other planets are connected with the orbiting of the earth … not only do their phenomena [movements] follow therefrom but also the order and size of all the planets and spheres, and heaven itself is so linked together that in no portion of it can anything be shifted without disrupting the remaining parts and the universe as a whole." Although he had formed his theory by around 1530, Copernicus did not publish his epochal work *On the Revolutions of the Celestial Spheres* until 1543, when he was on his deathbed and beyond the reach of critics (an extract is given in *Witnesses* on p. 486). The diagram on the right above illustrates Copernicus's ideas.

Against Copernicus' ideas were ranged centuries of tradition and the weight of orthodox Christian thought. The validation of his theory by later scientists over the following 150 years firmly established the new world order of the Scientific Revolution.

Brahe, Kepler, and Bruno   Born three years after Copernicus' death, the Danish nobleman Tycho Brahe (1546–1601) gathered meticulous astronomical records from a well-equipped observatory built to his own design. Situated in Brahe's castle on his private island—both gifts from his royal patron, Frederic II of Denmark, it contained a model of the globe 5 feet (1.5m) in diameter. While Brahe's astronomical observations, including sensational sightings of a supernova (a super-bright, exploding star) in 1572 and a new comet in 1577, led him to reject the Ptolemaic model, he never fully accepted the Copernican system. He maintained that the sun revolved around the earth, while the other planets revolved around the sun. Brahe nevertheless provided the data from which later scientists could pursue the implications of Copernicus' theory.

Some of the materials Brahe left unpublished on his death were edited by his assistant at the imperial court at Prague (where Brahe had settled in his last years), the German mathematician and mystic Johannes Kepler (1571–1630). Kepler employed Brahe's data of celestial motion to test the Copernican theory, concluding that nature operated in regular patterns that could be described mathematically. By 1619, Kepler

Pioneers of a New Cosmology

During the sixteenth and seventeenth centuries, European philosophers—the ancestors of modern scientists— fundamentally reconstructed the human understanding of the universe. Previously an expression of the divine will, the universe was now a giant machine that operated according to rational, indeed mathematical, principles. Nicolaus Copernicus was the first of a series of thinkers to generate this new cosmological understanding, which reached its culmination in Isaac Newton's work. Their principal claims are presented in brief in these passages.

Copernicus claims that the earth rotates (1543): [Copernicus criticizes earlier thinkers whose calculations did not explain planetary motion correctly and whose methods were inconsistent.] I pondered long upon this uncertainty of mathematical tradition in establishing the motion of the system of the spheres. ... I therefore took pains to read again the works of all the philosophers on whom I could lay hand to seek out whether any of them had ever supposed that the motions of the spheres were other than those demanded by the mathematical schools. ... [Copernicus soon finds that certain antique authors had suggested the earth itself moves.] Taking advantage of this I too began to think of the mobility of the Earth ... [and] ... by long and frequent observations I have at last discovered that, if the motions of the rest of the planets be brought into relation with the circulation of the Earth and be reckoned in proportion to the orbit of each planet, not only do their phenomena presently ensue, but the order and magnitudes of all stars and spheres, nay the heavens themselves, become so bound together that nothing in any part thereof could be moved from its place without producing confusion of all the other parts and the Universe as a whole. [Having established the motion of the earth, Copernicus carries on to describe other aspects of his cosmology including the order of the planets, with the sun at the center.]
(Copernicus, *On the Revolutions of the Celestial Spheres*, 1543; ed. M. Munitz, 1957)

Newton defines the whole burden of philosophy—to explain the universal system (1687): I offer this work as the mathematical principles of philosophy, for the whole burden of philosophy seems to consist in this: from the phenomena of motions to investigate the forces of nature, and then from these forces to demonstrate the other phenomena; and to this end the general propositions in the first and second Books are directed. In the third Book I give an example of this in the explication of the System of the World; for by the propositions mathematically demonstrated in the former Books, in the third I derive from the celestial phenomena the forces of gravity with which bodies tend to the sun and the several planets. Then from these forces, ... I deduce the motions of the planets, the comets, the moon, and the sea. I wish we could derive the rest of the phenomena of Nature by the same kind of reasoning from mechanical principles, for I am induced by many reasons to suspect that they may all depend upon certain forces by which the particles of bodies ... are either mutually impelled towards one another ... or are repelled and recede from one another. These forces being unknown, philosophers have hitherto attempted the search of Nature in vain; but I hope the principles here laid down will afford some light either to this or some truer method of philosophy.
(Isaac Newton, *Mathematical Principles of Natural Philosophy*, Vol. I, 1687; ed. Cajori, 1974)

An island of knowledge: *The astronomers of the sixteenth- and early-seventeenth centuries worked with relatively simple equipment. Tycho Brahe's observatory at Stjerneborg in Denmark was considered to be state-of-the-art in around 1600.*

had developed three principles or "laws" of planetary motion around the sun, still accepted today. The first demonstrated that the planets moved in ellipses, not circles around the sun. The second demonstrated that planets moved at varying speeds in their elliptical orbits, so that the area of the ellipse defined by their path and their radii drawn to the sun were equal in any period of time. The third revealed a mathematical harmony in cosmic relationships that was doubtless most gratifying to a mystic such as Kepler—namely that the square of the period of each planet's revolution is proportional to the cube of its mean distance from the sun. The planets danced like ballerinas according to a common script, written in numbers.

When Kepler was still a young man, the Italian philosopher and Dominican friar Giordano Bruno (?1548–1600) was burned at the stake, charged with pantheism (the concept that the universe and God are ultimately identical). Bruno's theories included the claim that the universe was infinite, and composed of innumerable irreducible elements. Bruno's theory of infinity was not based either on observations such as Brahe's or on the scholarly examination of ancient theories undertaken by Copernicus: he was an original thinker who believed that the perceptions of the human mind were conditioned by a person's spatial, chronological, and even psychological position. The universe might roll on for ever, and anything conceivable by the mind might be true, in some universe or other. Bruno's concept of an infinite universe contributed to the definitive revision of European ideas of the shape and extent of the cosmos, inaugurating the modern conception of the world.

MUST READS

Books that Made the Scientific Revolution

Nicholas Copernicus	*On the Revolutions of the Celestial Spheres* (1543)
Andreas Vesalius	*On the Structure of the Human Body* (1543)
Francis Bacon	*The Advancement of Learning* (1605)
William Harvey	*Circulation of the Blood* (1628)
Johannes Kepler	*New Astronomy* (1609)
Galileo Galilei	*The Starry Messenger* (1610)
Isaac Newton	*Mathematical Principles of Natural Philosophy* (1687)

Galileo Galilei   The new spirit of inquiry emphasised the need to support theories about the material world with observation—the basis of modern scientific method. To make possible more accurate observation of the heavens, the mathematician, musician, and philosopher Galileo Galilei (1564–1642) employed techniques learned from a Dutch lens-grinder to construct the first astronomical telescope, which is illustrated on the right. From 1609, he used this to verify Copernican theory and record many

Galileo's telescope: *Galileo's remarkable telescope changed forever people's long-standing beliefs in an earth-centered system. Revealing for the first time new heavenly bodies for which existing cosmologies did not allow, and unanticipated fluxes and imperfections in those already known, it lent support to the Copernican hypothesis that the earth and other planets orbited around the sun. (Galileo Galilei, telescope, 1609; Museo delle Scienza, Florence)*

Science and Religion in Conflict

As the astronomer and physicist Galileo Galilei was to learn most powerfully in 1633—when his views were condemned by a tribunal of the Inquisition and he was forced, if insincerely, to abjure them—religion could act most powerfully against science. In the first of these passages, Galileo explains to the duchess of Tuscany that the truths of scripture, which are for human salvation, are distinct from the truths of natural phenomena, which derive from the evidence of our senses. In the second, Newton assures a clerical correspondent that his principles of motion argue for causation by a rational divine power.

Writing to Grand Duchess Christina, Galileo distinguishes scientific from theological inquiry (1615): I am inclined to think that Holy Scripture is intended to convince men of those truths which are necessary for their salvation, and which being far above man's understanding cannot be made credible by any learning, or by any other means than revelation. But that the same God who has endowed us with senses, reason, and understanding, does not permit us to use them, and desires to acquaint us in another way with such knowledge as we are in a position to acquire for ourselves by means of those faculties—that, it seems to me I am not bound to believe, especially concerning those sciences about which the Holy Scriptures contain only small fragments and varying explanations; and this is precisely the case with astronomy, of which there is so little that the planets are not [even] all enumerated. ... I think that in discussing natural phenomena we ought not to begin with texts from Scripture but with experiment and demonstration, for from the Divine Word Scripture and nature do alike proceed.
(From J. J. Fahie ed., *Galileo: His Life and Work*, 1903)

Writing to Reverend Bentley, Newton explains God's indispensable role in the Newtonian universe (December 10, 1692): When I wrote my treatise about our system [*Mathematical Principles of Natural Philosophy*, published in 1687], I had an eye upon such principles as might work with considering men for the belief of a Deity; and nothing can rejoice me more than to find it useful for that purpose. ... The motions which the planets now have ... could not spring from any natural cause alone, but were impressed by an intelligent Agent. ... Nor is there any natural cause which could give the planets those just degrees of velocity, in proportion to their distances from the sun and other central bodies, which were requisite to make them move in such concentric orbs about those bodies. ... To make this system, therefore, with all its motions, required a cause which understood and compared together the quantities of matter in the several bodies of the sun and planets and the gravitating powers resulting from thence. ... [A]nd to compare and adjust all these things together, in so great a variety of bodies, argues that cause to be, not blind and fortuitous, but very well skilled in mechanics and geometry.
(From M. Munitz ed., *Theories of the Universe*, 1957)

---

other observations. He saw the spots on the sun and the mountainous surface of the moon; he found that Jupiter had satellites and Saturn rings, and that the Milky Way was made up of innumerable stars.

Galileo announced his discoveries in his *Starry Messenger* (1610), winning public applause and offers of patronage. He also gained enemies as the forces of intellectual and religious orthodoxy turned against him, in particular church leaders who, still engaged in the mission of Catholic Reformation (see Chapter 14), maintained that the Copernican theory was contrary to faith. In 1632, a generation after his observations had finally consigned the Ptolemaic cosmos to the realms of fiction, Galileo published his *Dialogue Concerning the Two Chief World Systems*. Constructed as a dialogue between proponents of the Ptolemaic and Copernican cosmic models, it unequivocally supported the latter. Galileo chose to write in Italian, rather than in Latin, the language still used for scholarly publications throughout Europe, which meant that his work could reach a wider audience in his own country. In 1633, a church court examined Galileo and ordered him to repudiate

his views. Threatened with torture, he acceded—an act that one modern philosopher termed "the crime of Galileo." (In 1992, more than six centuries later, the Church at last reversed Galileo's conviction.) Still, church condemnation did not halt the widespread circulation of Galileo's ideas. He had shattered existing frontiers to formulate the possibility of a universe that was wholly without center or boundary: an infinitude of bodies that was unthinkably remote.

Galileo was also a pioneer physicist. He used new equipment and experimentation to reveal flaws in prevailing beliefs about the nature and behavior of matter, which were largely derived from the writings of the Greek philosopher Aristotle (384–322 B.C.E.). Galileo described the law of falling bodies (that they fall at exactly the same rate of acceleration regardless of their weight) and discovered the law of pendular motion (that any pendulum takes the same amount of time to traverse its maximum and minimum arcs). He contested Aristotle's view that the natural condition of material bodies was to be at rest: according to Galileo (and modern physics since that time), matter was naturally in motion.

Isaac Newton It was the English scientist Isaac Newton (1642–1727) who went on to discover the principles that governed the limitless universe imagined by Bruno and investigated by Galileo, thus completing the early modern reconceptualization of the world system. In his *Mathematical Principles of Natural Philosophy* (1687; an extract from the introduction is given in *Witnesses* on p. 486), published in Latin, Newton defined the principle of universal gravitation. Gravity explained the movements of earthly and celestial bodies, providing the new world system with a unity and coherence that seemed to have been lost when Copernicus had removed the earth from the center of the cosmos a century and a half before. Newton further elaborated three laws of motion that have served as a framework for physical mechanics ever since. He also developed the branch of mathematics known as calculus and demonstrated using a glass prism that white light could be split into the sequence of colors that make up the spectrum.

Despite the breakthrough concepts they developed, early modern scientists worked squarely within the framework of the medieval intellectual tradition they transcended. They were considered "natural philosophers," whose range of inquiry embraced the whole material universe. This lack of more closely defined specialization helps explain the versatility of a Galileo or a Newton, who ranged easily from mathematics to physics to astronomy. Moreover, these early scientists used Latin, the universal language of learning in Europe, to communicate their findings across languages (Polish, Danish, German, Italian, English) and religious divides—Copernicus and Galileo were Roman Catholic; Brahe, Kepler, and Newton Protestant—while also permitting them to speak to the generalists among their educated public.

"Man the Machine": Exploration of the Human Body

Before about 1500 in Europe, the human body was unknown terrain. Ancient physicians had made extensive clinical observations and acquired some practical surgical experience, but they could not explain what they observed. In the sixteenth and seventeenth centuries, however, anatomists and physicians learned that the human being was an autonomous mechanism governed by natural laws. Exploration of the fabric of the body yielded a new model of the human being: in the words of one French writer, "man the machine." This breakthrough in medical thought was comparable to the breakthroughs in the realm of astronomy.

Ancient physicians had proposed the theory of **humors** to explain the functioning of the body. It was based on early Greek speculations, codified in the works of Galen (second century C.E.; see Chapter 6), and repeated by Arab and Christian followers. It held that each healthy body possessed a balance of four bodily fluids: blood, black and yellow bile, and phlegm. These governed in turn four temperamental tendencies or humors—sanguine ("bloody," connoting optimism or good spirits); the black bilious (melancholic, depressed); the yellow bilious (choleric, hostile); the phlegmatic (slow and complaisant). Physicians examined their patients' bodily fluids and drained their blood, confident in their theory although dubious about the prospects of a cure. But they did not understand how or why the blood circulated, or even how a baby was conceived.

The course of medicine changed with direct exploration of the body. Renaissance artists seeking accuracy in the representation of the human form (notably Leonardo da Vinci) began to draw careful studies of its visible parts. Physicians, meanwhile, began to dissect cadavers. Progress was rapid, resulting in a new understanding of the body as a complex natural machine made up of interacting systems.

Among the first to practice the dissection of human cadavers was the Flemish anatomist Andreas Vesalius (1514–1564). He demonstrated his art at the university of Padua in Italy. In 1543, the same year as the publication of the Copernican theory, Vesalius published his *On the Structure of the Human Body*, which helped dismantle the Galenic system. The illustration from its title page on p. 490 shows him performing a dissection.

The ancient humoral theory, meanwhile, had already been challenged by the Swiss physician Theophrastus von Hohenheim, known by his Latin name Paracelsus (1493–1541). A systematic observer, inspired though he was by the false science of **alchemy**, Paracelsus experimented with a number of chemicals as therapies and developed some effective new treatments, such as opiates to kill pain. An experienced surgeon, Paracelsus also compiled in the German of ordinary readers the first practical surgical manual.

Vesalius' approach was pursued by the English physician William Harvey (1578– 1657), who proclaimed: "I profess to learn and teach anatomy not from books but from dissections, not from the tenets of philosophers but from the fabric of nature (see *Witnesses*, p. 493)". Having acquired his medical degree in Padua, he returned to London to practice and teach, serving eventually as court physician to James I and Charles I. His most important discovery was that the blood circulated through the body via arteries and veins, propelled by the heart functioning as a pump, as shown in the diagram on the left. The implications of Vesalius' observations, Paracelsus' experiments, and Harvey's hypothesis were not to be fully realized until the nineteenth century. In the mean time, however, some patients began to benefit from their proposals. On the battlefields of sixteenth- and seventeenth-century Europe, surgeons learned to close wounds without cautery (sealing with a hot iron), to improve amputation techniques on limbs that could not be restored to function, and to apply prosthetic devices. And in the domestic realm, doctors, shouldering midwives aside, began to deliver babies.

For the first time, anatomists began to understand how the female body functioned differently from the male. Ancient tradition on this issue was divided: according to the Aristotelians, the female body was that of a "defective male," and the male sperm was the sole cause of the creation of new life. The woman's uterus merely housed the growing fetus until the moment of birth. The Galenists took a more positive view of the female role in conception and gestation, hypothesizing that the fetus was formed by the conjunction of the male sperm and "female seed." This theory accorded women's bodies greater respect than in the Aristotelian formulation, and was at least one step closer to what modern biology knows to be the case. In the seventeenth century, physicians began to develop the fields of gynecology and obstetrics (the study of the female body and of childbearing respectively). First among them was William Harvey, who made important observations of embryonic growth in animals, which resulted in a better understanding both of the female role in conception and gestation, and of general female dysfunctions and diseases.

At this point, the male medical establishment collided with the midwives. These were women who, over the generations, often from mother to daughter, transmitted what knowledge there was of the process of giving birth. Midwives guided women in their pregnancy and prepared them for labor; they knew when the fetus was well-positioned, and when its position needed to be adjusted by a skilled woman's hand (as shown in the woodcut above), and they knew when there was no hope, but that mother and child would perish. Midwives directed a team of female relatives and friends through the birth process. After the birth, they instructed the mother in the care of her child, and the personal care she needed to recover from the experience of giving birth.

Discovering the Human Body

Dissecting the body: *The sixteenth and seventeenth centuries saw a revolution in notions about human biology. An increasing reliance on experiment and empiricism began to replace subservience to the texts of the great anatomists of antiquity such as Aristotle and Galen. This illustration from the title page of Andreas Vesalius' On the Structure of the Human Body, 1543, shows Vesalius breaking with tradition by doing his own dissections.*

Over the early modern centuries, male physicians took over the power to manage birth. By the eighteenth century, the forceps had been developed to aid in the extraction of an infant in a difficult birth. Their use was limited to trained physicians, all male, who warned future mothers of the dangers they faced from "untrained" midwives.

Progress in medicine also made an impact in the treatment of disease. Although physicians did not yet know that microbes or viruses caused disease, they understood that disease had objective causes, and that it required strenuous treatment. In the early eighteenth century, during a stay in the Ottoman Empire, Lady Mary Wortley Montagu (1689–1762), wife of the English ambassador to Constantinople (modern Istanbul), observed the practice of smallpox inoculation, in effect the deliberate infection of the patient with a mild case of the disease. She had her own children vaccinated, and championed smallpox prevention in England on her return in 1721. Later in the century, Edward Jenner (1749–1823) refined the vaccine, and smallpox became the first disease to be conquered by medical science—both advances saving millions of lives.

Midwifery and childbirth: *Trained in the new culture of science, the male-dominated medical establishment frequently discredited earlier practices. In some cases, women were pushed out of fields they had traditionally dominated. Such is the case with midwifery, which had once been almost exclusively a female occupation, as shown here in this 1554 woodcut.*

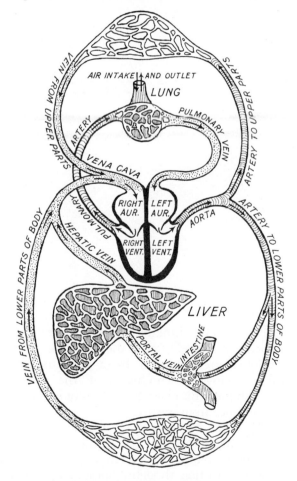

Circulation of the blood: *William Harvey's theories about the circulation of blood through veins and arteries, explained here in his diagram, were backed up by simple, yet highly effective empirical proofs.*

Hard Facts and Pure Reason: New Modes of Thinking

Advances in science in the early modern period owed much to the development of new modes of thinking. Trained in critical methods (and the Greek language) by Renaissance humanists (see Chapter 13), philosophers began to develop original systems of metaphysics. They created methods of reasoning that, unlike the propositions and syllogisms of medieval disputation, enabled scientific inquiry. They doubted everything, including the authority, once supreme, of Aristotle; and the assumptions, once self-evident, of Christianity. They studied nature more than reports of nature, and saw that its framework could be described in the language of mathematics. They accepted the evidence of indisputable facts, often gathered through experimentation. They trusted in, and could often demonstrate, the fundamental rationality of the world.

Aristotle continued to reign for 200 years after the humanist Lorenzo Valla (1405–1457) challenged his monopoly (see Chapter 13). While Aristotelianism stood for the old world order, it could also become a weapon against traditional ideas, as when the Italian

major religions in post-Reformation Europe

▢ Protestant	▲ birthplace of major Enlightenment thinker (with year of birth)
▢ Roman Catholic	▪ important university
▨ strong Protestant minorities within Roman Catholic areas	
▢ Eastern Orthodox	

Map 17.1 The Major Scientific Thinkers and Philosophes: *Both the Scientific Revolution and Enlightenment were transnational movements, whose major exponents hailed from a variety of national, cultural, and religious backgrounds. Though it is true that the culture of science flourished best in Protestant countries, many of the most important thinkers came from, lived in, and wrote in Catholic countries.*

Pietro Pomponazzi (1462–1524) challenged the central Christian doctrine of the immortality of the soul: how could the soul be immortal, when it was so thoroughly enmeshed with the material body?

Such explorations of the possibilities of Aristotelianism during the sixteenth century paved the way for the development in the seventeenth century of philosophies spun out of pure reason. For the French nobleman René Descartes, the Dutch-Jewish lens-grinder Benedict Baruch de Spinoza (1632–1677), and the German nobleman and politician Gottfried Wilhelm von Leibniz (1646–1716), the universe, or nature itself, was perfectly rational. According to Descartes, everything in the universe was either mind (a "thinking substance") or body (an "extended substance"), and the universe itself a vortex of matter directed by a thinking mind. Descartes' followers, who made up the Cartesian school, sustained this clean separation of matter from mind, substance from spirit.

For Spinoza, the universe was one single substance, alternately Nature or God himself, a perfect amalgam of matter and reason. In a significant break with Judeo-Christian thought, Spinoza saw God as enmeshed in nature, no longer a purely spiritual being capable of judging and directing the cosmos. His heterodoxy caused him to be expelled from the Jewish community of Amsterdam in 1656.

Leibniz, in contrast, won wide acclaim, and was courted by the princes of central Europe. He acknowledged the existence of a wholly immaterial God, the creator of the universe, and, like his own creation, infinite in space and time. But that universe was self-sufficient in its operations—consisting of a divinely ordained, perfectly ordered infinitude of immaterial particles, called "monads," each constituting a mirror of the whole, harmonious universe.

Other early modern thinkers, inspired by ancient texts, adopted the philosophical outlook of **skepticism**: an attitude of universal doubt. Whereas in the eleventh century the medieval philosopher Saint Anselm stated "I believe in order to understand," these men doubted in order to know. Descartes doubted the evidence of sense experience but proposed instead a logical method of **deducing**

further principles from essential first principles—this was the **deductive** method, based ironically on a faith in the capacity of pure reason.

French mathematician Blaise Pascal (1623–1662) doubted the capacity of reason to know anything: the only source of certainty for human beings, he argued, was a faith based not on tradition but on probability. For the Scots philosopher David Hume (1711–1776), even hard facts offered no truly dependable knowledge, let alone the vapors of mysticism. It may *appear* that the hammer strikes the nail, Hume argued, but the relationship can never be entirely proved, as the natural world is only a sequence of impressions.

Other early modern philosophers continued to believe in the reliability of sense perception, and in the evidence of hard facts. In late Renaissance Italy, the Dominican friar Bernardino Telesio (1509–1588)

WITNESSES

Pioneers of New Scientific Methodologies

How do we know what is true? Is it from the evidence of our senses, or reasoned demonstration—from an experiment, or from a logical proof? These were questions that occupied the philosophers of the new science in the seventeenth century. In these passages, two Englishmen, the philosopher Francis Bacon and physician William Harvey, argue for the empirical method, the derivation of knowledge from sense experience; and the French philosopher Descartes argues for the rational method, the deduction of true statements from prior truths.

From the senses to judgment—Francis Bacon advocates the Inductive Method (1620): There are and can be only two ways of searching into and discovering truth. The one flies from the senses and particulars to the most general axioms, and from these principles, the truth of which it takes for settled and immoveable, proceeds to judgment and to the discovery of middle axioms. And this way is now in fashion. The other derives axioms from the senses and particulars, rising by a gradual and unbroken assent, so that it arrives at the most general axioms last of all. This is the true way, but as yet untried.
(From H. G. Dick ed., *Selected Writings of Francis Bacon*, 1955)

Dissections not books—William Harvey defends the Empirical Method (1628): True philosophers, who are only eager for truth and knowledge, never regard themselves as already so thoroughly informed, but that they welcome further information from whomsoever and from whencesoever it may come; ... very many, on the contrary, maintain that all we know is still infinitely less than all that still remains unknown. ... Neither do they think it unworthy of them to change their opinion if truth and undoubted demonstration require them so to do. ... I profess both to learn and

to teach anatomy, not from books but from dissections; not from the positions of philosophers but from the fabric of nature. ... I avow myself the partisan of truth alone; and I can indeed say that I have used all my endeavors, bestowed all my pains on an attempt to produce something that should be agreeable to the good, profitable to the learned, and useful to letters.
(William Harvey, *Circulation of the Blood*, 1628; ed. C. D. Leake, 1931)

Truth firm and assured—the rationalism of René Descartes (1637): Inasmuch as I desired to devote myself wholly to the search for truth, I thought that I should ... reject as absolutely false anything of which I could have the least doubt, in order to see whether anything would be left after this procedure which could be called wholly certain. Thus, as our senses deceive us at times, I was ready to suppose that nothing was at all the way our senses represented them to be. As there are men who make mistakes in reasoning even on the simplest topics in geometry, I judged that I was as liable to error as any other, and rejected as false all the reasoning which I had previously accepted as valid demonstration. Finally, as the same percepts [i.e., perceptions] we have when awake may come to us when asleep without their being true, I decided to suppose that nothing that had ever entered my mind was more real than the illusions of my dreams. But I soon noticed that while I thus wished to think everything false, it was necessarily true that I who thought so was something. Since this truth, I think, therefore I am, was so firm and assured that all the most extravagant suppositions of the sceptics were unable to shake it, I judged that I could safely accept it as the first principle of the philosophy I was seeking.
(Descartes, *Philosophical Essays*, 1637; ed. J. Lafleur, 1964)

argued for a systematic understanding of nature based on experience and observation in his giant work *On Nature According to Its Own Principles* (1565). Circulating widely at the end of the sixteenth century, it encouraged a preference for experienced-based, or **empirical** knowledge of the kind essential to the whole process of scientific inquiry.

Bacon, Galileo, and Locke   The English philosopher, essayist, and statesman Francis Bacon (1561–1626) took up Telesio's mission. He declared war on traditional Aristotelian philosophy, constructed from mere tissues of words, which could neither harness nature nor benefit humanity. Bacon aimed to reshape philosophy, planning to publish a *Great Instauration*, or "re-establishment," of knowledge. Parts of that project appeared in such works as *The Advancement of Learning* (1605) and the *New Method* (*Novum Organum*) (1620, a passage from which is quoted in *Witnesses* on p. 493). For Bacon, knowledge would have to be established on the observation of hard facts, without which the human being "neither knows anything nor can do anything."

First of all, the human mind must be freed of its prejudices and presuppositions, the glittering but false "idols" that people continued to worship. Bacon defined four classes of idols: the "idols of the tribe," those inherent in the human condition because of its essential nature and cultural heritage; the "idols of the cave," or the particular prejudices of individuals; the "idols of the marketplace," those shared commonplaces that arise from inaccurate understanding of words; and the "idols of the theater," the mistaken beliefs learned from unworthy others, including "the various dogmas of philosophers."

According to Bacon, the mind was to be cleared of these prejudices and presuppositions, so that it could apprehend hard facts with pure reason. Then, it would proceed by **inductive** reasoning: from observed data to more generalized statements "rising by a gradual and unbroken ascent, so that it arrives at the most general axioms last of all." The observer would systematically gather information about a phenomenon until a regular pattern emerged. From that pattern, he would form a theory, or **hypothesis**, about the phenomenon, which could be tested, verified, and expressed as a general statement. The accumulation of those general statements would amount to knowledge—or "science"—itself.

In Italy, Galileo developed the method of reasoning that would come to be called "the scientific method." Like Bacon, he held that the observation of clear facts led to universal statements. From data gathered about the movement of bodies in space, for example, theories might be devised to explain them. Impatient of waiting for sufficient data, however, and dissatisfied with their quality in the imperfect world around him, Galileo developed the method of

experiment: the staged and repeated "experiencing" of phenomena, controlled so that the factors of greatest interest are isolated and made visible. This method of inductive reasoning based on data gathered from the controlled observation of nature or from experiment remains the method of modern science.

It was Bacon the theorist rather than Galileo the experimenter who provided the inspiration for the English philosopher John Locke (1632–1704) in his advancement of the cause of inductive logic. His *Essay Concerning Human Understanding* is as important for philosophy, pedagogy, and psychology as his *Two Treatises on Civil Government* (both published 1690) (see Chapter 15) is for the development of political thought. In the former he argued against Descartes' contention that the mind contained true ideas of reality even at birth. Instead, Locke proposed that the mind at birth contained no ideas at all—it was a "blank slate," a *tabula rasa* as empty of thought as a teacher's empty blackboard. It is written on by experience. As the mind experiences things through the five senses, it forms ideas about the material world. The things come first; the mind fits thought to them, and after that, words. Everything in the mind arrives first through experience.

Consequently, evil thoughts and actions derived not from an innate evil in the soul, but from unfortunate experience in the world of things. Such moral deficiencies could be repaired, Locke implied, by a new round of more positive experience. The implications of Locke's theory of learning for social change were immense: immorality was not rooted in the soul, the blood, or the social order. It resulted simply from exposure to a poor environment. A correction of the environment would necessarily result in an improvement in mental condition.

While Bacon, Galileo, and Locke grappled with theories aimed at explaining the hard facts of material reality, others rushed to collect the facts themselves. Historians amassed documents chronicling their city's, country's, or religion's past. Others, following but surpassing Classical and Renaissance models, catalogued famous men or famous women. Surveys of topography, botany, geography, and mineralogy poured off the presses. How-to books described methods of zinc-smelting, fishing, or housekeeping; the biology of bees, birds, and silkworms; drainage and irrigation systems; the making of glass.

Other "moderns" (those who hunted for new truths in the present, in contrast to admirers of the "ancients," who studied them in the past) not only described things but also invented them. New pieces of equipment, specially devised for investigating the world with greater detail and accuracy, included the telescope, microscope, thermometer, and barometer. Measuring and calculating devices included the pendulum clock and adding machine (the last by Pascal), the mechanical pump, the flexible hose for fighting fires and lightning rod for preventing them (by the American philosopher and statesman Benjamin Franklin, see Chapter 20), new uses for windmills, and early versions of the typewriter, the sock knitter, and the sewing machine.

The new curiosity about, and desire to master, material reality is evidenced in the rush of discovery, invention, and data-collection that characterized the seventeenth and eighteenth centuries. That absorption in the concrete, the manipulable, the massive, and the movable contrasted both with the passive contemplation of the Middle Ages and the intellectual and aesthetic values of the Renaissance, with its passion for the past and its idealizing quest for truth, beauty, and perfection. The new age was more concerned with how things worked than whether they had reached the highest pitch of perfection—more interested in science, in sum, than in art.

The End of Magic

In a new world where facts were hard and reason prevailed, magical explanations of events were doomed. During the Renaissance, the possibilities of magic had expanded, boosted by learned humanists for whom ancient magical beliefs were as intriguing as ancient knowledge. Two centuries later, however, confidence in magical constructs withered among the learned, and took a last refuge in peasant huts and villages. Reason was the solvent that put an end to magic.

The most widely accepted form of secular magical thought was **astrology**, the study of the ways in which heavenly bodies supposedly affected human life. Until well into the seventeenth century, astrology remained a respectable branch of knowledge. Physicians, especially, were likely to boast secondary expertise as astrologers, and rulers routinely consulted astrologers about the best place to build a palace or the best time for a military expedition. The citizens of the republic of Venice included a horoscope of their city in public chronicles, knowing that it promised Venice a long and prosperous future, while an English astrologer accurately predicted the critical but unlikely 1645 Parliamentary victory in England's Civil War and the later, unprecedented execution of the king.

By the time Newton published his *Mathematical Principles* (1687), however, it was no longer possible for the educated elites to accept the principles of astrology. In a universe systematically ordered and governed by laws expressed in mathematical relationships, there was no room for mysterious communications between the heavens and the earth. Astrology retreated to the margins, to become a lure to the untutored and a pastime for the privileged.

Meanwhile, science made other inroads on the domain of the occult. Occult or "hidden" knowledge at the beginning of the early modern period included

HOW MANY?

Witchcraft Trials: Centers of Activity, Numbers Tried, and Percentages Executed as a Result

Place	Dates	Number of people tried (where outcome is known)	% executed
Dept of the Nord, France	1542–1679	187	48
Essex	1560–1672	291	24
Finland	1520–1699	710	16
Fribourg	1607–83	162	33
Geneva	1537–1662	318	21
Guernsey	1563–1634	78	46
Hungary	1520–1777	932	48
Luxembourg	1509–1687	547	69
Namur	1509–1646	270	54
Neuchâtel	1568–1677	341	63
Norway	1551–1760	730	38
Pays de Vaud	1537–1630	102	90
Scotland	1563–1727	402	54

Distribution of Witches Between the Sexes

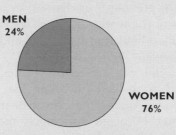

MEN 24%
WOMEN 76%

Based on a sample of 8,738 people tried for witchcraft in Southwest Germany, the bishopric of Basel, Franche-Comté, Geneva, Namur, Luxembourg, Dept of the Nord, Castile, Aragon, Venice, Finland, Estonia, Russia, Hungary and New England (U.S.A) in the sixteenth–eighteenth centuries. The lowest percentage of women tried for witchcraft is in Russia, 1622–1700, where out of 136 people accused, only 32 percent were female. In Basel, 1571–1670, on the other hand, out of 190 people tried, 95 percent were female. In New England, 1620–1725, out of 242 people tried, 78 percent were female.

Source: *Brian P. Levack, The Witch-Hunt in Early Modern Europe (2nd edition, Longman, 1995)*

much of what later became modern physics, chemistry, and biology. Occultists were mainstream thinkers who strove to learn much about many things: among them were Paracelsus, Brahe, and Kepler. Newton, proponent of a grandly rational view of the cosmos, was an alchemist who believed in the possibility of transforming elements into each other and creating more valuable substances from baser ones. The varied range of experiments conducted by alchemists, which involved heating, mixing, dissolving, and generally observing the behavior of many different substances, contributed directly to the development of the modern science of chemistry.

As astrology became distinct from astronomy, and chemistry from alchemy, the field of magic was shrinking. "White" magic, in other words those practices, including astrology and alchemy, by which the course of nature could be understood and altered, was yielding to science. "Black" magic, namely practices intended to cause harm, was already in deep disrepute—the "witches" condemned of such practices were hounded into obedience or tried and executed (see Chapter 14 and *How Many?* on p. 495). By the mid-seventeenth century in much of Europe, however, the prosecution of witches had ceased. Rational thought could no longer entertain the possibility of nocturnal black sabbaths or aerial broomstick escapades.

As witches disappeared from towns and villages, so monsters disappeared from maps. **Cartography**, the science of mapmaking, which had been immensely stimulated by the discoveries and voyages of the fifteenth and sixteenth century (see Chapter 16), now became rationalized and, like astronomy, mathematicized. Legendary monsters vanished from their positions at the previously uncharted ocean peripheries of the maps of the world to be replaced with the parallels and meridians that quantified and codified space and dealt magic another blow.

Magic did not die entirely. Uneducated people continued to believe in what the learned called superstitions. Among the educated, the figure of the practitioner of magic—so much more than what modern people think of as a "magician"—had an afterlife in literature and drama as the passion-stirred individualist, ceaselessly but fatally curious and creative. That figure, epitomizing heroic modern humanity in its desire to stretch the boundaries of what can be known or achieved, was immortalized in the play *Doctor Faustus* by the English author Christopher Marlowe (1564–1593). Three centuries later, Faust returned in German drama and French opera.

By 1750, for intellectuals and their audience, magic had largely died and credence in traditional authority had faded. Replacing them were faith in pure reason and a commitment to hard empirical facts, in an infinite world perceived through the senses of the body, which was in essence a machine. The "disenchantment" of the world, in the words of the twentieth-century German sociologist Max Weber, had finally been accomplished.

THE LIGHTS GO ON: THE ENLIGHTENMENT

Science and philosophy cleared away the magical beliefs and stale orthodoxies of an intellectual tradition dating back to antiquity. In the clean air and bright light of a new mental age, intellectuals in late seventeenth- and eighteenth-century Europe turned from science and metaphysics to society. Now they inquired into how people lived and how they were governed. These thinkers are known by the French term *philosophes* (the most important books they wrote are listed in *Must Reads* below). They created the era known as the "**Enlightenment**."

The Enlightenment was the predominant intellectual movement of the century extending from England's Glorious Revolution of 1688 (see Chapter 15) and the greatest works of Locke and Newton to the outbreak of the French Revolution in 1789 (see Chapter 20). Centered in France and England, it was also a powerful trend in Scotland, Italy, and the Netherlands, in some of the German courts and cities, and in the North American colonies. The *philosophes*

MUST READS

Books that Made the Enlightenment

Isaac Newton	*Mathematical Principles of Natural Philosophy* (1687)
John Locke	*Essay Concerning Human Understanding* (1690)
John Locke	*Two Treatises of Civil Government* (1690)
Voltaire	*Philosophical Letters* (1734)
Montesquieu	*The Spirit of Laws* (1748)
Jean-Jacques Rousseau	*The Social Contract* (1762)
Jean-Jacques Rousseau	*Émile: or On Education* (1762)
Denis Diderot and Jean d'Alembert	*Encyclopedia* (1751–81)
Condorcet	*Sketch for a Historical Picture of the Progress of the Human Mind* (1795)

Map 17.2
Subscriptions to Diderot and d'Alembert's Encyclopedia
Source: *Based on J. Merriman, A History of Europe,* Vol. I: From the Renaissance to the Age of Napoleon *(New York: W.W. Norton, 1996), p. 411.* Just as France had more than its share of intellectuals (see Map 17.1), it had more than its share of subscribers to the *Encyclopedia*–while eastern Europe, Spain, and Scandinavia are underrepresented. How would you explain this geography of readership?

redefined the terms of Western thought and experience, discovered new foundations for political life, looked afresh at non-European places, customs, and beliefs, and drafted new blueprints for the future of humanity. At the core of the Enlightenment was the relentless deployment of reason to confront reality and to challenge traditional authority. In his 1784 essay "What is Enlightenment?," the philosopher Immanuel Kant (1724–1804) summarized the movement's mission as well as anyone can in the ringing imperative: "Dare to know!"

Common Sense

"I offer nothing but plain facts and *common sense*," wrote the English journalist and professional revolutionary Thomas Paine (1737–1809), explaining the purpose of his incendiary pamphlet (1776) of that name. Just as Descartes had sought "clear and distinct" ideas about universal reality, Enlightenment thinkers sought truths so plain and simple that they could be understood by everyone. Mere common sense would suffice.

"Common sense" was a deceptively innocent concept, as Paine well knew. It could be used as a weapon to slash through the obfuscations and pretensions of traditional culture, as by the French Huguenot refugee Pierre Bayle (1647–1706) in his *Historical and Critical Dictionary* (1695–1697). Bayle wielded common sense to demolish traditional concepts of society and thought as he redefined the very words that Europeans used. Reprinted frequently, translated, abridged, and extracted, Bayle's *Dictionary* was, as one

modern historian has called it, "a great engine of skepticism," and a "ponderous machine of war." With a copy propped on a shelf in every major library, it detached a generation of European intellectuals from traditional pieties and prejudices alike.

Some fifty years later, the French essayist, playwright, and literary critic Denis Diderot (1713–1784) masterminded the creation of a huge *Encyclopedia* (subtitled *A Classified Dictionary of the Sciences, Arts, and Trades*) that, like Bayle's *Dictionary*, redefined the outlook of the European public. The largest publishing venture of the age, it contained 60,000 brilliantly illustrated articles written by a team of authors. Publication of its thirty-five volumes took more than thirty years, beginning in 1751. The *Encyclopedia* aimed to encapsulate human knowledge. Its effect was to alter the way people thought. It provided information about such diverse subjects as farming and the soul, with entries on "history," "humanity," and the "slave trade." With a novel emphasis on science, crafts, and technology (coin stamping is illustrated on p. 498), the *Encyclopedia* told a spellbound public that dikes and waterwheels were as important as the symbols of heraldry or the calendar of saints. It sold widely, mostly in France, but also reached Madrid, Naples, and St. Petersburg at the fringes of Enlightenment Europe, as Map 17.2 above shows. In North America, Thomas Jefferson (1743–1826) and Benjamin Franklin (1706–1790) subscribed. The *Encyclopedia* won profits for the publisher and notoriety for the editors at the same time as it made the Enlightenment message the common property of the learned.

Work and Leisure

***Diderot and d'Alembert's* Encyclopedia:** *Printed books and journals allowed a widespread diffusion of scientific ideas. The* Encyclopedia, *published in France beginning in 1751, gathered together in one easily accessible source virtually all the key ideas of the Scientific Revolution and Enlightenment. Practical subjects, such as coin stamping, illustrated here, were especially well represented.*

In his *Philosophical Letters*, Voltaire (1694–1778)— the most important *philosophe*—also sought to reinvent the universe of knowledge, urging his readers to cast off their inherited misconceptions. Its famous entry on "Religion," for example, blasted the injustices wrought in the name of God by Jews, Muslims, and especially Christians. Voltaire's savage criticism of traditional customs and beliefs is also the mainspring of his novellas *Candide, Zadig,* and *Micromégas.*

Voltaire's younger contemporary, the Swiss-born author Jean-Jacques Rousseau (1712–1778), saw in the human being an endless possibility for good that was stifled by the paraphernalia of schools, books, and teachers. In *Émile* (1762), a book now considered to be one of the foundations of modern pedagogy, Rousseau argued that the young child should learn from nature, not books, until the age of twelve. He should learn science by doing it, and history from his exploration of current issues: "It is not a question of knowing what is, but only what is useful." Tutored in this way, the child would gain a greater measure of self-confidence, as well as the good sense to learn whatever was necessary for success.

The war on tradition waged by Enlightenment thinkers necessarily involved a war on the Christian churches, whose whole history, they believed, was stained by indefensible notions and cruel practices. The whole Christian enterprise was snarlingly dubbed by Voltaire, "*l'infâme,*"—an infamous, or detestable thing. To the apostles of common sense, the acceptance of rigid dogmas, and the act of faith itself, went directly against the imperatives of reason. The churches, in turn, had generally been either slow to accept or downright hostile to the discoveries of science, as in Galileo's case. Even the instigator of the Protestant Reformation (see Chapter 14), Martin Luther (1483–1546), cried out on first hearing of Copernicus' theory: "This fool wants to turn the whole of astronomy upside down!" Newton, however, found no contradiction between physics and faith, declaring that "the most beautiful system of the sun, planets and comets could only proceed from the … dominion of an intelligent and powerful Being … [who] endures forever and is everywhere present."

Even so, few Enlightenment thinkers were ready to do without religion altogether, and many adopted the stance of **deism**. Deists believed in "nature and nature's God," in the words of the American author of the Declaration of Independence, Thomas Jefferson, a "supreme being" and benevolent creator, who permitted the universe to operate according to natural law. They rejected wholesale the doctrines, rituals, and hierarchies of the churches—"truth has no sect," pronounced Voltaire. Others were agnostics or atheists who viewed Christianity as wholly irrelevant to the pursuit of truth; a religion full of miracles, grumbled Hume, which required a miracle for a rational man to believe in it. In such a climate of opinion, the cause of religious toleration, which was already championed by some well-known Reformation figures (see Chapter 14), acquired new support: John Locke's *Letter Concerning Toleration* (1689) urged openness to all religious expressions—except those of Roman Catholics and atheists, whom this early liberal Protestant thinker considered to be outside the margins of what could be tolerated!

One alternative to Christianity was provided in eighteenth-century Europe by Freemasonry. Blending beliefs supposedly from ancient Egyptian polytheism with the mysteries of medieval guild organization, it retained a belief in divine power and propounded an ethic of brotherly love. Opposed alike to the ceremonies of the old Church and the tyranny of traditional monarchy, it nevertheless involved the performance of complex and secret initiation rituals.

Learning from nature: *An aristocratic family puts into practice the new educational philosophies of Jean-Jacques Rousseau in this 1778 print by J. B. Simonet entitled "Here is the Law of Nature....". Rousseau criticized the earlier stress on strict discipline and book learning from an early age and stressed instead the importance of allowing young children the freedom to interact with nature, learn by experience, and develop their own innate and individual personalities.* (Metropolitan Museum of Art, New York)

Its members, who ranged from artisans and sailors to the great Voltaire, were undismayed, and Masonic lodges proliferated throughout Europe—numbering 800 in France alone on the eve of the 1789 Revolution. Freemasonry seemed to offer a secular religion to those who craved common sense.

Social Contracts

Common sense provided a corrective not only to traditional beliefs and prejudices, but also to over-abstract theory and bookish rationality. It persuaded men and women to think and act in new ways and to question the established framework of society and government. Enlightenment thinkers used it to undermine political authority in their development of the concept of a "social contract" (see Chapter 15).

In his *Second Treatise of Civil Government*, which is quoted in *Witnesses* on p. 500, John Locke saw government as a contract created by male property-owners, powered by their consent, and responsible to their interests. If government was an arrangement of this kind, its object was not to extract obedience from the subject but to avoid tyranny by the ruler. Locke's eighteenth-century followers included Montesquieu, Rousseau, and Thomas Jefferson.

In his *Spirit of Laws* (1748) the nobleman and professional *philosophe* Montesquieu (Charles-Louis de Secondat, 1689–1755) argued that laws determined the spirit of a nation, having evolved over time according to local conditions and historical accident. Public assemblies should act, in the preferred system he called "constitutionalism," to safeguard the freedom of citizens both from the arbitrariness of kings and the chaos of too free a democracy: "the government [must] be so constituted," he advised, "that one man need not be afraid of another." He also formulated the principle of the "separation of powers," in which each of the government's three functions—executive, legislative, and judicial—acts as a check and balance to the others. This distinction that Montesquieu saw as essential to good government and the preservation of liberty later became central to the world's first written national constitution, that of the United States (see Chapter 19).

Rousseau's *Social Contract* (1762) was concerned with the relation between the individual and the whole of society, whose intentions were expressed as a "general will." Each person willingly surrendered some of his natural liberty to the community of the whole in order to gain protection and security. He could do so with confidence, because the state was guided not by a monarch but by "a moral and collective body" of citizens. The individual, "in giving himself to all, gives himself to nobody." Nevertheless, the effect of Rousseau's reasoning was to elevate the "state" in relation to the individual. Freed from the usual constraints of royal or divine authority, it defined itself and decreed its own laws.

While Rousseau's theory of social contract allowed the state more power than did Locke, the English philosopher's more libertarian view was adopted by his eloquent follower across the Atlantic, the Virginian lawyer Thomas Jefferson. The core attitudes of the Enlightenment toward government are succinctly expressed in the American Declaration of Independence, which Jefferson authored (although his original language was modified by a cautious committee). In a few sentences, he recapitulated Locke's notions of government by consent and the

right to dissolve a government usurped by tyranny. To secure their natural rights of life, liberty, and happiness, he wrote, "governments are instituted among men, deriving their just powers from the consent of the governed." When the government no longer serves those ends, "it is the right of the people to alter or abolish it," and to start anew to design a government as "shall seem to them most likely to effect their safety and happiness."

The social contract theories of Enlightenment thinkers did not create, nor did they even recommend, democracy, in which all the governed participate in the machinery of government. It was still to be

WITNESSES

Visions of a Just Society

Enlightenment thinkers brought the daring and rigor of scientific exploration to the issue of human society: on what sound principles can we build a just society, they asked, and just what are the prospects for the human species? Here, Voltaire calls for universal toleration of other customs, beliefs, and opinions, to undo the legacy of hatred and conflict from the past; Locke envisions government as an agreement, or contract, between an accountable ruler and sovereign citizens; and Condorcet finds in the perfectibility of the human being the prospect of unlimited human progress.

Voltaire calls for toleration (1763): I no longer address myself to man, but to You, eternal God of all beings and of all worlds. ... You have not given us a heart to hate each other, nor hands to strangle one another. ... May You prevent our different clothes, insufficient languages, ridiculous customs, imperfect laws and foolish opinions from becoming causes for hatred and persecution. Let those who light candles in broad daylight in Your honor cherish those who content themselves with the light of the sun. ... And may the poor look upon the rich without envy, for You know that wealth and titles are unworthy reasons for vanity and pride. Have all men remember that they are brothers! ... If the plague of war is inevitable, let us not hate one another and torture each other in times of peace. And let us employ the short period of our existence in thanking You, wherever we may reside, be it in Siam or California, and in whatever language we command, for the life You have granted us.
(From V. W. Topazio ed., *Voltaire: A Critical Study of his Major Works*, 1967)

Locke sees government as a revocable social contract between ruler and ruled (1690): The reason men enter into society [create governments and laws] is for the preservation of their property; and the reason they choose and authorize a legislature is that laws may be made ... as guards and fences for the properties of all the members of the society, to limit the power ... of

every part and member of the society. ... Whenever the legislators endeavor to ... destroy the property of the people, or to reduce them to slavery under arbitrary power, they put themselves into a state of war with the people, who are thereupon absolved from any farther obedience, and are left to the common refuge, which

God has provided for all men, against force and violence. Whensoever therefore the legislature ... endeavors to grasp themselves, or put into the hands of any other, an absolute power over the lives, liberties, and property of the people; by that breach of trust they forfeit the power the people had put into their hands for quite contrary ends, and it devolves to the people, who have a right to resume their original liberty, and, by the establishment of a new legislature ... provide for their own safety and security, which is the end for which they are in society.
(John Locke, *Two Treatises of Government*, 1690; ed. C. B. Macpherson, 1980)

Condorcet envisions reason as the basis for unlimited human progress (1794): The aim of the work that I have undertaken ... will be to show by appeal to reason and fact that nature has set no term to the perfection of human faculties; that the perfectibility of man is truly indefinite; and that the progress of this perfectibility, from now onwards independent of any power that might wish to halt it, has no other limit than the duration of the globe upon which nature has cast us. This progress will doubtless vary in speed, but it will never be reversed. ... The time will ... come when the sun will shine only on free men who know no other master but their reason; when tyrants and slaves, priests and their stupid or hypocritical instruments will exist only in works of history and on the stage; and when we shall ... learn how to recognize and destroy, by force of reason, the first seeds of tyranny and superstition, should they ever dare to reappear amongst us.
(Condorcet, *Sketch for a Historical Picture of the Progress of the Human Mind*, 1795; ed. J. Barraclough, 1955, reissued 1979)

a long time before women, or men who did not own land or property, were to have any voice in the processes of government. Nevertheless, these theories formed a first step in the development of genuinely democratic political systems.

Other Places, Other Customs

As Enlightenment authors hammered out new frameworks for political life, they sometimes looked to the experience of other peoples in other places, who acted according to very different customs and beliefs. Travel literature is an ancient genre, in which a distinctly new phase began with the opening of the New World to European explorers (see Chapter 16). Inevitably, eye-witness reports of the pre-Columbian civilizations of the Americas, which had evolved quite separately from those in Europe and the East, prompted Europeans to reflect on the meaning for their own society of the other cultures of humankind. Such works as the Italian Peter Martyr's *Chronicles of the New World* (1530), the French Jean de Léry's *History of a Voyage to the Land of Brazil* (1578), and the English Richard Hakluyt's *The Principal Navigations, Voyages, Traffics and Discoveries of the English Nation* (1589) forced Europeans to revise their notion of the heroic, now played out in distant wildernesses.

In her 1688 novel *Oroonoko*, the English novelist and playwright Aphra Behn (1640–89) depicted the courageous martyrdom of a noble African king caught in the violent trap of South American slavery. A generation or so later Daniel Defoe celebrated the conquest of nature and "savage" alike by his hero Robinson Crusoe (1719), who survived abandonment in the wilderness because of his superior mental and practical skills. In his novella *Candide*, Voltaire empathized with the Amerindians of Peru, in his view victims of the extraordinary cruelty of European Jesuits. Montaigne, Diderot, and Rousseau respected, and even celebrated, the "savages" of the other hemisphere—in direct contrast to the English lexicographer Samuel Johnson (1696–1772), who grumbled that "savages" made up four-fifths of the inhabitants of the globe.

Asian and Islamic cultures also found European interpreters. China's Confucian traditions, which resembled those of the contemporary West in their lucid rationality, impressed Enlightenment *philosophes*, and Hindu and Buddhist mysticism won sympathetic students. The East, especially the Ottoman Empire— still a formidable political presence in eastern Europe although languishing—provided an exotic contrast to prosaic European customs. Voltaire situated his comic hero Zadig in ancient Babylon, and Montesquieu's satirical *Persian Letters*, supposedly written by Asian observers of contemporary France, drew on contrasting Eastern and Western perspectives in its disguised attack on French royal absolutism (see Chapter 15).

The geographical explorations of the early modern era opened up realms of previously inconceivable possibility—to one commentator, a "horizon that recedes without end." Not surprisingly, the encounter with other real worlds encouraged the creation of fictitious ones. An early example is the English author and statesman Thomas More's *Utopia* (see Chapter 14), which certainly drew on New World themes: the work's narrator is a survivor of a shipwreck in unknown seas, so that a seemingly real journey introduces a plausible but imaginary one. The Dominican friar Tommaso Campanella (1568–1639), a prisoner of the Inquisition for twenty-seven years and possibly insane, described a more extensive utopia in his *City of the Sun*. The people inhabiting a world based on the astronomy of Copernicus, Bruno, and Galileo are transformed into what they know, a condition that is defined as the only form of eternal life. Campanella's contemporary, the English philosopher Francis Bacon constructed a utopian "New Atlantis" described in a book of the same title, whose citizens utilized scientific principles as they worked to improve their daily lives. And in the Enlightenment period, the Anglo-Irish author Jonathan Swift's satire *Gulliver's Travels* (1726) criticized contemporaries and explored the indeterminacy of moral values while depicting imaginary foreign realms.

These authors shared an awareness of other worlds beyond the limits of Western civilization—known, imaginary, and possible—which allowed them to reexamine their own. In the wider arena of the unfolded globe, the old European boundaries of identity faded: "Once past the equator," wrote Denis Diderot, "a man is neither English, nor Dutch, nor French, nor Spanish, nor Portuguese"; he has become "nothing." In these shifting realities, European assumptions could be shown for what they were— intrinsically no better, sometimes more deceptive or more shallow, than those of other cultures.

Encounters with other realities stimulated European reflection on the future of humankind. One popularizer of science announced fantastically (as it then seemed) that someday human beings might walk on the moon, while the French *philosophe*, the Marquis de Condorcet (Marie-Jean-Antoine Caritat, 1743–1794) predicted phenomenal advancements for the human race. He foresaw the elimination of poverty, the extension of human life, the establishment of mass education, and the equality of the sexes in his *Sketch for a Historical Account of the Progress of the Human Mind* (1795), an extract from which is given in *Witnesses* on p. 500. It was written, ironically, while Condorcet was evading the grip of the revolutionary Terror (see Chapter 20), which perhaps prompted his suicide.

Optimism like Condorcet's, based on secular faith in reason, suffuses the products of the Enlightenment. Fundamentally, all things in heaven and on earth were perceived to be orderly, splendid, and benign. "Whatever is," as the English poet Alexander Pope (1688–1744) declared, "is right."

A LITTLE LEARNING: LITERACY AND EDUCATION

The order of the world might be essentially right, according to Pope, but understanding it was still a matter for the select few: "A little learning is a dangerous thing," he warned. Enlightenment, in his view, was for the well-educated only—it was not enough to be able to read; one needed to be widely read and intellectually well-equipped. This exclusive view did not reflect the enormous broadening of the audience for science, literature, and ideas that occurred in the early modern centuries. While the ruling classes retained their privileged access to education (for their male offspring, at least) schools in general took on a broader mission, printshops poured out books, more people read, and many wrote. Teachers and bureaucrats, women and amateurs possessing what Pope dismissed as a "little learning" now participated in the intellectual world, which extended beyond the study and university to include learned and artistic academies, fashionable salons, and public as well as private museums.

Pleasure Reading

The creation of a broader audience for the intellectual products of the early modern era can be ascribed to two institutions: the school and the printshop. Where medieval schools had trained priests and monks, and Renaissance schools the sons of wealthy merchants, despots, and noblemen, from the sixteenth through eighteenth centuries, more people in general had the chance to go to school and learn to read (the growth in literacy is shown in the table on the right). They became the reading public of the Enlightenment era, avid consumers of many types of literature and new ideas propounded in cheap, easily available printed books.

The seventeenth and eighteenth centuries saw many, varied educational initiatives as the ability to read became an increasingly essential skill. In both England and France, private endowments established hundreds of different schools for the children of certain cities, craft professions, or religious denominations. In 1698, King Louis XIV of France (r. 1643–1715) ordered the establishment of a school in each rural district. In 1714, Peter the Great of Russia (r. 1682–1725) ordered the creation of "ciphering schools" throughout the realm, to train future technicians in arithmetic and geometry. In 1763, Frederick the Great of Prussia (r. 1740–1786) decreed that elementary education was obligatory, and the Habsburg emperor Joseph II (r. 1765–1790) created

---

Literacy Rates: France and the German States

Literacy in Urban France	
1683	51%
1770	60%

Source: *E. Le Roy Ladurie, The Ancien Regime: A History of France 1610–1774 (Cambridge, MA: Basil Blackwell, 1996), p. 309.*

Literacy in Rural Normandy	Males	Females
Late 17th Century	37%	7%
Late 18th Century	73%	46%

Source: *F. Furet and M. Ozouf, Reading and Writing Literacy in France from Calvin to Jules Ferry (New York: Cambridge University Press, 1982), p. 160.*

Literacy in the German States	
c. 1500	3–4%
c. 1800	50% (Males 50–66%; Females 33–50%)

Source: *J. Merriman, A History of Modern Europe: From the Renaissance to the Age of Napoleon (New York: W.W. Norton, 1996), pp. 38, 417.*

The eighteenth century was a time when great numbers of Europeans learned to read and write for the first time. Though measures of literacy are notoriously inaccurate (partly because of problems defining specifically what level of ability constitutes literacy), the figures above provide a good guide to overall trends.

---

state schools in which students destined for bureaucratic positions were trained to read and write their native languages (including the Magyar, Croatian, Slovak, Romanian, and Ruthenian of the empire's ethnic minorities, in addition to German).

Some privately endowed schools were created specifically for girls, including two of the most famous schools of the era, at Port-Royal and Saint-Cyr, both in France. A century later, in Russia, Empress Catherine the Great (r. 1763–1796) founded the Smolny Institute, a school for 500 daughters of noblemen, modeled on Saint-Cyr. All of these girls' schools aimed to prepare their students for marriage and polite society, rather than for scholarship or public life, since the future leaders of society were overwhelmingly male. Wealthy boys were often tutored at home, while their sisters sometimes listened in.

At the advanced level, the European universities continued to train physicians, lawyers, clergymen, and philosophers. Their enrollments grew, however, as more laymen and students from the lesser nobility and the middle classes attended. A university education was a prerequisite for entry to the professions. Hence women, barred from universities into modern times, failed to enter professional careers. While the older universities in Italy and France experienced some stagnation, others flourished, especially in the Dutch Republic and in Scotland. New universities continued to be founded notably in the German lands, Spain, Spanish America, and British North America.

Elementary schools succeeded in raising rates of literacy in the vernacular languages in western Europe. Overall, more than fifty percent of city dwellers gained basic literacy, and not all peasants (as was once the case) were illiterate. While men attained higher literacy rates, women too experienced rising literacy. Women became an important component of the reading audience, and tended to support women authors, to read novels about women's experience, and to subscribe to periodical publications pertaining to women's lives.

While the sons of elite groups learned Latin and perhaps Greek, for most people literacy meant the ability to read the vernacular language of their state. In the early modern centuries, these vernacular languages were just becoming standardized, as on form or regional dialect took precedence over others. This process can often be linked to the emergence of a preeminent literary figure and the adoption of his works as national "classics." Dante (1265–1321) performed this service for Italian, and Luther, in his translation of the Bible, for German. The dramatist William Shakespeare (1564–1616) was a key figure in the creation of modern English, and the French language reached a similar peak in the mock-heroic works of François Rabelais (c. 1494–c. 1553). For Spanish, the novel *Don Quixote* by Miguel de Cervantes (1547–1616) is central. Some of the major scientific and philosophical works of the early modern period were likewise also written in vernacular languages, for example those by Galileo in Italian and Descartes in French.

By the seventeenth century, standardization of the grammar and spelling of European languages followed. Vernacular dictionaries became available in some languages, and boards of experts such as the French Academy, established in 1634, met to regularize and safeguard the newly formed modern languages. Latin remained into the nineteenth century (into the twentieth in parts of eastern Europe) a useful language for communicating philosophy, science, medicine, theology, law, and sometimes history. But from the seventeenth century most literature, political theory, and other ideas were expressed in the vernacular whose readership formed the widest possible circle.

The development of vernacular languages was aided by the printing press, while printing establishments benefited from larger audiences. The scope of printed material expanded as vernacular readers bought more books.

In the sixteenth century—the first full century of printing—religious and classical works dominated. The Bible, saints' lives, prayerbooks and other devotional works, were initially the works most favoured by presses and sought by readers. The war between the Protestant Reformation and Roman Catholicism from the early sixteenth century was waged in print. With regard to Classical works, the first aim was to produce clear, legible, and accurate versions of ancient Latin and Greek texts. By 1500, however, vernacular translations were being produced, making such authors as Cicero, Plutarch, and Tacitus available to a wider public.

The vernacular readership was interested in a diverse range of subjects. They bought almanacs and books on etiquette and history, animal husbandry, beermaking or viniculture, and collections of choral hymns. They read fairy tales and novels, kept abreast of things with newspapers (published daily in the big cities of the later eighteenth century) and laughed at satirical cartoons. They studied the explorers' narratives of their journeys to the New World, and sought advice about marriage, childrearing, and childbirth. These books opened a world of knowledge to audiences beyond the university and the monastery: with the Enlightenment, for the first time in Europe, the lights turned on in the homes of ordinary folk.

Major printing centers included Venice, Rome, Basel (Switzerland), Strasbourg, Antwerp, Amsterdam, London, and Paris. These cities were magnets for editors, translators, and authors from many countries, who joined intellectuals and artists in a process that stimulated new understandings.

Such a lively intellectual milieu led to the expression of unconventional ideas that often provoked official censorship, which in turn broached the issue of free speech. Many of the *philosophes'* books were censored but continued to be distributed via a covert trade in prohibited books. Bayle and Locke published their work in the safe haven of the Dutch Republic, where dissent was tolerated, but Voltaire and Diderot, in France, found some of their works condemned. Rousseau learned from a bookseller friend of the fate of his book on educational proposals: "I saw your *Emile . . .* publicly consigned to the flames in Madrid," he wrote, in front of a Dominican church one Sunday "in the presence of a whole crowd of gaping imbeciles." Demand for the book soared.

The English Puritan poet John Milton (1608–1674) addressed the problem of the regulation of ideas, hurling against a recent act of Parliament to censor "scandalous, seditious and libellous works" an elegant and impassioned defense of free speech

In Defense of The Worth of Women

Juan Luis Vives	*The Instruction of a Christian Woman* (1523)
Henry Cornelius Agrippa von Nettesheim	*On the Nobility and Preeminence of the Female Sex* (1529)
Moderata Fonte	*The Worth of Women* (1600)
Lucrezia Marinella	*The Nobility and Excellence of Women* (1601)
Marie de Gournay	*The Equality of Men and Women* (1622)
Anna Maria van Schurman	*Whether a Christian Woman should be Educated* (1650)
François Poulain de la Barre	*On the Equality of the Two Sexes* (1674)

and free thought. "For books are not absolutely dead things, but do contain a potency of life in them to be as active as the soul was whose progeny they are," Milton argued in his *Areopagitica*. "Who kills a man kills a reasonable creature, … but he who destroys a good book, kills reason itself." It is no accident that, in this environment of intellectual debate women thinkers began actively to assert the worth of the female sex and the unacknowledged capacity of the female mind.

A Cat and a Catte: Women and Learning

Marie de Gournay (1565–1645), close associate of the French essayist Michel de Montaigne, observed of the graceful creature adorning her room that there was no difference between *un chat* ("a cat") and *une chatte* ("a catte," or female cat): "the human animal is neither male nor female." That conclusion was reached—and even then, accepted by few—only after a struggle over the nature of female identity known as the *querelle des femmes* ("the debate on women").

The *querelle* had its origins in the deep misogyny of medieval literature, which presented women as vain, self-centered, deceitful, corrupting, and lecherous. Beginning with Christine de Pisan (1364–c. 1430) (see Chapter 12), a series of authors in most of the

Women and Learning

Louis Michel Dumesnil, **Queen Christina of Sweden with Descartes:** *Only a minority of major scientific and philosophical figures during the seventeenth and eighteenth centuries considered women to be intellectually equal to men. One such was René Descartes, who is seen here, seated at a table, engaged in tutoring Queen Christina of Sweden.* (Palace of Versailles, France)

Attributed to Jan van Belcamp, The Clifford "Great Picture": *The Englishwoman Lady Clifford, seen in the panel at left with her books in a painting from around 1646, was a contemporary of Queen Christina of Sweden and profited from a similar sort of tutoring. Contrast the portrait of Margaret Cavendish on p. 507, depicted in her library amid her fantasies but without books!* (Collection of Abbot Hall Art Gallery, England)

European languages—some male but mostly female—wrote in defense of women. Their defenses elicited a correspondingly large group of responses. Through the course of this *querelle* may be traced an increasingly sophisticated justification for the spiritual and intellectual equality of the female to the male.

The first stage of the debate included many catalogues of "women worthies"—powerful and important women in history and legend. More serious issues pertaining to women's spiritual and intellectual equality were developed by Italian humanists, especially among women humanists (see "Nogarola" in Chapter 13), whose arguments were elaborated in the sixteenth century by Erasmus (c. 1466–1536) and Vives (1492–1540), and especially by Henry Cornelius Agrippa von Nettesheim (1486–1535), a philosopher and physician who also dabbled in alchemy. Agrippa not merely defended women but proposed their supremacy. His work *On the Nobility and Preeminence of the Female Sex* was widely translated and imitated, influencing two notable seventeenth-century works: Marie de Gournay's *The Equality of Men and Women* (1622) and Lucrezia Marinella's (1571–1653) *The Nobility and Excellence of Women*. With Mary Wollstonecraft's *A Vindication of the Rights of Woman* (1792), this tradition reaches its culmination.

A closely related issue was women's capacity for education. Their defenders include the influential Dutch scholar Anna Maria van Schurman (1607–1678), whose Latin treatise *On the Capacity of the Female Mind for Learning* was widely read in translation, and her contemporary, the Englishwoman Margaret Cavendish, Duchess of Newcastle (c. 1623–1673), depicted in *Windows On* on p. 507 who grumpily complained about the limitations of her own training: "As for learning, that I am not versed in it, no body, I hope, will blame me for it, since it is sufficiently known, that our sex is not brought up to it, as being not suffered to be instructed in schools and universities." Around 1700, Cavendish's compatriot Mary Astell (1666–1731) urged the higher education of women in a kind of Protestant nunnery, set apart from male-dominated society, in her *Serious Proposal to the Ladies*. In France, meanwhile, François Poulain de la Barre (1647–1723) presented a comprehensive defense of female capacity for advanced education in his book *On the Equality of the Two Sexes*, quoted in *Witnesses* on p. 506 while Bernard de Fontenelle (1657–1757) designed his work on scientific popularization, *Conversations on the Plurality of Worlds*, as a dialogue between a philosopher and a woman. Finally, the Marquis de Condorcet advocated not only women's equal capacity for advanced education, but, additionally and unprecedentedly, their participation as citizens in public affairs. The illustrations above and on p. 504 show two women who benefitted from private tutoring; Queen Christina was taught by Descartes himself.

Women Writers Even as the debate about women's nature and rationality reached a higher pitch, women had begun to write (see Chapters 10, 12, 13). Prior to the Renaissance, nearly all women's public writing

Women, Men, and Learning

The debate over women's capacity for knowledge began well before the Enlightenment. However, in an era that stressed reason as the essential human trait, it became all the more important for women to claim for themselves the capacity to reason. That claim is made effectively by two seventeenth-century thinkers, the male Poulain de la Barre, who argues the full equality of the sexes on the basis of their mental capacities, and Mary Astell, who advanced the argument that at least some women should pursue a serious education.

François Poulain de la Barre declares that the mind has no sex (1673): It is easy to see that sexual differences apply only to the body since ... it is only the body which is used for human reproduction; the mind is involved in reproduction only in giving its assent and, since it does this in the same way in everyone, one may conclude that it has no sex.

If one considers the mind in itself, one finds that it is equal and has the same nature in all human beings, and that it is capable of all kinds of thoughts. ... The difference between the sexes does not result from their minds. ...

This is even more obvious if we consider the head, which is the unique organ of the sciences and the place where the mind exercises all its functions. Our most accurate anatomical investigations do not uncover any difference between men and women in this part of the body. The brain of women is exactly like ours.

(François Poulain de la Barre, *On the Equality of the Two Sexes,* 1673; ed. D. M. Clarke, 1990)

Mary Astell explains why men seem to know more than women (c. 1700): There are strong and prevalent reasons which demonstrate the superiority and preeminence of the men. For in the first place, boys have much time and pains, care and cost bestowed on their education, girls have little or none. The former are early initiated in the sciences, are made acquainted with ancient and modern discoveries, they study books and men, have all imaginable encouragement. ... The latter are restrained, frowned upon, and beaten ...; laughter and ridicule, that never-failing scarecrow, is set up to drive them from the tree of knowledge. But if in spite of all difficulties nature prevails, and they can't be kept so ignorant as their masters would have them, they are stared upon as monsters, censured, envied, and every way discouraged.

(Mary Astell, *The First English Feminist: Reflections on Marriage and Other Writings;* ed. B. Hill, 1986)

was religious. Saints and nuns, writing themselves or through dictation to confessors or mentors, had contributed to the Western mystical tradition as well as to a female tradition of self-exploration. In the Renaissance, women humanists, while not departing from a Christian framework, used Classical models in their letters, orations, and dialogues, which often gave expression to strong feminist themes.

The next three centuries saw an explosion of female creativity, as the grip of a traditional intellectual culture, dominated by the university, Latin, and the priesthood, weakened. The humanist dethroning of medieval Scholasticism (see Chapter 13), the use of the vernacular, the proliferation of the printshop, the views of Locke and Descartes, which located the ability to think in a mind unformed by class, profession, or gender, and the new worlds opened by explorers or discovered by scientists, all combined to create a milieu in which women felt free to write and impelled to express themselves.

In Italy, the number of published women writers soared to around 250 for the period from 1500 to 1700. Of these, about a third continued to write on religious themes but others composed love poems (mostly courtesans), occasional letters, and moral treatises which were sought by publishers and purchased by the public in great quantity. In England and France, works by, for, and about women increased markedly in the seventeenth century.

What did women write about? Some wrote devotional works, but the proportion of these to the whole of women's production diminished sharply after 1600. Some wrote about the family, others wrote about themselves. Some joined in discussions of philosophy, science, language, and love; they wrote histories or biographies, or translated the works of famous men; they wrote poetry or **novels**, a genre which originated in the seventeenth century and was influenced by the need to address a female readership. One scholar counts 106 women authors of 568 novels writing in English before Jane Austen (1775–1817) became, as used to be thought, the "first" woman novelist.

Works about the family predominate. Women wrote diaries about their experience as mothers and wives, and guidebooks to life and manners for their children. The Jewish woman Glückel (1656–1724) of Hameln, a widow who had survived two husbands and raised twelve children, described in her memoirs the resourcefulness, diligence, and faith that allowed the family to survive in the world of seventeenth-century mid-European ghettoes. Arcangela Tarabotti (1604–1652) wrote in protest of "paternal tyranny" in Catholic Italy, where fathers disposed of superfluous daughters in convents. Women wrote against the constraints of marriage, as did Mary Astell in her *Reflections on Marriage,* quoted in *Witnesses* on the left, and the Italian Moderata Fonte (1555–1592) in her dialogue on *Women's Worth.* The chief speaker

Anna Morandi Manzolini

Elisabetha and Johannes Hevelius, 1673

Margaret Cavendish, Duchess of Newcastle

Among Western nations, Italy offered perhaps the best environment for women scientists. Anna Morandi Manzolini (top), for example, made several original discoveries in anatomy and held a professorship at the University of Bologna from 1760 until her death in 1774. In many cases, women accepted and repeated arguments about their intellectual inferiority to men. Margaret Cavendish, Duchess of Newcastle (left), herself an active participant in the important scientific debates of her time, nonetheless stated that women's brains were "cold" and "soft" compared to men's. Women often worked alongside their more celebrated husbands as scientific assistants or, occasionally, as full partners. In a print from 1673 (above) Elisabetha and Johannes Hevelius take astronomical readings together using a sextant.

Why might it be even more difficult for women to enter the sciences than other learned pursuits?

To continue your investigation of this topic, please go to www.prenhall.com/king for the related **WINDOWS** on the **WEB** activity

Discourse in Salons and Academies

A. Lemonnier, The Salon of Madame Geoffrin: *Educated women played a key role in spreading Enlightenment culture through the many salons they ran. In this painting from 1812 an actor reads from Voltaire at the salon of Madame Geoffrin. Some of the most famous philosophes found a congenial atmosphere for debate and philosophy.* (Châteaux de Malmaison et Bois-Préau, France)

Members of the French Royal Academy of Sciences: *During the eighteenth century, learning became an important cultural accomplishment among the well-to-do. New ideas and philosophies were spread via various media. Of great importance were the growing number of scientific academies established from the seventeenth century on. In this 1666 tapestry by Henri Testelin, members of the French Royal Academy of Sciences gather for their inaugural meeting.* (Palace of Versailles, France)

in the latter work proclaims proudly: "I would rather die than subordinate myself to any man."

Women also participated in the discussion of pedagogy, defending the educability of women. They debated the theories of Descartes in France and Italy, and studied Platonism in England. In Italy, Lucrezia Marinella demonstrated an encyclopedic command of contemporary philosophical debates in the seventeenth century, and Laura Bassi pursued a professional scientific career in the eighteenth. The French noblewoman Emilie du Châtelet (1706–1749), Voltaire's patron and lover, worked daily on the latest problems raised by science and philosophy. In England, Lady Mary Wortley Montagu published a newspaper that discussed current philosophical and political issues.

In France, meanwhile, women acted as literary critics and promoted an elaborate, stylized manner of speaking and writing that earned them the name *les précieuses* (the precious ones). Brilliant women hosted **salons**, sessions in their homes attended by the leading men of letters of the day in which new ideas were debated and criticized. Although not themselves *philosophes* or authors, Madame Geoffrin (1699–1777), Madame du Deffand (1697–1780), and the latter's former protegée Julie de Lespinasses (1732–1776), were leaders of intellectual conversation in Paris at a time when to think was to converse, and when Paris led Europe in the generation of ideas. Madame Geoffrin's salon is shown on p. 508.

The English playwright and novelist Aphra Behn presents an outstanding case of the woman author who recognized the predicament she faced as an educated woman in a society dominated by men. During her adventurous youth she lived in the Dutch colony of Surinam in South America, served as a spy in the Netherlands, and married a Dutch businessman, whose death in 1666 when she was twenty-five freed her for a writer's career. Behn's distinctively feminist plays (successfully staged in London in the 1670s and 1680s) explored the realms of marriage and adultery, featuring plucky heroines who defied male power and greed. Her plays were among the first on the English stage to employ female actresses. Her thirteen novels may perhaps establish her, 150 years before Austen, as the first woman novelist in English. Among these is the extraordinary *Oroonoko*, set in the New World, with its uncompromising repudiation of slavery. In her own words, she faulted the prejudices that had for too long kept women from receiving a serious education:

> *Permitting not the female sex to tread,*
> *The mighty paths of learned heroes dead …*

Conscious of her talents and ambitious to win the fame due to her, she sought above all the freedom that male writers enjoyed: "If I must not because of my sex, have this freedom, I lay down my quill and you shall hear no more of me … I value fame as much as if I had been born a hero." Seeing no difference between a catte and a cat, Behn claimed her due place in the world of letters.

In the early modern centuries, women began to emerge from the subordinate position in which they had previously been placed by custom and belief. Women thinkers and writers, who first confronted on the level of language the assumptions that had kept them imprisoned, were the pioneers of that advance. Wider social change would follow later; at the end of the twentieth century, that process was not yet everywhere completed.

Halls of Reason: The Social Context

If the disputation was characteristic of the intellectual life of the Middle Ages, the collection was characteristic of the early modern period: collections of books, natural objects, and scientific instruments; and collections of people interested in intellectual pursuits.

In the early modern era, the passion for collecting (previously confined to kings) spread to members of the nobility, bourgeoisie, and learned elite. Objects that were precious or unusual because of their antiquity, craftsmanship, or materials; items brought from across the wide oceans now navigated by European ships; and exotic plants and animals found their way into famous collections. The apartments of the Habsburg emperor Rudolph II (1576–1612) were littered with clocks and machinery, books and statues,

---

Official Scientific Academies in Europe During the Eighteenth Century

	Official Scientific Societies in all Europe (excluding colonies)	Official Scientific Societies in France
1700	5	2
1789	65	29

Much more than universities, scientific academies were the vital institutions of scientific discourse during the Scientific Revolution and Enlightenment. The great increase in their number during the eighteenth century testifies to the growing interest in science among the governments, crowns, and other elites who funded them. The table above shows only official societies (ones formally recognized or funded by their respective governments).

Source: *Based on J. E. McClellan III,* Science Reorganized: Scientific Societies in the Eighteenth Century *(New York: Columbia University Press, 1985), pp. 261–280.*

while paintings lined the walls. Remnants of antiquity, contemporary art works, and scientific and musical instruments were heaped together as a kind of summation of all that was known and valued. More specialized collections developed in the hands of scholars, scientists, or wealthy amateurs. The sixteenth-century Italian Ulisse Aldrovandi (1522–1605) gathered specimens of rare and exotic creatures, which were visited by at least the 1579 persons who signed his guest book (at least ten percent were members of the nobility). By the eighteenth century the gentleman-collector's study and the dilettante prince's palace crammed with curios had given rise to the first modern museums: the Ashmolean in Oxford, the British Museum in London, the Brera in Milan, the Louvre in Paris.

The society of the learned gathered together in a range of associations. In Renaissance Italy, humanists met in the gardens of their patrons for polite conversations; later, during the sixteenth century, they moved into academies. These were associations in which both noble and commoner, and male and female participants mingled to discuss ideas, the arts, or the news of the day. In the informal and vivid setting of the academy, ideas and styles originated that could not have been heard in the hierarchical setting of the university or court.

In the seventeenth century, north of the Alps, academies took a different direction. More official and formal, they served as laboratories for the creation of new knowledge. The French Royal Academy of Sciences, established by King Louis XIV in 1666 (its members are depicted on p. 508), was expected both to explore technologies useful to the state and to reflect glory upon the monarch. Provincial academies encouraged both literary and scientific activities, frequently sponsoring essay competitions or rewarding exceptional achievement. Private academies and literary societies on the Italian model also flourished, in France closely resembling private salons. The English Royal Society, founded like the French by royal initiative in 1662, left its members entirely free to pursue their own interests. By 1670 its membership numbered 200 and included, alongside amateur merchants and artisans, a number of the most prominent scientists, mathematicians, and philosophers in the nation.

Outside these gatherings of professional thinkers, people gathered informally in the hundreds of coffeehouses and clubs that sprang up in the cities of western Europe. The English insurance company Lloyds grew up in one London coffeehouse visited by businessmen engaged in international shipping; in another, courses on Newtonian mechanics and optics were available. Members of private clubs or Masonic lodges formed reading groups and developed lending libraries. The salons over which gifted women presided in the major European capitals brought together the wealthy, the learned, and the famous to discuss the latest literary or philosophical works.

Informal associations of the learned and talented, at first in Italy, subsequently in the Netherlands, France, and England, were the matrix of the new ideas and visions that fueled the Enlightenment. Superseding the monastery, the cathedral, and the court, more lively than the contemporary university, located in homes and shops that were magnets alike for those with a little or a great deal of learning, they were the halls of reason that characterize the age as much as the monarchs' halls of mirrors. Here the age of reason took form, guided by the transcendent discoveries of intellectual leaders and extended by the buzzing conversation of their readers, followers, and admirers.

Conclusion
DESCARTES' DILEMMA AND THE MEANING OF THE WEST

Because he thought, Descartes concluded, he must exist. And because he existed, he could know. It was confidence in the knowability of things that knit the intellectual world of the West into one system and that gave the Enlightenment its momentum. In the early modern centuries, the rationalism of Western culture that was already apparent in medieval thought was reaffirmed. But now reason reigned alone and triumphant, sharing no space with the Christian faith that had unified the West in the Middle Ages. Loosed from its moorings in faith, expanding around the globe, certain of the knowledge it garnered from the operations of reason, the civilization of the West approached the threshold of the modern age fired with confidence and titanic ambition.

QUESTIONS TO CONSIDER

1. Why does it make a difference whether the earth or the sun is at the center of the universe? Why does it make a difference if there are many or infinite universes, and not just one?

2. Why is it important that the astronomical patterns and events, as well as the movements of bodies on the Earth, can be expressed mathematically?

3. Why was the dissection of human bodies the key to opening up modern medicine? Is this step in any way comparable to contemporary astronomical explorations?

4. Why did many Enlightenment thinkers see the church as an enemy of reason? What is the relation between the increase in literacy and the increase in women's literacy?

SUGGESTED RESOURCES

Biagioli, Mario, *Galileo, Courtier: The Practice of Science in the Culture of Absolutism* (Chicago: University of Chicago Press, 1993). Explains how Galileo rose to prominence by relying on practices of patronage traditional in courtly society.

Brockliss, L. W. B., *Calvet's Web: Enlightenment and the Republic of Letters in Eighteenth-Century France* (Oxford: Oxford University Press, 2002). Traces the network of correspondence of an Avignon physician from 1750 until 1810, showing how a an Enlightenment community of the learned was welded out of words.

Chartier, Roger, *The Order of Books: Readers, Authors and Libraries in Europe between the 14th and 18th Centuries* (trans. Lydia G. Cochrane; Stanford: Stanford University Press, 1994). Relates how developments in the tracking, indexing, and ordering of books created a new world of knowledge between the late Middle Ages and the Enlightenment.

Christianson, John Robert, *On Tycho's Island: Tycho Brahe and his Assistants, 1570–1601* (Cambridge: Cambridge University Press, 2000). Reveals Brahe as a master administrator of a scientific research organization and publicist of a scientific world view.

Crosby, Alfred W., *The Measure of Reality: Quantification and Western Society, 1250–1600* (Cambridge: Cambridge University Press, 1997). By the sixteenth century, Europeans had exceeded every other civilization in its use of quantification—in map-making, clock-making, record-keeping, musical notation, painting, and numerous other endeavors—laying the basis for the distinctly Western path of modernization.

Dobbs, Betty Jo Teeter, *The Janus Faces of Genius: The Role of Alchemy in Newton's Thought* (Cambridge: Cambridge University Press, 1991). Far from being a rationalist who rejected religion, Newton is revealed in this major reconceptualization of his role as dedicated to bringing natural philosophical and religious truth together into one system.

Goldsmith, Elizabeth, ed., *Going Public: Women and Publishing in Early Modern France* (Ithaca: Cornell University Press, 1995). Essay collection exploring how French women writers "went public" in the 17th and 18th centuries, seeking wider audiences for the memoirs, novels, and poems that had previously circulated in coterie circles.

Goodman, Dena, *The Republic of Letters: A Cultural History of the French Enlightenment* (Ithaca: Cornell University Press, 1994). Focusing largely on salons, argues that women provided sociability, discussion, and civility to the overall culture of the Enlightenment.

Grafton, Anthony, *Cardano's Cosmos: the Worlds and Works of a Renaissance Astrologer* (Cambridge MA–London: Harvard University Press, 1999). Famed as a physician, mathematician, and scientist, Cardano was also known and courted throughout Europe as an astrologer, whose predictions were widely sought by the wealthy and powerful.

Lewalski, Barbara K., *Writing Women in Jacobean England* (Cambridge, MA: Harvard University Press, 1993). Focuses on educated, typically aristocratic, women and their relationship—either as patrons or writers—with print culture during the early 17th century.

Outram, Dorinda, *The Enlightenment* (Cambridge: Cambridge University Press, 1995). An up-to-date synthesis, placing the remarkable intellectual motor of the Enlightenment in the context of changing social structures, gender roles, and global ventures.

Porter, Roy, *The Creation of the Modern World: The Untold Story of the British Enlightenment* (New York: W.W. Norton, 2000). Whereas Enlightenment surveys often dwell on French giants like Montesquieu, Diderot, Voltaire, and Rousseau, Porter gives the credit for the development of a modern world view to Britain.

Ridley, Jasper, *The Freemasons: A History of the World's Most Powerful Secret Society* (New York: Arcade, 2002). History of a secret society emerging from a medieval craft guild, treasuring ancient Egyptian lore, and enrolling some of the major intellectuals and political actors in the century of the Enlightenment.

Sobel, Dava, *Longitude: the True Story of a Lone Genius Who Solved the Greatest Scientific Problem of his Time* (Walker & Co., 1995). A vivid narration of how one British clockmaker created the sea-borne chronometer, which permitted sailors to determine with accuracy the longitude of their ship.

Printing: history, resources, links:
http://www.digitalcentury.com/enyclo/update/print.html

Shakespeare's Globe Theater (University of Reading, UK):
http://www.rdg.ac.uk/globe/home.htm

Johann Kepler, 1571–1630 (Rice University):
http://es.rice.edu/ES/humsoc/Galileo/People/kepler.html

Early Modern Women Online: bibliography and web resources (Folger):
http://chnm.gmu.edu/emw/bibliography.htm

⚙ Western Civilization Documents CD-ROM

13.1 Francis Bacon: from First Book of Aphorisms
13.2 Miguel de Cervantes: Chapter 1 from Don Quixote
13.3 John Bunyan: from Pilgrim's Progress
13.5 Rejecting Aristotle: Galileo Defends the Heliocentric View
13.6 Rethinking the Bible: Galileo Confronts his Critics
18.1 John Locke: Essay Concerning Human Understanding
18.2 David Hume: Of the Dignity or Meanness of Human Nature
18.3 Charles Montesquieu: The Spirit of the Laws
18.4 The Encyclopedia
18.5 A Doctor Criticizes Midwives
18.6 Medicine from Turkey: The Small Pox Vaccination
18.7 Adam Smith: Division of Labor

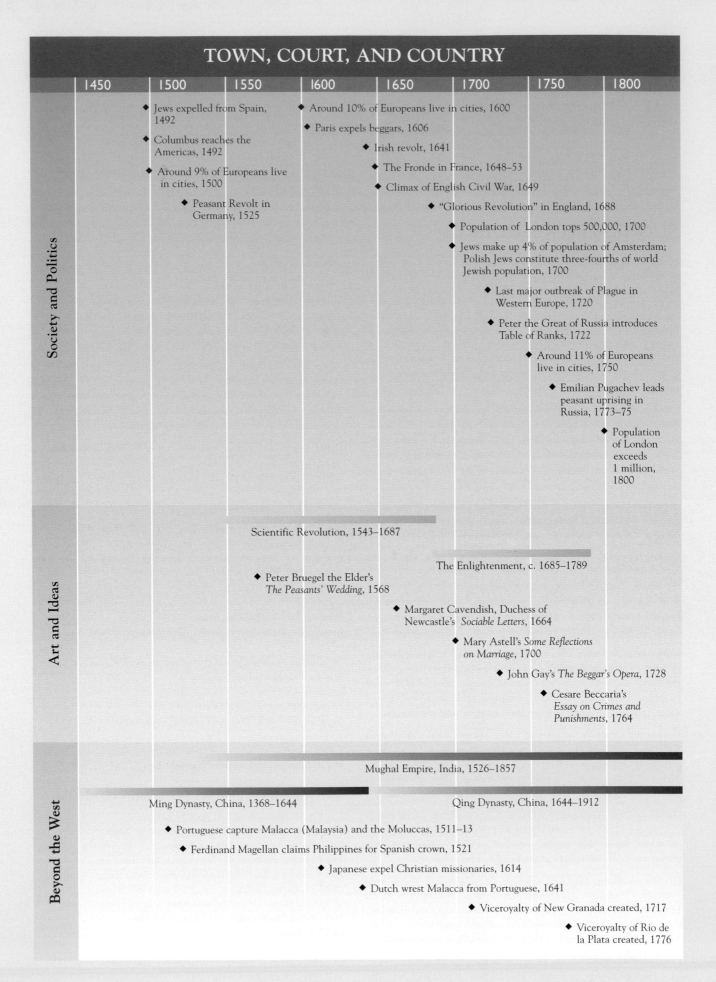

TOWN, COURT, AND COUNTRY

| | 1450 | 1500 | 1550 | 1600 | 1650 | 1700 | 1750 | 1800 |

Society and Politics

- Jews expelled from Spain, 1492
- Columbus reaches the Americas, 1492
- Around 9% of Europeans live in cities, 1500
- Peasant Revolt in Germany, 1525
- Around 10% of Europeans live in cities, 1600
- Paris expels beggars, 1606
- Irish revolt, 1641
- The Fronde in France, 1648–53
- Climax of English Civil War, 1649
- "Glorious Revolution" in England, 1688
- Population of London tops 500,000, 1700
- Jews make up 4% of population of Amsterdam; Polish Jews constitute three-fourths of world Jewish population, 1700
- Last major outbreak of Plague in Western Europe, 1720
- Peter the Great of Russia introduces Table of Ranks, 1722
- Around 11% of Europeans live in cities, 1750
- Emilian Pugachev leads peasant uprising in Russia, 1773–75
- Population of London exceeds 1 million, 1800

Art and Ideas

Scientific Revolution, 1543–1687

The Enlightenment, c. 1685–1789

- Peter Bruegel the Elder's *The Peasants' Wedding*, 1568
- Margaret Cavendish, Duchess of Newcastle's *Sociable Letters*, 1664
- Mary Astell's *Some Reflections on Marriage*, 1700
- John Gay's *The Beggar's Opera*, 1728
- Cesare Beccaria's *Essay on Crimes and Punishments*, 1764

Beyond the West

Mughal Empire, India, 1526–1857

Ming Dynasty, China, 1368–1644

Qing Dynasty, China, 1644–1912

- Portuguese capture Malacca (Malaysia) and the Moluccas, 1511–13
- Ferdinand Magellan claims Philippines for Spanish crown, 1521
- Japanese expel Christian missionaries, 1614
- Dutch wrest Malacca from Portuguese, 1641
- Viceroyalty of New Granada created, 1717
- Viceroyalty of Rio de la Plata created, 1776

18 TOWN, COURT, AND COUNTRY

Privilege and Poverty in Early Modern Europe

1500–1780

Europe in the 18th century

- areas with a population of over 40 per square km
- areas with a population of 20-40 per square km
- ● cities with populations of over 500,000
- • cities with populations of 100,000-500,000

KEY QUESTIONS

◆ **Honorable Pursuits:** How did monarchs exalt themselves above the nobility, and how did nobles reassert their worth and honor in an age of kings?

◆ **New Ways with New Wealth:** How did the advancing bourgeoisie live in the expanding cities? What were the circumstances of the urban poor?

◆ **Field and Village:** How did technological advances affect rural life in western Europe? Why did the condition of the eastern European peasantry deteriorate in the early modern period?

The Would-Be Gentleman The French playwright Molière (1622–1673) amused King Louis XIV (r. 1643–1715) with sprightly comedies lampooning hypocrites, pretentious ladies, hypochondriacs, and social-climbing members of the bourgeoisie—such as Monsieur Jourdain, the main character in The Would-Be Gentleman. In his desperate effort to turn himself into a nobleman, Jourdain hires a music master, a dancing master, and a philosopher—but fails hilariously. Molière's play, first performed in 1670, highlights the key social issue of the age: the exclusive hold on status and privilege retained by the nobility, and the subordination of all other social groups.

The would-be gentleman was laughable to his audience because he yearned to acquire a status to which he was not born. The early modern age (approximately the period from 1500 to 1750) was still one of social orders entered at birth, altered rarely, and only at great cost. The great representative assemblies of the emerging states of Europe (see Chapter 15) were constituted by delegates from the constituent orders of clergy (the first order or "Estate"), nobles (the second), and commoners (the third, understood to include everyone from the urban bourgeoisie to the peasant in the fields); the British Parliament reduced the three orders to two, creating a bicameral legislature of nobles or "Lords" and "Commoners." In terms of culture, too, each order had its customs. The aristocracy developed an elaborate code of behavior, that preserved their preeminence and set the standard for all subordinate classes. The artisans and merchants of growing towns and cities developed a new taste for luxury, education and the arts. The poor in town and country had neither the wealth nor leisure to cultivate a taste for luxury, but continued to engage in the rituals of village life, or to explore the new possibilities of gin lanes or the poorhouse.

The members of each order strove at least to maintain, or better, to surpass the social status they had inherited from their parents. As Molière's bourgeois gentleman strove to be like the nobility, nobles strove to be like kings, and kings raised themselves above humanity. Beneath the ranks of the bourgeoisie, artisans and shopkeepers also craved the marks of social prestige, lest they fall further down the ladder of social rank. There the quest for prestige dimmed. Workers, migrants, and servants fought to survive, along with deserted women and children and the destitute. The struggle of the poor for subsistence and the aspirations of the propertied for status in town, court, and country mark the social relations of the early modern era. They foreshadow the boundaries of social class that still prevail in the Western world today. The diagram on p. 515 show different patterns of social inequality.

HONORABLE PURSUITS: THE EUROPEAN NOBILITY OF THE EARLY MODERN AGE

Comprising between one and ten percent of the population in most parts of Europe, the nobility was the traditional landowning and military class. Noble prestige was defended by the idea of honor, which expressed pride in ancient heritage and moral code. Its status increased in the early modern era because of its monopoly of cultural refinement and its closeness to those who held real power: the kings.

Lines and Houses

Europe's most powerful noblemen came from ancient "**lines**" that held title to ancient "**houses**." The line was the series of family connections leading back through male ancestors to the earliest possessors of the land that gave the family its noble status. The "house" was the place or even the building with which the family was associated and from which it took its aristocratic title. For example, the Marquis de Lafayette (1757–1834), a participant in both the American and French revolutions (see Chapters 19, 20), was a member of the house of Lafayette; his family name, seldom used, was "du Motier."

The preeminence of the house in defining noble status stemmed from the nobility's original role in European society in the Middle Ages (see Chapter 9). Because land was originally the reward bestowed by a monarch for military service, it was the nobleman's identity as warrior that established his right as householder. It also provided the emblems of his high social status, the shield and the sword. The symbols decorating a nobleman's shield—his coat of arms—would once have served to identify fully-armed knights on the battlefield.

Shield and sword represented the value of **honor** that noblemen believed was uniquely theirs. To maintain noble status, it was not sufficient or even necessary to be wealthy; it was only necessary to preserve one's honor. In this cause, European aristocrats were willing to kill or be killed, often resorting to dueling as a ritualized form of private warfare. At the same time, the European nobleman could still win honor in the manner of his medieval forebears in the frequent real wars that engulfed Europe in the early modern era. The mounted knight became an army officer, in a transformation that helped the aristocracy to keep its hold into the twentieth century on senior military positions. Away from the battlefield, meanwhile, the nobleman was a hunter, intent on fine sport, good exercise, and dominion over the forest. When nobles entered their treed reserves, accompanied by their wives and servants, they were demonstrating their power over nature itself. Poor men might have the right to gather chestnuts or firewood

Social Inequalities

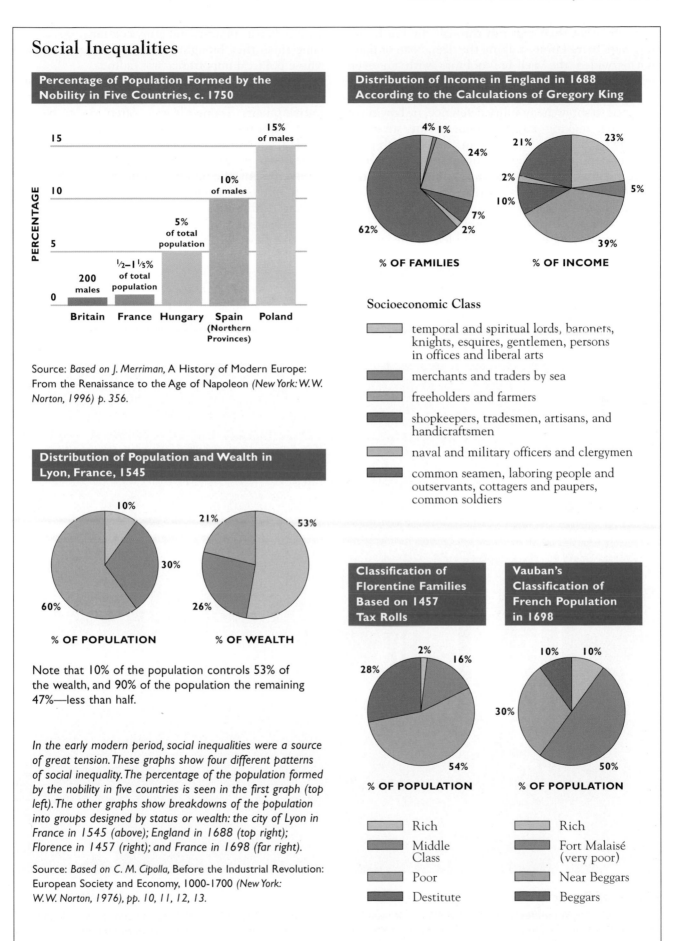

Percentage of Population Formed by the Nobility in Five Countries, c. 1750

Source: *Based on J. Merriman,* A History of Modern Europe: From the Renaissance to the Age of Napoleon *(New York: W.W. Norton, 1996) p. 356.*

Distribution of Population and Wealth in Lyon, France, 1545

Note that 10% of the population controls 53% of the wealth, and 90% of the population the remaining 47%—less than half.

In the early modern period, social inequalities were a source of great tension. These graphs show four different patterns of social inequality. The percentage of the population formed by the nobility in five countries is seen in the first graph (top left). The other graphs show breakdowns of the population into groups designed by status or wealth: the city of Lyon in France in 1545 (above); England in 1688 (top right); Florence in 1457 (right); and France in 1698 (far right).

Source: *Based on C. M. Cipolla,* Before the Industrial Revolution: European Society and Economy, 1000-1700 *(New York: W.W. Norton, 1976), pp. 10, 11, 12, 13.*

Distribution of Income in England in 1688 According to the Calculations of Gregory King

% OF FAMILIES

% OF INCOME

Socioeconomic Class

- temporal and spiritual lords, baronets, knights, esquires, gentlemen, persons in offices and liberal arts
- merchants and traders by sea
- freeholders and farmers
- shopkeepers, tradesmen, artisans, and handicraftsmen
- naval and military officers and clergymen
- common seamen, laboring people and outservants, cottagers and paupers, common soldiers

Classification of Florentine Families Based on 1457 Tax Rolls

% OF POPULATION

- Rich
- Middle Class
- Poor
- Destitute

Vauban's Classification of French Population in 1698

% OF POPULATION

- Rich
- Fort Malaisé (very poor)
- Near Beggars
- Beggars

there, or to let their pigs run through the brush, but they were barred from stalking the deer, boar, or hares that provided the well-fed nobility with an even richer diet of meat.

Men and women of other social groups were expected to show the nobility deference, by bowing or curtseying, making way for them in the street, or yielding to them the front pew in church. Such privileges of nobility were legally enforceable. The nobleman, in turn, was accustomed to wielding authority over those of lesser social status. The French writer Voltaire (see Chapter 17) had little recourse against a lofty nobleman who took revenge on him for insults in print by having him beaten and left in the street.

During the early modern era the intrusion into the old nobility of men possessed of wealth or professional skills changed the nature of the class. New nobles, called *noblesse de robe* ("of the robe") in France after the robes worn by judges, assimilated quickly to the old nobility "of the sword." They purchased land and

acquired coats of arms and army commissions. At the same time, they brought a new dynamism to a class whose political importance was fading.

Some commoners were ennobled because of service to the crown through their exceptional administrative talents. Trained lawyers often rose to become royal ministers and advisers. These new nobles swelled the bureaucracies of the nation states which increased in pace with royal budgets. Overall, the cost of government, the number of officials, and the size of the nobility, all tripled or quadrupled in the early modern centuries.

Townsmen who had grown numerous by commerce—an activity that was considered dishonorable for noblemen and in some places actually forbidden them—yearned to join the aristocracy. The cash-starved monarchs of Europe, with armies to supply and palaces to build, granted their wish through the sale of titles. This practice led to an increase in the nobility, which grew by one-half in seventeenth-century

Images of Power

Hall of Mirrors, Versailles: *In the Hall of Mirrors at Louis XIV's palace at Versailles, the king could see his sovereignty reflected as he proceeded from one formal appointment to the next. Versailles served to attract and distract nobles, who arrived from their country estates to vie with each other in elaborate rituals to win the king's favor.*

***François Marot*, Louis XIV Instituting the Order of Saint Louis:** *In this 1710 painting, Louis XIV exercises his function as royal patron and rewards the efforts of his nobles at Versailles by conferring the Order of Saint Louis.* (Palace of Versailles, France)

Spain and doubled in France between 1715 and 1789. In the republic of Venice, nobility admitted 127 new families to their ranks between 1646 and 1718 for the enormous sum of 100,000 ducats apiece.

In England, a unique case, it was virtually impossible for a commoner to buy or insinuate his way into the restricted noble elite called the peerage. There were only about 200 peers in a nation of several million. But wealthy commoners regularly purchased country estates and so became members of the gentry. This non-noble landowning elite had access to power and privilege in England comparable to that of the nobilities of continental European countries.

By the eighteenth century, the presence among the nobility of many people who had been born commoners gave strong cause for reflection on what nobility was: was it determined by birth, wealth, virtue, or education? Such discussions led to a profound criticism of noble privilege in the Enlightenment (see Chapter 17), and ultimately to the revolutionary rejection of all that it stood for.

In the meantime, Europeans generally accepted the nobility as a hereditary ruling class. The aim of new nobles was to become assimilated as quickly as possible to the old elite: they acquired estates and coats of arms; they enjoyed exemption from some taxes in a number of countries; and they sought to marry their children to the children of the old nobles. As newcomers gained high status, however, some members of the traditional nobility were experiencing

difficulties. Where income from land declined, nobles could fall into poverty, possessing little but their sword and their coat of arms and the threadbare costume of a magistrate.

Some noblemen met the challenges of the early modern period by engaging in commerce, by vigorously managing their estates, or by marrying a wealthy commoner's daughter. Their willingness to accept a redefinition of what it was to be an aristocrat permitted them to survive into a new age in the position of dominance to which they were accustomed. Not all noblemen were free to adapt in this way, however. In France and Spain, a nobleman who engaged in trade was liable to "derogation"—to be struck from the rolls of nobility. In some localities, marriages between nobles and commoners were illegal. Those noblemen who survived best the transition from medieval to early modern society did so by playing an active part in the more sophisticated royal administration and growing bureaucracy required by modern states, and by adapting to the needs of the marketplace, both in their land management and in their cash investments.

Though the nobility was an ancient class, it was a dynamic one in the early modern centuries. New members entered the nobility, while poor nobles struggled to maintain their hereditary status. The wealthiest nobles, of the old sword families, continued to dominate the choicest positions and access to power and privilege.

The Italian Court

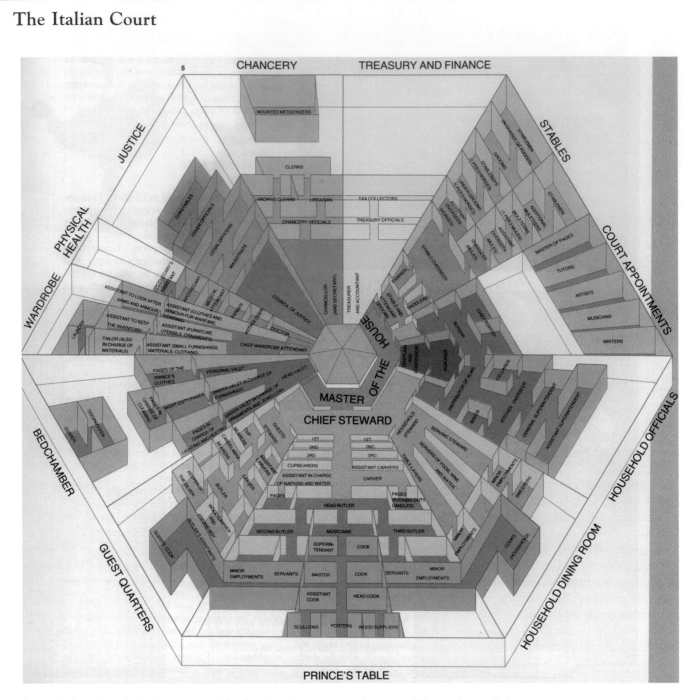

Just as Italy produced the classic manual (by Castiglione) instructing aristocrats of Europe how to behave at court, it also first elaborated the organization of the princely court. The courts of tiny Mantua, Ferrara, and Urbino (see Chapter 13) then served as models for the monarchical courts of France, England, Spain, and wealthier German states. Shown here is a structural representation of an Italian court.
Source: *S. Bertelli et al, The Courts of the Italian Renaissance (New York–Oxford: Facts on File Publications, 1986).*

Patterns of Nobility

The nature of the European nobility varied from region to region. Each community had its own particular set of relationships between nobleman and peasant, nobleman and king.

In Russia, an autocratic tsar distributed privileges to a nobility defined entirely by its service to the crown, and rewarded those servants with the right to dominate a nearly enslaved peasantry (**serfs**). Here the nobility originated not from the earlier landowning or military elite, known as the boyars, which had been suppressed, but from the decrees of the tsars. Ivan the Terrible (r. 1533–1584) and Peter the Great (r. 1682–1725) (see Chapter 15) transformed the Russian elite into a service nobility, a process culminating under Peter in the 1722 "Table of Ranks." The Table of Ranks set out the military and bureaucratic services in fourteen ascending categories. It was intended to replace promotion according to birth and ancestry by promotion according to a person's ability, and to open up the highest ranks of the nobility to those commoners who gave distinguished service as administrators or officers.

To compensate nobles for their lifelong commitment to government the tsars gave them total authority over their serfs, who became virtual slaves, bound not only to the land but also to their lords. Catherine the Great (r. 1762–1796), in her "Charter of the Nobility" of 1785, reaffirmed the privileges held by lords over serfs, and attempted to mold the Russian nobility into a cultural as well as political elite (constituting somewhere between two to three percent of the population).

In Prussia the ruler granted economic and judicial privileges to the nobles, called Junkers, in exchange for military service. Here, as in Russia, the near-total mobilization of the nation brought the interests of the nobility into line with national aims, at the expense of the peasant population.

Further east, in the aristocratic republic of Poland, a nobility comprising some ten to fifteen percent of the population tyrannized its peasantry while also having a say in the election of its king. Enriched by grain exports to the more urbanized areas of western Europe, the Polish nobility jealously guarded its medieval rights to assemble and vote on national issues. It possessed, in addition, the liberum veto ("free veto"), enabling any individual nobleman to thwart the intentions, for good or ill, of any monarch. This constitutional situation invited anarchy and contributed to the series of international maneuvers that culminated in the partition and final disappearance of the Polish nation in 1795.

Much of the rest of eastern Europe (excluding the Balkans, still largely under Ottoman rule) fell under the domination of the **Habsburg** dynasty. As in Poland, the Czech and Hungarian nobility constituted a large percentage of the population, and profited from commerce in grain. While they resented their subordination to German-speaking Habsburg emperors, they often filled posts in the royal administration. In the northern countries of Denmark and Sweden, as in Russia and Prussia, nobles received their privileges from the king in proportion to their service to the crown.

The principalities that made up the many German-speaking states of central Europe, as well as Sweden and Habsburg Austria, modeled themselves on the western absolute monarchies, and their

nobility also resembled those in the west. In northern Italy, Switzerland, and the Netherlands, the nobility were not a preeminent political class, but shared authority in various ways with the wealthy urban bourgeoisie who controlled civic affairs, and frequently engaged in commerce themselves. As landowners, they were concerned with agricultural productivity, but did not necessarily supervise the work of tenant farmers. Nobles of once-great mercantile centers such as Venice, whose ancestors had scoured the Mediterranean for profit, lived in the countryside in leisured detachment.

In England, the nobility consisted of some 200 peers with long medieval traditions who played an important role in Parliament. Despite owning fifteen to forty percent of the land, they had little direct authority over a largely free peasantry. Both this nobility and the gentry often took great interest in the productivity of their landholdings, which were farmed largely by tenant farmers employing landless day laborers. An exception to the general European pattern, the English nobility had surrendered its tax privileges, but voted in Parliament to tax itself as required to supplement the monarch's own funds. With the gentry, it was deeply involved in government and unafraid of the power of the crown, limited decisively by the two revolutions of 1649 and 1688 (see Chapter 15).

In France and Spain, nobles stood at the apex of a steep social hierarchy, overseen by monarchs jealous of their autonomy. In Spain, the nobility (totaling some 500,000 adult males) ranged from powerful grandees to simple *hidalgos*. Seeking to maintaining the purity and distinctiveness of noble lines, the crown supported the *hidalgos* with modest state pensions, and until 1773 barred noble participation in trade or manual labor. That prohibition was a disability for the *hidalgos*, many of whom were impoverished and unable to keep themselves as befitted their status.

The French nobility also considered commercial activity incompatible with high status. Poor nobles suffered as land values fell, while the "grand" nobility managed well on its vast estates, advantageous marriages, financial investments, and royal patronage. Altogether, from 25,000 to 55,000 families claimed noble status, and owned a quarter to a third of all cultivated land. Of these, up to sixty percent were poor.

In the 1630s, Cardinal Richelieu (1585–1642) tried to strengthen the power of the crown in relation to these grand nobles. He restricted their role as generals of private armies, ordered their fortified castles and towers destroyed, and prohibited their duels of honor, labeling them crimes against the state. Aristocrats chafed at these restrictions, and seized the opportunity to recover their lost autonomy shortly after the deaths of the Cardinal and of his master Louis XIII (r. 1610–1643). The young king Louis XIV was still a minor, and France was ruled by the queen mother, the regent Anne of Austria (1601–1666) and her lover, the Italian-born Cardinal Jules Mazarin (1602–1661). In 1648 a protest against royal financial policies grew into a full-scale insurrection that engaged not only the nobility but also townspeople and peasants. The Fronde, named after the slingshot used by Parisian children to shoot pebbles at rich folk in carriages, was suppressed in 1653, resulting in the humiliation of the aristocracy and the triumph of the crown. Traumatized by his experience at age twelve of rebellious Frondeurs, Louis XIV later distracted his potentially troublesome grand nobles in the salons and gardens of his huge palace of Versailles outside Paris. Meanwhile, robe nobles wielded regional power in their judicial assemblies, or *parlements*, or transacted with efficiency the business of government.

Courtiers and Kings

Some members of the aristocratic elite were not only nobles but courtiers too. They attended Europe's kings, princes, and prelates in palatial settings that expressed the ruler's glory. These courts had a dual function: they served to subordinate the nobility to the greater power of the monarch, and—increasingly in the early modern period—they were places where elite arts and social graces were nurtured, setting a new standard for European culture. Those monarchs who still aimed to possess absolute power needed to win the cooperation of their nobles, to reward loyalty, and to discipline resistance. To this end, they drew their nobles to court, where the monarch stood at the center controlling the courtier nobility who, like planets, circled around their sun. This court system had its roots less in the rough, itinerant councils of medieval monarchs than in the lavish ritual systems of the local despots of the Italian Renaissance (see Chapter 13 and the diagram on p. 518). The jewelbox courts of Ferrara and Mantua, Milan and Urbino, spawned imitations on the grand scale in Madrid, Prague and Vienna, St. Petersburg, and London, but above all at Versailles.

The sparkle of aristocratic activity heightened the grandeur of the monarch. A throng of courtiers and servants busily engaged in little of importance formed a kind of collective human prop for the symbolic authority of the prince. Courts also attracted artists and intellectuals with the promise of royal patronage: their brilliant productions added further luster to princely authority. Architecture and the arts were designed to reflect the monarch's grandeur—literally in the case of Louis XIV's Hall of Mirrors at Versailles, illustrated on p. 516. Conspicuous expressions of wealth and high culture ranged from the gems sewn on courtiers' clothes or hung about the necks of their wives, to the silver forks that, for the first time in the history of the West, were used for the delicate science of proper dining; in an older and cruder age, the elite ate with their fingers, just like their peasant subjects. The early modern court system evolved through the need of monarchs to engage the cooperation of their nobles in their determination to retain absolute power. At the same time, bureaucrats, accountants, and secretaries began to carry on more of the business of government. Guided in that direction by the Italian city states and the papal curia, Europe's monarchs made great progress by 1750 in developing centralized and efficient methods of government, staffed by administrators, like the *intendants* instituted by Richelieu. Even so, monarchs still relied on nobles to recruit armies, keep order, and deal out justice.

A great weakness of the court system was that it was precisely those nobles who resided at court, closest to the monarch, who often turned out to be most likely to disobey him. This made court society rife with suspicion, aspiration, and deception, the perfect breeding ground for intrigue and rebellion. Both women and men joined in this intrigue and deception involved in playing for power. In this setting, women's general exclusion from warfare or government was irrelevant: they, like their menfolk, became easy experts in such methods as innuendo and gossip. The aim of intrigue was to gain power and privilege in a system of patronage in which monarchs bestowed rewards on loyal nobles. While lesser offices were filled by members of the lower nobility, gentry, or bourgeoisie, high positions were generally reserved for the high nobility. Salaries dispensed in this way took on the nature of bribes, and the whole system was, to modern eyes, corrupt. While official state payments often lined the pockets of those entrusted with distributing them, nobles who depended on royal handouts often waited for months or years for their promised rewards.

Court life also served as a school, in which the self-willed nobles of Europe learned the new arts of civility. Civility entailed far more than showing reverence to a monarch: it involved a code of manners and attitudes that would become the standard of proper behavior for the next few centuries. Nobles at court needed to know how to behave at table, in the bedroom, in the garden, and in the great halls; in what way and where to bow, speak, or attend to bodily functions; how to address people of different ranks; how to dress for each occasion. To advise the aspiring courtier there were etiquette manuals, supplemented by letters from parents and advice from patrons. The classic manual, a Europe-wide bestseller, was *The Book of the Courtier* by the Italian diplomat Baldassare Castiglione (1478–1529), a passage from which is given in *Witnesses* on p. 521. Translated into five languages, and circulating in 115 editions before 1600, it provided a model for the ideal courtier, who should combine the qualities of a sportsman and a warrior, a musician and a poet, a conversationalist and a counsel to the prince. He should possess all these virtues lightly, with a quality Castiglione called *sprezzatura*, translatable as lively nonchalance, an effortless display of the most refined and developed abilities.

The great chasm that divided the early modern courtier from the warrior knight of the Middle Ages can now be understood. The nobleman who wished to succeed in the new game played in the corridors of power must learn cultural skills unknown in the earlier era. The modern courtier went to school, watched his manners, and participated in music, dance, and theatrical events as both performer and spectator.

Noblewomen Noblewomen too became expert courtiers. Except for female monarchs, women of the highest social class had been warriors only as surrogates for their husbands and held no public office. A woman's manners and artistry were her sole means of announcing high status, to which she claimed right through her father's line or the wealth of her husband. Woman's role as a civilizing force had roots in the

courtly games of the Middle Ages (see Chapter 9), in which a noblewoman might hold sway through the yearning love and admiration she inspired in young aristocrats and troubadours. Women's role as social arbiter persisted in the early modern era: in the model court described by Castiglione, women presided as moderators and judges of the conversation and behavior of men. "Society depends on women," Voltaire noted, however much men were the agents in realms outside the court. No wonder that the salon—a lady's sitting room—became in the Enlightenment the principal setting for the exchange of ideas (see Chapter 17).

Nevertheless, even noblewomen remained subject to their husbands, just as in the Middle Ages. Marriage choices were made by fathers, with an eye to family honor and prosperity. Women often were dispatched at young ages to older husbands. Bearing children in quick succession, who were quickly dispatched to wet nurses, they might find relief in early widowhood, or perhaps a discreet love affair—the

---

WITNESSES

Courtier Graces, Bourgeois Self Control

During the seventeenth and eighteenth centuries, the nobility and the bourgeoisie—two elite social groups—developed codes of behavior suitable for their members. Nobles, or "courtiers," who ideally spent their life at court in the presence of the monarch, refined their previous warrior ideal to include the possession of verbal fluency and effortless grace. The bourgeois ideal was to save time, money, and energy, in order to focus on the transcendent duty of obtaining "wealth and distinction." The first ideal is represented here by the tremendously successful Book of the Courtier; *the second by American leader Benjamin Franklin's* Autobiography.

Castiglione tells the would-be gentlemen of Europe how to live at the courts of princes (1528): Now your request is that I should describe what, in my view, is the form of courtiership most appropriate for a gentleman living at the Courts of princes ... in short, ... what kind of man must be one who deserves the name of a perfect courtier. ... I would have our courtier of noble birth and good family, since it matters far less to a common man if he fails to perform virtuously and well than to a nobleman. For if a gentleman strays from the path of his forebears, he dishonours his family name and not only fails to achieve anything but loses what has already been achieved. ... The first and true profession of the courtier must be that of arms; and this above everything else I wish him to pursue vigorously. Let him also stand out from the rest as enterprising, bold and loyal to whomever he serves. ... So I wish our courtier ... demonstrate strength and lightness and suppleness and be good at all the physical exercises befitting a warrior. Here, I believe, his first duty is to

know how to handle expertly every kind of weapon, either on foot or mounted. ... [One must always] steer away from affectation at all costs, as if it were a rough and dangerous reef, and ... practice in all things a certain nonchalance which conceals all artistry and makes whatever one says or does seem uncontrived and effortless. I am sure that grace springs especially from this, since everyone knows how difficult it is to accomplish some unusual feat perfectly, and so facility in such things excites the greatest wonder; whereas, in contrast, to labour at what one is doing and, as we say, to make bones over it, shows an extreme lack of grace. (Baldassare Castiglione, *The Book of the Courtier*, 1528; ed. G. Bull, 1967)

Benjamin Franklin recommends self-discipline and hard work (1771): Reading was the only amusement I allow'd myself. I spent no time in taverns, games or frolicks of any kind; and my industry in my business continu'd as indefatigable as it was necessary. ... My circumstances, however, grew daily easier. My original habits of frugality continuing, and my father having, among his instructions to me when a boy, frequently repeated a proverb of Solomon, "Seest thou a man diligent in his calling, he shall stand before kings, he shall not stand before mean men," I from thence considered industry as a means of obtaining wealth and distinction, which encourag'd me, tho' I did not think that I should ever literally *stand before kings*, which, however, has since happened; for I have stood before *five*, and even had the honor of sitting down with one, the King of Denmark, to dinner. (Benjamin Franklin, *The Autobiography of Benjamin Franklin*; ed. J. Bigelow, 1867)

Aristocratic Leisure

Giovanni Pannini, Gallery of Scenes from Ancient Rome: *During the seventeenth and eighteenth centuries, the European nobility enjoyed power, indulged in luxury, and consumed culture. Here, in a painting dated 1759, fashionably dressed aristocrats examine the accumulated artifacts and representations of Classical civilization, displayed floor to ceiling in the vast halls of an imaginary palace.* (Louvre, Paris)

latter a risky choice, since adultery on a wife's part was punishable in many places by death (although openly tolerated in high aristocratic circles). Or they might find amusement in court intrigue, salon conversations, or the world of fashion.

Fashion and Culture Fashion—the idea that we can choose what we wear and that this choice is meaningful—had arrived at the end of the Middle Ages, in courts and cities that had access to luxury fabrics, often obtained by foreign trade. First aristocratic, and then burgher dress became distinguished from that of peasants, the clergy, and lawyers and other professionals. The latter two groups continued to wear the long robe of the previous era, while peasants still dressed in homespun tunics and cloaks. The elites clothed themselves in silks, brocades, velvets, laces, luxury wools, and furs, adorned with jewels, ribbons, buttons, and clasps, as shown in *Windows On*, p. 600. Outlandish styles came and faded: shoes with long toes; detachable sleeves slashed to show the silk beneath; headdresses stacked high on wire frames

and wide skirts supported by wire basketwork; deep decolletés that revealed women's bosoms and stiff codpieces that accentuated, while covering, male genitals; stockings that ended below or over the knee, and breeches that closed over or above the stockings.

Amid this panoply, a few clear trends can be distinguished in upper-class fashion. First, at the beginning of the early modern era, men's clothing diverged from women's (they had both previously worn gowns, cassocks, robes, and cloaks). The main garment became the short doublet (a close-fitting jacket), while women's robes remained long. Then, toward the end of the seventeenth century, the doublet gave way to two garments, an inner sleeveless waistcoat and an outer coat, that are the forerunners of the modern vest and jacket. Finally, in the eighteenth century, women's dress for the first time became more elaborate and luxurious than men's.

In the realm of culture, the court replaced the church as the primary institution. It was initially through royal and noble patronage that modern European music, theater, dance, and the visual arts developed. During the early modern period, many of the great composers were still hired primarily to produce religious music, but the patronage of music was being assumed by the kings, princes, and prelates whose courts also supported the first orchestras of string, brass, and wind instruments. By the eighteenth century, most formal music was secular and performed in the courts. Elaborate festivals, ballets, and masques were organized for such occasions as weddings and victories, diplomatic visits and sacred events.

Art was also essential to the culture of the high nobility. Royal and aristocratic patrons competed with each other in amassing collections of works of art (an imaginary one is depicted on p. 522). These collections announced the good taste, learning, and wealth of the patron. Many works were created in styles that evoked the art of ancient Greece and Rome. A renewed interest in this art, gave birth to Renaissance Classicism. Classical features, such as balanced proportions and grand entrance porticos with columns, became the mark of high-prestige buildings, from country houses to churches and palaces.

In the seventeenth and eighteenth centuries the Baroque style prevailed, especially in Italy, Spain, Germany, and Austria. This was characterized by bold, dramatic rhythms, with strongly curving, often disrupted forms. A highly decorative variation of Baroque called Rococo won favor in France and eastern Europe in the early eighteenth century. Meanwhile, as the nobility and their favored architects and artists began to travel more widely, visiting ancient sites on the so-called Grand Tour, a more precise and scholarly form of Classicism, termed Neoclassicism, evolved. The Baroque style of architecture was especially suited for displaying the grandiose ambitions of the European royalty and nobility who commissioned the great building projects of the age. In Russia, Peter the Great constructed a whole new city, St. Petersburg, much of which was designed in the Baroque style by architects brought from western Europe. This gigantic enterprise was at once a display of the despotic power of an absolute monarch and an expression of civilized good taste on a grand scale.

Princes and nobles commissioned portraits of themselves and their families, which record the importance of the noble line and the luxury of the age. In England, Sir Anthony van Dyck (1599–1641) painted numerous portraits of Charles I (r. 1625–1649) and his family,

The Comédie Française, 1780: *Aristocratic culture found clear expression in theatrical performance, which in the early modern period became increasingly lavish, flamboyant, and formalized—as demonstrated in this contemporary drawing of the French national theater on the eve of the French Revolution.* (Paris, Bibliothèque Nationale)

while his contemporary in France, Pierre Mignard (1612–1695), immortalized the "Sun King" Louis XIV and his court. In Spain Diego Velázquez (1599–1660) painted forty portraits of King Philip IV. Family portraits carefully emphasize the role of the patriarch, and illustrate the fecundity and respectability of his wife.

Despite the changes forced on it during this period, the early modern nobility was a successful class. In many cases, it maintained its honor, its social and economic privileges, while ceding some political power to the monarch. At the same time, it had been transformed by the experience of the high noblemen and women who attended the kings of Europe at court. They created an ideal of behavior that set a new standard in European culture, at precisely that moment when European culture took precedence on a global stage. Into the twentieth century, to belong to the European elite was to possess as the accompaniments of power a superior education, refined manners, and cultivated taste.

NEW WAYS WITH NEW WEALTH: THE EARLY MODERN BOURGEOISIE

As the European nobility was transformed during the early modern era, so the bourgeoisie developed in size, complexity, wealth, and in the range of its aspirations. Europe's leading cities became cultural centers rivaling the kingly courts, as its once-modest private homes became showplaces of domestic virtues and lavish material consumption. Some members of the bourgeoisie, such as Molière's would-be gentleman, practiced the social and cultural skills that were now the earmarks of high status and sought to enter the ranks of the aristocracy. As they yearned to climb the social ladder, those beneath them sold their crafts in the shops and on the streets, labored in burgher homes as servants, or acquired their daily bread by theft or prostitution. Those who were idle and unpaid sought charity from the institutions that guarded well the wealth of riches commanded by urban patriciates.

The Ranks of the Bourgeoisie

The bourgeoisie derived from the merchants who lived as exceptions in a society that comprised clergy, nobles, and peasants—the three medieval social orders, or estates. They were called, in French, *bourgeois* (in English, German, and Italian: burgher, *Bürger*, *borghese*) because they lived in *bourgs* (borough, *Burg*, *borgo*), or towns. As towns multi-plied, the bourgeoisie also grew, early becoming an exceptionally prosperous and dynamic class in Italy and Flanders (see Chapter 11). By the seventeenth century, the bourgeoisie were the dominant social group in Europe's urban centers: in London and Amsterdam, for example, they rivaled the aristocracy in power and prestige.

The early modern bourgeoisie developed great social complexity. Constituting as much as ten percent of the population in England, France, and the Netherlands, although only a tiny percentage of the regions of eastern Europe, it included merchants, bankers, and entrepreneurs as well as patricians, professionals, guildsmen, and prosperous artisans. Among these were the dynamic leaders of Europe's economic expansion. Some were conservators of outmoded and restrictive mercantile traditions. And some, having amassed their wealth in commerce, invested it in land and lived like nobles. There was no longer a single but many bourgeois orders uncomfortably ranked among the commoners, mostly peasant, of the Third Estate.

The entrepreneurs and bankers, descendants of the great medieval merchant princes, were engaged in those activities that yielded the greatest profits: long-distance trade and the financial back-up that made it possible to fit out oceangoing ships and undertake other costly ventures. Resident mainly in the most populous cities of western Europe, these men invested in the joint stock companies that trade with Asia and the Americas, in the ships that carried African slaves across the Atlantic or wheat cargoes in the Baltic, and in the mines providing iron for guns and machinery. Bankers lent cash to monarchs and startup funds to other merchants. Energetic, creative, and risk-taking, these entrepreneurs opened up world markets and mapped out the commercial system that made Europe the foremost economic power in the world (see Chapter 16).

The patricians were the traditional elites of the European cities. These more conservative "city fathers" were outpaced in Amsterdam and London by dynamic entrepreneurs, but continued to flourish in smaller independent cities such as Strasbourg or Hamburg. Their merchant ancestors had accumulated the wealth that enabled later generations to live on rents and investments while maintaining control of town councils. Where the entrepreneurs drove forward the European economic engine, the patricians' outlook was often local and limited. Other members of the bourgeoisie whose prosperity was not primarily based on mercantile activity included bureaucrats and public officials, who were often trained lawyers.

In the frequent civic and religious processions that wound through streets and market squares, the patricians marched first, followed by guildsmen and artisans, costumed and accoutred according to their ranks. The guildsmen were artisans who were masters of their craft, as certified by the guild organization. Unlike entrepreneurs, whose mercantile activities had burst the bounds of guild-organized commerce, the guildsmen of the early modern period were a conservative force: they tended to resist change in production methods, trade patterns, and the social organization of industries. Below guildsmen in status

Going to market: *Trade and commerce (later industry) were the lifeblood and culture of Europe's urban bourgeoisie. In this anonymous contemporary painting buyers and sellers fill the cheese market in front of the Weighouse in the busy Dutch merchant city of Alkmaar.* (Stedelijk Museum, Alkmaar)

were journeymen ("day-laborers," from the French *journée*, a day) or craftspersons not admitted to guilds, or practicing crafts that had no guild structure. Very rarely, women workers, especially in such specialized textile crafts as gold embroidery or pursemaking, might belong to guilds in their own right, rather than as the widow or daughter of a master.

In Protestant regions, members of the clergy were considered as professionals with bourgeois or gentry status. In Catholic regions, they remained a class apart: privileged like most nobles, with freedom from taxation, they were accorded the highest social honors. In the nations of Catholic Europe, the clergy constituted the highest ranking social group, or "First Estate," technically followed by the nobility as second, although many high-ranking clergy were nobles.

The sons of the bourgeoisie—entrepreneurial, patrician, or artisan—often joined their fathers in commercial partnerships. But increasingly, following a pattern already seen in the towns of late medieval Italy, these young men proceeded from the elementary schooling that equipped them to be merchants to the secondary and advanced education that permitted them to be lawyers, clergymen, or physicians. From this professional order came not only most of Europe's administrators and bureaucrats, but nearly all its theorists and intellectuals. Other young men from wealthy bourgeois families sought to acquire the land that made it possible for a burgher to live like a nobleman, even without the official title of nobility. In the Dutch Republic, the distinction between wealthy landowner and nobleman was fine. In England, landownership of itself conferred social status, making it possible for a man rich from trade to become a member of the gentry: "Trade in England makes gentlemen and has peopled this nation with gentlemen," commented the novelist Daniel Defoe (1660–1731). The defection of successful bourgeois to the countryside, and worse, to the ranks of the nobility, tended to retard the development of the commercial classes and their most energetic members, the entrepreneurs.

At Home

Those wealthy bourgeois who did not emigrate to the countryside aimed, in town, to "live nobly"—which meant to have servants to do the menial work, and to spend lavishly on beautiful or useful things made by others' hands. In the intimacy of their well-furnished homes, however, townspeople seem to have experienced domestic lives more infused with sentiments of love and devotion than was typical of the aristocracy, or available to most of the laboring poor.

The interior spaces of burgher households began to shine with the kinds of luxuries—carved furniture, tiled or sculpted fireplaces, elegantly decorated chests, painted and glazed dishware, silver implements, and glass vessels—that had previously been the possessions of only wealthy nobles or the most successful of Italy's merchant princes. Less conspicuously lavish items were still expensive, including window glass, candles, and fine soap, and such foodstuffs as meat, fish, and cheeses in abundance, and imported wines, tea, and coffee. In a world where simply having enough to eat amounted to prosperity, bourgeois magnates reveled in material goods and consumables. In costume as in diet, they imitated aristocratic opulence, as far as their budgets and their mercantile prudence would allow.

Particularly in the Netherlands, where the bourgeoisie achieved a maximum of success in the seventeenth century, the contents of households and laden tables were enshrined in art. While painters elsewhere celebrated royalty and nobility, here such artists as Jan Vermeer (1632–1675) depicted the clean, ample, and tranquil space of the bourgeois household.

Already in the Middle Ages, the wealthier town-dwellers protected household wealth by adopting the system of giving daughters a "marriage portion," or dowry, and limiting inheritance either to the eldest son (primogeniture) or all males. Like noblemen (see Chapter 9), burgher patriarchs traced their descent in the male line, and carefully chose their children's marriage partners to enhance family status and prevent the drain of capital. Emotional ties between family members, including sentiments of affection for children, were often subordinated in these circumstances to the needs of household maintenance.

The prominent role of the father in this household system was further reinforced by the advent of the Reformation in some parts of Europe (see Chapter 14), and of absolutism in many (see Chapter 15). In Protestant families, the patriarch summoned the family to daily prayer and enforced discipline not just as the eldest male, but also as the minister of divine authority. The father was understood to be monarch in his family, as the ruler was in the state: to obey him was to learn to obey the king. "A family is . . . a little Commonwealth," wrote one English preacher, "a school wherein the first principles and grounds of government and subjection are learned."

In a family system dominated in this way by the husband and father, a wife's duty was to be subordinate—not a new obligation in the early modern era (see Chapter 12). Among the bourgeoisie, however, concerns for the preservation of family wealth and advancement of social status made marriage a business of critical importance for many persons other than the bride. The complete surrender of personality required of a woman in marriage was often made without the woman herself having actively made a decision to marry, or to marry the man chosen for her by her parents, who were not bound to consider their daughter's inclinations. Sadly, wrote the English aristocrat Margaret Cavendish, Duchess of Newcastle (1623–1673) "daughters are but branches which by marriage are broken off from the root whence they sprang and grafted onto the stock of another family."

Once married, a woman was largely defined by the interests of the new household. Her dowry wealth was generally given over to her husband to manage (not until modern times were women completely free to manage their own, or their family's, finances), while her behavior and costume were assumed to reflect her husband's social position. Adultery was seen as a woman's crime: a man who had sexual relations with other women outside of marriage committed no wrong, except against the honor of the other woman's husband. A married woman who committed adultery injured her husband so grievously that, in Spain, he was entitled to execute her with impunity and, in France, with slight or no consequence.

Married women had only limited claim to their children, or to their own or their husband's property. Children belonged to their fathers. Only rarely did a married woman leave a household with her children, who were understood to continue her husband's lineage. Wealthy widows were discouraged from marrying again, especially if there were young children who might suffer if a woman's dowry was removed from the household; they were often encouraged to remain in the deceased husband's house, maintaining a chaste condition. Depending on local law, a woman might be entitled to any portion of his property.

Some women protested against the restrictions of marriage and women's status, as the passages quoted in *Witnesses* on p. 527 show. In *Some Reflections on Marriage* (1700), quoted in *Witnesses* on p. 506. Mary Astell (1666–1731) offered a powerful critique, centered on the need for women to develop their own personalities and faculties prior to becoming a wife. Women should not rely only on beauty and adornments—nor should men be satisfied with these, but should seek real companionship with an educated comrade. In all, a woman should consider before she married, since once wed, she was in her husband's power, "and if the matrimonial yoke be grievous, neither law nor custom affords her that redress which a man obtains." Lady Mary Chudleigh (1656–1710) put the matter succinctly in her poem "To The Ladies":

Wife and Servant are the same,
But only differ in the Name.

Women Protest against Husbands and Predators

In the sixteenth century, women's voices were finally heard—after centuries of near silence. Their works were composed mostly in the vernacular, which unlike Latin did not require an advanced education. The printing press made possible the publication of many copies, circulated widely, as in the case of Moderata Fonte's The Worth of Women represented in the first excerpt here. Women artists, too, became more conspicuous, as in the case of Artemisia Gentileschi, represented in the second excerpt. Both women protest against the actions of men: the first, broadly and theoretically, condemning them for "usurping" women's rights; the second, concretely and particularly, testifying in a trial against a man who raped her.

A Venetian woman lambasts the tyranny of men (1592): If men usurp our rights, should we not complain and declare that they have wronged us? Or if we are their inferiors in status, but not in worth, this is an abuse that has been introduced into the world and that men have then, over time, gradually translated into law and custom; and it has become so entrenched that they claim … that the status they have gained through their bullying is theirs by right. … And we would suffer it. … if they did not insist on exerting such absolute control over us and in such an arrogant manner, treating us like slaves who cannot take a step without asking their permission or say a word without their jumping down our throats. … As fathers, as brothers, as sons or husbands or lovers or whatever other relationship they have to us, they all abuse us, humiliate us, and do all they can to harm and annihilate us.

(Moderata Fonte (Modesta da Pozzo), *The Worth of Women, Wherein is Clearly Revealed their Nobility and their Superiority to Men*, 1592; ed. and trs. V. Cox, 1997)

Artemisia Gentileschi, painter, testifies at the trial of her rapist (1612): Agostino put his head on my breast … and said: "Let's walk together a while, because I hate sitting down." … After we had walked around two or three times, each time going by the bedroom door, when we were in front of the bedroom door, he pushed me in and locked the door. He then threw me onto the edge of the bed, pushing me with a hand on my breast. … Lifting my clothes, which he had a great deal of trouble doing, he placed a hand with a handkerchief at my throat and on my mouth to keep me from screaming. … I felt a strong burning and it hurt very much, but because he held my mouth I couldn't cry out. However, I tried to scream as best I could.

I scratched his face and pulled his hair and … I even removed a piece of flesh. … And after he had done his business he got off me. When I saw myself free, I went to the table drawer and took a knife and moved toward Agostino saying: "I'd like to kill you with this knife because you have dishonored me."

(From M. D. Garrard, *Artemisia Gentileschi*, 1989)

The wife's condition might have been more like a prostitute's than a servant's, suggested the writer Daniel Defoe. In *Conjugal Lewdness, or Matrimonial Whoredom* he argued that marriage often amounted to the legally protected sexual exploitation of women.

High rates of child-bearing and high infant mortality were both accepted facts of existence (see Chapter 12). The children of elite families often spent their first years with wet nurses. Sons returned to their mothers only briefly before they again left their parents' homes—perhaps around age fourteen, but possibly as early as eight—to serve an apprenticeship in their destined occupation, to enter a military academy or religious institution, or in other ways to embark on adult life. In another sense, they did not achieve adulthood until their later twenties, when they married themselves (often to a much younger wife, or an older widow), set up their own households, and perhaps succeeded to their fathers' positions.

Despite these bleak realities, the bourgeois families of the early modern era began to reconceptualize childhood. Evidence exists in diaries and letters of a deepened emotional involvement of parents in childrearing, an increased concern for children's education and welfare. Around the mid-seventeenth century, the severe disciplining of children in school was questioned. Elite mothers increasingly breastfed their own babies; they also dressed them in special clothes (children had previously been dressed just like miniature adults), and supplied them with playthings. Mothers and fathers alike recorded their mourning for children who died, as so many did, by arranging elaborate funerals, commissioning monuments, or writing works describing their grief. In general, family life in the comfortable homes of bourgeois Europeans seems to have become more focused on personal identity and experience. Outside these homes, in the vibrant cities of early modern Europe, a new cultural world was also emerging.

Downtown

While some members of the bourgeoisie wished to buy land and noble status, those who remained based in the great European cities created a vital and refined cultural world that imitated, rivaled, and eventually replaced that of the court: the world of "downtown."

Medieval European cities had developed as autonomous commercial centers (see Chapter 11), in which merchant organizations determined the forms of town governments, which wrested political privileges from kings, bishops, and emperors. Each city developed distinctive social and cultural traditions, and different patterns of interaction with the immediate countryside, and with other independent cities.

By the sixteenth century, however, the medieval patterns were changing, in three ways (see also Chapter 16). First, the major urban concentrations shifted from the Mediterranean region to the Atlantic region, where new patterns of urbanization emerged, driven by explosive economic and population growth.

Second, the network of autonomous cities was replaced by networks of integrated regions, in which major cities were the economic focus of a large area that included many medium-sized and small towns. Often these regional supercities were also national capitals, as were London and Paris. As regional centers, these previously isolated centers of commercial endeavor now derived their wealth and resources from far beyond the urban core. They opened themselves up to the countryside beyond, whose goods they purchased and whose needs they supplied.

Third, the pace of urbanization accelerated overall. Not only did the populations of Europe's towns and cities increase, but the proportion of Europeans living in cities rose from under nine percent in 1500

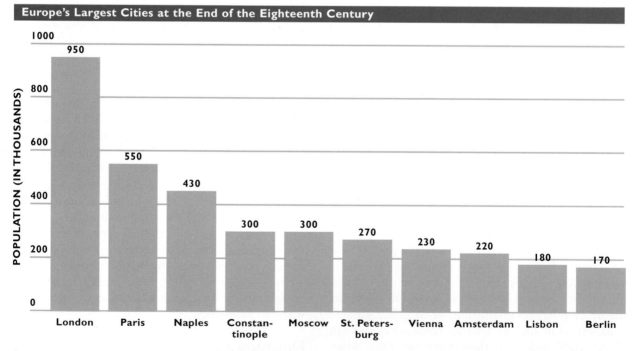

Population Takeoff in Europe

| | Approximate European Populations | | | | | |
	France	Prussia	Russia	Italy	Sweden	England
1600	10,500,000	N/A	10,000,000	12,000,000	1,000,000	4,066,000
1700	21,000,000	1,750,000	14,000,000	13,000,000	1,500,000	5,027,000
1800	29,000,000	9,000,000	30,000,000	19,000,000	2,500,000	8,728,000

Sources: *Based on* Atlas of World Population History *(New York: Facts on File, 1978) and B. R. Mitchell,* British Historical Statistics *(Cambridge: Cambridge University Press, 1988), pp. 7–9, 40–42, 52–54.*

Europe's Largest Cities at the End of the Eighteenth Century

Bar chart, POPULATION (IN THOUSANDS):
- London: 950
- Paris: 550
- Naples: 430
- Constantinople: 300
- Moscow: 300
- St. Petersburg: 270
- Vienna: 230
- Amsterdam: 220
- Lisbon: 180
- Berlin: 170

Source: *Based on J. Merriman,* A History of Modern Europe: From the Renaissance to the Age of Napoleon *(New York: W. W. Norton, 1996), p. 385.*

By 1500, Europe began to recover from the catastrophic population losses caused by the Black Death (see Chapter 12). After a slowdown in the rate of growth in the seventeenth century, steady gains were realized after 1700, and by 1800, Europe was densely populated. The first table shows the mounting population of selected European countries in 1600, 1700, and 1800, while the second shows the population attained by some of Europe's most important cities by around 1800.

to about twelve percent by 1750 overall (with a still higher proportion in the Mediterranean and north-western regions). The largest cities in the Middle Ages barely exceeded 100,000 inhabitants; by 1700, the largest broke the barrier of 500,000 and by 1800, approached 1 million, as the diagram on p. 528 shows. Smaller cities with fewer than 50,000 inhabitants continued to thrive. Constituting three-fourths of all European cities, they were hives of commercial activity and key to Europe's urbanism.

Increasing in size and in the range of their economic activity, the great European cities lost their walls: they were no longer the exceptional islands they had been in the sea of medieval society. No longer enclosed by gates and walls, the intensity of city life spilled out from busy port and market complexes into the surrounding region and beyond. Reflecting national and continental interests rather than merely local ones, urban planning and architecture adopted new forms. Broad avenues cut through the winding web of medieval streets to provide a stage for royal and religious processions and military parades, for personal communication and commercial traffic. Buildings sprouted up in the imposing Baroque and Neoclassical architectural styles borrowed from aristocratic mansions: official palaces, stock markets, and banks; the townhouses of the nobility and wealthy bourgeoisie. By 1750, the cities were displacing courts, palaces, cathedrals, and monasteries as centers of European civilization.

Against the backdrop of monumental buildings and planned streets, a new urban theater materialized. Medieval cities had been cultural centers, where ritual processions and special events occupied a good part of the annual calendar. Early modern cities engendered different forms of cultural activity. The elites travelled in carriages to visit government officials, business contacts, or personal friends. They promenaded in public gardens and along river embankments. They frequented coffeehouses and teashops, and went shopping on "high" streets lined with speciality shops, stocked with the manufactures of Europe and exotic produce from around the globe.

For the first time, the city also contained theaters in the modern sense. In the Middle Ages, plays based on Bible stories had been enacted in villages, monasteries, and courts, while the Italian Renaissance had seen the revival of Classical drama. In London from the late 1500s, and in Spain and France in the 1600s, dramatic performances moved into public theaters, where they were enjoyed by audiences mixed in gender and social origin, achieving glorious success. European playwrights of the early modern era included some of the greatest geniuses of the Western tradition: most notably William Shakespeare (1564–1616) in England; Lope de Vega (1562–1635) in Spain; Jean-Baptiste Racine (1639–1699), Pierre Corneille (1606–1684), and Molière in France.

Women also wrote for the stage, including the Italian Antonia Pulci (1452–1501) and the English Aphra Behn (1640–1689) (see Chapter 17).

The first operas had been staged for elite audiences in Renaissance Italy. By the 1700s, opera houses stood in most major European cities and played to crowds who came to applaud the brilliant virtuosity of the performers as much as to listen to the music. The Classical, tragic themes of the earliest operas were joined by comic themes, often boldly critical of contemporary society. One such was *The Beggar's Opera* by John Gay (1685–1732), which celebrated criminals and prostitutes in a subtle commentary on elite values, or *The Marriage of Figaro* by Wolfgang Amadeus Mozart (1756–1791), based on the play of the French adventurer Pierre-Augustin Caron de Beaumarchais (1732–1799), with its charms concealing a merciless critique of the aristocracy.

While theater developed in part from folk traditions, musical performance evolved from the royal and princely courts, which had provided patronage for composers and musicians. In bourgeois homes, meanwhile, families and friends joined in choral and solo singing, with amateur instrumental accompaniment.

This musical tradition erupted into the life of the city in the seventeenth century with the opening of public opera halls (such as Venice's Fenice), and in the eighteenth century with the creation of the concert hall. The virtuoso skills of composers, musicians, and singers could now be enjoyed by a bourgeois audience that did not reside at court.

The bourgeois outsiders of medieval society were the insiders of the early modern city. City-dwellers imitated the arts of the court to create the urban civilization of the modern Western world, centered not in halls of mirrors but amid the traffic of downtown. The bourgeoisie were not the only residents of the early modern cities, however: they shared their habitat with the poor, who, leaving the countryside, thronged there in search of work.

Workers and Strangers

The ranks of the bourgeois were the elites of the cities that they shared with a multiplicity of people, whose presence made urban life more turbulent and variable than life on the land. Migrants from towns and villages boosted the population levels of early modern cities, which could not be maintained by citizen births alone: migration accounts for much of the urban demographic growth in this period. Some migrants were educated professionals or skilled artisans, who found employment in the city councils, the schools and universities, or guild-regulated shops. But most were unskilled: they packed the streets and filled the rented rooms in cities that provided them with only limited opportunities and no remedies for the harsh realities of the marketplace.

Being Poor: in Town and Country

The condition of the poor remained dire in the early modern centuries, but had become more various than in the previous era. Some of that variety is indicated in the passages here. The first describes an attempt in the city of Venice to reduce the number of street beggars by removing those that had become sick to a hospital. In the second, the poor workers of Manchester, still angry and hungry in the aftermath of a harshly suppressed food riot, send a threatening letter to the local Justice of the Peace. In the third, a German poet gives expression to the plight of the peasant, as bleak as it had always been.

A view from the top—Sick beggars in Venice must enter the hospital of the *Incurabili* or be banished (1522): Many gentlemen and gentlewomen and others have been moved to take pity on numerous persons sick and sore of the French pox [i.e. syphilis] and other ills. Some of these persons in their bodily weakness languish in the streets and the doorways of churches and public places both at San Marco and at Rialto to beg for a living ... giving forth a terrible stench and infecting their neighbours and those with whom they live. ... Now, because the aforesaid charitable persons are making every possible effort to care for these sick people—who are plunged into the deepest destitution and misfortune—in a hospital of theirs at the Spirito Santo ... , we ... decree ... that, if from henceforth any men or women sore of the French pox or other ill are called upon by the agents of the aforesaid hospital to go and enter the place to be nursed and looked after, and yet refuse and will not go, ... they shall be ... banished from this our city.

(Decree of the *Provveditori alla Sanità*, February 22, 1522; eds. D. Chambers and B. Pullan, 1992)

The poor of Manchester write threateningly to Mr. James Bailey, J.P., following the violent repression of a food riot in July 1762: This is to asquaint you that We poor of Rosendale Rochdale Oldham Saddleworth Ashton have all mutaly and firmly agreed by Word and Covinent and Oath to Fight and Stand by Each Other as long as Life doth last for We may as well all be hanged as starved to Death and to see ower Children weep for Bread and none to give Them ... but take This for a shure Maxon, That if You dont put those good Laws in Execution against all Those Canables or Men Slayers That have the Curse of God and all honest Men both by Gods Laws and Mens Laws ... I know You all have Power to stop such vilonas Proceedings if You please and if You dont amaidatley put a Stopp and let hus feel it the next Saturday We will murder You all that We have down in Ower List and Wee will all bring a Faggot and burn down Your Houses and Wait Houses and make Your Wifes Widdows and Your Children Fatherless for ... Blood for Blood We Require. Take Care.

(From E. P. Thompson, "The Crime of Anonymity" in D. Hay, et al, *Albion's Fatal Tree*, 1975)

A German peasant describes his condition (1568):
    I am a peasant.
    My work is hard and bitter.
    I must plow, seed, and harrow,
    Then cut, reap, and beat.
    I gather wood and make hay and grain.
    Rents and taxes break my heart.
    I live on plain bread and water,
    As the Lord has commanded Adam.

(Jost Amman, "The Peasant"; ed. S. Ozment, 1980)

Unskilled men worked as common day-laborers who hauled goods, removed debris, swept chimneys, or groomed horses. Women worked as domestic servants, or as spinners, embroiderers, or seamstresses. Servants were a numerous (and increasingly female) class in all European cities of the early modern period, numbering in the tens of thousands in eighteenth-century London or Paris. Men and women alike were subject to economic cycles that brought high prices and unemployment: just as a migrant from the country could become a city worker, that worker might easily become one of the urban underclass of the desperately poor. After 1500, one of Europe's major problems was what to do with indigents.

Members of this impoverished underclass were variously called "beggars," "wanderers," "vagabonds," and "paupers." They were a significant presence, constituting about ten to thirty percent of urban population. In Roman Catholic cities especially, charitable institutions offered relief (such as the Venetian hospital cited in *Witnesses* above), though only to a very few, and almsgiving was still practiced. This vulnerable poor population was increasingly unwelcome, particularly in the Protestant cities of the north, which often expelled indigents. Even Catholic Paris ruled in 1606 that beggars should be whipped, branded, and driven out of town (and in 1749, imprisoned). In contrast to the medieval notion that poverty was an opportunity for compassion, poverty was redefined after 1500 as a criminal offense.

In England, poor laws dating from the reign of Elizabeth I (r. 1558–1603) distinguished the "deserving" from the "undeserving" poor. The former could be housed in workhouses (later poorhouses) supported by the local parish. The latter must be set to work, or expelled from the locality—as, frequently, were strangers and foreigners. Such regulations created two strata of poor folk: those immobilized in their

Artemisia Gentileschi, Judith Slaying Holofernes, *c. 1620*

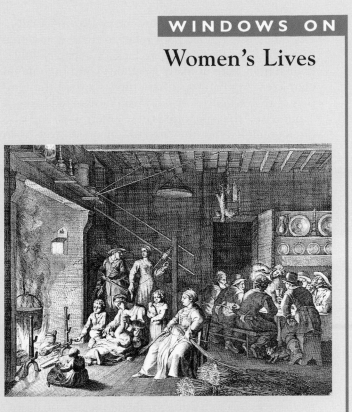

Claudine-Françoise Bouzonnet, after a drawing by Jacques Sella, Family Evening, *1667*

Attributed to the School of Murillo, Celestina and her Daughter

Women's lives in the early modern period revolved around their sexuality. In the engraving of a peasant family (top right), shadings of light and dark separate the world of women from the world of men. A harsher reality is indicated by the image of two prostitutes, young and old (or perhaps a prostitute and an aged procuress) looking out from a barred window—a stark and tragic reminder of their total isolation from the respectable world (above). In a dramatic painting by the renowned woman

artist Artemisia Gentileschi, a woman revenges herself on a tyrant (top left). The biblical heroine Judith slays Holofernes, who is an enemy not only of her nation but also of the women he victimizes. (above: State Hermitage Museum, St. Petersburg; top left: Uffizi, Florence)

What would have to change before women could seek identities based on characteristics other than sexuality?

To continue your investigation of this topic, please go to www.prenhall.com/king for the related **WINDOWS** on the **WEB** activity

parishes, and those adrift on the roads. In London, city officials extended poor relief to those considered "deserving" because of their lack of capacity (able-bodied men were unlikely to qualify) and high moral character. Applying such strictures soothed the tempers of the ordinary folk who paid designated taxes or "poor rents" that supported these enterprises, and who often grumbled that they had to support wastrels as an unwanted burden. The threat of social unrest stilled these complaints. It was better to pay the cost of poor relief than to suffer riot and upheaval.

In France, a workhouse system also supplemented the informal networks of private charity. The *hôpital* ("hospital") continued to house both the hopelessly poor and the hopelessly sick, two groups equally unsupported by home and family. Those able to work labored at menial tasks to pay the cost of their maintenance. Some of the able-bodied poor, willing to work but unable to find employment, were set to road-building and construction tasks organized by publicly funded "workshops." None of these institutions provided sufficient relief to fill the giant well of poverty.

Women and Children Women who had lost the protection of fathers (through abandonment or death) and husbands (through desertion or death) figured disproportionately among the poor. They had less opportunity than men to find well-paid work, and they bore the additional responsibility of caring for children that no one else wanted. In workhouses and poorhouses, they performed the low-level textile work that had traditionally been done by women, while male artisans took on the more highly-skilled jobs of weaving and finishing. Some regions had convent-style asylums where poor women performed low-paid work, perhaps acquired job skills, and engaged in frequent devotions. Despite the variety of these places of refuge, many poor women at the bottom of what one modern historian has called the "hierarchy of hunger" found no support except among the community of those equally adrift, and lived on the profits of begging.

Poor mothers, whether married or single, were especially vulnerable to variations in the supply and cost of the food they needed both for themselves and for their children. In line with new economic thinking, towns and cities sometimes withdrew from subsidizing grain, as they had in the Middle Ages, with the result that prices soared to a natural high in times of scarcity. High prices, in turn, provoked riot, as the passage reproduced in *Witnesses* on p. 530 and the print on p. 534 show. In the eighteenth century, women were often in the forefront of those who rioted, their explosive speech and physical unrestraint contrasting with their accustomed condition of controlled subservience.

Poor women often took to prostitution to save themselves from homelessness and destitution. During the Middle Ages, prostitution was generally

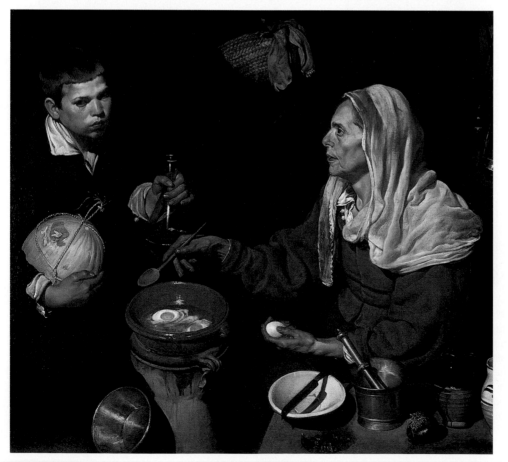

Ordinary Faces
Diego Velázquez, Old Woman Frying Eggs: *This 1618 painting by the Spanish baroque artist Diego Velázquez features both the shimmering eggs in a pan, representing the perfect, desirable nutrition provided by women everywhere, but especially among the poor, and the deep, mysterious gaze of woman and boy, united in a central ritual act of food-preparation. Velázquez, who would paint princes and popes, here elevates the food and its cook to solemn and imposing rank.* (National Galleries of Scotland)

legal, protected by civic authorities and kings alike as a way of forestalling more serious social problems. From the sixteenth century, that policy shifted: although prostitution was still tolerated and regulated in most urban areas, it was now perceived in both Roman Catholic and Protestant communities as a social evil that threatened the welfare of good citizens. A new category of institutions was created to house women who had been prostitutes, or who might turn to prostitution if not rescued from poverty and the streets. In late Renaissance Italy, asylums for the "badly married" allowed impoverished widows as well as former prostitutes to learn the skills that would enable them to leave the shelter for low-paying jobs.

Swift social intervention in the case of prostitution testifies that a social motive was at work beyond the desire to relieve poverty or punish crime. Measures taken to control prostitution attest to a readiness to discipline and monitor sexual behavior. That impulse is also evident in the intensified prosecution of sodomites (the term indiscriminately used for male homosexuals), infanticides, and alleged witches (the latter two groups mostly female). These trends mark an era also noted for the creation of modern science and Enlightenment rationalism.

Orphaned children formed another significant class of the poor. Orphanages had their roots in the early Christian era, but they were transformed in the eighteenth century by the number of abandoned infants they had to accommodate. Institutionalized in the first few months of life, most orphans were effectively presumed illegitimate, born as a result of rape or

William Hogarth, The Career of Gin: *William Hogarth's 1751 engraving is an indictment of the toxin of gin, to which the urban dwellers of eighteenth-century England became addicted, and the irresponsibility of the poor— drunken, suicidal, criminal, as seen in the many individual scenes that make up this unified image. At its center, representing the summit of irresponsibility, is the besotted woman, prominently seated on the stairs, her nursing breasts wantonly bared and legs scarred with syphilitic sores indicative of her manner of life, who allows her neglected infant to fall to his destruction over the railing.* (British Museum, London)

prostitution, or simply abandoned. With wet nursing still the only alternative to maternal breastfeeding, and with pediatric medicine still undeveloped, the orphanage system resulted in staggering death rates, in the range of fifty to ninety percent in European capitals. Those who survived the orphanage were placed still young as servants or apprentices.

Other children wandered the city, adrift and utterly alone. In many towns, most street beggars were children. Abandoned children swarmed down the roads that led to the cities, ideal recruits for the bands of beggars and thieves and disbanded mercenary soldiers whose gangs often "ruled" a whole neighborhood or district.

Crime and Disease The chronic poverty of so many encouraged crime, and elites suspected virtually all the poor of criminal intent. In cities, it is thought that crime was on a powerful upswing from as early as the seventeenth century. The increased incidence of crime stimulated the use of harsh punishments, such as physical mutilation, public humiliation, deportation overseas, and death. Judicially mutilated men and women could be seen everywhere, and capital punishment for minor property violations became common. Women were punished as harshly as, or more harshly than, men, unless they happened to be pregnant. The gallows alongside the gate reminded new arrivals of the judicial power of the city.

The gallows promised to bring order where society had descended to disorder. Critics horrified by this official use of violence, however, began to speak up against harsh punishment. The moral failing of the criminal, Sir Thomas More (1477–1535) pointed out in *Utopia*, was often a rational response to a harsh economic reality that made people choose between crime and starvation. The poor man stole, and was hanged, while wealthier offenders (often tried in different courts) might escape punishment altogether. A new generation of penologists, or experts on punishment, suggested that the end of justice was the reclamation of the criminal. In 1764, Italian jurist Cesare Beccaria published his influential *Essay on Crimes and Punishments* that heralded the end of torture and capital punishment. The English theoretician Jeremy Bentham later put Beccaria's views to work in his proposal for a model prison, the "Panopticon." Meaning "Total Surveillance," the Panopticon replaced the violence of the gallows with the relentless scrutiny of those committed to the rehabilitation and redemption, rather than the punishment, of criminals.

Early modern experts also sought remedies for disease. But the medicine of university-trained physicians, or surgeons with practical experience of wounds, or folk healers (mostly female) offered few remedies for illness (see also Chapter 17). Unaware of the real causes of infection, surgeons wielded a frightening array of unsanitary knives and scalpels to mend wounds or amputate limbs, or drained blood from patients already weakened by disease.

The main victory in the battle against illness was the end of bubonic plague in western Europe, a victory that owned everything to nature and nothing to health professionals. The plague, which had first arrived in 1347 and wrought unprecedented devastation on European populations (see Chapter 12), continued to return every few years to take new victims into the eighteenth century. When the plague exhausted itself in western Europe (although it remained endemic in eastern Europe into the nineteenth century, and in Africa and Asia into the twentieth). Its last outbreak was in 1720 in the French port of Marseilles. Thereafter, the disease faded out: by a

Urban Riots and Plague

The Fettmilch uprising in Frankfurt:
While drunkenness, crime, and disease oppressed the ordinary citizens, so too did the urban patriciate—an upper crust of the bourgeoisie that monopolized public magistracies. A ferocious urban riot in the city of Frankfurt in 1612–1616 was directed against the patriciate and, as often and tragically occurred, against the city's Jews. (Historisches Museum, Frankfurt-am-Main)

Stürmung der Iüdengasse zü Franckfürt am Mayn.

Plague ward in a Hamburg hospital: *Pre- and early-industrial cities were notoriously harsh, unwelcoming environments. Poverty, squalor, overcrowding, and crime were ever-constant problems. Due to their concentrated populations, cities were also disproportionately at risk for experiencing major outbreaks of infectious disease. This 1746 depiction of a plague ward in a hospital in Hamburg offers few comforts. Note the crude conditions of amputation in the center.* (Germanisches Nationalmuseum, Nürnberg)

benign historical accident, the black rat, which carried the flea that carried the killer bacillus, lost its ecological niche to a rival species. Meanwhile, prosperity (for some) and better nutrition also made it possible for the population to resist other diseases more successfully. Until just over a century ago, higher caloric consumption was the greatest cause of improved health for most Europeans.

Yet diseases still ravaged unprotected populations. The poorest Europeans, malnourished and badly housed, were the most vulnerable to such killers as typhus, typhoid, scarlet fever, and pneumonia, as well as the smallpox for which, at last, a preventive was found (see Chapter 17). Hospitals, which also housed the elderly and the destitute, were the refuge of the seriously ill whose own families could not assist them. A ward in a Hamburg hospital is illustrated above. At the margins of city life, the sick became strangers.

Other Outsiders The cities encompassed other outsiders: foreigners, dissenters, and Jews. Cosmopolitan centers such as Venice and Amsterdam had for years accommodated the needs of foreigners (Greeks and Turks, for example) by allowing them to build at their own expense a protected enclave, where they could pursue their own religion while trading with the local citizens. Dissenters were those adherents of minority (mostly Protestant) sects who were granted a grudging tolerance in England, and a more generous one in the Dutch Republic. Subject to various restrictions, they were at least protected by law, once Europe had weathered its outbreak of religious warfare.

The Jews formed another group of city dwellers whose presence of more than a thousand years among European Christians had won, at best, a reluctant tolerance. They had long since been expelled from some parts of western Europe, most recently (in 1492 and 1497) from Spain and Portugal (see Chapters 12, 14).

Still, large communities of Jews lived in the towns of the Holy Roman Empire, northern Italy, and the Netherlands. They flourished especially in Venice (where they were confined to the ghetto; see Chapter 12), and in Amsterdam, constituting in 1700 four percent of the population. In these regions, they enjoyed considerable freedom, although always subject to social restrictions. Further east, Jewish civic life thrived in the city of Prague in Bohemia. The strongest concentrations of Jewish population were to be found, however, in Poland, Lithuania, and the Balkans. By 1700, Poland alone probably sheltered more than three-fourths of the world's Jews, who constituted over four percent of the whole population.

Jewish communities from 1500 to 1750 benefited from the broadening of European culture stimulated by the Renaissance thirst for Classical learning and the Reformation rupture of Catholic uniformity. As those movements developed in scientific and enlightened directions, Jews continued to enjoy relative autonomy and security, while they were not yet liable, as later, to assimilation. Nevertheless, the horrors of the previous era, marked by anti-Semitic outbursts triggered especially by the Crusades and plague crises, did not wholly disappear. The Jews of Poland were harshly persecuted from 1648 into the 1650s, and blood-libel accusations by both Protestant and Catholic zealots pursued their communities in the Empire and Italy. As the modern age approached, the Jews were still strangers in Christian Europe.

FIELD AND VILLAGE: THE BOUNDARIES OF PEASANT LIFE

While city-dwellers enjoyed the riches of an urban environment now at the core of Western society, in the country, free peasants and bonded serfs, tenant farmers and sharecroppers, lost out both to the city and to enterprising landowners alike. For most of world history, most people were peasant farmers, and farming remained a struggle to wrest subsistence from the soil. Plowing, sowing, reaping, tool maintenance, and stock rearing were the framework of peasant life, as the passage quoted in *Witnesses* on p. 530 suggests. Changes in that great continuity in the early modern period allowed some Europeans to prosper as never before. Many others lost ground. Change and continuity characterized the rituals of village life, in which the sturdy cultural patterns of traditional Europe were both rehearsed and subverted.

Bread, Beans, and Flocks

The fields of grain—rye, barley, oats, wheat—that stretched across Europe's great plain provided the bread that led to improved health and increased population. Progress in medieval farming techniques lay behind the continent's demographic success: the use of the heavy plow, and the fallowing of one field in a two- or three-field system of rotation (see Chapter 9). After 1600 in the Netherlands and England, entrepreneurial landowners promoted farming techniques that further enhanced the fertility of the land, freeing some of it for the development of cash crops.

Urbanized from an early period, the Netherlands had scarcely enough land to grow the grain necessary for its ample population. In the seventeenth century, after the struggle of the largely Protestant northern provinces to free themselves from the rule of Catholic Spain had been resolved and the Dutch Republic created, Dutch landowners employed agricultural techniques that led to dramatically increased production of high-quality, high-priced agricultural goods. The merchant fleet that hauled grain from eastern Europe to home ports made these innovations possible. Freed from the need to produce wheat for bread, local farmers grew marketable vegetables and raised cows for dairy products. They rotated the sowing of crops in sequences planned so that nutrients lost in one planting would be restored to the soil in the next. In addition, ambitious land-drainage projects increased the amount of arable land that could be devoted to the new kinds of agricultural production. Fat cows and round, ripe cheeses, together with a variety of garden crops (among them the new species imported from the Americas), signified the improved diet and comfortable wealth of the Dutch. These innovations amounted to the first stage of what some historians have called the "Agricultural Revolution."

The English followed the Dutch in agricultural innovation, draining marshland, introducing crop rotation, and planning their agricultural ventures with an eye to the market. In so doing, landowners often displaced peasant cultivators, and installed tenant farmers directly responsible to them. Displaced peasants might become day-laborers or migrants to the cities.

The goal of landowner management was in some cases the increased cultivation of grain and vegetables. Often, though, it was to remove land from cultivation by erecting hedges or fences around common land previously used for grazing by an entire community or medieval-style open fields in the process known as enclosure. This made room for livestock—dairy cows, as in the Netherlands, and more importantly, sheep—which required only one man to oversee a whole herd or flock. English sheep had produced much of the wool woven into cloth in northern Europe throughout the Middle Ages. When an expanding market for wool led landlords to enclose the fields that had once supported numerous peasants, sheep grazed where once men had farmed.

Dutch and English landowners pioneered agricultural methods that would one day benefit farmers everywhere. In both countries, greater agricultural productivity freed land from grain production for the cultivation of high-profit cash crops, dairy products, and raw wool. While the changes had the potential to benefit all in the long run, they pressured some peasant farmers in the short run: many English farmers lost their land to the combined phenomenon of tenant farming and stock-raising. Many eastern European peasants suffered so that their masters might produce the quantities of grain that Dutch merchants paid well to acquire.

Elsewhere the pace of agricultural change was slow and uneven. In eastern Europe, landowners profited from the increased market for grain in the west. They increased their yields by extracting more labor from their serfs, rather than by improving their techniques. In Spain, increased acreage was devoted to sheep-farming organized by the guild of sheeptenders known as the Mesta. In Italy's rich Po river valley, maize (corn) and rice cultivation alongside traditional crops resulted in abundant harvests. Elsewhere, even in populous France, older farming methods remained in use up to the eighteenth century. Peasants living in manorial villages still plowed cooperatively, and grazed their animals on common land. Farmers eeking out a living on thin upland soil still used the wooden plow, and in the extensive forests of Russia and Sweden, slash and burn methods were used to carve out temporary farmlands.

Varieties of Labor

Alongside this great variety in the management of farmlands, a corresponding variety existed in the condition of farmers, as Map 18.1 on p. 537 shows. In the early modern centuries, differences in farmers' status became more pronounced, ranging from the prosperous English **yeoman** to the Russian serf. The most significant difference was between the mainly free peasantry of western Europe, and that of the oppressed serfs of eastern Europe. It is in this era that

Map 18.1 The Emancipation of the Peasantry up to 1812: *By 1812, almost all of Europe's peasantry had won their freedom. The exceptions were Russia and much of eastern Europe, Spain and Portugal, and southern Italy, where serfdom or other forms of unfree labor continued into the nineteenth century. Scandinavia (outside of Denmark) had never known serfdom. In Britain and the Netherlands (including Belgium) the peasants had emerged from serfdom after around 1200. The French Revolution (see Chapter 20) saw the destruction of the remnants of serfdom in France, and encouraged liberation in northern Italy, some of the Austrian lands, and Denmark.* **What factors permitted freedom to advance in some regions and not in others?**

a marked disparity between the economic condition of those two European zones appeared.

In the west, the progress out of serfdom that had begun in the Middle Ages was largely completed. Most farmers were free men or women, legally bound neither to the landowner nor the land. Best off were peasant proprietors, who were freehold owners of a plot sufficient to feed their families and yield a marketable surplus. Even tenant farmers, who paid a landowner for the use of their land, could prosper if their farms were large and fertile. Then came the smallholders and sharecroppers. Smallholders might own just enough land to provide subsistence for their families in good years. In bad years, they borrowed in order to survive, or they starved. Sharecroppers, who owed landowners a share of up to fifty percent of all they produced, lived in a constant state of indebtedness. Even more vulnerable was the condition of day-laborers, who neither owned nor rented land but, continually in search of work, survived from day to day on the wages gained by their labor.

All peasants paid for the land they worked. Their plight is satirized in the cartoon on p. 538. Some paid "dues" to the landowner, obligations descending from medieval contracts, involving a certain amount of labor or a payment of cash, crops, or livestock. Others paid rent or a percentage share of the produce. Landowners could also collect fees from peasants for the use of the mill to grind grain or the winepress. To the king peasants owed taxes on the land, in addition to direct taxes on such commodities as salt, a hated levy that disproportionately burdened the poor. In Catholic regions, the church also took its tenth share or tithe. By the early modern era this was no longer used to support the local priest but rather drained to the big cities or to Rome itself to help fund the great prelates.

Peasant Lives

Cultivating and processing flax: *For most peasants, life in early modern Europe continued to revolve around a few fundamental certainties: the seasonal agricultural cycle, the village, hard labor, and the continual threat of crop shortages or outright famine. In this 1791 engraving, an entire family—except the youngest child who plays with the dog—is engaged in combing, cutting, and preparing the fibers of flax to weave into linen cloth.* (Private Collection)

In England, farmers were free of the tithe, yeomen could with hard work and good fortune hope to join the gentry, and even tenant farmers could prosper. But the English peasantry suffered greatly from the waves of enclosure, speeded by laws passed by Parliament, that gathered pace from the sixteenth to the eighteenth century. Those who lost their land might work in their homes in the "cottage industries" of textile manufacture (see Chapters 16, 21), or they might seek employment as migrant day-laborers.

The condition of the laborers of eastern Europe, consigned to a "second serfdom" in the early modern era, was worse. In Russia, for example, the tsar granted noble landowners the right to enserf their peasantry in exchange for loyalty and service. Russian nobles measured their wealth not by the extent of their acreage but by the number of "souls"—adult male serfs—who owed them labor.

Polish nobles acquired the same prerogatives without any concessions to the crown, driven by the lure of profits to be gained by exporting grain to western Europe through Baltic ports. Throughout eastern Europe, obligatory labor for the lord was increased to such an extent that peasants could scarcely cultivate their own land use. In Bohemia and Moravia, labor service called the *robot* (meaning "work") left the serfs only one day a week to cultivate their own land. Our modern conception of the mechanical robot descends from these laborers whose spirits were crushed by excessive exploitation. Landowners retained many rights over the peasants, and could demand gifts or prohibit a daughter's marriage. In many regions, nobles exercised judicial powers over serfs, their capacity to exact capital

Plight of the peasant: *The seeming stability of rural life masked important, and ultimately revolutionary, changes. This cartoon by Bulloz shows a struggling, elderly French peasant—a "commoner"—who is having to bear the full weight of the other two main continental social orders, or "estates," the privileged aristocracy and clergy.*

punishment signaled ominously by the presence of the gallows standing near the manor house.

Russian landholders attempted to stem the flight of overburdened workers by declaring their serfs bound to their land and village. Desperate serfs and other fugitives ran for the "borderlands," the region of Ukraine between old Muscovy, Poland, and the Crimea. Those who remained were virtually slaves, as the landowners might sell not only their land, with attached serfs, but the serfs, bodily, themselves.

Festival and Riot

Even in oppressed Russian villages, people danced, sang, and celebrated special occasions. The village community helped its members weather famine, cold, war, disease, and taxes. Its leaders met regularly to plan planting or harvest, and to address the demands of the landlord, or the misbehavior of the villagers. The villagers shared in joys and sorrows, and proclaimed in story and song the clever wiles by which peasants maneuvered and survived. Customs of village carnival and riot, disdained by the grandees of the court and city patricians, gave expression to the energy and talents of those who could neither read

nor rule. The village celebrations of peasants and serfs are the matrix of national traditions that have been inherited by modern states.

The life of the village was a whole world to the peasants. Together they celebrated the festivals of the Christian year, in rituals that were not wholly purged of pre-Christian, pagan practices. Together they feasted at harvest time, and at ceremonies marking births, deaths, baptisms, and weddings. At these events, they engaged in wrestling matches and tugs-of-war, brutal blood sports, and lighthearted entertainments. Self-trained experts played melodies distinctive to the region—"folk" music—on simple string, wind, and percussion instruments, accompanying village singers and dancers drawn from young and old, and men and women.

The young people of the village found wives and husbands in the same community where their parents had found theirs. Groups of adolescent girls paraded in front of the young men in rituals of courtship. Groups of adolescent boys courted them—but also joined in drunken and violent sprees, creating social and sexual disorder. Village healers or "good" witches could provide potions that aroused love, it was believed, in the opposite sex. Engaged lovers might

***Pieter Bruegel the Elder,* The Peasants' Wedding:** *Festive times provided welcome relief from work and were an important part of the peasantry's social and cultural life. Laden with symbolic meanings, at its simplest level this painting by Pieter Bruegel the Elder from around 1568 depicts such a scene. (Kunsthistorisches Museum, Vienna)*

decide not to wait to take their marriage vows before they consummated their understanding.

The village controlled its own members. Most premarital pregnancies resulted in hasty weddings under the guidance of village elders—although some were ended upon consultation of the midwife with herbal concoctions, often dangerous to the mother if not the fetus. In ritual enactments, adolescent gangs mocked those members of the community whose behavior was considered out of bounds—cuckolded husbands, scolding women, men who married women too young or who beat their wives. Also part of the festival celebration was the ritual of role reversal, where women dressed like men, beggars like nobles, in a safe but probing critique of social norms.

The festivities of village life were overshadowed by austerity. Peasants dressed in drab tunics and robes of black or gray, often bequests from dead relatives who had also worn them for a whole lifetime. They lived in huts of wood, clay, or rubble, consisting of one or two small rooms shared with animals who needed shelter and provided a source of heat. Unlike the wealthy bourgeoisie or nobles, their homes had no ornament, in fact scarcely any furniture at all: a bench, a table, perhaps a bed, a pot to cook the daily soup that was the main accompaniment of bread. About a pound of bread (of barley, rye, or wheat), if it could be had, was the standard poor person's diet, or porridge or potatoes if grain for bread was scarce, enriched by thin soups of vegetables and occasional eggs.

A famous depiction of a peasant wedding by the Flemish artist Pieter Bruegel (c. 1525–1569; see p. 539) shows solid peasants at table, amply supplied with round loaves and cheeses (but, correctly, no meat), boisterous in their celebration of the ample fruits of the earth. But the painting deceives. For the average European peasant's experience was of scarcity rather than abundance.

In the eighteenth century, scarcity was still a problem. In the Middle Ages, local governments often stockpiled grain in the event of crisis, but now it was sold on the open market, to the highest bidder, and its cost pressed ever upward. Periods of scarcity, together with the harshness of landowner exactions, inflamed many to rebel. Peasant unrest—often sparked by crowds gathered for festivals or processions—was ceaseless: the German peasants in 1525; dispossessed Irish Roman Catholics in 1641; the Russian followers of the false tsars Stephen Razin in 1670–1671 and Emilian Pugachev in 1773–1775, convulsed their nations. Amid the pages of a famous genealogy of Venetian noble families may be found periodically the telling comment on the disappearance of a patriarch, "murdered by the peasants."

During the English Civil War, members of two groups put forward radical solutions for social ills. The Levellers and the Diggers proposed the elimination of social distinctions and the assumption of real power by those below the elites. The Leveller leader Henry Denne denied that he wished to turn "the world upside down," yet his proposals for social reform were profoundly unsettling to those who ruled.

Resisting the demands of the landowner, the authority of the church, the tyranny of gender roles, or the rigidity of the whole social hierarchy, villagers had views of their own about their world that were far from those of the educated bourgeoisie or courtly aristocrats. Nevertheless, the ability of the peasant to present his point of view was nullified by the extraordinary refinement of verbal expression possessed by social superiors. His stories would be bound in volumes of folktales, his songs and dances worked into symphonies and operas, but he himself was voiceless.

In the seventeenth and eighteenth centuries, the elites declared war on the popular culture of the villagers. Catholic and Protestant clerics insisted on a "higher" standard of sexual morality than village custom allowed, and oversaw the regular religious instruction of peasant youth. Agents of absolute states called for obedience to the king, the court, and his officials from those who already supported those dignitaries with their tax contributions. Reformers and intellectuals attacked surviving "pagan" and magical beliefs, and brought the standards of urban and courtly refinement to bear on peasant custom. Priests and philosophers, pastors and journalists insisted that peasant culture be modernized, nationalized, and standardized—the peasant, too, should become a gentleman.

Conclusion
THE PRIVILEGED, THE POOR, AND THE MEANING OF THE WEST

In the early modern age, the system of ranked social orders inherited from the Middle Ages became more complex and more dynamic. The gap between the elites and the poor widened as status came to be determined by cultural refinement, in addition to wealth. Being poor became a problem, a reproach, a threat. To escape poverty, to approach nobility, were the aspirations of those in the middle—Europe's would-be gentlemen. An expanding group with seemingly limitless ambitions, these would-be gentlemen began their advance, which still continues today.

QUESTIONS TO CONSIDER

1. How were nobles able to maintain their position and privileges even after the age of the mounted knight was over?

2. In what way did courts and cities serve as the centers of Western civilization in the seventeenth and eighteenth century?

3. If the bourgeoisie became as rich as the nobility, or even richer, why did they create forms of culture that were different from those of the nobility?

4. Did the condition and possibilities of the poor, the indigent, and the alien (including Jews and other religious minorities) improve during the seventeenth and eighteenth centuries?

5. How did the conditions of agricultural workers change from the sixteenth through eighteenth centuries? Why was their situation different in western and in eastern Europe?

SUGGESTED RESOURCES

Adams, Christine, *A Taste for Comfort and Status: A Bourgeois Family in Eighteenth-Century France* (University Park PA: Pennsylvania State University Press, 2000). Studies some 300 surviving letters written by members of the Lamothes family to reconstruct the social, professional, intellectual, and civic life of a bourgeois household in Bordeaux.

Arditi, Jorge, *A Genealogy of Manners: Transformations of Social Relations in France and England from the Fourteenth to the Eighteenth Century* (Chicago: University of Chicago Press, 1998). Examins etiquette manuals and courtesy books to show how the nobility of France and England created a code of behavior to assert social dominance.

Asch, Ronald and Adolf M. Birke, eds., *Princes, Patronage and the Nobility: The Court at the Beginning of the Early Modern Age* (London: German Historical Institute; Oxford: Oxford University Press, 1991). Focuses on the role of royal and princely courts as the contact point between rulers and local elites during the early modern era.

Beik, William, *Urban Protest in Seventeenth-Century France: the Culture of Retribution* (Cambridge: Cambridge University Press, 1997). Examines the struggle between angry crowd and town magistrates in more than 15 urban settings.

Dewald, Jonathan, *The European Nobility, 1400–1800* (Cambridge: Cambridge University Press, 1996). An up-to-date, comprehensive overview of Europe's nobility from the late Middle Ages to the time of nobility, stressing the resourcefulness and flexibility of this elite class.

Franits, Wayne E., *Paragons of Virtue: Women and Domesticity in Seventeenth-Century Dutch Art* (Cambridge: Cambridge University Press, 1995). Uncovers the bourgeois ideals of domesticity and gender relations embedded in the art of the Dutch Golden Age.

Hill, Bridget, *Servants: English Domestics in the Eighteenth Century* (Oxford: Oxford University Press, 1997). Examines diaries, journals, and memoirs to reconstruct the experience of male and female servants of all ranks in households both wealthy and modest.

Hoffman, Philip T., *Growth in a Traditional Society: The French Countryside, 1450–1815* (Princeton: Princeton University Press, 1996). Shows how village economy responded flexibly to changes in policies and market structures—which suggests that revolution was not, as some have argued, the only path for peasant advancement.

Le Roy Ladurie, Emmanuel, *The French Peasantry, 1450–1600* (Berkeley: University of California Press, 1987). Explores the relationship between demographic changes and alterations in patterns of marriage, landholding, rent, and violence.

Manning, Roger B., *Hunters and Poachers: A Cultural and Social History of Unlawful Hunting in England, 1485–1640* (Oxford: Clarendon Press of Oxford University Press, 1993). Since hunting was the aristocracy's leisured form of war, and deer-hunting remained an aristocratic preserve into the 18th century, poaching was available to the poor and not-so-poor as a way at once to obtain meat and to resist authority.

Safley, Thomas Max and Leonard N. Rosenband, eds., *The Workplace before the Factory: Artisans and Proletarians, 1500–1800* (Ithaca-London: Cornell University Press, 1993). Eleven essays examining the lives of early modern artisans in Europe (and New England), in such occupations as mining, textile manufacturing, shipbuilding, and printing.

Woolf, Stuart, *Domestic Strategies: Work and Family in France and Italy, 1600–1800* (Cambridge: Cambridge University Press, 1991). Explores how ordinary people dealt with markets and institutions in order to advance the interests of their households and families.

Wrightson, Keith, *Earthly Necessities: Economic Lives in Early Modern Britain* (New Haven: Yale University Press, 2000). How social systems adjusted to economic change between 1470 and 1750.

Almanach de la Cour—images and materials on nobility, royalty, and chivalry, from the Middle Ages through the 18th century:
http://www.chivalricorders.org

Vermeer, Dutch painter of scenes of daily life—images, some accompanied by commentary:
http://www.kfki.hu/~arthp/html/v/vermeer/index.html

William Hogarth, painter and satirist of contemporary English life—images and biography:
http://sunsite.dk/cgfa/hogarth

Western Civilization Documents CD-ROM

12.5 Putting the Poor to Work
16.1 Tortured Execution vs. Prison Rules
16.2 Life in the Eighteenth Century: An Artisan's Journey
16.3 Instructions for a New Law Code
16.4 Jonathan Swift: A Description of a City Shower
16.7 G.M. Trevelyan: Chapter XIII from English Social History

INALIENABLE RIGHTS

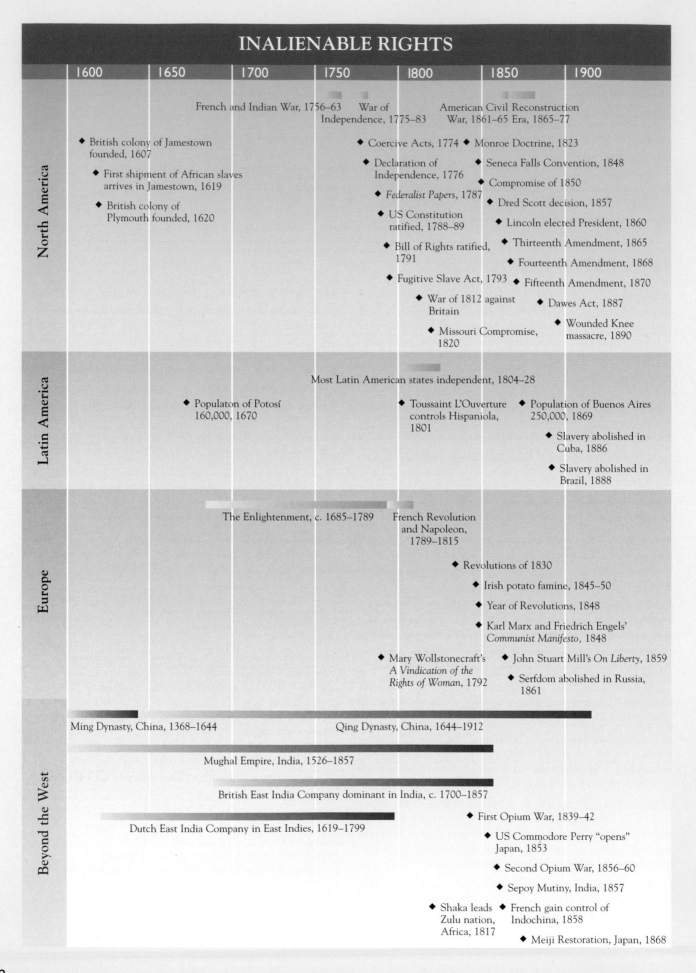

	1600	1650	1700	1750	1800	1850	1900

North America

French and Indian War, 1756–63   War of Independence, 1775–83   American Civil War, 1861–65   Reconstruction Era, 1865–77

- British colony of Jamestown founded, 1607
- First shipment of African slaves arrives in Jamestown, 1619
- British colony of Plymouth founded, 1620
- Coercive Acts, 1774
- Declaration of Independence, 1776
- *Federalist Papers*, 1787
- US Constitution ratified, 1788–89
- Bill of Rights ratified, 1791
- Fugitive Slave Act, 1793
- War of 1812 against Britain
- Missouri Compromise, 1820
- Monroe Doctrine, 1823
- Seneca Falls Convention, 1848
- Compromise of 1850
- Dred Scott decision, 1857
- Lincoln elected President, 1860
- Thirteenth Amendment, 1865
- Fourteenth Amendment, 1868
- Fifteenth Amendment, 1870
- Dawes Act, 1887
- Wounded Knee massacre, 1890

Latin America

Most Latin American states independent, 1804–28

- Populaton of Potosí 160,000, 1670
- Toussaint L'Ouverture controls Hispaniola, 1801
- Population of Buenos Aires 250,000, 1869
- Slavery abolished in Cuba, 1886
- Slavery abolished in Brazil, 1888

Europe

The Enlightenment, c. 1685–1789   French Revolution and Napoleon, 1789–1815

- Revolutions of 1830
- Irish potato famine, 1845–50
- Year of Revolutions, 1848
- Karl Marx and Friedrich Engels' *Communist Manifesto*, 1848
- Mary Wollstonecraft's *A Vindication of the Rights of Woman*, 1792
- John Stuart Mill's *On Liberty*, 1859
- Serfdom abolished in Russia, 1861

Beyond the West

Ming Dynasty, China, 1368–1644   Qing Dynasty, China, 1644–1912

Mughal Empire, India, 1526–1857

British East India Company dominant in India, c. 1700–1857

Dutch East India Company in East Indies, 1619–1799

- First Opium War, 1839–42
- US Commodore Perry "opens" Japan, 1853
- Second Opium War, 1856–60
- Sepoy Mutiny, India, 1857
- Shaka leads Zulu nation, Africa, 1817
- French gain control of Indochina, 1858
- Meiji Restoration, Japan, 1868

CHAPTER
19

INALIENABLE RIGHTS

Revolution and its Promises in
Anglo- and Latin America

1500–1880

extent of European settlement, 1750

Amerindian peoples

KEY QUESTIONS

◆ **Old and New in the New World:** How did the presence of multiple ethnicities and cultures—European, Amerindian, and African—make the New World fundamentally different from the Old? How did the conditions experienced by the forced laborers of the Americas, both native and slave, differ from those of European peasant workers?

◆ **Declarations of Independence:** What are the sources of the ideas embodied in the US Constitution? Why is it significant that the Constitution is a written document?

◆ **Fulfilling the Promise:** In North America in 1791, what groups still did not enjoy the freedoms announced in the Declaration of Independence? What progress had been attained toward that ideal by 1900? To what extent was the situation in Latin America comparable?

Jefferson's Promise Called upon to declare to the world why it was that North American colonists rebelled against their British masters, Thomas Jefferson (1743–1826) provided a concise statement of the political values of the Enlightenment (see Chapters 15, 17). Ironically a slaveowner himself, he asserted the "self-evident" truth that "all men are created equal," endowed with the "inalienable rights" of "life, liberty, and the pursuit of happiness." Government, said Jefferson, is created by men to protect these rights. When it fails to do so, "it is the right of the people to alter or abolish it," and to institute a new one.

The points Jefferson stated so concisely were a concentration of the inherited political traditions of the West: behind them stand Aristotle and Cicero, Thomas Aquinas and Marsilius of Padua, Hobbes and Locke, Montesquieu and Voltaire (see Chapters 4, 10, 15, and 17)—above all, Locke.

The United States of America was the first nation in the world to be founded on these ancient, medieval, and Enlightenment principles. Soon the nations of Latin America would also declare their independence on the same principles. In neither region was the Jeffersonian promise of civic equality fulfilled at first. Yet an ocean away from the European homeland where those ideals were born, some progress was made toward the goal of securing for at least some citizens their inalienable rights.

This chapter explores the career of the nations of the Western Hemisphere during the four centuries after Columbus' first journey, examining the impact of the European legacy upon a world where Europeans, Amerindians, and Africans met, and considering the extent to which the Enlightenment principles Jefferson announced were realized in the Americas.

OLD AND NEW IN THE NEW WORLD

During the colonial period, from 1492 to about 1800 (see Chapter 16), the old and the new converged in different ways in British North America and in Latin America (including those parts of South America, the Caribbean, and Mexico where Spanish, Portuguese, or French, all derived from Latin, are spoken).

In the south, the imprint of European social, religious, and political institutions was heavy; in the north, it was light. In the south, large indigenous Amerindian populations molded colonial culture; in the north, the native presence was slighter. The economy of the southern region depended on plantations, ranches, or mines sustained by impressed Indian or slave labor; the economy of the northern region was more varied. The proportions of old and new in New World civilizations help explain their development.

Brazil and the Caribbean: Plantation Nations

During the colonial era, Brazil and the Caribbean islands developed plantation economies of a type unknown in Europe, but dominated by European elites. From the outset, Christopher Columbus (1451–1506) began building a New World economy different from the old. The climate was favorable, and the wilderness beckoned with fantasies of countless stores of gold. Columbus established a fortified city, and set six Dominican friars to convert and "civilize" the native Tainos. Within a generation, ships laden with New World treasures sailed regularly to Spain.

The Caribbean Tobacco was the first cash crop farmed in the Spanish-ruled Caribbean islands, followed by sugar, brought by Dutch merchants by way of Brazil. Having learned to grow sugar in Asia, the Portuguese developed the plantation system, sustained by slave labor, in their Atlantic islands of the Madeiras and São Tomé. Sugar cultivation was imported into Brazil, along with cargoes of slaves. From there, it reached the Caribbean islands.

The Amerindians of the Caribbean—the Tainos, Caribs, and Arawaks—could not supply the huge labor force required to grow, harvest, and mill sugar cane. By around 1600, some ninety percent of the Caribbean natives had died from overwork, heartbreak, and disease. African slaves replaced the natives. These provided a labor pool that the armed Europeans managed brutally. Since neither women's labor nor their fertility was deemed valuable, male slaves outnumbered females two to one, which meant that the slave population could not maintain itself through reproduction. New shipments of African captives were constantly required. The increase in the numbers of slaves imported into the New World is shown in *How Many?* on p. 565.

The existence of slavery informed every aspect of the new Caribbean culture. African song, dance, and storytelling figured more powerfully than the Christian rituals or European refinements of the elite. A mixture developed of Christian and African customs, particularly in western Hispaniola (modern Haiti), where it became known as **voodoo**.

Soon Dutch, French, and English competitors challenged Spanish dominion of the Caribbean and its coastal rim. With the foothold of Dutch Guiana (later Surinam) on the northern coast of South America, the Dutch continued to play a significant role in Caribbean shipping. The French acquired half of Hispaniola, as well as the islands of Martinique and Guadeloupe, and the north coastal colony of French Guiana. The British controlled the Bahamas and Jamaica, as well as some islands of the Lesser Antilles, the colony of British Honduras on the mainland of Central America (later Belize), and a British sector of

Guiana. The small European landowner class that dominated a much larger slave population relied on its mother countries for defense and supplies.

By 1750, the Caribbean had changed dramatically from the early days of the Spanish conquest. The large population of Africans outnumbered whites and **mulattoes** (persons of mixed African and European parentage) about ten to one. The Amerindian natives had virtually disappeared. The economy was dominated by the production of sugar and the Spanish monopoly had been broken.

Brazil   Spain was the principal metropolitan power in the Caribbean, but Portugal dominated Brazil. Early explorers recognized growing near the coast of the new continent a tree used for dyes that Portuguese merchants had previously exported from Asia. Brazil itself was named after this breselwood, or brazilwood. For a generation, the shipping of dyewoods occupied the Portuguese exploiters of the new territory. Later, the Portuguese brought sugar to Brazil, along with the plantation system of sugar farming. On the plantation, slaves tended the sugar plants, cut the canes, and milled the sugar for which Europeans developed an insatiable demand. The plantation farming of sugar, then coffee, became the backbone of the Brazilian economy. As many as 3 to 5 million African slaves were imported to labor on Brazilian plantations from the early 1500s, about one-third to one-half of all slaves imported to the western hemisphere. By 1800, blacks and mulattoes comprised more than half of Brazil's population. The practice of frequent manumission (release from slavery) resulted in a large group of free blacks and mulattoes, who gathered in the cities and intermingled with white elites. The indigenous Amerindians, on the other hand, isolated in the tropical forests of the interior, had little contact with Europeans concentrated on the eastern shore.

The Brazilian economy was more diverse than the Caribbean, which was wholly dependent on plantation crops. In addition to dyewoods, Brazil exported other products from the tropical forest (especially the drugs curare and coca), and mined gold and diamonds. A late-colonial gold rush encouraged the growth of Brazil's southern cities of São Paulo and Rio de Janeiro, which supplanted the original port city of Bahía in importance. Brazilian products amounted to as much as two-thirds of Portugal's exports; as was the case elsewhere, metropolitan prosperity depended heavily on colonial produce.

All three major Brazilian cities also supported small manufacture, whose artisans were often black or mulatto. Blacks and mulattoes also worked in the cities as servants, carters, peddlers, and prostitutes. As one Brazilian observer noted, "it was the black who developed Brazil."

The Portuguese regime in Brazil was similar to that in Spanish South America, although less restrictive. Advised by his overseas Council on New World concerns, the king appointed a viceroy to govern Brazil, who was surrounded by the ceremony and luxury befitting a European monarch. Law courts were headed by royal officials, and a tax commission oversaw the farming of revenues (i.e. the granting to individuals of the lucrative right to collect taxes).

Regional administrators were military officials called captains, who enjoyed considerable latitude. They launched a tradition of military leadership in civilian affairs, which saw Brazil push its boundaries westward by the 1700s to the Andes Mountains and south to the Plata River.

Captains were often native Portuguese who later returned to more prominent positions at home, but some were creoles (white Americans descended from European forebears on both sides). Creoles were a social group of critical importance in both

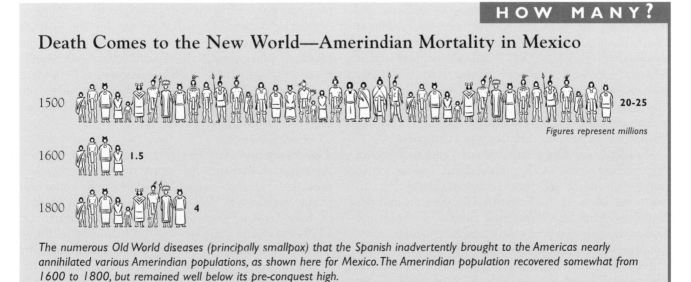

HOW MANY?

Death Comes to the New World—Amerindian Mortality in Mexico

1500   **20-25**

Figures represent millions

1600   **1.5**

1800   **4**

The numerous Old World diseases (principally smallpox) that the Spanish inadvertently brought to the Americas nearly annihilated various Amerindian populations, as shown here for Mexico. The Amerindian population recovered somewhat from 1600 to 1800, but remained well below its pre-conquest high.

Portuguese and Spanish America: from their ranks came the magistrates who headed the councils of local "municipalities," which dealt with land disputes, water supply, or security, in addition to various judicial procedures.

The Portuguese system of colonial rule had two main problems. The first was the inevitable tension between creoles and European-born *peninsulares* ("peninsulars," or people from the Iberian peninsula), who directed the colony's affairs. While creoles often believed that the peninsulars did not understand the American context, the peninsulars looked down on the creoles. The second problem was that of incompetence, caused by the neglect of duties or corruption. In the eighteenth century, the king's chief minister, the Marquis of Pombal (1699–1777) raised the standard of colonial administration, and reasserted the dominion of the motherland over the creole elite. Recognizing that Portugal's fortunes depended on Brazil's prosperity, he promoted industry and meticulously managed the royal treasury.

The Portuguese crown also closely monitored Brazil's economic life. It held monopolies of important commodities and collected tariffs on nearly all American imports. It permitted only Portuguese ships to carry Brazilian trade, and encouraged only those crops or manufactures that were considered to complement the Portuguese economy. Such restrictions were characteristic of **mercantilism** (see Chapter 16), and weighed heavily on colonial economies.

Nevertheless, some colonial landowners acquired immense wealth from estates as vast as whole provinces of the European homeland. Leading members of the creole elite resented their subordination to peninsular Portuguese and sought higher marks of status. The formation of militias for colonial defense provided an opportunity for such men, whose attainment of high military rank narrowed the social distance between them and peninsular governors.

Portugal also dominated Brazil's cultural and intellectual life, and saw to the firm establishment of Christianity. As elsewhere in Latin America, the conversion of the native Amerindians was a first priority. Unlike the placid Tainos that Columbus first encountered, Brazil's Amerindians resisted both Christianization and Europeanization into the eighteenth century, when decrees from Lisbon still called for natives to wear clothes like the Portuguese.

Brazilians of European descent remained within the cultural world of the motherland, journeying to Europe for study and intellectual discourse. By this route the ideas of the Scientific Revolution and the Enlightenment finally reached Brazil, which by the end of the colonial period still had not a single printing press or university, in contrast to the twenty-three universities in the Spanish zone. The Portuguese crown prohibited the establishment of printing, for fear of its revolutionary potential.

Spanish America: Mine, *Hacienda,* and Village

Spanish America stretched from California and Texas in North America to Cape Horn at the tip of South America. In this vast realm, as in the Caribbean and Brazil, explorers, conquerors, and settlers created a new economic and social system modeled on European patterns but shaped by local conditions.

Spanish settlements were concentrated in Mexico, called New Spain, and Peru (including also modern Bolivia, Ecuador, Colombia, and Chile), where the Aztec and Inca empires had flourished (see Chapter 16). In the pre-conquest era, the majority of Amerindians lived in this region, with sparser populations inhabiting Brazil, the Caribbean islands, and North America. During the first century of Spanish dominion, disease ravaged the native population, which in places sank to under ten percent of its former strength. While the native population recovered somewhat in the seventeenth century, their numbers remained low into the nineteenth century, well below their pre-conquest levels.

Mexico, for instance, had a population as high as 25 million at the time of the conquest. In the early 1800s, the population numbered no more than 8 million, counting European whites, mulattoes, **mestizos** (of European and Amerindian parentage) and Amerindians—the latter numbering about fifty percent of the whole. *How Many?* on p.545 shows this decline. In all of Spanish America at that date, the population numbered just under 17 million. Of this figure less than half was Indian, nearly one-third mestizo, one-fifth white, and a small minority African. Amerindians were the largest group in Mexico and Central America, while Indians and mestizos together constituted a majority elsewhere in Spanish America.

Changes in the ethnic composition of Mexico and Peru are shown in the graphs on p. 559. Low population and physical barriers discouraged the settlement of interior regions of South America. Instead Spanish settlers remained in the charted regions of the Mexican plateau and the Pacific coast (eventually extending along the Plata River, consisting of modern Argentina and Paraguay). Here they established an economy based on mining and agriculture, and oriented toward European markets.

The Economy   In the early years of the Spanish American settlement, the thirst for gold and silver prevailed. Hernán Cortés (1485–1547), the conqueror of the Aztecs, sent home shiploads of golden trinkets of native manufacture, while Francisco Pizarro (c. 1475–1541), the conqueror of the Inca empire, found the "silver mountain" at Potosí (modern Bolivia), one of the richest silver mines ever known. With a population of some 160,000 around 1670, Potosí became the largest city in the New World.

Native Laborers in Spanish America

Following quickly upon the Spanish and Portuguese exploration, then conquest, of large parts of the Americas were settlement and exploitation. The conquistadores and their successors acquired land and privileges, and put the native population to work in ways that pressed them into dependency. These passages report the conditions imposed on laborers subject to an encomienda, which resembled the European manorial system, and the reality of life in the mines, where laborers were essentially slaves.

What natives owed two *Encomenderos* who arrived with Hernando Cortés in 1517: [The Amerindians] are assessed each day two chickens and four loads of wood and two loads of maize, and fodder for the horses; and every eighty days twenty petticoats, and twenty shirts, and four loads of blankets of henequen [a plant fiber], and the labor on their plantings of peppers, beans, maize, and wheat, and the carrying of all this to the city, and the completion of the house, and they are not to be charged beyond this. ...

On April 21, 1553, by agreement, the services of the thirty-two Indians ... were commuted, so that instead ... they are to give from now on 192 common gold pesos per year in payments made every eighty days. ...
(Encomienda Records from Nestalpa, 1547–1553; ed. C. Gibson, 1968)

Miners of Potosí (Bolivia), described by a Spanish missionary (c. 1622): [Once] I went ... into the mine. ... The ore was very rich black flint, and the excavation so extensive that it held more than 3,000 Indians working away hard with picks and hammers, breaking up that flint ore; and when they have filled their little sacks, the poor fellows, loaded down with ore, climb up ... ladders or rigging, some like masts and others like cables, and so trying and distressing that a man empty-handed can hardly get up them. ... [To support the mine walls, the Indians] keep leaving supports or pillars of the ore itself. ... [Yet] There are men so heartless that for the sake of stealing a little rich ore, they go down out of hours and deprive the innocent Indians of this protection by hollowing into these pillars to steal the rich ore in them, and then a great section is apt to fall in and kill all the Indians, and sometimes the unscrupulous and grasping superintendents themselves....
(From Antonio Vazquez de Espinosa, *Compendium and Description of the West Indies*, 1942)

At first, native Amerindian laborers performed the dangerous work of mining, but as their numbers plummeted during the sixteenth century, African slaves were imported. Even so, the number of slaves brought to Spanish America was much lower than in the Caribbean and Brazil, and enforced Indian labor remained central to the mining enterprise.

Further gold and silver strikes were made, and the value of exports peaked in the period c. 1580–1630. Mining experts from Europe introduced the amalgamation process, which used mercury to separate silver from its alloy. At such ports as Havana in Cuba or San Juan in Puerto Rico, consignments of precious metals were loaded onto hefty Spanish ships that sailed in convoy twice a year, guarded by armed men-of-war from attack by Dutch and English privateers.

For nearly two centuries, gold and especially silver were Spanish America's major exports. They enriched neither the native population nor the people of Spain, but trickled through the royal treasury to profit merchants in Amsterdam or London. Later, other minerals, cacao beans and grain, and beef and hides were shipped to European markets. In the eighteenth century, trade increased from a few sailings per year around 1700 to 189 in 1760–1761. The Spanish government's "House of Trade" (*casa de contratación*), headed by the merchants of Seville or Cadiz, operated according to mercantilist principles and designated only a few ports of entry for European manufactures or for American exports.

Spanish America's second major economic activity was farming. Crops were sold locally, supplying villagers, city dwellers, and the large mining communities. European and creole elites sought to own farmland, a source of both wealth and prestige.

The first generation of settlers won **encomiendas** from the crown, which were similar to the medieval fief. These grants had been used as a tool of the Reconquest in Spain from the Moors in earlier centuries, and were now brought to the Americas. In exchange for military services, the recipient was granted land and the right to the labor of a certain number of native Indians. In a chronically depopulated region, land without the right to commandeer a workforce valued little. The effect of the encomienda contract was to enserf, if not enslave, the Amerindian workers, as suggested by the passage quoted in *Witnesses* above. It was controversial in Spain, where the king accepted the Church's arguments against the enslavement of native Americans.

In time, the encomienda gave way to the **hacienda**, a type of large farm, embracing the owner's "great house," family and servants, the workshop and stables, the fields and villages of native Indian farmers, as illustrated on p. 548. While neither serfs nor

Life on a Hacienda

1 Indian town
2 Hamlet of Indian town
3 Central site of hacienda
4 Quarters of permanent workers
5 Owner's residence
6 Farmland of hacienda
7 Town and market

The hacienda was more than a farm. It was a system for the exploitation of the labor of Indian villagers, some resident, some part-time, who were tied to the Spanish owner by contract and debt. A simplified scheme of a typical hacienda is shown here.
Source: *Based on J. Lockhart, S. B. Schwartz,* Early Latin America: A History of Colonial Spanish America and Brazil *(Cambridge: Cambridge University Press, 1983)*

slaves, villagers worked on the owner's land, in addition to farming their own plots. Owners provided tools and seeds, or made loans, for all of which repayment was expected. Villagers thus became bound as debt slaves—the **peons**, who soon constituted the majority of native Indians in Spanish America.

The more fortunate peons worked on lands owned by the Roman Catholic Church, which became the largest single landholder in the Americas. The clergy often proved more flexible creditors and sympathetic managers than their secular counterparts. When, in the late eighteenth century, crown-appointed reformers sought to limit church power, everyone suffered.

The Church in Spanish America played a complex role. The Christian clergy were both oppressors, who sought to suppress native culture, and liberators, who guided the people to the best possible life in the framework of the European conquest. They worked for the conversion of the natives, enforcing conformity to European norms, but they were also dispensers of charity, and the directors of hospitals and schools. They learned the Amerindian languages, and translated oral histories and folktales into Spanish. In the South American universities, they included courses in Indian languages to train new generations of pastors to native populations.

Organized by the very different pursuits of farming for local markets and mining for export, the Spanish American economy at first seems to have defined a

two-class society: that of farm and mine owners or managers, and workers. The real situation was more complicated due to the factor of race. Initially, the elite was white, of European descent, while the workers were mostly native Indian. Soon, those racial divisions blurred as a result of miscegenation, or racial intermixture. The shortage of European females encouraged concubinage, and even marriage was legally permitted across race lines as early as 1501. Spanish America was a truly trans-racial society, based on social and sexual contact between Caucasoid, Mongoloid, and Negroid peoples (often identified as the three principal races).

Racial mixing, however, did not yield social equalization. On the contrary, white elites maintained the distinction of their status from those of Amerindians, the majority group that possessed the lowest prestige, and of the intermediate group called **castas** (including Africans, mulattoes, and mestizos).

Government Europeans from the homeland, meanwhile, claimed superiority to creoles. Creoles might participate in government at the local level of the "municipality," serve as officers in the militia, or even hold high rank in the Church hierarchy. But nearly all the high positions in the government of Spanish America were entirely reserved for peninsulars. These social tensions persisted despite the fact that creoles and peninsulars often intermarried.

The exclusion of creoles from senior government positions mattered, since Spanish America was heavily governed. Two huge viceroyalties were formed in the first generation after the conquest: the Viceroyalty of New Spain, of which Cortés was the first viceroy; and that of Peru. All the affairs of the colonial empire flowed through the viceregal offices. Each viceroyalty was subdivided into regional governments, or **audiencias**, with only the smaller subdivision of the municipality left to creole governors. Sometimes prone to corruption, the Spanish colonial administration was on the whole efficiently managed.

In the eighteenth century, Spain experienced a change of royal dynasty, when a European war installed Bourbon kings related to the monarchs of France in place of the Habsburg line (see Chapter 15). The Spanish Bourbons brought to colonial administration the tools of government developed under the able ministers of the French king Louis XIV (r. 1643–1715). The viceroyalties were subdivided, and the two new ones of New Granada (1717) and La Plata (1776) added. A higher standard of efficiency was instituted just at the time, ironically, when both absolute monarchy and the policy of mercantilism were under fire from Enlightenment critics (see Chapters 16, 18).

The creole elites of Spanish America resisted the Bourbon "reforms." Some were critical of the monarchy, many more were critical of mercantilism, and most resented the imposition of peninsular officials upon a society that, they believed, could be better led by themselves. Creole officers grew bold in native militias, while creole leaders centered in Buenos Aires directed large-scale smuggling operations designed to evade prohibitions on imports by sea. Creole elites helped build city centers whose baroque palaces, churches, and other public buildings mimicked European capitals in their elegance and cosmopolitan air. Blind to the possibility of resistance to their regime by native Indian villagers, they were preparing to resist the monarchy and its peninsular minions when the opportunity arose.

At the same time, creole elites supported a Spanish American culture that was deeply attached to Europe. Schools and universities followed European models, while American-born historians, philosophers, and mathematicians kept abreast of European currents in thought. Mexico City and Lima had printing presses already in the 1500s, and by 1800, nearly twenty presses published books for the small confraternity of learned creoles. Entering a convent at age fifteen in preference to marriage, in a career typical of many learned European women, Sor Juana Inés de la Cruz (1651–1695) wrote verse in a classical Castilian that is indistinguishable from the best produced in Europe.

In Spanish America, creole women continued to pursue the roles that were traditional in European society, where male patriarchs administered property and made decisions. Creole men, however, had few women of European descent available to them—a shortage contributing to the practice of concubinage and the resulting racial mixtures. In licit and illicit relationships, Indian and *casta* women were subject to white males by gender and by race. A European system of gender discrimination was thus unfortunately reinforced by the American phenomenon of racial discrimination.

In this arena as in many others, Spanish America was a blend of European social hierarchies and cultural outlooks with New World peoples and environments. The two realities met in the person of the creole, who would soon take charge.

The North Atlantic Coast: The Beckoning Wilderness

On the eastern coast of North America, as in Latin America, European newcomers created new societies in the seventeenth and eighteenth centuries that preserved features of the customs and outlook of their homelands. The lands of the future United States of America employed English models of judicial procedure and governance. Religious groups that in Europe had coexisted with difficulty developed side by side in a new environment. In the absence of a hereditary nobility or standing army, and given a nearly limitless expanse of undeveloped territory extending to the west, European settlers sensed possibilities that were unknown on the far side of the Atlantic. As they pursued their goals, they intruded upon Amerindian natives who were compelled to yield their land to the newcomers; and upon African captives who were compelled to do their labor.

The French, Dutch, and English who followed the Portuguese and Spanish to the New World found a land thinly settled by Amerindian natives—no Inca or Aztec empires here—lacking conspicuous sources of wealth or any sign of a sea link to the riches of Asia. The first resource that Europeans exploited in North America was a humble one: fish. In the seas of the north Atlantic off modern Newfoundland (claimed by the English) and Nova Scotia (claimed by the French), schools of cod beckoned to merchant shippers. Soon European woodsmen (mostly French) searched the forests for furs, and European farmers (mostly English and Dutch) scratched the new soil to see what it would yield.

Early Settlements   The first enduring European settlements north of Spanish Florida were made after 1600. French expeditions reached from Canada to the Mississippi, establishing forts, trading depots, and missions. From Quebec, founded in 1608, French governors administered their American realm as an extension of the homeland. That realm numbered no more than 80,000 citizens in 1756, including fishermen, traders, and hunters clustered around fortified settlements. Valued as suppliers of furs and as wilderness guides, Amerindian natives were neither impressed into labor service, as in Spanish America, nor even displaced, as they were in the British colonies to the south.

In time, the British colonies of North America surpassed the French in population and importance. The first English colonies at Jamestown (1607) and Plymouth (1620) were agricultural ventures with modest aims. They were organized by the Virginia and Plymouth Companies, who provided funds and supplies to start the settlers off in a new land. The settlers too were modest people who sought land to farm and freedom from the economic and cultural restrictions of life in old Europe. These features of the first English settlements were to influence the whole later process of colonial formation.

Other colonies formed around the Chesapeake Bay and in Massachusetts, Rhode Island, Connecticut, and New Hampshire. South of these New England colonies, Dutch companies concentrating on the Hudson waterway founded the province of New Netherland in 1623, the capital of which, New Amsterdam, was seized by the British and renamed New York in 1664. Pennsylvania, New Jersey, and Delaware developed between New York and the Chesapeake region before 1700, absorbing Swedish and Dutch settlements. South of Virginia, the Carolinas were settled in part by migration from the British West Indies, features of whose economy the new colonies displayed. By 1700, all but Georgia (founded in 1732) of the eventual thirteen colonies had been established. They were sparsely populated communities, clinging to the ocean shore and the banks of rivers that emptied into the Atlantic. Several (Massachusetts and Georgia, for example) were assumed to extend from the Atlantic seaboard westward across the continent—from "sea to sea"— long before the nature of that expanse could be known.

Originally organized by joint stock companies or individual proprietors, the colonies built their own institutions of local government, which by 1700 displayed some common features. Most had a governor appointed by a far-away king. The colonists taxed themselves to pay the governor's salary. A legislature decided upon those tax levies and managed other local matters. Colonists meeting minimal property requirements voted for representatives (drawn from the wealthiest stratum of the population). These voters constituted only about forty percent of the adult male population; they excluded all slaves, Amerindians, and women, as well as the poor, the young, and recent immigrants. Experience in self-government over more than 150 years inclined many Anglo-Americans to resist new demands from Parliament in the decade before the eventual strike for independence.

No European-born nobility held sway in Anglo-American society. Immigrants were often fleeing poverty or repression. The nobility and the wealthier merchants stayed home. Even the governors did not form a cohesive elite, buttressed by ritual and luxury, as they did to the south. Instead, the colonial elite developed from within in a land where upward mobility was possible (see the diagram on p. 553). Colonial leaders were very different from the hereditary aristocracies who reigned in Europe.

No standing army policed the colonists. To defend against internal rebellion, foreign infringement, or Indian raids, the colonists raised their own militias. Regular army troops were not dispatched to the Americas until war broke out with the French in 1756 (see below). They provided a military education to the colonial militias, who would profit from their lessons a few years later.

At first, the colonial economy relied upon Britain's. Local artisans and merchants fulfilled local needs, although the colonies remained dependent on Britain (as the mother country wished) for manufactures. Mercantile restrictions encouraged the colonists were to produce goods useful to the metropolis, and to transport their goods on British ships. In the early years of colonial development, these restrictions were seen more as benefits than burdens.

The colonists lived in European-style villages, with central church, official buildings, and public spaces. As in Europe, all family members were expected to labor. Men were the main workers outside the house, assisted by the older boys. Women performed domestic chores, spun and wove cloth, tended the vegetable garden and small animals, and trained their daughters in these tasks. The products of their artistry, sold to supplement household income, included textiles, processed foods, soap, candles, and the like.

Families were larger, on the whole, than in the homeland. Once the hardships of the early years were past, families with six or eight surviving children were common. These patterns led to high rates of population growth: in 1700, the British colonies had a population of about 250,000 white Europeans; by 1800, about 5 million people of European descent resided in Britain's former colonies, almost one half of the total population of England. The custom of **primogeniture** that prevailed in Britain (see Chapter 18) was often bypassed, and family property was divided among all children, including girls. Women (especially widows) and children enjoyed a higher status than in British society.

The competition to inherit was eased in the colonies because of the open territory that lay beyond the last fenced plot in the village. Not even natural barriers restricted the opportunities for landownership: in eastern North America, there were no mountain ranges as high as the Andes, no rivers as vast as the Amazon, and no treacherous, disease-ridden jungles. The perceived promise of easy abundance just

African Laborers in a Harsh New World

Advertisement for sale of slaves, July 24, 1769

Eastman Johnson, **A Ride for Liberty—The Fugitive Slaves,** *c. 1862*

Slaves picking cotton

After early, unsuccessful attempts to impress Indians into labor service, Europeans in all parts of the Americas began to rely heavily on imported African slaves. A 1769 poster from Charleston advertises the sale of slaves originating in Sierra Leone (above left). The desperation of a slave family on the run in North America is captured in the dramatic image of A Ride for Liberty by the American painter Eastman Johnson (above right). Such attempts at escape rarely succeeded. In a more prosaic scene, slave women are shown working in the cotton fields, one accompanied by her child (right). (above right: Brooklyn Museum, New York)

In the sale announcement, what are the effects on the reader of precise wording (specifying how many slaves, where they are from, the master and owner of the ship), the characterization of the slaves as "prime, healthy," and the framing of the whole in a Greek key design border?

 To continue your investigation of this topic, please go to www.prenhall.com/king for the related **WINDOWS** on the **WEB** activity

Map 19.1 The European Presence in the Americas on the Eve of Independence (1750): By 1750, Europeans had staked their claim to most of the territory of the Americas. In the north, France held a vast American empire that dwarfed both Britain's and Spain's, but it was less settled and less developed than either of the latter. After 1763, France's North American territory passed to the British, while it retained control of colonies in the Caribbean and Guiana. With many of their earlier possessions denied them by the British, the Dutch still retained footholds in Guiana (Surinam) and the Caribbean. Britain held thirteen distinct colonies on North America's Atlantic seaboard and several in the Caribbean, while Portugal held the one mammoth colony of Brazil. Spain held the lion's share of South America and the southern and southwestern zones of North America, divided into the viceroyalties of New Spain, Peru, Chile, New Granada, and Rio de la Plata; as well as Caribbean territories, principally Cuba. What explanation can be found from this map, if any, of the rebirth of the thirteen British Atlantic colonies as a new nation destined to become the world's sole superpower?

beyond the next hill or stream shaped the American consciousness and persists to the present day.

Amerindians and Africans   That beckoning wilderness was not vacant, of course, but inhabited by some 1 million natives who possessed no concept of private property, considering the land to belong to their tribes and nations. In their first encounters with Amerindian natives, the colonists often established friendly relations. In some cases, settlers negotiated a contract with Indian tribes for the use of their land. The Dutch famously purchased Manhattan island from the Indians of that name, and the Quaker William Penn (1644–1718) bought land as needed from his Indian "Friends." Such peaceful exchanges gave way to conflict. Occasionally, natives displaced from their lands responded by raiding colonial settlements. The colonists replied, fighting small-scale wars

The Social Pyramid in Colonial North America, 1775

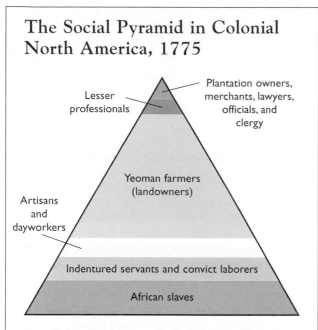

Britain's North American colonies did not avoid the social inequalities of the mother country, but exceeded them. "Merchant princes" and landed gentry sat at the very top of a pyramid that led all the way down to African slaves.
Source: *Based on T. A. Bailey, The American Pageant: A History of the Republic, Vol. I, 5th ed. (Lexington, MA: D. C. Heath and Co. 1975), p. 70.*

along the shores of the James or Connecticut rivers in Virginia and New England. Indian nations leagued together to protect their ancestral territories, sometimes allying with the French against British intruders, or with the British against the French.

Not all the interactions between Indian natives and European settlers involved violence, however. Religious and intellectual leaders called for the conversion and "civilization" of the Indians, and some were indeed converted to Christianity in the early decades of settlement. The Protestant missionary effort, however, was a lame thing in contrast to the extraordinarily successful conversion efforts of the Roman Catholic Church in Latin America.

New World Cultural Encounters

John White, Indian Woman and Child:
One of the earliest English observers of Amerindians and their culture, colonist John White painted this watercolor (far left) of an Amerindian mother and child—the latter holding a doll dressed in European style—in around 1585. (British Museum)

Albert Eckhout, Mulatto: *Whereas in the north, European settlers and natives kept their distance, in Spanish America, Africans, Amerindians, and Europeans mixed freely, so that individuals of mixed racial background, such as this mulatto soldier painted in around 1641 (left) were increasingly common. (The National Museum of Denmark)*

Native Removal in Anglo-America

In Anglo-American North America, Amerindian tribes and nations presented a singular difficulty to a new nation intent on territorial and economic expansion. Tragically, finding that Amerindians did not readily assimilate European patterns of life, national leaders made the decision to push them westward, with hopeful but empty promises of a satisfactory new homeland. In this new homeland, uprooted Amerindians would suffer violence, poverty, and isolation.

Lewis Cass, Governor of Michigan Territory 1813–1831, discusses the case for Indian Removal (1830): The destiny of the Indians, who inhabit the cultivated portions of the territory of the United States, or ... their borders, has long been a subject of deep solicitude to the American government and people. ...

[V]arious plans for their preservation and improvement were ... pursued. Many of them were carefully taught at our seminaries of education, in the hope that principles of morality and habits of industry would be acquired. ... Missionary stations were established among various tribes. ... Unfortunately, they are monuments ... of unsuccessful and unproductive efforts. What tribe has been civilized by all this expenditure of treasure, and labor, and care? ...

The cause of this total failure cannot be attributed to the nature of the experiment, or to ... [those] who have directed it. ... [T]here seems to be some insurmountable obstacle in the habits or temperament of the Indians. ... [I]f [the Indians] ... are anxious to escape ... [from United States states' laws] ample provision has been made ... A region is open to them, where they and their descendants can be secured in the enjoyment of every privilege which they may be capable of estimating and enjoying. If they choose to remain where they now are, they will be ... subject, as our citizens are, to the operation of just and wholesome laws.

(Lewis Cass, *Removal of the Indians*, January 1830; eds. T. Purdue and M. D. Green, 1995)

Andrew Jackson, President 1828–1837, on the need for and progress of Indian removal (1835): The plan of removing the aboriginal people who yet remain within the settled portions of the United States to the country west of the Mississippi River approaches its consummation. ... All preceding experiments for the improvement of the Indians have failed. It seems now to be an established fact that they cannot live in contact with a civilized community and prosper... .

The plan for their removal and reestablishment ... has been dictated by a spirit of enlarged liberality. [They are to be given ample lands, supplies of clothing and arms, and provisions sufficient for one year after their arrival.] In that time, from the nature of the country and of the products raised by them, they can subsist themselves by agricultural labor, if they choose to resort to that mode of life; if they do not they are upon the skirts of the great prairies, where countless herds of buffalo roam... .

[Arrangements have been made to build schools, churches, dwellings for the chiefs, and to provide funds for poor relief, tools, steel, and iron.] And besides these beneficial arrangements, annuities are in all cases paid ... in all cases sufficiently great, if justly divided and prudently expended, to enable them, in addition to their own exertions, to live comfortably.

(From J. D. Richardson ed., *A Compilation of the Messages and Pages of the Presidents 1787–1897*, 1896–1899)

Trade flowed between Europeans and Indians. The former craved hides and furs, and the latter sought guns and other manufactures. European settlers also transmitted their diseases to the natives, who as in Latin America had no natural immunity to smallpox, diphtheria, and other illnesses. Disease caused an absolute decline in the native populations, so that the demographic balance between the two races shifted: the handful of settlers, who multiplied and prospered, became a majority among a shrinking community of natives. Weakened in numbers, diminished by their need for Western goods, undermined by quasi-legal land grabs and patronizing attempts at conversion, Indian communities were vulnerable as the colonies expanded across a continent they came to see as theirs.

While Indians were not forced to labor on settlers' farms, as in Latin America, African slaves were. The first shipment of slaves arrived in Jamestown on a Dutch ship in 1619, only twelve years after the colony was founded. Thereafter, slaves trickled into British North America, mostly to the southern colonies, where a sub-tropical climate promoted the cultivation of cash crops—first tobacco, then rice and indigo, and finally cotton—in a plantation system similar to that in the Caribbean islands. By 1700, the foundations of a plantation economy had been laid in Virginia and the Carolinas. In the northern colonies, too, a few African slaves labored as domestic servants, sailors, and artisans.

The slave economy supported a social organization in which African people were assigned the lowest rank. British elites in the West Indies had elaborated this racial perspective, which was adopted by North American planters. Racial prejudices did not prevent racial mixing, however, as slaveholders demanded the sexual cooperation of female slaves and permitted the raising of mixed-race offspring on their plantations.

Racial mixture followed a course different from that in Spanish America, however. In British America, there was little miscegenation of Europeans and Indians. The offspring of European men and slave women, moreover, were considered to be slaves and to be black, regardless of the fairness of their skin.

Slavery developed slowly in the British colonies because of the availability of "indentured servants." These were Europeans, male or female, who had contracted to come to the New World. In return for their passage, they sold their labor for a set number of years—generally four to seven. Unlike the Amerindian peon of Spanish America, or the African slave, the indentured servant might anticipate social opportunity equal to that of any other New World settler when the terms of indenture had been fulfilled.

A New Society   The opportunities offered by flourishing British colonies, and by a seemingly limitless wilderness beyond, attracted Europeans other than the English. There came the Scots, Welsh, and Irish from the British Isles, as well as Swedes and Dutch. Even in its first century, although strongly imprinted by its English heritage, the culture of North America was open and pluralistic.

In contrast to European countries, where memories of religious war, and of the demand for conformity, enforced by violence, were still vivid, in British America there was no **established religion**. Some colonies did align themselves with one branch of Christianity, collecting taxes for its support, and inviting dissenters to depart; but they never knew the Inquisition, the demands of an overweening clergy, or the presence of a monolithic Church as chief landowner or creditor. Religion remained a powerful force in British America, but not a unitary power.

Nevertheless, in Puritan New England especially, religion ruled sternly, demanding conformity to its understanding of God's will. Puritan austerity gradually waned and during the 1730s and 1740s a tide of religious expression called the Great Awakening swept the colonies. It demanded of worshippers not merely an outward conformity to religious norms but a deep commitment stemming from an experience of transformation, of being "born again" in faith. That religious current has persisted in American life.

Unburdened by any single established church, a hereditary nobility, or the excessive control of royal government, the British colonists profited from their freedom. When, in the aftermath of the French and Indian War, the British crown imposed a new round of economic demands and mercantile restrictions upon its North American colonists, the latter were unwilling to accept them. The French and Indian War had been the American phase of a world-wide struggle between the two powers of Britain and France, then preeminent in Europe. In its European phase known as the Seven Years' War (1756–1763),

Britain struggled to snatch primacy from France and its ally Spain. At the same time, Britain wrested from France the controlling position in the sub-continent of India. In North America, Britain won Canada in the north, and vast unexplored territories to the west which restive colonists were ready to investigate.

The war also brought the British face to face with their own American colonists, whose wealth, military capacity, and incipient claims for cultural and political autonomy became apparent. British citizens shouldered one of the highest tax rates in Europe, and Parliament looked to the colonists to pay a fairer share of the costs of the recent war. Parliament's pursuit of this objective, coupled with its enforcement of mercantilist restraints, was to lead to another war in North America—one the British would lose.

By this time, however, key features of Britain's political and cultural life had been re-rooted on American soil. There they produced new fruit. In British North America, as in Latin America, those who transplanted features of European life into the western hemisphere created exactly what the explorers thought they had stumbled upon: a New World.

DECLARATIONS OF INDEPENDENCE

Map 19.1 on p. 552 shows the European presence in the Americas in 1750. Within two generations of the Treaty of Paris (1763) that ended the French and

---

WHO'S WHO

Liberators of Latin America

François Dominique Toussaint L'Ouverture (c. 1748–1803), leader of the African slaves of Saint-Dominique who created Haiti, the first republic in the western hemisphere.

Miguel Hidalgo (1753–1811), Mexican priest who led an insurgent army of thousands of native Indians against the capital city in 1810, in the opening bid for Mexican independence.

Pedro I, Brazilian king (r. 1822–1831) who declared Brazilian independence in 1822 and accepted the title of "Constitutional Emperor."

Simón de Bolívar (1783–1830)

Antonio José de Sucré (1794–1830)

Bernardo O'Higgins (c. 1777–1842)

José de San Martín (1778–1850)

four creole aristocrats who fought Spanish armies from 1810–1826, winning the independence of Venezuela, Colombia, Ecuador, Peru, Bolivia, Chile, and Argentina.

Indian War, most of the European New World colonies achieved independence. A North American rebellion against Britain unexpectedly succeeded, and led to the creation of a new nation. Fired by that example and by a favorable tide of events in Europe, the South American colonies rebelled a generation later. The monarchs of France, Spain, Portugal, and Great Britain were made to acknowledge that peoples who were once their subjects were now independent players in the concert of nations.

Atlantic North America: War for Independence

The United States of America was the first nation of the Western world successfully to graduate from colonial status to autonomy. The strength of its own, original institutions enabled the United States to win independence. So did the quality of its leaders, trained in European values and ideas which would soon find expression in a written constitution that was the legal foundation of the new nation.

The Roots of Revolution   The Treaty of Paris of 1763 granted Britain all the land between the Appalachians and the Mississippi River, as well as Quebec, the core of New France (in addition to Florida, ceded by Spain, France's ally). It also, as it turned out, laid the foundations for Britain's defeat in the American War for Independence that broke out twelve years later.

The Proclamation of 1763, as required by the Treaty of Paris, reserved the western territory to the Indian nations settled there, and denied it to angry colonists hopeful of expanding westward. In 1774, Britain further angered the mostly Protestant colonists by extending religious and civil liberties to the Roman Catholic French Canadians. Meanwhile, Parliament had imposed new taxes on the colonists, who believed themselves exempt from taxation, and Parliament powerless to tax them. Parliament for its part needed to repay the heavy costs of fighting the French and Indian War.

Parliament proceeded to levy a series of taxes, culminating in the Stamp Act of 1765, which required the purchase of a license or stamp to read a newspaper or send a letter or execute a legal document. After fierce and determined colonial resistance Parliament repealed the Stamp Act in 1766. At the same time, doggedly, it issued the Declaratory Act, a sullen piece of legislation that affirmed Britain's power to tax its colonies.

John Trumbull, **The Signing of the Declaration of Independence, July 4, 1776:** *This famous depiction (based on his own miniatures with portrait heads of Adams and Jefferson painted from life) of the moment of signing in Independence Hall in Philadelphia on the first July 4th was painted by John Trumbull, a veteran of the Revolutionary war, and mounted to much public acclaim in the United States Capitol in 1819. (Yale University Art Library)*

In 1767, Parliament imposed the Townshend Duties on imports. The new levies spurred a response from a network of cooperating colonial assemblies, led by Massachusetts. Active resistance in Massachusetts, punctuated by violence, led to military occupation. In 1770, British soldiers fired on unarmed protesters, killing five—the notorious "Boston Massacre."

By 1773, Parliament had removed all duties except a tax on tea, levied as a subsidy to the East India Company then suffering from foreign competition. American consumers protested by the ostentatious non-consumption of tea. The Boston Sons of Liberty, one of the groups of disciplined protesters the colonies had developed since the first resistance of 1765, responded colorfully to the arrival of a shipment in Boston Harbor. On December 16, 1773, dressed up like Indians, they slipped by night onto the anchored ships and threw the tea overboard. Parliament responded with the Coercive Acts of 1774, which ordered Boston Harbor closed until the tea was paid for and established martial law in the city.

The leaders of the colonial revolt against Parliament were members of the affluent merchant and planter classes, whose economic interests had been threatened by parliamentary actions since 1763. Yet it would be too simple to ascribe their opposition to Britain solely to economic self-interest. That would be to exclude the dimension of intellectual culture, at the very moment when, in Europe, its development was high in quality and particularly relevant to the American scene (see Chapter 17).

In America as in Europe, men gathered to discuss the latest ideas and world events in libraries, academies, and clubs. Schools and universities trained Americans on home soil, and literacy was high. American leaders were well-read, both in the Classics and in contemporary discussions of the purpose of government, individual rights, private property, and the social contract. Readers of John Locke (1632–1704) and the Enlightenment *philosophes*, they believed passionately in the quest for individual freedom, the need for toleration, the importance of representation and due process. They extended the Enlightenment analysis of the evils of despotism to the American context, where it no longer made any sense (they believed) for hereditary rulers to govern free men. Enlightenment theory combined with themes of resistance between 1763 and 1776, when the first modern nation declared its abdication from the world's first global empire.

It was not sufficient, however, for lofty minds to form theories; American leaders also had to unite and develop a sense of nationhood. A common purpose is evident in the Committees of Correspondence, established throughout the colonies to spread information about developments in Boston, and in 1774, twelve of the thirteen colonies (all but Georgia) sent fifty-six representatives to the First Continental Congress. Clearly, colonial leaders had begun to see their

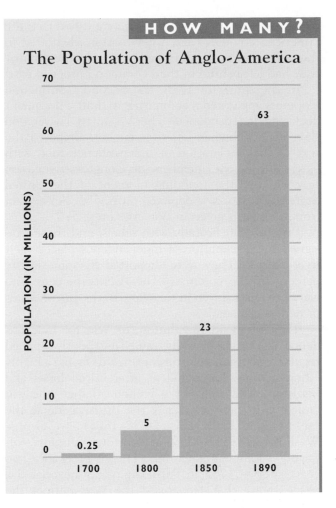

HOW MANY?

The Population of Anglo-America

enterprise as having national dimensions, distinct from its European roots. Then, in the spring of 1775, a swift series of events carried this movement forward.

Rebellion   Fearing a British offensive, Massachusetts militiamen had stockpiled ammunition at the town of Concord outside of Boston. The British dispatched troops to seize it. On April 19, as the redcoated soldiers marched through the village of Lexington, a shot rang out—the famous "shot heard round the world," prefiguring not only the American but subsequent revolutions around the globe. From Concord, where they faced American militiamen, the British returned to Boston harried by the local farmer-soldiers whose guerrilla tactics contrasted memorably with the strict order of the well-drilled redcoats. In Boston itself, martial law reigned.

The battles of Lexington and Concord forced the gentlemen in Congress to make some decisions during the winter of 1775–1776. Did they represent one nation or thirteen colonies? Did what happened in Massachusetts affect the other twelve colonies? If so, should they attempt to heal the break with Britain, or league together to oppose her? An impassioned printer, the recent immigrant Thomas Paine (1737–1809) sharply defined the issues in his pamphlet *Common Sense* (1776). An instant bestseller (some 100,000 copies were circulated), it called on the public to recognize what was already an accomplished fact: the American colonies were a new nation, dedicated to the pursuit of trade and liberation from the tyranny they had left behind in their common European past.

In the spring of 1776, the Second Continental Congress appointed a committee to draft a document declaring independence. The Virginian lawyer and slaveowner Thomas Jefferson largely composed the text of the Declaration of Independence that, with emendations, the members of Congress signed on July 4. This, the founding moment of the United States as a nation is depicted on p. 556. An extract from the text is given in *Witnesses* on p. 570.

Britain dealt brutally with rebels, and those who signed the Declaration of Independence placed their lives at risk. They were supported by some eighty percent of the colonists. The twenty percent who were **Loyalists** stayed in the wings of the British army, or fled to Canada.

The American Revolution, or War for Independence, was fought by badly trained and poorly supplied regular soldiers and militia contingents facing a highly efficient army. Nevertheless, after initial losses and hardships, and aided by a French alliance, the war ended with the surrender of the British general, the 1st Marquis Cornwallis (1738–1805), to George Washington (1732–1799) at Yorktown, Virginia, following a joint American and French blockade. Two years later in 1783 in Paris, diplomats negotiated a peace treaty that recognized the new nation, the United States of America, and granted it land from the Atlantic seaboard to the Mississippi River.

The New Nation   What kind of nation was the new United States to be? Would it be modeled on England, with a king and a parliament? Would the thirteen states be self-governing, or would they be subdivisions of one state, relating to each other through a central, or **federal** government? These issues were hammered out over the next generation.

Under the "Articles of Confederation" the thirteen former colonies each retained autonomy and cooperated in the war effort. In 1787, the Constitutional Convention convened at Philadelphia to consider a new framework for government. The former colonial leaders James Madison, John Jay, and Alexander Hamilton collaborated on the *Federalist Papers*, essays composed to convince the public of the need for a strong centralized, or federal government to guide foreign policy, oversee interstate commerce, adjudicate disputes between different states, and fund projects of interest to the whole nation. Despite a considerable amount of reluctance, the Constitution was adopted in 1788 after ratification by the necessary minimum of nine states.

The Constitution of the United States adopts principles from two political theorists of the Enlightenment: John Locke and Montesquieu (see Chapter 17). From Locke it takes the principle of rule by an assembly of representatives, whose interests must be respected by any executive power whose own potential for tyrannical rule is thereby curtailed. From Montesquieu it takes the principle of balancing the functions of government (executive, legislative, judicial), so that each checks and balances the others. These principles, committed to writing, have survived without serious challenge and have served as a model for emerging governments around the world.

In 1791, a Bill of Rights containing ten articles was ratified. These became the first ten amendments to the Constitution, guaranteeing freedom of speech, assembly, and the press; the right of citizens to bear arms and thus fight as a militia to defend the nation; the sanctity of the citizen's property and privacy; freedom in judicial matters from the requirement of self-incrimination, and from "cruel and unusual punishment," referring to the use of torture and abusive conditions of imprisonment in contemporary European judicial systems.

The American War of Independence, it has often been noted, was less a revolution than a nationalist revolt. Nothing was "turned over" except the leadership of the country: economy, society, and culture developed after 1783 along the same lines they had pursued prior to 1774. The leaders of the American Revolution nevertheless made two extraordinary conceptual leaps. For the first time in the history of the West, they had envisioned the possibility of a legitimate challenge to established political power by ordinary citizens. And they had created a written instrument of government, again the first in the history of the West, that guaranteed individual rights, guarded against arbitrary power, balanced the different functions of government, and provided a mechanism for its amendment. The government created by these programs was not yet a democracy; but it was a frame within which democracy could, and ultimately did, take form.

Revolution in Haiti and Mexico

The North American precedent of a war for independence soon found imitators in the Latin south. The first of the Latin American revolts occurred in the French Caribbean colony of Saint-Domingue (formerly part of the island of Hispaniola) renamed by the victorious rebels "Haiti." This, too, was a nationalist revolt, which replaced French colonial administrators with a local elite. It was even more a profound revolution, in which slaves rose up against masters, blacks against whites.

The revolution began in 1791, during the French revolution of which Caribbean slaves halfway around the world had heard. They rose up under the leadership of the educated son of African slaves, François Dominique Toussaint L'Ouverture (c. 1748–1803), a

Changes in the Ethnic Composition of Latin American Populations

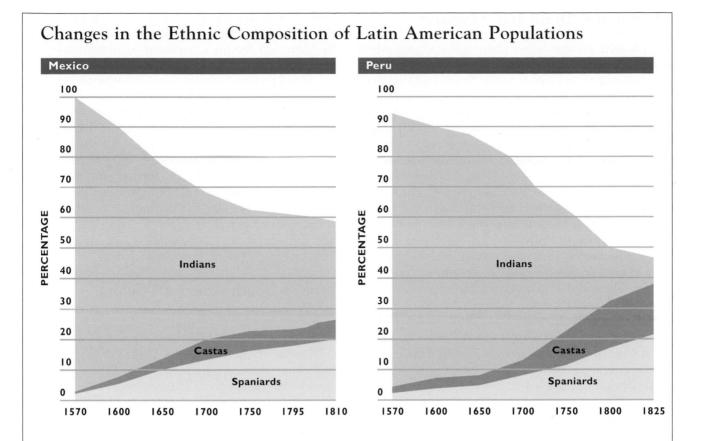

The heavy toll on Indian populations wrought by European diseases, the rise of immigration from the Old World to the New, and miscegenation among Spaniards, Amerindians, and African slaves profoundly altered the ethnic composition of Mexico and Peru during the colonial period. In both cases, the Amerindian component of the population fell markedly while the population of Spanish settlers rose. The population of castas (an intermediate group including Africans, mulattoes, and mestizos), a consequence of racial diversity and mixing, increased to form about fifteen percent of the Mexican, and thirty percent of the Peruvian population by their respective terminal dates.

Source: J. Lockhart, S. B. Schwartz, *Early Latin America: A History of Colonial Spanish America and Brazil (Cambridge: Cambridge University Press, 1983), pp. 320, 342*

slave himself. Leading a half-million slaves and some 25,000 mulattoes against 40,000 whites, by 1801 he had gained control of the whole of Hispaniola. The French, now ruled by Napoleon (1769–1821) (see Chapter 20), captured the insurgent slave. L'Ouverture died in 1803, a prisoner in France. His lieutenants persisted, and in 1804 they declared independence for the western half of the island, which they called Haiti. A state ruled by former slaves, Haiti became the second independent nation in the western hemisphere, the first in Latin America. Slaveowners everywhere trembled.

A struggle for independence in New Spain soon followed. This revolution remained unfinished, however, as more conservative forces seized power in the newly independent country, and creole and peninsular elites struggled for dominance in what later became Mexico. Their quarrel opened an opportunity for the priest Miguel Hidalgo (1753–1811), who in 1810 led an insurgent army of tens of thousands of native Indians against the capital city. He massacred the militia forces sent against him, abolished slavery, declared independence; then, believing his mission to be now fulfilled, he sent his followers home.

Captured and executed by the Spaniards in 1811, Hidalgo was the first leader of the Mexican revolution. The second was José María Morelos (1765–1815), also a priest. Following Hidalgo's lead, he raised an army, called for social equality and the redistribution of land; but in 1815 he, too, was captured and executed. In 1821, Mexico finally gained its independence from Spain. But independence was not accompanied by the social revolution envisioned by the priestly rebels Hidalgo and Morelos. A creole elite (who were joined by royalist peninsulars) established General Augustín de Iturbide (1783–1824) as emperor. Slavery continued, the Indians won no new land, and Mexico continued to swing from leader to leader for the next few decades.

Transition in Brazil and Paraguay

The violent revolution in Haiti and the unfinished one in Mexico contrast with peaceful transitions from colonial rule to independence in Brazil and Paraguay.

In 1807, as Napoleon blasted through the Iberian peninsula, the prince-regent of Portugal, John VI (r. 1799–1826), fled to take refuge in Brazil, where his presence united and animated the colony. When the king returned to Lisbon in 1821, he left his son and heir Pedro (r. 1822–1831) in Rio de Janeiro to preside over an American court now considered equal to the Portuguese. Creole officials were enthusiastic about the elevation of Brazil, but pressed for greater autonomy. Pedro yielded, declaring Brazil's independence in 1822 and accepting the title of "Constitutional Emperor." The constitution was ratified in 1824 and remained unchallenged until the monarchy fell in 1889. Local support for the constitutional monarchy increased in 1840, when Pedro's American-born son, Pedro II (1831–1889), ascended the throne. Brazil was now a wholly independent and wholly American nation.

Independence also came bloodlessly for Paraguay, accompanied by a profound social revolution. In 1811, while the king of Spain was a captive of Napoleon, a congress of Paraguayans declared their independence both from Spain and from the viceroyalty of La Plata. They chose a dictator: the lawyer and theologian José Gaspar Rodríguez de Francia (1766–1840), notoriously cruel but admired by historians for his competent administration of a poor and complex nation.

Aided by local creole elites, Francia nationalized the former crown and church lands, which he organized as a series of state ranches, rented for nominal fees to any Indians willing to labor there. Agricultural production increased, easing the poverty of the Indian population and enhancing the country's prosperity. With further improvements in education and manufacture to his credit, the unpleasant Francia emerges alongside the Portuguese monarchs, the former slave L'Ouverture, and the martyred priests Hidalgo and Morelos, as a hero of Latin American independence.

Spanish South America: Victory at Ayacucho

Spanish South America boasted heroes still more celebrated: Simón Bolívar (1783–1830) and his lieutenant Antonio José de Sucre (1795–1830) of Venezuela, Bernardo O'Higgins (c. 1777–1842) of Chile, and José de San Martín (1778–1850) of Argentina. From 1810 to 1826, these creole aristocrats fought Spanish armies and won independence for the regions of New Granada, Peru, and La Plata, from which were carved seven sovereign states

---

WITNESSES

A Different Path for Spanish America

In his address at Angostura in 1819, the South American revolutionary leader, Simón Bolívar, calls for a republican constitution for the new state of Venezuela. This was to be centered on the principle of equality, in order to build a liberal society that would fully embrace the multiethnic peoples of the region.

I must say that it has never for a moment entered my mind to compare the position and character of two states as dissimilar as the English-American [i.e. the United States] and the Spanish-American. Would it not be most difficult to apply to Spain the English system of political, civil, and religious liberty? Hence, it would be even more difficult to adapt to Venezuela the law of North America. Does not [the French *philosophe* Montesquieu] state that laws should be suited to the people for whom they are made ... [and] that they should be in keeping with ... their inclinations, resources, number, commerce, habits, and customs? This is the code we must consult, not the code of Washington! ...

Our people are neither European nor North American; rather, they are a mixture of African and the Americans who originated in Europe. ... The greater portion of the native Indians has been annihilated; Spaniards have mixed with Americans and Africans, and Africans with Indians and Spaniards. While we have all been born of the same mother, our fathers, different in origin and in blood, are foreigners, and all differ visibly as to the color of their skin: a dissimilarity which places upon us an obligation of the greatest importance.

Under the Constitution, which interprets the laws of Nature, all citizens of Venezuela enjoy complete political equality. Although equality may not have been the political dogma of Athens, France, or North America, we must consecrate it here in order to correct the disparity that apparently exists. My opinion, Legislators, is that the fundamental basis of our political system hinges directly and exclusively upon the establishment and practice of equality in Venezuela. ... By this step alone, cruel discord has been completely eliminated. How much jealousy, rivalry, and hate have thus been averted!

(From H. A. Bierck and V. Lecuña eds., *Selected Writings of Bolívar*, 1951; trs. L. Bertrand)

of modern South America: Venezuela, Colombia, Ecuador, Peru, Bolivia, Chile, and Argentina. Bolívar's aspirations for the new state of Venezuela are quoted in *Witnesses* on p. 560.

Argentina swiftly won its independence, then joined the western armies that freed Chile, Peru, and Bolívar's "Great Colombia" (Bolivia, Colombia, Ecuador, and Venezuela). In 1807, British warships sailed into Buenos Aires. The creole militia resisted the attack and took charge of the nation. In 1817, its leader San Martín marched the Argentine army across the Andes to support the Chileans under O'Higgins. In 1820, he pressed on to Peru, the center of Spanish power in America. There, in 1822, he joined Bolívar. The final destruction of Spanish forces was wrought by

Bolívar's Triumphal Entry into Caracas: *Born into an aristocratic Spanish family in Caracas, New Granada (today Venezuela) in 1783, Bolívar joined in the failed attempt to liberate his homeland in 1812, but succeeded in doing so in 1821. Here, Bolívar makes his triumphal entry. (Private Collection)*

Antonio de Sucre in 1824 at the battle of Ayacucho, which won independence for the new Latin states, and ensured the dominance of the creole elite.

The victory of these South American heroes was a victory for national autonomy, for Enlightenment values, and for free trade. It did not involve a social revolution, however, such as was dreamed of but abandoned in Mexico, and was secured for former slaves and Indian peons, respectively, in Haiti and Paraguay. The social and economic condition of the majority of the population was not affected by the achievement of independence.

As Map 19.2 on p. 562 shows, over the next generation, many of the modern nations of Spanish America emerged as free states, with the exceptions of Cuba, Panama, and Puerto Rico. The British, French, and Dutch retained their Caribbean and Guyanese possessions. As Europe, recovering from the Napoleonic wars (see Chapter 20), considered reviving its interests in the western hemisphere, the United States President issued a stern warning in 1823. The Monroe Doctrine stated that the Americas were not open "for future colonization by any European power," and that the United States would take any such attempt as "an unfriendly act." Protected by United States policy and, additionally, British interest in maintaining the Americas as a zone of free trade, the Latin American countries were free to pursue their own careers.

FULFILLING THE PROMISE

Both North and South America saw the triumph of liberal principles in the revolutions that occurred during the half-century following 1776. These enacted one of the ideals announced in the United States Declaration of Independence: the right of a people to abolish an abusive government, and institute a new one. They did not attempt to realize the other: the principle that all "men" are created equal. By 1880, the United States progressed some distance toward securing for all its citizens their "inalienable rights." In Latin America, that principle of liberalism was not yet even on the agenda.

The Reign of the *Caudillo*

From the 1820s through the 1880s, the nations of Latin America took form. Led by educated men descended from the creoles of the colonial era, economy, culture, and society were modernized. At the same time, traditional social patterns persisted, supported by two powerful conservative interests: the Church and the military. Consequently, most people found their condition no better, and perhaps worse, than it had been under colonial rule. To unify societies pulled between the ambitions of the elites and the needs of the masses, the autocratic strongman, or *caudillo*, stepped in. Backed up by the military, the caudillos promoted the construction of new societies while suppressing any signs of disorder.

Trade with the Old World

In 1800–1880, the Latin American landowning elite developed its existing agricultural and mining enterprises. Commodities carried from the interior to port cities were transshipped abroad: coffee from Brazil and Central America; beef and hides from Argentina and Uruguay; tin from Bolivia and nitrates from Chile; from the great landed estates, or *latifundia*, all over Latin America a cornucopia of corn, cacao beans, nuts and bananas, medicinal plants and dyestuffs.

These goods traveled by railroad to waiting steamships, some fitted, after 1876, with refrigerated compartments for the shipment of beef. This new transportation technology had recently been developed in Europe (see Chapter 21), and rapidly found its way to assist the western hemisphere as it enlarged its role in the world marketplace. In 1815–1820, as few as two or three ships each year left Chile for England; in 1850, the figure was at least 300. During the same period, the value of exports shipped from Buenos Aires tripled. Boosted by coffee production, Brazil increased its foreign trade six- or sevenfold between 1883 and 1889. Overall, Latin American trade increased forty-three percent between 1870 and 1884, a period in which British trade increased just twenty-seven percent. While foreign trade boomed, local commerce between the regions of Latin America, where overland transport was difficult, lagged.

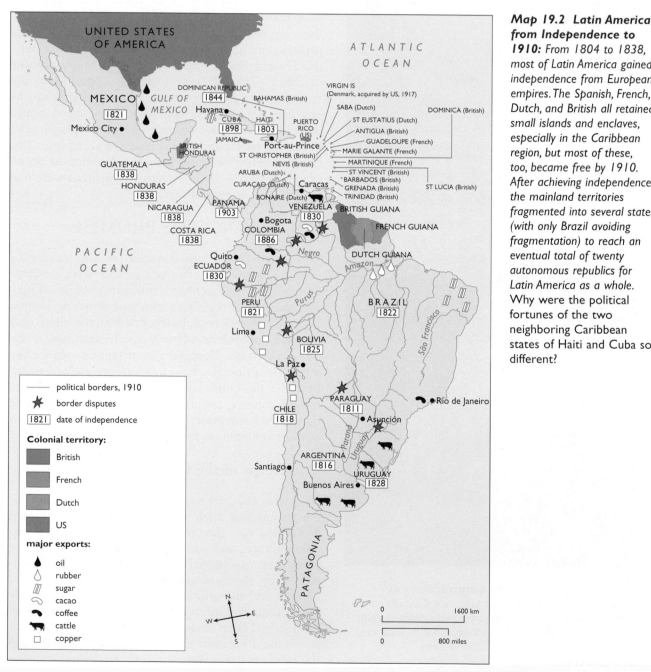

Map 19.2 Latin America from Independence to 1910: *From 1804 to 1838, most of Latin America gained independence from European empires. The Spanish, French, Dutch, and British all retained small islands and enclaves, especially in the Caribbean region, but most of these, too, became free by 1910. After achieving independence, the mainland territories fragmented into several states (with only Brazil avoiding fragmentation) to reach an eventual total of twenty autonomous republics for Latin America as a whole. Why were the political fortunes of the two neighboring Caribbean states of Haiti and Cuba so different?*

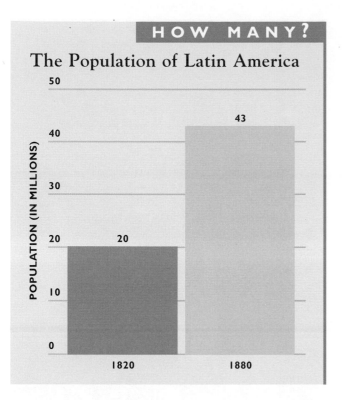

HOW MANY?

The Population of Latin America

Trade with Europe caused cities such as Buenos Aires, São Paulo, and Santiago to flourish. By 1869 the population of Buenos Aires rose to 250,000, then increased eightfold; by 1914, one of four Argentinians lived in that port city. In Chile, twenty-seven percent of the population was urban by 1875, forty-three percent by 1900. By 1850, Brazil's Atlantic coast was dotted with prosperous municipalities, with 500 more created between 1890 and 1914.

Some city-dwellers had migrated from the countryside, but many came from the impoverished zones of eastern and southern Europe in search of new opportunities. Those who succeeded joined native elites in striving to make their cities as much like European ones as possible. Adorned with grand boulevards and opera houses, railroad stations, senate buildings, and churches, these imitated the latest trends in European architecture and city planning, aspiring to be as grand as Paris.

Urban elites and landed proprietors purchased the manufactures of industrial Europe, especially Britain. In 1825, half of British exports to the western hemisphere were to Latin America, and half of these to Brazil alone. "Spanish America is free," one British official remarked considering the opportunities there for trade and investment, "and … she is English." With competition from the fine products of Europe's new factories (see Chapter 21), the wares produced by local artisans sank in value. Latin American manufactures, poorer in quality and prestige, were destined primarily for local markets.

The Latin American economy came to depend on European capital, and financiers set up banks in the expanding cities. They funded the building of roads, ports, and eventually railroads for transporting goods from the interior to the harbors. They also funded the emerging Latin American states, which were often unable to service their debts and suffered bankruptcy. Despite wealth accumulated in some social sectors, government and society remained insecure—one consequence of an economy that produced, as was often lamented, "growth without development."

Divided Societies The beneficiaries of economic growth were the same elite who resisted colonial rule and led their peers to rebellion. They now ruled the fragile nations that had been formed in revolution. Sharing power with them were the leaders of the Church and the army.

As before, the Church's role was complex. On the one hand, it was a major landowner and, before the advent of complex banking, a source of finance capital. On the other, it was attuned to the native Indian population. Nevertheless, while the clergy sometimes supported the villagers against the interests of the great landowners, the Church's role was more often conservative, seeking to defend itself against the encroachment of liberal values.

The military, meanwhile, played a major role in Latin American society—and so it remains to this day. Elegantly uniformed officers represented the self-sufficiency of the new, otherwise illegitimate revolutionary societies of America. Nearly everywhere, they propped up the authority of the president, the king, or the caudillo. Their support was well rewarded. In the first generation of independence, expenditure on the military often took up more than fifty percent of the new nations' budgets. Mexico's military budget between 1821 and 1845 exceeded the total of all government revenues on fourteen occasions.

If colonial social patterns persisted in the Church and the military, the pre-Columbian past endured in the customs of the native masses. Wherever possible, they lived in their ancestral villages, and when displaced to haciendas, mines, or cities they retained their traditional culture, which had survived conquest and revolution alike.

Especially foreign to that culture was any notion of private property. Indians possessed their village lands in common. They cooperated in tasks, rather than compete and stand out beyond their comrades. Despite attempts to integrate the Indians into an economy based on private ownership, their assumption that land existed for communal use remained unshaken. Their village management of land, largely respected in the colonial era, was targeted by the post-revolutionary elites and rulers, whose land grabs enriched those who exported goods to foreign markets.

Nor did the economic prosperity of the post-revolutionary period advance the condition of the slave, before slavery itself was ended. Slaves were a minority in much of Spanish America, but in Brazil and the

Caribbean, they predominated. Slave rebellions were frequent well into the nineteenth century, and bands of runaway slaves were common in the remote interior.

Persons of mixed race belonged to the group called the *castas*, or "castes," who possessed a social status above that of Indian natives, and who sometimes benefited from economic growth. Those who pursued artisan or merchant careers came to occupy a middling rank. European immigrants—Spanish, Italian, Irish, German, among others—included many skilled laborers or professionals, and could prosper in Latin American society.

Latin American societies were thus divided between the interests, on the one hand, of the educated elites, assisted by a middling sector of professionals and merchants, buttressed by the Church and army; and, on the other, by those of the masses, Indian, black, and mixed (except in those nations—Chile, Argentina, and Uruguay—whose populations were mostly European). They somewhat resembled the societies of Europe in the eighteenth century but were, in fact, more perilously divided. In Europe the poor were not separated from their rulers by differences of race, culture, and history.

The Latin American economy was linked to the European in a pattern, not easily broken, in which one partner exported resources, the other manufactures. Though the Latin American market was thus subordinated to the European, the owners of the

Juan O'Gorman, **Porfirio Díaz,** *1893: Political power in nineteenth-century Latin American states was generally monopolized by Creole elites and forceful* caudillos—*such as Mexico's Porfirio Díaz (r. 1876–1911) shown in this mural—who ruled primarily for the benefit of wealthy landowners, the church, and the military. (detail, Castillo de Chapultepec, Mexico City)*

mines, ranches, and *latifundia* reaped handsome profits and had no incentive to alter the arrangement. On the contrary: adopting the views of the French founder of **positivism**, Auguste Comte (1798–1857) (see Chapter 23), they held that an elite of highly trained experts justly led society to greater productivity, harmony, and happiness.

This program of "Order and Progress" would justify much of the social policy of the age, accepted by both "liberals" and "conservatives." Order meant the continuation of existing social patterns, and progress, the growth of profitable foreign trade in a free trade system. Liberals and conservatives were distinguished not by their economic strategies, but by their attitudes toward the Church. Liberals viewed the Church as an obstacle to progress, considered redistributing its property, and terminating its judicial and economic privileges. Conservatives saw the Church as a bulwark of the social order.

The dictatorial leaders who thrived in the first generation after independence would employ at will

Native and Elite Caudillos

Diego Rivera, A Sunday Afternoon in the Alameda Park: *Though Amerindians and* castas *were often marginalized within Latin American society, members of these "lower orders" did occasionally achieve political power. The Zapotec Indian lawyer Benito Juárez, for example, became President of Mexico in 1861 and is depicted at the center of this 1947 mural.*

both liberal and conservative stategies; the strong-men, or caudillos. These autocrats were usually drawn from the elite and nearly always promoted by the military. They well understood the effectiveness of the military in maintaining social order and protect-ing the interests of "civilization," as they saw it, over what they termed "barbarism." At the same time, caudillos of elite origin promoted the various

economic interests of their class by allowing land takeovers and the manipulation of labor contracts.

Some caudillos, however, often of mixed race, were considered "popular." The popular caudillos pur-sued land policies that benefited native or mestizo workers. Popular caudillos garnered success as they awakened among the millions of their constituents an appetite for justice. The "throng of aristocrats," one told his followers, takes all wealth and privileges, "leaving you only with misery, disgrace, and work. ..."

Unlike these populist leaders, most of the caudil-los stood for the maintenance of order. Typical is the Mexican caudillo Porfirio Díaz (1830–1915), a mes-tizo, who rose to the rank of general and battled his way to supremacy. He is depicted on p. 564. From 1876 to 1910, his autocratic, centralized government promoted economic growth while it protected the tra-ditional interests of landowners, Church, and army—the usual recipe for success in Latin America.

While the old elites retained control, most nations had forged satisfactory constitutions and created rep-resentative assemblies which achieved at last the abo-lition of slavery. Beginning with "free birth" laws early in the century, which held free anyone born on native soil of slave parentage, abolition was attained nearly everywhere by 1880. The last two nations in the west-ern hemisphere to accept abolition were Cuba (1886) and Brazil (1888).

Alone of the Latin American nations, Brazil was ruled by an emperor until the formation of a republic, one year after abolition. Cuba and Puerto Rico were the last of the old colonies to be ruled by Spain. While Haiti and the Dominican Republic were independent, most of the other Caribbean nations were under French, English, Dutch, or Danish rule. These regions did not experience the reign of the caudillo.

By the 1880s, most Latin American nations had developed governments based on limited representa-tion. The majority of the people, Christianized and hispanized though they were, had little role in that government. Jefferson's vision of 1776, resting on the assumption that "all men are created equal," remained entirely alien to Latin America's leaders whose high prosperity demanded that some men—and all women—be left unequal.

By the People

The citizens of the United States of America were conscious of their nationhood. That consciousness emerged from the shared tragedy of war and the shared creation of a written Constitution with its statement of fundamental, inalienable rights. Over the next three generations, the nation would draw closer to the ideal implied in its founding documents: that all people were equal, and that the government was theirs. By the 1880s, the United States was nearly but was not yet a government "by the people."

HOW MANY?

Unwilling Strangers—Trends in the Trade of African Slaves

Figures represent slaves in thousands

Although the marketing of African slaves by European entrepreneurs began even before 1500, it peaked in the eighteenth century, reaching an apex on the eve of the American revolution.
Source: H. Spodek, *The World's History (Upper Saddle River, NJ: Prentice Hall, 1998), p. 451.*

The Expansion of a Nation   In the interim, the difficult question posed itself: who, and what, was an American? As the nation grew, it absorbed new immigrants and repulsed its own Amerindian natives. It freed its African slaves, and heard the protests of women subordinated to male leadership in the state, church, and family. As Map 19.3 on p. 567 shows, it expanded territorially from the Atlantic seaboard 3000 miles west to the Pacific shore past the barriers of the Appalachian Mountains, the Mississippi River, the Great Plains, the Rocky Mountains. With each new territory, the definition continued to broaden of who was an "American."

The first frontier lay between the Appalachians and the Mississippi, acquired by the United States in the 1783 settlement of the War for Independence. Pioneers poured into the region and formed the new states of Tennessee, Kentucky, and Ohio. In 1787, the Northwest Ordinance established guidelines for the admission to the Union of states, declared slave-free, to be carved out of the territory bounded by the Ohio and Mississippi Rivers and the Great Lakes.

The remaining additions to the territories of the continental United States occurred in three stages. The first was the Louisiana Territory, an expanse of over 800,000 square miles between the Mississippi and the Rocky Mountains. It was purchased for $15 million from the cash-poor French Emperor Napoleon (see Chapter 20) in 1803, and charted from 1804 to 1806 by the officer Meriwether Lewis and his colleague William Clark. In 1819, with the Spanish cession of Florida, the eastern half of the continent south of British Canada belonged to the new United States.

In 1846, the United States made its second large territorial acquisition. This was the Oregon territory, defined by an agreement with Britain establishing the United States–Canadian border at the 49th parallel of latitude. A third set of territories was acquired by war from neighboring Mexico between 1845 and 1853. This territory included much of the future states of Texas (which had previously won its independence), Arizona, New Mexico, Utah, Nevada, and California. A small adjunct to these, including parts of Arizona and New Mexico, was acquired in 1853 as the Gadsden Purchase. (Further additions to United States territory, none contiguous, include Alaska; the Hawaiian islands; Puerto Rico; and scattered Pacific islands; see Chapter 29).

Into the unknown west opened to settlement by purchase, treaty, and war, American settlers moved: pioneers on foot, families in carriages, caravans of covered wagons. The century-long experience of the frontier affected the notion that Americans had of themselves. They had cut loose from the European past and all its restrictive hierarchies and systems of privilege. They were a people engaged in the discovery of the world and themselves.

As the settlers' fortunes rose, those of the native Indian peoples sank. During the first years of colonization, European impact on the Indian way of life was limited. Natives and newcomers sometimes cooperated and sometimes clashed. Until the end of the eighteenth century, however, the natives largely retained their land and their traditional culture.

That situation changed during the first decades of independence. The victors of the War for Independence imposed treaties that forced the east coast Indians to cede their lands. With a combined population of about 150,000, these tribes were docile. They had long lived in proximity to the settlers; some were Christian converts, and some had acquired literacy. Some of their leaders were the mixed-blood offspring of Indian women and men of European background. Their marginality enabled them to guide their people in negotiations with the new Americans—negotiations they were destined to lose.

In the Northwest Territory opened in 1787, settlers encountered tribes unfamiliar with the habits of white Americans who were more easily deceived into surrendering their land. One American governor purchased much of the future state of Indiana from Miami and Delaware Indians for a mere $10,000. Although the Shawnee chief Tecumseh and his charismatic medicine-man brother resisted such land grabs, Chief Black Hawk (1767–1838) of the Sauk tribe surrendered his people's hunting grounds when, touching the fateful "goose quill," he unknowingly ratified a treaty with the United States government.

Systematic displacement of Indian populations began in the 1820s. Passages concerning the official policies are quoted in *Witnesses* on p. 554. Whole peoples were forcibly resettled in strange and less desirable lands, remote from ancestral graves and memories. This new policy affected Indian tribes from Florida, Alabama, and Georgia, and others on the border of Illinois and Iowa. Many were driven west and south to reserved "Indian territory" in modern Oklahoma, an arid region utterly unlike their

---

MUST READS

Calls for Revolution, Abolition, and Women's Rights

Thomas Paine   *Common Sense* (1775)

Frederick Douglass   *Narrative of the Life of Frederick Douglass, an American Slave, written by himself* (1845)

Harriet Beecher Stowe   *Uncle Tom's Cabin* (1852)

Elizabeth Cady Stanton   *Eighty Years and More: Reminiscences* (1898)

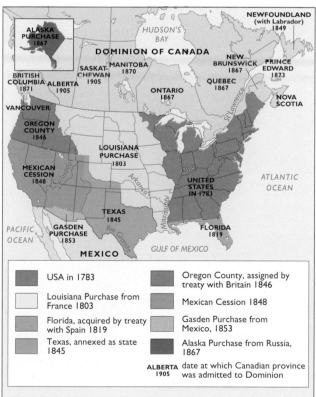

Map 19.3 (above and right) *Manifest Destiny: the Expansion of the United States, Amerindian Relocation, and Consolidation of Canada:*
After winning independence from Britain in 1783, and following its perceived "Manifest Destiny," the United States expanded westward at great speed. By expropriation, war, and purchase, it gained its present dimensions by 1898. Indigenous Amerindians paid a high price for the consolidation of the United States. Numerous battles, forced relocations, and the toll of Old World disease, reduced the pre-settlement population north of the Rio Grande from a peak of about 1 million—speaking 2000 languages—to just a few battered and isolated populations who were left languishing on reservations. Meanwhile, Canada expanded and consolidated as a dominion of the British Empire, with similar pressure on indigenous peoples (right). How did North Americans of European descent perceive the Amerindian population?

homelands. The illegal Cherokee forced migration along the Trail of Tears in the winter of 1838–1839, ordered by the Democratic President Andrew Jackson (1767–1845), is one of the saddest chapters in the history of the young United States.

After 1840, the conflict between American whites and native Indians shifted to the region between the Mississippi and the Pacific. While the southwest was home to **pueblo**-dwelling Indians with a long history of interaction with Mexican whites, on the Great Plains there roamed nomadic Indian peoples numbering about 360,000, whose limited contact with European peoples had enabled them to supply themselves with guns and horses. The Plains Indians used these to hunt bison herds, their main economic activity—the bison population of some 30 million could feed, clothe, and equip them indefinitely.

Mobile and aggressive, the Plains Indians resisted the advance of white settlers in a struggle which reached its final phase after 1865. As settlers streamed across the plains, they snapped up Indian land, confronted and killed Indians (who returned violence for violence), and slaughtered the bison. Railroad lines followed them, criss-crossing the Indians' realm in nine interlocking routes (see Chapter 21). Regular army cavalry and infantry, released from duty in the Civil War (see below), moved west to protect American migrants and their homes.

The last battles in this conflict occurred in the final decades of the nineteenth century. In 1881 the Sioux chief Sitting Bull (c. 1831–1890) surrendered his people and his lands to federal troops, by whose fire he was killed in 1890. The Apache leader Geronimo (c. 1829–1909) abandoned his long resistance in 1886. In 1890, at Wounded Knee, South Dakota, federal troops massacred 200 Indian worshipers who had gathered to dance the Ghost Dance, a newly invented ritual of desperation.

In Oregon, the salmon-hunting Nez Percé ("pierced nose," so named by French hunters for their distinctive form of adornment) refused to cooperate with federal officials. They fled to the north; weakened by starvation, just short of the Canadian border, their gifted leader Chief Joseph (c. 1840–1904) halted and surrendered, defeated by the suffering of his people. "I will fight no more forever," he announced in memorable words that seem to sum up the voice of the Indian peoples of North America.

By 1900, some four centuries after the Spanish conquest, the indigenous peoples of the Americas were no longer in possession of the lands that were the core of their identity. Nearly all the Indian nations under United States dominion had been relocated and dispirited, reduced permanently to a secondary status in the country that was once theirs.

Not all Americans approved of the government's "solution" for the Indian problem. Objections to the policy of Indian resettlement were voiced by Helen Hunt Jackson (1830–1885) in her explosive *A Century of Dishonor* published in 1881; and in 1883, the Women's National Indian Rights Association

Activists for Feminism and Abolition

Women's rights and abolitionism: *For women, and even more for former slaves, the full and equal inclusion into the American nation, as envisioned in the Declaration of Independence proved an elusive goal throughout the course of the nineteenth century. Shown as partners, Elizabeth Cady Stanton and Susan B. Anthony (left) supported both abolitionist and feminist causes, as did Frederick Douglass (right).*
(left: Library of Congress; right: National Portrait Gallery, Washington, D.C.)

count as three-fifths of a person for purposes of representation and taxation. The effect was to guarantee to the southern states, where slavery was concentrated, more representatives in Congress than they would have obtained if slaves were not counted at all. Article I.9 guaranteed that the slave trade would not be impeded by law before 1808 (after which it was indeed ended), while Article IV.2 assured that the United States government would assist those whose slaves had escaped in the recovery of their property. For these provisions, abolitionists viewed the Constitution as flawed. They were further enraged by the passing of the Fugitive Slave Law of 1793, which reaffirmed the slaveowners' right to recover escaped slaves.

Ironically, circumstances conspired to boost the growth of American slavery exactly when political developments might suggest it was due to expire. In 1793, the northerner Eli Whitney invented the **cotton gin**, which mechanized the process of removing the small seed pods that grew amid the cotton fibers, making the large-scale production of cotton possible. That capability coincided, by chance, with the moment when British textile mills were converted into factories driven by steam power. The British factories were hungry for raw cotton, and the fertile fields of the American south were ready to provide it. Slavery and cotton thus worked together to dominate the economy, the social relations, and the culture of the south, especially the states from South Carolina to Mississippi, where Africans often outnumbered white Americans. The slave population of the south soared from about 700,000 in 1790 to 4 million in 1860. That surge fired the enthusiasm of Northern abolitionists. Other Northerners opposed slavery on economic grounds and opposed its extension into new territories. Some proposed resettling slaves in Africa.

Slavery drove a wedge between the interests of those states whose economy depended upon slave labor, and those where it did not—between the southern and northern states. Those sectional differences

formed to battle for victims of western expansionism. In 1887, the Dawes Severalty Act attempted to make private farmers of Indians whose tradition of land management was communal. It proposed to make gifts of land in parcels of 160 acres, and to grant full citizenship to participants. Seeking to impose European norms on Indian natives, it was a failure.

Slavery and Abolitionism   The years of Indian displacement corresponded roughly to those of the rise and fall of African slavery in the United States. *Witnesses* on p. 571 and *Windows On* on p. 551 give insight into the lives of the slaves. Although at the foundation of the republic, most Americans accepted the institution of slavery, many deplored both the slave trade and the exploitation of unfree labor. Implicit in the statement that "all men are created equal" was the seed of **abolitionism**, the theory that slavery was morally wrong and should be abolished.

The Constitution, however, acknowledged and protected the institution of slavery at three critical points. Article I.2 contains the infamous "Three-Fifths Compromise," providing that a slave would

Foundations of Freedom in Anglo-America

The new United States based its constitution on a rich heritage of political philosophy. Yet a few fundamental documents from the era of its founding, and thereafter, encapsulate some of its essential principles. Represented here are the Declaration of Independence, *with its promise of equality and its assertion that government must protect the rights of citizens; the* Seneca Falls *Declaration, deriving from the earlier one, which extends the thinking about equality and rights to women citizens of the republic; and the speech delivered by Abraham Lincoln to commemorate the Gettysburg battlefield of the Civil War. The latter recalls the initial promise of 1776 and restates the mission of the United States: government of, by, and for the people.*

Separation from Britain: Thomas Jefferson's Declaration of Independence (1776): We hold these truths to be self-evident, that all men are created equal, that they are endowed by their Creator with certain unalienable Rights, that among these are Life, Liberty and the pursuit of Happiness. That to secure these rights, Governments are instituted among Men, deriving their just powers from the consent of the governed, That whenever any Form of Government becomes destructive of these ends, it is the Right of the People to alter or to abolish it, and to institute new Government, laying its foundation of such principles and organizing its powers in such form, as to them shall seem most likely to effect their Safety and Happiness... .

The history of the present King of Great Britain is a history of repeated injuries and usurpations all having in direct object the establishment of an absolute tyranny over these States... . [A list of "injuries and usurpations" follows.]

In every stage of these Oppressions We have Petitioned for Redress in the most humble terns: Our repeated Petitions have been answered only by repeated injury. A Prince, whose character is thus marked by every act which may define a Tyrant, is unfit to be the ruler of a free People... .

We, therefore, the Representatives of the United States of America, in General Congress, Assembled, appealing to the Supreme Judge of the World for the rectitude of our intentions, do, in the Name, and by Authority of the good People of the Colonies, solemnly publish and declare, That these United Colonies are, and of Right ought to be Free and Independent States; that they are Absolved from all Allegiance to the British Crown, and that all political connection between them and the State of Great Britain, is and ought to be totally dissolved... .
(The Declaration of Independence Made by the Original Thirteen States in Congress at Philadelphia, 1776)

Rights for women (1848): We hold these truths to be self-evident: that all men and women are created equal; that they are endowed by their Creator with certain inalienable rights; that among these are life, liberty, and the pursuit of happiness; that to secure these rights governments are instituted, deriving their just powers from the consent of the governed. Whenever any form of government becomes destructive of these ends, it is the right of those who suffer from it to refuse allegiance to it, and to insist upon the institution of a new government, laying its foundation on such principles, and organizing its power in such form, as to them shall seem most likely to effect their safety and happiness... .

The history of mankind is a history of repeated injuries and usurpations on the part of man toward woman, having in direct object the establishment of an absolute tyranny over her. To prove this, let facts be submitted... . [A list of "injuries and usurpations" follows.]

Now, in view of this entire disenfranchisement of one-half the people of the country ... in view of the unjust laws above mentioned, and because women do feel themselves aggrieved, oppressed, and fraudulently deprived of their most sacred right, we insist that they have immediate admission to all the rights and privileges which belong to them as citizens of the United States.
("Declaration of Sentiments and Resolutions, Seneca Falls, 1848". M. J. Gage, 1969, pp. 70–73)

The promise renewed: Abraham Lincoln's Gettysburg Address (1863): Four score and seven years ago our fathers brought forth on this continent, a new nation, conceived in Liberty, and dedicated to the proposition that all men are created equal.

Now we are engaged in a great civil war, testing whether that nation or any so conceived and so dedicated, can long endure. We are met on a battle-field of that war. We have come to dedicate a portion of that field, as a final resting place for those who gave their lives that that nation might live. It is altogether fitting and proper that we should do this.

But, in a larger sense, we can not dedicate—we can not consecrate—we can not hallow this ground. The brave men, living and dead, who struggled here, have consecrated it, far above our poor power to add or detract. The world will little note, nor long remember what we say here, but it can never forget what they did here. It is for us the living, rather, to be dedicated here to the unfinished work which they who fought here have thus far so nobly advanced. It is rather for us to be here dedicated to the great task remaining before us—that from these honored dead we take increased devotion to that cause for which they gave the last full measure of devotion—that we here highly resolve that these dead shall not have died in vain—that this nation, under God, shall have a new birth of freedom—and that government of the people, by the people, for the people, shall not perish from the earth.
(From R. P. Basler ed., *The Collected Works of Abraham Lincoln,* vol. 7, 1953)

ended in the **secession** of the southern states and the Civil War fought from 1861 to 1865. Even before that confrontation began, attempts had been made to deal with the issues of the abolition, preservation, and extension of slavery.

Twice, congressional leaders offered compromises in an attempt to silence the Sectionalist debates. In 1820–1821, the Missouri compromise provided that unorganized territory north of the 36°30′ parallel should remain free, while slavery could be extended to the south. Missouri would be admitted as a slave state, though north of that latitude, while Maine would be admitted as free.

The Compromise of 1850 reversed the principles of the Missouri Compromise. California was admitted as a free state, but the status of the Utah and New Mexico Territories were to be determined by the decision of the people. Among other provisions, slavery was allowed in Washington D.C., but the slave trade ended, and a stern fugitive-slave law was now imposed.

The 1850 Compromise did not settle the slavery issue for long. Four years later, a northern politician proposed the terms of the Kansas-Nebraska Act. It called upon the organization of Kansas and Nebraska as territories, with the slavery issue to be decided upon admission to statehood by the people there resident. Pro-slave and anti-slave activists rushed to Kansas, which became a battleground for the competing interests that soon turned to fraud and violence. "Bleeding Kansas" foreshadowed the horrors to come when, soon, the Civil War began.

The stiff fugitive slave rules of 1850 paved the way for the infamous Dred Scott case, upon which the Supreme Court ruled in 1857. Born a slave, Dred Scott had moved with his master to the Northwest Territory, where he lived for years on free soil. On that basis, he claimed his freedom upon his master's death. The Court ruled against him, and returned him to slavery.

The abolitionists were horrified by the ruling, which seemed to privilege slave-holders. Northerners in general now opposed the extension of slavery, though few favored its abolition where it already existed. That was the position held by Abraham Lincoln (1809–1865), an Illinois lawyer who in 1860 won the nomination for President of a new, northern political party; the Republican.

WITNESSES

African Bondage in Anglo-America

These two documents offer a glimpse of the two sides of slavery in the United States. The first, from the perspective of the slaveowner, calls for the recapture and punishment of runaway slaves. The second, from the perspective of those who had been enslaved, shows the determination to win freedom from slavery.

A colonial slave code (Virginia) aims to discourage runaway slaves: Whereas many times slaves run away and lie hid and lurking in swamps, woods, and other obscure places, killing hogs, and committing other injuries to the inhabitants ... if the slave does not immediately return, anyone whatsoever may kill or destroy such slaves by such ways and means as he ... shall think fit. ... If the slave is apprehended ... it shall ... be lawful for the county court, to order such punishment for the said slave, either by dismembering, or in any other way ... as they in their discretion shall think fit, for the reclaiming any such incorrigible slave, and terrifying others from the like practices. ...
(From H. Zinn ed., *A People's History of the United States*, 1980)

A former slave who had bought her own freedom in the antebellum South succeeds in buying her daughter's freedom, as recounted by abolitionist Laura S. Haviland (1889): We solicited over seventy dollars for a poor woman by the name of Jackson, from Marseilles, Kentucky, who had bought herself by washing and ironing of nights, after her mistress' work was done. During seven long years she did not allow herself to undress except to change. Her sleep was little naps over the ironing board. Seven years of night work brought the money that procured her freedom. She had a son and daughter nearly grown, and to purchase their freedom she was now bending her day and night energies. ... The master's indebtedness compelled him to sell one of them, and market was found for the girl of sixteen. Nine hundred dollars was offered, and the distressed mother had but four hundred dollars to pay. ...

In her distress she went from house to house, to plead for a buyer who would advance the five hundred dollars, and take a mortgage on her until she could make it. At length she found a Baptist deacon who purchased her daughter, and she paid him the four hundred dollars. He was to keep her until the mortgage was redeemed by her mother. ... After working very hard one year, she was able to pay but one hundred and fifty dollars toward the mortgage, when her health began to fail. The deacon told her ... he could not wait longer than another year, before he would have to sell her.

[Advised by sympathizers, the mother sought the aid of abolitionists in Cincinnati and Oberlin, including the author of the memoir.] A few weeks later the glad mother returned and redeemed the daughter. I saw them together ... happy in their freedom.
(Laura S. Haviland, *A Woman's Life: Work, Labors, and Experiences*, 1889; ed. G. S. Lerner, 1973)

Winslow Homer

The Bayonet Charge: *Winslow Homer's 1862 wood engraving of a bayonet charge captures the fury of a Civil War battlefield, yet still hints at the futility of an effort where brave men oppose hot guns with cold steel and face destruction.* (The Metropolitan Museum of Art, New York)

When Lincoln won the election, the slaveholding states of the lower south (South Carolina, Georgia, Florida, Texas, Mississippi, Louisiana, and Alabama) seceded from the Union, arguing the full sovereignty of each state within the nation. The secessionist states formed the Confederate States of America, loyal to all the principles of the United States polity except those related to slavery.

North Carolina, Virginia, Tennessee, and Arkansas soon joined the Confederacy. Four other slave states—Maryland, Delaware, Kentucky, and Missouri—which formed a border between the slaveholding regions and the north remained within the Union. In Western Virginia opponents of secession formed a new state, staunchly Unionist in allegiance.

Civil War and After   In 1861, South Carolina militia men fired on the federal garrison at Fort Sumter in Charleston harbor. Lincoln called a Special Session of Congress to ask for approval of the actions he had taken to counter the southern offensive. He argued against the theory of state sovereignty, calling

"States' Rights" a fiction—a "sophistry," or trick of logic. He called on Congress to reaffirm the supremacy of that nation which alone in human history, as he put it, had been called into existence to lighten its citizens' burdens. The Civil War began, the central and most tragic event in the nation's history (see Chapter 20).

It was not the purpose of the Civil War to put an end to American slavery. But that was its result. In 1863, the Emancipation Proclamation made all slaves in rebellious territories "forever free." That partial liberation affected neither northern states nor Confederate territory not under Union control. Yet it freed some half a million slaves by 1865 and struck a blow to the heart of the institution of slavery.

The war over, Congress set out both to reorganize and to punish the south. That mission they pursued until 1877 when "Reconstruction," as the process was called, ended. Former secessionists regained their civil rights. The crowds of reformers and opportunists who had streamed south dwindled, and the programs instituted to help freed men gain land and legal rights ceased.

In 1865, all slaves still in bondage were made free by the Thirteenth Amendment to the United States Constitution. In 1868, the Fourteenth Amendment guaranteed freed slaves the rights of citizens. In 1870, the Fifteenth assured them the right to vote.

Legislation could not adequately address the problems left by more than two centuries of slavery. Southern whites took steps to segregate blacks and deny them political rights. Black Codes, which reduced freed men to a condition of virtual serfdom, were banned, but their spirit prevailed and a host of customs and regulations barred African Americans from full civic participation. Black schools and black churches were targets for sporadic, illegal repression, and black leaders were victims of violence. Kept separate, illiterate, vulnerable, and poor, freed slaves did not yet benefit from the guarantee of rights found in the Declaration of Independence, the Bill of Rights, and the post-war amendments.

Yet the promise remained, as President Lincoln restated it in 1863 at the battlefield site of a recent Union victory in Gettysburg, Pennsylvania. In his brief speech honoring the thousands who died, quoted in *Witnesses* on p. 570, the president linked the moment to the moment of national founding: "Four score and seven years ago," which was to say in 1776, "our fathers brought forth upon this continent... ." He summoned his listeners to a second founding, there on the bloodied Pennsylvania fields, a sacred event. They were to "consecrate" themselves, pledging to fulfill the promise Jefferson once had made to create a government that nurtured the inalienable rights of all: one that was "of the people, by the people, for the people."

When Lincoln summoned Americans to fulfill that promise, slavery was not yet dead. The liberation of former slaves from the habits of discrimination that slavery had ingrained was still to come. Native Indians continued to languish in the bleak reservations built by federal officials. Other groups now sought inclusion in the circle of Americans. Poor white males, white immigrant males, and females of all origins claimed their place among those who called themselves "we, the people" of the United States.

In colonial America, as in England, property requirements limited the electorate. In seventeenth-century Massachusetts, just over half of all adult males

Winslow Homer, A New Field of Dead Men: *After the Civil War, soldiers who had been farmboys returned home to their farms; but they, and their fields, had changed—a metaphysical reality Winslow Homer captures splendidly in his huge 1865 painting of* The Veteran in a New Field. *The farmer back on the job is also the figure of Death wielding his scythe against innumerable, towering shafts of wheat, displayed in a brilliant yellow, who will each be cut down in their multitudes by the relentlessness of war.* (The Metropolitan Museum of Art, New York; Bequest of Adelaide Milton de Groot)

were eligible to vote; elsewhere the percentage approached twenty percent. After independence, the franchise gradually broadened. By the 1820s all white males had been granted **suffrage**, or the right to vote.

Immigrants, too, of whom some 5 million arrived between 1790 and 1860, sought inclusion in American civil life. Before the Civil War, they were mostly Irish or German, and often Catholics who found a hostile reception in a largely Protestant society. Later in the century, more waves of immigrants arrived from southern and eastern Europe as well as Asia and Latin America. Spurred by the discrimination they met, immigrants gained entry to politics in order to protect their communities as they struggled to succeed in a new world.

Women, like slaves, were denied full participation in American society; all, of whatever rank, were injured by the Jeffersonian statement that "all *men* are created equal." A feminist movement developed alongside abolitionism, leading to the 1848 meeting of women leaders and some male supporters at Seneca Falls, New York. Its outcome was the Declaration of Sentiments, quoted in *Witnesses* on p. 570, which called for an end to women's subordination to men. Prominent among the grievances were the limits on women's right to hold property or to have custody of their children; their prohibition from higher education or professional careers; their unequal status in the workplace and the unequal pay they received; and the sexual double standard that permitted males to ignore moral norms while requiring women to obey them. The most urgent issue was the right to vote, which some hoped would be achieved for women when it was granted to freed black slaves. Among those supporting the Seneca Falls declaration were male abolitionist leaders, white and black.

After the Civil War, women leaders observed bitterly that while former male slaves now possessed the right to vote (if only in theory), no woman did. This injustice shaped the American women's movement, which now focused almost entirely on suffrage (finally obtained only in 1920). The circle of American citizenship had already expanded, and would continue to do so despite the opposition of those who stood to lose a monopoly on political power.

By the late 1800s, the question "Who is an American?" might be answered as follows: anyone born on American soil or, if born abroad, **naturalized**, or officially accepted as a citizen upon the satisfaction of minimal requirements. A second question still remained: "*What* is an American?" If not of English descent, would he or she speak English? If not of European descent—as the descendants of Africans, Asians, or Amerindians were not—would he or she identify with European culture, the civilization of the West? Though the question remains open, certain facts are clear: the political ideals, and the moral values behind them, that guided the American experiment, were the product of Western thought, the children of Western civilization.

Conclusion
JEFFERSON'S PROMISE, LINCOLN'S PLEDGE, AND THE MEANING OF THE WEST

From independence through the late nineteenth century, the United States proceeded in the direction of the inclusion of all its peoples in the task of government, and the recognition of their inalienable rights —goals that Jefferson promised, and Lincoln pledged. The nations of Latin America, where the task of inclusion was more difficult, did not.

In the north, the majority of the population was of European descent at the time the United States was founded. Amerindians numbered a sparse few hundred thousand, and Africans, slave and free, amounted to perhaps ten percent of the population. The cultural imprint of the European old world was therefore powerful.

In most of Spanish America, in contrast, the Amerindian population was a majority at the time that independence was won, while Africans dominated the Caribbean and Brazil. The elites of European descent who created the economic, political, and social foundations of their nations were a minority, who imposed their language and religion as a standard for all. Yet to this day the traditional cultures of native peoples are not wholly merged with that of the elites. Is Latin America an heir to Western civilization? It seems so. Not all of its people, however, belong to that civilization. Nor will they, or should they, unless they acquire through schooling the cultural values of the West—values responsible both for their domination in the colonial era and, subsequently, their liberation.

QUESTIONS TO CONSIDER

1. Why was the plantation system so important in shaping the future of Brazil and the Caribbean on the one hand, and the southern part of Anglo-North America on the other?

2. Why did the colonial societies and states in Latin America develop a different relation with indigenous Amerindian populations than those in North America?

3. Why was a written constitution a breakthrough? Why did the new United States create a written constitution, when none of the major European states had one?

4. Why were Latin American states rather unsuccessful in the nineteenth century, relative to the expanding United States?

5. To what extent did the United States meet the challenge of its founding principles by the end of the nineteenth century?

SUGGESTED RESOURCES

Berlin, Ira, *Generations of Captivity: A History of African-American Slaves* (New Haven: Yale University Press, 2003). Masterful synthesis of the slave experience across the regions of the U.S. and over five generations.

Calloway, Colin G., *New Worlds for All: Indians, Europeans, and the Remaking of Early America* (Baltimore: Johns Hopkins University Press, 1997). Describes the long cultural interaction between Europeans and Amerindians, including North and South America, and the Spanish, French, Russian, English, invaders.

Coatsworth, John & Alan M. Taylor, eds., *Latin America and the World Economy since 1800* (Cambridge MA: Harvard University Press, 2000). Essays exploring how the Latin American economy, one of the world's strongest around 1800, steadily declined thereafter.

Draper, Theodore, *A Struggle for Power: The American Revolution* (New York: Time Books, 1996). Sees the Revolution as resulting from a struggle for power rather than from republican ideology or economic interest.

Harvey, Robert, *Liberators: Latin America's Struggle for Independence, 1810–1830* (London: John Murray, 2000). Vivid narrative of the process of liberation and state-formation in Latin America.

Kennedy, Roger G., *Burr, Hamilton, and Jefferson: A Study in Character* (Oxford: Oxford University Press, 2000). Thoughtful recent assessment of the unique personalities of three enormously important Americans in the era of founding.

Kukla, Jon, *A Wilderness So Immense: The Louisiana Purchase and the Destiny of America* (New York: Alfred A. Knopf. 2003). Focuses on the twenty years before the 1803 purchase, and the struggle for control of the Mississippi between the young US, Britain, Spain, and France.

Langley, Lester D., *The Americas in the Age of Revolution, 1750–1850* (New Haven, CT: Yale University Press, 1996). Offers a "comparative history of the revolutionary age," taking in both American continents.

Lynch, John, *Caudillos in Spanish America, 1800–1850* (Oxford: Clarendon Press of Oxford University Press, 1992). Traces the cultural, social, and political origins of the early caudillos.

Maier, Pauline, *American Scripture: Making the Declaration of Independence* (New York: Alfred A. Knopf, 1997). Views the creation of the epochal "Declaration of Independence" as a complex process involving many makers and ideas.

Noll, Mark A., *America's God: From Jonathan Edwards to Abraham Lincoln* (Oxford: Oxford University Press, 2002). Traces the evolution over a little more than a century of a new American religious tradition, appropriate to a new republic and distinct from its European matrix.

Stauffer, John, *The Black Hearts of Men: Radical Abolitionists and the Transformation of Race* (Cambridge MA: Harvard University Press, 2002). Shows how white abolitionists acquired "black hearts" by identifying with the condition and struggle of black slaves.

Twinam, Ann, *Private Lives, Public Secrets: Gender, Honor, Sexuality, and Illegitimacy in Colonial Spanish America* (Stanford: Stanford University Press, 1999). Explores how the colonial elite disciplined themselves in order to maintain group status.

Indigenous peoples of the Americas, all regions, articles, and resources:
http://www.hartford–hwp.com/archives/41/index.html

Thomas Jefferson: resources for his life and career, including electronic texts (University of Virginia):
http://etext.virginia.edu/jefferson

Jefferson's house at Monticello:
http://www.monticello.org

Abigail Adams Historical Society, resources in brief, with links:
http://www.abigailadams.org/Abigail/abigail.html

Frederick Douglass, National Historic Site (US NPS), biography and images of his home:
http://www.nps.gov/frdo/freddoug.html

Abraham Lincoln Online, texts and images, with links to further resources:
http://showcase.netins.net/web/creative/lincoln.html

Biblioteca virtual de Simon Bolivar, depicted to his political philosophy:
http://www.geocities.com/Athens/Acropolis/7609/eng

⊙ Western Civilization Documents CD-ROM

17.1 Slaves in the City
17.2 Demands from a Slave Rebellion
17.3 The Stamp Act
17.4 "Declaration of Sentiments": American Women Want Independence
17.5 Thomas Paine: Common Sense
17.6 John Adams: Thoughts on Government
21.1 "Sentiments of the Nation" A Mexican Call for Independence
21.2 Thomas MacAulay: A Radical War-Song
21.3 Alexis de Tocqueville: The New Social Morality
21.4 Simon Bolivar's Political Ideas

REVOLUTION

Revolution and Reorganization

American War of
Independence,
1775–83

French Revolution,1789–99

Napoleonic era, 1799–1815

◆ Storming of Bastille, July 14, 1789

◆ Declaration of the Rights of Man
and the Citizen, Aug 27, 1789

◆ March on Versailles, Oct 5–6, 1789

◆ Civil Constitution of the Clergy,
July 12, 1790

◆ Edmund Burke's Reflections on the
Revolution in France, 1790

◆ September Massacres, Sept 2–6, 1792

◆ Louis XVI executed, Jan 21, 1793

◆ Levée en masse, Aug 23, 1793

◆ Festival of Reason, Nov 10, 1793

◆ France ends slavery in colonies, 1794

◆ "Thermidor": fall of Robespiere,
July 28, 1794

◆ Condorcet's Progress of the
Human Mind, 1795

◆ Directory, 1795–99

◆ Napoleon becomes
First Consul, 1799

◆ Concordat between Napoleon
and Catholic Church, 1801

◆ Napoleon becomes
Emperor, 1804

◆ Civil Code established
in France, 1804

◆ Battles of Austerlitz
and Trafalgar, 1805

◆ Napoleon invades
Russia, 1812

◆ Congress of Vienna,
1814–1815

◆ Napoleon defeated
at Waterloo, 1815

Beyond the West

Mughal Empire, India, 1526–1857

British East India Company in India, c. 1700–1857

Qing Dynasty, China, 1644–1912

Dutch East India Company in East Indies, 1619–1799

CHAPTER 20

REVOLUTION:
The End of the Old Regime
1789–1815

Empire of Napoleon, 1812

KEY QUESTIONS

◆ **Preludes to Revolution:** Which groups joined together to resist the Old Regime? What were their different complaints against the king?

◆ **The Rights of Man:** How did ideas about the rights of men become incorporated in the French Revolution? Why did the rights of women not receive the same attention?

◆ **The Birth of a Nation:** What were the forces that radicalized the French Revolution beginning as early as 1789? What stopped the process of radicalization?

◆ **The Imperial Adventure:** Why was government by one man acceptable to the French after the experience of Revolution? In what ways did Napoleon support the revolutionary agenda? Which revolutionary principles did he oppose?

Thermidor On July 26, 1794—in the hot summer month the French revolutionaries had renamed "Thermidor"— Maximilien Robespierre (1758–1794) addressed the National Convention for the last time. For two years he had led that body of young radicals, unloosing a torrent of change and spilling a torrent of blood. But on this morning, a group of his former colleagues shouted him down. The next day, he was arrested and tried; the following morning, executed by the guillotine. The Terror he had launched with his decrees, and defended with his fiery orations, ended with his death.

Thermidor marked the end of the Revolution that destroyed absolute monarchy in France, along with the rest of the *ancien régime*, or "Old Regime", the social and political system previously established in that country. Yet it did not staunch the revolutionary impulse, which would erupt often in the next generations. In time, the French Revolution would transform all of Europe, inspiring bold hopes and triggering ruthless repression. It would lead to the creation of a new kind of nation, responsible not to a monarch but to its people—citizens now, not subjects. "The people" had made their presence felt and had announced their implacable demands.

Map 20.1 on p. 594 shows the progress of the Revolution. By 1789, the Old Regime was tottering. Nobles, burghers, peasants, and intellectuals had grown skeptical of kings, bureaucrats, the tax structure, and all the privileges and patronage that buttressed a failing system. Resistance broke out in 1789, and mounted rapidly, escalating in intensity over five years until the upheaval of Thermidor in 1794. Reaction then set in, but without wholly undoing the changes the Revolution had introduced. In 1799, the general

Napoleon Bonaparte seized leadership of France. Appropriating those features of the Revolution that suited him—while his armies exported throughout Europe the principles of "Liberty, Equality, Fraternity" that had energized revolt at home—he proceeded to impose strict control of the legal, political, and cultural life of the nation. Not a king, but a dictator, he transformed the revolutionary tradition and pointed it in the direction of the modern state.

PRELUDES TO REVOLUTION

The Enlightenment *philosophes* (see Chapter 17) had identified the faults of the French Old Regime and of similar despotic regimes elsewhere in Europe. Absolute monarchs, foolish laws, lazy aristocrats, intrusive clergy, and inquisitive censors all stifled human freedom and happiness. Their unjust dominion should be swept away. Attempts to do so were numerous in the years prior to the French Revolution. Nobles, gentry, peasants and intellectuals actively resisted those forces that stifled their freedom: absolutism, **seigneurialism**, mercantilism, and superstition.

Resistance to Absolutism

Even before Enlightenment thinkers framed their critique of absolute monarchy, the English had defied it. In 1649, the English Civil War culminated in the execution of Charles I by Parliamentarians (see Chapter 15). The principle that Parliament had authority even over the monarch was reaffirmed by the "Glorious Revolution" of 1689. During the following century, the influence of Britain's narrow aristocracy remained undiminished, and even representatives to the House of Commons were drawn from the wealthiest social strata. Still, the authority of the king was limited by Parliament.

Empty coffers: In this lampoon of the French financial crisis of the years before 1789, entitled "Le Défécit," Louis XVI and his chief finance minister contemplate the crown's empty coffers while a priest and an aristocrat exit with bags full of money. (British Museum, London)

In British North America the pretenses of monarchy received a more powerful rebuke in the War of Independence of 1776–1783 (see Chapter 19). Revolutionary leaders named as "tyrant" the same king whose powers, in Britain, were limited by its constitution, and their "Declaration of Independence" assailed him for violating their human rights.

Victory for the American colonists, in 1781, brought in its wake also victory for the republican ideas that had informed the debate about independence in 1776. The new nation rejected monarchy as its political form and created instead a government with balanced executive, judicial, and legislative powers defined by a written constitution. Thomas Paine, self-appointed scribe of both the American and French revolutions, proclaimed in his pro-independence tract *Common Sense* that in America, "the law is king".

Elsewhere, the challenge to monarchy was not nearly as strong as it was in the two English-speaking nations of Great Britain and the new United States. To be sure, the Italian republics (Venice, Genoa, Lucca) and the Swiss cantons managed without kings altogether, but only on the fringes of the main political currents of the age. The ailing Dutch Republic (created in the 1600s when the Northern Netherlands had gained independence from Habsburg Spain) was a republic still, though it was vulnerable to the aspirations of the princes of Orange, who sought to make their provincial title of *stadholder* hereditary. The once-mighty monarchs of Sweden and Poland were overshadowed by their nobles— those of Poland resisting not merely absolutism but any central order whatever. The refusal of its nobility to support a strong, centralized monarchy resulted in the annihilation of the Polish nation by its aggressive neighbors in the third partition of 1795 (see Chapter 15). The Hungarian nobles, fractious like the Polish and unconstrained by a monarch having no king of their own, resisted their Habsburg overlords. The Hungarians' struggle would erupt in the age of nationalism, during the next century.

A few "enlightened" monarchs adopted the *philosophes*' advice to promote the common welfare, fostering education, toleration, justice, and other human rights (see Chapter 17). In Prussia, Frederick II (r. 1740–1786) reformed the state bureaucracy and promoted industry and commerce. Yet he maintained a social system dominated by nobles, in which most people were voiceless. The Habsburg emperor Joseph II (r. 1765–1790) freed the Austrian serfs, among the most oppressed people of Europe. This farsighted action was undone by his brother and successor Leopold (r. 1790–1792), who, however, had some claim to the title of enlightened ruler, having introduced representative institutions when he ruled the Italian state of Tuscany (1765–1790).

In Russia, Catherine the Great (r. 1762–1796) supervised the reform of Russia's legal code, for which she personally composed an *Instruction* infused with Enlightenment principles. She promulgated the Statute of National Education, ordering the creation of state-funded schools. During her reign, more books were published in Russia than in all previous years combined. Yet much of what she started was left unfinished, and she was responsible for the extension of serfdom and deterioration of the condition of that already overburdened population.

"Enlightened" monarchs introduced reforms so long as they served the interests of the state and nurtured the institution of monarchy itself. They recognized that absolutism was unsustainable if it remained unleavened by any solicitude for its subjects. The monarch, as Catherine argued, "possesses all the means for the eradication of all harm and looks on the general good as its own."

In prerevolutionary France, aristocrats resisted the claims of absolute monarchy. In contrast to the era of Louis XIV (r. 1643–1715), when the most important noblemen of the realm were summoned to Versailles to dance attendance on the king, eighteenth-century aristocrats claimed greater independence. That independence was expressed through the *parlements*, or law courts, which often countered royal directives issued by centrally appointed administrators, or *intendants*. The Sun King's successors struggled to uphold royal authority over recalcitrant nobles.

In 1787, desperate for funds (in part because of the costly assistance lent to the American revolutionaries), the young king Louis XVI (r. 1774–1793) summoned an Assembly of Notables. He and his ministers hoped that these prominent men (including clergy, nobles, and bourgeois) would be willing to tax themselves in order to raise essential revenues. He was disappointed. The Assembly of Notables disbanded. Having nowhere else to turn, the king summoned the Estates-General, a legislative body of medieval origin which had not met since 1614, under his great-grandfather's grandfather, Henry IV. The principle function of this assembly was to vote tax levies. By forcing the king to take this step, the "notables" had, in effect, signed his death warrant—and that of many of their own class. For the summoning of the Estates-General was the trigger of the Revolution that swiftly followed.

Peasants Revolts and Free Trade

While landowning elites resisted the pretensions of absolute monarchs, peasants often rose up in armed revolt against landowners. Peasant revolts were numerous, violent, and unsuccessful in European history—just as they were in antiquity or contemporary China. Peasant militias fell regularly to the superior force of professional armies. As if without memory of these earlier defeats (most had left no trace beyond what community elders recalled, when they became stressed by famine or landowner abuse, the peasants arose (see Chapter 18).

Why did peasants revolt? Because of landowners' demands and scarcity of food. The eighteenth century (an era, some scholars contend, of "feudal reaction" against absolutist centralization) saw a hardening of the landlords' position (see Chapter 18). This process occurred in western as well as eastern Europe, where the establishment of a "second serfdom" crushed the spirit of the workers. In a free-market economy, where agricultural surpluses could be sold for profit, landlords strove to increase the productivity of their lands. They moved to limit common lands and rights, such as the rights to graze livestock or glean forest products. And they squeezed what labor they could from the peasantry, insisting on the performance of "servile duties"—such as wall repair and road building— traditionally attached to their plots of soil.

The *philosophes* (and the economic specialists among them, known as "**physiocrats**") denounced these labor services, relics of a medieval economy. Ironically, however, the economic strategies of economic Enlightenment thinkers exacerbated he hardships of the poor. The "free trade" policies they advocated (*laissez faire*, or "let it be") might lift barriers to commerce and ease regulations. But they also interfered with traditional anti-famine practices of grain hoarding by local lords or municipalities. Now, in periods of famine, people could obtain grain only by paying a steep price; those who could not pay starved. The urban poor, being remote from any source of agricultural products and wholly dependent on inadequate mechanisms of distribution, were especially vulnerable. Hunger was often more severe in the eighteenth-century than it had been in earlier times. Those who suffered such experiences nurtured a potentially explosive hatred for those whom they blamed for their poverty: the local landowners.

Although the poor might suffer from the cycles of the free market, bourgeois businessmen and physiocrats opposed the traditional policy of mercantilism (see Chapter 16). They deplored the tariffs and fees that burdened trade with unnecessary costs, the granting of monopolies to favored companies, the obsession with bullion the costly competition between nations. In 1776, the Scots economist Adam Smith presented the anti-mercantilist and free-trade positions eloquently and at length in ins influential *Inquiry into the Nature and Causes of the Wealth of Nations* (see Chapter 16). Mercantilism had been central to the foreign and domestic policies of absolute monarchs, and resistance to mercantilism as an important strike against the *ancien régime*.

The War of Ideas

As nobles and kings, landlords and peasants, mercantilist statesmen and entrepreneurs confronted each other, Enlightenment thinkers engaged in a war of ideas. Their enemies were superstition, ignorance, intolerance, and obfuscation, to which they opposed the probing force of reason.

Voltaire, the preeminent Enlightenment sage, had identified the Church as the sinister agent of superstition, and to his last moment he called for its destruction: *"Ecrasez l'infâme!"* (see Chapter 17). The objections to the privileged position accorded the Church in Roman Catholic countries were numerous. It promoted childish beliefs, critics argued, in saints and miracles. It persecuted heretics (the Inquisition was still busy in Spain and Portugal and their overseas colonies). It preached intolerance. It opposed the explorations of philosophy and social criticism. Above all, the clergy in general, and especially the elite order of Jesuits, were seen as defenders of absolute monarchy.

As two alternatives to established religion, Catholic or Protestant, intellectuals favored deism and Freemasonry. The first won favor because it was free of doctrine, positing only a "supreme being", the creator of the universe. The second gained adherents because it claimed authority in a pre-Christian and rationalist tradition, based on an ideal of brotherly love.

Both of these alternative "religious" movements formed part of a process of secularization that had been underway since the Italian Renaissance (see Chapter 13), when laymen in large numbers first joined the ranks of intellectuals. Thereafter, the growth of schooling, the spread of literacy, the advent of printing (which made cheap books, cartoons, and street ballads widely available) promoted a culture in which received dogmas were increasingly open to question (see Chapter 17). By the mid-eighteenth century, the cheap print media exposed even the poor to critiques of the powerful, and thus engaged them in the political debate.

By this time, a new form of subversive literature had emerged: pornography. Pornography not only busied the censors but also entered the realms of politics. What better way to sully the image of the mighty than by associating them with the prohibited fantasies of the pornographer? Among the targets was Marie Antoinette (1755–1793), the fastidious and hated consort of Louis XVI. According to the scandal-mongers, her lust was insatiable and her intimate "favorites" both male and female. Salacious accounts of her supposed debauchery inflamed popular resentment of the monarchy.

Thus, intellectuals, entrepreneurs, peasants, artisans, workers, and aristocrats all resisted, from their different motives, the established patterns of the old order. Although its vestiges would linger in places until World War I, it was already moribund by May 1789, in the more enlightened regions of western Europe. At that point, in France, there arrived at Versailles—the seat of the French court, situated at a distance of about 12 miles from Paris—the elected representatives to the Estates-General.

THE RIGHTS OF MAN

The arrival of these representatives opened the first phase of the Revolution: a liberal revolution which aimed to forge a government that would secure the "rights of man and the citizen." Those rights included the civil rights defined in the unwritten British constitution and the written American one. They also included more universal concepts of right derived from ancient philosophy via Thomas Hobbes (1588–1679), John Locke (1632–1704), and the *philosophes* (see Chapters 15, 17). These rights would be guaranteed in a newly framed constitution, to which the king would be subordinate.

A second phase of the Revolution began soon after the first and unfolded simultaneously: the radical revolution. Its effect was to transform French society. It would disenfranchise the "orders" or "estates" that had held sway for centuries and would reinvent the cultural values and religious beliefs of the people. These changes were to be achieved by the mobilization of masses of people, who, for the first time, gained access to the political process. The radical nature of revolution provided no role whatsoever for a king, and he would not succeed in surviving it.

The Work of the National Assembly

In 1788, Louis XVI unknowingly launched the first phase of the French Revolution when he summoned the Estates-General to Versailles. The assembly consisted of representatives from the First, Second, and Third **Estates** (respectively, the clergy, nobility, and all commoners). During the winter of 1788–1789, the electorate gathered to ponder the history of that body, choose representatives, and construct an agenda by compiling *cahiers de doléances*, or "notebooks of grievances." All adult male taxpayers were eligible to participate. They met according to their "estate" in different local settings. The clergy and nobility met in large, elegant rooms, the peasants in parish churches, artisans and merchants in their guildhalls.

Here they compiled some 40,000 *cahiers*, later digested into 615 general *cahiers*, of which most survive. The grievances included complaints about judicial incompetence, official misbehavior, the censorship of the press, religious intolerance, abuses by landlords, unjust taxation, and the condition of the roads. The *cahiers* amounted to a critique of the

Jacques-Louis David, Oath of the Tennis Court: *The Revolution proper began with the convocation of the Estates-General in May 1789 and the Third Estate's historic decision to constitute itself a National Assembly. Here in Jacques-Louis David's 1790 painting, members of the Third Estate, barred from the main meeting room, meet at a nearby tennis court and swear never to disband until a Constitution has been established. (Musée Carnavalet, Paris)*

Land Ownership by Social Category on the Eve of the French Revolution

	Clergy	Nobility	Bourgeoisie	Peasantry
Land in France owned by each group	6–10%	20–25%	30%	40–45%
Each group as a percentage of the total population	2%	1.5%	8.4%	82–87%

One of the long-term causes of revolution in France was the great inequality in wealth, measured in land ownership. This graph shows that two of the smallest groups in the population—clergy and nobility, or the First and Second Estates—together owned nearly one-third of all land in France.

existing political system, a critique that showed considerable agreement across class lines. A hefty seventy-four percent of the participants from the Third Estate demanded liberty of the press; and so did eighty-eight percent of the nobility. Free trade was advocated by forty-two percent of the Third and thirty-five percent of the nobility. The abolition of landlords' rights, in contrast, advocated by sixty-four percent of the Third, won the approval of only fourteen percent of the nobility, whose interests such a move would obviously injure.

One set of the complaints heard in that tense winter concerned the structure of the Estates-General itself. When it had last met, in 1614, it had consisted of the same number of representatives of each of the three estates, which voted as a body. As a result, the whole assembly produced only three votes, and (where there was not unanimity) always yielded a decision of two to one. Two estates could ally to determine the outcome, and often the First and Second Estates, the privileged orders, combined against the Third.

In 1788, these features of the composition and voting rules of the Estates-General aroused protest. A group composed largely of liberal aristocrats, called the "Society of Thirty", specially targeted for change these "forms of 1614"—and with good reason. Since 1614, the category of the Third Estate had become so complex that it could no longer be considered a single social order of "commoners." Comprising some ninety-eight percent of the French population, it included people from different regions, occupations, and levels of wealth, those who owned land and those who didn't; master craftsmen and unskilled laborers; those who wrote books and those who couldn't read; day workers and lawyers; entrepreneurs and servants. Nearly ten percent of the Third Estate consisted of members of the bourgeoisie, which was itself divided between merchants linked to the world of commerce, on the one hand, and the numerous public officials, *rentiers*, and professionals more closely tied to the traditional world of patronage relations, on the other.

How could so diverse a group be lumped together and given a single vote? Why should so large a group receive only one vote of three? The process of responding to the royal summons set in motion a series of provocative questions that would lead to the undoing of both the Estates-General and the monarchy.

As electors composed their *cahiers*, writers of tracts and pamphlets also explored the issues raised by the summoning of the Estates-General. One pamphlet, entitled *What is the Third Estate?*, stated the issues with particular clarity. Quoted in *Witnesses* on p. 584, it was the work of Emmanuel Joseph Sieyès (1748–1836), a young priest of bourgeois origin who began by championing the Revolution, then turned from its excesses, and finally supported its destroyer, Napoleon Bonaparte (see below). Sieyès concluded that the Third Estate had no need of the First and Second, but was in fact a complete nation in itself. Its members performed all the nation's productive work. On that account, they, and not idle clerics and aristocrats, were the nation. And they should be allotted votes accordingly.

Sieyès did not demand, as his argument suggested, the evisceration of the social elites. He modestly requested just two crucial changes—changes also requested by other pamphleteers and listed in many of the *cahiers*. The first was that the number of representatives of the Third Estate should equal the total number allotted to the other two. The second was that the votes be counted by head, rather than by order. The effect of these proposals would be that the Third Estate, by acquiring just one supporter from one of the other groups, would amount to a decisive majority.

Only the first of these proposals was approved. When the Estates-General arrived in Versailles, on May 5, 1789, the representatives of the Third Estate numbered about 600, double the number representing each of the other two. But when the elaborate preliminaries were over and the representatives of all three estates gathered, they were instructed by the king's ministers to vote by order and not by head.

The method of voting was accordingly the first item of business taken up by the Estates-General. Debates consumed several weeks. The king and his advisers contemplated the possibility of an assembly in which the Third Estate possessed a majority. On June 17, the Third Estate announced itself to be the National Assembly, a body representative of the people of France. Cornered, the king struck back. On June 21, the delegates of the Third found their meeting hall barred. They reconvened in a tennis court.

There, the stakes of the debate were raised. The issue before the angry representatives was no longer the structure of the Estates-General, nor even the method of voting. Those matters had been resolved, to their displeasure, by the king's action—they were allowed neither to meet nor to vote under his aegis. The angry representatives, shown in David's painting on p. 581, consequently declared their intention to act: they swore an oath that they would not disband until they had written a constitution for France. That constitution would secure the rights of man, and the demotion of the king.

The Estates-General was no more. From 1789 to 1791 the representatives to the National Assembly would compose the legislation defining the new government. Most of them came from the educated bourgeoisie; they were young; nearly two-thirds were lawyers. They addressed several key matters. The first was the issue of landlords' rights: What was to be done about the remnants of customary authority that some landowners still had over some tenants, including those who were not serfs? The second was the Church: What was to be done about the excessive authority (as these representatives believed) of the clergy, and the excessively large share that the Church enjoyed of the territorial wealth of France? The third had to do with civil rights: What provision should be made to protect the political and personal rights of all citizens? The last had to do with the king: Where would he fit into the new constitution? Would he agree to accept the subordinate position that such a constitution would accord a monarch?

The events of summer 1789 drove the agenda of the National Assembly forward. Peasant rebellions broke out in several regions. Armed bands roamed the countryside, some of the rebels broke into the castles of their masters in search of documents specifying labor and monetary dues. These were burned—and often the houses too. Frightened aristocrats packed their belongings and fled to friendlier nations, remaining in exile for the course of the Revolution. The swift, violent rebellion was dubbed the "Great Fear." In response, the Assembly met in a tense all-night session on August 4, 1789. Its result was the dismantling of landlords' customary rights and the abolition of the system of noble privilege that had prevailed for a millennium. Some of the decrees are listed in *Witnesses* on p. 584.

Later that month, the National Assembly addressed the issue of civil rights. Combining elements of the English and American constitutions with some major principles of Enlightenment political theory, they promulgated, on August 26, the "Declaration of the Rights of Man and the Citizen", quoted in *Witnesses* on p. 584. The rights defined in this document constitute a digest of liberal political principles and establish the theoretical framework of a future constitution. Later versions of the "Declaration" were included in subsequent constitutions, and it forms part of France's constitution today.

Opening with the statement that "ignorance, neglect, or contempt of human rights, are the sole causes of public misfortunes and corruptions of Government," the "Declaration" proceeds to define those rights in full. It affirms that "men are born, and always continue, free, and equal in respect of their rights" and that the purpose of government is to preserve "the natural and imprescriptible rights of man." Human liberty is unrestricted, except by the need to allow for the liberty of others, and must not be limited by systems of law. Free speech and freedom of worship are also to be guaranteed, along with the civil protections (like those long embedded in Anglo-Saxon law) against improper arrest and prosecution. Citizens are accorded the right to consent to taxes levied upon them, and private property is acknowledged and protected. For all its brevity— fewer than 1000 words— the "Declaration" states the main principles of modern liberalism as developed by Enlightenment thinkers.

Article X of the "Declaration" provides for freedom of conscience and worship. To achieve that goal, revolutionary leaders needed to rein in the Roman Catholic Church, powerful because of its wealth and its hold on the consciences of the faithful. On November 2, 1789, the Assembly (now established in Paris) confiscated all church property—amounting to fifteen percent of the land in France, which had yielded an immense, tax-free income in tithes. The following month, it issues a new paper currency, backed by the huge value of former church lands, now considered "*biens nationaux*" ("national property"). Peasant entrepreneurs and bourgeois speculators eagerly purchased the land itself at auction. These provisions effectively destroyed the economic power of the Roman Catholic Church in France.

During the following year, the Assembly issued more restrictions on Church and clergy. On February 13, 1790, it suppressed the religious houses in Paris. On July 12, 1790, it promulgated the Civil Constitution of the Clergy, quoted in *Witnesses* on p. 584. That legislation dismantled the institution of the Church, just as the legislation of August 4, 1789, had dismantled the privileges of the nobility. All priests (of whom there were some 40,000) would receive salaries from the new secular state (rather

The Collapse of the Old Regime

The Old Regime collapsed because of anger, violence, the class of personalities, and unpredictable circumstances—but also because of words. Presented here are some of the words that were powerful enough to remake an entire nation. Abbé Sieyès questions the privileges of the nobility, while in three acts of legislation, from 1789 and 1790, the National Assembly dismantles all feudal relations, defines the civil rights of all citizens, and secularizes the Church by making the clergy responsible to the state. In 1791, the feminist writer Olympe de Gouges responds to the Declaration of the Rights of Man and the Citizen with her own Declaration of the Rights of Woman and the Citizen, calling for a broadening of the concept of citizenship in a direction not before anticipated.

Abbé Sieyès asks: "What is the Third Estate?" (1789):
We have three questions to ask:

1st. What is the third estate? Everything.
2nd. What has it been heretofore in the political order? Nothing.
3rd. What does it demand? To become something therein. ...

What are the essentials of national existence and prosperity? *Private* enterprise and *public* functions. Private enterprise may be divided into four classes: [those engaged in agriculture; those engaged in industry and production; "dealers and merchants"; and the professional and service classes, ranging from scientists to domestic servants]. ... Such are the labors which sustain society. Who performs them? The third estate.

Public functions. ... may [also] be classified under four headings: the Sword, the Robe, the Church, and the Administration. ... [T]he third estate everywhere constitutes nineteen-twentieths of them, except that it is burdened with all that is really arduous, with all the tasks that the privileged order refuses to perform. ...

Who, then, would dare to say that the third estate has not within itself all that is necessary to constitute a complete nation?
(From J. H. Stewart ed., *A Documentary Survey of the French Revolution,* 1951)

Decrees passed the night of August 4, 1789, in response to the "Great Fear": 1. The National Assembly abolishes the feudal regime entirely, and decrees that both feudal and [other contractual] rights and dues ... are abolished without indemnity. ... 4. All seigneurial courts of justice are suppressed without any indemnity; nevertheless the officials of such courts shall continue in office until the National Assembly has provided for the establishment of a new judi-cial organization. 5. Tithes of every kind ... are abolished subject to the devising of means for providing in some other manner for the expenses of divine worship, ... and for all establishments, seminaries, schools, colleges, hospitals, communities and others, to the maintenance of which they are now assigned. ... 9. Pecuniary privileges, personal or real, in matters of taxation are abolished forever. Collection shall be made from all citizens and on all property, in the same manner and in the same form. ... 11. All citizens may be admitted, without distinction of birth, to all ecclesiastical, civil, and military employments and offices.
(From J. H. Stewart ed., *A Documentary Survey of the French Revolution,* 1951)

The foundations of liberal government are defined in the Declaration of the Rights of Man and the Citizen (1789): The Representatives of the French People, organized in National Assembly, considering that ignorance, forgetfulness, or contempt of the rights of man are the sole cause of public misfortunes and the corruption of governments, have resolved to set forth in a solemn declaration the natural, inalienable, and sacred rights of man, in order that such declaration, continually before all members of the social body, may be a perpetual reminder of their rights and duties. ... 1. Men are born and remain free and equal in rights; social distinctions may be based only upon general usefulness. 2. The aim of every political association is the preservation of the natural and inalienable rights of man; these rights are liberty, property, security, and resistance to oppression. 3. The source of all sovereignty resides essentially in the nation; no group, no individual may exercise authority not emanating expressly therefrom.
(From J. H. Stewart ed., *A Documentary Survey of the French Revolution,* 1951)

The "Civil Constitution of the Clergy" (1790) attempts to secularize the Church: The National Assembly, after having heard the report of the ecclesiastical committee, has decreed and do decree the following as constitutional articles: Title I, ARTICLE I. Each department shall form a single diocese, and each diocese shall have the same extent and the same limits as the department [thus bring the organization of the Church in line with the political organization of the nation. ... Title II, ARTICLE I. Beginning with the day of publication of the present decree, there shall be but one mode of choosing bishops and parish priests, namely that of election. II. All elections shall be by ballot and shall be decided by the absolute majority of the votes. ... [thus taking the selection of clergy out of the hands of the institutional Church.] Title III, ARTICLE I. The ministers of religion, performing as they do the first and most important functions of society and forced to live continuously in the place where they discharge the offices to which they have been called by the confidence of the people, shall be supported by the nation [thus secularizing the clergy, who become employees of the state]. II. Every bishop, priest, and officiating clergyman in a chapel of ease shall be furnished with a suitable dwelling. ... Salaries shall be assigned to each, as indicated below. ...
(From J. H. Robinson, ed., *Readings in European History,* 2 vols. [Boston: Ginn, 1906], 2: 423–427; taken from the website: http://history.hanover.edu/texts/civilcon.htm)

than from tithes levied on parishioners). Freedom of worship was extended to Protestants and Jews. By an addendum of November 27, 1790, priests were required to swear an oath of loyalty to the revolutionary government. Only about one-half complied. Many others, in hiding, continued to perform traditional religious functions for loyal parishioners and encouraged resistance to the Revolution.

On September 3, 1791, the Assembly approved in final form the constitution it had pledged in the tennis court to formulate. Reluctantly, the king acceded. Allowed to retain his title and permitted direct authority over foreign policy and the army, Louis XVI surrendered his claim to absolute power.

The Legislative Assembly and National Convention

At this point, the members of the Assembly surrendered some power of their own. Having completed their task, they intended to go home (thoughtfully awarding, before disbanding, a large gratuity to the owner of the tennis court where the critical oath had been sworn). A decree that none of their number would be eligible to serve in the next assembly (championed as a democratic measure by, among others, Robespierre) entailed the election of a new slate of delegates to a new institution. This new Legislative Assembly took up the reins of government in October. Its delegates were not only new, but also younger and less experienced that the representatives chosen in 1789.

The one-year term of the Legislative Assembly concluded in September 1792. At that point, a third assembly convened: the National Convention. Legislators who had served in the previous assemblies were eligible for election to this new body. Consequently, the National Convention included both experienced legislators from the original National Assembly and those with little or no legislative experience. It also included persons of different "parties," or sets of political beliefs and objectives. Since 1787, political clubs identified with different political viewpoints had sprung up all over Paris and in the provinces; by 1794 these would number some 4000. Among these clubs were the Girondins (named after the Gironde region in southwest France, from where the principles figures of this group hailed) and the Jacobins (named after the church of St. Jacques, or James, in which their party held its meetings, and led by Maximilien Robespierre). The average age of the delegates to the Convention was a youthful thirty-five, and most favored radical change.

The political clubs developed a range of rival strategies for the future of the Revolution. The more moderate Girondins had considerable influence from 1791 to 1792. But they were shouldered aside by the more extreme Jacobins, who emerged as leaders

of the Convention and of the Revolution in the fall of 1792. Over the next three years, these revolutionaries put aside the issues of human and civil rights that had previously absorbed the National Assembly to attend to the unseating of the king and the transformation of society.

Meanwhile, events in Paris had captured the attention of observers from abroad. In that busy capital, the "rights of man and citizen" had now been inscribed in blood. The end had come, it seemed, of the reigns of kings, strongmen, warriors, and priests who had saddled the human race since the curtain lifted on the story of civilization. One man who responded to the lure of Paris was the Englishman Tom Paine (1737–1809) (see Chapter 17), a professional revolutionary and an incendiary author.

Author of *Common Sense* and *The Crisis*, pamphlets supporting the cause of American independence against Britain, Paine worked on a larger canvas in his monumental *Rights of Man*, quoted in *Witnesses* on p. 588. This two-part work, published during his stay in France in 1791 and 1792, interpreted the Revolution as a necessary struggle between liberty and tyranny. Elected as a representative to the National Convention, Paine then found that his views were insufficiently radical for its Jacobin leaders. He was imprisoned from December 1793 to November 1794, during the height of the Terror and the execution of Robespierre; he emerged to find the Revolution over. Like Sieyès, Paine managed to survive the Revolution he celebrated in his works.

Like Paine, the English writer Mary Wollstonecraft (1759–1797) lived in Paris during the Revolution and acclaimed the French quest for political freedom. Her *Vindication of the Rights of Man*, written in 1790—and, like Paine's *The Rights of Man*, written in response to an anti-revolutionary treatise by the British statesman Edmund Burke—defended the principle that a new society could be successfully based on abstract conceptions of natural rights. When the National Convention voted to exclude women from political life, however, Wollstonecraft responded with her *Vindication of the Rights of Woman* (1792), a revolutionary work of a different sort. The first major work of Western feminism, it argues that women should define goals and achieve careers equivalent to those open to men.

In his earlier work *Reflections on the Revolution in France* (1790; see *Witnesses*, p. 588), Edmund Burke (1729–1797) had challenged the basic assumption of revolutionary activity: that it is possible, having destroyed a traditional political system, to create a new one that is better. It was the wisdom of human communities successively evolving over time, Burke argued, that had produced kings, nobles, religious values, the rituals of civilized human association. They had defects. But could a single generation concoct new social institutions without also simultaneously planting the seeds of what would become new forms of injustice and cruelty?

Burke wrote during the first year of the Revolution. He seemed to predict the turmoil that would break out shortly after his *Reflections* spoke of the flawed premises of revolutionary zeal. Although Paine and Wollstonecraft wrote eloquently of political ideals, Burke's view of the French Revolution was more accurate. For the Revolution did rip apart old customs and institutions; it did assault the fundamental structure of radical society; and it did create new governmental agencies as ruthless, perhaps more ruthless, than those they replaced. Soon after its inception, the Revolution grew violent. It turned even more violent as its locus shifted from the legislative assembles into the streets and fields where the poor and excluded, energized by change, pushed the Revolution in unanticipated directions, creating for themselves not a just society, but one that was novel and full of possibility.

THE BIRTH OF A NATION

From 1789 through 1794, a second, parallel and complementary, phase of the Revolution unfolded. Whereas the first aimed only to defeat tyranny, the second sought the transformation of society—a *total* revolution. The first was accomplished by the power of legislation and used the written word as its weapon. The second was accomplished by action and movement and symbol, while words were recruited to justify actions taken or planned. The architects of the first were mostly middle-class male professionals. The architects of the second were the crowds of people, and their self-appointed agents, who heretofore had occupied no place in the political hierarchy. Their activity in the French Revolution marks the entry into history of a new political class: the "people"—consisting of artisans, peasants and dayworkers, city folk and country folk, the shabby servant and the respectable householder, and women as well as men—all those who traditionally had been excluded from power. In 1789, from the margins of the political realm, they watched deputies to the Estates-General reinvent themselves as the National Assembly. By 1794, they *were* the nation, at home and on the march.

Peasants and Sans-Culottes

The agents of this popular revolution consisted of two groups: the peasants, themselves a disparate class including both proprietors and landless laborers from the various regions of France and the laborers, artisans and shopkeepers of the cities, primarily Paris. These were the "sans-culottes"—so called because they wore long trousers of crude cloth rather than the elegant knee breeches (*culottes*) and silk stockings worn by the bourgeois or nobleman. Their wives, daughters, and mothers also joined in the drama of revolution, and at times were principals in the action. Within the first six months of the Revolution, peasants and *sans-culottes*, both armed and dangerous, had burst onto the political stage.

Revolution in the streets: *Parisian citizens stormed the Bastille on July 14, 1789 and provided themselves with gunpowder with which to defend the revolution. In this contemporary illustration by Cholat, ordinary people, male and female, engage in decisive action. Contrast the image on page 581, where male members of a well-dressed elite dedicate themselves to the project of defining a new political order.* (Musée Carnavalet, Paris)

The March on the Bastille In June 1789, disturbing rumors reached Paris from Versailles of the struggle between the king and the delegates of the Third Estate. Would the king send an army to subdue the Parisians as he had, apparently, used armed guards to intimidate the National Assembly? Fear permeated the city. On July 11, the king dismissed his finance minister, Jacques Necker, an act the people of Paris found ominous. Then, on July 14, a crowd of 80,000 rushed to the Bastille, an ancient royal fortress. Commanded by an old governor in charge of a small garrison, it interested the crowd because of its ammunition stores. They stormed in, released the prisoners (there were only seven), and killed soldiers and the governor himself—whose severed head they displayed on a pike. The attack is depicted on p. 586.

The assault on the Bastille is for the French today the symbol of their Revolution, and its anniversary is celebrated as a national holiday. Just as in the United States, a July 4 celebration (the day of the signing of the Declaration of Independence) commemorates the Revolution against Great Britain.

News of the fall of the Bastille reached the delegates in Versailles along with reports of peasant uprisings around the nation, and these events, as we have seen, stimulated them to pass new legislation abolishing the whole apparatus of the Old Regime and to issue the "Declaration of the Rights of Man."

The possibility of royal repression was not the only threat confronting the people of Paris: famine now prevailed. the grain crop had failed in 1785, 1787, and 1788; stores of food had vanished, while shipments of grain were few; and the price of daily bread soared to eighty-eight percent of a worker's daily wage. As so often in traditional society, it was women—whose responsibility it was to feed the children—who raged most bitterly at the food shortage. On October 5, 1789, around 10,000 Parisian women, armed with pikes, knives, clubs, and muskets, marched in a driving rain on the royal palace at Versailles. Accompanying them was a contingent of 12,000 soldiers of the Paris town militia, the National Guard, under the command of the liberal nobleman the Marquis de Lafayette (1757–1834), who had once fought with George Washington in support of the American Revolution. (He would survive the Terror to espouse, in 1830, the succession of Louis-Philippe, the last king of France.)

The women burst into the palace, where they killed some guards. They compelled the king, the queen, and their son to return with them to Paris, shouting as they walked alongside the royal carriage that had gotten "the Baker, the Baker's wife, and the Baker's boy"—taunts voicing their hopes that the royal captive would somehow provide them with bread. With these words they accomplished not only the king's social demotion but his political demotion as well: he had been transferred from his zone of royal power at Versailles to the city of Paris, where the people held sway. The National Assembly followed soon afterward. Paris was now the center of the Revolution.

Defending the Revolution From October 1789 to September 1791, emotions in Paris simmered. Co-resident in the same city were the king, the National Assembly (and its successors), and the masses of the "people," the *sans-culottes*, both male and female, who milled in the streets and snatched up each morsel of news. The king aimed to preserve his authority and the remnants of the Old Regime. The Assembly attempted to design a new government through the mechanisms of proposal, debate, and vote. The people, now "citizens," demanded famine relief, a responsive government, and the destruction of their enemies. In revolutionary Paris, the people who had been ignored throughout the long story of civilization—the poor and the hungry—now entered history.

From 1791 to 1793, the presence of the king, the fervor of the crowd, and the anxieties of foreign monarchs reshaped the Revolution. On June 21, 1791, the king fled Paris with his family; caught and arrested at Varennes, near France's northeastern border, he returned five days later, a prisoner. All this time, aristocratic refugees urged other European rulers—who eyed nervously the events unfolding so near their borders—to intervene against the Revolution. On August 27, 1791, the monarchs of Prussia and Austria issued the Declaration of Pillnitz, announcing their intention to intervene in French affairs. Several months later, having joined into a coalition they provoked a French declaration of war (see *Witnesses*, p. 595). In August 1792, coalition forces crossed into France, and were met, and repulsed, by French armies (who, before the year was out, would be singing the angry battle anthem the "Marseillaise"). Here began France's military venture against the monarchies of Europe which was to last until 1815 and transform the shape of Europe.

As the coalition armies advanced, Paris responded. On August 10, 1792, Paris was declared a Commune, its citizens collectively dedicated to the defense of the revolutionary cause. Angry mobs stormed the royal Tuileries palace. In September, they invaded the prisons that held suspected enemies of the Revolution, whom they summarily tried and murdered with pikes, clubs, and knives. These September Massacres, shocking even to many revolutionary leaders, resulted in the slaughter of more than 1200 prisoners—one-half of those detained. On September 22, the day after its first meeting, the National Convention proclaimed France to be a republic. That day became the first day of the first month of the Year I of a new revolutionary calendar.

In December, the king faced trial. "The tree of liberty can only grow if watered by the blood of

The "True" Rights of Man—Burke vs. Paine

In 1790, having observed for himself events in France during the early stages of the Revolution, Edmund Burke published his Reflections on the Revolution in France, which questioned the legitimacy of the revolutionaries from a number of vantage points so thoroughly and subtly that his critique amounts to a foundation document of conservative thought. Two years later, Thomas Paine, who had already experienced the American Revolution firsthand and formulated important original arguments against mercantilism and hereditary monarchy responded to Burke in his Rights of Man. Presented here are sections of their two works pertaining to the issue of the true rights of "man."

Edmund Burke distinguishes between civil and natural rights, the latter necessarily surrendered in part upon entry into society (1790): Far am I from denying in theory, full as far as my heart from withholding in practice (if I were of power to give or to withhold), the real rights of men. ... Men have a right to live by that rule; they have a right to do justice, as between their fellows, whether their fellows are in public function or in ordinary occupation. They have a right to the fruits of their industry; and to the means of making their industry fruitful. They have a right to the acquisition of their parents; to the nourishment and improvement of their offspring; to instruction in life, and to consolation in death. Whatever each man can separately do, without trespassing upon others, he has a right to do for himself; and he has a right to a fair portion of all which society, with all its combinations of skill and force, can do in his favour. In this partnership all men have equal rights; but not to equal things. He that has but five shillings in the partnership, has a good a right to it, as he that has five hundred points has to his larger proportion. But he has not a right to an equal dividend in the product of the joint stock. and as to the share of power, authority, and direction which each individual ought to have in the management of the state, that I must deny to be amongst the direct original rights of man in civil society; for I have in my contemplation the civil social man, and no other. It is a thing to be settled by convention.

If civil society be the offspring of convention, that convention must be its law. That convention must limit and modify all the descriptions of constitution which are formed under it. Every sort of legislative, judicial, or executory power are its creatures. They can have no being in any other state of things; and how can any man claim under the conventions of civil society, rights which do not so much as suppose its existence? rights which are absolutely repugnant to it? ... Men cannot enjoy the rights of an uncivil and of a civil state together. That he may obtain justice, he gives up his right of determining what it is in points the most essential to him. That he may secure some liberty, he makes a surrender in trust of the whole of it.

Government is not made in virtue of natural rights, which may and do exist in total independence of it. Government is a contrivance of human wisdom to provide for human wants. Men have a right that these wants should be provided for by this wisdom. Among these wants is to be reckoned the want, out of civil society, of a sufficient restrain upon their passions. Society requires not only that the passions of individuals should be subjected, but that even in the mass and body, as well as in the individuals, the inclinations of men should frequently be thwarted, their will controlled, and their passions brought into subjection. This can only be done by a power out of themselves; and not, in the exercise of its function, subject to that will and to those passions which it is its office to bridle and subdue. In this sense the restraints on men, as well as their liberties, are to be reckoned among their rights. But as the liberties and the restrictions vary with times and circumstances, and admit of infinite modifications, they cannot be settled upon any abstract rule; and nothing is so foolish as to discuss them upon that principle.

Paine sees civil right as an extension of natural rights (1792): From this short review it will be easy to distinguish between that class of natural rights which man retains after entering into society and those which he throws into the common stock as a member of society.

The natural rights which he retains are all those in which the Power to execute is as perfect in the individual as the right itself. Among this class, as is before mentioned, are all the intellectual rights, or rights of the mind; consequently religion is one of those rights. The natural rights which are not retained, are all those in which, though the right is perfect in the individual, the power to execute them is defective. They answer not his purpose. A man, by natural right, has a right to judge in his own cause; and so far as the right of the mind is concerned, he never surrenders it. But what availeth it him to judge, if he has not power to redress? He therefore deposits this right in the common stock of society, and takes the arm of society, of which he is a part, in preference and in addition to his own. Society grants him nothing. Every man is a proprietor in society, and draws on the capital as a matter of right.

From these premises two or three certain conclusions will follow:

First, That every civil right grows out of a natural right; or, in other words, is a natural right exchanged.

Secondly, That civil power properly considered as such is made up of the aggregate of that class of the natural rights of man, which becomes defective in the individual in point of power, and answers not his purpose, but when collected to a focus becomes competent to the Purpose of every one.

Thirdly, That the power produced from the aggregate of natural rights, imperfect in power in the individual, cannot be applied to invade the natural rights which are retained in the individual, and in which the power to execute is as perfect as the right itself.

We have now, in a few words, traced man from a natural individual to a member of society, and shown, or endeavoured to show, the quality of the natural rights retained, and of those which are exchanged for civil rights.

[Note on sources: these are both taken from the Internet, which posts the documents from their original eighteenth-century editions.]

kings," asserted one deputy. By a majority of one, the Convention sentenced Louis XVI to death. On January 21, 1793, before 20,000 spectators, he was executed by a new invention, the guillotine designed to be relatively humane, as well as efficient and democratic, offering all its victims death by decapitation formerly reserved for aristocrats). The executioner displayed the royal head, for the "crowned fools" of Europe to see and reflect upon, as shown in *Windows On*, p. 592. The minutes of the Convention warned ponderously: "Peoples of Europe! Peoples of the World! Look carefully at the thrones and you will see that they are nothing but dust!" The European powers were completely undaunted: by early March, Britain, the Netherlands, Spain, and Sardinia had joined the First Coalition against France. Surrounded and isolated, the French mobilized furiously to defend their Revolution.

On April 6, 1793, the Committee of Public Safety was formed to do whatever was necessary to mobilize the nation. Its extraordinary actions had not only military, but also economic, psychological, and cultural dimensions. Led at first by the Jacobin Georges-Jacques Danton (1759–1794), it was soon taken over by Maximilien Robespierre, who, a year later, sent his rival to the guillotine. For a little over a year, Robespierre managed France and the Revolution, a single-minded dictator and ultimately the victim of his own stratagems.

On August 23, 1793, the Committee of Public Safety ordered a "mass levy" of troops—a target figure of 300,000 men. The decree is quoted in *Witnesses* on p. 595. Every adult male was eligible, with unmarried or childless men between eighteen and twenty-five to be called up first. The women were to be mobilized, too, "to make tents and clothes, and [to] serve in the hospitals." Even the old men had their assigned task: "to stimulate the courage of the warriors and preach the unity of the Republic and hatred of kings." The mass levy was a recipe for total war, calling for the dedication of each citizen of either gender and all ages to the success of the new **Republic**.

Robespierre's mass levy marks a new departure in warfare. Until now, the conduct of war had been primarily a nobleman's business. From the late fifteenth century, infantry and artillery forces had taken precedence over cavalry, and other changes in military organization occurred because of the crystallization of nations and constantly improving gun technology (see Chapter 15). But the men who led these forces, like those who commanded the cavalry, were almost invariably nobles—in Europe generally and in France, whose "nobility of the sword" were proud of their heroic past. These, however, were precisely the nobles who fled France in 1789. Some 60 percent of the officers in the royal army were now *émigrés*. With the ranks of noble officers drastically thinned, talented leaders had to be recruited from among the people and promoted on the basis of merit. The mass recruitment of French villagers resulted in the sudden democratization of the army.

The million men—out of a population of 28 million—who marched for the Republic in the 1790s were defenders not only of their land but also of revolutionary ideals. These *enfants de la patrie* ("children of the fatherland"), in the words of the fearsome "Marseillaise," fought for France, the Revolution, and the Republic. In these armies of the 1790s was that that nationalism—an ideology centered on allegiance to the nation, its culture, and its people—that would spread throughout Europe and figure centrally in its political history thereafter (see Chapters 23, 25).

The French army mobilized not only against foreign enemies but also against counter-revolutionaries who threatened the Republic from within. In March 1793, a revolt erupted in the Vendée region, in northwestern France. It continued until December and was not totally pacified for years. Ascribed by members of the Convention to "the ignorance, fanaticism and subservience of the country people" or "the criminality and hypocrisy of the priests," it involved 60–100,000 artisans and peasants, encouraged by dissident clergy. Loyalist soldiers of artisan and peasant origin brutally suppressed the uprising. Citizens shot citizens in the Vendée, in massacres that prefigured those of modern times.

The Terror   For Robespierre and his supporters, critics of the Revolution were as harmful to the Republic as armed counter-revolutionaries, and so must also be targeted for suppression. From June 1793 to July 1794, these presumed rebels, "guilty" only of political dissent, were hunted all over France. As many as 300,000 were imprisoned, and tens of thousands executed. (By contrast, not one person had suffered official execution for political crimes during the American Revolution; and all those who signed the Declaration of Independence died peacefully.) The victims included persons who were guilty only of having once been privileged—among them the chemist Antoine Laurent Lavoisier (1743–1794) and the *philosophe* Marie Jean Antoine-Nicholas Caritat, Marquis de Condorcet (1743–1794), author amid the violent torrent of a rosy *Sketch for a Historical Picture of the Progress of the Human Mind*. Condorcet died on his first night in prison, perhaps by suicide, cheating the guillotine.

Lavoisier and Condorcet were among a group of writers, intellectuals, and artists who, in 1789, constituted the 208 members, according to one scholar's count, of the French cultural elite. The Revolution hit them hard. Of those identified by this scholar, 19 were executed; 4 committed suicide; 25 were imprisoned; 17 were denounced, or "watched" by authorities; and 23 emigrated. Nearly half of France's cultural leaders suffered in the Revolution fought for, among other freedoms, that of expression.

This period of extreme repression is known as the Reign of Terror. Its main author, and last victim, was Maximilien Robespierre, whose activity foreshadows that of the totalitarian dictators of the twentieth century. Yet in his earlier career as a young provincial lawyer of poor family, Robespierre had been an idealist, a disciple of Rousseau. And in the National Assembly, where he pressed for the broadening of the electoral franchise, his principles stance won him the epithet "the Incorruptible." Assuming the leadership of the Jacobin club in 1791, he won election that same year as a delegate of the Paris Commune to the National Convention. In 1793, he supported the execution of the king and the purge of the Girondins. Elected to the Committee of Public Safety in July 1793, Robespierre became its spokesperson. In that role, he advocated the emergency measures undertaken to mobilize the nation and destroy political opponents, initiating the Reign of Terror—the perhaps inevitable consequence of his ominous creed that the Revolution was a "war waged by liberty against its enemies." The purges of the spring of 1794, consuming both his more moderate colleague Danton and the atheistic journalist Jacques René Hébert (1757–1794), worried even his supporters. A conspiracy of fearful members of the Convention had Robespierre arrested and tried on July 27, 1794 (9 Thermidor), in order to prevent more purges to come.

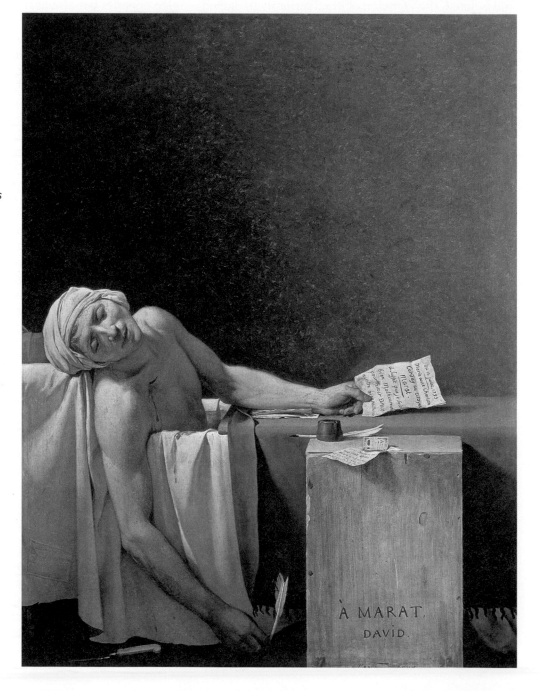

Jacques-Louis David, Death of Marat *(1793): The influential radical thinker Jean-Paul Marat, challenged by the more conservative Girondins, brought his Montagnard faction of the National Convention to its height early in 1793—just months before a young female opponent, Charlotte Corday, gained access to his rooms and stabbed him in his bath. David displays the 50-year-old martyr to the revolutionary cause with a stoic, Neoclassical starkness, all verticals (the arm holding the quill, the bathsheets, the rectangular block supporting the inkwell) and horizontals (the extended arm, the written sheet, the head that could no longer be supported by his body). (Musée Royaux des Beaux Arts de Belgique, Brussels)*

Along with more than a hundred of his supporters, he died the next day by the guillotine.

That the curtain fell thus swiftly on Robespierre's life was no doubt a blessing for the French people. Although Robespierre had capably managed the war effort and sustained the nation in a time of crisis, his call for the suppression of all dissent opened the path to even greater violence in an era already so stained by bloodshed that its epochal achievements could be called into question. In Robespierre's brilliant speeches, the fusion of democratic idealism and brutal repression is striking. His important speech of February 5, 1794, for example, identified democracy with virtue at the same time that it argued the need to defend virtue with "terror"—a theoretically just and ideal violence. The republic was in peril externally ("all the despots surround you") and internally ("all the friends of tyranny conspire"). It must "annihilate" both sets of enemies or "perish with its fall." The people must be guided by reason and the enemies of the people by terror." Both virtue and terror are essential in time of revolution: "virtue, without which terror is destructive; terror, without which virtue is impotent." In these startling phrases, linking the incongruous qualities of virtue and terror, Robespierre uses the manipulative language characteristic of the demagogue and dictator.

The Culture of Revolution

Amid the terror and political transformations of the early 1790s, revolutionary leaders also engineered a cultural revolution, which achieved the reshaping of religious and intellectual values, the democratization of society, and the remodeling of the family, which fell short, nevertheless, of obtaining for women full citizenship or sexual equality. It aimed to eradicate all the imprints of tradition on the human spirit, beginning with Christian belief and aristocratic privilege.

The attack on the property and privileges of the Roman Catholic Church had already begun in 1789. In the following year, the Civil Constitution of the Clergy secularized ecclesiastical institutions. In 1792, the Convention desanctified the church of Saint Geneviève, patron saint of Paris, and rededicated it to the celebration of "great men"; here Voltaire and Rousseau were honored. On October 5, 1793, in the midst of the Terror, Christianity was abolished. In November 1793, Hébert organized the Festival of Reason, which proclaimed the end of religion and the elevation of the human mind. Averse to atheism, Robespierre offered instead the deist "cult of the Supreme Being;" this was launched with the June 1794 Festival of the Supreme Being, shown in *Windows On* on p. 592, complete with its gaudy props designed by the quasi-official artist of the Revolution, Jacques-Louis David (1749–1825).

These efforts to deracinate Christianity from French soil and spirit did not succeed. Many people, especially in the villages, clung to their faith and their rituals. They protected the priests who had gone into hiding and they detested the Revolution. Later, Napoleon—who recognized that Christianity still lived and was useful to his purposes— permitted the Church a partial reestablishment.

The secularization and rationalization of values was pursued in the intellectual as in the religious sphere. The system of weights and measures was

FRENCH LIBERTY.   BRITISH SLAVERY.

James Gilray, cartoon on the French Revolution: *The pioneering Scottish cartoonist James Gilray satirizes the achievements of the French Revolution in this 1792 image of two grotesque figures: a starving Frenchman on the left feeding his emaciated body on raw grasses, the traditional famine food of premodern crisis; and a bloated Englishman on the right—presumably the victim of an oppressive monarchy—scarfing down a tankard of ale and a side of beef. Who won the Revolution?*

The Radical Revolution

Anonymous, Execution of King Louis XVI, January 21, 1793

The Abolition of Slavery Proclaimed to the Convention on 16 Pluviôse, Year II, c. 1794

Festival of the Supreme Being

Villeneuve, Something to Ponder for the Crowned Fools of Europe, 1793

The Revolution entered a more radical stage after August 1792. On January 21, 1793, the deposed King Louis XVI went to the guillotine, as depicted in a contemporary painting (top). Supporters of the revolution vaunted the regicide, in a tone that echoed the message of the image shown here (right). The French inscription that accompanied the bloody, severed head of the king challenged the "crowned fools" of Europe to reflect on the fate of those who opposed the revolution. The radical Revolution brought huge social and cultural changes. Among these was the abolition of slavery throughout the French Empire, proclaimed to the Convention on February 4, 1794 (left center). With the demotion of Roman Catholicism, Robespierre created a fully rational new kind of religion. The engraving here depicts the Festival of the Supreme Being held on June 8, 1794 (left). (top and left center: Musée Carnavalet, Paris; right and left: Bibliothèque Nationale, Paris)

What is the effect on the viewer, in the image at the upper left, of the portrayal of the executioners of the king as businesslike, dressed-for-success functionaries? Do the spectators appear to be troubled?

To continue your investigation of this topic, please go to www.prenhall.com/king for the related **WINDOWS** on the **WEB** activity

reorganized on a decimal basis, requiring the creation of new units of measurement. The "meter," for instance, currently the basis of measurements in most Western nations, was defined in 1791 by the French Academy of Sciences as a precise fraction of the quadrant of the Earth's circumference running from the North Pole through Paris to the equator.

The revolutionary spirit also called for the reorganization of the calendar, replacing names and dates derived from classical or Christian concepts with new ones. The names of months now reflect the natural year—"Germinal," or "budding," for mid-March to mid-April; "Thermidor," or "heat," for mid-July–mid-August; "Brumaire," or "foggy," for mid-October–mid-November. The years were renumbered to recognize revolutionary events. Year I was defined as beginning at the moment of the creation of the Republic (declared on September 22, 1792). This system of numeration, based on secular, political events, contrasted sharply with earlier calendrical schemes measured from a presumed date of the creation of the world (in the case of the Jewish calendar) or the irrelevant date, as it seemed to these deist revolutionaries, of the birth of Christ. In reordering the calendar, as in redefining measurements, the new government repudiated the experience of the past and began, brashly, anew.

The same outlook may explain the great burgeoning of newspapers and pamphlets. Even ordinary people could read, or have read to them, these digests of the revolutionary events of the day. Among the revolutionary leaders, both Hébert and Jean-Paul Marat (1743–1793) (each a victim of the Revolution: the former guillotined, the latter assassinated, as depicted on p. 590) were journalists who used the press to forge a national consciousness.

New outlooks also shaped daily behavior, transforming the manners and customs established under the Old Regime. The deference formerly shown to persons of high social status was abolished. And where it was previously customary to address someone as "*monsieur*" or "*madame*"—or, in the case of a lord, "*monsigneur*"—now it was decreed that people address each other, without regard to status, as "*citoyen*" ("citizen") and "*citoyenne*." And each would address the other with the familiar form of "you," "*tu*," rather than the formal "*vous*." Men of the bourgeoisie adopted the long trousers of the *sans-culottes*. Wealthy women followed the fashion of simple dressing with plain (and sometimes translucent) fabrics.

The democratization of society extended to the matter of slavery. In 1791, the National Assembly had abolished slavery within the boundaries of France. In 1794, the National Convention extended abolition to the colonial possessions, whose economies depended upon the institution (see Chapter 19). In the French Caribbean colony of Saint-Domingue, located on an island shared with Spanish Santo Domingo, the abolition of slavery stimulated an independence movement, under the capable leadership of a former slave, Toussaint L'Ouverture (c. 1748–1803). Although Toussaint would later become a victim of Napoleon's attempt to reconquer the colony, the new black nation of Haiti won and retained its independence.

The family according to the revolutionaries, embodied a different kind of slavery—the result of patriarchal arrangements for the preservation of property. Fathers controlled the marriages of their children. Further, they directed inheritances away from daughters and toward elder sons, in order to preserve over generations the wealth of favored males. The Revolution introduced several laws that undermined this patriarchal structure. It legalized divorce, enabling women to be released from family ties (as some 6000 did in Paris alone between 1793 and 1795). It insisted on the sharing of inheritance among all heirs, female as well as male, in the event of an intestate death. It even, briefly, declared equal inheritance rights for illegitimate, as for legitimate, offspring. Wives and children, especially daughters, won unprecedented rights by these changes.

Despite the granting of these unprecedented rights, women did not gain the right to participate in civic life. Olympe de Gouges (1748–1793), the self-educated daughter of a butcher, an actress and playwright, detected the bias of revolutionary legislators from an early moment. In response to promulgation of the "Declaration of the Rights of Man" in August 1789, she published, in 1791, her "Declaration of the Rights of Woman." Her point was twofold. In the first place, women had heretofore suffered a double deprivation of rights: by the state, on the one hand, and by their husbands and fathers, on the other. In the second place, the male delegates to the National Assembly, had disturbingly, not thought to do anything about this.

These arguments, containing stern admonitions about the deprivation of women's rights within the family, De Gouges presents mainly in the preface to

MUST READS

Books and Pamphlets from the French Revolution

Emmanuel Sieyès	*What Is the Third Estate?* (1789)
Edmund Burke	*Reflections on the Revolution in France* (1790)
Olympe de Gouges	*Declaration of the Rights of Woman and the Citizen* (1791)
Tom Paine	*Rights of Man* (1791)
Mary Wollstonecraft	*A Vindication of the Rights of Woman* (1792)

her "Declaration." The main text, consisting of 17 articles, amusingly parodies of the "Declaration of the Rights of Man," revealing its misogynist assumptions. According to De Gouges, women, as much as men, are "born free," with the right to have their "imprescriptible rights" preserved by a government whose sole purpose for existing is to guarantee such rights. De Gouges pursues the implications of her own logic. In matters of criminal law, where women had traditionally been exempt from prosecution because of their presumed incapacity, she insists on their responsibility. Women, like men, might be "accused, arrested, and detained" for violations of law; indeed, women have the right "to mount the scaffold," to face the supreme penalty. De Gouges herself was guillotined in 1793. Before she died, she had composed the first feminist critique of the relation between the family and the state.

De Gouges had dedicated her "Declaration of the Rights of Woman and the Citizen" to the queen, Marie Antoinette, who she hoped would, as a woman, be sympathetic to women's interests. Marie Antoinette was herself a target of public criticism, fired in part by her taste for luxury and rumors of her sexual promiscuity but also, apparently, by her being a woman and a foreigner. In at least 126 pamphlets, she was charged with adultery, lesbianism, and more bizarre forms of sexual misbehavior. Like her husband, she was accused of being an enemy of the new state, and on October 16, 1793, she followed him to the scaffold. In the same year, de Gouges, too, was sent to the guillotine, a victim of the Reign of Terror which saw an activist for women's rights, however revolutionary, as an enemy of the Revolution.

The failure of male revolutionaries to undertake the civil liberation of women was not, in 1793,

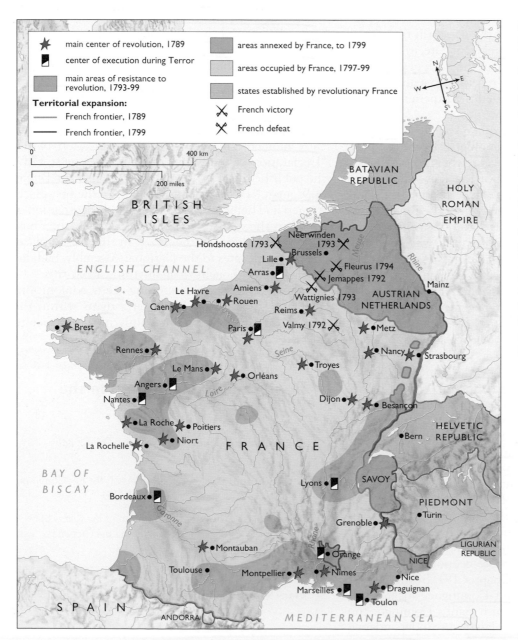

Map 20.1 The Revolution, 1789–1799: *The Revolution involved the whole of France, where entire regions were either loyal to the new government or in opposition. The Terror also affected the entire nation, although repression was centered in the capital. Even before Napoleon's advent, the revolutionary armies won victories against their European opponents. Shown here are main centers of revolutionary activity, executions during the Terror, and early battles. Among the areas that most resisted the Revolution are those centered on the three major cities outside of Paris: Lyons, Marseilles, and Bordeaux; why?*

Revolution Turns Radical

The Revolution might have ended in September 1791, when the National Assembly achieved its goal of promulgating a constitution approved and signed by the king. Instead, the Revolution took a radical turn, some indications of which are seen in the documents here. In the spring of 1792, with Austria and Prussia poised to invade France, the French preempt them by declaring war against Austria and "the unjust aggression of a [foreign] King." The following August, the Jacobin faction pledges to struggle in "mortal combat" against the machinations of the king they now name "Louis the Last." In December, the National Convention offers fraternal aid to the nations of Europe in their struggle against tyranny. After the king was condemned and guillotined in January 1793, the Terror prevailed; one spectator describes the fate of a few of its victims.

The National Assembly declares war on Austria (April 20 1792). The National Assembly declares that the French nation, faithful to the principles consecrated by its Constitution *not to undertake any war with a view to making conquests, and never to employ its forces against the liberty of any people,* takes arms only to maintain its liberty and independence; That the war which it is forced to undergo is not a war of nation against nation, but the just defense of a free people against the unjust aggression of a [foreign] king: That Frenchmen will never mistake their brothers for their real enemies. ... That it adopts in advance all foreigners who, abjuring the cause of its enemies, range themselves under its banners and consecrate their efforts to the defense of its liberty. ...
(From J. H. Stewart, trans., *A Documentary Survey of the French Revolution* [N.Y.: the Macmillan Co., 1951], pp. 287–288)

The radical Jacobin faction reviews its gains, but alerts its members to the designs of the king (1792). Since the 10th of August [the] conspirators have expiated their crimes; public spirit has risen again [and] triumphs at length over the scoundrels leagued against its liberty and its welfare. Nevertheless, the people of Paris have felt the necessity of preserving an imposing attitude and of exercising a strict surveillance over the connecting links and agents of the conspiracy of the traitor, Louis the last! ... The head, the cause, and the pretext of the machinations still breathes! Despotism moves in the shadows; let us stand fast to engage it in mortal combat, whatever form it assumes.
(From J. H. Stewart, trans., *A Documentary Survey of the French Revolution* [N.Y.: The Macmillan Co., 1951]. p. 321)

In December 1792, the National Convention issues this Proclamation to the Nations, promising the support of the French people to all those proposing to rid themselves of tyrants: the French people to the people of ... brothers and friends: We have conquered our liberty and we shall maintain it. We offer to bring this inestimable blessing to you, for it has always been rightly ours, and only by a crime have our oppressors robbed us of it. We have driven out your tyrants. Show yourselves free men and we will protect you from their vengeance, their machinations, or their return. From this moment the French nation proclaims the sovereignty of the people, the suppression of all civil and military authorities which have hitherto governed you and of all which the taxes which you bear, under whatever form, the abolition [Page 450] of the tithe, of feudalism, of seigniorial rights and monopolies of every kind, of serfdom, whether real or personal , of hunting and fishing privileges, of the corvee, the salt tax, the tolls and local imposts, and, in general, of all the various kinds of taxes with which you have been loaded by your usurpers; it also proclaims the abolition among you of all noble and ecclesiastical corporations and of all prerogatives and privileges opposed to equality. You are, from this moment, brothers and friends; all are citizens, equal in rights, and all are alike called to govern, to serve, and to defend your country.
(From J. H. Robinson, ed., *Readings in European History*, 2 vols. [Boston: Ginn, 1906], 2: 449–450; taken from the website: http://history.hanover.edu/TEXTS/natcom.htm)

Decree establishing the *Levée en masse,* or mass levy of troops (August 23, 1793): Henceforth, until the enemies have been driven from the territory of the Republic, the French people are in permanent requisition for army service. The young men shall go to battle; the married men shall forge arms and transport provisions; the women shall make tents and clothes, and shall serve in the hospitals; the children shall turn old linen into lint; the old men shall repair to the public places, to stimulate the courage of the warriors and preach the unity of the Republic and hatred of kings. ... The levy shall be general. Unmarried citizens or childless widowers, from eighteen to twenty-five years, shall go first; they shall meet, without delay, at the chief town of their districts. ... The battalion organized in each district shall be united under a banner bearing the inscription: *The French people risen against tyrants.*
(From J. H. Stewart ed., *A Documentary Survey of the French Revolution,* 1951)

The Abbé Carrichon describes the execution by guillotine of a group of nobles (1793–1794): At last we reached the fatal spot. ... The moment was overwhelming. ... The sacrifice was due to begin. The noisy merriment of the spectators and their ghastly jibes add to the sufferings of the victims. ... The executioner and his assistants climb on to the scaffold and arrange everything. The former puts on over his other clothes a blood-red overall. He places himself on the left ... while his assistants stand on the other side. ... When everything is ready ... [the first victim] goes up the steps with the help of the executioners. The chief headsman takes him by the left arm, the big assistant by the right and the other man by the legs. In a moment they lay him flat on his face and his head is cut off and thrown with his body into a great tumbril, where the bodies swam in blood: and so it goes on. ... The Maréchale was the third to go up. They had to make an opening in the top of her dress to uncover her neck. Mme d'Ayen was the tenth.
(From G. Pernoud and S. Flaissie eds., *The French Revolution*, 1961)

surprising. At that time, women's voices had only, and only faintly, begun to be heard (see Chapter 17). They fought a misogynist tradition that denied that women were truly human, or capable of education or understanding at the level of men. The demand for political rights was wholly new in the early 1790s—as new as the meter and the Year I. It could have arisen only in the context of a male revolution against illegitimate authority. Although men did not welcome feminist claims during the French Revolution, the Revolution made the articulation of those claims possible for the first time in the history of the West, or anywhere on the globe.

The cultural revolution was as profound as the political one and ultimately as irreversible. And so it was that Robespierre—that precocious master of the corruption of language—fell from power not on July 27, 1794, but during Thermidor of the Year II. The Revolution would soon, once more, change course.

Reaction Sets In: the Directory

On Robespierre's downfall, his opponents took control of the National Convention. By August 1795, it had framed a new constitution, providing for the creation of a "Directory" as the nation's chief executive; this became effective the following November. The Directory, a five-man executive committee, presided over an assembly elected by limited suffrage. (The election of 1792 had been, in contrast, by universal manhood suffrage.) It proceeded to limit the freedoms gained by the Revolution to members of the high bourgeoisie, to shed many of its cultural innovations, to repress dissent, and to prosecute abroad the war, whose aim had shifted from self-defense to expansion.

Luxury and gaiety returned in the circles of those who had profited from the Revolution, or whose wealth had survived it. Hardship returned to the circles of the now-tamed *sans-culottes*, for the Revolution had not tamed the monsters of scarcity and inflation. The secret police monitored both royalist and popular conspiracies against the state. Repression and reaction reigned.

The liberal phase of the Revolution that began in 1789 had won for the French the same kinds of rights that Anglo-Americans had achieved in their War for Independence and recently ratified Constitution (see Chapter 19). The catalogue of those rights had emerged from Anglo-Saxon law, English precedent, and the different social and political theories that the Enlightenment thinkers had derived from earlier Western intellectual traditions.

The radical phase of the Revolution, also begun in 1789, had been characterized by peremptory decrees, by the abolition of long-established customs and the imposition of new ones, and above all by violence, directed against citizens and strangers alike. It was accomplished by the people *en masse*—the peasants of the countryside and the Parisian *sans-culottes*, then unloosed by bourgeois members of the legislative assemblies, whose modest programs for change escalated rapidly and unstoppably.

The achievements of both phases, the liberal and the radical, would be undone as the Directory yielded to Napoleon. Yet both would have an afterlife, in France and beyond, in years to come.

THE IMPERIAL ADVENTURE

The Directory governed for only four years. On one side, it faced resistance from royalists who wished to dismantle the Revolution and reinstate the Old Regime. On the other, it faced disenfranchised commoners, afflicted once again by the soaring price of bread, who still believed that the Revolution was theirs. It suffered, too, from its own inefficiency, incompetence, and corruption. Financial problems, dating back to the creation of a paper currency in 1789, went unresolved. Bourgeois investors suffered when, in 1797, more than half the national debt was canceled. The demands of the army aggravated the financial crisis; yet, the army was the key to the future.

The war begun in 1792 to defend France from encircling monarchies had become a ceaseless, roaming venture, which broadcast revolutionary ideas as it shifted political boundaries. The army won fine territorial prizes for France and glory for its generals. Preeminent among these was Napoleon Bonaparte (1769–1821), portrayed on p. 598, whose career began to develop amid the smoke of the dying Revolution. In just over 15 years, he would lead France to autocracy and transform Europe.

The Coming of Napoleon

Had Napoleon Bonaparte served in the pre-Revolutionary army, where only men of high rank succeeded, he would have remained a nobody. He was descended from a minor noble family of Corsica, a tiny and newly acquired Mediterranean island, whose native dialect was closer to Italian than to French. At the French military academy where he was sent to prepare for the best career open to boys of his background, he suffered the humiliation of being poor, short, and foreign. Even as a child, however, he displayed his talent for leadership—directing his classmates in snowball combat. In 1785, at the age of 16, he won a commission in the artillery, and in 1793, at age 24, seized the fortified harbor of Toulon for the Revolution in the face of a British naval assault. In October 1795, he won the gratitude of the Directory when he dispersed a crowd of royalist dissidents (killing about 100 of them) with, as he is said to have remarked, "a whiff of grapeshot." Rewarded with high command, he departed for wars abroad, where the effects of the Revolution in France were beginning to be felt.

By 1795, the First Coalition which had been formed against Revolutionary France had expanded to include Russia, Britain, the Netherlands, Spain, and Sardinia, as well as Austria. (Prussia had withdrawn, having just gorged itself in an independent political agreement with one-third of what remained of Poland—the balance assigned to Russia and Austria; see Chapter 15.) However, the coalition did not last long. One by one, France defeated or formed new alliances with most of its members, until only Austria and Britain remained. During the next four years, the French would oppose the Austrians in Italy and the British wherever they had interests—on the Mediterranean Sea and in North Africa, India, and the Caribbean. Napoleon took part in some phases of the war with both of these adversaries.

From spring 1796 to winter 1797, Napoleon stormed through northern Italy, then occupied by Austria. As he went, he transformed his troops into a dauntless force, capable of deadly speed and compact, focused attack. They defeated Austrian regular forces as well as Italian militias. By the Treaty of Campo Formio (October 17, 1797), Napoleon became master of northern Italy, which he reorganized as the Cisalpine Republic, a satellite of France. The peace settled, Napoleon returned to France in order to win support for his project to defeat the crucial enemy, as he saw it: Britain.

Napoleon's career in Italy already displayed the features that would characterize his later military ventures. He did not merely win battles; he also reshaped states and principalities, and did so with a purpose beyond territorial gain. He built more coherent, more centralized, more governable states than those he had defeated. Meanwhile, Napoleon's extraordinary charisma won him the devotion of is troops and impressed observers throughout Europe.

He was also, in his way, a revolutionary. Although he had cast his lot with the conservative Directory, there were elements of the revolutionary agenda that Napoleon actively promoted in the lands over which he held authority. For example, he fully embraced the Revolution's anti-clericalism. Throughout northern Italy, he suppressed religious orders and tore down moldering churches or converted them to secular uses. He imposed French law upon subject lands, abolishing serfdom, limiting aristocratic privilege, and insisting upon the inheritance rights of children of both sexes. His soldiers broadcast the Revolution's ideals of "liberty, equality, and fraternity." At the same time, their fierce patriotism awakened sentiments of national and ethnic loyalty among the peoples they encountered—sentiments that would inspire some of the great political movements of the coming century.

After returning briefly to France, Napoleon set out again in 1798, this time for Egypt. (Here, one of his adjutants found and arranged for the transport home of the Rosetta Stone, with its key to the late ancient demotic Egyptian language; see Chapter 1.) He saw Egypt—then controlled by the Ottoman Empire (see Chapter 15) and allied with Britain—as a stepping-stone to India and the heart of the British Empire. He defeated a Mamluk army at the Battle of the Pyramids; but soon afterward the British admiral Horatio Nelson (1758–1805) destroyed the French fleet at the Battle of the Nile, leaving Napoleon stranded in Egypt. The following year, Napoleon, along with companions, slipped past the British fleet and sped to France, where conspiracy was afoot.

There, he found a situation favorable to his ambitions: the government was foundering and France was in disarray. He joined forces with Emmanuel-Joseph Sieyès, author of the inflammatory 1789 tract "What is the Third Estate?" (see above). Now one of the Directors, Sieyès believed that a strong leader was needed to bring order to the state. He helped plan the events that occurred on 18 Brumaire (by the revolutionary calendar still in force), or November 9, 1799. With a small group of armed supporters, Napoleon marched into the assembly of the two ruling councils and announced that he would take charge. The deputies discussed the possibility of arresting him, but before they could vote on the matter, Napoleon's brother Lucien (1775–1840), president of the lower council, ordered the soldiers to expel those in opposition.

In this *coup d'état* (sudden seizing of power), Napoleon proclaimed a new government, of which he would be "First Consul" (with Sieyès and another supporter, for the moment, the second and third). For the next sixteen years, the story of France is the story of Napoleon.

Napoleon's France

The inexorable rise of Napoleon Bonaparte accelerated. In 1802, he made himself sole Consul for life; in 1804, emperor. Along the way, he paused briefly to consult the people of France, who had the privilege of approving each of these appointments by plebiscite. Having achieved a *rapprochement* with the Church, he invited Pope Pius VII (whom he would dispossess of the Papal States in 1809 and subsequently place under house arrest) to perform the coronation ceremony in Paris. Upon prior agreement, he took the crown himself and placed it on his own head; then he placed the consort's crown on that of his wife, Josephine de Beauharnais (1763–1814). There could be no doubt where the power lay. The moment is commemorated in David's painting, reproduced on p. 602.

As Napoleon's titles accumulated, republican institutions wasted away. After 1799, when he imposed the constitution of the Year VIII, the elected assembly was replaced by an appointed Senate and a Tribunal (eliminated by 1808), chosen by the

Napoleon at War

Antoine-Jean Gros, Napoleon Bonaparte on Arcole Bridge (1790): *Though he studied with David, Gros did not adopt the master's cool Neoclassicism. Here a romantic young Napoleon is hero and victor, a dauntless energy conveyed by the swirling forms of his sash, his hair, and his standard. (Hermitage Museum)*

Senators from a list of 6000 "notabilities." Those two bodies together disposed of legislation proposed by a Council of State, chosen by Napoleon. This whole government apparatus was approved by a plebiscite in which all adult males were permitted to vote. An overwhelming majority—99 percent— voted "Yes" to an authoritarian constitution. A little more than a decade since the promulgation of the first republican constitution, nearly all of its elements had been abolished with the approval of the electorate.

Pursuing the goals his royal Bourbon predecessors had mapped, Napoleon centralized and bureaucratized the government. In each *département*, or district, an appointed prefect executed his orders. Napoleon recruited his magistrates, like his army officers, from all social classes (including former members of the nobility) and rewarded loyal and efficient service well. To stabilize the currency and support commerce, he established, in 1800, the Bank of France. To ensure a steady flow of revenues, he regularized the system of taxation, including both direct taxes on property and indirect taxes on salt, tobacco, and liquor. To promote trade, he abolished most internal customs tolls and standardized weights and measures. To control the circulation of ideas, he censored the theater and the press, shutting down all but 13 of 73 newspapers, and unleashed a secret police force under the direction of a former agent of the Terror, Joseph Fouché. To underscore his eminence and that of his court, he created a new nobility from an assortment of former *émigré* aristocrats, loyal magistrates, and army officers—bestowing 3600 titles between 1808 and 1814. The former revolutionary Sieyès, who had engineered his rise to power, was made a count.

Napoleon also revised the legal system, creating the *Code Napoléon* (Napoleonic, or Civil, Code). This massive document, containing more than 2,000 articles, is still in force in France today, as well as in many other countries. It combined the comprehensive approach of Roman law with Enlightenment and, to some extent, revolutionary principles. To anxious bourgeois survivors of the Revolution, the Civil Code guaranteed the sanctity of private property. By contrast, it limited the rights of workers to form associations, or even to move about the country without official identification.

Within the family, the Code reaffirmed the father's traditional rights over household property and persons. A wife could not buy or sell property without her husband's approval, and her income was

Gros, **Napoleon on the Battlefield of Eylau:** *A legislator, a critic, an educator, Napoleon was above all a war-maker—a successful one, too, until the last years of his career. In this 1808 painting he is seen with his loyal followers and soldiers on the field of the battle of Eylau in 1807.* (Louvre, Paris)

Revolution in Fashion

Pre-Revolution fashion worn by the upper-middle class, 1780

Pre-Revolution dress of the working class, c.1780

Fashion worn by the Incroyables, or Unbelievables, 1794

The momentous changes wrought by the French Revolution are written, among other ways, in how men and women dressed before and after the event. Shown here at top left are a representative couple of the upper-middle class just prior to the Revolution. She wears an elaborate flounced and frilled dress; he a vest, jacket, and culottes, or knee-length pants, which come to an end below the knee, atop silk stockings and elegant, heeled shoes. Modest though their dress is—aristocratic and courtly fashion was much more elaborate—it would become less showy after the Revolution ran its course. To their right is a working-class couple of the same era, dressed far more simply. Note especially the man's characteristic trousers, or sans-culottes, which extend, never gathered, below the knee to the ankles. The image upper right depicts soldiers and other participants in the Revolution in 1793–1794, the year of the Reign of Terror. Only the military drummer retains the culottes of the pre-Revolutionary era. At lower left, a wealthy couple strut the latest fashion at the climactic moment of the Revolution, 1794, just

Revolutionaries, 1793–94

before the fall of Robespierre and the institution of the Directory. These represent the Incroyables, or Unbelievables, the fast set of Revolutionary Paris at a tricky, transitional moment. At lower right, in a parlor scene from 1839, the effects of Revolution on fashion are displayed. The men, whether in military or sober civilian dress, now wear trousers like the proletarian sans-culottes *that their ancestors would have disdained, while the woman, still beautifully attired, has moderated her frills and flounces.* (top left: Private Collection; right: Costumes Historiques de la France; below left: Private Collection; Facing page, top: Private Collection; Facing page, below: Private Collection)

Did men's or women's fashions change more over these two generations? Why?

Post-Revolutionary fashion, 1839

To continue your investigation of this topic, please go to www.prenhall.com/king for the related WINDOWS on the WEB activity

considered to belong to him and his heirs. Divorce was possible but difficult, and, as in centuries past, adultery was considered a more serious violation for a woman than for a man. Napoleon thought little of women's rights, and saw their role as consisting chiefly in the bearing and rearing of children.

Thos children were, like their mothers, subordinated to their father's will, or that of their parents acting jointly. Parents could choose marriage partners for their children or reject their children's choices. Fathers could have their children jailed—one of the hated features of the Old Regime. The Code retained, however, the Revolution's bar against primogeniture (the practice by which the eldest son inherited the bulk of family property).

Just as he understood the importance of a coherent system of law, Napoleon also foresaw the need for a universal system of education. He did not institute such a system; nevertheless, under his guidance, France surpassed almost all other states in providing for the general education of the young. He ordered that each village should have a school for the elementary education of the young of both sexes. Secondary education was more limited; but the system of secondary schools, or *lycées* (open to boys— not to girls—who could afford the fees), was an

exceptional beginning to an educational system of high quality and, in time, universal access. Napoleon also organized a public university system.

Napoleon's settlement with the Roman Catholic Church was a complex matter. The Revolution had been anti-clerical from the start and, under Jacobin domination, wholly anti-religious. Its leaders had viewed priests and members of the religious orders as hypocritical, greedy, or superfluous, and the international church hierarchy as opposed to the interests of the French nation. One of the early acts of the National Assembly, moreover, had been to strip the Church of all its property. Yet many Frenchmen and women remained loyal Catholics, and even more wished to reestablish the Church to enforce moral standards, sanctify the key events of life—birth, marriage, and death—and to provide early schooling.

By the Concordat of 1801, the compromise negotiated with the Vatican, Napoleon reestablished the Roman Catholic Church in France under terms favorable to its ruler. The Church surrendered its claim to all property confiscated by the Revolution. Clergy must either swear allegiance to the state or resign. Priests could pursue their pastoral work unfettered, but were required to read official pronouncements

Jacques-Louis David, **Consecration of the Emperor Napoleon I and Coronation of the Empress Josephine in the Cathedral of Notre-Dame de Paris on December 2, 1804, 1806, and 1807:** *In an event of personal self-display that troubled Royalists and radicals alike, Napoleon brought the pope to Paris for his consecration and the coronation of his empress, Josephine de Beauharnais, in a moment that was to evoke memories of the papal crowning of Charlemagne in 800 C.E. Napoleon himself took the crown and placed it on his own head; then crowned Josephine, as is depicted here.* (Louvre)

Napoleon, According to Himself and to an Enemy

Although the emperor Napoleon thought of himself as a champion of the Revolution, a restorer of the nation, a hero "who extended the limits of glory," others saw him as a despot, a danger, an anomaly. In these passages, the sketch of Napoleon by the feminist Madame de Staël stands in clear contrast to Napoleon's own self-portrait.

Napoleon anticipates most of the charges that history will make against him, and defends his record (c. 1815): I closed the gulf and cleared the chaos. I purified the Revolution, dignified Nations and established Kings. I excited every kind of emulation, rewarded every kind of merit, and extended the limits of glory! This is at least something! And on what point can I be assailed on which an historian could not defend me? Can it be for my intentions? But even here I can find absolution. Can it be for my despotism? It may be demonstrated that the Dictatorship was absolutely necessary. Will it be said that I restrained liberty? It can be proved that the licentiousness, anarchy, and the greatest irregularities, still haunted the threshold of freedom. Shall I be accused of having been too fond of war? It can be shown that I always received the first attack. Will it be said that I aimed at universal monarchy? It can be proved that this was merely the result of fortuitous circumstances, and that our enemies themselves led me step by step to this determination. Lastly, shall I be blamed for my ambition? This passion I must doubtless be allowed to have possessed, and that in no small degree; but at the same time, my ambition was of the highest and noblest kind that ever, perhaps, existed—that of establishing the empire of reason, the full exercise and complete enjoyment of all the human faculties!

(From Marquis de Las Cases, Memoirs of the Life, Exile, and Conversations of the Emperor Napoleon, 1894; ed. J. K. Sowards, 1992)

Literary critic, novelist and *salonière* Madame de Staël (1766–1817) gives her impressions of the dictator (1816): I very quickly saw, in the various occasions I had to meet him during his stay in Paris, that his character could not be defined by the words we ordinarily use; he was neither good, nor fierce, nor gentle, nor cruel, like others we know. Such a being, having no equals, could neither feel nor arouse any sympathy: he was more than a human being or less than one. His appearance, his mind, and his speech were foreign in nature—an added advantage for subjugating the French.

Far from being reassured by seeing Bonaparte more often, I was made increasingly apprehensive. I had a vague feeling that no emotions of the heart could influence him. He considers a human being a fact or a thing, not a fellow man. He does not hate nor does he love. For him, there is nothing but himself; all others are ciphers.

Every time I heard him speak I was struck by his superiority: yet it had no resemblance to that of men educated and cultivated by study or by social intercourse, such as may be found in England or France. But his speech showed a feeling for the situation, like the hunter's for his prey.

(Madame de Staël, On Politics, Literature and National Character, 1818; ed. J. K. Sowards, 1992)

from the pulpit. At the same time, Napoleon guaranteed freedom of worship to all, including Protestants and Jews (who together numbered about five percent of the population). All clerical salaries, even those of Protestants, would be paid by the state. Loyal Catholics might return to their churches, but the Catholic behemoth that had saddled France, as the revolutionaries saw it, forever lost its privileges.

Did Napoleon restore the monarchy, buttressed by the nobility and Church? Not exactly. In the pattern of Robespierre, he was a new kind of ruler, more a prefiguration of a totalitarian dictator than a resurrection of ancient kingship. But his dictatorial intentions were expressed in his actions—in his undoing of the Revolution, his disenfranchisement of the people, his resurrection of court and nobility, his sweeping reconfiguration of government. Two views of him are given in *Witnesses* above.

Muscular, short and brilliant, Napoleon was a tireless worker, "never happier than in the silence of his own study," according to a modern historian, "surrounded by papers and documents." After a day full of responsibilities, he retired at ten, to awake a few hours later to write letters (80,000 or so in the course of his career) and composing orders. On this impressive schedule, he accomplished the reorganization of France and the conquest of most of Europe.

Napoleon and the *Grande Armée*

Map 20.2 on p. 604 shows the expansion of Napoleon's empire. If Robespierre, in mobilizing the nation, was technically the founder of the modern French army, Napoleon was its true creator—the adored leader of the *Grande Armée* (Great Army) and one of the greatest military commanders in history (see Gros' painting of him on p. 598). Already a hero by virtue of his Italian campaign of 1796–1797, Napoleon seemed, in his campaigns of 1800–1815, to be invincible. The German poet Goethe marveled that "his life was the stride of a demigod from victory to victory." The composer Beethoven planned to

Map 20.2 Napoleon's Empire and Major Battles, 1799–1815: *Napoleon's empire consisted of a core of areas conquered and annexed to France, others conquered and ruled by members of his family, and a periphery of dependencies.* What arguments did Napoleon give to the French people for the conquest of European neighbors?

write a symphony in his honor—though he became disillusioned, and changed the dedication of the "Eroica" symphony to read, "Composed in Memory of a hero." All of Europe admired or dreaded him, and it took most of Europe to defeat him.

From 1793, France faced a series of coalitions (the First, formed in 1793; the Second, formed in 1798; the Third, 1805–1815) united at first against the Revolution and then against Napoleon. The First Coalition derived from the Prussian–Austrian alliance of 1792, and by 1795 it also included Britain, Russia, the Netherlands, Spain, and Sardinia. The Second included Britain, Austria, and Russia. The Third Coalition included the same combatants as the Second, with the addition of Prussia in 1806. Other coalitions formed in response to new defeats. Prussia and Austria supported Napoleon in 1812, but both

joined Russia and Britain and other allied forces against France in 1813, the last phase of this struggle, and in a seventh and final coalition in 1815, the allies at last liberated Europe from Napoleon.

To oppose these enemies required constant readiness and constant recruitment. From 1798, the institution of an annual draft meant that every young Frenchman faced the prospect of conscription (a situation that had not prevailed in France before the Revolution, nor would it after 1815 until the next century brought the experience of two world wars). Over the 23 years of revolutionary and Napoleonic warfare, some 2 to 3 million men served in the army, of whom about half a million died. Some resisted conscription, especially in rebellious regions of the south, where over fifty percent of those called failed to comply; and some draftees deserted, often swelling the ranks of criminal bands. For those who supported the war effort and showed courage or talent, the opportunity for promotion was open.

Napoleon's army employed tactics that marked a new stage in the evolution of warfare. For the sake of speed, it lived flagrantly off the land. Even those natives who welcomed the French initially as "liberators" had second thoughts when they saw the resulting devastation of their fields and homes. Thus unencumbered by the need for supply lines, the French could move swiftly (as much as 20 miles per day), a second feature of Napoleon's toolkit. They struck where they were not expected and wrung victory even from superior forces. Assisting them in the bold game of sudden attack were ample cannon mounted on mobile carts, handled by skilled gunnery crews. The French bombardment exhausted the enemy, who then succumbed to a powerful charge. Napoleon grouped combined forces of infantry, cavalry, and artillery into combat divisions and larger corps. Each corps acted as a disciplined entity, united by pride in shared experience and common symbols and by gratitude for the rewards that the emperor distributed to those who served well.

Further, Napoleon exploited the possibilities of the infantry column. His opponents generally fought in line formation (even the British, whose excellent guns and peerless discipline allowed them withstand Napoleonic tactics), maneuvering into close formation for defense. Napoleon sent his soldiers forth in concentrated, marching columns, driven by drumbeat, terrible to behold and seemingly implacable. The powerful columns sliced through the lines of Austrian and Prussian opponents, scattering frightened soldiers, who now became the prey of the cavalry's sabers and their horses' hooves.

Napoleon's tactics were wasteful of men, as he knew. "A man such as I does not consider the deaths of a million men," he commented. Those in the front ranks were devastated by gunfire, but those in the rear moved up swiftly past their dead comrades to avenge them. It was France's large population—the largest of any European nation—that made Napoleon's tactics possible, while the emperor

Francisco Goya, The Executions of the Third of May, 1808: *Napoleon met his first serious setbacks in the Peninsular War in Spain, where French troops committed atrocities that aroused a significant amount of native resistance. Here in Francisco Goya's 1814 painting, a French firing squad executes guerrilla rebels, the chief victim's body extended in the form of the crucified Christ. (Prado, Madrid)*

succeeded in convincing the soldiers of this Grand Army that their sacrifice was warranted.

From 1800 to 1815, Napoleon's armies fought mainly in the German lands, Spain, and Russia. They won their greatest victory in the first area, where French armies absorbed the left bank of the Rhine, compensating Prussia, Austria, and some other German states for the loss of their domains. In 1798 Napoleon had imposed a constitution on Switzerland, now dubbed the Helvetic Republic, central Europe was briefly at peace.

At this juncture, some of Napoleon's troops attempted the reoccupation of Haiti and the reinstitution of slavery (see Chapter 19). The attempt failed—one of Napoleon's few early defeats. Although the architect of Haitian independence, Toussaint L'Ouverture, died in a French prison, Napoleon's soldiers died of disease; because of British intervention they could not be replaced. By the end of 1803, the island was lost. Meanwhile, Napoleon disposed of another colonial possession, the huge Louisiana Territory, which was sold in 1803 to the United States (see Chapter 19).

In 1805, returning to the German lands, Napoleon crushed Austrian and Russian forces at Ulm and Austerlitz. In 1806 he reorganized the hundreds of German principalities into the more rational Confederation of the Rhine, while overseeing the dissolution of the Holy Roman Empire, accomplished when its Habsburg emperor (Napoleon's future father-in-law) relinquished that title.

Alarmed by these new French victories, Prussia joined the Third Coalition; the next year it met, and lost to, Napoleon's army at Jena. In 1807, Napoleon defeated a Russian army at Friedland, forcing the tsar to agree to the Treaty of Tilsit, which made him France's reluctant ally. The three major continental powers had all been sidelined. Only Britain still stood undefeated against France.

The Tide Turns

It did so doggedly, benefiting from public support and the ingenuity of smugglers. In 1805, the naval commander Lord Nelson, who had previously chased Napoleon out of Egypt, destroyed the French fleet at Cape Trafalgar, near Gibraltar—and with it Napoleon's hopes of invading England. In 1806, Napoleon closed all continental ports to British ships, a strategy he called the Continental System. He aimed to cripple the British economy, already strained by military costs, by denying it European markets for its manufacturers and reexported colonial products. The painful effects for Britain included not only loss of income but an unsought war with the United States (the War of 1812). That young nation, a trading partner of France, bristled at British licensing demands and aggressive boarding and searching

of its ships. But smugglers managed to feed a trickle of British goods to the Continent, where demand was high, and Napoleon's Continental System failed.

Napoleon's will to conquer Britain led him south across the Pyrenees in 1808 to the Iberian Peninsula, where, beyond Spain, lay Britain's ally Portugal. A large French force marched toward the Portuguese capital, Lisbon, triggering the flight of the king to Brazil and the forced abdication of the Spanish king, Charles IV, and of his heir, Ferdinand VII, in favor of Napoleon's brother Joseph Bonaparte (1768–1844, r. 1808–1813). It also precipitated the combined opposition of Spain's powerful Church (resistant to Napoleon's plans for secularization), its nobility, and its peasantry, who, returning atrocity for atrocity, as shown in Goya's painting on p. 605, fought a modern guerilla war against the invaders. The British army, under Arthur Wellesley (1769–1852), later duke of Wellington, supported native resistance. It trapped more than 400,000 of Napoleon's Grand Army on the Iberian Peninsula and, in 1813, drove it out in tatters.

By this time, Napoleon's power had been fatally wounded elsewhere. His new alliance with the Habsburgs (divorcing Josephine, he had married the Habsburg princess Marie Louise) and his ambitions in the eastern Mediterranean, made Russia (which Austria viewed with distrust) his next target. In June 1812, with 450,000 men, he crossed the Polish border into Russia. Instead of the hoped-for rapid victory, however, he found himself pursuing the Russian army as it retreated, using scorched earth tactics, deep into the interior. After a costly and indecisive battle at Borodino, seventy miles to the west of Moscow, Napoleon captured the Russian capital in September. The city had been evacuated, and fire broke out the day the French entered. The Russian troops had escaped, with the tsar, to where the French could follow them no more. Napoleon was left stranded in hostile territory on the verge of the Russian winter. A 1500-mile retreat followed, fatal both to the emperor's men and to his ambitions. The abject Napoleon returned to Paris in December, ahead of the remnant of his army—130,000 soldiers. The others had died of cold and gunfire, disease and hunger in one of the worst episodes in the history of warfare.

The emperor's enemies were heartened by the Russian debacle. Wellington especially, fresh from his triumph in Spain, now concentrated all his military genius on securing the final defeat of Napoleon. The "Battle of the Nations" (Leipzig) in October 1813, was a resounding victory for the allies. Their armies pursued Napoleon back into France and, on March 31, 1814, entered Paris. From nearby Fontainebleau, Napoleon vainly tried to secure generous terms from the allies. In April, after a failed suicide attempt, he abdicated: first to his son then unconditionally. He was sent unharmed, an exile, to be the sovereign of the tiny island of Elba—tinier by far than Corsica, its neighbor in western Mediterranean waters. Then, after a few months he escaped.

Napoleon returned to France in March 1815, marching northward from the Mediterranean coast toward Paris. Troops and generals forgot their obligations to the restored Bourbon king, Louis XVIII, and joined his train, crying, as on the battlefield, "*Vive l'empereur!*" ("Long live the Emperor"). The allies were alarmed; though Wellington, at least, who did not underestimate his foe, was not surprised. Napoleon invited the next encounter, which took place at Waterloo, on the Belgian plains, where he had marched with 125,000 recruits. He was met by British forces, reinforced late in the day by Prussian allies who had been hastily summoned to the field. The French attack was fearsome, but the British would not fold. Victory went to the allies. "He has ruined us," a wounded French soldier lamented, "yet I love him still."

Napoleon was once again imprisoned, and once again exiled, unharmed. But instead of the quiet retirement in the United States or England that he had optimistically requested, he was exiled in the company of British guards to the remote island of St. Helena, in the south Atlantic. Located halfway between the west coast of Africa and the east coast of Brazil, it offered no chance of escape; had he escaped, there would have been no place to go. Napoleon sickened, lingered, and died six years later, still a British captive. The British feared even his corpse. They released it finally, in 1840, to the restored French monarch Louis Philippe (r. 1830–1840), who placed it reverently in the Hôtel des Invalides (formerly a military hospital), under the main dome. Thus did a descendant of Louis XVI, victim of the Revolution, honor the Corsican upstart who had appropriated the Revolution to further his own prodigious ambitions.

The victors of Waterloo, meanwhile, set about eradicating the joint legacies of the Revolution and Napoleon. Yet the impress of these phenomena on the consciousness of Europe could never be completely erased. Europe had seen monarchy bloodied and restored. It had beheld both liberation and conquest within an amazingly short timespan of just one generation. It had glimpsed the promise of universal rights and stirred with a new passion for national integrity. Which of these possibilities would bear fruit? "I live only for posterity," Napoleon said. His gift to posterity was a time bomb packed with a wealth of potentialities for both good and evil.

Conclusion
REVOLUTION, EMPIRE, AND THE MEANING OF THE WEST

The Revolution of 1789 ended with the fall of Robespierre, the installation of the Directory, and Napoleon's 1799 *coup d'état* and yet it did not end. From the Revolution in France burst the new flood tide of an awakened people eager for access to power. Over the next century, the people would often rush into the streets, raise their barricades, and fight for what they now saw as their rights. That expectation, the child of Revolution, is still alive in the West, and elsewhere, today.

Napoleon, too, contributed to the revolutionary legacy. By his legal, bureaucratic, and cultural initiatives, he acted to restore prerevolutionary social conditions, to maintain order, and to respect the privileges of rank. Yet the *grande armée* effected a massive dispersion of revolutionary ideals, promoted by the persuasive voices of those who believed that they had won liberation from the tyranny of the Old Regime. And Napoleon himself first disrupted, and then remade the political boundaries of Europe, discarding nations he deemed obsolete and creating new states from archaic ones. While he restored order and privilege at home, he unleashed forces for change abroad. It is Napoleon's Europe, refashioned by the destruction and renewal that he wrought, that became the foundation of the modern system of states which carried forward, in the century that followed, the traditions of the West.

Meanwhile, another agent of change had emerged, more disruptive and more violent than Robespierre's Revolution or Napoleon's wars: a machine, moved by non-human power, which, over that same century, would invade the fields and gardens of the nations of the Western world (see Chapter 21).

QUESTIONS TO CONSIDER

1. The French Revolution, unlike the American, seems to be not one revolution but several. Why?

2. How important were Enlightenment ideas in the French Revolution?

3. To what extent will all revolutions entail a Reign of Terror? How could it be avoided?

4. Why did the French Revolution end in the dictatorship of Napoleon?

5. Did Napoleon further, or reverse, the changes in society and culture brought about by the Revolution?

SUGGESTED RESOURCES

Andress, David, *Massacre at the Champ de Mars: Popular Dissent and Political Culture in the French Revolution* (London: Boydell & Brewer, 2000). Traces the cultural systems and events in Paris that create the massacre of July 1791, as the Revolution enters its radical phase.

Censer, Jack Richard & Lynn Hunt. *Liberty, Equality, Fraternity: Exploring the French Revolution* (State Park, PA: Pennsylvania State University Press, 2001). New, up-to-date synthesis, with good coverage of the colonial dimensions of the revolt and historians' debates about it.

Chartier, Roger, *The Cultural Origins of the French Revolution*, trans. Lydia Cochrane (Durham, NC: Duke University Press, 1991). An important book, which asserts that the Revolution was caused neither by the Enlightenment nor by class tensions, but on the growing secularism, cynicism, and politicization of the French masses.

De Baecque, Antoine, *Seven Deaths under the French Revolution* (London: Routledge, 2001). Brilliant exploration of the cultural significance for contemporaries of the dead bodies of seven revolutionary victims, including King Louis XVI, Robespierre, and Marie Antoinette.

Esdaile, Charles, *The Peninsular War: A New History* (New York: Palgrave Macmillan, 2003). Complete study of the war in Spain 1807–1813, with guerillas joining the Spanish and British against Napoleon, and winning.

Garrioch, David, *The Making of Revolutionary Paris* (Berkeley: University of California Press, 2002). Evokes the spectacle and culture of eighteenth-century Paris as a setting for Revolution.

Hampson, Norman, *The Terror in the French Revolution* (New York: St. Martin's Press, 1998). Account of the bloodiest stage of the Revolution.

Hardman, John, *French Politics, 1774–1789: From the Accession of Louis XVI to the Fall of the Bastille* (London; New York: Longman, 1995). A detailed treatment of the French monarchy on the eve of the Revolution, stressing considerations of political power and place.

Hufton, Olwen H., *Women and the Limits of Citizenship in the French Revolution* (Toronto; Buffalo: University of Toronto Press, 1992). Essays on the disillusionment of women participants in the Revolution.

Jones, Colin, *The Great Nation: France from Louis XV to Napoleon 1715–1799* (New York: Columbia University Press, 2002). An updated synthesis, surveying the whole period from the high tide of absolutism to the coming of Napoleon.

Markham, J. David, *Napoleon's Road to Glory: Triumphs, Defeats and Immortality* (London: Brassey's, 2003). Recent biography with emphasis on how Napoleon came to power, his long-goals, and how he ruled.

Roche, Daniel, *The Culture of Clothing: Dress and Fashion in the Ancient Regime*, trans. Jean Birrell (Cambridge: Cambridge University Press, 1994). Cultural history examining the production, distribution, and wearing of clothing for social, psychological, and other meanings.

Tackett, Timothy, *When the King Took Flight* (Cambridge MA: Harvard University Press, 2003). The story of Louis XVI's flight in 1791, and its consequences for the Revolution.

Wolloch, Isser, *Napoleon and his Collaborators: the Making of a Dictatorship* (New York: W. W. Norton, 2001). Study of how Napoleon addressed the political, social, and economic needs of the nation.

Notes and sources on Olympe des Gouges (Sunshine for Women):
http://www.pinn.net/~sunshine/march99/gouges2.html

Robespierre, full text of his speech at the Festival of the Supreme Being (The History Place):
http://www.historyplace.com/speeches/robespierre.htm

Napoleon Bonaparte Internet Guide:
http://www.napoleonbonaparte.nl

⦿ Western Civilization Documents CD-ROM

19.1 "The Declaration of the Rights of Man and the Citizen"
19.2 "The Declaration of the Rights of Women and the Female Citizen"
19.3 Petition of Women of the Third Estates
19.4 Robespierre: Justification of Terror
19.5 Louis XVI: A Royal Reform Proposal, 1787
19.6 Edmund Burke: The Moral Imagination
20.1 A View from the Field: A Napoleonic Soldier
20.2 A View from the Other Side: A British Soldier
20.3 The French View
20.4 The Arab View

PART SIX

THE WEST BECOMES MODERN

Industrialization, Imperialism, Ideologies (1750–1914)

The arrival of the machine set Western civilization on the path to modernity that was largely completed by 1914. In Britain at first, then in Belgium and France, Germany and the United States, and finally in the rest of Europe and Japan, human beings made machines that produced commodities for use and export in quantities never before conceivable. Machines transformed Western society, where distinctions between rich and poor shifted and deepened. An increasingly bourgeois elite enjoyed a level of comfort previously known only to royalty and aristocracy, while a vast industrial working class experienced the unprecedented hardships of industrial work and urban life.

As European merchants, administrators, and generals ventured abroad to establish colonies and protectorates all over the globe, they recreated far from home the social rifts found in industrial cities. A European elite delighted in luxury as it managed the transmutation of native societies according to Western expectations, and enlisted laborers of many colors and customs to produce cheap goods. Success abroad encouraged Western ideologues to think that people of European descent had gained supremacy over the other peoples of the world because of their inherent racial, or genetic, superiority.

Critics of both social systems, the industrial and the colonial, denounced these injustices. Other thinkers fought to preserve liberal principles, to promote nationalist causes, to advocate rights for women or slaves, or toleration for Catholics, Protestants, or Jews. They spoke and wrote in a rich cultural milieu where, as Classical style gave way to Romantic and Realist movements, the modern repudiation of ancestral norms was already visible. By the end of the nineteenth century, with the death of God proclaimed by the German philosopher Friedrich Nietzsche, the self had lost its coherence, and the ability of the mind to apprehend a certain fixed reality was wholly cast in doubt.

21 Machines in the Garden
The Industrialization of the West, 1750-1914

22 Lives of the Other Half
Western Society in an Industrial Age, 1750-1914

23 The Concert of Europe
Mass Politics and the Triumph of State, 1815-1914

24 The Western *Imperium*
European Expansion Around the Globe, 1750-1914

25 Storm, Stress, and Doubt
European Culture from Neoclassicism to Modernism, 1780-1914

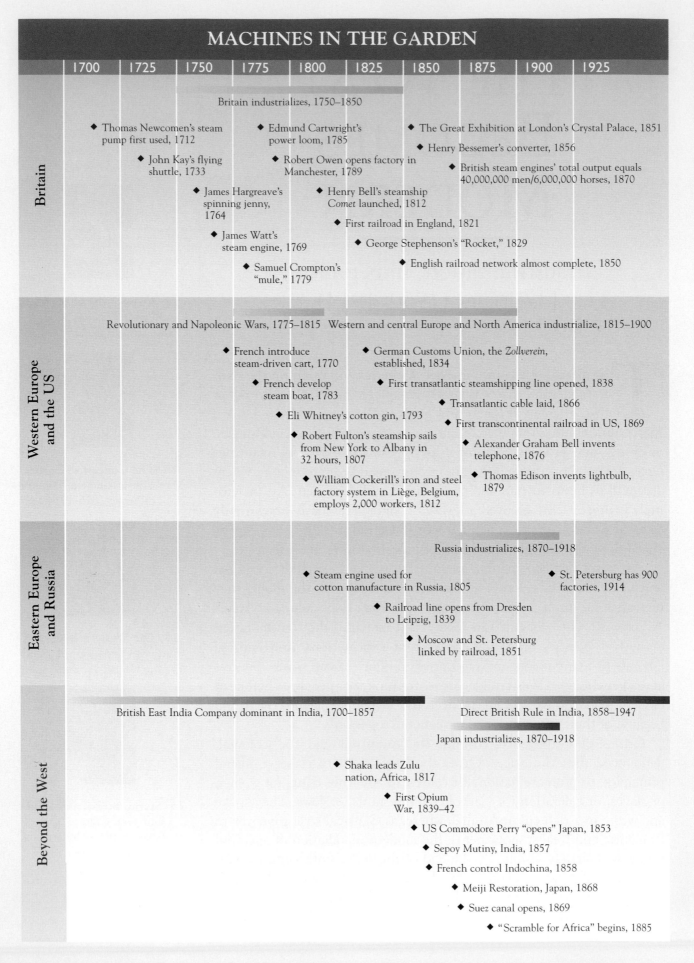

MACHINES IN THE GARDEN

| 1700 | 1725 | 1750 | 1775 | 1800 | 1825 | 1850 | 1875 | 1900 | 1925 |

Britain

Britain industrializes, 1750–1850

◆ Thomas Newcomen's steam pump first used, 1712

◆ Edmund Cartwright's power loom, 1785

◆ The Great Exhibition at London's Crystal Palace, 1851

◆ John Kay's flying shuttle, 1733

◆ Robert Owen opens factory in Manchester, 1789

◆ Henry Bessemer's converter, 1856

◆ James Hargreave's spinning jenny, 1764

◆ Henry Bell's steamship *Comet* launched, 1812

◆ British steam engines' total output equals 40,000,000 men/6,000,000 horses, 1870

◆ James Watt's steam engine, 1769

◆ First railroad in England, 1821

◆ Samuel Crompton's "mule," 1779

◆ George Stephenson's "Rocket," 1829

◆ English railroad network almost complete, 1850

Western Europe and the US

Revolutionary and Napoleonic Wars, 1775–1815   Western and central Europe and North America industrialize, 1815–1900

◆ French introduce steam-driven cart, 1770

◆ German Customs Union, the *Zollverein*, established, 1834

◆ French develop steam boat, 1783

◆ First transatlantic steamshipping line opened, 1838

◆ Eli Whitney's cotton gin, 1793

◆ Transatlantic cable laid, 1866

◆ Robert Fulton's steamship sails from New York to Albany in 32 hours, 1807

◆ First transcontinental railroad in US, 1869

◆ Alexander Graham Bell invents telephone, 1876

◆ William Cockerill's iron and steel factory system in Liège, Belgium, employs 2,000 workers, 1812

◆ Thomas Edison invents lightbulb, 1879

Eastern Europe and Russia

Russia industrializes, 1870–1918

◆ Steam engine used for cotton manufacture in Russia, 1805

◆ St. Petersburg has 900 factories, 1914

◆ Railroad line opens from Dresden to Leipzig, 1839

◆ Moscow and St. Petersburg linked by railroad, 1851

Beyond the West

British East India Company dominant in India, 1700–1857   Direct British Rule in India, 1858–1947

Japan industrializes, 1870–1918

◆ Shaka leads Zulu nation, Africa, 1817

◆ First Opium War, 1839–42

◆ US Commodore Perry "opens" Japan, 1853

◆ Sepoy Mutiny, India, 1857

◆ French control Indochina, 1858

◆ Meiji Restoration, Japan, 1868

◆ Suez canal opens, 1869

◆ "Scramble for Africa" begins, 1885

MACHINES IN THE GARDEN

The Industrialization of the West

1750–1914

areas of industrial concentration and development, 1914

KEY QUESTIONS

◆ **Before Industrialization:** What were the preconditions of industrialization, and how were they achieved in Europe before 1750?

◆ **Britain Industrializes:** What were the main steps towards industrialization in Britain? Why was the steam engine a crucial component of economic change?

◆ **Catching Up:** Why did other nations lag behind Britain in industrialization? When did continental Europe, the United States, and other regions of the world become industrialized?

Satanic Mills   The English author Charles Dickens (1812–1870) described in his novel *Hard Times* a town he dubbed "Coketown," transformed for the worse by the advent of the steam engine and the factory. "It was a town of machinery and tall chimneys," he wrote, "out of which interminable serpents of smoke trailed themselves for ever and ever, and never got uncoiled." It had a canal turned black, and a river turned purple from the pollutants that issued from the factory where a "steam-engine worked monotonously up and down like the head of an elephant in a state of melancholy madness." Into a peaceful natural world of clear sky and clean water, the machine had introduced poisons and dirt and demonic beasts—smoke serpents and mad elephants. Into the garden of pre-modern Europe the machine had burst with all its attendant maladies, staining the landscape of the pre-industrial paradise with, in the words of the visionary poet William Blake (1757–1827), "dark Satanic mills."

But the machine that despoiled the "garden," as wordsmiths nostalgically perceived it, of the pre-modern West was not simply destructive in its effects. Its arrival marked a new stage in the ability of the human species to create wealth and gain freedom from scarcity. Beginning in Britain in the late eighteenth century, the transformation of industrial production was accomplished on an astounding scale and with amazing speed, in barely a generation. This process of **industrialization**, often called the "Industrial Revolution," is the most significant change in the history of humankind since hunters and gatherers settled down to farm and live in villages at the end of the Neolithic era thousands of years earlier (see Chapter 1). For many historians and economists, it overshadows the French Revolution (see Chapter 20), or indeed any series of merely political events, in importance for the future of the human race.

This chapter explores the preconditions for industrialization in Britain and in Europe that existed well before 1780. It then describes the many innovations in technology and in the organization of work that together constituted the process of industrialization in Britain, well established by 1850. Finally, it traces the steps by which the industrial tide spread through Europe by around 1870, and thereafter to the rest of the globe where, far from Blake's England, there also sprang up "Satanic mills."

BEFORE INDUSTRIALIZATION

Long before Satanic forces, as Blake perceived them, planted machines in the garden of pre-industrial Europe, the foundations of an industrial economy and society had been laid. They were laid by men and women who could not have conceived of machine power, precision-made parts, or factory systems of production. Societies that had not pursued the European path of economic and social development were not, however, as well-equipped to develop new industrial methods. The features that made Europe the first region in the world to develop modern industry were these. First, from about the twelfth through the fifteenth centuries there developed an urban grid, home to extensive craft production, whose system of employment and distribution reached into the adjacent countryside (see Chapters 11, 12). Urban centers and their rural hinterland together provided a market for goods, stimulating production and exchange. Second, beginning in the sixteenth century, there occurred a rapid series of interconnected revolutionary developments in warfare, commerce, science, and agriculture (see Chapters 15, 16, 17, 18). Together, Europe's medieval social and economic framework, and the early modern advances in technology and knowledge, created the stage for industrialization.

Medieval Foundations: The Urban Grid

After the collapse of Roman power in western Europe during the fifth century C.E., Europe had few towns, and very few large ones. During the next several centuries, urban development ceased, as Europe fell prey to waves of invasion and suffered chronic economic recession. The exchange of goods never ceased, however, and as soon as circumstances permitted, it accelerated. Merchants who had previously journeyed with the goods they had for sale carried either on their own back or on that of a pack animal became sedentary. They settled in communities and the communities of merchants became the nuclei of European towns and cities.

In other civilizations—for example in China or Islam—a few enormous cities served as centers of political, religious, or intellectual life. Europe's cities, in contrast, were small, numerous, and commercial in character. They clustered in certain regions and exchanged goods among themselves, providing centers for both local and more extensive markets. Together, they formed a continuous urban grid that extended north to south from the lowland ports on the North Sea to the north Italian cities, both inland and coastal, of Tuscany, Lombardy, and Venetia. Numbering in the hundreds, most had only 2 to 3 thousand inhabitants; substantial towns had 20 to 30 thousand; and the biggest cities at their height reached about 100,000. At first, their residents were almost all artisans or merchants. In time, they also accommodated significant numbers of day workers, servants, migrants, vagrants, priests, and noblemen. But the merchants (who exchanged goods locally, regionally, and long-distance) and artisans (who produced and exchanged goods locally) were the key social groups in European cities, and impressed their character upon them.

By 1300, successful artisans and merchants formed craft guilds, associations of those engaged in the same kind of production or exchange. These self-governing associations established rules for the conduct of the craft or trade, defined procedures for training (apprenticeship) and entrance, and set standards for price and quality. The more important guilds and guildsmen were the city leaders, or "patriciate," who frequently negotiated **charters** with the noble or monarch who had sovereignty over the region. These charters made the towns independent of feudal networks, based on the exchange of land rights and services, and allowed townspeople to rule themselves.

Towns were centers of both trade and production. (A description of a cloth market is given in *Witnesses* on p. 614.) Merchants organized the import and export of raw materials, essential goods, and luxury commodities, the latter procured from distant locations in eastern Europe, Asia, and Africa. They developed commercial techniques that facilitated the keeping of accounts, the sale of goods, and the exchange of currencies. And they established networks of agents in remote European and non-European **entrepôts** or markets to manage long-distance trade. Those agents kept exquisite commercial records and wrote letters to their home offices describing foreign mercantile practices which their mastery of foreign languages permitted them to understand.

Artisans and merchants together participated in the production of Europe's main manufacture: textiles. Raw wool, especially from Spain and England, was processed in Flemish and Italian workshops, in grades ranging from the utilitarian to the highly refined. Linen and, in time, silk (from raw fiber processed in Italy and France) were also processed in similar ways. Metalwork was Europe's second most important manufacture. Swords and later guns joined bolts of cloth in the bellies of ships that traversed the Mediterranean to foreign markets.

The manufacture of both textile and metal products, though centered in towns, rested on an **infrastructure** that reached out to rural areas. Mining by its nature was a rural enterprise, that needed to be connected with purchasers and metalworkers in the towns. The raw materials for textile production, including not only the fiber itself, but also the materials for washing and dyeing, came from nearby as well as distant regions. Moreover, the country provided many of the textile workers, especially the myriad women who spun cloth on simple spindles or, after about 1300, the hand-operated spinning wheel.

In highly-urbanized Italy, the more advanced processes of textile production—weaving, fulling, dyeing, finishing—were performed in town, often in large workshops. In other less-urbanized areas (including parts of England, France, and central Europe), these processes might be performed in the cottages of workers in an arrangement called the **"putting-out system"** (see Chapter 16). Town and country were linked together, communicating through itinerant merchants or their agents, who distributed materials, collected finished products, and provided payment. These linkages multiplied and strengthened over time, and by the eighteenth century amounted to a **"protoindustrial"** system centered in towns and radiating out into adjacent rural areas.

The main features of Europe's urban grid were in place, and some were long-established, by 1500. They prepared the way for later industrialization, which harnessed merchant energies and commercial techniques while modernizing production methods.

Early Modern Changes

Soon after 1500, some revolutionary changes began to impact upon the social, economic, and intellectual realms, setting the stage for a later process of rapid industrialization. Historians sometimes refer to a "military," a "commercial," a "scientific," and an "agricultural" revolution. All occurred between 1500 and 1750, and all are preconditions for industrial development after 1780.

Changes in military technology and organization were developed especially by Italian generals and engineers just before 1500 (see Chapter 15). The cannon became more accurate and mobile, while improvements in hand-carried guns and muskets gave infantry an advantage over cavalry and precipitated changes in army organization. The plans of individual fortresses and strategies for national defense adjusted to new realities, guided by military theoreticians. Armies became larger and more expensive to equip and maintain, necessitating (as one among many factors) the centralization of nation states and the creation of new systems of taxation. By 1750, professional soldiers wore regimental uniforms, drilled in formation, fired in lines, and were subject to strict military discipline. Advanced gun technology and more intensive organization, discipline, and planning were related to the later process of industrialization.

Starting just before 1500, the Portuguese, Spanish, Dutch, English, and French—the Atlantic-facing nations of Europe—sent their ships around the globe in search of new commodities and new markets (see Chapter 16). The result was a remaking of the European economy, affecting prices, manufacturing methods, consumer habits, political administration, agricultural organization—just about every aspect of life. All of these were important for later industrialization, but none more important than the network of trade routes that now criss-crossed the globe like a web, and the ever-increasing value of foreign trade—effects sometimes called the "commercial" revolution.

Buying and Selling Before the Industrial Age

Since the earliest civilizations, and even before they formed, people have bought and sold commodities and crafted goods—artisans have sold their own wares; merchants have sold merchandise obtained from others; kings and states have sought to bolster the wealth of their nations, if only by excluding the goods of others to realize higher tax revenues. All these various activities were still ongoing in the eighteenth and nineteenth centuries when industrialization dramatically transformed first Europe's, then the world's, economies. In these passages, the English novelist Daniel Defoe describes a market scene in Yorkshire, England; the British government seeks to protect its domestic textile industries; and a German economist laments the tariffs that impede trade.

Daniel Defoe describes the Yorkshire cloth market (c. 1724): The Market itself is worth describing…. The street is a large, broad, fair and well-built Street, beginning … at the Bridge, and ascending gently to the North. Early in the Morning, there are Tressels placed in two Rows in the Street, sometimes two Rows on a Side …; then there are Boards laid cross those Tressels, so that the Boards lie like long Counters on either Side, from one end of the street to the other. The clothiers come early in the Morning with their Cloth; and as few clothiers bring more than one Piece, the Market being so frequent, they go into the Inns and Publick-Houses with it, and there set it down. At seven a Clock in the Morning … the Market Bell rings; … without hurry or noise, and not the least disorder, the whole Market is fill'd; all the Boards upon the Tressels are covered with Cloth … and behind every Piece of Cloth, the Clothier standing to sell it. As soon as the Bell has done Ringing, the Merchants and Factors, and Buyers of all Sorts, come down…. [T]hey reach over to the Clothier and whisper, and in the fewest Words imaginable the Price is stated; one asks, the other bids; and 'tis agree, or not agree, in a Moment…. [I]n less than half an Hour you will perceive the Cloths begin to move off, the Clothier taking it up upon his Shoulder to carry it to the Merchant's House; and by half an Hour after eight a Clock the Market Bell rings again; immediately the Buyers disappear, the Cloth is all sold, or if here and there a Piece happens not to be bought, 'tis carried back into the Inn, and, in a quarter of an Hour, there is not a Piece of Cloth to be seen in the Market.
(From D. B. Horn and M. Ransome eds., *English Historical Documents, 1714–1783*, 1957)

The British government moves to protect domestic wool and silk manufactures by banning the use of printed calicoes, imported from India (1721): Whereas it is most evident, that the wearing and using of printed, painted, stained and dyed callicoes in apparel, household stuff, furniture, and otherwise, does manifestly tend to the great detriment of the woollen and silk manufactures of this kingdom, and to the excessive increase of the poor, and if not effectually prevented, may be the utter ruin and destruction of the said manufactures, and of many thousands of your Majesty's subjects and their families, whose livelihoods do intirely depend thereupon: for remedy thereof may it please your most excellent Majesty, That it may be enacted … by and with the advice and consent of the lords spiritual and temporal, and commons, in the present parliament assembled, … That from and after [25 December 1722], it shall not be lawful for any person or persons whatsoever to use or wear in Great Britain, in any garment or apparel whatsoever, any printed, stained or dyed callico, under the penalty of forfeiting to the informer the sum of five pounds of lawful money of Great Britain for every such offense.
(From D. B. Horn and M. Ransome eds., *English Historical Documents, 1714–1783*, 1957)

The economist Friedrich List describes impediments to trade and industry in the German states (1819): Thirty-eight customs boundaries cripple inland commerce, and produce much the same effect as ligatures which prevent the free circulation of the blood. The merchant trading between Hamburg and Austria, or Berlin and Switzerland must traverse ten states, must learn ten customs tariffs, must pay ten successive transit dues. Anyone who is so unfortunate as to live on the boundary line between three or four states spends his days among hostile tax-gatherers and custom house officials; he is a man without a country…. Only the remission of the internal customs, and the erection of a general tariff for the whole Federation [of German states], can restore national trade and industry and help the working classes.
(From W. O. Henderson, *The Rise of German Industrial Power, 1834–1914*, 1975)

Meanwhile, the revolution in science (see Chapter 17), began with astronomy, physics, and mathematics, later embracing biology, medicine, and chemistry. New paradigms for the structure and workings of the universe encouraged the kind of thinking about complex systems that later informed industrial organization. The use of the experimental method, developed by Galileo Galilei (1564–1642) and other early scientists to test their theories, further encouraged the understanding of material objects and processes, and required scientists, or the artisans they employed, to design new artifacts and make things work. Pumps, thermometers, telescopes, microscopes, and other pieces of special equipment invented to aid experimentation, observation, and measuring, littered the scientist's laboratory. More widely, the idea that specific requirements could be met by the invention of completely new artifacts was to underpin important aspects of the coming industrial era. Accumulating knowledge of the properties of chemicals and gases would similarly prove useful in industrial processes. Just as important as the tinkering inspired by science were the habits of thought that accompanied it: the attention to quantity and number; the zeal to find a simpler, more direct or elegant explanation; the desire to know even more, in the words of one historian (referring to the medieval magician, Dr. Faustus, who sold his soul to the devil in order to obtain unlimited knowledge), the "Faustian spirit of mastery."

Related to these earlier "revolutions" were profound changes in agricultural techniques developed from the seventeenth century in the Netherlands and, soon afterward, in Britain (see Chapter 18). Networks of ditches and dikes for drainage and flood control, and canals for irrigation, required advanced engineering skills and encouraged practical thinking about water supply, transportation, and communication. The elimination of the **fallow**, in some regions, opened new fields for experimental techniques of crop rotation, quickly resulting in enormously increased productivity and fertility. Increased yields meant improved nutrition, at the same time that specialized agricultural management of restricted fields radically changed the pattern of rural labor.

Enclosure of previously open, communal fields, especially in England in the seventeenth and eighteenth centuries, resulted in large-scale dislocations in the life of rural communities. Overall, the effects of the many initiatives in agriculture during this period were population growth, the practice of using hired labor, and the availability of large numbers of landless day laborers for agriculture and manufacturing. All were important for the process of industrialization, which required a mobile, flexible labor force, and a mass market for manufactured goods.

By 1750, the impact of revolutionary changes in these different but interconnected areas had been felt, especially in the northwestern region of Europe that had surged ahead of the Mediterranean region both in wealth and creativity. By this date in Britain, the process of industrialization was already under way.

BRITAIN INDUSTRIALIZES

Beginning soon after 1700, Britain experienced the first stages of industrialization, which accelerated rapidly after about 1780. Map 21.1 on p. 616 shows its development. By 1850, the process of industrialization had peaked. Britain was now the foremost manufacturing and trading nation in the world. The miracle of British industrialization was born from the interconnected histories of basic substances: coal, water, iron, and cotton.

Cotton and Water

Wool, not cotton, had been the lynchpin of medieval manufacture in Europe. The raw fiber came from sheep who grazed abundantly on Europe's relatively cool, well-watered fields. Complex workshop systems evolved to process the raw wool into a range of textiles for local as well as foreign consumption. Around 1700, wool was Britain's major export, amounting to some eighty or ninety percent of the total. Around the same time, however, British consumers, more numerous and more affluent as agricultural conditions improved, developed a taste for cotton cloth.

Bright, washable calicoes (fabrics from Calicut) were produced in India and imported by the British East India Company, which had by that time established virtual sovereignty in the Asian subcontinent. Cotton grew easily in India's hot climate. Indian women spun fine, strong yarn, which they wove into lightweight yet durable fabrics. Imports of these fabrics more than tripled in the last third of the seventeenth century—861,000 pieces for the period 1699–1701, compared to 240,000 pieces for 1663–1669. The passage quoted in *Witnesses* on p. 614 reveals a government attempt to restrict such imports.

British manufacturers, hoping to compete with the desirable new import, acquired raw cotton from American colonies, whose sub-tropical climate proved favorable to the recently transplanted Asian crop. British workers, however, or British techniques, could not produce a satisfactory cotton textile. They succeeded in interweaving cotton yarn with linen to make a product called fustian. But consumers wanted unblended cotton.

The Beginnings of Industrialization   If there was no way to wean the public from a taste for cotton, could the means be developed to produce cotton cloth in Britain, entrepreneurs asked, so that they might reap the profit at home? The need for a solution to this problem stimulated a series of inventors to develop machinery that shattered traditional norms of textile manufacture once and for all. Those inventions were: the flying shuttle patented by John Kay (1704–1764) in 1733 and widely used from the 1750s; the spinning jenny, introduced in 1764 by James Hargreaves (d. 1778) and patented in 1770; the water frame, which automated the jenny, patented by Richard Arkwright (1732–1792) in 1769; the "mule," developed by Samuel Crompton (1753–1827) in 1779 (he couldn't afford to patent it), combining the jenny and the water frame to produce a fine, strong yarn; and the power loom, patented by Edmund Cartwright (1743–1823) in 1785.

Map 21.1 Great Britain Industrializes, 1750–1850: *From 1750 to 1850, Britain leaped ahead of the rest of Europe and the world in industrial production. Some of the causes for and consequences of that progress are illustrated here: natural resources (coal, iron, copper, lead, tin); natural and artificial waterways; large industrial and commercial centers; and a network of railroad links. Why were population concentrations important for industrialization?*

Spinning and weaving are the two major processes of textile manufacture. (Other ancillary processes include washing, combing, fulling, dyeing, etc.) For centuries, weaving had been accomplished on a loom, which permitted the horizontal weft to be laced through the stretched vertical fibers of the warp. Kay's flying shuttle mechanized that process. The laborer had only to pull a cord to push the shuttle, and it wove the yarn horizontally through the warp threads. Not only did this innovation greatly speed the process of weaving (provoking some wrathful handloom weavers to destroy the inventor's model). It also put pressure on spinning.

Spinning was the real bottleneck in textile production. Traditionally, it was performed by women who worked with two rod-like tools, the distaff and spindle. The former held the mass of raw fiber, drawn out by fingers and spun to produce a twisted length of thread. The latter held the finished, weavable yarn yielded by the repeated, tedious process of separating and twisting fiber into thread and winding fine thread into durable yarn.

The innovation of the crank-operated spinning wheel speeded up the spinning process. The spinning-wheel, however, still produced only one thread of yarn at a time; it took between six and ten spinners to produce the yarn for one loom operator. Hargreaves' spinning jenny, illustrated in *Windows On* on p. 618, produced the first major breakthrough in spinning since the earliest days of textile work. It enabled a single laborer to produce several threads at once: six, twelve, twenty-four—the only limit was the force that could be exerted on the cranking mechanism. British laborers could now produce pure cotton yarn comparable to that spun by practiced Indian spinners, in virtually unlimited quantity.

As jennies became larger, however, spinning could no longer be done in the workers' cottages. The workers had mostly been women, who won welcome distraction from the tedium of the task by chatting with daughters, kinfolk, and friends engaged in the same work, and by supervising younger children also assigned useful labor. The invention of the jenny disrupted cottage-based spinning. Soon the new machines were being installed in specially constructed manufacturing shops, alongside several others. Workers, still women, walked from their cottages to the shop on a specified schedule. The children they brought with them performed ancillary tasks. A new kind of workplace was taking form.

Soon the jenny was linked by Arkwright's water frame (and later Crompton's mule) to an alternative source of power—the wheel. Water wheels, and more rarely windmills, were the sole forms of machinery known in the Middle Ages that were not driven by either human or animal muscle. Used mostly for grinding grain, their capacity to perform repetitive work had been known for centuries. With the creation of the jenny, and its placement in a workshop rather than a cottage, the opportunity offered by the time-tested wheel became apparent. The workshop was located next to a running stream, which turned a wheel that transmitted power to the moving parts of the jenny. The human laborer was no longer needed to turn the jenny's crank, but only to tend the machine, feed it raw fiber, and replace its bobbins (the machine version of the spindle) on which the strong, uniform yarn was wound, as suggested by the passage quoted in *Witnesses* on p. 622. Cotton and water came together, marking an important step toward industrialization.

With the availability of an infinitely expandable supply of cotton yarn, the burden of further development in textile production fell on weaving. The male laborers who had installed a loom in their cottages were now kept busy, and new entrants to the field

learned the skill. For a generation more (up to three generations in some regions) the handloom weavers commanded high rates. Their labor was essential if cloth production was to rise to the level of the availability of raw cotton and processed yarn.

Effects at Home and Abroad   But how could weavers keep up with the enormous quantity of yarn spun by the tireless, ever-expandable jennies? Cartwright's power loom presented the solution. With water power driving the flying shuttle, little but supervisory attention was required from the laborer. As power-driven looms slowly took their place alongside jennies in the mills, weaving as well as spinning entered the industrial age. The handloom weavers lost their specialist niche in the manufacturing process, and faced demoralizing transformation into ordinary mill workers.

On two other continents, many more people suffered from the mechanization of cotton cloth production in English mills, which still nestled in the country alongside rushing streams. In India, the export trade in cotton cloth declined for a century and by 1830 was dead. For centuries, Indian spindles and looms had provided cottons throughout Asia and the Middle East. But with the advent of industrialization, these regions preferred to import cheap, durable cotton textiles from distant Britain. In India, workers lost employment in the textile sector, and the economy geared downward to export cash crops and resources. That shift amounted to the deindustrialization of India, which became a prelude to its political defeat (see Chapter 24).

In the British colonies of North America (more than the Caribbean, where sugar cultivation was the economic mainstay), increasing numbers of African slaves were imported to sow, tend, and harvest fields of cotton. The plant had only recently been introduced in the southern Atlantic colonies, where tobacco, indigo, and rice had preceded it as major cash crops. Cotton grew well in the Western Hemisphere, however. Its success encouraged the establishment of more and larger plantations, modeled on those created for the farming of Caribbean sugar and Virginian tobacco. British slave ships were never busier than in the century when cotton became established in the American south. By the late eighteenth century, Africans were a large minority of the residents of the continent, their enslavement encouraged by the yawning British market for raw fiber. And cotton production had not yet peaked.

The American phase of the story of cotton continued uninterrupted throughout the War for Independence (1775–1783). Not long after that conflict was resolved and the United States Constitution ratified, another invention, the creation of an American engineer, joined the new technologies that transformed cotton manufacture. In 1793, Eli

WHO'S WHO

Inventors of the Industrial Age: Textiles

John Kay (1704–1764) the flying shuttle

James Hargreaves (1720?–1778) the spinning jenny

Richard Arkwright (1732–1792) the water frame

Samuel Crompton (1753–1827) the "mule"

Edmund Cartwright (1743–1823) the power loom

Eli Whitney (1765–1825) the cotton gin

Power from Steam

Newcomen steam engine, 1717

Henry Cort's "puddling furnace," 1784

James Watt's design of a rotary engine, 1782

Bessemer converter, 1856

The development of the steam engine burst the bounds of previous technology, increasing the power available for work by a factor of thousands and tens of thousands. Whereas power historically had been limited by the capacity of muscle, wind, or water, now it was virtually unlimited. The amazing machine that turned ordinary water into limitless power is seen in its early stage of development in Newcomen's 1717 model (top left; note the human figure on the left for scale), and in its later refinement in James Watt's elegant 1782 plan of a rotary engine, capable of turning a shaft for advanced industrial applications (bottom left).

Besides their use in textile manufacture and transportation, steam engines powered the new "iron age" (approximately 1760–1856), speeding up and improving iron and steel production. Henry Cort's "puddling furnace," patented in 1784, removed the impurities introduced into molten iron by the coke used for smelting it (top right). The transition from iron to steel was made possible in large part by the invention of the Bessemer converter in 1856 (bottom right).

What kinds of jobs could be done once the rotary engine was invented?

To continue your investigation of this topic, please go to www.prenhall.com/king for the related **WINDOWS** on the **WEB** activity

Whitney (1765–1825) was staying with a friend in Georgia, the manager of a cotton plantation. There he learned that one task above all slowed the process by which the cotton fibers were plucked from the plant, cleaned, and packaged for export. When first picked, the cotton fibers were tangled with seed. Valuable labor time was devoted to plucking and pulling out the seeds.

Familiar with industrial organization in New England mills, Whitney understood the value of this lost time and set out to find a way to reduce it. Within ten days, he had designed a model of the "cotton gin," a simple machine operated by human or horse power that spun the raw cotton, agitating and extracting the seeds. The cotton gin did efficiently what human workers did poorly. From 1793 to 1800, the amount of cotton exported jumped from 18 to 83 million pounds, more than a fourfold increase. In the end, however, the machine meant not less work for African slaves, but more. Speeding up the processing of fiber only encouraged the growing, picking, ginning, baling, and shipping of more cotton in the quest for greater profits. The gin inaugurated the reign of King Cotton in the American south, that did not falter until the Civil War (1861–1865) finally brought an end to slavery.

Meanwhile, the series of revolutionary technical innovations in cotton cloth manufacture already discussed made Britain the leading world producer of the textile. In due course, the new technology would be adapted for the manufacture of wool, linen, and silk textiles. But first, the cotton mill would undergo a final transformation. The water wheel made way for the steam engine, the end product of another story of successful technological innovation. That story is important and must be told before we return to see the mill reborn as the modern factory.

Coal and Water

The creation of the cotton mill resulted from the marriage of cotton textile production with the water-driven wheel. The steam engine resulted from a different combination of natural resources: coal and water. Coal heated water to produce steam. Steam was used to power the pumps needed to remove water from deep mines where coal (the principal fuel of the era, at least in Britain) lay hidden in the earth. The elegant circularity of these relations is important. It is precisely where these two substances lay in close proximity that the steam engine was developed to provide a solution.

Coal mining accelerated in Britain from the seventeenth to the eighteenth centuries. Charcoal, derived from wood, was the fuel previously used for a major task of traditional manufacture: the smelting of iron. But charcoal was in short supply. Most of Britain's forests had long since been felled to clear fields for

cultivation, and to provide fuel and construction materials. Timber for housing and shipbuilding was imported, from Russia and the American colonies. Unlike wood, however, coal was plentiful. In the 1600s, it began to be used for metallurgical and domestic heating purposes. With the increased use of iron in both machines and manufactures, demand for iron rose, and consequently also for coal. Mining boomed.

At first, coal was easily removed from near the surface. As those seams were exhausted, however, miners dug deeper into the earth, until mineshafts and tunnels reached well below the water table, and became liable to flooding. Flooding both weakened the tunnels and made it harder to remove the coal. Workers removed the water in buckets and carts. In places they adapted pumps of the kind used in the ships of the British Navy to keep the water that seeped in from sinking the vessels. Pumping by hand was constant, tiresome work. The need became apparent for a way to power pumps without wasting human effort.

At this juncture, the British inventor Thomas Savery (c. 1650–1715) adapted the design for a steam-powered engine already explored by the French Huguenot immigrant Denis Papin (1647–c. 1712). It utilized simple principles. When water turns to steam, its volume expands 1600 times. The force generated by that expansion can move a piston back and forth in a cylinder, and the piston can drive a pump—or, in later applications, virtually any machinery. The materials needed were also basic, both found nearby in the flooded mine: water and coal. These were the building blocks of the gigantic steam engine that Savery designed. He displayed it to fellow scientists at a meeting of the Royal Society, where Britain's leading experts gathered (see Chapter 17), and to King William III (r. 1689–1702) at one of his country residences, Hampton Court, and patented it in 1698.

Thomas Newcomen (1663–1729) invented an improved engine (first used 1712), illustrated in *Windows On*, p. 621. For the next half-century, the huge, awkward steam engines created by Savery and Newcomen loomed over the lips of coal mines, and pumped out water from the deep galleries below.

The early steam engines were inefficient, however. After the water was heated, and the resultant steam did its work, it needed to be cooled, and then heated again. Both time and fuel were wasted in the process. Having been commissioned to repair a Newcomen engine, the Scottish instrument-maker James Watt (1736–1819) began his search for a solution to these problems. Working over twenty years, he developed an efficient steam engine that burned only half as much fuel as its predecessors. Not only more effective in mining operations, it could also be adapted for other settings—as it would be for textile and iron production and, eventually, transportation.

Watt introduced several improvements to the original steam engines. First, he designed a separate condensing chamber where the water could be cooled and then recirculated. Second, he mounted an air pump to move steam into the chamber. Third, he insulated parts of the engine to prevent energy loss. Watt patented his improved engine in 1769, and in the 1770s, in partnership with the engineer and entrepreneur Matthew Boulton (1728–1809), developed a new engine capable of delivering rotary power. It is illustrated in *Windows On*, p. 621.

One of the problems Watt faced in developing an efficient engine was the need for precisely measured cylinders. Without them, the steam was not sufficiently contained in the cylinder, so that force was lost and fuel wasted. The solution he found for this problem is yet another illustration of how different technologies cross-fertilized each other in the development of modern industry. Watt employed the skill of gunmakers to craft his cylinders (what is a gun, after all, but a cylinder through which a missile is channeled and exploded?). A precision-made gun barrel insured both accuracy and safety. Its qualities also served well in the operation of the steam engine.

The efficient new steam engine was important in coal mining, where the results were evident: by 1830, Britain was responsible for four-fifths of the world's coal production. But now the steam engine could assist with other tasks—virtually any task that presented itself—greatly outpowering human or animal workers, as the passage quoted in *Witnesses* on p. 622 and the illustration on p. 624 show. Attention turned to the textile mills, recent innovations themselves, where water power, transmitted from rushing stream to turning wheel, drove the machines that spun yarn and wove cloth. By the 1780s, steam engines were utilized to drive these machines, marking the beginning of the history of the "factory" (derived from "manufactory," a place where things were manufactured). In factories, machines made things; human "hands" (signified by the Latin "*manu*" of "manufacture") worked mainly to tend machines.

After 1785, when Edmund Cartwright patented his power loom, steam-powered textile factories multiplied. Factories no longer needed to be near streams. They could be established near to coal mines, and where bolts of finished cloth were easily transferred to canal barges or ships for export. Often they were near river or ocean ports or, in time, railroad depots. Profits were enormous. The industrialist Robert Owen (1771–1858) opened a factory in Manchester in 1789 for £100 in startup capital. Twenty years later, he paid £84,000 in cash to buy out his partners in the venture.

Outside of mining and textile manufacture, steam engines could be used to grind flour, brew beer, spin potting wheels, or prepare ceramic glazes, refine sugar, or power a printing press—and above all, to produce the parts of other machines. By 1800, 500 engines were at work in British factories, principally in the

heavy industries (metals and textiles). By 1870, Britain's steam engines produced as much power as could have been generated by 6 million horses, or 40 million people—more than the nation's population.

While machines for textile manufacture greatly increased Britain's industrial output, and the steam engine raised that output still further, the availability of more and better iron drove it astronomically higher. That effect was achieved when the steam engine was applied to the manufacture of iron.

Iron, Coal, and Steam

From the earliest use of iron (see Chapter 1), the smelting process involved using high heat to melt the metal, release it from its ore, and remove impurities. In pre-modern Europe, first charcoal, and much later coke, distilled from coal, were used as fuels in this process. The availability of the steam engine permitted new innovations in iron manufacture.

Britain's own iron ores were of inferior quality, laced with impurities that injured the resultant metal's strength and malleability. Iron ore was imported from Sweden, Russia, and (after 1776) the United States. Meanwhile, some manufacturers experimented with coke, as opposed to charcoal, as a fuel for the production of raw or "pig" iron. In 1784, Henry Cort (1740–1800) patented his technique of "puddling," which allowed coke to be used throughout the process of iron manufacture. The process is shown in the diagram in *Windows On*, p. 621. The pig iron was heated with the coke to form a paste, which was stirred with iron rods, allowing impurities to be burned away. The molten iron was then passed between rollers, which pressed out any remaining impurities. A means had been found to use native ores in the manufacture of top-grade iron.

Innovations in iron manufacture meant a surge in production as shown in *How Many?* on p. 623. In 1750, Britain produced 28,000 tons of pig iron. By 1790, after puddling had been introduced, that figure more than tripled, to 87,000 tons; in 1818, it was 325,000 tons, in 1830, 700,000 tons, and in 1870, 4 million tons. Over 120 years, these staggering figures amount to a sum 142 times the original value—a rate of increase immeasurably beyond what could be achieved by human or animal power alone.

The steam engine permitted further advances in metallurgy. The engine could operate bellows to blast hot air into the molten iron—work previously done by hand. By 1856, Henry Bessemer (1813–1898) developed a method of using the steam engine to operate bellows and rollers in the process of iron refining, making the use of expensive, skilled "puddlers" unnecessary, and, by reintroducing carbon to the refined iron, to produce steel—harder and finer than iron. The steam engine, illustrated in *Windows On* on p. 621, operated in one continuous process to

In the Factory

Interior of a cotton factory, Lancashire, England, 1835

Factory production brought new efficiencies to tasks that had been accomplished by individual artisans or by family groups in traditional cottage industry. Nowhere was this change more visible than in the textile industries, where technology previously had permitted only one thread, or only a few, to be spun at a time. Now, as depicted above in a mid-nineteenth-century British factory, with the use of the mass-output "mule," multiple strands of thread were wound on multiple spindles simultaneously. So fundamental to textile production was the multiplication of spindles that factory capacity was measured in "spindlage"—not the number of machines, or workers, or even bolts of cloth, but of the spindles on which was wound mechanically produced thread.

Iron and steel factories, now powered by steam engines, experienced similar efficiencies, as depicted in the illustration of an iron and steel factory.

By the 1870s, electricity was widely used for interior and street illumination and as a new source of power. Here a French factory is lit by electric "candles" in an 1883 illustration by Georges Dary.

Iron and steel factory, nineteenth century

 To continue your investigation of this topic, please go to www.prenhall.com/king for the related **WINDOWS** on the **WEB** activity

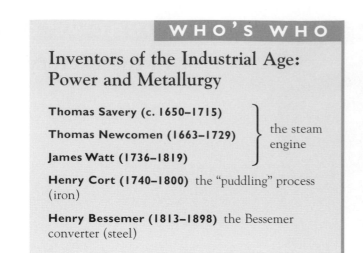

Inventors of the Industrial Age: Power and Metallurgy

Thomas Savery (c. 1650–1715)

Thomas Newcomen (1663–1729)   } the steam engine

James Watt (1736–1819)

Henry Cort (1740–1800) the "puddling" process (iron)

Henry Bessemer (1813–1898) the Bessemer converter (steel)

half-million tons worldwide in 1870 to almost thirty times that figure (14,600,000 tons) in 1895.

The iron and steel employed domestically or exported abroad had many uses. In Britain at first, and then elsewhere, these increasingly included the construction of new machines—steam engines to power factories, and the machines that produced goods in the factories. Once again, a circular process is observed: machines made it possible to produce the substance from which to make more machines. Interrelations such as this characterized the building of the industrial era, where each innovation was promptly applied to other purposes.

Railroad and Steamship

Just as the power of the steam engine could be used to drive machines that stood in place, it could also be adapted to machines that moved. The possibilities of using steam to revolutionize transportation presented themselves from the beginning. In 1770, the French had attempted to develop a rudimentary steam-driven

produce a high-grade metal capable of serving the needs of a machine age. Almost a luxury metal in the early years of industrialization, steel commanded a price more than ten times that of pig iron. But steel became cheap as production bounded from about a

The Coming of the Machine Age

The first observers of the machine-powered manufacturing process were often astonished by the speed, the capacity, and the productivity of the steam engine—a great beast with "iron fingers, teeth, and wheels," and "the noblest machine ever invented by man," as these two authors observe with understandable awe.

Edward Baines, a nineteenth-century student of industrialization, describes the great productivity of the machine-powered textile factory (1835): It is by iron fingers, teeth, and wheels, moving with exhaustless energy and devouring speed, that the cotton is opened, cleaned, spread, carded, drawn, roved, spun, wound, warped, dressed, and woven. ... All are moving at once—the operations chasing each other; and all derive their motion from the mighty engine, which, firmly seated in the lower part of the building, and constantly fed with water and fuel, toils through the day with the strength of perhaps a hundred horses. Men, in the meanwhile, have merely to check its slight and infrequent irregularities—each workman performing, or rather superintending, as much work as could have been done by *two or three hundred men* sixty years ago. ... When it is remembered that all these inventions have been made within the last seventy years it must be acknowledged that the cotton mill presents the most striking example of the dominion obtained by human science over the powers of nature, of which modern times can boast.
(Edward Baines, *History of the Cotton Manufacture in Great Britain*, 1835; ed. M. J. Daunton, 1995)

The steam engine as a living beast (1834): It is [in] the property which the steam-engine possesses of regulating itself, and providing for all its wants, that the great beauty of the invention consists. It has been said that nothing made by the hand of man approaches so near to animal life. Heat is the principle of its movements; there is in its tubes circulation, like that of the blood in the veins of animals, having valves which open and shut in proper periods; it feeds itself, evacuates such portions of its food as are useless, and draws from its own labours all that is necessary to its own subsistence. ... The motion of the fluids in the boiler represents the expanding and collapsing of the heart; the fluid that goes to it by one channel is drawn off by another, in part to be returned when condensed by the cold, similar to the operation of veins and arteries. Animals require long and frequent periods of relaxation from fatigue, and any great accumulation of their power is not obtained without great expense and inconvenience. The wind is uncertain; and water, the constancy of which is in few places equal to the wants of the machinist, can seldom be obtained on the spot, where other circumstances require machines to be erected. To relieve us from all these difficulties, the last century has given us the steam engine ... the noblest machine ever invented by man—the pride of the machinist, the admiration of the philosopher.
(M. A. Alderson, essay, 1834; ed. R. L. Hills, 1993)

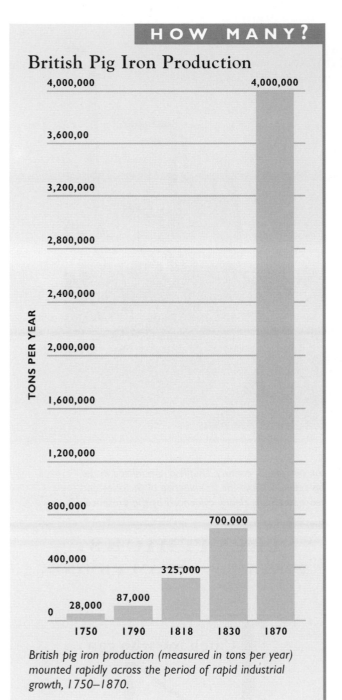

British Pig Iron Production

British pig iron production (measured in tons per year) mounted rapidly across the period of rapid industrial growth, 1750–1870.

ore from the rock face to the surface (when they did not carry baskets, or push crates). The rails, at first made of timber, were laid to permit the wheels of the carts to roll freely without becoming mired in mud. They were laid in the galleries of the mine or on the road from the mine to a depot by a river or canal, where the heavy mining products were loaded on barges for shipment to market. As early as 1556, a classic Renaissance treatise on metallurgy described the use of rails for just these purposes.

The carts, the rails, and the engine were first put together near the mines. They formed short railroad lines that ran from the mine to a coastal, river, or canal depot transporting coal. In 1804, the engineer Richard Trevithick (1771–1833) developed a locomotive, illustrated on p. 624, capable of carrying heavy loads on such truncated lines. The first expanded lines date from the 1820s, and in 1821, a rail line extended from Darlington, a mining center, to Stockton, a port; by 1825, this line was offering both freight and passenger services.

The next step in the development of the railroad came with the idea that the railroad could exist apart from the mine. It could link markets and ports, and could transport goods other than mining products. It might carry, for instance, bolts of cotton cloth, or loads of cabbages, to market centers. By 1829, George Stephenson (1781–1848) had developed the locomotive *Rocket* (which could clock a good 36 mph on a normal run—several times the speed of a horse pulling a cart). It operated on a line between the booming factory town of Manchester and the port of Liverpool, serving the Atlantic trade. By 1850, England was crisscrossed with a network of rail lines—an infrastructure that still exists in part 150 years later.

The railroad might be considered the most significant breakthrough in transportation since the days, millennia earlier, of the introduction of the wheel or the sail (see Chapter 1). Previously, in most parts of the world and certainly in Europe, the transportation of heavy materials over long distances was usually accomplished by water—whether on the sea or by river or canal. (Exceptions were the long pack animal trains that traversed the Silk Road in Asia, or the camel caravans across Middle Eastern deserts.) The railroad was faster, safer, and nearly limitless, reaching wherever rails could be laid. Railroad stations, the scenes of myriad comings and goings, as shown in Monet's painting on p. 625 became the new foci of industrial civilization. Timetables that clocked those goings and comings were objects of passionate scrutiny, offering the promise of arriving at a specified time at any given destination.

The steamship developed in tandem with the railroad, in due course replacing the sail, as rail replaced the wheeled cart. The American Robert Fulton (1765–1815) developed the prototype of the modern steamship from the unsuccessful design created by a

cart, followed by a steamboat in 1783. Useful steam-driven vehicles, however, were not developed until the early 1800s, when the necessary components—the steam engine, together with abundant supplies of iron and coal—were assembled.

A "railroad train" is a series of carts or carriages linked together (the train) whose wheels run on a pathway of parallel rails drawn by an engine (the locomotive). The steam engine itself, it has been seen, had origins intimately linked to the coal mine. Similarly, the railroad train was initially developed for mining work, assembling its parts from elements of the mining enterprise. The carts derived from those the miners used to transport coal or mineral-bearing

Steam Outdoes Men and Beasts

Sheffield, England, in 1879: *One of the industrial boom towns of the nineteenth century, Sheffield specialized in the production of steel and steel implements (such as cutlery and files). This scene displays the prominence of factories and belching smokestacks—and the continuity of traditional rural life in their midst, as is clearly evidenced by the presence of countryfolk and their cows.*

French inventor in 1783. In 1807, Fulton's 150-foot *Clermont*, powered by a Boulton and Watt engine, traveled upriver from New York City to Albany in thirty-two hours, averaging a little under five miles per hour. In Britain, Henry Bell (1767–1830) launched his steamship *Comet* in 1812. A steamship first crossed the Atlantic in 1819, powered partly by sail and partly by steam-driven paddlewheels, taking thirty days. The first transatlantic steamship line opened in 1838. By the 1850s, sturdy, reliable steamships fitted with screw propellers (which replaced the paddlewheel) were visiting all the major ports of the globe. The career of the sailing ship, which had opened the Atlantic and Pacific oceans to commerce, would soon close.

Industrialization took place in Britain first because of a number of favorable circumstances. Britain's colonial empire linked it with the cotton workshops

TREVITHICKS,
PORTABLE STEAM ENGINE.

Catch me who can.

Mechanical Power Subduing Animal Speed.

Advertisement for Trevithick's engine: *This advertisement for Richard Trevithick's primitive locomotive (developed in 1804, and called here a "portable steam engine") reads "Catch me who can!" and, even more defiantly, "Mechanical Power Subduing Animal Speed." This last concise phrase sums up the heroic achievement of industrialization.*

of India and the cotton fields of the Americas. Its own land yielded coal and iron in abundance, and its ample waterways and harbors made transportation and communication easy. Its sound banking system, ready capital, landlords friendly to profitable innovation, and entrepreneurs promoted investment in new ventures. Its government encouraged commerce but did not intervene too much to protect or restrict. Its large supply of unskilled laborers was available to work in the industries developed largely by a pool of talented artisans, who, unlike their continental colleagues, were unhampered by guild restrictions. Beyond these factors, a willingness to experiment seems to characterize the makers of what some historians call an industrial revolution in Britain.

By 1870, industrialization had transformed Britain. Machine power—"unconquer'd steam" (in the words of Erasmus Darwin, grandfather of naturalist Charles Darwin)—had demonstrated its superiority over animal strength, and machines were planted in the garden of the countryside. Over green fields loomed huge, brash factories (Blake's nightmare),

their smokestacks telling the tale of the storming, blasting steam engines within. Sleek, fast trains carried coal and iron, bolts of cloth, and the machines to make them to every corner of the country.

No other state could compete with Britain in output or market share, at home or abroad, as the passage quoted in *Witnesses* on p. 633 suggests. In 1851, the "Great Exhibition of the Works of Industry of all Nations" was held in London's Crystal Palace. In that building whose walls were fabrics of glass and steel, assembled on-site from factory-made components, more than 6 million visitors from around the globe admired 13,000 exhibits of British industrialization. After about a century of development, Britain remained unsurpassed in its industrial capacity. As the diagrams on p. 630 show, however, by 1870 four other nations had set out on the road to industrialization—Belgium, France, Germany, and the United States—two of which would overtake Britain in industrial capacity by 1900. Those other states had begun industrializing early, profiting from Britain's prior experience.

The Railroad and the Automobile

Claude Monet, Gare Saint-Lazare: *The 1877 work of French Impressionist painter Claude Monet captures the excitement of the railroad, which was the culminating symbol of triumphant industrialization. The huge and impressive Paris railroad station, with its multiple divergent tracks eliciting the wonder of distant lands, receives the mighty engine in its nimbus of gray smoke. (Musée d'Orsay, Paris)*

Karl Benz at the wheel: *The extraordinary century that opened with the development of the railroad closed with that of the internal combustion engine that powered the modern automobile, first available in the 1880s. Here is Karl Benz, creator of the Benz automobile, steering his new product in 1887.*

CATCHING UP

How does industrialization spread? Not like dye in water, or like an infection spread through droplets in the air. Each innovation in technology, in manufacture, in distribution had to be introduced on new ground by an individual engineer or merchant or investor. Energetic men (women did not figure noticeably in this process) from other nations visited, observed, and documented industrial processes in Britain. Or sometimes British experts, lured by the promise of bonuses or new opportunities, traveled abroad with a precious cargo of mental capital.

By a succession of such efforts—made covertly, as British law forbade the export of technology and the emigration of experts—other nations developed industrial foundations. As Map 21.2 on p. 627 shows, by 1870, much of western Europe and parts of North America were industrialized or had begun the process of industrialization. Between 1870 and 1914, other nations challenged and even surpassed the British lead, while other regions did not begin to industrialize until the twentieth century.

The First Imitators

The first imitators of industrial Britain were its neighbors in northwestern Europe—France, Belgium, and Germany—and its former North American colony, the United States. Beginning very soon after the Napoleonic settlement (see Chapter 20),

entrepreneurs in these regions began to expand the manufacture of textiles and metals, and to build railroad networks. By 1870, the industrial economies of these nations had developed to a point where they were competing directly with Britain. Germany and the United States proceeded to pass Britain's high-water mark by 1913. This later phase of industrialization, sometimes called the "Second Industrial Revolution," was characterized by the use of chemicals in manufacturing processes, electricity for power and light, and communication technologies.

France and Belgium   In the 1700s, France had been a vigorous producer of manufactures, but fell behind its rival Britain during the early industrial era of steam power. Until the late eighteenth century, France and Britain were not only the two main colonial powers, but the two leading manufacturing powers in Europe. Domestic or cottage industry flourished in France as well as Britain, producing textiles for local and foreign markets. France's iron production exceeded Britain's, while its cotton consumption was about the same.

Around 1760, Britain began to pull ahead in industrial capacity—even before the disruption caused after 1789 by the French Revolution. Signs of the quickening of Britain's economic progress are evident in the number of patents granted for new inventions, the volume of foreign trade, the rate of urbanization, and the production of textiles and iron. Though the French government actively intervened to promote the growth of manufactures, private entrepreneurship in Britain proved more effective, while economic blockades of revolutionary France reduced its ability to import raw materials. By 1800, Britain greatly exceeded France in all statistical measures of industrial activity.

Not only did Britain spurt forward at the end of the eighteenth century, but France dropped out of the race after 1789. Until Napoleon's defeat in 1815, France was preoccupied with a political and social transformation that left little opportunity, or wealth, for economic development. At the end of the revolutionary era, French manufacture had fallen below its level in 1789. In the meantime, Britain had enjoyed a near monopoly of foreign trade.

The period that followed, from the restoration of the monarchy through the inauguration of the Third Republic (1815–1871; see Chapter 20), was favorable to the development of an entrepreneurial bourgeoisie. Some of Napoleon's innovations proved helpful—the abolition of guilds, the removal of internal **tariffs**, and the standardization of commercial law. The mechanization of textile manufacture proceeded on the British model—French entrepreneurs often chose to hire skilled British workers, of whom there were as many as 15,000 working in France by 1830.

The French state actively intervened in economic matters. Through monarchical, republican, and imperial eras, official policy favored those who invested funds or launched companies, especially family firms. The government built the national railroad system (in place by the 1840s), then leased the component lines for terms of more than one hundred years to private companies. Napoleon III (r. 1850–1870) encouraged banking firms to invest in industrial ventures. Still, French industrialization was slowed by the commitment of so much of the economy to agriculture, and by the scarcity of coal and iron (exacerbated by the loss of Alsace and Lorraine to Germany in 1871, following the Franco-Prussian War). In 1870, France still lagged behind Britain, and would soon fall behind Germany and the United States.

The Belgian economy, which resembled that of France in 1789, followed its neighbor's lead and drew profitably on British expertise, in defiance of British law. A major coup was the enlistment of the Cockerill family of expert British manufacturers. William

Map 21.2 The Industrialization of Continental Europe, 1815–1860: *As in Great Britain, industrial concentration in continental Europe occurred in the vicinity of mineral deposits and major ports. The continued flow of goods was encouraged by the elimination of tariffs and customs. The German customs union (the Zollverein, 1834), which incorporated most of the German states, was one of the most effective of these various free trade systems. Why is the level of industrial activity relatively low in southern Europe (Spain, Portugal, Italy)?*

Cockerill (1759–1832) (honored with French citizenship by Napoleon in 1810 for his introduction of textile manufacture to France) built a factory system for the combined production of metals and machines in Liège (modern Belgium, under French domination 1797–1815 and Dutch domination 1815–1830). In 1812, it employed 2000 workers; by the 1830s, it was the largest such plant in the world—reflecting a mission, as one observer thought, "to fill the whole world with machinery." The machines built in Cockerill's factory permitted the rapid development of mining, shipbuilding, and railroad systems. To set up their railroad system, the Belgians hired Britain's first expert, George Stephenson.

Germany   The German nation was only constituted in 1871, at about the time that German industrial activities surged ahead to new highs of production. The earlier stages of German industrialization had been undertaken primarily by Prussia. In the eighteenth century, Frederick the Great of Prussia (1712–1786), whose talents encompassed military management, literature, and music, had also been alert to his small state's economic interests. He outlined his goals neatly: first, to bring money in from abroad; second, to prevent its seeping out to foreign countries. He promoted silk, wool, and cotton manufactures, welcomed French Huguenot and Jewish immigrants whose diligence contributed to economic development wherever they settled, and seized Silesia from neighboring Austria in part to acquire its

mineral resources, especially coal. Still, outside of the industrial regions of Saxony and the newly acquired Rhineland (1815), Prussia was primarily an agricultural nation; its prosperous manufactures formed only a small part of its economy.

Napoleon's consolidation of the German states in the early nineteenth century was, ironically, a spur not only to German nationalism but also to economic progress. (His abolition of guilds and serfdom also promoted innovation and labor mobility.) In 1834, a further consolidation for economic purposes only—the *Zollverein*, or "Customs Union"—was voluntarily adopted by nearly all the German states. With the elimination of customs barriers among these still autonomous states, new enterprises, such as modern textile factories, could flourish, and new industries find markets and resources. Among these resources were coal, which from the 1840s began to be mined intensively in the Ruhr, Silesia, and Saar regions, and iron, smelted with coke from the 1850s. Coal production increased steadily in volume (more than doubling in the period 1851–1857 alone), until Germany, having incorporated the valuable provinces of Alsace and Lorraine, became Europe's greatest producer. Bismarck had said that Germany would be unified by "blood and iron" but, a modern economist has observed, it could be more truly said to owe its success to "coal and iron."

At the same time, even before the German nation formally came into being, a German rail system developed. By 1839, with the opening of a railway from Dresden to Leipzig, the German states were on their way to the development of a mature railroad system. Construction proceeded in the 1840s, and by 1860 total German rail mileage surpassed that of any other nation of continental Europe. As elsewhere, the creation of a railroad network stimulated industry and the labor market.

At first, German observers faithfully pursued the British model of industrial development. Like the French and the Belgians, they traveled to Britain and came home with new ideas. Alfred Krupp (1812–1887), called the "Cannon King," was the most famous member of a dynasty that controlled one of Germany's largest firms into the mid-twentieth century. Krupp visited Britain in 1838 to learn about metallurgical techniques. He later established the major German steel company that made possible the new nation's rapid development of machines, ships, and weapons later in the century. At the Crystal Palace in 1851, Krupp showed off his own 4300-pound steel block, impressing even the British with the quality and mass of the product, and a gun barrel of brilliant cast steel. By 1862, he had installed a Bessemer converter at the Krupp works in the Ruhr.

Krupp's enormous metalworks were typical of German industrialization after 1871. Germany's industries grew swiftly, rivaling British capacity by

1900. German businesses tended to be on a large scale for several reasons: first, Germany possessed the natural resources that fed heavy industry; second, the state actively subsidized and promoted new enterprises and investment; and third, funding was readily provided by modern credit banks, which especially encouraged exports to foreign markets. Patterns of investment encouraged the formation of **cartels**, in which one or two large firms dominated a whole industrial sector. Only two firms, for instance, controlled ninety percent of the electrical industry, which was pioneered in Germany. Germany's rapid industrial growth can be measured in its changing share of the world output of manufactured goods: from thirteen percent in 1870 to sixteen percent in 1900, while Britain's output gradually slid from thirty-two to eighteen percent.

The United States   Like France, Belgium, and Germany, the fledgling United States learned to industrialize from Britain. Like Germany, its industrial economy surged in the last few decades of the nineteenth century during the "Second Industrial Revolution."

From early colonial days, the economy of the United States was tightly linked to Britain's. It had sent timber and tobacco to the motherland, and foodstuffs to her Caribbean colonies, enabling them to pursue the monoculture of sugar. By the middle of the eighteenth century, cotton cultivation in the southern Atlantic colonies grew steadily in volume, accelerating rapidly after the War for Independence. Cotton bound the United States economy to industrial Britain from 1783 until the 1860s, when the Civil War (1861–1865) disrupted the plantation system and put an end to slavery.

In the late eighteenth century, entrepreneurs returning from tours of inspection abroad established the first textile mills in the New England states. In 1793, Samuel Slater (1768–1835) established on the British model the first water-powered textile mill in the United States, in Rhode Island. Only fifteen more mills were built by 1808, but in 1809, eighty-seven additional mills were established. By 1814 in Waltham, Massachusetts, Francis Cabot Lowell (1775–1817) built a weaving factory designed on British models, its looms powered by steam engines. By 1831, the young industrial nation boasted 795 cotton factories, with a capacity of 1.2 million yarn spindles—nearly forty times the capacity of 1809. By the 1840s, sewing machines, invented by Isaac Singer (1811–1875), were busy in factories producing ready-made clothing.

British railroad construction won prompt attention from United States entrepreneurs. Beginning with the Baltimore and Ohio Railroad, local lines were already developed in the 1830s, and by the 1840s there were 3000 miles of interregional rail lines.

Private businessmen were the main developers of rail capacity, in contrast to France or Germany where the state dominated the establishment of railroad systems. The distances traversed by rail lines in the United States were huge, since railroads needed to carry manufactured products and migrating peoples from the Atlantic to the Pacific coast, 3000 miles away, and to return with grain and beef. The demand for boxcars and rails was consequently enormous, and stimulated steel and machine production.

Northern railroads supplied Union soldiers all along the battlefront and helped win the Civil War against the South, whose underdeveloped rail network served mostly to carry bales of cotton from farm areas to coastal ports. While the guns still roared, railroad companies began to stretch new lines across the belly of the nation. In 1869, with the war only four years over, rail lines extending from the Midwest and California met at Promontory Point, Utah, amid the peaks of the Rocky Mountains. The completion of the first transcontinental railroad anywhere on the globe was marked by the ceremonial driving of a golden spike, the hammer wielded by California entrepreneur John Leland Stanford (1824–1893). The Atlantic was now linked with the Pacific, from whose coast the West would find another vantagepoint on the East.

Railroad development encouraged other economic projects. It not only boosted machine and metal production, but facilitated the distribution of textiles and other manufactures, and foodstuffs. Another factor in industrial development was the existence of a large mobile labor force, augmented after the 1840s by immigration from Europe (especially refugees from the Irish famine) and, to a lesser extent, Asia. Government support in the form of federal land grants to entrepreneurs venturing westward was helpful, while government interference remained limited. By the 1870s, large corporations such as Andrew Carnegie's (1835–1919) steelworks employed hundreds or even thousands of workers, who shopped in company-run stores and were supervised by a private police force—maintained unapologetically by a man who would become one of the greatest United States philanthropists.

Although the economy of the United States remained heavily agricultural, its agricultural production was increasingly mechanized with the invention of tractors and harvesting machinery, and refrigeration systems for rail cars and steamships. The nation's seemingly limitless natural resources—both mineral and agricultural—and its ambitious, often ruthless entrepreneurs, had by 1914 made the United States the world's leading industrial nation.

The Second Phase   By this late date—more than a century after the founding of the first textile mills, or the refinement of the steam engine—industrialization on both sides of the Atlantic had entered a second

Patterns of European Economic Development: 1850–1873

	1850	1869	1873
Britain			
Railroad	6,621	15,145	16,082
Coal	37,500	97,066	112,604
Steam power	1,290	4,040	
Pig iron	2,249	5,446	6,566
Raw cotton	266.8	425.8	565.1
Germany			
Railroad	3,639	10,834	14,842
Coal	5,100	26,774	36,392
Steam power	260	2,480	
Pig iron	212	1,413	2,241
Raw cotton	17.1	64.1	117.8
France			
Railroad	1,869	10,518	11,500
Coal	7,225	21,432	24,702
Steam power	370	1,850	
Pig iron	406	1,381	1,382
Raw cotton	59.3	93.7	55.4
Belgium			
Railroad	531	1,800	2,335
Coal	3,481	7,822	10,219
Steam power	70	350	
Pig iron	145	535	607
Raw cotton	10.0	16.3	18.0

By five measures of economic development—total railroad mileage (statute miles), coal production (1000 metric tons), steam power capacity (1000 horsepower), pig iron output (1000 metric tons), and raw cotton consumption (1000 metric tons)—Britain outpaced her three leading European rivals from 1850 to 1873. The gap narrowed, however, especially between Germany and Britain. Note Germany's sevenfold increase in coal production, compared to Britain's threefold increase, and Germany's sevenfold increase in cotton consumption, compared to Britain's, which slightly more than doubled.
Source: Based on D. Landes, The Unbound Prometheus (Cambridge: Cambridge University Press, 1969), p. 194.

phase. Joining the heavy industries (metals and textiles) of early industrialization, were newer industries concerned with producing chemicals or providing gas and electrical power. Chemical products (often derived from petroleum) were employed in textile manufacture, agriculture, mining, and construction in the form of dyes, fertilizers, or explosives. From the early 1800s, gas lamps illuminated streets, shops,

Map 21.3 Industrialized Europe by 1914: *By 1914, areas of industrial concentration in Europe had increased in number and the railroad system was greatly expanded (compare Map 21.2, p. 627).* Why do railroads and industry go hand-in-hand in this era?

homes, and factories—"Gas has replaced the sun!" exclaimed one contemporary enthusiastically.

Electricity soon replaced gas as a source of power. In 1879, the American Thomas Edison (1847–1931) invented the incandescent light bulb, making electricity usable to light homes and public places. By the 1880s, electricity had taken over for the lighting of city streets, department stores, hotels, and public buildings. Gradually, ordinary homes were wired, and housewives felt privileged to have sewing machines, refrigerators, and vacuum cleaners that operated by electrical power. Electricity powered local transportation—the streetcars or "trolley" cars that first opened up suburban housing for workers, who were enabled to live in surroundings pleasanter than the immediate area of their industrial workplace. Bicycles, too, allowed workers to glide swiftly through city streets and in the countryside. By 1885, a workable internal combustion engine was available to power the first generation of automobiles. By 1909, a French observer announced: "It's finished, the tranquility of our streets, and the charm of promenading either on foot or in a carriage. ... Paris belongs to the machines."

Communications, meanwhile, had developed to meet the needs of entrepreneurs around the globe. First the telegraph (which could communicate even across the Atlantic ocean, thanks to a cable laid in 1866), then the telephone, patented by Alexander Graham Bell (1847–1922) in 1876, conquered the distances that modern economies traversed. From the

1890s, wireless communication was made possible by the work of Guglielmo Marconi (1874–1937), and by the early 1900s radio broadcasts could be received in ordinary households. During those same years, silent motion pictures began to be screened (by 1908, France had more than 1000 movie theaters), and couples could dance in their living rooms to music produced by the gramophone (see Chapter 26).

As Map 21.3 shows, by 1914, Western civilization had been transformed by industrialization, and could be called modern—for industry, which brought machines into the garden of traditional society, was in itself the creator of modernity.

The Rest of the West and the Asian Vanguard

By 1870, France, Belgium, Germany, and the United States had joined the select circle of industrialized nations. Over the next generation, other European nations entered—the Netherlands and Scandinavia, northern Italy, parts of Spain, Portugal, and Ireland, Poland and the region around Prague (the present-day Czech Republic), following in the footsteps of earlier neighbors. So too did Russia, as well as Canada, Australia, and Japan.

Tsar Peter the Great (r. 1682–1725) had put Russia on the path to industrialization. He traveled himself to western European nations, studying their military and shipbuilding technology especially. The

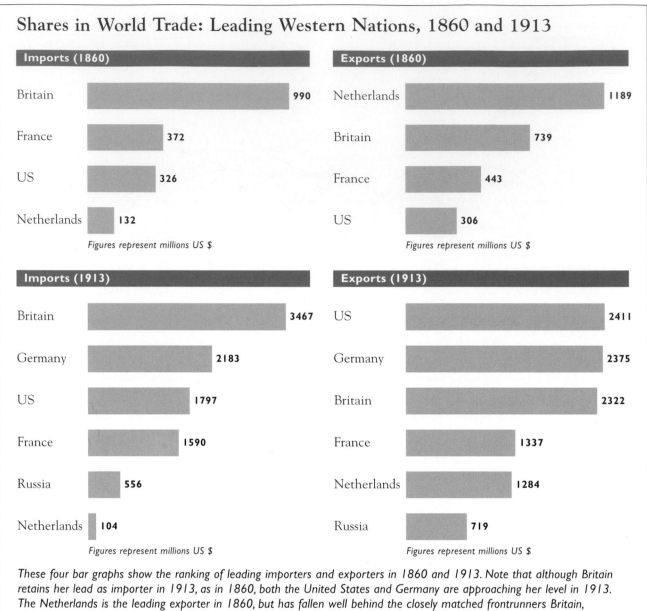

Shares in World Trade: Leading Western Nations, 1860 and 1913

Imports (1860)

Britain	990
France	372
US	326
Netherlands	132

Figures represent millions US $

Exports (1860)

Netherlands	1189
Britain	739
France	443
US	306

Figures represent millions US $

Imports (1913)

Britain	3467
Germany	2183
US	1797
France	1590
Russia	556
Netherlands	104

Figures represent millions US $

Exports (1913)

US	2411
Germany	2375
Britain	2322
France	1337
Netherlands	1284
Russia	719

Figures represent millions US $

These four bar graphs show the ranking of leading importers and exporters in 1860 and 1913. Note that although Britain retains her lead as importer in 1913, as in 1860, both the United States and Germany are approaching her level in 1913. The Netherlands is the leading exporter in 1860, but has fallen well behind the closely matched frontrunners Britain, Germany, and the United States—with the latter in the lead.

state supported the production of heavy manufactures, and eighty-six manufacturing enterprises were launched. By the end of the eighteenth century, Russia's iron production was second only to Britain's, and its urban populations had tripled.

These ventures had a limited impact, however, given the vastness of the nation and its entrenched system of agricultural production based on serf labor. In the nineteenth century, Russia industrialized but only slowly, on the model established by Britain in the previous century. In 1805, a steam engine was first used for cotton manufacture. In 1836, Cort's puddling process was introduced for the production of iron. Beginning in 1843, foreign consultants oversaw the importation and installation of updated machinery for textile manufacture, and planned the development of railroad and steamship systems. From 1820, a steamboat regularly plied the river Volga. By 1851, a rail line ran from St. Petersburg to Moscow. The numbers of factories and free (non-serf) laborers multiplied, while serf workers labored in industrial workshops and serf entrepreneurs built and extended them.

But the economic base on which these impressive increases rested was inadequate. The nation was overwhelmingly agricultural (and continued demand for basic commodities—timber, grain, wax—encouraged it to remain so). Moreover, Russia had no tradition of artisan manufacture and only a tiny merchant class—about one-fourth of one percent of the population. The tsars' earnest support and the purchased services of Western experts had slight impact.

A transformation of the Russian economy along modern lines would only begin in the last years of the nineteenth century. By that time, a full generation after the abolition of serfdom, large numbers of laborers released from the land were available. These joined the skilled, mobile workers clustered in those cities large enough to support full-scale industrialization, funded by foreign capital. The exploitation of coal fields near the Black Sea, oil wells near the Caspian Sea, and iron lodes in the Ural Mountains, linked now by railroad to western Russian centers, made Russia competitive with the most advanced nations of the West. Urbanization gathered pace, the urban population rising from under 6 million around 1860 to more than 23 million in 1913. During this period, the population of Moscow increased from 500,000 to more than 1.5 million, and that of St. Petersburg from about 500,000 to

2 million. Despite a slow start, St. Petersburg, boasting 900 factories in 1914, was an industrial center among the largest in Europe.

In the Russian industrialization of the 1890s, Minister of Finance Sergei Witte (1849–1915), quoted in *Witnesses* below, labored to promote important enterprises and to lure foreign capital to fund them. Above all, he saw to the construction of an improved railroad system that linked Moscow and St. Petersburg to ocean ports and navigable rivers, and to manufacturing, agricultural, and mining centers. In 1899, under his direction, more than 3000 miles of the Trans-Siberian railway line had been completed. Arching across the whole continent of Asia, it opened Siberia to colonization. When he was dismissed in 1906,

---

WITNESSES

Catching Up in Argentina, Germany, and Russia

By the middle and late nineteenth century, other nations of the Western world—including those across the Atlantic Ocean—were rushing in order to follow Britain's lead in industrialization. Here, policy advisers in Argentina, the German states, and the Russian empire greet with enthusiasm the challenge their nations faced to modernize and compete in a changed world.

Argentinian journalist and diplomat Juan Bautista Alberdi hails the railroad as a tool for unity and prosperity (1852): The railroad offers the means of righting the topsy-turvy order that Spain established in this continent. She placed the heads of our state where the feet should be. For her ends of isolation and monopoly this was a wise system; for our aims of commercial expansion and freedom it is disastrous. We must bring our capitals to the coast, or rather bring the coast into the interior of the continent. The railroad and the electric telegraph, the conquerors of space, work this wonder better than all the potentates on earth. The railroad changes, reforms, and solves the most difficult problems without decrees or mob violence. It will forge the unity of the Argentine Republic better than all our congresses. The congresses may declare it "one and indivisible," but without the railroad to connect its most remote regions it will always remain divided and divisible, despite all the legislative decrees.
(From B. Keen ed., *Latin American Civilization: History and Society, 1492 to the Present*, 4th ed., 1986)

Friedrich List on England's leadership in global industrialization (1841): Far from having been stopped in its progress by England, the world has received from her its strongest impulse. She has served as a model to all nations in her internal and external policy; in her great inventions and grand enterprises of every kind; in the advancement of the useful arts; in the construction of roads, railways and canals; in the discovery and cultivation of lands in a state of nature, particularly

in displaying and developing the natural wealth of tropical countries, and in the civilization of tribes, savage or subsiding into barbarism. Who can tell how far behind the world would have been if there had been no England?
(Friedrich List, *The National System of Political Development*, 1941; ed. T. H. von Laue, 1969)

Russian Finance Minister Sergei Witte argues that Russia must industrialize if it is to flourish (1900): The experience of all peoples clearly shows that only the economically independent countries are fully able to assert their political power. ... At present the political strength of the great powers which are called to fulfill great historical tasks in the world is created not only by the spiritual valor of their peoples but also by their economic organization. Even the military preparedness of a country is determined not only by the perfection of its military machine but by the degree of its industrial development. Russia ... needs ... a proper economic foundation for her national policy and her culture. ... International competition does not wait. If we do not take energetic and decisive measures so that in the course of the next decades our industry will be able to satisfy the need of Russia and of the Asiatic countries which are—or should be—under our influence, then the rapidly growing foreign industries will break through our tariff barriers and establish themselves in our fatherland and in the Asiatic countries mentioned above and drive their roots into the depths of our economy. This may gradually clear the way also for triumphant political penetration by foreign powers. ... It is possible that the slow growth of our industries will endanger the fulfillment of the great political tasks of the monarchy. Our economic backwardness may lead to political and cultural backwardness as well.
(Sergei Witte, "On the Condition of Our Industry," 1900; ed. T. H. von Laue, 1969)

WHO'S WHO

Inventors of the Industrial Age: Transportation and Communication

George Stephenson (1781–1848) the locomotive

Robert Fulton (1765–1815) the steamboat

Thomas Edison (1847–1931) the incandescent lightbulb

Alexander Graham Bell (1847–1922) the telephone

Guglielmo Marconi (1874–1937) the radio

Russian industrialization, though still lagging behind the leaders of western Europe, was well under way.

The economies of colonial Latin America—Spanish and Portuguese, Caribbean and continental—were firmly linked, like the English and French ones of North America, to Europe (see Chapters 16, 19). The trade in tobacco, rice, and indigo, timber, fur, and fish in the latter case; silver, gold, and sugar in the former, formed chains across the Atlantic.

The silver and gold extracted from South American mines, mainly with native Amerindian labor, flowed through Spain and Portugal for three centuries, and provided Europe generally with the bullion necessary to trade with the nations of Asia. Sugar from Brazil and the Caribbean islands, raised and harvested mainly by imported African slaves, fed European appetites no longer content with a diet of bread and soup. In all these cases, the pattern is the same: the fruits of the earth, the produce of the mine, or the bounty of the fields were sent to Europe. In return came manufactured goods, especially metal products and textiles, such as the cotton fabric used to clothe plantation slaves, purchased in the Americas primarily by those of European descent. Thus supplied, they spurned the cruder handicrafts produced by native artisans. This trading pattern was distinctly unbalanced to the disadvantage of the dark-skinned laborers of Latin America.

Although the commodities traded changed with time, the same pattern prevailed for a century after the 1820s, the point at which most Latin American nations (all but Cuba and Puerto Rico, and the English and French Caribbean colonies) achieved their independence (see Chapter 19). The exports of silver and gold dwindled, to be replaced by other profitable products of the mines and large landed estates (**latifundias**): nitrates and tin, coffee, beef, and grain, medicinal plants and dyestuffs. The manufactured goods received in return were now machine-made textiles and metals, which competed with, and

dispirited native artisans. Sugar exports from the Caribbean continued to flow, as Europeans continued to favor a variety of sweet treats and sweeteners for the exotic beverages, coffee and tea, that they had made their own.

In this context, Latin America failed to industrialize. Beginning in the 1850s, railroad lines were built to bring goods from the mines and the *latifundias* to the ports (see *Witnesses*, p. 633). Trade was directed toward Europe, and not toward the vast interior which remained largely untouched by the rail. Steam engines were employed in updated mines, thanks to foreign investment capital, mostly British. They also powered sugar refineries as early as 1815, requiring slaves to produce more and more raw cane to feed the vigorous new machines. But the failure to acquire the machinery for local manufacture was virtually total. As a consequence, Latin America as a whole lagged well behind the industrialized nations of the world into the twentieth century—despite its vigorous participation in foreign trade, and despite the wealth of a thin stratum of elite consumers, landowners, and entrepreneurs.

A quite different pattern holds for the far-flung British colonies of Australia, New Zealand, and Canada, later independent units of the Commonwealth, which was from 1931 the political association of former British colonies (see Chapter 27). These regions began to claim a stake in world trade (based at first on exports of abundant raw materials, such as foodstuffs, wool, and minerals) and industrial development by the late nineteenth century. As industrial powers, their fuller development, however, belongs to the twentieth century.

Apart from European nations, their colonies, and former colonies, Japan was the sole region to industrialize before the twentieth century. It did so because of the shocking challenge presented to its proud traditional culture by the advent, from the 1850s, of foreign economic intervention backed by the threat of force (see Chapter 24). Until that date, Japan, like China, considered itself economically self-sufficient. Although largely agricultural, it produced fine craft manufactures, and had some familiarity with Western gun technology (the gift of the Dutch merchants who, alone of Europeans, were allowed to deal with the Japanese through the port of Nagasaki).

Once "opened," however, by the arrival of the American Commodore Matthew Perry (1794–1858), the Japanese accomplished within a generation an astounding political and economic revolution. By the 1880s, Japan had established a textile-based industrial economy, which featured steam-driven factories, modern machinery, vigorous steel production, and an effective system of transportation by railroad and steamship. The Japanese economic miracle continued to flower into the next century, enabling it to defeat militarily a European rival—Russia—as early as 1905 (see Chapter 24).

Postponed Industrialization

By 1870, industrialization had reached maturity in several Western nations, and had begun in others, as it had in Japan. Elsewhere in Asia and Africa—in India, China, southeast Asia and Oceania; in the Middle East, North Africa, and Sub-Saharan Africa—industrialization had to wait until the twentieth century. During the 1800s, these regions exported cheaply-priced resources to the West, and in return purchased expensive manufactured goods, to their economic disadvantage (see Chapter 24).

Prior to the mechanization of British textile manufacture, as has been seen, India had been not only an active participant in Afro-Asian commerce, but also an active center as producer and exporter of cotton cloth. By the 1830s, it had become a consumer of British manufactures, including cotton textiles. In less than two generations, India had been transformed from a productive region to a non-productive one. The continued British presence (until 1947) meant that the Indian economy continued to serve British needs, as market and as provider of resources. The construction of a major railroad network from the 1850s, carrying both freight and passengers, increased mobility and stimulated commerce. But it did not encourage India to develop its own industries. Rather,

it facilitated the export of cash crops, including raw cotton, and the penetration of British manufacturers deep into the interior of the vast sub-continent.

Further east, China, like India, had played a central role in the Asian economy for many centuries. China produced prized manufactures, notably silk and porcelain, as well as tea, an expensive agricultural commodity. Her busy merchants carried these exports overland to India and western Asia, and shipped them throughout the South China Sea and western Pacific—to Korea and Japan, southeast Asia and Oceania. Despite China's strong economic position, however, it lagged behind with regard to the West at a critical juncture.

In China, the prevailing philosophy of Confucianism inhibited the development of industrialization. Confucianism denigrated merchants and profit-seeking, an attitude that was a disincentive to industrial development. Moreover, households with a surplus that could have been invested in commerce or manufacture generally preferred to invest in education for their sons, since the chief road to advancement was through the examination system to positions in government which conferred wealth and prestige. Any further surplus would have been invested in land, which became even more valuable as, especially with the demographic crisis of the

Liberia's first railway: Industrialization has achieved global proportions in the twentieth century, as suggested by this photograph of Liberian workers building that nation's first railroad in 1950—one hundred years after Britain, the homeland of the steam engine, had completed its essential railroad grid.

eighteenth century forward, population pressures made it a scarce commodity. Precisely when innovation was needed, the reigning Manchu or Qing dynasty (1644–1912) finally began to weaken.

Meanwhile, Western nations sought greater access to Chinese ports, jealously closed to foreigners (see Chapter 24). In 1793 and 1816, the British sent representatives to China seeking more favorable treaty arrangements. Huge quantities of tea, which the British public craved, triggered these overtures. In this period, tea made up about half of British imports from China, which increased nearly eightfold between the 1780s and 1815. In exchange for tea, the British offered textiles, lead, and tin—and, covertly and illegally, opium processed from the poppy crop grown in India. Chinese officials were uninterested in the former, and furious about the latter.

In 1837, the imperial official Lin Tse-Hsu (1785–1850) addressed to the British Queen Victoria (r. 1837–1901) a stern letter about the opium trade. Whereas the Chinese exported many goods, all of benefit to humanity, he wrote, the British sent to China, along with benign products, an addictive poison. How could they sanction exposing Chinese people to a dangerous substance not permitted to their own citizens? To stop the traffic in drugs, the Chinese would severely punish any foreigner found participating in it—the penalty being decapitation. Not long after, the First Opium War (1839–1842) broke out, in which British warships shelled several Chinese ports that were completely defenseless against superior Western weaponry. By the 1842 Treaty of Nanjing, the British gained access to Guangzhou (Canton), Shanghai, and other ports.

Thereafter, several Western nations followed the British in "opening up" China to trade. As in India, the influx of Western manufactures had the unfortunate effect of retarding China's own industrial development. The first successful railroad, which was simply a short line for hauling coal to port, dated only from 1882. No factories for the machine production of textiles were established until the end of the century. The lofty Chinese empire sank rapidly to economic dependence upon contact with the West.

The experience of the Ottoman states of North Africa and western Asia followed a similar trajectory. These regions considered themselves superior to Europe in every regard—in religion, in statecraft, and in commerce. In the course of the nineteenth century, however, Western manufactures had their now familiar, and fatal, effects on native economies. Despite attempts, especially in Egypt, to establish factories under the guidance of Western advisers, these regions continued to fail to industrialize. They became exporters of agricultural and mineral commodities, locked into an unfavorable trade relationship with the European nations.

The nations of Sub-Saharan Africa were even less able than India, China, or the Ottoman Empire to withstand the economic dominance of Europe. With the cessation of the slave trade during the nineteenth century, their merchants were starved for cash. Despite a strong commercial tradition, and long experience in the manufacture of iron, Africans, too, became suppliers of raw materials to the industrialized West. That economic subordination, as will be seen, was merely a prelude to an even more complete subordination to those nations.

Conclusion
DESPOILED GARDENS AND THE MEANING OF THE WEST

By 1870, the productivity of the Western world far exceeded any measure imaginable in 1770. More things were made than ever before; exchanged faster; and sent further afield. The agent of this nearly inconceivable jump in material capacity was the machine operating by non-human, non-animal power—this was the first important innovation in the human ability to produce since the first human ancestor wielded the first tool.

Henceforth, humankind would share its earthly domain with the machine. For Enlightenment thinkers, the human being was much like a machine—a wholly rational being, a mechanism governed by mind. Julien Offray de la Mettrie (1709–1751), a case in point, argued in his aptly titled *Man the Machine* (1748) that the soul was nothing more than an extension of the body, itself a mechanical system. Now the machine approached the realm of the human. Like their human inventors, machines made things, and machines made machines. The machine commanded its human operator to tend it and feed it. If the human was a machine, could the machine be seen as possessing spirit, as it possessed heat and locomotion? Could the machine do good or evil?

The new machines caused Enlightenment optimism to cloud over, giving way to a darker, indeed Satanic, vision. The machines that invaded and despoiled the gardens of Western civilization promised abundance, but they devastated nature and deformed human lives. The following chapters will consider the impact of the machine on human society in the West and beyond, and on the ideas and images created by those who lived under its sway.

QUESTIONS TO CONSIDER

1. Why did the Industrial Revolution happen first in England?

2. What is the relation between textile manufacture and industrialization? What role did cotton play in the preliminary stages of industrialization?

3. How did the same machine—the steam engine—revolutionize both manufacturing and transportation?

4. Why were some countries able to catch up quickly with England in industrial capacity, and others only more slowly?

5. Worldwide, to what extent was the state a major factor in industrialization? To what extent did industrialization come about because of individual initiative?

SUGGESTED RESOURCES

Auerbach, Jeffrey A., *The Great Exhibition of 1851: A Nation on Display* (New Haven: Yale University Press, 1999). Highlights the struggle by competing interests to define the Great Exhibition, with consequences for the future.

Hills, Richard, *Power from Steam: A History of the Stationary Steam Engine* (Cambridge: Cambridge University Press, 1993). A comprehensive history of the steam engine from Savery and Newcomen, to Watt, to the age of electricity.

Johnson, Christopher H., *The Life and Death of Industrial Languedoc, 1700–1920* (Oxford: Oxford University Press, 1995). Studies a case of deindustrialization in a region of southern France which had begun to introduce new technology and build a modern wool industry, but began to decline in the later 19th century.

Kemp, Tom, *Industrialization in the Non-Western World* (2nd ed.; London: Longman, 1989). Traces the path to industrialization in six non-Western nations: Japan, the Soviet Union, India, China, Brazil, and Nigeria.

Mazlish, Bruce, *The Fourth Discontinuity: The Co-Evolution of Humans and Machines* (New Haven: Yale University Press, 1993). Imaginative exploration of the interactive development of humans and machines.

Milward, Alan S. and S. B. Saul, *The Development of the Economies of Continental Europe, 1850–1914* (Cambridge, MA: Harvard University Press, 1977). Detailed study of the economic history of European industrialization.

Mokyr, Joel, ed., *The British Industrial Revolution: An Economic Perspective* (2nd ed.; Boulder: Westview Press, 1998). Five essays assessing recent views of the Industrial Revolution.

Morris-Suzuki, Tessa, *The Technological Transformation of Japan from the Seventeenth to the Twenty-First Century* (Cambridge: Cambridge University Press, 1994). Good, general economic history of Japan over several centuries. Synthesizes Japanese and Western scholarship.

Ogilvie, Sheilagh C. & Markus Cerman, eds., *European Proto-Industrialization: An Introductory Handbook* (Cambridge: Cambridge University Press, 1996). Essays tracing the development of small-scale export industries between 1500 and 1800, constituting a stage of economic activity preliminary to the so-called "Industrial Revolution."

Overton, Mark, *Agricultural Revolution in England: The Transformation of the Agrarian Economy 1500–1850* (Cambridge: Cambridge University Press, 1996). General introduction to the changes in farming that helped create Britain's rising wealth and which ultimately facilitated industrialization.

Smail, John, *Merchants, Markets and Manufacture: The English Wool Textile Industry in the Eighteenth Century* (New York: St. Martin's, 1999). Notes the importance of product innovation and of export trade, describing not only what merchants and producers did, but how they thought about it.

Stearns, Peter N., *The Industrial Revolution in World History* (Boulder, CO: Westview Press, 1993). Integrates and compares industrialization in Britain, Europe, the US, Russia, Japan, the Pacific Rim, Latin America, and elsewhere.

Timmins, Geoffrey, *The Last Shift: The Decline of Handloom Weaving in Nineteenth-Century Lancashire* (New York: St. Martins Press, 1993). Nineteenth-century handloom weavers are seen as the exemplar of skilled artisans replaced—and in many cases ruined—by technological advances in the textile industry.

Steam Engine Library, with links to contemporary texts about early industrialization:
http://www.history.rochester.edu/steam

Age of Industry, links to biographies and texts relevant to the Industrial Revolution (Northwestern University):
http://history.evansville.net/industry.html

Samuel Slater, Father of the American Industrial Revolution (geocities), text and images:
http://www.geocities.com/~woon_heritage/slater.htm

⊙ Western Civilization Documents CD-ROM

16.5 The Creation of the Steam Loom
16.6 Protesting the Machines
22.1 Extolling the Virtues of the Manufacturer

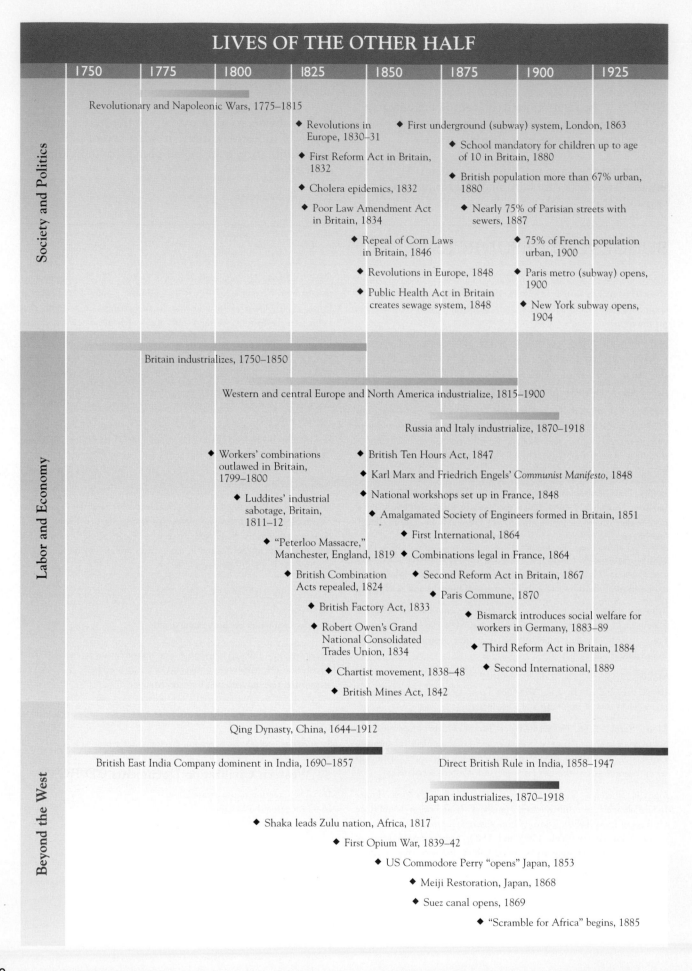

CHAPTER 222

LIVES OF THE OTHER HALF

| 1750 | 1775 | 1800 | 1825 | 1850 | 1875 | 1900 | 1925 |

Society and Politics

Revolutionary and Napoleonic Wars, 1775–1815

◆ Revolutions in Europe, 1830–31

◆ First underground (subway) system, London, 1863

◆ First Reform Act in Britain, 1832

◆ School mandatory for children up to age of 10 in Britain, 1880

◆ Cholera epidemics, 1832

◆ British population more than 67% urban, 1880

◆ Poor Law Amendment Act in Britain, 1834

◆ Nearly 75% of Parisian streets with sewers, 1887

◆ Repeal of Corn Laws in Britain, 1846

◆ 75% of French population urban, 1900

◆ Revolutions in Europe, 1848

◆ Paris metro (subway) opens, 1900

◆ Public Health Act in Britain creates sewage system, 1848

◆ New York subway opens, 1904

Labor and Economy

Britain industrializes, 1750–1850

Western and central Europe and North America industrialize, 1815–1900

Russia and Italy industrialize, 1870–1918

◆ Workers' combinations outlawed in Britain, 1799–1800

◆ British Ten Hours Act, 1847

◆ Karl Marx and Friedrich Engels' *Communist Manifesto*, 1848

◆ Luddites' industrial sabotage, Britain, 1811–12

◆ National workshops set up in France, 1848

◆ Amalgamated Society of Engineers formed in Britain, 1851

◆ "Peterloo Massacre," Manchester, England, 1819

◆ First International, 1864

◆ Combinations legal in France, 1864

◆ British Combination Acts repealed, 1824

◆ Second Reform Act in Britain, 1867

◆ Paris Commune, 1870

◆ British Factory Act, 1833

◆ Bismarck introduces social welfare for workers in Germany, 1883–89

◆ Robert Owen's Grand National Consolidated Trades Union, 1834

◆ Third Reform Act in Britain, 1884

◆ Second International, 1889

◆ Chartist movement, 1838–48

◆ British Mines Act, 1842

Beyond the West

Qing Dynasty, China, 1644–1912

British East India Company dominent in India, 1690–1857

Direct British Rule in India, 1858–1947

Japan industrializes, 1870–1918

◆ Shaka leads Zulu nation, Africa, 1817

◆ First Opium War, 1839–42

◆ US Commodore Perry "opens" Japan, 1853

◆ Meiji Restoration, Japan, 1868

◆ Suez canal opens, 1869

◆ "Scramble for Africa" begins, 1885

CHAPTER
22

LIVES OF THE OTHER HALF

Western Society in an Industrial Age

1750–1914

population density:

☐ under 50 per square mile	■ 100-200 per square mile
■ 50-100 per square mile	■ over 200 per square mile
■ cities with a population of over 1 million	

KEY QUESTIONS

◆ **Workers and Workplace:** How did the workers subjected to the harsh conditions imposed by industrialization respond? What benefits had they achieved by the eve of World War I?

◆ **The Industrial City:** What was the impact of industrialization on the life of the European city—population levels, street life, leisure activities, structures and infrastructures?

◆ **The Two Halves at Home:** What were the conditions in which the wealthy and the poor lived in townhouse and tenement? How did their experiences differ?

Domains of Rich and Poor   In his 1890 book How The Other Half Lives, *the photojournalist Jacob Riis (1849–1914) revealed to middle-class New Yorkers the unhappy and desperate lives of the laboring poor and the hopelessly poor trapped in the seamier districts of their city. Only a few steps away from prosperity, he wrote, we encounter poverty. "We stand upon the domain of the tenement. ... Suppose we look into one?" And so we shall.*

This chapter surveys the lives of rich and poor in nineteenth-century cities transformed by the advent of the machine. It peers into the places where workers labored and the places where they lived. Then it will cross town to visit other neighborhoods, not far away but a world apart, to consider the lives of the rich, whose wealth depended on the labor of those who owned nothing and commanded no one—those of the other half.

In industrial society, the poor were many and various. They were wageworkers who hauled loads and constructed homes, railroad stations, and public buildings; they were skilled **artisans** who tailored men's clothing or made precision tools; they were laundresses, prostitutes, thieves, and the jobless; and they were, most conspicuously, the new social group of **factory** workers, or **proletarians**. All lived together in the squalid streets of bursting cities, where they contended with filth, disease, and crime.

Across town (or sometimes just around the corner), lived the wealthy, not nearly so numerous, yet still various. Among the rich were the modern descendants of the old nobility, and the heirs of the old bourgeoisie—bankers, merchants, and professionals (including lawyers, physicians, engineers, accountants, and university professors). Preeminent among the bourgeoisie was a new group of factory owners, investors, and entrepreneurs: the capitalists, whose enterprises harnessed the power of machines to generate profits that were reinvested to create even more wealth. The rich lived in a world apart from the poor—a world filled with broad boulevards, grand homes, lavish consumption, and elaborate social ritual.

As the machine transformed the landscape of the Western world, it also transformed society, whose two halves in their separate domains, the rich and the poor, now faced each other in a new setting, across new and daunting barriers.

WORKERS AND WORKPLACE

As industrialization proceeded from the late eighteenth into the early nineteenth century (see Chapter 21), the nature of work changed. Machines established the framework of things, and workers obeyed the command of their clatter and roar. Machines transformed people just as they transformed the workplace, creating in the industrial proletariat a self-conscious working class—organized "labor."

Mine, Mill, and Factory

Workers in the mine pit, water-powered mill, and steam-driven factory experienced labor conditions harsher than those that rural workers knew in their villages, cottages, and fields. Workers of all ages and both sexes labored long days, in poor light and bad air, with little time to eat or rest. They were unprotected from dangerous equipment and subject to the peremptory commands and stern punishments of foremen or owners. Passages in *Witnesses* on p. 641 give an insight into the lives of factory workers.

The underground universe of the mine had always been a place of horror for those who probed the earth's recesses for tin and copper, gold and silver, iron and coal. In antiquity, slaves were employed to work the mines—an expendable workforce who could be subjected to heavy loads, noxious gases, and frequent cave-ins and explosions. The same risks attended mining in the early modern era, when heightened demand for iron and coal required deeper pits and more intensive production. These risks were often borne by the most fragile workers. Children, for example, were assigned to haul goods from the deepest mine tunnels because their slight bodies could adapt to the cramped underground spaces. Conditions in the mines only deteriorated as industrialization progressed and demand for their products increased.

Meanwhile, in the mills, rows of large machines wound newspun yarn on multiple spindles. Little was expected of their human operators, who were there to provide fresh raw fiber, realign yarn that had wandered or snapped, and keep up with the relentless pace of the machine. The machines themselves did the work, without artistry perhaps, but also without fatigue.

The relation between the worker and his work—more often her work in the early days of the mill—changed drastically. Previously a woman alone would spin all that was required for her family. Equipped with the simple distaff or spindle, she worked at home, amid childcare and household duties, assisted by unmarried female kin and neighbors. Her husband or some other local artisan would weave the thread into cloth in his cottage or workshop. In the proto-industrial "putting-out" system (see Chapter 16)—also called "domestic" or "cottage industry"—both spinning and weaving were performed on contract for production beyond household needs. The entrepreneur and his agents managed supplies, assigned fees, and collected profits, but left the village environment and the social world of the cottage unaltered.

With the advent of the mill, the cottage workers—men, women, and children—journeyed from the village to the river's edge. There they worked under the formal direction of an overseer and at the pace set by the machine. Just as, for centuries, many of the textile workers had been women, women were numerous among the employees of the mills. And just as their children had assisted with simpler tasks at home—washing, carrying, sorting—they, too, joined the labor force in the mill. The first generations of industrial workers consisted of all the members of the pre-industrial family, as yet unaltered by the requirements of modern industrial processes.

When the mills expanded to become factories—buildings containing many machines—the machine became a tyrant. Huge, belching, raucous steam engines, fed with mountains of coal by laborers' shovels, powered the machines which could be multiplied to the limit of the factory's power capacity. The workforce expanded to meet the demands of the machines. Battalions of workers streamed into the factories at a set hour, announced by the clocks and bells and whistles that governed precious industrial time.

Strict rules enforced by a system of fines and punishments disciplined this large and potentially restive labor force. Workers were required to report to work and depart at certain set hours. They were to avoid surly or aggressive behavior, keep their own workplace clean, and meet a work schedule. Corporal punishment, especially of children, kept the tired or the resistant properly at work, with summary dismissal as a final sanction. These oppressive regulations kept

---

WITNESSES

The Factory Observed

The first generations of factory labor were the harshest, as owners drove workers ruthlessly, and brought in women and young children to work under the most arduous conditions. Defenders of industry, like the author of the first excerpt given here, were not troubled by these conditions. The next two authors give the other, more accurate, view of the conditions of factory labor.

Andrew Ure, defender of industrialization, gives high marks to factory conditions for child laborers (1835): I have visited many factories ... entering the spinning rooms, unexpectedly, and often alone, at different times of the day, and I never saw a single instance of corporal chastisement inflicted on a child, nor indeed did I ever see children in ill-humour. They seemed to be always cheerful and alert, taking pleasure in the light play of their muscles,—enjoying the mobility natural to their age. ... It was delightful to observe the nimbleness with which they pieced the broken ends, as the mule-carriage began to recede from the fixed roller-beam. ... The work of these lively elves seemed to resemble a sport. ... As to exhaustion by the day's work, they evinced no trace of it on emerging from the mill in the evening; for they immediately began to skip about any neighboring playground, and to commence their little amusements with the same alacrity as boys issuing from a school.
(Andrew Ure, *The Philosophy of Manufactures*, 1835; eds. G. B. Kirsch et al, *ibid*, 1997)

P. Gaskell describes the appearance of English factory workers in 1833: Any man who has stood at twelve o'clock at the single narrow door-way, which serves as the place of exit for the hands employed in the great cotton-mills, must acknowledge, that an uglier set of men and women, of boys and girls, ... it would be impossible to congregate in a smaller compass. Their complexion is sallow and pallid—with a peculiar flatness of feature, caused by the want of a proper quantity of adipose substance to cushion out the cheeks. Their stature low—the average height of four hundred men, measured at different times, and different places, being five feet six inches. Their limbs slender, and playing badly and ungracefully. A very general bowing of the legs. Great numbers of girls and women walking lamely or awkwardly. ... Hair thin and straight—many of the men having but little beard, and that in patches of a few hairs. ... A spiritless and dejected air... .
(From P. Gaskell, *The Manufacturing Population of England*, London: Baldwin & Cradock, 1833
http://landow.stg.brown.edu/victorian/history/workers2.html)

Flora Tristan reports on conditions in English factories (1842): Most workers lack clothing, bed, furniture, fuel, wholesome food—even potatoes! They spend from twelve to fourteen hours each day shut up in low-ceilinged rooms where with every breath of foul air they absorb fibres of cotton, wool or flax, or particles of copper, lead or iron. They live suspended between an insufficiency of food and an excess of strong drink; they are all wizened, sickly and emaciated; their bodies are thin and frail, their limbs feeble, their complexions pale, their eyes dead. ... In English factories ... you will never hear snatches of song, conversation and laughter. The master does not like his workers to be distracted from their toil for one moment by any reminder they are living human beings; he insists on silence, and a deathly silence reigns. ... Between master and man there exist [no] ... bonds of familiarity, courtesy and concern ... bonds which soften the feelings of hatred and envy that the rich, with their disdain and harshness, their excessive demands and their love of luxury, always rouse in the hearts of the poor.
(*The London Journal of Flora Tristan*, 1842; ed. J. Hawkes, 1982)

workers in line although noise was deafening and light dim, meals swift and cheerless, and the machinery hazardous. Many workers lost fingers or limbs in the machinery, unshielded, unregulated by any law.

Even labor under these conditions, however, was preferable to the alternative—no work at all. Business cycles were volatile during the early expansion of factories. Workers often found themselves unemployed because of overproduction, when warehouses were full, or simply because of seasonal shifts in demand. As industrialization progressed, some craftsmen found their products, and their skills, became obsolete. Such was the fate of the English handloom weavers, who for a few brief decades had made out handsomely by processing into cloth the huge product of mechanized spinning jennies. Between 1805 and 1833 their wages fell by seventy-five percent.

Women and Children   Factories employed women and children well into the industrial era, an inheritance from the system of mill or cottage textile production. Owners found women to be useful employees on many counts. Women workers were strong enough to manage most machines, and offered little resistance to the demands of the workplace. They were cheap as well, earning as little as one-half a man's salary. During the early years of industrialization, they made up as much as one-third of the workforce. Yet in Britain, at least, women's factory labor was gradually curtailed. Legislation of the 1830s and 1840s limited their workday (and prohibited their employment in mines). After the mid-nineteenth century, British factory workers were overwhelmingly male. Women's labor did not end, however, but was transformed. In their homes, in the homes of others, and on the streets of the city, for lower pay and with lower status, they performed non-factory work.

The labor of children (technically those under age twenty, but in practice as young as eight or nine) was also essential in the early years of industrialization. One British historian has judged their exploitation "one of the most shameful events" of his nation's history, while a French scholar has termed it not only the exploitation but "martyrdom" of the young. Many children entered the factories alongside their parents, or at their bidding. Owners also procured child workers *en masse* by contracting with local orphanages and poorhouses. Children could be given simple jobs, such as sweeping or loading and switching bobbins of yarn. Their labor, like that of their mothers and older sisters, was cheap—a child earned about one-fourth the wage of an adult male. Like women, they were pliable and obedient to the commands of the foreman. If resistant, they could be physically punished, as children regularly were at home. Such abuse was only one aspect of their exploitation. The long hours of work, the lack of exercise, the absence of instruction and access to the open air, led to permanent physical and mental injury. The experiences of some children are narrated in *Witnesses* on p. 644.

Child labor was not officially or generally repudiated in the Western world until the twentieth century. It was, however, gradually restricted, at first in Britain and France. In 1833, the British Factory Act set a maximum of a nine-hour workday for children under thirteen. In 1847, further legislation reduced the workday of women and older children to ten and a half hours. In 1842, the Mines Act prohibited work for women and girls underground, as well as boys under ten. In France, where the state had never before intervened in employers' relations with their workers, a child labor law passed in 1841 banned factory work for children under eight, and limited the workday to eight and twelve hours respectively for children under and over age thirteen. Yet in Britain (as elsewhere), child labor remained an important component of the workforce as late as 1874, when fourteen percent of textile workers were children, and even 1900, when thousands of children under fourteen labored in mines and factories.

Children were not the only martyrs to industrialization. Workers throughout Europe suffered, especially in the early development of the iron and textiles production that made Europe the wealthiest region in the world. In the end, however, workers, too, benefited. They began to do so when they learned to join together to form organizations that could extract from a booming economy some fair share of the wealth that their labor helped generate.

The Birth of Labor

With industrialization, it became possible to produce and sell more goods. It was capitalism that made that potential actual. Capitalism is an economic system resting on the pre-industrial commercial achievements of European merchants, and theorized by Adam Smith in his embrace of market systems of supply and demand and his rejection of the state-managed economics of mercantilism (see Chapters 11, 16). In a capitalist system, entrepreneurs are free to invest their money, or capital, to acquire machines and factories (the astonishing capacity of which had only recently become a reality) and thereby to seek maximal profits with minimal government intervention. Proponents of capitalism argue that the great productivity achieved, and enormous profits gained, ultimately benefit every member of a society through an absolute increase in the amount of wealth, greater economic opportunity, increased availability of consumer products, and higher standards of living.

With industrialization, organized by capitalism, the history of the "working class" truly begins. Laborers began to think of themselves as a collective entity—as **"labor"** as opposed to "capital," the factory owners and entrepreneurs. They formed collective

Men and Work

Käthe Kollwitz, drawing from the series **A Weavers' Uprising,** *1897*

If the Industrial Revolution is the age of the voracious entrepreneur, it is also the age of the working man, the era when the "working class" took form—even though men, and women, had always worked throughout human history. The characteristic form of industrial labor was in the factory; yet factory labor was only one part of the story of work in an industrial age. Above, a group of determined weavers (whose artisan wages and conditions suffered from competition with factory machinery), their bodies expressive of the harsh conditions under which they lived, go out on strike in 1897, while at right, in 1895, three men with hand tools build the streets whose construction and repair was ceaseless in an era of exploding urbanization. Below right, workers at the Krupp plant in Essen, Germany, are seen tending to "Fritz," an enormous steam hammer originally invented in Britain. (top: Käthe-Kollwitz Museum, Berlin; center: Punch Magazine)

How do the conditions of work shown in these images differ from those of the guild artisans of earlier times?

This illustration from Punch magazine shows road construction workers, 1895

Workers at the Krupp plant, Germany, 1903

To continue your investigation of this topic, please go to www.prenhall.com/king for the related **WINDOWS** on the **WEB** activity

643

organizations to provide mutual support and to press for greater concessions from their employers. Eventually, **trade unions** gained the right to bargain collectively with their employers. Sometimes they used the device of the **strike**, withholding their labor in order to compel owners to accede to their demands. Trade unions worked toward two principal goals: to secure both better working conditions and higher living standards for their members. By 1900, industrial workers and their families lived significantly better than they did in 1800.

Early Labor Associations The formation of modern trade unions was a complex process involving several intermediate steps. First, associations of skilled artisans formed to fill the vacuum left by the waning of the medieval guilds (see Chapter 11), which by the late eighteenth century were under pressure, especially in Britain and France, for their resistance to the mechanisms of the **free market**. A system driven by supply and demand, contrary to the ideals of the guild, might threaten product quality (which had been carefully specified) or allow profits to exceed

WITNESSES

Workers' Lives

These excerpts provide glimpses into the varied work lives, always difficult, of a range of laborers—an English boy who was both farm laborer and textile worker; Irish laborers hauling heavy sacks of goods in the dockyards; an English girl mineworker; a German girl who worked at carding and spinning; the servants in a French household, as described in a housekeeping manual.

A Yorkshire Chartist recalls his boyhood and youth experiences during the 1820s–1840s: Tom Brown's Schooldays would have had no charm for me, as I had never been to a day school in my life; when very young I had to begin working, and was pulled out of bed between 4 and 5 o'clock … in summer time to go … take part in milking a number of cows. … I went to a card shop [i.e., textile workshop] afterwards, and there had to set 1500 card teeth for a ½d. … I have been a woollen weaver, a comber, a navvy on the railway, and a [quarryman] … [and so] I claim to know some little of the state of the working classes.
(B. Wilson, *The Struggles of an Old Chartist*, 1887; ed. E. P. Thompson, 1964)

Irish stevedores unload sacks of oats at the Liverpool docks (1830s): These men … received the ful sacks as they were lowered by the crane off the hitch on their shoulders and carried them across the road. They pursued their heavy task during the working hours of a summer's day at a uniform, unremitting pace, a trot of at least five miles an hour, the distance from the vessel to the storehouse being full fifty yards. … At this work a good labourer earned, at 16d. per 100 sacks, ten shillings a day; so that consequently he made seven hundred and fifty trips … thus performing a distance of … forty-three miles.
(Sir G. Head, *A Home Tour of Great Britain*, 1835; ed. E. P. Thompson, 1964)

Seventeen-year-old Patience Kershaw describes her work in the coal mines to a parliamentary committee of inquiry (1842): My father has been dead about a year; my mother is living and has ten children … three lasses go to mill; all the lads are colliers [i.e., coal mine workers]. … I never went to day-school; I go to Sunday-school, but I cannot read or write; I go to pit at five o'clock in the morning and come out at five in the evening; I get my breakfast of porridge and milk first; I take my dinner with me, a cake [a plain oatcake], and I eat as I go; I do not stop or rest any time for the purpose; I get nothing else until I get home, and then have potatoes and meat, not every day meat. I [work] in the clothes I have now got on, trousers and ragged jacket … sometimes they [the male workers] beat me, if I am not quick enough, with their hands; they strike upon my back; the boys take liberties with me … I am the only girl in the pit; there are about 20 boys and 15 men; all the men are naked; I would rather work in the mill than in coal-pit.
(Evidence given before Lord Ashley's Mines Commission, 1842; eds. G. B. Kirsch et al, 1997)

German socialist Luise Zietz (1865–1922) recalls her childhood in the 1870s: We had to pluck apart and oil the raw wool, to run it through the "wolf," which compressed it further, then it had to be put through the carding machine two times. A pair of dogs, who switched off, drove this machine by a large treadwheel, and when one of the large dogs died on us, we ourselves had to get down in the wheel. … Spinning was a terrible torture for us children. We crouched hour after hour on the low stool behind the spinning wheel at the horrible monotonous and exhausting work, just spinning, spinning, spinning.
(From B. S. Anderson and J. P. Zinsser, *A History of their Own: Women in Europe from Prehistory to the Present*, Vol. 2, 1988)

A French housekeeping manual describes the female servant's duties (1896): The maid of all work should get up at six, fix her hair, get herself ready, and not come down to the kitchen without being ready to go out to the market. From 6 to 9 o'clock, she has the time to do many things. She will light the furnace and the fires or get the stove going. She will prepare the breakfasts, do the dining room, brush the clothes and clean the shoes. When the masters arise, she will do their rooms, will put water in the water closets, carry up wood or coal, and carry down the excrement. For all these tasks, she will put on oversleeves and a white apron and take care to wash her hands. Then, … the dining room is restored to order, the tableware washed and put away, the cooking utensils cleaned.
(From B. S. Anderson and J. P. Zinsser, *ibid*)

what an older generation considered "just" (i.e. based on the cost of materials and labor rather than on the highest price obtainable in an open market). Guilds fought to retain their influence in many regions, but failed to do so in the wealthier nations. In Britain their power had faded by the late eighteenth century. In France, they fell victim to the Revolution, which tolerated no limitations on urban workers in the archaic name of quality.

Nevertheless, in the absence of any form of state welfare, workers still needed the protections the guilds had provided. The associations that emerged provided services to skilled artisans and their families, called "combinations," aroused alarm in the authorities. The British Combination Acts of 1799–1800 were intended to suppress them, while laws passed during the Revolution (1791) and under Napoleon outlawed them in France. Although these prohibitions were repealed in 1824 and 1864 respectively, workers' combinations continued to be suspect.

Skilled artisans often joined with their fellows to resist the mechanization of their trades. In Britain, France, and the German lands, such workers rioted. The English Luddites, textile-workers who rallied under the name of the (probably mythical) leader Ned Ludd, expressed their rage in 1811–1812 by smashing the machines that aimed to replace them. In 1831 and 1834 in the French city of Lyons, where thirty percent of the nation's exports were manufactured, journeymen weavers rose up against workshop owners (see *Windows On*, p. 643). During the same decade, the tailors of Paris, finding their incomes plunging as factory production undercut opportunities, took revenge on the machinery that threatened their economic status. In Prussian Silesia, linen-weavers rioted in 1844 against a factory-type system that threatened to turn high-skilled artisans into mere laborers.

Throughout the nineteenth century, the plight of the skilled artisan remained perilous. Tailors, shoemakers, and cabinetmakers figured among the leaders of revolutionary episodes and organizations—most conspicuously in Paris during the revolutions of 1830, 1848, and 1871 (see Chapter 20). It was precisely their kind of labor that was most threatened by competition from the factories that spewed out cheap goods at low prices.

Such outbreaks of violence fueled government determination to suppress workers' associations. At the same time, they prefigured the strikes of a more ordered labor movement that began to emerge around the mid-nineteenth century in Britain. There some groups of highly-skilled workers formed a new type of professional craft association, exemplified by the Amalgamated Society of Engineers, founded in 1851. A national organization supported by members' dues, it offered health benefits and unemployment protection, as well as a platform from which to negotiate for economic and political benefits. Such early trade unions sprang from the craft workshop tradition and not from the "Satanic mills" where unskilled workers still labored without any associations that could offer mutual consolation and assistance.

Skilled workers held high prestige and could command good wages (although these were still only a small fraction—one-third or one-fourth—of the income of a member of the bourgeoisie). Such privileges raised them well above the condition of the semi-skilled and unskilled workers whose numbers ballooned with the expansion of factory production, who earned only two-thirds or one-half as much. It is these new workers (called "proletarians" after the underclass of Roman citizens who were considered to serve the state only by reproducing and peopling the Republic) whose oppressed condition led to the formation of the modern labor movement.

The Proletariat   The condition of the proletarians, or proletariat, appeared permanent and inescapable. Not only did these workers labor long hours, in appalling conditions, for barely a subsistence wage, but they could aspire to little better. Moreover, they had no higher aspirations for their children, whom they generally introduced to the same form of employment. In the absence of any encouragement from employers or the state, and in the absence of a system of mass education, few workers expected their children to achieve greater wealth or status than they themselves possessed. It is unlikely that more than an exceptional few even pondered the possibility.

There were an exceptional few, however, who sought to improve their own understanding of the world to assist their advancement. They joined self-help movements, or attended voluntary lectures on science, business, and the arts, that offered a random but still advanced education. While working in his family's cotton mill in Manchester, the German industrialist and later **Communist** Friedrich Engels (1820–1895) was impressed by the popularity of such lectures, commenting in 1844, "I have sometimes come across workers, with their fustian jackets falling apart, who are better informed on geology, astronomy and other matters than many an educated member of the middle classes in Germany."

The workers who found their way to evening lectures on geology were greatly outnumbered by those who sought out taverns for relaxation or who returned to their beds to rest, after sixteen hours of labor. But even this more numerous group began, in the early years of industrialization, to seek each other out for solidarity, the necessary first step in the building of the labor movement. From the 1760s onward, they formed voluntary groups, variously called "friendly" or "mutual aid" or "cooperative" societies.

In the early nineteenth century, when such associations of workers were closely scrutinized by authorities, their objectives were limited. Funded by members' dues, they offered loans, unemployment and death benefits, and assistance to orphans. They established cooperative stores, where goods could be purchased at close to their wholesale cost, enabling working families to stretch their slight wages. By 1803, about 9600 friendly societies in Britain boasted over 700,000 members. By 1851, such organizations had founded 130 cooperative stores. The movement spread to the continent. By the mid-nineteenth century, cooperative banks sprang up in the German lands, with one in nearly every city by century's end. In France several thousand friendly societies enrolled about 800,000 workers by 1870, who constituted approximately thirteen percent of the workforce.

Utopia and Reform   The originators of **socialism** (see Chapter 24), joined by some sympathetic entrepreneurs, encouraged worker cooperation. Early socialist thinkers envisioned a future society where workers lived in dignity, harvesting the wealth that workshops and factories produced with their labor and sharing equally in those profits. Families would live and work together and children would be educated. The patriarchal strictures that bound traditional families—requiring female chastity and obedience—could be abolished or at least modified. Relationships between men and women could be founded in love, not necessity. Women would enjoy the same sexual freedoms that men had always claimed. The state itself would be altered. Engineers and scientists might take the lead, qualified for the undertaking by competence rather than social origin. They would displace traditional leaders chosen from members of noble or bourgeois elites.

While most such **utopian** societies remained merely theoretical, some visionaries attempted to give them reality. In Britain, the successful self-made industrialist Robert Owen (1771–1858), an artisan's son, devoted much of his career to bettering the condition of the worker. Owen had prospered in cotton manufacture in the last decade of the eighteenth century, turning a £100 investment into a huge fortune (see Chapter 21). In 1800, struck by the miserable living and working conditions of his textile workers, he moved his operation from Manchester, England's greatest boom town, to New Lanark, near Glasgow, Scotland. There he established not merely a factory but an entire community, including housing, cooperative stores, a sewage system, schools for workers' children, and a humane workplace. The whole experiment, eagerly viewed by European industrial experts and visitors, embodied a new moral code based on cooperation, rather than competition.

In the 1820s, Owen journeyed to North America, to launch new cooperative ventures in an unfinished country where anything might be possible. He established an experimental community of New Harmony in the state of Indiana, where agricultural and

WHO'S WHO

Chroniclers and Builders of the Industrial Age

Jeremy Bentham (1748–1832) English political theorist, proponent of "Utilitarianism," and designer of the model prison, the "Panopticon."

Edwin Chadwick (1800–1890) disciple of Jeremy Bentham; promoted the building of systems for the delivery of water and the removal of sewage in his 1842 *Report on the Sanitary Condition of the Labouring Population of Great Britain*.

Robert Owen (1771–1858) self-made English entrepreneur, factory owner, experimentalist in utopian community building, and founder of the Grand National Consolidated Trades Union.

Louis Blanc (1811–1882) French socialist theorist and proponent of "national workshops" that would provide unemployed laborers with work and a decent wage.

Karl Marx (1818–1883) German-born intellectual; author, in collaboration with Friedrich Engels, of the *Communist Manifesto*; creator of modern socialist theory and progenitor of all modern communist systems.

Friedrich Engels (1820–1895) German industrialist and later communist; author of a classic study of life in British Manchester during a period of rapid industrialization.

Georges Haussmann (1809–1891) pioneer urban designer and adviser to French emperor Napoleon III; recreated Paris by razing its old structures to make way for a planned system of streets and monumental buildings.

Josephine Butler (1828–1906) British philanthropist and feminist; battled for the repeal of the Contagious Diseases Act of 1864 (mandating the medical supervision of prostitutes).

Jacob Riis (1849–1914) Danish-born crime reporter turned photojournalist; chronicler of how "the other half" lived in New York City during the industrial age.

industrial workers came together to form a self-sufficient society. It later disintegrated, but by then Owen had moved on to other things.

After his return from the United States, Owen organized a mass workers' movement in 1834: the Grand National Consolidated Trades Union. This was meant to be a single organization that would unite all workers in the country, who would therefore wield the irresistible negotiating weapon of a general strike. Owen's aim was not merely to improve workers' pay and conditions, but also to influence the political process. His initiatives should be seen in the context of the politicization of labor (see below), that progressed as the century aged.

Owen's giant union soon collapsed, as had his perfect communities, and those of other designers of utopias. A new generation of social critics put utopianism aside and focused more concretely on solving immediate problems such as low wages and unemployment. In France, the socialist theorist Louis Blanc (1811–1882) proposed the creation of "national workshops." These would be funded by a benevolent state that guaranteed workers the right to work and a decent wage immune to the pressures of competition. The republican government formed in early 1848 committed huge sums to subsidize such workshops, intended to absorb workers unable to find employment elsewhere. They proved immensely popular, and their dissolution a few months later was one trigger of the workers' revolt and the suppression of the June Days (see Chapter 20).

In June, French workers' concerns turned from economic to political aims. Embittered by the closing of the national workshops, they exploded with anti-government feeling, setting up street barricades in the time-honored fashion of French revolutionaries. This uprising was suppressed with excessive violence in which 4000 died. That outbreak was a major episode in the political history of workers' movements, but it was not the only one. Throughout industrialized Europe, urbanized, unskilled workers constituted a huge and potentially volatile part of the population. Wherever their demands became assertive, the possibility of political revolution loomed.

Well before the uprisings that took place in France, Germany, and elsewhere in 1848 (see Chapter 20), British workers had joined middle-class reformers to agitate for the Reform Act of 1832 (which broadened the franchise to middle-class men and made electoral reforms) and the Factory Act of 1833 and subsequent workplace legislation. They opposed the Corn Laws, which protected high-cost, local grain against cheaper imports, to the disadvantage of the poor—their opposition peaking in the notorious "Peterloo Massacre" (named for St. Peter's Field, Manchester, and the battle of Waterloo) of 1819 when mounted soldiers charged on a mass meeting. Workers also opposed the 1834 Poor Law Amendment Act, which withdrew support for unemployed able-bodied adults unless they were employed in state-run workhouses.

From 1838 to 1848, a movement to petition Parliament to pass a "People's Charter" harnessed workers' aspirations, which they determined to pursue "Peaceably if we may, forcibly if we must." Drafted by the London Working Men's Association, the Charter contained six points that were sure to alarm lawmakers. In addition to petitioning for electoral reform, these included a call for universal manhood suffrage. Presented to Parliament and rejected in 1839, again in 1842, and a final time in 1848, the Charter represented the heroic attempt of British workers to gain political objectives. Though it failed, those who participated in the Chartist movement had gained valuable practical experience of the political process.

Workers in the industrializing nations of continental Europe learned that same lesson later in the century, as the utopian socialism of its early decades gave way to an urgent, militant socialism in its latter half. Workers leaned to a variety of "**social democratic**" political parties, which proposed to win benefits for their supporters by gaining majorities in representative assemblies. Some joined the Communists, a group of socialists to whom a mission and a program were provided by the German intellectuals Friedrich Engels and Karl Marx (1818–1883) in their *Communist Manifesto* of 1848 (see Chapter 25). Both analytical and inspiring, the brief *Manifesto* is one of the key monuments of modern politics. It marks the moment when the possibility was first voiced of a complete reversal of the social order. Workers should throw off the chains that bind them by abolishing private property, eliminating the capitalist bourgeoisie, and taking control of both the factories and the state. These ideals animated the Communist League established in London in 1847, and subsequently the much larger International Workingmen's Association, or "First International," in 1864, and the "Second International" in 1889.

Even more threatening than the Communists to established elites were the French syndicalists and Russian anarchists. The former urged that workers gain their ends through coordinated, violent strikes against the state. The latter urged the annihilation of the state itself, which they saw as inherently alien to human welfare. In autocratic Russia, and in France where workers' revolts had twice been bloodily suppressed, syndicalism and anarchism won followers. But in Britain and other industrializing nations, trade unions were the primary institutions upon which workers relied in their quest for betterment.

Trade Unions Trade unions can be distinguished from both the "friendly societies" and utopian communities. They are workers' organizations whose main goal is to negotiate with employers for wage and workplace improvements. Trade unions continued to provide the kinds of benefits that mutual aid societies had offered, but they also attempted to deal with the managers and owners of large enterprises in negotiations known as **collective bargaining**. While capitalist entrepreneurs resisted the formation of trade unions, the trade union movement encouraged an orderly approach to workers' rights and pay, in contrast to outbreaks of riot and revolution that had

The Matchgirls' Union on strike, 1888

Maidservants in the kitchen, 1860s–1870s

The Industrial Revolution created a variety of working environments for women, who constituted a major fraction of all industrial workers. They often worked long hours in poor conditions, like the women workers from the matchmaking factory who famously called a strike in 1888 (above). Many women were domestic servants, like the ones working in this kitchen (right). Others were pieceworkers, who, seated close to a small stove, sewed garments to be sold by the "piece" (below left).

Women of higher social standing tended not to work. Instead, they remained at home, where their main functions were to provide beauty, grace, and children. They could also go shopping in one of the new department stores, where they participated in a booming economy as consumers rather than laborers. The ribbons gallery of the great French department store, the Bon Marché was a vibrant, inviting space for those who had no need to work (below right).

(above: Hulton Getty; below left: Museum of the City of New York)

What differences in costume indicate to any observer the differences in status between women workers and shoppers?

Jacob Riis, **Sewing and Starving in an Elizabeth Street Attic,** *c. 1890*

Illustration of the **Bon Marché** *from* **Le Monde Illustré,** *c. 1875*

To continue your investigation of this topic, please go to www.prenhall.com/king for the related WINDOWS on the WEB activity

frightened entrepreneurs and only succeeded in stiffening their resolve to yield little to workers.

Where negotiation failed, trade unions wielded the weapon of the strike. In the early years of the labor movement, strikes were often violently suppressed, but by the late nineteenth century, they had matured to become a practical tool in the mission of organized labor to wrest from employers some of the wealth that their members' labors had generated.

The earliest trade unions formed in Britain soon after the repeal of the Combination Laws. Thus the National Union of Cotton Spinners was organized in 1829, the National Association for the Protection of Labor in 1830, and Owen's Grand National Consolidated Trades Union in 1834. But they soon collapsed, and from the later 1830s to 1848, the goals of Chartism took over from unionization. In the mid-century, skilled workers recruited from the artisan classes began to form crafts associations. After 1875, when the tactics of collective bargaining were finally recognized as legal, trade unions expanded in earnest. Their ranks were filled by unskilled and semi-skilled workers who were persuaded by such examples as the successful strikes of the London dockworkers in 1889, or the London match girls in 1888. By 1900, a century and a half after the beginnings of industrialization, membership in British trade unions had risen to over 2 million workers.

In Germany, too, union membership climbed from the 1860s to about 2 million around 1900, although the chancellor Otto von Bismarck (1815–1898) had tried to suppress the tactic of the strike. Here union members often supported the Social Democratic party, with a socialist, but not communist agenda, which militantly advocated workers' interests. In France, in the 1860s a nascent trade movement succumbed to the general repression following the 1871 Paris Commune (see Chapter 20). Driven underground, French unions or *syndicats* tended toward the violent solutions of syndicalism.

By the last two decades of the nineteenth century, workers had made considerable progress. Their standard of living had begun to rise. They now had more food and better food to eat than their fathers and grandfathers. Their wages were sufficient to purchase necessities and even to allow a small surplus for entertainment and brief vacations. If they suffered unemployment, or faced a strike, their trade union could assist with funds. They could not entirely put behind them the fear of want, nor had they yet attained the dignity that solid and regular pay afforded, but real gains had been made.

In the 1880s, the newly constituted state of Germany led the way to a new stage in the relations between workers and society. Bismarck instituted government insurance programs that would protect workers in the events of illness and disability, unemployment and old age. After 1900, Britain, France, the United States, and most other Western nations in turn instituted similar measures. Why was Bismarck, of all leaders the least indulgent to workers' petitions, the one to initiate a program of social insurance? He sought to lessen the momentum of social democracy by assuaging the workers with popular programs. Thus appeased, they might ignore calls for militant action against the state.

The modern working class suffered much in the formative stages of industrialization. Yet it achieved much before the end of the nineteenth century. Its members experimented with self-help groups and shopping cooperatives, utopian communes, riot and strike, with political initiatives and with collective bargaining. By 1900, although most still struggled to feed themselves and their families, the workers of the Western world had improved their standard of living beyond that achieved by any laborers of past ages.

THE INDUSTRIAL CITY

Cities had long been centrally important to the development of the European economy (see Chapters 11, 18). In the late eighteenth century, as population spurted as a result of improvements in agriculture, cities swelled prodigiously, as the table on p. 650 shows. Their populations approached and even (in the case of London) exceeded the 1 million mark that separates modern from pre-modern urban centers in the West. These already swollen cities, some of which became industrial centers after 1800, and others of which were major commercial centers, experienced an influx of workers that pushed population levels to several millions—exceeding those of any concentration of human beings previously known to have existed on the face of the globe. The table on p. 651 shows the changes in some major industrial nations.

As city populations exploded, urban structures and networks were transformed. The old, jumbled buildings and narrow, winding streets became overcrowded. As overcrowding fostered the spread of disease, the city developed systems of water supply and sewage removal. Streetcars moved people quickly across town, electric lighting made nighttime activities possible, and professional police and fire forces provided security. Neighborhoods developed distinctive personalities. Elegant boulevards designed by urban planners sliced through the districts where the wealthy resided. Narrow streets and alleyways, which the planners left untouched, snaked through the districts of the poor. These were an ideal setting for criminals and prostitutes—"streetwalkers"—who considered them their own. Whether they dwelled on mean streets or ample boulevards, city dwellers were prone to the **alienation** that haunted urban life, where the multiple goings and comings of many meant for some the atomization of humanity and the reduction of the human spirit.

Boom Towns

Already in the early modern era, streams of people flowed from the country to the city where jobs might be found. With the arrival of the factory, the din of the steam engines, the whirr of machinery, beckoned new throngs of migrants. The big cities which had reached nearly 1 million in 1800, reached several million by 1900, as shown in the table below.

The first nation to industrialize, Britain offers ample evidence of spectacular rates of urban growth. In 1750, Britain had only two cities with populations over 50,000. A century later, there were twenty-nine. The ten largest cities all at least doubled in the first half of the nineteenth century, with those centered in the new manufacturing regions near coalfields and seaports growing fastest. Leeds and Birmingham more than tripled; Manchester, Liverpool, and Glasgow more than quadrupled.

Manchester alone, nearly one-third of whose residents were engaged in the mechanized production of cotton cloth, doubled between 1801 and 1831 (from 70,000 to 142,000), then more than doubled again (to 409,000) over the next twenty years. Like "an industrious spider," as a contemporary remarked, from its

center Manchester spun a web of roads and railways reaching out to swelling towns from where it received supplies and workers. Engels' description of Manchester is quoted in *Witnesses* on p. 655. Another commentator marveled: "From this foul drain the greatest stream of human industry flows out to fertilize the whole world. From this filthy sewer pure gold flows."

Though it did not increase at the pace of the northern manufacturing centers, the population of London increased from about 1 to 5 million by the end of the nineteenth century, when it was home to more than one-sixth of the nation's people. By 1850, more than fifty percent of Britain's population lived in cities; by 1880, more than two-thirds.

Rates of growth outside of Britain were slower but still substantial. Paris nearly doubled between 1800 and 1850, then doubled again over the next thirty years. By 1900, a majority of France's population lived in cities. Berlin (Germany) and St. Petersburg (Russia) doubled in the first half of the nineteenth century, and St. Petersburg then quadrupled, reaching a population of 2 million by 1914. From an 1800 population figure of 170,000, Berlin reached a total of 1.6 million by 1890. Vienna (Austria) increased about eighty percent, while Budapest (Hungary) more than tripled

Population of Europe's Largest Cities, 1750–1950

Rank	1750 City	Population	1850 City	Population	1950 City	Population
1	London	676,000	London	2,320,000	London	8,860,000
2	Paris	560,000	Paris	1,314,000	Paris	5,900,000
3	Naples	324,000	St. Petersburg	502,000	Moscow	5,100,000
4	Amsterdam	219,000	Berlin	446,000	Ruhr	4,900,000
5	Lisbon	213,000	Vienna	426,000	Berlin	3,707,000
6	Vienna	169,000	Liverpool	422,000	Leningrad	2,700,000
7	Moscow	161,000	Naples	416,000	Manchester	2,382,000
8	Venice	158,000	Manchester	412,000	Birmingham	2,196,000
9	Rome	157,000	Moscow	373,000	Vienna	1,755,000
10	St. Petersburg	138,000	Glasgow	346,000	Rome	1,665,000

European cities grew enormously during the era of incipient and maturing industrialization. Simultaneously, their rank order often shifted. Note in this table the mounting importance of Moscow and St. Petersburg (Leningrad in the third column) and the new British industrial centers of Manchester and Birmingham. As they escalated, traditional centers like Vienna and Rome, although growing respectably, fell to a lower place in the ranking of top ten cities. And three giants of early modern commerce—Lisbon, Venice, and Amsterdam—disappeared entirely from the top ten. London and Paris, whose populations exploded, maintained their top-rank positions.

Source: P. M. Hohenberg and L. H. Lees, The Making of Urban Europe, 1000–1950 (Cambridge, MA: Harvard University Press, 1985; 2nd ed., 1995), p. 227.

Map 22.1 Charles Booth's Poverty Map, 1889: From 1886 to 1903, the philanthropist and businessman Charles Booth conducted a systematic and scientific survey of the condition of London's poor after three generations of rapid industrialization and urbanization. Where do most of the wealthy and middle class Londoners live? Where are the "poor" and the "very poor" concentrated?

from 287,000 in 1867 to nearly 1 million in 1914. (Elsewhere in east-central Europe, where industrialization had scarcely started, large cities were few and increased only slowly.) The percentage of people living in cities, and the numbers of Europeans overall, both increased, resulting in a growth of urban populations by 1910 to six times their 1800 level.

These increases were achieved, for the most part, not through a growth in the birthrate but through migration to the cities. Only about one-half of those who lived in nineteenth-century London and Paris had been born there. Until the twentieth century,

cities did not reproduce themselves. They required constant immigration from the countryside around, continuing on a larger scale a pattern that dated from the Middle Ages, when peasants sought employment and refuge in towns.

Urban migrants were of two sorts: those who came but left, and those who came and stayed. The former worked for a period in the city, then returned to country villages. When they did so, they brought with them the outlook of experienced urbanites, contributing to the increasing connectedness of country folk to city things. The second category of migrants came to

Levels of Urbanization in Leading European Nations (with the United States and Japan), 1800, 1850, 1910

	1800	1850	1910
Belgium	20	34	57
Britain	23	45	75
France	12	19	38
Germany	9	15	49
Italy	18	23	40
Netherlands	37	39	53
Russia	6	7	14
Spain	18	18	38
US	5	14	42
Japan	14	15	18

Figures represent approximate percentage of population living in cities

As industrialization developed, more workers moved to cities. This bar graph shows the increasing percentage of urban-dwellers relative to the whole population in ten countries at three junctures in time. Note Britain's rapid and huge urbanization, by which it surpassed the citified Netherlands within the fifty-year span of its peak industrialization (1800–1850). Belgium, too, leapt forward to take second place in 1910, also ahead of the Netherlands. The level of urbanization in Britain, Belgium, and France approximately tripled in 1800–1910. In Germany, it increased more than fivefold, and in the United States, more than eightfold. In contrast, Italy, Spain, Russia, and Japan—even the Netherlands, despite its initial advantage—are slower to increase their levels of urbanization.

Source: P. Bairoch, Cities and Economic Development: From the Dawn of History to the Present, trs. C. Braider (Chicago: University of Chicago Press, 1988), p. 221

the cities and stayed, driving down (since most migrants were young) the average age of city dwellers. These migrants often joined the armies of the poor: those who labored in workshops and factories, who hauled and lifted and hammered, who cleaned and cooked in the well-kept houses of professionals, merchants, bureaucrats, and nobles.

For not all jobs in the city were factory jobs. Only in the handful of cities, such as Manchester, that were created during the process of industrialization, did industrial workers constitute a majority of workers. In most cities, there was a greater mix of occupations. In London in 1891, for instance, factory workers comprised about thirty-eight percent of all male, and thirty-three percent of all female workers. But servants also constituted a large group, comprising only seven percent of the more numerous male laboring population, but fifty-four percent of female workers. A group of kitchen servants is illustrated in *Windows On* on p. 648. After factory workers, servants (who were mostly female) were the largest occupational group in European cities. By 1900 in Britain, half of all working women worked as servants.

A notable development was the emergence of the category of "**white-collar**" workers, as they were later designated because they wore the clean clothes of the respectable middle classes rather than the heavy, durable blue of those who worked with their hands. They were bank tellers, secretaries in utility and insurance companies, draughtsmen and bookkeepers, tax-collectors and food inspectors, sales clerks in the new department stores and teachers in newly-mandated public schools. Their recruitment to government offices was rapid in the last decades of the century, when state bureaucracies in the advanced countries came close to doubling. Most white-collar workers were men, but women also prospered, especially as teachers, nurses, and sales and office clerks.

Although white-collar workers often aspired to enter the middle classes themselves—and sometimes succeeded—most workers were poor. For them, the **demographic** patterns of urban life were remorseless. The poor were less likely to survive childhood,

and more likely to die young than the wealthy in the cities of nineteenth-century Europe. Although birthrates among the poor were very high, their infants often died, with infant mortality running at up to fifty percent of all births. Toward the end of the nineteenth century, cities became more healthful and these demographic trends improved. Death rates fell, including infant deaths, and life expectancy increased. Meanwhile, although birthrates fell overall due to the increased practice of birth control, out-of-wedlock births rose—a marked characteristic of the modern era. These patterns meant that by around 1900, the city at last reproduced itself. No longer a killer of people, the city had also become the norm, rather than an exception in the social fabric of life in many European countries.

Structure and Infrastructure

Some of the headiest urban growth of the early years of industrialization involved new cities that suddenly developed—as did Manchester—from mere villages. More often, however, the greatly expanded urban areas of the nineteenth century involved a medieval or even ancient city, whose familiar buildings, streets, and walls were inadequate to house the influx of newcomers. The structures and infrastructures of these established cities became greatly strained as populations grew.

Where were people to live? They crowded into the existing building stock, squeezing in unrelated groups into **tenement** rooms. Or they occupied new, cheap housing hastily constructed on city outskirts. In some cities, wageworkers stayed in the city's poor districts in the dilapidated remnants of its older buildings. They doubled up, sharing rooms and facilities with strangers. This was the case in Paris, for example,

On and Under City Streets

Gustave Caillebotte, Rainy Day: *Slum clearance and the creation of wide boulevards offered easier traffic flow and broad urban vistas, though at the expense of the old neighborhoods. Baron Haussmann's program of urban renewal during the 1850s and 1860s transformed Paris from a crowded medieval town to a spacious modern city, shown here in a work from 1876–1877 by the Impressionist painter Caillebotte. (Musée Marmottan, Paris)*

Above and below ground in Paris: *The mid- and late-nineteenth century saw substantial improvements in urban life. The installation of municipal sewage systems greatly improved public health. This contemporary sketch of the Parisian system shows the complex of drains and sewers constructed below street level that gradually extended throughout the entire city, eventually bringing clean water and removing waste in poor as well as privileged neighborhoods.*

where the population increased by twenty-five percent in the period 1817–1827, while housing capacity increased by only ten percent. In other cities, such as Manchester, where there was no ancient building stock into which the poor might flow, entrepreneurs hastily constructed large, cheap, and anonymous buildings on the outskirts of the industrial core. Outside French and German industrial towns straggled rows of company-built, barracks-like houses or high-rise multi-residential buildings.

While poor residents crowded into old buildings, or spilled outward in shapeless, spreading suburbs, the wealthy bourgeoisie and aristocracy also found new housing. They either pushed outward, establishing new neighborhoods beyond the haunts of the poor, or established themselves in elegant enclaves within the city. Among the latter were the areas around the grand boulevards of western Paris, as shown on p. 652. These had been opened up by Baron Georges Haussmann (1809–1891), Napoleon III's adviser and pioneer urban designer, by tearing down the cramped, old housing of workers' districts. (Haussmann's project not only beautified the city, but also helped to control civil unrest by depriving would-be revolutionaries of their defenses and exposing them, when necessary, to gunfire.) Other

such areas were the *Ringstrasse* ("ring street," formed on the pattern of the old walls that had ringed the medieval city) of Vienna, and the streets bordering London's fine parks. These new developments were graced by elegant public buildings—modern museums and hospitals, post offices and monuments.

Until the late nineteenth century, the wealthier urbanites traversed the city by carriage, while workers walked. The absence of affordable transport for the poor meant that they had to live within walking distance of their workplace. This situation changed in the last decades of the century. New forms of transportation including trolley car systems powered by electricity, underground railroads, for example in London (1863), Paris (1900), and New York (1904), and bicycles made it possible for working families to move out to choicer and relatively cheaper suburban areas. By the mid-nineteenth century in major cities, gas lamps lighted the streets (replaced by electrical lamps by the end of the century), so that citizens of all classes could stroll abroad with confidence. By that era as well, running water and sewage lines had begun to challenge that great specter of urban life: infectious disease.

Cholera, spread through contaminated food and water supplies, was the great killer of city dwellers. It arrived in the early 1830s and returned periodically throughout the century. It struck London first in 1832, and then again in 1847, when 53,000 died throughout the nation, of whom 14,000 died in London alone. It visited Paris in 1832 and 1849, striking the poor more viciously than the wealthy. The death statistics revealed the outlines of a pitiless social classification, remarked one horrified observer, in itself "a savage denial of the doctrines of equality" that had supposedly been secured by the sacrifices of the Revolution. From 1892 to 1895, again, cholera took the lives of 300,000 Europeans, the great majority (270,000) Russians.

By that time, the work of Louis Pasteur (1822–1895) had uncovered the bacterial origins of disease (see Chapter 24), and the role of water as a vehicle for bacterial transmission was understood. Social reformers began to rank water supply systems as an issue of prime importance. In Britain, Edwin Chadwick (1800–1890), a disciple of the radical thinker Jeremy Bentham (1748–1832; see Chapter 24), urged the building of systems for the delivery of water and the removal of sewage in his 1842 *Report on the Sanitary Condition of the Labouring Population of Great Britain*. Here he argued that the consequences of disease were "greater or less … according as there is more or less sufficient drainage of houses, streets, roads, and land, combined with more or less sufficient means of cleansing and removing solid refuse and impurities." According to the guidelines of the Public Health Act passed through Chadwick's advocacy in 1848, Britain built sewage lines, water delivery systems, and reservoirs. After the first cholera epidemic, the French slowly instituted a similar system. By mid-century, only one building in five in Paris received piped water, and sewage systems often served only privileged quarters of the city, leaving workers to use old collective toilets. By 1887, nearly three-quarters of Parisian streets had sewers.

Although cholera was the worst epidemic disease that Europeans faced in the nineteenth century, there were others. Smallpox still killed and destroyed, although vaccination, when used, was effective in controlling it. Venereal disease, whose spread was linked to the prostitution that thrived in cities, was a serious problem. Tuberculosis, which again ravaged the poor and malnourished far more cruelly than the wealthy, was judged responsible for about one-fifth of the deaths in England in 1839. The pollutants that increased mightily with industrialization also contributed to disease and death. These included the dyes and chemicals from shops and factories, as well as the black smoke produced by the coal burned to power the industrial machine.

On the Streets

Crime and Punishment Meanwhile, other dangers roamed the streets. The concentration of wealth that was essential to city life was an invitation to crime, with the anonymity of urban life allowing predator and prey to coexist. Citizens succumbed to paralyzing fears of a hold-up in the solitary darkness, or a surreptitious and deadly assault. "For the past month," noted a French observer to his correspondent in December, 1843, "the sole topic of conversation has been the nightly assaults, hold-ups, daring robberies … [The assailants] attack rich and poor alike. … At one time the advantage of being poor was that at least you were safe; it is so no longer."

Urban police forces were established, and police records reported mounting instances of assaults on the innocent—if only because their record-keeping methods had become more sophisticated, so that every instance was noted. Newspapers daily reported the crimes of the night before, and devoted much of their space and lurid description to the executions of condemned perpetrators.

Criminals who were not executed were incarcerated or deported. Around 1830 in Paris, about 43,000 people (more than eighty percent male) were shut in prisons, or more than one in every thousand adults. Of these, the majority (seventy-one percent) were guilty of crimes against property. Imprisonment was increasingly the preferred form of punishment, following the influential theories of the Enlightenment theorist Cesare Beccaria (1738–1794). His influential *Essay on Crimes and Punishments* (1764) had heralded the end of torture and routine capital punishment, and his views were taken up by Jeremy Bentham in his proposals for a new form of prison, the "Panopticon" (see below). Deportation to the more remote and deadly colonies (in the Caribbean, North Africa, Australia) was also a commonly imposed penalty in France and Britain.

As the numbers of the imprisoned increased, prison reform initiatives sprang up. Christian activists (especially in Britain and the young United States) urged that the aim of incarceration be redefined as the redemption of the convicted, rather than their mere immobilization. The use of solitary confinement, the requirement of strict silence, the assignment of uniforms, and the imposition of compulsory labor came to characterize prison life. In Jeremy Bentham's Panopticon, constant scrutiny by officials would ensure the proper behavior of the inmates. The name, meaning "a place where all can be seen," suggested a psychological control over deviant behavior that, despite the author's humane intentions, heralded devices of modern totalitarian control.

Though crime was reported more regularly, policed more thoroughly, and punished more effectively, it was no more frequent in urban than it had been in rural settings. It became more terrifying, it seems, merely because the numbers of urban residents meant the multiplication of the fear aroused by malefactors.

The nocturnal voyager along the city's streets, in fact, was more likely to encounter a drunkard or a vagrant than a thief. The consumption of distilled alcohol (gin, vodka, whiskey) became widespread in the nineteenth century, competing with the more familiar beverages of beer and wine. Consumption of these latter favorites also soared—workers disbursed a large fraction of their wages on drink consumed before, during, and after work, while the wealthy considered dining incomplete without a trail of fine vintages. Alcoholism became a serious problem, even among women, previously excluded from the convivial settings of tavern and café where heavy drinking took place. The frustrations of industrial employment or the isolation of urban existence—which Engels remarked upon (see *Witnesses*, p. 655)—may have promoted excessive drinking in both sexes. Conversation accompanied social drinking. An abundance of both sometimes stimulated the formation of political attitudes, especially among workers—to such an extent that, in Paris, the café was deemed "the parliament of the people."

A vagrant or beggar was often only an unemployed drifter. Others belonged to gang-like groups, which sought mutual assistance and occasionally veered into criminal activity. Since the early sixteenth century, vagrancy had been eyed suspiciously by city officials, who often refused to distinguish between thieves and itinerant traders such as peddlers. Selling portable, cheap items, peddlers too had a marginal role in the world of shops, factories, and public spaces that made up the modern city.

Prostitution Walking the streets of the city were also the least fortunate of the prostitutes, whose trade reached a new importance in the nineteenth century. The large modern city had tens of thousands of prostitutes (London, for example, as many as 80,000). These ranged from wealthy, pampered **courtesans** who received their clients in well-furnished apartments, to the occupants of a brothel under the command of a madam or pimp. And they also included the stray, impoverished or part-time, often married, sexworker who picked up clients on the street. Some prostitutes were initiated by their own mothers, often poor and desperate, or prostitutes themselves. Some were forcibly recruited by abduction and rape, or turned to the profession when, as unmarried domestic servants discovered to be pregnant, they were cast out of their employers' homes on to the streets. Some adopted the career freely because it offered higher wages, easier work, and shorter hours than unskilled female wageworkers could otherwise command. Some remained prostitutes for only a brief interlude, before accumulating a dowry and marrying. Others were trapped in the dim underworld where prostitution, crime, and addiction converged.

WITNESSES

Friedrich Engels' Portrait of the Industrial City (1844)

Engels' famous descriptions of urban life in an industrial age provided ammunition to those, like his associate Karl Marx, who saw unrestrained capitalism leading to the diminution of the human being, and the creation of a proletariat so hopeless that it would one day rise up and triumph over its exploiters.

Manchester: The view from the bridge—mercifully concealed from smaller mortals by a parapet as high as a man—is quite characteristic of the entire district. At the bottom the Irk flows, or rather stagnates. It is a narrow, coal-black stinking river full of filth and garbage … out of whose depths bubbles of miasmatic gasses constantly rise and give forth a stench that is unbearable even on the bridge forty or fifty feet above the level of the water. … Above Ducie Bridge there are tall tannery buildings, and further up are dye-works, bone mills and gasworks. The total entirety of the liquid wastes and solid offscourings of these works finds its way into the River Irk, which receives as well the contents of the adjacent sewers and privies. … Below Ducie Bridge, on the left, one looks into piles of rubbish, the refuse, filth and decaying matter of the courts on the steep left bank of the river. Here one house is packed very closely upon another, and because of the steep pitch of the bank a part of every house is visible. All of them are blackened with smoke, crumbling, old, with broken window panes and window frames. The background is formed by old factory buildings, which resemble barracks.—On the right, low-lying bank stands a long row of houses and factories. The second house is a roofless ruin, filled with rubble, and the third stands in such a low situation that the ground floor is uninhabitable and is as a result without windows and doors. The background here is formed by the paupers' cemetery and the stations of the railways to Liverpool and Leeds. Behind these is the workhouse, Manchester's "Poor Law Bastille." It is built on a hill, like a citadel, and from behind its high walls and battlements looks down threateningly upon the working-class quarter that lies below.

London: [T]he inhabitants of London have had to sacrifice the best part of their humanity. … The very bustle and tumult of the streets has something repugnant in it, something that human nature feels outraged by. Hundreds of thousands of people from all classes and ranks of society crowd by each other. Are they not all human beings with the same qualities and faculties: Do they not all have the same interest in being happy? Must they not in the end seek their happiness through the same means and methods? Yet they rush past each other as if they had nothing in common, nothing to do with one another. They are in (tacit) agreement on one thing only—that everyone keep to the right of the pavement so as not to interfere with the crowds that stream in the opposite direction. Meanwhile it occurs to no one that others are worth even a glance. The brutal indifference, the unfeeling isolation of each individual person in his private interest becomes the more repulsive and offensive, the more these individuals are packed into a tiny space. We know well enough that this isolation of the individual—this narrow-minded self-seeking—is everywhere the fundamental principle of modern society. But nowhere is it so shamelessly unconcealed … as in the tumultuous concourse of the great city. The dissolution of mankind into monads, each of which has a s eparate purpose, is carried here to its furthest point. It is the world of atoms.

From this it follows that the social war—the war of all against all—has been openly declared. … Men here regard each other only as useful objects. Each one exploits the other with the result that the stronger tramples the weaker underfoot, and that the few who are strong, the capitalists, seize everything for themselves, while for the many who are weak, the poor, there remains scarcely a bare existence.

(Friedrich Engels, *The Condition of the Working Class in England*, 1844; ed. S. Marcus, 1974)

All prostitutes depended on the demand created by men with money to purchase their services. These men came from all social classes, and, despite the rigid moral and social codes that governed, at least outwardly, the lives of the wealthier classes, their behavior was tolerated throughout most of Europe. Prostitution was considered (with the exception of some reformers) a necessary accommodation to the supposed realities of male sexual life.

If prostitution was tolerated, prostitutes themselves were kept under careful surveillance. As potential carriers of venereal disease, they posed a threat to public health. In many states (in France and Russia, for instance), brothels were frequently inspected by police, and prostitutes, who had to be licensed with the authorities, were examined for disease. (Their male associates, however, who were just as likely to be carriers, were spared the official scrutiny directed toward women sexworkers.)

In 1866–1869, the British parliament inaugurated the medical examination of prostitutes in garrison towns and seaports with the Contagious Diseases Acts, which provided for the isolation of those who proved to have the disease. The determined opposition of Josephine Butler (1828–1906), a clergyman's wife and an early campaigner for women's sexual freedom, led to the law's repeal in 1886. Still in Britain as elsewhere, the tendency was to isolate brothels to special "red light" districts where middle-class men would not willingly go.

The Problem of Poverty The high incidence of prostitution, like that of crime and vagrancy, mirrored the existence of widespread poverty (there is a poverty map of London on p. 651). Urban poverty took on new dimensions in the bloated industrial cities, putting many individuals at risk of incarceration, violence, and abandonment, and inviting new sets of social attitudes and social policy. Before 1800, poverty was the concern of the churches or of small local agencies of government. By 1900, it was seen as a problem to be managed by the national state.

Britain pioneered in creating a national system of poor relief. The Poor Law Amendment Act of 1834 established a series of residential workhouses, to which the unemployed poor could be forcibly removed. These functioned much like prisons (see the photograph on p. 660). Strict discipline prevailed, work obligations were heavy, and food was plain and meager. Worse still, the workhouse system resulted in the break-up of families. Able-bodied men, who were expected to seek and find employment, were excluded. Women, children, and the old or infirm became the main beneficiaries—or victims—of the workhouse.

The British workhouse system found few imitators in other nations where, by the late nineteenth century, legislation in favor of workers served to moderate the effects of poverty. In Germany, as has been seen,

Bismarck instituted a system of benefits that cushioned employed workers and their families from unemployment, disability, ill health, and lack of income in old age. That model would be followed by many modern states. Trade unions, in addition, offered help in the case of unemployment, strike, or the death of a primary wage-earner. Private charities of a traditional sort continued to serve the poor, as did a new set of **philanthropic organizations**, which won the active support especially of some middle- and upper-class women.

Nevertheless, the poor continued to suffer particular disabilities. They were often uneducated or even illiterate. They had higher rates of illegitimacy and infanticide, suicide and mental illness than the rest of the population, less resistance to disease and lower life expectancy. They more often committed crimes, and were more often its victims. They ate less than the affluent, their nutrition deficit evident to the eye— the average laborer was several inches shorter than the average member of the middle class. In this pattern of starvation, that of poor women who were mothers of children—an "autostarvation" for the sake of their offspring—was a constant.

The poor were seen by the wealthy not merely as a class apart, but almost as a separate race, with a distinct culture and society. If the city was the site of the "dissolution of mankind into monads [very small units]," as Friedrich Engels observed—or the place where, uniquely, "the human heart is sick," according to the Romantic poet William Wordsworth (1770–1850)—surely those who were most deprived of selfhood and burdened with sick hearts were the dispossessed poor of the modern city.

THE TWO HALVES AT HOME

Crowding a new generation of industrial workers into the existing frame of urban life had tremendous consequences. The effects could be seen out on the street. The cityscape displayed sharp contrasts between the lives of the rich and those of the "other half." Such contrasts gain deeper reality, however, when the observer turns from the streets to the homes of workers and their employers. A chasm yawned between the tenement and the townhouse.

In the Tenement

However miserable the peasant's hovel (and some were mere piles of mud, or ditches covered with entangled branches), a peasant family normally had a place to live within an established village. The newly urbanized workers of the industrial age had nothing of the sort. As the photograph on p. 658 shows, they lived in one or two rooms shared with kin or strangers in the aging building stock of established cities, or in hastily-erected tenements in new towns or suburbs destined soon to deteriorate into **slums**.

In those rooms, heated if at all by a fireplace also used for cooking, they ate, slept, and gathered together. There were generally no separate rooms for food-preparation or dining, for bathing or toileting, for sleeping, or for intimate relationships of body or mind, as the passage in *Witnesses* below reveals. There was neither running water nor artificial light (well after these had become available to the affluent). For the performance of bodily functions, there were outhouses, or a pot inside, the contents of which were disposed of from windows by a centuries-old custom to add to the muck in the streets below.

The peasant household, moreover, possessed a stability the worker's household often lacked. In the countryside, male and female roles were distinguished.

While both men and women worked, sometimes side by side in the fields, they had different jobs. Men more often handled heavy tools, especially the plow, while women more often took care of barnyard chickens and other small animals, a cottage garden, housekeeping tasks, and above all the ceaseless labor of cooking and spinning. The worker's household instead was characterized by shifting, uncertain relations between the genders. In the early years of industrialization, men worked in factories alongside their wives and children. As women left the factories, they took up other work, still essential to family fortunes, while children often stayed in the factory. There they labored under dangerous conditions, subject to abusive employers, for the sake of a meager wage donated to support the family as a whole.

WITNESSES

The Two Halves at Home

Not only were the conditions of work very different for the poor and the wealthy in Europe's industrial age, but their living conditions sharply differed as well. These two passages present the filth and squalor of the worker's home, and the cultural emptiness and repressiveness of the bourgeois household.

The urban poor: description of domestic conditions among workers in Lille, France (1832): In their obscure cellars, in their rooms, which one would take for cellars, the air is never renewed, it is infected; the walls are plastered with garbage. ... If a bed exists, it is a few dirty, greasy planks; it is damp and putrescent straw; it is a coarse cloth whose color and fabric are hidden by a layer of grime; it is a blanket that resembles a sieve. ... The windows, always closed, are covered by paper and glass, but so black, so smoke-encrusted, that the light is unable to penetrate ... everywhere are piles of garbage, of ashes, of debris. ... One is exhausted, in these hovels, by a stale, nauseating, somewhat piquant odor, odor of filth, odor of garbage. ...

... I have seen individuals of both sexes and of very different ages lying together, most of them without nightshirts and repulsively dirty. Father, mother, the aged, children, adults, all pressed, stacked together. I stop. The reader will complete the picture, but I warn him that if he wishes it to be accurate, his imagination must not recoil before any of the disgusting mysteries performed on these impure beds in the midst of obscurity and drunkenness.

(From W. H. Sewell, *Work and Revolution in France: The Language of Labor from the Old Regime to 1848*, 1980)

The wealthy: Flora Tristan describes the life of the bourgeois Englishwoman (1842): It has long been the fashion to extol English liberties, but England is the seat of the most abominable despotism, where laws and prejudices submit women to the most revolting inequality! A woman may inherit only if she has no brothers;

she has no civil or political rights and the law subjects her to her husband in every respect. ...

This is what happens in wealthy families: the children are confined to the third floor with their nurse, maid or governess; the mother asks for them when she wishes to see them ... [and] she addresses them in a formal manner. As the poor little girl is starved of affection, her capacity for loving is never awakened ..., while for the father she hardly knows, she has a respect mingled with fear, and for her brother she keeps the consideration and deference she has been obliged to show him from her earliest childhood.

The system followed for the education of young girls seems to me fit to turn the most intelligent child into a blockhead. ... It is concerned solely to imprint on these young minds the *words* of all the European languages without the slightest thought for the *ideas*. ...

Young ladies have very few amusements: as family life is formal, arid, and intolerably boring, they plunge headlong into the world of the novel. Unfortunately, these romances revolve around lovers such as England has never known, and their influence gives birth to hopes that can never be fulfilled. ... [T]he fate of the married woman is very much sadder than that of the spinster; at least the unmarried woman enjoys a certain freedom, she can enter society and travel with her family or with friends, whereas once a woman is married, she cannot stir from the house *without the permission of her husband*. The English husband is like the *lord and master* of feudal times. ...

The English husband sleeps with his servant, casts her out when she is pregnant or after she has given birth. ... In England the wife is not the mistress of the household as she would be in France. In fact she is almost a stranger in her own home; the husband holds the money and the keys. ... [H]e has sole charge of everything.

(*The London Journal of Flora Tristan*, 1842; ed. J. Hawkes, 1982)

Getting by: *Many workers could not afford housing, not even in a slum. In one of journalist Jacob Riis's now classic photographs of working class existence in New York City, dated c. 1890, lodgers on Bayard Street rent a spot to spend the night for 5 cents. (Museum of the City of New York)*

Male heads of households depended for income on their children and wives. Frequently the householder was himself unemployed—for unemployment was a common, cyclical reality in the early industrial era—while his wife and children worked.

These different relations to work were reflected in personal relationships within workers' families. Women continued to bear complete responsibility for housework, the burden of which was added to paid labor outside the home. Since it was they who shopped for necessary supplies, they often controlled family finances. Managing the money that their husbands and children brought home, they sometimes rescued it from the hands of a spouse hoping to spend it at the local tavern.

Workers' wives could find employment as laundresses, daily servants, pieceworkers, and, later in the nineteenth century, laborers in the "**sweated industries.**" Piecework entailed sewing items of clothing, such as shirts, embroidering luxury items, or knitting stockings or caps, as shown in *Windows On* on p. 648. They might also market these products in the streets, as peddlers. The sweated industries employed a few laborers in workshops, or "sweatshops," outside the factory, generally dedicated to clothing manufacture. In all these cases, the wages they received were lower than those earned by male factory workers, or indeed by men doing work of equal difficulty. Overall, women may have earned about one-half the wages that men did for comparable work and hours.

Lower wages were not the only disability that women in working-class households experienced. They were often left to support whole families when the male head of household was unemployed or, as happened quite frequently, when he deserted his family altogether. They were often the victims of physical abuse from desperate and drunken husbands.

Single women workers were freer to move about to seek employment. In Britain, they often worked as domestic servants in the homes of bourgeois or aristocratic families (see below). As servants, they were frequently made pregnant by their masters or their masters' sons—a familiar cause for dismissal and social disgrace. Unmarried women in other job categories

Occupations of Women Workers in Milan (1881), London (1891), and France (1906)

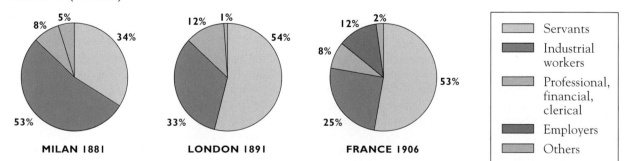

MILAN 1881

8% 5% 34% 53%

LONDON 1891

12% 1% 54% 33%

FRANCE 1906

12% 2% 8% 53% 25%

- ☐ Servants
- ☐ Industrial workers
- ☐ Professional, financial, clerical
- ☐ Employers
- ☐ Others

As in the early modern period, a great many of the women who worked found employment as servants. By the end of the nineteenth century, however, large numbers of women were working in factories, and in clerical and administrative positions in offices and stores—even as owners of shops and other enterprises.

Sources: *Based on P. M. Hohenberg and L. H. Lees,* The Making of Urban Europe, 1000–1950 *(Cambridge, MA: Harvard University Press, 1985; 2nd ed., 1995), p. 210, and R. Price,* A Social History of Nineteenth-Century France *(New York: Holmes & Meier, 1987), p. 213.*

also often found themselves pregnant in the industrial city, where the restraints of village life had withered and died. Women who gave birth out of wedlock frequently abandoned their babies to the care of foundling homes or orphanages, now become numerous, and sometimes killed them. Many such women were forced into prostitution.

Whatever their circumstances, the laboring poor shared this characteristic with the incarcerated prisoner or the workhouse resident: they had nowhere to go. They had little expectation that conditions would improve for them, or that their children could aspire to higher positions than those they themselves occupied. Their wages purchased little beyond food and that food was mostly bread. Well over half a workers' wage was spent on food, and, after expenses of housing and clothing, barely ten percent was left—often dispensed on drink and entertainment. After their long workday, male and female workers alike sought recreation in tavern, café, or **music hall**, the social clubs of the poor. If they spent too much of their meager supply of cash on these amusements, pawnbrokers and loansharks were always available to lend them more, and bind them even more firmly to an unending condition of poverty.

By the late nineteenth century, and a little earlier in Britain (where workers' diets and prospects were somewhat better), standards of living for the working poor in northern and western Europe began at last to rise. In Britain, real wages increased by one-third between 1850 and 1875, and by nearly one-half again between 1870 and 1900. Advances in Germany were nearly as great. Improvements in agriculture resulted in lower food costs, at least in these privileged regions, falling to about half of the family budget. More money became available for housing, for clothes (cheap, well-cut ready-mades were now widely available), and for entertainment. Workers' diets became more varied, including grain and even meat, shipped in refrigerated compartments from the Americas and Australia. No longer a luxury, meat consumption among workers rose steadily.

Another step toward the eventual advancement of the working class was the advent of public schooling for its children (see also Chapter 25). By the eighteenth century, elementary schooling had become more widely available for the young children of ordinary folk in such areas as Prussia, Scotland, and parts of Anglo-America. The nineteenth century saw the expansion of mass secular education. From the 1880s, Britain and France instituted mandatory, free public schools for all children; most states of the United States had already done so by the end of the nineteenth century. With access to public education in at least these leading nations, all children—the tenement dweller just as much as the child of privilege—had the valuable opportunity to gain the skills by which they could strive for greater success.

In the Townhouse

Out in the countryside in pre-modern Europe, the grand manor house or castle of the local landowner dominated the huts or cottages of the peasants. The gulf between rich and poor was equally apparent in the city, which contained both the opulent townhouse or apartment of the bourgeois or nobleman and the worker's rented room. In the industrial era, as the dwellings of the poor became even bleaker in the multi-storied anonymity of the tenement, the homes of the well-off became softer, warmer and more comfortable than ever.

Domestic comfort had only recently become an important consideration for the upper classes as the industrial age opened. Since the fifteenth century, aristocratic homes had developed differentiated private and public spaces, both suitably adorned with fine furniture and tapestries. By the seventeenth and eighteenth centuries, aristocratic homes in country and city featured lush furnishings and expensive adornments—and the great luxury of windows. As industrialization proceeded in the nineteenth century, the ever-larger and ever-wealthier bourgeoisie imitated the pacesetting nobility and furnished their townhouses and apartments to suit their enhanced social and economic position.

The number of rooms multiplied, and more things filled those rooms. The homes of the wealthy now possessed parlors and studies, bedrooms and nurseries, and formal dining-rooms. Walls lined with brocaded cloth or richly designed papers were hung with prints and paintings, and adorned with fine wood or plaster moldings. Candelabras hung from the ceiling or were mounted on the wall. Scattered about were fine musical instruments—such as a piano in the parlor—showpiece clocks on pedestals or mantels, and collections of small precious things—crystal, silver, porcelain. Furniture included elegant tables and wardrobes and soft, deep chairs, resting on patterned carpets.

The dusting and cleaning of such large houses stuffed with so many possessions were the constant care of servants, who served in European cities in veritable armies. Most domestic servants were women who lived in closets and attics, consumed the same food as their employers' families, and could expect reasonable conditions of life and work despite their meager pay. Even in less wealthy bourgeois households, a single maid-of-all-work might clean the house, tend the fires, and wait at table, among a variety of other tasks. Servant labor made the bourgeois style of life possible.

Ladies of Leisure Like their female servants, elite women were also dedicated to the maintenance of the bourgeois or aristocratic household. Their lives are described in *Witnesses* on p. 657. They were expected to avoid work themselves—exemption from labor was essential to the status of "lady"—but to manage the labor of servants in housekeeping and food preparation tasks. The boundaries between the privileged and those considered to be "inferior" lay in these delicate, clearly understood social distinctions between the housewife who labored and the one who, having at least one female servant, did not.

Bourgeois and aristocratic women turned their skills and aptitudes instead to other household functions. They exercised their taste in the choice of furnishings and works of art, in the selection of schools and tutors for their children, and in the arts of hospitality—the entertainment of neighbors and business associates with afternoon tea, elaborate dinners (served in multiple courses by servants in formal attire), or for extended visits, all arranged by the genteel exchange of invitations in person or through written notes on luxury stationery. The elite household consumed much—food and drink, furniture and furnishings, the labor of servants—and women were charged with procuring these consumables. They hired servants, dealt with tradesmen, and visited the new department stores (the first of which appeared in Paris soon after 1850)—those palaces of consumerism which, observed the French writer Emile Zola (1840–1902; see Chapter 25), threatened to replace the churches in the hearts of many.

When not shopping or visiting, elite women stayed current by reading sentimental novels or ladies' magazines which had been published since the eighteenth century, filled with articles about fashion, entertaining, and childcare. They employed their leisure with activities that produced little of practical use but much of beauty: embroidery, knitting, and other forms of needlework. One advice book for young ladies explained: "The intention of your being taught needlework, knitting and such like is not on account of the intrinsic values of all you can do with your hands, which is trifling, but to enable you to fill up, in a tolerably agreeable way, some of the many solitary hours you must necessarily pass at home."

Women of the elites were responsible for the households in which they led lives of ease. At the same time, they had little connection with the public world beyond the household—the realm of work, wealth, and power. The distinction between a woman's life close to the household and a man's apart from it was not new to the industrial age, but it was to become even sharper as the "separate spheres" of home and work involved wholly different activities. Work had been wholly removed from the household, which was once itself a zone of productive activity, and it moved to the factory, the bank, the office building. The household now became the site for recuperation from work, a place reserved for the consumption of goods and services. Here women bore the responsibility of equipping their male kin for the distant, different place of work.

The widening gap between home and work among the elites, the spheres of female and male, was expressed in the new fashions of the industrial age. Some of these developments are illustrated in *Windows On*, pp. 600–601. A generation after the French Revolution, driven forward by the rage of the *sans-culottes* (see Chapter 20), bourgeois and aristocratic men abandoned knee-breeches for trousers, a fashion associated with practical, serious work, rather than the frivolities of the court. At the same time, they gave up powdered wigs and perfume, silks (except in the relic of the tie) and velvets, jewelry and high-heeled shoes. They dressed in black or grey, suggesting sober attention to duty, with the distinction between the wealthier and the less-wealthy evident not in the style of clothing but only in such details as the cut of the garment and the quality of the fabric. Elite women, however, continued to wear (after an interlude of simplicity during the Napoleonic era) the huge skirts, tight bodices, and brilliant colors of female aristocrats of the previous era. Their dress proclaimed their leisured status and

Workhouse and Café

Dinnertime in St. Pancras workhouse: *Significant numbers of poorer urbanites lacked even the most basic housing, and made their homes instead at workhouses or other institutional refuges. Here, women eat in the St. Pancras, London workhouse, in a scene from around 1900.*

their mission to bear children—their fertility announced to the world by the contrast between full skirt and corseted waist. Indeed, hoops and crinolines made women gigantic, larger than their menfolk but frailer, physically absurd in a way that suggested their continued rootedness to a natural world amid the frantic pandemonium of modern industrial life.

Although women's reproductive mission was thus displayed in their costume, privileged women in the wealthier nations were in fact beginning to bear fewer children—especially in France, where birthrates dropped drastically toward the end of the nineteenth century. Such declining birthrates witness the practice of birth control, especially the traditional but unreliable method of *coitus interruptus*, or male withdrawal. Condoms, though known, were crude, and mostly used with prostitutes, and the other possibilities (herbal remedies and home surgery) were unpleasant, dangerous, and often deadly.

Family Life   A declining rate of infant mortality perhaps encouraged people to have fewer children. Economic factors were also important: increased costs associated with childrearing, especially private education, affected the middle classes, while, for working-class families, child labor laws and compulsory education meant that younger children could no longer contribute to family income. Whatever the case, fewer children in the family meant that non-working mothers could devote more time and care to their children's rearing. They worried over child health and education, seeking the opinion of experts and carefully selecting schools. For the first time in Western history, women of the elites breastfed their own infants, both to nourish them better, and to surround them with the maternal tenderness that so many infants through the ages had never known.

This trend toward the deepening attachment of middle-class women to their children (aristocratic women generally still consigned theirs to the care of servants) coincided with changes in the medical treatment of childbirth. Male midwives, and then male doctors, took over the business of supervising birth for women of the upper classes (although they did so in women's homes rather than in hospitals, where poor women suffered the dangers of infection and neglect). The development of the forceps in the eighteenth century had helped infants and mothers to survive difficult births. A century later, two other developments assisted the mother. The first was the adoption of the principle of antisepsis (see Chapter 25), by assuring the cleanliness of surgical instruments and environment, which greatly reduced the rate of maternal mortality. The second was the introduction of anesthesia, initially by the use of chloroform—an innovation that Britain's Queen Victoria (r. 1837–1901) personally experienced and approved enthusiastically.

The intensifying involvement of better-off women with their young children was one aspect of a general intensification of family feeling. More often than in the past, men and women married partners of their choosing. Encouraged in part by the powerful cultural movement of Romanticism (see Chapter 25), whose message resounded in books, opera, and theater, they sought marriages founded on love. Meanwhile, marital love was valued by the public consensus as it had not been in earlier ages, when duty, obedience, or mutual affection was the expressed ideal. Advice books glorified family life, and manuals on conjugal love encouraged both men and women to seek sexual gratification within marriage for the sake of the harmonious community of mother, father, and children.

In the intense theater of family life, privileged women were the source not only of heightened sentiment, but also of a "higher" morality. It was the women who conveyed moral lessons, and saw to

***Pierre-Auguste Renoir,* Le Moulin de la Galette:** *After dark, the city was full of opportunities. Working-class and middle-class urban-dwellers alike shopped, attended theaters and music halls, strolled in parks, and relaxed with friends in taverns and cafés. In Paris, cafés such as this one—painted by Impressionist artist Pierre-Auguste Renoir in 1876—were popular places to socialize. (Louvre, Paris)*

their children's moral as well as intellectual growth. Mothers supervised religious instruction, presiding over family prayers and seeking to instill the values of self-control and self-reliance that had become newly important in industrial society.

Women's association with the moral realm also reached beyond the household. Many engaged in charitable activities that took them across their own thresholds, and out beyond the boundaries of their neighborhood and caste to tend to the needs of those of the other half: orphans, unwed mothers, prostitutes, the sick, the poor. They gathered in clubs and organizations for charitable purposes, where as volunteer treasurers, secretaries, and presidents, they acquired the experience of management they were barred from in the professional world of work.

Despite their vigorous role in philanthropic activities (which also appealed to many men of the affluent classes), and their competence in running large and complex households, women were still expected to defer to men in matters concerning money. In most countries, a woman's dowry was still her husband's to use, if it was not absolutely his property. In some, women could own no property in their own name, and could negotiate loans only with the co-signature of a husband, father, or guardian. In France, where the Revolution had insisted on daughters' equal right to inherit, the Napoleonic Code (see Chapter 20) classed women as legal incompetents along with children, the insane, and criminals.

Nearly everywhere, a woman's adultery was still viewed by the law as a more serious offense than a man's—and in some countries, it was permissible for a husband who caught his wife in the adulterous act to kill her. Divorce, too (where it was obtainable at all), was more easily obtained by a man than a woman, who needed to prove amply and without question her husband's offenses. In the event of divorce or separation, it was fathers who generally held all custodial rights over children—and not their mothers, whose sentimental attachment to them was increasingly part of family life.

These barriers to women's independence would be resisted in the new feminist movement of the later 1800s (see Chapter 25). In the meantime, most propertied families functioned as though these problems did not exist, appearing to enjoy wholeheartedly the many opportunities their comfortable lives offered. Besides receiving visitors at home, and visiting others, men and women of the bourgeoisie and aristocracy eagerly attended concerts, the theater, and the opera, where they sat in halls among audiences who were much more orderly than in the past, and listened more attentively than had their ancestors— even entertainment was becoming a serious matter during the industrial age, requiring a disciplined and responsible attitude.

They also frequented teashops and cafés, strolled in well-groomed parks, borrowed books from libraries, attended lectures at literary or philosophical societies, and relaxed at their (mostly all-male) clubs. They traveled by the new railroad lines to the beach and to spas, where they bathed in and drank mineral-laden waters thought to be beneficial to their health. Equipped with guides to monuments, museums, and restaurants, they toured the cities of Europe, and, boarding steamships where they slept in luxurious staterooms and enjoyed elaborate dinners, they ventured to colonial centers abroad (see Chapter 24).

Far from home, the men and women of the privileged classes enjoyed comforts and refinements unthinkable in the tenements where the other half lived.

Conclusion

THE ONE HALF, THE OTHER HALF, AND THE MEANING OF THE WEST

During the nineteenth century, industrialization recreated the human and urban landscape of the wealthier Western nations. It created new social groups—that of the factory worker who bore the burden of the pain entailed by the reconstruction of the modern economy, and that of the capitalist, for whose profit the worker labored. At the same time, it created a new, previously inconceivable, kind of city—a huge and diverse place, embracing factories and libraries, department stores and brothels, all knit together by sewage and water pipes, gas lines, and electrical cable. Within that city the astoundingly rich coexisted with the desperately poor, and contrasts between wealth and poverty were vivid and shocking. The disparity between rich and poor, which had long been a concern of the Christian churches, would henceforth be taken up by the secular leaders of the Western world—a problem with moral, practical, and political dimensions, threatening both stability and conscience. At the dawn of the twenty-first century, the problem persists across the West still.

Even as rich and poor confronted each other in the different capitals of the Western world, the West was vigorously extending its influence in the world beyond the West, as the following chapter will show, confronting a different sort of poverty, and creating a new set of relationships between those who command and those who serve.

QUESTIONS TO CONSIDER

1. Why did working in factories have a different effect on children and families than work carried on in the household or on the farm?

2. Why are the industrial workers, or proletariat, of the modern age different from any of the groups of poor people encountered throughout earlier history?

3. Why does industrialization change the nature of workers' associations? How are the new trade unions different from medieval craft guilds?

4. Why were the lives of the urban poor so different from those of the rich and the middle class?

5. How did the family change in size and function during the nineteenth century? What was the impact on the education of children?

SUGGESTED RESOURCES

Biernacki, Richard, *The Fabrication of Labor: Germany and Britain, 1640–1914* (Berkeley: University of California Press, 1995). Explores national differences in concepts of labor and wages.

Clark, Anna, *The Struggle for the Breeches: Gender and the Making of the British Working Class* (Berkeley-Los Angeles; University of California Press, 1995). Describes how male and female workers competed for jobs and household authority in the early industrial era, with the result that women lost the struggle for the breeches.

Corbin, Alain, *The Lure of the Sea: The Discovery of the Seaside in the Western World 1750–1840* (Berkeley: University of California Press, 1994). Traces the significance of the sea-shore as both a physical destination and a cultural artifact.

Fuchs, Rachel G., *Poor and Pregnant in Paris: Strategies for Survival in the Nineteenth Century* (New Brunswick, NJ: Rutgers University Press, 1992). How poverty and abandonment led to bleak outcomes.

Haine, W. Scott, *The World of the Paris Café: Sociability Among the French Working Class, 1789–1914* (Baltimore: The Johns Hopkins University Press, 1996). Identifies the café as the cultural center of French workers' lives in the 19th century.

Horn, Pamela, *Children's Work and Welfare, 1780–1890* (Cambridge: Cambridge University Press, 1995). Useful introduction to an important and frequently under-examined area of industrial history.

Jordan, David P., *Transforming Paris: The Life and Labors of Baron Haussmann* (Chicago: University of Chicago Press, 1995). A biography of the man responsible for the transformation of Paris from a medieval to a modern reality, in tune with the social and economic transformations of the century.

Joyce, Patrick, *The Rule of Freedom: Liberalism and the Modern City* (New York: Verso, 2003). Looking at Manchester and London, with side glances at Vienna, Calcutta, and Los Angeles, explores how the modern city promotes the liberation and at the same time greater governmental control of the citizens.

Landers, John, *Death and the Metropolis: Studies in the Demographic History of London, 1670–1830* (Cambridge: Cambridge University Press, 1993). Seeks the cause of London's high mortality rates, focusing on unhealthy environmental conditions and disease.

Maynes, Mary Jo, *Taking the Hard Road: Life Course in French and German Workers' Autobiographies in the Era of Industrialization* (Durham: University of North Carolina Press, 1995). Sensitive study of autobiographies written by French and German workers, about one-third of them women, whose lives span the long 19th century, and whose memories help us to understand the impact of industrialization on the lives of real people.

Maza, Sarah, *The Myth of the French Bourgeoisie: An Essay on the Social Imaginary, 1750–1850* (Cambridge MA: Harvard University Press, 2003). Denies the existence of the French bourgeoisie in the sense of a group self-consciously defined, an argument calling for the rethinking of much recent work in social history.

Rappaport, Erika Diane, *Shopping for Pleasure: Women in the Making of London's West End* (Princeton: Princeton University Press, 2000). Describes how the habit of shopping developed by middle-class women transformed the life and the structure of London's West End.

Reid, Donald, *Paris Sewers and Sewermen: Realities and Representations* (Cambridge, MA: Harvard University Press, 1991). The sewer is the emblem of 19th-century city transformation, as public health experts learn that the inflow of clean water and removal of sewage are essential for the control of disease. Reid explores the men who took on the heroic task of installing and maintaining the sewer system in Paris.

Ross, Ellen, *Love and Toil: Motherhood in Outcast London, 1870–1918* (Oxford: Oxford University Press, 1993). Examines how mothers struggled to keep working families intact and nurture children.

The Plight of Women's Work in the Early Industrial Revolution in England and Wales (Women in World History Curriculum), brief history and texts:
http://www.womeninworldhistory.com/lesson7.html

Child Labor (Victorian Web, Hartwick College):
http://landow.stg.brown.edu/victorian/history/hist8.html

Jacob Riis, How the Other Half Lives: Studies among the Tenements of New York (New York: Charles Scribner's Sons, 1890), full-text hypertext edition:
http://www.yale.edu/amstud/inforev/riis/title.html

Western Civilization Documents CD-ROM

22.2 Child Labor Inquiry
22.3 Women Miners
22.4 A Factory Girl
22.5 A View from Downstairs
22.6 Improving the Poor?
23.2 Women Without Power Change the System
23.6 Gertrude Himmelfarb: from Poverty and Compassion

THE CONCERT OF EUROPE

1810	1830	1850	1870	1890	1910	1930

Revolution and Reorganization

◆ Congress of Vienna, 1814–15

◆ Carlsbad Decrees, 1819

◆ US Monroe Doctrine, 1823

◆ Decembrist Revolt in Russia, 1825

◆ Revolutions in Europe, 1830–31

◆ Greek independence, 1832

◆ Revolutions in Europe, 1848

◆ Louis Napoleon restores Empire in France, 1851

◆ Austro-Prussian War, 1866

◆ Dual Monarchy of Austria-Hungary established, 1867

◆ Unification of Italy, 1870

◆ Franco-Prussian War, 1870–71

◆ Paris Commune, 1870

◆ Unification of Germany, 1871

◆ Bismarck made Chancellor, 1871

◆ Congress of Berlin divides Ottoman empire, 1878

◆ Russo-Japanese War, 1904–5

◆ Balkan Wars, 1912–13

Society and Ideas

◆ Factory Act in Britain, 1833

◆ German customs Union, the Zollverein, formed, 1834

◆ Louis Blanc's The Organization of Work, 1839

◆ Potato Famine devastates Ireland, 1845–50

◆ Emancipation of serfs in Russia, 1861

◆ First International, 1864

◆ Slavery abolished in US, 1865

◆ School mandatory for British children up to 10, 1880

◆ Bismarck creates social welfare system for workers in Germany, 1883–89

◆ Second International, 1889

Beyond the West

Atlantic slave trade, 1500–1888

Qing Dynasty, China, 1644–1912

◆ Shaka leads Zulu nation, 1817

◆ First Opium War, 1839–42

◆ Second Opium War, 1856–60

◆ Sepoy Mutiny, India, 1857

◆ Meiji Restoration, Japan, 1868

◆ Suez canal opens, 1869

◆ Berlin Conference sets off "Scramble for Africa," 1884

◆ Indian National Congress founded, 1885

CHAPTER 23

THE CONCERT OF EUROPE:

Mass Politics and the Triumph
of the State

1815–1914

newly unified or established
states, with date

KEY QUESTIONS

◆ **Power to the People, 1815–1848:** Why were
there repeated revolutionary outbreaks in this
period, especially in 1830–1831 and 1848? What
attempts were made to prevent and suppress
them?

◆ **One People, One Nation: 1848–1871:** Which
European peoples came together as a nation for
the first time in this era, and which peoples found
themselves to be entrapped as minorities in
multiethnic states?

◆ **The State Triumphant: 1848–1914:** How did
the European states reassert their authority after
an era of revolution and turmoil?

The Paris Commune In 1870–1871, the workers of Paris resisted Prussian invaders and then their own countrymen, briefly creating the world's first socialist state amid the last spasms of the Franco-Prussian War. The Prussian siege brought starvation but did not quell the surge of political feeling within the city. Revolutionary clubs sprang up abundantly, while women's groups pressed for political and social rights, such as day care for working mothers. Workers' groups declared the "Paris Commune," a stateless society of free producers, engaged in what Vladimir Ilich Lenin (1876–1924) was later to call a "festival of the oppressed." In Versailles, in January 1871, the victors proclaimed the German Empire; in February, they settled an armistice with the French. In Paris, however, the war had not ended.

The attack on Paris that began in March 1871 was made not by Germans but by Frenchmen, the regular army of the new third Republic. In May they wrested Paris from its Communard defenders in the streets and marketplaces, neighborhood by neighborhood. It took a week—"Bloody Week," May 21–28—and the slaughter was immense. More than 20,000 Parisians were killed, both men and women, in the bloodiest episode in almost a century of sporadic revolution. As the photograph on p. 678 shows, their bodies were bundled into mass graves, dug in the lovely parks that the Emperor Napoleon had built for the recreation of the citizens.

The Paris Commune, crushed in March 1871, was the last of a series of revolts by the "people" against the "state" that mark the history of nineteenth-century Europe. Henceforth, the state would reign triumphant. But it could no longer do so without attending to the urgent needs of the people—which, if ignored, might erupt in violence. The age when kings and gentlemen could manage government by themselves was over, and the age of mass politics had begun.

The people raised their voices against their rulers, especially in the first half of the century, as they sought liberty from what they perceived as tyrannical regimes. Later in the century, it was often nationalist feelings that fired rebellions, and such uprisings were instrumental in creating the new unified states of Italy and Germany. By the last decades of the century, however, order prevailed, and the powerful states of Europe took up the task of governing and accommodating the masses of the people who had arrived at the political front and would not thereafter go home.

POWER TO THE PEOPLE: 1815–1848

In the waning days of Napoleon's empire, representatives of the nations who had defeated him came together in Vienna to create the "concert of Europe"—a harmonious balance among the most powerful nations, intended to secure a lasting peace. The plans devised at the Congress of Vienna (1814–1815) were, in fact, quite successful. They prevented war in Europe for more than half a century, and even managed to contain rebellious impulses for fifteen years. Thereafter, they could no longer mute the aspirations of bourgeois liberals, nationalists of all social classes, and workers. Most of the European monarchies that existed in 1815, or were reinstated thereafter, endured into the next century. But the people, seeking to be no longer subjects but citizens, demanded rights and recognition. Their aspirations exploded into action in 1830 and again, more forcefully, in 1848. These revolts were invariably suppressed. Yet they served to remind governments that peoples' demand for entry into the political arena could not be ignored or denied.

After Napoleon: The Conservative Response

To the representatives of the victor nations who met at the Congress of Vienna, Napoleon was the embodiment of all they disliked. The 1789 Revolution in France had tossed out monarchy, aristocracy, and Church. Under Napoleon, they were not restored, although the latter two received accommodations. In the eyes of the representatives, Napoleon was an illegitimate ruler whose intrusion among European leaders posed a profound threat, even after Napoleon himself had met his defeat.

The French Revolution itself presented an even greater threat. It had established a liberal agenda of human and civil rights, such as freedom of the press, freedom of assembly, freedom of religion, and the abrogation of class distinction, that challenged the authoritarian powers of European monarchs. Though the Revolution had foundered after the events of Thermidor, the French army had broadcast its message in all the lands it entered; and this message, it was feared, might inspire new revolutions abroad.

Moreover, the French Revolution had triggered a surge of patriotic sentiment, or **nationalism**, also exported by French soldiers alongside liberalism. To these two ideological threats, the diplomats of Vienna adopted an opposing ideological stance: that of **conservatism** (see Chapter 25).

The pioneering conservative Edmund Burke had cautioned against the destruction of institutions and beliefs built up over centuries, the work of multiple generations (see Chapter 20). He had foreseen what the consequences of revolution might be, but he died (in 1797) before they had materialized in the person of Napoleon. A harsher conservatism than Burke's emerged from the Vienna discussions, articulated by the principal Habsburg representative, Prince

Clemens von Metternich (1773–1859). Some of his ideas are noted in *Witnesses* on p. 682.

Metternich urged the following goals: to suppress revolutions everywhere; to restore legitimate rulers; to support the nobility and established churches; to limit dissent and even debate by controlling the press and establishing mechanisms of surveillance by secret police forces. Both liberal and nationalist movements threatened the stability of the allied nations; so they would have to be averted or destroyed. Just as Napoleon had suppressed the liberal aspirations of the Revolution, now monarchy, aristocracy, and Church would suppress the legacy of Napoleon.

By the time it ended, in June 1815, the Congress of Vienna had reestablished the monarchies disrupted by Napoleon and Revolution and the religious establishments that had supported them. Their distribution is shown on Map 23.1 below. As Map 23.2 on p. 672 shows, these governments set about suppressing liberalism and nationalism in the German and Italian states and in France; some anti-liberal measures were applied even in Britain, where the monarchy remained intact. European powers were, however, unable to stop revolutions in the colonies in South America and the Caribbean (see Chapter 19), and, ironically, supported a revolution in Greece against the Ottoman Empire. Within their own boundaries, they muzzled dissent by breaking up associations of workers and students, by censoring the press, and by unleashing secret police forces.

Liberalism and Nationalism in Central Europe

Austria was especially vulnerable to disruption by nationalist movements. Over the previous centuries, it had expanded from a mere duchy within the Holy Roman Empire to a principality; its Habsburg monarchs had held the imperial title virtually without interruption since the late 1400s. During the course of this expansion, Austria had absorbed a large part of central and southeastern Europe. Among its dominions were Bohemia, Moravia, and Hungary (including Transylvania); parts of Poland, Russia, and Italy; and the Ottoman Balkans, including parts of Croatia and Serbia. In addition to German-speaking Austrians, its

Map 23.1 Europe in 1815 as Established by the Congress of Vienna: *In 1815, the participants of the Congress of Vienna rearranged the map in order to achieve a European balance of power.* Given their geographical boundaries and subdivisions, which regions of Europe promise to be the most volatile in years to come?

peoples included Italians, Czechs, Slovaks, Magyars, Poles, Romanians, Slovenes, and Croats. They spoke at least twenty different languages, and adhered to Roman Catholicism, Eastern Orthodoxy, Judaism, Islam, and varieties of Protestantism. Different political agendas guided the actions of these different ethnic groups.

The Austrian and Czech bourgeoisie shared the outlook of western European liberals. They hoped to limit Habsburg autocracy, to gain political rights and secure freedom of the press. Czech liberals were moved by nationalism, as were the powerful nobles of Hungary and Croatia. These aristocrats could be persuaded to cooperate with the Austrian government, which supported their domination over a subject peasantry, but they still demanded greater independence within the Habsburg regime. Other regions were more resistant to Habsburg rule; in Serbia and Moldavia, rebellions broke out in 1817 and 1821.

Northern Italians sought freedom from Habsburg rule. In 1831, insurrections broke out in Italy against Austrian and papal domination, calling for a unified Italian nation. Although those rebellions were suppressed, their cause was given increased muscle by the ardent patriot Giuseppe Mazzini (1805–1872), who became their leader. Some of his ideas are noted in *Witnesses* on pp. 679 and 732. He organized disparate groups of **carbonari** ("charcoal-burners") into the liberal–nationalist organization "Young Italy." It was not sufficient to have rights, Mazzini told his followers; one must belong to a nation: "Without Country you have neither name, token, voice, nor rights, no admission as brothers into the fellowship of the People." Organized as a secret society, admission to which involved oaths hedged with threats of retribution, Young Italy grew into a major movement which spurred progress toward national unification—a goal achieved in 1870.

Nationalist movements inspired by liberal principles flourished in the German cities and principalities, as indicated in *Witnesses* on pp. 679 and 732. Continuing the work begun by Napoleon, the Congress of Vienna created a Confederation of 39 German states (including Prussia and Austria), whose representatives attended a Federal Diet at Frankfurt. Instead of unifying Germany, however, this reorganization actually underscored the autonomy of the component states.

It was, rather, a combination of university students and their professors who spearheaded liberal and nationalist sentiment in Germany; and they faced tough opposition. The Carlsbad Decrees of 1819, which were conceived by Metternich and proposed jointly by the rulers of both Prussia and Austria to the complaisant Diet of the German Confederation, abolished the student proto-revolutionary clubs, and silenced the press: "No [daily or serial] publication …," came the decree to muzzle that voice, "shall go to press in any state of the union without the previous knowledge and approval of the state officials."

Censorship, however, could not choke off news of the 1830 revolt in France (see below), which sparked further rebellions in the Netherlands, Poland, and elsewhere. At Heidelberg and Frankfurt, university students gathered to call for a united Germany. The "Ten Articles," issued by the Diet of the German Confederation, scripted the suppression of liberal movements throughout the German states, but failed to silence a generation of young men who would become lawyers, magistrates, and professors of a new nation. Meanwhile, although political unification was postponed, the customs union (Zollverein) formed in 1843, which eliminated internal tariffs and promoted the economic unity of many of the German states, was of great significance for Germany's future.

Another creation of the Congress of Vienna was a united kingdom of the Netherlands, which included both the northern, largely Protestant provinces and the southern Catholic ones formerly under Habsburg rule. The new king, William I (r. 1815–1840), of the line of the princes of Orange, consolidated his position in the north. The southern provinces resisted amalgamation, and they revolted in 1830 (in the wake of the French revolt of that year). They eventually organized the separate nation of Belgium, headed by its own constitutional monarch supported by a representative assembly.

Revolution in Russia, the Iberian Peninsula, and Greece

The Russian empire, like the Austrian, had expanded territorially over the previous centuries. It now contained many Asian minorities, of which some groups were Muslims; and in 1815 it absorbed part of the kingdom of Poland which Napoleon had briefly reconstituted as the Grand Duchy of Warsaw. These subject territories were not, however, the main source of difficulty for Tsar Alexander I (r. 1801–1825). Rather, it was his nation's social rigidity. The great majority of the Russian people were virtually serfs, the personal property of the nobility.

Russia's minuscule bourgeoisie could do little to resist the autocratic regime, but a handful of dissident nobles attempted a coup in December 1825, on Alexander's death. Their attempt to place the former tsar's brother Constantine (believed to be more liberal) on the throne failed, and Alexander's son Nicholas became tsar. Nicholas I (r. 1825–1855) subdued the "Decembrist Revolt" (as it was called) and executed or exiled its leaders, inaugurating an era of even fiercer repression.

"Serfdom is a powder keg under the state," warned one of the tsar's noble advisers in 1839. From 1826 to 1849, serfs rose up in revolt on nearly 2000 occasions—not always with the success of the 54 peasants

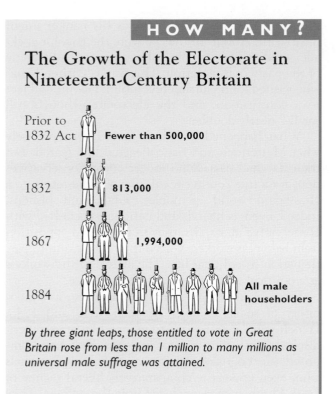

HOW MANY?

The Growth of the Electorate in Nineteenth-Century Britain

Prior to 1832 Act — Fewer than 500,000

1832 — 813,000

1867 — 1,994,000

1884 — All male householders

By three giant leaps, those entitled to vote in Great Britain rose from less than 1 million to many millions as universal male suffrage was attained.

who in 1835 managed to kill 144 estate owners and 29 stewards before their rebellion, like the others, was suppressed. Meanwhile, dissident intellectuals, mostly aristocrats, fed on the thousands of foreign books smuggled into Russia and pondered nightly by impassioned student ideologies (see Chapter 25).

In Spain and Portugal, whose monarchs were restored by the Congress of Vienna, dissent still simmered; liberal revolutions, begun in both countries in 1820, were suppressed in 1823 and 1824, respectively. Across the Atlantic, several of the Spanish colonies revolted more on the pattern of the North American revolt of 1775 than the French one of 1789 (see Chapter 19). By 1825, the continental Spanish American colonies, as well as Brazil (formerly Portuguese), had been constituted as independent nations. European efforts to reverse these changes were halted by the policy declared in 1823 by U.S. President James Monroe and known as the Monroe Doctrine: the Americas, it announced, "are henceforth not to be considered as subjects for future colonization by any European powers"; and any intervention by European powers in the affairs of the Western Hemisphere would be seen as an "unfriendly act."

European powers might have intervened in Greece, but they did not. Here, insurrection broke out in 1821 against the Muslim Ottoman regime, which had ruled Greece since the fifteenth century (see Chapters 14, 15). In this case, the anti-revolutionary principles of the European states conflicted with their anti-Turkish and pro-Christian sentiments. Liberal writers, intellectuals, and young people all over Europe, and especially in England, cheered on the Greek revolt, while their governments, though suspicious of all such movements, did nothing to protect the legitimate regime. By 1832, Greece had won its independence from the Ottoman Empire.

Pressure for Change in Great Britain

Britain, which had already undergone an industrial transformation (see Chapter 21), still shared the difficulties faced by the other principal nations during the post-Napoleonic period. Liberals demanded the broadening of the franchise and other civil rights, while workers sought to better their condition. As protest stirred, the Combination Acts of 1799 and 1800, which barred the formation of workers' organizations, were sternly enforced until their eventual repeal in 1824. "Corn Laws" (which protected landowners' profits) taxed grain imports, keeping the price of bread artificially high. The government suppressed mass protests against such restrictive tariffs and other inequalities. In 1819, in Manchester, soldiers fired on a crowd of 60,000 people gathered in St. Peter's Fields, demanding parliamentary reforms and repeal of the Corn Laws. Eleven people were killed in this "Peterloo Massacre" (named in imitation of Waterloo). Religious freedom was another contentious issue. Until 1829, Roman Catholics were barred from holding political office in Britain and Ireland. The Roman Catholic population of Ireland, subject to mostly Anglo-Irish Protestant landlords, suffered unremitting discrimination.

Over the next generation, however, Britain managed, without revolution, to open access to government and to nurse the wounds caused by economic change. The Reform Act of 1832 nearly doubled the franchise, as *How Many?* above shows. Now the wealthiest one-fifth of adult male citizens could vote for representatives in Parliament—an improvement, but still far short of universal suffrage.

The Poor Law of 1834 (see Chapter 22), which introduced new provisions for housing the destitute, signaled the government's readiness to address the social problem of poverty. In 1846, the repeal of the Corn Laws permitted the importation of cheaper grain; previously the Factory Act of 1833 and Mines Act of 1842 had done something to improve the conditions faced by the most exploited industrial workers.

More radical reforms were called for by the Chartist movement. This organization of working people acquired its name from a "People's Charter" drawn up in 1838 by the London Working Men's Association. The Charter demanded universal male suffrage, a secret ballot, and electoral reform, among other changes. Its supporters met and marched for ten years, engaging a generation of ordinary people in participatory democracy. Millions of citizens signed petitions, which were sent to Parliament in 1939 and

1842 but left unheeded. In 1848, stirred by news of continental revolutions, the Chartist movement culminated in a last great, but again futile, march.

Even more deeply estranged from British public life were the people of Ireland, saddled by absentee landlords and religious intolerance, unrepresented in Parliament, and unassisted by the government. In 1845, crisis struck (see Chapter 24).

Irish farmers had taken to growing potatoes (see Chapter 16), which grew easily and provided bountiful nourishment from a small area. In Ireland, where most peasants possessed only the tiniest of plots of soil from which to gain their whole sustenance, the potato took over, not merely as the chief but virtually as the sole crop. In 1845, the potato crop failed. A devastating famine, the "Great Hunger," seized Ireland, killing millions, leaving others malnourished, and driving hundreds of thousands more to emigrate (mostly to the United States). The long-standing hostility to British domination was to blaze still hotter among those who remembered the years of famine.

France: Laboratory of Revolution

In the years after Waterloo, France oscillated between revolution and reaction. In 1815 the Bourbon monarchy was again restored, in the person of Louis XVIII (r. 1814–1824), Louis XVI's younger brother, who had occupied the throne briefly the year before. (The young Louis XVII had died in prison in 1795.) He ruled subject to a constitution, appointing the upper chamber of a two-chamber assembly, while a tiny electorate of 100,000 adult males (in a nation of 30 million) chose the deputies to the lower chamber. The Napoleonic Code continued in force, and Napoleon's Concordat was retained, with modifications that effectively reestablished Roman Catholicism in France.

Upon Louis XVIII's death in 1824, his brother Charles X (1757–1836) succeeded him. Strongly supported by conservatives and royalists and determined to reinstate absolutism, Charles made new accommodations to the Roman Catholic Church, imposed stricter censorship, and generally protected the powerful. In July 1830, he issued the July Ordinances, which reduced the electorate even further to a thin stratum of wealthy men. The response was explosive: liberal bourgeois and angry workers spilled out into the streets of Paris. They threw together makeshift barricades of scrap wood and cast-off objects, and, in a pattern that would be repeated often in years to come, they faced, with their irregular weapons the king's regular troops.

Charles abdicated. In his place, Louis-Philippe (r. 1830–1848), member of a younger branch of the Bourbon dynasty, took the throne—without ceremony or pretense to absolutist principles. Unlike Charles X, he did not wear royal robes or a crown, but

the same kind of business suit as his banker might have worn. And in his hat he wore the tricolor cockade: a red, white, and blue ribbon rosette emblematic of the party of Revolution. This was a "Citizen King" who wished for no further revolution. He rules subject to a constitution, and the electorate—though still small—nearly doubled.

What happened in France in 1830 was precisely what Metternich and his colleagues had feared. But their day had passed; no longer could conservatives hope for a true counter-revolution and the return to a chessboard world of nobles, kings, and bishops. Indeed, even as liberals and nationalists clashed with conservative monarchs, they in turn faced opposition from below, as workers voiced their own claim to participation in political life. The arrival of the workers as a political force is viewed first in France.

France had not yet completed its career as a laboratory of social change. Between 1830 and 1848, French popular resistance to monarchial government displayed two main sets of interests. The first comprised the bourgeois businessmen and professionals who, even under the comparatively liberal regime of Louis-Philippe, were excluded from the suffrage. They sought the liberalization of the constitution and of economic policy.

The second set of interests was the growing class of urban workers, their ranks swollen by recent migrants from the countryside, who threatened disruption. They were encouraged by the theories of a new group of radical political thinkers, the socialists (see Chapters 22, 25). While embracing liberal notions of civil rights, socialists also maintained that states were responsible for improving the lives of their citizens through public policy and direct subsidies, requiring the redistribution of private property—a demand opposed by bourgeois liberals, who were disinclined to surrender a modicum of their accumulated wealth.

These two revolutionary streams—the bourgeois and the worker, the liberal and the radical— intersected in 1848. Late in February of that year, a mass demonstration turned into revolution when panicky soldiers fired on a crowd, killing 40 people. The crowd carried the martyred citizens through the streets, seized public buildings, and erected barricades to deter government troops. The events are described in *Witnesses* on page 671.

Louis-Philippe was forced to abdicate, and the Second French Republic was born. A provisional government proclaimed universal manhood suffrage and called for the election of a National Assembly to write a republican constitution. (It also abolished slavery in all French colonies—that institution having been reinstated by Napoleon.)

The February revolution was a bourgeois revolution. It would be followed by a revolt of workers and artisans, just as in 1789 the moderate revolution had given way to a radical one. From the onset, the

To The Barricades: Paris, France, 1848, 1871

In 1830 and 1848, the revolutionary impulse spread to the rest of Europe from France, as it had in the years after 1789—and indeed from Paris, where young bourgeois intellectuals and idealistic workers and artisans continued to take inspiration from the spirit of freedom and fraternity that the Revolution had embodied. In two of the passages presented here, Alexis de Tocqueville (1805–1859) and Alphonse de Lamartine (1790–1869), both writers of note, and both participants in republican government, comment on the 1848 revolt; de Tocqueville warns of its coming, and Lamartine describes its outbreak. In the third passage, a British journalist describes vividly what he saw during the suppression of the Commune in 1871, the last in the series of nineteenth-century revolts.

Alexis de Tocqueville, shortly before the Revolution of 1848, foretells its approach: I am told that there is no danger because there are no riots; I am told that, because there is no visible disorder on the surface of society, there is no revolution at hand. Gentlemen, permit me to say that I believe you are deceived. True, there is no actual disorder; but it has entered into men's minds. See what is passing in the breasts of the working classes, who, I grant, are at present quiet. ... Do you not see that there are gradually forming in their breasts opinions and ideas which are destined not only to upset this or that law, ministry, or even form of government, but society itself, until it totters upon the foundations on which it rests today? Do you not hear them repeating unceasingly that all that is above them is incapable and unworthy of governing them; that the present distribution of goods throughout the world is unjust; that property rests on a foundation which is not an equitable foundation? And do you not realize that when such opinions take root, when they spread in an almost universal manner, when they sink deeply into the masses, they are bound to bring with them sooner or later, I know not when nor how, a most formidable revolution?
(*The Recollections of Alexis de Tocqueville*, ed. A. T. de Mattos, 1896)

Alphonse de Lamartine, poet and politician, describes how the February revolution (1848) began: Towards ten o'clock in the evening, a small column of republicans of the young bourgeoisie passed through the rue Lepelletier. ... [soon] another column of workmen and men of the people presented itself, and halted there. ... A red flag floated amidst the smoke of torches over the foremost ranks of this multitude. Its numbers thickened as it continued to advance. A sinister curiosity became intent upon this cloud of men, which seemed to bear the mystery of the day.

In the front of the Hotel of Foreign Affairs, a battalion of the line, drawn up in battle array, with loaded arms, its commander at the head, barred the boulevard. The column suddenly halts before this hedge of bayonets. The floating of the flag and the gleaming of torches frighten the horse of the commander. Rearing and whirling on its hind legs, the horse throws itself back towards the battalion, which opens to surround its leader. A discharge of fire-arms resounds in the confusion of this movement. did it proceed, as has been said, from a concealed and perverse hand, fired upon the people by an agitator of the people, in order to revive by the sight of blood the cooling ardor of the struggle? Did it come from the hand of one of the insurgents upon the troop? In fine, what is more likely, did it come accidentally from the movement of some loaded weapon, or from the hand of some soldier who believed his commander was wounded when he saw the fright of his horse? No one knows. Crime or chance, that discharge of fire-arms rekindled a revolution.
(From Alphonse de Lamartine: *History of the Revolution of 1848* (Boston: Phillips, Sampson & Co., 1849.

A British journalist describes the collapse of the Paris Commune (1871): The Versaillist troops collected about the foot of the Rue St. Honoré, were enjoying the fine game of Communist hunting. The Parisians of civil life are caitiffs [scoundrels] to the last drop of their thin, sour, white blood. [Only] yesterday they had cried "Long live the Commune!". ... To-day they rubbed their hands with livid currish joy to have it in their power to denounce a Communist and reveal his hiding place. Very eager at this work are the dear creatures of women. They know the rat holes into which the poor devils have got, and they guide to them with a fiendish glee. ... They have found him, the miserable [fellow]! Yes; they drag him out ... and a guard of six of them hem him round as they march into the Rue St. Honoré. A tall, pale, hatless man, with something not ignoble in his carriage. His lower lip is trembling, but his brow is firm, and the eye of him has got some pride and defiance in it. They yell—the crowd—"Shoot him; shoot him!"—the demon-women most clamorous, of course. ... He is down; he is up again; he is down again. ... But it is useless. They are firing into the flaccid carcase [sic] now. ... His brains spurt on my boot and splash in the gutter.
(From R. M. Golden and T. Kuehn eds., *Western Societies: Primary Sources in Social History*, Vol. 2, 1993)

economy descended into crisis, while prices and taxes soared. Workers pressed the government to provide work for unemployed laborers in national workshops—a program devised by the socialist Louis Blanc (1811–1882) which the provisional government initially had undertaken, but would later repudiate. In the midst of this disorder, Parisians and provincials enlisted in hundreds of political clubs of varying ideologies: liberal, radical, and even feminist in orientation (see *Windows On*, p. 684). Women now insisted not only on civil rights but on rights specific to women—the right to divorce their husbands, female suffrage, the equality of women before the law.

In April, eighty-four percent of the electorate (all adult males were now eligible to vote) chose the legislature; It was strongly conservative and monarchist; socialists and radical republicans gained only one in nine seats. When the radicals attempted to unseat the Assembly, the new government turned against them. On June 23, 1848, this new National Assembly announced the dismantling of the national workshops. The workers took to the streets. Once again the barricades went up in the poorer sections of Paris,

defended by women as well as men, mostly workers and artisans, joined by a contingent of bourgeois sympathizers and intellectuals.

This three-day insurrection, known as the "June Days," was suppressed by the middle-class youth of the National Guard and by the lower-class youth of the Mobile Guard, a tactical force established by the Assembly to keep order—men as poor as those they faced across the barricades. The bourgeois Guardsmen shot hundreds of workers, and the Mobile Guard swept through the streets, killing about 1500 people, some of whom are shown in *Windows On*, p. 684. Some 12,000 insurgents were arrested, and about 8000 of these imprisoned; some 4000 were sent to penal colonies in Algeria and French Guiana, where they had but a scant chance of survival.

By November 1848, the political clubs had dissolved, censorship had been reinstated, women had withdrawn from view, and yet another constitution had been promulgated. Establishing France's Second Republic, it called for presidential elections the following month. On December 10, the victory went to Louis-Napoleon Bonaparte (1808–1837), nephew

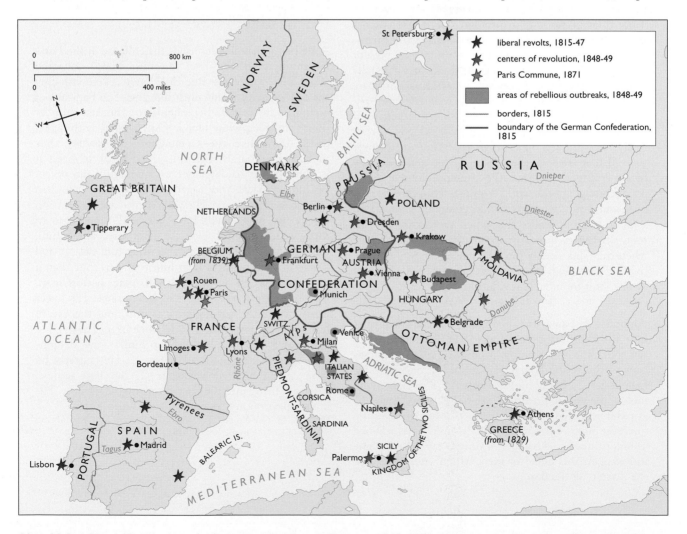

Map 23.2 Liberal, Nationalist, and Socialist Uprisings in Europe, 1815–1871: *Liberal, nationalist, and socialist revolts broke out between the Congress of Vienna settlement and 1871. Which areas of Europe were largely free of revolutionary activity, and why?*

of the defeated Napoleon. He would be reelected in 1851, with the approval of 90 percent of those voting; then, at the end of the year, he would dissolve the Second Republic he had twice been elected to lead. The following year, but another overwhelming vote, the empire was restored and Louis-Napoleon ascended the throne as Napoleon III (r. 1852–1870; the son of Napoleon I, had died in 1832). Having fought three revolutions and constructed two republics, the French, by the vote of a resounding majority, knelt once more to autocracy.

The rest of Europe studied Paris in 1848, as it had in 1789 and 1830. This revolt in France set off a series of insurrections in other European centers, reaching the Austrian empire, the German and Italian states, the Netherlands and Belgium, Russia, Spain, and Portugal—a total of more than fifty outbreaks (see Map 23.2, p. 672). In these places, bourgeois revolutionaries fought for written constitutions, freedom of the press, judicial equality, and a wider franchise. Nationalists in the Austrian empire and in German and Italian lands fought for autonomy. Students, professors, journalists, and workers took part in urban revolts which were violent and brutally suppressed.

Although not one of these 1848 revolts was successful, they left their mark upon Europe. While rejecting pleas for popular representation or autonomy, rulers nevertheless took note of the volcanic force that resided in the people, whose pleas could not go unheard forever. If 1789 spelled the beginning of a process that would put an end to the rule of kings, nobles, and bishops, 1848 offered further promise that that objective was in sight.

ONE PEOPLE, ONE NATION: 1848–1871

From 1815 to 1848, nationalism, as well as liberalism, was a spur to popular revolt. Nationalist impulses were especially strong in two settings: first, in the multinational Habsburg empire, where minority populations sough privileges or independence; later, in those regions united by language and culture but for centuries politically divided: Germany and Italy.

During the brief period from the 1848 revolutionary surge through the close of the Franco-Prussian War in 1871, nationalist aspirations were, to some extent, satisfied. The Habsburg empire was reorganized to give special status to the large Hungarian minority, and to recognize to a degree the separate cultures of Czech, Croat, and Slav minorities. The many component states of the Italian peninsula and of the German-speaking lands (except for Austria) achieved unification in the new nations of Italy and Germany. In both cases, though liberal nationalists had long championed the cause, unification was achieved from above by senior statesmen, who were themselves of noble birth. And in both cases, the

new nations were monarchies. In other respects, the Italian and German cases are distinct.

The Creation of Austria-Hungary

Within the multinational Austrian state, the numerous minority populations sought independence or some form of cultural autonomy. Their distribution is shown on Map 23.3 on p. 680. The Habsburg government ignored these aspirations, although it did encourage economic development. Emperor Francis Joseph (r. 1848–1916) addressed dissent by firing his unpopular head of government (who directed the secret police) and experimenting ineffectively with new constitutions which gave greater representation to subject nationalities. Meanwhile, the emperor's reputation plummeted as Austria suffered repeated battlefield losses against Piedmont and Prussia.

Not until 1867 did the emperor accede to nationalist demands, agreeing, reluctantly, to legislation creating the Dual Monarchy of Austria-Hungary. The newly constituted state had two separate parliaments under a single Habsburg ruler. He remained king of Hungary, as well as emperor of Austria, but Hungary gained a separate political identity and the right of self-rule, while the Hungarian language became the official language of government. Hungarian resistance to Habsburg rule was thus neutralized. Other minority peoples, especially Czechs, Slavs, and Croats, were permitted to use their native languages in schools and in churches. They remained dissatisfied and the Slav minorities, especially in Hungary, remained restless.

The Unification of Italy

The Italian provinces, shown in the inset to Map 23.3 on p. 680, had a proud history. Long before they were reduced to third-rate status and subjected to Austrian, Spanish, and papal domination, the Italian city-states and principalities had been thriving political powers in their own right and cradles of the Italian Renaissance (see Chapter 13). After Napoleon swept through the peninsula, Mazzini and Giuseppe Garibaldi (1807–1882) led a broad nationalist movement—known as the *Risorgimento*, or "Revival"—supported actively by bourgeois professionals. Joining these leaders after 1842 was the nobleman Camillo di Cavour (1810–1861), the new prime minister of Piedmont-Sardinia, a prosperous and constitutional monarchy. An intellectual with a taste for, and understanding of, economics, the graduate of a military academy, fired with republican sentiments, Count Cavour schemed, negotiated, and fought to achieve the unification of Italy.

Promising Napoleon III of France the provinces of Nice and Savoy, Cavour won the French emperor's support for his objective. A joint Piedmontese and French army pushed the Austrian army out of much of northern Italy in 1859, though Austria retained Venetia (the territory surrounding and including Venice). In 1860, several other states voluntarily ceded themselves to Piedmont. Meanwhile Garibaldi, a veteran Sardinian revolutionary, portrayed below, led an irregular volunteer force of 1000 "Red Shirts" in a daring invasion of Sicily. Joined by some of the men he had "liberated," Garibaldi then crossed to the mainland and swept up to Naples, bringing the whole of the south under Piedmontese dominion. The military victory was later confirmed by plebiscites. Before Garibaldi could reach Rome and challenge Cavour's monarchist state with a republican Italy, Cavour's troops rushed south to join Garibaldi in Naples.

Joseph Garibaldi

Garibaldi's March: *Giuseppe Garibaldi's series of military victories, culminating in the capture of Naples, became one of the great legends of the nineteenth century. He is seen here leading volunteer soldiers in his "March" across the Italian mainland, which was seen by many as a vindication of the right of the individual to political self-determination. (Private Collection)*

The Parliament that Failed: *In the grand interior of the Church of Saint Paul in Frankfurt-am-Main (modern Germany), more than 800 delegates from tens of German states met to create a constitution for a future nation. Their well-laid plans to create a liberal modern state based on the rule of law under a constitutional monarch failed, however, when in 1849 the Prussian king Frederick William IV declined to become the figurehead monarch of a Germany governed by a parliament.*

In 1861, Victor Emmanuel II, king of Piedmont-Sardinia, was declared king of Italy. In 1866, as a result of Italy's support of Prussia in the Austro-Prussian War, the new nation acquired Venetia. In 1870, when French troops defending the papacy vacated Rome to face Prussian forces at home, Italian troops moved in and took the city. The following year, with the assent of Roman people, Rome was declared the capital of Italy. The pope, previously the ruler of the central 15 percent of the peninsula, retreated to the tiny precinct of the Vatican on the west side of the river Tiber. The political unification of Italy had been achieved. The great disparities in economic level and linguistic and cultural differences among Italy's varied regions were not yet overcome, and would remain an issue at the end of the following century.

The Unification of Germany

It was through the inspired and often ruthless methods of the Prussian nobleman Otto von Bismarck

(1815–1896) that the unification of Germany was achieved. Bismarck completed a process begun by Napoleon and furthered by the Congress of Vienna, of rationalizing the many German cities and principalities into a coherent whole, as the inset to Map 23.3 on p. 680 shows. But the thirty-nine states of the German Confederation, established by the Congress, which included both Prussia and Austria, did not amount to a nation, as the events of the 1830s and 1840s demonstrated. In the spring of 1848, revolutions provided the impetus for a first attempt at unification. This forced promises of liberalization, which would be followed by the reassertion of central authority. In Frankfurt, in May 1848, more than 800 delegates from many of the German states met to design a constitution for a future nation, as depicted above. Over 80 percent of the delegates to this Frankfurt Parliament had attended universities, and two-thirds were judges, lawyers, professors, teachers, or bureaucrats—a cross-section of the liberal bourgeoisie, though tilted toward diligent and idealistic professionals, with few businessmen.

The liberalization of the Frankfurt delegates went only so far. Confining the franchise to propertied men, unfriendly to the needs of workers or peasants, and unwilling to admit to the union any state bringing with it territories having non-German populations, the Frankfurt Parliament had few supporters. In 1849, nevertheless, it promulgated a constitution for a united German state with a limited monarchy. When offered the crown of the new Germany, the Prussian king, Frederick William IV (r. 1840–1861), spurned it, and the bourgeois liberals who had made the offer, calling it a "crown from the gutter." The rejection of the new constitution by Prussia and (previously) by Austria, undermined the Frankfurt Parliament, and it dispersed.

In 1862, a struggle between the new king, William I (king of Prussia 1861–1888; German emperor 1871–1888) and the Prussian Parliament resulted in the appointment of Bismarck as prime minister. Aiming at any cost to defend the monarchy within Prussia, and Prussia's status in Germany and elsewhere in Europe, Bismarck pursued a strategy based on clear-sighted identification of the state's real interests, that would be dubbed *Realpolitik*. Accordingly, as a first step, he established the army's requirements as paramount within the state; he also suppressed liberalism in its various forms; liberal parties, supporters, and press. Next, he undertook war against Denmark (1864), Austria (1866), and France (1870–1871), in order to secure Prussian dominance within the German confederation and preeminence in a future united Germany.

The war against Denmark won the province of Schleswig-Holstein for Prussia. The Austro-Prussian War humiliated Austria militarily and resulted in the elimination of the German Confederation (which had included Austria) and the creation of the North German Confederation (which did not). The war against France saw Prussian forces defeat the French army, then besiege Paris—whose citizens responded by forming the revolutionary Commune (see above). The peace settlement of the Franco-Prussian War awarded Prussia the border provinces of Alsace and Lorraine, where many German speakers lived, and a cash indemnity. On January 18, 1871, in the palace of Versailles, the German Empire was officially proclaimed, with William I as emperor and Bismarck as chancellor (the event is depicted on p. 681). Bismarck's later speech to the German people, exhorting them to be strong, is quoted in *Witnesses* on p. 682.

THE STATE TRIUMPHANT: 1848–1914

Between 1848 and 1914, the political landscape of Europe fundamentally changed. German and Italy became nations; Austria-Hungary ceased to be the overweening power it once had been. France became a republic once again, and permanently, and Britain approached democracy. After 1861, Russia no longer rested on the shoulders of its serfs, and even in laggard Spain and Portugal, forces were in action that would lead to the modernization of these states. In most of the European nations, by 1914, all adult men could vote; parliaments met to debate principles or make laws, and growing swarms of bureaucrats administered offices responsible for commerce, transportation, and education. Meanwhile, industrialization and modernization encouraged a swelling proletariat of displaced artisans and aspiring workers to press for a better life. The clamor of peoples—for nationhood, for food, for land, for security, for glory—could not be ignored by powerful states, even as they encroached in new ways into the lives of their citizens.

Britain: The Challenge of Mass Politics

The modernization of the state in Britain was fundamentally connected to the nation's liberalization and, especially, the broadening of its franchise. It was here that the liberal agenda won its greatest victory, as the expansion of the franchise in 1832 set Britain on the path it would follow for decades.

Despite the cautions of wealthy businessmen, aristocrats, and Queen Victoria (r. 1837–1901), a second Reform Act, in 1867, extended the franchise yet again, more than doubling the number of those entitled to vote in 1832. This new bill, which admitted all but the poorest laborers to the electorate, resulted in a more liberal Parliament, which reformed the army, legalized trade unions, and limited the privileges of the Church of England. In 1884, the franchise was extended once more to include virtually all adult males—an additional 2 million voters. The foundations for modern democracy were now solidly laid.

Guiding Britain during this period were two capable prime ministers, William Gladstone (1809–1898) for the new Liberal party (which took the place of the former Whig party) and Benjamin Disraeli (1804–1881) for the Conservative (or Tory) party. Though responsible to very different constituencies, both supported the laissez-faire (free trade) policies which had prevailed in Britain since the repeal of the Corn Laws in 1846 (see above). Under Gladstone, whose speech to Parliament is quoted in *Witnesses* on p. 682, the Liberal party won broad support from the new voters admitted in 1867 and 1884. Under Disraeli, the Conservatives built nationalist and imperialist themes into their party platform in order to mobilize popular support outside of the landed elite and wealthiest business leaders. Other parties and interest groups pressed for a broader democracy—among them the suffragettes, who worked for women's political rights; reform-minded socialists (see Chapter 25); and, after 1901, the newly-formed Labour party. By the early twentieth century, British government was responsible to the masses of its people.

Russia: An Autocracy Attempts Reform

The autocratic Russian regime did not possess the flexibility of the British government. In 1848, the system was still based on a nobility whose loyalty was repaid with concessions over a serf population that included—since merchants and middle-class professional were few—nearly all of the Russian people.

By 1860, it was clear that serfdom must end. In a rapidly changing world, serfs had become inefficient: as workers, as soldiers, as citizens. Serf labor discouraged innovation—on the part of both landowners, who lived sufficiently on the labor of others, and serfs themselves, who clung to traditional methods of organization. Although freed serfs, as a large new class of taxpayers, might be a source of state revenue, escaped and rebellious serfs were a drain on the purse and a threat to order. If Russia were to rank alongside the great powers of the West, it was necessary to emancipate the serfs.

On March 3, 1861, Tsar Alexander II (r. 1855–1881) proclaimed the emancipation of the nation's 12 million serfs—roughly one half of all Russians then living. The state would recompense landowners for the loss of their land, which would be distributed among the former serfs by the village council of male householders. The former serfs would reimburse the state in forty-nine annual payments, with the village being collectively responsible for the debt. During that time, the serfs were rooted to their village. It would be almost two generations before large sections of the peasant population were truly free. In the meantime, former serfs were no longer counted among the "souls" with which landowners had reckoned their capital and could no longer be beaten or killed at a nobleman's nod.

Alexander also introduced further reforms. In 1864, he created village and regional *zemstvos*, or assemblies. In 1870, he created a similar structure of dumas, or councils, for cities. In both cases, the delegates were chosen by local officials and could not operate as representative institutions. Nevertheless, they were the first institutional structures of the kind in Russia and had potential for further political development. The tsar also instituted courts of justice (necessitated by the handover of judicial powers from landowners to the state) and reformed the army, which now relied on free peasant, rather than impressed serf, conscripts.

Freeing the serfs did not make Russia a liberal state. The tsarist Third Section (secret) police harried "political criminals" (anyone construed as an enemy of the regime) and tried to safeguard Russia from revolutionary ideas, which arrived between the covers of foreign books, smuggled in by the millions. In contrast to western Europe, where liberal intellectuals were often also teachers, journalists, or physicians, Russian society fostered the development of a permanent group of professional revolutionaries, largely from the nobility, many of whom became martyrs to the cause of social revolution. The benevolent tyrant himself, Alexander II, was also a martyr of sorts, assassinated in 1881 (after earlier attempts) by members of a radical political club.

From the 1880s until the outbreak of revolution in 1917 (see Chapter 26), a wide range of political activists and parties strove for preeminence—from democrats who wished to establish a parliamentary system to socialists representing the peasants' or workers' interests (see Chapter 25). Under Alexander's successor, Alexander III (r. 1881–1894), repression returned. The tsar launched a program of "Russification," supported by the Russian Orthodox Church, aimed at the 60 percent of the population that was not ethnically Russian (in Poland, Ukraine, and Belorussia; in the Baltic, the Caucasus, and Central Asia). Under Nicholas II (r. 1894–1917), Russia's expansionist policies led to the catastrophe of the Russo-Japanese War (1904–1905; see Chapter 24). Russia's defeat in that conflict, only 50 years after its defeat in the Crimea, pointed to the weakness of the regime and invited the revolutionary outbreak of 1905, to which the government offered only an inadequate response (see Chapter 26).

By the beginning of the twentieth century, attempts at reform in Russia had still failed to dismantle that nation's autocracy, increasingly untenable in an era of popular aspirations.

France: From Second Empire to Third Republic

While Russia remained in thrall to its long-established policy of repression, France might have been expected—in the light of its recent history—to be a model of political and social progress. But the government in power from 1851 (when the Second Republic was dissolved) to 1870 discouraged the liberalization for which many clamored. To be sure, there had been significant gains. Napoleon III ruled an empire in which all adult males were eligible to vote (the only nation in Europe that could so boast); where strikes were legal (after 1864); and where the government encouraged commerce, urban renewal, and the construction of railroads. Yet it was a nation where the wealthy lived to excess; where the press was censored; where the Roman Catholic Church was privileged; where political patronage and favoritism reigned. Nowhere in Europe were the bourgeoisie more solid or content (in Britain, they still lived in the shadow of aristocracy). And nowhere in Europe were the strivings of workers—not factory workers, who were few (see Chapter 21), but rather artisans such as shoemakers and tailors—more fierce or explosive.

In September 1870, Prussian armies blazed through northeastern France; captured, deposed, and exiled the emperor Napoleon III; and marched on Paris. In Paris, the French proclaimed the Third Republic, established a provisional government, and laid plans to elect a National Assembly which would create a new constitution. The provisional government then withdrew to Tours, as the Prussians besieged Paris, abandoned to its poorest citizens—the Communards (see above). In January 1871, in the Hall of Mirrors at Versailles, where Louis XIV had flaunted the glory of France, the victors proclaimed the German Empire. In February, the Germans settled an armistice with the French government in exile. In March, the French government sent the regular army of the newly declared Third Republic to destroy the Paris Commune—which had, not long before, stood alone to block the Prussian advance.

The dead buried, the Third Republic resumed course. In the French National Assembly, as in the British Parliament, liberal and conservative interests wrested with each other. The political parties competed for support from the increasingly influential middle bourgeoisie of shopowners, teachers, and prosperous peasants. Moderate republican leaders tried to steer a center course between monarchists, supported by the Church, on the right, and militant socialists on

the left. Liberals could rejoice that elections were based on universal manhood suffrage, that freedom of the press was guaranteed, that the Church was muzzled, and that a system of mass education had been instituted (see Chapter 25). Conservatives nursed nationalist sentiments and imperialist ambitions, stained by anti-Semitism (see Chapter 24).

Central Europe: The German and Austro-Hungarian Empires

The new German Empire was the old Prussian state writ large, even though individual states (there were twenty-five) were allowed considerable autonomy within their own boundaries. The parliament, or Reichstag, existed to approve what the emperor and his chief minister, the chancellor, proposed. It did not supply cabinet officers, nor did it propose legislation. Military and foreign policy were decided elsewhere, and positions in the army and civil service were staffed by members of the Prussian autocracy—the "Junker" elite. The preeminence of Prussian nobles in the administration of the German state was widely accepted by the high bourgeoisie, which in this period was engaged in the process of industrialization.

Corpses of the Communards: French politics continued along a radical path after the Congress of Vienna. The short-lived Paris Commune, an autonomous state created by left-wing intellectuals and urban workers, ended with the massacre of the defenders. Note the corpse of the young woman lined up with those of her companions, a few among the thousands who were executed by government soldiers and then prepared for mass burial. (Musée Carnavalet, Paris)

The Meaning of Country: German and Italian Nationalism

The French Revolution brought liberalism to all corners of Europe; and it brought nationalism as well. Just as the French gained a sense of themselves as a "people" when they became self-governing citizens, no longer subject to a king, they gained a sense of themselves as a nation, the patrie, or "fatherland." The foreign peoples whose lands they invaded—or "liberated"—learned from the French what it was to be a people, and longed for the true liberation of their nations, whether from the French invaders, or their own rulers. The passages here are by two nationalists whose compatriots struggled for and won independence by 1871: the German Johann Gottlieb Fichte (1762–1814) and the Italian Giuseppe Mazzini (1805–1872).

Johann Gottlieb Fichte examines the sentiment of love of country, which binds people on earth to an eternal principle (1807): Love that is truly love, and not a mere transitory lust, never clings to what is transient; only in the eternal does it awaken and become kindled, and there alone does it rest. Man is not able to love even himself unless he conceives himself as eternal; apart from that he cannot even respect, much less approve, of himself. Still less can be love anything outside himself without taking it up into the eternity of his faith and of his soul and binding it thereto. He who does not first regard himself as eternal has in him no love of any kind, and, moreover, cannot love a fatherland, a thing which for him does not exist. He who regards his invisible life as eternal, but not his visible life as similarly eternal, may perhaps have a heaven and therein a fatherland, but here below he has no fatherland, for this, too, is regarded only in the image of eternity—eternity visible and made sensuous, and for this reason also he is unable to love his fatherland. If none has been handed down to such a man, he is to be pitied. But he to whom a fatherland has been handed down, and in whose soul heaven and earth, visible and invisible meet and mingle, and thus, and only thus, create a true and enduring heaven—such a man fights to the last drop of his blood to hand on the precious possession unimpaired to his posterity.

Hence, the noble-minded man will be active and effective, and will sacrifice himself for his people. Life merely as such, the mere continuance of changing existence, has in any case never had any value for him, he has wished for it only as the source of what is permanent. But this permanence is promised to him only by the continuous and independent existence of his nation. In order to save his nation he must be ready even to die that it may live, and that he may live in it the only life for which he has ever wished.
(From Johann Gottlieb Fichte, Addresses to the German nation (New York: Funk & Wagnalls, 1898), trans. R. F. Jones & G. H. Turnbull (Chicago: University of Chicago Press, 1922).

Giuseppe Mazzini calls upon the workers of Italy to love their country, so as to serve all humanity (1844): O, my brothers, love your Country! Our country is our Home, a house God has given us, placing therein a numerous family that loves us, and whom we love. ... Our Country is our common workshop, whence the products of our activity are sent forth for the benefit of the whole world; wherein the tools and implements of labour we can most usefully employ are gathered together; nor may we reject them without disobeying the plan of the Almighty, and diminishing our own strength.

In labouring for our own country on the right principle, we labour for Humanity. Our country is the fulcrum of the lever we have to wield for the common good. If we abandon the fulcrum, we run the risk of rendering ourselves useless not only to Humanity but to our country itself. Before men can associate with the nations of which Humanity is composed, they must have a national existence. There is no true association except among equals. It is only through our country that we can have a recognized collective existence. Humanity is a vast army advancing to the conquest of lands unknown, against enemies both powerful and astute. ... Wheresoever you may be, in the centre of whatsoever people circumstances may have placed you, be ever ready to combat for the liberty of that people, should it be necessary, but combat in such wise that the blood you shed may reflect glory, not on yourself alone, but on your country. ... Your country is the sign of the Mission God has given you to fulfill towards Humanity. The faculties and forces of all her sons should be associated in the accomplishment of that mission. The true country is a community of free men and equals, bound together in fraternal concord to labour towards a common aim. ... Where the activity of a portion of the powers and faculties of the individual is either cancelled or dormant; where there is not a common Principle, recognized, accepted, and developed by all, there is no true Nation, no People; but only a multitude, a fortuitous agglomeration of men whom circumstances have called together and whom circumstances may again divide. ...
(From Joseph Mazzini, *An Essay On the Duties of Man Addressed to Workingmen* (New York: http://history.hanover.edu/texts/mazzini/mazzini5.htm)

Unification of Germany, to 1871
- Prussia, 1815
- territory acquired by Prussia, 1815-66
- other German states absorbed into empire
- → military campaigns, 1864-71
- —— boundary of North German Confederation, 1866
- —— boundary of German Empire, 1871

DENMARK

Austro-Prussian forces, 1864
SCHLESWIG-HOLSTEIN
POMERANIA   Danzig
WEST PRUSSIA   EAST PRUSSIA
MECKLENBURG
OLDENBURG   Hamburg
NETHERLANDS
HANOVER   Berlin   POSEN   Vistula   RUSSIA
BRUNSWICK   BRANDENBURG
BELGIUM   RHINELAND   WESTPHALIA
Austrian-Prussian war, 1866
Cologne   THURINGIA   SAXONY
HESSE   PRAGUE
Frankfurt   BOHEMIA
PALATINATE   Prague
Franco-Prussian war, 1871   LORRAINE   BAVARIA
FRANCE   ALSACE   WÜRTTEMBERG   Munich
BADEN   Danube
SWITZERLAND   AUSTRIA

National and ethnic groups within Habsburg Empire

Slavonic:
- Czech
- Slovak
- Polish
- Slovene
- Croatians and Serbians
- Ruthenians (Ukrainians)

Teutonic:
- German

Romanic:
- Italian
- Romanian

Finno-Ugrian:
- Magyars (Hungarians)
- —— border of Habsburg empire

0 ———— 300 km
0 ———— 150 miles

N / W / E / S

GERMAN EMPIRE

BOHEMIA   Prague

RUSSIA

Munich

MORAVIA   Kracow   GALICIA   Vistula

Vienna

BUKOVINA

AUSTRIA
STYRIA   Budapest
TYROL   CARINTHIA   HUNGARY
TRANSYLVANIA

Venice   Trieste
ITALY   CROATIA   SLAVONIA   VOJVODINA
ROMANIA
Belgrade   Bucharest

Unification of Italy, to 1870 (inset)
SWITZERLAND   AUSTRIA-HUNGARY
SAVOY   LOMBARDY   VENETIA
PIEDMONT   Milan   Venice
SARDINIA   MODENA   ROMAGNA
FRANCE   NICE   TUSCANY   Florence   ADRIATIC SEA
PAPAL STATES
CORSICA to France 1768   Rome
SARDINIA   Naples   KINGDOM OF THE TWO SICILIES
TYRRHENIAN SEA
MEDITERRANEAN SEA

BOSNIA

ADRIATIC SEA

SERBIA   Danube

OTTOMAN EMPIRE

Unification of Italy, to 1870
- kingdom of Piedmont-Sardinia
- territory lost to France, 1860
- territory annexed 1859
- annexed 1860
- annexed 1866
- annexed 1870
- → route of Garibaldi's forces
- —— Italian frontier, 1914

Map 23.3 Unification and Differentiation around 1870: *By 1871, both Italy and Germany achieved national unification. During the same years, Europe's eastern empires (Austro-Hungarian, Russian, and Ottoman) contained numerous ethnic, religious, and national minorities whose aspirations remained a source of tension well into the next century. Why was it seen as important to coerce diverse peoples into a unitary state?*

The Making of an Emperor, 1871: *Here, Prussian King William I and his Chancellor Otto von Bismarck celebrate the creation of the German empire, with the former as ruler, in January, 1871—even as Parisian workers and shopkeepers vowed to keep Paris free in the face of German invasion—in the Hall of Mirrors, a fitting setting from the age of absolutism, in the palace of Versailles built by an earlier absolute ruler, Louis XIV.*

Far more worrying to them than the pretensions of the nobles were the aspirations of the workers, which were voiced with increasing firmness after the German Social Democratic Party (or SPD) was founded in 1875. By 1912, this party would account for 35 percent of the popular vote.

Bismarck was extraordinarily effective in preventing further inroads of the SDP, instituting government-funded insurance programs which preempted the social democratic agenda (see Chapter 22). He also labored to limit the privileges enjoyed since antiquity by the Catholic Church in Germany—a church to which more than one-third of the population belonged. In his **Kulturkamfp**, or "culture war," he secularized marriage and the institution of the priesthood. In addition, he retained the ban on Catholic (and Jewish) participation in high government office and looked suspiciously at the center- and left-leaning Catholic political parties. In 1890, however, Bismarck's stern and vigorous management of the affairs of the Prussian state and the new German Empire came to an end. Unable to work with

the new emperor, William II (r. 1888–1917), a man of mediocre mind and lazy temperament, he resigned. Without his guidance, Germany became increasingly aggressive and nationalistic.

Whereas in Germany and other European countries, the struggles between liberals and conservatives, monarchists and republicans, Catholics and socialists were paramount, in Austria-Hungary the key issues remained ethnic: Where was there freedom, or even a sense of identity, for Slavs in a society dominated by Germans and Magyars, whose combined population amounted to less than one-fourth of the population. Croats and Czechs (the latter constituting the third-largest ethnic group in Austria-Hungary), especially, pressed for autonomy, their demands most strongly resisted by the Magyars, who launched a "Magyarization" campaign—resented all the more because the Magyar language, unrelated to the Slav or Germanic languages of other denizens of the Empire, was exceedingly difficult for non-natives to learn.

The task that fell to Emperor Francis Joseph was to hold the Empire together, in the face of these ethnic

Statesmen Look Ahead: Austria, Germany, Britain

Statesmen, diplomats, politicians won a new importance in the modernizing states of the nineteenth century. Here three such statesmen look to the future. Prince Clemens von Metternich (1773–1859), agent of the Habsburgs, urges the legitimate governments of Europe to band together to suppress the forces of liberalism and dissent. Otto von Bismarck (1815–1898), chancellor of the German Empire 1871–1890, urges the Germans, who were surrounded on all sides by "warlike neighbors," to be strong. William Ewart Gladstone (1809–1898), four times British prime minister and, from 1867, leader of the Liberal party, urges his listeners to accept the reality of mass politics and welcome the previously excluded working majority as participants in the nation-state.

Metternich calls on the states of Europe to save society from ruin (1820). Union between the monarchs is the basis of the policy which must now be followed to save society from total ruin. ...

The first principle to be followed by the monarchs, united as they are by the coincidence of their desires and opinions, should be that of maintaining the stability of political institutions against the disorganized excitement which has taken possession of men's minds. ...

Let [the Governments] in these troublous times be more than usually cautious in attempting real ameliorations, not imperatively claimed by the needs of the moment, to the end that good itself may not turn against them—which is the case whenever a Government measure seems to be inspired by fear. ...

Let them give minute attention to the financial state of their kingdoms, so that their people may enjoy, by the reduction of public burdens, the real, not imaginary, benefits of a state of peace.

Let them be just, but strong; beneficent, but strict.

Let them maintain religious principles in all their purity, and not allow the faith to be attacked and morality interpreted according to the social contract or the visions of foolish sectarians.

Let them suppress Secret Societies, that gangrene of society.

In short, let the great monarchs strengthen their union, and prove to the world that if it exists, it is beneficent, and ensures the political peace of Europe: that it is powerful only for the maintenance of tranquility at a time when so many attacks are directed against it; that the principles which they profess are paternal and protective, menacing only the disturbers of public tranquility. ...

(From Prince Klemens von Metternich, "Political Confession of Faith," 1820, in *Memoirs of Prince Metternich*, 1815–1829, ed. Prince Richard Metternich (New York: Scribner and Son 1881.)

Bismarck urges Germany, unified at last, to be strong (1888). When I say that it is our duty to endeavour to be ready at all times and for all emergencies, I imply that we must make greater exertions than other people for the same purpose, because of our geographical position. We are situated in the heart of Europe, and have at least three fronts open to an attack. France has only her eastern, and Russia only her western frontier where they may be attacked. We are also more exposed to the dangers of a coalition than any other nation. ... God has placed us where we are prevented, thanks to our neighbors, from growing lazy and dull. He has placed by our side the most warlike and restless of all nations, the French, and He has permitted warlike inclinations to grow strong in Russia, where formerly they existed to a lesser degree. Thus we are given the spur, so to speak, from both sides, and are compelled to exertions which we should perhaps not be making otherwise. The pikes in the European carp-pond are keeping us from being carps by making us feel their teeth on both sides. ... This will bring us to that state of being inseparable which all other nations possess, while we do not yet enjoy it. But we must respond to the intentions of Providence by making ourselves so strong that the pikes can do nothing but encourage us. ... Attack the German nation anywhere, and you will find it armed to a man, and every man with the firm belief in his heart: God will be with us.

(From Otto von Bismarck, "Speech to the Reichstag," 1888, in *The Age of Bismarck: Documents and Interpretations*, ed. T. S. Hamerow (New York: Harper & Row, 1973), pp. 290–293; from Rogers 2.218–20.)

William Gladstone asks the House of Commons to look into the future (1866). Let us for a moment consider the enormous and silent changes which have been going forward among the labouring population. ... Let us try and raise our views above the fears, the suspicions, he jealousies, the reproaches, and the recriminations of this place and this occasion. Let us look onward to the time of our children and our children's children. ... Is there or is there not, I ask, a steady movement of the labouring classes, and is or is not that movement a movement onwards and upwards? ...

But a very few words more, and I have done. May I speak briefly to honourable gentlemen opposite (i.e. the Conservative party]. ... You cannot fight against the future. Time is on our side. The great social forces which move onwards in their might and majesty, and which the tumult of our debates does not for a moment impede or disturb—those great social forces are against you; they are marshaled on our side; and the banner which we now carry in this fight, though perhaps at some moment it may droop over our sinking heads, yet it soon again will float in the eye of heaven, and it will be borne by the firm hands of the united people of the three kingdoms, perhaps not to an easy, but to a certain and not too distant victory.

(From Gladstone, "Speech to the House of Commons, 12 April 1866." http://www.csn.ul.ie/~debates/gladstone.htm.)

demands, by the symbolic power of his Habsburg ancestry and with support from the long-established Catholic Church. The army, too, was a force for unity, its soldiers drawn from the twelve different constituent nationalities of the empire (although a disproportionate number of its officers were German-speaking). A new threat to imperial unity emerged after 1878, when Austria-Hungary absorbed Bosnia and Herzegovina, which included a population of Muslims (in a Catholic empire) and Serbs (sentimentally linked to their kin in independent Serbia, and supported by the Russian Pan-Slavic policies). These tensions would lead to the Balkan wars of 1912–1913 and to a series of terrorist incidents, and would create the immediate conditions for the outbreak of war in 1914 (see Chapter 26).

Mediterranean Europe: Italy, Spain, and Portugal

In southern Europe, the patterns of democratization and modernization best seen in Britain, and recognizable elsewhere, are obscured.

The unification of Italy, completed in 1871, was imposed by a northern literate bourgeoisie upon the massive poor, illiterate, and fervently Catholic population of the southern part of the peninsula, who sought neither the culture nor the politics of a liberal age. Here, the authority of the local priest, landowner, and small merchant was respectfully acknowledged, with order maintained by the highly organized criminal networks, the Camorra (in Naples) or the Mafia (in Sicily). The northern regime brought taxation and conscription. The pope, meanwhile, forbade Catholics even to vote for federal politicians, while political leaders unseated the Church from the schools, from its land, and even from its jurisdiction over marriage and divorce and other areas traditionally subject to **canon law**.

In the north, under the aegis of the monarchs Victor Emmanuel II (r. 1861–1878), Umberto I (r. 1878–1900), and Victor Emmanuel II (r. 1900–1946), ministers and deputies came and went, knitting together loose political coalitions which opposed both militant workers and the disestablishment of the Church, while sometimes trumpeting nationalist and imperialist themes. When the liberal prime minister Giovanni Giolitti (1842–1928), the most successful of these transient figures, drew too close to an agreement with the Church after 1912, the socialists won an enormous victory, forcing Giolitti out—just on the eve of impending war (see Chapter 26). By that juncture, the Italians had not succeeded in democratizing, modernizing, or even truly unifying their state.

Church and monarchy also remained powerful forces in the two nations of the Iberian Peninsula. Spain under Queen Isabella II (r. 1833–1868) (who

had been preferred to her brother Don Carlos, promoted by a reactionary faction) was a turbulent scene of coup and counter-coup, in which monarchists, moderates, republicans, and separatists contended. The period from Isabella's death until 1876 oscillated between monarchy and republic, until a constitutional monarchy was established under King Alfonso XII (r. 1868–1885). Isabella's son. By this time, constitutional monarchists had to contend with socialist and anarchist parties which had begun to make inroads among enclaves of workers, especially in Asturias and the Basque region; the first socialists were elected to the Spanish Parliament in 1909. Frequent strikes were met with severe repression, and political life remained unstable well into the new century, up to the brink of the Civil War of the 1930s (see Chapter 28). Portugal, too, struggled between liberal and reactionary monarchical regimes throughout the nineteenth century.

Wars and Alliances

If the last decades of the nineteenth century were a period of state consolidation, they also saw the increasing belligerency of some European nations who sought to expand their territory or their military capacity. That belligerency expressed itself in wars, which broke out in the Balkans, in response to Russian ambitions, and also, spurred by Prussian aggression, in central and western Europe. In seeking protection from their neighbors' expansionist tendencies, European states cast about for friends and supporters, creating a network of alliances and counter-alliances which would themselves ultimately become a cause of political instability.

The Congress of Vienna of 1814–1815 had envisioned a grand "Concert of Europe," a peaceful coexistence of nations whose mutual difficulties would be resolved through diplomacy and compromise. To a greater extent, that vision had been realized. Congresses held at Berlin in 1878 and 1884–1885 attempted to settle Balkan affairs and to mediate among the European states pressing to enter and exploit Africa. Another international gathering held at The Hague in 1899, discussed the restraint of armament levels, and became the world body known as the International Court of Justice. Yet unresolved conflicts between states resulted in sporadic European wars: the Crimean War (1853–1856), concerned with Russian advances in the Balkans; the Prussian invasion of Denmark of 1864; and the Austro-Prussian (1866) and Franco-Prussian wars (1870–1871).

In 1853, the post-Napoleonic calm was first ruptured when Russia invaded the Ottoman principalities of Moldavia and Walachia in the Balkans. Russia sought to support its Slavic brethren in these lands and also to push its way to Constantinople, where the

The French Revolution of 1789 mothered many revolutions, most clustering around the sparkpoints of 1830 and 1848. In the illustration above right, Polish nationalists seeking independence from Russia establish a provisional government in 1831. A newly-installed bourgeois government sent the national army to suppress the revolt of Paris workers and artisans in 1848, of whom a few martyrs are depicted below left, fallen alongside the barricade built of cobbles spanning the narrow street of their humble quarter. A common theme in the Parisian revolts of 1789, 1848, and 1870–1871 was the assertion of women's rights and right to speak in the political clubs that sprung up spontaneously. Such a woman's club is depicted below right, as a woman of great personal presence addresses an audience of enthusiastic listeners. (top: National Museum, Cracow; below left: Louvre, Paris; below right: Musée d'Art Moderne de la Ville de Paris)

Why could masses of people be mobilized in this era, as never before, for national independence and economic and gender equity?

J. N. Lewicki, Great Saturday, *1831*

Ernest Meissonier, La Barricade, rue de la Mortellerie, Memory of the Civil War, *June 1848*

Women's Club, Paris, c. 1848

To continue your investigation of this topic, please go to www.prenhall.com/king for the related **WINDOWS** on the **WEB** activity

Turks held sway, and thus open the Mediterranean waters to the Russian navy. The British, who had friendly trade relations with the Ottomans and feared Russian encroachment in this region, soon came to the support of the Turks. Napoleon III of France, in turn, supported Britain, partly because he felt that a military victory abroad would be likely to play well at home. Camillo di Cavour, premier of Piedmont-Sardinia, lent his aid to France in exchange for French aid in the unification of Italy. And Austria-Hungary, always opposed to a strong Russian presence in the Balkans, also joined the allies.

Most of the fighting took place on the Crimean peninsula, then a Russian possession, on the Black Sea (hence the name "Crimean War" for this conflict). Poorly armed, Russia was unable to prevent the destruction of its naval base at Sevastopol; its defeat was total. Britain had demonstrated its leadership as much as Russia had its military weakness; the Ottoman Empire was saved; and, in 1858, the two principalities of Moldavia and Walachia, whose occupation by Russia had triggered the war, were united to form the independent state of Romania. The Russians returned home to digest the meaning of their failure, which would soon stimulate political reforms and an accelerated program of industrialization.

Ten years after the end of the Crimean War, Austria, too, would know defeat—at the hands of its rival Prussia. Whereas earlier in the century Austria had enjoyed ascendancy over Prussia in the German Confederation, now Prussia had become powerful; and in 1866, in a conflict lasting only seven weeks, it dismantled Austrian influence among the German states. That achieved, the way was prepared for the next step, which followed shortly, of German unification under Prussian auspices.

The political diminution of France, the plaything in the nineteenth century of two Napoleons, was accomplished by the Franco-Prussian War. It was fought over the same strip of territory west of the Rhine about which Charlemagne's grandsons had struggled in the ninth century, and it resulted in the annexation by Prussia of some of that corridor: the provinces of Alsace and Lorraine, including the prosperous cities of Strasbourg and Metz. The war also precipitated the collapse of the Second Empire, the departure of Emperor Napoleon III, and the inauguration of the French Third Republic.

On their own territory, the European states showed some restraint in confining themselves to these few wars. Abroad, they battled freely as they saw fit in pursuit of colonial interests (see Chapter 24). The swift, brisk wars of the nineteenth century, often won by simple superiority of firepower, were not greatly dangerous (except that they encouraged complacency about the frightening possibilities of full-scale war). Diplomats, meanwhile, labored to ward off potential conflicts by constructing complex (and

secret) defensive alliances. Toward the end of the nineteenth century, these began to proliferate.

An overview of the nineteenth century reveals two general patterns of alliance, one succeeding the other, with Russian Pan-Slavism serving as the hinge. Until the 1880s Austria and Prussia (later Germany) were allied with Russia, while France and Britain remained aloof. But from the 1880s, Russian Pan-Slav policies antagonized those central European empires. Russia eventually found support from France and Britain—the latter two nations, who had faced each other in the Hundred Years' War of the late Middle Ages and in the colonial struggles of the eighteenth century, finally uniting in an epochal joining of hands on the eve of world war.

The earlier of these two alliance systems began with the Holy Alliance (1815) of Austria, Prussia, and Russia, an immediate outgrowth of the counter-revolutionary agenda of the Congress of Vienna. Central to Metternich's strategy was the buttressing of monarchical power with the authority of the Church. In the Holy Alliance, the three emperors of central and eastern Europe sought to protect the interests of their churches and to gain enhanced reputation from their role as protectors of religion. The three-party alliance was revived at Bismarck's instigation in the Three Emperors' League of 1873 (renewed in 1881), even after Austria-Hungary had joined Britain and France in punishing Russia in the Crimea.

The later of the two alliance systems emerged in the aftermath of the Crimean War, with the development of Russian Pan-Slavism. Russia's earlier solidarity with the two central European emperors had been shaken in the Crimea and destroyed in 1878 by the Congress of Berlin (see Chapter 26). After 1890, which contained Russia's expansion on

---

HOW MANY?

Great Power Battle Deaths in European Wars, 1803–1918

Napoleonic Wars (1803–1815)	1,869,000
Crimean War (1853–1856)	217,000
Franco-Prussian War (1870–1871)	180,000
World War I (1914–1918)	7,734,300

Source: C. Tilly, *Coercion, Capital and European States, AD 990–1990* (Cambridge, MA: Basil Blackwell, 1990), pp. 165–166.

the Balkan peninsula, Russia sought the support of the two other great powers, France and Britain. France was a natural ally of Russia, as long-standing cultural ties bound the two nations together, recently strengthened by a flow of French capital eastward to fund Russia's railroads and burgeoning industries. By 1894, Russia and France had forged a joint defensive alliance.

At first, Britain, sheltered by the power of her navy, refused to join any of these alliance systems. Her natural sympathies lay with Germany, and she had long been hostile to France. However, rapid German naval buildup in the 1890s, seemingly aimed specifically at dismantling British superiority, eroded those sympathies. By 1904, Britain's diplomats had tilted to France, with whom it signed the Entente Cordiale (a "cordial agreement"). The European nations were rapidly becoming entangled in a complicated web of mutual assurance and fear.

Britain did not as yet turn to Russia, with whom it competed for influence in Persia and Afghanistan. To complicate matters, Britain supported the world's newest great power, Japan, after 1902, in response to Russia's new presence at Port Arthur, and Japan would best Russia in the conflict of 1905–1906. Nevertheless, by 1907, Britain had decided that Russia was less of a threat than Germany, and the two nations settled their differences over the Middle East. The Entente Cordiale with France was now enlarged by the participation of Russia, and renamed the Triple Entente. Meanwhile, in response to Russia's apparent hostility, Germany and Austria-Hungary formed between themselves the rock-solid Dual Alliance of 1879; three years later, Italy joined them to make the Triple Alliance. In the last years before 1914, when war would break out again, Triple Entente and Triple Alliance faced each other, tense with mutual fears (see Chapter 26).

Conclusion
THE TRIUMPHAL STATE AND THE MEANING OF THE WEST

The period from Napoleon's defeat to the outbreak of world war, nearly one hundred years later, was punctuated by confrontation between the state and its people: official power versus the power of populations energized by liberalism, nationalism, socialism, and other vision of self-advancement (see Chapter 25). In 1830, in 1848, in 1871, the power of the state reasserted itself. As the European nations crossed into the twentieth century, their leaders were wary but contented. They did not doubt the strength, the competence, the rightness of their governments to do what they were doing. The same confidence would be observed on the continents of Asia and Africa and in the Americas, as these triumphal modernized western states ventured out to control most of the rest of the globe.

At the same time, the European state system was fragile. Officials often held on to power by repressing opposition. Increasingly, that opposition came not from angry mobs of protestors, who could easily be shot down by a detachment of well-disciplined troops. Instead, it came through the organized institution of a political party—moderate, liberal, left, conservative; centrist, socialist, democratic, republican constitutionalist, anarchist, syndicalist, agrarian socialist, Christian democratic, Catholic worker. These, too, could be suppressed. But they could also negotiate and compromise and build new alliances, win seats in the national parliament, and bring the voice of the people to the chamber where decisions were made that impacted on the lives of all.

The state emerged triumphant from the trials of the century from 1815 to 1914. But the state had a new partner. The millions of citizens freed by the forces of modernization and industrialization from bondage to the land, and by the words of post-Enlightenment theorists from bondage to authority (see Chapter 25) would not willingly return to their former condition of servitude.

QUESTIONS TO CONSIDER

1. What were the main goals of the representatives to the Congress of Vienna? Were they more concerned with Napoleon, or with the Revolution?

2. How did the French Revolution and Napoleon both engender revolutionary movements in the Italian and German lands? What was the relation between these political events and the rise of nationalism?

3. How did the ethnic diversity of the Habsburg empire differ from our own? Did it have the same causes, and generate the same kinds of demands?

4. How did liberalism fare in the nineteenth century? Was Europe more liberal in 1871 than in 1789?

5. To what extent did Russia embrace liberalism during the nineteenth century?

SUGGESTED RESOURCES

Blackbourn, David & Geoff Eley, *The Peculiarities of German History: Bourgeois Society and Politics in Nineteenth-Century German* (Oxford: Oxford University Press, 1984). Seeks to understand German developments in terms of the specific nature of German society within the European setting.

Church, Clive H., *Europe 1830: Revolution and Political Change* (London–Boston: Allen & Unwin, 1983). Focuses on this often under-explored revolutionary year.

Feuchtwanger, Edgar J., *Bismarck* (London: Routledge, 2002). A new biography that seeks to understand the evolution of the Prussian aristocrat into a revolutionary creator of a new kind of state.

Gould, Roger V. *Insurgent Identities: Class, Community, and Protest in Paris from 1848 to the Commune* (Chicago: University of Chicago Press, 1995). Comparing the Revolution of 1848 with the Commune, finds that social class identity was critical in the first, but small-group and neighborhood solidarity more important in the later conflict.

Greenfield, Liah, *Nationalism: Five Roads to Modernity* (Cambridge, MA: Harvard University Press, 1992). The development of nationalism in four major European states and in the U.S., which argues that nationalism was an important factor promoting modernization, rather than a result thereof.

Hobsbawm, E. J., *Nations and Nationalism since 1780: Programme, Myth, Reality* (new ed.; Cambridge: Cambridge University Press, 1993). Explores the origins of nationalisms, its efflorescence during the period 1870–1914, and its twentieth-century consequences.

Nord, Philip G., *The Republican Moment: The Struggle for Democracy in Nineteenth-Century France* (Cambridge, MA: Harvard University Press, 1995). Explores how, after the shock of revolutions and the experience of authoritarian government in the Second Empire, France achieved democracy due to the civic-minded solidarity of the people at large.

Okey, Robin, *The Habsburg Empire: from Enlightenment to Eclipse* (New York: St. Martin's Press, 2000). Utilizing sources reflecting its diverse ethnicities, traces how the Habsburg empire responded to the challenges of revolution and nationalism from the reign of Joseph II to the end of World War I.

Riall, Lucy, *Italian Risorgimento: State, Society and National Unification* (London: Verso, 1994). A recent synthesis that incorporates recent studies and offers a thematic approach.

Rich, Norman, *Why the Crimean War? A Cautionary Tale* (Hanover, NH: University of New England Press for Brown University, 1985). Synthesizes recent historical studies why the war happened and who won, and points to the greater conflict of World War I.

Simpson, William, *The Second Reich, 1871–1918* (Cambridge: Cambridge University Press, 1995). Overview of the whole era, attending to the competing views of contemporary historians.

Smith, Dennis Mack. *Cavour* (New York: Knopf, 1985). Superior biography of a central figure in Italian unification.

Sperber, Jonathan, *The European Revolutions, 1848–1851* (Cambridge: Cambridge University Press, 1994). Synthesis of recent scholarship.

Traugott, Mark, *Armies of the Poor: Determinants of Working-Class participation in the Parisian Insurrection of June 1848* (New York: Transaction Publishers, 2000). A sociologist analyzes the effects of organization upon the political beliefs and behavior of rebellious workers and Mobile Guard soldiers in the 1848 Revolution.

Encyclopedia of the 1848 Revolutions—brief essays on scores of figures and problems pertaining to the 1848 revolutions, by an international set of contributors, with bibliographies (1999, Ohio State University): **http://www.cats.ohiou.edu/~Chastain/index.htm**

The Monroe Doctrine (Avalon Project, Yale Law): **http://www.yale.edu/lawweb/avalon/monroe.htm**

The Anthony P. Campanella Collection of Giuseppe Garibaldi—images and materials, originally exhibited summer-fall 1997 (University of South Carolina): **http://www.sc.edu/library/spcoll/hist/garib/garib.html**

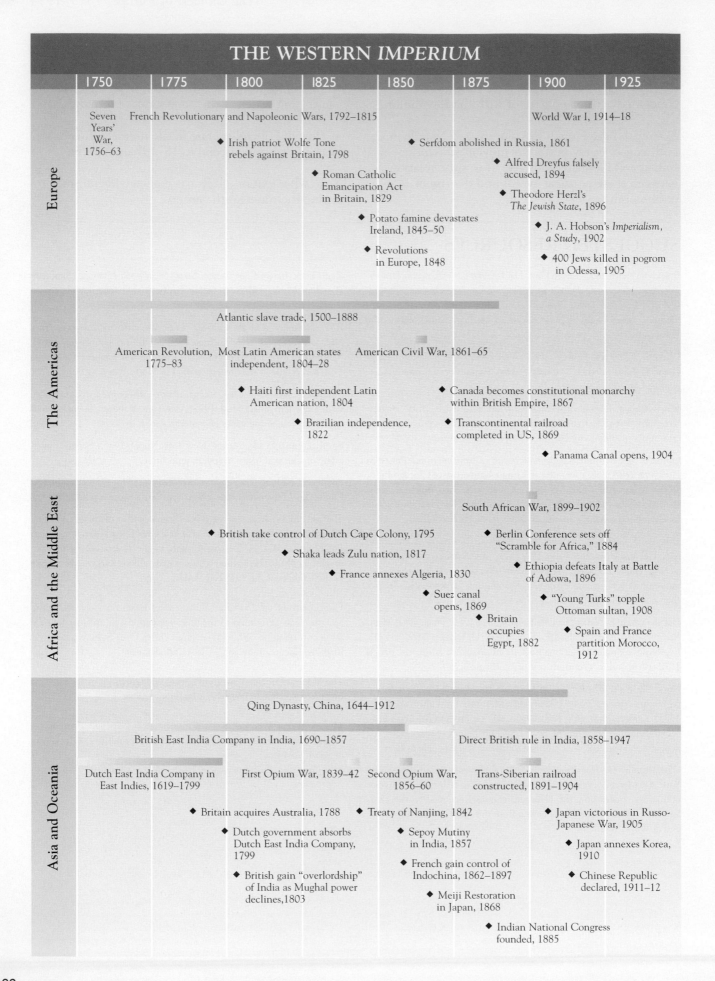

THE WESTERN *IMPERIUM*

	1750	1775	1800	1825	1850	1875	1900	1925

Europe

Seven Years' War, 1756–63

French Revolutionary and Napoleonic Wars, 1792–1815

World War I, 1914–18

◆ Irish patriot Wolfe Tone rebels against Britain, 1798

◆ Roman Catholic Emancipation Act in Britain, 1829

◆ Potato famine devastates Ireland, 1845–50

◆ Revolutions in Europe, 1848

◆ Serfdom abolished in Russia, 1861

◆ Alfred Dreyfus falsely accused, 1894

◆ Theodore Herzl's *The Jewish State*, 1896

◆ J. A. Hobson's *Imperialism, a Study*, 1902

◆ 400 Jews killed in pogrom in Odessa, 1905

The Americas

Atlantic slave trade, 1500–1888

American Revolution, 1775–83

Most Latin American states independent, 1804–28

American Civil War, 1861–65

◆ Haiti first independent Latin American nation, 1804

◆ Brazilian independence, 1822

◆ Canada becomes constitutional monarchy within British Empire, 1867

◆ Transcontinental railroad completed in US, 1869

◆ Panama Canal opens, 1904

Africa and the Middle East

South African War, 1899–1902

◆ British take control of Dutch Cape Colony, 1795

◆ Shaka leads Zulu nation, 1817

◆ France annexes Algeria, 1830

◆ Suez canal opens, 1869

◆ Britain occupies Egypt, 1882

◆ Berlin Conference sets off "Scramble for Africa," 1884

◆ Ethiopia defeats Italy at Battle of Adowa, 1896

◆ "Young Turks" topple Ottoman sultan, 1908

◆ Spain and France partition Morocco, 1912

Asia and Oceania

Qing Dynasty, China, 1644–1912

British East India Company in India, 1690–1857

Direct British rule in India, 1858–1947

Dutch East India Company in East Indies, 1619–1799

First Opium War, 1839–42

Second Opium War, 1856–60

Trans-Siberian railroad constructed, 1891–1904

◆ Britain acquires Australia, 1788

◆ Dutch government absorbs Dutch East India Company, 1799

◆ British gain "overlordship" of India as Mughal power declines,1803

◆ Treaty of Nanjing, 1842

◆ Sepoy Mutiny in India, 1857

◆ French gain control of Indochina, 1862–1897

◆ Meiji Restoration in Japan, 1868

◆ Indian National Congress founded, 1885

◆ Japan victorious in Russo-Japanese War, 1905

◆ Japan annexes Korea, 1910

◆ Chinese Republic declared, 1911–12

CHAPTER
24

THE WESTERN IMPERIUM

European Migration, Settlement,
and Domination around the Globe

1750–1914

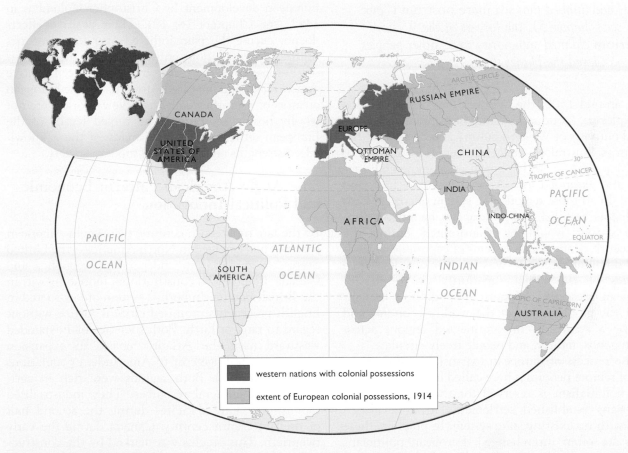

western nations with colonial possessions

extent of European colonial possessions, 1914

KEY QUESTIONS

◆ **Lands of European Settlement:** What parts of
the world outside of Europe became new
homelands of European, or Western, civilization?

◆ **Imperialism in Asia:** What was the role of
merchant companies in the extension of
European influence into Asia? What was the
response of China and Japan to Western bids for
commercial relations?

◆ **Imperialism in the Middle East:** How was the
European presence in the Middle East different

from that in south and east Asia? How did Africa,
known to Europeans for centuries, come to be
occupied and partitioned in the decades before
World War I?

◆ **Dominion Within:** What groups within Europe
were subjected to a domination tantamount to
that of imperialism abroad?

◆ **Migrants and Money:** What consequence did
imperialist ventures have on the worldwide
movement of money and people?

The Better Bookshelf In 1835, in a "Minute on Indian Education" prepared for the British Parliament, the English historian Thomas Babington Macaulay (1800–1859) declared that "a single shelf of a good European library was worth the whole native literature of India and Arabia." Thus he dismissed all of India's lofty literature, whose sacred texts rested on traditions at least as old as those of the Hebrew Bible. Although Macaulay promoted the cause of education in India, then part of the British Empire he betrayed an attitude characteristic of the Europeans who, by 1914, dominated much of the globe. Just as the Romans, who once ruled the ancient Mediterranean world, had dubbed that sea mare nostrum ("our sea"; see Chapter 5), the forgers of the Western **imperium** claimed superiority to all other peoples and considered the planet theirs.

From around 1500, the Western *imperium* expanded as explorers, conquerors and entrepreneurs established outposts of Western culture and customs in the Americas, Australasia, and elsewhere (see Chapter 16 and Map 24.1, p. 691). European commercial ventures also extended into Asia, the Middle East, and Africa. In all these regions, the system of coastal trading depots established by European merchants centuries earlier would be transformed during the nineteenth century into systems of economic or territorial domination, while Western thinkers developed theories of the racial superiority of peoples of European descent. Western imperialism brought about the globalization of the world's economy and culture: a system of interconnected regions across which goods, money, and people freely circulate.

The process of European expansion and domination of remote peoples is here called **imperialism**. The term **colonialism** is reserved for those cases where Europeans established settlements in undeveloped lands with no existing state system. In practice, these terms are often interchanged. European politicians might refer to their "colonial" policies, even in regions such as India, which was not a "colony"; and those who lived under European domination resisted "colonialism." More recently, the economic policies of the wealthier nations of the world are often referred to as "**neo-colonialism**."

Two contrasting views on imperialism are cited in *Witnesses* on p. 713. The Western *imperium* burdened the peoples and civilizations it engulfed. Yet the imperialist legacy is not entirely negative. The West spread abroad principles of human rights and parliamentary democracy, later embraced by non-Western nations as they forged their own liberation (see Chapter 29). And although the West imposed its own cultural norms on often unwilling peoples, these have

also led to improved health care, expanded educational systems, and agricultural and industrial modernization. The West has also learned much from the other cultures of the rest of the world, and became enriched by its global ventures.

LANDS OF EUROPEAN SETTLEMENT: COLONIAL VENTURES

In the lands settled by European migrants, the culture of the West developed new economic, social, and political patterns that would transform the world. Nowhere were these innovations more profound than in the Americas, the two continents first opened to European development by Christopher Columbus in 1492 (see Chapters 16, 19). Their positive effects do not excuse the pain inflicted over four centuries on the two populations enlisted to serve the interests of European settlers: those of displaced native Amerindians and imported Africans. Yet the European creators of what they called the New World were not wholly hostile in intent. The mixed legacy of the European settlement includes many of the acknowledged strengths and benefits of modern society.

The Anglo-American Pattern: Economic and Political Innovation

By the late nineteenth century, two Anglo-American societies had emerged in North America—the United States, from 1783 an independent republic, and Canada, from 1867 a constitutional monarchy within the British Empire. In both, a system of law rooted in English precedents promised citizens justice without regard to rank or birth. Both societies had expanded westward from the Atlantic coast, an expansion which came at huge cost to Amerindian populations (see Chapter 19). Both regions were rich in agricultural and mineral resources. They industrialized rapidly—the United States during the second half of the nineteenth century, Canada during the early twentieth. This process was marked by the construction of railroad lines extending across 3000 miles of mountain, plain, desert, and prairie. The more densely populated United States, especially its northern states, industrialized dramatically: by 1914 it had overtaken its European competitors to become the world's leading producer of steel.

From 1860 to 1865, those northern states fought a ferocious war with secessionist southern states whose economy depended on the plantation system of agricultural production, and thus on slave labor (see Chapter 19). In consequence, the southern states were returned to the Union and slavery was abolished, with pathbreaking legislation promising full citizenship rights, including the suffrage, to former slaves. Those promises were gainsaid by formal and informal systems

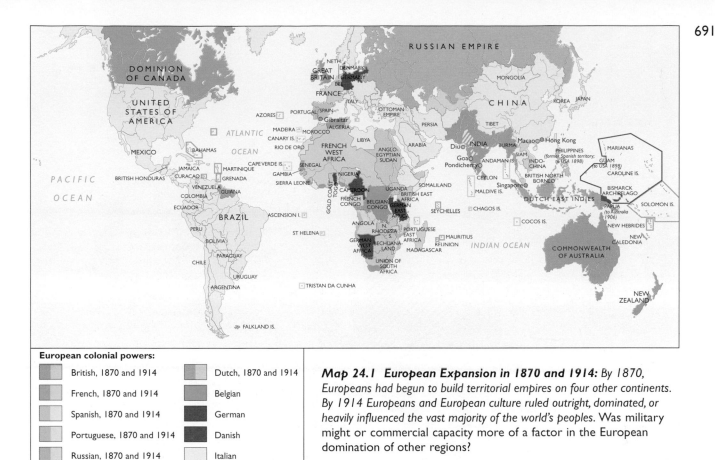

European colonial powers:

British, 1870 and 1914	Dutch, 1870 and 1914
French, 1870 and 1914	Belgian
Spanish, 1870 and 1914	German
Portuguese, 1870 and 1914	Danish
Russian, 1870 and 1914	Italian

Map 24.1 European Expansion in 1870 and 1914: *By 1870, Europeans had begun to build territorial empires on four other continents. By 1914 Europeans and European culture ruled outright, dominated, or heavily influenced the vast majority of the world's peoples. Was military might or commercial capacity more of a factor in the European domination of other regions?*

of segregation that barred those of African heritage from the enjoyment of their presumed civil rights. Women, too, in the United States as in Canada, did not enjoy political emancipation before the end of World War I (see Chapter 27). Yet by the early twentieth century Anglo-American societies had created vibrant economies and free polities, where opportunities abounded for many of those who sought them. Race, gender, and poverty kept some from reaching for those opportunities. Nevertheless these societies were more nearly free, and the principles upon which they rested embraced the principle of equality more firmly than any others in the world.

Both Anglo-American states respected and cultivated European traditions. During the colonial era, elementary and secondary education followed European patterns, while eleven universities, founded by the time of the American Revolution, authoritatively transmitted the heritage of European ideas to later generations. Cultural institutions such as academies and concert halls offered cultural opportunities available mostly to elites.

The English language created the cultural unification of North America, and was adopted even by immigrants from non-English speaking European regions. One significant exception was the Canadian province of Quebec, where French settlers taught their children the language and Roman Catholic religion of their forebears. Elsewhere, Anglo-Americans were generally Christians who came from a variety of Protestant denominations.

In language, religion, educational traditions, and political and social values, Anglo-America continued to remain firmly tied to established European patterns into the twentieth century.

The Spanish-American Pattern: Racial Mixture and Persistent Autocracy

In the Spanish-speaking regions of the Americas a new civilization also took form. By 1900, the colonies that Spain ruled for centuries had become independent nations. Cuba was the last to do so (while Puerto Rico was shifted from Spanish to United States rule) as a result of the Spanish–American war of 1898. At that point Spanish-American nations were only beginning to develop democratic institutions. Most were still ruled by despots and dominated by the military. A few had adopted constitutions that protected civil rights, limited church privileges, and abolished slavery.

The societies of these Spanish-American nations were also markedly different from those of Anglo-America. Centuries of cross-ethnic sexual relations meant that many Spanish-Americans had mixed Amerindian, African, and European ancestry. Persons of all skin colors were found among the ruling and commercial elites, as well as among the poor. In the country villages, however, peasant populations were heavily Amerindian.

The Spanish-American economies generally depended on the export of agricultural and mineral produce. They did not undergo the industrialization and consequent modernization that occurred in Europe and Anglo-America. This economic system

Map 24.2 Europeans in Asia: *European territorial expansion in Asia prior to 1914 includes gains made by the British, the French, the Russians, and the Dutch. The British dominated India in 1857 and parts of southeast Asia in 1826–1915. To the east of Burma in Indochina, the areas of Vietnam, Laos, and Cambodia long under Chinese influence fell to the French after 1884. Thailand, however (indicated on the map under its old name, Siam), remained independent. The lands of the Dutch East India Company in the East Indies were ceded in 1799 to the Dutch government, which by 1910 controlled most of Indonesia. Russia greatly expanded its authority in central and east Asia during the nineteenth century, building a contiguous empire with many parallels to those of other European powers. The United States played only a small role in territorial terms in the intrusion into Asia; why?*

benefited the owners of mines and land, who relied on the exploitation of impressed Amerindian workers.

As in Anglo-America, the cultural institutions of Spanish America were modeled on European ones. Roman Catholic priests, monks, and missionaries, saw to the creation of cathedrals and parish organization, monasteries and convents, and the Inquisition. Churchmen persuaded native peoples to accept Christianity, and where possible provided elementary education in the Spanish tradition. Male members of the creole elites often finished their education in European cities and universities. European traditions also prevailed in the realm of the arts (where native Amerindian artistic styles influenced the visual arts) and ideas, and Spanish-American capitals resembled the great cities of Europe.

By 1900, Spanish America had not entirely shaken off its colonial past. The economic and political innovations that had transformed Anglo-America failed to take root in its southern neighbors. The intermixture of peoples invigorated the civilization, but did not result in its democratization.

Much of the rest of Latin America followed the Spanish-American pattern. Exploited mainly for their sugar crop during the colonial era, the French, English and Dutch-speaking societies of the Caribbean and Central America were heavily populated by African slave laborers until abolition was finally achieved in 1886. African religions, speech, and customs strongly influenced the cultures of these regions, although Christian practices and European languages remained dominant.

In Portuguese-speaking Brazil, the plantation economy likewise resulted in a huge presence of Africans, and many Brazilians had some African ancestry. In contrast, the Amerindians of the Amazon resisted both Europeanization and Christianization. Although Brazil's ample mineral and agricultural resources contributed to a vigorous economy, it remained an economy dependent on the export of cash crops and minerals, and had comparatively few industrial manufactures to export.

Australasia: Another Anglophone Success

More than 200 years after the Spanish and Portuguese first settled in the Americas, Britain launched a similar undertaking in the south Pacific. Australasia (including Australia, the world's smallest continent, and the nearby islands of New Zealand) had first been sighted by the Dutch and was charted by the British navigator Captain James Cook (1728–1779).

Australasia resembled North America in that the indigenous peoples had attained only a simple level of technical development. The **Aborigines** (meaning "those there from the beginning"), were expelled from the most desirable lands as British migrants and deported criminals settled after formal possession by Britain in 1788. New Zealand was home to nearly 150,000 Maoris, a native group of Polynesian origin. Here British settlers established a colonial society based on an agreement in 1840 with native peoples (the Treaty of Waitangi), subsequently violated, assuring equal rights. In both regions European settlers developed a prosperous economy based on the exploitation of natural resources and the development of sheep and dairy ranches.

Australia and New Zealand remained British colonies during the nineteenth century, developing as European enclaves of Anglophone culture. Their vigorous cultural institutions resulted in the attainment of high levels of literacy and health for their European populations, although the New Zealand Maori and Australian aboriginal peoples remained largely excluded from these benefits.

The Russian Empire: Russification Across Five Thousand Miles

By 1500, Russia had become the largest nation in the world. Throwing off Mongol suzerainty (see Chapters 8, 9, 15), Muscovite rulers pressed into Asia, reaching the Caspian Sea with the conquests of Kazan (1552) and Astrakhan (1556) and then beyond the Urals to Siberia. In the seventeenth century, fur traders and explorers crossed Siberia to the Pacific.

In the eighteenth century, Tsars Peter I ("the Great"; r. 1682–1725) and Catherine II ("the Great"; r. 1762–1796) eroded Ottoman claims in the southeast while simultaneously intruding westward into Poland and the Baltic. In the later nineteenth century, recovering from the humiliation of the Crimean War (1853–1856; see Chapter 20), Tsars Alexander II (r. 1855–1881) and Alexander III (r. 1881–1894) advanced in the Caucasus, central Asia, Siberia, and even North America. With these gains, Russia established sovereignty across northern Asia and south to a belt of natural mountain, desert, and river borders with Persia, Afghanistan, India (later Pakistan), and China.

By 1914, the Russian empire's vast dimensions were nearly double those of any of the other modern behemoths—the United States, China, India, or Brazil. An expression of its gigantic stature and industrial capacity was the Trans-Siberian railroad. Constructed between 1891 and 1904, it joined lines earlier constructed to arch from the capital of St. Petersburg to Vladivostok, founded in 1860 on the Pacific coast. Russia's further aims in Asia met traumatic defeat during a conflict with newly-vigorous Japan—the Russo-Japanese war of 1904–1905.

Russian expansion in Asia involved the exploitation of ample natural resources and the imposition of European traditions on sparsely-settled peoples of different origins. The European nucleus of Russia was already well-endowed with mineral resources and fine, flat fields. Subsequent additions in the Caucasus, the Urals, and Siberia brought great wealth in the form of natural gas and oil, coal and iron, gold, diamonds, and furs—even though much of the eastern region is too cold for crop cultivation.

Resident in these Asian lands were peoples of nearly a hundred nationalities, ethnicities, or language groups. Many groups resisted Russian domination in an ongoing pattern of tension and rebellion that continues into the twentieth century, creating problems for tsarist, communist, and post-communist rulers. The largely Muslim peoples of south central Asia, dwelling along the route of the ancient Silk Road (see Chapters 5, 6, 8), had old and distinct cultural traditions, and remain unassimilated.

In the Asian zone of the Russian empire, as in Australasia and the Americas, European colonists opened huge regions to economic development and exploitation. One result was the displacement, or subjugation, of native peoples. Another was the implantation of European cultures in a distant and distinct context. In all these regions, Old World traditions developed under the stimulus of changed conditions, leading to the creation of new forms of wealth, new social structures, and new political traditions.

OLD WORLD ENCOUNTERS: IMPERIALISM IN ASIA

Europeans did not rest with the establishment of colonies in the remote and sparsely populated regions of the Americas, Australasia, and northern Asia. They also pressed their commercial interests in the crowded Old World zones where established states and advanced civilizations did not welcome intruders from the West, but were compelled to admit them.

Europeans had sought for centuries the luxury goods of Asia (see Chapters 5, 6, 8, 11). Merchants had traveled overland by foot, horse, or camel, or by ship across the Indian Ocean and on to the South China sea, to acquire expensive silks, perfumes, and spices. The quest for spices drove Portuguese navigators to hazard the Atlantic currents, and sent Columbus westward to seek a direct route, as he thought, to Japan (see Chapter 16).

During the sixteenth century, Portuguese, French, Dutch, Spanish, and English merchant depots dotted the coasts of India, the East Indies (the Malay archipelago and Indonesia), and the Philippines, and even remote China and Japan. By the eighteenth century, cotton textiles, porcelains, and tea joined the list of important commodities that the West sought in the East. European entrepreneurs and the states that backed them, responding to increased commercial demand, insisted upon greater access to the economies of the Asian nations and in some cases seized dominion over them. In this process of imperialism, here as elsewhere, European nations exploited the resources of other regions for their own benefit, and imposed upon other peoples European political, economic, and cultural systems.

The Western encounter with Asia is pursued here by examining, first, those regions where systems of trading depots became the basis for the later establishment of direct imperialist rule (the Indian sub-continent, and the island regions of the East Indies and the Philippines). The account then turns to those regions that were relatively isolated (China, Korea, Indochina, and Japan), resistant to penetration, and "opened up" to European trade only by the threat, or the reality, of force. Map 24.2 on p. 692 traces the spheres of European influence in Asia.

India: A Sub-continent Subdued

In 1500, various kingdoms, both Muslim and Hindu, flourished in the huge Indian sub-continent. In the 1700s, it fell increasingly under the control of the British East India Company. After 1858, it was directly ruled by the British government.

Established by Muslim Turkic invaders from central Asia, the Mughal Empire was the first large, centralized state on the Indian sub-continent since the Gupta empire more than one thousand years before (see Chapter 8). Its founder was the occasional poet and memoirist Babur (1483–1530), a remote descendant of the feared conqueror Tamurlane (1336?–1405) who had not so long before ravaged western Asia. Defeating native armies at Panipat in 1526, deep within the Ganges region, Babur united the squabbling Muslim princedoms of northern India into a state further consolidated by his successors.

Notable among these were Babur's grandson Akbar (r. 1556–1605), Akbar's grandson Shahjahan (r. 1627–1656), and Shahjahan's son Aurangzeb (r. 1658–1707). Akbar won the support of Hindu leaders from the Rajput region, thus forging a mixed Hindu–Muslim state efficiently managed by bureaucrats ranked in a hierarchy modeled on that of his army. Encouraging literature and the arts, he presided over a golden age which saw a synthesis, especially in miniature painting, of Persian and native forms.

Shahjahan shared Akbar's artistic tastes. He was renowned as the patron of the Taj Mahal which he had built as a mausoleum (completed in 1643) for his young wife (who had died prematurely in 1629). Symbolizing the paradise in which the royal couple would be reunited, the bejewelled monument is considered one of the world's finest buildings. Aurangzeb oversaw the expansion of the empire to its maximum by 1680, then faced the crises that pointed to its eventual decline. Rajput revolts in the northwest, and the sudden growth of the Marathas, a dynamic Hindu people of western India, undermined the Mughal system.

By that date, English officials of the East India Company had shouldered aside their Arab, Dutch, Portuguese, and French competitors (see Chapter 16). Soon after 1600, the merchants of the British East India Company arrived, establishing themselves at Bombay on the west coast, and on the east at Madras and Calcutta, where they founded an administrative center in 1690. Meanwhile, the French seized footholds at Pondicherry and Chandernagore (now Chandarnagar) in 1697. The military forces of the French and British merchant communities came into conflict after 1740, just as their national armies faced each other in the War of the Austrian Succession (1740–1748) and the Seven Years' War (1756–1763; see Chapter 15). In 1757, the British general Robert Clive (1725–1774) defeated a native force supported by the French at Plassey in Bengal. When the Seven Years' War was concluded by the Treaty of Paris of 1763, Britain gained Canada, territories in the Caribbean and Africa, and control of India. The British East India Company was now the chief European power on the Indian sub-continent, and would soon acquire mastery over native states as well.

This company of profit-seeking merchants dominated India from the 1700s, although increasingly regulated by the British government. Deploying an army of about 100,000 mostly native troops, the governors of the British East India Company absorbed

The importance of prestige: *European nations saw their empires—in Asia and elsewhere—as sources of both prestige and economic benefit. The benefit of prestige is well illustrated by A. E. Harris's illustration of the British King Edward VII as he receives a group of maharajahs and other dignitaries, who are clothed in their finest garments for the honor, in 1901. (Roy Miles Gallery, London)*

the native princedoms or reduced them to vassal status. As the Company's success mounted, and rumors of corruption surged, the British government intervened to supervise. As a result of the Regulating Act of 1773 and the East India Company Act of 1784, Parliament scrutinized the administration of Indian territories. By these steps, an imperial realm took form in the sub-continent (see *Witnesses*, p. 697).

India was a site of imperialism in action, as British officials exploited India economically, ruled it peremptorily, and often denigrated native culture— although many British officials and visitors admired India's civilization. The region's yield of spices, tea, and cotton textiles was cheaply purchased and sold profitably at home, without modernizing agricultural production in India itself (although British governors did promote the construction of irrigation and drainage systems). The trade in those commodities now left India poor as returns on agricultural commodities diminished, as the poet Dalpatram Kavi laments, in *Witnesses* on p. 697. Textile exports also dwindled as the Industrial Revolution (see Chapter 21) transformed British textile production and flooded world markets with cheap cotton cloth. Industrialization made India an importer of manufactured cottons, reversing for the first time in history its favorable balance of trade.

As India sank into the adverse economic relationship with a colonial power that characterized South America, its people became the target of European attitudes of racial superiority. Indian natives were barred from political decision-making, from military and administrative offices (although permitted to compete in examinations for lesser positions in the Civil Service, which grew to number about 1000 British and Indian members). They were excluded from the social circles of the resident British elite.

That elite also often dismissed India's impressive literary and religious heritage (see Chapter 1 and *Witnesses*, p. 697)—Hindu, Buddhist, Muslim—as alien and inferior. Missionaries converted few of these adherents of ancient faiths to Christianity. (Missionary efforts to improve health services and education did, however, bear fruit.) Certain customs that the British elite found repugnant—such as the caste system, that relegates millions to permanent social disability, or *suttee*, the supposedly voluntary burning of wives on a husband's funeral pyre—are still viewed as contrary to universal moral concepts. Others, such as the Hindu refusal to eat beef, or the Muslim refusal to eat pork, were rejected only because unfamiliar.

Economic exploitation, inflexible rule, and cultural incompatibilities stimulated the mutiny of native soldiers (called **sepoys**) in the Company's Indian army that erupted into war in 1857 and changed the nature of British sovereignty in India. Over the previous century, common soldiers had been recruited from among Hindu and Muslim natives, and trained to modern European standards. Some native soldiers rose in rebellion in May 1857, provoked perhaps by a perceived religious insult (their cartridges of ammunition, which they needed to break open with their teeth, were rumored to be coated with beef or pork fat, each kind offensive to either Hindu or Muslim troops) as well as deeper grievances.

Over the next fourteen months, sepoy rebels resisted British forces, while atrocities occurred on both sides. In the aftermath, the British Parliament instituted some reforms, including the guarantee of religious toleration, changes in land administration and military procedures, and the admission of Indian natives to some advisory councils and offices. In the India Act of 1858, having disposed of the British East India Company, the British Parliament declared it would henceforth administer India directly. In 1877, India was constituted as a monarchy subordinate to the British crown, and the British Queen Victoria (r. 1837–1901) was crowned empress. Some 1000 British administrators staffed the Indian Civil Service and lower offices, which ruled the sub-continent through the agency of hundreds of thousands of subordinate, native bureaucrats. Indian subjugation, as illustrated in the photograph above, was complete, and Indian nationalism was born.

From 1858 to 1917, though the British grip on India was firm, new cultural currents pointed toward eventual emancipation—a promise indeed envisioned by discussions between British and Indian leaders in 1917–1918. Extensive railroad construction facilitated interior trade and communication, and some native entrepreneurs were able to insert themselves in the foreign-dominated commercial system. These developments, together with the effects of the opening of the Suez Canal in 1869 (see below), resulted in a sevenfold increase in India's foreign trade.

For ordinary families, uncontrolled population increase outpaced gains in domestic product. The high-status natives who succeeded in entering the provincial civil service educated their children at schools recently instituted on the European model, or at British boarding schools and universities. This educated native elite was able to criticize British rule in its own terms. Its representatives in the Indian National Congress founded in 1885, the sub-continent's first national political movement, began to press for independence. Between 1907 and 1916, the Congress split into moderate and radical factions. Later on, Muslim–Hindu hostilities further split the Congress, fracturing the religious unity that Babur had tried to construct four centuries earlier. In the years following World War I (1914–1918), the Indian sub-continent nourished the intellectual and political leaders who would one day lead it to independence.

The Philippines and East Indies: Enduring Mercantile Empires

In the Philippines and the East Indies (including modern Malaysia and Indonesia), small European merchant settlements founded in the 1500s led, as in India, to enduring domination by European powers.

The huge tropical archipelago of the East Indies, extending more than 3000 miles west to east and lying on the sea route between India and China, was a magnet for merchant adventurers. It was originally populated around 1000 B.C.E. by migrants from the Asian mainland, and had seen the arrival of earlier traders in two waves: first, Indians around the seventh century C.E., who introduced Buddhism and Hinduism, and second, Arabs from the fourteenth century onward, who introduced Islam.

In contact with the advanced civilizations of the region, island natives developed states of their own. On Sumatra and Java, two native kingdoms emerged, respectively Buddhist (the Sri Vijaya) and Hindu (that of the Majapahits). These kingdoms flourished successfully from the seventh through the fifteenth centuries. Soon thereafter, Islam was established throughout the region, which splintered into separate political units.

The islands later named the Philippines (after King Philip II of Spain) form another tropical archipelago, extending about 1200 miles north to south. They were first populated about 30,000 years ago, and from about 1000 C.E. they had commercial relations with Chinese, Japanese, and Malaysian merchants (carriers of Buddhism), and with Arab merchants (who introduced Islam) from the fifteenth.

The first European to arrive was the Portuguese navigator Ferdinand Magellan (*c.* 1480–1521; see Chapter 16) who claimed the islands for Spain in 1521. In 1571, merchants established a permanent station at Manila, after which the "Manila galleon" regularly journeyed between New Spain (modern Mexico) and the Philippines. Filipino companies exchanged native commodities for American silver in a commerce protected from foreign interlopers into the 1830s: spices, sugar, and coffee.

Spanish governors and armies, meanwhile, established a regime that endured until 1898. Ruled by a viceroy advised by an appointed royal council, or *audiencia*, it fought off pirates and competitors, and was disturbed by stirrings of rebellion only in its last years. Just as nationalist forces were poised to win independence from their Spanish overlord, Spain lost a decisive naval battle in Manila Bay (1898) to the United States. Within the year the United States had acquired sovereignty over the Philippines, to the dismay of many public figures opposed to such foreign ventures.

Their dismay deepened when Filipino leaders turned to guerrilla warfare, capitulating only in 1901. The United States spent more money, and sacrificed more lives in suppressing the revolt than it had in the Spanish–American War (1898)—a measure of Filipino determination. In 1914, the largely Christian Filipinos (converted by Spanish missionaries) were English-speaking dependents of the United States.

The East Indies were colonies first of the Portuguese and then of the Dutch. Portuguese interest in the region came when spices were the most valued commodity in the European trading system and the East Indies archipelago was the world's principal source of spices (especially the sub-group of nearly 14,000 islands known as the Moluccas, and formerly as the Spice Islands). In 1511 the Portuguese captured the city-state of Malacca, poised on the Malay straits that were the gateway to the Indies. By 1513, they had reached the Moluccas, and controlled the spice trade.

In the seventeenth century, Portuguese mastery yielded to the merchants, admirals, and governors of the Dutch East India Company. Over the next three centuries they acquired in the East Indies a total dominion comparable to that achieved by the British East India Company in India. Establishing their headquarters at Batavia (present-day Jakarta), founded in 1619 on the island of Java, they seized Malacca from the Portuguese in 1641, then the Moluccas, outposts on the island of Sumatra, and, by stages, the whole of the islands of Java and Bali. In 1910, all of modern Indonesia (except for the Portuguese enclave of East Timor) was in Dutch hands. After 1799, when the Dutch East India Company was dissolved, the Dutch government took direct control.

The Dutch now possessed the world monopoly of the Moluccan spice trade. In the eighteenth century the Dutch also promoted a range of other exports: coffee, for which Europeans soon developed an enduring passion, along with tea and tobacco. As in Spanish America, an economy based on the processing of agricultural commodities succeeded in short-circuiting any native attempts at modernization or diversification. Native resistance to Dutch policies exploded in rebellion in Java in 1825–1830 and on all three major islands—Java, Bali, and Sumatra—from the 1880s. At the beginning of the twentieth century,

---

W I T N E S S E S

Britain's Empire in India

The British takeover of the various peoples and nations of India was entirely to the advantage of the Indians—or so the British argued, as do the first two authors here, for whom British institutions and the English language were self-evidently superior to any others. A different view is expressed in the third passage, by an Indian poet, who calls on his countrymen to industrialize and grow wealthy so that they may reclaim their own nation from foreigners.

Lord Wellesley defends the East India Company (1813): There never was an organ of government, in the history of the world, so administered, as to demand more of estimation than that of the East India Company. There might ... be points of error to correct; but if their Lordships looked at the general state of our Empire in India— ... if they adverted to the state of real solid peace, in which countries were now placed, that had in previous times been so constantly exposed to war and devastation ... they would see that ... the administration ... of the East India Company had been productive of strength, tranquillity and happiness. The situation of the natives had been meliorated and improved—the rights of property, before unknown, had been introduced and confirmed. ... A judicial system had been established which, though not perfect, contained with it all the essentials of British justice.
(Lord Wellesley, Speech in the House of Lords, April 9, 1813; *English Historical Documents*, 1959, vol. XI)

Historian and statesman Thomas B. Macaulay urges that the British Parliament establish an English-language educational system in colonial India (1835): We have a fund to be employed as Government shall direct for the intellectual improvement of the people of [India]. The simple question is, what is the most useful way of employing it?

All parties seem to be agreed on one point, that the dialects commonly spoken among the natives of this part of India, contain neither literary nor scientific information, and are, moreover, so poor and rude that, until they are enriched from some other quarter, it will not be easy to translate any valuable work into them. It seems to be admitted on all sides, that the intellectual improvement of those classes of the people who have the means of pursuing higher studies, can at present be effected only by means of some language not vernacular amongst them. ... The whole question seems to me to be, which language is the best worth knowing. ...

I have no knowledge of either Sanscrit or Arabic.—But I have done what I could to form a correct estimate of their value. I have read translations of the most celebrated Arabic and Sanscrit works. I have conversed ... with men distinguished by their proficiency in the Eastern tongues. ... I have never found one among them who could deny that a single shelf of a good European library was worth the whole native literature of India and Arabia. ...

How, then, stands the case? We have to educate a people who cannot at present be educated by means of their mother-tongue. We must teach them some foreign language. The claims of our own language it is hardly necessary to recapitulate. It stands preeminent even among the languages of the west. ... Whoever knows that language has ready access to all the vast intellectual wealth, which all the wisest nations of the earth have created and hoarded in the course of ninety generations. It may safely be said, that the literature now extant in that language is of far greater value than all the literature which three hundred years ago was extant in all the languages of the world together. ... The English tongue is that which would be the most useful to our native subjects.
(Thomas B. Macaulay, "Minute of 2 February 1835 on Indian Education"; ed. G. M. Young, 1957)

The Bombay poet Dalpatram Kavi laments "The Attack of King Industry," which has transferred all wealth into the hands of foreigners (1861):
Fellow countrymen, let us remove all the miseries of
  our country,
Do work, for the new kingdom has come, its king is
industry.

Our wealth has gone into the hands of foreigners. The
  great blunder is yours
For you did not unite yourselves—fellow countrymen.

Consider the time, see for yourselves, all our people
  have become poor,
Many men of business have fallen—fellow countrymen.

...

Introduce industry from countries abroad and achieve
  mastery of the modern machinery.
Please attend to this plea for the Poet Dalpat—fellow
  countrymen.
(Dalpatram Kavi, "The Attack of King Industry"—"Hunnarkhan-ni Chadayi"; eds. C. Trivedi and H. Spodek, 1998)

the so-called Ethical Policy provided greater educational and administrative opportunities for talented natives. But in 1914, Dutch imperialism in the region remained repressive and entirely unyielding.

China, Korea, and Indochina: Forced Entry

In India and the East Indies, European merchant depots were the wedges that opened vast regions to direct domination by European nations. That pattern was not repeated on the mainland of east and southeast Asia. Although merchant footholds were established from the 1500s at Malacca, Macao, and Nagasaki (in present-day Malaysia, China, and Japan), these were scant. Before 1800, the advanced societies of the Asian mainland were little affected by European presence in the South China Sea.

After 1800, however, when Asian nations faced European states possessing military and technological superiority, the situation changed. They were unable to withstand the insistent demand for access to sources of wealth as yet untapped by European commerce.

In 1800, China was the oldest and most secure monarchy in the world (see Chapters 2, 8, 16). For centuries, it had imposed its law on neighboring states in Korea, Indochina, and Mongolia—over which states, at times, it exercised sovereignty. China collected tribute from these and even more distant regions. It exported prized commodities and manufactures: silk textiles, porcelain and lacquer goods, tea and other agricultural produce. Its merchants carried on a busy commerce within China and abroad, reaching India, the East Indian archipelago, and parts of Oceania, as well as central Asia and Mediterranean ports via the ancient Silk Road.

Along these routes, China also diffused its high literary and philosophical culture—Buddhist, Taoist, and Confucian. Trained in that Confucian tradition, China's scholars and poets were also its government officials (if they succeeded in passing licensing examinations). They administered the mammoth empire for the most part judiciously and efficiently. Science and technology also flourished in China, the world leader in those endeavors until the seventeenth century. China first gave the world paper, gunpowder, and block printing, among other inventions.

These patterns prevailed over a series of dynasties extending back to the Shang, Zhou, and Qin of the Bronze and Iron Ages; and to the Han, Tang, Song, and Yüan that ruled from the period of ancient Rome to the threshold of the European Renaissance (see Chapters 1, 2, 8, 16). They continued thereafter under the Ming (1368–1644) and Qing, or Manchu rulers (1644–1912). With the latter, who were exhausted, corrupt, and subjected to European overlords, the venerable procession of emperors and dynasties ended.

In 1368, after thirty years of popular resistance to Mongol Yüan rule, rebel leader Chu Yan-chang established the Ming dynasty. He and his Ming successors rebuilt the region, which had been devastated by the wars leading to Mongol victory in 1279. The imperial economic policy favored agriculture over commerce. That decision resulted in conservative government in the countryside, exercised by gentry landowners who belonged to the same social stratum as Confucian political officials.

Under Ming rule the economy flourished. Textiles, raw cotton, and grain, the main domestic commodities, traveled to and from the major trading centers in the Yangzi delta (especially Nanjing) and the newly founded (1421) capital at Beijing, which provisioned a large network of frontier garrisons in the north. Population soared from a depressed 60 million at the time of Ming takeover to more than 100 million in the late 1500s. At that time more people lived in China than in all of Europe.

Early successes permitted the Ming to challenge the Mongols, invade Vietnam (in Indochina), and reduce Korea to vassalage. From the late sixteenth century, they withdrew to a defensive posture, as Japanese pirates harried their coasts, boldly entered the Yangzi, and challenged China's preeminence in Korea. Ineffective emperors ceded authority to corrupt eunuchs, who had withstood government reform efforts. From 1627, a rash of rebellions left China vulnerable to incursion once again from the north. In 1644, the Ming fell to a new dynasty which was to be China's last: the Qing.

The Manchu, a non-Chinese people who originated in Manchuria, swept into the Chinese region from the 1620s, established themselves as the Qing dynasty at Beijing in 1644, and consolidated their sovereignty in the resistant south and west by 1680. During the following century, they expanded into Mongolia, central Asia, and Indochina, as the costs of expansion injured an already precarious economy.

By 1800, economic crisis loomed. Virtually all the arable land of China was under cultivation, and had reached the limit of what it could produce. Food supply was further strained by a population increase from about 100 million in 1650 to more than 300 million by 1800 and 420 million by 1850. The hungry peasants rebelled, as did subject states corralled unwillingly into the Manchu Empire.

Meanwhile, by the 1830s, the importation of opium by the British had begun to destabilize the Chinese economy. Since the 17th century, the British had paid in silver coin for Chinese tea, as tea-drinking became a regular custom at home. Seeking to balance their trade deficit, the British had exported Indian-grown opium to China—an import which not only led to the depletion of Chinese silver reserves, but threatened to corrupt Chinese workers in seaport regions. The free-trade policies of the British collided with the

Confucian principles of Chinese officials, for whom government must exert a moral influence that included commercial relations. When Chinese officials acting on the highest authority confiscated and destroyed more than 19,000 chests of opium in 1839, the conflict between world views erupted into the First Opium War of 1839–1842. Its result was a mandate for the economic opening of China by European merchants and states.

Since 1557, Chinese officials had allowed the Portuguese to maintain a trading station at Macao on the southern coast. British and French merchants later obtained a foothold at nearby Guangzhou (Canton), and the Dutch, briefly, on the island of Taiwan. From these depots, they exported the Chinese tea and luxuries craved by Western elites. Unsatisfied, they sought greater access to Chinese markets. The British, particularly, hoped to gain buyers for cotton textiles from Britain's new mills (see Chapter 21); or opium, in quantities of close to 2000 tons annually, imported from British-held India.

The imperial government rebuffed British pleas for greater access. Opium carried on British ships, in violation of Chinese law, succeeded in corrupting port officials and causing the addiction of millions of natives. Chinese bureaucrats investigated and condemned the trade, and protested to Queen Victoria, advising her of the penalty decreed for European peddlers of opium: decapitation. In 1839, responding to Chinese confiscation of opium stores, British warships trained their cannon on several coastal cities. Overwhelmed by Western superiority in weaponry, as related in *Witnesses* on p. 700, the Chinese capitulated.

The Treaty of Nanjing (Nanking) of 1842 put an end to the First Opium War and compelled China to open its gates to Western commerce and control. Protected by the new policy of **"extraterritoriality"** (which exempted Westerners from Chinese law), European trading stations operated at Macao, Guangzhou (Canton), Shanghai, and other ports. In addition the British gained control of Hong Kong, an island later (1898) leased to Britain for ninety-nine years.

E. Duncan, painting of the steamer Nemesis: *Western warships wreaked havoc on traditional societies that had no weaponry to defend themselves. Here, the steam-powered Nemesis swiftly destroys Chinese junks at Guangzhou, China in 1843, as the British force the opening of China to Western trade. (National Maritime Museum, Canada)*

In 1856, the Second Opium War erupted as the Chinese attempted to block European encroachments. A British and French force destroyed the imperial summer palace outside Beijing, and occupied the city. In 1860, China backed down, accepting a treaty that delivered some fifty ports to foreign control, permitted European diplomatic residents in Beijing, allowed Christian missionary activity, and, a final blow, legalized the importation of opium.

The humiliation of China continued for another generation. From 1848 to 1865, the Chinese government spent its energies suppressing the massive Taiping Rebellion, whose leader, a Christian-trained mystic and moralist, offered promise of national regeneration. Between 1862 and 1897, the French seized Vietnam and Laos in Indochina, previously dominated by China. An updated Japanese army claimed Taiwan and other smaller territories in the Sino-Japanese War of 1894–1895. Russia, meanwhile, crept into the northeast and briefly dominated Manchuria. By 1900, France, Britain, Germany, and Russia had imposed on the Qing government a system of **concessions**, or economic spheres of influence. These effectively partitioned China, weakened by famine and unrest. Progressive officials attempted to modernize and reform the Chinese government, in a program known as "self-strengthening." Their efforts came too late. Western subjugation of a once great, now decadent state was nearly complete.

The expropriations of European merchants, the arrogance of military leaders, the contempt of European officials for an ancient civilization, and the alien promptings of Christian missionaries, stimulated explosive and violent native resistance movements. The most famous of these was the rebellion of the Boxers (1898–1901), as the Europeans called them. Properly named the "Righteous and Harmonious

Fists," this was a secret society hostile to all Western political and cultural influence encouraged by the dowager empress Tz'u-Hsi (1835–1908) and her conservative courtiers. The Boxers deplored not only China's political takeover by the West, but the demoralization of the Chinese by foreigners whose technical and military power they recognized but whose intellectual and religious culture they despised.

Although the Boxer rebellion failed, native intellectuals had begun to conceive of national independence—both from the failing Qing dynasts and from European interlopers. A series of uprisings in 1911 dismantled the Qing dynasty. Sun Yat-sen (1866–1925) became president of the resulting republic in 1912, but was pushed aside the next year by the dictator Yüan Shih-k'ai (1859–1916). That new government was forced to surrender some territories to Japan during World War I. In 1914, the great empire that had loomed over east Asia for more than two millennia faced an uncertain future.

The native kingdoms of Southeast Asia, meanwhile, which had for centuries been prey to Chinese incursions, fell to British and French expansionism. By 1885, Britain controlled all of Burma (now called Myanmar). In addition, between 1786 and 1819, she had acquired three strategic city-states on the Malay Peninsula (and a protectorate over the region) that assured access to Chinese ports: Penang, Malacca (by Dutch cession), and Singapore, the latter established as a free port. One of the four European concession powers in China, France took direct control of modern Laos, Vietnam, and Cambodia in a war waged from 1862 to 1897. By 1914, with the exception of Siam (modern Thailand), Indochina was part of the European *imperium*.

Japan: Point, Counterpoint

Alone of the non-Western nations of the globe, Japan successfully resisted Western encroachment, responding to aggression with a disciplined program of self-development that rendered it, by 1914, one of the major world powers. Unlike China, which suffered repeated disruptions between the fifteenth and nineteenth centuries, Japan was politically unified and well-poised to meet the challenge of Western intervention when it came in 1853.

In 1603, after the suppression of more than a century of disorder, the *samurai* Tokugawa Ieyasu (1543–1616) seized the supreme position of *shogun* (the military leader of Japan, appointed by the imperial court which itself wielded no effective power). He initiated a period of stability that lasted two and a half centuries, reining in the competing samurai

The European Arrival in East Asia

Two very different encounters of Asian peoples with the West are recorded here. The first passage describes the Chinese failure to resist British warships during the First Opium War. The second reports the success of a Japanese delegation which studied on-site the parliaments of Europe, to prepare for the creation of a Japanese constitution.

The futility of traditional resistance: a modern historian describes Chinese efforts to repel British ships during the First Opium War (1842):

[Chinese volunteer] Pei Ch'ing-ch'iao's ... assignment was to superintend the making of five hundred rocket mortars. The model was an ancient specimen supplied by the aged Commander Tuan Yung'fu, and came from Yünnan. Pei was ashamed, he says, that ... the best they could produce was a contrivance that looked as though it emanated from the pages of the *Fire-dragon Book*, a seventeenth-century treatise on artillery. These mortars were supposed to be used in setting fire to the sails and rigging of foreign ships, but do not seem ever to have come into action.

Someone suggested that fire-crackers should be tied to the backs of a number of monkeys, who would then be flung on board the English ships. The flames would spread rapidly in every direction and might with luck reach the powder-magazine, in which case the whole ship would blow up. Nineteen monkeys were bought, and ... were brought in litters to the advanced base. After the failure of the Chinese attack they accompanied the retreating armies. ...
(From A. Waley ed., *The Opium War Through Chinese Eyes*, 1958)

Ito Hirobumi, chief architect of Japan's modernizing Meiji Constitution of 1889, recounts his efforts to understand and learn from the West (1909): It was in the month of March, 1882, that His Majesty [the Japanese emperor] ordered me to work out a draft of a constitution to be submitted to his approval. No time was to be lost, so I started on ... an extended journey ... to make as thorough a study as possible of the actual workings of different systems of constitutional government . ... I took young men with me, who all belonged to the elite of the rising generation, to assist and to cooperate with me in my studies. I sojourned about a year and a half in Europe, and having gathered all the necessary materials ... I returned home in September, 1883. Immediately after my return I set to work to draw up the Constitution.
(Ito Hirobumi, *Reminiscences on the Drafting of the New Constitution*, 1909; ed. W. T. de Bary, 1958)

Commodore Perry's "Black Ship": *The threat of imminent attack on Japan was posed by the warship that the American Commodore Perry piloted into Japanese waters in 1853. Such naval force served ultimately to bring both China and Japan into the Western-dominated global economy during the nineteenth century.* (The Mariner's Museum, Virginia)

clan-leaders, or *daimyos*, who had established themselves as independent territorial lords. Rewarding loyal samurai with offices and privileges and suppressing those who resisted, he compelled the Japanese nobility to recognize a strongly centralized government: the *bakufu*, located in Edo (modern Tokyo), a capital distinct from the imperial court of Kyoto.

Tokugawa and his successors established a legal code, a highway system, and a network of fortifications from which to suppress any future challenge to the now-powerful state. Prosperity returned, and the population climbed from about 20 million in 1600 to about 30 million in the eighteenth century.

The Tokugawa shogunate enforced a policy of isolation, shunning the Western adventurers who sought a foothold in Japan. Portuguese traders had arrived in 1542, followed quickly by Jesuit missionaries. The Tokugawa expelled the missionaries in 1614, and Christianity was soon extirpated in a series of persecutions in the 1630s. Even Buddhism was subordinated to Shinto religious institutions (see Chapters 1, 8), which elevated the shogun (the emperor for the moment in eclipse) as a ritual leader. And Confucianism, an import from China, supported the development of a samurai code of conduct appropriate to the new regime. The shogunate discouraged all contact with Western customs and even Western technology. The European guns that Tokugawa forces used to gain sovereignty, quickly imitated by Japanese military technicians, were banned soon after.

The shoguns did, however, allow the Dutch, established in Nagasaki since 1567, to remain in carefully supervised isolation. The Japanese were instructed to have nothing to do with their culture, their religion, or even their method of writing with letters that ran oddly sideways, in contrast to the

vertical columns of Asian characters. Yet the West demanded access, as it had in China. Between 1793 and 1853, several Western ships visited Japan's key ports seeking permission to trade. The last and most famous visitor, in 1853, was the United States Commodore Matthew Perry (1794–1858), whose warship is shown on the left. Perry threatened the Japanese with bombardment if they did not cooperate. Japan admitted the foreigners, submitting to the humiliating Harris Treaty of 1858.

Nevertheless, the Japanese managed to avoid Western domination. By 1868, the capitulation had triggered a fantastic series of events. A group of young, determined samurai expelled the shogun and restored the emperor as titular ruler, removed from obscurity in Kyoto to the capital at Tokyo, and to power (although the revolutionary samurai continued to hold real power). This was the sixteen-year-old Mutsuhito (1852–1912) who, as the descendant of the sun goddess (according to tradition and official doctrine until 1945), was seen as destined to fulfill the divine plan for Japan's governance. The revolutionary event is known as the "Meiji" (the term means "enlightened rule") restoration.

These innovators created a new imperial bureaucracy in which promotion was based on talent, abolished feudalism, and created a conscript army (1873). They sent experts to the major Western capitals to study law codes and parliamentary constitutions, (see the passage reproduced in *Witnesses* on p. 700) and technicians to study industrial production. They introduced cabinet government, bicameral legislature, and a formal constitution (1885–1889). They set up schools (enrolling ninety percent of all school-age children by 1900) and universities to train future generations to manage a renewed Japan.

By 1914, Japan was a modern nation, having swiftly experienced the processes of industrialization and urbanization that had taken centuries in Europe. Using one-third of the revenues gathered from a reformed tax system, the government promoted industry, transportation, and communications. Textile and steel production sped forward in the 1880s and 1890s, boosting Japan's trade balance—the nation was now an exporter of manufactures, an importer of raw materials. Population continued to climb, and by 1914, about one-third lived in cities.

Streamlined, industrialized, and fully competitive with the West, Japan now pursued its own imperialist goals in east Asia. Seizing the adjacent Kuril and Ryukyu Islands in 1875 and 1879, as a result of the Sino-Japanese War of 1894–1895 she further acquired Taiwan and part of Manchuria. In the Russo-Japanese war of 1904–1905, the unanticipated Japanese victory announced that nation's entry to the circle of great world powers. In 1910, Japan annexed Korea and, as a participant in World War I, claimed for itself further

Chinese territories in its notorious Twenty-One Demands issued in 1915 (see Chapter 26).

Japan was the exception among Asian states. Not only did the Japanese resist foreign domination, but they acquired the military and technical skills that gave Europeans their edge in the age of imperialism. By 1914, Japan was an imperialist power, too.

OLD WORLD ENCOUNTERS: IMPERIALISM IN THE MIDDLE EAST AND AFRICA

More easily than in Asia, European powers came to dominate the native peoples of the Middle East and Africa. Map 24.3 on p. 704 shows how these regions were divided. In the Middle East, a weakening Ottoman Empire gave the principal imperialist nations opportunities to exert economic and political influence. In Africa, the European nations intruded swiftly and decisively in 1880–1900.

The Middle East: The Last Islamic Empire

From ancient times, a series of vigorous empires ruled the Middle East (see Chapters 1, 8). The last of these—that of the Turkish Ottoman dynasty—reached its peak in the sixteenth century, weakened in the seventeenth and eighteenth, and succumbed in the nineteenth to the commercial and military power of western European nations it once scorned.

From the seventh century, followers of the prophet Muhammad carried the religion of Islam (from the Arabic term for "submission" to God) through the Middle East and North Africa, into Spain, the Balkans, India, and the East Indies. From the eleventh century C.E., the regimes of the Arabic rulers, or caliphs, yielded to new incursions of Asian steppe nomads—Turkish and Mongol polytheists who converted to Islam and ruled in its name.

In 1500, three Islamic dynasties ruled in the Middle East: the Safavids in Persia (modern Iran); the Mamluks in Egypt and Syria (including modern Palestine/Israel, Lebanon, and Jordan); the Ottomans in Asia Minor (Anatolia, now Turkey) and south-east Europe, nearly as far north as modern Hungary (see also Chapters 14, 15, 16). By 1600, the Mamluk lands fell to the Ottomans, who had also absorbed the coastal regions of North Africa and the Black Sea while containing the Safavids to the southeast.

Meanwhile, the Ottoman navy seized most of the strategic island bases that were situated in the Mediterranean from Venice, Genoa, and Spain, capturing Euboea (Negroponte) (1470); Lemnos (1479); Rhodes (1522); Cyprus (1573); and Crete (1669). Their rivals stopped Ottoman maritime expansion only in 1571, at the battle of Lepanto off the Peloponnesian coast of Greece. On land, Ottoman armies had advanced by 1529 through Hungary as far as Vienna, where they were only narrowly repulsed by a combined force of European armies.

By 1600, however, the Ottoman Empire had already spent its first vigor. Over the next two centuries, the Austrian Habsburgs and the Russian tsars pushed back the Ottoman borders in southeastern Europe. In 1683, combined European armies repelled a second Ottoman attempt to take Vienna, and the Treaties of Karlowitz (1699) and Passarowitz (1718) opened southeastern Europe to Habsburg advance at Ottoman expense. From 1768 to 1783, Russia under Catherine the Great seized the northern shore of the Black Sea, finally acquiring an outlet to warm-water seas. Meanwhile, the British navy patrolled the Mediterranean to protect its trade link to India from pirate raids issuing from Ottoman-held ports.

By 1800, the Ottoman empire was, it was said, the "sick man of Europe"—a phrase repeated gleefully by several European monarchs who hoped to profit from its disease. The following century saw its disintegration. In 1914, the Ottoman Empire retained only one-third of the territory it had ruled in 1800. Moreover, the seeds had been planted for later resistance to Western intervention by Asian and African people previously under Ottoman rule.

In Europe, the dismantlement of Ottoman power began with the successful revolution from 1821–1830, by which Greece won its independence. The Balkan states to the north—Serbia, Montenegro, Albania, Bulgaria, and Romania—had all broken away from Ottoman dominion by 1914. Bosnia–Herzegovina and Bessarabia were wrested away from Ottoman rule and incorporated, respectively, by Austria and Russia.

In Syria, Ottoman officials continued to rule ineffectually (with Lebanon under Christian governors after 1861) as British, French, and Russian interests took hold. The regions further east and south—Iraq and the Arabian Peninsula—came under British influence during the years prior to 1914, while Russian influence prevailed in Iran and in the Caucasian states of Georgia, Armenia, and Azerbaijan.

In North Africa, independent local rulers asserted themselves in Egypt (which dominated Sudan to its south), Libya, Tunisia, and Algeria; Morocco, an independent sultanate, never fell under Ottoman rule. All of these, including Morocco, became subjected to European states as their economies faltered due to the disruption caused by foreign intervention. France annexed Algeria (1830) and Tunisia (1881); Britain dominated Egypt (1882); Spain and France together partitioned Morocco (1912); and Italy occupied Libya (1911). By 1914, European powers had absorbed the whole of North Africa.

Shocked into an awareness of modern warfare and administration by Napoleon's presence in 1798–1801 (see Chapter 20), the Ottoman governors of Egypt detached the region from the parent state. The Macedonian governor, Muhammad 'Ali (1769–1849)

Europe in Africa and the Middle East

Much misunderstanding and resentment accompanied Europeans in their contacts with the people of Africa and the Middle East. In the first passage here, a French missionary speaks admiringly, but patronizingly, of a native African leader and his people. In the second, an Islamic reformer urges his coreligionists to recover their ancient greatness in the sciences, the springboard of commerce and wealth, so as to compete with the European nations that have taken over so much of the world.

Ernest Linant de Fellefonds, a French Catholic missionary, recounts a conversation with Kabaka Mutesa (M'Tesa), the ruler of Buganda, East Africa (1875): In answer to all M'Tesa's questions concerning the earth, the sun, the moon, the stars and the sky and in order to make him understand the movement of the heavenly bodies, I had to make shapes on a board, the heavenly bodies being represented by little glass balls. The lecture took place today. ...

M'Tesa grasped everything perfectly. ... [and] was able to inspire ... in many of his people this quest for understanding, for self-instruction and for knowledge. ... They are an inquiring, observant, intelligent people with minds longing for the learning of white people whose superiority they recognize ...

(From D. A. Low, *Mind of Buganda: Documents of the Modern History of an African Kingdom*, 1971)

Jamal al-Din al-Afghani, an Islamic reformer, speaks on science (1882): The Europeans have now put their hands on every part of the world. The English have reached Afghanistan; the French have seized Tunisia. In reality this ... conquest has not come from the French or the English. Rather it is science that everywhere manifests its greatness and power. ...

If we study the riches of the world we learn that wealth is the result of commerce, industry, and agriculture. Agriculture is achieved only with agricultural science, botanical chemistry, and geometry. Industry is produced only with physics, chemistry, mechanics, geometry, and mathematics; and commerce is based on agriculture and industry.

Our *ulama* [Islamic leaders] ... have not understood that science is a noble thing that has no connection with any nation, and is not distinguished by anything but itself. ...

The father and mother of science is proof. ... The truth is where there is proof, and those who forbid science and knowledge in the belief that they are safeguarding the Islamic religion are really the enemies of that religion.

(Al-Afghani, *On the Importance of Science*, 1882; ed. M. R. Keddie, 1983, 2nd ed.)

---

reorganized the tax system, imported Western technology, encouraged factory construction, created public schools, modernized the army, and established his own dynasty—which failed to implement further the changes he had initiated. Under his successors, native entrepreneurs became financially dependent upon British and French bankers who poured into the European quarters of Alexandria. In 1882, the country went bankrupt. The British occupied this strategic region (extending into the Sudan) to protect its bankers' investments and its merchant navy's access to the Suez Canal.

Under the direction of the French entrepreneur Ferdinand de Lesseps (1805–1894), the Canal had been constructed to solve an ancient problem: how to connect the goods that came to Mediterranean ports from the interiors of Africa and Europe with the Indian Ocean trade routes that led to India, the East Indies, and east Asia? Portuguese explorers had a water route around the southern tip of Africa (see Chapter 16). But that journey was now shortened by the creation of a water link between the Mediterranean and the Red Sea—the Suez Canal—completed in 1869. A British-built rail link from Alexandria to Cairo and the Canal, completed in the 1850s, further facilitated the export of African goods to Asia.

The Middle Eastern regions of the failing Ottoman Empire had already lapsed into economic decline

before 1800. Thereafter, they further suffered from the **economic imperialism** of European companies and states. Their traditional crafts and artisanal organizations weakened as these regions became suppliers of primary materials for European factories. Middle Eastern workers produced cotton, most importantly, but also sugar and tobacco for export, in exchange for high-priced European manufactures. The resulting balance of trade favored European interests, while it was ruinous to the natives, creating underdevelopment where there had once been prosperity.

European economic domination aroused native resistance under the influence of Islamic leaders called **ulamâ**, and judges, or **qâdi** (see Chapter 8). Islamic rebellions erupted, especially following the French and British interventions in northern Africa in 1881 and 1882. In Egypt, there was a call for a revival of Islamic traditions, and a new **jihad**, or religious struggle, against the infidel intruders. An Islamic resistance inspired by the **Mahdi**, the charismatic prophet Muhammad Ahmad (1849–1885), controlled the Sudan from 1881 to 1898, targeting both Egyptians, who had subjugated their nation, and the Europeans who now ruled Egypt.

While popular resistance movements flared, Muslim intellectuals faced a stony reality: adherence to Islam meant clinging to tradition, but independence from European domination could only be achieved by

Map 24.3 Europeans in Africa and the Middle East: *As the Ottoman Empire disintegrated after 1800, European powers rushed in. In the former region, they established protectorates, direct dominion, or zones of influence by the post-World War I settlement of 1923. Africa in general, both northern and sub-Saharan, was partitioned by the European powers between 1880 and 1913. The national boundaries of modern African states reflect the interests of Western imperialists. They bear little relationship to pre-existing African political borders or to African boundaries of ethnicity, language, or tribal community (see Map 24.4 opposite). Why were African states and peoples not able to resist the European onslaught after 1880?*

modernization of ideas and institutions. The debate took place in schools and academies, and in the press, itself modeled on the traditions of Western journalism. The cultural elite was divided. Traditionalists looked backward to a purer era of Islam. Modernists, such as the teacher and journalist Jamal ad-Din al-Afghani (1838–1897), called for a new orientation of Islam in

scientific rationalism, recalling the great age in the ninth through twelfth centuries when Islamic scientists and philosophers were the world's most innovative thinkers (see Chapter 8 and *Witnesses*, p. 703).

Attempts to modernize through direct political action came in the early twentieth century. Protest following the 1890 concession to foreign merchants of

Map 24.4　African States and People Before 1880

other nations of the Middle East still lay under the sway of European entrepreneurs and governments.

Sub-Saharan Africa: Divided and Despoiled

By 1914, the economic exploitation of Africa south of the Sahara had resulted in its division. Every corner of the region, except the states of Ethiopia and Liberia had by this time fallen under European sovereignty, as Map 24.3 on p. 704 shows.

In 1500, the European presence in Africa was minimal (see Chapters 8, 16, 19). The Islamic states and settlements on the northern and eastern coasts were far more important for the internal development of the continent. From the north, Arab traders crossed the Sahara, visiting the rich cities of the Sudan to acquire gold, spices, the exotic products of the jungle, and slaves. These cities were not only commercial nodes stimulated by Arab trade, but also the religious and cultural capitals of Islamized native African states—including Songhay, the successor to Mali and Ghana—that had developed over previous centuries and now extended almost continuously across the grassland region to the south of the desert.

To the east, along the Red Sea and Indian Ocean coasts, stretched a string of Islamic centers that traded with the peoples of the interior. By 1500, Islamic Adal near the Horn of Africa was in stiff competition with Ethiopia just inland. Further south, intense commercial activity had stimulated the development of interior states, notably the rich, fortified center of Zimbabwe, whose exports were sent as far as China.

Other native states flourished in interior regions, created by the iron-using farmers and herders of sub-Saharan Africa, as yet untouched by Christianity or Islam (see Map 24.4 above). A cluster of small states developed between Lakes Tanganyika and Victoria. Further south, the Bantu states of Luba and Lunda supplied eastern coastal depots, but also the western native state of Kongo, just inland of the Atlantic coast south of the Congo river. North and west of Kongo, stretching west of the Niger delta along the "Gold" and "slave" coasts, native states developed after about 1500 (Benin, Oyo, Asante), stimulated by trade with Songhay and the Hausa states of the western and central Sudan, whose flourishing cities impressed European travelers.

In this western region, as well as around the Cape and, to a lesser extent, on the eastern coast near the mouth of the Zambezi River, European merchants established their trading centers. The process began with the Portuguese just before 1500. The Dutch, British, French, Spanish, Germans and even Danes followed in the seventeenth century. In 1652, the Dutch settled the Cape, and over the next centuries expanded toward the interior. Between 1795 and 1803, Britain occupied the Dutch settlement.

the tobacco production and export by the **shah** (ruler) of Iran culminated in the revolution of 1906, which established a representative assembly on Western models. The shahs subsequently suppressed the assembly and ruled autocratically until deposed decades later not by a liberal parliament but by an Islamic revolt that established a **theocracy** (see Chapter 29).

Modernization was desperately needed at the core of the Ottoman Empire, in what would in 1921 become the nation of Turkey. Here a succession of corrupt or ineffective sultans and advisers had permitted the empire to weaken. From 1839 to 1876, reformers introduced the policy of Tanzimat, or "reordering," which involved changes in areas of justice, taxation, education, and minority rights. But these did not stop the decline. In 1875, the Ottoman sultan declared that interest would no longer be paid on the public debt; the state was bankrupt. As in Egypt, that economic collapse opened the gates to European bankers. In 1881, a foreign commission undertook to supervise the imperial finances. In 1878, European powers at the Congress of Berlin saw to the further fragmentation of the Ottoman Empire, apportioning Bosnia-Herzegovina to Austria-Hungary, while Britain received Cyprus, and France, Tunisia.

These humiliations at last stimulated a movement of young native intellectuals, or "Young Turks." Their resistance culminated in a 1908 revolution that deposed and replaced the sultan, and eventually replaced his government by one that was more modern but not less brutal. Among the defeated nations in World War I (see Chapter 26), the last of the Islamic empires expired in 1918. Its remnant, Turkey, adopted a Western model of political order, and contended on equal ground with the nations of Europe, while the

European merchants sought the same commodities from African kings and chieftains as Arab merchants had long done. Following the European settlement of the Americas after 1500, however, one economic activity became preeminent: the trade in slaves (see Chapter 16). Kidnapped, captured, or purchased by native leaders, often from Arab intermediaries, and sold or resold to Europeans, some 10 million black slaves, mostly male, were compelled to sail the Atlantic "middle passage" in wretched conditions prior to further resale and lifelong unpaid labor. Arab merchants also dealt in slaves, transporting them in growing numbers from the east coast to Mediterranean and Indian Ocean ports.

After 1807, Western prohibitions of the slave trade pressured the economies of African states. Slave-trading now shifted south and eastward, where slave-hunters joined elephant hunters in the search for human beings and ivory tusks. Asian and European consumers wanted ivory for luxury objects such as billiard balls and piano keys, and native communities grew wealthy from the trade. A good share of the profit was spent on guns to equip the armies of militaristic native states springing up on the eastern coast to exercise dominion over the interior.

No longer in the market for slaves, nineteenth-century European merchants sought tropical products such as peanuts, palm oil, and rubber which they exchanged for European industrial manufactures—textiles, metals, and guns. There were goods more valuable still to be found. Gold and diamond deposits made the fortunes of many European companies formed to mine them—the source of the great wealth and influence of the British imperialist and entrepreneur Cecil Rhodes (1853–1902)—along with iron, coal, and copper. Entrepreneurs enlisted armies of migrant laborers to work their mines for starvation wages and in horrific conditions.

As knowledge of Africa grew, the extent of the continent's mineral wealth became clear. From the 1790s through the 1870s, the promise of the interior stimulated a series of expeditions (mostly by British explorers, with African guides and servants) to investigate its topography and peoples. (Such expeditions were made possible, in part, by the European discovery of **quinine**, derived from cinchona bark native to the Andes of South America, to control the effects of malaria.) The contribution of late nineteenth-century explorers was to map the major river highways that led to the African interior: the upper Nile, the Zambezi, the Zaire. Their aims were in part scientific, and their expeditions culminated in reports to learned societies; they were also in part religious, in part commercial. The missionary David Livingstone (1813–1873) explored the lakes and rivers of central Africa for more than twenty years, striving to promote the two civilizing forces, as he saw it, of Christianity and commerce. The journalist Henry Morton Stanley

(1841–1904), employed variously by United States, British, and Belgian interests, explored the Congo during the 1870s and 1880s to assess the commercial value of its jungle abundance.

Pressing further into the interior, Europeans sparked religious conflict. Christian missionaries established themselves in the vicinity of European settlements, especially in west Africa. They opened schools and hospitals, providing needed services even as they battled African **animist** and magical beliefs. Soon, native converts began missions of their own, adapting Christianity to local customary belief, song, and dance. Although many Africans resented the imposition of Western religious and cultural values, others were ardent converts themselves and proponents of Christian expansion. The Christian presence also encouraged Islamic jihads, especially in the central and western Sudan, where recently-converted Muslims sought zealously to impose a strict orthodoxy on nominal believers and proselytes. Islamic influences intensified on the eastern coast as the trade in ivory and slaves increased.

In only a few places did European states exercise direct domination over African territory before 1880: the French in Algeria; the Spanish in Guinea; the Portuguese in Angola and Mozambique; and the British at the Cape. The displaced Dutch settlers, called **Boers** (from the Dutch word for farmer), plunged in stages deep into the interior—most famously in the "Great Trek" of 1835–1837—where they founded the Orange Free State and the state of Transvaal, first recognized, then absorbed by the British. In these regions, they came in contact with several African peoples who, in their turn, were driven to migrate to distant lands by the consolidation of the Zulu nation in 1817 under their brilliant chief Shaka (c. 1787–1828). Shaka's Zululand, centrally administered, like his disciplined army of 40,000 conscripts, eventually fell to the British after the founder was treacherously murdered by his half-brothers.

From 1880, the major European powers effected the complete partition of Africa. The Berlin Conference of 1884 established the principle that sovereignty in Africa would be determined by "effective occupation." In the ensuing "scramble for Africa," the main feature of the "second" or "New" imperialism, all these European powers raced to occupy effectively what territory they could.

The occupation of the African interior swept inward from the coasts. The British and the French moved south from the Mediterranean coast, establishing colonies in the Sudan (French West Africa and, in condominium, the British–Egyptian Sudan). From the east, the Italians, Portuguese, Germans, and British snatched up the lands they called Eritrea and Somaliland, German and British East Africa (Tanganyika and Kenya), and Mozambique. From the Cape, the British expanded north to the Rhodesias

German invasion of Tanzania

Europeans and Africans

Europeans had a popular notion of themselves as bearers of civilization, commerce, and culture. Here, a less optimistic portrait of European–African relations—a battle between German and native troops in Tanzania—is drawn by early twentieth-century African artist Maru Bomera (left).

Most Africans were brought under European domination and integrated into the imperial economies. Here, African workers in Dakar, Senegal carry heavy sacks of peanuts for export (bottom). (left: Tanzania National Museum)

(named after Rhodes) and Bechuanaland. In the Anglo-Boer War (1899–1902), they recaptured the Orange Free State and Transvaal from the Boer or **Afrikaner** settlers (after the dialect they now spoke, which was composed of Dutch and African elements), who had once been permitted to settle there. Of these different units, it was the British who forged the Union of South Africa.

On the west, proceeding north from the Cape, the Germans, Portuguese, and French established German South West Africa, Angola, and French Equatorial Africa, while along the Congo river the Congo Free State fell to Belgium, and specifically to its king Leopold II (r. 1865–1909), who set a new and terrible standard for the brutal exploitation of native labor. Further north along the Atlantic coast, the British, Germans, Spanish, and French established, respectively, Nigeria and the Gold Coast; the Cameroons and Togoland; Rio de Oro and Spanish Morocco; French Morocco (as a protectorate, while Islamic sultans continued as nominal rulers) and Senegal. French, Italian, and British-dominated states, part of the Middle Eastern cultural zone, now stretched along the Mediterranean. In 1914, nothing of Africa was left to the Africans but Liberia, which had been founded by freed American slaves, and Christian Ethiopia, which repulsed Italian invasion at the Battle of Adowa in 1896.

The partition of Africa accomplished the final partition of the inhabited globe, reorganized as nation states according to European definitions made without regard to native custom or ethnicity. Domination stretched and altered the European consciousness; Europeans dominated everywhere, and they dominated even those, a little different from themselves, who dwelled within their own domains.

DOMINION WITHIN

By 1914, Europeans had spent four centuries establishing their dominion over other peoples of the world in Africa and the Americas, Asia and Oceania. Their imperialism was not restricted to these remote regions only. It also affected cultural, religious, or other types of minorities who existed within their own boundaries. Among those groups whose histories prepared them to be viewed as targets for oppression in Europe were the Irish and the Jews.

The Irish: Despised and Persecuted

In the early Middle Ages, after their conversion to Christianity under Saint Patrick (see Chapter 10), the Celtic peoples of Ireland created a splendid civilization that in many ways outshone those of the Anglo-Saxon, Frankish, and Lombard kingdoms. From these regions, a significant number of capable youths traveled to study in Irish monasteries, the most disciplined and productive in Europe, and home to an unrivaled school of manuscript illuminators. Ireland also sent its missionaries and teachers abroad. Outside of the monasteries, the chiefs of the Irish clans, though they fought each other, supported cultural development and patronized poets who served as historians and theologians as well, the scribes of national memory and conscience.

Struck hard by Viking raids in the eighth and ninth centuries (see Chapter 9), Ireland lost its cultural preeminence. In the twelfth century, the pope placed it under the protection of the king of England, Henry II (r. 1154–1189). English nobles acquired Irish lands and exploited the native peasantry. From

African workers

the twelfth through the sixteenth century, Ireland was England's colony. Engels' description of its subjugation is given in *Witnesses* on p. 709.

Ireland's subjugation took a harsher turn when, in the 1530s, King Henry VIII (r. 1509–1547) repudiated the pope and created a new Protestant Church of England, with himself as its head (see Chapter 14). As England's colony, Ireland, too, was supposed to accept the new religious settlement, which made the king supreme head of the Church of Ireland in 1537. As in England, monasteries were dissolved, nonconverting priests dismissed, and the people required to abandon ancient customs. But in Ireland, the people identified the new prayers and rites with their English oppressors. As often elsewhere, the attempt to convert a subjugated nation to the religion of its masters was unsuccessful. Religious difference added to the tension between the Irish and the English, whose domination was now not only political and military, but also cultural.

From 1537 until 1798, the discord was intense. English absentee landlords confiscated Irish lands and peonized the laborers. From the early seventeenth century, the English sent more willing colonists—loyal and Protestant—to settle in the remote north of the island, where their descendants live still. English monarchs and the English Parliament twice sent their armies across the Irish Sea to suppress rebellions and punish the population. The brutal occupation of Ireland in 1649–1650 by Oliver Cromwell (see Chapter 15), then head of the Parliamentary army, is unforgotten in that nation's history.

The worst period of anti-Catholic repression followed. British authorities shut down Roman Catholic schools, and hounded and slaughtered the priests, often hidden at great risk by peasants and nobles. In 1798, the Irish patriot Wolfe Tone (1763–1798), the Protestant founder of the Society of United Irishmen, received support from French revolutionary forces in launching a rebellion against their common enemy, the British. The rebellion was harshly suppressed, and Tone committed suicide in prison, evading the reprisals that once again ravaged Ireland.

The plan first outlined by the British prime minister William Pitt the Younger (1759–1806) for settling what was delicately called the "Irish problem" involved two key actions. By the first, taken in 1800, Ireland was incorporated into a new political entity, the United Kingdom of Great Britain and Ireland, and ruled directly by the British Parliament to which it would elect 100 members. Irish leaders condemned this coerced unification, and now pressed for "home rule" by their own national assembly.

The second, realized in the Roman Catholic Emancipation Act of 1829, was more conciliatory. For the first time, Roman Catholics were able to take a seat in Parliament. By 1800, Roman Catholics had already regained some economic and political rights denied them since the reign of Henry VIII: the rights to worship freely, and to educate their children, to marry, and to conduct their personal lives according to that faith. Further, they were permitted to hold some public offices, upon the taking of a loyalty oath, and to enter the military forces and the universities. Subsequently, in 1869, the resented Protestant Church of Ireland—to which some one million Irish Protestants adhered—was disestablished.

Some progress had been made in settling the differences between the British and the Irish when, in 1845, the great potato famine began. The Irish peasantry had become dependent upon the potato as a primary, often their sole crop. Introduced from the Americas and established as a field crop by the eighteenth century, it edged out the cultivation of grains that required fallowing if they were not to exhaust the soil (see Chapter 16). Infestation by a fungus specific to the potato resulted in catastrophe. Famine struck, and persisted for four years. An estimated 1 million died, and 1 million emigrated, causing the population of Ireland to drop by some twenty-five percent between 1845 and 1850. Over the next decades, 2 million more persons emigrated, leaving a population of about 4 million in 1900, half the pre-famine figure. The devastation was comparable to that wrought by the Black Death of 1348–1349, the greatest demographic catastrophe in European history.

Britain's perceived failure to assist Ireland, coupled with its record of persecution and oppression, convinced many Irish leaders of the necessity of national independence, even as significant progress was being made toward greater autonomy for Ireland within the United Kingdom. Indeed, Parliament voted to permit home rule in 1914. The coincident outbreak of World War I (see Chapter 26), however, prevented its enactment, and Ireland was poised for revolution.

The British who ruled Ireland came to detest the Irish peasantry. Their Roman Catholicism was seen as dangerous, their poverty an affront—even though it was British land policies and taxation that exacerbated it. The Anglo-Irish writer Jonathan Swift (1667–1745) had assailed British attitudes in his satirical essay "A Modest Proposal," which outlined a solution to the crisis of poverty and overpopulation: the children of poor parents might be boiled and eaten. Around 1800, as Britain industrialized, Irish immigrants squeezed into urban slums and performed the most despised jobs. Drunkenness, laziness, and criminality were all seen as the attributes of the Irish, the people whom the British had themselves reduced to desperation (see the cartoon in *Windows On*, p. 711).

The Jews: The Intimate Enemy

By 1750, European Jews had already experienced many centuries of persecution (see Chapters 12, 14, 18). They suffered mob violence; discrimination, including special dress requirements and exclusion from certain professions; and expulsion, from England and France in the thirteenth and fourteenth centuries, from the German lands in the fourteenth and fifteenth, and finally from the Iberian kingdoms in 1492 and 1497. Pushed into eastern Europe, by the eighteenth century most lived under the rule of Russian, Polish, Prussian, or Austrian monarchs. Here, in village *shtetls* or city ghettos, they labored as tailors, soapmakers, tanners, furriers, and as financiers, raising fortunes for kings, and moneylenders, serving the poor who resented their wealth.

During these years, Jews maintained their religious traditions. The center of every Jewish community was the synagogue: a place for learning, judgment, prayer, and the exercise of charity, supporting a sizeable elite of learned males—students, cantors, scribes, and rabbis—who committed themselves to learn and transmit the traditions of the Jewish people. The primacy of learning, and the respect for tradition, enabled an isolated people to survive and to flourish.

Since the fall of the Temple (see Chapter 7), the tradition of learned and logical commentary in Judaism coexisted with a mystical, more emotional tradition of worship. During the thirteenth century,

the former tradition reached its apogee in the work of Maimonides (Moses ben Maimon; 1138–1204). Maimonides presented the foundations of Jewish thought in his scholarly works including the classic *Guide of the Perplexed*, composed in Arabic but circulated in Hebrew and Latin translations. Combining Jewish law and Greek philosophy into one rational system, his work paralleled that of contemporary Islamic and Christian philosophers, who were also building rational theological systems on the foundations of ancient thought (see Chapters 8, 10).

Meanwhile, an alternative, mystical tradition flourished, based on the study of **kabbalah**, a body of orally-transmitted "secret" knowledge—expressed in patterns of ten divine numbers and the twenty-two letters of the Hebrew alphabet—that would allow the worshiper to approach directly to God. Such studies culminated in the Zohar, a thirteenth-century southern French work that presented a mystical interpretation of Old Testament passages and themes.

A series of messianic movements erupted in the seventeenth and eighteenth centuries, the most famous being that of Shabbetai Zevi (1626–1676). In 1665 in Smyrna (Izmir, modern Turkey), Zevi proclaimed himself to be the long-awaited Messiah. The

---

Dominion Within: The Jews and the Irish

Even as Europeans invaded the far corners of the globe and exploited the goods and labor of foreign peoples, at home they acted similarly towards two peoples in their midst: the Jews and the Irish. In the first of these passages, a German theorist warns his readers about the threat to German culture that he felt was posed by the Jews—a situation exacerbated by Jewish immigration. In the second passage, Friedrich Engels reflects on the destruction and demoralization brought about by the centuries-long British occupation of Ireland.

The German historian Heinrich von Treitschke condemns the "Jews Among Us" (1889): The instinct of the masses has ... identified a severe danger, a threat to the new life of Germans and one to be taken quite seriously. ...

Our Eastern border delivers year in, year out, a swarm of young [Jewish] men ... who are content for now to sell trousers but whose children and grandchildren will run stock exchanges and newspapers. Immigration grows before our eyes, and the question of how we can melt this alien folk element together with our own keeps getting more serious. ...

The loud agitation of the moment emerges as a brutal, but natural, reaction of German folk feeling against a foreign element which has begun to take up too much space. ... Let us not deceive ourselves: the movement is deep and strong. ... Even in the high-

est-educated circles, among men who would denounce every thought of religious intolerance or national arrogance, the words resound with a single voice: "The Jews are our misfortune!"
(Heinrich von Treitschke, *Ein Wort über unser Judenthum*, 1889; ed. P. Riley, 1998)

Friedrich Engels characterizes the centuries of British rule of Ireland: Characteristic of this country are its ruins. ... The most ancient are all churches; after 1100, churches and castles; after 1800 the houses of peasants. ...

The country has been completely ruined by the English wars of conquest from 1100 to 1850 ... [so that the people themselves] feel that they are no longer at home in their own country. ... The Irishman knows he cannot compete with the Englishman, who comes with means in every respect superior; emigration will go on until the predominantly ... Celtic character of the population is all to hell. How often have the Irish started to try and achieve something, and every time they have been crushed, politically and industrially! By consistent oppression they have been artificially converted into an utterly demoralized nation and now fulfill the notorious function of supplying England, America, Australia, etc., with prostitutes, casual labourers, pimps, thieves, swindlers, beggars and other rabble.
(*Marx–Engels, Selected Correspondence, 1846–95*, 1934; ed. N. Mansergh, 1965)

mystic and scholar Nathan of Gaza (1644–1680) promoted his cult in diaspora communities of the Ottoman Empire and Europe, resulting in mass enthusiasm and miraculous events across those regions. In 1666, Zevi journeyed north from Palestine to Smyrna. Denounced and imprisoned, he appeared before the sultan's court and was offered the choice of death or apostasy. Zevi chose the latter, converted to Islam, and snared a good job as the sultan's gatekeeper.

In the next century, **Hasidism** developed in eastern European regions of dense Jewish settlement. This was a modern religious movement growing out of earlier medieval seekings of the "pious" (the *hasid*) for spiritual comfort. The Ukrainian spiritual leader Israel ben Eliezer (c. 1700–1760) devoted himself to serving the needs of ordinary people, who awarded him the name Ba'al Shem Tov, or "Master of the Good Name." He and his followers held that the pious man could be a poor man who reached God not through years of study, but through zealous piety. Their celebrations marked by joyous and even ecstatic song and dance, Hasidic communities flourished and spread throughout eastern Europe and, later, the United States.

Meanwhile, the rational strain of Jewish thought also produced new fruit. In seventeenth-century Amsterdam, home to many Sephardic Jews (descended from those expelled from Spain and Portugal), Baruch Spinoza (1632–1677) developed a pantheistic philosophy grounded in Jewish thought but transformed by contemporary gentile philosophy (see Chapter 17). In his *Ethics*, *Treatise on the Correction of the Mind*, and *Theological–Political Treatise*, Spinoza demonstrated the continuities between human and divine, the compatibility of religion with political stability and with free thought, and the historical understanding of scripture. Yet the work of this proponent of philosophical freedom was condemned during his life by the Amsterdam Jewish community.

Spinoza's focus on freedom was characteristic of the mental world of the seventeenth and eighteenth centuries, during which ideas circulated more freely than ever before. In that open atmosphere, many Jews flourished. Some became wealthy serving as financiers for nobles and kings, and had adopted aspects of the dress, the behavior, and the outlook of their employers. Others, like Spinoza, had involved themselves in the intellectual debates of the age. The Enlightenment raised the prospect that Jews, too, might enter mainstream European society, and even attain equal civil rights. In the mid-seventeenth century, Cromwell's regime in England and, in the 1790s, the revolutionary regime in France moved to exclude religion from the public realm, facilitating Jewish **assimilation**.

In the eighteenth century, small circles of privileged Jews within major western European capitals were able to enter the mainstream of culture, such as

Moses Mendelssohn (1729–1786), who wrote rational explanations of Judaism in modern languages for the non-Jewish audience. In the following century, Jews and converted Jews were among Europe's leading poets, musicians, and political and scientific theorists—Heinrich Heine (1797–1856), Felix Mendelssohn (1809–1847, Moses' grandson), Karl Marx (1818–1883), and Sigmund Freud (1856–1939; see Chapter 24) are famous examples. Among other eminent Jews who remained fully committed to Judaism as a religion and a community were members of the Rothschild family of international bankers.

Yet discrimination continued and indeed intensified under the conservative monarchs of eastern Europe, as the passage quoted in *Witnesses* on p. 709 indicates. Even the cosmopolitan West saw outbreaks of virulent anti-Semitism, as in the case of the French army captain Alfred Dreyfus (1859–1935) who in 1894 was falsely accused of selling sensitive documents to the Germans (see *Windows On*, p. 711). Although the case against him was flimsy (he was later proved innocent), high-ranking generals allowed Dreyfus to be publicly degraded and exiled to a penal colony on Devil's Island off the South American coast. An outcry from the French intelligentsia followed, the highlight of which was the rebuttal by novelist Emile Zola (see Chapter 25), headlined "*J'Accuse*" ("I Accuse You") and dramatically displayed in 1898 on the front page of the newspaper *L'Aurore* ("The Dawn"). Dreyfus was eventually released.

In the Russian Empire, an outbreak of **pogroms** shattered the precarious security of the Jewish communities in rural villages and big cities. From 1881 until 1917, with the tsar, bureaucracy, and police failing to intervene in time, anti-Semitic riots caused the murder of many Jews and the destruction of their communities, as in Odessa during four days in 1905, when 400 Jews were murdered. A steady exodus of Russian Jews streamed to western Europe and the Americas.

The pogroms convinced many Jewish intellectuals that there could be no safety for the Jews in Europe. "In countries where we have lived for centuries we are still cried down as strangers," wrote the Hungarian journalist Theodor Herzl (1860–1904). Herzl proposed a solution: the evacuation of European Jews to their ancient homeland of Palestine. His arguments, outlined in his 1896 book *The Jewish State*, constitute the original document of the program of **Zionism**, largely realized after awesome struggles in the following century (see Chapter 29).

The Psychology of Domination

If anti-Semitism is an extreme case of hostility directed against a people because of their cultural distinctiveness, it is far from the only one. During the late nineteenth century, Western intellectuals inscribed in their speeches, letters, treatises, and

Thomas Nast, "The Day We Celebrate," 1867

"The Traitor—The Degradation of Alfred Dreyfus," cover of Le Petit Journal, January 13, 1895

Like few other events in modern history, the Dreyfus affair focused the attention of educated Europeans on questions of anti-Semitism. In this illustration (above left), Dreyfus, wrongfully convicted of treason, looks on as the French Ecole Militaire strips him of his buttons and braids and breaks his sword.

Jews were more often victims of harsher persecution. Here, victims of a pogrom (anti-Jewish riot) are laid out in the Ukraine in a scene from around the end of World War I (bottom).

The Irish also suffered from discrimination and negative stereotyping. Thomas Nast's satirical cartoon (above) depicts the Irish as irresponsible, unintelligent drunkards and ruffians. (bottom: The Jewish Museum, New York).

What characteristics made two such dissimilar groups the target of European hostility?

Pogrom victims in the Ukraine, 1881–1917

To continue your investigation of this topic, please go to www.prenhall.com/king for the related **WINDOWS** on the **WEB** activity

dispatches to the press the inferiority of other peoples of the world—those of other "races." The use of the term "**race**" in these decades has no scientific basis, but emerged from discussions of the theory of evolution recently proposed by Charles Darwin (1809–1882; see Chapter 25) and was colored by assumptions of Western superiority reinforced by the experience of imperialist ventures. Racial theory relates differences between peoples to their ancestry, rather than to differences in their culture or history.

Among those contributing to late nineteenth century racial thinking were the French politician Jules Ferry (1832–1893), architect of that nation's system of public education and advocate of colonial expansion, and the British entrepreneur Cecil Rhodes. Rhodes exemplifies that outlook: "I contend that we are the finest race in the world and that the more of the world we inhabit the better it is for the human race." Social Darwinists (see Chapter 25) looked for progress to emerge from the competition between "superior" and "inferior" peoples. The statistician Karl Pearson (1857–1936), an advocate of **eugenics**, urged the systematic "improvement" of populations. It was his "scientific view" that a nation's people should be "substantially recruited from the better stocks," and kept efficient through competition in war with "inferiors," and in commerce with equals. "This is the natural history view of mankind," he wrote, "and I do not think you can in its main features subvert it."

Imbued with such attitudes of racial superiority, many Europeans considered it their duty to introduce Western values to the world: it was the "white man's burden," the title of a poem by the muse of British imperialism, the Indian-born Rudyard Kipling (1865–1936), which is quoted in *Witnesses* on p. 713. Liberty of the press, religious toleration, representative government, impartial justice, were the exports that European elites could bring to Asian and African states.

Christian missionaries believed that they brought sound truths to the peoples of the rest of the world, and many dedicated men and women lost their lives in seeking to accomplish that purpose. In Africa, they won many converts; and though their contempt for native customs aroused resentment, mission schools trained many of the new African nations' future leaders, and mission hospitals provided services not otherwise available. In Asia, loyalty to ancient religious traditions—Hindu, Buddhist, Confucian, Taoist, Islamic—and outright hostility to the missionary effort, resulted in few conversions. Missionaries did not (at least at first) understand, however, that their benevolence implied their assumption of the preeminence of their customs and values—the assumption that their supremacy was due to their inherent superiority.

Writers, politicians, and generals, and even priests, pastors, nurses, and nuns shared in the assumption that Asians and Africans and Amerindians and other indigenous peoples would benefit by acquiring Western culture. Nevertheless, there were those who criticized imperialism and its racist assumptions. The Polish-born English novelist Joseph Conrad (1857–1924) described the corruption of the spirit that came from dominion over others as in his account of Belgian occupation of the Congo in the *Heart of Darkness* (1902). English author George Orwell (1903–1950), Indian-born and employed in his youth as a colonial policeman in Burma, repudiated imperialism as a crime against others and a poisoner of the European consciousness. Hilaire Belloc (1870–1953), another English anti-imperialist, sardonically identified the source of the European power to enslave others: the machine gun.

> *Whatever happens we have got*
> *The Maxim-gun; and they have not.*

In the United States, opposition arose to United States involvement in crushing the independence movement that broke out in the Philippines after the Spanish–American War (1898). In the Platform of the American Anti-Imperialist League, leading intellectuals, businessmen, and politicians argued that such imperialist aggression violated the fundamental principles of the United States Constitution: in the land of George Washington and Abraham Lincoln, it should not be necessary "to reaffirm that all men, of whatever race or color, are entitled to life, liberty and the pursuit of happiness," they wrote, insisting that "the subjugation of any people is … open disloyalty to the distinctive principles of our Government."

The British economist J. A. Hobson (1858–1940), in his *Imperialism, a Study* published in 1902 and later used by the Russian Marxist theorist Vladimir Ilyich Ulyanov, called Lenin (see Chapters 25, 26, 28),

MUST READS

Imperialism, For ...

Joseph Chamberlain   *Foreign and Colonial Speeches* (1897)

Rudyard Kipling   *"The White Man's Burden"* (1899)

Karl Pearson   *National Life from the Standpoint of Science* (1905)

and Against...

Joseph Conrad   *Heart of Darkness* (1902)

Vladimir Ilich Lenin   *Imperialism, the Highest Stage of Capitalism* (1916)

John Atkinson Hobson   *Imperialism* (1902)

Europe's "Burden" or Benefit? Contrasting Views of the Purpose and Morality of Imperialism

When Europeans intervened in the lives of peoples in remote parts of the world, were they conferring a benefit or laying a burden upon the unwilling targets of Western expansion? The two authors here, both English, differ on the question. For the poet Rudyard Kipling, the British were rightly seen as the civilizers of the "new-caught, sullen peoples" they had conquered. For historian J.A. Hobson, the British were less nobly engaged in a quest for economic profit, seeking markets for their goods that would otherwise fail in competition with newly unfolding industrial nations.

The poet of imperialism, Rudyard Kipling, proclaims it the "white man's burden" to bring civilization to the natives of other continents, viewed as "sullen" inferiors: "half devil and half child" (1899):
Take up the White Man's burden—
Send forth the best ye breed—
Go bind your sons to exile
To serve your captives' need;
To wait in heavy harness,
On fluttered fold and wild—

Your new-caught, sullen peoples,
Half devil and half-child.
(Rudyard Kipling, *Verse*, 1899)

It was this sudden demand for foreign markets for manufactures and for investments which was avowedly responsible for the adoption of Imperialism as a political policy. ... They needed Imperialism because they desired to use the public resources of their country to find profitable employment for their capital which otherwise would be superfluous. ... As one nation after another enters the machine economy and adopts advanced industrial methods, it becomes more difficult for its manufacturers, merchants, and financiers to dispose profitably of their economic resources, and they are tempted more and more to use their Governments in order to secure for their particular use some distant undeveloped country by annexation and protection.
(John A. Hobson, *Imperialism*, London: Allen and Unwin, 1948)

identified the greed of capitalist investors as the source of a baneful European expansionism, whose effect was the impoverishment of peoples abroad as well as at home (see *Witnesses* above). Racial theories propounded by intellectuals and politicians were only a disguise, he suggested, for mere acquisitiveness: "biology and sociology weave thin convenient theories of a race struggle for the subjugation of the inferior peoples, in order that we ... may take their lands and live upon their labours."

The spectacle of money and goods, workers and refugees, flowing to and from Europe lends support to the notion that imperialist expansion was essentially economic in motivation.

MIGRANTS AND MONEY

Prodded by entrepreneurs, "opened" by foreign states, menaced by gunfire, warships, and armies, by 1914 the nations of the world had been joined into a single economic system. Steamships journeyed between continents, exchanging copper, rubber, and silk for machine parts and cotton textiles. Telegraph cables linked distant regions, railroads spanned whole continents and blasted through and under mountains, and two great canals in two hemispheres (see below) abolished barriers to trade.

From the industrial centers of Europe money flowed to fund development in China or Chile, Russia or the Sudan. And money flowed back to Europe and

the United States, a rich return on their investments, as the graph on p. 714 shows. In antiquity and the Middle Ages, trade abroad had been trade in luxuries. The quantities were limited, the value small, producers and consumers few. In the modern age, a global economy involves huge quantities and astonishing sums, and affects everyone.

People moved, too, across the globe, in search of work, safety, or freedom. Their movements, indicated by the graph on p. 715, changed the distribution of cultures and skin colors on all the inhabited continents, as populations rose. The world's wealth multiplied, but unevenly, enriching those living in industrialized regions more than those who did not, whose poverty, relatively speaking, deepened.

The Global System: Money and Goods

The trading system across Europe, Africa, and Asia that developed in antiquity expanded after 1500 to include the Americas and the great oceans. It expanded again after 1750 to embrace the whole globe.

By 1900, a pattern was established in which the regions outside of Europe mostly provided raw materials and foodstuffs to the now industrialized giants of the West. China supplied silk, porcelain, and especially tea; India tea, cotton, spices, and jute; southeast Asia spices and coffee, rubber and tin; and Australasia minerals, including gold and copper, and foodstuffs, especially meat and dairy products.

The Middle East grew raw cotton for European factories, and Asian Russia yielded furs and minerals. Africa supplied gold, diamonds, and other minerals, rubber, palm oil, and other tropical produce. In all of Afro-Asia, Japan alone exported manufactured goods in quantity. By 1918, forty percent of all its exports were manufactures, and only fifteen percent of imports. The value of its foreign trade increased about sixty-fold between 1878 and 1918.

Latin America, whose main products at the outset were silver and gold (see Chapter 19), soon also produced sugar, tobacco, and coffee (the Caribbean and Brazil), nitrates and meat (Chile and Argentina), and other minerals and foodstuffs. North America at first supplied the West Indies with grain and fish, and later both Canada and the United States exported foodstuffs round the world. By 1914, the United States was highly industrialized and a net producer of manufactured goods. Within Europe itself, the eastern regions shipped grain to west, which exported industrial manufactures and the skills to the rest of the continent.

This gigantic exchange of commodities and manufactures was accomplished especially by steamship and railroad, two new forms of transportation. In the British merchant marine, steam replaced sailing ships rapidly; elsewhere, steam triumphed only in the last generation before 1914. Large and powerful steamships carried more goods than sailing ships, conquering distances that had once been nearly insuperable.

Railroads were also critical in the world trade network, and their web expanded wherever money, ships, and merchandise traveled. In 1870, more than ninety percent of all the rail mileage in the world was in western Europe and North America, which region also saw the first great transcontinental links—the United States in 1869, Canada in 1885. The next generation saw the trans-Siberian railroad reach Vladivostok (1916) and the trans-Andean line in South America (1910). Later, railroad lines spread across Africa and the Middle East, India, and China. By 1911, one-quarter of world rail mileage lay outside of Europe and North America.

The telegraph and telephone also helped shrink the world. By 1914, telegraph cables connected the Americas, Europe, the Middle East, and Africa; before long, the network extended to east Asia. Two great canals cut across slivers of land in the Mediterranean and Central America to connect on different poles the eastern and western halves of the globe. The Suez Canal (see above), connecting the Mediterranean with the Red Sea, opened in 1869; the Panama Canal, connecting Atlantic and Pacific Oceans, in 1914. The latter was a United States project, which united the two coasts of North America and opened Asia to eastern American ports.

From 1800 to 1914, the total value of world trade more than quintupled and foreign trade as a proportion of all trade increased from three to thirty-three

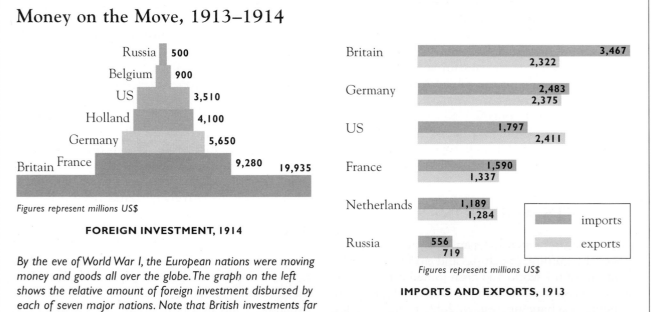

Money on the Move, 1913–1914

FOREIGN INVESTMENT, 1914

Russia	500
Belgium	900
US	3,510
Holland	4,100
Germany	5,650
France	9,280
Britain	19,935

Figures represent millions US$

IMPORTS AND EXPORTS, 1913

	imports	exports
Britain	3,467	2,322
Germany	2,483	2,375
US	1,797	2,411
France	1,590	1,337
Netherlands	1,189	1,284
Russia	556	719

Figures represent millions US$

By the eve of World War I, the European nations were moving money and goods all over the globe. The graph on the left shows the relative amount of foreign investment disbursed by each of seven major nations. Note that British investments far exceed those of the nearest competitor, France, and that those of the United States lag behind four European colonial powers. The graph on the right shows the value of imports and exports for each of six nations on the eve of World War I. Note that the leading importers of goods are Britain and Germany, while the United States surpasses the other European traders. In exports, however, the United States is at the head of the class, exporting a greater value of goods than any European nation in absolute terms, and a much greater value relative to imports. Germany, too, has become a strong competitor to Britain. The increasing economic strength of Germany and the United States would be displayed in the political sphere over the next decades (see Chapters 26, 28).

Source: Times Atlas of World History, 4th ed. (London: Times Books, 1993), pp. 256–257.

percent. In this vast marketplace, the largest single player was Britain, which in 1860 was responsible for the value of one-quarter of all the world's trade. It was the pivot of international commerce, and the largest banking center. The total value of Britain's investments abroad was only slightly less than the total value of the wealth invested by France, Germany, Belgium, the Netherlands, and the United States together—no other countries approached these in the magnitude of their foreign investments. The British were especially active in South America, the French and British in the Middle East, the British again in India, China, and Australia. In addition, Europeans invested in North America, Russia, the Balkans, as well as the Ottoman Empire.

The Global System: Peoples and Culture

While money invigorated the economies of emerging nations, so too did the arrivals in new lands of hunted, hungry, and restless peoples from the old regions of the globe. After 1500, the distribution of the peoples of the world shifted: people of different nationalities, religions, and civilizations resettled far away from their homelands. Between 1800 and 1914, the most dramatic migrations were those of Europeans, especially to the Americas. Asian emigration within Asia and to the Americas was also significant.

About 40 million Europeans resettled in other continents during this period of global reshuffling. After 1845, driven by the Great Famine (see above), about 3 million Irish left, mostly for North American cities. After 1848, traumatized by the failure of political revolution in central Europe, about 5 million Germans resettled in the United States and South America (especially Argentina). Poverty drove 5 million Italians to the United States and South America (especially Argentina) in the later nineteenth century. Between 1881 and 1917, during a surge of pogroms in the Russian Empire, nearly 2 million Jews fled, again, to the Americas.

More than 12 million English, Welsh, and Scots emigrants—constituting the single largest national group—journeyed to the Americas or to even more remote Australia and New Zealand. Lured by cheap land, nearly 2 million Scandinavians came to North America. After 1900, another 2 million Italians settled mostly in the coastal cities of North and South America. More than 1 million French migrants established themselves in Morocco and Algiers in North Africa.

Chinese emigrants settled on the west coast of the United States and in the Caribbean, where they often worked as indentured laborers. Indian emigrants, similarly, became indentured workers in the Caribbean, while, in their settlements in South Africa, they formed a thin merchant stratum between white European bosses and African natives. Both Chinese and Indian entrepreneurs moved into the East Indies, the Chinese also to Indochina, where they formed merchant communities. Until the 1880s, the waning

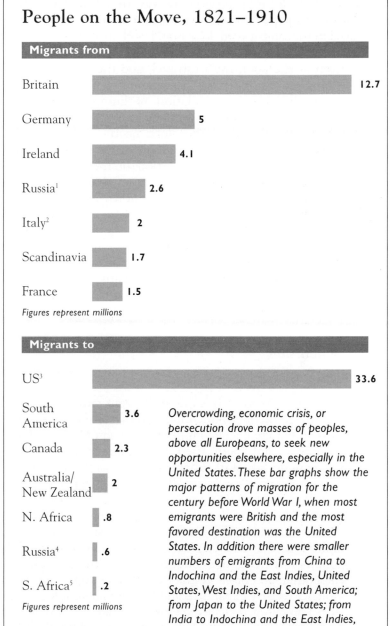

People on the Move, 1821–1910

Migrants from

Britain	12.7
Germany	5
Ireland	4.1
Russia[1]	2.6
Italy[2]	2
Scandinavia	1.7
France	1.5

Figures represent millions

Migrants to

US[3]	33.6
South America	3.6
Canada	2.3
Australia/ New Zealand	2
N. Africa	.8
Russia[4]	.6
S. Africa[5]	.2

Figures represent millions

Overcrowding, economic crisis, or persecution drove masses of peoples, above all Europeans, to seek new opportunities elsewhere, especially in the United States. These bar graphs show the major patterns of migration for the century before World War I, when most emigrants were British and the most favored destination was the United States. In addition there were smaller numbers of emigrants from China to Indochina and the East Indies, United States, West Indies, and South America; from Japan to the United States; from India to Indochina and the East Indies, east Africa, South America, and West Indies; and Africans as slaves to South America and the Middle East. Such patterns would change after the disturbance of world war.

Source: Times Atlas of World History, 4th ed. (London: Times Books, 1993), p.205.
[1] [1860–1910] [2] [1901–1910] [3] [1821–1920] [4] [Mostly Russian, to Asian Russia] [5] [1821–1888]

slave trade still operated across the Atlantic to Cuba and Brazil and to Arabian ports.

Within Europe, English factories employed a large population of Irish workers, and Polish peasants found opportunity in the new Ruhr industrial zone of western Germany. About 7 million European Russians resettled in the great expanse of Siberia. In addition, Russian peasants moved seasonally, streaming to St. Petersburg and Moscow to find factory work during the winter months, returning to the countryside come spring to work on the land. In 1900, such peasant workers constituted nearly 1 million, or two-thirds, of St. Petersburg's population. Italian migrant workers journeyed in the same way to do seasonal work in southern France and Germany—and even distant Argentina.

Even as the poor, the frustrated, and the endangered folk of Europe piled on steamers bound for other continents, the population of Europe itself increased—faster than any other region of the world. While the population of the globe nearly doubled (increasing from 900 to 1600 million between 1800 and 1900), the European proportion of the whole increased from about one-fifth to more than one-quarter of this total (about 423 million), and the white proportion to about one-third.

By 1910, the sparsely-inhabited lands that Europeans had settled in the Americas, the southern Pacific, and Asian Russia contained 200 million people, most of European descent—nearly half as many as in the European homelands. From 1800 to 1900, the population of the United States nearly quintupled, while that of Mexico doubled, that of Brazil quadrupled, and that of Argentina had risen tenfold, from about one-half million to almost 5 million. European domination of the globe was mirrored in a surge in the quantity of Europeans.

That surge correlated to disproportionate wealth, as imperialism shifted the world's balance of wealth and poverty. One thousand years earlier, Europe had been poor; Islamic, Indian, and Chinese civilizations had been wealthy. In 1914, Europe and its offshoots were wealthy; and so, too, the Japanese. But now the peoples of Africa, the Middle East, and Asia labored to grow, mine, and process those products needed to supply Europe and its children. Wealth had shifted to Europe, and poverty to the non-Western peoples of the Old World, the Americas, and Australasia.

By 1914, nevertheless, nearly all the globe's inhabitants were part of one integrated economic system which held the potential of greater wealth for all. In Europe and in lands of European settlement, previously unsurpassed standards of living had been attained, and were enjoyed by a larger part of the population. Famine had been conquered in western Europe, North America, and Australasia. In time, as the newly-poor regions of the globe struggled free of European domination (see Chapter 28), they would not spurn the wealth of the West, but would struggle to attain such well-being for themselves. If that goal is one day achieved, it would be a fine, if unintended consequence of the Western *imperium*.

Conclusion
THE WESTERN *IMPERIUM* AND THE MEANING OF THE WEST

Between 1500 and 1914, Europe brought most of the world under its control. By 1914, Germany, France, and the Netherlands ruled millions of non-Europeans in Africa, Asia, and the Americas. The sprawling Russian Empire engulfed millions of Asian Muslims. The United States had acquired dominion over the Philippines and Puerto Rico. Britain flew its nation's flag over one-fifth of the surface of the globe, and ruled one-fourth of its inhabitants. Just as the ancient Romans proclaimed the Mediterranean "our sea" (see Chapter 5), Europeans might survey the planet Earth and declare it theirs.

The effect of Europe's expansion was not merely to control, but also to unify. Imperialist ventures integrated the world's peoples, nations, and civilizations. This was not the first attempt to unify the corners of the earth. The Persians, Hellenistic Greeks, Romans, Islamic caliphs, and Mongol khans had understood that challenge (though their empires lacked the racial dimension of later Western rule). The dominion these earlier conquerors won through violence did much to make disparate nations aware of each other, and promote the exchange of important technologies. The European nations also employed violence as they expanded, and brought about integration.

The European *imperium* was more successful than its precursors; it was also undeniably brutal. That brutality was encouraged by assumptions of cultural superiority. Western elites dismissed the customs and ignored the genius of the peoples they encountered—as did the genial historian Macaulay in his characterization of Indian culture with which this chapter opened. Their arrogance and their brutality were neither unprecedented nor unique. A glance back at Roman campaigns of conquest, or Mongol raids that left no creature alive, dispels that notion. Nevertheless, they committed deep injustices that would demand, in time, painful remedies (see Chapter 29). Few concerned themselves with that possibility during an era when Western civilization, as the next chapter will show, seemed unassailable.

QUESTIONS TO CONSIDER

1. What are the differences between colonialism and imperialism?

2. Was Britain's eventual dominance of the Indian subcontinent clear from the early days of the British East India Company?

3. Why was Japan able to resist Western domination, and become a modern nation in its own right, while China declined as the authority of its rulers and traditions were eroded by the foreign presence?

4. What triggered the European rush to occupy the African interior, after centuries when Europeans were content to remain on the margins of the continent?

5. Why did some Europeans turn on their own neighbors, the Irish and the Jews, and make them particular targets of mockery, discrimination, and violence?

SUGGESTED RESOURCES

Arnold, David, *Colonizing the Body: State Medicine and Epidemic Disease in Nineteenth-Century India* (Berkeley: University of California Press, 1993). Explores how epidemic disease and ideas about its treatment shaped British conceptions of India and of their role as colonizers.

Beasley, W. G., *Japan Encounters the Barbarian: Japanese Travelers in America and Europe* (New Haven: Yale University Press, 1995). Describes the fact-finding mission in the 1860s and 1870s of Japanese observers in Europe and the United States, in the service of a modernized Japan.

Brustein, William I., *Roots of Hate: Anti-Semitism in Europe before the Holocaust* (Cambridge: Cambridge University Press. 2003). Examines the multiple strands of anti-Semitism in several European nations from the late nineteenth century to World War II.

Curtin, Philip D., *The World and the West: The European Challenge and the Overseas Response in the Age of Empire* (Cambridge: Cambridge University Press, 2000. Probes the interactions between Western societies and others around the globe during the nineteenth and twentieth centuries.

Frykenberg, Robert Eric, *Christians and Missionaries in India: Cross-Cultural Communication since 1500* (Grand Rapids, Mich.: William B. Eerdmans; London: Routledge Curzon, 2003). Essays explore the dynamic interaction between Christian missions and Indian society in the eighteenth and nineteenth centuries.

Goodwin, Jason, *Lords of the Horizons: A History of the Ottoman Empire* (New York: Henry Holt, 1999). An overview of the vast Ottoman Empire, which encompassed many ethnicities and religious groups, yet which thrived because of its tolerance and commitment to meritocracy, which allowed talented subjects to advance.

Hamilton, Carolyn, *Terrific Majesty: The Powers of Shaka Zulu and the Limits of Historical Invention* (Cambridge MA: Harvard University Press, 1998). Hamilton explores the figure of Shaka Zulu as a metaphor for leadership and national South African memory.

Khodarkovsky, Michael, *Russia's Steppe Frontier: the Making of a Colonial Empire, 1500–1800* (Bloomington: Indiana university Press, 2001). Traces the encounters between Russian officials and borderland peoples from the time of the Mongols to the beginning of modern times.

MacDonald, Robert H., *The Language of Empire: Myths and Metaphors of Popular Imperialism, 1880–1918* (New York: St. Martin's Press, 1994). Explores the production and consumption of concepts of "Empire".

O Grada, Cormac, *Black '47 and Beyond: the Great Irish Famine in History, Economy, and Memory* (Princeton: Princeton University Press, 1999). Uses interdisciplinary social science concepts and comparative studies to write a rich and comprehensive account of the great disaster.

Pakenham, Thomas, *The Scramble for Africa: 1876–1912* (New York: Random House, 1991). Comprehensive study.

Procida, Mary A., *Married to the Empire: Gender, Politics and Imperialism in India, 1883–1947* (Manchester: Manchester University Press, 2002). Investigates the role played by the wives of British civil servants and military officers in colonized India.

Smith, Helmut Walser, *The Butcher's Tale: Murder and Anti-Semitism in a German Town* (New York: W. W. Norton. 2002). Microhistory of a case in a West Prussian town in 1900, showing how a brutal murder of a Christian was recast as a Jewish ritual killing.

An On-Line History of the US: the Age of Imperialism (smplanet):
http://www.smplanet.com/imperialism/toc.html

Imperialism, the Highest Stage of Capitalism, by Vladimir Ilyich Lenin (Lenin Works Archive):
http://www.marxists.org/archive/lenin/works/1916

Joseph Conrad, *Heart of Darkness* (1899); (SUNY Buffalo):
http://www.acsu.buffalo.edu/~csicseri

Beyond the Pale: The History of the Jews in Russia—with sections on the Dreyfus affair and late-19th-century anti-Semitism:
http://www. friends-partners.org/partners/beyond-the-pale/index.html

National Archives of Ireland Research Guide, *The Great Famine, 1845–1850*:
http://www.nationalarchives.ie/famine.html

Western Civilization Documents CD-ROM

25.1 Confessions of Faith, Cecil Rhodes
25.2 Manifesto for the Society of German Colonization
25.3 A White Woman's Perspective of Africa
25.4 Black Man's Burden
25.5 Between Ruler and Ruled
25.6 Advocating Change

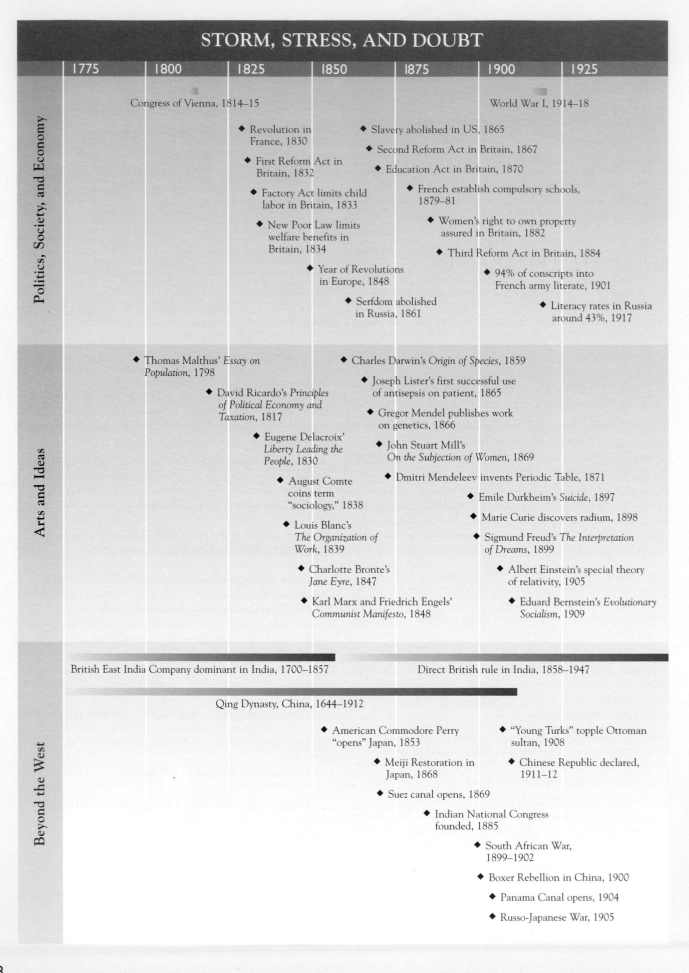

STORM, STRESS, AND DOUBT

1775	1800	1825	1850	1875	1900	1925

Politics, Society, and Economy

Congress of Vienna, 1814–15

World War I, 1914–18

◆ Revolution in France, 1830

◆ Slavery abolished in US, 1865

◆ Second Reform Act in Britain, 1867

◆ First Reform Act in Britain, 1832

◆ Education Act in Britain, 1870

◆ Factory Act limits child labor in Britain, 1833

◆ French establish compulsory schools, 1879–81

◆ New Poor Law limits welfare benefits in Britain, 1834

◆ Women's right to own property assured in Britain, 1882

◆ Third Reform Act in Britain, 1884

◆ Year of Revolutions in Europe, 1848

◆ 94% of conscripts into French army literate, 1901

◆ Serfdom abolished in Russia, 1861

◆ Literacy rates in Russia around 43%, 1917

Arts and Ideas

◆ Thomas Malthus' *Essay on Population*, 1798

◆ Charles Darwin's *Origin of Species*, 1859

◆ Joseph Lister's first successful use of antisepsis on patient, 1865

◆ David Ricardo's *Principles of Political Economy and Taxation*, 1817

◆ Gregor Mendel publishes work on genetics, 1866

◆ Eugene Delacroix' *Liberty Leading the People*, 1830

◆ John Stuart Mill's *On the Subjection of Women*, 1869

◆ August Comte coins term "sociology," 1838

◆ Dmitri Mendeleev invents Periodic Table, 1871

◆ Emile Durkheim's *Suicide*, 1897

◆ Louis Blanc's *The Organization of Work*, 1839

◆ Marie Curie discovers radium, 1898

◆ Sigmund Freud's *The Interpretation of Dreams*, 1899

◆ Charlotte Bronte's *Jane Eyre*, 1847

◆ Albert Einstein's special theory of relativity, 1905

◆ Karl Marx and Friedrich Engels' *Communist Manifesto*, 1848

◆ Eduard Bernstein's *Evolutionary Socialism*, 1909

Beyond the West

British East India Company dominant in India, 1700–1857

Direct British rule in India, 1858–1947

Qing Dynasty, China, 1644–1912

◆ American Commodore Perry "opens" Japan, 1853

◆ "Young Turks" topple Ottoman sultan, 1908

◆ Meiji Restoration in Japan, 1868

◆ Chinese Republic declared, 1911–12

◆ Suez canal opens, 1869

◆ Indian National Congress founded, 1885

◆ South African War, 1899–1902

◆ Boxer Rebellion in China, 1900

◆ Panama Canal opens, 1904

◆ Russo-Japanese War, 1905

CHAPTER
25

STORM, STRESS, AND DOUBT

European Culture from Classicism to Modernism

1780–1914

KEY QUESTIONS

◆ **From Romanticism to Realism:** Why did the calm elegance of Classicism give way to Romanticism and then Realism? What relation did changes in artistic and literary style have to political events?

◆ **The Sciences and the Schools:** What new disciplines in the sciences and social sciences took their place in the university curriculum? What steps were taken to school the children of workers and peasants, both male and female?

◆ **Ideals and Ideologies:** How did Enlightenment visions of ideal societies become expressed as ideologies? Why did liberalism, conservatism, socialism, feminism, and others appeal to the masses of men and women?

◆ *Fin-de-siècle* **and the Advent of the Modern:** What are the characteristics of Modernism in literature, the arts, and thought?

Notes from Underground In 1864, the Underground Man—the narrator of Notes from the Underground by Russian author Fyodor Dostoevsky (1821–1881)—announced the failure of the Enlightenment principle of rationality. Reason, he conceded, "is an excellent thing, there is no disputing that, but reason is only reason and can only satisfy man's rational faculty." The human being will never abandon sensation and impulse for the presumed good that reason supplies. Our life may be worthless, concedes the Underground Man, "… yet it is life nevertheless and not simply extracting square roots." Given the choice between feeling and reason, human beings will always choose feeling in the end—even if feeling means suffering: "man will never renounce real suffering, that is, destruction and chaos."

FROM ROMANTICISM TO REALISM

This terrible message from underground is the voice of the "Modern," a complex and doubt-tinged worldview that evolved between 1789 and 1914. During that long century, the West accumulated great wealth and power. Industrialization stimulated global trade, while colonial and imperial ventures resulted in the European domination of much of the world (see Chapters 21, 23). These changes reshaped Western consciousness, and gave rise to new artistic and intellectual visions. In the arts, **Classicism** gave way to **Romanticism**, which elevated feeling over reason; and Romanticism to **Realism**, which inspected the contemporary world without sentiment or illusion.

Romanticism and Revolt

Enlightenment rationalism and Classical style, which mirrored its calm certainty, did not long survive the French Revolution (see Chapter 20). The post-revolutionary world invited artists and thinkers to put down their books and seek not to know but to feel.

Painted by the French artist Eugène Delacroix (1798–1863), *The 28th July: Liberty Leading the People*, which is reproduced in *Windows On* on p. 722, exemplifies the new spirit of Romanticism. In Delacroix's *Liberty*, all is in motion. A fierce female figure symbolizing Liberty represents the savage mother of a revolutionary generation. She signals the crowd of revolutionaries onward, over the bodies of dead and wounded comrades: a child wielding two revolvers, an artisan in frock coat. Such a painting celebrates change, passion, and action.

In a similar vein, the English Romantic artists J. M. W. Turner (1775–1851) and John Constable (1776–1837). spurned the idealised landscapes of Classical

style, and depicted nature in its primal, disorderly condition—in wild forests, burgeoning gardens, in storms, or at night. In Constable's landscapes of spreading green fields enveloping a few anonymous figures, nature, though benign, engulfs the human realm. Turner's spraying seas, as in *Shipwreck* illustrated on p. 722, or roaring railroads dissolve into mist, as all that is solid melts into the ambient natural world. Romantic artists also inclined to historical and exotic subjects, such as ruined castles or harems drawn from their fantasies about the Middle East.

Romantic musical style was also characterised by stormy variations of mood and tempo. The innovative later works of the German composer Ludwig van Beethoven (1770–1827), whose career bridged from Classical to Romantic, shock and stimulate. Writing often for the voice, the Austrian composer Franz Schubert (1797–1828) crafted contemporary poetry, with its celebration of love and loss, into art songs.

Opera especially benefited from the transition to Romantic style. Opera's sung drama is the ideal medium for grand themes such as love, death, sacrifice and betrayal, that Romantic style could portray with rich emotional power. The operas of the Italian composer Giuseppe Verdi (1813–1901), convey passion and grand idealism, whether the world of the Italian Renaissance is painted in *Rigoletto* (1851) or that of an up-to-date Parisian courtesan in *La Traviata* (1853).

Romanticism also infused literature, and especially poetry, the preeminent vehicle for the expression of emotion and the exploration of the self. The work of the English poet William Wordsworth (1770–1850) exemplifies the centrality of nature for Romantic poets. His friend Samuel Taylor Coleridge (1772–1834) depicted the poet as an inspired genius in his "Kubla Khan":

> *Beware! Beware!*
> *His flashing eyes, his floating hair!*
> *Weave a circle round him thrice,*
> *And close your eyes with holy dread:*
> *For he on honey-dew hath fed,*
> *And drunk the milk of Paradise.*

The centrality of heterosexual love, both marital and adulterous, as a literary theme prompted the participation of women in the culture of Romanticism. Women were often the subjects of Romantic works—betrayed wives, dying lovers, tormented courtesans. But they were also often creators in their own right. The wife of the English poet Percy Bysshe Shelley (1792–1822) was also a writer—Mary Shelley (1797–1851), the daughter of early feminist Mary Wollstonecraft (1759–1797; see Chapter 17). Likewise, the wife of the German poet Wilhelm von Schlegel (1767–1845), whose translation of Shakespeare stirred the Romantic imagination, was Caroline Michaelis (1763–1809), who left her first husband for the German idealist philosopher Joseph von Schelling (1775–1854). As in the Enlightenment, learned women sparkled in salons, but were now more likely to be themselves thinkers of stature—as was Rahel Varnhagen von Ense (1771–1833). Born Rahel Levin, a Jew, she converted to Christianity and, hosted an important Berlin salon during the decades from the 1790s to the 1820s.

Germaine de Staël (1766–1817), a salonière but much more, was the daughter of Jacques Necker (1732–1804), the Swiss finance minister of the former French king Louis XVI. As both hostess and author, she surveyed a turbulent period of French history, from Revolution to Empire and Restoration, interrogating the meaning of it all. She wrote novels featuring female heroines in tragic situations, but was even more important as a literary critic and political commentator. After traveling through Germany and observing at first-hand developments in literary, musical, and philosophical circles, she introduced the rest of Europe to some of the pioneers of Romanticism, the creators of the movement known as **Sturm und Drang** ("Storm and Stress").

Romanticism had first emerged in the German states. The German language, with its complex consonant combinations and surging rhythms lends itself to a poetry that represents emotion. Thus Johann Wolfgang von Goethe (1749–1832) expressed the uncontrollable strivings of the human spirit in his verse drama *Faust* (completed 1832), and the fatal power of love in his novel *The Sorrows of Young Werther* (1774). In *Faust*, the legendary late medieval sage and magician, who wished to know the hidden mysteries of the universe, suffers the consequences of his unbridled ambitions: death and damnation. The tormented young Werther, failing in love, commits suicide.

Historical settings evoked a powerful response among Romantic authors, who were fasinated by the medieval past. An interest in the past also related Romanticism to the nationalist movements of the nineteenth century, especially German, Italian, Polish, Czech, and Hungarian (see Chapter 20). History abounded with national heroes from an epic past, a shared heritage for people who otherwise knew only that they spoke the same language and worshiped in the same faith.

Romanticism also impacted upon philosophy, and found an advocate above all in G. W. Friedrich Hegel (1770–1831). History and feeling both played a central part in his work. Throughout history, the realm of the spirit evolved, which would one day reach its final culmination in the political state of Germany. It was not reason that made that nation great, according to Hegel, but its spirit, or will, or passion.

Realism and Disenchantment

If the powerful emotion in Romantic works rediscovered the passion in a world that the Enlightenment

had demystified, Realism accomplished for a second time the world's disenchantment.

Realist painters depicted ordinary human beings in everyday settings, eating, working, burying their dead. *The Man with the Hoe* by the French artist Jean-François Millet (1814–1875) for example, depicts a nameless worker identified by his labor: by his bent back, his rugged tool, and the invincible toughness of the soil (see *Windows On*, p. 722). He is a figure of the present moment, whose image bespeaks the condition of the peasant wholly identified with the work he must do.

A new medium, perfectly suited to Realism, was developed in the 1830s by L. J. M. Daguerre (1789–1851)—photography. The camera recorded a segment of reality, as seen by the eye, unmediated—so it was believed—by the adornments or fantasies of the artist. Photography shops sprang up in major cities, while expert photographers employed the camera as a witness to contemporary events, for example Jacob Riis (1849–1914; see Chapter 22) in his narrative and photographic account of the poor in New York, *How the Other Half Lives*.

Realist literature found its ideal vehicle in the novel, which created a convincing background of events against which the stories of struggling individuals unfolded. The French novelist Honoré de Balzac (1799–1850), for example, drew more than 2000 portraits of contemporary Parisians in the roughly ninety novels of the series *The Human Comedy*. His compatriot Gustave Flaubert (1821–1880) looked to the stultifying life of the provinces, where his fictional character, the adulterous Madame Bovary lived. His novel of that title (1857) tells the story of a woman who is compelled by soul-deadening tedium to disrupt moral boundaries and eventually to destroy herself. The novels of Emile Zola (1840–1902) examine

The Cycle of Styles: Classicism, Romanticism, and Realism

Eugène Delacroix, **Liberty Leading the People**, *1830*

Jean-François Millet, **The Man with the Hoe**, *1860–1862*

Western art passed through three broad stages during the first several decades of the nineteenth century. The carefully controlled scenes created by Classicists such as the French Revolutionary-era artists Jacques-Louis David soon gave way to more emotional and romantic images. Eugène Delacroix's Liberty Leading the People *(top)— which emphasizes the passion and action of the 1830 Revolution in France—epitomizes the new movement. Similarly, the English painter J. M. W. Turner challenges Enlightenment notions of the order of nature in his* Shipwreck *(bottom), stressing instead uncontrollable power and majesty.*

By mid-century, however, Realist artists were turning from the heroic to the mundane and creating accurate depictions of the minutiae of ordinary life. Jean-François Millet's The Man with the Hoe *(above right) illustrates this trend.*

Photography, developed in the 1830s by L. J. M. Daguerre, provided a medium well suited for realism. It could capture life more or less in its actuality—as demonstrated here by the portrait of the American Lemuel Shaw (1851), when he was serving as chief justice of the Massachusetts supreme court (below right)—freeing artists later in the century to pursue more innovative approaches and styles referred to as Modernism.

(top: Louvre, Paris; bottom: British Museum, London; above right: The J. Paul Getty Museum, Los Angeles; below right: Metropolitan Museum of Art, New York)

Do you find any similarity between the visions of nature depicted by Millet and Turner in these illustrations?

J. M. W. Turner, **Shipwreck**, *1823*

Albert Sands Southworth and Josiah Johnson Hawes, **Lemuel Shaw**, *1851*

To continue your investigation of this topic, please go to www.prenhall.com/king for the related **WINDOWS** on the **WEB** activity

Pioneers of Literary Style: Romanticism and Realism

Whereas Romanticism appealed to the beauties of nature and the wisdom innate in each individual, Realism looked at life as it actually was—often sordid; and people as they actually were—often debased by circumstances they could not help. The two passages here are by two exemplars of each approach: the American poet Walt Whitman and the French novelist Emile Zola.

A manifesto of Romanticism—Walt Whitman would rather look at the stars than listen to an expert (c. 1864):
When I heard the learn'd astronomer,
When the proofs, the figures, were ranged in columns
   before me,
When I was shown the charts and diagrams,
   to add, divide,
and measure them,
When I sitting heard the astronomer where he
   lectured
with much applause in the lecture-room,
How soon unaccountable I became tired and sick,

Till rising and gliding out I wander'd off by myself,
In the mystical moist night-air, and from time to time,
Look'd up in perfect silence at the stars.
(Walt Whitman, "When I Heard the Learned Astronomer," c. 1864)

A *Miner's Life*—an extract from a Realist novel (1885): That started them all off, and each threw in his word, while the fumes of the oil lamp mingled with the reek of fried onions. You worked like a beast of burden at a job that used in the olden days to be a punishment for convicts, more often than not you died in harness, and with all that you could not even have meat on the table at night. Of course you had food of a kind, you did eat, but so little that it was just enough to keep you suffering without dying outright, weighed down by debts and hounded as though you had stolen the bread you ate. … The only pleasures in life were to get drunk or get your wife with a baby, and even then the beer made you too fat in the paunch, and when the child grew up he didn't care a bugger about you.
(Emile Zola, *Germinal*, 1885; trs. L. Tancock, 1954)

the lives of ordinary people—coal miners in his *Germinal* (1885), a passage from which is quoted in *Witnesses* above, a prostitute in *Nana* (1880)—as in a hostile environment. In England, Charles Dickens (1812–1870) depicted the squalor of the lives of the poor, the psychology of industrial capitalists, and the experiences of neglected or abandoned children.

Whereas Romanticism had resisted industrialization and retreated into nostalgia and the celebration of nature, Realism faced it ruthlessly. The ugliness of the physical environment, the deterioration of the laborer's body, the flattening of the spirit, and the endurance of the individual were grim subjects that called for unblinking investigation.

Did Realist writers have a political agenda? In their searing portrayals of poverty and exclusion, they present problems that begged for solutions. In the context of recurrent political revolution, and of the mounting force of socialism (see below), it would seem that literary Realism straddles the realms of art and politics. Some Realist authors indeed represented a new type of intellectual—an activist concerned with concrete and pressing issues. Zola's public championship of Alfred Dreyfus (see Chapter 24), a Jewish officer wrongfully convicted on charges of spying in 1894, marks the public birth of this phenomenon.

Novelists, among them women novelists, also considered the situation of women. The English novelist Jane Austen (1775–1817), focused on love and marriage as the central issues in women's lives and the social world. The sisters Charlotte (1816–1855),

Emily (1818–1848), and Anne Brontë (1820–1849), and George Eliot (the masculine pseudonym of Mary Ann Evans; 1819–1880) described the choices women made constrained by family demands and the desire for self-expression. In France, George Sand (a masculine pseudonym for Amandine A. L. D. Dudevant; 1804–1876) wore men's clothes and smoked cigars, while she pursued alliances with men of the intellectual elite and wrote novels, letters, and memoirs.

Music, too, took up some of the themes associated with Realism. Composers incorporated in their works melodic motifs from the song and dance of the peasants, or the "folk." Thus Polish and Hungarian motifs are showcased in the polonaises and mazurkas of Frédéric Chopin (1810–1849). Composers of Italian opera focused on contemporary settings and characters from the lower strata of society.

The Realists' immersion in the world linked them to socialism and **feminism** as it distanced them from both Classicism and the Romantics. Their role in literature was paralleled in the universities by the work of scientists, social scientists, and scholars.

THE SCIENCES AND THE SCHOOLS

Intellectuals promoted the development of new professional disciplines. Some of the principal ones are listed in *Who's Who* on p. 728. Meanwhile, the spread of public elementary education allowed talented young people access to professional careers.

The Past as It Really Was

The political and intellectual currents of nineteenth-century Europe are reflected in the writing of history, or **historiography**. In the Enlightenment, history was considered an art, and the author's opinions were allowed to color his view of the past. In the nineteenth century, historians saw themselves as the synthesizers of evidence, which, often in the form of original, official documents, bound them to the conclusions that emerged from their analysis. The product of this method, they believed, would be, in the famous words of the German historian Leopold von Ranke (1795–1886), a description of the past *wie es eigentlich gewesen ist*, "as it really happened." *Witnesses* on p. 725 quotes from his writings.

Pursuing this ideal, historians compiled extensive accounts of the development of major institutions, primarily the modern state. Von Ranke himself wrote histories of Germany, France, Italy, and England. Thomas Babington Macaulay (1800–1859) produced a history of England in five volumes; Jules Michelet (1798–1874) one of France in twenty-four volumes; and J.-C.-L. Simonde de Sismondi (1773–1842) one of Italy in sixteen volumes.

Historians also looked beyond the sphere of the state. The nature of the historical Jesus, for instance, intrigued the French historian Ernest Renan (1823–1892), whose *Life of Jesus* (1863) shocked Christian Europe with its realist, anti-Christian stance. The English historian George Grote (1794–1871) chronicled ancient Greece, at a time when the non-Christian, Classical antecedents of Western civilization intrigued many intellectuals. The Swiss historian Jacob Burckhardt (1818–1897) described the Italian Renaissance as the birthplace of the modern spirit.

In these endeavors, historians took possession of the European past which they interpreted in terms that were meaningful for their own age. They established the writing of history as an academic discipline on a level with the traditional subjects of theology, medicine, or law in university faculties. Germany led the way in creating a multi-departmental university, in which the new historical discipline found a home. There it was joined by other humanistic pursuits such as Classics, the study of the civilizations of ancient Greece and Rome, modern languages and linguistics.

The World as It Came to Be

In establishing history as an evidence-based inquiry, historians were imitating scientists, who tested and proved their theories, or hypotheses, with evidence. Science made important advances during the nineteenth century, especially in the field of biology. Investigations in microbiology and genetics and the theory of evolution fundamentally changed the way human beings understood their place in the cosmos.

Microbiology and Genetics Louis Pasteur (1822–1895) was the culminating figure in a sequence of scientists who located the living organisms that caused many infectious diseases. With the aid of the microscope, Dutch, Italian, German, and French scientists opened a world invisible to the unaided eye, gazing at the tiniest independent animals, or protozoa; the different cells found in the brain, the blood, or the parts of plants; and bacteria.

Continuing these investigators' earlier work, Pasteur explained the processes of fermentation in yeast, and the souring of milk, both the result of bacterial activity. He developed the process to destroy bacterial contaminants in milk, called after him "**pasteurization**," and demonstrated that the apparent self-generation of **microorganisms** in non-organic media in fact derived from microorganisms introduced by contamination. Subsequently, he identified the bacteria responsible for forms of anthrax and cholera affecting farm stock, and the pathogens that ravaged silkworm populations essential for the textile industry. Finally, he isolated the bacterium responsible for rabies, a disease that terrorized rural populations exposed to infected animals. Pasteur's development of vaccines to prevent these diseases opened the road to the conquest of infectious disease. (Before Pasteur, only smallpox could be prevented through vaccination; see Chapter 17.)

The Austrian monk Gregor Johann Mendel (1822–1884) investigated the role of genes in biological reproduction through observations he made in his monastery garden. Like Pasteur, his work rested on that of early microscopists. Their analyses of animal and plant forms had contributed to the work of eighteenth-century **taxonomists**, who grouped and ranked the species of living things. The question of inheritance then presented itself: how did species transmit to their descendants their characteristic features?

Mendel's study of ordinary garden peas led him to the genetic theory of inheritance. The plants were long or short; their seeds were smooth or wrinkled. By carefully arranged cross-pollination of the plants in various permutations, he pointed to the existence of paired genes, of which some were dominant, which determined the characteristics of offspring. His genetic theory countered the prevailing theory, associated with the French scientist Jean-Baptiste Lamarck (1744–1829), that acquired characteristics could be inherited. Although his work was published in 1866, Mendel's obscurity meant that it was not circulated until after 1900.

Darwin's Theory of Evolution The work of the English naturalist Charles Darwin (1809–1882) depended, like Mendel's, on systematic observation. In the 1831 voyage of the British ship *Beagle*, in which he traveled as ship's naturalist, Darwin recorded his observations of species from many regions, notably

Pioneers of the Intellectual Disciplines: History, Social Science, and Science

New fields of knowledge took their places in European universities during the nineteenth century, filling out a curriculum that, since antiquity, had been based on philosophy, languages, and literature. Here, the German scholar Leopold von Ranke defines a new, more rigorous mission for the discipline of history; the English theorist Thomas Malthus lays down principles fundamental to economics and demography; the French theorist Emile Durkheim defines the new realm of the "social" sciences; and the English naturalist Charles Darwin opens a new era for the life sciences with the announcement of the theory of evolution by means of natural selection.

The German historicist Leopold von Ranke calls for the critical evaluation of historical sources (1824): One who for the first time confronts the multitudinous monuments of modern history must [feel like one] who confronted a great collection of antiquities in which genuine and spurious, beautiful and repulsive, important and insignificant, from many nations and periods, were heaped together without order. ... The material confronted would speak in a thousand voices. ... Some of the specimens ... attempt to derive from the past theorems for the future. Many want to defend or to attack. Not a few are zealous to develop the explanation of occurrences ... from the basis of subjective conditions and emotions. Then there are some which have only the purpose of passing along what has [actually] happened. ... The persons participating in the action speak. Original sources, alleged and actual, are present in abundance. Before all the question arises, "Which among many is a source of original knowledge? From which can we be truly instructed?"
(Leopold von Ranke, *Towards a Critique of Modern Historiography*, 1824; ed. A. W. Small, 1924)

Thomas Malthus gauges the implications of unrestrained population increase (1798): I have read some of the speculations on the perfectibility of man and of society with great pleasure. ... I ardently wish for such happy improvements. But I see great, and to my understanding, unconquerable difficulties in the way to them. [Malthus defines two premises affecting population growth and its outcome.]

First, That food is necessary to the existence of man.
Secondly, That the passion between the sexes is necessary and will remain nearly in its present state. ...

Thus I say that the power of population is indefinitely greater than the power in the earth to produce subsistence for man. Population, when unchecked, increases in a geometrical ratio. Subsistence only increases in an arithmetical ratio. A slight acquaintance with numbers will show the immensity of the first power in comparison of the second. By the law of our nature which makes food necessary to the life of man, the effects of these two unequal powers must be kept equal. This implies a strong and constantly operating check on population from the difficulty of subsistence. This difficulty must fall somewhere and must necessarily be severely felt by a large proportion of mankind. ...
(Thomas Robert Malthus, *First Essay on Population*, 1798; Royal Economic Society, 1926)

Emile Durkheim insists that sociology is an independent science (c. 1901): A discipline may be called a "science" only if it has a definite field to explore. Science is concerned with things, realities. If it does not have a datum to describe and interpret, it exists in a vacuum. ... Before social science [or sociology] could begin to exist, it had first of all to be assigned a definite subject-matter. ... The subject-matter of social science is social things: that is, laws, customs, religions, etc. [which] are actual things, like all other things in nature; they have their own specific properties, and these call for sciences which can describe and explain them.
(Emile Durkheim, lecture, c. 1901; ed. A. Giddens, 1989)

Darwin outlines how species evolve by natural selection (1859): It has been seen ... that amongst organic beings in a state of nature there is some individual variability: ... But how is it that varieties, which I have called incipient species, become ultimately converted into good and distinct species... ? All these results ... follow from the struggle for life. Owing to this struggle, variations, however slight and from whatever cause proceeding, if they be in any degree profitable to the individuals of a species, in their infinitely complex relations to other organic beings and to their physical conditions of life, will tend to the preservation of such individuals, and will generally be inherited by the offspring. The offspring, also, will thus have a better chance of surviving, for, of the many individuals of any species which are periodically born, but a small number can survive. I have called this principle, by which each slight variation, if useful, is preserved, by the term Natural Selection.
(Charles Darwin, *The Origin of Species*, 1896; vol. 1)

the exotic species that had developed in isolation on the Galápagos islands (an archipelago 600 miles west of the coast of Ecuador). His observations led to questions: why and how did these creatures develop their distinctive characteristics? In response, he published in 1859 his *On the Origin of Species by Means of Natural Selection, or the Preservation of Favoured Races in the Struggle for Life.*

The theory of natural selection, summarized in *Witnesses* on p. 725, was an epochal breakthrough. It postulated that species of living things had constantly to struggle for existence. In the competition to eat and reproduce, individuals possessing certain biological characteristics were more successful than others. To the extent that those more desirable characteristics were inherited by subsequent generations, those descendants would win the struggle to survive, and accomplish the evolution of the species. Less desirable characteristics would result in the failure of individuals and of their offspring to compete successfully. Their biological future was bleak. No divine intervention, no special efforts of an individual to surpass his biological destiny, entered into the process. Nature itself made the decision.

Darwin's theory was the culmination of generations of biological and social thought. His understanding of the struggle for survival, for food and sexual reproduction, owed much to Malthus, while his understanding of the expanses of time over which species had evolved drew on the geological studies of Charles Lyell (1797–1875). His notion of a struggle for existence among competing animals had first been raised by his grandfather, Erasmus Darwin (1731–1802). Another influence was the work of Alfred Russel Wallace (1823–1913), who had studied the varied species of the Malay Peninsula, and was about to publish his account of biological evolution that threatened to preempt Darwin's.

The theory of natural selection explained, first, how existing species might have come into being

without specific acts of divine creation. Second, it explained how variations in species characteristics might have developed other than by acquisition—that is, by the inherited behavior of individuals. Third, it embraced the animal, the vegetable, and even the human realms, claiming that the human being was firmly embedded in the natural order and subject to processes of change. This controversial point Darwin stated explicitly in his 1871 volume *The Descent of Man, and Selection in Relation to Sex.*

Darwinian theory, satirized in the cartoon on p. 727, posed challenges to religion, to humanism, and to liberalism. If nature selected some species for survival and others for extinction, what became of God? If human beings were simply accidents thrown up by the evolutionary process, where was the dignity of Man? If the fittest species alone survive, what did that imply for the status of persons whose race, nationality, class, or sex varied from the norm that Darwin himself represented—an upper-class Englishman?

Darwinian theory would soon be challenged on all of these points. Religious leaders protested immediately, while Social Darwinism (see below) applied the Darwinian model to the competition between classes, nations, and races, and feminists challenged Darwin's argument that women had reached a level of biological evolution lower than that attained by men.

Other Scientific Advances The physical sciences also made advances, developing Newtonian principles in models of sub-molecular motion, of electricity, magnetism, and light. Chemists expanded the list of known elements ranked by atomic characteristics in the summary periodic table. The discovery of radium in 1898 by the Polish-born physicist Marie Curie (1867–1934) launched her and husband Pierre Curie (1859–1906) on the investigation of the phenomenon of radiation (the process by which energy is emitted from a body and absorbed by another). For this she received Nobel prizes in 1903 (with her husband) and 1911. On her husband's death in 1906, she assumed his university position, becoming the first woman to teach at the Sorbonne in Paris. The couple are portrayed on p. 727.

Of key importance for medicine was the development of antisepsis (killing or inhibiting bacteria). The British surgeon Joseph Lister (1827–1912), having studied with Pasteur, applied the principle of antisepsis to hospital environment. Now surgical patients would be treated in antiseptically clean hospital operating rooms, attended by teams of robed, masked physicians and assistants. From the 1840s, nitrous oxide, ether, or chloroform could achieve general anesthesia or mask the experience of pain. The physicians of the British Queen Victoria (r. 1837–1901) famously employed chloroform during her eighth childbirth in 1852: "the effect was soothing, quieting and delightful beyond measure," she reported.

WHO'S WHO

In the Sciences (1789–1914)

Charles Darwin (1809–1882) English naturalist; author of *Origin of Species*; created the theory of evolution by natural selection.

Gregor Mendel (1822–1884) Austrian monk and botanist; established the mathematical principles of the science of genetics.

Louis Pasteur (1822–1895) French biologist and pioneer of bacteriology; developed the concept and process of "pasteurization."

Joseph Lister (1827–1912) English surgeon and medical scientist; established the principles of antisepsis in hospitals.

Marie Curie (1867–1934) Nobel-prize-winning Polish-born French scientist; with her husband Pierre pioneered the study of radioactivity.

Albert Einstein (1879–1955) German physicist; creator of relativity theory and the notion that mass and energy are interconvertible.

Pioneers of Science

"Man is But a Worm": In 1859, Charles Darwin published his Origin of Species *establishing the theory of evolution, and in 1871, his* Descent of Man. *Darwinian theory, and especially its implications for the origins of humans, inspired frequent satire. One example is seen in this cover illustration from* Punch *magazine (December 6, 1881), where a circle of apes, having evolved initially from a worm, evolve in due course into a smartly dressed Englishman.*

Sciences of Society

Like history and the sciences, the social sciences found a place in nineteenth-century universities, with the emergence of political science, economics, sociology, psychology—fields of study that did not exist as such prior to the nineteenth century.

The science of economics had been pioneered by Adam Smith (1723–1790), author of *The Wealth of Nations* (see Chapter 16), who formulated the principles of supply and demand and the division of labor. Economics crystallized further because of the work of two Englishmen, the businessman David Ricardo (1772–1823), son of Dutch-Jewish immigrants, and the clergyman Thomas Malthus (1766–1834).

What gave a commodity value, Ricardo asked—its intrinsic worth, or something else? If the former, why did prices often exceed the cost of materials? In answer to these questions he developed in his *Principles of Political Economy and Taxation* (1817), the "labor theory of value," later utilized by Karl Marx (see below). The value of an item derived not only from materials, and from the owner's proprietary (overhead) costs, but also from the cost of hiring the labor necessary to produce it.

Since it was in the interest of sellers to keep prices low in order to sell more, they exerted a downward pressure on labor costs. Workers' wages were kept as low as possible—and the lowest possible figure was always exactly the same: that sum that would allow the worker to subsist, and no more. Ricardo's explanation accorded well with experience. Workers' wages tended to devolve to subsistence level by what Ricardo called the "iron law of wages."

In his 1798 *Essay on Population*, (see *Witnesses*, p. 725), Malthus explored the mechanisms of population growth and the question of human happiness—why it had not been obtained by the great mass of people. He discovered that irrepressible appetites for food and sex constrained human beings mercilessly, as though by an iron law such as the one Ricardo described. Sexual activity resulted in more births, which led to more mouths to feed, and the eventual exhaustion of the food supply. When food supply could not keep pace with human population growth, that population became vulnerable to disease and starvation (two terrible forces that Malthus called "positive checks" on population), and soon shrank.

Marie Curie and Pierre Curie: Nineteenth- and early twentieth-century women increasingly carved out places for themselves at the forefront of intellectual, scientific, and political life. The Polish-born French scientist Marie Curie, seen here in a scene from 1895 relaxing with her husband-collaborator Pierre, pioneered the study of radiation.

Human communities that wished to eat needed to restrict their rate of fertility. Malthus advised them to do so through late marriage or abstinence, as historically they had done for centuries.

Both Ricardo and Malthus, though amateurs, contributed to social and political thought, which soon branched into autonomous professional disciplines. Auguste Comte (1798–1857), was the founder of sociology, the term he coined in 1838, the scientific study of human social behavior. Comte was a proponent of **positivism**, the creation of knowledge based on concrete evidence. Positivism looked carefully at hard facts and aimed at practical ends. The positivist study of human societies would lead, Comte argued, to sociology, which could then point the way to the creation of optimal human communities. Later, the French sociologist Emile Durkheim (1858–1917; see *Witnesses*, p. 725) was less certain that positivism led to well-functioning communities. Rather, cohesiveness derived from the set of moral and religious assumptions that a community collectively shared. When those shared assumptions broke down, misery set in. In *Suicide* (1897), Durkheim ascribed the phenomenon of suicide to the fragmentation of social values.

WHO'S WHO

In Political, Philosophical, and Social Thought: the First Generation (1789–1914)

Edmund Burke (1729–1797) English statesman and philosopher of Conservatism.

Thomas Malthus (1766–1834) English clergyman, economist, and demographer; his *Essay on Population* (1798) foresaw the dangers of overpopulation.

Jeremy Bentham (1748–1832) English Utilitarian philosopher; argued that the only true standard for good was that which served the "greatest good for the greatest number."

G. W. Friedrich Hegel (1770–1831) German Idealist philosopher and important influence on Karl Marx.

F. M. Charles Fourier (1772–1837) Pioneer "Utopian" Socialist; proposed the creation of workers' communities based on a *phalange*, or communal association, of carefully selected personality types.

Auguste Comte (1798–1857) French Positivist thinker and founder of sociology.

Leopold von Ranke (1795–1886) German historian; promoted the use of official sources as the basis for writing history "as it really happened."

The English philosopher Herbert Spencer (1820–1903), less concerned with community, argued that superior individuals, derived from a superior inheritance—they were, in brief, racially superior. The most competent individuals—whom Spencer identified as those of the Anglo-Saxon race—would in time gain superiority over others. This theory of individual success based on competition and racial aptitude, seeming to mirror Darwin's theory of natural selection, acquired an air of scientific authority. Spencer's "Social Darwinism," however, has been repeatedly rejected by scientists, who note the confusion between Darwin's theory of the biological evolution of *species* and Spencer's notion of the willed competition between individuals *within* a species. Spencer's views, however, helped justify European imperial expansion over "races" presumed to be "inferior" (see Chapter 24).

The development of economics and sociology was important for political thinking, even as the liberalism that had displaced theories of monarchical rule was itself fragmented into conservatism and nationalism, socialism, communism, feminism, and anarchism (see below). Political thought, too, found a respectable university niche, and animated reformers and revolutionaries, whose work will be considered below. First, the system of schooling must be described by which youngsters were prepared to enter into the social mainstream.

Schooling the Masses

The principle of mass public elementary education is recent. Prior to the nineteenth century, nearly all elementary education was private. For the elites generally, such education aimed at Latin literacy. In some merchant circles, vernacular literacy was deemed sufficient, and mathematical skills were stressed. In Protestant communities, literacy was linked to Bible reading and basic religious instruction. Girls, along with literacy and perhaps some bookkeeping, needed to learn needlework skills. Privileged girls would also learn drawing, dancing, and music. Those at convent schools also received a thorough, and often tedious, religious training.

Most children, however, did not go to school. Children of working-class families might master a craft, do agricultural work, or labor as servants. Many did not learn to read, write, or perform arithmetic; many did not speak the official national language, but a non-standard dialect—as was the case with over ten percent of children in France as late as 1863.

The public schooling of the masses began in France and Britain in the late nineteenth century. It was schooling guided by a secular state that had begun to broaden its franchise, and looked to equip its citizens to participate in civil life. In France, anti-clerical republicanism called for a completely secular, public education. Its advocates wanted to terminate the clergy's long monopoly of the schools. From 1833 each commune (a local administrative unit) had been required to operate a primary school. Often the teachers were clergy who, though subject to secular standards, continued to teach religious doctrine. By 1847, nearly 4 million children attended these schools, and by 1875, literacy rates had climbed significantly.

From 1879 to 1881, the Minister of Education (later Premier) Jules Ferry (1832–1893) instituted a program of school reforms. These established free, secular, coeducational, and compulsory public schools in each village. Centrally-controlled teacher-training schools graduated idealistic school teachers of republican sympathies. By 1901, 83,700 primary schools of all types existed to instruct more than 5 million children (of a national population of 38.9 million) in basic subjects. By the same date an impressive ninety-four percent of army conscripts (a cross-section of the nation's male youth) were literate.

Secondary schools expanded as well, including girls as well as boys. Even so, few students, mostly from wealthy families, went on to secondary school (a fraction of a percent). Even fewer attended university (although attendance had tripled by 1900), the pathway to careers in law, medicine, and the civil service.

In Britain, Church-directed Sunday Schools were established from the late 1780s to provide poor children with basic skills. Hannah More (1745–1833), an early advocate, defined their aim "to train up the lower classes in habits of industry and piety." By 1833, nearly half of the school-age population was enrolled. The Sunday Schools could not by themselves produce educated workers (whose literacy rates in the early years of industrialization hovered depressingly around five percent for men, and two percent for women). Yet they laid the groundwork for a system of comprehensive, mass education.

Parliament mandated the operation of public schools by the Education Act of 1870. The Quaker member of Parliament William Foster (1818–1886), among others, had put the case: "On the speedy provision of elementary education depends our industrial prosperity, the safe working of our constitutional system, and our national power." In 1880, Parliament required school attendance for all children up to age ten; in 1899 it extended the requirement through age twelve; in 1891, it eliminated all fees. An educated citizenry and an educated workforce were now viewed as essential for an advanced nation.

Other European nations followed suit. In Italy prior to unification, the state of Piedmont in 1847 was the first to establish such a system. After unification, general progress was made, resulting in increasing the literacy rate from 1860 rates of about twenty-five percent for men and ten percent for women to an overall rate of seventy-five percent by 1914. That figure disguises the great division in Italy between the affluent, largely literate northern provinces, and the impoverished, southern ones, where fewer than one-half of all children attended schools.

In Germany after 1870, an affluent, newly unified nation moved swiftly to train its youth. By 1900, less than one percent of the population failed to meet the standard of literacy. In Russia, where serfdom had been abolished only in 1861, the general literacy rate had risen to forty-three percent by 1917, with the countryside still lagging behind the cities, and women behind men. The government attempted to close higher education in Russia to all but the nobility, although some non-nobles did succeed in attending secondary school and university.

Although secondary and higher education remained exclusive, the elementary education now available to many meant a transformation in the intellectual world. Readers of all classes consumed novels, magazines, and newspapers—the latter evolving from monthlies to weeklies to dailies. As a result, the gap between the culture of the learned and the "popular" culture of workers and peasants, which had opened wide since the age of the Renaissance (see Chapters 13, 17), narrowed considerably. Reading and schooling encouraged national consciousness and culture that complemented the spirit of nationalism and the democratization of politics that characterized the age.

The establishment of public schooling in the wealthier nations of western Europe meant even the children of the poor might someday attend university, participate in the creation of new knowledge, and read, view, and listen to the cultural products of artists and intellectuals in what was then the dynamic center of the world's civilizations.

IDEALS AND IDEOLOGIES

Public education was one fruit of **liberalism**, the dominant **ideology** of the nineteenth century. (An ideology is a set of ideas linked to a program of social or political action.) Liberalism was, however, only one of several ideologies in this complex century whose political systems ranged from tsarist autocracy in Russia to republicanism, in France. Others included conservatism and nationalism, socialism and its offshoots (including communism), and feminism. The diagram on p. 730 shows their relationships.

Liberalism: Freedom and Rights

The ideas fundamental to liberalism derived from ancient, medieval, and Renaissance traditions. They were crystallized around 1690 by the English philosopher John Locke (see Chapters 15, 17), and further developed by Enlightenment thinkers. Liberalism assumes the rationality of the universe and the human capacity for rational thought. It values individual

Modern Ideologies

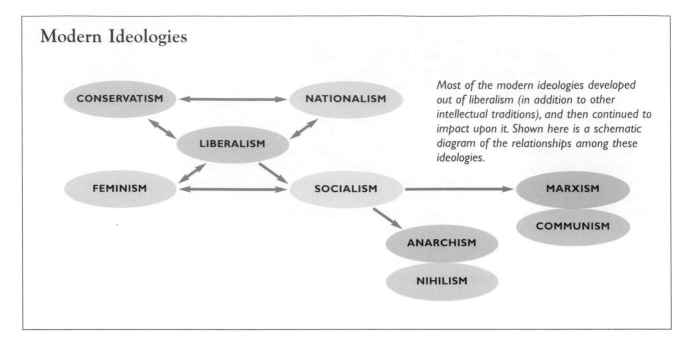

Most of the modern ideologies developed out of liberalism (in addition to other intellectual traditions), and then continued to impact upon it. Shown here is a schematic diagram of the relationships among these ideologies.

freedom, including the possession of private property; the protection of civil rights, including the right to remove an abusive government; and government by a representative assembly with decisions made by majority vote. These principles inspired the American, French, and Latin American revolutions (see Chapter 19).

During the nineteenth century, liberalism reached its zenith. Supporters of constitutional monarchy called upon its principles, and free trade. Liberalism encouraged the toleration of minority religions—leading in Britain, for example, to the admission of Catholics, Jews, and Dissenters to political office. In multinational regions, it promoted the rights of ethnic minorities. It invited the expansion of the suffrage (the right to vote), first to male property owners, then to all male citizens, and eventually to women. Finally, liberal principles, buttressed by religious arguments, underlay abolitionist arguments for the elimination of slavery and serfdom (see Chapters 16, 19). Nineteenth-century liberalism did not, however, insist on the participation of all citizens in the political process—the fundamental principle of democracy, in which power resides in the people, who exercise it either directly or through elected representatives.

Several British thinkers developed liberal theory in the direction of social reform. The formulator of **utilitarianism**, Jeremy Bentham (1748–1832), extended liberal principles to argue that society as a whole, through government mechanisms, should work to secure "the greatest good for the greatest number." Such reasoning reduced liberalism's focus on the individual, and extended existing concepts of government's responsibility to the governed. The teaching of Bentham and his disciples led to the regulation of factory conditions, prison reform, the

installation of water supply and sewage systems, and the establishment of mass public education.

The philosopher John Stuart Mill (1806–1873), was the conscience of liberalism. While supporting the activist morality of utilitarianism, he returned to the issue of individual freedom. In his essay *On Liberty* (1859), published in the same year as Darwin's *Origin of Species* and quoted in *Witnesses* on p. 732, he elevated the liberty of the individual above communitarian needs. Free speech, for instance, must remain uninfringed, even if the speaker gives voice to ideas that are dangerous, offensive, or wrong.

Mill further advocated the rights of women, based on the same assumptions of individual freedom, in his *On the Subjection of Women* (1869). Mill's feminism had profited from a twenty-year collaboration with Harriet Taylor (1807–1858), who had previously written in favor of female suffrage, to whom he was married after her first husband's death in 1851.

Conservatism: Valuing Tradition

While liberal thinkers reaffirmed the freedom of the individual, conservatism argued reverence for traditional institutions, obedience to authority, and resistance to change. Conservatism as a theoretical position first emerged in Edmund Burke's (1729–1797) critique of the French Revolution, the *Reflections on the Revolution in France* (1790), which is quoted in *Witnesses* on p. 732. Burke argued that political institutions evolved slowly and expressed accumulated wisdom of many generations. They might be changed slowly and cautiously; but if destroyed rapidly, they would give way to new institutions that were no better than the old and perhaps far worse.

Those who gathered at the Congress of Vienna (1814–1815) to arrange the post-Napoleonic peace settlement of Europe, still shaken by the Revolution in France, were conservatives who wished to erase the effects of recent change (see Chapter 23). They were determined to restore monarchy in France, and to guarantee its supremacy elsewhere. They vowed to counter all revolutionary activity wherever it occurred—as it soon did in Latin America. They disliked constitutions, they detested the Enlightenment, and they distrusted university students with their dangerous talk of freedom and equality. They hated newspapers, many in the despised languages of ethnic minorities, that promoted disorder and disobedience.

How could traditional authority fight such enemies? Prince Clemens von Metternich (1773–1859), the key Austrian official at the Congress of Vienna (see Chapter 23), pointed the way, urging legislation that would impose censorship and halt revolutionary activity. Those aims were achieved for the German states in the Carlsbad Decrees of 1819. In Austria, Prussia, and Russia the secret police (an institution Napoleon had pioneered) hovered over revolutionaries and intellectuals.

Nationalism: A Sacred Purpose

Among those watched by the secret police were advocates of nationalism. Nationalism emerged in the 1790s from the fervor of French armies that fought to defend their new revolutionary order (see Chapter 20). More than patriotism; it was a mere passion that enthused the masses, a sense of sacred purpose and unity.

Nationalism could also be a powerful force among those who aspired to nationhood. The German peoples, conscious of a common language and a common past, had been splintered for centuries into hundreds of states, then reorganized by the Congress of Vienna into thirty-eight (see Chapter 20). Now, many of them yearned to be one. Intellectuals looked to German history for heroes and memories, in order to create a cultural unity that prefigured a hoped-for political unification. When that unification was achieved in 1871, it could draw on a sense of nationhood constructed by poets and philosophers.

Italy's aspirations for nationhood likewise emerged some time before its ultimate unification in 1870 (see Chapter 20). For centuries, the region housed a multiplicity of city-states and despotisms, some ruled by foreigners. These were eventually unified by capable political and military leaders, but also through the efforts of committed idealists and intellectuals who stirred nationalist feeling in the acadamies, the universities, and the daily press, while dodging the Austrian secret police.

Nationalist sentiment was especially strong among those peoples who, though possessing a cultural and historical identity, were subject to another nation. In the Americas, new nations emerged as a result of the nationalist strivings of the British, Spanish, and Portuguese colonists (see Chapter 19). Minority nationalities within the multinational empires of Europe also sought autonomy. These included the Poles within Prussia and Russia; the Belgians subject to the Netherlands (until 1830); the Norwegians subject to Sweden (until 1905); the Jews and Muslims of Central Asia within the Russian empire; the Hungarians, Croats, Serbs, Slovaks, Slovenes, and others within the Austrian Empire; and the Bulgarians, Romanians, Albanians, Serbs, and Greeks within the Ottoman Empire. National aspirations precipitated the Greek war for independence, several Balkan wars and other rebellions and terrorist episodes, including the one that precipitated World War I (see Chapter 26).

Nationalist feeling within Europe's dominant nations often coincided with theories of racial supremacy (see Chapter 24) and militarism. These were in turn both related to the imperialist ventures of the European states which reached their height in the generations before 1914. For example, English advocates of the preeminence of the "Anglo-Saxon race"—a version of nationalist thinking—often also advocated the use of military force in defending British interests. Similar statements could be heard in all the major European languages during an era when both nationalist and racial concepts peaked.

Nationalism also had a complex relationship to the kindred ideologies of conservatism and liberalism. In some settings (the Serbs under Ottoman or Austrian rule, for instance), nationalism was conservative, looking toward a lost past of cultural freedom, and finding strength in traditional religious affiliations. In others, as in Italy, nationalism was liberal, seeking to affirm human rights and throw off the yoke of abusive government. Nationalism's ability to sustain very different political agendas would also reveal itself in the twentieth century, when it was linked with Fascism (see Chapter 28), and even, as in the Nazi (National Socialist) program, with socialism.

Socialism, however, was essentially international, or transnational. It looked to a human community that preceded the state, and repudiated the system of private property that had led, according to liberal theory, to the creation of the state (see Chapter 15). For communism, which developed from socialism, national boundaries were also meaningless. The state itself would be obliterated when the workers of the world acquired the reins of power. Feminism, linked to liberalism as well as socialism, also saw the state primarily as an obstacle to the advancement of women, who even in the most advanced states had historically been denied political rights.

Socialism: Sharing the Wealth

Rooted in the French Revolution, and given urgency by industrialization, socialism flowered in the years following Napoleon's defeat. It employed liberal principles of equality and justice to critique the concentration of wealth, and envisioned society as a community of workers capable of exercising political power. It differed from liberalism in its repudiation of the principle that the ownership of private property was an essential human right, and looked to the community or state to provide for the welfare of all.

Socialist principles began to be formulated during the Revolution's second, more violent and creative phase. The notion that the state was immediately responsible to the people at large—not just those in the Convention, but those in the street—was preliminary to socialism. So were the ideas of such revolutionaries as François-Noël Babeuf (1760–1797) (who survived Robespierre to be guillotined by the Directory) who argued that the wealth of the rich should be redistributed to the poor.

A generation later, Henri de Saint-Simon (1760–1825) announced that it was a function of the state to assure a certain minimum of material welfare for its populace. So that it could do so efficiently, the state should be controlled by those endowed with the highest rational and administrative capacities—a consortium of industrialists and scientists. These views he presented in several works, beginning with the audacious *On the Reorganization of European Society* (1814). The positivist philosopher and pioneer sociologist August Comte supported Saint-Simon in this political program, until the latter developed, just prior to his death, a new mystical religion, centered on the relief of the misery of the poor. Compassion for the poor in the Saint-Simonian system linked the medieval religious and the modern socialist traditions.

Saint-Simon's compatriots and contemporaries F. M. Charles Fourier (1772–1837) and Etienne Cabet (1788–1856) further developed a visionary, or "utopian" socialism. Fourier proposed the creation of communities of workers—each group of workers a *phalange* (or phalanx, after the ancient Greek military unit), accommodated in a *phalanstère* (phalanstery)—

WITNESSES

Idealists and Ideologues (I)

More than any previous century, the nineteenth century saw the airing of alternate and hostile views of society and politics. These passages represent three different currents: liberalism, in the words of John Stuart Mill; conservatism, in the words of Edmund Burke; and nationalism, both German and Italian, in the words of, respectively, Johann Gottlieb Fichte and Giuseppe Mazzini.

John Stuart Mill defines human liberty as limited only by the possibility of harm to others (1859): The sole end for which mankind are warranted, individually or collectively, in interfering with the liberty of action of any of their number is self protection. ... The only purpose for which power can be rightfully exercised over any member of a civilized community, against his will, is to prevent harm to others. His own good, either physical or moral, is not a sufficient warrant. He cannot rightfully be compelled to do or forbear because it will be better for him to do so, because it will make him happier, because, in the opinion of others, to do so would be wise or even right. ... The only part of the conduct of anyone for which he is amenable to society is that which concerns others. In the part which merely concerns himself, his independence is, of right, absolute.
(John Stuart Mill, *On Liberty*, 1859; Norton Critical Edition, 1975)

Edmund Burke warns of chaos to follow when the edifice of government is torn down (1790): The science of government ... [is] a matter which requires ... more experience than any person can gain in his whole life. ... It is [thus] with infinite caution that any man ought to venture upon pulling down an edifice which has answered in any tolerable degree for ages the common purposes of society, or on building it up again, without having models and patterns of approved utility before his eyes. ... When ancient opinions of life are taken away, the loss cannot possibly be estimated. From that moment we have no compass to govern us; nor can we know distinctly to what port we steer. ...
(Edmund Burke, *Reflections on the Revolution in France*, 1790)

Two nationalists see nationhood as language, tradition, and culture: *Johann Gottlieb Fichte:* The first, original, and truly natural boundaries of states are beyond doubt their internal boundaries. Those who speak the same language are joined to each other by a multitude of invisible bonds by nature herself, long before any human art begins; they understand each other and have the power of continuing to make themselves understood more and more clearly; they belong together and are by nature one and an inseparable whole. ... From this internal boundary, which is drawn by the spiritual nature of man himself, the marking of the external boundary by dwelling places results as a consequence. ...
(Johann Gottlieb Fichte, "Thirteenth Address," 1806; ed. G. A. Kelly, 1968)

Giuseppe Mazzini: [The people of one nation] speak the same language, they bear about them the impress of consanguinity, they kneel beside the same tombs, they glory in the same tradition; ... Nationality ought ... to be ... the assertion of the individuality of a human group called by its geographical position, its traditions, and its language, to fulfill a special function in the European work of civilization.
(Giuseppe Mazzini, "Europe: Its Condition and Prospects," 1852; ed. W. Clark, 1880)

who would live together, males and emancipated females, in harmony. They would engage in productive work, participate in artistic and musical projects, and enjoy fulfilling lives unfettered by conventional religious or moral restrictions.

Cabet also envisioned a harmonious workers' community. His *Voyage to Icaria* (1840) described an imaginary voyage to a workers' paradise organized by principles he called "communist" (the first use of the term). Cabet tried to put his ideas in action, setting off with hundreds of followers in 1848 to plant a communitarian settlement in Nauvoo, Illinois, on the site of one just abandoned by Mormon sectarians bound for Salt Lake City, Utah.

An opponent of the state (which he thought should be abolished) and of the capitalists who, he believed, were its principal beneficiaries, Pierre-Joseph Proudhon (1809–1865) envisioned workers' communities based on equity and justice. His 1840 book *What is Property?* posed that central question. Those who accumulate property, according to Proudhon, remove wealth from the common store and deprive the poor of basic necessities. He responded to his own question with an unequivocal reply: all property was theft. An extract from his writings on government is given in *Witnesses* on p. 734.

The attempts of Robert Owen (1771–1858) meanwhile to build real workers' communities in Britain and the United States (see Chapter 22) contributed to later socialist development. In France again, Louis Blanc (1811–1882) proposed in his 1840 book *The Organization of Work* a system of government-funded national workshops as a remedy for unemployment. These, too, were failures. At the same time, they were precedents for later workers' organizations. More, they announced the principle that government owed its citizens a right as substantial as the rights to free speech or worship: the right to work.

Marxism, Communism, Anarchism: Transfers of Power

After 1848, the utopian visions of the early socialists gave way to the pragmatic programs of workers' organizations, or trade unions, and social democratic political parties (see Chapter 22). Many of their leaders were influenced by the form of socialism that came to predominate in the latter half of the century, termed **Marxism** after its exponent Karl Marx (1818–1883).

Marxism combined economic analysis, social criticism, historical description, moral philosophy, and political theory into a weighty and complex intellectual system. It first appeared in a pamphlet written on the eve of the revolutions of 1848, the *Communist Manifesto*, on which Marx collaborated with fellow German intellectual Friedrich Engels (1820–1895). Together they had been founders of a political party that they called the "Communist League." Now,

dismissing as mere quackery the visionary socialism of Saint Simon or Owen, they outlined the fundamentals of a "scientific" socialism.

Surveying a society transformed by industrialization, they distinguished two major social groups, or classes: the bourgeoisie and the **proletariat**. For Marx and Engels, the term "**class**" denoted not merely a group of people, but a group that shared a certain relation to "the means of production," the tools for the creation of wealth. The "bourgeoisie" included those who manufactured on a vast scale in machine-powered factories, conducting business worldwide. It was the bourgeoisie who owned the "means of production"—the machines and factories of an industrial economy—and who used their financial resources (capital) in order to create even more wealth.

The workers whose labor was hired by bourgeois capitalists were themselves powerless and poor. These were the "proletariat," who participated in industrial society as mere "appendages" of the machines that made other people wealthy.

These two social classes were locked in an epochal battle; indeed it was history's final battle. All of history, Marx and Engels explained, was a history of "class struggle" (see *Witnesses*, p. 734). Earlier eras had seen the clash of landowners and slaves, of knights and serfs. In each age two primary classes emerged from the broader society to fight a duel, their struggle creating new social conditions that became the foundations of the next historical era. That process had continued to the present moment, when the class struggle was more intense than ever heretofore.

Its greater intensity derived from tangible, measurable conditions. Never before had so many people fallen into one of the two competing social classes. Never before had the wealthy been so powerful and their servants so deprived of power. History approached that moment when all but a few would be of one group—the proletariat—and only a few would oppose them—the bourgeoisie. At that moment, the many would seize power, and appropriate for themselves the means of production. Now wealth would belong to the workers, which is to say, to society as a whole. Socialism would have been achieved, and the resulting society, a workers' paradise, would be wholly classless, or communist.

Thus communism grew from socialism, systematized by Marx and Engels, who predicted as inevitable the destruction of private property and the victory of the industrial workers of the world. "Workers of the world, unite!," the *Manifesto* closes, "you have nothing to lose but your chains!"

Marx lived for thirty-five years after the publication of the *Manifesto*. During that time, he continued to write, (making regular use of the British Museum Reading Room in London, where he lived), and to organize, supported financially by Engels. Engels also contributed importantly to communist theory in his

The Conditions of the Working Class in England (1845) and *The Origin of the Family, Private Property, and the State* (1884). Marx's most important work was the three-volume *Capital*, an exhaustive analysis of the modern industrial economy. He also encouraged the formation of workers' unions and social democratic parties, and in 1864 organized the First International (the common name for the First Working Men's Association). After Marx's death in 1883, the Second International was formed in 1889.

In the late nineteenth century, Marxist theory developed most vigorously within the German workers' movement, where it branched in several directions. An "orthodox" school of thought, represented by Karl Kautsky (1854–1938) adhered to the original Marxian formulations. A "revisionist" school, represented by

Eduard Bernstein (1850–1932), while respectful of the Marxist analysis, urged socialists to respond flexibly to emerging new conditions. These now offered the possibility of an evolution through a series of parliamentary reforms in the direction of communism, rather than the violent revolution that Marx prophesied. Christian Socialists—a seeming paradox, as Marx himself was militantly atheist—urged blending Christian values of compassion and mutual assistance with a Marxist analysis of society.

Socialist parties flourished according to the German pattern in Austria, Belgium, the Netherlands, and the Scandinavian countries. That pattern failed to crystallize in the United States, where Marxian socialism had little appeal in an environment of relative ease and freedom. The broad and flexible

WITNESSES

Idealists and Ideologues (II)

Three further, this time "radical", outlooks on society and politics are represented here—"radical" because they challenged existing hierarchies and values. Karl Marx and Friedrich Engels define some basic principles of the communist agenda; Pierre-Joseph Proudhon, a proponent of anarchism, deplores all government control; and Emmeline Pankhurst explains why the goals of feminism may be won only with violence.

Karl Marx and Friedrich Engels define history as a series of class struggles (1848): The history of all hitherto existing society is the history of class struggles. Freeman and slave, patrician and plebeian, lord and serf, guild-master and journeyman, in a word, oppressor and oppressed, stood in constant opposition to one another, carried on an uninterrupted, now hidden, now open fight, a fight that each time ended, either in a revolutionary reconstitution of society at large, or in the common ruin of the contending classes. ... The modern bourgeois society that has sprouted from the ruins of feudal society has not done away with class antagonisms. ... Society as a whole is more and more splitting up into two great hostile camps, into two great classes directly facing each other—bourgeoisie and proletariat. ...
(Karl Marx and Friedrich Engels, *The Communist Manifesto*, 1848; ed. S. Moore, 1888)

Pierre-Joseph Proudhon—an anarchist—asks, "What is Government?" (1851): To be GOVERNED is to be kept under surveillance, inspected, spied upon, bossed, law-ridden, regulated, penned in, indoctrinated, preached at, registered, evaluated, appraised, censured, ordered about, by creatures who have neither the right, nor the knowledge, nor the virtue to do so. ... It is, under the pretense of public benefit and in the name of the general interest, to be ... extorted, squeezed,

hoaxed, robbed; then at the slightest resistance, ... to be squelched, corrected, vilified, bullied, hounded, tormented, bludgeoned, disarmed, strangled, imprisoned, shot down, judged, condemned, deported, sacrificed, sold, betrayed . ... That's government, that's its justice, that's its morality! And to think that there are democrats among us who claim that there is some good in government—socialists who support this infamy in the name of Liberty, Equality, and Fraternity—proletarians who proclaim their candidacy for the Presidency of the Republic! Hypocrisy!
(From R. Hoffman ed., *Anarchism*, 1970)

Emmeline Pankhurst, the English feminist and suffragette explains why women are militant (1913): The extensions of the franchise to the men of my country [Britain] have been preceded by very great violence, by something like a revolution, by something like civil war. In 1832 ... it was after the practice of arson on so large a scale that half the city of Bristol was burned down in a single night ... that the Reform Bill of 1832 was allowed to pass into law. [This enfranchised middle-class males.] In 1867 ... rioting went on all over the country, and as the result ... the Reform Act of 1867 was put upon the statute books. [This enfranchised urban working-class males.] In 1884 ... rioting was threatened and feared, and so the agricultural laborers got the vote. Meanwhile, during the '80s, women, like men, were asking for the franchise. ... Meetings of the great corporations, great town councils, and city councils, passed resolutions asking that women should have the vote. More meetings were held, and larger, for Woman Suffrage than were held for votes for men, and yet the women did not get it. Men got the vote because they were and would be violent. The women did not get it because they were constitutional and law abiding. ...
(Emmeline Pankhurst, speech, October 21, 1913; ed. J. Marcus, 1955)

principles of the Socialist Labor Party formed by Eugene Debs (1855–1926) were more popular. In Britain, despite the presence of Marx, Marxist principles did not catch hold as on the continent. In their place, the Fabian Society (founded 1883/84) urged the gradual introduction of socialist values.

In France and Russia, socialist movements and their offshoots inclined toward violence. France's revolutionary past, and the recent bloody suppression of the Paris Commune of 1871 (see Chapter 23) led socialists in that nation to view the Fabian gradualism or Bernstein's revisionism as unimpressive. While Jean Jaurès (1859–1914), the pacifist assassinated on the eve of World War I, worked to build a vigorous socialism through parliamentary means, French **Syndicalists** (the term derived from the French word for trade union, or *syndicat*) planned instead for a violent revolution, to be engineered by workers' associations and precipitated by a general strike.

Anarchists, mostly Russian, advocated an immediate, violent assault on all government authority as the only means of acquiring social and political liberty. The theorist Mikhail Bakunin (1814–1876), having outlined the essential principles of **anarchism**, was expelled from the First International. But anarchism won followers in Spain and Italy, whose undeveloped economies provided fertile soil for extremism. **Nihilists**, specifically Russian, posited the non-meaning of everything, and promoted a violent and terroristic attack on all authority. Not surprisingly, terror ensued (see Chapter 26).

Feminism: Rights for Women

As liberals and socialists posed their different visions of the ideal life, women claimed for themselves a full role in contemporary society. Their movement, called feminism, drew on ideas developed from Renaissance humanism and the Enlightenment. Mary Wollstonecraft's *A Vindication of the Rights of Woman* (1792) had summoned women to construct lives for themselves outside of marriage and regardless of their sexual destiny. In the next century, modern ideologies introduced a new dimension to women's aspirations.

The seventeenth and eighteenth centuries had seen at least some real progress for women (see Chapters 17, 18). Elite women gained prestige from the occupation of childrearing, while many also extended their educative and nurturing activities into the wider society, engaging in philanthropic work. A few participated in intellectual circles as authors, critics, or patrons. Further down the social scale, some women found employment in theatrical and dance companies— marginal professions viewed by many as not differing much from prostitution, but offering talented women, nevertheless, greater independence and visibility.

The French Revolution saw female activism emerge in social groups outside of the elites. For such women, food crisis riots had been a characteristic form of political participation (see Chapter 20). Now they became revolutionaries: they shouted slogans, stormed prisons, cheered executions, marched on Versailles, and formed a network of revolutionary clubs. Meanwhile, revolutionary leaders passed legislation favorable to women, permitting divorce and facilitating inheritance of property by women. It appeared briefly as though substantial rights for women might be secured in the flux of revolution.

The Revolution itself, however, put an end to what it began. Never admitting women to the franchise (even as universal male suffrage was briefly instituted), in 1793 it ordered the women's political clubs closed down. In the same year, Olympe de Gouges, author of the provocative *Declaration of the Rights of Women* (1790) went to the guillotine (see Chapter 20). As the painter Elisabeth Vigée-Lebrun remarked in her memoirs, women had ruled before 1789, but "the Revolution dethroned them."

The Revolution's retreat from the matter of women's rights was seconded by the Directory and reaffirmed in Napoleon's Civil Code of 1804. The Civil Code returned women to the rule of the patriarch. Their property rights and personal freedoms were again sharply restricted, and they were restored to political nullity.

The Struggle for Women's Suffrage From that nullity, liberalism and socialism offered different possibilities of emancipation. Liberalism seemed to promise women the same freedom and rights that it promised men. In Britain and the United States, progress was made toward achieving that goal. John Stuart Mill advocated women's complete civil equality, to be marked by voting rights and the ability to hold political office. In 1867 he proposed a woman's suffrage amendment to the Reform Bill that expanded the male franchise. The amendment's failure prompted the formation the following year of the National Society for Women's Suffrage that would lead a growing movement for voting rights.

The suffrage movement came to a head with the protests of Emmeline Pankhurst (1858–1928), joined by her own daughters and other followers, whose demands for political rights turned militant in the early twentieth century. A speech of hers is quoted on p. 734. Imitating tactics employed by agitators for Irish independence, they smashed windows, cut telegraph wires, and vandalized post boxes. "The argument of the broken pane of glass," proclaimed Pankhurst, "is the most valuable argument in modern politics." Their acts of civil disobedience resulted in imprisonment and, when they protested with hunger strikes, painful and demeaning forced feeding.

Progress was also made in areas besides the franchise. By 1865, twenty-nine states of the United States granted married women the right to own and administer property. The British Parliament followed suit in 1882. Before 1900, women's colleges were established at the old English universities (Girton and Newnham at Cambridge; Somerville and Lady Margaret Hall at Oxford), and women gained admittance to the University of London, as they did to some colleges and universities in the United States. The British philanthropist Josephine Butler (1828–1906) defended women's rights by opposing the Contagious Diseases Acts (in force 1864–1886), which instituted the medical regulation of prostitutes. The *Englishwomen's Journal* and other publications kept readers informed of issues important to women.

The Struggle for Social Equality   Feminists also turned to socialism for a more radical analysis of the sources of women's social inequality. Why were women still kept subordinate to men, principally fathers and husbands? Why were their rights to own and dispose of property, especially if married, still limited? Why did their husbands, not they, have custodial rights to children? Why was divorce largely unavailable in the event of marital breakdown? Why was adultery still seen as a woman's crime? Why should women not enjoy the same sexual liberty that men had always claimed? Why were all

---

WHO'S WHO

In Political, Philosophical, and Social Thought: the Second Generation (1789–1914)

Giuseppe Mazzini (1805–1872) Italian nationalist and founder of "Young Italy."

John Stuart Mill (1806–1873) English liberal philosopher; author of *On Liberty* (1859).

Mikhail Bakunin (1814–1876) Russian thinker and pioneer of the ideology of Anarchism.

Karl Marx (1818–1883) German philosopher; creator of Scientific Socialism and co-author (with Friedrich Engels) of the *Communist Manifesto*.

Herbert Spencer (1820–1903) English sociologist; best known for developing a theory of "Social Darwinism."

Friedrich Nietzsche (1844–1900) German anti-Christian philosopher who heralded the "Death of God."

Sigmund Freud (1856–1939) German psychologist and founder of psychoanalysis.

Emmeline Pankhurst (1858–1928) English radical feminist and suffragette; founder and leader of the Women's Social and Political Union.

---

women who lived outside the protected zone of the elite—servants and workers—considered the proper sexual prey of elite men?

Just as socialism, and especially Marxism, offered men of the laboring classes the dream of freedom from the domination by whose who monopolized the ownership of property, it offered women of all classes freedom from the domination of the very same men—as heads of propertied households, at once their employers and their male kin.

The early socialists already included the emancipation of women in their visionary plans to reform society. Though the household remained their fundamental unit, Fourier's phalansteries granted women complete economic and sexual freedom. Fourier himself saw the liberation of women as an index of human liberation, announcing that, as a general principle, "social progress and historic changes occur by virtue of the progress of women toward liberty." Saint-Simon and his followers posited women's right to inherit property and to full citizenship status. In 1832, the Saint-Simonian women's newspaper *La Tribune des Femmes* ("The Women's Tribune") argued for the combined struggle for emancipation of women and workers. After Marx's death, his benefactor and collaborator Engels delineated the historical progress of the subjugation of women in *The Origin of the Family, Private Property, and the State* (1884).

The confluence of socialism and feminism, seen especially in France, was most dramatically realized in the revolutions that periodically erupted there throughout the nineteenth century. In 1848, women's political clubs sprang up in Paris, much as they had after 1789. Their concerns were economic and political, but also addressed issues concerning the family and sexuality. In 1870, again, women's intense political activism embraced both the economic and political issues that concerned their male colleagues, and issues of particular interest for women. The suppression of the Commune marked a defeat not only for the working class, but for women as well.

Feminism drew on both liberal and socialist theory in its quest for the further liberation of human sexuality. Medieval restrictions on sexual expression were enforced by the Roman Catholic Church. Even harsher sanctions were introduced in the early modern era, which prosecuted the "crimes" of sodomy, infanticide, and witchcraft (linked to a variety of deviant sexual activities). The seventeenth and eighteenth centuries saw an upsurge of libertinism among the elites, accompanied by the circulation of pornography and obscene political art and writing. By the revolutionary era, the novels of the French nobleman, the Marquis de Sade (1740–1814), described practices, deemed deviant in the extreme, that caused pleasure through the infliction of pain.

During the nineteenth century, despite great reticence about sexual matters, evidence mounts of the increased intensity of romantic courtship and love within marriage; so does that of resistance to restrictions on premarital and homosexual activity, and on women's sexuality within and outside of marriage. During the last decades before 1914, at least among the vanguard urban elite of western Europe, an era of greater sexual freedom began to dawn.

FIN DE SIÈCLE AND THE ADVENT OF THE MODERN

The *fin de siècle* ("end of the century") and the first years of the new century saw a riotous repudiation of traditional restraints on behavior, thought, and expression. The long weekend was cut short by the outbreak of war in 1914 (see Chapter 26). By then, Europe's cultural world had cut loose from its past; its religious and moral systems crumbled. Their place was taken by new understandings of the human mind, new models of the structure of the universe, and new ways of seeing the world, supplied by the scientists, philosophers, writers, and artists who created the Modern.

The Death of God

During the nineteenth century, the religious outlook that had hitherto characterized Western civilization came under general attack. The eighteenth century saw the growth of evangelical movements that appealed to the poor and lower middle-class—the **Methodists** in England, and the **Pietists** in the German lands, for example. Post-revolutionary conservatism and Romantic nostalgia had promoted Catholic revivals in France and England, an Anglican revival in England, and an invigorated orthodoxy among German Lutherans. But these revivals did not prevent the decline of the churches whose attendance dropped, especially among men, as Christianity, especially Roman Catholicism, became a woman's concern. Judaism, meanwhile, tended to secularization as some successful Jews assimilated with a mainstream culture. By 1914, though religion remained important for the rural poor and bourgeois homemakers, urban workers, self-confident elites, and cultivated opinion-makers had largely abandoned it.

Profound religious faith did not die out entirely among intellectuals, however. The Danish theologian and philosopher Sören Kierkegaard (1813–1855) powerfully argued for the centrality of religious experience. Tormented by the disintegration of spiritual confidence, seeing no certain or concrete demonstration of God's existence, he nevertheless advocated a radical choice for Christian theism. In England, the sermons and tracts of John Henry Newman (1801–1890) guided a revival of Anglicanism (the "Oxford Movement"). Following his conversion to Catholicism in 1845, Newman led many of his followers back to that faith.

The "death of God"—for thus the philosopher Friedrich Nietzsche (1844–1900) hailed the downfall of the religious outlook—followed from the twin onslaught of science and revolution. By its nature, the scientific outlook disputes the religious. In search of system and certainty, scientists pushed aside the mysterious nebula that necessarily enfolds religious experience. The unavoidable rivalry between science and religion began with the first phases of the Scientific Revolution (see Chapter 17), and troubled the careers of Copernicus, Galileo, and Bruno.

A new phase of that conflict began with Darwin's announcement of his theory of evolution. The theory of evolution ruled out neither the existence of God nor the human experience of worship. But it did refute the notion of a divine creation at one moment and for all time. God's creative activity, if that notion was not abandoned altogether, was confined to an earlier moment in cosmic history than the creation of the biological species. Those evolved continuously over vast reaches of time, without divine intervention, through entirely natural mechanisms. **Darwinism** outraged traditionalists all over the West, and outrages many still. It constituted a revolution in thought; as some would claim, the single most important one of the nineteenth century.

Darwin was not himself an enemy of religion; Marx was. For him, religious institutions were at best instruments of the bourgeoise in their oppression of the proletariat. At worst, they promoted obfuscations that kept the defenseless poor enthralled—religion was, as he succinctly put it, the "opiate of the masses." Aside from some mystical elements in utopian socialism, and the compassionate radicalism of the Christian socialist parties, nineteenth-century socialism and its descendants were unswervingly atheistic.

Contemporary philosophy also dispensed with God. During the Enlightenment, philosopher Immanuel Kant (1724–1804) had both elevated rational criteria of judgment, and shown their compatibility with a secular morality. During the Romantic era, Hegel marked the progress through history of supreme spiritual values. Neither Kant nor Hegel anchored their moral or spiritual views to Christianity. A generation later, Arthur Schopenhauer (1788–1860), influenced by both Romanticism and Indian mysticism, described a universe driven alternatively by "will" or "idea"—by an emotion-laden driving force or by rational thought, severing the two tendencies of Western thought that medieval philosophers had coaxed into a synthesis.

The irrational tendencies of Schopenhauer's philosophy reappeared in extreme form in Nietzsche's. With penetrating insight, Nietzsche lambasted all the shaky preconceptions and prejudices of his day—including, or so it seemed to him, the trite promises of religion. He unwrapped the hypocrisy of moralistic bourgeois shopkeepers, of self-satisfied politicians, of slogan-spouting demagogues, of silken-tongued professors, of Christianity (a "slave religion") and Judaism. Above all these ordinary folk, he elevated the "superman" (*Übermensch*)—an individual of supreme will and daring, who disdained to be bound by any strictures of morality or tradition. Modernism found its epitome in Nietzsche, whose trenchant prose disposed of dead ideals and transported Western civilization beyond the rigors of Good and Evil.

New Visions

The new worldview, termed **Modernist**, that emerges in Nietzsche's work was not merely destructive. A new world was emerging, as new visions of reality formed. Among the heralds of a dawning twentieth-century worldview, Sigmund Freud (1856–1939) and Albert Einstein (1879–1955) stand out.

Sigmund Freud   A medical doctor specializing in neurology, Freud developed from his clinical work (notably with women suffering from mental illnesses that the nineteenth century diagnosed as "hysteria") the theory of the **unconscious**. This Modernist concept threw overboard the Western understanding of mind—that it was essentially rational. Instead, Freud described forces that operated below the level of consciousness—desires for pleasure, instincts of rage (the realm of the id, Latin for "it")—to modify behavior not quite successfully directed either by the rational, conscious self (the ego, or "I"), or the body of rules and conventions imprinted on the mind in early childhood (the superego, "above the ego").

From Freud's theories developed the modern fields of clinical psychology, psychiatry, and psychotherapy, with wide-ranging consequences for counseling, education, and social work. More, they yielded a more complex understanding of human personality as it functioned in life and in the arts. Modernism here gave birth to the modern human being.

Albert Einstein   Einstein reshaped the Western understanding of the universe as Freud did that of the self, rupturing the Newtonian cosmos and describing one more complex, more dynamic, and more fraught with uncertainty. Two major contributions can be noted which profoundly affected general culture as well as the more specialized concerns of physicists.

The first of these is the theory of **relativity**, explained in *Witnesses* on p. 778. If the speed of light is constant, and natural laws prevail, then time and motion will be relative to the observer. For the scientist, Einstein's theory explains observed cosmic phenomena. For the lay person, what once appeared to be true had become relative, or mutable. What seems true here is not necessarily true there; what is true now is not necessarily true later; even the ideas of here, there, now, and then are fluid and undefinable.

The second contribution was the principle that the relation between mass and energy could be expressed in an equation; thus they were convertible, and one could be changed into the other. The equation is the famous $e = mc^2$, stating that a quantity of energy (e) can be obtained which is equal to the mass of a particle (m) times the square of the velocity of light (c). For scientists, this principle had many applications. For the world at large, it underlay the development of the most terrible weapon ever known, the atomic bomb, whose explosive force derives from the release of tremendous energy from a small quantity of matter. An idealist and pacifist, Einstein was horrified by the prospect of a bomb, understanding from the first the destructive potential of his equation (see Chapter 30).

Modernism and the Arts   In a universe where things were relative and the human mind was not what it seemed, literature and the arts took new directions. Such writers as the Swedish dramatist August Strindberg (1849–1912), the American poet Ezra Pound (1885–1972), and the Irish novelist James Joyce (1882–1941), among others, hammered out forms of expression appropriate to a new age.

In the visual arts, Modernist tendencies appeared as early as the 1860s. From the Renaissance forward, the artist's skill was measured by his or her ability to represent clearly defined subjects—a building, a dramatic scene, or a beautiful woman (see Chapter 13). By the later nineteenth century, the primacy of the object yielded to a different imperative. The modern artist's goal became the depiction of the experience of a fleeting moment, to see with the artist's inner vision. The paraphernalia of daily life were matter to be manipulated by the artist's mind and hand.

The French Impressionists can be considered the first school of modern art, although this term is imprecise. Claude Monet (1840–1926) and Pierre Auguste Renoir (1841–1919), among others, painted domestic scenes, landscapes, and figures with a new intent. They studied the effects of light, which varies at different moments of the day, changing our perception of forms. In 1874, this group of young painters presented an exhibition of their paintings—disdaining the official annual Salon of the French Academy, which had previously refused their work. From the title of Monet's picture *Impression–Sunrise*, reproduced in *Windows On* on p. 740, they became known as Impressionists. Though attacked by art critics at first, by the 1880s the new style had triumphed; by 1886 it had been superseded.

Where the Impressionists tried to capture visual reality through the sparkling, momentary play of light, younger innovators focused on the turbulent inner world of emotions and the unconscious. The Dutch painter Vincent van Gogh (1853–1890) invested people, landscapes, and simple objects with

The *Fin de Siècle* and the Advent of the Modern

As the nineteenth century turned and the twentieth dawned, modernism was born, as thought and art boldly cast off the bonds of traditional European culture, including both the prohibitions of Christianity and the confidence of the Enlightenment. Here, novelist Fyodor Dostoevsky defends irrationalism; philosopher Friedrich Nietzsche repudiates moralism; physician Sigmund Freud reveals the aggressive impulses driving human behavior; and poet Guillaume Apollinaire celebrates the new abandonment in the arts of the representation of nature so as to provide a higher order of truth and of pleasure.

Fyodor Dostoevsky's "Underground Man" declares the primacy of the will, personality, and irrational urges (1864): Oh, tell me, who first declared ... that man only does nasty things because he does not know his own real interests; and that if he were enlightened, if his eyes were opened to his real normal interests, man would at once become good and noble. ... You see, gentlemen, reason, gentlemen, is an excellent thing, there is no disputing that, but reason is only reason and can only satisfy man's rational faculty, while will is a manifestation of all life, that is, of all human life including reason as well as all impulses. And although our life, in this manifestation of it, is often worthless, yet it is life nevertheless and not simply extracting square roots. ... But I repeat for the hundredth time, there is one case, one only, when man may purposely, consciously, desire what is injurious to himself, what is stupid. ... This very stupid thing ... this caprice of ours, may really be more advantageous for us, gentlemen, than anything else on earth ... because ... it preserves for us what is most precious and most important—that is, our personality, our individuality.
(Fyodor Dostoevsky, *Notes From the Underground*, 1864; ed. E. P. Dutton, 1988)

Friedrich Nietzsche repudiates morality and religion (1888):
What is good?—All that heightens the feeling of power, the will to power, power itself in man.
What is bad?—All that proceeds from weakness.
What is happiness?—The feeling that power *increases*— that a resistance is overcome.
Not contentment, but more power; *not* peace at all, but war; *not* virtue, but proficiency (virtue in the Renaissance style, *virtù*, virtue free of moralic acid).
The weak and ill-constituted shall perish: first principle of *our* philanthropy. And one shall help them to do so.
(Friedrich Nietzsche, *Twilight of the Idols/The Anti-Christ*, 1888; ed. R. J. Hollingdale, 1968)

The French poet Guillaume Apollinaire discusses the new trends in art (1913): [Modernist] painters, while they still look at nature, no longer imitate it, and carefully avoid any representation of natural scenes which they may have observed. ... Real resemblance no longer has any importance, since everything is sacrificed by the artist to truth, to the necessities of a higher nature whose existence he assumes, but does not lay bare. The subject has little importance any more. Generally speaking, modern art repudiates most of the techniques of pleasing devised by the great artists of the past. While the goal of painting is today, as always, the pleasure of the eye, the art-lover is henceforth asked to expect delights other than those which looking at natural objects can easily provide.
(Guillaume Apollinaire, *The Cubist Painters: Aesthetic Meditations*, 1913; ed. L. Abel, 1962)

---

the intensity of his personal world. His *Potato Eaters* (1885), portraying a family of miners, shows the impoverishment of the human spirit. His depictions of ordinary objects describe in worn leather and bent wood his own passionate and suffering nature. His *Starry Night* (1889), illustrated in *Windows On* on p. 740, portrays the modern cosmos, the explosive sky overwhelming the natural landscape, in which human beings must dwell.

In the twentieth century, artists turned from representationalism to paint **abstract** forms. The Russian Vasily Kandinsky (1866–1944) sought to express ideas and evoke emotions by the sheer power of line and color (see *Witnesses*, p. 778, and *Windows On*, p. 740). The Spanish master Pablo Picasso (1881–1973), who explored many stylistic approaches in the course of his long career, was a pioneer of

Cubism around 1907. This style fragmented forms into multiple facets, just as the eye in reality takes in objects from several angles. Like Kandinsky, he was painting a reality that dwelled in his mind alone—not what seemed, but what he knew to exist.

In music, also, where representation had never been a possibility, traditional norms fractured in the later nineteenth century. The operas of Richard Wagner (1818–1883) pushed to an extreme the Romantic understanding of music—that it was to express, and arouse, intense emotion. His overpowering musical compositions accompanied a vision of German history, the German soul, and German destiny informed by both Romanticism and nationalism. In this regard, Wagner is often seen as a forerunner of Nazism (see Chapter 28)—a possibility supported by his well-documented anti-Semitism.

Claude Monet, Impression–Sunrise, 1872

Fin de Siècle and the Advent of the Modern

Modernism arose as nineteenth-century notions of God, progress, order, and purpose collapsed before the twin onslaught of science (especially Darwinism) and Revolution. While Friedrich Nietzsche and Sigmund Freud helped dismantle the presuppositions of Western society—especially Christianity, traditional morality, and the presumption of human rationality—Impressionist, Post-Impressionist, Expressionist, and abstract styles inaugurated Modernism in the visual arts.

Impressionists such as Claude Monet—here represented by his Impression–Sunrise (top)—strove to describe their inner worlds rather than recreate the outer world represented by Western artists since the Renaissance. The Impressionists were soon overtaken by other artists and styles, each increasingly non-representational. In the Post-Impressionist Starry Night by Vincent Van Gogh (center), the heavens throb and pulse with light and energy, totally overwhelming the frail mortal realm that lies beneath.

During the twentieth century, artists including the Russian Vasily Kandinsky abandoned representation altogether in favor of purely abstract images (bottom).

(top: Musée Marmottan, Paris; center: Museum of Modern Art, New York; bottom: Städtische Galerie im Lenbachhaus, Munich)

To what extent are Monet's and van Gogh's paintings, like Kandinsky's, also exercises in abstraction?

Vincent van Gogh, Starry Night, 1889

Vasily Kandinsky, Study for Composition VII, 1913

 To continue your investigation of this topic, please go to www.prenhall.com/king for the related **WINDOWS** on the **WEB** activity

In the early twentieth century, Igor Stravinsky (1882–1971) and Arnold Schoenberg (1874–1951) took up a Modernist attack on traditional musical form that paralleled the rejection of representationalism in the visual arts. Stravinsky's ballet *The Rite of Spring*, performed in Paris in 1913, provoked the audience to outrage with its rhythmic and tonal violations of prevailing standards of composition, as well as its celebration of primal emotions and a pagan worldview. Audience members were horrified as dancers clad in bizarre costumes writhed obscenely, accompanied by music that to them was raucous and chaotic. It was the clarion call of the twentieth century.

Schoenberg's **atonal** music, the first examples of which were performed in 1909, aroused not so much horror as confusion. Listeners did not understand the composer's disavowal of the tonal structures that defied all previous Western music. The new, abstract structures of Schoenberg's compositions not only did not sound tuneful, but they did not seem to communicate any comprehensible human emotion or idea.

This creative ferment among artists and intellectuals scarcely affected the ordinary worker, or merchant, or leisured aristocrat—even as it transformed the mental universe their descendants would inhabit. To the extent that they could, they spent the last decades before World War I amusing themselves. The music halls and cabarets, theaters and beer halls provided light-hearted song and dance—heavily laden, nevertheless, with messages that overturned the moral values of an earlier era. Outside, and in the daylight, an equivalent disruption of norms was accomplished by the new world of speed. In automobiles and balloons, on motorcycles and bicycles, and especially in airplanes, people of all social classes and both genders soared beyond the confined worldview of their ancestors, who had been limited by the compass of nature to the speed of mammalian limbs.

In 1896, the Olympic Games were held again, for the first time since antiquity (see Chapter 4). But these were Modernist games. The ancient Greeks had competed to win glory and to worship their gods. The races run by modern Europeans were complicated by nationalist resentments and by the convulsive efforts by competitors to go faster and get further. Such were the ingredients, too, of the cataclysm that put a stop to the joyous rebellion of the *fin de siècle* and the experiments of Modernism: the first war to engulf the whole of the globe.

Conclusion
THE ADVENT OF THE MODERN AND THE MEANING OF THE WEST

A giant creativity marks the era of Western culture bounded by the French Revolution and the outbreak of World War I. Artists, and intellectuals leapt from Classical, to Romantic, to realist, to abstract styles, and from the mission of depicting a reality that existed in fact to one that existed in the mind of the subject. Scientists discovered radiation and the cell, and introduced the theories of evolution, genetic inheritance, and relativity. Biology, chemistry, and physics, along with history, psychology, sociology, and economics, became academic disciplines housed in university departments. The children of peasants and workers went to school in their millions, as they would soon go to war. Liberals, conservatives, nationalists, socialists, communists, anarchists, and feminists devised their competing ideologies and contended for followers and for power. By 1914, Western culture was Modern and modern people cast aside the traditions that had both guided and constrained them. In 1914, as the following chapter relates, the elders whose values they rejected led the children of the Western world into the cataclysm of world war.

QUESTIONS TO CONSIDER

1. Why was Romanticism a particularly appealing movement to Europeans who had just experienced the French Revolution?

2. Why did Darwinism pose a challenge both to religion on the one hand, and to liberalism on the other?

3. How was it possible that some European nations instituted systems of mass public education for the first time anywhere in the world? What were the likely effects of that cultural change?

4. Why were nationalism and socialism fundamentally opposed? How did Marx change the understanding of socialism?

5. What were the roots of modern feminism, and what was its relation to socialism?

6. How would you characterize the "modern" culture that arose in the last years of the nineteenth century?

SUGGESTED RESOURCES

Butler, Christopher, *Early Modernism: Literature, Music and Painting in Europe, 1900–1916* (Oxford: Oxford University Press, 1994). Synthetic examination of early modernism in painting, literature, and music.

Bynum, W. F., *Science and the Practice of Modern Medicine in the Nineteenth Century* (Cambridge: Cambridge University Press, 1994). Examines the interaction of scientific theory and medical practice.

Desmond, Adrian J. and James Moore, *Darwin* (New York: Viking Penguin, 1991). Perhaps the best biography of this important figure.

Donner, Wendy, *The Liberal Self: John Stuart Mill's Moral and Political Philosophy* (Ithaca–London: Cornell University Press, 1991). Updated study of the philosopher's contributions to 19th-century liberalism.

Fritzsche, Peter, *Reading Berlin 1900* (Cambridge: Harvard University Press, 1996). Examines daily newspapers in the first years of the 20th century to understand the exciting urbanism of Berlin, a magnet for artists and writers, in an age of modernism.

Geison, Gerald L., *The Private Science of Louis Pasteur* (Princeton: Princeton University Press, 1995). Examines Pasteur's personal laboratory notebooks to reconstruct the scientist's motives and intentions in the world of powerful and learned men he inhabited.

Gibson, Mary, *Born to Crime: Cesare Lombroso and the Origins of Biological Criminology* (Westport CT: Praeger, 2002). At the intersection of modern science and social science lies the nineteenth-century assumption of inborn criminal tendencies, explored here in the work of an Italian anthropologist.

Himmelfarb, Gertrude, *The De-Moralization of Society: From Victorian Virtues to Modern Values* (New York: Alfred A. Knopf, 1995). Stimulating comparison of Victorian and modern values.

Johnson, James H., *Listening in Paris: A Cultural History* (Berkeley: University of California Press, 1994). How and why people thronged to the concert hall in Paris during the years when Romanticism emerged, and how what they heard transformed contemporary culture.

Offen, Karen, *European Feminisms, 1700–1950: A Political History* (Stanford: Stanford University Press, 1998). A comparative account of the development of feminism in the West.

Quinn, Susan, *Marie Curie: A Life* (New York: Simon & Schuster, 1995). Comprehensive account of this major scientist, placing her firmly in the context of women's history.

Vitezslav, Orel, *Gregor Mendel: The First Geneticist* (Oxford: Oxford University Press, 1996). Excellent biography, covering most aspects of Mendel's life and work.

Wheen, Francis, *Karl Marx: A Life* (New York: W. W. Norton, 2000). The first major biography of Marx since the Cold War depicts him as a humane man whose aspirations summed up the issues of the century.

Wohl, Robert, *A Passion for Wings: Aviation and the Western Imagination, 1908–1918* (New Haven: Yale University Press, 1994). How flight captured the imagination of the adventurous minds of artists, intellectuals, and the leisured rich during one decade of the 20th century.

Romantic Chronology, timeline of major works and styles interspersed with events, late-18th century to 1851:
http://ucsb.edu.591/rchrono

Albert Einstein, Image and Impact (American Institute of Physics) resources and links:
http://www.aip.org/history/einstein

Guide to resources on Karl Marx, including electronic books (epistemelinks):
http://www.epistemelinks.com/Main/Philosophers. asp?PhilCode=Marx

And from Bjorn's guide to philosophy:
http://www.knuten.liu.se/~bjoch509/philosophers/mar.html

⊙ Western Civilization Documents CD-ROM

20.5 Jean-Jacques Rousseau: from Emile
20.6 Samuel Taylor Coleridge: From Aids to Reflection
20.7 Gothic Churches
20.8 Prometheus
21.5 Karl Marx and Friedrich Engels: The Communist Manifesto
21.6 Michael Harrington: Socialism: Past and Future
21.7 Anarchism: Michael Bakunin
23.3 Sex in Society
23.4 John Stuart Mill: from the Subjection of Women
23.5 Bernard Shaw: Act III from Mrs. Warren's Profession
24.1 George Eliot: Essay on Margaret Fuller and Mary Wollstonecraft
24.2 An Advocate for Science Education
24.3 Sexual Science?
24.4 Auguste Comte
24.5 Friedrich Nietzsche
24.5 Sir Edmund Gosse

PART SEVEN

TOWARD A
NEW WEST

Post-War, Post-Modern, Post-Industrial
(1914–2000)

Three enormous conflicts overshadow the twentieth century and put the whole project of Western civilization in jeopardy: World War I, World War II, and the Cold War. World War I marked the point at which the West was no longer in the ascendant over the other regions of the world. A wounded civilization limped on to confront the various crises of economic collapse, social upheavals, and the advance of totalitarian states.

World War II purchased the defeat of fascism, which had threatened to reverse the Western tradition, at the cost of more than 40 million lives. The victory over fascism, won by an alliance of the democratic United States and Britain and the Communist Soviet Union, was a vindication of the civilization of the West.

The Cold War pitched two of the victors of the prior conflict against each other in an epochal duel between communism and capitalism. The two Superpowers faced each other in a bi-polar system that split the world, armed with weapons that could not be used—for they threatened the annihilation of human life itself. The face-off continued until, in 1989, communism began to self-destruct in Europe and the Soviet Union. Meanwhile, the regions of the earth that, in 1900, had been dominated by Europeans had won their autonomy, and claimed their stake in the world of nations. The transmission of knowledge edged out industrial manufacture in the world economy, as systems of communication and transportation came to unite the most remote regions of the earth.

In 1900, the West was secure in its political, military, and cultural superiority. In 2000, after the shock of three massive conflicts, the West inhabits a global world. It is a post-war, post-modern, and post-industrial West that enters the new millennium. Whether it maintains its identity and rediscovers its mission through a reflection on its traditions and achievements is in the hands of the present generation.

THE MIGHTY ARE FALLEN

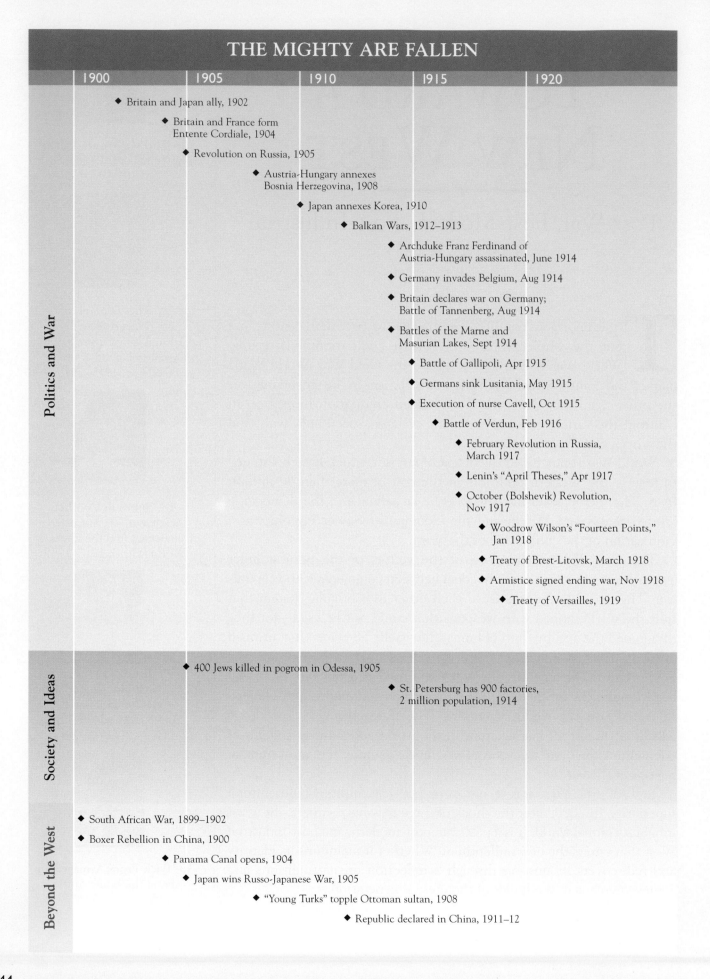

	1900	1905	1910	1915	1920

Politics and War

◆ Britain and Japan ally, 1902

◆ Britain and France form Entente Cordiale, 1904

◆ Revolution on Russia, 1905

◆ Austria-Hungary annexes Bosnia Herzegovina, 1908

◆ Japan annexes Korea, 1910

◆ Balkan Wars, 1912–1913

◆ Archduke Franz Ferdinand of Austria-Hungary assassinated, June 1914

◆ Germany invades Belgium, Aug 1914

◆ Britain declares war on Germany; Battle of Tannenberg, Aug 1914

◆ Battles of the Marne and Masurian Lakes, Sept 1914

◆ Battle of Gallipoli, Apr 1915

◆ Germans sink Lusitania, May 1915

◆ Execution of nurse Cavell, Oct 1915

◆ Battle of Verdun, Feb 1916

◆ February Revolution in Russia, March 1917

◆ Lenin's "April Theses," Apr 1917

◆ October (Bolshevik) Revolution, Nov 1917

◆ Woodrow Wilson's "Fourteen Points," Jan 1918

◆ Treaty of Brest-Litovsk, March 1918

◆ Armistice signed ending war, Nov 1918

◆ Treaty of Versailles, 1919

Society and Ideas

◆ 400 Jews killed in pogrom in Odessa, 1905

◆ St. Petersburg has 900 factories, 2 million population, 1914

Beyond the West

◆ South African War, 1899–1902

◆ Boxer Rebellion in China, 1900

◆ Panama Canal opens, 1904

◆ Japan wins Russo-Japanese War, 1905

◆ "Young Turks" topple Ottoman sultan, 1908

◆ Republic declared in China, 1911–12

THE MIGHTY ARE FALLEN

The Trauma of World War I

1914–1920

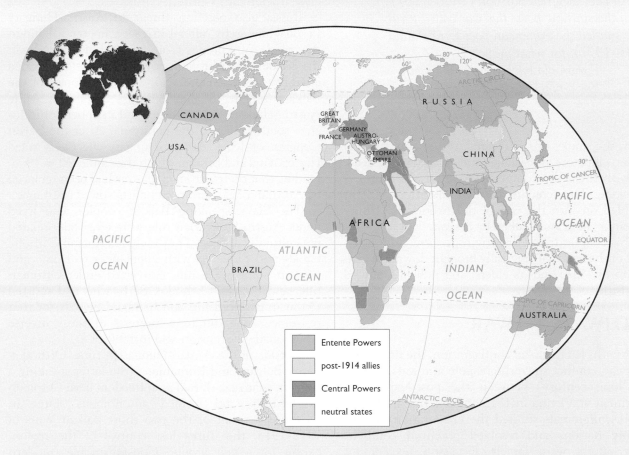

Entente Powers

post-1914 allies

Central Powers

neutral states

KEY QUESTIONS

◆ **Pathways to War:** How did the European states avoid conflict for nearly a century after the Congress of Vienna? What was the triggering event that drove them to war in 1914?

◆ **In the Midst of Battle:** What were the main differences between the kind of warfare on the Western and the Eastern fronts of the war? How important was the war at sea? What effect did the Russian Revolution have on the closing years of the war?

◆ **In Search of Peace:** What were the different intentions of the nations that gathered to discuss the peace settlement? What was the significance of Woodrow Wilson's "Fourteen Points"?

The Generation of 1914 In August 1914, European leaders sent a generation to war. In companies, brigades, and regiments, young men marched off to the cheers of parents, teachers, and kings, their minds set on honor and glory. Instead, they found slaughter, filth, vermin, starvation, and disease. More than 65 million fought. More than 21 million were wounded by bullets, bombs, and poison gas, or mentally ravaged by the horrors concocted by the most advanced civilization on the globe. More than 8 million died— "the unreturning army that was youth," wrote the English poet Siegfried Sassoon (1886–1967), one of the startling poets this war called forth. And, snarled the American poet Ezra Pound (1885–1972), for what purpose?

> For an old bitch gone in the teeth,
> For a botched civilization.

When the smoke finally cleared, the mighty too had fallen—emperors, politicians, and generals were dead, and with them the complacency of an age irretrievably gone. The remnant of the generation of 1914 stumbled on into the rest of the twentieth century without a guide and stalked by despair.

This chapter traces the origins, course, and settlement of the war that tragically brought down the generation of 1914, and its elders, and radically altered the history of the West.

PATHWAYS TO WAR

Many paths led to global conflagration, the first major European conflict since the Napoleonic wars. During the "long century" between the post-Napoleonic settlement at Vienna in 1815 and the first hostilities of 1914, diplomats secured the cooperation of contending nations and resolved potential conflicts. Their efforts were largely successful; except for colonial ventures and brief outbreaks of limited war, Europe was at peace (see Chapters 24, 25). Even so, as the old century turned, threats to peace, at home and in faraway continents, asserted themselves. The furious signing of treaties of alliance, accelerating as the new century turned, testified to mounting political tensions. These radiated from several troublespots. All would figure in the conflict of world war, as Map 26.2 on p. 757 shows.

Hot Spots

In the decades before the outbreak of World War I, the map of the globe was dotted with "hot spots," or danger zones where long resentment and counterposed interests provided fertile ground for conflict.

French and German interests collided in the area west of the Rhine. French leaders and patriots saw the German seizure of the provinces of Alsace and Lorraine following the Franco–Prussian War as a tragic and unforgivable provocation.

Germany also faced a rival to the east. Here Russia, long dependent on western European technology and experts, was beginning to modernize and industrialize. A formidable military power, it had lost face, nevertheless, by its defeats in the Crimea and by the Japanese, and was troubled by revolution in 1905. Russia still looked strong, however, and with its Polish and Ukrainian territories loomed dangerously close to Germany's eastern border.

Russia also posed a threat to Austria-Hungary (a "dual monarchy" after 1867; see Chapter 20) and to the whole of Europe as a result of its policies in the Balkans. As Ottoman power in the region waned after 1699 (see Chapters 15, 20), the peoples of the Balkans sought to gain national autonomy, while Austria-Hungary sought to extend its sphere of influence southward into the peninsula. After the Berlin Congress of 1878, Austria-Hungary effectively ruled Herzegovina and Bosnia, which they annexed in 1908. Finding that their Ottoman masters had been replaced by Austrian ones, Serb nationalists vowed resistance.

The Slavic-speaking Balkan peoples who lived under Austro-Hungarian rule were ethnically related but culturally diverse. They included Roman Catholic Croats and Slovenes with allegiances to Rome and western Europe; Muslims converted under Ottoman rule; and Eastern Orthodox Serbs who had resisted Ottoman overlordship and had paid heavily for that resistance. The different interests of these diverse groups made for tension and instability.

Outside of the Austro-Hungarian zone, Orthodox Serbs, Bulgars, and Romanians (the latter speaking a Romance language), had won freedom from Ottoman overlordship and formed autonomous states in 1878. As a result of the two short Balkan Wars of 1912–1913, the Turks lost control of the region, except for a belt around Constantinople (modern Istanbul). In addition, the boundaries of the Balkan nations were redefined to the disadvantage of Bulgaria and the advantage of Serbia, while Albania and Montenegro gained national autonomy. Thereafter Serbia supported Slav resistance to Austrian rule in Bosnia and Herzegovina. So did that other, much larger Orthodox and Slavic nation—the Russian Empire, protector of Pan-Slavic nationalist aspirations. In the Balkans, nationalism was a disruptive force that drove the world to war.

As Russia supported Pan-Slav objectives in the Balkans, it sought to wrest from the decaying Ottoman sultans their strategic post at Constantinople. Constantinople was one of the world's major ports, strategically positioned at the entrance to the Black Sea from the Mediterranean. It had particular interest

The Onset of War

As war loomed, observers responded variously depending on their nationality, their beliefs, and their occupations. In these three examples, a German theorist welcomes war as ennobling; the British Foreign Secretary outlines apprehensively the risks that lay ahead; and the British philosopher Bertrand Russell, a pacifist, is horror struck by how much ordinary people actually welcomed the excitement and violence of war.

On the eve of war, nationalist and militarist sentiments abounded, as expressed in these words of the German theorist Heinrich von Treitschke (1915): When the State exclaims: My very existence is at stake! Then social self-seeking must disappear and all party hatred be silent. The individual must forget his own ego and feel himself a member of the whole, he must recognize how negligible is his life compared with the good of the whole. Therein lies the greatness of war that the little man completely vanishes before the great thought of the State.
(Heinrich von Treitschke, *Die Politik*, 1915; eds. M. Perry et al, 1995)

On the eve of Britain's declaration of war British Foreign Secretary Sir Edward Grey explains to the House of Commons why war must be fought and what war might bring (August 4, 1914): We have great and vital interests in the independence ... of Belgium. If Belgium is compelled to submit to allow her neutrality to be violated, of course the situation is clear. ... [I]f her [Belgium's] independence goes, the independence of Holland will follow. I ask the House from the point of view of British interests, to consider what may be at stake. If France is beaten ... [and] becomes subordinate to the will and power of one greater than herself ... and if Belgium fell under the same dominating influence, and then Holland, and then Denmark. ... We are going to suffer, I am afraid, terribly in this war whether we are in it or whether we stand aside. ...
(*Hansard's Parliamentary Debates*, 5th Series, vol. 65, 1809–1827)

In London as war is declared, Bertrand Russell, British philosopher and mathematician, is troubled by the bloodthirstiness of the populace (August 15, 1914): Although I did not foresee anything like the full disaster of the war, I foresaw a great deal more than most people did. The prospect filled me with horror, but what filled me with even more horror was the fact that the anticipation of carnage was delightful to something like ninety per cent of the population. ... I had supposed that most people liked money better than almost anything else, but I discovered that they like destruction even better.
(Bertrand Russell, Letter to London's *Nation*, August 15, 1914; eds. M. Perry et al, 1995)

for Russia, whose only warm-water ports lay in the Black Sea, and whose free access through the Dardanelles strait commanded by Constantinople's fortresses was essential for international trade. While Russia had designs on Constantinople, the other European powers, propping up the empty Ottoman suit, worked industriously to keep the city Turkish.

Weakening Ottoman influence prompted European maneuvers at the extremities of the Ottoman Empire as in southeast Europe. In North Africa, European nations now sought to acquire footholds through military or economic means (see Chapter 23). To the west, Spain and France held protectorates in Morocco. In 1905 and 1911, Germany challenged French authority in Morocco with shows of support for Moroccan autonomy. These moves precipitated two crises and drove France and Britain into alliance. In 1911, the Italians invaded Libya in the center of the north African littoral, while Egypt, where British and French financial interests had long competed, was occupied by British troops from 1882, becoming a protectorate in 1914. In the Middle East, Britain and Russia competed for influence in Persia, Iraq, and Afghanistan.

Far to the east, Japan had acquired the Chinese island of Formosa (Taiwan) in the Sino-Japanese war of 1894–1895. Ten years later, in the Russo-Japanese war, it obtained footholds on the Asian continent, in South Manchuria and Kwantung, as well as the southern half of the island of Sakhalin (Karafuto). In 1910, Japan annexed Korea; in 1914, declaring support for the Entente powers when war broke out in Europe, she swiftly seized German protectorates in China: Manchuria, Shandong, and Fujian, as well as several Pacific islands. The Chinese simply acquiesced to the territorial claims Japan announced in the Twenty-One Demands, lands Japan was allowed to retain by the 1919 treaties of Paris (see below). Chinese popular outrage at these losses triggered the student-led May Fourth Movement, a focal point in the later revolutionary politics of that nation (see Chapter 29).

In Europe, meanwhile, political tensions would soon erupt into war. On June 26, 1914, in the Bosnian capital of Sarajevo, a nineteen-year-old terrorist of the secret "Black Hand" society shot the Archduke Franz Ferdinand (1863–1914), fifty-year-old sportsman and heir to the Austrian and Hungarian thrones, and his wife. The assassination gave Austrian diplomats an opportunity to put pressure on Serbia. Encouraged by Germany, Austria issued an ultimatum; Serbia prevaricated, and Austria declared war, provoking Russian mobilization. These rapid exchanges in late July triggered the activation in early

August of the European system of alliances for mutual defense. The Serbian assassination and the Austrian ultimatum together cut the cord. For the next four years, the nations of Europe were at war.

Men and Boys at War

With the onset of war, old and young prepared to fight. The different points of view expressed are examined in *Witnesses* on p. 747. Elderly diplomats and generals, their experience shaped by memories of such conflicts as the Crimean War and colonial campaigns where Europeans easily outgunned native forces, planned to mobilize a generation of young men.

Even the battle plans of the generals were, on the whole, old. Although Europe's military elite had fought few battles during the nineteenth century, they had constructed many battle plans. German planning was especially intense, both because of the traditional militarism of the old Prussian **Junker** generals, and because of Germany's understandable fear of encirclement. Planted in Europe's center, with neither mountains nor seas as buffers, Germans knew that in any war they might have to face an enemy on two fronts, both west and east.

Addressing this difficulty, Alfred von Schlieffen (1833–1913), veteran of the Franco-Prussian war and former chief of the German General Staff, devised by 1905 the most important of Europe's battle plans. Upon his death, in 1913, never having had the opportunity to use it, he bestowed the "Schlieffen plan" upon Field Marshal Helmuth von Moltke (1848–1916), himself a man of advanced age. Von Moltke understood it to be his duty to follow the Schlieffen plan faithfully. The grand design that would determine the destinies of Europe's youth was a decade old.

Other nations had their battle plans, too. The French Plan XVII urged an offensive posture. French generals bellowed—by striking into Alsace and Lorraine and then, from that vantagepoint west of the Rhine, boldly on to Berlin. The British trusted in their new Dreadnought battleships—so named after the first hefty Dreadnought launched in 1906, imposingly armed with heavy-caliber guns—and their traditional naval strength. To support their ally, they would dispatch a small expeditionary force to France. The Austrians had plans, too, but deferred to leadership from Berlin. The Russian army had plans to modernize its weaponry and its communications, goals not yet achieved when war erupted. Its generals sent millions of young peasants off to the front, desperately undersupplied.

In another, subtler way, old men held the fortunes of young men on the eve of world war. In schools and homes, the old taught the young the unhealthy message that their duty to their nation surpassed all other duties, that honor surpassed all other values, and that greatness displayed itself above all on the battlefield.

The pseudo-scientific theories that circulated among late nineteenth-century intellectuals (see Chapters 24, 25) taught that some "races" were superior to others, and that the conflicts of nations, were part of an epochal natural struggle in which the "fittest" would survive. Cultural habits reinforced these beliefs and encouraged an escalating militarism. In the time-honored tradition, boys from elite families played sports as a preparation for war. As though the violent defeat of an adversary could be an elegant game, they strove to fence, hunt, and shoot as gentlemen should, impeccably dressed and in fashion.

When orders for mobilization went up on walls and were broadcast in the newspapers, a generation of young men lined up for battle, democrats, socialists, and former pacifists together. In Britain, they volunteered. Elsewhere, they were drafted. They went in high spirits, cheered on by their mothers, unaware of the horrors they were to face. The war would be over "before the leaves fall," said the pundits in August; before Christmas, at the very latest. The young men left home trusting the words of their elders, and the war plans that lay ready in the desk drawers of graying generals born in an older Europe. Wrote Rudyard Kipling (1865–1936):

> If any question why we died,
> Tell them, because our fathers lied.

The generation of 1914 marched as children to the front. Only half returned whole. When they did return, they too were old, grayed by the memory of slaughter.

IN THE MIDST OF BATTLE

Map 26.1 on p. 749 shows the fronts and major battles of the war. Fronts formed immediately where invaders met defenders, but both sides held their ground. Germany faced France and Britain at the western front, parallel lines of fortified trenches stretching from Switzerland to the English Channel. Germany faced Russia on the eastern front, among ravaged villages, swamps, and forests. On the seas, around the world, merchant ships laden with military hardware and foodstuffs bound for Allied ports ran a gauntlet of German **U-boats** (*Unterseeboote*, or submarines), while British battleships choked off the flow of such goods to German ports. At home, women were employed in munitions factories, making the numberless bullets and bombs needed at the fronts, and hoarded food to feed their children. In Russia, soldiers without food to eat or bullets to defend themselves left the military front for the one back home— the struggle for peace, bread, and land.

Stalemate in the West

The Schlieffen plan called for a rapid, disabling blow at France, making possible the concentration of forces

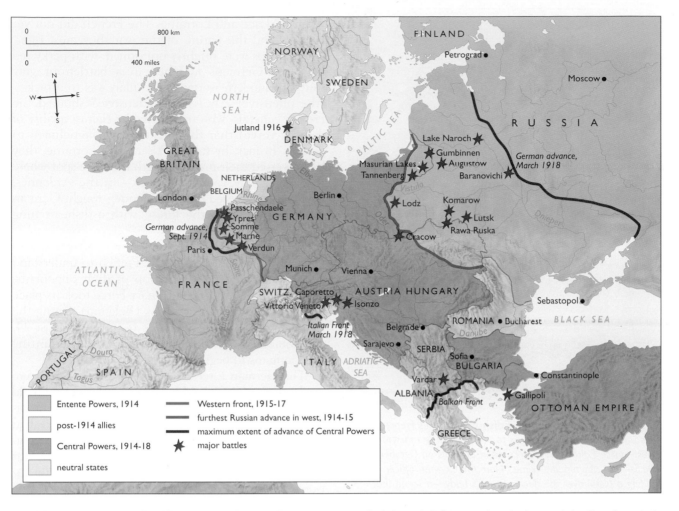

Map 26.1 Europe—A Two-Front War: *After the German army smashed through Belgium and pushed toward the French capital of Paris, war on the western front settled into a stalemate and was fought largely from trenches, with staggering loss of life. The eastern front was a different matter. While also a very deadly affair, war was fought here on the move, with trenches the exception rather than the rule. The Italians, however, were locked in futile combat with the Austrians during 1915 to 1917, fighting eleven battles at the river Isonzo with negligible result. Why did the Western front develop so quickly into a stalemate?*

on the east to deal with Russia, regarded as the major threat. Although France could be reached from Germany by crossing the Rhine and pounding through Alsace and Lorraine, that was not the route Schlieffen prescribed. Instead, he had proposed a giant encirclement of Paris from the north. German forces would cut through Belgium, violating that nation's neutrality, in a vast arc around Paris, edging so close to the coast that, as Schlieffen envisioned it, a soldier on the powerful right flank might "brush the Channel with his sleeve." Having taken Paris, they would swoop eastward to pounce on the French forces who, as it was rightly predicted, would have foolishly charged to Alsace-Lorraine, leaving the heart of their homeland undefended.

It was only a minor obstacle for the German general staff that Belgium was a neutral nation. When Belgium was constituted as a state in 1830, the combined nations of Europe had pledged themselves to protect its neutrality. As they grew aware of German designs, Belgian leaders attempted to convince their

incredulous allies of the impending crisis. By this time, the Germans were already on the move.

The First Moves The great fortifications at Liège, guarding the road to Brussels, were considered the best in Europe. The city was ringed by ramparts, and defended by a garrison; a circle of satellite fortresses surrounded it. It seemed, and should have been, impregnable. But the Belgian army had not yet moved up to defend it. And the Germans came with new long-range guns of an unprecedented destructive capacity. On August 16, 1914, the city surrendered, barely two weeks after the war began. The German invasion thrust on past the Belgian town of Namur, across the river Meuse and into the Ardennes forest.

The German advance through Belgium seemed to display a unique and novel brutality. The resisters who harassed the German advance provoked furious reprisals: the execution of hostages, including women and children, the burning of homes, the slaughter of livestock. At the university town of Louvain, angered

750

Execution of British nurse Edith Cavell: *This French poster calls upon that nation's citizens to remember the martyrdom of British nurse Edith Cavell, executed in Brussels on October 12, 1915—"an abominable crime." Note the German officer holding a pistol over the dead woman's body—a scene that aroused horror in an era when women were held properly to be exempt from the first-hand sufferings of war.*

by snipers, the German command ordered the citizens to be massacred and the city burned. The library was destroyed, a library that had guarded for centuries one of the finest collections in Europe.

The horrors of the German assault on Belgium were exaggerated further in the propaganda reports that circulated in Britain and France and beyond. Press reports, cartoons, and posters told of brutalized infants, and raped and murdered women, including the British nurse Edith Cavell (1865–1915), portrayed above, who was charged with assisting prisoners and refugees and executed in 1915. Propaganda aroused war fever among the allied nations of western Europe.

For by now, they had formally become military allies. For years, the French pressed the British to agree to a defensive treaty; for years, Britain evaded making that commitment. At last, the British recognized the threat to France, and thus to the Channel, and to themselves. How many men must they send the French as a sign of their support? Just one, responded the French, and we shall be sure that he gets killed—for one British soldier dead by a German bayonet would seal the alliance in the popular mind.

In the end, the British sent an expeditionary force across the Channel, while the French sent troops toward Alsace and Lorraine. The French did not yet comprehend the nature of the war they must fight. Their troops were brightly uniformed, with perky red hats; the Germans marched in a battlefront gray suited to modern warfare. The plan was to attack—"the offensive! Always the offensive!" shouted the French generals, who trusted in the *élan* (a quality of dash or verve) that they believed all Frenchmen to possess. In fact, by taking Alsace and Lorraine, they had diverted their main strength from the spot where the real enemy vanguard struck—in the Ardennes, where outnumbered French defenders fought German invaders blindly in the forest, with a disheartening number of casualties.

Meanwhile, the British were slow to arrive, slow to fight, and slower still than the French to understand the strength and determination of their opponents. At last, the British Expeditionary Force took its place alongside the French at Mons (Belgium), facing the right of the German offensive front. By August 24, this combined Allied force was in retreat, permitting the Germans to begin their arc toward Paris.

The German forces that set out on that arc were weaker than they should have been—weaker than old Schlieffen had wished, whose dying injunction was "only keep the right wing strong." Von Moltke had detached some troops to resist the French advance in Alsace-Lorraine, and he permitted one of his best generals to leave the western front and begin operations in the east. As a result, the German right wing did not, as intended, sweep west of Paris to encircle it, but slipped down to the east of the capital.

Informed of the German position, the general in charge of the Paris garrison acted promptly. Requisitioning whatever vehicles could be found—including famously the city's taxis—he sent soldiers from the garrison out to join with regular French forces and meet the Germans. Just thirty-five miles from Paris, on the river Marne, these French forces won on September 5–8 one of the most important Allied victories of the war. They stopped the German advance, denied them Paris, and forced them to retreat. Pushed back forty miles to the river Aisne, the Germans dug a trench, a fortification quickly available wherever there were soldiers with spades.

Digging In Before winter settled in 1914, the line of German trenches stretched from the Aisne north to the Channel, and south past the western face of Alsace to the Swiss border. Opposite those 466 miles of German fortifications stretched a parallel line of trenches dug with French and British spades. From 1914 until 1918, that line scarcely moved, though brave men on both sides hurled themselves repeatedly across the "no-man's land" that lay between the two lines of trenches. In 1915, French offensives in the north gained no ground. In February 1916, the Germans struck mightily at the border fortress of

The 1905 uprising, a scene from Battleship Potemkin, 1925

The assault on the Winter Palace, Petrograd 1917

Above, a scene from Sergei Eisenstein's 1925 film Battleship Potemkin—conceived as part of a film cycle to tell the story of the revolution—commemorates a failed 1905 uprising. Here, the film's most famous scene is shown—the panic on the Odessa Steps as troops open fire on the crowd.

In Petrograd (now, as it was before, St. Petersburg) in 1917, the masses of the people had spilled out into the street. A woman's food riot in winter led to the tsar's abdication and the institution of a Provisional Government. In the spring, the Bolshevik revolutionary Vladimir Ilich Lenin arrived, won the allegiance of the surging crowds of soldiers and sailors and workers, and in November led the charge on the Tsar's Winter Palace—the decisive blow which delivered a radical faction control of a vast state. Once won, it had to be defended against armies in the field and enemies of the state within. Below, in Moscow's Red Square, Lenin addresses the troops responsible for defending the new Bolshevik regime against separatist and Tsarist rivals.

How was Lenin's leadership different from that of the tsars who were expelled?

Lenin addresses the troops in Red Square, 1917

To continue your investigation of this topic, please go to www.prenhall.com/king for the related **WINDOWS** on the **WEB** activity

751

Verdun, killing so many French soldiers that their proclaimed goal to "bleed France white" seemed fulfilled. Yet in this protracted battle that engaged 2 million men, the "victors" suffered casualties nearly as high (350,000) as the French "losers" (400,000).

In July 1916, the British countered with a huge offensive along an eighteen-mile front on the river Somme, memorialized by the song in *Witnesses* on p. 753. Here preliminary bombardment by the British guns ripped up the ground, slowing their own men's assault across a stretch of no-man's land while fully exposed to German machine guns. Those British soldiers who did reach the German line were trapped and shot down on the barbed wire. In the first day of battle alone, over fifty percent of the British force of 110,000 were casualties; nearly twenty percent died.

By the end of the Somme offensive, the tally sheet of casualties was again nearly even: 620,000 British and French to 650,000 Germans. The next year, the news was worse. In 1917, half the French army mutinied when, after another failed offensive, yet another was ordered. Launching a third offensive from the same Belgian town of Ypres that had seen terrible slaughter in 1914 and 1915, the British hurled themselves suicidally at the Germans at Passchendaele (Belgium)—and gained four miles. The German generals who resisted them began, for the first time, to despair of winning.

From 1914 to 1918, there was stalemate on the western front, where millions of corpses lay buried, some in the trenches they had defended. The trenches, as deep as men were tall, sheltered soldiers on an open field and fortified their position. Trench warfare was not new: it had been used by Napoleon's soldiers, and by both Northern and Southern forces in the American Civil War. But the trench was the hallmark of the western front, where men battled for a few more yards of ground beyond the enemy's entrenched position. If those few yards were taken, a new trench was dug, perhaps to be surrendered to the enemy when he counter-attacked.

In all, some 25,000 miles of trench scarred the elongated front, dug in parallel networked systems between a few yards and a mile apart. The most advanced German position, achieved early in the war, yielded to an Allied advance only when fresh American divisions arrived late in 1917. In the final campaigns of 1918, the now superior Entente forces pushed the Germans back to the Belgian border.

British, French, and German soldiers ate, slept, and passed time in the trenches—aware that, in safe positions to the rear, their generals dined well and plotted out the battle with sets of colored pins. Conditions were repellent: mud and excrement, rats and lice (no one escaped the lice, thus all the soldiers were "lousy"—the original meaning of that term),

Soldiers and horses in gas masks: *Among the horrifying innovations of World War I combat was the use of nerve gas by both sides to gain an advantage over the enemy in the stalemate of trench warfare. This scene of German soldiers, equipped with gas masks, riding their horses, also equipped with protective muzzles, presents an almost unbearably ironic contrast between traditional warfare conducted with horse-drawn carts and modern, total war, waged without mercy by machine-propelled cannisters of toxic agents.*

At the Front

The shocked reactions to battlefield horrors come to us from an enormous literature of poems, diaries, and letters written in the midst of war, of which a few are excerpted here. They speak vividly of the pain of seeing young men die, the lack of awareness and self-absorption of leaders, the absurdity of patriotic sentiments that once seemed noble, the immense courage of the ordinary soldier, and the inability of those far from the front to understand the immensity of the tragedy.

English soldier and poet Wilfred Owen describes a German gas attack (1915):
Gas! GAS! Quick, boys! – An ecstasy of fumbling,
Fitting the clumsy helmets just in time;
But someone still was yelling out and stumbling,
And flound'ring like a man in fire or lime …
Dim, through the misty panes and thick green light,
As under a green sea, I saw him drowning.

In all my dreams, before my helpless sight,
He plunges at me, guttering, choking, drowning.

If in some smothering dreams you too could pace
Behind the wagon that we flung him in,
And watch the white eyes writhing in his face,
His hanging face, like a devil's sick of sin;
If you could hear, at every jolt, the blood
Come gargling from the froth-corrupted lungs,
Obscene as cancer, bitter as the cud
Of vile, incurable sores on innocent tongues,
My friend, you would not tell with such high zest,
To children ardent for some desperate glory
The old lie: *Dulce et decorum est*
Pro patria mori*.
[*"Pleasing and right it is to die for one's country."]
(Wilfred Owen, "Dulce et Decorum est …," 1915; ed. S. Sassoon, 1920)

Song sung by the British troops who took their positions on July 1, 1916 for the battle of the Somme, in which thousands were slaughtered:
We beat them on the Marne,
We beat them on the Aisne,
  We gave them hell
  At Neuve Chapelle
And here we are again!
(From M. Gilbert, *The First World War: A Complete History*, 1994)

Czech draftee Jaroslav Hasek remembers his commanding officer, with no fondness (c. 1914):
Apparently by way of encouraging the rank and file … [the commanding officer] asked where the young recruit came from, how old he was, and whether he had a watch. The young recruit … said he hadn't got one, whereupon the aged general gave a fatuous smile … and said, "That's fine, that's fine," whereupon he honored a young corporal, who was standing near, by asking him whether his wife was well.

"Beg to report, sir," bawled the corporal, "I'm not married."

Whereupon the general, with a patronizing smile, repeated, "That's fine, that's fine."

Then the general, lapsing still further [into] senile infantility, asked Captain Sagner to show him how his troops numbered off in twos from the right, and after a while, he heard them yelling, "One-two, one-two, one-two."

The aged general was very fond of this. At home he had two orderlies, and he used to line them up in front of him and make them number off: "One-two, one-two."

Austria had lots of generals like this.
(Jaroslav Hasek, *The Good Soldier Schweik*, c. 1914; ed. P. Selver, 1963)

A German soldier writes home from the trenches (1915): Our regiment has been transferred to this dangerous spot, Souchez. No end of blood has already flowed. … A week ago the 142nd attacked and took four trenches from the French. It is to hold these trenches that we have been brought here. … This letter has been interrupted no end of times. Shells began to pitch close to us—great English 12-inch ones. … One … struck the next house and buried four men, who were got out … horribly mutilated. I saw them and it was ghastly!

Everybody must now be prepared for death in some form or other. … [T]he newspapers have probably given you a different impression. They tell only of our gains and say nothing of the blood that has been shed, of the cries of agony that never cease. The newspaper doesn't give any description either of *how* the "heroes" are laid to rest. … [U]p here … one throws the bodies out of the trench and lets them lie there, or scatters dirt over the remains of those which have been torn to pieces by shells.
(Alfons Ankenbrand in A. F. Wedd, ed., *German Students' War Letters*, 1929)

Slaughter and horror are far from the mind of English poet Jessie Pope as she celebrates the women who will "keep their end up" until the khaki-uniformed soldiers come home (1916):
There's the girl who clips your ticket for the train,
  And the girl who speeds the lift from floor to floor,
There's the girl who does a milk-round in the rain,
  And the girl who calls for orders at your door.
    Strong, sensible, and fit,
    They're out to show their grit,
  And tackle jobs with energy and knack.
    No longer caged and penned up,
    They're going to keep their end up
Till the khaki soldier boys come marching back.
(Jessie Pope, "War Girls," 1916; ed. C. W. Reilly, 1981)

***Paul Nash*, We are Making a New World:** *Paul Nash's painting from 1918 of the battlefield near Ypres (Belgium), sardonically entitled* We Are Making a New World, *describes vividly with grotesquely exaggerated forms the devastation wrought by constant and massive bombardment.* (Imperial War Museum, London)

tedium, and fear. Ordered to attack, they climbed out of the trenches and went "over the top" across "no-man's land," in the face of enemy fire, as a German soldier describes in *Witnesses* on p. 753. That mad charge of exposed men against an enemy's fortified position, repeated again and again over four years, explains the resulting slaughter.

If the trench defined the war's western front, it was not its only military characteristic. Machine guns firing 600 rounds a minute were concentrated in nests that could annihilate waves of charging infantry. Developed by American inventors Richard Gatling (1818–1903) and Hiram Maxim (1840–1916), these guns were employed in colonial wars to wreak devastation on native armies. They caused high losses in Europe as well. "Three men and a machine gun can stop a battalion of heroes," observed a French general of the battle at Verdun.

Barbed wire, used on American ranches, helped defend the lines of trenches. Enemy soldiers had to stop and cut wire before they could continue their charge. As they worked, howitzers lobbed shells at them from distant, unseen positions. Explosive grenades varied in shape, range, and deadliness. Poison gas, a recent invention first used by the Germans in 1915 but quickly imitated, disabled the enemy who could then be overcome, or evaded, by masked troops—or such was the intention; in fact the flow of gas could not be controlled and often disabled the users. The poet Wilfred Owen describes a gas attack in *Witnesses* on p. 753. The British developed tanks, heavily armored vehicles that crawled on caterpillar treads over trenches, wire, and ground churned up by bombardment. Both sides used airplanes for reconnaissance; the Germans were the first to set machine guns to shoot in rhythm with the rotation of the propeller. Zeppelin airships dropped bombs on enemy cities. As the instruments of death multiplied, the numbers of the dead mounted.

The Eastern Steamroller

The eastern front was another scene of carnage. Here Austrian and German infantry faced the immense army of the Russian Empire, one of the world's four most populous nations. The rest of Europe regarded Russia as an enormous military steamroller that could burst out of the east and unstoppably roll westward. In reality, the Russian soldiers, who were mostly peasants, set out to war with too little food, and too few boots and bullets. And the Russian officers, all nobles, were a mixed lot of the heroic, the undisciplined, and the treacherous. Within a few months of the start of warfare in the east, the steamroller had paused, and Russia was in peril. By 1917, its prospects had become desperate.

In the summer of 1914 in Petrograd (formerly St. Petersburg, renamed that year), Russian officers gallantly welcomed the war. Spurred by Pan-Slavic enthusiasm, and French persuasion, they marched promptly to battle. Too promptly; for the Russians were unprepared. Their supply lines were unready (and hampered in any case by their rail lines, constructed to a different gauge than those in western Europe) and their supplies were inadequate.

Yet the Russian army's first strike had been successful—they won the battle of Gumbinnen over a small German army on August 20—and their swift penetration of the German **salient** in eastern Prussia alarmed von Moltke. Contrary to Schlieffen's principles, the German commander detached from the western campaign one of his most competent younger generals (not yet fifty), Erich Ludendorff (1865–1937), prominent in the capture of Liège, and sent him along with Paul von Hindenburg (1847–1934), aged sixty-seven, an elderly hero plucked out of retirement, to block the forward thrust of the Russian steamroller.

The Russian generals made it easy for the Germans. Not only did they send hungry men and starved horses to the front lines, but they broadcast to each other uncoded messages detailing their positions that the German radio corps happily intercepted. The Germans delivered the uncoordinated Russian armies a crushing defeat at the Battle of Tannenberg (August 26–31). The war had barely begun, and Russia's failed Prussian offensive cost around 250,000 casualties—a fraction of the bloodletting still to come that would leave nearly 2 million of Russia's 12 million soldiers dead.

The following January (1915), Germany's Austrian allies attacked a Russian army in the Carpathian Mountains on the Hungarian border. A winter war at those elevated altitudes brought new miseries—both guns and fingers froze. In the spring, the Germans arrived to do the job their allies could not, driving the Russians 100 miles back from the front. Having secured east Prussia on the north of the eastern front, and taken the Carpathians on the south, the victorious Germans pushed through the center of Poland beyond Warsaw to Brest-Litovsk. By the end of 1915, a new front ran from the Baltic to the Black Sea, leaving much of Russia's richest territory under German command.

The butchery continued. On the Russian side, generals and commanders were disgraced and replaced, while trainloads of fresh conscripts arrived at the front to freeze, starve, and bleed. On the German side, Hindenburg and Ludendorff were relentless.

In 1916, the energetic Russian general Aleksey Alekseyevich Brusilov (1853–1926) launched a serious offensive on the south of the front into Austrian Galicia and German-occupied Poland. In 1917, as the Germans pushed back in an offensive that, by 1918, brought them deep into the interior, Russian soldiers mutinied. In Petrograd, revolution was afoot. In March 1917, the Petrograd workers' Soviet (or council) issued Army Order No. 1. Those in the ranks, it stated, need no longer obey their commanders, but should form committees and take power into their own hands. Soldiers streamed home from the front, disgusted with war and ready to throw their lot in with the revolution (see below).

The Russian military disaster was complicated by the nature of the army. The British and French armies (the German and Austrian less so) were effectively popular, or citizen armies, whereas the Russian army reflected a more traditional society. The officers were nobles and the soldiers peasants. They shared an allegiance to the tsar and a profound religious tradition. But history divided them. The peasants had always obeyed, whether on the land or at the front, and the nobles commanded. The slaughter at the front, combined with starvation and disease, awakened in peasant conscripts the thought that perhaps they would obey no longer.

South of the Russian positions on the eastern front, Austro-Hungarian forces (with German assistance or, often, direction) battled in the Balkans and in Italy. Bulgaria and the Ottoman Empire had leagued with the Central Powers. Between these nations and the Austrian border lay Romania and Serbia, which joined the Entente, as did Greece, tempted by promises of key chunks of Ottoman territory at the war's end. By 1916, overcoming stiff resistance from Slav Serbs and Romanians, the Central Powers controlled the whole Balkan Peninsula north of Greece.

Further west lay Italy, which had secretly negotiated a favorable treaty with Britain and France which detached them from their prior allegiance to the Central Powers. Italian armies battled to regain the *terra irredenta* ("unredeemed land") arching north along the Adriatic toward Trieste which, their leaders held, was rightfully Italian. Eleven times they faced an Austro-German force at the Isonzo river from June 1915 to May 1917, where more than 500,000 Italians were wounded or killed while edging only a little closer to the Adriatic. Even that progress was reversed, when they were pushed back seventy-five miles from Caporetto to regroup only twenty miles from Venice; from there, in 1918, they plunged on to win, at last, a victory at Vittorio Veneto. With the eventual peace settlement, Italy recovered her *terra irredenta*, at the cost of hundreds of thousands of irredeemable lives.

At Sea and Abroad

Prior to World War I, the British navy was the most powerful in the world, and the British trusted it to shield their nation from European conflicts. But over the previous two decades, the Germans had begun to construct a naval force that rivaled Britain's, equipped with battleships that were modern and almost unsinkable. Alarmed, the British responded by developing the Dreadnought, launched in 1906, the fiercest battleship ever constructed, equipped with ten heavy guns of unprecedented 12-inch size.

Over the next years, German and British shipyards raced to build more ships on its pattern. At the same time, the Germans developed a fleet of more than 100 submarines (an American innovation) or U-boats. Capable of slipping secretly in and out of ports, their torpedoes threatened the enemy's mighty Dreadnoughts and the merchant carriers of its suppliers.

The big ships had few opportunities to meet each other in battle. They did so in only one significant open battle, at Jutland, off Denmark, in the North Sea on May 31, 1916. The British lost more ships and more men, but the Germans fled; the battle had no clear result. More serious than such encounters was the war of attrition in northern seas. In the North and Baltic seas, British ships blocked supplies—foodstuffs as well as military goods—from reaching German ports. British ships also brought European armies to fight the allies of the Central Powers in the Middle East, and to dismantle Germany's colonial empire, while distant Japan, an Allied power, seized German protectorates in the Chinese provinces of Shandong and Manchuria.

The blockade choked Germany and Austria-Hungary, whose citizens were near starvation by 1917. The Germans in return aimed to stop the flow of goods to British and Allied ports, targeting especially the richly-laden ships of the neutral United States (as that nation sought to retain its neutrality while continuing to reap profits from its Atlantic trade with European powers on both sides). In these attempts, the submarine was their best and only tool.

On May 7, 1915, a German U-boat sank the British liner *Lusitania* in the Irish Sea, as a result of which 1200 persons died (including 128 United States citizens). It was found to contain (although the United States denied it) American-produced ammunition bound for Allied use, encouraging Germany to view the United States as a potential enemy. In 1916, when more Americans were wounded in the

WHO'S WHO

"Winners and Losers"

Archduke Franz Ferdinand (1863–1914), heir to the Austrian and Hungarian thrones, assassinated on June 26, 1914, by a Serbian terrorist.

Helmuth von Moltke (1848–1916), German Field Marshal, inherited the Schlieffen Plan which directed the German advance through Belgium to France in 1914.

Edith Cavell (1865–1915), British nurse, charged with assassinating prisoners and refugees and executed by a German officer in 1915.

Rosa Luxemburg (1870–1919), a founder of the Polish socialist party, later German socialist leader, imprisoned in Germany for opposition to the war, and killed in 1919 during Spartacist (communist) uprising against the new government that had been installed at the war's end.

Woodrow Wilson (1856–1924), US President who, though he had campaigned against his country's involvement in the war, sent US soldiers to fight in Europe and, in 1918, worked vainly to negotiate a peace in line with the ideals expressed in his "Fourteen Points."

sinking of the French ship *Sussex*, President Woodrow Wilson (1856–1924) protested vigorously, eliciting a pledge from the Germans to renounce such tactics. In January 1917, nevertheless, Germany declared a policy of unrestricted submarine warfare against Allied shipping, and acted upon it. Until a convoy system was instituted in May of that year, one-fourth of all British ships that left port were sunk, as were one-fourth of all those seeking to make port.

Germany's U-boat tactics misfired. Now Britain was able to convince the United States that the Germans displayed a perfidy that could not be ignored with safety. Isolationist, pacifist, and even pro-German sentiments eventually yielded to such arguments. On April 6, 1917, the United States Congress declared war, sending the first United States forces (of an eventual total of about 4 million mobilized) to Europe the following summer.

Meanwhile, the war had expanded to other theaters. All the French and most British leaders thought it should be fought and won on the western front. Some British strategists, however, argued for pursuing hostile objectives further away from home. They would thus weaken their opponents on the European fronts, and at the same time secure some fine colonial territories abroad.

Their first objective was the Ottoman Empire, now under a military despotism headed by the Young Turks (see Chapter 24). The Ottoman navy attacked Russia's Black Sea ports in October 1914 and closed the Dardanelles straits in November, blocking Russia's access to the Mediterranean. A British strike at the Dardanelles would support their ally, and at the same time serve to protect British interests in the Mediterranean. In 1915, the British sent thirteen battleships and more than 400,000 men (mostly colonial troops from Australia and New Zealand) to take the straits. The infantry landed at Gallipoli, fought and lost horribly to Turkish defenders, and were forced to evacuate late in 1915 and early in 1916, after suffering casualties of fifty percent.

Assisted by the forces of rebellious Arabs from the Hejaz (the coastal region of the Arabian Peninsula), the British also fought Turkish armies in Palestine and Mesopotamia, eventually capturing Damascus and Baghdad. From the Mediterranean, the war spilled over to Africa and east Asia, where Germany's various colonies and protectorates fell to Britain (assisted by South African soldiers in Africa) or allied Japan (in China).

In still another way, the wider world contributed to the war centered in Europe. From all parts of the globe, the colonies supplied pack animals and automobiles, tools and blankets, guns and bullets. Colonial soldiers—from Senegal and South Africa, India, Australia, New Zealand, Canada, and Moroccoz fought alongside Europeans. More than 2 million were casualties.

Map 26.2 A World at War: *The truly global nature of World War I can be seen here. Note particulary the site of battles that took place in Germany's various African colonial holdings. Was World War I in fact the first world war?*

At Home

As the European conflict spread around the globe, changes were occurring at home. The demand for military supplies sent women into the factories. Capital, too, was put to work, as bankers, speculators, and smugglers aided the army in prosecuting the war. These changes were meant to last for the duration. Their effects were far greater and longer.

War meant an accelerated demand for virtually everything that factories produced—textiles for uniforms, blankets, and bandages in addition to normal civilian use; metals, machines, and tools; weapons and ammunition (see *How Many?*, p. 758); packaged and canned food and, for the blockaded Central Powers, food substitutes. War production required the service of bankers, who floated loans for the new factories and the purchase of supplies, and reaped their interest on the huge sales of factory products. As huge quantities of goods needed to be distributed within each country and abroad, more investment was required to fund packaging and transportation. On an unprecedented scale, money circulated to sustain the war effort.

As the diagram on p. 758 shows, stepped-up war production meant the mass employment of millions of women, many of whom had never before been wage-earners. Women stood in assembly lines to make guns and shells, drove trucks, collected tickets, and read gas meters (see *Witnesses*, p. 753). Jobs that once were filled only by the poor, male or female, were now often held by middle-class women, whose social awareness expanded. Many later became involved in social movements to remedy the conditions of work and home life for the laboring class.

Exposure to the world of work triggered changes in women's behavior and outlook. For the first time in the history of the West, women's skirts rose above their ankles. The fashion for voluminous petticoats and crinolines of not so long ago disappeared, along with stifling corsets, to be replaced by flowing clothes that followed the lines of the body. Women publicly took up smoking and drinking, stayed out late unescorted, and walked briskly and alone through the streets of the city. It was a modern woman who emerged from the war years, independent in outlook, and often of necessity, with the death of so many young men, self-supporting.

While many women worked in factories, others supported the war effort by working as nurses. Once the province of the religious orders, nursing had recently become a modern, secular profession—a transformation largely due to the pioneering work of one determined upper-class British woman, Florence Nightingale (1820–1910), who had volunteered to serve in a hospital in Scutari (in Turkey) during the Crimean War. As in other pre-modern wars, disease was as much a killer as gunfire: thousands died from infected wounds, cholera, and dysentery. Nightingale introduced standards for sanitation, acquired funding for proper equipment and medications, and trained other women to attend properly to the needs of the ill and wounded. Her example would be followed in the American Civil War by Clara Barton (1821–1912); and during World War I by the courageous, mostly privileged women who staffed the field hospitals erected immediately adjacent to the killing fields and cared for the dying, wounded, and diseased men sent back from the front lines.

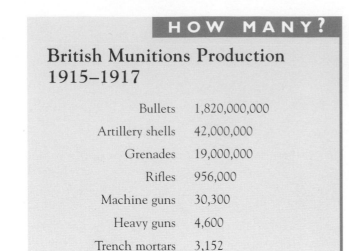

British Munitions Production 1915–1917

Bullets	1,820,000,000
Artillery shells	42,000,000
Grenades	19,000,000
Rifles	956,000
Machine guns	30,300
Heavy guns	4,600
Trench mortars	3,152

Among other features of life on the home front was the demoralization which followed upon the news of the mounting dead, when nearly every family lost a son, a father, a cousin, or a friend. The stresses of wartime encouraged behaviors that would have been condemned before 1914—heavy drinking and high rates of out-of-wedlock births. Food and other shortages meant rationing, price controls, and standing in line. Speculators profited from the shortages, and many became rich acquiring and selling such commodities as oil or rubber.

The mass mobilization required for world war had to be supported by the will of the whole nation—as the French revolutionary wars had been by drafted soldiers and commoner officers. Armies relied on conscripts (and in Britain, at the start, on volunteers), who could only be activated if their families stood behind the effort. Those families, safely at home, faced privations, too—especially in central Europe, where the peoples of the blockaded nations were starving by 1917. It was essential that the public of the combatant nations receive the right information—not always true information—circulated to the public in newspapers, through posters, and in broadcast speeches. Information, often sliding into propaganda, was a necessity on the home front. It was supplied by newswriters and war correspondents, whose new profession dated from the Crimean War.

Not all the news during the war years came from the battlefront. Much was going on at home. In Britain, the Liberal candidate David Lloyd George (1863–1945) became Prime Minister in a coalition government in 1916. Elsewhere, social democratic parties and labor organizations protested the war, at least at the outset—for many socialists believed, erroneously, that workers united to overthrow the capitalist order would never fire on each other. In Germany, the women pacifists and socialists Clara Zetkin (1857–1933) and Rosa Luxemburg (1870–1919) were imprisoned for their opposition to the war. Dutch socialists summoned an international peace conference. The French suffered a soldiers' mutiny, but German presence on their soil ultimately restored solidarity. Food shortages in Germany (caused by the British naval blockade) resulted in food riots in 1916, and the deaths of about 750,000 citizens by war's end. Domestic tensions, meanwhile, reached serious levels in Russia, which had already sacrificed millions of men to the butchery of the eastern front, when the soldiers made it known they would go on no longer.

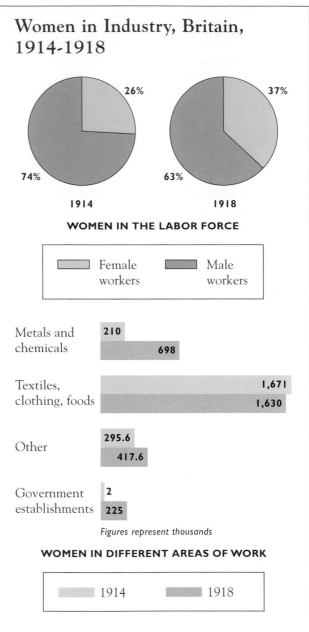

Women in Industry, Britain, 1914-1918

WOMEN IN THE LABOR FORCE

1914: 26% Female workers, 74% Male workers
1918: 37% Female workers, 63% Male workers

Female workers — Male workers

	1914	1918
Metals and chemicals	210	698
Textiles, clothing, foods	1,671	1,630
Other	295.6	417.6
Government establishments	2	225

Figures represent thousands

WOMEN IN DIFFERENT AREAS OF WORK

1914   1918

Labor shortages created by the mobilization of men for war brought huge numbers of women into a variety of employments during 1914–1918. Once hostilities ceased, however, the bulk of these new jobs disappeared again.
Source: Women in Industry: Report of the War Cabinet Committee on Women in Industry *(London: His Majesty's Stationery Office, 1919).*

Russia Turns Back

In Russia, as further west, the factories roared furiously to produce armaments and supplies for the soldiers at the front. Russian industrialization had progressed rapidly in the generation before 1914 (see Chapter 21), and millions of workers—fully one-third of them women—crowded into the poorer districts of Moscow and Petrograd. However, as famine struck an already restive peasantry, production quotas drove the workers, and wounded or renegade soldiers returned from the front with tales of starvation and mayhem, the conditions for revolution crystallized. By the end of the single thunderous year of 1917, tsarist monarchy had yielded to a communist dictatorship.

The 1905 Revolution These things might have happened otherwise if the tsar had responded differently to the upheaval of 1905. But Tsar Nicholas II (r. 1894–1918) learned to rule from his predecessor, Alexander III (r. 1881–1894), who had pursued a dual policy of the repression of political enemies and the Russification of ethnic minorities—policies resulting in a succession of riots and pogroms (see Chapter 24) and the exile or execution of radical intellectuals.

Succeeding to the monarchy in 1894, Nicholas was determined to uphold the tsarist system of terror and repression. Backed up by the army, the secret police, obsequious ministers, the fanatically nationalist Black Hundreds, and an imperious, apparently hysterical wife—the German-born Alexandra (1872–1918), granddaughter of Britain's Queen Victoria—he met the demands for reform posed in 1905 uncomprehendingly and inflexibly.

In 1905, with Russian military failure in the war with Japan as somber backdrop, the demands of liberal nobles and bourgeois for a national parliament on the western European model coincided with the petitions of workers for political reform. In January, a group of the 100,000 factory workers then on strike in St. Petersburg presented to the tsar at his Winter Palace their petition for better working conditions and the right to unionize. The police ordered the workers to disperse; they refused. The police fired, killing about 100 people, including women and children. This "Bloody Sunday" massacre triggered strikes and rebellions throughout Russia.

Advised by his reform-minded chief minister, Sergei Witte (1849–1915), who urged concessions to the progressive agenda, Nicholas issued his October Manifesto. It called for the formation of a national representative assembly, or **Duma**, to be chosen by universal male suffrage. In addition, it permitted the formation of local and municipal councils, and allowed freedom of the press. Further unrest in December, however, and the return of the army from Asia, encouraged the tsar to take back many of his concessions. He ordered workers' leaders arrested and

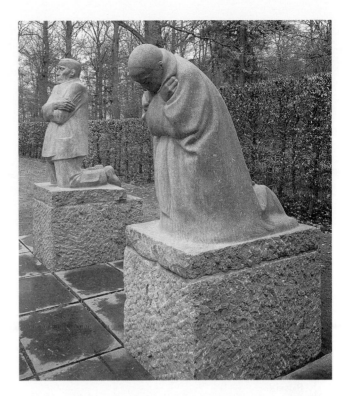

***Käthe Kollwitz*, Die Eltern (The Parents):** *As mothers, women mourned the millions of their sons, an unprecedented toll, who died terrifying deaths far from home. One such mother was the German artist Käthe Kollwitz, who tried to salve her grief after the conflict was over by producing a sculpture of the two stricken parents at their son's grave, forever weeping stone tears in his memory.*

minority uprisings suppressed, while unleashed forces of repression engaged in renewed anti-Semitic pogroms (see Chapter 24).

Nevertheless, the Duma met the following April (1906). Its largely liberal representatives (the more radical Social Democratic and Social Revolutionary delegates refused to participate) pressed for agrarian and political reform. To limit these reformist moves, the tsar created an upper assembly, of whom half the members were obedient appointees. When the Duma protested, it was dissolved. A second, more conservative Duma was elected. It, too, was dissolved. A third Duma elected in 1907 continued to press ineffectively for reform. Meanwhile, the reformist Witte had been dismissed and replaced by the more conservative chief minister Peter Stolypin (1862–1911).

In 1911, Stolypin himself was assassinated, having marked himself as too liberal by introducing reforms that allowed enterprising peasants (called *kulaks*) to establish their own farms. Nicholas retreated further into his circle of conservative supporters, who urged an ongoing campaign of repression and Russification and maintained a stubborn ignorance of the great storm that was brewing. Liberals and progressives chafed, while socialists of various shades of opinion discussed revolution.

Military Expenditures of the Great Powers, 1890 and 1914

	Year	Total Defense Expenditure ($ millions)	Cost per Capita Home Population
Japan	1890	24	0.6
	1914	96	1.75
Germany	1890	144	2.95
	1914	554	8.52
British Empire	1890	157	4.03
	1914	384	8.53
France	1890	186	4.87
	1914	287	7.33
Russia	1890	145	1.32
	1914	442	2.58
US	1890	67	1.06
	1914	314	3.20

The massive mobilization of people and resources in World War I meant a reorientation of economies and huge financial burdens on the citizenry. As this table shows, the increase in military costs per capita in wartime (1914 figure) ranged from about 150 percent (France) to about 300 percent (Japan and US) of their cost in peacetime (1890 figure).
Source: W. S. Morton, Japan: Its History and Culture, 3rd ed. (New York: McGraw Hill, 1994), p. 182.

Factions and Visionaries   Between 1905 and 1917, Russian political parties were active and multifarious. They shared a determined opposition to tsarist autocracy (the latter supported by the high clergy and conservative nobles, along with officials whose loyalty had been purchased with privileges); otherwise they disagreed.

They were arrayed in three main groups. The first included the progressive nobles and bourgeois, professionals and liberal intellectuals, of whom the foremost were the Kadets (Constitutional Democrats), who aimed to establish a constitutional monarchy on European models. The second consisted of the several socialist parties intent on land reform (addressing the still unresolved condition of the eighty-five percent of Russia's population composed of former serfs), of which the best known were the Social Revolutionaries. The third group was that of the

Marxist parties, who advanced the revolutionary potential of industrial workers (the proletariat; see Chapters 23, 25). These included the pacifist Internationalists, and the Marxian Social Democrats, themselves split into **Bolshevik** (meaning "majority," as this faction once held a majority at the 1903 party congress) and **Menshevik** (meaning "minority") factions. Other revolutionary groups also proliferated, including those of the anarchists (see Chapter 25). The different parties produced their own newspapers to interpret political events for their readership. These were produced irregularly and distributed secretly, evading the censors.

Russian politics were further complicated by the fact that most of the revolutionary leaders were not in Russia. By 1900, the Okhrana, the tsarist secret police, had tracked most of them and seen them banished to Siberia. Once released, they often sought refuge in London, Brussels, or Zurich. From these cities, they published articles of political analysis for the party press or telegraphed instructions to

WHO'S WHO

Russia: Makers of Revolution

Nicholas II (r. 1894–1918), Tsar of Russia, head of a repressive regime, ardent supporter of the war, he was away at the front when revolution broke out in St. Petersburg; subsequently imprisoned and murdered by the revolutionary regime.

Grigorii Rasputin (1872–1916), charismatic, probably fraudulent mystic and healer, protected by Tsarina Alexandra through whom he manipulated policy decisions until he was finally murdered by aristocratic opponents.

Alexander Kerensky (1881–1970), moderate social democrat who led the Provisional Government of Russia upon the Tsar's abdication, and was himself ousted by Lenin in the October Revolution (November 6, 1917).

Vladimir Ilyich Ulyanov, known as "Lenin" (1870–1924), leader while in exile of the Bolshevik faction of Marxian social democrats, who returned to Russia (with German assistance) in 1917 and soon took up leadership of the young revolution.

Lev Davidovich Bronstein, known as "Trotsky" (1879–1940), returned to Russia in 1917 from exile in the US and joined forces with Lenin; organizer of the Red Army and negotiator of the Treaty of Brest-Litovsk; murdered in 1940 at the command of Lenin's successor Stalin (see Chapter 28).

colleagues in St. Petersburg, and met with leaders of like-minded European parties at international congresses. Supported by party funds, parental largesse, or their own labor, they lived this existence of political exile for decades on end.

Such was the career pattern of Vladimir Ilyich Ulyanov (1870–1924), who adopted the revolutionary pseudonym "Lenin," the leader of the Bolshevik faction of Marxian social democrats. He is portrayed on p. 751. Radicalized by the execution in 1887 of his older brother, charged under Alexander III with participating in an assassination plot, Lenin committed himself to the career of professional revolutionary.

Arrested and exiled in 1895, Lenin departed in 1900 for Switzerland. A brilliant theorist as well as an active conspirator, Lenin produced analyses of capitalism and imperialism, and blueprints for revolution that adapted Marx to the circumstances of the Russian Empire. The essential points were outlined in his *What Is To Be Done?* (1902), quoted in *Witnesses* on p. 762. Revolution could be achieved in Russia, and a proletarian state created, but not by the workers alone. A disciplined **cadre**, or core group of committed and educated leaders, would lead the rank and file of workers, who would join with the peasantry (for Lenin, an unformed and unreliable group) to dethrone autocracy and create a revolutionary society.

Another exile who became a prominent leader of the Bolshevik revolt was Lev (Leon) Davidovich Bronstein (1879–1940), who adopted the pseudonym "Trotsky." In 1917, when news of mounting crisis arrived, he was living in the United States. Returning immediately to Petrograd, he joined with the Menshevik faction and became active as a leader of the Petrograd **Soviet**, an informal association of workers' councils. The Mensheviks hoped to work through such councils so as to be ready to act once bourgeois liberals had formed a constitutional government. As the events of 1917 unfolded, however, Trotsky joined with Lenin and the Bolsheviks.

Precipitating the Crisis The revolutionary year 1917 was preceded by the crisis of leadership of 1916, itself provoked by the experience of war. The tsar himself decided to go to the front to rally the troops, and left at the helm of the Russian Empire his obsequious ministers, his haughty wife, and her friend and counselor, the drunken, unstable but charismatic Grigorii Rasputin (1872–1916). Having won over the tsarina by convincing her that he alone could save her hemophiliac son, the heir to the throne, Rasputin exerted his influence in political affairs. Never has a state managed by such incompetents faced opponents of such intelligence and resolve.

In December 1916, a group of noble conspirators poisoned, shot, bludgeoned, and finally drowned Rasputin, who died at last beneath the ice of the Neva River. Now Russia was wholly without leadership. The pitiless winter descended, news from the front was bad, factory workers went on strike, and food shortages peaked. In March 1917, the women of Petrograd took to the streets—how often in the past women had rioted for bread! But rarely with such effect.

The women's protest turned into revolution—the "February" revolution by the old Russian calendar then in use. Workers joined the women, while mobs seized public buildings, and armed themselves with guns from the arsenal. Factory workers formed themselves into militias of self-appointed "Red Guards," and, prodded by Menshevik organizers, created the Petrograd Soviet of Workers' and Soldiers' Deputies. On March 12, Duma leaders created a Provisional Government to maintain order. Three days later, Tsar Nicholas abdicated, the last Romanov ruler of Russia, and the first emperor to lose his throne as a result of World War I.

Heading the Provisional Government was a committee of directors including both Kadets and socialists. Its aim was to restore order at home, manage food distribution, prosecute the war, introduce reforms, and arrange for the election of a constituent assembly that would, at long last, write a constitution. The moderate social democrat Alexander Kerensky (1881–1970), who emerged as its leader (and would die in exile in New York City fifty-three years later, one of the longest-lived of the generation of 1917), might have succeeded in meeting those goals had not the Petrograd Soviet formed other goals of its own.

In April 1917, Lenin returned from Switzerland. His triumphal arrival in Russia is described in *Witnesses* on p. 762. He had journeyed most of the overland distance in a sealed railroad car supplied by the German government, Russia's enemy, which recognized the profit to be gained from planting in Petrograd a Bolshevik agitator. The British politician Winston Churchill later described the transhipment of Lenin as a form of biological warfare—the transmission of a "plague bacillus" to destroy the enemy.

Safely arrived, Lenin joined the leaders of the Petrograd Soviet, which now had some 3000 members. By summer, his Bolsheviks controlled it. With their simple sociology (there were only two classes, the exploited proletariat and the exploiting bourgeoisie, and one must choose to serve one or the other) and their irresistible promises—"Land, Bread, Peace"—the Bolsheviks soon won influence in the workers' soviets of Moscow and other major cities. Taking the initiative, the Petrograd Soviet issued Army Order No. 1 (see above), an invitation to soldiers to disobey their officers with impunity. During the spring and summer of 1917, Russian soldiers "voted with their feet" (in Lenin's pungent phrase). They arrived in Petrograd from the front just in time to join the revolution.

Whereas Kerensky's Provisional Government wanted to win the war and secure a democratic constitution, the Bolsheviks wanted to end the war and

Revolution in Russia

Of the many ingredients of the Russian Revolution of 1917, the leadership of Vladimir Ilich Lenin, who became the first head of the new revolutionary state, was indispensable. In these passages, Lenin speaks—long before the Revolution broke out—of the need for a leadership group of professional revolutionaries; he is greeted by representatives of the volatile ranks of workers, soldiers, and sailors in Petrograd in April 1917; and, in the same month, he announces the strategy that the revolutionaries must follow in order to gain control.

Lenin defines the need for a Vanguard Party to lead the workers (1902): We have said that *there could not have been* Social-Democratic [revolutionary] consciousness among the workers. It would have to be brought to them from without. The history of all countries shows that the working class, exclusively of its own effort, is able to develop only trade-union consciousness. ...

I assert ... that no revolutionary movement can endure without a stable organization of leaders maintaining continuity ... that such an organization must consist chiefly of people professionally engaged in revolutionary activity. ... [who] will centralize all the secret aspects of the work—the drawing up of leaflets, the working out of approximate plans; and the appointing of bodies of leaders for each urban district, for each factory district, and for each educational institution. ...
(V. I. Lenin, *Collected Works*, vol. 5, 1973)

Nadezhda Krupskaya, Lenin's wife and secretary, describes their return to Russia (1917): The masses of Petrograd—workers, soldiers and sailors—came to welcome their leader. ... We were in the midst of a surging sea of people.

No one who has not lived through the revolution can have any idea of its solemn grandeur. Red banners, a guard of honor of Kronstadt sailors, searchlights from the Peter and Paul fortress ..., armoured cars, files of working men and women guarding the road. ...

When Ilyich stepped out on to the platform, a captain came up to him, stood at attention and reported. Taken by surprise, Ilyich returned the salute. A guard of honor was lined up on the platform, and Ilyich was led past it. ... Then we were seated in motor-cars, while Ilyich was placed on an armoured car ... "Long live the socialist world revolution!" Ilyich shouted into the vast crowd swarming around us.

Ilyich already felt the beginning of that revolution in every fibre of his being.
(Nadezhda Konstantinovna Krupskaya, *Lenin*; ed. B. Isaacs, 1960)

Upon his return to Russia following the collapse of the Tsarist regime, Lenin proclaims his revolutionary strategy in the April Theses (1917):

2. The specific feature of the present situation in Russia is that the country is *passing* from the first stage of the revolution—which ... placed power in the hands of the bourgeoisie—to its *second* stage, which must place power in the hands of the proletariat and the poorest sections of the peasants. ...
This peculiar situation demands of us an ability to adapt ourselves to the special conditions of Party work among unprecedentedly large masses of proletarians who have just awakened to political life.
3. No support for the Provisional Government. ...
4. ... The masses must be made to see that the Soviets of Workers' Deputies are the *only possible* form of revolutionary government, ... therefore our task is ... to present a patient, systematic, and persistent explanation of the errors of [the Provisional Government's] ... tactics, an explanation especially adapted to the practical needs of the masses.
(Lenin's April Theses, proclaimed 1917)

seize power. The two sets of aims competed, much as the crowds of frock-coated officials in the Winter Palace jostled against the crowds of workers and soldiers in the street. In July, the moderate forces gained the upper hand; soon, though, the Bolsheviks rebounded and gained control. In September, the reactionary general Lavr Kornilov (1870–1918) attempted a coup, which Kerensky suppressed. Thereafter, enemies of the revolution were branded "Kornilovites," whether or not they had joined in the attempt at military putsch.

In October, as Kerensky's supporters awaited the formation of a constituent assembly, and as Lenin's supporters awaited the arrival of the delegates to the All-Russian Congress of Soviets, Lenin saw a moment of opportunity and grabbed it. As the delegates of the soviets arrived, but before they had the opportunity to oppose Lenin's move, supported by squads of workers, soldiers (from the Petrograd garrison), and sailors (from the nearby naval base at Kronstadt) the Bolsheviks stormed the Winter Palace, described in *Windows On*, p. 751. Kerensky was expelled, and all power passed, as Lenin had wished, from the Provisional Government to the soviets. That event of November 6, 1917 marks the onset of the Bolshevik Revolution. By the old Russian calendar, the date was October 24; hence the event is known as the "October Revolution."

In Petrograd, the Bolsheviks seized the post office and telephone exchanges, government offices and ministries, the railroads, banks, and newspaper offices. In Moscow, they seized the Kremlin, the sacred center of the Russian state. Former Menshevik Leon Trotsky, head of the Military Revolutionary Committee that had coordinated the insurrection, organized the Red Army, and Felix Dzerzhinsky (1877–1926) the secret police, or Cheka.

The further course of the Bolshevik Revolution is a story to be told elsewhere (see Chapter 28). For the moment, its significance is that it resulted in Russia's withdrawal from the war. With the title People's Commissar for Foreign Affairs, Trotsky conducted the delicate negotiations with the Germans. An armistice was reached in December 1917. There remained the terms of the peace. When Trotsky rejected the German demands, they responded instantly by smashing into Ukraine, the Crimea, and Georgia to the east, and north to the Gulf of Finland, which lies barely 150 miles from Petrograd. Checked, desperate, on March 3, 1918 Trotsky signed at Brest-Litovsk in Belarus a peace treaty that left Russia mutilated. Russia sacrificed Poland, Moldova, Bessarabia, Ukraine, Georgia, the Baltic states, Finland—nearly one-fourth of the Russia the tsars had built, nearly one-third of its farmland, more than half of its industries, nearly all of its coal mines, cotton, and oil. The Bolsheviks who had wished to leave the war at any price paid a tremendous price; yet Lenin believed the losses unimportant, since they were bound to revert to Russia in the imminent world-wide communist revolution. Meanwhile, they were free to secure their revolution, and the Germans were free to return to the anguish of the western front.

Lenin the revolutionary was also a visionary. Seeing a new world ahead, he sacrificed all else—his own youth and livelihood, the lives of millions, the traditions of a nation—to make that vision real. Nearly halfway around the globe, a more prosperous nation with its own unique traditions had as its leader another visionary—the American president Woodrow Wilson (1856–1924)—for whom democracy and peace were imperatives that loomed as large as did revolution for Lenin. These two visionaries from the peripheries of the Western world foreshadowed its future more accurately than any of the leaders of the core nations of Europe, older now, after four years of war, exhausted, and transformed.

IN SEARCH OF PEACE

Woodrow Wilson was elected president in 1916 in part because he opposed American involvement in the war then raging in Europe—"He Kept Us Out of War" was his campaign slogan. The following year, he brought the United States into the war. As a fresh American army arrived in 1917 and, in 1918, swept German forces back through Belgium and across the Rhine, Wilson announced his blueprint for the future. Viewing this war as the "war to end all wars," he insisted that the settlement must provide for long-term goals: the establishment of democracy and the securing of a permanent peace.

In the event, the visionary Wilson did not succeed in realizing his plan. The peace settlement was achieved by deal-making and manipulations that left the work of building the future undone, and the defeated nations hungry for vengeance.

Peace Plans

On January 8, 1918, in an address to both houses of the United States Congress, President Wilson outlined his "Fourteen Points" (see *Witnesses*, p. 764). Underlying them were three fundamental principles. First, war must and could be avoided in the future if the nations in concert obeyed certain guidelines, above all the accomplishment of "open covenants of peace, openly arrived at." Second, national status should rest on ethnic self-determination—if a people considered themselves a unity, their living together "along historically established lines of allegiance and nationality" should be assured. Third (the substance of the crucial Fourteenth Point), an international body should be created, the League of Nations, to negotiate conflicts between nations before war erupted: "A general association of nations must be formed under specific covenants for the purpose of affording mutual guarantees of political independence and territorial integrity to great and small states alike."

Wilson's proposal also advocated free trade and freedom of the seas; a general disarmament "to the lowest point consistent with domestic safety"; the restoration of just boundaries and the protection of neutrality; an equitable settlement of colonial claims; and the relinquishing to Russia (then in the midst of civil war), in the spirit of self-determination, of its own destiny: "The treatment accorded Russia by her sister nations in the months to come will be the acid test of their good will, of their comprehension of her needs as distinguished from their own interests, and of their intelligent and unselfish sympathy."

Although Wilson's Fourteen Points may have been overly hopeful, he was the only world leader to grasp one essential desideratum: the avoidance of war in an age when war's destructive power could no longer be endured by humankind. To reach that end, he urged the embracing of democratic procedures under universal standards of justice.

The idealist Wilson was not alone in envisioning peace in 1918. On both sides of the conflict, people clamored for peace. In Britain, France, Italy, and Belgium they called for compensation and revenge.

MUST READS

Memories of War and Revolution

Erich Maria Remarque	*All Quiet on the Western Front* (1929)
Siegfried Sassoon	*The War Poems* (1983)
Wilfrid Owen	*Poems*
N.N. Sukhanov	*The Russian Revolution* (1917)

In Search of Peace

The idealistic president of the United States Woodrow Wilson saw an opportunity to make sense of the tragedy of World War I by establishing world politics on new principles of openness, freedom, self-determination, and negotiation. The treaties of Paris that were finally ratified—exemplified here by the Treaty of Versailles with Germany, designated the principal aggressor—instead aimed at containment and punishment, and thus pointed the way to an unstable peace and renewed war.

Woodrow Wilson's vision of the post-war order—the principles of justice and self-determination guide his "Fourteen Points" (1918): We [the US] entered this war because violations of right had occurred which touched us to the quick and made the life of our own people impossible unless they were corrected and the world secured once for all against their recurrence. What we demand in this war, therefore, ... is that the world be made fit and safe to live in; ... The program of the world's peace, therefore, is our program; and that program, the only possible program, as we see it, is this:
I. Open covenants of peace, openly arrived at, after which there shall be no private international understandings of any kind but diplomacy shall proceed always frankly and in the public view.
II. Absolute freedom of navigation upon the seas, outside territorial waters. ...
III. The removal ... of all economic barriers and the establishment of an equality of trade conditions among all the nations consenting to the peace. ...
IV. [International arms reductions]. ...
V. A free, open-minded, and absolutely impartial adjustment of all colonial claims, based upon a strict observance of the principle that ... the interests of the populations concerned must have equal weight with the equitable claims of the government whose title is to be determined.
VI. The evacuation of all Russian territory. ...
VII. Belgium ... must be evacuated and restored. ...
VIII. All French territory should be freed ... and the wrong done to France by Prussia in 1871 in the matter of Alsace-Lorraine ... should be righted. ...
IX. A readjustment of the frontiers of Italy should be effected along clearly recognizable lines of nationality.
X. The peoples of Austria-Hungary [including various Slavs] ... should be accorded the freest opportunity of autonomous development.
XI. Rumania, Serbia, and Montenegro should be evacuated; occupied territories restored; Serbia accorded free and secure access to the sea; and the relations of the several Balkan states ... determined ... along historically established lines of allegiance and nationality; ...
XII. The Turkish portions of the present Ottoman Empire should be assured a secure sovereignty, but the other nationalities which are now under Turkish rule should be assured ... an absolutely unmolested opportunity of autonomous development. ...
XIII. An independent Polish state should be erected. ...
XIV. A general association of nations must be formed under specific covenants for the purpose of affording mutual guarantees of political independence and territorial integrity to great and small states alike.
(*Congressional Record*, vol. 56, 1918, pt. 1)

From the Treaty of Versailles—guidelines for the containment and punishment of Germany as the instigator of war (1919):
Article 42. Germany is forbidden to maintain or construct any fortifications either on the left bank of the Rhine or on the right bank to the west of a [specified] line ...
Article 45. ... Germany cedes to France ... the coal mines situated in the Saar Basin. ...
Article 51. The territories [of Alsace and Lorraine] ... are restored to French sovereignty. ...
Article 80. Germany acknowledges and will respect strictly the independence of Austria. ...
Article 81. Germany ... recognizes the complete independence of the Czecho-Slovak State. ...
Article 84. German nationals habitually resident in ... the Czecho-Slovak State will obtain Czecho-Slovak nationality *ipso facto* and lose their German nationality. ...
Article 87. Germany ... recognizes the complete independence of Poland. ...
Article 116. Germany acknowledges ... the independence of all the territories which were part of the former Russian Empire on August 1, 1914.
Article 119. Germany renounces ... all her ... overseas possessions. ...
Article 159. The German military forces shall be demobilized and reduced. ...
Article 198. The armed forces of Germany must not include any military or naval air forces. ...
Article 231. The Allied and Associated Governments affirm and Germany accepts the responsibility of Germany and her allies for causing all the loss and damage to which the Allied and Associated Governments and their nationals have been subjected as a consequence of the war imposed upon them by the aggression of Germany and her allies.
Article 232. ... Germany undertakes that she will make compensation for all damage done to the civilian population of the Allied and Associated Powers and to their property ... as [elsewhere] defined. ...
(*Peace Treaty With Germany*, 66th Congress, 1st Session, Senate Document 49, 1919)

In Russia, sentiments for peace merged with the tide of revolution. Elsewhere in eastern Europe they were the platform of increasingly popular parties whose speakers called for peace without delay, without annexations of territory, without indemnities—a truce without winners or losers.

In Germany and Austria-Hungary, centrist socialists and republicans managed two revolutions during the last days of the war. These forced the expulsion of the Hohenzollern and Habsburg emperors, whose dynasties had reigned so long. The German revolution, sparked by naval mutinies and followed by general strikes, achieved the abdication of the emperor and the establishment of a democratic republic on November 9, 1918. The Austrians had already withdrawn from the war six days before. The flight of the last Habsburg, Charles (r. 1916–1918), who had succeeded Franz Joseph (r. 1848–1916) in 1918, meant the dismemberment of that multiethnic empire. Hungary and Austria declared themselves republics in October and November, free to pursue their separate paths.

These revolutions enabled new governments to sue for peace. But the transition from empire to republic in central Europe did not proceed without turmoil. As in Russia, a variety of political parties struggled to gain leadership. Whereas the Bolsheviks were victorious in Russia, moderate socialists held on to power in Germany and Austria. In Germany, centrist leaders weathered naval mutinies, a Bavarian socialist secessionist movement, and street rioting in Berlin. In that city, they faced the radical "Spartacist" faction of the Socialist Party (named after the slave who had led a revolt in ancient Rome; see Chapter 5). It was led by the brilliant theorists Karl Liebknecht (1871–1919) and Rosa Luxemburg, who guided the formation of workers' and soldiers' militias, modeled on those that had gained power in Petrograd in 1917. Fearful of a second Bolshevik revolution, the new German government unleashed the army to quell the uprising. Army agents were to murder Liebknecht and Luxemburg on January 15, 1919, just as the representatives of the victorious nations gathered at Versailles to decide on the terms of peace. The Spartacist socialists subsequently became the German Communist Party.

Meanwhile, the war reached closure on the military fronts. In a last, desperate offensive in March 1918, the Germans advanced westward with more than 1 million men, intending to finish what they had started in the fall of 1914. In June, some 300,000 still fresh United States troops responded with irresistible force, pushing the German armies back to Belgium, the Rhine, and beyond. In Germany, only the emperor and his generals still spoke of victory—and now the generals began to urge an armistice.

In October 1918, the German premier Prince Max von Baden (1867–1929) approached Wilson, expressing interest in the Fourteen Points and the promise of "peace without victory." But Wilson's patience had

HOW MANY?

What Germany Lost

100%	of her pre-war colonies
80%	of her pre-war fleet
48%	of all iron production
16%	of all coal production
13%	of her 1914 territory
12%	of her population

been tried by the loss of American lives. He left von Baden to deal with the British and the French, made pitiless by the experience of the slaughter on the western front. With these the Central Powers signed an armistice on November 11, 1918. Champagne flowed in London, Paris, and New York. The war was over, but peace would not easily follow. As the combatants had bloodied each other in battle, the victors now set out, with paper and pen, to bloody the losers at the conference called to set the terms of surrender.

Settlement at Paris

Attending the peace conference in Paris were the prime ministers of France, Britain, and Italy, and the president of the United States: respectively, Georges Clemenceau (1841–1929; known as "the tiger"), David Lloyd George, Vittorio Orlando (1860–1952), and Woodrow Wilson. In addition to these "Big Four," there were delegates from twenty-three other nations and four British dominions. No delegates represented the defeated powers; none were welcome from Russia, which had bled for the Allied cause but had exited the struggle early. The delegates wrangled, and the Big Four retired behind closed doors to work out the future of Europe. Clemenceau and Lloyd George looked for revenge and reparations; Orlando wanted land; and Wilson conceded much while fixing his sights on a future League of Nations.

The Peace of Paris resulted in a series of separate treaties with the defeated powers, each named after the Parisian suburb in which it was signed during 1919–1920. Of these the Treaty of Versailles, which settled affairs with Germany, overshadowed the others. In discussions held from January to June, these points emerged. First, Germany must be forced to admit its guilt as the aggressor and instigator of the terrible conflict. Second, it must repay the Allies the cost of war. Third, it must be demilitarized to the extent that it could cause no new conflict. Fourth, the defeated nations must surrender territory in Europe and possessions around the globe to the victor nations, who demanded a reward for their wartime sacrifice.

Germany, indeed, was humbled and stripped bare (see *Witnesses*, p. 764, and *How Many?*, p. 765). Article 231 of the Treaty of Versailles signed on June 28, 1919—the famous "war guilt" clause—stated that Germany accepted full responsibility for all losses and damages suffered by the Allies "as a consequence of the war imposed upon them by the aggression of Germany and her allies." Germany was ordered to pay a **reparation** of 132 billion gold marks (about $33 billion) over a period of years, a sum arrived at by rough calculation of the cost of war to the victor nations— a penalty of unimaginable dimension, little of which was ever paid. Their army was reduced to 100,000 volunteers, their airforce was eliminated, and their navy limited to six warships and no submarines. Even their merchant and fishing fleets were limited, and their shipyards assigned to supply the victor nations with new vessels at no cost. The Rhineland (the rich western sector) would be occupied by the French army until such date as the reparations were paid, and the coal-rich Saar region administered by an international committee until 1935, when a plebiscite would determine whether it became French or German. (The citizens of the Saar eventually chose German citizenship.) Kipling applauded the harsh settlement:

> *These were our Children who died for our Lands.*
> *   They were dear in our sight ...*
> *The Price of our Loss shall be paid to our Hands ...*
> *   That is our Right.*

Germany also accepted territorial concessions. The provinces of Alsace and Lorraine were returned to France; other German territory was ceded to Denmark, Belgium, and Poland, the latter reconstituted nation thus gaining "a corridor" to the Baltic Sea (except for the "free" city of Danzig, now Gdánsk) which divided East Prussia from the rest of the German homeland. German colonies in Africa and Asia were transferred to the Allied powers.

Austria, the remnant of the Austro-Hungarian Empire whose Balkan policies had triggered the war, gave up so much territory that its final dimensions were smaller than the crown lands the Habsburgs had ruled for centuries. From the lands it lost, whole new nations were constituted, their boundaries drawn (as much as possible) according to the Wilsonian principle of ethnic self-determination. Hungary became an independent republic. Czechoslovakia and Yugoslavia united, respectively, the Czechs and Slovaks and the southern Slavic Croatians, Slovenes, and Serbs. Romania doubled its territory. The south Tyrol (in the Alps) and parts of the Adriatic coast were conceded to Italy, which reclaimed thereby much of its *terra irredenta* but not enough to satisfy the Italian nationalists, who denounced this as a "mutilated peace."

A corridor of states was created of what was once western Russia—for, although the Brest-Litovsk treaty became invalid with the defeat of Germany,

Russia had still surrendered its destiny to the victorious powers. From its borderlands were formed the independent states of Poland, Lithuania, Latvia, Estonia, and Finland; while Bessarabia was ceded to Romania. Bulgaria gave up territory to Romania, Greece, and Yugoslavia.

The former Ottoman Empire, soon to be reconstituted as the modern nation of Turkey, was assigned to yield to Greece and Italy much of its European land, as well as key positions in Asia Minor and the island of Rhodes. These demands the Turks resisted, driving out the Greek forces that had rapidly moved into Asia Minor, and forcing the Europeans to accept a few Aegean islands in compensation. Leading the resistance was the young general Mustafa Kemal (1881–1938), who from 1923 until his death became Turkey's dictator (see Chapter 29).

The new state of Turkey was a truncated rump of the former Ottoman Empire. Although still a major power in the Middle East, on the European side of the straits (which were now open to all nations) it contained only the area around Constantinople (now Istanbul). Its North African and Middle Eastern territories were all lost. The belt from Morocco to Afghanistan became a patchwork of British, French, Spanish, and Italian colonies, protectorates, and "mandates." A mandate was the commission to administer a region (such as those of the former Ottoman Empire and former German colonies) under the auspices of the League of Nations, the institution Wilson had envisioned and which had a brief life between 1919 and 1939. It was the most hopeful, if flawed, outcome of the Paris conference.

The League of Nations was formed in 1919 to secure peace among nations so that the world, as Wilson had wished, would be made "safe for democracy." On its executive committee were British, French, Italian, and Japanese delegates. As at Versailles, delegates from the former Central Powers and communist Russia (now the Union of Soviet Socialist Republics, or USSR) were not represented. Neither was the United States. President Wilson had returned home from Paris to find his own nation in the grip of an isolationist mood. Republicans had a majority in the Senate (Wilson was a Democrat), while Irish, Italian, and German minority constituents all reported to their representatives their dissatisfactions with the peace settlement. In November 1919, the proposal that the United States join the League of Nations failed, and Wilson's spirits crumbled. Without American leadership, the League did not have the strength to fulfill its mission.

It certainly could not overcome the bitter feelings left by the peace treaties that the victor nations presented their former enemies: Versailles, with Germany, June 28, 1919; Saint-Germain, with Austria, September 10, 1919; Neuilly, with Bulgaria, November 27, 1919; Trianon, with Hungary, June 4,

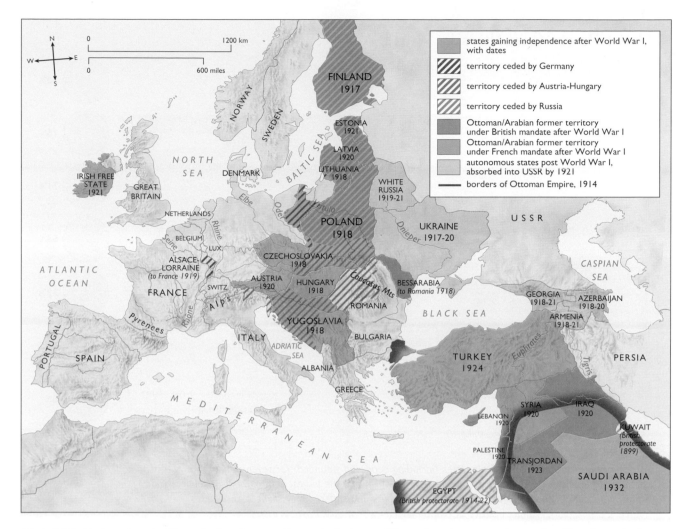

Map 26.3 Redrawing the Boundaries: *Post-war Europe looked very different from its pre-war incarnation. Negotiators broke up large multinational empires and created (or recreated) a swath of countries along supposed lines of "national self-determination." The settlement also destroyed, or weakened, European empires. The Ottoman Empire was one of the chief casualties. Germany was compelled to yield her colonies to the protection of victor nations. They were greedy to assume their new "mandates" but too exhausted to manage them effectively (see also Map 23.4 on p. 704). Why did Russia, which had not been one of the Central Powers blamed for the war, suffer the greatest loss of territory?*

1920; Sèvres, with Ottoman Turkey, August 10, 1920. No sooner issued, the treaties were challenged by the defeated nations. The next war was already in the making, as the French Marshal Ferdinand Foch (1851–1929) understood when he said of the Versailles agreement, "This isn't a peace, it's a twenty-year truce!" It lasted not quite twenty years.

Outcomes

In his 1865 Second Inaugural Address, President Abraham Lincoln reflected on the bitter experience of the American Civil War (see Chapter 19). It was longer and more cruel than anyone had anticipated. But its achievements were also monumental—the reestablishment of the American democracy, and the abolition of slavery. Had Lincoln spoken fifty-four years later of the record left by World War I, he would have noted a slaughter far greater, but an outcome less

hopeful. Its main effect was to increase, as the humanist Desiderius Erasmus (1469–1536) said of wars long before, the "empire of the dead."

Map 26.3 above shows the post-war boundaries. The chief outcome of World War I was the fall of the mighty—the rulers of four empires (German, Austro-Hungarian, Russian, and Ottoman); the values of European civilization that had reached its zenith in the century just ended; and an entire generation of young men. "How are the mighty fallen/ and the weapons of war perished!" (2 Samuel 1:25).

The first of these effects this chapter has already traced. The second will be described in Chapter 27. The third left a Europe populous with orphans, black-garbed widows, and mutilated men, who lived to visit the fresh-dug graves that crowded immense new cemeteries. Casualty rates in the armies of Germany, France, and Russia reached, respectively, sixty-three, seventy-one, and seventy-six percent; in Britain,

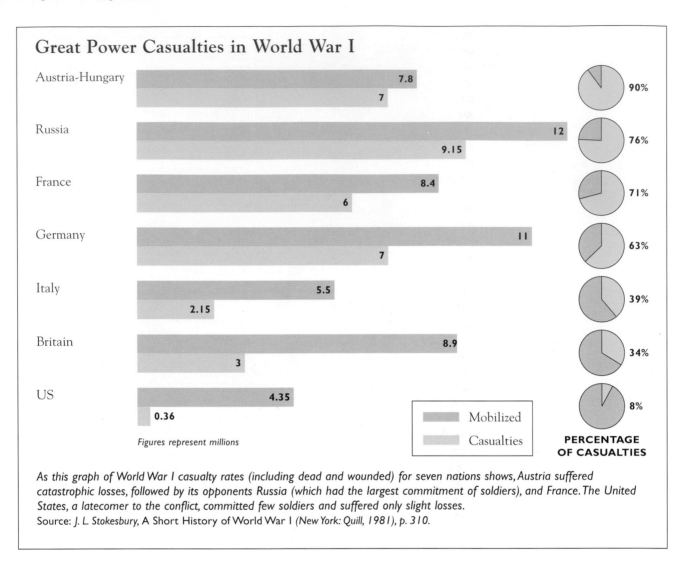

Great Power Casualties in World War I

	Mobilized	Casualties	Percentage of Casualties
Austria-Hungary	7.8	7	90%
Russia	12	9.15	76%
France	8.4	6	71%
Germany	11	7	63%
Italy	5.5	2.15	39%
Britain	8.9	3	34%
US	4.35	0.36	8%

Figures represent millions

As this graph of World War I casualty rates (including dead and wounded) for seven nations shows, Austria suffered catastrophic losses, followed by its opponents Russia (which had the largest commitment of soldiers), and France. The United States, a latecomer to the conflict, committed few soldiers and suffered only slight losses.
Source: J. L. Stokesbury, A Short History of World War I (New York: Quill, 1981), p. 310.

never invaded, and Italy, only peripherally engaged, the rates were thirty-four and thirty-nine percent. The United States, a late entrant, mobilized about 4 million men, and suffered only eight percent casualties. The Austro-Hungarian Empire suffered the highest rate of casualties, fighting simultaneously on two fronts, in cold, and amid mountains. Of the 7.8 million men mobilized, seven million—almost ninety percent—were killed or wounded.

Overall, some 8.5 million combatants died (not counting those dead of disease and other war-related causes)—thirteen percent of the 65 million mobilized. The French, German, Austrian, and Romanian dead were sixteen, sixteen, fifteen percent and a staggering forty-five percent of combatants respectively. The French dead, more than 1.3 million men of 8.4 million sent to war, were a number equivalent to one-half of all those who, in 1914, were between eighteen and thirty-two years of age—one-half a generation.

Thirty million more were to die in the aftermath of war—the victims of the worst ever influenza epidemic. Probably borne to Europe by United States soldiers in the spring of 1918, the disease raged among the undernourished survivors of war. The horrors of the battlefront nourished the still greater cataclysms that hostile Nature could wreak.

Conclusion
GLOBAL WAR AND THE MEANING OF THE WEST

World War I marked the point at which the West ceased to be in the ascendant over the other civilizations of the world. Its political influence had peaked and its cultural confidence was shattered—it seemed a "botched civilization," as Pound had written. Over the next three generations, though pressed by economic collapse (Chapter 27), the loss of empire (Chapter 29), the hell of totalitarianism (Chapter 28), and the joint terrors of genocide and the atomic bomb (Chapters 28, 30), the West would nevertheless endure.

QUESTIONS TO CONSIDER

1. Why was there so much support for war in 1914, among ordinary people as well as among states? Why might women be a special case in wartime, with particular motives for supporting or opposing war?

2. How did modern technology affect the course of the war, and which side made better use of it?

3. What was the relation between World War I and the Russian Revolution? Would the Bolsheviks have been able to succeed in the absence of war?

4. How did the ideals expressed in Wilson's "Fourteen Points" compare to the terms of the Treaty of Versailles? In 1918, which promised more success for a peaceful Europe and a peaceful world?

SUGGESTED RESOURCES

Clements, Barbara Evans, *Bolshevik Women* (Cambridge: Cambridge University Press, 1997). Studies of the women who made the Russian Revolution, from the pre-revolutionary generation of agitators to the death of the last female Bolshevik in the post-Stalinist era.

Ferguson, Niall, *The Pity of War: Explaining World War I* (New York: Basic Books, 1999). Daring new exploration of central issues pertaining to World War I, highlighting British and German mismanagement and the important new role of the U.S.

Fitzpatrick, Sheila, *The Russian Revolution*, 2nd ed. (Oxford: Oxford University Press, 1994). Assesses the revolutionary achievement from 1917 to the early 1930s, challenging notions of the Bolsheviks as merely totalitarian dictators.

Grayzel, Susan R., *Women's Identities at War: Gender, Motherhood, and Politics in Britain and France during the First World War* (Chapel Hill: University of North Carolina Press, 1999). While men were combatants, women during wartime were mothers.

Hamilton, Richard F. and Holger H. Herwig, *The Origins of World War I* (Cambridge: Cambridge University Press, 2003). Recent and systematic synthesis in comparative framework, putting the emphasis back on decision-makers and events, rather than big issues like imperialism or Social Darwinism.

Keegan, John, *The First World War* (New York: Alfred A. Knopf, 1999). Masterful account of the failure of diplomacy that led to the War, and the horrors that followed thereupon, marking the end of an era and the beginning of the modern age.

Kolata, Gina, *Flu: The Story of the Great Influenza Pandemic of 1918 and the Search for the Virus that Caused It* (New York: Farrar, Straus and Giroux, 2000). As though the devastations of the 1914–1918 period were not sufficient, while thoughts turned to peace, the flu epidemic of 1918 took 40 million lives worldwide, spreading in the wake of war.

Pipes, Richard, *The Russian Revolution* (New York: Knopf, 1990). Exhaustive and controversial account of the Revolution by one of its most outstanding and outspoken recent critics.

Read, Christopher, *From Tsar to Soviets: the Russian People and their Revolution, 1917–1921* (Oxford: Oxford University Press, 1996). A complex investigation of the revolution that recognizes both the propulsion given to events by a people detained too long by the tsarist authocracy, and a Bolshevik leadership intent on supreme power.

Service, Robert, *Lenin: A Biography* (Cambridge, MA: Harvard University Press, 2000). Brilliant and comprehensive post-Cold War biography that seeks to fathom Lenin's personality, formed in a vibrant home and fueled by immense ideas, while it does not excuse him from the decisions he made that led to oppression and devastation.

Stevenson, David, *Armaments and the Coming of War: Europe 1904–1914* (Oxford: Clarendon Press of Oxford University Press, 1996). Explores the military technologies of each of the major European powers during the late 19th and early 20th centuries.

Winter, Jay, *Sites of Memory, Sites of Mourning: The Great War in European Cultural History* (Cambridge: Cambridge University Press, 1995). The trauma of the war lingered long after the peace treaties were signed, marked by the cemeteries and monuments that sprang up as "sites of mourning" over the face of Europe.

Woollacott, Angela, *On Her Their Lives Depend: Munitions Workers in the Great War*, (Berkeley: University of California Press, 1994). Explores the lives, conditions, and consequences of women's work in munitions factories in Britain during the war.

Wright, Patrick, *Tank: the Progress of a Monstrous War Machine* (New York: Viking, 2002). A cultural history of the tank from steam-engine days, to its use in two world wars and recent appearance in 1989 in Tiananmen Square.

World War I: Trenches on the Web, a complete on-line resource for World War I (images, maps, sources, resources, bibliography, links): **http://www.worldwar1.com**

The Russian Revolution, on-line guide to sources, e-books, narrative, links: **http://www.barnsdle.demon.co.uk/russ/rusrev.hmtl**

Wilson on the Web, guide to resources, on Woodrow Wilson—speeches, bibliography, links (geocities): **http://www.geocities.com/Athens/2391**

Western Civilization Documents CD-ROM

26.1 Rupert Brooke: The Soldier
26.2 Siegfried Sasson
26.3 Isaac Rosenberg
26.4 Woodrow Wilson: Speech on the Fourteen Points
26.5 Anna Eisenmenger, A German Soldier Returns Home
26.6 A French Baker's Wife's Role in War
26.7 Non-European's View of the Start of World War I
26.8 Pressing for Peace
26.9 Georges Clemenceau Presents the French Demands at the Paris Peace Conference

THE TRIUMPH OF UNCERTAINTY

	1900	1910	1920	1930	1940	1950

Politics and War

World War I and the Russian Revolution, 1914–21   World War II, 1939–45

◆ Mussolini's fascists march on Rome, 1922

◆ Adolf Hitler achieves power in Germany, 1933

◆ Italy invades Ethiopia, 1935

◆ Germany rearms, 1936

Society, Economy, and Ideas

◆ Max Planck's concepts of quantum mechanics, 1900

◆ Ellen Key's *The Century of the Child*, 1900

◆ First films play in "nickleodeons," 1900s

◆ Albert Einstein's special theory of relativity, 1905

◆ D. W. Griffith's *The Birth of a Nation*, 1915

◆ Quantum theory established, 1926

◆ John Maynard Keynes' *The End of Laissez–Faire*, 1926

◆ Werner Heisenberg formulates "uncertainty principle," 1927

◆ Bertolt Brecht's *Threepenny Opera*, 1928

◆ Sergei Eisenstein's *October*, 1928

◆ Joseph Stalin launches First Five Year Plan in Soviet Union, 1928

◆ Alexandra Kollontaiforms *Zhenotdel* (Women's Department) in Soviet Russia, 1919

◆ US stockmarket crash and start of Depression, 1929

◆ Hawley-Smoot Tariff, 1930

◆ Austria's Creditanstalt bank fails, 1931

◆ 13 million Americans (30% of workforce) unemployed, 1932

◆ New Economic Policy (NEP) in Soviet Union, 1921–28

◆ Franklin Delano Roosevelt establishes New Deal, 1933

◆ James Joyce's *Ulysses*, 1922

◆ "Popular Front" alliances of Communists and Socialists, 1935

◆ Hyperinflation destroys German currency's value, 1923

◆ Leni Riefenstahl's *Triumph of the Will*, 1935

◆ Dawes Plan reschedules German reparations payments, 1924

◆ "Popular Front" left–liberal government under Léon Blum in France, 1936

◆ Jean Renoir's *La Grande Illusion*, 1937

◆ Sergei Eisenstein's *The Battleship Potemkin*, 1925

◆ Sergei Eisenstein's *Alexander Nevsky*, 1938

◆ Jean-Paul Sartre's *Being and Nothingness*, 1943

◆ Franz Kafka's *The Trial*, 1925

Beyond the West

◆ Amritsar Massacre, India, 1919

◆ British Commonwealth of Nations created, 1931

◆ Japan invades China, 1937

◆ Independence and partition of India, 1947

◆ UN partitions Palestine, Israel declares independence, 1947

◆ Communist victory in China, 1949

CHAPTER 27

THE TRIUMPH OF UNCERTAINTY

Cultural Innovation, Social Disruption, and Economic Collapse

1915–1945

GREENLAND

SWEDEN

NORWAY

NORTH SEA

GREAT BRITAIN

DENMARK

NETH.

GERMANY

BELGIUM

POLAND

CZECH

FRANCE

SWITZ.

USSR

BLACK SEA

ARMENIA

TURKEY

CANADA

UNITED STATES OF AMERICA

ATLANTIC OCEAN

GULF OF MEXICO

MEDITERRANEAN SEA

AFRICA

● US debtor nations, 1914-25

industrial unemployment, 1931-36:

☐ countries reaching a maximum of 15-25%

■ countries reaching a maximum of 26-50%

KEY QUESTIONS

◆ **Uncertainty in the Arts and Thought:** How were the uncertainties of the post-war period expressed in the arts, sciences, and philosophy, and in such new genres as cinema and jazz?

◆ **Uncertain Boundaries:** How were women liberated from traditional roles in the post-war years, and what was the impact on the family and state?

◆ **Economic Uncertainty:** What were the decisions made that caused, despite a post-war boom, the economic collapse of the 1920s and 1930s? What were the political implications of the desperate need of the shamed and doubt-ridden people who suffered its effects?

The Roll of Dice In 1930, the young physicist Werner Heisenberg (1901–1976) explained his "principle of indeterminacy" to a scientific gathering that included the giant of the scientific world Albert Einstein (1879–1955), creator of the theory of relativity (see Chapter 25). Since the behavior of subatomic particles could not be precisely known, Heisenberg reasoned, it should be described in terms of statistical probability. Einstein found the notion of a merely probable universe intolerable; a moral world, he insisted, depended on a rational universe. "God," he barked, "does not roll dice."

But Heisenberg's indeterminacy more accurately describes the realities in the Western world in the years after World War I (1914–1918) than does Einstein's vision of order. To most artists and intellectuals—for whom God had long since died (see Chapter 25)—the old certainties had vanished and the future was shadowy. Gender roles and social institutions were also in flux, as women sought personal freedom and citizenship, and as the traditional family lost many of its functions to social workers and state agencies. Western economies boomed and crashed, leaving millions without the savings that had promised security in old age, and millions more without work or without food. This catastrophe struck barely ten years after the close of a war that had left an unprecedented number mutilated and dead (see Chapter 26).

In this age of unknowns, the human condition was fragile. The mood of doubt and the tendency to irrationalism that had characterized the pre-war West mounted to a chronic condition of uncertainty. During the twenty years between the conclusion of the Paris peace treaties and the declarations that opened World War II, uncertainty triumphed in the arts and in thought, in social roles and institutions, and in economic life. Its shadow was not dispelled before the century ended.

UNCERTAINTY IN THE ARTS AND IN THOUGHT

The assault on rationalism that had begun with Romanticism around 1800 peaked in the early twentieth century. Pessimism prevailed about the nature of reality, the integrity of the self, as well as the limits of language. The visual arts abandoned linear narrative and realistic representation. Scientists and philosophers, despairing of certain knowledge, found a variety of ways to describe their uncertainty or even abandoned the search for absolute truths altogether. Literature looked inward, or focused on the perils of the human condition adrift in a world that was meaningless or menacing.

Montage: the Disrupted Narrative

Building on **avant-garde** developments in the last years of the nineteenth century, the pioneering artists of the twentieth no longer sought to represent objective reality. Whatever they painted, played, performed, or screened was not intended to imitate what existed in the world, but to present a creative reinvention of that reality. This Modernist project involved the abandonment of earlier artistic norms as new orthodoxies emerged in a rapidfire procession.

Moving Pictures Of the technical innovations, none was more novel than film. Its precursor the photograph had evolved from the 1830s to capture an image of objects in front of a camera—a great man, his family, a battlefield. Fifty years later, film was invented as a sequence of photographs, each viewed very rapidly in turn as the celluloid medium—the film—was drawn before the eye of the beholder. The effect was a moving picture created from the series of separate images. The art form popularly known as "the movies," "flicks," or "films" was more formally called **cinema**, short for "cinematograph" (from the Greek words for "motion" and for "drawing"), a picture engendered by motion.

The moving picture, however, existed nowhere on the film; It existed only in the mind of the viewer, whose brain supplied the continuity between separate still images. Whereas the photograph was the quintessential form of "Realist" art, claiming to reproduce perfectly the real object, film was essentially a modern medium, representing something that conceivably might exist but in fact did not.

In the 1900s and 1910s, fascinated viewers devoured early films in shopfront theaters called "nickelodeons" (because it cost a nickel, or five cents, to view) or peered into machines called "kinetoscopes" (from the Greek words for "motion" and "view"). An alternative to the live entertainment of the music hall or theater was provided by the soundless train rides, battles, robberies, or slapstick routines that formed the staple subjects of films. Studios sprang up as entrepreneurs sought to satisfy the public's appetite for the sixteen-minute-long films (the playing time of the celluloid strip that could be stored on one reel), of which hundreds, then thousands were produced each year. Mass entertainment had been born.

A motley cohort of artists turned film into the characteristic art form of the twentieth century. They were themselves actors, directors, or producers, with prior experience in provincial repertory, music hall, and circus. These were not intellectuals, but pragmatists willing to work fast and risk everything to exploit the moving image for expression and for profit.

Among the first great cinematographers were the American D. W. Griffith (1875–1948) and the

Russian Sergei Eisenstein (1898–1948), who boldly appropriated the technology of film to create a new kind of narrative form. Griffith was a Kentucky-born sentimentalist who longed for the patrician South of the United States before the Civil War—a culture based on slavery. His most famous film, *The Birth of a Nation* (1915), a still from which is illustrated below, was an American epic exploring the soul of the nation by retelling its history. It culminates with a scene repellent to modern audiences of the Ku Klux Klan (a secret society pledged to enforce the subordination of African Americans newly released from slavery) riding out on its nightmarish mission, and defeating the quintessential enemy—the African American soldiers of a United States Army force.

To arrive at his grandiose and unfortunate vision, Griffith introduced many innovations to the business of film-making. Films extended beyond their one-reel, sixteen-minute format to several reels, and two or three hours. And the photographic sequences were edited, so that the viewer saw an assemblage of images that did not necessarily occur in the same place or in sequence—a structural change that added a further element of unreality to the unreality that was already inherent in the medium. Griffith juxtaposed scenes that were to be understood as simultaneous in real time—robbers approaching, for instance, while the inhabitants of a house dread their arrival. Drama and suspense created by these juxtapositions enhanced the experience of viewing.

Eisenstein, making films under Communist rule from 1924 until his death in 1948, was a still more sophisticated manipulator of cinematic images. Eisenstein disrupted natural sequences, extracting images as his eye and his concept required to produce specific psychological effects in the viewer. This method of composition, based on disruption or discontinuity, is called **montage** (a French word referring to the ordering of images). The director rearranges reality to create a cinematic narrative that is abstract and idea-driven.

Using juxtapositions and interpolations in a pattern whose structure was rooted in the theory of **Marxian dialectic**, Eisenstein constructed sweeping, epic retellings of revolutionary events. His *Battleship Potemkin* (1925) retells an incident of the 1905 Revolution in Russia. Without sound or artificial lighting, or trained actors in major roles, by juxtaposing images of a sailors' rebellion, a popular demonstration, and the repressive violence of a military guard, he communicates the essentials of the revolutionary message: the innocence of the masses of the people, and the evil of those who hold power over them.

The work of Griffith, Eisenstein, and other early film-makers—German, French, Italian, and Swedish as well as American and Russian—paved the way for the mature cinema of the 1920s and 1930s (by which time it had acquired synchronous sound). Many films aimed merely to entertain: grandiose historical epics, westerns, and gangster movies. Others presented social critiques, as did the comic films of Charlie Chaplin (1889–1977). The English-born son of two circus performers, Chaplin was grounded in the high comic tradition and used the persona of the clown in many of his films (which he directed, and in which he often acted) to reveal the absurdities of modern times.

Less comic but equally profound, Jean Renoir (1894–1979), the son of the Impressionist painter Pierre-Auguste Renoir, explored the meaning of World War I in his *La Grande Illusion* ("The Great Illusion") of 1937. Not a wartime adventure story, but an analysis of the disintegration of the traditional European world during World War I, Renoir's film juxtaposes a German and a French aristocrat, and these in turn with a worker and a Jew. Although the French gentleman is the German's prisoner, both are equally the social superiors of the other two—who nevertheless represent the vigorous world of the future, and who alone will survive the reality.

Whereas some films offered a critique of contemporary society, others were created in order to to celebrate the prevailing political regime. These were

D. W. Griffith, Birth of a Nation: *Pioneer film-maker D. W. Griffith portrays in 1915 the birth of a nation with novel techniques and old hatreds. Here in the wake of the Civil War, members of the Ku Klux Klan (a racist paramilitary group active in the American south after Reconstruction and into the first decades of the twentieth century) "build" the new United States, as Griffith sees it, through terror.*

Uncertainty, Now and To Come

Like the performing arts, the visual arts reflected twentieth-century currents in thought and feeling. This painting by the Surrealist painter René Magritte (above) gives expression to the uncertainties of the age. A familiar object is labeled with a description that says it is not what it is: "Ceci n'est pas une pipe" ("This is not a pipe").

More confidently, Futurist artists looked ahead to new human triumphs over nature and history. In 1914, Antonio Sant'Elia imagined the city of the future—not very distant from our own cities today, but immensely different from those of Europe on the verge of World War I, where many buildings, streets, and squares were still defined by the architectural norms of previous centuries. (above: Los Angeles County Museum of Art; below: Paride Accetti Collection, Milan).

the propaganda films of the Communists and the German National Socialists, or Nazis, who recognized the capacity of the new medium to lend grandeur and conviction to their enterprise. In the Soviet Union, Lenin had recognized the importance of film (he called it the most important art form of the century), and his successor Joseph Stalin (1879–1953; see Chapters 26, 28) enlisted it to advance the interests of the new communist state. Filmmaking was placed under the supervision of an office of *agitprop*—the term abbreviating words meaning "agitation," denoting the arousal of revolutionary enthusiasm, and **propaganda**, meaning the diffusion of concepts favorable to the regime. Eisenstein, who had passionately hymned the Revolution in such films as *The Battleship Potemkin* and *October* (or *Ten Days that Shook the World*) (1928), was muzzled under Stalin by the artistic policy of **Socialist Realism**. Only as World War II approached (see Chapter 28) did his originality reappear in *Alexander Nevsky* (1938). Recalling a medieval confrontation between heroic defenders of Russian Muscovy and the faceless,

heartless ranks of Germanic invaders defeated in battle on a frozen lake, the film symbolized the imminent struggle with a modern enemy.

Similarly, the Nazi German leader Adolf Hitler (1889–1945) supported the creation of those films that advanced the Nazi agenda (see Chapter 28). He commissioned Leni Riefenstahl (1902–   ), Germany's first major woman director, to create the documentary film *Triumph of the Will* (1935), whose chilling message of German supremacy and romanticized aggression caused it to be banned in Britain, Canada, and the United States. Using unusual camera angles to maximize the awesome impression of Nazi leaders, and to announce the capacity for disciplined violence of massed Nazi troops, Riefenstahl advanced Hitler's project to install the third, final, and eternal Reich, or empire (the first was the medieval, Holy Roman Empire; the second lasted from 1871 to 1918).

Antonio Sant'Elia, **Electric Center**

Far from Russia and Germany during these interwar years, the film industry installed itself in Hollywood, part of Los Angeles, California, a new city where the weather was almost always good. Promiscuity and gangsterism flourished in this rootless society of instant celebrities, awash (especially during the years of Prohibition, 1920–1933, when alcohol was officially banned) in a flood of alcohol, nicotine, and drugs. Hollywood became the capital of mass communications. It would communicate to vast audiences the reconstructions of reality assembled in a montage from photographic fragments—an unreal representation of a concrete reality.

Other Visual Arts   Film may have been the most important medium of the visual arts in the twentieth century, as Lenin had said; but its career paralleled that of the others. In painting and sculpture, various schools of abstract art ("abstract" in that they considered themselves free from the "concreteness" of the represented object) flourished in the major artistic centers, especially Paris: Cubism, Expressionism, Surrealism, and others (see Chapter 25). Novel and original, the artistic works produced shared a more or less marked tendency to distort, segment, displace, superimpose, or otherwise violate the recognizable objects of the real environment.

In architecture, despite its "concreteness," innovations also abounded. Architects rejected the traditional vocabulary of building—the arches, columns, and domes, the grand entrances and decorated windows informed by Classical, Gothic, Renaissance, and Baroque forms. Instead, they designed the buildings needed by a modern age—factories, office blocks, railroad stations—that were expressive of their function, stripped of decoration, employing conspicuously the building materials of the modern age: concrete, glass, and steel (see *Electric Center* on p. 774).

The Jazz Age   Unlike painting and sculpture, seen only in museums, architecture reached the eyes of multitudes. Like film, it was a medium of mass communication. In the same way, while some forms of music remained esoteric in the interwar years, a new form of music—**jazz**—became truly popular. Heard in bars and restaurants, on phonographs or radios, it gave its name to the era. The Jazz Age marked a new musical genre, and a new kind of audience.

The new vocabulary of jazz distinguished it from the classical repertoire, naive folk song, and music hall ditties. North American in origin but quickly appreciated in Europe, jazz was a kind of musical montage derived from the experience of African Americans, based on the sounds invented during centuries of plantation slavery. A fusion of African harmony, melody, and rhythm with Western styles, these sounds were heard in work songs and lamentations, in field shouts and Christian spirituals, and later woven into the new forms of jazz—**blues**, ragtime, Dixieland, swing, bop, and successive styles.

Jazz diverged sharply from the classical tradition both in sound and culture. In contrast to the symphony orchestra, jazz was played by bands (playing such instruments as trumpet, trombone, and tuba, saxophone and clarinet, bass, banjo, and guitar, drums, and piano). It was improvisational: the lead performer invented and varied both melody and rhythm at will backed up by a band that spontaneously responded to the soloist's cues. Its rhythms were therefore freer than those heard in the concert hall, and its melodies featured non-standard repetitions, dissonances, improvisations, and the characteristic flattened thirds and sevenths of the chord that established the tonality of sadness supplied by the experience of slavery. The blues, generally vocal, highlighted that sadness in songs about poverty, abandonment, and despair.

Jazz came from the other side of town—from the slums, ghettos, and working-class districts alongside the railroad tracks and the docks. Most of its performers were black, although white bands and orchestras adopted the style and popularized it among audiences outside the South. At first, jazz was widely denounced by respectable people as music that celebrated sex

Louis Armstrong's jazz combo: *Just as film pieced together real images into a constructed new reality, modern dance and popular music utilized bits of classical art forms to construct patterns of movement and sound expressive of a modern age. Depicted here is Louis Armstrong (seated left), leader of the Hot Five combo that flourished in the 1920s, and the figure who brought the new sound of jazz from New Orleans in the American south to affluent urban audiences.*

Writers and Artists in an Age of Uncertainty

Luigi Pirandello (1867–1936) Italian novelist and playwright; his *Six Characters in Search of an Author* (1921) developed the technique of "theater within the theater."

D. W. Griffith (1875–1948) American pioneer motion-picture director; his *The Birth of a Nation* (1915) has been hailed for its innovative technique and condemned for its racist message.

Eugene O'Neill (1888-1953) Leading American dramatist; major works include *Long Day's Journey into Night* (produced posthumously in 1956) and *The Iceman Cometh* (1946).

Charlie Chaplin (1889–1977) British-born American actor and film director; his "lovable tramp" character earned him critical and popular acclaim; major films include *Modern Times* (1935) and *The Great Dictator* (1940).

Jean Renoir (1894–1979) French-born film director; son of the Impressionist painter Pierre-Auguste Renoir; his films—including *Madame Bovary* (1934) and *Grand Illusion* (1937)—are known for their dramatic realism.

Bertolt Brecht (1898–1956) German playwright and poet; author of *Threepenny Opera* (1928); pioneered the use of theater as a vehicle for leftist political criticism.

Sergei Eisenstein (1898–1948) Russian film director and Soviet propagandist; his *Battleship Potemkin* (1925), *October* (1928), and *Alexander Nevsky* (1938) combined major historical themes with ground-breaking cinematography.

and had wild jungle rhythms. Many of its performers, and many listeners, like the Hollywood stars and starlets, led a fast life that came to characterize the era: the 1920s are often called the "jazz age." Jazz was nevertheless a sophisticated musical form—popular in every sense—created by ordinary people, and from the experience of their unique past, and addressed directly to audiences of ordinary, untrained listeners; yet it was able to rival in expressive capacity and in audience appeal the classical forms of the high musical tradition.

At the same time that jazz challenged classical sound, the new compositions of classically-trained composers, now experimenting with atonality, were rapidly disenchanting concert audiences (see Chapter 25). As the new symphonies and operas became less comprehensible even to educated listeners, these demanded to hear the works of the older classical and Romantic repertory. Requiring a familiarity with a historical musical tradition, the concert hall became increasingly remote from contemporary experience—something to be enjoyed by well-to-do consumers of a specialized cultural product. Dance suffered a similar rupture: classical ballet was remote from the experience of most people, for whom dance meant the dances performed in music hall and cabaret, or by the audience of jazz bands, who became participants in the process of expressive improvisation. In the United States, modern dance freed itself from the rituals of ballet, formulated in royal courts, to incorporate some elements of folk dance movement, and convey emotion more expressively. In Europe, ballet continued to win popular attention in Russia, opera in Italy. Elsewhere, however, the repertoire of the Jazz Age dominated, as it did in the cabarets of Europe whose song and dance, jaded successors to the lighthearted fare of turn-of-the-century music halls, mocked society and its guardians.

The jazz idiom, and its message of a world where the disinherited and irreverent reigned was dramatized in the blazingly original plays of the German author Bertolt Brecht (1898–1956). Brecht's angry Marxism, seen in his savage critique of capitalists as exploiters of the poor, shocked his audience. So did his unblinking honesty which uncovered moral failings in the oppressed as well as the oppressor, and his break with the custom of theatrical illusion. Brechtian theater used some of the devices of cinematic montage. Narrative continuities were disrupted so as to arouse emotions—outrage, disgust, hostility—in the viewer. *Die Dreigroschenoper* (*The Threepenny Opera*, 1928), based on an eighteenth-century play about London's criminal underworld, *The Beggar's Opera* (1728), combines Brecht's drama with the jazz score of composer Kurt Weill (1900–1950) to yield a theatrical achievement—midway between the century's two world wars and on the eve of global economic crisis—that is the epitome of the Modern.

In challenging conventional morality, Brecht had allies in Britain and across the Atlantic. Irish-born playwright George Bernard Shaw (1856–1950) assaulted Victorian assumptions about class, religion, and sex in his plays, while American Eugene O'Neill (1888–1953) explored in his dramas the tragic hypocrisy of family relationships. Neither Shaw nor O'Neill, however, stabbed so viciously as Brecht at the comfortable assumptions of contemporary society.

Brecht's acid cynicism was more nearly matched by the humorous but black pessimism of the Italian author Luigi Pirandello (1867–1936). Pirandello's dramas are disturbing not because, like Brecht's, they violated moral and theatrical conventions, but because they invaded the boundary between reality and illusion and left viewers confused and doubt-ridden. Perhaps no play more accurately mirrors the uncertainty of the twentieth-century Western outlook than Pirandello's *Six Characters in Search of an Author* (1921), describing that world as a vacuum whose Creator has ceased to exist. Contemporary scientists and philosophers had similar doubts about a universe without author, purpose, or compassion.

Indeterminacy: the Limits of Knowledge and Action

In the nineteenth century, the biological sciences had flourished; the early twentieth century, in contrast, was the age of new discoveries in physics. These dismantled the Newtonian cosmos, which had affirmed the rationality, consistency, and predictability of all universal actions—a paradigm that had for two hundred years governed the thinking of experts and public alike. The cosmos that took its place was changing, bent, and uncertain.

The Anxieties of Science　The principle of relativity announced by Albert Einstein in 1905 (see Chapter 25) shattered Newtonian certainties. In Newton's universe, definable laws acted uniformly on objects that behaved predictably and consistently. Into this ordered world, Einstein introduced the element of uncertainty. Time and space were relative to the observer. What was true in one set of conditions was not true in another. Instead of inspiring

---

WHO'S WHO

Scientists and Philosophers in an Age of Uncertainty

Albert Einstein (1879–1955) German-born Jewish physicist; developed special and general theories of relativity, and the notion that mass and energy are interconvertible as expressed by the equation "e = mc²."

Werner Heisenberg (1901–1970) German physicist and philosopher; his Uncertainty Principle (1927) proposes that it is impossible accurately and simultaneously to measure the position and velocity of a particle.

Bertrand Russell (1872–1970) Nobel-Prize winning English philosopher and mathematician; ardent advocate of pacifism and nuclear disarmament.

Ludwig Wittgenstein (1889–1951) Austrian-born English philosopher, his *Tractatus Logico-Philosophicus* (1922) treated the nature and limits of language.

Jean-Paul Sartre (1905–1980) French novelist and existential philosopher; argued that the essential meaninglessness of existence presented humans with an opportunity for total freedom.

---

faith in a Creator, the new condition of the universe that Einstein introduced aroused people's anxiety.

That anxiety increased with the investigation of the **atom** by the scientists Neils Bohr (1885–1962), Max Planck (1858–1947), and Werner Heisenberg. Previously, the atom had been understood as the smallest particle, irreducible and changeless, of any substance. That notion had originated with the ancient Greek philosopher Democritus (see Chapter 4), but it rapidly disintegrated after 1895, when the discovery of X-rays and the investigation of radiation by the Curies (see Chapter 25) inaugurated a new scientific venture: the investigation of subatomic particles.

Within the atom, scientists discovered an inconceivably small universe anchored by a nucleus about which other particles whirled (the electrons); and within the nucleus, further particles (protons and neutrons). Over the next generation, they attempted to align the model of the motion of subatomic particles with that of planetary bodies in the solar system. They learned that the particles' electrical nature—they were positive (the protons), negative (the electrons), or neutral (the neutrons)—caused them to repel or attract each other and hold the system in balance. They learned that the disruption of the nucleus resulted in the release of enormous stored energy—the fundamental principle behind the atomic bomb (see Chapter 28).

Planck proposed that the energy emitted by atomic particles did not flow smoothly but jumped in discontinuous spurts, or quanta (hence "**quantum theory**"). And yet the wave theory of light, or electricity, could not be entirely abandoned for a particle theory, if all phenomena were to be explained. Scientists concluded that both wave and particle theories, though seemingly contradictory, were correct, and that the two coexisted logically though absurdly—the theory of "complementarity."

Werner Heisenberg's 1927 formulation of the awesome "principle of indeterminacy" or "uncertainty," pointed out the limits of knowledge. Heisenberg demonstrated that it was impossible to know certainly both the position and the velocity of a subatomic particle. The more precise knowledge of one attribute became, the less precise knowledge of the other was rendered. Since certainty was impossible, the investigator should describe each by a range of statistical possibility. In a universe that was indeterminate, or uncertain, the scientist could never attain more than probable knowledge. It was this surrender to a permanent condition of uncertainty that Einstein—refused to accept. One day, he preferred to hope, the rationality of the universe, and thus its moral center, would be reaffirmed.

Philosophical and Religious Responses　Philosophers studied the new science. In such an uncertain universe, some decided, philosophers should restrict

The World Becomes Uncertain

Modernism, which threw off traditional social and cultural norms, had already destabilized the European cultural world when war broke out in 1914, with traumatic effects. In these passages, the physician Freud and writer Valéry speak of the effect of war: it had caused "disillusionment" according to the former, and had "cruelly wounded" the mind according to the latter. The spirit of uncertainty that prevailed in the postwar era was also expressed in the science of the age, which departed from observable or inherited truths, and in the arts, which ceased to concentrate on depicting recognizable subject matter.

French writer and thinker Paul Valéry discusses the cultural and psychological effects of World War I (1922): We are a very unfortunate generation, whose lot has been to see the moment of our passage through life coincide with the arrival of great and terrifying events, the echo of which will resound through all our lives. ... You know how greatly the general economic situation has been disturbed, and the polity of states, and the very life of the individual; you are familiar with the universal discomfort, hesitation, apprehension. *But among all these injured things is the Mind.* The Mind has indeed been cruelly wounded; its complaint is heard in the hearts of intellectual man; it passes a mournful judgment on itself. It doubts itself profoundly.
(Paul Valéry, speech, 1922; ed. M. Cowley, 1954)

Albert Einstein's Theory of Relativity described by a peer (Lincoln Barnett) (1954): It [Einstein's Theory of Relativity] explains why all observers in all systems everywhere, regardless of their state of motion, will always find that light strikes their instruments and departs from their instruments at precisely the same velocity. For as their own velocity approaches that of light, their clocks slow down, their yardsticks contract, and all their measurements are reduced to the values obtained by a relatively stationary observer. ... From this it follows that nothing can move faster than light, no matter what forces are applied.
(Lincoln Barnett, *The Universe and Dr. Einstein*, 1954)

Sigmund Freud on civilization's discontent (1930): Men are not gentle creatures who want to be loved ... ; they are, on the contrary, creatures among whose instinctual endowments is to be reckoned a powerful share of aggressiveness. As a result, their neighbour is for them not only a potential helper or sexual object, but also someone who tempts them to satisfy their aggressiveness on him, to exploit his capacity for work without compensation, to use him sexually without his consent, to seize his possessions, to humiliate him, to cause him pain, to torture and to kill him. ... Civilization has to use its utmost efforts in order to set limits to man's aggressive instincts. ... Hence, therefore, the use of methods intended to incite people into ... relationships of love, hence the restriction upon sexual life, and hence too the ideal's commandment to love one's neighbour as oneself—a commandment which is really justified by the fact that nothing else runs so strongly counter to the original nature of man. ...
(Sigmund Freud, *Civilisation and its Discontents*, 1930; ed. J. Strachey, 1961)

Werner Heisenberg explains how war inspired his scientific thought (1952): When I left school in 1920 in order to attend the University of Munich, the position of our youth as citizens was very similar to what it is today. Our defeat in the first world war [*sic*] had produced a deep mistrust of all the ideals which had been used during the war and which had lost us that war. They seemed hollow now and we wanted to find out for ourselves what was of value in this world and what was not: we did not want to rely on our parents or our teachers. Apart from many other values we re-discovered science in this process.
(Werner Heisenberg, *Philosophical Problems of Nuclear Science*, 1952; ed. F. C. Hayes, 1966)

Painter Vasily Kandinsky learns that the artist's goal should be to express feeling and not represent objects, whose very existence science has called into doubt (1913): Previously I had only known realistic art ... and suddenly for the first time I saw a *painting.* That it was a haystack [by impressionist Claude Monet] the catalogue informed me. I could not recognize it. This nonrecognition was painful to me. I considered that the painter had no right to paint indistinctly. I dully felt that the object of the painting was missing. And I noticed with astonishment and confusion that the picture not only draws you but impresses itself indelibly on your memory. ... All this was unclear to me, and I could not draw the simple conclusions of this experience. But what was entirely clear to me— was the unsuspected power of the palette, which had up to now been hidden from me. ... And unconsciously the object was discredited as an indispensable element of a painting. ...
(Vasily Kandinsky, "Reminiscences," 1913; ed. R. Herbert, 1964)

themselves to discussing only what was indisputably true and knowable—only those logical deductions that were impenetrable to criticism, only those statements that were about things that were clearly "the case." Philosophy should cease to speculate about unseen or unknowable things, which should be left purely to spiritualists, novelists, and quacks.

These assumptions characterize the school of **logical positivism**, also called logical or scientific empiricism. Derived from the work on scientific logic of the British thinkers Bertrand Russell (1872–1970) and Alfred North Whitehead (1861–1947), and the investigations into the imprecision of language presented by George E. Moore (1873–1958), it was developed immediately following World War I by a group of mathematicians and philosophers known as the Vienna School. This circle published the writings of the Austrian Ludwig Wittgenstein (1889–1951), who had been Russell's student at Cambridge. Wittgenstein's *Tractatus Logico-Philosophicus* (1921) spelled out the philosopher's duty to clarify ideas, not to theorize about the unknown. Wittgenstein's understanding of the relations between language, the mind, and reality subsequently took root in Britain (where he taught from 1929 until his death) as well as the United States, where they are loosely described as the "analytic school."

Continental theorists who found Anglo-American logical positivism unsatisfying, offered different responses to the challenge of indeterminacy. **Existentialists** argued that, though the universe was admittedly unreliable and incoherent, and even the personal self was a great mystery, the actions taken by the conscious mind in themselves created a reality that, though dangerous, was genuine. Existentialism never formed a clearly demarcated school. Only the French thinker Jean-Paul Sartre (1905–1980) explicitly identified himself as an "existentialist." He expounded his view of the non-existence of God or meaning outside the unfettered, committed, acting self in novels and plays, as well as in his principal philosophical work *Being and Nothingness* (1943).

In the world presented by scientists and philosophers, either God did not exist or, if he existed, he did not control anarchic and obscure realities. Many turned from this psychological despair once again to religion and mysticism. Some embraced **spiritualism**, attempting to contact the spirits of the dead through professional mediums and special rituals. Others rediscovered the benefits of religious faith. Among Roman Catholics, interest in the miraculous swelled, and thousands sought healing and relief at shrines such as those at Lourdes (France) and Fátima (Portugal)—the latter founded as recently as 1917. In the United States, Protestant **fundamentalism** flourished in direct response to the destructive critique that Modernism made of religious principles and of the Bible.

Although most intellectuals remained aloof from orthodox religion, important exceptions included the French philosopher, paleontologist, and Jesuit priest Pierre Teilhard de Chardin (1881–1955). His views about cosmic evolution blended scientific theories of evolution with Christian humanist and cosmological views. Also French, the Jewish-born philosopher Simone Weil (1909–1943) turned to a mystical Roman Catholic Christianity in her quest for a greater closeness between humanity and God. In

Germany a series of Protestant thinkers, much influenced by existentialism, such as Dietrich Bonhoeffer (1906–1945), adhered to fundamental Christian principles while restating biblical concepts in the light of the modern critique of religious faith. The Austrian Jewish theologian Martin Buber (1878–1965), influenced by both existentialism and Hasidic pietism (see Chapter 24), described in his influential *I and Thou* (1923) the intimate relationship attainable between God and worshiper.

By the twentieth century, the official pronouncements of Europe's largest church, the Roman Catholic, had become more open to modernization than when, in 1870, Pope Pius IX (r. 1846–1878) defined the doctrine of "papal infallibility." Pius' successor Leo XIII (r. 1878–1903) encouraged both a deep spirituality and social reform. His encyclical, or pronouncement, *Rerum novarum* ("Of New Things") in 1891 spoke against revolution and socialist utopianism, but in favor of equity in worker–employer relations, and the need for a just and adequate wage. Subsequent popes continued to speak for social justice within Europe, and for the easing of poverty and the need for peace throughout the world.

Nevertheless, the Church represented moral views now widely perceived as rigid and outdated. They seemed absurd to the progressive writers who flourished in the interwar years. Works of fiction such as *Ulysses* (1922) by the Irish novelist James Joyce (1882–1941) or the seven-volume *Remembrance of Things Past* (1913–1927) by the French writer Marcel Proust (1871–1922) ruptured at once the narrative continuities and moral certainties of nineteenth-century literature. The symbolic, sometimes surreal, stories and novels of the Czech Jew Franz Kafka (1883–1924) centered on threatened, anxiety-ridden individuals who reveal the terrifying truths behind bourgeois appearances. The hero of Kafka's *The Trial* (1925) experiences the annihilation of his identity when, faced with a tribunal governed by no discernible rules, he is accused of a crime he cannot remember committing.

While Kafka pointed to the menace implied in the modern world, the American-born expatriate poet T. S. Eliot (1888–1965) saw modernity as not so much menacing as empty, a meaningless vacuum, sliding toward destruction. His poem "The Hollow Men" (1925) sums up the feelings of a generation, shortly after World War I:

> *This is the way the world ends*
> *This is the way the world ends*
> *This is the way the world ends*
> *Not with a bang but a whimper.*

Here Eliot doubts not merely the prospect of human survival but more, its significance. In the great uncertainty of the age, the harshest uncertainty was this: whether human life had any value at all.

UNCERTAIN BOUNDARIES: THE NEW WOMEN, THE SHRINKING FAMILY, THE NURTURANT STATE

Just as intellectual pessimism and artistic sabotage assailed old truths and disrupted old forms, familiar notions of the role of women, the function of the family, and the mission of the state dissolved in the face of new social realities. Over the next generation, a "new woman" emerged. Economically independent, sexually liberated, she was in appearance and behavior everything her mother was not. The dismantling of the traditional family that had begun with industrialization (see Chapter 23) proceeded apace as the family's social, economic, and cultural functions dwindled. At the same time, the state assumed duties of nurturing and protection that had once been provided (if at all) by the family or religious institutions.

The New Woman

During World War I, women quite suddenly acquired unprecedented freedom along with exceptional responsibilities (see Chapter 26). Their fathers, sons, and brothers were at war, and the conflict generated an insatiable need for guns, bullets, uniforms, and bandages. To supply these, and to sustain the civilians in whose name the slaughter was undertaken, factories must produce overtime, buses run, schools and hospitals function, foodstuffs reach shops and pantries. With millions of men called away from their work to fight, millions of women poured into the workforce. Their successful performance of essential tasks brought them welcome prestige, wages, and aspirations for a new future.

At war's end, men returned to the factories and women, for the most part, to their homes. Governments and employers pushed women out of their wartime occupations. The jobs were needed for the returning men. Married women were deemed to be dependents of their husbands, whose labors earned a "family wage." Resuming the traditional roles forgotten for the duration of the emergency, they nurtured the children whose numbers would partly compensate for wartime fatalities.

Women in Politics   Women returned home often with ballot in hand. In appreciation of their wartime contributions, and in response to sustained pressure from the **suffragist** movement, many nations awarded women the right to vote (see the chart below).

From one point of view, the granting of female suffrage marked the culmination of women's long-expressed aspirations. From another, it was an insufficient response to the intractable problem of women's unequal condition, rooted in their enduring experience of subordination to patriarchal families and societies. The first view was that of most bourgeois feminists, whose outlook was shaped by the prevailing liberalism of the governing classes (see Chapter 25). Liberal theorists had argued for women's right to be "active" citizens, a status marked by the right to vote. Bourgeois women had embraced that goal. By 1900, bourgeois feminism had narrowed almost entirely to the suffragist agenda.

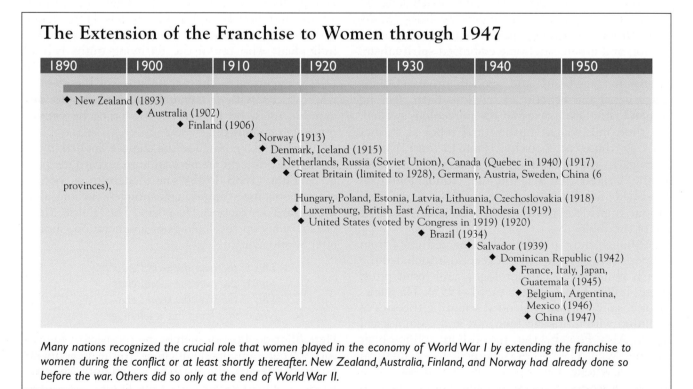

The Extension of the Franchise to Women through 1947

1890	1900	1910	1920	1930	1940	1950

◆ New Zealand (1893)
◆ Australia (1902)
◆ Finland (1906)
◆ Norway (1913)
◆ Denmark, Iceland (1915)
◆ Netherlands, Russia (Soviet Union), Canada (Quebec in 1940) (1917)
◆ Great Britain (limited to 1928), Germany, Austria, Sweden, China (6 provinces),
Hungary, Poland, Estonia, Latvia, Lithuania, Czechoslovakia (1918)
◆ Luxembourg, British East Africa, India, Rhodesia (1919)
◆ United States (voted by Congress in 1919) (1920)
◆ Brazil (1934)
◆ Salvador (1939)
◆ Dominican Republic (1942)
◆ France, Italy, Japan, Guatemala (1945)
◆ Belgium, Argentina, Mexico (1946)
◆ China (1947)

Many nations recognized the crucial role that women played in the economy of World War I by extending the franchise to women during the conflict or at least shortly thereafter. New Zealand, Australia, Finland, and Norway had already done so before the war. Others did so only at the end of World War II.

Many women of the laboring classes, in contrast, had aligned themselves with socialism and the social democratic parties that attracted large worker memberships during the late 1800s (see Chapters 22, 25). The socialist agenda for women was generally more ambitious than the liberal. It often included the right to divorce, to maternal custody of children, to property and contract, and to sexual freedom. In many social democratic parties, women met separately, created their own hierarchies, and had a significant role in the creation of policy. For socialist women, the granting of the right to vote in a political system they found inadequate offered little when compared to the elevation of the female condition.

German socialism was especially friendly to women's issues. Its early theoretician August Bebel (1840–1913) had written *Woman and Socialism* (1883), calling for women's civil, economic, and sexual rights, and dismissing as nonsense the notion that women were by nature limited to the tasks of childrearing and housekeeping. Later Karl Kautsky (1854–1938) predicted that by working alongside of men, women would gain equality with them: "[Woman] will be [man's] free companion, emancipated not only from the servitude of the house, but also from that of capitalism." On the eve of World War I, Clara Zetkin (1857–1933) criticized the suffragist movement as short-sighted, and called on women to fight for full economic and social freedom from both men and capitalism at once.

Russian socialism (which merged with the Bolshevik movement after 1917), was more militant than its counterparts (see Chapter 28). Women were prominent in the socialist parties active before World War I, as organizers, propagandists, agitators, and even assassins. Most notably, Alexandra Kollontai (1872–1952), an aristocratic Bolshevik advocate of free love, encouraged the factory women of St. Petersburg to embrace simultaneous feminist and socialist missions. An extract from her writings is given in *Witnesses* on p. 782. Some revolutionaries opposed Kollontai's approach, which they felt distracted everyone from the essential point, the class struggle. Kollontai survived the 1917 Revolution, however, to become a key figure in the new Communist government, whose leader Lenin (see Chapters 26, 28) detested women's subordination within the family and considered household drudgery to be "barbarously unproductive, petty, nerve-wracking, stultifying and crushing." As a leader of the Communist Party's Zhenotdel, or Women's Department (in existence 1919–1930), she was able to define feminist goals—female literacy and education, economic equality, freedom from housework and childcare, and sexual freedom—as part of that body's agenda.

The Bachelorette Few women, however, were socialist activists of the caliber of Zetkin or Kollontai.

The spur to more substantial change in women's lives came neither from socialism nor liberalism, but from the cultural explosions of the Jazz Age. Women's behavior—at least that of a vanguard of young, risk-taking women—reframed the issue of women's rights and women's place.

A New Woman emerged in the post-war years. She was a pleasure-seeking androgyne—a "*garçonne*" as the type was popularized in a daring 1922 French best-seller of that name, a "girl-boy" or "bachelorette." Her lean contours—a contrast to the bustled, corseted figure of her mother's generation—declared that her first function was not reproduction. She cut, or "bobbed," her hair, and applied lipstick, eyeshadow, rouge, and nail polish (previously regarded as the adornments of prostitutes). She wore slim skirts whose hemlines rose a shocking ten inches above her ankles, revealing more of the female body than had been seen (at least in fashionable dress) since antiquity. She was sexually liberated, and could use the devices and procedures made available by the medical profession to limit birth through **contraception** or **abortion**. Pressured by advertising and the advice of columnists in women's magazines, she might smoke cigarettes, drink cocktails, dance to the new sound of the jazz band, live alone or with a lover, have her own bank account, drive cars, and fly airplanes.

While the more expensive new recreations were restricted to rich young women, the attitudes of the New Woman were also adopted by working women. Such women might work in a shop, an office, or a profession. Certain professions enrolled large numbers of women, perhaps because of women's continued interest in gender-related matters. Teaching, nursing, and the new profession of social work were especially recognized as women's callings, where women could perform at the professional level the kinds of work seen as appropriate for women who, in the family framework, taught the young and cared for the sick and elderly. "She who cared only for her own flesh and blood," enthused the American economic theorist and feminist Charlotte Perkins Gilman (1860–1935), "is now active in all wide good works around the world."

The new field of social work emerged only after World War I in response to urban poverty in working-class and immigrant communities. Social workers aimed to assist individuals and families to improve their prospects by adapting to their communities and availing themselves of neighborhood resources. In the past, assistance of this sort had been provided by large family networks, or by religious institutions with long traditions of subventions to children, the poor, the elderly, the abandoned, the chronically ill, and socially-marginalized women—prostitutes, out-of-wedlock mothers, and widows. But family networks had often broken down among the urban poor and immigrant communities, and religious institutions

Rethinking Women's Roles and Possibilities

During the early twentieth century, feminist authors and activists conceived of deep reversals in the understanding of women's roles. Here, Charlotte Perkins Gilman posits the need for women's economic independence; Alexandra Kollontai announces the liberation of women from the anxieties of household management and childrearing; and Emma Goldman calls for women's freedom of choice in love, celebrating free love itself.

Charlotte Perkins Gilman criticizes women's economic dependence on men (1898): [M]en produce and distribute wealth; and women receive it at their hands. As men hunt, fish, keep cattle or raise corn, so do women eat game, fish, beef, or corn. ... The economic status of the human race in any nation, at any time, is governed mainly by the activities of the male. ... Although not producers of wealth, women [do, however] serve in the final processes of preparation and distribution. [Thus] their labor in the household has a genuine economic value. ... The labor of women in the house, certainly, enables men to produce more wealth than they otherwise could; and in this way women are economic factors in society. But so are horses. The labor of horses enables men to produce more wealth than they otherwise could. The horse is an economic factor in society. But the horse is not economically independent, nor is the woman. ...
(Charlotte Perkins Gilman, *Women and Economics*, 1898; ed. M. Schneir, 1972)

The end of women's work and the traditional family? Alexandra Kollontai describes life and work under Soviet communism (c. 1920): The individual household is dying. It is giving way ... to collective housekeeping. Instead of the working woman cleaning her flat, the communist society can arrange for men and women whose job is to go round in the morning cleaning rooms. ... Instead of the working woman having to struggle with the cooking ... communist society will organise public restaurants and communal kitchens. ... The working woman will not have to slave over the washtub any longer, or ruin her eyes darning her stockings and mending her linen. ...

[T]he workers' state will [even] come to replace the family; society will gradually take upon itself all the tasks that before the [Bolshevik] revolution fell to the individual parents. ... We already have homes for very small babies, creches, kindergartens, children's colonies and homes, hospitals and health resorts for sick children, restaurants, free lunches at school and free distribution of text books, warm clothing and shoes to school children. All this goes to show that the responsibility for the child is passing from the family to the collective. ...
(From A. Holt ed., *Selected Writings of Alexandra Kollontai*, 1977)

Russian anarchist and United States immigrant Emma Goldman celebrates free love and free women (1910): Free love? As if love is anything but free! ... Yes, love is free; it can dwell in no other atmosphere. In freedom it gives itself unreservedly, abundantly, completely. ... Love needs no protection; it is its own protection. So long as love begets life no child is deserted, or hungry, or famished for the want of affection. I know this to be true. I know women who became mothers in freedom by the men they loved. Few children in wedlock enjoy the care, the protection, the devotion free motherhood is capable of bestowing. ...
(Emma Goldman, "Marriage and Love," 1910; ed. M. Schneir, 1972)

---

had lost prestige and were insufficiently funded. Their place was taken by social workers.

Especially privileged and talented women sought careers as physicians, studying at those few European universities that from the 1890s opened their medical programs to women (or, in the United States, at the Women's Medical College of Philadelphia, established in 1851; the first medical program in the world available to female candidates). Women physicians inclined to those specializations which, like teaching and nursing, were extensions of activities traditional for females—pediatrics, gynecology, and obstetrics.

Although many working women of the post-war years pursued careers in teaching, nursing, medicine, and social work, most were office-workers, telephone operators, or shop-clerks. (Together with many male workers, they constituted the white-collar labor force, in contrast to blue-collar industrial workers.) Of these, many were young single women, who would cease work upon marriage and take up family responsibilities. But increasingly, they were married women who worked to supplement their family's income, or single women who chose not to marry (this group formed an increasingly large category).

Charlotte Perkins Gilman, editor of the journal *Forerunner* and author of *Women and Economics* (1898), quoted in *Witnesses* above, encouraged the trend for mature women to seek lifelong careers. Only financial independence, she argued, could give women genuine independence and dignity. Women who demonstrated their intellectual capacity and effectiveness in the workplace refuted the notions of nineteenth-century theorists (Darwin foremost among them; see Chapter 25) who held that women were biologically inferior to men. Men had reached a more advanced evolutionary stage, Darwin contended, than had women, children, or the pre-state peoples of the globe whom he termed "savages" (one instance of the linking of presuppositions about race or ethnicity with those about gender). Like proto-feminist thinkers from the Renaissance forward, Gilman rejoined that men and women shared a common, human nature. Women could as well as men, she argued, acquire the necessary expertise to work in the business and professional world.

Optional Motherhood   In order to do so, women might need to shed the burdens of housework, and postpone (or abjure) motherhood, or limit the number of births. Modern medicine made birth-control options available to women as never before in history: the use of the diaphragm that permitted safe, effective birth control without any requirement of abstinence; and safe surgical abortion by trained experts in antiseptic conditions. These breakthroughs provided release from the cycle of childbirth and lactation that had previously determined the lives of most women. They are, some experts suggest, the preconditions of women's liberation.

Some methods of birth control had been known for centuries (*coitus interruptus*, or male withdrawal before ejaculation, is described in the Bible and was regularly used throughout the European Middle Ages). But modern birth-control procedures had a short history. Underground information circulated during the 1800s about condoms, douches, and diaphragms. In 1882, Aletta Jacobs (1854–1929) established the first modern birth control clinic in Amsterdam. Over the next generation, Dutch clinics trained socialist and sexual radical advocates from Britain and the United States. One of these, Margaret Sanger (1879–1966) founded a clinic in Brooklyn,

New York in 1916—so that every woman might "control her own body"—and was imprisoned for thirty days for doing so. At first socialist in outlook (she urged working women not to propagate children who would slave in capitalist factories and die in capitalist wars), she broadened her message after World War I to invite all women to the sexual freedom that existed with the availability of birth control.

The birth control movement also flourished in Britain and northern Europe (though not in the Roman Catholic countries to the south). In 1921, a clinic was established in London by Marie Stopes (1880–1958), author of two widely-read books that advocated planned births. These pioneering establishments operated in a hostile environment, where religious stricture and national law condemned or forbade the distribution of birth-control information and devices. Sweden was an exception: here, from the 1930s, the state both permitted and subsidized the use of birth control.

The availability of birth control marks a watershed in the history of women's quest for equality and autonomy. The ability to control their bodies had the potential to free women more profoundly than the acquisition of civil or political rights. So momentous a social change aroused objections from different quarters. Many religious leaders protested contraception on moral grounds. The Roman Catholic Church forbade it, holding that the creation of new life fell under God's authority, and not that of the woman who might bear the child. Many political leaders, mostly male, also opposed birth limitation. They adhered to a traditional model of the family in which women remained subordinate members, with special responsibility for childrearing and housework.

Abortion aroused even greater alarm than contraception. It was condemned by most religious groups (the Roman Catholic Church forbade it under any circumstances in 1869), and was

The Great Procession: *On the home front, liberation meant women's ability to control her reproduction. On the political front, it meant suffrage—the right to vote. In the Great Procession on June 18, 1910, members and supporters of the Women's Social and Political Union organized by British feminist Emmeline Pankhurst march for women's suffrage. Note that the women still wear the long skirts that had been the fashion for centuries but which would soon rise during World War I, a costume change marking a radical shift in the public role of women.*

generally illegal. Nevertheless, women desiring abortions could generally obtain them. Poor women often fell victim to untrained or unscrupulous practitioners, who cheated them, seriously injured, or even killed them. Wealthy, well-informed women, in contrast, could achieve perfectly safe abortions clandestinely in properly-equipped clinics or hospitals.

However restricted, the capacity women acquired to control their reproductive lives enfranchised them as powerfully as did the right to vote. This capacity has enabled modern women to act as full and equal citizens of their nations and their world.

The Shrinking Family and the Nurturant State

The liberation of women was one of several circumstances that has led to the diminished importance of the parent-headed household in modern Western societies. The twentieth-century family has been a shrinking family—shrinking in size, shrinking in functions, shrinking in prestige, and shrinking in its capacity to socialize its children. As the family unit became less influential, the state was summoned to nurture its citizens and provide physical and emotional support to unprotected individuals or families in crisis.

New Patterns of Family Life   The average western European family had been shrinking since the nineteenth century. The utilization on a large scale of some method of birth control meant lower fertility. As improvements in nutrition and medicine enhanced survival rates for infants and children, families deliberately limited the number of children born. Parents were therefore less burdened by dependents who required care and expense. Family limitation seemed to be in the interests of both children and parents.

Among the elites, smaller families meant that children became the objects of intense concern. Their health, schooling, and well-being preoccupied parents, who lavished wealth on vacations, tutors, and amusements. Those privileged youngsters, in turn, could expect to inherit a larger share of family wealth than had their predecessors. Among the poor, smaller families meant a greater chance at survival. Scarce resources insufficient to nurture five or six children might adequately feed two, and permit better-nourished parents to withstand disease and live longer. Poor women eagerly sought the services of birth-control professionals, when these became available, not so much for the selfish indulgence in unregulated sexuality (as critics charged), but so as to protect children already born from the competition of those not yet conceived.

In Soviet Russia, women were promised that they did not need to forego marriage or pleasure or children; the state would feed, nurture, and school their offspring. The early radicalism of the Bolshevik

outlook of the 1920s on sex quickly waned, however, partly because the resources to set up the new forms of housing were simply not available. The promise of elaborate social support for women was in any case lost after 1930 when, under Stalin (see Chapter 28), the Women's Department was abolished, marriage laws were stiffened, abortion outlawed, and women told both to work and to clean, shop, and care for their children, somehow, at home.

Although the Soviet state urged its young families to reproduce, most European societies experienced the opposite phenomenon. The decline in birthrates continued, as the chart below shows. By 1900 in France, they had fallen nearly fifty percent since 1810. From highs of about thirty-five births annually per thousand population in France and Britain in the early 1800s, birthrates slipped below twenty by the interwar period. As women tended to marry earlier and have fewer children, they found they were still in the prime of life when they no longer had major responsibilities for the welfare of their families. These trends freed women to take on other tasks.

Families were also shrinking in the range of functions they performed, and in the prestige that they enjoyed. In the twentieth century, the functions performed by a family were very different from those of the noble clans that had organized social relations in ancient Greece and Rome and during the European

Declining Birthrates in France and Britain, 1801–1951

During the nineteenth and into the mid-twentieth century, birthrates declined in the most affluent Western nations. The main reason for this was that as mortality declined and the demand for consumer and cultural goods increased, families adopted strategies for the preservation of household resources.
Source: B. Mitchell, European Historical Statistics, 1750–1970 (Columbia University Press, 1975).

Middle Ages. These families had waged war, apprehended and punished criminals, settled disputes, and appeased gods or saints. In the modern age, families (or their male heads) no longer took responsibility for war, justice, and religion, but had delegated these to national armies, to legal professionals, and to the clergy. There was little left for families to do. Their remaining functions were primarily social (they participated in community affairs) and cultural (they transmitted values and knowledge to their children).

The diminution of family functions meant that the performance of those that remained was the focus for heightened attention. Concerns with the feeding and rearing of children became obsessive. Manuals compiled by "experts" told mothers what to do, implicitly doubting whether mother would be able to measure up to the task. The ability of the family to perform its cultural mission was disrupted, moreover, by the emergence of the youth peer group as a culturally influential section of society. While families tried to instill traditional values, young people looked to each other for standards of behavior that would define them as a group apart. Popular music, reshaped now by jazz, especially marked the world of the youth peer group, which distanced the family further from the social formation of its children.

Changes in the way families functioned meant that many families lost control over their children, or might be unable to feed and nurture an obstinate or rebellious child. The economic failures of the 1930s exacerbated these tendencies. Fathers might not be able to provide sustenance for their young, who in turn left the family home to fend for themselves.

The readjustment of such families, if they were poor, became the business of social workers. They attempted to teach, counsel, comfort, and heal the wounds caused by poverty, delinquency, and dysfunction. In her mission to the poor immigrants of Chicago, as an instance, the American Jane Addams (1860–1935) established Hull House in 1889, the prototype of the "settlement house," a community center that served as the site for the distribution of middle-class largesse. Providing classes in English and gymnastics, and opportunities for socialization as well as social services, it was an enormous success, drawing more than 1000 participants each week. By the 1920s, privately and publicly funded social work endeavors of this sort had outpaced those of religious organizations in attending to the needs of poor and troubled families.

As Western families diminished in size and in functions, many looked back nostalgically to the imagined warmth of traditional families. But many celebrated the freedom that could be enjoyed as the power waned of the father and head of household to dominate his wife and children. Those who hailed this new freedom were unconcerned when national states began to assume some of the functions the family had relinquished.

New Roles for the State   The growth of the nurturant, or "motherly" state—a state committed to the care of its citizens and not merely to their defense or moral discipline—was a phenomenon that marked the twentieth-century West. Earlier political theorists had proposed that the state might restrain the sinfulness of its members; or that it might act without regard to good and evil as a purely secular and autonomous entity; or that it must not intrude upon its citizens' private lives (see Chapter 15). In the nineteenth century, there developed the notion that the state was responsible for the welfare of every one of its citizens, and especially the weakest among them: the very young and very old, the disabled and the impoverished.

The modern state began to intervene in family life with the social welfare legislation of the late nineteenth century (see Chapter 22). In the 1880s in Germany, the chancellor Otto von Bismarck instituted programs that protected workers against loss of income due to disability, unemployment, or old age. Britain and France followed in the early 1900s. The experience of World War I stimulated further legislation in favor of the poor, of workers, and of families. So many millions had fought and suffered. The state, it was felt, must ease their financial pain and, however feebly, attempt to remedy their personal losses.

To this period may be traced the beginnings in the Western democracies of the modern **welfare state**. In addition to providing social insurance plans protecting workers against unemployment, disability, and old age, the state taxed its citizens—who were willing to bear the cost—to provide maternity leave, food subsidies, childcare centers and kindergartens, counseling, job training, and medical services, variously according to the customs and expectations of each society. The working-class population (lured away by such mechanisms from the bait of revolution) came to look to the state for support in the moments of crisis that had once been alleviated only by family or the Church.

Some theorists, while supporting state intervention in family life, resisted the trend toward a diminished maternal role in the socialization of children. The books of the Swedish writer Ellen Key (1849–1926) entitled *The Century of the Child* (1900) and *The Renaissance of Motherhood* (1914), both widely translated, elevated the role of the biological mother in childrearing at the same time that they called for the state to provide financial support for families and welfare guarantees for mothers without partners.

Proponents of **natalism**, especially in the fascist nations of Italy, Spain, and Germany, also stressed the mother's role and her need for state support. Their objectives were more complex than Key's. They sought to reaffirm the subordination of women within the family while encouraging the rapid birthing of new citizens (and new soldiers) for societies devastated by war fatalities. Birth control and abortion were accordingly banned. "The use of contraceptives means a violation of nature," announced German leader Adolf Hitler, "a degradation of womanhood, motherhood, and love."

In fascist societies, support of mothers was not part of a broader intervention in support of women, but was narrowly directed to bolstering the state's own aims. The Western nations under liberal or socialist governments also celebrated motherhood, awarding medals to mothers of multiple legitimate offspring and placing Mother's Day on the annual calendar. In these societies, support for mothers was balanced by support for other categories of the needy, including those who were outside of marital families.

For a variety of reasons, most Western nations took on nurturant functions in the decades after World War I. The reinvention of the state as the family of last resort was confirmed in the 1930s, at the nadir of worldwide economic catastrophe. How it did so will be observed in due course. First, it must be shown how that catastrophe came to be.

ECONOMIC UNCERTAINTY: FROM PROSPERITY TO THE BREADLINE

In the 1920s, the economies of Western nations and their allies, colonies, and trading partners around the globe struggled to recover from the dual trauma of world war and the Communist revolution (see Chapters 26, 28). Within a few years, prosperity, it

seemed, had returned. That prosperity was illusory. The nations of the West and the world followed the United States into a tenacious depression triggered by unrestrained speculation and a stock market crash. Efforts to tame the Great Depression failed until, ten years later, as another war began, military production defeated the monster of depression and put an end to the era of economic uncertainty.

Happy Days

After the war and the revolution, the shocked, grieving, and hungry peoples of the Western world longed to return to normalcy. The United States led them all as it rapidly recovered from a wartime economy and attained unprecedented prosperity. These were happy days for a young nation that had recently taken the lead in economic production and political affairs.

Boomtime in the United States   By the outbreak of World War I, the United States was world leader in industrial production and foreign trade. In the ten years following the Versailles settlement, United States production spurted forward. Its exports supplied half the manufactures produced in the world, as well as seventy percent of the oil and forty percent of the coal.

One of the secrets of that great productivity was the efficiency of American factories and their workforce. The assembly line, developed by entrepreneur Henry Ford (1863–1947) to speed up the manufacture of his automobiles, maximized the productivity of

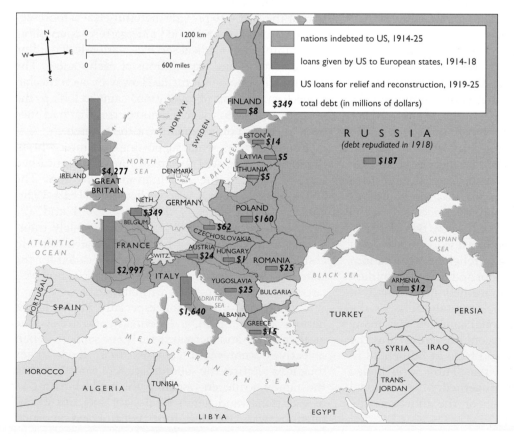

Map 27.1 European Debts to the United States, 1914–1925—War Loans and Loans for Relief and Reconstruction: *Europe's economic landscape was transformed by four years of war. Victors in battle, the Allied nations found themselves hugely in debt to the United States for war loans and other assistance. Of these nations, only Finland ever paid its debt in full. The Soviets repudiated their war debt, refusing to acknowledge their tsarist obligations. The vectors of capital transfer between Europe and North America are clear evidence of Europe's surrender of global economic leadership to the United States in the twentieth century. Why did the United States lend monies to a whole corridor of central-European states?*

industrial labor. So too did the methods of industrial organization advocated by Frederick Winslow Taylor (1856–1915). Closely observing workers' behavior in his famous time–motion studies, he showed how reorganization of space, tools, and procedures could lead to greater productivity.

The workers who accepted these regimens were organized in trade unions, which crystallized into two main groups representing skilled and unskilled workers respectively. The former of these, the American Federation of Labor (AFL), at its origin in 1886 a gathering of twenty-five unions of skilled laborers, had grown by 1901 to represent nearly one-third of all skilled workers. The latter, the Congress of Industrial Organizations, emerged only in 1935 in opposition to the AFL's exclusionary policies.

Labor unions resisted employers who demanded too much work, for too little pay, under unsafe conditions. A series of strikes and riots, violently suppressed, marked the formative years of the American labor movement: the Great Railroad Strike of 1877; the Haymarket Square Riot (between labor unionists and police) of 1886; the 1892 steelworkers' strike against the mill in Homestead, Pennsylvania; the 1894 strike of railroad Pullman workers. A new series of strikes erupted in the 1930s. By that era, the unions had retreated from militant demonstration and even political activity, and elevated "bread-and-butter" issues—salaries and benefits. The trade unionists pressed for a minimum wage, and restricted child labor. The number of laboring children aged from ten to fifteen dropped by 1930 to a third of its 1910 high, before it was at last made illegal in 1938.

United States trade unions avoided socialism. Some workers were intrigued by international socialism and supported the presidential ambitions of Eugene V. Debs (1855–1926), but most did not support the Bolshevik takeover in Russia in 1917. American workers remained within established political frameworks, voting for Democratic and Republican presidents, as did their employers.

As in Europe, many wage-earners were not industrial workers. Agricultural workers, mostly non-unionized, were already suffering from an agricultural depression which had set in during the 1920s. White collar workers—salesmen and women, managers, clerks, and secretaries, as well as professionals such as accountants and engineers, teachers and professors, nurses, lawyers, and physicians, often better paid than industrial workers—were generally not unionized.

In the prosperous 1920s, American consumers purchased the goods produced by American factories—phonographs, telephones, vacuum cleaners, sewing machines, and, especially, automobiles. Spending for consumption, for leisure, for the home, they fueled a rapidly growing economy (see *Witnesses*, p. 790).

The companies producing these goods were traded on the stock market, or required investment loans.

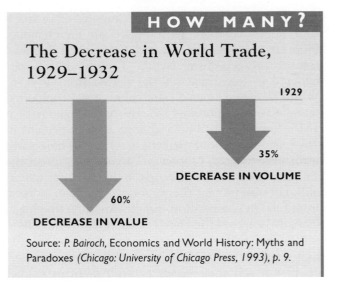

HOW MANY?

The Decrease in World Trade, 1929–1932

1929

35%
DECREASE IN VOLUME

60%
DECREASE IN VALUE

Source: P. Bairoch, Economics and World History: Myths and Paradoxes *(Chicago: University of Chicago Press, 1993), p. 9.*

These needs were handled by the brokers and bankers, many of them based in Wall Street, New York City, the home of the world's busiest exchanges.

The stock exchanges were closely linked with American banks, which purchased stocks, and made loans to domestic and foreign companies and governments. American bankers had by now displaced the British as the main players in an international money system. It was largely American money that had financed World War I, sending about $10 billion to some twenty nations. As those loans were repaid, others were issued. Gold flooded into the United States as a result of debt repayment, reaching unprecedented levels.

In 1900, the international currency system was anchored by the British pound sterling, itself tied to a gold standard—pounds were literally as good as gold. After World War I, the American dollar, also linked to gold, displaced the pound as the principal international currency. The gold standard supported the global trading system by ensuring convertibility among currencies. It was, however, inflexible. The supply of currency was limited to the value of gold the nation possessed. The government could not print more money to stimulate the economy. Without sufficient money to purchase goods and services, production could drop, and deflation follow.

As the world's greatest manufacturer and banker, the United States was central to the global trading system. So long as goods and money flowed smoothly out from the United States and back again, that commercial system was healthy. If the behavior of American investors or producers changed, the system was jeopardized. During the 1920s, trade barriers and the distractions of the stock market began to interfere with international commercial rhythms.

Many historians fault American foreign trade policy during the 1920s. It encouraged the export of manufactures and agricultural produce, and insisted that markets abroad should be kept open for all comers. But stiff tariffs limited imports of products that might compete with American merchandise. From its origins, the United States had inclined toward protectionism (while Britain in contrast adhered to free trade for the period from 1846 to World War I). Duties on the value of most imported manufactures amounted to thirty-five percent in 1816, forty percent by 1832, forty to fifty percent in 1875, and forty-four percent in 1913. These tariff walls were erected, proponents argued, to protect the "infant industries" of a newly industrializing nation and, later, to protect the wages of American workers from foreign competition. Employing the same logic, Congress enacted the Hawley-Smoot Tariff in 1930—raising the tariff rate on imports to the unprecedented high of about forty-eight percent. Foreign producers could not sell their goods in an American market which had made them artificially expensive; without those sales, they were unable to repay their debts to American bankers.

The investment mania that swept over Wall Street in the late 1920s further disrupted the free flow of global trade. Money that might otherwise have been sent abroad poured into American stocks and funds. From 1928 to 1929, the amount of capital sent abroad dropped sharply—loans to Germany, for instance, shrank from $277 to $29.5 million. Quick, dramatic returns appealed more to investors than the slow growth of distant enterprises. The richest people in the United States, the most powerful nation in the world, knew happy days were with them and did not consider that what went up fast might descend catastrophically.

Post-war Europe   As Americans rejoiced in their prosperity, Europe inched forward. Rebuilding commenced, and standards of living improved. By 1925, for the first time the production of food and raw materials surpassed their 1913 high.

Britain and France were strained by the need to assume the costs of new social programs. War debts burdened them. Productivity lagged. To protect manufactures, both nations imposed tariffs. In doing so, Britain broke with the free trade tradition in place since 1846. In the hope of bolstering British currency, in addition, the government returned in 1925 to the gold standard abandoned during the war (as did some forty nations in all); then repudiated it finally in 1931.

Both British and French governments also faced well-organized demands for higher wages and benefits from industrial workers. In Britain, the election of 1924 led to a Labour government (whose constituents were mostly union members) with Liberal support. Nevertheless, conservative interests continued to direct the economy. In 1931, a "National Government" (a coalition of Labour, Liberal, and Conservative ministers) took over, but failed to exercise effective leadership.

In France, socialist and communist parties competed, failing to capture a majority. Following the 1934 turnabout in policy announced by the Comintern (the Soviet organization monitoring extra-Soviet communist parties), communists, socialists, and other groups joined in a Popular Front against the menace of Fascism (see Chapter 28). In 1936, a left-liberal government was elected with a strong fifty-seven percent of the vote. One of the Popular Front governments linking left and central political parties, it was led by the Jewish socialist Léon Blum (1872–1950), who attempted to steer a course between the agendas of Left and Right. Although it liberalized the workplace, and established annual vacations and a forty-hour workweek, the Popular Front could not reverse an economic downturn, as productivity slipped and investment lagged.

Lackluster economic performance was the pattern in western Europe, as in France and Britain. Communist parties were springing up, branching off from social democratic parties, as communists and socialists competed for the loyalty of trade unionists.

In central Europe, the defeated nations of World War I faced disheartening economic problems. Germany, above all, was saddled with the burden of reparations—calculated so as to recompense the victor nations for the total expense of the war. These were not amounts that a demoralized and starving nation was willing to pay. To do so would have required a double sacrifice: a voluntary decrease in consumption of goods, and an increase in taxes. That two-pronged strategy was unacceptable. Instead, Germany defaulted through 1922. The next year French and Belgian forces occupied the coalfields of the buffer Ruhr region, intending to seize the value of the debt in the form of coal. Only the intervention of the United States and Britain in 1924 prevented a meltdown to violence (as the local population resisted) and chaos. By the terms of the Dawes Plan, a more acceptable payment plan was established. The United States would make loans to Germany according to a complex schedule, enabling Germany in turn to repay the French.

In the end, Germany never paid the reparations owed. Yet the reparations crisis had wreaked terrible damage upon the German economy. To raise funds to pay the Ruhr laborers while they resisted French occupation, the German government printed paper currency at will, shown in *Windows On*, p. 789. By November 15, 1923, the Deutschmark had fallen to twelve-billionths of its 1922 (July) value (from 493.2 to 4,200,000,000,000 marks per dollar). Viewed differently, it fell to a flabbergasting one-trillionth of its value of 4.2 marks per dollar in 1914 (July). This single fact bespeaks an economic trauma whose effects on the history of Germany and the world would be played out tragically over the next twenty-two years (see Chapter 28).

Highs and Lows

Issuing of the "Rentenmark," November 15, 1923

A first surge of prosperity following World War I preceded a decade of economic turmoil. Above, German officials are ready to dispose of chests of bills which have lost much of their value in an era of devastating inflation. The hyperinflation that struck Germany in the early 1920s was a premonition of the depression and deflation that struck worldwide after the crash of the New York stock market in 1929. On the eve of that crash, the Wall Street brokers in the image shown here (right) happily read the news on slender lengths of ticker tape of their ever-mounting profits. Those highs would soon give way to cataclysmic lows, and the worst depression of the modern era. Depression followed the stock market crash, bringing unemployment to millions of workers around the globe. Ten years later, the Depression still lingered. Hunger and unemployment threatened to trigger outbreaks of social unrest. Below, a watercolor painting shows hunger marchers in 1932 being dispersed by London police.

Wall Street, October 1929

How can similar political pressures give rise, in different settings, to hyperinflation or depression and deflation? What are their different effects on the masses?

Hunger marchers in London, 1932.

 To continue your investigation of this topic, please go to www.prenhall.com/king for the related **WINDOWS** on the **WEB** activity

Living Through the Great Depression

Americans were unprepared for the Great Depression. Here, President Calvin Coolidge, only months before the Depression began, expresses confidence in American wealth. Over the next years, ordinary people without jobs or cash suffered hunger and humiliation, like the author of the second excerpt, and the young African American later known as Malcolm X, author of the third.

United States president Calvin Coolidge speaks to Congress on the state of the American economy on the eve of the Crash and Great Depression (1928): No Congress of the United States ever assembled, on surveying the state of the Union, has met with a more pleasing prospect than that which appears at the present time. ... The great wealth created by our enterprise and industry, and saved by our economy, has had the widest distribution among our own people, and has gone out in a steady stream to serve the charity and the business of the world. ... The country can regard the present with satisfaction and anticipate the future with optimism.
(President Calvin Coolidge, Message to Congress, December 4, 1928; ed. E. Hobsbawm, 1996)

The American economy—the general condition of the unemployed multitudes (1932): You are a carpenter. Your last cent is gone. They have cut off the gas. ... You can't get a job now for love or money. What do you do? ... [Y]ou go to the cop. He pulls out his directory and sends you to one of the listed charitable societies. ... You draw the Episcopal Family Relief Society. The Relief Society clears your name through the central agency to see that you are not receiving help elsewhere. ... Eventually it will allot you $2 to $8 a week, depending on the locality and the funds available. If its funds are exhausted it asks you to wait.
(From *Fortune* magazine, September 1932; ed. J. A. Garraty, 1986)

African American leader Malcolm X recalls the Depression's effects on poor blacks in Michigan (1934): By 1934, we really began to suffer. This was about the worst depression year, and no one we knew had enough to eat or live on. Some old family friends visited us now and then. At first they brought food. Though it was charity, my mother took it. ... In Lansing, there was a bakery where, for a nickel, a couple of us children would buy a tall flour sack of day-old bread and cookies, and then walk the two miles back out into the country to our house. ... But there were times when there wasn't even a nickel and we would be so hungry we were dizzy. My mother would boil a big pot of dandelion greens and we would eat that.
(From J. A. Garraty ed., *The Great Depression*, 1986)

With cheap—indeed worthless—marks, the government paid the Ruhr workers. But in 1923 devaluation caused hyperinflation that terrified the German people. The sturdy, prudent middle class found that their lifesavings had been made worthless by unbridled inflation. Those on fixed incomes became paupers, while workers had to be paid several times per day with bills of rapidly declining worth—and to carry their wages home in a suitcase or wheelbarrow.

Those scarred by hyperinflation would not forget the crisis. Yet Germany revived later in the decade, and the young entrepreneurs and managers who benefited most from that boom reveled in a new, though limited, prosperity.

To stimulate production in the Soviet Union, in 1921 the Communist leader Lenin, loosened briefly the economic controls imposed after 1917 (see Chapter 28). Under Lenin's New Economic Policy (NEP), retail trade and light industry were returned to private ownership and peasants were allowed to cultivate their own land. By 1929, with Lenin dead (in 1924) and Stalin in power, that policy was reversed. A series of Five-Year Plans set production goals for state-controlled industry that boosted the Soviet Union to the forefront of the developed nations.

The Scandinavian nations of Denmark, Finland, Norway, and Sweden found a "middle way" between the imposition of state controls in the Soviet Union and the free-market principles of the western European nations. Here the government promised benefits to every citizen from cradle to grave, paying for them with heavy taxation. Some major industries were nationalized, but many others were permitted to flourish in free-market competition. Economic experimentation yielded both industrial growth and improved living conditions. The Scandinavian system posed an alternative to the hectic buying and selling and uncertainty of outcomes that characterized the United States economy at this period.

In 1929, on the far side of the Atlantic, speculation in stocks, the spawning of holding companies, and the multiplication of unsecured loans marked an economy that might, at any point, go haywire. Speculation soared in the period from 1923 to 1929, years that saw the quadrupling of the volume of shares traded. Investors believed the market would never go down. They borrowed in order to buy, the only collateral being the value of the shares purchased. Such an unprecedented "bull market" led to catastrophe as stocks became desperately overvalued, and finance capital outstripped the capacity of consumers to buy. On October 24, 1929, "Black Thursday," disaster struck. That day, on which nearly 13 million shares were sold, and losses mounted to 3 billion dollars, marks the beginning of the Great Crash. Another plunge came five days later. Stock prices plummeted from an index of 216 to 145 by the end of November, and over the next three years pursued an unsteady descent to bottom out at 34—from $87 billion at their peak to $18 billion at their low. The financial giants of Wall Street trembled, shocked by their own losses and uncertain about what was to come. What came was a broadening of economic crisis into every corner of the United States, Europe, and the world.

On the Dole

The collapse in stock values in October 1929 set off a chain of events culminating in a profound, stubborn depression—the Great Depression. Banks had been involved in the speculative excess of 1928–1929. Pressed by their losses, they called in the monumental loans they had issued to fund the investment frenzy. Their debtors could not pay. Banks fell, pre-

cipitating the failure of thousands of others, and cheating depositors of their savings. Those deposits were uninsured (insurance of small bank deposits was instituted only in 1933). Lifesavings were lost. Public confidence plummeted.

The banking crisis combined with larger economic trends to create monumental hardship. Production fell twenty percent from 1929 to 1930; by 1932, it stood at one-half its 1929 level. Wages fell, and workers were laid off. The passage in *Witnesses* on p. 790 describes their plight. The number of unemployed rose to more than 13 million by 1932—almost thirty percent of the workforce in the United States. Since workers were also consumers, spending slowed, especially on big-ticket items whose high rate of sales was an index of prosperity—housing and automobiles. Even necessities were expensive, and consumers bought on credit, accumulating unmanageable debt.

The emergency deepened. Warehouses packed full with merchandise canceled their factory orders.

Map 27.2 Maximum Unemployment Rates for Industrial Workers, 1930–1938: *The Great Depression hit different regions at different times and with varying intensity. Shown here are the year and approximate rate of maximum unemployment during the period 1930–1938 for fourteen nations. The Soviet Union, in the midst of its Five Year Plans, remained wholly insulated from the unemployment that the Great Depression brought other nations. Japan, engaged in industrial expansion, suffered less than most. The maxima for Germany and the United States exceeded all others. The great disruption unemployment caused in these nations was expressed in divergent social and political responses: for Germany, the rise of Fascism (see Chapter 28), and for the United States, the launching of the New Deal. What might explain relatively low rates of unemployment in France, Belgium, and Britain?*

The Shame of Need, the Dignity of Work

New York during the Depression: Unemployment forced millions of men and women into a poverty and degradation symbolized by, above all, the breadline. Scenes such as this one in New York were repeated in cities and towns around the world.

the burden of war debt. At a conference in Lausanne, Switzerland, in 1932, an attempt was made to unloose the knot of debt obligations. France agreed to end reparations with a final transfer from Germany—which Germany never made. France defaulted, in turn, on its debt to the United States, which continued to insist, even as the demand paralyzed European economies, that all war debts be honored.

European banks failed if they could not respond to American calls for funds. In 1931, the Austrian giant Creditanstalt, drained by withdrawals of foreign funds, closed its doors. That move set off financial panic in Europe as depositors rushed to their banks to withdraw their endangered funds. In Britain, they withdrew gold, depleting the supply. Humiliated, Britain was forced finally to repudiate the gold standard that had anchored the pound. Now the pound inflated heavily, losing twenty-eight percent of its value in 1931.

Britain and her trading partners (including members of the newly-founded Commonwealth of Nations) fled gold, but the United States maintained the gold standard (aside from a brief interlude, and

The unemployed could not pay their rent. Homeless, they moved out into the streets, building shanties for their families of scrap lumber and debris. Shanty towns grew up outside the cities which a few years earlier had beckoned to newcomers with the promise of work and good fortune. Called "Hoovervilles" after Herbert Hoover, president from 1929–1933 when the Depression settled on the nation, they were visible monuments to the plight of the dispossessed.

The central symbol of the Depression, however, was not the shanty town. It was the breadline, or the "dole," the food handout that signaled the degradation suffered by the millions. Relief organizations opened soup kitchens and distributed food. Every day, lines of hungry adults and children reached outside and snaked around corners, as the hopeless and dishonored waited to eat from the giving hands of strangers. A breadline in New York is depicted above.

Effects in Europe   The stock market crash rocketed around the globe. American investment overseas dropped drastically from 1929 to 1933, then virtually ceased for the rest of the decade. While the flow of dollars abroad dried up, American bankers called in their loans from foreign borrowers (mostly European). The flow of gold and coin to the United States swelled, while European stores were depleted, and they still groaned under

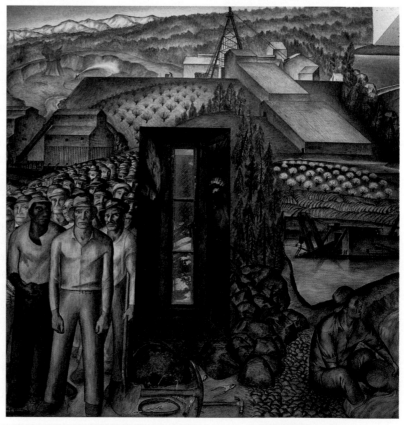

John Langley Howard, **California Industrial Scenes:** *The workers' faces painted in their honor by Paul Langley Howard in a mural series from around 1934 show great ethnic and racial variety but a single mood of determination, that is tinged by sadness.* (Coit Tower, San Francisco)

subsequent devaluation of the dollar), along with France, Belgium, the Netherlands, and Switzerland. These nations formed a separate trading bloc, distinct from the British. In addition to these two, a third bloc developed in central Europe, led by Germany. The barriers between these three isolated, exclusionary trading blocs were bolstered by high tariffs, installed to discourage foreign imports and protect domestic manufactures. The free and integrated trading network of the West in its boom years had vanished.

The remedies adopted for economic crisis only yielded more crisis. Currency inflation, economists reasoned, might help. With a cheaper currency, prices would decline and people could buy more goods. Protective tariffs would force them to purchase domestic manufactures, and sustain employment. These were illusions. Instead, trade declined, and production and employment levels fell, as Map 27.2 on p. 791 shows. At the depths of the Depression in the early 1930s, unemployment in the developed nations may have reached as high as 30 million—around one-fourth to one-fifth of the workforce, and in Germany as much as two-fifths (about 6 million workers)—with many others forced into part-time work.

The effects of stock market collapse, bank failure, production slowdown, and mass unemployment were felt around the globe. Many of the colonized nations of Asia, Africa, and Latin America were primary producers of agricultural commodities. Their fortunes had soared during World War I, when Europe needed their products. After the war, Europeans relied less on the importation of primary products from these markets. As the market became glutted with certain commodities, agricultural prices fell worldwide. The producers of wheat, sugar, rice, coffee, and other staples could not rapidly adjust to a changed marketplace. (India, an exception, took advantage of Britain's crisis to develop its own steel and textile industries.) The laborers deprived of the profits on their goods could not purchase the exports of the industrialized nations. Agricultural surplus and weakened sales exacerbated the international depression, as world trade sank by 1933 to nearly one-third of its 1929 level (see *How Many?* on p. 787).

The Soviet Union and Germany　The Great Depression never came to the Soviet Union. It struck Germany hard, but was defeated. Between 1929 and 1938, these two nations ruled by totalitarian governments (see Chapter 28) had annual growth rates per capita of 4.3 percent and 4.2 percent respectively—the highest in the Western world, or indeed anywhere in the world except Japan (where the figure was 5 percent). By the 1930s, the Soviet Union had experienced a brief return to capitalism under Lenin's NEP (New Economic Plan) and was suffering the forcible creation of a fully industrialized and fully socialized economy under the terms of Stalin's First Five Year

Plan (see Chapter 28). Workers and peasants labored to meet Stalin's high quotas for agricultural and industrial production. While agricultural output remained weak, industry boomed, constantly fed by massive capital reinvestment allocated by the central government. Although the Soviet people suffered grievously from Stalin's policies, they were isolated from the depression that gripped western Europe.

Similarly, Germany benefited from the policies of the Nazi leader Adolf Hitler. Of the Western nations, Germany was hardest hit by depression. It had suffered a staggering unemployment rate and a catastrophic thirty-nine percent drop in production. That misery was Hitler's opportunity; he seized power in 1933 and brought the Depression to an end. His Four Year Plan launched in 1936 (financed by deficit spending on the **Keynesian** model also adopted in the United States by Roosevelt) aimed at economic self-sufficiency and a rapid increase in industrial production—especially military production. Commercial agreements made with Poland, Hungary, and Romania in central and eastern Europe assured Germany a supply of agricultural products and raw materials for industrial use. Meanwhile, German industrial scientists developed synthetic substitutes for exotic resources (cotton, wool, rubber) to bypass the need for foreign imports. The total control that Hitler exercised over economic life allowed him to mobilize people, commodities, and money to enhance industrial growth and assure military readiness.

Searching for Remedies　Elsewhere the Depression persisted. People looked to their governments to take some action. Governments remained committed to deflation and steep tariffs. Workers defeated by hardship lined up for the dole.

In the United States, the election of Franklin Delano Roosevelt as president (1933–1945), brought fresh hope and the **New Deal**, which brought some relief and new aspirations. With an expression of compassion that had not been heard in American political life since perhaps Abraham Lincoln, Roosevelt defined the cause of the economic emergency, named the guilty parties, and announced the cure in his inaugural address as president. The cause was greed; the guilty parties were the rich speculators; and the cure was the largesse to be provided by the government for the "one-third of the nation" that was, as Roosevelt put it in his second inaugural address, "ill-housed, ill-clad, ill-nourished."

The first task was to organize cash relief. The Federal Emergency Relief Administration, created in 1933, handed out millions of dollars to states and agencies to help relieve hunger and homelessness. Two years later, the Social Security Act established for the first time in the United States the principle that those who could not work—children, the elderly, the disabled—should receive state benefits. It created a new social contract between government and people, superseding the system of private charity and self-help that had prevailed in the past.

In addition to these first steps toward establishing a modern welfare state—a state that assumes the obligation to sustain its citizens from cradle to grave—the New Deal set up programs to put the unemployed to work in public works projects and to sustain artists and writers by assigning them historical and cultural projects with a government salary. As a further measure to protect workers' interests, the New Deal created the National Labor Relations Act in 1935 that supervised unions and protected their right to engage in collective bargaining. To prevent future economic catastrophes, it passed legislation in 1933 and 1934 that insured bank deposits and supervised the stock exchanges.

All of these programs were expensive. Indeed, the New Deal sought to accomplish its goals by going into debt, with the government borrowing to support its programs. That tactic represented an abandonment of conventional views of government spending that dictated a balanced budget, especially during crisis periods. Instead, the New Deal embraced the novel economic theories of the British economist John Maynard Keynes (1883–1946), author of the 1926 work *The End of Laissez-Faire*. Keynes urged the state to engage in "counter-cyclical" activity: when times were hard, it should spend; when prosperity returned, it should raise taxes to enhance revenues and conserve wealth. The free market could not be relied upon to reequilibrate economic systems, which required the deliberate intervention of state spending stimuli and restraints. Keynes's theory seemed to offer a compromise position between capitalism, with its program of unrestrained profit-seeking, and socialism, with its tendency to deaden individual initiative. The New Deal set out to spend its way to recovery,

HOW MANY?

Rise and Fall of Annual Growth Rate in the United States, Japan, and the Soviet Union Before and After 1929

ANNUAL GROWTH RATE IN PER CAPITA GNP

Legend: ■ 1925–1929   ▨ 1929–1938

US: +2.3, -1.3
Japan: +1.1, +5.0
Soviet Union: +6.0, +4.3

The Great Depression played havoc with national rates of production and world trade (see Box on p. 820). Here the hard-hit United States suffers a steep decline in its annual growth rate, while the Soviet Union, turning from its NEP (New Economic Policy) developed under Lenin to the Five Year Plans developed under Stalin, suffers a more modest loss. Japan, arming itself for expansion in its Asian hinterland, experiences rapid growth.
Source: P. Bairoch, Economics and World History: Myths and Paradoxes *(Chicago: University of Chicago Press, 1993), p. 8.*

imbuing American liberalism with a new, pro-government ethos. As promised in Roosevelt's campaign song, "happy days" would come again, brought about by a newly activist state.

Conclusion
UNCERTAIN LIVES AND THE MEANING OF THE WEST

Roosevelt's Depression remedies may have alleviated some of the pain caused by economic collapse. But they did not reverse the economic trend. In 1938, unemployment was nearly as high as at the low point of Depression. World trade had stagnated, restricted by narrowly nationalistic economic policies. Only renewed military production was sufficient to stimulate the economy. By 1939, as European leaders rearmed their nations in preparation for another war, the factories hummed again, producing bullets, guns, and profits. The people of the Western world were able to go off the dole only because they were once again sent off to the front.

The economic volatility of the postwar years, and especially the Great Depression, had brought not only hardship but also anxiety to the people of the West and of the world. The era of the Modern had arrived—and then it crashed. Who, if anyone, was at fault? What, if anything, could be done? When would normalcy return? Amid the uncertainties born of economic crisis, many looked for strong leaders, who gave clear and positive answers, and promised that certainty would rise from despair. Those leaders came, promising the certainty that only totalitarian regimes can give a demoralized and disoriented populace; but with them came tragedy.

QUESTIONS TO CONSIDER

1. Why did artists in the 1920s and 1930s choose not to depict objective reality?

2. Why is cinema a particularly effective medium for shaping mass opinion?

3. Why is jazz an essentially "modern" artistic form? With its roots in African–American culture, why was it especially suited to an age of modernism?

4. How did World War I affect women and children for the better, and for the worse?

5. Both democratic and totalitarian states intervened in the lives of families after World War I. What were the benefits and dangers of those interventions?

6. What are the ways in which states might have acted to prevent the Great Depression?

SUGGESTED RESOURCES

Brendon, Piers, *The Dark Valley: A Panorama of the 1930s* (New York: Knopf, 2000). Panoramic look at the lives of people and states in the United States, Europe, Russia, and Japan involved in the economic and political crises of the second interwar decade.

Brian, Denis, *Einstein: A Life* (New York: J. Wiley, 1996). Comprehensive and up-to-date biography of this monumental figure.

Chauncey, George, *Gay New York: Gender, Urban Culture and the Making of the Gay Male World, 1890–1940* (1994). Explores the creation of a gay culture in New York in the late-19th and early-20th century.

Eichengreen, Barry, *Golden Fetters: The Gold Standard and the Great Depression, 1919–1939* (Oxford: Oxford University Press, 1992). Focuses on policy decisions regarding the gold standard as key to the onset and nature of the Depression.

Erenberg, Lewis A., *Swingin' the Dream: Big Band Jazz and the Rebirth of American Culture* (Chicago: University of Chicago Press, 1998). Shows how jazz became a popular music form that lifted the spirits of the depression generation, and came to represent America.

Golan, Romy, *Modernity and Nostalgia: Art and Politics in France between the Wars* (New Haven: Yale University Press, 1995). Argues that French Modernism, from World War I to Vichy was permeated with nostalgic and traditionalist longings deriving from the trauma of the war.

Jelavich, Peter, *Berlin Cabaret* (Cambrdige, MA: Harvard University Press, 1993). Jelavich sees *cabaret* as a reshaping of older, popular forms of entertainment by artistic elites searching for new ways to express the nature of life in this key "modern" city.

Kanigel, Robert, *The One Best Way: Frederick Winslow Taylor and the Enigma of Efficiency* (New York: Viking, 1997). Taylor pioneered time and motion studies and their application to work, helping create the 20th-century workplace.

Kennedy, David M., *Freedom from Fear: The American People in Depression and War, 1929–1945* (Oxford: Oxford University Press, 1999). Pulitzer-Prize-winning narrative of how Americans faced and faced down misery and danger over two critical decades.

Pedersen, Susan, *Family, Dependence, and the Origins of the Welfare State: 1914–1945* (Cambridge: Cambridge University Press, 1993). Comparative study of the movements pushing for family allowances in France and Britain during the first half of the 20th century.

Sklar, Robert, *Film: An International History of the Medium* (New York: Prentice Hall–H. N. Abrams, 1993). Surveys the development of cinema from its earliest days to the recent past, with an emphasis on the interaction of cinema, society, and technology.

Skocpol, Theda, *Protecting Soldiers and Mothers: The Political Origins of Social Policy in the United States* (Cambridge, MA: Belknap Press of Harvard University Press, 1992). Finds that the United States, although its "welfare state" was started later than European peers, nevertheless created many pioneering social support programs, especially maternalist ones, pressured by a multiplicity of vibrant interest groups.

Stites, Richard, *The Women's Liberation Movement in Russia: Feminism, Nihilism and Bolshevism, 1860–1930*, 2nd ed. (Princeton, NJ: Princeton University Press, 1991). Examines the historical development of the "woman question" in Russia during the 19th and early 20th centuries.

Weber, Eugen, *The Hollow Years: France in the 1930s* (New York: W. W. Norton, 1994). Informative study of Depression-era France treating in detail the arts, culture, and ordinary life.

Existentialism—links to essays and websites on existentialism: **http://www.knowdeep.org/existentialism**

Women's Studies Database: History (University of Maryland): **http:// www.inform.umd.edu/EdRes/Topic/WomensStudies/Reading Room/History**

America from the Great Depression to World War II: 1935–1945, prints and photographs (American Memory, Library of Congress): **http://memory.loc.gov/ammem/fsowhome.html**

● Western Civilization Documents CD-ROM

27.1 Werner Heisenberg: Uncertainty

27.2 Jean-Paul Sartre: Existentialism

27.3 A Room of One's Own

27.4 The Depression: Germany's Unemployed

27.5 Neville Chamberlain Defends the Policy of Appeasement

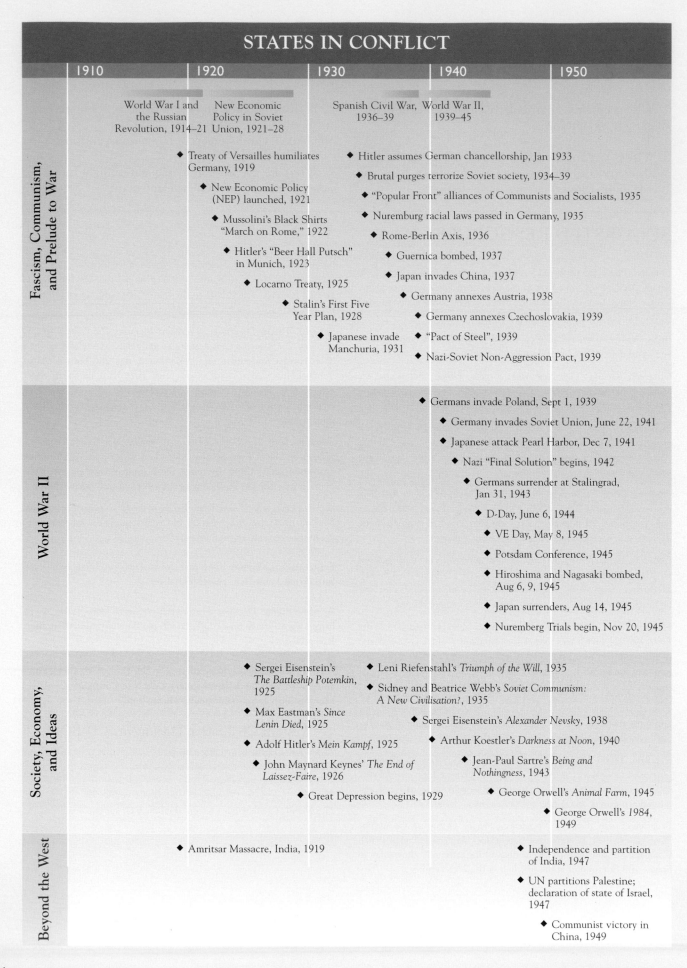

STATES IN CONFLICT

	1910	1920	1930	1940	1950

World War I and the Russian Revolution, 1914–21

New Economic Policy in Soviet Union, 1921–28

Spanish Civil War, 1936–39

World War II, 1939–45

Fascism, Communism, and Prelude to War

◆ Treaty of Versailles humiliates Germany, 1919

◆ New Economic Policy (NEP) launched, 1921

◆ Mussolini's Black Shirts "March on Rome," 1922

◆ Hitler's "Beer Hall Putsch" in Munich, 1923

◆ Locarno Treaty, 1925

◆ Stalin's First Five Year Plan, 1928

◆ Japanese invade Manchuria, 1931

◆ Hitler assumes German chancellorship, Jan 1933

◆ Brutal purges terrorize Soviet society, 1934–39

◆ "Popular Front" alliances of Communists and Socialists, 1935

◆ Nuremburg racial laws passed in Germany, 1935

◆ Rome-Berlin Axis, 1936

◆ Guernica bombed, 1937

◆ Japan invades China, 1937

◆ Germany annexes Austria, 1938

◆ Germany annexes Czechoslovakia, 1939

◆ "Pact of Steel", 1939

◆ Nazi-Soviet Non-Aggression Pact, 1939

World War II

◆ Germans invade Poland, Sept 1, 1939

◆ Germany invades Soviet Union, June 22, 1941

◆ Japanese attack Pearl Harbor, Dec 7, 1941

◆ Nazi "Final Solution" begins, 1942

◆ Germans surrender at Stalingrad, Jan 31, 1943

◆ D-Day, June 6, 1944

◆ VE Day, May 8, 1945

◆ Potsdam Conference, 1945

◆ Hiroshima and Nagasaki bombed, Aug 6, 9, 1945

◆ Japan surrenders, Aug 14, 1945

◆ Nuremberg Trials begin, Nov 20, 1945

Society, Economy, and Ideas

◆ Sergei Eisenstein's *The Battleship Potemkin*, 1925

◆ Max Eastman's *Since Lenin Died*, 1925

◆ Adolf Hitler's *Mein Kampf*, 1925

◆ John Maynard Keynes' *The End of Laissez-Faire*, 1926

◆ Great Depression begins, 1929

◆ Leni Riefenstahl's *Triumph of the Will*, 1935

◆ Sidney and Beatrice Webb's *Soviet Communism: A New Civilisation?*, 1935

◆ Sergei Eisenstein's *Alexander Nevsky*, 1938

◆ Arthur Koestler's *Darkness at Noon*, 1940

◆ Jean-Paul Sartre's *Being and Nothingness*, 1943

◆ George Orwell's *Animal Farm*, 1945

◆ George Orwell's *1984*, 1949

Beyond the West

◆ Amritsar Massacre, India, 1919

◆ Independence and partition of India, 1947

◆ UN partitions Palestine; declaration of state of Israel, 1947

◆ Communist victory in China, 1949

CHAPTER

28

STATES IN CONFLICT

Communism, Fascism, Democracy, and the Crisis of World War II

1917–1945

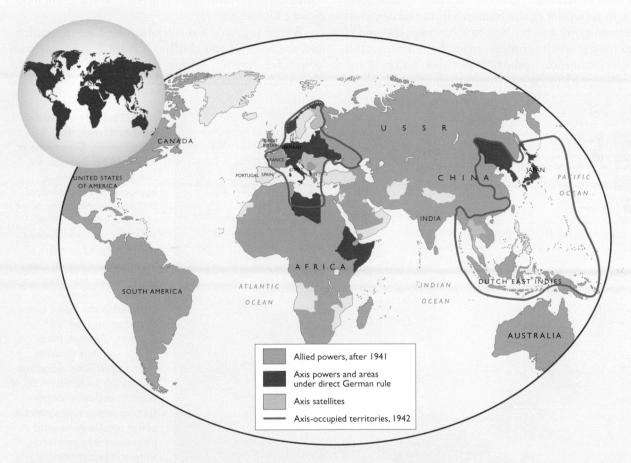

Allied powers, after 1941

Axis powers and areas under direct German rule

Axis satellites

Axis-occupied territories, 1942

KEY QUESTIONS

◆ **Bolsheviks and Communists:** To what extent was Stalin able to modernize the Soviet economy? What were the social and political consequences of his attempts to collectivize agriculture and increase industrial production?

◆ **The Faces of Fascism:** Why did Fascism develop differently in different cultural settings? What did the various Fascisms have in common, and how was Nazism unique?

◆ **The Second World War:** Should the democratic nations of Europe have responded more quickly to the menace of Fascism?

The Omnipotent State *"Everything within the state, nothing outside the state, nothing against the state!" With this summons, the Italian fascist leader Benito Mussolini (1883–1945) convinced the Italian people, in the uncertain years after World War I, to embrace the certainty that was offered by totalitarianism. The German Nazi leader Adolf Hitler (1889–1945) voiced a similar ideal: "Ein Reich, ein Volk, ein Führer!" ("one state, one people, one leader").*

These are the formulas of **totalitarianism**, a term often used to denote those regimes that demand the complete surrender of the human will to the demands of the omnipotent state. No state has ever succeeded in exercising such control over its citizens. But through persuasion, propaganda, and terror, some have attempted to do so. Totalitarian regimes (along with kindred despotisms or monarchies, often termed **authoritarian**) repudiate liberal principles of individual rights, freedom of conscience and expression, and access to political power.

As Map 28.1 shows, during the 1920s and 1930s, totalitarian governments came to power in many European nations: notably **fascism** in Italy and Germany (where it was known as Nazism); and communism in the Soviet Union (1917–1991, consisting of Russia and many of the lands of the former Russian Empire). In 1939, the aggressions of one of these states—Germany—provoked World War II. It ended in 1945 with the defeat of Nazi Germany, fascist Italy, and imperial Japan by the alliance of Britain and the United States, both democracies, and the communist Soviet Union.

Allied triumph was overshadowed by the matchless tragedies of the conflict. Of these one was mass **genocide**, directed against the Jews of Europe, the direct consequence of Nazi racial theory. The second

Map 28.1 Democratic, Authoritarian, and Totalitarian Government, 1919–1937: *Between the two great wars, most of Europe (and in Asia, Japan) drifted to authoritarian or totalitarian rule. Totalitarian governments—governments that attempted to direct all aspects of the lives of their citizens while repressing individual freedoms— prevailed in the Soviet Union (communism, from 1917), Germany (Nazism, from 1933), and Italy (fascism, from 1922). Other European nations fell for some period of years to authoritarianism— systems whose rulers came to power outside democratic procedures and governed without representative assemblies or through the manipulation of docile parliaments. Democracies survived, however, on the north and northwestern fringes of Europe and in Czechoslovakia—areas that had long parliamentary traditions, or had not suffered territorial loss as a result of World War I, or had advanced industrial bases. Why might advanced industrialization be a deterrent to dictatorship?*

was the explosion in two Japanese cities, in August 1945, of atomic bombs, with their consequences of mass death, mutilation, and disease, and the threat of universal destruction.

This catastrophic war brought an end, however, to the interwar era of uncertainty (see Chapter 27). Certainty returned as the nature of Nazism became clear: it was an evil that could not be tolerated. Reluctantly at first but decisively at last, its opponents massed to defeat it.

BOLSHEVIKS AND COMMUNISTS

In Russia, the Bolsheviks who seized power in 1917 in the name of desperate masses (see Chapter 26) established a totalitarian state that employed modern tools of regulation, propaganda, and terror in order to compel the obedience of its peasants, workers, and intellectuals.

A generation of brilliant leaders accomplished the transformation of Russia from autocracy to the communist dictatorship called the Soviet Union (properly the USSR, the Union of Soviet Socialist Republics). Foremost among them were Vladimir Ilyich Lenin (1870–1924) and Joseph Vissarionovich Dzhugashvili (1879–1953), known as Stalin ("man of steel").

Lenin had reconstructed Marxian socialism (see Chapter 25) to suit Russian circumstances, as he perceived them. Stalin derived from Lenin a model for the forcible imposition of socialism. He also learned—from Lenin but also from Mussolini and Hitler—strategies for seizing and maintaining power. By 1939, when war once again engulfed Europe, Russian communism had reached maturity.

Lenin: Rewriting Marx

By 1917, Lenin had reconstructed the theories of Marxian socialism to suit Russian realities: a semi-industrialized country with a minuscule bourgeoisie, a nascent proletariat, and a vast peasantry. In 1917, his version of Marxism (Marxist-Leninism) became the political orthodoxy of the new communist state.

In his 1902 book *What Is To Be Done?* (see Chapter 26), Lenin announced the key points in his rewriting of Marx. An elite of trained intellectuals was necessary, he argued, to instruct and lead the proletariat. **Trade union** organizations were immature. Russian industrialization had been laggard. Many of the workers were not truly urbanized proletarians but peasants who labored for a season in the factory, then returned to the fields. They needed, Lenin believed, to be guided by a cadre of intellectuals, committed to the cause, who would serve as permanent, professional revolutionaries. Lenin's Marxism was thus modified not only by the condition of Russian workers, but also by the Russian tradition of a radical, elite intelligentsia (see Chapter 25).

> ## MUST READS
>
> ## Key Books by Key Leaders
>
> | | |
> |---|---|
> | **Vladimir Ilyich Lenin** | *What Is To Be Done?* (1902) |
> | **Adolf Hitler** | *Mein Kampf (My Struggle)* (1925) |
> | **Winston Churchill** | *The Speeches of Winston Churchill* (1941–1945) |

When the revolution began in the spring of 1917 (see Chapter 26), Lenin expounded his principles in simple terms to mass audiences. At a ripe moment, the Bolsheviks acted, swiftly and almost unopposed, storming the Winter Palace and successfully ousting the provisional government. The Bolsheviks were only a faction of a faction, which in a nation of about 170 million had recruited perhaps 200,000 followers; now Bolshevism would shape the future of Russia. That nation was soon to learn that the dictatorship of the proletariat was, in the end, but another, and brutal, dictatorship.

War Communism and the New Economic Policy

It required three years of struggle to consolidate power, during which the Bolsheviks waged war against rival political factions, tsarist counterrevolutionaries, and foreign detachments. Even as Trotsky negotiated the Brest-Litovsk settlement (see Chapter 26), he built up the Red Army to safeguard the state Lenin had snatched in the October Revolution.

Establishing the Communist State   The Red Army faced a formidable task. In all directions, rival, or "White" organizations formed to oppose it. In the south, it faced troops of the general Lavr Georgyevich Kornilov (1870–1918; see Chapter 26) and his successors, joined at first by the Don Cossacks. In the Caucasus region, the Red Army needed to recover Georgia, Armenia, and Azerbaijan, which had declared their independence in 1918. In the east, they faced a conservative counter-government established at Omsk in Siberia, as well as an autonomous republic of social revolutionaries at Kuybyshev (now Samara). To the southwest, they aimed to recover Ukraine. In the north, Allied forces had occupied Murmansk and Archangel, ostensibly to protect Allied stores of war material. By 1920, the White opposition had been suppressed, rebellious nationalities brought to heel, and the foreigners dispersed. Russia was devastated. Between 10 and 30 million, mostly civilians, were dead.

Wartime atrocities, committed by both sides, were followed by the terror unleashed by the hated Cheka, a political police force organized in 1917 by the Bolshevik Felix Edmundovich Dzerzhinsky (1877–1926) to secure the new regime. The Cheka annihilated thousands of suspected enemies of the people, its persecutions mounting to 118 in the single month of February 1921. Modeled on its tsarist predecessor, the detested Okhrana, the Cheka surpassed that organization in the numbers of those executed, in the use of torture, and in the conditions of exile (now to forced labor camps) to which "politicals" (political prisoners) were subjected. The heritage of the Cheka endured in successor secret police organizations including: the GPU (State Political Administration), from 1922 (or OGPU, the word "united" added at the start, after 1923); the NKVD (People's Commissariat of Internal Affairs) from 1934; and the KGB (Committee of State Security) from 1953.

There remained the problem of disciplining not merely people, but thoughts. Censorship began promptly after the 1917 October Revolution with the closing of the "counterrevolutionary" press. By the summer of 1918, all independent dailies, weeklies, and monthlies had been suppressed. In 1920, suspect books were targeted. All but two copies each (these to be kept apart in "special reserve") of the works of ninety-four suspect authors—including Plato, Descartes, and Tolstoy—were removed from library shelves and destroyed. The instruction for this action proceeded directly from Nadezhda Krupskaya (1869–1939), member of the **commissariat** on education, and Lenin's wife and loyal companion during the years of exile.

WITNESSES

Bolsheviks and Communists: Forging Communist Society

Two themes of early Soviet society emerged in the first years of the regime: the need to extract more wheat from the peasants to feed the industrial workers, and the need to create a modern industrial society as rapidly as possible. These imperatives are illustrated here in a 1918 speech on food procurement; in a 1931 speech of Stalin's to the managers of Soviet industry; and in a 1926 rhapsody by a loyal servant of the state about the imminent industrialization of Soviet society.

Among the other harsh measures that constituted "War Communism," a decree on food procurement orders the extraction of grain supplies from peasant proprietors (May 13, 1918): DECREE OF THE ALL-RUSSIAN CENTRAL EXECUTIVE COMMITTEE … While the consuming provinces are starving, great stocks of cereals, including the 1916 harvest and the 1917 harvest which has not yet been threshed, lie, as habitually, in the producing provinces. These stocks are in the hands of rural *kulaks* [better-off peasants] and wealthy people, in the hands of the rural bourgeoisie. … [T]his rural bourgeoisie remains deaf and unresponsive in the face of the moanings of starving workers and poor peasants; it refuses to dispatch cereals to the state station points … while at the same time it sells for its own benefit … at fabulous prices to speculators and bagmen. The obstinacy of the greedy *kulaks* and wealthy peasants must be brought to an end. … The reply to the violence of grain holders upon the rural poor must be violence upon the bourgeoisie.

Not a single *pud* [unit of weight] of grain must remain in the hands of the grain holders, except the quantity needed for sowing and subsistence of the household until the next harvest.

(From R. A. Wade, ed., *Documents of Soviet History, vol. 1: The Triumph of Bolshevism, 1917–1919,* 1995)

In a speech to the Managers of Socialist Industry, Stalin urges ceaseless efforts to industrialize for the sake of the fatherland (1931): To slacken the tempo would mean falling behind. And those who fall behind get beaten. But we do not want to be beaten. No, we refuse to be beaten! One feature of the history of old Russia was the continual beatings she suffered for falling behind, for her backwardness. She was beaten by the Mongol Khans. She was beaten by the Turkish beys. She was beaten by the Swedish feudal lords. She was beaten by the Polish and Lithuanian gentry. She was beaten by the British and French capitalists. She was beaten by the Japanese barons. All beat her—for military backwardness, for cultural backwardness, for political backwardness, for industrial backwardness, for agricultural backwardness. …

We are fifty or a hundred years behind the advanced countries. We must make good this distance in ten years. Either we do it, or they crush us.

(J. V. Stalin, speech to Managers of Socialist Industry, 1931)

Writer V. Zazubrin celebrates the coming industrialization of the Soviet Union as a necessary step in the creation of socialist society (1926): Let the fragile green breast of Siberia be dressed in the cement armor of cities, armed with the stone muzzles of factory chimneys, and girded with iron belts of railroads. Let the *taiga* [Russian forest] be burned and felled, let the steppes be trampled. Let this be, and so it will be inevitably. Only in cement and iron can the fraternal union of all peoples, the iron brotherhood of all mankind be forged.

(V. Zazubrin, speech to the 1st Congress of Siberian Writers, 1926; ed. B. Komarov, 1980)

Krupskaya also supported the campaign for the "liquidation of illiteracy" launched in 1919 for all citizens between eight and fifty. In 1917, the Russian masses were largely (fifty-seven percent) illiterate. On farms and in workplaces, adults labored to learn to read. Some progress had been made by 1926, when just over half—fifty-one percent—of Russians had attained literacy.

The need to communicate socialist theory to an uninstructed population gave impetus to film, theater, and art, which were charged to "agitate" audiences to revolutionary zeal. Krupskaya promoted the director Sergei Eisenstein (1898–1948), whose pioneering films presented historical and theoretical concepts through purely visual means (see Chapter 27). Theatrical performances celebrated heroic peasants and derided counterrevolutionaries. Posters presented bold images of ideal types—workers, peasants, soldiers—selflessly laboring for the creation of a new society.

Economic Measures To establish the socialist foundations of the new Soviet state, stern measures were also required in the economic sphere, as the passages in *Witnesses* on p. 800 show. Lenin had promised land to his peasant supporters and saw to the redistribution of landowners' property. Much farmland, however, was ravaged by the battles of the Civil War; while peasants, compelled to surrender their grain stores, had reduced their sown acreage. The consequence was a great famine in 1921, resulting in 5 million deaths. As people died in the streets where packs of starving, abandoned children roamed, the new government sought and received international aid to ameliorate the crisis.

Even as famine struck the countryside, Lenin requisitioned grain for the cities—workers would eat at the expense of the peasants. The workers, meanwhile, had been organized into self-governing soviets, which were responsible for meeting the production quotas set by a supreme council that regulated the industrial economy. They labored hard, at low wages and under unsafe conditions, compelled to forego consumer goods—housing, food, and clothing—to support maximum reinvestment in manufacturing enterprises.

People resisted the heavy economic burdens imposed by what was called "War Communism." Moscow and Petrograd shriveled, and industrial production plummeted. In 1921, Lenin adopted the more moderate approach announced in his NEP (New Economic Policy). It permitted small entrepreneurs to operate freely and peasants to acquire their own farms and livestock. This strategy encouraged a stratum of landowning peasants, called **kulaks**, and won popular support for communism at a crucial moment.

Commissars and Comintern The Communist government system also took form during these years. Immediately following the October Revolution (see Chapter 26), Bolshevik leadership had been affirmed by the National Congress of soviets then meeting in Petrograd (although only after the Mensheviks and Socialist Revolutionaries walked out). Lenin took the chairmanship of the newly constituted Council of People's Commissars, or "ministers". This new government council and the Politburo (short for political bureau) or policy committee of the Bolshevik party, soon relocated to Moscow.

In January 1918, the newly elected Constituent Assembly convened for the first time. But the Bolsheviks had not obtained a majority of its delegates, and so immediately disbanded the assembly—the last chance Russia had for a democratic, constitutional, and representative government. Instead, by the principle of "democratic centralism," the hierarchy of local and regional soviets sent recommendations upward, ultimately to the Communist central committee, which made a final decision—the "party line," binding upon all. Lenin hoped to stimulate new communist revolutions abroad, reminding his followers "that the interests of socialism, the interests of world socialism, are superior to national interests, to the interests of the state." In 1919, he launched the Third, or Communist, International, the "Comintern," which was to consist of foreign delegations under strict Soviet leadership. Its task was to subject all foreign communist parties to the discipline of Soviet communism and so to promote world revolution.

By 1920, the Comintern's "Twenty-One Conditions" for parties seeking affiliation outlined the essentials of "true" communism. The Comintern communicated to foreign communist parties the Soviet "line," or policy on international and domestic matters. From 1928, it instructed them not to compromise with liberal or socialist parties—a bold stand, since social democrats alone outnumbered foreign communist party members more than fifteen to one. In 1935, in a policy reversal, the Comintern directed otherwise. It now encouraged communists abroad to join with center and left parties in Popular Front coalitions aimed at combating fascism.

By that time, under Lenin's successor Stalin, the hope for spontaneous, world-wide communist revolution had been set aside. From 1928, Stalin had proposed a different goal for which to strive: "socialism in one country." Lenin had wished to establish world-wide socialism; instead, Stalin established a national communist state, under one-party rule, disciplined by the threat of violence, and governed by the *nomenklatura* (those who held positions, or "names"), the obedient servitors of the Politburo. Stalin then turned to transform the stubborn Russian economy according to socialist principles.

Stalin: Gravedigger of the Revolution?

To do so, he enlisted the labor and the lives of the peasants, the workers, and his own revolutionary comrades. He compelled the peasantry to work on collective farms, dispossessing the one rural class that had shown enterprise and leadership—the now vilified kulaks. He subjected industrial workers to harsh conditions dictated by rigid production quotas, while denying them consumer goods. He bullied and silenced his Bolshevik comrades, veterans of the 1917 takeover and the harsh Civil War, as well as millions of party functionaries, military officers, and citizens. Shocked by his despotism, Leon Trotsky called him the "gravedigger" of the Revolution. Perhaps; but at the same time, Stalin was, with Lenin, the builder of Soviet communism.

Stalin had always been different from the other leading Old Bolsheviks. A native of Georgia (in the Caucasus, and then part of the Russian empire) and the son of a shoemaker, Stalin became a Bolshevik in 1903. But he was not an intellectual, and did not join in the esoteric debates enjoyed before 1917 of fine points of Marxian theory.

Stalin was an effective manager who by the early 1920s had demonstrated his ability to execute instructions ruthlessly. This quality Lenin appreciated until, at the edge of death, he learned that it was accompanied by self-serving ambition. In declining health, having suffered from several strokes, and communicating only through written memoranda, Lenin dictated a "political testament" during his last weeks urging Stalin's removal from his post as general secretary of the party. But Stalin had already asserted himself. The testament was ignored, and then suppressed (it was not publicized until after Stalin's death in 1956). At his lowest moment, Trotsky was given the task of denying to Western skeptics that such a document existed. Thus he rescued a man he saw as an enemy—the "gravedigger of the Revolution."

In 1924, Lenin's embalmed body was laid to rest in a mausoleum in Red Square, Moscow's civic center, to be venerated as a deity in the public religion of communism. Now Stalin began in earnest to maneuver for power, "exposing" each of his colleagues in turn as extremists or deviationists. By 1930, he had expelled them all from the Politburo, and surrounded himself with lackeys. By 1940, every one of the six men with whom he shared power in 1924 had been killed. Trotsky, the last, was tracked by Stalin's agents to Mexico, and murdered by a Spanish NKVD agent with a mountaineer's ice pick.

As Stalin rose, debate ceased. All decisions proceeded from him, as once from the tsars. Even the information presented to him, in time, was filtered so as not to disagree with the dictator's presuppositions.

Stalin now proceeded to target new groups of supposed opponents, extremists, and "enemies of the people," who were paraded in "show trials" put on to instruct the Soviet people and the watching world. There were trials of engineers, of industrial managers, of party leaders and officials. Disoriented or impassive

after torture and threats, strangely compliant defendants confessed to crimes against the state before being sent to the labor camps or to death. In the course of trial, some of the accused went insane, committed suicide, or mysteriously died.

After the murder in 1934 of the Old Bolshevik Sergei Mironovich Kirov (1888–1934), who had spoken critically of Stalin's despotism in party meetings, the killing mounted to a frenzy. The murder was probably ordered by Stalin (who subsequently disposed of all the principals in the plot, including the assassin and his NKVD directors). But at the time, Stalin mourned Kirov's loss, and proceeded to "investigate" the murder.

Between 1934 and 1939 hundreds of inner-circle Communists were arrested, tried, and executed. Those killed included 98 of 139, or seventy percent, of Central Committee members; and 1,108, or fifty-six percent, of the 1966 representatives to the 1934 XVIIth party congress held in 1934. Thousands, perhaps millions, of other public officials, artists, intellectuals, and ordinary people were also victims, (see *Witnesses* on p. 804). According to Roy Medvedev (1925–), a dissident survivor of the Soviet regime, the total arrested during 1934–1939 mounted to around 3 to 5 million, with hundreds of thousands shot. At the peak of the purge, over 200 executions were recorded per day in the Lubyanka, the NKVD central prison; "not streams, these were rivers of blood."

A purge of military officers in 1937–1938 complemented the purge of party officials. By 1939, Stalin had eliminated half of the Red Army officer corps—more than 40,000, of whom 400 were of the rank of colonel and above, including three of the five marshals, thirteen of the fifteen army commanders,

HOW MANY?

Stalin's Deathlist

Costs of collectivization, 1928–1933
People: about 10 million dead (the nation suffered a net loss in total population of 20 million from 1917–1934)
Livestock: 1 million head of cattle, pigs, sheep, and goats destroyed

Arrested, 1937–1938 5 million, of whom 1 million were executed

In jail, 1938 1 million

In gulags, 1935–1937: 6 million
1938: 7 million

Survival rate of purge-era prisoners: about 10%
Purged by 1939 of those active in 1934: Central Committee members: 98 of 139 (70%)
Representatives to the XVIIth Party Congress (1934): 1,108 of 1,966 (56%)

nine out of ten army generals, and six out of seven admirals. When the German army attacked the Soviet Union in 1941, two-thirds of its generals were novices.

Those arrested in the purges were imprisoned, tortured, sent to labor camps, or shot. Of these destinies, the labor camp or **gulag** is the special emblem of the Stalinist era (although its history begins under Lenin, with sixty-five in existence by 1922). Supervised by special government agencies, the labor-camp system went well beyond the penal regimes of the tsarist era. Prisoners worked at heavy tasks, for extraordinarily long work days under extreme conditions, especially of cold, as gulags were mostly in the Arctic. They were housed in barracks without heat or furnishings, denied adequate food (rations were deliberately withheld to present an incentive to productivity) and subjected to physical and psychological abuse. The labor of these prisoners dug canals, mined gold, and felled forests, contributing significantly if horribly to the nation's economic success.

Few survived. The camp served the combined purpose of work and extermination. Frequent shipments of fresh prisoners (criminals and politicals) restocked the labor gangs when their predecessors had died of hunger, exhaustion, or brutality. In just a few years, the special killing squads of the Nazi security force (the SS, or *Schutzsstaffel*)—these were the executioners, on the fronts or in the death camps, of Jews, Poles, and others—would show they had learned much from the Stalinist gulag.

Socialism in One Country

Among the political prisoners transported to the gulag were millions of kulaks. These small rural proprietors Stalin declared to be a peasant aristocracy that he would "liquidate as a class", as part of his program to attain "socialism in one country."

Small peasant proprietors were a relatively new social group. In the wake of the 1861 emancipation of the serfs, a handful of peasants had been able to establish themselves on small farms. With the Bolshevik confiscation of large estates in 1918, more were able to do so. The policies of War Communism bore heavily on this peasant elite, whose stores of grain were requisitioned for use by the Red Army and industrial workers. Under the NEP instituted in 1921, however, determined kulaks again increased their landholdings.

Even so, the peasant elite that existed in 1928 when Stalin launched his policy of **collectivization** was hardly a class of oppressors, as was charged. Kulaks (a term of abuse, signifying tight-fisted greed) typically owned seventy to eighty acres of land and two or three draught animals, and often hired their neighboring smaller peasants or day laborers to assist with farm tasks. Far from wealthy, kulaks more closely resembled a struggling middle class.

It was this social group that the collectivization campaign destroyed. Stalin's agents in the countryside demanded stated amounts of grain from each region. The grain was needed to feed the cities and industrial centers, where the proletariat labored to modernize a still-backward economy. The quotas were set so high that peasants were left with insufficient stores for themselves; at one point, the amount of grain requisitioned amounted to more than the total harvested.

The peasants resisted these demands. Sometimes they protested violently; sometimes they refused to grow the crops that they would not be allowed to enjoy. Inflamed, Stalin responded with a drive to remove the entire peasantry to collective farms, to be governed by soviets and supervised by official ideologues, or commissars. At the same time, he would boost grain yields (as he believed) by eliminating the kulaks who, he thought, clung to an outmoded, privatist model of rural production.

From 1928 to 1933, Communist officials confiscated kulak farms, seized grain stores, invaded cottages, and sent the occupants away homeless—if they did not shoot them or deport them to the gulag (see the photograph on p. 805 and *Witnesses* on p. 804). Millions starved to death, in their devastated villages or in the camps. Millions snatched their revenge in advance, burning their own farms and killing their livestock. In the winter of 1932–1933, this disruption of agriculture triggered famine. Peasants throughout Russia suffered through this induced scarcity which followed by only a few years the war-induced famine of 1921. The cost of collectivizing the countryside mounted to about 10 million deaths.

As Stalinist policies enforced socialism in the agricultural sphere, the industrial workforce also experienced the rigors imposed by a rapidly transforming economy. The workers, too, suffered shortages, and were harried by unrealistic production goals set by central economic planners. By their labors, nevertheless, Soviet Russia became a major world producer of steel, weapons, and machines. And a whole new elite of trained managers and engineers gained an autonomy their parents had never known.

The massive industrialization of the Soviet economy accomplished between 1928 and 1939 was guided by successive Five Year Plans. The first was approved in 1929, the second in 1933, the third in 1938, this last cut short by the outbreak of World War II. Each plan set production quotas to spur growth, especially in the heavy industries (metals, machines, and textiles). Although statistics were often falsified to give the illusion of success, the plans did lead to a dramatic expansion of Soviet infrastructure and industrial capacity.

The Five Year Plans accomplished nearly as much as they had ambitiously proposed. By 1938, the Soviet Union outdid Britain, and nearly equaled Germany, as a producer of pig-iron and steel. Agricultural production, too, eventually improved. But there had been deficits: rapid modernization required workers to endure low living standards, peasants to starve to feed the workers, and the most energetic stratum of the peasantry—the kulaks—to be sacrificed in order to achieve socialism in one country.

Socialist Realism, Soviet Realities

Social and cultural changes reshaped the lives of urbanized workers during the two interwar decades. Communism called for a transformation of the family and the repression of religion, the arts, and thought.

Communist Totalitarianism: Repression and Terror

Communism brought new opportunities to many Soviet citizens, especially by providing access to education and thereupon employment opportunities. Yet it was an undoubtedly, and horrifyingly, repressive regime. In these statements, the Kronstadt sailors who were eager participants in the 1917 Revolution denounce the communist dictatorship as it had emerged four years later; a novelist describes through fictional characters the brutal repression of the kulaks; a contemporary writer recalls the fear experienced by those who lived through the purges of the 1930s; and a Bolshevik hero, a victim of those purges, declares his innocence to posterity.

The Kronstadt sailors, participants in the 1917 October Revolution, denounce the communist dictatorship (March 1921): With the October Revolution the working class had hoped to achieve its emancipation. But there resulted an even greater enslavement of human personality. … [But now there is resistance.] Here and there the land is lit up by the fires of rebellion in a struggle against oppression and violence. … The Generals of Communism see clearly that it is the people who had risen, the people who have become convinced that the Communists have betrayed the ideas of Socialism. … [L]ife under the Communist dictatorship is more terrible than death. … [The Kronstadt rebellion was quickly crushed by Red troops.]
(Alexander Berkman, "The Kronstadt Rebellion," 1922)

An episode from the unpublished novel of M. N. Averbakh, member of a special brigade charged to liquidate the kulaks (1930): The door opened. The brigade burst into the house. The … officer in charge of the operation was in front, brandishing a revolver.

"Hands up!"

Morgunov was barely able, in the gloom, to make out the frail figure of the class enemy. He was wearing white drawers and a dark undershirt, and was barefoot. … The eyes, wide with terror, glanced from place to place. … He kept blinking and crossing himself, shifting from one foot to the other, … and suddenly be began to sob. … His wife, not a young woman, jumped down from the high sleeping bench and began to wail at the top of her voice. The children began crying. A calf lying beside the stove, apparently not in very good health, began to bawl.

Morgunov looked around, aghast. He saw that the hut contained nothing but the one room and the big Russian stove. In the front corner … were two simple wooden benches and a crude table made of planks. No chest of drawers, no beds, no chairs. …

The class enemy!
(From R. Medvedev, *Let History Judge: The Origins and Consequences of Stalinism*, rev. ed., ed. G. Shriver, 1989)

Writer Nadezhda Mandelstam, whose husband, the poet Osip Mandelstam, died a prisoner in 1938, recalls the Stalinist terror: Anybody who breathes the air of terror is doomed, even if nominally he manages to save his life. Everybody is a victim—not only those who die, but also the killers, ideologists, accomplices and sycophants who close their eyes or wash their hands. …

The principles and aims of mass terror have nothing in common with ordinary police work or with security. The only purpose of terror is intimidation. To plunge the whole country into a state of chronic fear, the number of victims must be raised to astronomical levels, and on every floor of every building there must always be several apartments from which the tenants have suddenly been taken away. The remaining inhabitants will be model citizens for the rest of their lives.
(Nadezhda Mandelstam, *Hope against Hope: A Memoir*, ed. M. Hayward, 1970)

Before his execution by Stalin's political police, Nikola Bukharin dictates to his wife a letter to a future generation of party leaders, to vindicate himself and testify to the terror (1938): I am leaving life. … I feel my helplessness before a hellish machine, which … has acquired gigantic power, fabricates organized slander, acts boldly and confidently. …

Storm clouds have risen over the party. My one head, guilty of nothing, will drag down thousands of guiltless heads. … I have been in the party since I was eighteen, and the purpose of my life has always been to fight for the interests of the working class, for the victory of socialism. …

I appeal to all party members! In these days, perhaps the last of my life, I am confident that sooner or later the filter of history will inevitably sweep the filth from my head. I was never a traitor; without hesitation I would have given my life for Lenin's, I loved Kirov, started nothing against Stalin. … Know, comrades, that on the banner, which you will be carrying in the victorious march to communism, is also my drop of blood.
(From R. Medvedev, *ibid*)

The war on the class enemy: "liquidate the kulaks": *Stalin's plan to build "socialism in one country" required the collectivization of agricultural production—which in turn required the elimination of small peasant proprietors (the kulaks). In this 1930 photograph, Russian villagers, who had been well-prompted by Soviet advisers, march with a banner asking to "liquidate the kulaks as a class."*

The Soviet Family Dismantling the family meant the liberation of women from male authority (see Chapter 27). The first steps in this direction were taken as early as 1918, when a new Family Code declared women's equality, erased the distinction between legitimate and illegitimate births, removed marriage from religious to civil jurisdiction, and permitted divorce. Two years later, a further decree made abortion legal if performed by a physician. Married or unmarried, women were to participate fully in society—their labor was required to build the socialist economy. Women were also active in the Communist Party, and worked as teachers and bureaucrats to build the new society that Lenin envisioned.

Many of these measures were revoked under Stalin, however, whose Family Code of 1936 made abortion illegal and divorce difficult, restored the category of illegitimacy, criminalized homosexuality, and sought to rehabilitate the family.

The nurture and instruction of children was a responsibility the Soviet state took seriously. It undertook to rear and educate all of its young. Neighborhood and factory nurseries cared for infants from birth onward. Well-run elementary schools trained the offspring of parents of whom many were themselves illiterate. In an egalitarian setting, these schools prepared children for the technical requirements of a modern society, at the upper levels training engineers, research scientists, teachers, and officers. At the same time, schools and Komsomol (youth organization) units instilled communist values into their young charges—some of whom won favor, during the purges, for denouncing their parents.

The Manipulation of Culture Those born in the early years of the Communist regime were raised to be uncritical supporters of the Soviet state. That state had replaced tsardom, aristocracy, and Church with a system that guaranteed social services to all and the opportunity for advancement to high position on the basis of merit.

As adults were retrained to participate in Soviet society, they were weaned from the Church that had for centuries been the mainstay of Russian culture. Official decrees desacralized churches, intimidated priests, and banned the performance of sacraments (restrictions briefly eased in 1941 when it was necessary to reaffirm traditional culture to support the "Great Patriotic War").

Communist censors understood very well the power of cultural expression in forming the minds of citizens. Writers, film-makers, and artists were gathered into unions that controlled the ideological content of books, plays, films, and paintings. Holding relatively high status in Soviet society, writers and artists largely followed the party line in matters of both taste and style.

So too did historians, linguists, psychologists, musicians, and even biologists, whose works were required to endorse the Soviet regime. Psychologists, for example, avoided Freudian psychoanalytic theories, as the notion of an unruly unconscious self countered Soviet understanding of the fully conscious and ideologically committed citizen. Biologists could not explore the field of genetics, as the notion of inherited characteristics countered the Soviet assumption of a wholly malleable human nature.

Stalin—father of his country: *This 1939 poster of Stalin as exultant master of an armed and ready Soviet Union expresses the nation's state on the eve of World War II—not a peaceful and democratic society but a militarist and despotic one. The words on the large unfurled banner exalt the leader: "Our army and our country are strengthened with the spirit of Stalin."*

By the 1930s, the bureaucratic control of the arts and ideas resulted in a serious loss of vitality. As the French author (formerly a communist sympathizer) André Gide (1869–1951) predicted, where there is no liberty, "art loses its meaning and its value … as … the assent of the greatest number … goes to the qualities the public is best able to recognize, that is to say conformity." In the visual arts, the officially sanctioned style of Socialist Realism prevailed, which celebrated the heroism of Soviet workers in a blandly academic manner. Film-making languished until, on the eve of World War II, Eisenstein produced his prophetic *Alexander Nevsky* (see Chapter 27).

The specter of the gulag kept many intellectuals in line. The novelist Maxim Gorky (1868–1936), an ardent participant in the debates of 1917, remained in favor as the leading intellectual of the new state that he never really endorsed. The poet Boris Pasternak (1890–1960), whose silence throughout the 1930s implied his hatred for the regime, was for the moment tolerated. The adventurous productions of the Old Bolshevik playwright Vsevolod Meyerhold (1874–1940?), however, invited repression in the

end; he was arrested, tortured, and probably executed. The poet Osip Mandelstam (1891–1938?), who had criticized Stalin, was exiled, and died *en route* to the gulag. The poet Anna Akhmatova (pseudonym of Anna Andreyevna Gorenko; 1889–1966)—whose two husbands were executed by Lenin and Stalin, whose son was exiled to the gulag, and who was herself twice denounced for the "bourgeois decadence" of her now widely-acclaimed work—succeeded in outliving the dictator.

Under Stalin, words were dangerous. For decades, some of the most important Soviet works of literature and thought were "published" only in manuscript and typescript, and circulated secretly (known as samizdat, "self-published"). Such was the case with the writings of Aleksandr Isayevich Solzhenitsyn (1918–), which at last escaped the censors to inform the peoples of the outside world about terror and the gulag in the world's first communist state.

Views from Abroad   Until the circulation abroad of Solzhenitsyn's *One Day in the Life of Ivan Denisovich* (1962) and *The Gulag Archipelago* (1973), exposing the Soviet labor camp system, ignorance about conditions in the Soviet Union was persistent. Idealistic sympathizers abroad, such as the British Fabian socialists Sidney and Beatrice Webb (see Chapter 25), enthusiastically praised the factories and labor camps in their *Soviet Communism: A New Civilisation?* (1935). The Dublin-born playwright George Bernard Shaw (1856–1950) approved of Stalin, who combined, he thought, the qualities of field marshal and pope. The novelist H. G. Wells (1866–1946) found him "candid, fair and honest," and the American industrialist Armand Hammer (1898–1990) commended his resourcefulness. These and other observers, including thousands of communist party workers around the world, ignored rumors and even hard evidence of the purges, the mass slaughter, and the bridling of free thought.

Some early followers did become disillusioned. The American writer Max Eastman (1883–1969), an enthusiastic supporter at first, soon renounced Bolshevism after visiting the Soviet Union in 1922. His *Since Lenin Died* (1925) unveiled the corrupt power plays of the 1920s. (It was to Eastman that an abject Trotsky denied the existence of Lenin's "testament" repudiating Stalin.) The English writer George Orwell (pseudonym of Eric Arthur Blair, 1903–1950), a socialist who had previously critiqued the hypocrisies of imperialism and absurdities of war, assailed communism for dehumanizing the individual in his epochal works *Animal Farm* (1945) and *Nineteen Eighty-Four* (1949).

The Yugoslav communist Anton Ciliga (1898–1992) clearly exposed the failures of Soviet society (where he lived from 1926 to 1936) in *The Russian Enigma* (1940). Arthur Koestler (1905–1983), a

Opponents of Totalitarianism

Arthur Koestler   *Darkness at Noon* (1940)

Anne Frank   *The Diary of Anne Frank* (1947)

George Orwell   *1984* (1949)

Alexander Solzhenitsyn   *The Gulag Archipelago* (1973)

Hungarian-born former Communist who was disillusioned by the 1930s purges, explored the phantom confessions of Stalin's victims in the classic *Darkness at Noon* (1940). Since the late 1980s, which brought the disintegration of the Soviet regime and the opening of the archives, scholars have been able to document the atrocities committed by a totalitarian state in the name of "the people."

Derived from the humane traditions of democratic socialism and liberalism, communism took a different turn in 1917, as Lenin and Stalin redefined its purposes. By the early 1920s, communism in the Soviet Union had crystallized as a totalitarian system sustained by terror and deception. The people it meant to serve benefited in many ways from its programs of economic modernization and mass education. But they suffered from the brutality of a state that elevated itself above the people it claimed to serve.

THE FACES OF FASCISM

In the decade after 1917, as Russian communism turned despotic, other European nations embraced different forms of fascism. Exalting a new type of charismatic leader—a *duce*, *Führer*, or *caudillo* (as these were named in Italian, German, and Spanish)—they chose nationalism, militarism, and corporatism over individual rights and freedom.

Why did so many Europeans abandon liberalism?—to the extent that, in 1938 when Hitler dismembered Czechoslovakia, it was the one remaining democracy, among all the nations of central or eastern Europe? The nations of Europe were unable to adjust to the outcomes of World War I. In some cases, their leaders were seen as having accepted too easily the grievous burdens of the Paris peace settlements. Or they could not manage the hammer blows in rapid succession, as in Germany, of inflation and economic depression. Or the people trusted too much the dynamic new leaders from the streets, who verged violence, youth, and unreason as antidotes to the ineptitudes of the politicians. For reasons such as these, support for fascist movements surged through Europe during the 1920s.

Fascism: an Ideology for the Twentieth Century

Fascism is a modern ideology, a child of the twentieth century. Unlike socialism or conservatism, rooted in a liberal past, it is the antithesis of liberalism, as the diagram on p. 816 illustrates. Fading toward monarchism or military despotism at one pole, toward anarchy at the other, but never toward democracy, the apparently inchoate phenomenon of fascism can be identified by some key features.

First, fascism is ultra-nationalistic—in contrast to the internationalism (or **cosmopolitanism**) of communism. It exhorts individuals to subordinate themselves to the whole "people." In the same anti-individualistic vein, fascism is **corporatist**, promoting identification with multi-class groups—industry-based councils or youth groups—which in turn support the nationalist agenda. Summoning individuals to identify themselves with nation rather than class, it is anti-socialist and anti-communist.

Second, fascism celebrates irrationalism, in contrast to communism's appeal to "scientific" theory. The elaborate symbols and images it devises appeal to myth rather than history, looking to memories of past greatness, and to premodern, even prehistoric episodes of heroic conquest. Fascism thrives on propaganda—the opposite of reasoned discourse—and specifically the propagation of pithy lies, slogans laden with hatred, resentment, or regret. Esteeming frenzy over reason, the will over the intellect, it prefers youth to age, and recruits its first followers among the discontented young.

Third, fascism promotes war and detests pacifism—in contrast, again, to Soviet communism, which came to power amid war's devastation promising "peace, land, bread." It exalts the qualities that accompany wartime heroism: courage, sacrifice, great efforts of will. "War alone brings all human energies to their highest state of tension," said Mussolini, "and stamps with the seal of nobility the nations which have to face it." Where war cannot be had, fascism admires bellicosity, if only in the form of terror.

Fourth, fascism advocates masculinism, and abhors any feminization of culture or politics. It upholds traditional gender roles in society—in contrast to communism which, in theory, denies gender inequality; or to liberalism, which must, in theory, recognize the rights of individuals irrespective of gender. Its vitalism and militarism are masculine ideals. It rejects pacifism and socialism as effeminate. Fascists are men. Women serve the fascist cause by tending to household needs and by bearing children, future mothers and soldiers.

Fifth, fascism is modernist—more so than communism, whose grand theoretical structures are rooted in nineteenth-century and even earlier streams of thought. The only one of the major Western ideologies to emerge in the twentieth century, fascism embraces novelty, especially new technologies and styles. Embracing **futurism**, it concocts visions of a mythicized future. It tends, consequently, to revolution, to the annihilation of existing structures and the fabrication of new ones: here, fascism does resemble communism, which also rejoices in the revolutionary meltdown of inherited institutions.

Finally, fascism is autocratic—at odds with communist theory, which promises power to a triumphant proletariat. It elevates an individual with charismatic qualities, who claims to represent the will of the people. To its *duce* or *Führer* it demonstrates allegiance in mass celebrations that turn the mere individual into a faceless servitor of his "leader" as of his state. It is by nature, therefore, anti-democratic (for democracy would give each person political power) and anti-liberal (for liberalism grants to each person inalienable rights).

Although fascism cannot coexist with communism ("the Left"), to which it is opposed in essence, it could and did make alliances with conservatism ("the Right"). Conservatism, which enlisted monarchists and militarists, honored the institutions and traditions that communism would dismantle. Accordingly fascists and conservatives could agree upon a nationalist, anti-communist, anti-pacifist program that excluded female activism and promoted a strong leader.

Europe's two principal fascist states arose in Italy and Germany. At the same time, Spain and Portugal, Hungary and Poland, Yugoslavia and Romania, and distant Japan among others had conservative governments with fascist components. By 1937, with the exception of the Soviet Union and the democracies of northwestern Europe (France, Britain, the Netherlands, Belgium, Switzerland, and the four Scandinavian nations), and Czechoslovakia, the sole democracy in central Europe, fascist or authoritarian governments ruled everywhere in Europe.

Mussolini and His Imitators

In Italy, the least of the Great Power victors of World War I, fascism first took form in the hands of Benito Mussolini, the least of the century's great dictators. A product of resentment, confusion, and force, Italian fascism was important as a role model for other authoritarian regimes.

Though a victor nation that gained territory as a result of the 1919 Paris treaties, Italy was disappointed with her reward for the terrible sacrifices made by her soldiers in the icy battlefields at the Isonzo River (see Chapter 26). Austria surrendered the Alto Adige (Italian Tyrol), the Triestino (Trieste and its environs), and Istria. But the newly-formed state of Yugoslavia incorporated a number of regions for which Italy felt it had bargained and bled.

Italians were also troubled by unrest in the streets and weakness in the parliament. Industrialized relatively late, the Italian economy had been greatly strained by wartime demands. Striking workers, often prodded into action by communist recruiters, poured into the streets. There they tangled with self-appointed black-shirted gangs of thugs and demobilized soldiers, the *fasci di combattimento* (combat "bundles," or squads) that sprang up in Italy after 1918. These *fascisti* ("fascists") detested communists and socialists, and suppressed their opponents by cudgeling, kidnapping, torture (castor oil, which they forced their victims to swallow in quantity, was a fascist trademark), and murder.

The Italian government—a constitutional monarchy dating only from the nation's unification in 1870—was dismayed by the disorder and looked for a leader who could contain it. King Victor Emmanuel III chose the easiest, most dangerous solution. He invited Benito Mussolini, leader of the black-shirted fascist gangs, and since 1921 a member of parliament for the new National Fascist party, to form a coalition government. Mussolini took a berth on the overnight train to Rome (this was his "March on Rome") to take up his appointment. By 1924, he personally dominated the government, having first dispatched by assassination his rival, the socialist leader Giacomo Matteotti (1885–1924), and quickly destroyed those who protested the act.

Mussolini in Genoa, 1938

The Duce: *Both Mussolini and Hitler were masters of self-presentation, staging spectacular processions and rallies that evoked high emotion and memories of past grandeur while they served to maximize the figure of the leader. Here, a triumphal Roman arch forms the theatrical backdrop to Mussolini's rousing public address in Genoa, underpinning the self-proclaimed magnificence of the* duce.

The man who acquired power so swiftly had been born poor. Like his proletarian father, a blacksmith, he was a committed socialist. From 1912, Mussolini edited the newspaper of the Italian socialist party *Avanti!* ("Forward"). He advocated worker activism and international pacifism until 1914, when, in an about-face, he joined those agitating for war. He fought, attaining (as did Hitler) the unexalted rank of corporal. After the war, he developed the political ideology of fascism (see *Witnesses* on p. 810), promoting it through violence and propaganda.

Once in power, Mussolini pursued a disparate agenda focused only in its ardent nationalism. He supported the large corporations by disabling trade unionism (while pretending to give workers a voice through corporation-based associations). In the Lateran Treaty of 1929, he forged an agreement with the papacy, which had lost the papal states in 1870. The pope was granted official recognition of his sovereignty over an autonomous Vatican state, and the Roman Catholic Church was permitted to resume its role in education while the state recognized the validity of Catholic marriage, which meant that there could be no divorce. In return for these concessions, the pope agreed to recognize the authority both of the Italian state and of Mussolini himself, who became the first leader of a unified Italy to be recognized by the Church.

In the arts, Mussolini promoted futurism, and cultural activities that magnified state interests. He centralized the bureaucracy and, famously, made the railroads run on time. He enforced the continued subordinate status of women, launching a natalist program, which encouraged women to reproduce prolifically in the interests of increasing national population (see Chapter 27). "Go back home," he told fascist party delegates in 1927, "and tell the women I need births, many births." As the photograph on p. 808 shows, he spoke to large, enthusiastic crowds gathered in vast cathedrals and arenas, monuments of past greatness, about Italy's ancient glory—Rome, he reminded them, had once ruled the Mediterranean world.

To recover that glory, Mussolini, too, must become a conqueror. He waited patiently to attain that status. In 1925, he took part with Britain, France, Belgium, and Germany in the agreement at Locarno (Switzerland) that guaranteed the maintenance of Germany's western (but not eastern) frontiers. In 1935, he joined once again with Britain and France in the agreement of Stresa (Italy), reaffirming the then allies' interest in preventing German aggrandizement. Later that year (on October 2, 1935), however, he struck at Ethiopia, which Italy had tried and failed to conquer in 1896 (see Chapter 24). The League of Nations punished Mussolini with weak economic sanctions; they did not, importantly, limit his access to oil, without which Mussolini could

not maintain his army. In 1939, Mussolini struck at Albania, across the Adriatic Sea.

Between Stresa in 1935 and the Albanian invasion in 1939, Italy edged gradually toward alliance with Germany. In the meantime, both Mussolini and Hitler had been sustaining a rebel Nationalist army in Spain as it battled the democratically elected Republican government (for the Spanish Civil War, see below). Mussolini sent divisions of "volunteers," fully equipped with aircraft and tanks, in support of the forces led by the Nationalist General Francisco Franco (1892–1975). In 1936, Mussolini and Hitler reached an agreement described as the Rome–Berlin Axis. In 1937, Italy joined Japan and Germany's Anti-Comintern Pact.

Other European nations followed the pattern of Mussolini's fascism, without necessarily adopting all of its ideological features. In the decade 1929–1939, they included Greece and the Balkan nations of Bulgaria and Yugoslavia; Hungary, Poland, and Austria; the Baltic states of Lithuania, Latvia, and Estonia; and Spain and Portugal. Here dictators with a nationalist agenda ruled in league with kings and military elites, sometimes, as in Italy, with the support of the Roman Catholic Church. Fascist movements surfaced even in democratic Britain (led by Sir Oswald Mosley, 1896–1980) and France.

Imperial Japan, Imperialist Ventures

Authoritarian government also took root in Japan, a country whose ancient imperial traditions and recent rapid modernization predisposed it toward despotism. Dominated by a military elite with expansionist plans and equipped with the latest technology, while Europe floundered, Japan was extending its power purposefully in east Asia.

In 1915 Japan imposed its Twenty-One Demands on China, claiming key footholds in Chinese territory and, in effect, made all China a Japanese dependency (see Chapter 25). Although Japan retained many of these claims in 1919, it was later forced to relinquish them. In 1921–1922, the Washington Conference, including Britain, France, Japan, and the United States, agreed to respect the independence and sovereignty of China. Japan agreed to restore the former German holding of Shandong to China, and to remove its troops from Siberia. It seemed that Japanese expansion had been contained.

The economic depression that gripped the Western world (see Chapter 27) also affected overpopulated Japan. Its poor peasants (its recent wealth was largely urban-based) could not afford to purchase Japanese products, and its industries relied on foreign markets. When the world demand for Japanese manufactures, especially silks, collapsed in the Depression, economic crisis in Japan followed. As in the West, crisis provided the cue for a militarist element to subvert the regular institutions of governance. A group of generals took over from the parliamentary regime that was reestablished after World War I. They now dealt directly with the emperor, believed to be the descendent of deities, who continued to inspire the sacrificial devotion of the Japanese people. They argued that Japan must expand on the mainland so that its people could eat. They were also concerned by the gathering strength of the Soviet Union to their north, and, to their west, by the concentration of power in the hands of the Chinese Nationalists under Chiang Kai-shek (Jiang Jieshi).

Upon the death in 1925 of revolutionary leader Sun Yat-sen (1866–1925; see Chapters 24, 29), Chiang took over the Nationalist, or Guomindang forces his predecessor had assembled. In 1926–1927,

with communist allies from whom he soon separated, Chiang drove north from Guangzhou on the South China Sea to the interior industrial center at Wuhan. His forces then wheeled eastward along the lower Yangzi River to prosperous Nanjing and the East China Sea port of Shanghai. By 1928, Chiang controlled a core of the eastern provinces from his capital at Nanjing. This regime he steadily expanded to the south and west, contending with local warlords, some his former allies. The rival communist factions withdrew into the countryside and began the recruitment of peasant supporters that would be the basis of their ultimate victory in 1949 (see Chapter 29).

Meanwhile, beginning in 1931, Japan began to tear at northeastern China, a region wedged between Soviet and Guomindang strongholds. Japanese forces

---

WITNESSES

Fascism and Nazism: the Flight from Reason

Fascism was not one ideology, but a potpourri of notions; Nazism included some of these, and added some others. Together, the two were lethal. In these passages, the Italian fascist leader Mussolini defines some features of fascism— its repudiation of pacifism, Marxism, and democracy, and its idolization of the state; the German Nazi leader Hitler attacks the Jews and calls for the appropriation of eastern European territories; and a young girl who witnessed the rise of Hitler recalls the terrible impact that he made.

Benito Mussolini defines the principles of Italian fascism (1932): Fascism ... repudiates the doctrine of Pacifism. ... War alone brings up to its highest tension all human energy and puts the stamp of nobility upon the peoples who have the courage to meet it. ...

Such a conception of life makes Fascism the complete opposite of ... so-called scientific and Marxian Socialism, the materialist conception of history. ...

Fascism combats the whole complex system of democratic ideology, and repudiates it. ... Fascism denies that the majority, by the simple fact that it is a majority, can direct human society; ... and it affirms the immutable, beneficial, and fruitful inequality of mankind. ...

The foundation of Fascism is the conception of the State, ... Fascism conceives of the State as an absolute, in comparison with which all individuals or groups are relative. ... The Fascist state is itself conscious, and has itself a will and a personality. ...
(Benito Mussolini with Giovanni Gentile, "The Political and Social Doctrine of Fascism," *Enciclopedia Italiana*, 1932)

Adolf Hitler on Aryans, Jews, and *Lebensraum* (1925): What we see before us of human culture today ... is almost exclusively the creative product of the Aryan. ... If one were to divide mankind into three groups: culture-founders, culture-bearers, and culture-destroyers, then as representative of the first kind,

only the Aryan would come in question. It is from him that the foundation and the walls of all human creations originate. ...

The Jew forms the strongest contrast to the Aryan. ... The Jewish people, with all its apparent intellectual qualities, is nevertheless without any true culture, especially without a culture of its own. ... He is and remains the typical parasite, a sponger who, like a harmful bacillus, spreads out more and more if only a favorable medium invites him to do so. ...

[W]e National Socialists must cling un-flinchingly to our foreign-policy aims, that is to guarantee the German nation the soil and territory to which it is entitled on this earth. ... We take up at the halting place of six hundred years ago. We terminate the endless German drive to the south and west of Europe, and direct our gaze towards the lands in the east ... and proceed to the territorial policy of the future.
(Adolf Hitler, *Mein Kampf*, 1925; trs. R. Mannheim, 1943, 1971)

Lilo Linke observes Hitler as a girl in Germany (1935): For an hour and a half Hitler spoke, every few minutes interrupted by fanatic acclamations. ... He thrust his chin forward. His voice, hammering the phrases with an obsessed energy, became husky and shrill and began to squeak more and more frequently. His whole face was covered with sweat. ...

The audience was breathlessly under his spell. This man expressed their thoughts, their feelings, their hopes; a new prophet had arisen ... and had the power to lead them into the promised land if they were only prepared to follow him. ...

A single question as to reason or proof or possibility would have shattered the whole argument, but nobody asked it—the majority because they had begun to think with their blood, which condemns all logic. ...
(Lilo Linke, *Restless Days*, 1935, 1963)

invaded Manchuria in 1931, which they organized in 1932 as the puppet state of Manchukuo (under the last emperor of China, who had abdicated in 1912, a member of the last imperial dynasty, the Qing, or Manchu). Japan paid little attention to the mild rebuke issued by the League of Nations in 1933 and withdrew from that body. Manchukuo, rich in resources and laced with railroad lines, sustained the Japanese economy. The military resumed its advance, controlling much of northern China by 1935. In 1937, Japan would seize the major Chinese cities of Beijing, Tientsin, Shanghai, Hangchow, and Nanjing—subjecting the last, the capital, to pillage and massacre, resulting in between 200,000 and 300,000 Chinese civilian deaths. Taking Tsintao and Guangzhou the following year, and the province of Hainan in February 1939, Japan controlled China's eastern provinces and most important ports. Like Europe at this date, Asia faced the prospect of domination by a mighty power that aimed to take from its neighbors what land and wealth it desired.

For by this point, Adolf Hitler and his Nazi party had achieved dominion in Germany, and had set out to dominate Europe, and the world.

Nazism: the German Form of Fascism

In Germany, fascism developed the distinctive form of Nazism, a product of Germany's particular history and Hitler's unique personality. The events of World War I, and the Versailles treaty imposed at its conclusion, had left Germany abject and defeated. By the late 1930s, Hitler led a prosperous, armed, and nazified Germany that was fully prepared to take the next step toward war and mastery.

The Roots of Nazism   Germany's military defeat in World War I had profound political consequences at home. Although the German generals had informed the government from the summer of 1918 that the war was unwinnable (see Chapter 26), the armistice of November 11 of that year was actually arranged by the centrist provisional government that had replaced that of Emperor William II (r. 1888–1918) only days earlier. Upon those Weimar politicians (named for the university town where the Constitutional Assembly of the new republic met) fell the duty of negotiating the Versailles peace treaty—a treaty that, its opponents felt, crippled and dishonored Germany. The generals who had failed to win the war presented themselves as having suffered a dastardly "stab in the back," when defeatist civilian leaders had signed the Armistice. The path was certainly now open to the rehabilitation of the military at the expense of parliamentary democracy.

The Versailles settlement stripped Germany of important territorial possessions. The industrial Saar district in the Ruhr region was placed (until a plebiscite in 1935) under international administration, the Rhineland was occupied and demilitarized, with Alsace and Lorraine, west of the Rhine, returned to France. The German army and navy were sharply cut back to the size of a police force barely capable of self-defense. Germany was effectively disarmed.

Moreover, the notorious "war guilt" clause in Article 231 of the Versailles treaty declared Germany responsible "for causing all the loss and damage" suffered by the Allies in a war "imposed upon them by the aggression of Germany and her allies." Crippled and starved by the conflict, Germany was to pay punitive "reparations." These provisions resulted in an ominous sense of national humiliation and deep resentment. Furthermore, the expense was unbearable. In an attempt to meet its costs, the government printed paper currency, leading to the ruinous hyperinflation of the 1920s (see Chapter 27).

In sum, the Versailles treaty amounted to a guarantee of renewed conflict. The Germans felt themselves dishonored, and plundered by the victor nations of World War I. Soon they would welcome a war of retaliation. But that war would be driven by other forces as well, including that of an explosive nationalism, fueled by popular racial theory.

Germany had only recently become a nation (see Chapter 23). It had developed an intense sense of nationhood from the experiences leading to unification in 1871: the Prussian resistance to Napoleon, the events of 1848, and Bismarck's construction of Prussian leadership (see Chapter 23). National pride was further bolstered by the cultural unity of the German-speaking domains.

The cohesion of German culture could be traced to the work of the reformer Martin Luther (1483–1546), who first distinguished national German interests from those of the cosmopolitan papacy. Since then, German-speakers had been among the leading figures of the scientific revolution and Enlightenment, and the Classical and Romantic movements in the arts (see Chapters 17, 25). In the nineteenth century, the German universities were the most advanced in Europe, training students in Classical and modern disciplines.

But German nationalism, as it emerged in the nineteenth century, also had deeper, troubling, dimensions. It was characterized by expansionist fantasies built on medieval precedents, and colored by racial theories. From the Middle Ages came the legacy of the "*Drang nach Osten,*" or "drive to the east," the movement of German-speaking peoples to open new territories in eastern Europe and to Christianize pagan Slavs. There lingered a sense of German entitlement to eastern lands, and of superiority over their peoples, who had indeed often been pressed into dependency in the Middle Ages.

German attitudes toward the Slavic peoples also had ideological origins. Imperialist ventures and

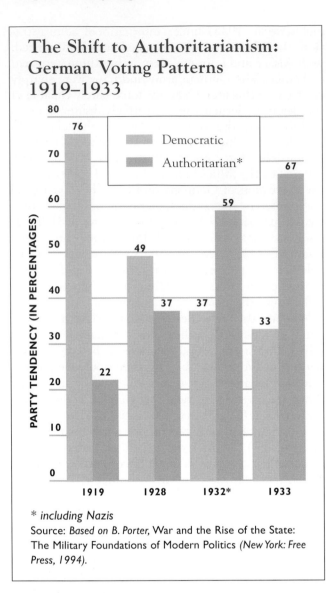

The Shift to Authoritarianism: German Voting Patterns 1919–1933

PARTY TENDENCY (IN PERCENTAGES)

- Democratic
- Authoritarian*

1919: 76, 22
1928: 49, 37
1932*: 37, 59
1933: 33, 67

* *including Nazis*

Source: *Based on B. Porter,* War and the Rise of the State: The Military Foundations of Modern Politics *(New York: Free Press, 1994).*

Darwinian theory encouraged the development of racial theories in the late nineteenth century (see Chapter 25). German academics constructed the notion of a superior Aryan race (related to ancient Indo-Aryan speakers of languages ancestral to those of modern Europe; see Chapters 1, 2). As Aryans, Germans were superior to Slavs, Jews, gypsies, and others, with a special place in the hierarchy of races.

The Rise of Hitler   These notions of German racial superiority, national destiny, the superiority of military to parliamentary rule, and the humiliations of the Versailles settlement, were the ingredients of the ideology of Nazism formulated by Adolf Hitler in his sprawling *Mein Kampf* ("My Struggle," 1925). To these Hitler added anti-Bolshevism and an economic justification for territorial expansion—the principle of Germany's need for (and hence entitlement to) *Lebensraum* ("living space").

Born in Austria–Hungary, the son of a government functionary and a doting mother, Adolf Hitler gave no evidence in his youth of the power he would wield.

With ambitions of becoming an artist, he gravitated to the political and cultural capital of Vienna. Living on the margins in those pre-war years, when philosophies stormed about, he picked up small jobs, slept in flophouses, and imbibed prevailing currents of thought (see Chapter 25): anti-Semitism, race theory, Nietzscheanism, socialism, and nationalism.

Hitler moved to Germany and joined the German army in Munich in 1914. He fought with distinction, achieving the rank of corporal and winning the Iron Cross. When an exhausted German government signed the armistice, Hitler, like his superiors, felt that he had been stabbed in the back.

With the war over, Hitler returned to Munich and became a political agent. In the confused, crisis-ridden 1920s, that meant recruiting like-minded comrades in beer halls and fostering squads of thugs who roamed the streets in search of enemies to maul. It also meant nursing the grievances the past had delivered: against Jews, against communists (among them, Jews), against rich speculators (among them, Jews), against the enemies of Germany, and politicians. As an informer in the pay of army intelligence, he infiltrated one of the fringe political parties—the NSDAP, or National-sozialistische deutsche Arbeiterpartei ("National-socialist German Workers' Party"), or Nazi for short—Hitler found a home.

Hitler was now a beer-hall orator, and commanded an armed gang of brown-shirted "stormtroopers," the later SA (*Sturmabteilungen*). In 1923, he led the Munich Nazis in a **putsch**, an attempted government takeover. Thrown in prison with a five-year sentence, he was released after a little more than six months. During that interlude, he wrote *Mein Kampf*. In contrast to the works of Lenin, characterized by their concision and logic, *Mein Kampf* impresses by the virulence of its ideas, the randomness of their expression, and the consistency of its maxims with the Nazi project Hitler later brought to culmination. A passage from it is reproduced in *Witnesses* on p. 810.

By the late 1920s, Nazis were as strong a presence as their chief political opponents, the communists, and began to win seats in the *Reichstag*, or parliament. When the Depression struck in 1929, Nazis and communists courted its victims. The communists recruited a following from among the industrial workers. The Nazis appealed to the lower and middle bourgeoisie, white-collar workers, small business proprietors, bureaucrats—those who were at once economically threatened, and fearful of Bolshevism.

By 1930, the Nazis gained a foothold in the Reichstag, winning 107 seats (of a total of 556) to the communists' 77; in July 1932, 196 seats. The graph above shows the shifts in voting patterns during these years. Meanwhile, the government floundered, as center-left leaders and ineffective chancellors came and went; the presidency remained in the hands of the elderly World War I veteran Paul von Hindenburg

(1847–1934; see Chapter 26), now nearly ninety. With conservative support, Hitler became chancellor on January 30, 1933, and formed a cabinet dominated by Nazis. It was to be the Weimar republic's last government. Twenty months later, after Hindenburg's death on August 2, 1934, the chancellorship and the presidency were merged. Hitler had reached the highest office in the German government by strictly legal means. He would now consolidate his power by force.

Hitler in Power On February 27, 1933, a fire broke out in the Reichstag building. Nazi arsonists were probably responsible, but blame was assigned to Hitler's communist opponents. The emergency gave Hitler the opportunity to suspend civil liberties and grab control. On March 23, 1933, the Enabling Act granted Hitler dictatorial powers. On August 19, 1934, a plebiscite approved the delegation of all executive power to Hitler as Führer, or "leader." Now Hitler moved to enact the nightmarish fantasies outlined so vividly—for any who had a mind to consult them—in *Mein Kampf*. "No human being has ever declared or recorded what he wanted more often than I," Hitler reminded an unseeing world.

Hitler's first goal was to climb out of the Depression (see Chapter 27). Two-fifths of German workers were without jobs, while production and foreign trade had dropped to disastrous lows. Hitler's solution for this crisis was threefold. First, he aimed at self-sufficiency, or **autarky**. With the institution of his Four Year Plan (October 19, 1936), the whole southeastern region of Europe was to trade almost exclusively with Germany. Second, Hitler encouraged barter exchange with other countries as an alternative to wealth-draining foreign trade, and had the chemical industries develop synthetic or "**ersatz**" equivalents of consumer staples and industrial supplies. Third, Hitler let loose the war machine. With factories producing guns, ammunition, and equipment, German workers found jobs, and a new appreciation for their Führer.

His economic program did not distract Hitler from the task of reshaping society. He encouraged groups of all sorts in a policy of *Gleichschaltung* (enforced conformity). Youth groups, choral groups, and sports clubs all offered opportunities for Nazi indoctrination and discouraged individualism. Christian organizations were a problem. Hitler did not like them; but many Germans did, and they were at least a force for social order. In 1933, Hitler made his peace with the Roman Catholics—and could not have been pleased to learn in 1937 that a papal encyclical denouncing Nazi racial policies had been read aloud in the churches. In 1933 he reorganized the mainstream Protestant churches into the nazified German Evangelical Church. More than sixty percent of German Protestants accepted the Nazi leader. Critics of Nazism formed a counter-church, the remnant of which resisted or fled.

Nazism promoted the sense of belonging to the *Volk*, or the people ("folk"), and history, legend, and song reinforced that sentiment. In art and in film, Hitler liked to see heroic images of the German people which defied the uncertainties of the twentieth-century world. In the painting reproduced on p. 814, he is shown as a knight in armor. In 1937, the Nazis mounted two art exhibitions: "German Art" paraded paintings of Aryan-type heroes, while "Degenerate Art" displayed the kind of images—Surrealist, Dadaist, Expressionist, Modernist, many by Jewish artists—that Hitler condemned.

In intellectual life, the Nazis required conformity, and burned books of which they disapproved. Some thinkers, such as the novelist Thomas Mann (1875–1955), refused to cooperate and lived in exile. Others, including the philosopher Martin Heidegger (1889–1976), gave the raised-arm Nazi salute on request and supported the regime.

Hitler directed women to resume their traditional roles. Central to Nazi ideology was the restriction of women to the realm of home and family—to *Kinder, Kirche, Küche* (children, church, kitchen). A Nazi "Women's Union," headed by the ideologue Gertrud Scholtz-Klink (1902–), supervised the political indoctrination of German women. In Nazi theory, the greatest service women performed for the state was bearing and rearing of Aryan children. The birthrate rose over forty percent between 1933 and 1939.

The Anti-Semitic Tide For none of Nazism's programs to promote fellowship and *völkisch* memory included Jews and other non-Aryans. Hitler's "racial laws" of 1935 were part of the process that became progressively uglier until it reached monstrous dimensions in the "Final Solution." This new era of persecution began with a call to boycott Jewish businesses. Jews were expelled from their positions in universities and the civil service. In time, they were denied citizenship; their properties were confiscated; they were forced to wear the yellow Star of David on their clothing. Slogans circulated: "The Jew is the cause and the beneficiary of our misery"; "The Jew is the plastic demon of the decline of mankind"; "The Jew is our greatest misfortune."

If it was still possible in 1933 for Jews to hope for a change of policy, over the next few years they should have abandoned all hope. Now stormtroopers beat up Jews on the street, destroyed Jewish places of business, and broke into Jewish houses to rob and rape. When Hitler seized Austria, Nazi agents burst into the Vienna residence of the founder of psychoanalysis, Sigmund Freud (see Chapter 25), a Jew. Mrs Freud, having watched the thugs tear apart her home, put some coins on the table and invited the brown-shirted gentlemen to take those as well. Freud himself was spirited out of the country to London. Less privileged Jews were left to face the full Nazi fury signaled by the

***Hubert Lanzinger*, Hitler as Knight:** *Like Russian artists who adopted the style of "Soviet Realism" to give expression to communist ideology, German artists celebrated Nazi themes. In this painting by Hubert Lanzinger from around 1936, Hitler is portrayed as a knight in shining armor, bearing a swastika standard, in a determined pose that echoes the medieval image of the Teutonic Order of Knights who conquered and converted the Slavic peoples of eastern Europe.*

horror of Kristallnacht ("Crystal Night," the night of broken glass, November 9–10, 1938). SS Hitler Youth squads gutted 7,500 Jewish business and destroyed 177 synagogues. Ninety-one Jews were killed, hundreds more injured, and hardly anyone protested.

Nazism also targeted other groups for exclusion and extinction. The communist members of the Reichstag were arrested in 1933, and along with those swept up from the streets and factories, sent to detention camps and prisons. Gypsies, homosexuals, the disabled and permanently ill were all marked for persecution. Influenced by the theories of eugenics then in vogue, which discouraged the propagation of those seen as "unfit," Hitler's race theory dictated that the lives only of healthy Aryans were valuable—those likely to reproduce. The others served no purpose, and should be eliminated. Scientists and physicians cooperated; even non-Nazis made no effective protest against orders to neglect or kill these unfortunates. They instituted a full-scale "euthanasia" program, which some scholars have seen as a pilot program for the wholesale killing of Jews undertaken in 1942.

Hitler's economic and social projects were publicized by speeches, radio announcements, and press features that broadcast Nazi propaganda. With their simple rhetoric and bald misrepresentation of truth, these effectively shaped popular attitudes. The impact

of Hitler himself is observed in *Witnesses* on p. 819. The aim was not to educate the elite, but to win instant recognition from the ignorant. "The larger the mass of men to be reached," Hitler advised in *Mein Kampf*, "the lower its purely intellectual level will have to be set." In view of the "primitive simplicity" of the mind of the mass of the people, Hitler argued, the true leader must use a "big lie" to win their trust. Deception on a grand scale was necessary if the German people were to accept Hitler's views about Jews, communists, the Aryan Master Race, and *Lebensraum*.

Even those unconvinced by Nazi propaganda were impressed by the ruthless brutality with which Nazism could act. In a preemptive stroke on June 30, 1934, Hitler used his private army, the SS, to purge the brown-shirted SA that had raised him to power—about 2 million strong, the scum of the streets, career criminals, habitual killers. In the "Night of the Long Knives," about eighty SA leaders were killed. By this massacre, Hitler detached himself from his early supporters and aligned himself with the interests of the industrial and military elite. In 1938, a more discreet purge of army officers followed, many of them from the old aristocracy.

At this juncture, Hitler needed to rid himself of upper-level officers whose patrician upbringing might have intruded a tradition of civility and even moral principles. For he was embarked on a program that required the violation of Germany's agreements with most of the nations of Europe. The German form of fascism had reached its maturity. Now Nazism would lead the world into war.

THE SECOND WORLD WAR: FASCISM DEFEATED

Having seized power in Germany, Hitler rearmed and allied with the Axis powers of Italy and Japan. The principal European democracies stood by, their inaction and incomprehension facilitating the arms buildup and first hostilities.

Fascism advanced to a high tide in 1942. Over the next three years, it was beaten back to a total defeat by the Allied powers—at first Britain alone, then Britain with two latecomer participants from the peripheries of the West, the Soviet Union and the United States.

In 1945, an era of Western history came to a close with the explosion of two atomic bombs in Japan and the liberation of the Nazi concentration camps, which had annihilated the targeted victims of Hitler's Final Solution.

The Dictatorships: Rearmament and Realignment

From 1933, Hitler rearmed Germany and allied with Italy and Japan. By 1936, all three Axis powers had undertaken expansionist projects in Europe, Africa, and Asia, as Map 28.2 below shows.

In 1925, representatives from Britain, France, Belgium, Italy, and Germany met at Locarno in Switzerland to put a close to the issues that the Versailles peace had left unresolved. Those discussions brought voluntary recognition by Germany of its borders in the west (though not the east), left the matter of unpaid reparations in genteel silence,

and welcomed Germany back into the community of European nations. In 1927, Germany gained admission to the League of Nations. It joined the ongoing series of disarmament conferences that many hoped would assure the goal United States president Wilson had enunciated, that the Great War would prove to be the war to end all wars. Amid the glorious prosperity that characterized the late 1920s, such hopes flourished.

Map 28.2 Expansion and Aggression West and East, 1930–1939: *Between 1930 and 1939, Germany, Italy, and Japan undertook programs of expansion in their separate spheres. Japan's expansion in east Asia and the Pacific had begun as early as 1895, advanced in 1905 as a result of the Russo-Japanese war, and culminated in the 1930s, with a push into Manchuria and northern and eastern China. Italy added to its existing African sphere of influence in Libya, Eritrea, and part of Somaliland by invading Ethiopia in 1935, and seized Albania in 1939, on the eve of war. Germany steadily followed up its first aggression of 1936—the remilitarization of the Rhineland—with annexations of Austria and the Sudetenland (Czechoslovakia) in 1938, and the rest of Czechoslovakia, the Baltic port of Memel, and Poland in 1939. The last aggression triggered the outbreak of war. What impels nations, at certain historical junctures, to attempt territorial expansion?*

International cooperation would not survive Hitler's advent to power. On July 15, 1933, Hitler joined with Britain, France, and Italy in signing the Four-Power Pact that affirmed adherence to the principles of the Locarno Treaty, the League covenant, and the Versailles treaty. But by the fall of that year, he began to repudiate all those principles and more. On October 14, 1933, Germany withdrew from disarmament discussions, and from the League of Nations itself. In 1934, the Soviet Union took Germany's place in the League of Nations.

Hitler rearmed. Army officers maximized the potential of the minimal forces allowed to Germany by the Versailles settlement, grooming an officer cadre and covertly sending pilots to train under Red Army instructors in the Soviet Union. On March 7, 1936, Hitler tested his military strength by reoccupying the Rhineland with a mere 22,000 troops (the Rhineland, German territory west of the Rhine, had been demilitarized by the terms of Versailles and evacuated by the French only in 1930). On March 16, he repudiated the disarmament clauses of the Versailles treaty. Hitler had sent a clear message to the European powers: he intended to take what he wished by force. They were surprisingly slow to grasp the reality of this message.

The remilitarization of the Rhineland challenged the authority of the Treaty of Versailles. In April, Hitler's former Locarno partners, Britain, France, and

Italy, met at Stresa in Italy to consider a possible response. France, meanwhile, signed a treaty of mutual assistance with the Soviet Union and explored treaties with Czechoslovakia, Yugoslavia, and Romania (the "Little Entente" from 1920). These diplomatic moves proved valueless. Hitler had negotiated an agreement (June 18, 1936) with the British, who sought to placate this alarming Führer, permitting Germany to build its navy up to thirty-five percent of British strength. The British government sought to use German strength as a bulwark against communism. The Soviet Union was seen as a greater threat than Germany, and there was considerable sympathy for Hitler at the highest levels of the administration. Thus was Hitler rewarded for invading the Rhineland and flouting international law.

In the fall of 1936, Hitler pursued alliances with Italy and Japan, who would become his partners in the coming war. On October 3, 1935, Mussolini had invaded Ethiopia. His democratic colleagues responded weakly; the League of Nations (before which the beleaguered emperor Haile Selassie, 1891–1975, had pleaded Ethiopia's cause), imposed toothless sanctions on Italy. Irritated, Mussolini secured the Ethiopian capital of Addis Ababa on May 5, 1936, and approached Hitler. The two agreed on an alliance, which Mussolini proclaimed on October 25, 1936 as the Rome–Berlin axis. A few weeks later (November 25), Germany and Japan joined in the

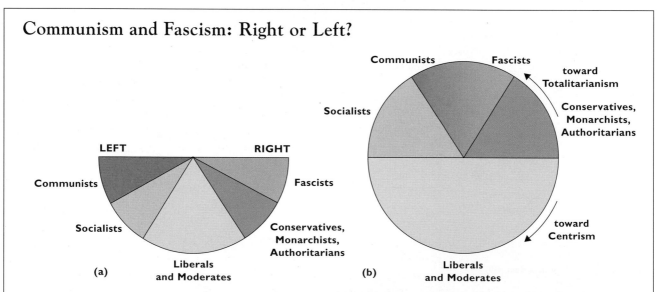

Communism and Fascism: Right or Left?

How are the phenomena of communism and fascism to be understood in relation to the more familiar spectrum of conservative and liberal political ideologies? A graphic representation can help, using the once again familiar categories of "left" for liberalism and socialism and their extremes, and "right" for conservatism and its extremes. For many scholars, communism, with its connection to democratic socialism, itself an outgrowth of liberalism, should lodge on the "left" of such a spectrum. Fascism, accordingly, with its links to conservative and authoritarian views, should lodge on the "right." These relationships are shown schematically in (a). Other scholars view communism and fascism as phenomena more closely related than that scheme implies, sharing such features as manipulation of mass sentiments through propaganda and indoctrination, futurism or modernism, anti-parliamentarianism, anti-liberalism, atheism, and inclination to violence. As totalitarian movements, then, they approach each other. This relationship is seen in (b).
Source: Based on H.R. Kedward, Fascism in Western Europe: 1900-1945 (Glasgow: Blackie and Son Ltd., 1971), pp. 240–241.

Anti-Comintern Pact that was ranged against the Soviet Union. Italy then joined a year later.

The Axis powers were now ready to expand. The Germans would recover what was justly theirs—its "unredeemed" lands that the last war had denied them, the lands of the Slavs, and racial and territorial dominance in Europe. The Italians would gain an overseas empire and the glory of the Roman Empire. Japan would seize dominion in eastern Asia so as to provide resources for its people and its factories, and achieve its supposed imperial destiny.

The Democracies: Frailty and Confusion

By the end of 1937, the Axis league had crystallized. Yet the Western democracies still misread the clear signal that catastrophe loomed. Were they misled? Were they inept? Were they so paralyzed by memories of the last war that they could not confront, when it was still possible to do so, those who would launch the next? These are difficult questions. Noting the following two factors may assist in finding answers.

First, the diplomacy of the principal democracies was aimed at maintaining the status quo achieved by the 1919 Paris treaties; the goal of their opponents, in contrast, was to subvert it. From 1919 through 1936, the League of Nations worked to achieve the "collective security" of Europe. In the 1920s, it sought to ease tensions in the Rhineland, and encouraged the settlement of the issues of reparations, war debt, and disarmament. In 1932, the League's Lytton Commission denounced the Japanese invasion of Manchuria as an "act of aggression." In 1935, when Italy invaded Ethiopia, the League imposed sanctions—but they were insufficient.

In each case, the League sought to diminish tensions, but nations set upon expansion reneged on international agreements. By 1936, the League had become ineffective. The nations that had depended upon it found themselves without a defender.

Second, political discussion in the free countries was marked by confusion and ideological fragmentation; in the Axis nations, in contrast, there was clarity of thought and unity of purpose. The major democracies cycled through coalition governments in the 1920s and 1930s; with the Popular Front coalitions of the 1930s, ideological variety reached a maximum, while the ineffectiveness of political leaders across the spectrum inspired little respect for any of the ideological alternatives represented.

Nor were those alternatives clearly distinguished. Apart from communists, there were on the left both democratic and anti-democratic socialists. Opposing them were conservatives and fascists. Fascism, however, in its appeals to group solidarity, and its repudiation of individualism, could tend toward socialism, in which it had its origins—Mussolini had really been a socialist; Nazism had originally embraced a working-class activism. Conservatives were so fearful of communism that they failed to see the more serious imminent threat of fascism. Liberal democrats, meanwhile, might be tempted by socialist, fascist, or communist alternatives, believing these to be the defenders of the working class, or the nation, or (as in the United States) of marginalized groups such as blacks and Jews.

Communism and fascism, finally, though viewed as opposites—both because of communist theory (which equated fascism with capitalism and imperialism) and fascist proximity to conservative aristocratic and clerical interests—had, ironically, strong resemblances. Both fascist states and the communist Soviet Union were ruled by dictators, repressed dissent, broadcast propaganda, and employed random terror to maintain control. Liberal democrats and democratic socialists occupied a weak center between wings that were not distinctly "right" or "left" on the political spectrum, but equally totalitarian.

In this stew of political alternatives, a well-meaning European could not easily make a rational choice. Neither could whole nations. They were rescued from perplexity by the advent of crisis: a preliminary crisis in Spain, followed by the graver one in central Europe.

The Spanish Civil War: Rehearsal for World War

From 1936 to 1939, civil war raged in Spain, on the periphery of continental politics. An elected center-left government faced a military revolt that eventually resulted in the creation of an authoritarian regime. While the European democracies stayed aloof, totalitarian powers both communist and fascist sent soldiers and supplies. Their intervention in the Spanish Civil War was a prologue to World War II.

The civil war was in origin a traditional conflict between liberalism on one side, and monarchy and entrenched elites on the other. Spain's era of greatness was long gone by 1898, when it lost the last of its major colonies (see Chapter 24). King Alfonso XIII (r. 1902–1931) ruled weakly thereafter as a constitutional monarch, bolstered by the Roman Catholic clergy and military leaders. Amid labor unrest and separatist revolts, Alfonso turned to the right and supported as prime minister José Antonio Primo de Rivera (1870–1930). In 1923, Primo de Rivera suspended the constitution, censored the press, and clamped down on the universities. When the Depression came in 1929, these tactics proved to be unsustainable.

In 1931, leftist Republican parties triumphed in municipal and national elections, forcing Alfonso to leave Spain. The new constituent assembly was dominated by socialists, communists, anarchists, and syndicalists. This body drafted a liberal constitution granting universal suffrage, basic freedoms, separation of Church and state, secular control of mass education, and the nationalization of church property. The disestablishment of the Roman Catholic Church was one platform on which nearly all agreed.

In 1933, new elections produced a rightist government which promptly undid earlier reforms. In 1936, the pendulum swung again; new elections yielded a left-center majority and a Popular Front government, alarming the wealthy, the clergy, and the military. On July 17, 1936, army officers in Spanish Morocco, North Africa, launched a revolt against the government. Ferried back to Spain in Italian ships, under the leadership of the general Francisco Franco, the Nationalists, as they were called, took control of the Spanish central region, which supported the rising. The Loyalists held the capital at Madrid, the Basque Country, and the developed eastern seaboard, including the region of Catalonia with its cosmopolitan capital at Barcelona.

By all rights, the legitimate, elected government should have won this struggle against a handful of insurgent generals. That it did not has to do with the behavior of the onlooker European nations. The ever-cautious democracies, fearful of war, would not intervene, even to provide the Spanish government with weapons and supplies. The dictatorships, however, intervened vigorously. Mussolini's Italy sent guns, tanks, planes, and men. Hitler unleashed his airforce, or Luftwaffe, including the elite Condor Legion, which practiced in Spain the tactics it would use in

the larger conflict to come. Stalin's Soviet Union fed the Loyalists supplies and armaments, for which it required payment in full, and in gold. These were delivered along with the usual political commissars, urging allegiance to the party line.

Loyalist volunteers arrived in Spain as well—the International Brigades, about 40,000 volunteers from Europe and the United States, democrats, socialists, communists, and workers eager to fight for a new order. Thus strengthened, the Loyalists fought desperately against Franco and his supporters (including the Roman Catholic Church, of whom they murdered more than 1000 priests and nearly 300 nuns).

The efficient Franco—a soldier rather than a fascist, but in league with fascism none the less—made steady progress. His German allies pursued their experiments. Their blanket bombing on April 26, 1937 of the Basque town of Guernica was a tragedy not only for the Basques, but for the whole world, now introduced to a new tactic—the deliberate bombing of unwarned civilians. Its cruelty is conveyed in the coldly eloquent monochrome of Picasso's painting *Guernica*.

By the end of 1938, Franco's forces seized Catalonia; by spring 1939, Valencia and the capital of Madrid. The Loyalists and their international volunteers fled, or were captured, tortured, and murdered. Fascism was on the march.

Still the democracies did not act, and would not do so until they were forced to go to war once again, war total and world-wide.

First Hostilities

In 1938, Hitler moved on two fronts, the opening sallies of the next world war. He took over two neighboring regions: the state of Austria and the Sudetenland region of Czechoslovakia. In justification, he could cite the Wilsonian principle of self-determination (see Chapter 26): the ethnic Germans of Austria (the majority of Austrians) and Czechoslovakia (a majority in the Sudetenland) rightly wished to be part of Germany rather than exist as a minority, subject people. In March 1938, he accomplished the *Anschluss*, or annexation, of Austria—a kindred nation already under its own fascist dictator, with a strong native Nazi party and compliant populace to support Hitler's arrival.

Hitler's ingestion of Austria was scarcely noted by European onlookers. They were more disturbed when later the same year he annexed the Czech Sudetenland, which had a German majority and was dominated by a Nazi party. Poland joined in to pick up the district of Czechoslovakia with a strong presence of ethnic Poles.

Alarmed, the British prime minister Neville Chamberlain (1869–1940) met with Hitler three times in 1938, pursuing a policy of **appeasement**.

A meeting of dictators: *Stalin and his advisers may also have been deceived by Hitler when they agreed to a pact in the summer of 1939. The absurdity of this Nazi–Communist marriage was generally noted, as in this cartoon from London's Evening Standard on September 20, 1939. On a corpse-littered battlefield the two armed dictators greet each other: "The scum of the earth, I believe," says Hitler cordially; "The bloody assassin of the workers, I presume?" says Stalin.*

Fighting the Second World War

As war burst, the intentions of the leaders of powerful states became painfully clear. Here, Hitler announces his ruthless intentions to dominate where he will; a Japanese nationalist argues for his nation's role as the unifier, and dominator, of all Asia; and a British statesman, the conservative, imperialist aristocrat Winston Churchill, rallies his countrymen to fight to the ultimate moment for victory over a "monstrous tyranny never surpassed in the dark and lamentable catalogue of human crime."

On the eve of war, Hitler muses on its future (1939): Since the autumn of 1938 … I decided to go with Stalin. After all there are only three great statesmen in the world, Stalin, I and Mussolini. Mussolini is the weakest. … So in a few weeks hence I shall stretch out my hand to Stalin at the common German–Russian frontier and with him undertake to re-distribute the world.

Our strength lies in our quickness and in our brutality; Genghis Khan has sent millions of women and children into death knowingly and with a light heart. History sees in him only the great founder of States. As to what the weak Western European civilisation asserts about me, that is of no account. I have given the command and I shall shoot everyone who utters one word of criticism. … Who after all is today speaking about the destruction of the Armenians?
(Speech by Adolf Hitler, as recorded by a witness; from E. L. Woodward and R. Butler, eds., *Documents on British Foreign Policy, 1919–1939*, 1954)

Japanese nationalist writer Tokutomi Iichirō comments on the Japanese Imperial Declaration of War (1941): In Nippon [Japan] resides a destiny to become the Light of Greater East Asia and to become ultimately the Light of the World. However, in order to become [the former] … we must have three qualifications. The first … is strength. … [W]e must expel Anglo-Saxon influence from East Asia with our strength. …

The second qualification is benevolence. Nippon must develop the various resources of East Asia and distribute them fairly to all the races within the Greater East Asian Co-Prosperity Sphere. …

The third qualification is virtue. … It was the favorite policy of the Anglo-Saxons to make the various races of East Asia compete and fight each other and make them mutually small and powerless. We must, therefore, console them, bring peace and friendship among them, and make them all live in peace with a boundlessly embracing virtue.
(From R. Tsunoda et al, *Sources of the Japanese Tradition*, 1958)

In speeches to the British Parliament, Churchill rallies the nation that would soon oppose Nazism alone (1940): *May 13, 1940:* … I have nothing to offer but blood and toil and tears and sweat. We have before all of us an ordeal of the most grievous kind. We have before us many, many long months of struggle and of suffering. If you ask what is our policy I will say it is to wage war … war by air, land and sea, war with all our might and with all the strength that God can give us, and to wage war against a monstrous tyranny never surpassed in the dark and lamentable catalogue of human crime. That is our policy. If you ask us, "What is your aim"? I can answer in one word—victory … victory however long and hard the road may be.
June 4, 1940 [after describing the evacuation of British forces from Dunkirk, on the far side of the Channel coast]:

We shall fight in France, we shall fight on the seas and oceans; we shall fight with growing confidence and growing strength in the air. We shall defend our island whatever the cost may be. We shall fight on the beaches, we shall fight on the landing grounds, in the fields, in the streets, and in the hills. We shall never surrender. …
(Winston Churchill, speeches to British Parliament, 1940)

Britain and France were determined to avoid war at all costs. Their citizens had not yet recovered from the slaughter of the previous war (see Chapter 26). Moreover, they hoped that a pacified Germany would serve as a bulwark against communism. In the culminating journey to Munich, Chamberlain obtained (along with French and Italian representatives) a commitment, signed September 29, 1938, that in return for permission to occupy the Sudetenland, Germany would make no further territorial demands.

On that promise the appeasers rested their hopes. Returning to Britain, Chamberlain waved the piece of paper and exulted that it meant "peace in our time." In fact, it meant peace for eleven months. For the following spring, Hitler returned to Czechoslovakia. He

engrossed what remained of the western part (the provinces of Bohemia and Moravia) on March 16, 1939, and organized the eastern sector as the puppet state of Slovakia. Czechoslovakia was no more. In exchange for a brief and specious peace, the Western democracies had delivered Czechoslovakia—and soon the Slavs, the Jews, and virtually all of Europe—to the Nazis.

Hitler's actions caused even Chamberlain's confidence to crumble, and stirred his British and French colleagues to confront Germany's aggressions. Poland would likely be his next target; on March 31, Britain certified to Poland that, if Germany invaded, it would declare war. In the meantime, stifling their distrust of communism, Britain and France would seek an alliance with Stalin's Soviet Union. A diplomatic party set out in August 1939. But the Germans got there first. On August 23, 1939, Hitler's representatives signed with Stalin a Non-Aggression Pact, assuring mutual neutrality if either party was attacked; and some Polish and Baltic territories for the Soviets if war did ensue. Hitler's reasons are outlined in *Witnesses* on p. 819. The Germans, who detested the Soviets both as Slavs and as Bolsheviks, had bought freedom for their invasion of Poland. The Soviets detested the fascists no more than the democrats—to them, "imperialists"—whose war they did not wish to fight. The Comintern was alerted. Communist officials dictated the new party line to their followers: they had fought fascism in Spain, but now they must support, or at least cease their criticism of Nazism, and remain aloof from the "imperialist war." Consternation also struck Western diplomats, who had hoped to play Germany against the Soviets, or the Soviets against Germany—and now awoke to find that their playthings were arrayed against them. A contemporary cartoon is reproduced on p. 818.

Meanwhile, Hitler seized the Baltic port of Memel; Italy seized Albania on April 7, and on May 22 formed a ten-year military alliance with Germany—the "Pact of Steel." On September 1, 1939, Hitler let loose **Blitzkrieg** ("lightning war," war as stupendous as a bolt of lightning) on Poland. (On that same day he ordered, his racial theories always in the forefront of his mind, the execution of some 70,000 mentally ill patients in German hospitals.) On September 3, Britain and France declared war on Germany.

From Appeasement to Victory

Appeasement failed less than one year after Chamberlain announced he had won "peace in our time." The world was at war again in a conflict that was to involve Europe, east and southeast Asia, North Africa, and the Middle East—with combatants recruited also from the United States and the British dominions (see Map 28.3, p. 822). World War I had been fought with trenches, barbed wire, and nerve gas. World War II would be fought with airplanes, aircraft carriers, and amphibious landings; codebreakers, spies, and radar; resistance cells, suicide missions, and covert operations; tanks and bombs, conventional and atomic. Never had so much wealth been channeled to produce so many machines that killed.

In the European theater of the war, the German offensive pressed forward to 1942 when it received setbacks in the Soviet Union and Africa. Thereafter the tide turned in favor of the Allies, who concluded the war with encirclement of Germany.

The Nazi Invasion of Poland and Western Europe
By the end of September 1939, the German invasion of Poland was virtually complete. Now the invaders

subjected that country to a savage occupation, killing in all about 3 million Poles. As an inferior race, according to Nazi ideology, the Slavic Poles were to be reduced to a docile, illiterate serfdom. Poles were barred from schools, denied privileges and position, subjected to arbitrary violence, or deported. Their leaders and intellectuals were slaughtered, and the large Jewish population ghettoized. Eastern Europe learned quickly the nature of Nazi conquest as it swept beyond Poland and into the Balkans.

Nazi occupation seemed gentler, at first, when it came to the western nations of Norway and Denmark, the Netherlands, and Belgium, nations Hitler gathered up in the first six months of 1940. On June 14, 1940, the Germans entered Paris, having breached the supposedly impregnable fortifications of the "Maginot Line." The French swiftly capitulated, while the government, headed by Marshal Philippe Pétain, an aging hero of the previous war, entered into collaboration with the Nazi victors. He would run a puppet French state from the southern resort town of Vichy, while Germans held the north and west. From France, Hitler determined to take Britain.

The Air War: Germany vs. Britain   From June 1940, when its Expeditionary Force escaped the continent from the northern French port of Dunkirk in fishing boats and yachts, until June 1941, when the Soviet Union joined the conflict, the British faced the Nazi behemoth alone. It was, as Sir Winston Churchill, prime minister from May 10, 1940, both the poet and the chief strategist of the conflict, intoned, "their finest hour." Extracts from his speeches are given in *Witnesses* on p. 819. Britain had a small army, a still vital navy, and a trained, eager airforce—fortunately, for the Channel, which had sheltered the island from invasion, could now be bridged by air. In what came to be known as the Battle of Britain, Royal Air Force (RAF) pilots, aided by the sinvention of radar, narrowly staved off invasion by the numerically superior Luftwaffe. Never, said Churchill, had so few done so much for so many.

The Luftwaffe commenced the bombing of British military targets in July 1940; soon it bombed cities as well, including Birmingham, Manchester, Liverpool, and Southampton. Above all, London was a target—its children preventively evacuated since 1939, and its citizens taking nightly refuge in subway stations. The "blitz" of London peaked in September but continued through spring 1941. London's great cathedral of St. Paul's survived amid the surrounding wreckage. In the industrial Midlands region, the lovely cathedral of Coventry was destroyed. Later in the war, strategic bombing by the Allies was to destroy great swathes of the German cities of Hamburg, Cologne, and Dresden, whose churches were reduced to scarred debris, and whose "unavoidable" civilian casualties included the elderly and infirm, women and children.

Although the British fought mostly in the air, they had other, secret weapons. These included a squad of cryptologists (Polish exiles broke the German cipher early in the war) who intercepted tens of thousands of German messages per month, and the best intelligence operation in Europe, which kept the Germans ignorant or deceived about their opponents' actions.

At sea, meanwhile, the Germans initially had the advantage as their U-boats preyed on shipping along the western approaches to Britain. After 1941, they moved out to the mid-Atlantic (safe from British aerial patrol). After the United States entered the war late in 1942, they found new targets further west and in the Caribbean. Eventually, long-range planes equipped with radar were able to track the U-boats, and settle the "battle of the Atlantic."

The Germans in the East and in North Africa By 1941, Hitler was planning a new venture for the spring: the invasion of his ally, the Soviet Union. On June 22, German armies launched a three-pronged assault on the Russian heartland. In the north, they targeted Leningrad; from the center, the capital, Moscow; to the south, the Crimean ports and lower river Don. The Germans dubbed this undertaking "Operation Barbarossa" in remembrance of the medieval German emperor Frederick I Barbarossa.

Until this moment, the Russians had observed their agreement with Germany. Two weeks after the Germans invaded Poland from the west, according to prior agreement, the Red Army did so from the east. One consequence of that invasion was the massacre in 1941, by Stalin's order, of 4443 Polish officers, in Katyn forest, near Smolensk. In 1944, Stalin shifted the blame for this massacre to the Nazis. Recent investigations assign it unequivocally to the Soviets—who were surely responsible also for 10,000 more Polish officers missing since the Soviet occupation. The incident is one relic of the brief period of Nazi–Soviet cooperation. In 1939–1940, Soviet forces allied with Germany also invaded the Baltic states, Finland, and Romania.

In June 1941, German forces smashed through the thin crust of Soviet defenses on the western frontier, taking Stalin thoroughly by surprise. The Red Army was not ready; it was in any case ill-trained. Stalin's Five Year Plans, however, had brought to a maximum the Soviet Union's capacity to produce armaments (it had nearly twice as many tanks at the front as the German attackers). And of people, it had an abundance. Communists around the globe celebrated Soviet strength—instructed now, after their abrupt about-face in 1939, to turn about once again.

In 1941 and 1942, the Germans advanced, tearing through Ukraine and the Crimea to the river Don, the Caucasus mountains, and almost to the Caspian Sea. But Soviet forces denied them Moscow, and the citizens and soldiers holding Leningrad—where a siege of almost 900 terrible days cost over 1 million lives—saved that city as well (the left photograph on p. 823 shows Leningrad during the seige). In August 1942, German forces reached the industrial center of Stalingrad, on the river Volga, gateway to the Caucasus oilfields. They struggled for months with the city's defenders, commanded by General Georgi Konstantinovich Zhukov (1896–1974), in the streets, face to face, from house to house.

As winter arrived, the battle hardened. Soviet armies encircled the Germans, who froze and starved, and were soon to die as newly minted tanks emerged from the Stalingrad factories. On January 31, 1943, the remnant of 91,000 German soldiers surrendered to the Soviet army. German military morale never recovered from the humiliating defeat at Stalingrad.

The following summer, the Germans met the Soviets at Kursk. Here 9000 tanks came to grips, tough German Panzers ("panthers") against even heavier Soviet tanks, which won the battle. From Kursk, the Red Army surged westward, its sights on Berlin. The Soviets had borne the brunt of the German war and sacrificed an estimated 20 to 28 million soldiers and civilians, dwarfing casualty rates for Britain or the United States, or even Germany. For the Soviets, this had not been simply a struggle between communism and fascism, or communism and imperialism. It had been a war for Mother Russia, the Great Patriotic War.

The year 1943 was pivotal in other theaters too. In North Africa, German forces under General Erwin G. Rommel (1891–1944) had arrived early in 1941 to blast through to Egypt and the Middle East. But at El Alamein in Egypt in October 1942, British general Bernard Montgomery (1887–1976) bested Rommel, the mastermind of tank warfare, with his own tactics. (Montgomery had profited from reading the book Rommel wrote on the subject.) Soon thereafter, United States forces landed in northwest Africa under General Dwight D. Eisenhower (1890–1969) to complete the German rout by the winter of 1943.

The War in Asia In east Asia also, 1942 was a turning point. In 1941, the Japanese had launched a campaign to control all the lands and islands of the western Pacific and southeast Asia (see *Witnesses*, p. 819). These were to form an outer zone of the Japanese Empire, complementary to the inner zone of home islands and Korean and Chinese possessions in a unified system called the Greater East Asia Co-Prosperity Sphere. Only the United States had a Pacific force capable of challenging them. To neutralize that potential enemy, the Japanese attacked, without warning, the United States naval base at Pearl Harbor in the Hawaiian islands, on December 7, 1941.

Until then, the United States had maintained an official neutrality, while supplying the Allies with armaments at first on a "cash and carry" basis, and after March 11, 1941 under the Lend-Lease program,

Map 28.3 Axis Advance and Allied Victory—World War II, 1939–1945: *The Axis powers expanded rapidly in the early years of the war. After 1943 turning points—the Russian victory at Stalingrad, the Allied invasion of Sicily and southern Italy—Axis-dominated Europe was put on the defensive. The June 1944 liberation of Rome and invasion of Normandy spelled the end of the Nazi empire, with final surrender in May 1945 following the Soviet sweep across eastern Europe and into Berlin. Meanwhile, the Allied war with Japan in the Pacific was effectively won by May 1945, although Japanese surrender followed only the epochal use of force—the release of two atom bombs—in August 1945.* **What was the nature of Allied progress in the Pacific from 1943 to 1945?**

on the promise of future payment. But the Pearl Harbor attack prompted an immediate response. The next day, Congress declared war on Japan; soon after, Germany declared war on the United States. American factories soared into full production, and by spring 1942, troops were pouring into Britain, Africa, and Asia while a fleet strong enough to patrol two oceans gathered in the south Pacific. After Pearl Harbor the vigilant Churchill, the lone fighter, then wary ally of the Soviets, relaxed.

From September 1941 to early 1942, the Japanese roared through Asia, defeating native and colonial defenders, deporting survivors to concentration camps where many were tortured and starved. When the first United States ships arrived to join Allied defenders (British, Dutch, New Zealand, and Australian) in

spring 1942, Japan controlled mainland and islands to a vast perimeter. Its dominions included much of eastern China, parts of Indochina and the East Indies, and many islands, including the Philippines, seized immediately after Pearl Harbor and the evacuation of United States general Douglas MacArthur (1880–1964).

After some initial defeats, and victories at Midway and Guadalcanal, United States forces drove the Japanese out of the Pacific islands over the next two years. Japanese defenders (whose casualties exceeded those of the Allies ten to one) dug into foxholes, hid in caves, rushed in desperate, futile charges. As their code of honor dictated, encircled garrisons stood to the death, and both combatants and civilians often chose suicide over capture. The last defenders were suicide bombers, who blew themselves up with the enemy ships they attacked—the *kamikaze*, named after the seemingly miraculous wind that in 1281 had saved Japan from a Mongol invasion.

By May 1945, the Allies had swept the Japanese from the open Pacific. The Japanese airforce and navy were largely destroyed. Japan's home islands, gripped by hunger, suffered steady United States bombardment from island bases. The British launched land attacks from India, and the Chinese fought where they could. Yet, cornered, the Japanese resisted.

Victory in Europe   The drive to free Europe began in earnest in 1943. In July of that year, Allied troops recently victorious in the North Africa campaign crossed the Mediterranean to land in Sicily and, on September 3, to the Italian mainland. Germany's ally, and a belligerent since June 1940, Italy surrendered; the Italian people welcomed the Allied soldiers as liberators. The now hated Mussolini was dismissed by the (still reigning) king Victor Emmanuel III, then arrested and imprisoned. He was subsequently rescued by the Germans, but finally shot, with his Jewish mistress, on April 28, 1945, after a hasty court-martial by **partisans** (unofficial **resistance** forces).

The final liberation of Italy from tenacious German forces took many months. By June 5, 1944, the Allies had fought their way to Rome, but the Germans still held the north. Venice, the last major city to fall, was taken only nine days before the German surrender on VE Day ("Victory in Europe"). In the Tuscan hills and the Po Valley, resistance forces linked up with the Allies and aided the liberation.

For there had been resistance groups in all the nations of occupied Europe. Active in many were communists receiving orders from Moscow; elsewhere nationalists who were instructed by governments-in-exile based in Britain; elsewhere Jews whose best choice was to fight Nazism wherever they could. The most effective were the Yugoslav partisans (divided between communist and monarchist units) who had fled to the mountains upon the German invasion of 1941, and there famously tied up twenty German divisions with their guerrilla tactics. Among the most daring perhaps were the German army officers whose attempt to assassinate Hitler on July 20, 1944, had it succeeded, might have saved the world millions of fatalities; but they were caught and savagely executed. The most ill-fated were the Poles of Warsaw, who perished on the brink of liberation in 1945, abandoned to Nazi fury by Stalin as he stalled outside the city. The French resistance groups pulled together at the end when on June 6, 1944, D-Day, Allied forces crossed the Channel to land on the Normandy coast, under the supreme command of United States general Eisenhower. In league with them were the forces of General Charles de Gaulle (1890–1970), who had escaped ahead of the Nazi takeover in 1940 and, from exile in Britain, organized the "Free French."

From Normandy, the Allied armies pushed eastward to meet the Soviets in Germany in April 1945. They moved swiftly, for the Soviets were storming westward, pushing the Germans out of Russia and Ukraine. By 1944, they had replaced the Germans as occupiers in Yugoslavia and Hungary, and, in 1945, Czechoslovakia and Poland. By April 30, 1945, the Soviets entered Berlin, and subdued it by May 2. On May 8, VE Day, with the surrender of German forces, the European war ended.

It was a dreadful liberation, accomplished with looting, terror, and the rape of tens of thousands, perhaps hundreds of thousands of women aged from ten

Starvation, Siege, and Sack

Leningrad and Shanghai: *Among the many images of the brutality of war, this one from Leningrad (left) in 1942 (where starvation and terror endured during a siege of almost 900 days) and another from Shanghai (right) in 1937 (where Japanese forces bombed and sacked the city) are particularly poignant. In the first, parents pull a sled laden with the body of their dead child down Leningrad's Nevsky Prospect. In the second, an infant sits amid the wreckage of a railroad station.*

to eighty in Germany alone. German prisoners could expect little mercy from Soviet avengers of their more than 20 million dead. But these cruelties could not equal what the Soviet troops found in the Nazi concentration camps they liberated—mass graves, machines of torture and death, a remnant of starved survivors—the evidence of unutterable evil, a secret and hideous **genocidal** war against the Jews.

FINAL SOLUTIONS

For the Jews, Hitler's chief advisers devised a "Final Solution," launched in spring 1942. The progress is shown on Map 28.4 below. From the start, Jews had been rounded up in the conquered nations. Some were shot, like the 100,000 at Babi Yar near Kiev in Ukraine, between 1941 and 1943 (see *Witnesses,* p. 827). A total of some 500,000 Jews would be killed in the Soviet Union before the German retreat. Some were ghettoized, like the 60,000 Jews of Warsaw, shown in *Windows On,* p. 825, who revolted in 1943 and were massacred, by April 20, to the last woman

and child. Others were transported to concentration camps—along with resisters, communists, gypsies, homosexuals, Russian and Polish prisoners, and others. There they were tormented, starved, and worked to death. Many died from the privations of the camps, the brutality of the guards, and the grotesque "scientific" experiments performed on these dehumanized subjects. The Final Solution was devised to ensure that they would all die. Its aim was to achieve the extermination of the Jews as a people—an aim it very nearly achieved.

The Germans established more than twenty concentration camps on German and Polish territory to warehouse their victims and extract what labor they could before they succumbed to starvation and disease. Of these, a few were designated as death camps—in German literally "places of annihilation"—whose purpose was the extermination of human beings: among them Auschwitz (which also served as a labor camp), Belsen (illustrated in *Windows On,* p. 825, Chelmno, Majdanek, Sobibor, and Treblinka. The Nazi extermination camps were unique. The Japanese,

Map 28.4 The Holocaust and the Bomb:
Hitler's Third Reich launched its "Final Solution" to the "Jewish question" in January 1942—the project to eliminate the Jews of Europe and their ancient culture, which continued until the Nazi defeat in 1945. One million Jews had already died, but now the killing became systematic: ghetto raids, massacres, deportations and death marches and, above all, the death camp, the machine designed especially for the destruction of human beings. The main map here shows the locations of the principal death camps, while the pie graphs document the extent of the destruction. The two atomic bombs that destroyed the Japanese cities of Hiroshima and Nagasaki on August 6 and 9, 1945, shown in the inset map, took fewer victims (see chart on p. 828), but aroused matchless terror. Why did some regions of Nazi-occupied Europe (Italy, Bulgaria) suffer relatively lesser injury to their Jewish populations?

Jews before their deportation, Amsterdam, 1943

Vicious anti-Semitism, culminating in the Final Solution (the attempt to exterminate all European Jewry) earned Nazism its special recognition as uniquely evil. Here, respectably dressed and unsuspecting Dutch Jews carry their belongings with them as they are about to board the train that will take them to concentration camps and, for most of them, their deaths (top left). Their clothes bear the yellow star they were required to display by Nazi regulations. Nazi soldiers supervised the massacre of Jews (top right), and the rounding-up and deportation of Jews to the Warsaw ghetto (bottom right). This last photograph was presented in evidence at the Nuremberg trial of those accused of war crimes. The Allied forces that liberated the Nazi death camps, such as the Belsen camp (bottom left), found a few starved survivors amid heaps of corpses and bones. The remains of some 9 million people were located, about 6 million of them Jews.

What was the response of the Allied powers, during and after World War II, to the German attempt to eradicate European Jewry?

Kovno pogrom, Lithuania, July 27, 1941

Belsen death camp, 1945

Jews removed to Warsaw ghetto, April 1943

 To continue your investigation of this topic, please go to www.prenhall.com/king for the related **WINDOWS** on the **WEB** activity

too, built concentration camps, and mistreated their prisoners of war—more than one-quarter of the Allied soldiers held captive died. But they did not use the camps for genocidal ends as the Nazis did.

Nazi managers invented a method of mass extermination: the gas chamber. SS guards packed hundreds, even thousands of prisoners at a time into the sealed rooms. They then introduced a precise quantity of Zyklon-B gas (crystallized prussic acid, normally used as a pesticide). Death followed in just a few minutes—between three and fifteen, reported a camp commander to the Nuremberg Tribunal for war crimes. His testimony is quoted in *Witnesses* on p. 827. Squads of Jewish slave laborers then ripped out gold teeth, and searched the bodies for gold, jewelry, and gems; then burned or buried them. In a few hours, all trace of the slaughter was removed—bones, blood, ashes, all vanished. At Auschwitz, the most efficient of the death camps, this pitiless system killed as many as 9000 people per day, and a total of perhaps 2.5 million during its years of operation.

Why did no one intervene to stop the slaughter? Much of it happened in secret. But enough was known. By 1942, the Allied governments knew that Jews were being killed on a large scale, but authorized no rescue missions. On the other hand, the occupied Danes managed brilliantly to ship most of their Jewish population to safety in neutral Sweden; and many individuals, at dire risk to themselves, from moral or religious motives, saved individual Jews.

Hiroshima bombed: *The devastation caused by the atomic bombs dropped by the United States planes on the Japanese cities of Hiroshima and Nagasaki was unprecedented, causing the obliteration of whole cities. This photograph shows the remains of Hiroshima after its bombing on August 6, 1945.*

The Nazis kept careful records of their extermination program. The death camps killed about 9 million people, of whom nearly 6 million were Jews (of these, more than 1 million were children, the first to be sent to die). Over the last half-century, some of the survivors have told their stories, and Jewish organizations have reconstructed the unforgettable part of the past now called the **Holocaust** (a Greek word meaning a sacrifice offered for burning, or a "sacred offering") or Shoah (a Hebrew word meaning "destruction"). Now schoolchildren and museumgoers learn, so that the events may never be repeated, of the unique evil rationally planned and deliberately executed by a presumably civilized people.

The deed did not go wholly unpunished. After the war, from November 1945 through October 1946, an international tribunal convened at Nuremberg in Germany to investigate the war crimes of Nazi leaders. Twelve were sentenced to death, others to long sentences; three were acquitted. A separate tribunal began early in 1946 to consider the crimes of twenty-five Japanese civil and military leaders, all of whom were found guilty, and of these seven executed. Of other collaborators tried in their own nations' tribunals, the eighty-nine-year old French general Pétain and the Nazi-appointed Norwegian president Vidkun Quisling (1887–1945), whose name has come to mean "traitor," were sentenced to death. (Pétain's life was spared at de Gaulle's request.) Hitler himself escaped. He had committed suicide in his Berlin bunker, to evade Soviet capture, on the night of April 28–29, 1945—the day after Mussolini's execution, and two weeks after president Roosevelt's peaceful death.

The discovery of the slaughter of the Jews began with the Soviet liberations of 1944–1945. Not long after its terrors began to be known, another horror was in preparation: the atomic bomb.

The lifelong pacifist Albert Einstein (1879–1955), who had foreseen the horror of the bomb (see Chapters 25, 27), wrote President Roosevelt in 1939, explaining how the power of nuclear fission could be harnessed to create a weapon of unprecedented force. Late in 1941, the "Manhattan Project" began for the development of that lethal device. A team of British, Canadian, and United States scientists labored over the next years to achieve its implementation. (Soviet, German, and Japanese scientists were also at work on the same project, but were well behind.) Roosevelt, Churchill, and their military strategists approved of the enterprise. It would be the weapon of weapons, the war-winner without equal, a tool that must be made and, if necessary, used.

On July 16, 1945, a test explosion showed the bomb was ready. At the Potsdam conference outside Berlin (July 17–August 2), the Soviet Union, United States, and Britain issued an ultimatum: Japan must surrender unconditionally. When Japan declined to do this, President Harry S. Truman (who had

Final Solutions

The end of the war was worse even than its outbreak, since it brought about two horrors barely conceivable in a world that had undergone many unbearable horrors: those of the Holocaust—the wilful attempt to exterminate the entire Jewish population of Europe—and of the atomic bombs dropped on two Japanese cities populated by non-combatants. These were the tragic "Final Solutions" of a war born more than anything else of the evil intent of individual men who rose to power. The first three passages describe a Nazi massacre of Jews and the administration of a German-run concentration camp, and argue the need to remember forever the terrible time when "law itself became immoral." The next two relate to the dropping of the atomic bomb: the reaction of President Truman to the announcement of the event, and a reporter's account of the devastation of Hiroshima, 30 days after the bomb changed its citizens' lives forever.

German engineer Hermann Graebe testifies at Nuremberg about a Nazi massacre of Jews in the Ukraine (1942): The people who had got off the trucks ... had to undress upon the orders of an SS man, who carried a riding or dog whip. They had to put down their clothes in fixed places, sorted according to shoes, top clothing and underclothing. ...

Without screaming or weeping, these people undressed, ... kissed each other, said farewells. ... I watched a family of about eight persons. ... An old woman with snow-white hair was holding the one-year-old child in her arms and singing it and tickling it. ... The couple were looking on with tears in their eyes. The father was holding the hand of a boy about ten years old and speaking to him softly. ...

At that moment the SS man at the pit shouted something to his comrade. The latter counted off about twenty persons and instructed them to go behind the earth mound. ... I walked around the mound and found myself confronted by a tremendous grave. ... [T]he pit was already two-thirds full. I estimated that it already contained about 1,000 people. ... The people, completely naked, went down some steps ... to the place to which the SS man directed them. ... Then I heard a series of shots.
(USGPO, *Nazi Conspiracy and Aggression* 1946; document PS 2992)

Concentration camp commander Rudolf Hoess testifies at Nuremberg (April 5, 1946): I was ordered to establish extermination facilities at Auschwitz in June 1941. ... The Camp Commander at Treblinka told me that he had liquidated 80,000 in the course of one-half year. ... He used monoxide gas and I did not think that his methods were very efficient. So when I set up the extermination building at Auschwitz, I used Cyclon B, which was a crystallized prussic acid which we dropped into the death chamber from a small opening. It took from 3 to 15 minutes to kill the people in the death chamber. ... We knew when the people were dead because their screaming stopped. ... After the bodies were removed our special commandos

took off the rings and extracted the gold from the teeth of the corpses. ... Another improvement we made over Treblinka was that we built our gas chambers to accommodate 2,000 people at one time, whereas at Treblinka their 10 gas chambers only accommodated 200 people each.
(USGPO, *Nazi Conspiracy and Aggression*, 1947; document PS 3868)

Survivor, author, and Noble Peace laureate Elie Wiesel reflects on the past (1987): In those days and nights, humanity was distorted and twisted in this city, the capital of a nation proud of its distant history, but struggling with its recent memories.

Everything human and divine was perverted then. The law itself became immoral. ... It became legal and praiseworthy to ... destroy human beings—sons and daughters of an ancient people—whose very existence was considered a crime. ...

Still, not all Germans alive then were guilty. ... Only the guilty were guilty.

Children of killers are not killers but children. I have neither the desire nor the authority to judge today's generation for the unspeakable crimes committed by the generation of Hitler.

But we may—and we must—hold it responsible, not for the past, but for the way it remembers the past. ... Memory is the keyword. ... [S]alvation, like redemption, can be found only in memory.
(Elie Wiesel, *The Kingdom of Memory*, 1990)

President Truman recalls the dropping of the atomic bomb (1945): On August 6 ... came the historic news that shook the world. I was eating lunch ... when Captain Frank Graham, White House Map Room watch officer, handed me the following message:

TO THE PRESIDENT
FROM THE SECRETARY OF WAR

Big bomb dropped on Hiroshima August 5 at 7:15 PM Washington time. First reports indicate complete success. ...

I was greatly moved. I ... said to the group of sailors around me, "This is the greatest thing in history. It's time for us to get home."
(*Memoirs by Harry S. Truman, I: Year of Decisions*, 1955)

English journalist Wilfred Burchett reports from Hiroshima (September 5, 1945): In Hiroshima, thirty days after the first atom bomb destroyed the city and shook the world, people are still dying, mysteriously and horribly, people who were uninjured in the cataclysm—from an unknown something which I can only describe as the atomic plague. Hiroshima does not look like a bombed city. It looks as if a monster steamroller had passed over it and squashed it out of existence. I write these facts as dispassionately as I can in the hope that they will act as a warning to the world.
(From P. Knightley, *The First Casualty: From the Crimea to Vietnam: The War Correspondent as Hero, Propagandist and Myth Maker*, 1975)

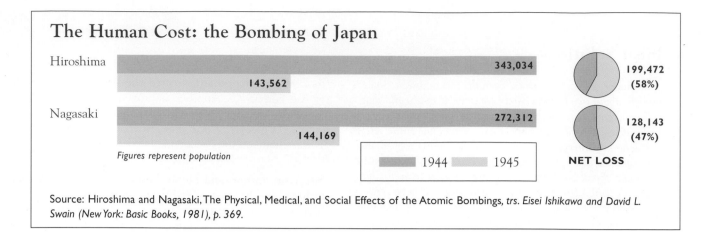

The Human Cost: the Bombing of Japan

Hiroshima — 343,034 / 143,562 — 199,472 (58%)

Nagasaki — 272,312 / 144,169 — 128,143 (47%)

Figures represent population

1944   1945

NET LOSS

Source: Hiroshima and Nagasaki, The Physical, Medical, and Social Effects of the Atomic Bombings, trs. Eisei Ishikawa and David L. Swain (New York: Basic Books, 1981), p. 369.

succeeded to the presidency on Roosevelt's death in April), ordered United States planes to drop on two Japanese cities the most powerful weapon ever made.

The bombs destroyed the cities in an instant, their destruction signaled by the mushroom-shaped cloud that immediately formed above the ruins. On August 6, the explosion of "Little Boy" (the bomb's name; the B-29 bomber was named Enola Gay, after the pilot's mother) immediately killed 78,000 of Hiroshima's 300,000 people—vaporized, burned, crushed. Many more were injured. The remainder lived to suffer mutilation and the horrible consequence of radiation (see *Witnesses*, p. 827). At Nagasaki, on August 9, "Fat Boy" killed more tens of thousands.

The deadly bombs brought a prompt result. Japanese leaders had already been discussing surrender before the bombing of Hiroshima. On August 10, the Japanese government communicated to the Allied command Japan's surrender, which Allied Supreme Commander General MacArthur accepted on September 2 on board the battleship *Missouri*.

No war tribunals gathered to judge the scientists and politicians who unleashed the power of the atomic bomb on the human race. They believed the use of the weapon was justified. Indeed, their arguments are powerful. An Allied invasion of Japan would almost certainly have cost more Japanese (and American) lives. All arguments diminish next to the sheer magnitude of the destruction caused by that unimaginable weapon, and the threat of annihilation it posed and poses to all subsequent human generations (see Chapter 30).

Conclusion
THE DEFEAT OF FASCISM AND THE MEANING OF THE WEST

Nazism sprang from a combination of the worst of the Western traditions—irrationalism, extreme nationalism, racism. It failed because of the best of them—the traditions of liberty and justice that had evolved over centuries and had been inscribed in the constitutions of the Western democracies. The struggle of committed democrats against all forms of fascism, joined by Russian communist defenders of their ideals and their soil, spelled its destruction in 1945.

The cost of the war was enormous. Combatant and civilian deaths came to an estimated total of 46 million. The Soviet Union alone suffered 11 million military, and between 10 and 20 million civilian deaths, a tremendous toll from a population of about 190 million. Germany suffered over 4 million deaths, civilian and military; the Chinese perhaps 15 million; the Japanese nearly 2 million (and scarcely any wounded—the Japanese preferred death); the Jewish dead came to nearly 6 million, the Polish 3 million. Most lightly touched, the British, the French, the Italians, and the Americans together suffered a little over 1 million combat deaths; among the occupied French, an additional 350,000 civilians died.

The slaughter purchased the defeat of fascism. Yet it did not spell the end of totalitarianism in the West, where fascism in Spain and Portugal, and communism in the Soviet Union, endured until 1974–1975 and 1991 (see Chapter 30). In the postwar decades, new non-Western nations often inclined toward authoritarian or communist governments (see Chapter 29).

The future would also be burdened by memories: the destruction of cities and the willful deaths of non-combatants; the Holocaust; the atomic bomb. These horrors would haunt future generations. For many, the West had been discredited. Certainly the old world-system was dead. Another world was about to emerge, in which the meaning of the West and its vaunted traditions would be subject to question.

QUESTIONS TO CONSIDER

1. To what extent was Lenin a Marxist? And to what extent was Stalin a Leninist?

2. Was Russia's rapid modernization in the 1920s and 1930s worth the cost of forced collectivization, the gulag system, and the purges of real and imagined enemies of the state?

3. Why did many Italians find Mussolini's fascism attractive? Why did they finally turn against it?

4. Why was Hitler able to garner the support of the German people? Would they have repudiated Hitler in the mid-1930s if they knew of his war plans and intentions for the Jews?

5. What made World War II a particularly brutal war? How would you compare the losses in World War II to those in World War I?

SUGGESTED RESOURCES

Bartov, Omer, *Murder in Our Midst: The Holocaust, Industrial Killing, and Representation* (Oxford: Oxford University Press, 1996). The term "Industrial Killing" refers to murder that is organized by the state.

Brooks, Jeffrey, *Thank you, Comrade Stalin! Soviet Public Culture from Revolution to Cold War* (Princeton: Princeton University Press, 2000). Examines newspaper accounts of Soviet life to track the phenomenon of ceaseless elevation of the Communist state and its leaders.

Browning, Christopher, *The Origins of the Final Solution: The Evolution of Nazi Jewish Policy, September 1939–March 1942* (Lincoln: University of Nebraska Press, 2004). Explains how the Nazi plan evolved from the expulsion to the annihilation of the Jews of Eastern Europe.

Duus, Peter, R. H. Myers, and M. R. Peattie, eds., *The Japanese Wartime Empire, 1931–1945* (Princeton, NJ: Princeton University Press, 1996). Essays on Japanese imperial practices in northeast and southeast Asia.

Fitzpatrick, Sheila, *Everyday Stalinism: Ordinary Life in Extraordinary Times: Soviet Russia in the 1930s* (Oxford: Oxford University Press, 2000). Argues that attention should be paid, with regard to this decade of Stalinist terror, to the elevation of a new class of trained technical experts and bureaucrats, who were able to live productive lives regardless of the nature of the regime.

Getty, J. Arch & Oleg V. Naumov, *The Road to Terror: Stalin and the Self-Destruction of the Bolsheviks, 1932–1939* (New Haven: Yale University Press, 1999). Analysis of documents released from the Soviet archives which make clear the extent of the Stalinist purges.

Gordetsky, Gabriel, *Grand Delusion: Stalin and the German Invasion of Russia* (New Haven: Yale University Press, 1999). Using recently-available archives, explains why Stalin trusted the German assurances of non-aggression.

Hicks, George, *The Comfort Women: Japan's Brutal Regime of Enforced Prostitution in the Second World War* (New York: W. W. Norton, 1995). Useful treatment of one of Japan's most notorious wartime activities.

Kaplan, Marion A., *Between Dignity and Despair: Jewish Life in Nazi Germany* (Oxford: Oxford University Press, 1998). Account of the attempts by Jews under German rule to maintain their traditions.

Kershaw, Ian, *Hitler 1889–1936: Hubris* (New York: W.W. Norton, 1998); *Hitler 1936–1945: Nemesis* (New York: W.W. Norton, 2000). Kershaw's comprehensive two-volume biography is likely to be the standard for years to come.

Mackay, Robert, *Half the Battle: Civilian Morale in Britain during the Second World War* (Manchester: Manchester University Press, 2002). Systematically assesses the morale of the British people ravaged by fear and uncertainty during World War II.

Mosse, George L., *The Fascist Revolution: Toward a General Theory of Fascism* (New York: Howard Fertig, 1999). Essays exploring the roots of fascism, focusing on the linked phenomena of nationalism, anti-Semitism, occultism, and the cult of the leader.

Radosh, Ronald, Mary R. Habeck, and Grigory Sevostianov, *Spain Betrayed: the Soviet Union in the Spanish Civil War* (New Haven: Yale University Press, 2001). Controversial exploration based on newly-opened Soviet archives, portraying the Soviet role in defending the Republic as more cynical than altruistic.

Service, Robert, *A History of Twentieth-Century Russia* (Cambridge, MA: Harvard University Press, 1998). Authoritative, balanced, and scholarly history of the Soviet Union.

Weitz, Margaret Collins, *Sisters in the Resistance: How Women fought to Free France, 1940–1945* (New York: J. Wiley, 1995). Examines the role of women and the limits and meaning of "resistance".

Joseph stalin, Biographical Chronicle:
http://www.stel.ru/stalin

The Rise of Adolf Hitler, an online narrative in 24 chapters (History Place):
http://www.bbc.co.uk/history
http://www.historyplace.com/worldwar2/riseofhitler

WWII oral history, women's experience of war:
http://www.stg.brown.edu/projects/WWII_Women/tocCS.html

⊙ Western Civilization Documents CD-ROM

28.1 Nadezhda K. Krupskaya
28.2 Benito Mussolini
28.3 Adolf Hitler: from Mein Kampf
28.4 Christopher Dawson: Religion and the Totalitarian State
28.5 The Russian Revolution
28.6 Socialist Marriage to Motherhood for the Fatherland
28.7 Stalin's First Five Year Plan
28.8 Leader of the NAZI Women's Organization
29.1 Adolf Hitler: The Obersalzberg Speech
29.2 Winston Churchill
29.3 Franklin D. Roosevelt
29.4 NAZI SS Officers
29.5 The Buchenwald Report
29.6 Notes from the Warsaw Ghetto
29.7 Surviving the Labor Camp

THE END OF IMPERIALISM

	1880	1900	1920	1940	1960	1980	2000

The Western World

World War I and the Russian Revolution, 1914–21

World War II, 1939–45

- ◆ "Easter Rising," Ireland, 1916
- ◆ Great Depression begins, 1929
- ◆ Commonwealth of Nations created, 1931
- ◆ UN Universal Declaration of Human Rights, 1948
- ◆ Cuban Missile Crisis, 1961
- ◆ Civil Rights Act, 1964
- ◆ Martin Luther King shot, 1968
- ◆ Helsinki Accords, 1975
- ◆ Soviet Union dissolved, 1991
- ◆ European Union created, 1994

Middle East and North Africa

- ◆ Balfour Declaration, 1917
- ◆ Ottoman Empire ends, 1919
- ◆ Egyptian independence ends, 1937
- ◆ UN partitions Palestine, 1947
- ◆ Nasser nationalizes Suez Canal, 1956
- ◆ Six-Day War, Israel, 1967
- ◆ Oil crisis, 1973–74
- ◆ Iranian Revolution, 1978
- ◆ Palestinian "Intifada," 1987
- ◆ Gulf War, 1991

Africa

- ◆ National party takes control, 1948
- ◆ Bantu Education Act, 1953
- ◆ Ghana independent, 1957
- ◆ Sharpeville massacre, 1960
- ◆ Nelson Mandela freed, 1990
- ◆ Mandela elected president of South Africa, 1994

India, Pakistan, and Bangladesh

- ◆ Indian National Congress Party founded, 1885
- ◆ Amritsar Massacre, India, 1919
- ◆ Gandhi's resistance campaign begins, 1919
- ◆ Independence and partition of India, 1947
- ◆ Gandhi assassinated, 1948
- ◆ Indira Gandhi prime minister of India, 1966
- ◆ Bangladesh established, 1971

East and Southeast Asia

Korean War, 1950–53   US military involvement in Vietnam, 1954–73

- ◆ Japanese annex Korea, 1910
- ◆ Chinese Revolution, 1911–12
- ◆ Japan invades China, 1937
- ◆ Nagasaki and Hiroshima bombed, 1945
- ◆ Vietnam declares independence, 1945
- ◆ French leave Indochina, 1954
- ◆ China's "Great Leap Forward," 1958–60
- ◆ Cultural Revolution begins in China, 1966
- ◆ Marcos regime overthrown, Philippines, 1986
- ◆ Tiananmen Square protests suppressed, 1989
- ◆ Hong Kong returns to Chinese control, 1997
- ◆ Indonesia's Suharto ousted, 1998

Latin America

- ◆ Spanish–American War, 1898
- ◆ Mexican Revolution, 1911
- ◆ FDR's "Good Neighbor" policy, 1933
- ◆ Organization of American States formed, 1948
- ◆ Castro seizes power in Cuba, 1959
- ◆ Bay of Pigs fiasco, 1961
- ◆ Chile's Salvador Allende overthrown, 1973
- ◆ Sandinistas take charge in Nicaragua, 1979
- ◆ Democratic elections in Argentina, Brazil, Mexico, Nicaragua, and Paraguay, 1980s

CHAPTER
29

THE END OF IMPERIALISM

Decolonization and Statebuilding
around the Globe

1914–1990s

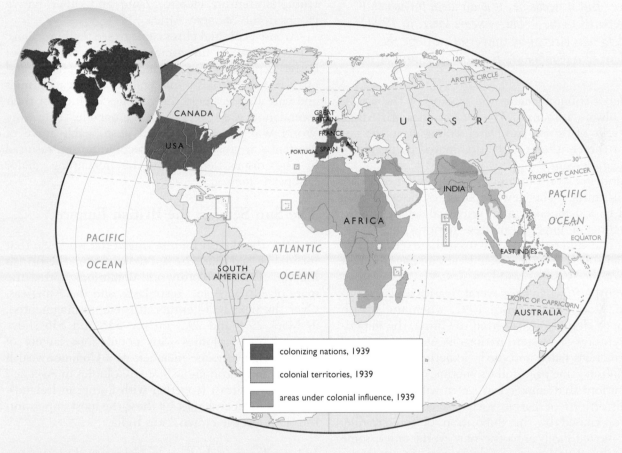

colonizing nations, 1939

colonial territories, 1939

areas under colonial influence, 1939

KEY QUESTIONS

◆ **Fading Empires:** Why did decolonization proceed
rapidly after World War II? How did the
European empires adjust to the post-imperial
reality?

◆ **New World Orders:** What kinds of governments
were established in the new states of Asia, Africa,
and the Middle East?

◆ **The Last Imperialists:** To what extent was the
United States an imperial power? What role
did it play abroad? How did the US government
respond to the minority populations within
its own borders in the generations after World
War II?

Sunset and Sunrise At his trial in 1964 for conspiracy against the government of South Africa, and on the eve of his imprisonment that would last twenty-six years, Nelson Mandela (1918–) spoke eloquently of his hopes for his people. All Africans should receive a living wage, have access to work and housing, be free to move about, and enjoy full civil rights, "because without them our disabilities will be permanent." Then he reaffirmed his commitment to democracy: "During my lifetime ... I have fought against white domination, and I have fought against black domination. I have cherished the ideal of a democratic and free society ... It is an ideal which I hope to live for and to achieve. But if needs be, it is an ideal for which I am prepared to die." Thirty years later, in 1994, Mandela was elected by universal suffrage the president of a democratic Republic of South Africa.

Mandela's triumph marks the passing of the age of imperialism—its sunset. The Union of South Africa was a relic of British and Dutch colonialism, the last area of the continent to be dominated by people of European descent. Now it would be African.

Mandela's words also mark the opening of a new age—a sunrise. The new Republic of South Africa would be a democracy with universal suffrage. With the fading of imperialism new nations were born, which had suffered tragically from the experience of colonial rule, but which would yet embrace the best ideals of the Western world.

From 1919, when the several treaties of Paris concluded World War I, until 1997, when the British colony of Hong Kong reverted to China, the imperialist ventures of Western nations in Asia, Africa, and the Americas faded and died. Sometimes the end of imperialism came peacefully, sometimes violently. The new nations that emerged struggled with its legacy—the distortions of native societies, economies, and cultures caused by the imposition of foreign rule. Some moved easily into the new world order; some have still not broken out of the impasse in which the colonial experience had left them. But the maps of the last decade of the twentieth century, in contrast to those of the first, display on every inhabited continent the free nations of a world that has outlived and surpassed imperialism.

FADING EMPIRES: ANTI-COLONIALISM AND DECOLONIZATION

By the outbreak of World War I, the principal European powers had devoured nearly all of the Old World (see Chapter 24). Exceptions were China, where the European presence was nevertheless strong,

Siam (now Thailand), Iran, Japan and its colonies in Asia; and Liberia and Ethiopia in Africa. Then the tide of empire-building turned. A first wave of colonial resistance to imperial claims swept through the Old World in response to World War I.

Even before 1914, European encroachment in Asia and Africa had not gone unchallenged. The British, Dutch, and French met fierce resistance, for example, to their dominion in the Sudan, Indonesia, and Indochina. So did the United States in its takeover of the Philippines. In India, as cultural elites pressed for independence, British rulers faced sporadic terrorist incidents. In North Africa and the Middle East, Islamic and nationalist movements threatened European suzerainty, as did revolts of Ashanti, Tutsi, Hutu, Hottentot, Herero, Zulu, and other native groups in sub-Saharan Africa.

Aroused colonial elites came to see the Europeans' political power as unwarranted, their exploitation of native economies unjust, and their imperialist and often racist outlooks intolerable. European armies and bureaucracies held the colonies in line, but their ascendancy was everywhere vulnerable. Following World War II, a second and unstoppable wave of resistance, a great quake of **decolonization**, resulted in the dismantlement of the remaining major European empires.

The Sun Sets on the British Empire

In 1919, the British Empire ringed the world, so that it could be said that "the sun never sets on the British Empire." British colonies and **dominions** dotted the maps of Africa, Asia, Australasia, and the Americas. Over the next half-century, this empire fragmented, as Maps 29.1 and 29.2 on pp. 833 and 836 show. Some former colonies with populations largely of British origin became members of a **Commonwealth** of equal and autonomous states. Colonies in Asia and Africa, in contrast (together with European Ireland), achieved independence. Of these the most important, the "jewel in the crown," was India.

Independence in India In India, an elite of a few thousand military officers, civil servants, missionaries, and teachers (which included both British and Indian members, in roughly equal numbers) ruled a nation of 300 million people, subdivided by political, regional, caste, and religious affiliations (see Chapter 24). The persistent poverty of the population aroused the concern of foreign administrators, but had positive uses. The British were the beneficiaries of an unequal economic strategy, whereby India exported agricultural commodities and raw resources, and purchased British manufactures in exchange. Poverty had other causes as well, including early marriage and high fertility, which led to insupportably high rates of population increase. The more India grew, the more it ate.

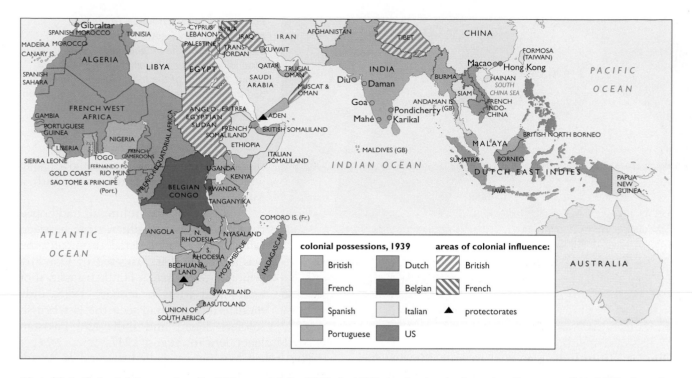

Map 29.1 Colonial Possessions in Africa and Asia, 1939: In 1939, despite the shocks and realignments of World War I, much of Asia and Africa still lay under the domination of a European power. What nationalist independence movements would arise especially in Asia and the Middle East during and after the end of the War?

From 1919 to 1947, India struggled toward independence. India's support of Britain in World War I— she supplied more than 1 million troops to serve with Allied forces—made Indian soldiers and political leaders more aware of their nation's place in the world system. After the war, British repression of popular political aspirations triggered outrage, as at Amritsar (April 13, 1919), when British troops fired on an assembly of unarmed civilians, killing 400 and injuring others. Nationalist leaders such as Subhas Bose (1897–1945) and Jawaharlal Nehru (1889–1964) called for independence, while Mohandas Gandhi (1869–1948) aroused popular support for nonviolent resistance to British domination. Nehru and Gandhi are seen in the photograph on p. 834.

Born a Hindu in India, trained as a barrister in London, Gandhi moved to South Africa in 1893 where he worked as an attorney. Shocked by the harsh discrimination suffered by Indians, he led a protest movement. From that experience he developed the strategy of nonviolent resistance against colonial rule, or *satyagraha*. It rested on an amalgamation of Hindu and Christian values and Western political philosophy. By suffering violence and causing none in return, his followers exposed their oppressors' injustice and their own righteousness.

Back in India in 1915, Gandhi instructed his followers in nonviolent resistance. Beginning in 1920, in response to British concessions he spurned as inadequate, Gandhi pursued his resistance campaign of protest marches and demonstrations. Although these sometimes broke down into rioting, they had the effect intended: a worldwide awakening to the injustice of continued British colonialism in India.

Gandhi's opposition to foreign rule included a critique of colonialist economies. He urged Indians to boycott British manufactures, and to reestablish native industrial production, as the passage quoted in *Witnesses* on p. 834 shows. Modeling the sacrificial behavior he expected of others, he labored constantly at cotton-spinning. Gandhi also wanted to purify (but not end) the caste system that was so central a feature of Indian (specifically Hindu) society, and called for the abolition of the status of "untouchability."

Gandhi's leadership was crucial during the interwar years, his great moral authority signaled by the title given him of "Mahatma," or "great soul." But such leaders as Bose and Nehru, whose approach was both more secular and more militant, also found supporters. Growing opposition convinced the British that they would have to yield. In 1942 they promised to grant independence as soon as the war was over. Nationalist leaders repulsed the offer, demanding immediate independence and launching a "Quit India" movement. In 1942, the British imprisoned these opposition leaders, and suppressed the strikes and riots that erupted in protest. Bose fled India and raised an Indian National Army in Singapore with the assistance of Britain's enemy Japan.

After the war, Britain did quit India. While diplomats worked out the terms of independence with Indian leaders, the tension between Muslims and

Forgers of Independence for India:
Mahatma Gandhi (seated on the right, in traditional garb), the prophet and builder of Indian national independence, confers with Jawaharlal Nehru, president of the India National Congress and the first elected Prime Minister of that nation on July 6, 1946.

the slaughter of 1 million. India became an overwhelmingly Hindu state with a Muslim minority.

Although Gandhi himself had hoped to avoid religious conflict, strife between religious groups persisted. Ironically, he was a victim of it. Angered by Gandhi's policy of tolerance, a Hindu assassin shot and killed him in January 1948, only months after he had seen the last British soldiers depart and India and Pakistan declared independent in August 1947.

The Indian experience spelled the end of British dominion in Asia. Independence followed for Ceylon (now Sri Lanka) and Burma (now Myanmar) in 1948, and Malaya in 1957 (in 1963 merged with Singapore and other entities, it was reconstituted as Malaysia). In 1997, according to the terms set out in their

Hindus within India remained an issue. Massive conflicts causing more than 200,000 deaths resulted in the partition of India and the creation of a new state (Muslim Pakistan, with territory on the Punjab in the northwest and eastern Bengal in the northeast), the wrenching dislocation of some 10 million people, and

---

WITNESSES

Asia: Independence for India and Vietnam

The end of World War II brought about enormous shifts in global power relations. Independence for India, gained immediately after the close of World War II, was a cause for which Mohandas Gandhi had struggled throughout his career. In the first of these passages, he speaks of the need for a genuine freedom, which must begin with freedom from want, of which political independence, although essential, can only be one part. Vietnam, under French control, declared independence in 1945, in the document excerpted in the second passage here. However, a unified nation of Vietnam only came into existence following years of struggle against France and the United States.

Mohandas Gandhi weighs what freedom means for the starving (1926): A starving man thinks first of satisfying his hunger. ... He will sell his liberty and all for the sake of getting a morsel of food. ... Such is the position of millions of the people of India. For them, liberty, God, and such words are merely letters ... without the slightest meaning. ... They will extend a welcome to any person who comes to them with a morsel of food. And if we want to give these people a sense of freedom we shall have to provide them with work which they can easily do in their desolate homes and which would give them at least the barest living.

This can only be done by the spinning wheel. And when they have become self-reliant and are able to support themselves, we are in a position to talk to them about freedom. ...
(M. K. Gandhi, "Young India," in *The Collected Works of Mahatma Gandhi*, Vol. 30, 1968)

The Vietnamese Declaration of Independence repeats the American and French Founding Declarations, and asks for the same rights (1945): "All men are created equal. They are endowed by their Creator with certain inalienable rights; among these are life, liberty and the pursuit of happiness."
This immortal statement was made in the Declaration of Independence of the United States of America in 1776. ...
[After a recitation of French and other violations of Vietnamese autonomy.] For these reasons, we ... solemnly declare to the world that Vietnam has the right to be a free and independent country—and in fact is so already. The entire Vietnamese people are determined to mobilize all their physical and mental strength, to sacrifice their lives and property in order to safeguard their independence and liberty.
(Ho Chi Minh, "Declaration of Independence of the Democratic Republic of Vietnam," 1945)

ninety-nine-year lease, the British surrendered Hong Kong, their last Asian possession, to China.

The Middle East and Africa   In the Middle East and North Africa, Britain retained control during the interwar years. Her most significant possession was Egypt, where the Suez Canal was the lifeline of her international commerce. Spurred by a 1919 revolt, Britain granted Egypt independence by stages between 1922 and 1936, while maintaining a garrison zone around the Canal. At the same time, Egypt and Britain jointly administered Sudan; Sudan subsequently became independent in 1956.

Britain also gained control of Palestine and Iraq as **mandates** under the 1919 Paris settlement (and had considerable influence in independent Iran). Iraq gained independence in stages between 1921 and 1932, though Britain maintained military bases there. Iran (Islamic but not Arab) acquired in 1925 a new monarch, or *shah*, friendly to the British (and United States)—Reza Khan (1878–1944), a military officer who seized the ancient Persian throne, installing by force the Páhlevi dynasty that would rule until 1979. In Palestine, however, the British unhappily remained, as an influx of Jewish Zionist settlers from Europe competed with indigenous Palestinian Arabs.

In 1946, Britain gave independence to the state of Jordan, and attempted to suppress the bloody struggles of Palestinians and Jewish settlers. On November 29, 1947, the United Nations (successor organization to the League of Nations; see Chapter 30), recommended the partition of Palestine, with the assignment of one part to the Jews. On May 14, 1948, Britain withdrew, and Israel declared herself an independent Jewish state. The Jews began to hope that their historic longing for this land might at last be satisfied, and resolved to fight for Israel's survival. The move was a guarantee of future anguish, however, as some 600,000 Palestinians fled Israel and Arab neighbor states resisted what they perceived as Israel's alien presence (see below). Britain further withdrew from the region, when, in 1967, her Arab **protectorates** on the Persian Gulf and Arabian Sea became the independent states of South Yemen in 1967, and Bahrain, Oman, Qatar, and the United Arab Emirates in 1971.

After World War II, an exhausted Britain also released its colonies in sub-Saharan Africa. In west Africa, the Gold Coast (formed from the native Ashanti, or Asante, nation, plus neighboring Togo) gained independence as Ghana in 1957—the first African nation to do so outside of South Africa. Nigeria, Sierra Leone, and Gambia followed in 1960, 1961, and 1965. In east Africa, the British colonies of Uganda, Kenya, and Tanganyika won independence in 1961 to 1963; so did the protectorates of British Somaliland (1960) and Zanzibar (1963), while Tanganyika later merged with adjacent Zanzibar to form Tanzania in 1964.

In the southeast, Northern Rhodesia and Nyasaland became independent as Zambia and Malawi in 1964, Botswana (formerly Bechuanaland) in 1966, and the tiny Lesotho (formerly Basutoland) and Swaziland in 1966 and 1968. Southern Rhodesia broke from Britain in 1965, its European planter elite clinging to policies of racial division similar to those of South Africa. After bitter guerrilla struggle against an unyielding white regime, its black African majority finally won black enfranchisement and in 1980 the state was renamed Zimbabwe. South Africa, formerly under British rule, had been since 1910 a dominion within the British Empire. It would follow its own unique course (see below). But adjacent Namibia, illegally occupied by South Africa since 1914, became independent in 1990.

The Commonwealth and Ireland   The creation of the Commonwealth of Nations in 1931 permitted some former colonies, though independent, to continue to enjoy the benefits of privileged economic relations with Britian. Canada, Australia, and New Zealand, lands largely populated by those of European descent, were Commonwealth members and supported the motherland vigorously during World War II. Other former British colonies that have joined the Commonwealth include India and several African and Caribbean states.

Ireland alone remained an intractable problem for post-imperial Britain (see Chapter 24). The British government finally approved Home Rule for Ireland in 1914; but the bill was suspended when World War I broke out, and was never subsequently enacted. Ireland was uninterested in the war that now occupied Britain's attention—except for Protestant northern Ireland, or Ulster. The Irish nationalists, meanwhile, had formed political parties—the Home Rule party and, after 1902, Sinn Fein ("We Ourselves")—and events moved rapidly toward the secession of southern Ireland from Britain. The British suppressed a rebellion that broke out on Easter Monday, 1916, and executed its leaders. Repression garnered a mass following for Sinn Fein, whose candidates won seats in Parliament in 1918 but refused to take them up, declaring themselves an independent Irish parliament. Outlawed, they went underground, warring against the detested Black and Tans, the special troops Britain dispatched to tame the rebellion.

The war over, saner heads sought a peaceful settlement. In 1920, a bill partitioned Ireland into two self-governing areas within the United Kingdom, Northern Ireland and Southern Ireland. In 1921, the Irish Free State in the south was declared a dominion within the British Empire, and in 1937, the British relinquished sovereignty altogether. After nearly eight centuries of British rule, Ireland was free. But it was not united, and not at peace: the internal struggle between British and Irish, Catholic and Protestant, would continue sporadically, and violently, through to the end of the century (see Chapter 30).

Reluctant Disengagement: the End of European Empires

In contrast to the British, the Dutch and French were determined to win back their colonies at the end of World War II. Portugal, Belgium, and Spain retained their African dominions as well. A defeated nation, Italy lost hers, which temporarily were granted as mandates to other states before being freed. In time, all yielded to the current of decolonization.

By 1900, the Dutch Empire had largely shrunk to its lucrative core of East Indian possessions (see Chapter 24). Frequent nationalist uprisings persisted despite the Dutch government's concessions. In the 1930s the Japanese swept the East Indies into the "Greater East Asia Co-Prosperity Sphere" and drove out its Dutch rulers. After the war, nationalists under Sukarno (1901–1970) took power.

The Dutch soon returned and attempted to reestablish their dominion. In 1949 they agreed to a Dutch–Indonesian union, an alliance Sukarno cast off in 1954. In 1957, when the Dutch refused to surrender Netherlands New Guinea to the new Indonesia, he ordered a billion dollars in Dutch assets seized and severed diplomatic relations. In 1963, Indonesia forcibly acquired that last Dutch colonial enclave. (The Dutch, meanwhile, had granted Suriname (in South America) a parliament in 1954, and full independence in 1975.)

The French masters of Indochina had also been displaced by the Japanese during World War II. Before the end of the conflict, the French proposed granting their colonies self-governing status within the French Union. Cambodia and Laos agreed, but Vietnamese nationalists under the leadership of Ho Chi Minh did not. In 1945 Vietnam declared independence (see *Witnesses*, p. 834), and war broke out between French and nationalist forces. In 1954, badly beaten at the climactic battle of Dien Bien Phu, the French withdrew. The 1954 settlement signed at Geneva granted Vietnam independence. But it also left the country disunified, with the north in Ho Chih Minh's control, and the south scheduled to determine its own future in a 1956 election. That election never occurred.

In the Middle East, the war-weary French could not maintain authority in their mandates of Syria and Lebanon against spirited opposition from the league of Arab states. Persuaded by the British, the French yielded. Both nations attained independence in 1945.

In 1956, the French surrendered their North African protectorates of Tunisia and Morocco, held since 1881 and 1912 respectively, to native rulers. But Algeria, which the French had ruled since 1830, was considered to be an extension of France. Here many European French had settled (constituting ten percent of the population) and created a colonial civilization, much like the Spanish settlers of the Americas. But nationalist and Islamist groups demanded that they leave and revolts broke out in 1954 after the French defeat in Indochina. The subsequent conflict, marked by mutual atrocities,

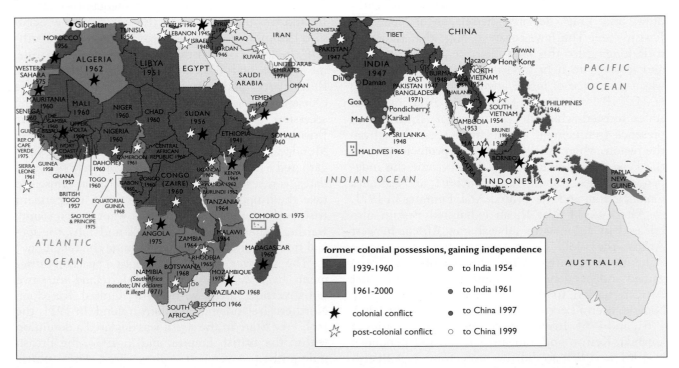

Map 29.2 Independence Gained in Africa and Asia 1939–1985: *The tired victors of World War II could not maintain their empires.* Which were the first European powers to relinquish their possessions in Africa and Asia? Which were the last?

resulted in the deaths of some 250,000 Algerians (of a population of 9 million) and nearly tore France apart as opinion at home polarized. In 1958, a revolt of the French army brought World War II hero Charles de Gaulle (1890–1970) back from retirement. He was elected president, his supporters believed, in order to maintain "*Algérie française,*" a French Algeria. Too good a strategist to battle in vain, de Gaulle returned Algeria to the Algerians in 1962.

The Algerian experience served as a model to avoid south of the Sahara. The French possessions of west and equatorial Africa (modern Guinea, Senegal, the Ivory Coast, Cameroon, Mali, Togo, Niger, Benin, Burkina Faso, Chad, Gabon, Mauritania, the Congo Republic, and the Central African Republic) gained their freedom with relative ease. Beginning in 1956, the French offered these colonies limited self-government within the French Union, an offer accepted by several. All had gained full independence by 1960 (but the east African colonies of the Comoros and Djibouti not until 1975 and 1977).

Portugal, the first of the European powers to win African and Asian footholds, was determined not to surrender colonies it had held so long and profitably. Nationalist movements in their colonies of Mozambique, Angola, and Guinea-Bissau, however, overwhelmed the military and economic capacity of Portuguese hard-liners. In 1974, military officers who recognized the impending failure of Portugal's colonial policy ousted the dictator Marcelo Caetano (1906–1980). With his fall came independence for Portugal's African colonies, as well as the island territories of Cape Verde and São Tomé and Principe. Portugal's neighbor Spain, having surrendered its section of Morocco, retained only a few African enclaves; nearly all were independent by 1968.

Belgium's African empire consisted of the great central Congo region and adjacent Rwanda and Burundi. Notorious exploiters of the people and resources of the Congo, the Belgians had failed to train a native managerial elite and the Congolese opposition was unprepared for political administration when the Belgians suddenly withdrew. The new nation achieved independence in 1960 as the state of Zaire (now the Democratic Republic of Congo), under Patrice Lumumba (1925–1961) as prime minister. Rival leaders representing ethnic minorities opposed Lumumba's nationalist strategy. They assassinated Lumumba and seized power. Rwanda and Burundi gained their independence in 1962.

In addition to their colonies in Asia, Africa, the Middle East, and the Americas, the European powers surrendered small islands in the Pacific, Atlantic, and Mediterranean. So passed the era of European imperialism. The new states that formed after independence repudiated that heritage. They found it was not easy to create better governments than those their masters had imposed upon them.

NEW WORLD ORDERS: STATEBUILDING IN AFRICA, THE MIDDLE EAST, AND ASIA

As the imperial powers exited, the stage was left to the premiers, presidents, and parliaments of the new nations of Asia and Africa. Newcomer states sought to form stable governments, stimulate economies, adopt new technologies, and provide for the health and education of their people, while still saddled with the legacies of imperial rule. Some met these goals readily; many others struggled or failed. In 1990, more nations lived under their own freely chosen leaders than ever before, and had begun the task of achieving security and prosperity for their peoples.

Statebuilding in Africa: from Village to Nation

Between 1945 and 1975, some forty independent states took form in Africa. (The African Resolution on Imperialism and Colonialism is cited in *Witnesses* on p. 841.) They experienced great disruption in their passage from subordinate colonies to modern democratic nations—even when the former colonial authority was supportive there was no easy transition.

The Legacy of Colonialism First, the national identities of the new states were inherently frail. Prior to the imperial scramble for Africa, the continent was governed by a variety of African kingdoms and pre-state, networked village communities. The European nations that partitioned Africa by 1914 created colonial territories whose boundaries were superimposed on traditional political divisions. When the European powers released their colonies, African nationalist leaders could not recover the political identities of pre-conquest times. But neither could they make the artificial new boundaries natural. Sometimes those borders divided ethnic or tribal groups, or encompassed two or more rival groups. Loyalty to the new nations was strained by ethnic tensions, linguistic divisions, and tribal memories. Pan-African congresses provided an important setting for the discussion of future projects, but did not lead to plans for political organizations larger than the colonial units.

Second, although colonialism had modernized the African economies, it had done so to benefit the metropolitan power rather than the colonized Africans. Once independence was won, the African nations found it difficult to reorient their economies in line with the broader needs of their peoples.

Colonized Africa had a cash crop economy. Peanuts, palm oil, coffee, cotton, and tobacco crops found foreign buyers. But the exclusive devotion of vast tracts of the best land to these profitable exports meant that less land was devoted to subsistence crops. The population was left vulnerable to food shortages, a situation exacerbated, as often in the 1970s and 1980s, by periodic drought. In addition, when the prices of export crops dipped, the whole economy staggered. From 1970 to 1990, food production declined, while the population grew unabatedly.

What was true of cash crops was also true of minerals. Their exploitation led to great wealth, but also to difficulties. Copper, gold, and diamonds were valuable exports, but these, too, were subject to commodity price fluctuation. Moreover, mineowners recruited large labor forces (generally all male) from the villages to work in the mines. With the men far from home, many women had to tend the fields alone. Not only did those women assume burdens of isolation and increased responsibility, but productivity often suffered, and the risk of famine increased.

New nationalist leaders found it difficult to shed the established model of the commodity economy—especially as it enriched an emerging urban elite of merchants, professionals, and bureaucrats. Turning to foreign capital to fund new enterprises led to

increased dependence on Western economies. Some leaders sought the solution of nationalizing some enterprises, or redistributing agricultural lands.

A third barrier to the establishment of modern democracy was cultural. Colonial administration had trained a small vanguard of Africans in European schools and universities. This elite was minuscule amid a vast sea of people untutored in political ideas. In the 1960s, at the peak of decolonization, scarcely three percent of the population had received a secondary education, and barely ten percent were literate. Religious allegiances—Muslim, Christian, polytheist, and **animist**—overlapped tribal and state boundaries, and did not serve to unify at the national level. Africa's divided, inexperienced, and ill-educated peoples were vulnerable to manipulation by propaganda and to control by dictators.

With these deficits, early efforts to establish democratic states understandably foundered. Nearly all the new African nations succumbed to authoritarian rulers who led one-party states that suppressed dissent. Their aims were not always malevolent: some pursued sound plans for economic development and human welfare. But even well-meaning dictators were tempted by wealth and power. Unchallenged by a democratic opposition, they became corrupt and inefficient. Often, these dictators were artificially sustained by Western nations or corporations which continued to seek advantage in the post-colonial era.

When corruption and inefficiency became intolerable, a military **coup** might oust a dictator and install the rule of generals—trained managers, but occasionally brutal ones, with little patience for claims of civil rights. Military governments might recivilianize the nation, once reform measures had been taken. But if the civilian governments failed again, military rule returned. During the 1950s and 1960s, military coups were frequent; during the 1970s and 1980s, they outpaced any other form of political change in Africa.

Several major African states experienced this rocky progression from hopeful independence to authoritarianism to military rule. Ghana, the former British Gold Coast colony, was governed by the pan-Africanist Kwame Nkrumah (1909–1972), a former teacher who studied in the United States and Britain. From 1948, he rallied urban elites and farmers to the cause of "Self-Government Now." Arrested, imprisoned, and released, he emerged in 1951 as key leader of the semi-autonomous state. Upon full independence in 1957, he became prime minister; in 1960, president (see *Witnesses*, p. 841). In that role, Nkrumah turned to authoritarianism and one-party rule. Having nearly bankrupted the nation with grandiose but often disastrous development projects, he was ousted by a military coup in 1966.

Patrice Lumumba, author, thinker, and nationalist leader, led an independent Zaire after the Belgian exodus in 1960. But leaders of tribal factions resisted

WHO'S WHO

Fading Empires in Africa

Patrice Lumumba (1925–1961), first premier of the state of Zaire (formerly the Congo) upon Belgian withdrawal in 1960, but assassinated by rivals in 1961.

Joseph (Sese Seko) Mobutu (1930–1997), seized power in Zaire after Lumumba's death, and held it for 32 years, with US support.

Kwame Nkrumah (1909–1972), pan-Africanist prime minister of Ghana upon its independence in 1957, and president in 1960; ousted by a military coup in 1967.

Robert Mugabe (1924–), Marxist leader of Rhodesian revolutionary party which ousted prime minister Ian Smith; became head of nation re-named Zimbabwe.

Desmond Tutu (1931–), South African Anglican archbishop who aroused world outrage against the segregationist apartheid policy of the white Afrikaner government of South Africa; winner of the 1984 Nobel Prize.

Nelson Mandela (1918–), leader of African National Congress imprisoned in 1964 and released in 1960; in 1994, won election to the presidency of South Africa.

Muammar el-Qaddafi (1942–), seized power in Libya in 1969 after toppling the pro-Western monarchy, nationalizing foreign petroleum assets, and, during the Cold War, accepting Soviet aid as well as Soviet arms.

Independence Day: *Independence came to most nations of Africa in the decades following World War II as colonial powers withdrew. As most African nations gained their independence, they began the process of state-building under their own leaders. South Africa, in contrast, had been under the control of white Europeans whose increasingly racist policies excluded African natives from power, education, and any type of high-paid employment. The opposition leader Nelson Mandela, imprisoned from 1964 and released after twenty-six years, is shown here speaking to the crowd in 1990. Mandela was elected President of the ANC (African National Congress) in 1991, at its first national conference. In 1994, he became president in South Africa's first post-apartheid elections.*

Lumumba's nationalist message, and one rich province seceded. In 1965, after Lumumba's assassination in 1961, a military coup put general Joseph (later Sese Seko) Mobutu (1930–1997) in power, in which position he remained propped up by the United States for thirty-two years.

These patterns reappeared in other settings. The brutal despot Idi Amin (1925–) held control of Uganda from 1971 until 1979; by then, he had caused the deaths of some 200,000 Ugandans, immigrants, and members of minority ethnicities. Nigeria, riven by tribal conflict, rocked between the corrupt authoritarianism of civilian and military governments.

In these states, authoritarian rule quickly descended into disorder and violence. In those nations where a large white settler caste had established itself in the pre-independence era, the potential for outbreaks of violence was even greater. In Kenya, African nationalists waged a guerrilla war for years before the settler elite finally yielded to native rule. In Southern Rhodesia, white settlers cut ties with Britain in 1965, before Britain could grant independence to the territory as a free African state in which blacks could vote. Rhodesian prime minister Ian Smith (1919–) fought guerrilla movements from 1973 until 1980, when Robert Mugabe (1924–), Marxist leader of one of the revolutionary parties, became head of the country that is now named Zimbabwe.

The Struggle against Apartheid The largest group of white settlers lived in the Union of South Africa, from 1910 an independent state, and the one fully industrialized nation in Africa. Here, as of the 1970s, those of European descent numbered 4 million, "coloreds" 2 million (including Asians and those of mixed identity), and black Africans some 20 million—yet a white ruling caste controlled every aspect of the economy and the government. In 1948, white voters installed the National Party, dominated by the Afrikaner descendants of the original Dutch settlers. Against their policies stood the African National Congress, founded in 1912. From the 1960s, the ANC organized resistance to National Party principles, publishing its own Freedom Charter in 1955.

The National Party's goal was to forestall black independence. The 1950 Population Registration Act and Group Areas Act assured the permanent economic disability of black South Africans. The first established classification by race. The second assigned those of the African classifications to live in "Bantustans," or tribal "homelands," constituting a mere fourteen percent of the land. By the Bantu Education Act of 1953, they were barred from excellent mission schools and compelled to attend government-run schools that enforced racial hierarchies and taught only rudimentary subjects. As workers, they received lower wages than whites for similar work.

Other laws established the social norms of **apartheid** ("separateness"), mimicking the segregation laws of the southern states of the United States. Such laws barred blacks from white-designated public facilities, banned interracial marriage, and required blacks to carry an identity card. The efforts of African nationalist leaders to resist apartheid resulted in their arrest, but also in the worldwide condemnation of the government of South Africa. The killing of unarmed demonstrators at Sharpeville in 1960 (leaving 67 dead, 180 wounded) and Soweto in 1976 (where police fired on a crowd of 15,000, killing 575, including 134 children) aroused world opinion against South Africa. The Anglican archbishop Desmond Tutu (1931–), winner of the 1984 Nobel Peace Prize, carried the story of racial injustice around the globe. His speech to the United Nations is quoted in *Witnesses* on p. 842.

World opinion strengthened by economic sanctions forced President Pieter W. Botha (1916–) to resign in 1989. His successor Frederik Willem de Klerk (1936–) searched for a compromise between black aspirations and Afrikaner obduracy. De Klerk lifted the ban on the African National Congress in 1990 and released its leader Nelson Mandela after twenty-six years of imprisonment (see the photograph above, and also *Witnesses*, p. 842). The two leaders worked together for a multiracial and democratic society, calling for elections based on universal suffrage. Held in 1994, that election made Mandela president, De Klerk one of two deputy presidents. An African pledged to win justice for both Africans and Afrikaners led South Africa for the first time.

Varying Models of Independence   In other states, where independence was attained only after guerrilla struggle—as in the former Portuguese colonies of Guinea-Bissau, Angola, and Mozambique, or the former French colony of Algeria—socialism appealed to the embittered nationalist victors. In addition, by the 1970s, the animosities between the United States and the Soviet Union generated by the Cold War (see Chapter 29) intruded upon African politics, as each antagonist funded and supplied friendly guerrilla forces and client states.

In Angola in 1975–1976, Soviet arms and some 45,000 troops from Cuba, then a Soviet client state, aided one guerrilla group against another supported by the United States. The Soviet protégés won, and a Marxist government was formed. In Algeria, upon the final departure of the French in 1962, a socialist government took over foreign interests and nationalized industries. In Libya, army colonel Muammar el-Qaddafi (1942–) toppled a pro-Western monarchy in 1969, nationalized foreign petroleum assets, removed United States and British military bases, and accepted Soviet aid and arms. In 1974, a self-proclaimed Marxist–Leninist regime took over in Ethiopia by overthrowing the last emperor Haile Selassie (r. 1930–1974). Ethiopia soon went to war with neighboring Somalia (pieced together in 1960 from former British and Italian Somalilands), also a Soviet client since 1974. For a while, the Soviet Union supplied both sides with arms and military experts. But on the whole, few African nations gravitated to the Soviet sphere of influence.

Among the conscientious African leaders who guided the continent into a modern age of political responsibility were the intellectuals Léopold Senghor (1906–) of Senegal, Patrice Lumumba of Zaire, and Jomo Kenyatta (c. 1893–1978) of Kenya. Senghor wrote several volumes of poetry; Lumumba wrote a study of his compatriots in *Congo: My Country* (1962); and Kenyatta wrote about the native traditions of his people in *Facing Mount Kenya* (1938) and *Suffering without Bitterness* (1968).

The socialist leaders Julius Nyerere (1922–) of Tanzania and Robert Mugabe (1924–) of Zimbabwe hoped to build African states on African principles, while serving citizens' welfare requirements according to Western political theory. Nyerere's controversial concept of *ujamaa* (familyhood), a politics based on village-centered popular rule, foundered in economic crisis, however. Mugabe's initial achievements, however—building bridges to the wealthy white minority of Zimbabwe, and seeking improved relations with South Africa—must now be negated by his usurpations of

Map 29.3 African Political Systems, 1996: *After more than 50 years since it came out from under the colonial yoke, Africa is not free. The political situation is heterogeneous and highly volatile, featuring a number of regimes which have not ascribed to the multiparty democratic model that appears today to be the preference of developing nations. This 1996 map shows a patchwork of authoritarian and democratic regimes, along with the many that are in transition. What conditions might be necessary for the continued democratization of Africa?*

white-owned lands and widespread corruption, which have resulted in his nation's impoverishment.

Under Nelson Mandela's leadership, notably, the African National Congress did not incline to Marxist socialism. Mandela staunchly adhered to democratic principles, displaying qualities for which, in 1993, he was recognized by the award of the Nobel Peace Prize. Mandela's 1994 election as president of South Africa with two-thirds of the popular vote was a triumph for democracy. But South Africa was not alone in the early 1990s. After decades of post-colonial experimentation and readjustment, and with the development of an indigenous educated and professional elite, many African states are moving in the direction of parliamentary procedures, multi-party elections, and economic privatization.

Africa: Post-Colonial Quandaries

As colonialist powers retreated, Africans considered the task that lay before them. Here the Ghanaian leader Nkrumah and the All-African People's Conference held at Accra in December 1958 call for a pan-African approach to end imperialism and promote economic development.

Kwame Nkrumah looks back to the past and ahead to the future, calling for an Africa that is politically unified and economically strong (1961): For centuries, Europeans dominated the African continent. The white man arrogated to himself the right to rule and to be obeyed by the non-white; his mission, he claimed, was to "civilise" Africa. Under this cloak, the Europeans robbed the continent of vast riches and inflicted unimaginable suffering on the African people.

All this makes a sad story, but now we must be prepared to bury the past with its unpleasant memories and look to the future. … It is clear that we must find an African solution to our problems, and that this can only be found in African unity. Divided we are weak; united, Africa could become one of the greatest forces for good in the world.

Although most Africans are poor, our continent is potentially extremely rich. Our mineral resources, which are being exploited with foreign capital only to enrich foreign investors, range from gold and diamonds to uranium and petroleum. Our forests contain some of the finest woods to be grown anywhere. Our cash crops include cocoa, coffee, rubber, tobacco and cotton. As for power, … Africa contains over 40 percent of the potential water power of the world. … Yet so far, less than 1 percent has been developed. This is one of the reasons why we have in Africa the paradox of poverty in the midst of plenty, and scarcity in the midst of abundance.

Never before have a people had within their grasp so great an opportunity for developing a continent endowed with so much wealth. Individually, the independent states of Africa, some of them potentially rich, others poor, can do little for their people. Together, by mutual help, they can achieve much. But the economic development of the continent must be planned and pursued as a whole. A loose confederation designed only for economic co-operation would not provide the necessary unity of purpose. Only a strong political union can bring about full and effective development of our natural resources for the benefit of our people.
(Kwame Nkrumah, *I Speak of Freedom: A Statement of African Ideology*, London: William Heinemann Ltd., 1961)

At Accra, December 5–13, 1958, more than 300 delegates to the All-African People's Conference, representing more than 200 million Africans, agreed on the following "Resolution on Imperialism and Colonialism:"
1. That the All-African People's Conference vehemently condemns colonialism and imperialism in whatever shape or form these evils are perpetuated.
2. That the political and economic exploitation of Africans by imperialist Europeans should cease forthwith.
3. That the use of African manpower in the nefarious game of power politics by imperialists should be a thing of the past.
4. That independent African States should pursue in their international policy principles which will expedite and accelerate the independence and sovereignty of all dependent and colonial African territories.
5. That fundamental human rights be extended to all men and women in Africa and that the rights of indigenous Africans to the fullest use of their lands be respected and preserved.
6. That universal adult franchise be extended to all persons in Africa regardless of race or sex.
7. That independent African states ensure that fundamental human rights and universal adult franchise are fully extended to everyone within their states as an example to imperial nations who abuse and ignore the extension of those rights to Africans.
8. That a permanent secretariat of the All-African People's Conference be set up to organise the All-African Conference on a firm basis.
9. That a human rights committee of the Conference be formed to examine complaints of abuse of human rights in every part of Africa and to take appropriate steps to ensure the enjoyment of the rights by everyone.
10. That the All-African People's Conference in Accra declares its full support to all fighters for freedom in Africa, to all those who resort to peaceful means of non-violence and civil disobedience, as well as to all those who are compelled to retaliate against violence to attain national independence and freedom for the people. …
(All-African People's Conference News Bulletin, Vol. I, No. 4, Accra: 1959

African Debates: Algeria and South Africa

Although a number of African nations were granted independence by colonial powers quickly after World War II, others underwent a longer and more painful experience. In Algeria, French settlers who had deep-rooted traditions as a colonial elite, refused to abandon the ideal of a "French Algeria," as a government official explains in the first of these excerpts. In the second, Frantz Fanon, a powerful anti-imperialist spokesperson, rejoices at Algeria's final victory. South Africa was already an independent nation when the War ended in 1945, but a nation whose native population was dominated by the descendants of older generations of European settlers from the Netherlands and Britain. The struggle of the African subjects of that colonial regime for civil rights in their own country lasted more than a generation, and was successful above all because of the sacrifice and determination of Nelson Mandela, eventually President of a renewed South African state, whose message was spread around the world by the native Anglican archbishop Desmond Tutu.

Jacques Soustelle, Governor-General of the French colony of Algeria, says France will never relinquish Algeria (1955): France is at home here, or rather, Algeria and all her inhabitants form an integral part of France, one and indivisible. All must know, here and elsewhere, that France will not leave Algeria any more than she will leave Provence and Brittany. Whatever happens, the destiny of Algeria is French.
(From K. Nkrumah, *I Speak of Freedom*, 1961)

Psychiatrist Frantz Fanon welcomes a new and autonomous Algeria (1959): On the Algerian soil a new society has come to birth. The men and women of Algeria today resemble neither those of 1930 nor those of 1954, nor yet those of 1957. The old Algeria is dead. All the innocent blood that has flowed on to the national soil [as a result of war with France] has produced a new humanity.
(Frantz Fanon, *A Dying Colonialism*, 1971)

Nelson Mandela speaks in his own defense at his trial at the Pretoria Supreme Court, Rivonia (1964): Africans want to be paid a living wage ... to live where they obtain work ... to be part of the general pop-

ulation, and not confined to living in their own ghettoes. ... Africans want to be allowed out after eleven o'clock at night and not to be confined to their rooms like little children. ... Africans want a just share in the whole of South Africa; they want security and a stake in society.

Above all, we want equal political rights, because without them our disabilities will be permanent. I know this sounds revolutionary to the whites in this country, because the majority of voters will be Africans. This makes the white man fear democracy. ...

During my lifetime I have dedicated myself to this struggle of the African people. I have fought against white domination and I have fought against black domination. I have cherished the ideal of democratic and free society in which all persons live together in harmony and with equal opportunities. It is an ideal which I hope to live for and to achieve. But if needs be, it is an ideal for which I am prepared to die.
(Nelson Mandela, *The Struggle is My Life*, 1990, 3rd ed.)

Archbishop Desmond Tutu implores the United Nations Security Council to help black South Africans gain their freedom (1984): White South Africans are not demons; they are ordinary human beings, scared human beings, many of them; who would not be, if they were outnumbered five to one? Through this lofty body, I wish to appeal to my white fellow South Africans to share in building a new society, for blacks are not intent on driving whites into the sea but on claiming only their rightful place in the sun in the land of their birth.

We deplore all forms of violence, the violence of an oppressive and unjust society and the violence of those seeking to overthrow that society, for we believe that violence is not the answer to the crisis of our land.

We dream of a new society that will be truly non-racial, truly democratic, in which people count because they are created in the image of God. ...

I say we will be free, and we ask you: Help us, that this freedom comes for all of us in South Africa, black and white, ... that it comes soon.
(Desmond Tutu, statement to the UN Security Council, October 23, 1984)

Statebuilding in the Middle East: Israel, Oil, and Islam

World War I accomplished the dismemberment of the last great Islamic empire in the Middle East—that of the Ottomans. Over the next decades, its component territories became independent states. After World War II, the inherent tension between Islamic traditions and modernization sharpened (see Chapter 24). The politics of oil, a sub-soil treasure concentrated

in the Arabian Peninsula, further destabilized the region. So too did the presence of Israel, created by European Zionists as a refuge for the Jewish people. These factors have made the Middle East a major trouble spot of the later twentieth century. Major Middle East leaders are listed in *Who's Who* on p. 843.

Turkey   The Ottoman Empire entered the twentieth century moribund. In 1914, it ruled only one-third of the lands it had held in 1800. Allied with the Central Powers in World War I, the Empire disintegrated at war's end. By the 1920 Treaty of Sèvres, it lost its North African, Middle Eastern, and European territories, along with some Aegean islands (confirmed as Italian possessions), leaving only Anatolia (in Asia Minor) as a homeland. Even in Anatolia, a valuable commercial strip near Smyrna was assigned to Greece, a reward for loyalty.

As Greek and Italian forces rushed to claim their prizes, Mustafa Kemal (1881–1938) led a swift counter-strike. An army commander during the recent war, Kemal was one of the Young Turks who had unseated the sultan in 1908. From 1919 to 1923, he recaptured Asia Minor and expelled the Greek occupiers. He won title not only to the whole of Anatolia, but also to a limited zone around Constantinople, now renamed Istanbul, on the European side of the Hellespont. The empire had been lost, but Turkey was born.

Made president in 1922 and henceforth known as Atatürk ("father of the Turks"), Kemal recast Turkey as a modern, secular state. He established compulsory public schools, for girls as well as boys, and by 1932 cut the illiteracy rate in half from its 1914 level. He established a civil law system (replacing traditional Muslim courts), discouraged Islamic customs, donned Western dress, made marriage a civil function, and transcribed the Turkish language in the West's Roman alphabet. He permitted elections (by universal suffrage) within a one-party system to a representative assembly whose decisions he consulted. By his death in 1938, Atatürk had transformed Turkey, which has since been further democratized by later constitutions (in 1961 and 1982).

Egypt While Atatürk reshaped Turkey, the Arab regions of the former Ottoman Empire gained new contours. The most successful of these was Egypt, technically independent since 1936 but retaining a "preferential alliance" with Britain which ensured the latter continued control of the Suez and port of Alexandria and certain military privileges. In 1952, a military coup forced out the reigning king and, in 1956, obtained the independence of Sudan. In 1956, Egyptian president Gamal Abdel Nasser (1918–1970) seized and nationalized the Canal, the conduit through which passed two-thirds of the oil used by western Europe. Nasser's provocative strike nearly precipitated a military confrontation with Britain and her allies (who were restrained by the United States).

Nasser proceeded to nationalize banks and industries, dispossess the great landowners, redistribute lands to the peasants, and promote higher education. Funded by the Soviet Union, he built the Aswan High Dam (completed 1970). Aswan controlled the Nile floods that had for centuries irrigated the land and made Egypt the granary of the Mediterranean. A great project that he likened in scale to the pyramid

"Fading Empires in the Middle East"

Mustafa Kemal (1881–1938), known as "Atatürk" ("Father of the Turks"), military creator of the new Turkish state (successor to the Ottoman Empire) of which he became president in 1922, promoting social and republican reforms within a one-party system.

Gamal Abdel Nasser (1918–1970), Egyptian president who repudiated the West by seizing and nationalizing the Suez Canal in 1956; he undertook massive programs of wealth redistribution, and built the Aswan High Dam (completed 1970) with Soviet funding.

Anwar Sadat (1918–1981), Egyptian president who attempted to reach a settlement with Israel, resulting in a 1979 treaty between Egypt and Israel, which triggered Sadat's assassination in 1981.

Yasir Arafat (1929–), leader of the Palestinian Liberation Organization, committed to achieving statehood for the Palestinian people and thus to obtaining concessions from the occupying nation of Israel.

Yitzhak Rabin (1922–1995)

Benjamin Netanyahu (1949–)

Ehud Barak (1942–)

Israeli prime ministers who have defended Israel's legitimacy while attempting to reach a settlement with Arafat and the PLO.

Ruhollah Khomeini (1902–1989), Iranian Shi'ite religious leader, entitled "ayatollah," who led a revolution ousting shah Muhammad Reza Pahlevi (1941–1979) in 1979 and then established an Islamist regime.

Saddam Hussein (1938–), dictator of Iraq, whose invasion of Kuwait in 1990 precipitated the Gulf War, fought victoriously by the US and its allies, which subsequently imposed harsh economic sanctions in an attempt to prevent further aggression from Iraq.

building of ancient pharaohs, it was intended to boost peasant productivity and generate electric power.

Nasser also galvanized the states of the Middle East, forging an international alliance for a pan-Arab, Islamic "socialism" that would be independent of both the West and communism. His successors have failed to resolve Egypt's economic problems, and face growing opposition from **Islamist** parties, which seek to unify Muslims and revitalize the religion and culture of Islam.

The Middle East   In the Middle East, Britain and France relinquished their post-World War I mandates and protectorates after World War II. Newly independent, these states confronted the tasks of creating a modern economy, transportation system, and institutions of health and education. Their accomplishment was complicated by the presence in the Middle East of the state of Israel, an abundance of oil, and increasing Islamic militancy.

A memo of November 2, 1917 by British minister Arthur Balfour (1848–1930) first approved the concept of a "national home for the Jewish people"— vague words that promised no support and gave no idea of how it would come into being. By 1917, Jewish immigrants had already founded a handful of settlements in Palestinian territory still under Ottoman rule (joining the approximately 68,000 Jews, mostly in Jerusalem, who had lived in Palestine for four centuries). From 1917 to 1948, tens of thousands of immigrants poured into Palestine, as Jewish settlers increased their share of the population from about one-tenth to a half.

The first settlers were committed Zionists (see Chapter 24) followed by refugees from Nazism. In time, these were joined by immigrants from other Middle Eastern states who had lived under Ottoman rule as a tolerated minority. With the financial assistance of Jews around the world, these pioneers installed irrigation systems and reclaimed once barren lands. When the new nation of Israel declared its independence in 1948 (see *Witnesses*, p. 845), it was more highly urbanized, better educated, better fed, and better armed than the surrounding Arab states.

Conflict was inevitable between the new state of Israel and its neighbors. Wars broke out in 1948, 1956, 1967, 1973, and 1982. In 1948, following the Israeli proclamation of independence on May 14, Arab forces from a league of neighboring states invaded the new nation. Highly motivated and better organized, the Israelis repulsed them. The territorial settlement based on the ceasefire lines gave them even more territory than had the United Nations' 1947 partition. Many Palestinian natives fled Israel; about half became refugees in neighboring Arab lands, while around 1 million still remain within Israel, as a significant minority in that nation whose population is currently about 5.5 million (see *How Many?* left).

Responding to border raids or threats of imminent invasion, Israel attacked Egypt in 1956, and its Arab neighbor states in 1967. At the close of the 1967 Six-Day War, Israel occupied lands south and west to the Suez Canal (the Sinai Peninsula) and east to the Jordan River (the region of the "West Bank," including the Old City of Jerusalem) as well as the Gaza Strip along the Mediterranean and the Golan Heights in Syria. Defying a United Nations injunction, Israel refused to leave until the Arab states agreed to negotiate; the Arabs refused to do so.

In 1973, after a six-year standoff, Egypt and Syria counterattacked. At the ceasefire they obtained a partial Israeli withdrawal from its 1967 high tide. In 1982, Israel invaded Lebanon to destroy the PLO headquarters. (The PLO, or Palestine Liberation Organization, was the official advocate of statehood for the uprooted Palestinians; some of its goals are listed in *Witnesses* on p. 845.) During these years, the United States provided Israel, and the Soviet Union its Arab opponents with arms, such activity serving to increase the volatility of the region's politics.

The problem remained that Israel occupied lands from which millions of now stateless Palestinians had been displaced. Over the next decades, some progress has been made toward resolving this intractable issue, which pits the moral right of the Jewish people to the homeland promised them against the moral right of Palestinian natives to the land which had long been theirs. In 1977, Egyptian president Anwar Sadat (1918–1981) bravely journeyed to Jerusalem to attempt to negotiate a settlement. That action culminated in the Camp David peace negotiations, hosted in 1978 by United States president Jimmy Carter (1924–). The resulting treaty between Egypt and Israel of March 26, 1979 obtained the complete Israeli

HOW MANY?

Palestinians Resident in the Middle East

Country	Resident Palestinians
Jordan	700,000
West Bank	675,000
Israel	350,000
Gaza	375,000
Lebanon	275,000
Syria	175,000
Egypt	25,000
Iraq	10,000
Persian Gulf countries	170,000
TOTAL	2,755,000

Estimated figures, March 1973

The destiny of 2.75 million stateless Palestinian Arabs, more than half of whom live as refugees in countries outside of Israel, is one of the greatest sources of tension in any region of the world.
Source: D. A. Schmidt, Armageddon in the Middle East *(New York: New York Times, 1974), p. 148.*

withdrawal from the Sinai. Egypt became the only Arab state to have made peace with Israel.

In 1981, Sadat was assassinated, the penalty for his peacemaking role. Fundamentalist groups, both Israeli and Arab, sprang up to resist the forces for peace. (Fundamentalists adhere strictly to the tenets of their religion and resist secular values and institutions; both Islamic and Jewish militancy may be linked to fundamentalist concerns.) In 1993, Israeli prime minister Yitzhak Rabin (1922–1995) and PLO chairman Yasir Arafat (1929–) signed a peace accord, following negotiations brokered by the United States and Norway. It allowed for Palestinian self-rule in the Gaza Strip and in the city of Jericho in the occupied West Bank, and called for a settlement by the end of a five-year transitional period. Further details within the same treaty framework were settled in 1995. These arrangements rankled nationalists on both sides. Recent years have seen a heightening of Arab resistance and Israeli nationalism. In 1987, young Palestinians in the Israeli-occupied territories of the West Bank and Gaza Strip launched the uprising called the *Intifada* ("shaking")—an informal campaign of stonethrowing, strikes, and demonstrations. In addition, Islamist groups (notably the Hamas and the Islamic Jihad) have launched random terrorist attacks, including suicide bombings, on Israeli civilians. These have inspired ferocious Israeli determination to resist. Assassinated in 1995, Rabin was replaced by Benjamin Netanyahu (1949–), of the conservative Likud Party, a figure reluctant to compromise with Palestinian groups. In 1999, the election of the moderate Ehud Barak (1942–) raised hopes for a new settlement.

WITNESSES

New Orders in the Middle East: Israel, the Palestine Liberation Organization, and Revolutionary Iran

In the troubled Middle East, one party's claim of justice often acts in contradiction to another's. That complexity is evident in the documents here. In the first, the nation of Israel—as the United Nations mandated—establishes itself as an independent state, claiming that it was "the natural right of the Jewish people to be masters of their own fate." In the second, a generation later, the Palestinian Liberation Organization, acting for the whole community of Palestinians (who had no state), declares the people's right of self-determination. In the third, the Iranian Ayatollah Khomeini, who had led his people in a successful revolution against rulers whose dynasty had been installed by Western governments, gives thanks for the nation's delivery from the power of the United States, that "global plunderer."

Declaration of the establishment of the State of Israel (1948): The land of Israel was the birthplace of the Jewish people. Here their spiritual, religious, and political identity was shaped. Here they first attained statehood, created cultural values of national and universal significance, and gave to the world the eternal Book of Books. …

On the 29th of November, 1947, the United Nations General Assembly passed a resolution calling for the establishment of a Jewish state in the land of Israel. … This recognition by the United Nations of the right of the Jewish people to establish their state is irrevocable. This right is the natural right of the Jewish people to be masters of their own fate, like all other nations, in their own sovereign state.

(From J. N. Moore, ed., *The Arab–Israeli Conflict: Readings and Documents*, 1977)

The goals of the Palestine Liberation Organization, founded to represent the interests of the Palestinians made stateless by the creation of Israel (1968):

#8: The Palestinian people is at the stage of national struggle for the liberation of its homeland. …

#9: Armed struggle is the only way of liberating Palestine. …

#26: The Palestine Liberation Organization … is responsible for the struggle of the Palestinian Arab people to regain, liberate and return to their homeland and to exercise the right of self-determination in that homeland.

(From Zuhair Diab, ed., *International Documents on Palestine*, document no. 360, 1971)

Iranian revolutionary leader, the Ayatollah Ruhollah Khomeini, defines the nature of the victory won (1980): God Almighty has willed—and all thanks are due Him—that this noble nation be delivered from the oppression and crimes inflicted on it by a tyrannical government and from the domination of the oppressive powers, especially America, the global plunderer. … It is our duty to stand firm against the superpowers, as we are indeed able to do, on condition that the intellectuals stop following and imitating either the West or the East, and adhere instead to the straight path of Islam and the nation. … Beloved youths, it is in you that I place my hopes. With the Qur'an in one hand and a gun in the other, defend your dignity and honor so well that your adversaries will be unable even to think of conspiring against you. … Know well that the world today belongs to the oppressed and sooner or later they will triumph. They will inherit the earth and build the government of God.

(Ayatollah Ruhollah Khomeini, "New Year's Message, 1980"; ed. M. Algar, 1981)

Oil and Fundamentalism Meanwhile, Israel's Arab neighbors had grown wealthy. Oil had become the chief fuel of the twentieth century, and sixty percent of the world's oil lay under the sands of the Arabian peninsula (with other rich deposits in the United States and Canada, Mexico, Venezuela, Nigeria, Indonesia, Russia, and Kazakhstan). Since World War II, as the West and Japan became increasingly dependent on oil, the oil-producing Arab states reasserted control of their reserves. Suddenly wealthy, their economy has been sustained by the export of a single precious commodity.

In Africa and Latin America, commodity-based economies suffered with fluctuations in world markets. To control that volatility, in 1961 the Arab states united (with other oil-rich nations) as the Organization of Petroleum Exporting Countries (OPEC), with the aim of preventing outsiders from dictating the value of their principal resource by collectively setting oil prices. Between 1973 and 1975, they quadrupled the cost of a barrel of oil, triggering hardship in the oil-consuming West.

The wealth derived from oil profits has flowed to a variety of projects: construction, health, education, wages—and the personal enrichment of elites and rulers. By the late 1990s, though they eluded the worst dangers of a free marketplace, the Arab states had not succeeded in using the profits from oil to diversify their economies or to establish industrialization.

In nearby Iran, under the autocratic rule of the shahs, modernization and secularization proceeded rapidly at the expense of the exploited and zealously religious masses. By the 1970s, religious leaders denounced the Western moral values that pervaded urbanized and industrialized society. They identified the West as the enemy of traditional Islamic culture—which in Iran was **Shi'ite**, as opposed to the Sunni form of Islam practiced in most of the region—and particularly the United States, a supporter of the shah and a major source of foreign capital and ideas.

The tension between Islamism and modernization erupted in 1979 in a coup that took the West by surprise (see *Witnesses*, p. 845). The elderly ayatollah (the title of a senior Shi'ite expert in Islamic law) Ruhollah Khomeini (1902–1989) ousted the brutal and corrupt regime of shah Muhammad Reza Pahlevi (1941–1979). Khomeini proceeded to reverse the course of Iranian development, leading a revolution which in November 1979 seized the United States embassy and held sixty-nine officials and workers hostage, most of them for fifteen months. Further, he dissolved the hated SAVAK (the foreign-bankrolled secret police); confiscated United States properties and expelled United States military personnel; restructured schools and universities, and restored Islamic law. His agents policed morals, censored newspapers and broadcast media, and banned alcohol. Women once again wore the veil in a wholesale repudiation of the cultural values of the West—the

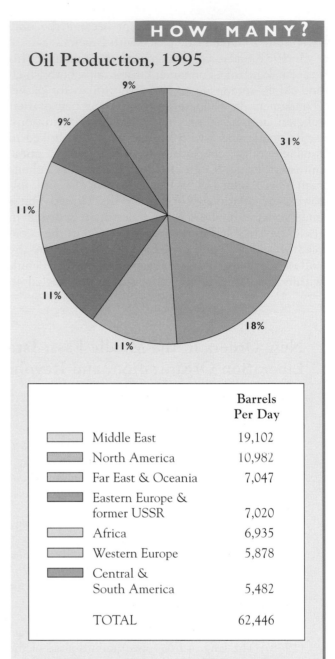

HOW MANY?

Oil Production, 1995

	Barrels Per Day
Middle East	19,102
North America	10,982
Far East & Oceania	7,047
Eastern Europe & former USSR	7,020
Africa	6,935
Western Europe	5,878
Central & South America	5,482
TOTAL	62,446

In 1995, world production of crude oil (still the most important source of fuel) reached 62,446 barrels per day. The chart above shows each region's share of global output, with the Middle East producing 19,102 barrels per day, or thirty-one percent of the total, compared to forty-one percent in 1929. In recent decades, Central and South America, western Europe, Africa, and the Far East and Oceania have significantly increased their share of world production.
Source: New York Times 1998 Almanac, p. 504.

homeland of the "Great Satan," the United States. After the death of Khomeini in 1989, deeply mourned by the Iranian people, his regime stayed the course, with recent elections and student resistance pointing toward a more moderate regime in the future.

Meanwhile, Islamic fundamentalism has proved to be a powerful force throughout North Africa and the

Middle East, and has been aimed not only at Western interests but also native, secular states. Islamist forces have supported terrorism in Egypt and Algeria, while in 1996, the Islamist Taliban faction fundamentalists swept into Afghanistan (previously a state within the Soviet sphere of influence) and transformed political culture and private life.

Not religion but nationalism and opportunism were the motives for the invasion by Iraqi leader Saddam Hussein (1938–) of adjoining Kuwait in 1990. His action provoked air attacks and ground invasion by the United States and allies (the Middle Eastern nations of Syria, Egypt, Saudi Arabia, and some smaller Gulf states as well as Western powers and Japan) in the second Gulf War. A swift victory for the Western forces in a fully televised conflict momentarily stymied Saddam's bid for territorial expansion and Arab leadership. The dictator contented himself with the brutal suppression of Shi'ite Muslim and Kurdish revolts at home.

By the end of the 1990s, the Middle East remains one of the world's most volatile regions. With the exception of Israel, its states are all dictatorships— military, princely, theocratic, oligarchic. Unifying forces include Islamic culture and pan-Arab nationalism—and the common hatred of Israel. But several factors destabilize the region: rivalries among even the Arab nations; the resurgence of Islamic fundamentalism; the abundance of oil, essential to power the industries of the West and Japan; the stockpile of sophisticated weapons supplied during the Cold War era by both superpowers and their allies; the presence of aggrieved minorities (Christian, Druze Muslims, Armenian, Kurd); and competing Israeli and Palestinian aspirations.

Statebuilding in Asia: Democracy, Communism, and Capitalism

The new post-colonial nations of Asia represent a variety of political forms. Some states (such as Pakistan and Indonesia) are reminiscent of those African nations that turned to autocracy when their colonial rulers left. But the major states of India and China offer contrasting models of democracy and communism, and the powerhouse micro-states of the Pacific Rim, resembling Japan more closely than India or China, are showcases of capitalism.

India and Pakistan India has maintained its democratic institutions, with a brief interruption, from independence in 1947 until the present day. Its first head was the nationalist leader Jawaharlal Nehru (1889–1964), an associate of Gandhi's who ruled for seventeen years. Attempting to remain "nonaligned" (independent of either of the two Cold War superpowers), he imitated features of both kinds of states in his administration of India—and unfortunately slid,

like many of his fellow dictators, toward cronyism, distributing key posts to family members and friends. In 1966, after a two-year interim, Nehru's daughter Indira Gandhi (1917–1984) became prime minister. By 1975, her economic policies (the nationalization of banks and control of private enterprise) aroused opposition, and she was charged with corruption. She

WHO'S WHO

Fading Empires in Asia

Mohandas Gandhi (1889–1948), Indian Nationalist opponent of British rule and creator of the philosophy and strategy of "civil disobedience" as a form of non-violent resistance to unjust power.

Jawaharlal Nehru (1889–1964), Indian Nationalist leader, and first prime minister of independent India (1947–1964).

Indira Gandhi (1917–1984), Nehru's daughter, Indian prime minister (1966–1984), charged with corruption and abuse of power; assassinated in 1984; as was her son Rajiv (1944–1991), who succeeded her, in 1991.

Sukarno (1901–1970), Indonesian Nationalist leader who took power after World War II, cooperating with the Dutch administration until it was finally ousted in 1963.

Suharto (1921–), Indonesian who took power from Sukarno in a US-backed military coup in 1965; established an authoritarian regime, and joined the Southeast Asian Treaty Organization, or SEATO, a regional defense organization; he was finally expelled in 1998 because of his corruption and failed policies.

Mao Zedong (1893–1976), Chinese communist revolutionary leader who seized power in 1949, presiding over radical social, economic, and cultural policies (which resulted in the death of millions of people) until his death.

Deng Xiaoping (1904–1997), already elderly, replaced Mao in 1976, and continued his policies, which called for, in 1989, the violent repression of the student-led revolt in Tiananmen Square.

Ferdinand Marcos (1917–1989), autocratic and increasingly corrupt president of the Philippines from 1965–1986, when he fled following the election of Corazon Aquino (1933–), the widow of his former opponent.

Ho Chi Minh (1890–1969), Vietnamese Nationalist leader who opposed French domination after World War I, and the US-supported South Vietnamese government after 1954, whose supporters eventually attained Vietnamese unification and independence in 1975.

responded by suspending the constitution and ruling personally. In elections in 1977, Gandhi and her party were repudiated and democratic institutions restored. She was reelected in 1980, but was assassinated during 1984 riots between Sikhs and Hindus by Sikh members of her own security guard. Gandhi's son Rajiv (1944–1991) succeeded her as prime minister and retained the ministry until 1989. He too, however, was assassinated, in 1991.

India's democracy remained intact through the Nehru–Gandhi years. The security of India's political institutions, however, continues to be menaced by enduring social and cultural problems. These include religious and ethnic conflicts (Hindu–Muslim violence flared up again in 1992); resentment against powerful elites, who dominate government and cultural life; and a runaway rate of population growth that threatens prosperity even as productivity grows in both agricultural and industrial domains.

Neighboring Pakistan, mainly ruled by military dictators since 1958, has not enjoyed India's democratic experience. East Pakistan, now Bangladesh, broke away in 1971 to form an independent state— one of the world's poorest. It too has been subject to authoritarian government and one-party rule.

Indonesia   The great archipelago of Indonesia also fell under authoritarian rule after winning liberation from the Dutch. Its president Sukarno, an architect of Indonesian independence, was still in power in the 1960s as that state slid into the orbit of communist China. In 1965, a United States-backed military coup under General Suharto (1921–) seized power (retaining Sukarno as figurehead until 1967), expelling communist officials and massacring their followers, along with about 750,000 ethnic Chinese. Suharto established an authoritarian regime, joining SEATO (the Southeast Asia Treaty Organization), a regional defense organization with close ties to the United States. He promoted economic modernization and attracted foreign investment, especially Japanese, while he suppressed dissent and restored Islamic law and customs. In 1998, mired in corruption and failed policies, Suharto was deposed by a mass movement led by university students demanding free elections and a democratic constitution.

China   In China, the revolution of 1911–1912 brought freedom from emperors and the intrusion of Western powers (see Chapter 24). From 1912 to 1927, the armies of the Nationalist or Guomindang Party, eventually trained and bankrolled by the Soviets, gradually won control of much of eastern and southern China (see Chapter 28). Their commander Chiang Kai-shek (Jiang Jieshi, 1887–1975) fought against local warlords. Meanwhile, communist leaders (the Chinese Communist Party was founded in 1921) built up their power-base among the peasants in the countryside, whose loyalty and cooperation they won through practical means, with land redistributions.

In 1927, Chiang expelled or murdered the communists in the Guomindang, who fled to the interior regions of south China. In 1934, he attacked their stronghold at Jiangxi. Some 100,000 people, including thirty-five women, fled to the north in the heroic "Long March" (more than 6000 miles) of 368 days. Harried by Guomindang pursuers, barely one-tenth survived to establish a secure base at Yan'an in Shaanxi Province. Led by Mao Zedong (1893–1976), pictured on p. 849, their forces of some 1 million men cooperated cautiously with Chiang's armies of 3 million when the Japanese invaded in 1937.

The Japanese occupation of the industrial zones of eastern China deprived Chiang of his supporters among the commercial elites. Following the Japanese surrender in 1945, he resumed his struggle with the communists. In 1948, with United States air and naval assistance, Chiang rashly attacked strong enemy positions in the north. Communist troops smashed and rolled past him, armed by the Soviets. They swept southward and fanned out over the whole of China. Chiang and his followers escaped to the island of Taiwan, removed by the peace settlement from Japanese domination. Chiang declared himself head of the Chinese state in exile. In 1949, Mao became the leader of the new, Communist People's Republic of China. His speech is quoted in *Witnesses* on p. 849. With fewer than 3 million Communist supporters, he had conquered a nation of 600 million people. After a century of fragmentation (see Chapter 24), China was united under one leader.

From 1949 until his death in 1976, Mao Zedong consolidated the Communist regime and transformed Chinese economy, society, and culture. Fittingly for a nation where peasants constituted eighty percent of the population, Mao's revised Marxist–Leninist principles made agricultural production a priority. Peasant collectives seized great estates, without compensation to the owners—who were "tried" and often executed by peasant tribunals. Productivity mounted during the 1950s. To boost it further, Mao launched the Great Leap Forward in 1958, whose goal was the complete collectivization of agriculture. The countryside was organized into large communes whose leaders directed the peasants' life and work. The experiment was a complete failure, undermined by floods, drought, and peasant resistance.

Some 10 million peasants died in the resulting famine. After 1961, the peasants returned to their smaller village collectives and generated modest gains in productivity, which gave them a living standard higher than in recent memory. Production in excess of the government-set quota was theirs to sell in local markets. Enhanced agricultural production promoted industrialization. Heavy industries (metals and machinery) in urban centers were developed first,

Chairman Mao and his Little Red Book: *Mao Zedong forged a unique form of communism in China based on peasant village organization and Marxist–Leninist principles. The poster shown here depicts youthful followers—with numberless others in the background—ardently studying the "Little Red Book" that contained the founder's philosophy. The poster gives an idealized vision of Mao's Communist regime.*

对伟大导师毛主席心怀一个"忠"字
对伟大毛泽东思想狠抓一个"用"字

He had the prerevolutionary intellectual and political elites arrested, "reeducated," or silenced. The press was censored, and religious groups, including numerous Christian missions, disbanded. Government officials supervised each village and household, seeking to break down traditions of family loyalty and social deference in favor of revolutionary and collective behavior. The advanced skills needed in a modern society, along with Maoist principles, were taught in schools that all children, male and female, were required to attend. Individuals selected for higher training or leadership positions were identified by party officials and notified of their destinies. Party

followed by more diversified factories in rural areas, offering employment alternatives for peasant workers. Organized as government-run enterprises, these industries invited foreign investment and trade.

Mao also undertook a profound reorientation of the traditions of ancient Chinese society and culture.

WITNESSES

Asia: Permanent Revolution in China

The communist revolution in China happened not once but at least twice: first in the aftermath of World War II, when Mao Zedong consolidated his power and established a new kind of economy and government; and second, in 1966, when the same leader launched the Great Proletarian Cultural Revolution, which would ensure the permanency of the revolution by eliminating cultural tendencies that had strayed away from the proletarian base of communist society. Here, Mao explains the first of these revolutions, in 1949; and the Central Committee of the Communist Party accepts the second, in 1966.

Mao Zedong explains the goals of the communist revolution (1949): "You are dictatorial." ... [T]hat is just what we are. ... [We must] deprive the reactionaries of the right to speak and let the people alone have that right.

"Who are the people?" At the present stage in China, they are the working class, the peasantry, the urban petty bourgeoisie and the national bourgeoisie. These classes, led by the working class and the Communist party, unite to form their own state and elect their own government: they enforce their dictatorship over the running dogs of imperialism—the landlord class and bureaucrat-bourgeoisie. ...

"Why must things be done this way?" ... If things were not done this way, the revolution would fail, the people would suffer, the country would be conquered. (Mao Zedong, speech, "In Commemoration of the 28th Anniversary of the Communist Party of China," June 30, 1949)

The Central Committee of the Chinese Communist party on the aims of the Great Proletarian Cultural Revolution (1966): The Great Proletarian Cultural Revolution now unfolding is a great revolution that ... constitutes a new stage in the development of the socialist revolution in our country. ... The proletariat must ... meet head-on every challenge of the bourgeoisie in the ideological field and use the new ideas, culture, customs and habits of the proletariat to change the mental outlook of the whole of society. At present, our objective is to struggle against and overthrow those persons in authority who are taking the capitalist road ... and all other exploiting classes and to transform education, literature and art and all other parts of the superstructure not in correspondence with the socialist economic base, so as to facilitate the consolidation and development of the socialist system. (From J. Robinson, *The Cultural Revolution in China*, 1969)

Tiananmen Square, 1989: More than twenty years after the Cultural Revolution, student-led demonstrations in Beijing's main Tiananmen Square protested against the repressive government that had succeeded Mao's regime. When on June 4, 1989, the government sent armed soldiers and tanks into the Square to end the protest, one lone and anonymous figure planted himself before the approaching column to prevent their advance. The famous photograph has captured a unique and moving moment of modern heroism.

members themselves—a mere one percent of this officially egalitarian society—submitted to programs of indoctrination that denigrated prerevolutionary assumptions and values.

In 1966, detecting an ebb of revolutionary energy especially among party leaders, Mao launched the Great Proletarian Cultural Revolution (see *Witnesses*, p. 849). Its aim was to achieve "permanent revolution"—a state of constant criticism, by the yardstick of Maoist doctrine, of all in authority. In schools and factories, young people formed into revolutionary squads (the "Red Guards") to spread propaganda and denounce those lagging in communist exuberance—targeting senior officials and members of their own families. Thousands of intellectuals and party functionaries were deported to the countryside for "reeducation" as manual laborers. Others were persecuted, imprisoned, tortured, or murdered. Mao's wife Jiang Qing (1914–1991) participated in the hunt, naming "counterrevolutionary" intellectuals. As the purges of the Cultural Revolution subsided, the stunned survivors waited, and the world watched, to see who might succeed the titanic Mao at his death in 1976.

That event brought Mao's now elderly companions of revolutionary days to power, foremost among them Deng Xiaoping (1904–1997). Survivors and in some cases victims of the Cultural Revolution, their first act was to oust from power Mao's widow and her three colleagues (publicly reviled as the "Gang of Four"). Deng proceeded to liberalize economic policy, permitting material incentives, a return to family-centered farming and factory-based (rather than centralized) decision-making. He encouraged foreign investment and trade, and promoted the scientific and technical training arrested by the anti-intellectualism of the Cultural Revolution. Resulting gains in productivity positioned China in the 1990s to participate actively in the modern system of global commerce. The price of this progress has been the continued curtailment of individual rights, backed up by censorship and repression of dissent. Especially controversial was the government's attempt to reverse rates of population growth by limiting family size to one child, with compulsory abortion for late pregnancies.

The children of the victims of the Cultural Revolution, who have no memory of the 1949 triumph, form a new generation. Many resist the regime of aging Communists who replaced Mao in 1976. In 1989, on the seventieth anniversary of the angry May Fourth Movement (see Chapter 26), university students led a massive demonstration in Tiananmen Square, the great central space of the capital of Beijing. The debates and demonstrations went on for weeks, and were televised worldwide, calling for an end to censorship and for free elections. Dissidents raised in the square a replica of the Statue of Liberty—a monument bestowed upon the United States by the French in 1886 to commemorate common republican traditions. Rechristened the "Goddess of Democracy," this icon made their provocative and dangerous message extremely clear.

China's leaders debated how they might respond, and decided, characteristically, on repression. The People's Liberation Army was dispatched to silence the dissidents. As the photograph above shows, tanks rolled into Tiananmen Square on June 4, 1989, crushing protestors who did not disperse, firing on unarmed demonstrators, killing about 1300, and arresting thousands more. Student leaders were rounded up and jailed without trial; some died from their injuries, some were executed. Witnesses to the repression told the story worldwide by telephone and fax machine; little was told through official channels. Since 1989, the government has released some of the jailed and tortured dissidents, but others are still held as political prisoners, even as China seeks admission to the club of modern nations who observe the rights of their citizens.

Japan and the Pacific Rim   Defeated in war, Japan sprang quickly to the first rank in the global market-place. With Japan occupied by Allied forces from 1945, under the command of United States general Douglas MacArthur (1880–1964), the revered emperor was permitted to remain, but as a figurehead, and only after he had publicly renounced the notion of his divinity. A new constitution emphasized that sovereignty lay with the people and parliament, founded an independent judiciary, and guaranteed civil rights for women as for men. Elementary and secondary education was made compulsory, labor unions made legal, landholding and corporate structures reshaped. The armed forces were disbanded (while the United States was permitted to maintain military bases on Japanese soil). In 1951, a peace treaty was signed and accepted by Japan and the Allies (except for the Soviet Union and China). National sovereignty was restored.

As a democratic, constitutional monarchy, Japan flourished. Its industries, banks, and commercial enterprises resumed their characteristic dynamism. Especially in the areas of electronics and automobile manufacture, Japan's products competed with the finest produced elsewhere, as enormous investment in research and development led to sophisticated technological products. By 1985, Japan was the world's second industrial power, after the United States. Wages were comparable to those in the affluent nations of the West. Until the slowdown that set in with the collapse of the Tokyo stock market in 1989, followed by a banking crisis in the late 1990s, Japan seemed to be on the way to claim first place.

Along with Japan, four other "Pacific Rim" states (so called because of their positioning on the east and southeast Asian coasts facing the Pacific) have emerged as economic powerhouses, albeit under authoritarian rule. Their activity, together with Japan's and China's, has nearly doubled East Asia's share of world production in the last generation, raising the region to parity with the West. From north to south, the first of these is South Korea. After recovering from the trauma of the Korean War in which one-tenth of its people died, it has flourished as a producer of electronic and automotive goods. The second is Taiwan, which has become a major commercial player under the Chinese Nationalist government established in 1949. The third is Hong Kong, British-owned from 1898 to 1997 and now reintegrated with China, an island-state that is a center of international finance capital. The fourth is Singapore, fully independent in 1965, another financial capital and exporter of labor-intensive manufactures. Especially in the latter two of these "Four Dragons" (or "Four Tigers") of the Pacific Rim, as they are called, forming a highly concentrated zone of economic endeavor, free enterprise reigns amid the ghosts of empires.

THE LAST IMPERIALIST

A latecomer to imperialism, the United States was among the last of the Western powers to renounce its dominion over other nations and peoples (see Chapter 19). After the war for independence from Britain (1776–1783), the new United States began a century of expansion across the North American continent, according to the self-defined privilege of **Manifest Destiny**. In that process of nation building, in the view of some observers, it acted as an imperialist power. It expropriated lands from native inhabitants, and annexed other territory from the independent nation of Mexico.

In the twentieth century, certainly, in Latin America, the Philippines, in Vietnam, and even its homeland, the United States has exercised dominion over unconsenting others, as Map 29.4 on p. 856 shows. In recent years, like its European peers, the United States has repudiated empire and its ambitions.

Good Neighbors: the United States in Latin America

The United States has played a contradictory role in Latin America (a region comprising Mexico and the nations of the Caribbean and South America whose people speak Spanish, Portuguese, or French, all derived from Latin). On the one hand, it has pretended to be a "good neighbor," the role urged by President Franklin Delano Roosevelt (1882–1945) in 1933. On the other hand, it has often intervened in the lives of the Latin American nations—to maintain order, to exclude other interests, to control the course of political events (even by invasion and occupation), to promote the economic interests of its entrepreneurs and investors, acting less like a "good neighbor" than the bully with a "big stick" envisioned by President Theodore Roosevelt (1858–1919).

Until 1898, the United States appeared to be a good, or at least an indifferent, neighbor toward the nations south of its borders. The Monroe Doctrine announced in 1823 declared the integrity of the Americas, warning that the United States would deem hostile any European attempt to recolonize the Western Hemisphere (see Chapters 19, 24). Except for the episode of the Mexican War, it remained detached over the next decades, engaged in its own expansion and traumatic Civil War (see Chapters 19, 24). After 1898, however, the United States frequently intervened in the political and economic life of the region.

The Spanish–American War of 1898 marked the shift in United States' strategy from indifference to intervention. Throughout the nineteenth century, the British had been the principal foreign presence in the region. British investors funded Latin America's mines and railroads, its manufactures flooded the

The Americas: a United States Protectorship in Cuba and the Mexican Nationalization of the Oil Industry

The United States' policy of interventionism—both official and commercial—with regard to Latin America is evident in these excerpts. In the first, the United States asserts its intent to remain involved, and in control, in a presumably independent Cuba. In the second, the Mexican president in 1938 offers as justification for his nation's takeover of foreign oil companies, including United States companies, their outrageous exploitation of the native population.

The Platt Amendment: United States conditions for the independence of Cuba (1902): I. ... [T]he government of Cuba shall never enter into any treaty or other compact with any foreign power or powers which will impair or tend to impair the independence of Cuba. ... III. ... [T]he Government of Cuba consents that the United States may exercise the right to intervene for the preservation of Cuban independence, [and for] the maintenance of a government adequate for the protection of life, property, and individual liberty. ... VII. ... [T]o enable the United States to maintain the independence of Cuba, and to protect the people thereof, as well as for its own defense, the government of Cuba will sell or lease to the United States lands necessary for coaling or naval stations at certain specified points to be agreed upon with the President of the United States.

(From C. I. Bevans, ed., *Treaties and Other International Agreements of the United States of America, 1776–1949*, vol. 8, 1971)

Lazlo Cardenas, president of Mexico 1934–1940, defends the nationalization of the oil industry (1938): It has been repeated *ad nauseam* that the oil industry has brought additional capital for the development and progress of the country. This assertion is an exaggeration. For many years, ... the oil companies have enjoyed great privileges for development and expansion ...; it is these factors of special privilege, together with the prodigious productivity of the oil deposits granted them by the Nation often against public will and law, that represent almost the total amount of this so-called capital.

Potential wealth of the Nation; miserably underpaid native labor; tax exemptions; economic privileges; governmental tolerance—these are the factors of the boom of the Mexican oil industry.

Let us now examine the social contributions of the companies. In how many of the villages bordering on the oil fields is there a hospital, or school or social center, or a sanitary water supply, or an athletic field ...?

Who is not aware of the irritating discrimination governing construction of the company camps? Comfort for the foreign personnel; misery, drabness, and insalubrity for the Mexicans. Refrigeration and protection against tropical insects for the former; indifference and neglect, medical service and supplies always grudgingly provided, for the latter; lower wages and harder, more exhausting labor for our people. ...

(From B. Keane, ed., *Readings in Latin American Civilization, 1942–Present*, 1967)

region's markets, and its navy protected British interests. After 1898, the United States replaced Britain as the region's main foreign investor, developer, exploiter, and master. It made the Caribbean its private lake, and the rest of the region its backyard.

After the 1898 war, Cuba and Puerto Rico, the last two Spanish colonies in the hemisphere, passed to the United States. Puerto Rico was ceded to the United States and, since 1953, has been a "commonwealth" under United States sovereignty. Cuba gained its independence as of 1898 under a constitution drafted according to United States guidelines. In 1901 the "Platt Amendment", part of which is quoted in *Witnesses* above, gave the United States the right to intervene in Cuban affairs in order to maintain order, and to keep a military force stationed at Cuba's Guantánamo Bay. The new state of Cuba was seen as a protectorate of the United States.

The terms of the Platt Amendment predicted future United States policy toward its Latin American neighbors. The point was reiterated in what is called the "Roosevelt Corollary to the Monroe Doctrine." In 1904 President Theodore Roosevelt defined

circumstances under which the United States might intervene in the internal affairs of a Latin American nation: evidence of "chronic wrongdoing," or an "impotence" that threatened civilized norms. Such wrongdoing and ineffectiveness, as defined by the United States, prompted that nation's takeover of Haiti and the Dominican Republic, making protectorates of those Caribbean states.

Panama also became a protectorate. In 1903, the United States encouraged Panama to break away from Colombia. When Panama became established as an independent nation, the United States secured from it on favorable terms (a rental of $250,000 per year, plus a $10 million one-time payment) the land needed to construct a canal across the fifty-mile waist of the isthmus. It obtained a perpetual lease to the ten-mile wide Canal Zone, over which it would exercise sovereign rights. The canal would be a major boon for United States and world shipping, which could span half the globe—from the Asian Pacific, to California, to Caribbean ports, to the European Atlantic ports—without the detour around South America's distant Cape Horn. It was the counterpart of the Suez Canal, built in Egypt by 1869 to link Mediterranean trade by way of the Red Sea with the Persian Gulf and Indian Ocean, avoiding the African Cape of Good Hope (see Chapter 24). Together, the two canals linked the oceans of the world.

When the Canal reached completion in 1914, the economic position of the United States in Latin America had strengthened. Between 1898 and 1914, United States investments in Latin America quintupled. Between 1914 and 1929, they tripled again, while British and other European interests receded. By 1929, almost forty percent of the region's imports came from the United States, which in turn absorbed almost thirty-three percent of its exports. United States businessmen funded copper factories in Chile, oil ventures in Mexico and Venezuela, tin mines in Bolivia, and two-thirds of Cuba's sugar production. Some companies—such as Boston's United Fruit, which built itself a "banana republic" in Central America—had huge territorial holdings.

Mexico   The stake that its investors had in Mexico prompted the United States to intervene when revolution broke out in 1910. The Mexican revolution was more than a revolt against the autocratic rule of Porfirio Díaz (1830–1915; see Chapter 19). It was also a broad protest of peasants and workers (mostly Indian and mestizo) against an oppressive social hierarchy topped by a landowner elite and foreign business interests.

Strongman Díaz had welcomed United States capital, and American citizens held Mexican land, mineral resources, and public utilities. Aiming to protect those interests and avoid disruption so close to its borders, the United States supported Mexican leaders it considered "moderate" and opposed those with revolutionary intentions—such as the peasant leader, Emiliano Zapata (1879–1913), and the colorful Francisco "Pancho" Villa (1877–1923), who headed a coalition of rebellious peasants, workers, and cowboys. In 1913, the United States President Woodrow Wilson (1856–1924) permitted arms shipments to the counterrevolutionaries. In 1914, with the unjustified arrest of United States sailors as a pretext, the United States navy occupied the port of Veracruz. In 1916, when Pancho Villa led a raid into New Mexico, Wilson dispatched General John J. Pershing (1860–1948) to capture him (which he failed to do).

These inglorious interventions altered nothing. Mexico formed a new government, whose 1917 constitution gravely threatened the interests of native and foreign elites. It seized estates and distributed land to the peasants; established collective organizations and a favorable labor code for workers; introduced limited suffrage (men could vote only for the official party's candidate, and women not until 1954); limited the role of the Roman Catholic Church; and confiscated without compensation all sub-soil rights,

including those of United States investors. Neither wholly revolutionary nor truly democratic, the new Mexican government achieved stability and promoted the general welfare, instituting public education, public health programs, and irrigation projects.

The Mexican revolution might have prompted a chain of revolutions in Latin America, as some feared. The Great Depression of the 1930s, which plunged the whole region into desperation (see Chapter 27), also threatened to do so. Dependent on the export of a few commodities, the Latin American economy suffered when demand sank. The elites found themselves without cash, while laborers and peasants grew restive as unemployment and hunger struck. Yet discontent did not lead to revolution. The region's strongmen, or *caudillos*, would not let it do so.

The Rule of the *Caudillos*   The enduring patterns of Latin American society—the intertwined elite of landowners, military officers, and churchmen—created the *caudillo* (see Chapter 19). The Latin American commodity economy called him into action. The wealth it generated was locked up for the consumption of the rich, and neither flowed to the poor nor stimulated more complex economic enterprises. This system yielded depressingly what some experts have termed "growth without development." It magnified social inequities and necessitated caudillo despots to keep order. From the 1930s through the 1970s, most nations of Latin America have experienced the rule of such bosses. Three may serve as examples: Argentina, Chile, and Brazil.

In Argentina, during the 1930s, dominated by landowning and military elites, the middle and working classes supported the rise to power of the army colonel Juan Perón (1895–1974), elected president in 1946. Backed by his dynamic and beautiful wife, Eva Duarte (1919–1952; "Evita," to her admirers), Perón redistributed wealth, promoted industrialization, and nationalized industries, measures that stimulated uncontrolled inflation and strained national finances. After 1949 the economy worsened, and Perón fled in the face of a military coup in 1955. For the next three decades, Argentina alternated between military and civilian strongmen (among them Perón and his second wife, who returned from 1973 to 1976). The vicious regime in power from 1976 to 1983 murdered more than 10,000 people, and imprisoned, tortured, and "disappeared" many more. The mothers of "missing" adult children, swept up in deadly raids by the military in charge, paraded regularly in the capital city of Buenos Aires to bear witness to their brutality. Since 1983, civilian, democratic governments have taken hold and spurred economic development.

In Brazil, a military coup elevated caudillo Getúlio Vargas (1883–1954), who ruled from 1930 to 1945, and again from 1951 to 1954. Vargas dismissed parliament and canceled elections, while he instituted censorship and a secret police force and encouraged rapid economic modernization. As leftist and liberal movements gained ground in the early 1960s, the military seized power in 1964 in a coup backed by the United States. Protests from the moderate middle class and the social revolutionary left were ruthlessly suppressed. Nevertheless, huge foreign investment spurred an economic miracle, in which industrial exports—rather than coffee and such commodities—generated real wealth for some Brazilians, without alleviating the poverty of others.

Brazil remained under military control from 1964 to 1985. Since then, democratically elected leaders have attempted to restore the free market, while confronting the problems of high inflation and debt. The exploitation of the Amazon River region, resulting in environmental degradation of global consequence, has raised concern, and prompted Brazil to host a United Nations conference on the environment in 1992. During its rocky postwar career, Brazil has industrialized and urbanized, its prosperity threatened still by the great poverty of the masses and rapid population growth.

In Chile, the working and middle classes forged coalition governments from the 1930s through the 1960s. In 1970, a moderate socialist government was elected with reformer Salvador Allende Gossens (1908–1973) as head. Allende's reforms included redistribution of land and the nationalization of banks and industries, especially copper-mining, in which United States entrepreneurs were heavily involved. But these measures triggered uncontrolled inflation and angered the middle classes.

In 1973, supported by the CIA (Central Intelligence Agency) of the United States, a military junta seized control, leaving Allende dead and his government finished. The new regime arrested 13,000 people immediately and, over the next seventeen years, killed some 2000. Under the repressive but modernizing regime of Augusto Pinochet (1915–), which lasted from 1973 until 1989, major industries were restored to the private sector, labor controlled, welfare services reduced, inflation lowered, exports increased, and the economy diversified. In 1989, free elections were reinstated.

The United States often supported the dictators and generals who protected the business interests of its nationals. Yet since the 1930s, it has moved away from the direct exploitation of the Latin American states. Franklin Delano Roosevelt announced the nation's benign intention to respect the rights of other nations in his "Good Neighbor" policy of 1933. In 1948, it helped form the Organization of American States to promote hemisphere solidarity against the threat of communist activity abroad. Postwar presidents Truman, Eisenhower, Kennedy, Johnson, and Nixon supported development in Latin America, as well as programs to bolster its military and police.

Response to Communism   In the 1950s and 1960s, the Cold War duel with the Soviet Union (see Chapter 30) added a new dimension to United States involvement in Latin America. Alert to the possibility of communist intervention in what it considered its own backyard, the United States assisted even corrupt and repressive anti-communist governments (see Chapter 30). **Counter-insurgency**—a crusade against leftist revolutionary activity—became a primary objective of United States foreign policy. The United States sent military advisers to lend assistance in Latin America, and trained and equipped native armies and police forces.

Occasionally United States forces intervened to direct the outcome of Latin American conflicts. In 1954, the United States sent troops to Guatemala to oust a left-leaning, reformist government. In 1979, it intervened in Nicaragua to prop up the conservative regime of Anastasio Somoza (1925–1980). The hostility aroused by this intervention boosted popular support for the Marxist regime of the Sandinistas who then took power. (The Sandinistas were named after the revolutionary hero Cesar Augusto Sandino, murdered in 1934.) Into the 1980s, through covert channels and without congressional approval, United States funds supported the Contra ("opponents") rebels against the Sandinista government. (In 1990, the Nicaraguan people themselves voted the Sandinistas out of power, electing a centrist government under Violeta Chamorro, b. 1929.) As recently as 1983, 1989, and 1993, United States troops intervened in the nations of Grenada, Panama, and Haiti.

Since 1960, the Latin American nation of greatest concern for United States policymakers has been Cuba, just ninety miles offshore of Florida. The United States managed the Cuban government during the early years of its nominal independence. In 1933, the strongman Fulgencio Batista (1901–1973) took over the government with United States support. For nearly thirty years, backed by the elites and the military, he ran a thoroughly corrupt administration deeply implicated with organized crime interests, which neglected and betrayed the island's already impoverished people.

In 1959, the revolutionary Fidel Castro (1927–), portrayed on p, 855, headed guerrilla forces that ousted Batista and his supporters; Cuba's wealthy and professional elites fled. Castro installed a socialist regime that redistributed land, nationalized industries, and established health services and universal education for the people Batista had despised. The local Communist party embraced Castro's government, while the Soviet Union supplied Cuba with arms and loans, and purchased its sugar. Tiny Cuba became a major center of world communism.

The displacement of a tame dictatorship by a Communist state in its own Caribbean lake alarmed United States officials. Cautious diplomacy broke

Castro's triumph: *In Cuba in 1959, the guerrilla forces of Fidel Castro drove out the corrupt government that had mortgaged the welfare of the people to American sugar companies. This photograph shows a triumphant Castro embracing one of his young supporters as he sweeps through Cuba to take power.*

down in 1961. The United States had backed an unsuccessful invasion by Cuban exiles at the Bay of Pigs. In response, the Soviets planted nuclear missiles on the island, which could easily reach the United States. In the tensest moment of his brief presidency, John F. Kennedy (1917–1963) "did not blink," as an adviser put it. His refusal to be intimidated forced the Soviets to back down. The United States agreed to plan no further invasions of Cuba.

The crisis past, relations between Cuba and the United States remained volatile, exacerbated by the activism of Cuban exiles who were now resident in the United States. By the 1990s, with the collapse of Soviet communism (see Chapter 30), together with the aging of the charismatic Castro, the tension of those relations finally eased.

Even in the early 1960s, at the zenith of the Cuban challenge, communism did not spread, as many had feared, to other Latin American nations. The containment of communism was due in part to United States-sponsored repression; but communism also failed because Latin American leaders made earnest efforts to reorient the economy so as to benefit the masses as well as the elites. They built new industries, adopted modern technologies, sought a broader spectrum of foreign investment, and diversified production. They accomplished the long-needed breakthrough, escaping the region's narrow dependence on a few export commodities. In addition, without taking the path of Cuban communism, they nationalized some economic functions, and instituted health and welfare programs.

By the 1980s, caudillism began to yield to democracy. A free electorate chose governments in

Argentina, Brazil, Mexico, Nicaragua, and Paraguay. Traces of older social hierarchies, concentrations of land ownership in elite circles, militarism, ethnic tensions, and abusive labor relationships persist in the region. But these appear to be yielding gradually to democratization and economic modernization. Whether Latin America's economic development can keep pace with its unrestrained population growth remains an open question.

The nationalist revolutions of the early 1800s promised an end to colonialism. That goal may at last have been accomplished at the close of the twentieth century. With the transfer of the Canal Zone to the nation of Panama in 1978 and the emancipation of a few Caribbean islands and mainland enclaves still in French, British, or Dutch hands, Latin America has crystallized as a region of largely independent, self-governing states. The United States, the last imperialist in the region, by its economic, political, and military interventions sometimes promoted, sometimes impeded, but in the end supports that achievement—as a good neighbor might.

The Domino Game: the United States in Asia

The United States might view the Caribbean as its lake, and the Americas as the paired continents of its hemisphere. But Asia was far away. Although the United States sought commercial access it had initially no large ambitions in that region. Yet the ideological struggles of the Cold War era defined Asia as a testing ground. The states of Asia were like dominoes, in the simile conceived in 1954 by United States president Dwight D. Eisenhower (1890–1969). If one fell to the alien destiny of communism, all would fall. To avert that outcome, the United States entered, and lost, the domino game.

The United States looked to Asia beginning in the 1850s, as it raced to share in the wealth that international commerce brought the old imperialists of Europe. Its goal, expressed in the "open door" policy enunciated in 1899, was commercial access to China, Japan, and other rich markets (see Chapter 24). Commercial activity, however, led to territorial acquisitions. To support its fleet in an age of steam power, the United States needed fueling stations and naval bases. It began to gather up Pacific islands. From 1851, the United States had a protectorate over Hawaii, acquiring the rights for a naval base at Pearl Harbor by 1887 and annexing the whole area in 1898. It also obtained rights to Midway (1867), Wake Island (1898), and American Samoa (1899). In 1898, it acquired the island of Guam and the archipelago of the Philippines.

The Philippines The Philippines, held by the United States from 1898 to 1946, was the United

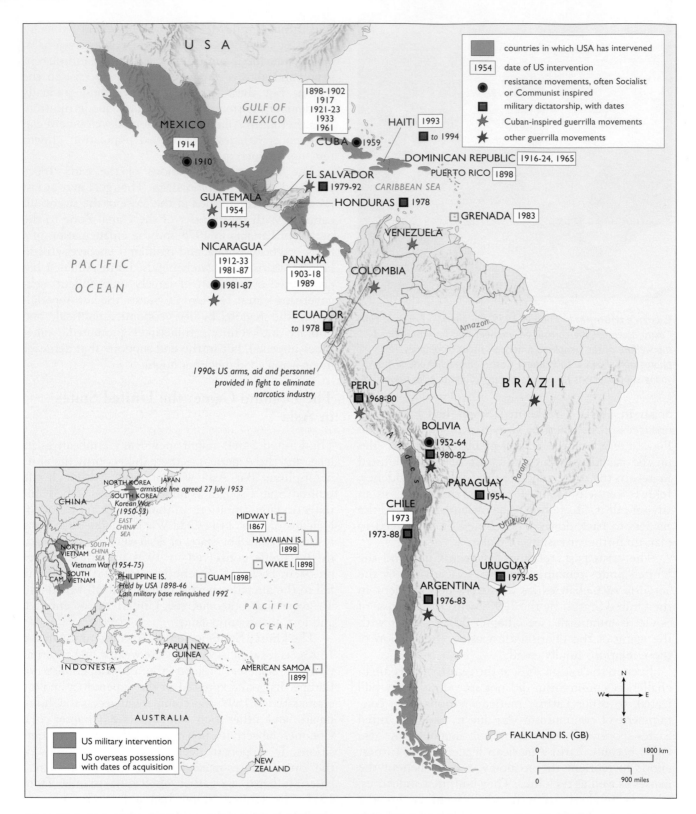

Map 29.4 United States Intervention in Latin America and Asia: *The imperialist ventures of the United States beyond the borders of North America began in 1898, with a series of interventions in Latin America. During the same period many guerrilla movements took form in resistance to established powers. These complex political changes are indicated in simplified form above. In the Pacific, meanwhile, the United States acquired several possessions between 1867 and 1899, and intervened militarily in Korea (1950–1953) and Vietnam (1954–1975), as shown in the inset map. What conditions might be necessary for the achievement of political stability throughout Latin America?*

States' first major non-continental territorial acquisition. The United States had claimed it with difficulty, overcoming ardent native resistance and opposition at home. During the 1930s, it negotiated with Filipino leaders a schedule for independence. In 1941, the Japanese invaded, causing the evacuation of the United States naval garrison and abandoning the inhabitants to a harsh occupation.

In 1946, the Philippines became independent according to schedule (although United States military bases remained until 1992). A landowning elite continued to exploit impoverished peasantry as parliamentary government gave way to increasingly despotic rule after 1965, with the election of Ferdinand Marcos (1917–1989). Marcos' regime became more and more corrupt and violent. Conservative elites supported his suppression of communist and Islamic opposition even as, in 1983, 1 million Filipinos defiantly marched in the funeral procession of his assassinated opponent Benigno Aquino. In 1986, Benigno's widow, Corazon Aquino (1933–), successfully challenged Marcos' reelection, which had been marred by irregularities. Marcos and his hated wife Imelda fled the country whose unsteady economic condition wad due in part to their depredations. Many social and economic problems remain unresolved, but the Philippines have attained democratic government under Aquino and her successors.

Korea The postwar involvement of the United States in Korea and Vietnam developed in response to the perceived threat of communism, which had expanded into eastern Europe and Asia (see Chapter 30). Policymakers feared that communism threatened Africa and the Americas as well.

The partition of Korea at the thirty-eighth parallel of latitude at the end of World War II had positioned two hostile regimes face to face: the communist People's Republic of Korea in the north; and the Republic of Korea in the south. The Korean War broke out suddenly in 1950 when 100,000 northern troops invaded the south and seized the capital Seoul. The North Korean leader, trained and installed by the Soviets, had likely acted at Stalin's prompting. The United States, with a large occupation force based in Japan (see above), saw the invasion as an act of communist aggression that, if not contained, could spread throughout east Asia. It called upon other nations of the recently-constituted United Nations (see Chapter 30) to join in the defense of South Korea. Although a joint effort, the commander-in-chief was the American Douglas MacArthur, and most of the troops came from the United States.

The United Nations forces repulsed the North Korean advance and moved northward toward the Chinese border. About 200,000 Chinese troops swept in from adjacent Manchuria, repelled MacArthur's forces, and, early in 1951, took Seoul a second time.

MacArthur freed Seoul and proposed extending the war to China, his aggressive approach leading to his dismissal by President Truman. Peace talks began in the summer of 1951, concluding only in 1953. A new boundary was drawn between south and north, with a demilitarized zone at the crucial border.

Although the United States had not fought alone in Korea, the war was in many ways an American war, not least because United States forces suffered 34,000 fatalities. In addition, the United States had instigated the military response to what might have remained a civil war, setting a precedent for intervention in the internal affairs of other Asian nations. And the United States had declared its determination to battle communist advance in Asia.

Vietnam The Korean war prefigured the Vietnam war, a conflict that occupied American attention for an entire generation. Part of the peninsula of Indochina, Vietnam had often suffered invasion—by the Chinese for centuries, and more recently by the French, who had seized almost all of Indochina by 1897 (see Chapters 8, 24). The French occupation triggered a nationalist movement, led by Ho Chi Minh (1890–1969) after World War I. In 1919, appealing to the principle of self-determination, Ho attempted and failed to persuade the drafters of the Paris treaties to free Vietnam as it had freed the subject nationalities of Europe (see Chapter 26). When they did not, he turned to communism, whose Comintern (see Chapter 28) offered friendly support to anti-colonial movements. In Moscow, Ho learned how to organize an insurgent struggle. In 1930, he formed the Indochinese Communist Party.

When the Japanese took over Indochina from the Vichy French during World War II, Ho formed the multi-party League for the Independence of Vietnam—the Viet Minh. In the meantime, nationalist fighters in Vietnam waged guerrilla war against the Japanese. Repatriated at war's end, Ho promulgated the Vietnamese Declaration of Independence, echoing principles drawn from the American Declaration and other classic sources of Western political thought. That document proclaimed the establishment of the Democratic Republic of Vietnam, with its capital at Hanoi.

Independence was not so easily won, however. Even as the Japanese evacuated, the British occupation forces yielded Vietnam to the French, who returned to reclaim their colonial rights. Vietnamese nationalists now fought the French in a prolonged struggle that ended only in 1954, with the obliteration of a French garrison at Dien Bien Phu, and the humiliation of that nation. Despite the sacrifice of tens of thousands of lives, the French had failed to quell the resistance of a people intent on independence, skilled in guerrilla tactics, and supported by the Chinese and the Soviets.

At first, the United States was also inclined to support Vietnamese independence. It reversed that policy and supported the French instead when the Korean War broke out in 1950. By 1954, the United States was paying seventy-eight percent of the costs of French operations in Vietnam. When the French pulled out, the United States went in.

The United States had no historic mission in Vietnam. What drove it to become involved in suppressing the Vietnamese struggle for independence? Why did a nation that had itself originated in a war for independence muster its resources to suppress another engaged in the same attempt?

The critical factor was the presence of communism. The Soviet Union's aims were patently expansionist. In 1949, moreover, a communist government had established itself in China, on Vietnam's border.

In 1950, a communist-inspired invasion of South Korea had dragged the United States into war. In 1954, president Eisenhower proposed his domino theory. Vietnam appeared to be the last bulwark against a communist Asia. The line, it was decided, must be drawn in Vietnam.

The 1954 Geneva Accords did not create an independent Vietnam, although Ho Chi Minh had badly beaten the French. It partitioned the nation at the seventeenth parallel of latitude, giving Ho the north, now communist. The last of the Accords, the Final Declaration, provided for elections throughout the country, north and south, in 1956. Without interference, the likely outcome in 1956 would have been a united Vietnam, under communist leadership. To forestall this event, the United States refused to sign the Final Declaration and assisted Ngo Dinh Diem (1901–1963) in his bid for power in the south.

Diem's actions triggered what came to be known as the Vietnam War. A French-educated Roman Catholic in a nation with a Buddhist majority, the corrupt autocrat Diem suppressed both political and religious opposition. He refused to hold the elections mandated by the Geneva settlement. That decision meant war. Ho Chi Minh's army mobilized. In 1960, thousands of pro-communist nationalists joined in the National Liberation Front to oppose Diem's autocratic government from within South Vietnam. They formed a guerrilla army supplied and guided from the north. These insurgents Diem contemptuously called the "Viet Cong" (Vietnamese communists). The combined activity of the North Vietnamese regular soldiers with the southern Viet Cong,

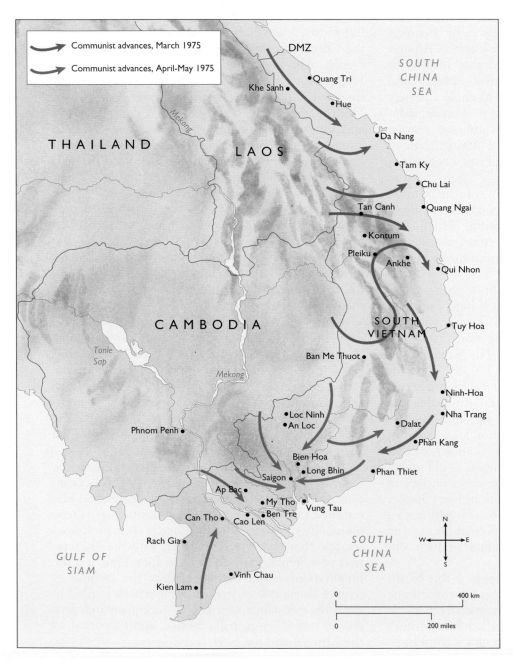

Map 29.5 The Fall of South Vietnam, 1975: *US forces left Vietnam in 1973, having achieved neither peace nor victory. In the spring of 1975, north Vietnamese troops and their southern allies swept rapidly from the north and from refuges in Laos and Cambodia to seize Saigon, capital of South Vietnam. What were the reasons for the United States' decision to leave Vietnam in 1973?*

Give Peace a Chance: *American involvement in Vietnam dragged on fruitlessly, leading the superpower to employ tactics that discredited the aggressor without damaging the defender. In this famous photograph from June 8, 1972 (left) that aroused horror worldwide (though the attack was accidental), young children flee from an American napalm bombing.*

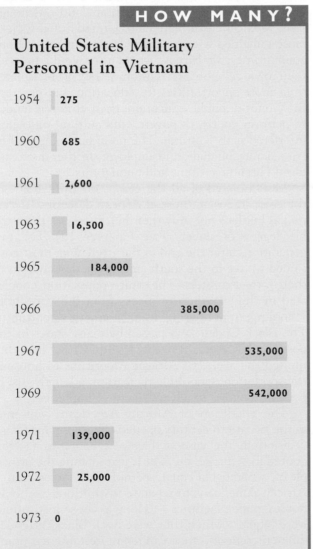

HOW MANY?

United States Military Personnel in Vietnam

Year	Personnel
1954	275
1960	685
1961	2,600
1963	16,500
1965	184,000
1966	385,000
1967	535,000
1969	542,000
1971	139,000
1972	25,000
1973	0

Source: W. R. Keylor, *The Twentieth-Century World: An International History,* 3rd ed. (Oxford: Oxford University Press, 1996), pp. 373, 375.

invisible within the southern population, frustrated all attempts to snatch the south from Ho's communist north.

Diem was a disappointment. Disgusted by his corruption, inefficiency, and intolerance—he ordered the destruction of Buddhist temples, among other atrocities—the United States withdrew support in 1963. That action encouraged a group of generals to assassinate Diem and seize power. A stream of generals ruled in turn in the south. The regime remained throughout an unsavory ally for the United States, difficult to defend to the public at home, and incapable of managing the war effort unassisted.

From 1954 to 1968, under presidents Eisenhower, Kennedy, and Johnson, the United States escalated its involvement in Vietnam, as *How Many?* left shows. In 1954, 275 Americans were advising the South Vietnamese army. By 1960, that figure had more than doubled to 685; by the end of 1961, it had risen to 2600; and by the time of President Kennedy's assassination in 1963, to 16,500. Meanwhile, the United States sent military aid rising to hundreds of millions of dollars annually. In 1965, the United States launched bombing raids in North Vietnam, and, for the first time, sent ground troops to the south—and the die was cast. By the end of 1965, there were 184,000 American soldiers in Vietnam; by 1966, 385,000; by early 1969, some 542,000. Now the United States was not merely an adviser to what it saw as the better side in a civil war. It was a combatant in an alien struggle on the other side of the globe.

As the numbers of ground forces mounted, Americans at home grew restive, then critical, then angry (see Chapter 30). A "credibility gap" grew wider as officials reported gains—measured in the daily "body count" of dead enemies, many of them civilian—while the Viet Cong and North Vietnamese regulars grew more numerous. Their Tet offensive of 1968, launched on a sacred Vietnamese holiday, showed that resistance was powerful and exposed the failure of United States officials to comprehend the depth of nationalist determination.

After 1968, the United States sought to find an exit from the Vietnam quagmire. President Johnson (1908–1973) signaled his awareness of the failure of his policies in Vietnam by withdrawing from the 1968 election. The new president Richard M. Nixon (1913–1994) promised to secure "peace with honor." By a policy of "Vietnamization," he gradually withdrew United States troops (only 25,000 remained at end 1972) and transferred military responsibilities to regular South Vietnamese forces. To cover the withdrawal, he intensified bombing in the north and in the contiguous states of Laos and Cambodia, thereby drawn into the maelstrom of the war. In 1973, Nixon accomplished the final withdrawal of United States troops—withdrawal, without honor or victory.

That withdrawal had the effect of abandoning the South Vietnamese to sure defeat. The 1973 settlement did not bring peace. By 1975, the North Vietnamese army had taken the southern capital of Saigon, and established dominion over a united Vietnam—an outcome for which Ho Chi Minh struggled for half a century before he died in 1969, just short of its fulfillment. Drawn into the conflict, Laos and Cambodia also fell to native communist movements, of which the Cambodian Khmer Rouge undertook an unprecidently vicious campaign against its own citizenry (see Chapter 30). Twenty years after the French withdrawal, a generation after the close of World War II, after nearly 58,000 American deaths and millions of Vietnamese deaths, after the rupture of confidence at home and the generation of implacable hostility abroad, Indochina (except for Thailand and Myanmar) was communist.

After Vietnam, the United States redefined its policy in Asia. Henceforth, it would seek commercial agreements, support friendly states, and promote a human rights agenda in the region. The domino game was over. The last imperialist limped home.

The Color Line: Conflict at Home

At home, the citizens and leaders of the United States faced the moral and social problems left by an earlier imperialist era. In pursuit of their Manifest Destiny, the European descendants of the first settlers, and the European immigrants who came in waves to join them, grabbed the land that stretched between the Atlantic and Pacific coasts. They seized it from peoples—Amerindian natives and Hispanic settlers of what had been Mexican territory—who became dispossessed of land and heritage alike. At the same time, the descendants of former slaves whose labor had sustained the economy of the old south remained still, as the twentieth century opened, unintegrated into society and barred from the means of progress.

A Visible Difference   Forgotten amid abundance, these groups shared one visible feature—their skin was ruddy, brown, or black. The exclusion of people of color from twealth and power in the world's wealthiest and most powerful nation became the foremost social issue of the century. Democratic principles and habits

of compassion for others alike had always faltered when they approached the color line.

By 1900, the Amerindian tribes of the United States had all been deprived of their lands and freedom (see Chapter 19). Some had been moved to territories set aside for the purpose; others resisted, and were forcibly driven into those **reservations**. They were wrested from the environment and the economy that had shaped their religion, language, and customs, and that were essential to their self-definition. In alien settings, they languished. Even when government programs offered opportunities for social and economic advancement, few individuals or tribes took advantage of them.

In the southwestern region of the United States, settlers wrested land from ranchers and planters of Mexican descent. Landless Mexican workers became subjects of the Anglophone United States. These were followed by waves of Mexican immigrants, for whom low-paid work in the United States offered a better opportunity than their homeland. Although some Mexicans assimilated into United States society, most remained a caste apart. Living in self-defined communities, or *barrios*, where they could practice their own religion and customs, they were isolated from most opportunities for education and progress. In systems of public education, their children tended to perform poorly, as poverty and cultural difference interfered with learning. The prejudice exhibited by bureaucrats, officials, and employers further disadvantaged Hispanic citizens and immigrants.

Most isolated of all the groups on the far side of the color line were those of African descent who carried as burdens not only their blackness but the terrible legacy of slavery (see Chapter 19). For two generations after the end of the Civil War, most continued to live in the south among the descendants of their former masters. The white population cooperated in the exclusion of blacks from the vote, from schooling, from housing, from economic opportunity. The Black Codes, laws passed by many states in the post-Civil War era, gave way to "Jim Crow" laws that limited the access of African Americans to housing, transportation, schooling, recreation, a lengthy list of possible avenues to advancement or happiness.

The condition of African Americans worsened as the twentieth century opened. The Supreme Court decision in the case of Plessy v. Ferguson (1896), quoted in *Witnesses* on p. 861, introducing the principle of "separate but equal," permitted the relegation of African Americans to separate institutions—schools, houses, public facilities—as long as those institutions were "equal" (which they were not). Blacks attended different schools, ate in different restaurants, drank from different water fountains, and sat in different sections of public buses.

Southern society prevented any deviation from these norms by a strategy of terror. The Ku Klux Klan, formed soon after the Civil War and reconstituted in 1915, was a loose network of secret societies that championed the white man's vision of the south. Disguised in fear-inspiring white robes and hoods, Klansmen terrorized blacks and their white supporters, leaving behind them as a sign of their implacable hostility a burning wooden cross. Klansmen often joined in lynchings, the illicit execution by hanging of those deemed guilty of crimes or hated without reason. In the 1880s, these had mounted to a high of over one hundred per year. They subsided, then returned, tripling in the key Depression year 1932–1933.

Despite terror, hatred, and discrimination, African Americans built their own neighborhoods and communities in the homeland they had never chosen. Christianized under slavery, they formed their own black churches (mostly Baptist and Methodist) headed by black pastors, who became the acknowledged leaders of African American communities. With the impediments to legal marriage and property ownership that slavery imposed now gone, they formed strong families and worked to secure land and housing, although they were more often forced into tenancy and sharecropping.

The Americas: Racial Equality and Racial Separatism in the United States

Between the end of the Civil War in 1865 and the Civil Rights Act of 1964 lay an interim of just under a century in which Americans of African descent, most the offspring of former slaves, suffered great wrongs, including discrimination in housing, employment, and education. A major victory in the battle to turn that tide of discrimination was won in 1954, with the United States Supreme Court decision in the case of Brown v. Board of Education, excerpted in the first passage here. Martin Luther King, Jr., was the principal figure in the African-American struggle to gain the rights promised by the Amendments 14 to 16 of the United States Constitution. The second passage contains one of his statements giving the reasons for his resistance. During the 1960s, the struggle for civil rights for African-Americans became increasingly bitter and sometimes violent. The Black Panther Party, self-styled as revolutionary, announced its principles in its founding document, a party platform in 1966, of which some points are given in the third passage.

The US Supreme Court decision in the case Brown v. Board of Education of Topeka, overturning the "separate but equal" principle established by Plessy v. Ferguson (1896), orders school integration "with all deliberate speed" (1954): Today, education is perhaps the most important function of state and local governments. Compulsory school attendance laws and the great expenditures for education both demonstrate our recognition of the importance of education to our democratic society. ... In these days, it is doubtful that any child may reasonably be expected to succeed in life if he is denied the opportunity of an education. Such an opportunity ... is a right which must be made available to all on equal terms.

We come then to the question presented: Does segregation of children in the public schools solely on the basis of race, even though the physical facilities and other "tangible" factors may be equal, deprive the children of the minority group of equal educational opportunities? We believe that it does.
(Brown v. Board of Education of Topeka, 347 US 483–496, 1954)

Martin Luther King, Jr.: a letter from Birmingham Jail (1963): My Dear Fellow Clergymen:
... I think I should indicate why I am here in Birmingham. ... I am in Birmingham because injustice is here. ...

You deplore the demonstrations taking place in Birmingham. ... It is unfortunate that demonstrations are taking place ... but it is even more unfortunate that the city's white power structure left the Negro community with no alternative.

We [Black Americans] have been waiting for more than 340 years for our constitutional and God-given rights. The nations of Asia and Africa are moving with jetlike speed toward gaining political independence, but we still creep at horse-and-buggy pace toward gaining a cup of coffee at a lunch counter.
(Martin Luther King, letter from Birmingham Jail, April 16, 1963; eds. A. P. Blaustein and R. L. Zangrando, 1968)

In 1966, the extreme Black Panther Party announced in its Platform its demands for autonomy and for compensation from "white racist" Americans:
1. *We want freedom. We want power to determine the destiny of our Black Community.* We believe that black people will not be free until we are able to determine our destiny.
2. *We want full employment for our people.* We believe that the federal government is responsible and obligated to give every man employment or a guaranteed income. ...
3. *We want an end to the robbery by the white man of our Black Community.* We believe that this racist government has robbed us and now we are demanding the overdue debt [projected during Reconstruction, after the Civil War] of forty acres and two mules as restitution for slave labor and mass murder of black people. ...
4. *We want decent housing, fit for shelter of human beings.* ...
5. *We want education for our people that exposes the true nature of this decadent American society. We want education that teaches us our true history and our role in the present-day society.* ...
(from http://lists.village.virginia.edu/sixties/HTML_docs/Resources/Primary/Manifestos/Panther_platform.html)

Martin Luther King, Jr., August 1963

Americans of African descent faced a long struggle for civil rights and guarantee of social and economic justice. Largely through the efforts of Martin Luther King, Jr.—shown here in August 1963 outside the White House (above)—a landmark Civil Rights Act was signed in 1964. The fiercely committed Malcolm X is seen here summoning his followers to action (below right). He holds aloft a newspaper with the headline "Our Freedom Can't Wait!" The unfinished nature of the quest for equality is illustrated in another photograph (below left), where striking Memphis (Tennessee) sanitation workers, most African American, wearing placards saying

"I am a man," parade in front of a row of National Guardsmen with rifles ready and bayonets affixed.

How do you think the soldiers regarded the strikers? And the strikers the soldiers?

Memphis sanitation workers' strike, March 1968

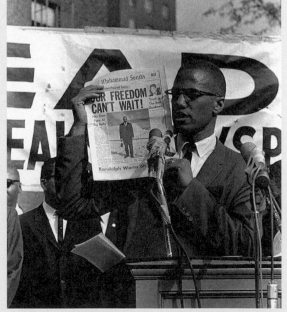

Malcolm X, New York, 1963

 To continue your investigation of this topic, please go to www.prenhall.com/king for the related **WINDOWS** on the **WEB** activity

Voices of Protest African American leaders had different visions of how best to promote their people. Scholars often note the classic opposition between two late nineteenth-century figures: Booker T. Washington (1856–1915), a freed slave; and William E. B. du Bois (1868–1963), the mixed descendent of Africans and Europeans, raised and educated in the north. Rising from the mine pits where he worked as a child immediately after emancipation, Washington became an educator, a reformer, and a public advocate on behalf of all African Americans and through his own efforts and intelligence. He urged upon his own community the values of hard work, especially in industrial tasks that would earn laborers respect and decent wages. He was cautiously non-revolutionary in his rhetoric, seeking to persuade white listeners of the diligence and benevolence of blacks rather than to frighten them with unsettling demands.

Du Bois took a different approach. A brilliant theorist and writer, he received a doctoral degree from Harvard (1895) and subsequently taught at Atlanta University in Georgia. Despite his mainstream credentials, Du Bois was no academic onlooker. He criticized Washington for kowtowing to white audiences and underestimating black competency. Calling on the "talented tenth" of black leaders to organize for political action, he formed the Niagara Movement in 1905, which in 1909, inspired the foundation of the National Association for the Advancement of Colored People (the NAACP), still a major force in the advocacy of equal rights for blacks. In 1961, concluding that American society would never truly welcome its black citizens, Du Bois joined the Communist Party, and moved to Ghana, in Africa, where he died in 1963. In such works as *The Souls of Black Folk* (1903) Du Bois argued for the radical emancipation of African Americans from deep-seated attitudes that he considered profoundly racist. In that work he diagnosed what he saw as the incapacity of white Americans to cross or erase the "color line," which he believed to be the defining issue of the twentieth century.

The color line grew bolder in the 1920s and 1930s when blacks emigrated in large numbers from the south to northern cities. As opportunities for unskilled workers shrank in the south (and most blacks were unskilled because segregation patterns barred them from high-quality schooling and training), they hoped to work in northern factories, on the railroads, and in the streets. Transplanted, they found that the north was also segregated. Denied access to the better schools and neighborhoods, they formed their own neighborhoods and church-centered communities. In isolated neighborhoods called ghettoes, African Americans led a life apart from other Americans—separate but not equal.

It was to these African Americans that Marcus Garvey (1887–1940) spoke most passionately. A Jamaica-born activist, Garvey lived in the United States from 1916 to 1927. Pointing to the long record of European mistreatment of non-Europeans, Garvey promoted rebellion and secession. He urged blacks "back to Africa," to build that continent from which their ancestors had been ripped centuries before. Convicted in 1925 of mail fraud in the management of his Black Star steamship line (founded to carry his followers back to Africa), Garvey was deported from the United States in 1927.

Among those who heard the voices of African American leaders calling for a new pride in the face of white dominance were the artists, performers, and writers of the Harlem Renaissance. The lights blazed nightly on New York City's Lenox Avenue and 135th Street where well-dressed blacks and radically chic whites visited clubs and theaters and conversed heatedly on the streets. Soon the voices were silenced by the Depression, which hurt black Americans even more than whites. Now movement leaders gathered into organizations such as the NAACP. The 1930s saw the political consciousness of the larger African American community broaden, as though in preparation for the vital struggles ahead.

The Harlem Renaissance was in full swing and the Great Depression had not yet stalled black progress when the greatest of African American leaders, Martin Luther King, Jr. (1929–1968), portrayed in *Windows On* on p. 862 was born. A minister and a minister's son, the recipient of a doctoral degree in theology, King was a worthy successor to Washington and du Bois. He combined Washington's understanding of the need to strive for advancement within a predominantly white society, with du Bois' deeper critique of that society's hostility to black success.

The Civil Rights Movement King began by protesting unjust barriers—the segregation of public transportation and public education. He became the prophet of the Civil Rights movement, which grew from resistance to bus segregation by a lone black woman, Rosa Parks (1913–), in 1955, to the high tide of 1964, when the Civil Rights Act was signed into law, barring discrimination by color in public facilities or in employment. More than any other single figure, he achieved widespread acknowledgment of the right—if not yet the reality—of black Americans to live, learn, and work as freely as their white counterparts. It may have been his great success that prompted an assassin to shoot King in 1968, when he was not yet forty and at the zenith of his career.

Du Bois' NAACP had prepared the way during the 1930s and 1940s for the drive against segregation that King led in the 1950s. Its team of lawyers brought cases that exposed segregationist practices. Chief counsel of the NAACP legal team from 1940 to 1961 was attorney Thurgood Marshall (1908–1993), appointed in 1967 the first African American justice of the Supreme Court. In 1954, the NAACP won a landmark judgment that effectively overturned Plessy v. Ferguson. In Brown v. Board of Education of Topeka, the Supreme Court ordered that "separate" schools were by nature unequal and discriminatory against black citizens. The next year, it ordered the twenty-one states that had segregated school systems to desegregate "with all deliberate speed." That mammoth victory opened the floodgates of reform.

In 1955, King led the boycott of the bus system of Montgomery, Alabama, that had been triggered by the arrest of Rosa Parks. In 1956, the Supreme Court vindicated that protest, declaring the segregation unconstitutional. The next year, with other leaders King worked to secure the enrollment of nine black students in the main white high school in Little Rock, Arkansas. A reluctant President Eisenhower sent federal troops to handle the crisis, which was resolved only in 1959.

These victories won, King and other civil rights leaders broadened their agenda. Through the SCLC (Southern Christian Leadership Conference), King urged a program of nonviolent resistance, based in part on the methods of Mohandas Gandhi. With the organizations CORE (Congress of Racial Equality) and SNCC (Student Nonviolent Coordinating Committee), activists confronted discrimination through nonviolent resistance. A dynamic coalition of young black southern activists, supported by northern white university students, won battles of conscience in lunch counters, waiting rooms, and polling booths across the south.

These resisters found violence turned against them, as segregationists with policemen and firemen fought against peaceful demonstrators. The rising tide of conflict compelled President John F. Kennedy to introduce a strong proposal for civil rights legislation. When King and 250,000 people came to Washington in August 1963, to proclaim their goal of racial justice, it was already in the works. By summer 1964, the Civil Rights bill was law—although Kennedy did not live to see its passage. The Voting Rights Act, passed the following year, added guarantees of access to the polls.

But these legislative victories seemed almost too late as the volume of protest rose. In the later 1960s, the militant Black Power movement rejected nonviolence and targeted the underlying racism that denied African Americans, even when accorded legal protections, their rights and their dignity (see *Witnesses*, p. 861). Riots broke out in urban centers from 1965 to 1967. The Black Muslim movement advocated black separatism. The courageous leader Malcolm X (1925–1965), a survivor of ghetto and prison cell, who is depicted in *Windows On* on p. 862. encouraged blacks to ceaseless struggle against white oppression, later accepting the possibility of racial integration. His former Black Muslim colleagues gunned him down in 1965. A lone gunman shot Martin Luther King in 1968.

In the end, the multiple movements for racial justice profoundly transformed the American consciousness. In 1964, activist Ella Baker (d. 1986) had proclaimed that seekers of freedom could not rest "until the killing of black mothers' sons becomes as important to the rest of the country as the killing of white mothers' sons." In time, it did. By the time of Malcolm X's death in 1965, by King's death in 1968, and certainly by Baker's death in 1986, most Americans had recognized the injustice of the tragic long night of exclusion, segregation, and prejudice. Government agencies officially repudiated those attitudes; in schools and houses of worship, they were assailed. A new liberal consensus had been established. Yet the full social and civil equality of African Americans was not yet a reality nor has it since been achieved. The color line still threads its way through the fabric of American life, the unlovely inheritance of slavery and the West's imperial ventures.

Conclusion
THE SHADOWS OF IMPERIALISM AND THE MEANING OF THE WEST

For 500 years, the most powerful Western nations imposed their will on the other regions of the globe. That age is over, but its shadows hover still. The exploitation of wealth that belonged to others, the coercive reshaping of societies and culture that had different roots and purposes, the demeaning of whole peoples—these actions performed by thousands of Westerners and approved by many millions have left deep wounds and great bitterness.

But though it imposed its will in ways now regretted, the reign of the West has not been without benefit for the other peoples of the world. Its industrial might, its political institutions, its cultural forms, even its religious values now have willing imitators around the globe, who can borrow from the West at will as they develop their own free and independent nations—just as dissident Chinese students, in Tiananmen Square in Beijing in 1989, erected a replica of the Statue of Liberty that stands in New York Harbor, and onlookers throughout the world beheld its message.

QUESTIONS TO CONSIDER

1. What was Gandhi's particular appeal to his Indian followers, and why were his tactics so effective against the British?

2. Why did some colonial powers quickly leave Africa following World War II, and why did others hold on to their colonies as long as possible?

3. What was the key feature of Atatürk's program to create a modern Turkey from the remains of the Ottoman empire?

4. Why, in East Asia, did Japan become a democracy while China did not?

5. To what extent should the United States be considered to have been an imperialist power in the nineteenth and twentieth centuries?

SUGGESTED RESOURCES

Ferguson, Niall, *Empire: The Rise and Demise of the British World Order and the Lessons for Global Power* (New York: Basic Books, 2003). Views Britain's immense empire at the opening of the twentieth century as a prologue to the globalized world of the next.

Frankel, Philip, *An Ordinary Atrocity: Sharpeville and its Massacre* (New Haven: Yale University Press, 2001). Comprehensive account of the Sharpeville massacre of March 21, 1960, the symbol to the onlooking world of the evils of apartheid in South Africa.

Gerges, Fawaz A., *The Superpowers and the Middle East: Regional and International Politics, 1955–1967* (Boulder, CO: Westview Press, 1994). Surveys this key geo-political relationship during the High Cold War.

Hargreaves, J. D., *Decolonization in Africa* (London–New York: Longman, 1988). Excellent survey, attending to Portuguese, Belgian, and Italian, as well as British and French empires.

Irokawa, Daikichi, *The Age of Hirohito: The Making of Modern Japan* (New York: Free Press, 1995). Critical assessment of Japanese history during the 62 years' reign of the Emperor Hirohito, who died in 1989.

Kaiser, David, *American Tragedy: Kennedy, Johnson, and the Origins of the Vietnam War* (Cambridge, MA: Belknap Press of Harvard University Press, 2000). First Vietnam history able to draw on a complete set of declassified documents. Kaiser argues that the roots of Vietnam policy date back to the Eisenhower era, and that Johnson, adopted the policy framework that Eisenhower had established, but Kennedy sidestepped.

Keay, John, *Empire's End: A History of the Far East from High Colonialism to Hong Kong* (New York: Scribner's, 1997). Covers the last 500 years, including the decline of foreign rule since the 1930s.

Leogrande, William M., *Our Own Backyard: the United States in Central America, 1977–1992* (Chapel Hill: University of North Carolina Press, 1998). Comprehensive overview of United States policy in Latin America during the last phase of the Cold War.

Lewis, Bernard, *What Went Wrong? Western Impact and Middle Eastern Response* (Oxford: Oxford University Press, 2002). Portrays the crisis of Islamic civilization as it lost ground to the West in technology and culture, by one of America's foremost historians of Islam.

Lischer, Richard, *The Preacher King: Martin Luther King, Jr. and the Word that Moved America* (Oxford: Oxford University Press, 1995). Examines the role played in King's thought by African-Baptist influences.

Meredith, Martin, *Nelson Mandela: A Biography* (New York: St. Martin's Press, 1998). Solid biography of this key figure of the late 20th century.

Read, Anthony & David Fisher, *The Proudest Day: India's Long Road to Independence* (New York: W. W. Norton, 1998). With a focus on liberation in 1947, the authors trace the British government's vacillation between benevolence and control in the preceding period, and the courage and determination of India's native leaders.

Spence, Jonathan, *Mao Zedong* (New York: Viking Penguin, 2000). Characterizes the revolutionary as committed to reform through upheaval, a theme borrowed from China's history and consistent with the subject's experience during the revolutionary struggle.

Wolpert, Stanley A., *Nehru: A Tryst with Destiny* (Oxford: Oxford University Press, 1996). Authoritative biography.

Young, Marilyn, *The Vietnam Wars, 1945–1990* (New York: Harper Trade, 1991). Unique account of the Vietnam conflict that gives equal consideration to the perspective of the Vietnamese themselves.

The United Nations and Decolonialization, current policies, declarations, and links (UN):
http://www.un.org/Depts/dpi/decolonization/main.htm

Mohandas Karamchand Gandhi, Man of Millennium, works, images, links (Institute of Advanced Studies, Nagpur, India):
http://www.mkgandhi.org

Nelson Mandela, biography and resources (African National Congress):
http://www.anc.org.za/people/mandela.hmtl

Martin Luther King, "I have a dream'" August 28, 1963:
http://odur.let.rug.nl/nusa

⬤ Western Civilization Documents CD-ROM

30.4 The Non-Aligned Movement
30.5 Stokley Carmichael: What We Want

BACK FROM ARMAGEDDON

1940	1950	1960	1970	1980	1990	2000

Korean War, 1950–53   Vietnam War, 1964–73

The Cold War and Global Politics

◆ Hiroshima and Nagasaki bombed, 1945

◆ United Nations founded, 1945

◆ Churchill's "Iron Curtain" speech, 1946

◆ Marshall Plan announced, 1947

◆ Truman Doctrine announced, 1947

◆ Berlin blockade and airlift, 1948

◆ UN Universal Declaration of Human Rights, 1948

◆ NATO formed, 1949

◆ China becomes Communist state. 1949

◆ Ethel and Julius Rosenberg executed, 1953

◆ Warsaw Pact formed, 1955

◆ Sukarno hosts Bandung, Indonesia, conference, 1955

◆ Nikita Khrushchev denounces Stalin, 1956

◆ Hungarian uprising, 1956

◆ Suez Crisis, 1956

◆ Soviet Union launches *Sputnik I*, 1957

◆ Berlin Wall erected, 1961

◆ Cuban Missile Crisis, 1961

◆ Nuclear test ban agreement, 1963

◆ Six-Day War, Israel, 1967

◆ Nuclear Non-Proliferation Treaty, 1968

◆ Prague Spring suppressed, Czechoslovakia, 1968

◆ *Apollo 11*, lunar landing, 1969

◆ Helsinki Accords, 1975

◆ Soviets invade Afghanistan, 1979

◆ Solidarity movement, Poland, 1980

◆ Marshall Tito dies, Yugoslavia, 1980

◆ Gorbachev launches *Perestroika* and *Glasnost*, 1985

◆ Chernobyl nuclear disaster, Ukraine, 1986

◆ Communism collapses in Eastern Europe, 1989

◆ Tiananmen Square protests suppressed, 1989

◆ UN Convention on the Rights of the Child, 1989

◆ START I treaty signed, 1991

◆ Yeltsin elected president of Russian Republic, 1991

◆ Anti-Gorbachev coup, Soviet Union, 1991

◆ Soviet Union dissolved, 1991

◆ Gulf War, 1991

◆ START II treaty signed, 1993

◆ Hutus massacre 500,000–800,000 Tutsis, Rwanda, 1994

◆ Bosnian Serbs massacre thousands in Srebenica, Bosnia-Herzegovina, 1995

◆ India and Pakistan carry out nuclear tests, 1998

◆ NATO bombs Serbia, 1999

Culture, Society, and Economy

◆ ENIAC computer developed, 1946

◆ Simone de Beauvoir's *The Second Sex*, 1949

◆ European Economic Community (Common Market) formed, 1957

◆ NOW (National Organization for Women) formed, 1966

◆ Beatles' "All You Need is Love" broadcast worldwide, 1967

◆ Stanley Kubrick's *2001: A Space Odyssey*, 1968

◆ Woodstock Festival, 1969

◆ First Earth Day celebration in US, 1970

◆ Alexander Solzhenitsyn's *The Gulag Archipelago*, 1973

◆ UN General Assembly establishes World Commission on Environment and Development, 1983

◆ Spain and Portugal join the Common Market, 1986

◆ "Earth Summit" meets, Brazil, 1992

◆ European Union created, 1994

◆ Kyoto Protocol commits industrial nations to reductions in greenhouse gas emissions, 1997

◆ Debut of the euro, 1999

BACK FROM ARMAGEDDON

From the Bomb to the Internet

1945–1990

USA and Cold War allies

USSR and Cold War allies

CANADA

UNITED KINGDOM

W. GER.

FRANCE

ITALY

SPAIN

USA

U S S R

CHINA

JAPAN

ATLANTIC OCEAN

CENTRAL AMERICA

A F R I C A

SOUTH AMERICA

INDIAN OCEAN

KEY QUESTIONS

◆ **Apocalypse Now?:** What was the reaction of the peoples of the non-Communist West to Soviet nuclear capacity? How did attitudes and relations change after the dissolution of the Soviet Union in 1991?

◆ **All You Need is Love:** How did the Sixties Generation—those born in the years following World War II—react to the prospect of nuclear war?; The Cold War?; The Vietnam War? What shifts in cultural values resulted from these stresses?

Reprieve from terror: 1989 On December 29, 1989, dissident playwright Václav Havel (1936–) became the first president of liberated Czechoslovakia as it set out on the path from dictatorship to democracy. "Your government, my people, has been returned to you," he proclaimed in his New Year's address a few days later.

Havel's ascendancy in a bloodless or "velvet" revolution marked the release of his nation from the Soviet-controlled communist regimes that had held sway since 1945. In 1989, Poland, Hungary, Bulgaria, East Germany (the German Democratic Republic), and Romania also threw off their former rulers, even as, in distant China, student democrats in Beijing's Tiananmen Square confronted the communist state (see Chapter 29). The events of 1989 preceded the dissolution in 1991 of the Soviet Union itself.

With its collapse, the terror eased that had gripped the nations of the West and of the world. From 1945 to 1989, two superpowers, the United States and the Soviet Union, both equipped with nuclear weapons, were locked in a condition of ideological stalemate and political confrontation known as the Cold War. For nearly fifty years, the prospect of Armageddon loomed—the great final battle of the nations of the world. That threat faded with the end of the Cold War, while internationalist movements to heal the Earth's ills flourished, rooted in the era of the 1960s when youthful activists proposed a worldwide agenda of human welfare and environmental concern.

APOCALPYSE NOW?

The last scene of World War II was the first scene of the age that followed. The atomic destruction of Hiroshima and Nagasaki in 1945 (see Chapter 28) struck a new kind of fear. "The life expectancy of the human species … [has] dwindled immeasurably," the *Washington Post* dismally announced. With the Soviet occupation of eastern Europe, the nations of the Western world divided into two hostile blocs—a communist East and a largely democratic West. For nearly fifty years, people wondered: would Apocalypse (a universal destruction prophesied in the Bible) come now? Or soon? Or could it be forestalled?

Postwar Polarization

From 1945 until 1953, the Soviet Union established its power in eastern Europe while the United States led an alliance of western European nations against further Soviet advance, pledging "massive retaliation" against any aggression.

Europe Divided By late 1945, the Soviet Union had already secured much of Europe. For two years after its

1943 victories at Stalingrad and Kursk (see Chapter 28), the Red Army swept German armies out of Russia and back to Berlin, where the enemy surrendered on May 8, 1945. The Soviet flag flew in Berlin and throughout the lands the Soviets now occupied.

Soviet territorial claims, rooted in older Russian ambitions, were sanctioned by wartime agreements between the Allies. The "Big Three"—United States president Franklin Delano Roosevelt (1882–1945), British prime minister Winston Churchill (1874–1965), and the Soviet leader Joseph Stalin (1879–1953)—convened twice during the war: at Teheran (Iran) in November and December 1943, and at Yalta in the Crimea in February 1945. (In addition, Churchill met with Stalin in October 1944 in Moscow.) A final meeting of the victors took place in Potsdam (Germany) in July 1945, where President Harry S. Truman (1887–1972) replaced Roosevelt, who had recently died; and Clement Attlee (1883–1967) replaced Churchill, defeated in British elections. These meetings yielded agreements that transferred to Soviet control a corridor of states from the Baltic to the Balkans—the European nations created in 1919 from the borderlands of fallen empires, promised by Hitler to Stalin in 1939.

This outcome was not what Roosevelt and Churchill had planned in the Atlantic Charter of August 1941. That charter stated that neither the United States nor Britain sought territorial aggrandizement, and called for the restoration of sovereign rights to nations that had been deprived of them, and the repudiation of the use of force to advance national interests—principles subsequently adopted by the twenty-six signatories of the January 1942 Declaration of the nascent United Nations. Those principles were ignored, however, as the Soviet Union, seeking to defend its borders and conscious of its extraordinary sacrifices in the battle against Nazism, took control of half of Europe. Now a communist megalith faced the nations to the west.

Between 1945 and 1949, Soviet-backed communist governments took over in East Germany, in Poland, Czechoslovakia, Hungary, Romania, Bulgaria, and Albania; Yugoslavia, alone, led by resistance hero Marshall Tito (Josip Broz, 1892–1980) broke with Moscow. In 1940, the Soviets had already annexed the Baltic states of Estonia, Lithuania, and Latvia; now they acquired parts of Finland, Romania, and Czechoslovakia. The citizens of these regions who had suffered Nazi brutality now lived under regimes answerable to the Soviet Union, a totalitarian state that imposed a command economy, agrarian collectives, press censorship, and one-party rule.

Western Europeans observed these developments with alarm. Having survived the Nazi threat, they now confronted a Soviet one. Their economies were in tatters, and their military capacity exhausted; Germany and Austria were wholly disarmed. They looked to the

Map 30.1 The Two Superpowers in a Bipolar World, 1955: *By 1955, Europe was divided between those states loyal to the Soviet Union (the members of the Warsaw Pact) and those aligned with the United States (members of NATO). Although many nations beyond Europe remained non-aligned, others also joined in alliances with one or another of the superpowers. The faceoff between the superpowers created, in effect, a "bipolar" world.* **Where were most of the "flashpoints" of conflict between the two powers located? Why?**

United States to guarantee their security. Would the United States renounce its former isolationism, and return to defend western Europe? In 1945, the answer was not yet clear. But the means were at hand with the terrible power of the atomic bomb.

European Recovery Meanwhile, the project of rebuilding Europe began. Nazi officials and collaborators were purged, and the destruction caused by bombs addressed. Cities were in ruins; some seventy to ninety percent of Germany's urban fabric had been destroyed, as had railroads and bridges, communications systems, and factories. Urban populations needed food and, for those driven to take shelter in warehouses or cellars, new housing. Millions of refugees awaited **repatriation**—Germans who had fled the advancing Red Army, forced laborers detained in Germany, former prisoners of war. Twelve million "displaced persons" were taken under the wing of Allied administrators.

German and Soviet prisoners of war unlucky enough to be released in the Red Army zone were shipped back to the Soviet Union; and then on to execution or the oblivion of the gulag.

In western Europe, parliamentary governments were restored and currencies stabilized—often at rates that caused the value of prewar bank accounts to plummet. British, French, and American armies settled down in western Germany and Austria. In the rest of Germany and eastern Europe, the Red Army dug in its heels.

Europe was vulnerable, analysts argued, its impoverished nations prone to communist takeover through open elections or covert design. Where the struggle against fascism had previously united the free world, now many saw communism as a primary global threat. American assistance would be needed for Europe's recuperation, not least as a counter-measure to communist influence. Proposed by Secretary of State

Weapons and Warriors

The Big Three: *The leaders of the major combatant nations— Churchill, Roosevelt, and Stalin (the so-called "Big Three")—met at Yalta in the Crimea in February 1945 to discuss Allied military strategy and the end of the war. At least as decisive—both in bringing the war in the Far East to a close and establishing post-War power relationships—was the atomic bomb.*

George C. Marshall (1880–1959) in 1947, the Marshall Plan (or "European Recovery Program") offered economic aid to any European nation—whatever its political commitments—upon the presentation of a reasonable proposal for its use. Prodded by their masters, the nations of the Soviet zone declined to participate; but the nations of western Europe responded enthusiastically, including the Germans whom Allied leaders had so recently labeled "beasts" and "barbarians."

Funneling United States wealth—$13.2 billion between 1948 and 1952—to the treasuries of non-communist Europe, the Marshall Plan became in effect an economic corollary of the political strategy announced in the Truman Doctrine.

Early Cold War Activity The Truman Doctrine, which energized foreign policy for more than two decades and culminated in the imbroglio of Vietnam (see Chapter 29), announced the strategy of "containment," outlined in 1947 by the State Department representative in Moscow, George F. Kennan (1904–).

Kennan viewed Soviet power as opportunistic and aggressive. The United States, he said, must offer an "unalterable counterforce" wherever the Soviets "show signs of encroaching upon the interests of a peaceful and stable world."

Crises in the eastern Mediterranean seemed to demand such a policy. In Turkey in 1946, the Soviet Union positioned itself to seize control of the Dardanelles, the straits connecting the Mediterranean and Black Seas for which the Russian tsars had long hungered. In response, President Truman deployed a naval force in the eastern Mediterranean. In Greece, meanwhile, communist opponents of the ruling monarchy were supplied by the new Balkan dictatorships. In 1947, the British Foreign Office informed the State Department that Britain could no longer afford to prop up its embattled ally. The United States assumed that task; communist opposition had failed by 1949.

These circumstances led Truman to define an aggressive international role for the United States. In March 1947, he announced that it "must be the policy of the United States to support free peoples who are resisting attempted subjugation by armed minorities or by outside pressures." This pledge to all nations confronted with the threat of communist takeover was the core of the "Truman Doctrine."

The mushroom-shaped cloud: *Hearing in 1939 that the Nazis had begun efforts to develop the world's first nuclear weapons, the United States strove successfully to beat them to the punch. By 1945 the United States had three bombs: one was tested at Alamagordo, New Mexico in July 1945, and the other two were dropped on Japanese cities in early August 1945. A later test of a similar device in the Nevada desert in 1946 is shown above.*

The Prospects of Nuclear War: Two Reflections

Fear of nuclear holocaust gripped a whole generation during the Cold War. In different ways, the words of author William Faulkner, at its outset, and songwriter Sting, near its end, express that fear.

Novelist William Faulkner speaks of the bomb during his Nobel Prize acceptance speech (1949): Our tragedy is a general and universal fear. ... There are no longer any problems of the spirit. There is only the question: when will I be blown up? ...

I decline to accept the end of man. It is easy enough to say that man is immortal simply because he will endure; that when the last ding-dong of doom has clanged and faded from the last worthless rock hanging tideless in the last red and dying evening, that even then there will still be one more sound: that of his puny inexhaustible voice, still talking. I refuse to accept this. I believe that man will not merely endure; he will prevail. He is immortal, not because he alone among creatures has an inexhaustible voice, but because he has a soul, a spirit capable of compassion and sacrifice and endurance.

(From Nobel Foundation, *Les Prix Nobel en 1950*, 1951)

Songwriter Sting considers the likelihood of war (1985):
How can I save my little boy
from Oppenheimer's deadly toy?
There is no monopoly on common sense
on either side of the political fence.
We share the same biology,
regardless of ideology.
Believe me when I say to you,
I hope the Russians love their children too.

[Sting's reference is to J. Robert Oppenheimer (1904–1967), one of the leading physicists on the atomic bomb project.]

("Russians," words and music by Sting, 1985)

Another early Cold War confrontation took place in the German capital of Berlin. In 1945, Britain, France, the United States, and the Soviet Union had occupied separate zones of Germany, as well as four separate sectors of Berlin—an awkward arrangement because the city was located 100 miles deep in the Soviet zone. By spring 1948, the division of Germany by four powers became a rupture between two: the consortium, on the one hand, of the British, French, and Americans in the west (who would organize the region as the Federal Republic of Germany the following year); and on the other, the Soviets in the east (who would respond by creating the German Democratic Republic).

In June 1948, wishing to isolate Berlin from the western zones of Germany (a policy to which the West Berlin municipal government refused to acquiesce), the Soviet Union shut down access to the city by road, rail, or waterway. For nearly a year the western powers organized an unprecedented airlift, supplying the besieged citizens with food and fuel. By May 1949, the Soviets dropped the blockade, having failed to detach Berlin from its ties to the West.

By the time of the Berlin crisis, the Western world had crystallized into two zones. The "free" and the "unfree" zones were separated by an "iron curtain" (in Churchill's phrase) constituted by the tanks and barbed wire that marked the borders between Soviet and non-Soviet states, and by the ideological gulf between them. As a response to the threat of aggression from the East, the United States, advised by Secretary of State Dean Acheson (1893–1971), guided the creation in 1949 of a multinational military alliance: the North Atlantic Treaty Organization (NATO).

The North Atlantic Treaty provided for mutual aid in case of attack against any of its members (originally twelve), with each nation later providing military units in proportion to its resources. It served not only a military purpose, but also provided a pattern for other cooperative projects. Just as the Marshall Plan had advanced the notion of economic cooperation, NATO nurtured the germs of political unity among the western European states. By 1951, several nations were cooperating in a European Coal and Steel Community, which led to the establishment of the European Economic Community [EEC], or Common Market, in 1957 (now the European Union).

In 1949, the achievement of NATO was to provide a "shield," and the nuclear-armed United States an atomic "sword" that could protect the continent from attack, delivering "massive retaliation"—"instantly, by means and at places of our own choosing," in the words of United States Secretary of State John Foster Dulles (1888–1959)—against any aggressor. This was not war, but it was like war, as both contenders (equally heirs to Western civilization) eyed each other warily.

Cold War Confrontations

In 1949, the year of NATO's creation, the Soviet Union demonstrated its nuclear capacity by exploding an atomic bomb. By 1952, the United States had developed the hydrogen bomb, 750 times more powerful than the one that destroyed Hiroshima. By 1953, the Soviets had one too. Now both superpowers were armed with weapons capable of annihilating the other—its cities, its people, its air and soil.

The citizens of the world took what comfort they could in the principle of "Mutual Assured Destruction," or MAD—an apt anagram, for the world certainly seemed to have become mad. With

Cold War Skies: Hope and Fear

The Berlin Airlift: *Angered by United States, British, and French plans to merge their zones of occupation in Germany, the Soviets attempted in 1948–1949 to blockade West Berlin— buried deep within the Soviet zone of occupation—and thus to cut it off from western Germany. The United States and Britain responded with the highly successful Berlin Airlift, making in all some 200,000 flights to drop off food and supplies to the besieged citizens, like those seen here.*

each superpower having the capability to annihilate the other, the reasoning went, neither would start a conflict; yet the possibility remained that one would. From 1948 into the 1960s, the tension between the two superpowers was at a zenith. It relaxed somewhat from the late 1960s into the 1970s, then mounted again during the 1980s.

In the early 1950s, both superpowers built up their arsenals. This "arms race" continued throughout the decades of the Cold War until the world had accumulated a total of some 50,000 nuclear weapons. Each contender had long-range bombers and radar detection systems to stop them. They had "inter-continental ballistic missiles" (ICBMs, developed in 1957) that could reach the enemy from a remote position of safety. They had intermediate-range ballistic missiles (IRBMs) that could be launched at an enemy from a nearby country. They had submarine-launched ballistic missiles (SLBMs), and anti-ballistic missiles that tried to find and stop incoming missiles (ABMs). Billions of dollars were dedicated each year to the goal of "Mutual Assured Destruction."

Each superpower mustered allies who might enhance its security. Already the chief figure in NATO, the United States promoted the organization of its non-European allies into a series of regional organizations. These included, in Asia, the Central Treaty Organization (CENTO) and Southeast Asia Treaty Organization (SEATO); and in the Americas, the Organization of American States (OAS). In 1955, the Soviets established the Warsaw

Treaty organization (or Warsaw Pact) with its east European allies, to defend the communist states from the West. In addition, it could rely on the support of the other major communist nations of the world— North Korea (from 1945), China (until 1960), Cuba (after 1960), and Vietnam (after 1976).

As the race for arms and allies spiraled upward, so too did technological competition in other strategically related areas—in space and in **cybernetics**. In October 1957, the Soviet Union sent up a first satellite, *Sputnik I*, to orbit the Earth. In January 1958, the United States responded to the challenge, sending *Explorer 1* into orbit. In April 1961, the Soviets again surpassed the Americans, launching a manned spacecraft. In July 1969, the United States upstaged the Soviets with the launching of Apollo 11, the first space mission to culminate in a lunar landing. From a lunar module detached from the spacecraft, astronaut Neil A. Armstrong (b. 1930) and his colleagues emerged and took "a giant step for mankind" on the moon's surface, watched on television by one-quarter of the people on earth. Thereafter, both superpowers maintained programs of space exploration, gathering information through satellites, probes, and space stations.

War stimulated the development of systems for the electronic storage and manipulation of data. The first computers were designed to help decipher intercepted messages during World War II. Such were Britain's pioneering Colossus, which could manipulate 5000 characters per second, or the massive ENIAC (Electronic Numerical Integrator and Computer) developed at the University of Pennsylvania in 1946.

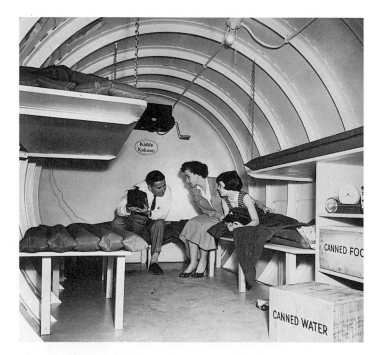

Fallout: *If western Berliners looked to the skies for assistance, many Americans, fearing a Soviet nuclear missile attack, sought the doubtful security of home-made basement fallout shelters during the early Cold War years.*

Thereafter, the United States led the world in the development of computer technology in the new field of cybernetics. The ENIAC weighed fifty tons, had 18,000 vacuum tubes, and could store the equivalent of just twenty words in memory. In the late 1990s, computers based on the silicon chip (about ¼ inch across) could store in memory the equivalent of more than 50 million words. This powerful chip has given its name to "Silicon Valley" (a region of northern California), a site of intense technological innovation. In 1968, the film *2001: A Space Odyssey*, directed by Stanley Kubrick (1928–1999) marked the arrival of the cybernetic space age in popular consciousness. It starred the supercomputer "Hal."

The buildup of arms and strategic technology made nuclear war seem likely. People sought to protect themselves as best they could. In civil defense programs citizens, including schoolchildren, practiced taking shelter, at a signal, from falling bombs—an absurd response to a weapon that could incinerate hundreds of thousands in an instant and kill any survivors with invisible radioactive fallout. Some United States families constructed "fallout shelters" in their basements or back yards, equipped with food and water supplies for long-term hibernation. Mass circulation magazines also offered guidance on planning a well-stocked shelter.

The battle for which these Cold Warriors prepared was a contest not merely between nations, but between two ideas, almost two religions. To many, communism seemed an absolute evil; liberal democracy and capitalism, absolute goods. Thus the military and political bifurcation of the Western world was paralleled by an ideological bifurcation, especially in the United States where an extreme, and unique, anti-communism took hold. In Europe, in contrast, outside of Spain and Portugal (where a lingering fascism silenced communist opposition), communist parties and adherents were accepted and active within a parliamentary setting.

From 1948, a committee of the United States House of Representatives known as the House Un-American Activities Committee (HUAC) investigated people associated in any way with the Communist party. Its improper tactics—pressuring witnesses to implicate others, and presuming guilt by association with suspect persons or organizations—were challenged at the time and subsequently condemned. Among HUAC's targets was Alger Hiss (1904–1996), a highly placed former State Department official, convicted of perjury in 1950. He had perjured himself, it was charged, by denying his guilt in spying for the Soviets; a charge of espionage could not be pursued because the statute of limitations had expired. Although many defended Hiss's innocence, recent revelations from materials previously barred to public examination appear to confirm his guilt.

HUAC's activities prepared the way for the emergence of Wisconsin senator Joseph McCarthy (1908–1957), the leader of a furious crusade against presumed communists. McCarthy chaired Senate committee hearings from 1953 to 1954, in which hysterical and unsubstantiated accusations ruined many careers and lives. Eventually, both his Senate colleagues (who censured him) and the public at large denounced McCarthy's "witchhunt" (so called because of its resemblance to the witch persecutions of earlier centuries).

Although McCarthy was repudiated, anti-communist feeling was widespread. Many states made a "loyalty oath" a condition for the employment of government personnel and teachers. In this tense climate, a couple convicted of betraying atomic secrets to the Soviets were executed in 1953: Ethel Rosenberg (1915–1953) and her husband Julius (1918–1953), considered wholly innocent by numerous supporters. As in the case of Hiss, recently-released evidence appears to confirm the guilt of these Cold War martyrs, although their punishment was surely exceptional: they were the first civilians in United States history executed for espionage.

The Cold War on the Global Stage

The Cold War Outside Europe The duel between the Soviet Union and the United States was fought in various settings around the world. In Latin America, the United States supported governments that took an anti-communist stance (see Chapter 29), including dictatorial regimes with unsavory reputations. It funded "counter-insurgency" programs to train military units in guerrilla tactics to be used against communist movements and states. Its CIA (Central Intelligence Agency) pursued the destabilization of pro-communist regimes, as in the coup that destroyed the elected government of Chilean socialist leader Salvador Allende Gossens (1908–1973) and in attempts to assassinate the Cuban communist leader Fidel Castro (b. 1927). In Cuba, an abortive invasion by an expatriate force (supported by the United States) and the Soviet installation on the island, in response, of missiles capable of carrying nuclear warheads triggered the most dangerous United States–Soviet confrontation of the era. The Cuban missile crisis of 1961 brought the two superpowers to the edge of nuclear war. A show of firmness by the United States persuaded the Soviets to dismantle their missile bases in exchange for an American promise not to invade Cuba again.

Although the emerging states of Africa were intent on their own internal problems (see Chapter 29), the Cold War contest between the United States and the Soviet Union inevitably intruded. From 1969, the Soviets supported strongman Colonel Muammar al-Qaddafi (b. 1942) in Libya. In 1974, it formed a pact with Somalia, providing weapons and military advice in exchange for naval and air footholds. In 1977, the Somalians cast off the Soviet alliance (and invited United States support) as it invaded neighboring Ethiopia, itself a Soviet client. The following year, Ethiopia defeated Somalia and compensated the Soviets with access to naval facilities. In 1975–1976, the Soviets sent weapons and some 19,000 Cuban troops to Angola to aid one group of insurgents against another supported by the United States. By the late 1970s, hundreds of Soviet advisers and more than 40,000 Cuban troops were deployed in a dozen African countries. The United States countered, enhancing its authority in Africa through programs providing economic advice and assistance. By the 1980s, the Soviets found it increasingly difficult to fund its African agenda. The Western bloc became the preeminent foreign influence on the continent.

In the Middle East, the United States backed Israel, while the Soviets embraced the cause of the dispossessed Palestinians, and supported the Arab states, especially Egypt (until its settlement with Israel in 1979), Syria, and Iraq (see Chapter 29). In east Asia a great communist state was formed in 1949, when Mao Zedong (1893–1976) led his triumphant forces into Beijing (see Chapter 29). Against this massive communist presence, the United States leagued with Japan, now a loyal ally after the period of postwar occupation. Another ally was the government of Taiwan (Formosa), established in 1949 by Chiang Kai-shek (Jiang Jieshi; 1887–1975) and the nationalist army that had taken refuge there from the communist forces that had overrun the mainland. Elsewhere in Asia, two major wars in Korea and Vietnam pitted revolutionary communist states against authoritarian, pro-Western ones backed by

---

WITNESSES

The Origins of the Cold War

World War II had barely ended when, like its afterword, the Cold War began. Winston Churchill's "iron curtain" speech of 1946, from which comes the first excerpt here, marks its beginning. The "Truman Doctrine" announced by the United States president who had authorized the use of the atomic bomb, in the second excerpt, depicts a struggle between a "free" West and an enslaved Soviet zone. The Soviet official Andrei Zhdanov, in the third, views United States activities in Europe and elsewhere as aggressive and imperialistic.

Winston Churchill, wartime British prime minister, notes the signs of Cold War (1946): From Stettin in the Baltic to Trieste in the Adriatic, an iron curtain has descended across the Continent. Behind that line lie all the capitals of ancient states of central and eastern Europe. Warsaw, Berlin, Prague, Vienna, Budapest, Belgrade, Bucharest and Sofia, all these famous cities ... lie in the Soviet sphere and all are subject in one form or another ... to a very high and increasing measure of control from Moscow. The Communist parties ... have been raised to pre-eminence and power far beyond their numbers and are seeking everywhere to obtain totalitarian control. ... This is certainly not the liberated Europe we fought to build up. Nor is it one which contains the essentials of permanent peace.
(From *New York Times*, March 4, 1946)

United States president Truman outlines the "Truman Doctrine" (March 12, 1947): At the present moment in world history nearly every nation must choose between alternative ways of life. The choice is too often not a free one. One way of life is based upon the will of the majority, and is distinguished by free institutions, representative government, free elections,

guaranties of individual liberty, freedom of speech and religion, and freedom from political oppression. The second way of life is based upon the will of a minority forcibly imposed upon the majority. It relies upon terror and oppression, a controlled press and radio, fixed elections, and the suppression of personal freedoms.

I believe that it must be the policy of the United States to support free peoples who are resisting attempted subjugation by armed minorities or by outside pressures. ...
(US Congress, Congressional Record, 80th Congress, 1st session, 1947)

Soviet official Andrei Zhdanov interprets United States "aid" as imperialism (1947): With a view to consolidating America's monopoly position in the markets gained as a result of the disappearance of her two biggest competitors, Germany and Japan [due to their defeat in the war], and the weakening of her capitalist partners, Great Britain and France [a result of the toll of winning the war], the new course of the United States' policy envisages a broad program of military, economic and political measures, designed to establish United States political and economic domination in all countries marked out for American expansion, to reduce these countries to the status of satellites of the United States and to set up regimes within them which would eliminate all obstacles on the part of labor and democratic movement to the exploitation of these countries by American capital. The United States is now endeavoring to extend this new line of policy not only to its enemies in the war and to neutral countries, but in an increasing degree to its wartime allies [also].
(Andrei Zhdanov, address to conference, September 22–23, 1947; ed. Kirsch et al., 1997)

Stalin is Dead, Europe Lives

Repression and revolution: *Upon becoming the Czechoslovak Communist party secretary in January 1968 Alexander Dubček led his country's efforts to implement pro-democratic reforms and abolish censorship. Warsaw Pact tanks brutally repressed this "Prague Spring" later the same year. Here, Czech patriots vent their anger on a Russian tank (right). Anti-communist protest and reform—all across the Eastern Bloc—met virtually no such opposition in 1989, however. In the photograph below, the Berlin Wall is hacked down by ordinary German citizens.*

the United States (see Chapter 29). In Korea, a communist state retained power in the north. After United States disengagement, Vietnam was finally unified as a communist state.

India and Indonesia avoided identification with either Cold War position in a policy of "non-alignment," which aimed to advance the interests of the developing nations of what was now called the **Third World** by trading with both superpowers but declining participation in Cold War struggles. Indonesian leader Sukarno (1901–1970), an advocate of non-alignment, hosted an historic meeting of

Asian and African leaders at Bandung in 1955. In the Middle East, Egyptian leader Colonel Gamal Abdel Nasser (1918–1970) also led a bloc of non-aligned Arab nations.

De-Stalinization and Repression in the East While Soviet and United States interests collided abroad, at home the United States presidents from 1952 to 1973 pursued resolutely anti-Communist policies. They faced a shifting Soviet policy as the regime of Joseph Stalin yielded to that of Nikita Khrushchev (1894–1971), and, in due course, Leonid Brezhnev (1906–1982).

After Stalin died in 1953, Khrushchev battled his way to preeminence by 1955. On February 25, 1956, he surprised the Twentieth Congress of the Communist Party with a denunciation of "the crimes of Stalin." Even in Moscow some began to hope that the purges were over, that censorship of the press and the arts would lighten, and that the horror of the gulag would cease.

De-Stalinization in Moscow meant a brief moment of relaxation of Soviet control in eastern Europe, where leaders took the initiative in reaching for greater autonomy. In Poland in 1956, the election as first secretary of Władisław Gomułka (1905–1982), a "national" communist thought to be independent of Moscow, went forward despite a frown from Khrushchev. The same year, a popular revolt in Hungary under the liberalizing prime minister Imre Nagy (1896–1958) threatened the Soviet-backed regime. When Hungary announced its withdrawal from the Warsaw Pact, Soviet forces invaded and crushed the revolution. The victors installed leaders loyal to Moscow, executing Nagy and 2000 supporters. Some 200,000 Hungarians fled to the West.

The suppression of the Hungarian revolt silenced eastern Europe. Five years later, the Soviet Union again made clear its intention to limit dissent. Deep inside the German Democratic Republic, Berlin was the weakest point in the Iron Curtain. Refugees streamed from the eastern Soviet zone to west Berlin—more than 3 million people, including skilled workers and professionals. In August 1961, East Germany closed this gap by constructing the Berlin Wall, a structure of barbed wire and concrete dividing the city. The flow of refugees ceased, while all of Germany could observe in the microcosm of Berlin the great barrier that separated East and West.

In 1968, after Khrushchev had been pushed aside and the bureaucrat Brezhnev had emerged as Soviet leader, the Czech reformer Alexander Dubček (1921–1992) offered a new challenge to Soviet rule. His promise of "socialism with a human face" aroused widespread support, including that of student activists. A Soviet-led Warsaw Pact army of some 175,000 troops invaded (in its only coordinated effort), the largest mobilization of ground forces on the European continent since World War II. It swiftly suppressed the "Prague Spring" that had seemed so hopeful.

Once again, force muzzled protest in eastern Europe. Only after an interlude of more than ten years did there arise another movement of resistance to communist rule, this time in Poland. Here in 1980 the workers in the Lenin Shipyard in Gdánsk (German Danzig), led by electrician and anti-government activist Lech Walesa (b. 1943), formed an independent labor union. It served as the nucleus for a federation of unions, Solidarity, which constituted a democratizing political movement that won 10 million adherents and finally celebrated the collapse of the communist government in 1989.

Talking About Disarmament By the time of Walesa's resistance, relations between the United States and the Soviet Union had experienced a period of easing tension, or **détente**. The notion of "peaceful coexistence" between the superpowers had been aired as early as the 1950s. In 1954 and 1955, the Soviets had called in the United Nations General Assembly for limitations on conventional and nuclear weapons. In 1959, aware of the strain that the arms race put on the Soviet economy, Khrushchev advocated total disarmament within four years. To secure such disarmament, however, the United States insisted on on-site inspections; and these the Soviet Union refused to allow.

After the Cuban showdown of 1961, both superpowers sought to restrict the testing of nuclear weapons and to prevent their proliferation. In 1963, the United States, the Soviet Union, and Britain agreed not to conduct nuclear tests in the atmosphere or in the sea. In 1967, with France, they agreed not to permit the introduction of nuclear weapons into the Earth's orbit or on the moon. The same year, most Latin American states agreed to keep their region nuclear-free.

In 1968, the three signatories of the 1963 partial test ban and fifty-nine other states signed a Nuclear Non-Proliferation Treaty (NNT, extended indefinitely in 1995), by which the participants pledged not to supply non-nuclear powers with nuclear weapons or the technology required to produce them. By 1970, additional countries had signed (the non-nuclear powers further agreeing not to acquire such weapons). It was eventually signed by most of the countries in the world, including France and China (but excluding South Africa, India, Pakistan, and Israel). In addition, Iran, Iraq, Libya, and North Korea, who had signed the treaty, were thought to be in violation. Compliance with NNT was to be enforced by an international inspection team under the aegis of the UN International Atomic Energy Administration. This mechanism meant that the non-nuclear nations would be policed, while the nuclear superpowers remained free to develop more weapons—and they did.

Further agreements were necessary to limit all arms development, as well as to prevent the further proliferation of nuclear arms. In seven sessions between 1969 and 1972 held in Helsinki (Finland) and Vienna (Austria), United States and Soviet officials participated in SALT (Strategic Arms Limitation Talks). SALT I limited each superpower to fixed quantities of certain kinds of missiles (while others remained unregulated) over a five-year term to expire in 1977. President Jimmy Carter (1924–) signed a SALT II treaty with Brezhnev in 1979, while President Ronald Reagan (1911–) participated in Intermediate-Range Nuclear Forces (INF) talks beginning in 1981 and START (Strategic Arms Reduction Talks) from 1982.

Despite promising first steps, détente stalled from 1975 to 1985, as both superpowers stockpiled new missiles and bombs. Warsaw Pact armaments in Europe rose to several times more than those available to NATO, though they were generally less powerful, while the United States developed a neutron bomb, or Enhanced Radiation Weapon, that killed with radiation rather than explosive force. In 1979, Islamist rebels threatened the Soviet client state of Afghanistan, provoking a Soviet invasion. Resuming the policy of military containment, President Reagan stirred his listeners to the task of defeating once and for all the "evil empire," as he provocatively termed the Soviet Union in 1983. Still unreconciled, East faced West with distrust and fear.

Armageddon Deferred: 1985–1991

In 1985, four decades from its inception, the Cold War lingered on. Then the Soviet bloc disintegrated, surprisingly and suddenly, without bombs and without tanks. In 1991, it ceased to be. With its collapse, the fear of imminent nuclear catastrophe abated.

By 1985, it was clear that the Soviet economy did not work. Consumer goods, and especially housing, were in insufficient supply. The ample produce of distant farms was poorly distributed. The eastern

European satellites, the annexed Baltic states, and the Soviet republics of Central Asia all sought greater independence. Experts in the Soviet bureaucracy wanted a freer hand to implement reforms, and even the long-muzzled Russian Orthodox Church raised its voice. The United States was winning the arms race. Change was imminent.

In 1985, Mikhail Gorbachev (1931–), the first Soviet leader to possess university training, launched the twin campaigns of **glasnost** ("openness") and **perestroika** ("restructuring"). By inviting the open discussion of political and economic realities, and then the cautious restructuring of public policy, Gorbachev hoped to save the world's first communist society from disintegration. Instead, open discussion turned to bitter criticism. It appeared that modest repairs could not rescue Soviet society from its path toward self-destruction. The breakdown of the Soviet system was foreshadowed in the disaster that occurred in Chernobyl (Ukraine) in 1986. There a partial meltdown at a badly managed nuclear power plant killed many swiftly, and contaminated vast areas with radioactivity.

A loyal communist but resolute reformer, Gorbachev followed where *glasnost* and *perestroika* led until, by 1989, the communist *imperium* fragmented. The Soviet Union relinquished its military commitments abroad, leaving the communist states of Cuba, North Korea, and Vietnam to fend for themselves (while China had since 1980 been moving in the direction of capitalism). Soviet troops came home from Afghanistan, abandoning the struggle against Islamist rebels who, in 1992, seized power.

Under Gorbachev's leadership, the Soviet Union ceased to monitor eastern Europe, where in a single year revolutions in all six satellite nations rejected pro-Soviet communist governments. In Poland, a newly legalized Solidarity party negotiated reforms that led to free elections and the establishment of a free market economy. In Hungary, a government committee declared independence from Communist party control, rehabilitated the leaders of the 1956 revolution and threw open the border with Austria.

In Czechoslovakia, Václav Havel (1936–) was elected President, while the parliament chose as its speaker the architect of the 1968 Prague Spring, Alexander Dubček. In East Germany, reformers forced the Soviet loyalist leader to resign, flung open the borders, and permitted the jubilant citizens to batter down the Berlin Wall with crowbars, pickaxes, and bare hands—"Stalin is dead; Europe lives!" someone scrawled on the Wall just before its demolition. Massive protests sent the communist strongman

---

WITNESSES

As the Cold War Ages: Two United States Presidents Discuss the Soviet Threat

By the 1970s—after the United States had lived through the trauma and humiliation of the Vietnam War—who still believed in the Cold War? Two United States presidents offered different and opposing views. Jimmy Carter urged the nation to turn away from the "inordinate fear of Communism" and return to basic American principles. Just a few years later, Ronald Reagan insisted that the battle had been, and was still, worth fighting—against an opponent that was an "evil empire."

We are not afraid: Jimmy Carter, University of Notre Dame, Commencement Address (May 22, 1977): Being confident of our own future, we are now free of that inordinate fear of Communism which once led us to embrace any dictator who joined us in our fear. For too many years we have been willing to adopt the flawed principles and tactics of our adversaries, sometimes abandoning our values for theirs. We fought fire with fire, never thinking that fire is better fought with water. This approach failed, with Vietnam the best example of its intellectual and moral poverty. But through failure we have found our way back to our own principles and values, and we have regained our lost confidence.
(From *New York Times*, May 23, 1977)

No compromise with an evil empire: Ronald Reagan (March 14, 1983): [The Soviet leadership has …] openly and publicly declared that the only morality they recognize is that which will further their cause, which is world revolution. … I think the refusal of many influential people to accept this elementary fact of Soviet doctrine illustrates an historical reluctance to see totalitarian powers for what they are. … I urge you to beware the temptation of pride—the temptation blithely to declare yourselves above it all and label both sides equally at fault, to ignore the facts of history and the aggressive impulses of an evil empire. …

I believe that communism is another sad, bizarre chapter in human history whose last pages even now are being written. I believe this because the source of our strength in the quest for human freedom is not material but spiritual, and, because it knows no limitation, it must terrify and ultimately triumph over those who would enslave their fellow man.
(Ronald Reagan, *Weekly Compilation of Presidential Documents*, March 14, 1983)

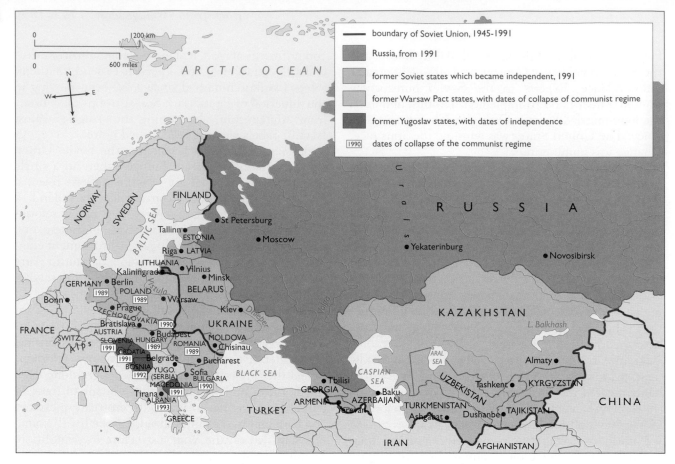

Map 30.2 Collapse of the Soviet Bloc, 1989–1991: *Soviet leader Mikhail Gorbachev's policy of glasnost permitted the rapid dissolution of the Soviet Union beginning in 1989. The nations of eastern Europe promptly declared their independence. In the Caucasus region and Central Asia, nationalist tensions accompanied the disaggregation of the former empire. By 1991, the USSR disappeared as a state and Russia reappeared on the map for the first time since the Russian Revolution (1917–1921). Why was it likely that, once Central authority weakened, the east European, Caucasian, and Asian regions would fragment?*

of Romania, Nicolae Ceauşescu (1918–1989) into flight. But he was caught, convicted hastily of "genocide," and shot on Christmas day, the grisly image of his corpse displayed on television screens worldwide to an astonished public. In 1990, the two halves of the German nation reunited, and in 1991 the Baltic states declared their independence along with the former Soviet republics of Belarus, Moldova, Ukraine, Armenia, Georgia, Azerbaijan, Kazakhstan, Kyrgyzstan, and Uzbekistan.

Meanwhile, Gorbachev was negotiating an end to the arms race. Discussions begun with Reagan in Reykyavik (Iceland) in 1986 culminated in 1991 in a treaty signed by Reagan's successor, George Bush (1924–) and Gorbachev: the START I treaty, which achieved a twenty-five percent reduction in the nuclear forces of the Soviet Union and fifteen percent in those of the United States. In the meantime, both nations agreed to the CFE (Conventional Forces in Europe) treaty of 1990, which required a balance of conventional forces which was to be attained by the elimination of much of the Soviet arsenal of tanks, aircraft, and artillery.

In Moscow, the economy continued to decline. Gorbachev encouraged greater efficiency in state-run enterprises, and permitted some free-market reforms.

But he would not abandon the command economy, which would have caused massive unemployment and monetary stress while, pro-capitalist advisers argued, it opened the road to economic renewal. And he continued to court communist advisers who opposed the turn to a free-market system.

Thus Gorbachev was caught between old-line communists and democratizing reformers. Prominent among the latter was Boris Yeltsin (1931–) elected president of the Russian Republic in 1991. When in August that year a group of military and secret police chiefs imprisoned Gorbachev and attempted to restore the old regime, Yeltsin opposed them, bravely announcing his defiance from atop a tank outside Moscow's parliament building. Together Yeltsin and the reinstated but debilitated Gorbachev watched as the constituent republics of the USSR declared their independence. Together they accepted the dissolution of the Soviet Union, and the end of the seventy-four-year Marxist-Leninist-Stalinist experiment.

With the disintegration of the Soviet Union, anticommunist sentiment swept the region. In parks and city centers, citizens tore down statues of Lenin and Felix Dzerzhinsky, head of the Bolshevik secret police. Worshipers returned to Russian churches, and former communists saw to the baptism of their children. The borders were opened. Jews in large numbers fled the endemic anti-Semitism of their homeland and emigrated to Israel and the United States. Islamic fundamentalism stirred in the newly independent republics of central Asia, supported by Afghan insurgents across the border, and the governments of Iran and Pakistan. Ethnic loyalties surged after the long Soviet interim among the disparate peoples of the Caucasus.

On December 25, 1991, having no nation over which to preside, Gorbachev resigned, Nobel Peace Prize (1990) in hand, to tour the lecture circuit and write his memoirs. Yeltsin managed the remnants of the dissolved Soviet Union, twelve of its fifteen now-independent states joined in the voluntary federation of the Commonwealth of Independent States (CIS). Its technological and military assets, including its stores of nuclear weapons, were reallocated to the member states. The nuclear arsenal of the former Soviet Union had been located in four of the republics—Ukraine, Belarus, Kazakhstan, and Russia itself—all of which cooperated with the commissions established to oversee arms limitation. In 1993, Yeltsin and Bush signed the START II treaty, which obtained the reduction of strategic weapons by twenty-five percent on both sides. In 1994, the United States airlifted from Kazakhstan, with Russia's permission, enough strategic enriched uranium to make twenty-four atomic bombs, lest it fall into the hands of renegade nations or illicit dealers.

In Russia, free-market speculators and corrupt bureaucrats reaped profits from the nation's reorganization. Protests against Yeltsin mounted as the currency collapsed, state employees went unpaid, and living conditions deteriorated. In 1993, communist opponents barricaded themselves in the parliament building, while their supporters fought outside.

The military police quelled the revolt, firing on the parliament complex and killing more than 100 people. Yeltsin survived to face a nationalist opponent later that year, and a reelection race against a communist challenger in 1996. Amid domestic crises, while suppressing a revolt in the Caucasian region of Chechnya, Yeltsin endured, health failing, as the economy—beset by corruption, gangsterism, scarcity, and inflation, fueled by the uncontrolled printing of new rubles—went into freefall in 1998.

The dissolution of the Soviet Union meant the dissolution of the Warsaw Pact. In 1999, the Czech Republic (Czechoslovakia had divided in 1993 into the Czech Republic and Slovakia), Poland, and Hungary were admitted to NATO. Russia itself, the chief member of the "evil empire" NATO had been born to combat, received associate status.

In 1999, as a new century and a new millennium approached, the nations of the world had begun to hope that the deadly logic of "mutual assured destruction" would not end in a final struggle between East and West, communism and capitalism, the perceived good and evil. The world had escaped the test of Armageddon, and the Apocalypse, for the moment, had been postponed.

ALL YOU NEED IS LOVE

It was a different world, though, from the one envisioned at Yalta by the victors of World War II. The generation born in the shadow of the bomb—the product of a postwar demographic bubble, bulging in numbers, unique in self-absorption—transformed the world. This "baby boom" cohort, the first ever threatened from birth by global annihilation, reached adolescence during the 1960s when, especially in the United States, they erupted in protest against the Cold War and its makers. Summoned to fight during the unpopular Vietnam War, they retorted "Hell no! We won't go!"; then impudently commanded their elders to "Make love, not war!" "All you need is love," the

A Changing of the Guard: *In many cases the collapse of Communism in Eastern Europe and the Soviet Union made outsiders insiders and vice-versa more or less overnight. Here, Czech dissident and renowned playwright Václav Havel— who under the Communists had spent time as a political prisoner— speaks as the newly elected president of Czechoslovakia in 1989.*

The Breakdown of Communism and the End of the Cold War

The "evil empire," as President Reagan had deemed it, crumbled of its own weight, but took more than a generation to fall. The descent began with premier Nikita Khrushchev's denunciation of Stalin in 1956, excerpted in the first passage below. More than 30 years later, premier Mikhail Gorbachev announces the need for "restructuring," as seen in the second passage. In the third, on New Year's Day, 1990, the new Czech president Václav Havel speaks of communism in his country as a system defeated, and in the fourth a historian writing that same year predicts a bleak future for socialism. In the last passage, a man born in the United States, who had defected to the Soviets in 1950, admits in 1998 that he had made a mistake.

Soviet premier Nikita Khrushchev denounces Stalin three years after the dictator's death (1956): The negative characteristics of Stalin ... transformed themselves during the last years into a grave abuse of power by Stalin, which caused untold harm to our Party. ... Stalin acted ... by imposing his concepts and demanding absolute submission to his opinion. Whoever opposed ... was doomed to removal from the leading collective and to subsequent moral and physical annihilation. ...

Stalin originated the concept "enemy of the people." This term ... made possible the usage of the most cruel repression, violating all norms of revolutionary legality against any one who in any way disagreed with Stalin. ... In ... actuality, the only proof of guilt used . . . was the "confession" of the accused himself; and, as subsequent probing proved, "confessions" were acquired through physical pressures [ie, torture] against the accused.

(Nikita Khrushchev, US Congress, 85th Congress, 1st session, 1957)

Soviet premier Mikhail Gorbachev on the background and need for *perestroika* (restructuring) (1987): The Soviet Union is a young state without analogues in history or in the modern world. Over the past seven decades ... our country has traveled a path equal to centuries. ... Huge productive forces, a powerful intellectual potential, a highly advanced culture, a unique community of over one hundred nations and nationalities, and firm social protection for 280 million people on a territory forming one-sixth of the Earth—such are our great and indisputable achievements and Soviet people are justly proud of them. ...

At some stage—this became particularly clear in the latter half of the seventies—something happened that was at first sight inexplicable. The country began to lose momentum. ... Difficulties began to accumulate and

deteriorate, and unresolved problems to multiply. ... We first discovered a slowing economic growth. In the last fifteen years the national income growth rates had declined by more than half. ... As time went on, material resources became harder to get and more expensive. ...

(Mikhail Gorbachev, *Perestroika: New Thinking for Our Country and the World*, 1987)

Czech president Václav Havel speaks of the past and present at a New Year's address shortly after the overthrow of communism in his country (1990): For 40 years you have heard on this day from the mouths of my predecessors ... the same thing: how our country is flourishing, how many more millions of tons of steel we have produced, how we are all happy, how we believe in our Government and what beautiful prospects are opening ahead of us. I assume you have not named me to this office so that I, too, should lie to you. Our country is not flourishing. ... The state, which calls itself a state of workers, is humiliating and exploiting them instead. ... [In education] we rank 72nd in the world. We have spoiled our land, rivers and forests ... and we have, today, the worst environment in the whole of Europe. ... The worst of it is that we live [also] in a spoiled moral environment. We have become morally ill because we are used to saying one thing and thinking another. We have learned not to believe in anything, not to care about each other, to worry only about ourselves. ...

(From *New York Times*, "Havel's Vision—Excerpts from Speech by the Czech President", January 2, 1990)

The economic historian Robert Heilbroner on the future prospects for Socialism (1990): I am not very sanguine about the prospect that socialism will continue as an important form of economic organization now that Communism is finished. ... [T]he collapse of the planned economies has forced us to rethink the meaning of socialism. As a semireligious vision of a transformed humanity, it has been dealt devastating blows in the twentieth century. As a blueprint for a rationally planned society, it is in tatters.

(Robert Heilbroner, "After Communism" in *The New Yorker*, September 10, 1990)

Joel Barr, American-born Soviet spy and defector to the Soviet Union (1950), explains why he renounced communism (1998): I believe that now history will show that the Russian Revolution was a tremendous mistake. ... It was a step backward. The real revolution for mankind that will go down for many, many years was the American Revolution.

(From *The New York Times*, August 16, 1998)

popular rock music group called the Beatles proclaimed in 1967, in a live performance broadcast worldwide via satellite to some 400 million listeners.

During the next decades, the Sixties generation and its imitators sought to bind up the world's wounds. The needs of others for food, security, and dignity engaged a generation that had become traumatized by Cold War brinkmanship. The Earth itself languished, ravaged by the deadly machines that powered the mindless quest for wealth and power. It, too, cried for love, not war.

Rolling Stones

The Power of Protest The Sixties generation, like "rolling stones" (featured in a song by Bob Dylan, b. Robert Zimmerman, 1941) that had shed the moss of the past, set out to transform the politics, society, and culture of the West. They began by protesting against the bomb, joining pacifists of an older generation such as philosopher Bertrand Russell and physicist Albert Einstein (see Chapter 27), inspired by Erich Maria Remarque's *All Quiet on the Western Front* (1929) about the futilities of the first World War, or Joseph Heller's *Catch-22* (1961) about the absurdities of the second.

From protesting against the bomb, young activists joined with the civil rights movement, seeking to end discrimination against those of African descent (see Chapter 29). Student leaders who had experienced the thrill of mass mobilization and commitment to a cause were determined to defy the conformist culture of their parents with a new militancy.

In 1964, students at the Berkeley campus of the University of California protested against college officials who had interfered, as they saw it, with their right to form political organizations. This Berkeley Free Speech movement, in which the university itself came to symbolize all the repressive forces of society, prefigured the movements soon to emerge to protest against United States involvement in the Vietnam War (see Chapter 29).

That war, billed by the "establishment" as a campaign against communism, was identified by the young as one more chapter in the tedious tale of the strong bullying the weak. By 1967, when large numbers of young men were being drafted to serve in Vietnam, anti-war protests flared on college campuses that housed one-third of the cohort born between 1945 and 1949. At teach-ins, faculty mentors explained to a younger generation raised on television and rock 'n' roll where Indochina was, and why Vietnamese independence mattered. At rallies, hundreds or thousands gathered at a chosen moment to witness their opposition to the war. Sometimes protest turned violent, when participants taunted the security forces sent to keep order, or disrupted traffic, or broke windows.

To student observers, the spectacle of a superpower unleashing its vast arsenal against impoverished Vietnamese peasants in order to deny them the independence they ardently sought was both horrible and absurd. A "credibility gap" yawned wide as televised announcements of specious victories, and exaggerated reports of the number of the slaughtered made politicized students enduringly skeptical of government. "Hey, hey, LBJ, how many kids have you killed today?" they taunted the president in one ditty from the angry repertoire of student protest.

The anti-war frenzy climbed from 1968 to 1972. In 1968, following the debacle of the Tet Offensive, the dispirited President Lyndon B. Johnson (1908–1973) announced that he would not seek another term in office. Later that year, the despair of many Americans intensified with the assassination of two respected leaders: Martin Luther King, Jr. (see Chapter 28), champion of civil rights; and presidential candidate Robert F. Kennedy (1925–1968), younger brother of the charismatic President John F. Kennedy (1917–1963), the victim of another assassin in 1963. Violence seemed to be winning.

Meanwhile, the American model of youth protest had impressed Europe. In Paris in May 1968, students protested against government cuts in funding for social spending and universities. Provoked by police intimidation of the Parisian Left Bank community of intellectuals and artists, students set up barricades in the streets and harassed the forces sent to maintain order. Many citizens supported the students; industrial workers struck in sympathy. By early June, however, the deft maneuvering of president Charles de Gaulle (1890–1970) brought the revolt to a quick close. The Parisian example of student resistance to government inspired student revolts in Britain, Italy, and, with greater consequence, in Czechoslovakia.

In the United States in 1969, the new president Richard Nixon (1913–1994) implemented "Vietnamization" (see Chapter 29), a dual strategy of escalated bombing and troop reduction leading to an eventual withdrawal of all United States forces in 1973. In 1970, at Kent State University (in Kent, Ohio), National Guardsmen shot at rock-throwing students—their contemporaries—killing four. It seemed as though the nation had reached a nadir of depravity; it devoured its own children, whose one crime was to hate war. Public opposition to the war surged. The Nixon administration quieted the protest by ending the draft, making the United States military a volunteer force. Those who "would not go" did not have to.

The youth of "the movement"—an affluent and largely white minority—won their battle against their elders. Poor white, black, or brown young men from inner cities and rural towns had no choice but to go. They fought a vicious war without popular support and returned to a nation embarrassed by their presence. They did not figure in the perceptions of the youth who forged the counter-culture of the Sixties founded on the right of each individual to unlimited self-expression. Nor did the "silent majority" of citizens, young and old, who were untouched or dismayed by student radicalism.

A Changing Culture The American youth rebellion, led by a privileged few, had wide-reaching social and cultural impact. During the 1950s, the men and women who had endured the Depression and defeated Nazism pursued their careers, bought houses and cars, populated the suburbs, and settled down to enjoy unprecedented economic prosperity. In the 1960s, their children—or at least a rebellious vanguard—spurned those careers, those neighborhoods, that complacency. In their dress, their tastes, and their sexual mores, they cast aside norms that had so recently triumphed with a stunning wartime victory, and replaced them with provocative new ones.

Costume and style tell the story of cultural transformation. Spurning their fathers' gray-flannel suits and their mothers' crinolined dresses, they dressed in stark black, or in exotic peasant frocks, or, most often, in blue jeans, the dark denim uniform of the working class. Movement pacesetters might favor bizarre hats, or accessories with a military theme (camouflage, knapsacks, boots), or non-precious jewelry crafted by the indigenes of the Americas, Africa, or Asia. They spurned steak and potatoes for international menus (Mexican, Chinese, Indian, Vietnamese), or chose a vegetarian regimen. Where older adults sipped cocktails, the student rebels of the Sixties took up drugs.

The psychoactive drugs adopted by the young induced mental conditions that mocked conventional standards of decorum, rationality, and responsibility. They included marijuana preeminently (a substance that produced mild effects comparable to those produced by moderate alcohol consumption), but also "hard drugs" such as LSD (lysergic acid diethylamide), heroin, and cocaine.

Drug use for vanguard rebels had a range of purposes. Drugs might create states of heightened sensitivity. Drug use allowed the avoidance of social responsibility, inviting the initiate to "turn on and drop out." It helped the young create an alternative culture, a moral universe distinct from that of the adults who wielded power and authority.

The Sixties produced a musical style of its own of superb quality and genuinely revolutionary effect—"rock," or "hard rock," evolved from the "rock 'n' roll" of the previous decade. The drug culture shaped rock music in several ways. Listeners and performers alike often used drugs, while song lyrics often celebrated drug use. The lack of restraint induced by drug use may have spurred the innovations of rock artists. The relations between the drug culture and rock are important; yet rock is much more than the musical accompaniment to the aimless leisure hours of the drug-consuming young generation.

Rock emerged from the American musical genres of the 1950s. "Pop," or popular music, featured easy melodies sung by polished performers—mainly white—for mainstream record companies. "Country and western" was a nostalgic regional style—also mainly white—that affirmed the customs of the old south and looked back to frontier days. "Rhythm and blues," or "blues," informed by jazz performance, communicated the depths of the African American experience (see Chapter 27). Spurned by most whites, it was the cultivated taste of an affluent few. Then in 1955, the southern white performer Elvis Presley (1935–1977) emerged to sing, gyrate, and sway a new kind of music, a compelling and shocking amalgam of black rhythms and sound.

By the 1960s, the generation formed by the experience of the Cold War had accepted Presley's musical challenge. Rock was not just a blend of musical motifs; it was social criticism. Adopting the simple, direct style of folk music traditions, such singers as Joan Baez (1941–) and Bob Dylan assailed the hypocrisy of mainstream culture. Meanwhile the British group the Beatles, which shot to stardom in 1962, developed Presley's style in a new mix of youth themes and counter-cultural challenges. Young people thronged to rock concerts and danced to the music of the Beatles and their disciples—as did the 450,000 who assembled in 1969, the apogee of rock, at the Woodstock Music Festival in New York State's gracious Catskill Mountains.

Rock's radical challenge to contemporary values was echoed in the cinema of the Sixties. In its visual reconstruction of reality, film had an inherently critical function (see Chapter 27), making it the ideal medium by which to convey the Sixties mood of rebellion. The anti-establishment heroes of *Bonnie and Clyde* (Arthur Penn, director; 1967), shockingly mutilated in the protracted montage of their death at the hands of police pursuers, and of *The Wild Bunch* (Sam Peckinpah, director; 1969), which opens and ends with brutal and senseless massacres, were emblems of the Sixties spirit.

European film had different concerns, elegantly communicated to select audiences while the larger public, fleeing such serious themes, sought primarily to be entertained. In France, Italy, and Sweden filmmakers meditated on the trauma of war and explored the deeper dimensions of the self. The films of Italian directors Federico Fellini (1920–1993) and Michelangelo Antonioni (1912–), notably *La dolce vita* ("The Good Life," 1960) and *L'avventura* ("The Adventure," 1959), evoke brilliantly the contradictions of postwar lives, while the Swedish director Ingmar Bergman (1918–) experimented with visual allegory to probe human emotion, as in *The Seventh Seal* (1956). The French directors of the *nouvelle vague* ("New Wave") that arrived in the 1950s celebrated human self-determination and freedom, as did *Les Quatre cents coups* ("The 400 Blows") by François Truffaut (1932–1984) and *À bout de souffle* ("Breathless") by Jean-Luc Godard (1930–), both released in 1959.

During the 1950s, the themes of human struggle against barbarism and death, a pensive reflection on the first half of a terrible century, found expression in a new generation of novelists, such as the French-Algerian Albert Camus (1913–1960), author of *The Plague* (1947). On the stage, the "theater of the absurd" is exemplified by the work of the Irish playwright Samuel Beckett (1906–1989), whose 1953 *Waiting for Godot* took up the theme of the dramatic exploration of meaning launched in the 1920s by Pirandello and Brecht (see Chapter 27). In the same way, the existentialism of Heidegger and Sartre (see Chapter 27), rooted in the 1930s and 1940s, found a new audience in the postwar era.

From the 1960s, the humanistic themes of the first flush of postwar culture shaded toward disillusionment. Many authors looked to Third World nations for models of political and cultural engagement, while others turned to revising or "deconstructing" established norms of thought and feeling. For instance, the French historian and philosopher Michel Foucault (1926–1984) exposed in his *Madness and Civilization* (1961) the repressive operation of common social practices.

On the other side of the Iron Curtain, where thought was governed by censors, cultural life was quite different (see Chapter 28). There novelists, poets, physicists, and historians covertly circulated in *samizdat* ("self-publication," by hand-delivered manuscript) their vision of a society distorted by communist repression. Boris Pasternak (1890–1960), an author who had experienced the 1917 revolution and its Stalinist aftermath, eluded the censors by publishing in Italy his *Doctor Zhivago* (1957), a novel breathing disillusionment with the whole Bolshevik experiment. *The Gulag Archipelago* by Alexander Solzhenitsyn (1918–), printed in Paris in 1973 after long *samizdat* currency, appalled the world with the story of Soviet forced-labor camps. The powerful voices of such dissidents as the physicist Andrei Sakharov (1921–1989) and historian Roy Medvedev (1925–) also circulated in secret.

Captivated by the popular culture that radiated from the United States, the commodified product of its protest movement, most Europeans were as indifferent to these trends in literature and thought as they were to art cinema. Rock music and movies, radio and television, the casual dress of anti-establishment youth, above all the uniform of blue jeans and T-shirts—these were the prizes consumers sought. Beyond the Iron Curtain, such treasures circulated in the underground, or "black" market.

To protest, drugs, music, film, and costume the youth movement added another ingredient: sexual revolution. In this most intimate sphere of human behavior, the young again defied the values of their elders. Courtship rituals, female chastity, monogamy, even fidelity in non-marital relationships—all these were questioned and rejected. Where the fear of unwanted pregnancy had once deterred women from the path of sexual radicalism, the new pharmacological discovery—the birth control "pill"—made it feasible. The custom of "swinging" gained popularity among some, which invited promiscuous and multiple sexual encounters, including adulterous, homosexual, and interracial relations.

The sexual radicalism of the Sixties accomplished a profound social revolution. In all previous civilizations, male elites had seen to the sexual regulation of their families. Now a vanguard group, harvesting the product of the socialist and feminist movements of the past two centuries, rejected all sexual regulation, with enduring effects on culture and society. "Your sons and your daughters are beyond your command …," Dylan hissed at the elders, "for the times they are a-changin'."

Women of Worth

The sexual revolution born of the Sixties movement in the United States allowed women to reject conventional restraints. It also encouraged the forging of a new feminism that sought freedoms for women of all social classes and of all nations, races, and religions. Now all women everywhere were deemed to be, in the biblical phrase, "women of worth."

The Demand for Equality The new feminism of the 1960s was the culmination of earlier feminist ideals, restated vigorously in two important books.

WITNESSES
Culture and Politics in the 1960s

Bob Dylan, The Times They are a-Changin' (1964):
Come mothers and fathers
Throughout the land
And don't criticize
What you can't understand
Your sons and your daughters
Are beyond your command
Your old road
Is rapidly agin'
Please get out of the new one
If you can't lend your hand
For the times they are a-changin'.
(Bob Dylan, *Lyrics, 1962–1985*, 1985)

Years of Protest

Flower power: *Fears of Communist expansion in Southeast Asia led the United States into a demoralizing and increasingly unpopular war in Vietnam, which aroused a whole generation to protest. In this photograph anti-war demonstrators in Washington, D.C. oppose guns with flowers.*

In 1949, the French writer Simone de Beauvoir's (1908–1986) brilliant manifesto, *The Second Sex*, made a post-war generation of women aware of the social denigration of women. In 1963, the American Betty Friedan's (1921–) *The Feminine Mystique* identified the cultural forces that denied women power and responsibility. The mirage of "femininity" controlled women's lives, Friedan argued. It confined their thoughts to their housecleaning and their hair-dos, and their days to shopping and self-doubt. In 1966, Friedan co-founded the National Organization of Women (NOW), the foremost institutional embodiment of the new feminism.

Women activists called for female autonomy in virtually every aspect of contemporary life. In the political sphere, women leaders pushed beyond the demand for suffrage, the key issue of earlier feminism (see Chapters 25, 27), to seek greater access to power. In many nations, women candidates were elected to political office, some reaching the highest political positions, as did Golda Meir (1898–1978) in Israel, Indira Gandhi (1917–1984) in India, and Margaret Thatcher (1925–) in Britain (1979–1990). Recently, women have gained the highest political positions in Iceland, Ireland, Norway, Portugal, and Poland in Europe; and in Argentina, Bangladesh, Dominica, Nicaragua, Pakistan, Sri Lanka, and Turkey elsewhere. In Europe, they have claimed twenty-five percent of the seats in the European Parliament; the percentage of women worldwide serving as national parliamentarians, in contrast, has changed little since 1975, remaining well under ten percent.

In the workplace as in politics, women's demands heightened. Although women made up an increasing proportion of the workforce in the postwar decades—they are now about one-half of all workers in the United States, about one-third in western Europe—they received lower wages than male workers. The demand for "equal pay for equal work" has brought about in some nations the narrowing, but not the elimination, of the "wage gap."

Expanded training opportunities gained women entrance to previously closed trades and professions. They now work in construction and trucking, as police and postal officials, in the armed forces, and as attorneys and judges, medical doctors and university professors. Professionalization of those careers that women traditionally had entered, such as teaching and nursing, has enhanced their status and salaries. Increasingly, women have reached executive

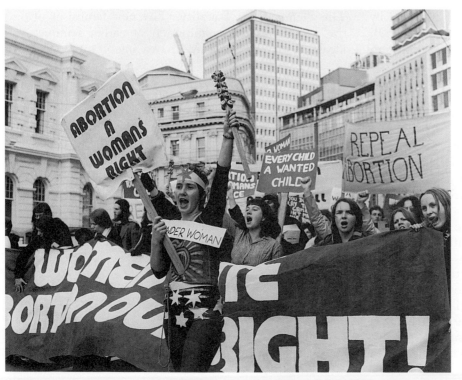

Pro-choice: *The Sixties gave rise to the sexual revolution, encouraging a new wave of feminist activism in support of abortion rights. Here, a star-spangled "Wonder Woman" leads an angry pro-choice rally in New Zealand, 1977, demanding a woman's right to bear only "wanted" children.*

levels of modern corporations where (although an invisible "glass ceiling" retards their entry to the highest positions or levels of compensation) they enjoy great authority and high salaries.

Western women increasingly insist on the right to work unimpeded by verbal or physical intimidation from male co-workers seeking sexual relations or expressing hostility to females. Activists have engaged employers and government in the crusade against "sexual harassment."

Risks to women outside of the workplace have also concerned female activists, where women are victims of rape, including marital rape, and domestic violence—the latter the leading cause, after war, of harm and death to women worldwide. In many countries, feminists have brought these violations into public consciousness, and have had them legally defined as crimes. Liberalized divorce laws in most Western nations enable women to escape abusive marriages.

The Politics of Reproduction Women's rights must include, feminists insist, the liberty to make choices about their bodies. Thus the drive undertaken by early-century feminists (see Chapter 27) to make contraception available to all women has culminated in the "pro-choice" movement of the century's last decades, whose activists have sought to make contraception safe, cheap, and available.

These goals put feminists at odds with the guardians of traditional society, mostly male. That conflict became especially sharp over the issue of abortion. In many countries, clinical abortion was and has remained illegal; in others, the right of abortion has broad acceptance. The development since 1988 of an effective oral abortifacient (RU 486) promises a greater ease of access to abortion than heretofore. In the United States, a struggle between advocates for the right to abort (the "pro-choice" faction) and those opposed (the "pro-life" faction) has been a prominent feature of contemporary life.

Paradoxically, the demands of contemporary feminism for women's complete liberation contradicts the **maternalist** goals advocated by earlier feminist leaders (see Chapter 27). These contended that women's most powerful role was in the family. Recent emphasis on women's reproductive rights, however, points away from maternalism, insisting that women be free to have few or no children; and to make those choices independently of their fathers, or the men whose offspring they carry. Advocates of traditional family generally oppose both these assumptions, as well as abortion and other mechanisms—easy divorce, certain tax measures—they perceive as undermining the stability of the family.

The feminist position dictates that unmarried women should be as free as married women to choose to bear children, and would wholly eliminate the distinction between "legitimate" and "illegitimate"

birth. The stigma associated with illegitimacy has largely faded in the developed nations, along with the economic sanctions and legal disabilities that "bastard" children so born once suffered. Furthermore, some feminist theorists argue that women who give birth outside of a marital family are entitled to government support for the raising of their children. Why, they ask, should some women be deprived of the right to raise future citizens merely because of their economic or social position, when modern democratic societies no longer bar access to educational or employment opportunities on those grounds?

The birthing of children, some feminists have argued, has been excessively medicalized. Whereas women in earlier societies (or outside of the West) often gave birth with the assistance of a female midwife, modernization has placed the process of birth in the hospital, frequently under the care of a male physician. Feminism has encouraged a revival of midwifery, and argued for a woman's right to safe and successful childbirth outside of the hospital environment. Where modern medicine may intervene too much with childbirth, however, it has not done enough for other aspects of women's health. Resources have been directed disproportionately to diseases suffered by men (prostate cancer), or to the male experience of diseases women also suffer (heart disease and stroke), and too little to diseases of women (breast cancer, osteoporosis).

Although feminists agree on most of these issues, they tend to disagree on two others: prostitution and pornography. Some feminists argue that prostitution degrades women. Others respond that women must be free to seek income from the use of their bodies, just as athletes or performers are. Similarly, some feminists see pornography as essentially antifemale, an extension of male acts of violence to representations of masculine power. Others see pornography as a form of expression that must be as free as all other forms of expression, and fear that imposing limits on pornography would open the way to reimposing restrictions on sexual expression so painfully and recently lifted.

Women Outside the West The feminist activists of the Western world have gained widespread support for women's freedoms. These are not equally recognized in other parts of the world. In communist and formerly communist states—the Soviet Union and its satellites, China, North Korea, Vietnam, and Cuba—women, in theory, possessed the same political and economic rights as men, and full freedom of reproductive choice. Yet women faced the dangers of sexual harassment, rape, and domestic abuse in communist societies as they did in the West. Despite official formulations, they have had a disproportionate responsibility for household tasks—housework, child-rearing, care of the elderly. Although abortion has

Women and the Post-War World: Manifestos, Achievements, Promises

Although the agenda for women was clear from the early years of the twentieth century, and international in scope, many goals—the vote, citizen rights, and reproductive freedoms—did not begin to be realized, even in the advanced countries of the West, until after World War II. Here, a New York group of women declare their demands for fundamental freedom in the Redstockings Manifesto of 1969. Meanwhile, the communist Chinese government act to protect women's interests in marriage in 1949, and the Islamic republic of Iran reassert in 1979, within the framework of a traditional theocracy, that culture's high valuation of women as mothers.

The Redstockings Manifesto by a New York organization of feminists (1969): Women are an oppressed class. Our oppression is total, affecting every facet of our lives. We are exploited as sex objects, breeders, domestic servants, and cheap labor ... whose only purpose is to enhance men's lives. ... Our prescribed behavior is enforced by the threat of physical violence. Because we have lived so intimately with our oppressors, in isolation from each other, we have been kept from seeing our personal suffering as a political condition. ... In reality, every such relationship is a *class* relationship, and the conflicts between individual men and women are political conflicts that can only be solved collectively.

(Circulated in typescript, July 7, 1969)

A new order for Chinese women: China's marriage law, passed by the Communists (1949): Article 1. The arbitrary and compulsory feudal marriage system, which is based on the superiority of man over woman and which ignores the children's interests, shall be abolished. The new democratic marriage system, which is based on free choice of partners, on monogamy, on equal rights for both sexes, and on protection of the lawful interests of women and children, shall be put into effect. ...

Article 7. Husband and wife are companions living together and shall enjoy equal status in the home.

(*The Marriage Law of the People's Republic of China*, 1959)

Women and the family in Revolutionary Iran: from the Constitution of the Islamic Republic of Iran (1979): The family unit is the foundation of society and the main institution for the growth and advancement of mankind. ... It is the principal duty of the Islamic government to regard women as the unifying factor of the family unit and its position. They are a factor in bringing the family out of the service of propagating consumerism and exploitation and renewing the vital and valuable duty of motherhood in raising educated human beings. ... As a result motherhood is accepted as a most profound responsibility in the Muslim viewpoint and will, therefore, be accorded the highest value and generosity.

(T. Y. Ismael, *Iraq and Iran: Roots of Conflict*, 1982)

---

been freely available, gynecological and contraceptive services have, in fact, been restricted.

In China, women's reproductive freedom has recently been constrained by state policy decreeing that no couple should have more than one child. Abortion has been imposed even when not desired, in as late as the ninth month of pregnancy. Yet these restrictions should be seen in the light of the great progress towards women's equality that has been made under communism. In traditional China, patriarchal authority was absolute; women's bodies bore its impress, as the traditional practice of the binding of feet from infancy produced the effect of disproportionately tiny feet in adult women.

Women, ironically, have suffered from the collapse of communism in the Soviet Union and eastern Europe, even as civil liberties have been restored. Communist governments had (in theory) guaranteed access to childcare, maternity benefits, and abortion, and had instituted quotas assuring women's representation in national assemblies. With their fall, women resumed burdens they thought they had lost, and have borne disproportionately the hardships of economic and cultural dislocation. In Poland, for example, the reinvigorated Roman Catholic Church has reaffirmed its uncompromising stand against birth control and abortion. In the central Asian republics of the former Soviet Union, where Islamic customs are being restored, many women are obliged to return to narrowly domestic roles.

Women of Islamic societies outside the communist realm also face special obstacles to their liberation. Islam is at once a faith and a way of life, and its law is both religious and civil (see Chapter 8). Its precepts with regard to women have not been secularized, as have been those of Western society. Women are understood to be under the protection of male kin at all times. In the more conservative Islamic societies, they are expected to be veiled in public, and may be barred from public life or even from such occupations as driving a car or going to university.

Non-Islamic Asian women also suffer disadvantages unknown in the West. In Japan, although some women obtain entry to elite universities and positions in a bustling corporate culture, traditional family norms keep many at home or, if in the workplace, in subordinate positions. In India, also, enduring social customs continue to disadvantage many women. Although the custom of *suttee*—where a widow went alive to the funeral pyre of her husband—has virtually disappeared, daughters are still valued less than their brothers in many Indian families. Often they are fed less, sold into prostitution (there are some 300,000 child prostitutes, mostly girls), or married to strangers for the advantage of other family members (and even murdered by their husbands if dowry demands are not met). The great poverty of peasant villagers exacerbates these problems. Women of the elite social strata, in contrast, are more likely to obtain secondary and university education, and to hold important public positions.

In Latin America, poverty also continues to disadvantage women, although maternal mortality rates are lower than in Africa, the Middle East, and southern Asia. A strong Catholic tradition has meant the limited availability of abortion, although contraception is widely used.

Perhaps the condition of women is nowhere more dismal than in Africa, where older social customs, including polygamy and slavery, burden many, and where exceptional poverty afflicts nearly all. Migrant labor patterns take men out of villages, and leave women behind to manage agricultural work and raise their children alone. Epidemic disease, including measles, tuberculosis, and AIDS (acquired immune deficiency syndrome; see below), has imposed upon women additional burdens of nursing and the trauma of child death. Most seriously, the rate of the heterosexual transmission of AIDS is higher in Africa than anywhere else in the world, resulting in the disproportionate infection of women. Of 3.8 million women worldwide who are infected with AIDS, 3.36 million, or eighty-eight percent, live in sub-Saharan Africa. Moreover, more women than men are carrying the HIV virus that promises the future development of the disease, implying that women will soon exceed men among the African victims of AIDS.

In a band of states cutting across Africa from Guinea in the west to Egypt, Ethiopia, and Somalia in the east, many women undergo at puberty the controversial surgical procedure of clitorectomy—also referred to as "female circumcision" or "genital mutilation". (In clitorectomy, the clitoris and all or part of the labia minora are excised; in the rarer practice of infibulation, part of the labia majora is excised as well, and most of the vaginal opening is stitched closed.) This operation is often performed by midwives without medical training and without anesthesia, in the absence of sterilized implements or a sanitary environment. It is estimated that 130 million women in the world today have undergone some form of genital cutting.

The consequence of clitorectomy performed by traditional methods is often infection and sometimes even death. In addition, the surgery results in the diminution of sensation in sexual contacts. That desensitization is at once the reason for clitorectomy, intended to promote the chastity of young brides; but also one reason for the opposition to it that has mounted in recent years. For feminists, clitorectomy is an assault on women's freedom and dignity. For members of those societies where the practice is common, it is a venerable tradition. The women concerned are themselves divided. Some have left their homelands in order to save themselves or their daughters from the experience. Others are proud to observe the customs of their people.

In a world still sharply divided into wealthier and poorer regions, women have different agendas. In the Western world (including Australia, New Zealand, and Japan), women are seeking equity in the workplace and in politics, reproductive rights, support in childcare and household responsibilities, and suitable medical attention. Elsewhere, women of the elites may share some of the concerns of their counterparts in the Western world. But most are poor, and suffer the greater likelihood that they will be undernourished, poorly educated, and exposed to epidemic disease; or sold into prostitution or slavery, or compelled to enter into unwanted or degrading marital relationships.

Perhaps the single greatest indicator of poor women's disadvantage in the developing world is their disappearance—for in several of these regions, women are missing in large numbers. Under normal circumstances, 95 girls are born for every 100 boys, and a similar sex ratio should be expected in the adult population. But there are ten percent fewer women than there should be in India, Burma, Pakistan in Asia; in Saudi Arabia, Kuwait, the United Arab Emirates, and Oman in the Middle East; and Libya in North Africa. In addition, several more nations have deficits of five percent, including China (where the deficit amounts to a monumental 20 million women), and several more with deficits up to that level. Almost all of the nations with such deficits are in the developing world (while many of the Western nations, in contrast, have a surplus of women). These aberrations result in a cumulative deficit of some 120 million women worldwide.

This disparity between the quantity of female and male life is an index of discrimination against women. More than men, women are denied nutrition, medical care, shelter, education, and other benefits. They are forced into servitude and prostitution, conditions often resulting in premature death. They are killed in childhood, or aborted prenatally, more often than male siblings. Whereas in affluent nations, abortion is a woman's choice, in poorer nations it is more often used to deny female life.

Abortion in general is more widely used in the emerging nations than in the wealthy nations of the world. Although twenty percent of pregnancies worldwide end in abortion, most abortions are performed outside of western Europe and North America. Ironically, the procedure is generally legal and medical facilities are advanced in those regions where abortions are less frequently performed. In regions with the highest rates of abortion, the procedure is more often illegal and improperly performed. Women in developing nations are 300 times more likely than their wealthier peers of the West and the North to experience complications (including death) as a consequence of abortion.

In the world's poorer regions, additionally, women are more likely to be pressed into prostitution and less likely to be educated. Especially in Asia, burdensome daughters are sold into sex slavery, and women without male protection seek income from prostitution. "Sex tourism," a custom where prosperous men from North America, western Europe, Saudi Arabia, and Australia seek recreational sex in certain cooperating markets in India, Indochina, Indonesia, and Brazil, has heightened the demand for child prostitutes.

Furthermore, women in Africa, the Middle East, and Asia show higher rates of illiteracy than men. Among the worst cases are Algeria and Zambia, where, respectively, eighty percent and seventy-four percent of adult women are illiterate, compared to thirty-eight and twenty-nine percent of adult men. These figures may be contrasted with those for most European nations and Japan, where fewer than one percent of women (but two percent in the United States) have failed to achieve literacy.

The disabilities suffered by those who are both female and poor have become the particular concerns of an international movement to uplift the condition of women around the globe. United Nations world conferences on women, attended by increasing numbers of women, met in Mexico in 1975, in Copenhagen in 1980, in Nairobi in 1985, and in Beijing in 1995. The last attracted an attendance of 30,000 women, and official delegates from 185 governments. Most nations of the world have signed the UN Convention on the Elimination of all Forms of Discrimination against Women. The recognition of the worth of women is now an international project.

Love Your Mother

Out on the American road in the 1980s, bumper stickers displayed a picture of the Earth, and beneath it the injunction: "Love your Mother." As family ties weakened and religious fervor waned, a devotion to the planet and the welfare of its peoples deepened among the activist young of the Western world.

Population, Disease, and Famine In an arithmetic to which the world was first alerted by Thomas Malthus (see Chapter 25), the welfare of human communities depends on the relation between two quantities: the size of the population and the resources that are

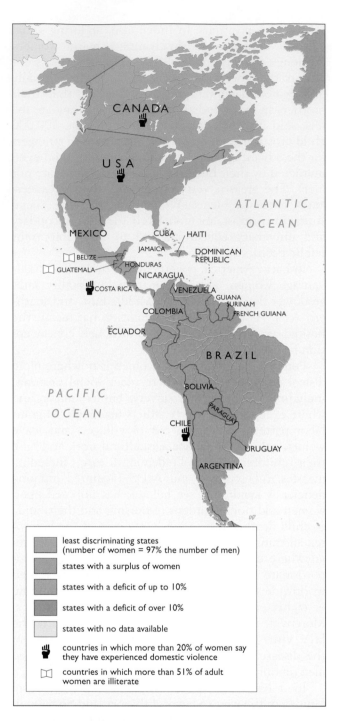

Map 30.3 (above and right) Women of the World, 1990s:
By the 1990s, the condition of women in the developed world (the West plus Japan) had improved greatly, while women in the rest of the world still suffered grave hardships. Some of the indices of women's welfare are indicated here: violence, literacy, and the female deficit. The female deficit is that number indicating "missing women": the shortfall in the number of women who should be alive given the number of men. What circumstances could account for a female deficit approaching or exceeding 10%?

available in order to sustain life. Where population exceeds available resources, disaster results.

Statisticians note with alarm recent population trends. More than 6.3 billion people lived on the earth in 2004; more than twice the 1950 figure of 2.5

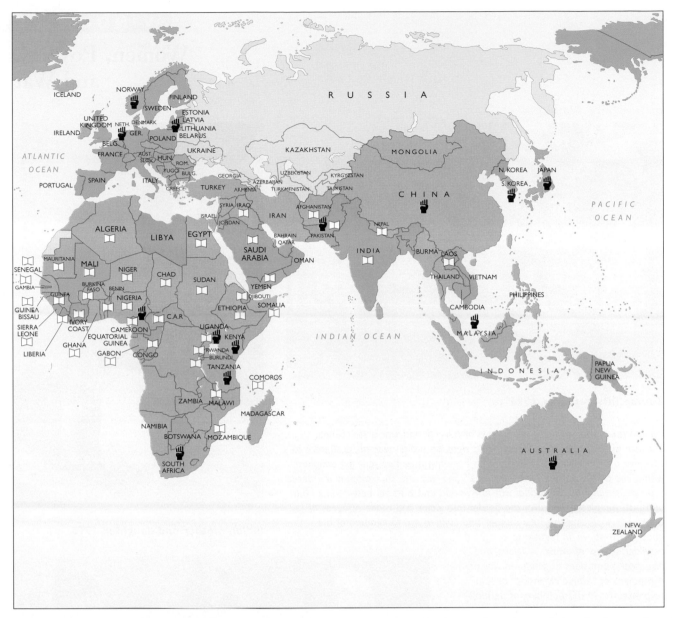

billion; nearly four times the 1900 figure of 1.6 billion; more than thirty times the 170 million in the heyday of the Roman Empire. Not only has population soared since 1750, but the rate of increase is itself increasing. Some regions are growing at annual rates of two or three percent, portending the doubling of the population, respectively, in thirty-four or twenty-three years. Some experts fear a "population bomb," population magnitudes that will threaten the welfare of all.

Population pressures vary regionally. In the developed world, population has slowed since a peak rate of growth after 1750. Birth rates declined, witnessing the practices of contraception and family planning. At present, these nations are experiencing a growth rate under one percent. Some are actually decreasing in population, as new childbirths fail to match deaths.

In the developing world (most of Asia, Africa, and Latin America), population growth rates are much higher. These regions contain eighty percent of world population, and account for ninety percent of all births. Here modernization has permitted populations

to increase far beyond traditional levels; but it has not progressed sufficiently to feed and nurture the resulting multitudes.

The most populous regions of the world experience deficits in the quality of life visible in lowered life expectancy, harsh conditions, and poor medical care. Whereas life expectancy is greater than seventy-five years in the world's wealthiest nations, it sinks to less than sixty-five in India, Indonesia, Egypt, and Peru, among others; to less than fifty-five in most of Africa; to less than forty-five in a few desperate states, including Afghanistan and Uganda; and to less than thirty-five in ten sub-Saharan African states ravaged by AIDS. High rates of child mortality correlate to decreased longevity. Among the nations with lowest life expectancy figures, as many as one in five of children under five years old die. That twenty percent rate of child mortality contrasts to a rate of one percent or less in the developed nations of the world. In 1993 in Great Britain and Germany, seven infants died per 1000 births, in Afghanistan, 163.

Zairian Tutsi refugees, 1996

Around the world, women's experience of poverty and war is sharpened because of their role as childbearers. At right, an Indian woman, desperate to conceive a male child, sits in 1993 with her unwanted two-year old daughter, whom she admits having "wanted to kill". She has, she says, already murdered a previous daughter. Genocidal war in Rwanda and Burundi between its Hutu and Tutsi peoples spilled over the border into Zaire and made refugees of thousands, including this Tutsi mother and child in the foreground of the photograph above. In Yugoslavia, a bewildering mix of ethnic, religious, and historical animosities engendered violent campaigns of "ethnic cleansing" and, in response, the NATO bombing of Serbia, perceived as the chief aggressor. In the photograph below an Albanian mother weeps for her son, killed in Kosovo in October 1998, by an explosive left by Serbian military police.

Indian mother and daughter, 1993

Now that women participate widely in war also as combatants, do you think that their attitudes toward war have changed? Will the increasing participation of women in political institutions have an impact on policies about poverty and war?

Albanian mother in mourning, 1998

To continue your investigation of this topic, please go to www.prenhall.com/king for the related **WINDOWS** on the **WEB** activity

Harsh conditions—poverty, war, hopelessness—impel people to migrate to places of greater opportunity. Migrants from India and China, for example, have moved to the Middle East and South Africa; to Canada, the United States, and the Caribbean; to Great Britain, Australia, and other Asian nations. In 1960, the United States housed 200,000 Asian immigrants; by 1998, 10 million. Sometimes whole communities of a particular national or ethnic group will migrate, in what is called a **diaspora**, or "scattering." The immigrants' new skills, as well as native customs and languages, serve to enrich the host nations where they settle, even as they often become the targets of ethnic or racial discrimination.

Overpopulation not only strains resources, but also encourages disease. The unprecedented advance of medical science in the twentieth century made it possible to prevent most childhood diseases; to cure many known bacterial infections; to repair broken limbs; to control bleeding; and to relieve pain to an extraordinary degree. By World War II, medical researchers had learned to cure (with antibiotics) or prevent (by immunization, sanitation, and pest control) most fatal epidemic diseases: among them, malaria, smallpox (now eradicated), syphilis, tuberculosis, typhoid, and yellow fever. The vaccination of children lowered the death toll caused by diphtheria, pertussis (whooping cough), and, more recently, measles. The control of influenza, which took by different estimates, 15 or 40 or more million lives in a pandemic at the end of World War I (see Chapter 26), is improving, but is frustrated by the mutability of the viral agent. More recently, progress has been made in the treatment of cancer; with early detection, many malignancies no longer kill.

Medical success in confronting the diseases of the past has not yet been equaled in the case of the deadliest plague of recent times: AIDS, developed by those infected with HIV (or human immunodeficiency virus). The disease originated in Africa, perhaps as a mutation of a dormant, endemic disease of a species of chimpanzee, and spread suddenly to the Americas around 1980. Since then, it has reached Asia, Europe, Australia, and New Zealand. By 1996, more than 6 million people had died of AIDS worldwide; in 2001, four nations (of which three were African) alone yielded more than 1 million deaths: South Africa, India, Zimbabwe, and Kenya; in the single year 2003, another 3 million died. In 2003, the UN's Joint Program on HIV/AIDS reported more than 40 million people worldwide were infected with HIV/AIDS including some 2.5 million children—figures predictive of millions more deaths in years to come. In that year alone, an additional five million were infected.

An HIV-infected person may not develop the disease itself for several years. In the wealthier nations, drug combinations are used to delay the disease's progress or, in some cases, prevent death. That therapy is not available to most people in the developing world, where both HIV infection and the number of AIDS cases are soaring. About sixty-three percent of those with HIV or AIDS worldwide live in Africa, already stressed by overpopulation and low levels of technical development. In the tiny nations of Rwanda and Burundi, twenty percent of pregnant women (who transmit the disease to their offspring in twenty-five to thirty-five percent of cases) test positive for the disease.

Unlucky Africa suffers other epidemics at the same time—principally measles and tuberculosis, resurgent wherever poverty and insanitary conditions give it leave, and newly virulent due to the development of drug-resistant strains of the bacillus.

Physicians cannot solve malnutrition, the principal cause of human misery, which still afflicts more than one in ten people worldwide. The conquest of malnutrition in the Western world and Japan is virtually complete. Not only is food produced in sufficient quantity in these regions, but it is generally made available even to the poorest citizens through government programs or private charity. Individuals still suffer hunger amid affluence; but their cases are unusual and often involve collateral problems such as mental illness and extreme isolation.

The poorer regions of the world are by definition those that fail to nourish their inhabitants. In 1992, daily caloric intake averaged 1883 in Peru; 1707 in Haiti; 1505 in Somalia (in contrast to 3671 in the United States; 3504 in Italy; and a magnificent 3778 in Ireland, previously devastated by the Great Famine of 1845). Low productivity remains the principal cause of hunger. In these poorer regions, a natural disaster—drought, flood, extreme cold—brings famine. It is in the regions where the margin of survival is narrowest that distribution mechanisms are poorest. Central governments or international agencies may be unable to deliver needed food and fuel supplies.

HOW MANY?

World Population Figures, 10,000 B.C.E.–2025 C.E.

Year	Population
10,000 B.C.E.	4 million
1 C.E.	170 million
1900	1,625 billion
1950	2,500 billion
2004	6,377 billion
2025 (projected)	7,824 billion

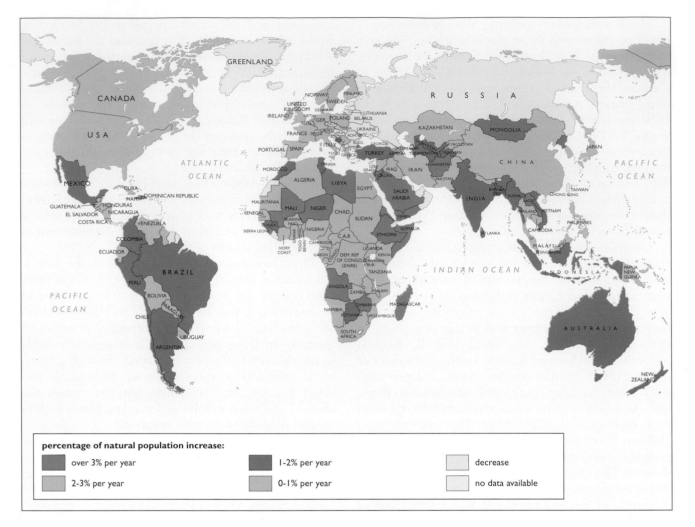

percentage of natural population increase:

over 3% per year

2-3% per year

1-2% per year

0-1% per year

decrease

no data available

Map 30.4 Rates of Population Growth, 1993: *Reaching a total of 5.5 billion in 1993, the world's population is unevenly distributed, as are rates of growth. In the lead for share of world population are China, with 21.4 percent, and India, with 16.3 percent. These nations are also growing at rapid rates of respectively one and two percent annually (with the effect that their populations will double in thirty-four and sixty-seven years respectively). What are the nations growing at the most rapid rates, and in what regions of the world are they located? What are the respective dangers of overpopulation and depopulation?* Source: M. Kidron and R. Segal, *The State of the World Atlas,* rev. 5th ed., (London: Penguin Reference, 1995) pp. 28–29.

Another kind of famine is caused not by natural disaster but by human decision-makers. Artificial famine seems all the more cruel because it is not merely preventable, but entirely willful. Warfare among private armies under fourteen different local strongmen led to mass hunger in Somalia, where over 300,000 starved in 1991–1992 as gunmen raided food shipments supplied by international agencies. In Sudan, the policies of strongman ruler Lt. Gen. Omar Ahmed al-Bashir who seized power in a 1989 coup have triggered a great famine, while his violations of human rights have led to the suspension of international aid efforts. These are small tragedies, however, next to those caused by collectivization of agriculture in the Soviet Union in the 1920s and in China in the 1950s, which each caused the deaths by starvation of some 10 million citizens (see Chapters 28, 29).

The Threat of Ecological Disaster Environmentalists are among the experts involved in the struggle against starvation, disease, and overpopulation. Environmentalism is a relatively new phenomenon, triggered by the brooding shadow of the atomic bomb. The possibility of the annihilation of humankind and the ruination of the planet moved a generation to arouse concern for the preservation of the earth which sustains us all.

In 1962, the publication *Silent Spring* by Rachel Carson (1907–1964) introduced a shocked audience to ecology, the beautiful (when undisturbed) interrelationships of plants, animals, and humans and to their natural environment. That wonderful equilibrium was jeopardized, Carson argued, by the use of toxic substances in materials used to promote agricultural productivity—chemicals that killed pests, fungi, and weeds. These agents entered and were retained by the soil, the water, and the air. They entered the tissues of plants and animals and, when ingested by humans, into our own bodies, where they caused disease. The protection of the environment became a pressing issue, especially for the young—whose perception was that their elders had irresponsibly plundered the natural world.

The environmentalist movement boomed as public education about endangered biological species and the benefits of recycling reshaped public consciousness. The first Earth Day celebration in 1970 (now celebrated annually in some 140 nations on April 22) defined the areas of concern. Earth Day was

HOW MANY?

AIDS Cases per 100,000 Population

50 or more cases		
Africa:	**Congo**	85
	Malawi	
	Namibia	103
	Zimbabwe	
Americas:	**Bahamas**	104

25 to 49 cases		
Africa:	Burkina Faso	
	Burundi	
	Cote d'Ivoire	
	Rwanda	
Americas:	Barbados	
	Bermuda	

15 to 24 cases		
Africa:	Ghana	
	Tanzania	
	Togo	
	Uganda	
Americas:	US	

Figures are per 100,000 population (1992, or latest available data). Nations with the three highest rates are indicated by bold text, with the absolute number of cases given.
Source: M. Kidron and R. Segal, The State of the World Atlas, rev. 5th ed., (London: Penguin Reference, 1995), p. 54.

WITNESSES

Love Your Mother: The Environmentalist Movement

The shocks of war in the twentieth century, accompanied by genocide and weapons of mass destruction, encouraged a renewed appreciation of the goods of the earth. Here, a United States official reflects on the origins of the environmentalist movement in 1969 and, in 1997, a journalist announces that global warming, with its threat of catastrophic climate shifts, has arrived.

Under Secretary of the Interior John C. Whitaker on the emergence of the modern environmental movement (1969): As Americans traveled in their automobiles, … they saw garish road signs, fields of junked automobiles, choked and dying streams, overgrazed and eroded hills and valleys, and roadsides lined with endless miles of beer cans, pop bottles, and the tin foil from candy wrappers and cigarette packages. They could no longer move a few hundred miles West: the frontiers were gone.
(From B. Kline, *First Along the River: A Brief History of the US Environmental Movement*, 1997)

Journalist Ross Gelbspan announces that global warming is here (1997): The recent weather record has been marked by more intense rainfalls and severe snowstorms; stronger hurricanes; unseasonal and prolonged droughts, resulting in crop failures and devastating forest fires from Texas to Mongolia; killer heat waves from India to Chicago; and record flooding from Yemen to Nepal. … Environmentalists have been warning us about global warming for years. What is news is that global warming is no longer merely a future possibility. The heat is on. Now. Its early impacts, in the form of more extreme and unstable climate, are being felt even as I write.
(Ross Gelbspan, *The Heat is On: The High Stakes Battle over Earth's Threatened Climate*, 1997)

followed by the United Nations Conference on the Human Environment, held in Stockholm (Sweden) in 1972, which resulted in the establishment of the United Nations Environment Program. In 1983, the General Assembly further established the World Commission on Environment and Development. In 1992, the United Nations Conference on Environment and Development (the "Earth Summit") met in Rio de Janeiro, attended by delegates from more than 178 countries. From the 1970s, "Green" parties joined the spectrum of political groups that contended for seats in European parliaments. The movement to protect the environment, in a brief generation, had leapt to the forefront of the international agenda.

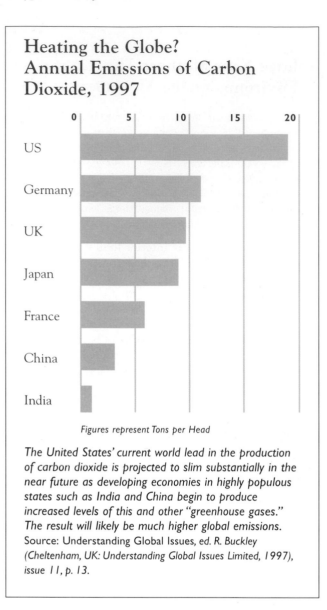

Heating the Globe?
Annual Emissions of Carbon Dioxide, 1997

Figures represent Tons per Head

The United States' current world lead in the production of carbon dioxide is projected to slim substantially in the near future as developing economies in highly populous states such as India and China begin to produce increased levels of this and other "greenhouse gases." The result will likely be much higher global emissions.
Source: Understanding Global Issues, ed. R. Buckley (Cheltenham, UK: Understanding Global Issues Limited, 1997), issue 11, p. 13.

chlorofluorocarbons, used in aerosol sprays and in refrigeration and air-conditioning systems, cause the degradation of the ozone layer.

The emission of carbon dioxide and other gases, an accompaniment of industrial processes, is a cause, environmentalists argue, of the tendency toward "global warming". The air thickened by gaseous emissions traps the sun's heat close to the surface of the earth. Temperatures rise as a result; as they have been rising throughout the century.

Living things have suffered from the poisons that modern life broadcasts into air, soil, and water. Environmentalists created lists of "endangered species" and launched campaigns to save those injured by commercial ventures—whales poisoned by oil leaks from tankers, seals cruelly hunted, dolphins trapped in nets. As species are endangered, so natural habitats are jeopardized by the encroachments of modern society. Wetlands and rainforests around the world are shrinking—25 million acres of trees are lost each year—and with them the capacity for vegetable and marine life to replenish the earth and atmosphere.

Non-Governmental Organizations   Just as an array of international organizations promote environmentalist agendas, others support a variety of humanitarian causes. These "non-governmental organizations" (NGOs), many of them private or Church-related, some sponsored by the United Nations, have guided the movements for human health, welfare, and

Among the many issues environmentalists raised were those of pollution, the depletion of the stratospheric ozone layer, global warming, and the endangerment of living species and habitats. Pollution accompanies industrialization. But Europe and the West generally, pioneers of industrialization, had cleaned up its environment to some extent. The major polluters were now in the newly industrializing nations of eastern Europe, India, and China. Yet the developed nations still polluted the air with chemical substances, spraying "acid rain" on humans, animals, and soil. They polluted the seas with waste from factories and naval vessels, imperiling whole categories of marine life. They built nuclear plants to generate power, which sometimes malfunctioned, releasing lethal radiation into the atmosphere.

Pollutants of a certain type, especially chlorofluorocarbons, have resulted in the thinning of the ozone layer, which is the protective gaseous zone of the earth's atmosphere that blocks the harmful effects of the sun's radiation. When released into the air, development. Constituting a new category of cooperative human effort—sometimes called "the third sector"—funded largely by grants from philanthropic foundations (notably the Ford or Rockefeller Foundations, both United States agencies) or private donations, they have become the primary agents of human welfare in a world that has turned from empire and values pluralism.

Senior among these NGOs is the International Red Cross, founded in 1864 (and since 1986 renamed the International Movement of the Red Cross and Red Crescent, to include Islamic national members), and honored with Nobel Peace Prizes in 1917, 1944, and 1963. The Red Cross serves the needs of the wounded and displaced in wartime, and brings food, clothing, medical care, and expert advisors to victims of natural disasters. Especially devoted to the medical needs of impoverished peoples or communities in crisis has been the French organization Médecins sans Frontières ("Doctors without Boundaries"), while CARE tends to the needs of children worldwide. Amnesty International has pursued the cause of identifying prisoners of conscience (those imprisoned for no crime but criticism of government policies) and organizing international support for their release.

In addition, many agencies and programs of the United Nations are devoted to the control and prevention of disease (the World Health Organization, or WHO); the increase and distribution of food supplies (the Food and Agriculture Organization, or FAO); the welfare of children (the United Nations International Children's Emergency Fund, or UNICEF); the facilitation of world trade (the World Trade Organization, or WTO); and the promotion of knowledge (the United Nations Educational, Scientific, and Cultural Organization, or UNESCO). Informing the work of its agencies is the general mission of the United Nations: "to save succeeding generations from the scourge of war," as its Charter reads; and to "reaffirm faith in fundamental human

---

WITNESSES

The Age of Human Rights

Since the close of World War II, more and more of the world's nations have been moving toward consensus on some fundamental human rights and obligations. Some of that thinking is evident in the following sections from key documents of the United Nations: its 1948 Declaration on Human Rights; its 1948 Convention on Genocide; and its 1989 Conventions on the Rights of the Child.

UN Universal Declaration of Human Rights (1948):
Article 1. All human beings are born free and equal in dignity and rights. ...
Article 2. Everyone is entitled to all the rights and freedoms set forth in this Declaration, without distinction of any kind, such as race, colour, sex, language, religion, political or other opinion, national or social origin, property, birth or other status. ...
Article 3. Everyone has the right to life, liberty and security of person. ...
(From *United Nations Publication* No. 63.1.13, 1963)

UN Convention on the Prevention and Punishment of the Crime of Genocide (1948):
Article 1. The Contracting Parties confirm that genocide whether in time of peace or in time of war, is a crime under international law which they undertake to prevent and to punish.
Article 2. ... [G]enocide means any of the following acts committed with intent to destroy, in whole or in part, a national, ethnical, racial or religious group, such as: (a) Killing members of the group; (b) Causing serious bodily or mental harm to members of the group; (c) Deliberately inflicting on the group conditions of life calculated to bring about its physical destruction in whole or in part; (d) Imposing measures intended to prevent births within the group; (e) Forcibly transferring children of the group to another group.
(From *Yearbook of the United Nations,* 1950)

UN Convention on the Rights of the Child (1989):
Principle 2. The child shall enjoy special protection, and shall be given opportunities and facilities, by law and by other means, to enable him to develop physically, mentally, morally, spiritually and socially in a healthy and normal manner and in conditions of freedom and dignity. ...
Principle 4. The child shall enjoy the benefits of social security. He shall be entitled to grow and develop in health; to this end, special care and protection shall be provided both to him and to his mother, including adequate pre-natal and post-natal care. The child shall have the right to adequate nutrition, housing, recreation and medical services. ...
Principal 6. The child ... needs love and understanding. He shall, wherever possible, grow up in the care and under the responsibility of his parents, and, in any case, in an atmosphere of affection and of moral and material security; a child of tender years shall not, save in exceptional circumstances, be separated from his mother. ...
Principle 7. The child is entitled to receive education, which shall be free and compulsory, at least in the elementary stages. ...
(From UN High Commissioner for Human Rights, 1997)

rights, in the dignity and worth of the human person, in the equal rights of men and women and of nations large and small."

Successor to the failed League of Nations, the United Nations was established in 1945, when representatives of fifty nations approved its charter. Consisting of a fifteen-member Security Council and a General Assembly, in which all member nations were to participate equally, the United Nations aimed to represent the concerted will of the nations of the globe in seeking peaceful resolution of conflicts and in promoting human welfare. By 1960, about fifty additional nations were admitted to membership, many of them newly independent states of Asia and Africa. By the late 1990s, the roster exceeded 180.

The United Nations has found multilateral solutions for several political confrontations in the postwar era, intervening in the Arab-Israeli crisis of 1947–1948, the Korean War in 1950, the Suez crisis in 1956, and the Congo crisis of 1960. Recently, it has coordinated international humanitarian and military "peace" forces, in the spirit of the 1992 "Agenda for Peace" outlined by Boutros Boutros-Ghali (1922–) of Egypt, UN Secretary-General 1992–1996. The World Court, the judicial organ of the United Nations, adjudicates disputes about territorial rights, sovereignty and nationality, immigration and asylum.

In December 1948, the United Nations adopted the Universal Declaration of Human Rights as a standard to which the nations of the world must be held. Among its principles were those contained in foundational documents of the liberal tradition such as the American Declaration of Independence and the French Declaration of the Rights of Man and the Citizen. To these were added guarantees of equality without distinctions of "race, color, sex, language,

religion, political or other opinion, national or social origin, property, birth or other status"; assurances of the enduring right to national citizenship, and the right to flee or return to one's own nation; the legitimation of government by the will of the people, expressed in free and fair elections; the prohibition of both slavery and torture. The UN Declaration notably includes provisions about private matters, likely to be affected by local belief and custom, as well as by marriage (which must rest on the consent of both man and woman) and childrearing (children must receive education that would expand and multiply their life chances, and training in respect for human rights and freedom).

The UN Declaration of Human Rights was adopted unanimously (the Soviet bloc nations, along with South Africa and Saudi Arabia, abstaining). A less ambitious, but still pathbreaking agreement was reached at Helsinki (Finland) in 1975. The United States, Canada, and all the countries of Europe, except Albania (including the Soviet Union and its satellites)—signed the Helsinki Accords, pledging their acceptance of human rights standards in validation of the principles of the UN document of 1948. Meanwhile, in November 1989, the United Nations issued a Convention on the Rights of the Child, which was a corollary to its universal Declaration of Human Rights.

By the time the Cold War ended, consensus had been reached among the world's major powers on the preeminent values of peace and human dignity. But far from the centers of wealth and technological competition for wealth and power produced new paradigms of war—tragic battles, and it is generally wished, the last battles, in the long history of human conflict (see Epilogue).

Conclusion

RETREAT FROM ARMAGEDDON AND THE MEANING OF THE WEST

For more than fifty years after the bombing of Hiroshima signaled the end of World War II, the peoples of the Western world lived in fear. Their world was split between a communist "East" and a "free West," both armed with weapons of mass destruction and locked in mutual hatred. After 1989, with the disintegration of Soviet communism, deadlock eased.

Meanwhile, a younger generation, led by a prosperous and willful vanguard of American students, turned from the Cold War to promote personal liberation, sexual revolution, and global activism. They have learned that the world is divided not so much between the chimeras of "East" and "West," as between North and South, the zones of the developed and developing nations. Disturbingly, that region, which is most burdened by poverty, disease, and overpopulation, also suffers disproportionately from injustice, terror, and war.

Among the questions that emerge from the second half of the twentieth century are these: will a renewed West, freed from the prospect of Armageddon, reassert its commitment to the finest values of the Western tradition? And will it—or can it, or should it—lead the way in the building of a humane and prosperous global civilization?

QUESTIONS TO CONSIDER

1. Could the Cold War have been avoided at the end of World War II?

2. How did the rivalry between the two superpowers create the "Third World"? Did the nations of the Third World have common interests?

3. Why did the Soviet Union collapse in 1991? Were internal failings, or external pressures more important?

4. Why did the Sixties movement emerge? Were political events, or ideologies, or cultural messages most critical in driving this generational shift? To what extent was the sexual revolution a necessary part of the Sixties project?

5. Why do the issues of overpopulation and environmentalism emerge from the Sixties movement?

SUGGESTED RESOURCES

Allyn, David, *Make Love, Not War: The Sexual Revolution: An Unfettered History* (London: Routledge, 2001). Consulting with advocates of sexual freedom, feminists, lawyers, prostitutes, and gays, Allyn retraces the history of the sexual revolution.

Boyer, Paul, *By the Bomb's Early Light: American Thought and Culture at the Dawn of the Atomic Age* (Chapel Hill, NC: University of North Carolina Press, 1994). Compelling exploration of the cultural and psychological impact of the bomb on Americans.

Courtois, Stephane, et al., *The Black Book of Communism: Crimes, Terror, Repression* (Cambridge, MA: Harvard University Press, 1999). Controversial exploration of the death toll of communism in its manifestations around the world.

Furet, François, *The Passing of an Illusion: the Idea of Communism in the Twentieth Century*, trans. Deborah Furet (Chicago: University of Illinois Press, 1999). Challenges the Left's Romantic and anti-liberal vision of the French Revolution, which as he sees it distorted political thought and action into modern times.

Fursenko, Aleksandr, and Timothy Naftali, *One Hell of a Gamble: Khrushchev, Castro, and Kennedy, 1958–1964* (New York: W. W. Norton, 1997). Gripping account of relations among Cuba, the USSR, and the US from the Cuban missile crisis to Khrushchev's fall.

Gaddis, John Lewis, Philip H. Gordon, Ernest R. May and Jonathan Rosenberg, *Cold War Statesmen Confront the Bomb: Nuclear Diplomacy since 1945* (Oxford: Clarendon Press, 2000). Studies the careers of ten statesmen to assess what role the existence of the bomb played in their political strategies.

Haynes, John Early and Harvey Klehr, *Venona: Decoding Soviet Espionage in America* (New Haven: Yale University Press, 1999). Based on United States files only opened in 1995, reveals the vast extent of the post-war Soviet espionage network.

Ignatieff, Michael, *The Warrior's Honor: Ethnic War and the Modern Conscience* (New York: Metropolitan, 1998). Contrasts the mercenaries and warlords committed to the ethnic tribalism which informs so many modern wars with the well-meaning peace interventionists, diplomats, journalists, and medical teams who share an ideal of universal human rights.

Isserman, Maurice & Michael Kazin, *America Divided: the Civil War of the 1960s* (Oxford: Oxford University Press, 1999). Well-researched comprehensive study of the different issues that sparked the divisions of the Sixties and which still continue to inform a cultural divide within American life.

Lomborg, Bjorn, *The Skeptical Environmentalist: Measuring the Real State of the World* (Cambridge: Cambridge University Press, 2001). A controversial work amply supported by statistical evidence, argues that the environmental crises regularly announced in the press are not problems at all.

McNeill, J.R., *Something New Under the Sun: An Environmental History of the Twentieth-Century World* (New York: W.W. Norton, 2000). Explores the progress of environmental degradation over the past century, and how it can be reversed without damaging the economy.

Nelson, Barbara J. and Najma Chowdhury, eds., *Women and Politics Worldwide* (New Haven, CT: Yale University Press, 1994). Vast essay collection, surveying women's varied experience in 44 countries around the world.

Volkogonov, Dmitri, *Autopsy for an Empire: The Seven Leaders who Built the Soviet Regime* (trans. Harold Shukman; New York: Free Press, 1998). The general who initiated the declassification of Soviet files narrates the Soviet story from the Bolshevik takeover to the regime's collapse in 1991.

Cold War International History Project, with document library, guides to institutes, links, resources (Woodrow Wilson International Center): **http://cwihp.si.edu**

The Sixties Project Website, documents, resources, links (University of Virginia): **http://lists.village.virginia.edu/sixties/HTML_docs/Scholar.html**

Women in Philosophy: Feminism—resources on feminist women thinkers: **http://www.eraticimpact.com/~feminism**

United Nations homepage (English), with links to reports and resources on Peace and Security, Economic and Social Development, Human Rights, Humanitarian Affairs, and International Law: **http://www.un.org/english**

Two approaches to environmentalism: Greenpeace International homepage: **http://www.greenpeace.org**

The New Environmentalism (RPPI/NEPI): **http://www.newenvironmentalism.org**

⊙ Western Civilization Documents CD-ROM

30.1 Nikita S. Khrushchev: Address to the Twentieth Party Congress
30.2 George Kennan, from Memoirs: 1925–1950
30.3 Bosnia: The Two Faces of War
30.6 The Wall in My Backyard

EPILOGUE:
THE FUTURE
OF THE WEST

The Westward Journey *When the Greek hero Ulysses (the Odysseus of Homer's Odyssey) returned home, after the Trojan war and twenty years of wandering, he did not, as imagined in a poem by the English poet Alfred, Lord Tennyson (1809–1892), stay there. Grizzled and old, yet "always roaming with a hungry heart," he set out to discover what lay beyond the western horizon of his Mediterranean world: "To strive, to seek, to find, and not to yield."*

Ulysses' journey brings to mind the condition of Western civilization as it enters the twenty-first millennium. The West is one of the world's youngest civilizations; but it is aging. Will it fade? Or will it continue the journey westwards, a "gray spirit yearning in desire," like Ulysses, venturing "to sail beyond the sunset":

> *To follow knowledge like a sinking star*
> *Beyond the utmost bound of human thought?*

What is the future of the West? Will there still be a distinctively Western world, and a Western civilization, in this third millennium of the Common Era? Or will the West shrink to "a small and inconsequential peninsula at the extremity of the Eurasian land mass," as Samuel Huntington has suggested? (see Witnesses p. 916).

We cannot answer this question. But we can consider some of the main lines of the world's economic, political, and cultural development over the fifteen years since the close of the Cold War in order to understand what may lie ahead for the civilization of the West. On the one hand, the world of nations appears to be moving towards greater political integration and economic globalization. On the other hand, some peoples and cultures and civilizations are striking out against precisely these trends, retreating to ancient customs and reviving ancient hostilities against those whose message of modernization—and Westernization—is viewed as threatening. Faced with this challenge, will the West lose its identity? Or will it strive aggressively—in the face, perhaps, of bitter criticism and daunting risks—for preeminence?

COMING TOGETHER

The breakup of the Soviet empire completed in the last days of 1991 (see Chapter 30) dramatically changed the world's political landscape. For nearly fifty years, two superpowers had faced each other with an intense antagonism; then one of those contestants slipped away. So momentous is the change that it can be said that the twentieth century ended in that year—in the same way that, in a sense, it began only in 1914 with the outbreak of World War I. This "short twentieth century" contrasts with the "long nineteenth century" (1789–1914), in which the nations of the West consolidated their power and prestige. Those nations then dragged the world into two calamitous world wars that resulted in mass slaughter and the prospect of universal destruction. Those conflicts in turn led to the Cold War and its bipolar geopolitical configuration that prevailed from the end of World War II until the moment when Gorbachev walked out of the Kremlin and the post-Soviet era began.

The end of the Cold War facilitated the coming together of nations, beginning with the nations of Europe, the matrix of Western civilization. In 1945, Europe was divided between victors and vanquished, those whose cities had been bombed and populations ravaged from those who had survived with lesser injuries. A new barrier of suspicion emerged between the nations of eastern Europe, which became satellites of the mammoth Soviet Union, and the nations of western Europe which aligned themselves with the giant across the Ocean, the United States (see Chapter 30).

European Recovery Since 1945

Yet from the exhausted, shattered European states that emerged from World War II in 1945, an increasingly united Europe formed. Those nations of western Europe which were free to do so proceeded to shape their futures through the parliamentary process. From the deep ideological rifts of the 1920s and 1930s, European politics have moved towards the center, with principal leaders chosen alternately from left-center and right-center parties. Thus Britain elected a Labour government in 1945, then shifted back and forth between Labour and Conservative governments over the next fifty years. The 1997 election made centrist, Europe-conscious Labour candidate Anthony Blair (b. 1953) Prime Minister. Since 1949, West Germany (and, after 1990, a united Germany) has shifted between Christian Democrat and Social Democrat leaders; the most recent elections, in 1998 and 2004, brought Social Democrat Gerhard Schröder (b. 1944) and a socialist-Green (environmentalist) coalition to power.

Italy was largely under Christian Democrat control until 1983, when a socialist coalition took over, to be repudiated in 2001 by the election of the right-leaning ("Forza Italia", or "Forwards, Italy!") leader Silvio Berlusconi. In 1958, shifting from the left-wing government installed in 1945, France changed course with the election of Charles de Gaulle (1890–1970) and, in 1959, the institution of the Fifth Republic. Since De Gaulle's resignation in 1969, first conservative and then socialist and centrist leaders held the reins. In 1995, conservative Jacques Chirac became president, sharing power with Jean-Pierre Raffarin as prime minister since 2002.

In these and other European nations outside the sphere once subject to Soviet power, transfers of power occur peacefully. Leaders of all parties preside over tax-heavy welfare states dedicated to protecting the citizens whose elders had begun, and suffered the consequences of, two world wars. In recent years, consensus has formed in western Europe for a non-ideological "Third Way," neither "Left" nor "Right," a pragmatic politics that both cherishes the citizens while it promotes the conditions that generate greater wealth for the nation. An exception is Ireland, which has adopted a pro-growth, low-tax economic orientation, and has enjoyed exceptional prosperity over the last decade.

Transnational Alliances

Over the same post-war period, two transnational alliances formed which pointed towards the political and economic unification of the continent: the Common Market, formed in 1957, and NATO, formed in 1949 (see Chapter 30). The first allowed for the free flow of goods across the borders of member nations. The latter, led by the United States, sought to defend its members against possible aggression from the Soviet Union and its satellites (which in 1955 organized the Warsaw Pact of allied eastern European states under its leadership).

The European Union

Since its founding, the Common Market has expanded to include more states and new forms of

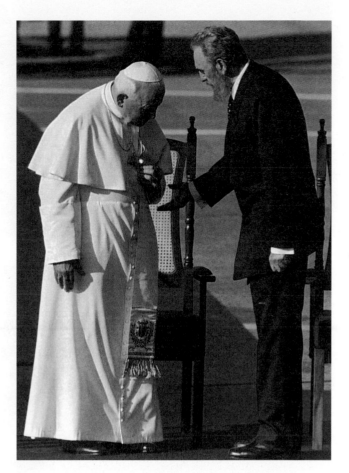

The Pope meets Castro: *The ending of the Cold War has brought into increasing contact societies and individuals long separated by mutual hostility and fear. Here, Pope John Paul II, the head of the Roman Catholic Church, meets Cuban leader Fidel Castro. Cuba is one of the last remaining communist states and is an officially atheist state.*

cooperation. It was replaced in 1967 by the European Community, and in 1993 became the European Union (EU). The EU is centered in Brussels (Belgium), with a written constitution and its own parliament (which meets in Brussels or Strasbourg, France) directly elected by popular vote. It aims to establish a common foreign policy for its members, and looks to their eventual political and economic integration. The collapse of communism in eastern Europe after 1989 made the vision of a united Europe seem even more plausible.

In May 2004, the EU admitted ten additional members, becoming a partnership of twenty-five states. The effect of the 2004 enlargement is to incorporate many nations that were isolated in the eastern bloc under Soviet domination until 1989. These states, on the whole, lag in wealth behind the older EU members. Their 75 million new citizens of Europe earn only 40% of the income, on average, of the citizens of established states. In addition, three more states— Bulgaria, Romania, and Turkey—have applied for EU membership. The date of 2007 has been set for the admission of Bulgaria and Romania.

Map 31.1 Europe: the Continent, the Union, the Alliance: *Europe is not only a continent and a set of nations as well as a unity created by the European Union and the eleven nations adopting a unitary currency, and the political alliance of NATO.*

Euroland

As of 2002, twelve of fifteen members of the European Union (all but the United Kingdom, Denmark, and Sweden) joined in the Economic and Monetary Union (EMU). Aiming to achieve the economic integration of the continent preparatory to its greater political integration, the EMU exercises strict discipline over member states in matters such as national indebtedness and monetary policy. On December 31, 1998, as one member proclaimed "the dawn of a new era in the integration of Europe," the EMU introduced its new currency, the "euro." In January 2002, the euro became Europe's single currency, and Europe was transformed into "Euroland," a vast new entity with some 300 million inhabitants and a twenty-five percent share of the world's economic output (nearly equal to the United States' share of twenty-eight percent).

Early in the third millennium, Europe was well on its way to continental unification at the levels of economic, political and cultural cooperation. It recalls the Europe of a millennium before, which, despite

impoverishment and political fragmentation, was building the cultural unity of Christianitas, or Christendom, based on a common faith, language, and intellectual traditions (see Chapter 10).

Post-Soviet States As the major states of western Europe have drawn more closely together over the last decade, they are readmitting to their midst, and to the concept of "Europe," eastern European states that lay under the Soviet aegis before 1989. In 1990, at sacrificial cost, the western German Federal Republic reunited with the eastern German Democratic Republic, which has begun to catch up with the economic powerhouse that is its western half. During the 1990s, Poland, Hungary, and the Czech Republic launched new economic policies. Painful at first, these policies have enabled those nations to become weaned from the command economies of the Soviet era and to compete and prosper in the European economic world. Russia itself lapsed into economic as well as constitutional confusion in 1992, its first post-Soviet year, and reached a nadir of misery in 1998. In 2001, at last, it began to

Through a Glass Darkly

Historians rarely dare to predict the future; but some do, and do so fearlessly. In these passages composed at the end of the twentieth century, historian Paul Kennedy in 1993 points to the need for technology to address the problem of population pressure; Czech president, author, and former dissident Václav Havel in 1999 envisions the creation of universal culture increasingly without political boundaries; and Nobel Prize-winning economist Amartya Sen in 2001 warns against the reduction of human nature to a single cultural identity.

Paul Kennedy on the Power of Technology versus the power of population (1993): The greatest test for human society as it confronts the twenty-first century is how to use "the power of technology" to meet the demands thrown up by "the power of population"; that is, how to find effective global solutions in order to free the poorer three-quarters of humankind from the growing Malthusian trap of malnutrition, starvation, resource depletion, unrest, enforced migration, and armed conflict ... The technology explosion is taking place overwhelmingly in economically advanced societies, many of which possess slow-growing or even declining populations. However, the demographic boom is occurring in countries with limited technological resources, very few scientists and skilled workers, inadequate investment in research and development, and few or no successful corporations; in many cases, their governing elites have no interest in technology, and cultural and ideological prejudices are ... tilted against change ... Simply because we do not know the future, it is impossible to say with certainty whether global trends will lead to terrible disasters or be diverted by astonishing advances in human adaption. What is clear is that as the Cold War fades away, we face not a "new world order" but a troubled and fractured planet, whose problems deserve the serious attention of politicians and publics alike. ...
(Paul Kennedy, *Preparing for the Twenty-First Century*, New York: Random House, 1993)

Václav Havel discusses the end of the nation-state and the coming of global society (1999): There is every indication that the glory of the nation-state as the culmination of every national community's history, and its highest earthly value—the only one, in fact, in the name of which it is permissible to kill, or for which people have been expected to die—has already passed its peak.

It would seem that the enlightened efforts of generations of democrats, the terrible experience of two world wars ... and the evolution of civilization have finally brought humanity to the recognition that human beings are more important than the state.

In this new world, people—regardless of borders—are connected in millions of different ways: through trade, finance, property, and information. Such relationships bring with them a wide variety of values and cultural models that have a universal validity. It is a world, moreover, in which a threat to some has an immediate impact on everyone ... in which all of us—whether we like it or not—must begin to bear responsibility for everything that occurs. In such a world, the idol of state sovereignty must inevitably dissolve. ...

If modern democratic states are usually defined by qualities such as their respect for human rights and liberties, the equality their citizens enjoy, and the existence of a civil society, then the condition toward which humanity will, and ... must, move will probably be characterized by a universal or global respect for human rights, by universal civic equality and the rule of law, and by a global civic society.
(Address to the Canadian Senate and House of Commons, April 29, 1999; pub. *New York Review of Books* (June 10, 1999); trans. from Czech by Paul Wilson)

Amartya Sen examines plural identities versus civilizational camps (2001): Dividing the world into discrete civilizations is not just crude. It propels us into the absurd belief that this partitioning is natural and necessary and must overwhelm all other ways of identifying people. That imperious view goes not only against the sentiment that "we human beings are all much the same," but also against the more plausible understanding that we are diversely different. ...

Each of us has many features in our self-conception. Our religion, important as it may be, cannot be an all-engulfing identity. Even a shared poverty can be a source of solidarity across the borders. The kind of division highlighted by, say, the so-called "antiglobalization" protesters—whose movement is, incidentally, one of the most globalized in the world—tries to unite the underdogs of the world economy and goes firmly against religious, national or "civilizational" lines of division.

The main hope of harmony lies not in any imagined uniformity, but in the plurality of our identities, which cut across each other and work against sharp divisions into impenetrable civilizational camps. Political leaders who think and act in terms of sectioning off humanity into various "worlds" stand to make the world more flammable—even when their intentions are very different. They also end up, in the case of civilizations defined by religion, lending authority to religious leaders seen as spokesmen for their "worlds." In the process, other voices are muffled and other concerns silenced. The robbing of our plural identities not only reduces us; it impoverishes the world.
("A World Not Neatly Divided," *The New York Times*, November 23, 2001)

show signs of economic recovery. At the same time, under president Vladimir Putin—upon whom Boris Yeltsin suddenly conferred the mantle of power shortly before midnight on December 31, 1999, a position later ratified by election—Russia has sought to rejoin Europe and the West. Putin's rapprochement in 2001 with newly-elected US President George W. Bush moved Russia forcefully in that direction.

The US and Europe

President Bush, meanwhile, saddled from the outset with a controversial election that he scantily won, began his term with an approach towards Europe more guarded than his predecessor's, William Jefferson Clinton (president 1993–2000). The terrorist attack of September 11, 2001 (see below) reestablished American solidarity with Britain, its traditional European ally, while leading to new frictions especially with the continental giants, France and Germany.

The Americas

In the Americas, both Clinton and Bush worked to build hemispheric cooperation during the 1990s. From the 1950s through the 1980s, The policies of the United States towards its Latin American neighbors had been colored by Cold War anxieties, resulting in the bolstering of authoritarian regimes and sporadic military interventions. At the same time, the United States extended assistance to emerging economies, and was the source of important financial investment.

By the 1990s, as the Cold War receded into memory, and leading Latin American states (Brazil, Argentina, Chile) developed powerful economies, these nations could better cooperate with the wealthier nations to the north. The Americas have also benefitted from NAFTA (North American Free Trade Agreement), enacted in 1994, which facilitated trade between Canada, the United States, and Mexico. A separate free trade agreement between the US and Chile is likely to profit both partners.

Many Latin American states have struggled with economic challenges over the last decade—inflation, budget deficits, excessive debt, and capital flight. These pressures have weakened some states whose democratic commitments have become fragile as they lean towards dictators both left and right. The possibility that some Latin American economies will "dollarize," or convert their currencies (already linked to the dollar) to United States dollars, suggests the consolidation of greater regional economic unity in the future, a goal called for at the Summit of the Americas held in Quebec in June 2000.

Both in Europe and the Americas, the quest for greater prosperity through barrier-free trade has helped bring nations together. That quest also drives the other nations of the world to embrace free market systems, and to bind them, if reluctantly at times, to the Western model of technological modernization, economic growth, and democratic values.

The Ties that Bind

The growing unity of the Western blocs, European and American, is part of a larger process towards the greater economic and cultural interconnectedness of the world—the process called globalization.

The Global Economy In economic terms, globalization means that the separate markets of the world—local, regional, and continental—are now linked into one. Not only do commodities purchased in the Western world, such as coffee, bananas, and oil, come from other continents, but clothing, carpets, and automobiles, among many other goods, are likely to have been manufactured in Asia, Africa, or South America where cheap labor markets lure Western investors. Jobs can be exported as well as materials, in a process called "outsourcing," whereby corporations minimize labor costs, depriving their own more highly-paid nationals of those jobs. Business is international, carried on by itinerant entrepreneurs and speeded by modern technologies of transportation, communication, and computerization.

Rich and poor nations In the global economy, the processes of industrialization and urbanization that began in Europe before 1800 have become the model for regions remote from that source (see Chapter 21). But progress has been irregular and incomplete. The "developed" world includes the industrialized nations of the West and Asia—Japan, China, and the Asian "dragons" or "tigers," now roaring back from the financial crisis of 1997 (see Chapter 29). It is far wealthier than the "developing" world, which includes many Asian, African, and Latin American nations.

That inequality is a source of resentment and unrest among the present losers in the globalization process, who suffer enormously during periods of economic transition or crisis caused by trade or currency imbalances—or by the corruption or inefficiency of local governments. The wealthier nations control the major international organizations that promote free trade and manage international loans and currency transfers; they express sympathy, but persist nevertheless to effect those changes that will facilitate free trade, based on sound currencies, across national boundaries. In the end, free markets and global trade networks, they promise, will generate economic growth and benefit all.

It was this promise of greater wealth after transitional pain that US President Clinton extended to the Bulgarians in November 1999, when he assured

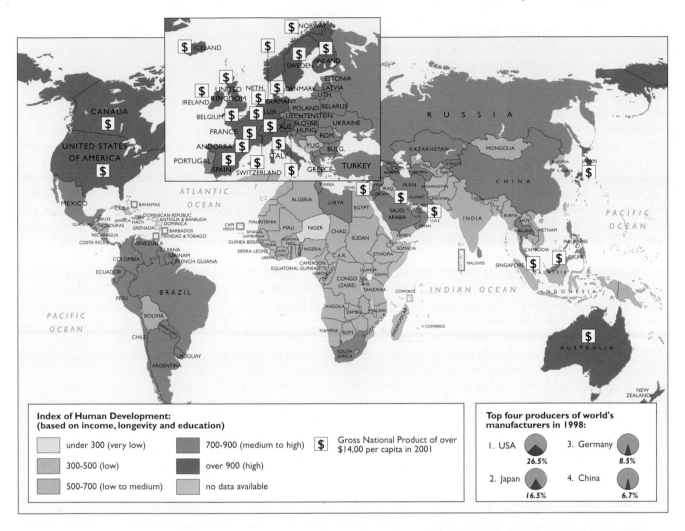

Map 31.2 The Wealth of Nations: Developed and Developing Nations of the World: *As the twenty-first century opens, the world appears to be divided between the wealthier nations, mostly Western, and poorer ones, mostly outside the West. With the exception of Japan, all the nations where the Gross National Product per capita in 1991 exceeded $10,000 were Western. Four nations—the United States, France, Germany, and Japan—produce over half of the value of the world's manufactured goods. The map shown here indicates relative levels of human welfare as indicated by the Human Development Index, a measure based on the three components of longevity, education, and income.*

them that "through freedom, you, too, shall overcome." A year later, he told the Vietnamese that "the key to the future" was "entrepreneurship, innovation, and competition," along with the free exchange of ideas. And British Prime Minister Tony Blair communicated a similar message in January 2000, addressing the annual meeting of the World Economic Forum in Davos, Switzerland: "far from impoverishing the world's poorer countries, trade liberalization is the only sure route to the kind of economic growth needed to bring their prosperity closer to that of the major developed economies."

Anti-globalization Protests The free trade consensus among the leaders of wealthy nations has recently fueled fierce protests from groups claiming to represent the world's poor and disenfranchised. Drawn from many nations and an enormous array of organizations from community groups to anarchist cells, these protestors have expressed themselves vigorously

and sometimes violently at several economists' gatherings. They have done so, most notably, at the meeting of the WTO (World Trade Organization) in Seattle (Washington, USA) in December 1999, of the World Bank and IMF (International Monetary Fund) in Prague (Czech Republic) in September 2000, and of the G8 (a summit meeting of the leaders of eight of the world's major industrial nations) in Genoa (Italy) in July 2001. In these settings, provocative and targeted acts of violence invited police repression, with consequent critiques by the press and the public. The Seattle meeting dissolved midway; the Genoa talks proceeded amid intense disturbance to their finish. This staged and bloodstained opposition to what protestors saw as an exploitative global capitalism did not deter the G8 leaders from their final statement—cushioned though it was with promises to assist heavily-indebted poor countries: "Sustained economic growth worldwide requires a renewed commitment to free trade."

Embracing Free Trade　The imperatives of free trade, open markets, fiscal discipline, and stability of currency, have been in different ways and to different degrees embraced by those Asian, African, and Latin American nations that wish to participate in the international trade network and, ultimately, in the wealth that it may generate. Russia is returning from several years of trauma, as it adjusts to a market economy, still lacking a commitment to free speech or the rules of property and procedure. China, still Communist, with an unyielding leadership committed to repressive practices, has a vigorous free market economy growing at unprecedented rates. Japan has reformed its over-protected economy and emerged from more than a decade of stagnation. The urban and technologically advanced sectors of India are flourishing and, as the promoters of the economic boom have said, "shining." The major nations of eastern Europe have already made the transition to a modern market economy, while several Latin American nations on that path have weathered currency collapse and economic stress. Despite much tension and difficulty, significant increases in levels of wealth, as well as improvements in health and welfare, have been made worldwide.

Technology and Globalization　The role of technology in economic globalization cannot be overstated. As manufacturing tasks have shifted to the "developing" zones of the world, the most highly developed have assumed the task of producing information and services rather than things. Rapid progress in cybernetics (see Chapter 30), with its origins in the military competition of World War II, has transformed the way business, government, and cultural institutions operate. The design and implementation of hardware and software systems require highly trained experts, while even the operation of these systems requires workers skilled beyond the level of the manual laborers who were once the core of the "working class." Those needs place huge demands on the educational systems of societies that aspire to excel in the enterprise of managing information: "in an economy dominated by information and knowledge," British prime minister Blair points out, "education is king." Those nations whose people are not only poor but also, as often follows, illiterate, are doubly burdened.

Transportation and Communication.　Technologically updated transportation and communication networks have also facilitated globalization. A dense network of air routes links once-remote entrepots, while increasing efficiency and commercial competition have reduced prices for business and leisure travelers. In populous regions, high-speed trains are convenient and accessible. The Channel tunnel, or "Chunnel," opened in 1994, provides a non-stop connection between Paris and London, two main poles of European culture—although it has not as yet met with the success for which its planners hoped. Even as these networks for high-speed movement link the world's capitals, truck roads and rail links slowly multiply in the isolated interiors of the developing world.

Communications technologies are able to link even these parts of the world not yet well served by transportation systems. By means of telephones, cellular phones, fax machines, the radio and above all, the Internet, vocal or digitalized information can be delivered almost instantaneously to governments, institutions, and individuals worldwide. In Africa, the radio has permitted long-distance communications where this was previously almost impossible. In China in 1989, fax machines distributed information about the Tiananmen Square demonstration and repression. In the late stages of the Yugoslav conflict, both Serbs and Kosovars communicated with outsiders by e-mail. E-mail also connects entrepreneurs and intellectuals in New York, Moscow, or Milan, who conclude sales or arrange conferences with their counterparts in Germany, India, or Colombia.

Space Programs　Technology brought the promise of taming the great distances not only of the globe but also of the universe. Space programs began in the context of the Cold War arms buildup of the 1950s and 1960s, as the Soviet Union and the United States sought to demonstrate their capacity to extend their presence beyond the limits of the terrestrial world (see Chapter 30). Space exploration has since evolved into a cooperative effort to study the nature of the universe, and to gauge the ways that human or animal life can survive in the alien environments of space. The Russian Mir space station, launched in 1986, was finally dismantled in 1999 after a series of mishaps. Before its termination, the seven-storey, 35-ton International Space Station with linked Russian and American modules was launched into orbit late in 1998. It is designed to accommodate an international team that will pursue Mir's goals in seeking knowledge about space.

American space ventures under the aegis of NASA (the National Aeronautics and Space Administration) have moved forward as well, achieving stunning new observations of the planet Mars. President Bush has made such ventures a priority with the establishment of the commission "Moon, Mars, and Beyond." In 2004, a privately-financed rocket plane soared above the earth's atmosphere for the first time. The journey of SpaceShipOne points to the new possibilities to emerge from private-sector ventures in space. Two tragic losses of manned spacecraft, however, also mark the recent history of American space exploration: in 1986, the destruction on takeoff of the space shuttle Challenger; and in 2003, the disintegration of the space shuttle Columbia on its return flight to Earth after a sixteen-day orbit.

Popular Culture While the Internet annihilates distance and space missions conquer it, perhaps nothing unifies peoples of the world as much as their participation in a common culture—a mass culture of television shows and rock music, of youth fashion, sport, and film. Although these trends first appeared in the free, exuberant 1920s, they developed their present form during the Sixties (see Chapter 30), an era marked by political protest, sexual liberation, and countercultural transformations. In the 1990s, mass cultural style continued to be dominated by United States youth. Their pursuits of "sex, drugs, and rock and roll" with the new admixture of "rap," now engage imitators on every continent. They also elicit protest from traditionalists who see American popular or "pop" culture as a threat to traditional religious values and models of the family.

Even traditionalists, however, now inhabit a globalized world where the narrow boundaries of the past—of village, nation, denomination, language—are dissolving. The world is not yet one, and conflicts and hatreds disrupt it. But it is certainly a linked system, in which no one part stands alone, and every thought or deed has potentially worldwide impact.

New Battles

Militarism, fanaticism, torture, genocide, and terror—these overshadowed the last decades of the twentieth century and the dawn of the twenty-first, even as the powerful nations of the developed world, the Cold War behind them, settled down to the business of building a prosperous global village based on technological innovation.

While proponents of theories of social justice sparred with proponents of globalization, opponents of modernization armed themselves to resist any universal notion of a just and prosperous society that was modeled on those of the Western world. The beliefs and infrastructures of traditional societies support them in this mission, and dictators, warlords, and strongmen goad them to violent resistance. Tribal hatreds, ethnic rivalries, and religious jihads caused intense destruction, at first, in pockets of the world remote from the Western gaze, and then in the very heartland of the West. Far from the centers of wealth and technological advance, competition for power produced new paradigms of war—numerous new battles, constituting a new chapter in the long history of human conflict.

Weapons of Mass Destruction As the superpowers disarmed after the Cold War, other states of the world acquired massive military capacity. China and India stockpiled powerful weapons; so did Israel, Pakistan, Libya, North Korea, Iran, and Iraq. India refused to sign the Nuclear Non-Proliferation treaty until its requirements were universal and equitable. On 11 May 1998, she demonstrated her independence by exploding nuclear devices about 70 miles from the Pakistani border. Also refusing to sign were India's neighbor Pakistan, South Africa, and Israel. Even without nuclear weapons, the militarized states of the developing world were dangerous. Some developed biological and chemical weapons (although international agreements prohibit their use), which are cheap, easily acquired, and difficult to monitor. Recently, these have been enumerated along with nuclear weapons among the WMDs, or "weapons of mass destruction," that fall into the hands of the untrustworthy leaders of "rogue" states.

Conventional arms, however, are the main material of war sought by the dictators and strongmen of the developing nations. These were acquired free from one or the other of the superpowers during the Cold War, or purchased on a growing open market. Armies as well as armaments are available for purchase, as mercenary bands, recruited from the veterans of military conflicts elsewhere in the world, take service under military strongmen who "buy war" in order to gain or keep power. Some states spend twice as much on the military as on health; others a mammoth ten times as much—Nigeria and Angola in Africa; Kuwait and Iraq under Saddam Hussein in the Middle East; Pakistan and the two Koreas in Asia.

Between 1900 and 1990, 237 wars had been fought worldwide, compared to 205 in the previous century, or 68 in the eighteenth century. Even relative to an increased population, the twentieth was the most violent century in human history. In the eighteenth century, wars caused about 5 deaths per 1000 people; in the nineteenth century, 6; in the twentieth century, 46.

Genocide When the military gain power—and some 40 percent of the world's states today are controlled by military men—not only is there more violence, but there are violations of the standards of human rights established by the United Nations in 1948. Torture—revived by the Cheka under the Bolsheviks, the Nazis, and French colonial forces—is inflicted on prisoners around the world; citizens are raped, beaten, and slain; political opponents are murdered; the press, radio, television, and the Internet are muzzled.

With the memory of the Nazi attempt to exterminate the Jews still vivid, the postwar world has also experienced recent episodes of genocide. Defined by the 1948 UN Convention on the Prevention and Punishment of the Crime of Genocide as "acts committed with intent to destroy, in whole or in part, a national, ethnical, racial, or religious group," modern genocide began early in the twentieth century with the Turkish persecution of their Armenian minority. More recently, genocidal warfare overwhelmed the neighboring African states of Rwanda and Burundi.

Why Some are So Rich and Some are So Poor

Greater productivity in the Western world, driven by technological innovation and especially modern information systems, have markedly increased the gap between rich and poor within nations, as well as between rich and poor nations. Some economic theorists predict disaster ahead, such as William Greider, or blame the economic policies on wealthy nations, private corporations, and the international monetary agencies that speak for them, as does Michel Chossudovsky. Others, like David Landes and Nancy Birdsall, recognize that chronic divisions of wealth are erosive of our human community, but see the solution in greater economic innovation and growth—and not in the greater regulation or redistribution of wealth.

William Greider examines the global market and the coming storm (1997): Imagine a wondrous new machine, strong and supple, a machine that reaps as it destroys. It is huge and mobile ... but no one is at the wheel. ... It is sustained by its own forward motion, guided mainly by its own appetites. And it is accelerating. ...

The machine is ... modern capitalism driven by the imperatives of global industrial revolution. ... a free-running economic system that is reordering the world. ...

... The symptoms of upheaval can be found almost anywhere ... The convergence has no fixed center, no reliable boundaries or settled outcomes. ... The earth's diverse societies are being rearranged and united in complicated ways by global capitalism. The idea evokes benumbed resignation among many. The complexity of it overwhelms. The enormity makes people feel small and helpless.
(William Greider, *One World, Ready or Not: The Manic Logic of Global Capitalism*, New York: Simon & Schuster, 1997)

Michel Chossudovsky discusses the globalization of poverty (1998): The late-twentieth century will go down in world history as a period of global impoverishment marked by the collapse of productive systems in the developing world, the demise of national institutions and the disintegration of health and education programs. This "globalization of poverty" ... was initiated in the Third World coinciding with the onslaught of the debt crisis. Since the 1990s, it has extended its grip to all major regions of the world ... Famines at the local level have erupted ... health clinics and schools have been closed down; hundreds of millions of children have been denied the right to primary education. ... there has been a resurgence of infectious diseases including tuberculosis, malaria and cholera. ...

... The increasing levels of global poverty resulting from economic restructuring are casually denied by G7 governments and international institutions ... social realities are concealed, official statistics are manipulated, economic concepts are turned upside down. In turn, public opinion is bombarded in the media with glowing images of global growth and prosperity. ...
(Michel Chossudovsky, "Global Poverty in the Late 20th Century," *Journal of International Affairs*, Vol. 52, no. 1, Fall 1998)

David S. Landes expresses concern over the futures of rich and poor (1998): The old division of the world into two power blocs, East and West, has subsided. Now the big challenge and threat is the gap in wealth and health that separates rich and poor. These are often styled North and South ... but a more accurate signifier would be the West and the Rest ... Here is the greatest single problem and danger facing the world in the Third Millennium. ...

... Our task (the rich countries), in our own interest as well as theirs, is to help the poor become healthier and wealthier. If we do not, they will seek to take what they cannot make; and if they cannot earn by exporting commodities, they will export people. In short, wealth is an irresistible magnet; and poverty is a potentially raging contaminant: it cannot be segregated, and our peace and prosperity depend in the long run on the well-being of others.
(David S. Landes, *The Wealth and Poverty of Nations: why Some are so Rich and Some So Poor*, New York–London: W.W. Norton, 1998)

Nancy Birdsall on learning to live with inequality (1998): Belying Marx, the biggest story of the last 150 years has been the emergence in the West of a prosperous and stable middle class. But it took time. During a long transition from agriculture to industry, changes in production and in the structure of employment caused wrenching inequality. Much inequality today may be the natural outcome of what is an analogous transition from an industrial to an information age.

Still, there is no reason to despair. Some inequality is healthy and will speed the transition. The rapidly growing wages of the educated and skilled are making education and training much more attractive personal investments. As more people get greater access to education, their relative income advantage over the unskilled will decline. ... More fundamentally, people may care less about their current ranking in a static picture of global income distribution than about just and fair access to a better future, especially for their children. In an unequal world, good opportunities represent fair rules and matter at least as much as current status. Greater opportunities—which can be delivered today—are a better guarantee of a socially coherent global community than improved distribution tomorrow.
(Nancy Birdsall, "Life is Unfair: Inequality in the World," *Foreign Policy*, No. 111, Summer 1998)

Rwanda For centuries, the Tutsi tribespeople of Rwanda and Burundi had dominated a Hutu majority (about 80 percent of the population), in a pattern encouraged by Belgian administrators after 1918. Upon the achievement of independence in 1962, the Hutus were granted political rights, yet persistent tensions erupted violently in 1965, 1969, 1972, and 1988, mounting to full civil war in 1994. As a Tutsi army drove Hutu forces to the frontier, fleeing Hutus massacred hundreds of thousands of Tutsi (and moderate Hutu) men, women, and children—at least 500,000, and perhaps as many as 800,000, out of a population of seven and a half million. Two million Hutus (including many of the killers) took refuge in Zaire and Tanzania, where, corralled in refugee camps, they suffered from starvation and disease. Most have since returned to Rwanda, where political reforms culminated in general elections in 2003, and attempts at reconciliation have achieved mixed success. The UN's International Criminal Tribunal for Rwanda has been in session since 1995, judging the cases of more than 70 individuals indicted for genocide. The first person to be convicted was the prime minister of the Rwandan government in 1994. He is the first head of state to be indicted, and then convicted, for genocide.

The Former Yugoslavia In the Balkans, on Europe's southeastern frontier, enduring hatreds flared up in the 1990s between orthodox Christian Serbs, Roman Catholic Croatians, and Muslim Bosnians, all southern Slavs speaking the same tongue (although using different alphabets). For 35 years, the independent communist leader Marshall Tito (Josip Broz, 1891–1980) had kept these mutually hostile groups together in a union of "all Slavs," or "Yugoslavia." When Tito died in 1980, the union was shaken. It disintegrated with the collapse of communism in 1989.

Yugoslavia dissolved into six federated republics—Croatia, Slovenia, Bosnia-Herzegovina, Montenegro, Macedonia, and Serbia. The two "autonomous regions" of Vojvodina and Kosovo lay within Serbia, which maintained the army of the former Yugoslav state. Slovenia and Croatia withdrew from the federation in 1991, and many of the Serb minority joined the Serbian army to prevent their secession.

Ethnic Cleansing Meanwhile, Bosnia-Herzegovina also sought to secede from the Serbian-led federation. Its Orthodox Serb minority (about 33 percent of a population that was also 44 percent Muslim Slav and 17 percent Catholic Croatian) resisted the March 1992 plebiscite in which a majority voted for independence. Bosnian Serbs, including many Yugoslav army veterans, constituted themselves the "Serbian Republic of Bosnia-Herzegovina" and besieged the capital of Sarajevo. Over the next three years, backed by Serbia under Slobodan Milosevic (b. 1941) and the regular Yugoslav army, they starved and bombed

the city. In a campaign of "ethnic cleansing"—the horrifying term born of this last European conflict—Serb forces persecuted, expelled, bullied, raped, and killed Bosnian Muslims. All contenders were guilty of atrocities, but the massacres by Serbs of some eight thousand victims in Srebenica in 1995 especially outraged international observers. The UN's International Criminal Tribunal for the former Yugoslavia, established at The Hague (The Netherlands) in 1993, declared the occurrence to be genocide, and indicted fourteen suspects. In 2004, an official Bosnian-Serb commission for the first time admitted that the atrocity had taken place.

The Dayton Accords The constituent nations of the European Union, NATO, and the United Nations (employing the US Air Force to enforce its decreed "no-fly zone") all attempted to halt the carnage in the Balkans. By the American-sponsored Dayton (Ohio) Peace Agreement of November 1995, the republic

From civilization to barbarism: *Heavy and protracted fighting in the Bosnian capital Sarajevo (in the former Yugoslavia) reduced much of that city, a center of European culture, to rubble. Here, a UN peace-keeper surveys the city's wrecked library in February 1994.*

Kostunica waving at crowds: *In October 2000, a coup in the capital of Belgrade resulted in the deposition of Serbian dictator Slobodan Milosevic (later extradited to the Hague, the Netherlands, to face trial for war crimes) and the election as president of Vajislav Kostunica, shown here greeting the crowd.*

was divided into Serbian and Muslim–Croat entities, to be ruled by a single parliament, elected under the eye of United Nations peacekeeping troops.

The Victory of Kostunica New Serb atrocities in 1999 against the Albanian Muslims of Kosovo provoked further warfare and refugee flight, as Milosevic pressed for ethnic Serb domination of an expanded Yugoslav state. The war finally ended only in October 2000, when a spontaneous coup in the capital at Belgrade resulted in the deposition of Milosevic and the election as president of Vojislav Kostunica, a professor of law. Apparent progress towards normalcy was interrupted, in 2003, by the assassination of prime minister Zoran Djindjic. However, in June 2004, the presidential election in Serbia was won by the pro-Western leader of the Democratic Party, Boris Tadic.

War Criminals Among the provisions of the Dayton accord was one that war criminals on both sides would be identified and prosecuted. Massacre, torture, and military rape, all considered illegal by international conventions., were prominent features of the "ethnic cleansing" of Bosnia-Herzegovina, as they were of most recent wars. The determination to bring to justice those who violate the limits of permissible military violence is another aspect of the gathering world consensus on issues of human dignity and freedom. Several Serbian generals were arrested and put on trial in the Hague by the UN International Criminal Tribune. In 2001, they were joined by Milosevic—who had been indicted in 1999 for war crimes committed by Serbian forces in the 1998–1999 conflict in Kosovo—including rape (first defined as a war crime

in international law in 1998), massacre, arson, and torture. Kostunica declined to send Milosevic abroad for trail, but his covert extradition was managed by Djindjic in 2001.

The prosecution of those who in positions of political or military leadership committed acts the world no longer deems acceptable or forgivable is a new feature of the international landscape, and promises to be frequent and diligent. Although the Cambodian Pol Pot (b. 1925/28) escaped prosecution (as leader of the Khmer Rouge faction he had been responsible for the death of nearly two million of the seven million Cambodian citizens between 1975 and 1979 by forced labor, starvation, disease, torture, or execution), having died peacefully of a heart attack in 1998, he was officially condemned for his actions. Similarly, the former Chilean president Augusto Pinochet (b. 1915), although excused from prosecution by a Chilean court, was held responsible by British and Spanish courts for violations of human rights committed following his 1973 rise to power.

The successful prosecution of those who have committed crimes against people subject to them helps establish the principle that leaders, no matter how powerful, cannot escape responsibility for their actions. It remains to be seen whether that principle is honored in years to come with regard to the ongoing genocide in the Sudan by the largely Arab and Muslim north against the non-Arab Christian south, with its toll of some two million lives and four million refugees; or in Zimbabwe, where the supporters of president Robert Mugabe are unlawfully seizing the land and property of his opponents, including the remaining white farmers of the former British colony.

Terrorism Over the last decades, outside the zone of the nation-state, terrorism has emerged as a threat to peace. Terrorism is perpetrated normally by individuals who do not have access to state power, and who attempt to gain their political or social ends by frightening innocents with horrific acts of violence. Among the perpetrators of terror are Italy's Red Brigades, responsible for the 1978 murder of premier Aldo Moro; Basque separatists in Spain; Kurdish rebels in Turkey; and the Shining Path in Peru, responsible since 1980 for some 69,000 civilian deaths. In recent years, Ireland, Israel, and the Islamic Middle East have been the main sites of terrorist activity.

The IRA Organized in the years after the Easter Rebellion of 1916, the Irish Republican Army (IRA) was dedicated to Irish independence from Britain. When the Irish Free State was formed in 1922, IRA militants still demanded the recovery of Northern Ireland from British control, and an end to dominion status under Great Britain. These goals they pursued in a series of bombings and riots during the early years of Irish independence. After 1949, after many Irish grievances had been addressed, the IRA was deemed an illegal organization and operated underground during the early 1950s. After 1969, the "provisional" branch of the IRA launched a determined campaign of terror in Northern Ireland, which spilled over to England. It resulted in, among other murderous acts, the assassination of a prominent British politician closely related to the Queen. After failed ceasefires, an accord was reached in 1998, which has been largely successful, although the violence has not entirely ceased.

The Israeli-Palestinian Conflict Whereas most of the demands of the IRA and their civilian supporters were realized by 1998, those of the landless Palestinians of the Middle East have not yet been addressed. For more than sixty years, a standoff has existed between Israel, constituted a state by action of the United Nations in 1949, and the Palestinian refugees thereby displaced (see Chapter 29). Although neighboring Arab states did not receive the Palestinian refugees, they have supported the Palestinian cause. For more than a decade, and most fiercely since 2000, mostly young male Palestinians have resisted what they perceive as Israeli abuses and even the presence of the state of Israel with assaults on Israeli soldiers and suicide bombings in Israeli cities. While supporters of Israel are shocked by the trail of assassination and murder, supporters of the Palestinian cause recall the massacre of 29 Arabs at prayer in a mosque in Hebron in January 1997 by an Israeli zealot and, more recently, the retaliatory strikes by Israeli forces against Palestinian terrorist acts.

THE "WAR ON TERROR"

In the greatest act of terrorism known to history, radical Islamists launched deadly attacks against American citizens and sites on September 11, 2001. Those attacks were the culmination of a sequence that began more than a decade earlier. The earlier strikes included the bombing of an American plane over Lockerbie, Scotland in December 1988 (by terrorists protected by Libya); the failed attempt to bomb the World Trade Center in New York City in 1993, masterminded by an Islamist cleric; and the bombing of a US Air Force base at Khobar Towers in Dharan, Saudi Arabia in June 1996, of American embassies in Kenya and Tanzania in August 1998, and of an American ship, the USS Cole, in Aden harbor, Yemen, in October 2000.

All of these events are linked to militant Islamist movements in North Africa and the Middle East, apparently engaged in a crusade against modernizing secular states seen as corrupt and decadent, and especially against the United States. Shocking as these earlier incidents were, they aroused little official response from the US government. Investigations were launched; American aircraft strafed an Afghan and a Sudanese target, without effect. The 9/11 attacks were more serious, however: in scope, certainly, but principally because they occurred on US soil.

The events of 9/11

Between 7:58 and 8:10 that morning, nineteen men boarded and commandeered four airplanes departing from Boston (two), Washington DC, and Newark NJ. They overpowered the crew and seized control of the cockpits, using for weapons ordinary boxcutters that had passed unnoticed through security gates. At 8:48, American Airlines 11 from Boston, with 92 persons on board, crashed into the north tower of the World Trade Center in the financial area of New York City. At 9:03, United Airlines 175 from Boston, with 65 persons on board, struck the south tower. With the upper storeys of both towers aflame, many of the occupants jumped to their deaths from above the 80th floor, their desperate suicides observed by terrified spectators and recorded by photographers. Thousands more—stock brokers and secretaries, cooks and janitors, firemen and policemen—were incinerated or crushed in the destroyed buildings. At 10:05 and 10:29, the two towers collapsed.

Meanwhile, at 9:40, American Airlines 77 from Washington, circled back to its base and crashed into the Pentagon, killing 64 persons on board and 190 inside the fortified building. Finally, at 10:03, United Airlines 93 from Newark, en route to Washington to strike the Capitol or White House,

Let's Roll: the War on Terror

On September 11, 2001, three of the four planes hijacked by terrorists of Osama Bin Laden's Al Quaeda organization hit their targets; one crashed, probably brought down by a few doomed passengers determined not to die without fighting, whose last words were heard by cell phone just before the plane exploded: "Let's roll!" Their action inaugurated the war soon launched officially by President George W. Bush against the terrorists and any nation that harbored them. Here are some voices from the early days of that struggle: of New York City mayor Rudolph Giuliani, whose heroic management of the catastrophic hit to the World Trade Center was admired across the US; of Muslim-born novelist Salman Rushdie, a victim and critic of militant Islamism; and of Bin Laden himself.

Rudolph Giuliani tells the United Nations that on the other side of democracy is tyranny (October 1, 2001): Our belief in religious freedom, political freedom, economic freedom—that's what makes an American. Our belief in democracy, the rule of law and respect for human life. That's how you become an American. ...

It's tragic and perverse that it's because of these very principles ... that we find ourselves under attack by terrorists. Our freedom threatens them because they know if our ideas of freedom gain a foothold among their people, it will destroy their power. ... The terrorists have no ideas or ideals with which to combat freedom and democracy. So their only defense is to strike out against innocent civilians, destroying human life in massive numbers and hoping to deter all of us from our pursuit ... of freedom. ...

But the long-term deterrent of spreading our ideals throughout the world is just not enough. ... The United Nations must hold accountable any country that supports or condones terrorism. ... It must ostracize any nation that supports terrorism. It must isolate any nation that remains neutral in the fight against terrorism. ... This is not a time for further study or vague directives.

The evidence of terrorism's brutality and inhumanity, of its contempt for life and the concept of peace is lying beneath the rubble of the World Trade Center less than two miles from where we meet today. Look at that destruction, that massive, senseless, cruel loss of human life and then I ask you to look in your hearts and recognize that there is no room for neutrality on the issue of terrorism. You're either with civilization or with terrorists. On one side is democracy, the rule of law and respect for human life. On the other is tyranny, arbitrary executions and mass murder.
(The New York Times, 10/2/01)

Salman Rushdie declares that, yes, this is about Islam: (November 2, 2001): "This isn't about Islam." The world's leaders have been repeating this mantra for weeks, partly in the virtuous hope of deterring reprisal attacks on innocent Muslims living in the West, partly because if the United States is to maintain its coalition against terror it can't afford to suggest that Islam and terrorism are in any way related.

The trouble with this necessary disclaimer is that it isn't true. If this isn't about Islam, why the worldwide Muslim demonstrations in support of Osama bin Laden and Al Qaeda? Why did those 10,000 men armed with swords and axes mass on the Pakistan–Afghanistan frontier, answering some mullah's call to jihad? Why are the war's first British casualties three Muslim men who died fighting on the Taliban side? ...

In recent weeks Muslim voices have everywhere been raised against the obscurantist hijacking of their religion. Yesterday's hotheads ... are improbably repackaging themselves as today's pussycats. ... If Islam is to be reconciled with modernity, these voices must be encouraged until they swell into a roar. ...

The restoration of religion to the sphere of the personal, its depoliticization, is the nettle that all Muslim societies must grasp in order to become modern. The only aspect of modernity interesting to the terrorists is technology ... a weapon that can be turned on its makers. If terrorism is to be defeated, the world of Islam must take on board the secularist-humanist principles on which the modern is based, and without which Muslim countries' freedom will remain a distant dream.
(The New York Times, 11/2/01)

Osama Bin Laden announces "Our Terrorism is Against America" (December 27, 2001): If their economy ends, they will busy themselves away from the enslavement of oppressed people ... It is important to concentrate on the destruction of the American economy.

Our terrorism is against America. Our terrorism is a blessed terrorism to prevent the unjust person from committing injustice and to stop American support for Israel, which kills our sons.

They (nineteen hijackers) used the enemy's planes and studied at enemy schools, without the need for training camps. But God helped them and taught this cruel lesson to those arrogant people who see freedom only for the white race and keep other nations humiliated and oppressed.
(Excerpts of Osama Bin Laden's videotaped comments aired on the Qatar-based Al-Jazeera television, December 27, 2001; The New York Times, 12/27/01)

Terrorist Attack on World Trade Centre: The horror and desolation of the scene in lower Manhattan, New York City, after the two great World Trade Center towers, emblems of American prosperity and daring, were struck by two different airplanes hijacked by squads of suicidal terrorists. Above, the upper floors of the towers are seen burning behind the landmark Brooklyn Bridge. Below, a lone observer in a wilderness of smoke and dust and the skeletal remains of the fallen towers.

crashed to the ground near Shanksville, southeast of Pittsburgh PA. Impelling the crash, which killed all 45 on board, was the heroic action of a few passengers who entered the cockpit to overpower the pilots. They had already learned by cellphone of the World Trade Center collapse. Phone calls to their wives from passengers Jeremy Glick and Thomas Burnett reveal the plan they hatched. "I know we're all going to die... ," said Burnett; "There's three of us who are going to do something about it." Their swift action prevented a much greater toll of death by taking down the plane.

At 22:30 the same day, President Bush announced that "our freedom, our way of life has come under attack," and that action would be taken against the terrorists and "those who harbor them." In all, nearly 3000 innocents, of whom many were foreigners, died in the 9/11 attacks.

What we Later Learned

On the day that these events occurred, neither media nor political leaders could well explain them. Gradually, a fuller story emerged. Since 1993, and protected after 1996 by the radically conservative Taliban regime in Afghanistan, various terrorist groups gelled under the leadership of the Saudi self-exile Osama Bin Laden in the Al Qaeda international terrorist organization. It was Bin Laden who ordered and approved the September 11 strike. His associates had carefully planned the attack for years, and the leaders had been schooled in the necessary tactics in Bin Laden's Afghan training camps, although they had completed the necessary flight training in the US. The 9/11 attacks were linked to the earlier attacks on US assets, and to several earlier and subsequent terrorist strikes around the world.

The 9/11 Response

The initial response to the 9/11 attacks was of horror and surprise, both at home and abroad—although Palestinian demonstrators, as well as Arab commentators and media reports, rejoiced. On September 20, President Bush, who had appeared profoundly shaken on the day of the catastrophe, made a first major statement about the US response. His first statement was repeated and amplified in later speeches and press conferences.

In sum, President Bush laid out the principles of an American "War on Terror." He pledged that the US would pursue, identify, and capture those behind the 9/11 attacks, at home and around the world; that extraordinary measures would be taken to do so, including expanded rights to detain citizen and noncitizen suspects accorded to the Attorney General in the Patriot Act; that the revenue streams flowing to terrorist organizations, and not only their personnel, would be tracked and halted; and that the US considered itself free to act not only against the terrorists, but against those sovereign states that promoted similar actions against the US and its citizens: "From this day forward, any nation that continues to harbor or support terrorism will be regarded by the United States as a hostile regime." Later, in his State of the Union Address of January 29, 2002, the President named three states of greatest concern, "arming to threaten the peace of the world," which he named the "axis of evil": Iran, Iraq, and North Korea (the latter especially dangerous because of its nuclear arms capacity and unstable, dictatorial government). In addition, with the official creation of a Department of Homeland Security, on January 24, 2003, he appointed former governor of Pennsylvania Tom Ridge as Secretary.

American Opinion

Initially, the American public opinion was solidly unified behind the President. Soon, however, fissures developed. The relatives of the victims of the 9/11 attacks, especially those at the World Trade Center, formed interest groups seeking maximum compensation for survivors, due memorialization of their relatives' sacrifice, and an investigation of the responses of local and national government to the disaster. Political opponents of President Bush questioned the effectiveness of the government's response, the sums earmarked to assist both survivors and the city, whose economy was severely damaged by the attacks, and even the quality of the air at Ground Zero, as the site of destruction was named. In 2003 and 2004, as preparations for the presidential election of fall 2004 geared up, relentless attacks on the management of the post-9/11 assailed Bush and his administration.

European Opinion

From Europe, meanwhile, were heard at the outset expressions of compassion for the American people who had suffered so stunning a blow. In time, that support frayed, as European leaders suggested the attacks were to some extent provoked by American policies in the Middle East. European criticism of the US mounted fiercely in 2002 and 2003 when the Americans pressed for military action against Iraq in the United Nations. Britain alone, and in Britain, it seemed at times only the prime minister Tony Blair, remained wholly supportive of President Bush.

Other Responses

Beyond Europe, Israel rallied to the support of the US, having itself long withstood vicious terrorist attacks from its Palestinian neighbors. Some Middle Eastern heads of state gave cautious support to US efforts to track terrorist activity in their realms. Among these, the cooperation of Pakistan's president Perez Musharref was critical, since Pakistan bordered Afghanistan, in 2001 the epicenter of Al Qaeda's terrorist network.

Afghanistan

Musharref's support was vital when, in October 2001, the US launched air strikes in Afghanistan. Its object was to pursue bin Laden and his organization, eradicate his terrorist training camps, and unseat the Taliban. Practitioners of an extreme form of Sunni Islam, repudiating everything Western, secular, and modern, the Taliban rulers of Afghanistan had, since 1996, confined women to their houses, disrupted schooling, and cut off free speech and press. In March 2001, in the face of international outrage, they destroyed two monumental statues of the Buddha, one 175 and one 120 feet tall, carved into a stony hillside in the fifth century. This iconoclast act broadcast their intolerance of objects held holy by others.

The US invasion of Afghanistan was marked by the highly focused and successful use of "smart" air power to obtain pinpoint objectives with minimum civilian or military casualties. By November 2001, the Taliban were toppled. By May 2002, Al Qaeda forces were expelled or driven underground (or across the border to Pakistan). In June 2002, the Loya Jirga, or traditional assembly, created the transitional government of the Islamic Republic of Afghanistan, with Hamid Karzai as president and former king Zahir Shah designated "father of the country." By 2004, although the capital at Kabul was largely secure and civil life was beginning to be restored, warlords and violence are still major features of the landscape.

John Walker Lindh

In November 2001, a rebellion broke out among prisoners captured in Afghanistan and held at a fortress in the northern region. One of the rebels was found to be a young American named John Walker Lindh, born and raised in northern California but now a Muslim convert and a Taliban soldier. He was subsequently charged and, as a result of a plea bargain, received a prison sentence of twenty years in prison. His case was the earliest indication of the complications that would arise from the capture, imprisonment, interrogation, and punishment of the prisoners of the "War on Terror."

Guantanamo

As an American citizen, Lindh's civil rights were correctly acknowledged. The Al Qaeda fighters captured in Afghanistan, however, as the Bush administration argued, were not to receive the rights of US citizens, nor even those of prisoners of war since Al Qaeda was not a state, and its fighters did not constitute an official army. They were designated "enemy combatants," and a special prison was constructed for these detainees near the American naval base at Guantanamo Bay in Cuba. American opinion was divided on the legitimacy of the Guantanamo Bay detentions. Further criticism mounted at home and abroad upon the circulation of rumors suggesting the maltreatment or abuse of Guantanamo prisoners. US officials pointed out, in their defense, that the detainees were accorded all due respect for their persons and their religious beliefs and practices.

The discovery of other terrorist plots in the US and abroad yielded more prisoners, who have been confined in the US, Germany, Spain, Britain, and elsewhere, according to the different legal practices of those jurisdictions. Within the US, it remains a matter of debate whether non-citizens indicted for terrorism must be accorded all civil rights normally extended to foreigners and immigrants, or whether their rights may be curtailed according to the limits of the Patriot Act.

The Iraq Connection

Iraq surfaced early in the post-9/11 discussions. Under totalitarian dictator Saddam Hussein, Iraq had invaded the neighboring nation of Kuwait in 1990. That act of aggression elicited US support in the 1991 Gulf War during the administration of the father of the current President Bush. US forces drove the Iraqi army out of Kuwait, but did not pursue Saddam Hussein to his capital at Baghdad. Since then, Saddam had continued and extended his abuse of his own people. That abuse included random arrests and executions, economic depredations, and the use of chemical and biological weapons on the Kurdish minority and Shi'ite majority, both subjected to Saddam's Sunni government.

Iraq and the UN

In 2002, the Bush administration identified Iraq as one of the three nations of the "axis of evil" (see above). Given that Iraq had once possessed WMDs considered illicit by the international community, and had never surrendered them to UN inspectors, and indeed had repeatedly ignored UN resolutions ordering it to do so, Bush representatives argued that the UN should proceed against Iraq. Although Iraq could not be identified as an ally of Bin Laden's, or as an instigator of the 9/11 attacks, its status as a rogue nation in the Middle East called for action, as the Bush administration viewed the situation, as part of the "War on Terror." The UN sent a new inspection team, which found no WMDs. When the US pushed for UN military action against Iraq the Security Council vetoed the request. Presumed European allies France and Germany were prominent among the critics of the US request.

The "Coalition of the Willing"

Despite the objections of the UN and much American public opinion, the Bush administration was determined to extend the War on Terror by targeting Iraq. It assembled during early 2003 a "Coalition of the Willing" of thirty-five nations sympathetic to American goals in the Middle East. Prominent among them was Britain, whose prime minister Tony Blair was as forceful as President Bush in asserting the principles of the War on Terror and identifying Iraq as a proper theater for its pursuit. In addition, Spain and Italy, both vulnerable to terrorist assault and, at the time, headed by pro-US leaders, several Eastern European nations (hailed as the "New Europe" by Bush officials), as well as Japan, South Korea, and Australia, among others, joined the American effort. The military forces contributed by these allies, however, were few; the US overwhelmingly, with the British secondarily, constituted the muscle in this coalition against terror in Iraq.

Woman and bakery: *Wars target young men, but kill indiscriminately—men, women, and children. They leave the survivors to struggle alone—often old women, like this one, who may be grieving those lost, or a hopeless future left in ruins like the destroyed bakery in the background.*

The Doctrine of Preemption

There remained the need for a theoretical justification of action against Iraq. The Bush administration proposed the doctrine of "preemption," starkly in contrast to the UN position that the exercise of military force was only legitimate in self-defense (aside from peace-keeping missions, or interventions to prevent further conflict). The doctrine of preemption stated instead that when threatened by terrorism, or state-wielded WMDs, sovereign nations may not be required to wait until they have been attacked, as such an attack could eliminate their ability to respond; instead, they may attack preemptively. The doctrine of preemption was judged slippery and risky not only by UN members and former European allies but by many American politicians and opinion-makers as well.

The Invasion of Iraq

On the argument of just preemption, nonetheless, American, British, and other coalition forces attacked Iraq on March 19, 2003. The invasion was fully televised by crews in Baghdad and elsewhere, and a slew of journalists "embedded" in various military units were able to give first-hand accounts of the hostilities. The anticipated difficulties were daunting: the use of chemical or biological weapons, guerrilla attacks, the destruction of vital bridges, roads, ports, and oil fields. In fact, as the regular Iraqi army melted away, progress was swift. The British struggled and won the port at Basra, on the Persian Gulf, and American forces reached Baghdad on April 5, 2003. The initial victory, although not unresisted, was easy. The subsequent occupation was long and bloody.

The Occupation

The US and Coalition occupation of Iraq was complicated by the fierce loyalty of Saddam Hussein's supporters, as well as by the centrifugal forces of Kurdish and Shi'ite interests. Although the Sunni Muslims are a minority in Iraq, they had long occupied a central zone attached to Baghdad—the "Sunni triangle." In this region, supporters of Saddam's regime continued to wage a guerrilla struggle against occupation forces. US missions found and killed Saddam's two sons, both of whom were deeply complicit in the atrocities of the regime. And finally, on December 13, 2003, it found Saddam Hussein, alive

Falling statue: *In a square in central Baghdad shortly after the arrival of triumphant American forces, a statue of Saddam Hussein is hauled off its pedestal—a sight that must have given great pleasure to the American marines who pulled it down, as yet unaware of the tremendous struggle that still lay ahead.*

and in hiding. In mid-2004, it was the stated US plan to convey the captured leader, under close guard, to a new Iraqi government. The capture of Saddam Hussein has not resulted in the cessation of terrorist activity, which rose with the approach of the date for the transference of power from the Coalition to a new Iraqi government.

Meanwhile, the Shi'ite minority, long repressed under Saddam, actively opposed US pressures for the establishment of a secular democratic government. Extended negotiations resulted in the Coalition obtaining the support of Shi'ite leaders for an autonomous Iraqi state with a constitution suited to an "Islamic democracy." The Kurdish minority, localized in the north of Iraq, has over the last decade, even under Saddam Hussein's regime, constituted itself as an autonomous entity within the state. It has negotiated for conditions that would permit it to remain as part of the Iraqi state, with guaranteed rights.

Trouble at Home

As American and Coalition casualties mounted in Iraq, as guerrilla resistance took a toll on morale, as the tasks of civil administration remained undone,

criticism of the Bush administration mounted at home. Even members of Bush's own Republican party expressed impatience with the administration's performance from 2003 to 2004. Democrats were largely hostile from the outset, and only confirmed in their opposition by the clumsiness and vacillation of the Iraq decision-makers, and their seeming inability to fix anything—the electrical system, the oil pipeline, and especially, security. In spring 2004, news of prisoner abuse by American guards at the fortress of Abu Ghraib exploded, seriously damaging the claim to legitimacy of the Bush administration's Iraq venture.

Seeding Democracy

Nonetheless, the clear if simple explanation offered by the President for US presence in Iraq wins the respect of some pundits and ordinary folk: a dangerous dictator was toppled, at the heart of a region that exports terror, and in place of his autocracy, a democratic state will take form. President Bush seemingly had gambled everything, including the success of his presidency, on the seeding of democracy in the Middle East, and specifically in Iraq.

The Future of the West

What role will the West play in the globalized world of the future? Here, Francis Fukayama argues that the Western liberal IDEA will continue to dominate in a new world; Bernard Lewis points out, in defense of the West, that it is the only civilization that has reflected upon and condemned its past errors; Samuel Huntington predicts a decline in the West, partly due to the failure of Western culture to value its own achievement; and Václav Havel pinpoints as the particular task of the West the dissemination of its "finest spiritual and intellectual traditions."

Francis Fukuyama looks at the future hegemony of Western Culture (1992): As mankind approaches the end of the millennium, the twin crises of authoritarianism and socialist central planning have left only one competitor standing in the ring as an ideology of potentially universal validity: liberal democracy, the doctrine of individual freedom and popular sovereignty. ...

What is emerging victorious ... is ... the liberal *idea*. That is to say, for a very large part of the world, there is now no ideology with pretensions to challenge liberal democracy, and no universal principle of legitimacy other than the sovereignty of the people. ...

(Francis Fukuyama, *The End of History and the Last Man*, Free Press, 1992)

Bernard Lewis asks if the place of the West in world history is a grossly undervalued achievement? (1994): In setting out to conquer, subjugate, and despoil other peoples, the Europeans were merely following the example set them by their neighbors and predecessors ... The interesting questions are not why they tried, but why they succeeded—and then why, having succeeded, they repented of their success as a sin. The success was unique in modern times; the repentance, in all of recorded history. ...

Imperialism, sexism, and *racism* are words of Western coinage—not because the West invented these evils, which are, alas, universal, but because the West recognized and named and condemned them as evils and struggled mightily to weaken their hold and to help their victims. If ... Western culture does indeed "go" [i.e. die out] imperialism, sexism, and racism will not go with it. More likely casualties will be the freedom to denounce them and the effort to end them.

(Bernard Lewis, "Eurocentrism Revisited, 1994" excerpted from *Commentary*, December 1994)

Samuel P. Huntington examines the decline of the West and the de-Westernization of the United States: (1996): Historically American national identity has been defined culturally by the heritage of Western civilization and politically by the principles of the American Creed on which Americans overwhelmingly agree: liberty, democracy, individualism, equality before the law, constitutionalism, private property. In the late twentieth century both components of American identity have come under concentrated and sustained onslaught from a small but influential number of intellectuals and publicists. In the name of multiculturalism they have attacked the identification of the United States with Western civilization, denied the existence of a common American culture, and promoted racial, ethnic, and other subnational cultural identities ...

The American multiculturalists ... reject their country's cultural heritage... [proposing] to create a country ... not belonging to any civilization and lacking a cultural core. History shows that no country so constituted can long endure as a coherent society. A multicivilizational United States will not be the United States; it will be the United Nations. ...

Rejection of the Creed and of Western civilization means the end of the United States of America as we have known it. It also means effectively the end of Western civilization. If the United States is de-Westernized, the West is reduced to Europe and a few lightly populated overseas European settler countries. Without the United States the West becomes a minuscule and declining part of the world's population on a small and inconsequential peninsula at the extremity of the Eurasian land mass.

(Samuel P. Huntington, *The Clash of Civilizations and the Remaking of World Order*, New York: Simon & Schuster, 1996)

Václav Havel discusses Europe's role for the twenty-first century (1996): Humanity is entering an era of multipolar and multicultural civilization. Europe is no longer the conductor of the global orchestra, but this does not mean it has nothing more to say to the world. A new task now presents itself, and with it a new meaning to Europe's very existence.

That task will no longer be to spread—violently or non-violently—its own religion, its own civilization, its own inventions, or its own power. Nor will it be to preach the rule of law, democracy, human rights, or justice to the rest of the world.

If Europe wishes, it can do something more modest yet more beneficial. It can become a model for how different peoples can work together in peace ... Moreover, Europe has one final possibility, if it so desires: it can reclaim its finest spiritual and intellectual traditions, ... and join ... in a search for the common moral minimum necessary to guide us all so that we may live side by side on one planet and confront jointly whatever threatens our lives together.

(*New York Review of Books*, 6/20/96, p. 41)

Sovereignty

On March 8, 2004, the Iraqi Governing Council signed an interim constitution for the new government to take power at the end of June. On June 28, 2004, a new sovereign Iraq stepped forth, governed by a council representing the major interests in the country. As of this writing, elections are planned for early 2005, to be supervised by the UN. The US military will remain in Iraq indefinitely to train an indigenous security force and to provide security during the transition.

Possible Outcomes of the "War on Terror"

American and world opinion is sharply divided on the preemptive war waged by the US in Iraq, and on American foreign policy generally. On the one hand, many European allies, led by France and Germany, as well as most Arab states, view recent US actions as unjustified and aggressive, a view also shared by about half of the American electorate. On the other hand, America's staunchest allies, led by Britain and Australia and including Italy, Poland, Japan, and South Korea, among others, view the radical Islamist threat combined with that of the proliferation of WMDs in the hands of untrustworthy states as a compelling cause for intervention. Unfavorable opinion, and a presidential election in November 2004 that may repudiate President Bush and his policies, may force the US to withdraw from Iraq and Afghanistan, and to retreat from its doctrine of preemption. The reaffirmation of the Bush position in November 2004 will make such retreat less likely.

The New Colossus

Whatever the course taken in the future, that taken in the past is certain, and has had important consequences. Islamist extremists attacked the US ruthlessly in 2001, and the US, in consequence, invaded Afghanistan that year and Iraq eighteen months later, in 2003. Terrorism awoke a sleeping giant. Without the provocation of the 9/11 attacks, the US would likely not have mobilized its forces or increased its defense infrastructure as it has recently done and will now probably do in the future. One consequence of the War on Terror has been the successful reassertion, as the world of nations opens a new century and a new millennium, of US primacy in military power. Whether that military primacy leads to a new imperialism, and creates of the US a new "colossus" comparable to the British empire from the eighteenth through early twentieth centuries, as Scottish historian Niall Ferguson has recently suggested, time will tell. Certainly, the US, one of the last-born children of Europe, accompanied by its British and Commonwealth allies, has become the principal bearer of the traditions of the West.

THE END OF THE WEST?

Where is the West in a global world? Has the West lost its importance, and its identity? Have its historical failings disqualified it for leadership, or required it to abandon its claims for greatness? Does the arrival of the post-Soviet, post-industrial, postmodern era mean the coming of the end of the West?

Western civilization has endured many vicissitudes, and will likely endure. In the twentieth century, two terrible wars threatened to destroy it. But the West has recovered, and the principles of human rights, individual freedom, and parliamentary democracy were vindicated. They are imitated worldwide. It is the primary goal of most of the nations of the developing world to establish civil societies on the model of those that exist in the Western world, resting on the core values of Western civilization.

Core Values

Western civilization has evolved its core values over more than a thousand years. They include: (1) the principle of human dignity: that all human beings

Astride the Prime Meridian: *These schoolchildren harbor no doubts about the meaning of the West. The West lies on one side of the line of longitude that runs through Greenwich, England, from pole to pole; on the other side is the East.*

are equal in worth, that they possess rights which cannot be taken away, and that to the greatest possible degree they are free; (2) the ideal of justice: that no person should be unfairly privileged above another; (3) the value of democracy: that the power to shape the future of a community belongs to its people as a whole and not to arbitrarily selected leaders; (4) the method of rationalism, which assumes that all phenomena (even those pertaining to God, essence, or spirit) may be subject to the critical scrutiny of the human mind; (5) the inclination to progress, to work towards goals to be achieved in the future; (6) the habit of self-examination, which encourages human beings to examine themselves seriously and often to test whether they have fulfilled their promise and their responsibilities.

Critiques of the West

The last of these—the habit of self-examination—has yielded a rich harvest of criticisms of Western societies. Over the last centuries, the nations of the West arrogated to themselves power over the other regions of the world, drained them of wealth, and subjected their peoples to inferior status. They created and defended the Atlantic system of slavery and more than a century after its abolition, have not yet wholly admitted the descendants of slaves into full participation in the societies to which they were forcibly brought. In the name of Christianity, those nations have waged wars against other nations and peoples, compelled conformity through terror and torture, and excluded dissenters, if they did not actively persecute them, from participation in political and social life. In the service of its ideologies, most notoriously Nazism, Western civilization has spawned episodes of genocide. Characterized by patriarchal family structures, Western societies have injured the women and children whose destinies have been determined by the status concerns of authoritative males. Western expansionism has led to the unrestrained industrialization of regions of the world, resulting in environmental degradation and human misery.

The Harvest

All of these charges are, to some extent, true. It is also true, however, that other civilizations have been brutal and aggressive, characterized by patriarchalism, and buttressed by slavery. The Western world, however, is alone in repudiating those behaviors that, by its own moral standards, it has come to condemn. The West has rejected intolerance, terror, torture, and tyranny; it has admitted women and the descendants of slaves to full participation in civic life; it has recognized the need to protect the natural environment and to foster health and education of all its citizens. These stances, more than the troubled legacy of past failings, are the harvest of the Western experience.

Conclusion
THE PAST, THE FUTURE, AND THE MEANING OF THE WEST

As Britain battled its way to world empire during the eighteenth century, the astronomers in the Royal Observatory at Greenwich (southeast London) resolved the thorny problem of longitude with the aid of newly refined chronometers. Their system was anchored by the time current in Greenwich, at a point which, as an international conference held in 1884 established, would define the Prime Meridian. The Prime Meridian is that line of longitude that divides East and West, and serves as a universal standard of space and time. It runs from pole to pole through Greenwich, thus conceived to be the preeminent point on Earth. Its creation was an act both of scientific imagination and astounding arrogance. It is a reminder of the ease with which the West could once partition the globe. Then there was no ambiguity about the question: "where, and what, is the West?"

Nor should there be now. The West is not so clearly a place as it once was. It is not simply the western part of Europe, or the western hemisphere; parts of the West (Australasia, for instance) are not in the "west" in any geographical sense at all. The West is its civilization, its cultural heritage, and the moral and intellectual values that heritage has nurtured. A consideration of the map of the world shows that the West is everywhere—not only in the core area of Europe where its civilization was first developed, but in the regions of European settlement, and ultimately in every part of the inhabited world to which Western influence has extended.

And so the West, while it is no longer anywhere in particular on the globe, is everywhere. As a civilization, a cultural tradition, a set of moral and intellectual values, it exists wherever people take positive steps to study its past, value its wealth of attainments, and work for its future—people like the students who read this book. The future of the West lies with you, who may choose to take up the exciting mission Ulysses embraced when he resolved to sail westward, striving, seeking, finding, not yielding, but roaming ever with a hungry heart.

SUGGESTED RESOURCES

Mazower, Mark, *Dark Continent: Europe's Twentieth Century* (New York: Alfred A. Knopf, 1999). Probes Europe's history across a brutal century, observing how Western values emerged and were preserved amid ambition, corruption, and totalitarianisms of all forms.

Trachtenberg, Marc, *A Constructed Peace: the Making of the European Settlement, 1945-1963* (Princeton: Princeton University Press, 1999). Patient narrative of how a stable European system was reached through diplomacy, with the need for a non-nuclear Germany defended by U.S. forces as its lynchpin.

Tiersky, Ronald, *Europe Today: National Politics, European Integration, and European Security* (Totowa NJ: Rowman & Littlefield, 2000). Synthesis of the post-Cold War European experience, focusing on east/west tensions and the need for security.

Norman M. Naimark and Holly Case, eds., *Yugoslavia and Its Historians: Understanding the Balkan Wars of the 1990s* (Stanford: Stanford University Press, 2003). Essays on various aspects of Yugoslav history providing context for discussions of the Balkan conflict usually described by journalists or government officials.

Rohde, David, *Endgame: The Betrayal and Fall of Srebrenica, Europe's Worst Massacre Since World War II* (New York: Farrar, Straus, and Giroux, 1997). Based on UN documents on hundreds of interviews, shows how the great nations involved in the former Yugoslavia, through incompetence and negligence, allowed 7,000 Muslims to be massacred by their Serbian captors.

Des Forges, Alison, et al., *Leave None to Tell the Story: Genocide in Rwanda* (New York: Human Rights Watch, 1999). Massive report on the Hutu massacre of hundreds of thousands of Tutsis in Rwanda in 1994.

Shawcross, William, *Deliver Us From Evil: Peacekeepers, Warlords, and a World of Endless Conflict* (New York: Simon & Schuster, 2000). Examining the vicious wars of the 1990s, often ethnic in origin, expresses caution about the usefulness of international intervention.

Power, Samantha, *A Problem From Hell: America and the Age of Genocide* (New York: HarperCollins, 2003). Pulitzer Prizewinning study of American failure, over the last century, to act decisively against genocide.

Harris, Lee, *Civilization and its Enemies: the Next Stage of History* (New York: Free Press, 2004). In a controversial interpretation, argues that the followers of Osama bin Laden are not political activists, but religious fanatics whose irrational goal is to kill Westerners.

Bhagwati, Jagdish, *In Defense of Globalization* (Oxford: Oxford University Press, 2004). An eminent economist explains why globalization is a force for social good, more than the source of exploitation.

Sen, Amartya, *Development as Freedom* (New York: Alfred A. Knopf, 1999). Nobel Prize-winning economist sees individual freedom as the goal of economic life, and the means by which abundance can be obtained.

Landes, David S, *the Wealth and Poverty of Nations: Why Some Are So Rich and Some So Poor* (New York: Norton, 1998). Thought-provoking study of the global distribution of wealth. Landes argues that what has made some nations rich and left others poor is their success in industrializing their economies.

De Soto, Hernando, *The Mystery of Capital: Why Capitalism Triumphs in the West and Fails Everywhere Else* (New York: Basic Books 2000). Argues that capitalism succeeds in the West because of its well-developed legal system founded on ideas of private property rights.

Ferguson, Niall, *Colossus: The Price of America's Empire* (Harmondsworth: Penguin, 2004). Views the U.S. as the heir to Britain's imperial tradition, if Americans are able to shoulder the burden of spreading democracy around the globe.

Mandelbaum, Michael, *The Ideas that Conquered the World: Peace, Democracy, and Free Markets in the Twenty-First Century* (New York: Public Affairs, 2002). Identifies three linked ideas that can form the basis of a new world order as they are accepted not only at the "core" but are diffused also to the periphery.

Jenkins, Philip, *The Next Christendom: The Coming of Global Christianity* (Oxford: Oxford University Press, 2002). Although the trend has gone unnoticed by most policymakers, Christianity has been spreading rapidly in South America, Africa, and Asia, making for a very different world Christendom in the twenty-first century.

World and political maps: http://www.atlapedia.com/

Elections around the world: www.election.world.org

The CIA's World Factbook : http://www.cia.gov/cia/publications/factbook/

Europa, Gateway to the European Union, by the EU: **http://europa.eu.int/index_en.htm**

Investigating Al-Qaeda, by BBC News: **http://news.bbc.co.uk/1/hi/in_depth/world/2001/war_on_terror/default.stm**

Iraq Time Line, by US Department of Defense: **http://www.defendamerica.mil/IraqTimeLine.html**

United Nations online: http://www.un.org/english/

War on Terrorism Resource Guides, by David Durant, Political Science and Government Documents Librarian, East Carolina University: **http://personal.ecu.edu/durantd/wot/index.html**

GLOSSARY

abolitionism: Designation for the movements in the United States and western Europe opposing the Atlantic slave trade and slavery.

Aborigines: The indigenous (native) or earliest-arrived peoples in any given area, especially the original Australian population.

abortion: The termination of pregnancy, spontaneous or contrived (through surgery or drugs), by the removal of embryo or fetus from the uterus.

absolute monarchy: Political system in which the powers of the monarch were theoretically "absolute," that is, not limited by any law or constitution. Absolute monarchs were limited in practice by the claims of the nobility, clergy, and tradition.

absolution: In some branches of Christianity, the act of pronouncing forgiveness and the remission of sins, performed by a priest in the sacrament of penance.

absolutism: A political system or project that concentrates power in the hands of the monarch. Absolutism came to prominence in Europe during the sixteenth through eighteenth centuries when monarchs sought to wrest power from the Church and the aristocracy, in order to create national states.

abstract art: Any of the various artistic styles or movements whose created images are non-representational, bearing little reference to actually-existing objects.

acropolis: The citadel of a Greek city, built at its highest point and containing the chief temples and public buildings.

Afrikaner: White resident of South Africa, typically of Dutch or Huguenot (French Protestant) descent, speaking the Afrikaans language (a variant of Dutch). *See also* **Boer**.

agnate: A relative on the father's side, from a male line of descent. A cognate is a relative whose kinship is on the mother's side.

agora: A central feature of the *polis*. Originally a marketplace, the *agora* also served as the main social and political meeting place. With the acropolis, the *agora* housed the most important buildings of the city-state.

alchemy/alchemist: Ancient mystical tradition involving the search for knowledge in order to transform base metals into gold.

alienation: From Marxist theory, the supposed disconnection of industrial workers from the product of their labor and from their human needs, as a result of the conditions of wage labor under capitalism. *See also* **proletarian**.

alumnus, alumna, alumni: In ancient Rome, abandoned infants who were picked up and "adopted" into families, usually as servants. In present-day usage, an alumnus or alumna is a person who has been graduated from a particular school or university.

ambassador: The highest-ranking diplomatic representative of one country to another, usually accorded the privilege of guaranteed personal security, or "diplomatic immunity."

ambulatory: A curved aisle running around the east end of a church, originally used for processions.

Amerindians: Aboriginal peoples of the Western Hemisphere, American Indians. Preferred to "Indian" (used to refer to the peoples of the Indian subcontinent) and "Native American" (an anti-immigrant American political party, called "the Know-Nothings").

anarchism: In political philosophy, the rejection of all government and law as the only means of acquiring social and political liberty.

Ancien Régime: Literally, "Old Regime," the term used to describe the traditional European system of legal, social, and political hierarchy which the French Revolution set out to destroy.

animism/animist: The belief that spirits or divinities dwell inside objects and living things, influencing or determining life and events in the natural world.

anthropomorphism: The assigning of human characteristics to animals, natural phenomena, or abstract ideas or, in religion, to a deity or spirit.

anti-Semitism: The discrimination against, prejudice or hostility toward Jews.

anti-trinitarianism: *See* **unitarianism**.

apartheid: Literally, "apartness;" in twentieth-century South Africa, the policy of segregating the black majority and white minority and granting to the latter the pre-ponderant political and economic power.

apostle: An early follower of Jesus, including the original twelve disciples and the first missionaries.

apotheosis: *See* **deification**.

appeasement: Policy of non-confrontation that was pursued by Britain toward Hitler's Germany in the 1930s, or any similar policy in general.

apprenticeship: Training in a craft or profession in which the master profits from the labor of the apprentice, and the apprentice receives training. *See also* **guild**, **master**.

apse: A domed or vaulted semicircular recess, especially at the east end of a church.

aristocracy: A government or social structure in which power and wealth is vested in a small minority, a hereditary nobility which claims to be best qualified to rule.

arquebus: A portable, long-barrelled gun, fired by a wheel-lock or match-lock, dating from the fifteenth century.

artisan: A skilled maker of things. Before the development of techniques of mass manufacture, artisans produced earthenware, tools, jewelry, etc. During the Industrial Revolution artisanal labor gave way to factory labor. *See also* **proletarian**.

Aryan: Formerly a term that referred to the Indo-European language family, and an assumed racial category which was composed of people of Indo-European "blood." The notion of an Aryan race was created by nineteenth-century race theorists and adopted by Adolf Hitler. "Aryan" is now used to designate the Indo-Iranian language group, or, more narrowly, the Indo-Aryan (Indic) branch and the group of Indo-Aryan speakers who invaded the Indian subcontinent c. 1500 B.C.E.

assimilation: The cultural, ethnic, linguistic, or other absorption of one or more peoples by another, dominant, group.

astrolabe: The most important instrument used by astronomers and navigators from antiquity through the sixteenth century, which enabled people to measure the altitudes of celestial bodies. The altitude of the North Star yields the latitude, and the altitude of the sun and stars yields the time. During the eighteenth century, the astrolabe was superseded by the sextant.

astrology: Pseudo-scientific study of the putative influence occasioned on individuals and societies by the planets. During the Scientific Revolution, the pursuit of astrology helped establish astronomy as a proper science.

atom: Smallest component of an element possessing all the chemical characteristics of that element, consisting of a nucleus and one or more electrons.

atonality: In music, this is the rejection of traditional harmonic elements including the diatonic scale and an obvious tonal center.

atrium: The central rectangular, interior open-air hall of the Etruscan and Roman house, usually considered the most important room.

audiencias: Governmental institutions or courts in colonial Spanish America designed to administer Spanish royal justice, including the protection of Amerindian rights.

autarky: Economic self-sufficiency. In Hitler's Germany, policy aimed at achieving political goals by establishing regional self-sufficiency.

authoritarianism/authoritarian: An anti-liberal governmental system wherein power resides in a single leader or narrow elite not responsible to the broader population, but which lacks the hallmarks of specifically fascist or other totalitarian regimes. *See also* **fascism**, **totalitarianism**.

auto-da-fé: An "act of faith," a penal sentence by the Spanish Inquisition; also, the execution of that sentence by burning at the stake.

avant-garde: Literally, "fore-guard," or vanguard; in the arts, this is the collective term for pioneers of innovative and unconventional styles.

barbarian: In ancient Greece, a word applied to non-Greek-speaking peoples, assumed to be inferior and uncivilized. Similarly used in Chinese civilization. Later and more generally, a person or group believed to lack cultural refinement.

basilica: An oblong building that ends in a semicircular protrusion (an apse), used in ancient Rome as a court of justice and place of public assembly; early Christians adapted this plan for their churches.

bastion: A projecting work in a castle wall or other fortification which allows the defenders to fire along the face of the wall.

bayonet: A short sword attached to the muzzle of a rifle. First used by European armies in the seventeenth century as an infantry weapon for close combat, eliminating the need for a corps of pikemen.

Bible: The sacred writings of Judaism and Christianity, known to Christians as the Bible, consisting of two parts. The first, called the Old Testament by Christians, stands alone for Jews as the Hebrew Bible. The second, called the New Testament, includes accounts of Jesus's life attributed to four of Jesus's disciples—Matthew, Mark, Luke, and John—known as Gospels (meaning "good news") or collectively as the Gospel.

Black Death: A fourteenth-century epidemic that killed one-fourth to one-third of the population of Europe (about 75 million people), caused by the bacterium *yersinia pestis* and spread by fleas harbored by the black rat.

Blitzkrieg: Literally, "lightning war," the tactic used by Nazi forces during World War II in which an invasion commences with aerial bombardment, followed by armored tank (or Panzer) divisions, then other motorized divisions and infantry.

blues: A musical form, generally vocal and expressing sadness or despair, characterized by the use of repeated "blues" tones.

Boer: Derived from Dutch word for "farmer," a white South African speaking Afrikaans, a Dutch dialect. *See also* **Afrikaner.**

Bolshevik: Literally, "majority persons," Lenin's faction of the Russian Social Democratic Party responsible for the Russian Revolution of 1917, the establishment of communism in Russia, and the creation of the Soviet Union.

bourgeoisie: Literally, "townspersons," including, in particular, artisans, merchants, lawyers, doctors, bankers, and, in the nineteenth century, factory-owners and industrial entrepreneurs. *See also* **burgher, class, proletarian.**

bourse: *See* **stock exchange.**

brahman: A priest or member of the priestly caste in Hinduism.

Bronze Age: An age in which bronze, an alloy of copper and tin, was used to manufacture tools, weapons, and other objects. The term originated as part of the nineteenth-century three-age system (Stone Age, Bronze Age, and Iron Age), but bronze technology actually appeared at different times in different parts of the world. Around 3000 B.C.E. in Mesopotamia and Egypt, bronze alloys were developed to make stronger tools, shields, and weapons.

bull: A letter issued by the pope stating a religious doctrine. In very early times, papal bulls (from Latin *bulla*, "leaden seal") were sealed with the imprint of the pope's signet ring. Today only the most solemn bulls carry a leaden seal.

bullion: Uncoined gold and silver, molded into bars or ingots.

burgher: In medieval Europe, a citizen of a town (*burg, borough, bourg, borgo*). Burghers were members of the class of enterprising merchants, bankers, and long-distance traders ("the bourgeoisie").

cadre: A core group within a larger political association or movement by whose activity the larger movement is organized, established, and expanded.

caliph: The supreme leader of the Islamic world after Muhammad's death in 632 C.E. Secular and religious authority were combined in the office of the caliph, who claimed to be appointed by God.

canon law: A single ecclesiastical rule or law, or the body of ecclesiastical law. By extension, a set of rules or fundamental texts pertinent in any art or discipline.

canton: In Switzerland, an independent unit of local government; the Swiss Confederation is divided into twenty-three cantons.

capitalism: An economic system organized around the profit motive and competition, in which the means of production are privately owned by businessmen and organizations which produce goods for a market guided by the forces of supply and demand.

caravel: A type of sailing ship, first developed in Portugal and widely used by fifteenth- and sixteenth-century explorers, equipped with square and lateen sails or entirely lateen rigged.

carbonari: In Italy, members of secret societies of liberals and nationalists opposed to the conservative order established at the Congress of Vienna in 1814–1815.

cartels: Voluntary associations of private corporations or individuals, aimed at achieving market dominance in a given sector or industry through violation of free-trade and competitive principles.

cartography: The research and drawing of maps. Begun in ancient times, cartography expanded during Europe's age of exploration from the late-fifteenth century, and became more accurate during the Scientific Revolution and Enlightenment.

castas: In Latin American history, intermediate social groups of mixed African, European, and Amerindian ancestry. *See also* **mulatto, mestizo.**

caste: A system of rigid hereditary social stratification, characterized by disparities of wealth and poverty, inherited occupations, and strict rules governing social contact.

castle: In the Middle Ages, the fortified residence of a European noble or monarch. At first only a wood or stone tower built on a mound encircled by walls or moat, castles later became more complex, with thick walls topped by a parapet.

catacombs: A complex of underground rooms and tunnels, especially in Rome, used as a cemetery, with niches for tombs and graves.

chancery: A record office; the court of a chancellor.

charter: Any written instrument establishing basic legal principles among the signing parties.

chivalry: The qualities that were expected of a knight; the code of values associated with the medieval nobility, developed in response to church strictures and elaborated at court.

Christendom: The part of the world in which Christianity predominates; the collective body of Christian believers.

cinema: Short for "cinematograph" (deriving from the Greek words for motion and for drawing), a picture engendered by motion, used popularly as the form of entertainment also called "film" and "the movies"; also the theater where such films are shown.

citizen: In ancient Greece, a free male inhabitant of a *polis*, with landowning and voting rights. In modern times, applied to any legal member of the state.

civic humanism: An engaged form of humanism that responded to the moral concerns of those who lived in cities. *See also* **humanism.**

civil law: *See jus civile*

civility: The set of manners and attitudes developed in European princely and royal courts from the later Middle Ages and into the early modern period.

civilization: A condition of society characterized by high cultural achievement and complex social development. A society is a civilization if it has (1) class stratification; (2) political and religious hierarchies; (3) a complex division of labor; (4) an economic system that creates agricultural surpluses; and (5) the skills to create architecture, tools, and weaponry.

clan: A number of households that claim descent from a common ancestor.

class: A social or economic group. In Marxist thought, specifically those individuals sharing a common relationship to the dominant means of production, such as the possessors (bourgeoisie, landlords, etc) or non-possessors (the proletariat, serfs).

Classicism/Classical: A term that refers to the ideals and styles of ancient Greek and Roman art, literature, and philosophy, and as reinterpreted by later generations. Classical ideals and styles have exemplified simplicity, harmony, restraint, proportion, and reason. Classicism also implies the finest period of artistic activity or the purest aesthetic. The era during which a society or art reaches its peak is often called classical, as in "Classical Greece" (fifth century B.C.E.).

clergy: A group ordained to perform religious functions. In Catholicism, the clergy is a hierarchical body headed by the pope.

cognate: *See* **agnate**.

cohort: A subdivision of the Roman legion, including infantry and cavalry.

collective bargaining: Process whereby workers negotiate collectively with their employer(s) or management via elected representatives. *See also* **strike, trade unions**.

collectivization: Under Stalin in the Soviet Union, the forced creation of a system of agricultural organization in which land was held in common under central control.

coloni: In imperial Rome, the class of poor tenant farmers, who were often the descendants of manumitted slaves. The *coloni* were the forerunners of the serfs of medieval Europe.

colonialism: The political, economic, or cultural expansion of national groups at the expense of others, and especially the process by which European nations came to dominate indigenous peoples in the Americas, northern Asia, and Australasia.

colony: an area or people beyond the borders of a state over which that state exercises control.

comedy: A genre of humorous drama, typically with a happy or absurd ending, sometimes critical of social and political institutions, that was first developed in ancient Greece.

commissariat: In the Soviet Union, name given to government departments until 1946, such as the People's Commissariat for Education.

Committee of Public Safety: During the radical phase of the French Revolution, executive body composed of nine men wielding total power as France faced counter-revolution and war with much of Europe. Under the leadership of Robespierre, it raised massive conscript armies and initiated the Terror. *See also* **Jacobins, Terror**.

common: In medieval Europe, a centrally located area of land that has been set aside for the free use of the community. Commons still exist in areas of England and the United States.

common law: A system of law developed after the Norman Conquest of England (1066), and still partly in use in most English-speaking countries. Unlike civil law (descended from the codified laws of the Roman Empire and from Napoleonic France), common law is not embodied in a text or code. Judges draw instead upon precedents set by earlier court decisions.

Commonwealth: Grouping of individual persons or of autonomous states into a consensual political community. The British Commonwealth, established in 1931, unites various former British colonies in a loose association paying varying levels of allegiance to the British Crown and sharing certain cultural and economic ties.

commune: In the Middle Ages, a self-governing municipality with the right to regulate trade, collect taxes, and operate its own system of justice within the town walls. In northern Europe, communes were often granted charters by the royal government or local court. In Italy, communes were sworn associations of townspeople that arose in the eleventh century to overthrow local bishops or feudal magnates.

communism: Socio-political system envisioned by Karl Marx and enacted in the twentieth century in Russia, China, and other countries.

compass: A device that indicates direction on the earth's surface; the principal instrument of navigation. A magnetic compass indicates movement relative to the earth's geomagnetic field.

concessions: Grants of land or of the right to engage in economic activities made to a second party by a government or other ruling body.

condottiere: *See* **mercenary**.

confraternity: An association of laypeople linked by a common mission, which combined spiritual and charitable service.

conquistadors: Military adventurers who led the Spanish exploration and conquest of the New World during the sixteenth century.

conservatism: Ideology, developed best by Edmund Burke, hostile to rapid change and esteeming traditional institutions, concepts, and strategies. Conservative principles underlay the order created by the Congress of Vienna in 1814–1815 following the defeat of Napoleon.

constitutional government: Government that rules according to an established body of basic laws, usually but not always written down, and whose power is thus limited.

consul: The two chief annual civil and military magistrates of Rome during the Republic.

contemplation: Quiet and solitary thought; the intellectual and religious ideal of medieval scholars who lived in monasteries and universities.

contraception: The prevention of pregnancy by any of a variety of sexual techniques, mechanical devices, or drugs.

conversion: The act or experience that is associated with the decisive adoption of a particular religion and set of beliefs, often entailing the rejection of a previous religious identity.

corporatism/corporatist: A hallmark of fascist states, corporatism describes a society based on cross-class grouping, especially the combining of the workers, administrators, and owners of a given enterprise into a single organization. It asserts the primacy of the "national community" and rejects the need for class-based organizations.

cosmopolis: A culturally prestigious city whose population is composed of peoples from many parts of the world; an urban center where a range of the most sophisticated customs, practices, and beliefs can be found.

cosmopolitanism: Belief in or advocacy of an international rather than national community, such as by Marxists, world religions, and so on.

cotton gin: Machine invented in 1793 in the United States by Eli Whitney to remove seeds mechanically from cotton fibers.

counter-insurgency: During the Cold War, term describing the United States' crusade against leftist revolutionary activities around the globe. In this context the United States sent experts to advise anti-communist rulers, equipped native armies and police forces, and set up programs to train foreign soldiers in modern military techniques.

coup d'état: The sudden, violent overthrow of a government by a small group.

courtesan: A kept woman or a prostitute, often highly skilled and capable of circulating among high-status patrons, typically associated with a royal court or clientele deriving from wealthy and powerful elites.

courtier: A person in attendance at a court, and who seeks the ruler's favor.

creole: A fully-formed language that develops from a pidgin language. Most creoles have vocabularies that are derived from major European languages; some of them exist only in spoken form. The word also refers to combinations of European and non-European cultures, especially cooking and music, and to people of mixed racial heritage. See *also* **mestizo**.

cubism: Art form pioneered immediately prior to World War I by Georges Braque and Pablo Picasso using fragmented images designed to show several sides of an object at the same time. *See also* **Modernism**.

culture: Learned behavior acquired by individuals as members of a particular group, in contrast to genetically endowed behavior. Each culture has different styles governing behavior and thought. "Culture" can include food preparation, politics, sculpture, architecture, painting, music, literature, philosophy, and a range of other civilized pursuits.

cuneiform: A system of writing from Sumer and used for various Middle Eastern languages from c. 3000 B.C.E. until c. 100 C.E. It consisted of wedge-shaped characters inscribed on clay, stone, wax, or metal.

curtain wall: The plain wall of a castle or other fortified place, connecting two towers.

cybernetics: From the Greek for "steersman," the science that studies control and communication systems in entities of any type—including social and business organizations, living organisms, machines, computers, the human brain, and so on.

Darwinism: Pertaining to the theory of Charles Darwin, who argued that organic forms, including humans, are the product of evolution by natural selection taking place over long periods of time.

decolonization: Process ending the control enjoyed by a metropolitan power over its colony, with the latter becoming fully independent. Decolonization of Europe's empires occurred during the post-World War II era. *See also* **metropolis**.

decurions: In cities of the Roman Empire, the elite hereditary class responsible for funding and administering municipal functions, and for collecting taxes.

deduction: In logic, the process of inferring specific cases from a general axiom or principle. *See also* **induction, empiricism**.

deification: The process of attributing god-like attributes to a human being. In ancient Rome, a deceased emperor was often deified in a ritual that was known as apotheosis.

deism: The belief that God created the universe as a perfect mechanism running according to mechanical laws discoverable through the use of reason rather than revelation.

demesne: That part of a medieval landholding cultivated exclusively for the lord's use.

democracy: Term from the Greek words for "people" and "power." A form of government in which citizens monitor the state; as opposed to oligarchy or monarchy, where the state is controlled by a small minority or individual. In a direct democracy citizens vote in an assembly, as in ancient Athens. In an indirect democracy citizens elect representatives.

demographic: Pertaining to the study of the structure and dynamics of human populations, including their distribution and movement by category (such as age, gender, ethnicity, occupation, nationality, and so on).

demotic: A simplified form of Egyptian hieroglyphic writing used for informal communication and by the masses; hieratic was a simplified form of writing used by the priesthood.

détente: Foreign policy designed to ease tensions with a rival state or bloc.

dhow: A type of sailing vessel with lateen sails, in common use from the Red Sea to the western coast of India.

dialectics: Logical argumentation, especially in the Western tradition according to the method of Aristotle and his followers. In modern times, the opposition or reconciliation of conflicting ideas or forces (as for Hegel and Marx).

dialogue: A literary genre favored by humanists, based on Classical models. Dialogue permitted an author to present two or more competing viewpoints and argue for each plausibly without committing himself.

diaspora: A Greek word meaning "dispersion," originally referring to the Jewish settlements of ancient Babylon and Egypt formed after the destruction of the Temple in 587 B.C.E. Later diasporas of Jews occurred, especially after Jewish revolts against Rome that took place in the first and second centuries C.E. Today, "diaspora" is a term used of Jewry outside of the state of Israel and is also applied to other dispersions of peoples.

Diet: In the Holy Roman Empire, the assembly of the representatives of the estates.

diplomacy: Conducting negotiations to resolve differences, regulate commerce, make alliances, etc. *See also* **ambassador**.

Directory: French revolutionary government from October 1795 to November 1799, comprising a bicameral legislature and five-man executive.

disputation: In medieval education, an exercise in logic that consists of arguments for and against a thesis, until a conclusion is reached. *See* **dialectics, scholasticism**.

distaff: A simple stick that is used in spinning. The distaff held raw fiber that was pulled and twisted into thread and wound on the spindle; later the spindle was the bobbin on the spinning machine that held spun thread.

dominion: Term describing the status, up to 1939, of the following members of the British Commonwealth: Australia, Canada, Eire, Newfoundland, New Zealand, and South Africa. Dominions were regarded as "autonomous communities" sharing equal status and close ties to the British Crown. *See also* **Commonwealth**.

dowry: The property a bride brings to her marriage. It correlates with the wealth or status of the bridegroom.

dualism: Any theory or system of philosophical or religious thought that recognizes two independent and mutually irreducible spiritual entities. The ancient Zoroastrian belief that the god of Good struggled against the god of Evil to determine human destiny was a form of dualism, influencing Judaism, Christianity, and Islam.

ducat: A gold coin with the portrait of the ruler (i.e. the duke, the doge) on it, first minted in 1284 by the city of Venice.

duchy: The territory of a duke or duchess.

Duma: From the Russian verb "to think" or "to reflect," the name of the Russian parliament, created for the first time as a consequence of the Revolution of 1905.

dynasty: A succession of monarchs of the same line of descent; a group or family that maintains power for a long period of time.

E = mc²: Energy = Mass multiplied by the square of the speed of light; Einstein's revolutionary equation showing that mass and energy are interconvertible and making possible the subsequent development of atomic bombs and atomic power.

economic imperialism: Economic—as opposed to political or military—hegemony of one state or culture over another, such as the dominance of foreign business interests within a developing country.

elite: A small group of persons who control major institutions, exercise military and/or political power, possess superior wealth, or enjoy elevated status and prestige.

empiricism: The use of observation and experiment to gain knowledge.

enclosure: In early modern Europe, process whereby common fields or separate holdings were consolidated into larger agricultural units.

encomienda: In colonial Spanish America, a grant made to an individual by the Spanish Crown of a certain number of Amerindians from whom he could exact tribute in gold, labor, or kind.

Enlightenment: Intellectual movement stressing the improvement of human society through the application of reason.

entrepôts: Ports, trading bases, warehouses, or other places into which goods and commodities are gathered prior to further distribution to sellers and consumers.

entrepreneur: A person who organizes and assumes the risks of a business.

epidemic: A contagious disease that periodically or episodically afflicts many people within a population, community, or region. Severe epidemics have killed large numbers of people, most notoriously the Black Death of fourteenth-century Europe.

ersatz: Hitler encouraged the chemical industries to develop synthetic or "ersatz" equivalents of normally traded goods.

established religion: Any religion sanctioned as the official religion of a given state, such as the Catholic faith in pre-Revolutionary France or the Anglican Church in England.

estate: A social group, legally defined, invested with distinct powers, possessions, and property.

Estate: In early modern Europe, one of three social orders (clergy, nobility, commoners). The Estates-General was an assembly of representatives of the three "Estates."

Eucharist: A central observance of the Christian churches, which is variously called the Lord's Supper, Holy Communion, and the Mass.

eugenics: Field of study or actual practice aimed at controlling human racial development, usually by means of selective breeding. Eugenics assumed probably its most extreme form in the hands of the Nazis, who strove for "Aryan purity" in and beyond Germany.

excommunication: The formal expulsion of a member from a religious group. In Roman Catholicism, the excommunicated are excluded from receiving the sacraments of the church.

existentialism/existentialist: Philosophical outlook positing the individual as the basic object of existence, and proposing the non-existence of any absolute values, truths, or meaning. Their absence was construed not as causes for despair but as opportunities for individuals to realize personal autonomy and freedom.

experiment: Procedure designed to test a specific principle or hypothesis by subjecting it to a carefully defined and repeatable test.

extraterritoriality: The condition of being subject to the laws of one's own country rather than those of the country within which one currently lives.

façade: A French word meaning "face" or "front." In architecture, a façade is the side of a structure, normally the front, that is architecturally or visually most significant.

factory: Especially in connection with the Industrial Revolution, an establishment equipped for the application of labor and machinery to the purpose of market-oriented mass production of goods.

fallow: Cultivated land deliberately allowed to lie idle during a growing season in order to prevent soil exhaustion.

famine: A shortage of food that is sufficient to cause widespread privation and a rise in mortality. Famine may be caused by natural events; by war; by political decisions; or by agricultural practices that cause soil erosion.

fascism/fascist: Form of political organization marked by anti-communism, anti-liberalism, governmental suppression of individual rights, militarism, the exaltation of a "national community," and rule of a charismatic leader.

federal: Relating to the central authority governing a federation of individual states, such as the federal government of the United States in relation to individual states.

feminism: Ideology founded in the perception of the unjust social subordination of women, which has had and continues to develop a variety of forms, including women's property and voting rights, abortion rights, or recognition of women's unique capacity to nurture children.

feudal: *See* **fief.**

fief, feudal: Medieval relationships of lordship, landholding, and service are often called "feudal," and depended on the granting of a unit of land, the "fief," in usufruct.

florin: A coin first minted in 1252 by the city of Florence; later, any of several gold coins patterned after the Florentine florin.

fluyt: A "flyboat;" in early modern Europe, a small, highly efficient vessel invented by the Dutch for inexpensive, utilitarian hauling.

folk: The people as a whole; those who bear and transmit the cultural values of a people.

free market: A market-place where goods and services may be freely exchanged at prices, in quantities, and on terms dictated only by factors of supply and demand, and where there is no regulation of such exchange by any government or other body.

fresco: Italian for "fresh," that is a technique of durable wall painting that is used extensively for murals. In pure (*buon*) fresco paint is applied to a fresh wet layer of plaster; painting on a dry (*secco*) surface with adhesive binder is not permanent.

fundamentalism/fundamentalist: In matters of religion or other ideology, an extreme conservative, and often one who is willing to attack any perceived deviation from a given orthodoxy.

futurism: Iconoclastic movement in art during the early twentieth century glorifying machinery, energy, and movement, and notably embraced by the Italian fascist movement under Mussolini.

galley: A warship driven by oars in battle and with sails for cruising. It was the standard European battle vessel until the late sixteenth century, when the sail-powered, more heavily armed, galleon replaced it.

genocide: Deliberate and systematic murder or attempted murder of an entire ethnic, racial, religious, or cultural group.

Gentile: A non-Jew, avoided by faithful Jews.

Geometric style: A style of Greek pottery produced in the ninth and eighth centuries B.C.E., marked by densely patterned lines, including zigzags and Greek key motifs.

ghetto: A segregated quarter where Jews were required to reside. In 1516, the first ghetto was established on the site of an iron foundry (the meaning of "ghetto") by the rulers of Venice. The term came to designate any urban area to which Jews were legally confined, or where Jews or any other socially marginalized group lived voluntarily.

glasnost: In Russian, "openness" or "publicity," the policy promoted in the 1980s by Soviet leader Mikhail Gorbachev in which the government's control of access to and exchange of information was to be slackened in order to stimulate debate and promote reform. *See also* **perestroika.**

Gospel: *See* **Bible.**

Gothic: An architectural style originating in twelfth-century France, which uses pointed arches and diagonal rib vaults.

grace: A central concept in Christian theology, referring to God's granting of salvation as a free and undeserved gift of love.

guerrilla: Derived from the Spanish resistance to Napoleon, literally a "little war," referring to the sometimes quite fierce struggle that is waged by non-regular soldiers, often in support of revolution or native resistance against imperialism. Also used as a personal noun, referring to the guerrilla warrior.

guild: An association of merchants or craftsmen. In medieval and early modern Europe, a guild normally comprised all self-employed members of an occupation in a town or district. Only guild members could practice that occupation.

gulag: Acronym of the Russian for "state camp," referring to the notorious network of Soviet prison camps where millions of Russians were forced to labor under extremely harsh conditions, especially during the Stalinist purges of the 1930s.

gymnasium: In ancient Greece, a place where athletes exercised in the nude. Gymnasia served as meeting places for social events and intellectual exchange.

gynaeceum: The "women's quarters" of a Greek citizen's house; the workshop for women textile workers on an early medieval estate.

Habsburg: Princely family, of German origin, prominent from the eleventh century until 1918 and whose members have been sovereigns of the Holy Roman Empire, Spain, and Austria.

hacienda: In colonial Spanish America, a large landed estate, often employing vast numbers of poor, heavily indebted agricultural laborers. *See also* **peons.**

Hasid/Hasidism: Member of the Jewish sect founded by Israel Baal Shem-Tov in Poland during the eighteenth century, and which emphasizes religious mysticism, zeal, and fervent prayer.

hegemony: The domination of one institution, sector, or state over others.

Hellas: The Greek name for Greece.

Hellenic: A term that designates the period of Greek culture and history from the Archaic Age (c. 700 to c. 500 B.C.E.) to the period of Alexander the Great (r. 336–323 B.C.E.).

Hellenistic: A term designating the period of Greek culture and history from the conquests of Alexander the Great until the eastern Mediterranean region fell under Roman domination (by 30 B.C.E.).

helot: In ancient Sparta, a serf who was forced to perform agricultural labor; originally, the Messenians, a group conquered by the Spartans and reduced to near slave status.

heresy: The rejection of the established doctrines of a group (e.g. a church) by a member or members of that group; from the Greek word meaning "to choose."

heterodoxy: Deviation from orthodoxy.

hierarchy: A series of persons, graded or ranked in order of authority.

hieratic: *See* **demotic.**

hieroglyph: Writing employing pictographic characters, developed in ancient Egypt.

historicism: The idea that any proper examination of history must take the period or subject under consideration absolutely in its own context while avoiding any prejudices or values connected to the historian him or herself or the historian's own time.

historiography: The writing of history, or any of its techniques and theories; the body of historical writing on any given subject.

Holocaust: Literally (from the Greek), "whole burning," or "burnt offering," term describing the Nazis' massacre of Jews during World War II. The notion of the Holocaust specifically as a "burnt offering" reflects the belief of some Jews that their people's suffering was a righteous punishment inflicted by God for the Jews' collective sins, especially assimilation. Uncapitalized, the term may describe any mass murder.

hominid: The genus of human-like animals, comprising modern humans (*Homo sapiens*) and ancestral and related human and human-like species (*Homo sapiens neanderthalensis, Homo erectus, Homo habilis*). *See* **species.**

Homo erectus: *See* **hominid.**

Homo habilis: See **hominid**.

Homo sapiens: See **hominid** and **species**.

honor: Form or measure of respect given (or withheld from) a person by his peers, especially among elite social groups. In early modern society, honor was often won in military combat or by duelling with an enemy or rival, by cleverness in speech, by the achievement of high office in government or the church, or by membership in prestigious organizations.

hoplite: A heavily armored foot soldier of ancient Greece, who fought in close formation, each carrying a heavy bronze shield (a *hoplon*), a short iron sword, and a long spear.

hospice: A place of refuge for travelers and pilgrims. In the medieval context, very similar to the non-specialized hospital.

hospital: Generally church-related and funded by bequests, the medieval hospital accommodated not only the sick but also abandoned children, "fallen" or deserted women, and the elderly. From the seventeenth century, it increasingly specialized in the treatment of the ill.

house: Stately home with which a particular noble family or "line" was associated and from which its name derived.

humanism: An intellectual movement that emerged in Italy in the late 1300s and spread throughout western and central Europe in the early modern period, centered around the revival of interest in ancient Greek and Roman literature, philosophy, and history.

humors: From ancient Greek medicine, these are the four elemental body fluids (blood, phlegm, black bile, yellow bile), the imbalance of which was treated by purging or blood-letting.

hypothesis: Proposition, usually intended provisionally. In science, hypotheses are either supported or falsified by experimental and other data. *See also* **experiment**.

icon: An image that represents a divine figure and is believed to possess some essential aspect of that divinity.

iconoclasm: A Christian religious movement opposed to the veneration of images (icons) of Christ and the saints. Controversy over the legitimacy of icons lasted for over a century (730–843 C.E.) in the Byzantine Empire. Iconoclasts (Greek for "image-breakers") often invaded churches, destroying the offending images.

ideology: The body of essential ideas, assumptions, and goals underlying a given movement or organization, such as Marxist ideology, capitalist ideology, and so on. *See also* **Marxism, capitalism**.

illuminated manuscript: A handwritten book with pictures and ornamentation, "illuminating," or lighting up, the page.

immortality: Being exempt from death, also human survival after physical death.

imperator: Originally, in ancient Rome, a person who commanded an army. Augustus Caesar was the *imperator* of all the armies and institutions of government, and thus of Rome and its territories.

imperialism: The process by which a state creates, expands, or defends its political or economic dominance over others, as in the domination by Europe of much of the rest of the world during the nineteenth and early twentieth centuries. *See also* **colonialism**.

imperium: Originally the supreme command in war, granted at Rome to consuls and other magistrates; later, authority over a region or empire.

indentured servant: In the early years of North American settlement, a European immigrant who worked without wages for a contracted period in exchange for the price of passage to the colonies and clothing, board, and lodging while in service.

Indo-European: An extensive language family, originally derived from a common ancestor, Proto-Indo-European. The surviving languages include Hindi, Persian, Russian, Polish, Armenian, Albanian, Greek, Italian, French, Spanish, Portuguese, German, English, Dutch, and the Scandinavian languages.

induction: In logic, the process of inferring general rules or axioms from specific cases, such as Newton's assertion of the law of gravitation based on numerous specific examples of motion. *See also* **deduction**.

indulgence: In medieval Catholicism, a document granting release from purgatorial punishment in recognition of service.

industrialization/Industrial Revolution: Process of technological, economic, and social transformation involving production for a mass market by means of heavy machinery and human labor deployed in factories. In the nineteenth century, industrializing nations experienced rapid economic growth, and the crystallization of two economic classes, the workers (proletariat) and industrialists (industrial bourgeoisie).

infantry: Armed foot soldiers, as distinct from cavalry, air, or sea forces.

infidel: In Islam, a nonbeliever, someone outside the faith.

infrastructure: The total of basic structures and services underlying an economy, including roads, railroads, bridges, electric grids, telephone cables, and power plants.

Inquisition: A church court to prosecute heretics. Inquisitory courts were harsh in their interrogation and punishment, obtaining confessions through torture.

intendant: In seventeenth- and eighteenth-century France, the absolute monarchy's key regional administrator, regarded by French monarchs as more reliable than hereditary officials.

investiture: The ceremonial conferring of high office and rank. The question as to which authority should have power to invest church officials provoked the "Investiture Controversy" during the high Middle Ages between the papacy and secular rulers.

Iron Age: The period when iron replaced bronze as the material for tools and weapons. Iron metallurgy began among the Hittites in eastern Anatolia, c. 1900–1400 B.C.E. and by 1000 B.C.E. had spread throughout the Middle East, Mediterranean region, and westward into Europe.

Islamist: Promotion of the civilization of Islam, whether by religious fundamentalists or secular activists; pertaining to any person or movement attempting to import Islamic religion, law, or moral values into political life.

isonomia: The principle in ancient Athenian society that citizens are entitled to equality before the law.

Jacobins: During the French Revolution, a political group of radical egalitarians who, under the determined leader Robespierre, orchestrated the Terror. The name derives from the church of Saint-Jacques, associated with a Dominican convent, in Paris. *See also* **Terror**.

jazz: Broad category of musical forms employing heavy improvization, complex harmonies and melodies, and in many cases unorthodox time signatures, pioneered at the turn of the twentieth century by African Americans.

jihad: An Arabic word meaning "striving"; according to the Qu'ran, the religious duty of Muslims. Often translated as "holy war," it can be interpreted as a personal or collective spiritual battle against evil, or as a physical battle against unbelievers.

joint-stock company: A type of partnership similar to a corporation. A joint-stock company has transferable shares which are sold at a stock exchange. It is managed by a board of directors elected by the partners (shareholders) who, unlike modern corporations, are personally liable for the company's debts. The joint-stock company was instrumental in the expansion of mercantile capitalism and European colonialism. *See also* **stock exchange**.

Junker: Especially in eastern Prussia, Germany, the class of aristocratic landholders, militaristic and authoritarian in disposition, from which many German officers were drawn.

jurisprudent: In ancient Rome, a citizen who was learned in law but who held no official position. Over time, jurisprudence came to mean a system or body of law, and jurisprudents became professionals in the imperial bureaucracy, whose documentation and analysis of past decisions constituted a system of law.

jus civile: In the Roman Empire, the "civil law," based primarily on codified statute, most famously the *Corpus Juris Civilis* of the sixth-century C.E. emperor Justinian, rather than court rulings and precedents. Today, used in the legal systems of certain western European countries and their offshoots in Latin America, Asia, and Africa. In contrast, the *jus gentium* ("law of nations") was based on unwritten customary practice and *jus naturale* ("law of nature") on an unwritten (and superior) divine or philosophical law.

justification: In Christianity, the process through which an individual, alienated from God by sin, is reconciled to God and becomes righteous through faith in Christ.

Kabbalah: Esoteric and mystical philosophical tradition within Judaism purporting to grant its initiates access to profound spiritual truths and knowledge of the future.

Keynesian: Pertaining to the ideas of the British economist Sir John Maynard Keynes, particularly his notion that free-market economies cannot always be relied on to self-correct, and must sometimes be actively managed by the central government. *See also* **New Deal**.

knight: In medieval Europe, a mounted warrior. Most were nobles of low rank who gave a military service to their lords in exchange for a land grant or maintenance. Higher-status nobles also acquired knighthood, by which they were admitted to military rank. A knight was named by a noble superior, and often went through an elaborate ceremony of knighthood.

koine: The form of Greek commonly spoken and written in the eastern Mediterranean in the Hellenistic and Roman periods, allowing people of many different cultures to communicate.

kore, pl. *korai*: A type of statue featuring a young, clothed female, developed in the Archaic Age (c. 700 B.C.E.).

kouros, pl. *kouroi*: A statue featuring a young, male nude, first introduced in the Archaic Age (c. 700 B.C.E.) and common in the Classical era.

kulak: In Russia and the Soviet Union, derogatory Russian term for a wealthy peasant. Literally "fists," kulaks were targeted by the communists for general destruction as a class during the late 1920s and early 1930s.

labor: An economic group whose members perform the basic functions of an economy. Key factors in the creation of industrial societies have included the harnessing of labor to specific productive purposes by an entrepreneurial class, the magnification of labor's productive powers by the application of increasingly powerful technologies, and the more efficient organization of labor in factories. *See also* **proletarian, factory**.

lateen sail: A triangular sail on a long yard, used by dhows and other light sailing vessels.

latifundia: In Roman times, a great landed estate, usually worked on by slaves. In Latin America, used to describe large ranches.

layperson: A person who is not a member of the clergy; now commonly meaning a person who is not a member of a specific profession.

legitimacy: The claim of a right to power, based on hereditary succession, electoral rules, or natural law.

liberalism: From the Enlightenment on, an ideology stressing individual liberty. In the economic sphere, liberalism, as championed by Adam Smith, demands that the state adopt a "hands-off" policy, allowing individuals the opportunity to pursue economic self-interest within a free market. In the political sphere, liberalism requires equal right to participate in the political process, and equal protection by the law, of all citizens.

line: The series of familial connections linking a noble to the ancestral founder of his family's noble status.

liturgy: The formal public rituals, prayers, and written texts of religious worship (from the Greek "people" and "work"), used of Christian services and the form of prayer in synagogues.

logical positivism: General term for the philosophies associated with the Vienna Circle, and which emphasize the verifiability of propositions, utility of empiricism, and logical analysis of language. *See also* **empiricism, positivism**.

Loyalists: Individuals or groups who remained faithful to the English Crown. The term is used primarily in the American Revolutionary context, in relation to the struggle between Crown and Parliament in Britain during the seventeenth century.

Lyceum: The philosophical school established by Aristotle; in the nineteenth century, the inspiration for secondary school education.

Mahdi: In Islam, title given to a leader combining temporal and spiritual authority who is expected to usher in a period of global righteousness.

man of war: An armed, combatant naval vessel.

mandate: In a system prevailing from 1919 to 1946, the grant of permission by the League of Nations to a member state to govern the affairs of a specific territory formerly under Ottoman Turkish or German control.

Manifest Destiny: Term proclaiming a belief that the westward expansion of the United States to the Pacific coast is both inevitable and divinely sanctioned. In some cases the term was also adopted by advocates of the annexation of Carribean and Pacific islands.

manor: In medieval Europe, a unit of social organization dominated by a lord, usually consisting of open fields, forest, and common grazing lands, a manor house and the lord's demesne, and one or more peasant villages. Peasants paid a portion of their produce and a number of days of labor each year to the lord. The lord was expected to provide military protection and to dispense justice.

manumission: The term for the formal act of emancipating a slave, sometimes by written agreement or payment by the slave to his master.

martyr: A person who suffers the penalty of death (and/or painful torture) for adhering to a religion or cause.

Marxian dialectic: From Marxist theory, the mechanism whereby historical change occurs, which Marx conceived as involving the opposition of a given basic socio-economic form—or "thesis"—with its opposite—or "antithesis." The tensions between these are supposedly ultimately resolved in their "synthesis"—or merging. The synthesis then constitutes a new "thesis," allowing the process to begin over again, and so on. The overall mechanism is likened to a conversation, thus the term "dialectic."

Marxism: Referring to or connected with the economic and political philosophy of Karl Marx. Marx, along with Friedrich Engels, believed that history was a "determined" (or inevitable) process involving struggle between opposing economic classes, and periodic revolution leading ultimately to a classless, communist society. *See also* **class**.

Mass: The celebration of the Eucharist, the central religious service of the Roman Catholic Church and some other Christian churches.

master: An artisan who is self-employed or who employs journeymen, usually a member of a guild. A journeyman who could demonstrate truly superior skills might be admitted to the guild as a master. In the later Middle Ages, the guild membership was often limited to the sons of masters.

materialism: A philosophical theory, first developed in ancient Greece, that physical matter is the only reality. In modern usage, this is also a term for a cultural style in which the goal is the satisfaction of physical desire and comfort.

maternalist: Pertaining to the belief that women's most powerful role is in the family. Maternalist thinking stresses that the mother who nurtures and instructs her children is the true creator of human society.

mendicant: Someone dependent on alms for sustenance. In the Middle Ages, the mendicant orders lived by begging or on charitable gifts. The first mendicant order grew out of the efforts of St. Francis of Assisi (c. 1182–1226).

Menshevik: Literally, "minority persons," the faction of Russian Social Democrats who in 1903 opposed Lenin's plans for a tightly-knit party organization comprising only professional revolutionaries, preferring a less rigid association of socialists.

mercantilism: An economic system developed in the early modern era to unify and increase the power and monetary wealth of a nation by regulating the entire national economy. From the sixteenth through the eighteenth century, western European governments practiced mercantilism to build up their military and industrial strength.

mercenary: A professional soldier who fights for pay in the army of a foreign country.

meridian: A great circle passing through both poles and any single point on earth. The meridian that passes through Greenwich, England, has been denoted the "prime," or first meridian.

Messiah: The prophesied king and redeemer of the Jews, who would restore the Jews to Israel and bring divine justice to the earth; derived from the Hebrew term for "anointed one." Translated into Greek as "Christos," the term was applied to Jesus.

mestizo: A term of biological and cultural classification used in the Spanish-speaking world for persons of mixed Amerindian and white ancestry.

metaphysics: The branch of philosophy concerned with ultimate universal principles such as being and purpose.

Methodism/Methodists: The branch of evangelical Christianity developed in the eighteenth century by the Englishman John Wesley and which appealed in particular to lower and lower-middle class audiences. *See also* **Pietism**.

metic: In ancient Greece, a merchant, usually a foreigner, who was a member of a class of resident non-citizens in the *polis*, with some, but not all, of the privileges of citizenship.

metropolis/metropolitan: A great city that is regarded as an important center of business or politics. Applied to the ancient world, the term means the "mother" *polis* that established a colony. In that sense, it continues to be applied to nations that establish colonies.

microorganisms: Generic term for any microscopic plants or animals, an understanding of the existence and actions of which—particularly bacteria—was a major scientific achievement during the nineteenth century. *See also* **pasteurization**.

Midrash: In Judaism, a method of interpreting biblical scriptures; later, compilations of stories and sermons commenting on, alluding to, or codifying biblical texts.

Milesian school: The first materialistic philosophers, Thales, Anaximander, and Anaximenes, who lived in the city of Miletus, in the sixth century B.C.E. They explained natural phenomena by reference to laws that governed growth and change, understood through observation and logic.

mintage, minting: The process by which metal money is coined by a government. A mint is the place where coins are manufactured from gold and silver bullion.

Mishnah: The oldest post-biblical codification of Jewish Oral Law, from the Hebrew "repetition" or "study." Together with the Gemara (later commentaries on the Mishnah), it forms the Talmud.

missionary: The missionary movement was the Christian effort to convert peoples. The first great missionary to the Gentiles, Paul, helped to spread Christianity until, by the end of the first century, it had reached most Mediterranean cities. The voyages of discovery in the fifteenth and sixteenth centuries and the expansion of European colonization began a surge of Roman Catholic missionary activity. Renewed missionary activity took place as part of nineteenth-century imperialism.

Modernism/Modernist: In art and culture, term for the many non-traditional styles and outlooks embraced by the avant-garde from the late nineteenth to the late twentieth century. *See also* **avant-garde**.

monarchy: Rule by a single individual, usually with life tenure and descended from a line of monarchs.

monasticism: The way of life of individuals who have chosen to pursue an ideal of perfection in a separate, dedicated religious setting. Monasticism is practiced in Buddhism, some forms of Christianity, and some other religions.

monotheism: Belief in a single God (as in Judaism, Christianity, and Islam). By contrast, polytheism is the belief that many gods exist; pantheism is the belief that God is suffused throughout, or is synonymous with, the universe; animism is the belief that spirits or divinities dwell inside objects and living things. Some religions are non-theistic (Confucianism, Buddhism), but permit belief in gods or spirits.

montage: In the arts, the technique of combining images from various sources into a single image or series of images.

Moor: In medieval and early modern Europe, an inhabitant of Muslim North Africa, and, by extension, the Arab and Arabicized conquerors and inhabitants of Spain.

mosque: The Islamic place of public worship (from the Arabic *masjid*, "a place to prostrate one's self [in front of God]"), always oriented toward Mecca, the holy city of Islam. A mosque must have a place for ritual washing, a place from which a leader (*imam*) can start the prayer, and a minaret, a tower from which Muslims are called to prayer.

mulatto: In former colonies of Spain, Portugal, and France, and in the United States, a term for a person of mixed Negro and European parentage.

museum: An institution where objects of aesthetic, educational, or historical value are preserved and displayed.

music hall: In British history, from the 1830s to around 1900, the most popular arena for mass entertainment. Often beginning as modest adjuncts to pubs, they later included large purpose-built structures, and featured song, dance, comedy, and other entertainments.

musket: A large-caliber, smooth-bore firearm aimed and fired from the shoulder, which first appeared in Spain in the mid-1500s and fired a lead ball.

Mycenae: An ancient Greek city which rose to military power around 1500 B.C.E. Mycenaean civilization, influenced by Minoan Crete and the ancient Middle East, flourished until about 1300 B.C.E.

mystery cults: In the ancient world, religious cults whose members believed that the performance of secret rituals would give them special knowledge and a mystical union with the divine. Initiates ritually reenacted the death and rebirth of the divinity at the center of the cult.

mysticism: Religious experience in which the believer has or claims direct contact with the sacred. In Christianity this can take the form of a vision of, or sense of union with, God.

myths: Stories that narrate in an imaginative and symbolic way the basic practices and beliefs upon which a culture rests. Mythology means either a certain body of myths (e.g. Greek or Scandinavian) or the study of myths.

natalism: In post-World War I Europe, the promotion of motherhood as a boon to the state. In fascist societies, this meant the encouragement or requirement of women to reproduce frequently in order to increase the national population, and thus war-readiness.

National Assembly: During the French Revolution, the revolutionary representative assembly of the entire nation largely comprising members of the Third Estate. Constituted on June 17, 1789, the National Assembly was reorganized as the National Convention, and later as the Legislative Assembly. *See also* **Estate**.

nationalism: A sense of community among individuals conceived as possessing similar "national" characteristics—history, religion, ethnicity, language, and so on—coupled with an ardent desire to manifest the community as an autonomous political nation.

naturalized: The condition of having gained citizenship through a legal process rather than by birth. Specific requirements for naturalization vary from nation to nation.

nave: The central space in a church, usually extending from the west door to the chancel, and often flanked by aisles.

neo-colonialism: International relationship characterized by one nation's dominance (usually economic) over another, but which lacks the formal, political, or legal hallmarks of outright colonialism. *See also* **colonialism, economic imperialism**.

Neolithic Period: The prehistoric development that followed the Paleolithic Period and preceded the Bronze Age. In the Neolithic ("New Stone Age," c. 9000–3000 B.C.E.), chipped stone tool manufacture became increasingly sophisticated; agriculture and the domestication of animals were introduced; and pottery and polished stone tools were developed.

Neoplatonism: An interpretation of Plato's philosophy that developed in the third century C.E., which influenced Christian and Islamic philosophy and theology. It holds that knowledge is possible only through the understanding of archetypes, essences that structure the objects and beings that make up the world of human experience. According to Neoplatonism, the human soul has within it a vision of these ideal forms, which are dependent on and created by the One (i.e. God).

nepotism: The practice of awarding jobs or privileges to a relative.

New Deal: The peacetime domestic program established during the 1930s by United States president Franklin D. Roosevelt to combat the Great Depression and provide work, assistance, and security to average Americans. Influenced by Keynesian economic ideas the New Deal established many new federal government programs and agencies including the Federal Deposit Insurance Corporation (FDIC), the Civilian Conservation Corps (CCC), the Work Projects Administration (WPA), and Social Security. *See also* **Keynesian**.

New Testament: *See* **Bible**.

nihilism/nihilist: In philosophy, the rejection of all established norms, laws, and institutions as meaningless, and of the possibility that absolute truths can ever be established.

nirvana: Release from bondage to physical desire and pain: a core belief of Buddhism, the ultimate state attained by the Buddha, and the goal of all Buddhists. In Hinduism, nirvana is achieved only through a complete cessation of the cycle of death and rebirth. In Buddhism a state of enlightenment can be achieved in this life, through spiritual or physical exercises.

notary: In medieval cities, a trained professional who drew up deeds, contracts, wills, and other documents essential for urban life.

novel: A literary form developed during the eighteenth century, a novel is a lengthy fictional narrative written in prose style.

oecumene: A Greek word referring to "the inhabited world"; in antiquity designating a distinct cultural community. The ecumenical councils in the early church were so called because they represented the whole church. Today, the term "ecumenical" is applied to the collective effort of all Christians to repair differences and manifest unity.

oikos: The household, the fundamental unit of private land and of domestic production in ancient Greece, consisting of a dominant man, his wife and children, and related and unrelated dependents, including slaves. The *oikos* was patrilineal and patriarchal.

Old Testament: *See* **Bible**.

oligarchy: A form of government in which a small minority holds ruling power in order to favor its own interests. Military dictatorships are often oligarchic, as are the political machines that sometimes run city governments in democracies.

Optimates: In late Republican Rome, die-hard defenders of patrician privilege (literally, the "best"). Opposing the Optimates were the Populares ("supporters of the people").

orthodoxy: The established (literally "correct") doctrine of a church or religious group.

ostracism: In ancient Athens, a method of banishment by popular vote, without trial.

Each year the citizens would vote on whether anyone was so dangerous to the state that he should be ostracized, or exiled for ten years. Later, ostracism came to mean any form of political or social exclusion.

Paleolithic Period: Prehistoric cultural development that preceded the Neolithic Period. In the Paleolithic ("Old Stone Age"), which lasted from about 2.5 million to about 10,000 years ago, hominids and humans developed the manufacture of chipped stone tools.

Pan-Slavism: Nationalistic ideology or movement stressing the unity and interests of various Slavic peoples, such as Russians, Ukrainians, and Serbs. Pan-Slavism originated in the 1830s as Slavic Balkan nations struggled for independence from Ottoman Turkish and Austrian control.

pantheism: *See* **monotheism**.

papacy: *See* **pope**.

papal bull: *See* **bull**.

papyrus: Writing paper made from the pith of a reed that grows wild in the Nile River, used from about 2400 B.C.E. by the people of Egypt, Palestine, Syria, and southern Europe. Connected together in strips and rolled up, it made scrolls, the books of antiquity.

parable: A brief moral tale (from the Greek *parabole*, "a setting beside"). In parables, a spiritual truth is articulated by telling a simple story. Well-known biblical examples include the Gospel stories of the Prodigal Son and of the Good Samaritan.

parlement: In medieval and early modern France, a regional supreme court of criminal and civil law. At first the *parlements* were staffed by royal appointees who supported medieval monarchs, but in the seventeenth and eighteenth centuries, they often obstructed the absolutist agenda of Bourbon kings. The revolutionary National Assembly of 1789 abolished the *parlements*.

parliamentary government: System of government in which power resides primarily in a legislative body or parliament.

partisan: Member of an unofficial resistance force, such as the French or Italian resistance; the zealous supporter of any given cause.

pasteurization: The process for destroying bacterial contaminants, developed by French nineteenth-century chemist Louis Pasteur.

pastor: In Protestantism, a leader or minister (Greek *pastor*, "shepherd") of a congregation who presides at the weekly Sunday celebration and whose role is to teach scripture, rather than to confer grace (the role of the priest in Catholicism). Pastors, unlike celibate priests, are allowed to marry.

patriarchy: Social organization marked by the supremacy of the father, the legal dependence of wives and children, and the reckoning of and inheritance from the male line.

patricians: The hereditary aristocratic class of ancient Rome, initially entitled to privileges denied to commoners (the plebeians). In medieval and early modern cities, a hereditary elite of bourgeois office-holders, *rentiers*, and high-status merchants, to be distinguished from ordinary guild merchants.

patrilineal: The tracing of ancestry and kinship through the male line. Female offspring are valued insofar as they help preserve the male line, mainly through marriage. Patrilineal families may also be patriarchal.

patrimony: The accumulation of familial wealth which can be inherited; originally the wealth that flows through the male line of descent.

patronage: The conferring of jobs, favors, and commissions by a powerful patron to a client in order to promote the patron's interests.

pax romana: Literally, "the Roman peace." Under the empire that was consolidated by Augustus Caesar (27 B.C.E.), Rome's total domination of Europe, the Mediterranean, and the Middle East brought about 250 years of peace, albeit a peace secured by conquest and bloodshed.

pedagogue: In ancient Greece, originally a slave who accompanied children to school. Later, pedagogue came to mean a theorist of education or a teacher.

penance: A sacrament of the Roman Catholic, Eastern Orthodox, and some Protestant churches. The rite consists in the confession of sins to a priest, who then assigns the repentant sinner an act of penance in order to obtain forgiveness.

peninsulares: Literally, "from the [Iberian] peninsula," residents of Latin America born in and loyal to Spain, and who dominated Spanish colonial offices up to the early nineteenth century.

peons: Poor agricultural laborers, typically indebted to their employers and thus essentially unable to contract as free workers or seek other employment. Peonage was a common form of labor in Latin America with roots extending back to the Conquest.

perestroika: In Russian, "restructuring," Soviet leader Mikhail Gorbachev's policy introduced in tandem with *glasnost* in 1985. *Perestroika* involved efforts to improve the economy and made modest concessions to private enterprise and property. *See also* **glasnost**.

perspective: In art, the techniques used to represent three-dimensional spatial relationships on a two-dimensional surface; from the fifteenth century, one of the principal characteristics of western European art.

peso: In the early modern era, a widely circulated coin minted from gold mined in Spanish America (also known as a "piece of eight," because it was worth eight *reales*).

phalanx: In ancient Greece, a military formation in which heavily armed infantrymen lined up close together in deep ranks, defended by a wall of shields.

Pharisees: A major Jewish sect (flourished c. 100 B.C.E.–100 C.E.), noted for strict observance of rites and ceremonies and for their insistence on the validity of their own oral traditions concerning the written law. Pharisaism arose in opposition to the Sadducees; Pharisees argued that religious authority was not the sole prerogative of the priesthood. The Pharisees developed the idea of an afterlife and the resurrection of the body, and the concept of the Messiah. Pharisaism profoundly influenced the rabbinical Judaism of later centuries.

philanthropic organization: Any one of the legally defined entities existing to collect, manage, and distribute private wealth to public causes including education, medical care, housing, and so on. Philanthropy literally means "love of humankind."

philosophy: The oldest form of systematic scholarly inquiry (from Greek *philosophos*, "lover of wisdom"). Today "philosophy" means: (1) the study of the principles underlying knowledge, being, and reality; (2) a particular system of philosophical doctrine; (3) the critical study of philosophical doctrines; (4) the study of the principles of a particular branch of knowledge; (5) a system of principles for guidance in everyday life.

phonogram: A character or symbol that represents a word, syllable, or language sound (phoneme) in writing.

physiocracy: Eighteenth-century school of thought, usually considered the scientific approach to economics in contrast to the mercantilist orthodoxies of the day. Physiocrats advocated a laissez-faire economy, and argued that land should be considered the basis of wealth and thus taxation. *See also* **mercantilism.**

pictograph: A simplified picture of an object that represents the object in writing.

*pietas***:** In Roman culture, the highest virtue, a selfless regard for the father and ancestors, with a determination to preserve the lineage. Our term "piety" is derived from *pietas*, but now means religious devotion.

Pietism/Pietists: Movement within the Lutheran church in Germany, dating from the 1600s, and which emphasized personal piety over ritual, formality, and orthodoxy.

pike: A weapon consisting of a long wooden shaft with a pointed steel head used by foot soldiers until superseded by the bayonet.

pilgrimage: The practice, common to many religions, of journeying to a holy place or shrine to obtain blessings from God or as an act of devotion or penance.

plantation system: Cultivating crops on extensive lands worked by slave labor, developed in the sixteenth century by the Portuguese settlers for sugar cultivation on São Tomé and elsewhere, and later adopted by other European colonizers.

plebeians: Most of the free citizens of ancient Rome, who were originally denied most of the rights accorded the privileged, hereditary patrician class.

*plebs***:** The ordinary people of Rome; by the last century B.C.E., this term referred to the increasingly dependent urban masses.

pluralism: In medieval and early modern Europe, the practice of holding several offices at the same time.

pogrom: From the Russian word for "thunder," a riot or violent attack directed against a minority group, especially Jews, or their property.

*polis***, pl.** *poleis***:** In ancient Greece, this was a city-state.

politiques: A faction that emerged in the sixteenth-century civil war between Protestants and Catholics in France, who rejected religious considerations in favor of the secular goal of order and national unity.

polyglot: A term describing geographical areas or states in which many different languages are spoken.

polytheism: *See* **monotheism.**

pope: The pope (literally, "father"), or bishop of Rome, is claimed by Roman Catholics as the successor to the apostle Peter, who is traditionally assigned preeminence over other apostles. The papacy comprises the pope and the system of ecclesiastical government of the Roman Catholic Church.

Populares: *See* **Optimates.**

portolan: From the thirteenth century on, charts that gave sailing distances in miles and bearings in straight lines. Lacking parallels and meridians, or any indication of the curvature of the earth, they could not be used on the open oceans.

positivism: Philosophical system developed by Auguste Comte in which the search for final causes and metaphysical knowledge is abandoned in favor of attaining certain or "positive" knowledge of physical matters by scientific methods of inquiry.

predestination: A Christian doctrine according to which a person's ultimate salvation or damnation is determined by God alone prior to, and apart from, any worth or merit on the person's part.

prelate: A clergyman of high rank.

Presocratic philosophy: Greek philosophy (c. 660–440 B.C.E.) prior to Socrates. The Presocratic philosophers challenged religious explanations of reality and sought to explain rationally the natural world and physical processes.

Prime Meridian: *See* **meridian.**

primogeniture: The preference given to the eldest son and his descendants in inheritance. Practiced in many regions of medieval Europe to maintain estates whole and intact.

*princeps***:** Literally, "first citizen," a title adopted by Augustus, the first Roman emperor. The system he created, based on the allegiance of the army and the people to the emperor (*imperator*) and on the collaboration between the emperor and the senatorial and equestrian classes, came to be known as the principate, the rule of the first citizen.

proletarian/proletariat: In ancient Rome, the poorest citizens, literally "bearer of children": the proletarian's only service to the state was to reproduce and provide new generations of citizens. In industrial society the term is used to describe the industrial working class which lives by selling its labor for wages to the bourgeoisie.

propaganda: Information disseminated to excite or intensify specific emotions and actions rather than specifically to educate or promote value-free, rational discourse. Propaganda often promotes half-truths or outright lies.

proscription: In ancient Rome, the posting of names of the opponents of a faction in the Forum. Those whose names were posted in the Forum were murdered and their wealth confiscated.

protectionism: The establishment of tariffs and other barriers to trade in order to protect domestic or local producers.

protectorate: Status or designation in international relations establishing the dominion of one state over another. The actual degree of control involved may vary.

protoindustrial: Literally, "first-" or "early-industrial," term applicable to the economic organization of areas of early modern Europe or to the early stages of industrialization, and based largely on the putting-out system. *See also* **putting-out system.**

Ptolemaic: Referring to Ptolemy, the second-century Greek astronomer and geographer, whose *Almagest* remained the authoritative explanation of the structure of the heavens until displaced by the Copernican system during the Scientific Revolution.

pueblo: A built structure of stone or adobe used for dwelling and defense by Amerindian groups of the American Southwest.

putsch: Literally, "thrust," any secretly plotted, suddenly carried-out attempt to overthrow a government, such as the Beer Hall Putsch in Germany during 1923.

putting-out system: Especially in early modern western Europe, a largely informal arrangement linking merchant-employers with laborers and craftspersons. Within this system, an entrepreneur purchased basic materials which would then be "put out" to local residents who would return finished products made at home on their own equipment. Also called "cottage" or "domestic" industry.

*qâdi***:** In Islam, a judge whose decisions are based on religious law.

quadrant: An instrument used by astronomers and navigators from medieval times to measure the altitude of the sun or a star and for surveying. At its simplest, the quadrant is a flat plate in the shape of a quarter circle marked with a degree scale along the curved side; two sights are attached to one of the radial sides and a plumb bob hangs from the apex.

quantum, pl. quanta: A quantity of energy, the smallest that can be absorbed or emitted as electromagnetic radiation.

quinine: Obtained from the bark of the Andean cinchona tree, a crystalline alkaloid used to treat malaria.

Qur'an: The sacred scripture of Islam. Muslims acknowledge the Qur'an, or Koran (Arabic, "reading" or "recital"), as the actual words of God that were given to the Prophet Muhammad between c. 610 and his death in 632.

rabbi: The title that is given to recognized Jewish religious teachers, sages, and leaders. Originally a term of respect (Hebrew, "my master"), around the first century C.E. it became a formal title for men who were authorized to interpret and expound Jewish law.

race: A population group, subspecies, or variety within the species *Homo sapiens*, set apart from other groups on the basis of arbitrarily selected, commonly visible criteria. The criteria most often selected are: skin color; "blood"; hair type; the shape and form of the body, head, and facial features; and alleged moral and/or behavioral attributes.

raison d'état: French for "reason of state," the justification given when the political interests of a nation-state override any moral principles governing the state's actions.

rationalism: The belief that the most fundamental knowledge is based on reason and that truth can be arrived at only by rational analysis of ideas, independent of empirical data, emotions, or prior authority.

real: In the early modern era, a small Spanish or Spanish-American silver coin, worth one-eighth of a peso.

Realism: In literature and the arts, the representation of objects as they really are or appear to be.

regent: A person appointed to govern during the absence, childhood, or incapacity of a monarch.

relativity: In physics, Einstein's 1905 theory that physical measurements are not absolute but vary depending on the relative position and motion of the observer and observed.

relic: An object esteemed and venerated because of its association with a saint or martyr, often a body-part. Relics are often credited with curative or miraculous powers.

relief: A mode of sculpture in which forms project outward from a plane surface.

reliquary: A receptacle, which is usually richly decorated and made of precious materials, and designed for the safekeeping or exhibition of a relic.

Renaissance: The period of European history from the early fourteenth to the mid-seventeenth century, derived from the French word for rebirth, originally referring to the revival of the values and artistic styles of Classical antiquity during that period, especially in Italy.

reparation: Money payments exacted by a victorious power from those it has defeated and reckoned as compensation to the former for the costs of war.

repatriation: The act or policy of returning immigrants, refugees, or other persons or groups considered foreign by legal, ethnic, religious, or other status to their home state. Repatriation can be forced or voluntary.

republic: Literally, "a thing of the public," a state or polity based on the notion that sovereignty resides with the people and which delegates the powers and responsibilities of rule to elected representatives.

reservation: Parcel of public land designated for the use of an Amerindian tribe.

resistance (forces): During World War II, any underground groups in Nazi-held Europe engaged in sabotage, intelligence, publishing, or other anti-Nazi activities.

resurrection: The "rising again" to life of a dead person in the future or in heaven. The concept of resurrection from death is found in several religions, but is associated particularly with Christianity because of the central belief in the resurrection of Jesus.

rhetoric: The branch of written and oral discourse that concerns persuasion (Greek *rhetor*, "speaker in the assembly").

Romance languages: The family of languages that developed out of the provincial Latin spoken in various sections of the Roman Empire after its fall: Italian, French, Spanish, Portuguese, Romanian, and Romansch (spoken in some parts of Switzerland).

Romanesque: A style of art and architecture that flourished throughout western Europe from about 1050 to about 1200. The word originally meant "in the Roman manner"; Romanesque church architecture characteristically employs the Roman round arch and the major forms of antique Roman vaulting, and retains the basic plan of the early Christian basilica.

Romanticism: Philosophical and artistic movement of the late eighteenth to mid-nineteenth century, rejecting the Enlightenment's exaltation of reason and stressing emotions and the imagination. As well as in painting, poetry, and literature, Romantic sentiments found expression in various nationalist platforms, such as Mazzini's Young Italy. *See also* **nationalism**.

rosary: A circular string of beads used by Roman Catholics for counting recitations of such prayers as the Hail Mary (Ave Maria), the Our Father (Lord's Prayer), and the Glory Be to the Father (Gloria Patri).

sacrament: In Christianity, a sacred ritual conferring grace.

Sadducees: A powerful Jewish religious sect, identified with the priesthood and aristocracy, that flourished from about 200 B.C.E. until the fall of Jerusalem in 70 C.E. Unlike the Pharisees, the Sadducees did not believe in resurrection and the immortality of the soul, and opposed the use of Oral Law, holding only to the Pentateuch (the first five books of the Old Testament).

saint: A holy person (from the Latin *sanctus*, "holy") who is credited with the ability to work miracles of healing, or to pray effectively for others. In the New Testament "saint" refers to a baptized follower of Jesus Christ. Later the phrase "communion of saints" was used to refer to all members of the Church, both living and dead. Still later, "saint" was defined as an individual who has either died a heroic death for Christ (i.e. a martyr), or whose life has been marked by unusual signs of compassion for others. The Church came to regulate cults venerating such individuals by instituting a system of canonization about 1000 C.E.

salient: In military terminology, the outward-projecting part of a troop formation.

salon: Especially in eighteenth-century France, a gathering of philosophers, writers, artists, and prominent members of society (or the room in which this usually occured) for the purpose of intellectual conversation or readings.

salvation: A religious concept that refers to the process through which a person is brought to ultimate, and eventually eternal, well-being. In Christianity, salvation (Latin *salus*, "health," "safety") refers to the process or state of being "saved" or "redeemed."

samurai: In medieval and early modern Japan, a class of warriors (from the Japanese *saburu*, "service"). The samurai were originally rural landowners who served as military retainers. Later they became military aristocrats and then military rulers.

Saracen: A term that Greek-speaking Byzantine chroniclers and other European peoples used for Muslim Arabs.

satrap: The governor of a province (satrapy) of the ancient Persian Empire.

schism: A formal division in a religious body. Two important schisms in the history of Christianity were the division between the Eastern (Orthodox) and Western (Roman) Churches (traditionally dated 1054), and the period (1378–1417) during which the Western Church had two, and later three, competing lines of popes.

Scholasticism: A philosophical movement that was dominant in medieval European universities and writing from about the ninth century through until the seventeenth century. Scholasticism combined Christian dogma, patristic philosophy (which was contained in the works of the Church Fathers), and the principles of Aristotelian philosophy.

Scientific Revolution: The period and process of the creation of modern science, especially astronomy and physics, usually dated from the publication of Copernicus's *On the Revolutions of the Celestial Spheres* (1543) to that of Newton's *Mathematical*

Principles of Natural Philosophy (1687), and which established classical physics.

secession: Official withdrawal from a state or other political entity, such as the withdrawal of several southern states from the United States during 1860–1861, which served as the cause of the American Civil War.

sect: A dissenting religious body or political faction, that is often regarded as heretical or blasphemous by the larger body of believers.

secular: Of or relating to the worldly or temporal. Specifically in Catholicism, the term "secular" refers to a category of clergy that is not bound by monastic vows or rules.

secularization: The process by which politics, economics, society, and culture are detached from religious influences or control; characteristic of Western civilization over the last two centuries and some contemporary Islamic societies.

Semitic: A branch of the Afroasiatic (or Hamito-Semitic) language group. Semites speak Semitic languages: Arabs, Aramaeans, Jews, and some Ethiopians, and in antiquity Babylonians, Assyrians, Phoenicians, Canaanites, and other groups. Speakers of a proto-Hamito-Semitic language may have migrated into Mesopotamia, the Middle East and the Arabian Peninsula from North Africa in the sixth millennium B.C.E.

Separatists: Seventeenth-century Puritans who separated from the Church of England and settled in North America to obtain freedom to practice their form of worship.

sepoy: Literally, "horseman," any Indian soldier, particularly an infantryman, in the service of the British or other European colonial army.

serf: In medieval Europe, a peasant who was legally bound to the soil and obligated to give a portion of his produce to his lord. Up until about 1200, most peasants in western Europe were serfs.

sexagesimal: A numerical system based on the number 60, used by the Babylonians. Largely supplanted by the number 10 (decimal system), sexagesimal arithmetic survives in the use of 60 for the minute and hour cycle, the dozen, the foot (divided into 12 inches), and the 360° circle.

sextant: An optical instrument used in navigation since the mid-eighteenth century to measure the angles of celestial bodies above the horizon from the observer's position.

shah: In Persia (modern Iran), the king or sovereign.

Shi'ite: One who practices Shi'ism, the smaller of the two main branches of Islam, and the dominant religious group in Persia (modern Iran). Shi'ites separated from Sunnism in the seventh century C.E. when, insisting that only descendants of Muhammad's son-in-law Ali could qualify, they rejected the fourth caliph accepted by the majority.

Shintoism: The indigenous religious tradition of Japan, based on the worship of gods, nature spirits, and ancestors. After the eighth century C.E., Shintoism coexisted and blended with Buddhism and Confucianism.

shuttle: In weaving, a device or object used for passing the thread of the woof between the threads of the warp.

Sikh: Member of a breakaway Hindu sect rejecting the caste system, Hindu mysticism and magic, idolatry, and pilgrimages. Sikhs have been at the forefront of Hindu opposition to Muslim domination.

simony: In Christian canon law, this is the term for the sale or purchase of a spiritual service or office.

skepticism: In philosophy, belief in the impossibility of obtaining certain knowledge.

slavery: A social practice in which a person is owned by and commanded to labor for the benefit of a master.

slum: Residential area, usually urban, characterized by a variety of social ills including the poverty of its residents, overcrowding, poor sanitation, and other unsafe or unpleasant conditions.

snuff: A preparation of dried, pulverized tobacco to be inhaled through the nostrils, chewed, or placed against the gums.

social democracy: From the late-nineteenth century in Europe and America, a philosophy and movement seeking the establishment of socialism not by revolution but by peaceful, evolutionary measures carried out within the existing non-socialist legal and political framework.

socialism: From the early nineteenth century on, any economic system or general philosophy emphasizing collective or state ownership of most forms of property, especially the means of production, and providing for the equitable and artificial rather than free-market distribution of wealth. *See also* **Marxism.**

Socialist Realism: In the Soviet Union, realistic art form glorifying proletarian values and serving as pro-communist and pro-government propaganda. Socialist Realism was established as the Soviet Union's official and only acceptable type of artistic expression during the 1930s.

Sophists: A group of ancient Greek teachers of rhetoric, philosophy, and the art of living, fifth–fourth centuries B.C.E., known for their adroit and specious reasoning. "Sophistry" is now applied to any form of devious, but convincing, argument.

Soviets: "Councils" of worker, soldier, and peasant deputies (chosen and controlled by the central authorities) who functioned as the primary governmental unit from the national to local levels from the Revolution of 1917 to the collapse of the Soviet Union.

specie: Money in the form of coinage.

species: A biological classification designating a type of organism or population of animals potentially capable of interbreeding.

spindle: *See* **distaff.**

spinster: In medieval Europe, an unmarried woman who maintained herself by spinning thread. Later, the term came to designate an unmarried woman who is past the common age for marrying.

spiritualism: The belief that the physical world is permeated by a deeper, ultimate reality defined as soul or spirit; popularly, the belief that the spirits of the dead can be accessed by the living with the assistance of an adept, or medium.

spiritualists: In sixteenth- and seventeenth-century Europe, inward-looking but radical Protestant sects, such as the Mennonites, Moravian Brethren, and English Society of Friends (Quakers). Spiritualist sects exalted the divine within the human and deliberately abstained from the demands of worldly existence.

spontaneous generation: In biology, the theory that microorganisms come into existence by themselves and from nothing. This belief was widespread until disproved by Louis Pasteur in the nineteenth century.

stele, pl. **stelae:** An upright stone slab or column, decorated with inscriptions or figures, common in prehistoric and early historic cultures.

steppes: The Slavic term for the vast grasslands, flat, semi-arid, and subject to extremes of temperature, that stretch across central Eurasia.

stoa: A freestanding porchlike structure that is usually walled at the back with a front colonnade, and which is designed to give pedestrians shelter and meeting places, often in the *agoras* of ancient Greek cities. The Stoic school of philosophy took its name from an Athenian stoa where its members first taught.

stock exchange/stock market: A place where brokers and dealers in stocks and bonds transact business together. Stock exchanges facilitated the financing of business and government activity by bringing together the buyers and sellers of the shares of joint-stock companies and, in later times, shares of corporations and bonds.

stratification: The division of society into separate groups, based on wealth, prestige, and/or ancestry.

strike: In industrial societies, a collective work stoppage initiated by workers, often via their unions, as a protest or weapon against their employer or general conditions of work. By causing economic pain to their employer, striking workers have typically sought to gain specified ends such as increased pay, safety improvements, or other benefits. *See also* **collective bargaining, trade unions.**

Sturm und Drang: Literally, "storm and stress," in literature, term describing the emotional turmoil that characterized not only German Romanticism, but Romanticism generally and the intellectual culture of Europe for at least the first half-century following the French Revolution. *See also* **Romanticism.**

suburb: A settlement immediately outside the walls of a city or fortification; in medieval Europe, sometimes the nucleus of a city.

suffrage: The right to vote officials into public office or to vote on specific legislation. In general, suffrage has increased during the late modern period to include wider groups of previously unenfranchised individuals.

suffragist: Pertaining to the struggle for suffrage, that is, the right of an individual or group to vote for their chosen political representatives, or an advocate of such rights.

sumptuary laws: Laws against luxury and extravagance (Latin *sumptus*, "expense"). Sumptuary laws prohibiting extravagance in dress or ceremony were designed to maintain moral standards and distinctions between social classes, and often particularly targeted women.

sunna: Literally, "way" or "path," the body of traditional Islamic law believed to derive directly from the words and actions of Muhammad.

Sunnite: A follower of the Sunni branch of Islam to which most Muslims belong. Sunnites claim to follow strictly the *sunna* (practices) of the Prophet Muhammad, as defined and elaborated by the religious authorities (*'ulama*).

surrogate: A person who acts on behalf of another.

sweated industries/sweatshops: Industries marked by especially oppressive and exploitative conditions including lack of basic safety standards, excessive hours of work, denial of legal rights, low pay, and curtailment of personal liberty.

symposium: Originally, in ancient Greece, an all-male drinking party, where men composed drinking songs and engaged in lively conversation. The term is now usually applied to a meeting where speeches are given and discussions are held.

synagogue: A building where Jews gather for worship and religious instruction; the focus of Jewish communal life. In ancient Judaism, worship centered on the Temple in Jerusalem, where sacrificial rites were performed by a special caste of priests, with the masses excluded. In contrast, the synagogue is open to all Jews for prayer, ceremony, the reading of the Torah, religious instruction, and preaching. The synagogue provided the model for the Christian church and Islamic mosque.

syncretism: The fusion of cultural forms of different origin and character into a new formation.

Syndicalism/Syndicalists: A form of unionism prominent in France, which aims at federated union control of the means of production and of society, to be obtained through general strike, sabotage, and terrorism. *See also* **trade unions**.

Talmud: A compendium of law and lore that is regarded in Judaism as the sequel to the Hebrew Bible and the basis of Jewish religious life. There are two Talmuds: the Palestinian, composed in the third and fourth centuries C.E., and the Babylonian, completed about 500 C.E., with some later additions.

tariff: Tax levied on goods traded across regional or national borders. The removal or reduction of tariffs during much of the nineteenth century facilitated increased economic and industrial growth.

Tartars, Tatars: Descendants of the Mongols, who ruled part of eastern Europe and central Asia.

tax farmer: A free agent contracted by a ruler or state to collect taxes, from which he takes an agreed-upon commission or, more often, whatever percentage he can expropriate.

taxonomy: Especially in biology, this is the science of organizing and classifying living organisms according to certain salient traits.

tenement: Literally, "that which is held by tenure," the designation for houses or other buildings leased as apartment dwellings, especially in poorer industrial towns and cities, to a number of separate tenants.

Terror, The: During the radical phase of the French Revolution, period of extreme, bloody, and summary revolutionary justice—from September 5, 1793 to July 27, 1794. The Terror, orchestrated by Robespierre and the Committee of Public Safety, resulted in the guillotining of tens of thousands of real and imagined enemies of the Revolution. *See also* **Committee of Public Safety**.

terrorism: The use of isolated, typically random acts of violence, often carried out against collateral or symbolic targets—such as national embassies and airlines—and intended primarily to instill fear and anxiety in a perceived enemy population.

theocracy: Governmental system in which civil law—as well as religious law—is understood as deriving from divine rather than secular sources, and in which ecclesiastical authorities may therefore play the role of legislature, executive, and judiciary.

Thermidor/Thermidorean Reaction: During the French Revolution, name given to the revolt on the ninth day of Thermidor (the "hot" month)—July 27, 1794 by the conventional calendar—leading to the downfall and execution of Robespierre and the cessation of the Terror. *See also* **Terror**.

Third World: Designation accorded in Western parlance to the "developing world" as a whole. The term originated in the context of the Cold War, when the notion was popular that the planet consisted of three "worlds"—the West (or First World), the Communist powers (or Second World), and the Third World of mostly non-aligned and poor states, most of whom had recently gained—or were in the process of gaining—independence from European empires.

tholos: The bee-hive shaped tombs of the Mycenaean kings.

tithe: A "tenth part" of agricultural or other produce, exacted to support the Church.

Torah: The entire body of Jewish teaching incorporated in the Hebrew Bible, the Talmud, and later rabbinical commentaries. Applied sometimes to the written Mosaic law contained in the first five books of the Bible.

totalitarianism: Governmental system and political culture which controls or attempts to control all aspects of life and suppress all forms of dissent. Nazi Germany and Stalinist Russia remain the classic examples of such a system.

trade unions: Workers' combinations dating from the industrial era. Unlike medieval guilds, unions do not regulate entry to trades, set prices, or establish quality standards but instead represent the interests of the workers in negotiation with employers. *See also* **collective bargaining, strike, Syndicalism**.

tragedy: A genre of drama, developed in ancient Greece, in which a hero meets death brought on by a flaw of character combined with events and circumstances beyond control.

transept: The part of the church that crosses the nave; also, either wing of the transept.

transubstantiation: In Roman Catholic or Eastern Orthodox church dogma, this is the miraculous change by which bread and wine at their consecration during the ritual of Mass become the body and blood of Christ.

Trinity: The Christian understanding of God as a unity of three persons (triune): Father, Son, and Holy Spirit. The idea of the Trinity is an attempt to reconcile the diverse statements about God contained in the Bible.

triumvirate: A ruling group of three persons; originally, in the last years of the Republic, Julius Caesar, Crassus, and Pompey.

tyranny: Rule by an illegitimate leader, the tyrant, who seizes power and holds it by violence. In ancient Greece, tyranny was seen as the opposite of monarchy. Both forms of rule, in fact, concentrate power in a single figure.

U-boat: Abbreviation of "Unterseeboot," German submarine, especially of the type first used in World War I, which inflicted heavy damage on Allied shipping.

'ulama: Teachers of Islamic law.

unconscious: In Freudian psychoanalysis, the aspect of the human mind from which derive instinctual ideas and impulses of which the conscious thinking mind is not directly aware. Freudian psychoanalytical theory describes complex interactions among three parts of the human psyche: the instinctual unconscious, or "id"; the conscious self, or "ego"; and the edifice of internalized social and cultural norms, or "superego."

unitarianism: A form of Protestant Christianity asserting that God is one person, rather than three persons in one (the Trinity).

United Kingdom: Officially the United Kingdom of Great Britain and Northern Ireland, comprising the countries of England, Scotland, Wales, and Northern Ireland, organized as a single political entity. The union of England with Wales took place in 1536; of these with Scotland in 1701; and with Ireland in 1801. The division of Ireland in 1922 left only Northern Ireland within the United Kingdom.

urban: Relating to the city. Urbanization is the process of becoming more urban through the concentration of population, the performance of economic tasks, and the progressive development of the mental outlook of a city.

usufruct: The legal right of using and enjoying the fruits or profits of something belonging to another. In medieval Europe, land held in usufruct and granted by another noble, or a king or an agent of the church, was often called a fief.

usury: Money-lending for profit.

utilitarianism: Ethical system developed by the English theorist Jeremy Bentham in which right is perceived as that which brings greatest happiness to the greatest number of persons.

utopia/utopian: Literally "no place," from the work of that name by sixteenth-century English theorist Thomas More, describing an ideal society. In recent times, often used pejoratively of goals considered unrealistic or unattainable in the real world. The word is often applied to pre-Marxist socialisms, to distinguish them from the more "scientific socialism" pioneered by Marx and Engels.

vassal: A person under the protection of a feudal lord, to whom he vows homage and fealty. The vassals of powerful rulers might also in turn have vassals.

vernacular: In medieval and early modern Europe, the native spoken language of a region or country; not Latin, which was the language used for the writing of high literary, scientific, legal, and religious works. In time the modern national vernaculars such as French, German, and Italian displaced Latin in most of these intellectual tasks.

voodoo: A hybrid religious-folkloric system widely practiced in Haiti, combining elements of Roman Catholicism (introduced by French colonialists) and African mysticism (introduced by slave populations from Dahomey—now Benin—in Africa).

warp, woof: The warp is a series of yarns that are extended lengthwise in a loom and crossed by the woof (or weft), together constituting, when it is complete, a woven textile.

welfare state: General term for the collection of laws, programs, and guarantees responsible for securing individuals' rights to a basic level of economic security, such as pensions, unemployment benefits, sick pay, and so on.

wergeld: Among the Germanic tribes that lived outside the borders of the Roman Empire, a vengence or compensation payment, which varied according to a person's status.

wet nurse: A lactating woman who is hired to breastfeed the baby of her employers.

white-collar: White-collar clerical or professional employees who do not perform manual labor (as do blue-collar workers).

yeoman: In British history, a farmer cultivating his own land.

Zionism: The movement or belief founded in 1896 by Theodore Herzl claiming Palestine as the rightful homeland of the Jews.

INDEX

SINGLE PC LICENSE AGREEMENT AND LIMITED WARRANTY